HOLT MATH

Holt Online Learning

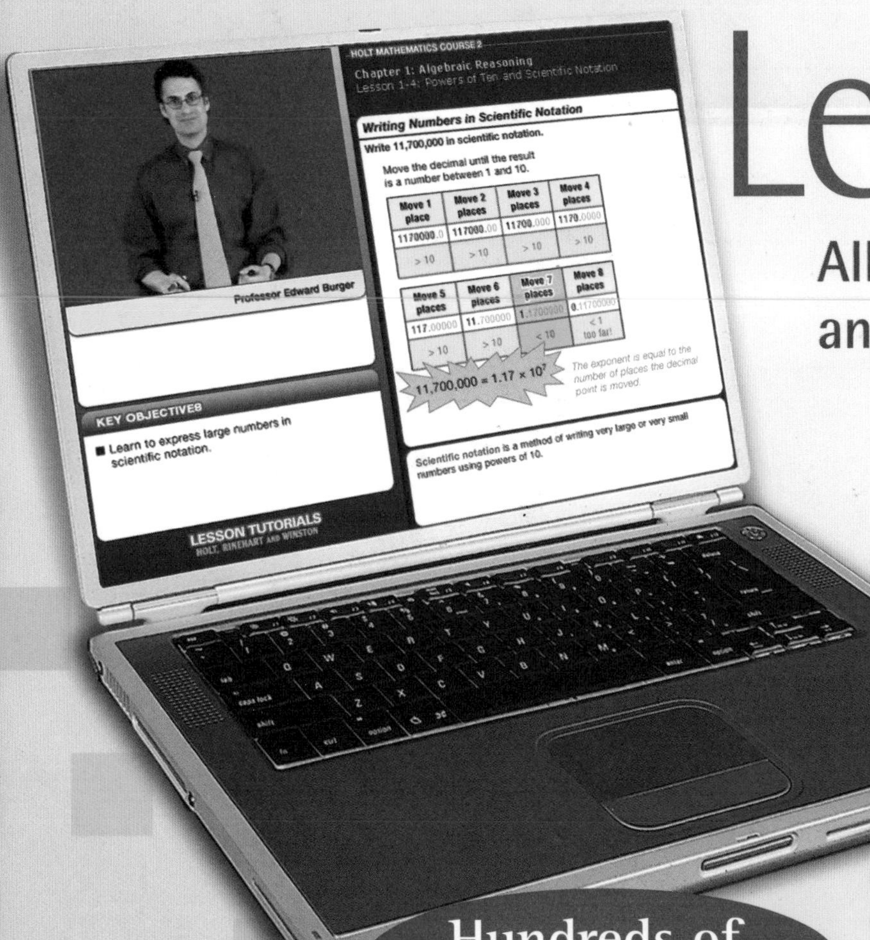

All the help you need, any time you need it.

go.hrw.com

Hundreds of videos online!

Lesson Tutorial Videos feature entertaining and enlightening videos that illustrate every example in your textbook!

Premier Online Edition

- Complete Student Edition
- **Lesson Tutorial Videos** for every example
  - > **Course 1**: 279 videos
  - > **Course 2**: 294 videos
  - > **Course 3**: 333 videos
- Interactive practice with feedback

Extra Practice

- Homework Help Online
- Intervention and enrichment exercises
- State test practice

Online Tools

- Graphing calculator
- TechKeys "How-to" tutorials on graphing calculators
- Virtual Manipulatives
- Multilingual glossary

For Parents

- Parent Resources Online

Log on to **www.go.hrw.com** to access Holt's online resources.

HOLT

Mathematics

Course 2

Jennie M. Bennett
Edward B. Burger
David J. Chard
Audrey L. Jackson
Paul A. Kennedy
Freddie L. Renfro
Janet K. Scheer
Bert K. Waits

HOLT, RINEHART AND WINSTON
A Harcourt Education Company
Orlando • Austin • New York • San Diego • London

Course 2 Contents in Brief

Student Handbook

Printed in the United States of America

ISBN 0-03-038512-1
2 3 4 5 073 09 08 07 06

Cover photo: The Stata enter at MIT, Boston, Massachustts, USA. © Scott Gilchrist/Master e

AUTHORS

Jennie M. Bennett, Ph.D. is a mathematics teacher at Hartman Middle School in Houston, Texas. Jennie is past president of the Benjamin Banneker Association, the Second Vice-President of NCSM, and a former board member of NCTM.

Paul A. Kennedy, Ph.D. is a professor in the Department of Mathematics at Colorado State University. Dr. Kennedy is a leader in mathematics education. His research focuses on developing algebraic thinking by using multiple representations and technology. He is the author of numerous publications.

Edward B. Burger, Ph.D. is Professor of Mathematics and Chair at Williams College and is the author of numerous articles, books, and videos. He has won several of the most prestigious writing and teaching awards offered by the Mathematical Association of America. Dr. Burger has appeared on NBC TV, National Public Radio, and has given innumerable mathematical performances around the world.

Freddie L. Renfro, BA, MA, has 35 years of experience in Texas education as a classroom teacher and director/coordinator of Mathematics PreK-12 for school districts in the Houston area. She has served as TEA TAAS/TAKS reviewer, team trainer for Texas Math Institutes, TEKS Algebra Institute writer, and presenter at math workshops.

David J. Chard, Ph.D., is an Associate Dean of Curriculum and Academic Programs at the University of Oregon. He is the President of the Division for Research at the Council for Exceptional Children, is a member of the International Academy for Research on Learning Disabilities, and is the Principal Investigator on two major research projects for the U.S. Department of Education.

Janet K. Scheer, Ph.D., Executive Director of Create A VisionTM, is a motivational speaker and provides customized K-12 math staff development. She has taught internationally and domestically at all grade levels.

Audrey L. Jackson is on the Board of Directors for NCTM. She is the Program Coordinator for Leadership Development with the St. Louis, public schools and is a former school administrator for the Parkway School District.

Bert K. Waits, Ph.D., is a Professor Emeritus of Mathematics at The Ohio State University and co-founder of T3 (Teachers Teaching with Technology), a national professional development program.

Contributing Authors

Linda Antinone
Fort Worth, TX
Ms. Antinone teaches mathematics at R. L. Paschal High School in Fort Worth, Texas. She has received the Presidential Award for Excellence in Teaching Mathematics and the National Radio Shack Teacher award. She has coauthored several books for Texas Instruments on the use of technology in mathematics.

Carmen Whitman
Pflugerville, TX
Ms. Whitman travels nationally helping districts improve mathematics education. She has been a program coordinator on the mathematics team at the Charles A. Dana Center, and has served as a secondary math specialist for the Austin Independent School District.

Reviewers

Thomas J. Altonjy
Assistant Principal
Robert R. Lazar Middle School
Montville, NJ

Jane Bash, M.A.
Math Education
Eisenhower Middle School
San Antonio, TX

Charlie Bialowas
District Math Coordinator
Anaheim Union High School District
Anaheim, CA

Lynn Bodet
Math Teacher
Eisenhower Middle School
San Antonio, TX

Debbie Brown
Mathematics Teacher
Eanes ISD
Austin, TX

Louis D'Angelo, Jr.
Math Teacher
Archmere Academy
Claymont, DE

Troy Deckebach
Math Teacher
Tredyffrin-Easttown Middle School
Berwyn, PA

Mary Gorman
Math Teacher
Sarasota, FL

Brian Griffith
Supervisor of Mathematics, K–12
Mechanicsburg Area School District
Mechanicsburg, PA

Ruth Harbin-Miles
District Math Coordinator
Instructional Resource Center
Olathe, KS

Anastasia Hay-Shelton
Mathematics Department Chair
San Antonio ISD
San Antonio, TX

Kim Hayden
Math Teacher
Milford Jr. High School
Milford, OH

Emily Hodges
Mathematics Teacher
Austin ISD
Austin, TX

Susan Howe
Math Teacher
Lime Kiln Middle School
Fulton, MD

Paula Jenniges
Austin, TX

Martha Krauss
Mathematics Teacher
Round Rock ISD
Round Rock, TX

Ronald J. Labrocca
District Mathematics Coordinator
Manhasset Public Schools
Manhasset, NY

Brenda Law
Mathematics Department Chair
Corpus Christi ISD
Corpus Christi, TX

Victor R. Lopez
Math Teacher
Washington School
Union City, NJ

George Maguschak
Math Teacher/Building Chairperson
Wilkes-Barre Area
Wilkes-Barre, PA

Dianne McIntire
Math Teacher
Garfield School
Kearny, NJ

Kenneth McIntire
Math Teacher
Lincoln School
Kearny, NJ

Francisco Pacheco
Math Teacher
IS 125
Bronx, NY

Vivian Perry
Edwards, IL

Vicki Perryman Petty
Math Teacher
Central Middle School
Murfreesbro, TN

Danielle Robles
Mathematics TAKS Coordinator
El Paso ISD
El Paso, TX

Jennifer Sawyer
Math Teacher
Shawboro, NC

Russell Sayler
Math Teacher
Longfellow Middle School
Wauwatosa, WI

Raymond Scacalossi
Math Chairperson
Hauppauge Schools
Hauppauge, NY

Richard Seavey
Math Teacher, retired
Metcalf Jr. High
Eagan, MN

Sherry Shaffer
Math Teacher
Honeoye Central School
Honeoye Falls, NY

Gail M. Sigmund
Math Teacher
Charles A. Mooney Preparatory School
Cleveland, OH

Jonathan Simmons
Math Teacher
Manor Middle School
Killeen, TX

Jeffrey L. Slagel
Math Department Chair
South Eastern Middle School
Fawn Grove, PA

Karen Smith, Ph.D.
Math Teacher
East Middle School
Braintree, MA

Traci Smith
Mathematics Teacher
Spring ISD
Spring, TX

Sonia Soto
Mathematics Teacher
El Paso ISD
El Paso, TX

Bonnie Thompson
Math Teacher
Tower Heights Middle School
Dayton, OH

Mary Thoreen
Mathematics Subject Area Leader
Wilson Middle School
Tampa, FL

Ann-Marie Torres
Mathematics Teacher
Round Rock ISD
Round Rock, TX

Paul Turney
Math Teacher
Ladue School District
St. Louis, MO

Preparing for Standardized Tests

Holt Mathematics provides many opportunities for you to prepare for standardized tests.

Test Prep Exercises

Use the Test Prep Exercises for daily practice of standardized test questions in various formats.

Multiple Choice—choose your answer.

Gridded Response—write your answer in a grid and fill in the corresponding bubbles.

Short Response—write open-ended responses that are scored with a 2-point rubric.

Extended Response—write open-ended responses that are scored with a 4-point rubric.

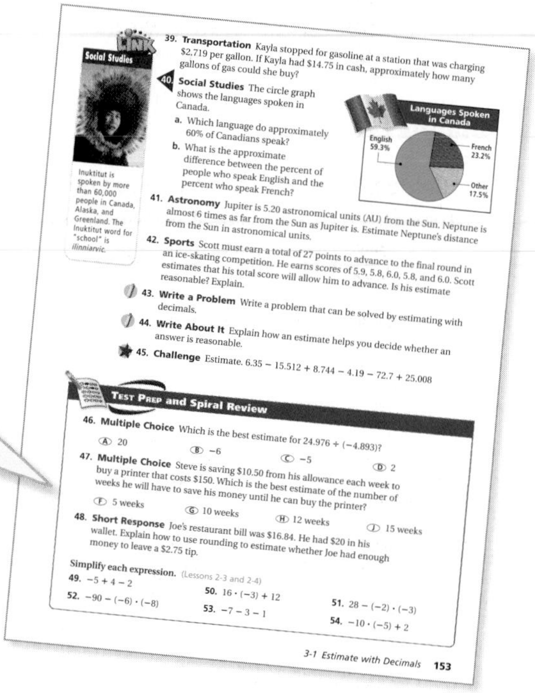
39. **Transportation** Kayla stopped for gasoline at a station that was charging $2.719 per gallon. If Kayla had $14.75 in cash, approximately how many gallons of gas could she buy?

40. **Social Studies** The circle graph shows the languages spoken in Canada.
a. Which language do approximately 60% of Canadians speak?
b. What is the approximate difference between the percent of people who speak English and the percent who speak French?

Inuktitut is spoken by more than 60,000 people in Canada, Alaska, and Greenland. The Inuktitut word for "school" is ilinniarvic.

41. **Astronomy** Jupiter is 5.20 astronomical units (AU) from the Sun. Neptune is almost 6 times as far from the Sun as Jupiter is. Estimate Neptune's distance from the Sun in astronomical units.

42. **Sports** Scott must earn a total of 27 points to advance to the final round in an ice-skating competition. He earns scores of 5.9, 5.8, 6.0, 5.8, and 6.0. Scott estimates that his total score will allow him to advance. Is his estimate reasonable? Explain.

43. **Write a Problem** Write a problem that can be solved by estimating with decimals.

44. **Write About It** Explain how an estimate helps you decide whether an answer is reasonable.

45. **Challenge** Estimate. 6.35 − 15.512 + 8.744 − 4.19 − 72.7 + 25.008

Test Prep and Spiral Review

46. **Multiple Choice** Which is the best estimate for 24.976 + (−4.893)?
Ⓐ 20 Ⓑ −6 Ⓒ −5 Ⓓ 2

47. **Multiple Choice** Steve is saving $10.50 from his allowance each week to buy a printer that costs $150. Which is the best estimate of the number of weeks he will have to save his money until he can buy the printer?
Ⓕ 5 weeks Ⓖ 10 weeks Ⓗ 12 weeks Ⓙ 15 weeks

48. **Short Response** Joe's restaurant bill was $16.84. He had $20 in his wallet. Explain how to use rounding to estimate whether Joe had enough money to leave a $2.75 tip.

Simplify each expression. (Lessons 2-3 and 2-4)

49. −5 + 4 − 2 50. 16 · (−3) + 12 51. 28 − (−2) · (−3)
52. −90 − (−6) · (−8) 53. −7 − 3 − 1 54. −10 · (−5) + 2

3-1 Estimate with Decimals 153

Test Tackler

Use the Test Tackler to become familiar with and practice test-taking strategies.

The first page of this feature explains and shows an example of a test-taking strategy.

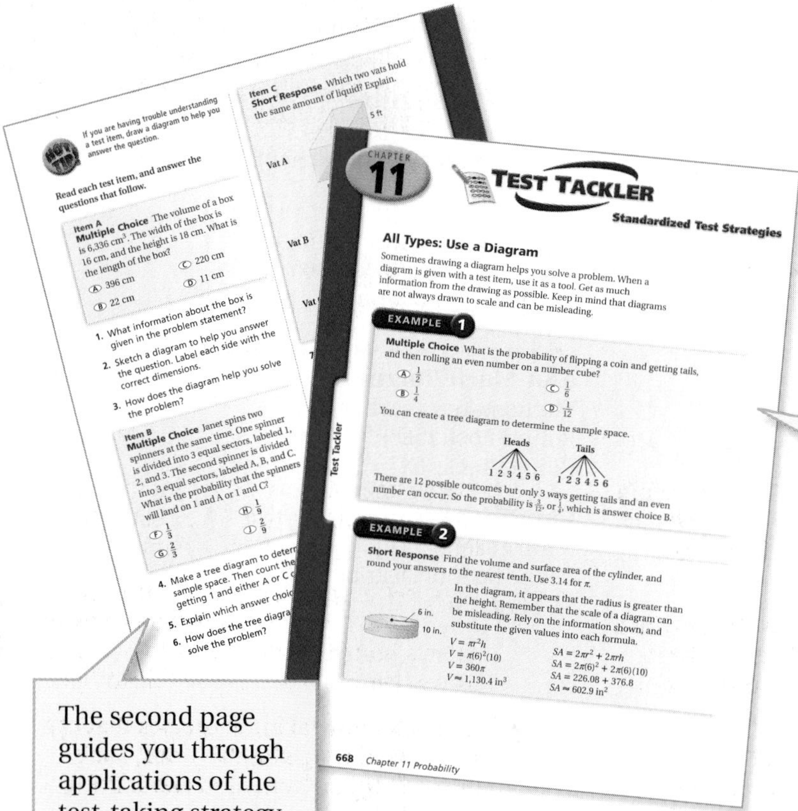
Chapter 11

Test Tackler

Standardized Test Strategies

All Types: Use a Diagram

Sometimes drawing a diagram helps you solve a problem. When a diagram is given with a test item, use it as a tool. Get as much information from the drawing as possible. Keep in mind that diagrams are not always drawn to scale and can be misleading.

EXAMPLE 1

Multiple Choice What is the probability of flipping a coin and getting tails, and then rolling an even number on a number cube?

Ⓐ $\frac{1}{2}$ Ⓒ $\frac{1}{6}$
Ⓑ $\frac{1}{4}$ Ⓓ $\frac{1}{12}$

You can create a tree diagram to determine the sample space.

There are 12 possible outcomes but only 3 ways getting tails and an even number can occur. So the probability is $\frac{3}{12}$, or $\frac{1}{4}$, which is answer choice B.

EXAMPLE 2

Short Response Find the volume and surface area of the cylinder, and round your answers to the nearest tenth. Use 3.14 for π.

In the diagram, it appears that the radius is greater than the height. Remember that the scale of a diagram can be misleading. Rely on the information shown, and substitute the given values into each formula.

$V = \pi r^2 h$ $SA = 2\pi r^2 + 2\pi rh$
$V = \pi(6)^2(10)$ $SA = 2\pi(6)^2 + 2\pi(6)(10)$
$V = 360\pi$ $SA = 226.08 + 376.8$
$V \approx 1{,}130.4 \text{ in}^3$ $SA \approx 602.9 \text{ in}^2$

668 Chapter 11 Probability

If you are having trouble understanding a test item, draw a diagram to help you answer the question.

Read each test item, and answer the questions that follow.

Item A
Multiple Choice The volume of a box is 6,336 cm³. The width of the box is 16 cm, and the height is 18 cm. What is the length of the box?
Ⓐ 396 cm Ⓒ 220 cm
Ⓑ 22 cm Ⓓ 11 cm

1. What information about the box is given in the problem statement?
2. Sketch a diagram to help you answer the question. Label each side with the correct dimensions.
3. How does the diagram help you solve the problem?

Item B
Multiple Choice Janet spins two spinners at the same time. One spinner is divided into 3 equal sectors, labeled 1, 2, and 3. The second spinner is divided into 3 equal sectors, labeled A, B, and C. What is the probability that the spinners will land on 1 and A or 1 and C?
Ⓕ $\frac{1}{3}$ Ⓗ $\frac{1}{9}$
Ⓖ $\frac{2}{3}$ Ⓙ $\frac{2}{9}$

4. Make a tree diagram to deter[…] sample space. Then count the[…] getting 1 and either A or C […]
5. Explain which answer choi[…]
6. How does the tree diagra[…] solve the problem?

Item C
Short Response Which two vats hold the same amount of liquid? Explain.

The second page guides you through applications of the test-taking strategy.

Standardized Test Prep

Use the Standardized Test Prep to apply test-taking strategies.

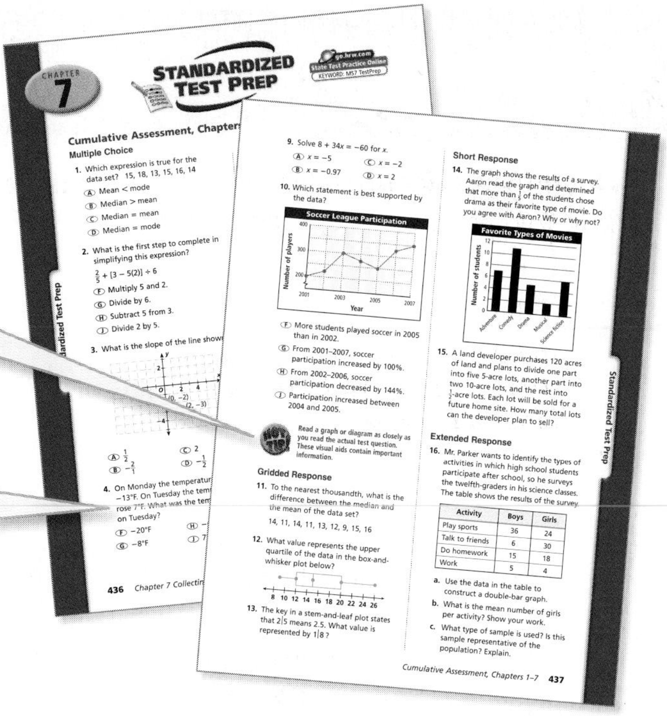

The Hot Tip provides test-taking tips to help you succeed on your tests.

These pages include practice with multiple choice, gridded response, short response, and extended response test items.

Countdown to Testing

Use the Countdown to Testing to practice for your state test every day.

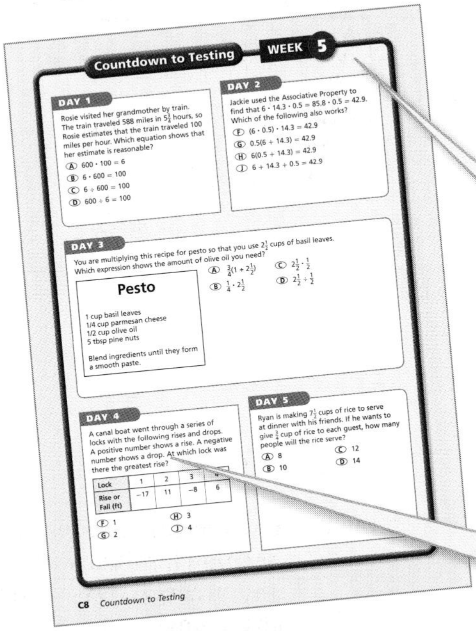

There are 24 pages of practice for your state test. Each page is designed to be used in a week so that all practice will be completed before your state test is given.

Each week's page has five practice test items, one for each day of the week.

Test-Taking Tips

- ☑ Get plenty of sleep the night before the test. A rested mind thinks more clearly and you won't feel like falling asleep while taking the test.
- ☑ Draw a figure when one is not provided with the problem. If a figure is given, write any details from the problem on the figure.
- ☑ Read each problem carefully. As you finish each problem, read it again to make sure your answer is reasonable.
- ☑ Review the formula sheet that will be supplied with the test. Make sure you know when to use each formula.
- ☑ First answer problems that you know how to solve. If you do not know how to solve a problem, skip it and come back to it when you have finished the others.
- ☑ Use other test-taking strategies that can be found throughout this book, such as working backward and eliminating answer choices.

COUNTDOWN TO TESTING

WEEK 1

DAY 1

What is the value of the expression $3(15 - 6) + (18 - 12)^2$?

Ⓐ 36
Ⓑ 45
Ⓒ 63
Ⓓ 75

DAY 2

Kyle buys 3 CDs for \$7 each and 2 DVDs for \$18 each. He pays \$3.42 in tax. Evaluate the expression $3 \cdot 7 + 2 \cdot 18 + 3.42$ to find how much money Kyle spent.

Ⓕ \$60.42
Ⓖ \$71.34
Ⓗ \$80.42
Ⓙ \$88.34

DAY 3

Derek made this sketch for a bulletin board in his room.

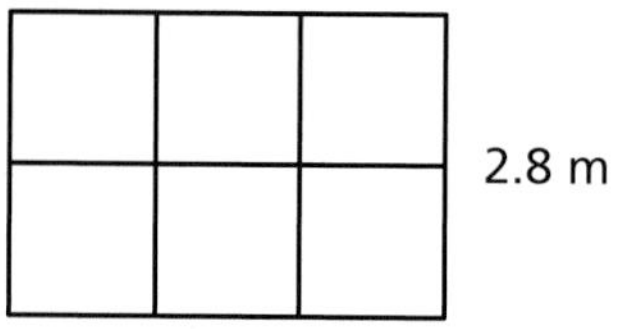

If Derek is using 8.4 square meters of wood to build the board, what is the best estimate of the board's length?

Ⓐ 1 meter
Ⓑ 2 meters
Ⓒ 3 meters
Ⓓ 4 meters

DAY 4

Estimate the volume of the square prism.

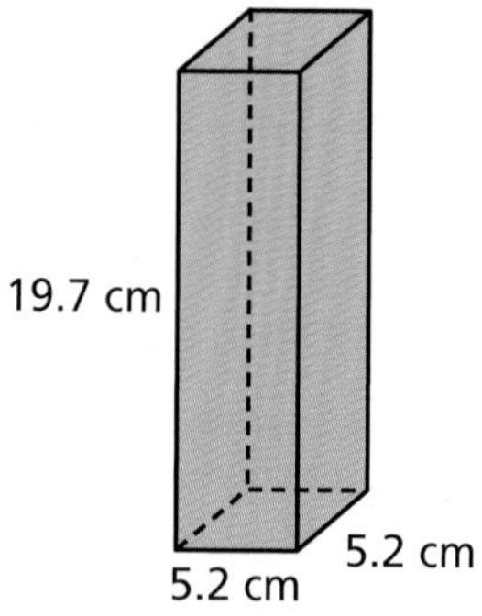

Ⓕ 300 cubic centimeters
Ⓖ 400 cubic centimeters
Ⓗ 500 cubic centimeters
Ⓙ 600 cubic centimeters

DAY 5

Willy is 25 inches tall. His brother Carlos is $2\frac{1}{4}$ times as tall. Which is the best estimate of Carlos's height?

Ⓐ 23 inches
Ⓑ 50 inches
Ⓒ 25 inches
Ⓓ 56 inches

Countdown to Testing WEEK 23

DAY 1

What is the rule for the pattern in the table below?

x	1	2	3	4
y	1	4	7	10

Ⓐ $y = 2x + 2$

Ⓑ $y = 3x - 2$

Ⓒ $y = \frac{x}{2} \cdot 5$

Ⓓ $y = 2x + 1$

DAY 2

Which pair contains similar figures?

Ⓕ 

Ⓖ 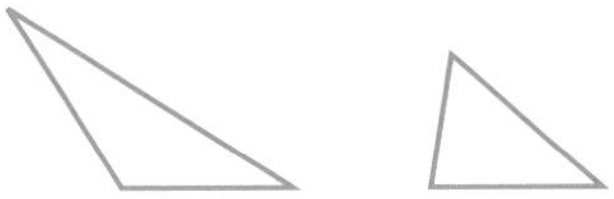

Ⓗ 

Ⓙ 

DAY 3

Which of the following describes this figure?

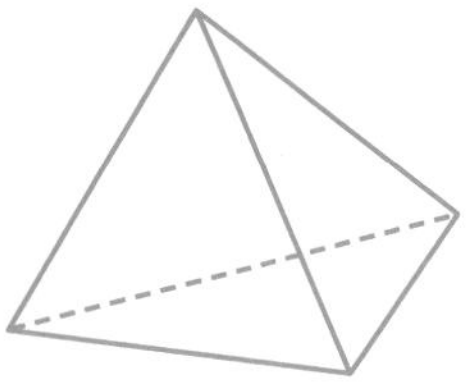

Ⓐ triangular prism

Ⓑ triangular pyramid

Ⓒ rectangular pyramid

Ⓓ cone

DAY 4

Danny needs to add the following lengths together so that he can buy enough wood for a project. What decimal number should Danny use to replace $12\frac{3}{8}$ m?

2.5 m, 6.75 m, 10.425 m, $12\frac{3}{8}$ m

Ⓕ 12.375 m

Ⓖ 12.75 m

Ⓗ 14.7 m

Ⓙ 15.7 m

DAY 5

Which of the following angle measures is supplementary to the measure of angle *ABC*?

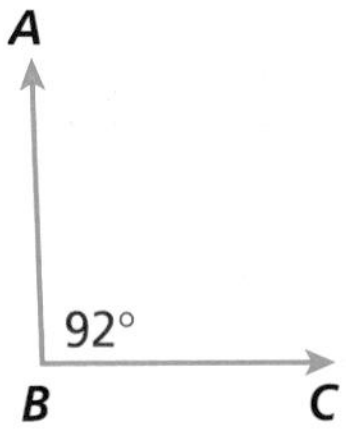

Ⓐ 3°

Ⓑ 28°

Ⓒ 88°

Ⓓ 90°

Countdown to Testing — WEEK 22

DAY 1

Which point is described by (−4, 3)?

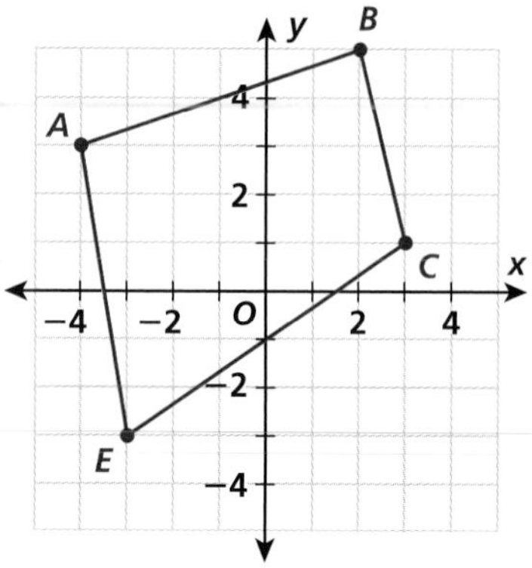

Ⓐ *D*

Ⓑ *A*

Ⓒ *B*

Ⓓ *C*

DAY 2

William received the following blueprint for a building. What is the area of this building?

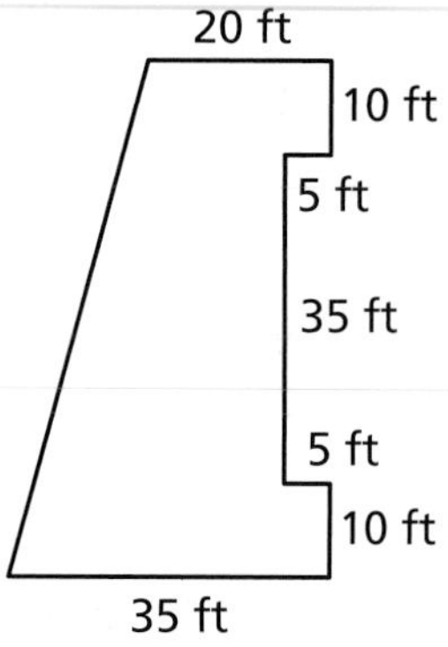

Ⓕ 1,258.5 square feet

Ⓖ 1,337.5 square feet

Ⓗ 1,425.5 square feet

Ⓙ 1,512.5 square feet

DAY 3

Which of the following is an isosceles triangle that is not equilateral?

Ⓐ 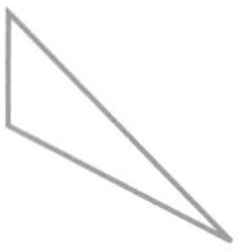

Ⓑ 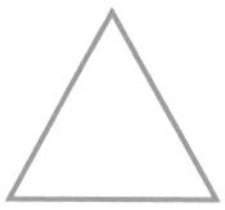

Ⓒ 

Ⓓ 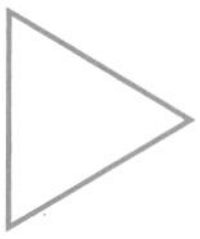

DAY 4

Kenny is building a compost bin. What is the best estimate of the volume of the bin?

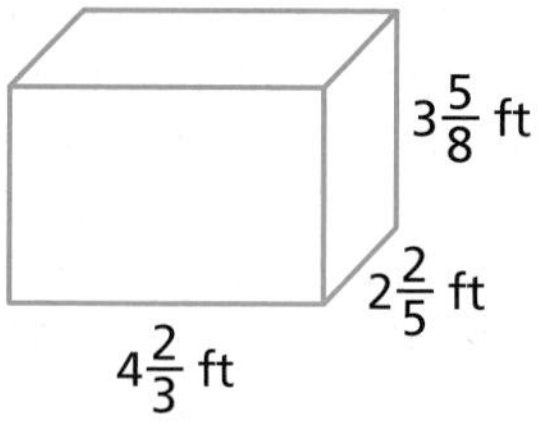

Ⓕ 11 cubic feet

Ⓖ 24 cubic feet

Ⓗ 40 cubic feet

Ⓙ 60 cubic feet

DAY 5

What is the value of this expression?

$(12 \div 3)^2 + 50 \div 2.5 - 10$

Ⓐ 16

Ⓑ 22.7

Ⓒ 26

Ⓓ 46

Countdown to Testing WEEK 21

DAY 1

If figure *ABCDE* is reflected across the *x*-axis, what will the new coordinates of *E* be?

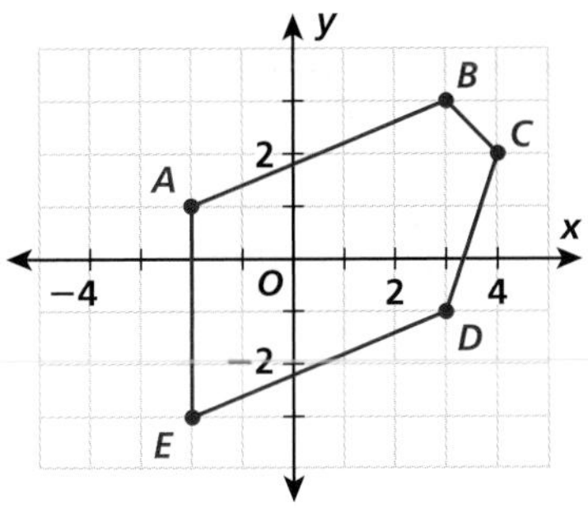

Ⓐ (−2, 3)
Ⓑ (2, 3)
Ⓒ (−3, 2)
Ⓓ (2, −3)

DAY 2

Which of the following figures is a parallelogram?

Ⓕ 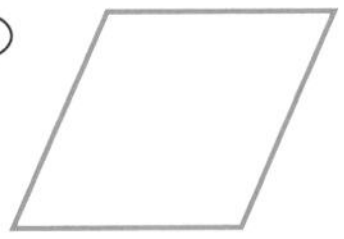
Ⓗ 
Ⓖ 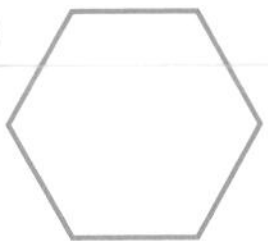
Ⓙ 

DAY 3

Which of the following best describes the angles below?

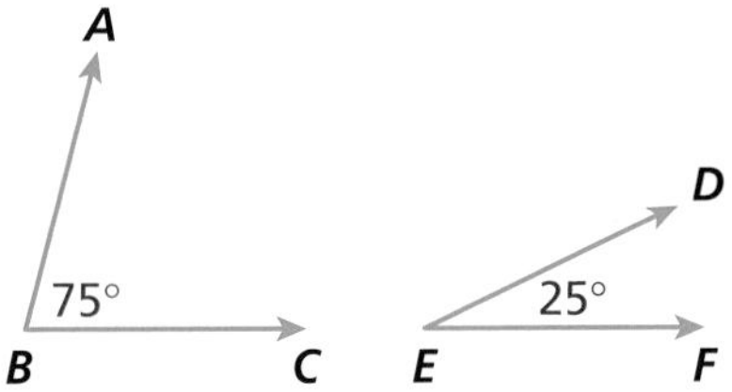

Ⓐ They are congruent.
Ⓑ They are supplementary.
Ⓒ They are complimentary.
Ⓓ None of the above.

DAY 4

What is the price of the most expensive TV?

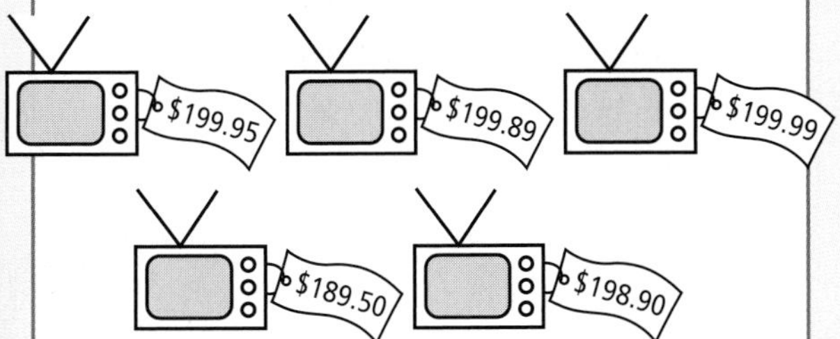

Ⓕ $199.89
Ⓖ $199.99
Ⓗ $189.50
Ⓙ $198.90

DAY 5

Carrie is designing a mosaic wall for her school's library. The wall measures 4 meters by 8 meters. The tiles she is using are 10 centimeters by 10 centimeters. If the tiles come 600 to a package, how many packages will Carrie need to cover the wall?

Ⓐ 4
Ⓑ 5
Ⓒ 6
Ⓓ 7

DAY 1

If figure *FGHJ* is reflected across the *x*-axis, what will the new coordinates of *J* be?

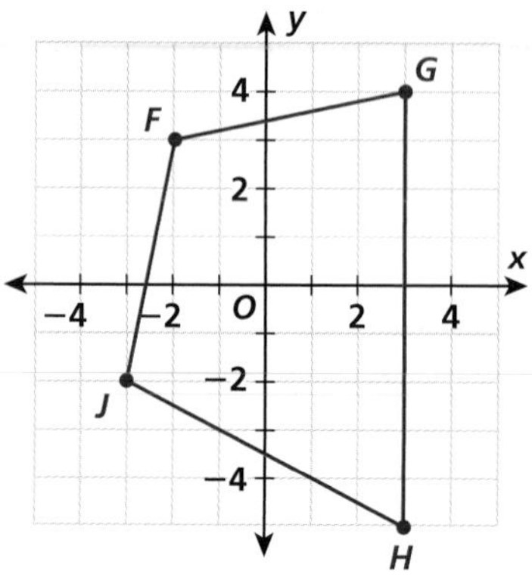

Ⓐ (−3, 2) Ⓒ (−3, −2)

Ⓑ (3, −2) Ⓓ (2, −3)

DAY 2

Each of the four triangles has the same area. If one bag of stones will cover an area of 25 square feet, how many bags will it take to cover the design?

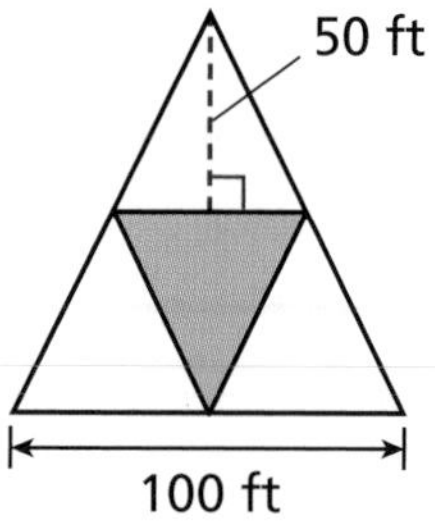

Ⓕ 25 Ⓗ 100

Ⓖ 75 Ⓙ 150

DAY 3

If ∠*ABC* and ∠*DEF* are supplementary and the measure of ∠*ABC* is 65°, what is the measure of ∠*DEF*?

Ⓐ 25° Ⓒ 105°

Ⓑ 35° Ⓓ 115°

DAY 4

Which of the following figures does not belong in the group if the triangles are classified by angles?

Ⓕ 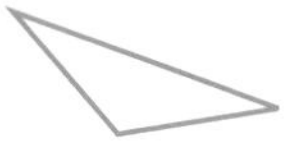 Ⓗ 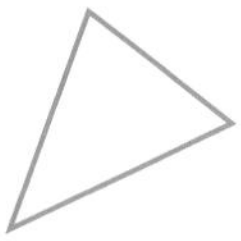

Ⓖ  Ⓙ 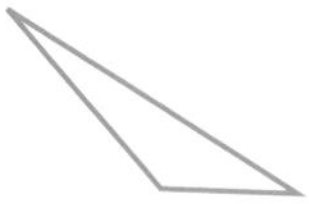

DAY 5

Four shovels of sand are mixed with 5 shovels of gravel to make cement. About how many shovels of gravel are needed for 45 shovels of sand?

Ⓐ 20 Ⓒ 45

Ⓑ 55 Ⓓ 75

Countdown to Testing WEEK 19

DAY 1

Henry is designing the lobby of an office building. He wants a tile pattern that will tessellate. Which tile can he use?

Ⓐ 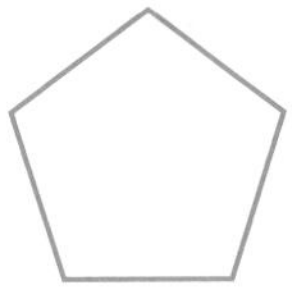

Ⓒ 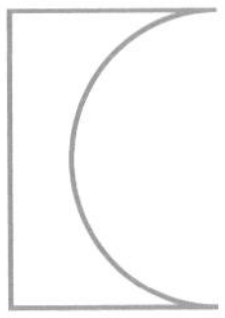

Ⓑ 

Ⓓ 

DAY 2

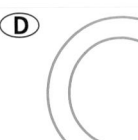

Ellis listed the following shapes as parallelograms: square, rectangle, trapezoid, and rhombus. He made one mistake. Which shape is not a parallelogram?

Ⓕ square Ⓗ trapezoid

Ⓖ rectangle Ⓙ rhombus

DAY 3

If figure *ABCD* is reflected across the *y*-axis, what will the new coordinates of *D* be?

Ⓐ (3, 1) Ⓒ (−3, −1)

Ⓑ (2, 2) Ⓓ (−3, 1)

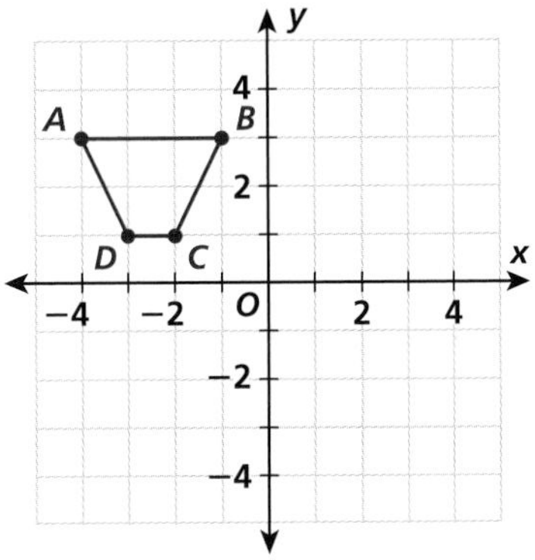

DAY 4

Which of the following angle measures is complementary to the measure of angle *ABC*?

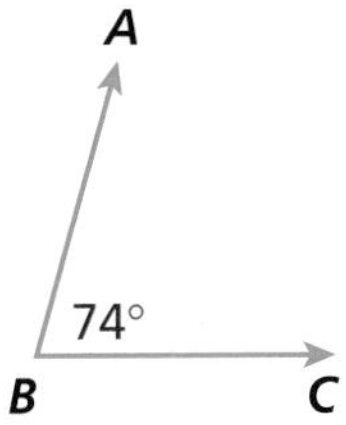

Ⓕ 6° Ⓗ 36°

Ⓖ 16° Ⓙ 106°

DAY 5

What is the mean of this set of data?

90, 108, 67, 84, 90, 82, 73, 90

Ⓐ 41 Ⓒ 87

Ⓑ 85.5 Ⓓ 90

DAY 1

What type of triangle is formed when you connect the three points?

Ⓐ equilateral
Ⓑ isosceles
Ⓒ right
Ⓓ obtuse

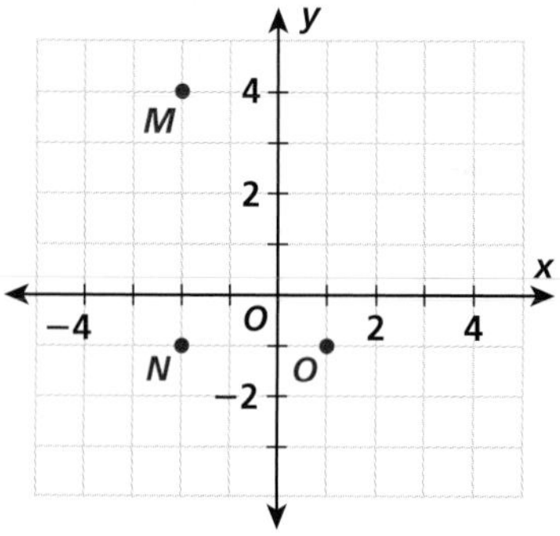

DAY 2

Alex kept track of the number of telemarketing calls he received each month for 6 months.

14, 10, 17, 12, 10, 15

Which of the following would not change if Alex decided to add the data value 11 for a seventh month?

Ⓕ median
Ⓖ range
Ⓗ mode
Ⓙ mean

DAY 3

Which two angles are supplementary?

Ⓐ
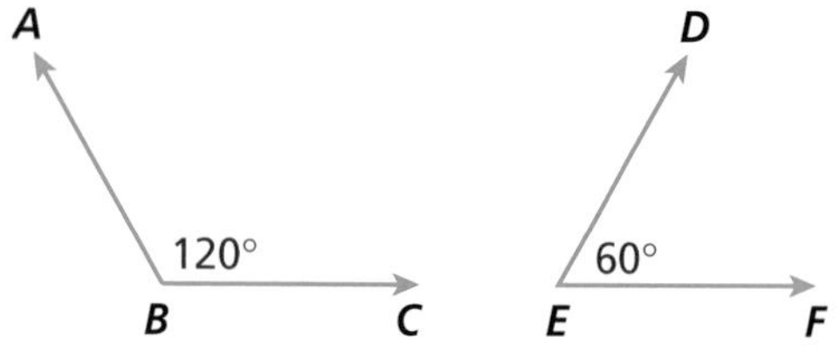

Ⓒ
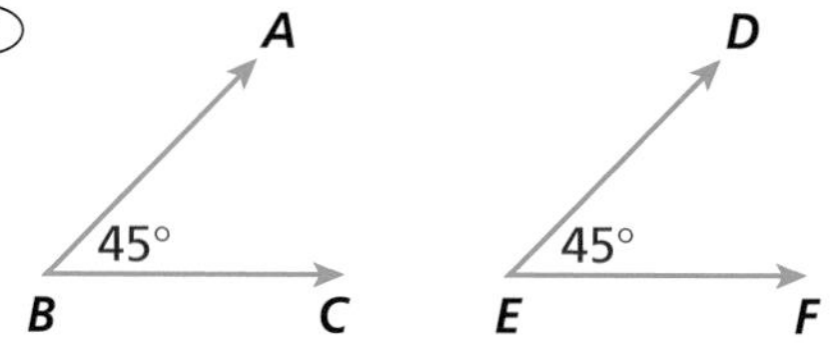

Ⓑ
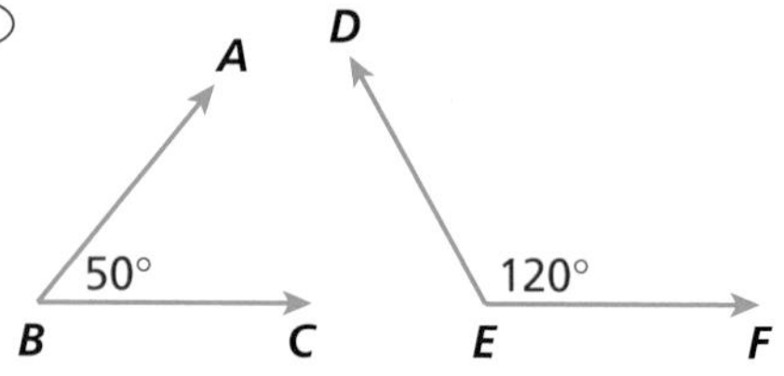

Ⓓ
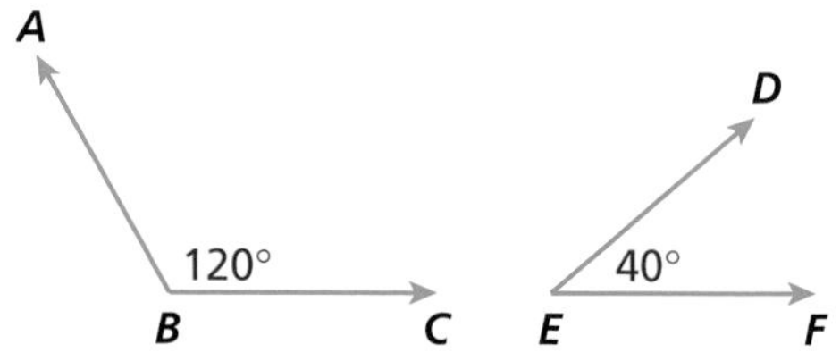

DAY 4

The line plot shows the daily low temperatures during one week. What is the mean low temperature for the entire week?

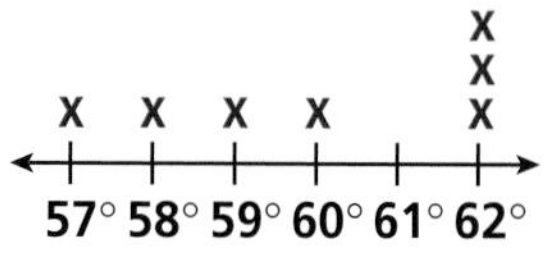

Ⓕ 60°F
Ⓖ 61°F
Ⓗ 62°F
Ⓙ 63°F

DAY 5

If a car is traveling at a speed of 48 miles per hour, how far can it travel in $1\frac{7}{8}$ hours?

Ⓐ 50 miles
Ⓑ 80 miles
Ⓒ 90 miles
Ⓓ 100 miles

Countdown to Testing WEEK 17

DAY 1

Which of the following is the greatest number for this data set?

32, 35, 19, 26, 40, 32, 18, 32, 16, 18

(A) median (C) mean

(B) mode (D) range

DAY 2

Naomi surveyed a group of people about their favorite movie genre: comedy, drama, action, musical, or science-fiction. Which of the following would be the best way for Naomi to display her results?

(F) line graph

(G) line plot

(H) circle graph

(J) scatter plot

DAY 3

Which two angles are complementary?

(A)

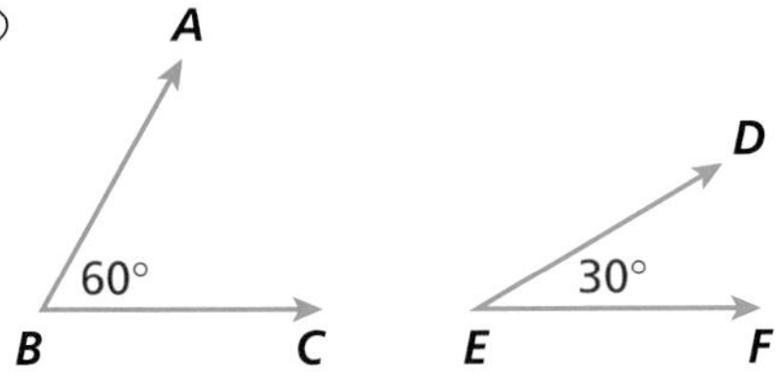

(C)

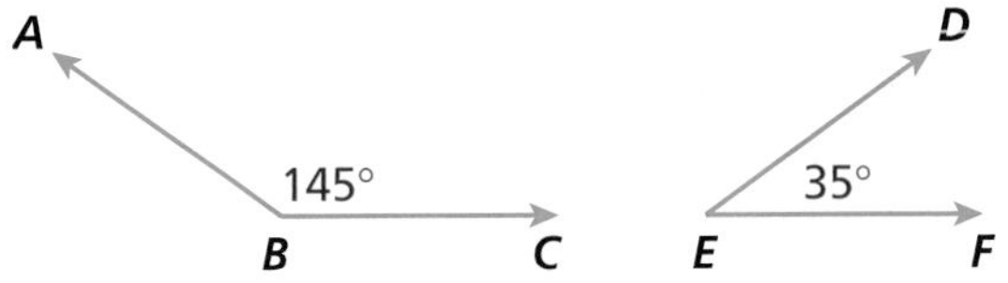

(B)

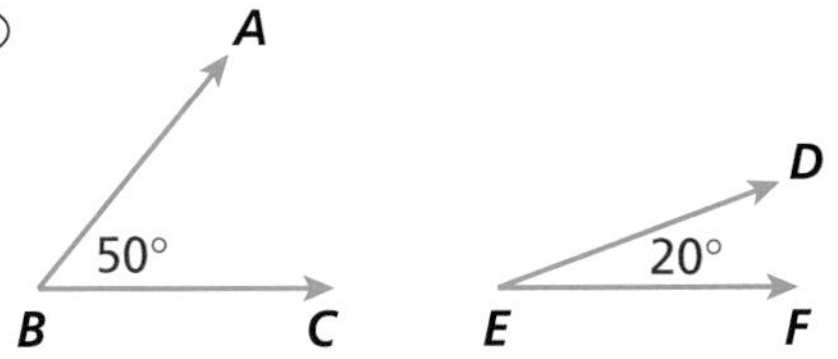

(D)

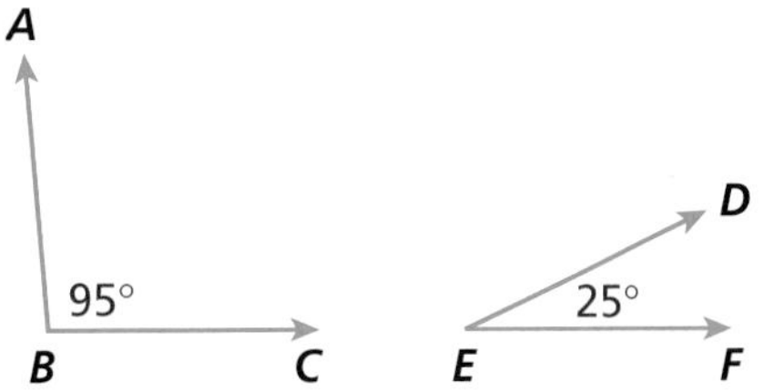

DAY 4

Jason recorded the number of cardinals he saw each month during his nature hikes. What is the mean number of cardinals Jason saw? Round your answer to the nearest whole number.

Stems	Leaves
0	6 6 8 9
1	2 4 5 8 8 8 9
2	1

(F) 6 (H) 15

(G) 14 (J) 18

DAY 5

The median of 4 numbers is 48. If three of the numbers are 42, 45, and 52, what is the other number?

(A) 43 (C) 51

(B) 47 (D) 55

Countdown to Testing WEEK 16

DAY 1

You are conducting a survey to see if the amount of hours of sleep that people need each night is related to their age. What type of diagram would you use to display some of the data you found?

Ⓐ line plot

Ⓑ circle graph

Ⓒ stem-and-leaf plot

Ⓓ scatter plot

DAY 2

What kind of data is most likely represented by this plot?

Stems	Leaves
7	2 2 4 4 5 7
8	1 3 5 5 7 8 8 8 9
9	0 2

Ⓕ cost of a movie ticket at local theaters

Ⓖ average height (in.) of students in a class

Ⓗ average daily temperatures at the beach

Ⓙ ages of students in a class

DAY 3

What is the measure 33 for this set of data?

33, 33, 66, 33

Ⓐ mode and mean

Ⓑ median and mean

Ⓒ mean and range

Ⓓ median and mode

DAY 4

What is the mean weight of these packages?

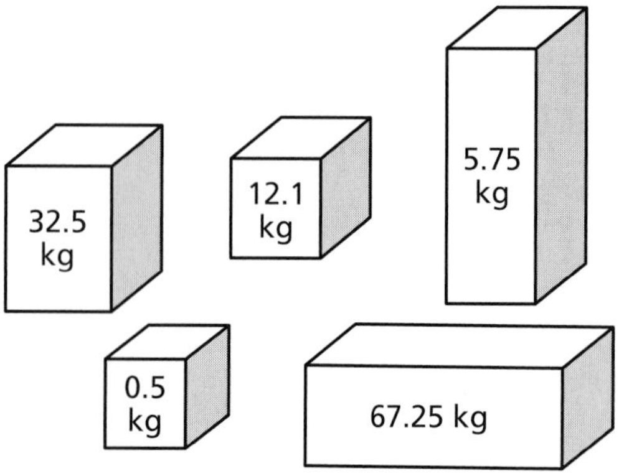

Ⓕ 21 kilograms

Ⓖ 23.62 kilograms

Ⓗ 25.13 kilograms

Ⓙ 118.10 kilograms

DAY 5

You buy a book for \$24.75 and pay 6.25% sales tax. What is the total cost of the book?

Ⓐ \$1.55

Ⓑ \$26.30

Ⓒ \$32.75

Ⓓ \$40.00

Countdown to Testing WEEK 15

DAY 1

What is the median of this data set?

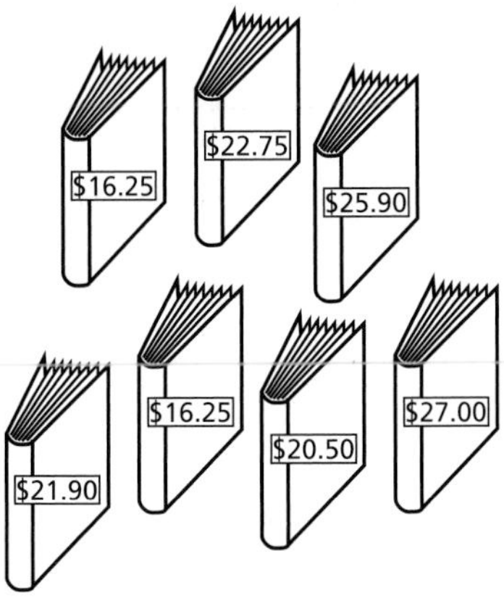

Ⓐ $10.75
Ⓑ $16.25
Ⓒ $21.90
Ⓓ $27.00

DAY 2

Louis received the following scores on his English quizzes this semester: 95, 95, 80, 70, 60. Which description of this data set would make Louis' results look best?

Ⓕ the mean of his scores
Ⓖ the median of his scores
Ⓗ the mode of his scores
Ⓙ the range of his scores

DAY 3

Nora wants to display data about the amount of time it took each runner to complete a race. What type of graph should she use?

Ⓐ bar graph
Ⓑ line graph
Ⓒ histogram
Ⓓ frequency table

DAY 4

The price of a meal came to $11.82 without tax or tip. Which is the best estimate of the cost of the meal if the tip is 15% and the tax is 8%? (Figure the tax and the tip on the base price of the meal.)

Ⓕ $10
Ⓖ $12
Ⓗ $15
Ⓙ $20

DAY 5

What is the mean of this set of data?

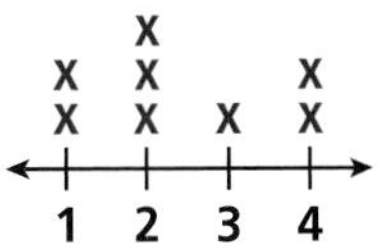

Ⓐ 1
Ⓑ 2
Ⓒ 3
Ⓓ 4

Countdown to Testing WEEK 14

DAY 1

Which point is described by the ordered pair (2, −2)?

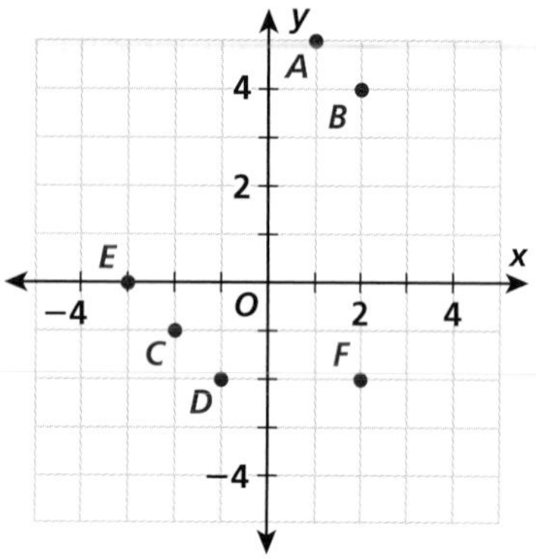

Ⓐ *B*
Ⓑ *D*
Ⓒ *E*
Ⓓ *F*

DAY 2

Which of the following describes the relationship between the numbers in this sequence?

$$\frac{1}{2}, \frac{1}{4}, \frac{1}{8}, \frac{1}{16}, \ldots$$

Ⓕ Each number is twice the number before it.
Ⓖ Each number is two more than the number before it.
Ⓗ Each number is one-half the number before it.
Ⓙ Each number is two less than the number before it.

DAY 3

Two similar figures

Ⓐ have the same size.
Ⓑ have the same shape.
Ⓒ have the same size and shape.
Ⓓ are congruent.

DAY 4

April is standing next to a tree. The length of April's shadow is 4 feet, and the length of the tree's shadow is 32 feet. If April is 5 feet tall, how tall is the tree?

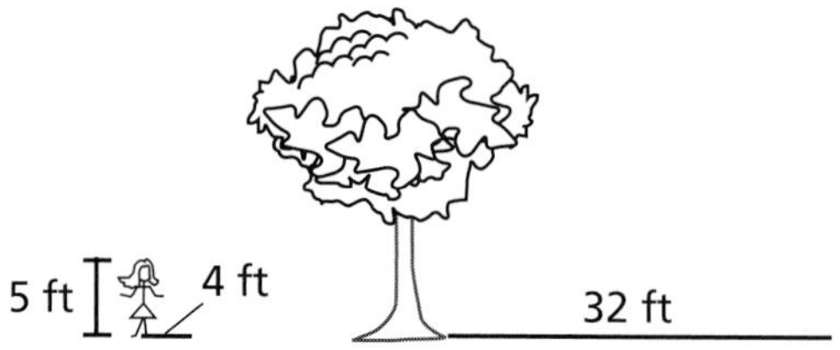

Ⓕ 18 feet
Ⓖ 24 feet
Ⓗ 32 feet
Ⓙ 40 feet

DAY 5

Susan buys leather purses from the manufacturer for $11.90 each and sells them to the public at 425% the price she paid. About how much do Susan's customers pay for a purse?

Ⓐ $15.50
Ⓑ $42.00
Ⓒ $51.00
Ⓓ $437.00

Countdown to Testing WEEK 13

DAY 1

A model car and a real car have the given dimensions. What is the length of the real car if the scale factor is 1:30?

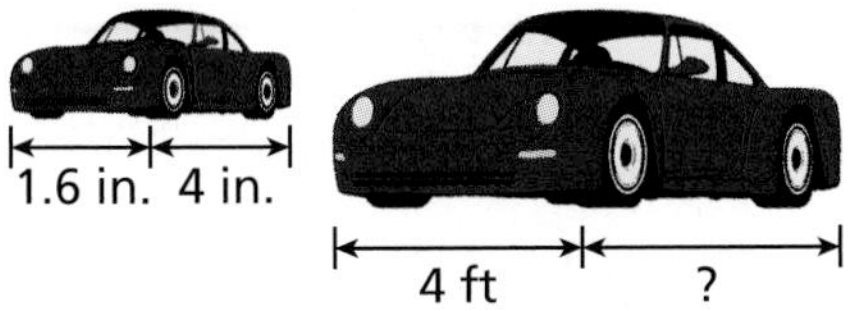

Ⓐ 8 feet
Ⓑ 9 feet
Ⓒ 10 feet
Ⓓ 12 feet

DAY 2

Which pair of triangles are similar?

Ⓕ
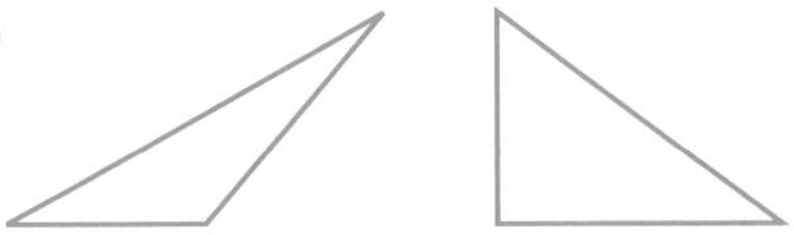

Ⓖ
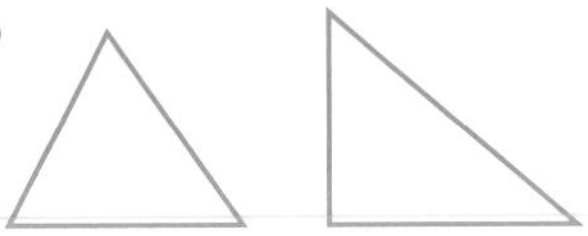

Ⓗ
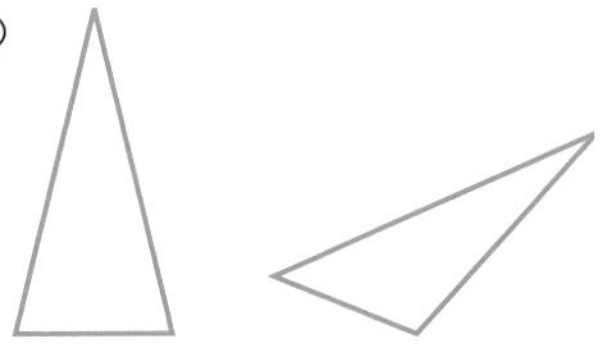

Ⓙ
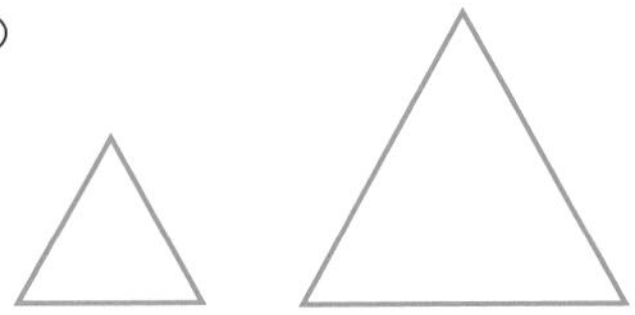

DAY 3

Which point is described by the ordered pair (−1, −1)?

Ⓐ *B*
Ⓑ *D*
Ⓒ *E*
Ⓓ *F*

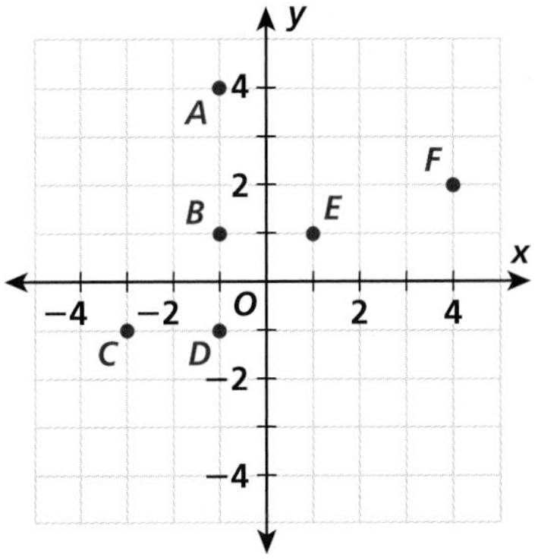

DAY 4

Randy wants to buy an MP3 player for $98.99, and it is on sale for 37% off. About how much money will Randy pay for the MP3 player before tax?

Ⓕ $40
Ⓖ $60
Ⓗ $70
Ⓙ $80

DAY 5

Julie goes mountain biking every Saturday. Last week, she rode 36 kilometers in 3 hours. What was her average rate of speed?

Ⓐ 8 kilometers per hour
Ⓑ 9 kilometers per hour
Ⓒ 12 kilometers per hour
Ⓓ 18 kilometers per hour

DAY 1

Which number best completes the pattern?

2, 5, 11, ___, 47, 95

Ⓐ 19
Ⓑ 22
Ⓒ 23
Ⓓ 31

DAY 2

Which of the following describes the relationship between the numbers in this sequence?

243, 81, 27, 9, …

Ⓕ A number is three more than the preceding number.
Ⓖ A number is three less than the preceding number.
Ⓗ A number is one-third of the preceding number.
Ⓙ A number is three times more than the preceding number.

DAY 3

Which two of the figures below are similar?

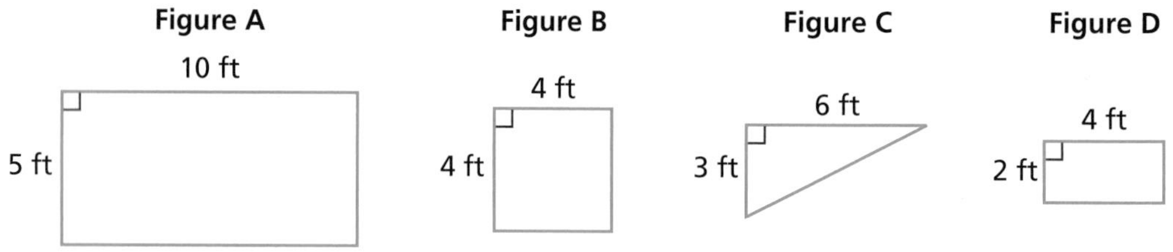

Ⓐ Figures A and D
Ⓑ Figures A and B
Ⓒ Figures B and D
Ⓓ Figures B and C

DAY 4

A discount store is selling a case of 24 bottles of water for $12.99. What is the unit price of a bottle of water to the nearest cent?

Ⓕ $0.27
Ⓖ $0.54
Ⓗ $1.85
Ⓙ $11.01

DAY 5

The shadow of a 4-foot-tall mailbox is 2 feet long. If the shadow of a tree is 16 feet long, what is the height of the tree?

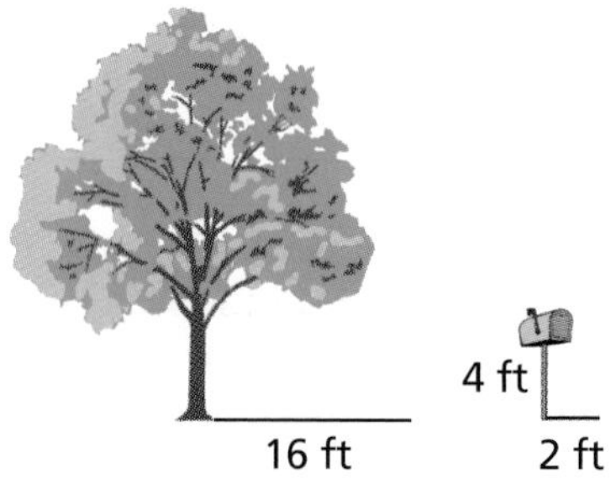

Ⓐ 18 feet
Ⓑ 24 feet
Ⓒ 32 feet
Ⓓ 64 feet

DAY 1

Which of the following describes the relationship between the numbers in this sequence?

145, 115, 85, 55, ...

Ⓐ A number is 30 less than the preceding number.

Ⓑ A number is half the preceding number.

Ⓒ A number is 30 more than the preceding number.

Ⓓ A number is 15 less than the preceding number.

DAY 2

Using the following pattern, which figure comes next?

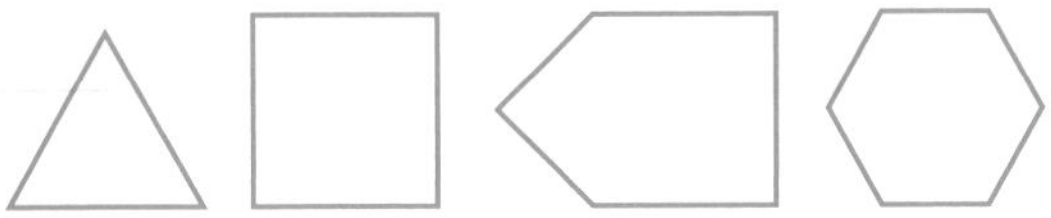

Ⓕ 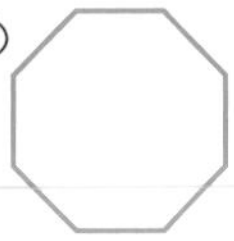

Ⓗ 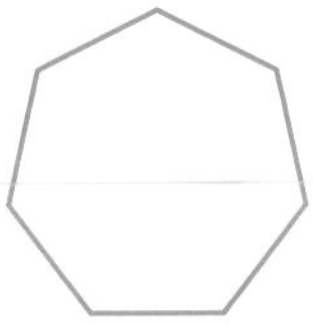

Ⓖ 

Ⓙ  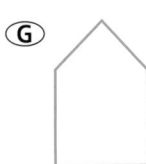

DAY 3

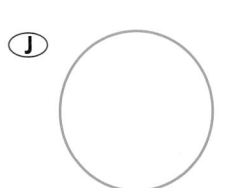

Which point is described by the ordered pair (−3, 2)?

Ⓐ *B*

Ⓑ *C*

Ⓒ *D*

Ⓓ *E*

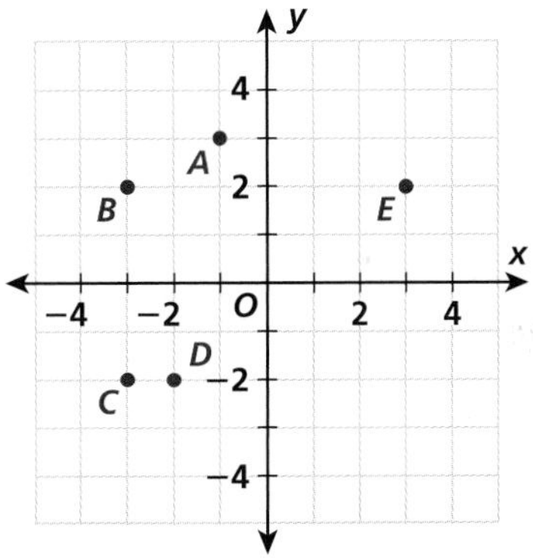

DAY 4

Dante recorded the following information about a seedling's growth for science class. How many inches did the seedling grow in three weeks?

Week	1	2	3
Inches Grown	$\frac{7}{8}$	$\frac{5}{6}$	$\frac{7}{24}$

Ⓕ $1\frac{1}{6}$ inches

Ⓖ $1\frac{17}{24}$ inches

Ⓗ 2 inches

Ⓙ 48 inches

DAY 5

Olivia read 125 pages of her medical textbook in 4 hours. What is her average rate of reading in pages per hour?

Ⓐ 1.25 pages per hour

Ⓑ 13 pages per hour

Ⓒ 31.25 pages per hour

Ⓓ 62.5 pages per hour

Countdown to Testing WEEK 10

DAY 1

Which point is described by the ordered pair (–4, 2)?

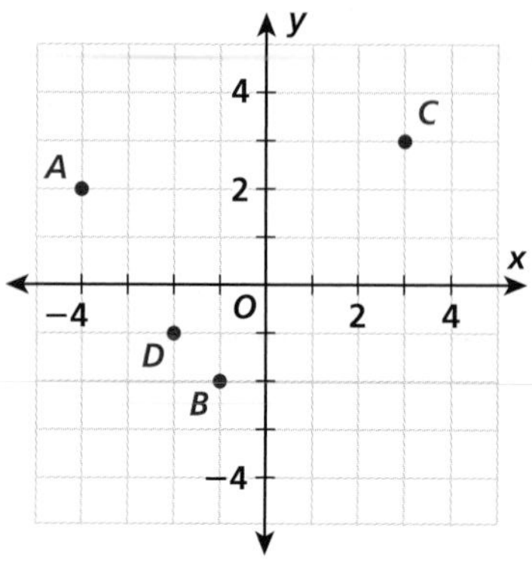

Ⓐ *A*　　Ⓒ *C*

Ⓑ *B*　　Ⓓ *D*

DAY 2

What is the pattern in the following table?

Input *x*	5	10	15	20
Output *y*	25	50	75	100

Ⓕ $y = x^2$　　Ⓗ $y = 5x$

Ⓖ $y = 3x$　　Ⓙ $y = 2x$

DAY 3

Which of the following describes the relationship between the numbers in this sequence?

2, 8, 32, 128, ...

Ⓐ A number is four more than the number preceding it.

Ⓑ A number is four times greater than the preceding number.

Ⓒ A number is one-fourth the preceding number.

Ⓓ A number is the square of the preceding number.

DAY 4

Mrs. Reese is taking a trip to visit her sister. If she drives 162 miles in 3 hours, what is her average rate of speed?

Ⓕ 3 miles per hour

Ⓖ 54 miles per hour

Ⓗ 162 miles per hour

Ⓙ 486 miles per hour

DAY 5

Sandy and his father built a tree house for Sandy's sister. How tall is the tree?

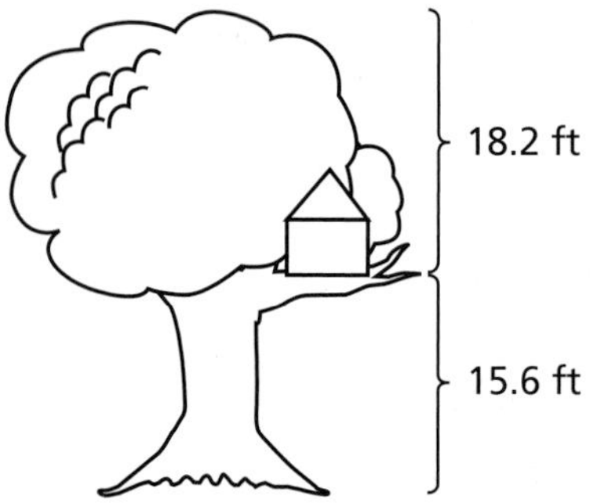

Ⓐ 2.6 feet　　Ⓒ 33.8 feet

Ⓑ 23.8 feet　　Ⓓ 34.8 feet

Countdown to Testing WEEK 9

DAY 1

What is the value of this expression?

$3 + 4 \cdot (2^2 + 21 \div 3)$

Ⓐ 26 Ⓒ 47

Ⓑ 36 Ⓓ 77

DAY 2

Diane is buying 4 DVDs for \$15.40 each. She calculates that she will spend \$61.60. Which of the following justifies Diane's solution?

Ⓕ $4(15 + 0.40) = 60 + 1.60 = 61.60$

Ⓖ $61.60 \div 0.4 = 15.4$

Ⓗ $4 \cdot 15 + 2 - 0.40 = 62 - 0.40 = 61.60$

Ⓙ $4(15.40 + 15.40 + 15.40 + 15.40) = 61.60$

DAY 3

Marc needs $\frac{5}{8}$ pound of blueberries to make a batch of muffins and another $\frac{1}{3}$ pound to make blueberry pancakes. How many pounds of blueberries does Marc need?

Ⓐ $\frac{2}{9}$ pound Ⓒ $\frac{7}{12}$ pound

Ⓑ $\frac{10}{13}$ pound Ⓓ $\frac{23}{24}$ pound

DAY 4

In the morning, Steve drives to his job at the bookstore. After work, he drives to the college where he takes classes. Then he drives back home. Which is the best estimate of the distance Steve travels each day?

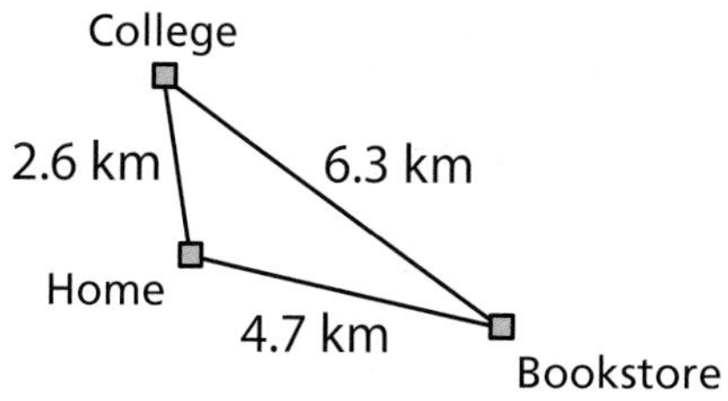

Ⓕ 8 kilometers

Ⓖ 10 kilometers

Ⓗ 12 kilometers

Ⓙ 14 kilometers

DAY 5

Brian is building a small reflecting pool. Which is the best estimate of the amount of water the pool will hold?

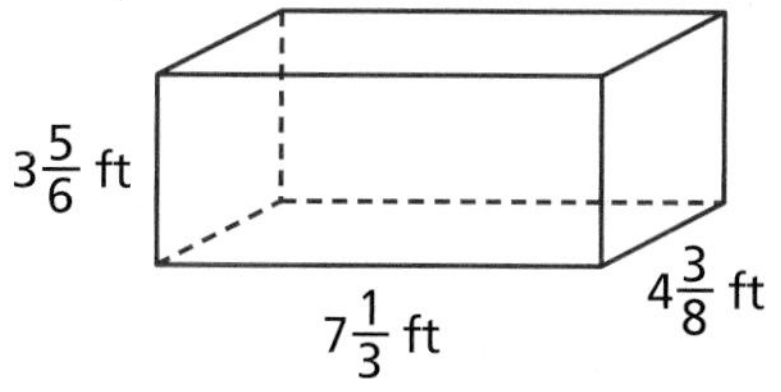

Ⓐ 84 cubic feet

Ⓑ 112 cubic feet

Ⓒ 140 cubic feet

Ⓓ 160 cubic feet

Countdown to Testing WEEK 8

DAY 1

The table shows the number of students in four different classes at Park Street Middle School who take the bus to school. Which class has the greatest fraction of students who take the bus to school?

Class	A	B	C	D
Students Who Take Bus	$\frac{15}{20}$	$\frac{20}{25}$	$\frac{12}{18}$	$\frac{12}{24}$

(A) Class A
(B) Class B
(C) Class C
(D) Class D

DAY 2

Tim and Sue are setting up a tent at a campground. Tim estimates that the tent will cover an area of 190 square feet, while Sue estimates the area will be 220 square feet. Whose estimate is better and why?

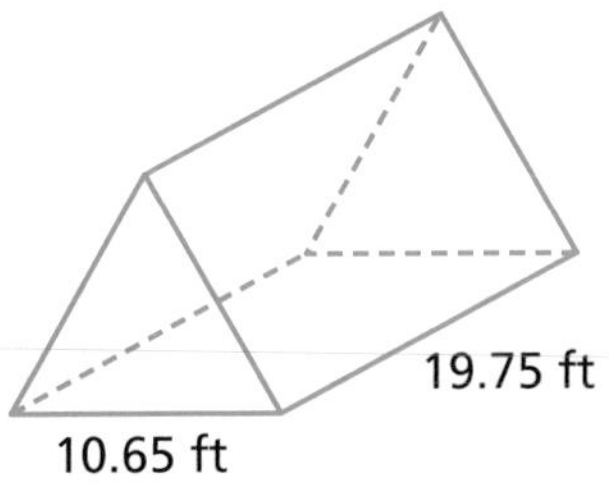

(F) Tim's; 19 · 10 = 190
(G) Sue's; 20 · 11 = 220
(H) Tim's; 10 ÷ 19 = 190
(J) Sue's; 2(11 + 20) = 220

DAY 3

Mrs. Robbins is knitting a scarf for her niece. She knitted $1\frac{7}{8}$ feet yesterday and $1\frac{2}{3}$ feet today. How many feet did Mrs. Robbins knit in both days?

(A) $\frac{5}{24}$ foot
(B) $1\frac{3}{4}$ feet
(C) $2\frac{9}{11}$ feet
(D) $3\frac{13}{24}$ feet

DAY 4

Which decimal completes this equivalency?

$$\frac{3}{4} = 75\% = ?$$

(F) 0.34
(G) 0.43
(H) 0.75
(J) 1.75

DAY 5

Mr. Reyes wants to fence in the area behind his house. How many meters of fencing does he need to buy?

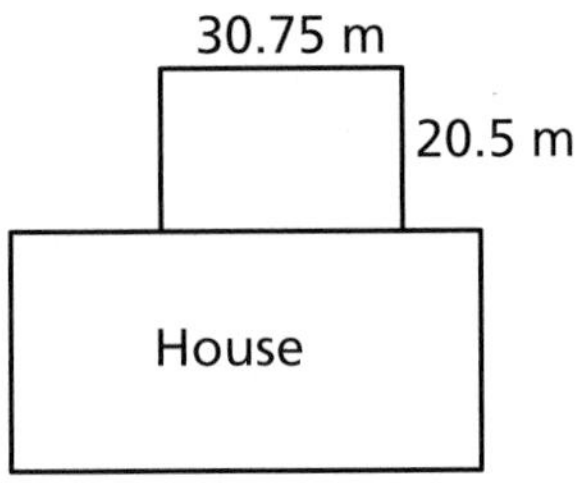

(A) 51.25 meters
(B) 71.75 meters
(C) 102.5 meters
(D) 630.38 meters

Countdown to Testing WEEK 7

DAY 1

Which of the following is the least number?

0.305 0.02 0.10 0.081

Ⓐ 0.305
Ⓑ 0.081
Ⓒ 0.10
Ⓓ 0.02

DAY 2

If it takes 5 buses to carry 225 passengers, how many passengers will 3 buses carry?

Ⓕ 45
Ⓖ 135
Ⓗ 170
Ⓙ 222

DAY 3

Sandra read a survey that found that 82.5% of people polled believed that volunteering one's time was the best way to serve one's community. What is this percent written as a fraction?

Ⓐ $82\frac{5}{10}$
Ⓑ $8\frac{25}{100}$
Ⓒ $\frac{33}{40}$
Ⓓ $8\frac{1}{4}$

DAY 4

Peter and a friend share a pizza. Peter eats 2 slices and his friend eats 3 slices. What fraction represents the amount of pizza both boys ate?

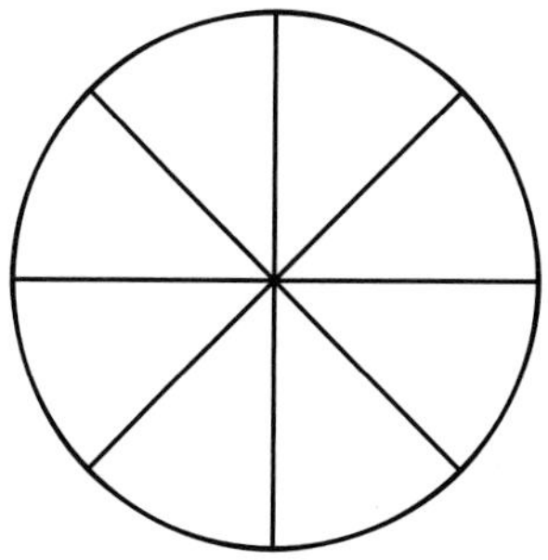

Ⓕ $\frac{1}{8}$
Ⓖ $\frac{1}{4}$
Ⓗ $\frac{3}{8}$
Ⓙ $\frac{5}{8}$

DAY 5

What is the best estimate of the volume of this figure?

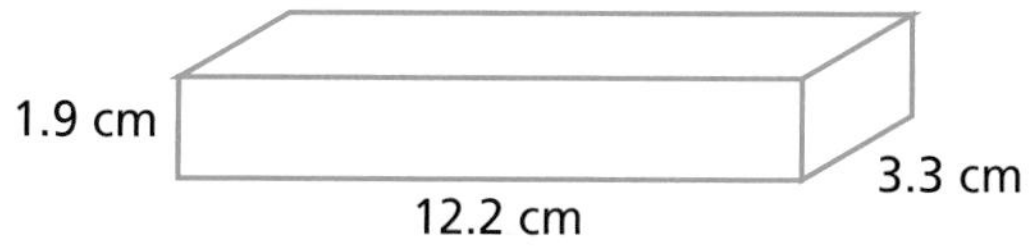

Ⓐ 24 cubic centimeters
Ⓑ 36 cubic centimeters
Ⓒ 72 cubic centimeters
Ⓓ 80 cubic centimeters

Countdown to Testing WEEK 6

DAY 1

Jeff runs 8.077 miles in an hour. Tina runs 8.102 miles in an hour. Jade runs 8.05 miles in an hour. Andy runs 8.032 miles in an hour. If they all started a race at the same time, who will finish first?

Ⓐ Tina Ⓒ Jade
Ⓑ Andy Ⓓ Jeff

DAY 2

Kevin simplified the problem $\frac{3}{4} + 3 - 1\frac{1}{2}$ on the chalkboard. Where was his first mistake?

Step 1: $\frac{3}{4} + 3\left(\frac{4}{4}\right) - \frac{3}{2}$

Step 2: $\frac{3}{4} + 3\left(\frac{4}{4}\right) - \frac{3}{2}\left(\frac{2}{2}\right)$

Step 3: $\frac{3}{4} + \frac{12}{4} - \frac{6}{4}$

Step 4: $\frac{15}{4} - \frac{6}{4}$

Step 5: $\frac{9}{4}$, which is $1\frac{3}{4}$

Ⓕ Step 2 Ⓗ Step 4
Ⓖ Step 3 Ⓙ Step 5

DAY 3

Jon has 4 shelves with 52 CDs on each shelf. He multiplies 50 by 4 and 2 by 4 to find that he has 208 CDs in all. Which property justifies Jon's solution?

Ⓐ Associative Ⓒ Distributive
Ⓑ Commutative Ⓓ Identity

DAY 4

Nate is buying a shirt that is on sale, but part of the tag is ripped off. What is the amount off written as a percent?

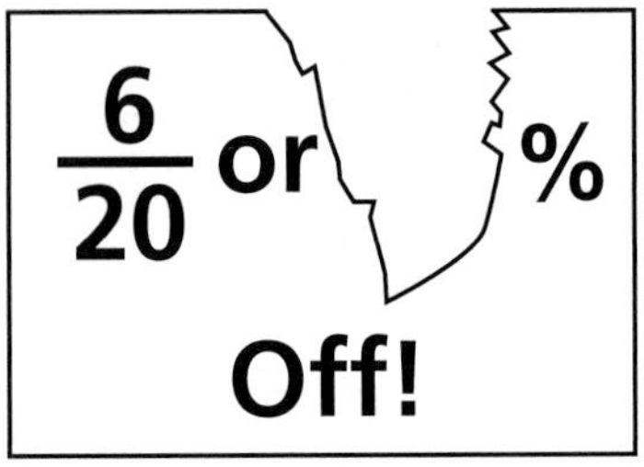

Ⓕ 0.3% Ⓗ 13%
Ⓖ 3% Ⓙ 30%

DAY 5

Tom is creating a model of a building. What is the height of the real building?

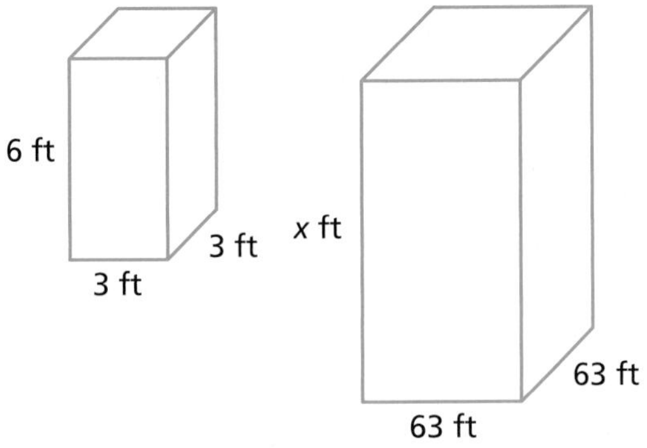

Ⓐ 54 feet Ⓒ 126 feet
Ⓑ 63 feet Ⓓ 3,969 feet

Countdown to Testing WEEK 5

DAY 1

Rosie visited her grandmother by train. The train traveled 588 miles in $5\frac{3}{4}$ hours, so Rosie estimates that the train traveled 100 miles per hour. Which equation shows that her estimate is reasonable?

Ⓐ $600 \cdot 100 = 6$

Ⓑ $6 \cdot 600 = 100$

Ⓒ $6 \div 600 = 100$

Ⓓ $600 \div 6 = 100$

DAY 2

Jackie used the Associative Property to find that $6 \cdot 14.3 \cdot 0.5 = 85.8 \cdot 0.5 = 42.9$. Which of the following also works?

Ⓕ $(6 \cdot 0.5) \cdot 14.3 = 42.9$

Ⓖ $0.5(6 + 14.3) = 42.9$

Ⓗ $6(0.5 + 14.3) = 42.9$

Ⓙ $6 + 14.3 + 0.5 = 42.9$

DAY 3

You are multiplying this recipe for pesto so that you use $2\frac{1}{2}$ cups of basil leaves. Which expression shows the amount of olive oil you need?

Pesto

1 cup basil leaves
1/4 cup parmesan cheese
1/2 cup olive oil
5 tbsp pine nuts

Blend ingredients until they form a smooth paste.

Ⓐ $\frac{3}{4}(1 + 2\frac{1}{2})$

Ⓑ $\frac{1}{4} \cdot 2\frac{1}{2}$

Ⓒ $2\frac{1}{2} \cdot \frac{1}{2}$

Ⓓ $2\frac{1}{2} \div \frac{1}{2}$

DAY 4

A canal boat went through a series of locks with the following rises and drops. A positive number shows a rise. A negative number shows a drop. At which lock was there the greatest rise?

Lock	1	2	3	4
Rise or Fall (ft)	−17	11	−8	6

Ⓕ 1

Ⓖ 2

Ⓗ 3

Ⓙ 4

DAY 5

Ryan is making $7\frac{1}{2}$ cups of rice to serve at dinner with his friends. If he wants to give $\frac{3}{4}$ cup of rice to each guest, how many people will the rice serve?

Ⓐ 8

Ⓑ 10

Ⓒ 12

Ⓓ 14

DAY 1

Which value does NOT make the following statement true?

$$0.028 < \square < 0.064$$

Ⓐ 0.027
Ⓑ 0.029
Ⓒ 0.043
Ⓓ 0.062

DAY 2

Six friends equally share the cost of a breakfast. The breakfast costs $42.30. Which expression shows each person's share?

Ⓕ 42.30 · 6
Ⓖ 42.30 − 6
Ⓗ 42.30 ÷ 6
Ⓙ 42.30 + 6

DAY 3

Ann buys 3 black candles, 2 white candles, and 4 striped candles. She gives the cashier a $50 bill and estimates that she will get about $8 in change. Which of the following shows that Ann's estimate is reasonable?

Ⓐ 15 + 11 + 16 = 42
Ⓑ 26 − 18 = 8
Ⓒ 50 − 8 = 42
Ⓓ 12 + 10 + 12 = 34

DAY 4

Miguel recorded the distances he ran each month. What is the total number of miles he ran?

Month	May	June	July
Miles	22.5	20.8	25.2

Ⓕ 43.3 miles
Ⓖ 46 miles
Ⓗ 68.5 miles
Ⓙ 69 miles

DAY 5

Martin is filling a trough with water. If the pail he is using can hold 9 cubic feet of water, how many times will he need to empty his pail into the trough in order to fill the trough completely?

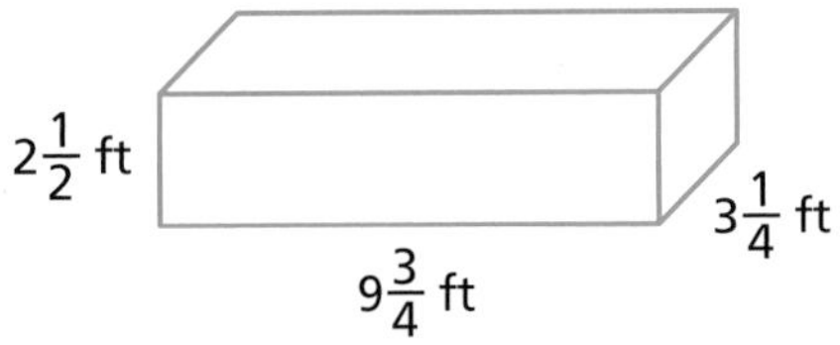

Ⓐ 6
Ⓑ 7
Ⓒ 8
Ⓓ 9

Countdown to Testing — WEEK 3

DAY 1

Which expression shows the fraction of flowerpots that have polka dots in both groups?

Ⓐ $\frac{1}{6} + \frac{1}{7}$

Ⓑ $\frac{6}{7} - \frac{4}{5}$

Ⓒ $\frac{3}{7} - \frac{4}{5}$

Ⓓ $\frac{4}{7} + \frac{5}{6}$

DAY 2

Jake estimates that the answer to 25 • 10.6 is between 250 and 275. Which of the following shows that Jake's estimate is reasonable?

Ⓕ $250 \div 10 = 25$; $275 \div 10 = 27.5$

Ⓖ $250 + 275 = 525$

Ⓗ $25 \cdot 10 = 250$; $25 \cdot 11 = 275$

Ⓙ $250 \div 11 = 23$

DAY 3

June surveyed her class and found that 45% of her classmates have visited the Grand Canyon. With 20 students in her class, June calculated that 9 students have visited the Grand Canyon. Which of the following shows that June's answer is reasonable?

Ⓐ $0.45 \cdot 100 = 45$

Ⓑ $4.5 \cdot 20 = 9$

Ⓒ $9 \cdot 20 \cdot 4.5 = 81$

Ⓓ $0.45 \cdot 20 = 9$

DAY 4

What is the value of the expression $(16 - 8) \cdot 3 + (10 \div 100)$?

Ⓕ 8.3

Ⓖ 24.1

Ⓗ 24.8

Ⓙ 34

DAY 5

Estimate the volume of the figure below.

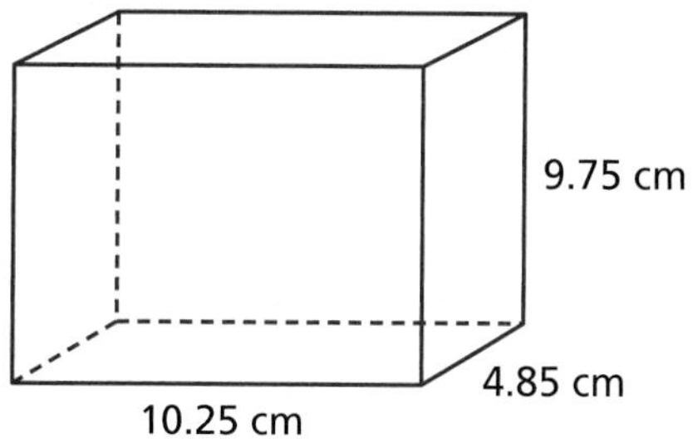

Ⓐ 300 cubic centimeters

Ⓑ 450 cubic centimeters

Ⓒ 500 cubic centimeters

Ⓓ 650 cubic centimeters

DAY 1

Rose's Bakery uses these apples to make one small apple tart.

Which expression represents the number of apples used in 4 small tarts?

(A) $4 \cdot 2\frac{1}{2}$

(B) $4 \div 2\frac{1}{2}$

(C) $4 + 2\frac{1}{2}$

(D) $4 - 2\frac{1}{2}$

DAY 2

Gil wants to fill his fish tank with water. Which is the best estimate of the volume of water he needs?

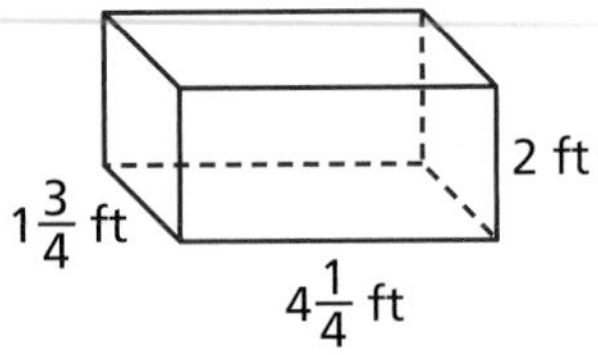

(F) 8 cubic feet

(G) 16 cubic feet

(H) 24 cubic feet

(J) 32 cubic feet

DAY 3

Tim's pet frog will grow 2.25 times in size in one month. If the frog is 4.7 centimeters long right now, which is the best estimate of its length after one month?

(A) 6 centimeters

(B) 8 centimeters

(C) 10 centimeters

(D) 15 centimeters

DAY 4

What is the value of the expression $4(8 - 3)^2 - 10 \cdot (25 \div 5)$?

(F) 50

(G) 150

(H) 200

(J) 350

DAY 5

The window box measures $4\frac{6}{8}$ inches × $4\frac{6}{8}$ inches × $10\frac{1}{4}$ inches. Which is the best estimate for the amount of soil that will fill the window box?

(A) 100 cubic inches

(B) 150 cubic inches

(C) 250 cubic inches

(D) 350 cubic inches

Countdown to Testing WEEK 24

DAY 1

Isaac had to draw four different pyramids for math class. He drew the figures below. Which figure is not a pyramid?

Ⓐ
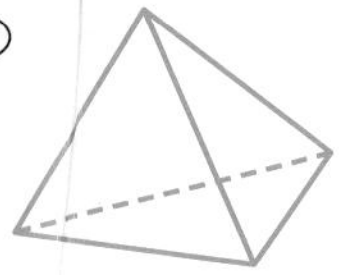

Ⓒ
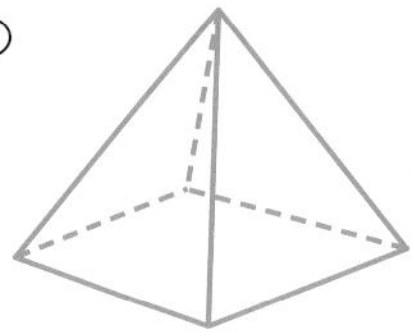

Ⓑ
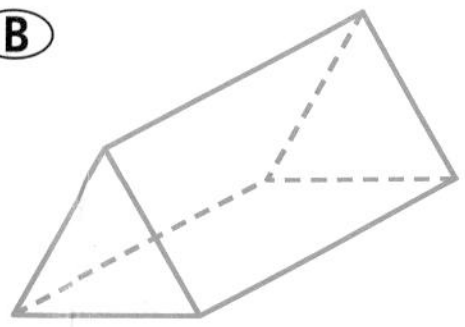

Ⓓ
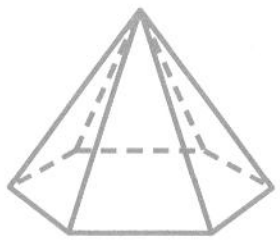

DAY 2

What object is represented by this net?

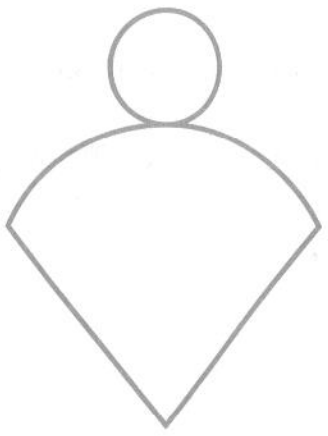

Ⓕ cone
Ⓗ cylinder
Ⓖ sphere
Ⓙ prism

DAY 3

Record the scores you've received on science quizzes this semester. If you want to see the shape of the data set, which of the following is the best way to display the data?

Ⓐ circle graph
Ⓑ double-bar graph
Ⓒ number line
Ⓓ line plot

DAY 4

Mrs. Minato's math class took a test yesterday. Any student who scored below 76 will have to take a make-up test. How many students in the class will **not** have to take the make-up test?

Stems	Leaves
9	2 4 4 6
8	0 0 3 4 7 9
7	2 2 5 6
6	3 8

Ⓕ 5
Ⓗ 11
Ⓖ 7
Ⓙ 16

DAY 5

Tamara uses 0.8 pound of mango to make a mango-banana fruit shake. How many shakes can Tamara make with 3.6 pounds of mango?

Ⓐ 3.5
Ⓒ 4.5
Ⓑ 4
Ⓓ 5

CHAPTER 1

Algebraic Reasoning

go.hrw.com
Online Resources
KEYWORD: MS7 TOC

Career: Cosmologist

Tools for Success

Reading and Writing Math

Study Skills

TEST PREP

Integers and Rational Numbers

CHAPTER 2

go.hrw.com
Online Resources
KEYWORD: MS7 TOC

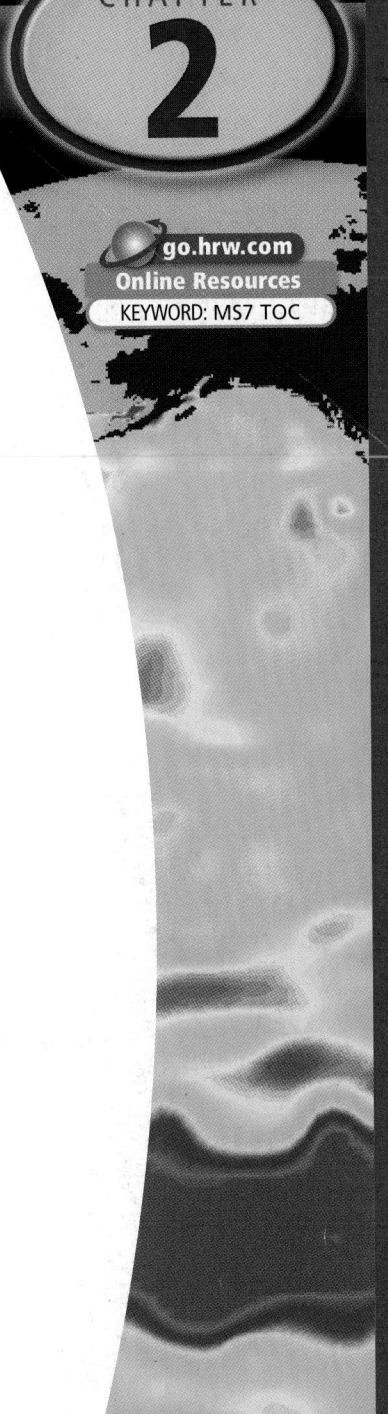

Career: Oceanographer

Table of Contents

Tools for Success

Reading and Writing Math

Study Skills

TEST PREP

CHAPTER 3

Applying Rational Numbers

go.hrw.com
Online Resources
KEYWORD: MS7 TOC

Career: Chef

Tools for Success

Reading and Writing Math

Study Skills

TEST PREP

CHAPTER 8

Geometric Figures

go.hrw.com
Online Resources
KEYWORD: MS7 TOC

Career: Bridge Designer

Tools for Success

CHAPTER 9

Measurement: Two-Dimensional Figures

Career: Fruit Tree Grower

go.hrw.com
Online Resources
KEYWORD: MS7 TOC

Tools for Success

Reading and Writing Math

Reading Math 517, 535
Writing Math 521, 527, 533, 537, 541, 545, 553, 559
Vocabulary 518, 524, 530, 556, 562

Study Skills

Know-It Notebook Chapter 9
Homework Help Online 520, 526, 532, 536, 540, 544, 552, 558
Student Help 538, 562

TEST PREP

Test Prep and Spiral Review 521, 527, 533, 537, 541, 545, 553, 559
Multi-Step Test Prep 561
Test Tackler 570
Standardized Test Prep 572

Measurement: Three-Dimensional Figures

CHAPTER 10

go.hrw.com
Online Resources
KEYWORD: MS7 TOC

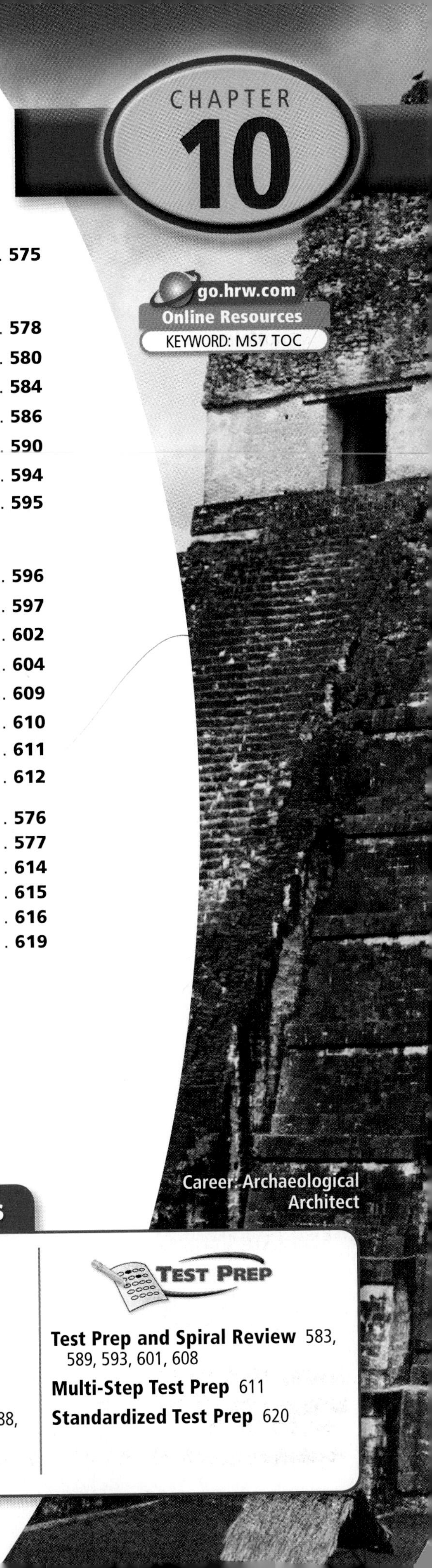

Career: Archaeological Architect

Tools for Success

Reading and Writing Math

Study Skills

TEST PREP

CHAPTER

11 Probability

go.hrw.com
Online Resources
KEYWORD: MS7 TOC

Career: Demographer

Tools for Success

Reading and Writing Math

Study Skills

TEST PREP

CHAPTER 12

Multi-Step Equations and Inequalities

go.hrw.com
Online Resources
KEYWORD: MS7 TOC

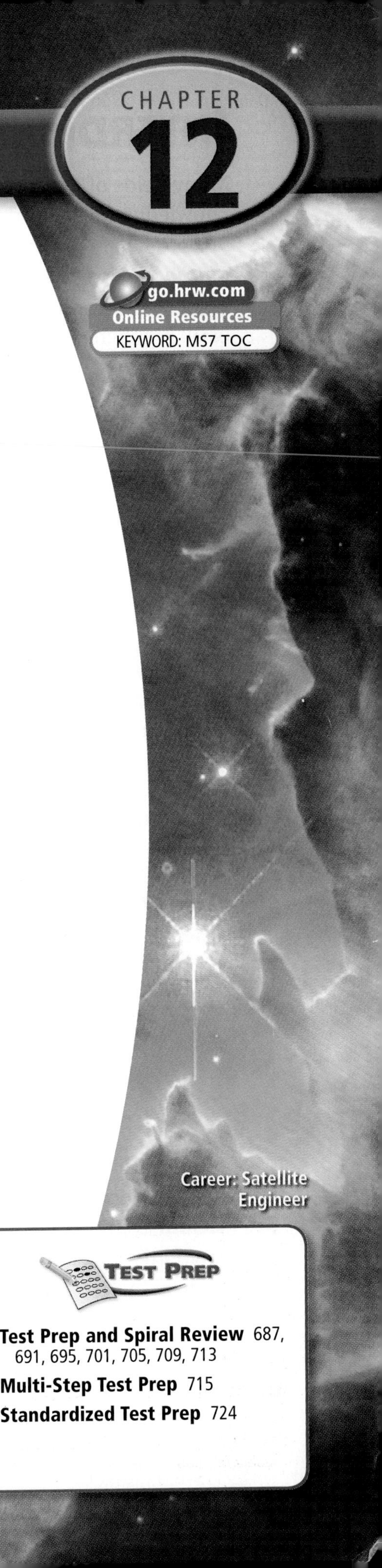
Career: Satellite Engineer

Tools for Success

Reading and Writing Math

Study Skills

TEST PREP

INTERDISCIPLINARY CONNECTIONS

Many fields of study require knowledge of the mathematical skills and concepts taught in ***Holt Mathematics Course 2***. Examples and exercises throughout the book highlight the math you will need to understand in order to study other subjects, such as Earth science or art, or to pursue a career in fields such as the environment or economics.

Fitness Four friends had a competition to see how far they could walk while spinning a hoop around their waists. The table shows how far each friend walked. Use the table for Exercises 51–53.

Person	Distance (mi)
Rosalyn	$\frac{1}{8}$
Cai	$\frac{3}{4}$
Lauren	$\frac{2}{3}$
Janna	$\frac{7}{10}$

51. How much farther did Lauren walk than Rosalyn?

52. What is the combined distance that Cai and Rosalyn walked?

53. Who walked farther, Janna or Cai?

54. Measurement A shrew weighs $\frac{3}{16}$ lb. A hamster weighs $\frac{1}{4}$ lb.

a. How many more pounds does a hamster weigh than a shrew?

b. There are 16 oz in 1 lb. How many more ounces does the hamster weigh than the shrew?

55. Multi-Step To make $\frac{3}{4}$ lb of mixed nuts, how many pounds of cashews would you add to $\frac{1}{8}$ lb of almonds and $\frac{1}{4}$ lb of peanuts?

56. Write a Problem Use facts you find in a newspaper or magazine to write a problem that can be solved using addition or subtraction of fractions.

57. Write About It Explain the steps you use to add or subtract fractions that have different denominators.

58. Challenge The sum of two fractions is 1. If one fraction is $\frac{3}{8}$ greater than the other, what are the two fractions?

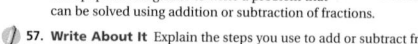

WHY LEARN MATHEMATICS?

Throughout the text, links to interesting application topics, such as architecture, music, and sports, will help you see how math is used in the real world. Some of the links have additional information and activities at go.hrw.com. For a complete list of all real-world problems in **Holt Mathematics Course 2,** see page 823 in the Index.

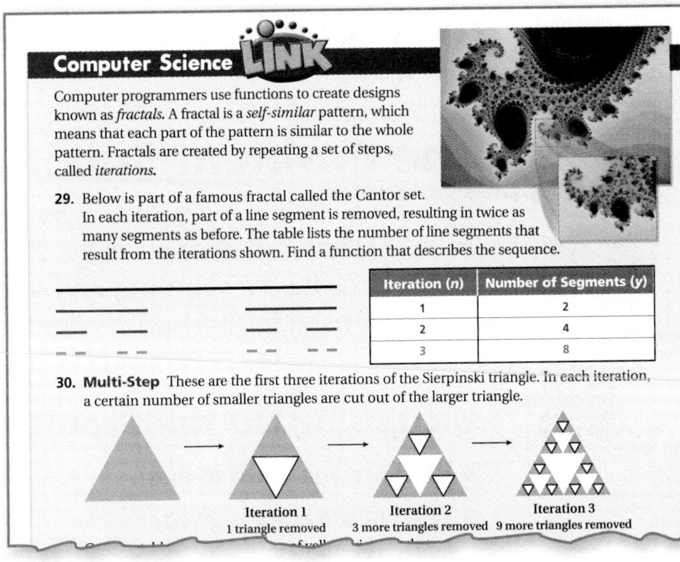

Computer Science LINK

Computer programmers use functions to create designs known as *fractals*. A fractal is a *self-similar* pattern, which means that each part of the pattern is similar to the whole pattern. Fractals are created by repeating a set of steps, called *iterations*.

29. Below is part of a famous fractal called the Cantor set. In each iteration, part of a line segment is removed, resulting in twice as many segments as before. The table lists the number of line segments that result from the iterations shown. Find a function that describes the sequence.

Iteration (n)	Number of Segments (y)
1	2
2	4
3	8

30. Multi-Step These are the first three iterations of the Sierpinski triangle. In each iteration, a certain number of smaller triangles are cut out of the larger triangle.

Real-World LINKS

LINK Agriculture

The owner of this 1,009.6 lb pumpkin won the New England Giant Pumpkin Weigh-Off in September 2000.

LINK Environment

About 15% of the methane gas in the atmosphere comes from farm animals.

LINK Weather

When the wind speed of a tropical storm reaches 74 mi/h, it is classified as a hurricane.

Focus on Problem Solving

PROBLEM SOLVING

The Problem Solving Plan

In order to be a good problem solver, you first need a good problem-solving plan. A plan or strategy will help you to understand the problem, to work through a solution, and to check that your answer makes sense. The plan used in this book is detailed below.

UNDERSTAND the Problem

- **What are you asked to find?** Restate the problem in your own words.
- **What information is given?** Identify the important facts in the problem.
- **What information do you need?** Determine which facts are needed to solve the problem.
- **Is all the information given?** Determine whether all the facts are given.

Make a PLAN

- **Have you ever solved a similar problem?** Think about other problems like this that you successfully solved.
- **What strategy or strategies can you use?** Determine a strategy that you can use and how you will use it.

SOLVE

- **Follow your plan.** Show the steps in your solution. Write your answer as a complete sentence.

LOOK BACK

- **Have you answered the question?** Be sure that you answered the question that is being asked.
- **Is your answer reasonable?** Your answer should make sense in the context of the problem.
- **Is there another strategy you could use?** Solving the problem using another strategy is a good way to check your work.
- **Did you learn anything while solving this problem that could help you solve similar problems in the future?** Try to remember the problems you have solved and the strategies you used to solve them.

PROBLEM SOLVING

Using the Problem Solving Plan

During summer vacation, Ricardo will go to space camp and then to visit his relatives. He will be gone for 5 weeks and 4 days and will spend 11 more days with his relatives than at space camp. How long will Ricardo stay at each place?

UNDERSTAND the Problem

List the important information.

- Ricardo will be gone for 5 weeks and 4 days.
- He will spend 11 more days with his relatives than at space camp.

The answer will be how long Ricardo stays at each place.

Make a PLAN

You can **draw a diagram** to show how long he will stay at each place. Use boxes for the length of each stay. The length of each box will represent the length of each stay.

SOLVE

Think: There are 7 days in a week, so 5 weeks and 4 days is a total of 39 days. Your diagram might look like this:

Relatives	**? days**	**11 days**	} = 39 days
Space camp	**? days**		

$39 - 11 = 28$ *Subtract 11 days from the total number of days.*

$28 \div 2 = 14$ *Divide this number by 2 for the 2 places he visits.*

Relatives	**14 days**	**11 days**	= 25 days
Space camp	**14 days**		= 14 days

So Ricardo will stay with his relatives for 25 days and at space camp for 14 days.

LOOK BACK

Twenty-five days is 11 days longer than 14 days. The total length of the two stays is $25 + 14 = 39$ days, or 5 weeks and 4 days. This solution fits the information given in the problem.

Using Your Book for Success

This book has many features designed to help you learn and study math. Becoming familiar with these features will prepare you for greater success on your exams.

Learn

Preview new **vocabulary** terms listed at the beginning of every lesson.

Look for the **Student Help** for hints and reminders.

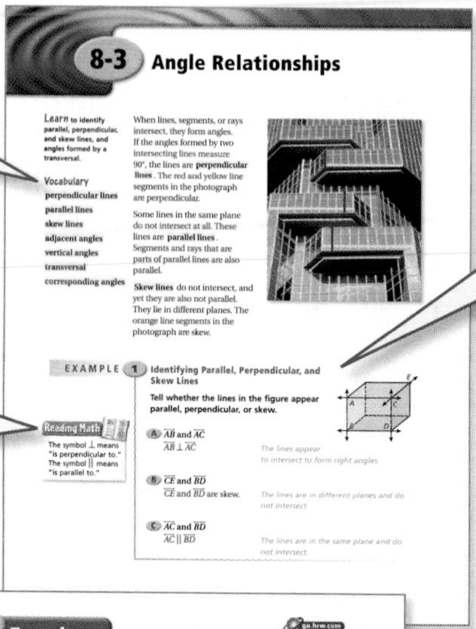

Study the **examples** to learn new math ideas and skills. The examples include step-by-step solutions.

Practice

Look back at examples from the lesson to solve the **Guided Practice** exercises.

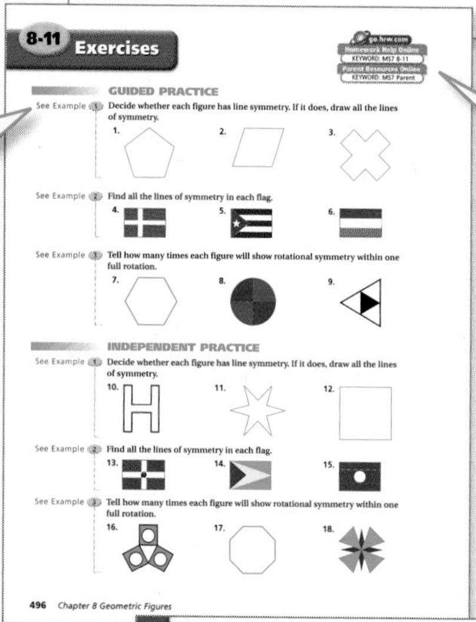

If you get stuck, use the internet for **Homework Help Online**.

Review

Study and review **vocabulary** from the entire chapter.

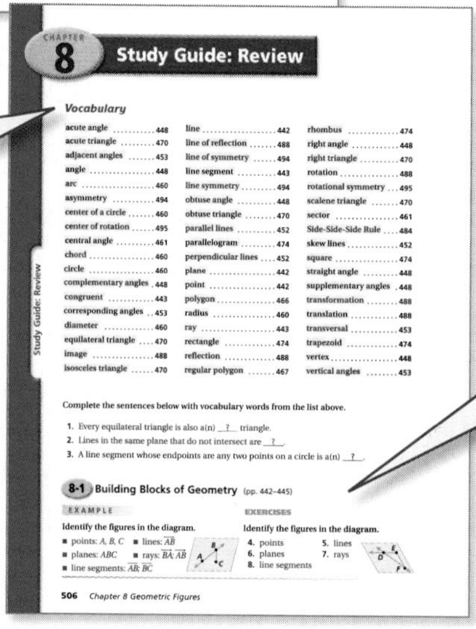

Test yourself with **practice problems** from every lesson in the chapter.

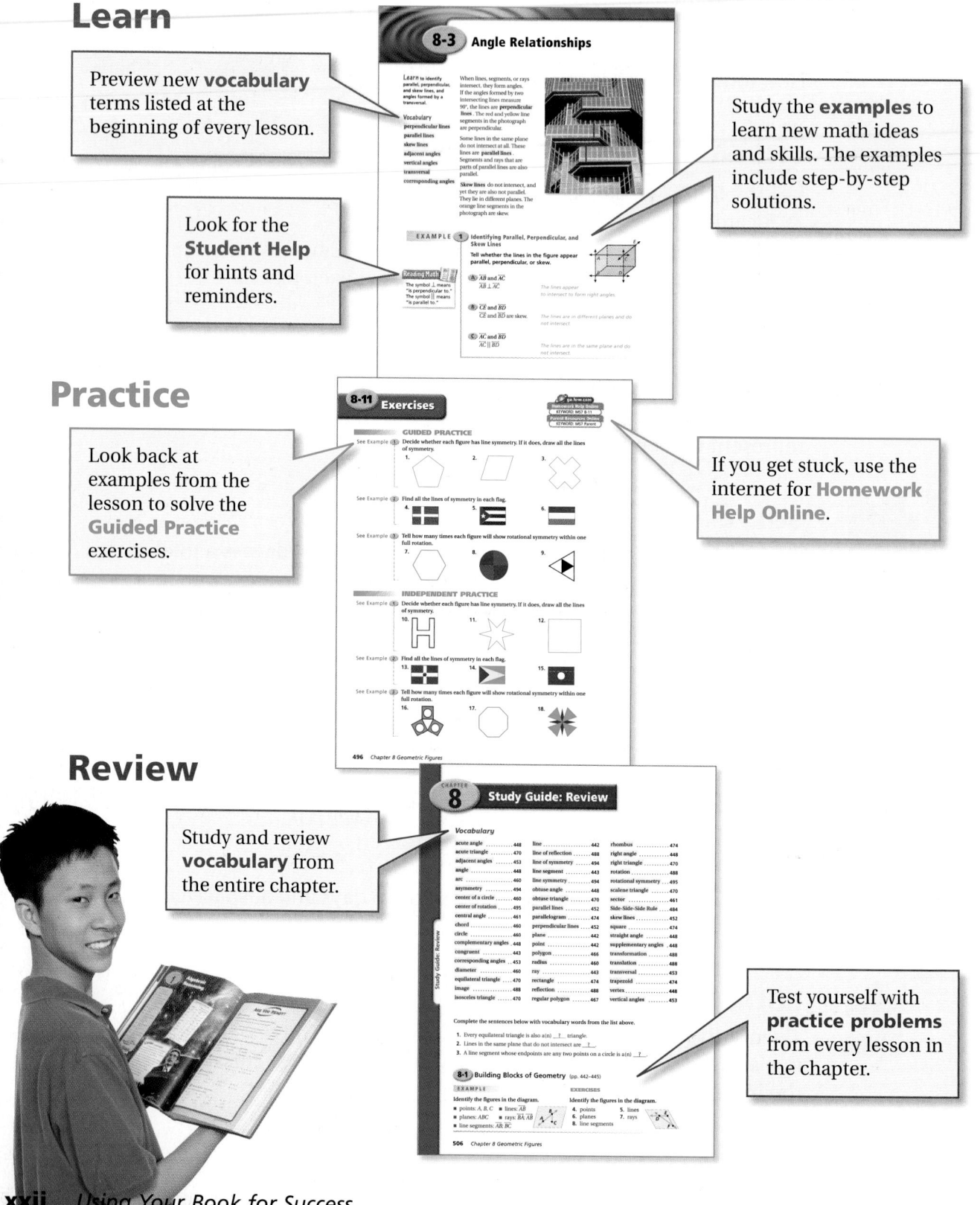

Scavenger Hunt

Holt Mathematics is your resource to help you succeed. Use this scavenger hunt to discover some of the many tools Holt provides to help you be an independent learner.

On a separate sheet of paper, fill in the blanks to answer each question below. In each answer, one letter will be in a yellow box. When you have answered every question, use the letters to fill in the blank at the bottom of the page.

1. What is the first key **vocabulary** term in the Study Guide: Preview for chapter 8?

2. What is the last key **vocabulary** term in the Study Guide: Review for chapter 7?

3. What game is featured in chapter 2 **Game Time**?

4. What keyword should you enter for **Parent Resources Online** on page 338?

5. What project is outlined in chapter 7 **It's in the Bag**?

6. What **career** is spotlighted on page 438?

7. What annual summer event is featured in chapter 2 **Problem Solving on Location**?

8. The chapter 5 **Test Tackler** gives strategies for what kind of standardized test item?

Math Humor

Why did the chicken add its opposite to itself? To get to the other side of the?...

CHAPTER 1

Algebraic Reasoning

go.hrw.com
Chapter Project Online
KEYWORD: MS7 Ch1

Astronomical Distances

Object	Distance from the Sun (km)*
Mercury	5.80×10^7
Venus	1.082×10^8
Earth	1.495×10^8
Mars	2.279×10^8
Jupiter	7.780×10^8
Saturn	1.43×10^9
Uranus	2.90×10^9
Neptune	4.40×10^9
Pluto	5.80×10^9
Nearest star	3.973×10^{13}

*Distances of planets from the Sun are average distances.

Career Cosmologist

Dr. Stephen Hawking is a cosmologist. Cosmologists study the universe as a whole. They are interested in the origins, the structure, and the interaction of space and time.

The invention of the telescope has extended the vision of scientists far beyond nearby stars and planets. It has enabled them to view distant galaxies and structures that at one time were only theorized by astrophysicists such as Dr. Hawking. Astronomical distances are so great that we use scientific notation to represent them.

ARE YOU READY?

Vocabulary

Choose the best term from the list to complete each sentence.

1. The operation that gives the quotient of two numbers is __?__.
2. The __?__ of the digit 3 in 4,903,672 is thousands.
3. The operation that gives the product of two numbers is __?__.
4. In the equation 15 ÷ 3 = 5, the __?__ is 5.

division
multiplication
place value
product
quotient

Complete these exercises to review skills you will need for this chapter.

Find Place Value

Give the place value of the digit 4 in each number.

5. 4,092	**6.** 608,241	**7.** 7,040,000	**8.** 4,556,890,100
9. 3,408,289	**10.** 34,506,123	**11.** 500,986,402	**12.** 3,540,277,009

Use Repeated Multiplication

Find each product.

13. $2 \cdot 2 \cdot 2$	**14.** $9 \cdot 9 \cdot 9 \cdot 9$	**15.** $14 \cdot 14 \cdot 14$	**16.** $10 \cdot 10 \cdot 10 \cdot 10$
17. $3 \cdot 3 \cdot 5 \cdot 5$	**18.** $2 \cdot 2 \cdot 5 \cdot 7$	**19.** $3 \cdot 3 \cdot 11 \cdot 11$	**20.** $5 \cdot 10 \cdot 10 \cdot 10$

Division Facts

Find each quotient.

21. $49 \div 7$	**22.** $54 \div 9$	**23.** $96 \div 12$	**24.** $88 \div 8$
25. $42 \div 6$	**26.** $65 \div 5$	**27.** $39 \div 3$	**28.** $121 \div 11$

Whole Number Operations

Add, subtract, multiply, or divide.

29. $\begin{array}{r} 425 \\ +\ 12 \\ \hline \end{array}$	**30.** $\begin{array}{r} 619 \\ +\ 254 \\ \hline \end{array}$	**31.** $\begin{array}{r} 62 \\ -\ 47 \\ \hline \end{array}$	**32.** $\begin{array}{r} 373 \\ +\ 86 \\ \hline \end{array}$
33. $\begin{array}{r} 62 \\ \times\ 42 \\ \hline \end{array}$	**34.** $\begin{array}{r} 122 \\ \times\ 15 \\ \hline \end{array}$	**35.** $7\overline{)623}$	**36.** $24\overline{)149}$

CHAPTER 1

Study Guide: Preview

Where You've Been

Previously, you

- used order of operations to simplify whole number expressions without exponents.
- used multiplication and division to solve problems involving whole numbers.
- converted measures within the same measurement system.
- wrote large numbers in standard form.

In This Chapter

You will study

- simplifying numerical expressions involving order of operations and exponents.
- using concrete models to solve equations.
- finding solutions to application problems involving related measurement units.
- writing large numbers in scientific notation.

Where You're Going

You can use the skills learned in this chapter

- to express distances and sizes of objects in scientific fields such as astronomy and biology.
- to solve problems in math and science classes such as Algebra and Physics.

Key Vocabulary/Vocabulario

algebraic expression	expresión algebraica
Associative Property	propiedad asociativa
Commutative Property	propiedad conmutativa
Distributive Property	propiedad distributiva
equation	ecuación
exponent	exponente
numerical expression	expresión numérica
order of operations	orden de las operaciones
term	término
variable	variable

Vocabulary Connections

To become familiar with some of the vocabulary terms in the chapter, consider the following. You may refer to the chapter, the glossary, or a dictionary if you like.

1. The words *equation, equal,* and *equator* all begin with the Latin root *equa-,* meaning "level." How can the Latin root word help you define **equation**?
2. The word *numerical* means "of numbers." How might a **numerical expression** differ from an expression such as "the sum of two and five"?
3. When something is *variable,* it has the ability to change. In mathematics, a **variable** is an algebraic symbol. What special property do you think this type of symbol has?

Study Guide: Preview

Reading and Writing Math

Reading Strategy: Use Your Book for Success

Understanding how your textbook is organized will help you locate and use helpful information.

As you read through an example problem, pay attention to the **margin notes**, such as Helpful Hints, Reading Math notes, and Caution notes. These notes will help you understand concepts and avoid common mistakes.

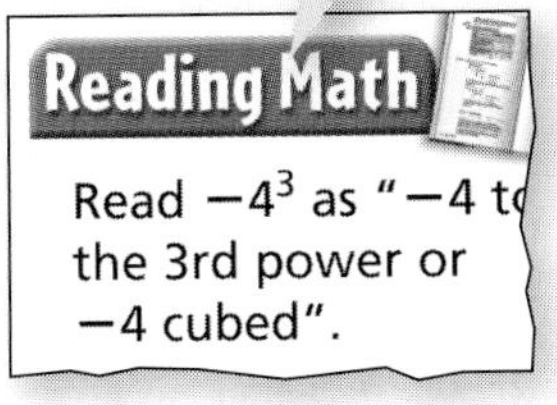
Reading Math
Read -4^3 as "−4 to the 3rd power or −4 cubed".

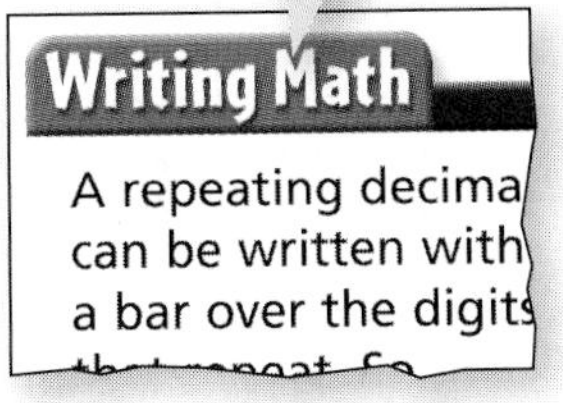
Writing Math
A repeating decima
can be written with
a bar over the digits

Helpful Hint
In Example 1A,
parentheses are not
needed because

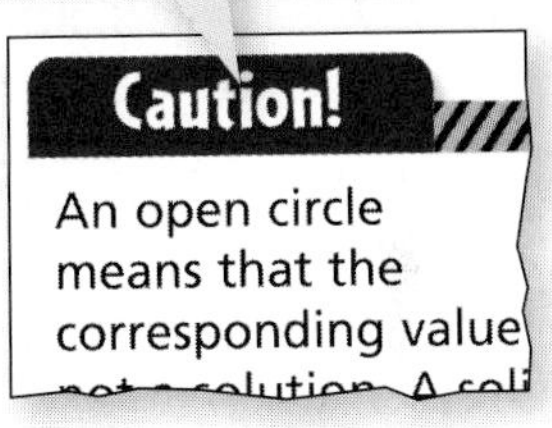
Caution!
An open circle
means that the
corresponding value

The **glossary** is found in the back of your textbook. Use it to find definitions and examples of unfamiliar words or properties.

The **index** is located at the end of your textbook. Use it to find the page where a particular concept is taught.

The **Skills Bank** is found in the back of your textbook. These pages review concepts from previous math courses.

Glossary/Glosario
Glossary/Glos
B
bar graph A graph that uses vertical or horizontal bars to display data. (p. 284)

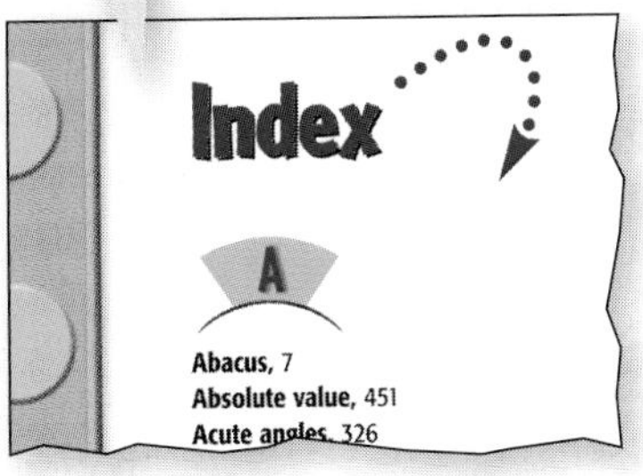
Index
A
Abacus, 7
Absolute value, 451

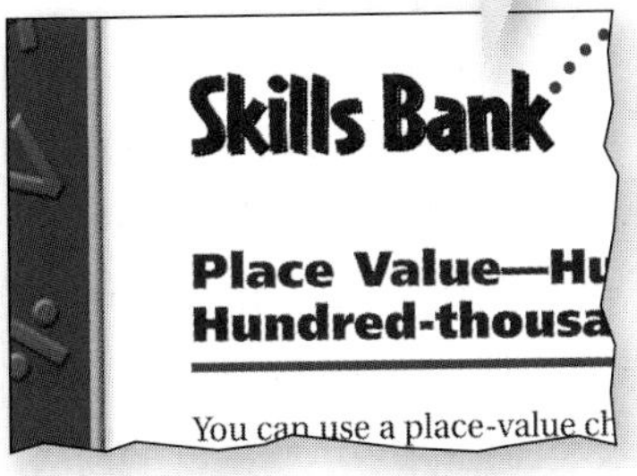
Skills Bank
Place Value—Hu
Hundred-thousa

Try This

Use your textbook for the following problems.

1. Use the index to find the page where *exponent* is defined.
2. In Lesson 1-9, what does the Remember box, located in the margin of page 43, remind you about the perimeter of a figure?
3. Use the glossary to find the definition of each term: *order of operations, numerical expression, equation.*
4. Where can you review how to multiply whole numbers?

1-1 Numbers and Patterns

Learn to identify and extend patterns.

Each year, football teams battle for the state championship. The table shows the number of teams in each round of a division's football playoffs. You can look for a pattern to find out how many teams are in rounds 5 and 6.

Football Playoffs

Round	1	2	3	4	5	6
Number of Teams	64	32	16	8	▮	▮

EXAMPLE 1 Identifying and Extending Number Patterns

Identify a possible pattern. Use the pattern to write the next three numbers.

A 64, 32, 16, 8, ▮, ▮, ▮, . . .

64 32 16 8 ▮ ▮ ▮

÷ 2 ÷ 2 ÷ 2 ÷ 2 ÷ 2 ÷ 2

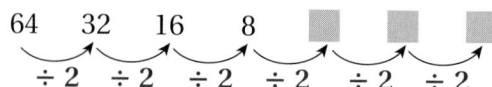

A pattern is to divide each number by 2 to get the next number.

$8 \div 2 = 4$ $4 \div 2 = 2$ $2 \div 2 = 1$

The next three numbers will be 4, 2, and 1.

B 51, 44, 37, 30, ▮, ▮, ▮, . . .

51 44 37 30 ▮ ▮ ▮

− 7 − 7 − 7 − 7 − 7 − 7

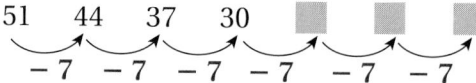

A pattern is to subtract 7 from each number to get the next number.

$30 - 7 = 23$ $23 - 7 = 16$ $16 - 7 = 9$

The next three numbers will be 23, 16, and 9.

C 2, 3, 5, 8, 12, ▮, ▮, ▮, . . .

2 3 5 8 12 ▮ ▮ ▮

+ 1 + 2 + 3 + 4 + 5 + 6 + 7

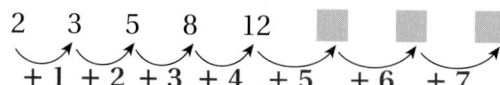

A pattern is to add one more than you did the time before.

$12 + 5 = 17$ $17 + 6 = 23$ $23 + 7 = 30$

The next three numbers will be 17, 23, and 30.

EXAMPLE 2 Identifying and Extending Geometric Patterns

Identify a possible pattern. Use the pattern to draw the next three figures.

A 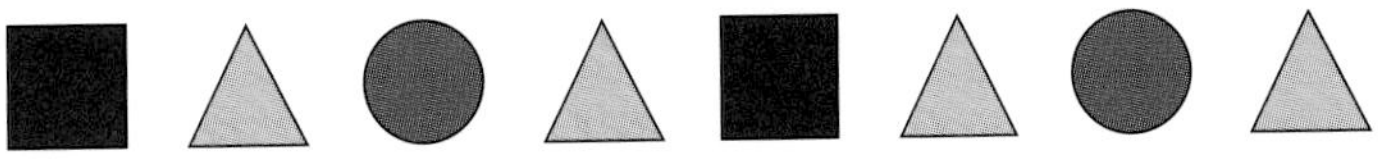

The pattern is alternating squares and circles with triangles between them.
The next three figures will be 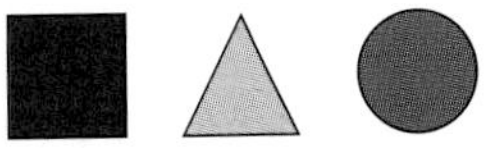.

B 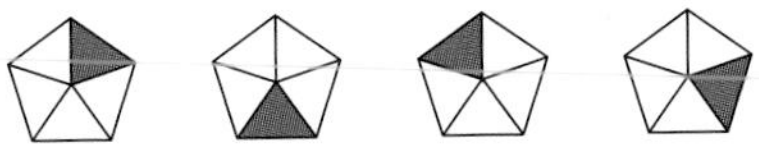

The pattern is to shade every other triangle in a clockwise direction.

The next three figures will be .

EXAMPLE 3 Using Tables to Identify and Extend Patterns

Make a table that shows the number of triangles in each figure. Then tell how many triangles are in the fifth figure of the pattern. Use drawings to justify your answer.

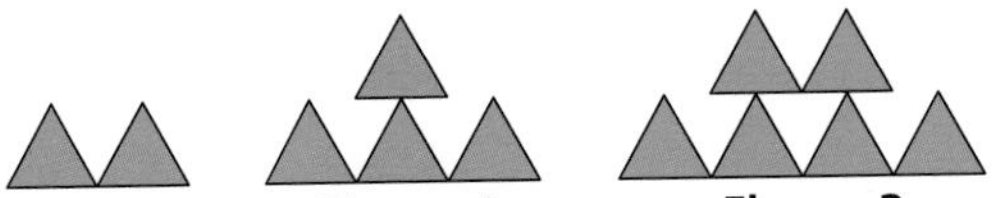

Figure 1 Figure 2 Figure 3

The table shows the number of triangles in each figure.

Figure	1	2	3	4	5
Number of Triangles	2	4	6	8	10

+ 2 + 2 + 2 + 2

The pattern is to add 2 triangles each time.

Figure 4 has $6 + 2 = 8$ triangles.

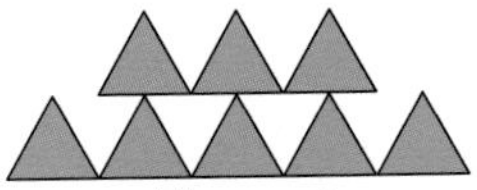

Figure 4

Figure 5 has $8 + 2 = 10$ triangles.

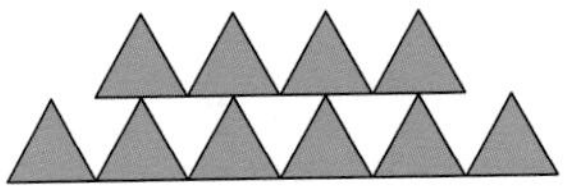

Figure 5

Think and Discuss

1. **Describe** two different number patterns that begin with 3, 6, . . .
2. **Tell** when it would be useful to make a table to help you identify and extend a pattern.

1-1 Exercises

go.hrw.com
Homework Help Online
KEYWORD: MS7 1-1
Parent Resources Online
KEYWORD: MS7 Parent

GUIDED PRACTICE

See Example 1 **Identify a possible pattern. Use the pattern to write the next three numbers.**

1. 6, 14, 22, 30, ■, ■, ■, . . .

2. 1, 3, 9, 27, ■, ■, ■, . . .

3. 59, 50, 41, 32, ■, ■, ■, . . .

4. 8, 9, 11, 14, ■, ■, ■, . . .

See Example 2 **Identify a possible pattern. Use the pattern to draw the next three figures.**

5. 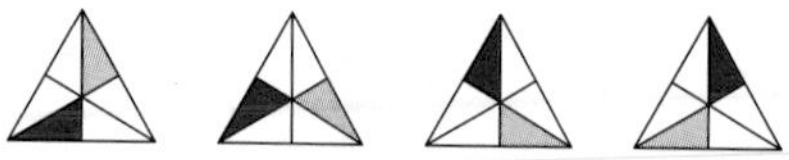

6. 

See Example 3 **7.** Make a table that shows the number of green triangles in each figure. Then tell how many green triangles are in the fifth figure of the pattern. Use drawings to justify your answer.

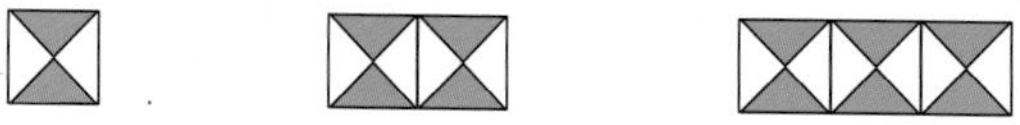

Figure 1 Figure 2 Figure 3

INDEPENDENT PRACTICE

See Example 1 **Identify a possible pattern. Use the pattern to write the next three numbers.**

8. 27, 24, 21, 18, ■, ■, ■, . . .

9. 4,096, 1,024, 256, 64, ■, ■, ■, . . .

10. 1, 3, 7, 13, 21, ■, ■, ■, . . .

11. 14, 37, 60, 83, ■, ■, ■, . . .

See Example 2 **Identify a possible pattern. Use the pattern to draw the next three figures.**

12. 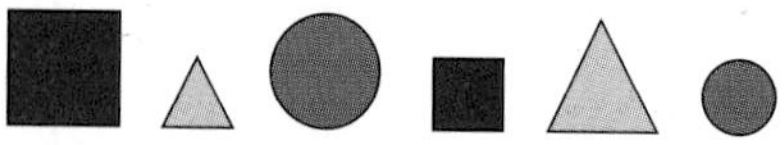

13. 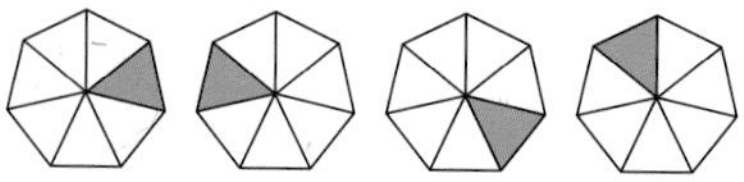

See Example 3 **14.** Make a table that shows the number of dots in each figure. Then tell how many dots are in the sixth figure of the pattern. Use drawings to justify your answer.

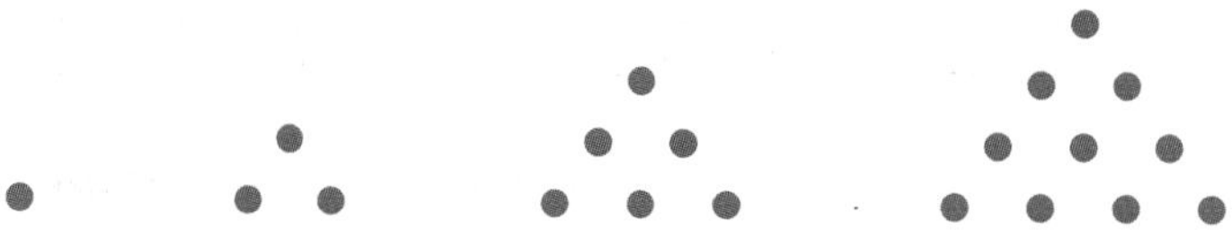

Figure 1 Figure 2 Figure 3 Figure 4

PRACTICE AND PROBLEM SOLVING

Extra Practice
See page 724.

Use the rule to write the first five numbers in each pattern.

15. Start with 7; add 16 to each number to get the next number.

16. Start with 96; divide each number by 2 to get the next number.

17. Start with 50; subtract 2, then 4, then 6, and so on, to get the next number.

18. Critical Thinking Suppose the pattern 3, 6, 9, 12, 15 . . . is continued forever. Will the number 100 appear in the pattern? Why or why not?

Identify a possible pattern. Use the pattern to find the missing numbers.

19. 3, 12, ■, 192, 768, ■, ■, . . .

20. 61, 55, ■, 43, ■, ■, 25, . . .

21. ■, ■, 19, 27, 35, ■, 51, . . .

22. 2, ■, 8, ■, 32, 64, ■, . . .

23. Health The table shows the target heart rate during exercise for athletes of different ages. Assuming the pattern continues, what is the target heart rate for a 40-year-old athlete? a 65-year-old athlete?

Target Heart Rate

Age	Heart Rate (beats per minute)
20	150
25	146
30	142
35	138

Draw the next three figures in each pattern.

24. 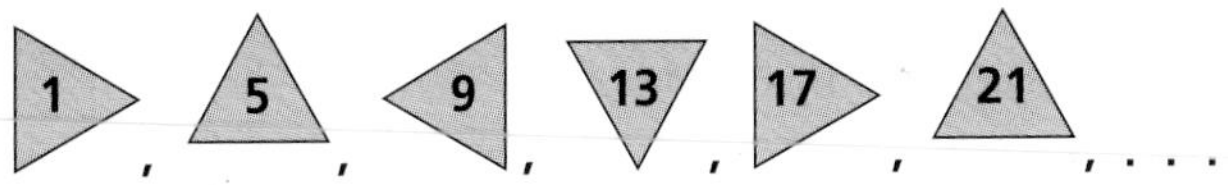

25. 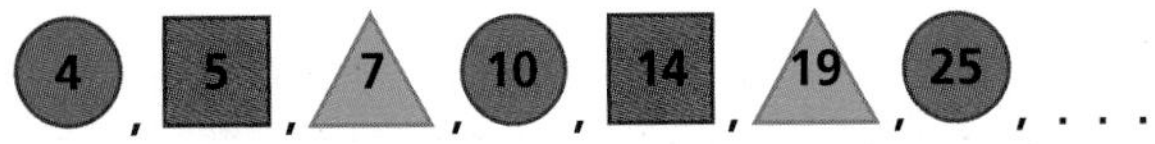

26. Social Studies In the ancient Mayan civilization, people used a number system based on bars and dots. Several numbers are shown below. Look for a pattern and write the number 18 in the Mayan system.

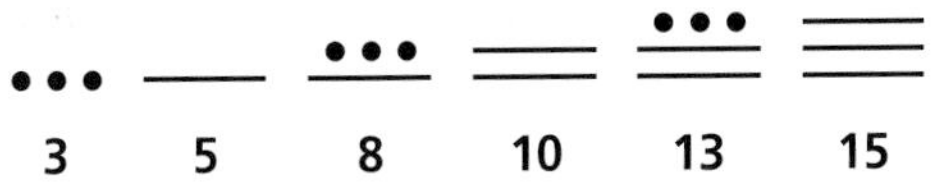

27. What's the Error? A student was asked to write the next three numbers in the pattern 96, 48, 24, 12, ... The student's response was 6, 2, 1. Describe and correct the student's error.

28. Write About It A school chess club meets every Tuesday during the month of March. March 1 falls on a Sunday. Explain how to use a number pattern to find all the dates when the club meets.

29. Challenge Find the 83rd number in the pattern 5, 10, 15, 20, 25, ...

TEST PREP and Spiral Review

30. Multiple Choice Which is the missing number in the pattern 2, 6, ■, 54, 162, . . . ?

Ⓐ 10 Ⓑ 18 Ⓒ 30 Ⓓ 48

31. Gridded Response Find the next number in the pattern 9, 11, 15, 21, 29, 39, ...

Round each number to the nearest ten. (Previous course)

32. 61 **33.** 88 **34.** 105 **35.** 2,019 **36.** 11,403

Round each number to the nearest hundred. (Previous course)

37. 91 **38.** 543 **39.** 952 **40.** 4,050 **41.** 23,093

1-2 Exponents

Learn to represent numbers by using exponents.

Vocabulary

power

exponent

base

A DNA molecule makes a copy of itself by splitting in half. Each half becomes a molecule that is identical to the original. The molecules continue to split so that the two become four, the four become eight, and so on.

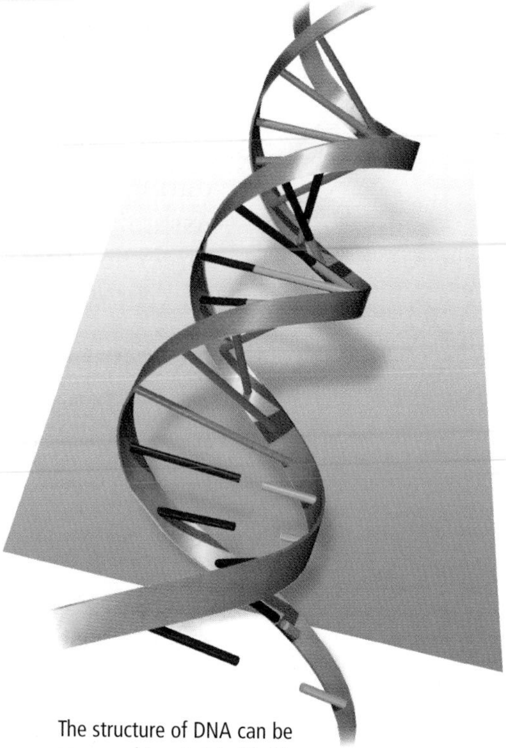

The structure of DNA can be compared to a twisted ladder.

Each time DNA copies itself, the number of molecules doubles. After four copies, the number of molecules is $2 \cdot 2 \cdot 2 \cdot 2 = 16$.

This multiplication can also be written as a **power**, using a base and an *exponent.* The **exponent** tells how many times to use the **base** as a factor.

Reading Math

Read 2^4 as "the fourth power of 2" or "2 to the fourth power."

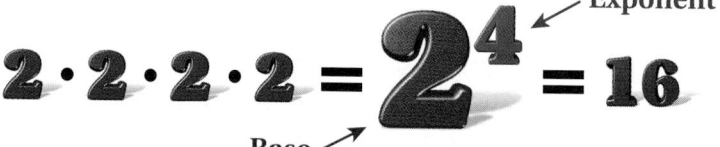

$$2 \cdot 2 \cdot 2 \cdot 2 = 2^4 = 16$$

Exponent (4)

Base (2)

EXAMPLE 1 Evaluating Powers

Find each value.

A 5^2

$5^2 = 5 \cdot 5$ *Use 5 as a factor 2 times.*

$= 25$

B 2^6

$2^6 = 2 \cdot 2 \cdot 2 \cdot 2 \cdot 2 \cdot 2$ *Use 2 as a factor 6 times.*

$= 64$

C 25^1

$25^1 = 25$ *Any number to the first power is equal to that number.*

Any number to the zero power, except zero, is equal to 1.

$6^0 = 1$ $10^0 = 1$ $19^0 = 1$

Zero to the zero power is *undefined,* meaning that it does not exist.

To express a whole number as a power, write the number as the product of equal factors. Then write the product using the base and an exponent. For example, $10{,}000 = 10 \cdot 10 \cdot 10 \cdot 10 = 10^4$.

EXAMPLE 2 Expressing Whole Numbers as Powers

Write each number using an exponent and the given base.

A **49, base 7**

$49 = 7 \cdot 7$ *7 is used as a factor 2 times.*

$= 7^2$

B **81, base 3**

$81 = 3 \cdot 3 \cdot 3 \cdot 3$ *3 is used as a factor 4 times.*

$= 3^4$

EXAMPLE 3 *Earth Science Application*

LINK Earth Science

An earthquake measuring 7.2 on the Richter scale struck Duzce, Turkey, on November 12, 1999.

The Richter scale measures an earthquake's strength, or magnitude. Each category in the table is 10 times stronger than the next lower category. For example, a large earthquake is 10 times stronger than a moderate earthquake. How many times stronger is a great earthquake than a moderate one?

Earthquake Strength	
Category	**Magnitude**
Moderate	5
Large	6
Major	7
Great	8

An earthquake with a magnitude of 6 is 10 times stronger than one with a magnitude of 5.

An earthquake with a magnitude of 7 is 10 times stronger than one with a magnitude of 6.

An earthquake with a magnitude of 8 is 10 times stronger than one with a magnitude of 7.

$$10 \cdot 10 \cdot 10 = 10^3 = 1{,}000$$

A great earthquake is 1,000 times stronger than a moderate one.

Think and Discuss

1. **Describe** a relationship between 3^5 and 3^6.
2. **Tell** which power of 8 is equal to 2^6. Explain.
3. **Explain** why any number to the first power is equal to that number.

1-2 Exercises

go.hrw.com
Homework Help Online
KEYWORD: MS7 1-2
Parent Resources Online
KEYWORD: MS7 Parent

GUIDED PRACTICE

See Example 1
Find each value.

1. 2^5 **2.** 3^3 **3.** 6^2 **4.** 9^1 **5.** 10^6

See Example 2
Write each number using an exponent and the given base.

6. 25, base 5 **7.** 16, base 4 **8.** 27, base 3 **9.** 100, base 10

See Example 3
10. Earth Science On the Richter scale, a great earthquake is 10 times stronger than a major one, and a major one is 10 times stronger than a large one. How many times stronger is a great earthquake than a large one?

INDEPENDENT PRACTICE

See Example 1
Find each value.

11. 11^2 **12.** 3^5 **13.** 8^3 **14.** 4^3 **15.** 3^4

16. 2^5 **17.** 5^1 **18.** 2^3 **19.** 5^3 **20.** 30^1

See Example 2
Write each number using an exponent and the given base.

21. 81, base 9 **22.** 4, base 4 **23.** 64, base 4

24. 1, base 7 **25.** 32, base 2 **26.** 128, base 2

27. 1,600, base 40 **28.** 2,500, base 50 **29.** 100,000, base 10

See Example 3
30. In a game, a contestant had a starting score of one point. He tripled his score every turn for four turns. Write his score after four turns as a power. Then find his score.

PRACTICE AND PROBLEM SOLVING

Extra Practice
See page 724.

Give two ways to represent each number using powers.

31. 81 **32.** 16 **33.** 64 **34.** 729 **35.** 625

Compare. Write <, >, or =.

36. 4^2 ▒ 15 **37.** 2^3 ▒ 3^2 **38.** 64 ▒ 4^3 **39.** 8^3 ▒ 7^4

40. 10,000 ▒ 10^5 **41.** 6^5 ▒ 3,000 **42.** 9^3 ▒ 3^6 **43.** 5^4 ▒ 7^3

44. To find the volume of a cube, find the third power of the length of an edge of the cube. What is the volume of a cube that is 6 inches long on an edge?

45. Patterns Domingo decided to save $0.03 the first day and to triple the amount he saves each day. How much will he save on the seventh day?

46. Life Science A newborn panda cub weighs an average of 4 ounces. How many ounces might a one-year-old panda weigh if its weight increases by the power of 5 in one year?

47. Social Studies If the populations of the cities in the table double every 10 years, what will their populations be in 2034?

City	Population (2004)
Yuma, AZ	86,070
Phoenix, AZ	1,421,298

48. Critical Thinking Explain why $6^3 \neq 3^6$.

49. Hobbies Malia is making a quilt with a pattern of rings. In the center ring, she uses four stars. In each of the next three rings, she uses three times as many stars as in the one before. How many stars does she use in the fourth ring? Write the answer using a power and find its value.

Order each set of numbers from least to greatest.

50. 29, 2^3, 6^2, 16, 3^5 **51.** 4^3, 33, 6^2, 5^3, 10^1 **52.** 7^2, 2^4, 80, 10^2, 1^8

53. 2, 1^8, 3^4, 16^1, 0 **54.** 5^2, 21, 11^2, 13^1, 1^9 **55.** 2^5, 3^3, 9, 5^2, 8^1

56. Life Science The cells of some kinds of bacteria divide every 30 minutes. If you begin with a single cell, how many cells will there be after 1 hour? 2 hours? 3 hours?

57. What's the Error? A student wrote 64 as 8 · 2. How did the student apply exponents incorrectly?

58. Write About It Is 2^5 greater than or less than 3^3? Explain your answer.

59. Challenge What is the length of the edge of a cube if its volume is 1,000 cubic meters?

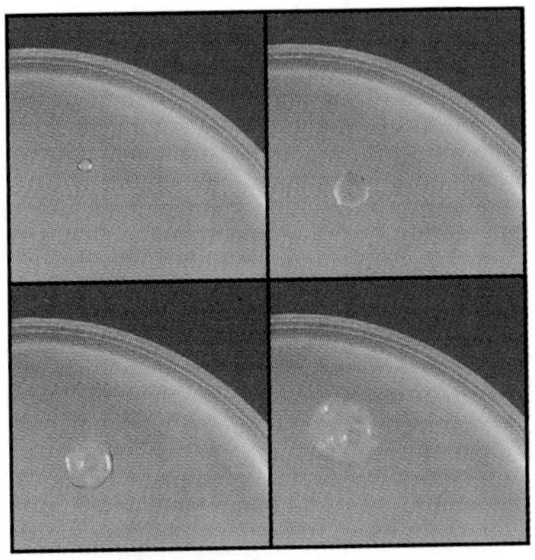

Bacteria divide by pinching in two. This process is called binary fission.

TEST PREP and Spiral Review

60. Multiple Choice What is the value of 4^6?

Ⓐ 24 Ⓑ 1,024 Ⓒ 4,096 Ⓓ 16,384

61. Multiple Choice Which of the following is NOT equal to 64?

Ⓕ 6^4 Ⓖ 4^3 Ⓗ 2^6 Ⓙ 8^2

62. Gridded Response Simplify $2^3 + 3^2$.

Simplify. (Previous course)

63. 15 + 27 + 5 + 3 + 11 + 16 + 7 + 4 **64.** 2 + 6 + 5 + 7 + 100 + 1 + 75

65. 2 + 9 + 8 + 12 + 6 + 8 + 5 + 6 + 7 **66.** 9 + 30 + 4 + 1 + 4 + 1 + 7 + 5

Identify a possible pattern. Use the pattern to write the next three numbers. (Lesson 1-1)

67. 100, 91, 82, 73, 64, . . . **68.** 17, 19, 22, 26, 31, . . . **69.** 2, 6, 18, 54, 162, . . .

1-3 Metric Measurements

Learn to identify, convert, and compare metric units.

The Micro Flying Robot II is the world's lightest helicopter. Produced in Japan in 2004, the robot is 85 millimeters tall and has a mass of 8.6 grams.

You can use the following benchmarks to help you understand millimeters, grams, and other metric units.

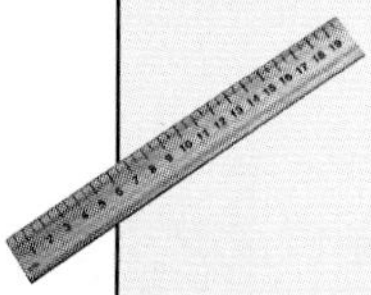

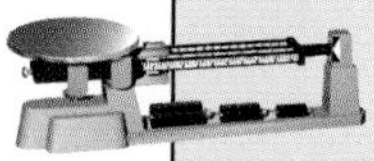

	Metric Unit	Benchmark
Length	Millimeter (mm)	Thickness of a dime
	Centimeter (cm)	Width of your little finger
	Meter (m)	Width of a doorway
	Kilometer (km)	Length of 10 football fields
Mass	Milligram (mg)	Mass of a grain of sand
	Gram (g)	Mass of a small paperclip
	Kilogram (kg)	Mass of a textbook
Capacity	Milliliter (mL)	Amount of liquid in an eyedropper
	Liter (L)	Amount of water in a large water bottle
	Kiloliter (kL)	Capacity of 2 large refrigerators

EXAMPLE 1 Choosing the Appropriate Metric Unit

Choose the most appropriate metric unit for each measurement. Justify your answer.

A The length of a car

Meters—the length of a car is similar to the width of several doorways.

B The mass of a skateboard

Kilograms—the mass of a skateboard is similar to the mass of several textbooks.

C The recommended dose of a cough syrup

Milliliters—one dose of cough syrup is similar to the amount of liquid in several eyedroppers.

Reading Math

Prefixes:
Milli- means "thousandth"
Centi- means "hundredth"
Kilo- means "thousand"

The prefixes of metric units correlate to place values in the base-10 number system. The table shows how metric units are based on powers of 10.

1,000	100	10	1	0.1	0.01	0.001
Thousands	Hundreds	Tens	Ones	Tenths	Hundredths	Thousandths
Kilo-	*Hecto-*	*Deca-*	Base unit	*Deci-*	*Centi-*	*Milli-*

You can convert units within the metric system by multiplying or dividing by powers of 10. To convert to a smaller unit, you must multiply. To convert to a larger unit, you must divide.

EXAMPLE 2 Converting Metric Units

Convert each measure.

A 510 cm to meters

510 cm = (510 ÷ 100) m *100 cm = 1 m, so divide by 100.*
= 5.1 m *Move the decimal point 2 places left: 510.*

B 2.3 L to milliliters

2.3 L = (2.3 × 1,000) mL *1 L = 1,000 mL, so multiply by 1,000.*
= 2,300 mL *Move the decimal point 3 places right: 2.300*

EXAMPLE 3 Using Unit Conversion to Make Comparisons

Mai and Brian are measuring the mass of rocks in their earth science class. Mai's rock has a mass of 480 g. Brian's rock has a mass of 0.05 kg. Whose rock has the greater mass?

You can convert the mass of Mai's rock to kilograms.

480 g = (480 ÷ 1,000) kg *1,000 g = 1 kg, so divide by 1,000.*
= 0.48 kg *Move the decimal point 3 places left: 480.*

Since 0.48 kg > 0.05 kg, Mai's rock has the greater mass.

Check

Use number sense. There are 1,000 grams in a kilogram, so the mass of Mai's rock is about half a kilogram, or 0.5 kg. This is much greater than 0.05 kg, the mass of Brian's rock, so the answer is reasonable.

Think and Discuss

1. **Tell** how the metric system relates to the base-10 number system.
2. **Explain** why it makes sense to multiply when you convert to a smaller unit.

1-3 Exercises

go.hrw.com
Homework Help Online
KEYWORD: MS7 1-3
Parent Resources Online
KEYWORD: MS7 Parent

GUIDED PRACTICE

See Example 1

Choose the most appropriate metric unit for each measurement. Justify your answer.

1. The mass of a pumpkin
2. The amount of water in a pond
3. The length of an eagle's beak
4. The mass of a penny

See Example 2

Convert each measure.

5. 12 kg to grams
6. 4.3 m to centimeters
7. 0.7 mm to centimeters
8. 3,200 mL to liters

See Example 3

9. On Sunday, Li ran 0.8 km. On Monday, she ran 7,200 m. On which day did Li run farther? Use estimation to explain why your answer makes sense.

INDEPENDENT PRACTICE

See Example 1

Choose the most appropriate metric unit for each measurement. Justify your answer.

10. The capacity of a teacup
11. The mass of 10 grains of salt
12. The height of a palm tree
13. The distance between your eyes

See Example 2

Convert each measure.

14. 0.067 L to milliliters
15. 1.4 m to kilometers
16. 900 mg to grams
17. 355 cm to millimeters

See Example 3

18. Carmen pours 75 mL of water into a beaker. Nick pours 0.75 L of water into a different beaker. Who has the greater amount of water? Use estimation to explain why your answer makes sense.

PRACTICE AND PROBLEM SOLVING

Extra Practice
See page 724.

Convert each measure.

19. 1.995 m = ▒ cm
20. 0.00004 kg = ▒ g
21. 2,050 kL = ▒ L
22. 0.002 mL = ▒ L
23. 3.7 mm = ▒ cm
24. 61.8 g = ▒ mg

Compare. Write <, >, or =.

25. 0.1 cm ▒ 1 mm
26. 25 g ▒ 3,000 mg
27. 340 mg ▒ 0.4 g
28. 0.05 kL ▒ 5 L
29. 0.3 mL ▒ 0.005 L
30. 1.3 kg ▒ 1,300 g

31. **Art** The *Mona Lisa* by Leonardo da Vinci is 77 cm tall. *Starry Night* by Vincent Van Gogh is 0.73 m tall. Which is the taller painting? How much taller is it?

Write each set of measures in order from least to greatest.

32. 0.005 kL; 4.1 L; 6,300 mL

33. 1.5 m; 1,200 mm; 130 cm

34. 4,000 mg; 50 kg; 70 g

35. 9.03 g; 0.0008 kg; 1,000 mg

36. Measurement Use a ruler to measure the line segment at right in centimeters. Then give the length of the segment in millimeters and meters.

LINK

Life Science

Bats consume up to 25% of their mass at each feeding.

Life Science **The table gives information about several species of Vesper, or Evening, bats. Use the table for Exercises 37 and 38.**

37. Which bat has the greatest mass?

38. Which bat has a longer wingspread, the Red Bat or the Big Brown Bat? How much longer is its wingspread?

U.S. Vesper Bats

Name	Wingspread	Mass
Red Bat	0.3 m	10.9 g
Silver-Haired Bat	28.7 cm	8,500 mg
Big Brown Bat	317 mm	0.01 kg

39. Critical Thinking One milliliter of water has a mass of 1 gram. What is the mass of a liter of water?

40. What's the Error? A student converted 45 grams to milligrams as shown below. Explain the student's error.

$$45 \text{ g} = (45 \div 1{,}000) \text{ mg} = 0.045 \text{ mg}$$

41. Write About It Explain how to decide whether milligrams, grams, or kilograms are the most appropriate unit for measuring the mass of an object.

42. Challenge A decimeter is $\frac{1}{10}$ of a meter. Explain how to convert millimeters to decimeters.

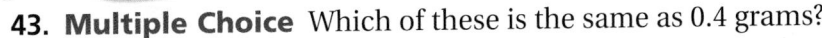

Test Prep and Spiral Review

43. Multiple Choice Which of these is the same as 0.4 grams?

Ⓐ 0.0004 mg   Ⓑ 0.004 mg   Ⓒ 400 mg   Ⓓ 4,000 mg

44. Short Response Which has a greater capacity, a measuring cup that holds 250 mL or a measuring cup that holds 0.5 L? Justify your answer.

Identify a possible pattern. Use the pattern to write the next three numbers. (Lesson 1-1)

45. 19, 16, 13, 10, ■, ■, ■, . . .

46. 5, 15, 45, 135, ■, ■, ■, . . .

47. 5, 6, 8, 11, 15, ■, ■, ■, . . .

48. 256, 128, 64, 32, ■, ■, ■, . . .

Find each value. (Lesson 1-2)

49. 9^2 **50.** 12^1 **51.** 2^7 **52.** 7^3 **53.** 3^4

1-4 Applying Exponents

Learn to multiply by powers of ten and express large numbers in scientific notation.

Vocabulary
scientific notation

The distance from Venus to the Sun is greater than 100,000,000 kilometers. You can write this number as a power of ten by using a base of ten and an exponent.

$$10 \cdot 10 \cdot 10 \cdot 10 \cdot 10 \cdot 10 \cdot 10 \cdot 10 = \mathbf{10^8}$$

Power of ten ↑

The table shows several powers of ten.

Power of 10	Meaning	Value
10^1	10	10
10^2	$10 \cdot 10$	100
10^3	$10 \cdot 10 \cdot 10$	1,000
10^4	$10 \cdot 10 \cdot 10 \cdot 10$	10,000

Astronomers estimate that there are 100 billion billion, or 10^{20}, stars in the universe.

You can find the product of a number and a power of ten by multiplying or by moving the decimal point of the number. For powers of ten with positive exponents, move the decimal point to the right.

EXAMPLE 1 Multiplying by Powers of Ten

Multiply $137 \cdot 10^3$.

A Method 1: Evaluate the power.

$137 \cdot 10^3 = 137 \cdot (10 \cdot 10 \cdot 10)$ *Multiply 10 by itself 3 times.*

$= 137 \cdot 1{,}000$ *Multiply.*

$= 137{,}000$

B Method 2: Use mental math.

$137 \cdot 10^3 = 137.000$ *Move the decimal point 3 places.*

$= 137{,}000$ ← 3 places *(You will need to add 3 zeros.)*

Remember!

A factor is a number that is multiplied by another number to get a product.

Scientific notation is a kind of shorthand that can be used to write large numbers. Numbers expressed in scientific notation are written as the product of two *factors*.

Writing Math

In scientific notation, it is customary to use a multiplication cross (×) instead of a dot.

In scientific notation, 17,900,000 is written as

$$1.79 \times 10^7$$

A number greater than or equal to 1 but less than 10 → 1.79; *A power of 10* → 10^7

EXAMPLE 2 **Writing Numbers in Scientific Notation**

Write 9,580,000 in scientific notation.

$9{,}580{,}000 = 9{,}580{,}000.$ — *Move the decimal point to get a number between 1 and 10.*

$= 9.58 \times 10^6$ — *The exponent is equal to the number of places the decimal point is moved.*

EXAMPLE 3 **Writing Numbers in Standard Form**

Pluto is about 3.7×10^9 miles from the Sun. Write this distance in standard form.

$3.7 \times 10^9 = 3.700000000$ — *Since the exponent is 9, move the decimal point 9 places to the right.*

$= 3{,}700{,}000{,}000$

Pluto is about 3,700,000,000 miles from the Sun.

EXAMPLE 4 **Comparing Numbers in Scientific Notation**

Mercury is 9.17×10^7 kilometers from Earth. Jupiter is 6.287×10^8 kilometers from Earth. Which planet is closer to Earth?

To compare numbers written in scientific notation, first compare the exponents. If the exponents are equal, then compare the decimal portion of the numbers.

Mercury: 9.17×10^7 km

Jupiter: 6.287×10^8 km — *Compare the exponents.*

Notice that $7 < 8$. So $9.17 \times 10^7 < 6.287 \times 10^8$.

Mercury is closer to Earth than Jupiter.

Think and Discuss

1. **Tell** whether 15×10^9 is in scientific notation. Explain.
2. **Compare** 4×10^3 and 3×10^4. Explain how you know which is greater.

1-4 Exercises

go.hrw.com
Homework Help Online
KEYWORD: MS7 1-4
Parent Resources Online
KEYWORD: MS7 Parent

GUIDED PRACTICE

See Example 1

Multiply.

1. $15 \cdot 10^2$ **2.** $12 \cdot 10^4$ **3.** $208 \cdot 10^3$ **4.** $113 \cdot 10^7$

See Example 2

Write each number in scientific notation.

5. 3,600,000 **6.** 214,000 **7.** 8,000,000,000 **8.** 42,000

See Example 3

9. A drop of water contains about 2.0×10^{21} molecules. Write this number in standard form.

See Example 4

10. Astronomy The diameter of Neptune is 4.9528×10^7 meters. The diameter of Mars is 6.7868×10^6 meters. Which planet has the larger diameter?

INDEPENDENT PRACTICE

See Example 1

Multiply.

11. $21 \cdot 10^2$ **12.** $8 \cdot 10^4$ **13.** $25 \cdot 10^5$ **14.** $40 \cdot 10^4$

15. $268 \cdot 10^3$ **16.** $550 \cdot 10^7$ **17.** $2{,}115 \cdot 10^5$ **18.** $70{,}030 \cdot 10^1$

See Example 2

Write each number in scientific notation.

19. 428,000 **20.** 1,610,000 **21.** 3,000,000,000 **22.** 60,100

23. 52.000 **24.** $29.8 \cdot 10^7$ **25.** 8,900,000 **26.** $500 \cdot 10^3$

See Example 3

27. History Ancient Egyptians hammered gold into sheets so thin that it took 3.67×10^5 sheets to make a pile 2.5 centimeters high. Write the number of sheets in standard form.

See Example 4

28. Astronomy Mars is 7.83×10^7 kilometers from Earth. Venus is 4.14×10^7 kilometers from Earth. Which planet is closer to Earth?

PRACTICE AND PROBLEM SOLVING

Extra Practice
See page 724.

Find the missing number or numbers.

29. $24{,}500 = 2.45 \times 10^{■}$ **30.** $16{,}800 = ■ \times 10^4$ **31.** $■ = 3.40 \times 10^2$

32. $280{,}000 = 2.8 \times 10^{■}$ **33.** $5.4 \times 10^8 = ■$ **34.** $60{,}000{,}000 = ■ \times 10^{■}$

Tell whether each number is written in scientific notation. Then order the numbers from least to greatest.

35. 43.7×10^6 **36.** 1×10^7 **37.** 2.9×10^7 **38.** 305×10^6

39. Physical Science In a vacuum, light travels at a speed of about nine hundred and eighty million feet per second. Write this speed in scientific notation.

Earth Science LINK

40. The earliest rocks native to Earth formed during the Archean eon. Calculate the length of this eon. Write your answer in scientific notation.

41. Dinosaurs lived during the Mesozoic era. Calculate the length of the Mesozoic era. Write your answer in scientific notation.

42. Tropites were prehistoric marine animals whose fossil remains can be used to date the rock formations in which they are found. Such fossils are known as *index fossils.* Tropites lived between 2.08×10^8 and 2.30×10^8 years ago. During what geologic time period did they live?

Geologic Time Scale

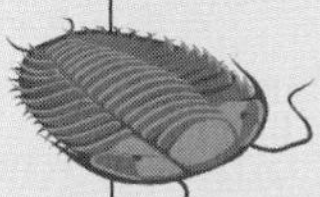

Eon	Era	Period
Phanerozoic (540 mya*–present)	**Cenozoic** (65 mya–present)	**Quaternary** (1.8 mya–present) **Holocene epoch** (11,000 yrs ago–present) **Pleistocene epoch** (1.8 mya–11,000 yrs ago) **Tertiary** (65 mya–1.8 mya) **Pliocene epoch** (5.3 mya–1.8 mya) **Miocene epoch** (23.8 mya–5.3 mya) **Oligocene epoch** (33.7 mya–23.8 mya) **Eocene epoch** (54.8 mya–33.7 mya) **Paleocene epoch** (65 mya–54.8 mya)
	Mesozoic (248 mya–65 mya)	**Cretaceous** (144 mya–65 mya) **Jurassic** (206 mya–144 mya) **Triassic** (248 mya–206 mya)
	Paleozoic (540 mya–248 mya)	**Permian** (290 mya–248 mya) **Pennsylvanian** (323 mya–290 mya) **Mississippian** (354 mya–323 mya) **Devonian** (417 mya–354 mya) **Silurian** (443 mya–417 mya) **Ordovician** (490 mya–443 mya) **Cambrian** (540 mya–490 mya)
Proterozoic (2,500 mya–540 mya)		
Archean (3,800 mya–2,500 mya)		
Hadean (4,600 mya–3,800 mya)		

*mya = million years ago

43. **Write About It** Explain why scientific notation is especially useful in earth science.

44. **Challenge** We live in the Holocene epoch. Write the age of this epoch in scientific notation.

TEST PREP and Spiral Review

45. **Multiple Choice** Kaylee wrote in her dinosaur report that the Jurassic period was 1.75×10^8 years ago. According to Kaylee's report, how many years ago was the Jurassic period?

(A) 1,750,000 (B) 17,500,000 (C) 175,000,000 (D) 17,500,000,000

46. **Multiple Choice** What is 2,430,000 in scientific notation?

(F) 243×10^4 (G) 24.3×10^5 (H) 2.43×10^5 (J) 2.43×10^6

Write each number using an exponent and the given base. (Lesson 1-2)

47. 625, base 5
48. 512, base 8
49. 512, base 2

Convert each measure. (Lesson 1-3)

50. 2.87 kg to grams
51. 1,700 m to kilometers
52. 8 L to milliliters

Technology LAB 1-4

Scientific Notation with a Calculator

Use with Lesson 1-4

go.hrw.com
Lab Resources Online
KEYWORD: MS7 Lab1

Scientists often have to work with very large numbers. For example, the Andromeda Galaxy contains over 200,000,000,000 stars. Scientific notation is a compact way of expressing large numbers such as this.

Activity

1 Show 200,000,000,000 in scientific notation.

Enter 200,000,000,000 on your graphing calculator. Then press ENTER.

2 E 11 on the calculator display means 2×10^{11}, which is 200,000,000,000 in scientific notation. Your calculator automatically puts very large numbers into scientific notation.

You can use the **EE** function to enter 2×10^{11} directly into the calculator. Enter 2×10^{11} by pressing 2 2nd EE , 11 ENTER.

2 Simplify $2.31 \times 10^4 \div 525$.

Enter 2.31×10^4 into your calculator in scientific notation, and then divide by 525. To do this, press 2.31 2nd use EE , key 4 ÷ 525 ENTER.
Your answer should be 44.

Think and Discuss

1. Explain how scientific notation and calculator notation are similar. What could the "E" possibly stand for in calculator notation?

Try This

Use the calculator to write each number in scientific notation.

1. 6,500,000
2. 15,000,000
3. 360,000,000,000

Simplify each expression, and express your answer in scientific notation.

4. $8.4 \times 10^6 \div 300$
5. $9 \times 10^3 - 900$
6. $2.5 \times 10^9 \times 10$
7. $3 \times 10^2 + 6000$
8. $2.85 \times 10^8 \div 95$
9. $1.5 \times 10^7 \div 150$

1-5 Order of Operations

Learn to use the order of operations to simplify numerical expressions.

Vocabulary

numerical expression

order of operations

When you get ready for school, you put on your socks *before* you put on your shoes. In mathematics, as in life, some tasks must be done in a certain order.

A **numerical expression** is made up of numbers and operations. When simplifying a numerical expression, rules must be followed so that everyone gets the same answer. That is why mathematicians have agreed upon the **order of operations**.

ORDER OF OPERATIONS

1. Perform operations within grouping symbols.
2. Evaluate powers.
3. Multiply and divide in order from left to right.
4. Add and subtract in order from left to right.

EXAMPLE 1 Using the Order of Operations

Simplify each expression.

A $27 - 18 \div 6$

$27 - 18 \div 6$	*Divide.*
$27 - 3$	*Subtract.*
24	

B $36 - 18 \div 2 \cdot 3 + 8$

$36 - 18 \div 2 \cdot 3 + 8$	*Divide and multiply from left to right.*
$36 - 9 \cdot 3 + 8$	
$36 - 27 + 8$	*Subtract and add from left to right.*
$9 + 8$	
17	

C $5 + 6^2 \cdot 10$

$5 + 6^2 \cdot 10$	*Evaluate the power.*
$5 + 36 \cdot 10$	*Multiply.*
$5 + 360$	*Add.*
365	

EXAMPLE 2 Using the Order of Operations with Grouping Symbols

Simplify each expression.

A $36 - (2 \cdot 6) \div 3$

$36 - (2 \cdot 6) \div 3$ *Perform the operation in parentheses.*

$36 - 12 \div 3$ *Divide.*

$36 - 4$ *Subtract.*

32

Helpful Hint

When an expression has a set of grouping symbols within a second set of grouping symbols, begin with the innermost set.

B $[(4 + 12 \div 4) - 2]^3$

$[(4 + 12 \div 4) - 2]^3$ *The parentheses are inside the brackets, so perform the operations inside the parentheses first.*

$[(4 + 3) - 2]^3$

$[7 - 2]^3$

5^3

125

EXAMPLE 3 *Career Application*

Maria works part-time in a law office, where she earns $20 per hour. The table shows the number of hours she worked last week. Simplify the expression $(6 + 5 \cdot 3) \cdot 20$ to find out how much money Maria earned last week.

Day	Hours
Monday	6
Tuesday	5
Wednesday	5
Thursday	5

$(6 + 5 \cdot 3) \cdot 20$ *Perform the operations in parentheses.*

$(6 + 15) \cdot 20$ *Add.*

$21 \cdot 20$ *Multiply.*

420

Maria earned $420 last week.

Think and Discuss

1. **Apply** the order of operations to determine if the expressions $3 + 4^2$ and $(3 + 4)^2$ have the same value.
2. **Give** the correct order of operations for simplifying $(5 + 3 \cdot 20) \div 13 + 3^2$.
3. **Determine** where grouping symbols should be inserted in the expression $3 + 9 - 4 \cdot 2$ so that its value is 13.

1-5 Exercises

go.hrw.com
Homework Help Online
KEYWORD: MS7 1-5
Parent Resources Online
KEYWORD: MS7 Parent

GUIDED PRACTICE

See Example 1
Simplify each expression.

1. $43 + 16 \div 4$
2. $28 - 4 \cdot 3 \div 6 + 4$
3. $25 - 4^2 \div 8$

See Example 2

4. $26 - (7 \cdot 3) + 2$
5. $(3^2 + 11) \div 5$
6. $32 + 6(4 - 2^2) + 8$

See Example 3

7. **Career** Caleb earns \$10 per hour. He worked 4 hours on Monday, Wednesday, and Friday. He worked 8 hours on Tuesday and Thursday. Simplify the expression $(3 \cdot 4 + 2 \cdot 8) \cdot 10$ to find out how much Caleb earned in all.

INDEPENDENT PRACTICE

See Example 1
Simplify each expression.

8. $3 + 7 \cdot 5 - 1$
9. $5 \cdot 9 - 3$
10. $3 - 2 + 6 \cdot 2^2$

See Example 2

11. $(3 \cdot 3 - 3)^2 \div 3 + 3$
12. $2^5 - (4 \cdot 5 + 3)$
13. $(3 \div 3) + 3 \cdot (3^3 - 3)$
14. $4^3 \div 8 - 2$
15. $(8 - 2)^2 \cdot (8 - 1)^2 \div 3$
16. $9{,}234 \div [3 \cdot 3(1 + 8^3)]$

See Example 3

17. **Consumer Math** Maki paid a \$14 basic fee plus \$25 a day to rent a car. Simplify the expression $14 + 5 \cdot 25$ to find out how much it cost her to rent the car for 5 days.
18. **Consumer Math** Enrico spent \$20 per square yard for carpet and \$35 for a carpet pad. Simplify the expression $35 + 20(12^2 \div 9)$ to find out how much Enrico spent to carpet a 12 ft by 12 ft room.

PRACTICE AND PROBLEM SOLVING

Extra Practice
See page 725.

Simplify each expression.

19. $90 - 36 \times 2$
20. $16 + 14 \div 2 - 7$
21. $64 \div 2^2 + 4$
22. $10 \times (18 - 2) + 7$
23. $(9 - 4)^2 - 12 \times 2$
24. $[1 + (2 + 5)^2] \times 2$

Compare. Write <, >, or =.

25. $8 \cdot 3 - 2$ ▒ $8 \cdot (3 - 2)$
26. $(6 + 10) \div 2$ ▒ $6 + 10 \div 2$
27. $12 \div 3 \cdot 4$ ▒ $12 \div (3 \cdot 4)$
28. $18 + 6 - 2$ ▒ $18 + (6 - 2)$
29. $[6(8 - 3) + 2]$ ▒ $6(8 - 3) + 2$
30. $(18 - 14) \div (2 + 2)$ ▒ $18 - 14 \div 2 + 2$

Critical Thinking **Insert grouping symbols to make each statement true.**

31. $4 \cdot 8 - 3 = 20$
32. $5 + 9 - 3 \div 2 = 8$
33. $12 - 2^2 \div 5 = 20$
34. $4 \cdot 2 + 6 = 32$
35. $4 + 6 - 3 \div 7 = 1$
36. $9 \cdot 8 - 6 \div 3 = 6$

37. Bertha earned \$8.00 per hour for 4 hours babysitting and \$10.00 per hour for 5 hours painting a room. Simplify the expression $8 \cdot 4 + 10 \cdot 5$ to find out how much Bertha earned in all.

38. **Consumer Math** Mike bought a painting for \$512. He sold it at an antique auction for 4 times the amount that he paid for it, and then he purchased another painting with half of the profit that he made. Simplify the expression $(512 \cdot 4 - 512) \div 2$ to find how much Mike paid for the second painting.

39. **Multi-Step** Anelise bought four shirts and two pairs of jeans. She paid \$6 in sales tax.
    a. Write an expression that shows how much she spent on shirts.
    b. Write an expression that shows how much she spent on jeans.
    c. Write and evaluate an expression to show how much she spent on clothes, including sales tax.

40. **Choose a Strategy** There are four children in a family. The sum of the squares of the ages of the three youngest children equals the square of the age of the oldest child. How old are the children?

    Ⓐ 1, 4, 8, 9 Ⓑ 1, 3, 6, 12 Ⓒ 4, 5, 8, 10 Ⓓ 2, 3, 8, 16

41. **Write About It** Describe the order in which you would perform the operations to find the correct value of $[(2 + 4)^2 - 2 \cdot 3] \div 6$.

42. **Challenge** Use the numbers 3, 5, 6, 2, 54, and 5 in that order to write an expression that has a value of 100.

Test Prep and Spiral Review

43. **Multiple Choice** Which operation should be performed first to simplify the expression $18 - 1 \cdot 9 \div 3 + 8$?

    Ⓐ Addition Ⓑ Subtraction Ⓒ Multiplication Ⓓ Division

44. **Multiple Choice** Which expression does NOT simplify to 81?

    Ⓕ $9 \cdot (4 + 5)$ Ⓖ $7 + 16 \cdot 4 + 10$ Ⓗ $3 \cdot 25 + 2$ Ⓙ $10^2 - 4 \cdot 5 + 1$

45. **Multiple Choice** Quinton bought 2 pairs of jeans for \$30 each and 3 pairs of socks for \$5 each. Which expression can be simplified to determine the total amount Quinton paid for the jeans and socks?

    Ⓐ $2 \cdot 3(30 + 5)$ Ⓑ $(2 + 3) \cdot (30 + 5)$ Ⓒ $2 \cdot (30 + 5) \cdot 3$ Ⓓ $2 \cdot 30 + 3 \cdot 5$

Find each value. (Lesson 1-2)

46. 8^6 47. 9^3 48. 4^5 49. 3^3 50. 7^1

Multiply. (Lesson 1-4)

51. $612 \cdot 10^3$ 52. $43.8 \cdot 10^6$ 53. $590 \cdot 10^5$ 54. $3.1 \cdot 10^7$ 55. $1.91 \cdot 10^2$

Technology LAB 1-5

Explore Order of Operations

Use with Lesson 1-5

go.hrw.com
Lab Resources Online
KEYWORD: MS7 Lab1

REMEMBER

The order of operations
1. Perform operations within grouping symbols.
2. Evaluate powers.
3. Multiply and divide in order from left to right.
4. Add and subtract in order from left to right.

Many calculators have an x^2 key that allows you to find the square of a number. On calculators that do not have this key, or to use exponents other than 2, you can use the caret key, ^ .

For example, to evaluate 3^5, press 3 ^ 5, and then press ENTER .

Activity

1 Simplify $4 \cdot 2^3$ using paper and pencil. Then check your answer with a calculator.

First simplify the expression using paper and pencil:
$4 \cdot 2^3 = 4 \cdot 8 = 32.$

Then simplify $4 \cdot 2^3$ using your calculator.

Notice that the calculator automatically evaluates the power first. If you want to perform the multiplication first, you must put that operation inside parentheses.

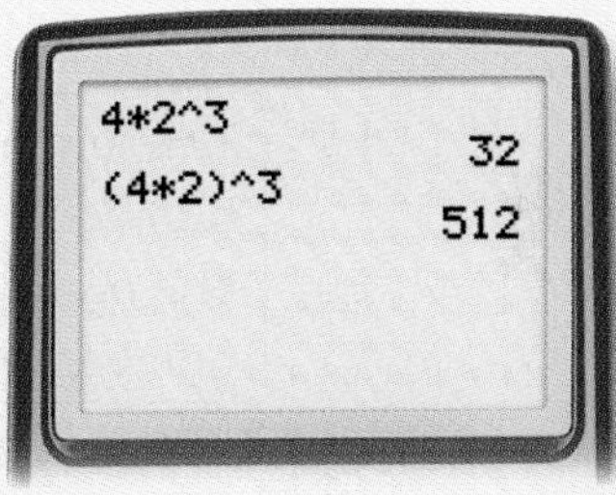

2 Use a calculator to simplify $\frac{(2 + 5 \cdot 4)^3}{4^2}$.

Think and Discuss

1. Is $2 + 5 \cdot 4^3 + 4^2$ equivalent to $(2 + 5 \cdot 4^3) + 4^2$? Explain.

Try This

Simplify each expression with pencil and paper. Check your answers with a calculator.

1. $3 \cdot 2^3 + 5$
2. $3 \cdot (2^3 + 5)$
3. $(3 \cdot 2)^2$
4. $3 \cdot 2^2$
5. $2^{(3 \cdot 2)}$

Use a calculator to simplify each expression. Round your answers to the nearest hundredth.

6. $(2.1 + 5.6 \cdot 4^3) \div 6^4$
7. $[(2.1 + 5.6) \cdot 4^3] \div 6^4$
8. $[(8.6 - 1.5) \div 2^3] \div 5^2$

1-6 Properties

Learn how to identify properties of rational numbers and use them to simplify numerical expressions.

Vocabulary

Commutative Property

Associative Property

Identity Property

Distributive Property

In Lesson 1-5 you learned how to use the order of operations to simplify numerical expressions. The following properties of rational numbers are also useful when you simplify expressions.

Commutative Property		
Words	**Numbers**	**Algebra**
You can add numbers in any order and multiply numbers in any order.	$3 + 8 = 8 + 3$ $5 \cdot 7 = 7 \cdot 5$	$a + b = b + a$ $ab = ba$

Associative Property		
Words	**Numbers**	**Algebra**
When you add or multiply, you can group the numbers together in any combination.	$(4 + 5) + 1 = 4 + (5 + 1)$ $(9 \cdot 2) \cdot 6 = 9 \cdot (2 \cdot 6)$	$(a + b) + c = a + (b + c)$ $(a \cdot b) \cdot c = a \cdot (b \cdot c)$

Identity Property		
Words	**Numbers**	**Algebra**
The sum of 0 and any number is the number. The product of 1 and any number is the number.	$4 + 0 = 4$ $8 \cdot 1 = 8$	$a + 0 = a$ $a \cdot 1 = a$

EXAMPLE 1 Identifying Properties of Addition and Multiplication

Tell which property is represented.

A $2 + (7 + 8) = (2 + 7) + 8$

$2 + (7 + 8) = (2 + 7) + 8$ *The numbers are regrouped.*

Associative Property

B $25 \cdot 1 = 25$

$25 \cdot 1 = 25$ *One of the factors is 1.*

Identity Property

C $xy = yx$

$xy = yx$ *The order of the variables is switched.*

Commutative Property

You can use properties and mental math to rearrange or regroup numbers into combinations that are easier to work with.

EXAMPLE 2 Using Properties to Simplify Expressions

Simplify each expression. Justify each step.

A $12 + 19 + 18$

$12 + 19 + 18 = 19 + 12 + 18$	*Commutative Property*
$= 19 + (12 + 18)$	*Associative Property*
$= 19 + 30$	*Add.*
$= 49$	

B $25 \cdot 13 \cdot 4$

$25 \cdot 13 \cdot 4 = 25 \cdot 4 \cdot 13$	*Commutative Property*
$= (25 \cdot 4) \cdot 13$	*Associative Property*
$= 100 \cdot 13$	*Multiply.*
$= 1{,}300$	

You can use the Distributive Property to multiply numbers mentally by breaking apart one of the numbers and writing it as a sum or difference.

Distributive Property		
Numbers	$6 \cdot (9 + 14) = 6 \cdot 9 + 6 \cdot 14$	$8 \cdot (5 - 2) = 8 \cdot 5 - 8 \cdot 2$
Algebra	$a \cdot (b + c) = ab + ac$	$a \cdot (b - c) = ab - ac$

EXAMPLE 3 Using the Distributive Property to Multiply Mentally

Use the Distributive Property to find 7(29).

Method 1

$7(29) = 7(20 + 9)$	*Rewrite 29.*
$= (7 \cdot 20) + (7 \cdot 9)$	*Use the Distributive Property.*
$= 140 + 63$	*Multiply.*
$= 203$	*Simplify.*

Method 2

$7(29) = 7(30 - 1)$

$= (7 \cdot 30) - (7 \cdot 1)$

$= 210 - 7$

$= 203$

Think and Discuss

1. **Describe** two different ways to simplify the expression $7 \cdot (3 + 9)$.
2. **Explain** how the Distributive Property can help you find $6 \cdot 102$ using mental math.

1-6 Exercises

go.hrw.com
Homework Help Online
KEYWORD: MS7 1-6
Parent Resources Online
KEYWORD: MS7 Parent

GUIDED PRACTICE

See Example 1
Tell which property is represented.

1. $1 + (6 + 7) = (1 + 6) + 7$ **2.** $1 \cdot 10 = 10$ **3.** $3 \cdot 5 = 5 \cdot 3$

4. $6 + 0 = 6$ **5.** $4 \cdot (4 \cdot 2) = (4 \cdot 4) \cdot 2$ **6.** $x + y = y + x$

See Example 2
Simplify each expression. Justify each step.

7. $8 + 23 + 2$ **8.** $2 \cdot (17 \cdot 5)$ **9.** $(25 \cdot 11) \cdot 4$

10. $17 + 29 + 3$ **11.** $16 + (17 + 14)$ **12.** $5 \cdot 19 \cdot 20$

See Example 3
Use the Distributive Property to find each product.

13. 2(19) **14.** 5(31) **15.** (22)2

16. (13)6 **17.** 8(26) **18.** (34)6

INDEPENDENT PRACTICE

See Example 1
Tell which property is represented.

19. $1 + 0 = 1$ **20.** $xyz = x \cdot (yz)$ **21.** $9 + (9 + 0) = (9 + 9) + 0$

22. $11 + 25 = 25 + 11$ **23.** $7 \cdot 1 = 7$ **24.** $16 \cdot 4 = 4 \cdot 16$

See Example 2
Simplify each expression. Justify each step.

25. $50 \cdot 16 \cdot 2$ **26.** $9 + 34 + 1$ **27.** $4 \cdot (25 \cdot 9)$

28. $27 + 28 + 3$ **29.** $20 + (63 + 80)$ **30.** $25 + 17 + 75$

See Example 3
Use the Distributive Property to find each product.

31. 9(15) **32.** (14)5 **33.** 3(58)

34. 10(42) **35.** (23)4 **36.** (16)5

PRACTICE AND PROBLEM SOLVING

Extra Practice
See page 725.

Write an example of each property using whole numbers.

37. Commutative Property **38.** Identity Property

39. Associative Property **40.** Distributive Property

41. Architecture The figure shows the floor plan for a studio loft. To find the area of the loft, the architect multiplies the length and the width: $(14 + 8) \cdot 10$. Use the Distributive Property to find the area of the loft.

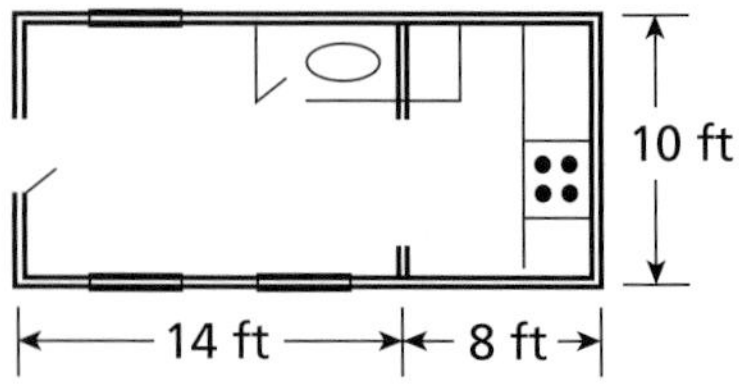

Simplify each expression. Justify each step.

42. $32 + 26 + 43$ **43.** $50 \cdot 45 \cdot 4$ **44.** $5 + 16 + 25$ **45.** $35 \cdot 25 \cdot 20$

Complete each equation. Then tell which property is represented.

46. $5 + 16 = 16 + \square$

47. $15 \cdot 1 = \square$

48. $\square \cdot (4 + 7) = 3 \cdot 4 + 3 \cdot 7$

49. $20 + \square = 20$

50. $2 \cdot \square \cdot 9 = (2 \cdot 13) \cdot 9$

51. $8 + (\square + 4) = (8 + 8) + 4$

52. $2 \cdot (6 + 1) = 2 \cdot \square + 2 \cdot 1$

53. $(12 - 9) \cdot \square = 12 \cdot 2 - 9 \cdot 2$

54. Sports Janice wants to know the total number of games won by the Denver Nuggets basketball team over the three seasons shown in the table. What expression should she simplify? Explain how she can use mental math and the properties of this lesson to simplify the expression.

Denver Nuggets

Season	Won	Lost
2001–02	27	55
2002–03	17	65
2003–04	43	39

55. What's the Error? A student simplified the expression $6 \cdot (9 + 12)$ as shown. What is the student's error?

$6 \cdot (9 + 12) = 6 \cdot 9 + 12$
$= 54 + 12$
$= 66$

56. Write About It Do you think there is a Commutative Property of Subtraction? Give an example to justify your answer.

57. Challenge Use the Distributive Property to simplify $\frac{1}{6} \cdot (36 + \frac{1}{2})$.

TEST PREP and Spiral Review

58. Multiple Choice Which is an example of the Associative Property?

Ⓐ $4 + 0 = 4$

Ⓑ $9 + 8 + 2 = 9 + (8 + 2)$

Ⓒ $5 + 7 = 7 + 5$

Ⓓ $5 \cdot (12 + 3) = 5 \cdot 12 + 5 \cdot 3$

59. Multiple Choice Which property is $2 \cdot (3 + 7) = (2 \cdot 3) + (2 \cdot 7)$ an example of?

Ⓕ Associative Ⓖ Commutative Ⓗ Distributive Ⓙ Identity

60. Short Response Show how to use the Distributive Property to simplify the expression 8(27).

Write each number using an exponent and the given base. (Lesson 1-2)

61. 36, base 6 **62.** 64, base 2 **63.** 9, base 3 **64.** 1,000, base 10

Simplify each expression. (Lesson 1-5)

65. $25 + 5 - (6^2 - 7)$ **66.** $3^3 - (6 + 3)$ **67.** $(4^2 + 5) \div 7$ **68.** $(5 - 3)^2 \div (3^2 - 7)$

CHAPTER 1

READY TO GO ON?

SECTION 1A

Quiz for Lessons 1-1 Through 1-6

1-1 Numbers and Patterns

Identify a possible pattern. Use the pattern to write the next three numbers or figures.

1. 8, 15, 22, 29, . . .

2. 79, 66, 53, 40, . . .

3. 

1-2 Exponents

Find each value.

4. 8^4

5. 7^3

6. 4^5

7. 6^2

8. The number of bacteria in a sample doubles every hour. How many bacteria cells will there be after 8 hours if there is one cell at the beginning? Write your answer as a power.

1-3 Metric Measurements

Convert each measure.

9. 17.3 kg to grams

10. 540 mL to liters

11. 0.46 cm to millimeters

12. Cat ran in the 400-meter dash and the 800-meter run. Hilo ran in the 2-kilometer cross-country race. All together, who ran the farthest, Cat or Hilo?

1-4 Applying Exponents

Multiply.

13. $456 \cdot 10^5$

14. $9.3 \cdot 10^2$

15. $0.36 \cdot 10^8$

Write each number in scientific notation.

16. 8,400,000

17. 521,000,000

18. 29,000

19. In May 2005, the world's population was over 6,446,000,000 and was increasing by 140 people each minute! Write this population in scientific notation.

1-5 Order of Operations

Simplify each expression.

20. $8 - 14 \div (9 - 2)$

21. $54 - 6 \cdot 3 + 4^2$

22. $4 - 24 \div 2^3$

23. $4(3 + 2)^2 - 9$

1-6 Properties

Simplify each expression. Justify each step.

24. $29 + 50 + 21$

25. $5 \cdot 18 \cdot 20$

26. $34 + 62 + 36$

27. $3 \cdot 11 \cdot 20$

Focus on Problem Solving

Solve

- **Choose an operation: multiplication or division**

To solve a word problem, you must determine which mathematical operation you can use to find the answer. One way of doing this is to determine the action the problem is asking you to take. If you are putting equal parts together, then you need to multiply. If you are separating something into equal parts, then you need to divide.

Decide what action each problem is asking you to take, and tell whether you must multiply or divide. Then explain your decision.

1. Judy plays the flute in the band. She practices for 3 hours every week. Judy practices only half as long as Angie, who plays the clarinet. How long does Angie practice playing the clarinet each week?

2. Each year, members of the band and choir are invited to join the bell ensemble for the winter performance. There are 18 bells in the bell ensemble. This year, each student has 3 bells to play. How many students are in the bell ensemble this year?

3. For every percussion instrument in the band, there are 4 wind instruments. If there are 48 wind instruments in the band, how many percussion instruments are there?

4. A group of 4 people singing together in harmony is called a quartet. At a state competition for high school choir students, 7 quartets from different schools competed. How many students competed in the quartet competition?

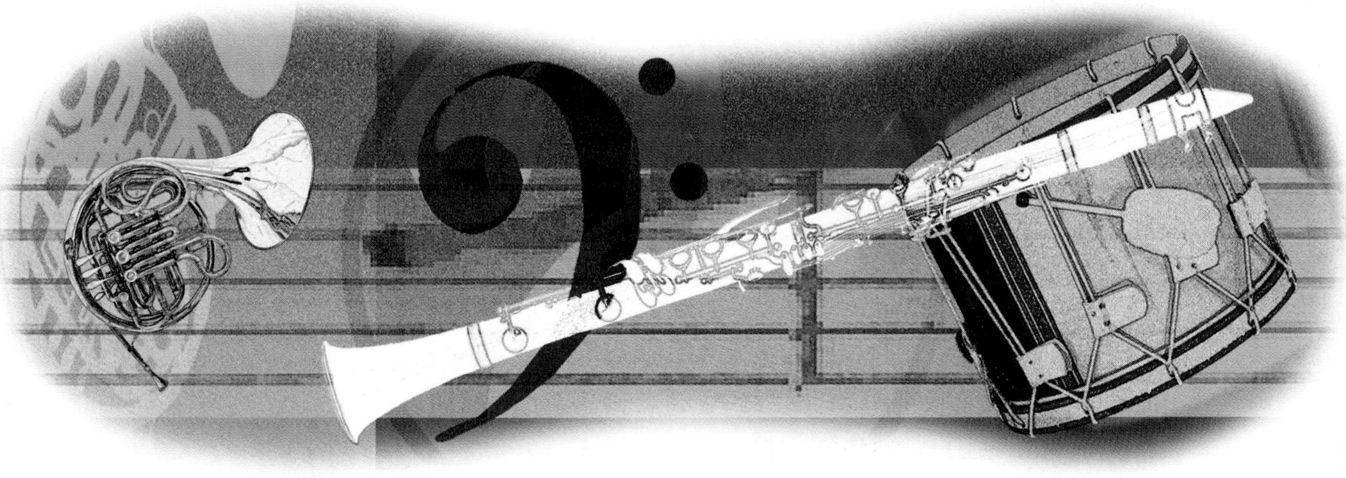

1-7 Variables and Algebraic Expressions

Learn to evaluate algebraic expressions.

Vocabulary
variable
constant
algebraic expression
evaluate

Ron Howard was born in 1954. You can find out what year Ron turned 16 by adding 16 to the year he was born.

$$1954 + 16$$

In algebra, letters are often used to represent numbers. You can use a letter such as a to represent Ron Howard's age. When he turns a years old, the year will be

$$1954 + \boldsymbol{a}.$$

The letter a has a value that can change, or vary. When a letter represents a number that can vary, it is called a **variable**. The year 1954 is a **constant** because the number cannot change.

Age	Year born + age = year at age	
16	1954 + 16	1970
18	1954 + 18	1972
21	1954 + 21	1975
36	1954 + 36	1990
a	1954 + a	

An **algebraic expression** consists of one or more variables. It usually contains constants and operations. For example, $1954 + a$ is an algebraic expression for the year Ron Howard turns a certain age.

To **evaluate** an algebraic expression, substitute a number for the variable.

EXAMPLE 1 **Evaluating Algebraic Expressions**

Evaluate $n + 7$ for each value of n.

A $n = 3$

$n + 7$
$3 + 7$ *Substitute 3 for n.*
10 *Add.*

B $n = 5$

$n + 7$
$5 + 7$ *Substitute 5 for n.*
12 *Add.*

Multiplication and division of variables can be written in several ways, as shown in the table.

When evaluating expressions, use the order of operations.

Multiplication		Division	
$7t$	$7 \cdot t$	$\frac{q}{2}$	$q/2$
$7(t)$	$7 \times t$	$q \div 2$	
ab	$a \cdot b$	$\frac{s}{r}$	s/r
$a(b)$	$a \times b$	$s \div r$	

EXAMPLE 2 Evaluating Algebraic Expressions Involving Order of Operations

Evaluate each expression for the given value of the variable.

A $3x - 2$ for $x = 5$

$3(5) - 2$	*Substitute 5 for x.*
$15 - 2$	*Multiply.*
13	*Subtract*

B $n \div 2 + n$ for $n = 4$

$4 \div 2 + 4$	*Substitute 4 for n.*
$2 + 4$	*Divide.*
6	*Add.*

C $6y^2 + 2y$ for $y = 2$

$6(2)^2 + 2(2)$	*Substitute 2 for y.*
$6(4) + 2(2)$	*Evaluate the power.*
$24 + 4$	*Multiply.*
28	*Add.*

EXAMPLE 3 Evaluating Algebraic Expressions with Two Variables

Evaluate $\frac{3}{n} + 2m$ for $n = 3$ and $m = 4$.

$\frac{3}{n} + 2m$	
$\frac{3}{3} + 2(4)$	*Substitute 3 for n and 4 for m.*
$1 + 8$	*Divide and multiply from left to right.*
9	*Add.*

Think and Discuss

1. Write each expression another way. **a.** $12x$ **b.** $\frac{4}{y}$ **c.** $\frac{3xy}{2}$

2. Explain the difference between a variable and a constant.

1-7 Exercises

go.hrw.com
Homework Help Online
KEYWORD: MS7 1-7
Parent Resources Online
KEYWORD: MS7 Parent

GUIDED PRACTICE

See Example 1
Evaluate $n + 9$ for each value of n.

1. $n = 3$
2. $n = 2$
3. $n = 11$

See Example 2
Evaluate each expression for the given value of the variable.

4. $2x - 3$ for $x = 4$
5. $n \div 3 + n$ for $n = 6$
6. $5y^2 + 3y$ for $y = 2$

See Example 3
Evaluate each expression for the given values of the variables.

7. $\frac{8}{n} + 3m$ for $n = 2$ and $m = 5$
8. $5a - 3b + 5$ for $a = 4$ and $b = 3$

INDEPENDENT PRACTICE

See Example 1
Evaluate $n + 5$ for each value of n.

9. $n = 17$
10. $n = 9$
11. $n = 0$

See Example 2
Evaluate each expression for the given value of the variable.

12. $5y - 1$ for $y = 3$
13. $10b - 9$ for $b = 2$
14. $p \div 7 + p$ for $p = 14$
15. $n \div 5 + n$ for $n = 20$
16. $3x^2 + 2x$ for $x = 10$
17. $3c^2 - 5c$ for $c = 3$

See Example 3
Evaluate each expression for the given values of the variables.

18. $\frac{12}{n} + 7m$ for $n = 6$ and $m = 4$
19. $7p - 2t + 3$ for $p = 6$ and $t = 2$
20. $9 - \frac{3x}{4} + 20y$ for $x = 4$ and $y = 5$
21. $r^2 + 15k$ for $r = 15$ and $k = 5$

PRACTICE AND PROBLEM SOLVING

Extra Practice
See page 725.

Evaluate each expression for the given values of the variables.

22. $20x - 10$ for $x = 4$
23. $4d^2 - 3d$ for $d = 2$
24. $22p \div 11 + p$ for $p = 3$
25. $q + q^2 + q \div 2$ for $q = 4$
26. $\frac{16}{k} + 7h$ for $k = 8$ and $h = 2$
27. $f \div 3 + f$ for $f = 18$
28. $3t \div 3 + t$ for $t = 13$
29. $9 + 3p - 5t + 3$ for $p = 2$ and $t = 1$
30. $108 - 12j + j$ for $j = 9$
31. $3m^3 + \frac{y}{5}$ for $m = 2$ and $y = 35$

32. The expression $60m$ gives the number of seconds in m minutes. Evaluate $60m$ for $m = 7$. How many seconds are there in 7 minutes?

33. **Money** Betsy has n quarters. You can use the expression $0.25n$ to find the total value of her coins in dollars. What is the value of 18 quarters?

34. **Physical Science** A color TV has a power rating of 200 watts. The expression $200t$ gives the power used by t color TV sets. Evaluate $200t$ for $t = 13$. How much power is used by 13 TV sets?

35. Physical Science The expression $1.8c + 32$ can be used to convert a temperature in degrees Celsius c to degrees Fahrenheit. What is the temperature in degrees Fahrenheit if the temperature is 30°C?

36. Physical Science The graph shows the changes of state for water.

a. What is the boiling point of water in degrees Celsius?

b. Use the expression $1.8c + 32$ to find the boiling point of water in degrees Fahrenheit.

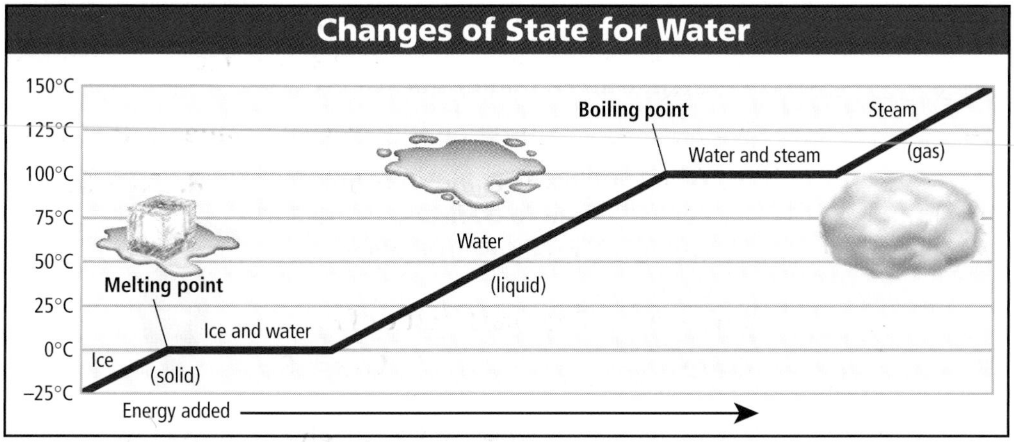

37. What's the Error? A student was asked to identify the variable in the expression $72x + 8$. The student answered $72x$. What was the student's error?

38. Write About It Explain why letters such as x, p, and n used in algebraic expressions are called variables. Use examples to illustrate your response.

39. Challenge Evaluate the expression $\frac{x + y}{y - x}$ for $x = 6$ and $y = 8$.

Test Prep and Spiral Review

40. Multiple Choice Which expression does NOT equal 15?

Ⓐ $3t$ for $t = 5$ Ⓑ $3 + t$ for $t = 12$ Ⓒ $t \div 3$ for $t = 60$ Ⓓ $t - 10$ for $t = 25$

41. Multiple Choice A group of 11 students go rock climbing at a local gym. It costs \$12 per student plus \$4 for each shoe rental. If only 8 students rent shoes, what is the total cost for the group to go climbing? Use the expression $12x + 4y$, where x represents the total number of students and y represents the number of students who rent shoes.

Ⓕ \$132 Ⓖ \$140 Ⓗ \$164 Ⓙ \$176

Write each number in scientific notation. (Lesson 1-4)

42. 102.45 **43.** 62,100,000 **44.** 769,000 **45.** 800,000

Use the Distributive Property to find each product. (Lesson 1-6)

46. 5(16) **47.** (17)4 **48.** 7(23) **49.** (29)3

1-8 Translate Words into Math

Problem Solving Skill

Learn to translate words into numbers, variables, and operations.

Although they are closely related, a Great Dane weighs about 40 times as much as a Chihuahua. An expression for the weight of the Great Dane could be $40c$, where c is the weight of the Chihuahua.

When solving real-world problems, you will need to translate words, or verbal expressions, into algebraic expressions.

Operation	Verbal Expressions	Algebraic Expression
+	• add 3 to a number • a number plus 3 • the sum of a number and 3 • 3 more than a number • a number increased by 3	$n + 3$
−	• subtract 12 from a number • a number minus 12 • the difference of a number and 12 • 12 less than a number • a number decreased by 12 • take away 12 from a number • a number less 12	$x - 12$
×	• 2 times a number • 2 multiplied by a number • the product of 2 and a number	$2m$ or $2 \cdot m$
÷	• 6 divided into a number • a number divided by 6 • the quotient of a number and 6	$a \div 6$ or $\frac{a}{6}$

EXAMPLE 1 **Translating Verbal Expressions into Algebraic Expressions**

Write each phrase as an algebraic expression.

A the product of 20 and t

product means "multiply"

$20t$

B 24 less than a number

less than means "subtract from"

$n - 24$

Write each phrase as an algebraic expression.

C **4 times the sum of a number and 2**

4 times the **sum** of a number and 2

$4 \cdot \quad n + 2$

$4(n + 2)$

D **the sum of 4 times a number and 2**

the **sum** of 4 times a number and 2

$4 \cdot n \quad + 2$

$4n + 2$

When solving real-world problems, you may need to determine the action to know which operation to use.

Action	Operation
Put parts together	Add
Put equal parts together	Multiply
Find how much more or less	Subtract
Separate into equal parts	Divide

EXAMPLE 2 Translating Real-World Problems into Algebraic Expressions

A **Jed reads p pages each day of a 200-page book. Write an algebraic expression for how many days it will take Jed to read the book.**

You need to *separate* the total number of pages *into equal parts.* This involves division.

$$\frac{\text{total number of pages}}{\text{pages read each day}} = \frac{200}{p}$$

B **To rent a certain car for a day costs \$84 plus \$0.29 for every mile the car is driven. Write an algebraic expression to show how much it costs to rent the car for a day.**

The cost includes \$0.29 per mile. Use m for the number of miles.

Multiply to *put equal parts together:* $0.29m$

In addition to the fee per mile, the cost includes a flat fee of \$84.

Add to *put parts together:* $84 + 0.29m$

Think and Discuss

1. **Write** three different verbal expressions that can be represented by $2 - y$.
2. **Explain** how you would determine which operation to use to find the number of chairs in 6 rows of 100 chairs each.

1-8 Exercises

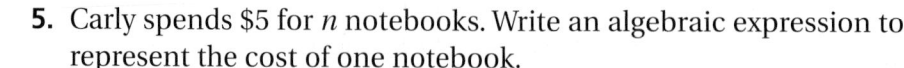

go.hrw.com
Homework Help Online
KEYWORD: MS7 1-8
Parent Resources Online
KEYWORD: MS7 Parent

GUIDED PRACTICE

See Example 1

Write each phrase as an algebraic expression.

1. the product of 7 and p

2. 3 less than a number

3. 12 divided into a number

4. 3 times the sum of a number and 5

See Example 2

5. Carly spends \$5 for n notebooks. Write an algebraic expression to represent the cost of one notebook.

6. A company charges \$46 for cable TV installation and \$21 per month for basic cable service. Write an algebraic expression to represent the total cost of m months of basic cable service, including installation.

INDEPENDENT PRACTICE

See Example 1

Write each phrase as an algebraic expression.

7. the sum of 5 and a number

8. 2 less than a number

9. the quotient of a number and 8

10. 9 times a number

11. 10 less than the product of a number and 3

See Example 2

12. Video Express sells used tapes. Marta bought v tapes for \$45. Write an algebraic expression for the average cost of each tape.

13. A 5-foot pine tree was planted and grew 2 feet each year. Write an algebraic expression for the height of the tree after t years.

PRACTICE AND PROBLEM SOLVING

Extra Practice
See page 725.

Write each phrase as an algebraic expression.

14. m plus the product of 6 and n

15. the quotient of 23 and u minus t

16. 14 less than the quantity k times 6

17. 2 times the sum of y and 5

18. the quotient of 100 and the quantity 6 plus w

19. 35 multiplied by the quantity r less 45

20. Multi-Step An ice machine can produce 17 pounds of ice in one hour.

a. Write an algebraic expression to describe the number of pounds of ice produced in n hours.

b. How many pounds of ice can the machine produce in 4 hours?

21. Career Karen earns \$65,000 a year as an optometrist. She received a bonus of b dollars last year and expects to get double that amount as a bonus this year. Write an algebraic expression to show the total amount Karen expects to earn this year.

Write a verbal expression for each algebraic expression.

22. $h + 3$ **23.** $90 \div y$ **24.** $s - 405$ **25.** $16t$

26. $5(a - 8)$ **27.** $4p - 10$ **28.** $(r + 1) \div 14$ **29.** $\frac{m}{15} + 3$

LINK
Life Science

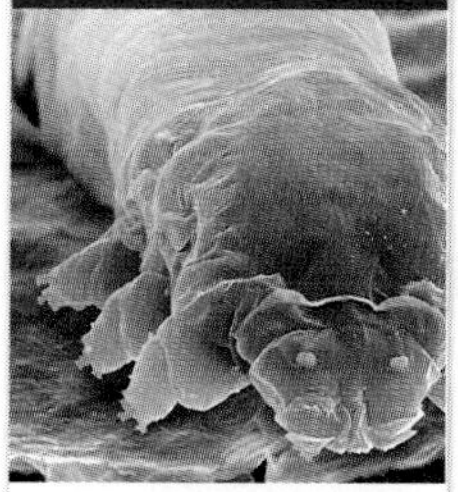

Up to 25 follicle mite nymphs can hatch in a single hair follicle.

30. Life Science Tiny and harmless, follicle mites live in our eyebrows and eyelashes. They are relatives of spiders and like spiders, they have eight legs. Write an algebraic expression for the number of legs in m mites.

Nutrition The table shows the estimated number of grams of carbohydrates commonly found in various types of foods.

Food	Carbohydrates
1 c skim milk	12 g
1 piece of fruit	15 g
1 slice of bread	15 g
1 oz lean meat	0 g

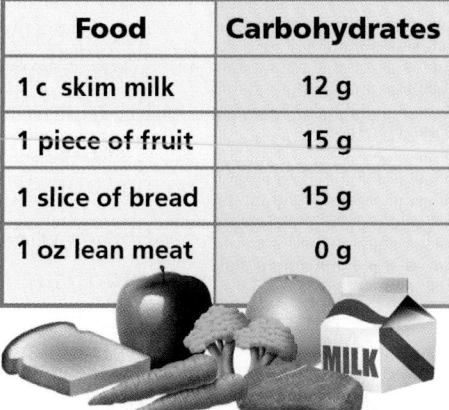

31. Write an algebraic expression for the number of grams of carbohydrates in y pieces of fruit and 1 cup of skim milk.

32. How many grams of carbohydrates are in a sandwich made from t ounces of lean meat and 2 slices of bread?

33. What's the Question? Al has twice as many baseball cards as Frank and four times as many football cards as Joe. The expression $2x + 4y$ can be used to show the total number of baseball and football cards Al has. If the answer is y, then what is the question?

34. Write About It If you are asked to compare two numbers, what two operations might you use? Why?

35. Challenge In 1996, one U.S. dollar was equivalent, on average, to $1.363 in Canadian money. Write an algebraic expression for the number of U.S. dollars you could get for n Canadian dollars.

TEST PREP and Spiral Review

36. Multiple Choice Which verbal expression does NOT represent $9 - x$?

(A) x less than nine

(B) x decreased by nine

(C) subtract x from nine

(D) the difference of nine and x

37. Short Response A room at the Oak Creek Inn costs $104 per night for two people. There is a $19 charge for each extra person. Write an algebraic expression that shows the cost per night for a family of four staying at the inn. Then evaluate your expression for 3 nights.

Simplify each expression. (Lesson 1-5)

38. $6 + 4 \div 2$ **39.** $9 \cdot 1 - 4$ **40.** $5^2 - 3$ **41.** $24 \div 3 + 3^3$

42. Evaluate $b - a^2$ for $a = 2$ and $b = 9$. (Lesson 1-7)

1-9 Simplifying Algebraic Expressions

Learn to simplify algebraic expressions.

Vocabulary

term

coefficient

Individual skits at the talent show can last up to x minutes each, and group skits can last up to y minutes each. Intermission will be 15 minutes. The expression $7x + 9y + 15$ represents the maximum length of the talent show if 7 individuals and 9 groups perform.

In the expression $7x + 9y + 15$, $7x$, $9y$, and 15 are *terms*. A **term** can be a number, a variable, or a product of numbers and variables. Terms in an expression are separated by plus or minus signs.

Caution!

A variable by itself, such as y, has a coefficient of 1. So $y = 1y$.

In the term $7x$, 7 is called the *coefficient*. A **coefficient** is a number that is multiplied by a variable in an algebraic expression.

Like terms are terms with the same variable raised to the same power. The coefficients do not have to be the same. Constants, like 5, $\frac{1}{2}$, and 3.2, are also like terms.

Like Terms	$3x$ and $2x$	w and $\frac{w}{7}$	5 and 1.8
Unlike Terms	$5x^2$ and $2x$ *The exponents are different.*	$6a$ and $6b$ *The variables are different.*	3.2 and n *Only one term contains a variable.*

EXAMPLE 1 Identifying Like Terms

Identify like terms in the list.

$5a \quad \frac{t}{2} \quad 3y^2 \quad 7t \quad x^2 \quad 4z \quad k \quad 4.5y^2 \quad 2t \quad \frac{2}{3}a$

Look for like variables with like powers.

$5a \quad \frac{t}{2} \quad 3y^2 \quad 7t \quad x^2 \quad 4z \quad k \quad 4.5y^2 \quad 2t \quad \frac{2}{3}a$

Like terms: $5a$ and $\frac{2}{3}a$ $\quad \frac{t}{2}$, $7t$, and $2t$ $\quad 3y^2$ and $4.5y^2$

Helpful Hint

Use different shapes or colors to indicate sets of like terms.

To simplify an algebraic expression that contains like terms, combine the terms. Combining like terms is like grouping similar objects.

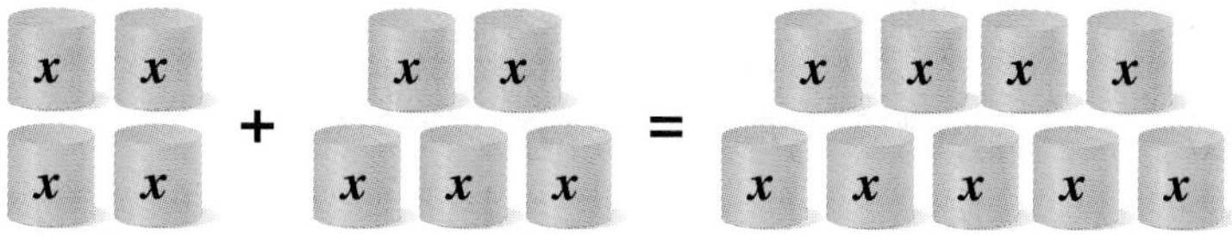

$4x \quad + \quad 5x \quad = \quad 9x$

To combine like terms that have variables, add or subtract the coefficients.

EXAMPLE 2 Simplifying Algebraic Expressions

Simplify. Justify your steps using the Commutative, Associative, and Distributive Properties when necessary.

A $7x + 2x$

$7x + 2x$	*7x and 2x are like terms.*
$9x$	*Add the coefficients.*

B $5x^3 + 3y + 7x^3 - 2y - 4x^2$

$5x^3 + 3y + 7x^3 - 2y - 4x^2$	*Identify like terms.*
$5x^3 + 7x^3 + 3y - 2y - 4x^2$	*Commutative Property*
$(5x^3 + 7x^3) + (3y - 2y) - 4x^2$	*Associative Property*
$12x^3 + y - 4x^2$	*Add or subtract the coefficients.*

C $2(a + 2a^2) + 2b$

$2(a + 2a^2) + 2b$	
$2a + 4a^2 + 2b$	*Distributive Property*

There are no like terms to combine.

EXAMPLE 3 *Geometry Application*

Remember!

To find the perimeter of a figure, add the lengths of the sides.

Write an expression for the perimeter of the rectangle. Then simplify the expression.

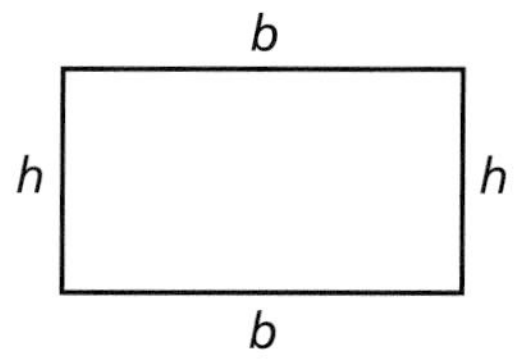

$b + h + b + h$	*Write an expression using the side lengths.*
$(b + b) + (h + h)$	*Identify and group like terms.*
$2b + 2h$	*Add the coefficients.*

Think and Discuss

1. Explain whether $5x$, $5x^2$, and $5x^3$ are like terms.

2. Explain how you know when an expression cannot be simplified.

1-9 Exercises

go.hrw.com
Homework Help Online
KEYWORD: MS7 1-9
Parent Resources Online
KEYWORD: MS7 Parent

GUIDED PRACTICE

See Example 1

Identify like terms in each list.

1. $6b \quad 5x^2 \quad 4x^3 \quad \frac{b}{2} \quad x^2 \quad 2e$

2. $12a^2 \quad 4x^3 \quad b \quad 4a^2 \quad 3.5x^3 \quad \frac{5}{6}b$

See Example 2

Simplify. Justify your steps using the Commutative, Associative, and Distributive Properties when necessary.

3. $5x + 3x$

4. $6a^2 - a^2 + 16$

5. $4a^2 + 5a + 14b$

See Example 3

6. Geometry Write an expression for the perimeter of the rectangle. Then simplify the expression.

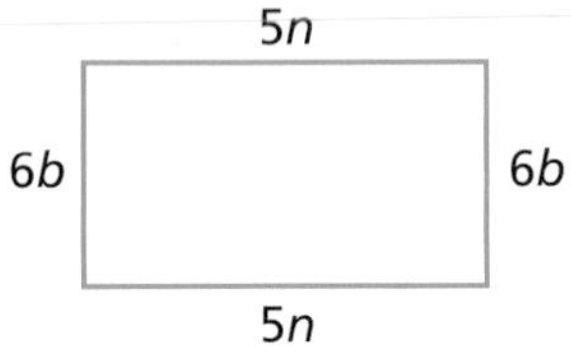

INDEPENDENT PRACTICE

See Example 1

Identify like terms in each list.

7. $2b \quad b^6 \quad b \quad x^4 \quad 3b^6 \quad 2x^2$

8. $6 \quad 2n \quad 3n^2 \quad 6m^2 \quad \frac{n}{4} \quad 7$

9. $10k^2 \quad m \quad 3^3 \quad \frac{p}{6} \quad 2m \quad 2$

10. $6^3 \quad y^3 \quad 3y^2 \quad 6^2 \quad y \quad 5y^3$

See Example 2

Simplify. Justify your steps using the Commutative, Associative, and Distributive Properties when necessary.

11. $3a + 2b + 5a$

12. $5b + 7b + 10$

13. $a + 2b + 2a + b + 2c$

14. $y + 4 + 2x + 3y$

15. $q^2 + 2q + 2q^2$

16. $18 + 2d^3 + d + 3d$

See Example 3

17. Geometry Write an expression for the perimeter of the given figure. Then simplify the expression.

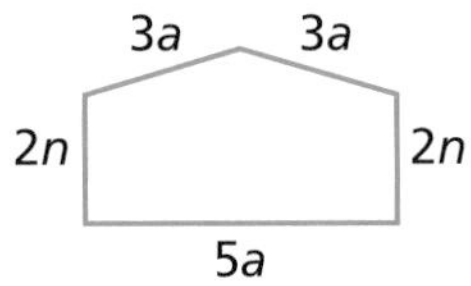

PRACTICE AND PROBLEM SOLVING

Extra Practice
See page 726.

Simplify each expression.

18. $4x + 5x$

19. $32y - 5y$

20. $4c^2 + 5c + 2c$

21. $5d^2 - 3d^2 + d$

22. $5f^2 + 2f + f^2$

23. $7x + 8x^2 - 3y$

24. $p + 9q + 9 + 14p$

25. $6b + 6b^2 + 4b^3$

26. $a^2 + 2b + 2a^2 + b + 2c$

27. Geometry Write an expression for the perimeter of the given triangle. Then evaluate the perimeter when n is 1, 2, 3, 4, and 5.

n	1	2	3	4	5
Perimeter ■	■	■	■	■	■

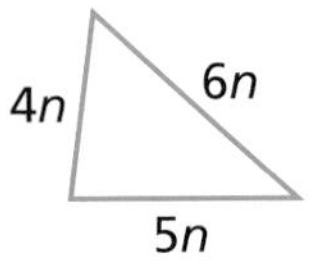

LINK

Business

The winner of each year's National Best Bagger Competition gets a bag-shaped trophy and a cash prize.

28. **Critical Thinking** Determine whether the expression $9m^2 + k$ is equal to $7m^2 + 2(2k - m^2) + 5k$. Use properties to justify your answer.

29. **Multi-Step** Brad makes d dollars per hour as a cook at a deli. The table shows the number of hours he worked each week in June.

    a. Write and simplify an expression for the amount of money Brad earned in June.

    b. Evaluate your expression from part **a** for $d = \$9.50$.

    c. What does your answer to part **b** represent?

Hours Brad Worked

Week	Hours
1	21.5
2	23
3	15.5
4	19

30. **Business** Ashley earns \$8 per hour working at a grocery store. Last week she worked h hours bagging groceries and twice as many hours stocking shelves. Write and simplify an expression for the amount Ashley earned.

31. **Critical Thinking** The terms $3x$, $23x^2$, $6y^2$, $2x$, y^2 and one other term can be written in an expression which, when simplified, equals $5x + 7y^2$. Identify the term missing from the list and write the expression.

32. **What's the Question?** At one store, a pair of jeans costs \$29 and a shirt costs \$25. At another store, the same kind of jeans costs \$26 and the same kind of shirt costs \$20. The answer is $29j - 26j + 25s - 20s = 3j + 5s$. What is the question?

33. **Write About It** Describe the steps for simplifying the expression $2x + 3 + 5x - 15$.

34. **Challenge** A rectangle has a width of $x + 2$ and a length of $3x + 1$. Write and simplify an expression for the perimeter of the rectangle.

TEST PREP and Spiral Review

35. **Multiple Choice** Translate "six times the sum of x and y" and "five less than y." Which algebraic expression represents the sum of these two verbal expressions?

    (A) $6x + 5$ (B) $6x + 2y - 5$ (C) $6x + 5y + 5$ (D) $6x + 7y - 5$

36. **Multiple Choice** The side length of a square is $2x + 3$. Which expression represents the perimeter of the square?

    (F) $2x + 12$ (G) $4x + 6$ (H) $6x + 7$ (J) $8x + 12$

Compare. Write <, >, or =. (Lesson 1-3)

37. 2.3 mm ▢ 23 cm 38. 6 km ▢ 600 m 39. 449 mg ▢ 0.5 g

Evaluate the expression $9y - 3$ for each given value of the variable. (Lesson 1-7)

40. $y = 2$ 41. $y = 6$ 42. $y = 10$ 43. $y = 18$

1-10 Equations and Their Solutions

Learn to determine whether a number is a solution of an equation.

Vocabulary

equation

solution

Ella has 22 CDs. This is 9 more than Kay has.

This situation can be written as an *equation*. An **equation** is a mathematical statement that two expressions are equal in value.

An equation is like a balanced scale.

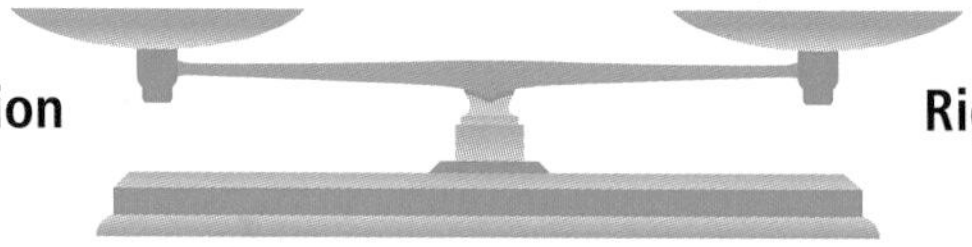

Just as the weights on both sides of a balanced scale are exactly the same, the expressions on both sides of an equation represent exactly the same value.

When an equation contains a variable, a value of the variable that makes the statement true is called a **solution** of the equation.

Reading Math

The symbol $\neq$ means "is not equal to."

$22 = j + 9$ $\quad$ $j = 13$ is a solution because $22 = 13 + 9$.

$22 = j + 9$ $\quad$ $j = 15$ is not a solution because $22 \neq 15 + 9$.

EXAMPLE 1 Determining Whether a Number Is a Solution of an Equation

Determine whether the given value of the variable is a solution.

A $18 = s - 7; s = 11$

$18 = s - 7$

$18 \stackrel{?}{=} 11 - 7$ *Substitute 11 for s.*

$18 \stackrel{?}{=} 4$ ✗

11 **is not** a solution of $18 = s - 7$.

B $w + 17 = 23; w = 6$

$w + 17 = 23$

$6 + 17 \stackrel{?}{=} 23$ *Substitute 6 for w.*

$23 \stackrel{?}{=} 23$ ✓

6 **is** a solution of $w + 17 = 23$.

EXAMPLE 2 Writing an Equation to Determine Whether a Number Is a Solution

Tyler wants to buy a new skateboard. He has \$57, which is \$38 less than he needs. Does the skateboard cost \$90 or \$95?

You can write an equation to find the price of the skateboard. If s represents the price of the skateboard, then $s - 38 = 57$.

\$90

$s - 38 = 57$

$90 - 38 \stackrel{?}{=} 57$ *Substitute 90 for s.*

$52 \stackrel{?}{=} 57$ ✗

\$95

$s - 38 = 57$

$95 - 38 \stackrel{?}{=} 57$ *Substitute 95 for s.*

$57 \stackrel{?}{=} 57$ ✔

The skateboard costs \$95.

EXAMPLE 3 Deriving a Real-World Situation from an Equation

Which problem situation best matches the equation $3x + 4 = 22$?

Situation A:

Harvey spent \$22 at the gas station. He paid \$4 per gallon for gas and \$3 for snacks. How many gallons of gas did Harvey buy?

The variable x represents the number of gallons of gas that Harvey bought.

\$4 per gallon ⟶ $4x$

Since $4x$ is not a term in the given equation, Situation A does not match the equation.

Situation B:

Harvey spent \$22 at the gas station. He paid \$3 per gallon for gas and \$4 for snacks. How many gallons of gas did Harvey buy?

\$3 per gallon ⟶ $3x$

\$4 on snacks ⟶ $+ 4$

Harvey spent \$22 in all, so $3x + 4 = 22$. Situation B matches the equation.

Think and Discuss

1. **Compare** equations with expressions.
2. **Give an example** of an equation whose solution is 5.

1-10 Exercises

go.hrw.com
Homework Help Online
KEYWORD: MS7 1-10
Parent Resources Online
KEYWORD: MS7 Parent

GUIDED PRACTICE

See Example 1

Determine whether the given value of the variable is a solution.

1. $19 = x + 4; x = 23$ **2.** $6n = 78; n = 13$ **3.** $k \div 3 = 14; k = 42$

See Example 2

4. Mavis wants to buy a book. She has \$25, which is \$9 less than she needs. Does the book cost \$34 or \$38?

See Example 3

5. Which problem situation best matches the equation $10 + 2x = 16$?

Situation A: Angie bought peaches for \$2 per pound and laundry detergent for \$10. She spent a total of \$16. How many pounds of peaches did Angie buy?

Situation B: Angie bought peaches for \$10 per pound and laundry detergent for \$2. She spent a total of \$16. How many pounds of peaches did Angie buy?

INDEPENDENT PRACTICE

See Example 1

Determine whether the given value of the variable is a solution.

6. $r - 12 = 25; r = 37$ **7.** $39 \div x = 13; x = 4$ **8.** $21 = m + 9; m = 11$

9. $\frac{a}{18} = 7; a = 126$ **10.** $16f = 48; f = 3$ **11.** $71 - y = 26; y = 47$

See Example 2

12. Curtis wants to buy a new snowboard. He has \$119, which is \$56 less than he needs. Does the snowboard cost \$165 or \$175?

See Example 3

13. Which problem situation best matches the equation $2m + 10 = 18$?

Situation A: A taxi service charges a \$2 fee, plus \$18 per mile. Jeremy paid the driver \$10. How many miles did Jeremy ride in the taxi?

Situation B: A taxi service charges a \$10 fee, plus \$2 per mile. Jeremy paid the driver \$18. How many miles did Jeremy ride in the taxi?

PRACTICE AND PROBLEM SOLVING

Extra Practice
See page 726.

Determine whether the given value of the variable is a solution.

14. $j = 6$ for $15 - j = 21$ **15.** $x = 36$ for $48 = x + 12$

16. $m = 18$ for $16 = 34 - m$ **17.** $k = 23$ for $17 + k = 40$

18. $y = 8$ for $9y + 2 = 74$ **19.** $c = 12$ for $100 - 2c = 86$

20. $q = 13$ for $5q + 7 - q = 51$ **21.** $w = 15$ for $13w - 2 - 6w = 103$

22. $t = 12$ for $3(50 - t) - 10t = 104$ **23.** $r = 21$ for $4r - 8 + 9r - 1 = 264$

24. Hobbies Monique has a collection of stamps from 6 different countries. Jeremy has stamps from 3 fewer countries than Monique does. Write an equation showing this, using j as the number of countries from which Jeremy has stamps.

Earth Science LINK

25. The diagram shows approximate elevations for different climate zones in the Colorado Rockies. Use the diagram to write an equation that shows the vertical distance d from the summit of Mount Evans (14,264 ft) to the tree line, which marks the beginning of the alpine tundra zone.

Source: Colorado Mall

26. The top wind speed of an F5 tornado, the strongest known kind of tornado, is 246 mi/h faster than the top wind speed of an F1 tornado, the weakest kind of tornado. The top wind speed of an F1 tornado is 72 mi/h. Is the top wind speed of an F5 tornado 174 mi/h, 218 mi/h, or 318 mi/h?

27. **Write a Problem** The mean surface temperature of Earth increased about 1°F from 1861 to 1998. In 1998, the mean surface temperature was about 60°F. Use this data to write a problem involving an equation with a variable.

28. **Challenge** In the 1980s, about 9.3×10^4 acres of tropical forests were destroyed each year due to deforestation. About how many acres of tropical forests were destroyed during the 1980s?

Maroon Bells in the Colorado Rockies

go.hrw.com
Web Extra!
KEYWORD: MS7 Storms

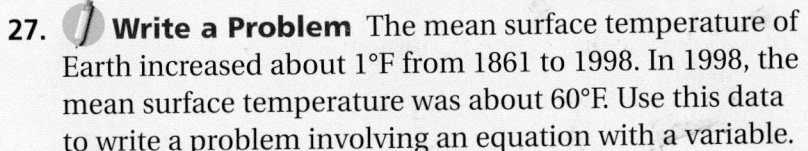

TEST PREP and Spiral Review

29. **Multiple Choice** Jack's rectangular bedroom has a length of 10 feet. He used the formula $A = 10w$ to find the area of his room. He found that his bedroom had an area of 150 square feet. What was the width of his bedroom?

Ⓐ 15 feet Ⓑ 25 feet Ⓒ 30 feet Ⓓ 15,000 feet

30. **Multiple Choice** The number of seventh-graders at Pecos Middle School is 316. This is 27 more than the number of eighth-graders. How many eighth-graders are enrolled?

Ⓕ 289 Ⓖ 291 Ⓗ 299 Ⓙ 343

Write each number in scientific notation. (Lesson 1-4)

31. 10,850,000
32. 627,000
33. 9,040,000

Tell which property is represented. (Lesson 1-6)

34. $(7 + 5) + 3 = 7 + (5 + 3)$
35. $181 + 0 = 181$
36. $bc = cb$

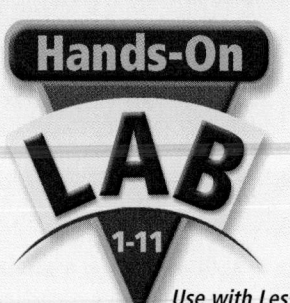

Hands-On LAB 1-11

Model Solving Equations

Use with Lessons 1-11 and 1-12

go.hrw.com
Lab Resources Online
KEYWORD: MS7 Lab1

KEY	REMEMBER
[+] = 1 [+] = variable	• In an equation, the expressions on both sides of the equal sign are equivalent. • A variable can have any value that makes the equation true.

You can use balance scales and algebra tiles to model and solve equations.

Activity

1 Use a balance scale to model and solve the equation $3 + w = 11$.

a. On the left side of the scale, place 3 unit weights and one variable weight. On the right side, place 11 unit weights. This models $3 + w = 11$.

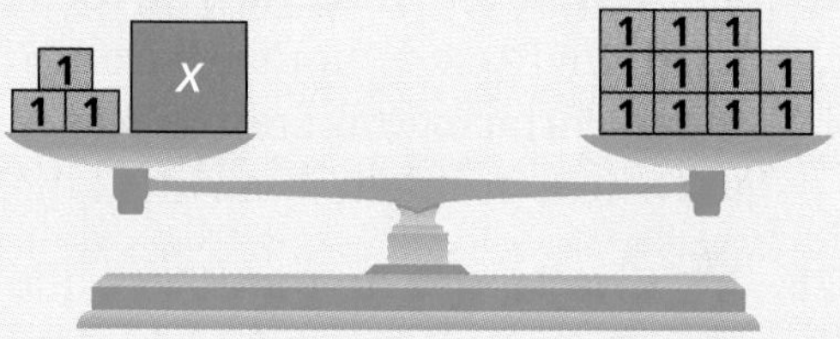

$3 + w = 11$

b. Remove 3 of the unit weights from each side of the scale to leave the variable weight by itself on one side.

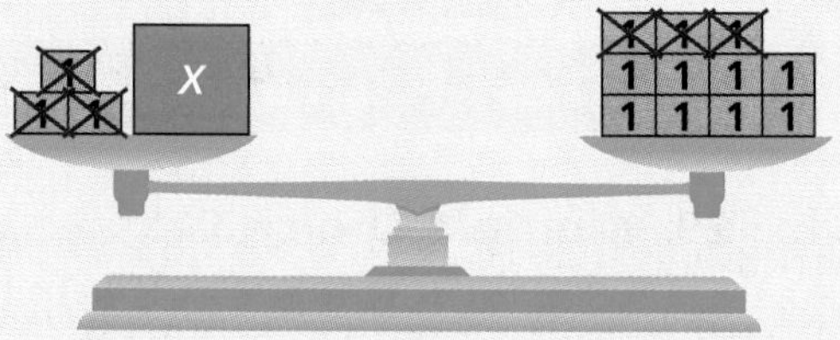

$$\begin{array}{rcl} 3 + w & = & 11 \\ -3 \quad & & -3 \end{array}$$

c. Count the remaining unit weights on the right side of the scale. This number represents the solution of the equation.

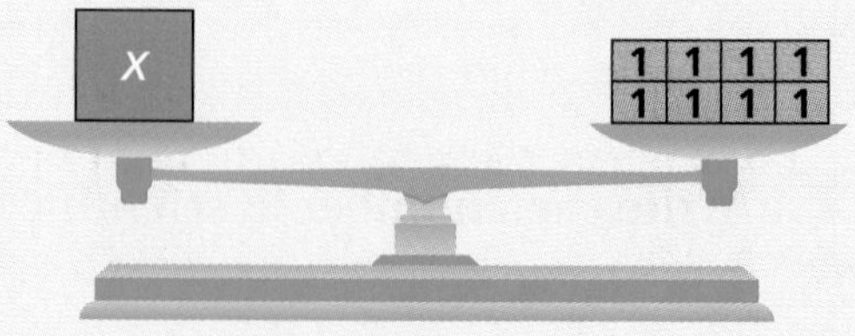

$w = 8$

The model shows that if $3 + w = 11$, then $w = 8$.

2 Use algebra tiles to model and solve the equation $3y = 15$.

a. On the left side of the mat, place 3 variable tiles. On the right side, place 15 unit tiles. This models $3y = 15$.

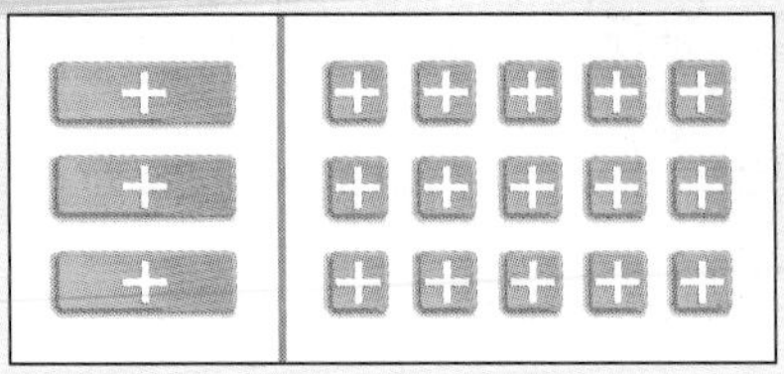

$$3y = 15$$

b. Since there are 3 variable tiles, divide the tiles on each side of the mat into 3 equal groups.

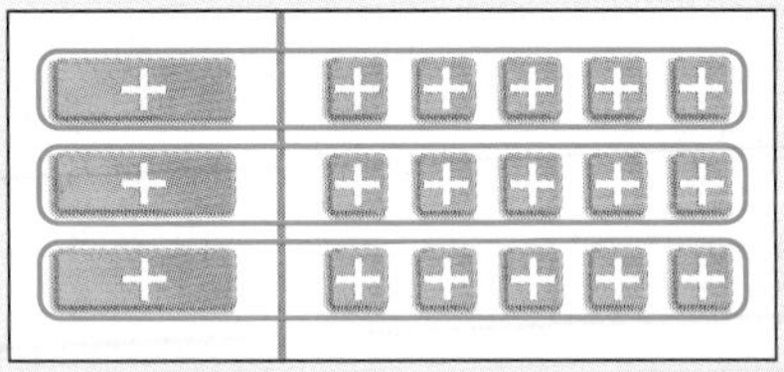

$$\frac{3y}{3} = \frac{15}{3}$$

c. Count the number of square tiles in one of the groups. This number represents the solution of the equation.

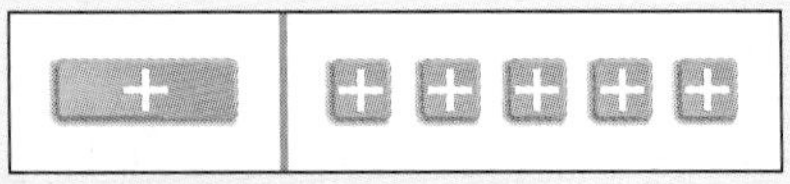

$$y = 5$$

The model shows that if $3y = 15$, then $y = 5$.

To check your solutions, substitute the variable in each equation with your solution. If the resulting equation is true, your solution is correct.

$3 + w = 11$	$3y = 15$
$3 + 8 \stackrel{?}{=} 11$	$3 \cdot 5 \stackrel{?}{=} 15$
$11 \stackrel{?}{=} 11$ ✔	$15 \stackrel{?}{=} 15$ ✔

Think and Discuss

1. What operation did you use to solve the equation $3 + w = 11$ in **1**? What operation did you use to solve $3y = 15$ in **2**?
2. Compare using a balance scale and algebra tiles with using a mat and algebra tiles. Which method of modeling equations is more helpful to you? Explain.

Try This

Use a balance scale or algebra tiles to model and solve each equation.

1. $4x = 16$
2. $3 + 5 = n$
3. $5r = 15$
4. $n + 7 = 12$
5. $y + 6 = 13$
6. $8 = 2r$
7. $9 = 7 + w$
8. $18 = 6p$

1-11 Addition and Subtraction Equations

Learn to solve one-step equations by using addition or subtraction.

Vocabulary

Addition Property of Equality

inverse operations

Subtraction Property of Equality

To solve an equation means to find a solution to the equation. To do this, isolate the variable—that is, get the variable alone on one side of the equal sign.

The variables are isolated.	The variables are *not* isolated.
$x = 8 - 5$	$x + 5 = 8$
$7 - 3 = y$	$7 = 3 + y$

Recall that an equation is like a balanced scale. If you increase or decrease the weights by the same amount on both sides, the scale will remain balanced.

ADDITION PROPERTY OF EQUALITY

Words	Numbers	Algebra
You can add the same amount to both sides of an equation, and the statement will still be true.	$\begin{array}{rcr} 2+3 & = & 5 \\ \underline{+4} & & \underline{+4} \\ 2+7 & = & 9 \end{array}$	$\begin{array}{rcr} x & = & y \\ \underline{+z} & & \underline{+z} \\ x+z & = & y+z \end{array}$

Use *inverse operations* when isolating a variable. Addition and subtraction are **inverse operations**, which means that they "undo" each other.

2 +5 = 7 ⟷ 7 −5 = 2

EXAMPLE 1 Solving an Equation by Addition

Solve the equation $x - 8 = 17$. Check your answer.

$$\begin{array}{rcl} x - 8 & = & 17 \\ \underline{+8} & & \underline{+8} \\ x & = & 25 \end{array}$$

*Think: 8 is **subtracted** from x, so **add** 8 to both sides to isolate x.*

Check

$x - 8 = 17$

$25 - 8 \stackrel{?}{=} 17$ — *Substitute 25 for x.*

$17 \stackrel{?}{=} 17$ ✔ — *25 is a solution.*

SUBTRACTION PROPERTY OF EQUALITY

Words	Numbers	Algebra
You can subtract the same amount from both sides of an equation, and the statement will still be true.	$\begin{aligned} 4 + 7 &= 11 \\ -3 \quad & \quad -3 \\ 4 + 4 &= 8 \end{aligned}$	$\begin{aligned} x &= y \\ -z \quad & \quad -z \\ x - z &= y - z \end{aligned}$

EXAMPLE 2 Solving an Equation by Subtraction

Solve the equation $a + 5 = 11$. Check your answer.

$$\begin{aligned} a + 5 &= 11 \\ -5 \quad & \quad -5 \\ a &= 6 \end{aligned}$$

*Think: 5 is **added** to a, so **subtract** 5 from both sides to isolate a.*

Check

$a + 5 = 11$

$6 + 5 \stackrel{?}{=} 11$ — *Substitute 6 for a.*

$11 \stackrel{?}{=} 11$ ✔ — *6 is a solution.*

EXAMPLE 3 *Sports Application*

Michael Jordan's highest point total for a single game was 69. The entire team scored 117 points in that game. How many points did his teammates score?

Let p represent the points scored by the rest of the team.

Jordan's points	+	Teammates' points	=	Final score
69	+	p	=	117

$$\begin{aligned} 69 + p &= 117 \\ -69 \quad & \quad -69 \\ p &= 48 \end{aligned}$$

Subtract 69 from both sides to isolate p.

His teammates scored 48 points.

Think and Discuss

1. **Explain** how to decide which operation to use in order to isolate the variable in an equation.
2. **Describe** what would happen if a number were added or subtracted on one side of an equation but not on the other side.

1-11 Exercises

go.hrw.com
Homework Help Online
KEYWORD: MS7 1-11
Parent Resources Online
KEYWORD: MS7 Parent

GUIDED PRACTICE

See Example 1
Solve each equation. Check your answer.

1. $r - 77 = 99$
2. $102 = v - 66$
3. $x - 22 = 66$

See Example 2

4. $d + 83 = 92$
5. $45 = 36 + f$
6. $987 = 16 + m$

See Example 3

7. After a gain of 9 yards, your team has gained a total of 23 yards. How many yards had your team gained before the 9-yard gain?

INDEPENDENT PRACTICE

See Example 1
Solve each equation. Check your answer.

8. $n - 36 = 17$
9. $t - 28 = 54$
10. $p - 56 = 12$
11. $b - 41 = 26$
12. $m - 51 = 23$
13. $k - 22 = 101$

See Example 2

14. $x + 15 = 43$
15. $w + 19 = 62$
16. $a + 14 = 38$
17. $110 = s + 65$
18. $x + 47 = 82$
19. $18 + j = 94$
20. $97 = t + 45$
21. $q + 13 = 112$
22. $44 = 16 + n$

See Example 3

23. Hank is on a field trip. He has to travel 56 miles to reach his destination. He has traveled 18 miles so far. How much farther does he have to travel?
24. Sandy read 8 books in April. If her book club requires her to read 6 books each month, how many more books did she read than what was required?

PRACTICE AND PROBLEM SOLVING

Extra Practice
See page 726.

Solve each equation. Check your answer.

25. $p - 7 = 3$
26. $n + 17 = 98$
27. $23 + b = 75$
28. $356 = y - 219$
29. $105 = a + 60$
30. $g - 720 = 159$
31. $651 + c = 800$
32. $f - 63 = 937$
33. $59 + m = 258$
34. $16 = h - 125$
35. $s + 841 = 1{,}000$
36. $711 = q - 800$
37. $63 + x = 902$
38. $z - 712 = 54$
39. $120 = w + 41$

40. **Physical Science** An object weighs less when it is in water. This is because water exerts a buoyant force on the object. The weight of an object out of water is equal to the object's weight in water plus the buoyant force of the water. Suppose an object weighs 103 pounds out of water and 55 pounds in water. Write and solve an equation to find the buoyant force of the water.

41. **Banking** After Lana deposited a check for \$65, her new account balance was \$315. Write and solve an equation to find the amount that was in Lana's account before the deposit.

42. **Music** Jason wants to buy the trumpet advertised in the classified ads. He has saved \$156. Using the information from the ad, write and solve an equation to find how much more money he needs to buy the trumpet.

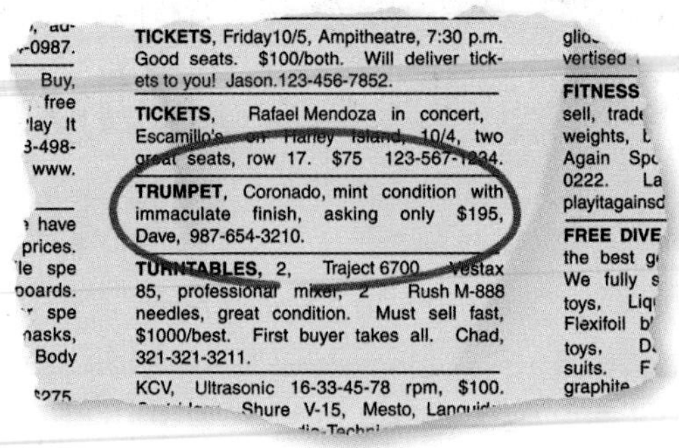
TICKETS, Friday10/5, Ampitheatre, 7:30 p.m. Good seats. \$100/both. Will deliver tickets to you! Jason.123-456-7852.

TICKETS, Rafael Mendoza in concert, Escamillo's on Harley Island, 10/4, two great seats, row 17. \$75 123-567-1234.

TRUMPET, Coronado, mint condition with immaculate finish, asking only \$195, Dave, 987-654-3210.

TURNTABLES, 2, Traject 6700 Vestax 85, professional mixer, 2 Rush M-888 needles, great condition. Must sell fast, \$1000/best. First buyer takes all. Chad, 321-321-3211.

KCV, Ultrasonic 16-33-45-78 rpm, \$100. Shure V-15, Mesto, Languid

43. **What's the Error?** Describe and correct the error. $x = 50$ for $(8 + 4)2 + x = 26$

44. **Write About It** Explain how you know whether to add or subtract to solve an equation.

45. **Challenge** Kwan keeps a record of his football team's gains and losses on each play of the game. The record is shown in the table. Find the missing information by writing and solving an equation.

Play	Play Gain/Loss	Overall Gain/Loss
1st down	Gain of 2 yards	Gain of 2 yards
2nd down	Loss of 5 yards	Loss of 3 yards
3rd down	Gain of 7 yards	Gain of 4 yards
4th down	■	Loss of 7 yards

Test Prep and Spiral Review

46. **Gridded Response** Morgan has read 78 pages of *Treasure Island.* The book has 203 pages. How many pages of the book does Morgan have left to read?

47. **Multiple Choice** Which problem situation best represents the equation $42 - x = 7$?

Ⓐ Craig is 42 years old. His brother is 7 years older than he is. How old is Craig's brother?

Ⓑ Dylan has 42 days to finish his science fair project. How many weeks does he have left to finish his project?

Ⓒ The total lunch bill for a group of 7 friends is \$42. If the friends split the cost of the meal evenly, how much should each person pay?

Ⓓ Each student in the Anderson Junior High Spanish Club has paid for a club T-shirt. If there are 42 students in the club and only 7 shirts are left to be picked up, how many students have already picked up their shirts?

Write each phrase as an algebraic expression. (Lesson 1-8)

48. the product of 16 and n 49. 17 decreased by k 50. 8 times the sum of x and 4

Simplify each expression. (Lesson 1-9)

51. $6(2 + 2n) + 3n$ 52. $4x - 7y + x$ 53. $8 + 3t + 2(4t)$

1-12 Multiplication and Division Equations

Learn to solve one-step equations by using multiplication or division.

Vocabulary

Multiplication Property of Equality

Division Property of Equality

Like addition and subtraction, multiplication and division are inverse operations. They "undo" each other.

$2 \cdot 5 = 10$

$10 \div 5 = 2$

MULTIPLICATION PROPERTY OF EQUALITY		
Words	**Numbers**	**Algebra**
You can multiply both sides of an equation by the same number, and the statement will still be true.	$3 \cdot 4 = 12$ $2 \cdot 3 \cdot 4 = 2 \cdot 12$ $6 \cdot 4 = 24$	$x = y$ $zx = zy$

If a variable is divided by a number, you can often use multiplication to isolate the variable. Multiply both sides of the equation by the number.

EXAMPLE 1 Solving an Equation by Multiplication

Solve the equation $\frac{x}{7} = 20$. Check your answer.

$\frac{x}{7} = 20$

$(7)\frac{x}{7} = 20(7)$ — *Think: x is **divided** by 7, so **multiply** both sides by 7 to isolate x.*

$x = 140$

Check

$\frac{x}{7} = 20$

$\frac{140}{7} \stackrel{?}{=} 20$ — *Substitute 140 for x.*

$20 \stackrel{?}{=} 20$ ✔ — *140 is a solution.*

DIVISION PROPERTY OF EQUALITY		
Words	**Numbers**	**Algebra**
You can divide both sides of an equation by the same nonzero number, and the statement will still be true.	$5 \cdot 6 = 30$ $\frac{5 \cdot 6}{3} = \frac{30}{3}$ $5 \cdot \frac{6}{3} = 10$ $5 \cdot 2 = 10$	$x = y$ $\frac{x}{z} = \frac{y}{z}$ $z \neq 0$

Remember!

You cannot divide by 0.

If a variable is multiplied by a number, you can often use division to isolate the variable. Divide both sides of the equation by the number.

EXAMPLE 2 Solving an Equation by Division

Solve the equation 240 = 4*z*. Check your answer.

$240 = 4z$ — *Think: z is **multiplied** by 4, so **divide** both sides by 4 to isolate z.*

$\frac{240}{4} = \frac{4z}{4}$

$60 = z$

Check

$240 = 4z$

$240 \stackrel{?}{=} 4(\mathbf{60})$ — *Substitute 60 for z.*

$240 \stackrel{?}{=} 240$ ✔ — *60 is a solution.*

EXAMPLE 3 *Health Application*

LINK

Health

In 2005, Lance Armstrong won his seventh consecutive Tour de France. He is the first person to win the 2,051-mile bicycle race more than five years in a row.

go.hrw.com
Web Extra!
KEYWORD: MS7 Lance

If you count your heartbeats for 10 seconds and multiply that number by 6, you can find your heart rate in beats per minute. Lance Armstrong, who won the Tour de France seven years in a row, from 1999 to 2005, has a resting heart rate of 30 beats per minute. How many times does his heart beat in 10 seconds?

Use the given information to write an equation, where *b* is the number of heartbeats in 10 seconds.

Beats in 10 s	·	6	=	beats per minute
b	·	6	=	30

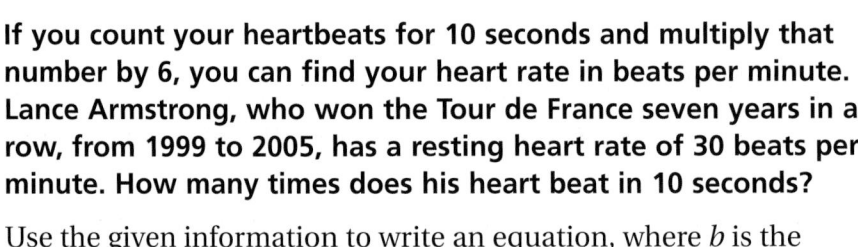

$6b = 30$ — *Think: b is **multiplied** by 6, so **divide** both sides by 6 to isolate b.*

$\frac{6b}{6} = \frac{30}{6}$

$b = 5$

Lance Armstrong's heart beats 5 times in 10 seconds.

Think and Discuss

1. Explain how to check your solution to an equation.

2. Describe how to solve $13x = 91$.

3. When you solve $5p = 35$, will p be greater than 35 or less than 35? **Explain** your answer.

4. When you solve $\frac{p}{5} = 35$, will p be greater than 35 or less than 35? **Explain** your answer.

1-12 Exercises

go.hrw.com
Homework Help Online
KEYWORD: MS7 1-12
Parent Resources Online
KEYWORD: MS7 Parent

GUIDED PRACTICE

See Example 1

Solve each equation. Check your answer.

1. $\frac{s}{77} = 11$ **2.** $b \div 25 = 4$ **3.** $y \div 8 = 5$

See Example 2

4. $72 = 8x$ **5.** $3c = 96$ **6.** $x \cdot 18 = 18$

See Example 3

7. On Friday nights, a local bowling alley charges $5 per person to bowl all night. If Carol and her friends paid a total of $45 to bowl, how many people were in their group?

INDEPENDENT PRACTICE

See Example 1

Solve each equation. Check your answer.

8. $12 = s \div 4$ **9.** $\frac{k}{18} = 72$ **10.** $13 = \frac{z}{5}$

11. $\frac{c}{5} = 35$ **12.** $\frac{w}{11} = 22$ **13.** $17 = n \div 18$

See Example 2

14. $17x = 85$ **15.** $63 = 3p$ **16.** $6u = 222$

17. $97a = 194$ **18.** $9q = 108$ **19.** $495 = 11d$

See Example 3

20. It costs $6 per ticket for groups of ten or more people to see a minor league baseball game. If Albert's group paid a total of $162 for game tickets, how many people were in the group?

PRACTICE AND PROBLEM SOLVING

Extra Practice
See page 726.

Solve each equation. Check your answer.

21. $9 = g \div 3$ **22.** $150 = 3j$ **23.** $68 = m - 42$

24. $7r = 84$ **25.** $5x = 35$ **26.** $9 = \frac{s}{38}$

27. $b + 33 = 95$ **28.** $\frac{p}{15} = 6$ **29.** $12f = 240$

30. $504 = c - 212$ **31.** $8a = 288$ **32.** $157 + q = 269$

33. $21 = d \div 2$ **34.** $\frac{h}{20} = 83$ **35.** $r - 92 = 215$

Multi-Step **Translate each sentence into an equation. Then solve the equation.**

36. A number d divided by 4 equals 3.

37. The sum of 7 and a number n is 15.

38. The product of a number b and 5 is 250.

39. Twelve is the difference of a number q and 8.

40. **Consumer Math** Nine weeks from now Susan hopes to buy a bicycle that costs $180. How much money must she save per week?

41. **School** A school club is collecting toys for a children's charity. There are 18 students in the club. The goal is to collect 216 toys. Each member will collect the same number of toys. How many toys should each member collect?

42. **Travel** Lissa drove from Los Angeles to New York City and averaged 45 miles per hour. Her driving time totaled 62 hours. Write and solve an equation to find the distance Lissa traveled.

43. **Business** A store rents space in a building at a cost of $19 per square foot. If the store is 700 square feet, how much is the rent?

44. **What's the Error?** For the equation $7x = 56$, a student found the value of x to be 392. What was the student's error?

45. **Write About It** How do you know whether to use multiplication or division to solve an equation?

46. **Challenge** The graph shows the results of a survey about electronic equipment used by 8,690,000 college students. If you multiply the number of students who use portable CD players by 5 and then divide by 3, you get the total number of students represented by the survey. Write and solve an equation to find the number of students who use portable CD players.

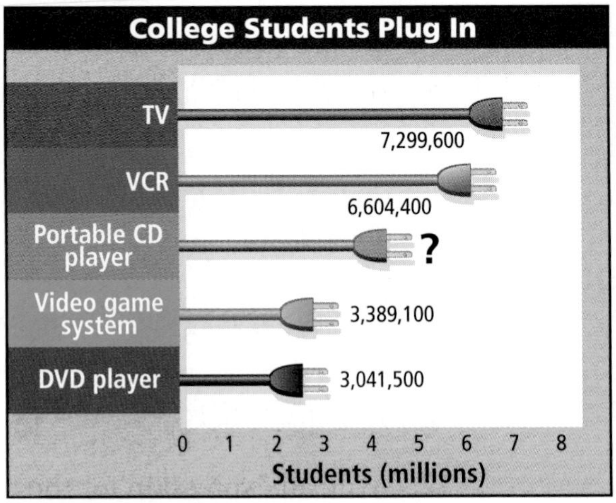

Test Prep and Spiral Review

47. **Multiple Choice** Mr. Tomkins borrowed $1,200 to buy a computer. He wants to repay the loan in 8 equal payments. How much will each payment be?

Ⓐ $80 Ⓑ $100 Ⓒ $150 Ⓓ $200

48. **Multiple Choice** Solve the equation $16x = 208$.

Ⓕ $x = 11$ Ⓖ $x = 12$ Ⓗ $x = 13$ Ⓙ $x = 14$

49. **Extended Response** It costs $18 per ticket for groups of 20 or more people to enter an amusement park. If Celia's group paid a total of $414 to enter, how many people were in her group?

Determine whether the given value of the variable is a solution. (Lesson 1-10)

50. $x + 34 = 48$; $x = 14$

51. $d - 87 = 77$; $d = 10$

Solve each equation. (Lesson 1-11)

52. $76 + n = 115$

53. $j - 97 = 145$

54. $t - 123 = 455$

55. $a + 39 = 86$

CHAPTER 1

READY TO GO ON?

SECTION 1B

Quiz for Lessons 1-7 Through 1-12

1-7 Variables and Algebraic Expressions

Evaluate each expression for the given values of the variable.

1. $7(x + 4)$ for $x = 5$

2. $11 - n \div 3$ for $n = 6$

3. $p + 6t^2$ for $p = 11$ and $t = 3$

1-8 Translate Words into Math

Write each phrase as an algebraic expression.

4. the quotient of a number and 15

5. a number decreased by 13

6. 10 times the difference of p and 2

7. 3 plus the product of a number and 8

8. A long-distance phone company charges a \$2.95 monthly fee plus \$0.14 for each minute. Write an algebraic expression to show the costof calling for t minutes in one month.

1-9 Simplifying Algebraic Expressions

Simplify each expression. Justify your steps.

9. $2y + 5y^2 - 2y^2$

10. $x + 4 + 7x + 9$

11. $10 + 9b - 6a - b$

12. Write an expression for the perimeter of the given figure. Then simplify the expression.

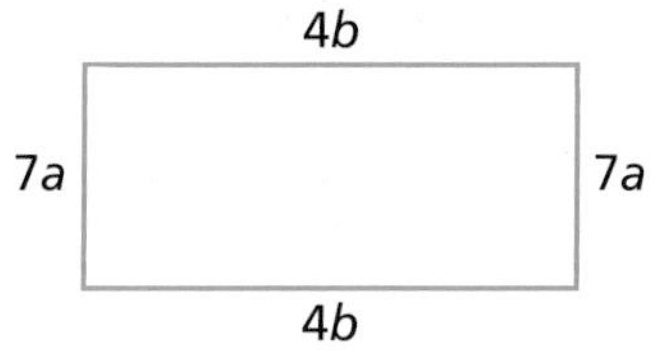

1-10 Equations and Their Solutions

Determine whether the given value of the variable is a solution.

13. $22 - x = 7; x = 15$

14. $\frac{56}{r} = 8; r = 9$

15. $m + 19 = 47; m = 28$

16. Last month Sue spent \$147 on groceries. This month she spent \$29 more on groceries than last month. Did Sue spend \$118 or \$176 on groceries this month?

1-11 Addition and Subtraction Equations

Solve each equation.

17. $g - 4 = 13$

18. $20 = 7 + p$

19. $t - 18 = 6$

20. $m + 34 = 53$

1-12 Multiplication and Division Equations

Solve each equation.

21. $\frac{k}{8} = 7$

22. $3b = 39$

23. $n \div 16 = 7$

24. $330 = 22x$

25. A water jug holds 128 fluid ounces. How many 8-ounce servings of water does the jug hold?

MULTI-STEP TEST PREP

Have a Heart Chuck's family decides to begin a fitness program. Their doctor encourages each family member to determine his or her maximum heart rate and then exercise at a lower rate.

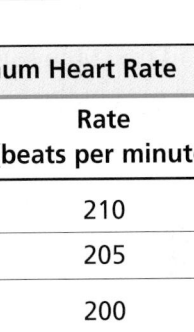

1. The table shows the recommended maximum heart rate for people of various ages. Describe the pattern in the table. Then find the maximum heart rate for Chuck's father, who is 45 years old.

2. There is another way to find a person's maximum heart rate. The sum of the maximum heart rate, h, and the person's age, a, should be 220. Write an equation that relates h and a.

3. Chuck's mother used the equation from problem 2 to determine that her maximum heart rate is 174 beats per minute. How old is Chuck's mother?

4. Chuck's mother counts the number of heartbeats in 10 seconds and multiplies by 6 to find her heart rate. Write and solve an equation to find the number of times her heart beats in 10 seconds when she is at her maximum heart rate.

5. The family doctor recommends warming up before exercise. The expression $110 - a \div 2$ gives a warm-up heart rate based on a person's age, a. Find the warm-up heart rate for Chuck's mother.

Maximum Heart Rate

Age	Rate (beats per minute)
10	210
15	205
20	200
25	195
30	190
35	185

Game Time

Jumping Beans

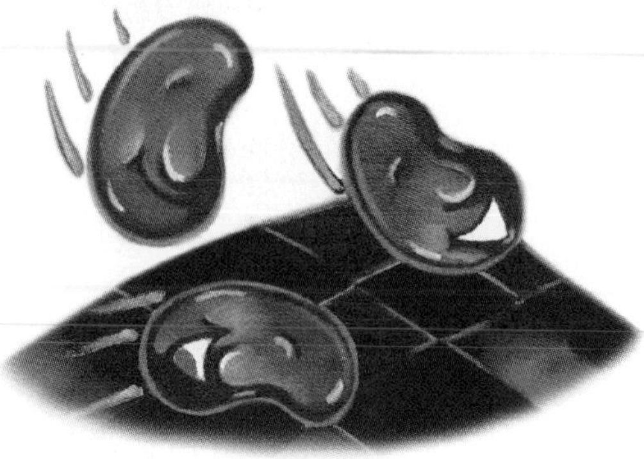

You will need a grid that is 4 squares by 6 squares. Each square must be large enough to contain a bean. Mark off a 3-square by 3-square section of the grid. Place nine beans in the nine spaces, as shown below.

You must move all nine beans to the nine marked-off squares in the fewest number of moves.

Follow the rules below to move the beans.

1. You may move to any empty square in any direction.
2. You may jump over another bean in any direction to an empty square.
3. You may jump over other beans as many times as you like.

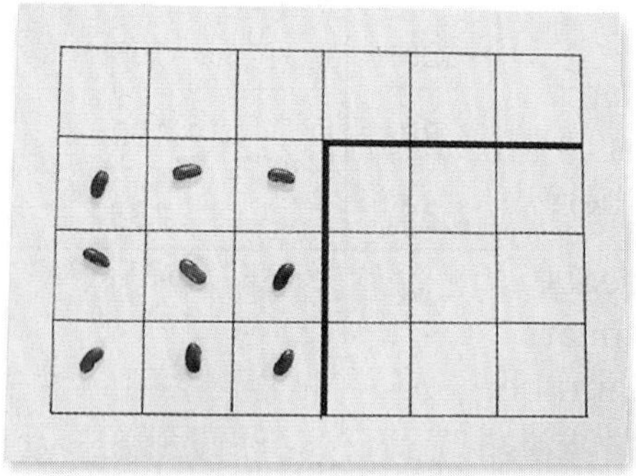

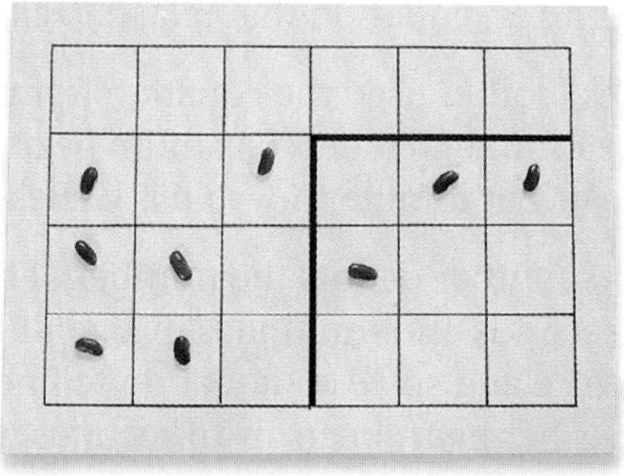

Moving all the beans in ten moves is not too difficult, but can you do it in nine moves?

Trading Spaces

The purpose of the game is to replace the red counters with the yellow counters, and the yellow counters with the red counters, in the fewest moves possible. The counters must be moved one at a time in an L-shape. No two counters may occupy the same square.

A complete copy of the rules and a game board are available online.

go.hrw.com
Game Time Extra
KEYWORD: MS7 Games

FOLDNOTES

It's in the Bag!

Materials
- 1 full sheet of decorative paper
- 3 smaller pieces of decorative paper
- stapler
- scissors
- markers
- pencil

PROJECT Step-by-Step Algebra

This "step book" is a great place to record sample algebra problems.

Directions

1. Lay the $11\frac{1}{2}$-by-$7\frac{3}{4}$-inch sheet of paper in front of you. Fold it down $2\frac{1}{2}$ inches from the top and make a crease. **Figure A**

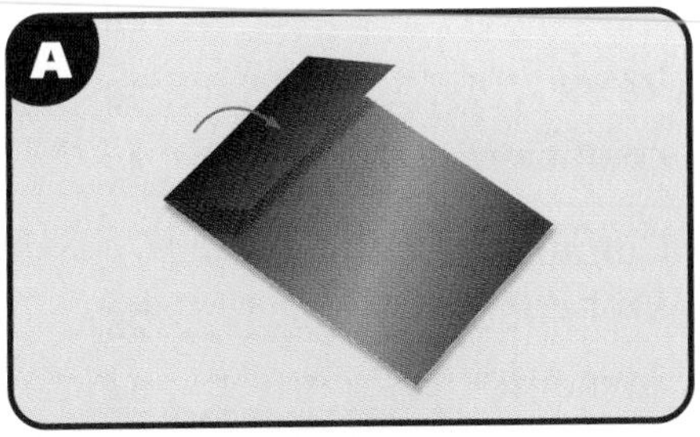
A

2. Slide the $7\frac{1}{4}$-by-$7\frac{3}{4}$-inch sheet of paper under the flap of the first piece. Do the same with the $5\frac{1}{2}$-by-$7\frac{3}{4}$-inch and $3\frac{3}{4}$-by-$7\frac{3}{4}$-inch sheets of paper to make a step book. Staple all of the sheets together at the top. **Figure B**

B

3. Use a pencil to divide the three middle sheets into thirds. Then cut up from the bottom along the lines you drew to make slits in these three sheets. **Figure C**

C

4. On the top step of your booklet, write the number and title of the chapter.

Taking Note of the Math

Label each of the steps in your booklet with important concepts from the chapter: "Using Exponents," "Expressing Numbers in Scientific Notation," and so on. On the bottom sheet, write "Solving Equations." Write sample problems from the chapter on the appropriate steps.

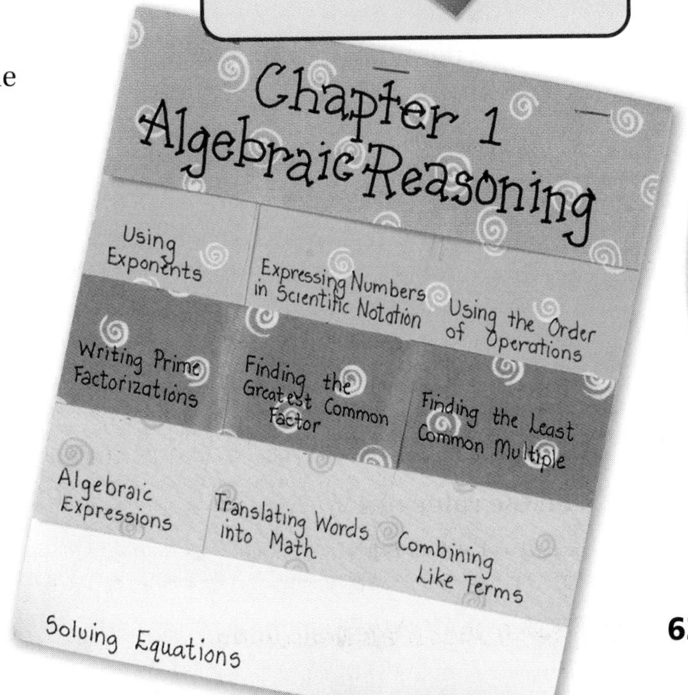

CHAPTER 1

Study Guide: Review

Vocabulary

Complete the sentences below with vocabulary words from the list above.

1. The __?__ tells how many times to use the __?__ as a factor.
2. A(n) __?__ is a mathematical phrase made up of numbers and operations.
3. A(n) __?__ is a mathematical statement that two expressions are equal in value.
4. A(n) __?__ consists of constants, variables, and operations.

1-1 Numbers and Patterns (pp. 6–9)

EXAMPLE

- **Identify a possible pattern. Use the pattern to write the next three numbers.**

  2, 8, 14, 20, . . .

  $2 + 6 = 8$ $\quad 8 + 6 = 14$ $\quad 14 + 6 = 20$

  A possible pattern is to add 6 each time.

  $20 + 6 = 26$ $\quad 26 + 6 = 32$ $\quad 32 + 6 = 38$

EXERCISES

Identify a possible pattern. Use the pattern to write the next three numbers.

5. 6, 10, 14, 18, . . .
6. 15, 35, 55, 75, . . .
7. 7, 14, 21, 28, . . .
8. 8, 40, 200, 1,000, . . .
9. 41, 37, 33, 29, . . .
10. 68, 61, 54, 47, . . .

1-2 Exponents (pp. 10–13)

EXAMPLE

- **Find the value of 4^3.**

  $4^3 = 4 \cdot 4 \cdot 4 = 64$

EXERCISES

Find each value.

11. 9^2
12. 10^1
13. 2^7
14. 1^7
15. 11^2

1-3 Metric Measurements (pp. 14–17)

EXAMPLE

- **Convert 63 m to centimeters.**

$63 \text{ m} = (63 \times 100) \text{ cm}$ *100 cm = 1 m*

$= 6{,}300 \text{ cm}$

EXERCISES

Convert each measure.

16. 18 L to mL **17.** 720 mg to g

18. 5.3 km to m **19.** 0.6 cm to mm

1-4 Applying Exponents (pp. 18–21)

EXAMPLE

- **Multiply $157 \cdot 10^4$.**

$157 \cdot 10^4 = 1570000$

$= 1{,}570{,}000$

EXERCISES

Multiply.

20. $144 \cdot 10^2$ **21.** $1.32 \cdot 10^3$ **22.** $22 \cdot 10^7$

Write each number in scientific notation.

23. 48,000 **24.** 7,020,000 **25.** 149,000

1-5 Order of Operations (pp. 23–26)

EXAMPLE

- **Simplify $(18 + 6) \cdot 5$.**

$(18 + 6) \cdot 5 = 24 \cdot 5 = 120$

EXERCISES

Simplify each expression.

26. $2 + (9 - 6) \div 3$ **27.** $12 \cdot 3^2 - 5$

28. $11 + 2 \cdot 5 - (9 + 7)$ **29.** $75 \div 5^2 + 8^2$

1-6 Properties (pp. 28–31)

EXAMPLE

- **Tell which property is represented.**

$(10 \cdot 13) \cdot 28 = 10 \cdot (13 \cdot 28)$

Associative Property

EXERCISES

Tell which property is represented.

30. $42 + 17 = 17 + 42$

31. $m + 0 = m$

32. $6 \cdot (x - 5) = 6 \cdot x - 6 \cdot 5$

1-7 Variables and Algebraic Expressions (pp. 34–37)

EXAMPLE

- **Evaluate $5a - 6b + 7$ for $a = 4$ and $b = 3$.**

$5a - 6b + 7$

$5(4) - 6(3) + 7$

$20 - 18 + 7$

9

EXERCISES

Evaluate each expression for the given values of the variables.

33. $4x - 5$ for $x = 6$

34. $8y^3 + 3y$ for $y = 4$

35. $\frac{n}{5} + 6m - 3$ for $n = 5$ and $m = 2$

1-8 Translate Words into Math (pp. 38–41)

EXAMPLE

- **Write as an algebraic expression.**

  5 times the sum of a number and 6

  $5(n + 6)$

EXERCISES

Write as an algebraic expression.

36. 4 divided by the sum of a number and 12

37. 2 times the difference of t and 11

1-9 Simplifying Algebraic Expressions (pp. 42–45)

EXAMPLE

- **Simplify the expression.**

  $4x^3 + 5y + 8x^3 - 4y - 5x^2$

  $4x^3 + 5y + 8x^3 - 4y - 5x^2$

  $12x^3 + y - 5x^2$

EXERCISES

Simplify each expression.

38. $7b^2 + 8 + 3b^2$

39. $12a^2 + 4 + 3a^2 - 2$

40. $x^2 + x^3 + x^4 + 5x^2$

1-10 Equations and Their Solutions (pp. 46–49)

EXAMPLE

- **Determine whether 22 is a solution.**

  $24 \stackrel{?}{=} s - 13$

  $24 \stackrel{?}{=} 22 - 13$

  $24 \stackrel{?}{=} 9$ ✗ 22 is not a solution.

EXERCISES

Determine whether the given value of the variable is a solution.

41. $36 = n - 12;\ n = 48$

42. $9x = 117;\ x = 12$

1-11 Addition and Subtraction Equations (pp. 52–55)

EXAMPLE

- **Solve the equation. Then check.**

$$\begin{aligned} b + 12 &= 16 \\ \underline{-12} \quad &\underline{-12} \\ b &= 4 \end{aligned} \qquad \begin{aligned} b + 12 &\stackrel{?}{=} 16 \\ 4 + 12 &\stackrel{?}{=} 16 \\ 16 &\stackrel{?}{=} 16 \checkmark \end{aligned}$$

EXERCISES

Solve each equation. Then check.

43. $8 + b = 16$

44. $20 = n - 12$

45. $27 + c = 45$

46. $t - 68 = 44$

1-12 Multiplication and Division Equations (pp. 56–59)

EXAMPLE

- **Solve the equation. Then check.**

$$\begin{aligned} 2r &= 12 \\ \frac{2r}{2} &= \frac{12}{2} \\ r &= 6 \end{aligned} \qquad \begin{aligned} 2r &= 12 \\ 2(6) &\stackrel{?}{=} 12 \\ 12 &\stackrel{?}{=} 12 \checkmark \end{aligned}$$

EXERCISES

Solve each equation. Then check.

47. $n \div 12 = 6$

48. $3p = 27$

49. $\frac{d}{14} = 7$

50. $6x = 78$

51. Lee charges $8 per hour to baby-sit. Last month she earned $136. How many hours did Lee baby-sit last month?

CHAPTER TEST

CHAPTER 1

Identify a possible pattern. Use the pattern to write the next three numbers.

1. 24, 32, 40, 48, . . . **2.** 6, 18, 54, 162, . . . **3.** 64, 58, 52, 46, . . . **4.** 13, 30, 47, 64, . . .

Find each value.

5. 6^2 **6.** 7^5 **7.** 8^6 **8.** 3^5

Convert each measure.

9. 180 mL to liters **10.** 7.8 m to centimeters **11.** 23.4 kg to grams

12. Jesse is 1,460 millimeters tall. Her sister is 168 centimeters tall, and her brother is 1.56 meters tall. Who is the tallest?

Multiply.

13. $148 \cdot 10^2$ **14.** $56.3 \cdot 10^3$ **15.** $6.89 \cdot 10^4$ **16.** $7.5 \cdot 10^4$

Write each number in scientific notation.

17. 406,000,000 **18.** 1,905,000 **19.** 22,400 **20.** 500,000

Simplify each expression.

21. $18 \cdot 3 \div 3^3$ **22.** $36 + 16 - 50$ **23.** $149 - (2^8 - 200)$ **24.** $(4 \div 2) \cdot 9 + 11$

Tell which property is represented.

25. $0 + 45 = 45$ **26.** $(r + s) + t = r + (s + t)$ **27.** $84 \cdot 3 = 3 \cdot 84$

Evaluate each expression for the given values of the variables.

28. $4a + 6b + 7$ for $a = 2$ and $b = 3$ **29.** $7y^2 + 7y$ for $y = 3$

Write each phrase as an algebraic expression.

30. a number increased by 12 **31.** the quotient of a number and 7

32. 5 less than the product of 7 and *s* **33.** the difference between 3 times *x* and 4

Simplify each expression. Justify your steps.

34. $b + 2 + 5b$ **35.** $16 + 5b + 3b + 9$ **36.** $5a + 6t + 9 + 2a$

Solve each equation.

37. $x + 9 = 19$ **38.** $21 = y - 20$ **39.** $m - 54 = 72$ **40.** $136 = y + 114$

41. $16 = \frac{y}{3}$ **42.** $102 = 17y$ **43.** $\frac{r}{7} = 1{,}400$ **44.** $6x = 42$

45. A caterer charged $15 per person to prepare a meal for a banquet. If the total catering charge for the banquet was $1,530, how many people attended?

TEST TACKLER

Standardized Test Strategies

Multiple Choice: Eliminate Answer Choices

With some multiple-choice test items, you can use mental math or number sense to quickly eliminate some of the answer choices before you begin solving the problem.

EXAMPLE 1

Which is the solution to the equation $x + 7 = 15$?

Ⓐ $x = 22$ Ⓑ $x = 15$ Ⓒ $x = 8$ Ⓓ $x = 7$

READ the question.
Then try to **eliminate** some of the answer choices.

Use number sense:

When you add, you get a greater number than what you started with. Since $x + 7 = 15$, 15 must be greater than x, or x must be less than 15. Since 22 and 15 are not less than 15, you can eliminate answer choices A and B.

The correct answer choice is C.

EXAMPLE 2

Arnold measured 0.15 L of water and then poured the water into a beaker labeled only in milliliters. What did the measurement read on the beaker?

Ⓕ 0.015 mL Ⓖ 0.15 mL Ⓗ 15 mL Ⓙ 150 mL

LOOK at the choices.
Then try to **eliminate** some of the answer choices.

Use mental math:

A milliliter is smaller than a liter, so the answer is greater than 0.15. You can eliminate answer choices F and G.

The prefix *milli-* means "thousandth," so multiply 0.15 by 1,000 to get 150 mL, which is answer choice J.

HOT TIP! Before you work a test question, use mental math to help you decide if there are answer choices that you can eliminate right away.

Read each test item and answer the questions that follow.

Item A

During the August back-to-school sale, 2 pairs of shoes cost $34, a shirt costs $15, and a pair of pants costs $27. Janet bought 2 pairs of shoes, 4 shirts, and 4 pairs of pants and then paid an additional $7 for tax. Which expression shows the total that Janet spent?

Ⓐ 34 + 4(15 + 27)

Ⓑ 34 + 4(15 + 27) + 7

Ⓒ 4(34 + 15 + 27) + 7

Ⓓ 34 + 15 + 4 · 27

1. Can any of the answer choices be eliminated immediately? If so, which choices and why?
2. Describe how you can determine the correct answer from the remaining choices.

Item B

Anthony saved $1 from his first paycheck, $2 from his second paycheck, then $4, $8, and so on. How much money did Anthony save from his tenth paycheck?

Ⓕ $10 Ⓗ $512

Ⓖ $16 Ⓙ $1,023

3. Are there any answer choices you can eliminate immediately? If so, which choices and why?
4. What common error was made in finding answer choice F?

Item C

Craig has three weeks to read an 850-page book. Which equation can be used to find the number of pages Craig has to read each day?

Ⓐ $\frac{x}{3} = 850$ Ⓒ $3x = 850$

Ⓑ $21x = 850$ Ⓓ $\frac{x}{21} = 850$

5. Describe how to use number sense to eliminate at least one answer choice.
6. What common error was made in finding answer choice D?

Item D

A window in a treehouse measures 56 centimeters wide. Samantha wants to build a seat along the window that is 35 centimeters wider than the window is. How wide, in meters, would the window seat need to be?

Ⓕ 91 m Ⓗ 0.21 m

Ⓖ 21 m Ⓙ 0.91 m

7. Which two choices can be eliminated by using mental math?
8. Explain how to convert from centimeters to meters.

Item E

What is the value of the expression $(1 + 2)^2 + 14 \div 2 + 5$?

Ⓐ 0 Ⓒ 17

Ⓑ 11 Ⓓ 21

9. Use mental math to quickly eliminate one answer choice. Explain your choice.
10. What common error was made in finding answer choice B?
11. What common error was made in finding answer choice C?

STANDARDIZED TEST PREP

go.hrw.com
State Test Practice Online
KEYWORD: MS7 TestPrep

Cumulative Assessment, Chapter 1

Multiple Choice

1. Which expression has a value of 74 when $x = 10$, $y = 8$, and $z = 12$?

   (A) $4xyz$
   (B) $x + 5y + 2z$
   (C) $2xz - 3y$
   (D) $6xyz + 8$

2. What is the next number in the pattern?

   $3, 3^2, 27, 3^4, 3^5, \ldots$

   (F) 729
   (G) 3^7
   (H) 243
   (J) 3^8

3. A contractor charges $22 to install one miniblind. How much does the contractor charge to install *m* miniblinds?

   (A) $22m$
   (B) $\frac{m}{22}$
   (C) $22 + m$
   (D) $\frac{22}{m}$

4. Which of the following is an example of the Commutative Property?

   (F) $20 + 10 = 2(10 + 5)$
   (G) $20 + 10 = 10 + 20$
   (H) $5 + (20 + 10) = (5 + 20) + 10$
   (J) $20 + 0 = 20$

5. Which expression simplifies to $9x + 3$ when you combine like terms?

   (A) $10x^2 - x^2 - 3$
   (B) $3x + 7 - 4 + 3x$
   (C) $18 + 4x - 15 + 5x$
   (D) $7x^2 + 2x + 6 - 3$

6. What is the solution to the equation $810 = x - 625$?

   (F) $x = 185$
   (G) $x = 215$
   (H) $x = 845$
   (J) $x = 1,435$

7. Tia maps out her jogging route as shown in the table. How many kilometers does Tia plan to jog?

Tia's Jogging Route	
Street	**Meters**
1st to Park	428
Park to Windsor	112
Windsor to East	506
East to Manor	814
Manor to Vane	660
Vane to 1st	480

   (A) 3,000 km
   (B) 300 km
   (C) 30 km
   (D) 3 km

8. To make a beaded necklace, Kris needs 88 beads. If Kris has 1,056 beads, how many necklaces can she make?

   (F) 968
   (G) 12
   (H) 264
   (J) 8

9. What are the next two numbers in the pattern?

   75, 70, 60, 55, 45, 40, . . .

   (A) 35, 30
   (B) 30, 20
   (C) 30, 25
   (D) 35, 25

10. Marc spends $78 for *n* shirts. Which expression can be used to represent the cost of one shirt?

   (F) $\frac{n}{78}$
   (G) $78n$
   (H) $\frac{78}{n}$
   (J) $78 + n$

11. Which situation best matches the expression $0.29x + 2$?

(A) A taxi company charges a \$2.00 flat fee plus \$0.29 for every mile.

(B) Jimmy ran 0.29 miles, stopped to rest, and then ran 2 more miles.

(C) There are 0.29 grams of calcium in 2 servings of Hearty Health Cereal.

(D) Amy bought 2 pieces of gum for \$0.29 each.

12. Which of the following should be performed first to simplify this expression?

$$16 \cdot 2 + (20 \div 5) - 3^2 \div 3 + 1$$

(F) $3^2 \div 3$

(G) $20 \div 5$

(H) $16 \cdot 2$

(J) $3 + 1$

HOT TIP! When you read a word problem, cross out any information that is not needed to solve the problem.

Gridded Response

13. If $x = 15$ and $y = 5$, what is the value of $\frac{2x}{y} + 3y$?

14. What is the exponent when you write the number 23,000,000 in scientific notation?

15. An airplane has seats for 198 passengers. If each row seats 6 people, how many rows are on the plane?

16. What is the value of the expression $3^2 \times (2 + 3 \times 4) - 5$?

17. What is the solution to the equation $10 + s = 42$?

18. What is the sum of 4 and the product of 9 and 5?

Short Response

19. Luke can swim 25 laps in one hour. Write an algebraic expression to show how many laps Luke can swim in *h* hours. How many hours will it take Luke to swim 100 laps?

20. An aerobics instructor teaches a 45-minute class at 9:30 A.M., three times a week. She dedicates 12 minutes during each class to stretching. The rest of the class consists of aerobic dance. How many minutes of each class does the instructor spend teaching aerobic dance? Write and solve an equation to explain how you found your answer.

21. Ike and Joe ran the same distance but took different routes. Ike ran 3 blocks east and 7 blocks south. Joe ran 4 blocks west and then turned north. How far north did Joe run? Show your work.

Extended Response

22. The Raiders and the Hornets are buying new uniforms for their baseball teams. Each team member will receive a new cap, a jersey, and a pair of pants.

Uniform Costs

	Raiders	Hornets
Cap	\$15	\$15
Jersey	\$75	\$70
Pants	\$60	\$70

a. Let *r* represent the number of Raiders team members, and let *h* represent the number of Hornets team members. For each team, write an expression that gives the total cost of the team's uniforms.

b. If the Raiders and the Hornets both have 12 team members, how much will each team spend on uniforms? Which team will spend the most, and by how much? Show your work.

CHAPTER 2

Integers and Rational Numbers

go.hrw.com
Chapter Project Online
KEYWORD: MS7 Ch2

Speed of Sound Through Different Materials

Material	Speed (m/s)
Air at 20°C	344
Water at 20°C	1,500
Wood (oak) at 20°C	3,850
Glass at 20°C	4,540
Steel at 20°C	5,200

Career *Oceanographer*

Is Earth warming? Or is it cooling? The temperature of the oceans is a very important factor in answering these questions. Oceanographers have been studying the temperature of the Pacific Ocean by measuring the speed of sound waves in the water.

How does this work? The speed of sound is affected by the temperature of the material through which the sound travels. In air, for example, the speed of sound increases about 0.6 meter per second for every degree Celsius that the temperature rises. By measuring the speed of sound in water, scientists can tell the water's temperature.

ARE YOU READY?

Vocabulary

Choose the best term from the list to complete each sentence.

1. To ___?___ a number on a number line, mark and label the point that corresponds to that number.

2. The expression $1 < 3 < 5$ tells the ___?___ of these three numbers on a number line.

3. A(n) ___?___ is a mathematical statement showing two things are equal.

4. Each number in the set 0, 1, 2, 3, 4, 5, 6, 7, . . . is a(n) ___?___.

5. To ___?___ an equation, find a value that makes it true.

whole number
expression
graph
solve
equation
order

Complete these exercises to review skills you will need for this chapter.

Order of Operations

Simplify.

6. $7 + 9 - 5 \cdot 2$	**7.** $12 \cdot 3 - 4 \cdot 5$
8. $115 - 15 \cdot 3 + 9(8 - 2)$	**9.** $20 \cdot 5 \cdot 2(7 + 1) \div 4$
10. $300 + 6(5 - 3) - 11$	**11.** $14 - 13 + 9 \cdot 2$

Find Multiples

Find the first five multiples of each number.

12. 2	**13.** 9	**14.** 15	**15.** 1
16. 101	**17.** 54	**18.** 326	**19.** 1,024

Find Factors

List all the factors of each number.

20. 8	**21.** 22	**22.** 36	**23.** 50
24. 108	**25.** 84	**26.** 256	**27.** 630

Use Inverse Operations to Solve Equations

Solve.

28. $n + 3 = 10$	**29.** $x - 4 = 16$	**30.** $9p = 63$	**31.** $\frac{t}{5} = 80$
32. $x - 3 = 14$	**33.** $\frac{q}{3} = 21$	**34.** $9 + r = 91$	**35.** $15p = 45$

CHAPTER 2

Study Guide: Preview

Where You've Been

Previously, you

- compared and ordered non-negative rational numbers.
- generated equivalent forms of rational numbers including whole numbers, fractions, and decimals.
- used integers to represent real-life situations.

In This Chapter

You will study

- comparing and ordering integers and rational numbers.
- converting between fractions and decimals mentally, on paper, and with a calculator.
- using models to add, subtract, multiply, and divide integers.
- finding the prime factorization, greatest common factor, and least common multiple.

Where You're Going

You can use the skills learned in this chapter

- to express negative numbers related to scientific fields such as marine biology or meteorology.
- to find equivalent measures.

Key Vocabulary/Vocabulario

equivalent fraction	fraccion equivalente
greatest common factor (GCF)	maximo comun divisor (MCD)
improper fraction	fraccion impropia
integer	entero
least common multiple (LCM)	minimo comun multipulo (mcm)
mixed number	numero mixto
prime factorization	factorizacion prima
rational number	numero racional
repeating decimal	decimal periodico
terminating decimal	decimal cerrado

Vocabulary Connections

To become familiar with some of the vocabulary terms in the chapter, consider the following. You may refer to the chapter, the glossary, or a dictionary if you like.

1. The word *common* means "belonging to or shared by two things." How can you use this definition to explain what the **least common multiple** of two numbers is?
2. Rational numbers come in many forms, including whole numbers and fractions. *Mixed* means "made up of more than one kind." What do you think a **mixed number** might be?
3. A decimal is a number that has digits to the right of the decimal point. What might you predict about those digits in a **repeating decimal**?

Reading and Writing Math

Writing Strategy: Translate Between Words and Math

As you read a real-world math problem, look for key words to help you translate between the words and the math.

Example

At FunZone the cost to play laser tag is \$8 per game. The cost to play miniature golf is \$5 per game. The one-time admission fee to the park is \$3. Jonna wants to play both laser tag and miniature golf. Write an algebraic expression to find the total amount Jonna would pay to play ℓ laser tag games and m golf games at FunZone.

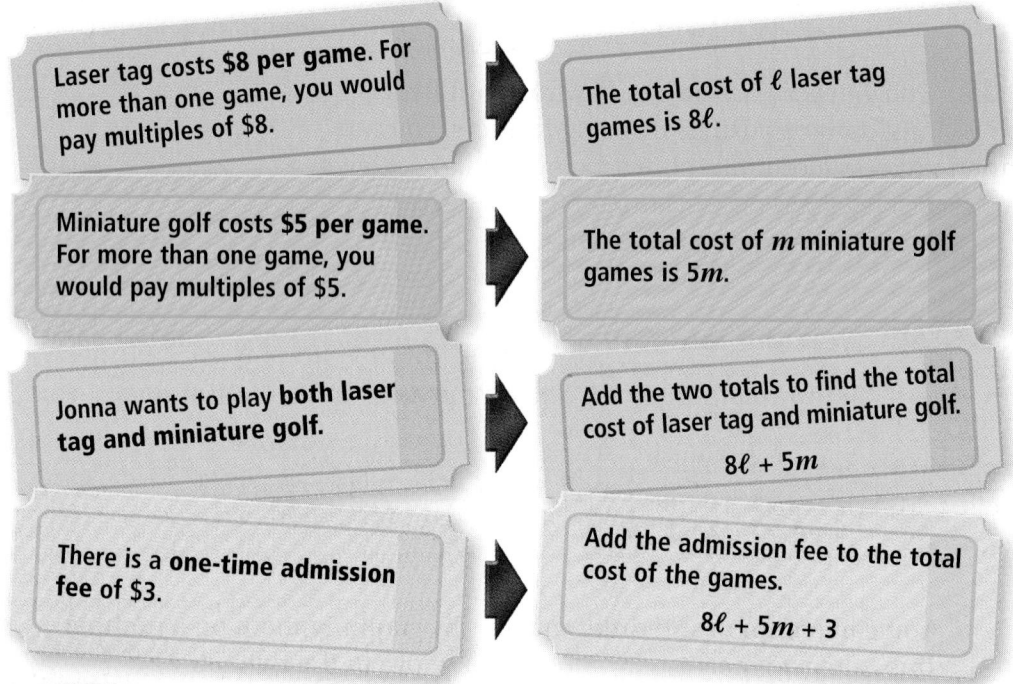

Laser tag costs **\$8 per game.** For more than one game, you would pay multiples of \$8. → The total cost of ℓ laser tag games is 8ℓ.

Miniature golf costs **\$5 per game.** For more than one game, you would pay multiples of \$5. → The total cost of m miniature golf games is $5m$.

Jonna wants to play **both laser tag and miniature golf.** → Add the two totals to find the total cost of laser tag and miniature golf.

$$8\ell + 5m$$

There is a **one-time admission** fee of \$3. → Add the admission fee to the total cost of the games.

$$8\ell + 5m + 3$$

Try This

Write an algebraic expression that describes the situation. Explain why you chose each operation in the expression.

1. School supplies are half-price at Bargain Mart this week. The original prices were \$2 per package of pens and \$4 per notebook. Cally buys 1 package of pens and n notebooks. How much does Cally spend?
2. Fred has f cookies, and Gary has g cookies. Fred and Gary each eat 3 cookies. How many total cookies are left?

2-1 Integers

Learn to compare and order integers and to determine absolute value.

Vocabulary
- opposite
- integer
- absolute value

The **opposite** of a number is the same distance from 0 on a number line as the original number, but on the other side of 0. Zero is its own opposite.

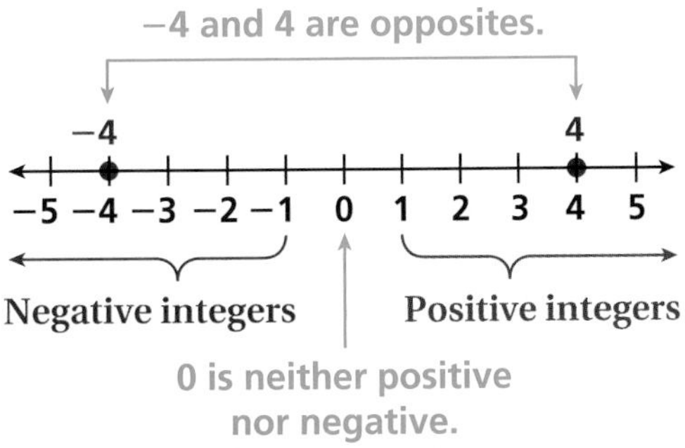

Dr. Sylvia Earle holds the world record for the deepest solo dive.

Remember!
The whole numbers are the counting numbers and zero: 0, 1, 2, 3, ...

The **integers** are the set of whole numbers and their opposites. By using integers, you can express elevations above, below, and at sea level. Sea level has an elevation of 0 feet. Sylvia Earle's record dive was to an elevation of $-1{,}250$ feet.

EXAMPLE 1 Graphing Integers and Their Opposites on a Number Line

Graph the integer -3 and its opposite on a number line.

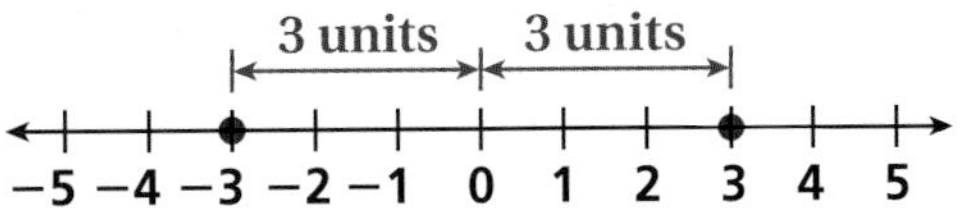

The opposite of -3 is 3.

You can compare and order integers by graphing them on a number line. Integers increase in value as you move to the right along a number line. They decrease in value as you move to the left.

EXAMPLE 2 Comparing Integers Using a Number Line

Remember!
The symbol < means "is less than," and the symbol > means "is greater than."

Compare the integers. Use < or >.

A 2 ▢ -2

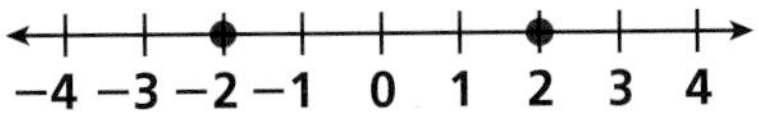

2 is farther to the right than -2, so $2 > -2$.

Compare the integers. Use $<$ or $>$.

B -10 ▒ -7

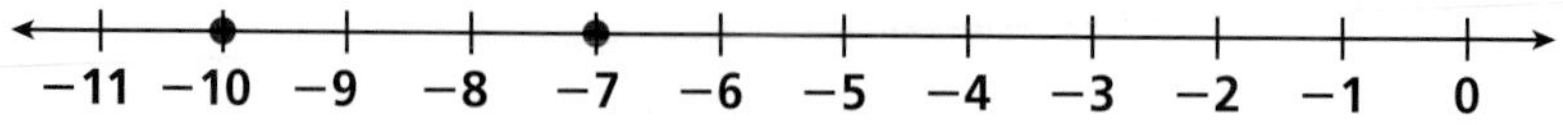

-10 is farther to the left than -7, so $-10 < -7$.

EXAMPLE 3 Ordering Integers Using a Number Line

Use a number line to order the integers −2, 5, −4, 1, −1, and 0 from least to greatest.

Graph the integers on a number line. Then read them from left to right.

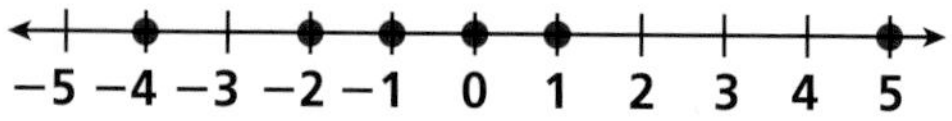

The numbers in order from least to greatest are −4, −2, −1, 0, 1, and 5.

A number's **absolute value** is its distance from 0 on a number line. Since distance can never be negative, absolute values are never negative. They are always positive or zero.

EXAMPLE 4 Finding Absolute Value

Reading Math

The symbol | | is read as "the absolute value of." For example, $|-3|$ means "the absolute value of −3."

Use a number line to find each absolute value.

A $|7|$

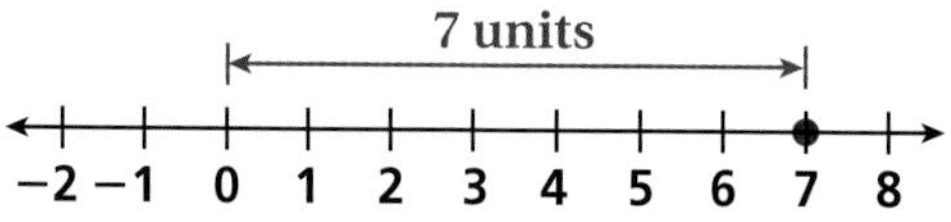

7 is 7 units from 0, so $|7| = 7$.

B $|-4|$

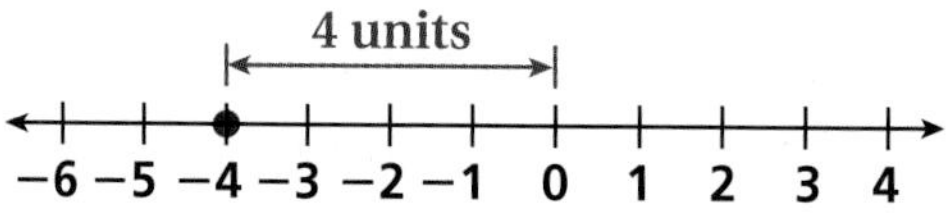

-4 is 4 units from 0, so $|-4| = 4$.

Think and Discuss

1. **Tell** which number is greater: −4,500 or −10,000.
2. **Name** the greatest negative integer and the least nonnegative integer. Then compare the absolute values of these integers.

2-1 Exercises

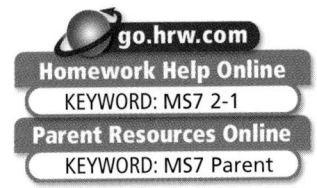

go.hrw.com
Homework Help Online
KEYWORD: MS7 2-1
Parent Resources Online
KEYWORD: MS7 Parent

GUIDED PRACTICE

See Example 1
Graph each integer and its opposite on a number line.

1. 2 **2.** −9 **3.** −1 **4.** 6

See Example 2
Compare the integers. Use < or >.

5. 5 □ −5 **6.** −9 □ −18 **7.** −21 □ −17 **8.** −12 □ 12

See Example 3
Use a number line to order the integers from least to greatest.

9. 6, −3, −1, −5, 4 **10.** 8, −2, 7, 1, −8 **11.** −6, −4, 3, 0, 1

See Example 4
Use a number line to find each absolute value.

12. $|-2|$ **13.** $|8|$ **14.** $|-7|$ **15.** $|-10|$

INDEPENDENT PRACTICE

See Example 1
Graph each integer and its opposite on a number line.

16. −4 **17.** 10 **18.** −12 **19.** 7

See Example 2
Compare the integers. Use < or >.

20. −14 □ −7 **21.** 9 □ −9 **22.** −12 □ 12 **23.** −31 □ −27

See Example 3
Use a number line to order the integers from least to greatest.

24. −3, 2, −5, −6, 5 **25.** −7, −9, −2, 0, −5 **26.** 3, −6, 9, −1, −2

See Example 4
Use a number line to find each absolute value.

27. $|-16|$ **28.** $|12|$ **29.** $|-20|$ **30.** $|15|$

PRACTICE AND PROBLEM SOLVING

Extra Practice
See page 727.

Compare. Write <, >, or =.

31. −25 □ 25 **32.** 18 □ −55 **33.** $|-21|$ □ 21 **34.** −9 □ −27

35. 34 □ $|34|$ **36.** 64 □ $|-75|$ **37.** $|-3|$ □ $|3|$ **38.** −100 □ −82

39. Earth Science The table shows the average temperatures in Vostok, Antarctica from March to October. List the months in order from coldest to warmest.

Month	Mar	Apr	May	Jun	Jul	Aug	Sep	Oct
Temperature (°F)	−72	−84	−86	−85	−88	−90	−87	−71

40. What is the opposite of $|32|$? **41.** What is the opposite of $|-29|$?

42. Business A company reported a net loss of $2,000,000 during its first year. In its second year it reported a profit of $5,000,000. Write each amount as an integer.

LINK

Sports

In wakeboarding, a rider uses the waves created by a boat, the wake, to jump into the air and perform tricks such as rolls and flips.

43. Critical Thinking Give an example in which a negative number has a greater absolute value than a positive number.

44. Social Studies Lines of latitude are imaginary lines that circle the globe in an east-west direction. They measure distances north and south of the equator. The equator represents 0° latitude.

a. What latitude is opposite of 30° north latitude?

b. How do these latitudes' distances from the equator compare?

Sports The graph shows how participation in several sports changed between 1999 and 2000 in the United States.

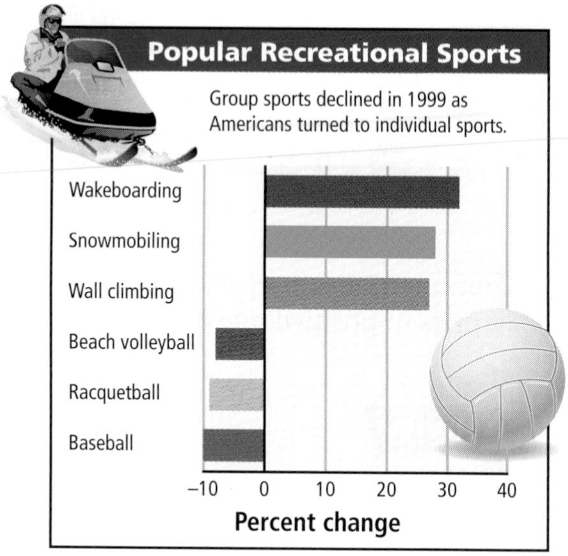

Source: USA Today, July 6, 2001

45. By about what percent did participation in racquetball increase or decrease?

46. By about what percent did participation in wall climbing increase or decrease?

47. What's the Error? At 9 A.M. the outside temperature was −3°F. By noon, the temperature was −12°F. A newscaster said that it was getting warmer outside. Why is this incorrect?

48. Write About It Explain how to compare two integers.

49. Challenge What values can x have if $|x| = 11$?

Test Prep and Spiral Review

50. Multiple Choice Which list shows the integers in order from least to greatest?

Ⓐ −5, −6, −7, 2, 3 Ⓑ 2, 3, −5, −6, −7 Ⓒ −7, −6, −5, 2, 3 Ⓓ 3, 2, −7, −6, −5

51. Multiple Choice The table shows the average temperatures in Barrow, Alaska, for several months. In which month is the average temperature lowest?

Ⓕ January Ⓗ May

Ⓖ March Ⓙ July

Monthly Temperatures	
January	−12°F
March	−13°F
May	20°F
July	40°F

Convert each measure. (Lesson 1-3)

52. 3.2 kg to g **53.** 167 cm to m **54.** 18 cm to mm **55.** 10.3 L to mL

Use the Distributive Property to find each product. (Lesson 1-6)

56. 3(12) **57.** 2(56) **58.** (27)6 **59.** (34)5

Hands-On LAB 2-2

Model Integer Addition

Use with Lesson 2-2

go.hrw.com
Lab Resources Online
KEYWORD: MS7 Lab2

KEY

= 1

= –1

\+ = 0

REMEMBER

- Adding or subtracting zero does not change the value of an expression.

You can model integer addition by using integer chips. Yellow chips represent positive numbers and red chips represent negative numbers.

Activity

When you model adding numbers with the same sign, you can count the total number of chips to find the sum.

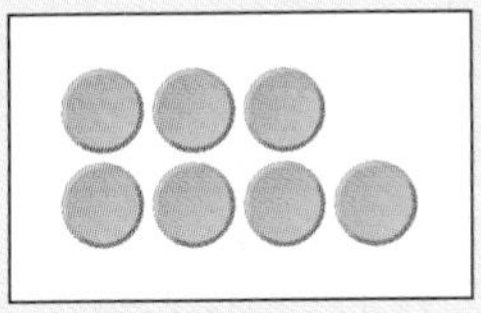

The total number of positive chips is 7.

$3 + 4 = 7$

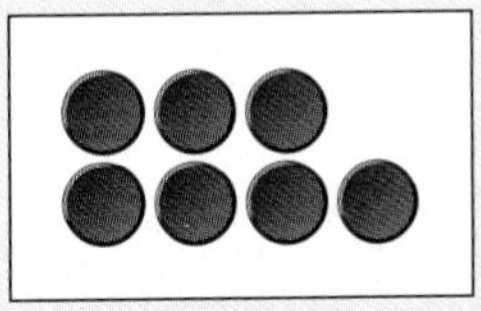

The total number of negative chips is 7.

$-3 + (-4) = -7$

1 Use integer chips to find each sum.

a. $2 + 4$ **b.** $-2 + (-4)$ **c.** $6 + 3$ **d.** $-5 + (-4)$

When you model adding numbers with different signs, you cannot count the chips to find their sum.

\+ = 2 and + = -2

but + = 0 *A red chip and a yellow chip make a neutral pair.*

When you model adding a positive and a negative number, you need to remove all of the zero pairs that you can find—that is, all pairs of 1 red chip and 1 yellow chip. These pairs have a value of zero, so they do not affect the sum.

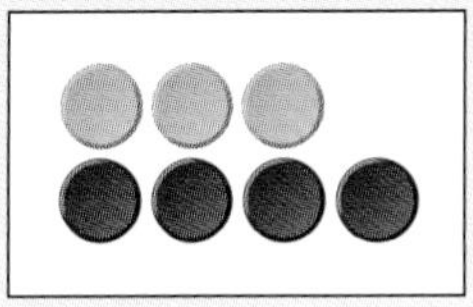

You cannot just count the colored chips to find their sum.

3 + (−4) = ▢

Before you count the chips, you need to remove all of the zero pairs.

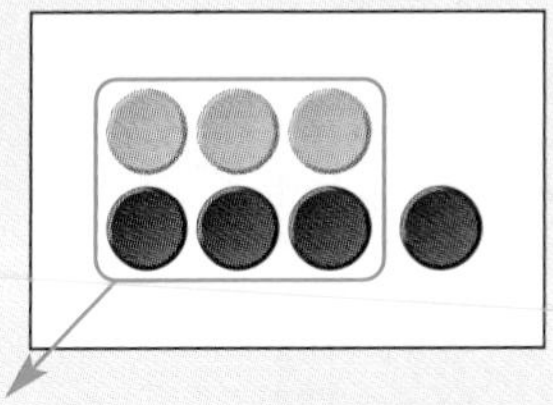

When you remove the zero pairs, there is one red chip left. So the sum of the chips is −1.

3 + (−4) = −1

2 Use integer chips to find each sum.

a. 4 + (−6) **b.** −5 + 2 **c.** 7 + (−3) **d.** −6 + 3

Think and Discuss

1. Will 8 + (−3) and −3 + 8 give the same answer? Why or why not?
2. If you have more red chips than yellow chips in a group, is the sum of the chips positive or negative?
3. If you have more yellow chips than red chips in a group, is the sum of the chips positive or negative?
4. Make a rule for the sign of the answer when negative and positive integers are added. Give examples.

Try This

Use integer chips to find each sum.

1. 4 + (−7) **2.** −5 + (−4) **3.** −5 + 1 **4.** 6 + (−4)

Write the addition problems modeled below.

5.

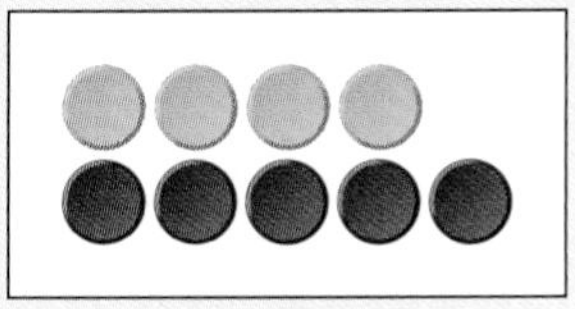

6.

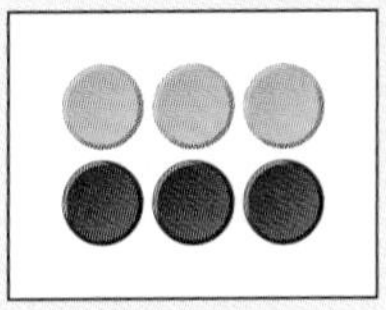

7.

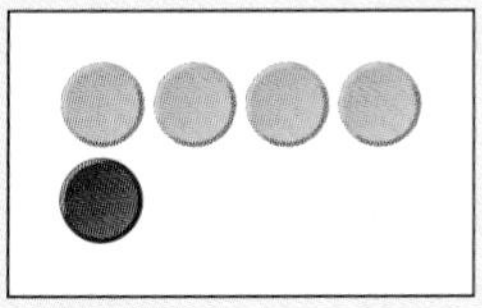

8.

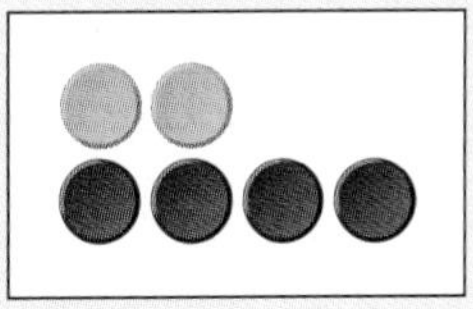

2-2 Adding Integers

Learn to add integers.

The Debate Club wanted to raise money for a trip to Washington, D.C. They began by estimating their income and expenses.

Income items are positive, and expenses are negative. By adding all your income and expenses, you can find your total earnings or losses.

One way to add integers is by using a number line.

Club Ledger

Estimated Income and Expenses

Description	Amount
Car wash supplies	−$25.00
Car wash earnings	$300.00
Bake sale supplies	−$50.00
Bake sale earnings	$250.00

EXAMPLE 1 Modeling Integer Addition

Use a number line to find each sum.

A $-3 + (-6)$

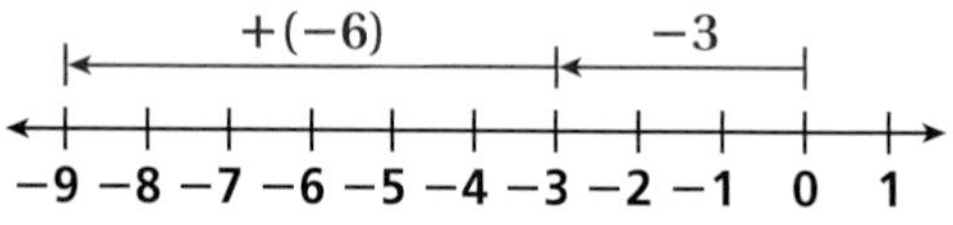

Start at 0. Move left 3 units. Then move left 6 more units.

$-3 + (-6) = -9$

B $4 + (-7)$

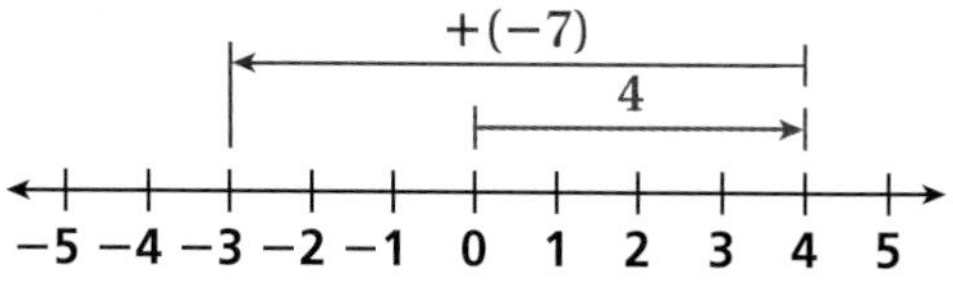

Start at 0. Move right 4 units. Then move left 7 units.

$4 + (-7) = -3$

You can also use absolute value to add integers.

Adding Integers

To add two integers with the same sign, find the sum of their absolute values. Use the sign of the two integers.

To add two integers with different signs, find the difference of their absolute values. Use the sign of the integer with the greater absolute value.

EXAMPLE 2 Adding Integers Using Absolute Values

Find each sum.

A $-7 + (-4)$

The signs are the **same**. Find the **sum** of the absolute values.

$-7 + (-4)$	*Think: 7 + 4 = 11.*
-11	*Use the sign of the two integers.*

B $-8 + 6$

The signs are **different**. Find the **difference** of the absolute values.

$-8 + 6$	*Think: 8 − 6 = 2.*
-2	*Use the sign of the integer with the greater absolute value.*

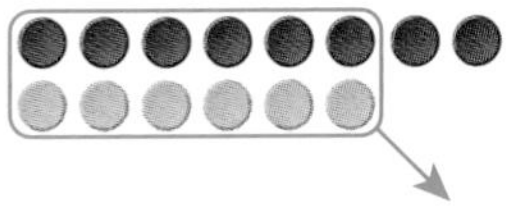

EXAMPLE 3 Evaluating Expressions with Integers

Helpful Hint

When adding integers, think: If the signs are the *same*, find the *sum*. If the signs are *different*, find the *difference*.

Evaluate $a + b$ for $a = 6$ and $b = -10$.

$a + b$	
$6 + (-10)$	*Substitute 6 for **a** and −10 for **b**.*
	*The signs are **different**. Think: 10 − 6 = 4.*
-4	*Use the sign of the integer with the greater absolute value **(negative)**.*

EXAMPLE 4 *Banking Application*

The Debate Club's income from a car wash was $300, including tips. Supply expenses were $25. Use integer addition to find the club's total profit or loss.

$300 + (-25)$	*Use negative for the expenses.*
$300 - 25$	*Find the difference of the absolute values.*
275	*The answer is positive.*

The club earned $275.

Think and Discuss

1. **Explain** whether $-7 + 2$ is the same as $7 + (-2)$.
2. **Use** the Commutative Property to write an expression that is equivalent to $3 + (-5)$.

2-2 Exercises

go.hrw.com
Homework Help Online
KEYWORD: MS7 2-2
Parent Resources Online
KEYWORD: MS7 Parent

GUIDED PRACTICE

See Example 1

Use a number line to find each sum.

1. $9 + 3$ **2.** $-4 + (-2)$ **3.** $7 + (-9)$ **4.** $-3 + 6$

See Example 2

Find each sum.

5. $7 + 8$ **6.** $-1 + (-12)$ **7.** $-25 + 10$ **8.** $31 + (-20)$

See Example 3

Evaluate $a + b$ for the given values.

9. $a = 5, b = -17$ **10.** $a = 8, b = -8$ **11.** $a = -4, b = -16$

See Example 4

12. Sports A football team gains 8 yards on one play and then loses 13 yards on the next. Use integer addition to find the team's total yardage.

INDEPENDENT PRACTICE

See Example 1

Use a number line to find each sum.

13. $-16 + 7$ **14.** $-5 + (-1)$ **15.** $4 + 9$ **16.** $-7 + 8$

17. $10 + (-3)$ **18.** $-20 + 2$ **19.** $-12 + (-5)$ **20.** $-9 + 6$

See Example 2

Find each sum.

21. $-13 + (-6)$ **22.** $14 + 25$ **23.** $-22 + 6$ **24.** $35 + (-50)$

25. $-81 + (-7)$ **26.** $28 + (-3)$ **27.** $-70 + 15$ **28.** $-18 + (-62)$

See Example 3

Evaluate $c + d$ for the given values.

29. $c = 6, d = -20$ **30.** $c = -8, d = -21$ **31.** $c = -45, d = 32$

See Example 4

32. The temperature dropped 17°F in 6 hours. The final temperature was −3°F. Use integer addition to find the starting temperature.

PRACTICE AND PROBLEM SOLVING

Extra Practice
See page 727.

Find each sum.

33. $-8 + (-5)$ **34.** $14 + (-7)$ **35.** $-41 + 15$

36. $-22 + (-18) + 22$ **37.** $27 + (-29) + 16$ **38.** $-30 + 71 + (-70)$

Compare. Write $<$, $>$, or $=$.

39. $-23 + 18$ ▒ -41 **40.** $59 + (-59)$ ▒ 0 **41.** $31 + (-20)$ ▒ 9

42. $-24 + (-24)$ ▒ 48 **43.** $25 + (-70)$ ▒ -95 **44.** $16 + (-40)$ ▒ -24

45. Personal Finance Cody made deposits of \$45, \$18, and \$27 into his checking account. He then wrote checks for \$21 and \$93. Write an expression to show the change in Cody's account. Then simplify the expression.

LINK

Recreation

The Appalachian Trail extends about 2,160 miles from Maine to Georgia. It takes about 5 to 7 months to hike the entire trail.

Evaluate each expression for $w = -12$, $x = 10$, and $y = -7$.

46. $7 + y$ **47.** $-4 + w$ **48.** $w + y$ **49.** $x + y$ **50.** $w + x$

51. Recreation Hikers along the Appalachian Trail camped overnight at Horns Pond, at an of elevation 3,100 ft. Then they hiked along the ridge of the Bigelow Mountains to West Peak, which is one of Maine's highest peaks. Use the diagram to determine the elevation of West Peak.

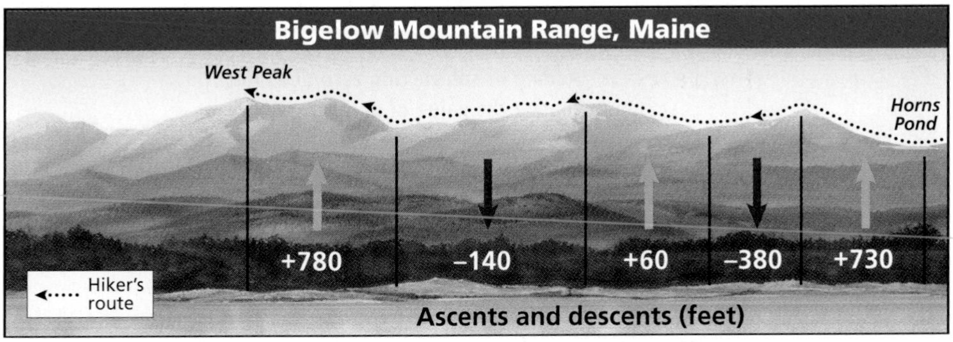

52. Multi-Step Hector and Luis are playing a game. In the game, each player starts with 0 points, and the player with the most points at the end wins. Hector gains 5 points, loses 3, loses 2, and then gains 3. Luis loses 5 points, gains 1, gains 5, and then loses 3. Determine the final scores by modeling the problem on a number line. Then tell who wins the game and by how much.

53. What's the Question? The temperature was −8°F at 6 A.M. and rose 15°F by 9 A.M. The answer is 7°F. What is the question?

54. Write About It Compare the method used to add integers with the same sign and the method used to add integers with different signs.

55. Challenge A business had losses of $225 million, $75 million, and $375 million and profits of $15 million and $125 million. How much was its overall profit or loss?

Test Prep and Spiral Review

56. Multiple Choice Which expression is represented by the model?

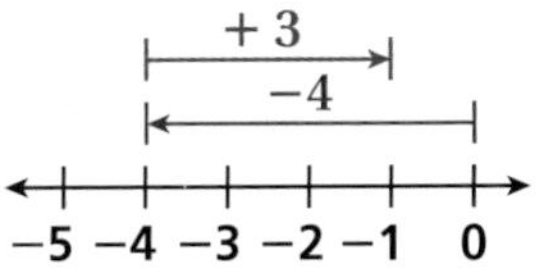

Ⓐ $-4 + (-1)$ Ⓒ $-4 + 3$

Ⓑ $-4 + 0$ Ⓓ $-4 + 4$

57. Multiple Choice Which expression has the greatest value?

Ⓕ $-4 + 8$ Ⓖ $-2 + (-3)$ Ⓗ $1 + 2$ Ⓙ $4 + (-6)$

Simplify each expression. (Lesson 1-5)

58. $2 + 5 \cdot 2 - 3$ **59.** $3^3 - (6 \cdot 4) + 1$ **60.** $30 - 5 \cdot (3 + 2)$ **61.** $15 - 3 \cdot 2^2 + 1$

Compare. Write <, >, or =. (Lesson 2-1)

62. -14 ▒ -12 **63.** $|-4|$ ▒ 3 **64.** $|-6|$ ▒ 6 **65.** -9 ▒ -11

Hands-On LAB 2-3

Model Integer Subtraction

Use with Lesson 2-3

go.hrw.com
Lab Resources Online
KEYWORD: MS7 Lab2

KEY

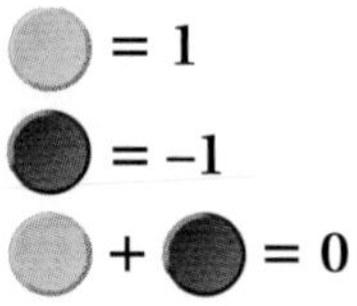

REMEMBER

- Adding or subtracting zero does not change the value of an expression.

You can model integer subtraction by using integer chips.

Activity

These groups of chips show three different ways of modeling 2.

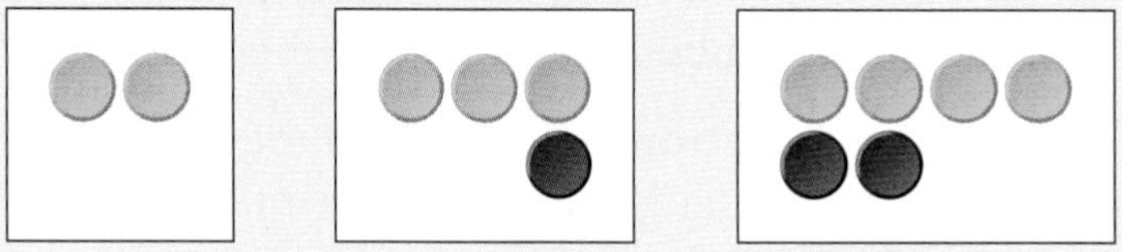

1 Show two other ways of modeling 2.

These groups of chips show two different ways of modeling −2.

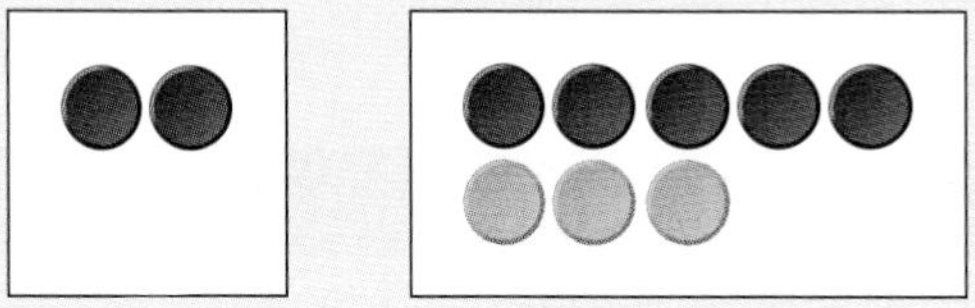

2 Show two other ways of modeling −2.

You can model subtraction problems involving two integers with the same sign by taking away chips.

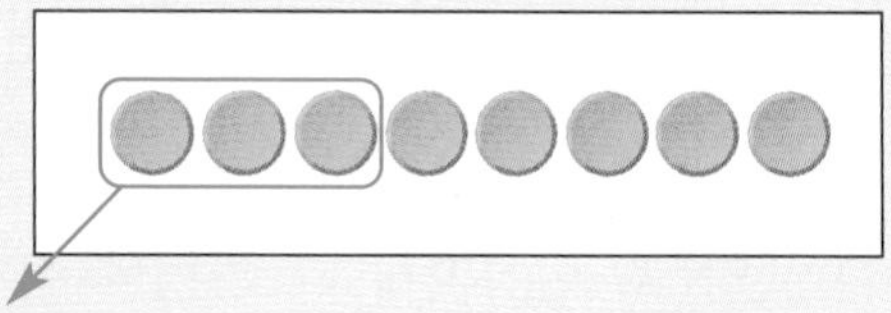

$8 - 3 = 5$

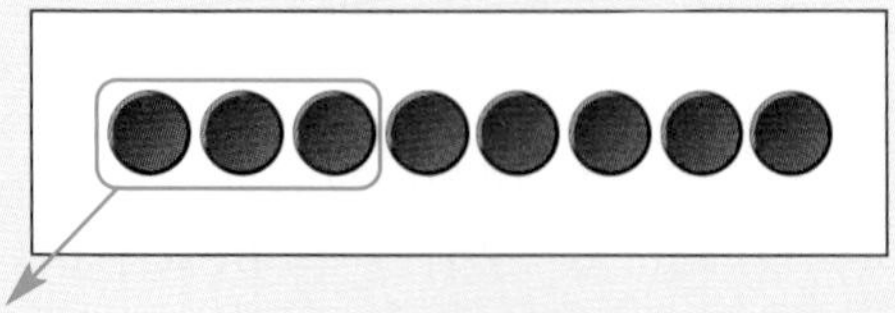

$-8 - (-3) = -5$

3 Use integer chips to find each difference.

a. $6 - 5$ **b.** $-6 - (-5)$ **c.** $10 - 7$ **d.** $-7 - (-4)$

To model subtraction problems involving two integers with different signs, such as $-6 - 3$, you will need to add zero pairs before you can take chips away.

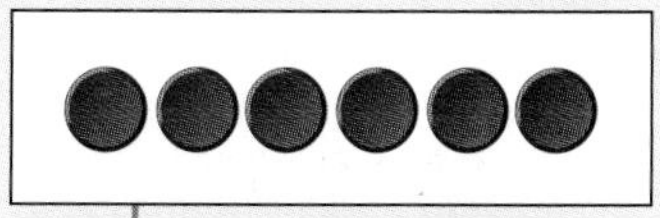

Use 6 red chips to represent -6.

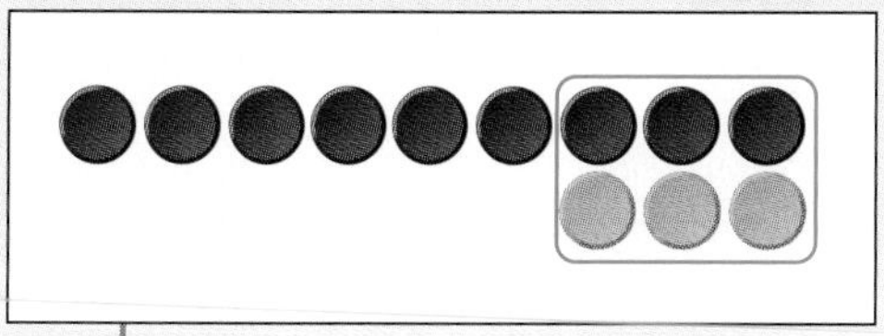

Since you cannot take away 3 yellow chips, add 3 yellow chips paired with 3 red chips.

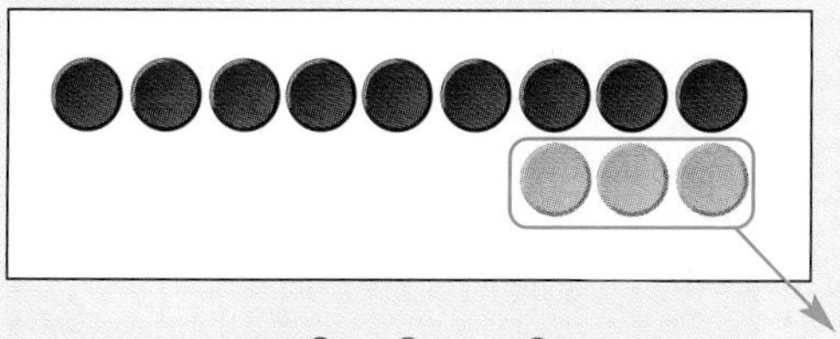

Now you can take away 3 yellow chips.

$-6 - 3 = -9$

4 Use integer chips to find each difference.

a. $-6 - 5$ **b.** $5 - (-6)$ **c.** $4 - 7$ **d.** $-2 - (-3)$

Think and Discuss

1. How could you model the expression $0 - 5$?
2. When you add zero pairs to model subtraction using chips, does it matter how many zero pairs you add?
3. Would $2 - 3$ have the same answer as $3 - 2$? Why or why not?
4. Make a rule for the sign of the answer when negative and positive integers are subtracted. Give examples.

Try This

Use integer chips to find each difference.

1. $4 - 2$ **2.** $-4 - (-2)$ **3.** $-2 - (-3)$

4. $3 - 4$ **5.** $2 - 3$ **6.** $0 - 3$

7. $5 - 3$ **8.** $-3 - (-5)$ **9.** $6 - (-4)$

2-3 Subtracting Integers

Learn to subtract integers.

During flight, the space shuttle may be exposed to temperatures as low as −250°F and as high as 3,000°F.

To find the difference in these temperatures, you need to know how to subtract integers with different signs.

You can model the difference between two integers using a number line. When you subtract a positive number, the difference is *less* than the original number, so you move to the *left*. To subtract a negative number, move to the *right*.

EXAMPLE 1 **Modeling Integer Subtraction**

Use a number line to find each difference.

A $3 - 8$

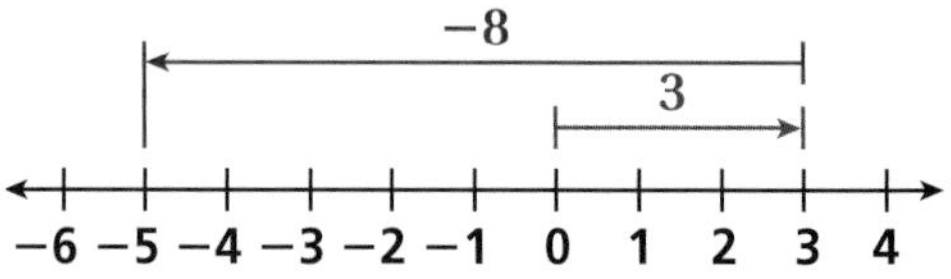

Start at 0.
Move right 3 units.
To subtract 8,
move to the left.

$3 - 8 = -5$

Helpful Hint

If the number being subtracted is less than the number it is subtracted from, the answer will be positive. If the number being subtracted is greater, the answer will be negative.

B $-4 - 2$

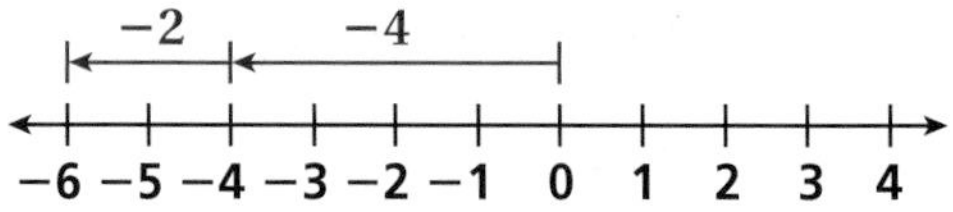

Start at 0.
Move left 4 units.
To subtract 2,
move to the left.

$-4 - 2 = -6$

C $2 - (-3)$

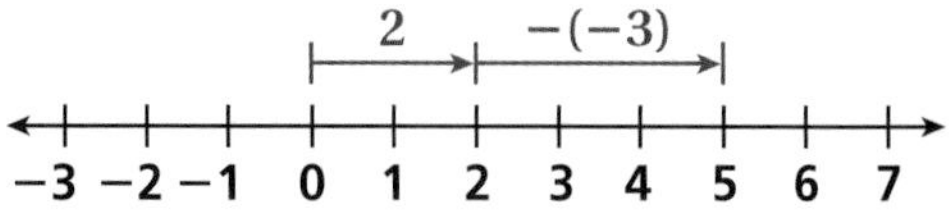

Start at 0.
Move right 2 units.
To subtract −3,
move to the right.

$2 - (-3) = 5$

Addition and subtraction are inverse operations—they "undo" each other. Instead of subtracting a number, you can *add its opposite.*

EXAMPLE 2 Subtracting Integers by Adding the Opposite

Find each difference.

A $5 - 9$

$5 - 9 = 5 + (-9)$ *Add the opposite of 9.*

$= -4$

B $-9 - (-2)$

$-9 - (-2) = -9 + 2$ *Add the opposite of −2.*

$= -7$

C $-4 - 3$

$-4 - 3 = -4 + (-3)$ *Add the opposite of 3.*

$= -7$

EXAMPLE 3 Evaluating Expressions with Integers

Evaluate *a* − *b* for each set of values.

A $a = -6, b = 7$

$a - b$

$-6 - 7 = -6 + (-7)$ *Substitute for a and b. Add the opposite of 7.*

$= -13$

B $a = 14, b = -9$

$a - b$

$14 - (-9) = 14 + 9$ *Substitute for a and b. Add the opposite of −9.*

$= 23$

EXAMPLE 4 *Temperature Application*

Find the difference between 3,000°F and −250°F, the temperatures the space shuttle must endure.

$3{,}000 - (-250)$

$3{,}000 + 250 = 3{,}250$ *Add the opposite of −250.*

The difference in temperatures the shuttle must endure is 3,250°F.

Think and Discuss

1. Suppose you subtract one negative integer from another. Will your answer be greater than or less than the number you started with?

2. Tell whether you can reverse the order of integers when subtracting and still get the same answer. Why or why not?

2-3 Exercises

go.hrw.com
Homework Help Online
KEYWORD: MS7 2-3
Parent Resources Online
KEYWORD: MS7 Parent

GUIDED PRACTICE

See Example 1
Use a number line to find each difference.

1. $4 - 7$ **2.** $-6 - 5$ **3.** $2 - (-4)$ **4.** $-8 - (-2)$

See Example 2
Find each difference.

5. $6 - 10$ **6.** $-3 - (-8)$ **7.** $-1 - 9$ **8.** $-12 - (-2)$

See Example 3
Evaluate $a - b$ for each set of values.

9. $a = 5, b = -2$ **10.** $a = -8, b = 6$ **11.** $a = 4, b = 18$

See Example 4
12. In 1980, in Great Falls, Montana, the temperature rose from −32°F to 15°F in seven minutes. How much did the temperature increase?

INDEPENDENT PRACTICE

See Example 1
Use a number line to find each difference.

13. $7 - 12$ **14.** $-5 - (-9)$ **15.** $2 - (-6)$ **16.** $7 - (-8)$

17. $9 - (-3)$ **18.** $-4 - 10$ **19.** $8 - (-8)$ **20.** $-3 - (-3)$

See Example 2
Find each difference.

21. $-22 - (-5)$ **22.** $-4 - 21$ **23.** $27 - 19$ **24.** $-10 - (-7)$

25. $30 - (-20)$ **26.** $-15 - 15$ **27.** $12 - (-6)$ **28.** $-31 - 15$

See Example 3
Evaluate $a - b$ for each set of values.

29. $a = 9, b = -7$ **30.** $a = -11, b = 2$ **31.** $a = -2, b = 3$

32. $a = 8, b = 19$ **33.** $a = -10, b = 10$ **34.** $a = -4, b = -15$

See Example 4
35. In 1918, in Granville, North Dakota, the temperature rose from −33°F to 50°F in 12 hours. How much did the temperature increase?

PRACTICE AND PROBLEM SOLVING

Extra Practice
See page 727.

Simplify.

36. $2 - 8$ **37.** $-5 - 9$ **38.** $15 - 12 - 8$

39. $6 + (-5) - 3$ **40.** $1 - 8 + (-6)$ **41.** $4 - (-7) - 9$

42. $(2 - 3) - (5 - 6)$ **43.** $5 - (-8) - (-3)$ **44.** $10 - 12 + 2$

Evaluate each expression for $m = -5$, $n = 8$, and $p = -14$.

45. $m - n + p$ **46.** $n - m - p$ **47.** $p - m - n$ **48.** $m + n - p$

49. Patterns Find the next three numbers in the pattern 7, 3, −1, −5, −9 . . . . Then describe the pattern.

Astronomy LINK

50. The temperature of Mercury, the planet closest to the Sun, can be as high as 873°F. The temperature of Pluto, the planet farthest from the Sun, is −393°F. What is the difference between these temperatures?

51. One side of Mercury always faces the Sun. The temperature on this side can reach 873°F. The temperature on the other side can be as low as −361°F. What is the difference between the two temperatures?

Maat Mons volcano on Venus
Source: NASA (computer-generated from the *Magellan* probe)

52. Earth's moon rotates relative to the Sun about once a month. The side facing the Sun at a given time can be as hot as 224°F. The side away from the Sun can be as cold as −307°F. What is the difference between these temperatures?

53. The highest recorded temperature on Earth is 136°F. The lowest is −129°F. What is the difference between these temperatures?

Use the graph for Exercises 54 and 55.

54. How much deeper is the deepest canyon on Mars than the deepest canyon on Venus?

55. **Challenge** What is the difference between Earth's highest mountain and its deepest ocean canyon? What is the difference between Mars' highest mountain and its deepest canyon? Which difference is greater? How much greater is it?

Highest and Lowest Points on Venus, Earth, and Mars

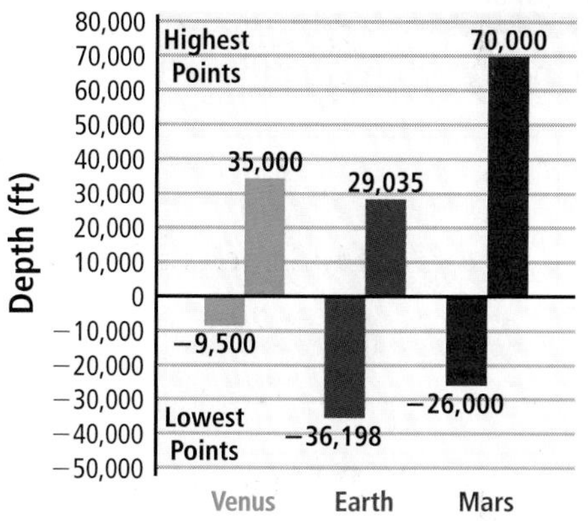

TEST PREP and Spiral Review

56. **Multiple Choice** Which expression does NOT have a value of −3?

Ⓐ $-2 - 1$ Ⓑ $10 - 13$ Ⓒ $5 - (-8)$ Ⓓ $-4 - (-1)$

57. **Extended Response** If $m = -2$ and $n = 4$, which expression has the least absolute value: $m + n$, $n - m$, or $m - n$? Explain your answer.

Evaluate each expression for the given values of the variables. (Lesson 1-7)

58. $3x - 5$ for $x = 2$
59. $2n^2 + n$ for $n = 1$
60. $4y^2 - 3y$ for $y = 2$
61. $4a + 7$ for $a = 3$
62. $x^2 + 9$ for $x = 1$
63. $5z + z^2$ for $z = 3$

64. **Sports** In three plays, a football team gained 10 yards, lost 22 yards, and gained 15 yards. Use integer addition to find the team's total yardage for the three plays. (Lesson 2-2)

Hands-On LAB 2-4

Model Integer Multiplication and Division

Use with Lesson 2-4

go.hrw.com
Lab Resources Online
KEYWORD: MS7 Lab2

KEY

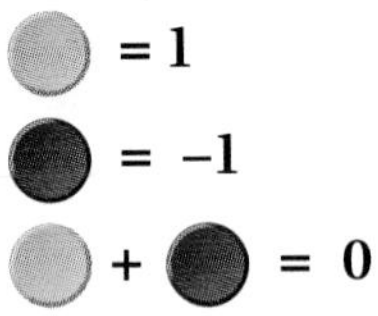

REMEMBER

- The Commutative Property states that two numbers can be multiplied in any order without changing the product.
- Multiplication is repeated addition.
- Multiplication and division are inverse operations.

You can model integer multiplication and division by using integer chips.

Activity 1

Use integer chips to model $3 \cdot (-5)$.

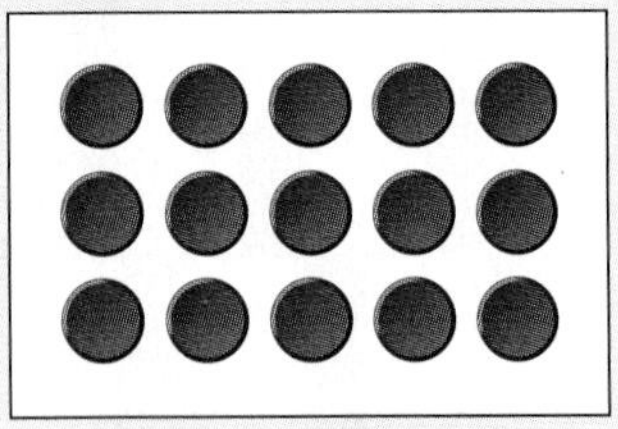

Think: $3 \cdot (-5)$ means 3 groups of -5.

Arrange 3 groups of 5 red chips.
There are a total of 15 red chips.

$3 \cdot (-5) = -15$

1 Use integer chips to find each product.

a. $2 \cdot (-2)$ **b.** $3 \cdot (-6)$ **c.** $5 \cdot (-4)$ **d.** $6 \cdot (-3)$

Use integer chips to model $-4 \cdot 2$.

Using the Commutative Property, you can write $-4 \cdot 2$ as $2 \cdot (-4)$.

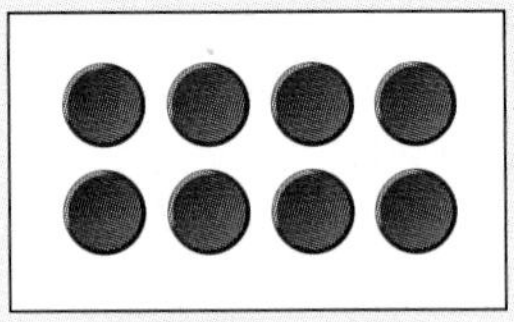

Think: $2 \cdot (-4)$ means 2 groups of -4.

Arrange 2 groups of 4 red chips.
There are a total of 8 red chips.

$-4 \cdot 2 = -8$

2 Use integer chips to find each product.

a. $-6 \cdot 5$ **b.** $-4 \cdot 6$ **c.** $-3 \cdot 4$ **d.** $-2 \cdot 3$

Think and Discuss

1. What is the sign of the product when you multiply two positive numbers? a negative and a positive number? two negative numbers?
2. If 12 were the answer to a multiplication problem, list all of the possible factors that are integers.

Try This

Use integer chips to find each product.

1. $4 \cdot (-5)$ **2.** $-3 \cdot 2$ **3.** $1 \cdot (-6)$ **4.** $-5 \cdot 2$

5. On days that Kathy has swimming lessons, she spends $2.00 of her allowance on snacks. Last week, Kathy had swimming lessons on Monday, Wednesday, and Friday. How much of her allowance did Kathy spend on snacks last week? Use integer chips to model the situation and solve the problem.

Activity 2

Use integer chips to model $-15 \div 3$.

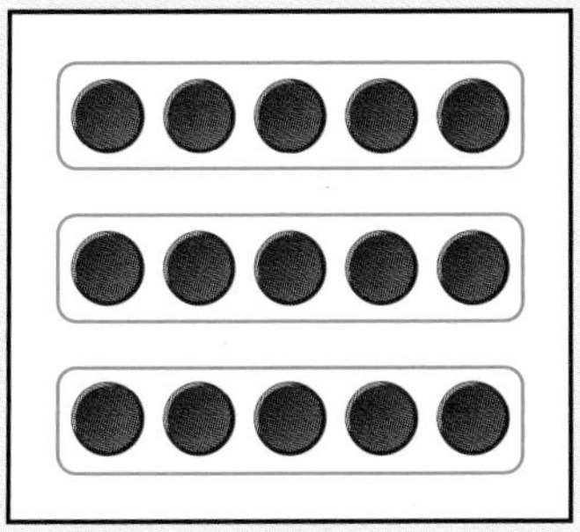

Think: −15 is separated into 3 equal groups.

Arrange 15 red chips into 3 equal groups.

There are 5 red chips in each group.

$-15 \div 3 = -5$

1 Use integer chips to find each quotient.

a. $-20 \div 5$ **b.** $-18 \div 6$ **c.** $-12 \div 4$ **d.** $-24 \div 8$

Think and Discuss

1. What is the sign of the answer when you divide two negative integers? a negative integer by a positive integer? a positive integer by a negative integer?
2. How are multiplication and division of integers related?

Try This

Use integer chips to find each quotient.

1. $-21 \div 7$ **2.** $-12 \div 4$ **3.** $-8 \div 2$ **4.** $-10 \div 5$

5. Ty spent $18 of his allowance at the arcade. He hit baseballs, played pinball, and played video games. Each of these activities cost the same amount at the arcade. How much did each activity cost? Use integer chips to model the situation and solve the problem.

2-4 Multiplying and Dividing Integers

Learn to multiply and divide integers.

You can think of multiplication as repeated addition.

$$3 \cdot 2 = 2 + 2 + 2 = 6 \text{ and } 3 \cdot (-2) = (-2) + (-2) + (-2) = -6$$

EXAMPLE 1 Multiplying Integers Using Repeated Addition

Use a number line to find each product.

A $3 \cdot (-3)$

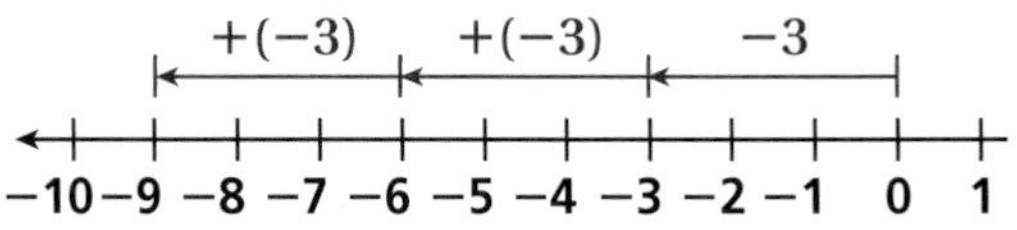

Think: Add −3 three times.

$3 \cdot (-3) = -9$

B $-4 \cdot 2$

$-4 \cdot 2 = 2 \cdot (-4)$ *Use the Commutative Property.*

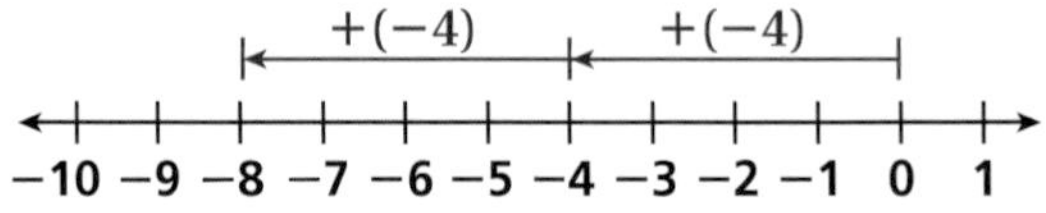

Think: Add −4 two times.

$-4 \cdot 2 = -8$

Remember!

Multiplication and division are inverse operations. They "undo" each other. Notice how these operations undo each other in the patterns shown.

The patterns below suggest that when the signs of two integers are different, their product or quotient is negative. The patterns also suggest that the product or quotient of two negative integers is positive.

$-3 \cdot 2 = -6$	$-6 \div (-3) = 2$
$-3 \cdot 1 = -3$	$-3 \div (-3) = 1$
$-3 \cdot 0 = 0$	$0 \div (-3) = 0$
$-3 \cdot (-1) = 3$	$3 \div (-3) = -1$
$-3 \cdot (-2) = 6$	$6 \div (-3) = -2$

Multiplying and Dividing Integers

If the signs are:		Your answer will be:
the same	⟶	positive
different	⟶	negative

EXAMPLE 2 Multiplying Integers

Find each product.

A $-4 \cdot (-2)$

$-4 \cdot (-2)$ *Both signs are negative, so the product is positive.*

8

B $-3 \cdot 6$

$-3 \cdot 6$ *The signs are different, so the product is negative.*

-18

EXAMPLE 3 Dividing Integers

Find each quotient.

A $72 \div (-9)$

$72 \div (-9)$ *Think: $72 \div 9 = 8$.*

-8 *The signs are different, so the quotient is negative.*

B $-144 \div 12$

$-144 \div 12$ *Think: $144 \div 12 = 12$.*

-12 *The signs are different, so the quotient is negative.*

C $-100 \div (-5)$

$-100 \div (-5)$ *Think: $100 \div 5 = 20$.*

20 *The signs are the same, so the quotient is positive.*

EXAMPLE 4 *Earth Science Application*

Jonie recorded the temperature change every hour for 4 hours as a cold front approached. The temperature dropped steadily a total of 24°F over the 4-hour period. What was the change in temperature during the first hour?

The temperature dropped 24°F. You can write this as -24.

$-24 \div 4 = -6$ *Divide the total drop in temperature by the total recording time.*

The temperature change during the first hour was -6°F.

Earth Science LINK

Each year there are about 16 million thunderstorms around the globe. Thunderstorms develop when moist air rises and encounters cooler air.

Think and Discuss

1. **List** at least four different multiplication examples that have 24 as their product. Use both positive and negative integers.
2. **Explain** how the signs of two integers affect their products and quotients.

2-4 Exercises

go.hrw.com
Homework Help Online
KEYWORD: MS7 2-4
Parent Resources Online
KEYWORD: MS7 Parent

GUIDED PRACTICE

See Example 1
Use a number line to find each product.

1. $5 \cdot (-3)$ **2.** $5 \cdot (-2)$ **3.** $-3 \cdot 5$ **4.** $-4 \cdot 6$

See Example 2
Find each product.

5. $-5 \cdot (-3)$ **6.** $-2 \cdot 5$ **7.** $3 \cdot (-5)$ **8.** $-7 \cdot (-4)$

See Example 3
Find each quotient.

9. $32 \div (-4)$ **10.** $-18 \div 3$ **11.** $-20 \div (-5)$ **12.** $49 \div (-7)$

13. $-63 \div (-9)$ **14.** $-50 \div 10$ **15.** $63 \div (-9)$ **16.** $-45 \div (-5)$

See Example 4
17. Angelina hiked down a 2,250-foot mountain trail. She stopped 5 times along the way to rest, walking the same distance between each stop. How far did Angelina hike before the first stop?

INDEPENDENT PRACTICE

See Example 1
Use a number line to find each product.

18. $2 \cdot (-1)$ **19.** $-5 \cdot 2$ **20.** $-4 \cdot 2$ **21.** $3 \cdot (-4)$

See Example 2
Find each product.

22. $4 \cdot (-6)$ **23.** $-6 \cdot (-8)$ **24.** $-8 \cdot 4$ **25.** $-5 \cdot (-7)$

See Example 3
Find each quotient.

26. $48 \div (-6)$ **27.** $-35 \div (-5)$ **28.** $-16 \div 4$ **29.** $-64 \div 8$

30. $-42 \div (-7)$ **31.** $81 \div (-9)$ **32.** $-77 \div 11$ **33.** $27 \div (-3)$

See Example 4
34. A scuba diver descended below the ocean's surface in 35-foot intervals as he examined a coral reef. He dove to a total depth of 140 feet. In how many intervals did the diver make his descent?

PRACTICE AND PROBLEM SOLVING

Extra Practice
See page 727.

Find each product or quotient.

35. $-4 \cdot 10$ **36.** $-3 \cdot (-9)$ **37.** $-45 \div 15$ **38.** $-3 \cdot 4 \cdot (-1)$

39. $-500 \div (-10)$ **40.** $5 \cdot (-4) \cdot (-2)$ **41.** $225 \div (-75)$ **42.** $-2 \cdot (-5) \cdot 9$

Evaluate each expression for $a = -5$, $b = 6$, and $c = -12$.

43. $-2c + b$ **44.** $4a - b$ **45.** $ab + c$ **46.** $ac \div b$

47. Earth Science A scuba diver is swimming at a depth of −12 feet in the Flower Garden Banks National Marine Sanctuary. She dives down to a coral reef that is at five times this depth. What is the depth of the coral reef?

Simplify each expression. Justify your steps using the Commutative, Associative, and Distributive Properties when necessary.

48. $(-3)^2$ **49.** $-(-2+1)$ **50.** $8+(-5)^3+7$ **51.** $(-1)^5 \cdot (9+3)$

52. $29-(-7)-3$ **53.** $-4 \cdot 14 \cdot (-25)$ **54.** $25-(-2) \cdot 4^2$ **55.** $8-(6 \div (-2))$

56. Earth Science The table shows the depths of major caves in the United States. Approximately how many times deeper is Jewel Cave than Kartchner Caverns?

Depths of Major U.S. Caves

Cave	Depth (ft)
Carlsbad Caverns	–1,022
Caverns of Sonora	–150
Ellison's Cave	–1,000
Jewel Cave	–696
Kartchner Caverns	–137
Mammoth Cave	–379

Source: NSS U.S.A. Long Cave List, Caves over one mile long as of 10/18/2001

Personal Finance Does each person end up with more or less money than he started with? By how much?

57. Kevin spends \$24 a day for 3 days.

58. Devin earns \$15 a day for 5 days.

59. Evan spends \$20 a day for 3 days. Then he earns \$18 a day for 4 days.

60. What's the Error? A student writes, "The quotient of an integer divided by an integer of the opposite sign has the sign of the integer with the greater absolute value." What is the student's error?

61. Write About It Explain how to find the product and the quotient of two integers.

62. Challenge Use > or < to compare $-2 \cdot (-1) \cdot 4 \cdot 2 \cdot (-3)$ and $-1+(-2)+4+(-25)+(-10)$.

Test Prep and Spiral Review

63. Multiple Choice Which of the expressions are equal to -20?

I $-2 \cdot 10$ **II** $-40 \div (-2)$ **III** $-5 \cdot (-2)^2$ **IV** $-4 \cdot 2 - 12$

(A) I only (B) I and II (C) I, III, and IV (D) I, II, III, IV

64. Multiple Choice Which expression has a value that is greater than the value of $-25 \div (-5)$?

(F) $36 \div (-6)$ (G) $-100 \div 10$ (H) $-50 \div (-10)$ (J) $-45 \div (-5)$

Write each phrase as an algebraic expression. (Lesson 1-8)

65. the sum of a number and 6 **66.** the product of -3 and a number

67. 4 less than twice a number **68.** 5 more than a number divided by 3

Find each difference. (Lesson 2-3)

69. $3-(-2)$ **70.** $-5-6$ **71.** $6-8$ **72.** $2-(-7)$

Hands-On LAB 2-5

Model Integer Equations

Use with Lesson 2-5

go.hrw.com
Lab Resources Online
KEYWORD: MS7 Lab2

KEY

[+] = 1

[−] = −1

[+] + [−] = 0

[+] (long tile) = x

REMEMBER

- Adding or subtracting zero does not change the value of an expression.

You can use algebra tiles to model and solve equations.

Activity

To solve the equation $x + 2 = 3$, you need to get x alone on one side of the equal sign. You can add or remove tiles as long as you add the same amount or remove the same amount on both sides.

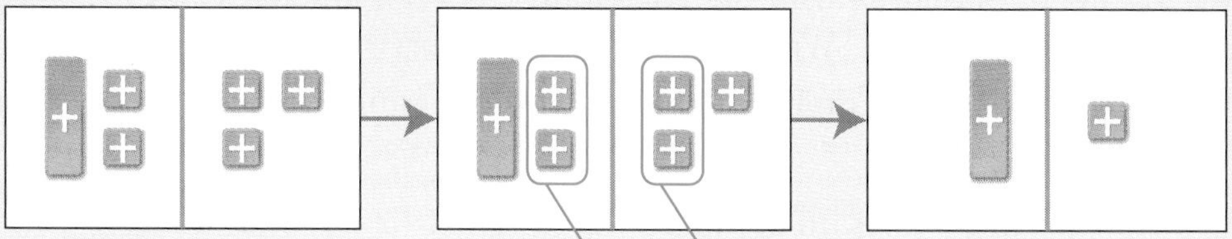

$x + 2 = 3$ *Remove 2 from each side.* $x = 1$

1 Use algebra tiles to model and solve each equation.

a. $x + 3 = 5$ **b.** $x + 4 = 9$ **c.** $x + 5 = 8$ **d.** $x + 6 = 6$

The equation $x + 6 = 4$ is more difficult to model because there are not enough tiles on the right side of the mat to remove 6 from each side.

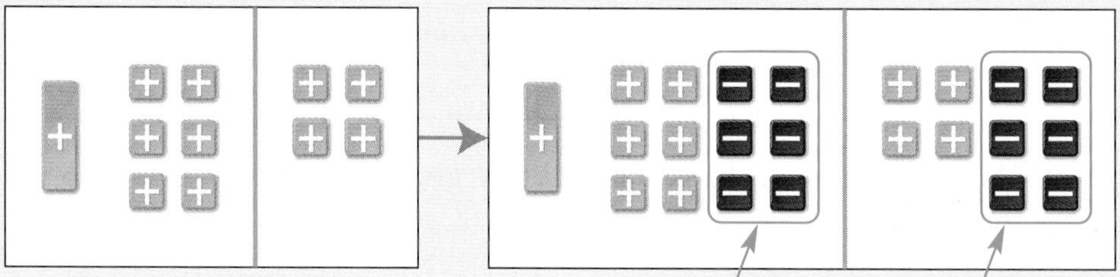

$x + 6 = 4$ *Add −6 to each side.*

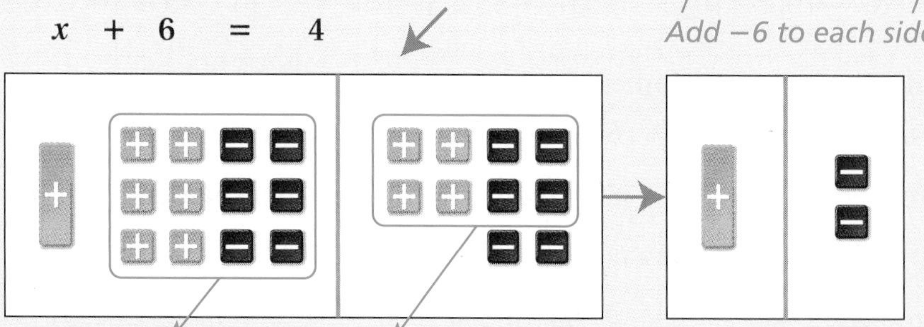

Remove zero pairs from each side. $x = -2$

2 Use algebra tiles to model and solve each equation.

a. $x + 5 = 3$ **b.** $x + 4 = 2$ **c.** $x + 7 = -3$ **d.** $x + 6 = -2$

When modeling an equation that involves subtraction, such as $x - 6 = 2$, you must first rewrite the equation as an addition equation. For example, the equation $x - 6 = 2$ can be rewritten as $x + (-6) = 2$.

Modeling equations that involve addition of negative numbers is similar to modeling equations that involve addition of positive numbers.

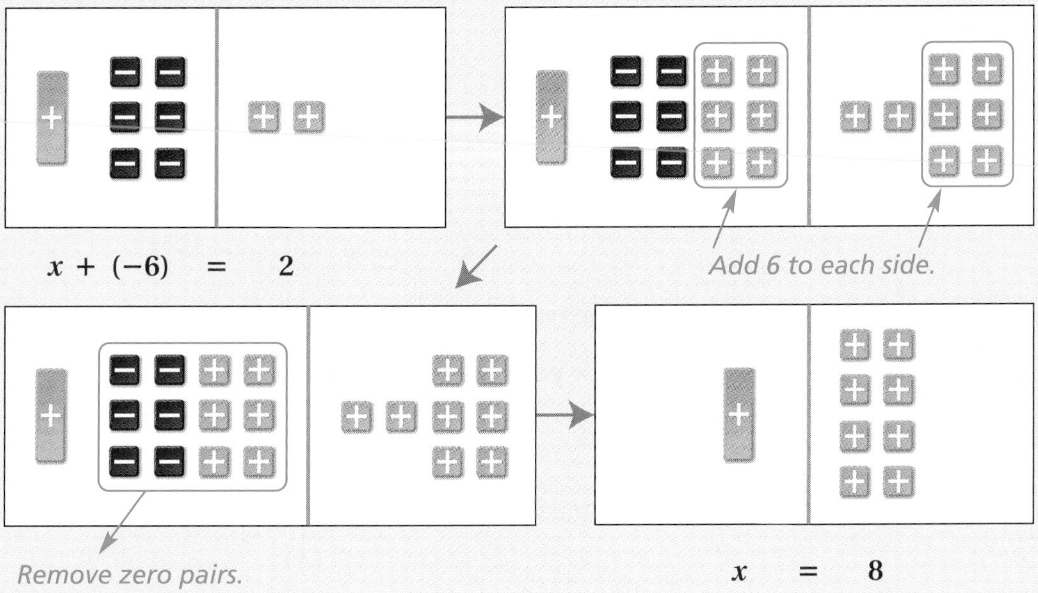

x + (−6) = 2
Add 6 to each side.
Remove zero pairs.
x = 8

3 Use algebra tiles to model and solve each equation.

a. $x - 4 = 3$ **b.** $x - 2 = 8$ **c.** $x - 5 = -5$ **d.** $x - 7 = 0$

Think and Discuss

1. When you remove tiles, what operation are you modeling? When you add tiles, what operation are you modeling?
2. How can you use the original model to check your solution?
3. To model $x - 6 = 2$, you must rewrite the equation as $x + (-6) = 2$. Why are you allowed to do this?

Try This

Use algebra tiles to model and solve each equation.

1. $x + 7 = 10$ **2.** $x - 5 = -8$ **3.** $x + (-5) = -4$ **4.** $x - 2 = 1$

5. $x + 4 = 8$ **6.** $x + 3 = -2$ **7.** $x + (-1) = 9$ **8.** $x - 7 = -6$

2-5 Solving Equations Containing Integers

Learn to solve one-step equations with integers.

To solve integer equations such as $x - 2 = -3$ you must isolate the variable on one side of the equation. One way to isolate the variable is to add opposites. Recall that the sum of a number and its opposite is 0.

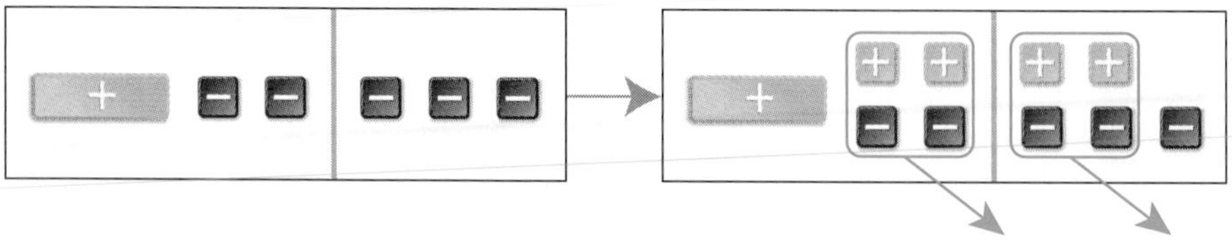

EXAMPLE 1 Solving Addition and Subtraction Equations

Helpful Hint

$3 + (-3) = 0$
3 is the opposite of −3.

Solve each equation. Check your answer.

A $-3 + y = -5$

$$\begin{aligned} -3 + y &= -5 \\ \underline{+3} \quad & \quad \underline{+3} \\ y &= -2 \end{aligned}$$

Add 3 to both sides to isolate the variable.

Check

$$-3 + y = -5$$

$$-3 + (-2) \stackrel{?}{=} -5$$ *Substitute −2 for y in the original equation.*

$$-5 \stackrel{?}{=} -5 \checkmark$$ *True. −2 is the solution to −3 + y = −5.*

B $n + 3 = -10$

$$\begin{aligned} n + 3 &= -10 \\ \underline{+(-3)} \quad & \quad \underline{+(-3)} \\ n &= -13 \end{aligned}$$

Add −3 to both sides to isolate the variable.

Check

$$n + 3 = -10$$

$$-13 + 3 \stackrel{?}{=} -10$$ *Substitute −13 for n in the original equation.*

$$-10 \stackrel{?}{=} -10 \checkmark$$ *True. −13 is the solution to n + 3 = −10.*

C $x - 8 = -32$

$$\begin{aligned} x - 8 &= -32 \\ \underline{+8} \quad & \quad \underline{+8} \\ x &= -24 \end{aligned}$$

Add 8 to both sides to isolate the variable.

Check

$$x - 8 = -32$$

$$-24 - 8 \stackrel{?}{=} -32$$ *Substitute −24 for x in the original equation.*

$$-32 \stackrel{?}{=} -32 \checkmark$$ *True. −24 is the solution to x − 8 = −32.*

EXAMPLE 2 Solving Multiplication and Division Equations

Solve each equation. Check your answer.

A $\frac{a}{-3} = 9$

$$\frac{a}{-3} = 9$$

$$(-3)\left(\frac{a}{-3}\right) = (-3)9$$ *Multiply both sides by −3 to isolate the variable.*

$$a = -27$$

Check $\frac{a}{-3} = 9$

$\frac{-27}{-3} \stackrel{?}{=} 9$ *Substitute −27 for a.*

$9 \stackrel{?}{=} 9$ ✔ *True. −27 is the solution.*

B $-120 = 6x$

$$-120 = 6x$$

$$\frac{-120}{6} = \frac{6x}{6}$$ *Divide both sides by 6 to isolate the variable.*

$$-20 = x$$

Check $-120 = 6x$

$-120 \stackrel{?}{=} 6(-20)$ *Substitute −20 for x.*

$-120 \stackrel{?}{=} -120$ ✔ *True. −20 is the solution.*

EXAMPLE 3 *Business Application*

A shoe manufacturer made a profit of $800 million. This amount is $200 million more than last year's profit. What was last year's profit?

Let p represent last year's profit (in millions of dollars).

This year's profit	is	$200 million	more than	last year's profit.
800	=	200	+	p

$$\begin{aligned} 800 &= 200 + p \\ \underline{-200} & \quad \underline{-200} \\ 600 &= p \end{aligned}$$

Last year's profit was $600 million.

Think and Discuss

1. Tell what value of n makes $-n + 32$ equal to zero.

2. Explain why you would or would not multiply both sides of an equation by 0 to solve it.

2-5 Exercises

go.hrw.com
Homework Help Online
KEYWORD: MS7 2-5
Parent Resources Online
KEYWORD: MS7 Parent

GUIDED PRACTICE

See Example 1
Solve each equation. Check your answer.

1. $w - 6 = -2$
2. $x + 5 = -7$
3. $k = -18 + 11$

See Example 2

4. $\frac{n}{-4} = 2$
5. $-240 = 8y$
6. $-5a = 300$

See Example 3

7. **Business** Last year, a chain of electronics stores had a loss of \$45 million. This year the loss is \$12 million more than last year's loss. What is this year's loss?

INDEPENDENT PRACTICE

See Example 1
Solve each equation. Check your answer.

8. $b - 7 = -16$
9. $k + 6 = 3$
10. $s + 2 = -4$
11. $v + 14 = 10$
12. $c + 8 = -20$
13. $a - 25 = -5$

See Example 2

14. $9c = -99$
15. $\frac{t}{8} = -4$
16. $-16 = 2z$
17. $\frac{n}{-5} = -30$
18. $200 = -25p$
19. $\frac{l}{-12} = 12$

See Example 3

20. The temperature in Nome, Alaska, was −50°F. This was 18°F less than the temperature in Anchorage, Alaska, on the same day. What was the temperature in Anchorage?

PRACTICE AND PROBLEM SOLVING

Extra Practice
See page 728.

Solve each equation. Check your answer.

21. $9y = 900$
22. $d - 15 = 45$
23. $j + 56 = -7$
24. $\frac{s}{-20} = 7$
25. $-85 = -5c$
26. $v - 39 = -16$
27. $11y = -121$
28. $\frac{n}{36} = 9$
29. $w + 41 = 0$
30. $\frac{r}{238} = 8$
31. $-23 = x + 35$
32. $0 = -15m$
33. $4x = 2 + 14$
34. $c + c + c = 6$
35. $t - 3 = 4 + 2$
36. **Geometry** The three angles of a triangle have equal measures. The sum of their measures is 180°. What is the measure of each angle?
37. **Sports** Herb has 42 days to prepare for a cross-country race. During his training, he will run a total of 126 miles. If Herb runs the same distance every day, how many miles will he run each day?
38. **Multi-Step** Jared bought one share of stock for \$225.
    a. He sold the stock for a profit of \$55. What was the selling price of the stock?
    b. The price of the stock dropped \$40 the day after Jared sold it. At what price would Jared have sold it if he had waited until then?

Translate each sentence into an equation. Then solve the equation.

39. The sum of -13 and a number p is 8.

40. A number x divided by 4 is -7.

41. 9 less than a number t is -22.

42. **Physical Science** On the Kelvin temperature scale, pure water boils at 373 K. The difference between the boiling point and the freezing point of water on this scale is 100 K. What is the freezing point of water?

Recreation The graph shows the most popular travel destinations over the 2001 Labor Day weekend. Use the graph for Exercises 43 and 44.

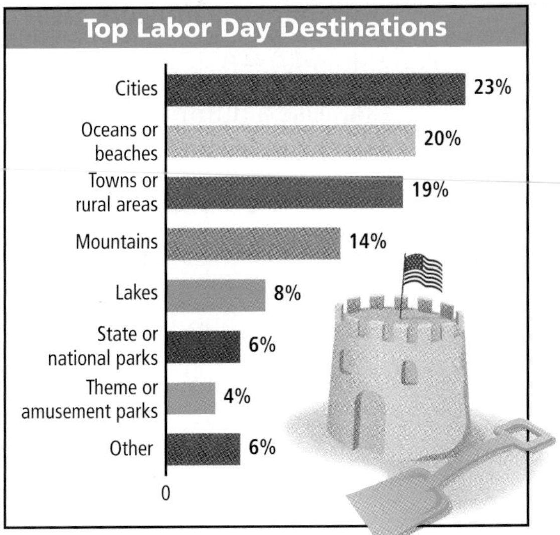

Source: AAA

43. Which destination was 5 times more popular than theme or amusement parks?

44. According to the graph, the mountains were as popular as state or national parks and what other destination combined?

45. **Choose a Strategy** Matthew (M) earns \$23 less a week than his sister Allie (A). Their combined salaries are \$93. How much does each of them earn per week?

(A) A: \$35; M: \$12 (B) A: \$35; M: \$58 (C) A: \$58; M: \$35

46. **Write About It** Explain how to isolate a variable in an equation.

47. **Challenge** Write an equation that includes the variable p and the numbers 5, 3, and 31 so that the solution is $p = 16$.

TEST PREP and Spiral Review

48. **Multiple Choice** Solve $-15m = 60$.

(A) $m = -4$ (B) $m = 5$ (C) $m = 45$ (D) $m = 75$

49. **Multiple Choice** For which equation does $x = 2$?

(F) $-3x = 6$ (G) $x + 3 = -5$ (H) $x + x = 4$ (J) $\frac{x}{4} = -8$

Identify a possible pattern. Use the pattern to write the next three numbers. (Lesson 1-1)

50. 26, 21, 16, 11, 6, . . . **51.** 1, 2, 4, 8, 16, . . . **52.** 1, 4, 3, 6, 5, . . .

Compare. Write <, >, or =. (Lessons 2-1, 2-2, and 2-3)

53. $-5 \;\square\; -8$ **54.** $4 \;\square\; |-4|$ **55.** $|-7| \;\square\; |-9|$

56. $-10 \;\square\; |-10|$ **57.** $-7 - 8 \;\square\; -15$ **58.** $-12 \;\square\; 10 + (-12)$

CHAPTER 2

READY TO GO ON?

SECTION 2A

Quiz for Lessons 2-1 Through 2-5

2-1 Integers

Compare the integers. Use < or > .

1. 5 ▢ −8
2. −2 ▢ −6
3. −4 ▢ 3
4. Use a number line to order the integers −7, 3, 6, −1, 0, 5, −4, and 8 from least to greatest.

Use a number line to find each absolute value.

5. $|-23|$
6. $|17|$
7. $|-10|$

2-2 Adding Integers

Find each sum.

8. −6 + 3
9. 5 + (−9)
10. −7 + (−11)

Evaluate $p + t$ for the given values.

11. $p = 5, t = -18$
12. $p = -4, t = -13$
13. $p = -37, t = 39$

2-3 Subtracting Integers

Find each difference.

14. −21 − (−7)
15. 9 − (−11)
16. 6 − 17
17. When Cai traveled from New Orleans, Louisiana, to the Ozark Mountains in Arkansas, the elevation changed from 7 ft below sea level to 2,314 ft above sea level. How much did the elevation increase?

2-4 Multiplying and Dividing Integers

Find each product or quotient.

18. $-7 \cdot 3$
19. $30 \div (-15)$
20. $-5 \cdot (-9)$
21. After reaching the top of a cliff, a rock climber descended the rock face using a 65 ft rope. The distance to the base of the cliff was 585 ft. How many rope lengths did it take the climber to complete her descent?

2-5 Solving Equations Containing Integers

Solve each equation. Check your answer.

22. $3x = 30$
23. $k - 25 = 50$
24. $y + 16 = -8$
25. This year, 72 students completed projects for the science fair. This was 23 more students than last year. How many students completed projects for the science fair last year?

Focus on Problem Solving

Make a Plan

• Choose a method of computation

When you know the operation you must use and you know exactly which numbers to use, a calculator might be the easiest way to solve a problem. Sometimes, such as when the numbers are small or are multiples of 10, it may be quicker to use mental math.

Sometimes, you have to write the numbers to see how they relate in an equation. When you are working an equation, using a pencil and paper is the simplest method to use because you can see each step as you go.

For each problem, tell whether you would use a calculator, mental math, or pencil and paper to solve it. Explain your answer. Then solve the problem.

1. A scouting troop is collecting aluminum cans to raise money for charity. Their goal is to collect 3,000 cans in 6 months. If they set a goal to collect an equal number of cans each month, how many cans can they expect to collect each month?

2. The Grand Canyon is 29,000 meters wide at its widest point. The Empire State Building, located in New York City, is 381 meters tall. Laid end to end, how many Empire State Buildings would fit across the Grand Canyon at its widest point?

3. On a piano keyboard, all but one of the black keys are arranged in groups so that there are 7 groups with 2 black keys each and 7 groups with 3 black keys each. How many black keys are there on a piano?

4. Some wind chimes are made of rods. The rods are usually of different lengths, producing different sounds. The frequency (which determines the pitch) of the sound is measured in hertz (Hz). If one rod on a chime has a frequency of 55 Hz and another rod has a frequency that is twice that of the first rod's, what is the frequency of the second rod?

2-6 Prime Factorization

Learn to find the prime factorizations of composite numbers.

Vocabulary
prime number
composite number
prime factorization

In June 1999, Nayan Hajratwala discovered the first known *prime number* with more than one million digits. The new prime number, $2^{6,972,593} - 1$, has 2,098,960 digits.

Nayan Hajratwala received a $50,000 award for discovering a new prime number.

A **prime number** is a whole number greater than 1 that has exactly two factors, 1 and itself. Three is a prime number because its only factors are 1 and 3.

A **composite number** is a whole number that has more than two factors. Six is a composite number because it has more than two factors—1, 2, 3, and 6. The number 1 has exactly one factor and is neither prime nor composite.

EXAMPLE 1 Identifying Prime and Composite Numbers

Tell whether each number is prime or composite.

A 19

The factors of 19 are 1 and 19.

So 19 is prime.

B 20

The factors of 20 are 1, 2, 4, 5, 10, and 20.

So 20 is composite.

A composite number can be written as the product of its prime factors. This is called the **prime factorization** of the number. You can use a factor tree to find the prime factors of a composite number.

EXAMPLE 2 Using a Factor Tree to Find Prime Factorization

Writing Math

You can write prime factorizations by using exponents. The exponent tells how many times to use the base as a factor.

Write the prime factorization of each number.

A 36

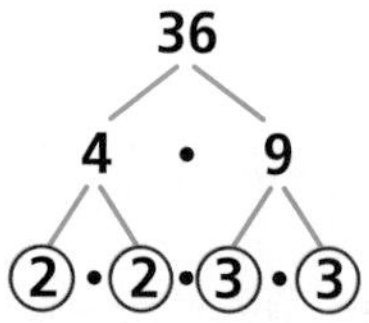

Write 36 as the product of two factors.

Continue factoring until all factors are prime.

The prime factorization of 36 is $2 \cdot 2 \cdot 3 \cdot 3$, or $2^2 \cdot 3^2$.

Write the prime factorization of each number.

B 280

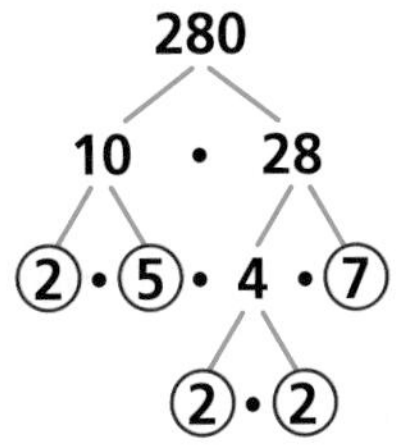

Write 280 as the product of two factors.

Continue factoring until all factors are prime.

The prime factorization of 280 is $2 \cdot 2 \cdot 2 \cdot 5 \cdot 7$, or $2^3 \cdot 5 \cdot 7$.

You can also use a step diagram to find the prime factorization of a number. At each step, divide by a prime factor. Continue dividing until the quotient is 1.

EXAMPLE 3 Using a Step Diagram to Find Prime Factorization

Write the prime factorization of each number.

A 252

```
2 | 252
 2 | 126
  3 | 63
   3 | 21
    7 | 7
        1
```

Divide 252 by 2. Write the quotient below 252. Keep dividing by a prime factor.

Stop when the quotient is 1.

The prime factorization of 252 is $2 \cdot 2 \cdot 3 \cdot 3 \cdot 7$, or $2^2 \cdot 3^2 \cdot 7$.

B 495

```
3 | 495
 3 | 165
  5 | 55
  11 | 11
        1
```

Divide 495 by 3. Keep dividing by a prime factor.

Stop when the quotient is 1.

The prime factorization of 495 is $3 \cdot 3 \cdot 5 \cdot 11$, or $3^2 \cdot 5 \cdot 11$.

There is only one prime factorization for any given composite number. Example 3B began by dividing 495 by 3, the smallest prime factor of 495. Beginning with any prime factor of 495 gives the same result.

```
5 | 495
 3 | 99
  3 | 33
  11 | 11
        1
```

```
11 | 495
  3 | 45
   5 | 15
    3 | 3
        1
```

Think and Discuss

1. Explain how to decide whether 47 is prime.

2. Compare prime numbers and composite numbers.

2-6 Exercises

go.hrw.com
Homework Help Online
KEYWORD: MS7 2-6
Parent Resources Online
KEYWORD: MS7 Parent

GUIDED PRACTICE

See Example 1
Tell whether each number is prime or composite.

1. 7 **2.** 15 **3.** 49 **4.** 12

See Example 2
Write the prime factorization of each number.

5. 16

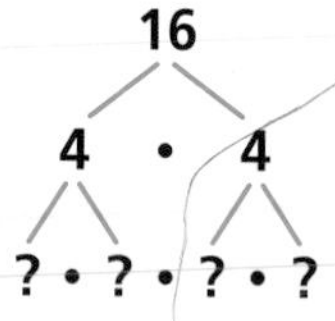

6. 54

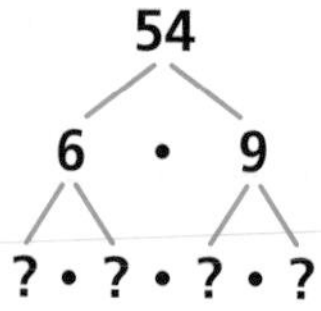

7. 81

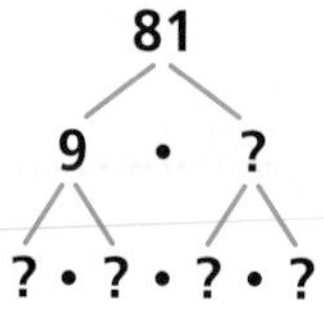

8. 105

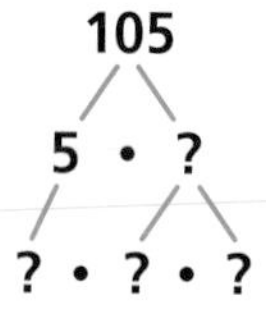

9. 18 **10.** 26 **11.** 45 **12.** 80

See Example 3
13. 250 **14.** 190 **15.** 100 **16.** 360
17. 639 **18.** 414 **19.** 1,000 **20.** 140

INDEPENDENT PRACTICE

See Example 1
Tell whether each number is prime or composite.

21. 31 **22.** 18 **23.** 67 **24.** 8
25. 77 **26.** 5 **27.** 9 **28.** 113

See Example 2
Write the prime factorization of each number.

29. 68 **30.** 75 **31.** 120 **32.** 150
33. 135 **34.** 48 **35.** 154 **36.** 210
37. 800 **38.** 310 **39.** 625 **40.** 2,000

See Example 3
41. 315 **42.** 728 **43.** 189 **44.** 396
45. 242 **46.** 700 **47.** 187 **48.** 884
49. 1,225 **50.** 288 **51.** 360 **52.** 1,152

PRACTICE AND PROBLEM SOLVING

Extra Practice
See page 728.

Complete the prime factorization for each composite number.

53. $180 = 2^2 \cdot \blacksquare \cdot 5$ **54.** $462 = 2 \cdot 3 \cdot 7 \cdot \blacksquare$ **55.** $1{,}575 = 3^2 \cdot \blacksquare \cdot 7$

56. $117 = 3^2 \cdot \blacksquare$ **57.** $144 = \blacksquare \cdot 3^2$ **58.** $1{,}300 = 2^3 \cdot \blacksquare \cdot 13$

59. Critical Thinking One way to factor 64 is $1 \cdot 64$.
  a. What other ways can 64 be written as the product of two factors?
  b. How many prime factorizations of 64 are there?

60. Critical Thinking If the prime factors of a number are all the prime numbers less than 10 and no factor is repeated, what is the number?

61. Critical Thinking A number n is a prime factor of 28 and 63. What is the number?

62. A rectangular area on a farm has side lengths that are factors of 308. One of the side lengths is a prime number. Which of the areas in the diagram have the correct dimensions?

63. Business Eric is catering a party for 152 people. He wants to seat the same number of people at each table. He also wants more than 2 people but fewer than 10 people at a table. How many people can he seat at each table?

64. Write a Problem Using the information in the table, write a problem using prime factorization that includes the number of calories per serving of the melons.

65. Write About It Describe how to use factor trees to find the prime factorization of a number.

66. Challenge Find the smallest number that is divisible by 2, 3, 4, 5, 6, 7, 8, 9, and 10.

Fruit	Calories per Serving
Cantaloupe	66
Watermelon	15
Honeydew	42

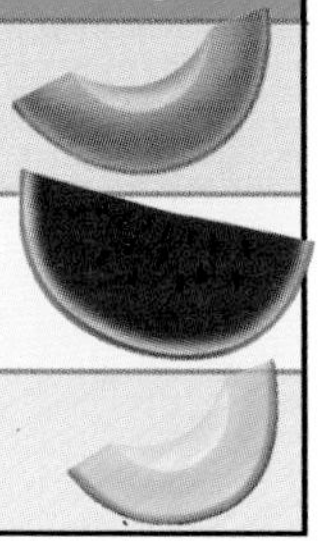

TEST PREP and Spiral Review

67. Multiple Choice Which is the prime factorization of 75?

Ⓐ $3^2 \cdot 5$ Ⓑ $3 \cdot 5^2$ Ⓒ $3^2 \cdot 5^2$ Ⓓ $3 \cdot 5^3$

68. Multiple Choice Write the composite number for $2 \cdot 3^3 \cdot 5^2$.

Ⓕ 84 Ⓖ 180 Ⓗ 450 Ⓙ 1,350

69. Short Response Create two different factor trees for 120. Then write the prime factorization for 120.

Multiply. (Lesson 1-4)

70. $2.45 \cdot 10^3$ **71.** $58.7 \cdot 10^1$ **72.** $200 \cdot 10^2$ **73.** $1{,}480 \cdot 10^4$

Solve each equation. Check your answer. (Lesson 2-5)

74. $3x = -6$ **75.** $y - 4 = -3$ **76.** $z + 4 = 3 - 5$ **77.** $0 = -4x$

2-7 Greatest Common Factor

Learn to find the greatest common factor of two or more whole numbers.

Vocabulary

greatest common factor (GCF)

When getting ready for the Fall Festival, Sasha and David used the greatest common factor to make matching party favors. The **greatest common factor (GCF)** of two or more whole numbers is the greatest whole number that divides evenly into each number.

One way to find the GCF of two or more numbers is to list all the factors of each number. The GCF is the greatest factor that appears in all the lists.

EXAMPLE 1 **Using a List to Find the GCF**

Find the greatest common factor (GCF) of 24, 36, and 48.

Factors of 24: 1, 2, 3, 4, 6, 8, 12, 24 — *List all the factors of each number.*

Factors of 36: 1, 2, 3, 4, 6, 9, 12, 18, 36

Factors of 48: 1, 2, 3, 4, 6, 8, 12, 16, 24, 48 — *Circle the greatest factor that is in all the lists.*

The GCF is 12.

A second way to find the GCF is to use prime factorization.

EXAMPLE 2 **Using Prime Factorization to Find the GCF**

Find the greatest common factor (GCF).

A **60, 45**

$60 = 2 \cdot 2 \cdot 3 \cdot 5$ — *Write the prime factorization of each number and circle the common prime factors.*

$45 = 3 \cdot 3 \cdot 5$

$3 \cdot 5 = 15$ — *Multiply the common prime factors.*

The GCF is 15.

B **504, 132, 96, 60**

$504 = 2 \cdot 2 \cdot 2 \cdot 3 \cdot 3 \cdot 7$ — *Write the prime factorization of each number and circle the common prime factors.*

$132 = 2 \cdot 2 \cdot 3 \cdot 11$

$96 = 2 \cdot 2 \cdot 2 \cdot 2 \cdot 2 \cdot 3$

$60 = 2 \cdot 2 \cdot 3 \cdot 5$

$2 \cdot 2 \cdot 3 = 12$ — *Multiply the common prime factors.*

The GCF is 12.

EXAMPLE 3 PROBLEM SOLVING APPLICATION

PROBLEM SOLVING

Sasha and David are making centerpieces for the Fall Festival. They have 50 small pumpkins and 30 ears of corn. What is the greatest number of matching centerpieces they can make using all of the pumpkins and corn?

1 Understand the Problem

Rewrite the question as a statement.

- Find the greatest number of centerpieces they can make.

List the **important information:**

- There are 50 pumpkins.
- There are 30 ears of corn.
- Each centerpiece must have the same number of pumpkins and the same number of ears of corn.

The **answer** will be the GCF of 50 and 30.

2 Make a Plan

You can write the prime factorizations of 50 and 30 to find the GCF.

3 Solve

$50 = \textcircled{2} \cdot \textcircled{5} \cdot 5$

$30 = \textcircled{2} \cdot 3 \cdot \textcircled{5}$ *Multiply the prime factors that are*

$2 \cdot 5 = 10$ *common to both 50 and 30.*

Sasha and David can make 10 centerpieces.

4 Look Back

If Sasha and David make 10 centerpieces, each one will have 5 pumpkins and 3 ears of corn, with nothing left over.

Think and Discuss

1. **Tell** what the letters GCF stand for and explain what the GCF of two numbers is.
2. **Discuss** whether the GCF of two numbers could be a prime number.
3. **Explain** whether every factor of the GCF of two numbers is also a factor of each number. Give an example.

2-7 Exercises

go.hrw.com
Homework Help Online
KEYWORD: MS7 2-7
Parent Resources Online
KEYWORD: MS7 Parent

GUIDED PRACTICE

See Example 1

Find the greatest common factor (GCF).

1. 30, 42 **2.** 36, 45 **3.** 24, 36, 60, 84

See Example 2

4. 60, 231 **5.** 12, 28 **6.** 20, 40, 50, 120

See Example 3

7. The Math Club members are preparing identical welcome kits for the sixth-graders. They have 60 pencils and 48 memo pads. What is the greatest number of kits they can prepare using all of the pencils and memo pads?

INDEPENDENT PRACTICE

See Example 1

Find the greatest common factor (GCF).

8. 60, 126 **9.** 12, 36 **10.** 75, 90

11. 22, 121 **12.** 28, 42 **13.** 38, 76

See Example 2

14. 28, 60 **15.** 54, 80 **16.** 30, 45, 60, 105

17. 26, 52 **18.** 11, 44, 77 **19.** 18, 27, 36, 48

See Example 3

20. Hetty is making identical gift baskets for the Senior Citizens Center. She has 39 small soap bars and 26 small bottles of lotion. What is the greatest number of baskets she can make using all of the soap bars and bottles of lotion?

PRACTICE AND PROBLEM SOLVING

Extra Practice
See page 728.

Find the greatest common factor (GCF).

21. 5, 7 **22.** 12, 15 **23.** 4, 6

24. 9, 11 **25.** 22, 44, 66 **26.** 77, 121

27. 80, 120 **28.** 20, 28 **29.** 2, 3, 4, 5, 7

30. 4, 6, 10, 22 **31.** 14, 21, 35, 70 **32.** 6, 10, 11, 14

33. 6, 15, 33, 48 **34.** 18, 45, 63, 81 **35.** 13, 39, 52, 78

36. Critical Thinking Which pair of numbers has a GCF that is a prime number, 48 and 90 or 105 and 56?

37. Museum employees are preparing an exhibit of ancient coins. They have 49 copper coins and 35 silver coins to arrange on shelves. Each shelf will have the same number of copper coins and the same number of silver coins. How many shelves will the employees need for this exhibit?

38. Multi-Step Todd and Elizabeth are making treat bags for the hospital volunteers. They have baked 56 shortbread cookies and 84 lemon bars. What is the greatest number of bags they can make if all volunteers receive identical treat bags? How many cookies and how many lemon bars will each bag contain?

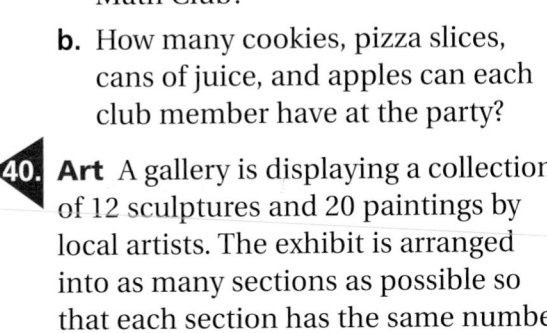

39. **School** Some of the students in the Math Club signed up to bring food and drinks to a party.

Food and Drink
Sign-up Sheet
Student
Item
Amount
Erica
Apples
14
Alejandro
Pizza
21 Slices
Michael
Juice
7 cans
Jennifer
Gingerbread Cookies
35

a. If each club member gets the same amount of each item at the party, how many students are in the Math Club?

b. How many cookies, pizza slices, cans of juice, and apples can each club member have at the party?

LINK

Art

The sculpture *Spoonbridge and Cherry* by Claes Oldenburg and Coosje van Bruggen is 30 ft high and over 50 ft long.

40. **Art** A gallery is displaying a collection of 12 sculptures and 20 paintings by local artists. The exhibit is arranged into as many sections as possible so that each section has the same number of sculptures and the same number of paintings. How many sections are in the exhibit?

41. **What's the Error?** A student used these factor trees to find the GCF of 50 and 70. The student decided that the GCF is 5. Explain the student's error and give the correct GCF.

42. **Write About It** The GCF of 1,274 and 1,365 is 91, or $7 \cdot 13$. Are 7, 13, and 91 factors of both 1,274 and 1,365? Explain.

43. **Challenge** Find three *composite* numbers that have a GCF of 1.

Test Prep and Spiral Review

44. **Gridded Response** What is the greatest common factor of 28 and 91?

45. **Multiple Choice** Which pair of numbers has a greatest common factor that is NOT a prime number?

Ⓐ 15, 20 Ⓑ 18, 30 Ⓒ 24, 75 Ⓓ 6, 10

Find each value. (Lesson 1-2)

46. 10^3 47. 13^1 48. 6^3 49. 3^4

Use a number line to find each sum or difference. (Lessons 2-2 and 2-3)

50. $-5 + (-3)$ 51. $2 - 7$ 52. $4 + (-8)$ 53. $-3 - (-5)$

Complete the prime factorization for each composite number. (Lesson 2-6)

54. $100 = \square \cdot 5^2$ 55. $147 = 3 \cdot \square$ 56. $270 = 2 \cdot 3^3 \cdot \square$ 57. $140 = \square \cdot 5 \cdot 7$

2-8 Least Common Multiple

Learn to find the least common multiple of two or more whole numbers.

Vocabulary

multiple

least common multiple (LCM)

The maintenance schedule on Kendra's pickup truck shows that the tires should be rotated every 7,500 miles and that the oil filter should be replaced every 5,000 miles. What is the lowest mileage at which both services are due at the same time? To find the answer, you can use *least common multiples.*

A **multiple** of a number is the product of that number and a nonzero whole number. Some multiples of 7,500 and 5,000 are as follows:

7,500: 7,500, **15,000**, 22,500, **30,000**, 37,500, 45,000, . . .
5,000: 5,000, 10,000, **15,000**, 20,000, 25,000, **30,000**, . . .

A common multiple of two or more numbers is a number that is a multiple of each of the given numbers. So **15,000** and **30,000** are common multiples of 7,500 and 5,000.

The **least common multiple (LCM)** of two or more numbers is the common multiple with the least value. The LCM of 7,500 and 5,000 is **15,000**. This is the lowest mileage at which both services are due at the same time.

EXAMPLE 1 Using a List to Find the LCM

Find the least common multiple (LCM).

A 3, 5

Multiples of 3: 3, 6, 9, 12, (15), 18
Multiples of 5: 5, 10, (15), 20, 25

List multiples of each number. Find the least value that is in both lists.

The LCM is 15.

B 4, 6, 12

Multiples of 4: 4, 8, (12), 16, 20, 24, 28
Multiples of 6: 6, (12), 18, 24, 30
Multiples of 12: (12), 24, 36, 48

List multiples of each number. Find the least value that is in all the lists.

The LCM is 12.

Sometimes, listing the multiples of numbers is not the easiest way to find the LCM. For example, the LCM of 78 and 110 is 4,290. You would have to list 55 multiples of 78 and 39 multiples of 110 to reach 4,290!

EXAMPLE 2 Using Prime Factorization to Find the LCM

Find the least common multiple (LCM).

A 78, 110

$78 = \boxed{2} \cdot 3 \cdot 13$	*Write the prime factorization of each number.*
$110 = \boxed{2} \cdot 5 \cdot 11$	*Circle the common prime factors.*
②, 3, 13, 5, 11	*List the prime factors of the numbers, using the circled factors only once.*
$2 \cdot 3 \cdot 13 \cdot 5 \cdot 11$	*Multiply the factors in the list.*

The LCM is 4,290.

B 9, 27, 45

$9 = \boxed{3} \cdot \boxed{3}$	*Write the prime factorization of each number.*
$27 = \boxed{3} \cdot \boxed{3} \cdot 3$	*Circle the common prime factors.*
$45 = \boxed{3} \cdot \boxed{3} \cdot 5$	
③, ③, 3, 5	*List the prime factors of the numbers, using the circled factors only once.*
$3 \cdot 3 \cdot 3 \cdot 5$	*Multiply the factors in the list.*

The LCM is 135.

EXAMPLE 3 *Recreation Application*

Charla and her little brother are walking laps on a track. Charla walks one lap every 4 minutes, and her brother walks one lap every 6 minutes. They start together. In how many minutes will they be together at the starting line again?

Find the LCM of 4 and 6.

$4 = \boxed{2} \cdot 2$

$6 = \boxed{2} \cdot 3$

The LCM is ② $\cdot\, 2 \cdot 3 = 12$.

They will be together at the starting line in 12 minutes.

Think and Discuss

1. **Tell** what the letters LCM stand for and explain what the LCM of two numbers is.
2. **Describe** a way to remember the difference between GCF and LCM.
3. **List** four common multiples of 6 and 9 that are not the LCM.

2-8 Exercises

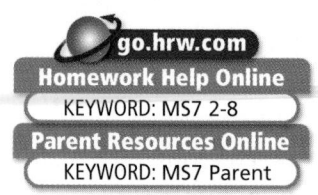

go.hrw.com
Homework Help Online
KEYWORD: MS7 2-8
Parent Resources Online
KEYWORD: MS7 Parent

GUIDED PRACTICE

See Example 1

Find the least common multiple (LCM).

1. 4, 7
2. 14, 21, 28
3. 4, 8, 12, 16

See Example 2

4. 30, 48
5. 3, 9, 15
6. 10, 40, 50

See Example 3

7. Jerry and his dad are walking around the track. Jerry completes one lap every 8 minutes. His dad completes one lap every 6 minutes. They start together. In how many minutes will they be together at the starting line again?

INDEPENDENT PRACTICE

See Example 1

Find the least common multiple (LCM).

8. 6, 9
9. 8, 12
10. 15, 20
11. 6, 14
12. 18, 27
13. 8, 10, 12

See Example 2

14. 6, 27
15. 16, 20
16. 12, 15, 22
17. 10, 15, 18, 20
18. 11, 22, 44
19. 8, 12, 18, 20

See Example 3

20. **Recreation** On her bicycle, Anna circles the block every 4 minutes. Her brother, on his scooter, circles the block every 10 minutes. They start out together. In how many minutes will they meet again at the starting point?
21. Rod helped his mom plant a vegetable garden. Rod planted a row every 30 minutes, and his mom planted a row every 20 minutes. If they started together, how long will it be before they both finish a row at the same time?

PRACTICE AND PROBLEM SOLVING

Extra Practice
See page 729.

Find the least common multiple (LCM).

22. 3, 7
23. 4, 6
24. 9, 12
25. 22, 44, 66
26. 80, 120
27. 10, 18
28. 3, 5, 7
29. 3, 6, 12
30. 5, 7, 9
31. 24, 36, 48
32. 2, 3, 4, 5
33. 14, 21, 35, 70
34. Jack mows the lawn every three weeks and washes the car every two weeks. If he does both today, how many days will pass before he does them both on the same day again?
35. **Critical Thinking** Is it possible for two numbers to have the same LCM and GCF? Explain.
36. **Multi-Step** Milli jogs every day, bikes every 3 days, and swims once a week. She does all three activities on October 3. On what date will she next perform all three activities?

Social Studies LINK

The Mayan, the Chinese, and the standard western calendar are all based on cycles.

37. The Mayan ceremonial calendar, or *tzolkin,* was 260 days long. It was composed of two independent cycles, a 13-day cycle and a 20-day cycle. At the beginning of the calendar, both cycles are at day 1. Will both cycles be at day 1 at the same time again before the 260 days are over? If so, when?

38. The Chinese calendar has 12 months of 30 days each and 6-day weeks. The Chinese New Year begins on the first day of a month and the first day of a week. Will the first day of a month and the first day of a week occur again at the same time before the 360-day year is over? If so, when? Explain your answer.

39. **Write About It** The Julian Date calendar assigns each day a unique number. It begins on day 0 and adds 1 for each new day. So JD 2266296, or October 12, 1492, is 2,266,296 days from the beginning of the calendar. What are some advantages of using the Julian Date calendar? What are some advantages of using calendars that are based on cycles?

40. **Challenge** The Mayan Long Count calendar used the naming system at right. Assuming the calendar began on JD 584285, express JD 2266296 in terms of the Mayan Long Count calendar. Start by finding the number of pictun that had passed up to that date.

Mayan Long Count Calendar
1 Pictun = 20 Baktun = 2,880,000 days
1 Baktun = 20 Katun = 144,000 days
1 Katun = 20 Tun = 7,200 days
1 Tun = 18 Winal = 360 days
1 Winal = 20 Kin = 20 days
1 Kin = 1 day

TEST PREP and Spiral Review

41. Multiple Choice Which is the least common multiple of 4 and 10?

Ⓐ 2 Ⓑ 10 Ⓒ 20 Ⓓ 40

42. Multiple Choice Which pair of numbers has a least common multiple of 150?

Ⓕ 10, 15 Ⓖ 150, 300 Ⓗ 2, 300 Ⓙ 15, 50

Simplify each expression. (Lesson 1-9)

43. $3c + 2c - 2$ **44.** $5x + 3x^2 - 2x$ **45.** $7u + 3v - 4$ **46.** $m + 1 - 6m$

Find the greatest common factor (GCF). (Lesson 2-7)

47. 12, 28 **48.** 16, 24 **49.** 15, 75 **50.** 28, 70

CHAPTER 2

READY TO GO ON?

SECTION 2B

Quiz for Lessons 2-6 Through 2-8

2-6 Prime Factorization

Complete each factor tree to find the prime factorization.

1. 24 → 6 • 4 → ? • ? • ? • ?

2. 140 → 14 • 10 → ? • ? • ? • ?

3. 45 → 3 • ? → 3 • ? • ?

4. 42 → ? • ? → 3 • 7 • ?

Write the prime factorization of each number.

5. 96	**6.** 125	**7.** 99
8. 105	**9.** 324	**10.** 500

2-7 Greatest Common Factor

Find the greatest common factor (GCF).

11. 66, 96	**12.** 18, 27, 45	**13.** 16, 28, 44
14. 14, 28, 56	**15.** 85, 102	**16.** 76, 95
17. 52, 91, 104	**18.** 30, 75, 90	**19.** 118, 116

20. Yasmin and Jon have volunteered to prepare snacks for the first-grade field trip. They have 63 carrot sticks and 105 strawberries. What is the greatest number of identical snacks they can prepare using all of the carrot sticks and strawberries?

2-8 Least Common Multiple

Find the least common multiple (LCM).

21. 35, 40	**22.** 8, 25	**23.** 64, 72
24. 12, 20	**25.** 21, 33	**26.** 6, 30
27. 20, 42	**28.** 9, 13	**29.** 14, 18

30. Eddie goes jogging every other day, lifts weights every third day, and swims every fourth day. If Eddie begins all three activities on Monday, how many days will it be before he does all three activities on the same day again?

31. Sean and his mom start running around a 1-mile track at the same time. Sean runs 1 mile every 8 minutes. His mom runs 1 mile every 10 minutes. In how many minutes will they be together at the starting line again?

Focus on Problem Solving

Look Back

• Check that your answer is reasonable

In some situations, such as when you are looking for an estimate or completing a multiple-choice question, check to see whether a solution or answer is reasonably accurate. One way to do this is by rounding the numbers to the nearest multiple of 10 or 100, depending on how large the numbers are. Sometimes it is useful to round one number up and another down.

Read each problem, and determine whether the given solution is too high, is too low, or appears to be correct. Explain your answer.

1. The cheerleading team is preparing to host a spaghetti dinner as a fund-raising project. They have set up and decorated 54 tables in the gymnasium. Each table can seat 8 people. How many people can be seated at the spaghetti dinner?

   Solution: 432 people

2. The cheerleaders need to raise $4,260 to attend a cheerleader camp. How much money must they charge each person if they are expecting 400 people at the spaghetti dinner?

   Solution: $4

3. To help out the fund-raising project, local restaurants have offered $25 gift certificates to give as door prizes. One gift certificate will be given for each door prize, and there will be six door prizes in all. What is the total value of all of the gift certificates given by the restaurants?

   Solution: $250

4. The total cost of hosting the spaghetti dinner will be about $270. If the cheerleaders make $3,280 in ticket sales, how much money will they have after paying for the spaghetti dinner?

   Solution: $3,000

5. Eighteen cheerleaders and two coaches plan to attend the camp. If each person will have an equal share of the $4,260 expense money, how much money will each person have?

   Solution: $562

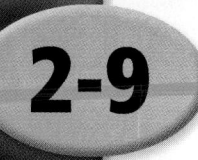

2-9 Equivalent Fractions and Mixed Numbers

Learn to identify, write, and convert between equivalent fractions and mixed numbers.

Vocabulary

equivalent fractions

improper fraction

mixed number

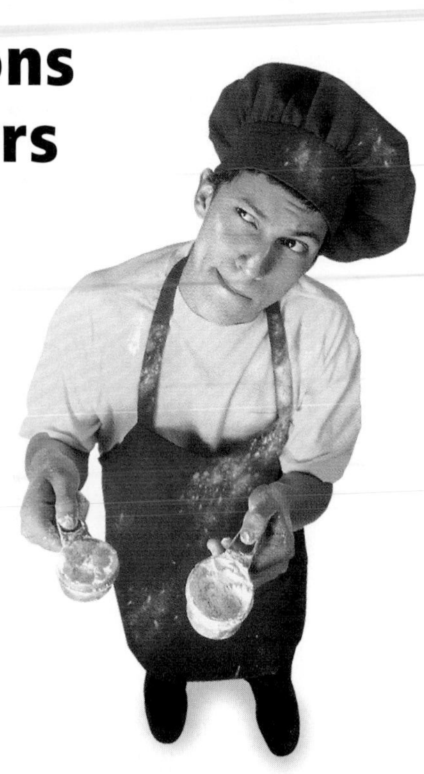

In some recipes the amounts of ingredients are given as fractions, and sometimes those amounts don't equal the fractions on a measuring cup. Knowing how fractions relate to each other can be very helpful.

Different fractions can name the same number.

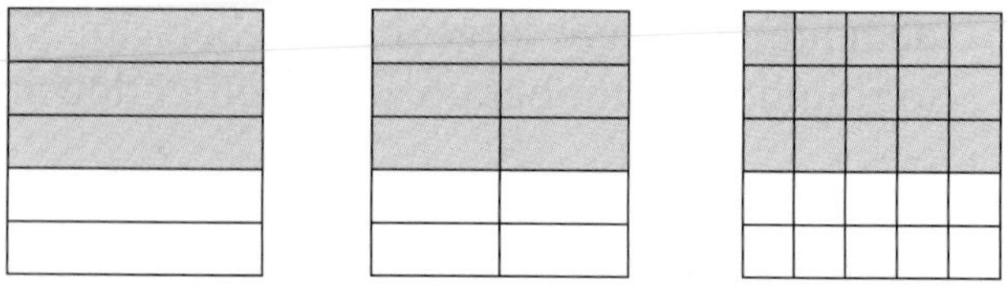

$$\frac{3}{5} = \frac{6}{10} = \frac{15}{25}$$

In the diagram, $\frac{3}{5} = \frac{6}{10} = \frac{15}{25}$. These are called **equivalent fractions** because they are different expressions for the same nonzero number.

To create fractions equivalent to a given fraction, multiply or divide the numerator and denominator by the same number.

EXAMPLE 1 Finding Equivalent Fractions

Find two fractions equivalent to $\frac{14}{16}$.

$\frac{14}{16} = \frac{14 \cdot 2}{16 \cdot 2} = \frac{28}{32}$ *Multiply the numerator and denominator by 2.*

$\frac{14}{16} = \frac{14 \div 2}{16 \div 2} = \frac{7}{8}$ *Divide the numerator and denominator by 2.*

The fractions $\frac{7}{8}$, $\frac{14}{16}$, and $\frac{28}{32}$ in Example 1 are equivalent, but only $\frac{7}{8}$ is in simplest form. A fraction is in simplest form when the greatest common factor of its numerator and denominator is 1.

EXAMPLE 2 Writing Fractions in Simplest Form

Write the fraction $\frac{24}{36}$ in simplest form.

Find the GCF of 24 and 36.

$24 = 2 \cdot 2 \cdot 2 \cdot 3$ *The GCF is $12 = 2 \cdot 2 \cdot 3$.*

$36 = 2 \cdot 2 \cdot 3 \cdot 3$

$\frac{24}{36} = \frac{24 \div 12}{36 \div 12} = \frac{2}{3}$ *Divide the numerator and denominator by 12.*

To determine if two fractions are equivalent, find a common denominator and compare the numerators.

EXAMPLE 3 Determining Whether Fractions Are Equivalent

Determine whether the fractions in each pair are equivalent.

A $\frac{6}{8}$ **and** $\frac{9}{12}$

Both fractions can be written with a denominator of 4.

$\frac{6}{8} = \frac{6 \div 2}{8 \div 2} = \frac{3}{4}$ $\qquad$ $\frac{9}{12} = \frac{9 \div 3}{12 \div 3} = \frac{3}{4}$

The numerators are equal, so the fractions are equivalent.

B $\frac{18}{15}$ **and** $\frac{25}{20}$

Both fractions can be written with a denominator of 60.

$\frac{18}{15} = \frac{18 \cdot 4}{15 \cdot 4} = \frac{72}{60}$ $\qquad$ $\frac{25}{20} = \frac{25 \cdot 3}{20 \cdot 3} = \frac{75}{60}$

The numerators are *not* equal, so the fractions are *not* equivalent.

$\frac{8}{5}$ is an **improper fraction**. Its numerator is greater than its denominator.

$\frac{8}{5} = 1\frac{3}{5}$

$1\frac{3}{5}$ is a **mixed number**. It contains both a whole number and a fraction.

EXAMPLE 4 Converting Between Improper Fractions and Mixed Numbers

Remember!

Quotient → 5
$4\overline{)21}$
−20
Remainder → 1

A **Write** $\frac{21}{4}$ **as a mixed number.**

First divide the numerator by the denominator.

$\frac{21}{4} = 5\frac{1}{4}$ *Use the quotient and remainder to write the mixed number.*

B **Write** $4\frac{2}{3}$ **as an improper fraction.**

First multiply the denominator and whole number, and then add the numerator.

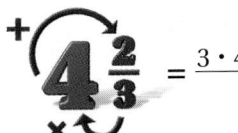

$4\frac{2}{3} = \frac{3 \cdot 4 + 2}{3} = \frac{14}{3}$ *Use the result to write the improper fraction.*

Think and Discuss

1. **Explain** a process for finding common denominators.
2. **Describe** how to convert between improper fractions and mixed numbers.

2-9 Exercises

go.hrw.com
Homework Help Online
KEYWORD: MS7 2-9
Parent Resources Online
KEYWORD: MS7 Parent

GUIDED PRACTICE

See Example 1
Find two fractions equivalent to the given fraction.

1. $\frac{21}{42}$ **2.** $\frac{33}{55}$ **3.** $\frac{10}{12}$ **4.** $\frac{15}{40}$

See Example 2
Write each fraction in simplest form.

5. $\frac{13}{26}$ **6.** $\frac{54}{72}$ **7.** $\frac{12}{15}$ **8.** $\frac{36}{42}$

See Example 3
Determine whether the fractions in each pair are equivalent.

9. $\frac{3}{9}$ and $\frac{6}{8}$ **10.** $\frac{10}{12}$ and $\frac{20}{24}$ **11.** $\frac{8}{6}$ and $\frac{20}{15}$ **12.** $\frac{15}{8}$ and $\frac{19}{12}$

See Example 4
Write each as a mixed number.

13. $\frac{15}{4}$ **14.** $\frac{22}{5}$ **15.** $\frac{17}{13}$ **16.** $\frac{14}{3}$

Write each as an improper fraction.

17. $6\frac{1}{5}$ **18.** $1\frac{11}{12}$ **19.** $7\frac{3}{5}$ **20.** $2\frac{7}{16}$

INDEPENDENT PRACTICE

See Example 1
Find two fractions equivalent to the given fraction.

21. $\frac{18}{20}$ **22.** $\frac{25}{50}$ **23.** $\frac{9}{15}$ **24.** $\frac{42}{70}$

See Example 2
Write each fraction in simplest form.

25. $\frac{63}{81}$ **26.** $\frac{14}{21}$ **27.** $\frac{34}{48}$ **28.** $\frac{100}{250}$

See Example 3
Determine whether the fractions in each pair are equivalent.

29. $\frac{5}{10}$ and $\frac{14}{28}$ **30.** $\frac{15}{20}$ and $\frac{20}{24}$ **31.** $\frac{125}{100}$ and $\frac{40}{32}$ **32.** $\frac{10}{5}$ and $\frac{18}{8}$

33. $\frac{2}{3}$ and $\frac{12}{18}$ **34.** $\frac{8}{12}$ and $\frac{24}{36}$ **35.** $\frac{54}{99}$ and $\frac{84}{132}$ **36.** $\frac{25}{15}$ and $\frac{175}{75}$

See Example 4
Write each as a mixed number.

37. $\frac{19}{3}$ **38.** $\frac{13}{9}$ **39.** $\frac{81}{11}$ **40.** $\frac{71}{8}$

Write each as an improper fraction.

41. $25\frac{3}{5}$ **42.** $4\frac{7}{16}$ **43.** $9\frac{2}{3}$ **44.** $4\frac{16}{31}$

PRACTICE AND PROBLEM SOLVING

Extra Practice
See page 729.

45. Personal Finance Every month, Adrian pays for his own long-distance calls made on the family phone. Last month, 15 of the 60 minutes of long-distance charges were Adrian's, and he paid $2.50 of the $12 long-distance bill. Did Adrian pay his fair share?

Write a fraction equivalent to the given number.

46. 8 **47.** $6\frac{1}{2}$ **48.** $2\frac{2}{3}$ **49.** $\frac{8}{21}$ **50.** $9\frac{8}{11}$

51. $\frac{55}{10}$ **52.** 101 **53.** $6\frac{15}{21}$ **54.** $\frac{475}{75}$ **55.** $11\frac{23}{50}$

LINK

Food

A single bread company can make as many as 1,217 loaves of bread each minute.

Find the equivalent pair of fractions in each set.

56. $\frac{6}{15}, \frac{21}{35}, \frac{3}{5}$ **57.** $\frac{7}{12}, \frac{12}{20}, \frac{6}{10}$ **58.** $\frac{2}{3}, \frac{12}{15}, \frac{20}{30}, \frac{15}{24}$ **59.** $\frac{7}{4}, \frac{9}{5}, \frac{32}{20}, \frac{72}{40}$

There are 12 inches in 1 foot. Write a mixed number to represent each measurement in feet. (Example: 14 inches = $1\frac{2}{12}$ feet or $1\frac{1}{6}$ feet)

60. 25 inches **61.** 100 inches **62.** 362 inches **63.** 42 inches

64. Social Studies A dollar bill is $15\frac{7}{10}$ centimeters long and $6\frac{13}{20}$ centimeters wide. Write each number as an improper fraction.

65. Food A bakery uses $37\frac{1}{2}$ cups of flour to make 25 loaves of bread each day. Write a fraction that shows how many $\frac{1}{4}$ cups of flour are used to make bread each day at the bakery.

66. Write a Problem Cal made the graph at right. Use the graph to write a problem involving fractions.

67. Write About It Draw a diagram to show how you can use division to write $\frac{25}{3}$ as a mixed number. Explain your diagram.

68. Challenge Kenichi spent $\frac{2}{5}$ of his \$100 birthday check on clothes. How much did Kenichi's new clothes cost?

How Cal Spends His Day

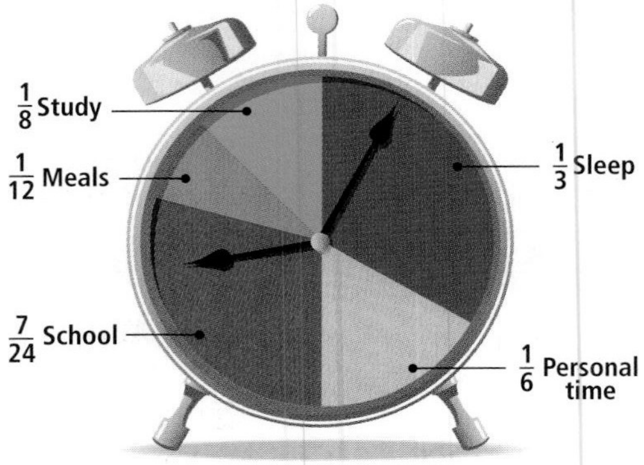

Test Prep and Spiral Review

69. Multiple Choice Which improper fraction is NOT equivalent to $2\frac{1}{2}$?

(A) $\frac{5}{2}$ (B) $\frac{10}{4}$ (C) $\frac{20}{6}$ (D) $\frac{25}{10}$

70. Multiple Choice Which fraction is equivalent to $\frac{5}{6}$?

(F) $\frac{20}{24}$ (G) $\frac{10}{18}$ (H) $\frac{6}{7}$ (J) $\frac{6}{5}$

71. Short Response Maria needs $\frac{4}{3}$ cups of flour, $\frac{11}{4}$ cups of water, and $\frac{3}{2}$ tablespoons of sugar. Write each of these measures as a mixed number.

Solve each equation. Check your answer. (Lessons 1-11 and 1-12)

72. $5b = 25$ **73.** $6 + y = 18$ **74.** $k - 57 = 119$ **75.** $\frac{z}{4} = 20$

Find the least common multiple (LCM). (Lesson 2-8)

76. 2, 3, 4 **77.** 9, 15 **78.** 15, 20 **79.** 3, 7, 8

2-10 Equivalent Fractions and Decimals

Learn to write fractions as decimals, and vice versa, and to determine whether a decimal is terminating or repeating.

Vocabulary

terminating decimal

repeating decimal

In baseball, a player's batting average compares the number of hits with the number of times the player has been at bat. The statistics below are for the 2004 Major League Baseball season.

Lance Berkman had 172 hits in the 2004 season.

Player	Hits	At Bats	$\frac{\text{Hits}}{\text{At Bats}}$	Batting Average (thousandths)
Lance Berkman	172	544	$\frac{172}{544}$	$172 \div 544 \approx 0.316$
Alex Rodriguez	172	601	$\frac{172}{601}$	$172 \div 601 \approx 0.286$

To convert a fraction to a decimal, divide the numerator by the denominator.

EXAMPLE 1 Writing Fractions as Decimals

Write each fraction as a decimal. Round to the nearest hundredth, if necessary.

A $\frac{3}{4}$

$$\begin{array}{r} 0.75 \\ 4\overline{)3.00} \\ \underline{-28} \\ 20 \\ \underline{-20} \\ 0 \end{array}$$

$\frac{3}{4} = 0.75$

B $\frac{6}{5}$

$$\begin{array}{r} 1.2 \\ 5\overline{)6.0} \\ \underline{-5} \\ 10 \\ \underline{-10} \\ 0 \end{array}$$

$\frac{6}{5} = 1.2$

C $\frac{1}{3}$

$$\begin{array}{r} 0.333\ldots \\ 3\overline{)1.000} \\ \underline{-9} \\ 10 \\ \underline{-9} \\ 10 \\ \underline{-9} \\ 1 \end{array}$$

$\frac{1}{3} = 0.333\ldots$
≈ 0.33

Helpful Hint

You can use a calculator to check your division:

3 ÷ 4 = 0.75
6 ÷ 5 = 1.2
1 ÷ 3 = 0.333...

The decimals 0.75 and 1.2 in Example 1 are **terminating decimals** because the decimals come to an end. The decimal 0.333... is a **repeating decimal** because the decimal repeats a pattern forever. You can also write a repeating decimal with a bar over the repeating part.

$0.333\ldots = 0.\overline{3}$ $\quad 0.8333\ldots = 0.8\overline{3}$ $\quad 0.727272\ldots = 0.\overline{72}$

You can use place value to write some fractions as decimals.

EXAMPLE 2 Using Mental Math to Write Fractions as Decimals

Write each fraction as a decimal.

A $\frac{2}{5}$

$\frac{2}{5} \times \frac{2}{2} = \frac{4}{10}$ *Multiply to get a power of ten in the denominator.*

$= 0.4$

B $\frac{7}{25}$

$\frac{7}{25} \times \frac{4}{4} = \frac{28}{100}$ *Multiply to get a power of ten in the denominator.*

$= 0.28$

You can also use place value to write a terminating decimal as a fraction. Use the place value of the last digit to the right of the decimal point as the denominator of the fraction.

EXAMPLE 3 Writing Decimals as Fractions

Reading Math

You read the decimal 0.036 as "thirty-six thousandths."

Write each decimal as a fraction in simplest form.

A 0.036

$0.036 = \frac{36}{1{,}000}$ *6 is in the thousandths place.*

$= \frac{36 \div 4}{1{,}000 \div 4}$

$= \frac{9}{250}$

B 1.28

$1.28 = \frac{128}{100}$ *8 is in the hundredths place.*

$= \frac{128 \div 4}{100 \div 4}$

$= \frac{32}{25}$, or $1\frac{7}{25}$

EXAMPLE 4 *Sports Application*

During a football game, Albert completed 23 of the 27 passes he attempted. Find his completion rate to the nearest thousandth.

Fraction	What the Calculator Shows	Completion Rate
$\frac{23}{27}$	23 ÷ 27 ENTER 0.851851852	0.852

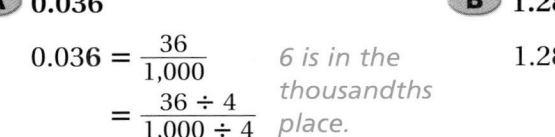

His completion rate is 0.852.

Think and Discuss

1. Tell how to write a fraction as a decimal.

2. Explain how to use place value to convert 0.2048 to a fraction.

2-10 Exercises

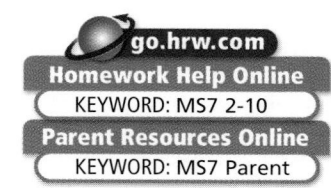

go.hrw.com
Homework Help Online
KEYWORD: MS7 2-10
Parent Resources Online
KEYWORD: MS7 Parent

GUIDED PRACTICE

See Example 1
Write each fraction as a decimal. Round to the nearest hundredth, if necessary.

1. $\frac{4}{7}$ **2.** $\frac{21}{8}$ **3.** $\frac{11}{6}$ **4.** $\frac{7}{9}$

See Example 2
Write each fraction as a decimal.

5. $\frac{3}{25}$ **6.** $\frac{7}{10}$ **7.** $\frac{1}{20}$ **8.** $\frac{3}{5}$

See Example 3
Write each decimal as a fraction in simplest form.

9. 0.008 **10.** −0.6 **11.** −2.05 **12.** 3.75

See Example 4
13. Sports After sweeping the Baltimore Orioles at home in 2001, the Seattle Mariners had a record of 103 wins out of 143 games played. Find the Mariners' winning rate. Write your answer as a decimal rounded to the nearest thousandth.

INDEPENDENT PRACTICE

See Example 1
Write each fraction as a decimal. Round to the nearest hundredth, if necessary.

14. $\frac{9}{10}$ **15.** $\frac{32}{5}$ **16.** $\frac{18}{25}$ **17.** $\frac{7}{8}$

18. $\frac{16}{11}$ **19.** $\frac{500}{500}$ **20.** $\frac{17}{3}$ **21.** $\frac{23}{12}$

See Example 2
Write each fraction as a decimal.

22. $\frac{5}{4}$ **23.** $\frac{4}{5}$ **24.** $\frac{15}{25}$ **25.** $\frac{11}{20}$

See Example 3
Write each decimal as a fraction in simplest form.

26. 0.45 **27.** 0.01 **28.** −0.25 **29.** −0.08

30. 1.8 **31.** 15.25 **32.** 5.09 **33.** 8.375

See Example 4
34. School On a test, Caleb answered 73 out of 86 questions correctly. What portion of his answers was correct? Write your answer as a decimal rounded to the nearest thousandth.

PRACTICE AND PROBLEM SOLVING

Extra Practice
See page 729.

Give two numbers equivalent to each fraction or decimal.

35. $8\frac{3}{4}$ **36.** 0.66 **37.** 5.05 **38.** $\frac{8}{25}$

39. 15.35 **40.** $8\frac{3}{8}$ **41.** $4\frac{3}{1,000}$ **42.** $3\frac{1}{3}$

Determine whether the numbers in each pair are equivalent.

43. $\frac{3}{4}$ and 0.75 **44.** $\frac{7}{20}$ and 0.45 **45.** $\frac{11}{21}$ and 0.55 **46.** 0.8 and $\frac{4}{5}$

47. 0.275 and $\frac{11}{40}$ **48.** $1\frac{21}{25}$ and 1.72 **49.** 0.74 and $\frac{16}{25}$ **50.** 0.35 and $\frac{7}{20}$

Economics LINK

Traders watch the stock prices change from the floor of a stock exchange.

Before the days of computer technology, ticker-tape machines were used to punch the stock prices onto paper strands.

Use the table for Exercises 51 and 52.

XYZ Stock Values (October 2001)				
Date	**Open**	**High**	**Low**	**Close**
Oct 16	17.89	18.05	17.5	17.8
Oct 17	18.01	18.04	17.15	17.95
Oct 18	17.84	18.55	17.81	18.20

51. Write the highest value of stock XYZ for each day as a mixed number in simplest form.

52. On which date did the price of stock XYZ rise by $\frac{9}{25}$ of a dollar between the open and close of the day?

53. **Write About It** Until recently, prices of stocks were expressed as mixed numbers, such as $24\frac{15}{32}$ dollars. The denominators of such fractions were multiples of 2, such as 2, 4, 6, 8, and so forth. Today, the prices are expressed as decimals to the nearest hundredth, such as 32.35 dollars.

a. What are some advantages of using decimals instead of fractions?

b. The old ticker-tape machine punched stock prices onto a tape. Perhaps because fractions could not be shown using the machine, the prices were punched as decimals. Write some decimal equivalents of fractions that the machine might print.

54. **Challenge** Write $\frac{1}{9}$ and $\frac{2}{9}$ as decimals. Use the results to predict the decimal equivalent of $\frac{8}{9}$.

go.hrw.com
Web Extra!
KEYWORD: MS7 Stock

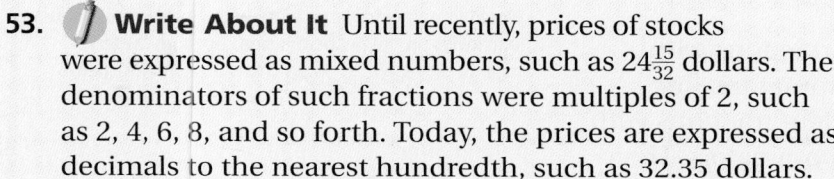

TEST PREP and Spiral Review

55. **Multiple Choice** Which is NOT equivalent to 0.35?

Ⓐ $\frac{35}{100}$ Ⓑ $\frac{7}{20}$ Ⓒ $\frac{14}{40}$ Ⓓ $\frac{25}{80}$

56. **Gridded Response** Write $\frac{6}{17}$ as a decimal rounded to the nearest hundredth.

Determine whether the given value of the variable is a solution. (Lesson 1-10)

57. $x = 2$ for $3x - 4 = 1$ **58.** $x = 3$ for $5x + 4 = 19$ **59.** $x = 14$ for $9(4 + x) = 162$

Write each as an improper fraction. (Lesson 2-9)

60. $4\frac{1}{5}$ **61.** $3\frac{1}{4}$ **62.** $1\frac{2}{3}$ **63.** $6\frac{1}{4}$

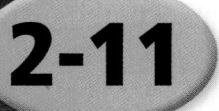

2-11 Comparing and Ordering Rational Numbers

Learn to compare and order fractions and decimals.

Vocabulary

rational number

Which is greater, $\frac{7}{9}$ or $\frac{2}{9}$?

To compare fractions with the same denominator, just compare the numerators.

$\frac{7}{9} > \frac{2}{9}$ because $7 > 2$.

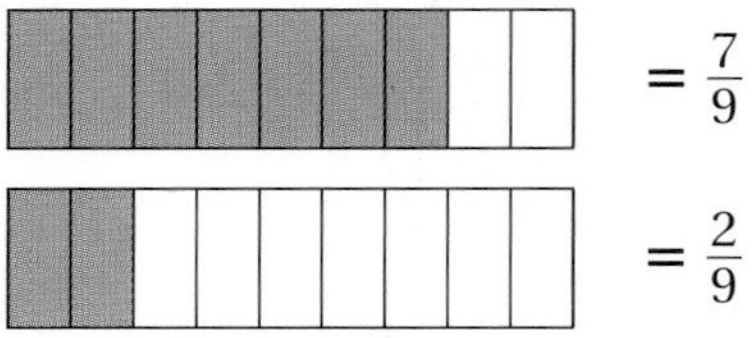

I would like an extra-large pizza with $\frac{1}{2}$ pepperoni, $\frac{4}{5}$ sausage, $\frac{1}{3}$ anchovies on the pepperoni side, $\frac{3}{8}$ peanut butter fudge, $\frac{5}{11}$ pineapple, $\frac{2}{13}$ doggy treats…and extra cheese.

To compare fractions with unlike denominators, first write equivalent fractions with common denominators. Then compare the numerators.

EXAMPLE 1 Comparing Fractions

Compare the fractions. Write < or >.

A $\frac{5}{6}$ ▢ $\frac{7}{10}$

The LCM of the denominators 6 and 10 is 30.

$$\frac{5}{6} = \frac{5 \cdot 5}{6 \cdot 5} = \frac{25}{30}$$

$$\frac{7}{10} = \frac{7 \cdot 3}{10 \cdot 3} = \frac{21}{30}$$

Write equivalent fractions with 30 as the denominator.

$$\frac{25}{30} > \frac{21}{30}, \text{ and so } \frac{5}{6} > \frac{7}{10}.$$

Compare the numerators.

B $-\frac{3}{5}$ ▢ $-\frac{5}{9}$

Both fractions can be written with a denominator of 45.

$$-\frac{3}{5} = \frac{-3 \cdot 9}{5 \cdot 9} = \frac{-27}{45}$$

$$-\frac{5}{9} = \frac{-5 \cdot 5}{9 \cdot 5} = \frac{-25}{45}$$

Write equivalent fractions with 45 as the denominator. Put the negative signs in the numerators.

$$\frac{-27}{45} < \frac{-25}{45}, \text{ and so } -\frac{3}{5} < -\frac{5}{9}.$$

Helpful Hint

A fraction less than 0 can be written as $-\frac{3}{5}$, $\frac{-3}{5}$, or $\frac{3}{-5}$.

To compare decimals, line up the decimal points and compare digits from left to right until you find the place where the digits are different.

EXAMPLE 2 Comparing Decimals

Compare the decimals. Write < or >.

A **0.81 ▢ 0.84**

0.81 ↕ 0.84 *Line up the decimal points.*
The tenths are the same.
Compare the hundredths: 1 < 4.

Since 0.01 < 0.04, 0.81 < 0.84.

B **$0.\overline{34}$ ▢ 0.342**

$0.\overline{34}$ = 0.3434 . . . *$0.\overline{34}$ is a repeating decimal.*
↕ *Line up the decimal points.*
0.342 *The tenths and hundredths are the same.*
Compare the thousandths: 3 > 2.

Since 0.003 > 0.002, $0.\overline{34}$ > 0.342.

A **rational number** is a number that can be written as a fraction with integers for its numerator and denominator. When rational numbers are written in a variety of forms, you can compare the numbers by writing them all in the same form.

EXAMPLE 3 Ordering Fractions and Decimals

Order $\frac{3}{5}$, $0.\overline{77}$, −0.1, and $1\frac{1}{5}$ from least to greatest.

$\frac{3}{5} = 0.60$ $0.\overline{77} \approx 0.78$ *Write as decimals with the same number of places.*

$-0.1 = -0.10$ $1\frac{1}{5} = 1.20$

Graph the numbers on a number line.

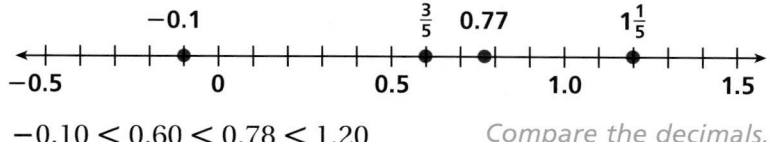

$-0.10 < 0.60 < 0.78 < 1.20$ *Compare the decimals.*

From least to greatest, the numbers are −0.1, $\frac{3}{5}$, $0.\overline{77}$, and $1\frac{1}{5}$.

Remember!

The values on a number line increase as you move from left to right.

Think and Discuss

1. Tell how to compare two fractions with different denominators.

2. Explain why −0.31 is greater than −0.325 even though 2 > 1.

2-11 Exercises

go.hrw.com
Homework Help Online
KEYWORD: MS7 2-11
Parent Resources Online
KEYWORD: MS7 Parent

GUIDED PRACTICE

See Example 1
Compare the fractions. Write < or >.

1. $\frac{3}{5}$ ▒ $\frac{4}{5}$ **2.** $-\frac{5}{8}$ ▒ $-\frac{7}{8}$ **3.** $-\frac{2}{3}$ ▒ $-\frac{4}{7}$ **4.** $3\frac{4}{5}$ ▒ $3\frac{2}{3}$

See Example 2
Compare the decimals. Write < or >.

5. 0.622 ▒ 0.625 **6.** 0.405 ▒ $0.\overline{45}$ **7.** −3.822 ▒ −3.819

See Example 3
Order the numbers from least to greatest.

8. $0.\overline{55}$, $\frac{3}{4}$, 0.505 **9.** 2.5, 2.05, $-\frac{13}{5}$ **10.** $\frac{5}{8}$, −0.875, 0.877

INDEPENDENT PRACTICE

See Example 1
Compare the fractions. Write < or >.

11. $\frac{6}{11}$ ▒ $\frac{7}{11}$ **12.** $-\frac{5}{9}$ ▒ $-\frac{6}{9}$ **13.** $-\frac{5}{6}$ ▒ $-\frac{8}{9}$ **14.** $10\frac{3}{4}$ ▒ $10\frac{3}{5}$

15. $\frac{5}{7}$ ▒ $\frac{2}{7}$ **16.** $-\frac{3}{4}$ ▒ $\frac{1}{4}$ **17.** $\frac{7}{4}$ ▒ $-\frac{1}{4}$ **18.** $-\frac{2}{3}$ ▒ $\frac{4}{3}$

See Example 2
Compare the decimals. Write < or >.

19. 3.8 ▒ 3.6 **20.** 0.088 ▒ 0.109 **21.** $4.\overline{26}$ ▒ 4.266

22. −1.902 ▒ 0.920 **23.** −0.7 ▒ −0.07 **24.** $3.\overline{08}$ ▒ 3.808

See Example 3
Order the numbers from least to greatest.

25. 0.7, 0.755, $\frac{5}{8}$ **26.** 1.82, 1.6, $1\frac{4}{5}$ **27.** −2.25, 2.05, $\frac{21}{10}$

28. $-3.\overline{02}$, −3.02, $1\frac{1}{2}$ **29.** 2.88, −2.98, $-2\frac{9}{10}$ **30.** $\frac{5}{6}$, $\frac{4}{5}$, 0.82

PRACTICE AND PROBLEM SOLVING

Extra Practice
See page 729.

Choose the greater number.

31. $\frac{3}{4}$ or 0.7 **32.** 0.999 or 1.0 **33.** $\frac{7}{8}$ or $\frac{13}{20}$ **34.** −0.93 or 0.2

35. 0.32 or 0.088 **36.** $-\frac{1}{2}$ or −0.05 **37.** $-\frac{9}{10}$ or $-\frac{7}{8}$ **38.** 23.44 or 23

39. Earth Science Density is a measure of the amount of matter in a specific unit of space. The mean densities (measured in grams per cubic centimeter) of the planets of our solar system are given in order of the planets' distance from the Sun. Rearrange the planets from least to most dense.

Planet	Density	Planet	Density	Planet	Density
Mercury	5.43	Mars	3.93	Uranus	1.32
Venus	5.20	Jupiter	1.32	Neptune	1.64
Earth	5.52	Saturn	0.69	Pluto	2.05

LINK — Life Science

An algae that grows in sloths' fur makes them look slightly green. This helps them blend into the trees and stay out of sight from predators.

40. Multi-Step Twenty-four karat gold is considered pure.

a. Angie's necklace is 22-karat gold. What is its purity as a fraction?

b. Luke's ring is 0.75 gold. Whose jewelry contains more gold, Angie's or Luke's?

41. Life Science Sloths are tree-dwelling animals that live in South and Central America. They generally sleep about $\frac{3}{4}$ of a 24-hour day. Humans sleep an average of 8 hours each day. Which sleep the most each day, sloths or humans?

42. Ecology Of Beatrice's total household water use, $\frac{5}{9}$ is for bathing, toilet flushing, and laundry. How does her water use for these purposes compare with that shown in the graph?

Average Daily Household Use of Water

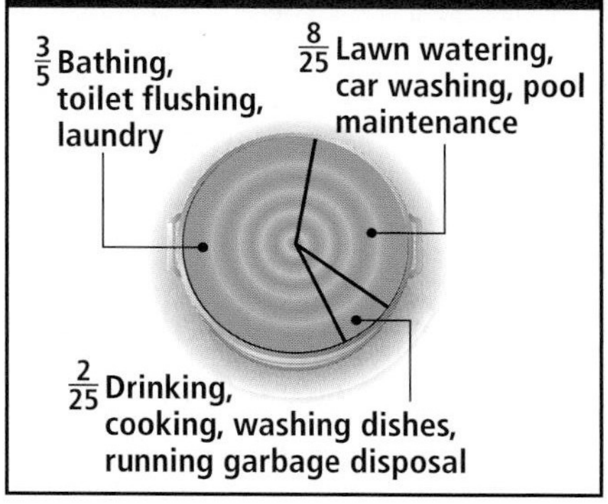

43. What's the Error? A recipe for a large cake called for $4\frac{1}{2}$ cups of flour. The chef added 10 one-half cupfuls of flour to the mixture. What was the chef's error?

44. Write About It Explain how to compare a mixed number with a decimal.

45. Challenge Scientists estimate that Earth is approximately 4.6 billion years old. We are currently in what is called the Phanerozoic eon, which has made up about $\frac{7}{60}$ of the time that Earth has existed. The first eon, called the Hadean, made up approximately 0.175 of the time Earth has existed. Which eon represents the most time?

Test Prep and Spiral Review

46. Multiple Choice Which number is the greatest?

Ⓐ 0.71 Ⓑ $\frac{5}{8}$ Ⓒ 0.65 Ⓓ $\frac{5}{7}$

47. Multiple Choice Which shows the order of the animals from fastest to slowest?

Ⓕ Spider, tortoise, snail, sloth

Ⓖ Snail, sloth, tortoise, spider

Ⓗ Tortoise, spider, snail, sloth

Ⓙ Spider, tortoise, sloth, snail

Maximum Speed (mi/h)				
Animal	Snail	Tortoise	Spider	Sloth
Speed	0.03	0.17	1.17	0.15

Compare. Write <, >, or =. (Lesson 2-1)

48. $|-14| \ \square \ -12$ **49.** $-7 \ \square \ -8$ **50.** $-4 \ \square \ 0$ **51.** $3 \ \square \ -5$

Simplify. (Lessons 2-2 and 2-3)

52. $-13 + 51$ **53.** $142 - (-27)$ **54.** $-118 - (-57)$ **55.** $-27 + 84$

CHAPTER 2

READY TO GO ON?

SECTION 2C

Quiz for Lessons 2-9 Through 2-11

2-9 Equivalent Fractions and Mixed Numbers

Determine whether the fractions in each pair are equivalent.

1. $\frac{3}{4}$ and $\frac{2}{3}$ **2.** $\frac{3}{12}$ and $\frac{4}{16}$ **3.** $\frac{7}{25}$ and $\frac{6}{20}$ **4.** $\frac{5}{9}$ and $\frac{25}{45}$

5. There are $2\frac{54}{100}$ centimeters in an inch. When asked to write this value as an improper fraction, Aimee wrote $\frac{127}{50}$. Was she correct? Explain.

2-10 Equivalent Fractions and Decimals

Write each fraction as a decimal. Round to the nearest hundredth, if necessary.

6. $\frac{7}{10}$ **7.** $\frac{5}{8}$ **8.** $\frac{2}{3}$ **9.** $\frac{14}{15}$

Write each decimal as a fraction in simplest form.

10. 0.22 **11.** −0.135 **12.** −4.06 **13.** 0.07

14. In one 30-gram serving of snack crackers, there are 24 grams of carbohydrates. What fraction of a serving is made up of carbohydrates? Write your answer as a fraction and as a decimal.

15. During a softball game, Sara threw 70 pitches. Of those pitches, 29 were strikes. What portion of the pitches that Sara threw were strikes? Write your answer as a decimal rounded to the nearest thousandth.

2-11 Comparing and Ordering Rational Numbers

Compare the fractions. Write < or >.

16. $\frac{3}{7}$ ▒ $\frac{2}{4}$ **17.** $-\frac{1}{8}$ ▒ $-\frac{2}{11}$ **18.** $\frac{5}{4}$ ▒ $\frac{4}{5}$ **19.** $-1\frac{2}{3}$ ▒ $\frac{1}{2}$

Compare the decimals. Write < or >.

20. 0.521 ▒ 0.524 **21.** 2.05 ▒ −2.50 **22.** 3.001 ▒ 3.010 **23.** −0.26 ▒ −0.626

Order the numbers from least to greatest.

24. $\frac{3}{7}$, −0.372, $-\frac{2}{3}$, 0.5 **25.** $2\frac{9}{11}$, $\frac{4}{5}$, 2.91, 0.9

26. −5.36, 2.36, $-5\frac{1}{3}$, $-2\frac{3}{6}$ **27.** 8.75, $\frac{7}{8}$, 0.8, $\frac{8}{7}$

28. Rafael measured the rainfall at his house for 3 days. On Sunday, it rained $\frac{2}{5}$ in. On Monday, it rained $\frac{5}{8}$ in. On Wednesday, it rained 0.57 in. List the days in order from the least to the greatest amount of rainfall.

MULTI-STEP TEST PREP

Ups and Downs Plaza Tower is a recently completed skyscraper in the downtown business district. To serve each of its 60-story towers, the building has multiple banks of elevators.

1. Eleven people get on one of the skyscraper's elevators. At the first stop, 5 people get off. At the second stop, 7 people get on. At the third stop, 8 people get off. How many people remain on the elevator? Use a number line to model and solve the problem.

2. On a different trip, the number of people getting on and off the elevator is modeled by $12 + (-5) + (-3) + 4$. How many people remain on the elevator?

3. The tower has two express elevators. One stops at the first floor and at floors that are multiples of 6. The other stops at the first floor and at floors that are multiples of 8. On which floors can you catch both express elevators? Explain.

4. The table shows the times that it takes four of the tower's elevators to travel various distances. The speed of each elevator is the distance divided by the time. Which elevator is fastest? slowest? Explain your reasoning.

	Distance (ft)	Time (s)	Speed (ft/s)
Elevator A	600	29	$\frac{600}{29}$
Elevator B	574	28	$\frac{574}{28}$
Elevator C	207	10	20.7
Elevator D	$20\frac{4}{5}$	1	$20\frac{4}{5}$

EXTENSION

Negative Exponents

Learn to evaluate negative exponents and use them to write numbers in scientific notation and in standard form.

When a whole number has a positive exponent, the value of the power is greater than 1. When a whole number has a negative exponent, the value of the power is less than 1. When any number has a zero exponent, the value of the power is equal to 1.

Do you see a pattern in the table at right? The negative exponent becomes positive when it is in the denominator of the fraction.

Power	Value	
10^2	100	$\div 10$
10^1	10	$\div 10$
10^0	1	$\div 10$
10^{-1}	$\frac{1}{10^1}$ or 0.1	$\div 10$
10^{-2}	$\frac{1}{10^2}$ or 0.01	$\div 10$
10^{-3}	$\frac{1}{10^3}$ or 0.001	

EXAMPLE 1 Evaluating Negative Exponents

Evaluate 10^{-4}.

$10^{-4} = \frac{1}{10^4}$ *Write the fraction with a positive exponent in the denominator.*

$= \frac{1}{10{,}000}$ *Evaluate the power.*

$= 0.0001$ *Write the decimal form.*

In Chapter 1, you learned to write large numbers in scientific notation using powers of ten with positive exponents. In the same way, you can write very small numbers in scientific notation using powers of ten with negative exponents.

EXAMPLE 2 Writing Small Numbers in Scientific Notation

Write 0.000065 in scientific notation.

$0.000065 = 0.000065$ *Move the decimal point 5 places to the right.*

$= 6.5 \times 0.00001$ *Write as a product of two factors.*

$= 6.5 \times 10^{-5}$ *Write in exponential form. Since the decimal point was moved 5 places, the exponent is −5.*

Remember!

Move the decimal point to get a number that is greater than or equal to 1 and less than 10.

EXAMPLE 3 Writing Small Numbers in Standard Form

Write 3.4×10^{-6} in standard form.

$3.4 \times 10^{-6} = 0000003.4$ — *Since the exponent is −6, move the decimal point 6 places to the left.*

$= 0.0000034$

When comparing numbers in scientific notation, you may need to compare only the powers of ten to see which value is greater.

EXAMPLE 4 Comparing Numbers Using Scientific Notation

Compare. Write <, >, or =.

A 3.7×10^{-8} ▢ 6.1×10^{-12}

$10^{-8} > 10^{-12}$ — *Compare the powers of ten.*

Since $10^{-8} > 10^{-12}$, $3.7 \times 10^{-8} > 6.1 \times 10^{-12}$.

B 4.9×10^{-5} ▢ 7.3×10^{-5}

$10^{-5} = 10^{-5}$ — *Compare the powers of ten.*

Since the powers of ten are equal, compare the decimals.

$4.9 < 7.3$ — *4 is less than 7.*

Since $4.9 < 7.3$, $4.9 \times 10^{-5} < 7.3 \times 10^{-5}$.

EXTENSION Exercises

Find each value.

1. 10^{-8}
2. 10^{-6}
3. 10^{-5}
4. 10^{-10}
5. 10^{-7}

Write each number in scientific notation or standard form.

6. 0.00000021
7. 0.00086
8. 0.0000000066
9. 0.007
10. 0.0009
11. 0.0453
12. 0.0701
13. 0.00003021
14. 5.8×10^{-9}
15. 4.5×10^{-5}
16. 3.2×10^{-3}
17. 1.4×10^{-11}
18. 2.77×10^{-1}
19. 9.06×10^{-2}
20. 7×10^{-10}
21. 8×10^{-8}

Compare. Write <, >, or =.

22. 7.6×10^{-1} ▢ 7.7×10^{-1}
23. 8.2×10^{-7} ▢ 8.1×10^{-6}
24. 2.8×10^{-6} ▢ 2.8×10^{-7}
25. 5.5×10^{-2} ▢ 2.2×10^{-5}
26. **Write About It** Explain the effect that a zero exponent has on a power.

Game Time

Magic Squares

A magic square is a grid with numbers, such that the numbers in each row, column, and diagonal have the same "magic" sum. Test the square at right to see an example of this.

You can use a magic square to do some amazing calculations. Cover a block of four squares (2 × 2) with a piece of paper. There is a way you can find the sum of these squares without looking at them. Try to find it. (*Hint:* What number in the magic square can you subtract from the magic sum to give you the sum of the numbers in the block? Where is that number located?)

Here's the answer: To find the sum of any block of four numbers, take 65 (the magic sum) and subtract from it the number that is diagonally two squares away from a corner of the block.

18	10	22	14	1
12	4	16	8	25
6	23	15	2	19
5	17	9	21	13
24	11	3	20	7

$65 - 21 = 44$

18	10	22	14	1
12	4	16	8	25
6	23	15	2	19
5	17	9	21	13
24	11	3	20	7

$65 - 1 = 64$

The number you subtract must fall on an extension of a diagonal of the block. For each block that you choose, there will be only one direction you can go.

Try to create a 3 × 3 magic square with the numbers 1–9.

Modified Tic-Tac-Toe

The board has a row of nine squares numbered 1 through 9. Players take turns selecting squares. The goal of the game is for a player to select squares such that any three of the player's squares add up to 15. The game can also be played with a board numbered 1 through 16 and a sum goal of 34.

A complete copy of the rules and a game board are available online.

go.hrw.com
Game Time Extra
KEYWORD: MS7 Games

FOLDNOTES

It's in the Bag!

Materials
- 3 sheets of decorative paper ($8\frac{1}{2}$ in. by $8\frac{1}{2}$ in.)
- scissors
- clear tape
- markers

PROJECT Flipping Over Integers and Rational Numbers

Create your own flip-flop-fold book and use it to write definitions, sample problems, and practice exercises.

Directions

1. Stack the sheets of decorative paper. Fold the stack into quarters and then unfold it. Use scissors to make a slit from the edge of the stack to the center of the stack along the left-hand crease. **Figure A**

2. Place the stack in front of you with the slit on the left side. Fold the top left square over to the right side of the stack. **Figure B**

3. Now fold down the top two squares from the top right corner. Along the slit, tape the bottom left square to the top left square. **Figure C**

4. Continue folding around the stack, always in a clockwise direction. When you get to the second layer, tape the slit in the same place as before.

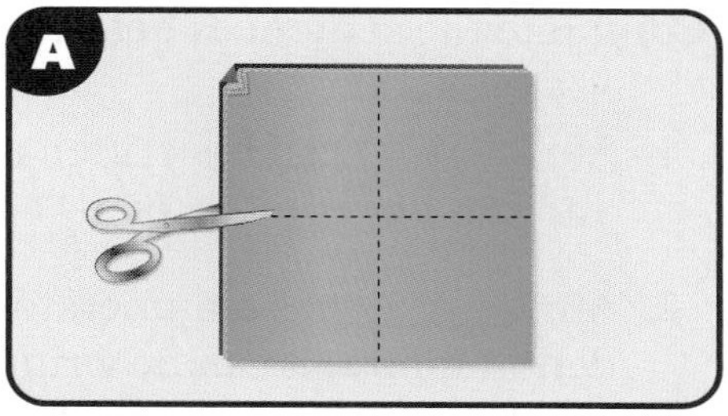
A

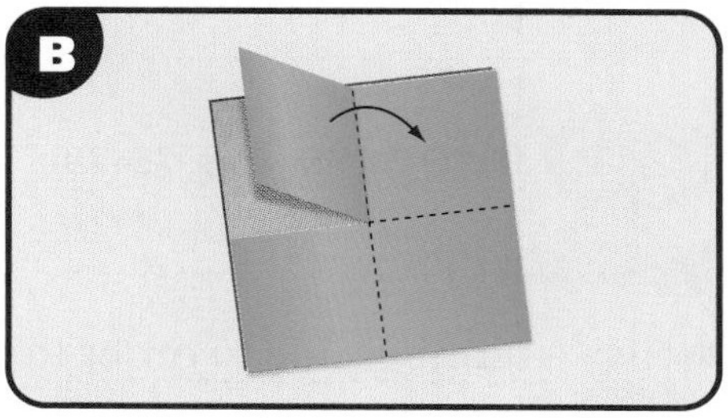
B

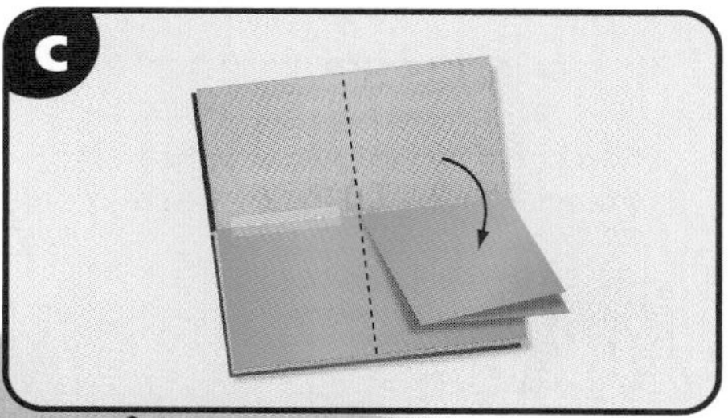
C

Taking Note of the Math

Unfold your completed booklet. This time, as you flip the pages, add definitions, sample problems, practice exercises, or any other notes you need to help you study the material in the chapter.

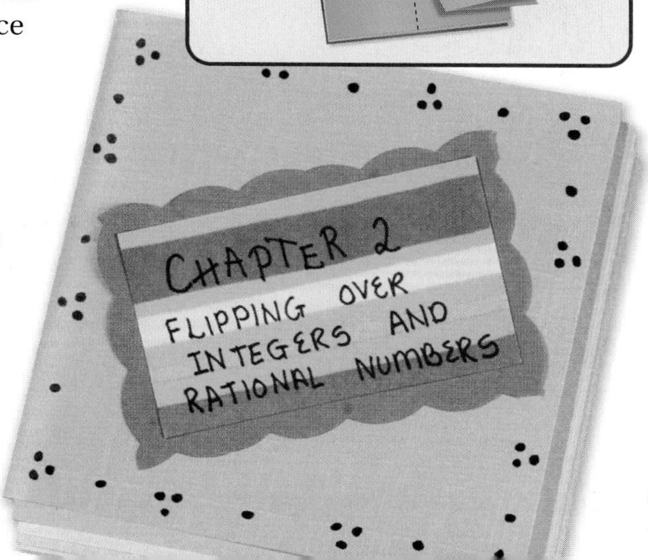

CHAPTER 2

Study Guide: Review

Vocabulary

absolute value 77	integer 76	prime factorization 106
composite number 106	least common multiple (LCM) 114	prime number 106
equivalent fractions ... 120	mixed number 121	rational number 129
greatest common factor (GCF) 110	multiple 114	repeating decimal 124
improper fraction 121	opposite 76	terminating decimal ... 124

Complete the sentences below with vocabulary words from the list above.

1. A(n) __?__ can be written as the ratio of one __?__ to another and can be represented by a repeating or __?__.
2. A(n) __?__ has a numerator that is greater than its denominator; it can be written as a(n) __?__, which contains both a whole number and a fraction.

2-1 Integers (pp. 76–79)

EXAMPLE

■ **Use a number line to order the integers from least to greatest.**

3, 4, −2, 1, −3

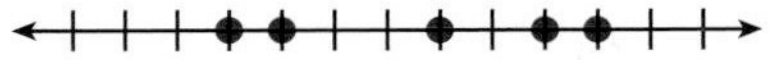

−3, −2, 1, 3, 4

EXERCISES

Compare the integers. Use $<$ or $>$.

3. -8 ▢ -15
4. -7 ▢ 7

Use a number line to order the integers from least to greatest.

5. −6, 4, 0, −2, 5
6. 8, −3, 2, −8, 1

Use a number line to find each absolute value.

7. $|0|$
8. $|-17|$
9. $|6|$

2-2 Adding Integers (pp. 82–85)

EXAMPLE

■ **Find the sum.**

−7 + (−11)

−7 + (−11) *The signs are the same.*

−18

EXERCISES

Find each sum.

10. −8 + 5
11. 7 + (−6)
12. −16 + (−40)
13. −9 + 18
14. −2 + 16
15. 12 + (−18)

2-3 Subtracting Integers (pp. 88–91)

EXAMPLE

■ **Find the difference.**

$-5 - (-3)$

$-5 + 3 = -2$ *Add the opposite of −3.*

EXERCISES

Find each difference.

16. $8 - 2$ **17.** $10 - 19$

18. $-6 - (-5)$ **19.** $-5 - 4$

2-4 Multiplying and Dividing Integers (pp. 94–97)

EXAMPLE

Find each product or quotient.

■ $12 \cdot (-3)$ *The signs are different, so the product is negative.*

-36

■ $-16 \div (-4)$ *The signs are the same, so the quotient is positive.*

4

EXERCISES

Find each product or quotient.

20. $5 \cdot (-10)$ **21.** $-27 \div (-9)$

22. $-2 \cdot (-8)$ **23.** $-40 \div 20$

24. $-3 \cdot 4$ **25.** $45 \div (-15)$

2-5 Solving Equations Containing Integers (pp. 100–103)

EXAMPLE

Solve.

■ $x - 12 = 4$

$\underline{+12} \quad \underline{+12}$ *Add 12 to each side.*

$x = 16$

■ $-10 = -2f$

$\frac{-10}{-2} = \frac{-2f}{-2}$ *Divide each side by −2.*

$5 = f$

EXERCISES

Solve.

26. $7y = 70$ **27.** $d - 8 = 6$

28. $j + 23 = -3$ **29.** $\frac{n}{36} = 2$

30. $-26 = -2c$ **31.** $28 = -7m$

32. $-15 = \frac{y}{7}$ **33.** $g - 12 = -31$

34. $-13 + p = 8$ **35.** $-8 + f = 8$

2-6 Prime Factorization (pp. 106–109)

EXAMPLE

■ **Write the prime factorization of 56.**

$56 = 8 \cdot 7 = 2 \cdot 2 \cdot 2 \cdot 7$, or $2^3 \cdot 7$

EXERCISES

Write the prime factorization.

36. 88 **37.** 27 **38.** 162 **39.** 96

2-7 Greatest Common Factor (pp. 110–113)

EXAMPLE

■ **Find the GCF of 32 and 12.**

Factors of 32: 1, 2, (4), 8, 16, 32
Factors of 12: 1, 2, 3, (4), 6, 12
The GCF is 4.

EXERCISES

Find the greatest common factor.

40. 120, 210 **41.** 81, 132

42. 36, 60, 96 **43.** 220, 440, 880

2-8 Least Common Multiple (pp. 114–117)

EXAMPLE

- **Find the LCM of 8 and 10.**

  Multiples of 8: 8, 16, 24, 32, (40)
  Multiples of 10: 10, 20, 30, (40)
  The LCM is 40.

EXERCISES

Find the least common multiple.

44. 5, 12 **45.** 4, 32 **46.** 3, 27
47. 15, 18 **48.** 6, 12 **49.** 5, 7, 9

2-9 Equivalent Fractions and Mixed Numbers (pp. 120–123)

EXAMPLE

- **Write $5\frac{2}{3}$ as an improper fraction.**

  $5\frac{2}{3} = \frac{3 \cdot 5 + 2}{3} = \frac{17}{3}$

- **Write $\frac{17}{4}$ as a mixed number.**

  $\frac{17}{4} = 4\frac{1}{4}$ *Divide the numerator by the denominator.*

EXERCISES

Write each as an improper fraction.

50. $4\frac{1}{5}$ **51.** $3\frac{1}{6}$ **52.** $10\frac{3}{4}$

Write each as a mixed number.

53. $\frac{10}{3}$ **54.** $\frac{5}{2}$ **55.** $\frac{17}{7}$

Find two fractions equivalent to the given fraction.

56. $\frac{16}{18}$ **57.** $\frac{21}{24}$ **58.** $\frac{48}{63}$

2-10 Equivalent Fractions and Decimals (pp. 124–127)

EXAMPLE

- **Write 0.75 as a fraction in simplest form.**

  $0.75 = \frac{75}{100} = \frac{75 \div 25}{100 \div 25} = \frac{3}{4}$

- **Write $\frac{5}{4}$ as a decimal.**

  $\frac{5}{4} = 5 \div 4 = 1.25$

EXERCISES

Write each decimal as a fraction in simplest form.

59. 0.25 **60.** −0.004 **61.** 0.05

Write each fraction as a decimal.

62. $\frac{7}{2}$ **63.** $\frac{3}{5}$ **64.** $\frac{2}{3}$

2-11 Comparing and Ordering Rational Numbers (pp. 128–131)

EXAMPLE

- **Compare. Write < or >.**

  $-\frac{3}{4}$ ▒ $-\frac{2}{3}$

  $-\frac{3}{4} \cdot \frac{3}{3}$ ▒ $-\frac{2}{3} \cdot \frac{4}{4}$ *Write as fractions with common denominators.*

  $-\frac{9}{12} < -\frac{8}{12}$

EXERCISES

Compare. Write < or >.

65. $\frac{4}{5}$ ▒ 0.81 **66.** 0.22 ▒ $\frac{3}{20}$
67. $-\frac{3}{5}$ ▒ −1.5 **68.** $1\frac{1}{8}$ ▒ $1\frac{2}{9}$

69. Order $\frac{6}{13}$, 0.58, −0.55, and $\frac{1}{2}$ from least to greatest.

CHAPTER TEST

CHAPTER 2

Use a number line to order the integers from least to greatest.

1. $-4, 3, -2, 0, 1$ **2.** $7, -6, 5, -8, -3$

Use a number line to find each absolute value.

3. $|11|$ **4.** $|-5|$ **5.** $|-74|$ **6.** $|-1|$

Find each sum, difference, product, or quotient.

7. $-7 + (-3)$ **8.** $-6 - 3$ **9.** $17 - (-9) - 8$ **10.** $102 + (-97) + 3$

11. $-3 \cdot 20$ **12.** $-36 \div 12$ **13.** $-400 \div (-10)$ **14.** $-5 \cdot (-2) \cdot 9$

Solve.

15. $w - 4 = -6$ **16.** $x + 5 = -5$ **17.** $-6a = 60$ **18.** $\frac{n}{-4} = 12$

19. Kathryn's tennis team has won 52 matches. Her team has won 9 more matches than Rebecca's team. How many matches has Rebecca's team won this season?

Write the prime factorization of each number.

20. 30 **21.** 66 **22.** 78 **23.** 110

Find the greatest common factor (GCF).

24. 18, 27, 45 **25.** 16, 28, 44 **26.** 14, 28, 56 **27.** 24, 36, 64

Find the least common multiple (LCM).

28. 24, 36, 64 **29.** 24, 72, 144 **30.** 12, 15, 36 **31.** 9, 16, 25

Determine whether the fractions in each pair are equivalent.

32. $\frac{6}{12}$ and $\frac{13}{26}$ **33.** $\frac{17}{20}$ and $\frac{20}{24}$ **34.** $\frac{30}{24}$ and $\frac{35}{28}$ **35.** $\frac{5}{3}$ and $\frac{8}{5}$

Write each fraction as a decimal. Write each decimal as a fraction in simplest form.

36. $\frac{3}{50}$ **37.** $\frac{25}{10}$ **38.** 3.15 **39.** 0.004

40. The Drama Club has 52 members. Of these members, 18 are in the seventh grade. What fraction of the Drama Club is made up of seventh-graders? Write your answer as a fraction and a decimal. Round the decimal to the nearest thousandth.

Compare. Write $<$ or $>$.

41. $\frac{2}{3} \blacksquare 0.62$ **42.** $1.5 \blacksquare 1\frac{6}{20}$ **43.** $-\frac{9}{7} \blacksquare -1$ **44.** $\frac{11}{5} \blacksquare 1\frac{2}{3}$

Chapter Test

CHAPTER 2

STANDARDIZED TEST PREP

Cumulative Assessment, Chapters 1–2

Multiple Choice

1. During a week in January in Cleveland, Ohio, the daily high temperatures were −4°F, −2°F, −12°F, 5°F, 12°F, 16°F, and 20°F. Which expression can be used to find the difference between the highest temperature of the week and the lowest temperature of the week?

Ⓐ 20 − 2 Ⓒ 20 − 12

Ⓑ 20 − (−2) Ⓓ 20 − (−12)

2. Find the greatest common factor of 16 and 32.

Ⓕ 2 Ⓗ 32

Ⓖ 16 Ⓙ 512

3. The fraction $\frac{3}{5}$ is found between which pair of fractions on a number line?

Ⓐ $\frac{1}{2}$ and $\frac{2}{10}$

Ⓑ $\frac{1}{2}$ and $\frac{7}{10}$

Ⓒ $\frac{3}{10}$ and $\frac{5}{15}$

Ⓓ $\frac{3}{10}$ and $\frac{8}{15}$

4. Maxie earns $210 a week working as a lifeguard. After she gets paid, she gives each of her three sisters $20, and her mom $120 for her car payment. Which equation can be used to find *p*, the amount of money Maxie has left after she pays her mom and sisters?

Ⓕ $p = 210 - (3 \times 20) - 120$

Ⓖ $p = 210 - 20 - 120$

Ⓗ $p = 120 - (3 \times 20) - 120$

Ⓙ $p = 3 \times (210 - 20 - 120)$

5. Which expression can be used to represent a pattern in the table?

x	?
−3	4
−5	2
−7	0
−9	−2

Ⓐ $x + 2$ Ⓒ $x - (-7)$

Ⓑ $-2x$ Ⓓ $x - 7$

6. Which of the following shows a list of numbers in order from least to greatest?

Ⓕ −1.05, −2.55, −3.05

Ⓖ −2.75, $2\frac{5}{6}$, 2.50

Ⓗ −0.05, −0.01, $3\frac{1}{4}$

Ⓙ $-1\frac{2}{8}$, $-1\frac{4}{8}$, 1.05

7. Which of the following is an example of the Associative Property?

Ⓐ $5 + (4 + 1) = (5 + 4) + 1$

Ⓑ $32 + (2 + 11) = 32 + (11 + 2)$

Ⓒ $(2 \times 10) + (2 \times 4) = 2 \times 14$

Ⓓ $4(2 \times 7) = (4 \times 2) + (4 \times 7)$

8. There are 100 centimeters in 1 meter. Which mixed number represents 625 centimeters in meters?

Ⓕ $6\frac{1}{4}$ m Ⓗ $6\frac{2}{5}$ m

Ⓖ $6\frac{2}{4}$ m Ⓙ $6\frac{3}{5}$ m

9. An artist is creating a design with 6 stripes. The first stripe is 2 meters long. The second stripe is 4 meters long, the third stripe is 8 meters long, and the fourth stripe is 16 meters long. If the pattern continues, how long is the sixth stripe?

Ⓐ 24 m　　Ⓒ 64 m

Ⓑ 32 m　　Ⓓ 128 m

10. Simplify the expression $(-5)^2 - 3 \cdot 4$.

Ⓕ −112　　Ⓗ 13

Ⓖ −37　　Ⓙ 88

11. Evaluate $a - b$ for $a = -5$ and $b = 3$.

Ⓐ −8　　Ⓒ 2

Ⓑ −2　　Ⓓ 8

HOT TIP! **Gridded responses cannot be negative numbers. If you get a negative value, you likely made an error. Check your work!**

Gridded Response

12. Find the missing value in the table.

t	$-t + 3 \cdot 5$
5	10
10	?

13. Solve for x and y in each equation. Grid the sum of x and y.

$x + 6 = -4$　　$-3y = -39$

14. Garrett dusts his bedroom every four days and sweeps his bedroom every three days. If he does both today, how many days will pass before he does them both on the same day again?

15. What is the power of 10 if you write 5,450,000,000 in scientific notation?

16. What is the value of 8^3 ?

Short Response

17. The sponsors of the marching band provided 128 sandwiches for a picnic. After the picnic, s sandwiches were left.

 a. Write an expression that shows how many sandwiches were handed out.

 b. Evaluate your expression for $s = 15$. What does your answer represent?

18. Casey said the solution to the equation $x + 42 = 65$ is 107. Identify the error that Casey made. Explain why this answer is unreasonable. Show how to solve this equation correctly. Explain your work.

Extended Response

19. Mary's allowance is based on the amount of time that she spends practicing different activities each week. This week Mary spent 12 hours practicing and earned $12.00.

 a. Mary spent the following amounts of time on each activity: $\frac{1}{5}$ practicing flute, $\frac{1}{6}$ studying Spanish, $\frac{1}{3}$ playing soccer, and $\frac{3}{10}$ studying math. Write an equivalent decimal for the amount of time that she spent on each activity. Round to the nearest hundredth, if necessary.

 b. For each activity, Mary earned the same fraction of her allowance as the time spent on a particular activity. This week, she was paid $3.60 for math practice. Was this the correct amount? Explain how you know.

 c. Order the amount of time that Mary spent practicing each activity from least to greatest.

 d. Write a decimal to represent the fraction of time Mary would have spent practicing soccer for 5 hours instead of 6 hours this week.

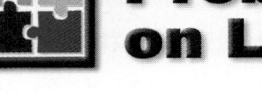

Problem Solving on Location

OHIO

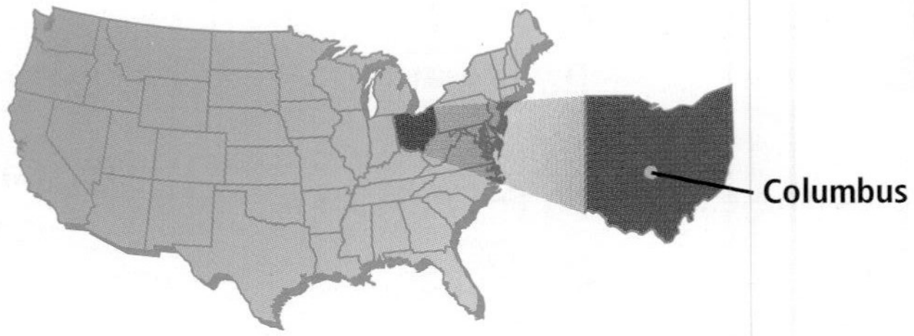

Covered Bridges

There are dozens of historic covered bridges located throughout Ohio. Each year, Ashtabula County holds a Covered Bridge Festival on the second weekend in October to coincide with the spectacular fall foliage.

Choose one or more strategies to solve each problem.

1. Netcher Road Bridge in Jefferson Township is 5 times as long as it is wide. The sum of its length and width is 132 feet. What are the bridge's length and width?

2. Olin Bridge in Plymouth Township is 115 feet long. It has several windows, evenly spaced, along one side of the bridge. Each window is 5 feet wide, and there is 15 feet of space between each of them. The distance between the last window on either side and the end of the bridge is 15 feet. How many windows are there?

For 3, use the graph.

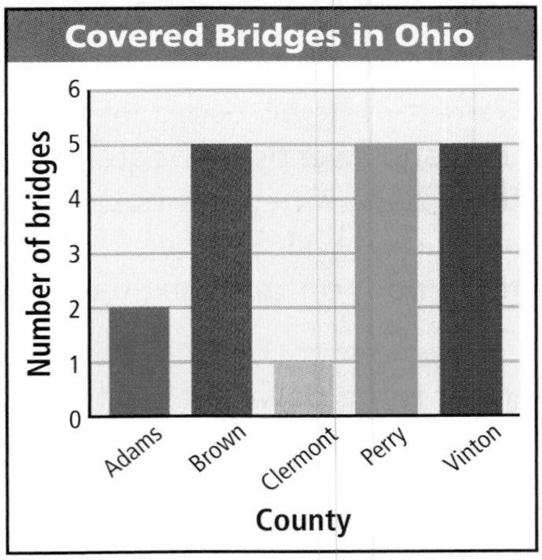

3. Ashtabula County has the greatest number of covered bridges in the state. Use the following information to determine the number of covered bridges in Ashtabula County.
   - Ashtabula County has more than 3 times the number of covered bridges Perry County has.
   - The number of covered bridges in Ashtabula County is a multiple of the number of covered bridges in Adams County.
   - Ashtabula County has fewer covered bridges than the five counties in the table combined have.

Draw a Diagram
Make a Model
Guess and Test
Work Backward
Find a Pattern
Make a Table
Solve a Simpler Problem
Use Logical Reasoning
Act It Out
Make an Organized List

The Ohio State Fair

For over 150 years, the Ohio State Fair in Columbus has celebrated the state's agricultural heritage. Each summer, the capital city hosts a diverse collection of exhibits, contests, and thrill rides. For more than one million annual visitors, the fair is an entertaining way to learn about Ohio's crops and livestock.

Choose one or more strategies to solve each problem.

1. Tickets to the fair cost \$8 for adults and \$7 for children. A group of visitors bought 7 tickets for \$52. How many adults and how many children were in the group?

The fair features exhibits about Ohio's most important crops. For 2–4, use the table.

2. Ohio ranks third in the nation for production of one of the crops shown in the table. In 2002, more than 5,000 acres but less than 1,000,000 acres of the crop were harvested. Production of the crop decreased in 2003. Which crop is it?
3. Assuming the same decrease in tomato production each year as in 2003, how many acres of tomatoes will be harvested in 2010?
4. Assuming the same increase in wheat production each year as in 2003, in what year will the wheat harvest be more than 2 million acres?

Ohio Crop Production

Crop	2002 Harvest (acres)	2003 Increase/Decrease (acres)
Potatoes	4.4×10^3	−100
Soybeans	4.7×10^6	−440,000
Tomatoes	6.7×10^3	−100
Wheat	8.1×10^5	+190,000

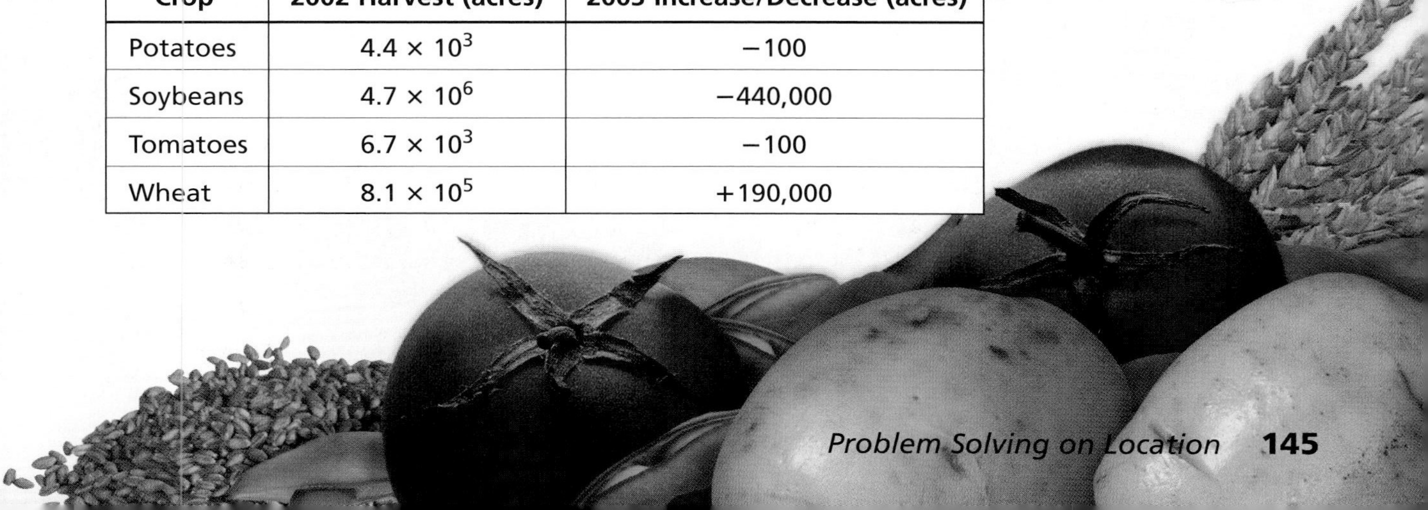

CHAPTER 3

Applying Rational Numbers

go.hrw.com
Chapter Project Online
KEYWORD: MS7 Ch3

Ingredients	10 Waffles	25 Waffles	50 Waffles
Flour	2 c	5 c	10 c
Salt	$\frac{3}{4}$ tsp	$1\frac{7}{8}$ tsp	$3\frac{3}{4}$ tsp
Baking powder	3 tsp	$7\frac{1}{2}$ tsp	15 tsp
Milk	$1\frac{2}{3}$ c	$4\frac{1}{6}$ c	$8\frac{1}{3}$ c
Butter (melted)	$\frac{1}{2}$ c	$1\frac{1}{4}$ c	$2\frac{1}{2}$ c

Career *Chef*

Tom Culbertson is a pastry chef. He develops and prepares all of the baked goods for his restaurant. In his work, Tom often uses fractions when measuring ingredients. He must also multiply and divide fractions to increase or decrease the number of servings for a recipe. In addition to the breads and desserts that he creates, Tom is famous for his breakfast waffles. Tom often adds fresh fruits, such as blueberries, strawberries, or bananas, to his waffles.

ARE YOU READY?

Vocabulary

Choose the best term from the list to complete each sentence.

1. A(n) __?__ is a number that is written using the base-ten place value system.	**decimal**
2. An example of a(n) __?__ is $\frac{14}{5}$.	**fraction**
3. A(n) __?__ is a number that represents a part of a whole.	**improper fraction**
	mixed number
	simplest form

Complete these exercises to review the skills you will need for this chapter.

Simplify Fractions

Write each fraction in simplest form.

4. $\frac{24}{40}$ **5.** $\frac{64}{84}$ **6.** $\frac{66}{78}$ **7.** $\frac{64}{192}$

8. $\frac{21}{35}$ **9.** $\frac{11}{99}$ **10.** $\frac{16}{36}$ **11.** $\frac{20}{30}$

Write Mixed Numbers as Fractions

Write each mixed number as an improper fraction.

12. $7\frac{1}{2}$ **13.** $2\frac{5}{6}$ **14.** $1\frac{14}{15}$ **15.** $3\frac{2}{11}$

16. $3\frac{7}{8}$ **17.** $8\frac{4}{9}$ **18.** $4\frac{1}{7}$ **19.** $5\frac{9}{10}$

Write Fractions as Mixed Numbers

Write each improper fraction as a mixed number.

20. $\frac{23}{6}$ **21.** $\frac{17}{3}$ **22.** $\frac{29}{7}$ **23.** $\frac{39}{4}$

24. $\frac{48}{5}$ **25.** $\frac{82}{9}$ **26.** $\frac{69}{4}$ **27.** $\frac{35}{8}$

Add, Subtract, Multiply, or Divide Integers

Find each sum, difference, product, or quotient.

28. $-11 + (-24)$ **29.** $-11 - 7$ **30.** $-4 \cdot (-10)$

31. $-22 \div (-11)$ **32.** $23 + (-30)$ **33.** $-33 - 74$

34. $-62 \cdot (-34)$ **35.** $84 \div (-12)$ **36.** $-26 - 18$

CHAPTER 3

Study Guide: Preview

Where You've Been

Previously, you

- added, subtracted, multiplied, and divided whole numbers.
- used models to solve equations with whole numbers.

In This Chapter

You will study

- using models to represent multiplication and division situations involving fractions and decimals.
- using addition, subtraction, multiplication, and division to solve problems involving fractions and decimals.
- solving equations with rational numbers.

Where You're Going

You can use the skills learned in this chapter

- to estimate total cost when purchasing several items at the grocery store.
- to find measurements in fields such as carpentry.

Key Vocabulary/Vocabulario

compatible numbers	números contabiles
reciprocal	reciproco

Vocabulary Connections

To become familiar with some of the vocabulary terms in the chapter, consider the following. You may refer to the chapter, the glossary, or a dictionary if you like.

1. When two things are compatible, they make a good match. You can match a fraction with a number that is easier to work with, such as 1, $\frac{1}{2}$, or 0, by rounding up or down. How could you use these **compatible numbers** to estimate the sums and differences of fractions?
2. When fractions are **reciprocals** of each other, they have a special relationship. The fractions $\frac{3}{5}$ and $\frac{5}{3}$ are reciprocals of each other. What do you think the relationship between reciprocals is?

Reading and Writing Math

Study Strategy: Use Your Notes Effectively

Taking notes helps you understand and remember information from your textbook and lessons in class. Listed below are some steps for effectively using your notes before and after class.

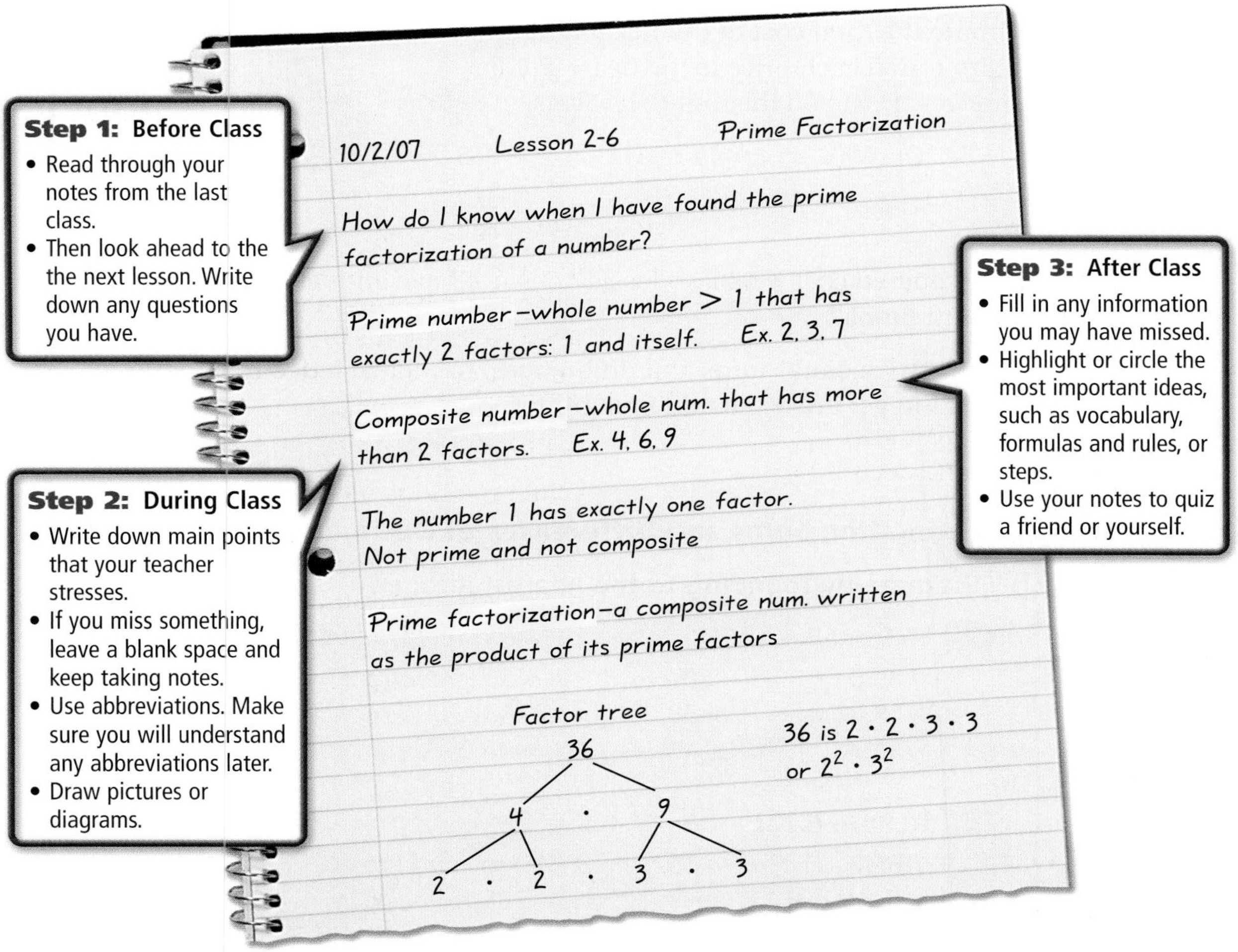
Step 1: Before Class
• Read through your notes from the last class.
• Then look ahead to the the next lesson. Write down any questions you have.
10/2/07 Lesson 2-6 Prime Factorization
How do I know when I have found the prime factorization of a number?
Prime number – whole number > 1 that has exactly 2 factors: 1 and itself. Ex. 2, 3, 7
Composite number – whole num. that has more than 2 factors. Ex. 4, 6, 9
The number 1 has exactly one factor. Not prime and not composite
Prime factorization – a composite num. written as the product of its prime factors
Factor tree
36
4 · 9
2 · 2 · 3 · 3
36 is 2 · 2 · 3 · 3 or 2² · 3²
Step 2: During Class
• Write down main points that your teacher stresses.
• If you miss something, leave a blank space and keep taking notes.
• Use abbreviations. Make sure you will understand any abbreviations later.
• Draw pictures or diagrams.
Step 3: After Class
• Fill in any information you may have missed.
• Highlight or circle the most important ideas, such as vocabulary, formulas and rules, or steps.
• Use your notes to quiz a friend or yourself.

Try This

1. Look at the next lesson in your textbook. Think about how the new vocabulary terms relate to previous lessons. Write down any questions you have.
2. With a classmate, compare the notes you took during the last class. Are there differences in the main points that you each recorded? Then brainstorm two ways you can improve your note-taking skills.

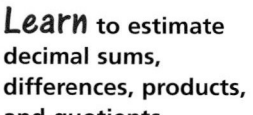

3-1 Estimate with Decimals

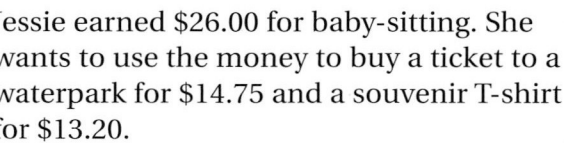

Problem Solving Skill

Learn **to estimate decimal sums, differences, products, and quotients.**

Vocabulary

compatible numbers

Jessie earned \$26.00 for baby-sitting. She wants to use the money to buy a ticket to a waterpark for \$14.75 and a souvenir T-shirt for \$13.20.

To find out if Jessie has enough money to buy both items, you can use estimation. To estimate the total cost of the ticket and the T-shirt, round each price to the nearest dollar, or integer. Then add the rounded values.

\$14.75	*7 > 5, so round to \$15.*	\$15
\$13.20	*2 < 5, so round to \$13.*	+ \$13
		\$28

The estimated cost is \$28, so Jessie does not have enough money to buy both items.

To estimate decimal sums and differences, round each decimal to the nearest integer and then add or subtract.

EXAMPLE 1 Estimating Sums and Differences of Decimals

Estimate by rounding to the nearest integer.

A **86.9 + 58.4**

86.9	⟶	87	*9 > 5, so round to 87.*
+ 58.4	⟶	+ 58	*4 < 5, so round to 58.*
		145	⟵ ***Estimate***

B **10.38 − 6.721**

10.38	⟶	10	*3 < 5, so round to 10.*
− 6.721	⟶	− 7	*7 > 5, so round to 7.*
		3	⟵ ***Estimate***

C **−26.3 + 15.195**

−26.3	⟶	−26	*3 < 5, so round to −26.*
+ 15.195	⟶	+ 15	*1 < 5, so round to 15.*
		−11	⟵ ***Estimate***

Remember!

To round to the nearest integer, look at the digit in the tenths place. If it is greater than or equal to 5, round to the next integer. If it is less than 5, keep the same integer.

You can use *compatible numbers* when estimating. **Compatible numbers** are numbers that replace the numbers in the problem and are easy to use.

Guidelines for Using Compatible Numbers	
When multiplying . . .	**When dividing . . .**
round numbers to the nearest nonzero integer or to numbers that are easy to multiply.	round numbers so that they divide without leaving a remainder.

EXAMPLE 2 Estimating Products and Quotients of Decimals

Use compatible numbers to estimate.

A $32.66 \cdot 7.69$

32.66	⟶	30	*Round to the nearest multiple of 10.*
$\times$ 7.69	⟶	$\times$ 8	*6 > 5, so round to 8.*
		240 ⟵	***Estimate***

Remember!

A prime number has exactly two factors, 1 and itself. So the factors of 37 are 1 and 37.

B $36.5 \div (-8.241)$

36.5	⟶	36	*37 is a prime number, so round to 36.*
-8.241	⟶	-9	*−9 divides into 36 without a remainder.*

$36 \div (-9) = -4$ ⟵ ***Estimate***

When you solve problems, using an estimate can help you decide whether your answer is reasonable.

EXAMPLE 3 *School Application*

On a math test, a student worked the problem $6.2\overline{)55.9}$ and got the answer 0.9. Use estimation to check whether the answer is reasonable.

6.2	⟶	6	*2 < 5, so round to 6.*
55.9	⟶	60	*6 divides into 60 without a remainder.*

$60 \div 6 = 10$ ⟵ ***Estimate***

The estimate is more than ten times the student's answer, so 0.9 is not a reasonable answer.

Think and Discuss

1. Explain whether your estimate will be greater than or less than the actual answer when you round both numbers down in an addition or multiplication problem.

2. Describe a situation in which you would want your estimate to be greater than the actual amount.

3-1 Exercises

go.hrw.com
Homework Help Online
KEYWORD: MS7 3-1
Parent Resources Online
KEYWORD: MS7 Parent

GUIDED PRACTICE

See Example 1

Estimate by rounding to the nearest integer.

1. 37.2 + 25.83 **2.** 18.256 − 5.71 **3.** −9.916 + 12.4

See Example 2

Use compatible numbers to estimate.

4. 8.09 · 28.32 **5.** −3.45 · 73.6 **6.** 41.9 ÷ 6.391

See Example 3

7. School A student worked the problem 35.8 · 9.3. The student's answer was 3,329.4. Use estimation to check whether this answer is reasonable.

INDEPENDENT PRACTICE

See Example 1

Estimate by rounding to the nearest integer.

8. 5.982 + 37.1 **9.** 68.2 + 23.67 **10.** −36.8 + 14.217

11. 15.23 − 6.835 **12.** 6.88 + (−8.1) **13.** 80.38 − 24.592

See Example 2

Use compatible numbers to estimate.

14. 51.38 · 4.33 **15.** 46.72 ÷ 9.24 **16.** 32.91 · 6.28

17. −3.45 · 43.91 **18.** 2.81 · (−79.2) **19.** 28.22 ÷ 3.156

See Example 3

20. Ann has a piece of rope that is 12.35 m long. She wants to cut it into smaller pieces that are each 3.6 m long. She thinks she will get about 3 smaller pieces of rope. Use estimation to check whether her assumption is reasonable.

PRACTICE AND PROBLEM SOLVING

Extra Practice
See page 730.

Estimate.

21. 5.921 − 13.2 **22.** −7.98 − 8.1 **23.** −42.25 + (−17.091)

24. 98.6 + 43.921 **25.** 4.69 · (−18.33) **26.** 62.84 − 35.169

27. −48.28 + 11.901 **28.** 31.53 ÷ (−4.12) **29.** 35.9 − 24.71

30. 69.7 − 7.81 **31.** −6.56 · 14.2 **32.** 4.513 + 72.45

33. −8.9 · (−24.1) **34.** 6.92 · (−3.714) **35.** −78.3 ÷ (−6.25)

36. Jo needs 10 lb of ground beef for a party. She has packages that weigh 4.23 lb and 5.09 lb. Does she have enough?

37. Consumer Math Ramón saves $8.35 each week. He wants to buy a video game that costs $61.95. For about how many weeks will Ramón have to save his money before he can buy the video game?

38. Multi-Step Tickets at a local movie theater cost $7.50 each. A large bucket of popcorn at the theater costs $4.19, and a large soda costs $3.74. Estimate the amount that 3 friends spent at the theater when they saw one movie, shared one large bucket of popcorn, and had one large soda each.

LINK
Social Studies

Inuktitut is spoken by more than 60,000 people in Canada, Alaska, and Greenland. The Inuktitut word for "school" is *ilinniarvic*.

39. **Transportation** Kayla stopped for gasoline at a station that was charging \$2.719 per gallon. If Kayla had \$14.75 in cash, approximately how many gallons of gas could she buy?

40. **Social Studies** The circle graph shows the languages spoken in Canada.

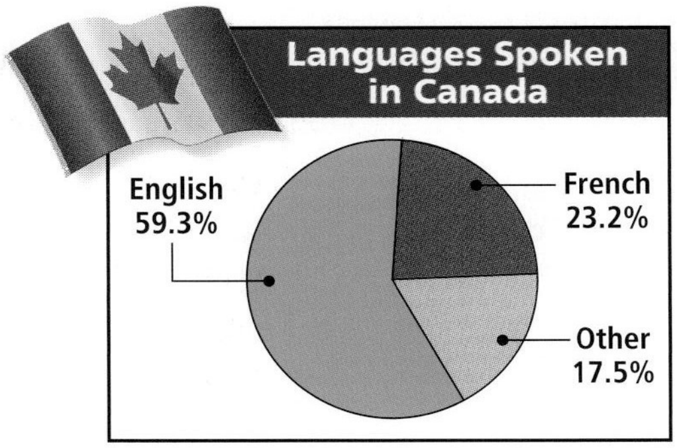

a. Which language do approximately 60% of Canadians speak?

b. What is the approximate difference between the percent of people who speak English and the percent who speak French?

41. **Astronomy** Jupiter is 5.20 astronomical units (AU) from the Sun. Neptune is almost 6 times as far from the Sun as Jupiter is. Estimate Neptune's distance from the Sun in astronomical units.

42. **Sports** Scott must earn a total of 27 points to advance to the final round in an ice-skating competition. He earns scores of 5.9, 5.8, 6.0, 5.8, and 6.0. Scott estimates that his total score will allow him to advance. Is his estimate reasonable? Explain.

43. **Write a Problem** Write a problem that can be solved by estimating with decimals.

44. **Write About It** Explain how an estimate helps you decide whether an answer is reasonable.

45. **Challenge** Estimate. $6.35 - 15.512 + 8.744 - 4.19 - 72.7 + 25.008$

Test Prep and Spiral Review

46. **Multiple Choice** Which is the best estimate for $24.976 \div (-4.893)$?

Ⓐ 20   Ⓑ −6   Ⓒ −5   Ⓓ 2

47. **Multiple Choice** Steve is saving \$10.50 from his allowance each week to buy a printer that costs \$150. Which is the best estimate of the number of weeks he will have to save his money until he can buy the printer?

Ⓕ 5 weeks   Ⓖ 10 weeks   Ⓗ 12 weeks   Ⓙ 15 weeks

48. **Short Response** Joe's restaurant bill was \$16.84. He had \$20 in his wallet. Explain how to use rounding to estimate whether Joe had enough money to leave a \$2.75 tip.

Simplify each expression. (Lessons 2-3 and 2-4)

49. $-5 + 4 - 2$
50. $16 \cdot (-3) + 12$
51. $28 - (-2) \cdot (-3)$
52. $-90 - (-6) \cdot (-8)$
53. $-7 - 3 - 1$
54. $-10 \cdot (-5) + 2$

3-2 Adding and Subtracting Decimals

Learn to add and subtract decimals.

One of the coolest summers on record in the Midwest was in 1992. The average summertime temperature that year was 66.8°F. Normally, the average temperature is 4°F higher than it was in 1992.

To find the normal average summertime temperature in the Midwest, you can add 66.8°F and 4°F.

$$\begin{array}{r} 66.8 \\ +\ 4.0 \\ \hline 70.8 \end{array}$$

Use zero as a placeholder so that both numbers have the same number of digits after their decimal points.

Add each column just as you would add integers.

Line up the decimal points.

The normal average summertime temperature in the Midwest is 70.8°F.

EXAMPLE 1 Adding Decimals

Add. Estimate to check whether each answer is reasonable.

A **3.62 + 18.57**

3.62	*Line up the decimal points.*
+ 18.57	
22.19	*Add.*

Estimate

4 + 19 = 23 *22.19 is a reasonable answer.*

B **9 + 3.245**

9.000	*Use zeros as placeholders.*
+ 3.245	*Line up the decimal points.*
12.245	*Add.*

Estimate

9 + 3 = 12 *12.245 is a reasonable answer.*

Remember!

When adding numbers with the same sign, find the sum of their absolute values. Then use the sign of the numbers.

Add. Estimate to check whether each answer is reasonable.

C $-5.78 + (-18.3)$

$-5.78 + (-18.3)$	*Think: 5.78 + 18.3.*
5.78	*Line up the decimal points.*
$+18.30$	*Use zero as a placeholder.*
24.08	*Add.*
$-5.78 + (-18.3) = -24.08$	*Use the sign of the two numbers.*

Estimate

$-6 + (-18) = -24$ *−24.08 is a reasonable answer.*

EXAMPLE 2 **Subtracting Decimals**

Subtract.

A $12.49 - 7.25$

12.49	*Line up the decimal points.*
$-\ 7.25$	
5.24	*Subtract.*

Caution!

You will need to regroup numbers in order to subtract in Example 2B.

B $14 - 7.32$

13 9 10 ~~14.00~~	*Use zeros as placeholders.*
$-\ 7.32$	*Line up the decimal points.*
6.68	*Subtract.*

EXAMPLE 3 ***Transportation Application***

During one month in the United States, 492.23 million commuter trips were taken on buses, and 26.331 million commuter trips were taken on light rail. How many more trips were taken on buses than on light rail? Estimate to check whether your answer is reasonable.

492.230	*Use zero as a placeholder.*
$-\ 26.331$	*Line up the decimal points.*
465.899	*Subtract.*

Estimate

$490 - 30 = 460$ *465.899 is a reasonable answer.*

465.899 million more trips were taken on buses than on light rail.

Think and Discuss

1. **Tell** whether the addition is correct. If it is not, explain why not.

$$\begin{array}{r} 12.3 \\ +\ 4.68 \\ \hline 5.91 \end{array}$$

2. **Describe** how you can check an answer when adding and subtracting decimals.

3-2 Exercises

go.hrw.com
Homework Help Online
KEYWORD: MS7 3-2
Parent Resources Online
KEYWORD: MS7 Parent

GUIDED PRACTICE

See Example 1 **Add. Estimate to check whether each answer is reasonable.**

1. 5.37 + 16.45 **2.** 2.46 + 11.99 **3.** 7 + 5.826 **4.** −5.62 + (−12.9)

See Example 2 **Subtract.**

5. 7.89 − 5.91 **6.** 17 − 4.12 **7.** 4.97 − 3.2 **8.** 9 − 1.03

See Example 3

9. In 1990, international visitors to the United States spent $58.3 billion. In 1999, international visitors spent $95.5 billion. By how much did spending by international visitors increase from 1990 to 1999?

INDEPENDENT PRACTICE

See Example 1 **Add. Estimate to check whether each answer is reasonable.**

10. 7.82 + 31.23 **11.** 5.98 + 12.99 **12.** 4.917 + 12 **13.** −9.82 + (−15.7)

14. 6 + 9.33 **15.** 10.022 + 0.11 **16.** 8 + 1.071 **17.** −3.29 + (−12.6)

See Example 2 **Subtract.**

18. 5.45 − 3.21 **19.** 12.87 − 3.86 **20.** 15.39 − 2.6 **21.** 21.04 − 4.99

22. 5 − 0.53 **23.** 14 − 8.9 **24.** 41 − 9.85 **25.** 33 − 10.23

See Example 3

26. Angela runs her first lap around the track in 4.35 minutes and her second lap in 3.9 minutes. What is her total time for the two laps?

27. A jeweler has 122.83 grams of silver. He uses 45.7 grams of the silver to make a necklace and earrings. How much silver does he have left?

PRACTICE AND PROBLEM SOLVING

Extra Practice
See page 730.

Add or subtract. Estimate to check whether each answer is reasonable.

28. −7.238 + 6.9 **29.** 4.16 − 9.043 **30.** −2.09 − 15.271

31. 5.23 − (−9.1) **32.** −123 − 2.55 **33.** 5.29 − 3.37

34. 32.6 − (−15.86) **35.** −32.7 + 62.82 **36.** −51 + 81.623

37. 5.9 − 10 + 2.84 **38.** −4.2 + 2.3 − 0.7 **39.** −8.3 + 5.38 − 0.537

40. Multi-Step Students at Hill Middle School plan to run a total of 2,462 mi, which is the distance from Los Angeles to New York City. So far, the sixth grade has run 273.5 mi, the seventh grade has run 275.8 mi, and the eighth grade has run 270.2 mi. How many more miles must the students run to reach their goal?

41. Critical Thinking Why must you line up the decimal points when adding and subtracting decimals?

Weather The graph shows the five coolest summers recorded in the Midwest. The average summertime temperature in the Midwest is 70.8°F.

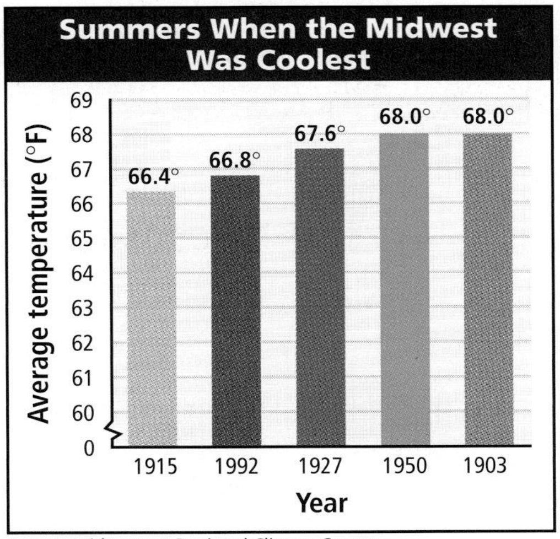

Source: Midwestern Regional Climate Center

LINK Physical Science

Egg-drop competitions challenge students to build devices that will protect eggs when they are dropped from as high as 100 ft.

42. How much warmer was the average summertime temperature in 1950 than in 1915?

43. In what year was the temperature 4.4°F cooler than the average summertime temperature in the Midwest?

44. Physical Science To float in water, an object must have a density of less than 1 gram per milliliter. The density of a fresh egg is about 1.2 grams per milliliter. If the density of a spoiled egg is about 0.3 grams per milliliter less than that of a fresh egg, what is the density of a spoiled egg? How can you use water to tell whether an egg is spoiled?

45. Choose a Strategy How much larger in area is Agua Fria than Pompeys Pillar?

Ⓐ 6.6 thousand acres

Ⓑ 20.1 thousand acres

Ⓒ 70.59 thousand acres

Ⓓ 71.049 thousand acres

National Monument	Area (thousand acres)
Agua Fria	71.1
Pompeys Pillar	0.051

46. Write About It Explain how to find the sum or difference of two decimals.

47. Challenge Find the missing number. $5.11 + 6.9 - 15.3 + \square = 20$

Test Prep and Spiral Review

48. Multiple Choice In the 1900 Olympic Games, the 200-meter dash was won in 22.20 seconds. In 2000, the 200-meter dash was won in 20.09 seconds. How many seconds faster was the winning time in the 2000 Olympics?

Ⓐ 1.10 seconds Ⓑ 2.11 seconds Ⓒ 2.29 seconds Ⓓ 4.83 seconds

49. Multiple Choice John left school with $2.38. He found a quarter on his way home and then stopped to buy a banana for $0.89. How much money did he have when he got home?

Ⓕ $1.24 Ⓖ $1.74 Ⓗ $3.02 Ⓙ $3.52

Solve each equation. Check your answer. (Lesson 2-5)

50. $x - 8 = -22$ **51.** $-3y = -45$ **52.** $\frac{z}{2} = -8$ **53.** $29 = -10 + p$

Estimate. (Lesson 3-1)

54. $15.85 \div 4.01$ **55.** $18.95 + 3.21$ **56.** $44.217 - 19.876$ **57.** $21.43 \cdot 1.57$

Hands-On LAB 3-3

Model Decimal Multiplication

Use with Lesson 3-3

go.hrw.com
Lab Resources Online
KEYWORD: MS7 Lab3

KEY

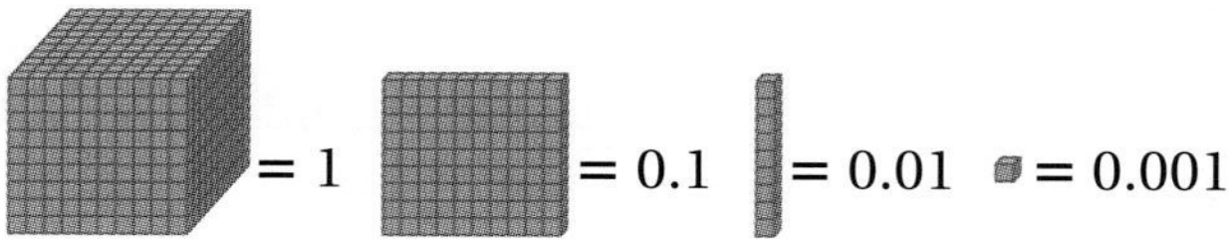

REMEMBER

- When using base-ten blocks, always use the largest value block possible.

You can use base-ten blocks to model multiplying decimals by whole numbers.

Activity 1

1 Use base-ten blocks to find $3 \cdot 0.1$.

Multiplication is repeated addition, so $3 \cdot 0.1 = 0.1 + 0.1 + 0.1$.

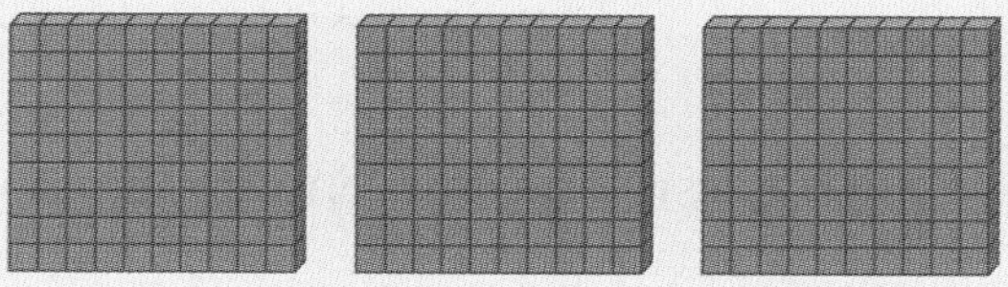

$3 \cdot 0.1 = 0.3$

2 Use base-ten blocks to find $5 \cdot 0.03$.

$5 \cdot 0.03 = 0.03 + 0.03 + 0.03 + 0.03 + 0.03$

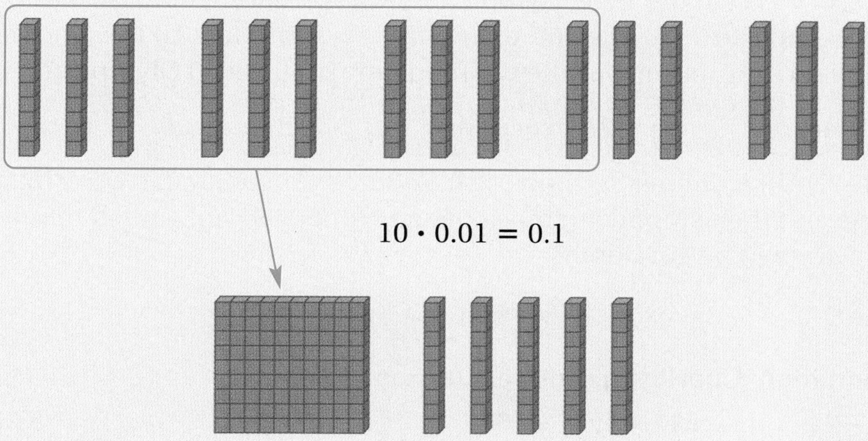

$5 \cdot 0.03 = 0.15$

Think and Discuss

1. Why can't you use base-ten blocks to model multiplying a decimal by a decimal?
2. Is the product of a whole number and a decimal less than or greater than the whole number? Explain.

Try This

Use base-ten blocks to find each product.

1. 4 · 0.5	**2.** 2 · 0.04	**3.** 3 · 0.16	**4.** 6 · 0.2
5. 3 · 0.33	**6.** 0.25 · 5	**7.** 0.42 · 3	**8.** 1.1 · 4

You can use decimal grids to model multiplying decimals by decimals.

Activity 2

1 Use a decimal grid to find 0.4 · 0.7.

Shade **0.4** horizontally. Shade **0.7** vertically. The area where the shaded regions overlap is the answer.

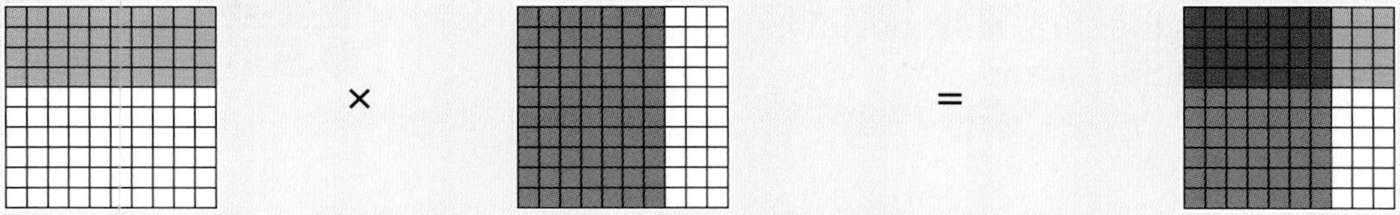

0.4 × 0.7 = 0.28

Think and Discuss

1. Explain the steps you would take to model 0.5 · 0.5 with a decimal grid.
2. How could you use decimal grids to model multiplying a decimal by a whole number?

Try This

Use decimal grids to find each product.

1. 0.6 · 0.6	**2.** 0.5 · 0.4	**3.** 0.3 · 0.8
4. 0.2 · 0.8	**5.** 3 · 0.3	**6.** 0.8 · 0.8
7. 2 · 0.5	**8.** 0.1 · 0.9	**9.** 0.1 · 0.1

3-3 Multiplying Decimals

Learn **to multiply decimals.**

You can use decimal grids to model multiplication of decimals. Each large square represents 1. Each row and column represents 0.1. Each small square represents 0.01. The area where the shading overlaps shows the product of the two decimals.

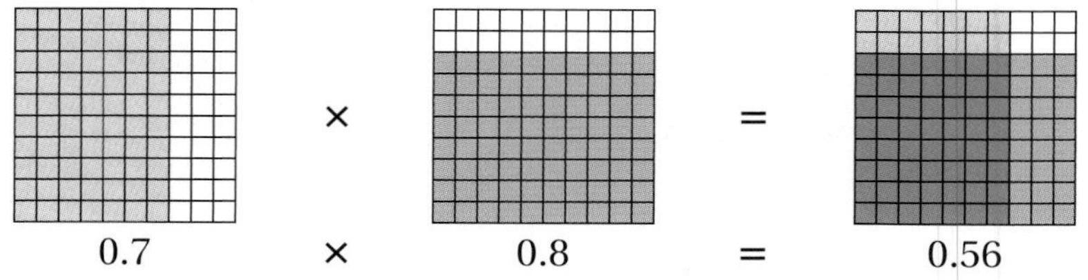

To multiply decimals, multiply as you would with integers. To place the decimal point in the product, count the number of decimal places in each factor. The product should have the same number of decimal places as the sum of the decimal places in the factors.

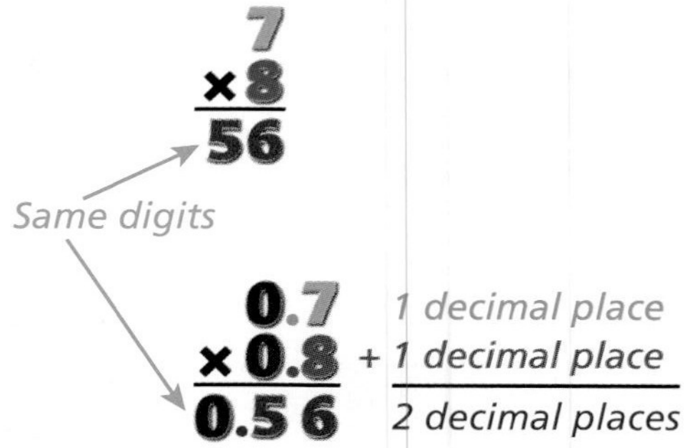

EXAMPLE 1 **Multiplying Integers by Decimals**

Multiply.

A $6 \cdot 0.1$

6	*0 decimal places*
× 0.1	*1 decimal place*
0.6	*0 + 1 = 1 decimal place*

B $-2 \cdot 0.04$

−2	*0 decimal places*
× 0.04	*2 decimal places*
−0.08	*0 + 2 = 2 decimal places. Use zero as a placeholder.*

C $1.25 \cdot 23$

1.25	*2 decimal places*
× 23	*0 decimal places*
3 75	
+ 25 00	
28.75	*2 + 0 = 2 decimal places*

EXAMPLE 2 Multiplying Decimals by Decimals

Multiply. Estimate to check whether each answer is reasonable.

A $1.2 \cdot 1.6$

1.2	*1 decimal place*
$\times\ 1.6$	*1 decimal place*
72	
120	
1.92	*1 + 1 = 2 decimal places*

Estimate

$1 \cdot 2 = 2$ *1.92 is a reasonable answer.*

B $-2.78 \cdot 0.8$

-2.78	*2 decimal places*
$\times\ 0.8$	*1 decimal place*
-2.224	*2 + 1 = 3 decimal places*

Estimate

$-3 \cdot 1 = -3$ *−2.224 is a reasonable answer.*

EXAMPLE 3 *Earth Science Application*

On average, 0.36 kg of carbon dioxide is added to the atmosphere for each mile a single car is driven. How many kilograms of carbon dioxide are added for each mile the 132 million cars in the United States are driven?

132	*0 decimal places*
$\times\ 0.36$	*2 decimal places*
792	
3960	
47.52	*0 + 2 = 2 decimal places*

Estimate

$130 \cdot 0.5 = 65$ *47.52 is a reasonable answer.*

Approximately 47.52 million (47,520,000) kilograms of carbon dioxide are added to the atmosphere for each mile driven.

Think and Discuss

1. Explain whether the multiplication $2.1 \cdot 3.3 = 69.3$ is correct.

2. Compare multiplying integers with multiplying decimals.

3-3 Exercises

go.hrw.com
Homework Help Online
KEYWORD: MS7 3-3
Parent Resources Online
KEYWORD: MS7 Parent

GUIDED PRACTICE

See Example 1

Multiply.

1. $-9 \cdot 0.4$ **2.** $3 \cdot 0.2$ **3.** $0.06 \cdot 3$ **4.** $-0.5 \cdot 2$

See Example 2

Multiply. Estimate to check whether each answer is reasonable.

5. $1.7 \cdot 1.2$ **6.** $2.6 \cdot 0.4$ **7.** $1.5 \cdot (-0.21)$ **8.** $-0.4 \cdot 1.17$

See Example 3

9. If Carla is able to drive her car 24.03 miles on one gallon of gas, how far could she drive on 13.93 gallons of gas?

INDEPENDENT PRACTICE

See Example 1

Multiply.

10. $8 \cdot 0.6$ **11.** $5 \cdot 0.07$ **12.** $-3 \cdot 2.7$ **13.** $0.8 \cdot 4$

14. $6 \cdot 4.9$ **15.** $1.7 \cdot (-12)$ **16.** $43 \cdot 2.11$ **17.** $-7 \cdot (-1.3)$

See Example 2

Multiply. Estimate to check whether each answer is reasonable.

18. $2.4 \cdot 3.2$ **19.** $2.8 \cdot 1.6$ **20.** $5.3 \cdot 4.6$ **21.** $4.02 \cdot 0.7$

22. $-5.14 \cdot 0.03$ **23.** $1.04 \cdot (-8.9)$ **24.** $4.31 \cdot (-9.5)$ **25.** $-6.1 \cdot (-1.01)$

See Example 3

26. Nicholas bicycled 15.8 kilometers each day for 18 days last month. How many kilometers did he bicycle last month?

27. While walking, Lara averaged 3.63 miles per hour. How far did she walk in 1.5 hours?

PRACTICE AND PROBLEM SOLVING

Extra Practice
See page 730.

Multiply. Estimate to check whether each answer is reasonable.

28. $-9.6 \cdot 2.05$ **29.** $0.07 \cdot 0.03$ **30.** $4 \cdot 4.15$

31. $-1.08 \cdot (-0.4)$ **32.** $1.46 \cdot (-0.06)$ **33.** $-3.2 \cdot 0.9$

34. $-325.9 \cdot 1.5$ **35.** $14.7 \cdot 0.13$ **36.** $-28.5 \cdot (-1.07)$

37. $-7.02 \cdot (-0.05)$ **38.** $1.104 \cdot (-0.7)$ **39.** $0.072 \cdot 0.12$

40. Multi-Step Bo earns $8.95 per hour plus commission. Last week, he worked 32.5 hours and earned $28.75 in commission. How much money did Bo earn last week?

41. Weather As a hurricane increases in intensity, the air pressure within its eye decreases. In a Category 5 hurricane, which is the most intense, the air pressure measures approximately 27.16 inches of mercury. In a Category 1 hurricane, which is the least intense, the air pressure is about 1.066 times that of a Category 5 hurricane. What is the air pressure within the eye of a Category 1 hurricane? Round your answer to the nearest hundredth.

42. **Estimation** The graph shows the results of a survey about river recreation activities.

a. A report claimed that about 3 times as many people enjoyed canoeing in 1999–2000 than in 1994–1995. According to the graph, is this claim reasonable?

b. Suppose a future survey shows that 6 times as many people enjoyed kayaking in 2009–2010 than in 1999–2000. About how many people reported that they enjoyed kayaking in 2009–2010?

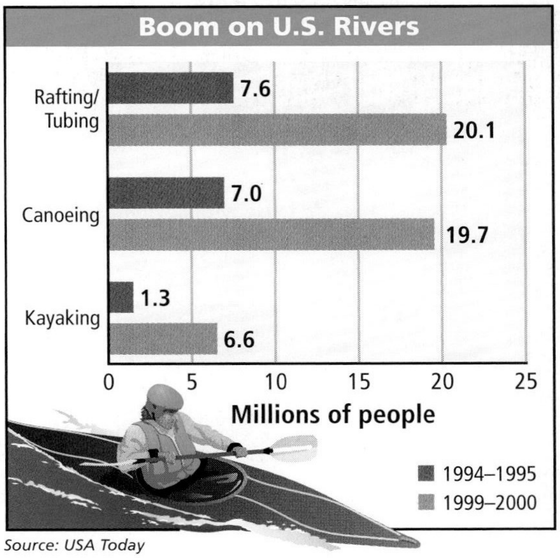

Source: USA Today

Multiply. Estimate to check whether each answer is reasonable.

43. 0.3 · 2.8 · (−10.6)

44. 1.3 · (−4.2) · (−3.94)

45. 0.6 · (−0.9) · 0.05

46. −6.5 · (−1.02) · (−12.6)

47. −22.08 · (−5.6) · 9.9

48. −63.75 · 13.46 · 7.8

49. What's the Question? In a collection, each rock sample has a mass of 4.35 kilograms. There are a dozen rocks in the collection. If the answer is 52.2 kilograms, what is the question?

50. Write About It How do the products 4.3 · 0.56 and 0.43 · 5.6 compare? Explain.

51. Challenge Evaluate $(0.2)^5$.

Test Prep and Spiral Review

52. Multiple Choice Which expression is equal to −4.3?

Ⓐ 0.8 · (−5.375) Ⓑ −1.2 · (−3.6) Ⓒ −0.75 · 5.6 Ⓓ 2.2 · (−1.9)

53. Gridded Response Julia walked 1.8 mi each day from Monday through Friday. On Saturday, she walked 2.3 mi. How many miles did she walk in all?

Write the prime factorization of each number. (Lesson 2-6)

54. 20 **55.** 35 **56.** 120 **57.** 64

Add or subtract. Estimate to check whether each answer is reasonable. (Lesson 3-2)

58. −4.875 + 3.62 **59.** 5.83 − (−2.74) **60.** 6.32 + (−3.62) **61.** −8.34 − (−4.6)

62. 9.3 + 5.88 **63.** 32.08 − 12.37 **64.** 19 − 6.92 **65.** −75.25 + 6.382

Hands-On LAB 3-4

Model Decimal Division

Use with Lessons 3-4 and 3-5

go.hrw.com
Lab Resources Online
KEYWORD: MS7 Lab3

KEY

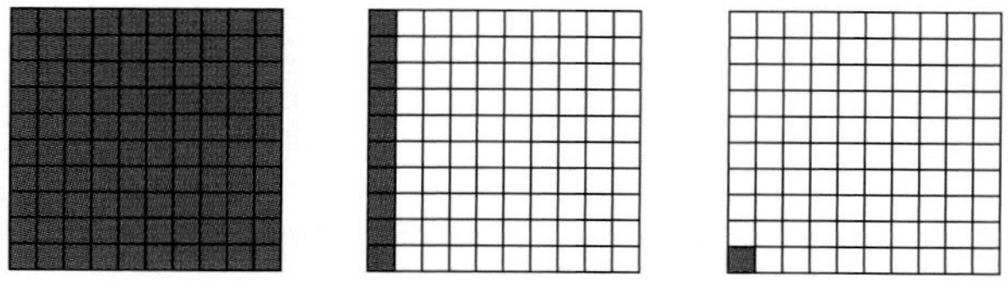

1	0.1	0.01
one	1 tenth	1 hundredth

You can use decimal grids to model dividing decimals by integers and by decimals.

Activity

1 Use a decimal grid to find $0.6 \div 2$.

Shade 6 columns to represent 0.6.

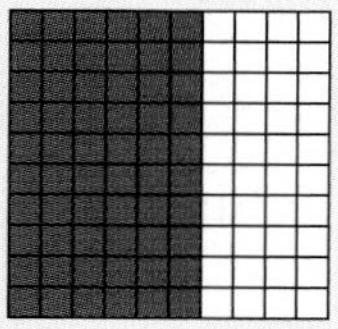

Divide the 6 columns into 2 equal groups.

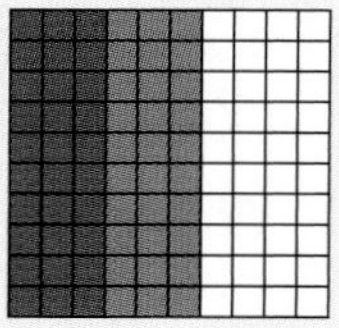

There are 3 columns, or 30 squares, in each group. 3 columns = 0.3

$0.6 \div 2 = 0.3$

2 Use decimal grids to find $2.25 \div 5$.

Shade 2 grids and 25 squares of a third grid to represent 2.25.

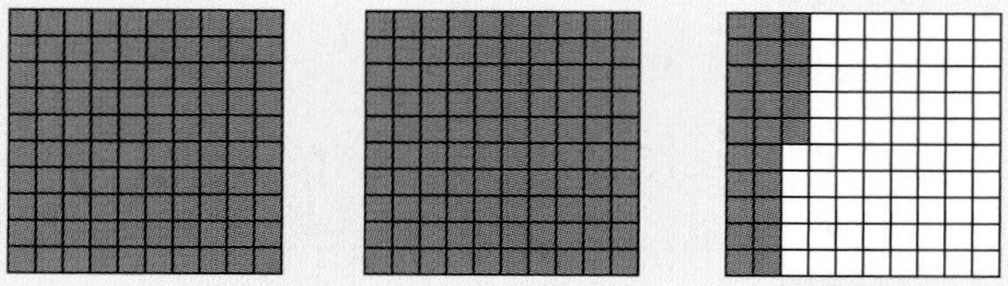

Divide the grids and squares into 5 equal groups. Use scissors to cut apart the grids. Think: 225 squares ÷ 5 = 45 squares.

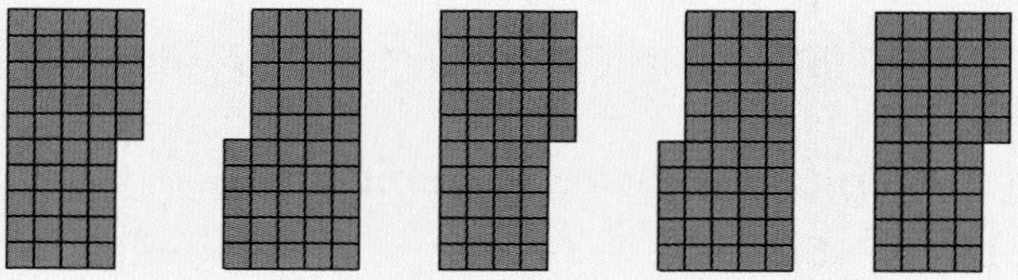

There are 45 squares, or 4.5 columns, in each group. 4.5 columns = 0.45

$2.25 \div 5 = 0.45$

3 Use decimal grids to find 0.8 ÷ 0.4.

Shade 8 columns to represent 0.8.

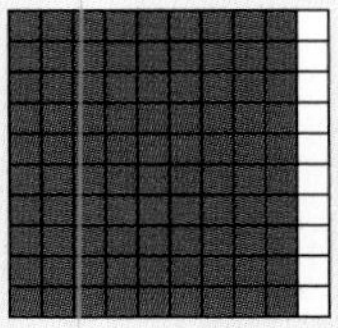

Divide the 8 columns into groups that each contain 0.4 of a decimal grid, or 4 columns.

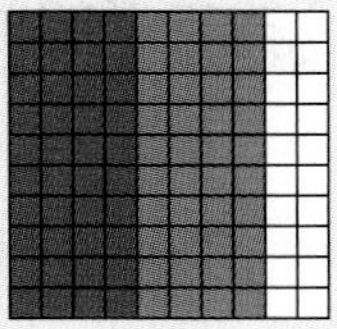

There are 2 groups that each contain 0.4 of a grid.

0.8 ÷ 0.4 = 2

4 Use decimal grids to find 3.9 ÷ 1.3.

Shade 3 grids and 90 squares of a fourth grid to represent 3.9.

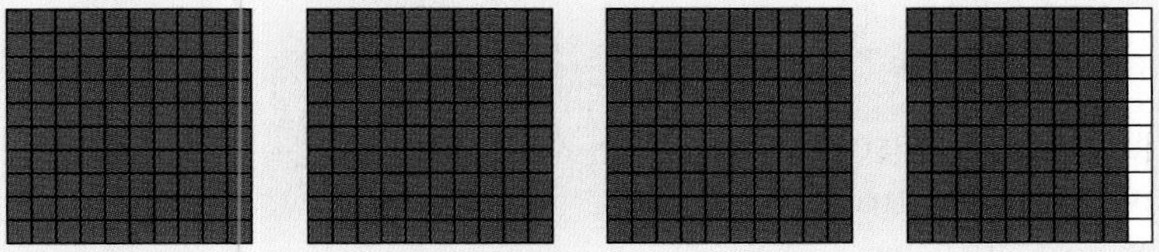

Divide the grids and squares into groups that each contain 1.3 of a decimal grid, or 13 columns.

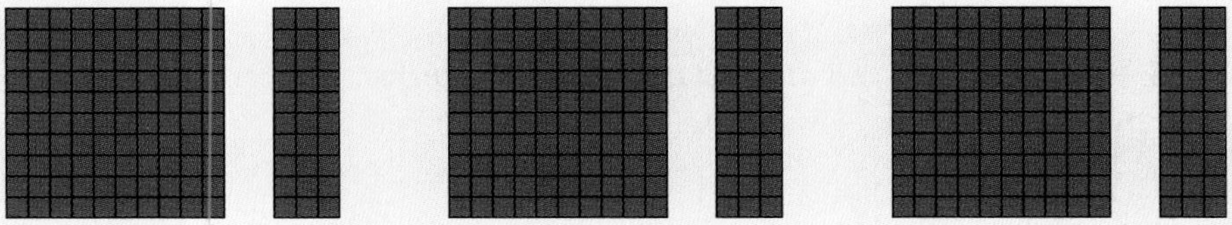

There are 3 groups that each contain 1.3 grids.

3.9 ÷ 1.3 = 3

Think and Discuss

1. Explain why you think division is or is not commutative.

2. How is dividing a decimal by a whole number different from dividing a decimal by another decimal?

Try This

Use decimal grids to find each quotient.

1. 0.8 ÷ 4 **2.** 0.6 ÷ 4 **3.** 0.9 ÷ 0.3 **4.** 0.6 ÷ 0.4

5. 4.5 ÷ 9 **6.** 1.35 ÷ 3 **7.** 3.6 ÷ 1.2 **8.** 4.2 ÷ 2.1

3-4 Dividing Decimals by Integers

Learn to divide decimals by integers.

Elena received scores of 6.85, 6.95, 7.2, 7.1, and 6.9 on the balance beam at a gymnastics meet. To find her average score, add her scores and then divide by 5.

$6.85 + 6.95 + 7.2 + 7.1 + 6.9 = 35$

$35 \div 5 = 7$

Elena's average score was 7, or 7.0.

Notice that the sum of Elena's scores is an integer. But what if the sum is not an integer? You can find the average score by dividing a decimal by a whole number.

Remember!

Division can undo multiplication.
$0.2 \cdot 4 = 0.8$ and
$0.8 \div 4 = 0.2$

$0.8 \div 4$ — *0.8 divided into 4 equal groups.*

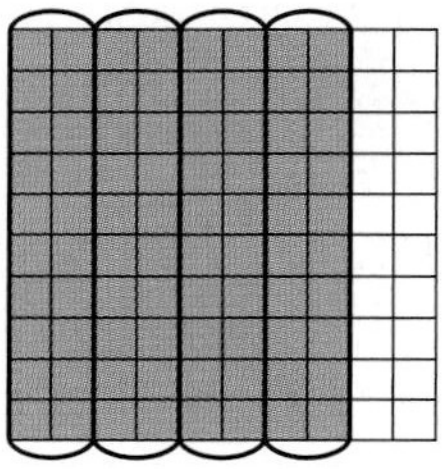

$0.8 \div 4 = 0.2$ — *The size of each group is the answer. Each group is 2 columns, or 0.2.*

EXAMPLE 1 Dividing Decimals by Integers

Remember!

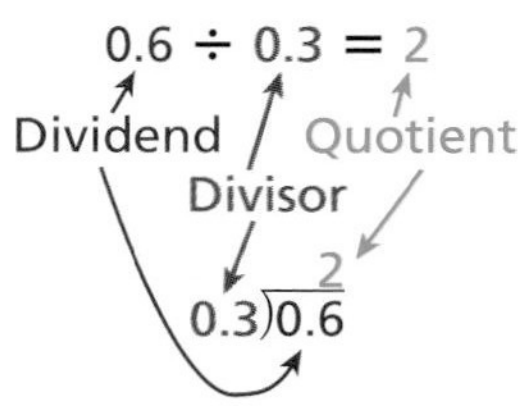

Divide. Estimate to check whether each answer is reasonable.

A **48.78 ÷ 6**

```
   8.13
6)48.78
 -48
   0 7
   -6
    18
   -18
     0
```

Place the decimal point in the quotient directly above the decimal point in the dividend.

Divide as with whole numbers.

Estimate

$48 \div 6 = 8$ — *8.13 is a reasonable answer.*

Remember!

When you divide two numbers with different signs, the quotient is negative.

Divide. Estimate to check whether each answer is reasonable.

B $0.18 \div 2$

$$\begin{array}{r} 0.09 \\ 2\overline{)0.18} \\ -18 \\ \hline 0 \end{array}$$

Place the decimal point in the quotient directly above the decimal point in the dividend. Add a zero as a placeholder in the quotient.

Estimate

$0.2 \div 2 = 0.1$ *0.09 is a reasonable answer.*

C $71.06 \div (-34)$

$$\begin{array}{r} 2.09 \\ 34\overline{)71.06} \\ -68 \\ \hline 3\ 06 \\ -3\ 06 \\ \hline 0 \end{array}$$

The signs are different. Think: 71.06 ÷ 34. Place the decimal point in the quotient directly above the decimal point in the dividend.

$71.06 \div (-34) = -2.09$

Estimate

$68 \div (-34) = -2$ *–2.09 is a reasonable answer.*

EXAMPLE 2 *Money Application*

For Mrs. Deece's birthday, her class bought her a pendant for \$76.50 and a card for \$2.25. If there are 25 students in the class, what is the average amount each student paid for the gift?

First find the total cost of the gift. Then divide by the number of students.

$76.50 + 2.25 = 78.75$ *The gift cost a total of \$78.75.*

$$\begin{array}{r} 3.15 \\ 25\overline{)78.75} \\ -75 \\ \hline 3\ 7 \\ -2\ 5 \\ \hline 1\ 25 \\ -1\ 25 \\ \hline 0 \end{array}$$

Place the decimal point in the quotient directly above the decimal point in the dividend.

Each student paid an average of \$3.15 for the gift.

Think and Discuss

1. Describe how to place the decimal point in the quotient when you divide a decimal by an integer.

2. Explain how to divide a positive decimal by a negative integer.

3-4 Exercises

GUIDED PRACTICE

See Example 1

Divide. Estimate to check whether each answer is reasonable.

1. $42.98 \div 7$ **2.** $24.48 \div 8$ **3.** $64.89 \div (-21)$

4. $-94.72 \div 37$ **5.** $0.136 \div 8$ **6.** $1.404 \div 6$

See Example 2

7. Hobbies Members of a reading group order books for \$89.10 and bookmarks for \$10.62. If there are 18 people in the reading group, how much does each person owe on average?

INDEPENDENT PRACTICE

See Example 1

Divide. Estimate to check whether each answer is reasonable.

8. $12.8 \div 4$ **9.** $80.1 \div (-9)$ **10.** $14.58 \div 3$

11. $-62.44 \div 7$ **12.** $7.2 \div 12$ **13.** $33.6 \div (-7)$

14. $0.108 \div 6$ **15.** $65.28 \div 32$ **16.** $-0.152 \div 8$

17. $21.47 \div 19$ **18.** $0.148 \div 4$ **19.** $79.82 \div (-26)$

See Example 2

20. Cheryl ran three laps during her physical education class. If her times were 1.23 minutes, 1.04 minutes, and 1.18 minutes, what was her average lap time?

21. Consumer Math Randall spent \$61.25 on some CDs and a set of headphones. All of the CDs were on sale for the same price. The set of headphones cost \$12.50. If he bought 5 CDs, what was the sale price of each CD?

22. In qualifying for an auto race, one driver had lap speeds of 195.3 mi/h, 190.456 mi/h, 193.557 mi/h, and 192.575 mi/h. What was the driver's average speed for these four laps?

PRACTICE AND PROBLEM SOLVING

Extra Practice
See page 730.

Divide. Estimate to check whether each answer is reasonable.

23. $-9.36 \div (-6)$ **24.** $48.1 \div (-13)$ **25.** $20.95 \div 5$

26. $0.84 \div 12$ **27.** $-39.2 \div 14$ **28.** $9.45 \div (-9)$

29. $47.75 \div (-25)$ **30.** $-94.86 \div (-31)$ **31.** $-0.399 \div 21$

Simplify each expression.

32. $0.29 + 18.6 \div 3$ **33.** $1.1 - 7.28 \div 4 + 0.9$

34. $(19.2 \div 16)^2$ **35.** $-63.93 \cdot (-12.3) \div (-3)$

36. $-2.7 \div 9 \div 12$ **37.** $5 \cdot [-99.25 \div (-5)] \cdot 20$

38. Multi-Step A ticket broker bought two dozen concert tickets for \$455.76. To resell the tickets, he will include a service charge of \$3.80 for each ticket. What is the resale price of each ticket?

39. **Recreation** The graph shows the number of visitors to the three most visited U.S. national parks in 2000. What was the average number of visitors to these three parks? Round your answer to the nearest hundredth.

40. **Nutrition** On average, each American consumed 261.1 lb of red meat and poultry in 2000. How many pounds of red meat and poultry did the average American eat during each month of 2000? Round your answer to the nearest tenth.

41. **Critical Thinking** Explain why using estimation to check the answer to $56.21457 \div 7$ is useful.

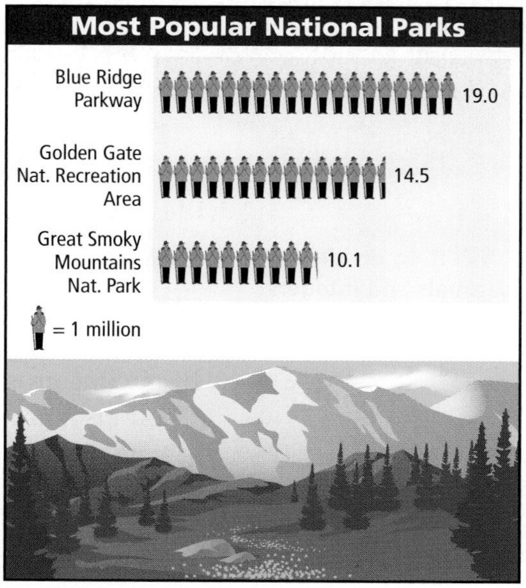

Source: USA Today

42. **Write a Problem** Find some supermarket advertisements. Use the ads to write a problem that can be solved by dividing a decimal by a whole number.

43. **Write About It** Compare dividing integers by integers with dividing decimals by integers.

44. **Challenge** Use a calculator to simplify the expression $(2^3 \cdot 7.5 + 3.69) \div 48.25 \div [1.04 - (0.08 \cdot 2)]$.

Test Prep and Spiral Review

45. **Multiple Choice** Which expression is NOT equal to -1.34?

Ⓐ $-6.7 \div 5$ Ⓑ $16.08 \div (-12)$ Ⓒ $-12.06 \div (-9)$ Ⓓ $-22.78 \div 17$

46. **Multiple Choice** Simplify $-102.45 \div (-15)$.

Ⓕ -8.25 Ⓖ -7.37 Ⓗ 5.46 Ⓙ 6.83

47. **Gridded Response** Rujuta spent a total of \$49.65 on 5 CDs. What was the average cost per CD?

Simplify each expression. (Lesson 1-5)

48. $2 + 6 \cdot 2$
49. $3^2 - 8 \cdot 0$
50. $(2 - 1)^5 + 3 \cdot 2^2$
51. $10 - (5 - 3)^2 + 4 \div 2$
52. $2^5 \div (7 + 1)$
53. $6 - 2 \cdot 3 + 5$

Multiply. Estimate to check whether each answer is reasonable. (Lesson 3-3)

54. $-2.75 \cdot 6.34$
55. $0.2 \cdot (-4.6) \cdot (-2.3)$
56. $1.3 \cdot (-6.7)$
57. $-6.87 \cdot (-2.65)$
58. $9 \cdot 4.26$
59. $7.13 \cdot (-14)$

3-5 Dividing Decimals and Integers by Decimals

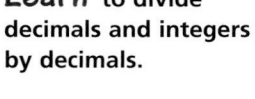

Learn to divide decimals and integers by decimals.

How many groups of 0.3 are in 0.6?

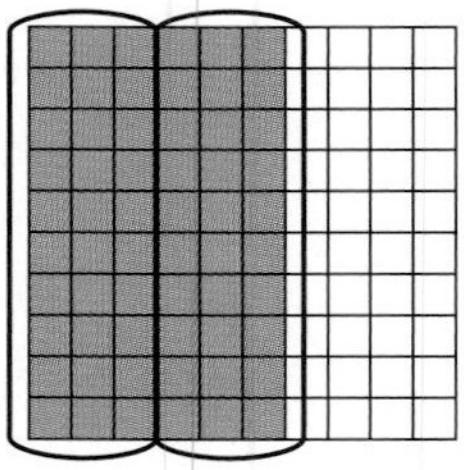

This problem is equivalent to $0.6 \div 0.3$. You can use a grid to model this division by circling groups of 0.3 and counting the number of groups.

There are 2 groups of 0.3 in 0.6, so $0.6 \div 0.3 = 2$.

When you divide two numbers, you can multiply *both numbers* by the same power of ten without changing the final answer.

Multiply both 0.6 and 0.3 by 10: $\mathbf{0.6 \cdot 10 = 6}$ and $\mathbf{0.3 \cdot 10 = 3}$

$$\mathbf{0.6 \div 0.3 = 2} \quad \text{and} \quad \mathbf{6 \div 3 = 2}$$

By multiplying both numbers by the same power of ten, you can make the divisor an integer. Dividing by an integer is much easier than dividing by a decimal.

EXAMPLE 1 Dividing Decimals by Decimals

Helpful Hint

Multiply both numbers by the least power of ten that will make the divisor an integer.

Divide.

A $\mathbf{4.32 \div 3.6}$

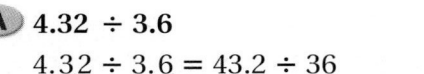

$4.32 \div 3.6 = 43.2 \div 36$ — *Multiply both numbers by 10 to make the divisor an integer.*

$$\begin{array}{r} 1.2 \\ 36\overline{)43.2} \\ -36 \\ \hline 7\,2 \\ -7\,2 \\ \hline 0 \end{array}$$

Divide as with whole numbers.

B $\mathbf{12.95 \div (-1.25)}$

$12.95 \div (-1.25) = 1295 \div (-125)$ — *Multiply both numbers by 100 to make the divisor an integer.*

$$\begin{array}{r} 10.36 \\ 125\overline{)1{,}295.00} \\ -1\,25 \\ \hline 45\,0 \\ -37\,5 \\ \hline 7\,50 \\ -7\,50 \\ \hline 0 \end{array}$$

Use zeros as placeholders.
Divide as with whole numbers.

$12.95 \div (-1.25) = -10.36$ — *The signs are different.*

EXAMPLE 2 Dividing Integers by Decimals

Divide. Estimate to check whether each answer is reasonable.

A $9 \div 1.25$

$9.00 \div 1.25 = 900 \div 125$ — *Multiply both numbers by 100 to make the divisor an integer.*

$$\begin{array}{r} 7.2 \\ 125\overline{)900.0} \\ -875 \\ \hline 25\ 0 \\ -25\ 0 \\ \hline 0 \end{array}$$

Use zero as a placeholder. Divide as with whole numbers.

Estimate $9 \div 1 = 9$ — *7.2 is a reasonable answer.*

B $-12 \div (-1.6)$

$-12.0 \div (-1.6) = -120 \div (-16)$ — *Multiply both numbers by 10 to make the divisor an integer.*

$$\begin{array}{r} 7.5 \\ 16\overline{)120.0} \\ -112 \\ \hline 8\ 0 \\ -8\ 0 \\ \hline 0 \end{array}$$

Divide as with whole numbers.

$-12 \div (-1.6) = 7.5$ — *The signs are the same.*

Estimate $-12 \div (-2) = 6$ — *7.5 is a reasonable answer.*

EXAMPLE 3 *Transportation Application*

If Sandy used 15.45 gallons of gas to drive her car 370.8 miles, how many miles per gallon did she get?

$370.80 \div 15.45 = 37{,}080 \div 1{,}545$ — *Multiply both numbers by 100 to make the divisor an integer.*

$$\begin{array}{r} 24 \\ 1{,}545\overline{)37{,}080} \\ -30\ 90 \\ \hline 6\ 180 \\ -6\ 180 \\ \hline 0 \end{array}$$

Divide as with whole numbers.

Sandy got 24 miles per gallon.

Helpful Hint

To calculate miles per gallon, divide the number of miles driven by the number of gallons of gas used.

Think and Discuss

1. **Explain** whether $4.27 \div 0.7$ is the same as $427 \div 7$.
2. **Explain** how to divide an integer by a decimal.

3-5 Exercises

go.hrw.com
Homework Help Online
KEYWORD: MS7 3-5
Parent Resources Online
KEYWORD: MS7 Parent

GUIDED PRACTICE

See Example 1

Divide.

1. $3.78 \div 4.2$ **2.** $13.3 \div (-0.38)$ **3.** $14.49 \div 3.15$

4. $1.06 \div 0.2$ **5.** $-9.76 \div 3.05$ **6.** $263.16 \div (-21.5)$

See Example 2

Divide. Estimate to check whether each answer is reasonable.

7. $3 \div 1.2$ **8.** $84 \div 2.4$ **9.** $36 \div (-2.25)$

10. $24 \div (-1.2)$ **11.** $-18 \div 3.75$ **12.** $189 \div 8.4$

See Example 3

13. Transportation Samuel used 14.35 gallons of gas to drive his car 401.8 miles. How many miles per gallon did he get?

INDEPENDENT PRACTICE

See Example 1

Divide.

14. $81.27 \div 0.03$ **15.** $-0.408 \div 3.4$ **16.** $38.5 \div (-5.5)$

17. $-1.12 \div 0.08$ **18.** $27.82 \div 2.6$ **19.** $14.7 \div 3.5$

See Example 2

Divide. Estimate to check whether each answer is reasonable.

20. $35 \div (-2.5)$ **21.** $361 \div 7.6$ **22.** $63 \div (-4.2)$

23. $5 \div 1.25$ **24.** $14 \div 2.5$ **25.** $-78 \div 1.6$

See Example 3

26. Transportation Lonnie used 26.75 gallons of gas to drive his truck 508.25 miles. How many miles per gallon did he get?

27. Mitchell walked 8.5 laps in 20.4 minutes. If he walked each lap at the same pace, how long did it take him to walk one full lap?

PRACTICE AND PROBLEM SOLVING

Extra Practice
See page 731.

Divide. Estimate to check whether each answer is reasonable.

28. $-24 \div 0.32$ **29.** $153 \div 6.8$ **30.** $-2.58 \div (-4.3)$

31. $4.12 \div (-10.3)$ **32.** $-17.85 \div 17$ **33.** $64 \div 2.56$

Simplify each expression.

34. $-4.2 + (11.5 \div 4.6) - 5.8$ **35.** $2 \cdot (6.8 \div 3.4) \cdot 5$

36. $(6.4 \div 2.56) - 1.2 - 2.5$ **37.** $11.7 \div (0.7 + 0.6) \cdot 2$

38. $4 \cdot (0.6 + 0.78) \cdot 0.25$ **39.** $(1.6 \div 3.2) \cdot (4.2 + 8.6)$

40. Critical Thinking A car loan totaling $13,456.44 is to be paid off in 36 equal monthly payments. Lin Yao can afford no more than $350 per month. Can she afford the loan? Explain.

Earth Science LINK

41. Glaciers form when snow accumulates faster than it melts and thus becomes compacted into ice under the weight of more snow. Once the ice reaches a thickness of about 18 m, it begins to flow. If ice were to accumulate at a rate of 0.0072 m per year, how long would it take to start flowing?

42. An alpine glacier is estimated to be flowing at a rate of 4.75 m per day. At this rate, how long will it take for a marker placed on the glacier by a researcher to move 1,140 m?

A glacier in Col Ferret, a pass in the Swiss Alps

43. If the Muir Glacier in Glacier Bay, Alaska, retreats at an average speed of 0.73 m per year, how long will it take to retreat a total of 7.9 m? Round your answer to the nearest year.

44. **Multi-Step** The table shows the thickness of a glacier as measured at five different points using radar. What is the average thickness of the glacier?

Location	Thickness (m)
A	180.23
B	160.5
C	210.19
D	260
E	200.22

45. The Harvard Glacier in Alaska is advancing at a rate of about 0.055 m per day. At this rate, how long will it take the glacier to advance 20 m? Round your answer to the nearest hundredth.

46. **Challenge** Hinman Glacier, on Mount Hinman, in Washington State, had an area of 1.3 km^2 in 1958. The glacier has lost an average of 0.06875 km^2 of area each year. In what year was the total area 0.2 km^2?

go.hrw.com
Web Extra!
KEYWORD: MS7 Ice

TEST PREP and Spiral Review

47. **Multiple Choice** Simplify $-4.42 \div 2.6 - 4.6$.

(A) -6.3 (B) -2.9 (C) 1.4 (D) 5.7

48. **Multiple Choice** A deli is selling 5 sandwiches for $5.55, including tax. A school spent $83.25 on roast beef sandwiches for its 25 football players. How many sandwiches did each player get?

(F) 1 (G) 2 (H) 3 (J) 5

Write each decimal or improper fraction as a mixed number. (Lessons 2-9 and 2-10)

49. $\frac{28}{3}$ 50. 6.29 51. $\frac{17}{5}$ 52. 5.7

Simplify each expression. (Lesson 3-4)

53. $6.3 + (-2.5) \div 2$ 54. $-5.38 \cdot 2.6 \div 4$ 55. $16.2 \div (-6)$ 56. $5.6 - 3.2 \div 2$

3-6 Solving Equations Containing Decimals

Learn to solve one-step equations that contain decimals.

Students in a physical education class were running 40-yard dashes as part of a fitness test. The slowest time in the class was 3.84 seconds slower than the fastest time of 7.2 seconds.

You can write an equation to represent this situation. The slowest time s minus 3.84 is equal to the fastest time of 7.2 seconds.

$$s - 3.84 = 7.2$$

EXAMPLE 1 Solving Equations by Adding or Subtracting

Remember!

You can solve an equation by performing the same operation on both sides of the equation to isolate the variable.

Solve.

A $\mathbf{s - 3.84 = 7.2}$

$$\begin{aligned} s - 3.84 &= 7.20 \\ \underline{+\,3.84} &\quad \underline{+\;3.84} \\ s \quad &= 11.04 \end{aligned}$$

Add to isolate s.

B $\mathbf{y + 20.51 = 26}$

$$\begin{aligned} y + 20.51 &= 2\overset{5}{\not{6}}.\overset{9}{\not{0}}\overset{10}{\not{0}} \\ \underline{-\,20.51} &\quad \underline{-\,20.51} \\ y \quad &= 5.49 \end{aligned}$$

Subtract to isolate y.

EXAMPLE 2 Solving Equations by Multiplying or Dividing

Solve.

A $\mathbf{\frac{w}{3.9} = 1.2}$

$$\frac{w}{3.9} = 1.2$$

$$\frac{w}{3.9} \cdot \mathbf{3.9} = 1.2 \cdot \mathbf{3.9}$$ *Multiply to isolate w.*

$$w = 4.68$$

B $\mathbf{4 = 1.6c}$

$$4 = 1.6c$$

$$\frac{4}{\mathbf{1.6}} = \frac{1.6c}{\mathbf{1.6}}$$ *Divide to isolate c.*

$$\frac{4}{1.6} = c$$ *Think: 4 ÷ 1.6 = 40 ÷ 16.*

$$2.5 = c$$

Focus on Problem Solving

Look Back

- **Does your solution answer the question in the problem?**

Sometimes, before you solve a problem, you first need to use the given data to find additional information. Any time you find a solution for a problem, you should ask yourself if your solution answers the question being asked, or if it just gives you the information you need to find the final answer.

Read each problem, and determine whether the given solution answers the question in the problem. Explain your answer.

1. At one store, a new CD costs $15.99. At a second store, the same CD costs 0.75 as much. About how much does the second store charge?

   Solution: The second store charges about $12.00.

2. Bobbie is 1.4 feet shorter than her older sister. If Bobbie's sister is 5.5 feet tall, how tall is Bobbie?

   Solution:
   Bobbie is 4.1 feet tall.

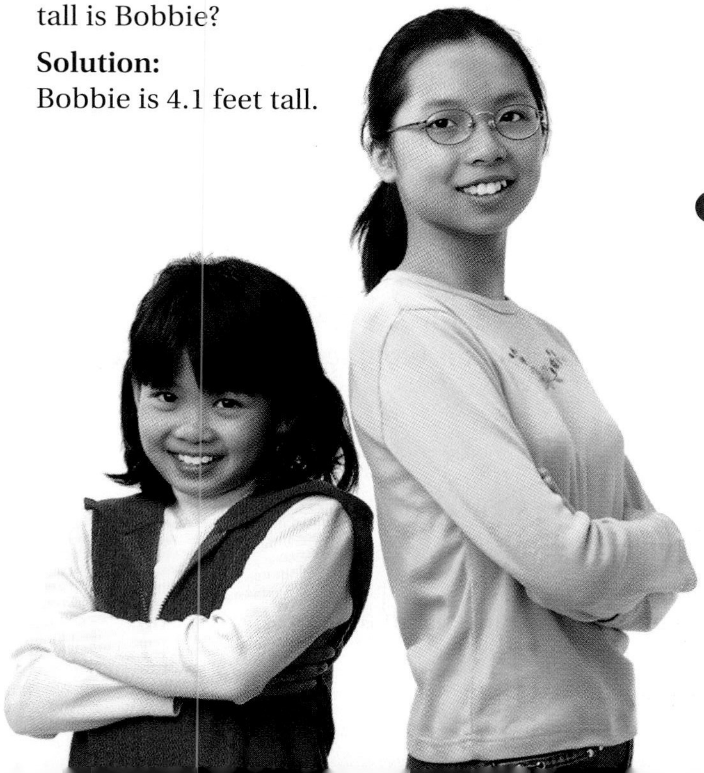

3. Juanita ran the 100-yard dash 1.12 seconds faster than Kellie. Kellie's time was 0.8 seconds faster than Rachel's. If Rachel's time was 15.3 seconds, what was Juanita's time?

   Solution: Kellie's time was 14.5 seconds.

4. The playscape at a local park is located in a triangular sandpit. Side A of the sandpit is 2 meters longer than side B. Side B is twice as long as side C. If side C is 6 meters long, how long is side A?

   Solution: Side B is 12 meters long.

5. Both Tyrone and Albert walk to and from school every day. Albert has to walk 1.25 miles farther than Tyrone does each way. If Tyrone's house is 0.6 mi from school, how far do the two boys walk altogether?

   Solution: Albert lives 1.85 mi from school.

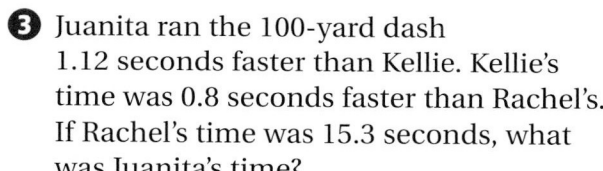

3-7 Estimate with Fractions

Problem Solving Skill

Learn to estimate sums, differences, products, and quotients of fractions and mixed numbers.

One of the largest lobsters ever caught was found off the coast of Nova Scotia, Canada, and weighed $44\frac{3}{8}$ lb. About how much heavier was this than an average lobster, which may weigh $3\frac{1}{4}$ lb?

Sometimes, when solving problems, you may not need an exact answer. To estimate sums and differences of fractions and mixed numbers, round each fraction to 0, $\frac{1}{2}$, or 1. You can use a number line to help.

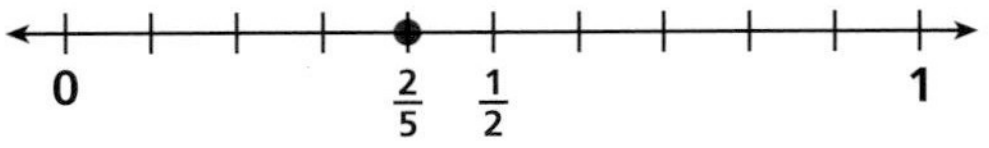

$\frac{2}{5}$ is closer to $\frac{1}{2}$ than to 0.

You can also round fractions by comparing numerators with denominators.

Benchmarks for Rounding Fractions		
Round to **0** if the numerator is much smaller than the denominator. Examples: $\frac{1}{9}, \frac{3}{20}, \frac{2}{11}$	Round to $\mathbf{\frac{1}{2}}$ if the numerator is about half the denominator. Examples: $\frac{2}{5}, \frac{5}{12}, \frac{7}{13}$	Round to **1** if the numerator is nearly equal to the denominator. Examples: $\frac{8}{9}, \frac{23}{25}, \frac{97}{100}$

EXAMPLE 1 ***Measurement Application***

One of the largest lobsters ever caught weighed $44\frac{3}{8}$ lb. Estimate how much more this lobster weighed than an average $3\frac{1}{4}$ lb lobster.

$44\frac{3}{8} - 3\frac{1}{4}$

$44\frac{3}{8} \longrightarrow 44\frac{1}{2}$ $\quad 3\frac{1}{4} \longrightarrow 3\frac{1}{2}$ *Round each mixed number.*

$44\frac{1}{2} - 3\frac{1}{2} = 41$ *Subtract.*

The lobster weighed about 41 lb more than an average lobster.

Helpful Hint

Round $\frac{1}{4}$ to $\frac{1}{2}$, round $\frac{1}{3}$ to $\frac{1}{2}$, and round $\frac{3}{4}$ to 1.

EXAMPLE 2 Estimating Sums and Differences

Estimate each sum or difference.

A $\frac{4}{7} - \frac{13}{16}$

$\frac{4}{7} \longrightarrow \frac{1}{2}$ $\quad \frac{13}{16} \longrightarrow 1$ *Round each fraction.*

$\frac{1}{2} - 1 = -\frac{1}{2}$ *Subtract.*

B $3\frac{3}{8} + 3\frac{1}{3}$

$3\frac{3}{8} \longrightarrow 3\frac{1}{2}$ $\quad 3\frac{1}{3} \longrightarrow 3\frac{1}{2}$ *Round each mixed number.*

$3\frac{1}{2} + 3\frac{1}{2} = 7$ *Add.*

C $5\frac{7}{8} + \left(-\frac{2}{5}\right)$

$5\frac{7}{8} \longrightarrow 6$ $\quad -\frac{2}{5} \longrightarrow -\frac{1}{2}$ *Round each number.*

$6 + \left(-\frac{1}{2}\right) = 5\frac{1}{2}$ *Add.*

Helpful Hint

In the fraction $\frac{7}{8}$, the numerator is close in value to the denominator. So round $\frac{7}{8}$ to 1.

You can estimate products and quotients of mixed numbers by rounding to the nearest whole number. If the fraction in a mixed number is greater than or equal to $\frac{1}{2}$, round the mixed number up to the next whole number. If the fraction is less than $\frac{1}{2}$, round down to a whole number by dropping the fraction.

EXAMPLE 3 Estimating Products and Quotients

Estimate each product or quotient.

A $4\frac{2}{7} \cdot 6\frac{9}{10}$

$4\frac{2}{7} \longrightarrow 4$ $\quad 6\frac{9}{10} \longrightarrow 7$ *Round each mixed number to the nearest whole number.*

$4 \cdot 7 = 28$ *Multiply.*

B $11\frac{3}{4} \div 2\frac{1}{5}$

$11\frac{3}{4} \longrightarrow 12$ $\quad 2\frac{1}{5} \longrightarrow 2$ *Round each mixed number to the nearest whole number.*

$12 \div 2 = 6$ *Divide.*

Think and Discuss

1. Demonstrate how to round $\frac{5}{12}$ and $5\frac{1}{5}$.

2. Explain how you know that $25\frac{5}{8} \cdot 5\frac{1}{10} > 125$.

3-7 Exercises

go.hrw.com
Homework Help Online
KEYWORD: MS7 3-7
Parent Resources Online
KEYWORD: MS7 Parent

GUIDED PRACTICE

See Example 1

1. The length of a large SUV is $18\frac{9}{10}$ feet, and the length of a small SUV is $15\frac{1}{8}$ feet. Estimate how much longer the large SUV is than the small SUV.

See Example 2

Estimate each sum or difference.

2. $\frac{5}{6} + \frac{5}{12}$
3. $\frac{15}{16} - \frac{4}{5}$
4. $2\frac{1}{6} + 3\frac{6}{11}$
5. $5\frac{2}{7} - 2\frac{7}{9}$

See Example 3

Estimate each product or quotient.

6. $1\frac{3}{25} \cdot 9\frac{6}{7}$
7. $21\frac{2}{7} \div 7\frac{1}{3}$
8. $31\frac{7}{8} \div 4\frac{1}{5}$
9. $12\frac{2}{5} \cdot 3\frac{6}{9}$

INDEPENDENT PRACTICE

See Example 1

10. **Measurement** Sarah's bedroom is $14\frac{5}{6}$ feet long and $12\frac{1}{4}$ feet wide. Estimate the difference between the length and width of Sarah's bedroom.

See Example 2

Estimate each sum or difference.

11. $\frac{4}{9} + \frac{3}{5}$
12. $2\frac{5}{9} + 1\frac{7}{8}$
13. $8\frac{3}{4} - 6\frac{2}{5}$
14. $6\frac{1}{3} + \left(-\frac{5}{6}\right)$
15. $\frac{7}{8} - \frac{2}{5}$
16. $15\frac{1}{7} - 10\frac{8}{9}$
17. $8\frac{7}{15} + 2\frac{7}{8}$
18. $\frac{4}{5} + 7\frac{1}{8}$

See Example 3

Estimate each product or quotient.

19. $23\frac{5}{7} \div 3\frac{6}{9}$
20. $10\frac{2}{5} \div 4\frac{5}{8}$
21. $2\frac{1}{8} \cdot 14\frac{5}{6}$
22. $7\frac{9}{10} \cdot 11\frac{3}{4}$
23. $5\frac{3}{5} \div 2\frac{2}{3}$
24. $12\frac{4}{6} \cdot 3\frac{2}{7}$
25. $8\frac{1}{4} \div 1\frac{7}{8}$
26. $15\frac{12}{15} \cdot 1\frac{5}{7}$

PRACTICE AND PROBLEM SOLVING

Extra Practice
See page 731.

Estimate each sum, difference, product, or quotient.

27. $\frac{7}{9} - \frac{3}{8}$
28. $\frac{3}{5} + \frac{6}{7}$
29. $2\frac{5}{7} \cdot 8\frac{3}{11}$
30. $16\frac{7}{20} \div 3\frac{8}{9}$
31. $-1\frac{3}{5} \cdot 4\frac{6}{13}$
32. $5\frac{3}{5} - 4\frac{1}{3}$
33. $3\frac{7}{8} + \frac{2}{15}$
34. $19\frac{5}{7} \div \left(-5\frac{2}{5}\right)$
35. $\frac{3}{8} + 3\frac{5}{7} + 6\frac{7}{8}$
36. $8\frac{4}{5} + 6\frac{1}{12} + 3\frac{2}{5}$
37. $14\frac{2}{3} + 1\frac{7}{9} - 11\frac{14}{29}$

38. Kevin has $3\frac{3}{4}$ pounds of pecans and $6\frac{2}{3}$ pounds of walnuts. About how many more pounds of walnuts than pecans does Kevin have?

39. **Business** October 19, 1987, is known as Black Monday because the stock market fell 508 points. Xerox stock began the day at $\$70\frac{1}{8}$ and finished at $\$56\frac{1}{4}$. Approximately how far did Xerox's stock price fall during the day?

40. **Recreation** Monica and Paul hiked $5\frac{3}{8}$ miles on Saturday and $4\frac{9}{10}$ miles on Sunday. Estimate the number of miles Monica and Paul hiked.

41. **Critical Thinking** If you round a divisor down, is the quotient going to be less than or greater than the actual quotient? Explain.

Life Science The diagram shows the wingspans of different species of birds. Use the diagram for Exercises 42 and 43.

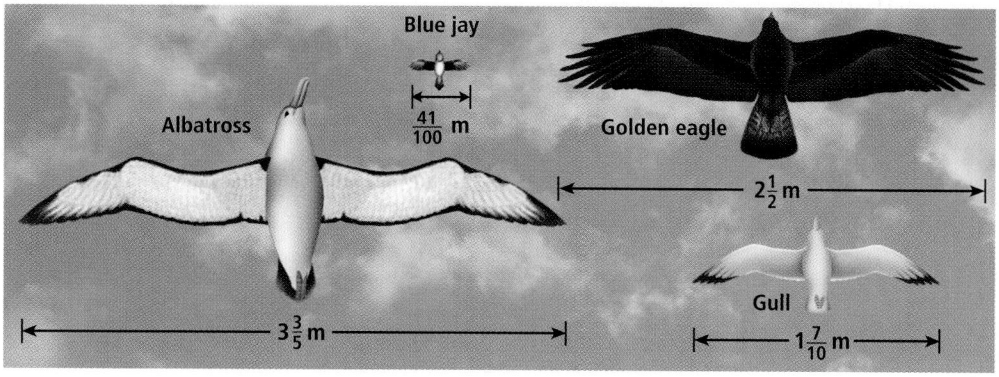

42. Approximately how much longer is the wingspan of an albatross than the wingspan of a gull?

43. Approximately how much longer is the wingspan of a golden eagle than the wingspan of a blue jay?

44. Write a Problem Using mixed numbers, write a problem in which an estimate is enough to solve the problem.

45. Write About It How is estimating fractions or mixed numbers similar to rounding whole numbers?

46. Challenge Suppose you had bought 10 shares of Xerox stock on October 16, 1987, for $73 per share and sold them at the end of the day on October 19, 1987, for $56\frac{1}{4}$ per share. Approximately how much money would you have lost?

Test Prep and Spiral Review

47. Multiple Choice For which of the following would 2 be the best estimate?

(A) $8\frac{7}{9} \cdot 4\frac{2}{5}$ (B) $4\frac{1}{5} \div 2\frac{5}{9}$ (C) $8\frac{7}{9} \cdot 2\frac{1}{5}$ (D) $8\frac{1}{9} \div 4\frac{2}{5}$

48. Multiple Choice The table shows the distance Maria biked each day last week.

Day	Mon	Tue	Wed	Thu	Fri	Sat	Sun
Distance (mi)	$12\frac{3}{8}$	$9\frac{11}{15}$	$3\frac{1}{4}$	$8\frac{1}{2}$	0	$4\frac{3}{4}$	$5\frac{2}{5}$

Which is the best estimate for the total distance Maria biked last week?

(F) 40 mi (G) 44 mi (H) 48 mi (J) 52 mi

Solve each equation. Check your answer. (Lessons 1-11 and 1-12)

49. $x + 16 = 43$ **50.** $y - 32 = 14$ **51.** $5m = 65$ **52.** $\frac{n}{3} = 18$

Solve. (Lesson 3-6)

53. $-7.1x = -46.15$ **54.** $8.7 = y + (-4.6)$ **55.** $\frac{q}{-5.4} = 3.6$ **56.** $r - 4 = -31.2$

Hands-On LAB 3-8

Model Fraction Addition and Subtraction

Use with Lesson 3-8

go.hrw.com
Lab Resources Online
KEYWORD: MS7 Lab3

Fraction bars can be used to model addition and subtraction of fractions.

Activity

You can use fraction bars to find $\frac{3}{8} + \frac{2}{8}$.

Use fraction bars to represent both fractions. Place the fraction bars side by side.

$\frac{3}{8} + \frac{2}{8} = \frac{5}{8}$

1 Use fraction bars to find each sum.

a. $\frac{1}{3} + \frac{1}{3}$ **b.** $\frac{2}{4} + \frac{1}{4}$ **c.** $\frac{3}{12} + \frac{2}{12}$ **d.** $\frac{1}{5} + \frac{2}{5}$

You can use fraction bars to find $\frac{1}{3} + \frac{1}{4}$.

Use fraction bars to represent both fractions. Place the fraction bars side by side. Which kind of fraction bar placed side by side will fit below $\frac{1}{3}$ and $\frac{1}{4}$? (*Hint:* What is the LCM of 3 and 4?)

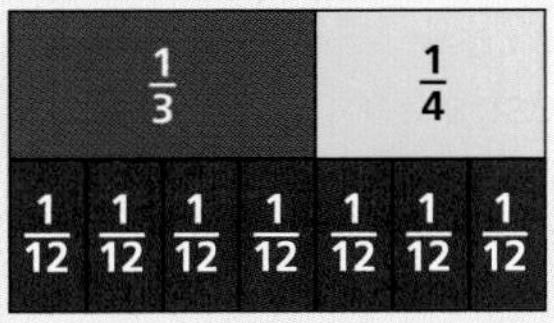

$\frac{1}{3} + \frac{1}{4} = \frac{7}{12}$

2 Use fraction bars to find each sum.

a. $\frac{1}{2} + \frac{1}{3}$ **b.** $\frac{1}{2} + \frac{1}{4}$ **c.** $\frac{1}{3} + \frac{1}{6}$ **d.** $\frac{1}{4} + \frac{1}{6}$

You can use fraction bars to find $\frac{1}{3} + \frac{5}{6}$.

Use fraction bars to represent both fractions. Place the fraction bars side by side. Which kind of fraction bar placed side by side will fit below $\frac{1}{3}$ and $\frac{5}{6}$? (*Hint:* What is the LCM of 3 and 6?)

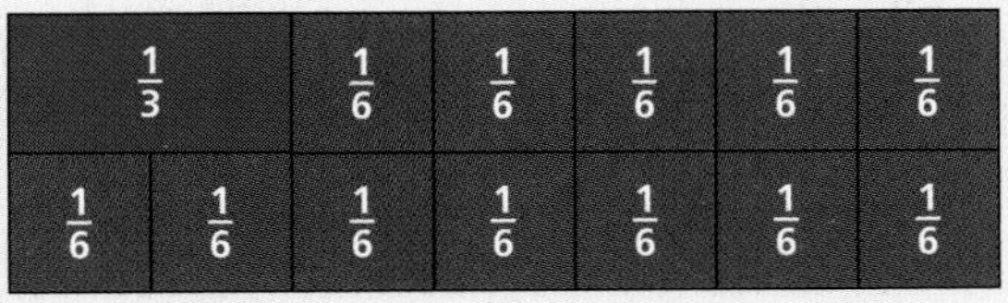

$\frac{1}{3} + \frac{5}{6} = \frac{7}{6}$

When the sum is an improper fraction, you can use the 1 bar along with fraction bars to find the mixed-number equivalent.

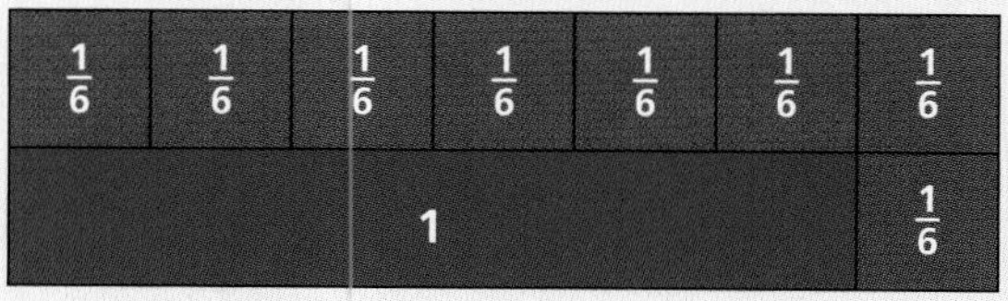

$\frac{7}{6} = 1\frac{1}{6}$

3 Use fraction bars to find each sum.

a. $\frac{3}{4} + \frac{3}{4}$ **b.** $\frac{2}{3} + \frac{1}{2}$ **c.** $\frac{5}{6} + \frac{1}{4}$ **d.** $\frac{3}{8} + \frac{3}{4}$

You can use fraction bars to find $\frac{2}{3} - \frac{1}{2}$.

Place a $\frac{1}{2}$ bar beneath bars that show $\frac{2}{3}$, and find which fraction fills in the remaining space.

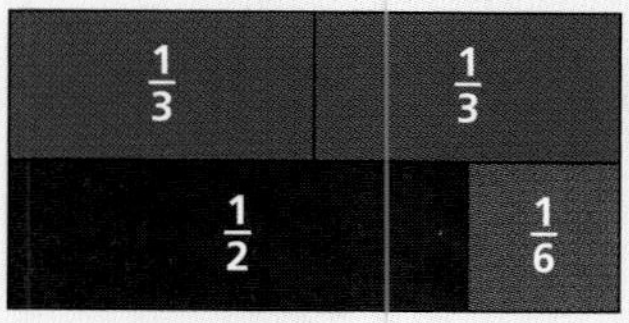

4 Use fraction bars to find each difference.

a. $\frac{2}{3} - \frac{1}{3}$ **b.** $\frac{1}{4} - \frac{1}{6}$ **c.** $\frac{1}{2} - \frac{1}{3}$ **d.** $\frac{3}{4} - \frac{2}{3}$

Think and Discuss

1. Model and solve $\frac{3}{4} - \frac{1}{6}$. Explain your steps.
2. Two students solved $\frac{1}{4} + \frac{1}{3}$ in different ways. One got $\frac{7}{12}$ for the answer, and the other got $\frac{2}{7}$. Use models to show which student is correct.
3. Find three different ways to model $\frac{1}{2} + \frac{1}{4}$.

Try This

Use fraction bars to find each sum or difference.

1. $\frac{1}{2} + \frac{1}{2}$ **2.** $\frac{2}{3} + \frac{1}{6}$ **3.** $\frac{1}{4} + \frac{1}{6}$ **4.** $\frac{1}{3} + \frac{7}{12}$

5. $\frac{5}{12} - \frac{1}{3}$ **6.** $\frac{1}{2} - \frac{1}{4}$ **7.** $\frac{3}{4} - \frac{1}{6}$ **8.** $\frac{2}{3} - \frac{1}{4}$

9. You ate $\frac{1}{4}$ of a pizza for lunch and $\frac{5}{8}$ of the pizza for dinner. How much of the pizza did you eat in all?

10. It is $\frac{5}{6}$ mile from your home to the library. After walking $\frac{3}{4}$ mile, you stop to visit a friend on your way to the library. How much farther must you walk to reach the library?

3-8 Adding and Subtracting Fractions

Learn to add and subtract fractions.

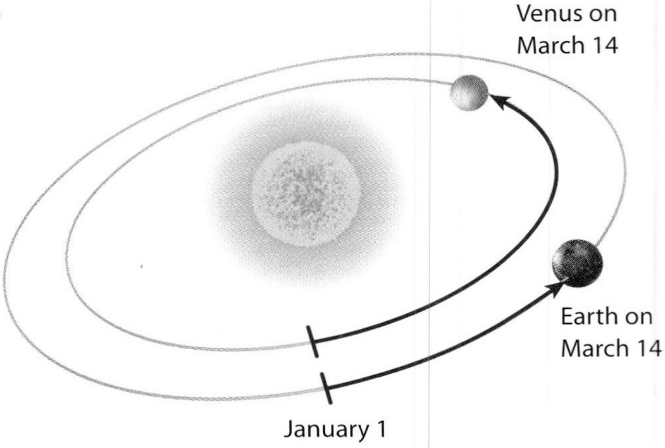

From January 1 to March 14 of any given year, Earth completes approximately $\frac{1}{5}$ of its orbit around the Sun, while Venus completes approximately $\frac{1}{3}$ of its orbit. The illustration shows what the positions of the planets would be on March 14 if they started at the same place on January 1 and their orbits were circular. To find out how much more of its orbit Venus completes than Earth, you need to subtract fractions.

EXAMPLE 1 Adding and Subtracting Fractions with Like Denominators

Add or subtract. Write each answer in simplest form.

A $\frac{3}{10} + \frac{1}{10}$

$\frac{3}{10} + \frac{1}{10} = \frac{3+1}{10}$ *Add the numerators and keep the common denominator.*

$= \frac{4}{10} = \frac{2}{5}$ *Simplify.*

B $\frac{7}{9} - \frac{4}{9}$

$\frac{7}{9} - \frac{4}{9} = \frac{7-4}{9}$ *Subtract the numerators and keep the common denominator.*

$= \frac{3}{9} = \frac{1}{3}$ *Simplify.*

To add or subtract fractions with different denominators, you must rewrite the fractions with a common denominator.

Helpful Hint

The LCM of two denominators is the lowest common denominator (LCD) of the fractions.

Two Ways to Find a Common Denominator

- Find the LCM (least common multiple) of the denominators.
- Multiply the denominators.

EXAMPLE 2 Adding and Subtracting Fractions with Unlike Denominators

Add or subtract. Write each answer in simplest form.

A $\frac{3}{8} + \frac{5}{12}$

$\frac{3}{8} + \frac{5}{12} = \frac{3 \cdot 3}{8 \cdot 3} + \frac{5 \cdot 2}{12 \cdot 2}$ *The LCM of the denominators is 24.*

$= \frac{9}{24} + \frac{10}{24}$ *Write equivalent fractions using a common denominator.*

$= \frac{19}{24}$ *Add.*

B $\frac{1}{10} - \frac{5}{8}$

$\frac{1}{10} - \frac{5}{8} = \frac{1 \cdot 4}{10 \cdot 4} - \frac{5 \cdot 5}{8 \cdot 5}$ *The LCM of the denominators is 40.*

$= \frac{4}{40} - \frac{25}{40}$ *Write equivalent fractions using a common denominator.*

$= -\frac{21}{40}$ *Subtract.*

C $-\frac{2}{3} + \frac{5}{8}$

$-\frac{2}{3} + \frac{5}{8} = -\frac{2 \cdot 8}{3 \cdot 8} + \frac{5 \cdot 3}{8 \cdot 3}$ *Multiply the denominators.*

$= -\frac{16}{24} + \frac{15}{24}$ *Write equivalent fractions using a common denominator.*

$= -\frac{1}{24}$ *Add.*

EXAMPLE 3 *Astronomy Application*

From January 1 to March 14, Earth completes about $\frac{1}{5}$ of its orbit, while Venus completes about $\frac{1}{3}$ of its orbit. How much more of its orbit does Venus complete than Earth?

$\frac{1}{3} - \frac{1}{5} = \frac{1 \cdot 5}{3 \cdot 5} - \frac{1 \cdot 3}{5 \cdot 3}$ *The LCM of the denominators is 15.*

$= \frac{5}{15} - \frac{3}{15}$ *Write equivalent fractions.*

$= \frac{2}{15}$ *Subtract.*

Venus completes $\frac{2}{15}$ more of its orbit than Earth does.

Think and Discuss

1. **Describe** the process for subtracting fractions with different denominators.
2. **Explain** whether $\frac{3}{4} + \frac{2}{3} = \frac{5}{7}$ is correct.

3-8 Exercises

go.hrw.com
Homework Help Online
KEYWORD: MS7 3-8
Parent Resources Online
KEYWORD: MS7 Parent

GUIDED PRACTICE

See Example 1

Add or subtract. Write each answer in simplest form.

1. $\frac{2}{3} - \frac{1}{3}$ **2.** $\frac{1}{12} + \frac{1}{12}$ **3.** $\frac{16}{21} - \frac{7}{21}$ **4.** $\frac{4}{17} + \frac{11}{17}$

See Example 2

5. $\frac{1}{6} + \frac{1}{3}$ **6.** $\frac{9}{10} - \frac{3}{4}$ **7.** $\frac{2}{3} + \frac{1}{8}$ **8.** $\frac{5}{8} - \frac{3}{10}$

See Example 3

9. Parker spends $\frac{1}{4}$ of his earnings on rent and $\frac{1}{6}$ on entertainment. How much more of his earnings does Parker spend on rent than on entertainment?

INDEPENDENT PRACTICE

See Example 1

Add or subtract. Write each answer in simplest form.

10. $\frac{2}{3} + \frac{1}{3}$ **11.** $\frac{3}{20} + \frac{7}{20}$ **12.** $\frac{5}{8} + \frac{7}{8}$ **13.** $\frac{6}{15} + \frac{3}{15}$

14. $\frac{7}{12} - \frac{5}{12}$ **15.** $\frac{5}{6} - \frac{1}{6}$ **16.** $\frac{8}{9} - \frac{5}{9}$ **17.** $\frac{9}{25} - \frac{4}{25}$

See Example 2

18. $\frac{1}{5} + \frac{2}{3}$ **19.** $\frac{1}{6} + \frac{1}{12}$ **20.** $\frac{5}{6} + \frac{3}{4}$ **21.** $\frac{1}{2} + \frac{2}{8}$

22. $\frac{21}{24} - \frac{1}{2}$ **23.** $\frac{3}{4} - \frac{11}{12}$ **24.** $\frac{1}{2} - \frac{2}{7}$ **25.** $\frac{7}{10} - \frac{1}{6}$

See Example 3

26. Seana picked $\frac{3}{4}$ quart of blackberries. She ate $\frac{1}{12}$ quart. How much was left?

27. Armando lives $\frac{2}{3}$ mi from his school. If he has walked $\frac{1}{2}$ mi already this morning, how much farther must he walk to get to his school?

PRACTICE AND PROBLEM SOLVING

Extra Practice
See page 731.

Find each sum or difference. Write your answer in simplest form.

28. $\frac{4}{5} + \frac{6}{7}$ **29.** $\frac{5}{6} - \frac{1}{9}$ **30.** $\frac{1}{2} - \frac{3}{4}$ **31.** $\frac{2}{3} + \frac{2}{15}$

32. $\frac{5}{7} + \frac{1}{3}$ **33.** $\frac{1}{2} - \frac{7}{12}$ **34.** $\frac{3}{4} + \frac{2}{5}$ **35.** $\frac{9}{14} - \frac{1}{7}$

36. $\frac{7}{8} + \frac{2}{3} + \frac{5}{6}$ **37.** $\frac{3}{5} + \frac{1}{10} - \frac{3}{4}$ **38.** $\frac{3}{10} + \frac{5}{8} + \frac{1}{5}$ **39.** $\frac{2}{5} - \frac{1}{6} + \frac{7}{10}$

40. $-\frac{1}{2} + \frac{3}{8} + \frac{2}{7}$ **41.** $\frac{1}{3} + \frac{3}{7} - \frac{1}{9}$ **42.** $\frac{2}{9} - \frac{7}{18} + \frac{1}{6}$ **43.** $\frac{2}{15} + \frac{4}{9} + \frac{1}{3}$

44. $\frac{9}{35} - \frac{4}{7} - \frac{5}{14}$ **45.** $\frac{1}{3} - \frac{5}{7} + \frac{8}{21}$ **46.** $-\frac{2}{9} - \frac{1}{12} - \frac{7}{18}$ **47.** $-\frac{2}{3} + \frac{4}{5} + \frac{5}{8}$

48. **Cooking** One fruit salad recipe calls for $\frac{1}{2}$ cup of sugar. Another recipe calls for 2 tablespoons of sugar. Since 1 tablespoon is $\frac{1}{16}$ cup, how much more sugar does the first recipe require?

49. It took Earl $\frac{1}{2}$ hour to do his science homework and $\frac{1}{3}$ hour to do his math homework. How long did Earl work on homework?

50. **Music** In music written in $^4/_4$ time, a half note lasts for $\frac{1}{2}$ measure and an eighth note lasts for $\frac{1}{8}$ measure. In terms of a musical measure, what is the difference in the duration of the two notes?

Fitness Four friends had a competition to see how far they could walk while spinning a hoop around their waists. The table shows how far each friend walked. Use the table for Exercises 51–53.

Person	Distance (mi)
Rosalyn	$\frac{1}{8}$
Cai	$\frac{3}{4}$
Lauren	$\frac{2}{3}$
Janna	$\frac{7}{10}$

51. How much farther did Lauren walk than Rosalyn?

52. What is the combined distance that Cai and Rosalyn walked?

53. Who walked farther, Janna or Cai?

54. Measurement A shrew weighs $\frac{3}{16}$ lb. A hamster weighs $\frac{1}{4}$ lb.

a. How many more pounds does a hamster weigh than a shrew?

b. There are 16 oz in 1 lb. How many more ounces does the hamster weigh than the shrew?

55. Multi-Step To make $\frac{3}{4}$ lb of mixed nuts, how many pounds of cashews would you add to $\frac{1}{8}$ lb of almonds and $\frac{1}{4}$ lb of peanuts?

56. Write a Problem Use facts you find in a newspaper or magazine to write a problem that can be solved using addition or subtraction of fractions.

57. Write About It Explain the steps you use to add or subtract fractions that have different denominators.

58. Challenge The sum of two fractions is 1. If one fraction is $\frac{3}{8}$ greater than the other, what are the two fractions?

TEST PREP and Spiral Review

59. Multiple Choice What is the value of the expression $\frac{3}{7} + \frac{1}{5}$?

Ⓐ $\frac{1}{3}$ Ⓑ $\frac{22}{35}$ Ⓒ $\frac{2}{3}$ Ⓓ $\frac{26}{35}$

60. Gridded Response Grace has $\frac{1}{2}$ pound of apples. Julie has $\frac{3}{8}$ pound of apples. They want to combine their apples to use in a recipe that calls for 1 pound of apples. How many more pounds of apples do they need?

Find the greatest common factor (GCF). (Lesson 2-7)

61. 5, 9 **62.** 6, 54 **63.** 18, 24 **64.** 12, 36, 50

Estimate each sum or difference. (Lesson 3-7)

65. $\frac{4}{7} + \frac{1}{9}$ **66.** $4\frac{2}{3} - 2\frac{3}{5}$ **67.** $7\frac{5}{9} - \left(-3\frac{2}{7}\right)$ **68.** $6\frac{1}{8} + 2\frac{4}{7}$

3-9 Adding and Subtracting Mixed Numbers

Learn to add and subtract mixed numbers.

Beetles can be found all over the world in a fabulous variety of shapes, sizes, and colors. The giraffe beetle from Madagascar can grow about $6\frac{2}{5}$ centimeters longer than the giant green fruit beetle can. The giant green fruit beetle can grow up to $1\frac{1}{5}$ centimeters long. To find the maximum length of the giraffe beetle, you can add $6\frac{2}{5}$ and $1\frac{1}{5}$.

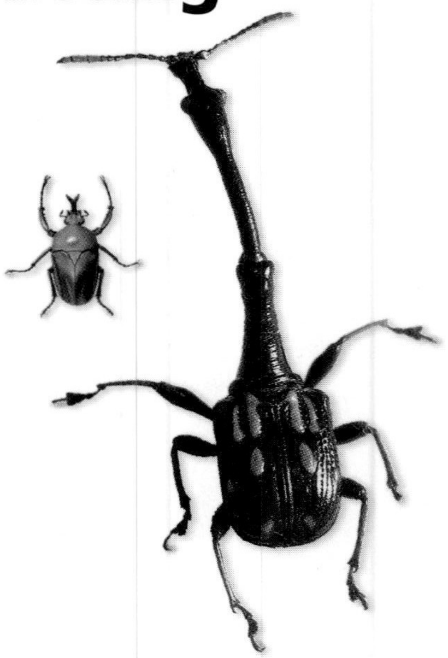

Helpful Hint

A mixed number is the sum of an integer and a fraction: $3\frac{4}{5} = 3 + \frac{4}{5}$.

EXAMPLE 1 *Measurement Application*

The giraffe beetle can grow about $6\frac{2}{5}$ centimeters longer than the giant green fruit beetle can. The giant green fruit beetle can grow up to $1\frac{1}{5}$ centimeters long. What is the maximum length of the giraffe beetle?

$6\frac{2}{5} + 1\frac{1}{5} = 7 + \frac{3}{5}$ *Add the integers, and then add the fractions.*

$= 7\frac{3}{5}$ *Add.*

The maximum length of the giraffe beetle is $7\frac{3}{5}$ centimeters.

EXAMPLE 2 Adding Mixed Numbers

Add. Write each answer in simplest form.

A $3\frac{4}{5} + 4\frac{2}{5}$

$3\frac{4}{5} + 4\frac{2}{5} = 7 + \frac{6}{5}$ *Add the integers, and then add the fractions.*

$= 7 + 1\frac{1}{5}$ *Rewrite the improper fraction as a mixed number.*

$= 8\frac{1}{5}$ *Add.*

B $1\frac{2}{15} + 7\frac{1}{6}$

$1\frac{2}{15} + 7\frac{1}{6} = 1\frac{4}{30} + 7\frac{5}{30}$ *Find a common denominator.*

$= 8 + \frac{9}{30}$ *Add the integers, and then add the fractions.*

$= 8\frac{9}{30} = 8\frac{3}{10}$ *Add. Then simplify.*

Sometimes, when you subtract mixed numbers, the fraction portion of the first number is less than the fraction portion of the second number. In these cases, you must regroup before subtracting.

Remember!

Any fraction in which the numerator and denominator are the same is equal to 1.

REGROUPING MIXED NUMBERS

Words	Numbers
Regroup.	$7\frac{1}{8} = 6 + 1 + \frac{1}{8}$
Rewrite 1 as a fraction with a common denominator.	$= 6 + \frac{8}{8} + \frac{1}{8}$
Add.	$= 6\frac{9}{8}$

EXAMPLE 3 Subtracting Mixed Numbers

Subtract. Write each answer in simplest form.

A $10\frac{7}{9} - 4\frac{2}{9}$

$10\frac{7}{9} - 4\frac{2}{9} = 6\frac{5}{9}$ *Subtract the integers, and then subtract the fractions.*

B $12\frac{7}{8} - 5\frac{17}{24}$

$12\frac{7}{8} - 5\frac{17}{24} = 12\frac{21}{24} - 5\frac{17}{24}$ *Find a common denominator.*

$= 7\frac{4}{24}$ *Subtract the integers, and then subtract the fractions.*

$= 7\frac{1}{6}$ *Simplify.*

C $72\frac{3}{5} - 63\frac{4}{5}$

$72\frac{3}{5} - 63\frac{4}{5} = 71\frac{8}{5} - 63\frac{4}{5}$ *Regroup.* $72\frac{3}{5} = 71 + \frac{5}{5} + \frac{3}{5}$

$= 8\frac{4}{5}$ *Subtract the integers, and then subtract the fractions.*

Think and Discuss

1. **Describe** the process for subtracting mixed numbers.
2. **Explain** whether $2\frac{3}{5} + 1\frac{3}{5} = 3\frac{6}{5}$ is correct. Is there another way to write the answer?
3. **Demonstrate** how to regroup to simplify $6\frac{2}{5} - 4\frac{3}{5}$.

3-9 Exercises

go.hrw.com
Homework Help Online
KEYWORD: MS7 3-9
Parent Resources Online
KEYWORD: MS7 Parent

GUIDED PRACTICE

See Example 1

1. **Measurement** Chrystelle's mother is $1\frac{2}{3}$ ft taller than Chrystelle. If Chrystelle is $3\frac{1}{2}$ ft tall, how tall is her mother?

See Example 2

Add. Write each answer in simplest form.

2. $3\frac{2}{5} + 4\frac{1}{5}$
3. $2\frac{7}{8} + 3\frac{3}{4}$
4. $1\frac{8}{9} + 4\frac{4}{9}$
5. $5\frac{1}{2} + 2\frac{1}{4}$

See Example 3

Subtract. Write each answer in simplest form.

6. $6\frac{2}{3} - 5\frac{1}{3}$
7. $8\frac{1}{6} - 2\frac{5}{6}$
8. $3\frac{2}{3} - 2\frac{3}{4}$
9. $7\frac{5}{8} - 3\frac{2}{5}$

INDEPENDENT PRACTICE

See Example 1

10. **Sports** The track at Daytona International Speedway is $\frac{24}{25}$ mi longer than the track at Atlanta Motor Speedway. If the track at Atlanta is $1\frac{27}{50}$ mi long, how long is the track at Daytona?

See Example 2

Add. Write each answer in simplest form.

11. $6\frac{1}{4} + 8\frac{3}{4}$
12. $3\frac{3}{5} + 7\frac{4}{5}$
13. $3\frac{5}{6} + 1\frac{5}{6}$
14. $2\frac{3}{5} + 4\frac{1}{3}$
15. $2\frac{3}{10} + 4\frac{1}{2}$
16. $6\frac{1}{8} + 8\frac{9}{10}$
17. $6\frac{1}{6} + 5\frac{3}{10}$
18. $1\frac{2}{5} + 9\frac{1}{4}$

See Example 3

Subtract. Write each answer in simplest form.

19. $2\frac{1}{14} - 1\frac{3}{14}$
20. $4\frac{5}{12} - 1\frac{7}{12}$
21. $8 - 2\frac{3}{4}$
22. $7\frac{3}{4} - 5\frac{2}{3}$
23. $8\frac{3}{4} - 6\frac{2}{5}$
24. $3\frac{1}{3} - 2\frac{5}{8}$
25. $4\frac{2}{5} - 3\frac{1}{2}$
26. $11 - 6\frac{5}{9}$

PRACTICE AND PROBLEM SOLVING

Extra Practice
See page 732.

Add or subtract. Write each answer in simplest form.

27. $7\frac{1}{3} + 8\frac{1}{5}$
28. $14\frac{3}{5} - 8\frac{1}{2}$
29. $9\frac{1}{6} + 4\frac{6}{9}$
30. $21\frac{8}{12} - 3\frac{1}{2}$
31. $3\frac{5}{8} + 2\frac{7}{12}$
32. $25\frac{1}{3} + 3\frac{5}{6}$
33. $1\frac{7}{9} - \frac{17}{18}$
34. $3\frac{1}{2} + 5\frac{1}{4}$
35. $1\frac{7}{15} + 2\frac{7}{10}$
36. $12\frac{4}{6} - \frac{2}{5}$
37. $4\frac{2}{3} + 1\frac{7}{8} + 3\frac{1}{2}$
38. $5\frac{1}{6} + 8\frac{2}{3} - 9\frac{1}{2}$

Compare. Write <, >, or =.

39. $12\frac{1}{4} - 10\frac{3}{4}$ ▒ $5\frac{1}{2} - 3\frac{7}{10}$
40. $4\frac{1}{2} + 3\frac{4}{5}$ ▒ $4\frac{5}{7} + 3\frac{1}{2}$
41. $13\frac{3}{4} - 2\frac{3}{8}$ ▒ $5\frac{5}{6} + 4\frac{2}{9}$
42. $4\frac{1}{3} - 2\frac{1}{4}$ ▒ $3\frac{1}{4} - 1\frac{1}{6}$

43. The liquid ingredients in a recipe are water and olive oil. The recipe calls for $3\frac{1}{2}$ cups of water and $1\frac{1}{8}$ cups of olive oil. How many cups of liquid ingredients are included in the recipe?

Travel The table shows the distances in miles between four cities. To find the distance between two cities, locate the square where the row for one city and the column for the other city intersect.

	Atherton	Baily	Charleston	Dixon
Atherton	X	$40\frac{2}{3}$	$100\frac{5}{6}$	$16\frac{1}{2}$
Baily	$40\frac{2}{3}$	X	$210\frac{3}{8}$	$30\frac{2}{3}$
Charleston	$100\frac{5}{6}$	$210\frac{3}{8}$	X	$98\frac{3}{4}$
Dixon	$16\frac{1}{2}$	$30\frac{2}{3}$	$98\frac{3}{4}$	X

44. How much farther is it from Charleston to Dixon than from Atherton to Baily?

45. If you drove from Charleston to Atherton and then from Atherton to Dixon, how far would you drive?

LINK **Agriculture**

The Netherlands produces more than 3 billion tulips each year.

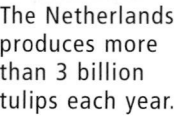

46. Agriculture In 2003, the United States imported $\frac{97}{100}$ of its tulip bulbs from the Netherlands and $\frac{1}{50}$ of its tulip bulbs from New Zealand. What fraction more of tulip imports came from the Netherlands?

47. Recreation Kathy wants to hike to Candle Lake. The waterfall trail is $1\frac{2}{3}$ miles long, and the meadow trail is $1\frac{5}{6}$ miles long. Which route is shorter and by how much?

48. Choose a Strategy Spiro needs to draw a 6-inch-long line. He does not have a ruler, but he has sheets of notebook paper that are $8\frac{1}{2}$ in. wide and 11 in. long. Describe how Spiro can use the notebook paper to measure 6 in.

49. Write About It Explain why it is sometimes necessary to regroup a mixed number when subtracting.

50. Challenge Todd had d pounds of nails. He sold $3\frac{1}{2}$ pounds on Monday and $5\frac{2}{3}$ pounds on Tuesday. Write an expression to show how many pounds he had left and then simplify it.

Test Prep and Spiral Review

51. Multiple Choice Which expression is NOT equal to $2\frac{7}{8}$?

Ⓐ $1\frac{1}{2} + 1\frac{3}{8}$ Ⓑ $5\frac{15}{16} - 3\frac{1}{16}$ Ⓒ $6 - 3\frac{1}{8}$ Ⓓ $1\frac{1}{8} + 1\frac{1}{4}$

52. Short Response Where Maddie lives, there is a $5\frac{1}{2}$-cent state sales tax, a $1\frac{3}{4}$-cent county sales tax, and a $\frac{3}{4}$-cent city sales tax. The total sales tax is the sum of the state, county, and city sales taxes. What is the total sales tax where Maddie lives? Show your work.

Find each sum. (Lesson 2-2)

53. $-3 + 9$ **54.** $6 + (-15)$ **55.** $-4 + (-8)$ **56.** $-11 + 5$

Find each sum or difference. Write your answer in simplest form. (Lesson 3-8)

57. $\frac{2}{5} + \frac{7}{20}$ **58.** $\frac{3}{7} - \frac{1}{3}$ **59.** $\frac{3}{4} + \frac{7}{18}$ **60.** $\frac{1}{3} - \frac{4}{5}$

Hands-On LAB 3-10

Model Fraction Multiplication and Division

Use with Lessons 3-10 and 3-11

go.hrw.com
Lab Resources Online
KEYWORD: MS7 Lab3

You can use grids to model fraction multiplication and division.

Activity 1

Use a grid to model $\frac{3}{4} \cdot \frac{1}{2}$.

Think of $\frac{3}{4} \cdot \frac{1}{2}$ as $\frac{3}{4}$ of $\frac{1}{2}$.

Model $\frac{1}{2}$ by shading half of a grid.

The denominator tells you to divide the grid into 2 parts.
The numerator tells you how many parts to shade.

Divide the grid into 4 equal horizontal sections.

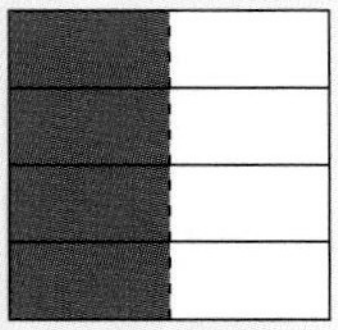

Use a different color to shade $\frac{3}{4}$ of the same grid.

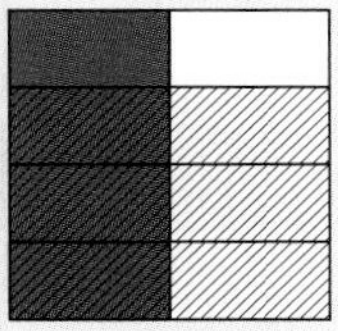

The denominator tells you to divide the grid into 4 parts.
The numerator tells you how many parts to shade.

What fraction of $\frac{1}{2}$ is shaded?

To find the numerator, think: How many parts overlap?
To find the denominator, think: How many total parts are there?

$\frac{3}{4} \cdot \frac{1}{2} = \frac{3}{8}$

Think and Discuss

1. Are $\frac{2}{3} \cdot \frac{1}{5}$ and $\frac{1}{5} \cdot \frac{2}{3}$ modeled the same way? Explain.
2. When you multiply a positive fraction by a positive fraction, the product is less than either factor. Why?

Try This

Use a grid to find each product.

1. $\frac{1}{2} \cdot \frac{1}{2}$
2. $\frac{3}{4} \cdot \frac{2}{3}$
3. $\frac{5}{8} \cdot \frac{1}{3}$
4. $\frac{2}{5} \cdot \frac{5}{6}$

Activity 2

Use grids to model $4\frac{1}{3} \div \frac{2}{3}$.

Divide 5 grids into thirds. Shade 4 grids and $\frac{1}{3}$ of a fifth grid to represent $4\frac{1}{3}$.

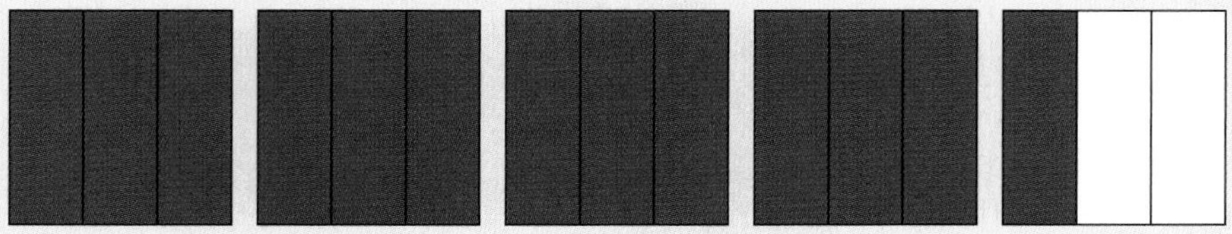

Think: How many groups of $\frac{2}{3}$ are in $4\frac{1}{3}$?

Divide the shaded grids into equal groups of 2.

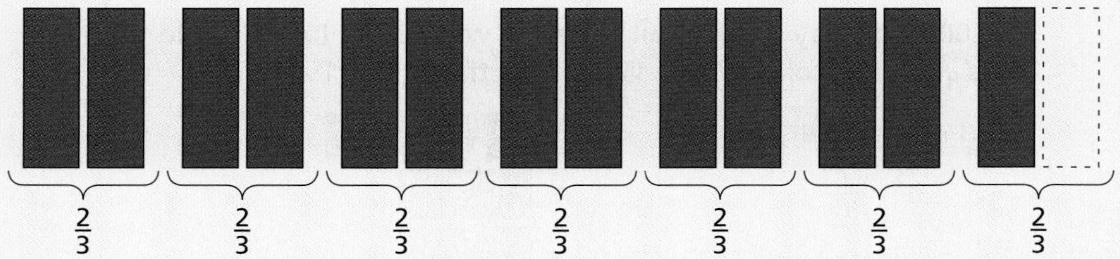

There are 6 groups of $\frac{2}{3}$, with $\frac{1}{3}$ left over. This piece is $\frac{1}{2}$ of a group of $\frac{2}{3}$.

Thus there are $6 + \frac{1}{2}$ groups of $\frac{2}{3}$ in $4\frac{1}{3}$.

$4\frac{1}{3} \div \frac{2}{3} = 6\frac{1}{2}$

Think and Discuss

1. Are $\frac{3}{4} \div \frac{1}{6}$ and $\frac{1}{6} \div \frac{3}{4}$ modeled the same way? Explain.
2. When you divide fractions, is the quotient greater than or less than the dividend and the divisor? Explain.

Try This

Use grids to find each quotient.

1. $\frac{7}{12} \div \frac{1}{6}$
2. $\frac{4}{5} \div \frac{3}{10}$
3. $\frac{2}{3} \div \frac{4}{9}$
4. $3\frac{2}{5} \div \frac{3}{5}$

3-10 Multiplying Fractions and Mixed Numbers

Learn to multiply fractions and mixed numbers.

The San Francisco–Oakland Bay Bridge, which opened in 1936, is a toll bridge used by drivers traveling between the two cities. In 1939, the toll for a car crossing the bridge was $\frac{2}{15}$ of the toll in 2005. To find the toll in 1939, you will need to multiply the toll in 2005 by a fraction.

EXAMPLE 1 *Transportation Application*

In 2005, the Bay Bridge toll for a car was \$3.00. In 1939, the toll was $\frac{2}{15}$ of the toll in 2005. What was the toll in 1939?

$3 \cdot \frac{2}{15} = \frac{2}{15} + \frac{2}{15} + \frac{2}{15}$

$= \frac{6}{15}$

$= \frac{2}{5}$ *Simplify.*

$= 0.40$ *Divide 2 by 5 to write the fraction as a decimal.*

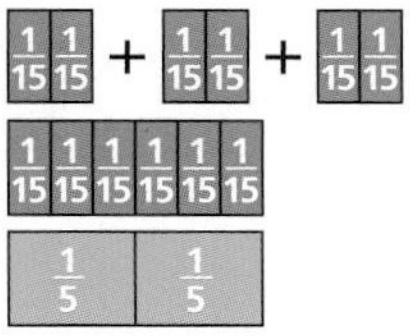

The Bay Bridge toll for a car was \$0.40 in 1939.

To multiply fractions, multiply the numerators to find the product's numerator. Then multiply the denominators to find the product's denominator.

EXAMPLE 2 Multiplying Fractions

Remember!

You can write any integer as a fraction with a denominator of 1.

Multiply. Write each answer in simplest form.

A $-15 \cdot \frac{2}{3}$

$-15 \cdot \frac{2}{3} = -\frac{15}{1} \cdot \frac{2}{3}$ *Write −15 as a fraction.*

$= -\frac{\overset{5}{\cancel{15}} \cdot 2}{1 \cdot \underset{1}{\cancel{3}}}$ *Simplify.*

$= -\frac{10}{1} = -10$ *Multiply numerators. Multiply denominators.*

Multiply. Write each answer in simplest form.

B $\frac{1}{4} \cdot \frac{4}{5}$

$\frac{1}{4} \cdot \frac{4}{5} = \frac{1 \cdot \cancel{4}^{1}}{{}_{1}\cancel{4} \cdot 5}$ *Simplify.*

$= \frac{1}{5}$ *Multiply numerators. Multiply denominators.*

C $\frac{3}{4} \cdot \left(-\frac{1}{2}\right)$

$\frac{3}{4} \cdot \left(-\frac{1}{2}\right) = -\frac{3 \cdot 1}{4 \cdot 2}$ *The signs are different, so the answer will be negative.*

$= -\frac{3}{8}$ *Multiply numerators. Multiply denominators.*

EXAMPLE 3 Multiplying Mixed Numbers

Multiply. Write each answer in simplest form.

A $8 \cdot 2\frac{3}{4}$

$8 \cdot 2\frac{3}{4} = \frac{8}{1} \cdot \frac{11}{4}$ *Write mixed numbers as improper fractions.*

$= \frac{{}^{2}\cancel{8} \cdot 11}{1 \cdot \cancel{4}_{1}}$ *Simplify.*

$= \frac{22}{1} = 22$ *Multiply numerators. Multiply denominators.*

B $\frac{1}{3} \cdot 4\frac{1}{2}$

$\frac{1}{3} \cdot 4\frac{1}{2} = \frac{1}{3} \cdot \frac{9}{2}$ *Write the mixed number as an improper fraction.*

$= \frac{1 \cdot \cancel{9}^{3}}{{}_{1}\cancel{3} \cdot 2}$ *Simplify.*

$= \frac{3}{2}$ or $1\frac{1}{2}$ *Multiply numerators. Multiply denominators.*

C $3\frac{3}{5} \cdot 1\frac{1}{12}$

$3\frac{3}{5} \cdot 1\frac{1}{12} = \frac{18}{5} \cdot \frac{13}{12}$ *Write mixed numbers as improper fractions.*

$= \frac{{}^{3}\cancel{18} \cdot 13}{5 \cdot \cancel{12}_{2}}$ *Simplify.*

$= \frac{39}{10}$ or $3\frac{9}{10}$ *Multiply numerators. Multiply denominators.*

Think and Discuss

1. Describe how to multiply a mixed number and a fraction.

2. Explain why $\frac{1}{2} \cdot \frac{1}{3} \cdot \frac{1}{4} = \frac{1}{24}$ is or is not correct.

3. Explain why you may want to simplify before multiplying $\frac{2}{3} \cdot \frac{3}{4}$. What answer will you get if you don't simplify first?

3-10 Exercises

go.hrw.com
Homework Help Online
KEYWORD: MT7 3-10
Parent Resources Online
KEYWORD: MT7 Parent

GUIDED PRACTICE

See Example 1

1. On average, people spend $\frac{1}{4}$ of the time they sleep in a dream state. If Maxwell slept 10 hours last night, how much time did he spend dreaming? Write your answer in simplest form.

See Example 2

Multiply. Write each answer in simplest form.

2. $-8 \cdot \frac{3}{4}$
3. $\frac{2}{3} \cdot \frac{3}{5}$
4. $\frac{1}{4} \cdot \left(-\frac{2}{3}\right)$
5. $\frac{3}{5} \cdot (-15)$

See Example 3

6. $4 \cdot 3\frac{1}{2}$
7. $\frac{4}{9} \cdot 5\frac{2}{5}$
8. $1\frac{1}{2} \cdot 1\frac{5}{9}$
9. $2\frac{6}{7} \cdot (-7)$

INDEPENDENT PRACTICE

See Example 1

10. Sherry spent 4 hours exercising last week. If $\frac{5}{6}$ of the time was spent jogging, how much time did she spend jogging? Write your answer in simplest form.

11. **Measurement** A cookie recipe calls for $\frac{1}{3}$ tsp of salt for 1 batch. Doreen is making cookies for a school bake sale and wants to bake 5 batches. How much salt does she need? Write your answer in simplest form.

See Example 2

Multiply. Write each answer in simplest form.

12. $5 \cdot \frac{1}{8}$
13. $4 \cdot \frac{1}{8}$
14. $3 \cdot \frac{5}{8}$
15. $6 \cdot \frac{2}{3}$
16. $\frac{2}{5} \cdot \frac{5}{7}$
17. $\frac{3}{8} \cdot \frac{2}{3}$
18. $\frac{1}{2} \cdot \left(-\frac{4}{9}\right)$
19. $-\frac{5}{6} \cdot \frac{2}{3}$

See Example 3

20. $7\frac{1}{2} \cdot 2\frac{2}{5}$
21. $6 \cdot 7\frac{2}{5}$
22. $2\frac{4}{7} \cdot \frac{1}{6}$
23. $2\frac{5}{8} \cdot 6\frac{2}{3}$
24. $\frac{2}{3} \cdot 2\frac{1}{4}$
25. $1\frac{1}{2} \cdot 1\frac{5}{9}$
26. $7 \cdot 5\frac{1}{8}$
27. $3\frac{3}{4} \cdot 2\frac{1}{5}$

PRACTICE AND PROBLEM SOLVING

Extra Practice
See page 732.

Multiply. Write each answer in simplest form.

28. $\frac{5}{8} \cdot \frac{4}{5}$
29. $4\frac{3}{7} \cdot \frac{5}{6}$
30. $-\frac{2}{3} \cdot 6$
31. $2 \cdot \frac{1}{6}$
32. $\frac{1}{8} \cdot 5$
33. $-\frac{3}{4} \cdot \frac{2}{9}$
34. $4\frac{2}{3} \cdot 2\frac{4}{7}$
35. $-\frac{4}{9} \cdot \left(-\frac{3}{16}\right)$
36. $3\frac{1}{2} \cdot 5$
37. $\frac{1}{2} \cdot \frac{2}{3} \cdot \frac{3}{5}$
38. $\frac{6}{7} \cdot 5$
39. $1\frac{1}{2} \cdot \frac{3}{5} \cdot \frac{7}{9}$
40. $-\frac{2}{3} \cdot 1\frac{1}{2} \cdot \frac{2}{3}$
41. $\frac{8}{9} \cdot \frac{3}{11} \cdot \frac{33}{40}$
42. $\frac{1}{6} \cdot 6 \cdot 8\frac{2}{3}$
43. $-\frac{8}{9} \cdot \left(-1\frac{1}{8}\right)$

Complete each multiplication sentence.

44. $\frac{1}{2} \cdot \frac{\blacksquare}{8} = \frac{3}{16}$
45. $\frac{2}{3} \cdot \frac{\blacksquare}{4} = \frac{1}{2}$
46. $\frac{\blacksquare}{3} \cdot \frac{5}{8} = \frac{5}{12}$
47. $\frac{3}{5} \cdot \frac{\blacksquare}{7} = \frac{3}{7}$
48. $\frac{5}{6} \cdot \frac{3}{\blacksquare} = \frac{1}{4}$
49. $\frac{4}{\blacksquare} \cdot \frac{4}{5} = \frac{8}{15}$
50. $\frac{2}{3} \cdot \frac{9}{\blacksquare} = \frac{3}{11}$
51. $\frac{\blacksquare}{15} \cdot \frac{3}{5} = \frac{1}{25}$

52. **Measurement** A standard paper clip is $1\frac{1}{4}$ in. long. If you laid 75 paper clips end to end, how long would the line of paper clips be?

53. **Physical Science** The weight of an object on the moon is $\frac{1}{6}$ its weight on Earth. If a bowling ball weighs $12\frac{1}{2}$ pounds on Earth, how much would it weigh on the moon?

54. In a survey, 200 students were asked what most influenced them to buy their latest CD. The results are shown in the circle graph.

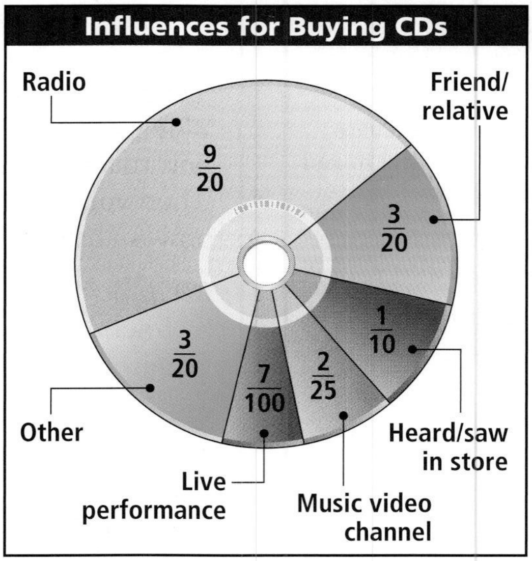

   a. How many students said radio most influenced them?
   b. How many more students were influenced by radio than by a music video channel?
   c. How many said a friend or relative influenced them or they heard the CD in a store?

55. The Mississippi River flows at a rate of 2 miles per hour. If Eduardo floats down the river in a boat for $5\frac{2}{3}$ hours, how far will he travel?

56. **Choose a Strategy** What is the product of $\frac{1}{2} \cdot \frac{2}{3} \cdot \frac{3}{4} \cdot \frac{4}{5}$?

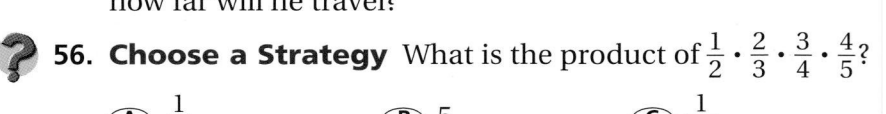

   (A) $\frac{1}{5}$ (B) 5 (C) $\frac{1}{20}$ (D) $\frac{3}{5}$

57. **Write About It** Explain why the product of two positive proper fractions is always less than either fraction.

58. **Challenge** Write three multiplication problems to show that the product of two fractions can be less than, equal to, or greater than 1.

Test Prep and Spiral Review

59. **Multiple Choice** Which expression is greater than $5\frac{5}{8}$?

   (A) $8 \cdot \frac{9}{16}$ (B) $-\frac{7}{9} \cdot \left(-8\frac{2}{7}\right)$ (C) $3\frac{1}{2} \cdot \frac{5}{7}$ (D) $-\frac{3}{7} \cdot \frac{14}{27}$

60. **Multiple Choice** The weight of an object on Mars is about $\frac{3}{8}$ its weight on Earth. If Sam weighs 85 pounds on Earth, how much would he weigh on Mars?

   (F) 11 pounds (G) $31\frac{7}{8}$ pounds (H) $120\frac{4}{5}$ pounds (J) $226\frac{2}{3}$ pounds

Use a number line to order the integers from least to greatest. (Lesson 2-1)

61. −7, 5, −3, 0, 4
62. −5, −10, −15, −20, 0
63. 9, −9, −4, 1, −1

Add or subtract. Write each answer in simplest form. (Lesson 3-9)

64. $4\frac{3}{5} + 2\frac{1}{5}$
65. $2\frac{3}{4} - 1\frac{1}{3}$
66. $5\frac{1}{7} + 3\frac{5}{14}$
67. $4\frac{5}{6} + 2\frac{5}{8}$

3-11 Dividing Fractions and Mixed Numbers

Learn **to divide fractions and mixed numbers.**

Vocabulary

reciprocal

When you divide 8 by 4, you find how many 4's there are in 8. Similarly, when you divide 2 by $\frac{1}{3}$, you find how many $\frac{1}{3}$'s there are in 2.

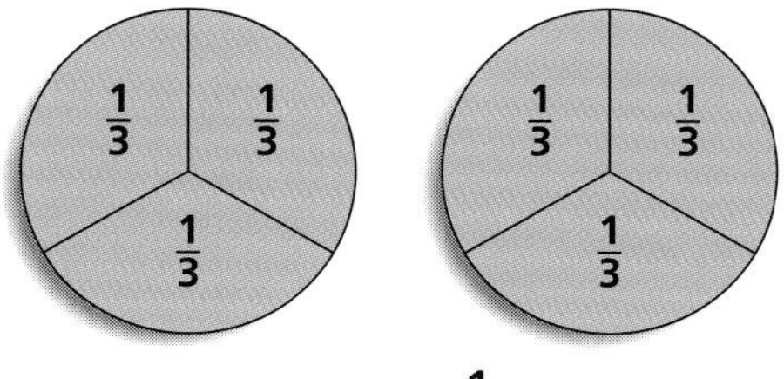

There are six $\frac{1}{3}$'s in 2.

Reciprocals can help you divide by fractions. Two numbers are **reciprocals** if their product is 1. The reciprocal of $\frac{1}{3}$ is 3 because

$\frac{1}{3} \cdot 3 = \frac{1}{3} \cdot \frac{3}{1} = \frac{3}{3} = 1.$

To divide by a fraction, find its reciprocal and then multiply.

$$2 \div \frac{1}{3} = 2 \cdot 3 = 6$$

EXAMPLE 1 Dividing Fractions

Divide. Write each answer in simplest form.

A $\frac{2}{3} \div \frac{1}{5}$

$\frac{2}{3} \div \frac{1}{5} = \frac{2}{3} \cdot \frac{5}{1}$ *Multiply by the reciprocal of $\frac{1}{5}$.*

$= \frac{2 \cdot 5}{3 \cdot 1}$

$= \frac{10}{3}$ or $3\frac{1}{3}$

B $\frac{3}{5} \div 6$

$\frac{3}{5} \div 6 = \frac{3}{5} \cdot \frac{1}{6}$ *Multiply by the reciprocal of 6.*

$= \frac{\overset{1}{\cancel{3}} \cdot 1}{5 \cdot \cancel{6}_2}$ *Simplify.*

$= \frac{1}{10}$

EXAMPLE 2 Dividing Mixed Numbers

Divide. Write each answer in simplest form.

A $4\frac{1}{3} \div 2\frac{1}{2}$

$4\frac{1}{3} \div 2\frac{1}{2} = \frac{13}{3} \div \frac{5}{2}$ *Write mixed numbers as improper fractions.*

$= \frac{13}{3} \cdot \frac{2}{5}$ *Multiply by the reciprocal of $\frac{5}{2}$.*

$= \frac{26}{15}$ or $1\frac{11}{15}$

Divide. Write each answer in simplest form.

B $\frac{5}{6} \div 7\frac{1}{7}$

$\frac{5}{6} \div 7\frac{1}{7} = \frac{5}{6} \div \frac{50}{7}$ *Write $7\frac{1}{7}$ as an improper fraction.*

$= \frac{5}{6} \cdot \frac{7}{50}$ *Multiply by the reciprocal of $\frac{50}{7}$.*

$= \frac{{}^{1}\cancel{5} \cdot 7}{6 \cdot \cancel{50}_{10}}$ *Simplify.*

$= \frac{7}{60}$

C $4\frac{4}{5} \div \frac{6}{7}$

$4\frac{4}{5} \div \frac{6}{7} = \frac{24}{5} \div \frac{6}{7}$ *Write $4\frac{4}{5}$ as an improper fraction.*

$= \frac{24}{5} \cdot \frac{7}{6}$ *Multiply by the reciprocal of $\frac{6}{7}$.*

$= \frac{{}^{4}\cancel{24} \cdot 7}{5 \cdot \cancel{6}_{1}}$ *Simplify.*

$= \frac{28}{5}$ or $5\frac{3}{5}$

EXAMPLE 3 Social Studies Application

LINK

Social Studies

The German monetary unit, the mark, plummeted in value following World War I. By November 1923, a single loaf of bread cost 2,000,000,000 marks. People used the worthless paper money for many unusual purposes, such as building kites.

Use the bar graph to determine how many times longer a $100 bill is expected to stay in circulation than a $1 bill.

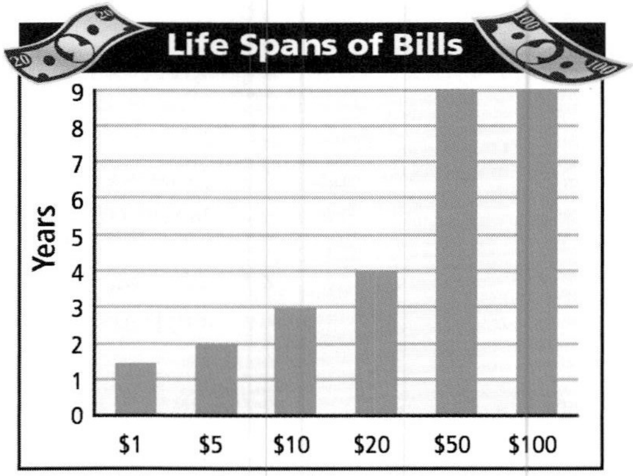

The life span of a $1 bill is $1\frac{1}{2}$ years. The life span of a $100 bill is 9 years.

Think: How many $1\frac{1}{2}$'s are there in 9?

$9 \div 1\frac{1}{2} = \frac{9}{1} \div \frac{3}{2}$ *Write both numbers as improper fractions.*

$= \frac{9}{1} \cdot \frac{2}{3}$ *Multiply by the reciprocal of $\frac{3}{2}$.*

$= \frac{{}^{3}\cancel{9} \cdot 2}{1 \cdot \cancel{3}_{1}}$ *Simplify.*

$= \frac{6}{1}$ or 6

A $100 bill is expected to stay in circulation 6 times longer than a $1 bill.

Think and Discuss

1. **Explain** whether $\frac{1}{2} \div \frac{2}{3}$ is the same as $2 \cdot \frac{2}{3}$.

2. **Compare** the steps used in multiplying mixed numbers with those used in dividing mixed numbers.

3-11 Exercises

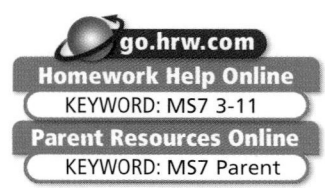

go.hrw.com
Homework Help Online
KEYWORD: MS7 3-11
Parent Resources Online
KEYWORD: MS7 Parent

GUIDED PRACTICE

See Example 1

Divide. Write each answer in simplest form.

1. $6 \div \frac{1}{3}$
2. $\frac{3}{5} \div \frac{3}{4}$
3. $\frac{3}{4} \div 8$
4. $-\frac{5}{9} \div \frac{2}{5}$

See Example 2

5. $\frac{5}{6} \div 3\frac{1}{3}$
6. $5\frac{5}{8} \div 4\frac{1}{2}$
7. $10\frac{4}{5} \div 5\frac{2}{5}$
8. $2\frac{1}{10} \div \frac{3}{5}$

See Example 3

9. Kareem has $12\frac{1}{2}$ yards of material. A cape for a play takes $3\frac{5}{6}$ yards. How many capes can Kareem make with the material?

INDEPENDENT PRACTICE

See Example 1

Divide. Write each answer in simplest form.

10. $2 \div \frac{7}{8}$
11. $10 \div \frac{5}{9}$
12. $\frac{3}{4} \div \frac{6}{7}$
13. $\frac{7}{8} \div \frac{1}{5}$
14. $\frac{8}{9} \div \frac{1}{4}$
15. $\frac{4}{9} \div 12$
16. $\frac{9}{10} \div 6$
17. $-16 \div \frac{2}{5}$

See Example 2

18. $\frac{7}{11} \div 4\frac{1}{5}$
19. $\frac{3}{4} \div 2\frac{1}{10}$
20. $22\frac{1}{2} \div 4\frac{2}{7}$
21. $-10\frac{1}{2} \div \frac{3}{4}$
22. $3\frac{5}{7} \div 9\frac{1}{7}$
23. $14\frac{2}{3} \div 1\frac{1}{6}$
24. $7\frac{7}{10} \div 2\frac{2}{5}$
25. $8\frac{2}{5} \div \frac{7}{8}$

See Example 3

26. A juicer holds $43\frac{3}{4}$ pints of juice. How many $2\frac{1}{2}$-pint bottles can be filled with that much juice?
27. **Measurement** How many $24\frac{1}{2}$ in. pieces of ribbon can be cut from a roll of ribbon that is 147 in. long?

PRACTICE AND PROBLEM SOLVING

Extra Practice
See page 732.

Evaluate. Write each answer in simplest form.

28. $6\frac{2}{3} \div \frac{7}{9}$
29. $9 \div 1\frac{2}{3}$
30. $\frac{2}{3} \div \frac{8}{9}$
31. $-1\frac{7}{11} \div \left(-\frac{9}{11}\right)$
32. $\frac{1}{2} \div 4\frac{3}{4}$
33. $\frac{4}{21} \div 3\frac{1}{2}$
34. $4\frac{1}{2} \div 3\frac{1}{2}$
35. $-1\frac{3}{5} \div 2\frac{1}{2}$
36. $\frac{7}{8} \div 2\frac{1}{10}$
37. $1\frac{3}{5} \div \left(2\frac{2}{9}\right)$
38. $\left(\frac{1}{2} + \frac{2}{3}\right) \div 1\frac{1}{2}$
39. $\left(2\frac{3}{4} + 3\frac{2}{3}\right) \div \frac{11}{18}$
40. $2\frac{2}{3} \div \left(\frac{1}{5} \cdot \frac{2}{3}\right)$
41. $\frac{4}{5} \cdot \frac{3}{8} \div \frac{9}{10}$
42. $-\frac{12}{13} \cdot \frac{13}{18} \div 1\frac{1}{2}$
43. $\frac{3}{7} \div \frac{15}{28} \div \left(-\frac{4}{5}\right)$

44. **Multi-Step** Three friends will be driving to an amusement park that is $226\frac{4}{5}$ mi from their town.
    a. If each friend drives the same distance, how far will each drive?
    b. Since the first driver will be in rush hour traffic, the friends agree the first driver will drive only $\frac{1}{3}$ of the distance found in part **a**. How far will the first driver drive?

45. **Multi-Step** How many $\frac{1}{4}$ lb hamburger patties can be made from a $10\frac{1}{4}$ lb package and an $11\frac{1}{2}$ lb package of ground meat?

Industrial Arts LINK

46. Multi-Step The students in Mr. Park's woodworking class are making birdhouses. The plans call for the side pieces of the birdhouses to be $7\frac{1}{4}$ inches long. If Mr. Park has 6 boards that are $50\frac{3}{4}$ inches long, how many side pieces can be cut?

47. For his drafting class, Manuel is drawing plans for a bookcase. Because he wants his drawing to be $\frac{1}{4}$ the actual size of the bookcase, Manuel must divide each measurement of the bookcase by 4. If the bookcase will be $3\frac{2}{3}$ feet wide, how wide will Manuel's drawing be?

48. The table shows the total number of hours that the students in each of Mrs. Anwar's 5 industrial arts classes took to complete their final projects. If the third-period class has 17 students, how many hours did each student in that class work on average?

Period	Hours
1st	$200\frac{1}{2}$
2nd	$179\frac{2}{5}$
3rd	$199\frac{3}{4}$
5th	$190\frac{3}{4}$
6th	$180\frac{1}{4}$

49. Critical Thinking Brandy is stamping circles from a strip of aluminum. If each circle is $1\frac{1}{4}$ inches tall, how many circles can she get from an $8\frac{3}{4}$-inch by $1\frac{1}{4}$-inch strip of aluminum?

50. Challenge Alexandra is cutting wood stencils to spell her first name with capital letters. Her first step is to cut a square of wood that is $3\frac{1}{2}$ in. long on a side for each letter in her name. Will Alexandra be able to make all of the letters of her name from a single piece of wood that is $7\frac{1}{2}$ in. wide and 18 in. long? Explain your answer.

Test Prep and Spiral Review

51. Multiple Choice Which expression is NOT equivalent to $2\frac{2}{3} \div 1\frac{5}{8}$?

(A) $\frac{8}{3} \cdot \frac{8}{13}$ (B) $2\frac{2}{3} \div \frac{13}{8}$ (C) $\frac{8}{3} \div \frac{13}{8}$ (D) $\frac{8}{3} \cdot 1\frac{5}{8}$

52. Multiple Choice What is the value of the expression $\frac{3}{5} \cdot \frac{1}{6} \div \frac{2}{5}$?

(F) $\frac{1}{25}$ (G) $\frac{1}{4}$ (H) $\frac{15}{22}$ (J) 25

53. Gridded Response Each cat at the animal shelter gets $\frac{3}{4}$ c of food every day. If Alysse has $16\frac{1}{2}$ c of cat food, how many cats can she feed?

Find the least common multiple (LCM). (Lesson 2-8)

54. 2, 15 **55.** 6, 8 **56.** 4, 6, 18 **57.** 3, 4, 8

Multiply. Write each answer in simplest form. (Lesson 3-10)

58. $-\frac{2}{15} \cdot \frac{5}{8}$ **59.** $1\frac{7}{20} \cdot 6$ **60.** $1\frac{2}{7} \cdot 2\frac{3}{4}$ **61.** $\frac{1}{8} \cdot 6 \cdot 2\frac{5}{9}$

3-12 Solving Equations Containing Fractions

Learn to solve one-step equations that contain fractions.

Gold classified as 24 karat is pure gold, while gold classified as 18 karat is only $\frac{3}{4}$ pure. The remaining $\frac{1}{4}$ of 18-karat gold is made up of one or more different metals, such as silver, copper, or zinc. The color of gold varies, depending on the type and amount of each metal added to the pure gold.

Equations can help you determine the amounts of metals in different kinds of gold. The goal when solving equations that contain fractions is the same as when working with other kinds of numbers—*to isolate the variable* on one side of the equation.

EXAMPLE 1 Solving Equations by Adding or Subtracting

Solve. Write each answer in simplest form.

A $x - \frac{1}{5} = \frac{3}{5}$

$$x - \frac{1}{5} = \frac{3}{5}$$

$$x - \frac{1}{5} + \frac{1}{5} = \frac{3}{5} + \frac{1}{5}$$ *Add to isolate x.*

$$x = \frac{4}{5}$$ *Add.*

B $\frac{5}{12} + y = \frac{2}{3}$

$$\frac{5}{12} + y = \frac{2}{3}$$

$$\frac{5}{12} + y - \frac{5}{12} = \frac{2}{3} - \frac{5}{12}$$ *Subtract to isolate y.*

$$y = \frac{8}{12} - \frac{5}{12}$$ *Find a common denominator.*

$$y = \frac{3}{12} = \frac{1}{4}$$ *Subtract. Then simplify.*

Helpful Hint

You can also isolate the variable y by adding the opposite of $\frac{5}{12}$, $-\frac{5}{12}$, to both sides.

C $\frac{7}{18} + u = -\frac{14}{27}$

$$\frac{7}{18} + u = -\frac{14}{27}$$

$$\frac{7}{18} + u - \frac{7}{18} = -\frac{14}{27} - \frac{7}{18}$$ *Subtract to isolate u.*

$$u = -\frac{28}{54} - \frac{21}{54}$$ *Find a common denominator.*

$$u = -\frac{49}{54}$$ *Subtract.*

EXAMPLE 2 Solving Equations by Multiplying

Solve. Write each answer in simplest form.

Caution!

To undo multiplying by $\frac{2}{3}$, you must divide by $\frac{2}{3}$ or multiply by its reciprocal, $\frac{3}{2}$.

A $\frac{2}{3}x = \frac{4}{5}$

$$\frac{2}{3}x = \frac{4}{5}$$

$$\frac{2}{3}x \cdot \frac{3}{2} = \frac{\overset{2}{\cancel{4}}}{5} \cdot \frac{3}{\cancel{2}_1}$$ *Multiply by the reciprocal of $\frac{2}{3}$. Then simplify.*

$$x = \frac{6}{5} \text{ or } 1\frac{1}{5}$$

B $3y = \frac{6}{7}$

$$3y = \frac{6}{7}$$

$$3y \cdot \frac{1}{3} = \frac{\overset{2}{\cancel{6}}}{7} \cdot \frac{1}{\cancel{3}_1}$$ *Multiply by the reciprocal of 3. Then simplify.*

$$y = \frac{2}{7}$$

EXAMPLE 3 *Physical Science Application*

Pink gold is made of pure gold, silver, and copper. There is $\frac{11}{20}$ more pure gold than copper in pink gold. If pink gold is $\frac{3}{4}$ pure gold, what portion of pink gold is copper?

Let c represent the amount of copper in pink gold.

$$c + \frac{11}{20} = \frac{3}{4}$$ *Write an equation.*

$$c + \frac{11}{20} - \frac{11}{20} = \frac{3}{4} - \frac{11}{20}$$ *Subtract to isolate c.*

$$c = \frac{15}{20} - \frac{11}{20}$$ *Find a common denominator.*

$$c = \frac{4}{20}$$ *Subtract.*

$$c = \frac{1}{5}$$ *Simplify.*

Pink gold is $\frac{1}{5}$ copper.

Think and Discuss

1. **Show** the first step you would use to solve $m + 3\frac{5}{8} = 12\frac{1}{2}$.
2. **Describe** how to decide whether $\frac{2}{3}$ is a solution of $\frac{7}{8}y = \frac{3}{5}$.
3. **Explain** why solving $\frac{2}{5}c = \frac{8}{9}$ by multiplying both sides by $\frac{5}{2}$ is the same as solving it by dividing both sides by $\frac{2}{5}$.

3-12 Exercises

go.hrw.com
Homework Help Online
KEYWORD: MS7 3-12
Parent Resources Online
KEYWORD: MS7Parent

GUIDED PRACTICE

See Example 1

Solve. Write each answer in simplest form.

1. $a - \frac{1}{2} = \frac{1}{4}$ **2.** $m + \frac{1}{6} = \frac{5}{6}$ **3.** $p - \frac{2}{3} = \frac{5}{6}$

See Example 2

4. $\frac{1}{5}x = 8$ **5.** $\frac{2}{3}r = \frac{3}{5}$ **6.** $3w = \frac{3}{7}$

See Example 3

7. Kara has $\frac{3}{8}$ cup less oatmeal than she needs for a cookie recipe. If she has $\frac{3}{4}$ cup of oatmeal, how much oatmeal does she need?

INDEPENDENT PRACTICE

See Example 1

Solve. Write each answer in simplest form.

8. $n - \frac{1}{5} = \frac{3}{5}$ **9.** $t - \frac{3}{8} = \frac{1}{4}$ **10.** $s - \frac{7}{24} = \frac{1}{3}$

11. $x + \frac{2}{3} = 2\frac{7}{8}$ **12.** $h + \frac{7}{10} = \frac{7}{10}$ **13.** $y + \frac{5}{6} = \frac{19}{20}$

See Example 2

14. $\frac{1}{5}x = 4$ **15.** $\frac{1}{4}w = \frac{1}{8}$ **16.** $5y = \frac{3}{10}$

17. $6z = \frac{1}{2}$ **18.** $\frac{5}{8}x = \frac{2}{5}$ **19.** $\frac{5}{8}n = 1\frac{1}{5}$

See Example 3

20. Earth Science Carbon-14 has a half-life of 5,730 years. After 17,190 years, $\frac{1}{8}$ of the carbon-14 in a sample will be left. If 5 grams of carbon-14 are left after 17,190 years, how much was in the original sample?

PRACTICE AND PROBLEM SOLVING

Extra Practice
See page 732.

Solve. Write each answer in simplest form.

21. $\frac{4}{5}t = \frac{1}{5}$ **22.** $m - \frac{1}{2} = \frac{2}{3}$ **23.** $\frac{1}{8}w = \frac{3}{4}$

24. $\frac{8}{9} + t = \frac{17}{18}$ **25.** $\frac{5}{3}x = 1$ **26.** $j + \frac{5}{8} = \frac{11}{16}$

27. $\frac{4}{3}n = 3\frac{1}{5}$ **28.** $z + \frac{1}{6} = 3\frac{9}{15}$ **29.** $\frac{3}{4}y = \frac{3}{8}$

30. $-\frac{5}{26} + m = -\frac{7}{13}$ **31.** $-\frac{8}{77} + r = -\frac{1}{11}$ **32.** $y - \frac{3}{4} = -\frac{9}{20}$

33. $h - \frac{3}{8} = -\frac{11}{24}$ **34.** $-\frac{5}{36}t = -\frac{5}{16}$ **35.** $-\frac{8}{13}v = -\frac{6}{13}$

36. $4\frac{6}{7} + p = 5\frac{1}{4}$ **37.** $d - 5\frac{1}{8} = 9\frac{3}{10}$ **38.** $6\frac{8}{21}k = 13\frac{1}{3}$

39. Food Each person in Finland drinks an average of $24\frac{1}{4}$ lb of coffee per year. This is $13\frac{1}{16}$ lb more than the average person in Italy consumes. On average, how much coffee does an Italian drink each year?

40. Weather Yuma, Arizona, receives $102\frac{1}{100}$ fewer inches of rain each year than Quillayute, Washington, which receives $105\frac{9}{50}$ inches per year. (*Source:* National Weather Service). How much rain does Yuma get in one year?

41. Life Science Scientists have discovered $1\frac{1}{2}$ million species of animals. This is estimated to be $\frac{1}{10}$ the total number of species thought to exist. About how many species do scientists think exist?

42. History The circle graph shows the birthplaces of the United States' presidents who were in office between 1789 and 1845.

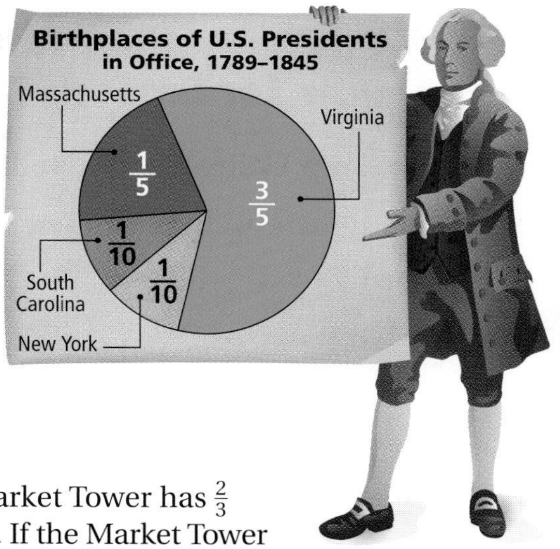

a. If six of the presidents represented in the graph were born in Virginia, how many presidents are represented in the graph?

b. Based on your answer to **a**, how many of the presidents were born in Massachusetts?

43. Architecture In Indianapolis, the Market Tower has $\frac{2}{3}$ as many stories as the Bank One Tower. If the Market Tower has 32 stories, how many stories does the Bank One Tower have?

44. Multi-Step Each week, Jennifer saves $\frac{1}{5}$ of her allowance and spends some of the rest on lunches. This week, she had $\frac{2}{15}$ of her allowance left after buying her lunch each day. What fraction of her allowance did she spend on lunches?

45. What's the Error? A student solved $\frac{3}{5}x = \frac{2}{3}$ and got $x = \frac{2}{5}$. Find the error.

46. Write About It Solve $3\frac{1}{3}z = 1\frac{1}{2}$. Explain why you need to write mixed numbers as improper fractions when multiplying and dividing.

47. Challenge Solve $\frac{3}{5}w = 0.9$. Write your answer as a fraction and as a decimal.

Test Prep and Spiral Review

48. Multiple Choice Which value of y is the solution to the equation $y - \frac{7}{8} = \frac{3}{5}$?

Ⓐ $y = -\frac{11}{40}$ Ⓑ $y = \frac{10}{13}$ Ⓒ $y = 1\frac{19}{40}$ Ⓓ $y = 2$

49. Multiple Choice Which equation has the solution $x = -\frac{2}{5}$?

Ⓕ $\frac{2}{5}x = -1$ Ⓖ $-\frac{3}{4}x = \frac{6}{20}$ Ⓗ $-\frac{4}{7} + x = \frac{2}{3}$ Ⓙ $x - 3\frac{5}{7} = 3\frac{1}{2}$

Order the numbers from least to greatest. (Lesson 2-11)

50. $-0.61, -\frac{3}{5}, -\frac{4}{3}, -1.25$ **51.** $3.25, 3\frac{2}{10}, 3, 3.02$ **52.** $\frac{1}{2}, -0.2, -\frac{7}{10}, 0.04$

Estimate. (Lesson 3-1)

53. $5.87 - 7.01$ **54.** $4.0387 + (-2.13)$ **55.** $6.785 \cdot 3.01$

CHAPTER 3

READY TO GO ON?

SECTION 3B

Quiz for Lessons 3-7 Through 3-12

3-7 Estimate with Fractions

Estimate each sum, difference, product, or quotient.

1. $\frac{3}{4} - \frac{2}{9}$
2. $-\frac{2}{7} + 5\frac{6}{11}$
3. $4\frac{9}{15} \cdot 3\frac{1}{4}$
4. $9\frac{7}{9} \div 4\frac{3}{5}$

3-8 Adding and Subtracting Fractions

Add or subtract. Write each answer in simplest form.

5. $\frac{5}{8} + \frac{1}{8}$
6. $\frac{14}{15} - \frac{11}{15}$
7. $-\frac{1}{3} + \frac{6}{9}$
8. $\frac{5}{8} - \frac{2}{3}$

3-9 Adding and Subtracting Mixed Numbers

Add or subtract. Write each answer in simplest form.

9. $6\frac{1}{9} + 2\frac{2}{9}$
10. $1\frac{3}{6} + 7\frac{2}{3}$
11. $5\frac{5}{8} - 3\frac{1}{8}$
12. $8\frac{1}{12} - 3\frac{1}{4}$
13. A mother giraffe is $13\frac{7}{10}$ ft tall. She is $5\frac{1}{2}$ ft taller than her young giraffe. How tall is the young giraffe?

3-10 Multiplying Fractions and Mixed Numbers

Multiply. Write each answer in simplest form.

14. $-12 \cdot \frac{5}{6}$
15. $\frac{5}{14} \cdot \frac{7}{10}$
16. $8\frac{4}{5} \cdot \frac{10}{11}$
17. $10\frac{5}{12} \cdot 1\frac{3}{5}$
18. A recipe calls for $1\frac{1}{3}$ cups flour. Tom is making $2\frac{1}{2}$ times the recipe for his family reunion. How much flour does he need? Write your answer in simplest form.

3-11 Dividing Fractions and Mixed Numbers

Divide. Write each answer in simplest form.

19. $\frac{1}{6} \div \frac{5}{6}$
20. $\frac{2}{3} \div 4$
21. $5\frac{3}{5} \div \frac{4}{5}$
22. $4\frac{2}{7} \div 1\frac{1}{5}$
23. Nina has $9\frac{3}{7}$ yards of material. She needs $1\frac{4}{7}$ yards to make a pillow case. How many pillow cases can Nina make with the material?

3-12 Solving Equations Containing Fractions

Solve. Write each answer in simplest form.

24. $x - \frac{2}{3} = \frac{2}{15}$
25. $\frac{4}{9} = -2q$
26. $\frac{1}{6}m = \frac{1}{9}$
27. $\frac{3}{8} + p = -\frac{1}{6}$
28. A recipe for Uncle Frank's homemade hush puppies calls for $\frac{1}{8}$ teaspoon of cayenne pepper. The recipe calls for 6 times as much salt as it does cayenne pepper. How much salt does Uncle Frank's recipe require?

MULTI-STEP TEST PREP

Heading South The Estrada family is planning to vacation at the beach in Corpus Christi, Texas. The Estradas live in Fort Worth and are considering different ways to make the trip. Corpus Christi is 372 miles south of Fort Worth.

1. A roundtrip airfare is available on the Internet for \$139.55. How much would it cost all four family members to fly to Corpus Christi?
2. Gasoline costs \$2.31 per gallon, and the family's car gets 21 miles to the gallon. How much does it cost the family to drive 1 mile?
3. How much would the family pay to drive roundtrip to Corpus Christi? Explain.
4. How much money can the family save by driving instead of flying?
5. The Estradas decide to drive and stop for a break in Waco. What fraction of the trip will be completed when they reach Waco?
6. The distance from Waco to San Antonio is $\frac{9}{20}$ of the trip. What fraction of the trip will be completed when the family reaches San Antonio?
7. The Estradas extend their trip to Raymondville, which is $1\frac{1}{4}$ times farther from Fort Worth than Corpus Christi is. How far is Raymondville from Fort Worth?

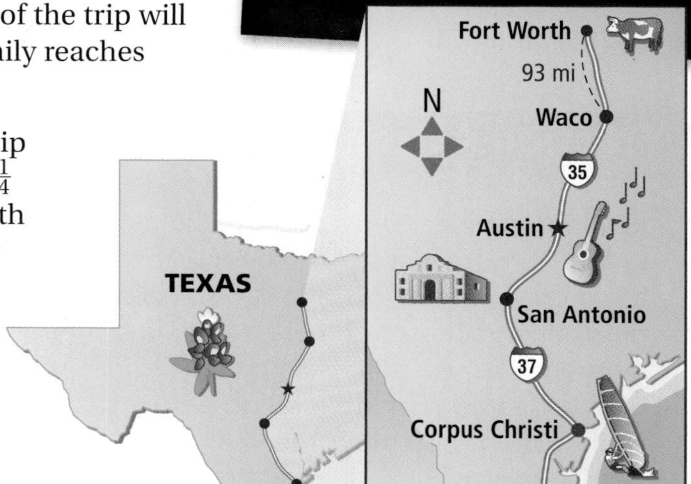

Game Time

Number Patterns

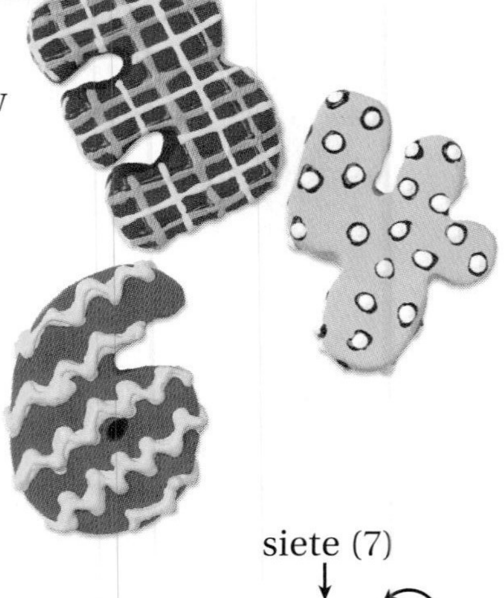

The numbers one through ten form the pattern below. Each arrow indicates some kind of relationship between the two numbers. Four relates to itself. Can you figure out what the pattern is?

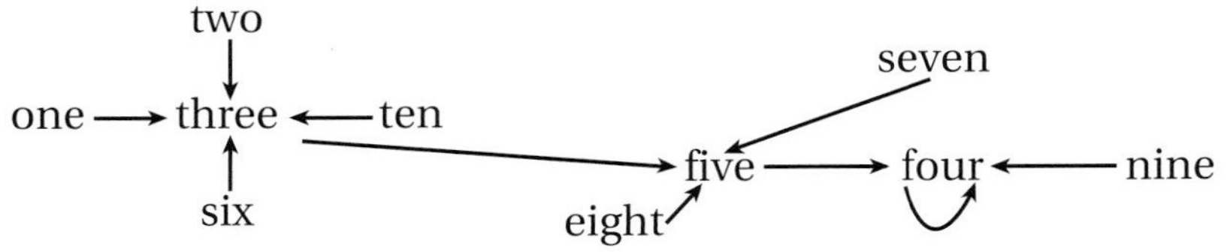

The Spanish numbers *uno* through *diez* form a similar pattern. In this case, *cinco* relates to itself.

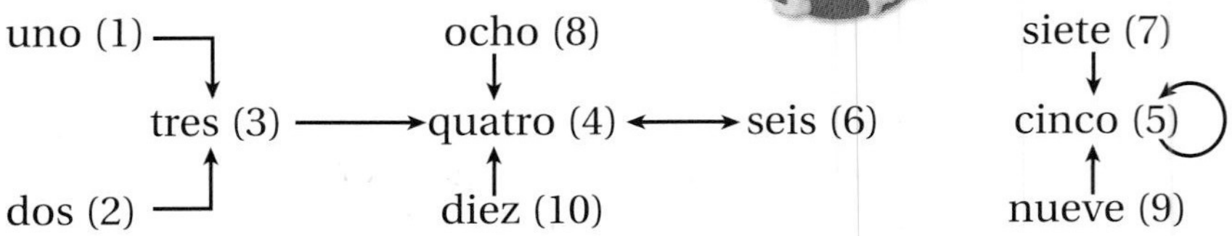

Other interesting number patterns involve cyclic numbers. Cyclic numbers sometimes occur when a fraction converts to a repeating nonterminating decimal. One of the most interesting cyclic numbers is produced by converting the fraction $\frac{1}{7}$ to a decimal.

$\frac{1}{7} = 0.\mathbf{142857}142857142\ldots$

Multiplying 142857 by the numbers 1–6 produces the same digits in a different order.

$1 \cdot 142857 = \mathbf{142857}$

$2 \cdot 142857 = \mathbf{285714}$

$3 \cdot 142857 = \mathbf{428571}$

$4 \cdot 142857 = \mathbf{571428}$

$5 \cdot 142857 = \mathbf{714285}$

$6 \cdot 142857 = \mathbf{857142}$

Fraction Action

Roll four number cubes and use the numbers to form two fractions. Add the fractions and try to get a sum as close to 1 as possible. To determine your score on each turn, find the difference between the sum of your fractions and 1. Keep a running total of your score as you play. The winner is the player with the lowest score at the end of the game.

go.hrw.com
Game Time Extra
KEYWORD: MS7 Games

A complete copy of the rules are available online.

It's in the Bag!

FOLDNOTES

Materials
- file folder
- ruler
- pencil
- scissors
- markers

PROJECT Operation Slide Through

Slide notes through the frame to review key concepts about operations with rational numbers.

Directions

1. Keep the file folder closed throughout the project. Cut off a $3\frac{1}{2}$-inch strip from the bottom of the folder. Trim the remaining folder so that is has no tabs and measures 8 inches by 8 inches. **Figure A**

2. Cut out a thin notch about 4 inches long along the middle of the folded edge. **Figure B**

3. Cut a $3\frac{3}{4}$-inch slit about 2 inches to the right of the notch. Make another slit, also $3\frac{3}{4}$ inches long, about 3 inches to the right of the first slit. **Figure C**

4. Weave the $3\frac{1}{2}$-inch strip of the folder into the notch, through the first slit, and into the second slit. **Figure D**

A
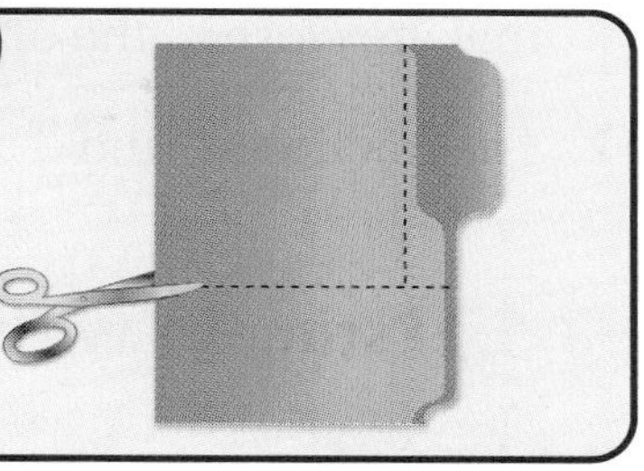

B
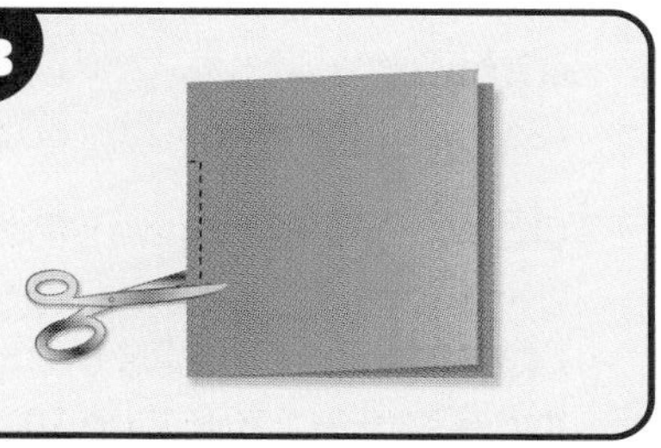

C
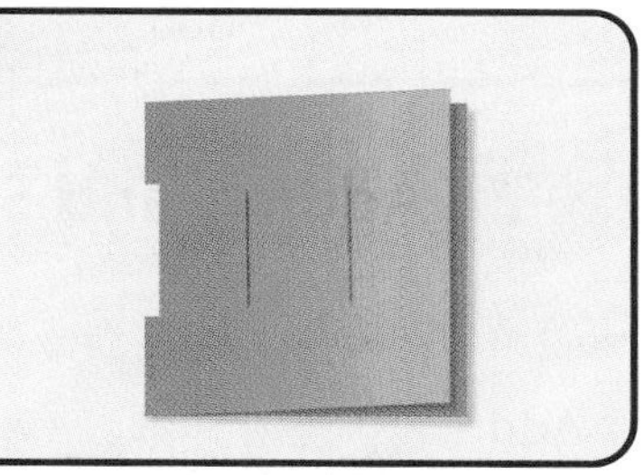

D
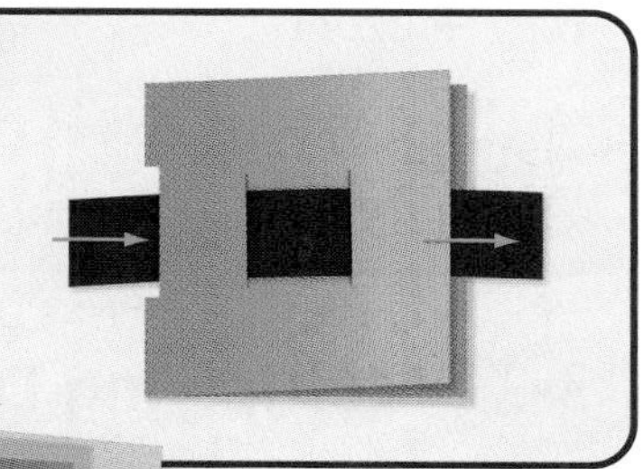

Taking Note of the Math

As you pull the strip through the frame, divide the strip into several sections. Use each section to record vocabulary and practice problems from the chapter.

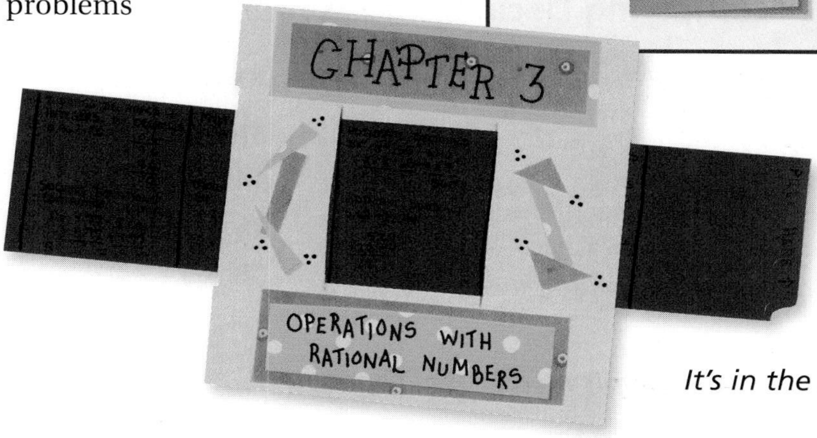

CHAPTER 3 Study Guide: Review

Vocabulary

compatible numbers . . . . 150 | reciprocal 200

Complete the sentences below with vocabulary words from the list above.

1. When estimating products or quotients, you can use ___?___ that are close to the original numbers and easy to use.
2. The fractions $\frac{3}{8}$ and $\frac{8}{3}$ are ___?___ because they multiply to give 1.

3-1 Estimate with Decimals (pp. 150–153)

EXAMPLE

■ **Estimate.**

$$\begin{array}{r} 63.28 \\ +\ 16.52 \end{array} \longrightarrow \begin{array}{r} 63 \\ +\ 17 \\ \hline 80 \end{array}$$ *Round each decimal to the nearest integer.*

$$\begin{array}{r} 43.55 \\ \times\ 8.65 \end{array} \longrightarrow \begin{array}{r} 40 \\ \times\ 9 \\ \hline 360 \end{array}$$ *Use compatible numbers.*

EXERCISES

Estimate.

3. 54.4 + 55.99
4. 11.48 − 5.6
5. 24.77 · 3.45
6. 37.8 ÷ 9.3
7. Helen saves $7.85 each week. She wants to buy a TV that costs $163.15. For about how many weeks will Helen have to save her money before she can buy the TV?

3-2 Adding and Subtracting Decimals (pp. 154–157)

EXAMPLE

■ **Add.**

5.67 + 22.44

$$\begin{array}{r} 5.67 \\ +\ 22.44 \\ \hline 28.11 \end{array}$$

Line up the decimal points.

Add.

EXERCISES

Add or subtract.

8. 4.99 + 22.89
9. −6.7 + (−44.5)
10. 18.09 − 11.87
11. 47 + 5.902
12. 23 − 8.905
13. 4.68 + 31.2

3-3 Multiplying Decimals (pp. 160–163)

EXAMPLE

■ **Multiply.**

1.44 · 0.6

$$\begin{array}{r} 1.44 \\ \times\ 0.6 \\ \hline 0.864 \end{array}$$

2 decimal places
1 decimal place
2 + 1 = 3 decimal places

EXERCISES

Multiply.

14. 7 · 0.5
15. −4.3 · 9
16. 4.55 · 8.9
17. 7.88 · 7.65
18. 63.4 · 1.22
19. −9.9 · 1.9

3-4 Dividing Decimals by Integers (pp. 166–169)

EXAMPLE

■ **Divide.**

$2.8 \div 7$

$$\begin{array}{r} 0.4 \\ 7\overline{)2.8} \\ -2\,8 \\ \hline 0 \end{array}$$

Place the decimal point in the quotient directly above the decimal point in the dividend.

EXERCISES

Divide.

20. $16.1 \div 7$

21. $102.9 \div (-21)$

22. $0.48 \div 6$

23. $17.4 \div (-3)$

24. $8.25 \div (-5)$

25. $81.6 \div 24$

3-5 Dividing Decimals and Integers by Decimals (pp. 170–173)

EXAMPLE

■ **Divide.**

$0.96 \div 1.6$

$$\begin{array}{r} 0.6 \\ 16\overline{)9.6} \\ -9\,6 \\ \hline 0 \end{array}$$

Multiply both numbers by 10 to make the divisor an integer.

EXERCISES

Divide.

26. $7.65 \div 1.7$

27. $9.483 \div (-8.7)$

28. $126.28 \div (-8.2)$

29. $2.5 \div (-0.005)$

30. $9 \div 4.5$

31. $13 \div 3.25$

3-6 Solving Equations Containing Decimals (pp. 174–177)

EXAMPLE

■ **Solve.**

$$\begin{array}{rcr} n - 4.77 & = & 8.60 \\ +\,4.77 & & +\,4.77 \\ \hline n & = & 13.37 \end{array}$$

Add to isolate n.

EXERCISES

Solve.

32. $x + 40.44 = 30$

33. $\frac{s}{1.07} = 100$

34. $0.8n = 0.0056$

35. $k - 8 = 0.64$

36. $3.65 + e = -1.4$

37. $\frac{w}{-0.2} = 15.4$

3-7 Estimate with Fractions (pp. 180–183)

EXAMPLE

■ **Estimate.**

$7\frac{3}{4} - 4\frac{1}{3}$

$7\frac{3}{4} \longrightarrow 8 \qquad 4\frac{1}{3} \longrightarrow 4\frac{1}{2}$

$8 - 4\frac{1}{2} = 3\frac{1}{2}$

$11\frac{7}{12} \div 3\frac{2}{5}$

$11\frac{7}{12} \longrightarrow 12 \qquad 3\frac{2}{5} \longrightarrow 3$

$12 \div 3 = 4$

EXERCISES

Estimate each sum, difference, product, or quotient.

38. $11\frac{1}{7} + 12\frac{3}{4}$

39. $5\frac{5}{7} - 13\frac{10}{17}$

40. $9\frac{7}{8} + \left(-7\frac{1}{13}\right)$

41. $11\frac{8}{9} - 11\frac{1}{20}$

42. $5\frac{13}{20} \cdot 4\frac{1}{2}$

43. $-6\frac{1}{4} \div \left(-1\frac{5}{8}\right)$

44. Sara ran $2\frac{1}{3}$ laps on Monday and $7\frac{3}{4}$ laps on Friday. About how many more laps did Sara run on Friday?

Study Guide: Review

3-8 Adding and Subtracting Fractions (pp. 186–189)

EXAMPLE

■ **Add.**

$\frac{1}{3} + \frac{2}{5} = \frac{5}{15} + \frac{6}{15}$

$= \frac{11}{15}$

Write equivalent fractions using a common denominator.

EXERCISES

Add or subtract. Write each answer in simplest form.

45. $\frac{3}{4} - \frac{1}{3}$

46. $\frac{1}{4} + \frac{3}{5}$

47. $\frac{4}{11} + \frac{4}{44}$

48. $\frac{4}{9} - \frac{1}{3}$

3-9 Adding and Subtracting Mixed Numbers (pp. 190–193)

EXAMPLE

■ **Add.**

$1\frac{1}{3} + 2\frac{1}{2} = 1\frac{2}{6} + 2\frac{3}{6}$

$= 3 + \frac{5}{6}$

$= 3\frac{5}{6}$

Add the integers, and then add the fractions.

EXERCISES

Add or subtract. Write each answer in simplest form.

49. $3\frac{7}{8} + 2\frac{1}{3}$

50. $2\frac{1}{4} + 1\frac{1}{12}$

51. $8\frac{1}{2} - 2\frac{1}{4}$

52. $11\frac{3}{4} - 10\frac{1}{3}$

3-10 Multiplying Fractions and Mixed Numbers (pp. 196–199)

EXAMPLE

■ **Multiply. Write the answer in simplest form.**

$4\frac{1}{2} \cdot 5\frac{3}{4} = \frac{9}{2} \cdot \frac{23}{4}$

$= \frac{207}{8}$ or $25\frac{7}{8}$

EXERCISES

Multiply. Write each answer in simplest form.

53. $1\frac{2}{3} \cdot 4\frac{1}{2}$

54. $\frac{4}{5} \cdot 2\frac{3}{10}$

55. $4\frac{6}{7} \cdot 3\frac{5}{9}$

56. $3\frac{4}{7} \cdot 1\frac{3}{4}$

3-11 Dividing Fractions and Mixed Numbers (pp. 200–203)

EXAMPLE

■ **Divide.**

$\frac{3}{4} \div \frac{2}{5} = \frac{3}{4} \cdot \frac{5}{2}$

$= \frac{15}{8}$ or $1\frac{7}{8}$

Multiply by the reciprocal of $\frac{2}{5}$.

EXERCISES

Divide. Write each answer in simplest form.

57. $\frac{1}{3} \div 6\frac{1}{4}$

58. $\frac{1}{2} \div 3\frac{3}{4}$

59. $\frac{11}{13} \div \frac{11}{13}$

60. $2\frac{7}{8} \div 1\frac{1}{2}$

3-12 Solving Equations Containing Fractions (pp. 204–207)

EXAMPLE

■ **Solve. Write the answer in simplest form.**

$\frac{1}{4}x = \frac{1}{6}$

$\frac{4}{1} \cdot \frac{1}{4}x = \frac{1}{6} \cdot \frac{4}{1}$

$x = \frac{4}{6} = \frac{2}{3}$

Multiply by the reciprocal of $\frac{1}{4}$.

EXERCISES

Solve. Write each answer in simplest form.

61. $\frac{1}{5}x = \frac{1}{3}$

62. $\frac{1}{3} + y = \frac{2}{5}$

63. $\frac{1}{6}x = \frac{2}{7}$

64. $\frac{2}{7} + x = \frac{3}{4}$

CHAPTER TEST

CHAPTER 3

Estimate.

1. 19.95 + 21.36 **2.** 49.17 − 5.88 **3.** $3.21 \cdot 16.78$ **4.** $49.1 \div 5.6$

Add or subtract.

5. 3.086 + 6.152 **6.** 5.91 + 12.8 **7.** 3.1 − 2.076 **8.** 14.75 − 6.926

Multiply or divide.

9. $3.25 \cdot 24$ **10.** $-3.79 \cdot 0.9$ **11.** $3.2 \div 16$ **12.** $3.57 \div (-0.7)$

Solve.

13. $w - 5.3 = 7.6$ **14.** $4.9 = c + 3.7$ **15.** $b \div 1.8 = 2.1$ **16.** $4.3h = 81.7$

Estimate each sum, difference, product, or quotient.

17. $\frac{3}{4} + \frac{3}{8}$ **18.** $5\frac{7}{8} - 3\frac{1}{4}$ **19.** $6\frac{5}{7} \cdot 2\frac{2}{9}$ **20.** $8\frac{1}{5} \div 3\frac{9}{10}$

Add or subtract. Write each answer in simplest form.

21. $\frac{3}{10} + \frac{2}{5}$ **22.** $\frac{11}{16} - \frac{7}{8}$ **23.** $7\frac{1}{3} + 5\frac{11}{12}$ **24.** $9 - 3\frac{2}{5}$

Multiply or divide. Write each answer in simplest form.

25. $5 \cdot 4\frac{1}{3}$ **26.** $2\frac{7}{10} \cdot 2\frac{2}{3}$ **27.** $\frac{3}{10} \div \frac{4}{5}$ **28.** $2\frac{1}{5} \div 1\frac{5}{6}$

29. A recipe calls for $4\frac{4}{5}$ tbsp of butter. Nasim is making $3\frac{1}{3}$ times the recipe for his soccer team. How much butter does he need? Write your answer in simplest form.

30. Brianna has $11\frac{2}{3}$ cups of milk. She needs $1\frac{1}{6}$ cups of milk to make a pot of hot cocoa. How many pots of hot cocoa can Brianna make?

Solve. Write each answer in simplest form.

31. $\frac{1}{5}a = \frac{1}{8}$ **32.** $\frac{1}{4}c = 980$ **33.** $-\frac{7}{9} + w = \frac{2}{3}$ **34.** $z - \frac{5}{13} = \frac{6}{7}$

35. Alan finished his homework in $1\frac{1}{2}$ hours. It took Jimmy $\frac{3}{4}$ of an hour longer than Alan to finish his homework. How long did it take Jimmy to finish his homework?

36. Mya played in two softball games one afternoon. The first game lasted 42 min. The second game lasted $1\frac{2}{3}$ times longer than the first game. How long did Mya's second game last?

CHAPTER 3

TEST TACKLER

Standardized Test Strategies

Gridded Response: Write Gridded Responses

When responding to a test item that requires you to place your answer in a grid, you must fill in the grid on your answer sheet correctly, or the item will be marked as incorrect.

EXAMPLE 1

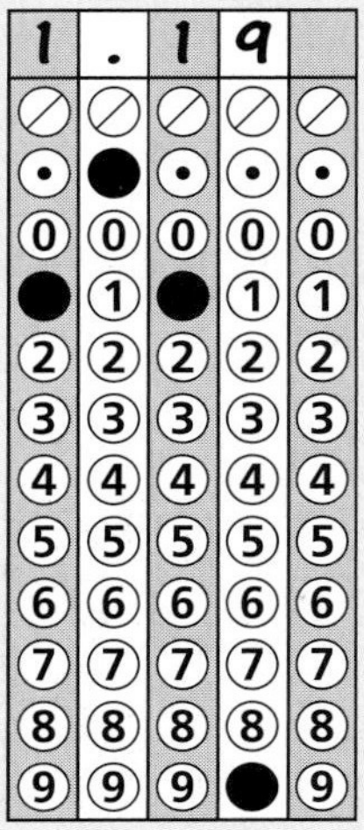

Gridded Response: Solve the equation $0.23 + r = 1.42$.

$$\begin{array}{rcr} 0.23 + r &=& 1.42 \\ -0.23 & & -0.23 \\ \hline r &=& 1.19 \end{array}$$

- Using a pencil, write your answer in the answer boxes at the top of the grid. Put the first digit of your answer in the leftmost box, or put the last digit of your answer in the rightmost box. On some grids, the fraction bar and the decimal point have a designated box.
- Put only one digit or symbol in each box. Do not leave a blank box in the middle of an answer.
- Shade the bubble for each digit or symbol in the same column as in the answer box.

EXAMPLE 2

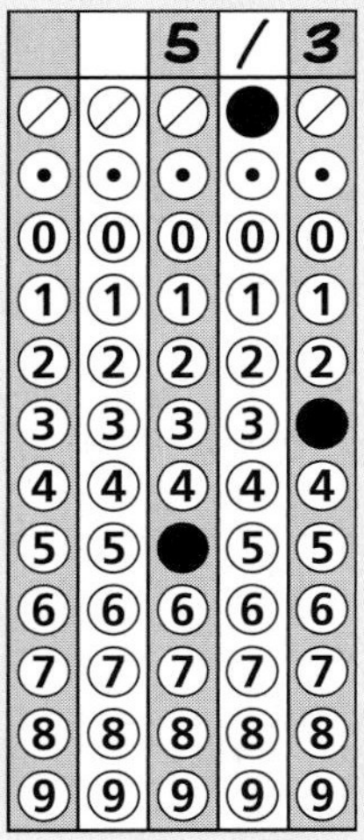

Gridded Response: Divide. $3 \div 1\frac{4}{5}$

$$3 \div 1\frac{4}{5} = \frac{3}{1} \div \frac{9}{5}$$
$$= \frac{3}{1} \cdot \frac{5}{9}$$
$$= \frac{15}{9} = \frac{5}{3} = 1\frac{2}{3} = 1.\overline{6}$$

The answer simplifies to $\frac{5}{3}$, $1\frac{2}{3}$, or $1.\overline{6}$.

- Mixed numbers and repeating decimals cannot be gridded, so you must grid the answer as $\frac{5}{3}$.
- Write your answer in the answer boxes at the top of the grid.
- Put only one digit or symbol in each box. Do not leave a blank box in the middle of an answer.
- Shade the bubble for each digit or symbol in the same column as in the answer box.

Test Tackler

HOT TIP! If you get a negative answer to a gridded response item, rework the problem carefully. Response grids do not include negative signs, so if you get a negative answer, you probably made a math error.

Read each statement, and then answer the questions that follow.

Sample A

A student correctly solved an equation for x and got 42 as a result. Then the student filled in the grid as shown.

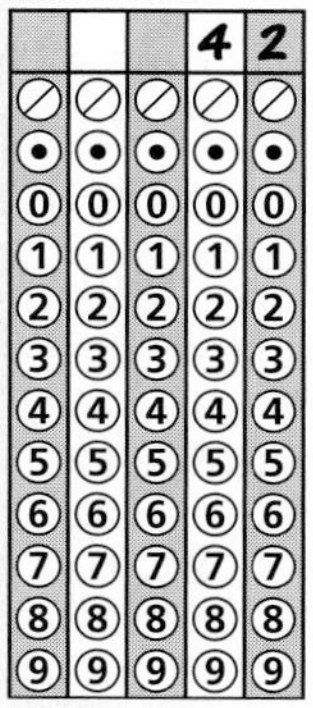

1. What error did the student make when filling in the grid?
2. Explain a second method of filling in the answer correctly.

Sample B

A student correctly multiplied 0.16 and 0.07. Then the student filled in the grid as shown.

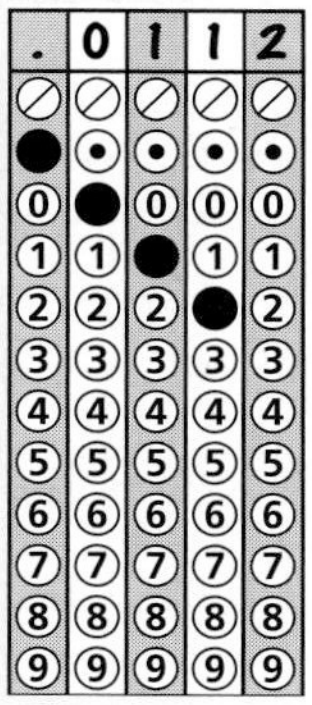

3. What error did the student make when filling in the grid?
4. Explain how to fill in the answer correctly.

Sample C

A student subtracted −12 from 5 and got an answer of −17. Then the student filled in the grid as shown.

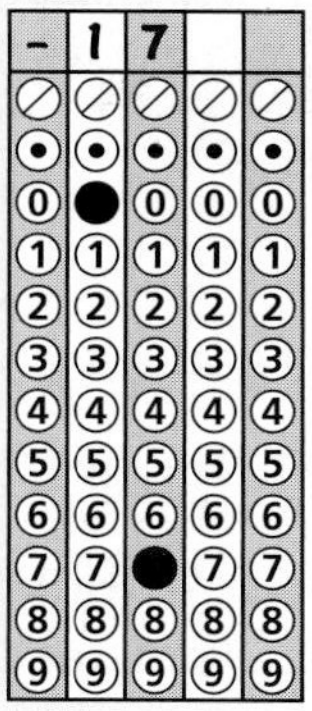

5. What error did the student make when finding the answer?
6. Explain why you cannot fill in a negative number on a grid.
7. Explain how to fill in the answer to 5 − (−12) correctly.

Sample D

A student correctly simplified $\frac{5}{6} + \frac{11}{12}$ and got $1\frac{9}{12}$ as a result. Then the student filled in the grid as shown.

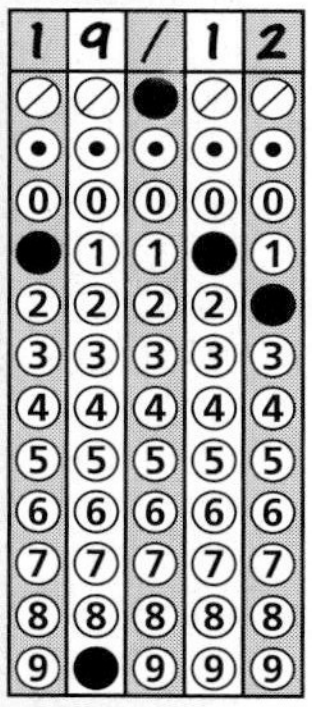

8. What answer is shown in the grid?
9. Explain why you cannot show a mixed number in a grid.
10. Write two equivalent forms of the answer $1\frac{9}{12}$ that could be filled in the grid correctly.

CHAPTER 3

STANDARDIZED TEST PREP

go.hrw.com
State Test Practice Online
KEYWORD: MS7 TestPrep

Cumulative Assessment, Chapters 1–3

Multiple Choice

1. A cell phone company charges $0.05 per text message. Which expression represents the cost of t text messages?

Ⓐ $0.05t$ Ⓒ $0.05 - t$

Ⓑ $0.05 + t$ Ⓓ $0.05 \div t$

2. Ahmed had $7.50 in his bank account on Sunday. The table shows his account activity for each day last week. What was the balance in Ahmed's account on Friday?

Day	Deposit	Withdrawal
Monday	$25.25	none
Tuesday	none	−$108.13
Wednesday	$65.25	none
Thursday	$32.17	none
Friday	none	−$101.50

Ⓕ −$86.96 Ⓗ $0

Ⓖ −$79.46 Ⓙ $96.46

3. Natasha is designing a doghouse. She wants the front of the doghouse to be $3\frac{1}{2}$ feet wide, and she wants the side of the doghouse to be $2\frac{3}{4}$ feet wider than the front. Which equation can be used to find x, the length of the side of the doghouse?

Ⓐ $3\frac{1}{2} + 2\frac{3}{4} = x$ Ⓒ $3\frac{1}{2} \cdot 2\frac{3}{4} = x$

Ⓑ $3\frac{1}{2} - 2\frac{3}{4} = x$ Ⓓ $3\frac{1}{2} \div 2\frac{3}{4} = x$

4. What is the value of $5\frac{2}{3} \div \frac{3}{9}$?

Ⓕ 17 Ⓗ 10

Ⓖ $\frac{17}{9}$ Ⓙ $5\frac{1}{3}$

5. Mrs. Herold has $5\frac{1}{4}$ yards of material to make two dresses. The larger dress requires $3\frac{3}{4}$ yards of material. Which equation can be used to find t, the number of yards of material remaining to make the smaller dress?

Ⓐ $3\frac{3}{4} - t = 5\frac{1}{4}$ Ⓒ $3\frac{3}{4} \div t = 5\frac{1}{4}$

Ⓑ $3\frac{3}{4} \cdot t = 5\frac{1}{4}$ Ⓓ $3\frac{3}{4} + t = 5\frac{1}{4}$

6. Carl is building a picket fence. The first picket in the fence is 1 m long, the second picket is $1\frac{1}{4}$ m long, and the third picket is $1\frac{1}{2}$ m long. If the pattern continues, how long is the seventh picket?

Ⓕ $1\frac{3}{4}$ m Ⓗ $2\frac{1}{4}$ m

Ⓖ 2 m Ⓙ $2\frac{1}{2}$ m

7. Daisy the bulldog weighs $45\frac{13}{16}$ pounds. Henry the beagle weighs $21\frac{3}{4}$ pounds. How many more pounds does Daisy weigh than Henry?

Ⓐ $23\frac{15}{16}$ pounds Ⓒ $24\frac{1}{16}$ pounds

Ⓑ $24\frac{5}{6}$ pounds Ⓓ $67\frac{9}{16}$ pounds

8. What is the prime factorization of 110?

Ⓕ $55 \cdot 2$ Ⓗ $11 \cdot 5 \cdot 2$

Ⓖ $22 \cdot 5 \cdot 2$ Ⓙ $110 \cdot 1$

9. Joel threw a shot put $24\frac{2}{9}$ yards. Jamil threw the shot put $33\frac{10}{11}$ yards. Estimate how much farther Jamil threw the shot put than Joel did.

Ⓐ 8 yards Ⓒ 12 yards

Ⓑ 10 yards Ⓓ 15 yards

HOT TIP! When possible, use logic to eliminate at least two answer choices.

10. Which model best represents the expression $\frac{6}{8} \times \frac{1}{2}$?

(F) 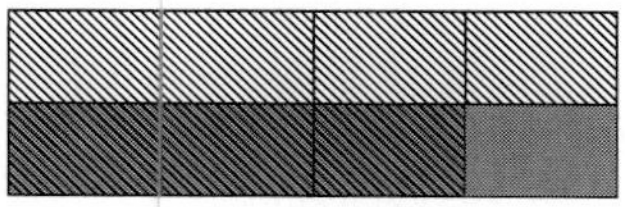

(G) 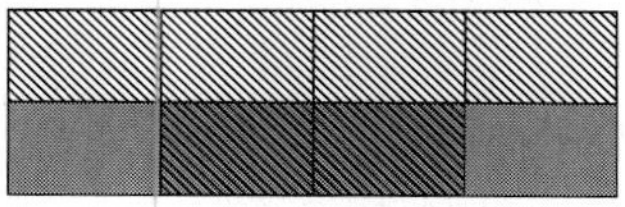

(H) 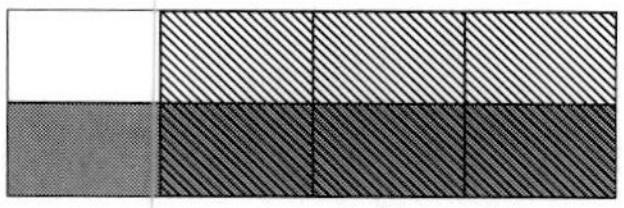

(J) 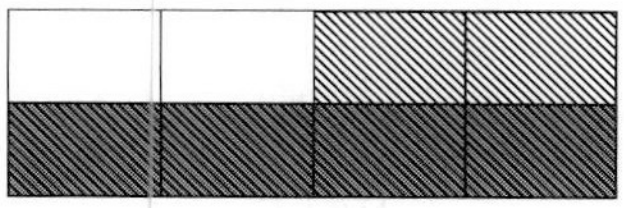

11. The table shows the different types of pets owned by the 15 students in Mrs. Sizer's Spanish class. What fraction of the students listed own a dog?

Type of Pet	Number of Students
Cat	5
Dog	9
Hamster	1

(A) $\frac{3}{5}$

(B) $\frac{1}{5}$

(C) $\frac{1}{15}$

(D) $\frac{1}{9}$

Gridded Response

12. In 2004, the minimum wage for workers was \$5.85 per hour. To find the amount of money someone earning this rate makes working x hours, use the equation $y = 5.85x$. How many dollars does Frieda earn if she works 2.4 hours?

13. Solve the equation $\frac{5}{12}x = \frac{1}{4}$ for x.

14. What is the value of the expression $2(3.1) + 1.02(-4) - 8 + 3^2$?

Short Response

15. Louise is staying on the 22nd floor of a hotel. Her mother is staying on the 43rd floor. Louise wants to visit her mother, but the elevator is temporarily out of service. Write and solve an equation to find the number of floors that Louise must climb if she takes the stairs.

16. Mari bought 3 packages of colored paper. She used $\frac{3}{4}$ of a package to make greeting cards and used $1\frac{1}{6}$ packages for an art project. She gave $\frac{2}{3}$ of a package to her brother. How much colored paper does Mari have left? Show the steps you used to find the answer.

17. A building proposal calls for 6 acres of land to be divided into $\frac{3}{4}$-acre lots. How many lots can be made? Explain your answer.

Extended Response

18. A high school is hosting a triple-jump competition. In this event, athletes make three leaps in a row to try to cover the greatest distance.

a. Tony's first two jumps were $11\frac{2}{3}$ ft and $11\frac{1}{2}$ ft. His total distance was 44 ft. Write and solve an equation to find the length of his final jump.

b. Candice's three jumps were all the same length. Her total distance was 38 ft. What was the length of each of her jumps?

c. The lengths of Davis's jumps were 11.6 ft, $11\frac{1}{4}$ ft, and $11\frac{2}{3}$ ft. Plot these lengths on a number line. What was the farthest distance he jumped? How much farther was this distance than the shortest distance Davis jumped?

CHAPTER 4

Patterns and Functions

go.hrw.com
Chapter Project Online
KEYWORD: MS7 Ch4

Fastest U.S. Roller Coasters

Roller Coaster	Speed (mi/h)
Superman the Escape	100
Millennium Force	92
Goliath	85
Titan	85

Career *Roller Coaster Designer*

Traditional roller-coaster designs rely on gravity for a coaster to gain speed. Some of these designs include loops and turns to make rides more exciting.

Jim Seay is a roller-coaster designer who uses high-tech methods to create exhilarating rides. His designs include a system that can propel a coaster from 0 to 70 miles per hour in less than four seconds!

ARE YOU READY?

Vocabulary

Choose the best term from the list to complete each sentence.

1. A(n) __?__ states that two expressions are equivalent.
2. To __?__ an expression is to substitute a number for the variable and simplify.
3. A value of the variable in an equation that makes the statement true is a(n) __?__ of the equation.
4. A(n) __?__ is a number that can be written as a ratio of two integers.

equation
evaluate
irrational number
rational number
solution

Complete these exercises to review skills you will need for this chapter.

Evaluate Expressions

Evaluate each expression.

5. $x + 5$ for $x = -18$
6. $-9y$ for $y = 13$
7. $\frac{z}{-6}$ for $z = 96$
8. $w - 9$ for $w = -13$
9. $-3z + 1$ for $z = 4$
10. $3w + 9$ for $w = 7$
11. $5 - \frac{y}{3}$ for $y = -3$
12. $x^2 + 1$ for $x = -2$

Solve Equations

Solve each equation.

13. $y + 14 = -3$
14. $-4y = -72$
15. $y - 6 = 39$
16. $\frac{y}{3} = -9$
17. $56 = 8y$
18. $26 = y + 2$
19. $25 - y = 7$
20. $\frac{121}{y} = 11$
21. $-72 = 3y$
22. $25 = \frac{150}{y}$
23. $15 + y = 4$
24. $-120 = -2y$

Number Patterns

Find the next three numbers in the pattern.

25. 95, 112, 129, 146, . . .
26. 85, 65, 60, 40, 35, . . .
27. 20, 20, 100, 100, 500, . . .
28. 12, 14, 17, 21, 26, . . .
29. 1, 3, 5, 7, . . .
30. −19, −12, −5, 2, . . .
31. 5, −10, 20, −40, 80, . . .
32. 0, −10, −5, −15, −10, . . .

CHAPTER 4

Study Guide: Preview

Where You've Been

Previously, you

- graphed ordered pairs of non-negative rational numbers on a coordinate plane.
- used tables to generate formulas representing relationships.
- formulated equations from problem situations.

In This Chapter

You will study

- plotting and identifying ordered pairs of integers on a coordinate plane.
- graphing to demonstrate relationships between data sets.
- describing the relationship between the terms in a sequence and their positions in a sequence.
- formulating problem situations when given a simple equation.

Where You're Going

You can use the skills learned in this chapter

- to sketch or interpret a graph that shows how a measurement such as distance, speed, cost, or temperature changes over time.
- to interpret patterns and make predictions in science, business, and personal finance .

Key Vocabulary/Vocabulario

coordinate plane	plano cartesiano
function	función
linear equation	ecuación lineal
linear function	función lineal
ordered pair	par ordenado
origin	origen
quadrant	cuadrante
sequence	sucesión
x-axis	eje de las x
y-axis	eje de las y

Vocabulary Connections

To become familiar with some of the vocabulary terms in the chapter, consider the following. You may refer to the chapter, the glossary, or a dictionary if you like.

1. A **sequence** is an ordered list of numbers, such as 2, 4, 6, and 8. Can you make up a sequence with a pattern and describe the pattern?
2. The word "linear" comes from the word *line.* What do you think the graph of a **linear equation** looks like?
3. An *origin* is the point at which something begins. Can you describe where to begin when you plot a point on a coordinate plane? Can you guess why the point where the x-axis and y-axis cross is called the **origin** ?
4. *Quadrupeds* are animals with four feet, and a *quadrilateral* is a four-sided figure. A coordinate plane has sections called **quadrants** . What does this word imply about the number of sections in a coordinate plane?

Study Guide: Preview

Reading and Writing Math

Writing Strategy: Write a Convincing Argument

A convincing argument or explanation should include the following:

- The problem restated in your own words
- A short response
- Evidence to support the response
- A summary statement

Example

Write About It

Explain how to find the next three integers in the pattern $-43, -40, -37, -34, \ldots$.

Step 1 **Identify the goal.**

Explain how to find the next three integers in the pattern $-43, -40, -37, -34, \ldots$.

Step 2 **Provide a short response.**

As the pattern continues, the integers increase in value. Find the amount of increase from one integer to the next. Then add that amount to the last integer in the pattern. Follow this step two more times to get the next three integers in the pattern.

Step 3 **Provide evidence to support your response.**

$-43 \quad -40 \quad -37 \quad -34 \quad \blacksquare \quad \blacksquare \quad \blacksquare$

$+3 \quad +3 \quad +3 \quad +3 \quad +3 \quad +3$

Find the amount of increase from one integer to the next.

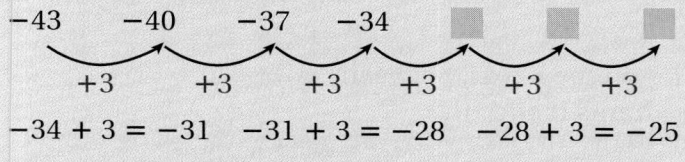

$-34 + 3 = -31 \quad -31 + 3 = -28 \quad -28 + 3 = -25$

The next three integers are -31, -28, and -25.

The pattern is to add 3 to each integer to get the next integer.

Step 4 **Summarize your argument.**

To find the next three integers in the pattern $-43, -40, -37, -34, \ldots,$ find the amount that is added to each integer to get the next integer in the pattern.

Try This

Write a convincing argument using the method above.

1. Explain how to find the next three integers in the pattern $0, -2, -4, -6, \ldots$.
2. Explain how to find the seventh integer in the pattern $-18, -13, -8, -3, \ldots$.

4-1 The Coordinate Plane

Learn to plot and identify ordered pairs on a coordinate plane.

Vocabulary

coordinate plane

***x*-axis**

***y*-axis**

origin

quadrant

ordered pair

A **coordinate plane** is a plane containing a horizontal number line, the ***x*-axis**, and a vertical number line, the ***y*-axis**. The intersection of these axes is called the **origin**.

The axes divide the coordinate plane into four regions called **quadrants**, which are numbered I, II, III, and IV.

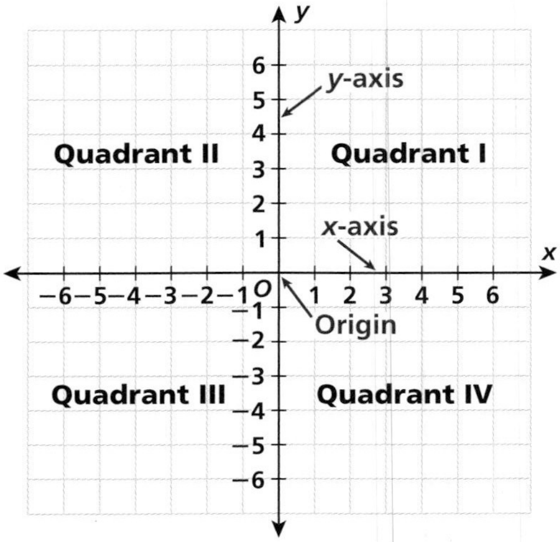

EXAMPLE 1 Identifying Quadrants on a Coordinate Plane

Identify the quadrant that contains each point.

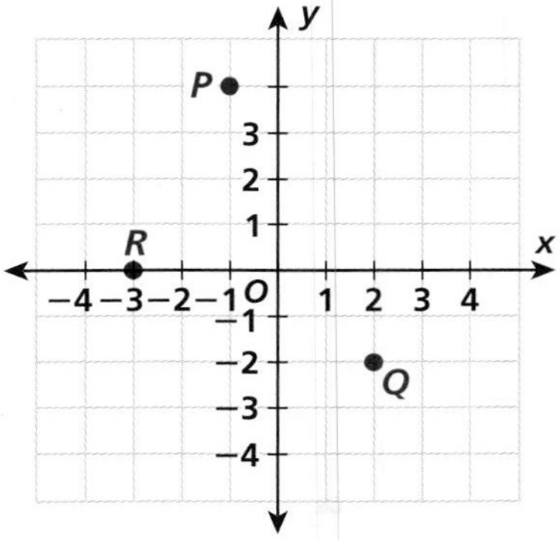

A *P*

P lies in Quadrant II.

B *Q*

Q lies in Quadrant IV.

C *R*

R lies on the *x*-axis, between Quadrants II and III.

An **ordered pair** is a pair of numbers that can be used to locate a point on a coordinate plane. The two numbers that form the ordered pair are called coordinates. The origin is identified by the ordered pair (0, 0).

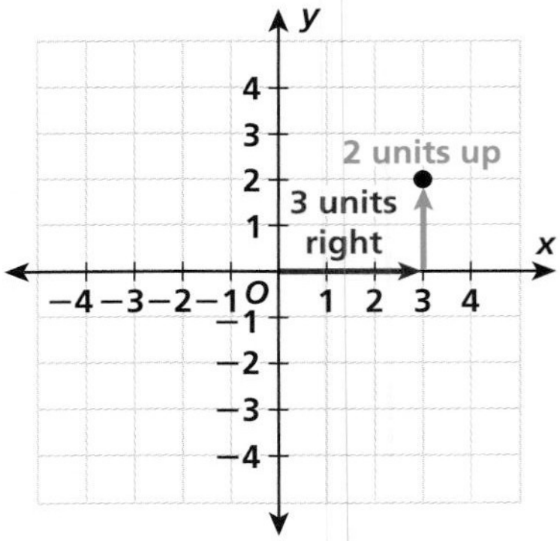

Ordered pair

(3, 2)

***x*-coordinate**: **Units right or left from 0**

***y*-coordinate**: **Units up or down from 0**

EXAMPLE 2 Plotting Points on a Coordinate Plane

Plot each point on a coordinate plane.

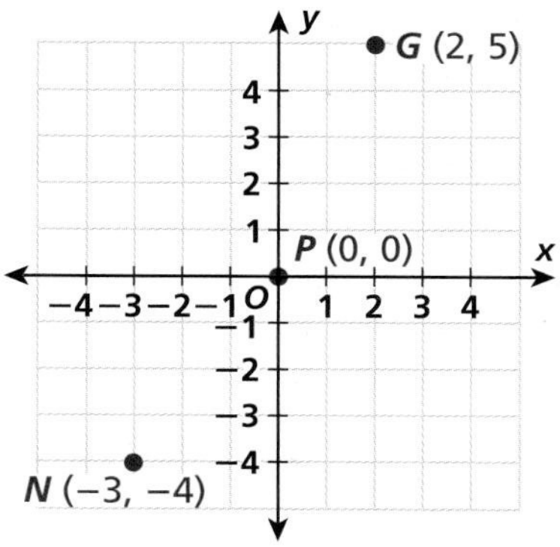

A G (2, 5)

Start at the origin. Move 2 units right and 5 units up.

B N (−3, −4)

Start at the origin. Move 3 units left and 4 units down.

C P (0, 0)

Point P is at the origin.

EXAMPLE 3 Identifying Points on a Coordinate Plane

Give the coordinates of each point.

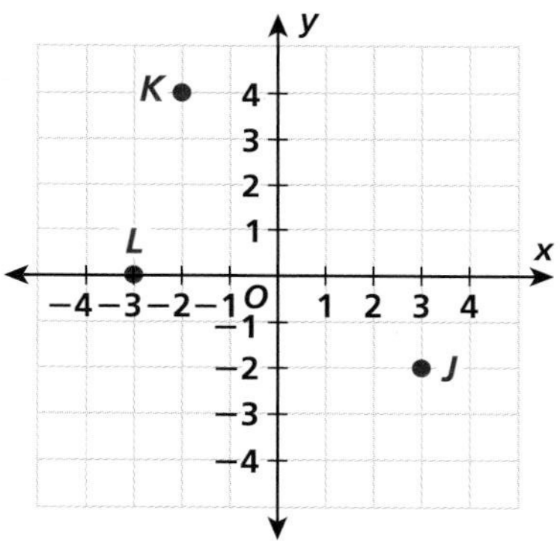

A J

Start at the origin. Point J is 3 units right and 2 units down.

The coordinates of J are (3, −2).

B K

Start at the origin. Point K is 2 units left and 4 units up.

The coordinates of K are (−2, 4).

C L

Start at the origin. Point L is 3 units left on the x-axis.

The coordinates of L are (−3, 0).

Think and Discuss

1. **Explain** whether point (4, 5) is the same as point (5, 4).
2. **Name** the x-coordinate of a point on the y-axis. Name the y-coordinate of a point on the x-axis.
3. **Suppose** the equator represents the x-axis on a map of Earth and a line called the *prime meridian,* which passes through England, represents the y-axis. Starting at the origin, which of these directions —east, west, north, and south—are positive? Which are negative?

4-1 Exercises

go.hrw.com
Homework Help Online
KEYWORD: MS7 4-1
Parent Resources Online
KEYWORD: MS7 Parent

GUIDED PRACTICE

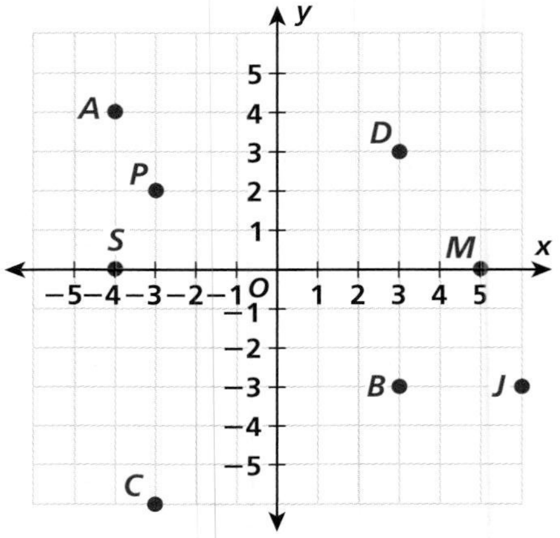

See Example 1 **Identify the quadrant that contains each point.**

1. *A* **2.** *B*

3. *C* **4.** *D*

See Example 2 **Plot each point on a coordinate plane.**

5. $E(-1, 2)$ **6.** $N(2, -4)$

7. $H(-3, -4)$ **8.** $T(5, 0)$

See Example 3 **Give the coordinates of each point.**

9. *J* **10.** *P*

11. *S* **12.** *M*

INDEPENDENT PRACTICE

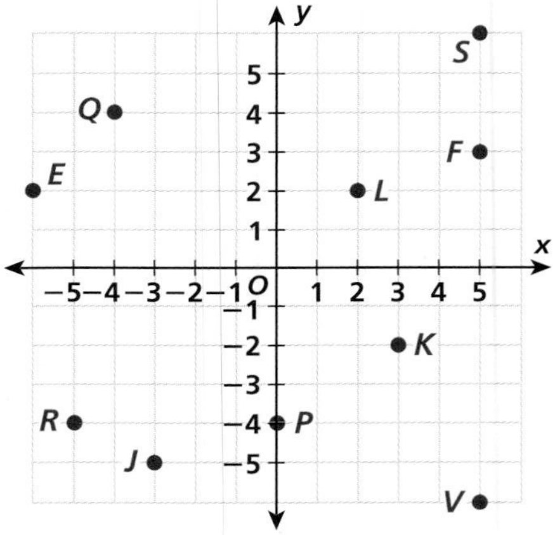

See Example 1 **Identify the quadrant that contains each point.**

13. *F* **14.** *J*

15. *K* **16.** *E*

See Example 2 **Plot each point on a coordinate plane.**

17. $A(-1, 1)$ **18.** $M(2, -2)$

19. $W(-5, -5)$ **20.** $G(0, -3)$

See Example 3 **Give the coordinates of each point.**

21. *Q* **22.** *V* **23.** *R*

24. *P* **25.** *S* **26.** *L*

PRACTICE AND PROBLEM SOLVING

Extra Practice
See page 733.

For Exercises 27 and 28, use graph paper to graph the ordered pairs. Use a different coordinate plane for each exercise.

27. $(-8, 1)$; $(4, 3)$; $(-3, 6)$ **28.** $(-8, -2)$; $(-1, -2)$; $(-1, 3)$; $(-8, 3)$

29. Geometry Connect the points in Exercise 27. Identify the figure and the quadrants in which it is located.

30. Geometry Connect the points in Exercise 28 in the order listed. Identify the figure and the quadrants in which it is located.

Identify the quadrant of each point described below.

31. The x-coordinate and the y-coordinate are both negative.

32. The x-coordinate is negative and the y-coordinate is positive.

LINK

Weather

When the wind speed of a tropical storm reaches 74 mi/h, it is classified as a hurricane.

go.hrw.com
Web Extra!
KEYWORD: MS7 Hurricane

33. What point is 9 units right and 3 units up from point (3, 4)?

34. **Critical Thinking** After being moved 6 units right and 4 units down, a point is located at (6, 1). What were the original coordinates of the point?

35. **Weather** The map shows the path of Hurricane Andrew. Estimate to the nearest integer the coordinates of the storm for each of the times below.

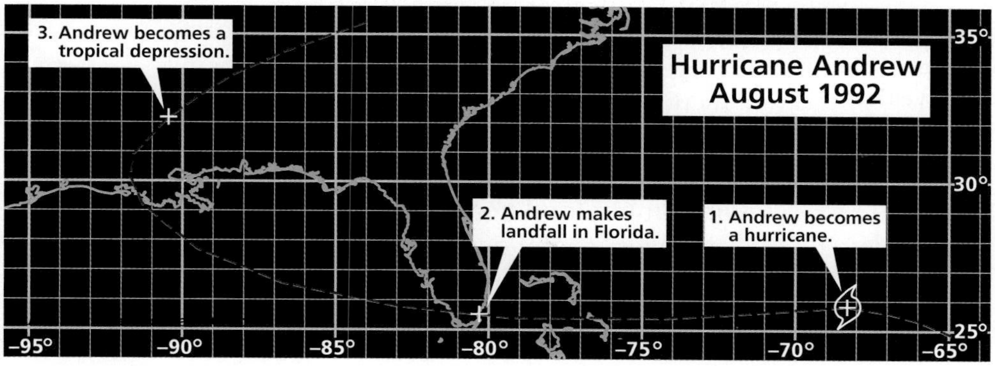

a. when Andrew first became a hurricane

b. when Andrew made landfall in Florida

c. when Andrew weakened to a tropical depression

36. **What's the Error?** To plot (−12, 1), a student started at (0, 0) and moved 12 units right and 1 unit down. What did the student do wrong?

37. **Write About It** Why is order important when graphing an ordered pair on a coordinate plane?

38. **Challenge** Armand and Kayla started jogging from the same point. Armand jogged 4 miles south and 6 miles east. Kayla jogged west and 4 miles south. If they were 11 miles apart when they stopped, how far west did Kayla jog?

TEST PREP and Spiral Review

39. **Multiple Choice** Which of the following points lie within the circle graphed at right?

Ⓐ (2, 6) Ⓑ (−4, 4) Ⓒ (0, −4) Ⓓ (−6, 6)

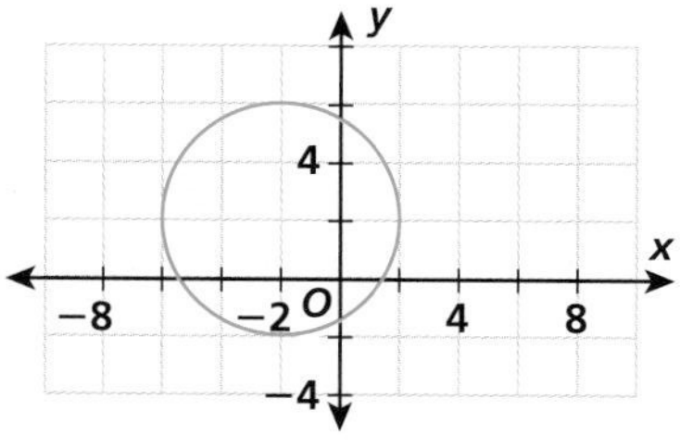

40. **Multiple Choice** Which point on the x-axis is the same distance from the origin as (0, −3)?

Ⓕ (0, 3) Ⓖ (3, 0) Ⓗ (3, −3) Ⓙ (−3, 3)

Find each sum. (Lesson 2-2)

41. $-17 + 11$ 42. $29 + 8$ 43. $40 + (-64)$ 44. $-55 + (-32)$

Divide. Write each answer in simplest form. (Lesson 3-11)

45. $8 \div 1\frac{1}{4}$ 46. $\frac{3}{5} \div \frac{6}{15}$ 47. $2\frac{1}{3} \div 1\frac{2}{3}$ 48. $\frac{5}{8} \div \frac{3}{4}$

4-2 Tables and Graphs

Learn to identify and graph ordered pairs from a table of values.

In October 2004, five lion cubs were born at Henry Vilas Zoo in Madison, Wisconsin. By the time the cubs were three months old, they were each eating $2\frac{1}{2}$ pounds of food per day. The table shows the amount of food needed to feed one cub over several days.

Number of Days	1	2	3	4
Amount of Food (lb)	2.5	5	7.5	10

EXAMPLE 1 Identifying Ordered Pairs from a Table of Values

Write the ordered pairs from the table.

x	y
5	6
7	7
9	7
11	9

→

(x, y)
(5, 6)
(7, 7)
(9, 7)
(11, 9)

The ordered pairs are (5, 6), (7, 7), (9, 7), and (11, 9).

EXAMPLE 2 Graphing Ordered Pairs from a Table of Values

Write and graph the ordered pairs from the table.

x	−3	−1	1	3
y	4	1	−2	−5

The ordered pairs are (−3, 4), (−1, 1), (1, −2), and (3, −5).

Plot the points on a coordinate plane.

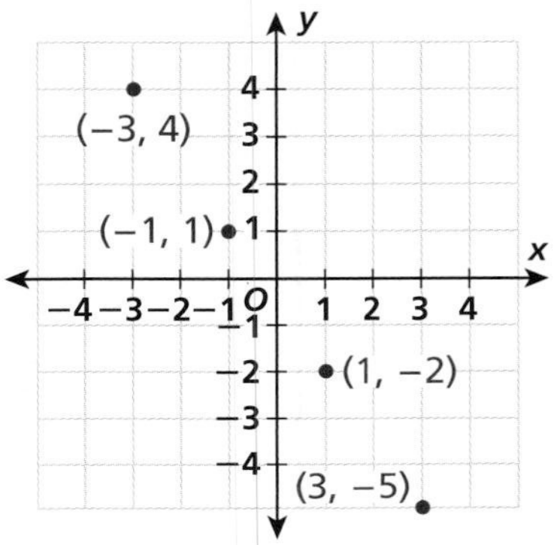

EXAMPLE 3 *Life Science Application*

The zookeepers at Henry Vilas Zoo are buying food for the lion cubs. The table shows the amount of food needed to feed one cub for 4 days. Graph the data. What appears to be the relationship between the number of days and the amount of food?

Number of Days	1	2	3	4
Amount of Food (lb)	2.5	5	7.5	10

Write the ordered pairs from the table.

Number of Days	1	2	3	4
Amount of Food (lb)	2.5	5	7.5	10
(x, y)	(1, 2.5)	(2, 5)	(3, 7.5)	(4, 10)

The ordered pairs are (1, 2.5), (2, 5), (3, 7.5), and (4, 10).

Now plot the points on a coordinate plane. Label the axes.

The graph shows that for each additional day, $2\frac{1}{2}$ additional pounds of food are needed for one lion cub.

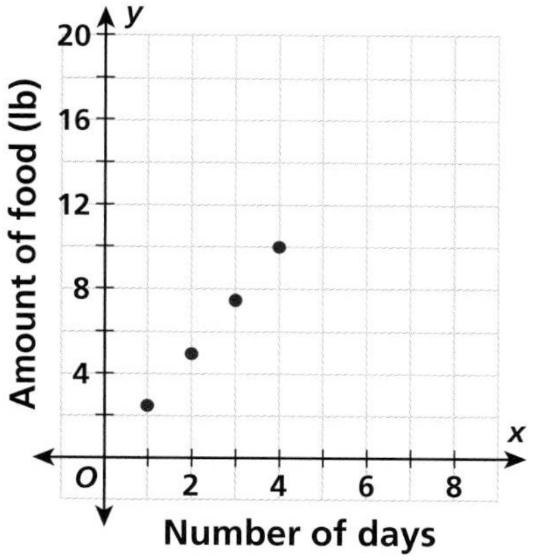

Think and Discuss

1. **Give an example** of a table that includes the origin as one of its ordered pairs.
2. **Explain** whether you could use the graph in Example 3 to find the amount of food needed to feed one cub for 14 days.
3. **Describe** a real-world situation that could be represented by a graph that has distinct points.

4-2 Exercises

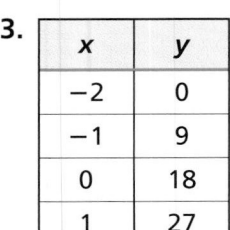

go.hrw.com
Homework Help Online
KEYWORD: MS7 4-2
Parent Resources Online
KEYWORD: MS7 Parent

GUIDED PRACTICE

See Example 1

Write the ordered pairs from each table.

1.

x	*y*
1	1
2	1
3	1
4	1

2.

x	*y*
8	4
10	5
12	6
14	7

3.

x	*y*
−2	0
−1	9
0	18
1	27

See Example 2

Graph the ordered pairs from each table.

4.

x	1	2	3	4
y	−2	−1	0	1

5.

x	−5	−3	−1	1
y	4	2	0	−2

See Example 3

6. The table shows the total cost of buying different numbers of drinks. Graph the data. What appears to be the relationship between the number of drinks and the total cost?

Number of Drinks	1	2	3	4
Total Cost ($)	1.50	3.00	4.50	6.00

INDEPENDENT PRACTICE

See Example 1

Write the ordered pairs from each table.

7.

x	*y*
−15	15
−10	10
−5	5
0	0

8.

x	*y*
−2	0
0	−1
4	−2
6	−3

9.

x	*y*
−11	−6
−9	−5
−7	−4
−5	−3

See Example 2

Graph the ordered pairs from each table.

10.

x	0	2	4	6
y	−1	1	3	5

11.

x	−3	−1	1	3
y	3	1	1	3

See Example 3

12. The table shows the total cost of an international phone call for different numbers of minutes. Graph the data. What appears to be the relationship between the number of minutes and the cost of a phone call?

Number of Minutes	2	4	6	8
Total Cost ($)	2	3	4	5

PRACTICE AND PROBLEM SOLVING

Extra Practice
See page 733.

13. **Business** An accountant uses 3.5 gallons of gas each day driving to and from her office.
    a. Make a table showing the total number of gallons of gas she uses for each of 5 days.
    b. Graph the data from your answer to **a**.

14. **Crafts** Candle makers calculate the burn time for a candle by lighting the candle and recording the amount of wax remaining at various times. The table shows data for a 6-ounce candle.

Elapsed Time (hr)	Wax Remaining (oz)
0	6
7	5
14	4
21	3

    a. Make a graph of the data.
    b. Explain how you can use the graph to find the amount of wax remaining after 35 hours.

15. **Write a Problem** Create a table of data representing the number of hours of homework you do for each of 5 days. Graph the data from your table.

16. **Write About It** A table of data shows the number of times a whale's heart beats in 3, 4, 5, and 6 minutes. Describe how to make a graph to show the relationship between the number of minutes and the number of heartbeats.

17. **Challenge** A table of data has the ordered pairs $(-2, 5)$, $(1, 4)$, and $(4, 3)$. Kim plots the points and connects them with a straight line. At what point does the line cross the x-axis?

TEST PREP and Spiral Review

18. **Multiple Choice** Miguel plotted the ordered pairs $(-3, -5)$, $(-2, -1)$, $(-1, 3)$, and $(0, 7)$. How many points did he plot in Quadrant III?

    Ⓐ 0   Ⓑ 1   Ⓒ 2   Ⓓ 3

19. **Short Response** The table shows the perimeters and areas of several rectangles. Make a graph of the data.

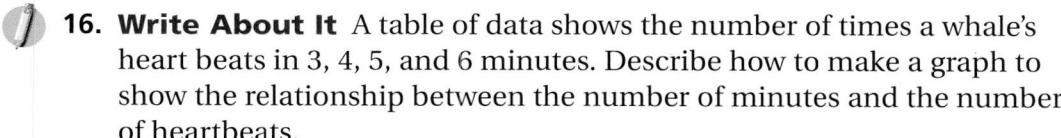

Perimeter (in.)	6	10	14	18
Area (in^2)	2	6	12	20

Divide. Estimate to check whether each answer is reasonable. (Lesson 3-4)

20. $48.6 \div 6$ 21. $31.5 \div (-5)$ 22. $-8.32 \div 4$ 23. $-74.1 \div 6$

Add. Write each answer in simplest form. (Lesson 3-9)

24. $1\frac{1}{5} + 3\frac{3}{5}$ 25. $7\frac{2}{3} + 8\frac{2}{3}$ 26. $9\frac{1}{4} + 6\frac{2}{3}$ 27. $4\frac{7}{10} + 3\frac{1}{8}$

Plot each point on a coordinate plane. (Lesson 4-1)

28. $A(-4, 1)$ 29. $B(0, 3)$ 30. $C(2, -2)$ 31. $D(1, 5)$

4-3 Interpreting Graphs

Learn to relate graphs to situations.

You can use a graph to show the relationship between speed and time, time and distance, or speed and distance.

The graph at right shows the varying speeds at which Emma exercises her horse. The horse walks at a constant speed for the first 10 minutes. Its speed increases over the next 7 minutes, and then it gallops at a constant rate for 20 minutes. Then it slows down over the next 3 minutes and then walks at a constant pace for 10 minutes.

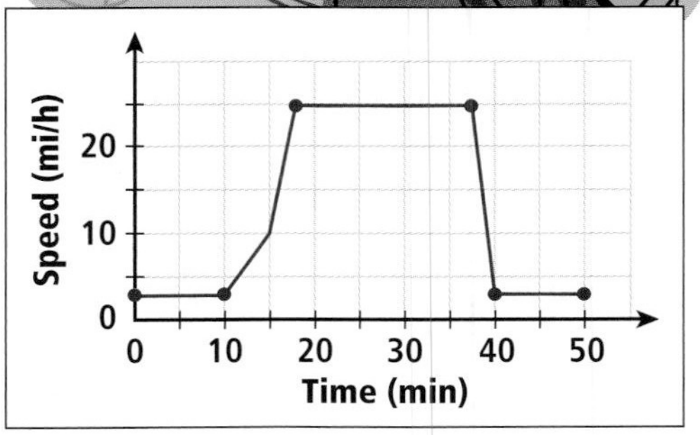

EXAMPLE 1 Relating Graphs to Situations

Jenny leaves home and drives to the beach. She stays at the beach all day before driving back home. Which graph best shows the situation?

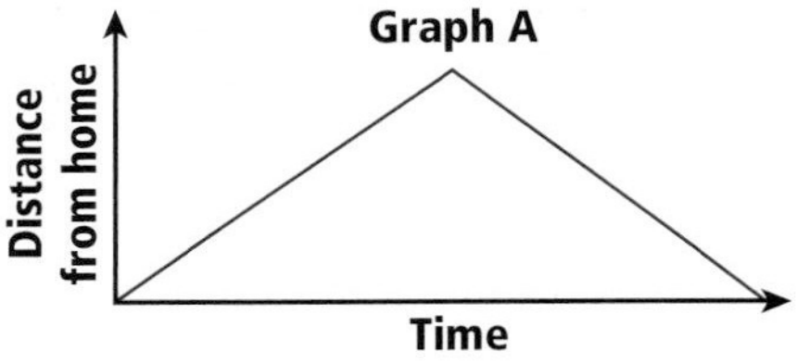

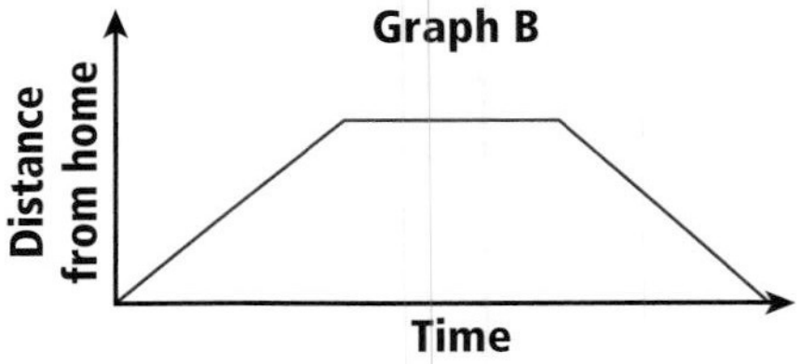

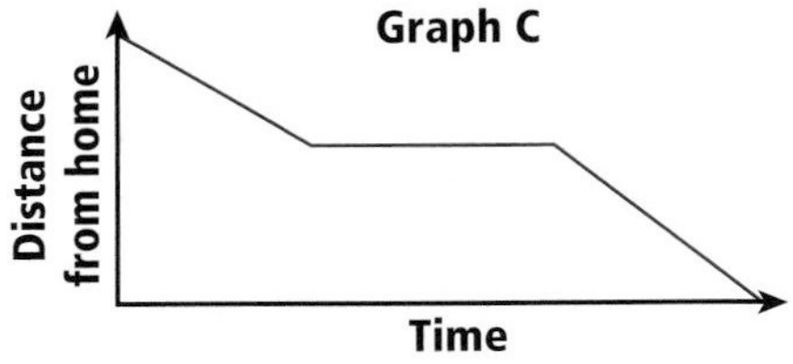

As Jenny drives to the beach, her distance from home *increases*. While she is at the beach, her distance from home is *constant*. As she drives home, her distance from home *decreases*. The answer is graph b.

EXAMPLE 2 PROBLEM SOLVING APPLICATION

PROBLEM SOLVING

Maili and Katrina traveled 10 miles from Maili's house to the movie theater. They watched a movie, and then they traveled 5 miles farther to a restaurant to eat lunch. After eating they returned to Maili's house. Sketch a graph to show the distance that the two friends traveled compared to time. Use your graph to find the total distance traveled.

1 Understand the Problem

The answer will be the total distance that Katrina and Maili traveled.

List the **important information:**

- The friends traveled 10 miles from Maili's house to the theater.
- They traveled an additional 5 miles and then ate lunch.
- They returned to Maili's house.

2 Make a Plan

Sketch a graph that represents the situation. Then use the graph to find the total distance Katrina and Maili traveled.

3 Solve

The distance from Maili's house increases from 0 to 10 miles when the friends travel to the theater. The distance increases from 10 to 15 miles when they go to the restaurant. The distance does not change while the friends watch the movie and eat lunch. The distance decreases from 15 to 0 miles when they return home.

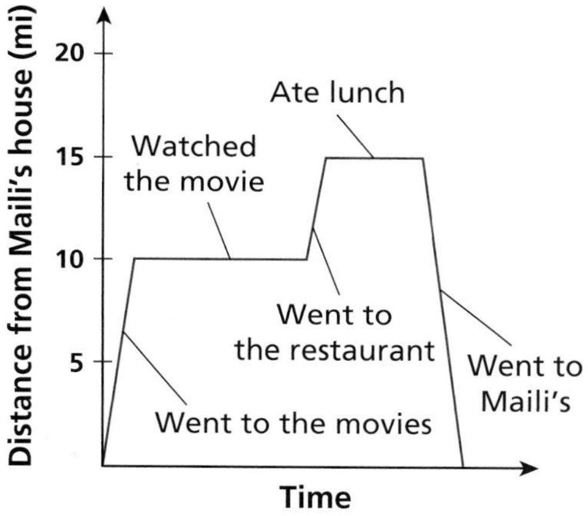

Maili and Katrina traveled a total of 30 miles.

4 Look Back

The theater is 10 miles away, so the friends must have traveled twice that distance just to go to the theater and return. The answer, 30 miles, is reasonable since it is greater than 20 miles.

Think and Discuss

1. **Explain** the meaning of a horizontal segment on a graph that compares distance to time.
2. **Describe** a real-world situation that could be represented by a graph that has connected lines or curves.

4-3 Exercises

go.hrw.com
Homework Help Online
KEYWORD: MS7 4-3
Parent Resources Online
KEYWORD: MS7 Parent

GUIDED PRACTICE

See Example 1

1. The temperature of an ice cube increases until it starts to melt. While it melts, its temperature stays constant. Which graph best shows the situation?

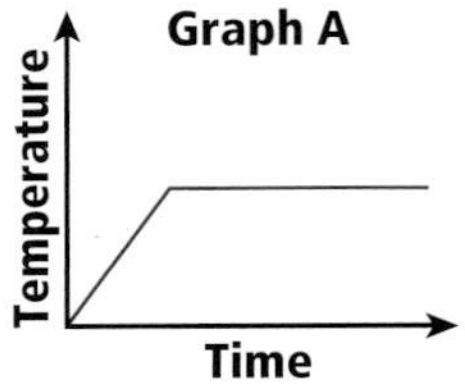

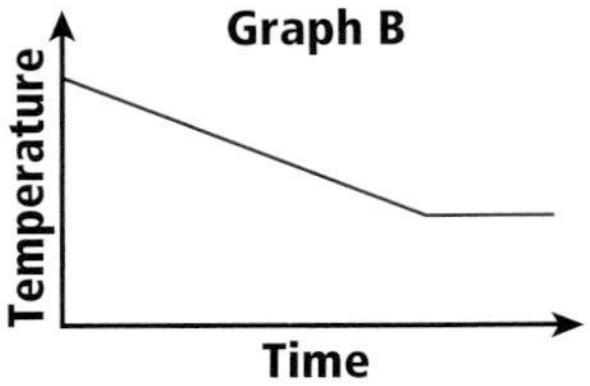

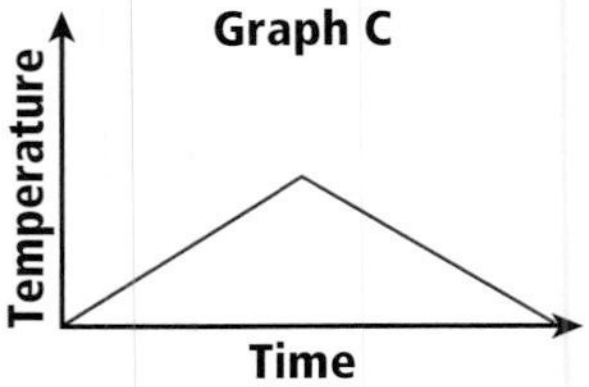

See Example 2

2. Mike and Claudia rode a bus 15 miles to a wildlife park. They waited in line to ride a train, which took them on a 3-mile ride around the park. After the train ride, they ate lunch, and then they rode the bus home. Sketch a graph to show the distance Mike and Claudia traveled compared to time. Use your graph to find the total distance traveled.

INDEPENDENT PRACTICE

See Example 1

3. The ink in a printer is used until the ink cartridge is empty. The cartridge is refilled, and the ink is used up again. Which graph best shows the situation?

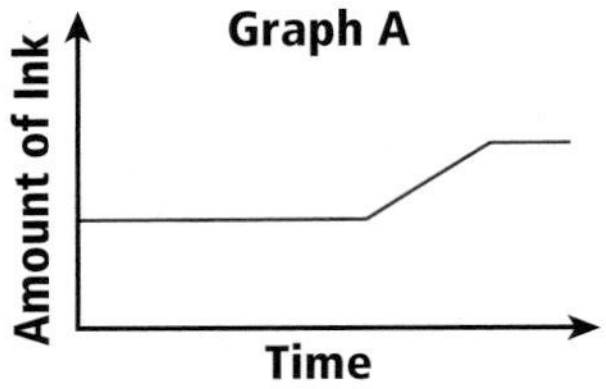

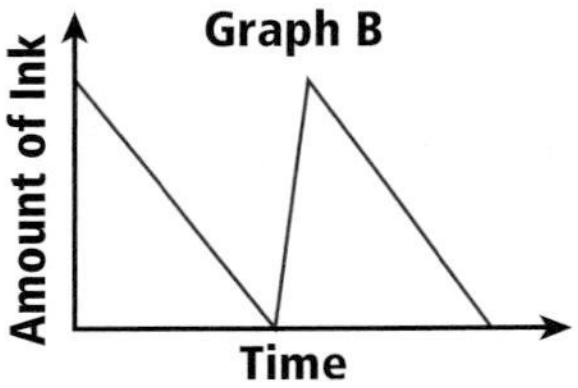

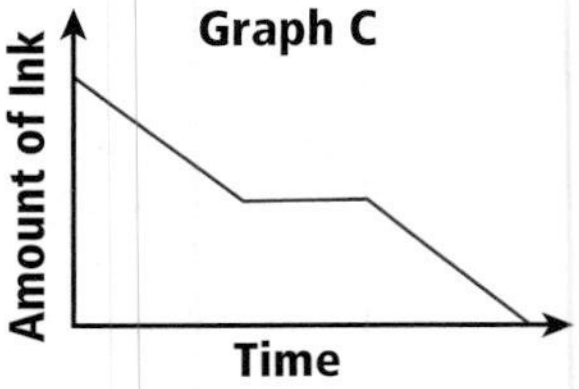

See Example 2

4. On her way from home to the grocery store, a 6-mile trip, Veronica stopped at a gas station to buy gas. After filling her tank, she continued to the grocery store. She then returned home after shopping. Sketch a graph to show the distance Veronica traveled compared to time. Use your graph to find the total distance traveled.

PRACTICE AND PROBLEM SOLVING

Extra Practice
See page 733.

5. Tell a story that fits the graph at right.

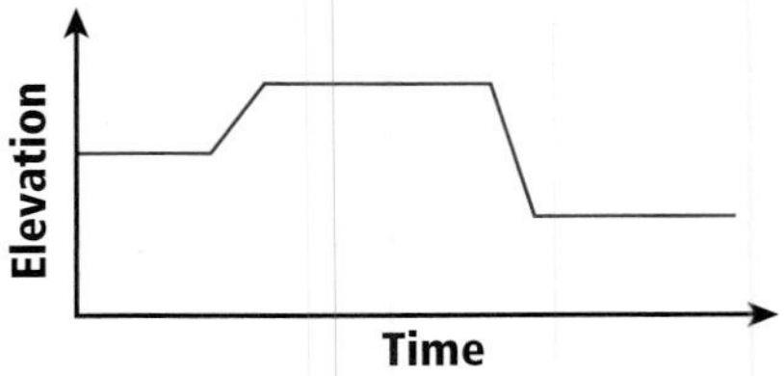

6. Lynn jogged for 2.5 miles. Then she walked a little while before stopping to stretch. Sketch a graph to show Lynn's speed compared to time.

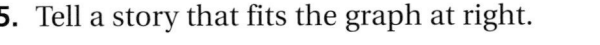

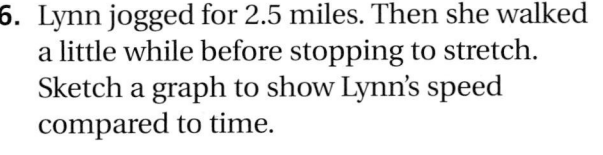

7. On his way to the library, Jeff runs two blocks and then walks three more blocks. Sketch a graph to show the distance Jeff travels compared to time.

8. **Critical Thinking** The graph at right shows high school enrollment, including future projections.

   a. Describe what is happening in the graph.

   b. Does it make sense to connect the points in the graph? Explain.

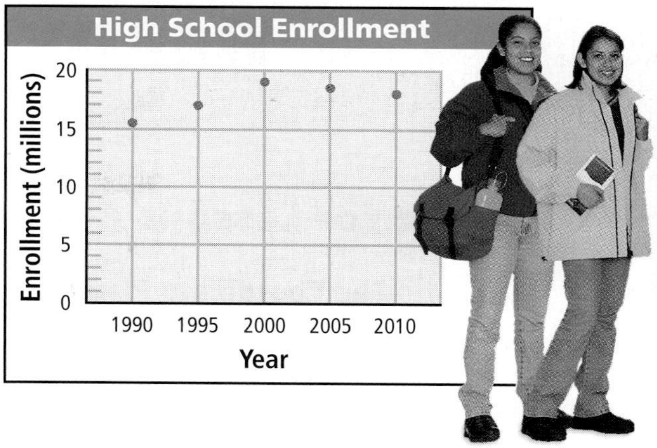

9. **Choose a Strategy** Three bananas were given to two mothers who were with their daughters. Each person had a banana to eat. How is that possible?

10. **Write About It** A driver sets his car's cruise control to 55 mi/h. Describe a graph that shows the car's speed compared to time. Then describe a second graph that shows the distance traveled compared to time.

11. **Challenge** The graph at right shows the temperature of an oven after the oven is turned on. Explain what the graph shows.

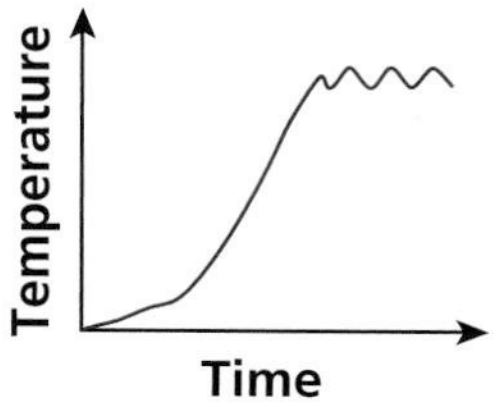

Test Prep and Spiral Review

12. **Multiple Choice** How does speed compare to time in the graph at right?

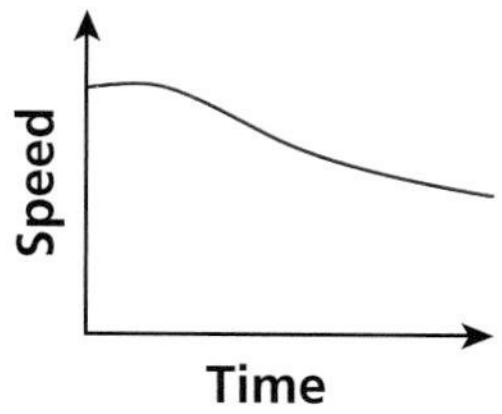

   Ⓐ It increases.   Ⓒ It stays the same.

   Ⓑ It decreases.   Ⓓ It fluctuates.

13. **Short Response** Keisha takes a big drink from a bottle of water. She sets the bottle down to tie her shoe and then picks up the bottle to take a small sip of water. Sketch a graph to show the amount of water in the bottle over time.

Find each absolute value. (Lesson 2-1)

14. $|9|$ **15.** $|-3|$ **16.** $|-15|$ **17.** $|0|$ **18.** $|5|$

Find the greatest common factor. (Lesson 2-7)

19. 12, 45   **20.** 33, 110   **21.** 6, 81   **22.** 24, 36

Write the ordered pairs from each table. (Lesson 4-2)

23.

x	1	3	5	7
y	4	6	8	10

24.

x	−6	0	6	12
y	0	6	−12	18

CHAPTER 4

READY TO GO ON?

SECTION 4A

Quiz for Lessons 4-1 Through 4-3

4-1 The Coordinate Plane

Plot each point on a coordinate plane. Then identify the quadrant that contains each point.

1. $W(1, 5)$ **2.** $X(5, -3)$ **3.** $Y(-1, -5)$ **4.** $Z(-8, 2)$

Give the coordinates of each point.

5. A **6.** B

7. C **8.** D

9. E **10.** F

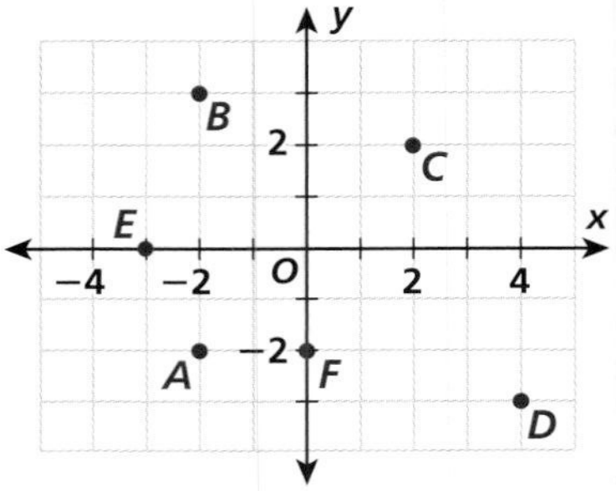

4-2 Tables and Graphs

Write and graph the ordered pairs from each table.

11.

x	y
1	5
−3	0
2	−5

12.

x	y
7	4
0	0
−4	3

13.

x	y
0	2
−6	6
−1	−2

14. The table shows the number of quarts there are in each number of gallons. Graph the data. What appears to be the relationship between the number of quarts and the number of gallons?

Quarts	8	12	16
Gallons	2	3	4

4-3 Interpreting Graphs

15. Raj climbs to the top of a cliff. He descends a little bit to another cliff, and then he begins to climb again. Which graph best shows the situation?

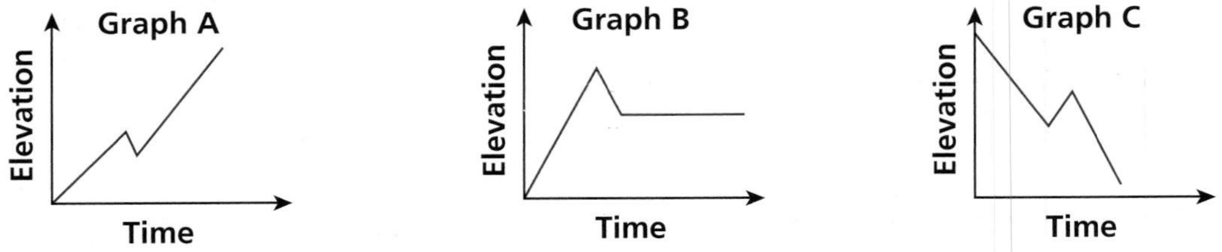

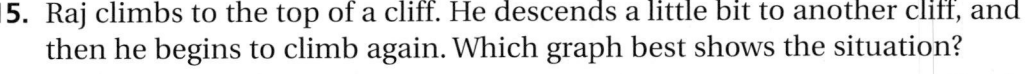

16. Ty walks 1 mile to the mall. An hour later, he walks $\frac{1}{2}$ mile farther to a park and eats lunch. Then he walks home. Sketch a graph to show the distance Ty traveled compared to time. Use your graph to find the total distance traveled.

Focus on Problem Solving

Understand the Problem

• **Sequence and prioritize information**

When you are reading a math problem, putting events in order, or in *sequence,* can help you understand the problem better. It helps to *prioritize* the information when you put it in order. To prioritize, you decide which of the information in your list is most important. The most important information has highest priority.

Use the information in the list or table to answer each question.

1 The list at right shows all of the things that Roderick has to do on Saturday. He starts the day without any money.

a. Which two activities on Roderick's list must be done before any of the other activities? Do these two activities have higher or lower priority?

b. Is there more than one way that he can order his activities? Explain.

c. List the order in which Roderick's activities could occur on Saturday.

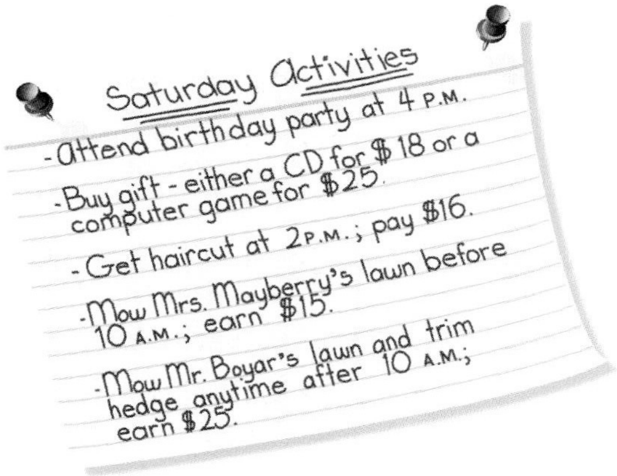
Saturday Activities
-Attend birthday party at 4 P.M.
-Buy gift - either a CD for $18 or a computer game for $25.
-Get haircut at 2 P.M.; pay $16.
-Mow Mrs. Mayberry's lawn before 10 A.M.; earn $15.
-Mow Mr. Boyar's lawn and trim hedge anytime after 10 A.M.; earn $25.

2 Tara and her family will visit Ocean World Park from 9:30 to 4:00. They want to see the waterskiing show at 10:00. Each show in the park is 50 minutes long. The time they choose to eat lunch will depend on the schedule they choose for seeing the shows.

a. Which of the information given in the paragraph above has the highest priority? Which has the lowest priority?

b. List the order in which they can see all of the shows, including the time they will see each.

c. At what time should they plan to have lunch?

Show Times at Ocean World Park	
9:00, 12:00	Underwater acrobats
9:00, 3:00	Whale acts
10:00, 2:00	Dolphin acts
10:00, 1:00	Waterskiing
11:00, 4:00	Aquarium tour

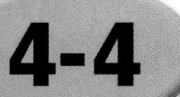

4-4 Functions, Tables, and Graphs

Learn to use function tables to generate and graph ordered pairs.

Vocabulary

function

input

output

As you raise spoon of soup (A) to your mouth, it pulls string (B), thereby jerking ladle (C), which throws cracker (D) past parrot (E). Parrot jumps after cracker, and perch (F) tilts, upsetting seeds (G) into pail (H). Extra weight in pail pulls cord (I), which opens and lights automatic cigar lighter (J), setting off sky rocket (K), which causes sickle (L) to cut string (M) and allow pendulum with attached napkin to swing back and forth, thereby wiping off your chin.

Rube Goldberg, a famous cartoonist, invented machines that perform ordinary tasks in extraordinary ways. Each machine operates according to a rule, or a set of steps, to produce a particular *output.*

In mathematics, a **function** operates according to a rule to produce exactly one output value for each input value. The **input** is the value substituted into the function. The **output** is the value that results from the substitution of a given input into the function.

A function can be represented by a rule written in words, such as "double the number and then add nine to the result," or by an equation with two variables. One variable represents the input, and the other represents the output.

Function Rule

$$y = 2x + 9$$

Output variable (y) **Input variable** (x)

You can use a table to organize and display the input and output values of a function.

EXAMPLE 1 **Completing a Function Table**

Find the output for each input.

A $y = 4x - 2$

Input	Rule	Output
x	$4x - 2$	y
−1	4(−1) − 2	−6
0	4(0) − 2	−2
3	4(3) − 2	10

Substitute −1 for x. Then simplify.

Substitute 0 for x. Then simplify.

Substitute 3 for x. Then simplify.

Find the output for each input.

B $y = 6x^2$

Input	Rule	Output
x	$6x^2$	y
−5	$6(-5)^2$	150
0	$6(0)^2$	0
5	$6(5)^2$	150

Substitute −5 for x. Then simplify.
Substitute 0 for x. Then simplify.
Substitute 5 for x. Then simplify.

Remember!

An ordered pair is a pair of numbers that represents a point on a graph.

You can also use a graph to represent a function. The corresponding input and output values together form unique ordered pairs.

Helpful Hint

When writing an ordered pair, write the input value first and then the output value.

EXAMPLE 2 Graphing Functions Using Ordered Pairs

Make a function table, and graph the resulting ordered pairs.

A $y = 2x$

Input	Rule	Output	Ordered Pair
x	$2x$	y	(x, y)
−2	$2(-2)$	−4	(−2, −4)
−1	$2(-1)$	−2	(−1, −2)
0	$2(0)$	0	(0, 0)
1	$2(1)$	2	(1, 2)
2	$2(2)$	4	(2, 4)

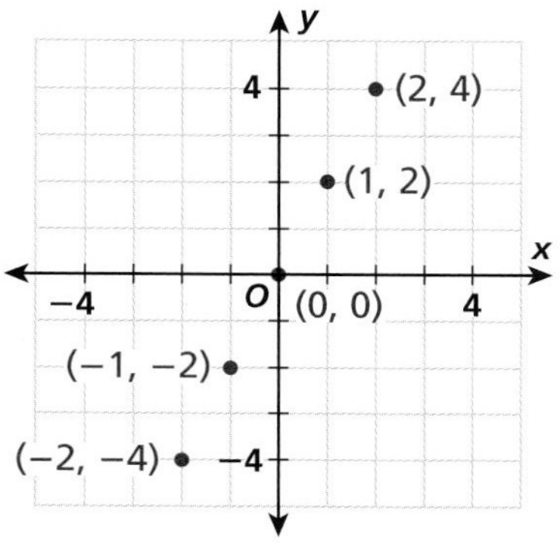

B $y = x^2$

Input	Rule	Output	Ordered Pair
x	x^2	y	(x, y)
−2	$(-2)^2$	4	(−2, 4)
−1	$(-1)^2$	1	(−1, 1)
0	$(0)^2$	0	(0, 0)
1	$(1)^2$	1	(1, 1)
2	$(2)^2$	4	(2, 4)

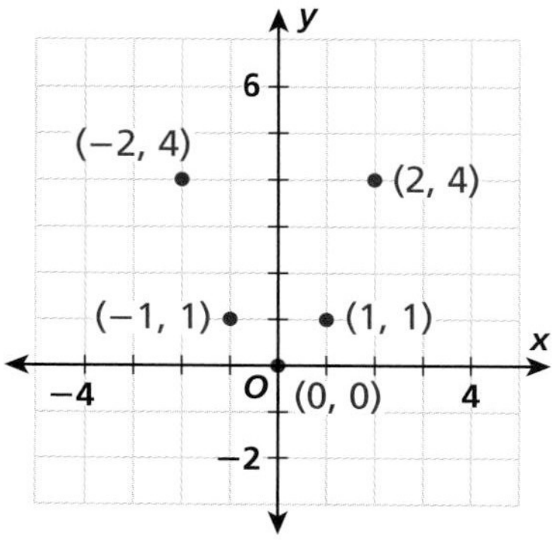

Think and Discuss

1. **Describe** how a function works like a machine.
2. **Give an example** of a rule that takes an input value of 4 and produces an output value of 10.

4-4 Exercises

go.hrw.com
Homework Help Online
KEYWORD: MS7 4-4
Parent Resources Online
KEYWORD: MS7 Parent

GUIDED PRACTICE

See Example 1 **Find the output for each input.**

1. $y = 2x + 1$

Input	Rule	Output
x	$2x + 1$	y
−3		
0		
1		

2. $y = -x + 3$

Input	Rule	Output
x	$-x + 3$	y
−2		
0		
2		

3. $y = 2x^2$

Input	Rule	Output
x	$2x^2$	y
−5		
1		
3		

See Example 2 **Make a function table, and graph the resulting ordered pairs.**

4. $y = 3x - 2$

Input	Rule	Output	Ordered Pair
x	$3x - 2$	y	(x, y)
−1			
0			
1			
2			

5. $y = x^2 + 2$

Input	Rule	Output	Ordered Pair
x	$x^2 + 2$	y	(x, y)
−1			
0			
1			
2			

INDEPENDENT PRACTICE

See Example 1 **Find the output for each input.**

6. $y = -2x$

Input	Rule	Output
x	$-2x$	y
−2		
0		
4		

7. $y = 3x + 2$

Input	Rule	Output
x	$3x + 2$	y
−3		
−1		
2		

8. $y = 3x^2$

Input	Rule	Output
x	$3x^2$	y
−10		
−6		
−2		

See Example 2 **Make a function table, and graph the resulting ordered pairs.**

9. $y = x \div 2$

Input	Rule	Output	Ordered Pair
x	$x \div 2$	y	(x, y)
−1			
0			
1			
2			

10. $y = x^2 - 4$

Input	Rule	Output	Ordered Pair
x	$x^2 - 4$	y	(x, y)
−1			
0			
1			
2			

PRACTICE AND PROBLEM SOLVING

Extra Practice
See page 734.

11. **Weather** The Northeast gets an average of 11.66 inches of rain in the summer.
    a. Write an equation that can be used to find y, the difference in rainfall between the average amount of summer rainfall and x, a given year's summer rainfall.
    b. Make a function table using each year's summer rainfall data.

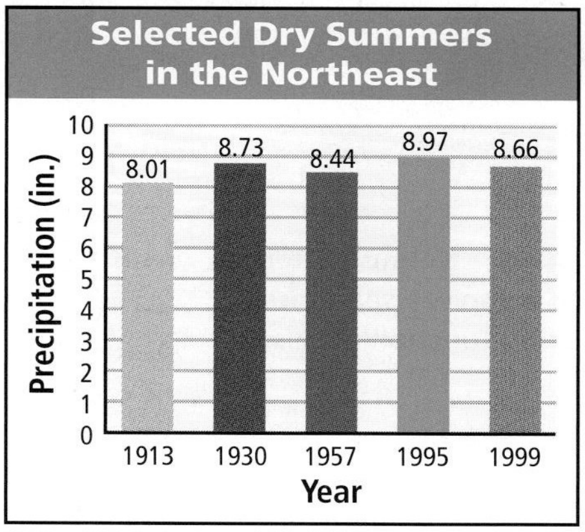

Source: USA Today, August 17, 2001

12. **Physical Science** The equation $F = \frac{9}{5}C + 32$ gives the Fahrenheit temperature F for a given Celsius temperature C. Make a function table for the values $C = -20°, -5°, 0°, 20°$, and $100°$.

13. **What's the Error?** What is the error in the function table at right?

x	$y = -x - 5$	y
−2	$y = -(-2) - 5$	−7
−1	$y = -(-1) - 5$	−6
0	$y = -(0) - 5$	−5
1	$y = -(1) - 5$	−6
2	$y = -(2) - 5$	−7

14. **Write About It** Explain how to make a function table for $y = 2x + 11$.

15. **Challenge** Mountain Rental charges a $25 deposit plus $10 per hour to rent a bicycle. Write an equation that gives the cost y to rent a bike for x hours. Then write the ordered pairs for $x = \frac{1}{2}$, 5, and $8\frac{1}{2}$.

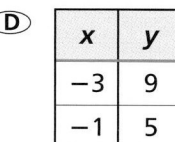

TEST PREP and Spiral Review

16. **Multiple Choice** Which table shows correct input and output values for the function $y = -2x + 3$?

Ⓐ

x	y
−1	−1
0	0

Ⓑ

x	y
−3	−2
−2	−1

Ⓒ

x	y
−5	−7
−1	1

Ⓓ

x	y
−3	9
−1	5

17. **Multiple Choice** Which function matches the function table?

x	0	1	2
y	3	4	11

Ⓕ $y = x + 3$ Ⓗ $y = 5x + 1$

Ⓖ $y = x^2 + 7$ Ⓙ $y = x^3 + 3$

Simplify. (Lesson 2-3)

18. $43 - (-18)$
19. $3 - (-2) - (5 + 1)$
20. $-4 - 8 - (-3)$

Solve. Write each answer in simplest form. (Lesson 3-12)

21. $\frac{1}{7}x = \frac{6}{7}$
22. $4z = \frac{4}{5}$
23. $\frac{6}{9}y = 3$
24. $\frac{1}{10}x = \frac{7}{8}$

4-5 Find a Pattern in Sequences

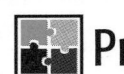

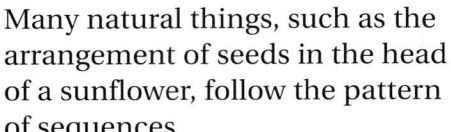

Problem Solving Skill

Learn to find patterns to complete sequences using function tables.

Vocabulary

sequence

term

arithmetic sequence

geometric sequence

Many natural things, such as the arrangement of seeds in the head of a sunflower, follow the pattern of sequences.

A **sequence** is an ordered list of numbers. Each number in a sequence is called a **term**. When the sequence follows a pattern, the terms in the sequence are the output values of a function, and the value of each term depends on its position in the sequence.

You can use a variable, such as n, to represent a number's position in a sequence.

n (position in the sequence)	1	2	3	4
y (value of term)	2	4	6	8

In an **arithmetic sequence**, the same amount is added each time to get the next term in the sequence. In a **geometric sequence**, each term is multiplied by the same amount to get the next term in the sequence.

EXAMPLE 1 Identifying Patterns in Sequences

Tell whether each sequence of y-values is arithmetic or geometric. Then find y when $n = 5$.

A

n	1	2	3	4	5
y	−12	−5	2	9	▒

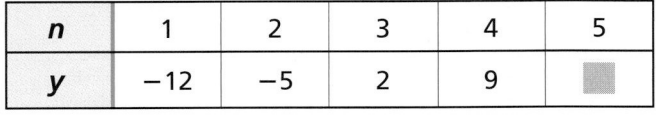

In the sequence $-12, -5, 2, 9,$ ▒$, \ldots,$ 7 is added to each term.

$9 + 7 = 16$ *Add 7 to the fourth term.*

The sequence is arithmetic. When $n = 5$, $y = 16$.

B

n	1	2	3	4	5
y	4	−12	36	−108	▒

In the sequence $4, -12, 36, -108,$ ▒$, \ldots,$ each term is multiplied by -3.

$-108 \cdot (-3) = 324$ *Multiply the fourth term by −3.*

The sequence is geometric. When $n = 5$, $y = 324$.

EXAMPLE 2 Identifying Functions in Sequences

Write a function that describes each sequence.

A 2, 4, 6, 8, . . .

Make a function table.

n	Rule	*y*
1	1 • 2	2
2	2 • 2	4
3	3 • 2	6
4	4 • 2	8

Multiply n by 2.

The function $y = 2n$ describes this sequence.

B 4, 5, 6, 7, . . .

Make a function table.

n	Rule	*y*
1	1 + 3	4
2	2 + 3	5
3	3 + 3	6
4	4 + 3	7

Add 3 to n.

The function $y = n + 3$ describes this sequence.

EXAMPLE 3 Using Functions to Extend Sequences

Sara has one week to read a book. She plans to increase the number of chapters that she reads each day. Her plan is to read 3 chapters on Sunday, 5 on Monday, 7 on Tuesday, and 9 on Wednesday. Write a function that describes the sequence. Then use the function to predict how many chapters Sara will read on Saturday.

Write the number of chapters she reads each day: 3, 5, 7, 9, . . .

Make a function table.

n	Rule	*y*
1	1 • 2 + 1	3
2	2 • 2 + 1	5
3	3 • 2 + 1	7
4	4 • 2 + 1	9

Multiply n by 2. Then add 1.

$y = 2n + 1$ *Write the function.*

Saturday corresponds to $n = 7$. When $n = 7$, $y = 2 \cdot 7 + 1 = 15$.

Sara plans to read 15 chapters on Saturday.

Think and Discuss

1. **Give an example** of a sequence involving addition, and give the rule you used.
2. **Describe** how to find a pattern in the sequence 1, 4, 16, 64, ...

4-5 Exercises

go.hrw.com
Homework Help Online
KEYWORD: MS7 4-5
Parent Resources Online
KEYWORD: MS7 Parent

GUIDED PRACTICE

See Example 1

Tell whether each sequence of y-values is arithmetic or geometric. Then find y when $n = 5$.

1.

n	1	2	3	4	5
y	−4	9	22	35	■

2.

n	1	2	3	4	5
y	8	4	2	1	■

See Example 2

Write a function that describes each sequence.

3. 3, 6, 9, 12, . . .
4. 3, 4, 5, 6, . . .
5. 0, 1, 2, 3, . . .
6. 5, 10, 15, 20, . . .

See Example 3

7. In March, WaterWorks recorded $195 in swimsuit sales. The store recorded $390 in sales in April, $585 in May, and $780 in June. Write a function that describes the sequence. Then use the function to predict the store's swimsuit sales in July.

INDEPENDENT PRACTICE

See Example 1

Tell whether each sequence of y-values is arithmetic or geometric. Then find y when $n = 5$.

8.

n	1	2	3	4	5
y	13	26	52	104	■

9.

n	1	2	3	4	5
y	14	30	46	62	■

See Example 2

Write a function that describes each sequence.

10. 5, 6, 7, 8, . . .
11. 7, 14, 21, 28, . . .
12. −2, −1, 0, 1, . . .
13. 20, 40, 60, 80, . . .
14. $\frac{1}{2}, 1, \frac{3}{2}, 2, \ldots$
15. 1.5, 2.5, 3.5, 4.5, . . .

See Example 3

16. The number of seats in the first row of a concert hall is 6. The second row has 9 seats, the third row has 12 seats, and the fourth row has 15 seats. Write a function to describe the sequence. Then use the function to predict the number of seats in the eighth row.

PRACTICE AND PROBLEM SOLVING

Extra Practice
See page 734.

Write a rule for each sequence in words. Then find the next three terms.

17. 35, 70, 105, 140, . . .
18. 0.7, 1.7, 2.7, 3.7, . . .
19. $\frac{3}{2}, \frac{5}{2}, \frac{7}{2}, \frac{9}{2}, \ldots$
20. −1, 0, 1, 2, . . .
21. $\frac{1}{3}, \frac{2}{3}, 1, \frac{4}{3}, \ldots$
22. 6, 11, 16, 21, . . .

Write a function that describes each sequence. Use the function to find the tenth term in the sequence.

23. 0.5, 1.5, 2.5, 3.5, . . .
24. 0, 2, 4, 6, . . .
25. 5, 8, 11, 14, . . .
26. 3, 8, 13, 18, . . .
27. 1, 3, 5, 7, . . .
28. 6, 10, 14, 18, . . .

Computer Science LINK

Computer programmers use functions to create designs known as *fractals.* A fractal is a *self-similar* pattern, which means that each part of the pattern is similar to the whole pattern. Fractals are created by repeating a set of steps, called *iterations.*

29. Below is part of a famous fractal called the Cantor set. In each iteration, part of a line segment is removed, resulting in twice as many segments as before. The table lists the number of line segments that result from the iterations shown. Find a function that describes the sequence.

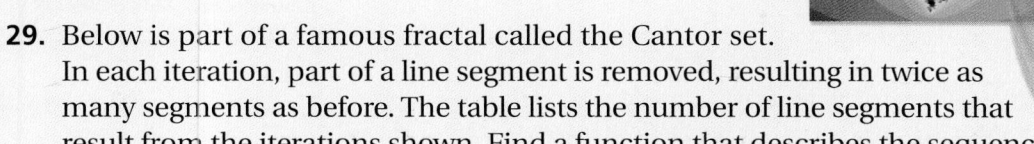

Iteration (n)	Number of Segments (y)
1	2
2	4
3	8

30. Multi-Step These are the first three iterations of the Sierpinski triangle. In each iteration, a certain number of smaller triangles are cut out of the larger triangle.

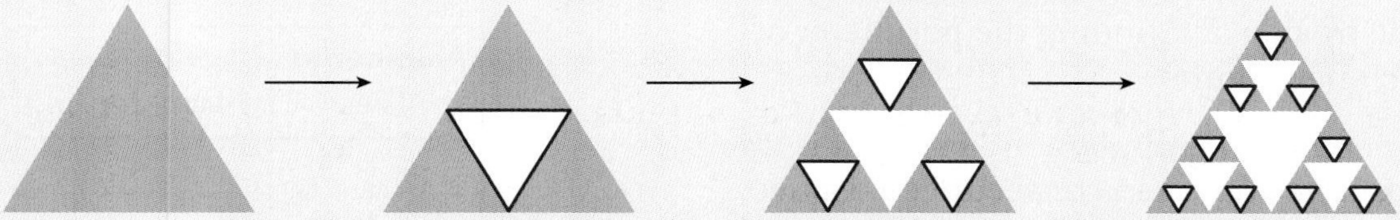

Iteration 1 1 triangle removed

Iteration 2 3 more triangles removed

Iteration 3 9 more triangles removed

Create a table to list the number of yellow triangles that exist after each iteration. Then find a function that describes the sequence.

31. Challenge Find a function that describes the number of triangles removed in each iteration of the Sierpinski triangle.

go.hrw.com
Web Extra!
KEYWORD: MS7 Fractals

TEST PREP and Spiral Review

32. Multiple Choice Which function describes the sequence 1, 4, 7, 10, . . . ?

Ⓐ $y = 3n$ Ⓑ $y = n + 3$ Ⓒ $y = 3n - 2$ Ⓓ $y = 2n$

33. Extended Response Create a sequence, and then write a function that describes it. Use the function to find the ninth term in the sequence.

Find each value. (Lesson 1-2)

34. 15^2 **35.** 10^7 **36.** 7^4 **37.** 9^3

Find each product. (Lesson 2-4)

38. $-16 \cdot 2$ **39.** $-40 \cdot (-5)$ **40.** $4 \cdot (-11)$ **41.** $-5 \cdot (-21)$

Hands-On LAB 4-6

Explore Linear Functions

Use with Lesson 4-6

go.hrw.com
Lab Resources Online
KEYWORD: MS7 Lab4

When the graph of a function is a line or a set of points that lie on a line, the function is *linear*. You can use patterns to explore linear functions.

Activity

1 The perimeter of a 1-inch-long square tile is 4 inches. Place 2 tiles together side by side. The perimeter of this figure is 6 inches.

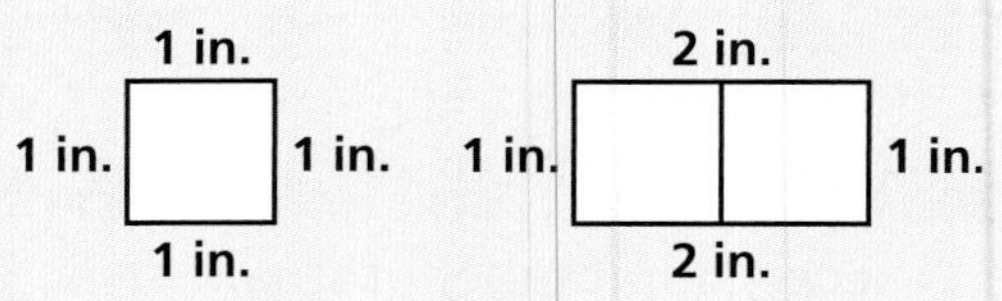

a. Complete the table at right by adding tiles side by side and finding the perimeter of each new figure.

Number of Tiles	Perimeter (in.)
1	4
2	6
3	
4	
5	

b. If x equals the number of tiles, what is the difference between consecutive x-values? If y equals the perimeter, what is the difference between consecutive y-values? How do these differences compare?

c. Graph the ordered pairs from your table on a coordinate plane. Is the graph linear? What does the table indicate about this function?

2 Draw the pattern at right and complete the next two sets of dots in the pattern.

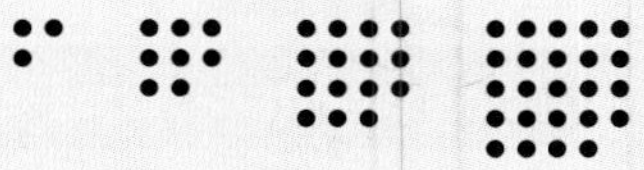

a. Complete the table at right. Let x equal the number of dots in the top row of each set. Let y equal the total number of dots in the set.

x	y
2	3
3	
4	
5	
6	

b. What is the difference between consecutive x-values? What is the difference between consecutive y-values? How do these differences compare?

c. Graph the ordered pairs on a coordinate plane. Is the graph linear? What does the table indicate about this function?

❸ Use square tiles to model rectangles with the following dimensions: 2 × 1, 2 × 2, 2 × 3, 2 × 4, and 2 × 5. The first three rectangles are shown.

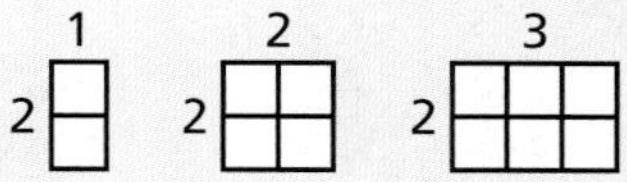

a. Find the perimeter and area of each rectangle. Complete the table at right. Let x equal perimeter and y equal area. (To find the area of a rectangle, multiply its length by its width. The areas of the first two rectangles are shown in the table.)

Rectangle	Perimeter x	Area y
2 × 1		2
2 × 2		4
2 × 3		
2 × 4		
2 × 5		

b. What is the difference between consecutive x-values? What is the difference between consecutive y-values? How do these differences compare?

c. Using what you have observed in ❶ and ❷, tell whether the relationship between x and y in the table is linear.

d. Graph the ordered pairs from your table on a coordinate plane. Does the shape of your graph agree with your answer to **c**?

Think and Discuss

1. How can you tell by looking at a function table whether the graph of the function is a line?
2. Is $y = x^2$ a linear function? Explain your answer.

Try This

1. Use square tiles to model each of the patterns shown below.
2. Model the next two sets in each pattern using square tiles.
3. Complete each table.
4. Graph the ordered pairs in each table, and then tell whether the function is linear.

Pattern 1

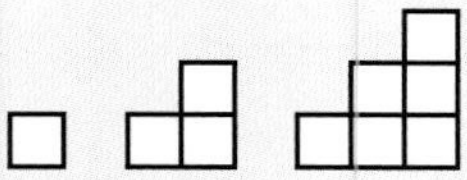

Number of Tiles x	Perimeter y
	4
	8
	12

Pattern 2

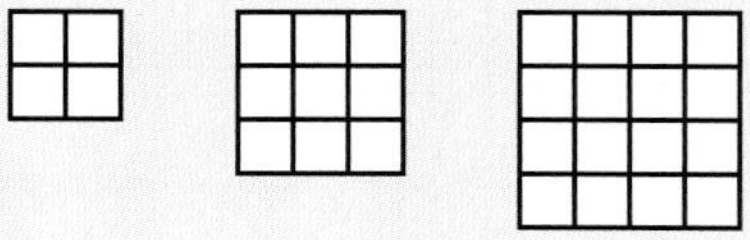

Perimeter x	Area y
8	
12	
16	

Pattern 3

Perimeter x	Area y
4	
6	
8	

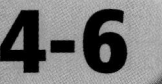

4-6 Graphing Linear Functions

Learn to identify and graph linear equations.

Vocabulary

linear equation

linear function

The graph below shows how far an inner tube travels down a river if the current flows 2 miles per hour. The graph is linear because all of the points fall on a line. It is part of the graph of a *linear equation.*

A **linear equation** is an equation whose graph is a line. The solutions of a linear equation are the points that make up its graph. Linear equations and linear graphs can be different representations of *linear functions.* A **linear function** is a function whose graph is a nonvertical line.

Only two points are needed to draw the graph of a linear function. However, graphing a third point serves as a check. You can use a function table to find each ordered pair.

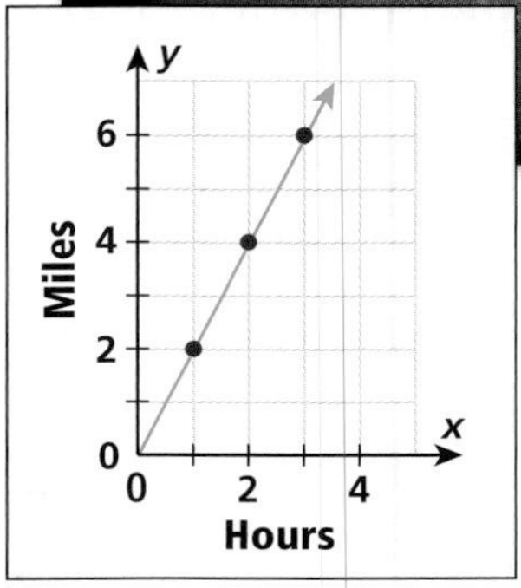

EXAMPLE 1 Graphing Linear Functions

Graph the linear function $y = 2x + 1$.

Input	Rule	Output	Ordered Pair
x	$2x + 1$	y	(x, y)
-1	$2(-1) + 1$	-1	$(-1, -1)$
0	$2(0) + 1$	1	(0, 1)
1	$2(1) + 1$	3	(1, 3)

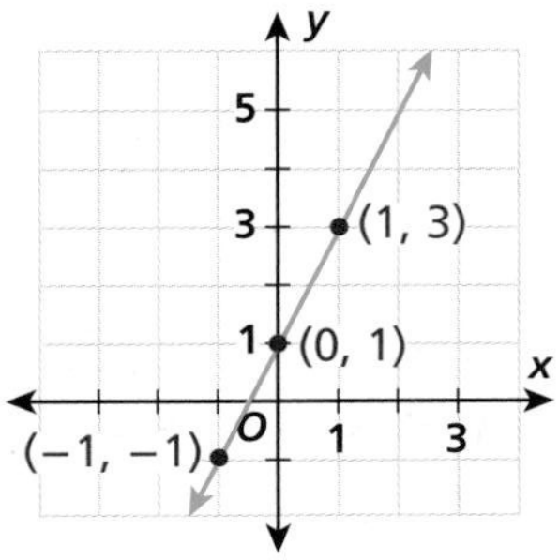

Place each ordered pair on the coordinate grid. Then connect the points to form a line.

EXAMPLE 2 *Physical Science Application*

For every degree that temperature increases on the Celsius scale, the temperature increases by 1.8 degrees on the Fahrenheit scale. When the temperature is 0°C, it is 32°F. Write a linear function that describes the relationship between the Celsius and Fahrenheit scales. Then make a graph to show the relationship.

Let x represent the input, which is the temperature in degrees Celsius. Let y represent the output, which is the temperature in degrees Fahrenheit.

The function is $y = 1.8x + 32$.

Make a function table. Include a column for the rule.

Input	Rule	Output
x	$1.8x + 32$	y
0	1.8(0) + 32	32
15	1.8(15) + 32	59
30	1.8(30) + 32	86

Multiply the input by 1.8 and then add 32.

Graph the ordered pairs (0, 32), (15, 59), and (30, 86) from your table. Connect the points to form a line.

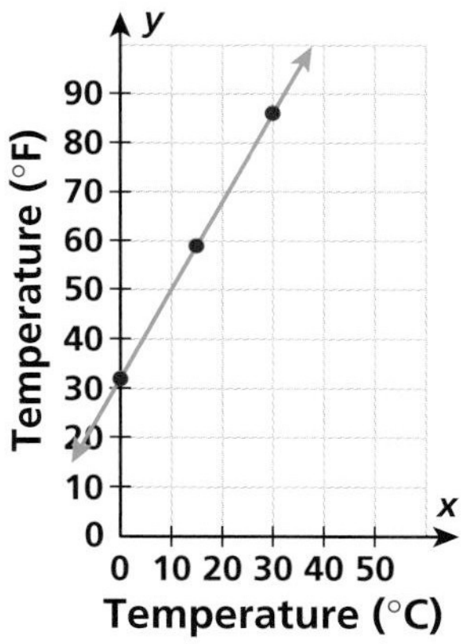

Since each output y depends on the input x, y is called the *dependent variable* and x is called the *independent variable.*

Think and Discuss

1. **Describe** how a linear equation is related to a linear graph.
2. **Explain** how to use a graph to find the output value of a linear function for a given input value.

4-6 Exercises

GUIDED PRACTICE

See Example 1

Graph each linear function.

1. $y = x + 3$

Input	Rule	Output	Ordered Pair
x	$x + 3$	y	(x, y)
−2			
0			
2			

2. $y = 2x - 2$

Input	Rule	Output	Ordered Pair
x	$2x - 2$	y	(x, y)
−1			
0			
1			

See Example 2

3. A water tanker is used to fill a community pool. The tanker pumps 750 gallons of water per hour. Write a linear function that describes the amount of water in the pool over time. Then make a graph to show the amount of water in the pool over the first 6 hours.

INDEPENDENT PRACTICE

See Example 1

Graph each linear function.

4. $y = -x - 2$

Input	Rule	Output	Ordered Pair
x	$-x - 2$	y	(x, y)
0			
1			
2			

5. $y = x - 1$

Input	Rule	Output	Ordered Pair
x	$x - 1$	y	(x, y)
3			
4			
5			

6. $y = 3x - 1$

Input	Rule	Output	Ordered Pair
x	$3x - 1$	y	(x, y)
−4			
0			
4			

7. $y = 2x + 3$

Input	Rule	Output	Ordered Pair
x	$2x + 3$	y	(x, y)
−2			
−1			
0			

See Example 2

8. Physical Science The temperature of a liquid is increasing at the rate of 3°C per hour. When Joe begins measuring the temperature, it is 40°C. Write a linear function that describes the temperature of the liquid over time. Then make a graph to show the temperature over the first 12 hours.

Extra Practice
See page 734.

LINK
Environment

About 15% of the methane gas in the atmosphere comes from farm animals.

PRACTICE AND PROBLEM SOLVING

9. **Earth Science** The water level in a well is 100 m. Water is seeping into the well and raising the water level by 10 cm per year. Water is also draining out of the well at a rate of 2 m per year. What will the water level be in 10 years?

10. **Multi-Step** Graph the function $y = -2x + 1$. If the ordered pair $(x, -5)$ lies on the graph of the function, what is the value of x? Use your graph to find the answer.

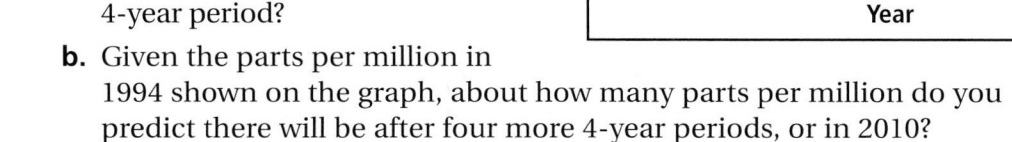

11. **Environment** The graph shows the amount of carbon dioxide in the atmosphere from 1958 to 1994.

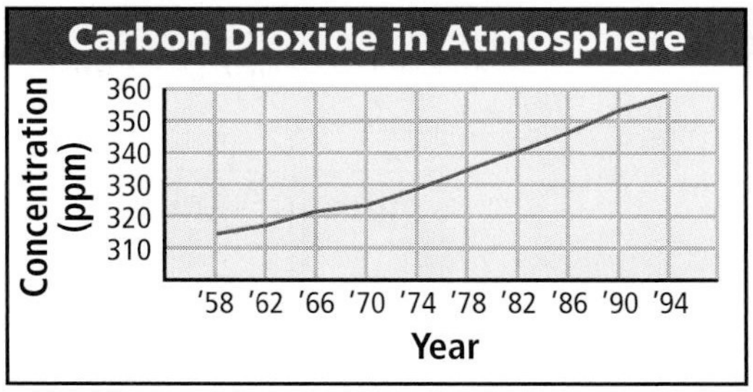

 a. The graph is approximately linear. About how many parts per million (ppm) were added each 4-year period?

 b. Given the parts per million in 1994 shown on the graph, about how many parts per million do you predict there will be after four more 4-year periods, or in 2010?

12. **What's the Question** Tron used the equation $y = 100 + 25x$ to track his savings y after x months. If the answer is $250, what is the question?

13. **Write About It** Explain how to graph $y = 2x - 5$.

14. **Challenge** Certain bacteria divide every 30 minutes. You can use the function $y = 2^x$ to find the number of bacteria after each half-hour period, where x is the number of half-hour periods. Make a table of values for $x = 1, 2, 3, 4,$ and 5. Graph the points. How does the graph differ from those you have seen so far in this lesson?

TEST PREP and Spiral Review

15. **Multiple Choice** The graph of which linear function passes through the origin?

 Ⓐ $y = x + 2$ Ⓑ $y = 3x$ Ⓒ $y = x - 1$ Ⓓ $y = 2x + 4$

16. **Short Response** Simon graphed the linear function $y = -x + 3$ at right. Explain his error, and graph $y = -x + 3$ correctly on a coordinate grid.

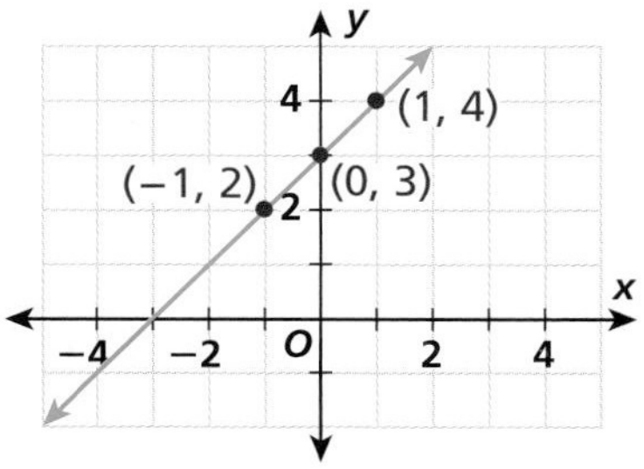

17. Tell a story that fits the graph. (Lesson 4-3)

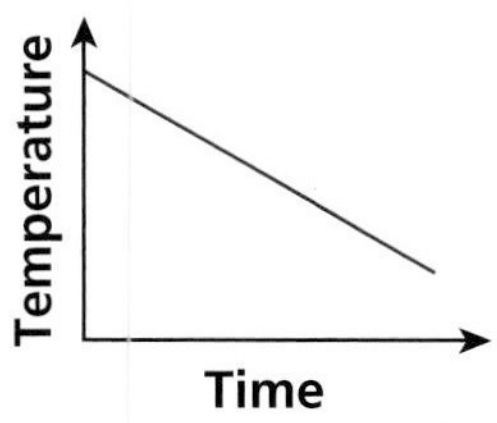

Write a function that describes each sequence. (Lesson 4-5)

18. 15, 10, 5, 0, . . .

19. −4, −2, 0, 2, . . .

20. 0.2, 1.2, 2.2, 3.2, . . .

READY TO GO ON?

SECTION 4B

Quiz for Lessons 4-4 Through 4-6

4-4 Functions, Tables, and Graphs

Find the output for each input.

1. $y = -3x + 2$

Input	Rule	Output
x	$-3x + 2$	y
−1		
0		
1		

2. $y = x \div 2$

Input	Rule	Output
x	$x \div 2$	y
−10		
2		
6		

Make a function table, and graph the resulting ordered pairs.

3. $y = -6x$ **4.** $y = 4x - 3$ **5.** $y = 4x^2$

4-5 Find a Pattern in Sequences

Tell whether the sequence of *y*-values is arithmetic or geometric. Then find *y* when $n = 5$.

6.

n	1	2	3	4	5
y	−2	7	16	23	■

7.

n	1	2	3	4	5
y	30	60	120	240	■

8.

n	1	2	3	4	5
y	16	9	2	−5	■

9.

n	1	2	3	4	5
y	−5	15	−45	135	■

Write a function that describes each sequence. Use the function to find the eleventh term in the sequence.

10. 1, 2, 3, 4, . . . **11.** 4, 8, 12, 16, . . . **12.** 11, 21, 31, 41, . . . **13.** 1, 4, 9, 16, . . .

4-6 Graphing Linear Functions

Graph each linear function.

14. $y = x - 4$ **15.** $y = 2x - 5$ **16.** $y = -x + 7$ **17.** $y = -2x + 1$

18. A freight train travels 50 miles per hour. Write a linear function that describes the distance the train travels over time. Then make a graph to show the distance the train travels over the first 9 hours.

MULTI-STEP TEST PREP

Going for a Ride Shauna and her family are planning to spend a day at a local amusement park. The park charges an admission fee and sells tickets for the rides.

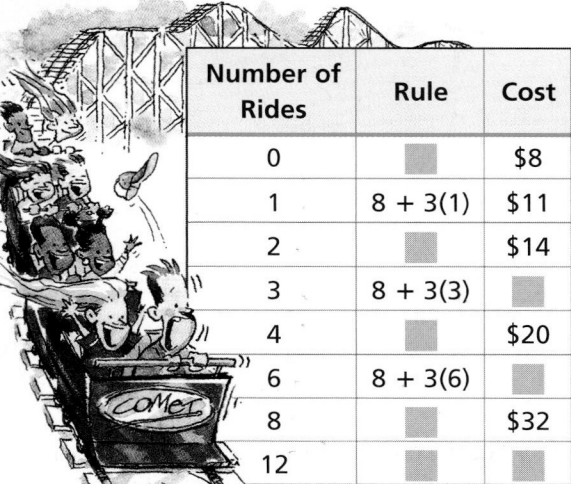

Number of Rides	Rule	Cost
0		$8
1	8 + 3(1)	$11
2		$14
3	8 + 3(3)	
4		$20
6	8 + 3(6)	
8		$32
12		

1. The table at right can be used to determine how much Shauna and her family could spend in a day at the park. Complete the table.
2. What is the park's admission fee? How much does it cost to go on each ride?
3. Suppose x represents the number of rides and y represents the cost. Write a function that describes the data in the table.
4. Use the function you wrote in Problem 3 to find the cost of 14 rides.
5. Make a graph that shows the cost as a function of the number of rides.
6. The park offers a flat-rate "ride all day" pass for $38. Explain when this is a better deal than paying for each individual ride.
7. Shauna and her brother each plan to go on 15 rides. Her parents will each go on 6 rides. Find the cost for the family to go to the park. Explain your answer.

EXTENSION

Nonlinear Functions

Learn to identify nonlinear functions.

Vocabulary

nonlinear function

As you inflate a balloon, its volume increases. The table at right shows the increase in volume of a round balloon as its radius changes. Do you think a graph of the data would or would not be a straight line? You can make a graph to find out.

Radius (in.)	Volume (in^3)
1	4.19
2	33.52
3	113.13
4	268.16
5	523.75

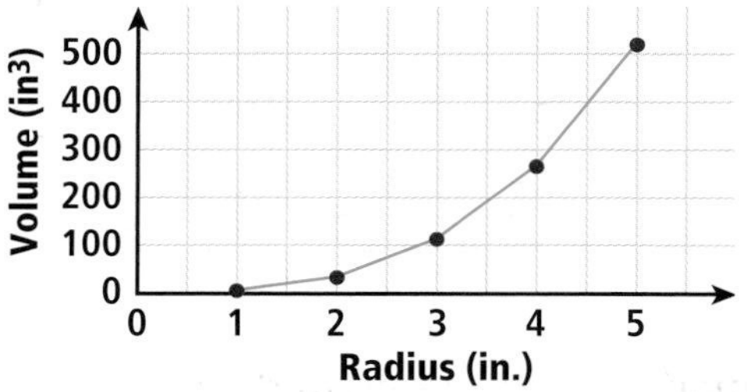

A **nonlinear function** is a function whose graph is not a straight line.

EXAMPLE 1 Identifying Graphs of Nonlinear Functions

Tell whether the graph is linear or nonlinear.

A

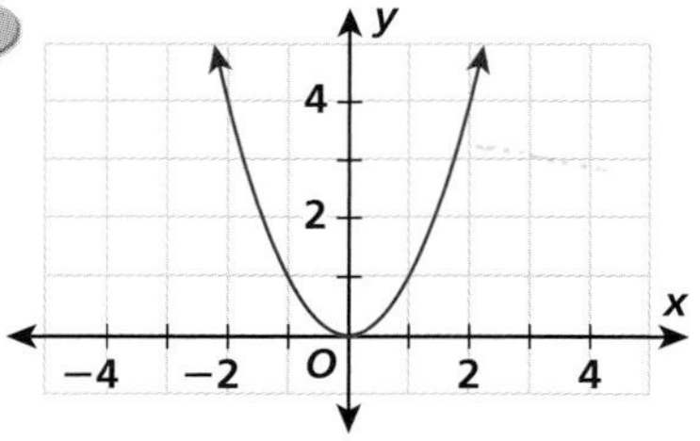

The graph is not a straight line, so it is nonlinear.

B

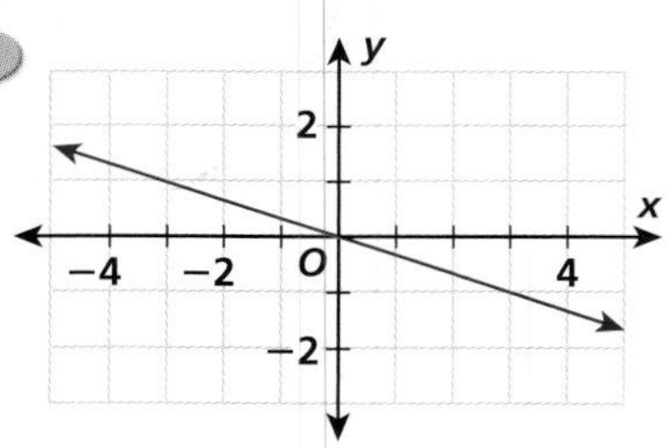

The graph is a straight line, so it is linear.

You can use a function table to determine whether ordered pairs describe a linear or a nonlinear relationship.

For a function that has a linear relationship, when the difference between each successive input value is constant, the difference between each corresponding output value is *constant.*

For a function that has a nonlinear relationship, when the difference between each successive input value is constant, the difference between each corresponding output value *varies.*

EXAMPLE 2 Identifying Nonlinear Relationships in Function Tables

Tell whether the function represented in each table has a linear or nonlinear relationship.

A

Input	Output
1	4
2	6
3	10

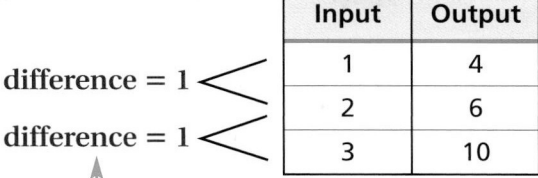

Input: difference = 1, difference = 1 — *The difference is constant.*

Output: difference = 2, difference = 4 — *The difference varies.*

The function represented in the table has a nonlinear relationship.

B

Input	Output
3	4
6	8
9	12

Input: difference = 3, difference = 3 — *The difference is constant.*

Output: difference = 4, difference = 4 — *The difference is constant.*

The function represented in the table has a linear relationship.

EXTENSION Exercises

Tell whether the graph is linear or nonlinear.

1.

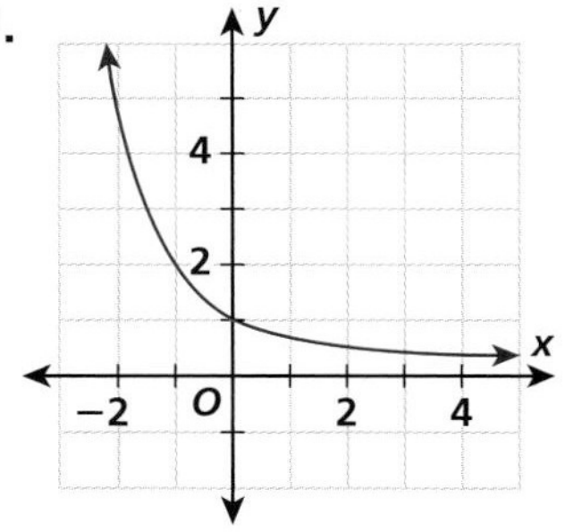

2.

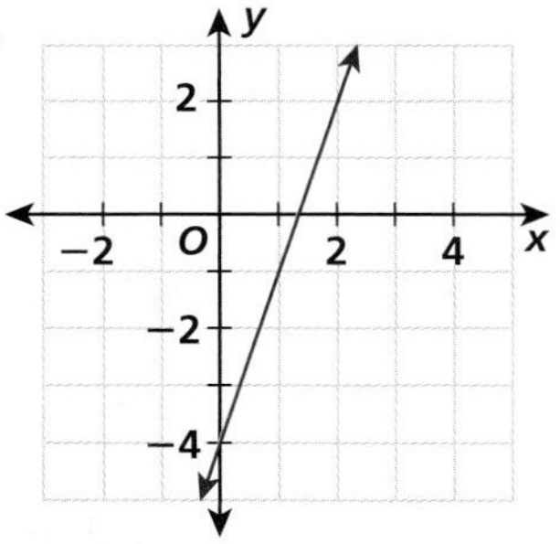

3.

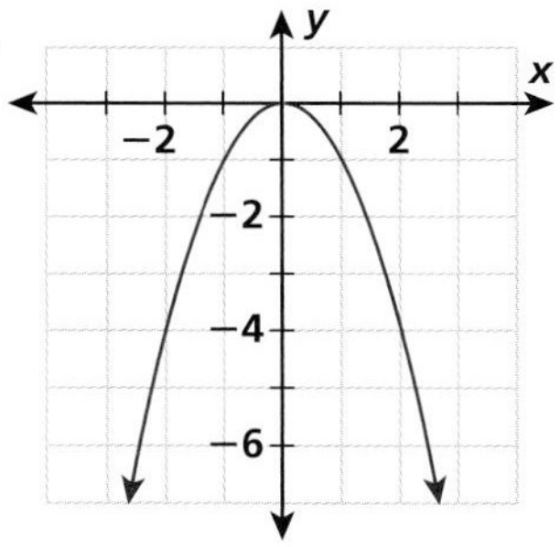

Tell whether the function represented in each table has a linear or nonlinear relationship.

4.

Input	Output
2	5
4	7
6	9

5.

Input	Output
1	6
2	9
3	14

6.

Input	Output
4	25
8	36
12	49

Game Time

Clothes Encounters

Five students from the same math class met to study for an upcoming test. They sat around a circular table with seat 1 and seat 5 next to each other. No two students were wearing the same color of shirt or the same type of shoes. From the clues provided, determine where each student sat, each student's shirt color, and what type of shoes each student was wearing.

1. The girls' shoes were sandals, flip-flops, and boots.
2. Robin, wearing a blue shirt, was sitting next to the person wearing the green shirt. She was not sitting next to the person wearing the orange shirt.
3. Lila was sitting between the person wearing sandals and the person in the yellow shirt.
4. The boy who was wearing the tennis shoes was wearing the orange shirt.
5. April had on flip-flops and was sitting between Lila and Charles.
6. Glenn was wearing loafers, but his shirt was not brown.
7. Robin sat in seat 1.

You can use a chart like the one below to organize the information given. Put *X*'s in the spaces where the information is false and *O*'s in the spaces where the information is true. Some of the information from the first two clues has been included on the chart already. You will need to read through the clues several times and use logic to complete the chart.

	Seat 1	Seat 2	Seat 3	Seat 4	Seat 5	Blue shirt	Green shirt	Orange shirt	Yellow shirt	Brown shirt	Sandals	Flip-flops	Boots	Tennis shoes	Loafers
Lila						X								X	X
Robin						O	X	X	X	X				X	X
April						X								X	X
Charles						X									
Glenn						X									

Materials
- 6 sheets of unlined paper
- scissors
- markers

FOLDNOTES

It's in the Bag!

PROJECT Patterns and Functions Fold-A-Books

These handy books will store your notes from each lesson of the chapter.

Directions

1. Fold a sheet of paper in half down the middle. Then open the paper and lay it flat so it forms a peak. **Figure A**

2. Fold the left and right edges to the crease in the middle. When you're done, the paper will be folded into four sections, accordion-style. **Figure B**

3. Pinch the middle sections together. Use scissors to cut a slit down the center of these sections, stopping when you get to the folds. **Figure C**

4. Hold the paper on either side of the slit. As open the slit, the paper will form a four-pa book. **Figure D**

5. Crease the top edges and fold the book closed. Repeat all the steps to make five more books.

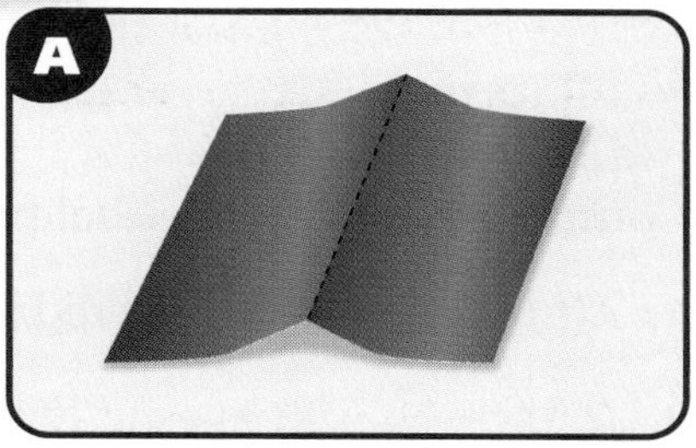

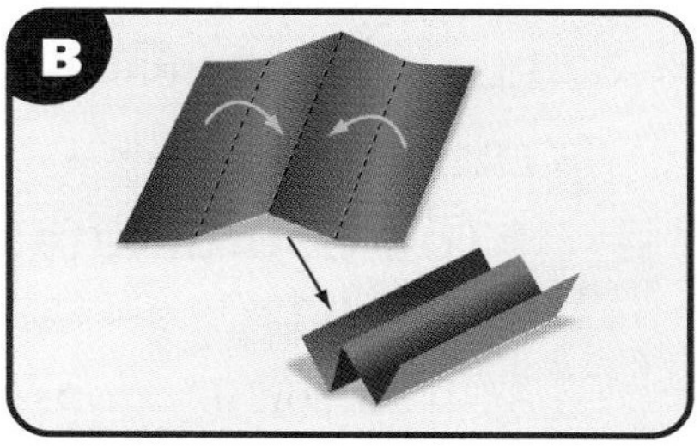

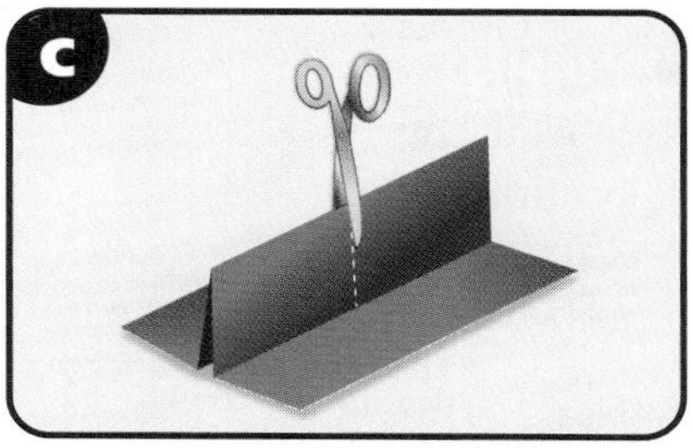

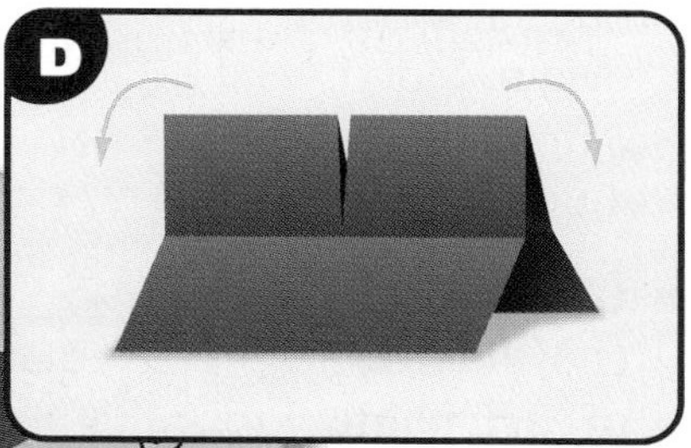

Taking Note of the Math

On the cover of each book, write the number and name of a lesson from the chapter. Use the remaining pages to take notes on the lesson.

CHAPTER 4

Study Guide: Review

Vocabulary

Complete the sentences below with vocabulary words from the list above.

1. A(n) __?__ is an ordered list of numbers.

2. A(n) __?__ gives exactly one output for every input.

3. A(n) __?__ is a function whose graph is a nonvertical line.

4-1 The Coordinate Plane (pp. 224–227)

EXAMPLE

Plot each point on a coordinate plane.

- ***M*(−3, 1)** Start at the origin. Move 3 units left and 1 unit up.
- ***R*(3, −4)** Start at the origin. Move 3 units right and 4 units down.

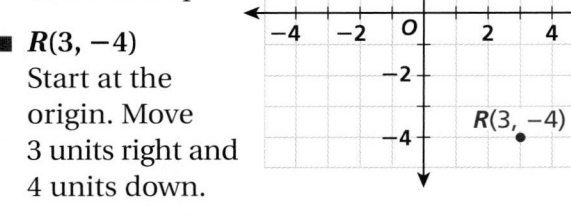

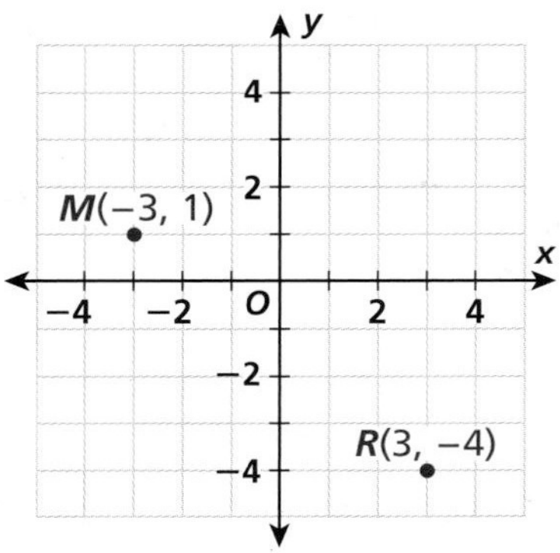

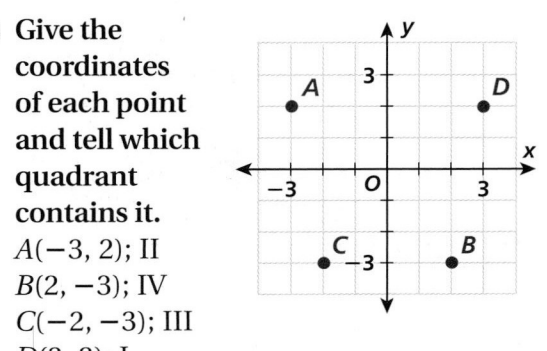

- **Give the coordinates of each point and tell which quadrant contains it.**
  A(−3, 2); II
  B(2, −3); IV
  C(−2, −3); III
  D(3, 2); I

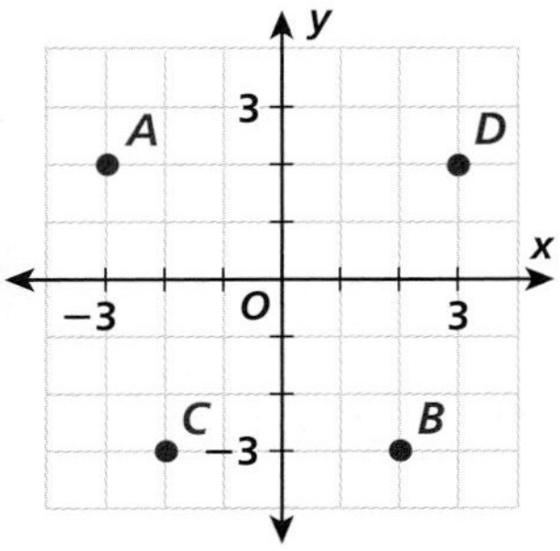

EXERCISES

Plot each point on a coordinate plane.

4. *A*(4, 2) **5.** *B*(−4, −2)

6. *C*(−2, 4) **7.** *D*(2, −4)

Give the coordinates of each point and tell which quadrant contains it.

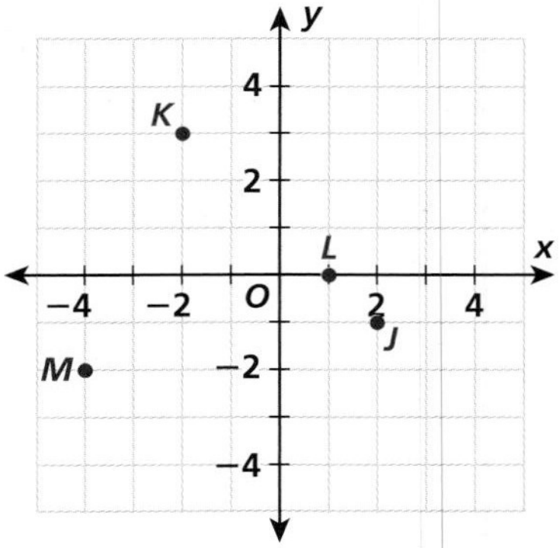

8. *J* **9.** *K*

10. *L* **11.** *M*

4-2 Tables and Graphs (pp. 228–231)

EXAMPLE

- **Write the ordered pairs from the table.**

x	*y*
3	1
2	4
5	7

The ordered pairs are (3, 1), (2, 4), and (5, 7).

EXERCISES

Write and graph the ordered pairs from each table.

12.

x	*y*
−2	0
1	1
3	−4

13.

x	*y*
5	2
−2	−6
0	3

4-3 Interpreting Graphs (pp. 232–235)

EXAMPLE

- **Ari visits his grandmother, who lives 45 miles away. After the visit, he returns home, stopping for gas along the way. Sketch a graph to show the distance Ari traveled compared to time. Use your graph to find the total distance traveled.**

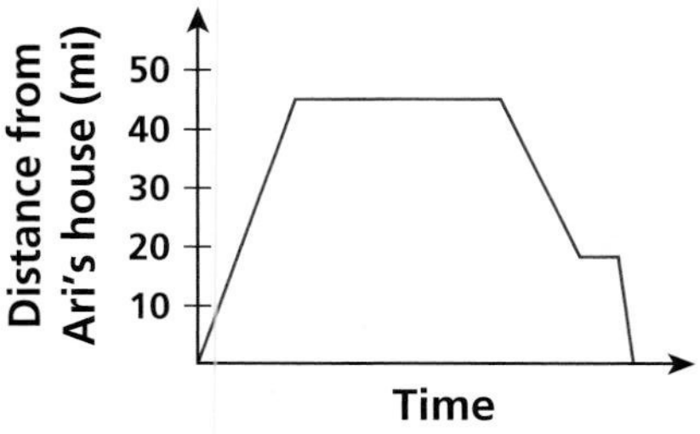

The graph increases from 0 to 45 miles and then decreases from 45 to 0 miles. The distance does not change while Ari visits his grandmother and stops for gas. Ari traveled a total of 90 miles.

EXERCISES

14. Amanda walks 1.5 miles to school in the morning. After school, she walks 0.5 mile to the public library. After she has chosen her books, she walks home. Sketch a graph to show the distance Amanda traveled compared to time. Use your graph to find the total distance traveled.

15. Joel rides his bike to the park, 12 miles away, to meet his friends. He then rides an additional 6 miles to the grocery store and returns home with groceries. Sketch a graph to show the distance Joel traveled compared to time. Use your graph to find the total distance traveled.

4-4 Functions, Tables, and Graphs (pp. 238–241)

EXAMPLE

- **Find the output for each input.**

$y = 3x + 4$

Input	Rule	Output
x	$3x + 4$	y
−1	3(−1) + 4	1
0	3(0) + 4	4
2	3(2) + 4	10

EXERCISES

Find the output for each input.

16. $y = x^2 - 1$

Input	Rule	Output
x	$x^2 - 1$	y
−2		
3		
5		

Study Guide: Review

4-5 Find a Pattern in Sequences (pp. 242–245)

EXAMPLE

■ **Tell whether the sequence of *y*-values is arithmetic or geometric. Then find *y* when $n = 5$.**

n	1	2	3	4	5
y	−1	3	7	11	

In the sequence, 4 is added to each term.

$11 + 4 = 15$ *Add 4 to the fourth term.*

The sequence is arithmetic.
When $n = 5$, $y = 15$.

■ **Write a function that describes the sequence. Use the function to find the eighth term in the sequence.**

3, 6, 9, 12, . . .

n	Rule	*y*
1	1 · 3	3
2	2 · 3	6
3	3 · 3	9
4	4 · 3	12

Function: $y = 3n$
When $n = 8$, $y = 24$.

EXERCISES

Tell whether each sequence of *y*-values is arithmetic or geometric. Then find *y* when $n = 5$.

17.

n	1	2	3	4	5
y	3	9	27	81	

18.

n	1	2	3	4	5
y	14	3	−8	−19	

Write a function that describes each sequence. Use the function to find the eighth term in the sequence.

19. 25, 50, 75, 100, . . .
20. −3, −2, −1, 0, . . .
21. −4, −1, 2, 5, . . .
22. 4, 6, 8, 10, . . .

4-6 Graphing Linear Functions (pp. 248–251)

EXAMPLE

■ **Graph the linear function $y = -x + 2$.**

Input	Rule	Output	Ordered Pair
x	$-x + 2$	*y*	(*x*, *y*)
−1	−(−1) + 2	3	(−1, 3)
0	−(0) + 2	2	(0, 2)
2	−(2) + 2	0	(2, 0)

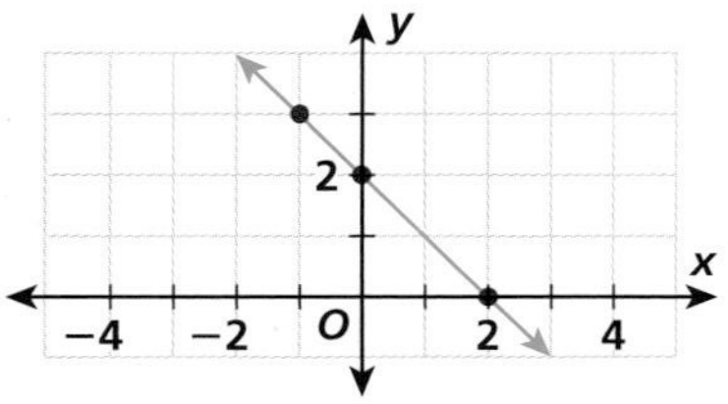

EXERCISES

Graph each linear function.

23. $y = 2x - 1$
24. $y = -3x$
25. $y = x - 3$
26. $y = 2x + 4$
27. $y = x - 6$
28. $y = 3x - 9$

CHAPTER TEST

Plot each point on a coordinate plane. Then identify the quadrant that contains each point.

1. $L(4, -3)$ **2.** $M(-5, 2)$ **3.** $N(7, 1)$ **4.** $O(-7, -2)$

Give the coordinates of each point.

5. A **6.** B **7.** C

8. D **9.** E **10.** F

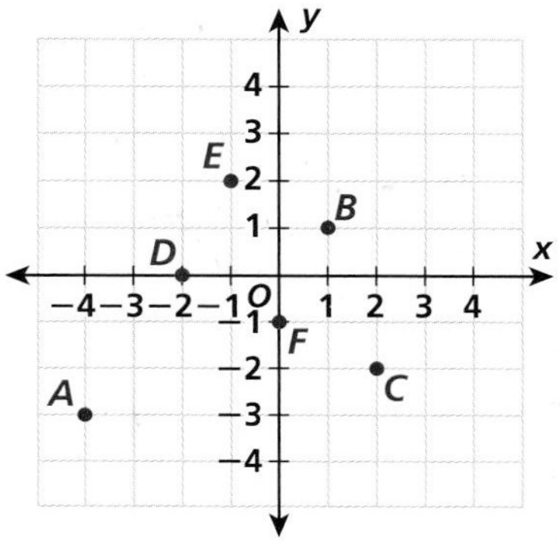

Write and graph the ordered pairs from each table.

11.

x	y
1	5
−3	0
2	−5

12.

x	y
0	2
−6	6
−1	−2

13. Ian jogs 4 miles to the lake. He swims a 1 mile loop and then jogs home. Sketch a graph to show the distance Ian traveled compared to time. Use your graph to find the total distance traveled.

Find the output for each input.

14. $y = -2x + 5$

Input	Rule	Output
x	−2x + 5	y
−1		
0		
1		

15. $y = x \div 4$

Input	Rule	Output
x	x ÷ 4	y
−8		
0		
4		

Tell whether each sequence of y-values is arithmetic or geometric. Then find y when $n = 5$.

16.

n	1	2	3	4	5
y	−2	8	−32	128	

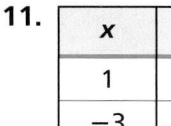

17.

n	1	2	3	4	5
y	−27	−16	−5	6	

Write a function that describes each sequence. Use the function to find the eleventh term in the sequence.

18. 1, 3, 5, 7 . . . **19.** 11, 21, 31, 41 . . . **20.** 0, 3, 8, 15 . . .

Graph each linear function.

21. $y = 3x - 4$ **22.** $y = x - 8$ **23.** $y = 2x + 7$

STANDARDIZED TEST PREP

go.hrw.com
State Test Practice Online
KEYWORD: MS7 TestPrep

Cumulative Assessment, Chapters 1–4

Multiple Choice

1. The fraction $\frac{7}{12}$ is found between which pair of numbers on a number line?

(A) $\frac{5}{12}$ and $\frac{1}{2}$

(B) $\frac{13}{24}$ and $\frac{3}{4}$

(C) $\frac{1}{3}$ and $\frac{11}{24}$

(D) $\frac{2}{3}$ and $\frac{5}{6}$

2. Which description shows the relationship between a term and *n*, its position in the sequence?

Position	Value of Term
1	0.25
2	1.5
3	4
4	9
n	

(F) Add 1.25 to *n*.

(G) Add 1 to *n* and multiply by 2.

(H) Multiply *n* by 1 and add 1.25.

(J) Multiply *n* by 2 and add 1.

3. For which equation is $x = -10$ the solution?

(A) $2x - 20 = 0$

(B) $\frac{1}{5}x + 2 = 0$

(C) $\frac{1}{5}x - 2 = 0$

(D) $-2x + 20 = 0$

4. What is the least common multiple of 10, 25, and 30?

(F) 5 (H) 150

(G) 50 (J) 200

5. Which problem situation matches the equation below?

$$x + 55 = 92$$

(A) Liam has 55 tiles but needs a total of 92 to complete a project. How many more tiles does Liam need?

(B) Cher spent $55 at the market and has only $92 left. How much did Cher start with?

(C) Byron drove 55 miles each day for 92 days. How many total miles did he drive?

(D) For every 55 students who buy "spirit wear," the boosters donate $92. How many students have bought spirit wear so far?

6. A recipe that makes 2 cups of guacamole dip calls for $1\frac{3}{4}$ cups of mashed avocados. How much avocado is needed to make 4 cups of dip with this recipe?

(F) 3.25 cups (H) 3.75 cups

(G) 3.5 cups (J) 4 cups

7. Which ordered pair is located on the *x*-axis?

(A) $(0, -5)$ (C) $(-5, 0)$

(B) $(5, -5)$ (D) $(1, -5)$

8. Which ordered pair is NOT a solution of $y = 5x - 4$?

(F) $(2, 6)$ (H) $(1, 0)$

(G) $(0, -4)$ (J) $(-1, -9)$

HOT TIP! Work backward from the answer choices if you cannot remember how to solve a problem.

9. Carolyn makes between \$5.75 and \$9.50 per hour baby-sitting. Which is the best estimate of the total amount she makes for 9 hours of baby-sitting?

(A) From \$30 to \$55

(B) From \$55 to \$80

(C) From \$80 to \$105

(D) From \$105 to \$130

Gridded Response

10. Patrick plans to spend the next 28 days preparing for a weight-lifting competition. He plans to spend a total of 119 hours at the gym. If Patrick is at the gym for the same amount of time every day, how many hours will he be at the gym each day?

11. Solve the equation $-4.3x = -0.215$ for x.

12. Determine the y-coordinate of the point.

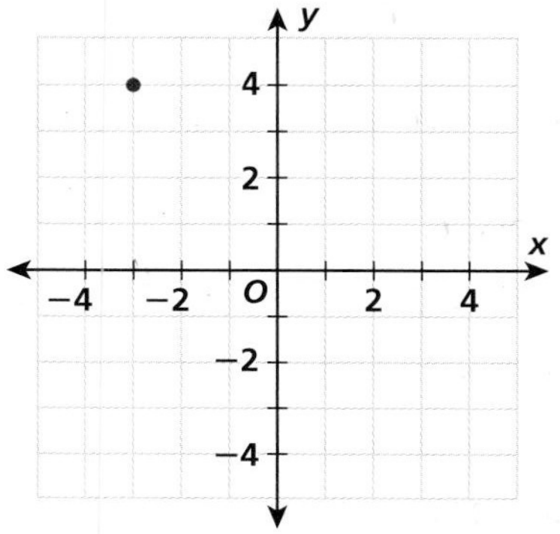

13. What is the sixth term in the following sequence?

$\frac{1}{2}, 1\frac{1}{4}, 2, 2\frac{3}{4}, \ldots$

Short Response

14. A teacher discussed 112 of the 164 pages of the textbook. What portion of the pages did the teacher discuss? Write your answer as a decimal rounded to the nearest thousandth and as a fraction in simplest form.

15. A bag of nickels and quarters contains four times as many nickels as quarters. The total value of the coins in the bag is \$1.35.

a. How many nickels are in the bag?

b. How many quarters are in the bag?

16. Describe in what order you would perform the operations to find the value of $(4 \cdot 4 - 6)^2 + (5 \cdot 7)$.

17. A recipe calls for $\frac{3}{4}$ cup flour and $\frac{2}{3}$ cup butter. Does the recipe require more flour or butter? Is this still true if the recipe is doubled? Explain how you determined your answer.

Extended Response

18. A bus travels at an average rate of 50 miles per hour from Nashville, Tennessee, to El Paso, Texas. To find the distance y traveled in x hours, use the equation $y = 50x$.

a. Make a table of ordered pairs using the domain $x = 1, 2, 3, 4,$ and 5.

b. Graph the solutions from the table of ordered pairs on a coordinate plane.

c. Brett leaves Nashville by bus at 6:00 A.M. He needs to be in El Paso by 5:00 A.M. the following day. If Nashville is 1,100 miles from El Paso, will Brett make it on time? Explain how you determined your answer.

Problem Solving on Location

UTAH

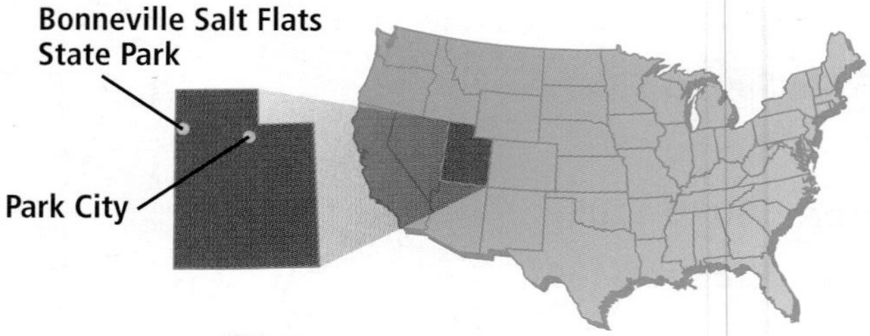

The Bonneville Salt Flats

The Bonneville Salt Flats are a barren stretch of land in northwest Utah covering more than 30,000 acres. The area may be desolate, but its flat surface makes it an ideal location for high-speed automobile racing. In fact, dozens of land speed records have been set at the salt flats.

Choose one or more strategies to solve each problem.

1. In 1965, Art Arfons set a speed record at the salt flats. The table shows the distances his car covered in various lengths of time. What was Arfons's speed in miles per hour?

The 1965 Speed Record

Time (min)	Distance (mi)
2	19.22
3	28.83
4	38.44

2. The surface of the Bonneville Salt Flats is approximately rectangular, and its length is twice its width. To prepare for racing, a crew sets out 22 pylons: one at each of three corners of the racing surface and one at every mile between the three corners along the edges. What are the length and width of the salt flats?

3. Teddy Tezlaff set the first land speed record at the Bonneville Salt Flats in 1914. A record set in 1963 was 265.7 mi/h faster than Tezlaff's record, and a record set in 1964 was 129.3 mi/h faster than the 1963 record. The 1964 record was 536.7 mi/h. What was Tezlaff's record-breaking speed?

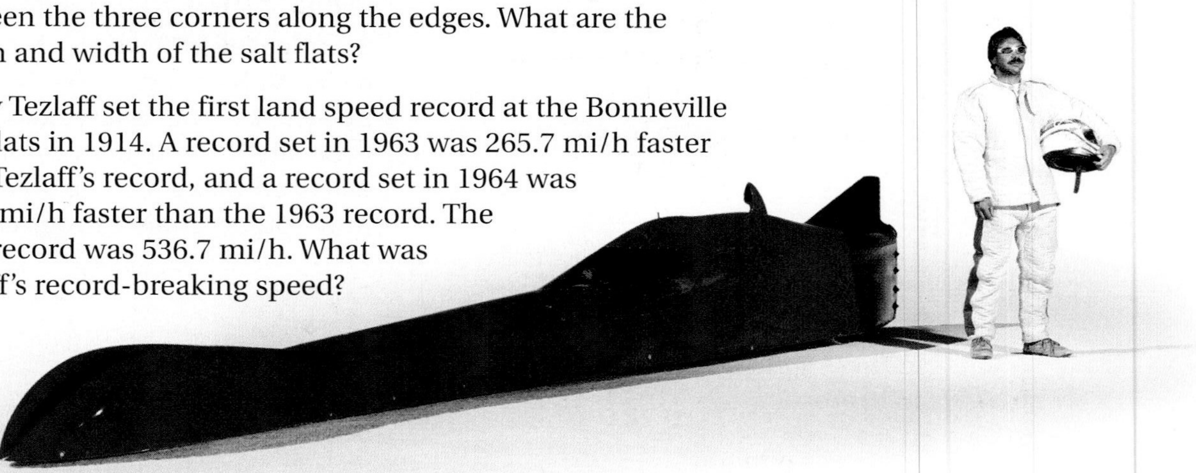

Problem Solving Strategies

Draw a Diagram
Make a Model
Guess and Test
Work Backward
Find a Pattern
Make a Table
Solve a Simpler Problem
Use Logical Reasoning
Act It Out
Make an Organized List

Park City

Park City, Utah, first gained fame as a silver-mining town. In recent years, the town has become better known as a world-class destination for winter sports. As one of the venues for the 2002 Winter Olympics, Park City was the site of the ski jumping and slalom events.

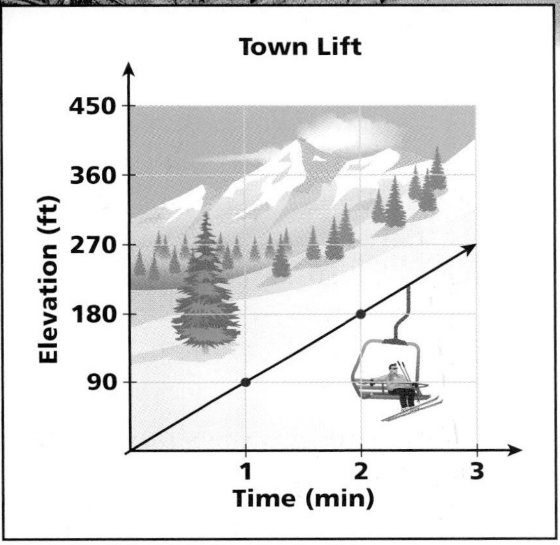

Choose one or more strategies to solve each problem. For 1 and 2, use the graph.

1. Park City features a ski lift, called the Town Lift, which begins on Main Street. The graph illustrates a person's elevation as he or she rides the lift from Main Street. Predict the rider's elevation after 9 minutes.

2. The Town Lift takes riders to the beginning of a trail that has an elevation of 1,170 feet. Predict how long the ride is from Main Street to the beginning of the trail.

3. One of the town's ski resorts offers private skiing lessons. The cost is \$53 for the first person and \$13 for each additional person. If your group has a budget of \$130 for lessons, how many people can take the private lesson?

4. A Park City resort has 100 ski trails. Each trail is classified as beginner, intermediate, or advanced. There are 44 intermediate trails, and there are 20 more advanced trails than beginner trails. How many advanced trails are there?

CHAPTER 5

Proportional Relationships

go.hrw.com
Chapter Project Online
KEYWORD: MS7 Ch5

Lengths of Ships and Their Models

Ship	Length of Ship (m)	Scale	Length of Model (mm)
Santa Maria	36.4	$\frac{1}{65}$	560
Golden Hind	25.9	$\frac{1}{72}$	360
HMS Bounty	47.0	$\frac{1}{48}$	980
Mayflower	38.7	$\frac{1}{64}$	605

Career *Model Builder*

When creating models of historical ships, model builders are careful to build their models to scale and with as much detail as possible. Model ships that are built for movies are much smaller than the original ships, while those built for display are often the same size as the original ships.

In the table, the scales show how the sizes of some models compare with the sizes of the original ships.

ARE YOU READY?

Vocabulary

Choose the best term from the list to complete each sentence.

1. A(n) __?__ is a number that represents a part of a whole.
2. A closed figure with three sides is called a(n) __?__.
3. Two fractions are __?__ if they represent the same number.
4. One way to compare two fractions is to first find a(n) __?__.

common denominator
equivalent
fraction
quadrilateral
triangle

Complete these exercises to review skills you will need for this chapter.

Write Equivalent Fractions

Find two fractions that are equivalent to each fraction.

5. $\frac{2}{5}$ **6.** $\frac{7}{11}$ **7.** $\frac{25}{100}$ **8.** $\frac{4}{6}$

9. $\frac{5}{17}$ **10.** $\frac{15}{23}$ **11.** $\frac{24}{78}$ **12.** $\frac{150}{325}$

Compare Fractions

Compare. Write $<$ or $>$.

13. $\frac{5}{6}$ ■ $\frac{2}{3}$ **14.** $\frac{3}{8}$ ■ $\frac{2}{5}$ **15.** $\frac{6}{11}$ ■ $\frac{1}{4}$ **16.** $\frac{5}{8}$ ■ $\frac{11}{12}$

17. $\frac{8}{9}$ ■ $\frac{12}{13}$ **18.** $\frac{5}{11}$ ■ $\frac{7}{21}$ **19.** $\frac{4}{10}$ ■ $\frac{3}{7}$ **20.** $\frac{3}{4}$ ■ $\frac{2}{9}$

Solve Multiplication Equations

Solve each equation.

21. $3x = 12$ **22.** $15t = 75$ **23.** $2y = 14$ **24.** $7m = 84$

25. $25c = 125$ **26.** $16f = 320$ **27.** $11n = 121$ **28.** $53y = 318$

Multiply Fractions

Solve. Write each answer in simplest form.

29. $\frac{2}{3} \cdot \frac{5}{7}$ **30.** $\frac{12}{16} \cdot \frac{3}{9}$ **31.** $\frac{4}{9} \cdot \frac{18}{24}$ **32.** $\frac{1}{56} \cdot \frac{50}{200}$

33. $\frac{1}{5} \cdot \frac{5}{9}$ **34.** $\frac{7}{8} \cdot \frac{4}{3}$ **35.** $\frac{25}{100} \cdot \frac{30}{90}$ **36.** $\frac{46}{91} \cdot \frac{3}{6}$

CHAPTER 5

Study Guide: Preview

Where You've Been

Previously, you

- used ratios to describe proportional situations.
- used ratios to make predictions in proportional situations.
- used tables to describe proportional relationships involving conversions.

In This Chapter

You will study

- using division to find unit rates and ratios in proportional relationships.
- estimating and finding solutions to application problems involving proportional relationships.
- generating formulas involving unit conversions.
- using critical attributes to define similarity.
- using ratios and proportions in scale drawings and scale models.

Where You're Going

You can use the skills learned in this chapter

- to read and interpret maps.
- to find heights of objects that are too tall to measure.

Key Vocabulary/Vocabulario

corresponding angles	ángulos correspondientes
corresponding sides	lados correspondientes
equivalent ratios	razones equivalentes
proportion	proporción
rate	tasa
ratio	razón
scale	escala
scale drawing	dibujo a escala
scale model	modelo a escala
similar	semejante
slope	pendiente

Vocabulary Connections

To become familiar with some of the vocabulary terms in the chapter, consider the following. You may refer to the chapter, the glossary, or a dictionary if you like.

1. "Miles per hour," "students per class," and "Calories per serving" are all examples of *rates*. What other rates can you think of? How would you describe a **rate** to someone if you couldn't use examples in your explanation?

2. *Similar* means "having characteristics in common." If two triangles are **similar**, what might they have in common?

3. The *slope* of a mountain trail describes the steepness of a climb. What might the **slope** of a line describe?

Reading and Writing Math

Writing Strategy: Use Your Own Words

Using your own words to explain a concept can help you understand the concept. For example, learning how to solve equations might seem difficult if the textbook does not explain solving equations in the same way that you would.

As you work through each lesson:

- Identify the important ideas from the explanation in the book.
- Use your own words to explain these ideas.

What Sara Reads	What Sara Writes
An **equation** is a mathematical statement that two expressions are equal in value.	*An <u>equation</u> has an equal sign to show that two expressions are equal to each other.*
When an equation contains a variable, a value of the variable that makes the statement true is called a **solution** of the equation.	*The <u>solution</u> of an equation that has a variable in it is the number that the variable is equal to.*
If a variable is multiplied by a number, you can often use division to isolate the variable. Divide both sides of the equation by the number.	*When the variable is multiplied by a number, you can undo the multiplication and get the variable alone by dividing both sides of the equation by the number.*

Try This

Rewrite each sentence in your own words.

1. When solving addition equations involving integers, isolate the variable by adding opposites.
2. When you solve equations that have one operation, you use an inverse operation to isolate the variable.

5-1 Ratios

Learn to identify, write, and compare ratios.

Vocabulary
ratio

In basketball practice, Kathlene made 17 baskets in 25 attempts. She compared the number of baskets she made to the total number of attempts she made by using the *ratio* $\frac{17}{25}$. A **ratio** is a comparison of two quantities by division.

Kathlene can write her ratio of baskets made to attempts in three different ways.

$\frac{17}{25}$ **17 to 25** **17:25**

EXAMPLE 1 Writing Ratios

A basket of fruit contains 6 apples, 4 bananas, and 3 oranges. Write each ratio in all three forms.

A bananas to apples

$$\frac{\text{number of bananas}}{\text{number of apples}} = \frac{4}{6}$$

There are 4 bananas and 6 apples.

The ratio of bananas to apples can be written as $\frac{4}{6}$, 4 to 6, or 4:6.

B bananas and apples to oranges

$$\frac{\text{number of bananas and apples}}{\text{number of oranges}} = \frac{4 + 6}{3} = \frac{10}{3}$$

The ratio of bananas and apples to oranges can be written as $\frac{10}{3}$, 10 to 3, or 10:3.

C oranges to total pieces of fruit

$$\frac{\text{number of oranges}}{\text{number of total pieces of fruit}} = \frac{3}{6 + 4 + 3} = \frac{3}{13}$$

The ratio of oranges to total pieces of fruit can be written as $\frac{3}{13}$, 3 to 13, or 3:13.

Sometimes a ratio can be simplified. To simplify a ratio, first write it in fraction form and then simplify the fraction.

EXAMPLE 2 Writing Ratios in Simplest Form

Remember!

A fraction is in simplest form when the GCF of the numerator and denominator is 1.

At Franklin Middle School, there are 252 students in the seventh grade and 9 seventh-grade teachers. Write the ratio of students to teachers in simplest form.

$\frac{\text{students}}{\text{teachers}} = \frac{252}{9}$ *Write the ratio as a fraction.*

$= \frac{252 \div 9}{9 \div 9}$ *Simplify.*

$= \frac{28}{1}$ *For every 28 students, there is 1 teacher.*

The ratio of students to teachers is 28 to 1.

To compare ratios, write them as fractions with common denominators. Then compare the numerators.

EXAMPLE 3 Comparing Ratios

Tell whether the wallet size photo or the portrait size photo has the greater ratio of width to length.

	Width (in.)	Length (in.)
Wallet	3.5	5
Personal	4	6
Desk	5	7
Portrait	8	10

Wallet: $\frac{\text{width (in.)}}{\text{length (in.)}} = \frac{3.5}{5}$ *Write the ratios as fractions with common denominators.*

Portrait: $\frac{\text{width (in.)}}{\text{length (in.)}} = \frac{8}{10} = \frac{4}{5}$

Because $4 > 3.5$ and the denominators are the same, the portrait size photo has the greater ratio of width to length.

Think and Discuss

1. **Explain** why you think the ratio $\frac{10}{3}$ in Example 1B is not written as a mixed number.
2. **Tell** how to simplify a ratio.
3. **Explain** how to compare two ratios.

5-1 Exercises

go.hrw.com
Homework Help Online
KEYWORD: MS7 5-1
Parent Resources Online
KEYWORD: MS7 Parent

GUIDED PRACTICE

See Example 1

Sun-Li has 10 blue marbles, 3 red marbles, and 17 white marbles. Write each ratio in all three forms.

1. blue marbles to red marbles
2. red marbles to total marbles

See Example 2

3. In a 40-gallon aquarium, there are 21 neon tetras and 7 zebra danio fish. Write the ratio of neon tetras to zebra danio fish in simplest form.

See Example 3

4. Tell whose DVD collection has the greater ratio of comedy movies to adventure movies.

	Joseph	Yolanda
Comedy	5	7
Adventure	3	5

INDEPENDENT PRACTICE

See Example 1

A soccer league has 25 sixth-graders, 30 seventh-graders, and 15 eighth-graders. Write each ratio in all three forms.

5. 6th-graders to 7th-graders
6. 6th-graders to total students
7. 7th-graders to 8th-graders
8. 7th- and 8th-graders to 6th-graders

See Example 2

9. Thirty-six people auditioned for a play, and 9 people got roles. Write the ratio in simplest form of the number of people who auditioned to the number of people who got roles.

See Example 3

10. Tell whose bag of nut mix has the greater ratio of peanuts to total nuts.

	Dina	Don
Almonds	6	11
Cashews	8	7
Peanuts	10	18

PRACTICE AND PROBLEM SOLVING

Extra Practice
See page 735.

Use the table for Exercises 11–13.

11. Tell whether group 1 or group 2 has the greater ratio of the number of people for an open-campus lunch to the number of people with no opinion.

Opinions on Open-Campus Lunch			
	Group 1	Group 2	Group 3
For	9	10	12
Against	14	16	16
No Opinion	5	6	8

12. Which group has the least ratio of the number of people against an open-campus lunch to the total number of survey responses?

13. **Estimation** For each group, is the ratio of the number of people for an open-campus lunch to the number of people against it less than or greater than $\frac{1}{2}$?

Physical Science LINK

The pressure of water at different depths can be measured in *atmospheres,* or atm. The water pressure on a scuba diver increases as the diver descends below the surface. Use the table for Exercises 14–20.

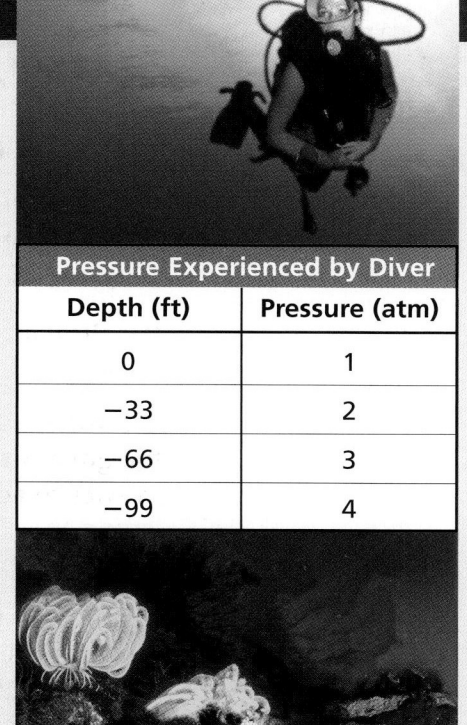

Pressure Experienced by Diver

Depth (ft)	Pressure (atm)
0	1
−33	2
−66	3
−99	4

Write each ratio in all three forms.

14. pressure at −33 ft to pressure at surface

15. pressure at −66 ft to pressure at surface

16. pressure at −99 ft to pressure at surface

17. pressure at −66 ft to pressure at −33 ft

18. pressure at −99 ft to pressure at −66 ft

19. Tell whether the ratio of pressure at −66 ft to pressure at −33 ft is greater than or less than the ratio of pressure at −99 ft to pressure at −66 ft.

20. ★ **Challenge** The ratio of the beginning pressure and the new pressure when a scuba diver goes from −33 ft to −66 ft is less than the ratio of pressures when the diver goes from the surface to −33 ft. The ratio of pressures is even less when the diver goes from −66 ft to −99 ft. Use the ratios that you wrote in Exercises 14–18 to explain why this is true.

go.hrw.com
Web Extra!
KEYWORD: MS7 Pressure

Test Prep and Spiral Review

21. Multiple Choice Johnson Middle School has 125 sixth-graders, 150 seventh-graders, and 100 eighth-graders. Which statement is NOT true?

Ⓐ The ratio of sixth-graders to seventh-graders is 5 to 6.

Ⓑ The ratio of eighth-graders to seventh-graders is 3:2.

Ⓒ The ratio of sixth-graders to students in all three grades is 1:3.

Ⓓ The ratio of eighth-graders to students in all three grades is 4 to 15.

22. Short Response A pancake recipe calls for 4 cups of pancake mix for every 3 cups of milk. A biscuit recipe calls for 2 cups of biscuit mix for every 1 cup of milk. Which recipe has a greater ratio of mix to milk? Explain.

Solve. (Lesson 3-6)

23. $1.23 + x = -5.47$ **24.** $3.8y = 27.36$ **25.** $v - 3.8 = 4.7$

26. Identify the quadrant in which the point $(5, -7)$ lies. (Lesson 4-1)

5-2 Rates

Learn to find and compare unit rates, such as average speed and unit price.

Vocabulary

rate

unit rate

The Lawsons are going camping at Rainbow Falls, which is 288 miles from their home. They would like to reach the campground in 6 hours of driving so that they can set up their campsite while it is still light. What should their average speed be in miles per hour?

A **rate** is a ratio that compares two quantities measured in different units. In order to answer the question above, you need to find the family's rate of travel.

Their rate is $\frac{288 \text{ miles}}{6 \text{ hours}}$.

A **unit rate** is a rate whose denominator is 1. To change a rate to a unit rate, divide both the numerator and denominator by the denominator.

EXAMPLE 1 Finding Unit Rates

A During exercise, Sonia's heart beats 675 times in 5 minutes. How many times does it beat per minute?

$\frac{675 \text{ beats}}{5 \text{ minutes}}$ *Write a rate that compares heart beats and time.*

$\frac{675 \text{ beats} \div 5}{5 \text{ minutes} \div 5}$ *Divide the numerator and denominator by 5.*

$\frac{135 \text{ beats}}{1 \text{ minute}}$ *Simplify.*

Sonia's heart beats 135 times per minute.

B To make 4 large pizza pockets, Paul needs 14 cups of broccoli. How much broccoli does he need for 1 large pizza pocket?

$\frac{14 \text{ cups broccoli}}{4 \text{ pizza pockets}}$ *Write a rate that compares cups to pockets.*

$\frac{14 \text{ cups broccoli} \div 4}{4 \text{ pizza pockets} \div 4}$ *Divide the numerator and denominator by 4.*

$\frac{3.5 \text{ cups broccoli}}{1 \text{ pizza pocket}}$ *Simplify.*

Paul needs 3.5 cups of broccoli to make 1 large pizza pocket.

An average rate of speed is the ratio of distance traveled to time. The ratio is a rate because the units in the numerator and denominator are different.

EXAMPLE 2 Finding Average Speed

The Lawsons want to drive the 288 miles to Rainbow Falls in 6 hours. What should their average speed be in miles per hour?

$\frac{288 \text{ miles}}{6 \text{ hours}}$ *Write the rate as a fraction.*

$\frac{288 \text{ miles} \div 6}{6 \text{ hours} \div 6} = \frac{48 \text{ miles}}{1 \text{ hour}}$ *Divide the numerator and denominator by the denominator.*

Their average speed should be 48 miles per hour.

A unit price is the price of one unit of an item. The unit used depends on how the item is sold. The table shows some examples.

Type of Item	Examples of Units
Liquid	Fluid ounces, quarts, gallons, liters
Solid	Ounces, pounds, grams, kilograms
Any item	Bottle, container, carton

EXAMPLE 3 *Consumer Math Application*

The Lawsons stop at a roadside farmers' market. The market offers lemonade in three sizes. Which size lemonade has the lowest price per fluid ounce?

Size	Price
12 fl oz	$0.89
18 fl oz	$1.69
24 fl oz	$2.09

Divide the price by the number of fluid ounces (fl oz) to find the unit price of each size.

$\frac{\$0.89}{12 \text{ fl oz}} \approx \frac{\$0.07}{\text{fl oz}}$ $\frac{\$1.69}{18 \text{ fl oz}} \approx \frac{\$0.09}{\text{fl oz}}$ $\frac{\$2.09}{24 \text{ fl oz}} \approx \frac{\$0.09}{\text{fl oz}}$

Since $\$0.07 < \$0.09$, the 12 fl oz lemonade has the lowest price per fluid ounce.

Think and Discuss

1. **Explain** how can you tell whether an expression represents a unit rate.
2. **Suppose** a store offers cereal with a unit price of $0.15 per ounce. Another store offers cereal with a unit price of $0.18 per ounce. Before determining which is the better buy, what variables must you consider?

5-2 Exercises

go.hrw.com
Homework Help Online
KEYWORD: MS7 5-2
Parent Resources Online
KEYWORD: MS7 Parent

GUIDED PRACTICE

See Example 1

1. A faucet leaks 668 milliliters of water in 8 minutes. How many milliliters of water does the faucet leak per minute?
2. A recipe for 6 muffins calls for 360 grams of oat flakes. How many grams of oat flakes are needed for each muffin?

See Example 2

3. An airliner makes a 2,748-mile flight in 6 hours. What is the airliner's average rate of speed in miles per hour?

See Example 3

4. **Consumer Math** During a car trip, the Webers buy gasoline at three different stations. At the first station, they pay \$18.63 for 9 gallons of gas. At the second, they pay \$29.54 for 14 gallons. At the third, they pay \$33.44 for 16 gallons. Which station offers the lowest price per gallon?

INDEPENDENT PRACTICE

See Example 1

5. An after-school job pays \$116.25 for 15 hours of work. How much money does the job pay per hour?
6. It took Samantha 324 minutes to cook a turkey. If the turkey weighed 18 pounds, how many minutes per pound did it take to cook the turkey?

See Example 2

7. **Sports** The first Indianapolis 500 auto race took place in 1911. The winning car covered the 500 miles in 6.7 hours. What was the winning car's average rate of speed in miles per hour?

See Example 3

8. **Consumer Math** A supermarket sells orange juice in three sizes. The 32 fl oz container costs \$1.99, the 64 fl oz container costs \$3.69, and the 96 fl oz container costs \$5.85. Which size orange juice has the lowest price per fluid ounce?

PRACTICE AND PROBLEM SOLVING

Extra Practice
See page 735.

Find each unit rate. Round to the nearest hundredth, if necessary.

9. 9 runs in 3 games
10. \$207,000 for 1,800 ft^2
11. \$2,010 in 6 mo
12. 52 songs on 4 CDs
13. 226 mi on 12 gal
14. 324 words in 6 min
15. 12 hr for \$69
16. 6 lb for \$12.96
17. 488 mi in 4 trips
18. 220 m in 20 s
19. 1.5 mi in 39 min
20. 24,000 km in 1.5 hr
21. In Grant Middle School, each class has an equal number of students. There are 38 classes and a total of 1,026 students. Write a rate that describes the distribution of students in the classes at Grant. What is the unit rate?
22. **Estimation** Use estimation to determine which is the better buy: 450 minutes of phone time for \$49.99 or 800 minutes for \$62.99.

Find each unit price. Then decide which is the better buy.

23. $\frac{\$2.52}{42\text{ oz}}$ or $\frac{\$3.64}{52\text{ oz}}$

24. $\frac{\$28.40}{8\text{ yd}}$ or $\frac{\$55.50}{15\text{ yd}}$

25. $\frac{\$8.28}{0.3\text{ m}}$ or $\frac{\$13.00}{0.4\text{ m}}$

26. Sports In the 2004 Summer Olympics, Justin Gatlin won the 100-meter race in 9.85 seconds. Shawn Crawford won the 200-meter race in 19.79 seconds. Which runner ran at a faster average rate?

27. Social Studies The population density of a country is the average number of people per unit of area. Write the population densities of the countries in the table as unit rates. Round your answers to the nearest person per square mile. Then rank the countries from least to greatest population density.

Country	Population	Land Area (mi^2)
France	60,424,213	210,669
Germany	82,424,609	134,836
Poland	38,626,349	117,555

28. Write a Problem A store sells paper towels in packs of 6 and packs of 8. Use this information to write a problem about comparing unit rates.

29. Write About It Michael Jordan has the highest scoring average in NBA history. He played in 1,072 games and scored 32,292 points. Explain how to find a unit rate to describe his scoring average. What is the unit rate?

30. Challenge Mike fills his car's gas tank with 20 gallons of regular gas at \$2.01 per gallon. His car averages 25 miles per gallon. Serena fills her car's tank with 15 gallons of premium gas at \$2.29 per gallon. Her car averages 30 miles per gallon. Compare the drivers' unit costs of driving one mile.

TEST PREP and Spiral Review

31. Multiple Choice What is the unit price of a 16-ounce box of cereal that sells for \$2.48?

Ⓐ \$0.14 Ⓑ \$0.15 Ⓒ \$0.0155 Ⓓ \$0.155

32. Short Response A carpenter needs 3 minutes to cut a board into 5 equal sections. If each cut takes the same length of time, at what rate is the carpenter cutting?

Compare. Write $<$, $>$, or $=$. (Lesson 1-3)

33. 600 mL ___ 5 L **34.** 0.009 mg ___ 8.91 g **35.** 254 cm ___ 25.4 mm

36. Julita's walking stick is $3\frac{2}{3}$ feet long, and Toni's walking stick is $3\frac{3}{8}$ feet long. Whose walking stick is longer and by how much? (Lesson 3-9)

5-3 Slope and Rates of Change

In Chichén Itzá, Mexico, during the spring and fall equinoxes, shadows fall on the pyramid El Castillo, giving the illusion of a snake crawling down the steps.

Learn **to determine the slope of a line and to recognize constant and variable rates of change.**

Vocabulary

slope

The steepness of the pyramid steps is measured by dividing the height of each step by its depth. Another way to express the height and depth is with the words *rise* and *run.*

The **slope** of a line is a measure of its steepness and is the ratio of rise to run:

$$\textbf{slope} = \frac{\textbf{rise}}{\textbf{run}}$$

If a line rises from left to right, its slope is positive. If a line falls from left to right, its slope is negative.

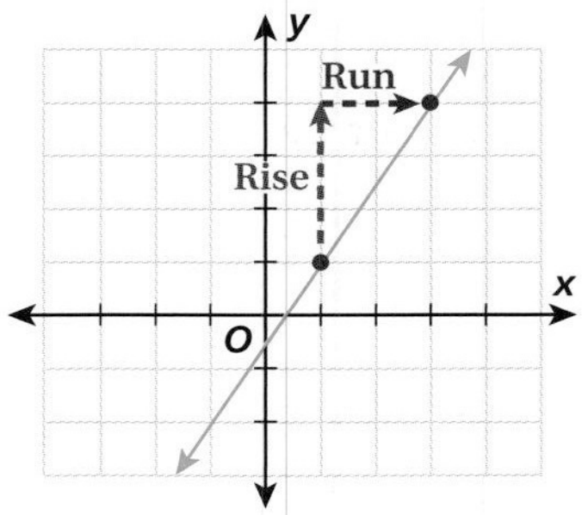

EXAMPLE 1 Identifying the Slope of the Line

Tell whether the slope is positive or negative. Then find the slope.

A

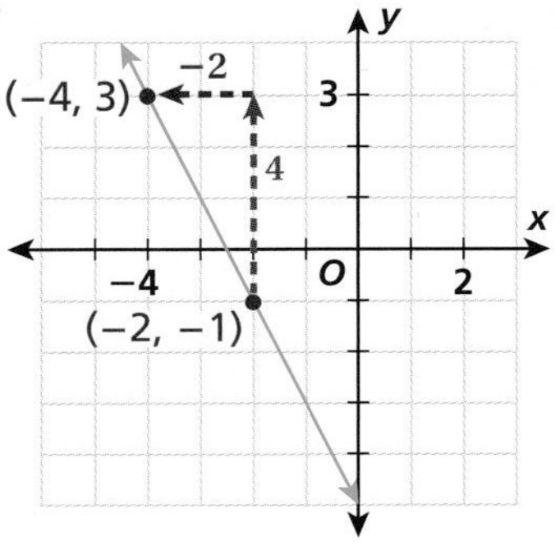

The line falls from left to right.

The slope is negative.

$\text{slope} = \frac{\textbf{rise}}{\textbf{run}}$

$= \frac{4}{-2}$ *The rise is 4. The run is –2.*

$= -2$

B

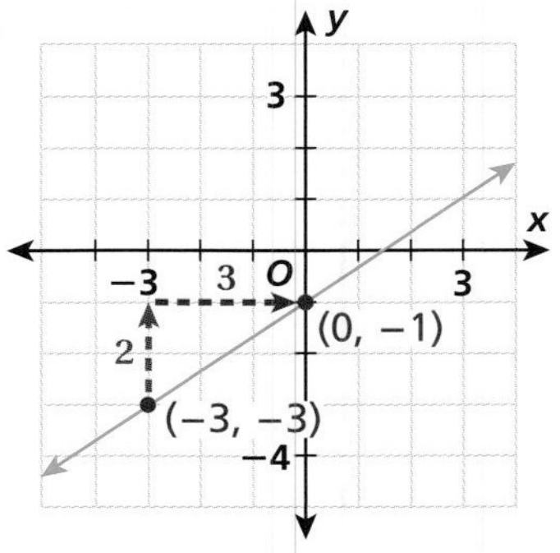

The line rises from left to right.

The slope is positive.

$\text{slope} = \frac{\textbf{rise}}{\textbf{run}}$

$= \frac{2}{3}$ *The rise is 2. The run is 3.*

You can graph a line if you know its slope and one of its points.

EXAMPLE 2 Using Slope and a Point to Graph a Line

Use the given slope and point to graph each line.

A $-\frac{3}{4}$; $(-3, 2)$

$$\text{slope} = \frac{\text{rise}}{\text{run}} = \frac{-3}{4} \text{ or } \frac{3}{-4}$$

From point $(-3, 2)$, move 3 units down and 4 units right, or move 3 units up and 4 units left. Mark the point where you end up, and draw a line through the two points.

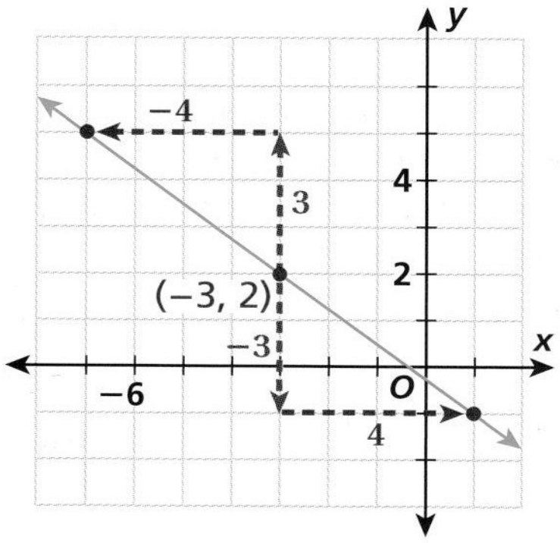

Remember!

You can write an integer as a fraction by putting the integer in the numerator of the fraction and a 1 in the denominator.

B 3; $(-1, -2)$

$3 = \frac{3}{1}$ *Write the slope as a fraction.*

$$\text{slope} = \frac{\text{rise}}{\text{run}} = \frac{3}{1}$$

From point $(-1, -2)$, move 3 units up and 1 unit right. Mark the point where you end up, and draw a line through the two points.

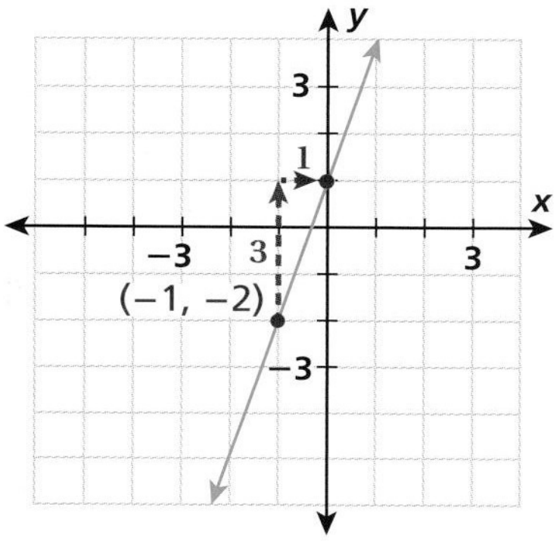

The ratio of two quantities that change, such as slope, is a *rate of change.*

A *constant rate of change* describes changes of the same amount during equal intervals. A *variable rate of change* describes changes of a different amount during equal intervals.

The graph of a constant rate of change is a line, and the graph of a variable rate of change is not a line.

EXAMPLE 3 Identifying Rates of Change in Graphs

Tell whether each graph shows a constant or variable rate of change.

A

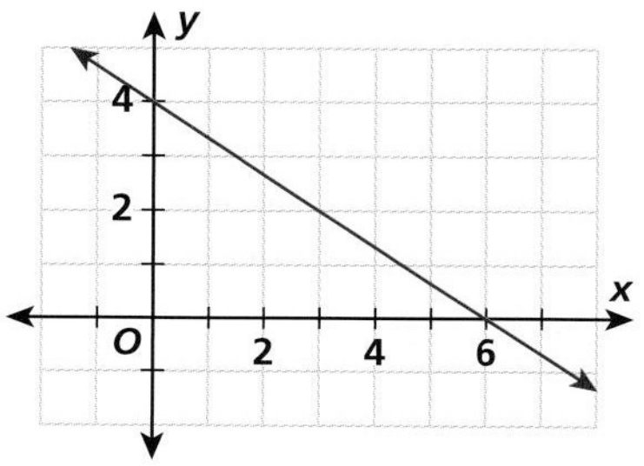

The graph is a line, so the rate of change is constant.

B

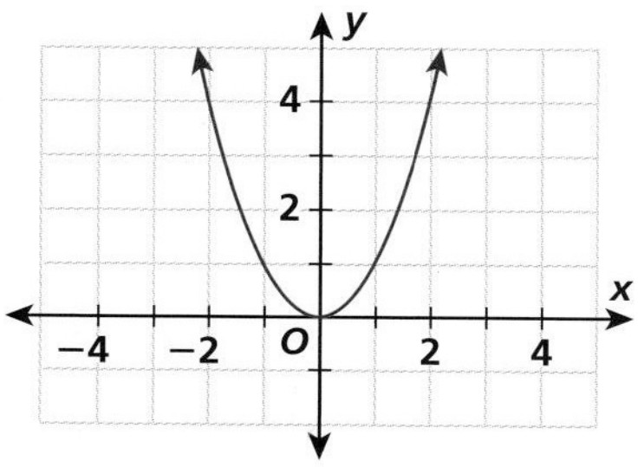

The graph is not a line, so the rate of change is variable.

EXAMPLE 4 Using Rate of Change to Solve Problems

The graph shows the distance a bicyclist travels over time. Does the bicyclist travel at a constant or variable speed? How fast does the bicyclist travel?

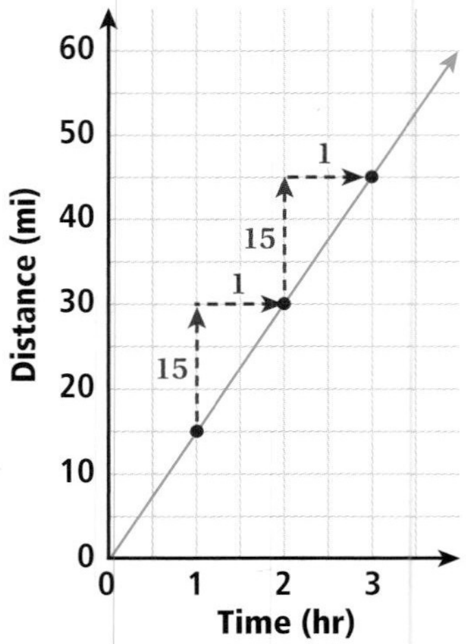

The graph is a line, so the bicyclist is traveling at a constant speed.

The amount of distance is the rise, and the amount of time is the run. You can find the speed by finding the slope.

$$\text{slope (speed)} = \frac{\text{rise (distance)}}{\text{run (time)}} = \frac{15}{1}$$

The bicyclist travels at 15 miles per hour.

Think and Discuss

1. **Describe** a line with a negative slope.
2. **Compare** constant and variable rates of change.
3. **Give an example** of a real-world situation involving a rate of change.

5-3 Exercises

go.hrw.com
Homework Help Online
KEYWORD: MS7 5-3
Parent Resources Online
KEYWORD: MS7 Parent

GUIDED PRACTICE

See Example 1

Tell whether the slope is positive or negative. Then find the slope.

1.

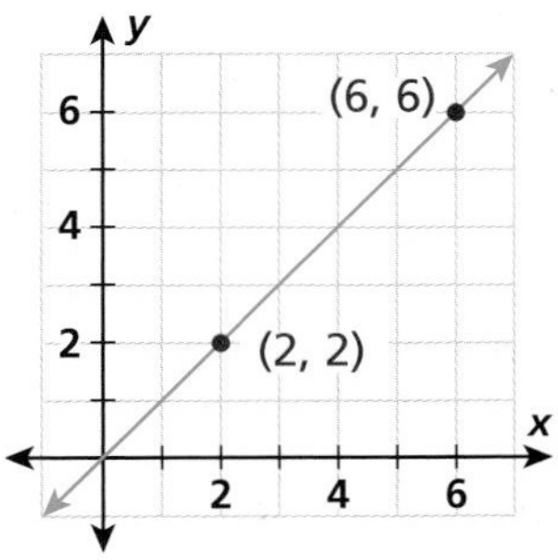

2.

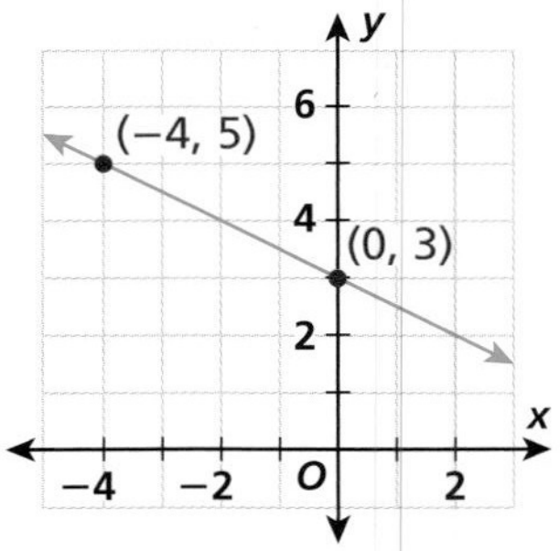

See Example 2

Use the given slope and point to graph each line.

3. 3; (4, −2)
4. −2; (−3, −2)
5. $-\frac{1}{4}$; (0, 5)
6. $\frac{3}{2}$; (−1, 1)

See Example 3

Tell whether each graph shows a constant or variable rate of change.

7.

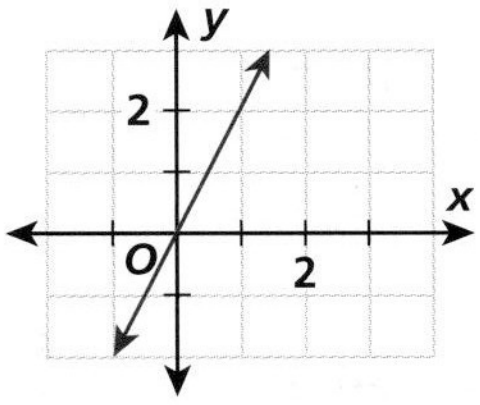

8.

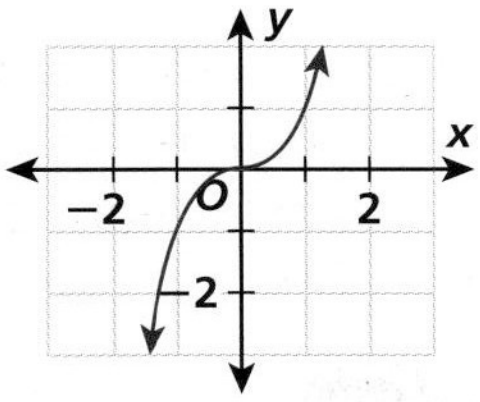

9.

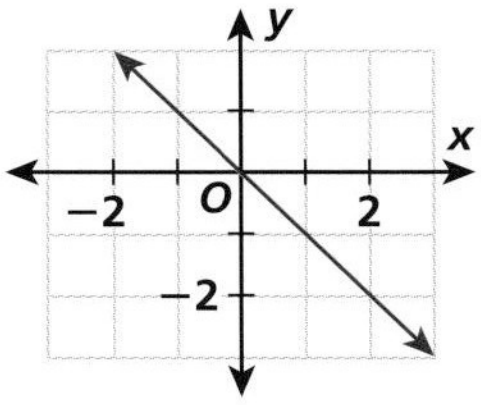

See Example 4

10. The graph shows the distance a trout swims over time. Does the trout swim at a constant or variable speed? How fast does the trout swim?

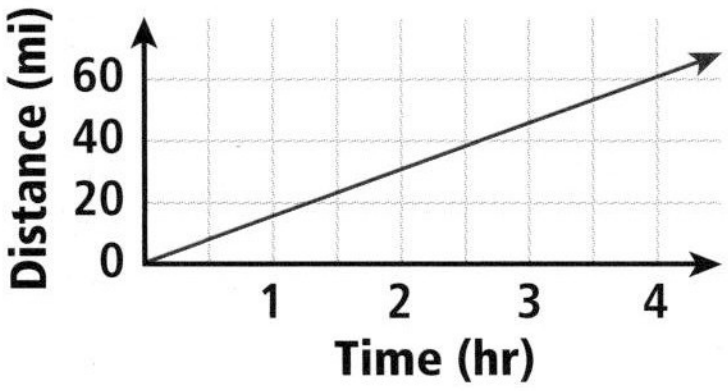

INDEPENDENT PRACTICE

See Example 1

Tell whether the slope is positive or negative. Then find the slope.

11.

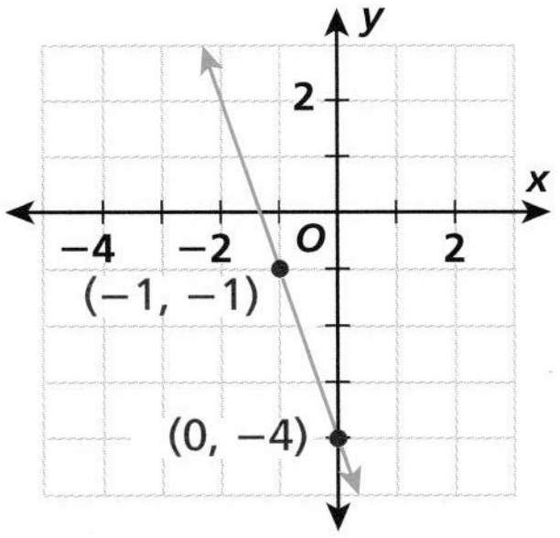

12.

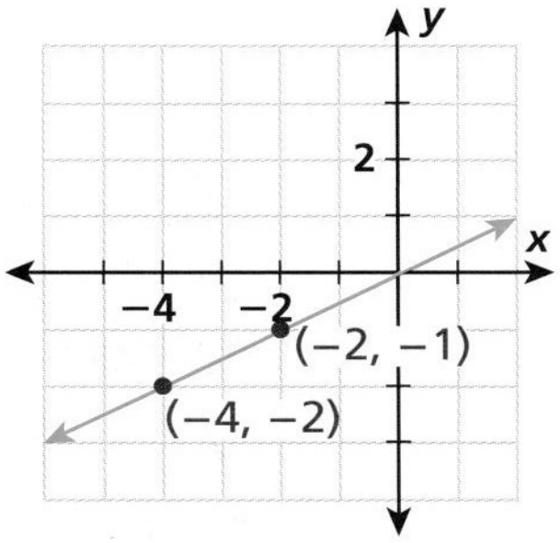

See Example 2

Use the given slope and point to graph each line.

13. -1; $(-1, 4)$ **14.** 4; $(-1, -3)$ **15.** $\frac{3}{5}$; $(3, -1)$ **16.** $\frac{2}{3}$; $(0, 5)$

See Example 3

Tell whether each graph shows a constant or variable rate of change.

17.

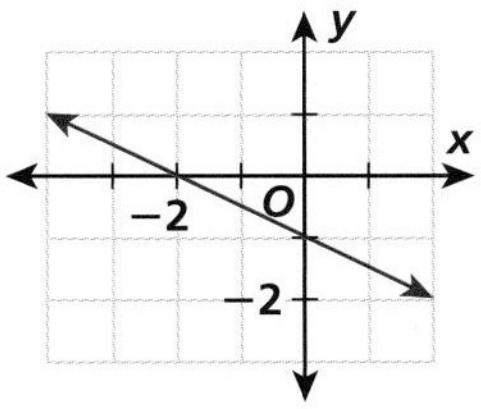

18.

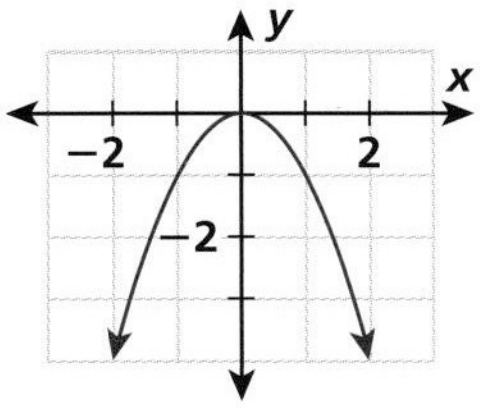

19.

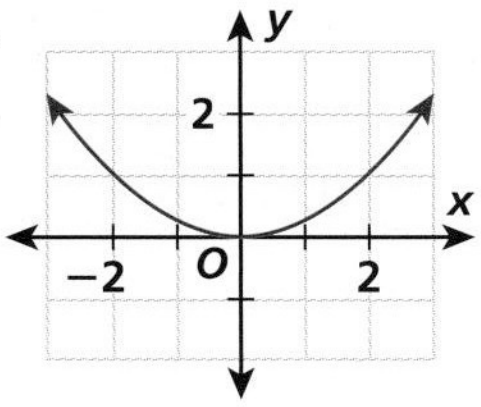

See Example 4

20. The graph shows the amount of rain that falls over time. Does the rain fall at a constant or variable rate? How much rain falls per hour?

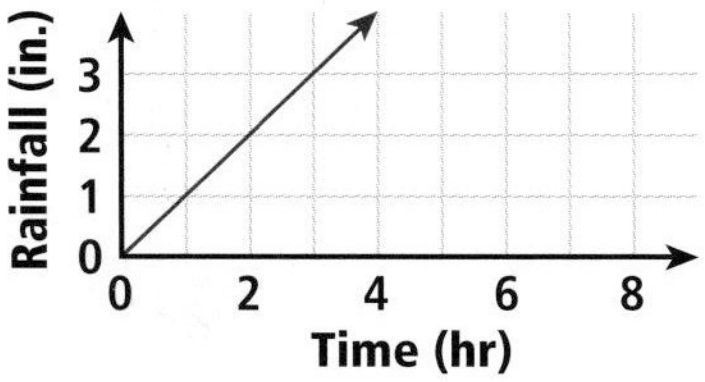

PRACTICE AND PROBLEM SOLVING

Extra Practice

See page 735.

21. Multi-Step A line has a slope of 5 and passes through the points $(4, 3)$ and $(2, y)$. What is the value of y?

22. A line passes through the origin and has a slope of $-\frac{3}{2}$. Through which quadrants does the line pass?

LINK

Agriculture

This water tower can be seen in Gaffney, South Carolina, where the South Carolina Peach Festival is held every year.

Graph the line containing the two points, and then find the slope.

23. $(-2, 13), (1, 4)$ **24.** $(-2, -6), (2, 2)$ **25.** $(-2, -3), (2, 3)$ **26.** $(2, -3), (3, -5)$

27. Explain whether you think it would be more difficult to run up a hill with a slope of $\frac{1}{3}$ or a hill with a slope of $\frac{3}{4}$.

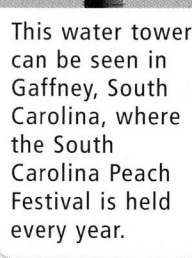

28. Agriculture The graph at right shows the cost per pound of buying peaches.

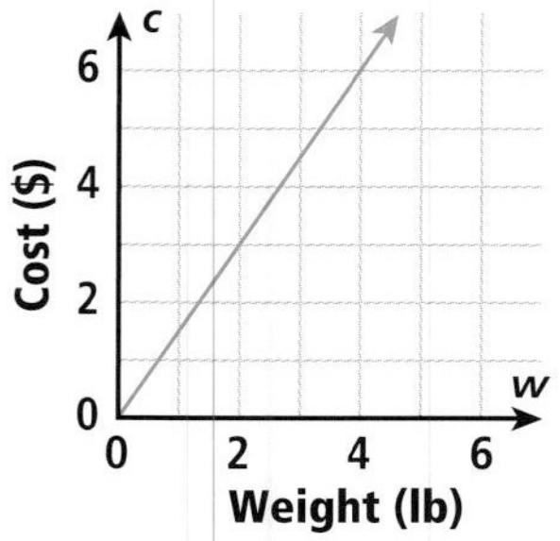

a. Is the cost per pound a constant or variable rate?

b. What is the cost per pound of peaches?

29. Critical Thinking A line has a negative slope. Explain how the y-values of the line change as the x-values increase.

30. What's the Error? Kyle graphed a line, given a slope of $-\frac{4}{3}$ and the point (2, 3). When he used the slope to find the second point, he found (5, 7). What error did Kyle make?

31. Write About It Explain how to graph a line when given the slope and one of the points on the line.

32. Challenge The population of prairie dogs in a park doubles every year. Does this population show a constant or variable rate of change? Explain.

Test Prep and Spiral Review

33. Multiple Choice To graph a line, Caelyn plotted the point (2, 1) and then used the slope $-\frac{1}{2}$ to find another point on the line. Which point could be the other point on the line that Caelyn found?

Ⓐ (1, 3) Ⓑ (4, 0) Ⓒ (1, −1) Ⓓ (0, 0)

34. Multiple Choice A line has a positive slope and passes through the point (−1, 2). Through which quadrant can the line NOT pass?

Ⓕ Quadrant I Ⓖ Quadrant II Ⓗ Quadrant III Ⓙ Quadrant IV

35. Short Response Explain how you can use three points on a graph to determine whether the rate of change is constant or variable.

Find each value. (Lesson 1-2)

36. 3^5 **37.** 5^3 **38.** 4^1 **39.** 10^5

Write a rule for each sequence in words. Then find the next three terms. (Lesson 4-5)

40. 3.7, 3.2, 2.7, 2.2, . . . **41.** $-\frac{3}{2}, 0, \frac{3}{2}, 3, \ldots$ **42.** $3, -1, \frac{1}{3}, -\frac{1}{9}, \ldots$

5-4 Identifying and Writing Proportions

Learn to find equivalent ratios and to identify proportions.

Vocabulary

equivalent ratios

proportion

Students in Mr. Howell's math class are measuring the width w and the length ℓ of their heads. The ratio of ℓ to w is 10 inches to 6 inches for Jean and 25 centimeters to 15 centimeters for Pat.

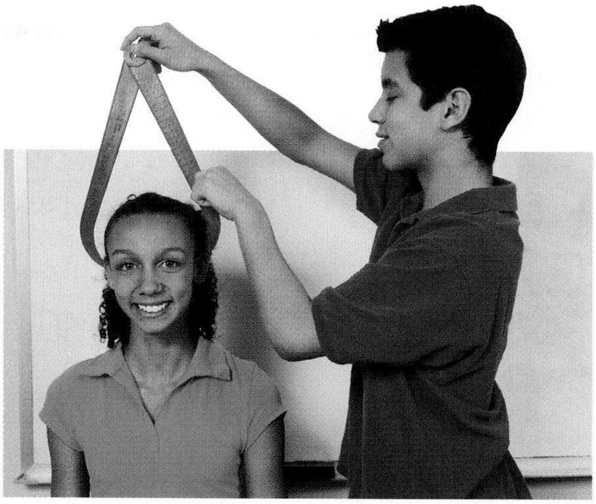

Calipers have adjustable arms that are used to measure the thickness of objects.

These ratios can be written as the fractions $\frac{10}{6}$ and $\frac{25}{15}$. Since both ratios simplify to $\frac{5}{3}$, they are equivalent. **Equivalent ratios** are ratios that name the same comparison.

Reading Math

Read the proportion $\frac{10}{6} = \frac{25}{15}$ by saying "ten is to six as twenty-five is to fifteen."

An equation stating that two ratios are equivalent is called a **proportion**. The equation, or proportion, below states that the ratios $\frac{10}{6}$ and $\frac{25}{15}$ are equivalent.

$$\frac{10}{6} = \frac{25}{15}$$

If two ratios are equivalent, they are said to be *proportional* to each other, or *in proportion.*

EXAMPLE 1 Comparing Ratios in Simplest Form

Determine whether the ratios are proportional.

A $\frac{2}{7}, \frac{6}{21}$

$\frac{2}{7}$ — *$\frac{2}{7}$ is already in simplest form.*

$\frac{6}{21} = \frac{6 \div 3}{21 \div 3} = \frac{2}{7}$ — *Simplify $\frac{6}{21}$.*

Since $\frac{2}{7} = \frac{2}{7}$, the ratios are proportional.

B $\frac{8}{24}, \frac{6}{20}$

$\frac{8}{24} = \frac{8 \div 8}{24 \div 8} = \frac{1}{3}$ — *Simplify $\frac{8}{24}$.*

$\frac{6}{20} = \frac{6 \div 2}{20 \div 2} = \frac{3}{10}$ — *Simplify $\frac{6}{20}$.*

Since $\frac{1}{3} \neq \frac{3}{10}$, the ratios are *not* proportional.

EXAMPLE 2 Comparing Ratios Using a Common Denominator

Use the data in the table to determine whether the ratios of oats to water are proportional for both servings of oatmeal.

Servings of Oatmeal	Cups of Oats	Cups of Water
8	2	4
12	3	6

Write the ratios of oats to water for 8 servings and for 12 servings.

Ratio of oats to water, 8 servings: $\frac{2}{4}$ — *Write the ratio as a fraction.*

Ratio of oats to water, 12 servings: $\frac{3}{6}$ — *Write the ratio as a fraction.*

$\frac{2}{4} = \frac{2 \cdot 6}{4 \cdot 6} = \frac{12}{24}$

$\frac{3}{6} = \frac{3 \cdot 4}{6 \cdot 4} = \frac{12}{24}$

Write the ratios with a common denominator, such as 24.

Since both ratios are equal to $\frac{12}{24}$, they are proportional.

You can find an equivalent ratio by multiplying or dividing the numerator and the denominator of a ratio by the same number.

EXAMPLE 3 Finding Equivalent Ratios and Writing Proportions

Find a ratio equivalent to each ratio. Then use the ratios to write a proportion.

A $\frac{8}{14}$

$\frac{8}{14} = \frac{8 \cdot 20}{14 \cdot 20} = \frac{160}{280}$ — *Multiply both the numerator and denominator by any number, such as 20.*

$\frac{8}{14} = \frac{160}{280}$ — *Write a proportion.*

B $\frac{4}{18}$

$\frac{4}{18} = \frac{4 \div 2}{18 \div 2} = \frac{2}{9}$ — *Divide both the numerator and denominator by a common factor, such as 2.*

$\frac{4}{18} = \frac{2}{9}$ — *Write a proportion.*

Life Science LINK

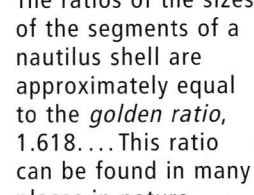

The ratios of the sizes of the segments of a nautilus shell are approximately equal to the *golden ratio*, 1.618.... This ratio can be found in many places in nature.

go.hrw.com
Web Extra!
KEYWORD: MS7 Golden

Think and Discuss

1. **Explain** why the ratios in Example 1B are not proportional.
2. **Describe** what it means for ratios to be proportional.
3. **Give an example** of a proportion. Then tell how you know it is a proportion.

5-4 Exercises

go.hrw.com
Homework Help Online
KEYWORD: MS7 5-4
Parent Resources Online
KEYWORD: MS7 Parent

GUIDED PRACTICE

See Example 1

Determine whether the ratios are proportional.

1. $\frac{2}{3}, \frac{4}{6}$ **2.** $\frac{5}{10}, \frac{8}{18}$ **3.** $\frac{9}{12}, \frac{15}{20}$ **4.** $\frac{3}{4}, \frac{8}{12}$

See Example 2

5. $\frac{10}{12}, \frac{15}{18}$ **6.** $\frac{6}{9}, \frac{8}{12}$ **7.** $\frac{3}{4}, \frac{5}{6}$ **8.** $\frac{4}{6}, \frac{6}{9}$

See Example 3

Find a ratio equivalent to each ratio. Then use the ratios to write a proportion.

9. $\frac{1}{3}$ **10.** $\frac{9}{21}$ **11.** $\frac{8}{3}$ **12.** $\frac{10}{4}$

INDEPENDENT PRACTICE

See Example 1

Determine whether the ratios are proportional.

13. $\frac{5}{8}, \frac{7}{14}$ **14.** $\frac{8}{24}, \frac{10}{30}$ **15.** $\frac{18}{20}, \frac{81}{180}$ **16.** $\frac{15}{20}, \frac{27}{35}$

See Example 2

17. $\frac{2}{3}, \frac{4}{9}$ **18.** $\frac{18}{12}, \frac{15}{10}$ **19.** $\frac{7}{8}, \frac{14}{24}$ **20.** $\frac{18}{54}, \frac{10}{30}$

See Example 3

Find a ratio equivalent to each ratio. Then use the ratios to write a proportion.

21. $\frac{5}{9}$ **22.** $\frac{27}{60}$ **23.** $\frac{6}{15}$ **24.** $\frac{121}{99}$

25. $\frac{11}{13}$ **26.** $\frac{5}{22}$ **27.** $\frac{78}{104}$ **28.** $\frac{27}{72}$

PRACTICE AND PROBLEM SOLVING

Extra Practice

See page 735.

Complete each table of equivalent ratios.

29.

angelfish	4	8	■	20
tiger fish	■	6	18	■

30.

squares	2	4	6	8
circles	■	16	■	■

Find two ratios equivalent to each given ratio.

31. 3 to 7 **32.** 6:2 **33.** $\frac{5}{12}$ **34.** 8:4

35. 6 to 9 **36.** $\frac{10}{50}$ **37.** 10:4 **38.** 1 to 10

39. Ecology If you recycle one aluminum can, you save enough energy to run a TV for four hours.

a. Write the ratio of cans to hours.

b. Marti's class recycled enough aluminum cans to run a TV for 2,080 hours. Did the class recycle 545 cans? Justify your answer using equivalent ratios.

40. Critical Thinking The ratio of girls to boys riding a bus is 15:12. If the driver drops off the same number of girls as boys at the next stop, does the ratio of girls to boys remain 15:12? Explain.

41. **Critical Thinking** Write all possible proportions using only the numbers 1, 2, and 4.

42. **School** Last year in Kerry's school, the ratio of students to teachers was 22:1. Write an equivalent ratio to show how many students and teachers there could have been at Kerry's school.

43. **Life Science** Students in a biology class surveyed four ponds to determine whether salamanders and frogs were inhabiting the area.

Pond	Number of Salamanders	Number of Frogs
Cypress Pond	8	5
Mill Pond	15	10
Clear Pond	3	2
Gill Pond	2	7

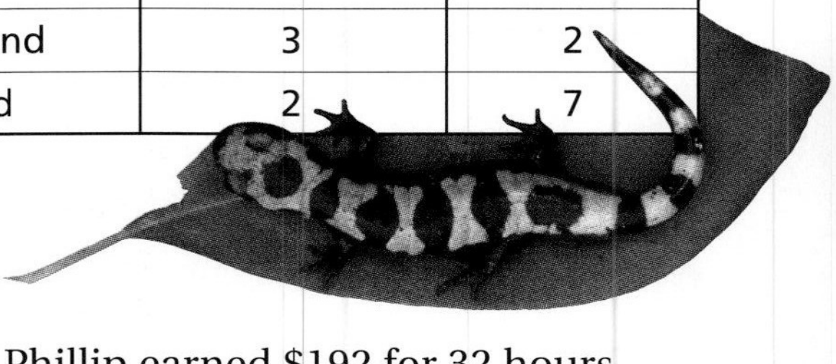

a. What was the ratio of salamanders to frogs in Cypress Pond?

b. In which two ponds was the ratio of salamanders to frogs the same?

44. Marcus earned $230 for 40 hours of work. Phillip earned $192 for 32 hours of work. Are these pay rates proportional? Explain.

45. **What's the Error?** A student wrote the proportion $\frac{13}{20} = \frac{26}{60}$. What did the student do wrong?

46. **Write About It** Explain two different ways to determine if two ratios are proportional.

47. **Challenge** A skydiver jumps out of an airplane. After 0.8 second, she has fallen 100 feet. After 3.1 seconds, she has fallen 500 feet. Is the rate (in feet per second) at which she falls the first 100 feet proportional to the rate at which she falls the next 400 feet? Explain.

Test Prep and Spiral Review

48. **Multiple Choice** Which ratio is NOT equivalent to $\frac{32}{48}$?

Ⓐ $\frac{2}{3}$ Ⓑ $\frac{8}{12}$ Ⓒ $\frac{64}{96}$ Ⓓ $\frac{128}{144}$

49. **Multiple Choice** Which ratio can form a proportion with $\frac{5}{6}$?

Ⓕ $\frac{13}{18}$ Ⓖ $\frac{25}{36}$ Ⓗ $\frac{70}{84}$ Ⓙ $\frac{95}{102}$

Divide. Estimate to check whether each answer is reasonable. (Lesson 3-5)

50. $14.35 \div 0.7$ 51. $-9 \div 2.4$ 52. $12.505 \div 3.05$ 53. $427 \div (-5.6)$

Make a function table. (Lesson 4-4)

54. $y = 2x - 1$ 55. $y = -x + 3$ 56. $y = \frac{x}{3} - 2$ 57. $y = -3x + 4$

5-5 Solving Proportions

Learn to solve proportions by using cross products.

Vocabulary

cross product

Density is a ratio that compares a substance's mass to its volume. If you are given the density of ice, you can find the mass of 3 mL of ice by solving a proportion.

Ice floats in water because the density of ice is less than the density of water.

For two ratios, the product of the numerator in one ratio and the denominator in the other is a **cross product**. If the cross products of the ratios are equal, then the ratios form a proportion.

$$\frac{2}{5} = \frac{6}{15} \qquad 5 \cdot 6 = 30 \qquad 2 \cdot 15 = 30$$

CROSS PRODUCT RULE

In the proportion $\frac{a}{b} = \frac{c}{d}$, where $b \neq 0$ and $d \neq 0$, the cross products, $a \cdot d$ and $b \cdot c$, are equal.

You can use the cross product rule to solve proportions with variables.

EXAMPLE 1 Solving Proportions Using Cross Products

Use cross products to solve the proportion $\frac{p}{6} = \frac{10}{3}$.

$\frac{p}{6} = \frac{10}{3}$

$p \cdot 3 = 6 \cdot 10$ *The cross products are equal.*

$3p = 60$ *Multiply.*

$\frac{3p}{3} = \frac{60}{3}$ *Divide each side by 3 to isolate the variable.*

$p = 20$

When setting up proportions that include different units of measurement, either the units in the numerators must be the same and the units in the denominators must be the same or the units within each ratio must be the same.

$$\frac{16 \text{ mi}}{4 \text{ hr}} = \frac{8 \text{ mi}}{x \text{ hr}} \qquad \frac{16 \text{ mi}}{8 \text{ mi}} = \frac{4 \text{ hr}}{x \text{ hr}}$$

EXAMPLE 2 PROBLEM SOLVING APPLICATION

PROBLEM SOLVING

Density is the ratio of a substance's mass to its volume. The density of ice is 0.92 g/mL. What is the mass of 3 mL of ice?

1 Understand the Problem

Rewrite the question as a statement.

- Find the mass, in grams, of 3 mL of ice.

List the **important information:**

- density $= \frac{\text{mass (g)}}{\text{volume (mL)}}$
- density of ice $= \frac{0.92 \text{ g}}{1 \text{ mL}}$

2 Make a Plan

Set up a proportion using the given information. Let m represent the mass of 3 mL of ice.

$$\frac{0.92 \text{ g}}{1 \text{ mL}} = \frac{m}{3 \text{ mL}} \begin{array}{l} \leftarrow \textit{mass} \\ \leftarrow \textit{volume} \end{array}$$

3 Solve

Solve the proportion.

$\frac{0.92}{1} = \frac{m}{3}$ *Write the proportion.*

$1 \cdot m = 0.92 \cdot 3$ *The cross products are equal.*

$m = 2.76$ *Multiply.*

The mass of 3 mL of ice is 2.76 g.

4 Look Back

Since the density of ice is 0.92 g/mL, each milliliter of ice has a mass of a little less than 1 g. So 3 mL of ice should have a mass of a little less than 3 g. Since 2.76 is a little less than 3, the answer is reasonable.

Think and Discuss

1. **Explain** how the term *cross product* can help you remember how to solve a proportion.
2. **Describe** the error in these steps: $\frac{2}{3} = \frac{x}{12}$; $2x = 36$; $x = 18$.
3. **Show** how to use cross products to decide whether the ratios 6:45 and 2:15 are proportional.

5-5 Exercises

go.hrw.com
Homework Help Online
KEYWORD: MS7 5-5
Parent Resources Online
KEYWORD: MS7 Parent

GUIDED PRACTICE

See Example 1

Use cross products to solve each proportion.

1. $\frac{6}{10} = \frac{36}{x}$
2. $\frac{4}{7} = \frac{5}{p}$
3. $\frac{12.3}{m} = \frac{75}{100}$
4. $\frac{t}{42} = \frac{1.5}{3}$

See Example 2

5. A stack of 2,450 one-dollar bills weighs 5 pounds. How much does a stack of 1,470 one-dollar bills weigh?

INDEPENDENT PRACTICE

See Example 1

Use cross products to solve each proportion.

6. $\frac{4}{36} = \frac{x}{180}$
7. $\frac{7}{84} = \frac{12}{h}$
8. $\frac{3}{24} = \frac{r}{52}$
9. $\frac{5}{140} = \frac{12}{v}$
10. $\frac{45}{x} = \frac{15}{3}$
11. $\frac{t}{6} = \frac{96}{16}$
12. $\frac{2}{5} = \frac{s}{12}$
13. $\frac{14}{n} = \frac{5}{8}$

See Example 2

14. Euro coins come in eight denominations. One denomination is the one-euro coin, which is worth 100 cents. A stack of 10 one-euro coins is 21.25 millimeters tall. How tall would a stack of 45 one-euro coins be? Round your answer to the nearest hundredth of a millimeter.
15. There are 18.5 ounces of soup in a can. This is equivalent to 524 grams. If Jenna has 8 ounces of soup, how many grams does she have? Round your answer to the nearest whole gram.

PRACTICE AND PROBLEM SOLVING

Extra Practice
See page 735.

Solve each proportion. Then find another equivalent ratio.

16. $\frac{4}{h} = \frac{12}{24}$
17. $\frac{x}{15} = \frac{12}{90}$
18. $\frac{39}{4} = \frac{t}{12}$
19. $\frac{5.5}{6} = \frac{16.5}{w}$
20. $\frac{1}{3} = \frac{y}{25.5}$
21. $\frac{18}{x} = \frac{1}{5}$
22. $\frac{m}{4} = \frac{175}{20}$
23. $\frac{8.7}{2} = \frac{q}{4}$
24. $\frac{r}{84} = \frac{32.5}{182}$
25. $\frac{76}{304} = \frac{81}{k}$
26. $\frac{9}{500} = \frac{p}{2{,}500}$
27. $\frac{5}{j} = \frac{6}{19.8}$
28. A certain shade of paint is made by mixing 5 parts blue paint with 2 parts white paint. To get the correct shade, how many quarts of white paint should be mixed with 8.5 quarts of blue paint?
29. **Measurement** If you put an object that has a mass of 8 grams on one side of a balance scale, you would have to put about 20 paper clips on the other side to balance the weight. How many paper clips would balance the weight of a 10-gram object?
30. Sandra drove 126.2 miles in 2 hours at a constant speed. Use a proportion to find how long it would take her to drive 189.3 miles at the same speed.
31. **Multi-Step** In June, a camp has 325 campers and 26 counselors. In July, 265 campers leave and 215 new campers arrive. How many counselors does the camp need in July to keep an equivalent ratio of campers to counselors?

Arrange each set of numbers to form a proportion.

32. 10, 6, 30, 18 **33.** 4, 6, 10, 15 **34.** 12, 21, 7, 4

35. 75, 4, 3, 100 **36.** 30, 42, 5, 7 **37.** 5, 90, 108, 6

38. Life Science On Monday a marine biologist took a random sample of 50 fish from a pond and tagged them. On Tuesday she took a new sample of 100 fish. Among them were 4 fish that had been tagged on Monday.

a. What comparison does the ratio $\frac{4}{100}$ represent?

b. What ratio represents the number of fish tagged on Monday to n, the estimated total number of fish in the pond?

c. Use a proportion to estimate the number of fish in the pond.

39. Chemistry The table shows the type and number of atoms in one molecule of citric acid. Use a proportion to find the number of oxygen atoms in 15 molecules of citric acid.

Composition of Citric Acid	
Type of Atom	**Number of Atoms**
Carbon	6
Hydrogen	8
Oxygen	7

40. Earth Science You can find your distance from a thunderstorm by counting the number of seconds between a lightning flash and the thunder. For example, if the time difference is 21 s, then the storm is 7 km away. How far away is a storm if the time difference is 9 s?

41. What's the Question? There are 20 grams of protein in 3 ounces of sautéed fish. If the answer is 9 ounces, what is the question?

42. Write About It Give an example from your own life that can be described using a ratio. Then tell how a proportion can give you additional information.

43. Challenge Use the Multiplication Property of Equality and the proportion $\frac{a}{b} = \frac{c}{d}$ to show that the cross product rule works.

Test Prep and Spiral Review

44. Multiple Choice Which proportion is true?

Ⓐ $\frac{4}{8} = \frac{6}{10}$ Ⓑ $\frac{2}{7} = \frac{10}{15}$ Ⓒ $\frac{7}{14} = \frac{15}{30}$ Ⓓ $\frac{16}{25} = \frac{13}{18}$

45. Gridded Response Find a ratio to complete the proportion $\frac{2}{3} = \frac{?}{?}$ so that the cross products are equal to 12. Grid your answer in the form of a fraction.

Estimate. (Lesson 3-1)

46. 16.21 − 14.87 **47.** 3.82 · (−4.97) **48.** −8.7 · (−20.1)

Find each unit rate. (Lesson 5-2)

49. 128 miles in 2 hours **50.** 9 books in 6 weeks **51.** $114 in 12 hours

Hands-On LAB 5-6

Generate Formulas to Convert Units

Use with Lesson 5-6

go.hrw.com
Lab Resources Online
KEYWORD: MS7 Lab5

Activity

Publishers, editors, and graphic designers measure lengths in *picas*. Measure each of the following line segments to the nearest inch, and record your results in the table.

Segment	Length (in.)	Length (picas)	Ratio of Picas to Inches
1		6	
2		12	
3		24	
4		30	
5		36	

1 ______

2 ____________

3 ________________________

4 ______________________________

5 ____________________________________

Think and Discuss

1. Make a conjecture about the relationship between picas and inches.
2. Use your conjecture to write a formula relating inches n to picas p.
3. How many picas wide is a sheet of paper that is $8\frac{1}{2}$ in. wide?

Try This

Using inches for *x*-coordinates and picas for *y*-coordinates, write ordered pairs for the data in the table. Then plot the points and draw a graph.

1. What shape is the graph?
2. Use the graph to find the number of picas that is equal to 3 inches.
3. Use the graph to find the number of inches that is equal to 27 picas.
4. A designer is laying out a page in a magazine. The dimensions of a photo are 18 picas by 15 picas. She doubles the dimensions of the photo. What are the new dimensions of the photo in inches?

5-6 Customary Measurements

Learn to identify and convert customary units of measure.

The king cobra is one of the world's most poisonous snakes. Just 2 fluid ounces of the snake's venom is enough to kill a 2-ton elephant.

You can use the following benchmarks to help you understand fluid ounces, tons, and other customary units of measure.

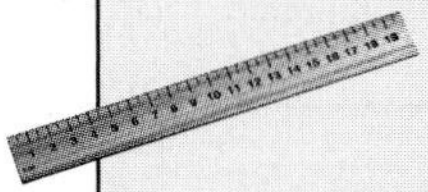

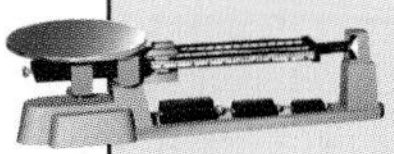

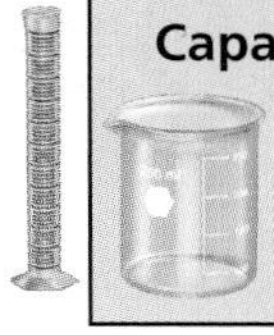

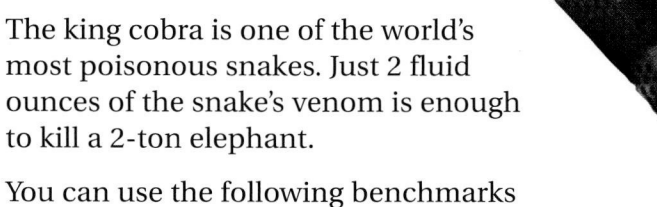

	Customary Unit	Benchmark
Length	Inch (in.)	Length of a small paper clip
	Foot (ft)	Length of a standard sheet of paper
	Mile (mi)	Length of about 18 football fields
Weight	Ounce (oz)	Weight of a slice of bread
	Pound (lb)	Weight of 3 apples
	Ton	Weight of a buffalo
Capacity	Fluid ounce (fl oz)	Amount of water in 2 tablespoons
	Cup (c)	Capacity of a standard measuring cup
	Gallon (gal)	Capacity of a large milk jug

EXAMPLE 1 Choosing the Appropriate Customary Unit

Choose the most appropriate customary unit for each measurement. Justify your answer.

A the length of a rug

Feet—the length of a rug is similar to the length of several sheets of paper.

B the weight of a magazine

Ounces—the weight of a magazine is similar to the weight of several slices of bread.

C the capacity of an aquarium

Gallons—the capacity of an aquarium is similar to the capacity of several large milk jugs.

The following table shows some common equivalent customary units. You can use equivalent measures to convert units of measure.

Length	Weight	Capacity
12 inches (in.) = 1 foot (ft) 3 feet = 1 yard (yd) 5,280 feet = 1 mile (mi)	16 ounces (oz) = 1 pound (lb) 2,000 pounds = 1 ton	8 fluid ounces (fl oz) = 1 cup (c) 2 cups = 1 pint (pt) 2 pints = 1 quart (qt) 4 quarts = 1 gallon (gal)

EXAMPLE 2 Converting Customary Units

Convert 19 c to fluid ounces.

Method 1: Use a proportion.

Write a proportion using a ratio of equivalent measures.

$$\frac{\text{fluid ounces}}{\text{cups}} \rightarrow \frac{8}{1} = \frac{x}{19}$$

$$8 \cdot 19 = 1 \cdot x$$

$$152 = x$$

Method 2: Multiply by 1.

Multiply by a ratio equal to 1, and cancel the units.

$$19 \text{ c} = \frac{19 \not{c}}{1} \times \frac{8 \text{ fl oz}}{1 \not{c}}$$

$$= \frac{19 \cdot 8 \text{ fl oz}}{1}$$

$$= 152 \text{ fl oz}$$

Nineteen cups is equal to 152 fluid ounces.

EXAMPLE 3 Adding or Subtracting Mixed Units of Measure

A carpenter has a wooden post that is 4 ft long. She cuts 17 in. off the end of the post. What is the length of the remaining post?

First convert 4 ft to inches.

$$\frac{\text{inches}}{\text{feet}} \rightarrow \frac{12}{1} = \frac{x}{4}$$ *Write a proportion using 1 ft = 12 in.*

$$x = 48 \text{ in.}$$

The carpenter cuts off 17 in., so subtract 17 in.

$$4 \text{ ft} - 17 \text{ in.} = 48 \text{ in.} - 17 \text{ in.}$$

$$= 31 \text{ in.}$$

Write the answer in feet and inches.

$$31 \text{ in.} \times \frac{1 \text{ ft}}{12 \text{ in.}} = \frac{31}{12} \text{ ft}$$ *Multiply by a ratio equal to 1.*

$$= 2\frac{7}{12} \text{ ft, or } 2 \text{ ft } 7 \text{ in.}$$

Think and Discuss

1. Describe an object that you would weigh in ounces.

2. Explain how to convert yards to feet and feet to yards.

5-6 Exercises

go.hrw.com
Homework Help Online
KEYWORD: MS7 5-6
Parent Resources Online
KEYWORD: MS7 Parent

GUIDED PRACTICE

See Example 1

Choose the most appropriate customary unit for each measurement. Justify your answer.

1. the width of a sidewalk
2. the amount of water in a pool
3. the weight of a truck
4. the distance across Lake Erie

See Example 2

Convert each measure.

5. 12 gal to quarts
6. 8 mi to feet
7. 72 oz to pounds
8. 3.5 c to fluid ounces

See Example 3

9. A pitcher contains 4 c of pancake batter. A cook pours out 5 fl oz of the batter to make a pancake. How much batter remains in the pitcher?

INDEPENDENT PRACTICE

See Example 1

Choose the most appropriate customary unit for each measurement. Justify your answer.

10. the weight of a watermelon
11. the wingspan of a sparrow
12. the capacity of a soup bowl
13. the height of an office building

See Example 2

Convert each measure.

14. 28 pt to quarts
15. 15,840 ft to miles
16. 5.4 tons to pounds
17. $6\frac{1}{4}$ ft to inches

See Example 3

18. A sculptor has a 3 lb block of clay. He adds 24 oz of clay to the block in order to make a sculpture. What is the total weight of the clay before he begins sculpting?

PRACTICE AND PROBLEM SOLVING

Extra Practice
See page 736.

Compare. Write <, >, or =.

19. 6 yd ▒ 12 ft
20. 80 oz ▒ 5 lb
21. 18 in. ▒ 3 ft
22. 5 tons ▒ 12,000 lb
23. 8 gal ▒ 30 qt
24. 6.5 c ▒ 52 fl oz
25. 10,000 ft ▒ 2 mi
26. 20 pt ▒ 40 c
27. 1 gal ▒ 18 c

28. **Literature** The novel *Twenty Thousand Leagues Under the Sea* was written by Jules Verne in 1873. One league is approximately 3.45 miles. How many miles are in 20,000 leagues?

29. **Earth Science** The average depth of the Pacific Ocean is 12,925 feet. How deep is this in miles, rounded to the nearest tenth of a mile?

LINK

Agriculture

The owner of this 1,009.6 lb pumpkin won the New England Giant Pumpkin Weigh-Off in September 2000.

Order each set of measures from least to greatest.

30. 8 ft; 2 yd; 60 in.

31. 5 qt; 2 gal; 12 pt; 8 c

32. $\frac{1}{2}$ ton; 8,000 oz; 430 lb

33. 2.5 mi; 12,000 ft; 5,000 yd

34. 63 fl oz; 7 c; 1.5 qt

35. 9.5 yd; 32.5 ft; 380 in.

36. Agriculture In one year, the United States produced nearly 895 million pounds of pumpkins. How many ounces were produced by the state with the lowest production shown in the table?

U.S. Pumpkin Production

State	Pumpkins (million pounds)
California	180
Illinois	364
New York	114
Pennsylvania	109

37. Multi-Step A marathon is a race that is 26 miles 385 yards long. What is the length of a marathon in yards?

38. In 1998, a 2,505-gallon ice cream float was made in Atlanta, Georgia. How many 1-pint servings did the float contain?

39. Critical Thinking Explain why it makes sense to divide when you convert a measurement to a larger unit.

40. What's the Error? A student converted 480 ft to inches as follows. What did the student do wrong? What is the correct answer?

$$\frac{1\text{ ft}}{12\text{ in.}} = \frac{x}{480\text{ ft}}$$

41. Write About It Explain how to convert 1.2 tons to ounces.

42. Challenge A dollar bill is approximately 6 in. long. A radio station gives away a prize consisting of a mile-long string of dollar bills. What is the value of the prize?

Test Prep and Spiral Review

43. Multiple Choice Which measure is the same as 32 qt?

Ⓐ 64 pt Ⓑ 128 gal Ⓒ 16 c Ⓓ 512 fl oz

44. Multiple Choice Judy has 3 yards of ribbon. She cuts off 16 inches of the ribbon to wrap a package. How much ribbon does she have left?

Ⓕ 1 ft 8 in. Ⓖ 4 ft 8 in. Ⓗ 7 ft 8 in. Ⓙ 10 ft 4 in.

45. A store sells a television for $486.50. If that price is 3.5 times what the store paid, what was the store's cost? (Lesson 3-6)

Determine whether the ratios are proportional. (Lesson 5-4)

46. $\frac{20}{45}, \frac{8}{18}$

47. $\frac{6}{5}, \frac{5}{6}$

48. $\frac{11}{44}, \frac{7}{28}$

49. $\frac{9}{6}, \frac{27}{20}$

READY TO GO ON?

Quiz for Lessons 5-1 Through 5-6

5-1 Ratios

1. A concession stand sold 14 strawberry, 18 banana, 8 grape, and 6 orange fruit drinks during a game. Tell whether the ratio of strawberry to orange drinks or the ratio of banana to grape drinks is greater.

5-2 Rates

2. Shaunti drove 621 miles in 11.5 hours. What was her average speed in miles per hour?
3. A grocery store sells a 7 oz bag of raisins for $1.10 and a 9 oz bag of raisins for $1.46. Which size bag has the lowest price per ounce?

5-3 Slope and Rates of Change

Tell whether each graph shows a constant or variable rate of change. If constant, find the slope.

4. 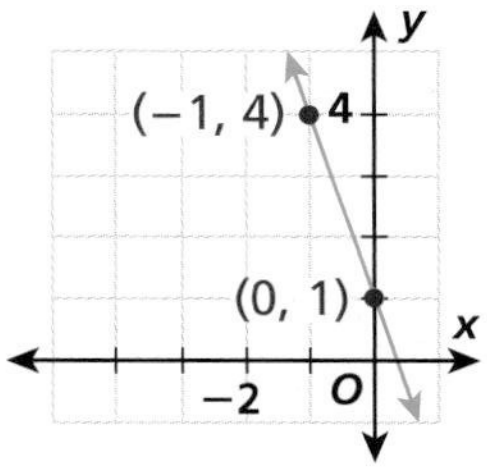

5. 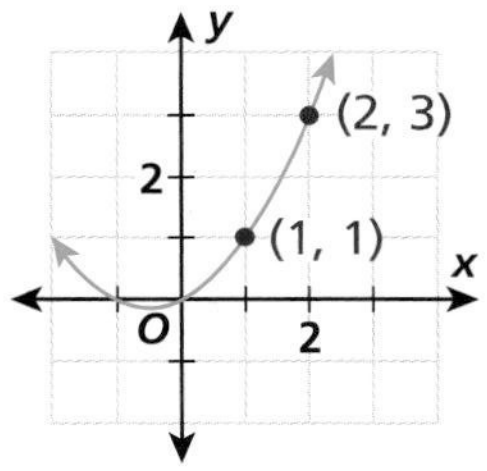

6. 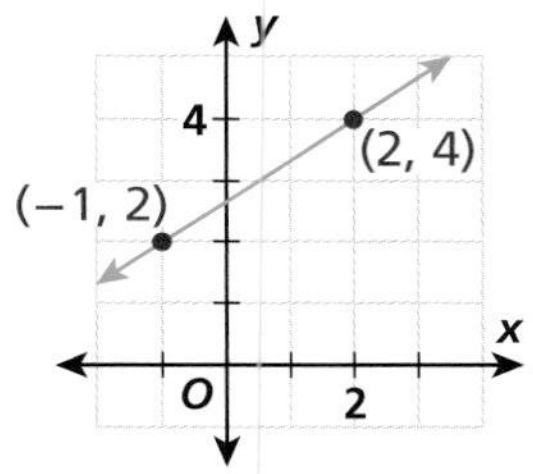

5-4 Identifying and Writing Proportions

Find a ratio equivalent to each ratio. Then use the ratios to write a proportion.

7. $\frac{10}{16}$
8. $\frac{21}{28}$
9. $\frac{12}{25}$
10. $\frac{40}{48}$

5-5 Solving Proportions

Use cross products to solve each proportion.

11. $\frac{n}{8} = \frac{15}{4}$
12. $\frac{20}{t} = \frac{2.5}{6}$
13. $\frac{6}{11} = \frac{0.12}{z}$
14. $\frac{15}{24} = \frac{x}{10}$
15. One dog year is said to equal 7 human years. If Cliff's dog is 5.5 years old in dog years, what is his dog's age in human years?

5-6 Customary Measurements

Convert each measure.

16. 7 lb to ounces
17. 15 qt to pints
18. 3 mi to feet
19. 20 fl oz to cups
20. 39 ft to yards
21. 7,000 lb to tons

Focus on Problem Solving

Make a Plan

• Choose a problem-solving strategy

The following are strategies that you might choose to help you solve a problem:

- Make a table
- Find a pattern
- Make an organized list
- Work backward
- Act it out
- Draw a diagram
- Guess and test
- Use logical reasoning
- Solve a simpler problem
- Make a model

Tell which strategy from the list above you would use to solve each problem. Explain your choice.

1. A recipe for blueberry muffins calls for 1 cup of milk and 1.5 cups of blueberries. Ashley wants to make more muffins than the recipe yields. In Ashley's muffin batter, there are 4.5 cups of blueberries. If she is using the recipe as a guide, how many cups of milk will she need?

2. The length of a rectangle is 8 cm, and its width is 5 cm less than its length. A larger rectangle with dimensions that are proportional to those of the first has a length of 24 cm. What is the width of the larger rectangle?

3. Jeremy is the oldest of four brothers. Each of the four boys gets an allowance for doing chores at home each week. The amount of money each boy receives depends on his age. Jeremy is 13 years old, and he gets \$12.75. His 11-year-old brother gets \$11.25, and his 9-year-old brother gets \$9.75. How much money does his 7-year-old brother get?

4. According to an article in a medical journal, a healthful diet should include a ratio of 2.5 servings of meat to 4 servings of vegetables. If you eat 7 servings of meat per week, how many servings of vegetables should you eat?

Hands-On LAB 5-7

Make Similar Figures

Use with Lesson 5-7

go.hrw.com
Lab Resources Online
KEYWORD: MS7 Lab5

Similar figures are figures that have the same shape but not necessarily the same size. You can make similar figures by increasing or decreasing both dimensions of a rectangle while keeping the ratios of the side lengths proportional. Modeling similar figures using square tiles can help you solve proportions.

Activity

A rectangle made of square tiles measures 5 tiles long and 2 tiles wide. What is the length of a similar rectangle whose width is 6 tiles?

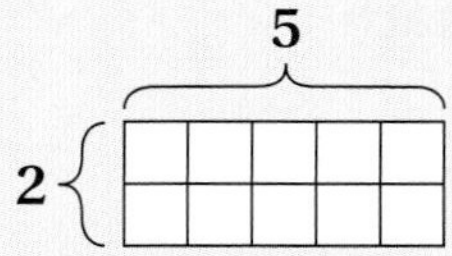

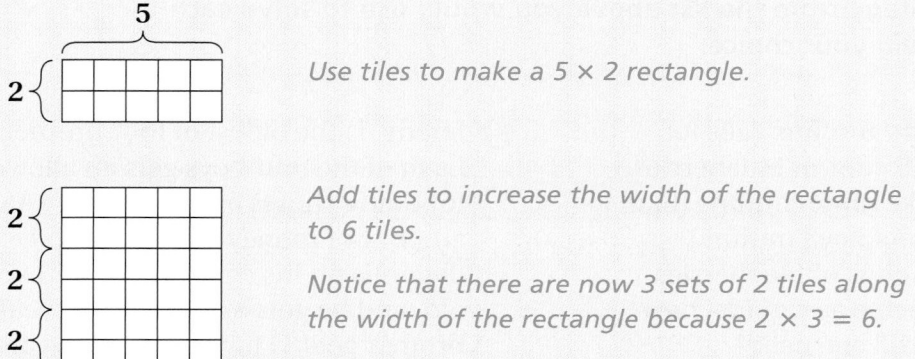

Use tiles to make a 5 × 2 rectangle.

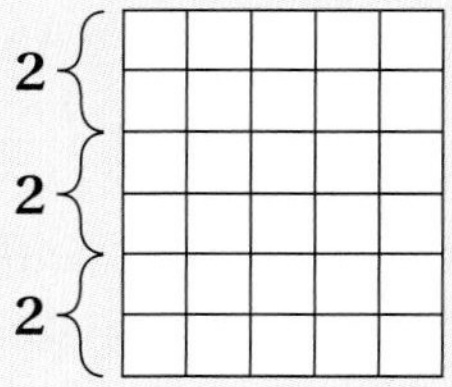

Add tiles to increase the width of the rectangle to 6 tiles.

Notice that there are now 3 sets of 2 tiles along the width of the rectangle because 2 × 3 = 6.

The width of the new rectangle is three times greater than the width of the original rectangle. To keep the ratios of the side measures proportional, the length must also be three times greater than the length of the original rectangle.

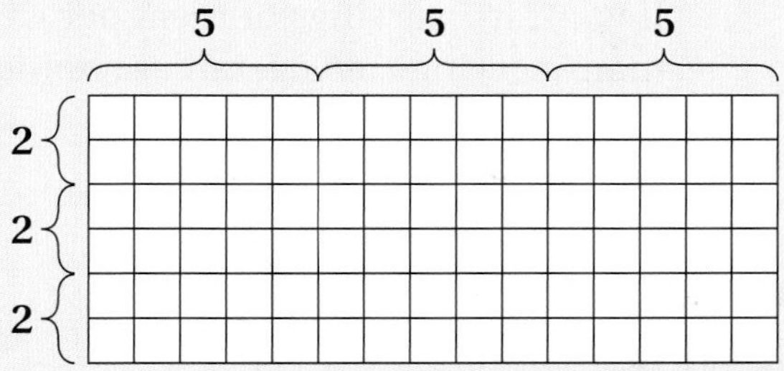

5 × 3 = 15

Add tiles to increase the length of the rectangle to 15 tiles.

The length of the similar rectangle is 15 tiles.

To check your answer, you can use ratios.

$\frac{2}{6} \stackrel{?}{=} \frac{5}{15}$ *Write ratios using the corresponding side lengths.*

$\frac{1}{3} \stackrel{?}{=} \frac{1}{3}$ ✔ *Simplify each ratio.*

1 Use square tiles to model similar figures with the given dimensions. Then find the missing dimension of each similar rectangle.

a. The original rectangle is 4 tiles wide by 3 tiles long. The similar rectangle is 8 tiles wide by x tiles long.

b. The original rectangle is 8 tiles wide by 10 tiles long. The similar rectangle is x tiles wide by 15 tiles long.

c. The original rectangle is 3 tiles wide by 7 tiles long. The similar rectangle is 9 tiles wide by x tiles long.

Think and Discuss

1. Sarah wants to increase the size of her rectangular backyard patio. Why must she change both dimensions of the patio to create a patio similar to the original?

2. In a backyard, a plot of land that is 5 yd × 8 yd is used to grow tomatoes. The homeowner wants to decrease this plot to 4 yd × 6 yd. Will the new plot be similar to the original? Why or why not?

Try This

1. A rectangle is 3 feet long and 7 feet wide. What is the width of a similar rectangle whose length is 9 feet?

2. A rectangle is 6 feet long and 12 feet wide. What is the length of a similar rectangle whose width is 4 feet?

Use square tiles to model similar rectangles to solve each proportion.

3. $\frac{4}{5} = \frac{8}{x}$ **4.** $\frac{5}{9} = \frac{h}{18}$ **5.** $\frac{2}{y} = \frac{6}{18}$ **6.** $\frac{1}{t} = \frac{4}{16}$

7. $\frac{2}{3} = \frac{8}{m}$ **8.** $\frac{9}{12} = \frac{p}{4}$ **9.** $\frac{6}{r} = \frac{9}{15}$ **10.** $\frac{k}{12} = \frac{7}{6}$

5-7 Similar Figures and Proportions

Learn to use ratios to determine if two figures are similar.

Vocabulary

similar

corresponding sides

corresponding angles

Octahedral fluorite is a crystal found in nature. It grows in the shape of an octahedron, which is a three-dimensional figure with eight triangular faces. The triangles in different-sized fluorite crystals are *similar* figures. **Similar** figures have the same shape but not necessarily the same size. The symbol ~ means "is similar to."

Corresponding angles of two or more polygons are in the same relative position. **Corresponding sides** of two or more polygons are in the same relative position.

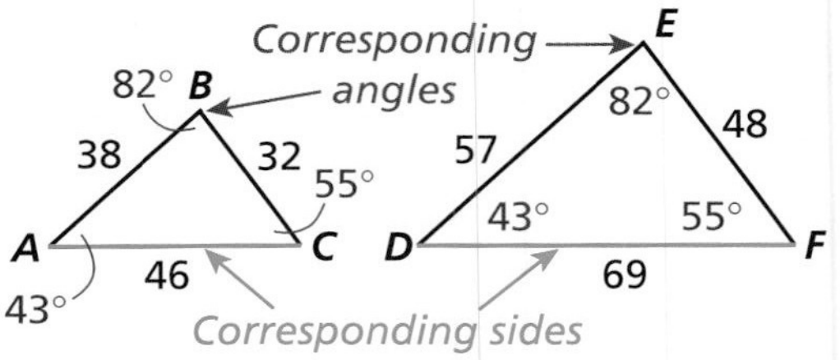

Writing Math

When naming similar figures, list the letters of the corresponding vertices in the same order. In Example 1, $\triangle DEF \sim \triangle QRS$.

SIMILAR FIGURES

Two figures are similar if

- the measures of their corresponding angles are equal.
- the ratios of the lengths of their corresponding sides are proportional.

EXAMPLE 1 Determining Whether Two Triangles Are Similar

Reading Math

A side of a figure can be named by its endpoints, with a bar above.

$\overline{AB}$

Without the bar, the letters indicate the *length* of the side.

Tell whether the triangles are similar.

The corresponding angles of the figures have equal measures.

$\overline{DE}$ corresponds to $\overline{QR}$.
$\overline{EF}$ corresponds to $\overline{RS}$.
$\overline{DF}$ corresponds to $\overline{QS}$.

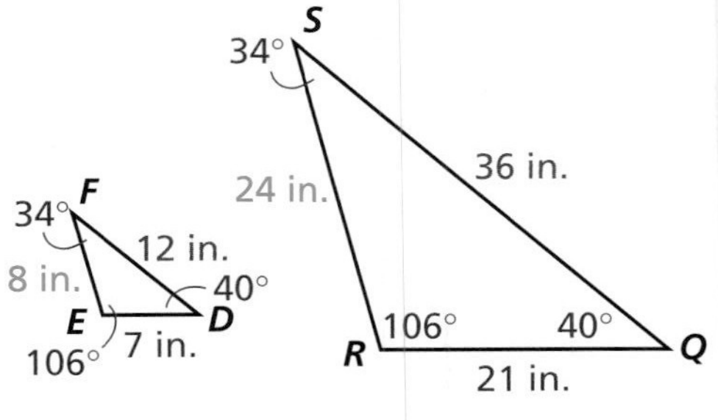

$\frac{DE}{QR} \stackrel{?}{=} \frac{EF}{RS} \stackrel{?}{=} \frac{DF}{QS}$ *Write ratios using the corresponding sides.*

$\frac{7}{21} \stackrel{?}{=} \frac{8}{24} \stackrel{?}{=} \frac{12}{36}$ *Substitute the lengths of the sides.*

$\frac{1}{3} = \frac{1}{3} = \frac{1}{3}$ *Simplify each ratio.*

Since the measures of the corresponding angles are equal and the ratios of the corresponding sides are equivalent, the triangles are similar.

With triangles, if the corresponding side lengths are all proportional, then the corresponding angles *must* have equal measures. With figures that have four or more sides, if the corresponding side lengths are all proportional, then the corresponding angles *may or may not* have equal angle measures.

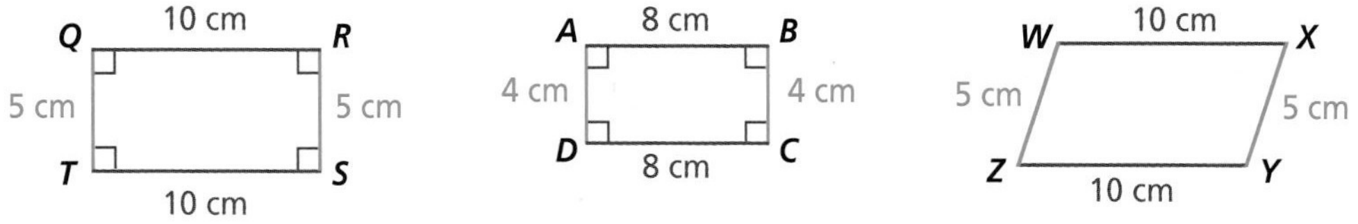

ABCD and QRST ***are*** *similar.*

ABCD and WXYZ ***are not*** *similar.*

EXAMPLE 2 Determining Whether Two Four-Sided Figures Are Similar

Tell whether the figures are similar.

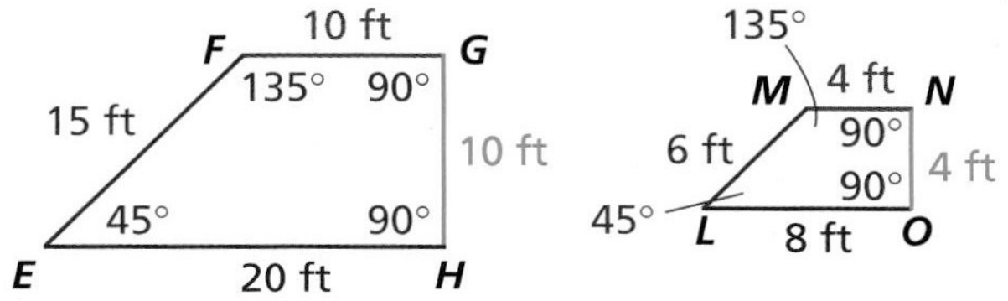

The corresponding angles of the figures have equal measures. Write each set of corresponding sides as a ratio.

$\frac{EF}{LM}$ *$\overline{EF}$ corresponds to $\overline{LM}$.* $\frac{FG}{MN}$ *$\overline{FG}$ corresponds to $\overline{MN}$.*

$\frac{GH}{NO}$ *$\overline{GH}$ corresponds to $\overline{NO}$.* $\frac{EH}{LO}$ *$\overline{EH}$ corresponds to $\overline{LO}$.*

Determine whether the ratios of the lengths of the corresponding sides are proportional.

$\frac{EF}{LM} \stackrel{?}{=} \frac{FG}{MN} \stackrel{?}{=} \frac{GH}{NO} \stackrel{?}{=} \frac{EH}{LO}$ *Write ratios using the corresponding sides.*

$\frac{15}{6} \stackrel{?}{=} \frac{10}{4} \stackrel{?}{=} \frac{10}{4} \stackrel{?}{=} \frac{20}{8}$ *Substitute the lengths of the sides.*

$\frac{5}{2} = \frac{5}{2} = \frac{5}{2} = \frac{5}{2}$ *Write the ratios with common denominators.*

Since the measures of the corresponding angles are equal and the ratios of the corresponding sides are equivalent, $EFGH \sim LMNO$.

Think and Discuss

1. Identify the corresponding angles of $\triangle JKL$ and $\triangle UTS$.

2. Explain whether all rectangles are similar. Give specific examples to justify your answer.

5-7 Exercises

go.hrw.com
Homework Help Online
KEYWORD: MS7 5-7
Parent Resources Online
KEYWORD: MS7 Parent

GUIDED PRACTICE

See Example 1 **Tell whether the triangles are similar.**

1.

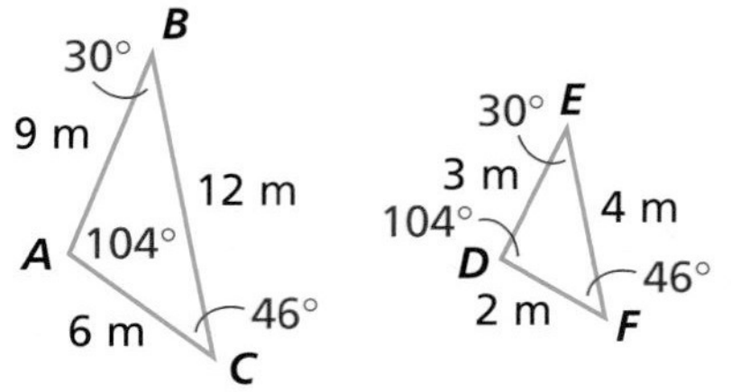

2.

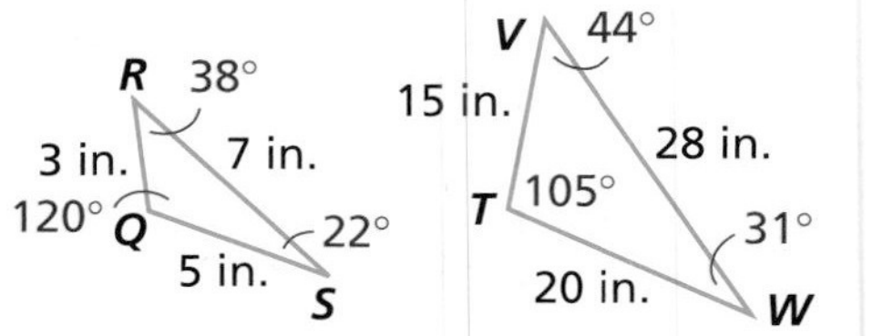

See Example 2 **Tell whether the figures are similar.**

3.

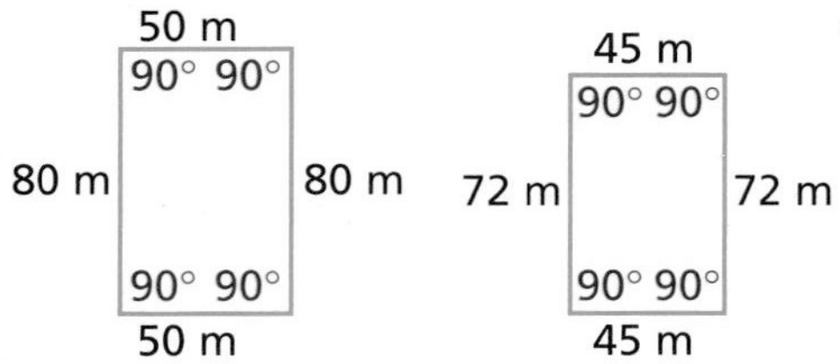

4.

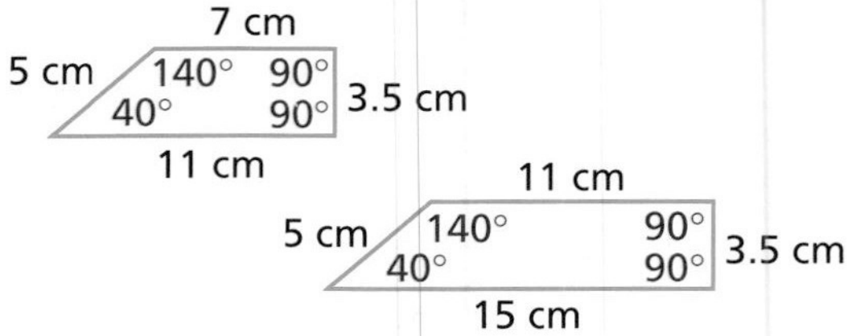

INDEPENDENT PRACTICE

See Example 1 **Tell whether the triangles are similar.**

5.

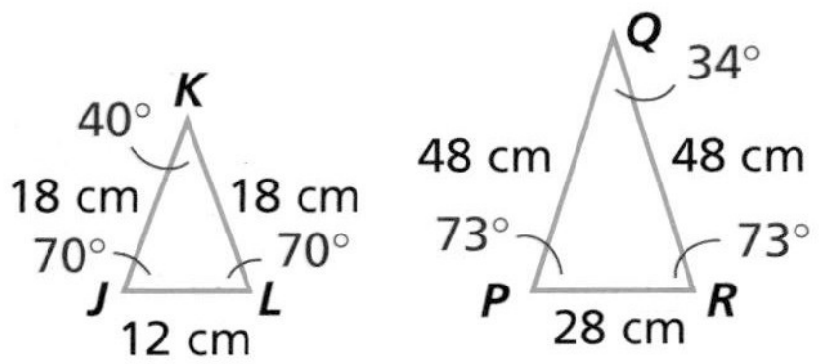

6.

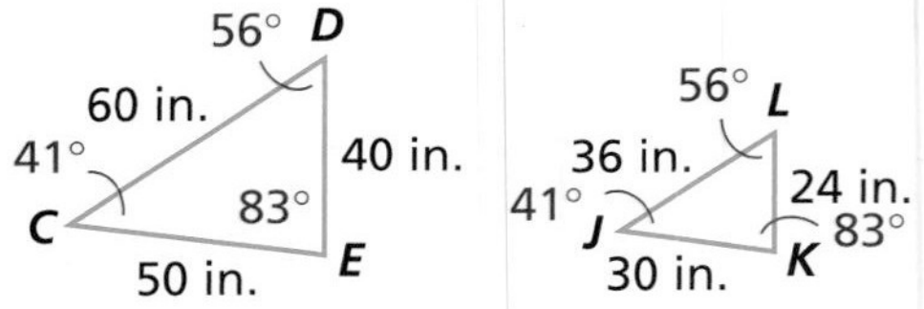

See Example 2 **Tell whether the figures are similar.**

7.

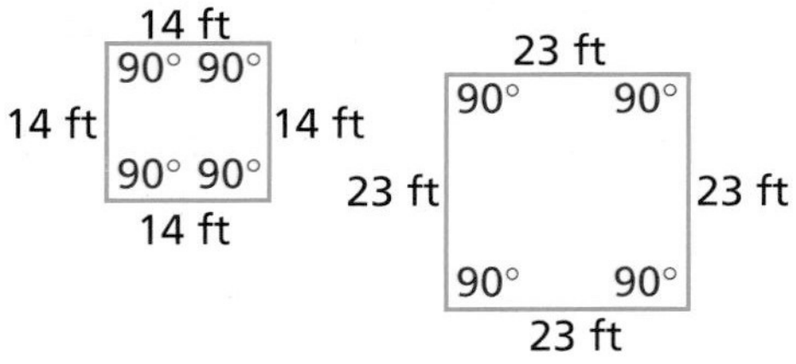

8.

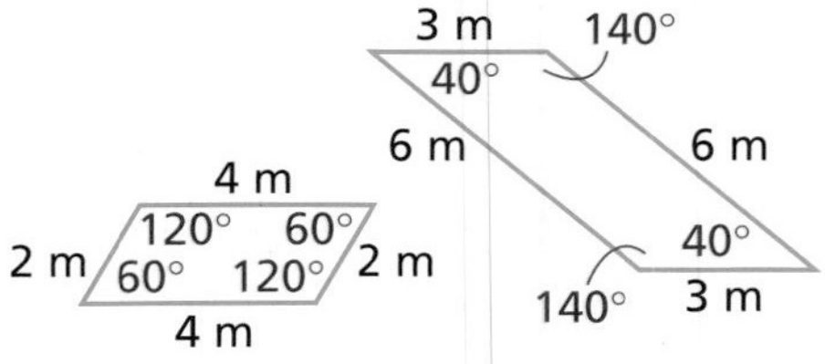

PRACTICE AND PROBLEM SOLVING

Extra Practice
See page 736.

9. Tell whether the parallelogram and trapezoid could be similar. Explain your answer.

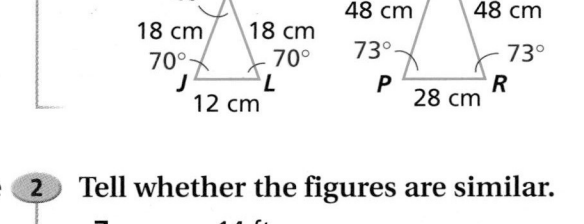

10. Kia wants similar prints in small and large sizes of a favorite photo. The photo lab sells prints in these sizes: 3 in. × 5 in., 4 in. × 6 in., 8 in. × 18 in., 9 in. × 20 in., and 16 in. × 24 in. Which could she order to get similar prints?

Tell whether the triangles are similar.

11.
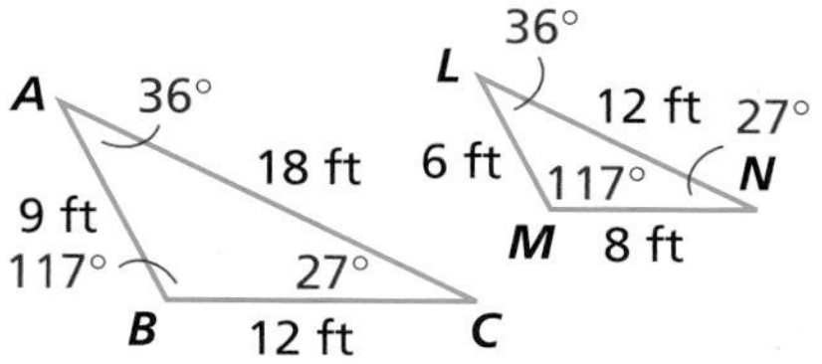

12.
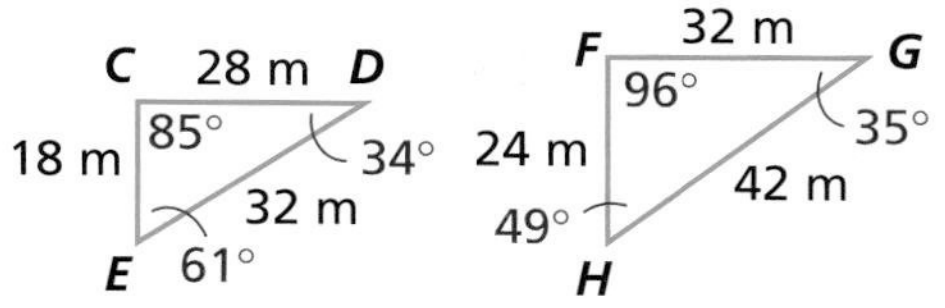

The figure shows a 12 ft by 15 ft rectangle divided into four rectangular parts. Explain whether the rectangles in each pair are similar.

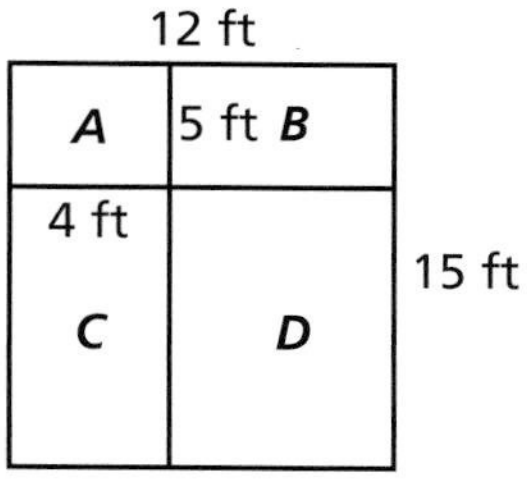

13. rectangle A and the original rectangle

14. rectangle C and rectangle B

15. the original rectangle and rectangle D

Critical Thinking **For Exercises 16–19, justify your answers using words or drawings.**

16. Are all squares similar?

17. Are all parallelograms similar?

18. Are all rectangles similar?

19. Are all right triangles similar?

20. **Choose a Strategy** What number gives the same result when multiplied by 6 as it does when 6 is added to it?

21. **Write About It** Tell how to decide whether two figures are similar.

22. **Challenge** Two triangles are similar. The ratio of the lengths of the corresponding sides is $\frac{5}{4}$. If the length of one side of the larger triangle is 40 feet, what is the length of the corresponding side of the smaller triangle?

Test Prep and Spiral Review

23. **Multiple Choice** Luis wants to make a deck that is similar to an 8-foot-by-10-foot deck. If Luis's deck must be 18 feet long, what must its width be?

Ⓐ 20 feet Ⓑ 16 feet Ⓒ 14.4 feet Ⓓ 22.5 feet

24. **Short Response** If a real dollar bill measures 2.61 in. by 6.14 in. and a play dollar bill measures 3.61 in. by 7.14 in., is the play money similar to the real money? Explain your answer.

Multiply. Write each answer in simplest form. (Lesson 3-10)

25. $-\frac{3}{4} \cdot 14$

26. $2\frac{1}{8} \cdot (-5)$

27. $\frac{1}{4} \cdot 1\frac{7}{8} \cdot 3\frac{1}{5}$

28. Tell whether 5:3 or 12:7 is a greater ratio. (Lesson 5-1)

5-8 Using Similar Figures

Learn to use similar figures to find unknown lengths.

Vocabulary

indirect measurement

Native Americans of the Northwest, such as the Tlingit tribe of Alaska, carved totem poles out of tree trunks. These poles, sometimes painted with bright colors, could stand up to 80 feet tall. Totem poles include carvings of animal figures, such as bears and eagles, which symbolize traits of the family or clan who built them.

Measuring the heights of tall objects, like some totem poles, cannot be done by using a ruler or yardstick. Instead, you can use *indirect measurement.*

Indirect measurement is a method of using proportions to find an unknown length or distance in similar figures.

EXAMPLE 1 Finding Unknown Lengths in Similar Figures

$\triangle ABC \sim \triangle JKL$. Find the unknown length.

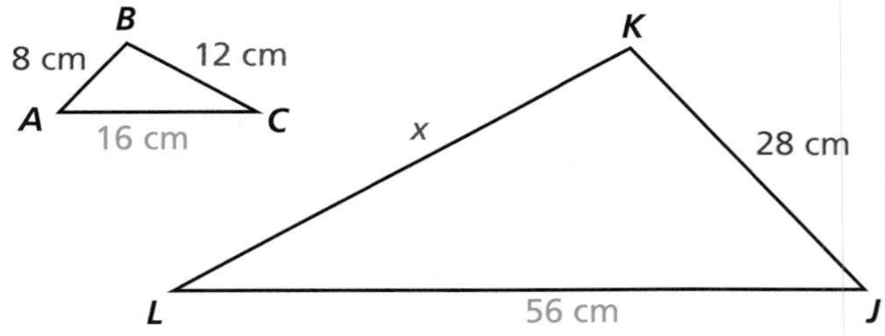

$\frac{AB}{JK} = \frac{BC}{KL}$ *Write a proportion using corresponding sides.*

$\frac{8}{28} = \frac{12}{x}$ *Substitute the lengths of the sides.*

$8 \cdot x = 28 \cdot 12$ *Find the cross products.*

$8x = 336$ *Multiply.*

$\frac{8x}{8} = \frac{336}{8}$ *Divide each side by 8 to isolate the variable.*

$x = 42$

KL is 42 centimeters.

EXAMPLE 2 Measurement Application

A volleyball court is a rectangle that is similar in shape to an Olympic-sized pool. Find the width of the pool.

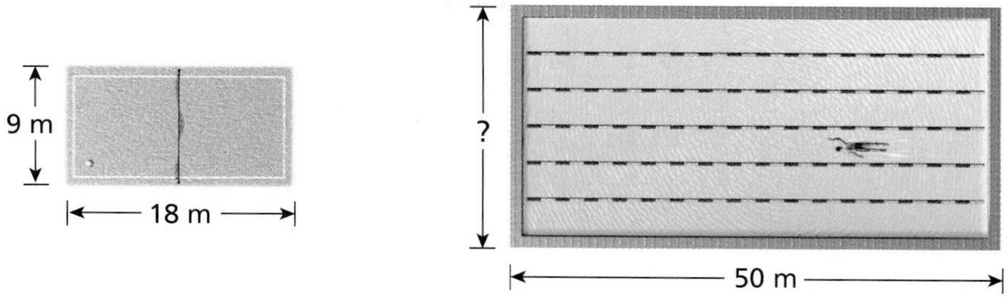

Let w = the width of the pool.

$\frac{18}{50} = \frac{9}{w}$ *Write a proportion using corresponding side lengths.*

$18 \cdot w = 50 \cdot 9$ *Find the cross products.*

$18w = 450$ *Multiply.*

$\frac{18w}{18} = \frac{450}{18}$ *Divide each side by 18 to isolate the variable.*

$w = 25$

The pool is 25 meters wide.

EXAMPLE 3 Estimating with Indirect Measurement

Estimate the height of the birdhouse in Chantal's yard, shown at right.

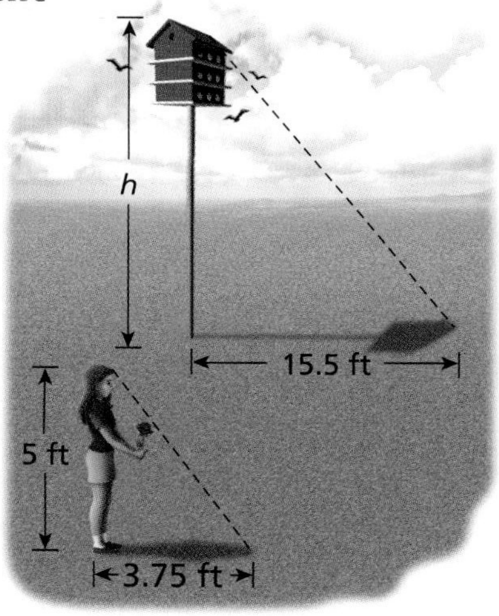

$\frac{h}{5} = \frac{15.5}{3.75}$ *Write a proportion.*

$\frac{h}{5} \approx \frac{16}{4}$ *Use compatible numbers to estimate.*

$\frac{h}{5} \approx 4$ *Simplify.*

$5 \cdot \frac{h}{5} \approx 5 \cdot 4$ *Multiply each side by 5 to isolate the variable.*

$h \approx 20$

The birdhouse is about 20 feet tall.

Think and Discuss

1. Write another proportion that could be used to find the value of x in Example 1.

2. Name two objects that it would make sense to measure using indirect measurement.

5-8 Exercises

go.hrw.com
Homework Help Online
KEYWORD: MS7 5-8
Parent Resources Online
KEYWORD: MS7 Parent

GUIDED PRACTICE

See Example 1

$\triangle XYZ \sim \triangle PQR$ in each pair. Find the unknown lengths.

1.
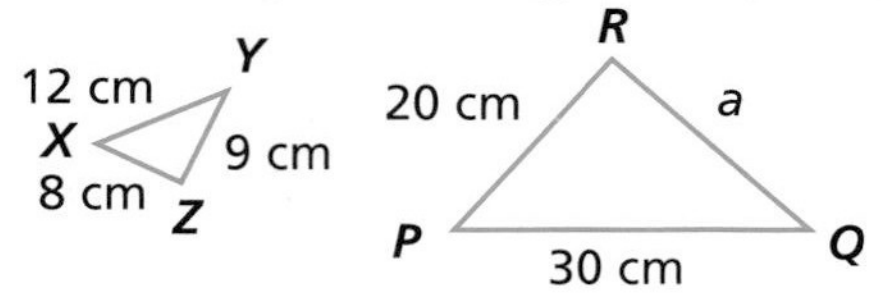

2.
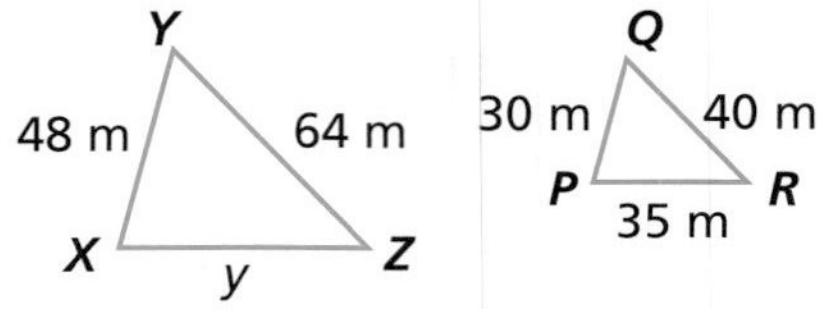

See Example 2

3. The rectangular gardens at right are similar in shape. How wide is the smaller garden?

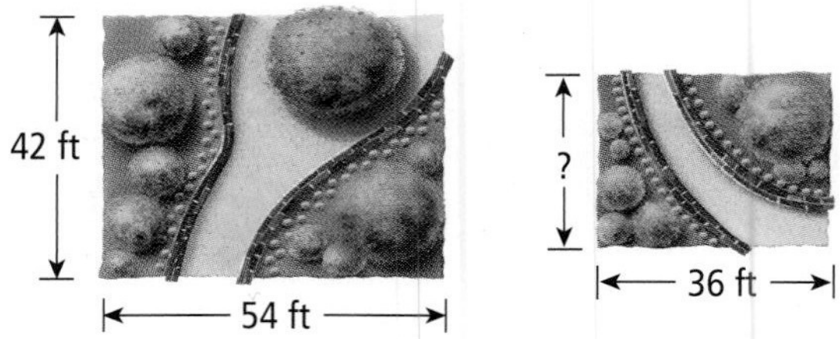

See Example 3

4. A water tower casts a shadow that is 21 ft long. A tree casts a shadow that is 8 ft long. Estimate the height of the water tower.

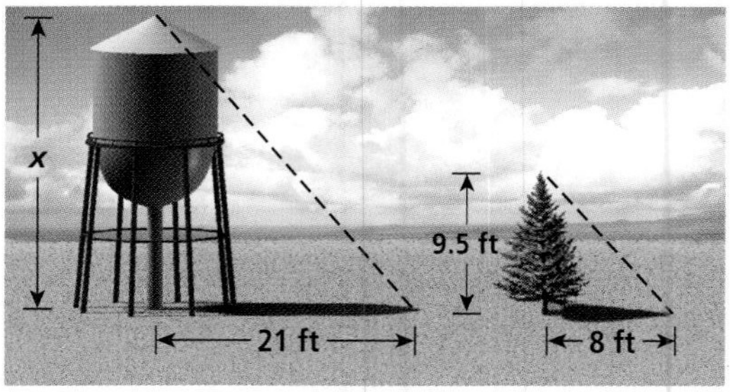

INDEPENDENT PRACTICE

See Example 1

$\triangle ABC \sim \triangle DEF$ in each pair. Find the unknown lengths.

5.
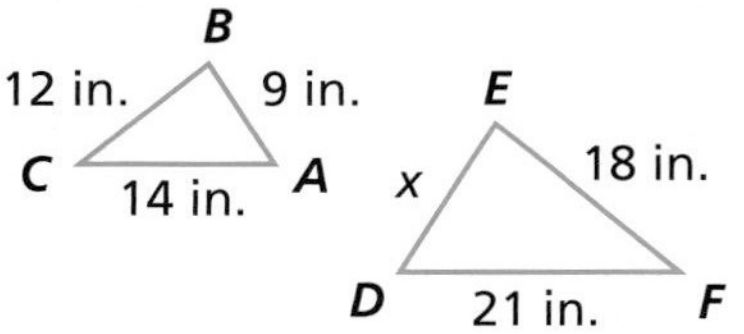

6.
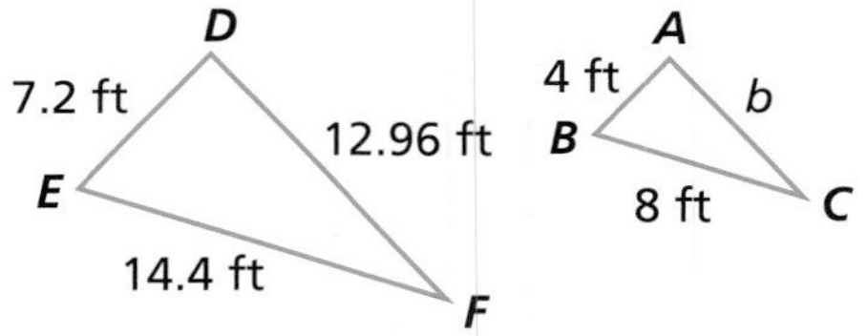

See Example 2

7. The two rectangular windows at right are similar. What is the height of the bigger window?

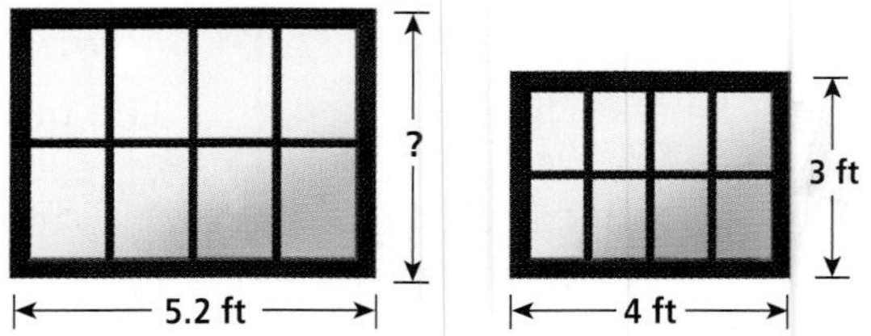

See Example 3

8. A cactus casts a shadow that is 14 ft 7 in. long. A gate nearby casts a shadow that is 5 ft long. Estimate the height of the cactus.

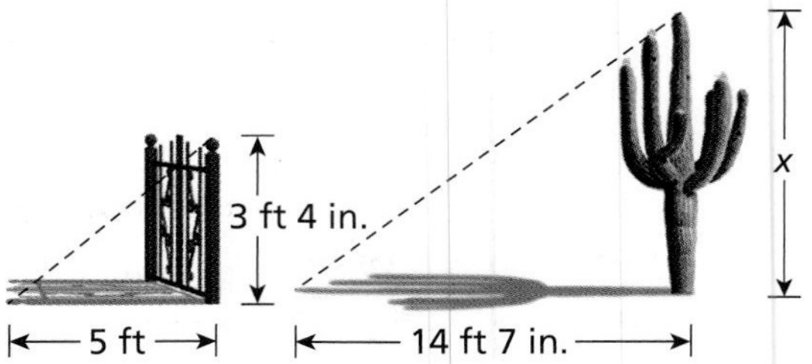

PRACTICE AND PROBLEM SOLVING

Extra Practice
See page 736.

9. A building with a height of 14 m casts a shadow that is 16 m long while a taller building casts a 24 m long shadow. What is the height of the taller building?

10. Two common envelope sizes are $3\frac{1}{2}$ in. × $6\frac{1}{2}$ in. and 4 in. × $9\frac{1}{2}$ in. Are these envelopes similar? Explain.

11. Art An art class is painting a mural composed of brightly colored geometric shapes. The class has decided that all the right triangles in the design will be similar to the right triangle that will be painted fire red. Find the measures of the right triangles in the table. Round your answers to the nearest tenth.

Triangle Color	Length (in.)	Height (in.)
Fire Red	12	16
Blazing Orange	7	■
Grape Purple	■	4
Dynamite Blue	15	■

12. Write a Problem Write a problem that can be solved using indirect measurement.

13. Write About It Assume you know the side lengths of one triangle and the length of one side of a second similar triangle. Explain how to use the properties of similar figures to find the unknown lengths in the second triangle.

14. Challenge $\triangle ABE \sim \triangle ACD$. What is the value of y in the diagram?

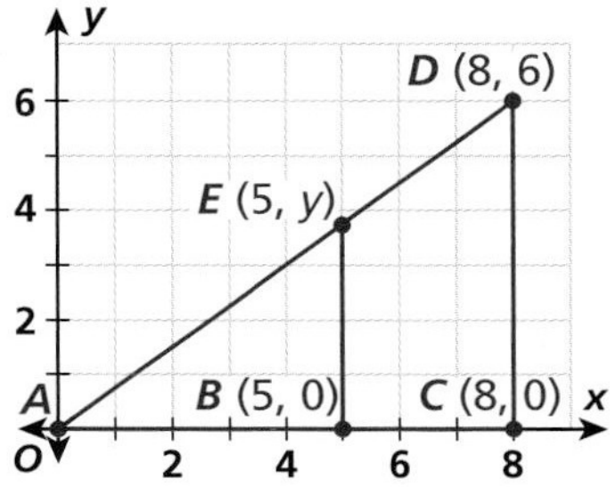

TEST PREP and Spiral Review

15. Multiple Choice Find the unknown length in the similar figures.

Ⓐ 10 cm
Ⓑ 12 cm
Ⓒ 15 cm
Ⓓ 18 cm

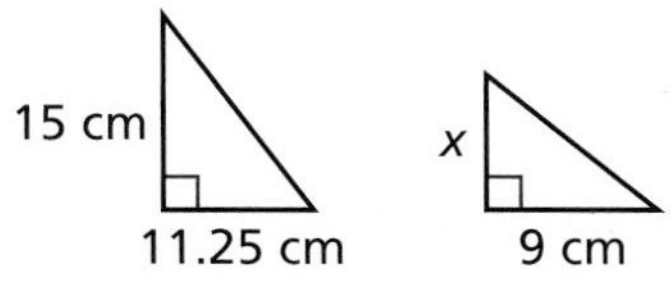

16. Gridded Response A building casts a 16-foot shadow. A 6-foot man standing next to the building casts a 2.5-foot shadow. What is the height, in feet, of the building?

Write each phrase as an algebraic expression. (Lesson 1-8)

17. the product of 18 and y
18. 5 less than a number
19. 12 divided by z

Choose the most appropriate customary unit for each measurement. Justify your answer. (Lesson 5-6)

20. weight of a cell phone
21. height of a dog
22. capacity of a gas tank

5-9 Scale Drawings and Scale Models

Learn to understand ratios and proportions in scale drawings. Learn to use ratios and proportions with scale.

Vocabulary

scale model

scale factor

scale

scale drawing

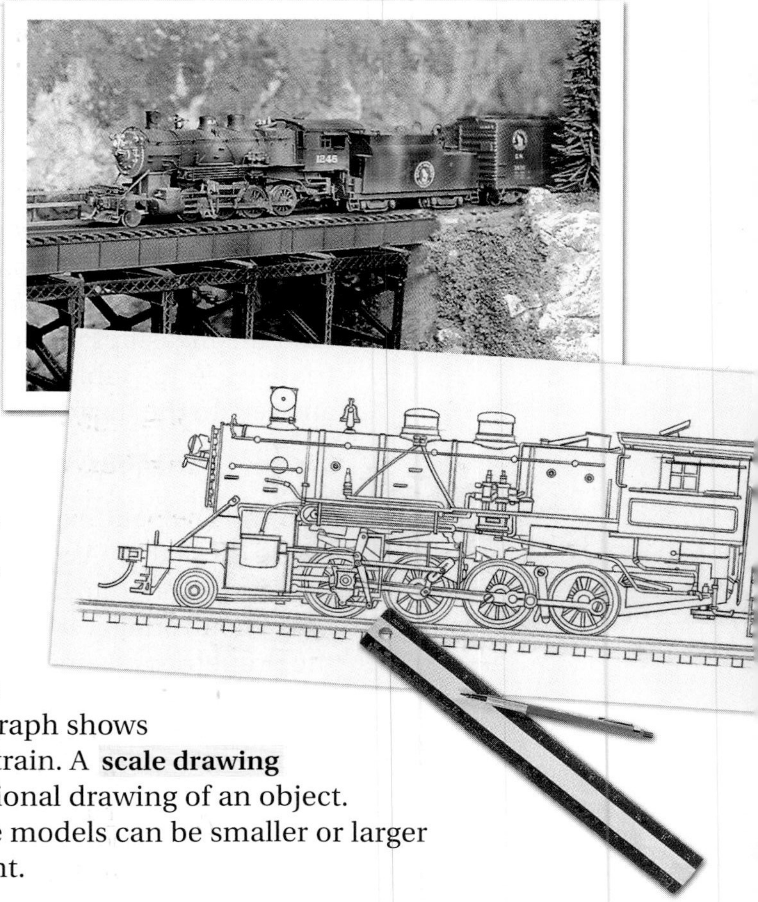

This HO gauge model train is a *scale model* of a historic train. A **scale model** is a proportional three-dimensional model of an object. Its dimensions are related to the dimensions of the actual object by a ratio called the **scale factor**. The HO scale factor is $\frac{1}{87}$. This means that each dimension of the model is $\frac{1}{87}$ of the corresponding dimension of the actual train.

A **scale** is the ratio between two sets of measurements. Scales can use the same units or different units. The photograph shows a *scale drawing* of the model train. A **scale drawing** is a proportional two-dimensional drawing of an object. Both scale drawings and scale models can be smaller or larger than the objects they represent.

EXAMPLE 1 Finding a Scale Factor

Identify the scale factor.

	Race Car	Model
Length (in.)	132	11
Height (in.)	66	5.5

You can use the lengths *or* heights to find the scale factor.

$$\frac{\text{model length}}{\text{race car length}} = \frac{11}{132} = \frac{1}{12}$$ *Write a ratio. Then simplify.*

$$\frac{\text{model height}}{\text{race car height}} = \frac{5.5}{66} = \frac{1}{12}$$

The scale factor is $\frac{1}{12}$. This is reasonable because $\frac{1}{10}$ the length of the race car is 13.2 in. The length of the model is 11 in., which is less than 13.2 in., and $\frac{1}{12}$ is less than $\frac{1}{10}$.

Caution!

A scale factor is always the ratio of the model's dimensions to the actual object's dimensions.

EXAMPLE 2 Using Scale Factors to Find Unknown Lengths

A photograph of Vincent van Gogh's painting *Still Life with Irises Against a Yellow Background* has dimensions 6.13 cm and 4.90 cm. The scale factor is $\frac{1}{15}$. Find the size of the actual painting, to the nearest tenth of a centimeter.

Think: $\frac{\text{photo}}{\text{painting}} = \frac{1}{15}$

$\frac{6.13}{\ell} = \frac{1}{15}$ *Write a proportion to find the length ℓ.*

$\ell = 6.13 \cdot 15$ *Find the cross products.*

$\ell = 92.0$ cm *Multiply and round to the nearest tenth.*

$\frac{4.90}{w} = \frac{1}{15}$ *Write a proportion to find the width w.*

$w = 4.90 \cdot 15$ *Find the cross products.*

$w = 73.5$ cm *Multiply and round to the nearest tenth.*

The painting is 92.0 cm long and 73.5 cm wide.

EXAMPLE 3 *Measurement Application*

On a map of Florida, the distance between Hialeah and Tampa is 10.5 cm. What is the actual distance *d* between the cities if the map scale is 3 cm = 80 mi?

Think: $\frac{\text{map distance}}{\text{actual distance}} = \frac{3}{80}$

$\frac{3}{80} = \frac{10.5}{d}$ *Write a proportion.*

$3 \cdot d = 80 \cdot 10.5$ *Find the cross products.*

$3d = 840$

$\frac{3d}{3} = \frac{840}{3}$ *Divide both sides by 3.*

$d = 280$ mi

The distance between the cities is 280 miles.

Think and Discuss

1. **Explain** how you can tell whether a model with a scale factor of $\frac{5}{3}$ is larger or smaller than the original object.
2. **Describe** how to find the scale factor if an antenna is 60 feet long and a scale drawing shows the length as 1 foot long.

5-9 Exercises

go.hrw.com
Homework Help Online
KEYWORD: MS7 5-9
Parent Resources Online
KEYWORD: MS7 Parent

GUIDED PRACTICE

See Example 1 **Identify the scale factor.**

1.

	Grizzly Bear	Model
Height (in.)	84	6

2.

	Moray Eel	Model
Length (ft)	5	$1\frac{1}{2}$

See Example 2 3. In a photograph, a sculpture is 4.2 cm tall and 2.5 cm wide. The scale factor is $\frac{1}{16}$. Find the size of the actual sculpture.

See Example 3 4. Ms. Jackson is driving from South Bend to Indianapolis. She measures a distance of 4.3 cm between the cities on her Indiana road map. What is the actual distance between the cities if the map scale is 1 cm = 30 mi?

INDEPENDENT PRACTICE

See Example 1 **Identify the scale factor.**

5.

	Eagle	Model
Wingspan (in.)	90	6

6.

	Dolphin	Model
Length (cm)	260	13

See Example 2 7. On a scale drawing, a tree is $6\frac{3}{4}$ inches tall. The scale factor is $\frac{1}{20}$. Find the height of the actual tree.

See Example 3 8. **Measurement** On a road map of Virginia, the distance from Alexandria to Roanoke is 7.6 cm. What is the actual distance between the cities if the map scale is 2 cm = 50 mi?

PRACTICE AND PROBLEM SOLVING

Extra Practice
See page 736.

The scale factor of each model is 1:12. Find the missing dimensions.

	Item	Actual Dimensions	Model Dimensions
9.	Lamp	Height: ▒	Height: $1\frac{1}{3}$ in.
10.	Couch	Height: 32 in. Length: 69 in.	Height: ▒ Length: ▒
11.	Table	Height: ▒ Width: ▒ Length: ▒	Height: 6.25 cm Width: 11.75 cm Length: 20 cm
12.	Chair	Height: $51\frac{1}{2}$ in.	Height: ▒

13. **Critical Thinking** A countertop is 18 ft long. How long is it on a scale drawing with the scale 1 in. = 3 yd?

14. **Write About It** A scale for a scale drawing is 10 cm = 1 mm. Which will be larger, the actual object or the scale drawing? Explain.

History LINK

Use the map for Exercises 15–16.

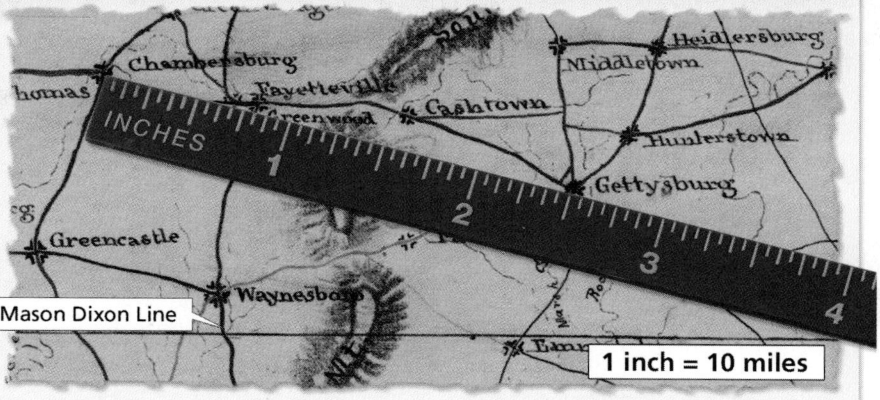

15. In 1863, Confederate troops marched from Chambersburg to Gettysburg in search of badly needed shoes. Use the ruler and the scale of the map to estimate how far the Confederate soldiers, many of whom were barefoot, marched.

16. Before the Civil War, the Mason-Dixon Line was considered the dividing line between the North and the South. If Gettysburg is about 8.1 miles north of the Mason-Dixon Line, how far apart in inches are Gettysburg and the Mason-Dixon Line on the map?

17. **Multi-Step** Toby is making a scale model of the battlefield at Fredericksburg. The area he wants to model measures about 11 mi by 7.5 mi. He plans to put the model on a 3.25 ft by 3.25 ft square table. On each side of the model he wants to leave at least 3 in. between the model and the table edges. What is the largest scale he can use?

18. ★ **Challenge** A map of Vicksburg, Mississippi, has a scale of "1 mile to the inch." The map has been reduced so that 5 inches on the original map appears as 1.5 inches on the reduced map. If the distance between two points on the reduced map is 1.75 inches, what is the actual distance in miles?

This painting by H.A. Ogden depicts General Robert E. Lee at Fredericksburg in 1862.

Test Prep and Spiral Review

19. **Multiple Choice** On a scale model with a scale of $\frac{1}{16}$, the height of a shed is 7 inches. What is the approximate height of the actual shed?

Ⓐ 2 feet Ⓑ 9 feet Ⓒ 58 feet Ⓓ 112 feet

20. **Gridded Response** On a map, the scale is 3 cm = 75 mi. If the distance between two cities on the map is 6.8 cm, what is the distance between the actual cities in miles?

Order the numbers from least to greatest. (Lesson 2-11)

21. $\frac{4}{7}$, 0.41, 0.054 **22.** $\frac{1}{4}$, 0.2, -1.2 **23.** 0.7, $\frac{7}{9}$, $\frac{7}{11}$ **24.** 0.3, $-\frac{5}{6}$, 0.32

Divide. Estimate to check whether each answer is reasonable. (Lesson 3-4)

25. $0.32 \div 5$ **26.** $78.57 \div 9$ **27.** $40.5 \div 15$ **28.** $29.68 \div 28$

CHAPTER 5

READY TO GO ON?

SECTION 5B

Quiz for Lessons 5-7 Through 5-9

5-7 Similar Figures and Proportions

1. Tell whether the triangles are similar.

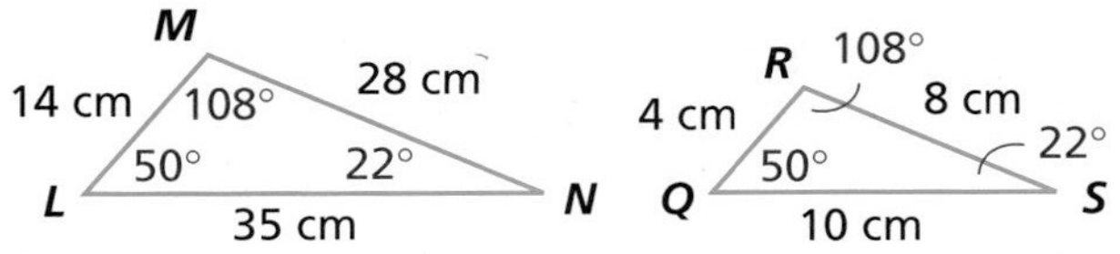

2. Tell whether the figures are similar.

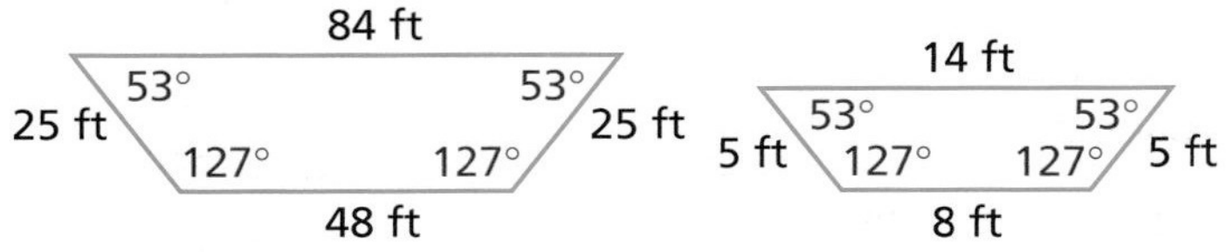

5-8 Using Similar Figures

$\triangle ABC \sim \triangle XYZ$ in each pair. Find the unknown lengths.

3.

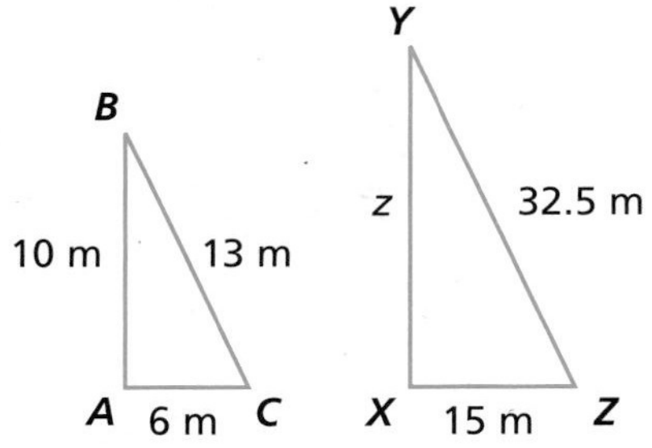

4.

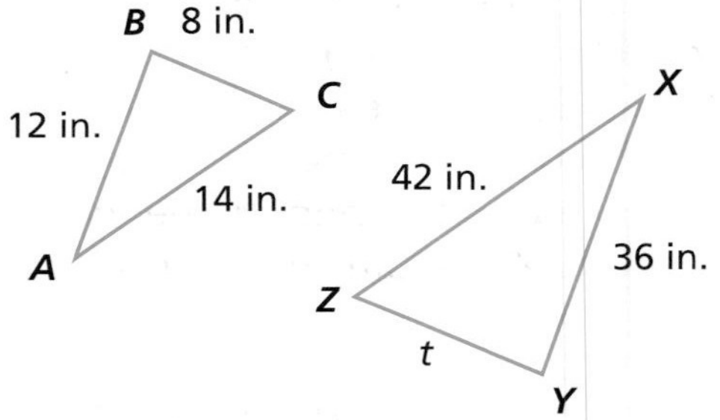

5. Reynaldo drew a rectangular design that was 6 in. by 8 in. He used a copy machine to enlarge the rectangular design so that the width was 10 inches. What was the length of the enlarged design?

6. Redon is 6 ft 2 in. tall, and his shadow is 4 ft 1 in. long. At the same time a building casts a shadow that is 19 ft 10 in. long. Estimate the height of the building.

5-9 Scale Drawings and Scale Models

7. An actor is 6 ft tall. On a billboard for a new movie, the actor's picture is enlarged so that his height is 16.8 ft. What is the scale factor?

8. On a scale drawing, a driveway is 6 in. long. The scale factor is $\frac{1}{24}$. Find the length of the actual driveway.

9. A map of Texas has a scale of 1 in. = 65 mi. If the distance from Dallas to San Antonio is 260 mi, what is the distance in inches between two cities on the map?

MULTI-STEP TEST PREP

CHAPTER 5

Bug Juice When campers get thirsty, out comes the well-known camp beverage bug juice! The recipes show how two camps, Camp Big Sky and Camp Wild Flowers, make their bug juice. Each camp has 180 campers. During a typical day, each camper drinks two 8-ounce cups of bug juice.

1. How many ounces of bug juice are consumed at each camp each day?
2. How much does it cost to make two quarts of bug juice at each camp?
3. Each camp has budgeted $30 per day for bug juice. Is $30 a day enough? How do you know? Show your work.
4. Campers begin to complain. They want their bug juice "buggier." How could each camp change its recipe, continue to serve 180 campers two 8-ounce cups of bug juice daily, and not spend more than $40 per day for bug juice? Explain your reasoning.

Camp Big Sky Bug Juice Recipe

- One 4 oz packet of mix A
- Add tap water to make 2 quarts of bug juice.

Camp Wild Flowers Bug Juice Recipe

- One 0.14 oz packet of mix B
- 4 oz sugar
- Add tap water to make 2 quarts of bug juice.

Prices

4 oz packet of mix A	$0.78
0.14 oz packet of mix B	$0.20
1 lb of sugar	$0.36

EXTENSION

Dimensional Analysis

Learn to use dimensional analysis to make unit conversions.

Vocabulary

unit conversion factor

You can use a *unit conversion factor* to change, or convert, measurements from one unit to another. A **unit conversion factor** is a fraction in which the numerator and denominator represent the same quantity but are in different units. The fraction $\frac{5{,}280 \text{ ft}}{1 \text{ mi}}$ is a unit conversion factor that can be used to convert miles to feet. Notice that because 1 mi = 5,280 ft, the conversion factor can be simplified to 1.

$$\frac{5{,}280 \text{ ft}}{1 \text{ mi}} = \frac{5{,}280 \text{ ft}}{5{,}280 \text{ ft}} = 1$$

When you multiply a quantity by a unit conversion factor, only the units change, not the quantity's value. Choosing an appropriate conversion factor is called *dimensional analysis.*

EXAMPLE 1 Making Unit Conversions

A bucket holds 16 quarts. How many gallons of water will fill the bucket? Use a unit conversion factor to convert the units.

There are 4 quarts per gallon, so a unit conversion factor is $\frac{1 \text{ gal}}{4 \text{ qt}}$ or $\frac{4 \text{ qt}}{1 \text{ gal}}$. Choose the one that allows the quart units to "cancel."

$$16 \cancel{\text{qt}} \cdot \frac{1 \text{ gal}}{4 \cancel{\text{qt}}} = \frac{16 \text{ gal}}{4} \quad \text{Multiply.}$$

$$= 4 \text{ gal}$$

Four gallons will fill the 16-quart bucket.

EXAMPLE 2 Making Rate Conversions

Use a unit conversion factor to convert 80 miles per hour to feet per hour.

There are 5,280 feet per mile, so use $\frac{5{,}280 \text{ ft}}{1 \text{ mi}}$ to cancel the miles.

$$\frac{80 \cancel{\text{mi}}}{1 \text{ hr}} \cdot \frac{5{,}280 \text{ ft}}{1 \cancel{\text{mi}}} = \frac{80 \cdot 5{,}280 \text{ ft}}{1 \text{ hr}} \quad \text{Multiply.}$$

$$= \frac{422{,}400 \text{ ft}}{1 \text{ hr}}$$

Eighty miles per hour is 422,400 feet per hour.

EXTENSION Exercises

Write the appropriate unit conversion factor for each conversion.

1. inches to feet
2. meters to centimeters
3. minutes to hours
4. yards to feet

Use a unit conversion factor to convert the units.

5. A bag of apples weighs 64 ounces. How many pounds does it weigh?
6. You need 48 inches of ribbon. How many feet of ribbon do you need?
7. A soup recipe calls for 3.5 quarts of water. How many pints of water are needed?

Use a unit conversion factor to convert the units within each rate.

8. Convert 32 feet per second to inches per second.
9. A craft store charges $1.75 per foot for lace. How much per yard is this?
10. A company rents boats for $9 per hour. How much per minute is this?
11. **Earth Science** The amount of time it takes for a planet to revolve around the Sun is called a period of revolution. The period of revolution for Earth is one Earth year, and the period of revolution for any other planet is one year on that planet.
    a. How many Earth years does it take Venus to revolve around the Sun?
    b. Use a unit conversion factor to find the number of Venus years equivalent to 3 Earth years. Round to the nearest tenth.
    c. Find your age on each planet to the nearest year.

Periods of Revolution Compared to Earth's

Planet	One Revolution in Earth Years
Venus	0.615
Mars	1.88
Neptune	164.79

12. In England, a commonly used unit of measure is the stone. One stone is equivalent to 14 pounds. If Jo weighs 95 pounds, how many stone does she weigh? Round your answer to the nearest tenth of a stone.
13. **Money** Fencing costs $3.75 per foot. Harris wants to enclose his rectangular garden, which measures 6 yards by 4 yards. How much will fencing for the garden cost?
14. **What's the Error?** Janice converted 56 gallons per second to quarts per minute using the unit conversion factors $\frac{4 \text{ quarts}}{1 \text{ gallon}}$ and $\frac{60 \text{ seconds}}{1 \text{ minute}}$. Her result was 13,440 quarts per minute. Was her answer reasonable? Explain.
15. **Challenge** Your car gets 32 miles per gallon of gasoline. You have $15, and gasoline costs $2.50 per gallon. How far can you travel on $15?

Game Time

Water Works

You have three glasses: a 3-ounce glass, a 5-ounce glass, and an 8-ounce glass. The 8-ounce glass is full of water, and the other two glasses are empty. By pouring water from one glass to another, how can you get exactly 6 ounces of water in one of the glasses? The step-by-step solution is described below.

1. Pour the water from the 8 oz glass into the 5 oz glass.
2. Pour the water from the 5 oz glass into the 3 oz glass.
3. Pour the water from the 3 oz glass into the 8 oz glass.

You now have 6 ounces of water in the 8-ounce glass.

Start again, but this time try to get exactly 4 ounces of water in one glass. (*Hint:* Find a way to get 1 ounce of water. Start by pouring water into the 3-ounce glass.)

Next, using 3-ounce, 8-ounce, and 11-ounce glasses, try to get exactly 9 ounces of water in one glass. Start with the 11-ounce glass full of water. (*Hint:* Start by pouring water into the 8-ounce glass.)

Look at the sizes of the glasses in each problem. The volume of the third glass is the sum of the volumes of the first two glasses: $3 + 5 = 8$ and $3 + 8 = 11$. Using any amounts for the two smaller glasses, and starting with the largest glass full, you can get any multiple of the smaller glass's volume. Try it and see.

Concentration

Each card in a deck of cards has a ratio on one side. Place each card face down. Each player or team takes a turn flipping over two cards. If the ratios on the cards are equivalent, the player or team can keep the pair. If not, the next player or team flips two cards. After every card has been turned over, the player or team with the most pairs wins.

A complete copy of the rules and the game pieces are available online.

go.hrw.com
Game Time Extra
KEYWORD: MS7 Games

It's in the Bag!

FOLDNOTES

Materials
- 2 paper plates
- scissors
- markers

PROJECT Paper Plate Proportions

Serve up some proportions on this book made from paper plates.

1. Fold one of the paper plates in half. Cut out a narrow rectangle along the folded edge. The rectangle should be as long as the diameter of plate's inner circle. When you open the plate, you will have a narrow window in the center. **Figure A**

2. Fold the second paper plate in half and then unfold it. Cut slits on both sides of the crease beginning from the edge of the plate to the inner circle. **Figure B**

3. Roll up the plate with the slits so that the two slits touch each other. Then slide this plate into the narrow window in the other plate. **Figure C**

4. When the rolled-up plate is halfway through the window, unroll it so that the slits fit on the sides of the window. **Figure D**

5. Close the book so that all the plates are folded in half.

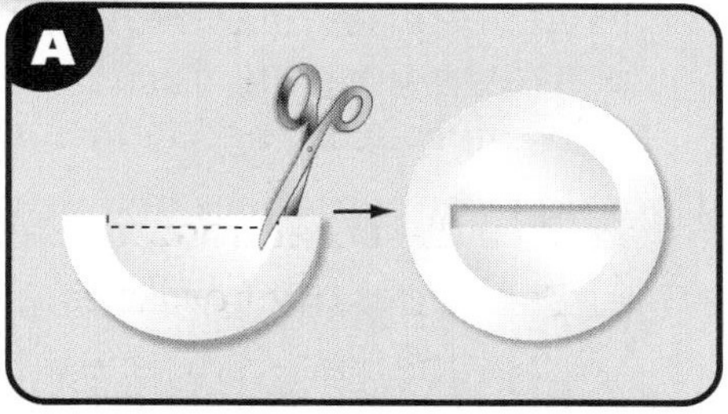

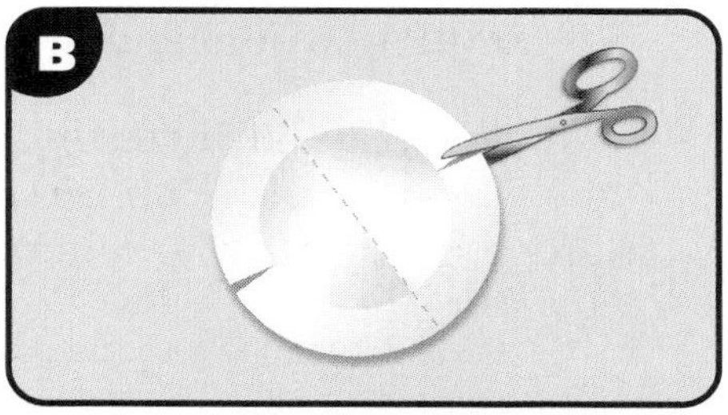

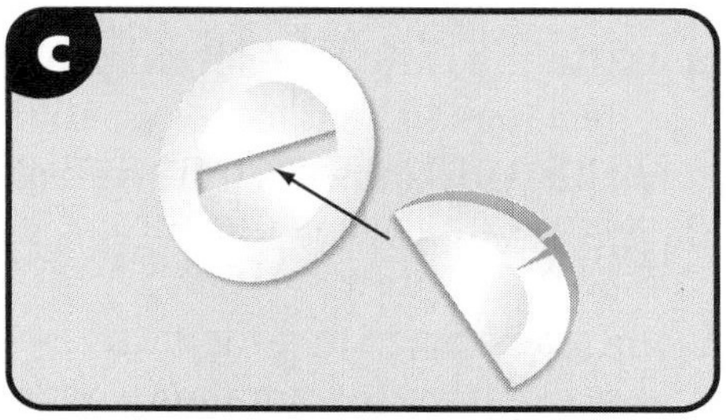

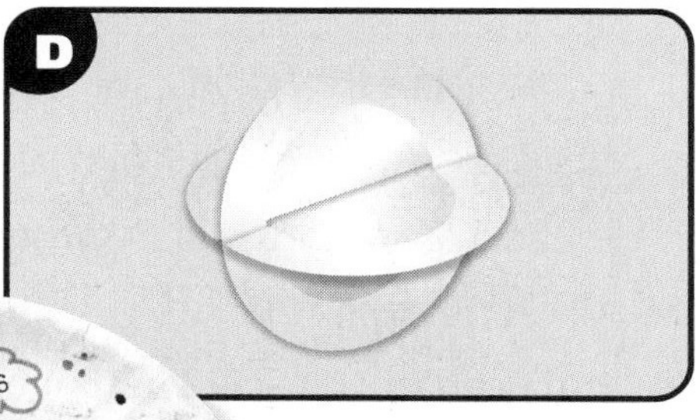

Taking Note of the Math

Write the number and name of the chapter on the cover of the book. Then review the chapter, using the inside pages to take notes on ratios, rates, proportions, and similar figures

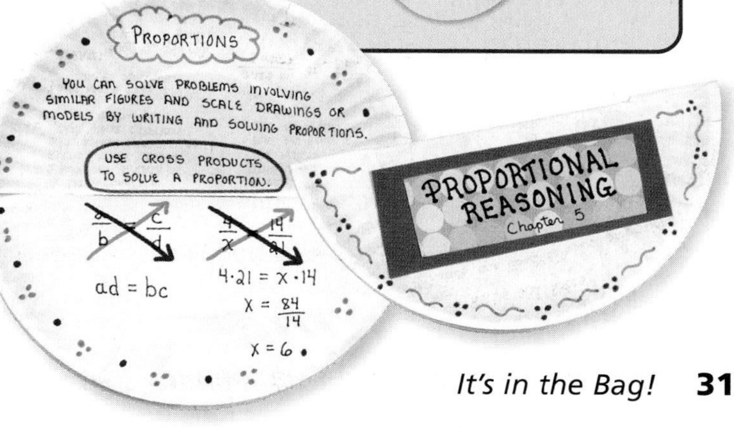

CHAPTER 5

Study Guide: Review

Vocabulary

corresponding angles	300	**proportion**	283	**scale factor**	308
corresponding sides	300	**rate**	274	**scale model**	308
cross product	287	**ratio**	270	**similar**	300
equivalent ratios	283	**scale**	308	**slope**	278
indirect measurement	304	**scale drawing**	308	**unit rate**	274

Complete the sentences below with vocabulary words from the list above.

1. __?__ figures have the same shape but not necessarily the same size.
2. A(n) __?__ is a comparison of two numbers, and a(n) __?__ is a ratio that compares two quantities measured in different units.
3. The ratio used to enlarge or reduce similar figures is a(n) __?__ .

5-1 Ratios (pp. 270–273)

EXAMPLE

■ **Write the ratio of 2 servings of bread to 4 servings of vegetables in all three forms. Write your answers in simplest form.**

$\frac{2}{4} = \frac{1}{2}$ *Write the ratio 2 to 4 in simplest form.*

$\frac{1}{2}$, 1 to 2, 1:2

EXERCISES

There are 3 red, 7 blue, and 5 yellow balloons.

4. Write the ratio of blue balloons to total balloons in all three forms. Write your answer in simplest form.
5. Tell whether the ratio of red to blue balloons or the ratio of yellow balloons to total balloons is greater.

5-2 Rates (pp. 274–277)

EXAMPLE

■ **Find each unit price. Then decide which has the lowest price per ounce.**

$\frac{\$2.70}{5\text{ oz}}$ or $\frac{\$4.32}{12\text{ oz}}$

$\frac{\$2.70}{5\text{ oz}} = \frac{\$0.54}{\text{oz}}$ and $\frac{\$4.32}{12\text{ oz}} = \frac{\$0.36}{\text{oz}}$

Since $0.36 < 0.54$, $\frac{\$4.32}{12\text{ oz}}$ has the lowest price per ounce.

EXERCISES

Find each average rate of speed.

6. 540 ft in 90 s
7. 436 min in 4 hr

Find each unit price. Then decide which is the better buy.

8. $\frac{\$56}{25\text{ gal}}$ or $\frac{\$32.05}{15\text{ gal}}$
9. $\frac{\$160}{5\text{ g}}$ or $\frac{\$315}{9\text{ g}}$

5-3 Slope and Rates of Change (pp. 278–282)

EXAMPLE

■ **Tell whether the graph shows a constant or variable rate of change. If constant, find the slope.**

The graph is a line, so the rate of change is constant.

$$\text{slope} = \frac{\text{rise}}{\text{run}} = \frac{-4}{1} = -4$$

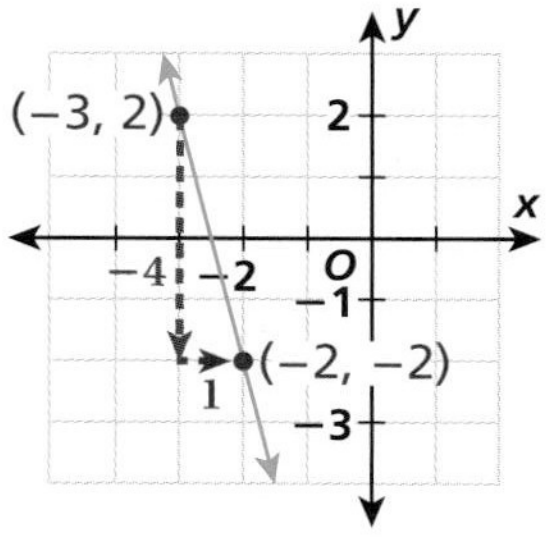

EXERCISES

Tell whether each graph shows a constant or variable rate of change. If constant, find the slope.

10.

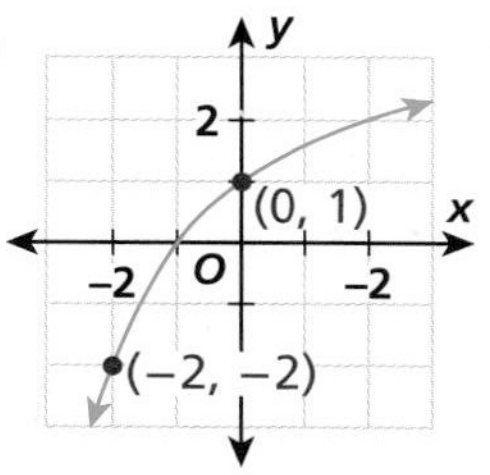

11.

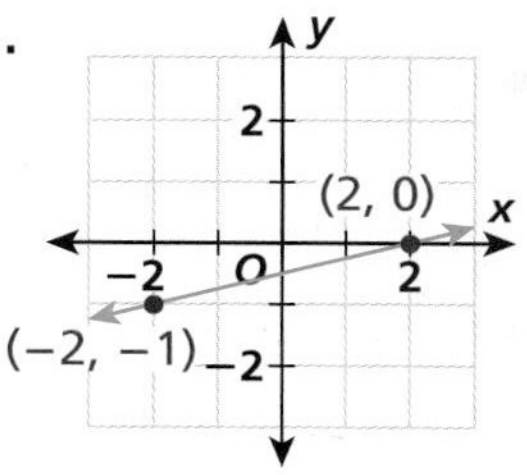

5-4 Identifying and Writing Proportions (pp. 283–286)

EXAMPLE

■ **Determine if $\frac{5}{12}$ and $\frac{3}{9}$ are proportional.**

$\frac{5}{12}$ — *$\frac{5}{12}$ is already in simplest form.*

$\frac{3}{9} = \frac{1}{3}$ — *Simplify $\frac{3}{9}$.*

$\frac{5}{12} \neq \frac{1}{3}$ — *The ratios are not proportional.*

EXERCISES

Determine if the ratios are proportional.

12. $\frac{9}{27}, \frac{6}{20}$ **13.** $\frac{15}{25}, \frac{20}{30}$ **14.** $\frac{21}{14}, \frac{18}{12}$

Find a ratio equivalent to the given ratio. Then use the ratios to write a proportion.

15. $\frac{10}{12}$ **16.** $\frac{45}{50}$ **17.** $\frac{9}{15}$

5-5 Solving Proportions (pp. 287–290)

EXAMPLE

■ **Use cross products to solve $\frac{p}{8} = \frac{10}{12}$.**

$\frac{p}{8} = \frac{10}{12}$

$p \cdot 12 = 8 \cdot 10$ — *Multiply the cross products.*

$12p = 80$

$\frac{12p}{12} = \frac{80}{12}$ — *Divide each side by 12.*

$p = \frac{20}{3}$, or $6\frac{2}{3}$

EXERCISES

Use cross products to solve each proportion.

18. $\frac{4}{6} = \frac{n}{3}$ **19.** $\frac{2}{a} = \frac{5}{15}$

20. $\frac{b}{1.5} = \frac{8}{3}$ **21.** $\frac{16}{11} = \frac{96}{x}$

22. $\frac{2}{y} = \frac{1}{5}$ **23.** $\frac{7}{2} = \frac{70}{w}$

5-6 Customary Measurements (pp. 292–295)

EXAMPLE

■ **Convert 5 mi to feet.**

$$\frac{\text{feet} \rightarrow 5{,}280}{\text{miles} \rightarrow 1} = \frac{x}{5}$$

$x = 5{,}280 \cdot 5 = 26{,}400$ ft

EXERCISES

Convert each measure.

24. 32 fl oz to pints
25. 1.5 tons to pounds
26. 13,200 ft to miles

5-7 Similar Figures and Proportions (pp. 300–303)

EXAMPLE

■ **Tell whether the figures are similar.**

The corresponding angles of the figures have equal measures.

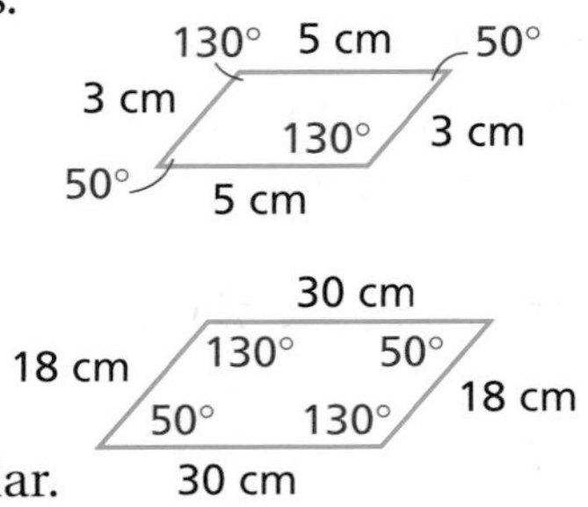

$\frac{5}{30} \stackrel{?}{=} \frac{3}{18} \stackrel{?}{=} \frac{5}{30} \stackrel{?}{=} \frac{3}{18}$

$\frac{1}{6} = \frac{1}{6} = \frac{1}{6} = \frac{1}{6}$

The ratios of the corresponding sides are equivalent. The figures are similar.

EXERCISES

Tell whether the figures are similar.

27.

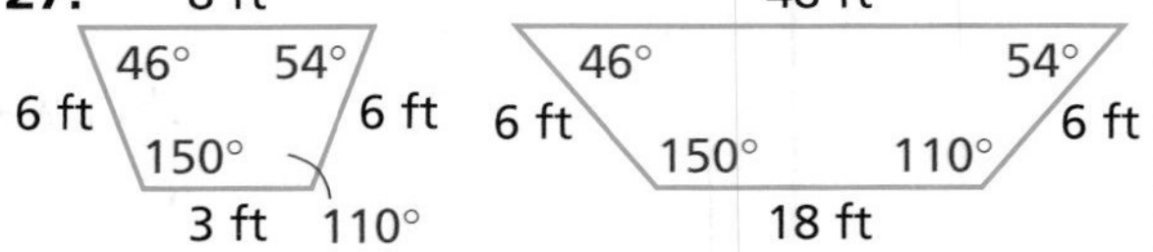

28.

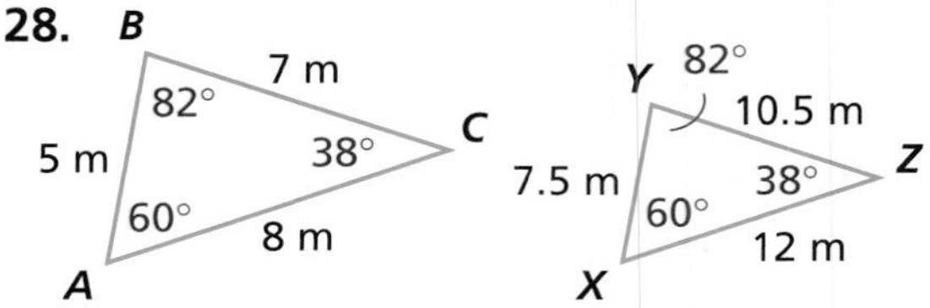

5-8 Using Similar Figures (pp. 304–307)

EXAMPLE

■ **$\triangle ABC \sim \triangle LMN$. Find the unknown length.**

$\frac{AB}{LM} = \frac{AC}{LN}$

$\frac{8}{t} = \frac{11}{44}$

$8 \cdot 44 = t \cdot 11$

$352 = 11t$

$\frac{352}{11} = \frac{11t}{11}$

$32 \text{ in.} = t$

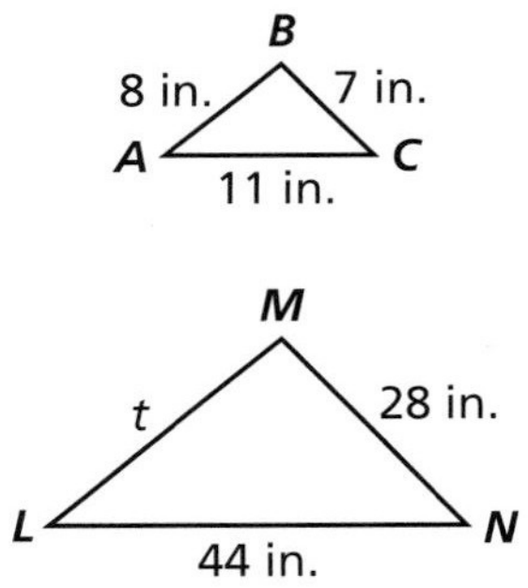

EXERCISES

$\triangle JKL \sim \triangle DEF$. Find the unknown length.

29.

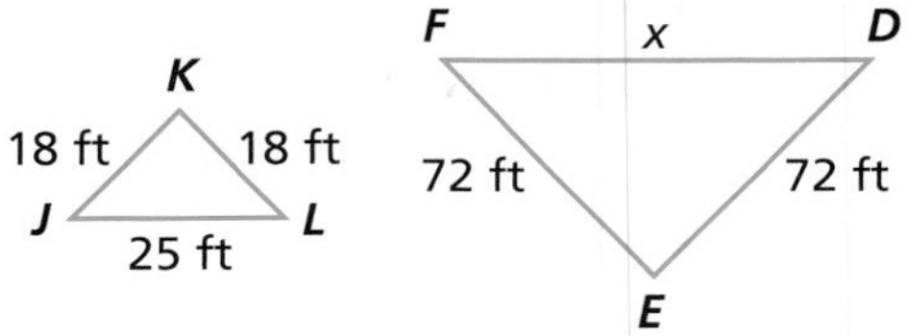

30. A tree casts a $30\frac{1}{2}$ ft shadow at the time of day when a 2 ft stake casts a $7\frac{2}{3}$ ft shadow. Estimate the height of the tree.

5-9 Scale Drawings and Scale Models (pp. 308–311)

EXAMPLE

■ **A model boat is 4 inches long. The scale factor is $\frac{1}{24}$. How long is the actual boat?**

$\frac{\text{model}}{\text{boat}} = \frac{1}{24}$

$\frac{4}{n} = \frac{1}{24}$ *Write a proportion.*

$4 \cdot 24 = n \cdot 1$ *Find the cross products.*

$96 = n$ *Solve.*

The boat is 96 inches long.

EXERCISES

31. The Wright brothers' *Flyer* had a 484-inch wingspan. Carla bought a model of the plane with a scale factor of $\frac{1}{40}$. What is the model's wingspan?

32. The distance from Austin to Houston on a map is 4.3 inches. The map scale is 1 inch = 38 miles. What is the actual distance?

CHAPTER TEST

1. Stan found 12 pennies, 15 nickels, 7 dimes, and 5 quarters. Tell whether the ratio of pennies to quarters or the ratio of nickels to dimes is greater.
2. Lenny sold 576 tacos in 48 hours. What was Lenny's average rate of taco sales?
3. A store sells a 5 lb box of detergent for $5.25 and a 10 lb box of detergent for $9.75. Which size box has the lowest price per pound?

Tell whether each graph shows a constant or variable rate of change. If constant, find the slope.

4.

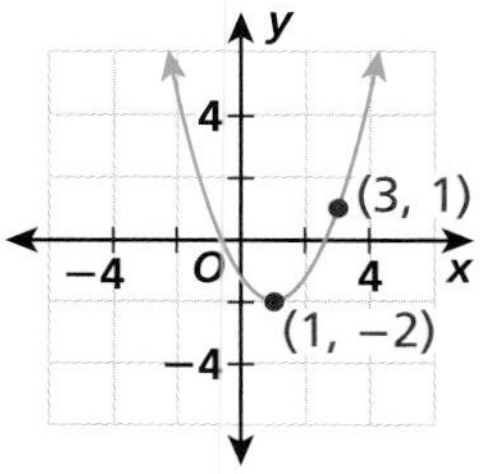

5.

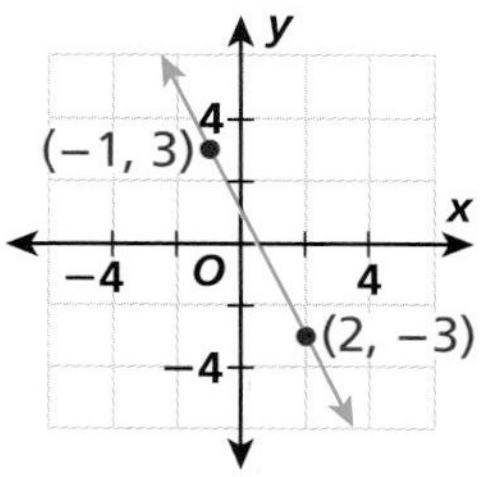

Find a ratio equivalent to each ratio. Then use the ratios to write a proportion.

6. $\frac{22}{30}$ 7. $\frac{7}{9}$ 8. $\frac{18}{54}$ 9. $\frac{10}{17}$

Use cross products to solve each proportion.

10. $\frac{9}{12} = \frac{m}{6}$ 11. $\frac{x}{2} = \frac{18}{6}$ 12. $\frac{3}{7} = \frac{21}{t}$ 13. $\frac{5}{p} = \frac{10}{2}$

Convert each measure.

14. 13,200 ft to miles 15. 3.5 lb to ounces 16. 17 qt to gallons

Tell whether the figures are similar.

17.

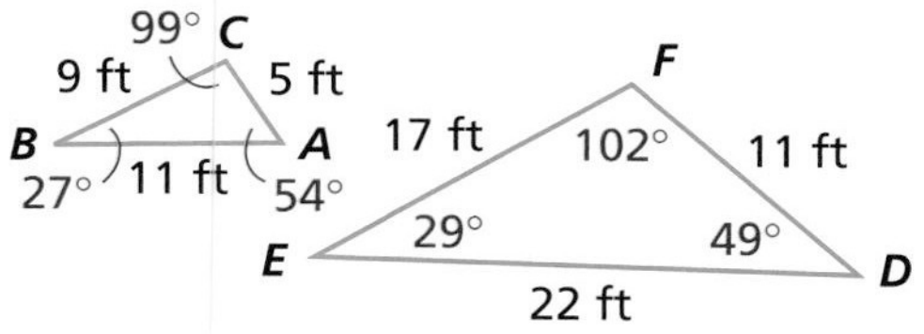

18.

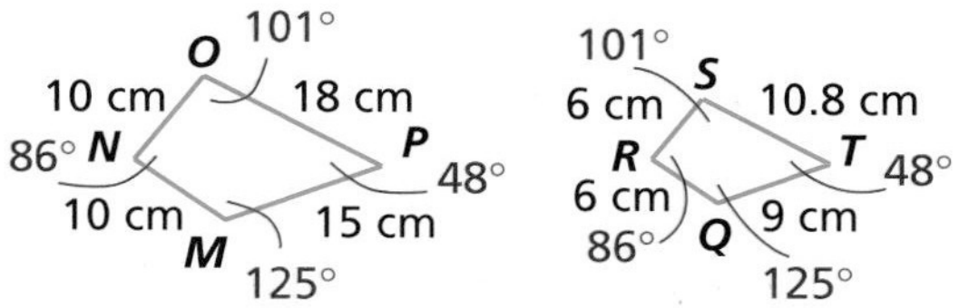

$\triangle WYZ \sim \triangle MNO$ in each pair. Find the unknown lengths.

19.

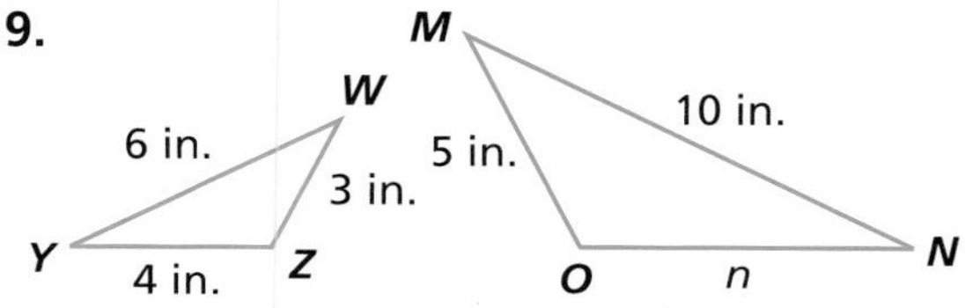

20.

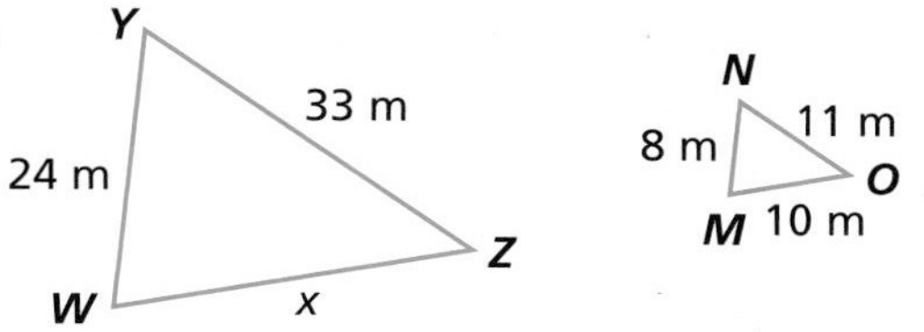

21. A scale model of a building is 8 in. by 12 in. If the scale is 1 in. = 15 ft, what are the dimensions of the actual building?
22. The distance from Portland to Seaside is 75 mi. What is the distance in inches between the two towns on a map if the scale is $1\frac{1}{4}$ in. = 25 mi?

CHAPTER 5

TEST TACKLER

Standardized Test Strategies

Extended Response: Understand the Scores

Extended-response test items usually involve multiple steps and require a detailed explanation. The items are scored using a 4-point rubric. A complete and correct response is worth 4 points, a partial response is worth 2 to 3 points, an incorrect response with no work shown is worth 1 point, and no response at all is worth 0 points.

EXAMPLE

Extended Response A 10-pound bag of apples costs \$4. Write and solve a proportion to find how much a 15-pound bag of apples would cost at the same rate. Explain how the increase in weight is related to the increase in cost.

Here are examples of how different responses were scored using the scoring rubric shown.

4-point response:

Let c = the cost of the 15 lb bag.

$$\frac{10 \text{ pounds}}{\$4} = \frac{15 \text{ pounds}}{c}$$

$$10 \cdot c = 4 \cdot 15$$

$$\frac{10c}{10} = \frac{60}{10}$$

$$c = 6$$

The 15 lb bag costs \$6.

For every additional 5 pounds, the cost increases by 2 dollars.

3-point response:

Let c = the cost of the 15 lb bag.

$$\frac{10 \text{ pounds}}{\$4} = \frac{15 \text{ pounds}}{c}$$

$$10 \cdot c = 4 \cdot 15$$

$$\frac{10c}{10} = \frac{60}{10}$$

$$c = 6$$

The 15 lb bag costs \$6.

For every additional 5 pounds, the cost increases by 6 dollars.

The proportion is set up and solved correctly, and all work is shown, but the explanation is incorrect.

2-point response:

Let c = the cost of the apples.

$$\frac{10 \text{ pounds}}{\$4} = \frac{c}{15 \text{ pounds}}$$

$$10 \cdot 15 = 4 \cdot c$$

$$\frac{150}{4} = \frac{4c}{4}$$

$$37.5 = c$$

The proportion is set up incorrectly, and no explanation is given.

1-point response:

$$37.5 = c$$

The answer is incorrect, no work is shown, and no explanation is given.

HOT TIP! After you complete an extended-response test item, double-check that you have answered all parts.

Read each test item and answer the questions that follow using the scoring rubric below.

Scoring Rubric

4 points: The student correctly answers all parts of the question, shows all work, and provides a complete and correct explanation.

3 points: The student answers all parts of the question, shows all work, and provides a complete explanation that demonstrates understanding, but the student makes minor errors in computation.

2 points: The student does not answer all parts of the question but shows all work and provides a complete and correct explanation for the parts answered, or the student correctly answers all parts of the question but does not show all work or does not provide an explanation.

1 point: The student gives incorrect answers and shows little or no work or explanation, or the student does not follow directions.

0 points: The student gives no response.

Item A
Extended Response Alex drew a model of a birdhouse using a scale of 1 inch to 3 inches. On the drawing, the house is 6 inches tall. Define a variable, and then write and solve a proportion to find how many inches tall the actual birdhouse is.

1. Should the response shown receive a score of 4 points? Why or why not?

$$\frac{1 \text{ inch}}{6 \text{ inches}} = \frac{3 \text{ inches}}{h}$$

$$1 \cdot h = 3 \cdot 6$$

$$h = 18$$

The actual birdhouse is 18 inches tall.

Item B
Extended Response Use a table to find a rule that describes the relationship between the first four terms of the sequence 2, 4, 8, 16, . . . and their positions in the sequence. Then find the next three terms in the sequence.

2. What should you add to the response shown, if anything, so that it receives full credit?

n	1	2	3	4
Rule	2^1	2^2	2^3	2^4
y	2	4	8	16

Each term is 2 times as great as the term before it. The rule is 2^n.

Item C
Extended Response The figures are similar. Find the value of x and the sum of the side lengths of one of the figures.

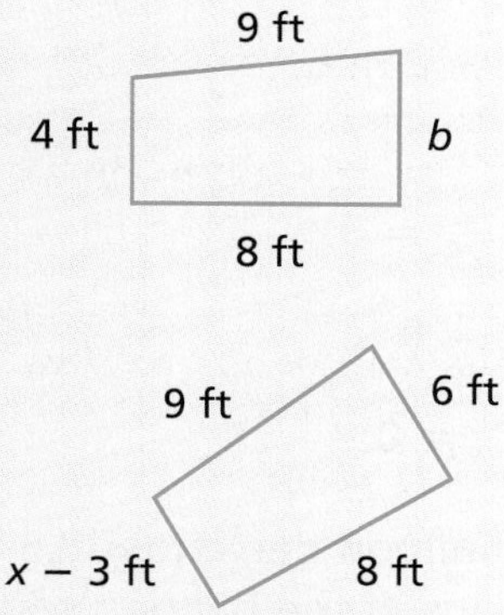

3. What needs to be included in a response that would receive 4 points?

4. Write a response that would receive full credit.

CHAPTER 5

STANDARDIZED TEST PREP

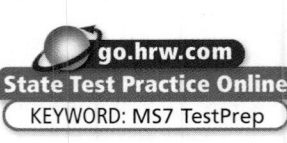

go.hrw.com
State Test Practice Online
KEYWORD: MS7 TestPrep

Cumulative Assessment, Chapters 1–5

Multiple Choice

1. What is the unknown length b in similar triangles ABC and DEF?

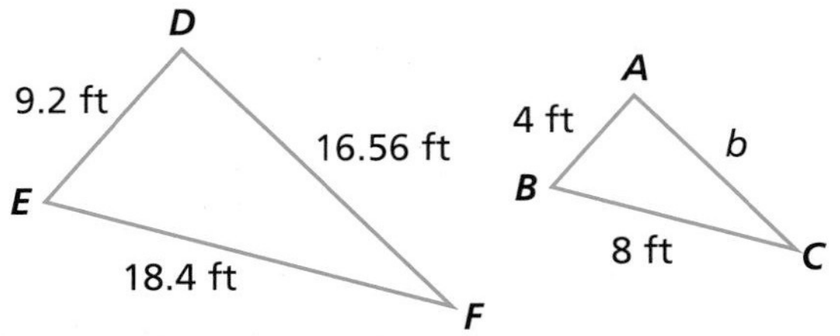

Ⓐ 7.2 feet
Ⓑ 6 feet
Ⓒ 4 feet
Ⓓ 5.6 feet

2. The total length of the Golden Gate Bridge in San Francisco, California, is 8,981 feet. If a car is traveling at a speed of 45 miles per hour, how many minutes would it take the car to cross the bridge?

Ⓕ 0.04 minute
Ⓖ 1.28 minutes
Ⓗ 1.7 minutes
Ⓙ 2.27 minutes

3. For which equation is $x = \frac{2}{5}$ the solution?

Ⓐ $5x - \frac{25}{2} = 0$

Ⓑ $-\frac{1}{5}x + \frac{2}{25} = 0$

Ⓒ $\frac{1}{5}x - 2 = 0$

Ⓓ $-5x + \frac{1}{2} = 0$

4. A hot air balloon descends 38.5 meters in 22 seconds. If the balloon continues to descend at this rate, how long will it take to descend 125 meters?

Ⓕ 25.25 seconds
Ⓖ 86.5 seconds
Ⓗ 71.43 seconds
Ⓙ 218.75 seconds

5. Which value completes the table of equivalent ratios?

Microphones	3	9	15	36
Karaoke Machines	1	3	?	12

Ⓐ 5
Ⓑ 7
Ⓒ 8
Ⓓ 9

6. On a baseball field, the distance from home plate to the pitcher's mound is $60\frac{1}{2}$ feet. The distance from home plate to second base is about $127\frac{7}{24}$ feet. What is the difference between the two distances?

Ⓕ $61\frac{1}{3}$ feet
Ⓖ $66\frac{5}{6}$ feet
Ⓗ $66\frac{19}{24}$ feet
Ⓙ $66\frac{5}{24}$ feet

7. Which word phrase best describes the expression $n - 6$?

Ⓐ 6 more than a number
Ⓑ A number less than 6
Ⓒ 6 minus a number
Ⓓ A number decreased by 6

8. A football weighs about $\frac{3}{20}$ kilogram. If a coach has 15 footballs in a large bag, which estimate best describes the total weight of the footballs?

Ⓕ Not quite 3 kilograms
Ⓖ A little more than 2 kilograms
Ⓗ Almost 1 kilogram
Ⓙ Between 1 and 2 kilograms

9. Which point lies on the line $y = 4x + 2$?

Ⓐ (2, 10) Ⓒ (−4, 2)

Ⓑ (0, −2) Ⓓ (−2, 6)

10. On a scale drawing, a cell phone tower is 1.25 feet tall. The scale factor is $\frac{1}{150}$. What is the height of the actual cell phone tower?

Ⓕ 37.5 ft Ⓗ 148 ft

Ⓖ 120 ft Ⓙ 187.5 ft

HOT TIP! If a diagram or graph is not provided, quickly sketch one to clarify the information provided in the test item.

Gridded Response

11. The Liberty Bell, a symbol of freedom in the United States, weighs 2,080 pounds. How many tons does the Liberty Bell weigh?

12. Find the quotient of $-51.03 \div (-8.1)$.

13. What is the slope of the line shown?

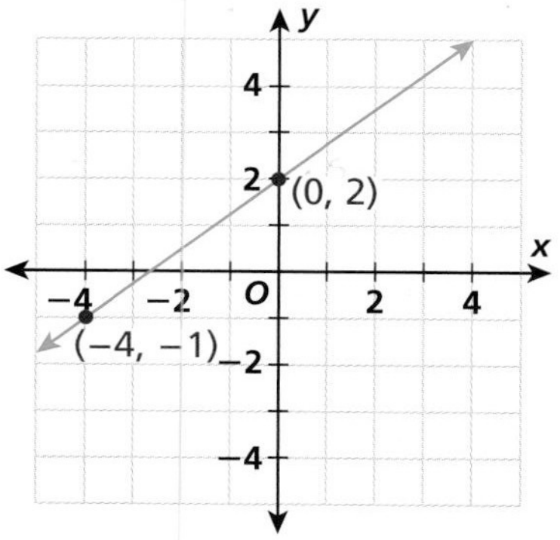

14. A florist is preparing bouquets of flowers for an exhibit. The florist has 84 tulips and 56 daisies. Each bouquet will have the same number of tulips and the same number of daisies. How many bouquets can the florist make for this exhibit?

Short Response

15. Jana began the month with \$102.50 in her checking account. During the month, she deposited \$8.50 that she earned from baby-sitting, withdrew \$9.75 to buy a CD, deposited \$5.00 that her aunt gave her, and withdrew \$6.50 for a movie ticket. Using compatible numbers, write and evaluate an expression to estimate the balance in Jana's account at the end of the month.

16. A lamppost casts a shadow that is 18 feet long. At the same time of day, Alyce casts a shadow that is 4.2 feet long. Alyce is 5.3 feet tall. Draw a picture of the situation. Set up and solve a proportion to find the height of the lamppost to the nearest foot. Show your work.

Extended Response

17. Riley is drawing a map of the state of Virginia. From east to west, the greatest distance across the state is about 430 miles. From north to south, the greatest distance is about 200 miles.

    a. Riley is using a map scale of 1 inch = 24 miles. Find the length of the map from east to west and the length from north to south. Round your answers to the nearest tenth.

    b. The length between two cities on Riley's map is 9 inches. What is the distance between the cities in miles?

    c. If an airplane travels at a speed of 520 miles per hour, about how many minutes will it take for the plane to fly from east to west across the widest part of Virginia? Show your work.

CHAPTER

6

Percents

go.hrw.com
Chapter Project Online
KEYWORD: MS7 Ch6

Annual Urban Waste Deposited in U.S. Landfills (million tons)			
Soil	**Wood**	**Concrete**	**Household Refuse**
107.6	87.6	22.5	32.7

Career *Urban Archaeologist*

Have you ever wanted to study the lifestyles of people who lived long ago? If so, becoming an archaeologist might be for you. Archaeologists learn about past civilizations by excavating cities and examining artifacts. They even examine garbage!

From 1973 to 2003, the urban archaeologists of the Garbage Project learned about the habits of present-day societies by excavating landfills and studying the things we throw away. They found that over 80% of urban waste in the United States is deposited in landfills.

ARE YOU READY?

Vocabulary

Choose the best term from the list to complete each sentence.

1. A statement that two ratios are equivalent is called a(n) __?__.

2. To write $\frac{2}{3}$ as a(n) __?__, divide the numerator by the denominator.

3. A(n) __?__ is a comparison by division of two quantities.

4. The __?__ of $\frac{9}{24}$ is $\frac{3}{8}$.

decimal
equation
fraction
proportion
ratio
simplest form

Complete these exercises to review skills you will need for this chapter.

Write Fractions as Decimals

Write each fraction as a decimal.

5. $\frac{8}{10}$ **6.** $\frac{53}{100}$ **7.** $\frac{739}{1,000}$ **8.** $\frac{7}{100}$

9. $\frac{2}{5}$ **10.** $\frac{5}{8}$ **11.** $\frac{7}{12}$ **12.** $\frac{13}{20}$

Write Decimals as Fractions

Write each decimal as a fraction in simplest form.

13. 0.05 **14.** 0.92 **15.** 0.013 **16.** 0.8

17. 0.006 **18.** 0.305 **19.** 0.0007 **20.** 1.04

Solve Multiplication Equations

Solve each equation.

21. $100n = 300$ **22.** $38 = 0.4x$ **23.** $16p = 1,200$

24. $9 = 72y$ **25.** $0.07m = 56$ **26.** $25 = 100t$

Solve Proportions

Solve each proportion.

27. $\frac{2}{3} = \frac{x}{12}$ **28.** $\frac{x}{20} = \frac{3}{4}$ **29.** $\frac{8}{15} = \frac{x}{45}$

30. $\frac{16}{28} = \frac{4}{n}$ **31.** $\frac{p}{100} = \frac{12}{36}$ **32.** $\frac{42}{12} = \frac{14}{n}$

33. $\frac{8}{y} = \frac{10}{5}$ **34.** $\frac{6}{9} = \frac{d}{24}$ **35.** $\frac{21}{a} = \frac{7}{5}$

CHAPTER 6

Study Guide: Preview

Where You've Been

Previously, you

- modeled percents.
- wrote equivalent fractions, decimals, and percents.
- solved percent problems involving discounts, sales tax, and tips.

In This Chapter

You will study

- modeling and estimating percents.
- writing equivalent fractions, decimals, and percents, including percents less than 1 and greater than 100.
- solving percent problems involving discounts, sales tax, tips, profit, percent of change, and simple interest.
- comparing fractions, decimals, and percents.

Where You're Going

You can use the skills learned in this chapter

- to find or estimate discounts, sales tax, and tips when shopping and eating out.
- to solve problems involving banking.

Key Vocabulary/Vocabulario

interest	interés
percent	por ciento
percent of change	porcentaje de cambio
percent of decrease	porcentaje de disminución
percent of increase	porcentaje de aumento
principal	capital
simple interest	interés simple

Vocabulary Connections

To become familiar with some of the vocabulary terms in the chapter, consider the following. You may refer to the chapter, the glossary, or a dictionary if you like.

1. The Italian word *cento* and the French term *cent* mean "hundred." What do you think **percent** means?
2. The word *interest* stems from Latin (*inter-* + *esse*) and means "to be between" and "to make a difference." In business, interest is an amount collected or paid for the use of money. How can you relate the Latin roots and meanings to the business definition of **interest**?
3. *Principal* is the amount of money deposited or borrowed. Interest builds upon the principal. How might common definitions of *principal*, such as "leader of a school" and "a matter of primary importance," help you remember this business meaning of **principal**?

Reading and Writing Math

Study Strategy: Use Multiple Representations

When a new math concept is introduced, the explanation given often presents the topic in more than one way. As you study, pay attention to any models, tables, lists, graphs, diagrams, symbols, and words used to describe a concept.

In this example, the concept of finding equivalent fractions is represented in model, number, and word form.

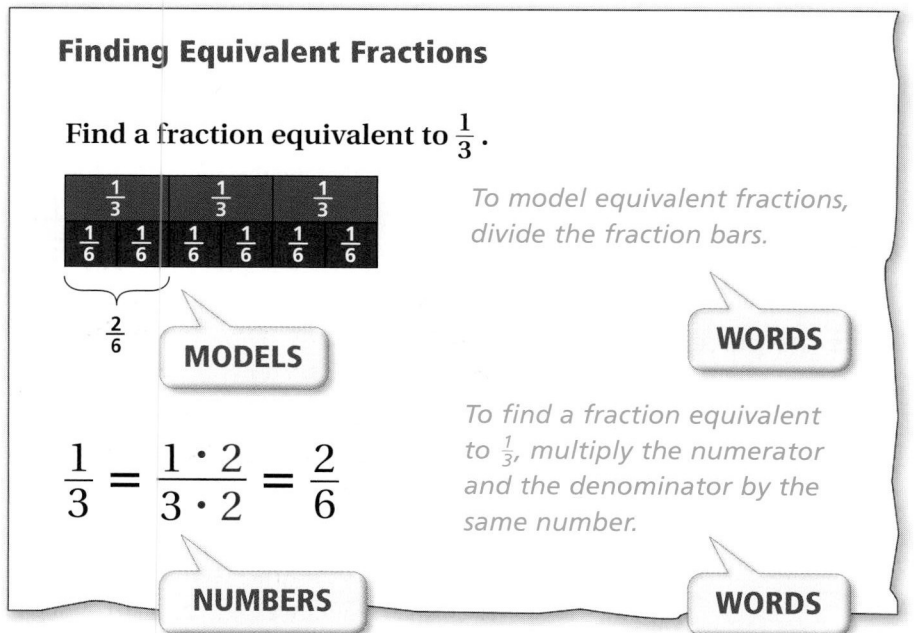

Finding Equivalent Fractions

Find a fraction equivalent to $\frac{1}{3}$.

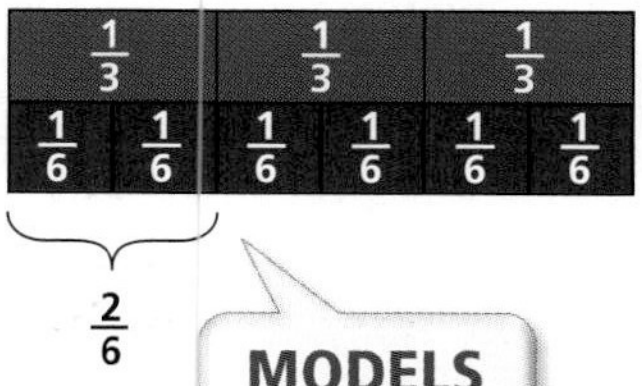

MODELS

To model equivalent fractions, divide the fraction bars.

WORDS

$$\frac{1}{3} = \frac{1 \cdot 2}{3 \cdot 2} = \frac{2}{6}$$

NUMBERS

To find a fraction equivalent to $\frac{1}{3}$, multiply the numerator and the denominator by the same number.

WORDS

Try This

1. Explain why it could be beneficial to represent a new idea in more than one way when taking notes.
2. Explain how you can use models and numbers to find equivalent fractions. Which method do you prefer? Explain.

6-1 Percents

Learn to model percents and to write percents as equivalent fractions and decimals.

Vocabulary

percent

It is estimated that over half the plant and animal species on Earth live in rain forests. However, rain forests cover less than 6 out of every 100 square miles of Earth's land. You can write this ratio, 6 to 100, as a *percent*, 6%.

A **percent** is a ratio of a number to 100. The symbol % is used to indicate that a number is a percent.

$\frac{6}{100} = 6\%$

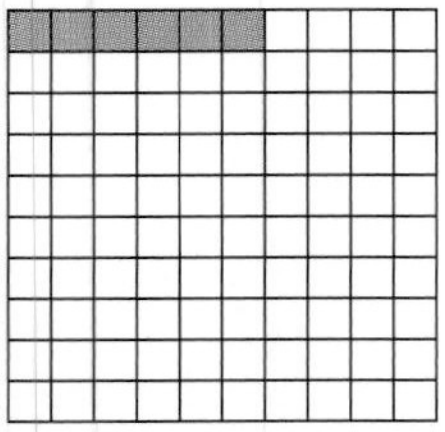

EXAMPLE 1 Modeling Percents

Reading Math

The word *percent* means "per hundred." So 6% means "6 out of 100."

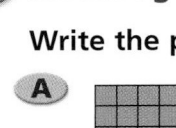

Write the percent modeled by each grid.

A

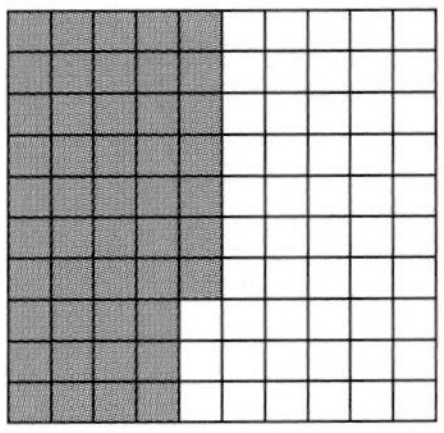

$\frac{\text{shaded}}{\text{total}} \rightarrow \frac{47}{100} = 47\%$

B

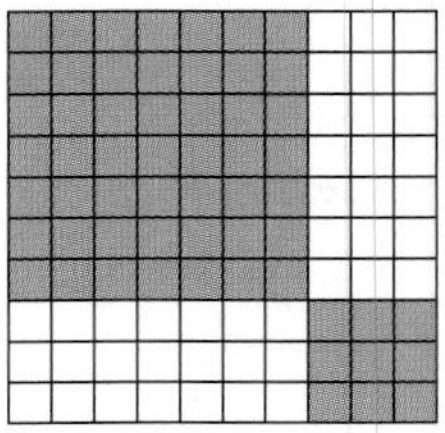

$\frac{\text{shaded}}{\text{total}} \rightarrow \frac{49 + 9}{100} = \frac{58}{100} = 58\%$

You can write percents as fractions or decimals.

EXAMPLE 2 Writing Percents as Fractions

Write 35% as a fraction in simplest form.

$35\% = \frac{35}{100}$ *Write the percent as a fraction with a denominator of 100.*

$= \frac{7}{20}$ *Simplify.*

So 35% can be written as $\frac{7}{20}$.

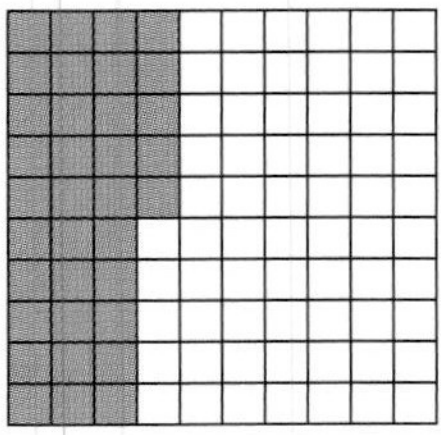

EXAMPLE 3 Writing Percents as Decimals

Write 43% as a decimal.

Method 1: Use pencil and paper.

$43\% = \frac{43}{100}$ *Write the percent as a fraction.*

$= 0.43$ *Divide 43 by 100.*

Method 2: Use mental math.

$43.\% = 0.43$ *Move the decimal point two places to the left.*

Think and Discuss

1. **Tell** in your own words what *percent* means.
2. **Explain** how to write 5% as a decimal.

6-1 Exercises

go.hrw.com
Homework Help Online
KEYWORD: MS7 6-1
Parent Resources Online
KEYWORD: MS7 Parent

GUIDED PRACTICE

See Example 1

Write the percent modeled by each grid.

1. 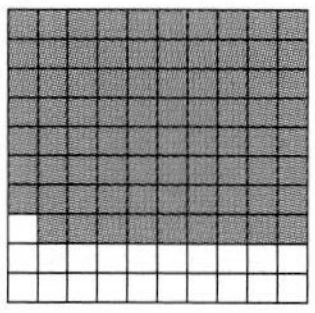

2. 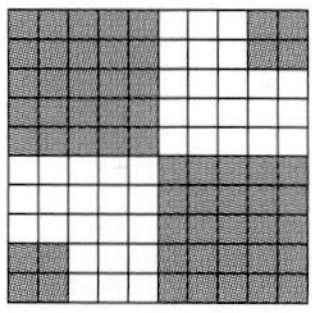

3. 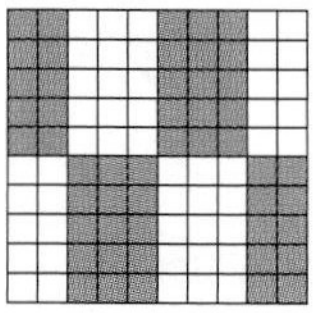

See Example 2

Write each percent as a fraction in simplest form.

4. 65% **5.** 82% **6.** 12% **7.** 38% **8.** 75%

See Example 3

Write each percent as a decimal.

9. 22% **10.** 51% **11.** 8.07% **12.** 1.6% **13.** 11%

INDEPENDENT PRACTICE

Write the percent modeled by each grid.

See Example 1

14. 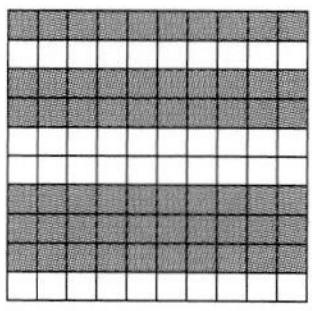

15. 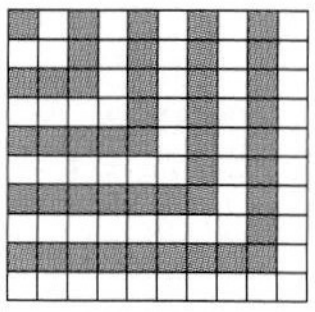

16. 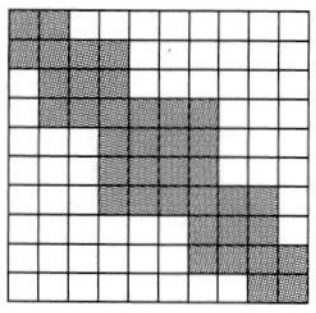

See Example 2
Write each percent as a fraction in simplest form.

17. 55% **18.** 34% **19.** 83% **20.** 53% **21.** 81%

See Example 3
Write each percent as a decimal.

22. 48% **23.** 9.8% **24.** 30.2% **25.** 66.3% **26.** 8.39%

PRACTICE AND PROBLEM SOLVING

Extra Practice
See page 737.

Write each percent as a fraction in simplest form and as a decimal.

27. 2.70% **28.** 7.6% **29.** 44% **30.** 3.148% **31.** 10.5%

Compare. Write <, >, or =.

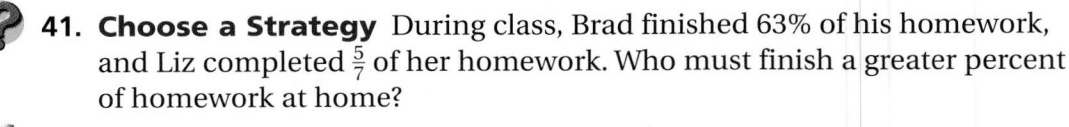

32. $\frac{18}{100}$ ▒ 22% **33.** $\frac{35}{52}$ ▒ 72% **34.** $\frac{10}{50}$ ▒ 22% **35.** $\frac{11}{20}$ ▒ 56%

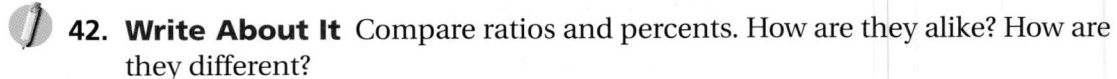

36. 41% ▒ $\frac{13}{30}$ **37.** $\frac{17}{20}$ ▒ 85% **38.** $\frac{3}{5}$ ▒ 60% **39.** 15% ▒ $\frac{4}{30}$

40. Multi-Step A nutrition label states that one serving of tortilla chips contains 7 grams of fat and 11% of the recommended daily allowance (RDA) of fat.

a. Write a ratio that represents the percent RDA of fat in one serving of tortilla chips.

b. Use the ratio from part **a** to write and solve a proportion to determine how many grams of fat are in the recommended daily allowance.

41. Choose a Strategy During class, Brad finished 63% of his homework, and Liz completed $\frac{5}{7}$ of her homework. Who must finish a greater percent of homework at home?

42. Write About It Compare ratios and percents. How are they alike? How are they different?

43. Challenge Write each of the following as a percent: 0.4 and 0.03.

Test Prep and Spiral Review

44. Multiple Choice Which inequality is a true statement?

Ⓐ $24\% > \frac{1}{4}$ Ⓑ $0.76 < 76\%$ Ⓒ $8\% < 0.8$ Ⓓ $\frac{1}{5} < 5\%$

45. Short Response Nineteen out of the 25 students on Sean's team sold mugs, and 68% of the students on Chi's team sold caps. Which team had a greater percent of students participate in the fundraiser?

Estimate each sum or difference. (Lesson 3-7)

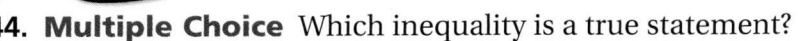

46. $\frac{7}{8} - \frac{3}{7}$ **47.** $6\frac{1}{10} + 5\frac{7}{9}$ **48.** $5\frac{2}{3} - \left(-\frac{3}{4}\right)$ **49.** $\frac{5}{12} + 2\frac{4}{5}$

Plot each point on a coordinate plane. (Lesson 4-1)

50. $A(2, 3)$ **51.** $B(-1, 4)$ **52.** $C(-2, -6)$ **53.** $D(0, -3)$

6-2 Fractions, Decimals, and Percents

Learn to write decimals and fractions as percents.

The students at Westview Middle School are collecting cans of food for the local food bank. Their goal is to collect 2,000 cans in one month. After 10 days, they have 800 cans of food.

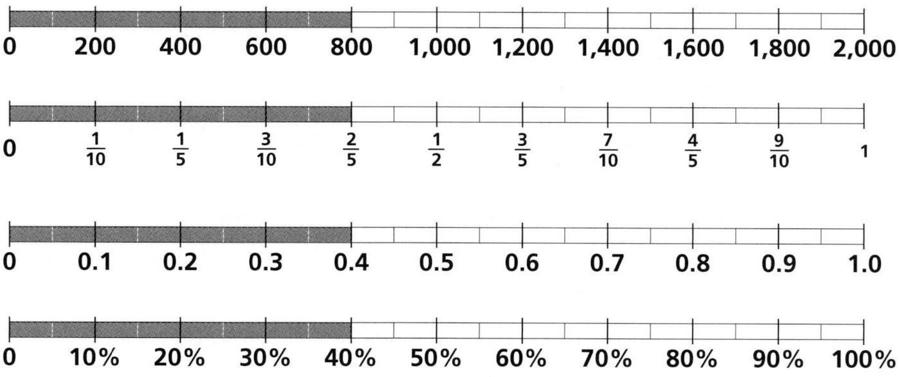

The models show that 800 out of 2,000 can be written as $\frac{800}{2,000}$, $\frac{2}{5}$, 0.4, or 40%. The students have reached 40% of their goal.

EXAMPLE 1 Writing Decimals as Percents

Write 0.2 as a percent.

Method 1: Use pencil and paper.

$0.2 = \frac{2}{10} = \frac{20}{100}$ *Write the decimal as a fraction with a denominator of 100.*

$= 20\%$ *Write the numerator with a percent sign.*

Method 2: Use mental math.

$0.20 = 20.0\%$ *Move the decimal point two places to the right and add a percent sign.*

$= 20\%$

EXAMPLE 2 Writing Fractions as Percents

Write $\frac{4}{5}$ as a percent.

Remember!

To divide 4 by 5, use long division and place a decimal point followed by a zero after the 4.

$5\overline{)4.0}$ = 0.8

Method 1: Use pencil and paper.

$\frac{4}{5} = 4 \div 5$ *Use division to write the fraction as a decimal.*

$= 0.8$

$= 0.80$

$= 80\%$ *Write the decimal as a percent.*

Method 2: Use mental math.

$\frac{4 \cdot 20}{5 \cdot 20} = \frac{80}{100}$ *Write an equivalent fraction with a denominator of 100.*

$= 80\%$ *Write the numerator with a percent sign.*

EXAMPLE 3 Choosing a Method of Computation

Decide whether using pencil and paper, mental math, or a calculator is most useful when solving the following problem. Then solve.

In a survey, 55 people were asked whether they prefer cats or dogs. Twenty-nine people said they prefer cats. What percent of the people surveyed said they prefer cats?

29 out of 55 = $\frac{29}{55}$ *Think: Since 29 ÷ 55 does not divide evenly, pencil and paper is not a good choice.*
Think: Since the denominator is not a factor of 100, mental math is not a good choice.

Using a calculator is the best method.

29 [÷] 55 [ENTER] [0.5272727273]

$0.5272727273 = 52.72727273\%$ *Write the decimal as a percent.*

$\approx 52.7\%$ *Round to the nearest tenth of a percent.*

About 52.7% of the people surveyed said they prefer cats.

Think and Discuss

1. **Describe** two methods you could use to write $\frac{3}{4}$ as a percent.
2. **Write** the ratio 25:100 as a fraction, as a decimal, and as a percent.

6-2 Exercises

go.hrw.com
Homework Help Online
KEYWORD: MS7 6-2
Parent Resources Online
KEYWORD: MS7 Parent

GUIDED PRACTICE

See Example 1 **Write each decimal as a percent.**

1. 0.6 2. 0.32 3. 0.544 4. 0.06 5. 0.087

See Example 2 **Write each fraction as a percent.**

6. $\frac{1}{4}$ 7. $\frac{3}{25}$ 8. $\frac{11}{20}$ 9. $\frac{7}{40}$ 10. $\frac{5}{8}$

See Example 3
11. **Decide whether using pencil and paper, mental math, or a calculator is most useful when solving the following problem. Then solve.**
In a survey, 50 students were asked whether they prefer pepperoni pizza or cheese pizza. Twenty students said they prefer cheese pizza. What percent of the students surveyed said they prefer cheese pizza?

INDEPENDENT PRACTICE

See Example 1

Write each decimal as a percent.

12. 0.15 **13.** 0.83 **14.** 0.325 **15.** 0.081 **16.** 0.42

See Example 2

Write each fraction as a percent.

17. $\frac{3}{4}$ **18.** $\frac{2}{5}$ **19.** $\frac{3}{8}$ **20.** $\frac{3}{16}$ **21.** $\frac{7}{25}$

See Example 3

22. **Decide whether using pencil and paper, mental math, or a calculator is most useful when solving the following problem. Then solve.**

In a theme-park survey, 75 visitors were asked whether they prefer the Ferris wheel or the roller coaster. Thirty visitors prefer the Ferris wheel. What percent of the visitors surveyed said they prefer the Ferris wheel?

PRACTICE AND PROBLEM SOLVING

Extra Practice
See page 737.

Compare. Write <, >, or =.

23. 45% ▒ $\frac{2}{5}$ **24.** 9% ▒ 0.9 **25.** $\frac{7}{12}$ ▒ 60% **26.** 0.037 ▒ 37%

27. **Multi-Step** One-half of the 900 students at Jefferson Middle School are boys. One-tenth of the boys are in the band, and one-fifth of those play the trumpet. What percent of the students at Jefferson are boys who play the trumpet in the band?

28. **Life Science** Rain forests are home to 90,000 of the 250,000 identified plant species in the world. What percent of the world's identified plant species are found in rain forests?

29. **What's the Error?** A student wrote $\frac{2}{5}$ as 0.4%. What was the error?

30. **Write About It** Describe two ways to change a fraction to a percent.

31. **Challenge** A desert area's average rainfall is 12 inches a year. This year the area received 15 inches of rain. What percent of the average rainfall amount is 15 inches?

TEST PREP and Spiral Review

32. **Multiple Choice** Which value is NOT equivalent to 45%?

Ⓐ $\frac{9}{20}$ Ⓑ 0.45 Ⓒ $\frac{45}{100}$ Ⓓ 0.045

33. **Short Response** Melanie's room measures 10 ft by 12 ft. Her rug covers 90 ft^2. Explain how to determine the percent of floor covered by the rug.

Make a function table for $x = -2, -1, 0, 1,$ and 2. (Lesson 4-4)

34. $y = 5x + 2$ **35.** $y = -2x$ **36.** $y = -\frac{2}{3}x - 4$

37. The actual length of a room is 6 m. The scale factor of a model is 1:15. What is the length of the room in the model? (Lesson 5-9)

6-3 Estimate with Percents

Problem Solving Skill

Learn to estimate percents.

A hair dryer at Hair Haven costs \$14.99. Carissa's Corner is offering the same hair dryer at 20% off the regular price of \$19.99. To find out which store is offering the better deal on the hair dryer, you can use estimation.

The table shows common percents and their fraction equivalents. You can estimate the percent of a number by substituting a fraction that is close to a given percent.

Percent	10%	20%	25%	$33\frac{1}{3}$%	50%	$66\frac{2}{3}$%
Fraction	$\frac{1}{10}$	$\frac{1}{5}$	$\frac{1}{4}$	$\frac{1}{3}$	$\frac{1}{2}$	$\frac{2}{3}$

EXAMPLE 1 Using Fractions to Estimate Percents

Remember!
Compatible numbers are close to the numbers in a problem and help you use mental math to find a solution.

Use a fraction to estimate 48% of 79.

$48\% \text{ of } 79 \approx \frac{1}{2} \cdot 79$ *Think: 48% is about 50% and 50% is equivalent to $\frac{1}{2}$.*

$\approx \frac{1}{2} \cdot 80$ *Change 79 to a compatible number.*

≈ 40 *Multiply.*

48% of 79 is about 40.

EXAMPLE 2 *Consumer Math Application*

Carissa's Corner is offering 20% off a hair dryer that costs \$19.99. The same hair dryer costs \$14.99 at Hair Haven. Which store offers the better deal?

First find the discount on the hair dryer at Carissa's Corner.

$20\% \text{ of } \$19.99 = \frac{1}{5} \cdot \$19.99$ *Think: 20% is equivalent to $\frac{1}{5}$.*

$\approx \frac{1}{5} \cdot \$20$ *Change \$19.99 to a compatible number.*

$\approx \$4$ *Multiply.*

The discount is approximately \$4. Since \$20 − \$4 = \$16, the \$14.99 hair dryer at Hair Haven is the better deal.

Another way to estimate percents is to find 1% or 10% of a number. You can do this by moving the decimal point in the number.

1% of 45 = 45.0

= 0.45

To find 1% of a number, move the decimal point two places to the left.

10% of 45 = 45.0

= 4.5

To find 10% of a number, move the decimal point one place to the left.

EXAMPLE 3 Estimating with Simple Percents

Use 1% or 10% to estimate the percent of each number.

A **3% of 59**

59 is about 60, so find 3% of 60.

1% of 60 = 60.0

3% of 60 = 3 · 0.60 = 1.8 *3% equals 3 · 1%.*

3% of 59 is about 1.8.

B **18% of 45**

18% is about 20%, so find 20% of 45.

10% of 45 = 45.0

20% of 45 = 2 · 4.5 = 9.0 *20% equals 2 · 10%.*

18% of 45 is about 9.

EXAMPLE 4 *Consumer Math Application*

Eric and Selena spent $25.85 for their meals at a restaurant. About how much money should they leave for a 15% tip?

Since $25.85 is about $26, find 15% of $26.

15% = 10% + 5% *Think: 15% is 10% plus 5%.*

10% of $26 = $2.60

5% of $26 = $2.60 ÷ 2 = $1.30 *5% is $\frac{1}{2}$ of 10%, so divide $2.60 by 2.*

$2.60 + $1.30 = $3.90 *Add the 10% and 5% estimates.*

Eric and Selena should leave about $3.90 for a 15% tip.

Think and Discuss

1. **Describe** two ways to estimate 51% of 88.
2. **Explain** why you might divide by 7 or multiply by $\frac{1}{7}$ to estimate a 15% tip.
3. **Give an example** of a situation in which an estimate of a percent is sufficient and a situation in which an exact percent is necessary.

6-3 Exercises

go.hrw.com
Homework Help Online
KEYWORD: MS7 6-3
Parent Resources Online
KEYWORD: MS7 Parent

GUIDED PRACTICE

See Example 1

Use a fraction to estimate the percent of each number.

1. 30% of 86 **2.** 52% of 83 **3.** 10% of 48 **4.** 27% of 63

See Example 2

5. Darden has $35 to spend on a backpack. He finds one on sale for 35% off the regular price of $43.99. Does Darden have enough money to buy the backpack? Explain.

See Example 3

Use 1% or 10% to estimate the percent of each number.

6. 5% of 82 **7.** 39% of 19 **8.** 21% of 68 **9.** 7% of 109

See Example 4

10. Mrs. Coronado spent $23 on a manicure. About how much money should she leave for a 15% tip?

INDEPENDENT PRACTICE

See Example 1

Use a fraction to estimate the percent of each number.

11. 8% of 261 **12.** 34% of 93 **13.** 53% of 142 **14.** 23% of 98

15. 51% of 432 **16.** 18% of 42 **17.** 11% of 132 **18.** 54% of 39

See Example 2

19. Consumer Math A pair of shoes at The Value Store costs $20. Fancy Feet has the same shoes on sale for 25% off the regular price of $23.99. Which store offers the better price on the shoes?

See Example 3

Use 1% or 10% to estimate the percent of each number.

20. 41% of 16 **21.** 8% of 310 **22.** 83% of 70 **23.** 2% of 634

24. 58% of 81 **25.** 24% of 49 **26.** 11% of 99 **27.** 63% of 39

See Example 4

28. Marc's lunch cost $8.92. He wants to leave a 15% tip for the service. About how much should his tip be?

PRACTICE AND PROBLEM SOLVING

Extra Practice
See page 737.

Estimate.

29. 31% of 180 **30.** 18% of 150 **31.** 3% of 96 **32.** 2% of 198

33. 78% of 90 **34.** 52% of 234 **35.** 19% of 75 **36.** 4% of 311

37. The new package of Marti's Snacks contains 20% more snack mix than the old package. There were 22 ounces of snack mix in the old package. About how many ounces are in the new package?

38. Frameworks charges $60.85 for framing. Including the 7% sales tax, about how much will it cost to have a painting framed?

39. Multi-Step Camden's lunch cost $11.67, and he left a $2.00 tip. About how much more than 15% of the bill did Camden leave for the tip?

40. Sports Last season, Ali had a hit 19.3% of the times he came to bat. If Ali batted 82 times last season, about how many hits did he have?

41. Business The table shows the results of a survey about the Internet. The number of people interviewed was 391.

a. Estimate the number of people willing to give out their e-mail address.

b. Estimate the number of people not willing to give out their credit card number.

Information People Are Willing to Give Out on the Internet

Information	Percent of People
E-mail address	78
Work phone number	53
Street address	49
Home phone number	35
Credit card number	33
Social Security number	11

42. Multi-Step Sandi earns $43,000 per year. This year, she plans to spend about 27% of her income on rent.

a. About how much does Sandi plan to spend on rent this year?

b. About how much does she plan to spend on rent each month?

43. Write a Problem Use information from the table in Exercise 41 to write a problem that can be solved by using estimation of a percent.

44. Write About It Explain why it might be important to know whether your estimate of a percent is too high or too low. Give an example.

45. Challenge Use the table from Exercise 41 to estimate how many more people will give out their work phone number than their Social Security number. Show your work using two different methods.

TEST PREP and Spiral Review

46. Multiple Choice About 65% of the people answering a survey said that they have read a "blog," or Web log, online. Sixty-six people were surveyed. Which is the best estimate of the number of people surveyed who have read a blog?

Ⓐ 30 Ⓑ 35 Ⓒ 45 Ⓓ 50

47. Short Response Ryan's dinner bill is $35.00. He wants to leave a 15% tip. Explain how to use mental math to determine how much he should leave as a tip.

Find each product. (Lesson 3-3)

48. $0.8 \cdot 96$ **49.** $30 \cdot 0.04$ **50.** $1.6 \cdot 900$ **51.** $0.005 \cdot 75$

52. Brandi's room was painted in a color that is a blend of 3 parts red paint and 2 parts white paint. How many quarts of white paint does Brandi need to mix with 6 quarts of red paint to match the paint in her room? (Lesson 5-5)

Hands-On LAB 6-4

Explore Percents

Use with Lesson 6-4

go.hrw.com
Lab Resources Online
KEYWORD: MS7 Lab6

REMEMBER

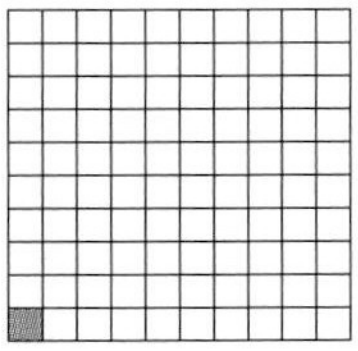
1% is 1 out of 100.

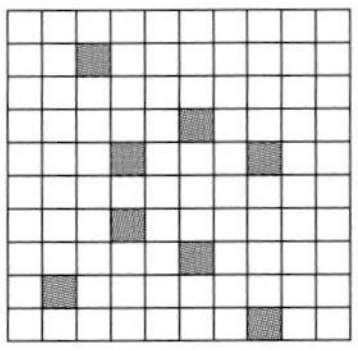
8% is 8 out of 100.

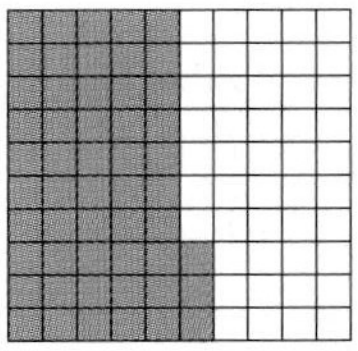
53% is 53 out of 100.

You can use 10-by-10 grids to model percents, including those less than 1 or greater than 100.

Activity 1

1. Use 10-by-10 grids to model 132%.

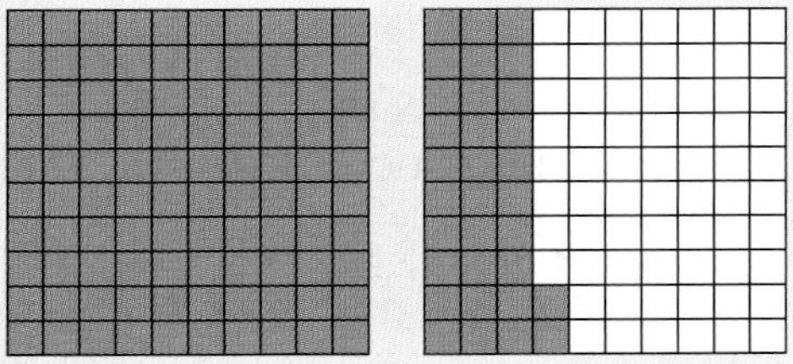

Think: 132% means 132 out of 100.

Shade 100 squares plus 32 squares to model 132%.

2. Use a 10-by-10 grid to model 0.5%.

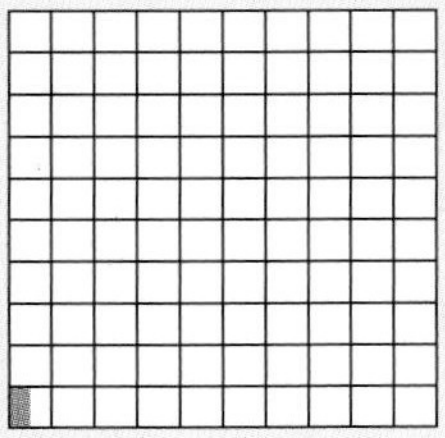

Think: One square equals 1%, so $\frac{1}{2}$ of one square equals 0.5%.

Shade $\frac{1}{2}$ of one square to model 0.5%.

Think and Discuss

1. Explain how to model 36.75% on a 10-by-10 grid.

2. How can you model 0.7%? Explain your answer.

Try This

Use 10-by-10 grids to model each percent.

1. 280% **2.** $16\frac{1}{2}$% **3.** 0.25% **4.** 65% **5.** 140.75%

You can use a percent bar and a quantity bar to model finding a percent of a number.

Activity 2

1 Find 65% of 60.

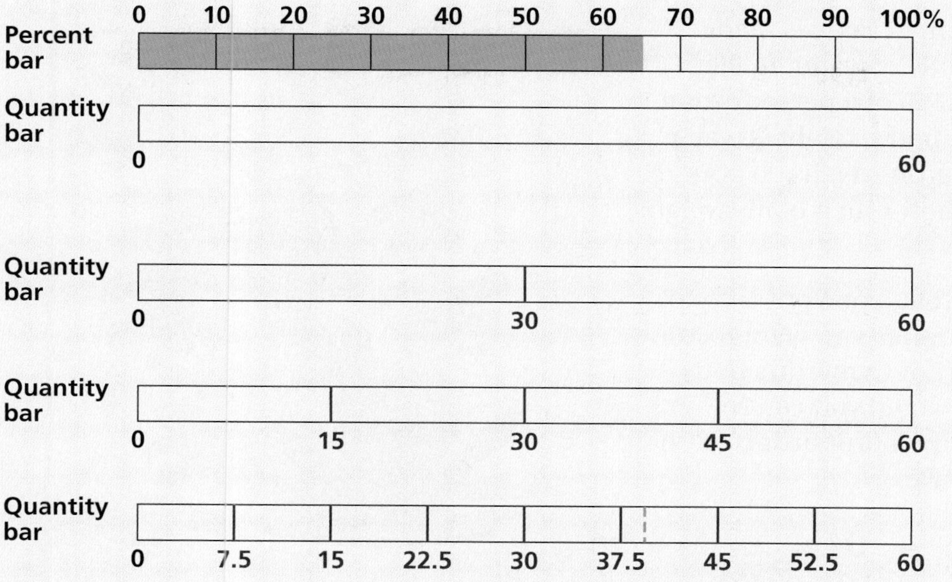

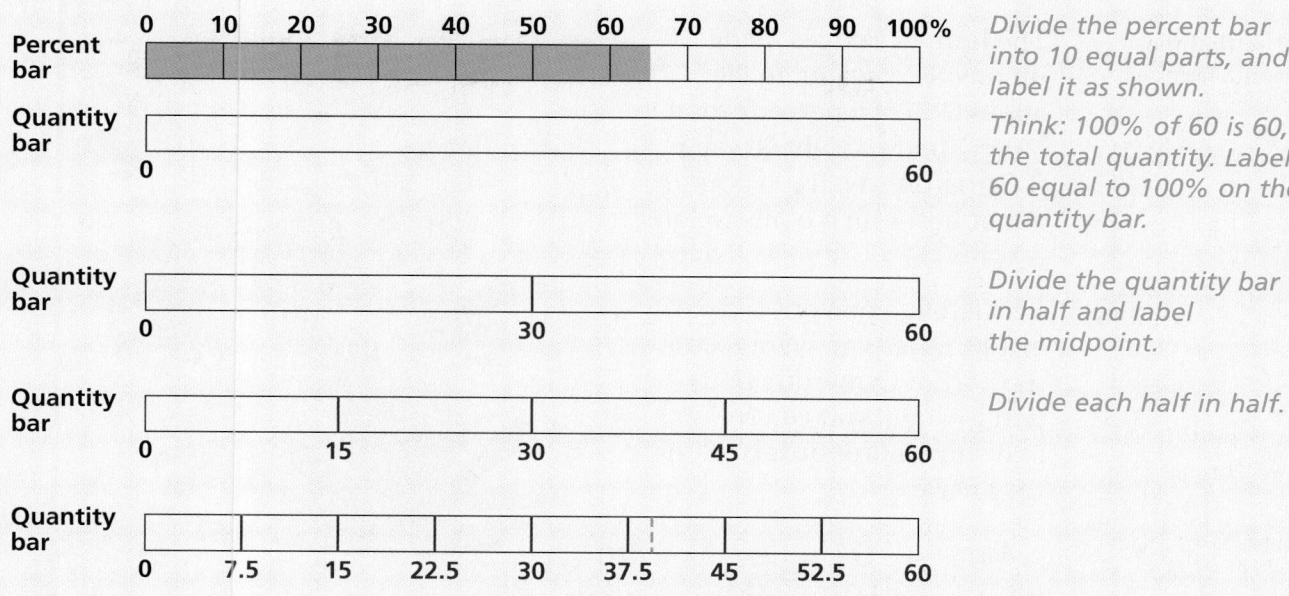

Divide the percent bar into 10 equal parts, and label it as shown.

Think: 100% of 60 is 60, the total quantity. Label 60 equal to 100% on the quantity bar.

Divide the quantity bar in half and label the midpoint.

Divide each half in half.

What point on the quantity bar lines up with 65% on the percent bar?
It appears that 65% of 60 is about 39. *Check by multiplying: 0.65 • 60 = 39.*

2 Find 125% of 60. *Think: 125% of a whole is greater than the whole.*
Extend the bars to find 125% of a number.

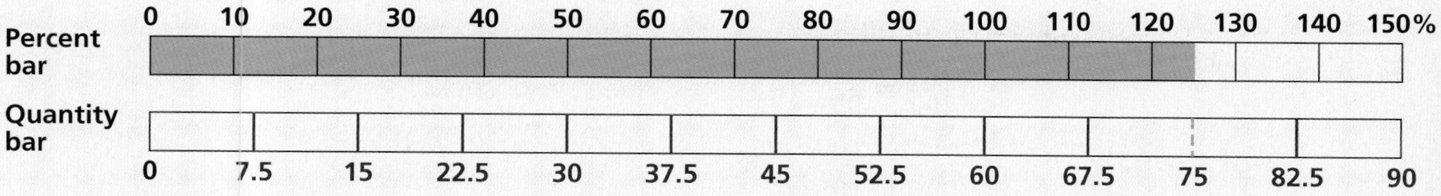

What point on the quantity bar lines up with 125% on the percent bar?
It appears that 125% of 60 is about 75. *Check by multiplying 1.25 • 60 = 75.*

Think and Discuss

1. Explain how to use a percent bar and a quantity bar to find a percent of a number.
2. Explain how using a percent bar and a quantity bar to model finding a percent of a number involves estimation.

Try This

Use a percent bar and a quantity bar to find the percent of each number. Use a calculator to check your answers.

1. 75% of 36 **2.** 60% of 15 **3.** 135% of 40 **4.** 112% of 25 **5.** 25% of 75

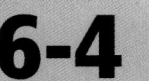

6-4 Percent of a Number

Learn to find the percent of a number.

The human body is made up mostly of water. In fact, about 67% of a person's total (100%) body weight is water. If Cameron weighs 90 pounds, about how much of his weight is water?

Recall that a percent is a part of 100. Since you want to know the part of Cameron's body that is water, you can set up and solve a proportion to find the answer.

$$\text{Part} \rightarrow \frac{67}{100} = \frac{n}{90} \leftarrow \text{Part}$$
$$\text{Whole} \rightarrow \qquad \qquad \leftarrow \text{Whole}$$

EXAMPLE 1 Using Proportions to Find Percents of Numbers

Find the percent of each number.

A 67% of 90

$\frac{67}{100} = \frac{n}{90}$ *Write a proportion.*

$67 \cdot 90 = 100 \cdot n$ *Set the cross products equal.*

$6{,}030 = 100n$ *Multiply.*

$\frac{6{,}030}{100} = \frac{100n}{100}$ *Divide each side by 100 to isolate the variable.*

$60.3 = n$

67% of 90 is 60.3.

B 145% of 210

$\frac{145}{100} = \frac{n}{210}$ *Write a proportion.*

$145 \cdot 210 = 100 \cdot n$ *Set the cross products equal.*

$30{,}450 = 100n$ *Multiply.*

$\frac{30{,}450}{100} = \frac{100n}{100}$ *Divide each side by 100 to isolate the variable.*

$304.5 = n$

145% of 210 is 304.5.

Helpful Hint

When solving a problem with a percent greater than 100%, the *part* will be greater than the *whole*.

In addition to using proportions, you can find the percent of a number by using decimal equivalents.

EXAMPLE 2 Using Decimal Equivalents to Find Percents of Numbers

Find the percent of each number. Check whether your answer is reasonable.

A **8% of 50**

8% of $50 = 0.08 \cdot 50$ — *Write the percent as a decimal.*

$= 4$ — *Multiply.*

Model

Since 10% of 50 is 5, a reasonable answer for 8% of 50 is 4.

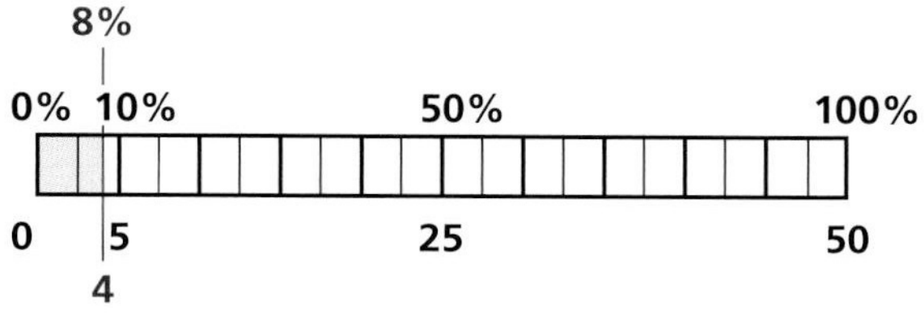

B **0.5% of 36**

0.5% of $36 = 0.005 \cdot 36$ — *Write the percent as a decimal.*

$= 0.18$ — *Multiply.*

Estimate

1% of 36 = 0.36, so 0.5% of 36 is half of 0.36. Thus 0.18 is a reasonable answer.

EXAMPLE 3 *Geography Application*

Earth's total land area is about 57,308,738 mi^2. The land area of Asia is about 30% of this total. What is the approximate land area of Asia to the nearest square mile?

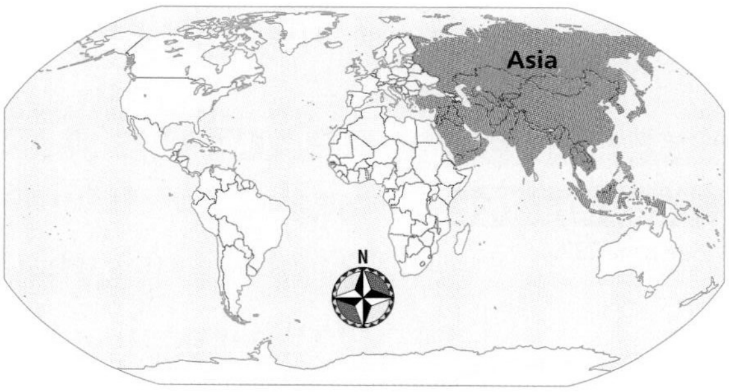

Find 30% of 57,308,738.

$0.30 \cdot 57{,}308{,}738$ — *Write the percent as a decimal.*

$= 17{,}192{,}621.4$ — *Multiply.*

The land area of Asia is about 17,192,621 mi^2.

Think and Discuss

1. **Explain** how to set up a proportion to find 150% of a number.
2. **Describe** a situation in which you might need to find a percent of a number.

6-4 Exercises

go.hrw.com
Homework Help Online
KEYWORD: MS7 6-4
Parent Resources Online
KEYWORD: MS7 Parent

GUIDED PRACTICE

See Example 1

Find the percent of each number.

1. 30% of 80 **2.** 38% of 400 **3.** 200% of 10 **4.** 180% of 90

See Example 2

Find the percent of each number. Check whether your answer is reasonable.

5. 16% of 50 **6.** 7% of 200 **7.** 47% of 900 **8.** 40% of 75

See Example 3

9. Of the 450 students at Miller Middle School, 38% ride the bus to school. How many students ride the bus to school?

INDEPENDENT PRACTICE

See Example 1

Find the percent of each number.

10. 80% of 35 **11.** 16% of 70 **12.** 150% of 80 **13.** 118% of 3,000

14. 5% of 58 **15.** 1% of 4 **16.** 103% of 50 **17.** 225% of 8

See Example 2

Find the percent of each number. Check whether your answer is reasonable.

18. 9% of 40 **19.** 20% of 65 **20.** 36% of 50 **21.** 2.9% of 60

22. 5% of 12 **23.** 220% of 18 **24.** 0.2% of 160 **25.** 155% of 8

See Example 3

26. In 2004, there were 19,396 bulldogs registered by the American Kennel Club. Approximately 86% of this number were registered in 2003. About how many bulldogs were registered in 2003?

PRACTICE AND PROBLEM SOLVING

Extra Practice
See page 737.

Solve.

27. 60% of 10 is what number? **28.** What number is 25% of 160?

29. What number is 15% of 30? **30.** 10% of 84 is what number?

31. 25% of 47 is what number? **32.** What number is 59% of 20?

33. What number is 125% of 4,100? **34.** 150% of 150 is what number?

Find the percent of each number. If necessary, round to the nearest tenth.

35. 160% of 50 **36.** 350% of 20 **37.** 480% of 25 **38.** 115% of 200

39. 18% of 3.4 **40.** 0.9% of 43 **41.** 98% of 4.3 **42.** 1.22% of 56

43. Consumer Math Fun Tees is offering a 30% discount on all merchandise. Find the amount of discount on a T-shirt that was originally priced at $15.99.

44. Multi-Step Shoe Style is discounting everything in the store by 25%. What is the sale price of a pair of flip-flops that was originally priced at $10?

LINK

Physical Science

Pure gold is a soft metal that scratches easily. To make the gold in jewelry more durable, it is often combined with other metals, such as copper and nickel.

45. Nutrition The United States Department of Agriculture recommends that women should eat 25 g of fiber each day. A granola bar provides 9% of that amount. How many grams of fiber does it contain?

46. Physical Science The percent of pure gold in 14-karat gold is about 58.3%. A 14-karat gold ring weighs 5.6 grams. About how many grams of pure gold are in the ring?

47. Earth Science The apparent magnitude of the star Mimosa is 1.25. Spica, another star, has an apparent magnitude that is 78.4% of Mimosa's. What is Spica's apparent magnitude?

48. Multi-Step Trahn purchased a pair of slacks for \$39.95 and a jacket for \$64.00. The sales tax rate on his purchases was 5.5%. Find the total cost of Trahn's purchases, including sales tax.

49. The graph shows the results of a student survey about computers. Use the graph to predict how many students in your class have a computer at home.

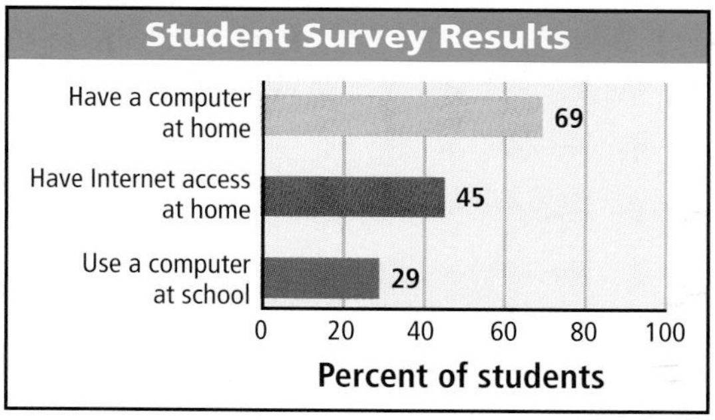

50. What's the Error? A student used the proportion $\frac{n}{100} = \frac{5}{26}$ to find 5% of 26. What did the student do wrong?

51. Write About It Describe two ways to find 18% of 40.

52. Challenge François's starting pay was \$6.25 per hour. During his annual review, he received a 5% raise. Find François's pay raise to the nearest cent and the amount he will earn with his raise. Then find 105% of \$6.25. What can you conclude?

Test Prep and Spiral Review

53. Multiple Choice Of the 875 students enrolled at Sycamore Valley Middle School, 48% are boys. How many of the students are boys?

Ⓐ 250 Ⓑ 310 Ⓒ 420 Ⓓ 440

54. Gridded Response A children's multivitamin has 80% of the recommended daily allowance of zinc. The recommended daily allowance is 15 mg. How many milligrams of zinc does the vitamin provide?

Find each unit rate. (Lesson 5-2)

55. Monica buys 3 pounds of peaches for \$5.25. What is the cost per pound?

56. Kevin types 295 words in 5 minutes. At what rate does Kevin type?

Write each decimal as a percent. (Lesson 6-2)

57. 0.0125 **58.** 0.26 **59.** 0.389 **60.** 0.099 **61.** 0.407

6-5 Solving Percent Problems

Learn to solve problems involving percents.

Sloths may seem lazy, but their extremely slow movement helps them seem almost invisible to predators. Sloths sleep an average of 16.5 hours per day. To find out what percent of a 24-hour day 16.5 hours is, you can use a proportion or an equation.

Proportion method

$$\text{Part} \rightarrow \frac{n}{100} = \frac{16.5}{24} \leftarrow \text{Part}$$
$$\text{Whole} \rightarrow 100 \qquad 24 \leftarrow \text{Whole}$$

$$n \cdot 24 = 100 \cdot 16.5$$
$$24n = 1{,}650$$
$$n = 68.75$$

Equation method

What **percent** of **24** is **16.5**?

$$n \cdot 24 = 16.5$$
$$n = \frac{16.5}{24}$$
$$n = 0.6875$$

Sloths spend about **69%** of the day sleeping!

EXAMPLE 1 Using Proportions to Solve Problems with Percents

Solve.

A What percent of 90 is 45?

$\frac{n}{100} = \frac{45}{90}$ *Write a proportion.*

$n \cdot 90 = 100 \cdot 45$ *Set the cross products equal.*

$90n = 4{,}500$ *Multiply.*

$\frac{90n}{90} = \frac{4{,}500}{90}$ *Divide each side by 90 to isolate the variable.*

$n = 50$

50% of 90 is 45.

B 12 is 8% of what number?

$\frac{8}{100} = \frac{12}{n}$ *Write a proportion.*

$8 \cdot n = 100 \cdot 12$ *Set the cross products equal.*

$8n = 1{,}200$ *Multiply.*

$\frac{8n}{8} = \frac{1{,}200}{8}$ *Divide each side by 8 to isolate the variable.*

$n = 150$

12 is 8% of 150.

EXAMPLE 2 Using Equations to Solve Problems with Percents

Solve.

A **What percent of 75 is 105?**

$n \cdot 75 = 105$ *Write an equation.*

$\frac{n \cdot 75}{75} = \frac{105}{75}$ *Divide each side by 75 to isolate the variable.*

$n = 1.4$

$n = 140\%$ *Write the decimal as a percent.*

140% of 75 is 105.

B **48 is 20% of what number?**

$48 = 20\% \cdot n$ *Write an equation.*

$48 = 0.2 \cdot n$ *Write 20% as a decimal.*

$\frac{48}{0.2} = \frac{0.2 \cdot n}{0.2}$ *Divide each side by 0.2 to isolate the variable.*

$240 = n$

48 is 20% of 240.

EXAMPLE 3 Finding Sales Tax

Helpful Hint

The *sales tax rate* is the percent used to calculate sales tax.

Ravi bought a T-shirt with a retail sales price of $12 and paid $0.99 sales tax. What is the sales tax rate where Ravi bought the T-shirt?

Restate the question: What percent of $12 is $0.99?

$\frac{n}{100} = \frac{0.99}{12}$ *Write a proportion.*

$n \cdot 12 = 100 \cdot 0.99$ *Set the cross products equal.*

$12n = 99$ *Multiply.*

$\frac{12n}{12} = \frac{99}{12}$ *Divide each side by 12.*

$n = 8.25$

8.25% of $12 is $0.99. The sales tax rate where Ravi bought the T-shirt is 8.25%.

Think and Discuss

1. **Describe** two methods for solving percent problems.
2. **Explain** whether you prefer to use the proportion method or the equation method when solving percent problems.
3. **Tell** what the first step is in solving a sales tax problem.

6-5 Exercises

go.hrw.com
Homework Help Online
KEYWORD: MS7 6-5
Parent Resources Online
KEYWORD: MS7 Parent

GUIDED PRACTICE

Solve.

See Example 1
1. What percent of 100 is 25?
2. What percent of 5 is 4?
3. 6 is 10% of what number?
4. 8 is 20% of what number?

See Example 2
5. What percent of 50 is 9?
6. What percent of 30 is 27?
7. 7 is 14% of what number?
8. 30 is 15% of what number?

See Example 3
9. The sales tax on a $120 skateboard at Surf 'n' Skate is $9.60. What is the sales tax rate?

INDEPENDENT PRACTICE

Solve.

See Example 1
10. What percent of 60 is 40?
11. What percent of 48 is 16?
12. What percent of 45 is 9?
13. What percent of 6 is 18?
14. 56 is 140% of what number?
15. 45 is 20% of what number?

See Example 2
16. What percent of 80 is 10?
17. What percent of 12.4 is 12.4?
18. 18 is 15% of what number?
19. 9 is 30% of what number?
20. 210% of what number is 147?
21. 8.8 is 40% of what number?

See Example 3
22. A 12-pack of cinnamon-scented pencils sells for $3.00 at a school booster club sale. What is the sales tax rate if the total cost of the pencils is $3.21?

PRACTICE AND PROBLEM SOLVING

Extra Practice
See page 738.

Solve. Round to the nearest tenth, if necessary.

23. 5 is what percent of 9?
24. What is 45% of 39?
25. 55 is 80% of what number?
26. 12 is what percent of 19?
27. What is 155% of 50?
28. 5.8 is 0.9% of what number?
29. 36% of what number is 57?
30. What percent of 64 is 40?

31. **Multi-Step** The advertised cost of admission to a water park in a nearby city is $25 per student. A student paid $30 for admission and received $3.75 in change. What is the sales tax rate in that city?

32. **Consumer Math** The table shows the cost of sunscreen purchased in Beach City and Desert City with and without sales tax. Which city has a greater sales tax rate? Give the sales tax rate for each city.

	Cost	Cost + Tax
Beach City	$10	$10.83
Desert City	$5	$5.42

LINK

Music

The viola family is made up of the cello, violin, and viola. Of the three instruments, the cello is the largest.

33. **Critical Thinking** What number is always used when you set up a proportion to solve a percent problem? Explain.

34. **Health** The circle graph shows the approximate distribution of blood types among people in the United States.

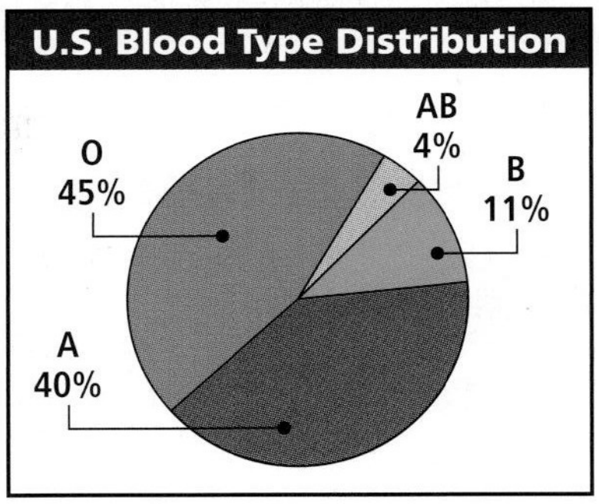

   a. In a survey, 126 people had type O blood. Predict how many people were surveyed.

   b. How many of the people surveyed had type AB blood?

35. **Music** Beethoven wrote 9 trios for the piano, violin, and cello. These trios make up 20% of the chamber music pieces Beethoven wrote. How many pieces of chamber music did he write?

36. **History** The length of Abraham Lincoln's first inaugural speech was 3,635 words. The length of his second inaugural speech was about 19.3% of the length of his first speech. About how long was Lincoln's second speech?

37. **What's the Question?** The first lap of an auto race is 2,500 m. This is 10% of the total race distance. The answer is 10. What is the question?

38. **Write About It** If 35 is 110% of a number, is the number greater than or less than 35? Explain.

39. **Challenge** Kayleen has been offered two jobs. The first job offers an annual salary of $32,000. The second job offers an annual salary of $10,000 plus 8% commission on all of her sales. How much money per month would Kayleen need to make in sales to earn enough commission to make more money at the second job?

Test Prep and Spiral Review

40. **Multiple Choice** Thirty children from an after-school club went to the matinee. This is 20% of the children in the club. How many children are in the club?

   Ⓐ 6   Ⓑ 67   Ⓒ 150   Ⓓ 600

41. **Gridded Response** Jason saves 30% of his monthly paycheck for college. He earned $250 last month. How many dollars did he save for college?

Divide. (Lessons 3-4 and 3-5)

42. −3.92 ÷ 7   43. 10.68 ÷ 3   44. 23.2 ÷ 0.2   45. 19.52 ÷ 6.1

Find the percent of each number. If necessary, round to the nearest hundredth. (Lesson 6-4)

46. 45% of 26   47. 22% of 30   48. 15% of 17   49. 68% of 98

READY TO GO ON?

Quiz for Lessons 6-1 Through 6-5

6-1 Percents

Write each percent as a fraction in simplest form.

1. 9% **2.** 43% **3.** 5% **4.** 18%

Write each percent as a decimal.

5. 22% **6.** 90% **7.** 29% **8.** 5%

6-2 Fractions, Decimals, and Percents

Write each decimal as a percent.

9. 0.85 **10.** 0.026 **11.** 0.1111 **12.** 0.56

Write each fraction as a percent. Round to the nearest tenth of a percent, if necessary.

13. $\frac{14}{81}$ **14.** $\frac{25}{52}$ **15.** $\frac{55}{78}$ **16.** $\frac{13}{32}$

6-3 Estimate with Percents

Estimate.

17. 49% of 46 **18.** 9% of 25 **19.** 36% of 150 **20.** 5% of 60

21. 18% of 80 **22.** 26% of 115 **23.** 91% of 300 **24.** 42% of 197

25. Carlton spent $21.85 on lunch for himself and a friend. About how much should he leave for a 15% tip?

6-4 Percent of a Number

Find the percent of each number.

26. 25% of 84 **27.** 52% of 300 **28.** 0.5% of 40 **29.** 160% of 450

30. 41% of 122 **31.** 178% of 35 **32.** 29% of 88 **33.** 80% of 176

34. Students get a 15% discount off the original prices at the Everything Fluorescent store during its back-to-school sale. Find the amount of discount on fluorescent notebooks originally priced at $7.99.

6-5 Solving Percent Problems

Solve. Round to the nearest tenth, if necessary.

35. 14 is 44% of what number? **36.** 22 is what percent of 900?

37. 99 is what percent of 396? **38.** 75 is 24% of what number?

39. The sales tax on a $105 digital camera is $7.15. What is the sales tax rate?

Focus on Problem Solving

Make a Plan

- **Estimate or find an exact answer**

Sometimes an estimate is sufficient when you are solving a problem. Other times you need to find an exact answer. Before you try to solve a problem, you should decide whether an estimate will be sufficient. Usually if a problem includes the word *about,* then you can estimate the answer.

Read each problem. Decide whether you need an exact answer or whether you can solve the problem with an estimate. Explain how you know.

1. Barry has $21.50 left from his allowance. He wants to buy a book for $5.85 and a CD for $14.99. Assuming these prices include tax, does Barry have enough money left to buy both the book and the CD?

2. Last weekend Valerie practiced playing the drums for 3 hours. This is 40% of the total time she spent practicing last week. How much time did Valerie spend practicing last week?

3. Amber is shopping for a winter coat. She finds one that costs $157. The coat is on sale and is discounted 25% today only. About how much money will Amber save if she buys the coat today?

4. Marcus is planning a budget. He plans to spend less than 35% of his allowance each week on entertainment. Last week Marcus spent $7.42 on entertainment. If Marcus gets $20.00 each week, did he stay within his budget?

5. An upright piano is on sale for 20% off the original price. The original price is $9,840. What is the sale price?

6. The Mapleton Middle School band has 41 students. Six of the students in the band play percussion instruments. Do more than 15% of the students play percussion instruments?

6-6 Percent of Change

Learn to solve problems involving percent of change.

Vocabulary

percent of change

percent of increase

percent of decrease

The U.S. Consumer Product Safety Commission has reported that, in 2000, 4,390 injuries related to motorized scooters were treated in hospital emergency rooms. This was a 230% increase from 1999's report of 1,330 injuries.

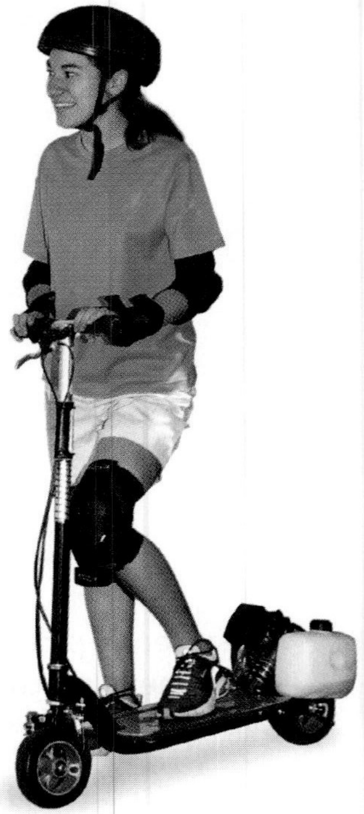

A percent can be used to describe an amount of change. The **percent of change** is the amount, stated as a percent, that a number increases or decreases. If the amount goes up, it is a **percent of increase**. If the amount goes down, it is a **percent of decrease**.

You can find the percent of change by using the following formula.

$$\text{percent of change} = \frac{\text{amount of change}}{\text{original amount}}$$

EXAMPLE 1 **Finding Percent of Change**

Find each percent of change. Round answers to the nearest tenth of a percent, if necessary.

A **27 is decreased to 20.**

$27 - 20 = 7$ *Find the amount of change.*

$\text{percent of change} = \frac{7}{27}$ *Substitute values into formula.*

≈ 0.259259 *Divide.*

$\approx 25.9\%$ *Write as a percent. Round.*

The percent of decrease is about 25.9%.

B **32 is increased to 67.**

$67 - 32 = 35$ *Find the amount of change.*

$\text{percent of change} = \frac{35}{32}$ *Substitute values into formula.*

$= 1.09375$ *Divide.*

$\approx 109.4\%$ *Write as a percent. Round.*

The percent of increase is about 109.4%.

Helpful Hint

When a number is decreased, subtract the new amount from the original amount to find the amount of change. When a number is increased, subtract the original amount from the new amount.

EXAMPLE 2 Using Percent of Change

The regular price of an MP3 player at TechSource is $79.99. This week the MP3 player is on sale for 25% off. What is the sale price?

Step 1: Find the amount of the discount.

$25\% \cdot 79.99 = d$ *Think: 25% of $79.99 is what number?*

$0.25 \cdot 79.99 = d$ *Write the percent as a decimal.*

$19.9975 = d$

$\$20.00 \approx d$ *Round to the nearest cent.*

The amount of the discount is $20.00.

Step 2: Find the sale price.

regular price	−	amount of discount	=	sale price
$79.99	−	$20.00	=	$59.99

The sale price is $59.99.

EXAMPLE 3 *Business Application*

Winter Wonders buys snow globes from a manufacturer for $9.20 each and sells them at a 95% increase in price. What is the retail price of the snow globes?

Step 1: Find the amount n of increase.

Think: 95% of $9.20 is what number?

$95\% \cdot 9.20 = n$

$0.95 \cdot 9.20 = n$ *Write the percent as a decimal.*

$8.74 = n$

Step 2: Find the retail price.

wholesale price	+	amount of increase	=	retail price
$9.20	+	$8.74	=	$17.94

The retail price of the snow globes is $17.94 each.

Think and Discuss

1. **Explain** what is meant by a 100% decrease.
2. **Give an example** in which the amount of increase is greater than the original amount. What do you know about the percent of increase?

6-6 Exercises

go.hrw.com
Homework Help Online
KEYWORD: MS7 6-6
Parent Resources Online
KEYWORD: MS7 Parent

GUIDED PRACTICE

See Example 1

Find each percent of change. Round answers to the nearest tenth of a percent, if necessary.

1. 25 is decreased to 18.

2. 36 is increased to 84.

3. 62 is decreased to 52.

4. 28 is increased to 96.

See Example 2

5. The regular price of a sweater is \$42.99. It is on sale for 20% off. Find the sale price.

See Example 3

6. Business The retail price of a pair of shoes is a 98% increase from its wholesale price. The wholesale price of the shoes is \$12.50. What is the retail price?

INDEPENDENT PRACTICE

See Example 1

Find each percent of change. Round answers to the nearest tenth of a percent, if necessary.

7. 72 is decreased to 45.

8. 55 is increased to 90.

9. 180 is decreased to 140.

10. 230 is increased to 250.

See Example 2

11. A skateboard that sells for \$65 is on sale for 15% off. Find the sale price.

See Example 3

12. Business A jeweler buys a ring from an artisan for \$85. He sells the ring in his store at a 135% increase in price. What is the retail price of the ring?

PRACTICE AND PROBLEM SOLVING

Extra Practice
See page 738.

Find each percent of change, amount of increase, or amount of decrease. Round answers to the nearest tenth, if necessary.

13. \$8.80 is increased to \$17.60.

14. 6.2 is decreased to 5.9.

15. 39.2 is increased to 56.3.

16. \$325 is decreased to \$100.

17. 75 is decreased by 40%.

18. 28 is increased by 150%.

19. A water tank holds 45 gallons of water. A new water tank can hold 25% more water. What is the capacity of the new water tank?

20. Business Marla makes stretchy beaded purses and sells them to Bangles ‘n’ Beads for \$7 each. Bangles ‘n’ Beads makes a profit of 28% on each purse. Find the retail price of the purses.

21. Multi-Step A store is discounting all of its stock. The original price of a pair of sunglasses was \$44.95. The sale price is \$26.97. At this discount rate, what was the original price of a bathing suit that has a sale price of \$28.95?

22. Critical Thinking Explain why a change in price from \$20 to \$10 is a 50% decrease, but a change in price from \$10 to \$20 is a 100% increase.

Economics LINK

23. The information at right shows the expenses for the Kramer family for one year.
    a. The Kramers spent \$2,905 on auto expenses. What was their income for the year?
    b. How much money was spent on household expenses?
    c. The Kramers pay \$14,400 per year on their mortgage. What percent of their household expenses is this? Round your answer to the nearest tenth.

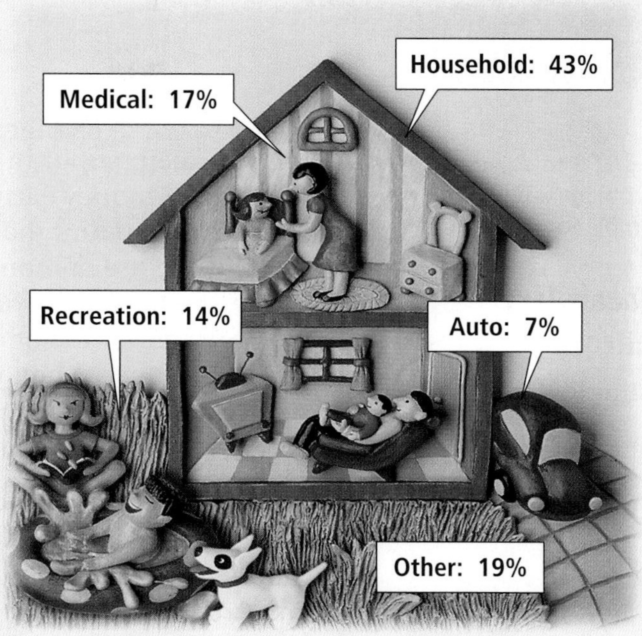

24. United States health expenses were \$428.7 billion in 1985 and \$991.4 billion in 1995. What was the percent of increase in health expenses during this ten-year period? Round your answer to the nearest tenth of a percent.

25. In 1990, the total amount of energy consumed for transportation in the United States was 22,540 trillion British thermal units (Btu). From 1950 to 1990, there was a 165% increase in energy consumed for transportation. About how many Btu of energy were consumed in 1950?

26. **Challenge** In 1960, 21.5% of U.S. households did not have a telephone. This statistic decreased by 75.8% between 1960 and 1990. In 1990, what percent of U.S. households had a telephone?

TEST PREP and Spiral Review

27. **Multiple Choice** Find the percent of change if the price of a 20-ounce bottle of water increases from \$0.85 to \$1.25. Round to the nearest tenth.

    (A) 47.1% (B) 40.0% (C) 32.0% (D) 1.7%

28. **Extended Response** A store buys jeans from the manufacturer for \$30 each and sells them at a 50% increase in price. At the end of the season, the store puts the jeans on sale for 50% off. Is the sale price \$30? Explain your reasoning.

Write each mixed number as an improper fraction. (Lesson 2-9)

29. $3\frac{2}{9}$ 30. $6\frac{2}{3}$ 31. $7\frac{1}{4}$ 32. $3\frac{2}{5}$ 33. $24\frac{1}{3}$

Convert each measure. (Lesson 5-6)

34. 34 mi to feet 35. 52 oz to pounds 36. 164 lb to tons

6-7 Simple Interest

Learn to solve problems involving simple interest.

Vocabulary

interest

simple interest

principal

When you keep money in a savings account, your money earns *interest*. **Interest** is an amount that is collected or paid for the use of money. For example, the bank pays you interest to use your money to conduct its business. Likewise, when you borrow money from the bank, the bank collects interest on its loan to you.

One type of interest, called **simple interest**, is money paid only on the *principal*. The **principal** is the amount of money deposited or borrowed. To solve problems involving simple interest, you can use the following formula.

$$I = P \cdot r \cdot t$$

Interest — I

Principal — P

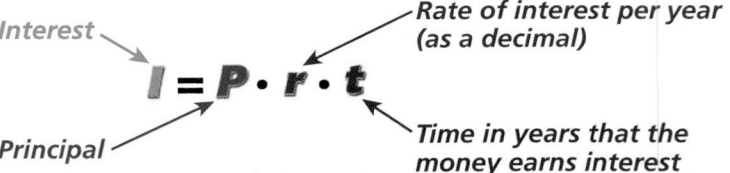

Rate of interest per year (as a decimal) — r

Time in years that the money earns interest — t

EXAMPLE 1 Using the Simple Interest Formula

Find each missing value.

A $I = \square$, $P = \$225$, $r = 3\%$, $t = 2$ years

$I = P \cdot r \cdot t$

$I = 225 \cdot 0.03 \cdot 2$ *Substitute. Use 0.03 for 3%.*

$I = 13.5$ *Multiply.*

The simple interest is \$13.50.

B $I = \$300$, $P = \$1{,}000$, $r = \square$, $t = 5$ years

$I = P \cdot r \cdot t$

$300 = 1{,}000 \cdot r \cdot 5$ *Substitute.*

$300 = 5{,}000r$ *Multiply.*

$\frac{300}{5{,}000} = \frac{5{,}000r}{5{,}000}$ *Divide by 5,000 to isolate the variable.*

$0.06 = r$

The interest rate is 6%.

EXAMPLE 2 **PROBLEM SOLVING APPLICATION**

PROBLEM SOLVING

Olivia deposits \$7,000 in an account that earns 7% simple interest. About how long will it take for her account balance to reach \$8,000?

1 Understand the Problem

Rewrite the question as a statement:

- Find the number of years it will take for Olivia's account balance to reach \$8,000.

List the **important information:**

- The principal is \$7,000.
- The interest rate is 7%.
- Her account balance will be \$8,000.

2 Make a Plan

Olivia's account balance A includes the principal plus the interest: $A = P + I$. Once you solve for I, you can use $I = P \cdot r \cdot t$ to find the time.

3 Solve

$$\begin{aligned} A &= P + I \\ 8{,}000 &= 7{,}000 + I && \textit{Substitute.} \\ \underline{-7{,}000} &\quad \underline{-7{,}000} && \textit{Subtract to isolate the variable.} \\ 1{,}000 &= I \end{aligned}$$

$$\begin{aligned} I &= P \cdot r \cdot t \\ 1{,}000 &= 7{,}000 \cdot 0.07 \cdot t && \textit{Substitute. Use 0.07 for 7\%.} \\ 1{,}000 &= 490t && \textit{Multiply.} \\ \frac{1{,}000}{\mathbf{490}} &= \frac{490t}{\mathbf{490}} && \textit{Divide to isolate the variable.} \\ 2.04 &\approx t && \textit{Round to the nearest hundredth.} \end{aligned}$$

It will take just over 2 years.

4 Look Back

The account earns 7% of \$7,000, which is \$490, per year. So after 2 years, the interest will be \$980, giving a total account balance of \$7,980. An answer of just over 2 years for the account to reach \$8,000 makes sense.

Think and Discuss

1. Write the value of t for a time period of 6 months.

2. Show how to find r if $I = \$10$, $P = \$100$, and $t = 2$ years.

6-7 Exercises

go.hrw.com
Homework Help Online
KEYWORD: MS7 6-7
Parent Resources Online
KEYWORD: MS7 Parent

GUIDED PRACTICE

See Example 1

Find each missing value.

1. $I = \square$, $P = \$300$, $r = 4\%$, $t = 2$ years
2. $I = \square$, $P = \$500$, $r = 2\%$, $t = 1$ year
3. $I = \$120$, $P = \square$, $r = 6\%$, $t = 5$ years
4. $I = \$240$, $P = \$4{,}000$, $r = \square$, $t = 2$ years

See Example 2

5. Scott deposits $8,000 in an account that earns 6% simple interest. How long will it be before the total amount is $10,000?

INDEPENDENT PRACTICE

See Example 1

Find each missing value.

6. $I = \square$, $P = \$600$, $r = 7\%$, $t = 2$ years
7. $I = \square$, $P = \$12{,}000$, $r = 3\%$, $t = 9$ years
8. $I = \$364$, $P = \$1{,}300$, $r = \square$, $t = 7$ years
9. $I = \$440$, $P = \square$, $r = 5\%$, $t = 4$ years
10. $I = \$455$, $P = \square$, $r = 7\%$, $t = 5$ years
11. $I = \$231$, $P = \$700$, $r = \square$, $t = 3$ years

See Example 2

12. Broderick deposits $6,000 in an account that earns 5.5% simple interest. How long will it be before the total amount is $9,000?
13. Teresa deposits $4,000 in an account that earns 7% simple interest. How long will it be before the total amount is $6,500?

PRACTICE AND PROBLEM SOLVING

Extra Practice
See page 738.

Complete the table.

	Principal	Interest Rate	Time	Simple Interest
14.	$2,455	3%	▒	$441.90
15.	▒	4.25%	3 years	$663
16.	$18,500	▒	42 months	$1,942.50
17.	$425.50	5%	10 years	▒
18.	▒	6%	3 years	$2,952

19. **Finance** How many years will it take for $4,000 to double at a simple interest rate of 5%?
20. **Banking** After 2 years, a savings account earning simple interest held $585.75. The original deposit was $550. What was the interest rate?

LINK

Art

The Flemish artist Marinus van Reymerswaele painted scenes of tax collectors and bankers. *The Money-Changer and His Wife* was finished in 1539.

go.hrw.com
Web Extra!
KEYWORD: MS7 Reserve

Use the graph for Exercises 21–23.

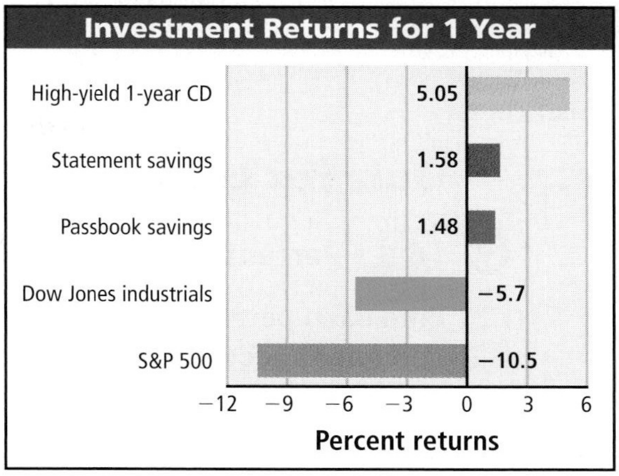

21. How much more interest was earned on $8,000 deposited for 6 months in a statement savings account than in a passbook savings account?

22. How much money was lost on $5,000 invested in S&P 500 stocks for one year?

23. Compare the returns on $12,000 invested in the high-yield 1-year CD and the Dow Jones industrials for one year.

24. Art Alexandra can buy a movable artist's-work-and-storage furniture set from her art instructor. She would buy it on credit for $5,000 at a simple interest rate of 4% for 3 years. She can purchase a similar furniture set online for $5,500 plus a $295 shipping and handling fee. Including interest, which set costs less? How much would Alexandra pay for the set?

25. Write a Problem Use the graph in Exercises 21–23 to write a problem that can be solved by using the simple interest formula.

26. Write About It Explain whether you would pay more simple interest on a loan if you used plan A or plan B.

Plan A: $1,500 for 8 years at 6% **Plan B:** $1,500 for 6 years at 8%

27. Challenge The Jacksons are opening a savings account for their child's college education. In 18 years, they will need about $134,000. If the account earns 6% simple interest, how much money must the Jacksons invest now to cover the cost of the college education?

TEST PREP and Spiral Review

28. Multiple Choice Julian deposits $4,500 in a bank account that pays 3% simple interest. How much interest will he earn in 5 years?

Ⓐ $135 Ⓑ $485 Ⓒ $675 Ⓓ $5,175

29. Short Response Susan deposits $3,000 in the bank at 6.5% simple interest. How long will it be before she has $3,500 in the bank?

30. Small book covers are $1\frac{1}{3}$ ft long. How many book covers can be made out of 40 ft of book cover material? (Lesson 3-11)

Find each percent of change. Round answers to the nearest tenth of a percent, if necessary. (Lesson 6-6)

31. 154 is increased to 200. **32.** 95 is decreased to 75. **33.** 88 is increased to 170.

READY TO GO ON?

Quiz for Lessons 6-6 Through 6-7

6-6 Percent of Change

Find each percent of change. Round answers to the nearest tenth of a percent, if necessary.

1. 37 is decreased to 17.
2. 121 is increased to 321.
3. 89 is decreased to 84.
4. 45 is increased to 60.
5. 61 is decreased to 33.
6. 86 is increased to 95.

When customers purchase a contract for cell phone service, providers often include the phone at a discounted price. Prices for cell phones from On-the-Go Cellular are listed in the table. Use the table for Exercises 7–9.

On-the-Go Cellular Phones	
Regular Price	Price with 2-year Contract
$49	Free
$99	$39.60
$149	$47.68
$189	$52.92
$229	$57.25

7. Find the percent discount on the $99 phone with a 2-year contract.
8. Find the percent discount on the $149 phone with a 2-year contract.
9. What happens to the percent discount that On-the-Go Cellular gives on its phones as the price of the phone increases?
10. Since Frank is increasing the distance of his daily runs, he needs to carry more water. His current water bottle holds 16 ounces. Frank's new bottle holds 25% more water than his current bottle. What is the capacity of Frank's new water bottle?

6-7 Simple Interest

Find each missing value.

11. $I =$ ▒, $P = \$750$, $r = 4\%$, $t = 3$ years
12. $I = \$120$, $P =$ ▒, $r = 3\%$, $t = 5$ years
13. $I = \$180$, $P = \$1500$, $r =$ ▒, $t = 2$ years
14. $I = \$220$, $P = \$680$, $r = 8\%$, $t =$ ▒
15. Leslie wants to deposit $10,000 in an account that earns 5% simple interest so that she will have $12,000 when she starts college. How long will it take her account to reach $12,000?
16. Harrison deposits $345 in a savings account that earns 4.2% simple interest. How long will it take for the total amount in the account to reach $410?

Multi-Step Test Prep

Bargain Shopping Shannon and Mary are training for a triathlon. Mary notices that a local sporting goods store is having a weekend sale on bike helmets. Both girls decide to replace their old helmets.

The girls see two signs when they enter the store on Saturday morning. One sign advertises the weekend sale. A second sign notes an early morning special.

END OF WEEK
SALE
40%
off the regular price of all bike helmets.
EARLY BIRD SPECIAL!
8:00 A.M. – 11:00 A.M.
Take an extra $\frac{1}{3}$ off the END of WEEK SALE price of all bike helmets!

1. The helmet Shannon wants has a regular price of \$54. What is the cost of this helmet during the weekend sale?
2. How much money will Shannon save off the weekend sale price if she buys her favorite helmet before 11:00 A.M.?
3. The helmet that Mary prefers regularly costs \$48. What is the cost of this helmet during the weekend early shopper special?
4. Shannon thinks that with the combined sales the bike helmets are now 70% off the regular price. Mary disagrees. She thinks the total discount is less than 70%. Who has figured the discount correctly, Shannon or Mary? Explain your answer.

Game Time

Lighten Up

On a digital clock, up to seven light bulbs make up each digit on the display. You can label each light bulb as shown below.

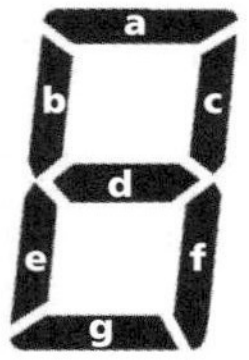

If each number were lit up for the same amount of time, you could find out which light bulb is lit the greatest percent of the time. You could also find out which light bulb is lit the least percent of the time.

For each number 0–9, list the letters of the light bulbs that are used when that number is showing. The first few numbers have been done for you.

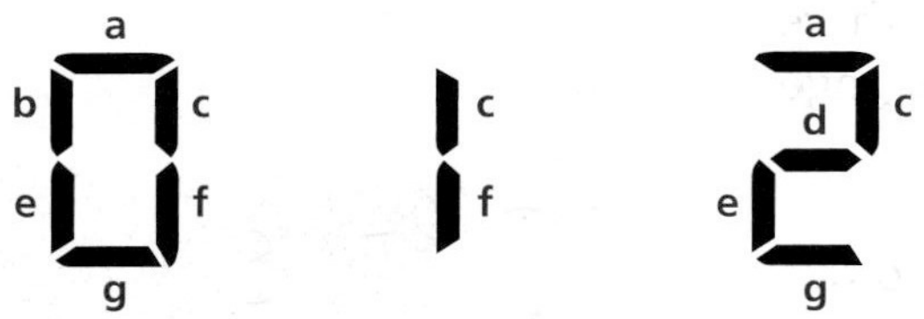

Once you have determined which bulbs are lit for each number, count how many times each bulb is lit. What percent of the time is each bulb lit? What does this tell you about which bulb will burn out first?

Percent Bingo

Use the bingo cards with numbers and percents provided online. The caller has a collection of percent problems. The caller reads a problem. Then the players solve the problem, and the solution is a number or a percent. If players have the solution on their card, they mark it off. Normal bingo rules apply. You can win with a horizontal, vertical, or diagonal row.

go.hrw.com
Game Time Extra
KEYWORD: MS7 Games

A complete copy of the rules and game pieces is available online.

FOLDNOTES

It's in the Bag!

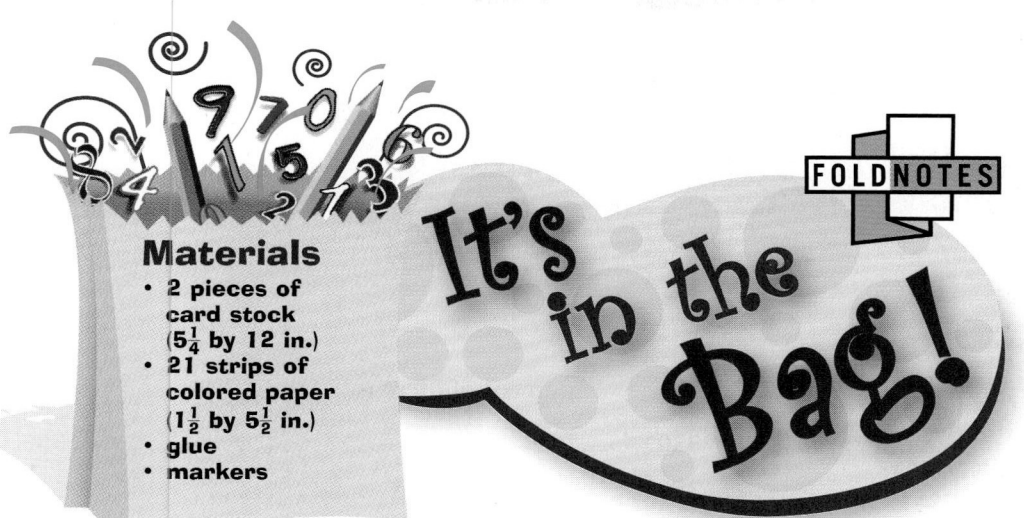

Materials
- 2 pieces of card stock ($5\frac{1}{4}$ by 12 in.)
- 21 strips of colored paper ($1\frac{1}{2}$ by $5\frac{1}{2}$ in.)
- glue
- markers

PROJECT Percent Strips

This colorful booklet holds questions and answers about percents.

Directions

1. Fold one piece of card stock in half. Cut along the crease to make two rectangles that are each $5\frac{1}{4}$ inches by 6 inches. You will use these later as covers for your booklet.

2. On the other piece of card stock, make accordion folds about $\frac{3}{4}$-inch wide. When you are done, there should be 16 panels. These panels will be the pages of your booklet. **Figure A**

3. Fold up the accordion strip. Glue the covers to the top and bottom panels of the strip. **Figure B**

4. Open the front cover. Glue a strip of colored paper to the top and bottom of the first page. **Figure C**

5. Turn the page. Glue a strip of colored paper to the back of the first page between the other two strips. **Figure D**

6. Glue strips to the other pages in the same way.

A

B
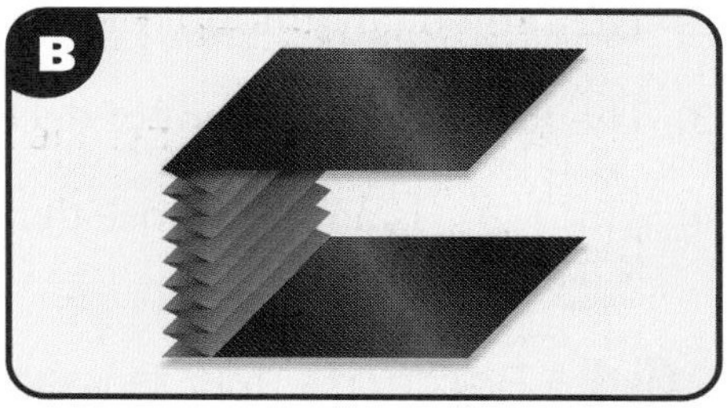

C
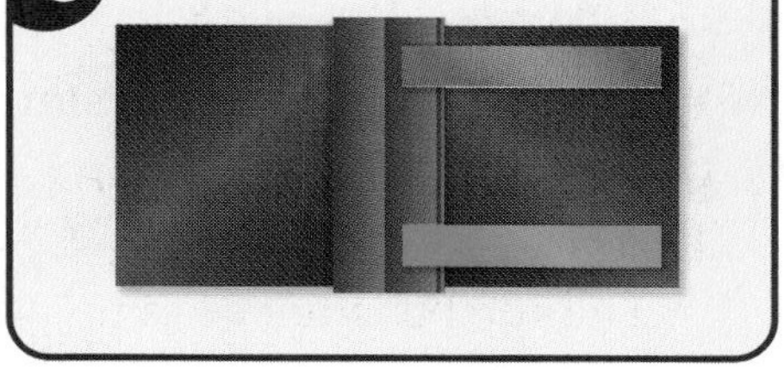

D
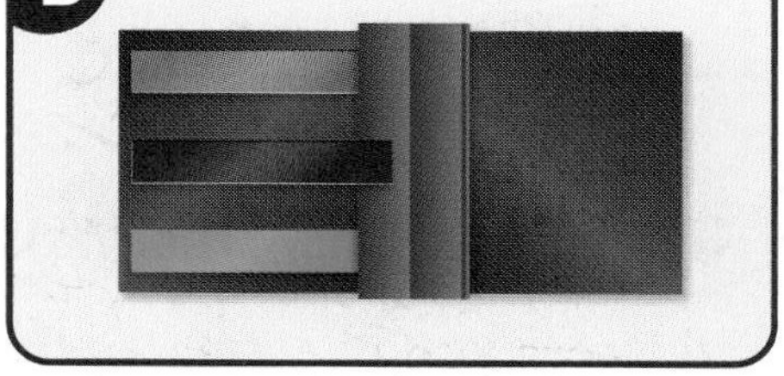

Putting the Math into Action

Write a question about percents on the front of each strip. Write the answer on the back. Trade books with another student and put your knowledge of percents to the test.

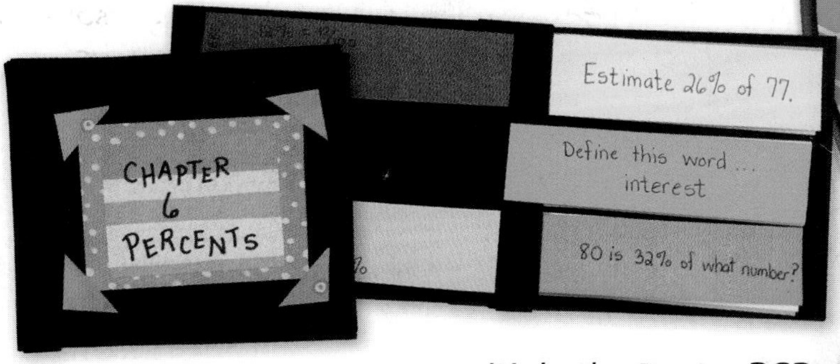

CHAPTER 6

Study Guide: Review

Vocabulary

Complete the sentences below with vocabulary words from the list above.

1. __?__ is an amount that is collected or paid for the use of money. The equation $I = P \cdot r \cdot t$ is used for calculating __?__. The letter P represents the __?__ and the letter r represents the annual rate.

2. The ratio of an amount of increase to the original amount is the __?__.

3. The ratio of an amount of decrease to the original amount is the __?__.

4. A(n) __?__ is a ratio whose denominator is 100.

6-1 Percents (pp. 330–332)

EXAMPLE

■ **Write 12% as a fraction in simplest form and as a decimal.**

$$12\% = \frac{12}{100} = \frac{12 \div 4}{100 \div 4} = \frac{3}{25}$$

$$12\% = \frac{12}{100} = 0.12$$

EXERCISES

Write each percent as a fraction in simplest form and as a decimal.

5. 78% **6.** 40%

7. 5% **8.** 16%

9. 65% **10.** 89%

6-2 Fractions, Decimals, and Percents (pp. 333–335)

EXAMPLE

Write as a percent.

■ $\frac{7}{8}$

$$\frac{7}{8} = 7 \div 8 = 0.875 = 87.5\%$$

■ **0.82**

$$0.82 = \frac{82}{100} = 82\%$$

EXERCISES

Write as a percent. Round to the nearest tenth of a percent, if necessary.

11. $\frac{3}{5}$ **12.** $\frac{1}{6}$

13. 0.06 **14.** 0.8

15. $\frac{2}{3}$ **16.** 0.0056

6-3 Estimate with Percents (pp. 336–339)

EXAMPLE

■ **Estimate 26% of 77.**

$26\% \text{ of } 77 \approx \frac{1}{4} \cdot 77$ *26% is about 25% and 25% is equivalent to $\frac{1}{4}$.*

$\approx \frac{1}{4} \cdot 80$ *Change 77 to 80.*

≈ 20 *Multiply.*

26% of 77 is about 20.

EXERCISES

Estimate.

17. 22% of 44

18. 74% of 120

19. 43% of 64

20. 31% of 97

21. 49% of 82

22. 6% of 53

23. Byron and Kate's dinner cost $18.23. About how much money should they leave for a 15% tip?

6-4 Percent of a Number (pp. 342–345)

EXAMPLE

■ **Find the percent of the number.**

125% of 610

$\frac{125}{100} = \frac{n}{610}$ *Write a proportion.*

$125 \cdot 610 = 100 \cdot n$

$76{,}250 = 100n$

$\frac{76{,}250}{100} = \frac{100n}{100}$

$762.5 = n$

125% of 610 is 762.5.

EXERCISES

Find the percent of each number.

24. 16% of 425

25. 48% of 50

26. 7% of 63

27. 96% of 125

28. 130% of 21

29. 72% of 75

30. Canyon Middle School has 1,247 students. About 38% of the students are in the seventh grade. About how many seventh-graders currently attend Canyon Middle School?

6-5 Solving Percent Problems (pp. 346–349)

EXAMPLE

■ **Solve.**

80 is 32% of what number?

$80 = 32\% \cdot n$ *Write an equation.*

$80 = 0.32 \cdot n$ *Write 32% as a decimal.*

$\frac{80}{0.32} = \frac{0.32 \cdot n}{0.32}$ *Isolate the variable.*

$250 = n$

80 is 32% of 250.

EXERCISES

Solve.

31. 20% of what number is 25?

32. 4 is what percent of 50?

33. 30 is 250% of what number?

34. What percent of 96 is 36?

35. 6 is 75% of what number?

36. 200 is what percent of 720?

37. The sales tax on a $25 shirt purchased at a store in Oak Park is $1.99. What is the sales tax rate in Oak Park?

6-6 Percent of Change (pp. 352–355)

EXAMPLE

Find each percent of change. Round answers to the nearest tenth, if necessary.

- **25 is decreased to 16.**

  $25 - 16 = 9$

  $$\text{percent of change} = \frac{9}{25} = 0.36 = 36\%$$

  The percent of decrease is 36%.

- **13.5 is increased to 27.**

  $27 - 13.5 = 13.5$

  $$\text{percent of change} = \frac{13.5}{13.5} = 1 = 100\%$$

  The percent of increase is 100%.

EXERCISES

Find each percent of change. Round answers to the nearest tenth, if necessary.

38. 54 is increased to 81.

39. 14 is decreased to 12.

40. 110 is increased to 143.

41. 90 is decreased to 15.2.

42. 26 is increased to 32.

43. 84 is decreased to 21.

44. The regular price of a new pair of skis is \$245. This week the skis are on sale for 15% off. Find the sale price.

45. Bianca makes beaded bracelets. Each bracelet costs \$3.25 to make. Bianca sells them at a 140% increase in price. What is the price of each bracelet?

6-7 Simple Interest (pp. 356–359)

EXAMPLE

Find each missing value.

- **$I = \square$, $P = \$545$, $r = 1.5\%$, $t = 2$ years**

  $I = P \cdot r \cdot t$

  $I = 545 \cdot 0.015 \cdot 2$ *Substitute.*

  $I = 16.35$ *Multiply.*

  The simple interest is \$16.35.

- **$I = \$825$, $P = \square$, $r = 6\%$, $t = 11$ years**

  $I = P \cdot r \cdot t$

  $825 = P \cdot 0.06 \cdot 11$ *Substitute.*

  $825 = P \cdot 0.66$ *Multiply.*

  $\frac{825}{0.66} = \frac{P \cdot 0.66}{0.66}$ *Isolate the variable.*

  $1{,}250 = P$

  The principal is \$1,250.

EXERCISES

Find each missing value.

46. $I = \square$, $P = \$1{,}000$, $r = 3\%$, $t = 6$ months

47. $I = \$452.16$, $P = \$1{,}256$, $r = 12\%$, $t = \square$

48. $I = \square$, $P = \$675$, $r = 4.5\%$, $t = 8$ years

49. $I = \$555.75$, $P = \$950$, $r = \square$, $t = 15$ years

50. $I = \$172.50$, $P = \square$, $r = 5\%$, $t = 18$ months

51. Craig deposits \$1,000 in a savings account that earns 5% simple interest. How long will it take for the total amount in his account to reach \$1,350?

52. Zach deposits \$755 in an account that earns 4.2% simple interest. How long will it take for the total amount in the account to reach \$1,050?

CHAPTER TEST

CHAPTER 6

Write each percent as a fraction in simplest form and as a decimal.

1. 95% **2.** 37.5% **3.** 4% **4.** 0.01%

Write as a percent. Round to the nearest tenth of a percent, if necessary.

5. 0.75 **6.** 0.06 **7.** 0.8 **8.** 0.0039

9. $\frac{3}{10}$ **10.** $\frac{9}{20}$ **11.** $\frac{5}{16}$ **12.** $\frac{7}{21}$

Estimate.

13. 48% of 8 **14.** 3% of 119 **15.** 26% of 32 **16.** 76% of 280

17. The Pattersons spent $47.89 for a meal at a restaurant. About how much should they leave for a 15% tip?

Find the percent of each number.

18. 90% of 200 **19.** 35% of 210 **20.** 16% of 85

21. 250% of 30 **22.** 38% of 11 **23.** 5% of 145

Solve.

24. 36 is what percent of 150? **25.** What percent of 145 is 29?

26. 51 is what percent of 340? **27.** 36 is 40% of what number?

28. 70 is 14% of what number? **29.** 25 is 20% of what number?

30. Hampton Middle School is expecting 376 seventh-graders next year. This is 40% of the expected school enrollment. How many students are expected to enroll in the school next year?

Find each percent of change. Round answers to the nearest tenth, if necessary.

31. 30 is increased to 45. **32.** 115 is decreased to 46.

33. 116 is increased to 145. **34.** 129 is decreased to 32.

35. A community theater sold 8,500 tickets to performances during its first year. By its tenth year, ticket sales had increased by 34%. How many tickets did the theater sell during its tenth year?

Find each missing value.

36. $I =$ ▒, $P = \$500$, $r = 5\%$, $t = 1$ year **37.** $I = \$702$, $P = \$1{,}200$, $r = 3.9\%$, $t =$ ▒

38. $I = \$468$, $P = \$900$, $r =$ ▒, $t = 8$ years **39.** $I = \$37.50$, $P =$ ▒, $r = 10\%$, $t = 6$ months

40. Kate invested $3,500 at a 5% simple interest rate. How many years will it take for the original amount to double?

STANDARDIZED TEST PREP

go.hrw.com
State Test Practice Online
KEYWORD: MS7 TestPrep

Cumulative Assessment, Chapters 1–6

Multiple Choice

1. Which ratio corresponds to the similar figures shown?

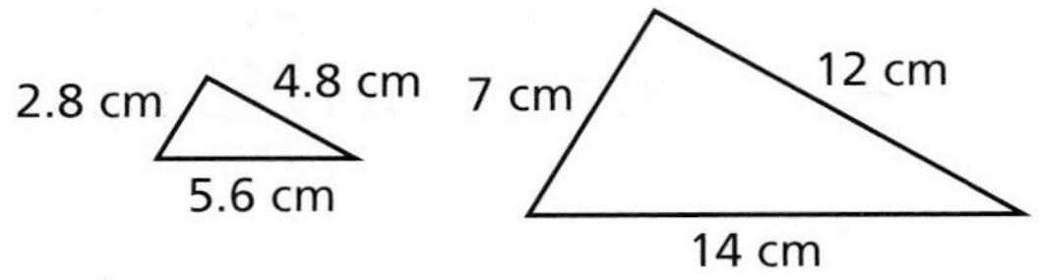

Ⓐ $\frac{4.2}{1}$ Ⓒ $\frac{1}{2}$

Ⓑ $\frac{2.5}{1}$ Ⓓ $\frac{1}{4}$

2. Which of the following is NOT equivalent to 12%?

Ⓕ 0.012 Ⓗ 0.12

Ⓖ $\frac{12}{100}$ Ⓙ $\frac{3}{25}$

3. Which situation corresponds to the graph?

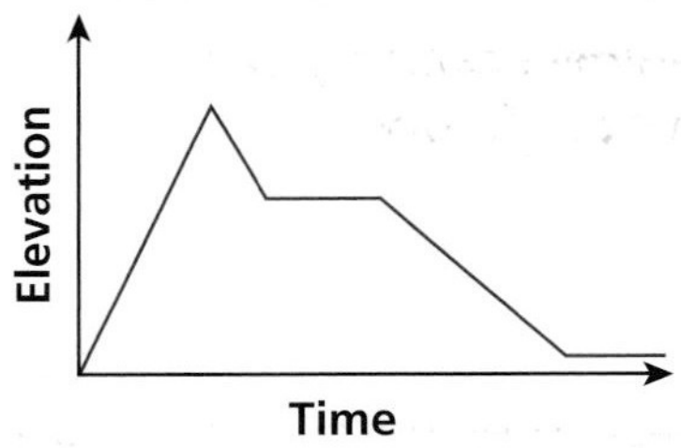

Ⓐ Ty rides his bike up a hill, immediately heads back down, stops and rests for a while, continues down the hill, and then rests.

Ⓑ Paul runs up a hill, stops a while for a water break, and then jogs back down the hill.

Ⓒ Sue rollerskates down a hill, stops for lunch, and then continues along a flat course for a while.

Ⓓ Eric swims across a pool, rests for a while when he gets to the other side, and then swims numerous laps without stopping.

4. Which point is not on the graph of $y = x^2 - 3$?

Ⓕ (0, −3) Ⓗ (−2, −7)

Ⓖ (2, 1) Ⓙ (−1, −2)

5. Which equation is an example of the Identity Property?

Ⓐ 100 + 10 = 2(50 + 5)

Ⓑ 50 + 10 = 10 + 50

Ⓒ 25 + (50 + 10) = (25 + 50) + 10

Ⓓ 50 + 0 = 50

6. A basketball goal that usually sells for $825 goes on sale for $650. What is the percent of decrease, to the nearest whole percent?

Ⓕ 12% Ⓗ 27%

Ⓖ 21% Ⓙ 79%

7. In Oregon, about 40 of the state's nearly 1,000 public water systems add fluoride to their water. What percent best represents this situation?

Ⓐ 0.4% Ⓒ 40%

Ⓑ 4% Ⓓ 400%

8. The number of whooping cranes wintering in Texas reached an all time high in 2004 at 213. The lowest number ever recorded was 15 whooping cranes in 1941. What is the percent of increase of whooping cranes wintering in Texas from 1941 to 2004?

Ⓕ 7% Ⓗ 198%

Ⓖ 91% Ⓙ 1,320%

9. What is the value of $8\frac{2}{5} - 2\frac{3}{4}$?

Ⓐ $5\frac{9}{20}$ Ⓒ $6\frac{1}{9}$

Ⓑ $5\frac{13}{20}$ Ⓓ $6\frac{7}{20}$

10. Which point lies outside of the circle?

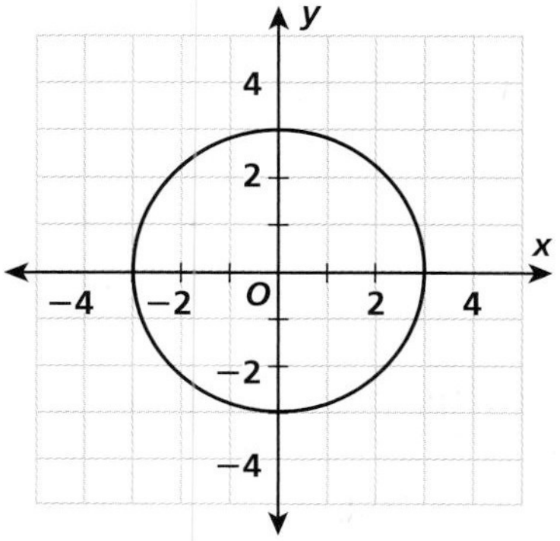

Ⓕ (−3, 0) Ⓗ (3, 3)

Ⓖ (1, 2) Ⓙ (−2, 1)

HOT TIP! **Make sure that your answer makes sense before marking it as your response. Reread the question and determine whether your answer is reasonable.**

Gridded Response

11. Jarvis deposits $1,200 in an account that earns 3% simple interest. How many years will it take him to earn $432 in interest?

12. Sylas finished a 100-meter freestyle swim in 80.357 seconds. The winner of the race finished in 79.222 seconds. How many seconds faster was the winning time than Sylas's time?

13. A baseball coach has a rule that for every time a player strikes out, that player has to do 12 push ups. If Cal strikes out 27 times, how many push ups will he be required to do?

14. Write a decimal equivalent to 60.5%.

15. What is the denominator of the value of $\frac{3}{2} + \frac{5}{6}$ when written in simplest form?

Short Response

16. The graph shows the number of boys and the number of girls who participated in a talent show.

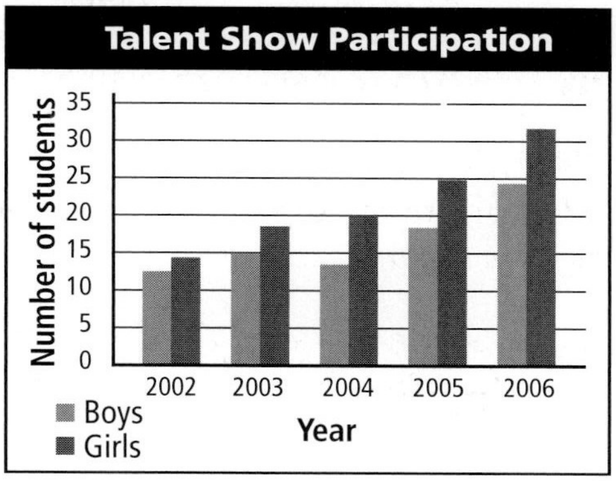

a. What is the approximate percent of increase of girls participating in the talent show from 2002 to 2005?

b. What percent of students participating in the talent show in 2006 were boys? Explain how you found your answer.

17. A homemaker association has 134 members. If 31 of these members are experts in canning vegetables, are more or less than 25% of the members canning experts? Explain how you know.

Extended Response

18. Riley and Louie each have $5,000 to invest. They both invest at a 2.5% simple interest rate.

a. Riley keeps her money invested for 7 years. How much interest will she earn? How much will her investment be worth?

b. What is the value of Louie's investment if he invests for 3 years, then removes and spends $1,000, and then invests what is remaining for 4 more years at a rate of 4%?

c. Using the information from parts **a** and **b**, who makes the most money in 7 years, Louie or Riley? Explain your reasoning.

Standardized Test Prep

Problem Solving on Location

MICHIGAN

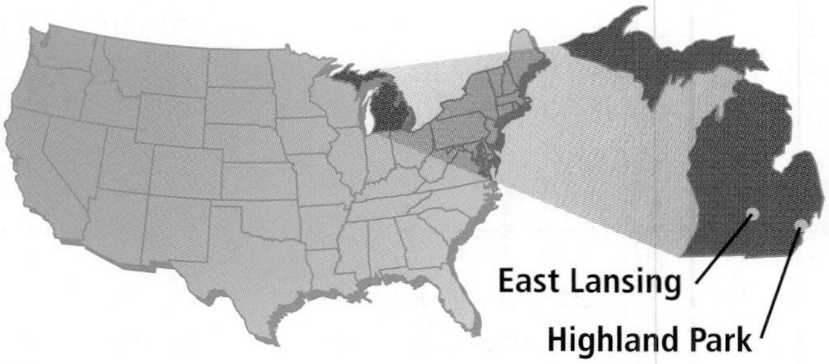

The First Assembly Line

In 1913, an engineer named Henry Ford revolutionized the auto industry when he installed the world's first automated assembly line in his Highland Park factory. Before the assembly line, building the frame of a car took longer than 12 hours. By keeping the workers in one place and bringing the parts to them on a moving conveyor belt, Ford could manufacture an entire car every 24 seconds!

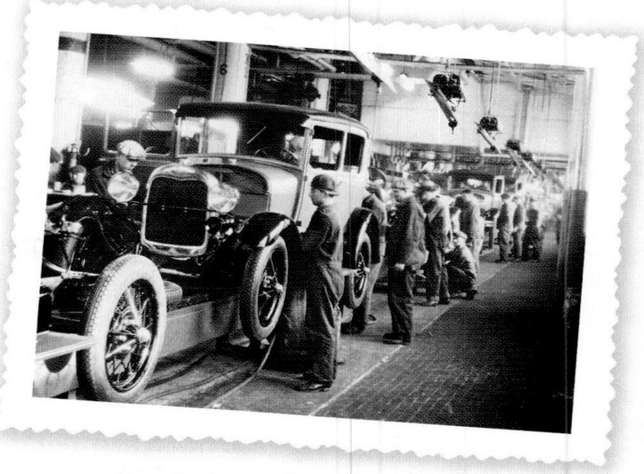

Choose one or more strategies to solve each problem.

1. Ford first used the assembly line to build a car part called a magneto. The ratio of the time it took to build a magneto before the assembly line was introduced to the time it took to build one after the assembly line was introduced is 4:1. With the assembly line, this car part could be completed 15 minutes faster. How long did it take to build a magneto before the introduction of the assembly line?

2. Car prices dropped as mass production of cars improved. The 1914 price of a Model T was 53% of the 1908 price. The 1925 price was 59% of the 1914 price. Given that a Model T sold for $260 in 1925, what was the price of a Model T in 1908?

For 3, use the table.

3. The assembly line made it possible to produce more cars each year. Predict the number of Model T's that were manufactured in 1918.

Ford's Model T

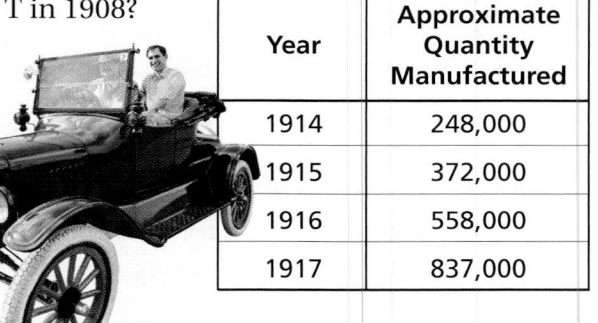

Year	Approximate Quantity Manufactured
1914	248,000
1915	372,000
1916	558,000
1917	837,000

Problem Solving Strategies

- Draw a Diagram
- Make a Model
- Guess and Test
- Work Backward
- Find a Pattern
- Make a Table
- Solve a Simpler Problem
- Use Logical Reasoning
- Act It Out
- Make an Organized List

Michigan State University

Michigan State University, located in East Lansing, was founded in 1855 as the nation's first agricultural college. Classes began in 1857 with just 63 students and 5 faculty members. Today, Michigan State is one of the largest universities in the United States, with more than 200 programs of study.

Choose one or more strategies to solve each problem.

1. In 2005, the total number of students at Michigan State University was about 45,000. The number of undergraduate students was 350% of the number of graduate students. How many undergraduate students were there? How many graduate students were there?

For 2–4, use the table.

2. Suppose expenses for room and board increase by 6% per year. What would room and board cost in 2010?

3. Suppose the tuition for Michigan residents increases by 8% per year. What would be the first year in which the tuition for Michigan residents is more than $10,000?

4. Jamal, Kyle, and Lisa are students at Michigan State University. Each student pays tuition, a matriculation fee, room and board, and taxes. The matriculation fee is about 6% of Jamal's expenses, room and board are about 23% of Kyle's expenses, and tuition is about 49% of Lisa's expenses. Which student is not a Michigan resident?

Annual Expenses at Michigan State University (2004)

Tuition for Michigan Residents	$6,188
Tuition for Out-of-State Students	$17,033
Matriculation Fee	$812
Room and Board	$5,458
Taxes	$44

CHAPTER 7

Collecting, Displaying, and Analyzing Data

go.hrw.com
Chapter Project Online
KEYWORD: MS7 Ch7

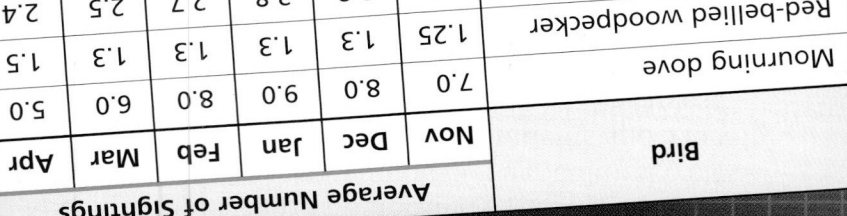

Bird	Average Number of Sightings					
	Nov	Dec	Jan	Feb	Mar	Apr
Mourning dove	7.0	8.0	9.0	8.0	6.0	5.0
Red-bellied woodpecker	1.25	1.3	1.3	1.3	1.3	1.5
Carolina chickadee	2.8	2.8	2.8	2.7	2.5	2.4

Career *Field Biologist*

Field biologists spend time outdoors studying populations of fish, birds, and other living things. The information they collect is often used to determine whether populations are growing or declining.

Sometimes, amateur naturalists help scientists collect information. For example, people with bird feeders can report to Project FeederWatch the number and kinds of birds that they see at their feeders throughout the winter.

ARE YOU READY?

Vocabulary

Choose the best term from the list to complete each sentence.

1. A part of a line consisting of two endpoints and all points between those endpoints is called a(n) __?__.

2. A(n) __?__ is the amount of space between the marked values on the __?__ of a graph.

3. The number of times an item occurs is called its __?__.

circle
frequency
interval
line segment
scale

Complete these exercises to review skills you will need for this chapter.

Order Whole Numbers

Order the numbers from least to greatest.

4. 45, 23, 65, 15, 42, 18

5. 103, 105, 102, 118, 87, 104

6. 56, 65, 24, 19, 76, 33, 82

7. 8, 3, 6, 2, 5, 9, 3, 4, 2

Whole Number Operations

Add or subtract.

8. 18 + 26 **9.** 23 + 17 **10.** 75 + 37 **11.** 98 + 64

12. 133 − 35 **13.** 54 − 29 **14.** 200 − 88 **15.** 1,055 − 899

Locate Points on a Number Line

Copy the number line. Then graph each number.

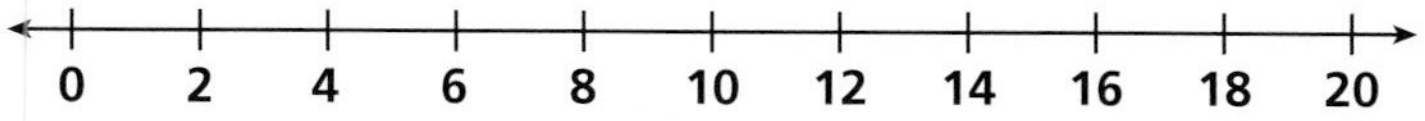

16. 15 **17.** 2 **18.** 18 **19.** 7

Read a Table

Use the data in the table for Exercises 20 and 21.

20. Which animal is the fastest?

21. Which animal is faster, a rabbit or a zebra?

Top Speeds of Some Animals

Animal	Speed (mi/h)
Elephant	25
Lion	50
Rabbit	35
Zebra	40

CHAPTER 7

Study Guide: Preview

Where You've Been

Previously, you

- used an appropriate representation for displaying data.
- identified mean, median, mode, and range of a set of data.
- solved problems by collecting, organizing, and displaying data.

In This Chapter

You will study

- selecting an appropriate representation for displaying relationships among data.
- choosing among mean, median, mode, or range to describe a set of data.
- making inferences and convincing arguments based on analysis of data.

Where You're Going

You can use the skills learned in this chapter

- to analyze trends and make business and marketing decisions.
- to strengthen a persuasive argument by presenting data and trends in visual displays.

Key Vocabulary/Vocabulario

bar graph	gráfica de barras
circle graph	gráfica circular
frequency table	tabla de frecuencias
line graph	gráfica lineal
line plot	diagrama de acumulación
mean	media
median	mediana
mode	moda
scatter plot	diagrama de dispersión
stem-and-leaf plot	tabla arborescente

Vocabulary Connections

To become familiar with some of the vocabulary terms in the chapter, consider the following. You may refer to the chapter, the glossary, or a dictionary if you like.

1. The word *median* comes from the Latin word *medius,* meaning "middle." What is the **median** value in a set of data? What other words come from this Latin root?
2. *Scatter* can mean "to spread out" or "to occur at random." What might the data points on a **scatter plot** look like?
3. *Frequency* is a measure of how often an event occurs or the number of like objects that are in a group. What do you think a **frequency table** might show?

Reading and Writing Math

Reading Strategy: Read a Lesson for Understanding

Before you begin reading a lesson, find out what its main focus, or objective, is. Each lesson is centered on a specific objective, which is located at the top of the first page of the lesson. Reading with the objective in mind will help guide you through the lesson material. You can use the following tips to help you follow the math as you read.

Learn to find the percent of a number.

→ Identify the objective of the lesson. Then skim through the lesson to get a sense of where the objective is covered.

"How do I find the percent of a number?"

→ As you read through the lesson, write down any questions, problems, or trouble spots you may have.

Find the percent of each number.

8% of 50

8% of 50 $= 0.08 \cdot 50$ *Write the percent as a decimal.*

$= 4$ *Multiply.*

→ Work through each example, as the examples help demonstrate the objectives.

Think and Discuss

1. Explain how to set up a proportion to find 150% of a number.

→ Check your understanding of the lesson by answering the Think and Discuss questions.

Try This

Use Lesson 6-1 in your textbook to answer each question.

1. What is the objective of the lesson?
2. What new terms are defined in the lesson?
3. What skills are being taught in Example 3 of the lesson?
4. Which parts of the lesson can you use to answer Think and Discuss question 1?

7-1 Frequency Tables, Stem-and-Leaf Plots, and Line Plots

Learn to organize and interpret data in frequency tables, stem-and-leaf plots, and line plots.

Vocabulary

frequency table
cumulative frequency
stem-and-leaf plot
line plot

IMAX® theaters, with their huge screens and powerful sound systems, make viewers feel as if they are in the middle of the action. In 2005, the classic IMAX film *The Dream Is Alive* had total box office receipts of over $149 million.

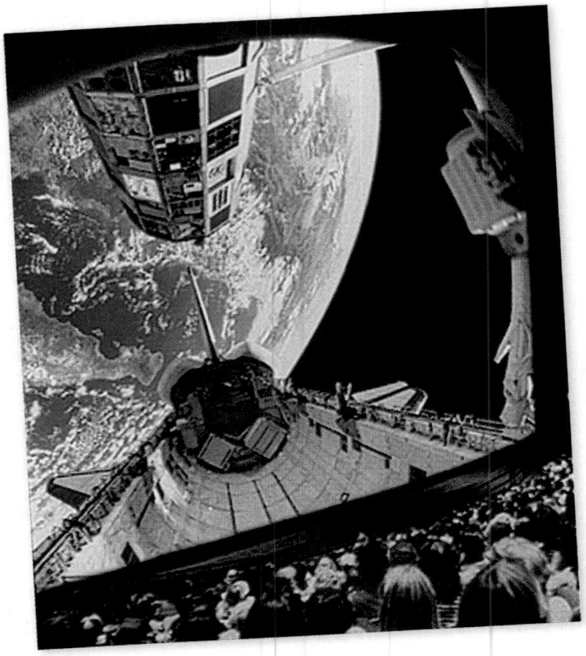

To see how common it is for an IMAX movie to attract such a large number of viewers, you could use a *frequency table*. A **frequency table** is a way to organize data into categories or groups. By including a **cumulative frequency** column in your table, you can keep a running total of the number of data items.

EXAMPLE 1 Organizing and Interpreting Data in a Frequency Table

The list shows box office receipts in millions of dollars for 20 IMAX films. Make a cumulative frequency table of the data. How many films earned under $40 million?

76, 51, 41, 38, 18, 17, 16, 15, 13, 13, 12, 12, 10, 10, 6, 5, 5, 4, 4, 2

Step 1: Choose a scale that includes all of the data values. Then separate the scale into equal intervals.

Step 2: Find the number of data values in each interval. Write these numbers in the "Frequency" column.

Step 3: Find the cumulative frequency for each row by adding all the frequency values that are above or in that row.

IMAX Films

Receipts ($ million)	Frequency	Cumulative Frequency
0–19	16	16
20–39	1	17
40–59	2	19
60–79	1	20

The number of films that earned under $40 million is the cumulative frequency of the first two rows: 17.

A **stem-and-leaf plot** uses the digits of each number to organize and display a set of data. Each *leaf* on the plot represents the right-hand digit in a data value, and each *stem* represents the remaining left-hand digits. The key shows the values of the data on the plot.

Stems	Leaves
2	4 7 9
3	0 6

Key: 2|7 means 27

EXAMPLE 2 Organizing and Interpreting Data in a Stem-and-Leaf Plot

The table shows the number of minutes students spent doing their Spanish homework. Make a stem-and-leaf plot of the data. Then find the number of students who studied longer than 45 minutes.

Minutes Spent Doing Homework					
38	48	45	32	29	48
32	45	36	22	21	64
35	45	47	26	43	29

Step 1: Order the data from least to greatest. Since the data values range from 21 to 64, use tens digits for the stems and ones digits for the leaves.

Step 2: List the stems from least to greatest on the plot.

Step 3: List the leaves for each stem from least to greatest.

Step 4: Add a key and title the graph.

Minutes Spent Doing Homework

The stems are the tens digits.

Stems	Leaves
2	1 2 6 9 9
3	2 2 5 6 8
4	3 5 5 5 7 8 8
5	
6	4

Key: 3|2 means 32

The leaves are the ones digits.

The entries in the second row represent the data values 32, 32, 35, 36, and 38.

The stem 5 has no leaves, so there are no data values in the 50's.

One student studied for **47** minutes, 2 students studied for **48** minutes, and 1 student studied for **64** minutes.
A total of 4 students studied longer than 45 minutes.

Helpful Hint

To represent 5 minutes in the stem-and-leaf plot in Example 2, you would use 0 as the stem and 5 as the leaf.

Similar to a stem-and-leaf plot, a **line plot** can be used to show how many times each data value occurs. Line plots use a number line and **X**'s to show frequency. By looking at a line plot, you can quickly see the *distribution*, or spread, of the data.

EXAMPLE 3 Organizing and Interpreting Data in a Line Plot

Make a line plot of the data. How many miles per day did Trey run most often?

Number of Miles Trey Ran Each Day During Training								
5	6	5	5	3	5	4	4	6
8	6	3	4	3	2	16	12	12

Step 1: The data values range from 2 to 16. Draw a number line that includes this range.

Step 2: Put an **X** above the number on the number line that corresponds to the number of miles Trey ran each day.

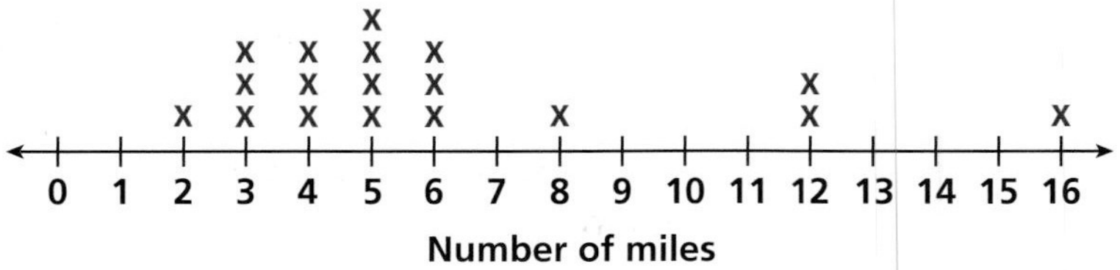

The greatest number of **X**'s appear above the number 5. This means that Trey ran 5 miles most often.

Think and Discuss

1. **Tell** which you would use to determine the number of data values in a set: a cumulative frequency table or a stem-and-leaf plot. Explain.

7-1 Exercises

go.hrw.com
Homework Help Online
KEYWORD: MS7 7-1
Parent Resources Online
KEYWORD: MS7 Parent

GUIDED PRACTICE

Number of Electoral Votes for Select States (2004)											
CA	55	GA	15	IN	11	MI	17	NY	31	PA	21
NJ	15	IL	21	KY	8	NC	15	OH	20	TX	34

See Example 1
1. Make a cumulative frequency table of the data. How many of the states had fewer than 20 electoral votes in 2004?

See Example 2
2. Make a stem-and-leaf plot of the data. How many of the states had more than 30 electoral votes in 2004?

See Example 3
3. Make a line plot of the data. For the states shown, what was the most common number of electoral votes in 2004?

INDEPENDENT PRACTICE

The table shows the ages of the first 18 U.S. presidents when they took office.

President	Age	President	Age	President	Age
Washington	57	Jackson	61	Fillmore	50
Adams	61	Van Buren	54	Pierce	48
Jefferson	57	Harrison	68	Buchanan	65
Madison	57	Tyler	51	Lincoln	52
Monroe	58	Polk	49	Johnson	56
Adams	57	Taylor	64	Grant	46

See Example 1

4. Make a cumulative frequency table of the data. How many of the presidents were under the age of 65 when they took office?

See Example 2

5. Make a stem-and-leaf plot of the data. How many of the presidents were in their 40s when they took office?

See Example 3

6. Make a line plot of the data. What was the most common age at which the presidents took office?

PRACTICE AND PROBLEM SOLVING

Extra Practice
See page 739.

Use the stem-and-leaf plot for Exercises 7–9.

Stems	Leaves
0	4 6 6 9
1	2 5 8 8 8
2	0 3
3	1

Key: 1|2 means 12

7. What is the least data value?
What is the greatest data value?

8. Which data value occurs most often?

9. **Critical Thinking** Which of the following is most likely the source of the data in the stem-and-leaf plot?

Ⓐ Shoe sizes of 12 middle school students

Ⓑ Number of hours 12 adults exercised in one month

Ⓒ Number of boxes of cereal per household at one time

Ⓓ Monthly temperatures in degrees Fahrenheit in Chicago, Illinois

10. **Earth Science** The table shows the masses of the largest meteorites found on Earth.

Largest Meteorites			
Meteorite	**Mass (kg)**	**Meteorite**	**Mass (kg)**
Armanty	23.5	Chupaderos	14
Bacubirito	22	Hoba	60
Campo del Cielo	15	Mbosi	16
Cape York (Agpalilik)	20	Mundrabilla	12
Cape York (Ahnighito)	31	Willamette	15

a. Use the data in the table to make a line plot.

b. How many of the meteorites have a mass of 15 kilograms or greater?

Life Science LINK

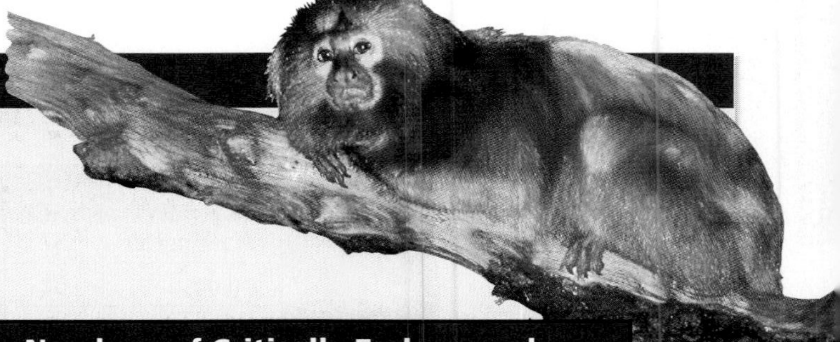

The map shows the number of critically endangered animal species in each country in South America. A species is critically endangered when it faces a very high risk of extinction in the wild in the near future.

Numbers of Critically Endangered Animal Species in South America

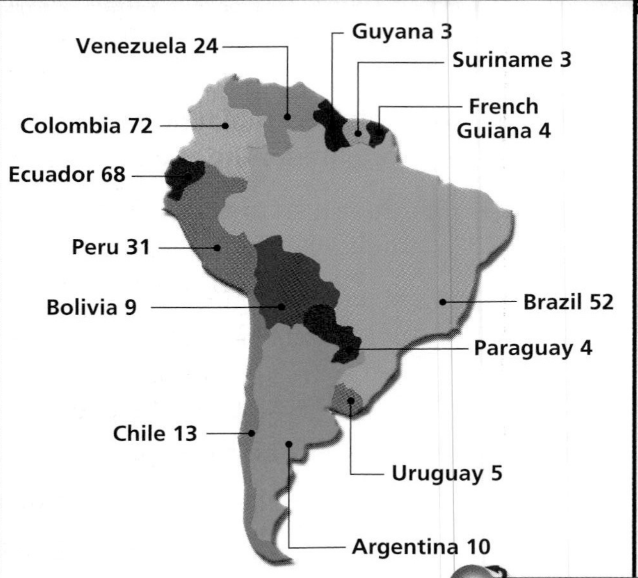

Source: International Union for Conservation of Nature and Natural Resources

go.hrw.com Web Extra! KEYWORD: MS7 Endangered

11. Which country has the fewest critically endangered species? Which has the most?

12. Make a cumulative frequency table of the data. How many countries have fewer than 20 critically endangered species?

13. Make a stem-and-leaf plot of the data.

14. **Write About It** Explain how changing the size of the intervals you used in Exercise 12 affects your cumulative frequency table.

15. **Challenge** In a recent year, the number of endangered animal species in the United States was 190. Show how to represent this number on a stem-and-leaf plot.

Test Prep and Spiral Review

Use the data for Exercises 16 and 17.

20	30	9	25	28
8	11	12	7	18
33	26	10	9	2

16. **Multiple Choice** How many stems would a stem-and-leaf plot of the data in the table have?

Ⓐ 1 Ⓒ 3

Ⓑ 2 Ⓓ 4

17. **Extended Response** Make a stem-and-leaf plot and a line plot of the data in the table. Which data display best shows the distribution of data? Explain.

18. Maria has 18 yards of fabric. A pillowcase takes $1\frac{1}{5}$ yards. How many pillowcases can Maria make with the fabric? (Lesson 3-11)

Find each unit rate. Round to the nearest hundredth if necessary. (Lesson 5-2)

19. 12 hr for \$102 **20.** \$2,289 in 7 mo **21.** 48 points in 3 games

7-2 Mean, Median, Mode, and Range

Learn to find the mean, median, mode, and range of a data set.

Vocabulary
mean
median
mode
range
outlier

To crack secret messages in code, you can list the number of times each symbol of the code appears in the message. The symbol that appears the most often represents the *mode*, which likely corresponds to the letter *e*.

Navajo Code Talkers used the Navajo language as the basis of a code in World War II.

The mode, along with the *mean* and the *median*, is a measure of *central tendency* used to represent the "middle" of a data set.

- The **mean** is the sum of the data values divided by the number of data items.
- The **median** is the middle value of an odd number of data items arranged in order. For an even number of data items, the median is the mean of the two middle values.
- The **mode** is the value or values that occur most often. When all the data values occur the same number of times, there is no mode.

The **range** of a set of data is the difference between the greatest and least values.

EXAMPLE 1 Finding the Mean, Median, Mode, and Range of a Data Set

Find the mean, median, mode, and range of the data set.

2, 1, 8, 0, 2, 4, 3, 4

Helpful Hint
The mean is sometimes called the *average*.

mean:

$2 + 1 + 8 + 0 + 2 + 4 + 3 + 4 = 24$ *Add the values.*

$24 \div 8 = 3$ *Divide the sum by the number of items.*

The mean is 3.

median:

0, 1, 2, 2, 3, 4, 4, 8 *Arrange the values in order.*

$\frac{2 + 3}{2} = 2.5$ *There are two middle values, so find the mean of these values.*

The median is 2.5.

mode:

0, 1, 2, 2, 3, 4, 4, 8 *The values 2 and 4 occur twice.*

The modes are 2 and 4.

range: $8 - 0 = 8$ *Subtract the least value from the greatest value.*

The range is 8.

Often one measure of central tendency is more appropriate for describing a set of data than another measure is. Think about what each measure tells you about the data. Then choose the measure that best answers the question being asked.

EXAMPLE 2 Choosing the Best Measure to Describe a Set of Data

The line plot shows the number of hours 15 people exercised in one week. Which measure of central tendency best describes these data? Justify your answer.

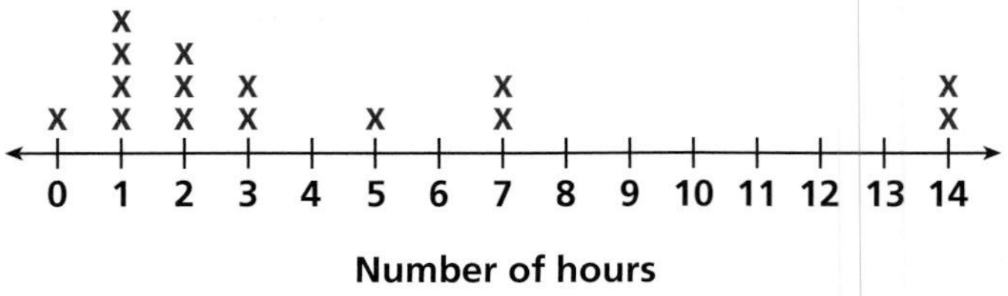

mean:

$$\frac{0+1+1+1+1+2+2+2+3+3+5+7+7+14+14}{15} = \frac{63}{15} = 4.2$$

The mean is 4.2.

Most of the people exercised fewer than 4 hours, so the mean does not describe the data set best.

median:

0, 1, 1, 1, 1, 2, 2, 2, 3, 3, 5, 7, 7, 14, 14

The median is 2.

The median best describes the data set because a majority of the data is clustered around the data value 2.

mode:

The greatest number of **X**'s occur above the number 1 on the line plot.

The mode is 1.

The mode represents only 4 of the 15 people. The mode does not describe the entire data set.

In the data set in Example 2, the value 14 is much greater than the other values in the set. An extreme value such as this is called an **outlier**. Outliers can greatly affect the mean of a data set.

Measure	Most Useful When
mean	the data are spread fairly evenly
median	the data set has an outlier
mode	the data involve a subject in which many data points of one value are important, such as election results

EXAMPLE 3 Exploring the Effects of Outliers on Measures of Central Tendency

The table shows the number of art pieces created by students in a glass-blowing workshop. Identify the outlier in the data set, and determine how the outlier affects the mean, median, and mode of the data. Then tell which measure of central tendency best describes the data with and without the outlier.

Name	Number of Pieces
Suzanne	5
Glen	1
Charissa	3
Eileen	4
Hermann	14
Tom	2

The outlier is 14.

Without the Outlier

mean:

$$\frac{5 + 1 + 3 + 4 + 2}{5} = 3$$

The mean is 3.
The outlier increases the mean of the data by about 1.8.

median:

1, 2, 3, 4, 5

The median is 3.
The outlier increases the median of the data by 0.5.

mode:

There is no mode.
The outlier does not change the mode of the data.

With the Outlier

mean:

$$\frac{5 + 1 + 3 + 4 + 14 + 2}{6} \approx 4.8$$

The mean is about 4.8.

median:

1, 2, 3, 4, 5, 14

$$\frac{3 + 4}{2} = 3.5$$

The median is 3.5.

mode:

There is no mode.

The median best describes the data with the outlier. The mean and median best describe the data without the outlier.

Caution!

Since all the data values occur the same number of times, the set has no mode.

Think and Discuss

1. **Describe** a situation in which the mean would best describe a data set.
2. **Tell** which measure of central tendency must be a data value.
3. **Explain** how an outlier affects the mean, median, and mode of a data set.

7-2 Exercises

go.hrw.com
Homework Help Online
KEYWORD: MS7 7-2
Parent Resources Online
KEYWORD: MS7 Parent

GUIDED PRACTICE

See Example 1

Find the mean, median, mode, and range of each data set.

1. 5, 30, 35, 20, 5, 25, 20

2. 44, 68, 48, 61, 59, 48, 63, 49

See Example 2

3. The line plot shows cooking temperatures required by different recipes. Which measure of central tendency best describes the data? Justify your answer.

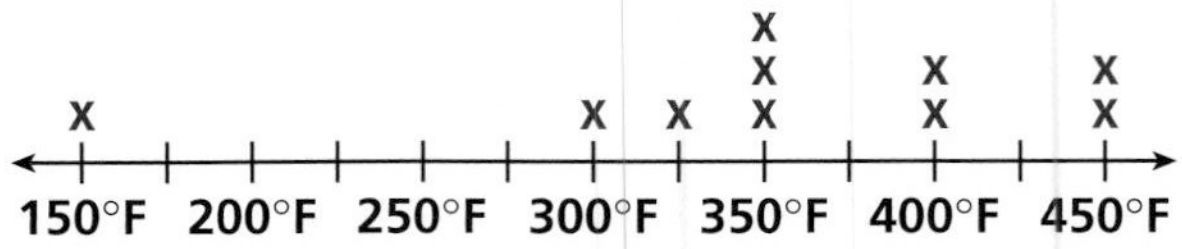

See Example 3

4. The table shows the number of glasses of water consumed in one day. Identify the outlier in the data set. Then determine how the outlier affects the mean, median, and mode of the data. Then tell which measure of central tendency best describes the data with and without the outlier.

Water Consumption

Name	Randy	Lori	Anita	Jana	Sonya	Victor	Mark	Jorge
Glasses	4	12	3	1	4	7	5	4

INDEPENDENT PRACTICE

See Example 1

Find the mean, median, mode, and range of each data set.

5. 92, 88, 65, 68, 76, 90, 84, 88, 93, 89

6. 23, 43, 5, 3, 4, 14, 24, 15, 15, 13

7. 2.0, 4.4, 6.2, 3.2, 4.4, 6.2, 3.7

8. 13.1, 7.5, 3.9, 4.8, 17.1, 14.6, 8.3, 3.9

See Example 2

9. The line plot shows the number of letters in the spellings of the 12 months. Which measure of central tendency best describes the data set? Justify your answer.

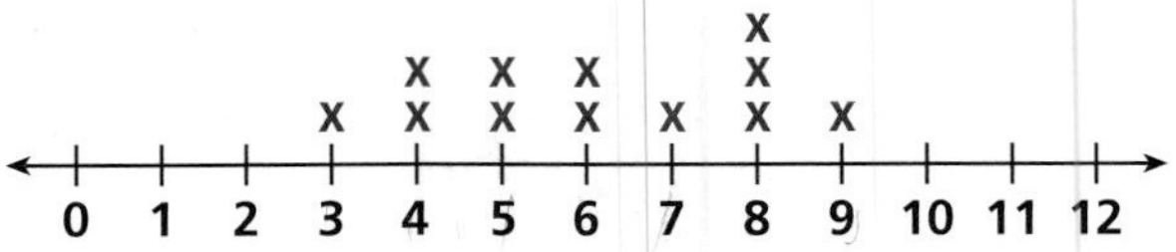

See Example 3

Identify the outlier in each data set. Then determine how the outlier affects the mean, median, and mode of the data. Then tell which measure of central tendency best describes the data with and without the outlier.

10. 13, 18, 20, 5, 15, 20, 13, 20

11. 45, 48, 63, 85, 151, 47, 88, 44, 68

PRACTICE AND PROBLEM SOLVING

Extra Practice
See page 739.

12. Health Based on the data from three annual checkups, Jon's mean height is 62 in. At the first two checkups Jon's height was 58 in. and 61 in. What was his height at the third checkup?

13. Find the mean, median, and mode of the data displayed in the line plot. Then determine how the outlier affects the mean.

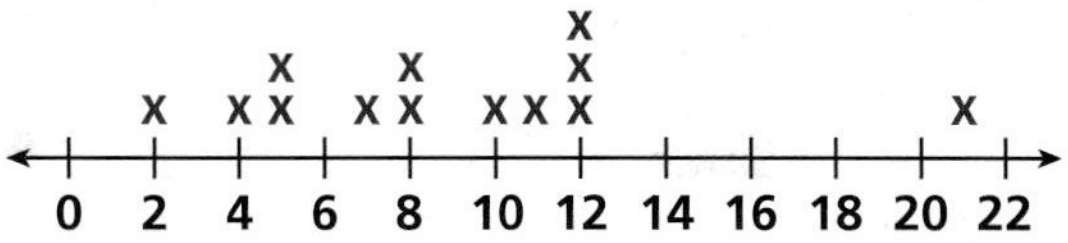

LINK

Sports

Mountain bikes account for over 50% of bicycle sales in the United States.

14. **Critical Thinking** The values in a data set are 95, 93, 91, 95, 100, 99, and 92. What value can be added to the set so that the mean, median, and mode remain the same?

15. **Sports** The ages of the participants in a mountain bike race are 14, 23, 20, 24, 26, 17, 21, 31, 27, 25, 14, and 28. Which measure of central tendency best represents the ages of the participants? Explain.

16. **Estimation** The table shows the monthly rainfall in inches for six months. Estimate the mean, median, and range of the data.

Month	Rainfall (in.)
Jan	4.33
Feb	1.62
Mar	2.17
Apr	0.56
May	3.35
Jun	1.14

17. **What's the Question?** The values in a data set are 10, 7, 9, 5, 13, 10, 7, 14, 8, and 11. What is the question about central tendency that gives the answer 9.5 for the data set?

18. **Write About It** Which measure of central tendency is most often affected by including an outlier? Explain.

19. **Challenge** Pick a measure of central tendency that describes each situation. Explain your choice.

a. the number of siblings in a family

b. the number of days in a month

Test Prep and Spiral Review

20. **Multiple Choice** What is the mean of the winning scores shown in the table?

Ⓐ 276 Ⓑ 276.8 Ⓒ 282.1 Ⓓ 285

Masters Tournament Winning Scores					
Year	2001	2002	2003	2004	2005
Score	272	276	281	279	276

21. **Multiple Choice** In which data set are the mean, median, and mode all the same number?

Ⓕ 6, 2, 5, 4, 3, 4, 1

Ⓖ 4, 2, 2, 1, 3, 2, 3

Ⓗ 2, 3, 7, 3, 8, 3, 2

Ⓙ 4, 3, 4, 3, 4, 6, 4

22. Brett deposits $4,000 in an account that earns 4.5% simple interest. How long will it be before the total amount is $4,800? (Lesson 6-7)

23. Make a stem-and-leaf plot of the following data: 48, 60, 57, 62, 43, 62, 45, and 51. (Lesson 7-1)

7-3 Bar Graphs and Histograms

Learn to display and analyze data in bar graphs and histograms.

Vocabulary
bar graph
double-bar graph
histogram

Hundreds of different languages are spoken around the world. The graph shows the numbers of native speakers of four languages.

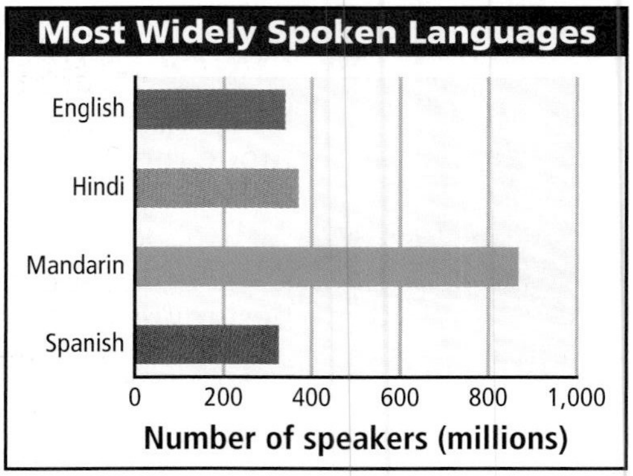

A **bar graph** can be used to display and compare data. The scale of a bar graph should include all the data values and be easily divided into equal intervals.

EXAMPLE 1 Interpreting a Bar Graph

Use the bar graph to answer each question.

A **Which language has the most native speakers?**
The bar for Mandarin is the longest, so Mandarin has the most native speakers.

B **About how many more people speak Mandarin than speak Hindi?**
About 500 million more people speak Mandarin than speak Hindi.

You can use a **double-bar graph** to compare two related sets of data.

EXAMPLE 2 Making a Double-Bar Graph

The table shows the life expectancies of people in three Central American countries. Make a double-bar graph of the data.

Country	Male	Female
El Salvador	67	74
Honduras	63	66
Nicaragua	65	70

Step 1: Choose a scale and interval for the vertical axis.

Step 2: Draw a pair of bars for each country's data. Use different colors to show males and females.

Step 3: Label the axes and give the graph a title.

Step 4: Make a key to show what each bar represents.

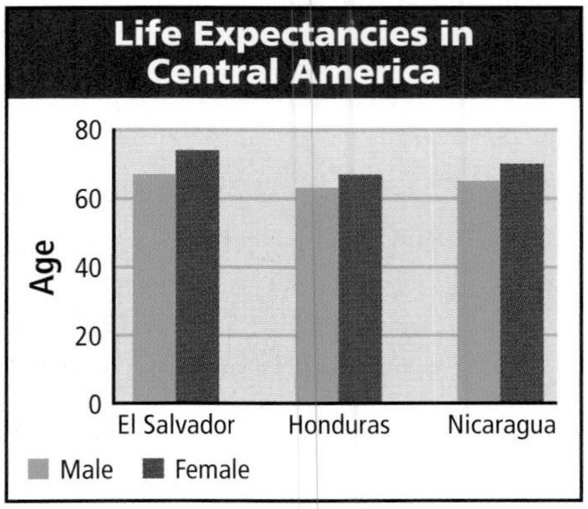

A **histogram** is a bar graph that shows the frequency of data within equal intervals. There is no space between the bars in a histogram.

EXAMPLE 3 Making a Histogram

The table below shows survey results about the number of CDs students own. Make a histogram of the data.

Number of CDs									
1	III	5	𝍸 I	9	𝍸 I	13	𝍸 IIII	17	𝍸 IIII
2	II	6	III	10	𝍸 𝍸	14	𝍸 𝍸 I	18	𝍸 II
3	𝍸	7	𝍸 III	11	𝍸 𝍸 I	15	𝍸 𝍸 I	19	II
4	𝍸 I	8	𝍸 II	12	𝍸 𝍸	16	𝍸 𝍸 I	20	𝍸 I

Step 1: Make a frequency table of the data. Be sure to use a scale that includes all of the data values and separate the scale into equal intervals. Use these intervals on the horizontal axis of your histogram.

Number of CDs	Frequency
1–5	22
6–10	34
11–15	52
16–20	35

Step 2: Choose an appropriate scale and interval for the vertical axis. The greatest value on the scale should be at least as great as the greatest frequency.

Step 3: Draw a bar for each interval. The height of the bar is the frequency for that interval. Bars must touch but not overlap.

Step 4: Label the axes and give the graph a title.

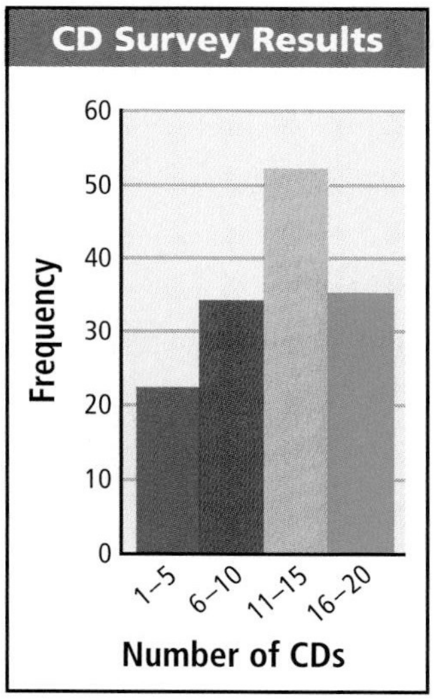

Think and Discuss

1. **Explain** how to use the frequency table in Example 3 to find the number of students surveyed.
2. **Explain** why you might use a double-bar graph instead of two separate bar graphs to display data.
3. **Describe** the similarities and differences between a bar graph and a histogram.

7-3 Exercises

go.hrw.com
Homework Help Online
KEYWORD: MS7 7-3
Parent Resources Online
KEYWORD: MS7 Parent

GUIDED PRACTICE

See Example 1

The bar graph shows the average amount of fresh fruit consumed per person in the United States in 1997. Use the graph for Exercises 1–3.

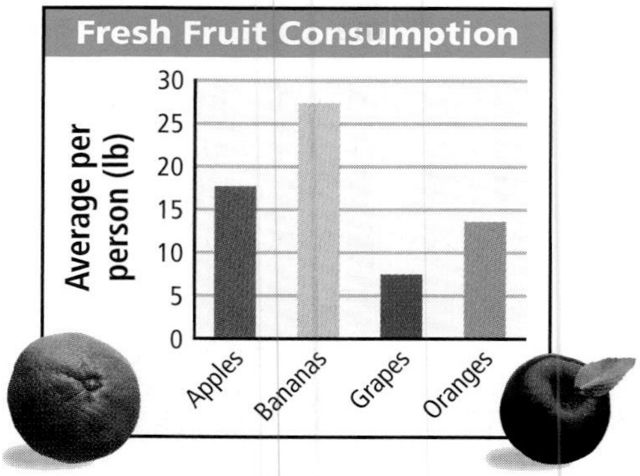

1. Which fruit was eaten the least?
2. About how many pounds of apples were eaten per person?
3. About how many more pounds of bananas than pounds of oranges were eaten per person?

See Example 2

4. The table shows national average SAT scores for three years. Make a double-bar graph of the data.

Year	Verbal	Math
1980	502	492
1990	500	501
2000	505	514

See Example 3

5. The list below shows the ages of musicians in a local orchestra. Make a histogram of the data.

14, 35, 22, 18, 49, 38, 30, 27, 45, 19, 35, 46, 27, 21, 32, 30

INDEPENDENT PRACTICE

See Example 1

The bar graph shows the maximum precipitation in 24 hours for several states. Use the graph for Exercises 6–8.

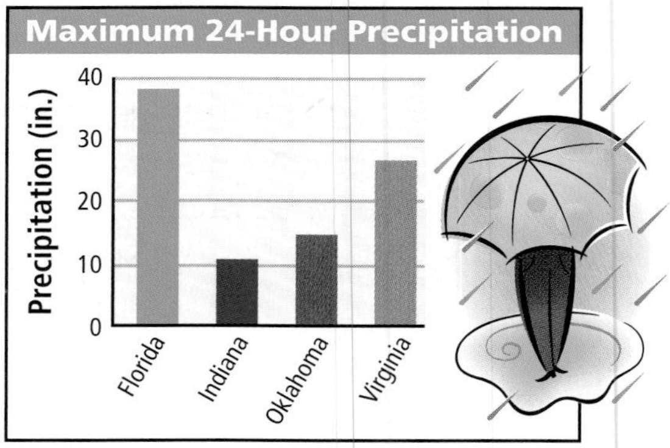

6. Which state received the most precipitation in 24 hours?
7. About how many inches of precipitation did Virginia receive?
8. About how many more inches of precipitation did Oklahoma receive than Indiana?

See Example 2

9. The table shows the average annual income per capita for three Chinese cities. Make a double-bar graph of the data.

City	1994	2000
Beijing	$614	$1,256
Shanghai	$716	$1,424
Shenzhen	$1,324	$2,626

See Example 3

10. The list below shows the results of a typing test in words per minute. Make a histogram of the data.

62, 55, 68, 47, 50, 41, 62, 39, 54, 70, 56, 47, 71, 55, 60, 42

Extra Practice
See page 739.

Social Studies LINK

William Jennings Bryan

In 1896 and 1900, William McKinley, a Republican, and William Jennings Bryan, a Democrat, ran for president of the United States. The table shows the number of electoral votes each man received in these elections.

11. Use the data in the table to make a double-bar graph. Label the horizontal axis with the years.

Candidate	1896	1900
McKinley	271	292
Bryan	176	155

12. Estimation In 1896, about how many more electoral votes did McKinley get than Bryan?

13. The frequency table shows the number of years the first 42 presidents spent in office. Can you tell how many presidents spent exactly six years in office? Explain.

Years in Office	Frequency
0–2	7
3–5	22
6–8	12
9–11	0
12–14	1

William McKinley

14. Use the frequency table to make a histogram.

15. Write About It What does your histogram show you about the number of years the presidents spent in office?

TEST PREP and Spiral Review

Use the graph for Exercises 16 and 17.

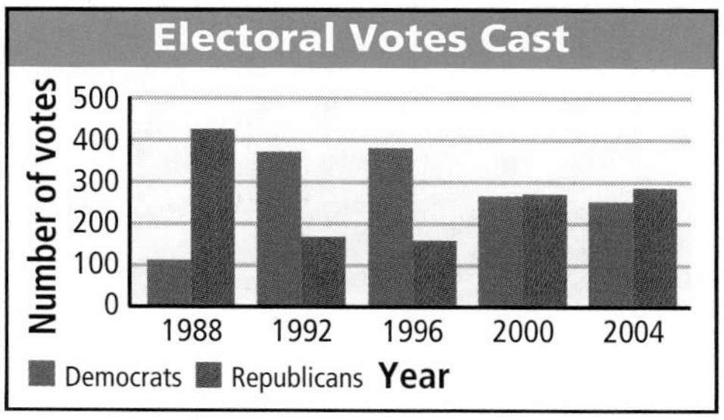

16. Multiple Choice In which year did the Democrats get the fewest number of electoral votes?

Ⓐ 1988 Ⓒ 2000

Ⓑ 1996 Ⓓ 2004

17. Multiple Choice In which year was the difference between the number of electoral votes for the Republicans and Democrats the least?

Ⓕ 1988 Ⓖ 1992 Ⓗ 2000 Ⓙ 2004

Determine whether the ratios are proportional. (Lesson 5-4)

18. $\frac{10}{24}, \frac{15}{36}$ **19.** $\frac{5}{22}, \frac{10}{27}$ **20.** $\frac{2}{20}, \frac{3}{30}$ **21.** $\frac{72}{96}, \frac{9}{12}$

Find the mean, median, mode, and range of each data set. (Lesson 7-2)

22. 42, 29, 49, 32, 19 **23.** 15, 34, 26, 15, 21, 30 **24.** 4, 3, 3, 3, 3, 4, 1

7-4 Reading and Interpreting Circle Graphs

Learn to read and interpret data presented in circle graphs.

Vocabulary
circle graph
sector

A **circle graph**, also called a pie chart, shows how a set of data is divided into parts. The entire circle contains 100% of the data. Each **sector**, or slice, of the circle represents one part of the entire data set.

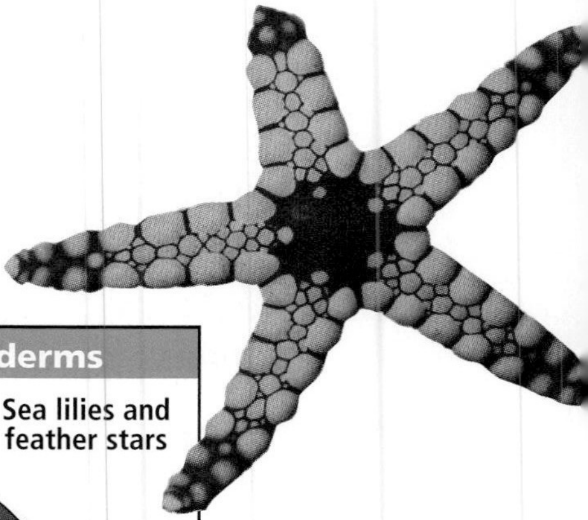

The circle graph compares the number of species in each group of echinoderms. Echinoderms are marine animals that live on the ocean floor. The name *echinoderm* means "spiny-skinned."

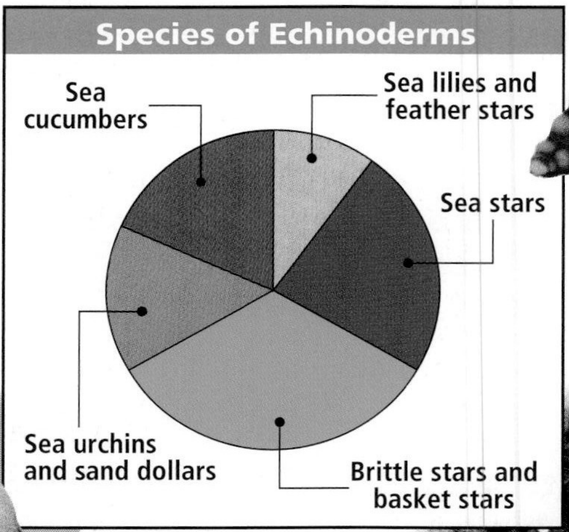

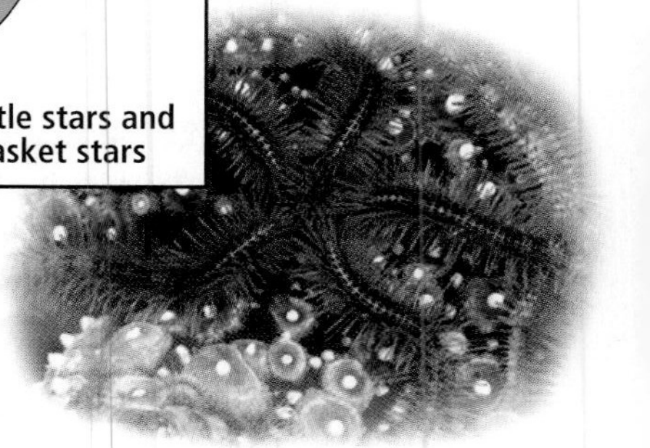

EXAMPLE 1 ***Life Science Application***

Use the circle graph to answer each question.

A **Which group of echinoderms includes the greatest number of species?**

The sector for brittle stars and basket stars is the largest, so this group includes the greatest number of species.

B **Approximately what percent of echinoderm species are sea stars?**

The sector for sea stars makes up about one-fourth of the circle. Since the circle shows 100% of the data, about one-fourth of 100%, or 25%, of echinoderm species are sea stars.

C **Which group is made up of fewer species—sea cucumbers or sea urchins and sand dollars?**

The sector for sea urchins and sand dollars is smaller than the sector for sea cucumbers. This means there are fewer species of sea urchins and sand dollars than species of sea cucumbers.

EXAMPLE 2 Interpreting Circle Graphs

Leon surveyed 30 people about pet ownership. The circle graph shows his results. Use the graph to answer each question.

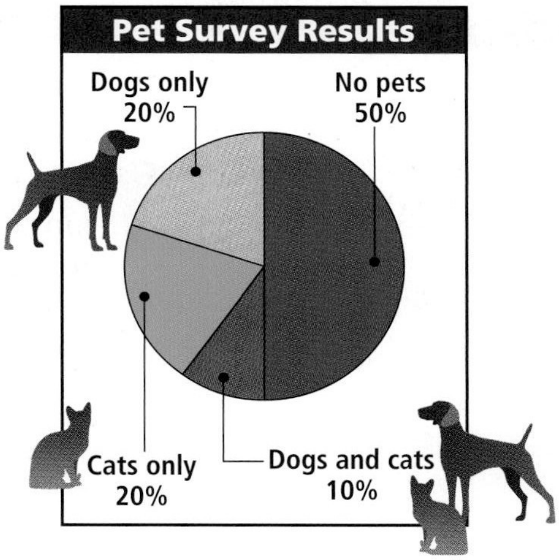

A How many people do not own pets?

The circle graph shows that 50% of the 30 people do not own pets.

$50\% \text{ of } 30 = 0.5 \cdot 30$

$= 15$

Fifteen people do not own pets.

B How many people own cats only?

The circle graph shows that 20% of the 30 people own cats only.

$20\% \text{ of } 30 = 0.2 \cdot 30$

$= 6$

Six people own cats only.

EXAMPLE 3 Choosing an Appropriate Graph

Decide whether a bar graph or a circle graph would best display the information. Explain your answer.

A the percent of a nation's electricity supply generated by each of several fuel sources

A circle graph is the better choice because it makes it easy to see what part of the nation's electricity comes from each fuel source.

B the number of visitors to Arches National Park in each of the last five years

A bar graph is the better choice because it makes it easy to see how the number of visitors has changed over the years.

C the comparison between the time spent in math class and the total time spent in school each day

A circle graph is the better choice because the sector that represents the time spent in math class could be compared to the entire circle, which represents the total time spent in school.

Earth Science LINK

Arches National Park, located in southeastern Utah, covers 73,379 acres. The park is famous for its natural sandstone arches.

Think and Discuss

1. **Describe** two ways a circle graph can be used to compare data.
2. **Compare** the use of circle graphs with the use of bar graphs to display data.

7-4 Exercises

go.hrw.com
Homework Help Online
KEYWORD: MS7 7-4
Parent Resources Online
KEYWORD: MS7 Parent

GUIDED PRACTICE

The circle graph shows the estimated spending on advertising in 2000. Use the graph for Exercises 1–3.

Money Spent on Advertising

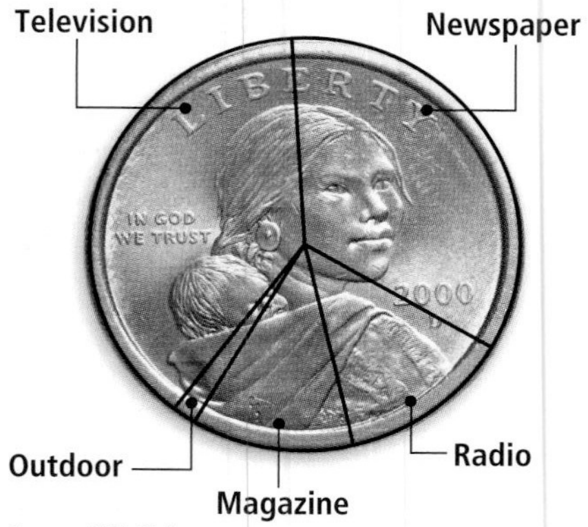

Source: USA Today

See Example 1

1. On which type of advertising was the least amount of money spent?
2. Approximately what percent of spending was on radio and magazine advertising?

See Example 2

3. Television and magazine advertising made up about 50% of all advertising spending in 2000. If the total amount spent was $100,000, about how much was spent on television and magazine advertising?

See Example 3

Decide whether a bar graph or a circle graph would best display the information. Explain your answer.

4. the lengths of the five longest rivers in the world
5. the percent of citizens who voted for each candidate in an election

INDEPENDENT PRACTICE

The circle graph shows the results of a survey of 100 teens who were asked about their favorite sports. Use the graph for Exercises 6–8.

Sports Survey Results

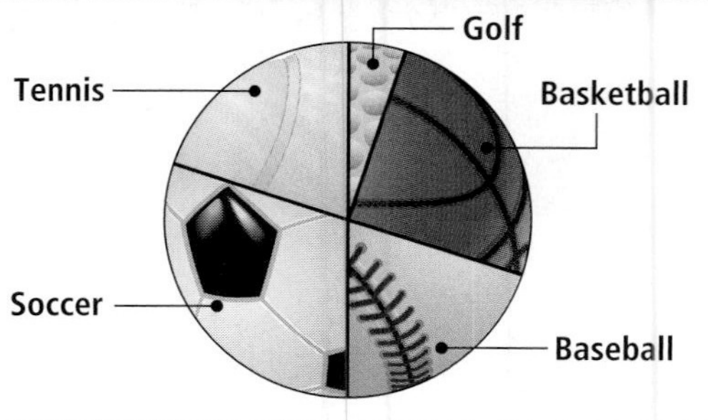

See Example 1

6. Did more teens pick basketball or tennis as their favorite sport?
7. Approximately what percent of teens picked soccer as their favorite sport?

See Example 2

8. According to the survey, 5% of teens chose golf. What is the number of teens who chose golf?

See Example 3

Decide whether a bar graph or a circle graph would best display the information. Explain your answer.

9. the number of calories eaten at breakfast compared with the total number of calories eaten in one day
10. the number of inches of rain that fell each month in Honolulu, Hawaii, during one year

PRACTICE AND PROBLEM SOLVING

Extra Practice
See page 739.

Geography The circle graph shows the percent of Earth's land area covered by each continent. Use the graph for Exercises 11–13.

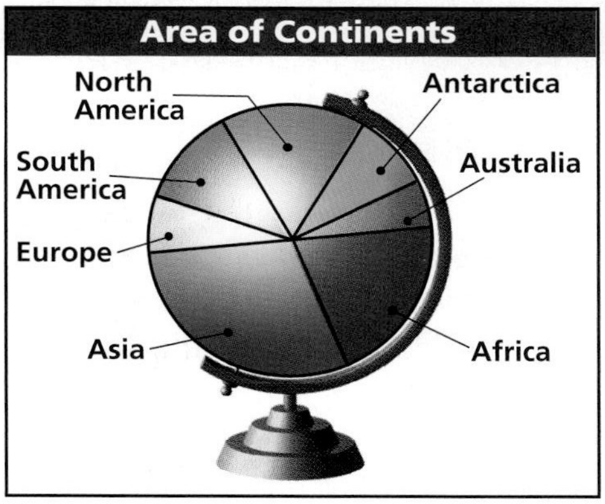

11. List the continents in order of size, from largest to smallest.

12. Approximately what percent of Earth's total land area is Asia?

13. Approximately what percent of Earth's total land area is North America and South America combined?

14. Critical Thinking A group of 200 students were asked how they like to spend their free time. Of the students surveyed, 47% said they like to play on the computer, 59% said they like to go to the mall, 38% said they like to go to the movies, and 41% said they like to play sports. Can you make a circle graph to display this data? Explain.

15. What's the Error? The table shows the types of pets owned by a group of students. A circle graph of the data shows that 25% of the students surveyed own a dog. Why is the graph incorrect?

Pet	Number of Students
Cat	卌 卌 卌
Dog	卌 卌 I
Fish	卌
Other	卌

16. Write About It What math skills do you use when interpreting information in a circle graph?

17. Challenge Earth's total land area is approximately 57,900,000 square miles. Antarctica is almost 10% of the total area. What is the approximate land area of Antarctica in square miles?

Test Prep and Spiral Review

Use the graph for Exercises 18 and 19.

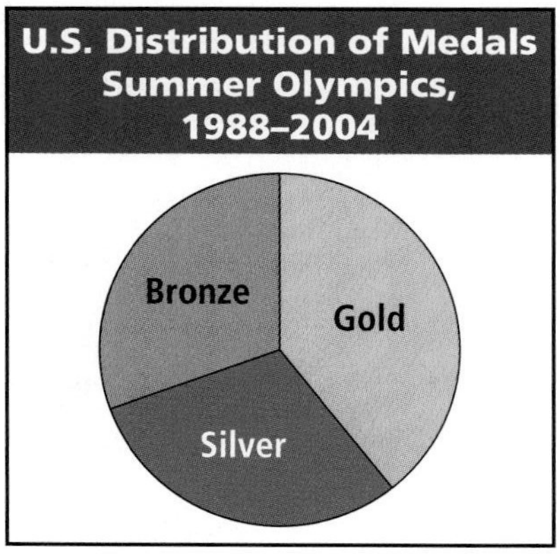

18. Multiple Choice Approximately what percent of the medals won by the United States were gold?

Ⓐ 25% Ⓑ 40% Ⓒ 50% Ⓓ 75%

19. Short Response The United States won a total of 502 medals in the Summer Olympics from 1988 to 2004. About how many of these were bronze medals? Show your work.

20. José has an American flag that measures 10 inches by 19 inches. He paints a picture of a flag that is 60 inches by 114 inches. Will his painted flag be similar to the American flag? (Lesson 5-7)

Compare. Write <, >, or =. (Lesson 6-2)

21. 0.1 ▒ 0.09 **22.** 1.71 ▒ $\frac{24}{11}$ **23.** 1.25 ▒ 125% **24.** 32.5 ▒ 69%

7-5 Box-and-Whisker Plots

Learn to display and analyze data in box-and-whisker plots.

Vocabulary

box-and-whisker plot

lower quartile

upper quartile

interquartile range

Carson is planning a deep-sea fishing trip. He chooses a fishing charter based on the number of fish caught on different charters.

A **box-and-whisker plot** uses a number line to show the distribution of a set of data.

To make a box-and-whisker plot, first divide the data into four parts using *quartiles.* The median, or *middle quartile,* divides the data into a lower half and an upper half. The median of the lower half is the **lower quartile**, and the median of the upper half is the **upper quartile**.

EXAMPLE 1 **Making a Box-and-Whisker Plot**

Use the data to make a box-and-whisker plot.

26, 17, 21, 23, 19, 28, 17, 20, 29

Step 1: Order the data from least to greatest. Then find the least and greatest values, the median, and the lower and upper quartiles.

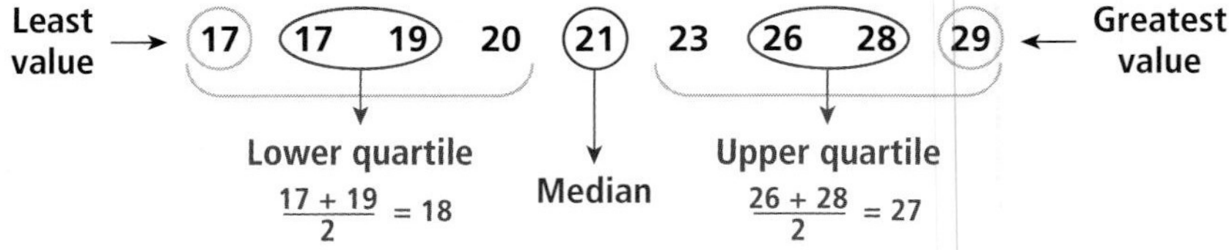

Caution!

To find the median of a data set with an even number of values, find the mean of the two middle values.

Step 2: Draw a number line. Above the number line, plot a point for each value in Step 1.

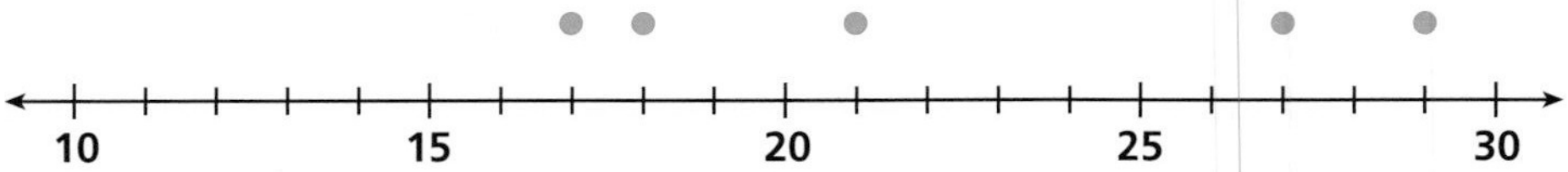

Step 3: Draw a box from the lower to the upper quartile. Inside the box, draw a vertical line through the median. Then draw the "whiskers" from the box to the least and greatest values.

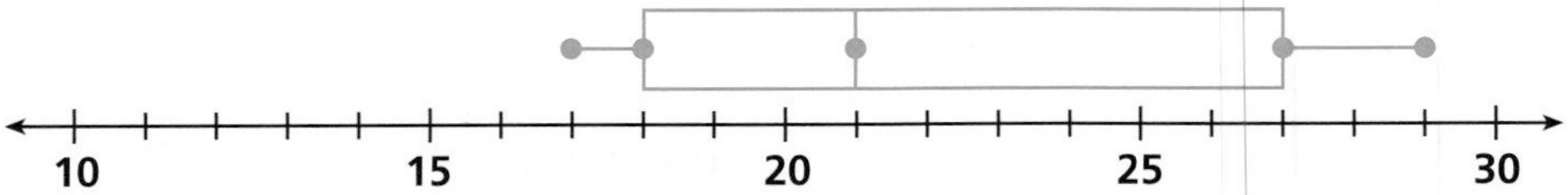

The **interquartile range** of a data set is the difference between the lower and upper quartiles. It tells how large the spread of data around the median is.

You can use a box-and-whisker plot to analyze how data in a set are distributed. You can also use box-and-whisker plots to help you compare two sets of data.

EXAMPLE 2 Comparing Box-and-Whisker Plots

The box-and-whisker plots below show the distribution of the number of fish caught per trip by two fishing charters.

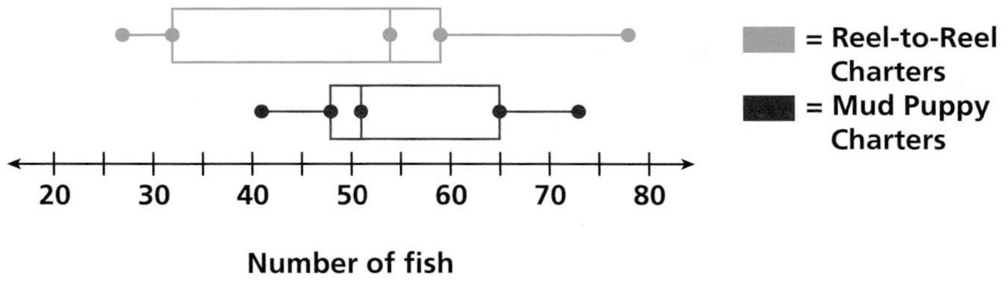

A Which fishing charter has a greater median?

The median number of fish caught on Reel-to-Reel Charters, about 54, is greater than the median number of fish caught on Mud Puppy Charters, about 51.

B Which fishing charter has a greater interquartile range?

The length of the box in a box-and-whisker plot indicates the interquartile range. Reel-to-Reel Charters has a longer box, so it has a greater interquartile range.

C Which fishing charter appears to be more predictable in the number of fish that might be caught on a fishing trip?

The range and interquartile range are smaller for Mud Puppy Charters, which means that there is less variation in the data. So the number of fish caught on Mud Puppy Charters is more predictable.

Think and Discuss

1. **Describe** what you can tell about a data set from a box-and-whisker plot.
2. **Explain** how the range and the interquartile range of a set of data are different. Which measure tells you more about central tendency?

7-5 Exercises

go.hrw.com
Homework Help Online
KEYWORD: MS7 7-5
Parent Resources Online
KEYWORD: MS7 Parent

GUIDED PRACTICE

See Example 1
Use the data to make a box-and-whisker plot.

1. 46 35 46 38 37 33 49 42 35 40 37

See Example 2
Use the box-and-whisker plots of inches flown by two different paper airplanes for Exercises 2–4.

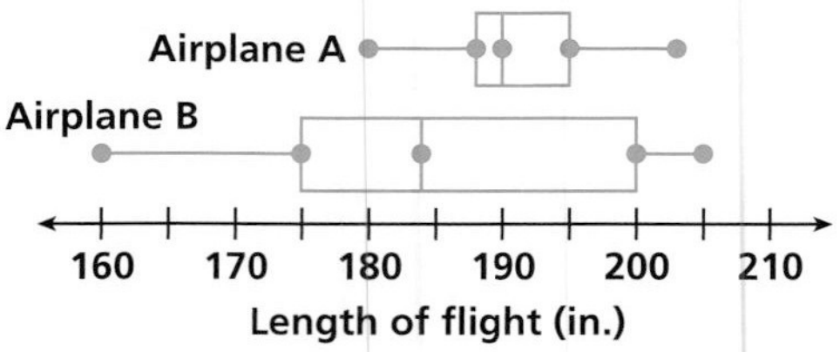

2. Which paper airplane has a greater median flight length?
3. Which paper airplane has a greater interquartile range of flight lengths?
4. Which paper airplane appears to have a more predictable flight length?

INDEPENDENT PRACTICE

See Example 1
Use the data to make a box-and-whisker plot.

5. 81 73 88 85 81 72 86 72 79 75 76

See Example 2
Use the box-and-whisker plots of apartment rental costs in two different cities for Exercises 6–8.

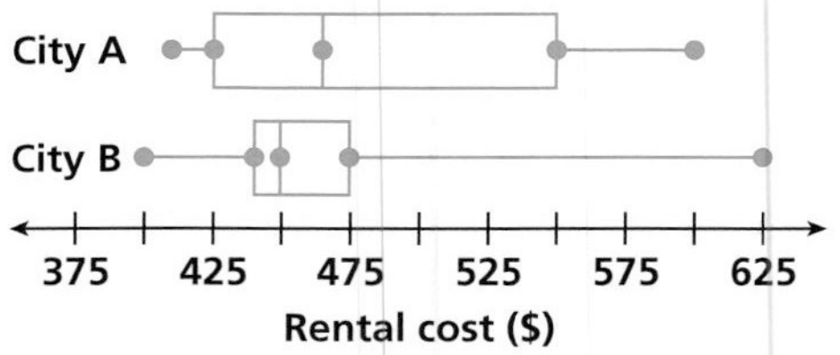

6. Which city has a greater median apartment rental cost?
7. Which city has a greater interquartile range of apartment rental costs?
8. Which city appears to have a more predictable apartment rental cost?

PRACTICE AND PROBLEM SOLVING

Extra Practice
See page 739.

The points scored per game by a basketball player are shown below. Use the data for Exercises 9–11.

12 7 15 23 10 18 39 15 20 8 13

9. Make two box-and-whisker plots of the data on the same number line: one plot with the outlier and one plot without the outlier.
10. How does the outlier affect the interquartile range of the data?
11. Which is affected more by the outlier: the range or the interquartile range?
12. Make a box-and-whisker plot of the data shown in the line plot.

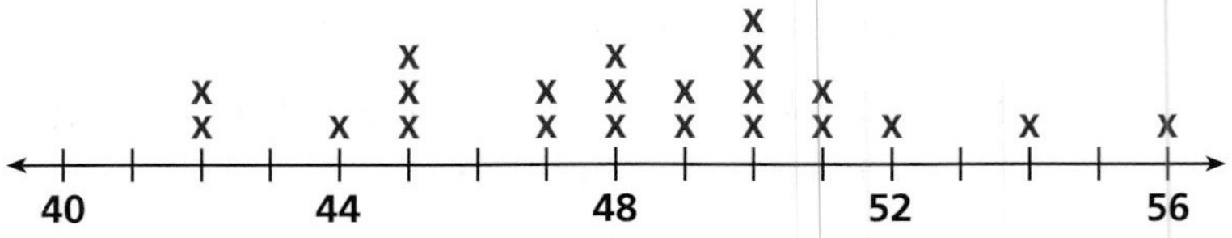

13. **Sports** The table shows the countries that were the top 15 medal winners in the 2004 Olympics.

Country	Medals	Country	Medals	Country	Medals
USA	103	Russia	92	China	63
Australia	49	Germany	48	Japan	37
France	33	Italy	32	Britain	30
Korea	30	Cuba	27	Ukraine	23
Netherlands	22	Romania	19	Spain	19

a. Make a box-and-whisker plot of the data.

b. Describe the distribution of the number of medals won.

14. **Measurement** The stem-and-leaf plot shows the heights in inches of a class of seventh graders.

a. Make a box-and-whisker plot of the data.

b. Three-fourths of the students are taller than what height?

c. Three-fourths of the students are shorter than what height?

Student Heights

Stems	Leaves
5	3 5 6 6 8 8 8 9 9
6	0 0 1 1 1 1 1 2 2 2 4

Key: 5|3 means 53

15. **What's the Error?** Using the data 2, 9, 5, 14, 8, 13, 7, 5, and 8, a student found the upper quartile to be 9. What did the student do wrong?

16. **Write About It** Two box-and-whisker plots have the same median and equally long whiskers. If the box of one plot is longer, what can you say about the difference between the two data sets?

17. **Challenge** An outlier is defined to be at least 1.5 times the interquartile range. Name the value that would be considered an outlier in the data set 1, 2, 4, 2, 1, 0, 6, 8, 1, 6, and 2.

Test Prep and Spiral Review

Use the graph for Exercises 18 and 19.

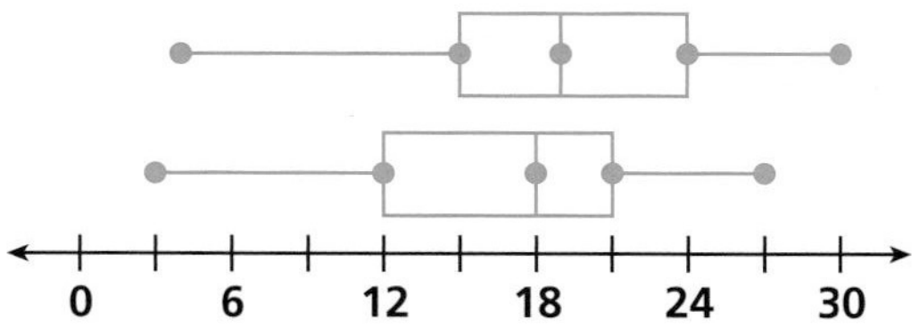

18. **Multiple Choice** What is the difference between the interquartile ranges for the two data sets?

(A) 21 (C) 9

(B) 18 (D) 0

19. **Gridded Response** What is the lower quartile of the box-and-whisker plot with the greater range?

20. A tree casts a 21.25 ft shadow, while a 6 ft tall man casts a 10.5 ft shadow. Estimate the height of the tree. (Lesson 5-8)

21. Mari spent $24.69 on lunch with her mom. About how much should she leave for a 15% tip? (Lesson 6-3)

Hands-On LAB 7-5

Use Venn Diagrams to Display Collected Data

Use with Lesson 7-5

go.hrw.com
Lab Resources Online
KEYWORD: MS7 Lab7

You can use a Venn diagram to display relationships in data. Use ovals, circles, or other shapes to represent individual data sets.

Activity 1

At Landry Middle School, 127 students play a team sport, 145 play a musical instrument, and 31 do both. Make a Venn diagram to display the relationship in the data.

1. Draw and label two overlapping circles to represent the sets of students who play a team sport and a musical instrument. Label one "Team sport" and the other "Musical instrument."

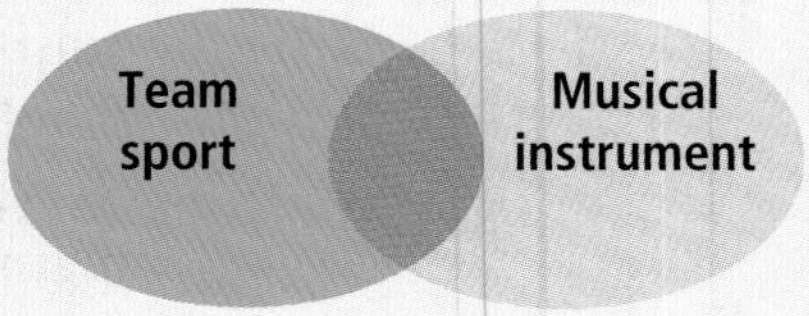

2. Write "31" in the area where the circles overlap. This is the number of students who play a musical instrument and a team sport.

3. To find the number of students who play a team sport *only*, begin with the number of students who play a team sport, 127, and subtract the number of students who do both, 31.

team sport	−	**both**	=	**team sport *only***
127	−	31	=	96

Use the same process to find the number of students who play a musical instrument *only*.

musical instrument	−	**both**	=	**musical instrument *only***
145	−	31	=	114

4. Complete the Venn diagram by adding the number of students who play *only* a team sport and the number of students who play *only* a musical instrument to the diagram.

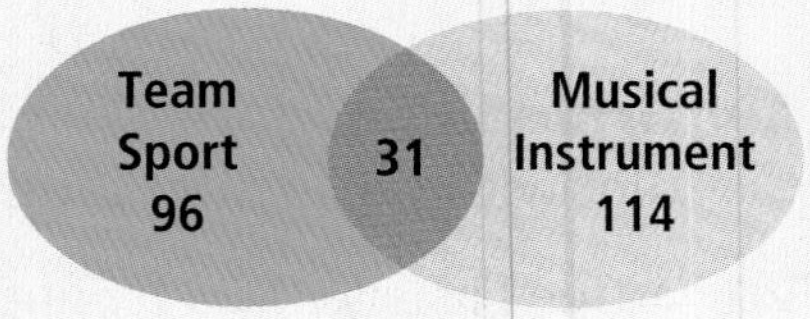

Think and Discuss

1. Explain why some of the numbers that were given in Activity 1, such as 127 and 145, do not appear in the Venn diagram.
2. Describe a Venn diagram that has three individual data sets. How many overlapping areas does it have?

Try This

Responding to a survey about favorite foods, 60 people said they like pasta, 45 said they like chicken, and 70 said they like hot dogs. Also, 15 people said they like both chicken and pasta, 22 said they like both hot dogs and chicken, and 17 said they like both hot dogs and pasta. Only 8 people said they like all 3 foods.

1. How many people like only pasta?
2. How many people like only chicken?
3. How many people like only hot dogs?
4. Make a Venn diagram to show the relationships in the data.

Activity 2

1. Interview your classmates to find out what kinds of movies they like (for example, action, comedy, drama, and horror).
2. Make a Venn diagram to show the relationships in the collected data.

Think and Discuss

1. Tell how many individual sets and how many overlapping areas a Venn diagram of the movie data will have.
2. Describe what a Venn diagram of student ages might look like. Would there be any overlapping sets? Explain.

Try This

1. Interview your classmates to find out what kinds of sports they like to play. Make a Venn diagram to show the relationships in the data.
2. The Venn diagram shows the types of exercise that some students do.
   a. How many students were surveyed?
   b. How many students jog?
   c. How many students like to both bike and walk?

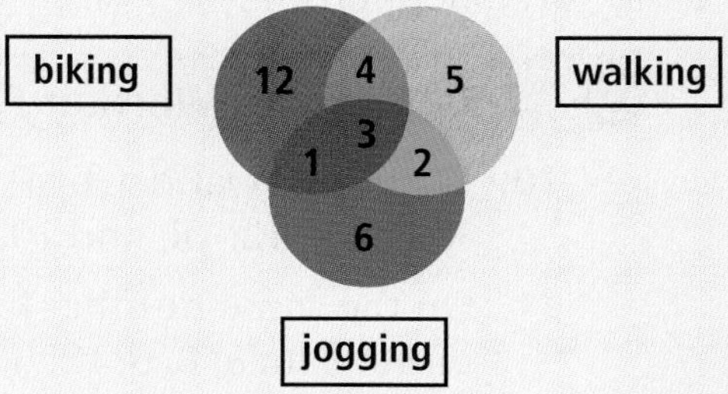

CHAPTER 7

READY TO GO ON?

SECTION 7A

Quiz for Lessons 7-1 Through 7-5

7-1 Frequency Tables, Stem-and-Leaf Plots, and Line Plots

The list shows the top speeds of various land animals.

42 55 62 48 65 51 47 59 67 61 49 54 55 52 44

1. Make a cumulative frequency table of the data.
2. Make a stem-and-leaf plot of the data.
3. Make a line plot of the data.

7-2 Mean, Median, Mode, and Range

The list shows the life spans in years of vampire bats in captivity.

18 22 5 21 19 21 17 3 19 20 29 18 17

4. Find the mean, median, mode, and range of the data. Round your answers to the nearest tenth of a year.
5. Which measure of central tendency best represents the data? Explain.

7-3 Bar Graphs and Histograms

6. The table shows the numbers of students in the sixth and seventh grades who participated in school fairs. Make a double-bar graph of the data.

School Fair Participation

Fair	Sixth Grade	Seventh Grade
Book	55	76
Health	69	58
Science	74	98

7. The list below shows the numbers of tracks on a group of CDs. Make a histogram of the data.

   13, 7, 10, 8, 15, 17, 22, 9, 11, 10, 16, 12, 9, 20

7-4 Reading and Interpreting Circle Graphs

Use the circle graph for problems 8 and 9.

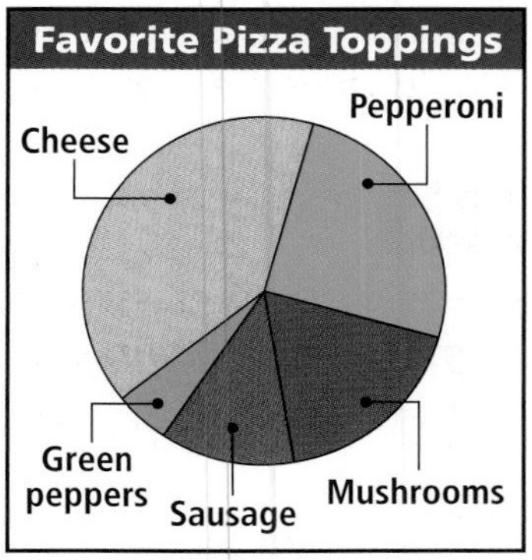

8. Approximately what percent of students picked cheese as their favorite topping?
9. Out of 200 students, 25% picked pepperoni as their favorite pizza topping. How many students picked pepperoni?

7-5 Box-and-Whisker Plots

10. Make a box-and-whisker plot of the data 14, 8, 13, 20, 15, 17, 1, 12, 18, and 10.
11. On the same number line, make a box-and-whisker plot of the data 3, 8, 5, 12, 6, 18, 14, 8, 15, and 11.
12. Which box-and-whisker plot has a greater interquartile range?

Focus on Problem Solving

Solve

• Choose an operation: addition or subtraction

In order to decide whether to add or subtract to solve a problem, you need to determine what action is taking place in the problem. If you are combining or putting together numbers, you need to add. If you are taking away or finding how far apart two numbers are, you need to subtract.

Determine the action in each problem. Then determine which operation could be used to solve the problem. Use the table for problems 5 and 6.

1. Betty, Raymond, and Helen ran a three-person relay race. Their individual times were 48 seconds, 55 seconds, and 51 seconds. What was their total time?

2. The Scots pine and the sessile oak are trees native to Northern Ireland. The height of a mature Scots pine is 111 feet, and the height of a mature sessile oak is 90 feet. How much taller is the Scots pine than the sessile oak?

3. Mr. Hutchins has $35.00 to buy supplies for his social studies class. He wants to buy items that cost $19.75, $8.49, and $7.10. Does Mr. Hutchins have enough money to buy all of the supplies?

4. The running time for the 1998 movie *Antz* is 83 minutes. Jordan has watched 25 minutes of the movie. How many minutes does he have left to watch?

Sizes of Marine Mammals

Mammal	Weight (kg)
Killer whale	3,600
Manatee	400
Sea lion	200
Walrus	750

5. The table gives the approximate weights of four marine mammals. How much more does the killer whale weigh than the sea lion?

6. Find the total weight of the manatee, the sea lion, and the walrus. Do these three mammals together weigh more or less than the killer whale?

7-6 Line Graphs

Learn to display and analyze data in line graphs.

Vocabulary

line graph

double-line graph

You can use a *line graph* to show how data changes over a period of time. In a **line graph**, line segments are used to connect data points on a coordinate grid. The result is a visual record of change.

Line graphs can be used for a variety of reasons, including showing the growth of a cat over time.

EXAMPLE 1 Making a Line Graph

Make a line graph of the data in the table. Use the graph to determine during which 2-month period the kitten's weight increased the most.

Age (mo)	Weight (lb)
0	0.2
2	1.7
4	3.8
6	5.1
8	6.0
10	6.7
12	7.2

Step 1: Determine the scale and interval for each axis. Place units of time on the horizontal axis.

Step 2: Plot a point for each pair of values. Connect the points using line segments.

Step 3: Label the axes and give the graph a title.

Helpful Hint

To plot each point, start at zero. Move *right* for the time and *up* for the weight.

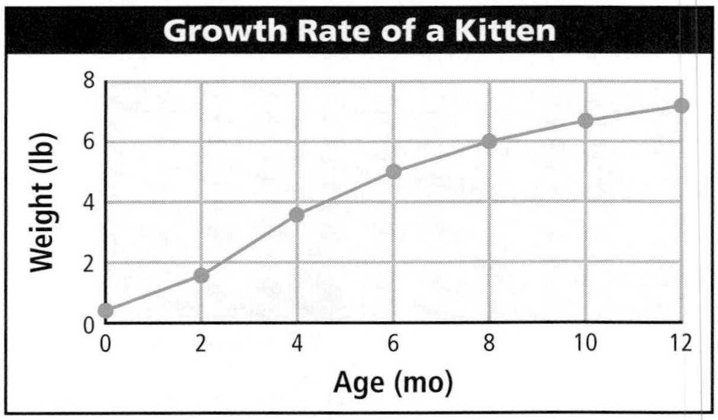

The graph shows the steepest line segment between 2 and 4 months. This means the kitten's weight increased most between 2 and 4 months.

A **biased sample** does not fairly represent the population. A study of 50 elk belonging to a breeder could be biased because the breeder's elk might be less likely to have Mad Elk Disease than elk in the wild.

EXAMPLE 2 Identifying Potentially Biased Samples

Determine whether each sample may be biased. Explain.

A **The first 50 people exiting a movie are surveyed to find out what type of movie people in the town like to see.**

The sample is biased. It is likely that not everyone in the town likes to see the same type of movie that those 50 people just saw.

B **A librarian randomly chooses 100 books from the library's database to calculate the average length of a library book.**

The sample is not biased. It is a random sample.

Given data about a random sample, you can use proportional reasoning to make predictions or verify claims about the entire population.

EXAMPLE 3 Verifying Claims Based on Statistical Data

A biologist estimates that more than 700 of the 4,500 elk at a wildlife preserve are infected with a parasite. A random sample of 50 elk shows that 8 of them are infected. Determine whether the biologist's estimate is likely to be accurate.

Set up a proportion to predict the total number of infected elk.

$$\frac{\text{infected elk in sample}}{\text{size of sample}} = \frac{\text{infected elk in population}}{\text{size of population}}$$

$$\frac{8}{50} = \frac{x}{4{,}500}$$ *Let x represent the number of infected elk at the preserve.*

$$8 \cdot 4{,}500 = 50 \cdot x$$ *The cross products are equal.*

$$36{,}000 = 50x$$ *Multiply.*

$$\frac{36{,}000}{50} = \frac{50x}{50}$$ *Divide each side by 50 to isolate x.*

$$720 = x$$

Based on the sample, you can predict that there are 720 infected elk at the preserve. The biologist's estimate is likely to be accurate.

Remember!

In the proportion $\frac{a}{b} = \frac{c}{d}$, the cross products, $a \cdot d$ and $b \cdot c$ are equal.

Think and Discuss

1. **Describe** a situation in which you would want to use a sample rather than survey the entire population.
2. **Explain** why it might be difficult to obtain a truly random sample of a very large population.

7-8 Exercises

go.hrw.com
Homework Help Online
KEYWORD: MS7 7-8
Parent Resources Online
KEYWORD: MS7 Parent

GUIDED PRACTICE

See Example 1

1. Determine which sampling method will better represent the entire population. Justify your answer.

Lone Star Cars: Customer Satisfaction	
Sampling Method	**Results of Survey**
Nadia surveys 200 customers on the car lot one Saturday morning.	92% are satisfied
Daria mails surveys to 100 randomly-selected customers.	68% are satisfied

See Example 2

Determine whether each sample may be biased. Explain.

2. A company randomly selects 500 customers from its computer database and then surveys those customers to find out how they like their service.
3. A city-hall employee surveys 100 customers at a restaurant to learn about the jobs and salaries of city residents.

See Example 3

4. A factory produces 150,000 light bulbs per day. The manager of the factory estimates that fewer than 1,000 defective bulbs are produced each day. In a random sample of 250 light bulbs, there are 2 defective bulbs. Determine whether the manager's estimate is likely to be accurate. Explain.

INDEPENDENT PRACTICE

See Example 1

5. Determine which sampling method will better represent the entire population. Justify your answer.

Midville Morning News: Subscription Renewals	
Sampling Method	**Results of Survey**
Suzanne surveys 80 subscribers in her neighborhood.	61% intend to renew subscription
Vonetta telephones 150 randomly-selected subscribers.	82% intend to renew subscription

See Example 2

Determine whether each sample may be biased. Explain.

6. A disc jockey asks the first 10 listeners who call in if they liked the last song that was played.
7. Members of a polling organization survey 700 registered voters by randomly choosing names from a list of all registered voters.

See Example 3

8. A university has 30,600 students. A survey is mailed to a random sample of 240 students, 20 of whom speak three or more languages. Predict the number of students at the university who speak three or more languages.

PRACTICE AND PROBLEM SOLVING

Extra Practice
See page 740.

Explain whether you would survey the entire population or use a sample.

9. You want to know the favorite painters of employees at a local art museum.

10. You want to know the types of calculators used by middle school students across the country.

11. You want to know how many hours per week the students in your social studies class spend on their homework.

12. **Life Science** A biologist chooses a random sample of 50 out of 750 fruit flies. She finds that 2 of them have mutated genes causing deformed wings. The biologist claims that approximately 30 of the 750 fruit flies have deformed wings. Do you agree? Explain.

LINK

Life Science

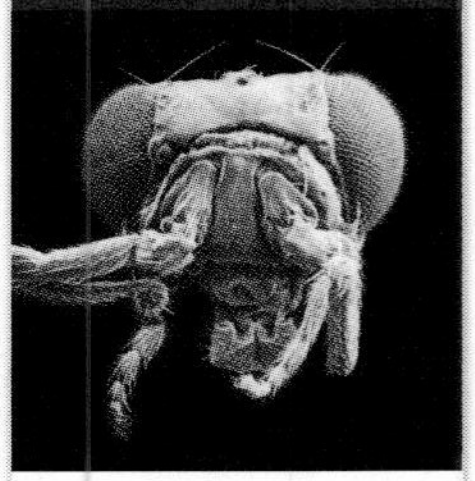

North American fruit flies are known to damage cherries, apples, and blueberries. In the Mediterranean, fruit flies are a threat to citrus fruits.

13. **Critical Thinking** Explain why surveying 100 people who are listed in the phone book may not be a random sample.

14. **What's the Error?** The students in Jacy's science class put their names in a hat. Of the 28 names in the hat, Jacy draws 5 names. She finds that 2 of those 5 students say that their favorite subject is science. Jacy predicts that 254 students of the 635 students at her school would say that their favorite subject is science. What is the error in Jacy's prediction?

15. **Write About It** Suppose you want to know whether the seventh-grade students at your school spend more time watching TV or using a computer. How might you choose a random sample from the population?

16. **Challenge** A manager at XQJ Software surveyed 200 company employees to find out how many of the employees walk to work. The results are shown in the table. Do you think the manager chose a random sample? Why or why not?

Employees at XQJ Software

	Total Number	Number Who Walk to Work
Population	9,200	300
Sample	200	40

TEST PREP and Spiral Review

17. **Multiple Choice** Banneker Middle School has 580 students. Wei surveys a random sample of 30 students and finds that 12 of them have pet dogs. How many students at the school are likely to have pet dogs?

Ⓐ 116 Ⓑ 232 Ⓒ 290 Ⓓ 360

18. **Short Response** Give an example of a biased sample. Explain why it is biased.

Write each percent as a decimal. (Lesson 6-1)

19. 52% 20. 7% 21. 110% 22. 0.4%

Find the percent of each number. (Lesson 6-4)

23. 11% of 50 24. 48% of 600 25. 0.5% of 82 26. 210% of 16

7-9 Scatter Plots

Learn to display and analyze data in scatter plots.

Vocabulary

scatter plot

positive correlation

negative correlation

no correlation

The supersaurus, one of the largest known dinosaurs, could weigh as much as 55 tons and grow as long as 100 feet from head to tail. The tyrannosaurus, a large meat-eating dinosaur, was about one-third the length of the supersaurus.

Two sets of data, such as the length and the weight of dinosaurs, may be related. To find out, you can make a *scatter plot* of the data values in each set. A **scatter plot** has two number lines, called *axes*—one for each set of data values. Each point on the scatter plot represents a pair of data values. These points may appear to be scattered or may cluster in the shape of a line or a curve.

EXAMPLE 1 Making a Scatter Plot

Use the data to make a scatter plot. Describe the relationship between the data sets.

Name	Length (ft)	Weight (tons)
Triceratops	30	6
Tyrannosaurus	39	7
Euhelopus	50	25
Brachiosaurus	82	50
Supersaurus	100	55

Step 1: Determine the scale and interval for each axis. Place units of length on the horizontal axis and units of weight on the vertical axis.

Step 2: Plot a point for each pair of values.

Step 3: Label the axes and title the graph.

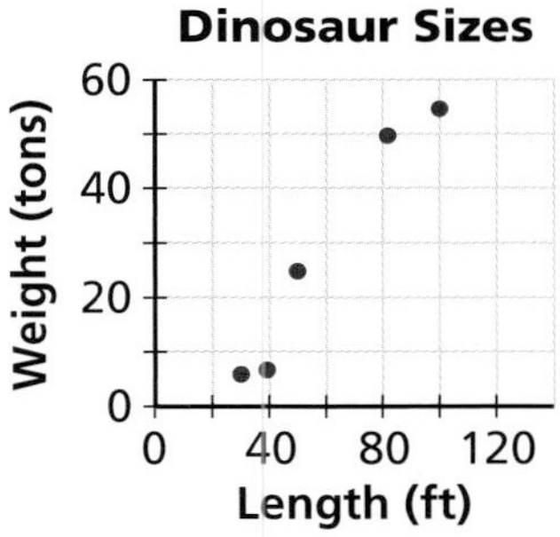

The scatter plot shows that a dinosaur's weight tends to increase as its length increases.

There are three ways to describe data displayed in a scatter plot.

Positive Correlation

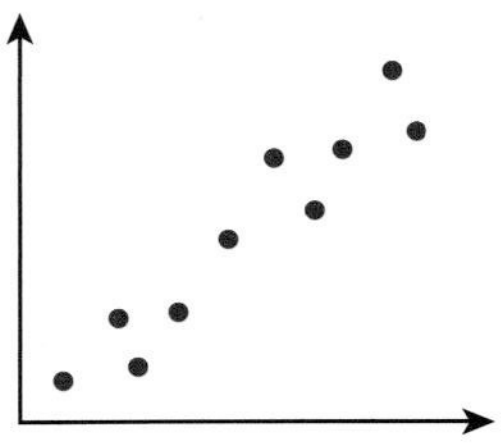

The values in both data sets increase at the same time.

Negative Correlation

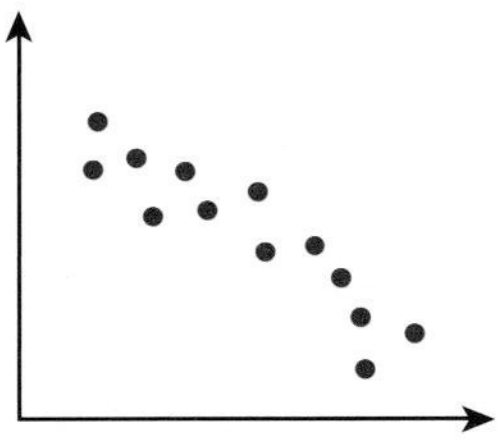

The values in one data set increase as the values in the other set decrease.

No Correlation

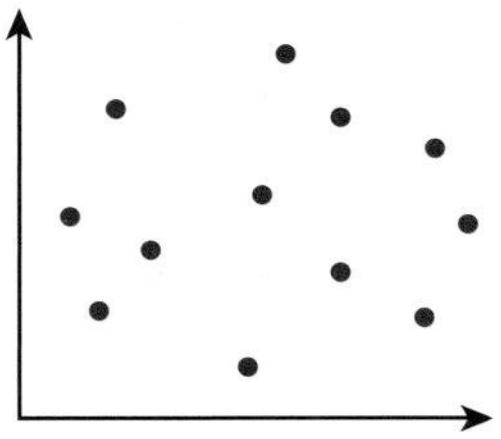

The values in both data sets show no pattern.

EXAMPLE 2 Determining Relationships Between Two Sets of Data

Write *positive correlation, negative correlation,* or *no correlation* to describe each relationship. Explain.

A

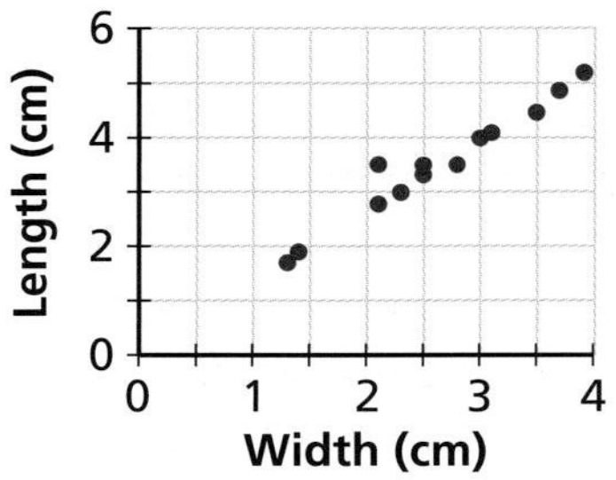

The graph shows that as width increases, length increases. So the graph shows a positive correlation between the data sets.

B

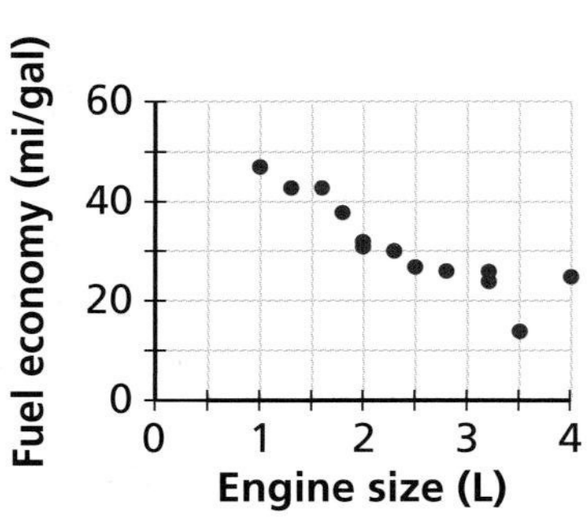

The graph shows that as engine size increases, fuel economy decreases. So the graph shows a negative correlation between the data sets.

C **the ages of people and the number of pets they own**

The number of pets a person owns is not related to the person's age. So there seems to be no correlation between the data sets.

Think and Discuss

1. **Describe** the type of correlation you would expect between the number of absences in a class and the grades in the class.
2. **Give an example** of a relationship between two sets of data that shows a negative correlation. Then give an example of a positive correlation.

7-9 Exercises

go.hrw.com
Homework Help Online
KEYWORD: MS7 7-9
Parent Resources Online
KEYWORD: MS7 Parent

GUIDED PRACTICE

See Example 1

1. The table shows the typical weights (in kilograms) and heart rates (in beats per minute) of several mammals. Use the data to make a scatter plot. Describe the relationship between the data sets.

Mammal	Weight	Heart Rate
Ferret	0.6	360
Human	70	70
Llama	185	75
Red deer	110	80
Rhesus monkey	10	160

See Example 2

Write *positive correlation, negative correlation,* or *no correlation* to describe each relationship. Explain.

2. 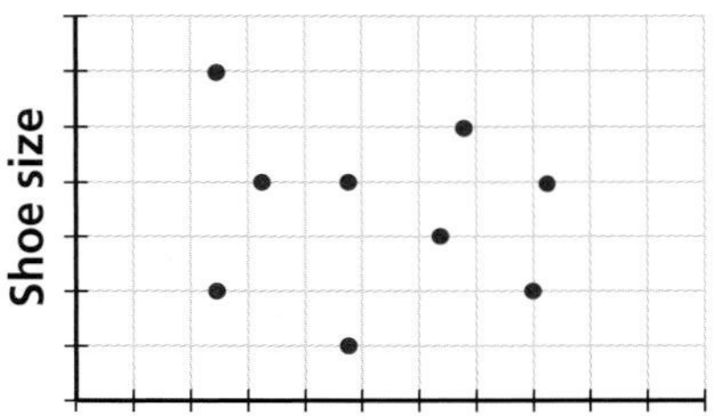

3. 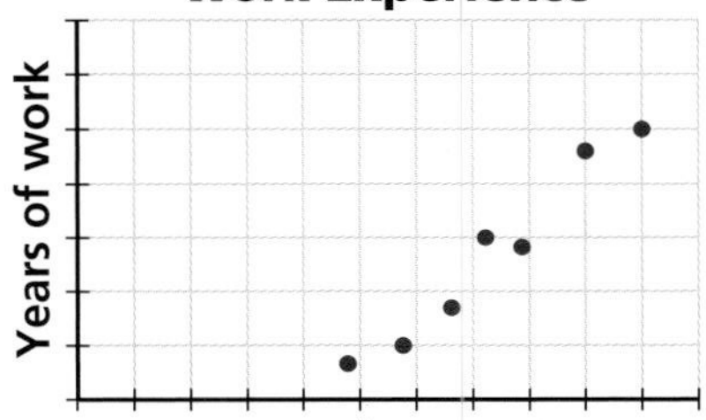

4. the time it takes to drive 100 miles and the driving speed

INDEPENDENT PRACTICE

See Example 1

5. The table shows solar energy cell capacity (in megawatts) over several years. Use the data to make a scatter plot. Describe the relationship between the data sets.

Year	Capacity	Year	Capacity
1990	13.8	1993	21.0
1991	14.9	1994	26.1
1992	15.6	1995	31.1

See Example 2

Write *positive correlation, negative correlation,* or *no correlation* to describe each relationship. Explain.

6. 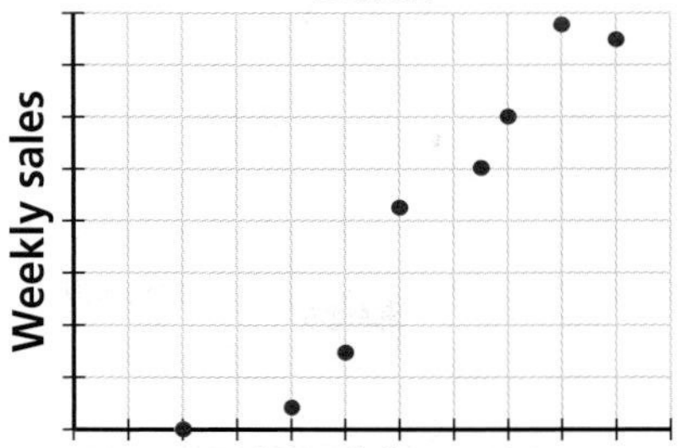

7. 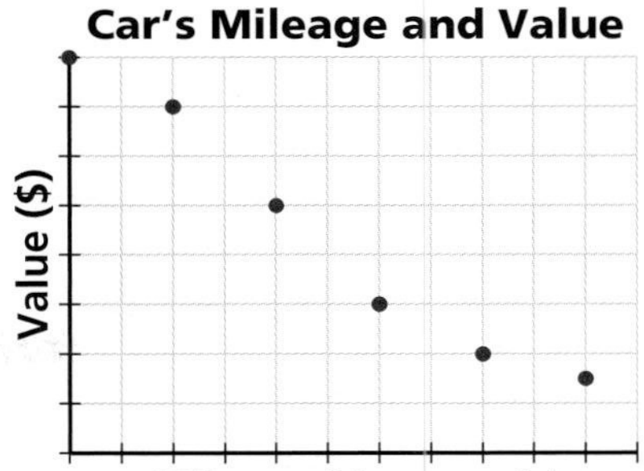

8. the number of students in a district and the number of buses in the district

Extra Practice
See page 740.

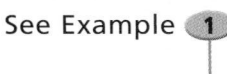

Science LINK

Critical Thinking **For Exercises 9–11, tell whether you would expect a positive correlation, a negative correlation, or no correlation. Explain your answers.**

9. the average temperature of a location and the amount of rainfall it receives each year
10. the latitude of a location and the amount of snow it receives each year
11. the number of hours of daylight and the amount of rainfall in a day
12. The table shows the approximate latitude and average temperature for several locations in the Southern Hemisphere. Construct a scatter plot of the data. What can you conclude from this data?
13. **Challenge** A location's elevation is negatively correlated to its average temperature and positively correlated to the amount of snow it receives. What kind of correlation would you expect between temperature and the amount of snowfall? Explain.

A scientist launching a weather balloon in Antarctica

Location	Latitude	Temperature
Quito, Ecuador	0° S	55°F
Melbourne, Australia	38° S	43°F
Tucuman, Argentina	27° S	57°F
Tananarive, Madagascar	19° S	60°F
Halley Research Station, Antarctica	76° S	20°F

TEST PREP and Spiral Review

14. **Multiple Choice** Use the scatter plot to determine which statements are true.
    - I The data shows a positive correlation.
    - II The data shows a negative correlation.
    - III The data shows no correlation.
    - IV As the years increase, the prize money increases.

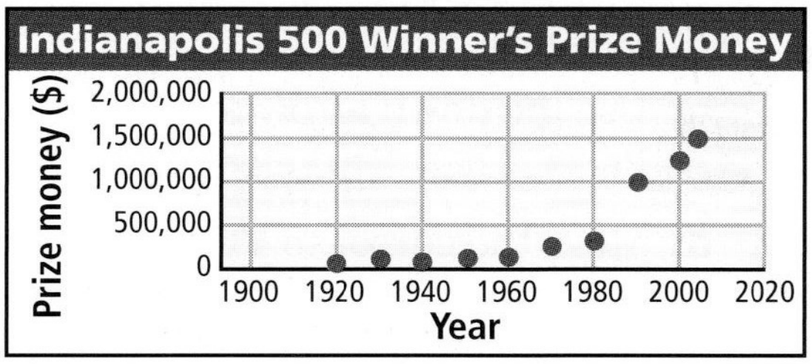

Ⓐ I only　　Ⓑ I and IV　　Ⓒ II and IV　　Ⓓ III only

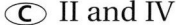

15. **Short Response** Give an example of two data sets that you would expect to have a positive correlation. Explain your answer.

Find the percent of each number. If necessary, round to the nearest tenth. (Lesson 6-4)

16. 95% of 80　　17. 120% of 63　　18. 62% of 14　　19. 7% of 50

20. The regular price of a computer monitor at the electronics store is $499. This month the monitor is on sale for 15% off. Find the sale price of the monitor. (Lesson 6-6)

Technology LAB 7-9

Samples and Lines of Best Fit

Use after Lesson 7-9

go.hrw.com
Lab Resources Online
KEYWORD: MS7 Lab7

You can use a graphing calculator to display relationships between variables in a scatter plot.

Activity 1

1. Survey at least 30 students in your grade to find the following information. Record your data in a table like the one below. (Your table will have at least 30 rows of data.) For **L5**, use numbers for the month. For example, enter "1" for January, "2" for February, etc.

L1 Height (in.)	L2 Age (mo)	L3 Length of Foot (in.)	L4 Length of Forearm (in.)	L5 Month of Birth
66	12	11	10	3
63	13	8	9	10
65	12	10	9.5	7

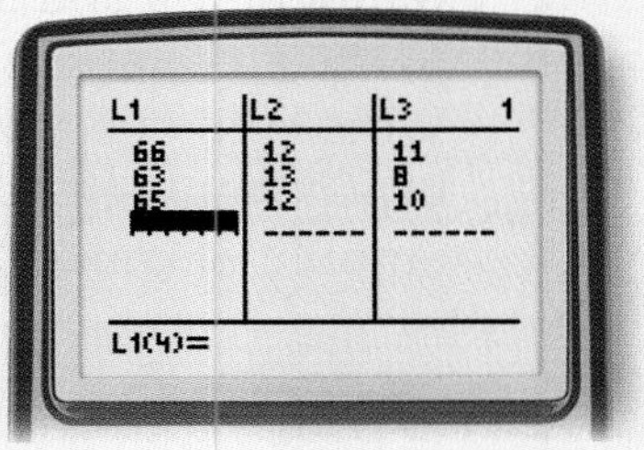

2. Press STAT ENTER to enter all the data into a graphing calculator.

3. Create a scatter plot for height and length of foot.

   a. Press 2nd Y= (STAT PLOT) ENTER for **Plot 1**.

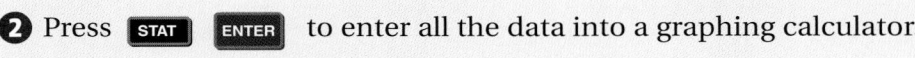

   b. Select ON, and use the arrow keys to select the scatter plot for **Type**.

   c. Use the down arrow to move the cursor to **Xlist**. Press 2nd 1 to select **L1**.

   d. Move the cursor to **Ylist**. Press 2nd 3 to select **L3**.

   e. Press ZOOM and then **9: ZoomStat** to view your graph.

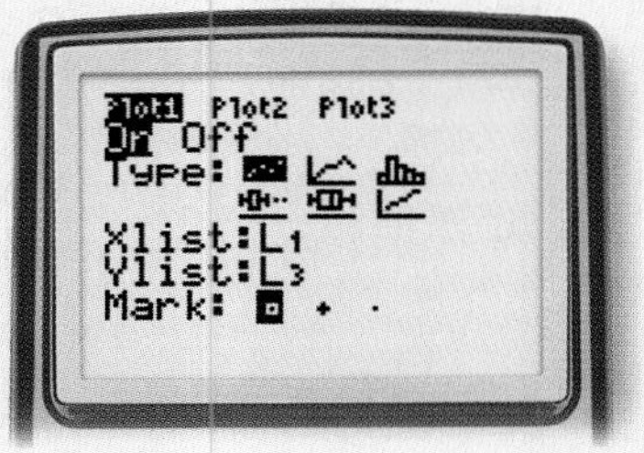

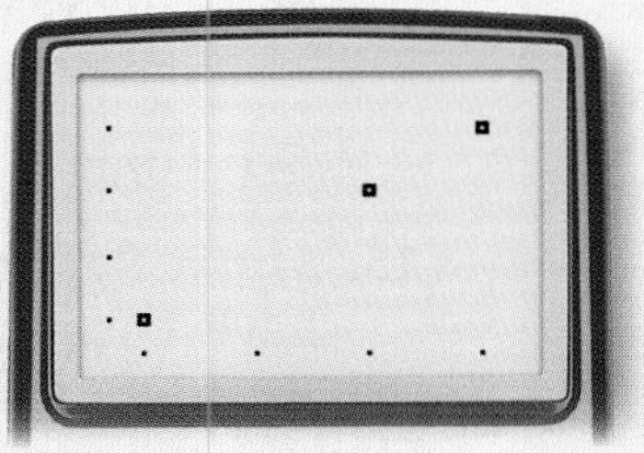

Think and Discuss

1. Describe the relationship between height and length of foot that is shown in the scatter plot from Activity 1.
2. What relationships would you expect to see between the other variables in the table?

Try This

1. Create a scatter plot of each of the other pairs of variables in your data-collection table. Which variables show a positive correlation? a negative correlation? no correlation?

Activity 2

1 Follow the steps from Activity 1, part 3 to display a scatter plot that shows the relationship between height and length of forearm.

2 Use TRACE to move the cursor between points on the graph. Use the coordinates of two points to estimate the slope of a line that would best fit through the data points on the graph.

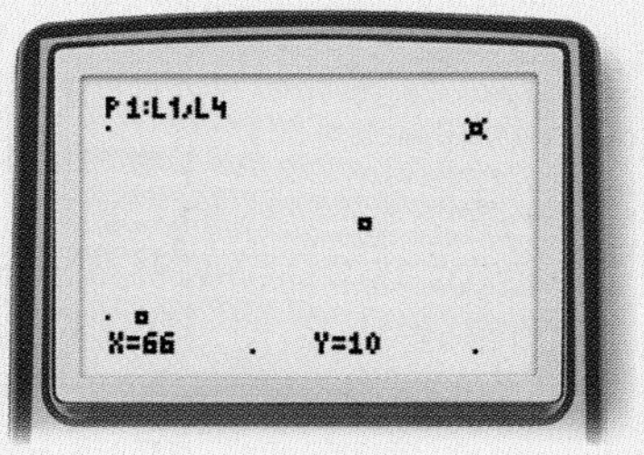

3 Press STAT and then use the right arrow key to select **CALC 4: LinReg (*ax* + *b*)**. Then press 2nd 1 , 2nd 4 ENTER to find the equation of the line of best fit.

4 Press Y= VARS **5: Statistics....** Use the right arrow key to select **EQ 1: RegEQ** and press ENTER to put the equation for the line of best fit into the equation editor.

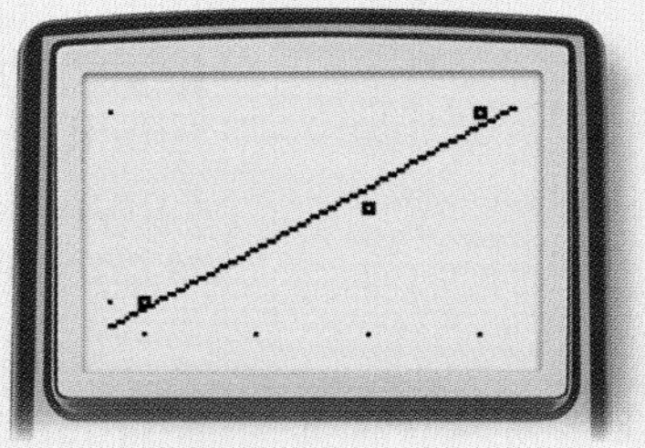

5 Press GRAPH to see the line of best fit graphed with the data points on the scatter plot.

Think and Discuss

1. Discuss how estimating the line of best fit gets easier the more data points you have.
2. Explain whether the sample from your class is representative of the population.

Try This

1. **a.** Press 2nd STAT MATH **3: mean (** 2nd 1 ENTER to find the mean height of your 30 classmates.

   b. Calculate the mean height of three students from the original survey who sit closest to you. What kind of sample is this? How does the mean height of this sample compare to the mean of the population from part **a**? Explain why they might be different.

   c. Calculate the mean height of 15 students form the original survey. How does this number compare with the mean of the population? Is it closer to the mean than the answer you got in part **b**?

7-10 Misleading Graphs

Learn **to identify and analyze misleading graphs.**

Advertisements and news articles often use data to support a point. Sometimes the data is presented in a way that influences how the data is interpreted. A data display that distorts information in order to persuade can be *misleading.*

An axis in a graph can be "broken" to make the graph easier to read. However, a broken axis can also be misleading. In the graph at right, the cost per minute for service with Company B looks like it is twice as much as the cost for service with Company A. In fact, the difference is only $0.10 per minute.

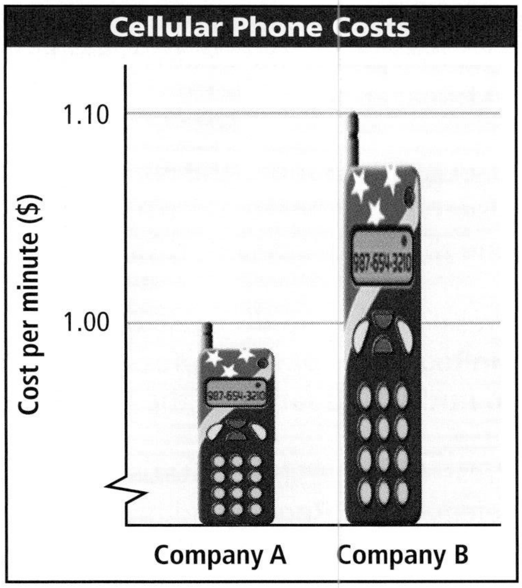

EXAMPLE 1 ***Social Studies Application***

Both bar graphs show the percent of people in California, Maryland, Michigan, and Washington who use seat belts. Which graph could be misleading? Why?

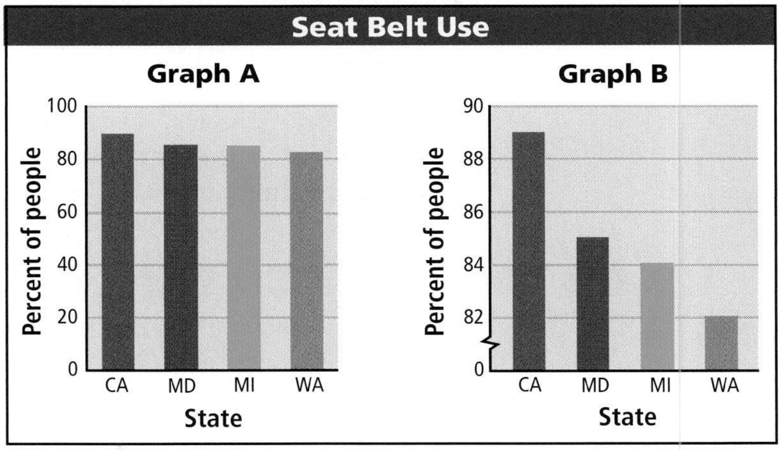

Graph B could be misleading. Because the vertical axis on graph B is broken, it appears that the percent of people in California who wear seat belts is twice as great as the percent in Michigan. In fact, it is only 5% greater. People might conclude from graph B that the percent of people in California who wear seat belts is much greater than the percents in the other states.

EXAMPLE 2 Analyzing Misleading Graphs

Explain why each graph could be misleading.

A

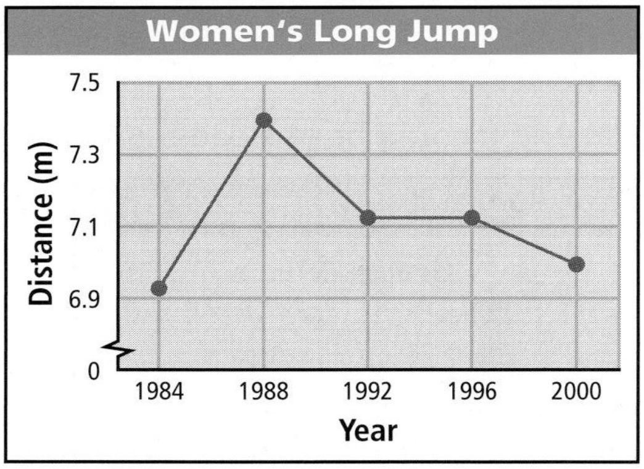

Because the vertical axis is broken, the distance jumped in 1988 appears to be over two times as far as in 1984. In fact, the distance jumped in 1988 is less than 0.5 meter greater than in the other years.

B

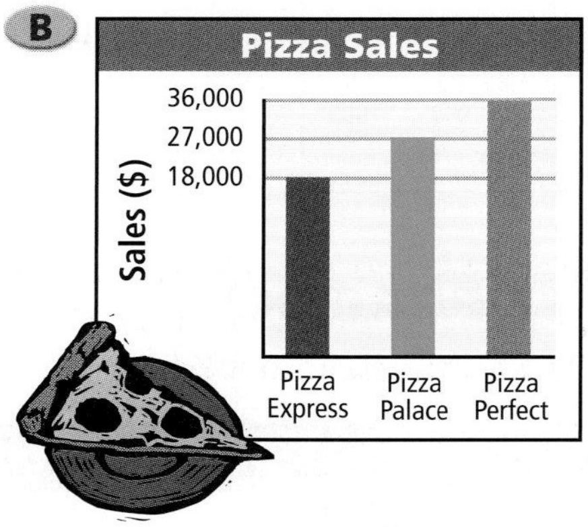

The scale of the graph is wrong. Equal distances on the vertical axis should represent equal intervals of numbers, but in this graph, the first $18,000 in sales is larger than the next $18,000. Because of this, you can't tell from the bars that Pizza Perfect's sales were twice those of Pizza Express.

Think and Discuss

1. **Explain** how to use the scale of a graph to decide if the graph is misleading.
2. **Describe** what might indicate that a graph is misleading.
3. **Give an example** of a situation in which a misleading graph might be used to persuade readers.

7-10 Exercises

go.hrw.com
Homework Help Online
KEYWORD: MS7 7-10
Parent Resources Online
KEYWORD: MS7 Parent

GUIDED PRACTICE

See Example 1

1. Which graph could be misleading? Why?

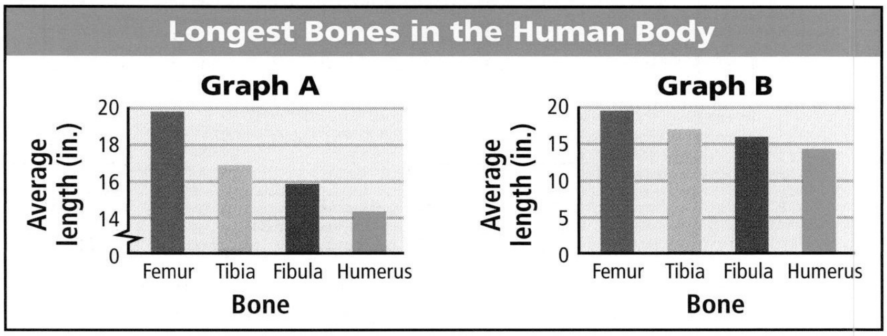

See Example 2

Explain why each graph could be misleading.

2.

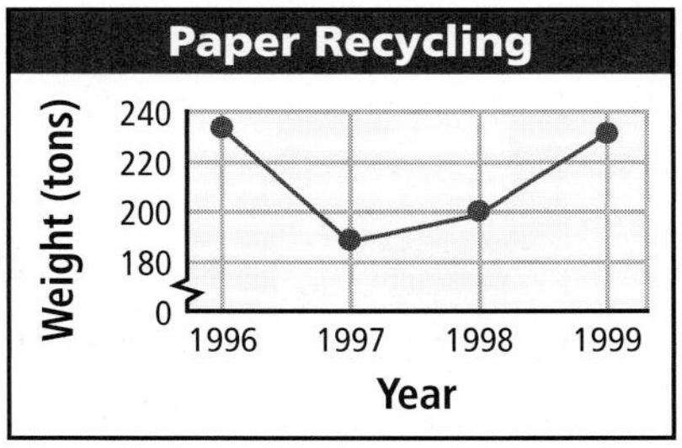

3.

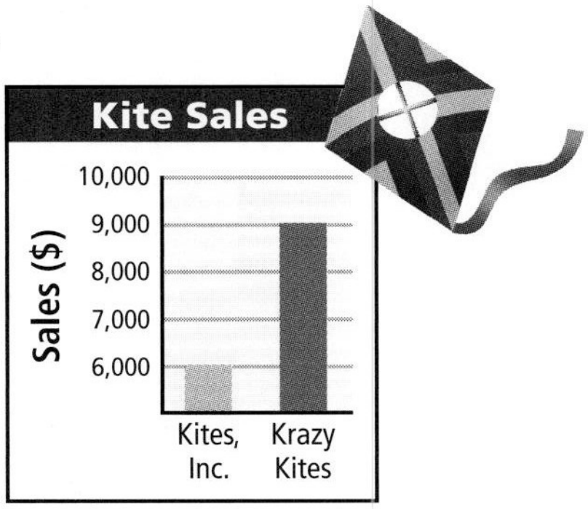

INDEPENDENT PRACTICE

See Example 1

4. Which graph could be misleading? Why?

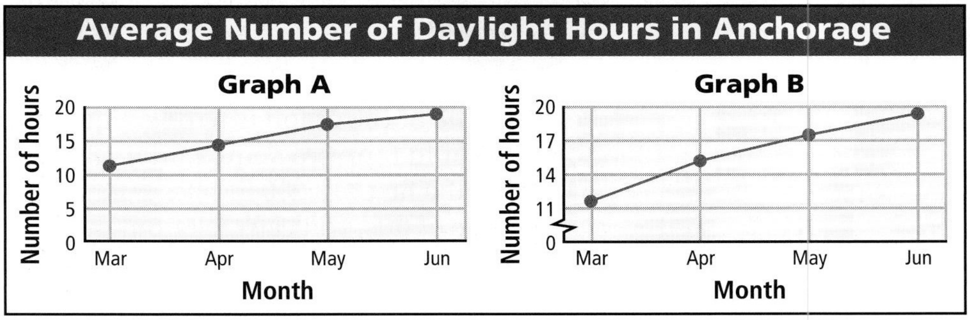

See Example 2

Explain why each graph could be misleading.

5.

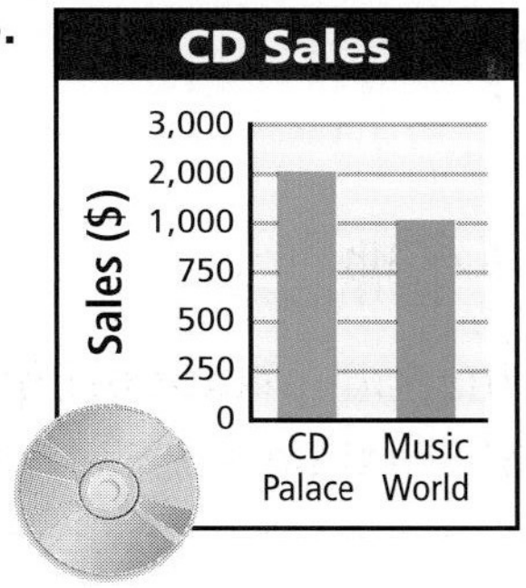

6.

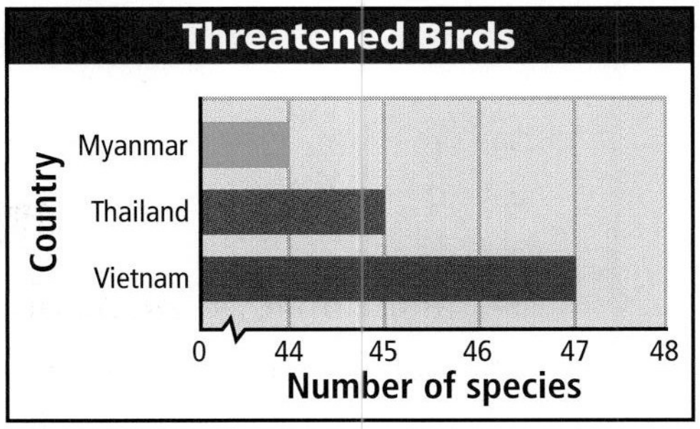

PRACTICE AND PROBLEM SOLVING

Extra Practice
See page 740.

7. **Business** Explain why the graphs below are misleading. Then tell how you can redraw them so that they are not misleading.

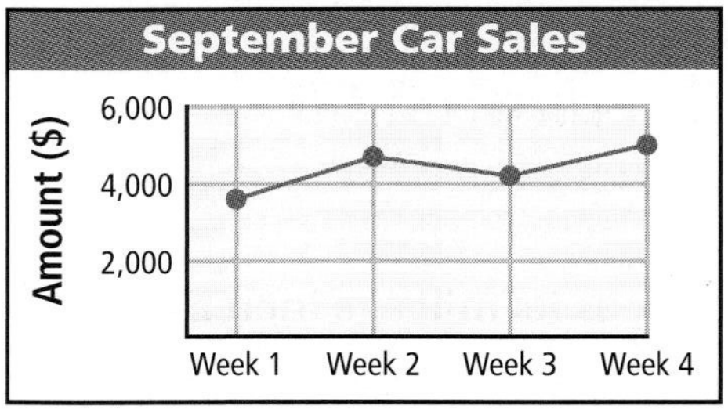

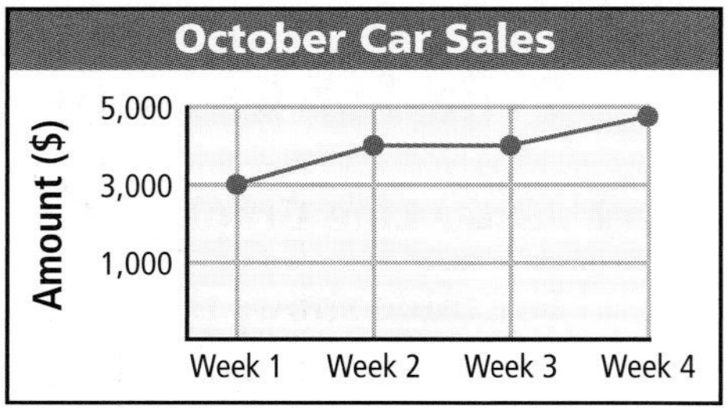

8. **Social Studies** The Appalachian Trail is a 2,160-mile footpath that runs from Maine to Georgia. The bar graph shows the number of miles of trail in three states. Redraw the graph so that it is not misleading. Then compare the two graphs.

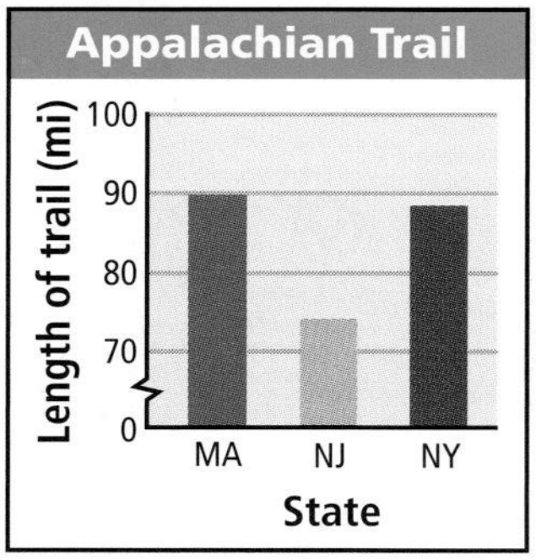

9. **Choose a Strategy** Tanya had $1.19 in coins. None of the coins were dollars or 50-cent pieces. Josie asked Tanya for change for a dollar, but she did not have the correct change. Which coins did Tanya have?

10. **Write About It** Why is it important to closely examine graphs in ads?

11. **Challenge** A company asked 10 people about their favorite brand of toothpaste. Three people chose Sparkle, one chose Smile, and six chose Purely White. An advertisement for Sparkle states, "Three times as many people prefer Sparkle over Smile!" Explain why this statement is misleading.

TEST PREP and Spiral Review

Use the graph for Exercises 12 and 13.

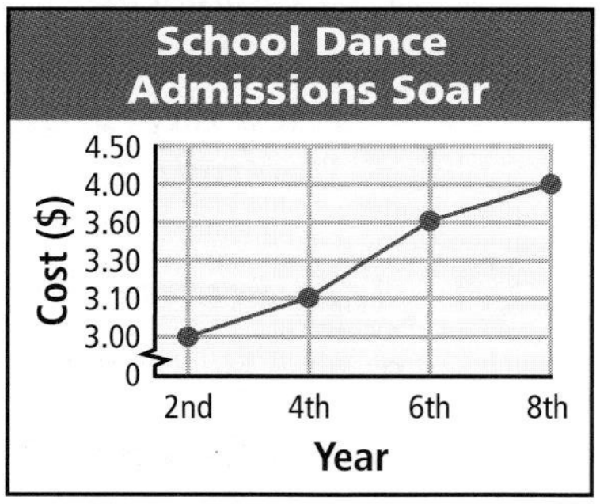

12. **Multiple Choice** Which statement is NOT a reason that the graph is misleading?

  (A) Broken interval on the vertical axis

  (B) The title

  (C) Vertical scale is not small enough

  (D) Intervals are not equal

13. **Short Response** Redraw the graph so that it is not misleading.

Solve. Write each answer in simplest form. (Lesson 3-12)

14. $\frac{3}{5}x = \frac{1}{5}$ 15. $x + \frac{2}{3} = \frac{5}{6}$ 16. $-\frac{1}{8}x = \frac{3}{4}$ 17. $x - \frac{3}{8} = -\frac{5}{6}$

Write *positive, negative,* or *no correlation* to describe each relationship. (Lesson 7-9)

18. height and test scores   19. speed of a car and time required to travel a distance

READY TO GO ON?

Quiz for Lessons 7-6 Through 7-10

7-6 Line Graphs

The table shows the value of a truck as its mileage increases.

Mileage (thousands)	Value of Truck ($)
0	20,000
20	18,000
40	14,000
60	11,000
80	10,000

1. Make a line graph of the data.
2. Use the graph to estimate the value of the truck when it has 12,000 miles.

7-7 Choosing an Appropriate Display

The table shows worldwide earthquake frequency.

Earthquake Frequency	
Category	Annual Frequency
Great	1
Major	18
Strong	120
Moderate	800

3. Choose the type of graph that would best display this data.
4. Create the graph that would best display the data.

7-8 Populations and Samples

Determine whether each sample may be biased. Explain.

5. Rickie surveys people at an amusement park to find out the average size of people's immediate family.
6. Theo surveys every fourth person entering a grocery store to find out the average number of pets in people's homes.
7. A biologist estimates that there are 1,800 fish in a quarry. To test this estimate, a student caught 150 fish from the quarry, tagged them, and released them. A few days later, the student caught 50 fish and noted that 4 were tagged. Determine whether the biologist's estimate is likely to be accurate.

7-9 Scatter Plots

8. Use the data to make a scatter plot.
9. Write *positive correlation, negative correlation,* or *no correlation* to describe the relationship between the data sets.

Cost ($)	2	3	4	5
Number of Purchases	12	8	6	3

7-10 Misleading Graphs

10. Which graph is misleading? Explain.

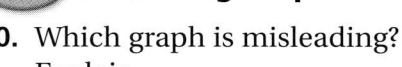

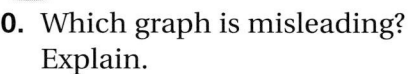

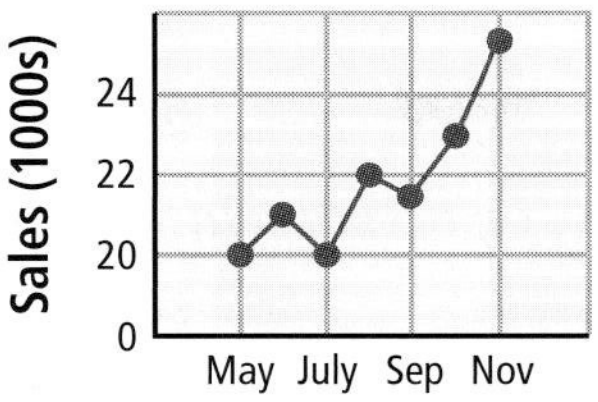

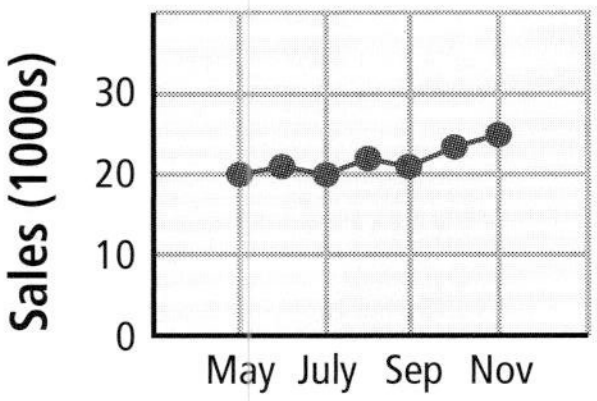

MULTI-STEP TEST PREP

Big Money Prizes A radio station is planning a contest. Each winner will select a money envelope. The station is planning on having 150 winners and giving away $6,000. The table shows the plan for filling the envelopes.

Number of Envelopes	Amount of Money
1	$5,000
2	$250
4	$50
12	$10
6	$5
25	$2
100	$1

1. The station wants to describe the typical amount of money a winner will receive. What are the mean, median, mode, and range of the amounts won?

2. The sponsors decide to double the amount of money they give away. The station manager wants to do this by doubling the amount of money in each envelope. Make a table showing how much money would be in each envelope.

3. How does the station manager's plan affect the mean, median, mode, and range of the amounts won?

4. The DJs think it would be better to double the number of winners rather than doubling the amount of money in each envelope. They want to double the number of envelopes containing each amount of money. Make a new table that shows their plan.

5. How does the DJs' plan affect the mean, median, mode, and range of the amounts won?

Game Time

Code Breaker

A *cryptogram* is a message written in code. One of the most common types of codes is a substitution code, in which each letter of a text is replaced with a different letter. The table shows one way to replace the letters in a text to make a coded message.

Original Letter	A	B	C	D	E	F	G	H	I	J	K	L	M
Code Letter	J	E	O	H	K	A	U	B	L	Y	V	G	P
Original Letter	N	O	P	Q	R	S	T	U	V	W	X	Y	Z
Code Letter	X	N	S	D	Z	Q	M	W	C	R	F	T	I

With this code, the word MATH is written PJMB. You can also use the table as a key to decode messages. Try decoding the following message.

J EJZ UZJSB OJX EK WQKH MN HLQSGJT HJMJ.

Suppose you want to crack a substitution code but are not given the key. You can use letter frequencies to help you. The bar graph below shows the number of times each letter of the English language is likely to appear in a text of 100 letters.

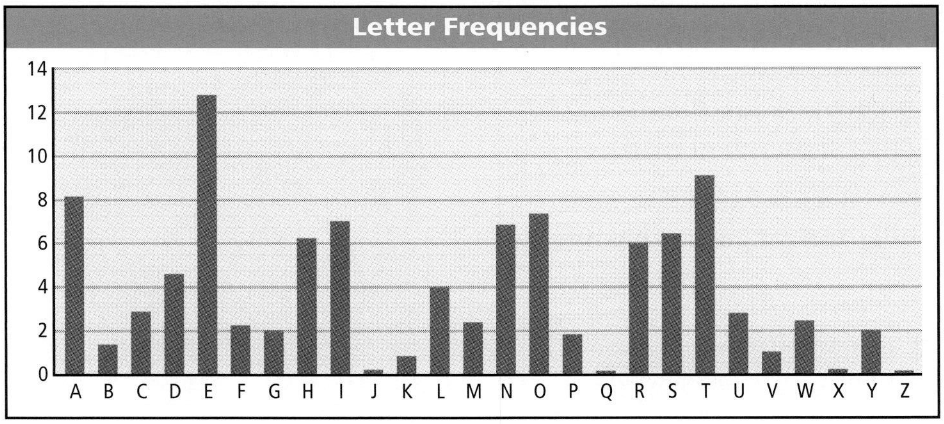

From the graph, you can see that E is the mode. In a coded text, the letter that appears most frequently is likely to represent the letter E. The letter that appears the second most frequently is likely to represent the letter T. Count the number of times each letter appears in the following message. Then use the letter frequencies and a bit of guesswork to decode the message. (*Hint:* In this code, P represents the letter M.)

KSQ PQUR, KSQ PQHGUR, URH KSQ PXHQ KQWW VXE DXPQKSGRT UCXEK U DQK XZ HUKU.

It's in the Bag!

FOLDNOTES

Materials
- card stock
- scissors
- glue
- colored paper
- magnetic strip
- tape
- empty CD case
- graph paper
- stapler

PROJECT Graph Match

Use an empty CD case to make a magnetic matching game about different types of graphs.

Directions

1. Trim the card stock to $4\frac{1}{2}$ inches by 5 inches. On the card stock, write "Match the Name and Number" and list the numbers 1 through 5 as shown. Cut small rectangles from the magnetic strip and glue these next to the numbers. **Figure A**

2. Glue colored paper to the rest of the magnetic strip. Write the names of five different types of graphs on the strip. Cut these apart to form magnetic rectangles with the names of the graphs. **Figure B**

3. Put a magnetic name of a graph next to each number on the card stock. Then tape the card stock to the inside back cover of an empty CD case. **Figure C**

4. Cut out five squares of graph paper that are each $4\frac{1}{2}$ inches by $4\frac{1}{2}$ inches. Label the squares 1 through 5. Draw a different type of graph on each square, making sure to match the types that are named on the magnetic rectangles.

5. Staple the graphs together to make a booklet. Insert the booklet into the cover of the CD case.

A

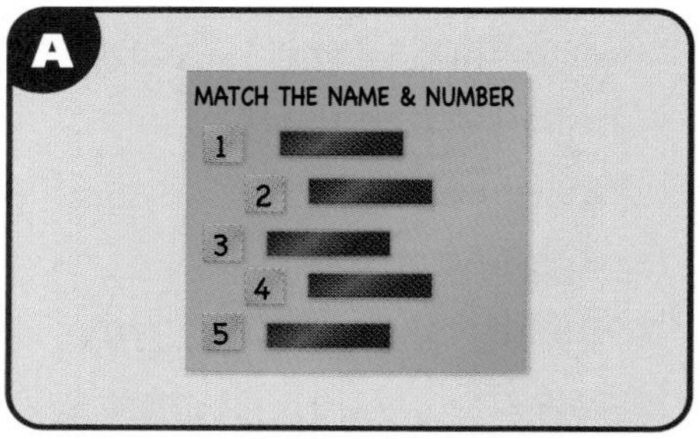

B

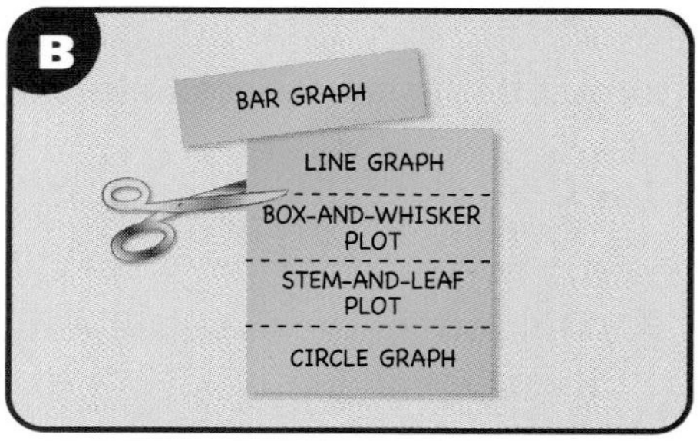

C

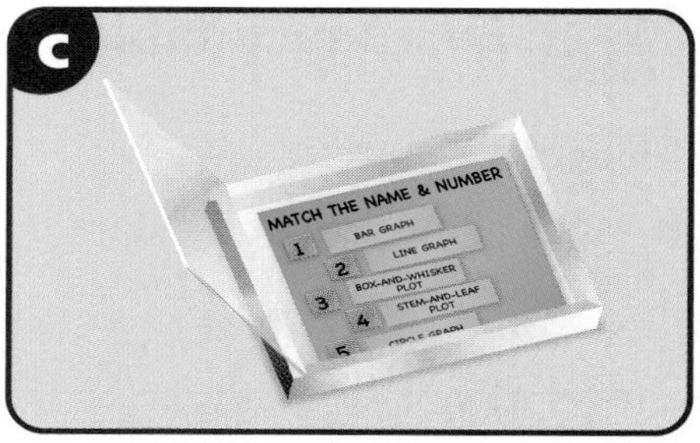

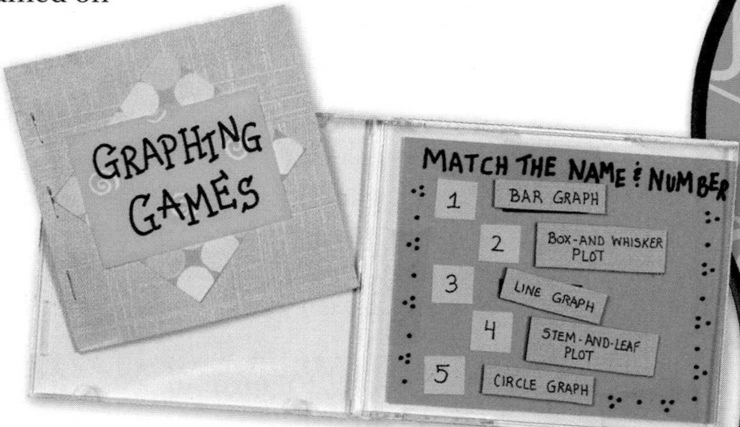

Putting the Math into Action

Exchange your game with a partner. Can you match each graph with its name?

CHAPTER 7 Study Guide: Review

Vocabulary

bar graph 386	interquartile range 395	population 412
biased sample 413	line graph 402	positive correlation 417
box-and-whisker plot ..394	line plot 377	random sample 412
circle graph 390	lower quartile 394	range 381
convenience sample ...412	mean 381	sample 412
cumulative frequency ..376	median 381	scatter plot 416
double-bar graph 386	mode 381	sector 390
double-line graph 403	negative correlation 417	stem-and-leaf plot 377
frequency table 376	no correlation 417	upper quartile 394
histogram 387	outlier 382	

Complete the sentences below with vocabulary words from the list above.

1. When gathering information about a(n) ___?___, researchers often study part of the group, called a(n) ___?___.

2. The sum of the data values divided by the number of data items is called the ___?___ of the data.

7-1 Frequency Tables, Stem-and-Leaf Plots, and Line Plots (pp. 376–380)

EXAMPLE

■ **Make a line plot of the data.**

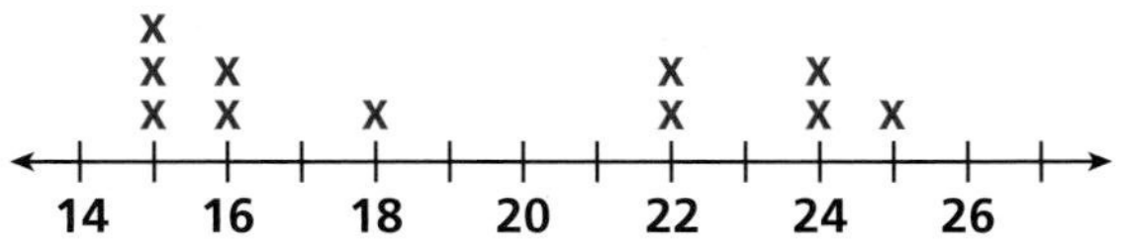

15, 22, 16, 24, 15, 25, 16, 22, 15, 10, 24, 18

EXERCISES

Use the data set 35, 29, 14, 19, 32, 25, 27, 16, and 8 for Exercises 3 through 5.

3. Make a cumulative frequency table.
4. Make a stem-and-leaf plot of the data.
5. Make a line plot of the data.

7-2 Mean, Median, Mode, and Range (pp. 381–385)

EXAMPLE

■ **Find the mean, median, mode, and range of the data set 3, 7, 10, 2, and 3.**

Mean: $3 + 7 + 10 + 2 + 3 = 25 \quad \frac{25}{5} = 5$

Median: 2, 3, 3, 7, 10

Mode: 3 Range: $10 - 2 = 8$

EXERCISES

Find the mean, median, mode, and range of each data set.

6. 324, 233, 324, 399, 233, 299
7. 48, 39, 27, 52, 45, 47, 49, 37

7-3 Bar Graphs and Histograms (pp. 386–389)

EXAMPLE

■ **Make a bar graph of the chess club's results: W, L, W, W, L, W, L, L, W, W, W, L, W.**

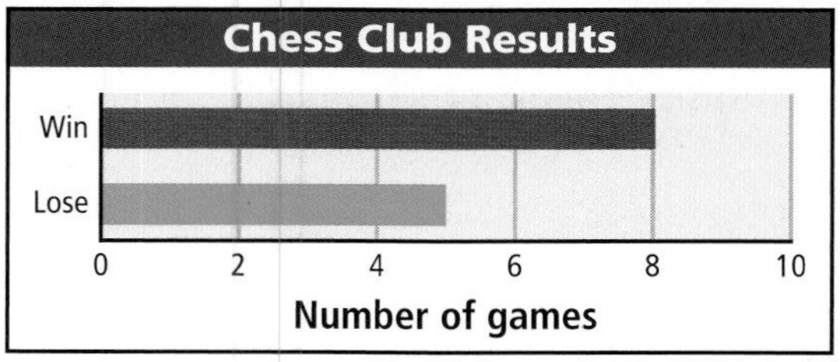

EXERCISES

8. Make a double-bar graph of the data.

Favorite Pet	Girls	Boys
Cat	42	31
Dog	36	52
Fish	3	10
Other	19	7

7-4 Reading and Interpreting Circle Graphs (pp. 390–393)

EXAMPLE

■ **About what percent of people said yellow was their favorite color?**
about 25%

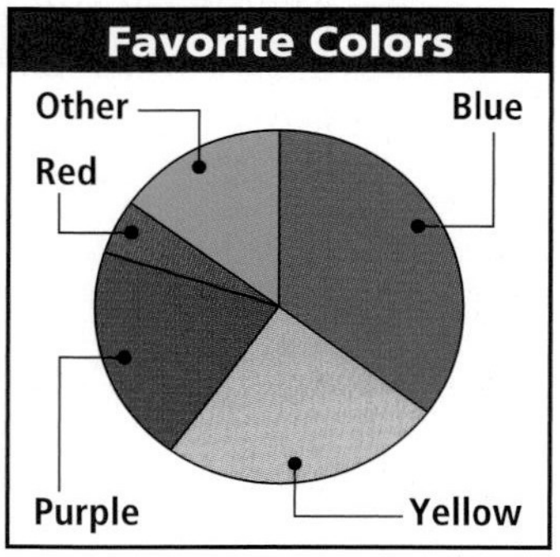

EXERCISES

Use the circle graph at left for Exercises 9 and 10.

9. Did more people choose purple or yellow as their favorite color?

10. Out of the 100 people surveyed, 35% chose blue as their favorite color. How many people chose blue?

7-5 Box-and-Whisker Plots (pp. 394–397)

EXAMPLE

■ **Use the data to make a box-and-whisker plot: 14, 10, 23, 16, 21, 26, 23, 17, and 25.**

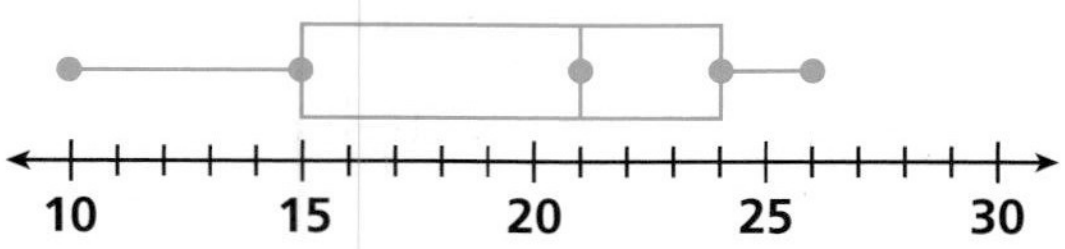

EXERCISES

Use the following data for Exercises 11–12: 33, 38, 43, 30, 29, 40, 51, 27, 42, 23, and 31.

11. Make a box-and-whisker plot.

12. What is the interquartile range?

7-6 Line Graphs (pp. 402–405)

EXAMPLE

■ **Make a line graph of the rainfall data: Apr, 5 in.; May, 3 in.; Jun, 4 in.; Jul, 1 in.**

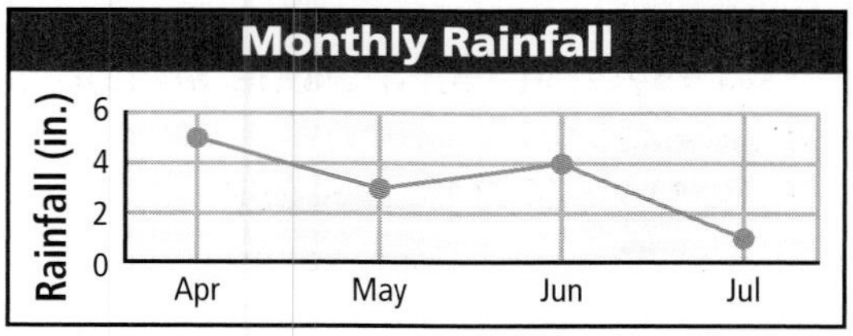

EXERCISES

13. Make a double-line graph of the data in the table.

U. S. Open Winning Scores					
	1995	1996	1997	1998	1999
Men	280	278	276	280	279
Women	278	272	274	290	272

7-7 Choosing an Appropriate Display (pp. 408–411)

EXAMPLE

- **Choose the type of graph that would best represent the population of a town over a 10-year period.**

  Line graph

EXERCISES

Choose the type of graph that would best represent these data.

14. number of dogs in a kennel each day

15. number of exports from different countries

7-8 Populations and Samples (pp. 412–415)

EXAMPLE

- **In a random sample of 50 pigeons at a park, 4 are found to have a beak deformation. Is it reasonable to claim that about 20 of the pigeon population of 2,000 have this deformation? Explain.**

  No; $\frac{4}{50}$ is not closely proportional to $\frac{20}{2,000}$.

EXERCISES

16. Fourteen out of 35 people surveyed prefer Brand X detergent. Is it reasonable for the store manager to claim that about 2,500 of the town's 6,000 residents will prefer Brand X detergent?

7-9 Scatter Plots (pp. 416–419)

EXAMPLE

- **Write *positive, negative,* or *no correlation* to describe the relationship between date of birth and eye color.**

  There seems to be no correlation between the data sets.

EXERCISES

17. Use the data to make a scatter plot. Write *positive, negative,* or *no correlation.*

Customers	47	56	35	75	25
Sales ($)	495	501	490	520	375

7-10 Misleading Graphs (pp. 422–425)

EXAMPLE

- **Explain why the graph could be misleading.**

  The vertical axis is broken, so it appears that A's sales are twice more than B's.

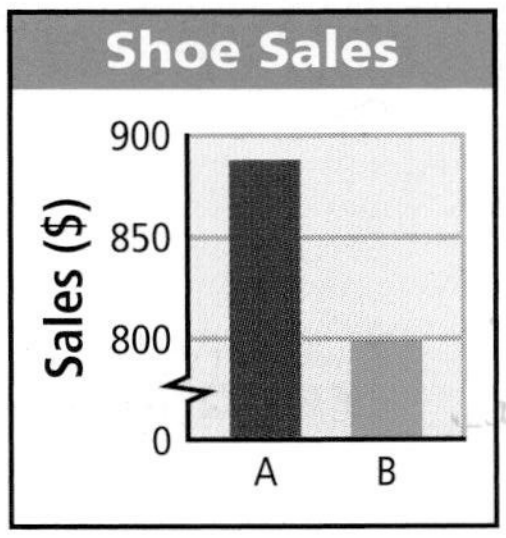

EXERCISES

18. Explain why the graph could be misleading.

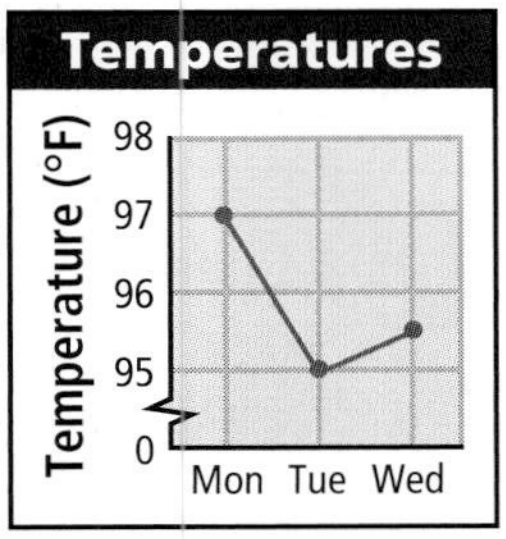

CHAPTER TEST

Use the data set 12, 18, 12, 22, 28, 23, 32, 10, 29, and 36 for problems 1–8.

1. Find the mean, median, mode, and range of the data set.
2. How would the outlier 57 affect the measures of central tendency?
3. Make a cumulative frequency table of the data.
4. Make a stem-and-leaf plot of the data.
5. Make a line plot of the data.
6. Make a histogram of the data.
7. Make a box-and-whisker plot of the data.
8. What is the interquartile range?

Use the table for problems 9 and 10.

9. The table shows the weight in pounds of several mammals. Make a double-bar graph of the data.
10. Which mammal shows the greatest weight difference between the male and the female?

Mammal	Male	Female
Gorilla	450	200
Lion	400	300
Tiger	420	300

Use the circle graph for problems 11 and 12.

11. Approximately what percent of the students are seventh graders?
12. If the school population is 1,200 students, are more than 500 students in eighth grade? Explain.

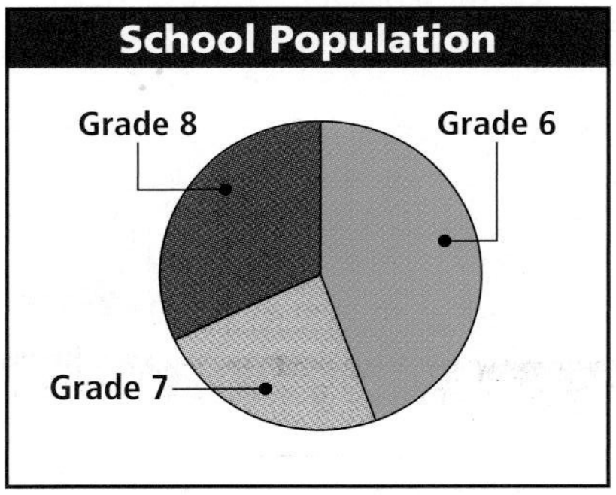

Use the table for problems 13 and 14.

13. The table shows passenger car fuel rates in miles per gallon for several years. Make a line graph of the data. During which 2-year period did the fuel rate decrease?
14. Estimate the fuel rate in 1997.
15. What type of graph would best display student attendance at various sporting events?

Year	1992	1994	1996	1998
Rate	21.0	20.7	21.2	21.6

For problems 16 and 17, write *positive correlation, negative correlation,* or *no correlation* to describe each relationship.

16. size of hand and typing speed
17. height from which an object is dropped and time it takes to hit the ground
18. Explain why the graph at right could be misleading.

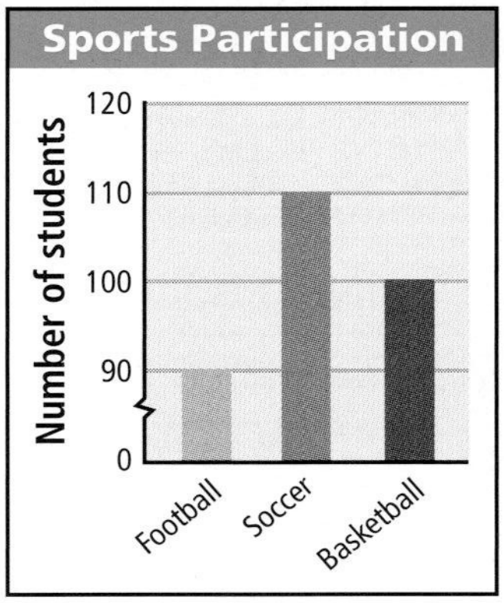

CHAPTER 7

TEST TACKLER

Standardized Test Strategies

Short Response: Write Short Responses

Short-response test items are designed to test your understanding of a math concept. In your response, you usually have to show your work and explain your answer. Scores are based on a 2-point scoring chart called a rubric.

EXAMPLE 1

Short Response The following data represents the number of hours Leann studied each day after school for her history test.

0, 1, 0, 1, 5, 3, 4

Find the mean, median, and mode for the data set. Which measure of central tendency best represents the data? Explain your answer.

Here are some responses scored using the 2-point rubric.

2-point response:

$\frac{0+1+0+1+5+3+4}{7} = 2$ *The mean is 2.*

0 0 1 (1) 3 4 5 *The median is 1.*

(0 0)(1 1) 3 4 5 *The modes are 0 and 1.*

The measure of central tendency that best represents the data is the mean, because it shows the average number of hours that Leann studied before her test.

1-point response:

$\frac{0+1+0+1+5+3+4}{7} = 2$ *The mean is 2.*

0 0 1 (1) 3 4 5 *The median is 1.*

(0 0)(1 1) 3 4 5 *The modes are 0 and 1.*

Notice that there is no explanation given about the measure of central tendency that best represents the data.

0-point response:

The mean is 2, the median is 2, and the mode is 0.

Notice that the answer is incorrect and there is no explanation.

Scoring Rubric

2 points: The student correctly answers the question, shows all work, and provides a complete and correct explanation.

1 point: The student correctly answers the question but does not show all work or does not provide a complete explanation; or the student makes minor errors resulting in an incorrect solution but shows all work and provides a complete explanation.

0 points: The student gives an incorrect answer and shows no work or explanation, or the student gives no response.

Underline or highlight what you are being asked to do in each question. Be sure to explain how you get your answer in complete sentences.

Read each test item and use the scoring rubric to answer the questions that follow.

Item A
Short Response The box-and-whisker plot shows the height in inches of seventh-grade students. Describe the spread of the data.

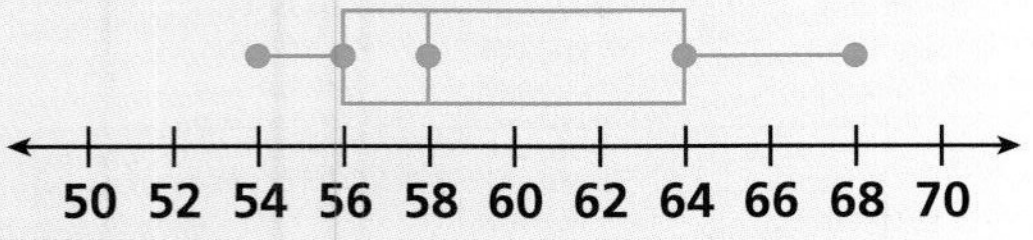

Student's Answer

There are more students between 58 and 70 inches tall than there are between 50 and 58 inches tall because the third quartile is farther from the median than the first quartile is.

1. What score should the student's answer receive? Explain your reasoning.
2. What additional information, if any, should the student's answer include in order to receive full credit?

Item B
Short Response Explain the type of graph you would use to represent the number of each type of car sold at a car dealership in May.

Student's Answer

I would use a bar graph to show how many of each car model was sold during the month.

3. What score should the student's answer receive? Explain your reasoning.
4. What additional information, if any, should the student's answer include in order to receive full credit?

Item C
Short Response Create a scatter plot of the data and describe the correlation between the outside temperature and the number of people at the public pool.

Temperature (°F)	70	75	80	85	90
Number of People	20	22	40	46	67

Student's Answer

There is a positive correlation between the temperature and the number of people at the public pool because as it gets hotter, more people want to go swimming.

5. What score should the student's answer receive? Explain your reasoning.
6. What additional information, if any, should the student's answer include in order to receive full credit?

Item D
Short Response A survey was conducted to determine which age group attended the most movies in November. Fifteen people at a movie theater were asked their age, and their responses are as follows: 6, 10, 34, 22, 46, 11, 62, 14, 14, 5, 23, 25, 17, 18, and 55. Make a cumulative frequency table of the data. Then explain which group saw the most movies.

Student's Answer

Age Groups	*Frequency*	*Cumulative Frequency*
0–13	4	4
14–26	7	11
27–40	1	12
41–54	1	13
55–68	2	15

7. What score should the student's answer receive? Explain your reasoning.
8. What additional information, if any, should the student's answer include in order to receive full credit?

STANDARDIZED TEST PREP

go.hrw.com
State Test Practice Online
KEYWORD: MS7 TestPrep

Cumulative Assessment, Chapters 1–7

Multiple Choice

1. Which expression is true for the data set? 15, 18, 13, 15, 16, 14

Ⓐ Mean $<$ mode

Ⓑ Median $>$ mean

Ⓒ Median $=$ mean

Ⓓ Median $=$ mode

2. What is the first step to complete in simplifying this expression?

$\frac{2}{5} + [3 - 5(2)] \div 6$

Ⓕ Multiply 5 and 2.

Ⓖ Divide by 6.

Ⓗ Subtract 5 from 3.

Ⓙ Divide 2 by 5.

3. What is the slope of the line shown?

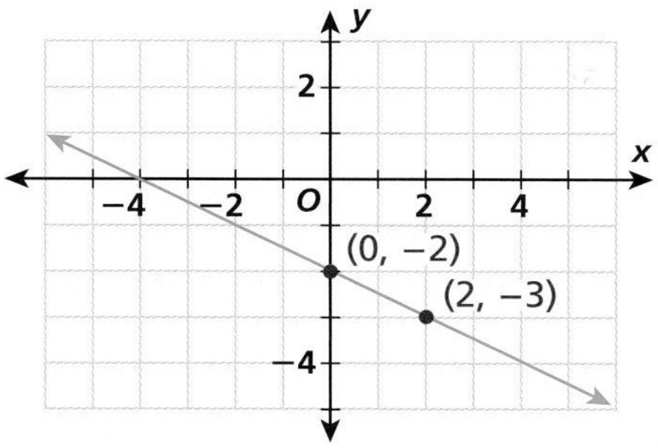

Ⓐ $\frac{1}{2}$

Ⓑ $-\frac{2}{1}$

Ⓒ 2

Ⓓ $-\frac{1}{2}$

4. On Monday the temperature was −13°F. On Tuesday the temperature rose 7°F. What was the temperature on Tuesday?

Ⓕ −20°F

Ⓖ −8°F

Ⓗ −6°F

Ⓙ 7°F

5. Which model best represents the fraction $\frac{5}{8}$?

Ⓐ 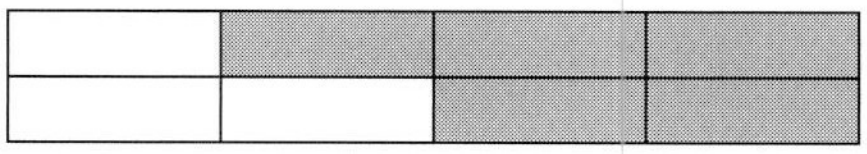

Ⓑ 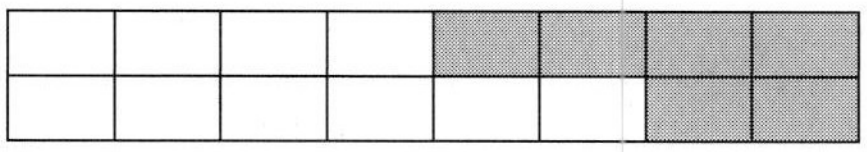

Ⓒ 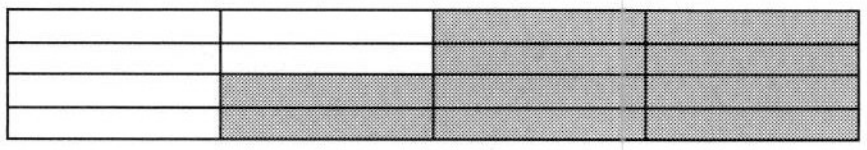

Ⓓ 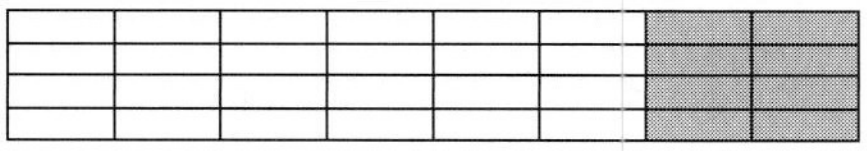

6. Ron eats $\frac{1}{4}$ cup of cereal every day as part of his breakfast. He has had a total of 16 cups of cereal this year. How many days has he eaten cereal?

Ⓕ 4 days

Ⓖ 16 days

Ⓗ 32 days

Ⓙ 64 days

7. A store is offering lip gloss at 25% off its original price. The original price of lip gloss is \$7.59. What is the sale price?

Ⓐ \$5.69

Ⓑ \$4.93

Ⓒ \$3.80

Ⓓ \$1.90

8. What is the mode of the data given in the stem-and-leaf plot?

Stems	Leaves
6	1 2 2 5 9
7	0 4 6 7 8
8	3 3 3 5 6

Key: 7|0 means 70

Ⓕ 25

Ⓖ 62

Ⓗ 76

Ⓙ 83

9. Solve $8 + 34x = -60$ for x.

(A) $x = -5$ (C) $x = -2$

(B) $x = -0.97$ (D) $x = 2$

10. Which statement is best supported by the data?

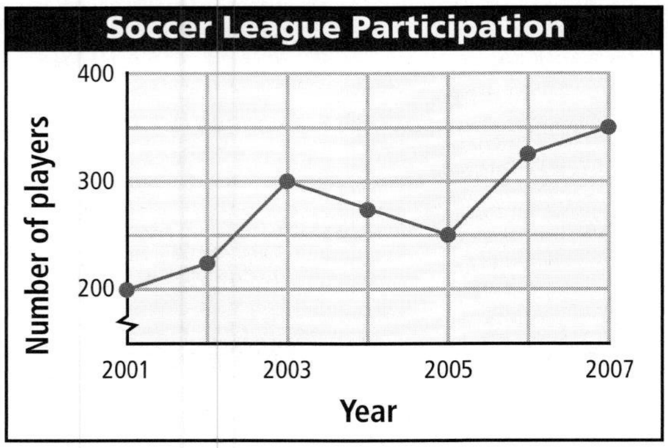

(F) More students played soccer in 2005 than in 2002.

(G) From 2001–2007, soccer participation increased by 100%.

(H) From 2002–2006, soccer participation decreased by 144%.

(J) Participation increased between 2004 and 2005.

Read a graph or diagram as closely as you read the actual test question. These visual aids contain important information.

Gridded Response

11. To the nearest thousandth, what is the difference between the median and the mean of the data set?

14, 11, 14, 11, 13, 12, 9, 15, 16

12. What value represents the upper quartile of the data in the box-and-whisker plot below?

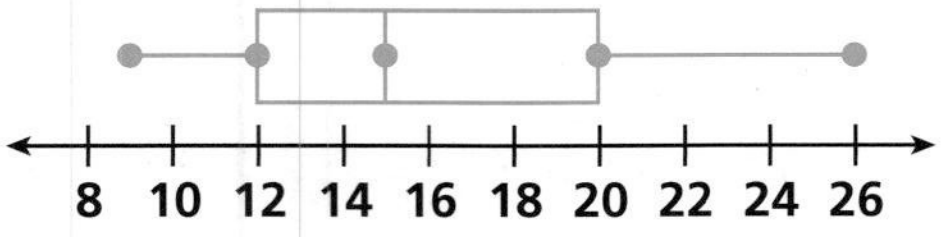

13. The key in a stem-and-leaf plot states that 2|5 means 2.5. What value is represented by 1|8 ?

Short Response

14. The graph shows the results of a survey. Aaron read the graph and determined that more than $\frac{1}{5}$ of the students chose drama as their favorite type of movie. Do you agree with Aaron? Why or why not?

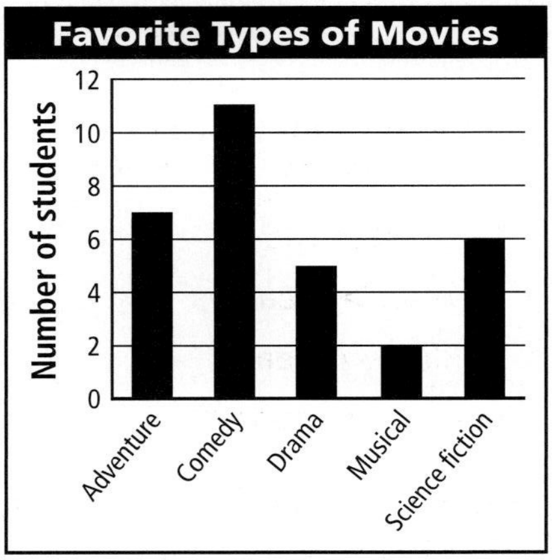

15. A land developer purchases 120 acres of land and plans to divide one part into five 5-acre lots, another part into two 10-acre lots, and the rest into $\frac{1}{2}$-acre lots. Each lot will be sold for a future home site. How many total lots can the developer plan to sell?

Extended Response

16. Mr. Parker wants to identify the types of activities in which high school students participate after school, so he surveys the twelfth-graders in his science classes. The table shows the results of the survey.

Activity	Boys	Girls
Play sports	36	24
Talk to friends	6	30
Do homework	15	18
Work	5	4

a. Use the data in the table to construct a double-bar graph.

b. What is the mean number of girls per activity? Show your work.

c. What type of sample is used? Is this sample representative of the population? Explain.

CHAPTER 8

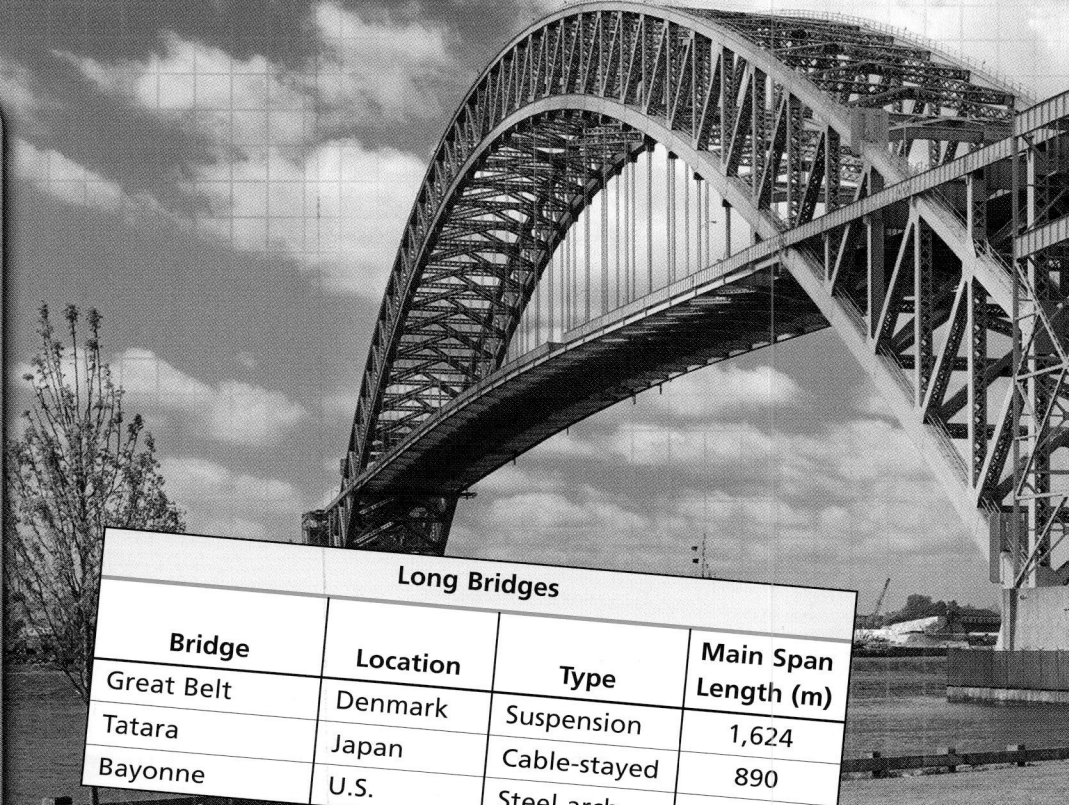

Geometric Figures

MULTI-STEP TEST PREP

go.hrw.com
Chapter Project Online
KEYWORD: MS7 Ch8

Long Bridges

Bridge	Location	Type	Main Span Length (m)
Great Belt	Denmark	Suspension	1,624
Tatara	Japan	Cable-stayed	890
Bayonne	U.S.	Steel arch	511

Career *Bridge Designer*

Many factors influence the way a bridge is constructed. A bridge must be able to withstand winds, snow, and the weight of traffic while supporting its own weight.

Bridge designers also have to consider the distance that a bridge must cross (called the *span*), the nature of the land, and the look of the structure. Bridge designers often combine technological know-how with artistry to create structures that are both functional and beautiful.

EXAMPLE 2 Identifying the Most Appropriate Display

The table shows the amount of time the students spent at the different exhibits at the butterfly park. Explain why each display does or does not appropriately represent the data.

Exhibit	Time (min)
Butterflies	60
Insects	45
Invertebrates	30
Birds	15

A

Stems	Leaves
1	5
2	
3	0
4	5
5	
6	0

Key: 2|0 means 20

A stem-and-leaf plot shows how often data values occur and how they are distributed.

There are only four data values, and how often they occur and how they are distributed are not important.

B

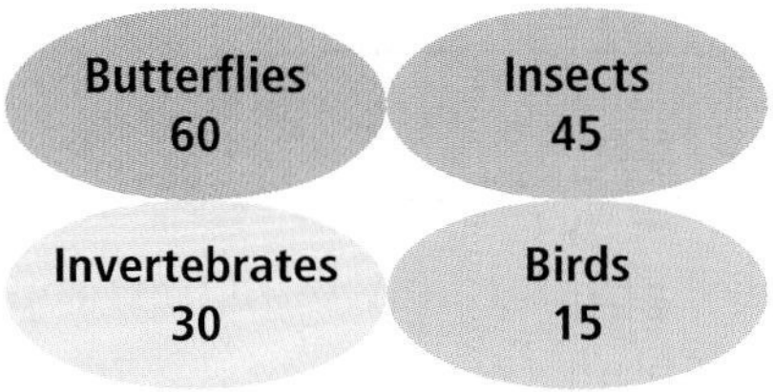

A Venn diagram shows the relationship between two or more data sets.

There is no relationship among the times spent at each exhibit.

C

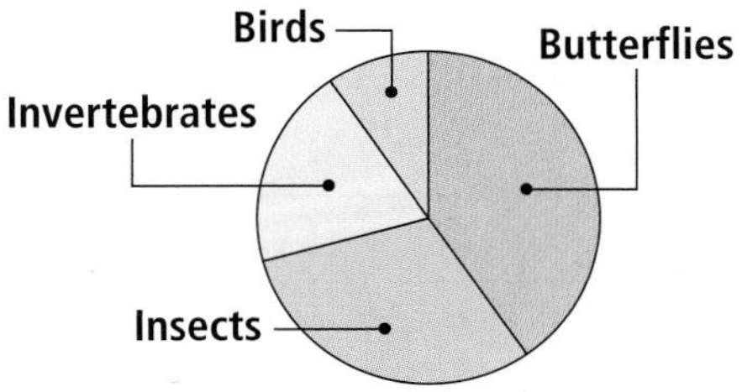

A circle graph shows how a set of data is divided into parts.

This circle graph appropriately shows the proportionate amount of time spent at each exhibit.

D

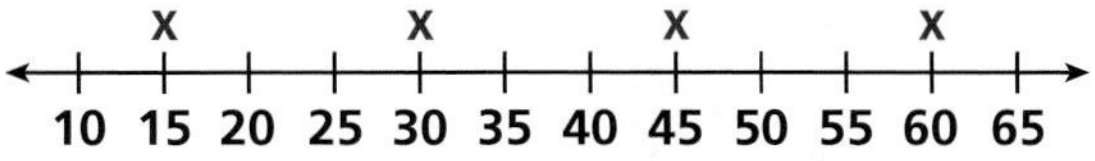

A line plot shows frequency of values.

How often the data values occur is not important.

Think and Discuss

1. **Explain** how data displayed in a stem-and-leaf plot and data displayed in a line plot are similar.
2. **Describe** a set of data that could best be displayed in a line graph.

7-7 Exercises

go.hrw.com
Homework Help Online
KEYWORD: MS7 7-7
Parent Resources Online
KEYWORD: MS7 Parent

GUIDED PRACTICE

See Example 1

Choose the type of graph that would best represent each type of data.

1. the prices of the five top-selling 42-inch plasma televisions
2. the height of a person from birth to age 21

See Example 2

The table shows Keiffer's earnings for a month. Explain why each display does or does not appropriately represent the data.

Week	1	2	3	4
Earnings ($)	20	30	15	25

3.

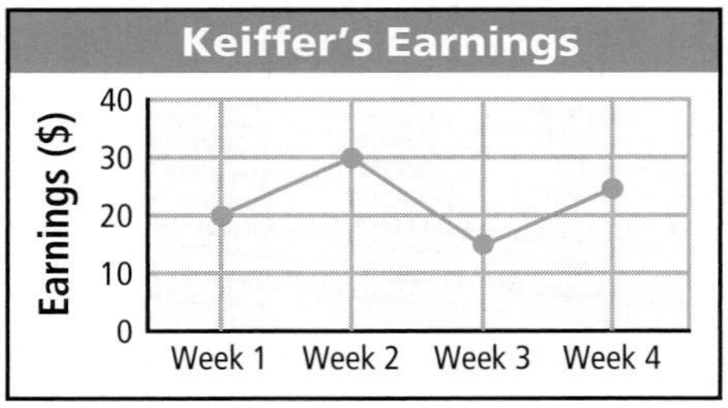

4.

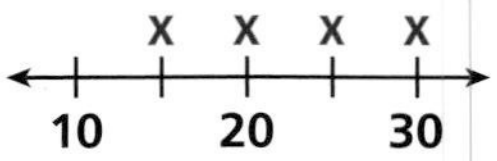

INDEPENDENT PRACTICE

See Example 1

Choose the type of graph that would best represent each type of data.

5. the number of tracks on each of the 50 CDs in a CD collection
6. the number of runners in a marathon for the last five years

See Example 2

The table shows the number of people who participate in various activities. Explain why each display does or does not appropriately represent the data.

Activity	Biking	Hiking	Skating	Jogging
Number of People	35	20	25	15

7.

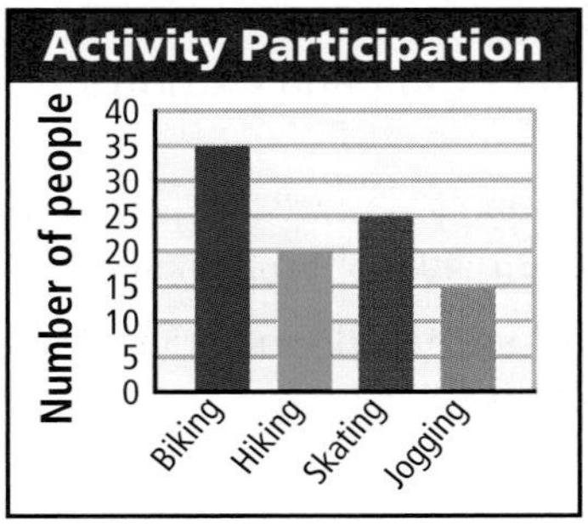

8.

Stems	Leaves
1	5
2	0 5
3	5

Key: 1|5 means 15

PRACTICE AND PROBLEM SOLVING

Extra Practice
See page 740.

9. The data gives the number of books 25 students read last summer.
7, 10, 8, 6, 0, 5, 3, 8, 12, 7, 2, 5, 9, 10, 15, 8, 3, 1, 0, 4, 7, 10, 8, 2, 11
Make the type of graph that would best represent the data.

10. **Life Science** Komodo Dragons are the world's largest lizard species. The table shows the weights of some adult male Komodo Dragons. Make the type of graph that would best represent the information.

Weight (lb)	Frequency
161–170	4
171–180	8
181–190	12
191–200	11
201–210	7

11. Yoko wants to use a stem-and-leaf plot to show the growth of the sweet peas that she planted last year. She measured how much the vines grew each month. Explain why Yoko's display choice may or may not best represent the data.

12. **Nutrition** The table shows the amount of protein per serving in various foods. Draw two different displays to represent the data. Explain your choices.

Food	Protein (g)
Egg	6
Milk	8
Cheese	24
Roast beef	28

13. **Choose a Strategy** Five friends worked together on a project. Matti, Jerad, and Stu all worked the same length of time. Tisha worked a total of 3 hours, which was equal to the total amount of time that Matti, Jerad, and Stu worked. Pablo and Matti together worked $\frac{1}{2}$ of the total amount of time that the five friends worked. Make the type of graph that would best represent the information.

14. **Write About It** Is a circle graph always appropriate to represent data stated in percents? Explain your answer.

15. **Challenge** The table shows the results of a survey of 50 people about their favorite color. What type of display would you choose to represent the data of those who chose blue, green, or red? Explain.

Color	Blue	Yellow	Green	Red	Other
Number	14	4	6	14	12

Test Prep and Spiral Review

16. **Multiple Choice** Which type of display would be most appropriate to compare the monthly rainfall for five cities?

Ⓐ Line graph Ⓑ Bar graph Ⓒ Circle graph Ⓓ Stem-and-leaf plot

17. **Extended Response** Nathan's family budgets $1,000 a month for expenses. They budget $250 for food, $500 for rent, $150 for transportation, and $100 for utilities. Tell which type of graph would best represent the data, justify your response, and draw the display.

Write each decimal as a percent. (Lesson 6-2)

18. 0.27
19. 0.9
20. 0.02
21. 0.406

22. Of the 75 campers at Happy Trails Summer Camp, 36% are scheduled to go horseback riding on Tuesdays. How many campers are scheduled to go horseback riding on Tuesdays? (Lesson 6-4)

7-8 Populations and Samples

Learn to compare and analyze sampling methods.

Vocabulary

population

sample

random sample

convenience sample

biased sample

In 2002, there were claims that Chronic Wasting Disease (CWD), or Mad Elk Disease, was spreading westward across North America. In order to verify claims such as these, the elk population had to be tested.

When information is gathered about a group, such as all the elk in North America, the entire group is called the **population**. Because testing each member of a large group can be difficult or impossible, researchers often study a part of the population, called a **sample**.

Helpful Hint

A random sample is more likely to be representative of a population than a convenience sample is.

For a **random sample**, members of the population are chosen at random. This gives every member of the population an equal chance of being chosen. A **convenience sample** is based on members of the population that are readily available, such as 30 elk in a wildlife preservation area.

EXAMPLE 1 Analyzing Sampling Methods

Determine which sampling method will better represent the entire population. Justify your answer.

Football Game: Student Attendance

Sampling Method	Results of Survey
Arnie surveys 80 students by randomly choosing names from the school directory.	62% attend football games
Vic surveys 28 students that were sitting near him during lunch.	81% attend football games

Arnie's method produces results that better represent the entire student population because he uses a random sample.

Vic's method produces results that are not as representative of the entire student population because he uses a convenience sample.

7-7 Choosing an Appropriate Display

Learn to select and use appropriate representations for displaying data.

On a field trip to a butterfly park, students recorded the number of species of each butterfly family they saw. Which type of graph would best display the data they collected?

There are several ways to display data. Some types of displays are more appropriate than others, depending on how the data is to be analyzed.

Use a **bar graph** to display and compare data.

Use a **circle graph** to show how a set of data is divided into parts.

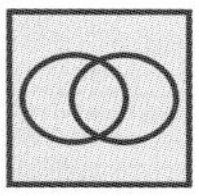

Use a **Venn diagram** to show relationships between two or more data sets.

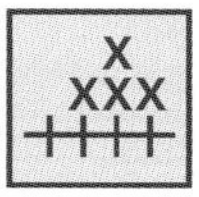

Use a **line plot** to show the frequency of values.

Use a **line graph** to show how data change over a period of time.

Use a **stem-and-leaf plot** to show how often data values occur and how they are distributed.

EXAMPLE 1 Choosing an Appropriate Display

A **The students want to create a display to show the number of species of each butterfly family they saw. Choose the type of graph that would best represent the data in the table. Explain.**

Butterfly Family	Number of Species
Gossamer-wing	7
Skippers	10
Swallowtails	5
Whites and sulphurs	4

There are distinct categories showing the number of species seen in each butterfly family.

A bar graph can be used to display data in categories.

B **The students want to create a display to show the population of butterflies in the park for the past few years. Choose the type of graph that would best represent this data. Explain.**

A line graph would best represent data that gives population over time.

3 The bar graph of the data appears as shown. Resize or reposition the graph, if necessary.

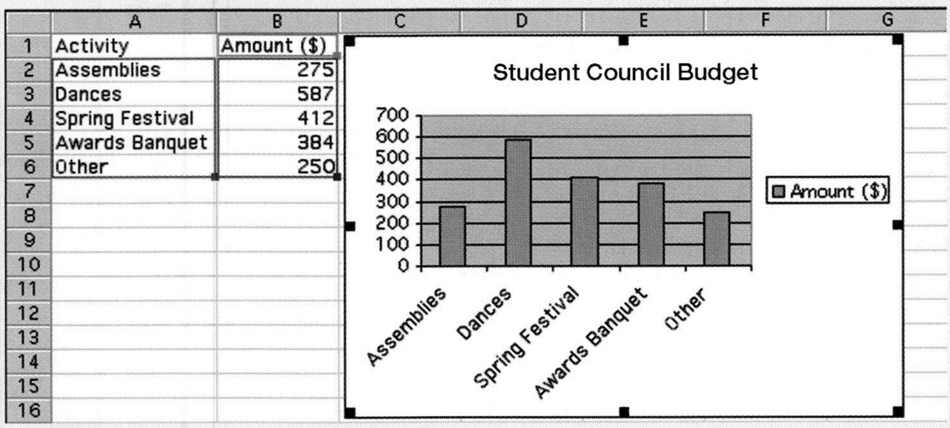

To see a circle graph of the data, select the bar graph (as shown above). Click the Chart Wizard icon and choose "Pie," which is the circle graph. Then click **FINISH** to choose the first type of circle graph.

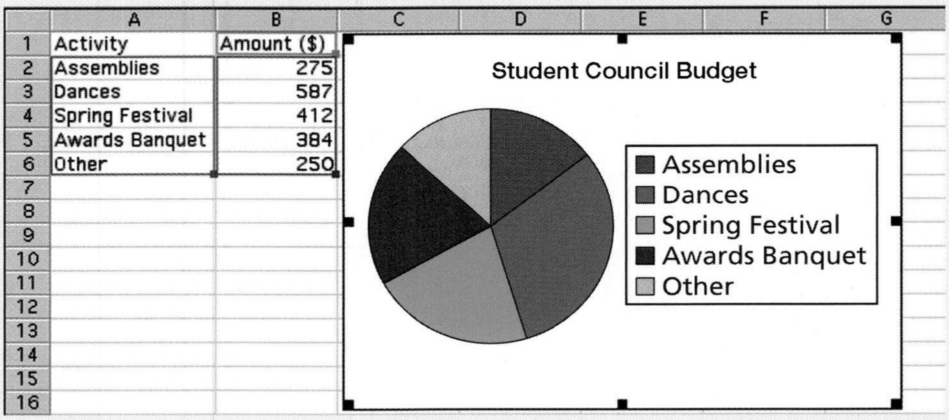

Think and Discuss

1. Which graph best displays the Student Council budget? Why?

2. Would a line graph be an appropriate display of the Student Council budget data? Explain.

Try This

1. The table shows the number of points scored by members of a girls' basketball team in one season. Use a spreadsheet to create a bar graph and a circle graph of the data.

Player	Ana	Angel	Mary	Nia	Tina	Zoe
Points Scored	201	145	89	40	21	8

2. Which type of graph is a better display of the data? Why?

Technology LAB 7-6

Use Technology to Display Data

Use after Lesson 7-6

go.hrw.com
Lab Resources Online
KEYWORD: MS7 Lab7

There are several ways to display data, including bar graphs, line graphs, and circle graphs. A spreadsheet provides a quick way to create these graphs.

Activity

Use a spreadsheet to display the Kennedy Middle School Student Council budget shown in the table at right.

Student Council Budget	
Activity	**Amount ($)**
Assemblies	275
Dances	587
Spring Festival	412
Awards Banquet	384
Other	250

1 Open the spreadsheet program, and enter the data as shown below. Enter the activities in column A and the amount budgeted in column B. Include the column titles in row 1.

	A	B	C
1	Activity	Amount ($)	
2	Assemblies	275	
3	Dances	587	
4	Spring Festival	412	
5	Awards Banquet	384	
6	Other	250	
7			

2 Highlight the data by clicking on cell A1 and dragging the cursor to cell B6. Click the Chart Wizard icon. Then click **FINISH** to choose the first type of column graph.

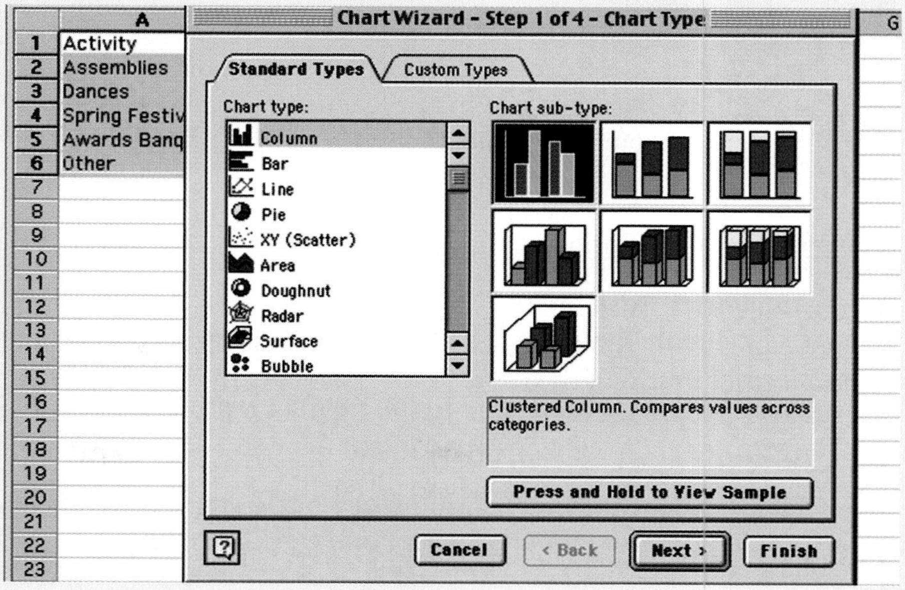

LINK

Earth Science

In 1988, forest fires burned millions of acres in Yosemite and Yellowstone National Parks.

9. Life Science The table shows the numbers of endangered species of vertebrates for selected years between 1998 and 2004.

	1998	2000	2002	2003	2004
Number of Species (thousands)	3.31	3.51	3.52	3.52	5.19

a. Make a line graph of the data in the table.

b. Estimate the number of endangered species of vertebrates in 1999.

10. Earth Science The graph shows the number of acres burned by wildfires in the United States from 1995 to 2000.

a. During which years did wildfires burn more than 6 million acres?

b. Explain whether the graph would be useful in predicting future data values.

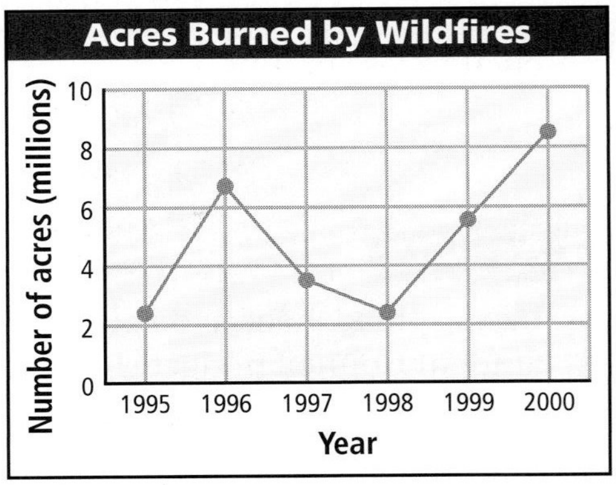

Source: National Interagency Fire Center

11. What's the Error? Denise makes a line plot to display how her town's population has changed over 10 years. Which type of graph would be more appropriate to display this data? Explain.

12. Write About It Explain the benefit of drawing a double-line graph rather than two single-line graphs for related sets of data.

13. Challenge A line graph shows that a town's population was 4,500 in 1980, 5,300 in 1990, and 6,100 in 2000. Assuming the population continues to grow at the same rate, what population will the line graph show in 2010?

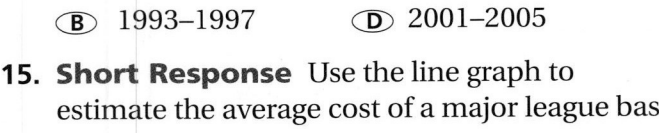

TEST PREP and Spiral Review

Use the graph for Exercises 14 and 15.

14. Multiple Choice During which period did the average cost of a major league baseball ticket increase the most?

Ⓐ 1991–1993   Ⓒ 1997–2001

Ⓑ 1993–1997   Ⓓ 2001–2005

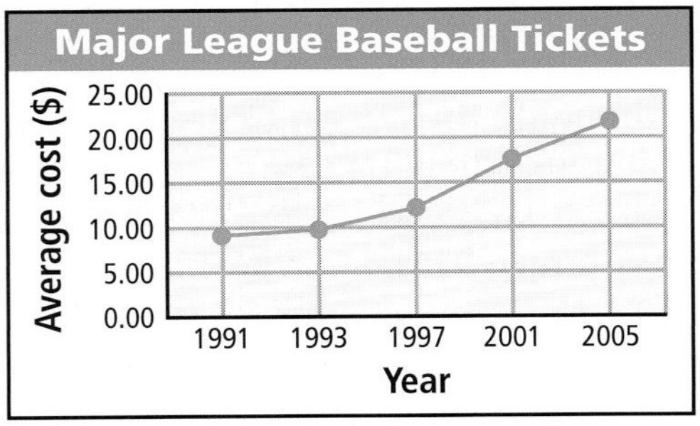

15. Short Response Use the line graph to estimate the average cost of a major league baseball ticket in 2003. Explain.

Write as a percent. Round to the nearest tenth of a percent, if necessary. (Lesson 6-2)

16. 0.15   **17.** 1.36   **18.** $\frac{2}{3}$ **19.** $\frac{11}{20}$

20. Decide whether a bar graph or a circle graph would best display the average temperature for each day of one week. Explain your answer. (Lesson 7-4)

7-6 Exercises

go.hrw.com
Homework Help Online
KEYWORD: MS7 7-6
Parent Resources Online
KEYWORD: MS7 Parent

GUIDED PRACTICE

The table at right shows average movie theater ticket prices in the United States. Use the table for Exercises 1 and 2.

Year	Price ($)
1965	1.01
1970	1.55
1975	2.05
1980	2.69
1985	3.55
1990	4.23
1995	4.35
2000	5.39
2005	6.41

See Example 1

1. Make a line graph of the data. Use the graph to determine during which 5-year period the average ticket price increased the least.

See Example 2

2. Use the graph to estimate the average ticket price in 1997.

See Example 3

3. The table below shows the amount of apple juice and raw apples in pounds consumed per person in the United States. Make a double-line graph of the data.

	2001	2002	2003	2004	2005
Apple Juice	21.4	21.3	21.4	23.1	24.0
Raw Apples	17.5	15.6	16.0	16.9	19.1

INDEPENDENT PRACTICE

The table at right shows the number of teams in the National Basketball Association (NBA). Use the table for Exercises 4–6.

Year	Teams
1965	9
1970	14
1975	18
1980	22
1985	23
1990	27
1995	27
2000	29
2005	30

See Example 1

4. Make a line graph of the data. Use the graph to determine during which 5-year period the number of NBA teams increased the most.
5. During which 5-year period did the number of teams increase the least?

See Example 2

6. **Estimation** Use the graph to estimate the number of NBA teams in 1988.

See Example 3

7. The table below shows the normal daily temperatures in degrees Fahrenheit in Peoria, Illinois, and Portland, Oregon. Make a double-line graph of the data.

	Jul	Aug	Sept	Oct	Nov	Dec
Peoria	76	73	66	54	41	27
Portland	68	69	63	55	46	40

PRACTICE AND PROBLEM SOLVING

Extra Practice
See page 740.

8. **Critical Thinking** Explain how the intervals on the vertical axis of a line graph affect the look of the graph.

You can use a line graph to estimate values between data points.

EXAMPLE 2 Using a Line Graph to Estimate Data

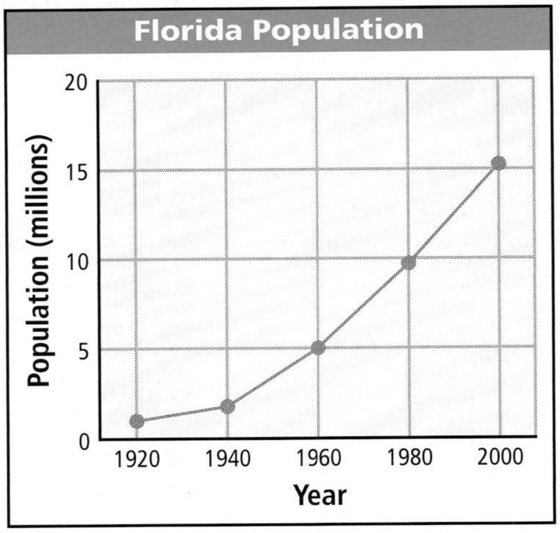

Use the graph to estimate the population of Florida in 1990.

To estimate the population in 1990, find the point on the line between 1980 and 2000 that corresponds to 1990.

The graph shows about 12.5 million. In fact, the population was 12.9 million in 1990.

A **double-line graph** shows change over time for two sets of data.

EXAMPLE 3 Making a Double-Line Graph

The table shows the normal daily temperatures in degrees Fahrenheit in two Alaskan cities. Make a double-line graph of the data.

Month	Nome	Anchorage
Jan	7	15
Feb	4	19
Mar	9	26
Apr	18	36
May	36	47
Jun	46	54

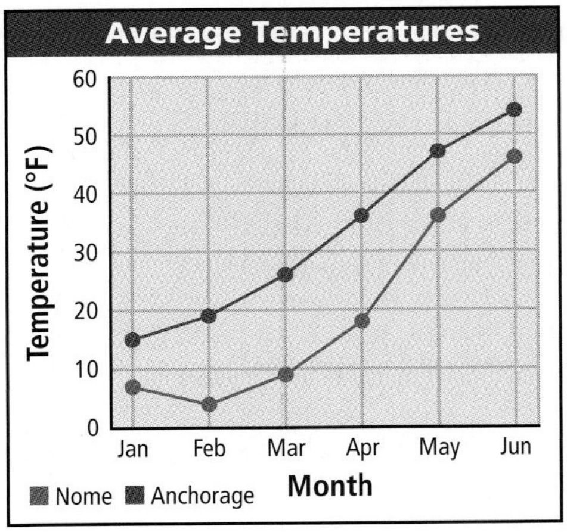

Plot a point for each temperature in Nome and connect the points. Then, using a different color, plot a point for each temperature in Anchorage and connect the points. Make a key to show what each line represents.

Think and Discuss

1. **Describe** how a line graph would look for a set of data that increases and then decreases over time.
2. **Give an example** of a situation that can be described by a double-line graph in which the two sets of data intersect at least once.

ARE YOU READY?

Vocabulary

Choose the best term from the list to complete each sentence.

decimal
integer
percent
proportion
ordered pair

1. An equation showing that two ratios are equal is a(n) __?__.

2. The coordinates of a point on a grid are written as a(n) __?__.

3. A(n) __?__ is a special ratio that compares a number to 100 and uses the symbol %.

4. The number −3 is a(n) __?__.

Complete these exercises to review skills you will need for this chapter.

Percents and Decimals

Write each decimal as a percent.

5. 0.77 **6.** 0.06 **7.** 0.9 **8.** 1.04

Write each percent as a decimal.

9. 42% **10.** 80% **11.** 1% **12.** 131%

Find the Percent of a Number

Solve.

13. What is 10% of 40? **14.** What is 12% of 100? **15.** What is 99% of 60?

16. What is 100% of 81? **17.** What is 45% of 360? **18.** What is 55% of 1,024?

Inverse Operations

Use the inverse operation to write an equation. Solve.

19. $45 + n = 97$ **20.** $n - 18 = 100$ **21.** $n - 72 = 91$ **22.** $n + 23 = 55$

23. $5 \times t = 105$ **24.** $b \div 13 = 8$ **25.** $k \times 18 = 90$ **26.** $d \div 7 = 8$

Graph Ordered Pairs

Use the coordinate plane at right. Write the ordered pair for each point.

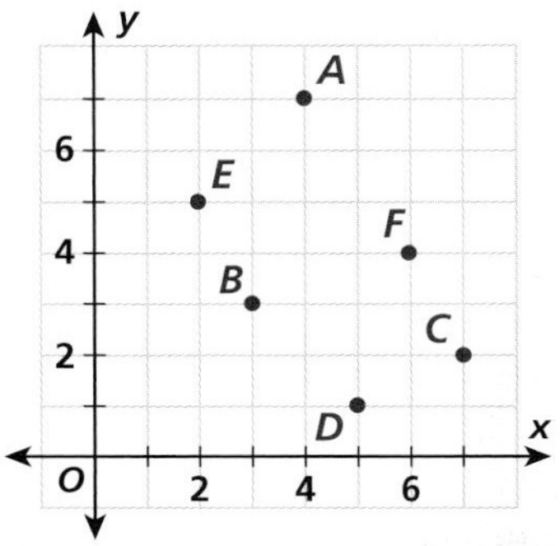

27. point A **28.** point B

29. point C **30.** point D

31. point E **32.** point F

CHAPTER 8

Study Guide: Preview

Where You've Been

Previously, you

- identified relationships involving angles in triangles and quadrilaterals.
- identified similar figures.
- graphed points on a coordinate plane.

In This Chapter

You will study

- classifying pairs of angles as complementary or supplementary.
- classifying triangles and quadrilaterals.
- graphing translations and reflections on a coordinate plane.
- using congruence and similarity to solve problems.

Where You're Going

You can use the skills learned in this chapter

- to solve problems related to architecture and engineering.
- to use transformations to create patterns in art classes.

Key Vocabulary/Vocabulario

angle	ángulo
congruent	congruente
line symmetry	simetría axial
parallel lines	líneas paralelas
perpendicular lines	rectas perpendiculares
polygon	polígono
quadrilateral	cuadrilátero
rotation	rotación
transformation	transformación
vertex	vértice

Vocabulary Connections

To become familiar with some of the vocabulary terms in the chapter, consider the following. You may refer to the chapter, the glossary, or a dictionary if you like.

1. *Congruent* comes from the Latin word *congruere,* meaning "to agree or correspond." If two figures are **congruent**, do you think they look the same or different?
2. *Polygon* comes from the Greek words *polus,* meaning "many," and *gonia,* meaning "angle." What do you think a shape called a **polygon** includes?
3. *Quadrilateral* comes from the Latin words *quadri,* meaning "four," and *latus,* meaning "sides." How many sides do you think a **quadrilateral** has?
4. *Rotation* can mean "the act of spinning or turning." How do you think a figure is moved when you perform a **rotation** on it?

Reading and Writing Math

Writing Strategy: Keep a Math Journal

Keeping a math journal can help you improve your writing and reasoning skills and help you make sense of math topics that might be confusing.

You can use your journal to reflect on what you have learned in class or to summarize important concepts and vocabulary. Most important, though, your math journal can help you see your progress throughout the year.

Journal Entry: Read the entry Lydia wrote in her math journal about similar figures.

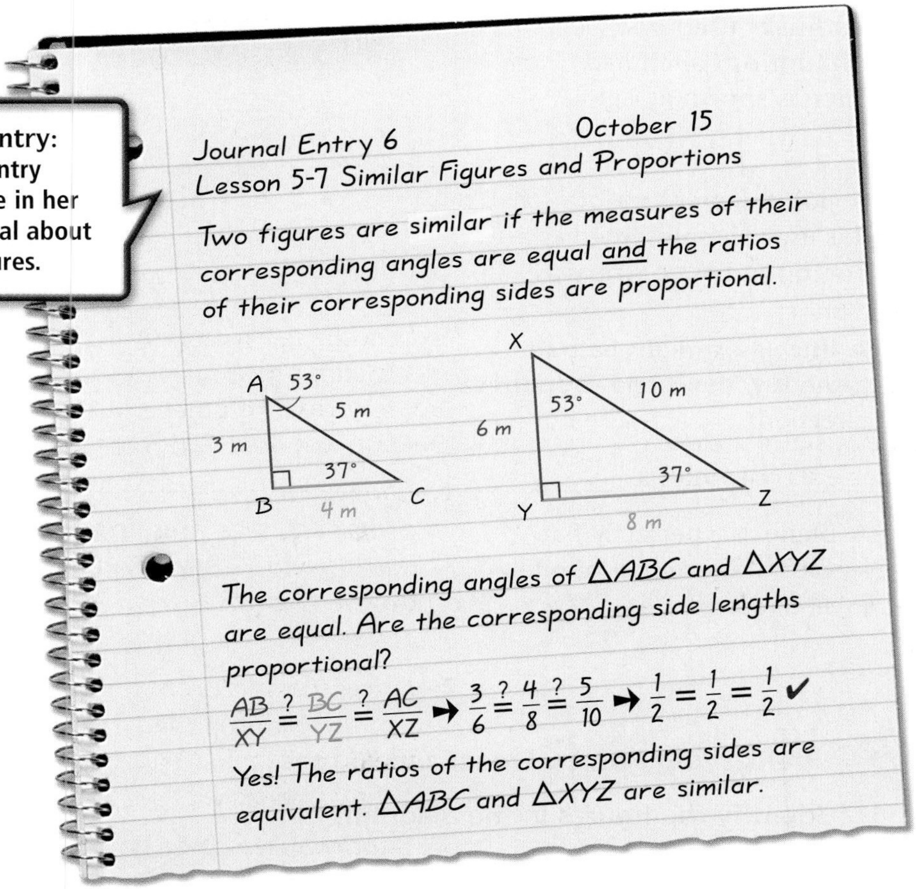
Journal Entry 6
October 15
Lesson 5-7 Similar Figures and Proportions
Two figures are similar if the measures of their corresponding angles are equal and the ratios of their corresponding sides are proportional.
A 53°
5 m
3 m
37°
B
4 m
C
X
53°
10 m
6 m
37°
Y
8 m
Z
The corresponding angles of ΔABC and ΔXYZ are equal. Are the corresponding side lengths proportional?
AB/XY ?= BC/YZ ?= AC/XZ → 3/6 ?= 4/8 ?= 5/10 → 1/2 = 1/2 = 1/2 ✓
Yes! The ratios of the corresponding sides are equivalent. ΔABC and ΔXYZ are similar.

Try This

Begin a math journal. Make an entry every day for one week. Use the following ideas to begin your entries. Be sure to date each entry.

- What I already know about this lesson is . . .
- The skills I need to be successful in this lesson are . . .
- What challenges did I have? How did I handle these challenges?

8-1 Building Blocks of Geometry

Learn to identify and describe geometric figures.

Vocabulary

point
line
plane
ray
line segment
congruent

Points, lines, and *planes* are the most basic figures of geometry. Other geometric figures, such as *line segments* and *rays,* are defined in terms of these building blocks.

Artists often use basic geometric figures when creating their works. For example, Wassily Kandinsky used *line segments* in his painting called *Red Circle,* which is shown at right.

Helpful Hint

A number line is an example of a line, and a coordinate plane is an example of a plane.

A **point** is an exact location. It is usually represented as a dot, but it has no size at all.		point A *Use a capital letter to name a point.*
A **line** is a straight path that extends without end in opposite directions.	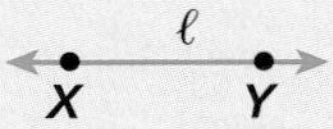	$\overleftrightarrow{XY}$, $\overleftrightarrow{YX}$, or ℓ *Use two points on the line or a lowercase letter to name a line.*
A **plane** is a perfectly flat surface that extends infinitely in all directions.	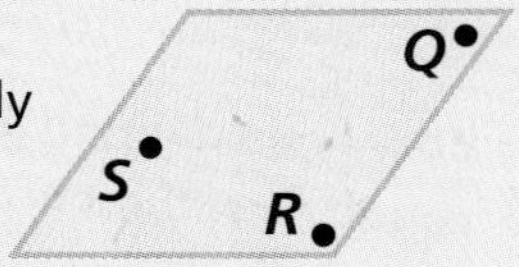	plane QRS *Use three points in any order, not on the same line, to name a plane.*

EXAMPLE 1 Identifying Points, Lines, and Planes

Identify the figures in the diagram.

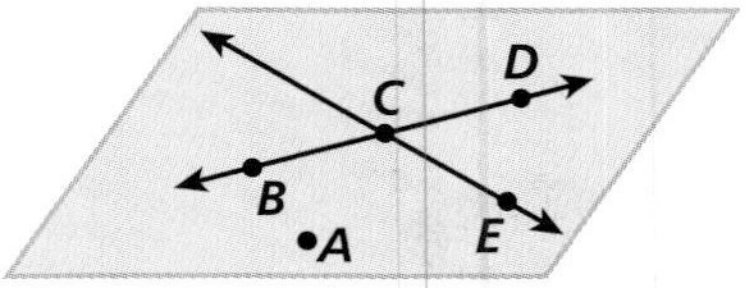

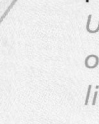

A three points

A, E, and D *Choose any three points.*

B two lines

$\overleftrightarrow{BD}$, $\overleftrightarrow{CE}$ *Choose any two points on a line to name a line.*

C a plane

plane ABC *Choose any three points not on the same line to name a plane.*

A **ray** is a part of a line. It has one endpoint and extends without end in one direction.

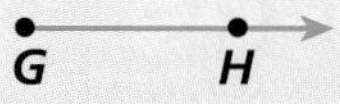

$\overrightarrow{GH}$

Name the endpoint first when naming a ray.

A **line segment** is a part of a line or a ray that extends from one endpoint to another.

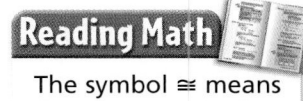

$\overline{LM}$ or $\overline{ML}$

Use the endpoints to name a line segment.

EXAMPLE 2 Identifying Line Segments and Rays

Identify the figures in the diagram.

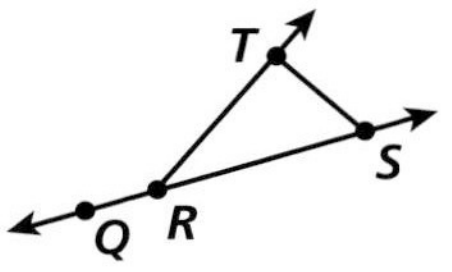

A **three rays**

$\overrightarrow{RQ}$, $\overrightarrow{RT}$, and $\overrightarrow{SQ}$ — *Name the endpoint of a ray first.*

B **three line segments**

$\overline{RQ}$, $\overline{QS}$, and $\overline{ST}$ — *Use the endpoints in any order to name a line segment.*

Figures are **congruent** if they have the same shape and size. Line segments are congruent if they have the same length.

You can use tick marks to indicate congruent line segments. In the triangle at right, line segments AB and BC are congruent.

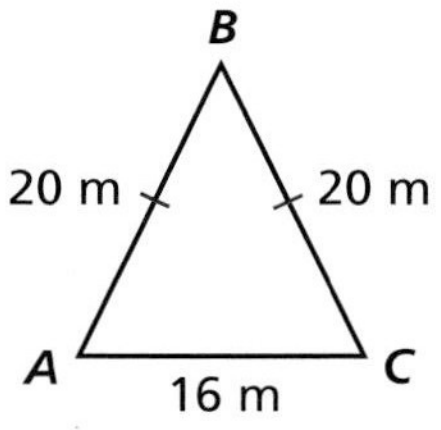

EXAMPLE 3 Identifying Congruent Line Segments

Reading Math

The symbol ≅ means "is congruent to."

Identify the line segments that are congruent in the figure.

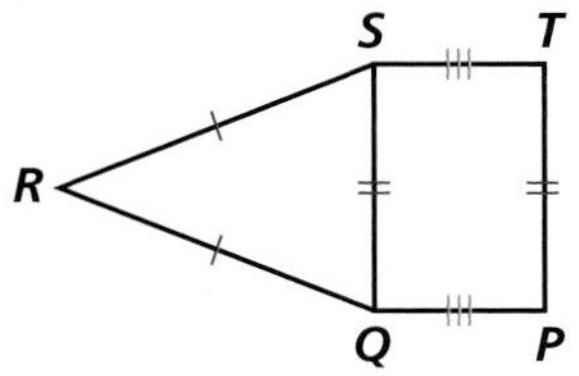

$\overline{QR} \cong \overline{SR}$ — *One tick mark*

$\overline{QS} \cong \overline{PT}$ — *Two tick marks*

$\overline{QP} \cong \overline{ST}$ — *Three tick marks*

Think and Discuss

1. **Explain** why a line and a plane can be named in more than two ways. How many ways can a line segment be named?
2. **Explain** why it is important to choose three points that are not on the same line when naming a plane.

8-1 Exercises

go.hrw.com
Homework Help Online
KEYWORD: MS7 8-1
Parent Resources Online
KEYWORD: MS7 Parent

GUIDED PRACTICE

See Example 1 **Identify the figures in the diagram.**

1. three points
2. two lines
3. a plane

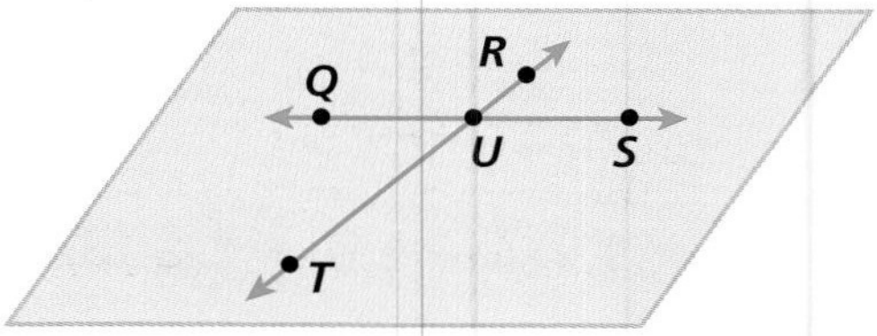

See Example 2
4. three rays
5. three line segments

See Example 3
6. Identify the line segments that are congruent in the figure.

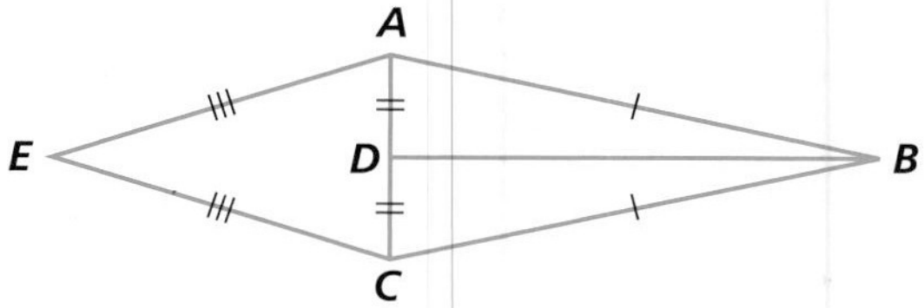

INDEPENDENT PRACTICE

See Example 1 **Identify the figures in the diagram.**

7. three points
8. two lines
9. a plane

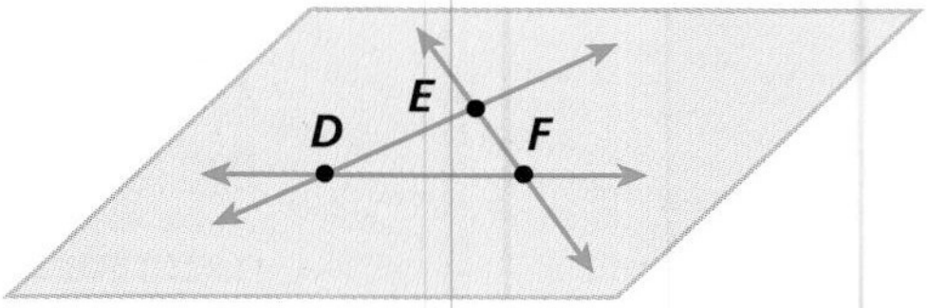

See Example 2
10. three rays
11. three line segments

See Example 3
12. Identify the line segments that are congruent in the figure.

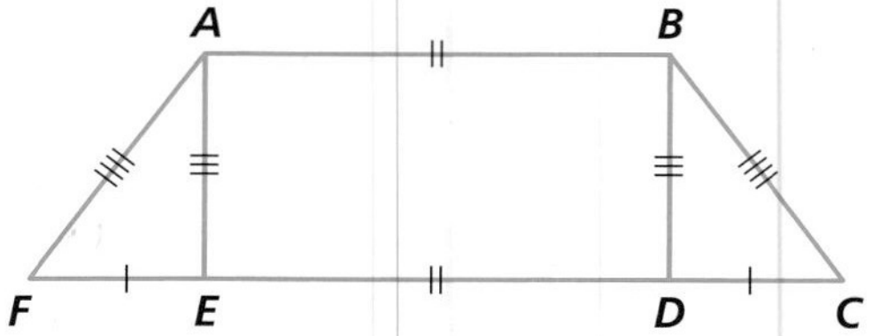

PRACTICE AND PROBLEM SOLVING

Extra Practice
See page 741.

13. Identify the points, lines, line segments, and rays that are represented in the illustration, and tell what plane each is in. Some figures may be in more than one plane.

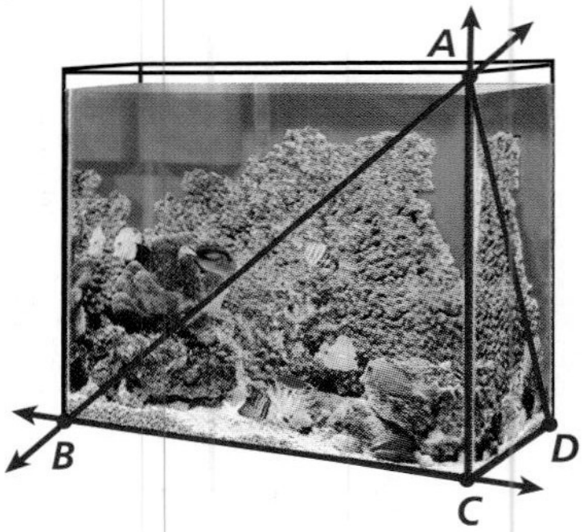

14. **Critical Thinking** How many different line segments can be named in the figure below? Name each segment.

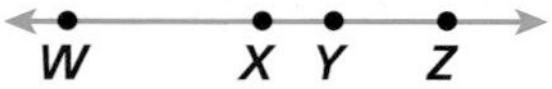

15. Draw a diagram in which a plane, 5 points, 4 rays, and 2 lines can be identified. Then identify these figures.

Art LINK

16. The painting at right, by Piet Mondrian, is called *Composition with Red, Yellow, and Blue*.
    a. Copy the line segments in the painting. Add tick marks to show line segments that appear to be congruent.
    b. Label the endpoints of the segments, including the points of intersection. Then name five pairs of congruent line segments.
17. Draw a figure that includes at least three sets of congruent line segments. Label the endpoints and use notation to tell which line segments are congruent.
18. **Critical Thinking** Can two endpoints be shared by two different line segments? Make a drawing to illustrate your answer.
19. **Write About It** Explain the difference between a line, a line segment, and a ray. Is it possible to estimate the length of any of these figures? If so, tell which ones and why.

20. **Challenge** The wooden sculpture at right, by Georges Vantongerloo, is called *Interrelation of Volumes.* Explain whether two separate faces on the front of the sculpture could be in the same plane.

Test Prep and Spiral Review

21. **Multiple Choice** Identify the line segments that are congruent in the figure.

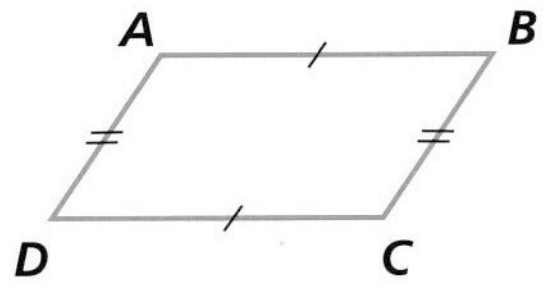

I $\overline{AB}, \overline{BC}$ II $\overline{AB}, \overline{CD}$

III $\overline{BC}, \overline{CD}$ IV $\overline{BC}, \overline{AD}$

Ⓐ I only   Ⓑ I and III   Ⓒ II and IV   Ⓓ II only

22. **Short Response** Draw a plane that contains each of the following: points *A*, *B*, and *C*; line segment *AB*; ray *BC*; and line *AC*.

Find each product or quotient. (Lesson 2-4)

23. $-48 \div (-3)$ 24. $-2 \cdot (-6)$ 25. $-56 \div 8$ 26. $5 \cdot (-13)$

Find each percent of change. Round answers to the nearest tenth of a percent, if necessary. (Lesson 6-6)

27. 85 is decreased to 60.   28. 35 is increased to 120.   29. 6 is decreased to 1.

Hands-On LAB 8-2

Explore Complementary and Supplementary Angles

Use with Lesson 8-2

go.hrw.com
Lab Resources Online
KEYWORD: MS7 Lab8

REMEMBER
- **An angle is formed by two rays with a common endpoint, called the vertex.**

Activity 1

You can use a *protractor* to measure angles in units called *degrees*. Find the measure of $\angle AVB$.

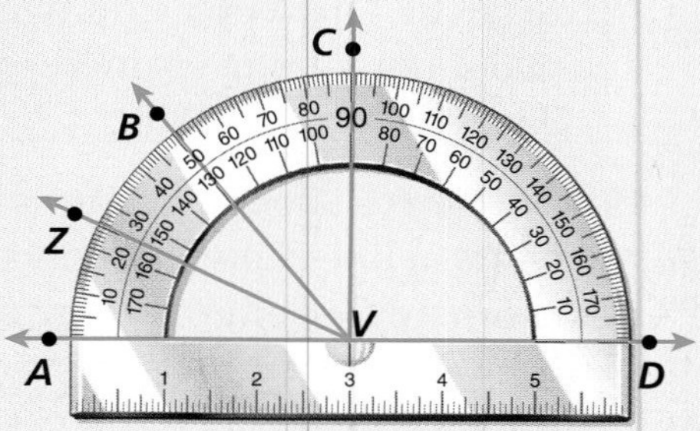

1. Place the center point of the protractor on the vertex of the angle.
2. Place the protractor so that $\overrightarrow{AV}$ passes through the 0° mark.
3. Using the scale that starts with 0° along $\overrightarrow{AV}$, read the measure where $\overrightarrow{VB}$ crosses the scale. The measure of $\angle AVB$ is 50°.

Think and Discuss

1. Explain how to find the measure of $\angle BVC$ without moving the protractor.

Try This

Use the protractor in Activity 1 to find the measure of each angle.

1. $\angle AVC$ **2.** $\angle AVZ$ **3.** $\angle DVC$

Activity 2

Copy and measure each pair of angles.

Type of Angle Pair	Examples	Nonexamples
Complementary	**1.** 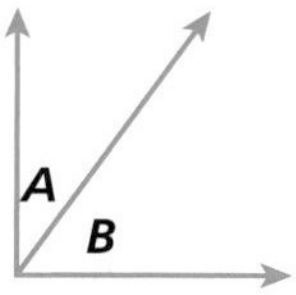	**2.** 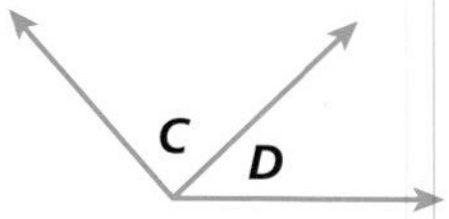
	3. 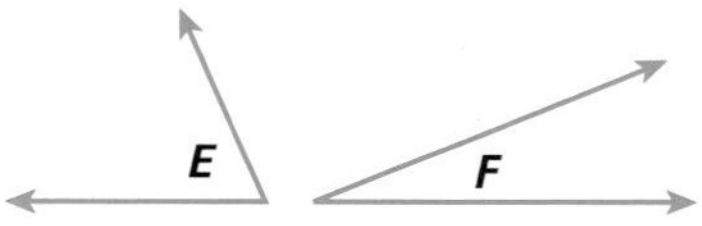	**4.** 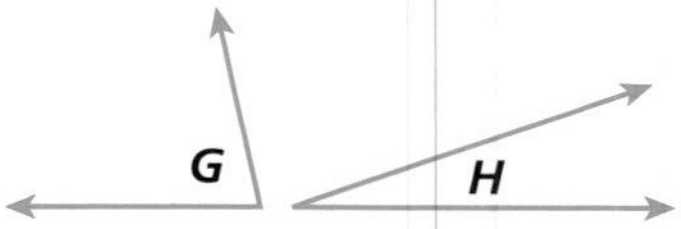

Type of Angle Pair	Examples	Nonexamples
Supplementary	**5.** 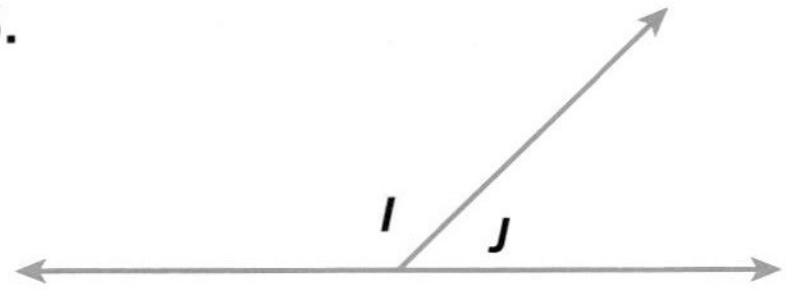 **7.** 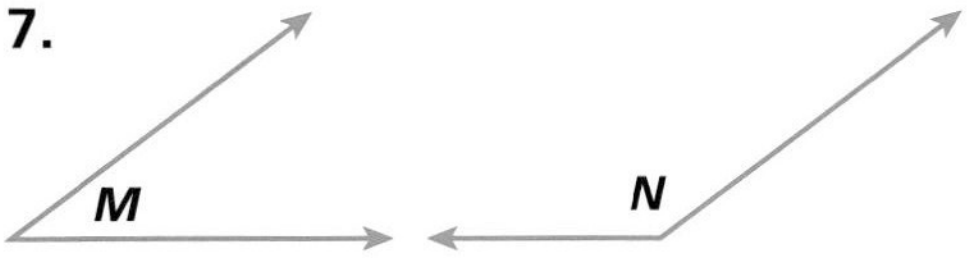	**6.** 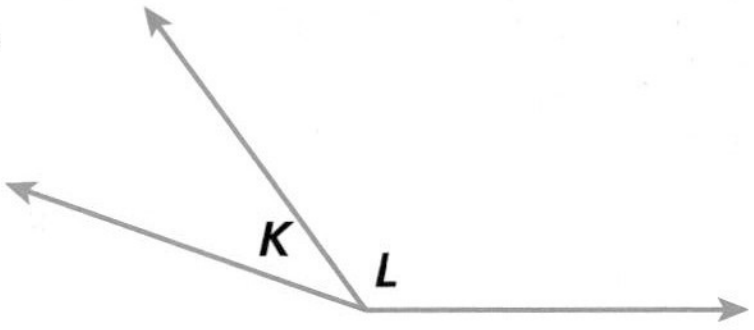 **8.** 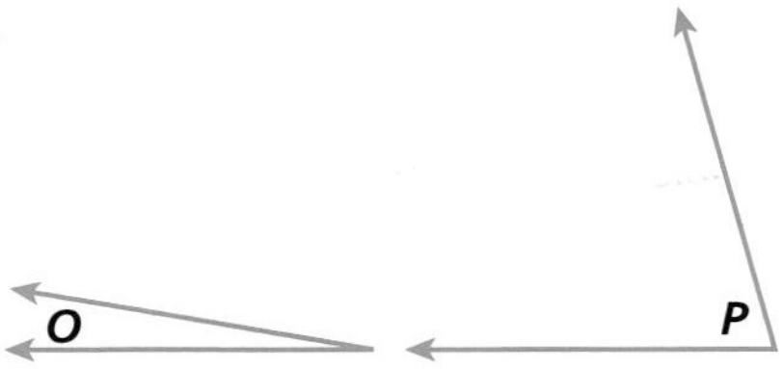

Think and Discuss

1. For each type of angle pair, complementary and supplementary, write a rule that relates the angle measurements.

Try This

Use a protractor to measure each of the angle pairs below. Tell whether the angle pairs are complementary, supplementary, or neither.

1.

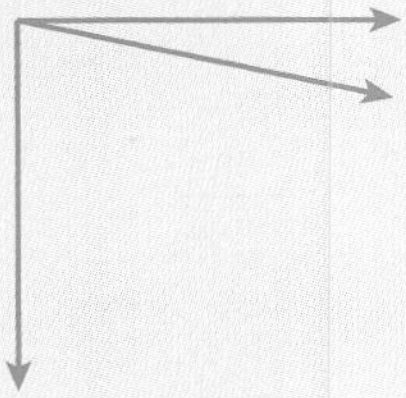

2.

3.

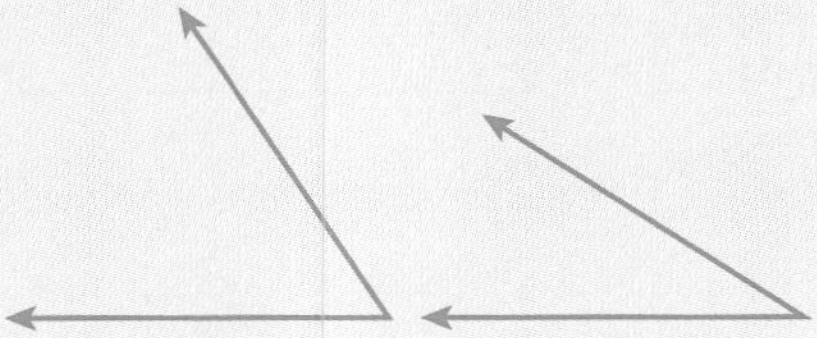

4.

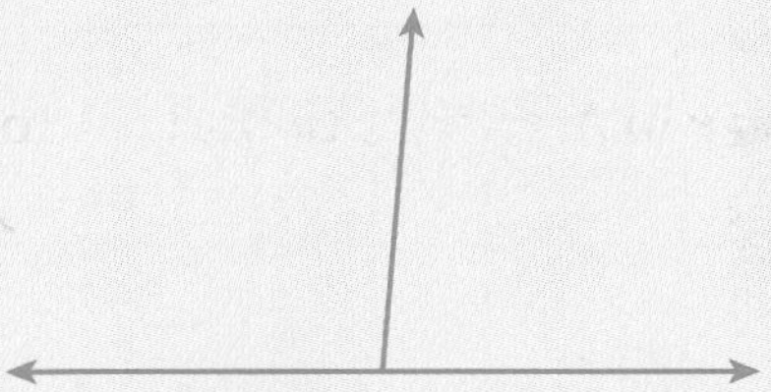

5. How can you tell that the angle pairs in exercise 4 are supplementary without using a protractor?

6. Use a protractor to find all the pairs of complementary and supplementary angles in the figure at right.

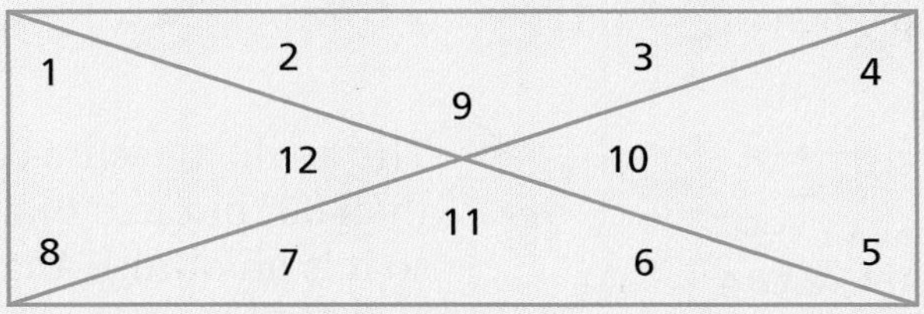

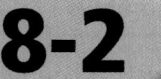

8-2 Classifying Angles

Learn to identify angles and angle pairs.

Vocabulary

angle
vertex
right angle
acute angle
obtuse angle
straight angle
complementary angles
supplementary angles

When riding down a ramp on a skateboard, the speed you gain depends partly on the *angle* that the ramp makes with the ground.

An **angle** is formed by two rays with a common endpoint. The two rays are the sides of the angle. The common endpoint is the **vertex**.

Angles are measured in degrees (°). An angle's measure determines the type of angle it is.

A **right angle** is an angle that measures exactly 90°. The symbol ⌉ indicates a right angle.

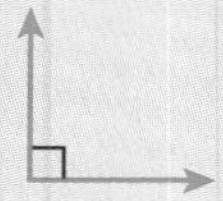

An **acute angle** is an angle that measures less than 90°.

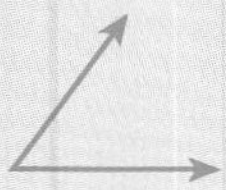

An **obtuse angle** is an angle that measures more than 90° but less than 180°.

A **straight angle** is an angle that measures exactly 180°.

EXAMPLE 1 Classifying Angles

Tell whether each angle is acute, right, obtuse, or straight.

A

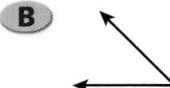

The angle measures greater than 90° but less than 180°, so it is an obtuse angle.

B

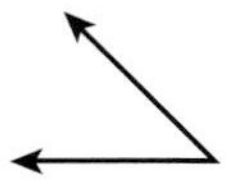

The angle measures less than 90°, so it is an acute angle.

Writing Math

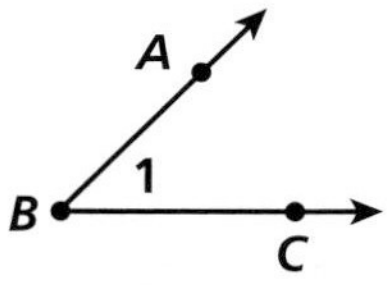

You can name this angle $\angle ABC$, $\angle CBA$, $\angle B$, or $\angle 1$.

If the sum of the measures of two angles is 90°, then the angles are **complementary angles**. If the sum of the measures of two angles is 180°, then the angles are **supplementary angles**.

EXAMPLE 2 Identifying Complementary and Supplementary Angles

Helpful Hint

If the angle you are measuring appears obtuse, then its measure is greater than 90°. If the angle is acute, its measure is less than 90°.

Use the diagram to tell whether the angles are complementary, supplementary, or neither.

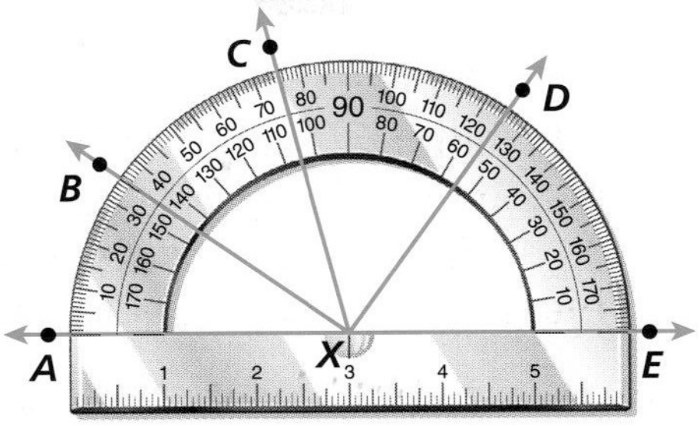

A $\angle DXE$ **and** $\angle AXB$

m$\angle DXE$ = 55° and m$\angle AXB$ = 35°

Since 55° + 35° = 90°, $\angle DXE$ and $\angle AXB$ are complementary.

Reading Math

Read m$\angle DXE$ as "the measure of angle *DXE*."

B $\angle DXE$ **and** $\angle BXC$

m$\angle DXE$ = 55°. To find m$\angle BXC$, start with the measure that $\overrightarrow{XC}$ crosses, 75°, and subtract the measure that $\overrightarrow{XB}$ crosses, 35°.
m$\angle BXC$ = 75° − 35° = 40°.

Since 55° + 40° = 95°, $\angle DXE$ and $\angle BXC$ are neither complementary nor supplementary.

C $\angle AXC$ **and** $\angle CXE$

m$\angle AXC$ = 75° and m$\angle CXE$ = 105°

Since 75° + 105° = 180°, $\angle AXC$ and $\angle CXE$ are supplementary.

EXAMPLE 3 Finding Angle Measures

Angles *R* and *V* are supplementary. If m$\angle R$ is 67°, what is m$\angle V$?

Since $\angle R$ and $\angle V$ are supplementary, m$\angle R$ + m$\angle V$ = 180°.

$$m\angle R + m\angle V = 180°$$
$$67° + m\angle V = 180° \qquad \textit{Substitute 67° for m}\angle R.$$
$$\underline{-\ 67°\qquad\qquad -\ 67°} \qquad \textit{Subtract 67° from both sides to isolate m}\angle V.$$
$$m\angle V = 113°$$

The measure of $\angle V$ is 113°.

Think and Discuss

1. **Describe** three different ways to classify an angle.
2. **Explain** how to find the measure of $\angle P$ if $\angle P$ and $\angle Q$ are complementary angles and m$\angle Q$ = 25°.

8-2 Exercises

go.hrw.com
Homework Help Online
KEYWORD: MS7 8-2
Parent Resources Online
KEYWORD: MS7 Parent

GUIDED PRACTICE

See Example 1
Tell whether each angle is acute, right, obtuse, or straight.

1. 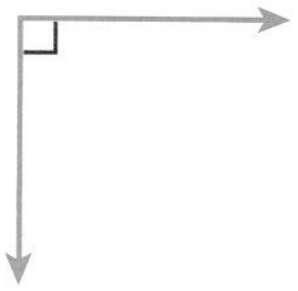

2. 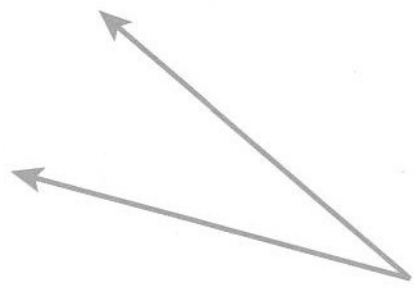

3. 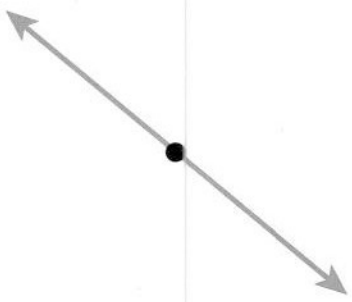

See Example 2
Use the diagram to tell whether the angles are complementary, supplementary, or neither.

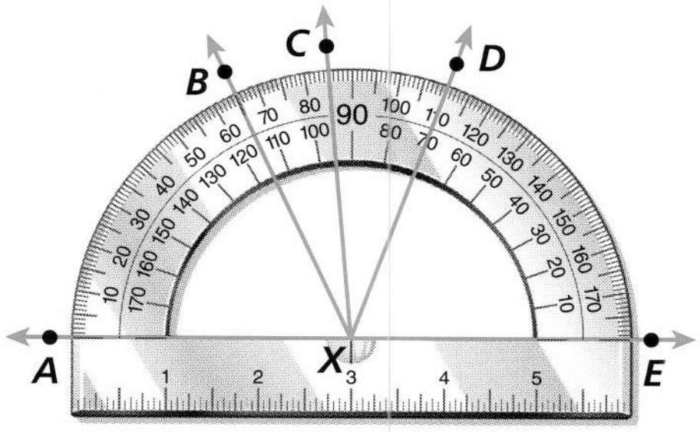

4. $\angle AXB$ and $\angle BXC$ **5.** $\angle BXC$ and $\angle DXE$

6. $\angle DXE$ and $\angle AXD$ **7.** $\angle CXD$ and $\angle AXB$

See Example 3

8. Angles L and P are complementary. If $m\angle P$ is 34°, what is $m\angle L$?

9. Angles B and C are supplementary. If $m\angle B$ is 119°, what is $m\angle C$?

INDEPENDENT PRACTICE

See Example 1
Tell whether each angle is acute, right, obtuse, or straight.

10. 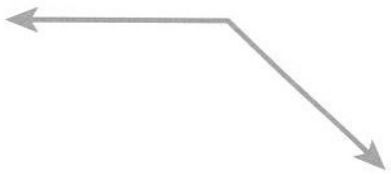

11. 

12. 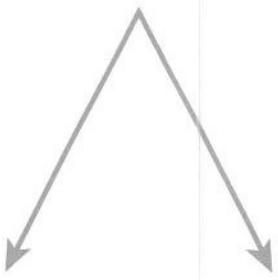

See Example 2
Use the diagram to tell whether the angles are complementary, supplementary, or neither.

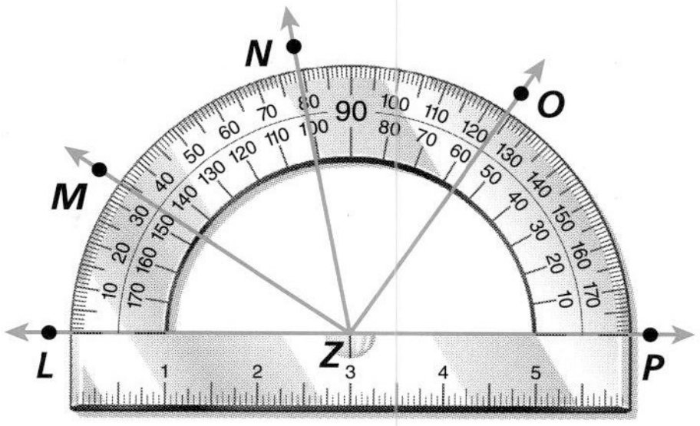

13. $\angle NZO$ and $\angle MZN$ **14.** $\angle MZN$ and $\angle OZP$

15. $\angle LZN$ and $\angle NZP$ **16.** $\angle NZO$ and $\angle LZM$

See Example 3

17. Angles F and O are supplementary. If $m\angle F$ is 85°, what is $m\angle O$?

18. Angles J and K are complementary. If $m\angle K$ is 22°, what is $m\angle J$?

PRACTICE AND PROBLEM SOLVING

Extra Practice
See page 741.

Classify each pair of angles as complementary or supplementary. Then find the missing angle measure.

19. 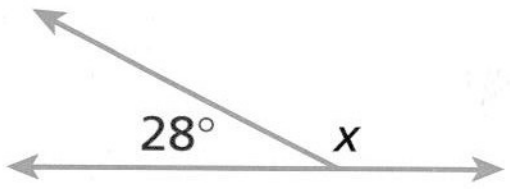

20. 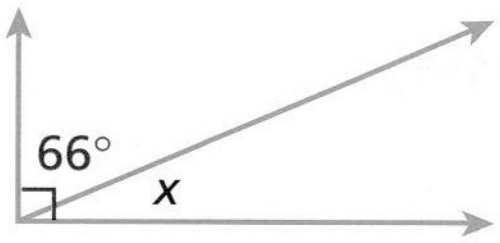

21. 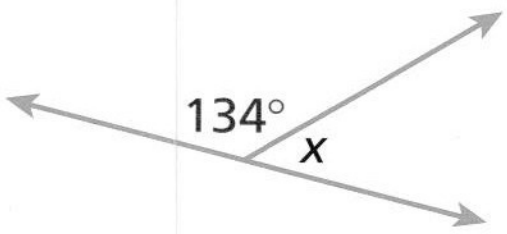

22. **Critical Thinking** The hands of a clock form an acute angle at 1:00. What type of angle is formed at 6:00? at 3:00? at 5:00?

23. **Geography** Imaginary curves around Earth show distances in degrees from the equator and Prime Meridian. On a flat map, these curves are displayed as horizontal lines (latitude) and vertical lines (longitude).

    a. What type of angle is formed where a line of latitude and a line of longitude cross?

    b. Estimate the latitude and longitude of Washington, D.C.

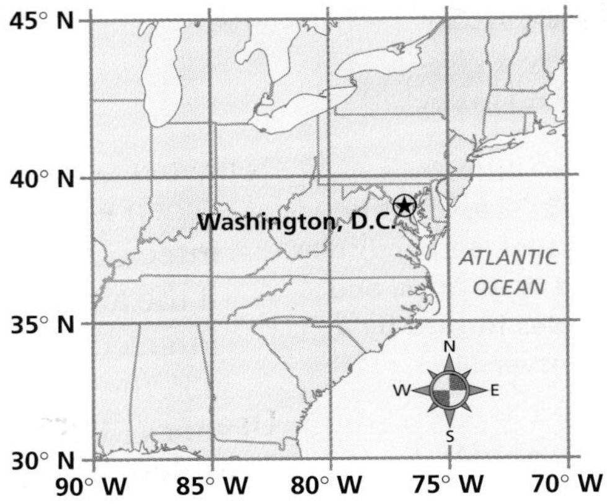

24. **What's the Error?** A student states that when the sum of two angles equals the measure of a straight angle, the two angles are complementary. Explain why the student is incorrect.

25. **Write About It** Explain why two obtuse angles cannot be supplementary to one another.

26. **Challenge** Find m∠*BAC* in the figure.

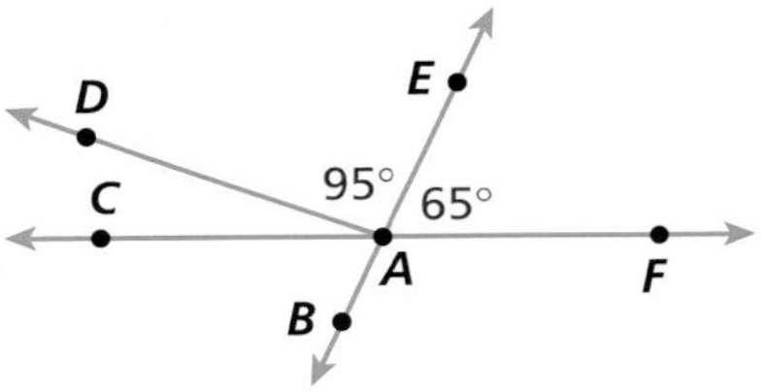

Test Prep and Spiral Review

Use the diagram for Exercises 27 and 28.

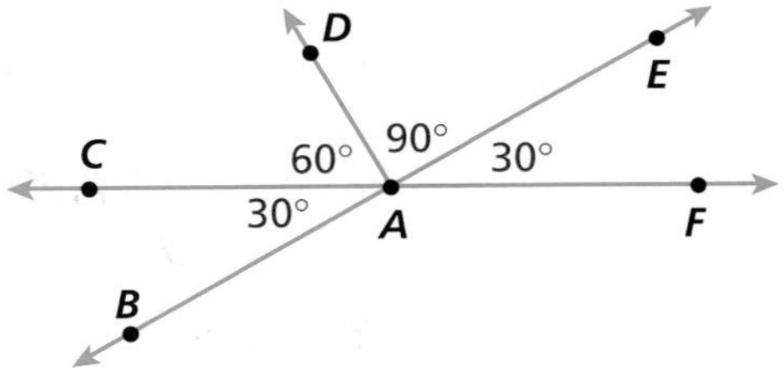

27. **Multiple Choice** Which statement is NOT true?

    Ⓐ ∠*BAC* is acute.

    Ⓑ ∠*DAE* is a right angle.

    Ⓒ ∠*FAE* and ∠*EAD* are complementary angles.

    Ⓓ ∠*FAD* and ∠*DAC* are supplementary angles.

28. **Multiple Choice** What is the measure of ∠*FAD*?

    Ⓕ 30° Ⓖ 120° Ⓗ 150° Ⓙ 180°

Find the mean, median, mode, and range of each data set. (Lesson 7-2)

29. 6, 3, 5, 6, 8

30. 14, 18, 10, 20, 23

31. 41, 35, 29, 41, 58, 24

32. Identify and name the figure at right. (Lesson 8-1)

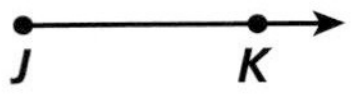

8-3 Angle Relationships

Learn to identify parallel, perpendicular, and skew lines, and angles formed by a transversal.

Vocabulary

perpendicular lines

parallel lines

skew lines

adjacent angles

vertical angles

transversal

corresponding angles

When lines, segments, or rays intersect, they form angles. If the angles formed by two intersecting lines measure 90°, the lines are **perpendicular lines**. The red and yellow line segments in the photograph are perpendicular.

Some lines in the same plane do not intersect at all. These lines are **parallel lines**. Segments and rays that are parts of parallel lines are also parallel.

Skew lines do not intersect, and yet they are also not parallel. They lie in different planes. The orange line segments in the photograph are skew.

EXAMPLE 1 **Identifying Parallel, Perpendicular, and Skew Lines**

Tell whether the lines in the figure appear parallel, perpendicular, or skew.

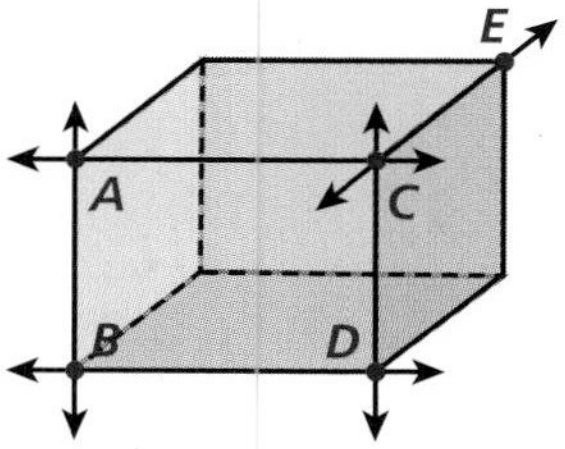

Reading Math

The symbol ⊥ means "is perpendicular to." The symbol || means "is parallel to."

A $\overleftrightarrow{AB}$ **and** $\overleftrightarrow{AC}$

$\overleftrightarrow{AB} \perp \overleftrightarrow{AC}$ *The lines appear to intersect to form right angles.*

B $\overleftrightarrow{CE}$ **and** $\overleftrightarrow{BD}$

$\overleftrightarrow{CE}$ and $\overleftrightarrow{BD}$ are skew. *The lines are in different planes and do not intersect.*

C $\overleftrightarrow{AC}$ **and** $\overleftrightarrow{BD}$

$\overleftrightarrow{AC} \parallel \overleftrightarrow{BD}$ *The lines are in the same plane and do not intersect.*

Reading Math

Angles with the same number of tick marks are congruent.

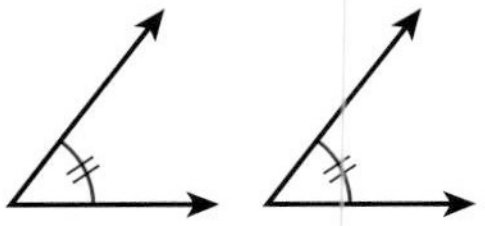

Adjacent angles have a common vertex and a common side, but no common interior points. Angles 2 and 3 in the diagram are adjacent. Adjacent angles formed by two intersecting lines are supplementary.

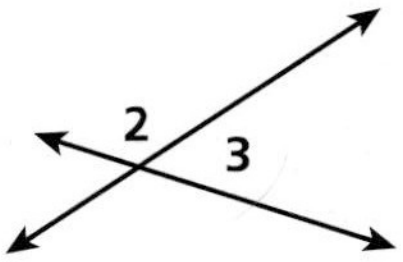

Vertical angles are the opposite angles formed by two intersecting lines. Angles 1 and 3 in the diagram are vertical angles. Vertical angles have the same measure, so they are congruent.

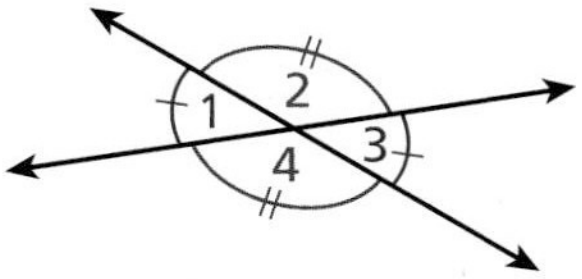

A **transversal** is a line that intersects two or more lines. Line t is a transversal. When the lines that are intersected are parallel, four pairs of *corresponding angles* are formed. **Corresponding angles** are on the same side of the transversal and are both above or both below the parallel lines. Angles 1 and 5 are corresponding angles. Corresponding angles are congruent.

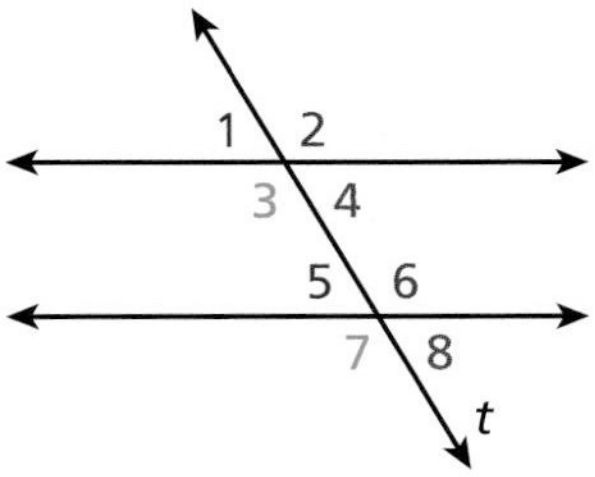

EXAMPLE 2 Using Angle Relationships to Find Angle Measures

Line $n \parallel$ line p. Find the measure of each angle.

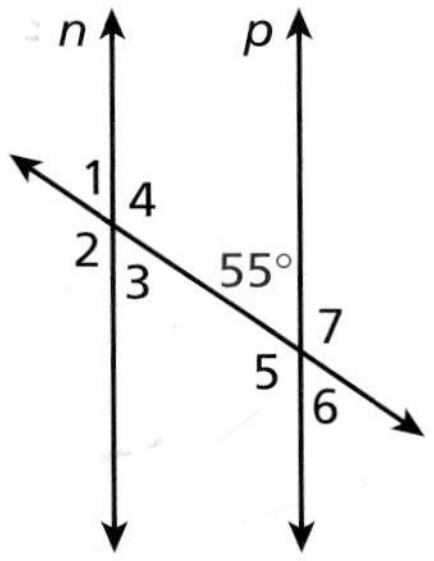

A $\angle 6$

$\angle 6$ and the 55° angle are vertical angles. Since vertical angles are congruent, $m\angle 6 = 55°$.

B $\angle 1$

$\angle 1$ and the 55° angle are corresponding angles. Since corresponding angles are congruent, $m\angle 1 = 55°$.

C $\angle 7$

$\angle 7$ and the 55° angle are adjacent, supplementary angles.

$$\begin{aligned} m\angle 7 + 55° &= 180° \\ \underline{\quad -55°} &\quad \underline{-55°} \\ m\angle 7 &= 125° \end{aligned}$$

The sum of the measures of supplementary angles is 180°.

Think and Discuss

1. **Draw** a pair of parallel lines intersected by a transversal. Use tick marks to indicate the congruent angles.
2. **Give** some examples in which parallel, perpendicular, and skew relationships can be seen in the real world.

8-3 Exercises

GUIDED PRACTICE

See Example 1

Tell whether the lines appear parallel, perpendicular, or skew.

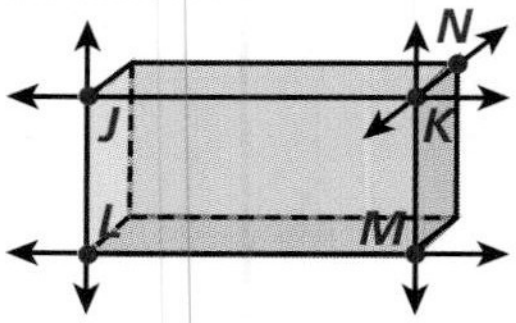

1. $\overleftrightarrow{JL}$ and $\overleftrightarrow{KM}$
2. $\overleftrightarrow{LM}$ and $\overleftrightarrow{KN}$
3. $\overleftrightarrow{LM}$ and $\overleftrightarrow{KM}$

See Example 2

Line $r \parallel$ line s. Find the measure of each angle.

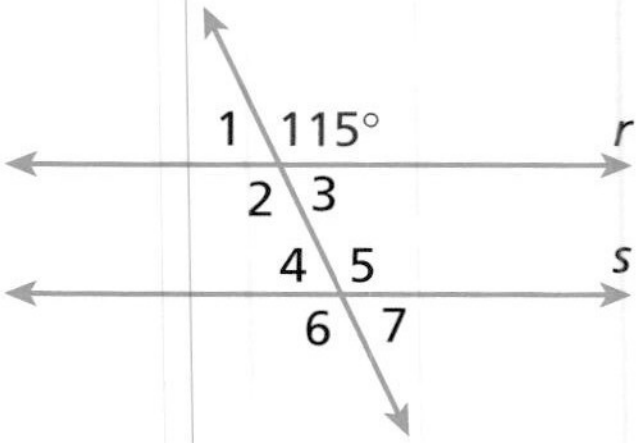

4. $\angle 5$
5. $\angle 2$
6. $\angle 7$

INDEPENDENT PRACTICE

See Example 1

Tell whether the lines appear parallel, perpendicular, or skew.

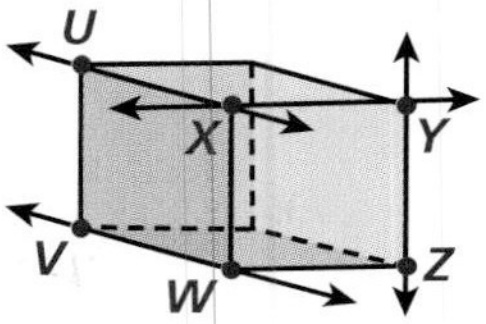

7. $\overleftrightarrow{UX}$ and $\overleftrightarrow{YZ}$
8. $\overleftrightarrow{YZ}$ and $\overleftrightarrow{XY}$
9. $\overleftrightarrow{UX}$ and $\overleftrightarrow{VW}$

See Example 2

Line $k \parallel$ line m. Find the measure of each angle.

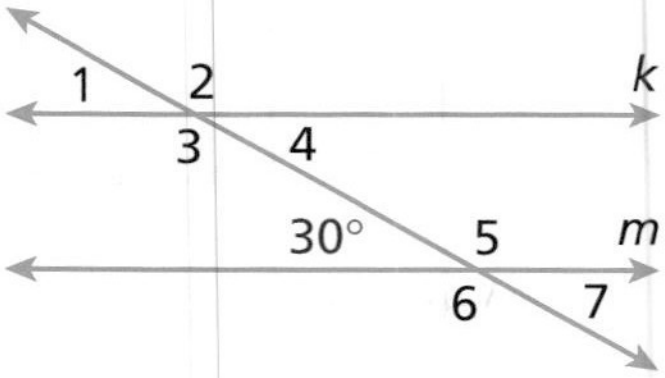

10. $\angle 1$
11. $\angle 3$
12. $\angle 6$

PRACTICE AND PROBLEM SOLVING

Extra Practice
See page 741.

For Exercises 13–16, use the figure to complete each statement.

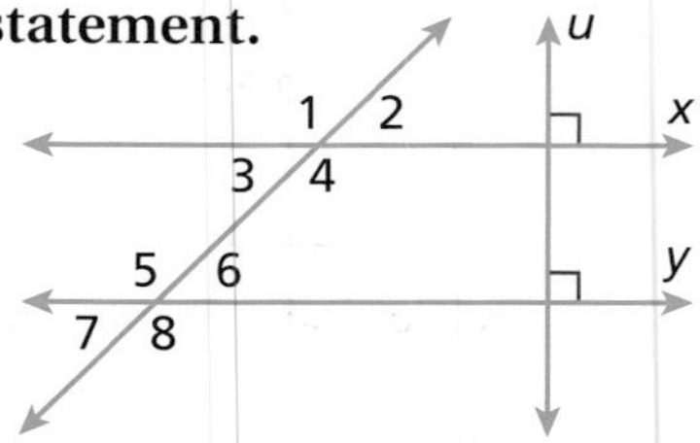

13. Lines x and y are ___?___.
14. Lines u and x are ___?___.
15. $\angle 3$ and $\angle 4$ are ___?___. They are also ___?___.
16. $\angle 2$ and $\angle 6$ are ___?___. They are also ___?___.
17. **Critical Thinking** A pair of complementary angles are congruent. What is the measure of each angle?
18. **Multi-Step** Two lines intersect to form four angles. The measure of one angle is 27°. Draw a diagram to show the measures of the other three angles. Explain your answer.

LINK

Construction

Construction workers use a tool called a *square* to make sure boards are perpendicular.

Tell whether each statement is always, sometimes, or never true.

19. Adjacent angles are congruent.

20. Intersecting lines are skew.

21. Vertical angles are congruent.

22. Parallel lines intersect.

23. Construction In the diagram of the partial wall frame shown, the vertical beams are parallel.

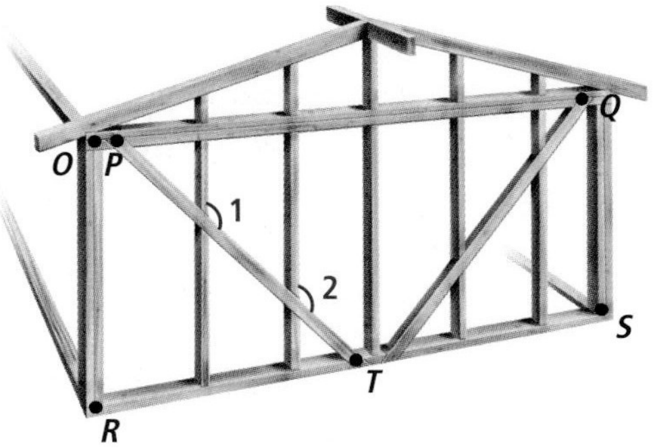

a. Angle ORT measures 90°. How are $\overline{OR}$ and $\overline{RS}$ related?

b. $\overline{PT}$ crosses two vertical crossbeams. What word describes $\overline{PT}$?

c. How are $\angle 1$ and $\angle 2$ related?

24. Critical Thinking Two lines intersect to form congruent adjacent angles. What can you say about the two lines?

25. Choose a Strategy Trace the dots in the figure. Draw all the lines that connect three dots. How many pairs of perpendicular lines have you drawn?

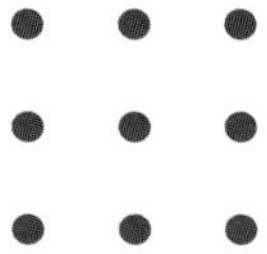

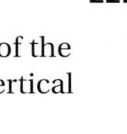

Ⓐ 8 Ⓑ 9 Ⓒ 10 Ⓓ 14

26. Write About It Use the definition of a straight angle to explain why adjacent angles formed by two intersecting lines are supplementary.

27. Challenge The lines in the parking lot appear to be parallel. How could you check that the lines are parallel?

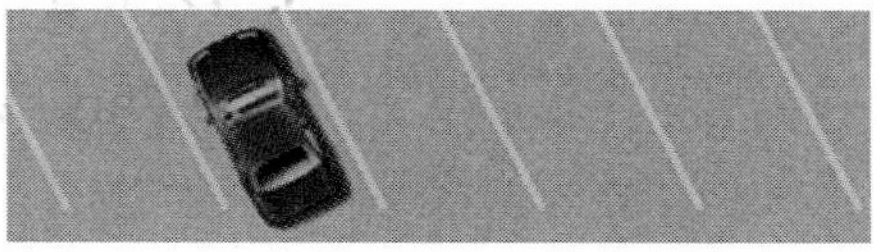

Test Prep and Spiral Review

Use the diagram for Exercises 28 and 29.

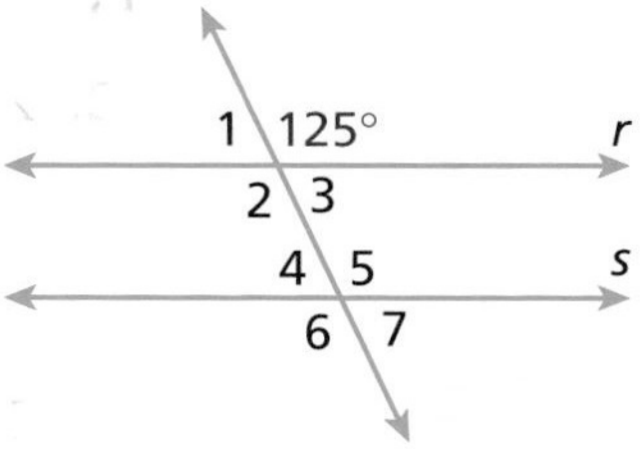

28. Multiple Choice What is the measure of $\angle 3$?

Ⓐ 125° Ⓑ 75° Ⓒ 65° Ⓓ 55°

29. Multiple Choice What is the measure of $\angle 6$?

Ⓕ 125° Ⓖ 75° Ⓗ 65° Ⓙ 55°

Add or subtract. Estimate to check whether each answer is reasonable. (Lesson 3-2)

30. $3.583 - (-2.759)$

31. $-9.43 + 7.68$

32. $-1.03 + (-0.081)$

Classify each pair of angles as complementary or supplementary. Then find the missing angle measure. (Lesson 8-2)

33.

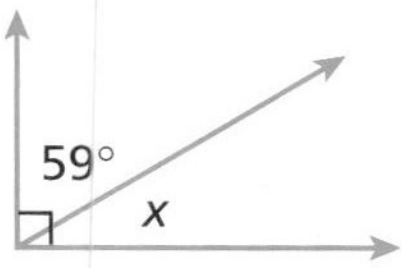

34.

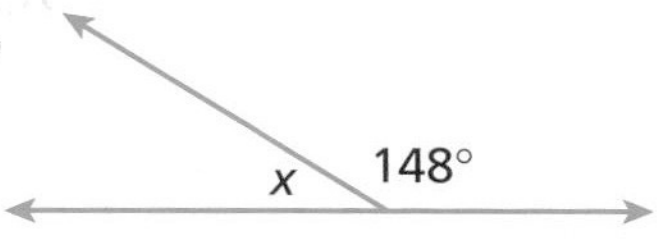

35.

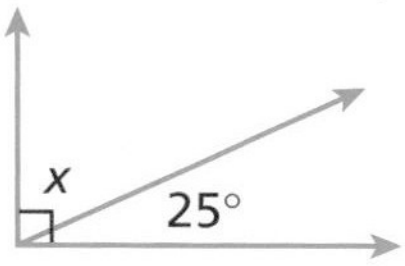

Hands-On LAB 8-3

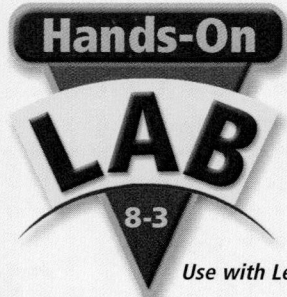

Construct Bisectors and Congruent Angles

Use with Lesson 8-3

go.hrw.com
Lab Resources Online
KEYWORD: MS7 Lab8

REMEMBER
- Congruent angles have the same measure, and congruent segments are the same length.

To bisect a segment or an angle is to divide it into two congruent parts. You can bisect segments and angles, and construct congruent angles without using a protractor or ruler. Instead, you can use a compass and a straightedge.

Activity

1 Bisect a line segment.

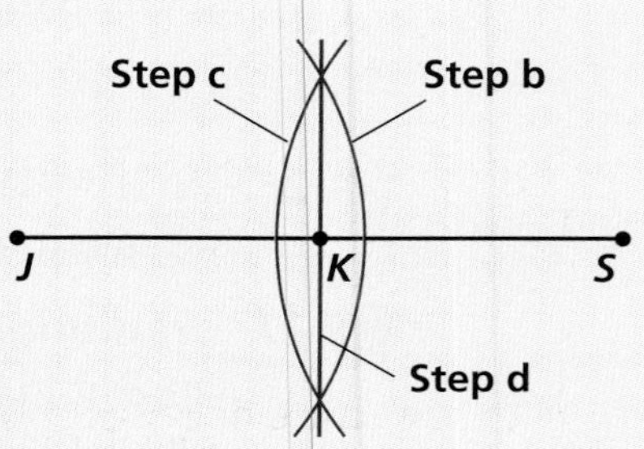

a. Draw a line segment $\overline{JS}$ on a piece of paper.

b. Place your compass on endpoint J and, using an opening that is greater than half the length of $\overline{JS}$, draw an arc that intersects $\overline{JS}$.

c. Place your compass on endpoint S and draw an arc using the same opening as you did in part **b.** The arc should intersect the first arc at both ends.

d. Draw a line to connect the intersections of the arcs. Label the intersection of $\overline{JS}$ and the line point K.

Measure $\overline{JS}$, $\overline{JK}$, and $\overline{KS}$. What do you notice?

The bisector of $\overline{JS}$ is a *perpendicular bisector* because all of the angles it forms with $\overline{JS}$ measure 90°.

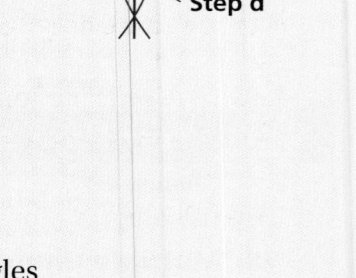

2 Bisect an angle.

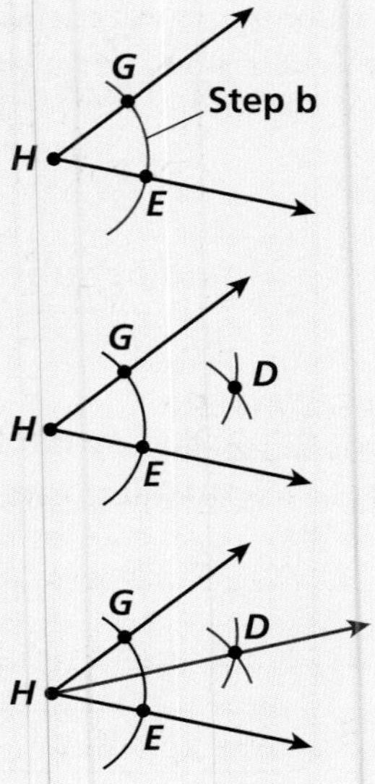

a. Draw an acute angle GHE on a piece of paper. Label the vertex H.

b. Place the point of your compass on H and draw an arc through both sides of the angle. Label points G and E where the arc crosses each side of the angle.

c. Without changing your compass opening, draw intersecting arcs from point G and point E. Label the point of intersection D.

d. Draw $\overrightarrow{HD}$.

Use your protractor to measure angles GHE, GHD, and DHE. What do you notice?

3 Construct congruent angles.

a. Draw angle *ABM* on your paper.

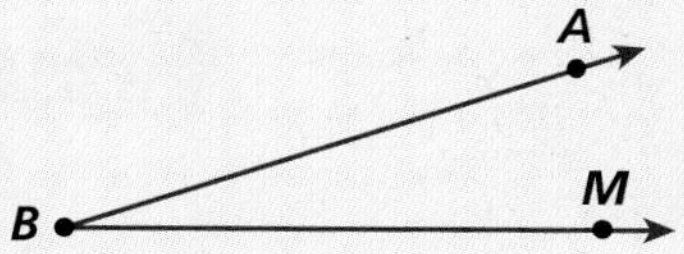

b. To construct an angle congruent to angle *ABM*, begin by drawing a ray, and label its endpoint *C*.

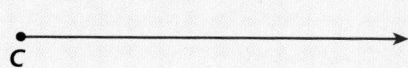

c. With your compass point on *B*, draw an arc through angle *ABM*.

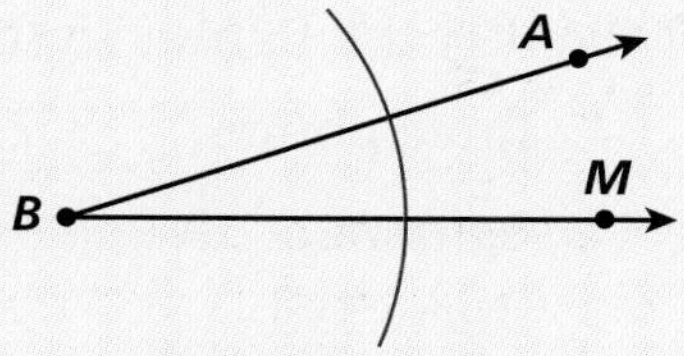

d. With the same compass opening, place the compass point on *C* and draw an arc through the ray. Label point *D* where the arc crosses the ray.

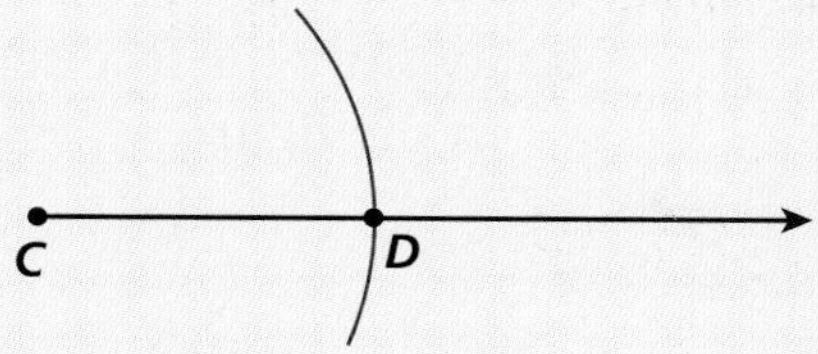

e. With your compass, measure the arc in angle *ABM*.

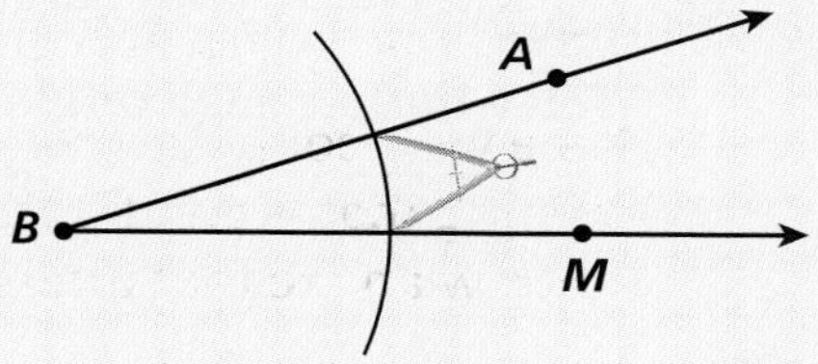

f. With the same opening, place your compass point on *D*, and draw another arc intersecting the first one. Label the intersection *F*. Draw $\overrightarrow{CF}$.

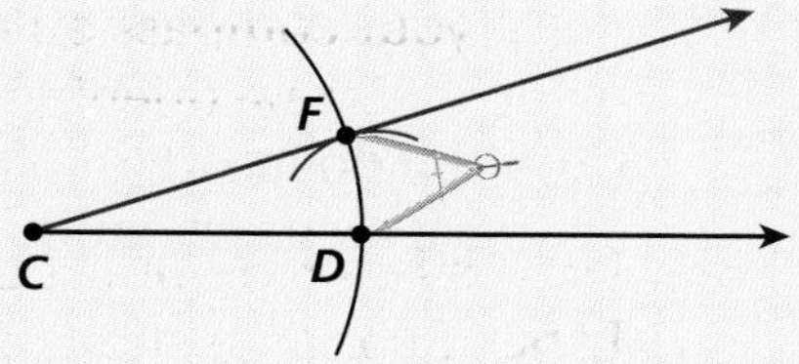

Use your protractor to measure angle *ABM* and angle *FCD*. What do you find?

Think and Discuss

1. How many bisectors would you use to divide an angle into four equal parts?
2. An 88° angle is bisected, and then each of the two angles formed are bisected. What is the measure of each of the smaller angles formed?

Try This

Use a compass and a straightedge to perform each construction.

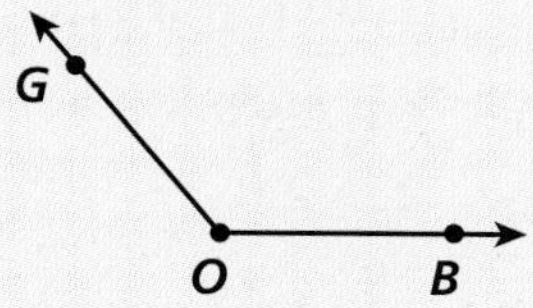

1. Bisect a line segment.
2. Trace and then bisect angle *GOB*.
3. Draw an angle congruent to angle *GOB*.

READY TO GO ON?

Quiz for Lessons 8-1 Through 8-3

8-1 Building Blocks of Geometry

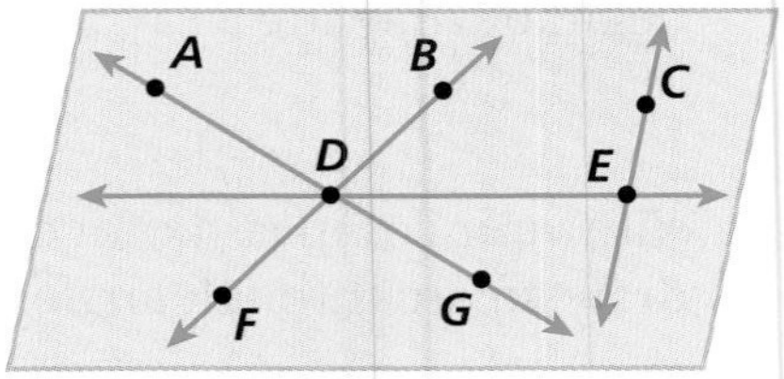

Identify the figures in the diagram.

1. three points
2. three lines
3. a plane
4. three line segments
5. three rays
6. Identify the line segments that are congruent in the figure.

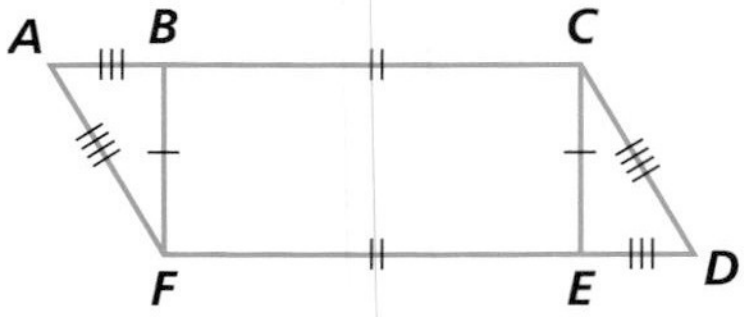

8-2 Classifying Angles

Tell whether each angle is acute, right, obtuse, or straight.

7. 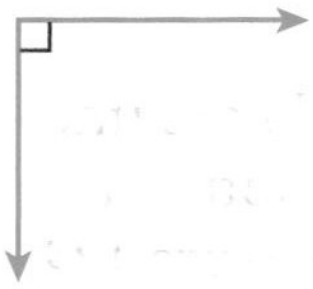
8. 
9. 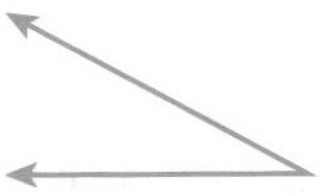
10. 

Use the diagram to tell whether the angles are complementary, supplementary, or neither.

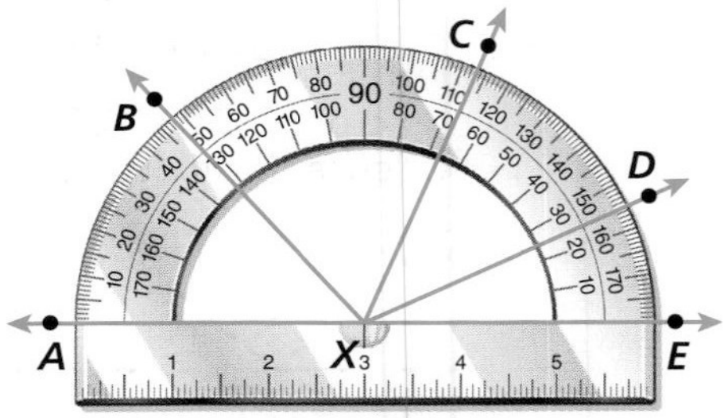

11. $\angle DXE$ and $\angle AXD$
12. $\angle AXB$ and $\angle CXD$
13. $\angle DXE$ and $\angle AXB$
14. $\angle BXC$ and $\angle DXE$
15. Angles R and S are complementary. If $m\angle S$ is 17°, what is $m\angle R$?
16. Angles D and F are supplementary. If $m\angle D$ is 45°, what is $m\angle F$?

8-3 Angle Relationships

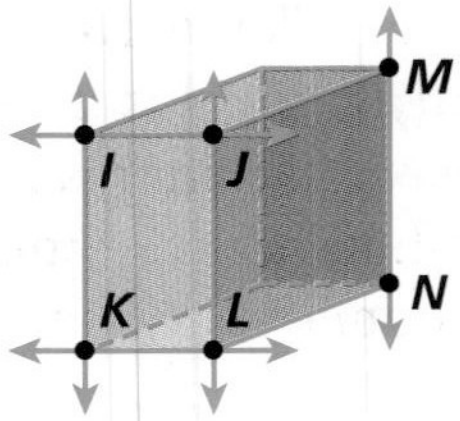

Tell whether the lines appear parallel, perpendicular, or skew.

17. $\overleftrightarrow{KL}$ and $\overleftrightarrow{MN}$
18. $\overleftrightarrow{JL}$ and $\overleftrightarrow{MN}$
19. $\overleftrightarrow{KL}$ and $\overleftrightarrow{JL}$
20. $\overleftrightarrow{IJ}$ and $\overleftrightarrow{MN}$

Line $a \parallel$ line b. Find the measure of each angle.

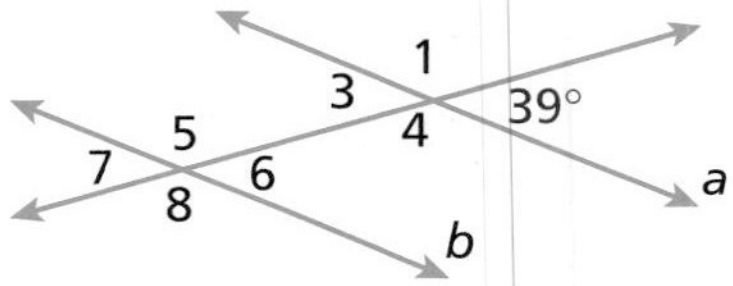

21. $\angle 3$
22. $\angle 4$
23. $\angle 8$
24. $\angle 6$
25. $\angle 1$
26. $\angle 5$

Focus on Problem Solving

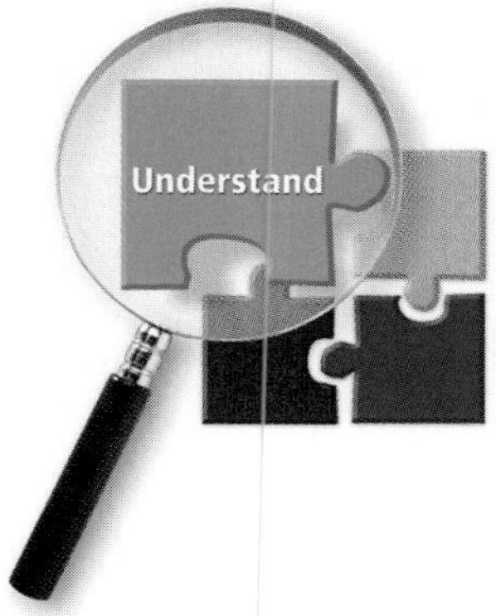

Understand the Problem

- **Restate the problem in your own words**

By writing a problem in your own words, you may understand it better. Before writing the problem, you may need to reread it several times, perhaps aloud, so that you can hear yourself saying the words.

Once you have written the problem in your own words, check to make sure you included all of the necessary information to solve it.

Write each problem in your own words. Check to make sure you have included all of the information needed to solve the problem.

1. The diagram shows a ray of light being reflected off a mirror. The angle of reflection is congruent to the angle of incidence. Use the diagram to find the measure of the obtuse angle formed by the reflected light.

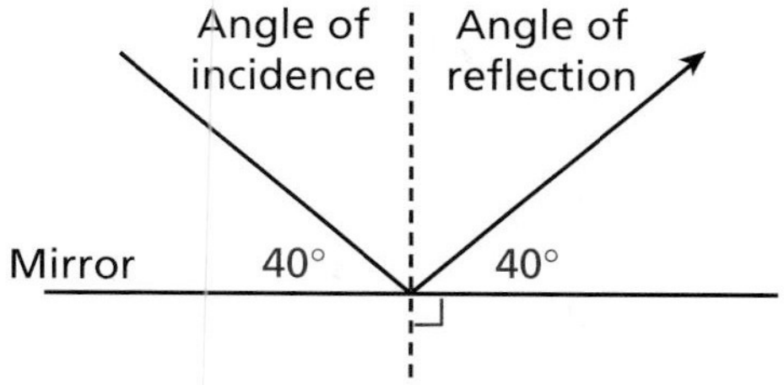

2. At the intersection shown, the turn from northbound Main Street left onto Jefferson Street is dangerous because the turn is too sharp. City planners have decided to change the road to increase the angle of the turn. Explain how the measures of angles 1, 3, and 4 change as the measure of angle 2 increases.

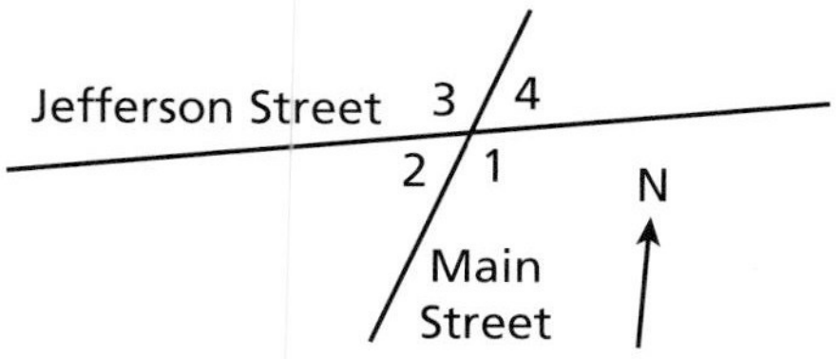

3. Parallel lines s and t are intersected by a transversal r. The obtuse angles formed by lines s and t measure 134°. Find the measure of the acute angles formed by the intersection of lines t and r.

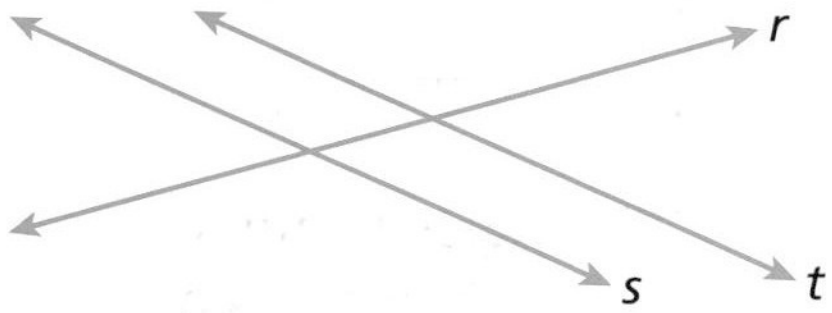

4. Many fashion designers use basic geometric shapes and patterns in their textile designs. In the textile design shown, angles 1 and 2 are formed by two intersecting lines. Find the measures of ∠1 and ∠2 if the angle adjacent to ∠2 measures 88°.

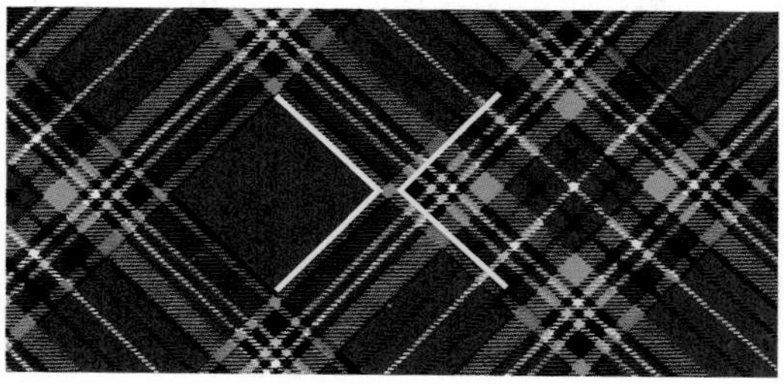

8-4 Properties of Circles

Learn to identify parts of a circle and to find central angle measures.

Vocabulary

circle

center of a circle

arc

radius

diameter

chord

central angle

sector

The wheel is one of the most important inventions of all time. Vehicles with wheels—from ancient chariots to modern bicycles and cars—rely on the idea of a *circle*.

A **circle** is the set of all points in a plane that are the same distance from a given point, called the **center of a circle**.

A circle is named by its center. For example, if point A is the center of a circle, then the name of the circle is circle A. There are special names for the different parts of a circle.

This relief sculpture was made around 645 C.E., and shows King Ashurbanipal of Nineveh riding on his chariot.

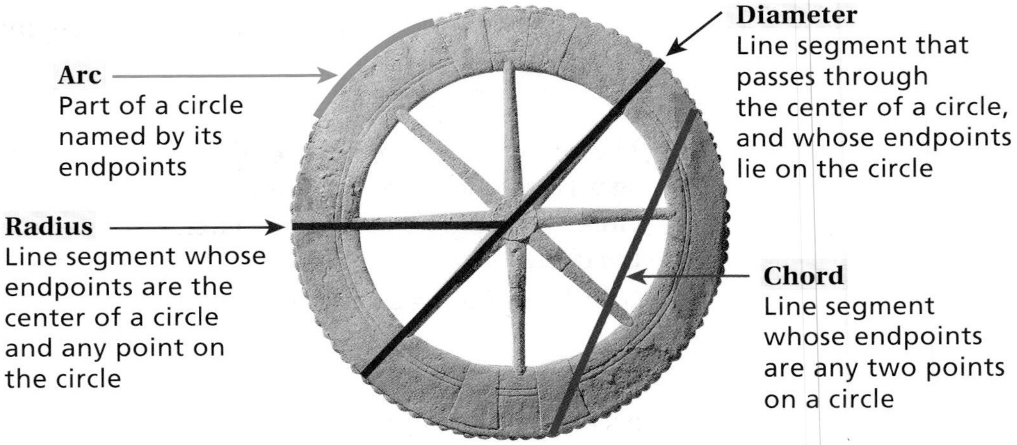
Arc
Part of a circle named by its endpoints
Radius
Line segment whose endpoints are the center of a circle and any point on the circle
Diameter
Line segment that passes through the center of a circle, and whose endpoints lie on the circle
Chord
Line segment whose endpoints are any two points on a circle

EXAMPLE 1 Identifying Parts of Circles

Reading Math

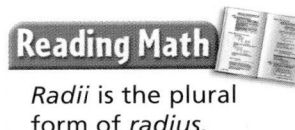

Radii is the plural form of *radius*.

Name the parts of circle P.

A radii

$\overline{PA}, \overline{PB}, \overline{PC}, \overline{PD}$

B diameter

$\overline{BD}$

C chords

$\overline{AD}, \overline{DC}, \overline{AB}, \overline{BC}, \overline{BD}$

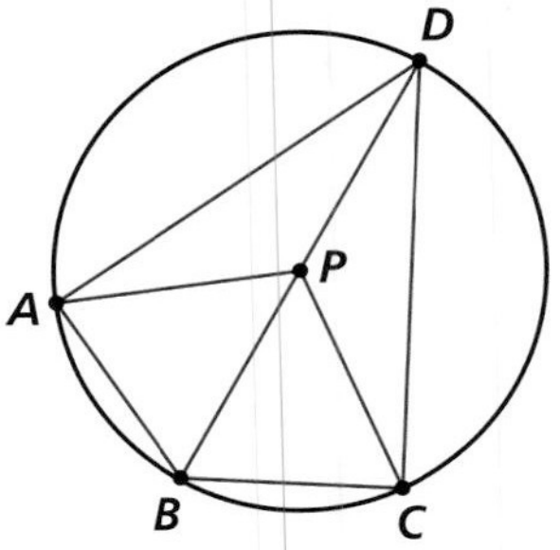
D
P
A
B
C

A **central angle** of a circle is an angle formed by two radii. A **sector** of a circle is the part of the circle enclosed by two radii and an arc connecting them.

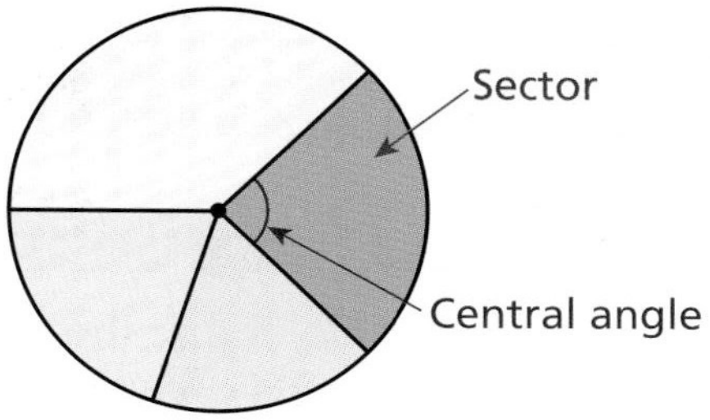

The sum of the measures of all of the nonoverlapping central angles in a circle is 360°. We say that there are 360° in a circle.

EXAMPLE 2 PROBLEM SOLVING APPLICATION

PROBLEM SOLVING

The circle graph shows the results of a survey to determine how people feel about keeping the penny. Find the central angle measure of the sector that shows the percent of people who are against keeping the penny.

Source: USA Today, 2001

1 Understand the Problem

List the **important information:**

- The percent of people who are against keeping the penny is 32%.

2 Make a Plan

The central angle measure of the sector that represents those people against keeping the penny is 32% of the angle measure of the whole circle. The angle measure of a circle is 360°. Since the sector is 32% of the circle graph, the central angle measure is 32% of 360°.

$32\% \text{ of } 360° = 0.32 \cdot 360°$

3 Solve

$0.32 \cdot 360° = 115.2°$ *Multiply.*

The central angle of the sector measures 115.2°.

4 Look Back

The 32% sector is about one-third of the graph, and 120° is one-third of 360°. Since 115.2° is close to 120°, the answer is reasonable.

Think and Discuss

1. Explain why a diameter is a chord but a radius is not.

2. Draw a circle with a central angle of 90°.

8-4 Exercises

go.hrw.com
Homework Help Online
KEYWORD: MS7 8-4
Parent Resources Online
KEYWORD: MS7 Parent

GUIDED PRACTICE

See Example 1

Name the parts of circle *O*.

1. radii
2. diameter
3. chords

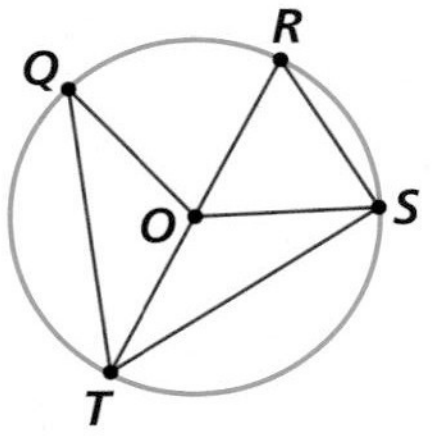

See Example 2

4. The circle graph shows the results of a survey in which the following question was asked: "If you had to describe your office environment as a type of television show, which would it be?" Find the central angle measure of the sector that shows the percent of people who described their workplace as a courtroom drama.

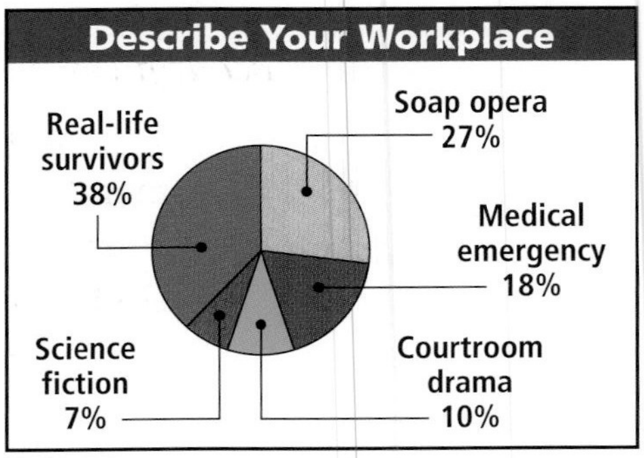

Source: *USA Today*

INDEPENDENT PRACTICE

See Example 1

Name the parts of circle *C*.

5. radii
6. diameters
7. chords

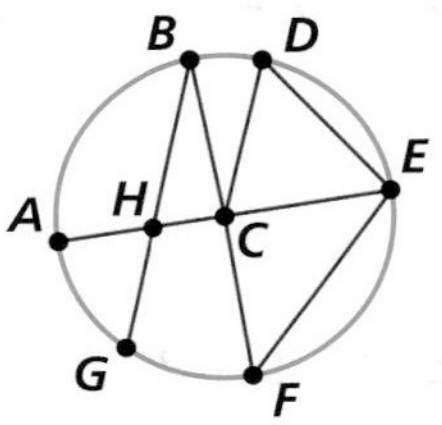

See Example 2

8. The circle graph shows the areas from which the United States imports bananas. Find the central angle measure of the sector that shows the percent of banana imports from South America.

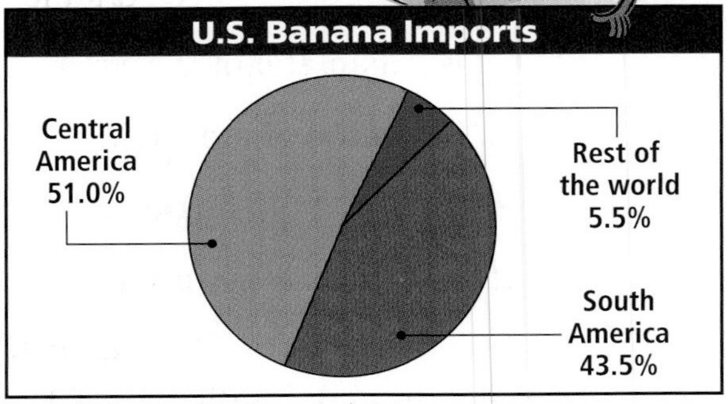

Source: US Bureau of the Census Trade Data

PRACTICE AND PROBLEM SOLVING

Extra Practice
See page 742.

9. What is the distance between the centers of the circles at right?

10. A circle is divided into five equal sectors. Find the measure of the central angle of each sector.

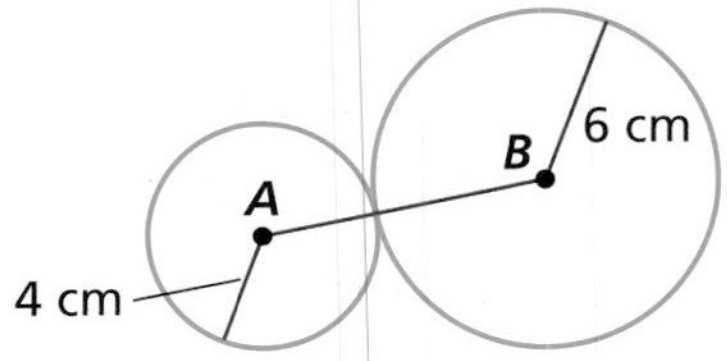

Music **Citizens of the United States were asked to choose a national song and a national anthem. The circle graph shows the results of the survey. Use the graphs for Exercises 11 and 12.**

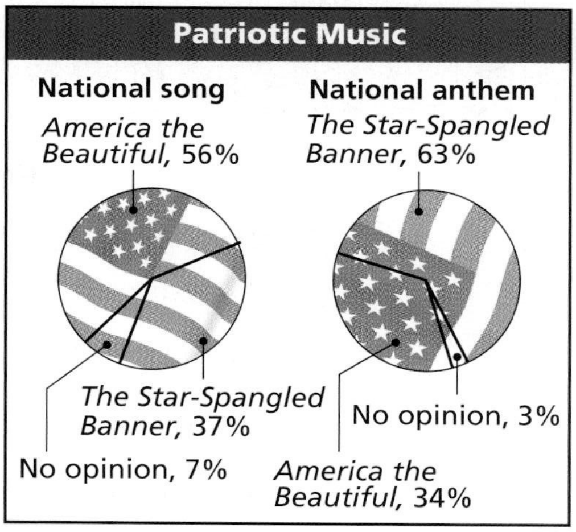

11. Find the central angle measure of the sector that shows the percent of people who chose *The Star-Spangled Banner* as the song they prefer.

12. Find the central angle measure of the sector that shows the percent of people who prefer *America the Beautiful* as the national anthem.

13. If $\overline{AB} \parallel \overline{CD}$ in the circle at right, what is the measure of $\angle 1$? Explain your answer.

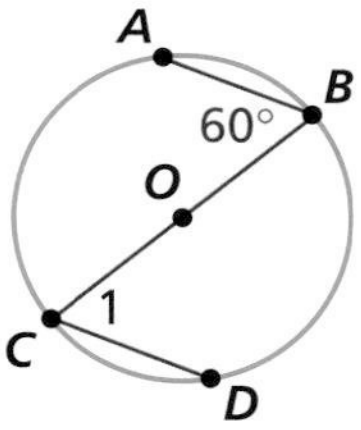

14. Write a Problem Find a circle graph in your science or social studies textbook. Use the graph to write a problem that can be solved by finding the central angle measure of one of the sectors of the circle.

15. Write About It Compare central angles of a circle with sectors of a circle.

16. Challenge Find the angle measure between the minute and hour hands on the clock at right.

Test Prep and Spiral Review

Use the figure for Exercises 17 and 18.

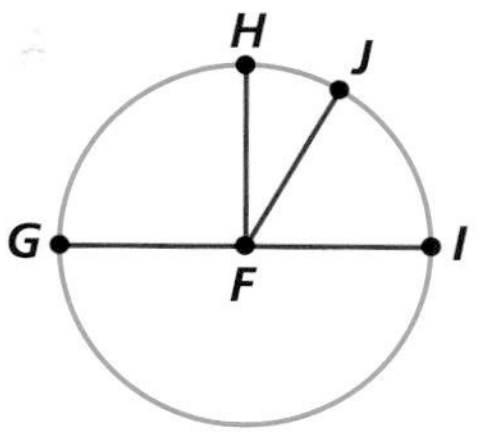

17. Multiple Choice Which statement is NOT true about the figure?

Ⓐ $\overline{GI}$ is a diameter of the circle.

Ⓑ $\overline{GI}$ is a chord of the circle.

Ⓒ $\angle GIJ$ is a central angle of the circle.

Ⓓ $\angle GFH$ and $\angle HFI$ are supplementary angles.

18. Gridded Response The diameter of the circle is perpendicular to chord HF. What is the measure of $\angle HFI$ in degrees?

Estimate. (Lesson 6-3)

19. 28% of 150 **20.** 21% of 90 **21.** 2% of 55 **22.** 53% of 72

Use the alphabet at right. (Lesson 8-3)

ABCDEFGH
IJKLMN
OPQRST
UVWXYZ

23. Identify the letters that appear to have parallel lines.

24. Identify the letters that appear to have perpendicular lines.

Hands-On LAB 8-4

Construct Circle Graphs

Use with Lesson 8-4

go.hrw.com
Lab Resources Online
KEYWORD: MS7 Lab8

REMEMBER
- There are 360° in a circle.
- A radius is a line segment with one endpoint at the center of a circle and the other endpoint on the circle.

A circle graph can be used to compare data that are parts of a whole.

Activity

You can make a circle graph using information from a table.

At Booker Middle School, a survey was conducted to find the percent of students who favor certain types of books. The results are shown in the table below.

To make a circle graph, you need to find the size of each part of your graph. Each part is a *sector*.

To find the size of a sector, you must find the measure of its angle. You do this by finding what percent of the whole circle that sector represents.

Find the size of each sector.

a. Copy the table at right.

b. Find a decimal equivalent for each percent given, and fill in the decimal column of your table.

c. Find the fraction equivalent for each percent given, and fill in the fraction column of your table.

d. Find the angle measure of each sector by multiplying each fraction or decimal by 360°. Fill in the last column of your table.

Students' Favorite Types of Books

Type of Book	Percent	Decimal	Fraction	Degrees
Mysteries	35%			
Science Fiction	25%			
Sports	20%			
Biographies	15%			
Humor	5%			

Follow the steps below to draw a circle graph.

a. Using a compass, draw a circle. Using a straightedge, draw one radius.

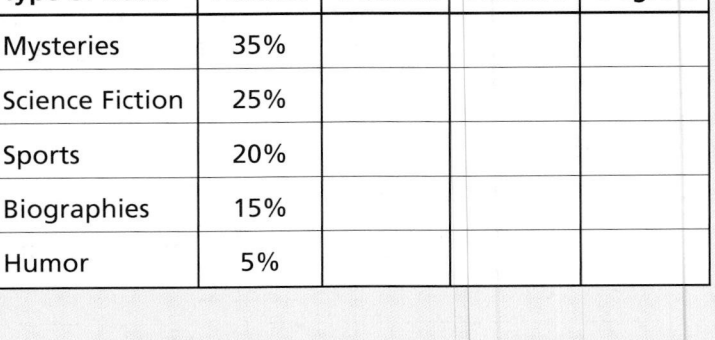

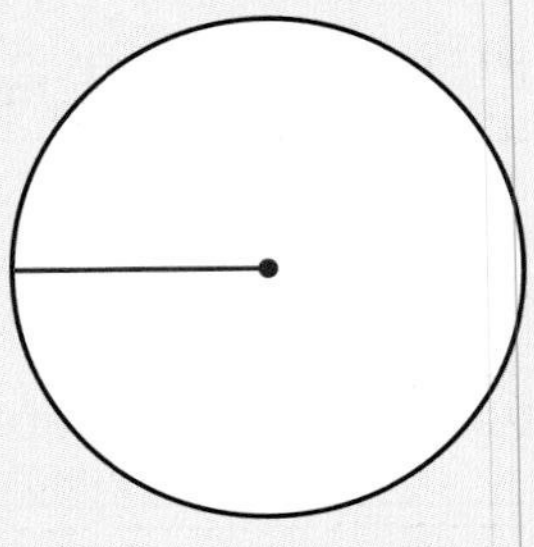

b. Use a protractor to measure the angle of the first sector. Draw the angle.

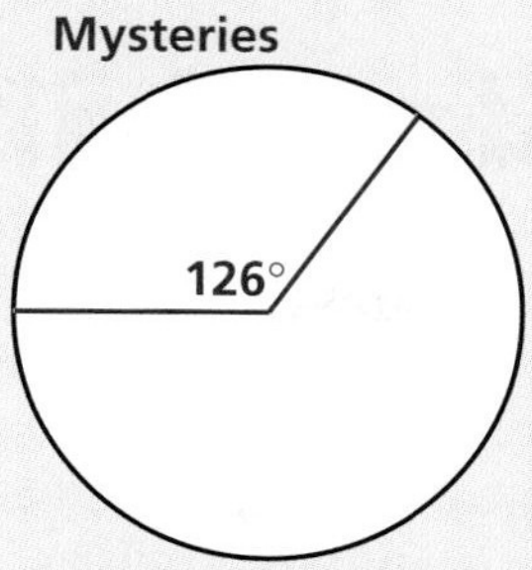

c. Use a protractor to measure the angle of the next sector. Draw the angle.

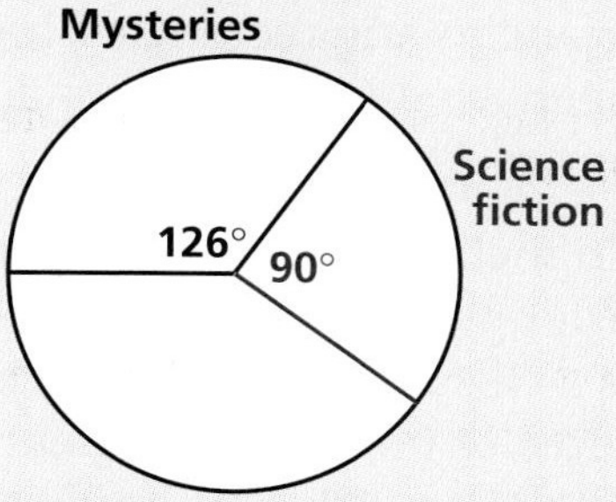

d. Continue until your graph is complete. Label each sector with its name and percent.

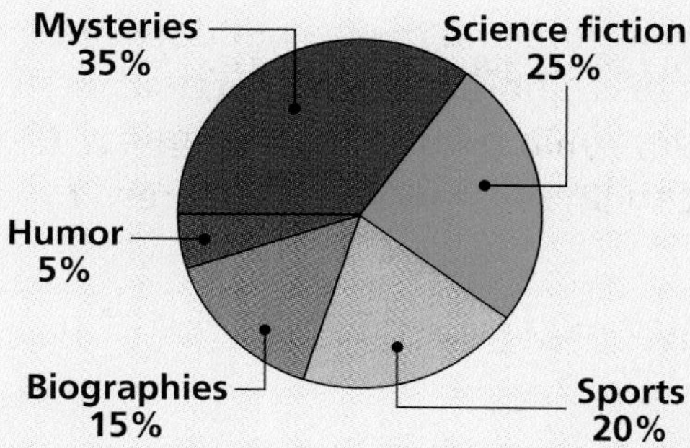

Think and Discuss

1. Total each column in the table from the beginning of the activity. What do you notice?
2. What type of data would you want to display using a circle graph?
3. How does the size of each sector of your circle graph relate to the percent, the decimal, and the fraction in your table?

Try This

1. Complete the table below and use the information to make a circle graph.

   On a typical Saturday, Alan divides his leisure time and spends it in the following ways:

Time Spent for Leisure

Activity	Percent	Decimal	Fraction	Degrees
Reading	30%			
Playing sports	25%			
Working on computer	40%			
Watching TV	5%			

8-5 Classifying Polygons

Learn to identify and name polygons.

Vocabulary

polygon

regular polygon

From the earliest recorded time, geometric shapes, such as triangles and rectangles, have been used to decorate buildings and works of art.

Triangles and rectangles are examples of *polygons*. A **polygon** is a closed plane figure formed by three or more line segments. Each line segment forms a side of the polygon, and meets, but does not cross, another line segment at a common point. This common point is a vertex of a polygon.

The Paracas were an ancient native culture of Peru. Among the items that have been excavated from their lands are color tapestries, such as this one.

Reading Math

Vertices is the plural form of *vertex*.

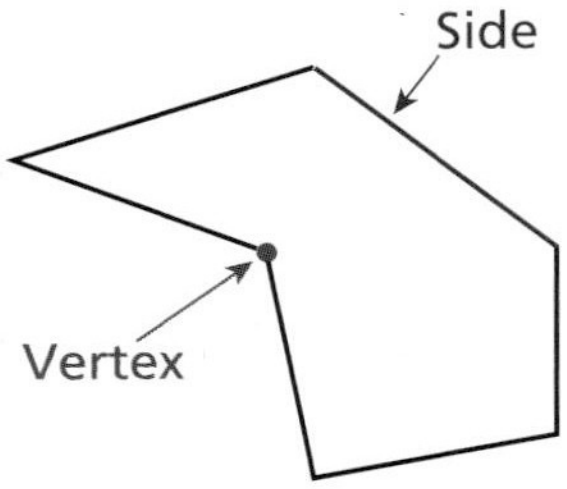

The polygon at left has six sides and six vertices.

EXAMPLE 1 Identifying Polygons

Determine whether each figure is a polygon. If it is not, explain why not.

A

The figure is a polygon.
It is a closed figure with 5 sides.

B

The figure is not a polygon.
It is not a closed figure.

C

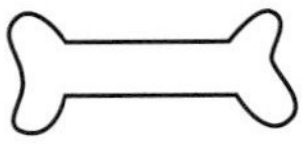

The figure is not a polygon.
Not all of the sides of the figure are line segments.

D

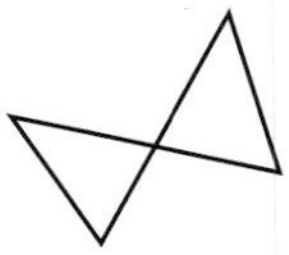

The figure is not a polygon.
There are line segments in the figure that cross.

Polygons are classified by the number of sides and angles they have.

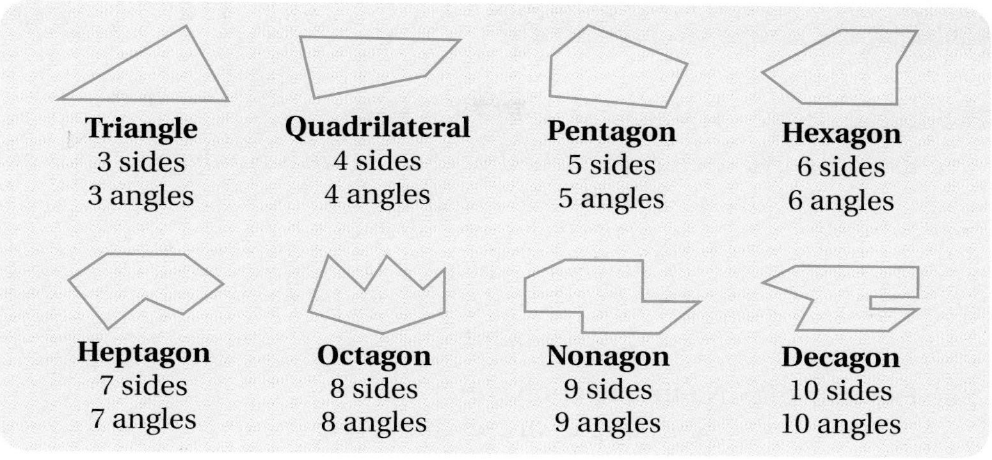

EXAMPLE 2 Classifying Polygons

Name each polygon.

A

10 sides, 10 angles

Decagon

B

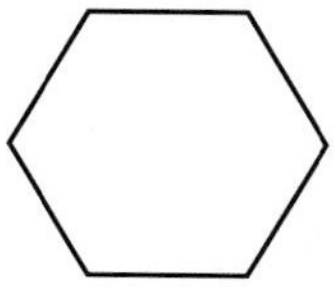

6 sides, 6 angles

Hexagon

A **regular polygon** is a polygon in which all sides are congruent and all angles are congruent.

EXAMPLE 3 Identifying and Classifying Regular Polygons

Name each polygon, and tell whether it is a regular polygon. If it is not, explain why not.

Caution!

A polygon with congruent sides is not necessarily a regular polygon. Its angles must also be congruent.

A

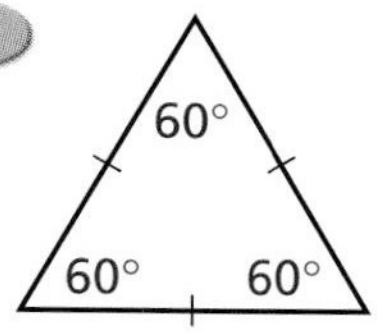

The figure has congruent angles and congruent sides. It is a regular triangle.

B

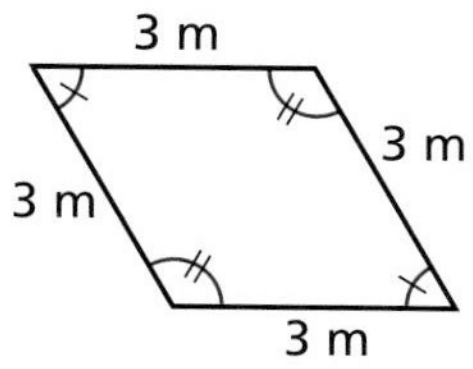

The figure is a quadrilateral. It is not a regular polygon because not all of the angles are congruent.

Think and Discuss

1. **Explain** why a circle is not a polygon.
2. **Name** three reasons why a figure would not be a polygon.

8-5 Exercises

go.hrw.com
Homework Help Online
KEYWORD: MS7 8-5
Parent Resources Online
KEYWORD: MS7 Parent

GUIDED PRACTICE

See Example 1 — Determine whether each figure is a polygon. If it is not, explain why not.

1. 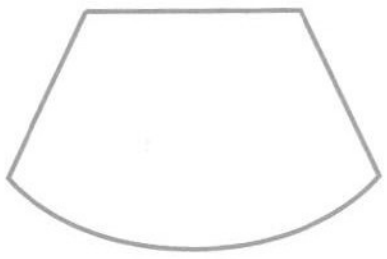

2. 

3. 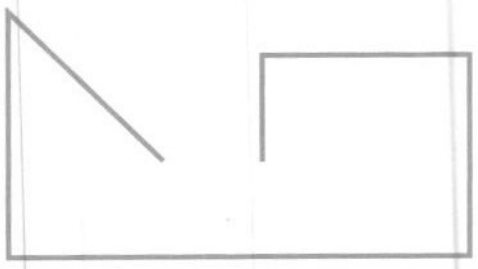

See Example 2 — Name each polygon.

4. 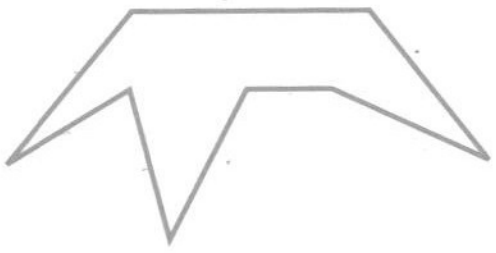

5. 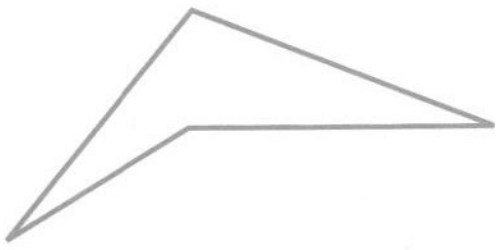

6. 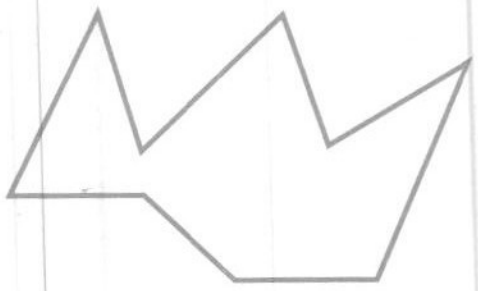

See Example 3 — Name each polygon, and tell whether it is a regular polygon. If it is not, explain why not.

7. 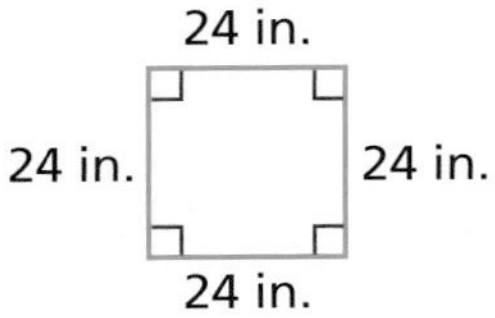

8. 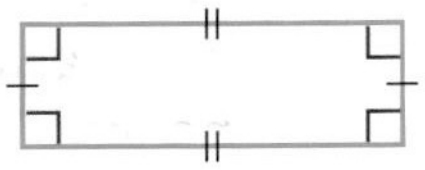

9. 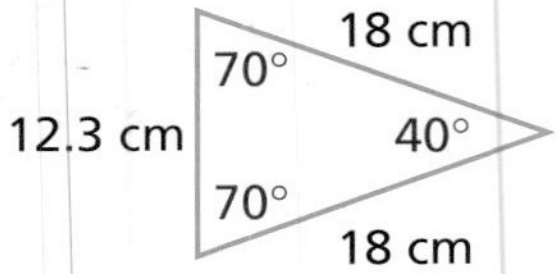

INDEPENDENT PRACTICE

See Example 1 — Determine whether each figure is a polygon. If it is not, explain why not.

10. 

11. 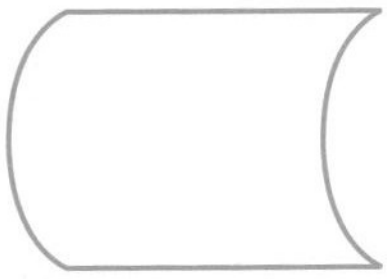

12. 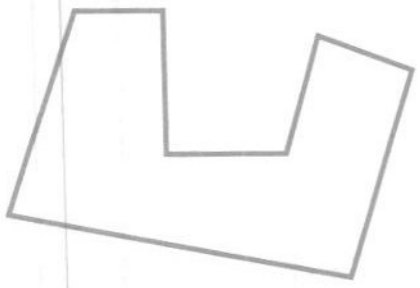

See Example 2 — Name each polygon.

13. 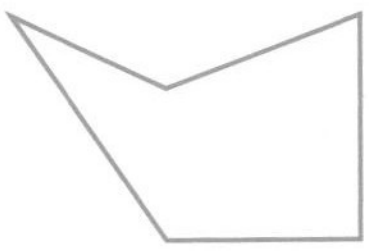

14. 

15. 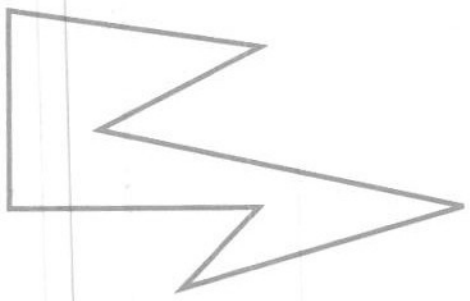

See Example 3 — Name each polygon, and tell whether it is a regular polygon. If it is not, explain why not.

16. 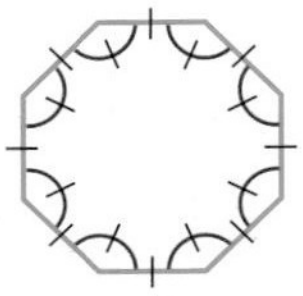

17. 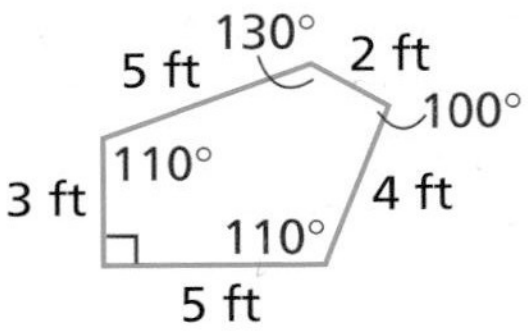

18. 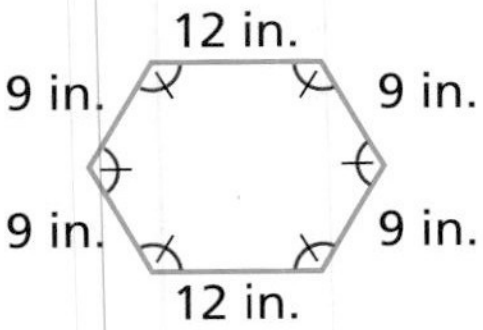

Extra Practice
See page 742.

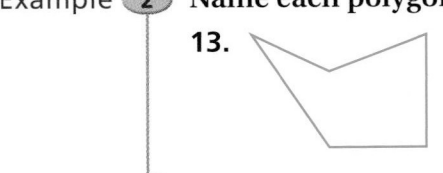

Art LINK

Quilting is an art form that has existed in many countries for hundreds of years. Some cultures record their histories and traditions through the colors and patterns in quilts.

19. The design of the quilt at right is made of triangles.

a. Name two other polygons in the pattern.

b. Which of the polygons in the pattern appear to be regular?

Use the photograph of the star quilt for Exercises 20 and 21.

20. The large star in the quilt pattern is made of smaller shapes stitched together. These smaller shapes are all the same type of polygon. What type of polygon are the smaller shapes?

21. A polygon can be named by the number of its sides followed by *-gon*. For example, a polygon with 14 sides is called a 14-gon. What is the name of the large star-shaped polygon on the quilt?

22. ★ **Challenge** The quilt at right has a modern design. Find and copy one of each type of polygon, from a triangle up to a decagon, onto your paper from the design. Write the name of each polygon next to its drawing.

go.hrw.com
Web Extra!
KEYWORD: MS7 Quilt

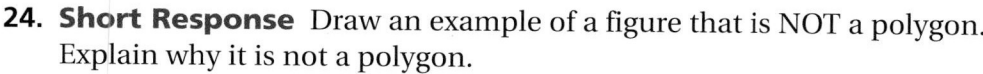

TEST PREP and Spiral Review

23. Multiple Choice What is true about the figure?

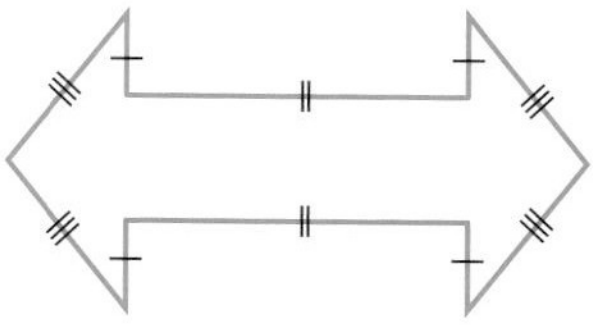

Ⓐ It is a polygon. Ⓒ It is a quadrilateral.

Ⓑ It is a regular polygon. Ⓓ It is a nonagon.

24. Short Response Draw an example of a figure that is NOT a polygon. Explain why it is not a polygon.

Write a function that describes each sequence. (Lesson 4-5)

25. 4, 7, 10, 13,...

26. −1, 1, 3, 5,...

27. 2.3, 3.3, 4.3, 5.3,...

Solve. Round answers to the nearest tenth, if necessary. (Lesson 6-5)

28. 8 is what percent of 15?

29. What is 35% of 58?

30. 63 is 25% of what number?

31. 22 is what percent of 85?

8-6 Classifying Triangles

Learn to classify triangles by their side lengths and angle measures.

Vocabulary

scalene triangle
isosceles triangle
equilateral triangle
acute triangle
obtuse triangle
right triangle

A harnessed rider uses the triangle-shaped control bar on a hang glider to steer. The framework of most hang gliders is made up of many types of triangles. One way to classify triangles is by the lengths of their sides. Another way is by the measures of their angles.

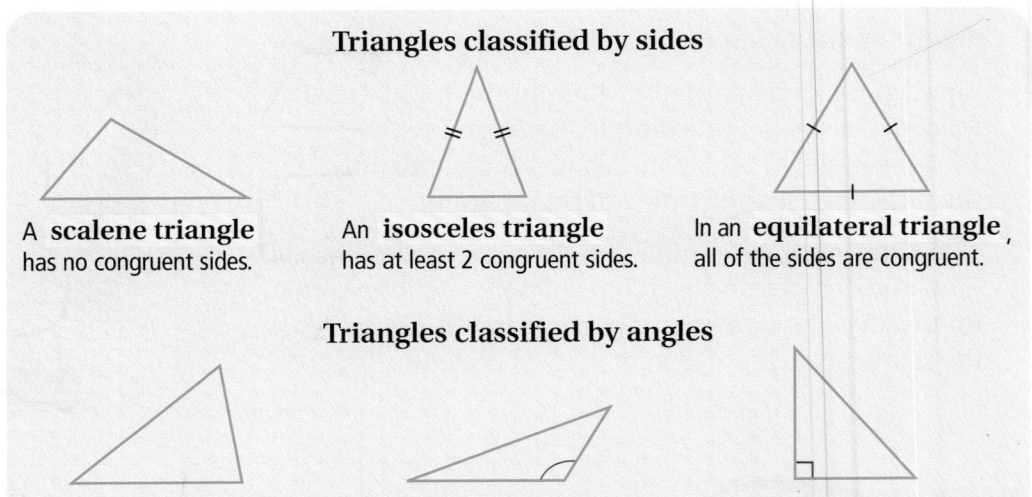

Triangles classified by sides

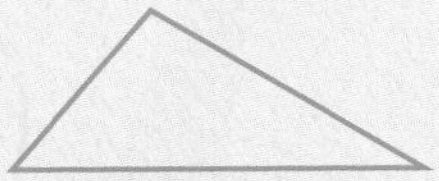

A **scalene triangle** has no congruent sides.

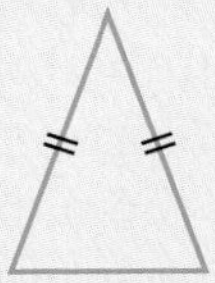

An **isosceles triangle** has at least 2 congruent sides.

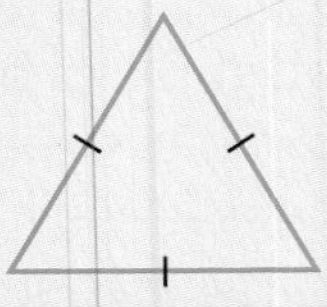

In an **equilateral triangle**, all of the sides are congruent.

Triangles classified by angles

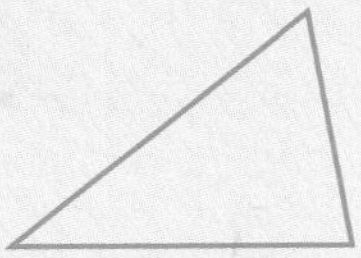

In an **acute triangle**, all of the angles are acute.

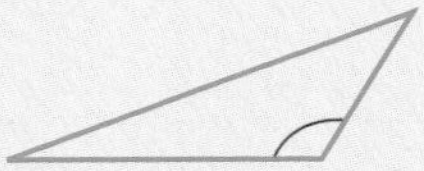

An **obtuse triangle** has exactly one obtuse angle.

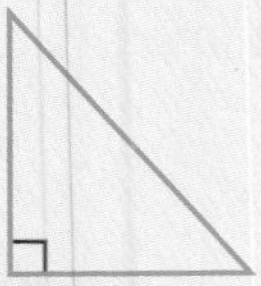

A **right triangle** has exactly one right angle.

EXAMPLE 1 Classifying Triangles

Classify each triangle according to its sides and angles.

A

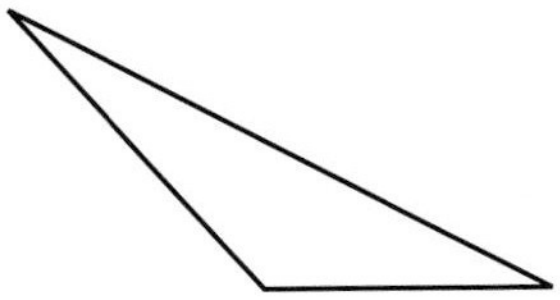

scalene *No congruent sides*
obtuse *One obtuse angle*

This is a scalene obtuse triangle.

B

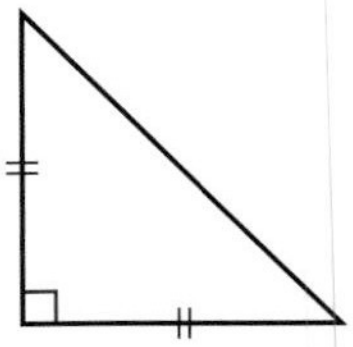

isosceles *Two congruent sides*
right *One right angle*

This is an isosceles right triangle.

Classify each triangle according to its sides and angles.

C

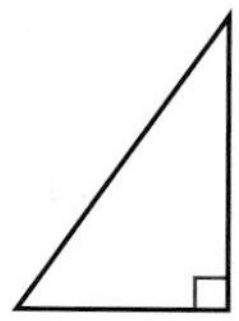

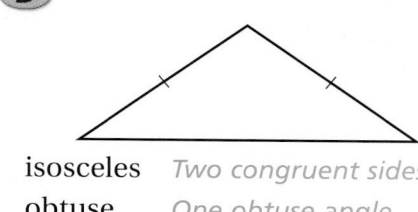

scalene	*No congruent sides*
right	*One right angle*

This is a scalene right triangle.

D

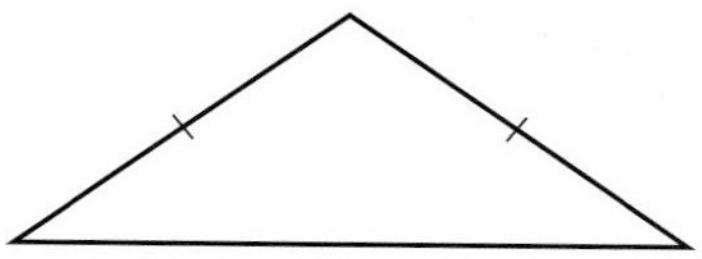

isosceles	*Two congruent sides*
obtuse	*One obtuse angle*

This is an isosceles obtuse triangle.

EXAMPLE 2 Identifying Triangles

Identify the different types of triangles in the figure, and determine how many of each there are.

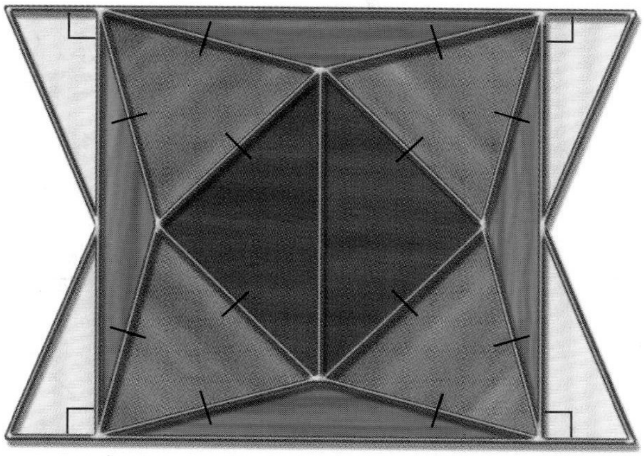

Type	How Many	Colors	Type	How Many	Colors
Scalene	4	Yellow	Right	6	Purple, yellow
Isosceles	10	Green, pink, purple	Obtuse	4	Green
Equilateral	4	Pink	Acute	4	Pink

Think and Discuss

1. **Draw** an isosceles acute triangle and an isosceles obtuse triangle.
2. **Draw** a triangle that is right and scalene.
3. **Explain** why any equilateral triangle is also an isosceles triangle, but not all isosceles triangles are equilateral triangles.

8-6 Exercises

go.hrw.com
Homework Help Online
KEYWORD: MS7 8-6
Parent Resources Online
KEYWORD: MS7 Parent

GUIDED PRACTICE

See Example 1

Classify each triangle according to its sides and angles.

1.

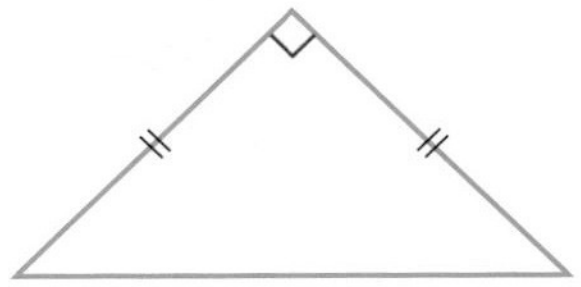

2.

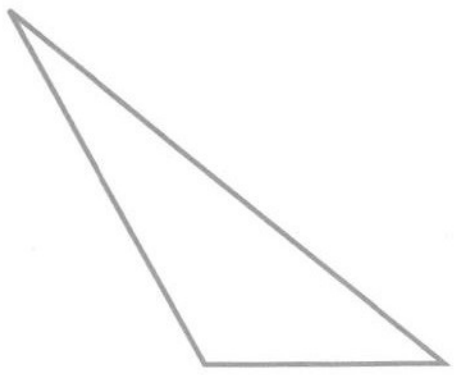

3.

See Example 2

4. Identify the different types of triangles in the figure, and determine how many of each there are.

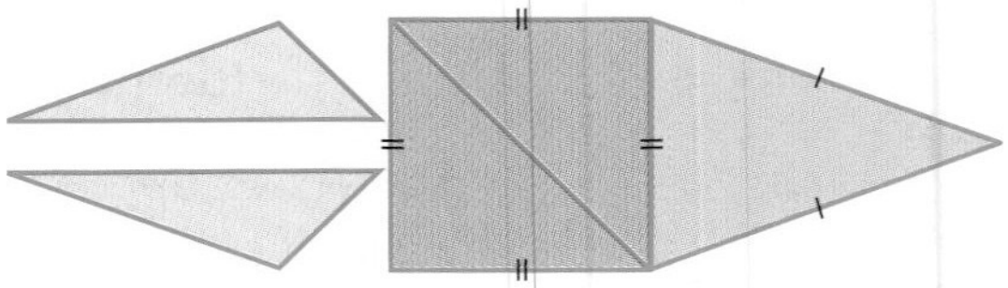

INDEPENDENT PRACTICE

See Example 1

Classify each triangle according to its sides and angles.

5.

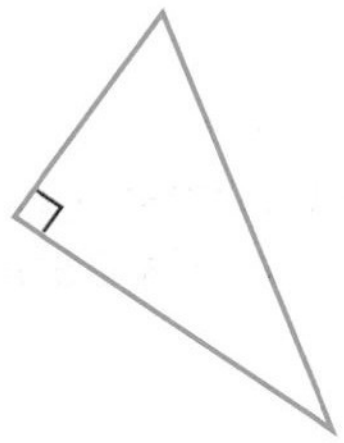

6.

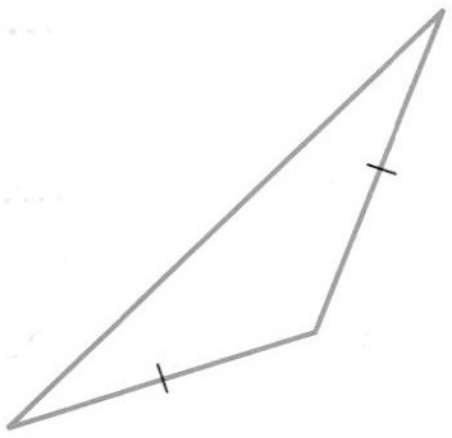

7.

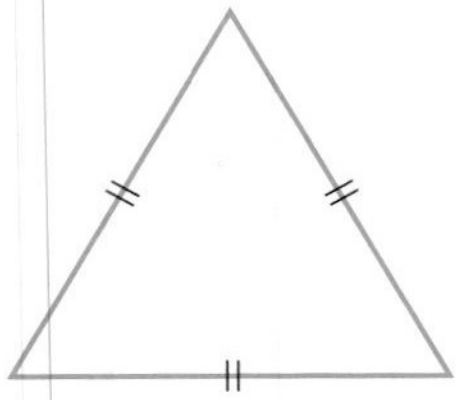

See Example 2

8. Identify the different types of triangles in the figure, and determine how many of each there are.

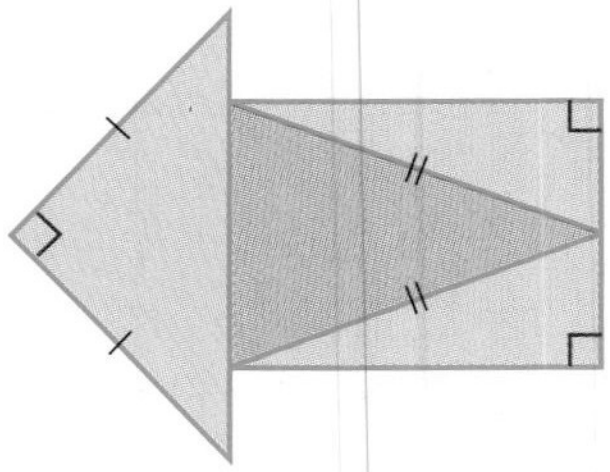

PRACTICE AND PROBLEM SOLVING

Extra Practice
See page 742.

Classify each triangle according to the lengths of its sides.

9. 6 ft, 9 ft, 12 ft **10.** 2 in., 2 in., 2 in. **11.** 7.4 mi, 7.4 mi, 4 mi

Classify each triangle according to the measures of its angles.

12. 105°, 38°, 37° **13.** 45°, 90°, 45° **14.** 40°, 60°, 80°

15. Multi-Step The sum of the lengths of the sides of triangle ABC is 25 in. The lengths of sides $\overline{AB}$ and $\overline{BC}$ are 9 inches and 8 inches. Find the length of side $\overline{AC}$ and classify the triangle.

16. Draw a square. Divide it into two triangles. Describe the triangles.

LINK

Architecture

The Washington Monument opened in 1888—105 years after Congress proposed a memorial to honor the first president of the United States.

Classify each triangle according to its sides and angles.

17.

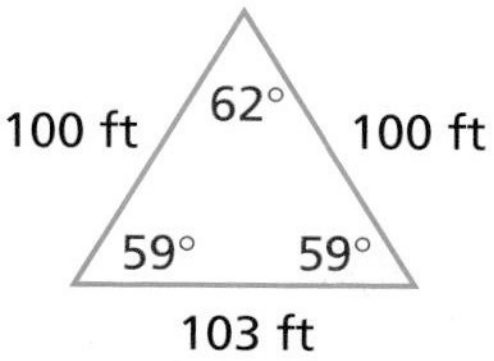

18.

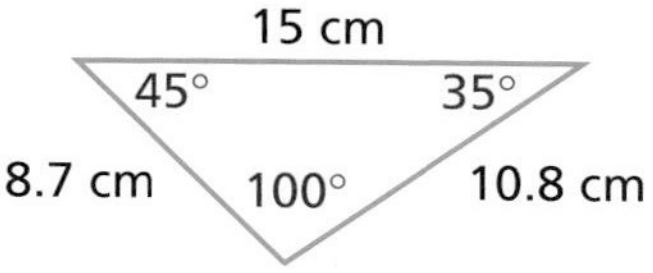

19.

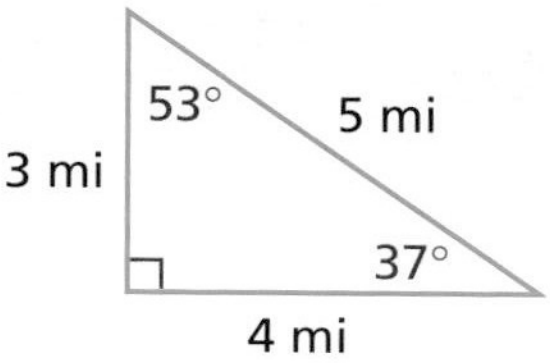

20. Geology Each face of a topaz crystal is a triangle whose sides are all different lengths. What kind of triangle is each face of a topaz crystal?

21. Architecture The Washington Monument is an obelisk, the top of which is a pyramid. The pyramid has four triangular faces. The bottom edge of each face measures 10.5 m. The other edges measure 17.0 m. What kind of triangle is each face of the pyramid?

22. Critical Thinking A line segment connects each vertex of a regular octagon to the vertex opposite it. How many triangles are within the octagon? What type of triangles are they?

23. Choose a Strategy How many triangles are in the figure?

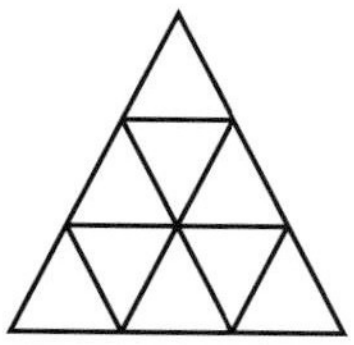

Ⓐ 6 Ⓑ 9 Ⓒ 10 Ⓓ 13

24. Write About It Is it possible for an equilateral triangle to be obtuse? Explain your answer.

25. Challenge The centers of circles *A*, *B*, *C*, *D*, and *E* are connected by line segments. Classify each triangle in the figure, given that the diameter of circle *D* is 4 and $DE = 5$, $BD = 6$, $CB = 8$, and $AC = 8$.

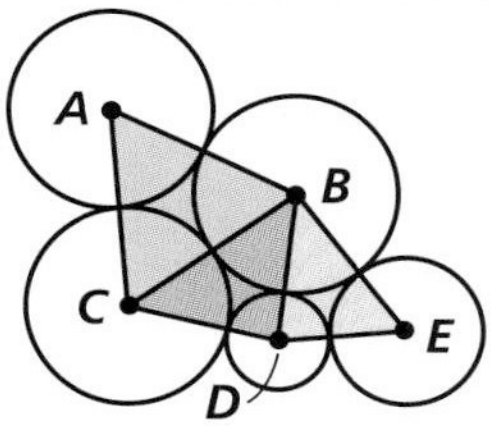

TEST PREP and Spiral Review

26. Multiple Choice Based on the angle measures given, which triangle is NOT acute?

Ⓐ 60°, 60°, 60° Ⓑ 90°, 45°, 45° Ⓒ 54°, 54°, 72° Ⓓ 75°, 45°, 60°

27. Multiple Choice Which of the following best describes the triangle?

Ⓕ Scalene, right triangle Ⓗ Isosceles, obtuse triangle

Ⓖ Isosceles, acute triangle Ⓙ Equilateral, acute triangle

28. Order the numbers $\frac{3}{7}$, -0.4, 2.3, and $1\frac{3}{10}$ from least to greatest. (Lesson 2-11)

Name each polygon, and tell whether it is a regular polygon. If it is not, explain why not. (Lesson 8-5)

29.

30.

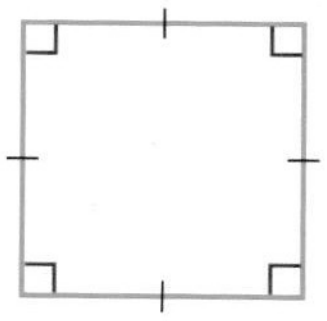

31.

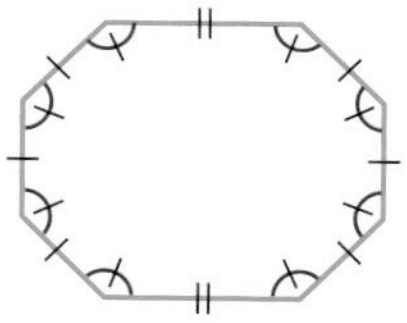

8-7 Classifying Quadrilaterals

Learn to name, identify, and draw types of quadrilaterals.

Vocabulary

parallelogram
rectangle
rhombus
square
trapezoid

College campuses are often built around an open space called a "quad" or "quadrangle." A quadrangle is a four-sided enclosure, or a quadrilateral.

Some quadrilaterals have properties that classify them as *special quadrilaterals.*

The Liberal Arts Quadrangle at the University of Washington, Seattle

Parallelogram		Both pairs of opposite sides are parallel and congruent. Both pairs of opposite angles are congruent.
Rectangle	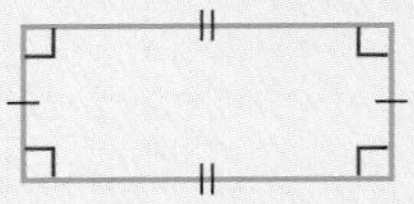	Parallelogram with four right angles.
Rhombus	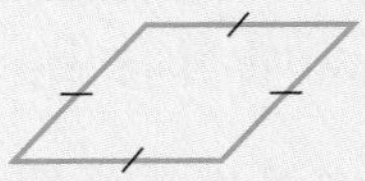	Parallelogram with four congruent sides.
Square	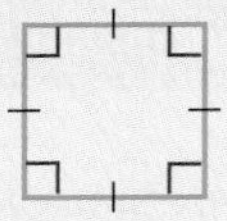	Parallelogram with four congruent sides and four right angles.
Trapezoid		Exactly one pair of opposite sides is parallel.

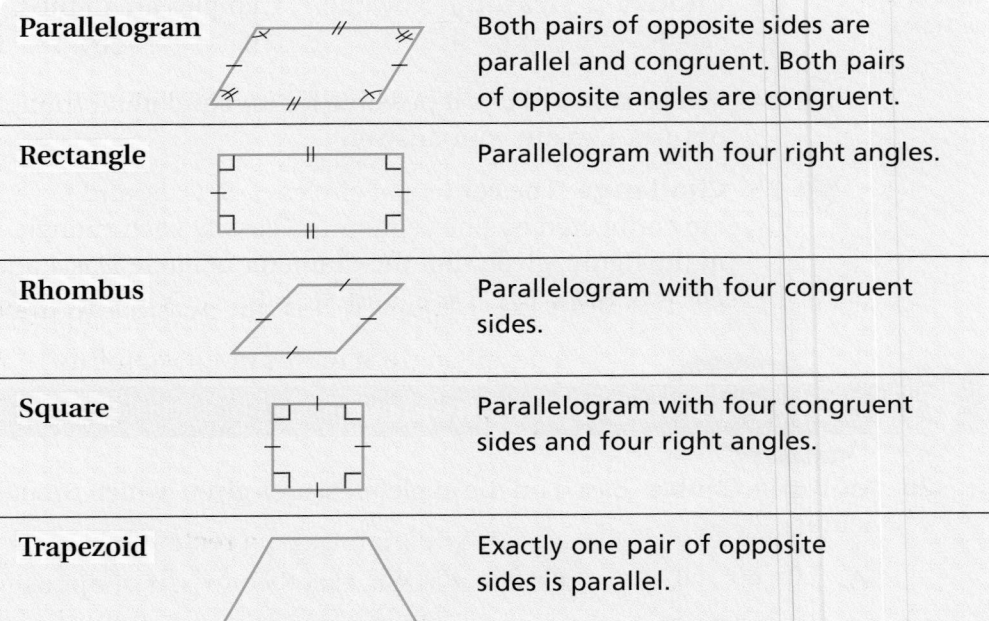

Quadrilaterals can have more than one name because the special quadrilaterals sometimes share properties.

EXAMPLE 1 Classifying Quadrilaterals

Give all of the names that apply to each quadrilateral. Then give the name that best describes it.

A

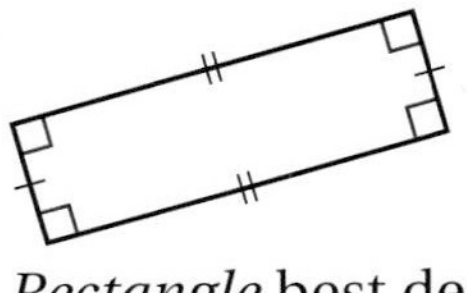

The figure has opposite sides that are parallel, so it is a parallelogram. It has four right angles, so it is also a rectangle.

Rectangle best describes this quadrilateral.

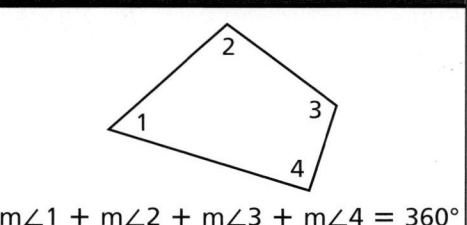

Angles of a Quadrilateral	
The sum of the measures of the angles in a quadrilateral is 360°.	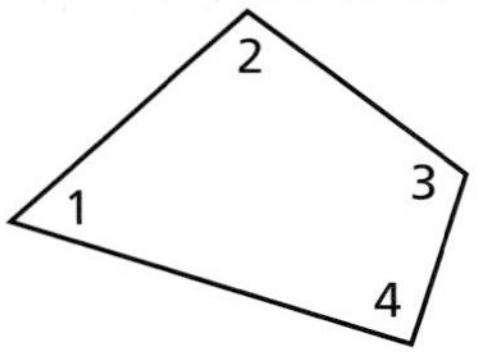 $m\angle 1 + m\angle 2 + m\angle 3 + m\angle 4 = 360°$

EXAMPLE 2 Finding an Angle Measure in a Quadrilateral

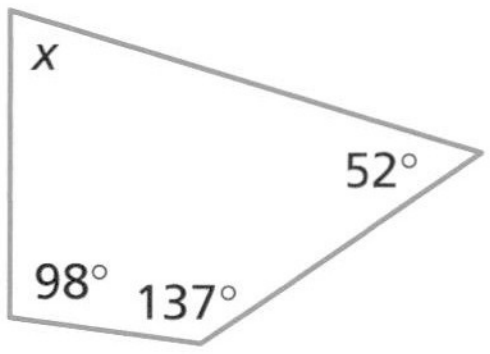

Find the unknown angle measure in the quadrilateral.

$98° + 137° + 52° + x = 360°$ *The sum of the angle measures is 360°.*

$287° + x = 360°$ *Combine like terms.*

$\underline{-287°} \quad \underline{-287°}$ *Subtract 287° from both sides.*

$x = 73°$

The unknown angle measure is 73°.

By dividing any figure into triangles, you can find the sum of its angle measures.

EXAMPLE 3 Drawing Triangles to Find the Sum of Interior Angles

Divide the polygon into triangles to find the sum of its angle measures.

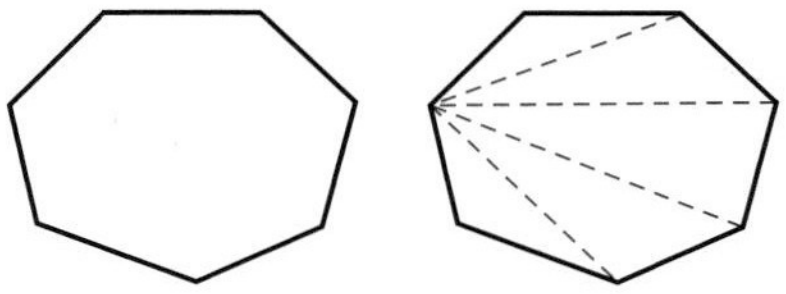

There are 5 triangles.

$5 \cdot 180° = 900°$

The sum of the angle measures of a heptagon is 900°.

Think and Discuss

1. **Explain** how to find the measure of an angle in a triangle when the measures of the two other angles are known.
2. **Determine** for which polygon the sum of the angle measures is greater, a pentagon or an octagon.
3. **Explain** how the measure of each angle in a regular polygon changes as the number of sides increases.

8-8 Exercises

go.hrw.com
Homework Help Online
KEYWORD: MS7 8-8
Parent Resources Online
KEYWORD: MS7 Parent

GUIDED PRACTICE

See Example 1

Find the unknown angle measure in each triangle.

1. 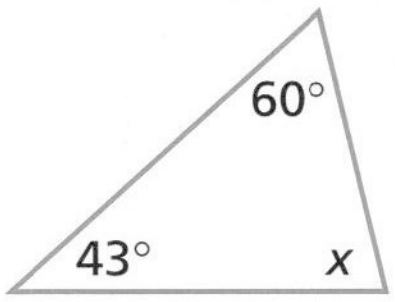

2. 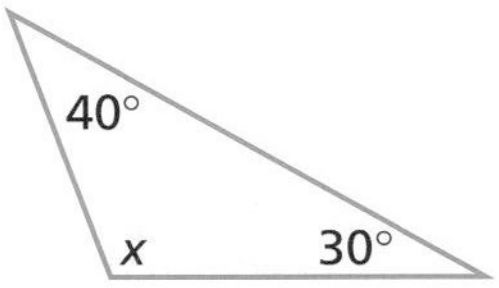

3. 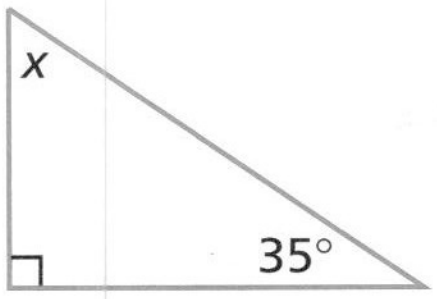

See Example 2

Find the unknown angle measure in each quadrilateral .

4. 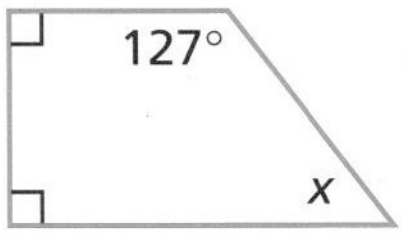

5. 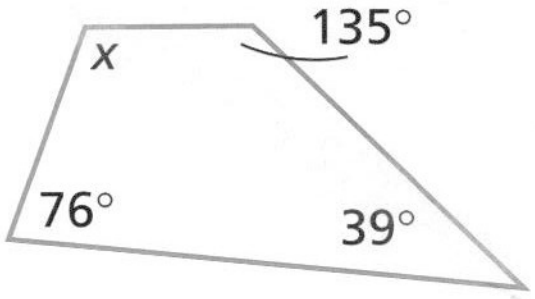

6. 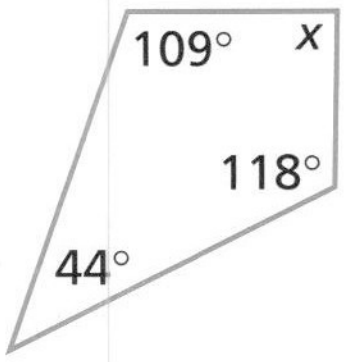

See Example 3

Divide each polygon into triangles to find the sum of its angle measures.

7. 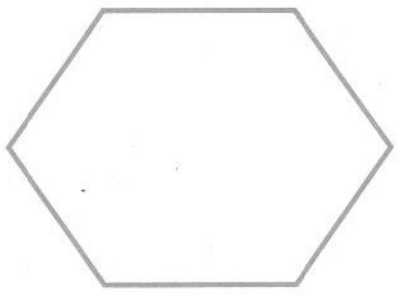

8. 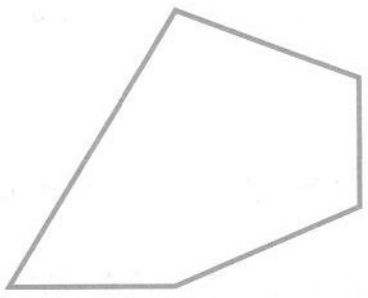

9. 

INDEPENDENT PRACTICE

See Example 1

Find the unknown angle measure in each triangle.

10. 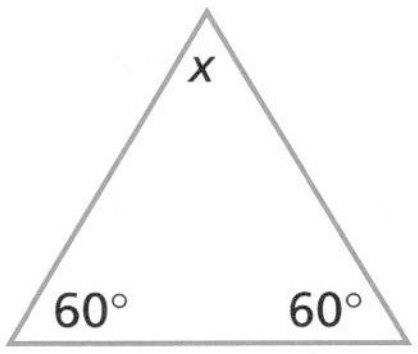

11. 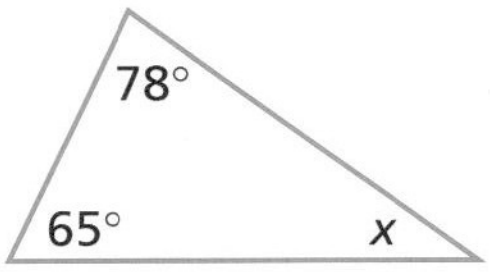

12. 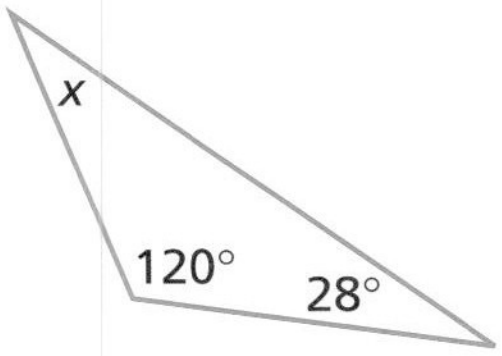

See Example 2

Find the unknown angle measure in each quadrilateral.

13. 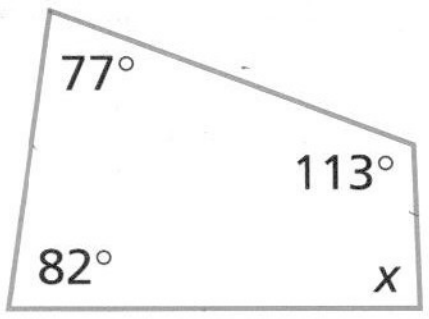

14. 

15. 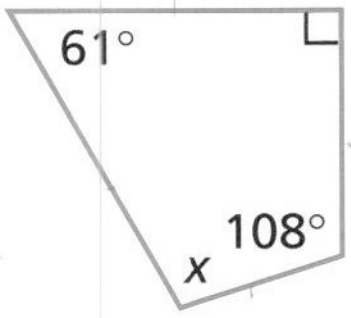

See Example 3

Divide each polygon into triangles to find the sum of its angle measures.

16. 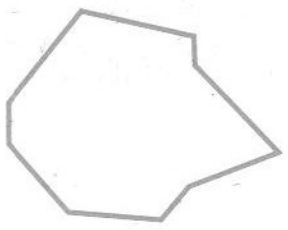

17. 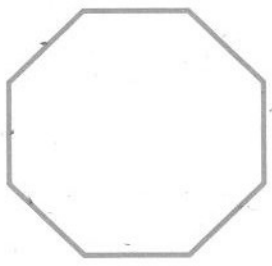

18. 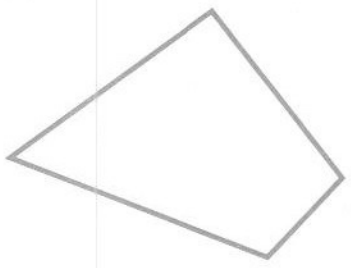

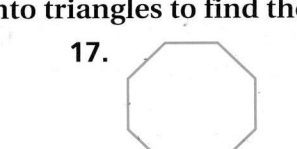

PRACTICE AND PROBLEM SOLVING

Extra Practice
See page 742.

19. **Earth Science** A sundial consists of a circular base and a right triangle mounted upright on the base. One acute angle in the right triangle is 52°. What is the measure of the other acute angle?

Find the measure of the third angle in each triangle, given two angle measures. Then classify the triangle.

20. 56°, 101° **21.** 18°, 63° **22.** 62°, 58° **23.** 41°, 49°

24. Multi-Step Each outer wall of the Pentagon in Washington, D.C., measures 921 feet. What is the measure of each angle made by the Pentagon's outer walls?

25. Critical Thinking A truss bridge is supported by triangular frames called trusses. If every truss in a truss bridge is an isosceles right triangle, what is the measure of each angle in one of the trusses? (*Hint:* Two of the angles in each truss are congruent.)

26. What's the Error? A student finds the sum of the angle measures in an octagon by multiplying 7 · 180°. What is the student's error?

27. Write About It Explain how to find the sum of the angle measures in a quadrilateral by dividing the quadrilateral into triangles.

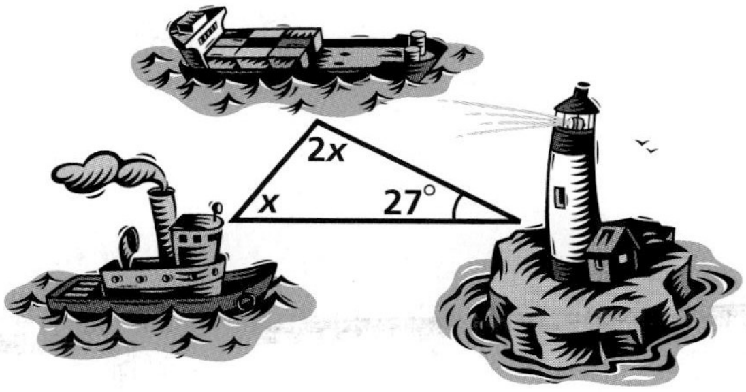

28. Challenge The angle between the lines of sight from a lighthouse to a tugboat and to a cargo ship is 27°. The angle between the lines of sight at the cargo ship is twice the angle between the lines of sight at the tugboat. What are the angles at the tugboat and at the cargo ship?

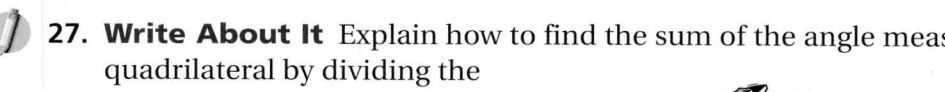

TEST PREP and Spiral Review

29. Multiple Choice A triangle has three congruent angles. What is the measure of each angle?

Ⓐ 50° Ⓑ 60° Ⓒ 75° Ⓓ 100°

30. Gridded Response Two angles of a triangle measure 58° and 42°. What is the measure, in degrees, of the third angle of the triangle?

Solve each proportion. (Lesson 5-5)

31. $\frac{x}{3} = \frac{30}{18}$ **32.** $\frac{8}{p} = \frac{24}{27}$ **33.** $\frac{4}{3} = \frac{t}{21}$ **34.** $\frac{0.5}{1.8} = \frac{n}{9}$

Name the types of quadrilaterals that have each property. (Lesson 8-7)

35. two pairs of opposite, congruent sides **36.** four congruent sides

CHAPTER 8

READY TO GO ON?

SECTION 8B

Quiz for Lessons 8-4 Through 8-8

8-4 Properties of Circles

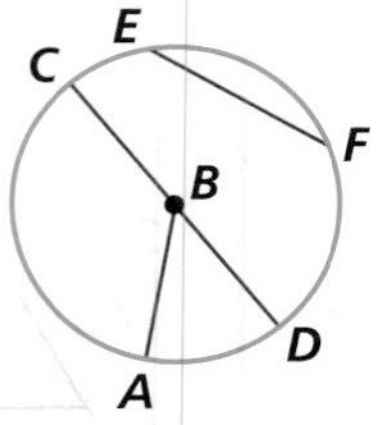

Name the parts of circle B.

1. radii
2. diameter
3. chords
4. A circle is divided into 6 equal sectors. Find the measure of the central angle of each sector.

8-5 Classifying Polygons

Name each polygon, and tell whether it is a regular polygon. If it is not, explain why not.

5. 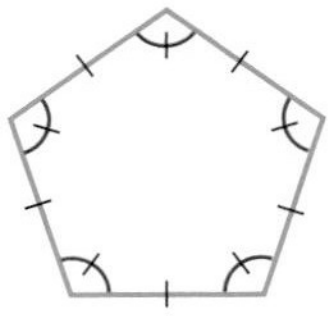

6. 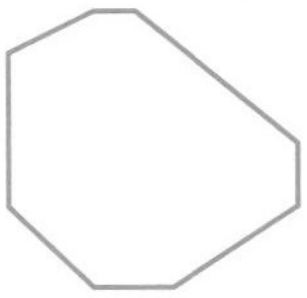

7. 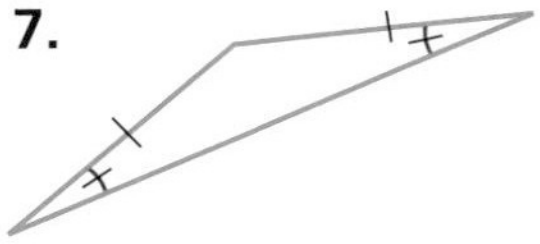

8. 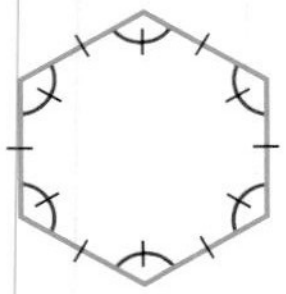

8-6 Classifying Triangles

Classify each triangle according to its sides and angles.

9. 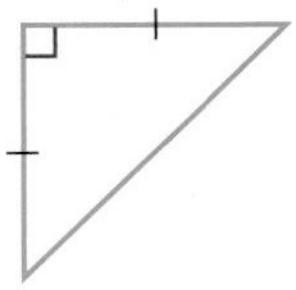

10. 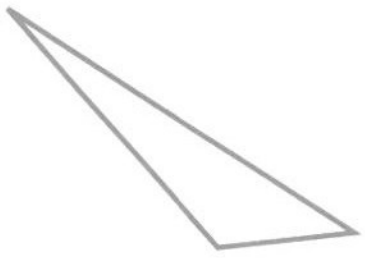

11. 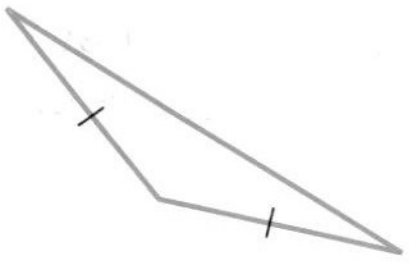

12. 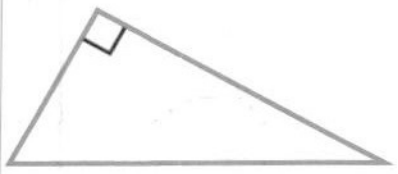

8-7 Classifying Quadrilaterals

Give all of the names that apply to each quadrilateral. Then give the name that best describes it.

13. 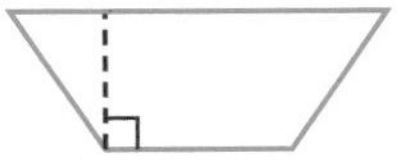

14. 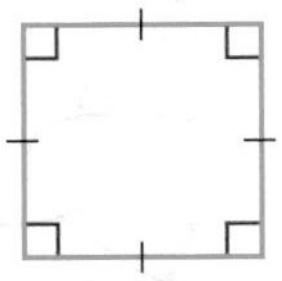

15. 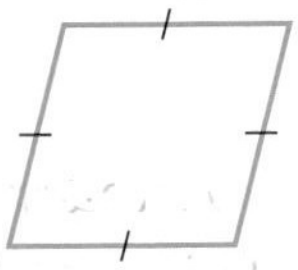

16. 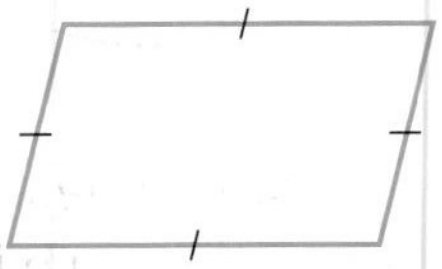

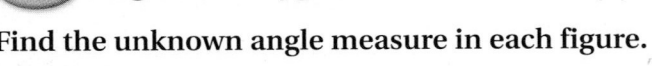

8-8 Angles in Polygons

Find the unknown angle measure in each figure.

17. 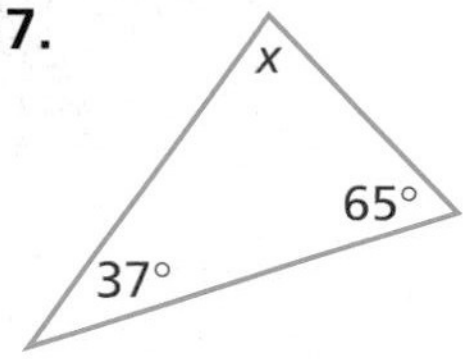

18. 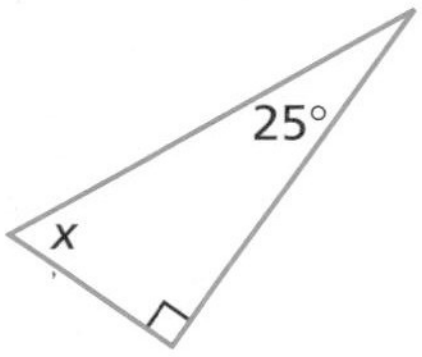

19. 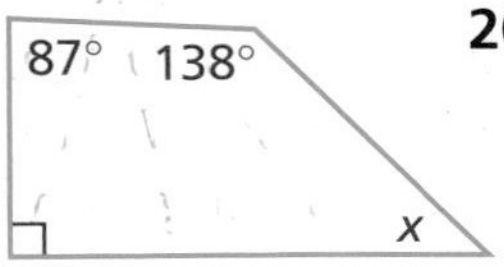

20. 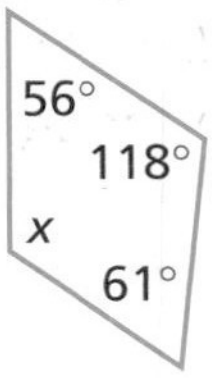

Focus on Problem Solving

Understand the Problem

• Understand the words in the problem

Words that you do not understand can sometimes make a simple problem seem difficult. Some of those words, such as the names of things or persons, may not even be necessary to solve the problem. If a problem contains an unfamiliar name, or one that you cannot pronounce, you can substitute another word for it. If a word that you don't understand is necessary to solve the problem, look the word up to find its meaning.

Read each problem, and make a list of unusual or unfamiliar words. If a word is not necessary to solve the problem, replace it with a familiar one. If a word is necessary, look up the word and write its meaning.

1. Using a pair of calipers, Mr. Papadimitriou measures the diameter of an ancient Greek amphora to be 17.8 cm at its widest point. What is the radius of the amphora at this point?

2. Joseph wants to plant gloxinia and hydrangeas in two similar rectangular gardens. The length of one garden is 5 ft, and the width is 4 ft. The other garden's length is 20 ft. What is the width of the second garden?

3. Mr. Manityche is sailing his catamaran from Kaua'i to Ni'ihau, a distance of about 12 nautical miles. If his speed averages 10 knots, how long will the trip take him?

4. Aimee's lepidoptera collection includes a butterfly with dots that appear to form a scalene triangle on each wing. What is the sum of the angles of each triangle on the butterfly's wings?

5. Students in a physics class use wire and resistors to build a Wheatstone bridge. Each side of their rhombus-shaped design is 2 cm long. What angle measures would the design have to have for its shape to be a square?

8-9 Congruent Figures

Learn to identify congruent figures and to use congruence to solve problems.

Side-Side-Side Rule

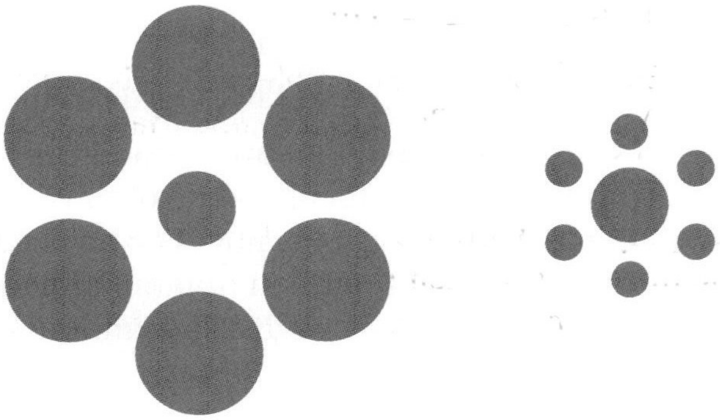

Look at the two patterns. Which center circle do you think is bigger? In spite of appearances, the two center circles are congruent. They are the same size and shape. Their apparent differences are optical illusions. One way to determine whether figures are congruent is to see whether one figure will fit exactly over the other one.

EXAMPLE 1 Identifying Congruent Figures in the Real World

Identify any congruent figures.

A

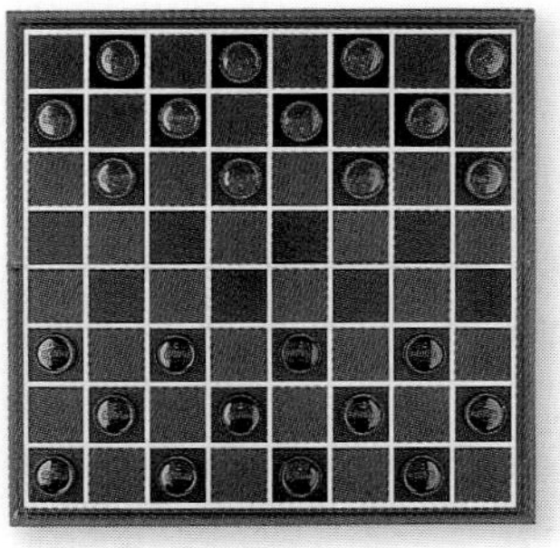

The squares on a checkerboard are congruent. The checkers are also congruent.

B

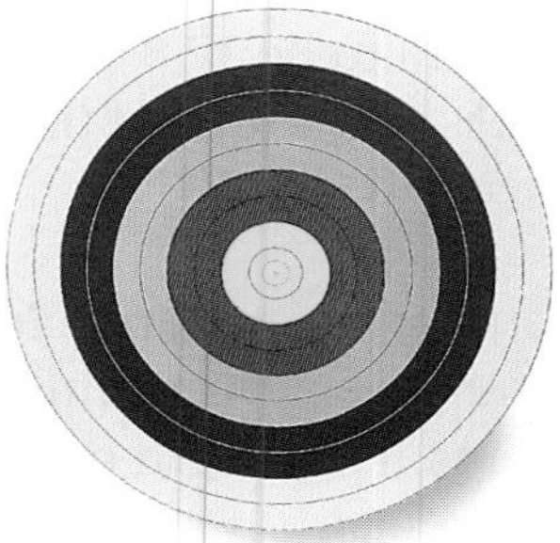

The rings on a target are not congruent. Each ring is larger than the one inside of it.

If all of the corresponding sides and angles of two polygons are congruent, then the polygons are congruent. For triangles in particular, if the corresponding sides are congruent, then the corresponding angles will always be congruent. This is called the **Side-Side-Side Rule**. Because of this rule, when determining whether triangles are congruent, you only need to determine whether the sides are congruent.

EXAMPLE 2 Identifying Congruent Triangles

Determine whether the triangles are congruent.

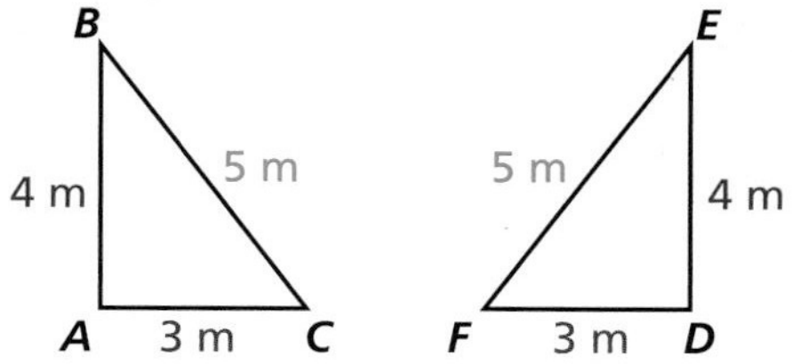

$AC = 3$ m $DF = 3$ m
$AB = 4$ m $DE = 4$ m
$BC = 5$ m $EF = 5$ m

By the Side-Side-Side Rule, $\triangle ABC$ is congruent to $\triangle DEF$, or $\triangle ABC \cong \triangle DEF$. If you flip one triangle, it will fit exactly over the other.

Reading Math

The notation $\triangle ABC$ is read "triangle *ABC*."

For polygons with more than three sides, it is not enough to compare the measures of their sides. For example, the corresponding sides of the figures below are congruent, but the figures are not congruent.

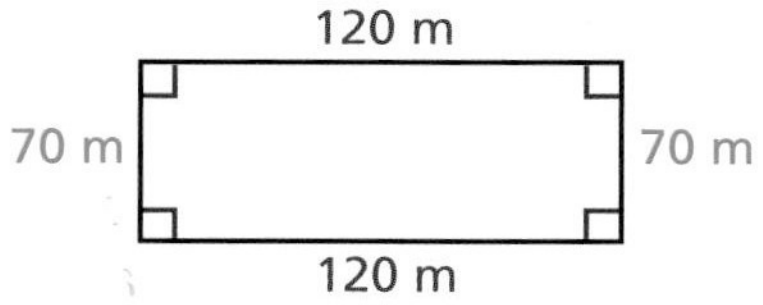

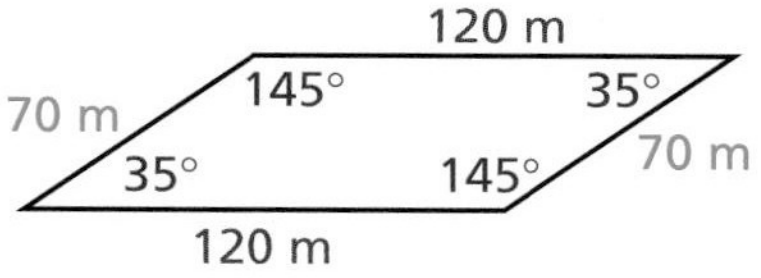

If you know that two figures are congruent, you can find missing measures in the figures.

EXAMPLE 3 Using Congruence to Find Missing Measures

Determine the missing measure in each set of congruent polygons.

A

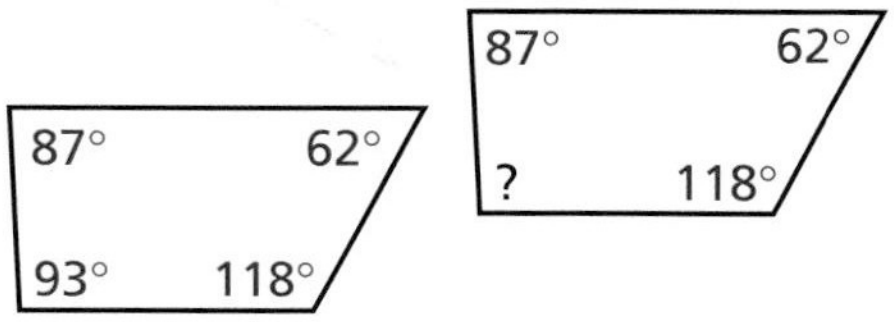

The corresponding angles of congruent polygons are congruent.

The missing angle measure is 93°.

B

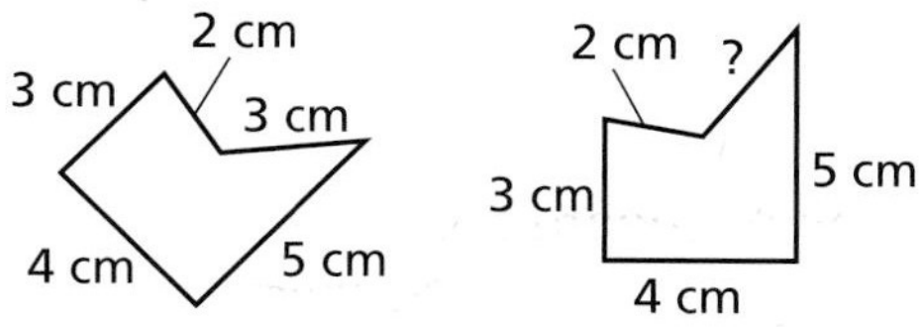

The corresponding sides of congruent polygons are congruent.

The missing side length is 3 cm.

Think and Discuss

1. **Draw** an illustration to explain whether an isosceles triangle can be congruent to a right triangle.
2. **Explain** why congruent figures are always similar figures.

8-9 Exercises

go.hrw.com
Homework Help Online
KEYWORD: MS7 8-9
Parent Resources Online
KEYWORD: MS7 Parent

GUIDED PRACTICE

See Example 1 **Identify any congruent figures.**

1. 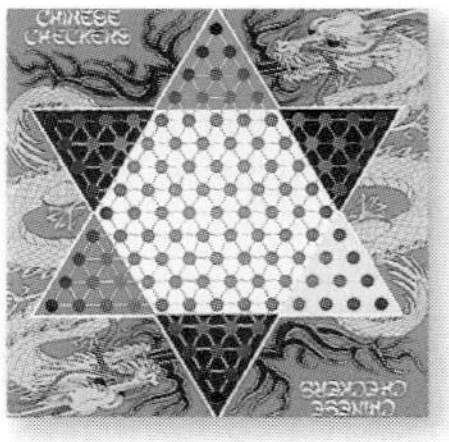

2. 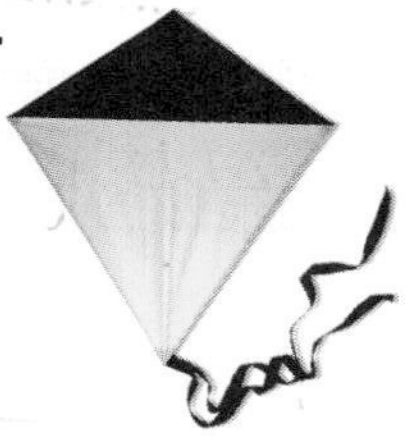

3. 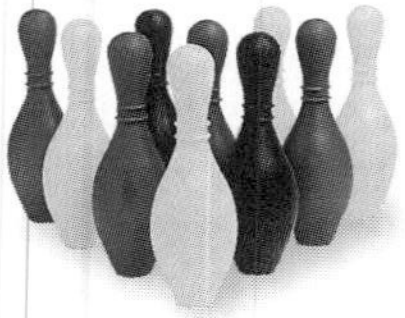

See Example 2 **Determine whether the triangles are congruent.**

4. 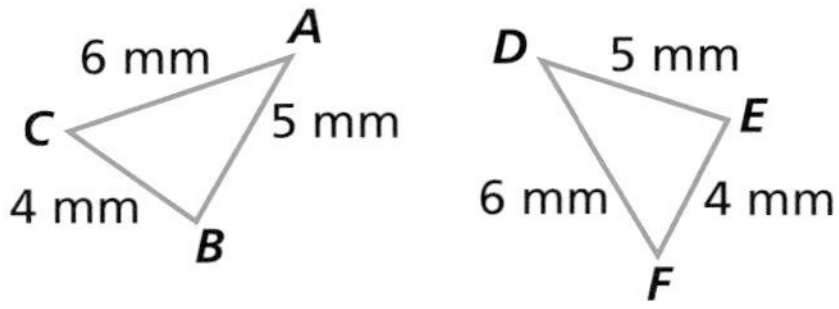

5. 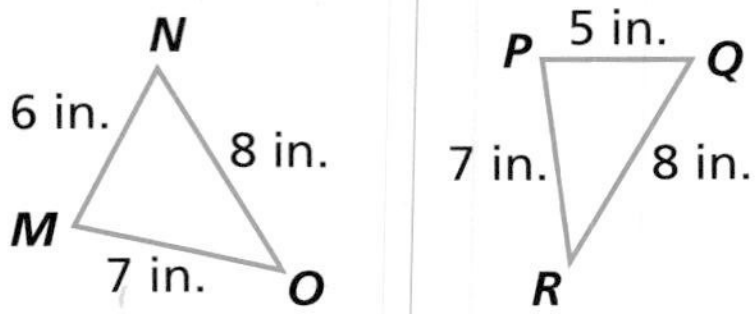

See Example 3 **Determine the missing measure in each set of congruent polygons.**

6. 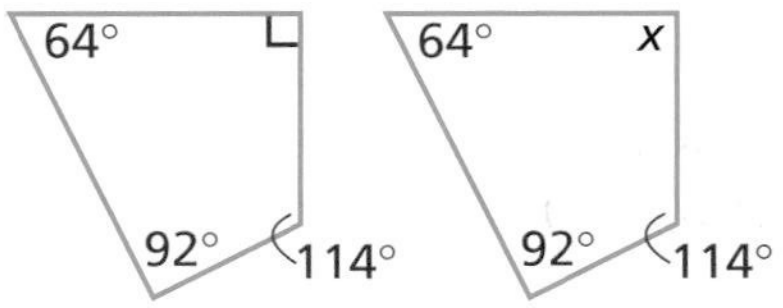

7. 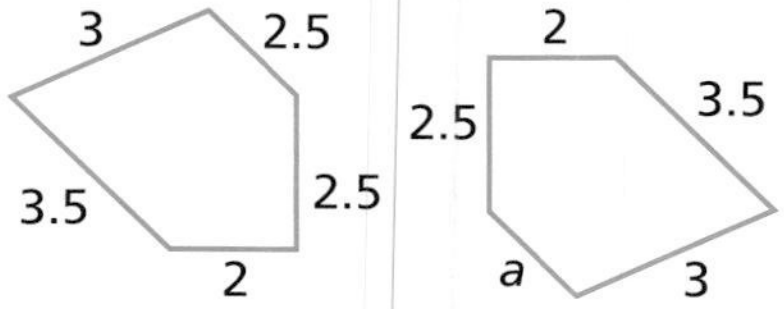

INDEPENDENT PRACTICE

See Example 1 **Identify any congruent figures.**

8. 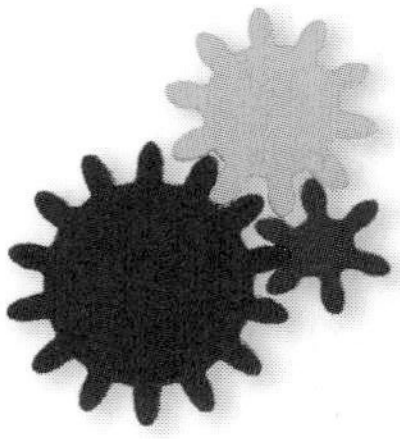

9. 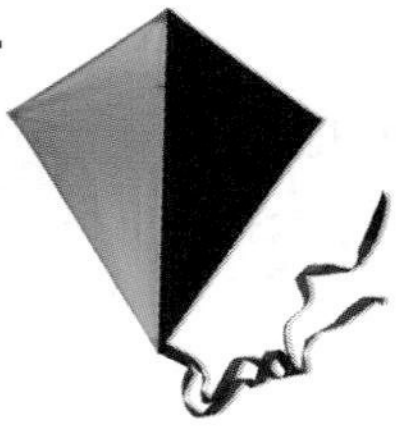

10. 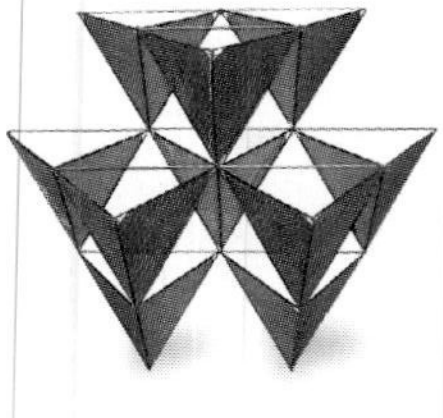

See Example 2 **Determine whether the triangles are congruent.**

11. 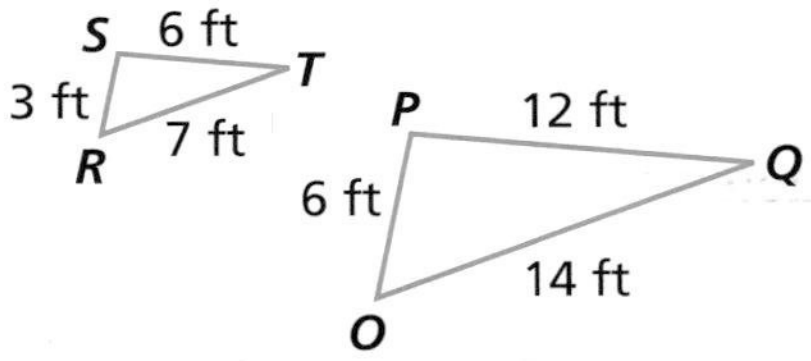

12. 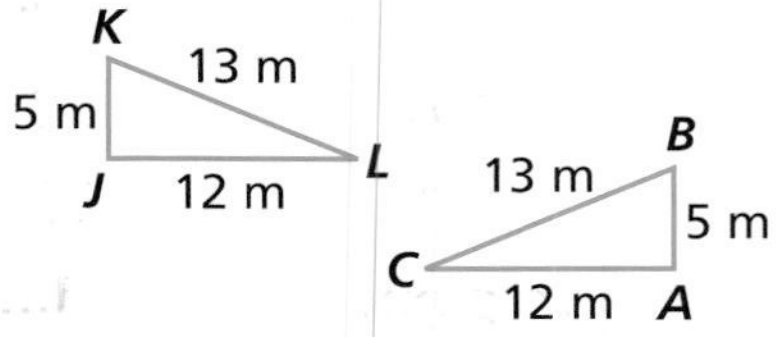

See Example 3 **Determine the missing measures in each set of congruent polygons.**

13. 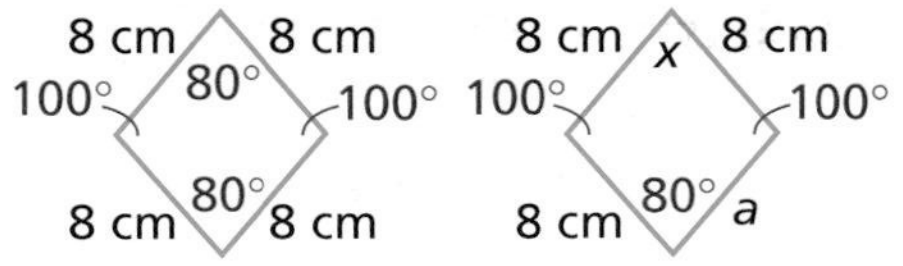

14. 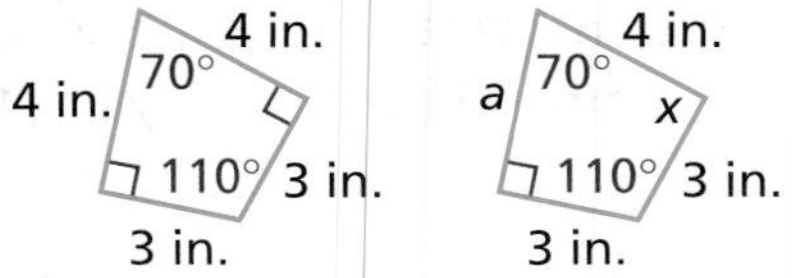

PRACTICE AND PROBLEM SOLVING

Extra Practice
See page 743.

Tell the minimum amount of information needed to determine whether the figures are congruent.

15. two triangles **16.** two squares **17.** two rectangles **18.** two pentagons

19. Surveying In the figure, trees A and B are on opposite sides of the stream. Jamil wants to string a rope from one tree to the other. Triangles ABC and DEC are congruent. What is the distance between the trees?

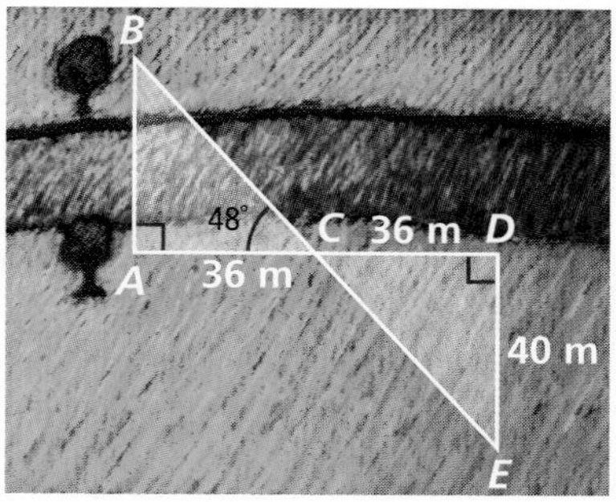

20. Hobbies In the quilt block, which figures appear congruent?

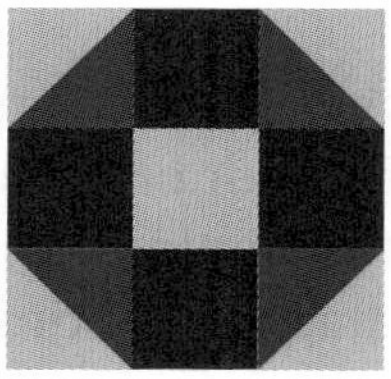

21. Choose a Strategy Anji and her brother Art walked to school along the routes in the figure. They started at 7:40 A.M. and walked at the same rate. Who arrived first?

Ⓐ Anji Ⓑ Art Ⓒ They arrived at the same time.

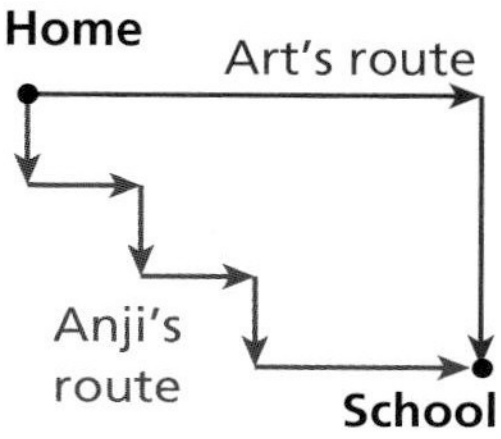

22. Write About It Explain how you can determine whether two triangles are congruent.

23. Challenge If all of the angles in two triangles have the same measure, are the triangles necessarily congruent?

TEST PREP and Spiral Review

24. Multiple Choice Which figures are congruent?

Ⓐ 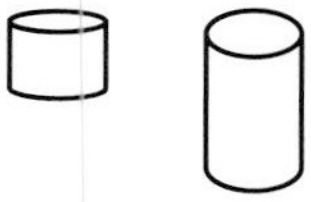 Ⓑ  Ⓒ 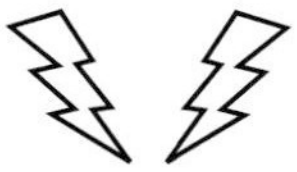 Ⓓ 

25. Multiple Choice Determine the missing measure in the congruent triangles.

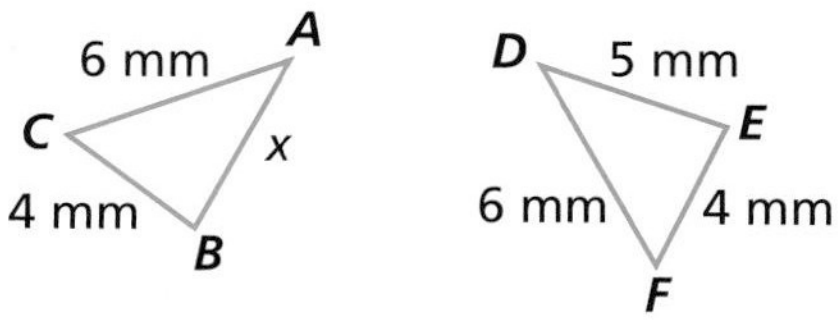

Ⓕ 4 mm Ⓗ 6 mm

Ⓖ 5 mm Ⓙ Cannot be determined

Plot each point on a coordinate plane. (Lesson 4-1)

26. $A\ (-4, 3)$ **27.** $B\ (1, -4)$ **28.** $C\ (-2, 0)$ **29.** $D\ (3, 2)$

Find the measure of the third angle in each triangle, given two angle measures. Then classify the triangle. (Lesson 8-8)

30. 25°, 48° **31.** 125°, 30° **32.** 60°, 60° **33.** 72°, 18°

8-10 Translations, Reflections, and Rotations

Learn to recognize, describe, and show transformations.

Vocabulary

transformation
image
translation
reflection
line of reflection
rotation

In the photograph, Michelle Kwan is performing a *layback spin*. She is holding her body in one position while she rotates. This is an example of a *transformation.*

In mathematics, a **transformation** changes the position or orientation of a figure. The resulting figure is the **image** of the original. Images resulting from the transformations described below are congruent to the original figures.

Types of Transformations

Translation	Reflection	Rotation
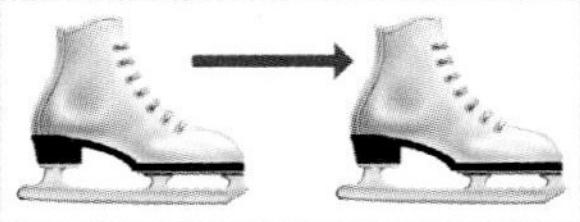	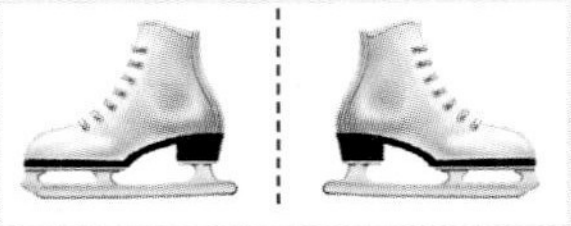	
The figure slides along a straight line without turning.	The figure flips across a **line of reflection**, creating a mirror image.	The figure turns around a fixed point.

EXAMPLE 1 Identifying Types of Transformations

Helpful Hint

The point that a figure rotates around may be on the figure or away from the figure.

Identify each type of transformation.

A

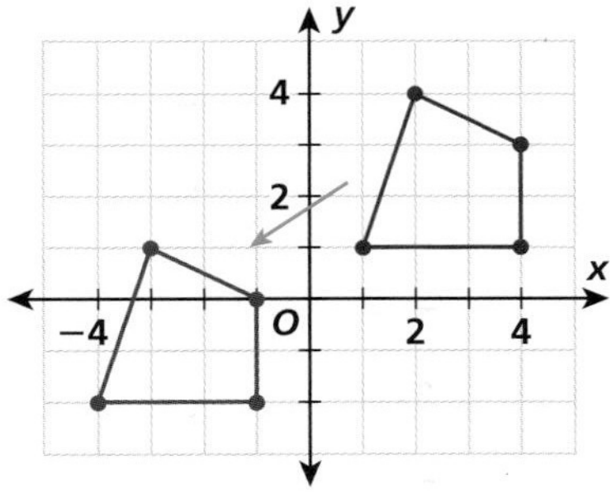

The figure slides along a straight line.
It is a translation.

B

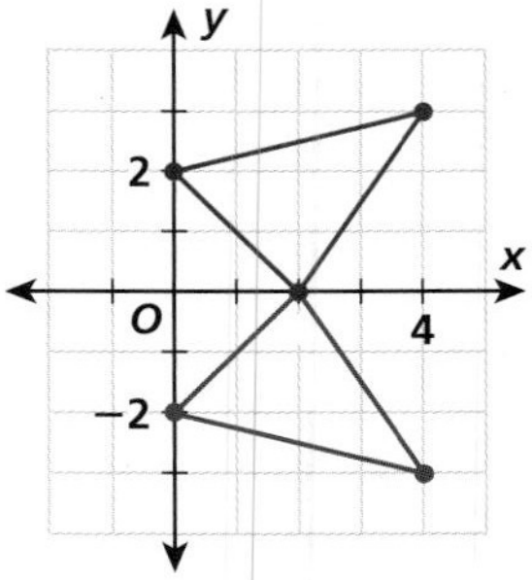

The figure flips across the x-axis.
It is a reflection.

EXAMPLE 2 Graphing Translations on a Coordinate Plane

Reading Math

A' is read "A prime" and is used to represent the point on the image that corresponds to point A of the original figure.

Graph the translation of $\triangle ABC$ 6 units right and 4 units down.

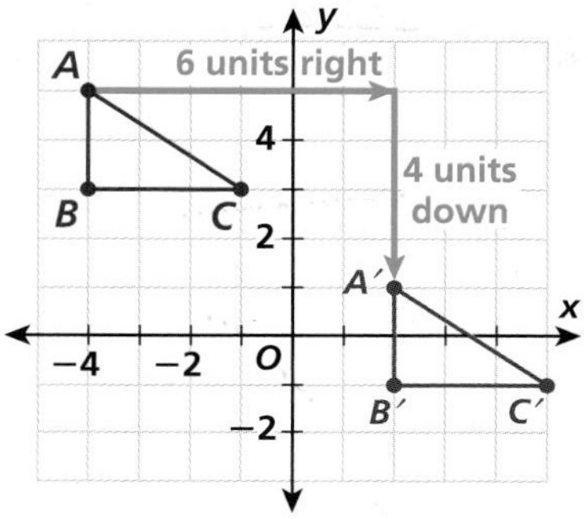

Each vertex is moved 6 units right and 4 units down.

EXAMPLE 3 Graphing Reflections on a Coordinate Plane

Graph the reflection of each figure across the indicated axis. Write the coordinates of the vertices of the image.

A x-axis

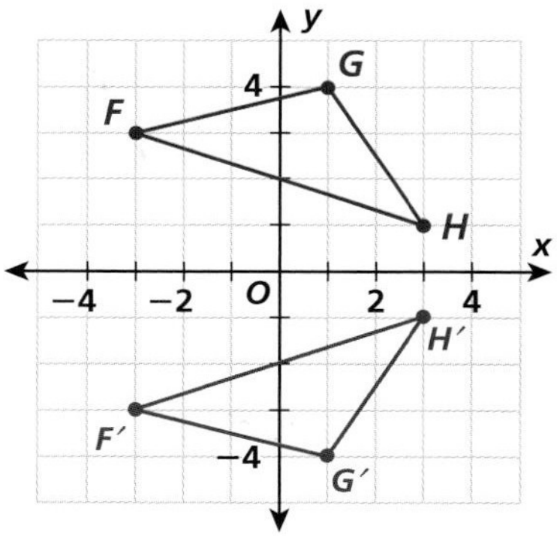

The x-coordinates of the corresponding vertices are the same, and the y-coordinates of the corresponding vertices are opposites.

The coordinates of the vertices of triangle $F'G'H'$ are $F'(-3, -3)$, $G'(1, -4)$, and $H'(3, -1)$.

B y-axis

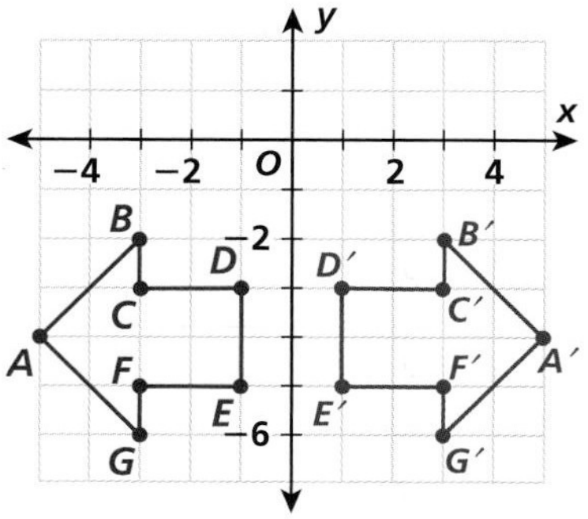

The y-coordinates of the corresponding vertices are the same, and the x-coordinates of the corresponding vertices are opposites.

The coordinates of the vertices of figure $A'B'C'D'E'F'G'$ are $A'(5, -4)$, $B'(3, -2)$, $C'(3, -3)$, $D'(1, -3)$, $E'(1, -5)$, $F'(3, -5)$, and $G'(3, -6)$.

EXAMPLE 4 Graphing Rotations on a Coordinate Plane

Triangle *JKL* has vertices *J*(−3, 1), *K*(−3, −2), and *L*(1, −2). Rotate △*JKL* 90° counterclockwise about the vertex *J*.

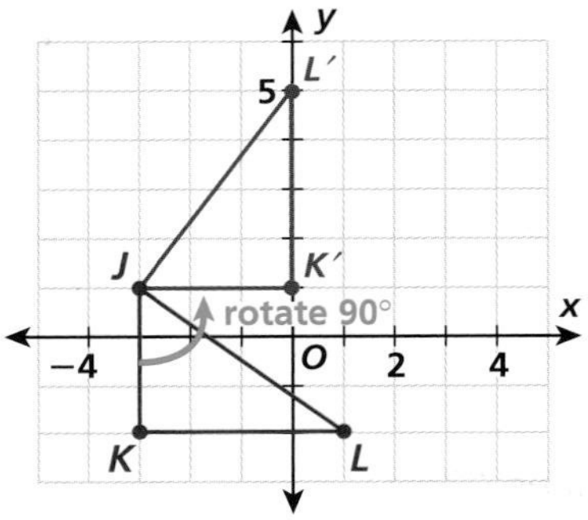

The corresponding sides, $\overline{JK}$ and $\overline{JK'}$, make a 90° angle.

Notice that vertex K is 3 units below vertex J, and vertex K′ is 3 units to the right of vertex J.

Think and Discuss

1. **Describe** a classroom situation that illustrates a translation.
2. **Explain** how a figure skater might perform a translation and a rotation at the same time.

8-10 Exercises

go.hrw.com
Homework Help Online
KEYWORD: MS7 8-10
Parent Resources Online
KEYWORD: MS7 Parent

GUIDED PRACTICE

See Example 1

Identify each type of transformation.

1.

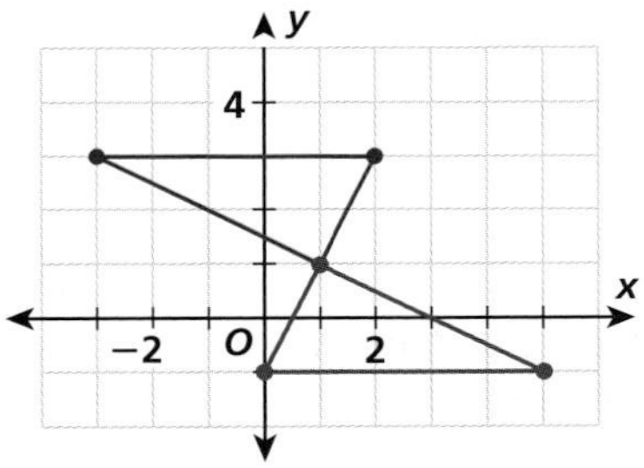

2.

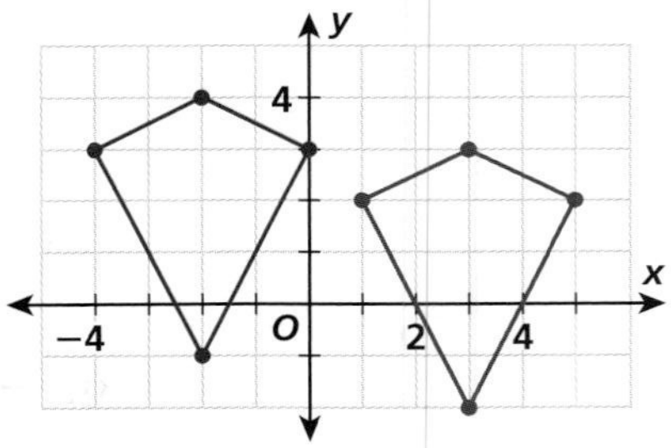

See Example 2

Graph each translation.

3. 2 units left and 3 units up

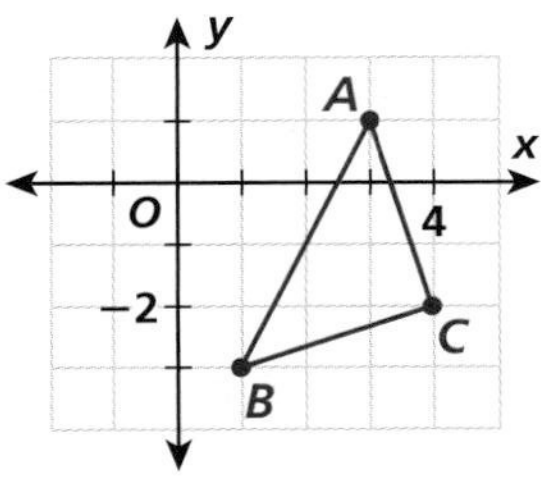

4. 3 units right and 4 units down

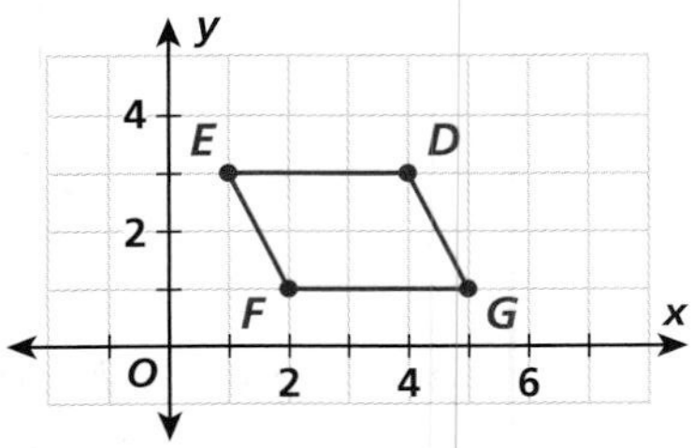

See Example 3

Graph the reflection of each figure across the indicated axis. Write the coordinates of the vertices of the image.

5. x-axis

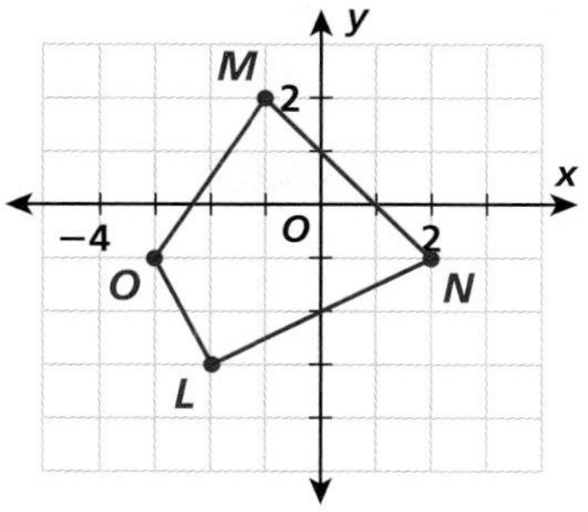

6. y-axis

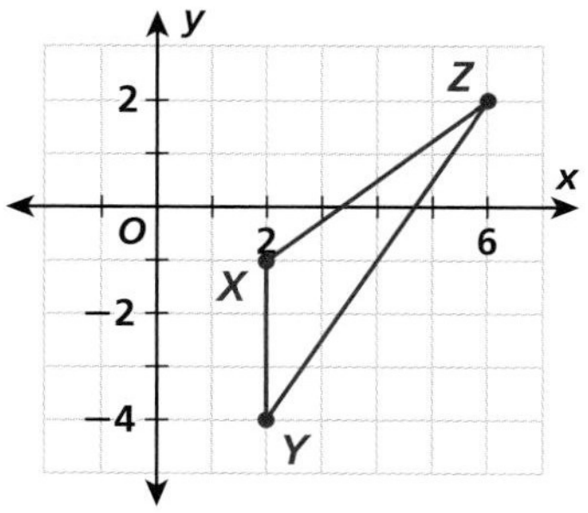

See Example 4

7. Triangle LMN has vertices $L(0, 1)$, $M(-3, 0)$, and $N(-2, 4)$. Rotate $\triangle LMN$ 180° about the vertex L.

INDEPENDENT PRACTICE

See Example 1

Identify each type of transformation.

8.

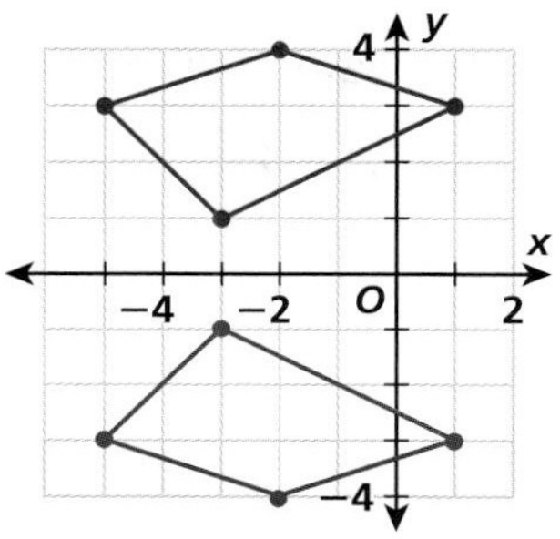

9.

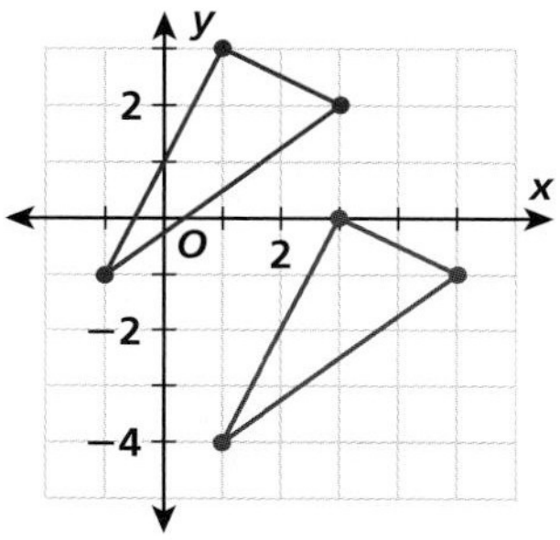

See Example 2

Graph each translation.

10. 5 units right and 1 unit down

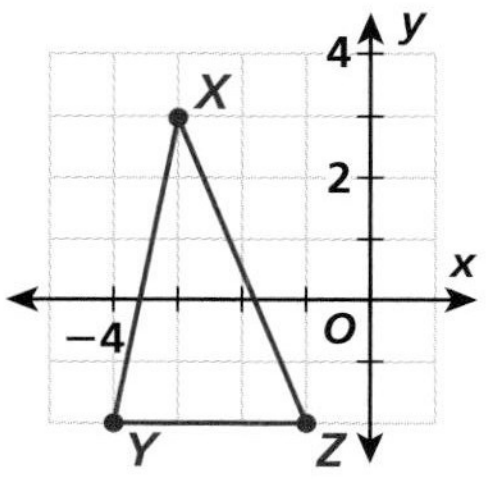

11. 4 units left and 3 units up

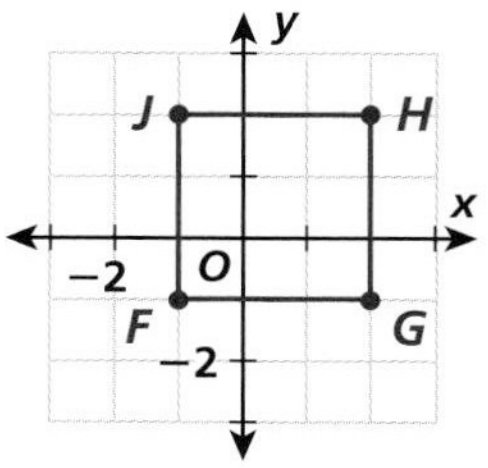

See Example 3

Graph the reflection of each figure across the indicated axis. Write the coordinates of the vertices of the image.

12. y-axis

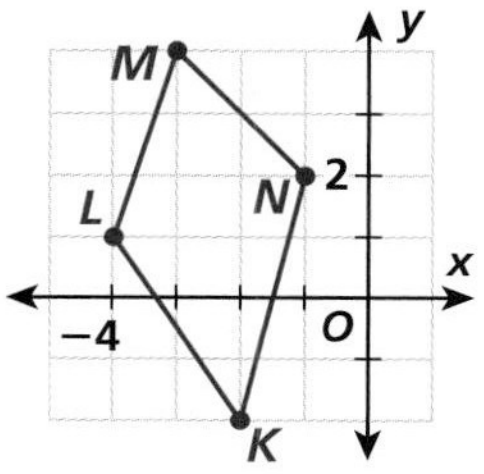

13. x-axis

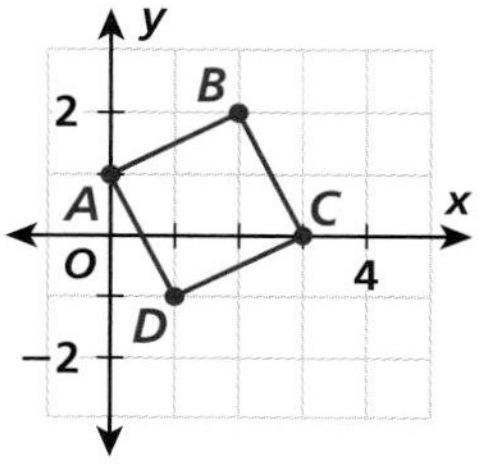

Extra Practice
See page 743.

See Example 4

14. Triangle MNL has vertices $M(0, 4)$, $N(3, 3)$, and $L(0, 0)$. Rotate $\triangle MNL$ 90° counterclockwise about the vertex L.

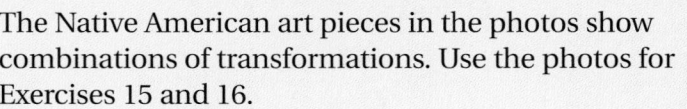

Social Studies LINK

The Native American art pieces in the photos show combinations of transformations. Use the photos for Exercises 15 and 16.

15. **Write About It** The Navajo blanket at right has a design based on a sand painting. The two people in the design are standing next to a stalk of corn, which the Native Americans called *maize*. The red, white, and black stripes represent a rainbow. Tell how the design shows reflections. Also explain what parts of the design do not show reflections.

16. **Challenge** What part of the bead design in the saddle bag at right can be described as three separate transformations? Draw diagrams to illustrate your answer.

Test Prep and Spiral Review

17. **Multiple Choice** What will be the coordinates of point X after a translation 2 units down and 3 units to the right?

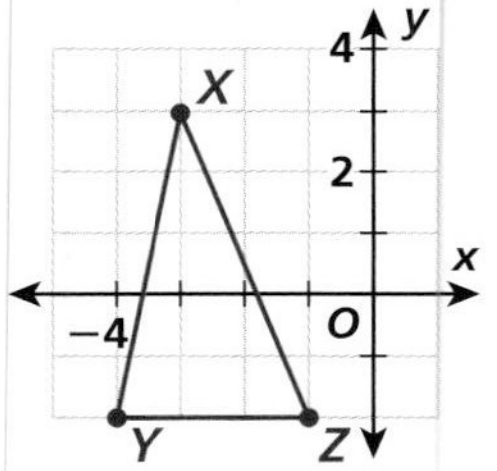

Ⓐ (0, 1)   Ⓑ (1, 0)   Ⓒ (−1, 0)   Ⓓ (0, −1)

18. **Short Response** Triangle ABC has vertices $A(-3, 1)$, $B(0, 1)$, and $C(0, 6)$. Rotate $\triangle ABC$ 90° clockwise around vertex B. Draw $\triangle ABC$ and its image.

Use the box-and-whisker plot for Exercises 19 and 20. (Lesson 7-5)

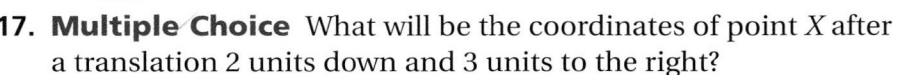

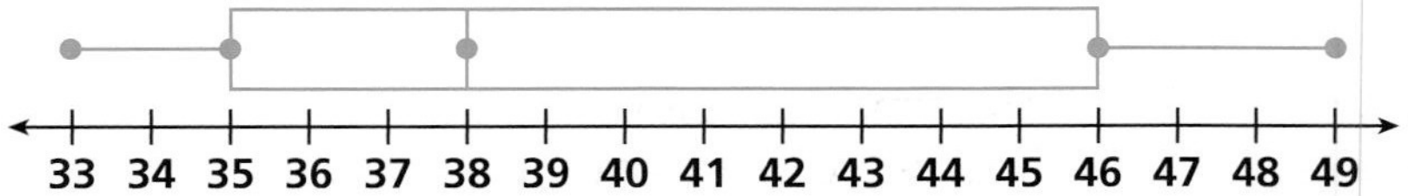

19. What is the median of the data?

20. What is the range of the data?

Determine the missing measure in each set of congruent polygons. (Lesson 8-9)

21.

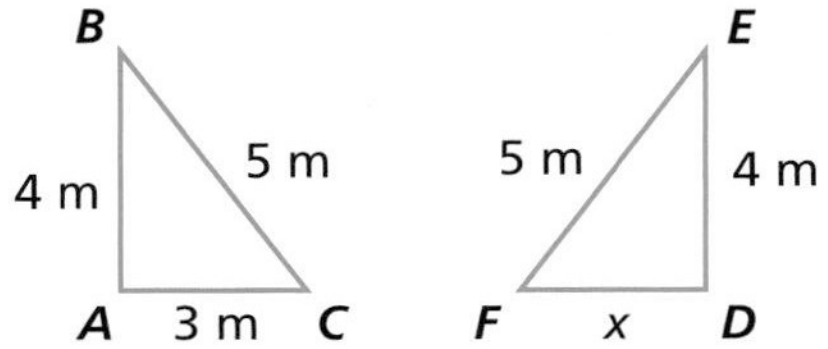

22.

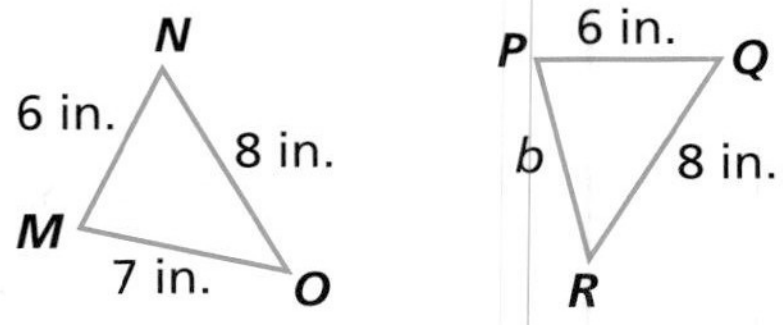

Technology LAB 8-10

Explore Transformations

Use with Lesson 8-10

go.hrw.com
Lab Resources Online
KEYWORD: MS7 Lab8

You can use geometry software to perform transformations of geometric figures.

Activity

1 Use your dynamic geometry software to construct a 5-sided polygon like the one below. Label the vertices *A, B, C, D,* and *E.* Use the translation tool to translate the polygon 2 units right and $\frac{1}{2}$ unit up.

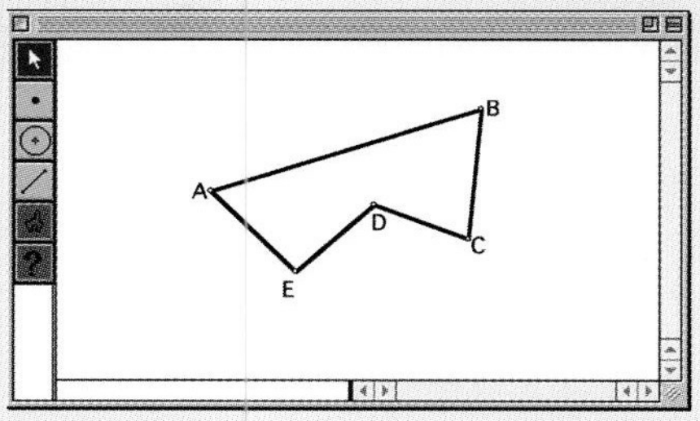

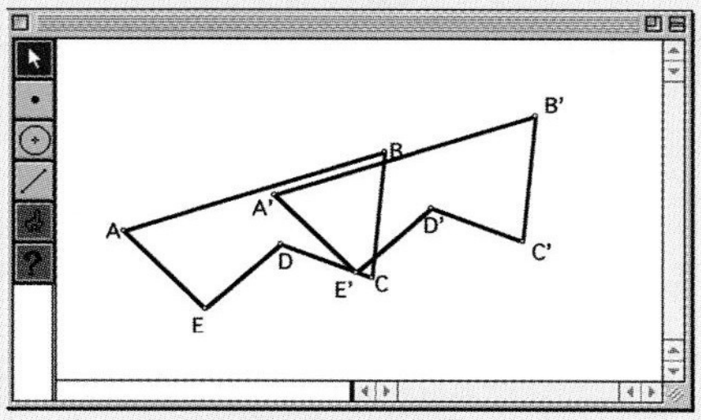

2 Start with the polygon from **1**. Use the rotation tool to rotate the polygon 30° and then 150°, both about the vertex *C.*

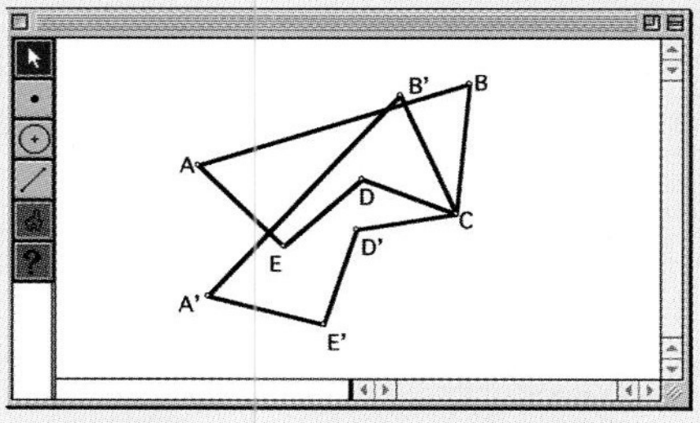

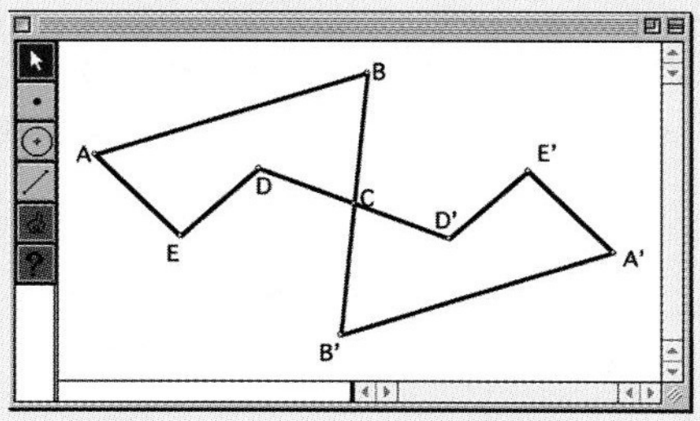

Think and Discuss

1. Rotate a triangle 30° about a point outside the triangle. Can this image be found by combining a vertical translation (slide up or down) and a horizontal translation (slide left or right) of the original triangle?
2. After what angle of rotation will the rotated image of a figure have the same orientation as the original figure?

Try This

1. Construct a quadrilateral *ABCD* using the geometry software.
   - **a.** Translate the figure 2 units right and 1 unit up.
   - **b.** Rotate the figure 30°, 45°, and 60°.

8-11 Symmetry

Learn to identify symmetry in figures.

Vocabulary

line symmetry
line of symmetry
asymmetry
rotational symmetry
center of rotation

Many architects and artists use symmetry in their buildings and artwork because symmetry is pleasing to the eye.

The Taj Mahal in Agra, India, is an example of Mughal architecture.

When you can draw a line through a plane figure so that the two halves are mirror images of each other, the figure has **line symmetry**, or is symmetrical. The line along which the figure is divided is called the **line of symmetry**.

When a figure is not symmetrical, it has **asymmetry**, or is asymmetrical.

The structure of the Taj Mahal is symmetrical. You can draw a line of symmetry down the center of the building. Also, each window in the building has its own line of symmetry.

EXAMPLE 1 Identifying Line Symmetry

Decide whether each figure has line symmetry. If it does, draw all the lines of symmetry.

A

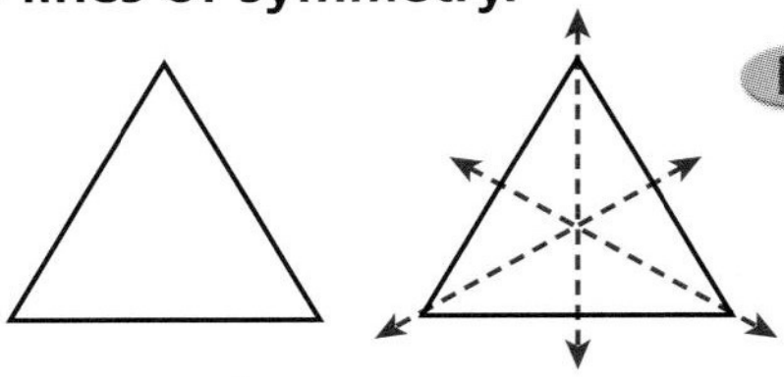

3 lines of symmetry

B

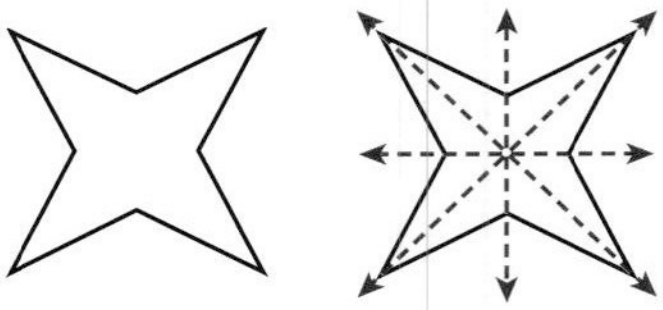

4 lines of symmetry

EXAMPLE 2 *Social Studies Application*

Find all the lines of symmetry in each flag.

A

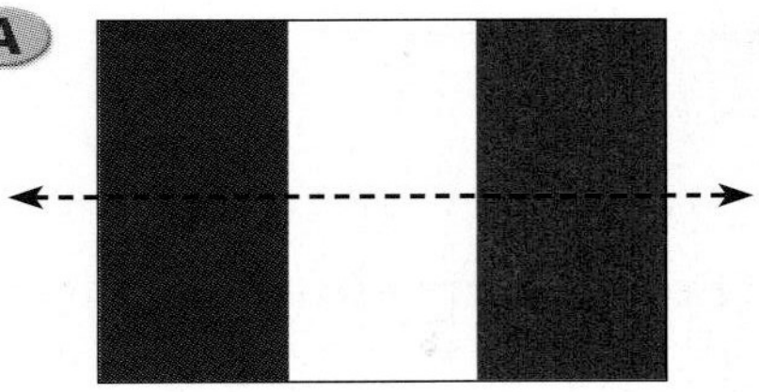

There is 1 line of symmetry.

B

There are no lines of symmetry.

A figure has **rotational symmetry** if, when it is rotated less than 360° around a central point, it coincides with itself. The central point is called the **center of rotation**.

If the stained glass window at right is rotated 90°, as shown, the image looks the same as the original stained glass window. Therefore the window has rotational symmetry.

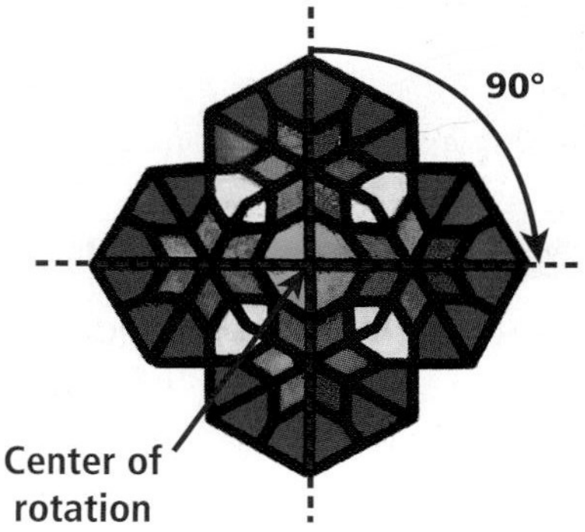

EXAMPLE 3 Identifying Rotational Symmetry

Tell how many times each figure will show rotational symmetry within one full rotation.

A

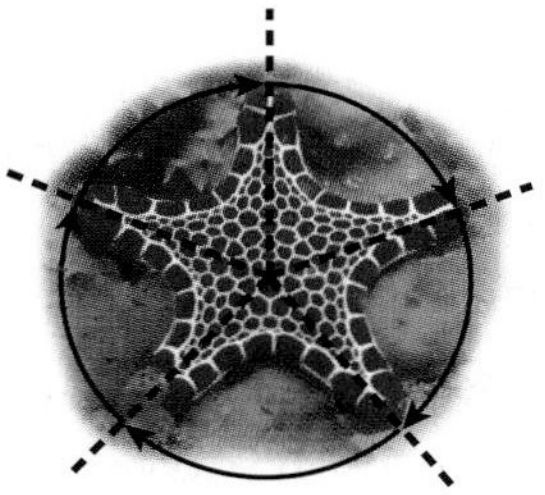

Draw lines from the center of the figure out through identical places in the figure.

The starfish will show rotational symmetry 5 times within a 360° rotation.

Count the number of lines drawn.

B

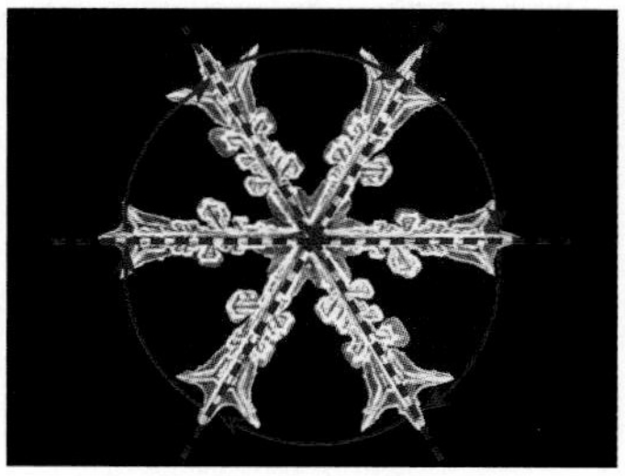

Draw lines from the center of the figure out through identical places in the figure.

The snowflake will show rotational symmetry 6 times within a 360° rotation.

Count the number of lines drawn.

Think and Discuss

1. **Draw** a figure that does not have rotational symmetry.
2. **Determine** whether an equilateral triangle has rotational symmetry. If so, tell how many times it shows rotational symmetry within one full rotation.

8-11 Exercises

go.hrw.com
Homework Help Online
KEYWORD: MS7 8-11
Parent Resources Online
KEYWORD: MS7 Parent

GUIDED PRACTICE

See Example 1 — **Decide whether each figure has line symmetry. If it does, draw all the lines of symmetry.**

1. 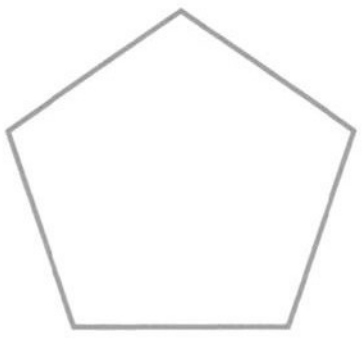

2. 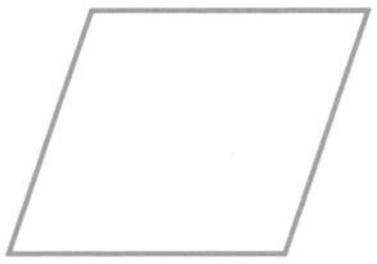

3. 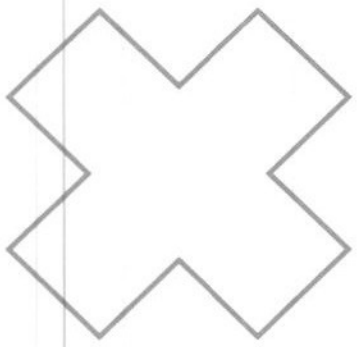

See Example 2 — **Find all the lines of symmetry in each flag.**

4. 

5. 

6. 

See Example 3 — **Tell how many times each figure will show rotational symmetry within one full rotation.**

7. 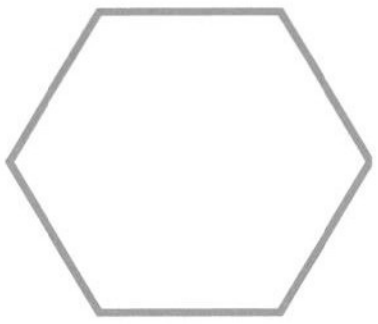

8. 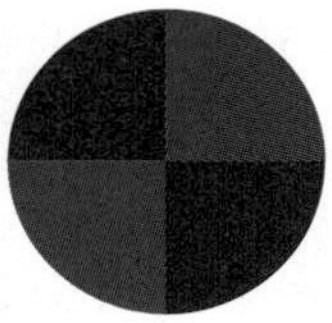

9. 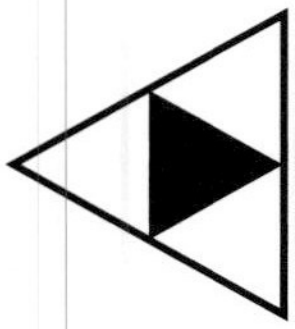

INDEPENDENT PRACTICE

See Example 1 — **Decide whether each figure has line symmetry. If it does, draw all the lines of symmetry.**

10. 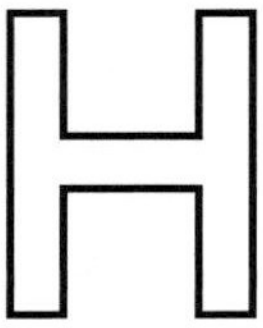

11. 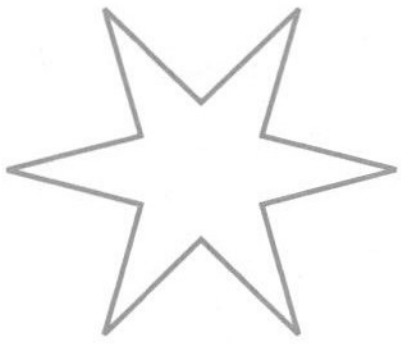

12. 

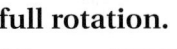

See Example 2 — **Find all the lines of symmetry in each flag.**

13. 

14. 

15. 

See Example 3 — **Tell how many times each figure will show rotational symmetry within one full rotation.**

16. 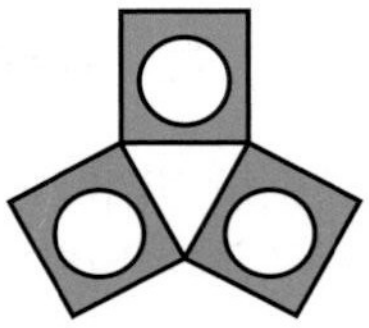

17. 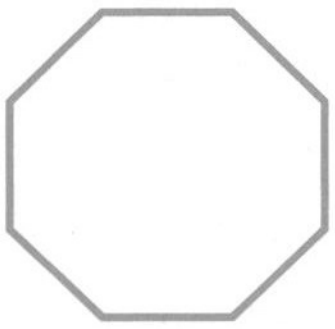

18. 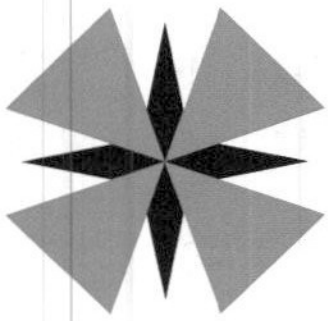

PRACTICE AND PROBLEM SOLVING

Extra Practice
See page 743.

19. Critical Thinking Which regular polygon shows rotational symmetry 9 times within one full rotation?

20. Life Science How many lines of symmetry does the photo of the moth have?

21. Fold a piece of paper in half vertically and then in half horizontally. Cut or tear a design into one of the folded edges. Then unfold the paper. Does the design have a vertical or horizontal line of symmetry? rotational symmetry? Explain your answer.

22. Art Tell how many times the stained glass image at right shows rotational symmetry in one full rotation if you consider only the shape of the design. Then tell how many times the image shows rotational symmetry if you consider both the shape and the colors in the design.

23. What's the Question? Marla drew a square on the chalkboard. As an answer to Marla's question about symmetry, Rob said "90°." What question did Marla ask?

24. Write About It Explain why an angle of rotation must be less than 360° for a figure to have rotational symmetry.

25. Challenge Print a word in capital letters, using only letters that have horizontal lines of symmetry. Print another word using only capital letters that have vertical lines of symmetry.

TEST PREP and Spiral Review

26. Multiple Choice How many lines of symmetry does the figure have?

Ⓐ None　　Ⓑ 1　　Ⓒ 2　　Ⓓ 4

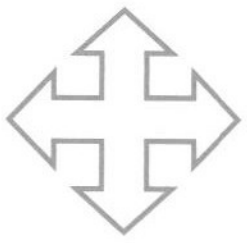

27. Gridded Response How many times will the figure show rotational symmetry within one full rotation?

28. A bridge in an architectural model is 22 cm long. The model scale is 2 cm = 30 m. Find the length of the actual bridge. (Lesson 5-9)

Triangle *JKL* has vertices $J(-3, -1)$, $K(-1, -1)$, and $L(-1, -4)$. Give the coordinates of the vertices of the triangle after each transformation. (Lesson 8-10)

29. Translate the triangle 4 units right and 2 units down.

30. Reflect the triangle across the *y*-axis.

Hands-On LAB 8-11

Create Tessellations

Use with Lessons 8-10 and 8-11

go.hrw.com
Lab Resources Online
KEYWORD: MS7 Lab8

Tessellations are patterns of identical shapes that completely cover a plane with no gaps or overlaps. The artist M. C. Escher created many fascinating tessellations.

Activity

1. Create a translation tessellation.

The tessellation by M. C. Escher shown at right is an example of a *translation tessellation*. To create your own translation tessellation, follow the steps below.

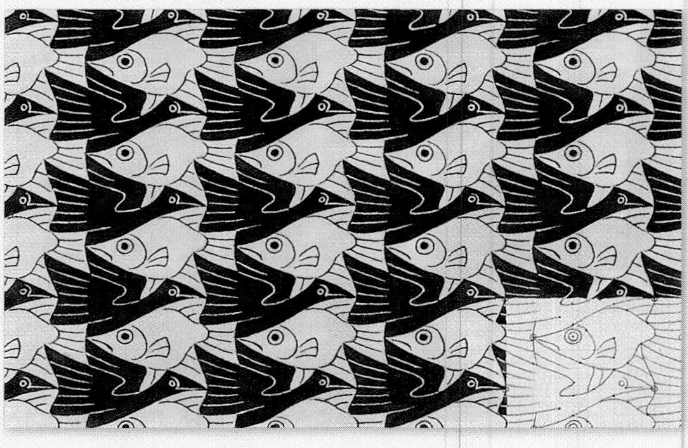

a. Start by drawing a square, rectangle, or other parallelogram. Replace one side of the parallelogram with a curve, as shown.

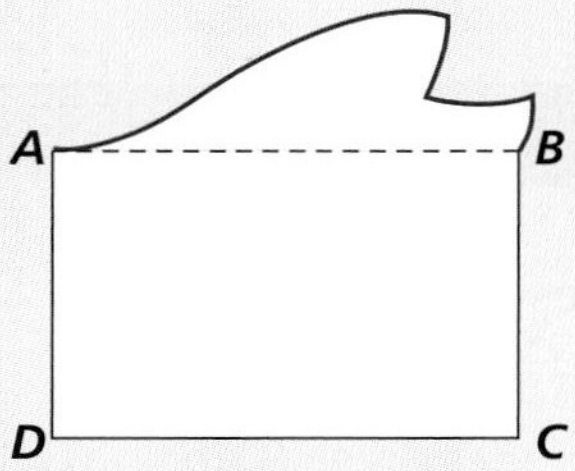

b. Translate the curve to the opposite side of the parallelogram.

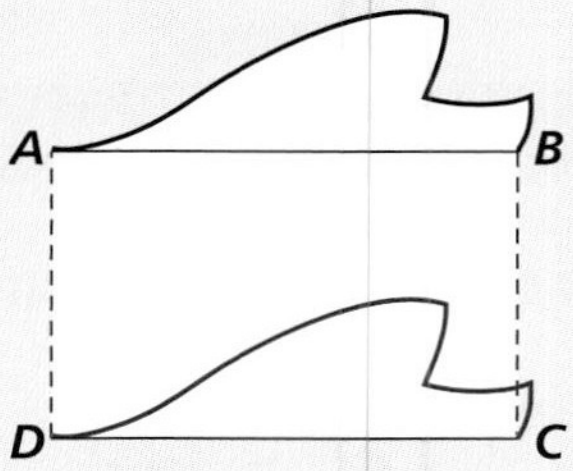

c. Repeat steps **a** and **b** for the other two sides of your parallelogram.

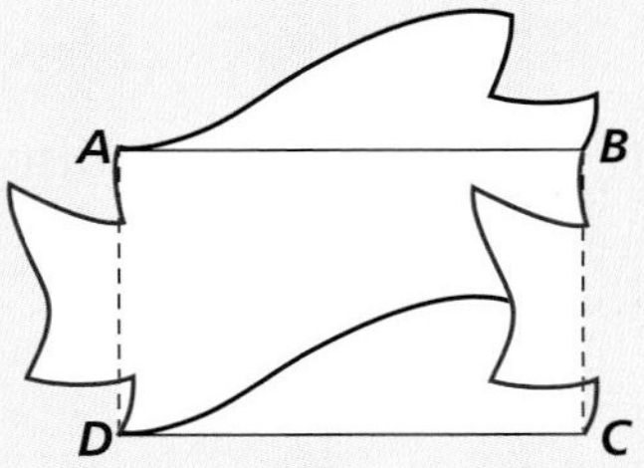

d. The figure can be translated to create an interlocking design, or tessellation. You can add details to your figure or divide it into two or more parts, as shown below.

2 Create a rotation tessellation.

The tessellation by M. C. Escher shown at right is an example of a *rotation tessellation*. To create your own rotation tessellation, follow the steps below.

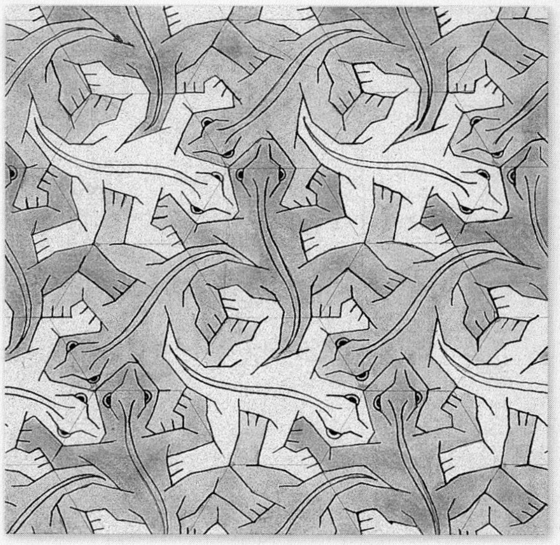

a. Start with a regular hexagon. Replace one side of the hexagon with a curve. Rotate the curve about point B so that the endpoint at point A is moved to point C.

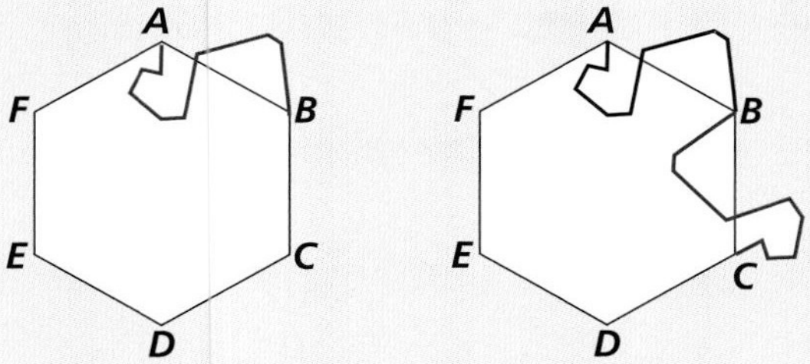

b. Replace side $\overline{CD}$ with a new curve, and rotate it about point D to replace side $\overline{DE}$.

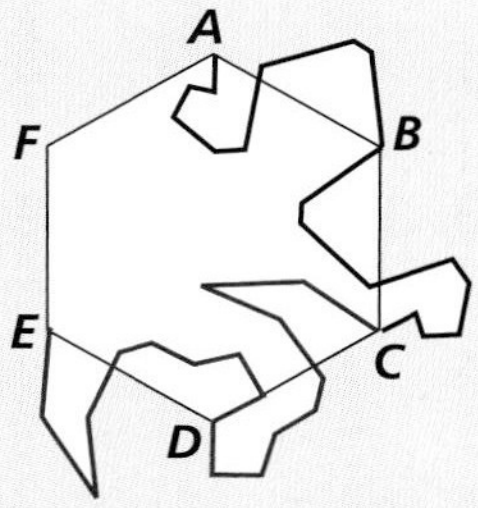

c. Replace side $\overline{EF}$ with a new curve, and rotate it about point F to replace side $\overline{FA}$.

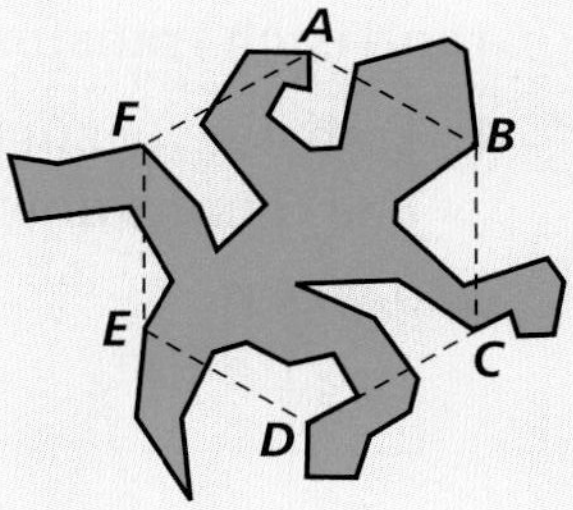

The figure can be rotated and fitted together with copies of itself to create an interlocking design, or tessellation. You can add details to your figure, if desired.

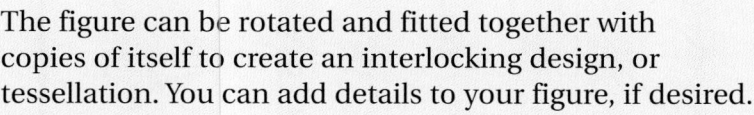

Think and Discuss

1. Explain why the two types of tessellations in this activity are known as translation and rotation tessellations.

Try This

1. Create your own design for a translation or rotation tessellation.
2. Cut out copies of your design from **1** and fit them together to fill a space with your pattern.

READY TO GO ON?

SECTION 8C

Quiz for Lessons 8-9 Through 8-11

8-9 Congruent Figures

Determine whether the triangles are congruent.

1.

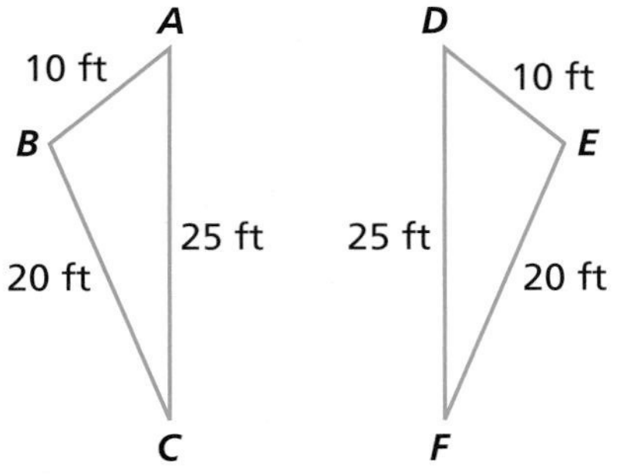

2.

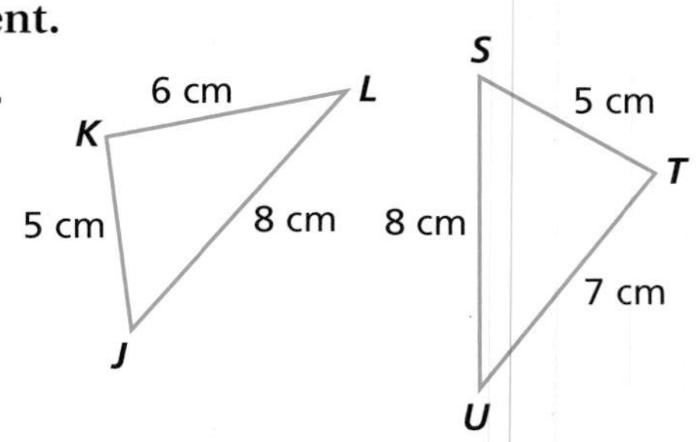

3. Determine the missing measure in the pair of congruent polygons.

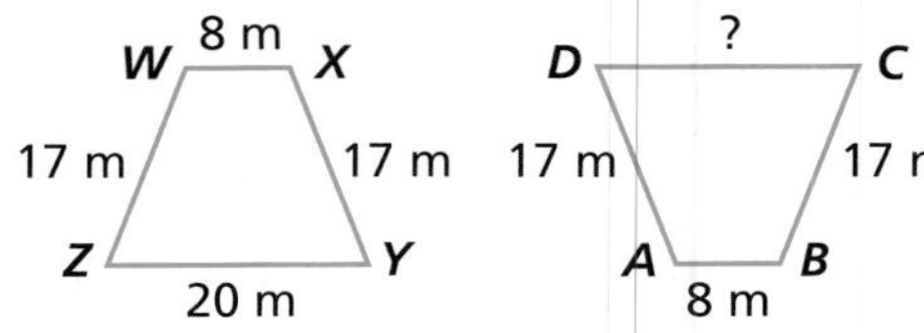

8-10 Translations, Reflections, and Rotations

Graph each transformation. Give the coordinates of the image's vertices.

4. Translate triangle *RST* 5 units down.

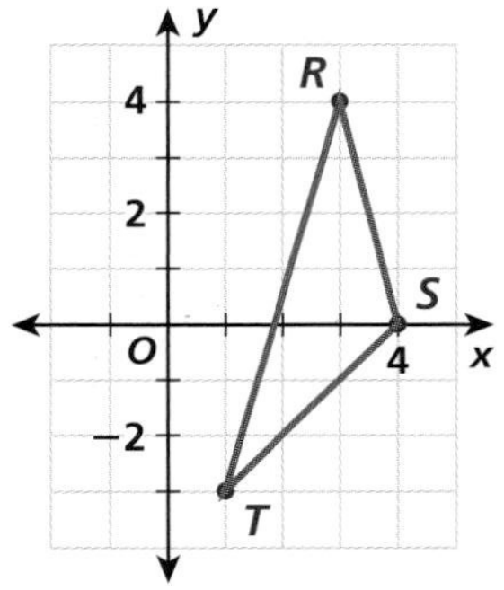

5. Reflect the figure across the x-axis.

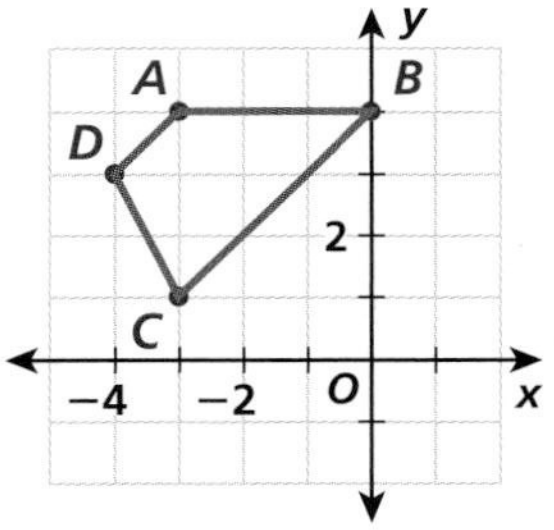

6. Rotate triangle *JKL* 90° clockwise about vertex *L*.

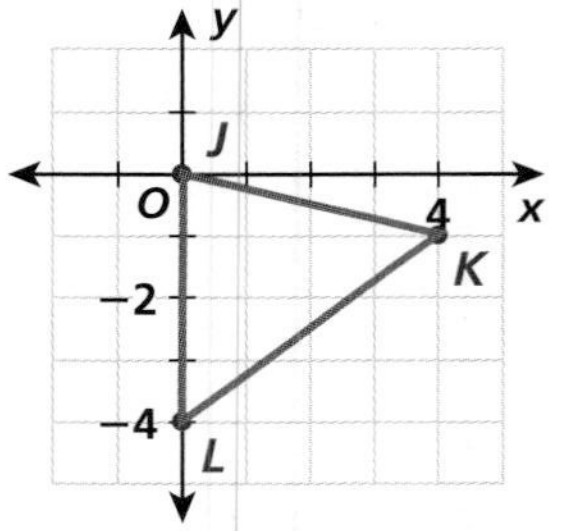

8-11 Symmetry

7. Decide whether the figure has line symmetry. If it does, draw all the lines of symmetry.

8. Tell how many times the figure will show rotational symmetry within one full rotation.

MULTI-STEP TEST PREP

Start Your Engines Several friends are racing remote-controlled cars. They use chalk to lay out the race course shown in the figure. Kendall examines the course beforehand to prepare for the race.

1. Kendall knows that figure *ABCD* is a trapezoid. What can he conclude about $\overline{AB}$ and $\overline{DC}$?
2. Using a protractor, Kendall measures $\angle ADF$ as 81° and $\angle DFA$ as 66°. He wants to know the angle at which he should turn his car as he goes from *C* to *A* to *D*. Explain how he can find the measure of $\angle CAD$ without using a protractor. Then find the angle measure.
3. Triangle *DEC* is equilateral. How long is the section of the course from *E* to *D*?
4. $\overline{AC}$ is congruent to $\overline{DB}$, and $\overline{AC}$ is 33 feet long. What is the total length of the course?
5. Kendall's car moves at about 10 feet per second. Estimate the time it will take his car to complete the course.

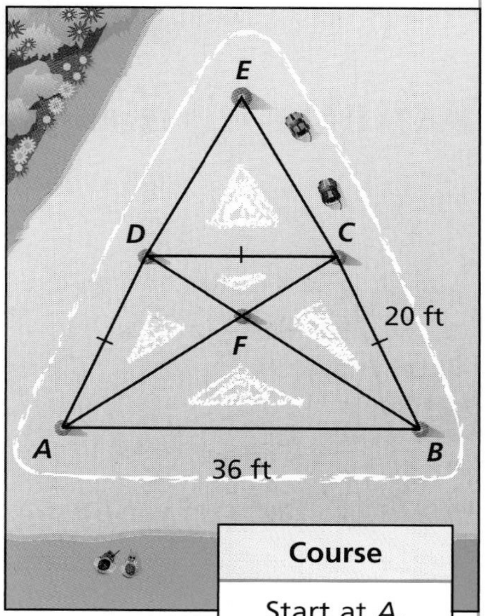

Course
Start at *A*.
A to *B*
B to *C*
C to *A*
A to *D*
D to *C*
C to *E*
E to *D*
D to *B*
End at *B*.

EXTENSION Dilations

Learn to explore similar figures through dilations.

Vocabulary
dilation

You can use computer software to *dilate* an image, such as a photograph. A **dilation** is a transformation that changes the size, but not the shape, of a figure. After a dilation, the image of a figure is similar to the original figure.

EXAMPLE 1 Identifying Dilations

Tell whether each transformation is a dilation.

Remember!
Similar figures have the same shape but not necessarily the same size.

A

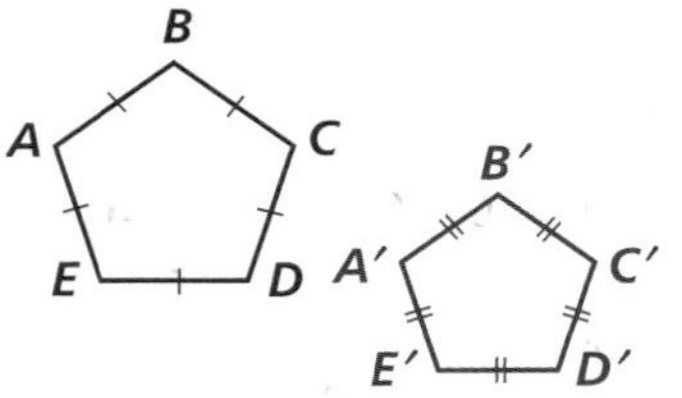

The figures are similar, so the transformation is a dilation.

B

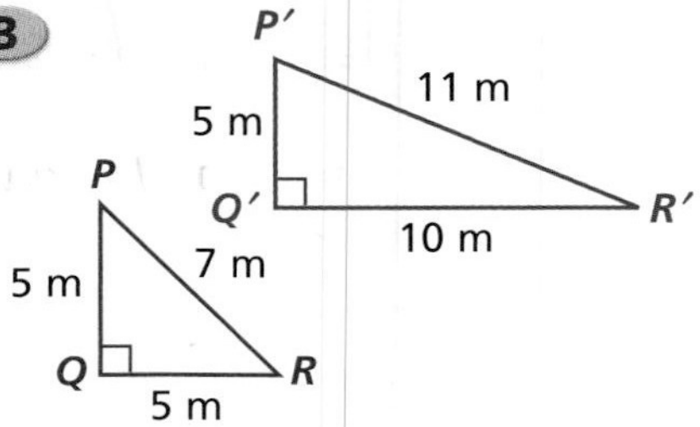

The figures are not similar, so the transformation is not a dilation.

A dilation enlarges or reduces a figure. The scale factor tells you how much the figure is enlarged or reduced. On a coordinate plane, you can find the image of a figure after a dilation by multiplying the coordinates of the vertices by the scale factor.

EXAMPLE 2 Using a Dilation to Enlarge a Figure

Draw the image of $\triangle ABC$ after a dilation by a scale factor of 2.

Write the coordinates of the vertices of $\triangle ABC$. Then multiply the coordinates by 2 to find the coordinates of the vertices of $\triangle A'B'C'$.

$A(1, 3) \rightarrow A'(1 \cdot 2, 3 \cdot 2) = A'(2, 6)$

$B(4, 3) \rightarrow B'(4 \cdot 2, 3 \cdot 2) = B'(8, 6)$

$C(4, 1) \rightarrow C'(4 \cdot 2, 1 \cdot 2) = C'(8, 2)$

Plot A', B', and C' and draw $\triangle A'B'C'$.

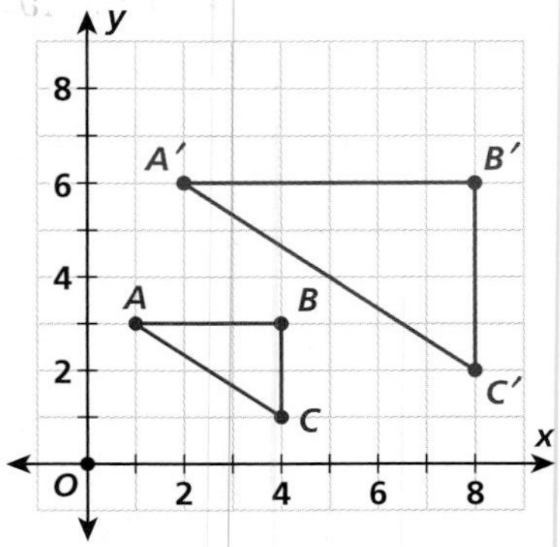

EXAMPLE 3 Using a Dilation to Reduce a Figure

Draw the image of $\triangle DEF$ after a dilation by a scale factor of $\frac{1}{3}$.

Write the coordinates of the vertices of $\triangle DEF$. Then multiply the coordinates by $\frac{1}{3}$ to find the coordinates of the vertices of $\triangle D'E'F'$.

$D(3, 3) \rightarrow D'(3 \cdot \frac{1}{3}, 3 \cdot \frac{1}{3}) = D'(1, 1)$

$E(9, 6) \rightarrow E'(9 \cdot \frac{1}{3}, 6 \cdot \frac{1}{3}) = E'(3, 2)$

$F(6, 0) \rightarrow F'(6 \cdot \frac{1}{3}, 0 \cdot \frac{1}{3}) = F'(2, 0)$

Plot D', E', and F' and draw $\triangle D'E'F'$.

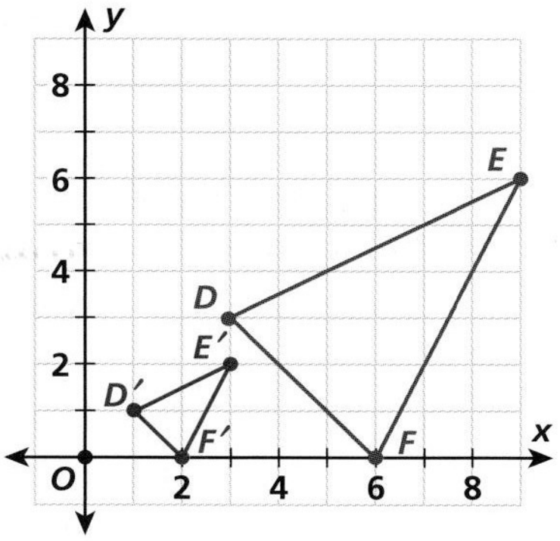

EXTENSION Exercises

Tell whether each transformation is a dilation.

1.

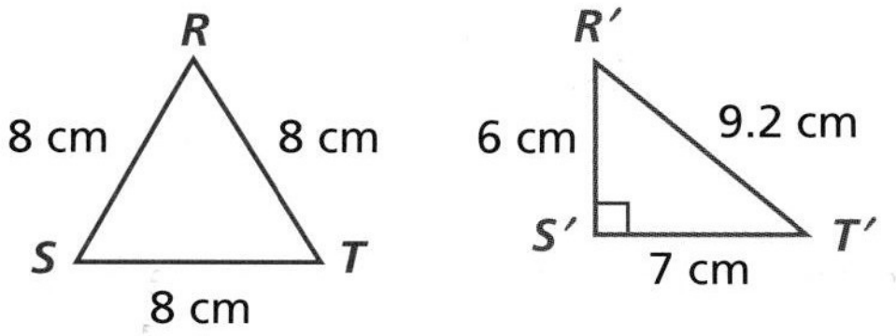

2.

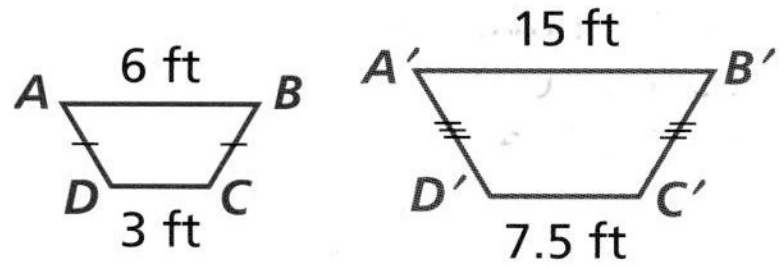

Draw the image of each figure after a dilation by the given scale factor.

3. scale factor 3

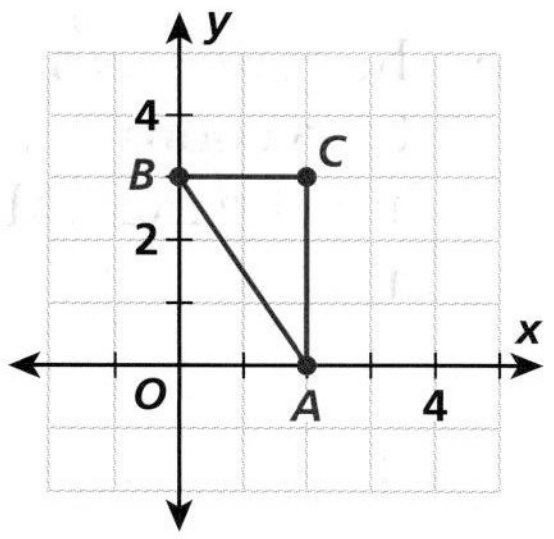

4. scale factor 2

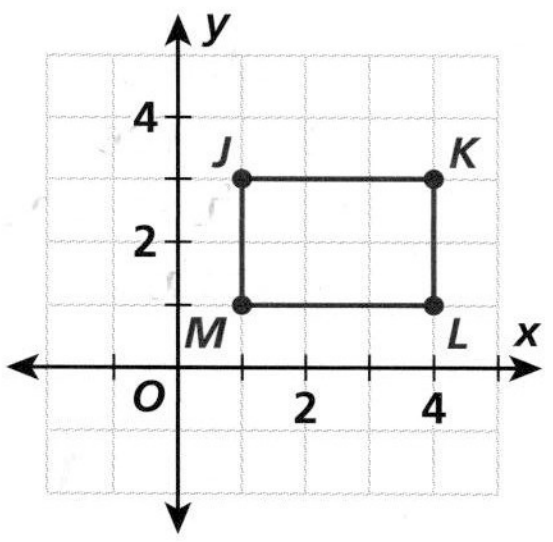

5. scale factor $\frac{1}{2}$

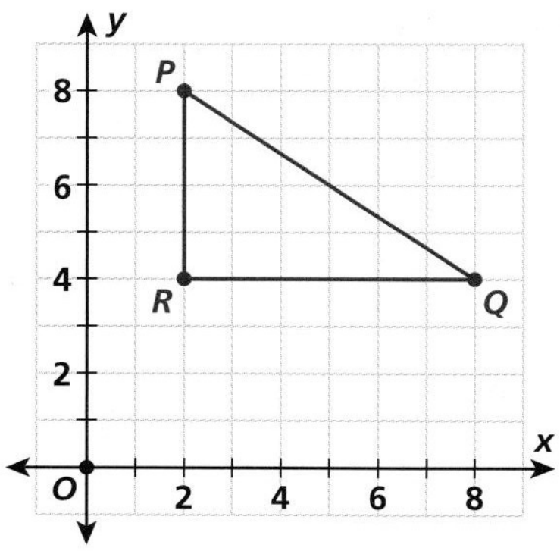

6. scale factor $\frac{1}{3}$

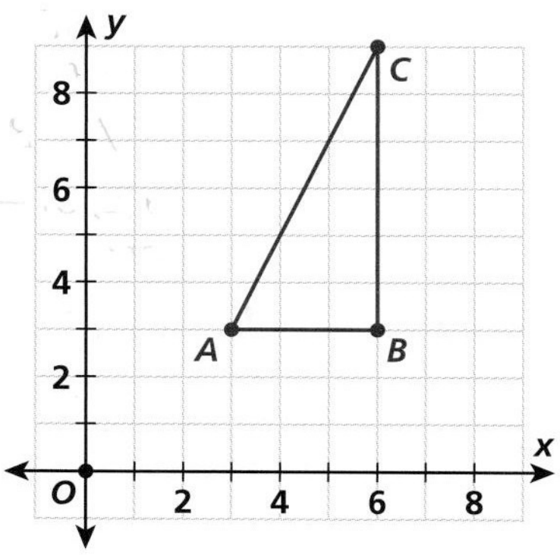

Game Time

Networks

A network is a figure that uses vertices and segments to show how objects are connected. You can use a network to show distances between cities. In the network at right, the vertices identify four cities in North Carolina, and the segments show the distances in miles between the cities.

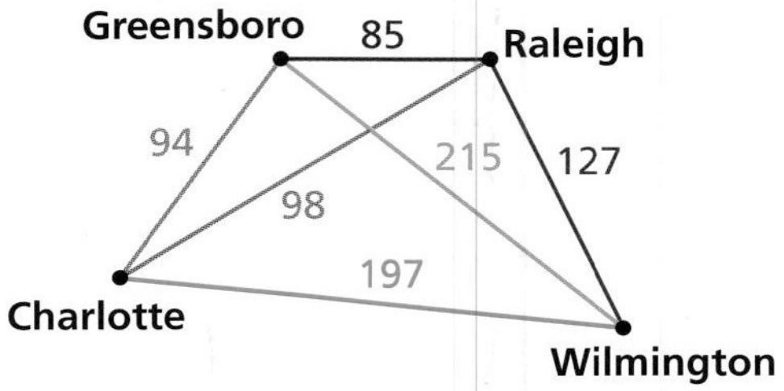

You can use the network to find the shortest route from Charlotte to the other three cities and back to Charlotte. First find all the possible routes. Then find the distance in miles for each route. One route has been identified below.

CGRWC $94 + 85 + 127 + 197 = 503$

Which is the shortest route, and what is the distance?

Color Craze

You can use rhombus-shaped tiles to build a variety of polygons. Each side of a tile is a different color. Build each design by matching the same-colored sides of tiles. Then see if you can create your own designs with the tiles. Try to make designs that have line or rotational symmetry.

A complete set of tiles is available online.

go.hrw.com
Game Time Extra
KEYWORD: MS7 Games

FOLDNOTES

It's in the Bag!

Materials
- 6 sheets of construction paper
- card stock
- scissors
- hole punch
- 4 electrical ties
- white paper
- markers

PROJECT Brochure Book of Geometric Figures

Make an organizer to hold brochures that summarize each lesson of the chapter.

Directions

1. Start with sheets of construction paper that are 12 inches by 18 inches. Fold one sheet in half to make it 12 inches by 9 inches and then in half again to make it 6 inches by 9 inches. **Figure A**

2. Hold the paper with the folds at the bottom and on the right-hand side. Turn the top left-hand corner back and under to form a pocket. **Figure B**

3. Turn the whole thing over and fold the top right-hand corner back and under to form a pocket. Repeat steps 1–3 with the other sheets of construction paper.

4. Cut out two pieces of card stock that are 6 inches by 9 inches. Punch four equally spaced holes down the length of each piece. Similarly, punch four equally spaced holes on each pocket as shown. **Figure C**

5. Stack the six pockets and put the card stock covers on the front and back of the stack. Insert electrical ties into the holes to hold everything together.

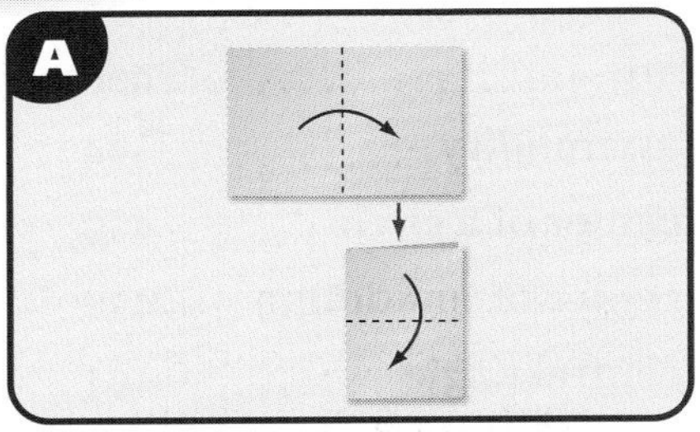

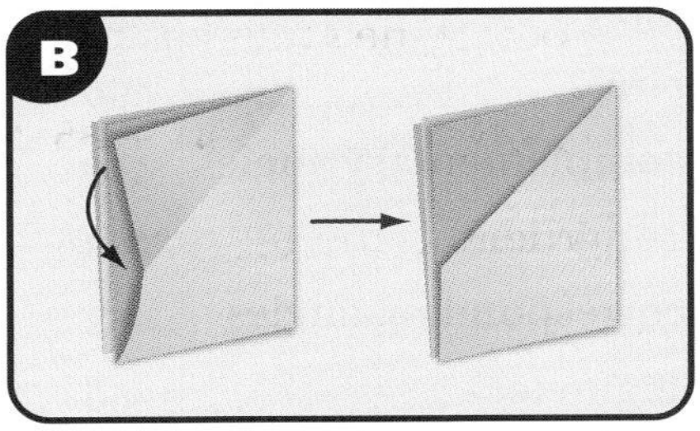

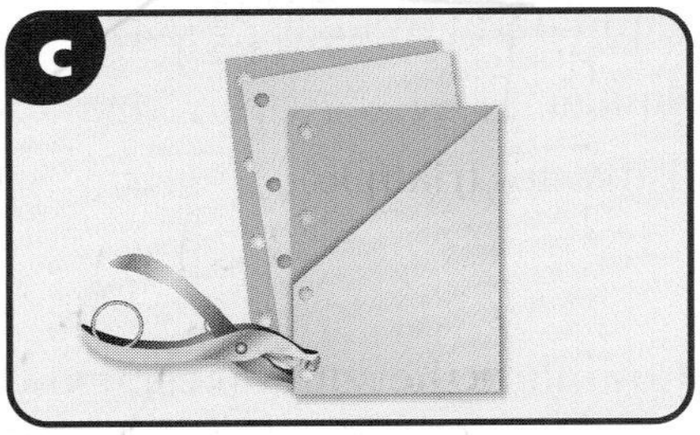

Taking Note of the Math

Fold sheets of plain white paper into thirds like a brochure. Use the brochures to take notes on the lessons of the chapter. Store the brochures in the pockets of your organizer.

CHAPTER 8 Study Guide: Review

Vocabulary

acute angle 448
acute triangle 470
adjacent angles 453
angle 448
arc 460
asymmetry 494
center of a circle 460
center of rotation 495
central angle 461
chord 460
circle 460
complementary angles . 448
congruent 443
corresponding angles . . 453
diameter 460
equilateral triangle 470
image 488
isosceles triangle 470
line 442
line of reflection 488
line of symmetry 494
line segment 443
line symmetry 494
obtuse angle 448
obtuse triangle 470
parallel lines 452
parallelogram 474
perpendicular lines 452
plane 442
point 442
polygon 466
radius 460
ray 443
rectangle 474
reflection 488
regular polygon 467
rhombus 474
right angle 448
right triangle 470
rotation 488
rotational symmetry . . . 495
scalene triangle 470
sector 461
Side-Side-Side Rule 484
skew lines 452
square 474
straight angle 448
supplementary angles . 448
transformation 488
translation 488
transversal 453
trapezoid 474
vertex 448
vertical angles 453

Complete the sentences below with vocabulary words from the list above.

1. Every equilateral triangle is also a(n) __?__ triangle.
2. Lines in the same plane that do not intersect are __?__.
3. A line segment whose endpoints are any two points on a circle is a(n) __?__.

8-1 Building Blocks of Geometry (pp. 442–445)

EXAMPLE

Identify the figures in the diagram.

- points: A, B, C
- lines: $\overleftrightarrow{AB}$
- planes: ABC
- rays: $\overrightarrow{BA}; \overrightarrow{AB}$
- line segments: $\overline{AB}; \overline{BC}$

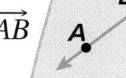

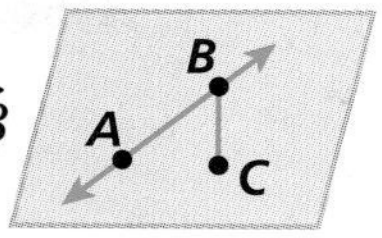

EXERCISES

Identify the figures in the diagram.

4. points
5. lines
6. planes
7. rays
8. line segments

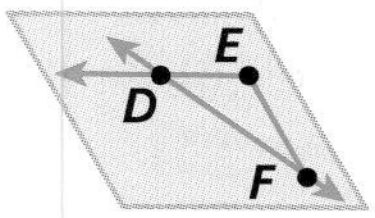

8-2 Classifying Angles (pp. 448–451)

EXAMPLE

- **Tell whether the angle is acute, right, obtuse, or straight.**

The angle is a right angle.

EXERCISES

Tell whether each angle is acute, right, obtuse, or straight.

9. 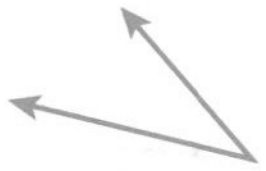

10. 

8-3 Angle Relationships (pp. 452–455)

EXAMPLE

- **Tell whether the lines appear parallel, perpendicular, or skew.**

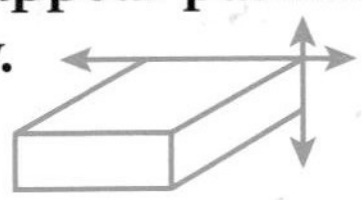

perpendicular

EXERCISES

Tell whether the lines appear parallel, perpendicular, or skew.

11. 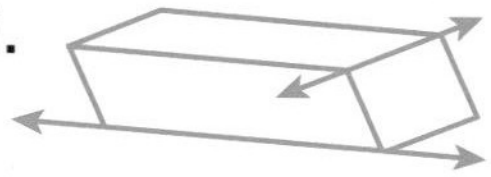

12. 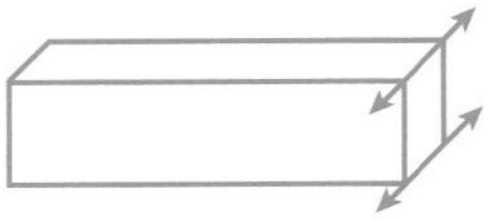

8-4 Properties of Circles (pp. 460–463)

EXAMPLE

Name the parts of circle *D*.

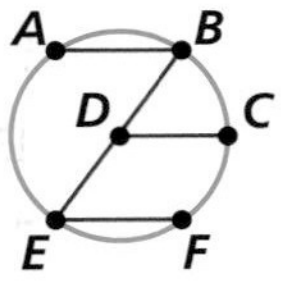

- radii: $\overline{DB}, \overline{DC}, \overline{DE}$
- diameter: $\overline{EB}$
- chords: $\overline{AB}, \overline{EB}, \overline{EF}$

EXERCISES

Name the parts of circle *F*.

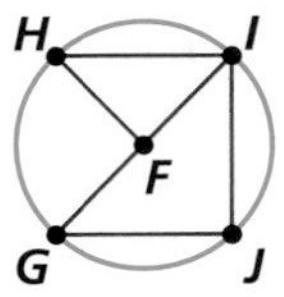

13. radii

14. diameter

15. chords

8-5 Classifying Polygons (pp. 466–469)

EXAMPLE

- **Tell whether the figure is a regular polygon. If it is not, explain why not.**
  No, all the angles in the polygon are not congruent.

EXERCISES

Tell whether each figure is a regular polygon. If it is not, explain why not.

16. 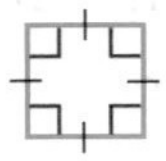

17. 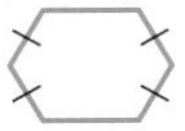

8-6 Classifying Triangles (pp. 470–473)

EXAMPLE

- **Classify the triangle according to its sides and angles.**

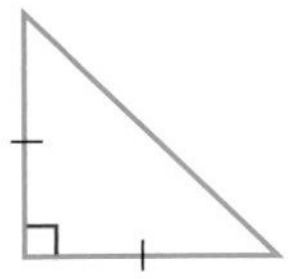

Isosceles right

EXERCISES

Classify each triangle according to its sides and angles.

18. 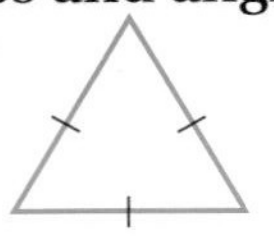

19. 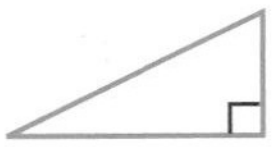

8-7 Classifying Quadrilaterals (pp. 474–477)

EXAMPLE

- **Give all of the names that apply to the quadrilateral.**

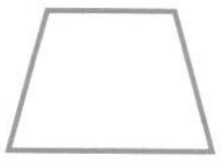

trapezoid

EXERCISES

Give all of the names that apply to each quadrilateral.

20. 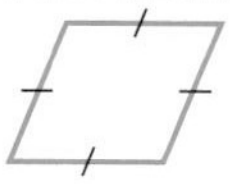

21. 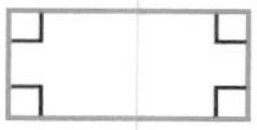

8-8 Angles in Polygons (pp. 478–481)

EXAMPLE

- **Find the measure of the unknown angle.**

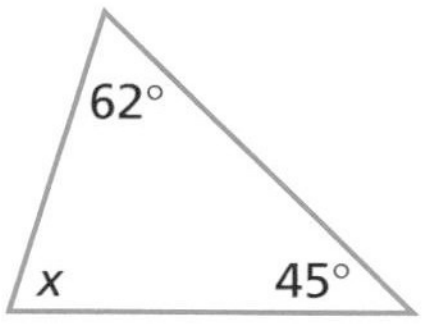

$62° + 45° + x = 180°$

$107° + x = 180°$

$x = 73°$

EXERCISES

Find the measure of the unknown angle.

22. 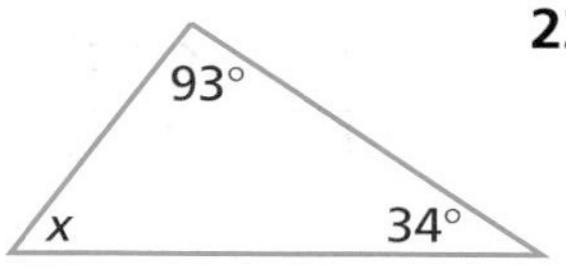

23. 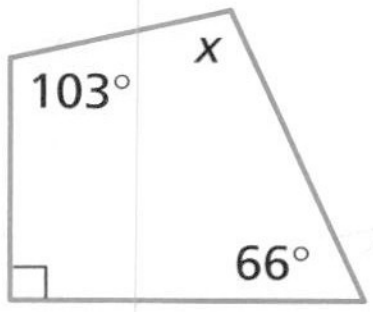

8-9 Congruent Figures (pp. 484–487)

EXAMPLE

- **Determine the missing measure in the set of congruent polygons.**

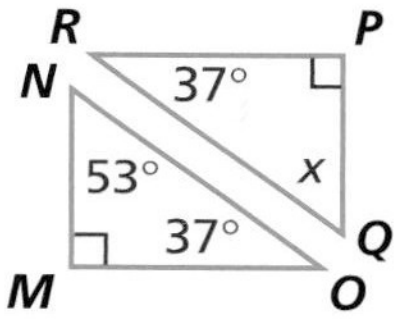

The angle measures 53°.

EXERCISES

24. Determine the missing measure in the set of congruent polygons.

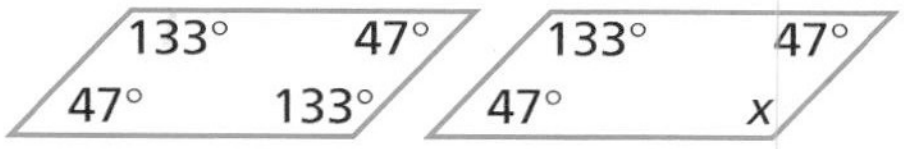

8-10 Translations, Reflections, and Rotations (pp. 488–492)

EXAMPLE

- **Graph the translation.**

Translate △*ABC* 1 unit right and 3 units down.

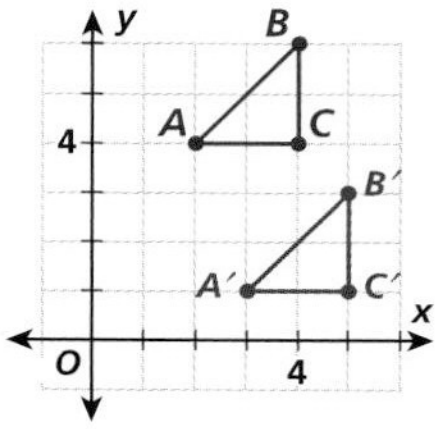

EXERCISES

Graph the translation.

25. Translate △*BCD* 2 units left and 4 units down.

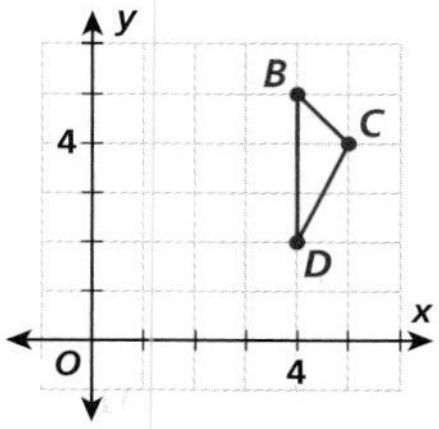

8-11 Symmetry (pp. 494–497)

EXAMPLE

- **Find all the lines of symmetry in the flag.**

The flag has four lines of symmetry.

EXERCISES

26. Find all the lines of symmetry in the flag.

CHAPTER TEST

Identify the figures in the diagram.

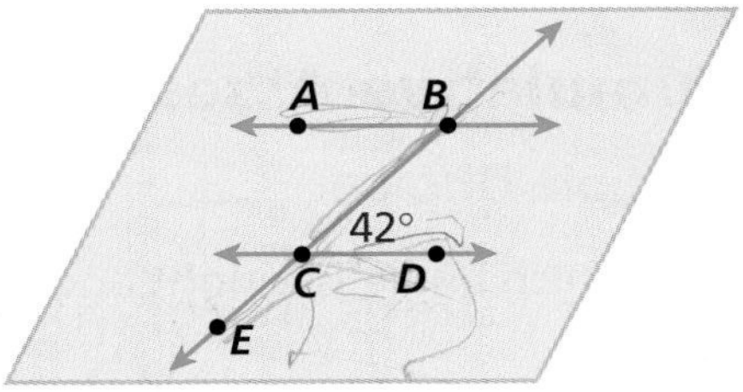

1. 4 points
2. 3 lines
3. a plane
4. 5 line segments
5. 6 rays

Line *AB* || line *CD* in the diagram. Find the measure of each angle and tell whether the angle is acute, right, obtuse, or straight.

6. $\angle ABC$
7. $\angle BCE$
8. $\angle DCE$

Tell whether the lines appear parallel, perpendicular, or skew.

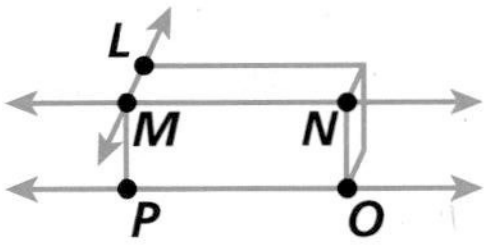

9. $\overleftrightarrow{MN}$ and $\overleftrightarrow{PO}$
10. $\overleftrightarrow{LM}$ and $\overleftrightarrow{PO}$
11. $\overleftrightarrow{NO}$ and $\overleftrightarrow{MN}$

Name the parts of circle *E*.

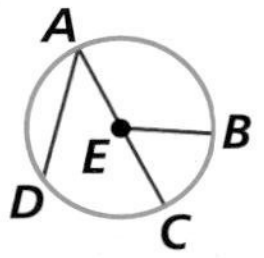

12. radii
13. chords
14. diameter

Tell whether each figure is a regular polygon. If it is not, explain why not.

15. 
16. 
17. 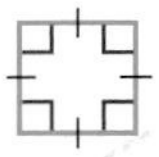

Classify each triangle according to its sides and angles.

18. 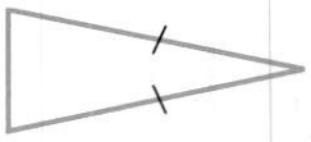
19. 
20. 

Give all the names that apply to each quadrilateral.

21. 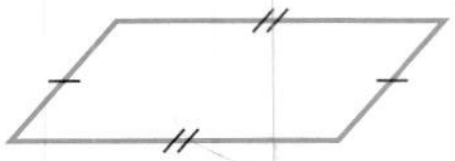
22. 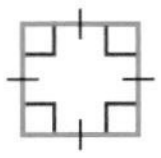
23. 

Find the measure of each unknown angle.

24. 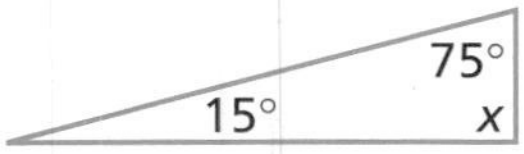

25. 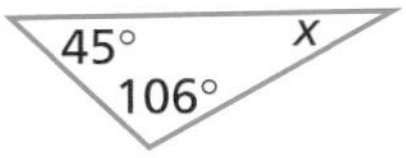

26. 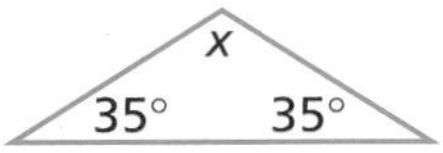

27. Determine the missing measure in the congruent polygons.

28. The vertices of a triangle have the coordinates $A(-1, -3)$, $B(-4, -1)$, and $C(-1, -1)$. Graph the triangle after a translation 3 units left.

Find all the lines of symmetry in each flag.

29. 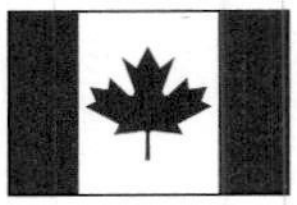
30. 

STANDARDIZED TEST PREP

Cumulative Assessment, Chapters 1–8

Multiple Choice

1. Which angle is a right angle?

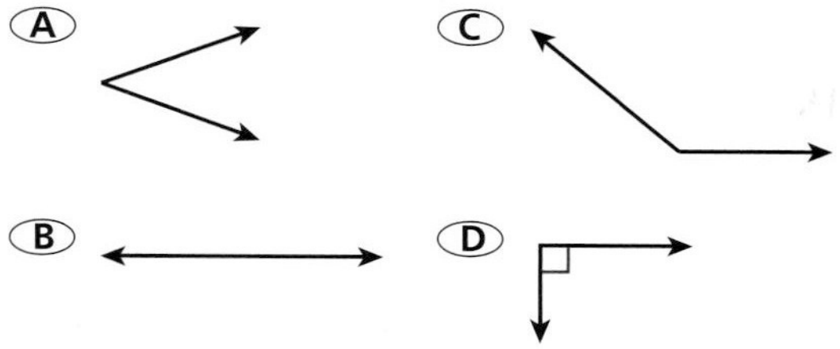

2. What is the number 8,330,000,000 written in scientific notation?

   F 0.83×10^{10} H 83.3×10^{8}
   G 8.33×10^{9} J 833×10^{7}

3. If point *A* is translated 5 units left and 2 units up, what will point *A*'s new coordinates be?

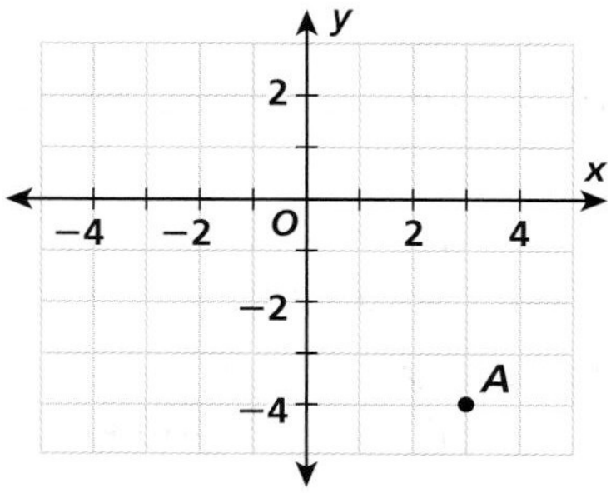

   A (−2, −2) C (−2, −6)
   B (8, −2) D (0, 1)

4. Nolan spent $\frac{1}{2}$ hour traveling to his orthodontist appointment, $\frac{3}{5}$ hour at his appointment, and $\frac{3}{4}$ hour traveling home. What is the total amount of time Nolan spent for this appointment?

   F $\frac{7}{11}$ hour H $1\frac{17}{20}$ hours
   G $\frac{37}{60}$ hour J $\frac{13}{5}$ hours

5. A store sells two dozen rolls of toilet paper for $4.84. What is the unit rate for one roll of toilet paper?

   A $0.13/roll of toilet paper
   B $0.20/roll of toilet paper
   C $0.40/roll of toilet paper
   D $1.21/roll of toilet paper

6. Which of the following best describes the triangle below?

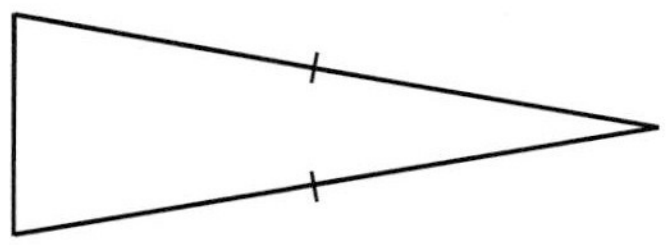

   F Acute isosceles triangle
   G Equilateral triangle
   H Obtuse right triangle
   J Obtuse scalene triangle

7. Which expression represents "twice the difference of a number and 8"?

   A $2(x + 8)$ C $2(x - 8)$
   B $2x - 8$ D $2x + 8$

8. For which equation is $x = 1$ NOT the solution?

   F $3x + 8 = 11$
   G $8 - x = 9$
   H $-3x + 8 = 5$
   J $8 + x = 9$

9. Which ratios form a proportion?

   A $\frac{4}{8}$ and $\frac{3}{6}$ C $\frac{4}{10}$ and $\frac{6}{16}$
   B $\frac{4}{12}$ and $\frac{6}{15}$ D $\frac{2}{3}$ and $\frac{5}{8}$

10. The graph shows how Amy spends her earnings each month. Amy earned $100 in May. How much did she spend on transportation and clothing combined?

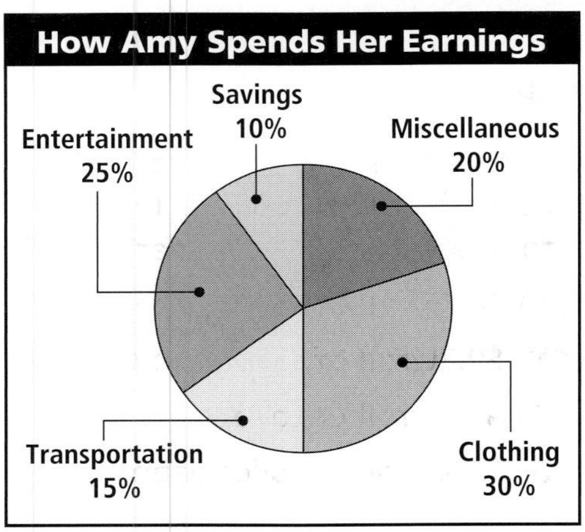

(F) $15
(G) $30
(H) $45
(J) $55

Once you have answered a short- or extended-response question, check to make sure you have answered all parts of the question.

Gridded Response

11. What is the unknown angle measure in degrees?

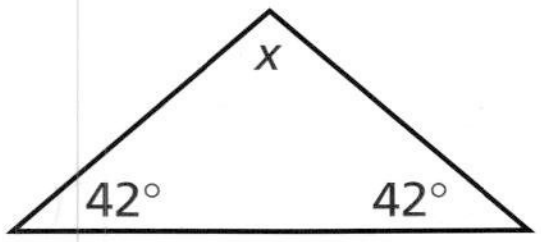

12. A figure has vertices $A(-4, -4)$, $B(-3, -2)$, and $C(-3, -6)$. What will the x-coordinate of point A' be after the figure is reflected across the y-axis?

13. An antiques dealer bought a chair for $85. The dealer sold the chair at her shop for 45% more than what she paid. To the nearest whole dollar, what was the price of the chair?

14. What is the value of the expression $-4x^2y - y$ for $x = -2$ and $y = -5$?

Short Response

15. Triangle ABC, with vertices $A(2, 3)$, $B(4, 0)$, and $C(0, 0)$, is translated 2 units left and 6 units down to form triangle $A'B'C'$.
    a. On a coordinate plane, draw and label triangle ABC and triangle $A'B'C'$.
    b. Give the coordinates of the vertices of triangle $A'B'C'$.

16. Taylor's goal is to spend less than 35% of her allowance each month on cell phone bills. Last month, Taylor spent $45 on cell phone bills. If she gets $120 each month as her allowance, did she achieve her goal? Explain your answer.

17. Consider the sequence 4, 8, 12, 16, 20, ...
    a. Write a rule for the sequence. Use n to represent the position of the term in the sequence.
    b. What is the 8th term in the sequence?

Extended Response

18. Four of the angles in a pentagon measure 74°, 111°, 145°, and 95°.
    a. How many sides and how many angles does a pentagon have?
    b. Is the pentagon a regular pentagon? How do you know?
    c. What is the sum of the angle measures of a pentagon? Include a drawing as part of your answer.
    d. Write and solve an equation to determine the missing angle measure of the pentagon.

Problem Solving on Location

PENNSYLVANIA

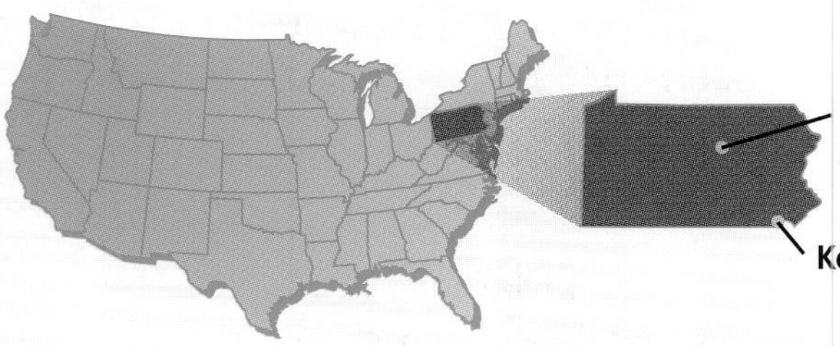

The Little League World Series

In 1938, Carl Stoltz created a baseball league for children in his hometown of Williamsport, Pennsylvania. A year later, the first Little League baseball game was played. Today, Williamsport remains the site of the annual Little League World Series, an event that attracts the best teams from around the globe.

Choose one or more strategies to solve each problem.

1. The Little League World Series features 8 teams from the United States and 8 teams from other countries. In the championship game, a U.S. team plays against one of the teams from another country. How many different matchups are possible?

For 2, use the graph.

2. Use the following information to determine which team won the championship in 2004.
   - The team that won the championship in 2004 won 5% of the championships from 1985 to 2004.
   - Mexico won the championship in 1997.
   - The team that won the championship in 2004 was not from Asia.

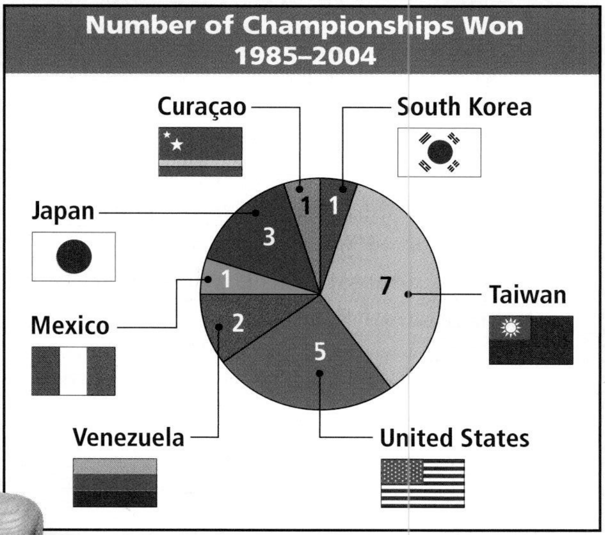

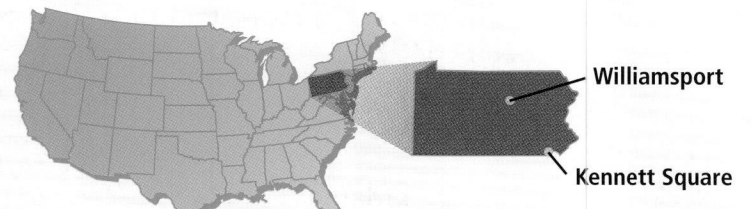

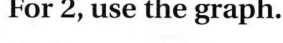

Problem Solving Strategies

- Draw a Diagram
- Make a Model
- Guess and Test
- Work Backward
- Find a Pattern
- Make a Table
- Solve a Simpler Problem
- Use Logical Reasoning
- Act It Out
- Make an Organized List

Longwood Gardens

Longwood Gardens in Kennett Square, Pennsylvania, is one of the largest display gardens in the world. With 20 outdoor gardens, 20 indoor gardens, and more than 11,000 varieties of plants, it's not surprising that the site attracts nearly one million visitors per year.

Choose one or more strategies to solve each problem.

1. The Italian Water Garden has 18 blue-tiled pools. The ratio of small pools to large pools is 2:1. How many of each size pool are there?
2. The garden's square fountain is 30 feet long on each side. A gardener plants tulip bulbs 6 inches apart around the edge of the fountain. How many bulbs does the gardener plant?

For 3, use the graph.

3. New information cards are being printed for the plants shown in the graph. Each card can hold information about 7 varieties of plants at most. Different types of plants (for example, water lilies and lilacs) cannot be mixed on a single card. How many cards will need to be printed?

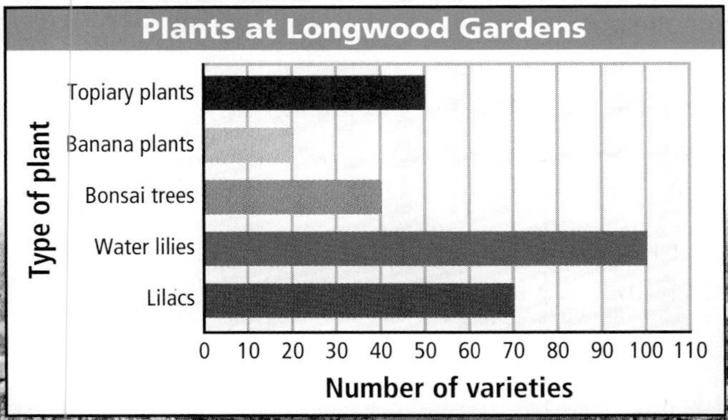

CHAPTER 9

Measurement: Two-Dimensional Figures

go.hrw.com
Chapter Project Online
KEYWORD: MS7 Ch9

Florida Tropical Fruit Tree Inventory

Tree Type	Number of Trees	Number of Trees per Acre
Grapefruit	14,751,000	181
Lemon	178,800	173
Lime	502,400	159
Orange	84,200,000	128

Career *Fruit Tree Grower*

Growing fruit trees requires diverse knowledge and skills. A fruit tree grower needs to know how to prepare soil, plant and care for trees, and guard the trees against insects and diseases.

To be successful, a fruit tree grower must also try to maximize the size and quantity of the fruit produced. Growers measure their land to determine the number of trees to plant and where each tree should be planted. The table shows the number and distribution of certain types of fruit trees in Florida.

ARE YOU READY?

Vocabulary

Choose the best term from the list to complete each sentence.

diameter
parallelogram
radius
right triangle
trapezoid

1. A(n) __?__ is a quadrilateral with exactly one pair of parallel sides.
2. A(n) __?__ is a four-sided figure with opposite sides that are congruent and parallel.
3. The __?__ of a circle is one-half the __?__ of the circle.

Complete these exercises to review skills you will need for this chapter.

Round Whole Numbers

Round each number to the nearest ten and nearest hundred.

4. 1,535 **5.** 294 **6.** 30,758 **7.** 497

Round Decimals

Round each number to the nearest whole number and nearest tenth.

8. 6.18 **9.** 10.50 **10.** 513.93 **11.** 29.06

Multiply with Decimals

Multiply.

12. $5.63 \cdot 8$ **13.** $9.67 \cdot 4.3$ **14.** $8.34 \cdot 16$ **15.** $6.08 \cdot 0.56$

16. $0.82 \cdot 21$ **17.** $2.74 \cdot 6.6$ **18.** $40 \cdot 9.54$ **19.** $0.33 \cdot 0.08$

Order of Operations

Simplify each expression.

20. $2 \cdot 9 + 2 \cdot 6$ **21.** $2(15 + 8)$ **22.** $4 \cdot 6.8 + 7 \cdot 9.3$

23. $14(25.9 + 13.6)$ **24.** $(27.3 + 0.7) \div 2^2$ **25.** $5 \cdot 3^3 - 8.02$

26. $(63 \div 7) \cdot 4^2$ **27.** $1.1 + 3 \cdot 4.3$ **28.** $66 \cdot [5 + (3 + 3)^2]$

Identify Polygons

Name each figure.

29. 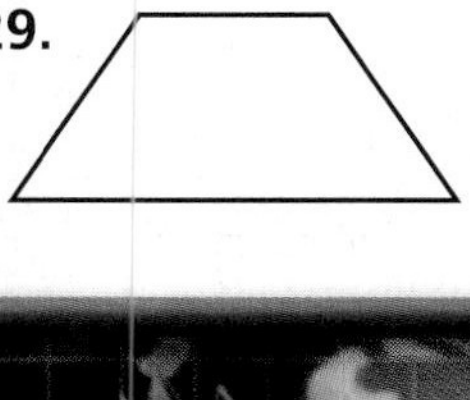

30. 

31. 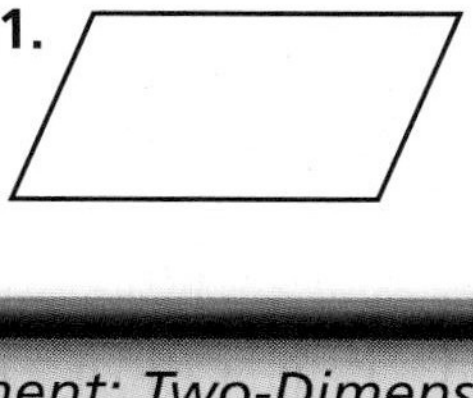

CHAPTER 9

Study Guide: Preview

Where You've Been

Previously, you

- found the perimeter or circumference of geometric figures.
- explored customary and metric units of measure.
- used proportions to convert measurements within the customary system and within the metric system.

In This Chapter

You will study

- comparing perimeter and circumference with the area of geometric figures.
- finding the area of parallelograms, triangles, trapezoids, and circles.
- finding the area of irregular figures.
- using powers, roots, and the Pythagorean Theorem to find missing measures.

Where You're Going

You can use the skills learned in this chapter

- to create an architectural floor plan.
- to design a building access ramp that meets government regulations.

Key Vocabulary/Vocabulario

area	área
circumference	circunferencia
hypotenuse	hipotenusa
perfect square	cuadrado perfecto
perimeter	perímetro
Pythagorean Theorem	teorema de Pitágoras
significant digits	dígitos significativos
square root	raíz cuadrada

Vocabulary Connections

To become familiar with some of the vocabulary terms in the chapter, consider the following. You may refer to the chapter, the glossary, or a dictionary if you like.

1. The *square root* of a number is one of the two equal factors of the number. For example, 3 is a square root because $3 \cdot 3 = 9$. How might picturing plant roots help you remember the meaning of **square root** ?
2. The word *perimeter* comes from the Greek roots *peri,* meaning "all around," and *metron,* meaning "measure." What do the Greek roots tell you about the **perimeter** of a geometric figure?
3. To *square a number* means "to multiply the number by itself," as in $2 \cdot 2$. Keeping this idea of *square* in mind, what do you think a **perfect square** might be?
4. The word *circumference* comes from the Latin word *circumferre,* meaning "to carry around." How does the Latin meaning help you define the **circumference** of a circle?

Reading and Writing Math

Reading Strategy: Read and Interpret Graphics

Figures, diagrams, tables, and graphs provide important data. Knowing how to read these graphics will help you understand and solve related problems.

Similar Figures

$\triangle ABC$ and $\triangle JKL$ are similar.

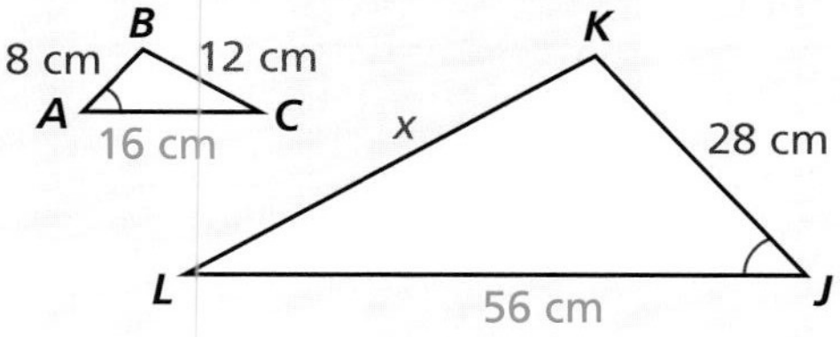

How to Read

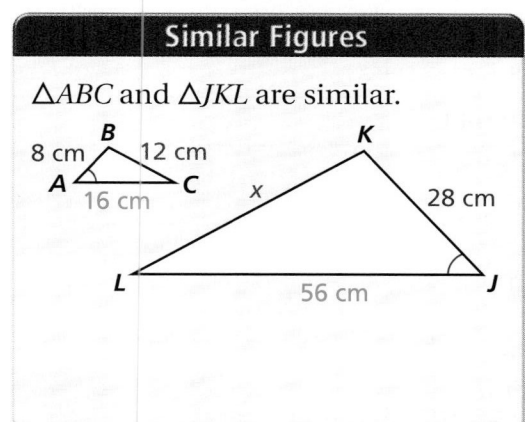

Read all labels.
$AB = 8$ cm; $AC = 16$ cm; $BC = 12$ cm; $JK = 28$ cm; $JL = 56$ cm; $KL = x$ cm; $\angle A$ corresponds to $\angle J$.

Be careful about what you assume.
You may think $\overline{AB}$ corresponds to $\overline{LK}$, but this is not so. Since $\angle A$ corresponds to $\angle J$, you know $\overline{AB}$ corresponds to $\overline{JK}$.

Double-Bar Graph

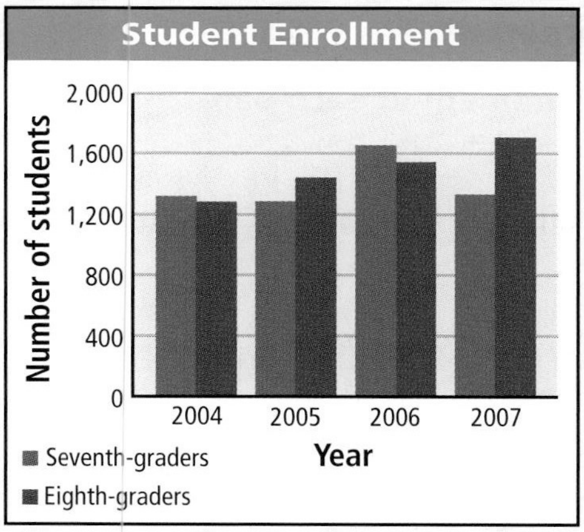

How to Read

Read the title of the graph and any special notes.
Blue indicates seventh-graders. Purple indicates eighth-graders.

Read each axis label and note the intervals of each scale.
***x*-axis**—year increases by 1.
***y*-axis**—enrollment increases by 400 students.

Determine what information is presented.
student enrollment for seventh- and eighth-graders per year

Try This

Look up each graphic in your textbook and answer the following questions.

1. Lesson 5-7 Exercise 1: Which side of the smaller triangle corresponds to $\overline{BC}$? Can you assume that $\angle BAC$ and $\angle EDF$ are right angles? Explain.
2. Lesson 7-3 Example 1: By what interval does the x-axis scale increase? About how many people speak Hindi?

9-1 Accuracy and Precision

Learn to compare the precision of measurements and to determine acceptable levels of accuracy.

Vocabulary

precision

accuracy

significant digits

Ancient Greeks used measurements taken during lunar eclipses to determine that the Moon was 240,000 miles from Earth. In 1969, the distance was measured as 221,463 miles.

At the University of Texas McDonald Observatory, a laser is used to measure the distance from Earth to the Moon.

There is a difference between these measurements because modern scientists conducted the measurement with greater *precision*. **Precision** is the level of detail an instrument can measure.

The smaller the unit an instrument can measure, the more precise its measurements will be. For example, a millimeter ruler has greater precision than a centimeter ruler because it can measure smaller units.

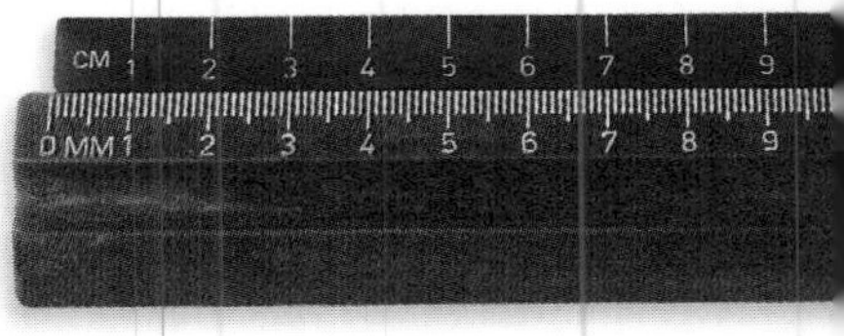

EXAMPLE 1 Judging Precision of Measurements

Choose the more precise measurement in each pair.

A **37 in., 3 ft**

Since an inch is a smaller unit than a foot, 37 in. is more precise.

B **5 km, 5.8 km**

Since tenths are smaller than ones, 5.8 km is more precise.

In the real world, no measurement is exact. The relative exactness of a measurement is its **accuracy**. In a measured value, all the digits that are known with certainty are called **significant digits**. Zeros at the end of a whole number are assumed to be nonsignificant. The table shows the rules for identifying significant digits.

Rule	Example	Number of Significant Digits
• Nonzero digits	45.7	3 significant digits
• Zeros between significant digits	78,002	5 significant digits
• Zeros after the last nonzero digit and to the right of a decimal point	0.0040	2 significant digits

EXAMPLE 2 Identifying Significant Digits

Determine the number of significant digits in each measurement.

A **120.1 mi**

The digits 1 and 2 are nonzero digits, and 0 is between two nonzero digits.

So 120.1 mi has 4 significant digits.

B **0.0350 kg**

The digits 3 and 5 are nonzero digits, and 0 is to the right of the decimal after the last nonzero digit.

So 0.0350 kg has 3 significant digits.

When you are adding and subtracting measurements, the answer should have the same number of digits to the right of the decimal point as the measurement with the least number of digits to the right of the decimal point.

EXAMPLE 3 Using Significant Digits in Addition or Subtraction

Calculate 45 mi − 0.9 mi. Use the correct number of significant digits in the answer.

45	*0 digits to the right of the decimal point*
$-\ 0.9$	*1 digit to the right of the decimal point*
$44.1 \approx 44$ mi	*Round the difference so that it has no digits to the right of the decimal point.*

When you are multiplying and dividing measurements, the answer must have the same number of significant digits as the measurement with the least number of significant digits.

EXAMPLE 4 Using Significant Digits in Multiplication or Division

Calculate 32.8 m · 1.5 m. Use the correct number of significant digits in the answer.

32.8	*3 significant digits*
$\times\ 1.5$	*2 significant digits*
$49.2 \approx 49\ m^2$	*Round the product so that it has 2 significant digits.*

Think and Discuss

1. Tell how many significant digits there are in 380.102.

2. Choose the more precise measurement: 18 oz or 1 lb. Explain.

9-1 Exercises

GUIDED PRACTICE

See Example 1
Choose the more precise measurement in each pair.

1. 4 ft, 1 yd **2.** 2 cm, 21 mm **3.** $5\frac{1}{2}$ in., $5\frac{1}{4}$ in.

See Example 2
Determine the number of significant digits in each measurement.

4. 2.703 g **5.** 0.02 km **6.** 28,000 lb

See Example 3
Calculate. Use the correct number of significant digits in each answer.

7. 16 − 3.8 **8.** 3.5 + 0.66 **9.** 11.3 − 4

See Example 4
10. 47.9 · 3.8 **11.** 7.0 · 3.6 **12.** 50.2 ÷ 8.0

INDEPENDENT PRACTICE

See Example 1
Choose the more precise measurement in each pair.

13. 11 in., 1 ft **14.** 7.2 m, 6.2 cm **15.** 14.2 km, 14 km

16. $4\frac{3}{8}$ in., $4\frac{7}{16}$ in. **17.** 2.8 m, 3 m **18.** 37 g, 37.0 g

See Example 2
Determine the number of significant digits in each measurement.

19. 0.00002 kg **20.** 10,000,000 lb **21.** 200.060 m

22. 4.003 L **23.** 0.230 cm **24.** 940.0 ft

See Example 3
Calculate. Use the correct number of significant digits in each answer.

25. 6.2 + 8.93 **26.** 7.02 + 15 **27.** 8 − 6.6

28. 29.1 − 13.204 **29.** 8.6 + 9.43 **30.** 43.5 + 876.23

See Example 4
31. 17 · 104 **32.** 21.8 · 10.9 **33.** 7.0 ÷ 3.11

34. 1,680 ÷ 5.025 **35.** 14.2 ÷ 0.05 **36.** 5.22 · 6.3

PRACTICE AND PROBLEM SOLVING

Extra Practice
See page 744.

Which unit is more precise?

37. foot or mile **38.** centimeter or millimeter

39. liter or milliliter **40.** minute or second

Calculate. Use the correct number of significant digits in each answer.

41. 38,000 · 4.8 **42.** 2.879 + 113.6 **43.** 290 − 6.1

44. 5.6 ÷ 0.6 **45.** 40.29 − 18.5 **46.** 24 ÷ 6.02

47. Multi-Step Jay estimates that he walks 15 miles each week. He walks 1.55 miles to school and then 0.4 miles to his aunt's house after school.

a. Is Jay's estimate reasonable? Explain.

b. How many miles does Jay walk during a 5-day school week? Use the correct number of significant digits in your answer.

Health LINK

The food labels at right give information about two types of soup: cream of tomato and minestrone. Use the labels for Exercises 48 and 49.

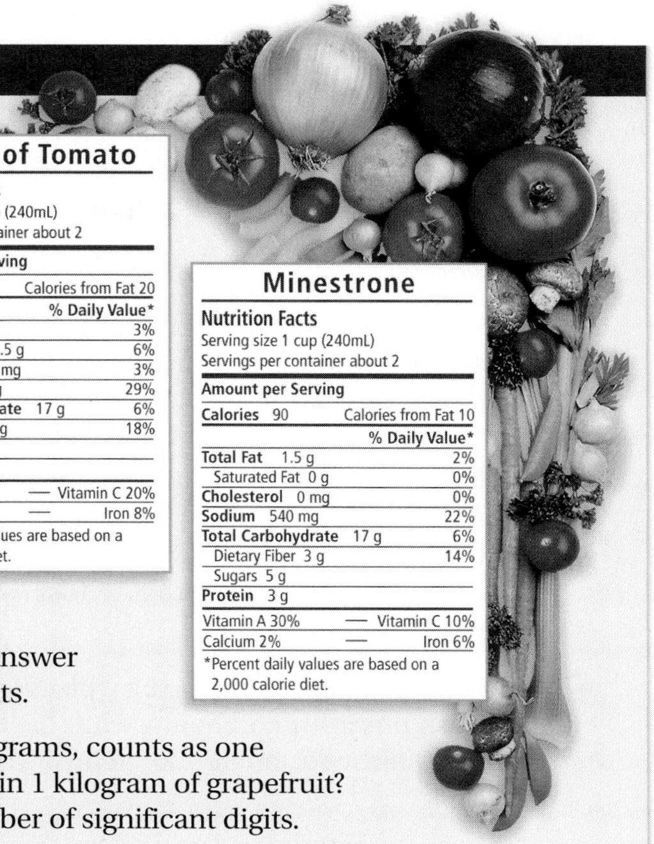

Cream of Tomato

Nutrition Facts	
Serving size 1 cup (240mL)	
Servings per container about 2	
Amount per Serving	
Calories 100	Calories from Fat 20
	% Daily Value*
Total Fat 2 g	3%
Saturated Fat 1.5 g	6%
Cholesterol 10 mg	3%
Sodium 690 mg	29%
Total Carbohydrate 17 g	6%
Dietary Fiber 4 g	18%
Sugars 11 g	
Protein 2 g	
Vitamin A 20% — Vitamin C 20%	
Calcium 0% — Iron 8%	
*Percent daily values are based on a 2,000 calorie diet.	

Minestrone

Nutrition Facts	
Serving size 1 cup (240mL)	
Servings per container about 2	
Amount per Serving	
Calories 90	Calories from Fat 10
	% Daily Value*
Total Fat 1.5 g	2%
Saturated Fat 0 g	0%
Cholesterol 0 mg	0%
Sodium 540 mg	22%
Total Carbohydrate 17 g	6%
Dietary Fiber 3 g	14%
Sugars 5 g	
Protein 3 g	
Vitamin A 30% — Vitamin C 10%	
Calcium 2% — Iron 6%	
*Percent daily values are based on a 2,000 calorie diet.	

48. Which measurement is more precise, the total amount of fat in cream of tomato soup or the total amount in minestrone? Explain.

49. One serving of cream of tomato soup contains 29% of the recommended daily value of sodium for a 2,000-calorie diet. What is the recommended daily value for sodium, in milligrams? Express your answer with the appropriate number of significant digits.

50. One-half of a medium-sized grapefruit, or 154 grams, counts as one serving of fruit. How many servings of fruit are in 1 kilogram of grapefruit? Express your answer with the appropriate number of significant digits.

51. ★ **Challenge** The greatest possible error of any measurement is half of the smallest unit used in the measurement. For example, 1 pt of juice may actually measure between $\frac{1}{2}$ pt and $1\frac{1}{2}$ pt. What is the range of possible actual weights for a watermelon that was weighed at $19\frac{1}{4}$ lb?

Test Prep and Spiral Review

52. Multiple Choice Which is the most precise measurement?

Ⓐ 1 mile Ⓑ 1,758 yards Ⓒ 5,281 feet Ⓓ 63,355 inches

53. Multiple Choice Which measurement does NOT have three significant digits?

Ⓕ 63.2 cm Ⓖ 0.08 ft Ⓗ 0.00500 m Ⓙ 4.06 yd

For Exercises 54–56, tell whether you would expect a positive correlation, a negative correlation, or no correlation. (Lesson 7-8)

54. the price of a car and the number of windows it has

55. the speed a car travels and the amount of time it takes to go 100 miles

56. the price per gallon of gasoline and the cost for a tank of gas

Determine whether each figure is a polygon. If it is not, explain why. (Lesson 8-5)

57. 

58. 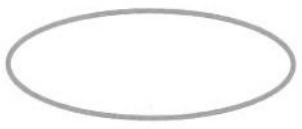

59. 

Hands-On LAB 9-2

Explore Perimeter & Circumference

Use with Lesson 9-2

go.hrw.com
Lab Resources Online
KEYWORD: MS7 Lab9

The distance around a figure is its perimeter. You can use a loop of string to explore the dimensions of a rectangle with a perimeter of 18 inches.

Activity 1

1. Cut a piece of string that is slightly longer than 18 inches. Tie the ends together to form an 18-inch loop.

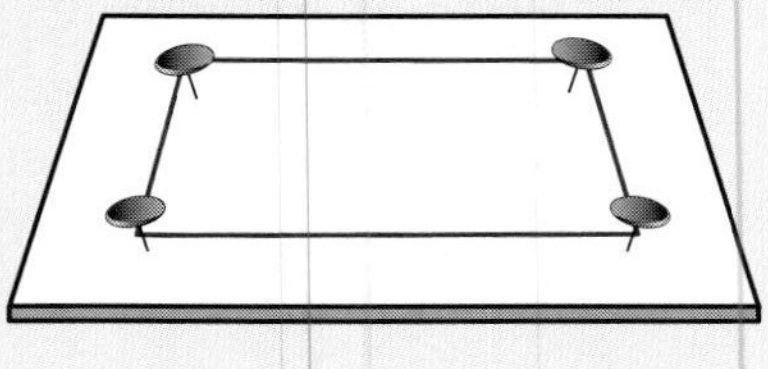

2. Make the loop into a rectangle by placing it around four push pins on a corkboard. Both the length and the width of the rectangle should be a whole number of inches.

3. Make different rectangles with whole-number lengths and widths. Record the lengths and widths in a table.

Length (in.)	1	2	3	■	■	■	■	■
Width (in.)	8	■	■	■	■	■	■	■

4. Graph the data in your table by plotting points on a coordinate plane like the one shown.

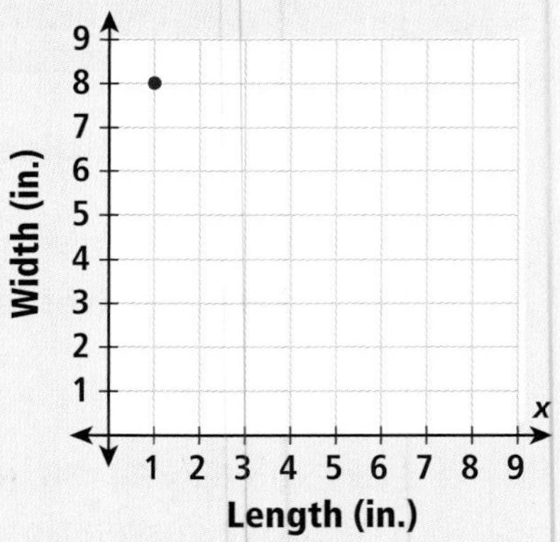

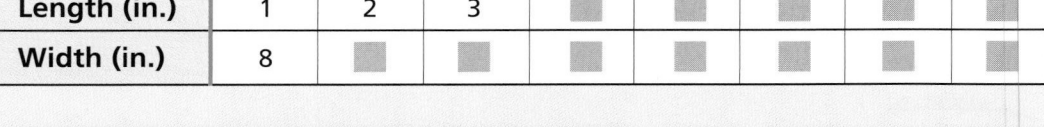

Think and Discuss

1. What pattern is made by the points on your graph?

2. How is the sum of the length and width of each rectangle related to the rectangle's perimeter of 18 inches?

3. Suppose a rectangle has length ℓ and width w. Write a rule that you can use to find the rectangle's perimeter.

Try This

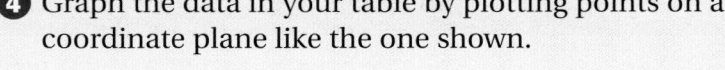

Use the rule you discovered to find the perimeter of each rectangle.

1.

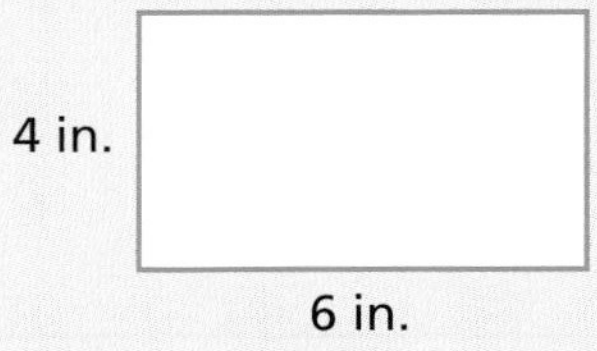

2.

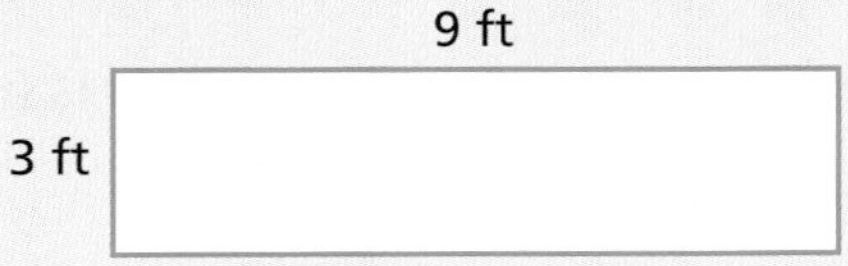

3.

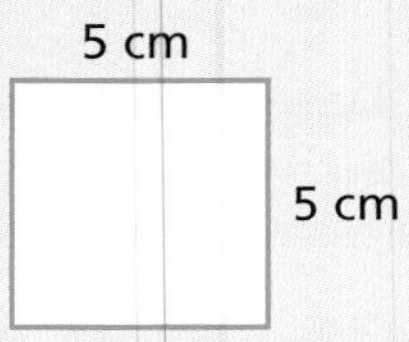

The perimeter of a circle is called the *circumference*. You can explore the relationship between a circle's circumference and its diameter by measuring some circles.

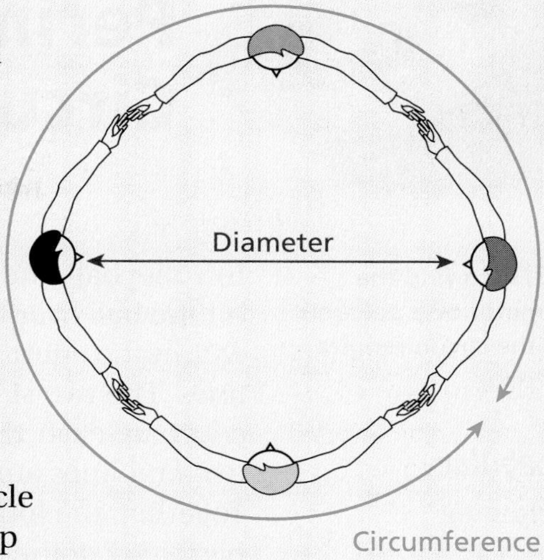

Activity 2

1. Four students should stand in a circle with their arms outstretched, as shown in the diagram.
2. Another student should find the diameter of the circle by measuring the distance across the middle of the circle with a tape measure.
3. The student should also find the circumference of the circle by measuring the distance around the circle from fingertip to fingertip across the backs of the students.
4. Record the diameter and circumference in a table like the one below.

Diameter (ft)	▒	▒	▒	▒	▒
Circumference (ft)	▒	▒	▒	▒	▒

5. Add one or more students to the circle and repeat the process. Record the diameter and circumference for at least five different circles.
6. Graph the data in your table by plotting points on a coordinate plane like the one shown.

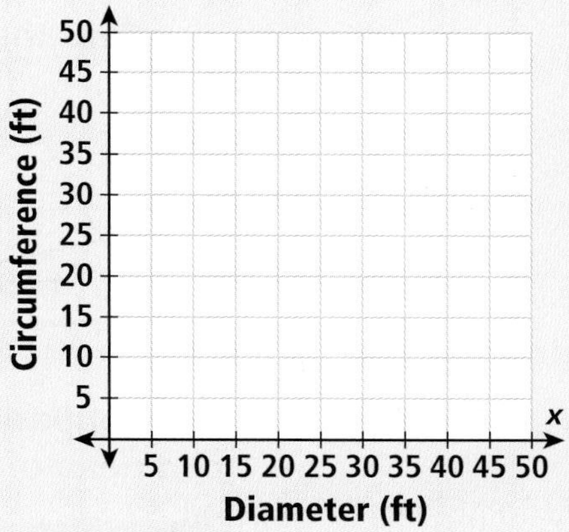

Think and Discuss

1. In general, what do you notice about the points on your graph? What shape or pattern do they seem to form?
2. Calculate the ratio of the circumference to the diameter for each of the data points. Then calculate the mean of these ratios. For any circle, the ratio of the circumference to the diameter is a constant, known as *pi* (π). Give an estimate for π based on your findings.

Try This

1. For a circle with circumference C and diameter d, the ratio of the circumference to the diameter is $\frac{C}{d} = \pi$. Use this to write a formula that you can use to find the circumference of a circle when you know its diameter.
2. Use your estimate for the value of π to find the approximate circumference of the circle at right.

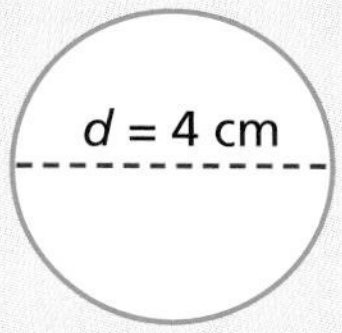

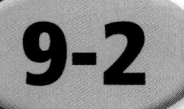

9-2 Perimeter and Circumference

Learn to find the perimeter of a polygon and the circumference of a circle.

Vocabulary
perimeter
circumference

In volleyball, the player serving must hit the ball over the net but keep it within the court's sidelines and end lines. The two sidelines on a volleyball court are each 18 meters long, and the two end lines are each 9 meters long. Together, the four lines form the *perimeter* of the court.

Perimeter is the distance around a geometric figure. To find the perimeter P of a rectangular volleyball court, you can add the lengths of its sides.

EXAMPLE 1 Finding the Perimeter of a Polygon

Find the perimeter.

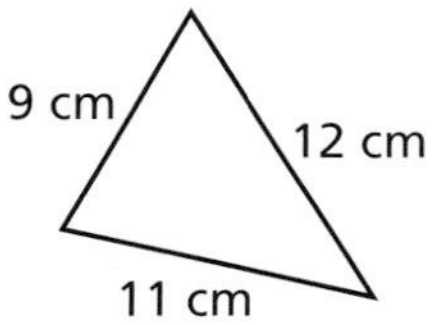

$P = 9 + 12 + 11$ *Use the side lengths.*

$P = 32$ *Add.*

The perimeter of the triangle is 32 cm.

Since opposite sides of a rectangle are equal in length, you can find the perimeter of a rectangle by using a formula.

PERIMETER OF A RECTANGLE		
The perimeter P of a rectangle is the sum of twice its length ℓ and twice its width w.	$P = 2\ell + 2w$	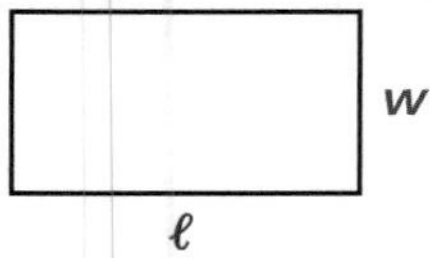

EXAMPLE 2 Using Properties of a Rectangle to Find Perimeter

Find the perimeter.

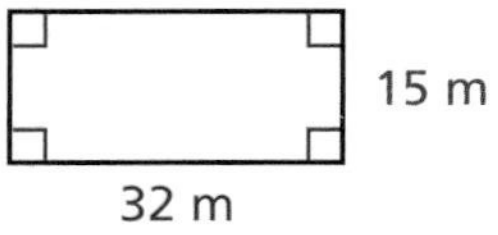

$P = 2\ell + 2w$ *Use the formula.*

$P = (2 \cdot 32) + (2 \cdot 15)$ *Substitute for ℓ and w.*

$P = 64 + 30$ *Multiply.*

$P = 94$ *Add.*

The perimeter of the rectangle is 94 m.

The distance around a circle is called **circumference**. For every circle, the ratio of circumference C to diameter d is the same. This ratio, $\frac{C}{d}$, is represented by the Greek letter π, called *pi*. *Pi* is approximately equal to 3.14 or $\frac{22}{7}$. By solving the equation $\frac{C}{d} = \pi$ for C, you get the formula for circumference.

CIRCUMFERENCE OF A CIRCLE		
The circumference C of a circle is π times the diameter d, or 2π times the radius r.	$C = \pi d$ or $C = 2\pi r$	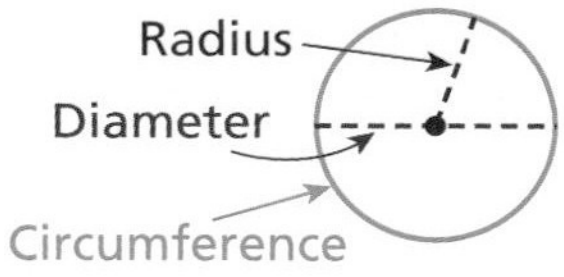

EXAMPLE 3 Finding the Circumference of a Circle

Find the circumference of each circle to the nearest tenth, if necessary. Use 3.14 or $\frac{22}{7}$ for π.

Helpful Hint

If the diameter or radius of a circle is a multiple of 7, use $\frac{22}{7}$ for π.

A

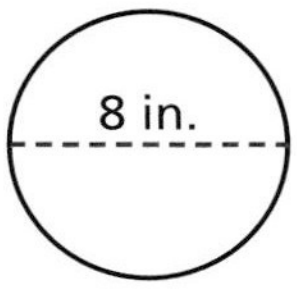

$C = \pi d$ — *You know the diameter.*

$C \approx 3.14 \cdot \mathbf{8}$ — *Substitute 3.14 for π and 8 for d.*

$C \approx 25.12$ — *Multiply.*

The circumference of the circle is about 25.1 in.

B

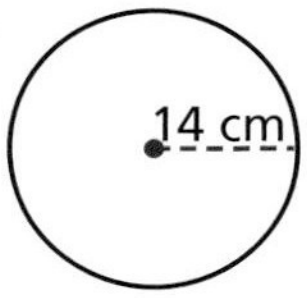

$C = 2\pi r$ — *You know the radius.*

$C \approx 2 \cdot \frac{22}{7} \cdot \mathbf{14}$ — *Substitute $\frac{22}{7}$ for π and 14 for r.*

$C \approx 88$ — *Multiply.*

The circumference of the circle is about 88 cm.

EXAMPLE 4 *Design Application*

Lily is drawing plans for a circular fountain. The circumference of the fountain is 63 ft. What is its approximate diameter?

$C = \pi d$ — *You know the circumference.*

$63 \approx 3.14 \cdot d$ — *Substitute 3.14 for π and 63 for C.*

$\frac{63}{\mathbf{3.14}} \approx \frac{3.14 \cdot d}{\mathbf{3.14}}$ — *Divide both sides by 3.14 to isolate the variable.*

$20 \approx d$

The diameter of the fountain is about 20 ft.

Think and Discuss

1. Describe two ways to find the perimeter of a volleyball court.

2. Explain how to use the formula $C = \pi d$ to find the circumference of a circle if you know the radius.

9-2 Exercises

go.hrw.com
Homework Help Online
KEYWORD: MS7 9-2
Parent Resources Online
KEYWORD: MS7 Parent

GUIDED PRACTICE

Find each perimeter.

See Example 1

1.

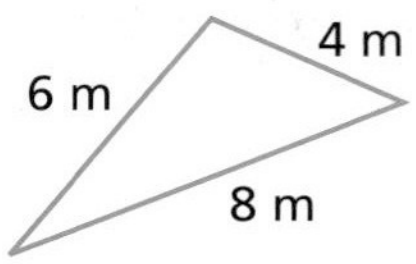

2.

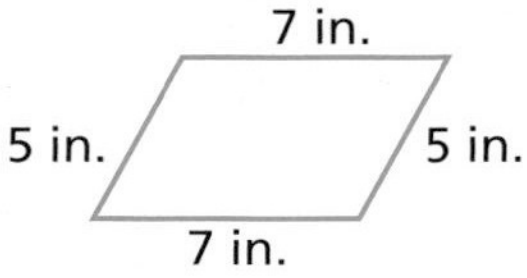

3.

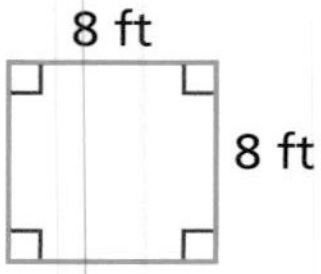

See Example 2

4.

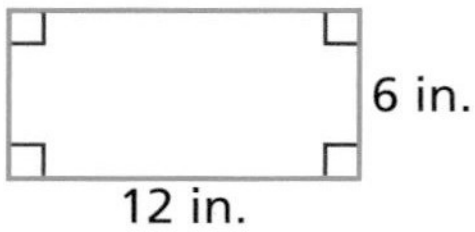

5.

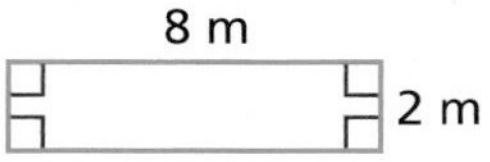

6.

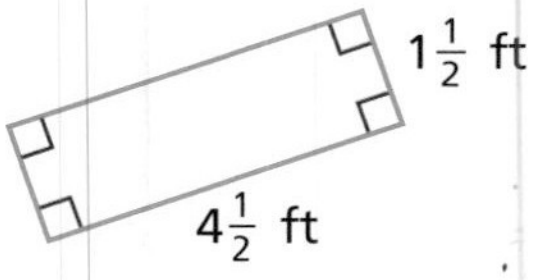

See Example 3

Find the circumference of each circle to the nearest tenth, if necessary. Use 3.14 or $\frac{22}{7}$ for π.

7.

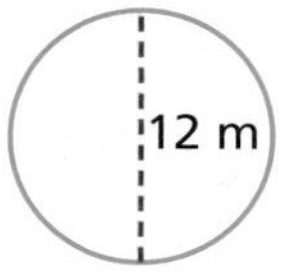

8.

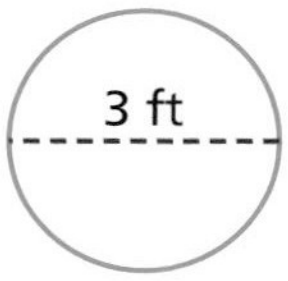

9.

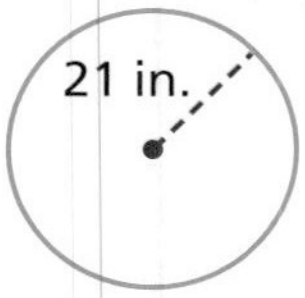

See Example 4

10. A Ferris wheel has a circumference of 440 feet. What is the approximate diameter of the Ferris wheel? Use 3.14 for π.

INDEPENDENT PRACTICE

Find each perimeter.

See Example 1

11.

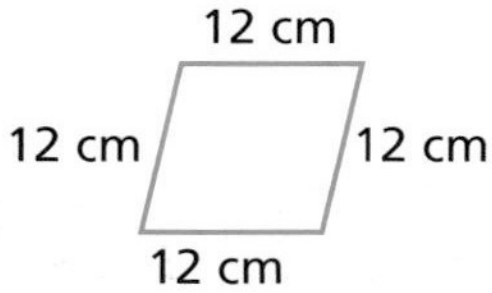

12.

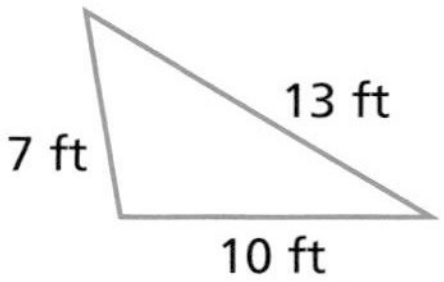

13.

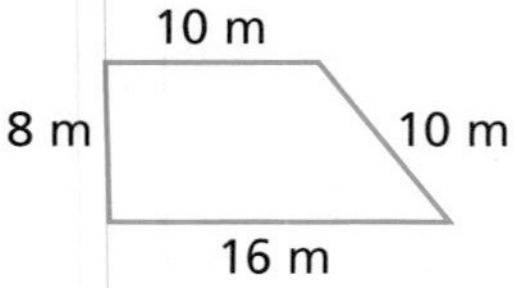

See Example 2

14.

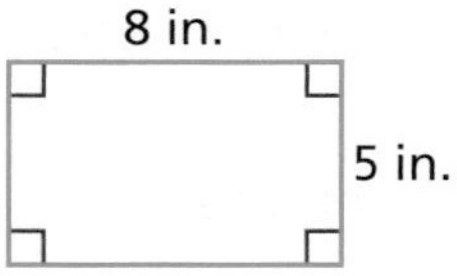

15.

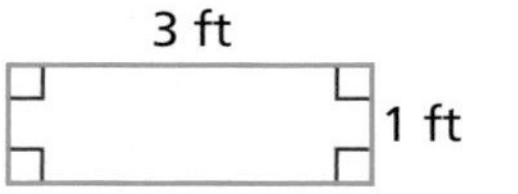

16.

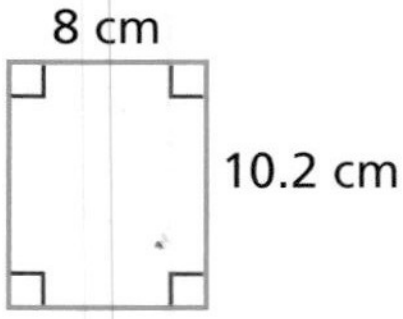

See Example 3

Find the circumference of each circle to the nearest tenth, if necessary. Use 3.14 or $\frac{22}{7}$ for π.

17.

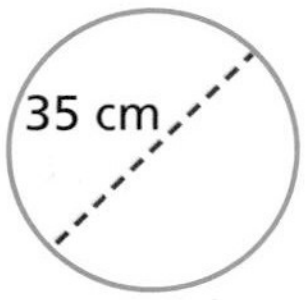

18.

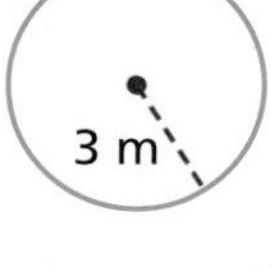

19.

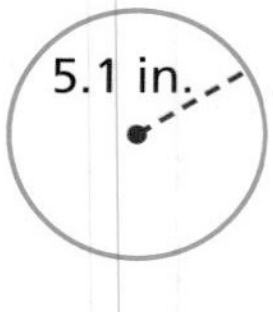

See Example 4

20. The circumference of Kayla's bicycle wheel is 91 inches. What is the approximate diameter of her bicycle wheel? Use 3.14 for π.

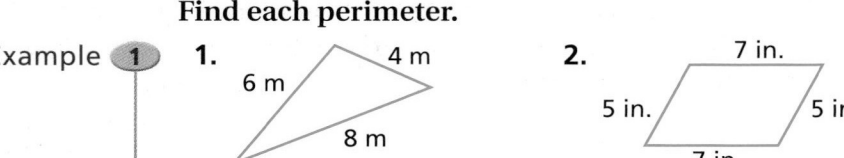

PRACTICE AND PROBLEM SOLVING

Extra Practice

See page 744.

Find each missing measurement to the nearest tenth. Use 3.14 for π.

21. $r =$ ■; $d =$ ■; $C = 17.8$ m

22. $r = 6.7$ yd; $d =$ ■; $C =$ ■

23. $r =$ ■; $d = 10.6$ in.; $C =$ ■

24. $r =$ ■; $d =$ ■; $C = \pi$

25. Critical Thinking Ben is placing rope lights around the edge of a circular patio with a 24.2 ft diameter. The lights are in lengths of 57 inches. How many strands of lights does he need to surround the patio edge?

26. Geography The map shows the distances in miles between the airports on the Big Island of Hawaii. A pilot flies from Kailua-Kona to Waimea to Hilo and back to Kailua-Kona. How far does he travel?

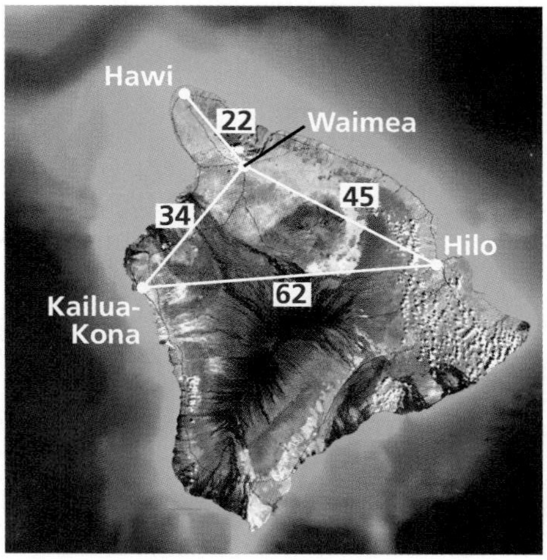

27. Architecture The Capitol Rotunda connects the House and Senate sides of the U.S. Capitol. The rotunda is 180 feet tall and has a circumference of about 301.5 feet. What is its approximate diameter, to the nearest foot?

28. Write a Problem Write a problem about finding the perimeter or circumference of an object in your school or classroom.

29. Write About It Explain how to find the width of a rectangle if you know its perimeter and length.

30. Challenge The perimeter of a regular nonagon is $25\frac{1}{2}$ in. What is the length of one side of the nonagon?

TEST PREP and Spiral Review

31. Multiple Choice Which is the best estimate for the circumference of a circle with a diameter of 15 inches?

Ⓐ 18.1 inches Ⓑ 23.6 inches Ⓒ 32.5 inches Ⓓ 47.1 inches

32. Multiple Choice John is building a dog pen that is 6 feet by 8 feet. How much fencing material will he need to go all the way around the pen?

Ⓕ 48 feet Ⓖ 28 feet Ⓗ 20 feet Ⓙ 14 feet

Solve. (Lesson 6-5)

33. 18 is 20% of what number?

34. 78% of 65 is what number?

Calculate. Use the correct number of significant digits in each answer. (Lesson 9-1)

35. $5.8 + 3.27$

36. $6 - 2.5$

37. $22.3 \cdot 6.2$

38. $60.6 \div 15$

Hands-On LAB 9-3

Explore Area of Polygons

Use with Lessons 9-3, 9-4, and 9-5

go.hrw.com
Lab Resources Online
KEYWORD: MS7 Lab9

You can use a parallelogram to find the area of a triangle or a trapezoid. To do so, you must first know how to find the area of a parallelogram.

Activity 1

1. On a sheet of graph paper, draw a parallelogram with a base of 10 units and a height of 6 units.

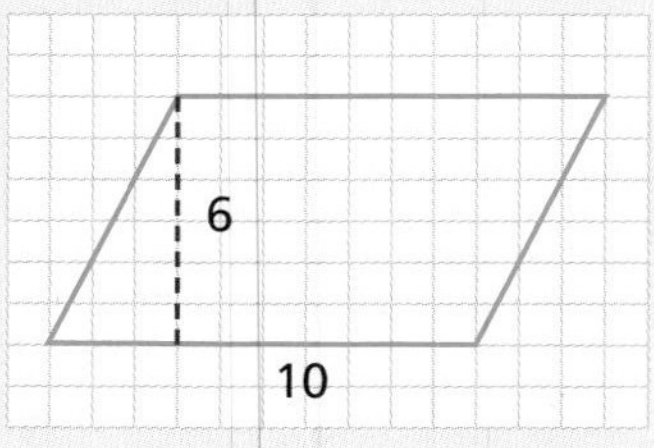

2. Cut out the parallelogram. Then cut a right triangle off the end of the parallelogram by cutting along the altitude.

3. Move the triangle to the other side of the figure to make a rectangle.

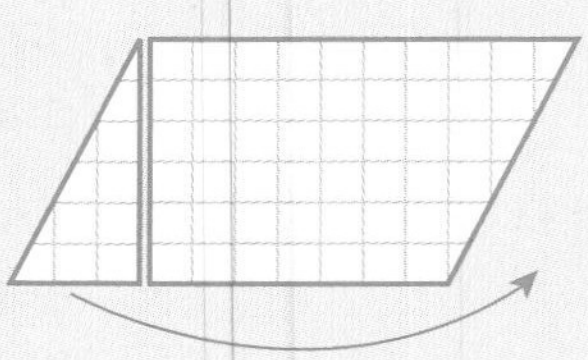

4. How is the area of the parallelogram related to the area of the rectangle?

5. What are the length and width of the rectangle? What is the area of the rectangle?

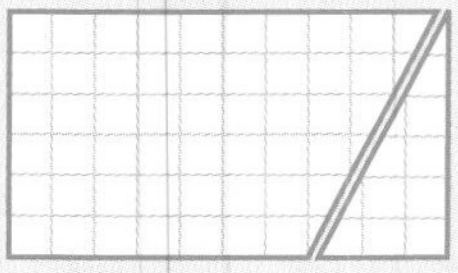

6. Find the area of the parallelogram.

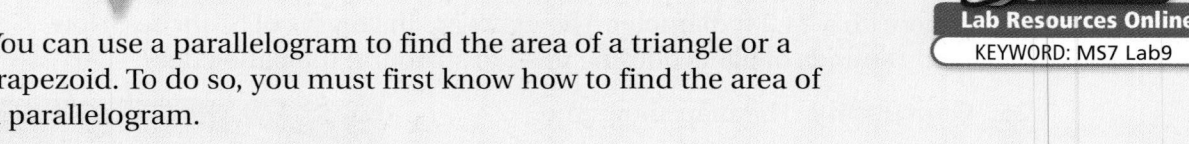

Think and Discuss

1. How are the length and width of the rectangle related to the base and height of the parallelogram?
2. Suppose a parallelogram has base b and height h. Write a formula for the area of the parallelogram.

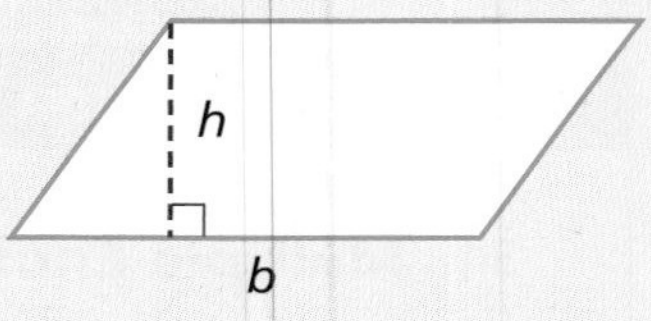

Try This

1. Does your formula work for any parallelogram? If so, show how to use the formula to find the area of the parallelogram at right.

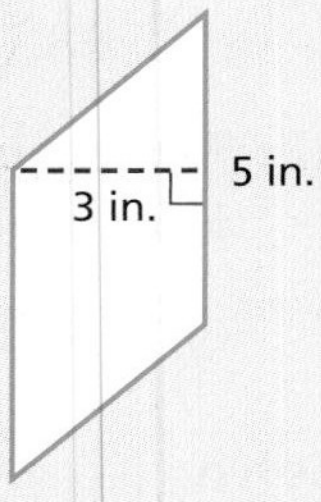

2. Explain what must be true about the areas of the parallelograms below.

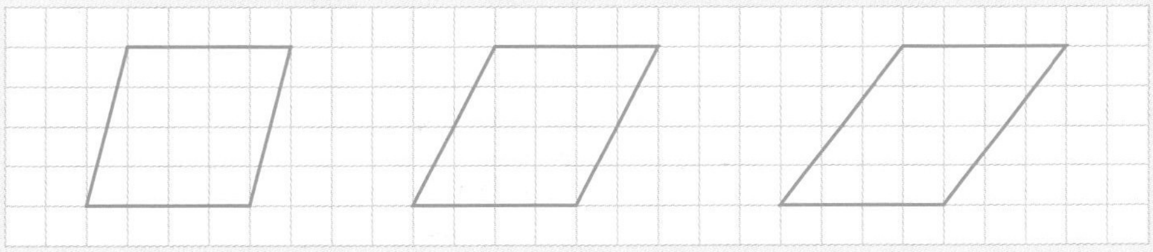

Activity 2

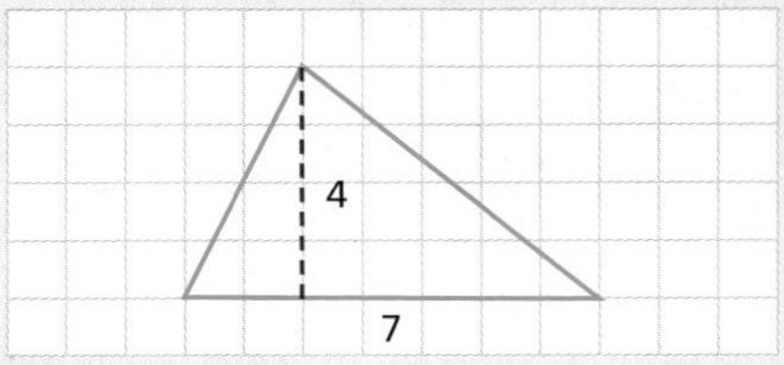

1. On a sheet of graph paper, draw a triangle with a base of 7 units and a height of 4 units.
2. Cut out the triangle. Then use the triangle to trace and cut out a second triangle that is congruent to it.
3. Arrange the two triangles to form a parallelogram.

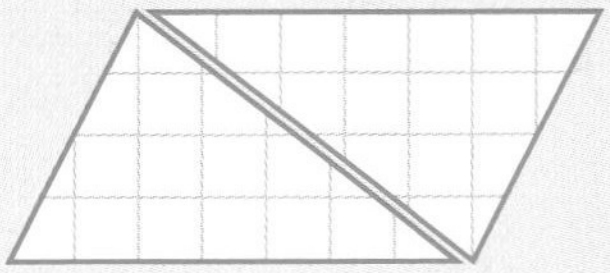

4. How is the area of the triangle related to the area of the parallelogram?
5. Find the areas of the parallelogram and the triangle.

Think and Discuss

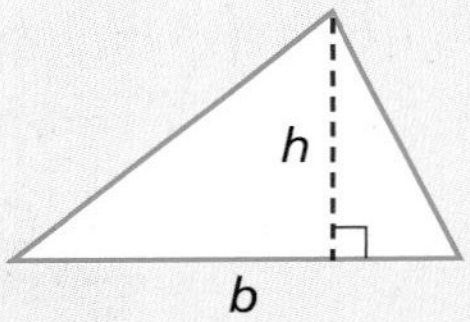

1. How are the base and height of the triangle related to the base and height of the parallelogram?
2. Suppose a triangle has base b and height h. Write a formula for the area of the triangle.

Try This

1. Find the area of a triangle with a base of 10 ft and a height of 5 ft.

Activity 3

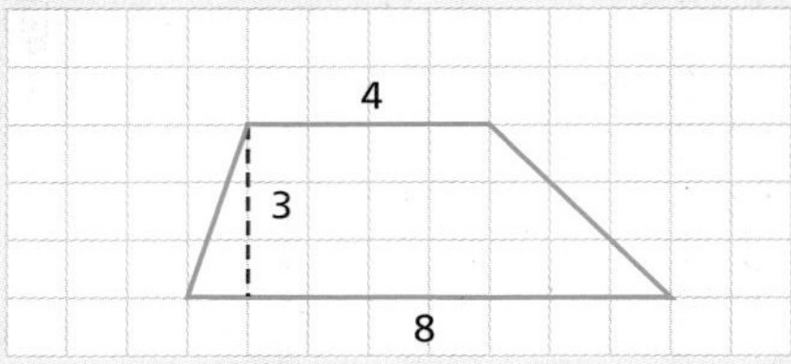

1. On a sheet of graph paper, draw a trapezoid with bases 4 units and 8 units long and a height of 3 units.
2. Cut out the trapezoid. Then use the trapezoid to trace and cut out a second trapezoid that is congruent to it.
3. Arrange the two trapezoids to form a parallelogram.

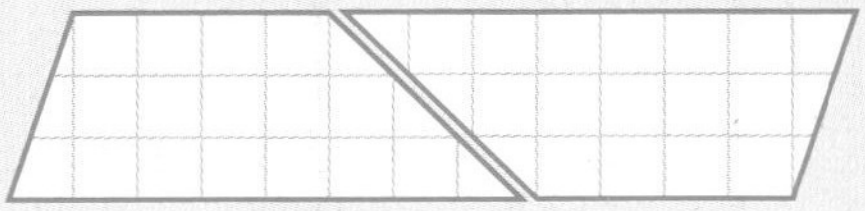

4. How is the area of the trapezoid related to the area of the parallelogram?
5. Find the areas of the parallelogram and the trapezoid.

Think and Discuss

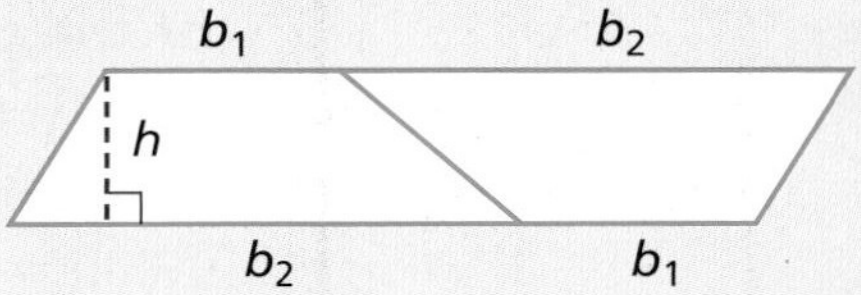

1. What is the length of the base of the parallelogram at right? What is the parallelogram's area?
2. What is the area of one of the trapezoids in the figure?

Try This

1. Find the area of a trapezoid with bases 4 in. and 6 in. and a height of 8 in.

9-3 Area of Parallelograms

Learn to find the area of rectangles and other parallelograms.

Vocabulary
area

The **area** of a figure is the number of unit squares needed to cover the figure. Area is measured in square units. For example, the area of a chessboard can be measured in square inches. The area of a lawn chessboard is much larger than a regular chessboard, so it can be measured in square feet or square yards.

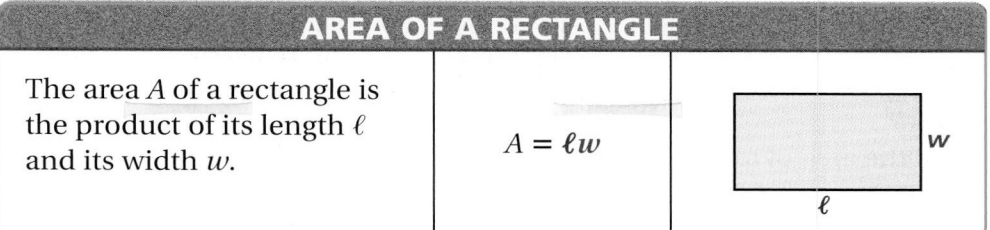

AREA OF A RECTANGLE		
The area A of a rectangle is the product of its length ℓ and its width w.	$A = \ell w$	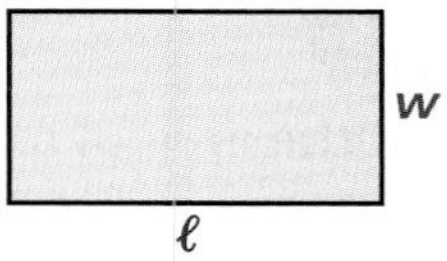

EXAMPLE 1 Finding the Area of a Rectangle

Find the area of the rectangle.

$A = \ell w$ *Use the formula.*

$A = 10 \cdot 7.5$ *Substitute for ℓ and w.*

$A = 75$ *Multiply.*

The area of the rectangle is 75 ft^2.

EXAMPLE 2 Finding Length or Width of a Rectangle

Bethany and her dad are planting a rectangular garden. The area of the garden is 1,080 ft^2, and the width is 24 ft. What is the length of the garden?

$A = \ell w$ *Use the formula for the area of a rectangle.*

$1{,}080 = \ell \cdot 24$ *Substitute 1,080 for A and 24 for w.*

$\frac{1{,}080}{24} = \frac{\ell \cdot 24}{24}$ *Divide both sides by 24 to isolate ℓ.*

$45 = \ell$

The length of the garden is 45 ft.

The base of a parallelogram is the length of one side. Its height is the perpendicular distance from the base to the opposite side.

AREA OF A PARALLELOGRAM		
The area A of a parallelogram is the product of its base b and its height h.	$A = bh$	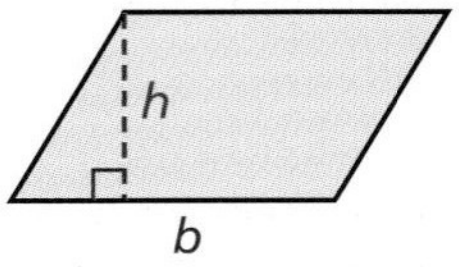

EXAMPLE 3 Finding the Area of a Parallelogram

Find the area of the parallelogram.

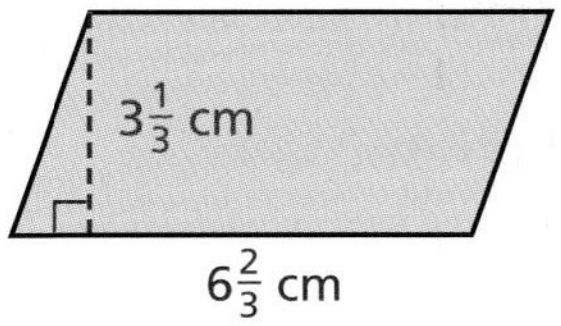

$A = bh$ *Use the formula.*

$A = 6\frac{2}{3} \cdot 3\frac{1}{3}$ *Substitute for b and h.*

$A = \frac{20}{3} \cdot \frac{10}{3}$ *Convert to improper fractions.*

$A = \frac{200}{9}$ or $22\frac{2}{9}$ *Multiply.*

The area of the parallelogram is $22\frac{2}{9}$ cm^2.

EXAMPLE 4 *Landscaping Application*

Birgit and Mark are building a rectangular patio measuring 9 yd by 7 yd. How many square feet of tile will they need?

First draw and label a diagram. Look at the units. The patio is measured in yards, but the answer should be in square feet.

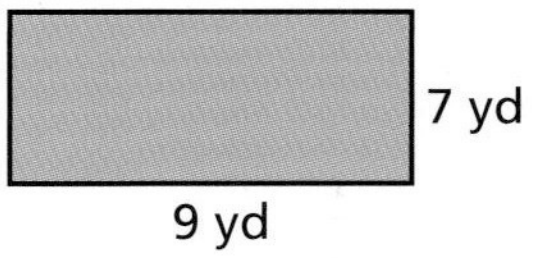

$9 \text{ yd} \cdot \frac{3 \text{ ft}}{1 \text{ yd}} = 27 \text{ ft}$ *Convert yards to feet by using a unit conversion factor.*

$7 \text{ yd} \cdot \frac{3 \text{ ft}}{1 \text{ yd}} = 21 \text{ ft}$

Now find the area of the patio in square feet.

$A = \ell w$ *Use the formula for the area of a rectangle.*

$A = 27 \cdot 21$ *Substitute 27 for ℓ and 21 for w.*

$A = 567$ *Multiply.*

Birgit and Mark need 567 ft^2 of tile.

Think and Discuss

1. Write a formula for the area of a square, using an exponent.

2. Explain why the area of a nonrectangular parallelogram with side lengths 5 in. and 3 in. is not 15 in^2.

9-3 Exercises

go.hrw.com
Homework Help Online
KEYWORD: MS7 9-3
Parent Resources Online
KEYWORD: MS7 Parent

GUIDED PRACTICE

See Example 1 **Find the area of each rectangle.**

1.

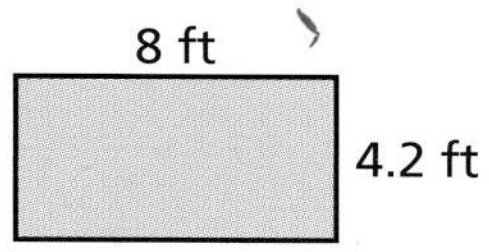

2.

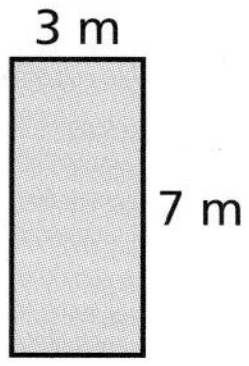

3.

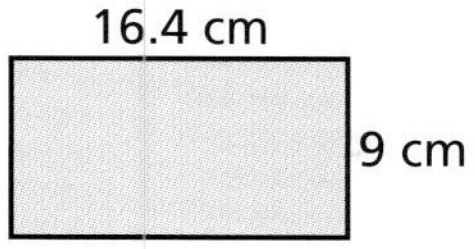

See Example 2 **4.** Kara wants a rug for her bedroom. She knows the area of her bedroom is 132 ft^2. The length of her room is 12 ft. What is the width of Kara's bedroom?

See Example 3 **Find the area of each parallelogram.**

5.

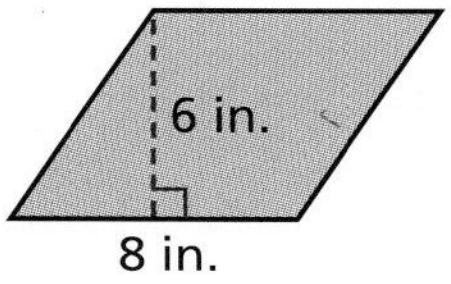

6.

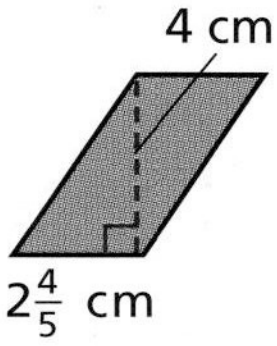

7.

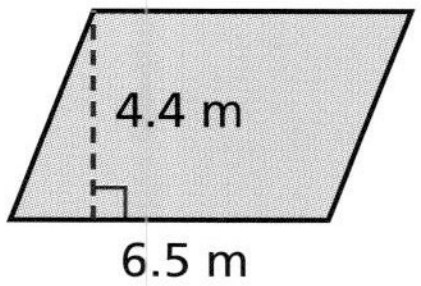

See Example 4 **8.** Anna is mowing a rectangular field measuring 120 yd by 66 yd. How many square feet will Anna mow?

INDEPENDENT PRACTICE

See Example 1 **Find the area of each rectangle.**

9.

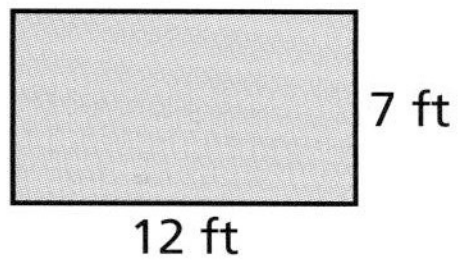

10.

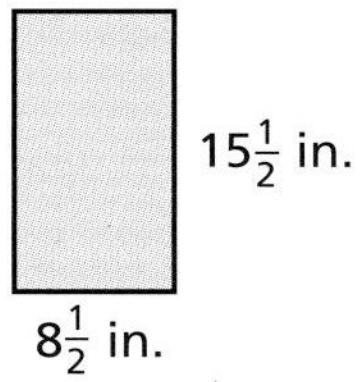

11.

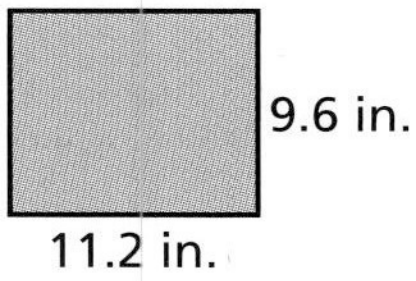

See Example 2 **12.** James and Linda are fencing a rectangular area of the yard for their dog. The width of the dog yard is 4.5 m. Its area is 67.5 m^2. What is the length of the dog yard?

See Example 3 **Find the area of each parallelogram.**

13.

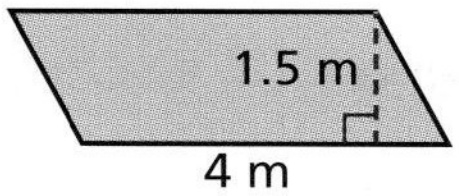

14.

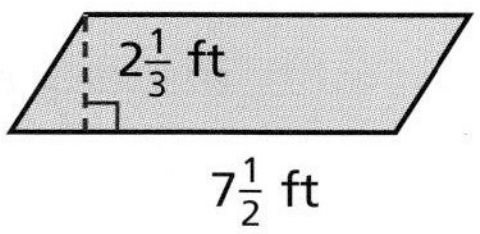

15.

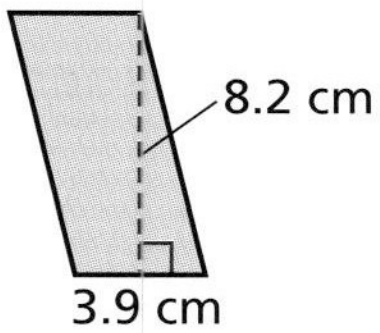

See Example 4 **16.** Abby is painting rectangular blocks on her bathroom walls. Each block is 15 in. by 18 in. What is the area of one block in square feet?

PRACTICE AND PROBLEM SOLVING

Extra Practice
See page 744.

Find the area of each polygon.

17. rectangle: $\ell = 9$ yd; $w = 8$ yd

18. parallelogram: $b = 7$ m; $h = 4.2$ m

Graph the polygon with the given vertices. Then find the area of the polygon.

19. (2, 0), (2, −2), (9, 0), (9, −2)

20. (4, 1), (4, 7), (8, 4), (8, 10)

21. Art Without the frame, the painting *Girl of Tehuantepec* by Diego Rivera measures about 23 in. by 31 in. The width of the frame is 3 in.

a. What is the area of the painting?

b. What is the perimeter of the painting?

c. What is the total area covered by the painting and the frame?

Girl of Tehuantepec by Diego Rivera

22. What is the height of a parallelogram with an area of 66 in^2 and a base of 11 in.?

23. Choose a Strategy The area of a parallelogram is 84 cm^2. If the base is 5 cm longer than the height, what is the length of the base?

Ⓐ 5 cm Ⓑ 7 cm Ⓒ 12 cm Ⓓ 14 cm

24. Write About It A rectangle and a parallelogram have sides that measure 3 m, 4 m, 3 m, and 4 m. Do the figures have the same area? Explain.

25. Challenge Two parallelograms have the same base length, but the height of the first is half that of the second. What is the ratio of the area of the first parallelogram to that of the second? What would the ratio be if both the height and the base of the first parallelogram were half those of the second?

TEST PREP and Spiral Review

26. Multiple Choice Find the area of the parallelogram.

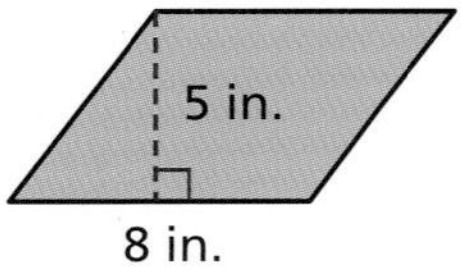

Ⓐ 13 in^2 Ⓑ 26 in^2 Ⓒ 40 in^2 Ⓓ 56 in^2

27. Extended Response Kiana is helping her dad build a deck. The plans they have are for a 6-foot-by-8-foot deck, but her dad wants a deck that has twice as much area. He suggests doubling the length of each side of the deck. Will this double the area? If not, suggest another method for doubling the area of the deck.

Tell whether each angle is acute, obtuse, right or straight. (Lesson 8-2)

28. 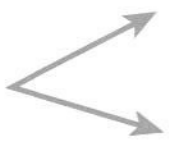

29. 

30. 

31. 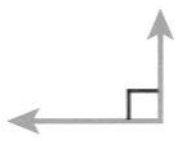

Find the perimeter of each rectangle, given the dimensions. (Lesson 9-2)

32. 6 in. by 12 in.

33. 2 m by 8 m

34. 16 cm by 3 cm

35. $4\frac{4}{5}$ ft by $1\frac{3}{8}$ ft

9-4 Area of Triangles and Trapezoids

Learn to find the area of triangles and trapezoids.

The Bermuda Triangle is a triangular region between Bermuda, Florida, and Puerto Rico. To find the area of this region, you could use the formula for the area of a triangle.

The base of a triangle can be any side. The height of a triangle is the perpendicular distance from the base to the opposite vertex.

AREA OF A TRIANGLE		
The area A of a triangle is half the product of its base b and its height h.	$A = \frac{1}{2}bh$	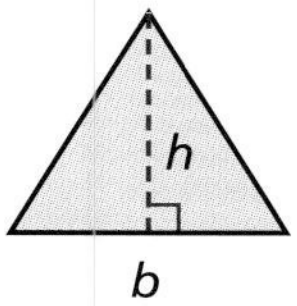

EXAMPLE 1 Finding the Area of a Triangle

Find the area of each triangle.

A

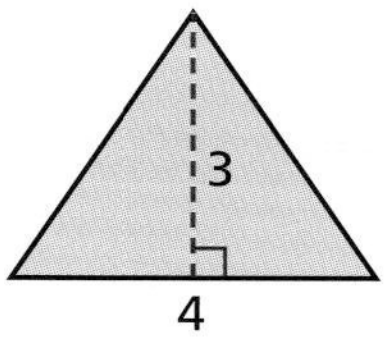

$A = \frac{1}{2}bh$ *Use the formula.*

$A = \frac{1}{2}(4 \cdot 3)$ *Substitute 4 for b and 3 for h.*

$A = 6$

The area of the triangle is 6 square units.

B

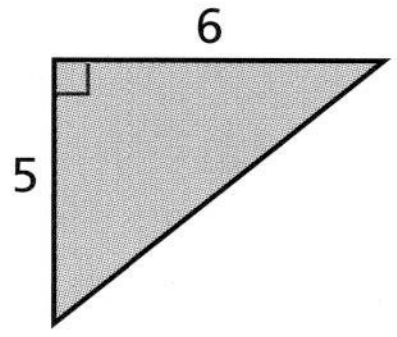

$A = \frac{1}{2}bh$ *Use the formula.*

$A = \frac{1}{2}(6 \cdot 5)$ *Substitute 6 for b and 5 for h.*

$A = 15$

The area of the triangle is 15 square units.

The two parallel sides of a trapezoid are its bases, b_1 and b_2. The height of a trapezoid is the perpendicular distance between the bases.

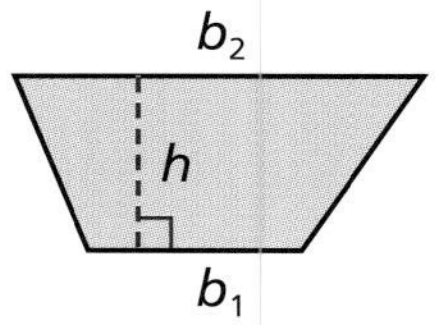

AREA OF A TRAPEZOID

The area of a trapezoid is half its height multiplied by the sum of the lengths of its two bases.	$A = \frac{1}{2}h(b_1 + b_2)$	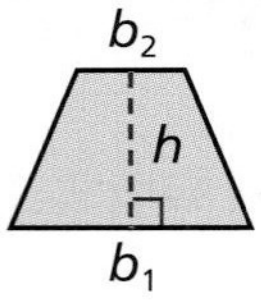

EXAMPLE 2 Finding the Area of a Trapezoid

Reading Math

In the term b_1, the number 1 is called a *subscript.* It is read as "*b*-one" or "*b* sub-one."

Find the area of each trapezoid.

A

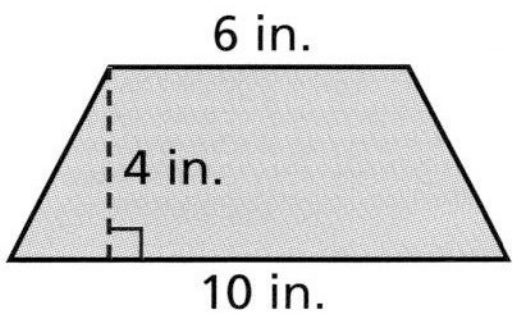

$A = \frac{1}{2}h(b_1 + b_2)$ *Use the formula.*

$A = \frac{1}{2} \cdot 4(10 + 6)$ *Substitute.*

$A = \frac{1}{2} \cdot 4(16)$ *Add.*

$A = 32$ *Multiply.*

The area of the trapezoid is 32 in^2.

B

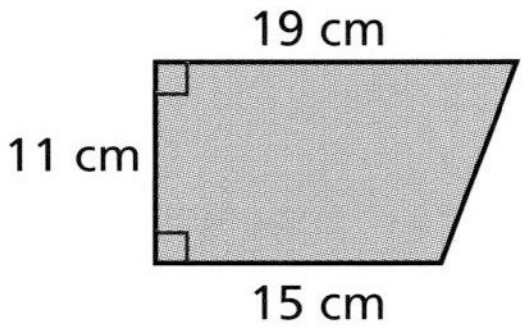

$A = \frac{1}{2}h(b_1 + b_2)$ *Use the formula.*

$A = \frac{1}{2} \cdot 11(15 + 19)$ *Substitute.*

$A = \frac{1}{2} \cdot 11(34)$ *Add.*

$A = 187$ *Multiply.*

The area of the trapezoid is 187 cm^2.

EXAMPLE 3 *Geography Application*

The state of Nevada is shaped somewhat like a trapezoid. What is the approximate area of Nevada?

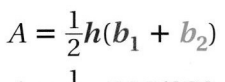

$A = \frac{1}{2}h(b_1 + b_2)$ *Use the formula.*

$A = \frac{1}{2} \cdot 320(200 + 475)$ *Substitute.*

$A = \frac{1}{2} \cdot 320(675)$ *Add.*

$A = 108{,}000$ *Multiply.*

The area of Nevada is approximately 108,000 square miles.

Think and Discuss

1. Tell how to use the sides of a right triangle to find its area.

2. Explain how to find the area of a trapezoid.

9-4 Exercises

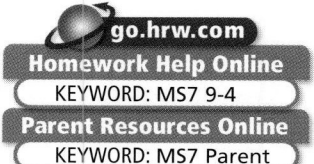

go.hrw.com
Homework Help Online
KEYWORD: MS7 9-4
Parent Resources Online
KEYWORD: MS7 Parent

GUIDED PRACTICE

See Example 1 **Find the area of each triangle.**

1.
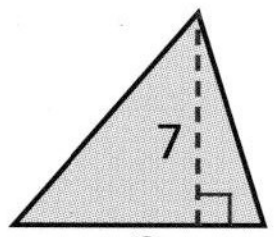

2.
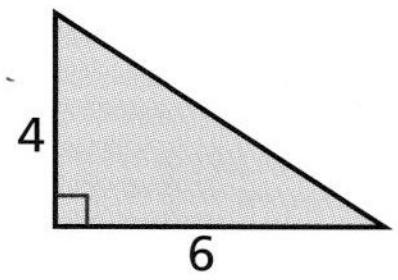

3.
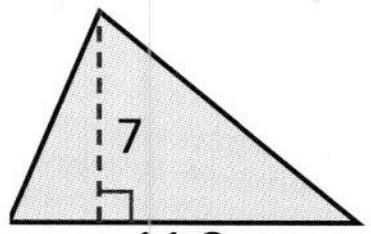

See Example 2 **Find the area of each trapezoid.**

4.
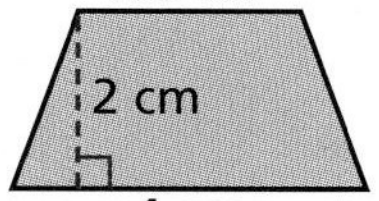

5.
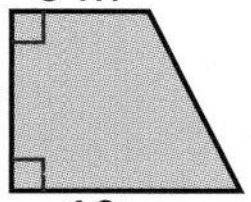

6.
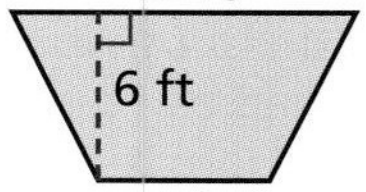

See Example 3 **7.** The state of Tennessee is shaped somewhat like a parallelogram. What is the approximate area of Tennessee?

INDEPENDENT PRACTICE

See Example 1 **Find the area of each triangle.**

8.
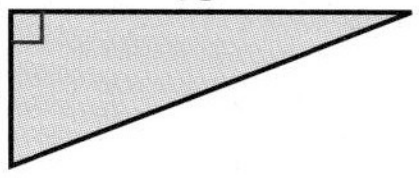

9.
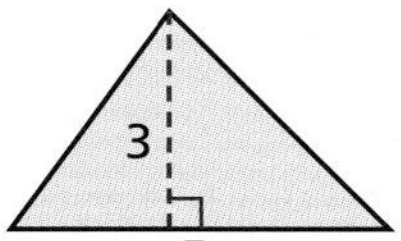

10.
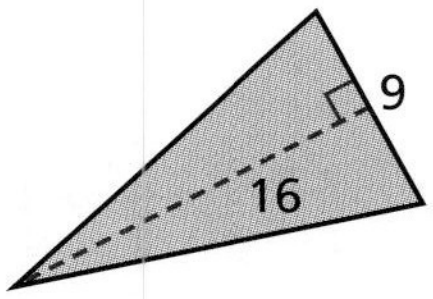

See Example 2 **Find the area of each trapezoid.**

11.
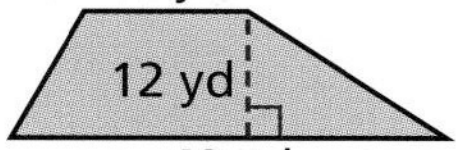

12.
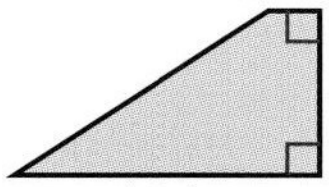

13.

See Example 3 **14.** The state of New Hampshire is shaped somewhat like a right triangle. What is the approximate area of New Hampshire?

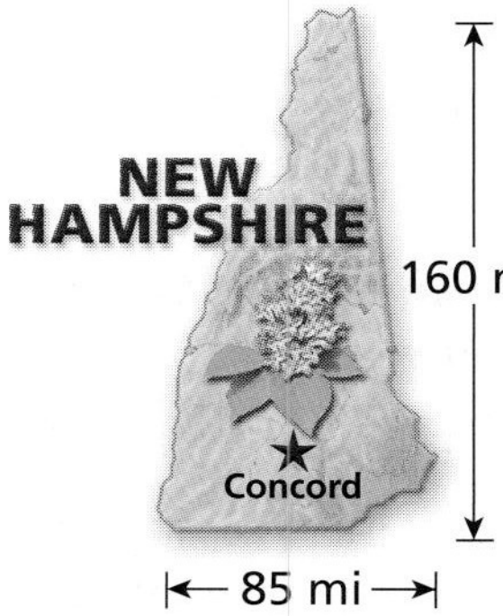

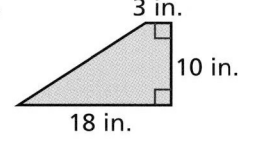

PRACTICE AND PROBLEM SOLVING

Extra Practice
See page 744.

Find the missing measurement of each triangle.

15. $b = 8$ cm
$h = \square$
$A = 18 \text{ cm}^2$

16. $b = 16$ ft
$h = 0.7$ ft
$A = \square$

17. $b = \square$
$h = 95$ in.
$A = 1{,}045 \text{ in}^2$

Graph the polygon with the given vertices. Then find the area of the polygon.

18. (1, 2), (4, 5), (8, 2), (8, 5)

19. (1, −6), (5, −1), (7, −6)

20. (2, 3), (2, 10), (7, 6), (7, 8)

21. (3, 0), (3, 4), (−3, 0)

22. What is the height of a trapezoid with an area of 9 m^2 and bases that measure 2.4 m and 3.6 m?

23. Multi-Step The state of Colorado is somewhat rectangular in shape. Estimate the perimeter and area of Colorado.

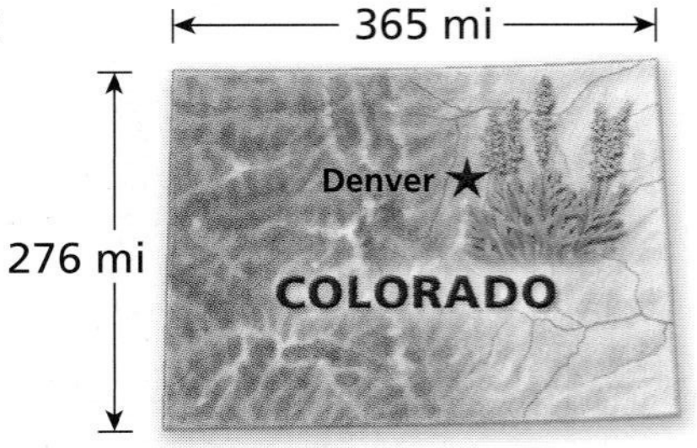

24. What's the Error? A student says the area of the triangle shown at right is 33 cm^2. Explain why the student is incorrect.

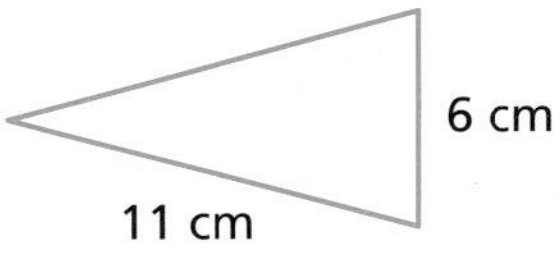

25. Write About It Explain how to use the formulas for the area of a rectangle and the area of a triangle to estimate the area of Nevada.

26. Challenge The state of North Dakota is trapezoidal in shape and has an area of 70,704 mi^2. If the southern border is 359 mi and the distance between the northern border and the southern border is 210 mi, what is the approximate length of the northern border?

TEST PREP and Spiral Review

27. Multiple Choice Find the area of the trapezoid.

Ⓐ 8 cm^2
Ⓑ 16 cm^2
Ⓒ 17 cm^2
Ⓓ 30 cm^2

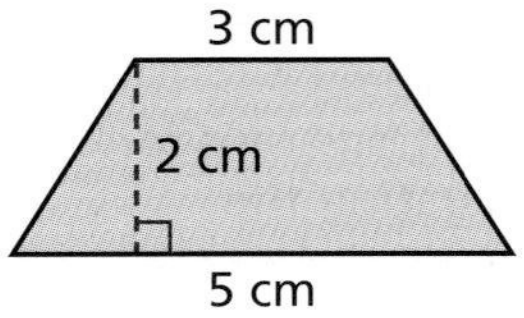

28. Short Response Graph the triangle with vertices (0, 0), (2, 3), and (6, 0). Then find the area of the triangle.

Find the measure of the third angle in each triangle, given two angle measures. (Lesson 8-8)

29. 45°, 45°

30. 71°, 57°

31. 103°, 28°

32. 62°, 19°

33. Justin is laying a tile floor in a room that measures 5 yd by 6 yd. How many square feet of tile does he need? (Lesson 9-3)

9-5 Area of Circles

Learn to find the area of circles.

A circle can be cut into equal-sized sectors and arranged to resemble a parallelogram. The height h of the parallelogram is equal to the radius r of the circle, and the base b of the parallelogram is equal to one-half the circumference C of the circle. So the area of the parallelogram can be written as

$A = bh$, or $A = \frac{1}{2}Cr$.

Since $C = 2\pi r$, $A = \frac{1}{2}(2\pi r)r = \pi r^2$.

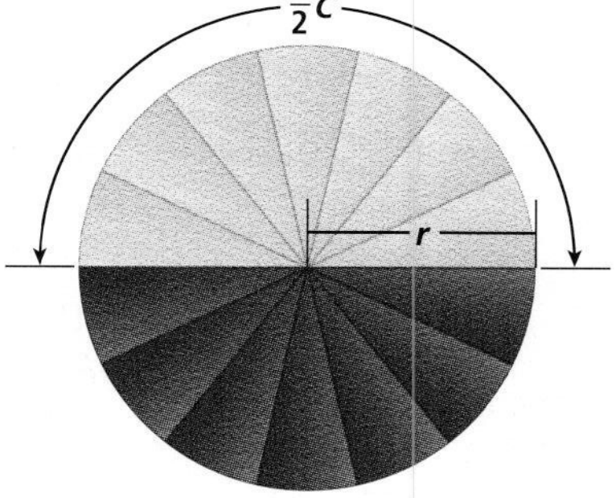

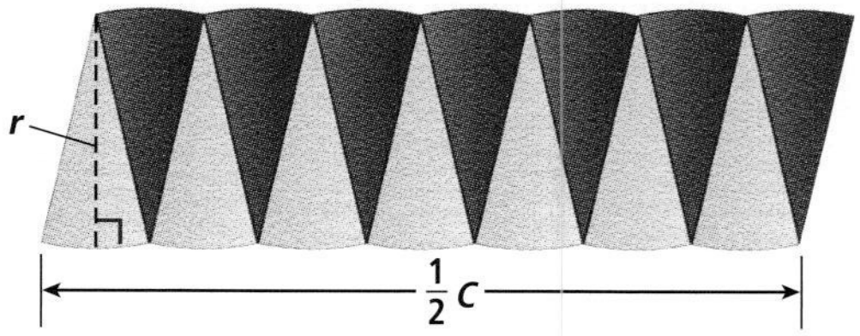

AREA OF A CIRCLE		
The area A of a circle is the product of π and the square of the circle's radius r.	$A = \pi r^2$	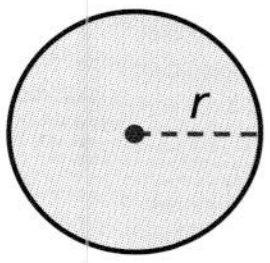

EXAMPLE 1 Finding the Area of a Circle

Remember!

The order of operations calls for evaluating the exponents before multiplying.

Find the area of each circle to the nearest tenth. Use 3.14 for π.

A

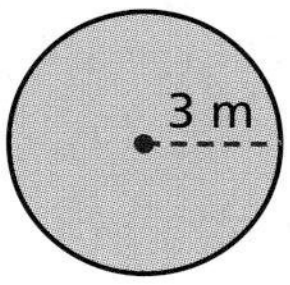

$A = \pi r^2$ *Use the formula.*

$A \approx 3.14 \cdot 3^2$ *Substitute. Use 3 for r.*

$A \approx 3.14 \cdot 9$ *Evaluate the power.*

$A \approx 28.26$ *Multiply.*

The area of the circle is about 28.3 m^2.

B

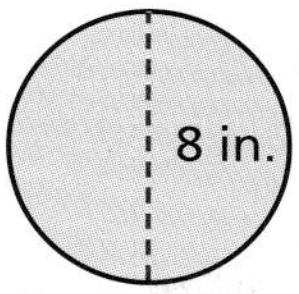

$A = \pi r^2$ *Use the formula.*

$A \approx 3.14 \cdot 4^2$ *Substitute. Use 4 for r.*

$A \approx 3.14 \cdot 16$ *Evaluate the power.*

$A \approx 50.24$ *Multiply.*

The area of the circle is about 50.2 in^2.

EXAMPLE 2 *Social Studies Application*

A group of historians are building a yurt to display at a local multicultural fair. The yurt has a height of 8 feet 9 inches at its center, and it has a circular floor of radius 7 feet. What is the area of the floor of the yurt? Use $\frac{22}{7}$ for π.

$A = \pi r^2$	*Use the formula for the area of a circle.*
$A \approx \frac{22}{7} \cdot 7^2$	*Substitute. Use 7 for r.*
$A \approx \frac{22}{\cancel{7}_1} \cdot \cancel{49}^{7}$	*Evaluate the power. Then simplify.*
$A \approx 22 \cdot 7$	
$A \approx 154$	*Multiply.*

The area of the floor of the yurt is about 154 ft^2.

Social Studies LINK

Nomads in Mongolia carried their homes wherever they roamed. These homes, called *yurts*, were made of wood and felt.

EXAMPLE 3 *Measurement Application*

Use a centimeter ruler to measure the radius of the circle. Then find the area of the shaded region of the circle. Use 3.14 for π. Round your answer to the nearest tenth.

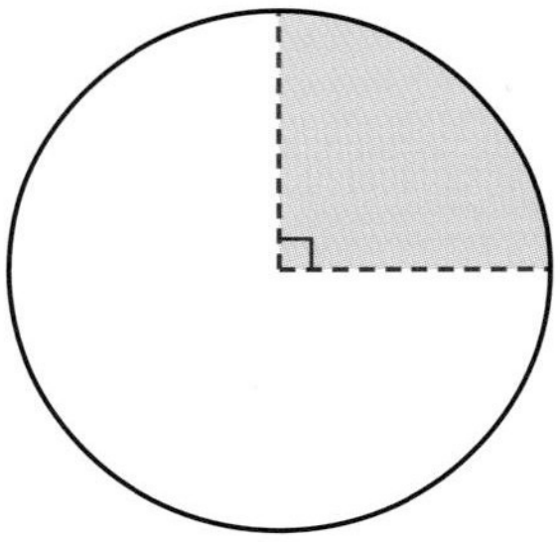

First measure the radius of the circle: It measures 1.8 cm.

Now find the area of the entire circle.

$A = \pi r^2$	*Use the formula for the area of a circle.*
$A \approx 3.14 \cdot 1.8^2$	*Substitute. Use 1.8 for r and 3.14 for π.*
$A \approx 3.14 \cdot 3.24$	*Evaluate the power.*
$A \approx 10.1736$	*Multiply.*

Since $\frac{1}{4}$ of the circle is shaded, divide the area of the circle by 4.

$10.1736 \div 4 = 2.5434$

The area of the shaded region of the circle is about 2.5 cm^2.

Helpful Hint

To estimate the area of a circle, you can square the radius and multiply by 3.

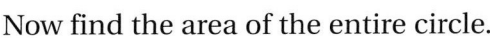

Think and Discuss

1. **Compare** finding the area of a circle when given the radius with finding the area when given the diameter.
2. **Give an example** of a circular object in your classroom. Tell how you could estimate the area of the object, and then estimate.

9-5 Exercises

go.hrw.com
Homework Help Online
KEYWORD: MS7 9-5
Parent Resources Online
KEYWORD: MS7 Parent

GUIDED PRACTICE

See Example 1

Find the area of each circle to the nearest tenth. Use 3.14 for π.

1. 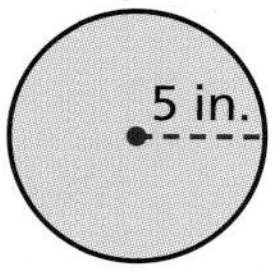

2. 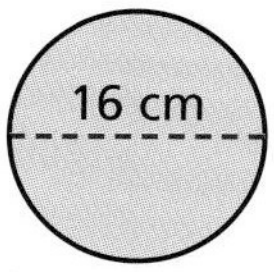

3. 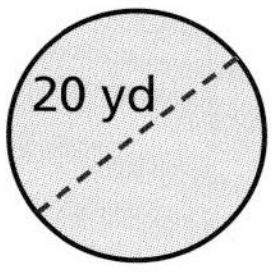

4. 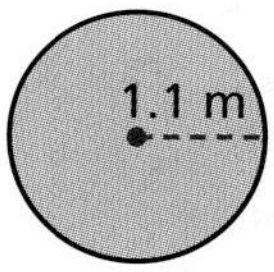

See Example 2

5. The most popular pizza at Sam's Pizza is the 14-inch pepperoni pizza. What is the area of a pizza with a diameter of 14 inches? Use $\frac{22}{7}$ for π.

See Example 3

6. **Measurement** Use a centimeter ruler to measure the diameter of the circle. Then find the area of the shaded region of the circle. Use 3.14 for π. Round your answer to the nearest tenth.

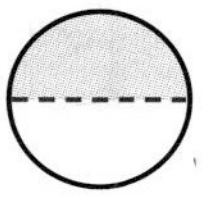

INDEPENDENT PRACTICE

See Example 1

Find the area of each circle to the nearest tenth. Use 3.14 for π.

7. 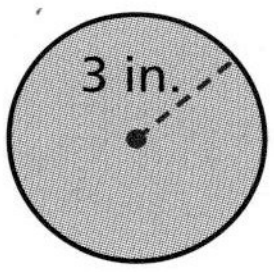

8. 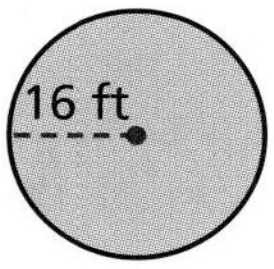

9. 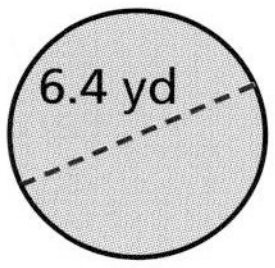

10. 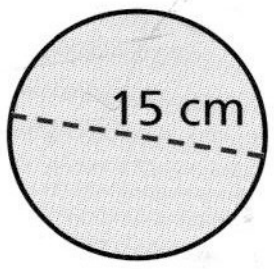

See Example 2

11. A wheel has a radius of 14 centimeters. What is the area of the wheel? Use $\frac{22}{7}$ for π.

See Example 3

12. **Measurement** Use a centimeter ruler to measure the radius of the circle. Then find the area of the shaded region of the circle. Use 3.14 for π. Round your answer to the nearest tenth.

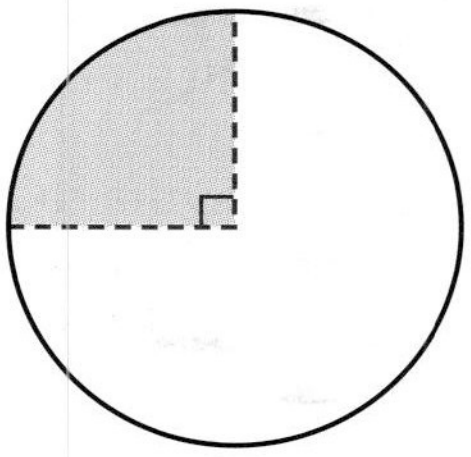

PRACTICE AND PROBLEM SOLVING

Extra Practice
See page 744.

13. A radio station broadcasts a signal over an area with a 75-mile radius. What is the area of the region that receives the radio signal?

14. A circular flower bed in Kay's backyard has a diameter of 8 feet. What is the area of the flower bed? Round your answer to the nearest tenth.

15. A company is manufacturing aluminum lids. The radius of each lid is 3 cm. What is the area of one lid? Round your answer to the nearest tenth.

Given the radius or diameter, find the circumference and area of each circle to the nearest tenth. Use 3.14 for π.

16. $r = 7$ m
17. $d = 18$ in.
18. $d = 24$ ft
19. $r = 6.4$ cm

Given the area, find the radius of each circle. Use 3.14 for π.

20. $A = 113.04 \text{ cm}^2$
21. $A = 3.14 \text{ ft}^2$
22. $A = 28.26 \text{ in}^2$

23. A hiker was last seen near a fire tower in the Catalina Mountains. Searchers are dispatched to the surrounding area to find the missing hiker.

a. Assume the hiker could walk in any direction at a rate of 3 miles per hour. How large an area would searchers have to cover if the hiker was last seen 2 hours ago? Use 3.14 for π. Round your answer to the nearest square mile.

b. How much additional area would the searchers have to cover if the hiker was last seen 3 hours ago?

24. **Physical Science** The tower of a wind turbine is about the height of a 20-story building. Each turbine can produce 24 megawatt-hours of electricity in one day. Find the area covered by the turbine when it is rotating. Use 3.14 for π. Round your answer to the nearest tenth.

25. **Critical Thinking** Two circles have the same radius. Is the combined area of the two circles the same as the area of a circle with twice the radius?

26. **What's the Question?** Chang painted half of a free-throw circle that has a diameter of 12 ft. The answer is 56.52 ft^2. What is the question?

27. **Write About It** Describe how to find the area of a circle when given only the circumference of the circle.

28. **Challenge** How does the area of a circle change if you multiply the radius by a factor of n, where n is a whole number?

Test Prep and Spiral Review

29. **Multiple Choice** The area of a circle is 30 square feet. A second circle has a radius that is 2 feet shorter than that of the first circle. What is the area, to the nearest tenth, of the second circle? Use 3.14 for π.

(A) 3.7 square feet (B) 10.0 square feet (C) 38.0 square feet (D) 179.2 square feet

30. **Short Response** A pizza parlor offers a large pizza with a 12-inch diameter. It also offers a "mega" pizza with a 24-inch diameter. The slogan used to advertise the mega pizza is "Twice the pizza of a large, and twice the fun." Is the mega pizza twice as big as the large? If not, how much bigger is it? Explain.

Line a || line b. Use the diagram to find each angle measure. (Lesson 8-3)

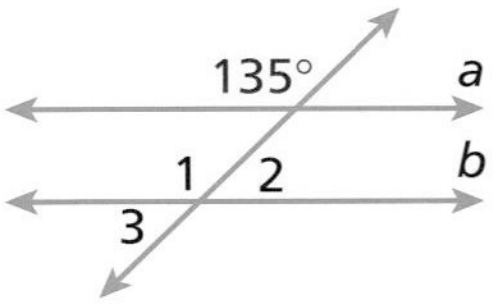

31. m∠1 32. m∠2 33. m∠3

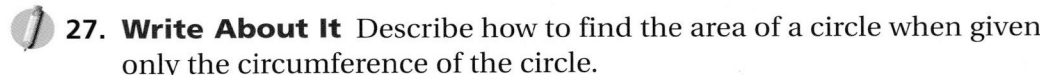

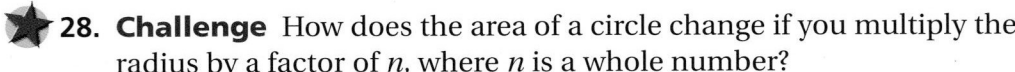

Graph the polygon with the given vertices. Then find the area of the polygon. (Lesson 9-4)

34. (−1, 1), (0, 4), (4, 1) 35. (−3, 3), (2, 3), (1, −1), (−1, −1)

9-6 Area of Irregular Figures

Learn to find the area of irregular figures.

You can find the area of an irregular figure by separating it into non-overlapping familiar figures. The sum of the areas of these figures is the area of the irregular figure. You can also estimate the area of an irregular figure by using graph paper.

EXAMPLE 1 Estimating the Area of an Irregular Figure

Estimate the area of the figure. Each square represents 1 ft^2.

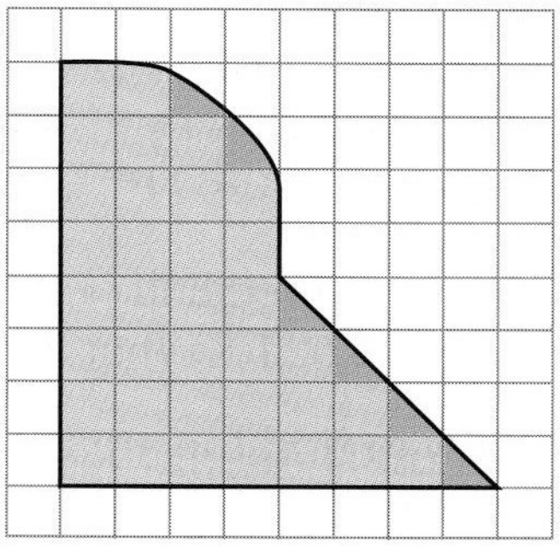

Count the number of filled or almost-filled squares: 35 yellow squares.

Count the number of squares that are about half-filled: 6 blue squares.

Add the number of filled squares plus $\frac{1}{2}$ the number of half-filled squares:

$35 + \left(\frac{1}{2} \cdot 6\right) = 35 + 3 = 38.$

The area of the figure is about 38 ft^2.

EXAMPLE 2 Finding the Area of an Irregular Figure

Find the area of the irregular figure. Use 3.14 for π.

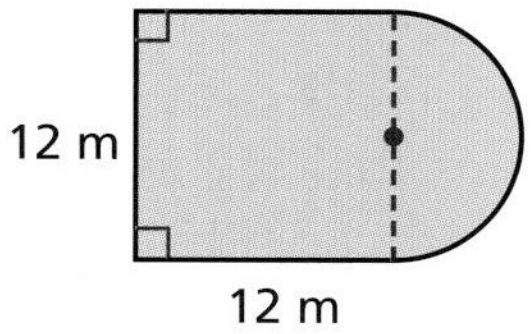

Step 1: Separate the figure into smaller, familiar figures.

Step 2: Find the area of each smaller figure.

Area of the square:

$A = s^2$ — *Use the formula for the area of a square.*

$A = 12^2 = 144$ — *Substitute 12 for s. Multiply.*

Area of the semicircle:

$A = \frac{1}{2}(\pi r^2)$ — *The area of a semicircle is $\frac{1}{2}$ the area of a circle.*

$A \approx \frac{1}{2}(3.14 \cdot 6^2)$ — *Substitute 3.14 for π and 6 for r.*

$A \approx \frac{1}{2}(113.04) \approx 56.52$ — *Multiply.*

Step 3: Add the areas to find the total area.

$A \approx 144 + 56.52 = 200.52$

The area of the irregular figure is about 200.52 m^2.

EXAMPLE 3 PROBLEM SOLVING APPLICATION

PROBLEM SOLVING

Chandra wants to carpet the floor of her closet. A floor plan of the closet is shown at right. How much carpet does she need?

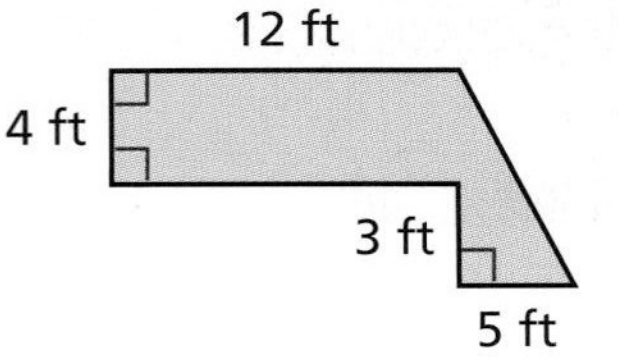

1 Understand the Problem

Rewrite the question as a statement:

- Find the amount of carpet needed to cover the floor of the closet.

List the **important information:**

- The floor of the closet is an irregular figure.
- The amount of carpet needed is equal to the area of the floor.

Helpful Hint

There are often several different ways to separate an irregular figure into familiar figures.

2 Make a Plan

Find the area of the floor by separating the figure into familiar figures: a rectangle and a triangle. Then add the areas of the rectangle and triangle to find the total area.

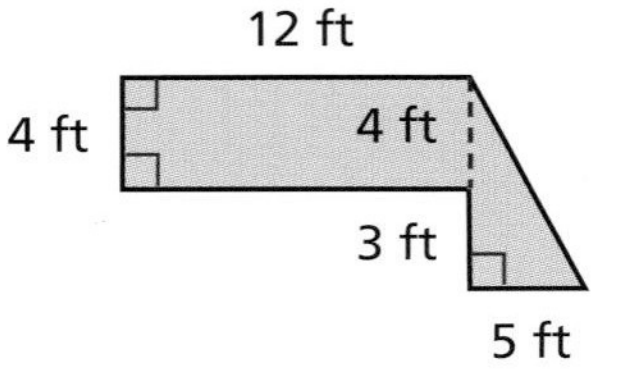

3 Solve

Find the area of each smaller figure.

Area of the rectangle:	Area of the triangle:
$A = \ell w$	$A = \frac{1}{2}bh$
$A = 12 \cdot 4$	$A = \frac{1}{2}(5)(3 + 4)$
$A = 48 \text{ ft}^2$	$A = \frac{1}{2}(35) = 17.5 \text{ ft}^2$

Add the areas to find the total area.

$A = 48 + 17.5 = 65.5$

Chandra needs 65.5 ft^2 of carpet.

4 Look Back

The area of the closet floor must be greater than the area of the rectangle (48 ft^2), so the answer is reasonable.

Think and Discuss

1. **Describe** two different ways to find the area of the irregular figure at right.
2. **Explain** why the area of the figure at right must be less than 32 in^2.

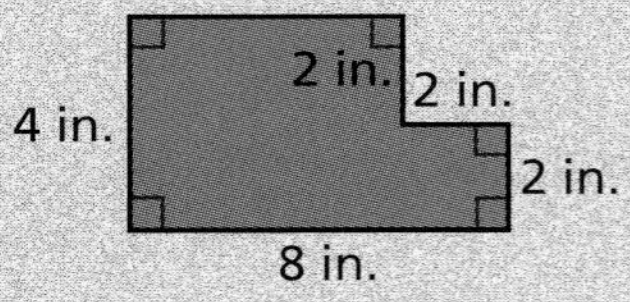

9-6 Exercises

go.hrw.com
Homework Help Online
KEYWORD: MS7 9-6
Parent Resources Online
KEYWORD: MS7 Parent

GUIDED PRACTICE

See Example 1

Estimate the area of each figure. Each square represents 1 ft^2.

1. 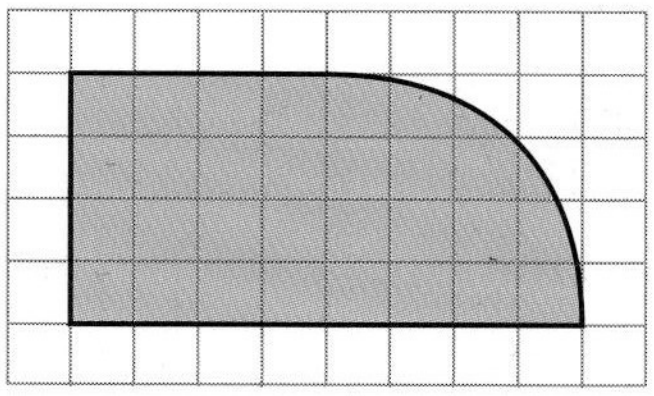

2. 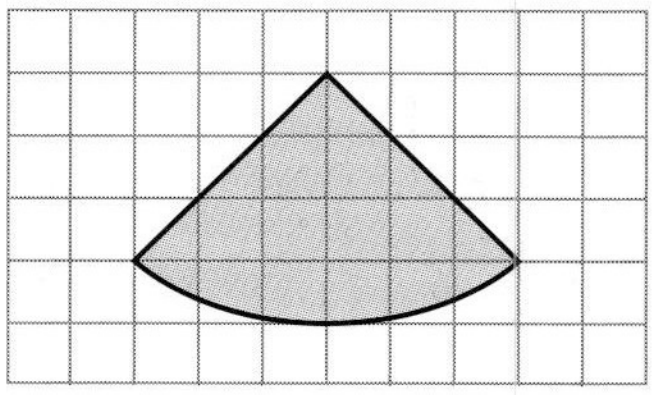

See Example 2

Find the area of each figure. Use 3.14 for π.

3. 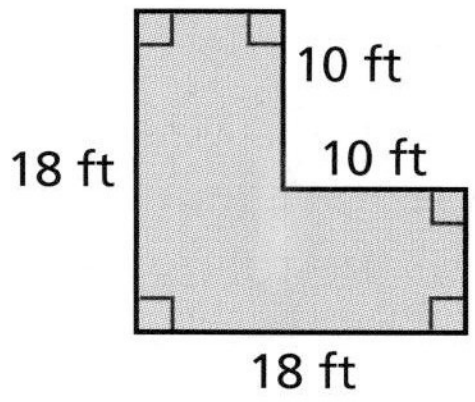

4. 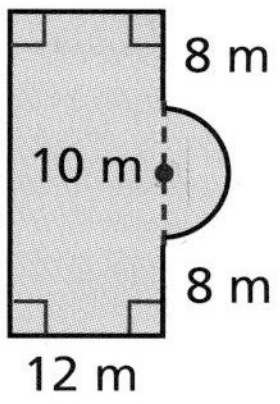

5. 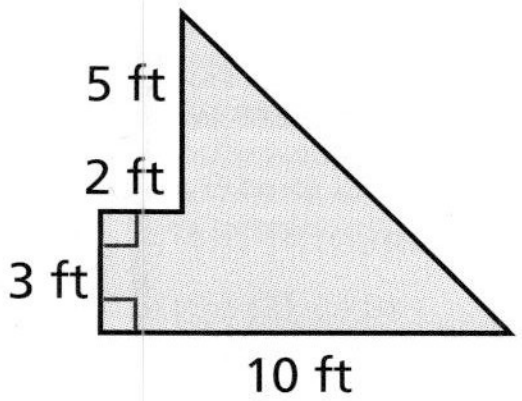

See Example 3

6. Luis has a model train set. The layout of the track is shown at right. How much artificial grass does Luis need in order to fill the interior of the layout? Use 3.14 for π.

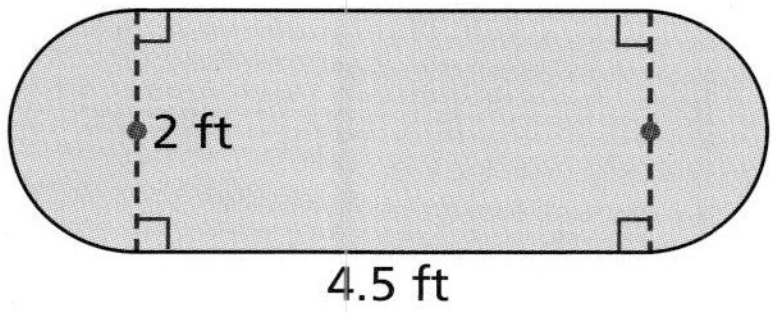

INDEPENDENT PRACTICE

See Example 1

Estimate the area of each figure. Each square represents 1 ft^2.

7. 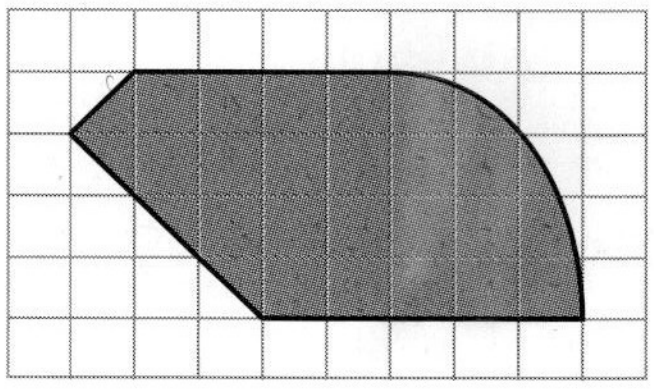

8. 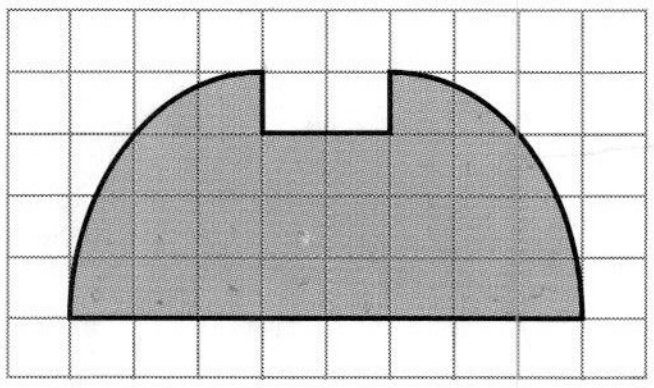

See Example 2

Find the area of each figure. Use 3.14 for π.

9. 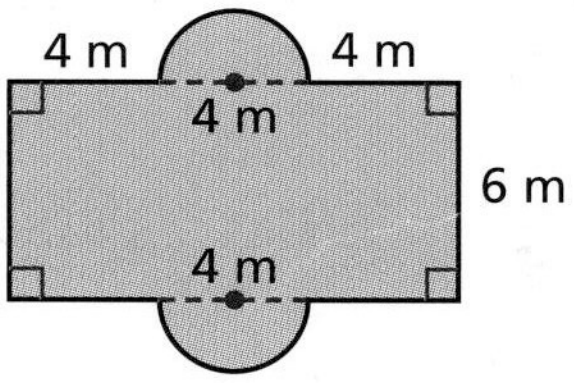

10. 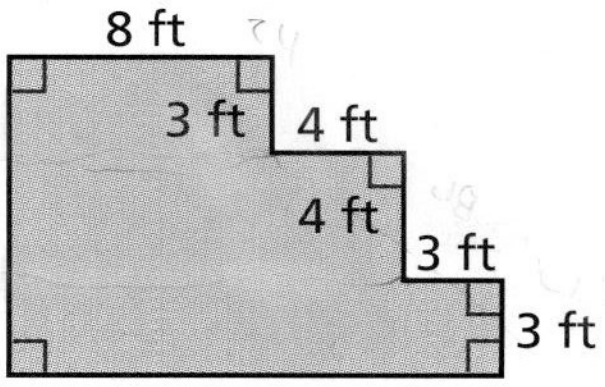

11. 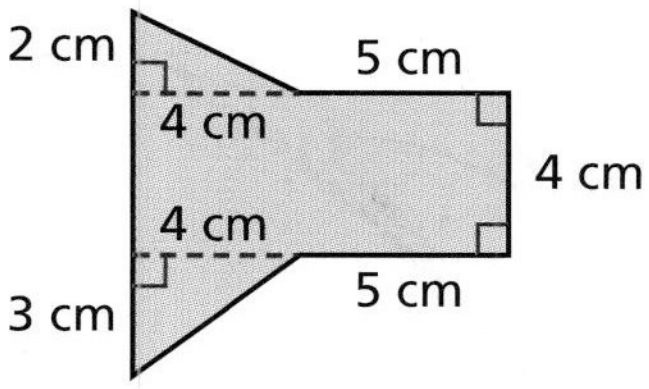

See Example 3

12. The figure shows the floor plan for a gallery of a museum. The ceiling of the gallery is to be covered with soundproofing material. How much material is needed? Use 3.14 for π.

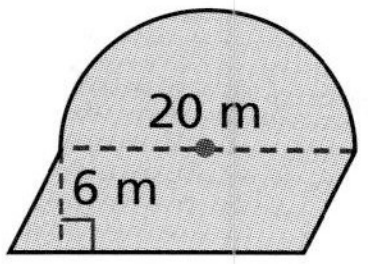

PRACTICE AND PROBLEM SOLVING

Extra Practice
See page 745.

Find the area and perimeter of each figure. Use 3.14 for π.

13.

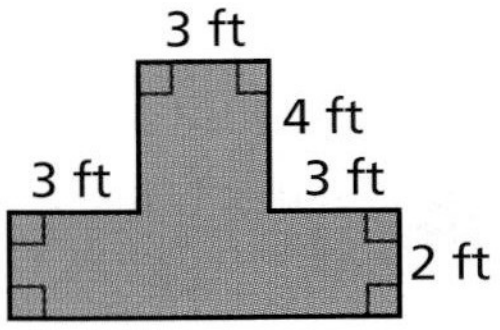

14.

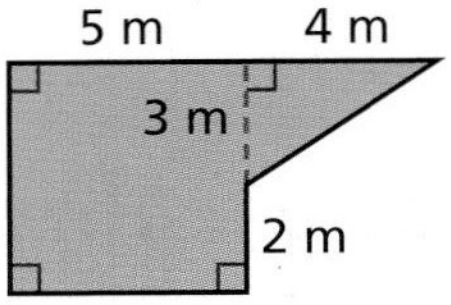

15.

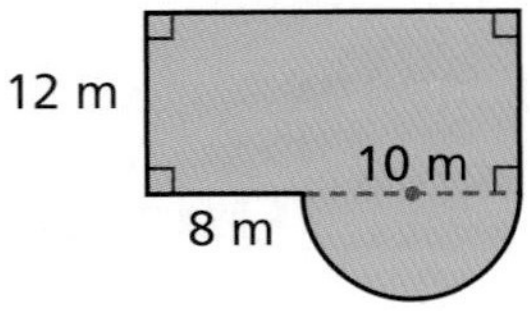

16. Multi-Step A figure has vertices $A(-8, 5)$, $B(-4, 5)$, $C(-4, 2)$, $D(3, 2)$, $E(3, -2)$, $F(6, -2)$, $G(6, -4)$, and $H(-8, -4)$. Graph the figure on a coordinate plane. Then find the area and perimeter of the figure.

17. Critical Thinking The figure at right is made up of an isosceles triangle and a square. The perimeter of the figure is 44 feet. What is the value of x?

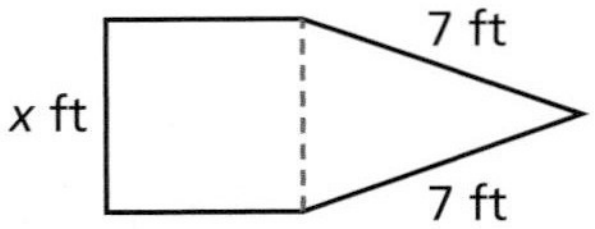

18. Choose a Strategy A figure is formed by combining a square and a triangle. Its total area is 32.5 m^2. The area of the triangle is 7.5 m^2. What is the length of each side of the square?

(A) 5 m (B) 15 m (C) 16.25 m (D) 25 m

19. Write About It Describe how to find the area of the irregular figure at right.

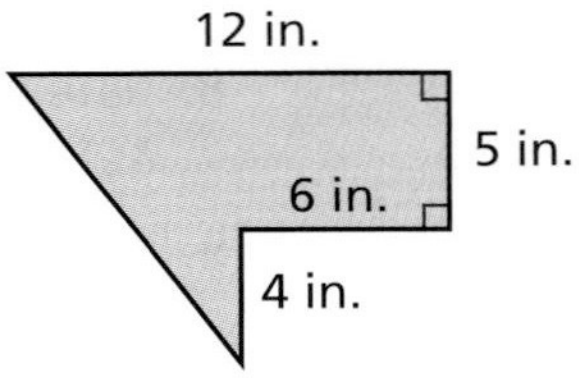

20. Challenge Find the area and perimeter of the figure at right. Use 3.14 for π.

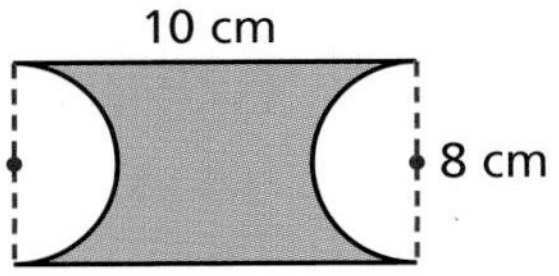

TEST PREP and Spiral Review

21. Multiple Choice A rectangle is formed by two congruent right triangles. The area of each triangle is 6 in^2. Each side of the rectangle is a whole number of inches. Which of these CANNOT be the perimeter of the rectangle?

(A) 26 in. (B) 24 in. (C) 16 in. (D) 14 in.

22. Extended Response The shaded area of the garden represents a patch of carrots. Veronica estimates that she will get about 12 carrots from this patch. Veronica is going to plant the rest of her garden with carrots. Estimate the total number of carrots she can expect to grow.

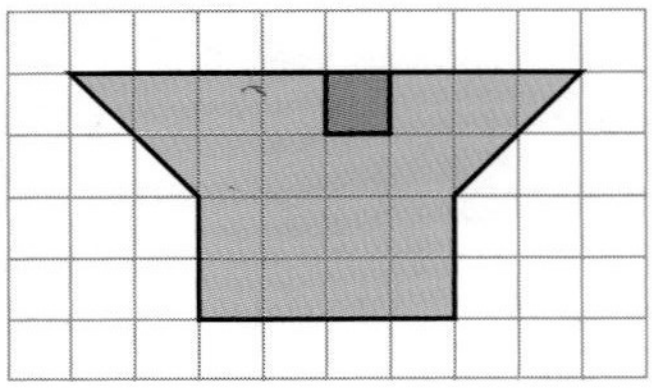

$\angle 1$ and $\angle 2$ are complementary angles. Find $m\angle 2$. (Lesson 8-2)

23. $m\angle 1 = 33°$ **24.** $m\angle 1 = 46°$ **25.** $m\angle 1 = 60°$ **26.** $m\angle 1 = 25.5°$

Given the diameter, find the area of each circle to the nearest tenth. Use 3.14 for π. (Lesson 9-5)

27. $d = 30$ m **28.** $d = 5.5$ cm **29.** $d = 18$ in. **30.** $d = 11$ ft

READY TO GO ON?

SECTION 9A

Quiz for Lessons 9-1 Through 9-6

9-1 Accuracy and Precision

1. Which measurement is more precise—5 in. or 56 ft?

Calculate. Use the correct number of significant digits in each answer.

2. 329 + 640
3. 5.6 • 2.59
4. 82.5 ÷ 16
5. 27.1 − 4

9-2 Perimeter and Circumference

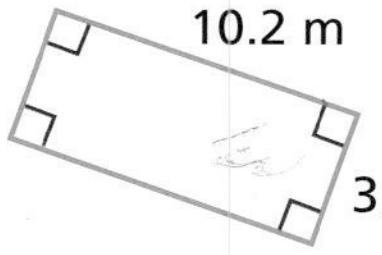

6. Find the perimeter of the figure at right.
7. If the circumference of a wheel is 94 cm, what is its approximate diameter?

9-3 Area of Parallelograms

8. The area of a rectangular courtyard is 1,508 m^2, and the length is 52 m. What is the width of the courtyard?
9. Jackson's kitchen is 8 yd by 3 yd. What is the area of his kitchen in square feet?

9-4 Area of Triangles and Trapezoids

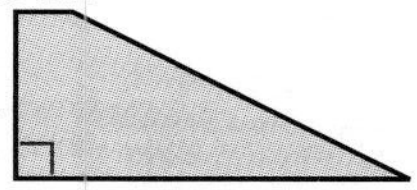

10. Find the area of the trapezoid at right.
11. A triangle has an area of 45 cm^2 and a base of 12.5 cm. What is the height of the triangle?

9-5 Area of Circles

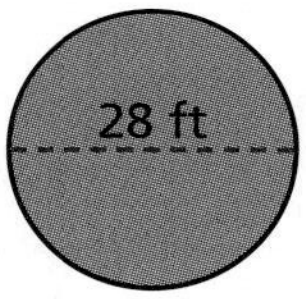

12. Find the area of the circle to the nearest tenth. Use 3.14 or $\frac{22}{7}$ for π.
13. The radius of a clock face is $8\frac{3}{4}$ in. What is its area to the nearest whole number?

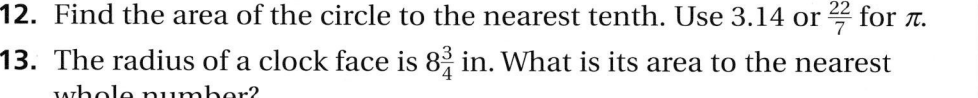

9-6 Area of Irregular Figures

Find the area of each figure to the nearest tenth. Use 3.14 for π.

14. 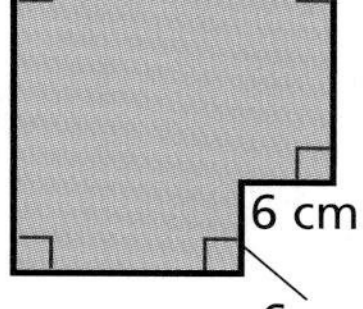

15. 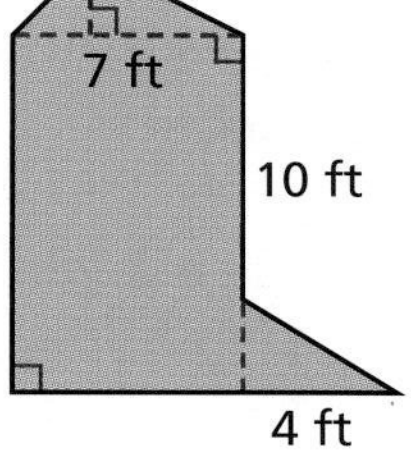

16. 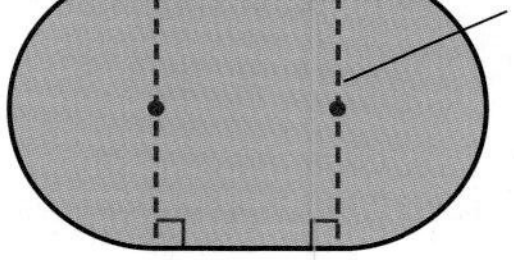

Focus on Problem Solving

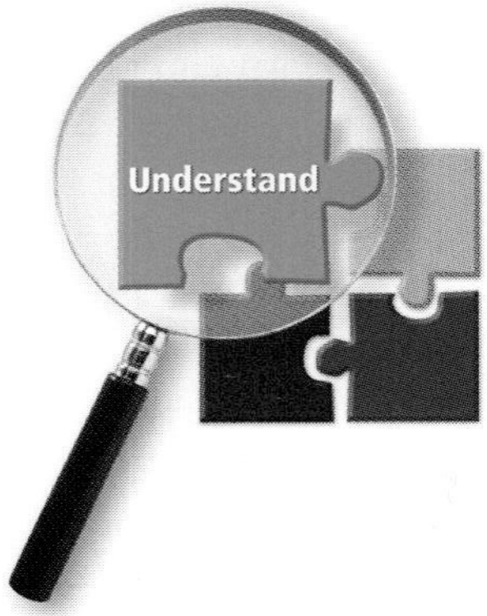

Understand the Problem

- **Identify too much or too little information**

Problems involving real-world situations sometimes give too much or too little information. Before solving these types of problems, you must decide what information is necessary and whether you have all the necessary information.

If the problem gives too much information, identify which of the facts are really needed to solve the problem. If the problem gives too little information, determine what additional information is required to solve the problem.

Copy each problem and underline the information you need to solve it. If necessary information is missing, write down what additional information is required.

1. Mrs. Wong wants to put a fence around her garden. One side of her garden measures 8 feet. Another side measures 5 feet. What length of fencing does Mrs. Wong need to enclose her garden?

2. Two sides of a triangle measure 17 inches and 13 inches. The perimeter of the triangle is 45 inches. What is the length in feet of the third side of the triangle? (There are 12 inches in 1 foot.)

3. During swim practice, Peggy swims 2 laps each of freestyle and backstroke. The dimensions of the pool are 25 meters by 50 meters. What is the area of the pool?

4. Each afternoon, Curtis walks his dog two times around the park. The park is a rectangle that is 315 yards long. How far does Curtis walk his dog each afternoon?

5. A trapezoid has bases that measure 12 meters and 18 meters and one side that measures 9 meters. The trapezoid has no right angles. What is the area of the trapezoid?

Hands-On LAB 9-7

Explore Square Roots and Perfect Squares

Use with Lesson 9-7

go.hrw.com
Lab Resources Online
KEYWORD: MS7 Lab9

You can use geometric models such as tiles or graph paper to represent squares and square roots.

Activity 1

1. Copy the three square arrangements below on graph paper. Continue the pattern until you have drawn 10 square arrangements.

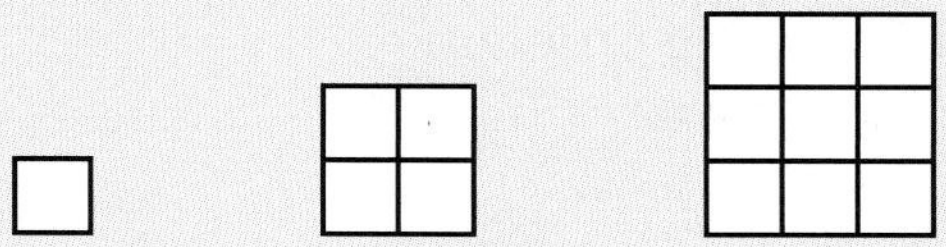

2. Copy and complete the table below. In the first column, write the number of small squares in each figure you drew. To complete the second column, use a calculator to find the square root.

   (To find the square root of 4, press 2nd $\sqrt{\ }$ x^2 4) ENTER .)

Total Number of Small Squares	Square Root
1	1
4	2
9	3
■	■
■	■
■	■
■	■
■	■
■	■
■	■

3. Shade in one column of each square arrangement that you drew in 1.

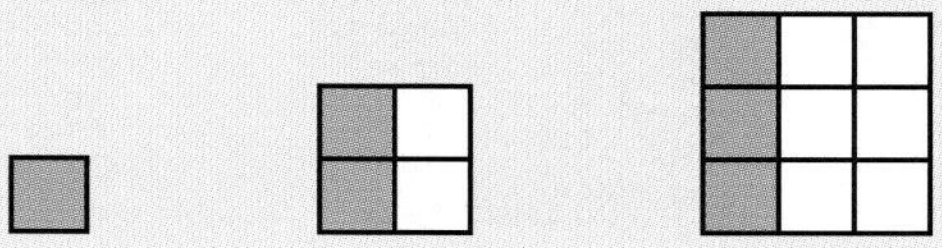

Think and Discuss

1. How does the square root relate to the total number of small squares in a figure?
2. How does the square root in the table relate to the shaded portion of each figure?

Try This

Use graph paper to find each square root.

1. 121 **2.** 144 **3.** 196

Activity 2

Follow the steps below to estimate $\sqrt{14}$.

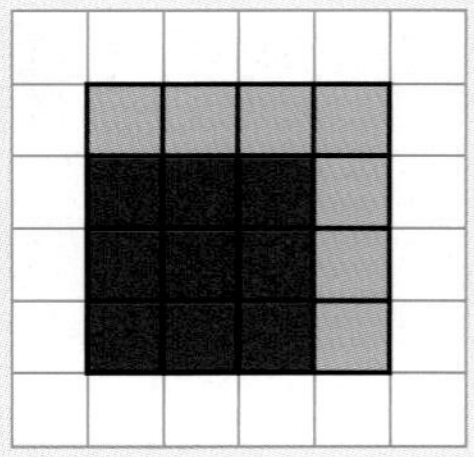

1 On graph paper, use one color to draw the smallest possible square arrangement using at least 14 small squares.

2 On the same arrangement, draw the largest possible square arrangement using less than 14 small squares.

3 Count the number of squares in each arrangement. Notice that 14 is between these numbers.

Number in small arrangement ***Number in large arrangement***

$$9 < 14 < 16$$

4 Use a calculator to find $\sqrt{14}$ to the nearest tenth. $\sqrt{14} = 3.7$. Use inequality symbols to compare the square roots of 9, 14, and 16.

$\sqrt{9} < \sqrt{14} < \sqrt{16}$

$3 < 3.7 < 4$ *The square root of 9 is less than the square root of 14, which is less than the square root of 16.*

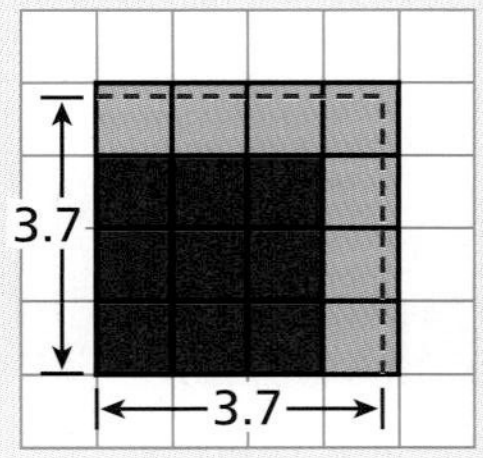

5 Use dashed lines on the figure to sketch a square that is 3.7 units on each side.

Think and Discuss

1. Describe how to use two numbers to estimate the square roots of nonperfect squares without using a calculator.
2. Explain how you can use graph paper to estimate $\sqrt{19}$.
3. Name three numbers that have square roots between 5 and 6.

Try This

Use graph paper to estimate each square root. Then use a calculator to find the square root to the nearest tenth.

1. $\sqrt{19}$ **2.** $\sqrt{10}$ **3.** $\sqrt{28}$ **4.** $\sqrt{35}$

9-7 Squares and Square Roots

Learn to find and estimate square roots of numbers.

Vocabulary

perfect square

square root

radical sign

A square with sides that measure 3 units each has an area of $3 \cdot 3$, or 3^2. Notice that the area of the square is represented by a power in which the base is the side length and the exponent is 2. A power in which the exponent is 2 is called a *square.*

EXAMPLE 1 Finding Squares of Numbers

Find each square.

A 6^2

Method 1: Use a model.

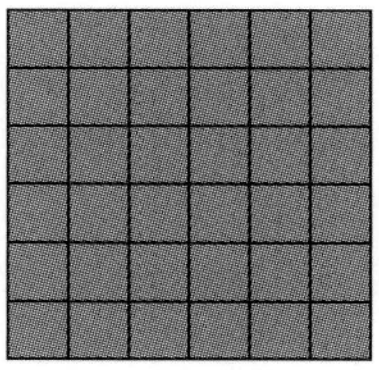

$A = \ell w$

$A = 6 \cdot 6$

$A = 36$

The square of 6 is 36.

B 14^2

Method 2: Use a calculator.

Press 14 x^2 ENTER.

$14^2 = 196$

The square of 14 is 196.

A **perfect square** is the square of a whole number. The number 36 is a perfect square because $36 = 6^2$ and 6 is a whole number.

Reading Math

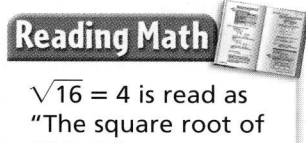

$\sqrt{16} = 4$ is read as "The square root of 16 is 4."

The **square root** of a number is one of the two equal factors of the number. Four is a square root of 16 because $4 \cdot 4 = 16$. The symbol for a square root is $\sqrt{\ }$, which is called a **radical sign**.

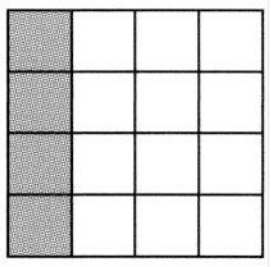

EXAMPLE 2 Finding Square Roots of Perfect Squares

Find each square root.

A $\sqrt{64}$

Method 1: Use a model.

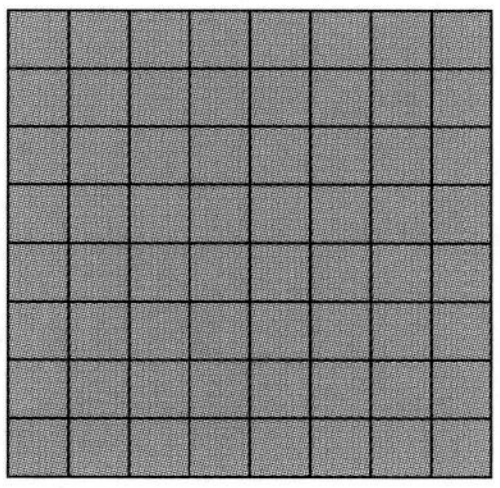

The square root of 64 is 8.

Find each square root.

B $\sqrt{324}$

Method 2: Use a calculator. Press 2nd x^2 324 ENTER.

$\sqrt{324} = 18$

The square root of 324 is 18.

You can use perfect squares to estimate the square roots of nonperfect squares.

EXAMPLE 3 Estimating Square Roots

Estimate $\sqrt{30}$ to the nearest whole number. Use a calculator to check your answer.

1, 4, 9, 16, 25, 36, . . . — *List some perfect squares.*

$25 < 30 < 36$ — *Find the perfect squares nearest 30.*

$\sqrt{25} < \sqrt{30} < \sqrt{36}$

$5 < \sqrt{30} < 6$ — *Find the square roots of 25 and 36.*

$\sqrt{30} \approx 5$ — *30 is closer to 25 than to 36.*

Check

$\sqrt{30} \approx 5.477225575$ — *Use a calculator to approximate $\sqrt{30}$. 5 is a reasonable estimate.*

EXAMPLE 4 *Recreation Application*

While searching for a lost hiker, a helicopter pilot covers a square area of 150 mi^2. What is the approximate length of each side of the square area? Round your answer to the nearest mile.

The length of each side of the square is $\sqrt{150}$.

$144 < 150 < 169$ — *Find the perfect squares nearest 150.*

$\sqrt{144} < \sqrt{150} < \sqrt{169}$

$12 < \sqrt{150} < 13$ — *Find the square roots of 144 and 169.*

$\sqrt{150} \approx 12$ — *150 is closer to 144 than to 169.*

Each side of the search area is about 12 miles long.

Think and Discuss

1. **Explain** how to estimate $\sqrt{75}$.
2. **Explain** how you might find the square root of 3^2.

9-7 Exercises

go.hrw.com
Homework Help Online
KEYWORD: MS7 9-7
Parent Resources Online
KEYWORD: MS7 Parent

GUIDED PRACTICE

See Example 1
Find each square.

1. 4^2 **2.** 17^2 **3.** 9^2 **4.** 15^2

See Example 2
Find each square root.

5. $\sqrt{400}$ **6.** $\sqrt{9}$ **7.** $\sqrt{144}$ **8.** $\sqrt{529}$

See Example 3
Estimate each square root to the nearest whole number. Use a calculator to check your answer.

9. $\sqrt{20}$ **10.** $\sqrt{45}$ **11.** $\sqrt{84}$ **12.** $\sqrt{58}$

See Example 4
13. A Coast Guard ship patrols an area of 125 square miles. The area the ship patrols is a square. About how long is each side of the area? Round your answer to the nearest mile.

INDEPENDENT PRACTICE

See Example 1
Find each square.

14. 3^2 **15.** 16^2 **16.** 8^2 **17.** 11^2

See Example 2
Find each square root.

18. $\sqrt{361}$ **19.** $\sqrt{16}$ **20.** $\sqrt{169}$ **21.** $\sqrt{441}$

See Example 3
Estimate each square root to the nearest whole number. Use a calculator to check your answer.

22. $\sqrt{12}$ **23.** $\sqrt{39}$ **24.** $\sqrt{73}$ **25.** $\sqrt{109}$

See Example 4
26. The area of a square field is 200 ft^2. What is the approximate length of each side of the field? Round your answer to the nearest foot.

PRACTICE AND PROBLEM SOLVING

Extra Practice
See page 745.

Estimate each square root to the nearest whole number.

27. $\sqrt{6}$ **28.** $\sqrt{180}$ **29.** $\sqrt{145}$ **30.** $\sqrt{216}$

31. $\sqrt{300}$ **32.** $\sqrt{420}$ **33.** $\sqrt{700}$ **34.** $\sqrt{1,500}$

Use a calculator to find each square root to the nearest tenth.

35. $\sqrt{44}$ **36.** $\sqrt{253}$ **37.** $\sqrt{87}$ **38.** $\sqrt{125}$

39. $\sqrt{380}$ **40.** $\sqrt{94}$ **41.** $\sqrt{202}$ **42.** $\sqrt{571}$

43. Critical Thinking An artist is making two square stained-glass windows. One window has a perimeter of 48 inches. The other has an area of 110 square inches. Which window is bigger? Explain.

LINK

Earth Science

To find the distance at which an object becomes visible, you can use your distance to the horizon and the object's distance to the horizon.

Given the area, find the missing value for each circle. Use 3.14 for π.

44. $A = 706.9\text{ m}^2$; $r =$ ____

45. $A = 615.44\text{ yd}^2$; $C =$ ____

46. $A = 28.26\text{ ft}^2$; $d =$ ____

47. $A = 3.14\text{ in}^2$; $r =$ ____

Order the numbers from least to greatest.

48. $\sqrt{49}, \frac{17}{3}, 6.5, 8, \frac{25}{4}$

49. $5\frac{2}{3}, \sqrt{25}, 3^2, 7.15, \frac{29}{4}$

50. Find the perimeter of a square whose area is 49 square inches.

51. Earth Science The formula $D = 3.56 \cdot \sqrt{A}$ gives the distance D in kilometers to the horizon from an airplane flying at an altitude A in meters. If a pilot is flying at an altitude of 1,800 m, about how far away is the horizon? Round your answer to the nearest kilometer.

52. Multi-Step For his new room, Darien's grandmother gave him a handmade quilt. The quilt is made up of 16 squares set in 4 rows of 4. The area of each square is 324 in^2. What are the dimensions of the quilt in inches?

53. Choose a Strategy The figure shows how two squares can be formed by drawing only seven lines. Show how two squares can be formed by drawing only six lines.

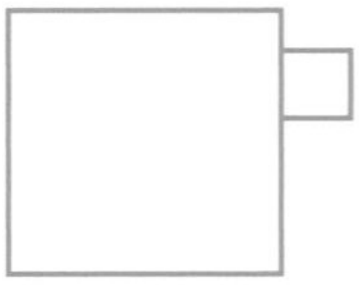

54. Write About It Explain the difference between finding the square of a number and finding the square root of a number. Use models and numbers in your explanation.

55. Challenge Find the value of $\sqrt{5^2 + 12^2}$.

TEST PREP and Spiral Review

56. Multiple Choice Which model represents 5^2?

Ⓐ

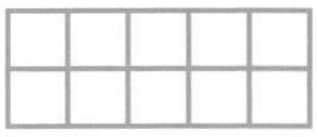

Ⓑ

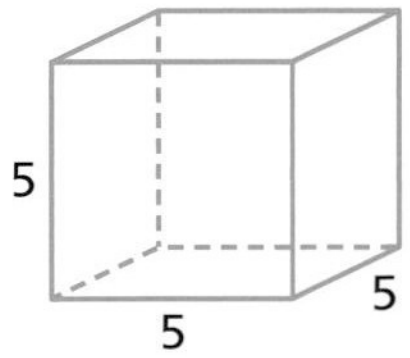

Ⓒ

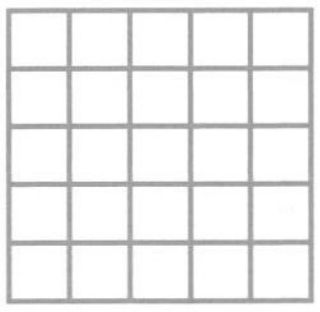

Ⓓ

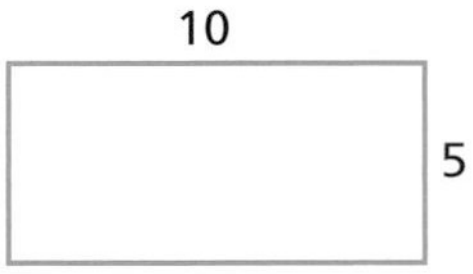

57. Multiple Choice Estimate the value of $\sqrt{87}$ to the nearest whole number.

Ⓕ 9　Ⓖ 10　Ⓗ 11　Ⓙ 12

Classify each triangle according to the lengths of its sides. (Lesson 8-6)

58. 2 in., 3 in., 4 in.

59. 5 cm, 5 cm, 5 cm

60. 8 ft, 6 ft, 8 ft

Given the radius or diameter, find the circumference and area of each circle to the nearest tenth. Use 3.14 for π. (Lesson 9-5)

61. $r = 11$ in.

62. $d = 25$ cm

63. $r = 3$ ft

Hands-On LAB 9-8

Explore the Pythagorean Theorem

Use with Lesson 9-8

go.hrw.com
Lab Resources Online
KEYWORD: MS7 Lab9

An important and famous relationship in mathematics, known as the Pythagorean Theorem, involves the three sides of a right triangle. Recall that a right triangle is a triangle that has one right angle. If you know the lengths of two sides of a right triangle, you can find the length of the third side.

Activity 1

1. The drawing at right shows an isosceles right triangle and three squares. Make your own drawing similar to the one shown. (Recall that an isosceles right triangle has two congruent sides and a right angle.)

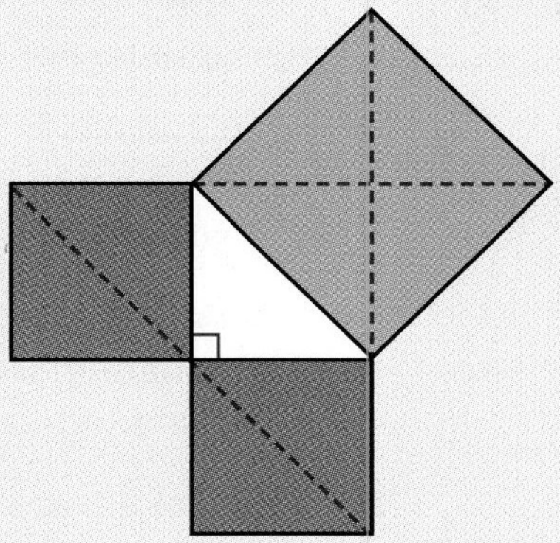

Cut out the two smaller squares of your drawing, then cut those squares in half along a diagonal. Fit the pieces of the smaller squares on top of the blue square.

Think and Discuss

1. What can you tell about the relationship between the areas of the squares?

2a. How does the side length of a square relate to the area of the square?

b. How do the side lengths of the triangle in your drawing relate to the areas of the squares around it?

c. Write an equation that shows the relationship between the lengths of the sides of the triangle in your drawing. Use the variables a and b to represent the lengths of the two shorter sides of your triangle, and c to represent the length of the longest side.

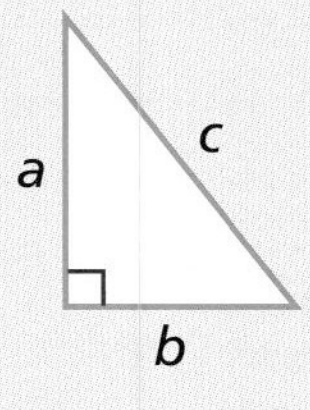

Try This

1. Repeat Activity 1 for other isosceles right triangles. Is the relationship that you found true for the areas of the squares around each triangle?

Activity 2

1 On graph paper, draw a segment that is 3 units long. At one end of this segment, draw a perpendicular segment that is 4 units long. Draw a third segment to form a triangle. Cut out the triangle.

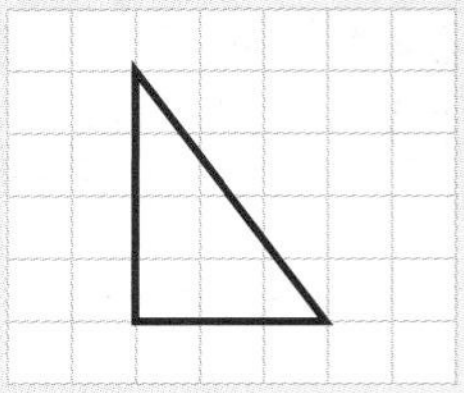

Cut out a 3-by-3 square and a 4-by-4 square from the same graph paper. Place the edges of the squares against the corresponding sides of the right triangle.

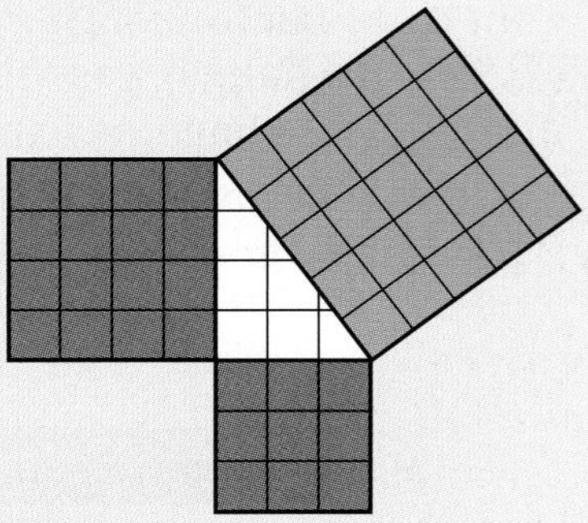

Cut the two squares into individual squares or strips. Arrange the squares into a large square along the third side of the triangle.

Think and Discuss

1. What is the area of each of the three squares? What relationship is there between the areas of the small squares and the area of the large square?
2. What is the length of the third side of the triangle?
3. Substitute the side lengths of your triangle into the equation you wrote in Think and Discuss Problem **2c** in Activity 1. What do you find?
4. Do you think the relationship is true for triangles that are not right triangles?

Try This

1. Use graph paper to cut out three squares with sides that are 3 units, 4 units, and 6 units long. Fit the squares together to form a triangle as shown at right. Is the relationship between the areas of the red squares and the area of the blue square the same as the relationship shown in Activity 2? Explain.

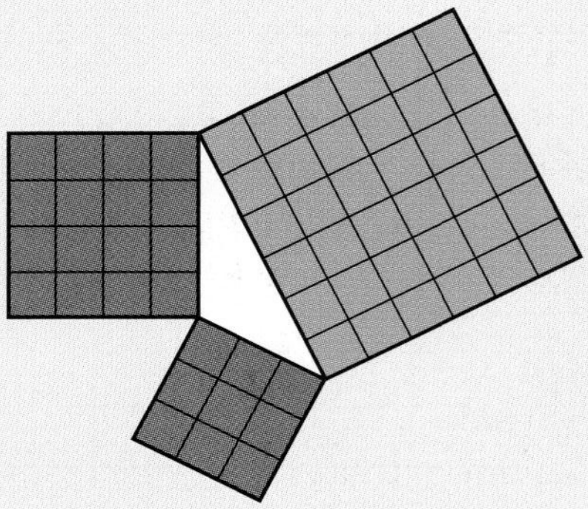

2. If you know the lengths of the two short sides of a right triangle are 9 and 12, can you find the length of the longest side? Show your work.
3. If you know the length of the longest side of a right triangle and the length of one of the shorter sides, how would you find the length of the third side?

9-8 The Pythagorean Theorem

Learn to use the Pythagorean Theorem to find the length of a side of a right triangle.

Vocabulary

leg

hypotenuse

Pythagorean Theorem

One of the first people to recognize the relationship between the sides of a right triangle was the Greek mathematician Pythagoras. This special relationship is called the *Pythagorean Theorem.*

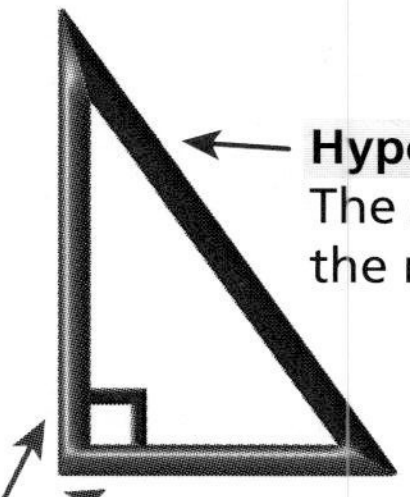

PYTHAGOREAN THEOREM		
In a right triangle, the sum of the squares of the lengths of the legs is equal to the square of the length of the hypotenuse.	$a^2 + b^2 = c^2$	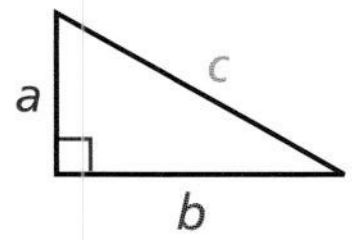

You can use the Pythagorean Theorem to find the length of any side of a right triangle.

EXAMPLE 1 Calculating the Length of a Side of a Right Triangle

Use the Pythagorean Theorem to find each missing measure.

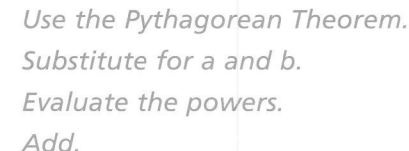

A

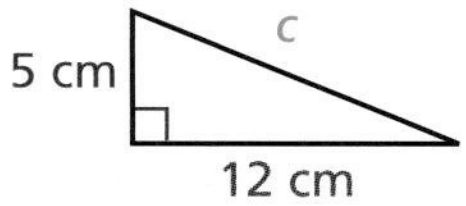

$a^2 + b^2 = c^2$ *Use the Pythagorean Theorem.*

$5^2 + 12^2 = c^2$ *Substitute for a and b.*

$25 + 144 = c^2$ *Evaluate the powers.*

$169 = c^2$ *Add.*

$\sqrt{169} = \sqrt{c^2}$ *Take the square root of both sides.*

$13 = c$

The length of the hypotenuse is 13 cm.

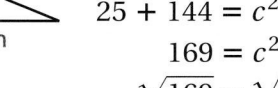

B

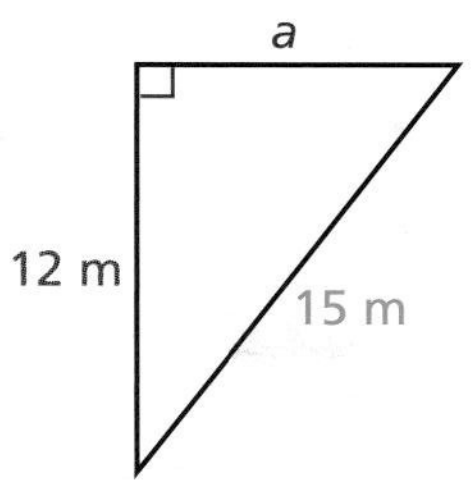

$a^2 + b^2 = c^2$ *Use the Pythagorean Theorem.*

$a^2 + 12^2 = 15^2$ *Substitute for b and c.*

$a^2 + 144 = 225$ *Evaluate the powers.*

$-144 \quad -144$ *Subtract 144 from both sides.*

$a^2 = 81$

$\sqrt{a^2} = \sqrt{81}$ *Take the square root of both sides.*

$a = 9$

The length of the leg is 9 m.

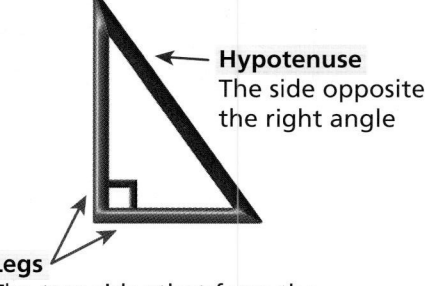

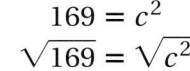

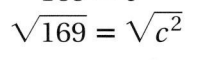

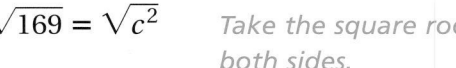

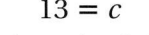

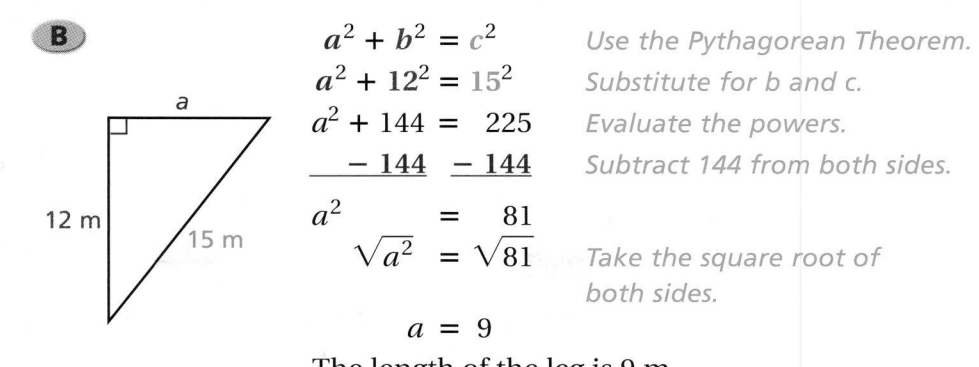

EXAMPLE 2

PROBLEM SOLVING

PROBLEM SOLVING APPLICATION

A regulation baseball diamond is a square with sides that measure 90 feet. About how far is it from home plate to second base? Round your answer to the nearest tenth.

1 Understand the Problem

Rewrite the question as a statement.

- Find the distance from home plate to second base.

List the **important information:**

- Drawing a segment between home plate and second base divides the diamond into two right triangles.
- The angle at first base is the right angle, so the segment between home plate and second base is the hypotenuse.
- The base lines are legs, and they are each 90 feet long.

2 Make a Plan

You can use the Pythagorean Theorem to write an equation.

3 Solve

$a^2 + b^2 = c^2$	*Use the Pythagorean Theorem.*
$90^2 + 90^2 = c^2$	*Substitute for the known variables.*
$8{,}100 + 8{,}100 = c^2$	*Evaluate the powers.*
$16{,}200 = c^2$	*Add.*
$127.279 \approx c$	*Take the square root of both sides.*
$127.3 \approx c$	*Round.*

The distance from home plate to second base is about 127.3 ft.

4 Look Back

The hypotenuse is the longest side of a right triangle. Since the distance from home plate to second base is greater than the distance between the bases, the answer is reasonable.

Think and Discuss

1. Explain whether it is ever possible to use the Pythagorean Theorem to find an unknown side length of a scalene triangle.

2. Demonstrate whether a leg of a right triangle can be longer than the hypotenuse.

9-8 Exercises

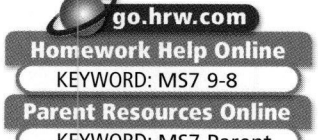

go.hrw.com
Homework Help Online
KEYWORD: MS7 9-8
Parent Resources Online
KEYWORD: MS7 Parent

GUIDED PRACTICE

See Example 1

Use the Pythagorean Theorem to find each missing measure.

1. 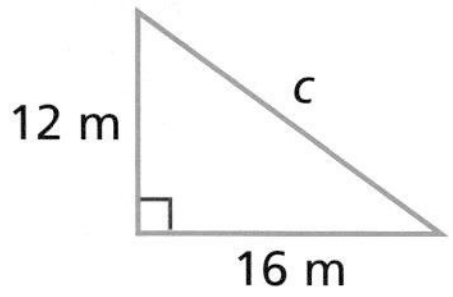

2. 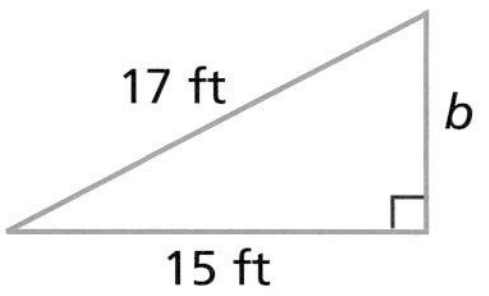

3. 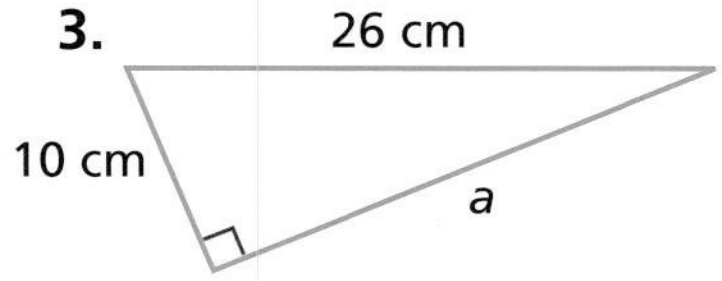

See Example 2

4. A 10 ft ladder is leaning against a wall. If the ladder is 5 ft from the base of the wall, how far above the ground does the ladder touch the wall? Round your answer to the nearest tenth.

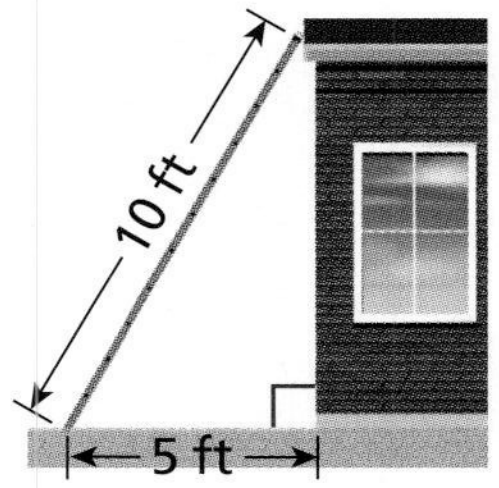

INDEPENDENT PRACTICE

See Example 1

Use the Pythagorean Theorem to find each missing measure.

5. 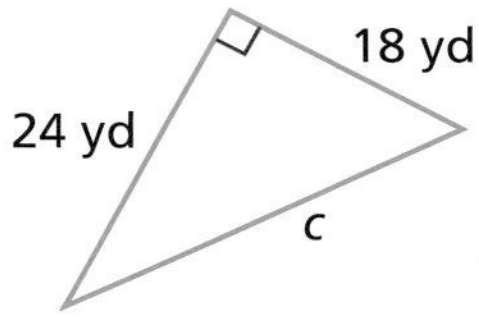

6. 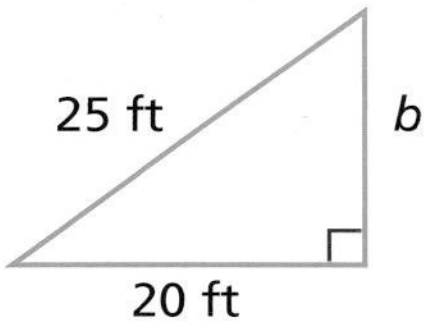

7. 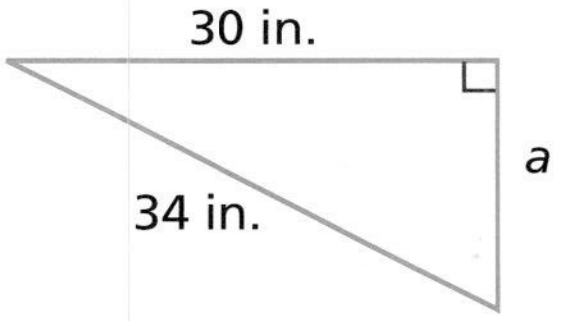

See Example 2

8. James rides his bike 15 miles west. Then he turns north and rides another 15 miles before he stops to rest. How far is James from his starting point when he stops to rest? Round your answer to the nearest tenth.

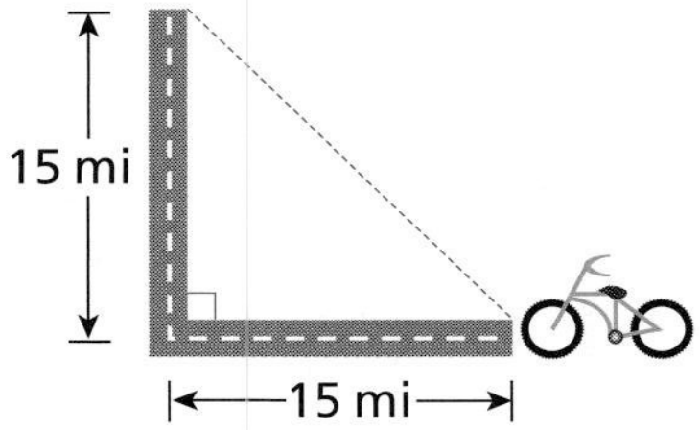

PRACTICE AND PROBLEM SOLVING

Extra Practice
See page 745.

The lengths of two sides of a right triangle are given. Find the length of the third side to the nearest tenth.

9. legs: 5 ft and 8 ft
10. leg: 10 mm; hypotenuse: 15 mm
11. leg: 19 m; hypotenuse: 31 m
12. legs: 21 yd and 20 yd
13. legs: 13.5 in. and 18 in.
14. leg: 13 cm; hypotenuse: 18 cm
15. **Critical Thinking** The numbers 3, 4, and 5 form a Pythagorean triple because $3^2 + 4^2 = 5^2$. When you double each of these values, does the resulting set of numbers also form a Pythagorean triple? Explain.

History LINK

16. Ancient Egyptians built pyramids to serve as tombs for their kings. One pyramid, called Menkaure, has a square base with an area of about 12,100 m^2.

a. What is the length of each side of the base?

b. What is the length of a diagonal of the base? Round your answer to the nearest tenth.

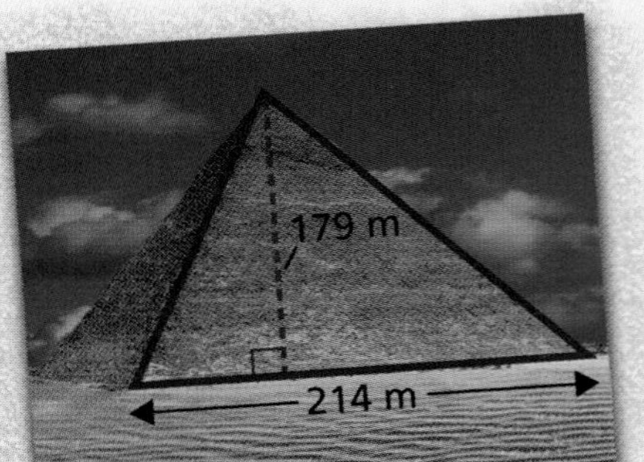

17. The photograph shows the Pyramid of Khafre in Egypt. Each side of its square base is about 214 meters long. Each triangular side is an isosceles triangle with a height of about 179 meters. What is the area of one side of the pyramid?

18. Use the Pythagorean Theorem to find the distance from one corner of the Pyramid of Khafre to its peak. Round your answer to the nearest tenth.

go.hrw.com
Web Extra!
KEYWORD: MS7 Egypt

19. Multi-Step The pyramids were constructed using a unit of measurement called a cubit. There are about 21 inches in 1 cubit. If the height of a pyramid is 471 feet, what is its height in cubits?

20. Write About It Given a right triangle, explain how you know which values to substitute into the equation $a^2 + b^2 = c^2$.

21. Challenge The pyramid at right has a square base. Find the height of the pyramid to the nearest tenth.

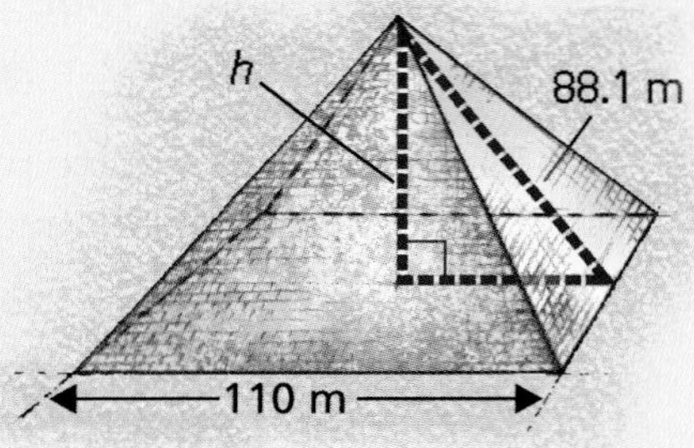

TEST PREP and Spiral Review

22. Multiple Choice Find the missing measure to the nearest tenth.

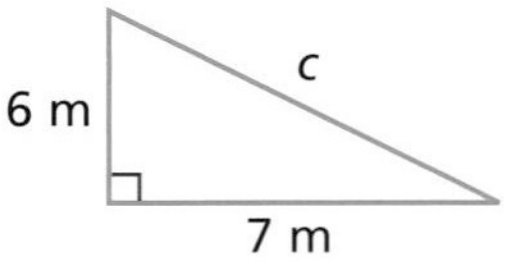

Ⓐ 3.6 m Ⓒ 11.8 m

Ⓑ 9.2 m Ⓓ 85 m

23. Gridded Response A 10-foot ladder is leaning against a wall. The bottom of the ladder is 2 feet away from the bottom of the wall. To the nearest tenth, how many feet up the wall will the ladder reach?

Find the measure of the angle formed by the hour and minute hands of a clock at each time. (Lesson 8-4)

24. 6:00 **25.** 3:00 **26.** 5:00 **27.** 2:00

Estimate each square root to the nearest whole number. (Lesson 9-7)

28. $\sqrt{140}$ **29.** $\sqrt{60}$ **30.** $\sqrt{200}$ **31.** $\sqrt{30}$

READY TO GO ON?

Quiz for Lessons 9-7 Through 9-8

9-7 Squares and Square Roots

Find each square.

1. 21^2
2. 7^2
3. 12^2
4. 13^2

Name the square and the square root represented by each model.

5. 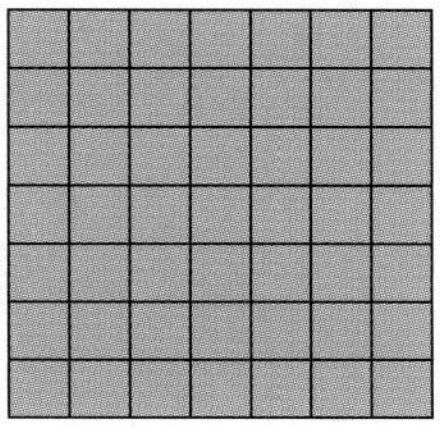

6. 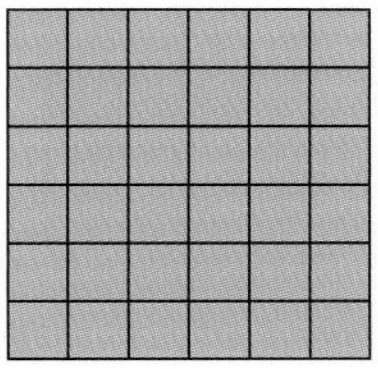

7. 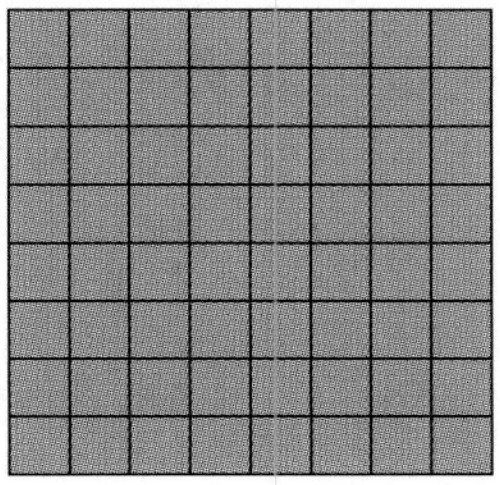

Find each square root.

8. $\sqrt{841}$
9. $\sqrt{1{,}089}$
10. $\sqrt{81}$
11. $\sqrt{576}$

Estimate each square root to the nearest whole number. Use a calculator to check your answer.

12. $\sqrt{40}$
13. $\sqrt{85}$
14. $\sqrt{12}$
15. $\sqrt{33}$

9-8 The Pythagorean Theorem

Use the Pythagorean Theorem to find each missing measure.

16. 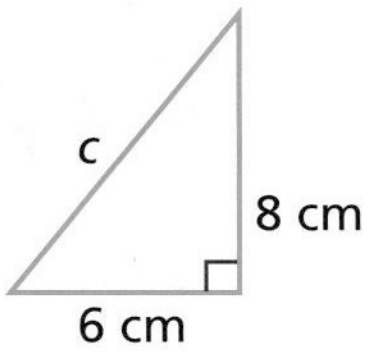

17. 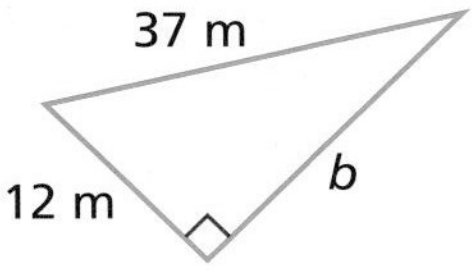

18. 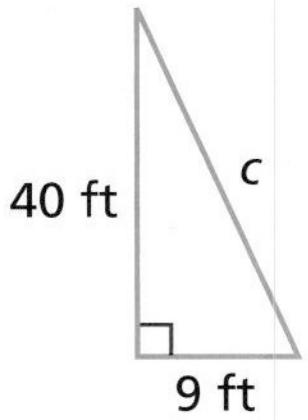

19. Thomas likes to jog at Memorial Park. The running trail he follows is in the shape of a right triangle. He knows one leg of the path is 1.8 miles, and the other leg is 3.2 miles. What is the distance of the third side of the trail to the nearest tenth of a mile?

20. Audrey built a ramp for the set of the new musical at her school. The height of the ramp is 8 feet, and the hypotenuse is 17 feet. What is the length of the ramp's base?

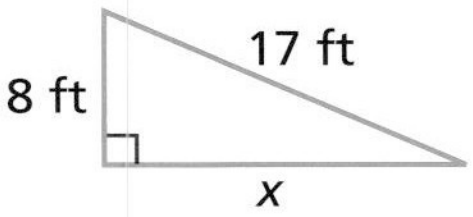

The lengths of two sides of a right triangle are given. Find the length of the third side to the nearest tenth.

21. leg: 14.3 m; hypotenuse: 22 m
22. legs: 10 yd and 24 yd
23. legs: 12.4 in. and 9.0 in.
24. leg: 2.5 cm; hypotenuse: 8 cm

MULTI-STEP TEST PREP

Gabriella's Garden Gabriella is designing a rectangular garden for her school. As shown in the figure, the garden will be surrounded by a walkway that is 5 feet wide.

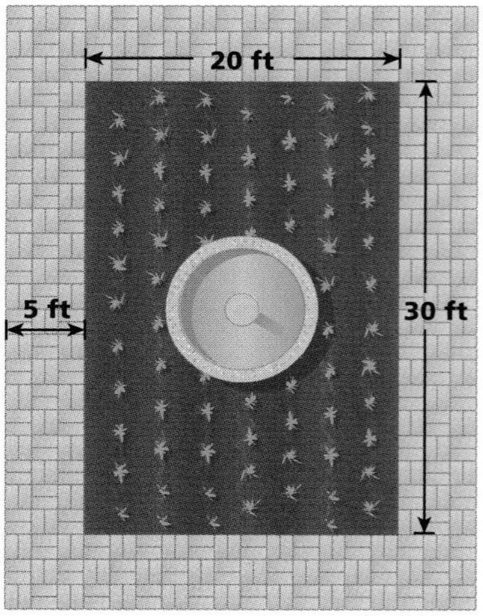

1. Gabriella wants to put a fence around the outside of the walkway. How much fencing does she need?
2. Gabriella is going to plant cabbage seedlings around the inside edge of the walkway. The seedlings should be planted 12 inches apart. How many seedlings will she need?
3. The design calls for a circular fountain in the center of the garden. The fountain's diameter will be 10 feet. To the nearest tenth of a foot, what will be the length of the concrete border that forms the edge of the fountain?
4. What is the area of the remaining land that is available for plants? Explain.
5. To help protect and enrich the soil, Gabriella plans to cover the planted part of the garden with mulch. One bag of mulch covers 18 square feet. How many bags should she buy?
6. To celebrate the opening of the garden, Gabriella wants to hang streamers from poles at the outer corners of the walkway, creating an X. How many feet of streamers will Gabriella need?

EXTENSION

Identifying and Graphing Irrational Numbers

Learn to classify numbers as rational or irrational and graph them on a number line.

Vocabulary

irrational numbers

Recall from Lesson 2-11 that a rational number can be written as a fraction with integers for its numerator and denominator. When rational numbers are written in decimal form, the decimal may be terminating or nonterminating. If a rational number is nonterminating, then it has a repeating pattern.

A decimal that is nonterminating with no repeating pattern is an **irrational number**.

Rational		Irrational
Terminating	**Nonterminating, Repeating**	**Nonterminating, Nonrepeating**
$\frac{1}{8} = 0.125$	$\frac{1}{3} = 0.333\ldots$, or $0.\overline{3}$	$\sqrt{2} = 1.414213562\ldots$
$\sqrt{9} = 3$	$\frac{2}{11} = 0.181818\ldots$, or $0.\overline{18}$	$\pi = 3.1415926\ldots$

EXAMPLE 1 Identifying Rational and Irrational Numbers

Identify each number as rational or irrational. Justify your answer.

A $\frac{2}{5}$

$\frac{2}{5} = 0.4$ *Write the number in decimal form.*

Because its decimal form is terminating, $\frac{2}{5}$ is rational.

B $\frac{5}{6}$

$\frac{5}{6} = 0.8333\ldots$, or $0.8\overline{3}$ *Write the number in decimal form.*

Because its decimal form is nonterminating and repeating, $\frac{5}{6}$ is rational.

C $\sqrt{16}$

$\sqrt{16} = 4$ *Write the number in decimal form.*

Because its decimal form is terminating, $\sqrt{16}$ is rational.

D $\sqrt{7}$

$\sqrt{7} = 2.645751311\ldots$ *Write the number in decimal form.*

There is no pattern in the decimal form of $\sqrt{7}$. It is a nonterminating, nonrepeating decimal. So $\sqrt{7}$ is irrational.

Remember!

By definition, any ratio of integers is a rational number.

Every point on the number line corresponds to a real number, either a rational number or an irrational number. Between every two real numbers there is always another real number.

EXAMPLE 2 Graphing Rational and Irrational Numbers

Graph the list of numbers on a number line. Then order the numbers from least to greatest.

$1.4, \sqrt{5}, \frac{3}{8}, \pi, -\frac{2}{3}, \sqrt{4}, \sqrt{16}$

Write all the numbers in decimal form, and then graph them.

$1.4, \sqrt{5} \approx 2.236, \frac{3}{8} = 0.375, \pi \approx 3.14, -\frac{2}{3} = -0.\overline{6}, \sqrt{4} = 2.0, \sqrt{16} = 4.0$

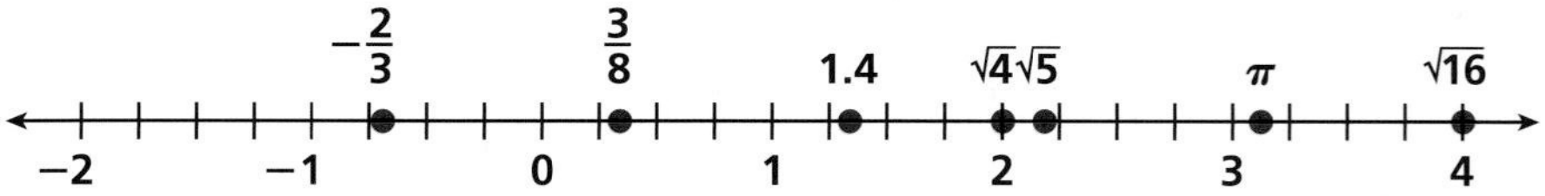

From left to right on the number line, the numbers appear from least to greatest: $-\frac{2}{3} < \frac{3}{8} < 1.4 < \sqrt{4} < \sqrt{5} < \pi < \sqrt{16}$.

EXTENSION Exercises

Identify each number as rational or irrational. Justify your answer.

1. $\sqrt{8}$ **2.** $\frac{5}{11}$ **3.** $\frac{7}{8}$ **4.** $\sqrt{36}$

5. $\frac{3}{13}$ **6.** $\sqrt{14}$ **7.** 2.800 **8.** $\frac{5}{6}$

9. $\sqrt{5}$ **10.** $\frac{6}{24}$ **11.** $\frac{10}{33}$ **12.** $\sqrt{18}$

Graph each list of numbers on a number line. Then order the numbers from least to greatest.

13. $2.6, 0.5, \sqrt{3}, -\frac{7}{10}, \frac{1}{3}$

14. $\sqrt{12}, \frac{3}{8}, -0.65, \frac{5}{9}, \sqrt{11}$

15. $-1.3, \sqrt{15}, 3.1, -\frac{2}{5}, \sqrt{4}$

16. $-2.1, -\frac{9}{10}, \sqrt{1}, -1.5, \sqrt{9}$

Name the two perfect squares that each square root lies between. Then graph the square root on a number line, and justify its placement.

17. $\sqrt{34}$ **18.** $\sqrt{46}$ **19.** $\sqrt{14}$ **20.** $\sqrt{6}$

21. $\sqrt{99}$ **22.** $\sqrt{63}$ **23.** $\sqrt{71}$ **24.** $\sqrt{13}$

25. What's the Error? A classmate tells you that the square root of any number is irrational. Explain why the classmate is incorrect.

Game Time

Shape Up

Rectangles

The square below has been divided into four rectangles. The areas of two of the rectangles are given. If the length of each of the segments in the diagram is an integer, what is the area of the original square?

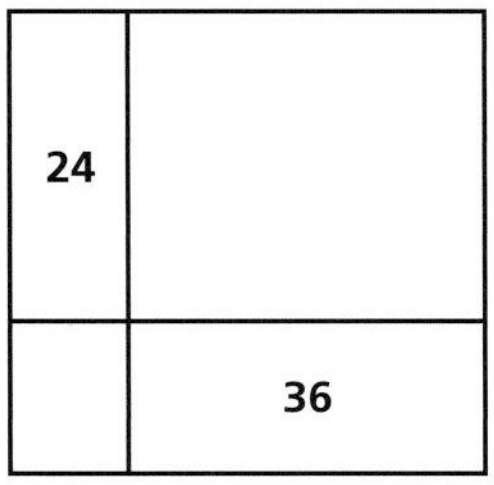

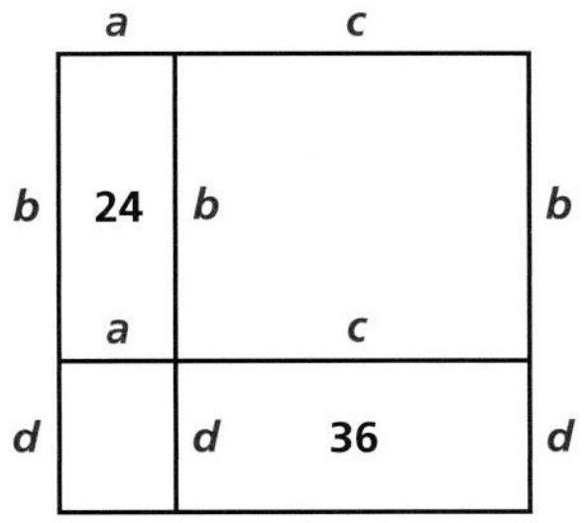

(*Hint:* Remember $a + c = b + d$.)

Use different lengths and a different answer to create your own version of this puzzle.

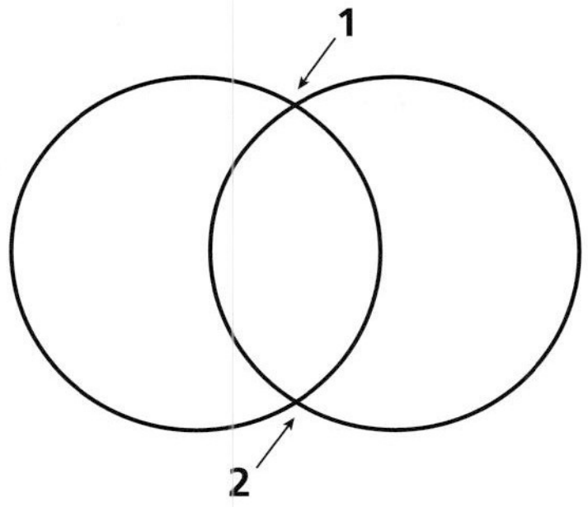

Circles

What is the maximum number of times that six circles of the same size can intersect? To find the answer, start by drawing two circles that are the same size. What is the greatest number of times they can intersect? Add another circle, and another, and so on.

Circles and Squares

Two players start with a sequence of circles and squares. Before beginning the game, each player chooses whether to be a "circle" or a "square." The goal of the game is to have the final remaining shape be the shape you chose to be. Shapes are removed from the sequence according to the following rules: On each move, a player selects two shapes. If the shapes are identical, they are replaced with one square. If the shapes are different, they are replaced with one circle.

go.hrw.com
Game Time Extra
KEYWORD: MS7 Games

A complete copy of the rules and game pieces are available online.

FOLDNOTES

It's in the Bag!

Materials
- lunch bag
- scissors
- tape
- markers
- index cards

PROJECT Bag o' Measurement

This bag of index cards will help you organize your notes on measuring two-dimensional figures.

1. Hold the lunch bag with the flap facing you at the top. Cut a thin strip from the flap as shown. **Figure A**
2. Cut along the sides of the flap so you can open it up. Then use your scissors to round off the corners at the top of the flap. **Figure B**
3. Fold up the bottom part of the flap. Then trim this part of the flap by cutting out a trapezoid as shown. **Figure C**
4. Cut another trapezoid from the bottom edge of the bag by cutting through all the layers. Then fold up the bottom of the bag to make two pockets, one below the other. **Figure D**
5. Tape the sides of the bag together to close the pockets. Fold down the flap and label it with the number and title of the chapter.

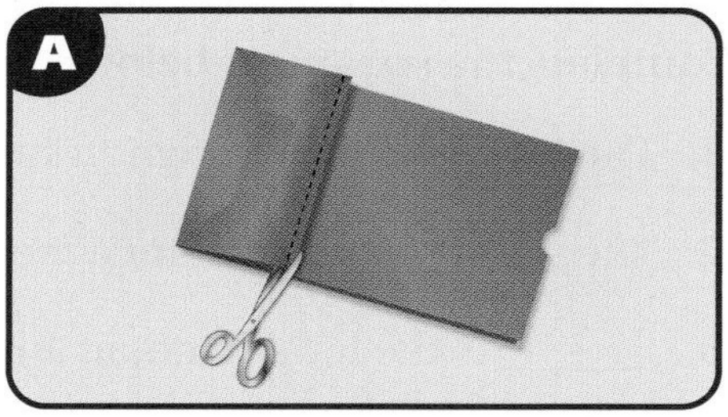
A

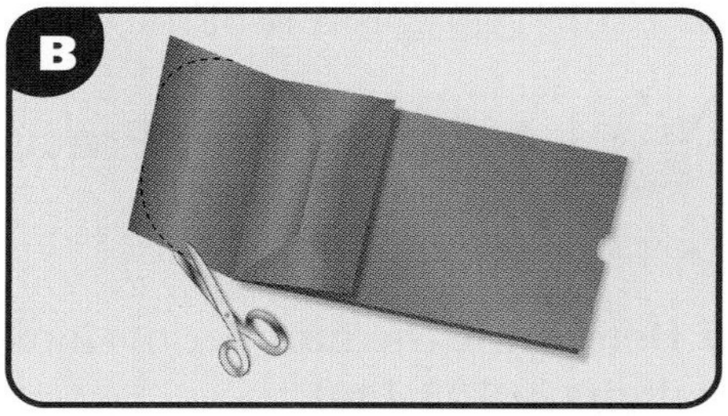
B

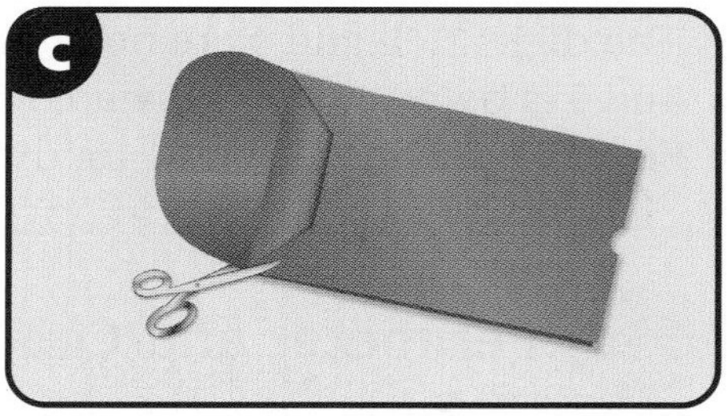
C

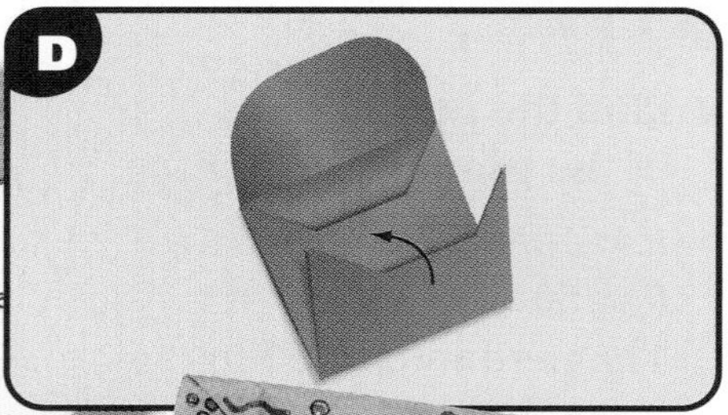
D

Taking Note of the Math

Use index cards to record measurement formulas, the Pythagorean Theorem, and other important facts from the chapter. Store the cards in the pockets of the bag.

CHAPTER 9 Study Guide: Review

Vocabulary

accuracy 518	leg 556	Pythagorean Theorem . 556
area 530	perfect square 550	radical sign 550
circumference 525	perimeter 524	significant digits 518
hypotenuse 556	precision 518	square root 550

Complete the sentences below with vocabulary words from the list above.

1. The longest side of a right triangle is called the ___?___.
2. The ___?___ is the distance around a circle.
3. ___?___ is the level of detail an instrument can measure.
4. A(n) ___?___ is one of the two equal factors of a number.

9-1 Accuracy and Precision (pp. 518–521)

EXAMPLE

■ **Determine the number of significant digits in 705.4 mL.**

The digits 7, 5, and 4 are nonzero digits, and 0 is between two nonzero digits. So 705.4 mL has 4 significant digits.

EXERCISES

Determine the number of significant digits in each measurement.

5. 0.450 kg
6. 6,703.0 ft
7. 30,000 lb
8. 0.00078 g
9. 900.5 cm
10. 1,204 gal

9-2 Perimeter and Circumference (pp. 524–527)

EXAMPLE

■ **Find the perimeter of the triangle.**

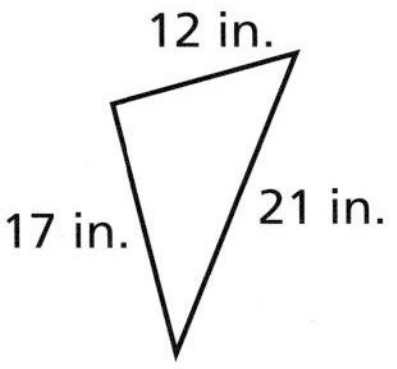

$P = 12 + 17 + 21$

$P = 50$

The perimeter is 50 in.

■ **Find the circumference of the circle. Use 3.14 for π.**

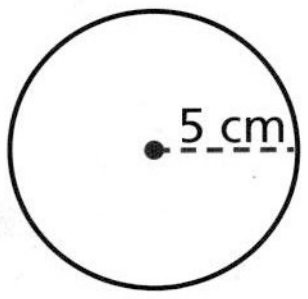

$C = 2\pi r$

$C \approx 2 \cdot 3.14 \cdot 5$

$C \approx 31.4$

The circumference is about 31.4 cm.

EXERCISES

Find the perimeter of each polygon.

11.

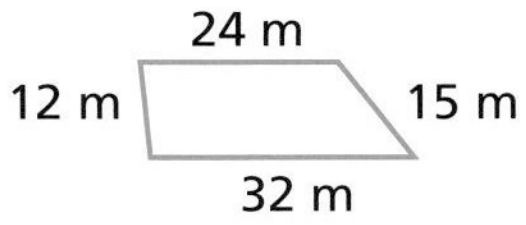

12.

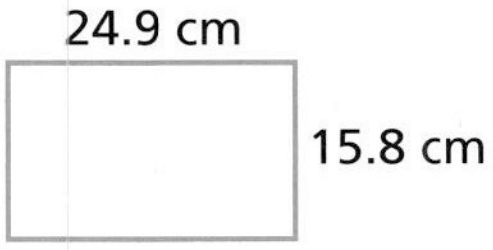

Find the circumference of each circle to the nearest tenth. Use 3.14 for π.

13.

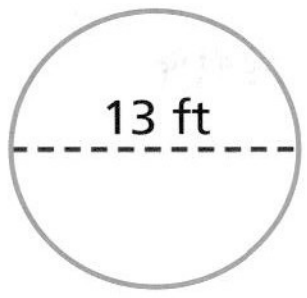

14.

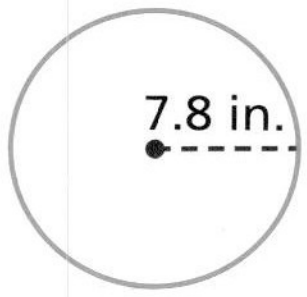

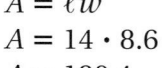

9-3 Area of Parallelograms (pp. 530–533)

EXAMPLE

- **Find the area of the rectangle.**

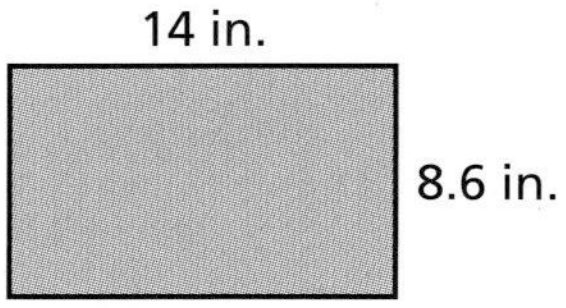

$A = \ell w$

$A = 14 \cdot 8.6$

$A = 120.4$

The area of the rectangle is 120.4 in^2.

EXERCISES

Find the area of each polygon.

15.

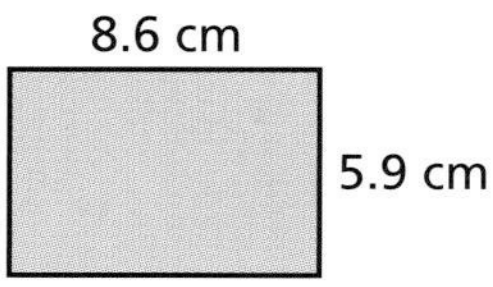

16.

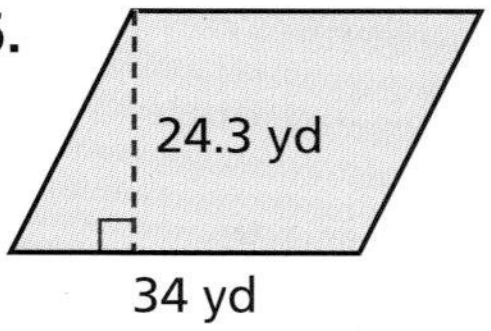

17. Rose is drawing a portrait for her art class. She is using a sheet of paper that is 6 inches wide and 12 inches long. What is the area of the art paper in square inches?

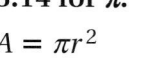

9-4 Area of Triangles and Trapezoids (pp. 534–537)

EXAMPLE

- **Find the area of the triangle.**

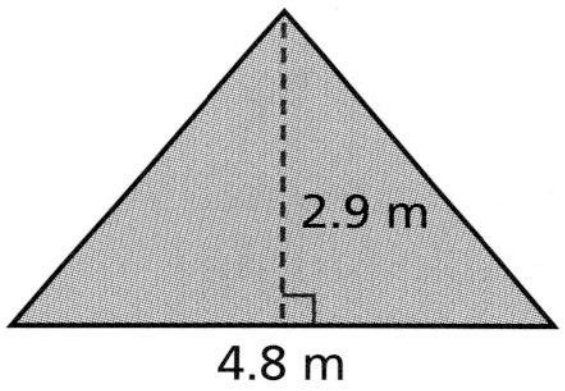

$A = \frac{1}{2}bh$

$A = \frac{1}{2}(4.8 \cdot 2.9)$

$A = \frac{1}{2}(13.92)$

$A = 6.96$

The area of the triangle is 6.96 m^2.

EXERCISES

Find the area of each polygon.

18.

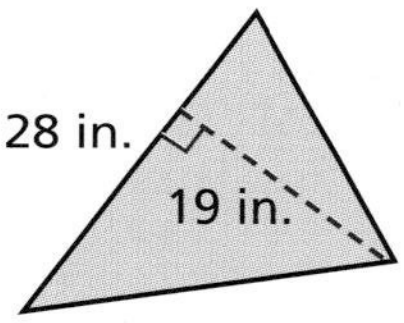

19.

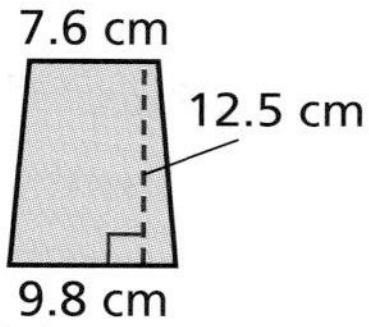

20.

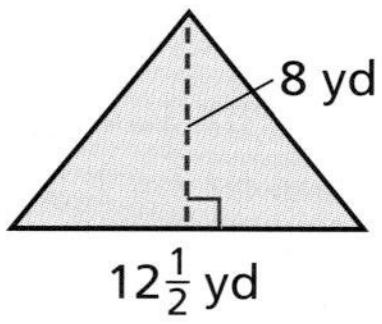

21.

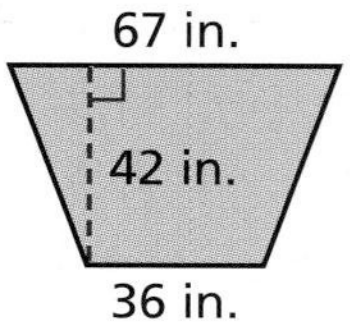

9-5 Area of Circles (pp. 538–541)

EXAMPLE

- **Find the area of the circle to the nearest tenth. Use 3.14 for π.**

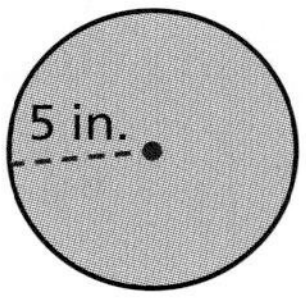

$A = \pi r^2$

$A \approx 3.14 \cdot 5^2$

$A \approx 3.14 \cdot 25$

$A \approx 78.5$

The area of the circle is about 78.5 in^2.

EXERCISES

Find the area of each circle to the nearest tenth. Use 3.14 for π.

22.

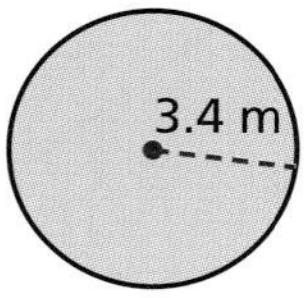

23.

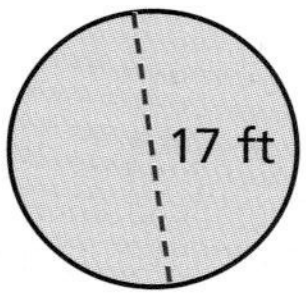

24. The minute hand on a clock is 9 inches long. What is the area of the circle the minute hand covers after one hour? Give your answer in square inches.

9-6 Area of Irregular Figures (pp. 542–545)

EXAMPLE

■ **Find the area of the irregular figure.**

Separate the figure into a rectangle and a triangle.

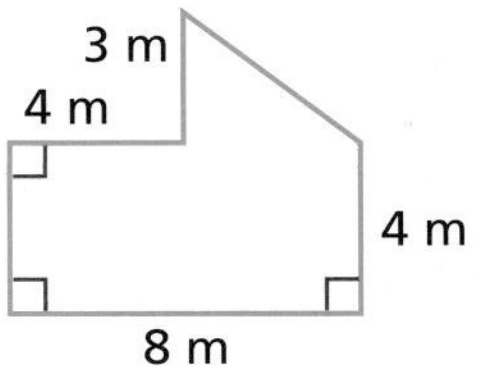

$A = \ell w$

$= 4 \cdot 8 = 32 \text{ m}^2$

$A = \frac{1}{2}bh$

$= \frac{1}{2}(3 \cdot 4) = 6 \text{ m}^2$

$A = 32 + 6 = 38 \text{ m}^2$

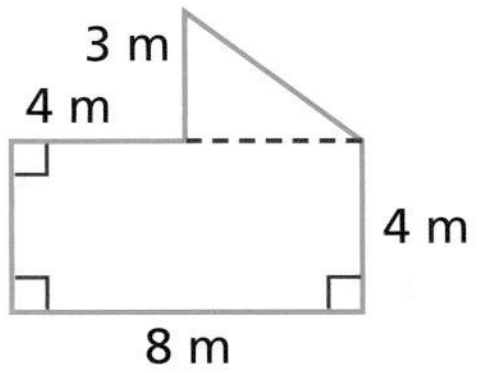

EXERCISES

Find the area of each figure. Use 3.14 for π.

25.

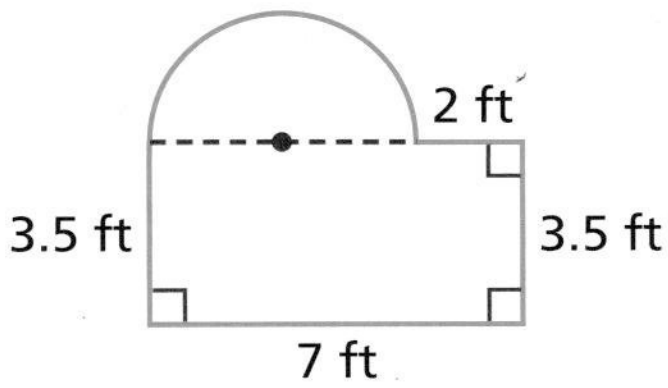

26.

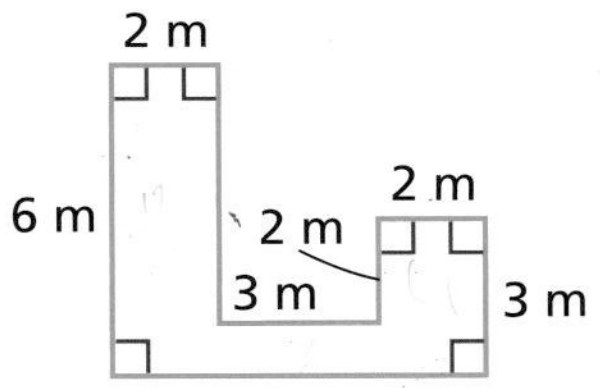

9-7 Squares and Square Roots (pp. 550–553)

EXAMPLE

■ **Estimate $\sqrt{71}$ to the nearest whole number.**

$64 < 71 < 81$ *Find the perfect squares nearest 71.*

$\sqrt{64} < \sqrt{71} < \sqrt{81}$

$8 < \sqrt{71} < 9$ *Find the square roots of 64 and 81.*

Since 71 is closer to 64 than to 81, $\sqrt{71} \approx 8$.

EXERCISES

Estimate each square root to the nearest whole number.

27. $\sqrt{29}$ **28.** $\sqrt{92}$

29. $\sqrt{106}$ **30.** $\sqrt{150}$

31. The area of Rita's square vegetable garden is 265 ft^2. What is the length of each side of the garden to the nearest foot?

9-8 Pythagorean Theorem (pp. 556–559)

EXAMPLE

■ **Use the Pythagorean Theorem to find the missing measure.**

$a^2 + b^2 = c^2$

$9^2 + 12^2 = c^2$

$81 + 144 = c^2$

$225 = c^2$

$\sqrt{225} = \sqrt{c^2}$

$15 = c$

The hypotenuse is 15 in.

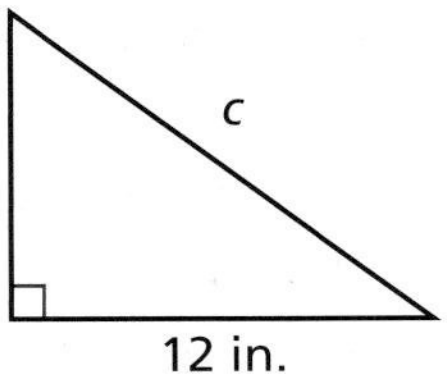

EXERCISES

Use the Pythagorean Theorem to find each missing measure.

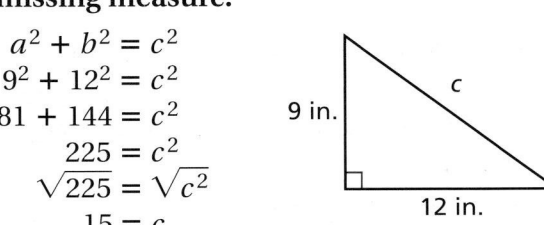

32.

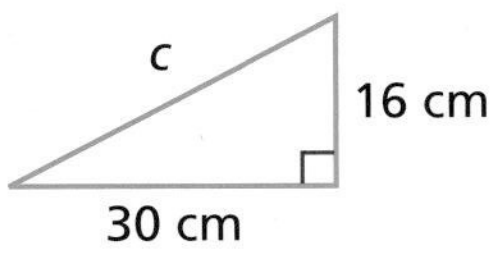

33.

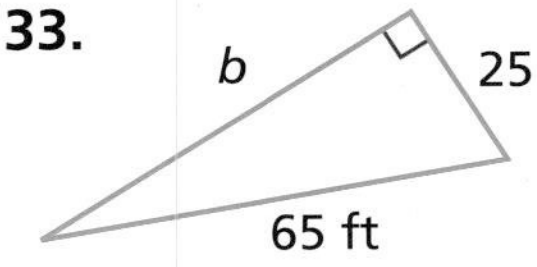

34.

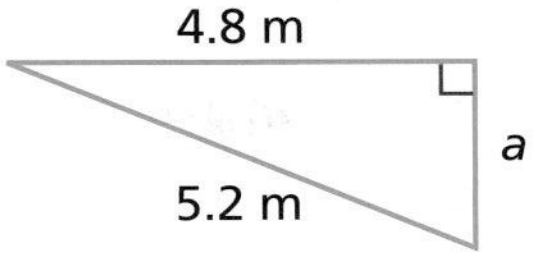

35.

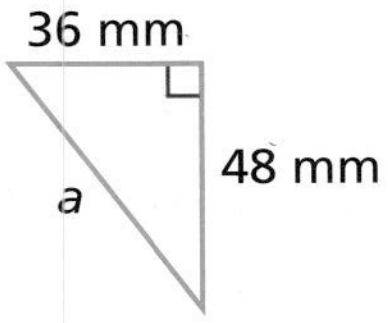

CHAPTER TEST

CHAPTER 9

Choose the more precise measurement in each pair.

1. 80 m, 7.9 cm
2. 18 yd, 5 mi
3. 500 lb, 18 oz

Calculate. Use the correct number of significant digits in each answer.

4. 5.6 lb ÷ 2.59
5. 3.14 · 125 cm
6. 5.882 in. + 5.17 in.

7. Find the perimeter of the trapezoid.

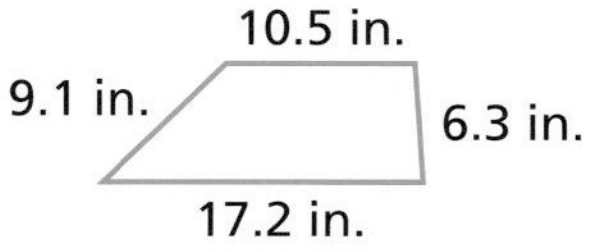

8. The opening of a playscape tunnel has a circumference of 25 ft. What is the radius of the tunnel to the nearest tenth?

Find the area of each figure.

9.

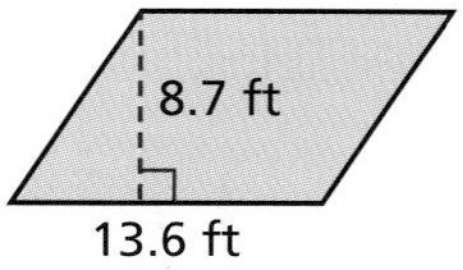

10.

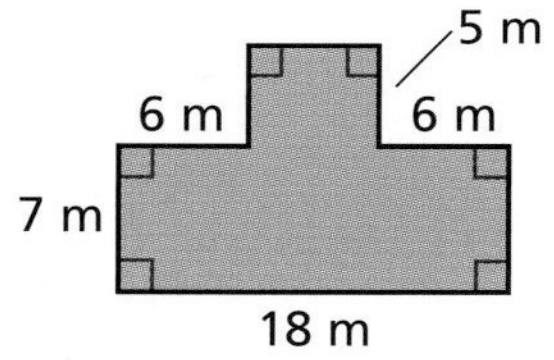

11.

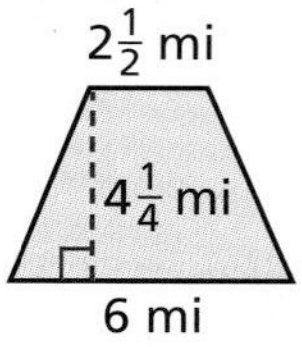

12. The area of a rectangular computer lab is 660 ft^2, and the width is 22 ft. What is the length of the computer lab?
13. The area of a circular fountain is 66 cm^2. What is its radius to the nearest tenth?

Use the diagram for Items 14 and 15.

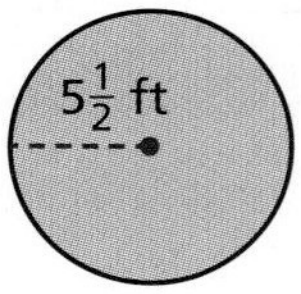

14. Find the circumference of the circle to the nearest tenth.
15. Find the area of the circle to the nearest tenth.

Find each square or square root.

16. 15^2
17. 23^2
18. $\sqrt{1,600}$
19. $\sqrt{961}$

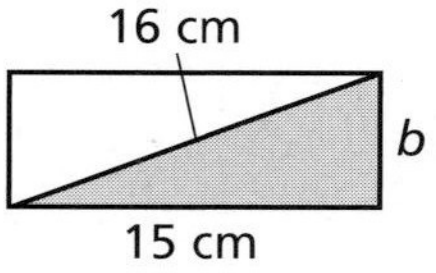

20. The tiles of Sara's new floor are black and white as shown. What is the missing length to the nearest tenth?
21. Triangle Park has a trail that follows the path of a right triangle. One leg of the trail is 2.1 miles, and the other leg is 3.0 miles. What is the distance of the third side of the trail to the nearest tenth of a mile?

Use the diagram at right for Items 22 and 23.

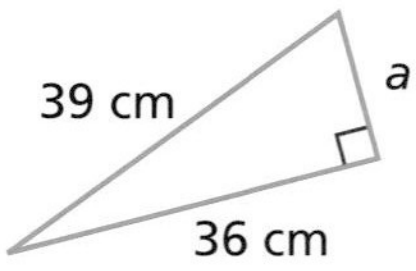

22. Use the Pythagorean Theorem to find the missing measure.
23. Find the area of the triangle.

Chapter Test

CHAPTER 9

TEST TACKLER

Standardized Test Strategies

Test Tackler

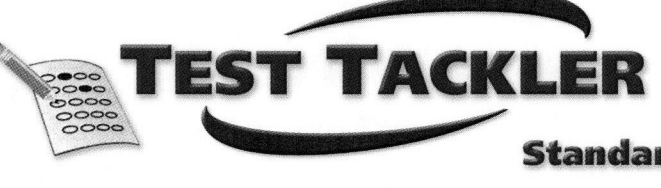

Multiple Choice: Context-Based Test Items

Sometimes a multiple-choice test item requires you to use information in the answer choices to determine which choice fits the context of the problem.

EXAMPLE 1

Which statement is supported by the figure?

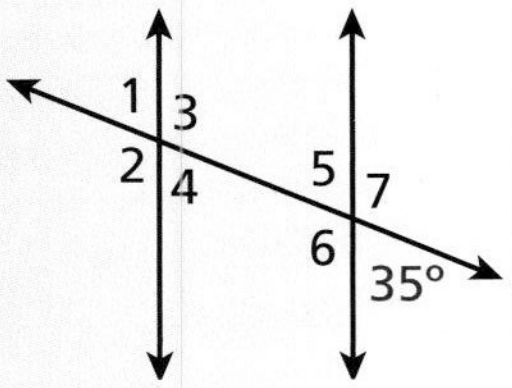

Ⓐ $\angle 1$ and $\angle 4$ are supplementary.

Ⓑ $\angle 3$ and $\angle 2$ are vertical angles.

Ⓒ The measure of $\angle 7$ is 35°.

Ⓓ $\angle 5$ and $\angle 6$ are congruent.

Read each answer choice to find the best answer.

Choice A: $\angle 1$ and $\angle 4$ are vertical angles and therefore, congruent. Congruent angles are supplementary only if they are right angles. $\angle 1$ and $\angle 4$ measure 35°.

Choice B: $\angle 3$ and $\angle 2$ are vertical angles. This is the correct answer choice.

Choice C: The measure of $\angle 7$ cannot be 35° because $\angle 7$ is supplementary to a 35° angle. Therefore, $\angle 7$ has a measure of 145°.

Choice D: $\angle 5$ and $\angle 6$ are supplementary angles but not right angles. Supplementary angles are congruent only if they are both right angles.

EXAMPLE 2

Which two figures have the same area?

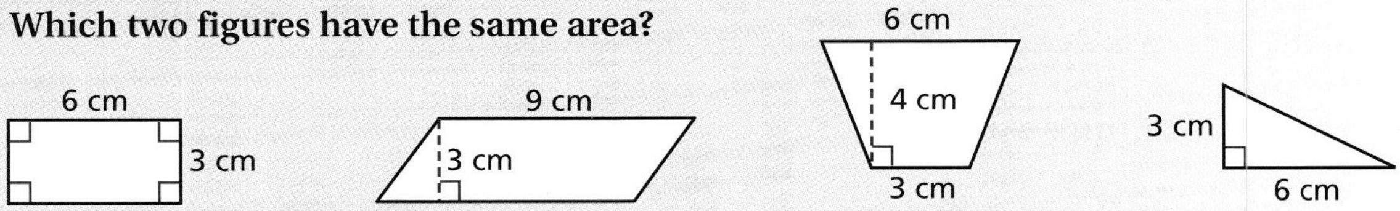

Figure I | Figure II | Figure III | Figure IV

Ⓕ Figure I and Figure II

Ⓖ Figure I and Figure III

Ⓗ Figure II and Figure III

Ⓙ Figure I and Figure IV

Find the areas of all four figures and compare them.

Figure I: $3 \cdot 6 = 18 \text{ cm}^2$

Figure II: $3 \cdot 9 = 27 \text{ cm}^2$

Figure III: $\frac{1}{2} \cdot 4(3 + 6) = 18 \text{ cm}^2$

Figure IV: $\frac{1}{2} \cdot 6 \cdot 3 = 9 \text{ cm}^2$

Figures I and III have the same area. Choice G is correct.

HOT TIP! Do not choose an answer until you have read all of the answer choices.

Read each test item and answer the questions that follow.

Item A

The area of the square is 16 cm^2. Which of the following is NOT correct about the circle?

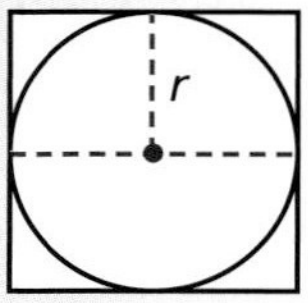

Ⓐ $C = 4\pi$ cm

Ⓑ $A = 16\pi$ cm^2

Ⓒ $d = 4$ cm

Ⓓ $r = 2$ cm

1. Since only one answer choice has incorrect information, why can you automatically eliminate answer choices C and D?
2. How can you find the side length of the square? What does the side length tell you about the circle?
3. Use your answer to Problem 2 to determine whether answer choice A has correct information.
4. How can you tell that choice B is the correct answer?

Item B

Which figure is an acute isosceles triangle?

Ⓕ 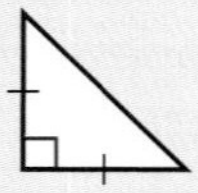

Ⓗ 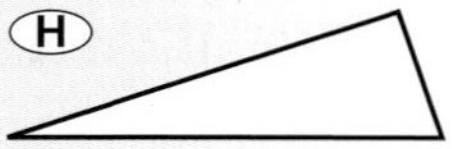

Ⓖ 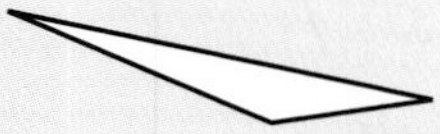

Ⓙ 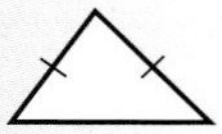

5. What is an acute triangle?
6. What is an isosceles triangle?
7. Why is choice F incorrect?

Item C

Which graph represents a reflection across the x-axis?

Ⓐ 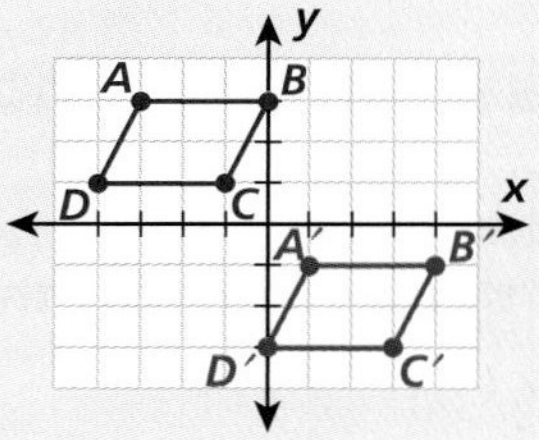

Ⓒ 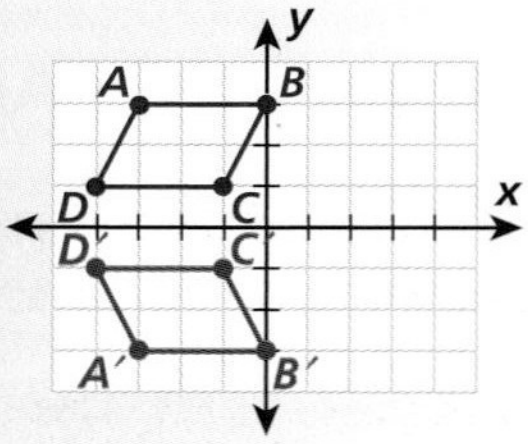

Ⓑ 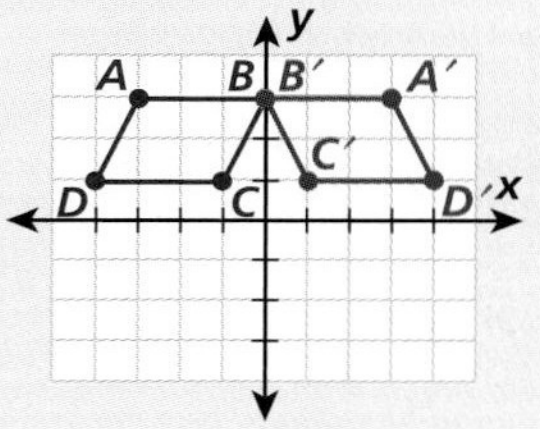

Ⓓ 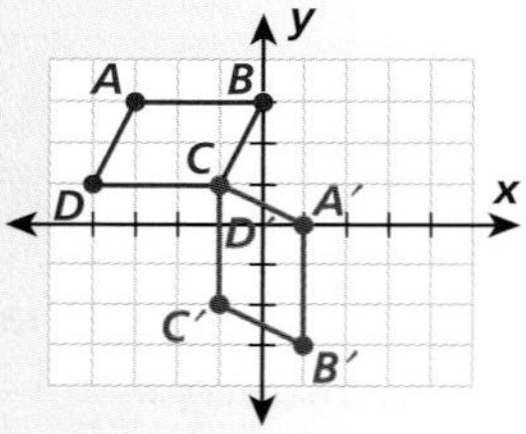

8. Which answer choices do NOT show reflections?
9. What is a reflection across the x-axis?

Item D

The area of the trapezoid is 30 in^2. Which equation CANNOT be used to find the height of the trapezoid?

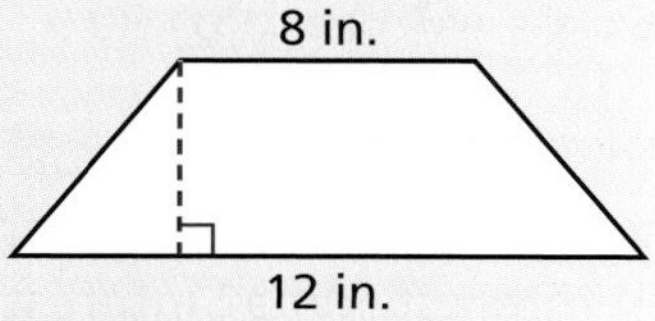

Ⓕ $30 = \frac{1}{2}(8 + 12)h$

Ⓖ $60 = (8 + 12)h$

Ⓗ $30 = \frac{1}{2}(8 - 12)h$

Ⓙ $\frac{1}{2}(8 + 12)h = 30$

10. What is the formula for the area of a trapezoid?
11. What steps would you take to solve the formula for h?

STANDARDIZED TEST PREP

go.hrw.com
State Test Practice Online
KEYWORD: MS7 TestPrep

Cumulative Assessment, Chapters 1–9

Multiple Choice

1. Which expression is represented by the model below?

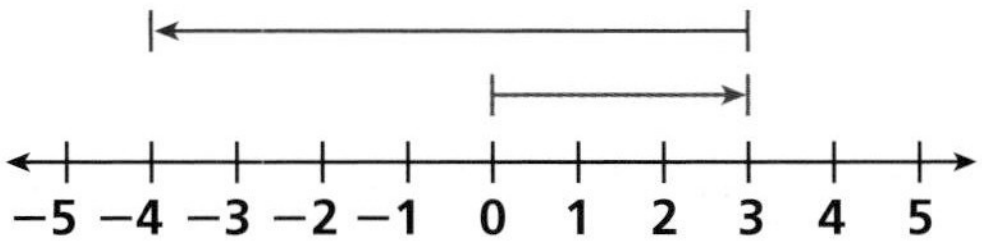

Ⓐ $3 + (-7)$　Ⓒ $-3 + 7$
Ⓑ $3 + 7$　Ⓓ $-3 + (-7)$

2. Which figure has only one line of symmetry?

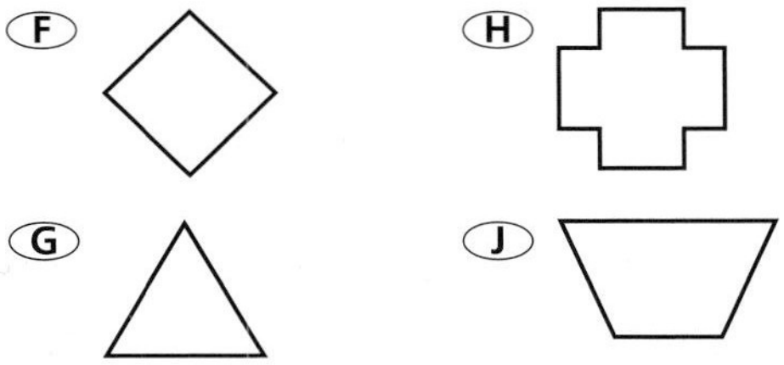

3. If $x + 2 = y$ and $y = 4^2$, what is the value of $x + y$?

Ⓐ 14　Ⓒ 22
Ⓑ 16　Ⓓ 30

4. You invest $200 into a simple interest savings account for 5 years and earn $60 in interest. What interest rate did you earn?

Ⓕ 1.5%　Ⓗ 30%
Ⓖ 6%　Ⓙ 33.3%

5. A color printer is designed to print 8 pages per minute. How many pages can the printer print in 13 minutes?

Ⓐ 1.6 pages　Ⓒ 84 pages
Ⓑ 21 pages　Ⓓ 104 pages

6. For which radius r is the area of a circle equal to 153.86 square inches?

Ⓕ $r = 7$ in.　Ⓗ $r = 24.5$ in.
Ⓖ $r = 12.5$ in.　Ⓙ $r = 49$ in.

7. Which equation describes the graph?

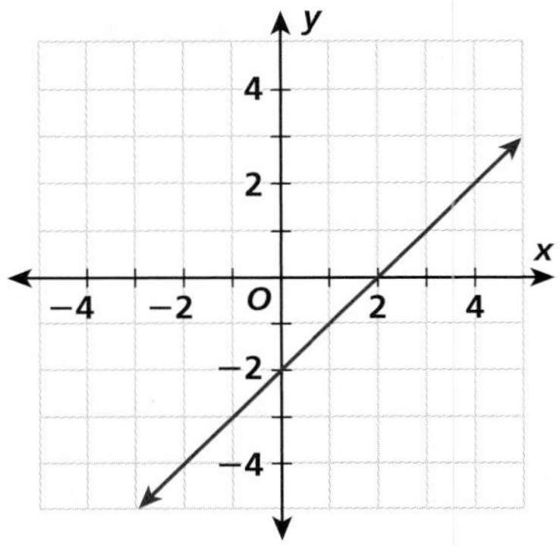

Ⓐ $y = x - 2$　Ⓒ $y = 2x + 1$
Ⓑ $y = x + 2$　Ⓓ $y = 2x - 2$

8. Seventy percent of historical figures pictured on U.S. currency do not have facial hair. What is the decimal equivalent of this value?

Ⓕ 0.07　Ⓗ 7.0
Ⓖ 0.70　Ⓙ 70

9. What is the area of the trapezoid?

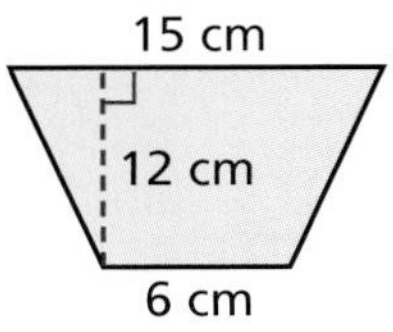

Ⓐ 81 cm^2　Ⓒ 135 cm^2
Ⓑ 126 cm^2　Ⓓ 252 cm^2

10. Paul plans to build a fence around the perimeter of his property. How much fencing does he need?

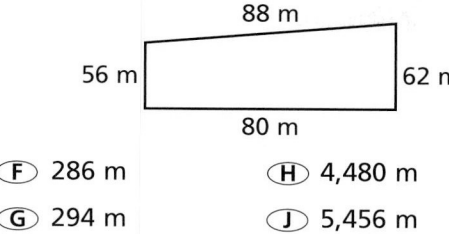

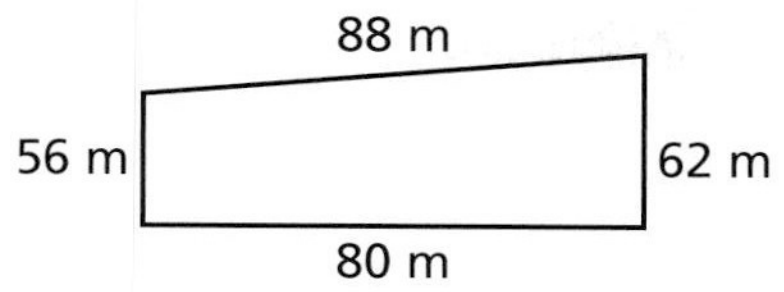

Ⓕ 286 m
Ⓖ 294 m
Ⓗ 4,480 m
Ⓙ 5,456 m

11. Gretchen bought six muffins for \$3.19, four bottles of juice at \$1.25 each, and a bag of apples at \$0.89 per pound. She gave the cashier \$20. What other information is necessary to find Gretchen's correct change?

Ⓐ Cost of one muffin
Ⓑ Total cost of the juice
Ⓒ Number of pounds of apples bought
Ⓓ Reason for buying the food

HOT TIP! **Write your explanations to short- and extended-response questions as complete sentences.**

Gridded Response

12. How many significant digits are in the measurement 0.00410 milligrams?

13. The diameter of a CD is about 12 cm. What is the circumference of the CD to the nearest tenth of a centimeter? Use 3.14 for π.

14. What is the x-coordinate of the point $(-2, 6)$ after it is translated 5 units right and 7 units down?

15. What is the measure in degrees of $\angle x$ in the triangle below?

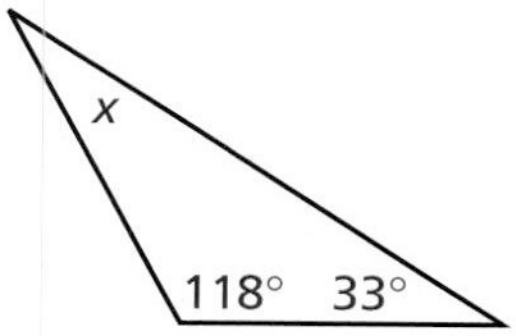

Short Response

16. The tennis team had a pizza party at the end of the season. The 17 team members spent a total of \$51.95 on pizza and \$6.70 on drinks. What is the average amount each team member spent for the party? Show your work.

17. Laurie wants to paste a circular photo onto a rectangular piece of cardboard. The area of the photo is 50.24 in^2. What are the smallest possible dimensions the piece of cardboard can have and still hold the entire photo? Use 3.14 for π and explain your answer.

18. Find the perimeter and area of a rectangle with length 12 m and width 7 m. Then find the side length of a square that has the same area as the rectangle. Round your answers to the nearest meter, and show your work.

Extended Response

19. Use $\triangle ABC$ and $\triangle STU$ for the following problems.

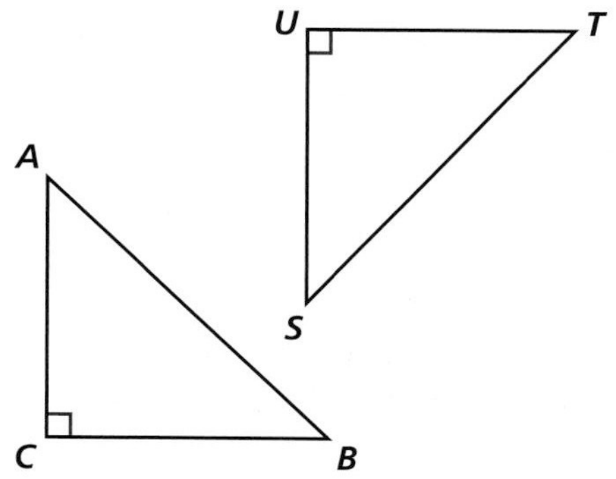

a. If $AB = 17$ m and $AC = 8$ m, what theorem can you use to find CB? Find CB, and show your work.

b. If $ST = 10$ m and $\triangle ABC$ is similar to $\triangle STU$, what ratio can you use to find SU and UT? Show how to find SU and UT to the nearest tenth of a meter.

c. Find the difference in the areas of the two triangles.

CHAPTER 10

Measurement: Three-Dimensional Figures

MULTI-STEP TEST PREP

go.hrw.com
Chapter Project Online
KEYWORD: MS7 Ch10

Pyramid	Location	Height (m)	Base Length (m)
El Castillo	Chichén Itzá, Mexico	55.5	79.0
Tikal	Tikal, Guatemala	30.0	80.0
Pyramid of the Sun	Teotihuácan, Mexico	63.0	225.0

Career *Archaeological Architect*

Did you ever wonder how the pyramids were built? Archaeologists who are also architects combine a love of the past with the skills of a building designer to study the construction of ancient buildings.

In recent years, archaeological architects have built machines like those used in ancient times to demonstrate how the pyramids might have been constructed. The table shows the dimensions of a few famous pyramids.

ARE YOU READY?

Vocabulary

Choose the best term from the list to complete each sentence.

1. A polygon with six sides is called a(n) __?__.
2. __?__ figures are the same size and shape.
3. A(n) __?__ is a ratio that relates the dimensions of two similar objects.
4. The formula for the __?__ of a circle can be written as πd or $2\pi r$.
5. __?__ figures are the same shape but not necessarily the same size.
6. A polygon with five sides is called a(n) __?__.

area
circumference
congruent
hexagon
pentagon
scale factor
similar

Complete these exercises to review skills you will need for this chapter.

Area of Squares, Rectangles, Triangles

Find the area of each figure.

7.

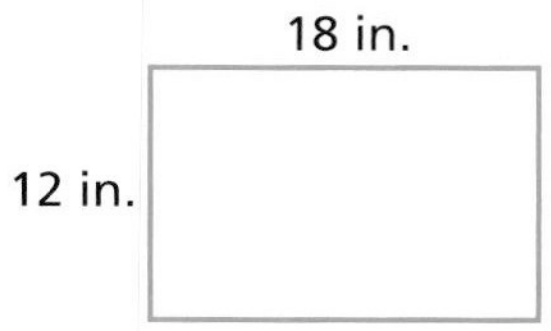

8.

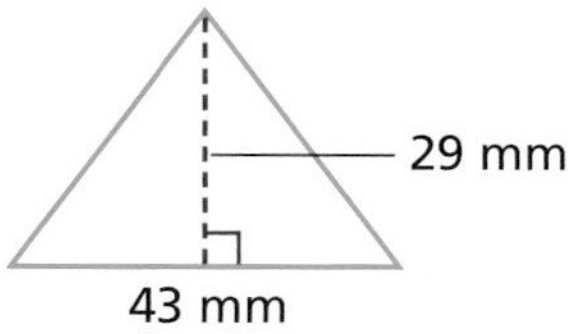

9.

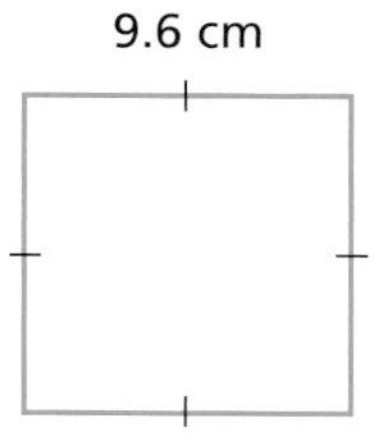

Area of Circles

Find the area of each circle to the nearest tenth. Use 3.14 for π.

10.

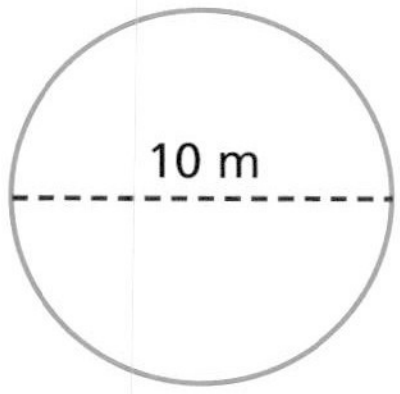

11.

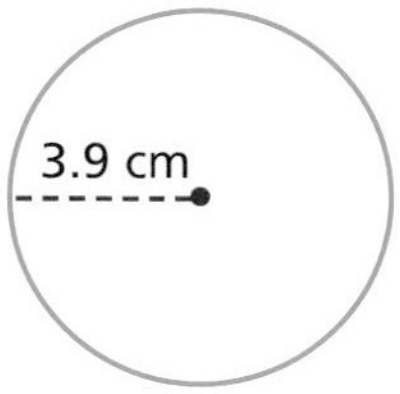

12.

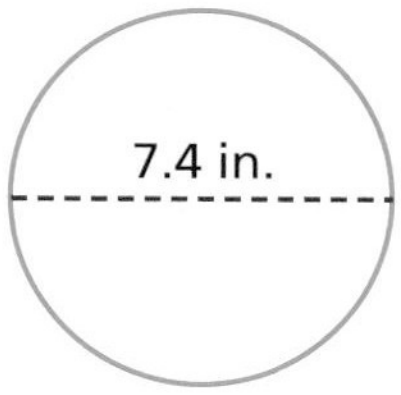

Find the Cube of a Number

Find each value.

13. 3^3 **14.** 8^3 **15.** 2.5^3 **16.** 6.2^3

17. 10^3 **18.** 5.9^3 **19.** 800^3 **20.** 98^3

CHAPTER 10

Study Guide: Preview

Where You've Been

Previously, you

- found the area of polygons and irregular figures.
- compared the relationship between a figure's perimeter and its area.

In This Chapter

You will study

- finding the volume of prisms, cylinders, pyramids, and cones.
- using nets to find the surface area of prisms and cylinders.
- finding the volume and surface area of similar three-dimensional figures.

Where You're Going

You can use the skills learned in this chapter

- to determine the amount of materials needed to build a doghouse.
- to convert dimensions of a model to real-world dimensions.

Key Vocabulary/Vocabulario

base	base de una figura tridimensional
edge	arista
face	cara
net	plantilla
polyhedron	poliedro
prism	prisma
surface area	área total
vertex of a polyhedron	vértice de un poliedro
volume	volumen

Vocabulary Connections

To become familiar with some of the vocabulary terms in the chapter, consider the following. You may refer to the chapter, the glossary, or a dictionary if you like.

1. Note the Spanish translation of *surface area* in the table above. What does the term *área total* tell you about the meaning of **surface area**?
2. The word *edge* comes from the Latin word *acer,* meaning "sharp." How does the Latin root help you define an **edge** of a three-dimensional figure?
3. The word *vertex* can mean "peak" or "highest point." What part of a cone or pyramid is the **vertex**?
4. The word *prism* comes from the Greek word *priein,* meaning "to saw." How might you describe a **prism** in terms of something sawn or cut off?

Reading and Writing Math

Study Strategy: Learn and Use Formulas

Throughout this chapter, you will be introduced to many formulas. Although memorizing these formulas is helpful, understanding the concepts on which they are based will help you to re-create the formula if you happen to forget.

One way to memorize a formula is to use flash cards. Write the formula on an index card and review it often. Include a diagram and an example. Add any notes that you choose, such as when to use the formula.

In Lesson 9-3, you learned the formula for area of a rectangle.

Sample Flash Card

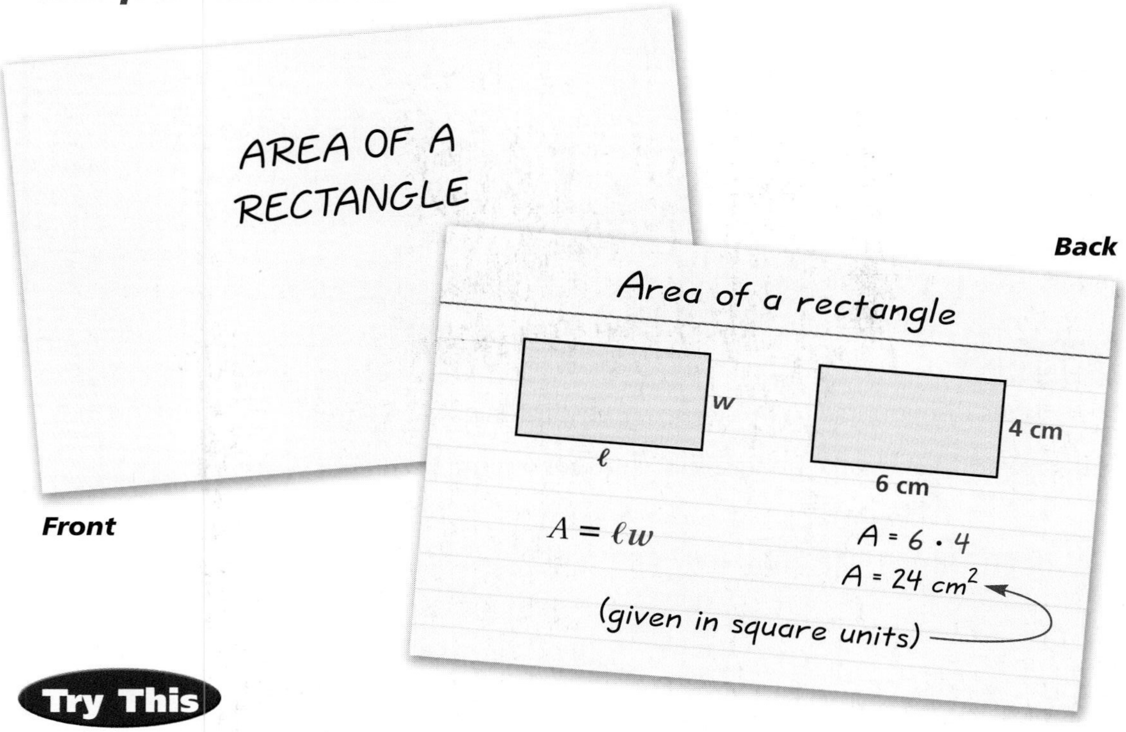

Try This

1. Create flash cards for some of the formulas from the previous chapters.
2. Describe a plan to help you memorize the formulas in Chapters 9 and 10.

Hands-On LAB 10-1

Sketch Three-Dimensional Figures from Different Views

Use with Lesson 10-1

go.hrw.com
Lab Resources Online
KEYWORD: MS7 Lab10

Three-dimensional figures often look different from different points of view. You can use centimeter cubes to help you visualize and sketch three-dimensional figures.

Activity 1

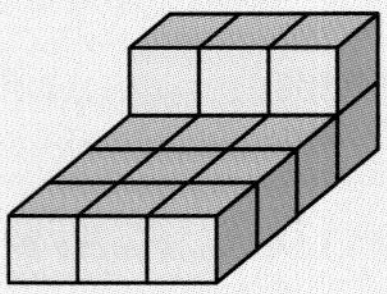

1. Use centimeter cubes to build the three-dimensional figure at right.
2. Now view the figure from the front and draw what you see. Then view the figure from the top and draw what you see. Finally, view the figure from the side and draw what you see.

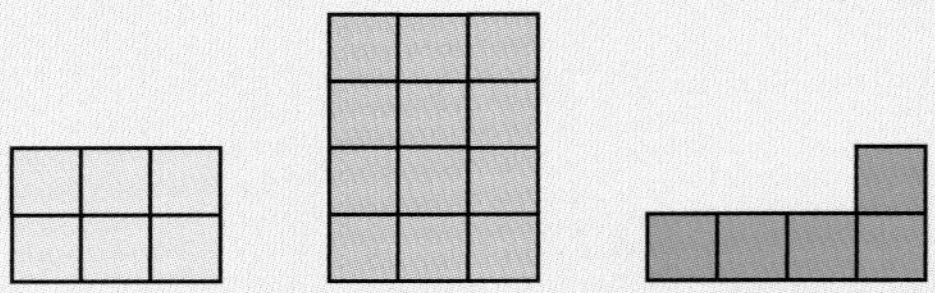

Think and Discuss

1. How many cubes did you use to build the three-dimensional figure?
2. How could you add a cube to the figure without changing the top view?
3. How could you remove a cube from the figure without changing the side view?

Try This

Use centimeter cubes to build each three-dimensional figure. Then sketch the front, top, and side views.

1. 

2. 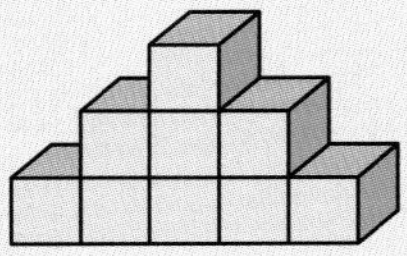

3. 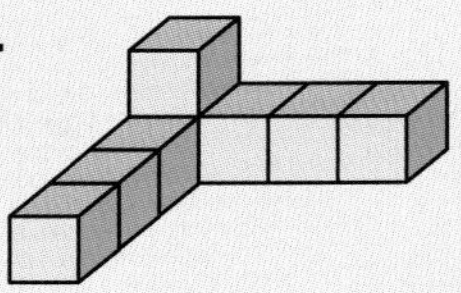

4. 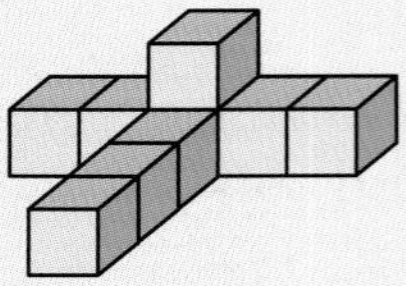

Activity 2

1 Use centimeter cubes to build a figure that has the front, top, and side views shown.

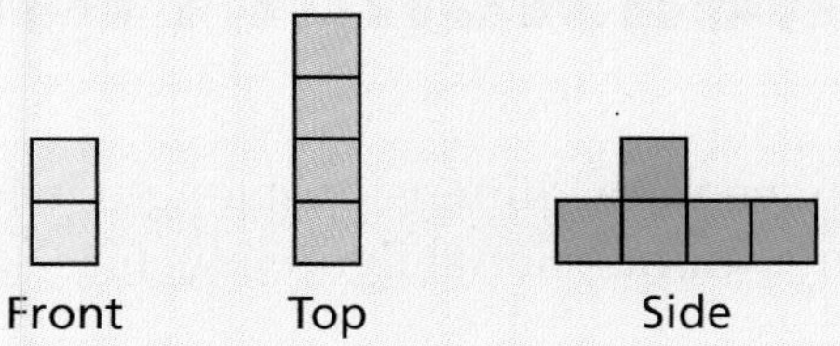

2 You can build the figure by first making a simple figure that matches the front view.

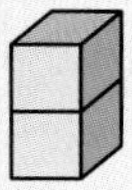

3 Now add cubes so that the figure matches the top view.

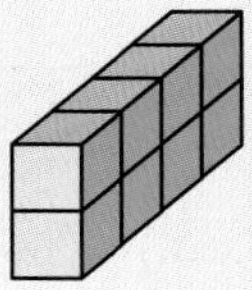

4 Finally, remove cubes so that the figure matches the side view. Check that the front and top views are still correct for the figure that you built.

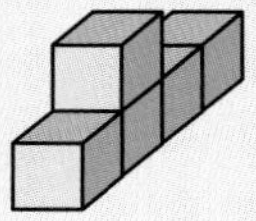

Think and Discuss

1. Discuss whether there is another step-by-step method for building the above figure. If so, is the final result the same?

Try This

The front, top, and side views of a figure are shown. Use centimeter cubes to build the figure. Then sketch the figure.

1.

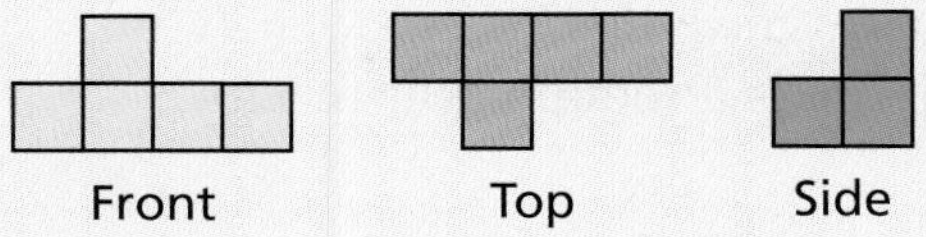

2.

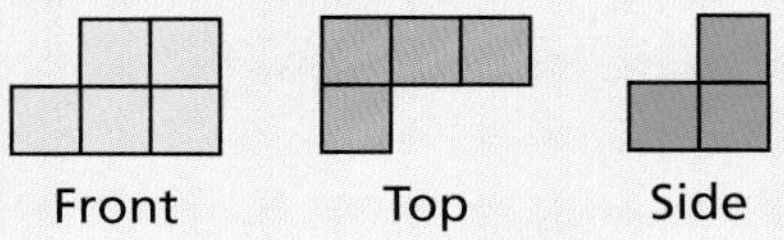

3. The views below represent a three-dimensional figure that cannot be built from cubes. Determine which three-dimensional figure matches the views.

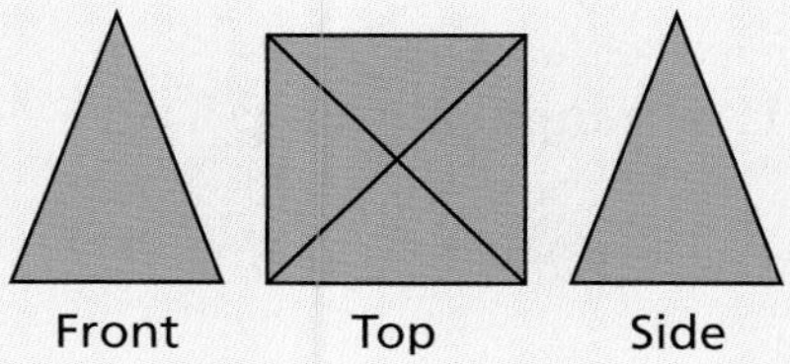

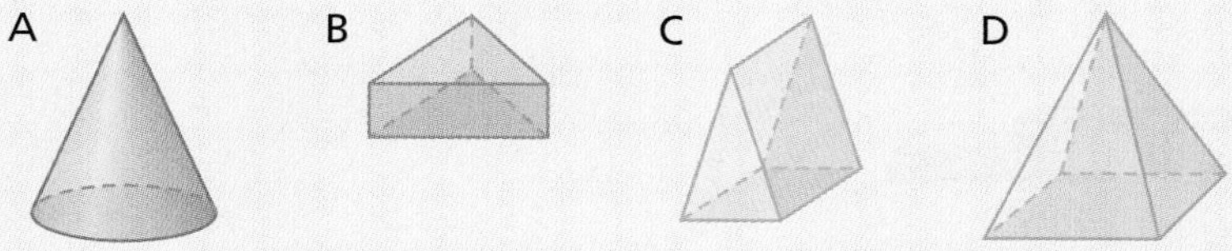

10-1 Introduction to Three-Dimensional Figures

Learn to identify various three-dimensional figures.

Vocabulary
face
edge
polyhedron
vertex
base
prism
pyramid
cylinder
cone

Three-dimensional figures have three dimensions: length, width, and height. A flat surface of a three-dimensional figure is a **face**. An **edge** is where two faces meet.

A **polyhedron** is a three-dimensional figure whose faces are all polygons. A **vertex** of a polyhedron is a point where three or more edges meet. The face that is used to name a polyhedron is called a **base**.

A *prism* has two bases, and a *pyramid* has one base.

Prisms	Pyramids
A **prism** is a polyhedron that has two parallel, congruent bases. The bases can be any polygon. The other faces are parallelograms. 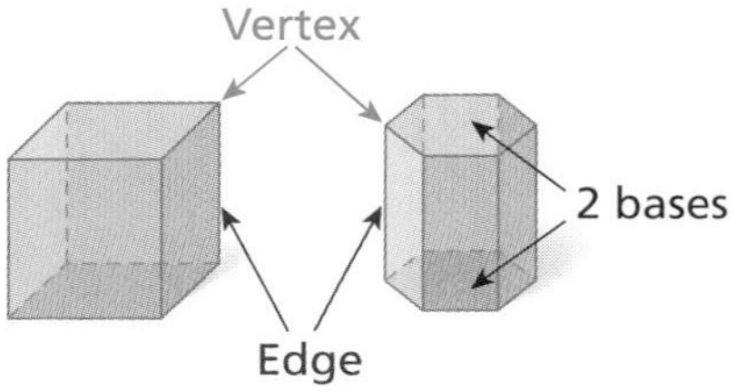	A **pyramid** is a polyhedron that has one base. The base can be any polygon. The other faces are triangles. 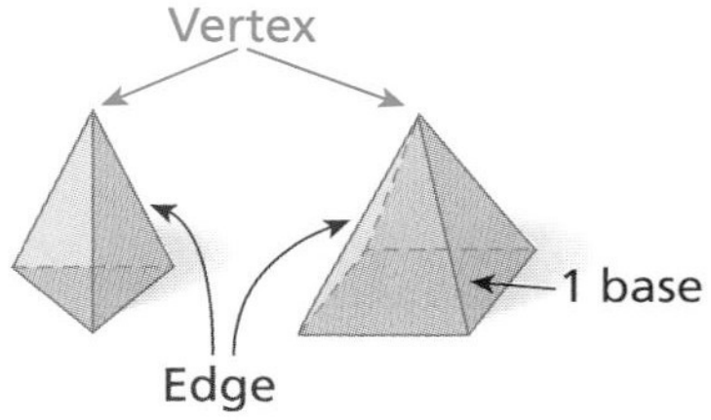

EXAMPLE 1 Naming Prisms and Pyramids

Identify the bases and faces of each figure. Then name the figure.

A 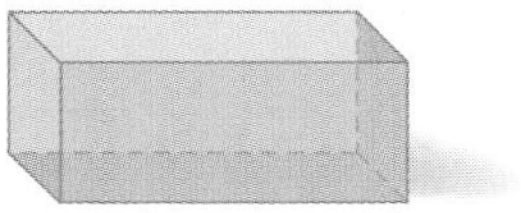

There are two rectangular bases.
There are four other rectangular faces.
The figure is a rectangular prism.

B 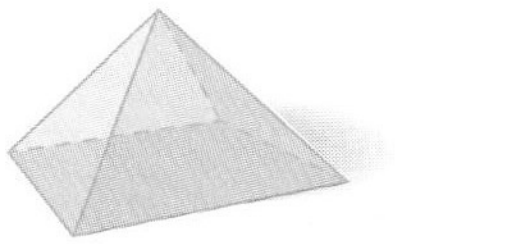

There is one rectangular base.
There are four triangular faces.
The figure is a rectangular pyramid.

C 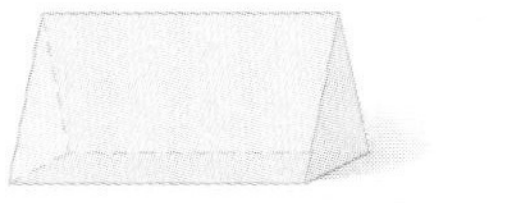

There are two triangular bases.
There are three rectangular faces.
The figure is a triangular prism.

D 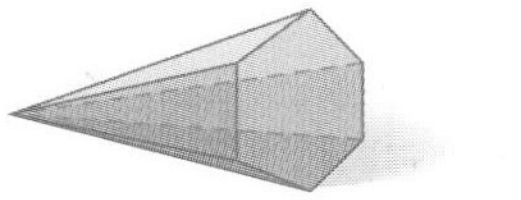

There is one hexagonal base.
There are six triangular faces.
The figure is a hexagonal pyramid.

Remember!
A polygon with six sides is called a hexagon.

Other three-dimensional figures include *cylinders* and *cones*. These figures are not polyhedrons because they are not made of faces that are all polygons.

Cylinders	Cones
A **cylinder** has two parallel, congruent bases that are circles. 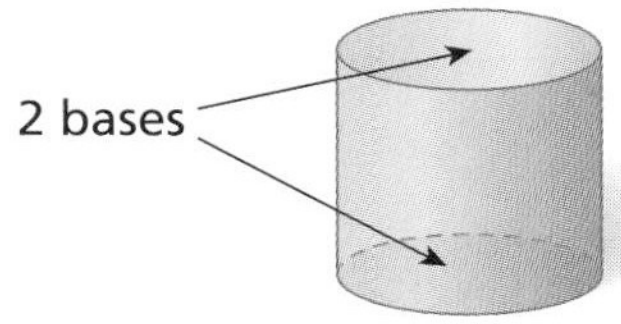	A **cone** has one base that is a circle and a surface that comes to a point called the vertex. 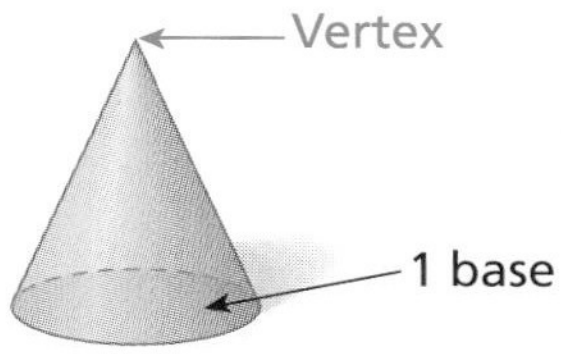

You can use properties to classify three-dimensional figures.

EXAMPLE 2 Classifying Three-Dimensional Figures

Classify each figure as a polyhedron or not a polyhedron. Then name the figure.

A 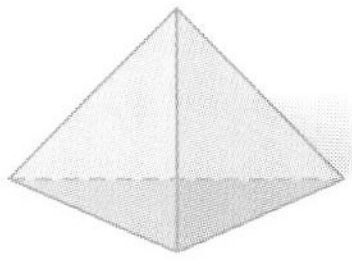

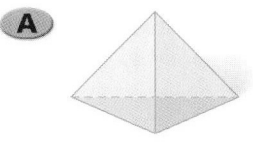

The faces are all polygons, so the figure is a polyhedron.
There is one triangular base.
The figure is a triangular pyramid.

B 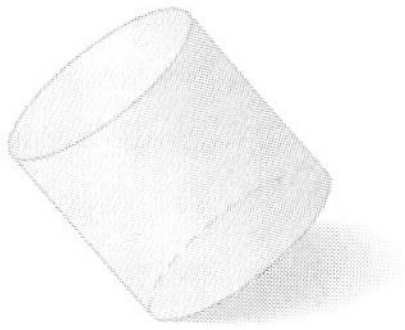

The faces are not all polygons, so the figure is not a polyhedron.
There are two circular bases.
The figure is a cylinder.

C 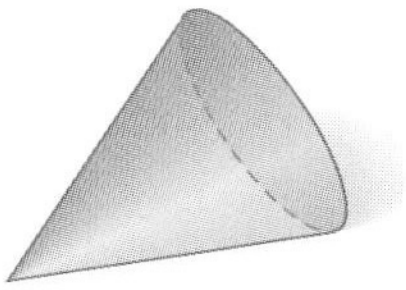

The faces are not all polygons, so the figure is not a polyhedron.
There is one circular base.
The figure is a cone.

Think and Discuss

1. Explain how to identify a prism or a pyramid.

2. Compare and contrast cylinders and prisms. How are they alike? How are they different?

3. Compare and contrast pyramids and cones. How are they alike? How are they different?

10-1 Exercises

go.hrw.com
Homework Help Online
KEYWORD: MS7 10-1
Parent Resources Online
KEYWORD: MS7 Parent

GUIDED PRACTICE

See Example 1

Identify the bases and faces of each figure. Then name the figure.

1. 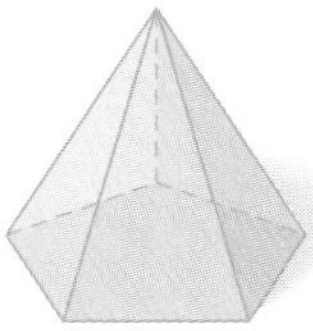

2. 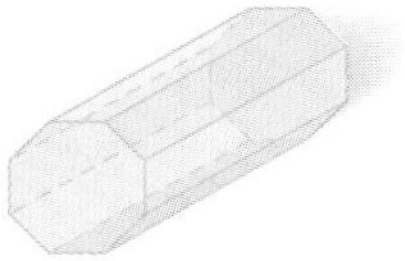

3. 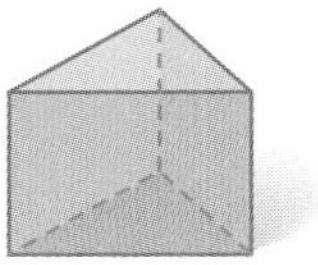

See Example 2

Classify each figure as a polyhedron or not a polyhedron. Then name the figure.

4. 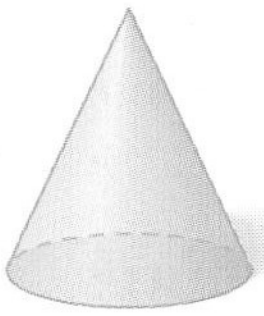

5. 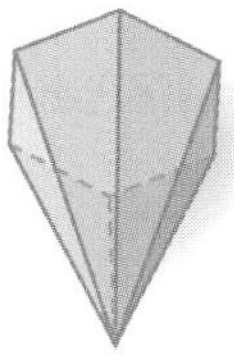

6. 

INDEPENDENT PRACTICE

See Example 1

Identify the bases and faces of each figure. Then name the figure.

7. 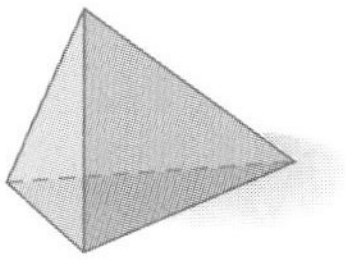

8. 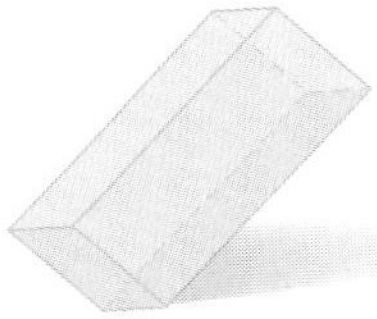

9. 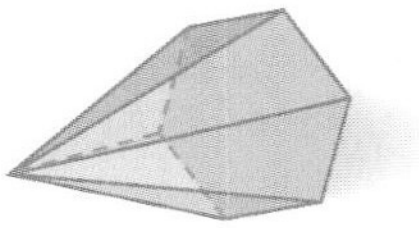

See Example 2

Classify each figure as a polyhedron or not a polyhedron. Then name the figure.

10. 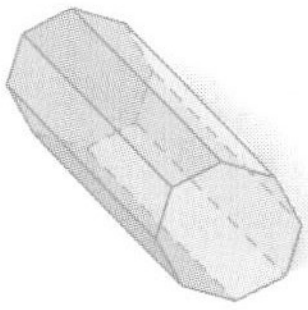

11. 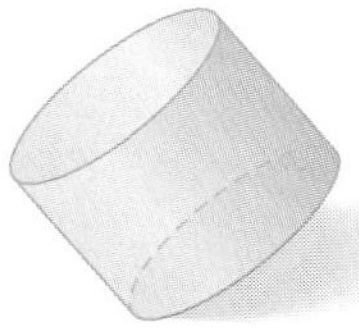

12. 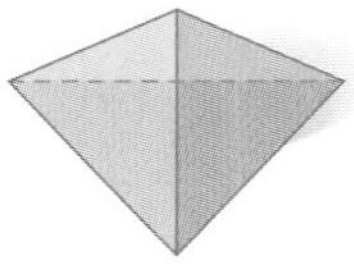

PRACTICE AND PROBLEM SOLVING

Extra Practice
See page 746.

Identify the three-dimensional figure described.

13. two parallel, congruent square bases and four other polygonal faces

14. two parallel, congruent circular bases and one curved surface

15. one triangular base and three other triangular faces

16. one circular base and one curved surface

Name two examples of the three-dimensional figure described.

17. two parallel, congruent bases

18. one base

History LINK

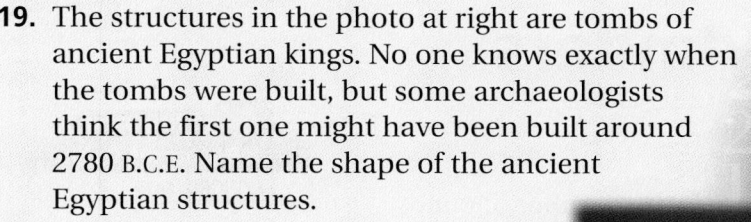

19. The structures in the photo at right are tombs of ancient Egyptian kings. No one knows exactly when the tombs were built, but some archaeologists think the first one might have been built around 2780 B.C.E. Name the shape of the ancient Egyptian structures.

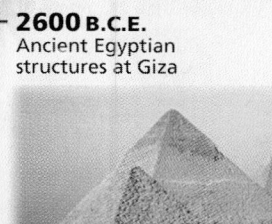

2600 B.C.E.
Ancient Egyptian structures at Giza

20. The Parthenon was built around 440 B.C.E. by the ancient Greeks. Its purpose was to house a statue of Athena, the Greek goddess of wisdom. Describe the three-dimensional shapes you see in the structure.

440 B.C.E.
Parthenon

21. The Leaning Tower of Pisa began to lean as it was being built. To keep the tower from falling over, the upper sections (floors) were built slightly off center so that the tower would curve away from the way it was leaning. What shape is each section of the tower?

1173
Leaning Tower of Pisa

22. **Challenge** The stainless steel structure at right, called the Unisphere, became the symbol of the New York World's Fair of 1964–1965. A sphere is a three-dimensional figure with a surface made up of all the points that are the same distance from a given point. Explain why the structure is not a sphere.

1964
Unisphere

go.hrw.com
Web Extra!
KEYWORD: MS7 Structures

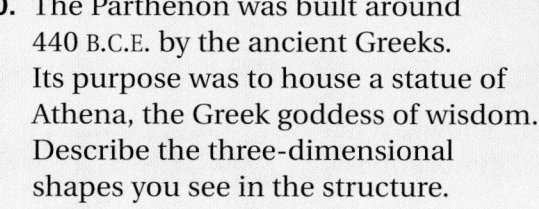

Test Prep and Spiral Review

23. **Multiple Choice** Which figure has six rectangular faces?

Ⓐ Rectangular prism Ⓒ Triangular pyramid

Ⓑ Triangular prism Ⓓ Rectangular pyramid

24. **Multiple Choice** Which figure does NOT have two congruent bases?

Ⓕ Cube Ⓖ Pyramid Ⓗ Prism Ⓙ Cylinder

Estimate each sum. (Lesson 3-7)

25. $\frac{2}{5} + \frac{3}{8}$ 26. $\frac{1}{16} + \frac{4}{9}$ 27. $\frac{7}{9} + \frac{11}{12}$ 28. $\frac{1}{10} + \frac{1}{16}$

29. A store sells two sizes of detergent: 300 ounces for $21.63 and 100 ounces for $6.99. Which size detergent has the lowest price per ounce? (Lesson 5-2)

Hands-On LAB 10-2

Explore the Volume of Prisms and Cylinders

Use with Lesson 10-2

go.hrw.com
Lab Resources Online
KEYWORD: MS7 Lab10

The volume of a three-dimensional figure is the number of cubes that it can hold. One cube represents one cubic unit of volume.

Activity 1

1. Use centimeter cubes to build the rectangular prism shown. What are the length, width, and height of the prism? How many cubes does the prism hold?

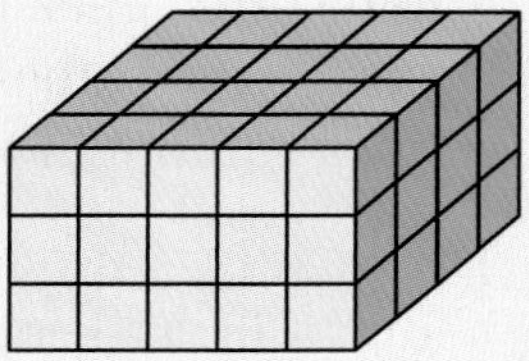

2. You can find out how many cubes the prism holds without counting every cube. First look at the prism from above. How can you find the number of cubes in the top layer without counting every cube?

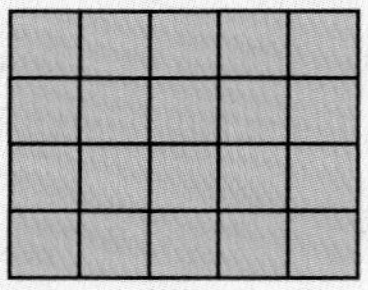

Top

3. Now look at the prism from the side. How many layers does the prism have? How can you use this to find the total number of cubes in the prism?

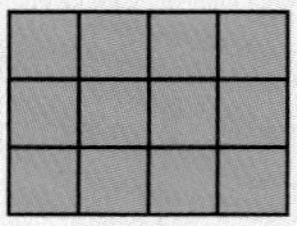

Side

Think and Discuss

1. Describe a shortcut for finding the number of cubes in a rectangular prism.
2. Suppose you know the area of the base of a prism and the height of the prism. How can you find the prism's volume?
3. Let the area of the base of a prism be B and the height of the prism be h. Write a formula for the prism's volume V.

Try This

Use the formula you discovered to find the volume of each prism.

1.

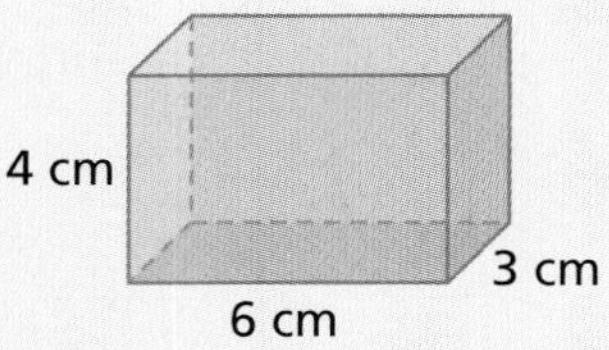

2.

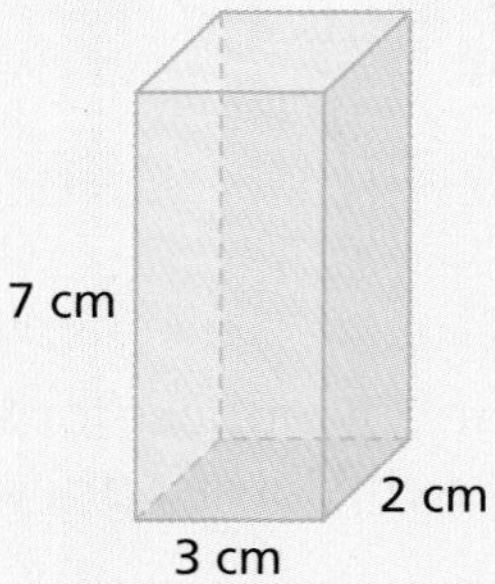

3.

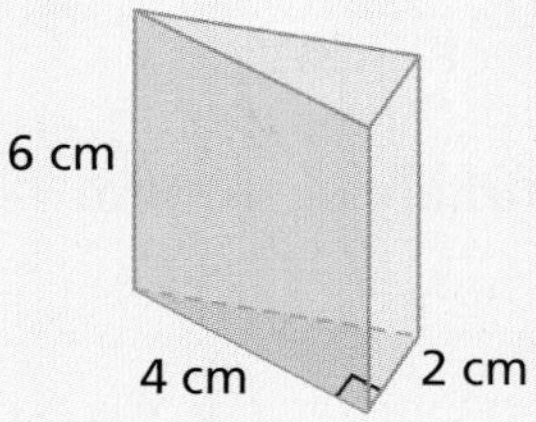

Activity 2

1. You can use a process similar to that in Activity 1 to develop the formula for the volume of a cylinder. You will need an empty soup can or other cylindrical container. Remove one of the bases.

2. Arrange centimeter cubes in a single layer at the bottom of the cylinder. Fit as many cubes into the layer as possible. How many cubes are in this layer?

3. To find how many layers of cubes would fit in the cylinder, make a stack of cubes along the inside of the cylinder. How many layers would fit in the cylinder?

4. How can you use what you know to find the approximate number of cubes that would fit in the cylinder?

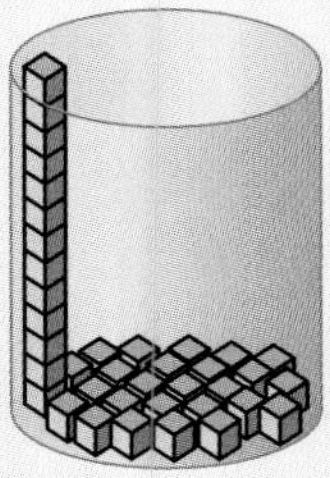

Think and Discuss

1. Suppose you know the area of the base of a cylinder and the height of the cylinder. How can you find the cylinder's volume?
2. Let the area of the base of a cylinder be B and the height of the cylinder be h. Write a formula for the cylinder's volume V.
3. The base of a cylinder is a circle with radius r. How can you find the area of the base? How can you use this in your formula for the volume of a cylinder?

Try This

Use the formula you discovered to find the volume of each cylinder. Use 3.14 for π and round to the nearest tenth.

1.

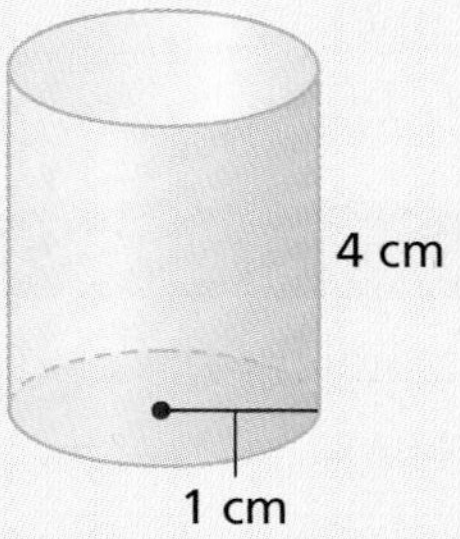

2.

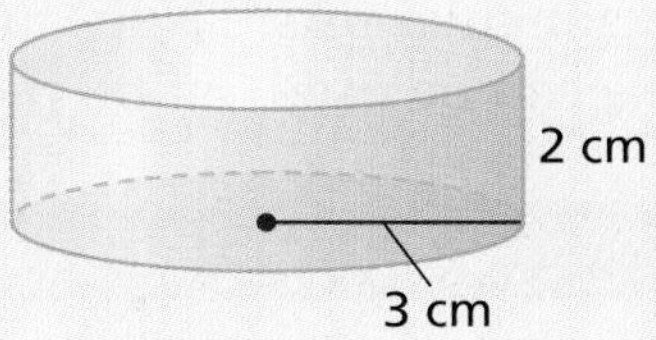

3.

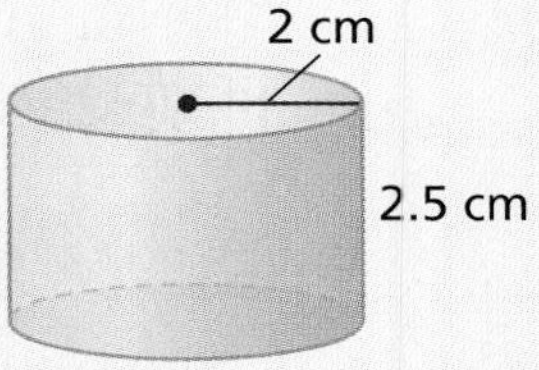

10-2 Volume of Prisms and Cylinders

Learn to find the volume of prisms and cylinders.

Vocabulary

volume

Any three-dimensional figure can be filled completely with congruent cubes and parts of cubes. The **volume** of a three-dimensional figure is the number of cubes it can hold. Each cube represents a unit of measure called a cubic unit.

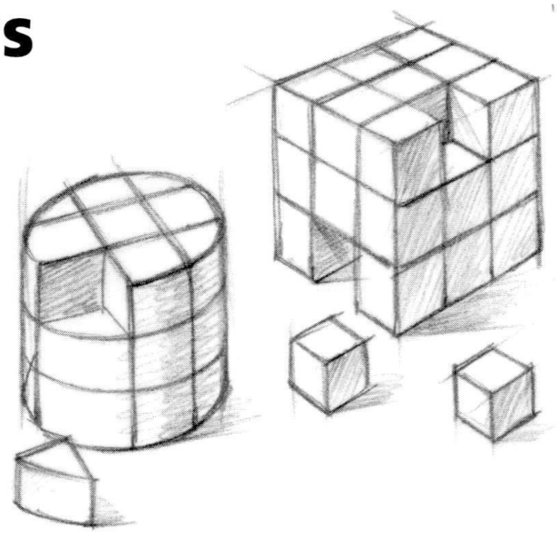

EXAMPLE 1 **Using Cubes to Find the Volume of a Rectangular Prism**

Find how many cubes the prism holds. Then give the prism's volume.

You can find the volume of this prism by counting how many cubes tall, long, and wide the prism is and then multiplying.

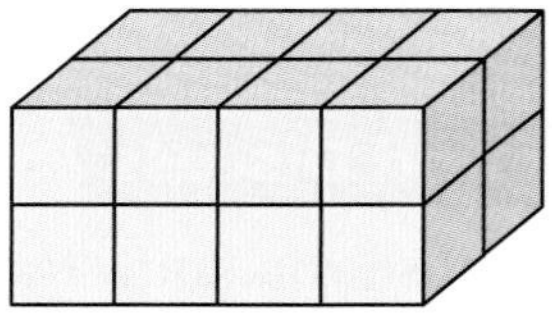

$2 \cdot 4 \cdot 2 = 16$

There are 16 cubes in the prism, so the volume is 16 cubic units.

Reading Math

Any unit of measurement with an exponent of 3 is a cubic unit. For example, m^3 means "cubic meter," and in^3 means "cubic inch."

To find a prism's volume, multiply its length by its width by its height.

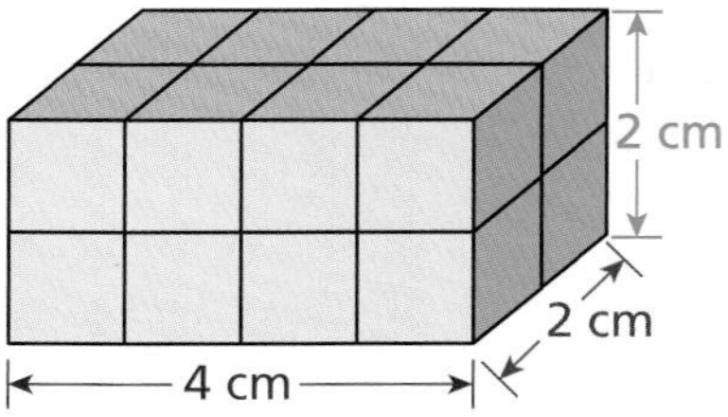

4 cm · **2 cm** · 2 cm = 16 cm^3

length · **width** · height = volume

area of base · height = volume

The volume of a rectangular prism is the area of its base times its height. This formula can be used to find the volume of any prism.

VOLUME OF A PRISM

The volume V of a prism is the area of its base B times its height h.

$$V = Bh$$

EXAMPLE 2 Using a Formula to Find the Volume of a Prism

Find the volume of each figure.

A

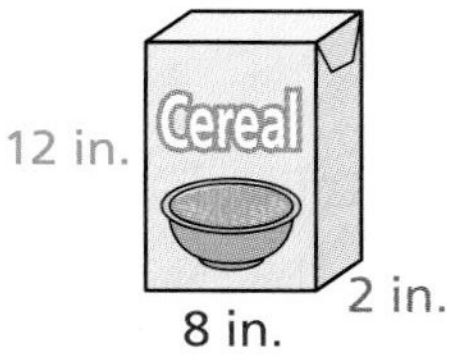

$V = Bh$ *Use the formula.*

The base is a rectangle: $B = \mathbf{8} \cdot \mathbf{2} = \mathbf{16}$.

$V = \mathbf{16} \cdot 12$ *Substitute for B and h.*

$V = 192$ *Multiply.*

The volume of the cereal box is 192 in^3.

B

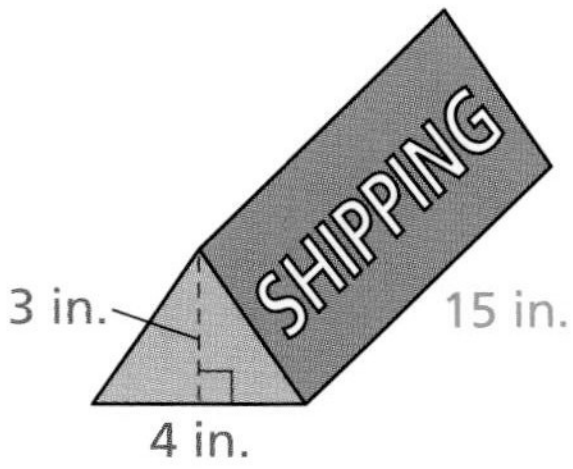

$V = Bh$ *Use the formula.*

The base is a triangle: $B = \frac{1}{2} \cdot \mathbf{4} \cdot \mathbf{3} = \mathbf{6}$.

$V = \mathbf{6} \cdot 15$ *Substitute for B and h.*

$V = 90$ *Multiply.*

The volume of the shipping carton is 90 in^3.

Finding the volume of a cylinder is similar to finding the volume of a prism.

VOLUME OF A CYLINDER

The volume V of a cylinder is the area of its base B times its height h.

$V = Bh$ or $V = \pi r^2 h$, where $B = \pi r^2$

EXAMPLE 3 Using a Formula to Find the Volume of a Cylinder

A can of shoe polish is shaped like a cylinder. Find its volume to the nearest tenth. Use 3.14 for π.

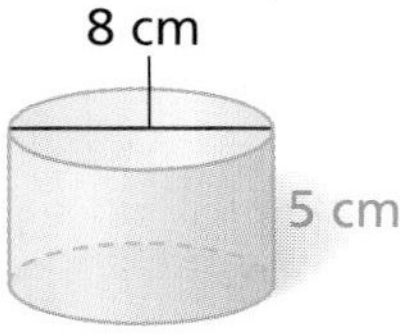

$V = Bh$ *Use the formula.*

The base is a circle: $B = \pi \cdot 4^2 \approx \mathbf{50.24}$ cm^2.

$V \approx \mathbf{50.24} \cdot 5$ *Substitute for B and h.*

$V \approx 251.2$ *Multiply.*

The volume of the shoe polish can is about 251.2 cm^3.

Think and Discuss

1. **Explain** what a cubic unit is. What units would you use for the volume of a figure measured in yards?
2. **Compare and contrast** the formulas for volume of a prism and volume of a cylinder. How are they alike? How are they different?

10-2 Exercises

go.hrw.com
Homework Help Online
KEYWORD: MS7 10-2
Parent Resources Online
KEYWORD: MS7 Parent

GUIDED PRACTICE

See Example 1 **Find how many cubes each prism holds. Then give the prism's volume.**

1.
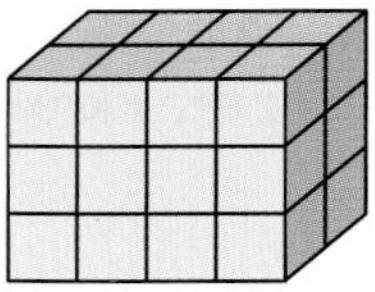

2.
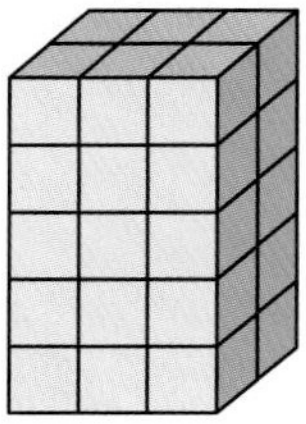

3.
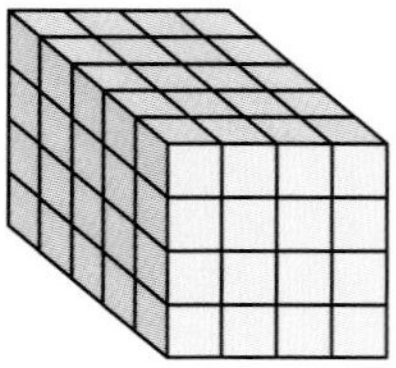

See Example 2 **Find the volume of each figure.**

4.
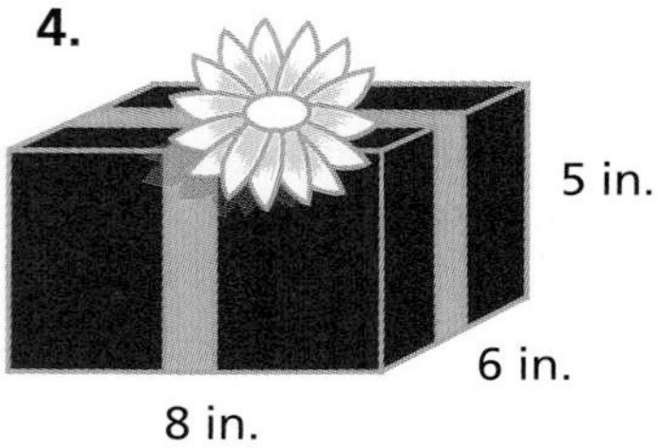

5.
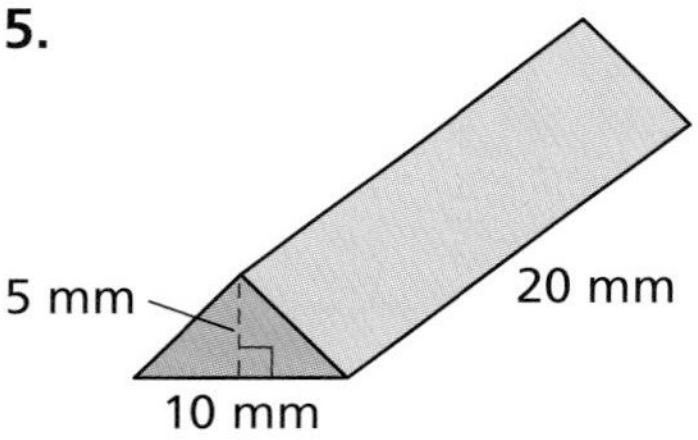

6.
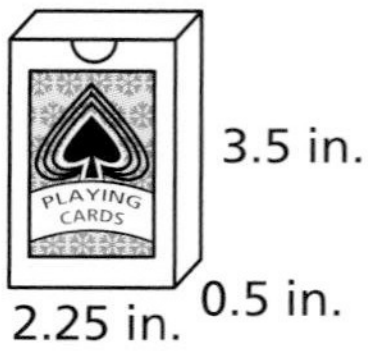

See Example 3 **7.** A can of tomato paste is shaped like a cylinder. It is 4 cm wide and 6 cm tall. Find its volume to the nearest tenth. Use 3.14 for π.

INDEPENDENT PRACTICE

See Example 1 **Find how many cubes each prism holds. Then give the prism's volume.**

8.
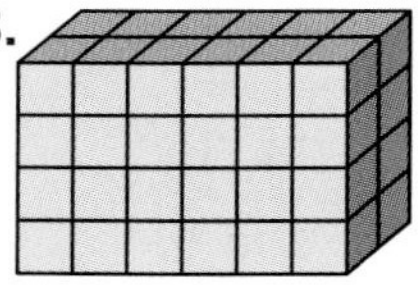

9.
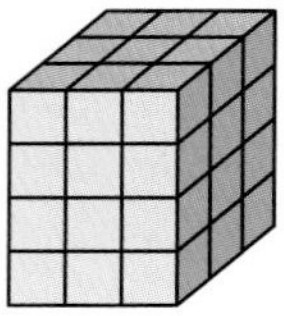

10.
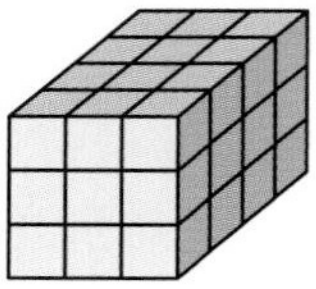

See Example 2 **Find the volume of each figure.**

11.
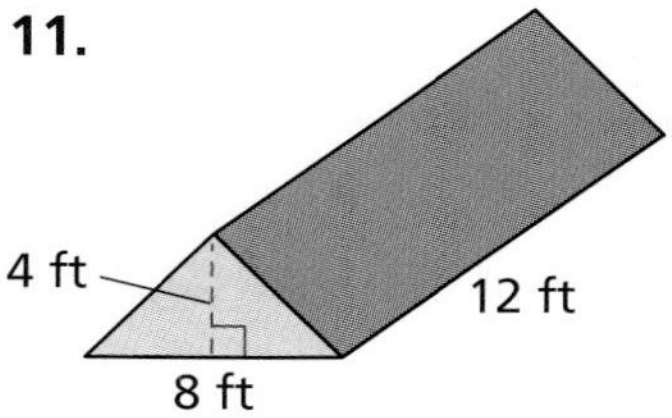

12.
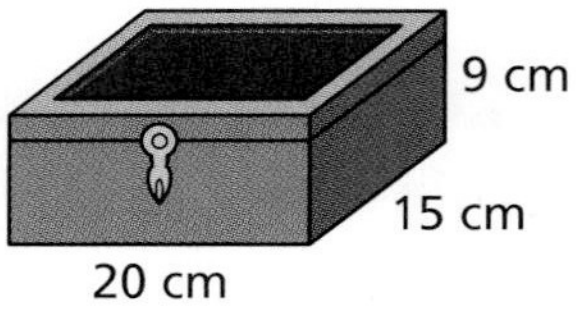

13.
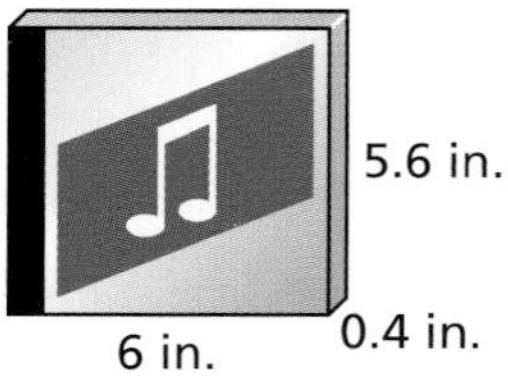

See Example 3 **14.** A paper towel roll is shaped like a cylinder. It is 4 cm wide and 28 cm tall. Find its volume to the nearest tenth. Use 3.14 for π.

PRACTICE AND PROBLEM SOLVING

Extra Practice
See page 746.

15. Multi-Step The base of a triangular prism is a right triangle with hypotenuse 10 m long and one leg 6 m long. If the height of the prism is 12 m, what is the volume of the prism?

LINK: Life Science

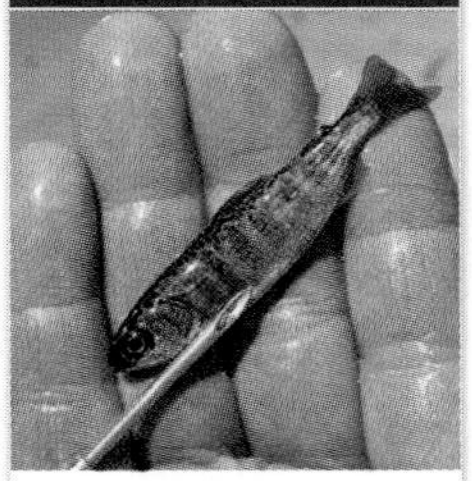

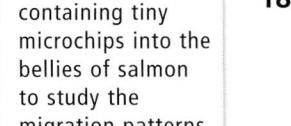

Marine biologists insert tags containing tiny microchips into the bellies of salmon to study the migration patterns of these fish.

go.hrw.com
Web Extra!
KEYWORD: MS7 Tags

16. Life Science An ID tag containing a microchip can be injected into a pet, such as a dog or cat. These microchips are cylindrical and can be as small as 12 mm in length and 2.1 mm in diameter. Use rounding to estimate the volume of one of these microchips. Then find the volume to the nearest tenth. Use 3.14 for π.

17. Recreation The tent shown is in the shape of a triangular prism. How many cubic feet of space are in the tent?

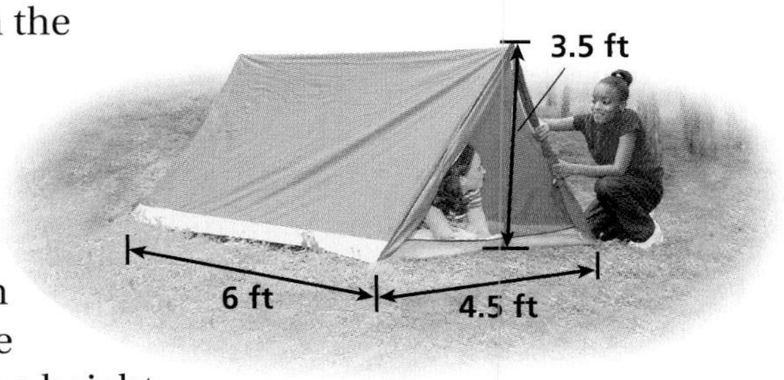

18. What's the Error? A student said the volume of a cylinder with a 3-inch diameter is two times the volume of a cylinder with the same height and a 1.5-inch radius. What is the error?

19. Write About It Explain the similarities and differences between finding the volume of a cylinder and finding the volume of a triangular prism.

20. Challenge Find the volume, to the nearest tenth, of the material that makes up the pipe shown. Use 3.14 for π.

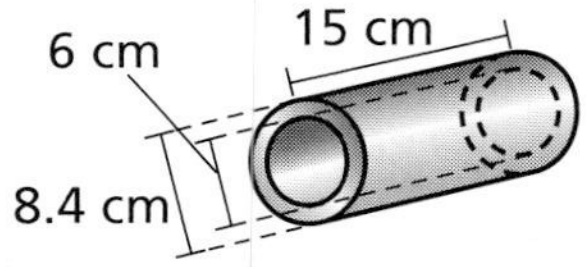

Test Prep and Spiral Review

21. Multiple Choice What is the volume of a triangular prism that is 10 in. long, 7 in. wide, and 4 in. high?

Ⓐ 110 in^2 Ⓑ 140 in^2 Ⓒ 205 in^2 Ⓓ 280 in^2

22. Multiple Choice Which figures have the same volume?

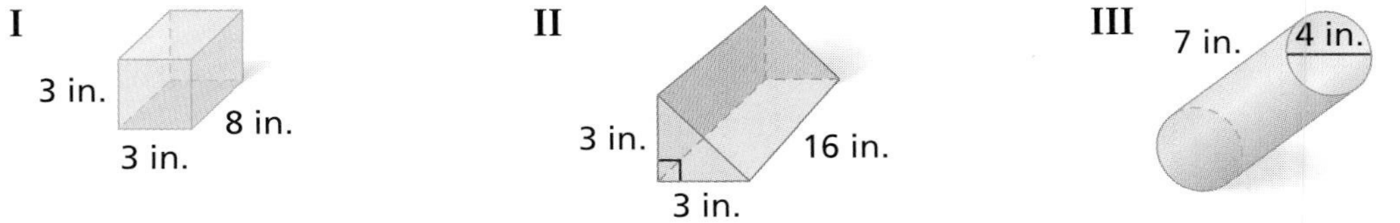

Ⓕ I and II Ⓖ I and III Ⓗ II and III Ⓙ I, II, and III

Find the simple interest. (Lesson 6-7)

23. $P = \$3{,}600$; $r = 5\%$; $t = 1.5$ years **24.** $P = \$10{,}000$; $r = 3.2\%$; $t = 2$ years

25. Students collected data on the number of visitors to an amusement park over a period of 30 days. Choose the type of graph that would best represent the data. (Lesson 7-7)

10-3 Volume of Pyramids and Cones

Learn to find the volume of pyramids and cones.

Suppose you have a square-pyramid-shaped container and a square-prism-shaped container, and the bases and heights are the same size. If you pour sand from the pyramid into the prism, it appears that the prism holds three times as much sand as the pyramid.

In fact, the volume of a pyramid is exactly one-third the volume of a prism if they have the same height and same-size base.

The height of a pyramid is the perpendicular distance from the pyramid's base to its vertex.

VOLUME OF A RECTANGULAR PYRAMID

The volume V of a rectangular pyramid is one-third the area of its base B times its height h.

$V = \frac{1}{3}Bh$ or $V = \frac{1}{3}\ell wh$, where $B = \ell w$

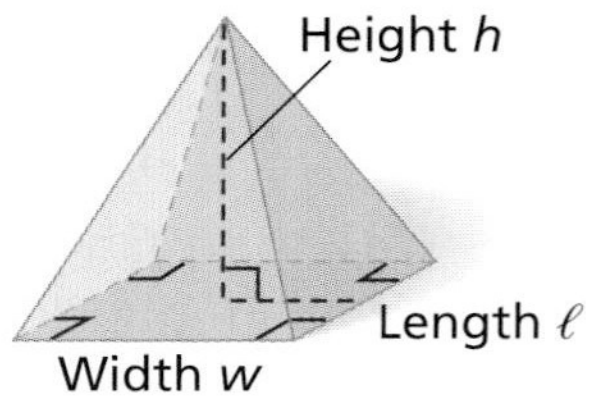

EXAMPLE 1 Finding the Volume of a Rectangular Pyramid

Find the volume of the pyramid to the nearest tenth. Estimate to check whether the answer is reasonable.

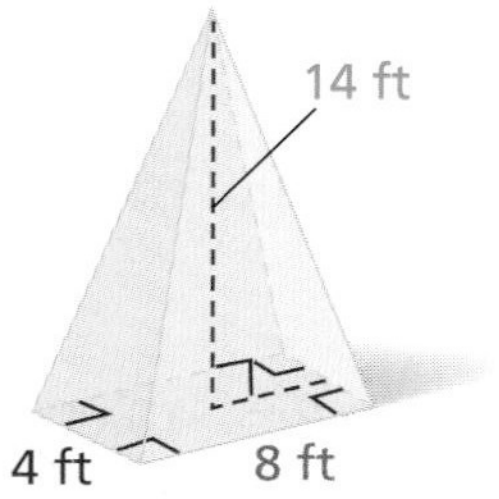

$V = \frac{1}{3}Bh$ *Use the formula.*

The base is a rectangle, so $B = \mathbf{4} \cdot \mathbf{8} = \mathbf{32}$.

$V = \frac{1}{3} \cdot 32 \cdot 14$ *Substitute for B and h.*

$V \approx 149.3 \text{ ft}^3$ *Multiply.*

Estimate $V \approx \frac{1}{3} \cdot 30 \cdot 15$ *Round the measurements.*

$= 150 \text{ ft}^3$ *The answer is reasonable.*

Similar to the relationship between volumes of prisms and pyramids, the volume of a cone is one-third the volume of a cylinder with the same height and a congruent base.

The height of a cone is the perpendicular distance from the cone's base to its vertex.

VOLUME OF A CONE

The volume V of a cone is one-third the area of its base B times its height h.

$V = \frac{1}{3}Bh$ or $V = \frac{1}{3}\pi r^2 h$, where $B = \pi r^2$

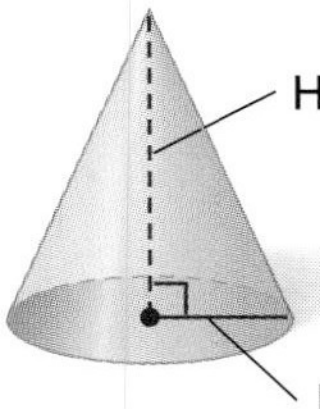

EXAMPLE 2 **Finding the Volume of a Cone**

Find the volume of each cone to the nearest tenth. Use 3.14 for π. Estimate to check whether the answer is reasonable.

Helpful Hint

To estimate the volume of a cone, round π to 3 so that $\frac{1}{3} \cdot \pi$ becomes $\frac{1}{3} \cdot 3$, which is 1.

A

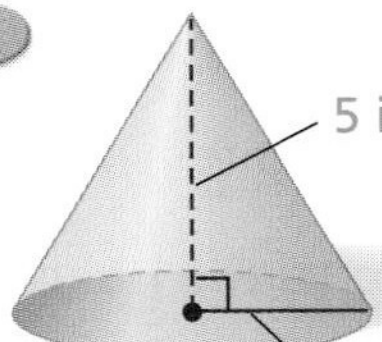

$V = \frac{1}{3}Bh$ *Use the formula.*

The base is a circle, so $B = \pi \cdot r^2 = 3.14 \cdot \mathbf{3}^2 \approx \mathbf{28.27}$.

$V \approx \frac{1}{3} \cdot \mathbf{28.27} \cdot 5$ *Substitute for B and h.*

$V \approx 47.1 \text{ in}^3$ *Multiply.*

Estimate $V \approx \left(\frac{1}{3} \cdot \pi\right) 3^2 \cdot 5$ $\quad \frac{1}{3} \cdot \pi \approx 1$

$\approx 45 \text{ in}^3$ *The answer is reasonable.*

B

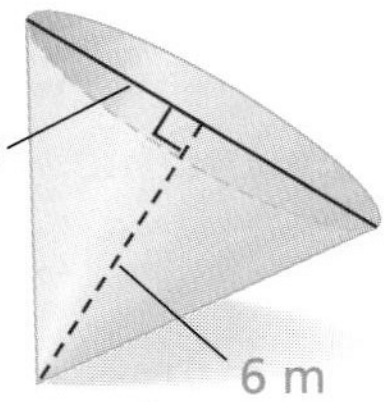

$V = \frac{1}{3}Bh$ *Use the formula.*

The base is a circle, so $B = \pi \cdot r^2 = 3.14 \cdot \left(\frac{\mathbf{8}}{2}\right)^2 \approx \mathbf{50.3}$.

$V \approx \frac{1}{3} \cdot \mathbf{50.3} \cdot 6$ *Substitute for B and h.*

$V \approx 100.6 \text{ m}^2$ *Multiply.*

Estimate $V \approx \left(\frac{1}{3} \cdot \pi\right) 4^2 \cdot 6$ $\quad \frac{1}{3} \cdot \pi \approx 1$

$\approx 96 \text{ m}^2$ *The answer is reasonable.*

Think and Discuss

1. **Explain** how to find the volume of a cone given the diameter of the base and the height of the cone.

2. **Compare and contrast** the formulas for volume of a pyramid and volume of a cone. How are they alike? How are they different?

10-3 Exercises

go.hrw.com
Homework Help Online
KEYWORD: MS7 10-3
Parent Resources Online
KEYWORD: MS7 Parent

GUIDED PRACTICE

See Example 1

Find the volume of each pyramid to the nearest tenth. Estimate to check whether the answer is reasonable.

1.

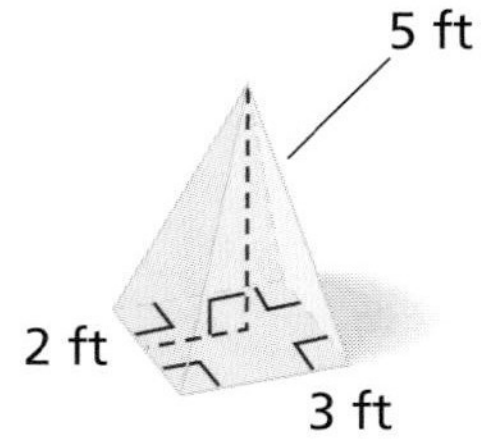

2.

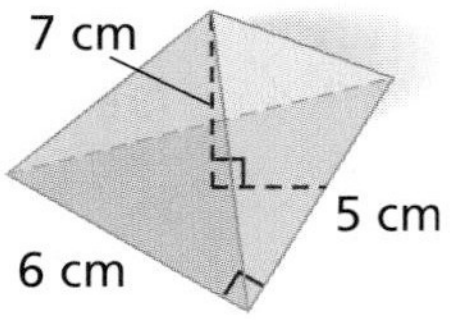

3.

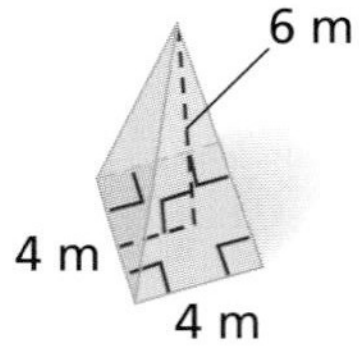

See Example 2

Find the volume of each cone to the nearest tenth. Use 3.14 for π. Estimate to check whether the answer is reasonable.

4.

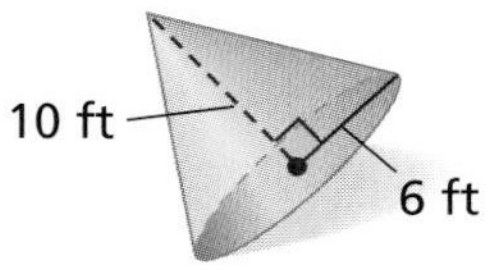

5.

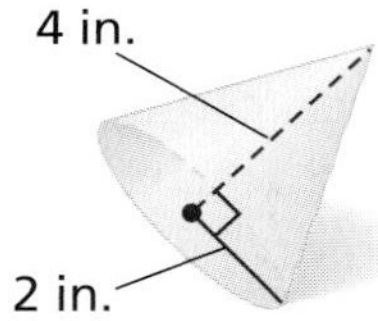

6.

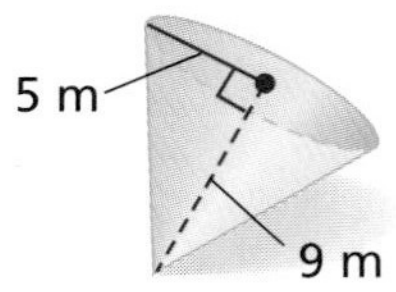

INDEPENDENT PRACTICE

See Example 1

Find the volume of each pyramid to the nearest tenth. Estimate to check whether the answer is reasonable.

7.

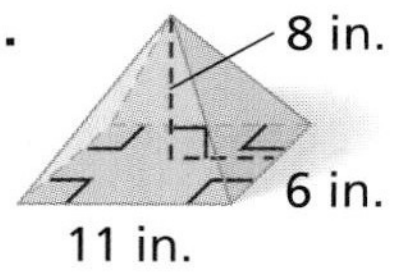

8.

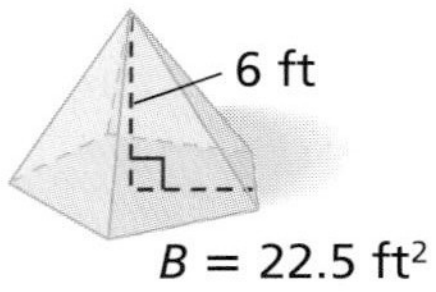

9.

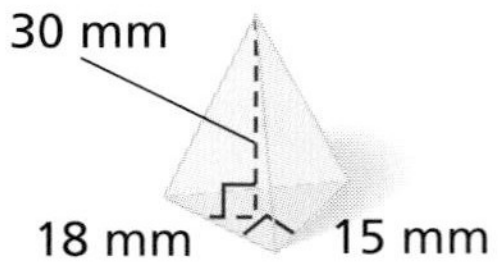

See Example 2

Find the volume of each cone to the nearest tenth. Use 3.14 for π. Estimate to check whether the answer is reasonable.

10.

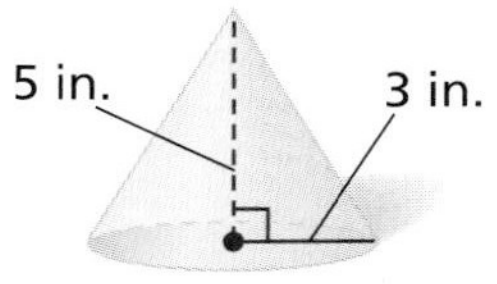

11.

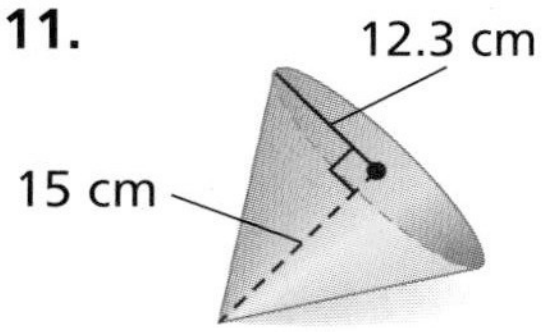

12.

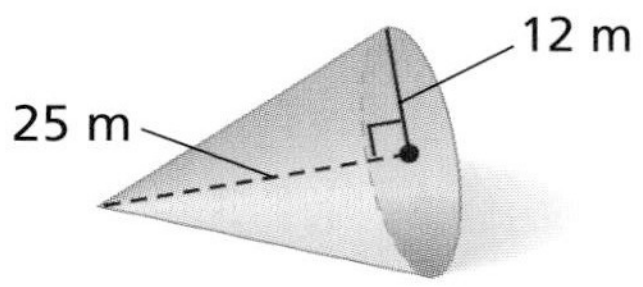

PRACTICE AND PROBLEM SOLVING

Extra Practice
See page 746.

Find the volume of each figure to the nearest tenth. Use 3.14 for π.

13. a 7 ft tall rectangular pyramid with base 4 ft by 5 ft

14. a cone with radius 8 yd and height 12 yd

15. Multi-Step Find the volume of an 8 in. tall right triangular pyramid with a base hypotenuse of 5 in. and base leg of 3 in.

16. Architecture The steeple on a building is a square pyramid with a base area of 12 square feet and a height of 15 feet. How many cubic feet of concrete was used to make the steeple?

17. Multi-Step A snack bar sells popcorn in the containers shown at right.

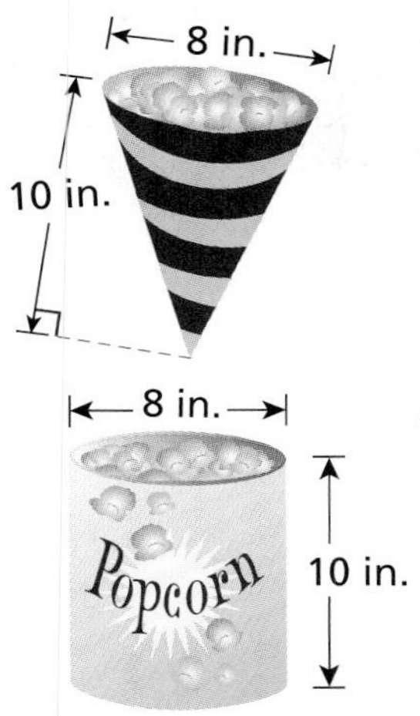

a. Based on the formulas for volume of a cylinder and a cone, how many times as much popcorn does the larger container hold?

b. How many cubic inches of popcorn, to the nearest tenth, does the cone-shaped container hold? Use 3.14 for π.

c. How many cubic inches of popcorn does the cylinder-shaped container hold? Use 3.14 for π.

d. Do your answers to parts **b** and **c** confirm your answer to part **a**? If not, find the error.

18. Critical Thinking Write a proportion of volumes for the given figures.

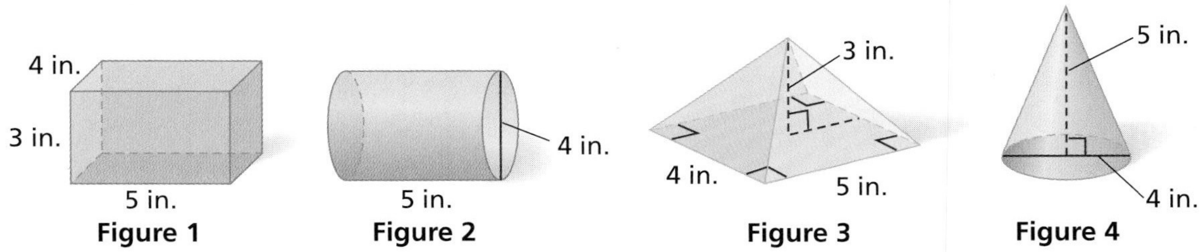

19. What's the Question? The answer is: The volume of figure A is $\frac{1}{3}$ the volume of figure B. What's the question?

20. Write About It Compare finding the volume of a cylinder with finding the volume of a cone that has the same height and base.

21. Challenge What effect does doubling the radius of a cone's base have on the cone's volume?

Test Prep and Spiral Review

22. Multiple Choice Which is the best estimate for the volume of a cone with a radius of 5 cm and a height of 8 cm?

Ⓐ 40 cm^3 Ⓑ 80 cm^3 Ⓒ 200 cm^3 Ⓓ 800 cm^3

23. Short Response A rectangular prism and a square pyramid both have a square base with side lengths of 5 inches and heights of 7 inches. Find the volume of each figure. Then explain the relationship between the volume of the prism and the volume of the pyramid.

Name the types of quadrilaterals that have each property. (Lesson 8-7)

24. four congruent sides

25. two sets of parallel sides

Find the volume of each figure to the nearest tenth. Use 3.14 for π. (Lesson 10-2)

26. cylinder: $d = 6$ m, $h = 8$ m

27. triangular prism: $B = 22$ ft^2, $h = 5$ ft

CHAPTER 10

READY TO GO ON?

SECTION 10A

Quiz for Lessons 10-1 Through 10-3

10-1 Introduction to Three-Dimensional Figures

Classify each figure as a polyhedron or not a polyhedron. Then name the figure.

1. 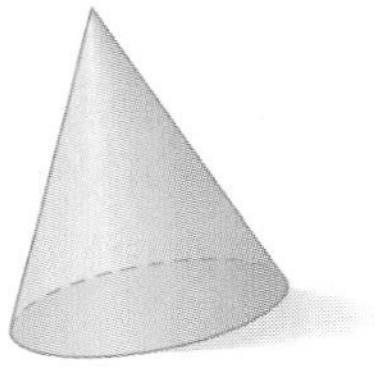

2. 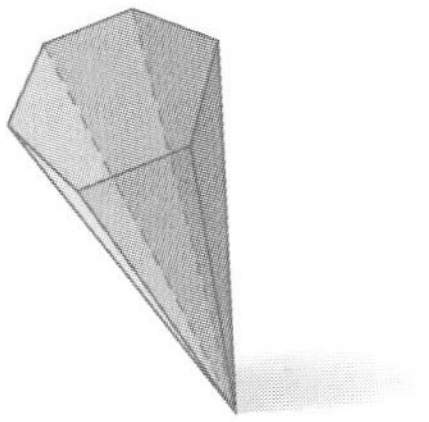

3. 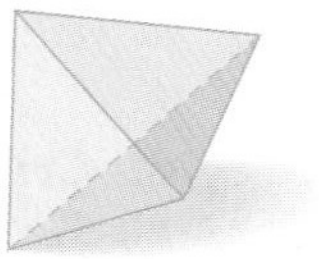

10-2 Volume of Prisms and Cylinders

Find how many cubes each prism holds. Then give the prism's volume.

4. 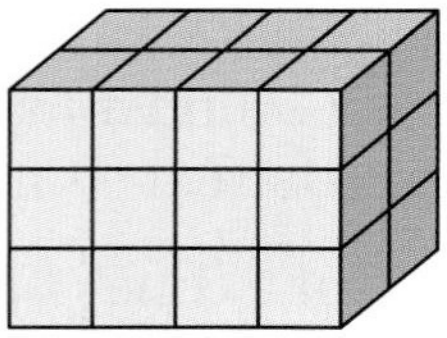

5. 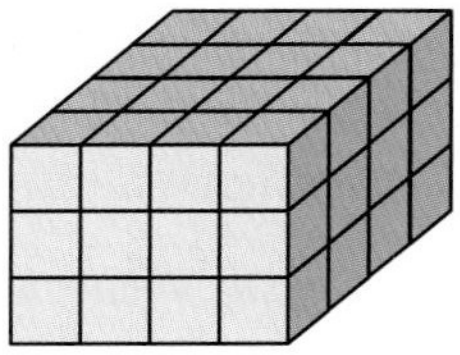

6. A box is shaped like a rectangular prism. It is 6 ft long, 2 ft wide, and 3 ft high. Find its volume.

7. A can is shaped like a cylinder. It is 5.2 cm wide and 2.3 cm tall. Find its volume. Use 3.14 for π.

10-3 Volume of Pyramids and Cones

Find the volume of each figure to the nearest tenth. Use 3.14 for π.

8. 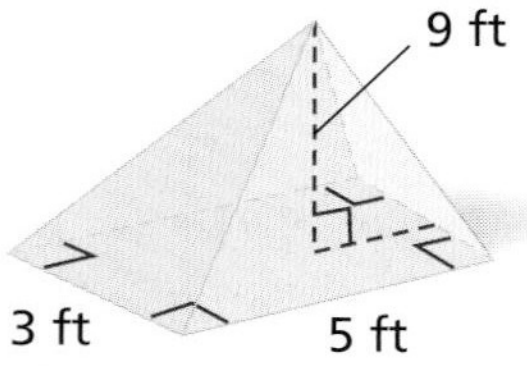

9. 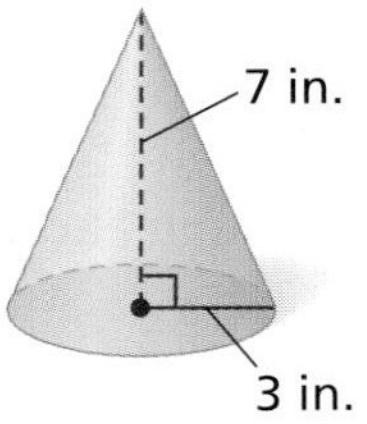

10. 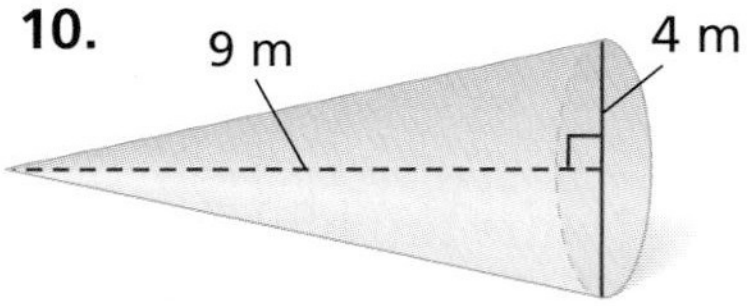

11. A cone has a radius of 2.5 cm and a height of 14 cm. What is the volume of the cone to the nearest hundredth? Use 3.14 for π.

Focus on Problem Solving

Solve

• **Choose an operation**

When choosing an operation to use when solving a problem, you need to decide which action the problem is asking you to take. If you are asked to combine numbers, then you need to add. If you are asked to take away numbers or to find the difference between two numbers, then you need to subtract. You need to use multiplication when you put equal parts together and division when you separate something into equal parts.

Determine the action in each problem. Then tell which operation should be used to solve the problem. Explain your choice.

1. Jeremy filled a sugar cone completely full of frozen yogurt and then put one scoop of frozen yogurt on top. The volume of Jeremy's cone is about 20.93 in^3, and the volume of the scoop that Jeremy used is about 16.75 in^3. About how much frozen yogurt, in cubic inches, did Jeremy use?

2. The volume of a cylinder equals the combined volumes of three cones that each have the same height and base size as the cylinder. What is the volume of a cylinder if a cone of the same height and base size has a volume of 45.2 cm^3?

3. The biology class at Jefferson High School takes care of a family of turtles that is kept in a glass tank with water, rocks, and plants. The volume of the tank is 2.75 cubic feet. At the end of the year, the baby turtles will have grown and will be moved into a tank that is 6.15 cubic feet. How much greater will the volume of the new tank be than that of the old tank?

4. Brianna is adding a second section to her hamster cage. The two sections will be connected by a tunnel that is made of 4 cylindrical parts, all the same size. If the volume of the tunnel is 56.52 cubic inches, what is the volume of each part of the tunnel?

Hands-On LAB 10-4

Use Nets to Build Prisms and Cylinders

Use with Lesson 10-4

go.hrw.com
Lab Resources Online
KEYWORD: MS7 Lab10

A net is a pattern of two-dimensional figures that can be folded to make a three-dimensional figure. You can use $\frac{1}{4}$-inch graph paper to help you make nets.

Activity

1 Use a net to construct a rectangular prism.

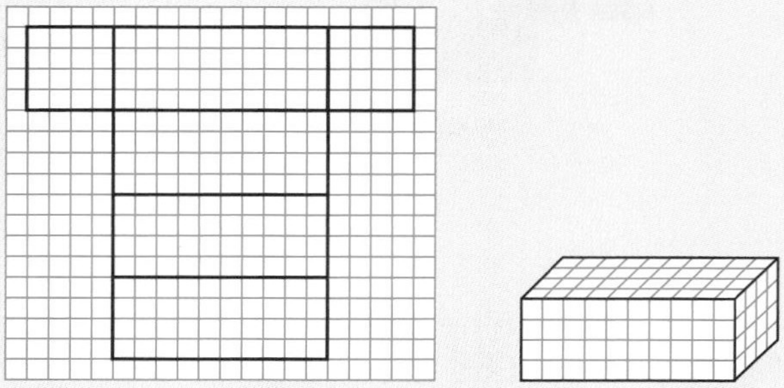

a. Draw the net at right on a piece of graph paper. Each rectangle is 10 squares by 4 squares. The two squares are 4 small squares on each side.

b. Cut out the net. Fold the net along the edges of each rectangle to make a rectangular prism. Tape the edges to hold them in place.

2 Use a net to construct a cylinder.

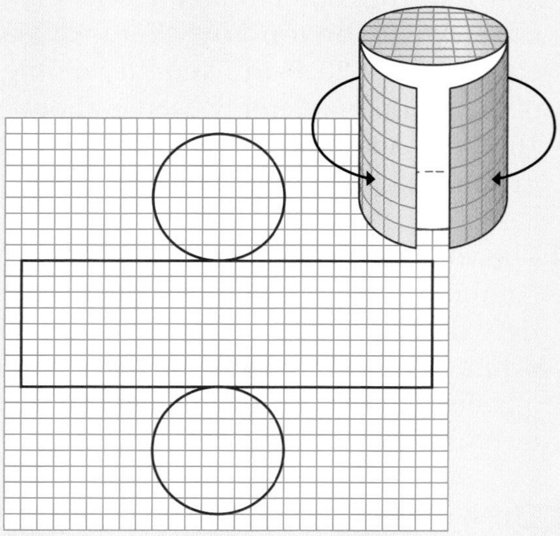

a. Draw the net at right on a piece of graph paper. The rectangle is 25 squares by 8 squares. Use a compass to make the circles. Each circle has a radius of 4 squares.

b. Cut out the net. Fold the net as shown to make a cylinder. Tape the edges to hold them in place.

Think and Discuss

1. What are the dimensions, in inches, of the rectangular prism that you built?
2. What is the height, in inches, of the cylinder that you built? What is the cylinder's radius?

Try This

1. Use a net to construct a rectangular prism that is 1 inch by 2 inches by 3 inches.
2. Use a net to construct a cylinder with a height of 1 inch and a radius of $\frac{1}{2}$ in. (*Hint:* The length of the rectangle in the net must match the circumference of the circles, so the length should be $2\pi r = 2\pi\left(\frac{1}{2}\right) \approx 3.14$ inches.)

10-4 Surface Area of Prisms and Cylinders

Learn to find the surface area of prisms and cylinders.

Vocabulary

net

surface area

If you remove the surface from a three-dimensional figure and lay it out flat, the pattern you make is called a **net**.

Nets allow you to see all the surfaces of a solid at one time. You can use nets to help you find the *surface area* of a three-dimensional figure. **Surface area** is the sum of the areas of all of the surfaces of a figure.

You can use nets to write formulas for the surface area of prisms. The surface area S of a prism is the sum of the areas of the faces of the prism. For the rectangular prism shown:

$S = \ell w + \ell h + wh + \ell w + \ell h + wh = 2\ell w + 2\ell h + 2wh$

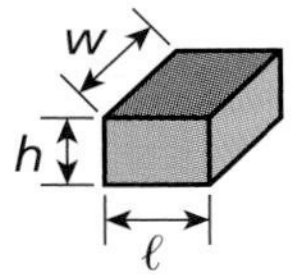

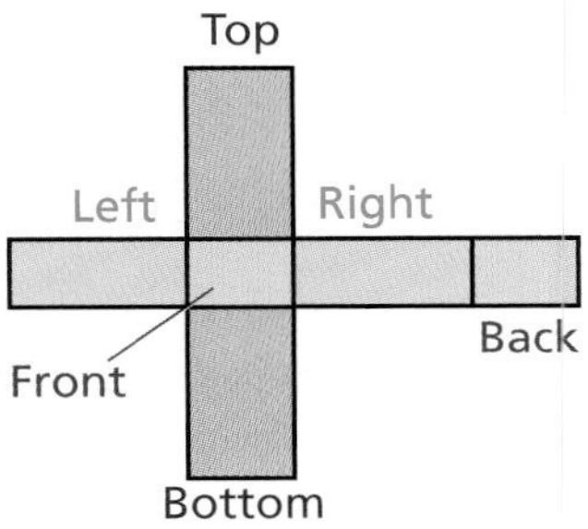

SURFACE AREA OF A RECTANGULAR PRISM

The surface area of a rectangular prism is the sum of the areas of each face.

$$S = 2\ell w + 2\ell h + 2wh$$

EXAMPLE 1 Finding the Surface Area of a Prism

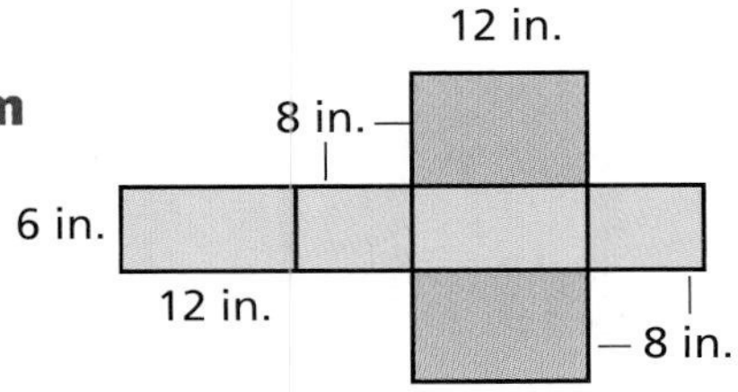

Find the surface area of the prism formed by the net.

$S = 2\ell w + 2\ell h + 2wh$

$S = (2 \cdot 12 \cdot 8) + (2 \cdot 12 \cdot 6) + (2 \cdot 8 \cdot 6)$ *Substitute.*

$S = 192 + 144 + 96$ *Multiply.*

$S = 432$ *Add.*

The surface area of the prism is 432 in^2.

If you could remove the curved surface from a cylinder, like peeling a label from a can, you would see that it has the shape of a rectangle when flattened out.

You can draw a net for a cylinder by drawing the circular bases (like the ends of a can) and the rectangular curved surface as shown below. The length of the rectangle is the circumference, $2\pi r$, of the base of the cylinder. So the area of the curved surface is $2\pi r \cdot h$. The area of each base is πr^2.

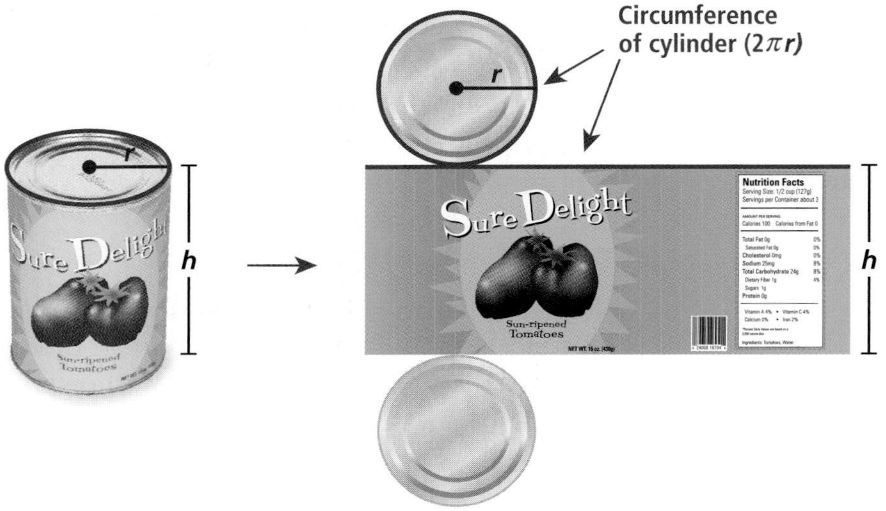

$$\begin{aligned}\text{Surface area} &= \text{area of top} + \text{area of bottom} + \text{area of curved surface}\\ &= \pi r^2 + \pi r^2 + (2\pi r)h\\ &= 2\pi r^2 + 2\pi rh\end{aligned}$$

SURFACE AREA OF A CYLINDER

The surface area S of a cylinder is the sum of the areas of its bases, $2\pi r^2$, plus the area of its curved surface, $2\pi rh$.

$$S = 2\pi r^2 + 2\pi rh$$

EXAMPLE 2 Finding the Surface Area of a Cylinder

Find the surface area of the cylinder formed by the net to the nearest tenth. Use 3.14 for π.

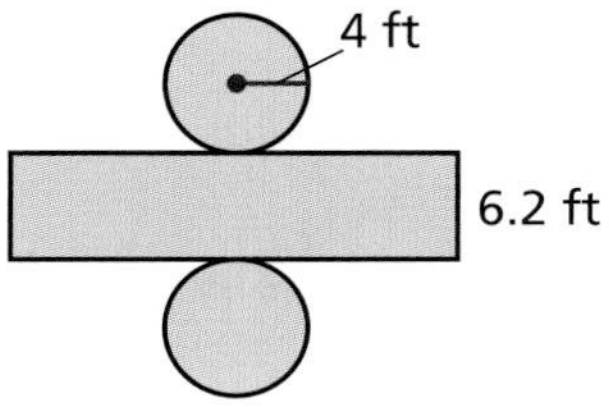

$S = 2\pi r^2 + 2\pi rh$ *Use the formula.*

$S \approx (2 \cdot 3.14 \cdot 4^2) + (2 \cdot 3.14 \cdot 4 \cdot 6.2)$ *Substitute.*

$S \approx 100.48 + 155.744$ *Multiply.*

$S \approx 256.224$ *Add.*

$S \approx 256.2$ *Round.*

The surface area of the cylinder is about 256.2 ft^2.

EXAMPLE 3 PROBLEM SOLVING APPLICATION

PROBLEM SOLVING

What percent of the total surface area of the tennis ball can is covered by the label? Use 3.14 for π.

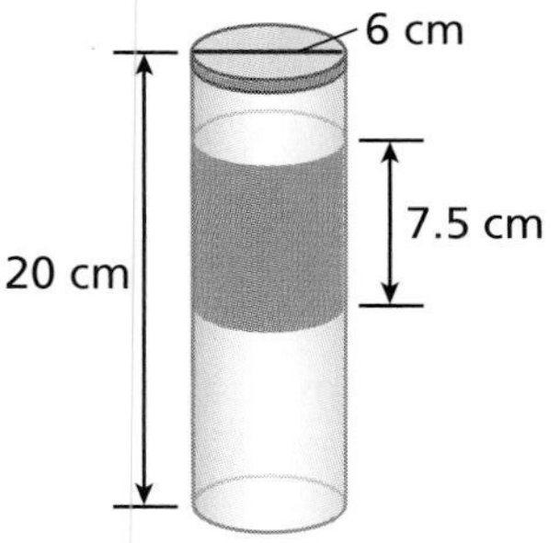

1 Understand the Problem

List the **important information:**

- The can is approximately cylinder-shaped.
- The height of the can is 20 cm.
- The diameter of the can is 6 cm.
- The height of the label is 7.5 cm.

2 Make a Plan

Find the surface area of the can and the area of the label. Divide to find the percent of the surface area covered by the label.

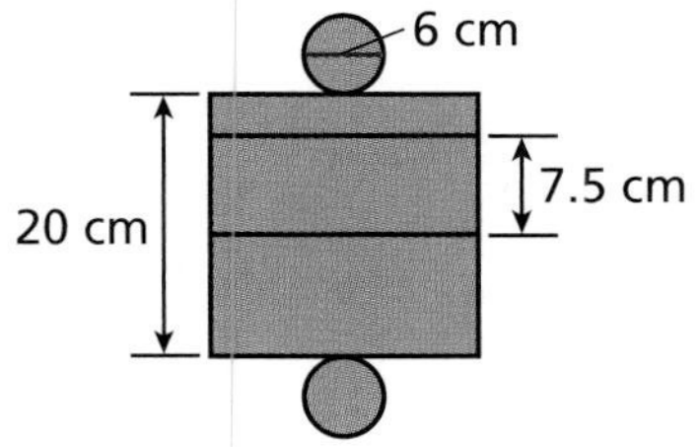

3 Solve

$$S = 2\pi r^2 + 2\pi rh$$
$$\approx 2(3.14)(3)^2 + 2(3.14)(3)(20) \quad \textit{Substitute for } r \textit{ and } h.$$
$$\approx 433.32 \text{ cm}^2$$
$$A = \ell w$$
$$= (2\pi r)w \quad \textit{Substitute } 2\pi r \textit{ for } \ell.$$
$$\approx 2(3.14)(3)(7.5) \quad \textit{Substitute for } r \textit{ and } w.$$
$$\approx 141.3 \text{ cm}^2$$

Percent of the surface area covered by the label: $\frac{141.3 \text{ cm}^2}{433.32 \text{ cm}^2} \approx 32.6\%$.

About 32.6% of the can's surface area is covered by the label.

4 Look Back

Estimate and compare the areas of the two rectangles in the net.

Label: $2(3)(3)(8) = 144 \text{ cm}^2$ $\quad \frac{144 \text{ cm}^2}{360 \text{ cm}^2} = 40\%$

Can: $2(3)(3)(20) = 360 \text{ cm}^2$

The answer should be less than 40% because you did not consider the area of the two circles. So 32.6% is reasonable.

Think and Discuss

1. **Explain** how you would find the surface area of an open-top box that is shaped like a rectangular prism.
2. **Describe** the shapes in a net used to cover a cylinder.

10-4 Exercises

go.hrw.com
Homework Help Online
KEYWORD: MS7 10-4
Parent Resources Online
KEYWORD: MS7 Parent

GUIDED PRACTICE

See Example 1
Find the surface area of the prism formed by each net.

1.

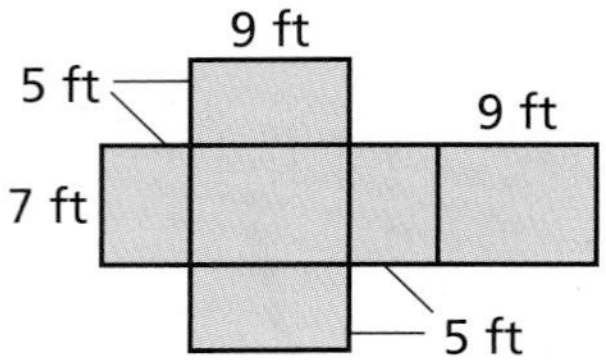

2.

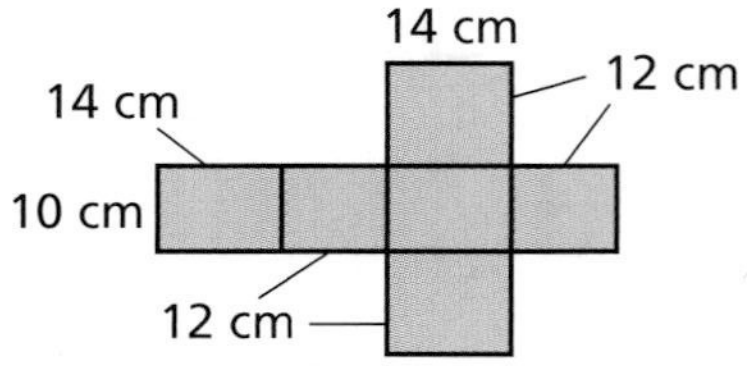

See Example 2
Find the surface area of the cylinder formed by each net to the nearest tenth. Use 3.14 for π.

3.

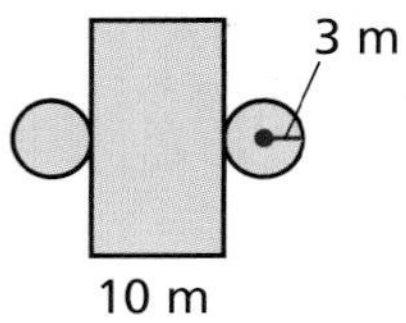

4.

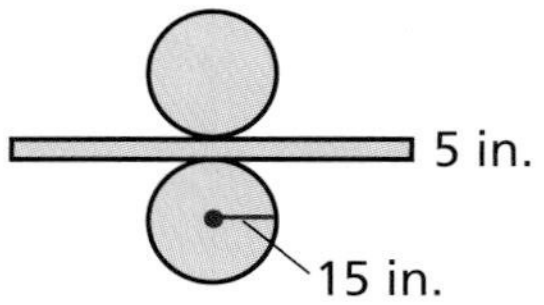

See Example 3
5. A travel mug is cylindrical, and its $2\frac{1}{2}$ in. width fits into most drink holders. What percent of the total surface area of the mug is covered by the 2 in. wide grip? Use 3.14 for π.

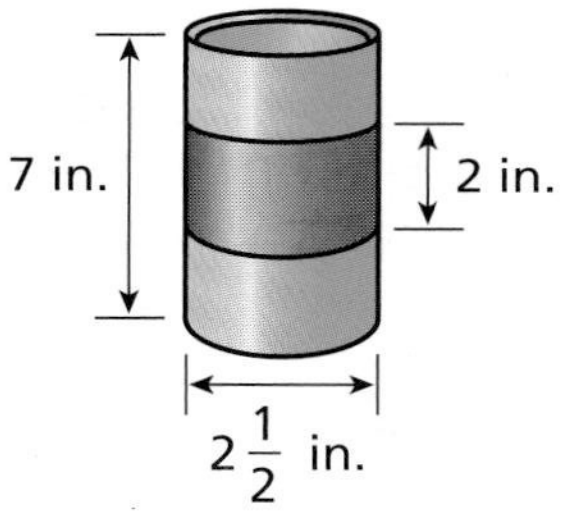

INDEPENDENT PRACTICE

See Example 1
Find the surface area of the prism formed by each net.

6.

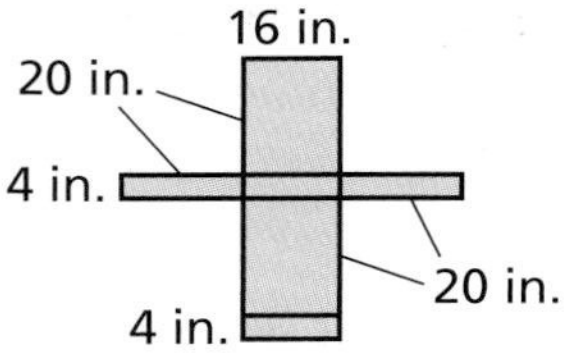

7.

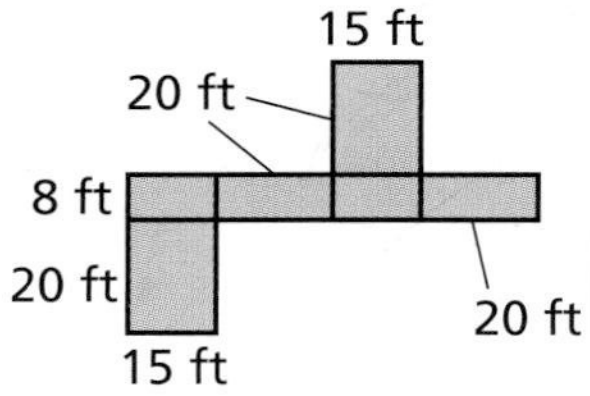

See Example 2
Find the surface area of the cylinder formed by each net to the nearest tenth. Use 3.14 for π.

8.

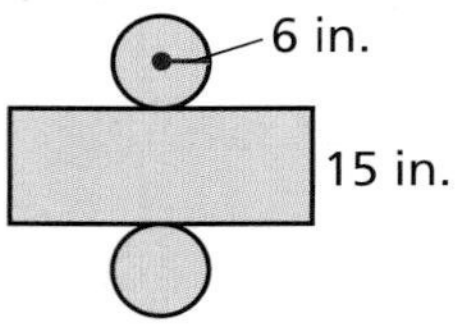

9.

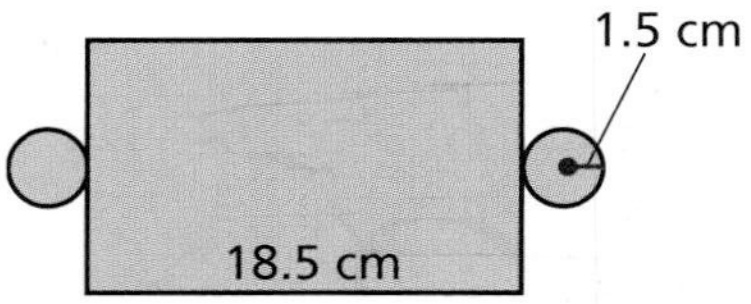

See Example 3
10. A stack of DVDs sits on a base and is covered by an 11 cm tall cylindrical lid. What percent of the surface area of the lid is covered by the label? Use 3.14 for π. (*Hint:* The lid has no bottom.)

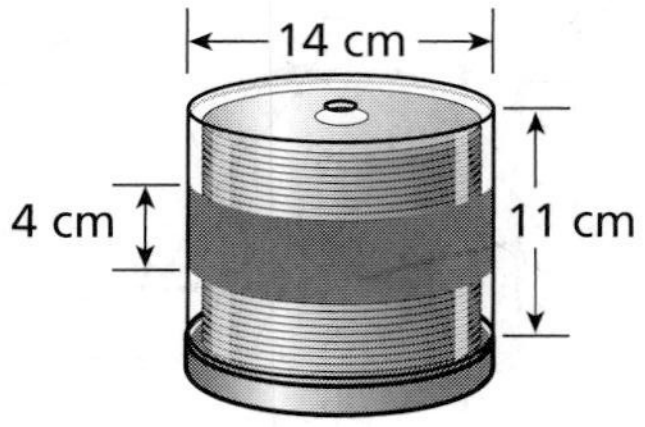

PRACTICE AND PROBLEM SOLVING

Extra Practice
See page 747.

11. A cannery packs tuna into metal cans like the one shown. Round your answers to the nearest tenth, if necessary. Use 3.14 for π.

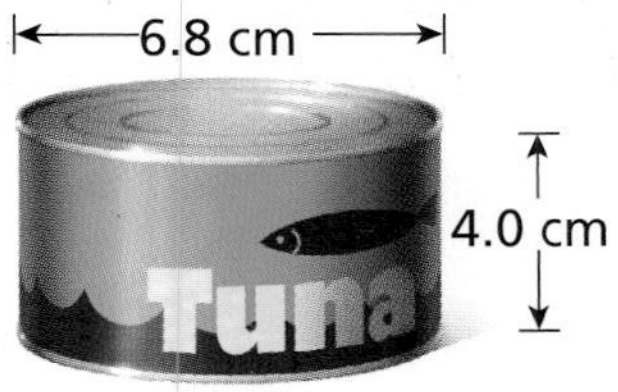

a. Draw and label a net for the cylinder.

b. About how many square centimeters of metal are used to make each can?

c. The label for each can goes all the way around the can. About how many square centimeters of paper are needed for each label?

12. The table shows the dimensions of two rectangular prism boxes with equal volumes. Which box requires more material to wrap? Explain.

	Length	Width	Depth
Box 1	20 in.	5 in.	3 in.
Box 2	10 in.	6 in.	5 in.

13. Choose a Strategy A Rubik's Cube® appears to be built of 27 smaller cubes. Only the outside faces are colored. How many of the "cubes" on a Rubik's Cube have only 2 colored faces?

14. Write About It Explain how you would find the side lengths of a cube with a surface area of 512 ft^2.

15. Challenge Find the surface area of the rectangular prism shown with a rectangular-prism-shaped hole all the way through it.

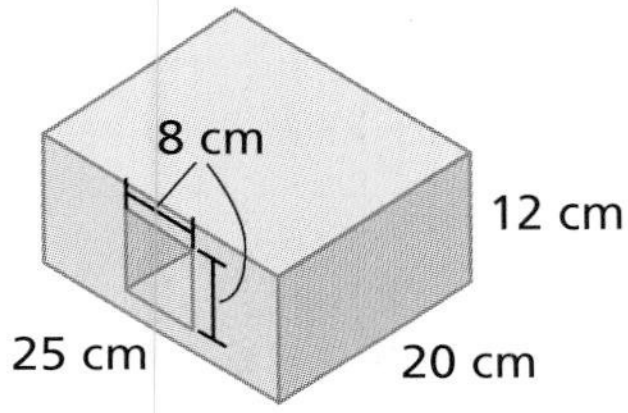

TEST PREP and Spiral Review

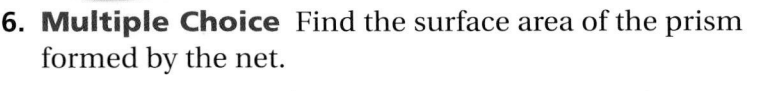

16. Multiple Choice Find the surface area of the prism formed by the net.

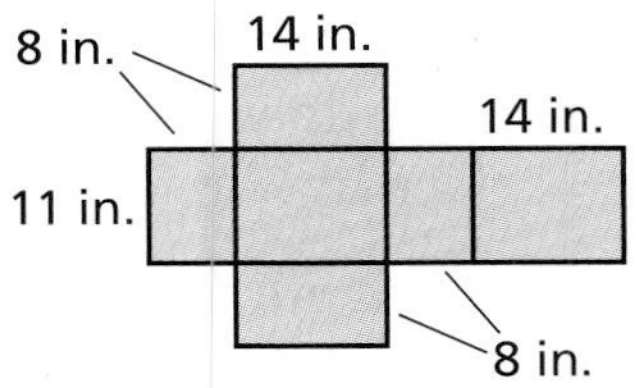

Ⓐ 286 in^3 Ⓒ 708 in^3

Ⓑ 310 in^3 Ⓓ 1,232 in^3

17. Gridded Response Find the number of square centimeters in the surface area of a cylinder with a 5 cm radius and a 15 cm height. Use 3.14 for π.

Find the measure of the third angle in each triangle, given two angle measures. (Lesson 8-8)

18. 83°, 28° **19.** 65°, 36° **20.** 22°, 102°

Find the volume of each figure to the nearest tenth.

21. a 4 in. tall rectangular prism with base 7 in. by 8 in. (Lesson 10-2)

22. a 9 cm tall square pyramid with base 6 cm by 6 cm (Lesson 10-3)

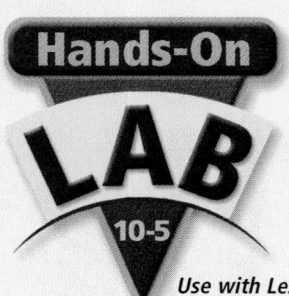

Hands-On LAB 10-5

Investigate the Surface Areas of Similar Prisms

Use with Lesson 10-5

go.hrw.com
Lab Resources Online
KEYWORD: MS7 Lab10

Recall that the surface area of a three-dimensional figure is the sum of the areas of all of its surfaces. You can use centimeter cubes to explore the surface areas of prisms.

Activity 1

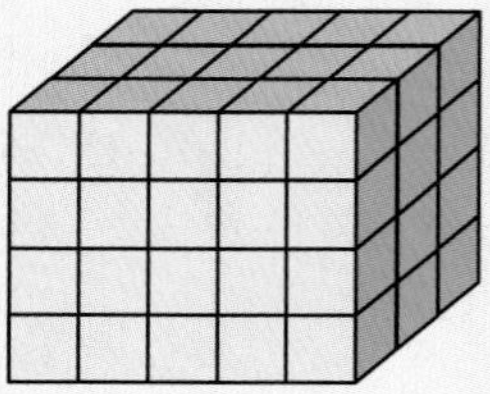

1. Use centimeter cubes to build the rectangular prism shown here.

2. You can find the surface area of the prism by first finding the areas of its front face, top face, and side face. Look at the prism from each of these views. Count the exposed cube faces to find the area of each face of the prism. Record the areas in the table.

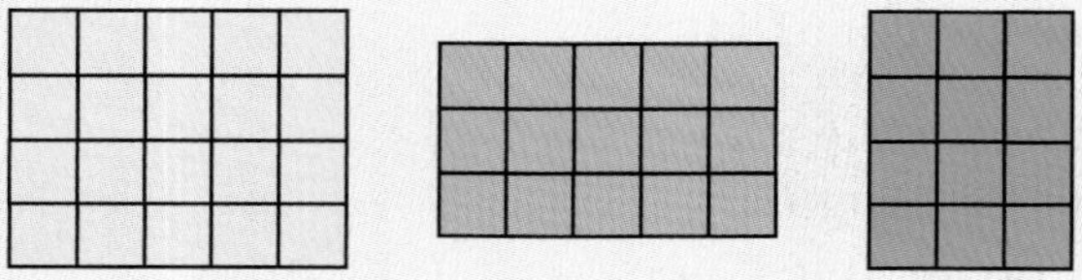

Front Top Side

	Front Face	Top Face	Side Face
Area			

3. Find the surface area of the prism as follows:
surface area = 2 · (area of front face) + 2 · (area of top face) + 2 · (area of side face)

Think and Discuss

1. Why do you multiply the areas of the front face, top face, and side face by 2 to find the surface area of the prism?
2. What are the length, width, and height of the prism in centimeters? What surface area do you get when you use the formula $S = 2\ell w + 2\ell h + 2wh$?

Try This

Use centimeter cubes to build each prism. Then find its surface area.

1. 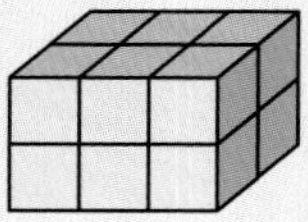

2. 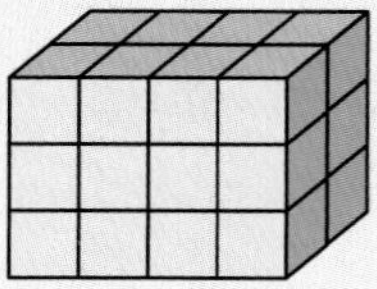

3. 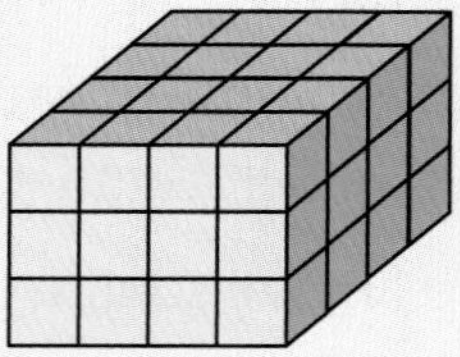

Activity 2

1 Use centimeter cubes to build rectangular prism A as shown.

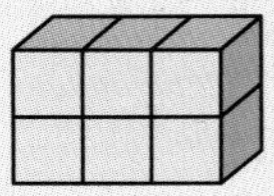

Prism *A*

2 Now use centimeter cubes to build a prism B that is similar to prism A by a scale factor of 2. Each dimension of the new prism should be 2 times the corresponding dimension of prism A.

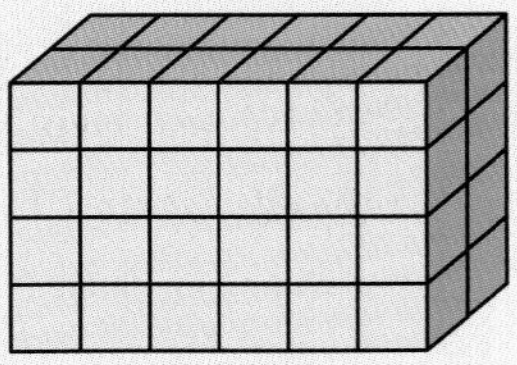

Prism *B*

3 Use the method from Activity 1 to find the areas of the front face, top face, and side face of each prism. Record the areas in the table.

	Area of Front Face	Area of Top Face	Area of Side Face
Prism *A*	▒	▒	▒
Prism *B*	▒	▒	▒

4 Find the surface area of prism A and the surface area of prism B.

5 Repeat the above process, this time building a prism C that is larger than prism A by a scale factor of 3. Add a row to your table for prism C, and find the areas of the front face, top face, and side face of prism C.

Think and Discuss

1. In **4**, how does the surface area of prism B compare with the surface area of prism A? How is this related to the scale factor?
2. In **5**, how does the surface area of prism C compare with the surface area of prism A? How is this related to the scale factor?
3. Suppose three-dimensional figure Y is similar to three-dimensional figure X by a scale factor of k. How are the surface areas related?

Try This

1. Find the surface area of prism R.
2. Prism S is larger than prism R by a scale factor of 4. Use what you discovered to find the surface area of prism S.

Prism *R*

10-5 Changing Dimensions

Learn **to find the volume and surface area of similar three-dimensional figures.**

Recall that similar figures have proportional side lengths. The surface areas of similar three-dimensional figures are also proportional. To see this relationship, you can compare the areas of corresponding faces of similar rectangular prisms.

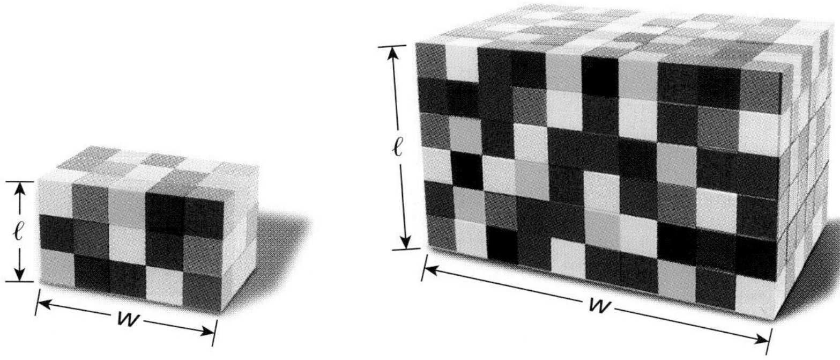

Remember!

A scale factor is a number that every dimension of a figure is multiplied by to make a similar figure.

Area of front of smaller prism	**Area of front of larger prism**	
$\ell \cdot w$	$\ell \cdot w$	
$3 \cdot 5$	$6 \cdot 10$	
15	$(3 \cdot 2) \cdot (5 \cdot 2)$	⟵ Each dimension is multiplied by a scale factor of 2.
	$(3 \cdot 5) \cdot (2 \cdot 2)$	
	$15 \cdot 2^2$	

The area of the front face of the larger prism is 2^2 times the area of the front face of the smaller prism. This is true for the entire surface area of the prisms.

SURFACE AREA OF SIMILAR FIGURES

If three-dimensional figure *B* is similar to figure *A* by a scale factor, then the surface area of *B* is equal to the surface area of *A* times the square of the scale factor.

$$\text{surface area of figure } A = \text{surface area of figure } B \cdot (\text{scale factor})^2$$

EXAMPLE 1 **Finding the Surface Area of a Similar Figure**

A **The surface area of a box is 27 in^2. What is the surface area of a similar box that is larger by a scale factor of 5?**

$S = 27 \cdot 5^2$ *Multiply by the square of the scale factor.*

$S = 27 \cdot 25$ *Evaluate the power.*

$S = 675 \text{ in}^2$ *Multiply.*

B **The surface area of the Great Pyramid was originally 1,160,280 ft^2. What is the surface area, to the nearest tenth, of a model of the pyramid that is smaller by a scale factor of $\frac{1}{500}$?**

$S = 1{,}160{,}280 \cdot \left(\frac{1}{500}\right)^2$ *Multiply by the square of the scale factor.*

$S = 1{,}160{,}280 \cdot \frac{1}{250{,}000}$ *Evaluate the power.*

$S = 4.64112$ *Multiply.*

$S \approx 4.6 \text{ ft}^2$

The volumes of similar three-dimensional figures are also related.

Remember!

$2 \cdot 2 \cdot 2 = 2^3$

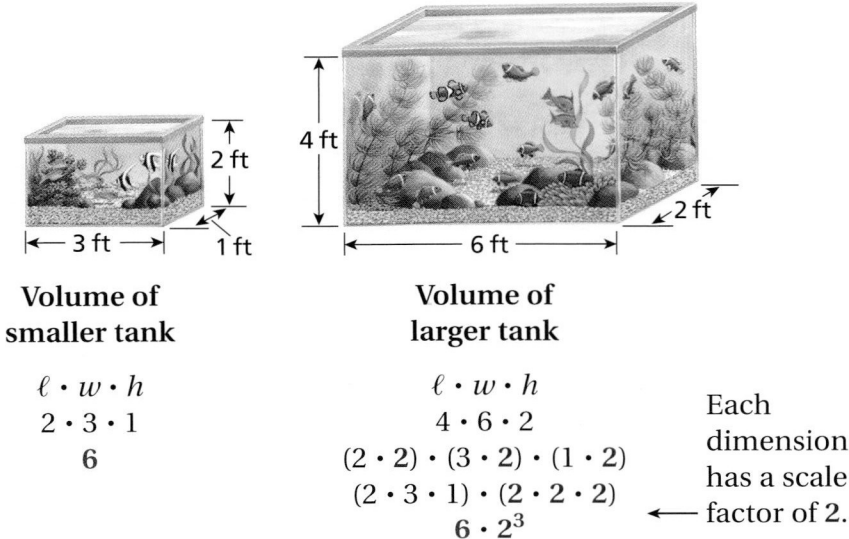

Volume of smaller tank	**Volume of larger tank**	
$\ell \cdot w \cdot h$	$\ell \cdot w \cdot h$	
$2 \cdot 3 \cdot 1$	$4 \cdot 6 \cdot 2$	
6	$(2 \cdot 2) \cdot (3 \cdot 2) \cdot (1 \cdot 2)$	
	$(2 \cdot 3 \cdot 1) \cdot (2 \cdot 2 \cdot 2)$	← Each dimension has a scale factor of 2.
	$6 \cdot 2^3$	

The volume of the larger tank is 2^3 times the volume of the smaller tank.

VOLUME OF SIMILAR FIGURES

If three-dimensional figure B is similar to figure A by a scale factor, then the volume of B is equal to the volume of A times the cube of the scale factor.

volume of figure A = volume of figure B · (scale factor)^3

EXAMPLE 2 Finding Volume Using Similar Figures

The volume of a bucket is 231 in^3. What is the volume of a similar bucket that is larger by a scale factor of 3?

$V = 231 \cdot 3^3$ *Multiply by the cube of the scale factor.*

$V = 231 \cdot 27$ *Evaluate the power.*

$V = 6{,}237 \text{ in}^3$ *Multiply.*

Estimate $V \approx 230 \cdot 30$ *Round the measurements.*

$= 6{,}900 \text{ in}^3$ *The answer is reasonable.*

EXAMPLE 3 PROBLEM SOLVING APPLICATION

PROBLEM SOLVING

Elise has a fish tank that measures 10 in. by 23 in. by 5 in. She builds a larger tank by doubling each dimension. There are 231 in^3 in 1 gallon. Estimate how many more gallons the larger tank holds.

1 Understand the Problem

Rewrite the question as a statement.

- Compare the capacities of two similar fish tanks, and estimate how much more water the larger tank holds.

List the **important information:**

- The small tank is 10 in. × 23 in. × 5 in.
- The large tank is similar to the small tank by a scale factor of 2.
- $231 \text{ in}^3 = 1 \text{ gal}$

2 Make a Plan

You can write an equation that relates the volume of the large tank to the volume of the small tank. Volume of large tank = Volume of small tank · (scale factor)^3. Then convert cubic inches to gallons to compare the capacities of the tanks.

3 Solve

Volume of small tank = $10 \times 23 \times 5 = \mathbf{1{,}150} \text{ in}^3$

Volume of large tank = $\mathbf{1{,}150} \cdot 2^3 = 9{,}200 \text{ in}^3$

Convert each volume into gallons:

$1{,}150 \text{ in}^3 \times \frac{1 \text{ gal}}{231 \text{ in}^3} \approx 5 \text{ gal}$ $\quad 9{,}200 \text{ in}^3 \times \frac{1 \text{ gal}}{231 \text{ in}^3} \approx 40 \text{ gal}$

Subtract the capacities: $40 \text{ gal} - 5 \text{ gal} = 35 \text{ gal}$

The large tank holds about 35 gallons more water than the small tank.

4 Look Back

Double the dimensions of the small tank and find the volume: $20 \times 46 \times 10 = 9{,}200 \text{ in}^3$. Subtract the volumes of the two tanks: $9{,}200 - 1{,}150 = 8{,}050 \text{ in}^3$. Convert this measurement to gallons: $8{,}050 \times \frac{1 \text{ gal}}{231 \text{ in}^3} \approx 35 \text{ gal}$.

Think and Discuss

1. **Tell** whether a figure's surface area has increased or decreased if each dimension of the figure is changed by a factor of $\frac{1}{3}$.
2. **Explain** how the surface area of a figure is changed if the dimensions are each multiplied by a factor of 3.
3. **Explain** how the volume of a figure is changed if the dimensions are each multiplied by a factor of 2.

10-5 Exercises

go.hrw.com
Homework Help Online
KEYWORD: MS7 10-5
Parent Resources Online
KEYWORD: MS7 Parent

GUIDED PRACTICE

See Example 1

1. The surface area of a box is 10.4 cm^2. What is the surface area of a similar box that is larger by a scale factor of 3?

2. The surface area of a ship's hull is about 11,000 m^2. What is the surface area, to the nearest tenth, of the hull of a model ship that is smaller by a scale factor of $\frac{1}{150}$?

See Example 2

3. The volume of an ice chest is 2,160 in^3. What is the volume of a similar ice chest that is larger by a scale factor of 2.5?

See Example 3

4. A fish tank measures 14 in. by 13 in. by 10 in. A similar fish tank is larger by a scale factor of 3. Estimate how many more gallons the larger tank holds.

INDEPENDENT PRACTICE

See Example 1

5. The surface area of a triangular prism is 13.99 in^2. What is the surface area of a similar prism that is larger by a scale factor of 4?

6. The surface area of a car frame is about 200 ft^2. What is the surface area, to the nearest tenth of a square foot, of a model of the car that is smaller by a scale factor of $\frac{1}{12}$?

See Example 2

7. The volume of a cylinder is about 523 cm^3. What is the volume, to the nearest tenth, of a similar cylinder that is smaller by a scale factor of $\frac{1}{4}$?

See Example 3

8. A tank measures 27 in. by 9 in. by 12 in. A similar tank is reduced by a scale factor of $\frac{1}{3}$. Estimate how many more gallons the larger tank holds.

PRACTICE AND PROBLEM SOLVING

Extra Practice
See page 747.

For each figure shown, find the surface area and volume of a similar figure that is larger by a scale factor of 25. Use 3.14 for π.

9. 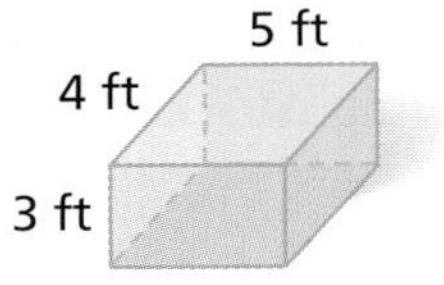

10. 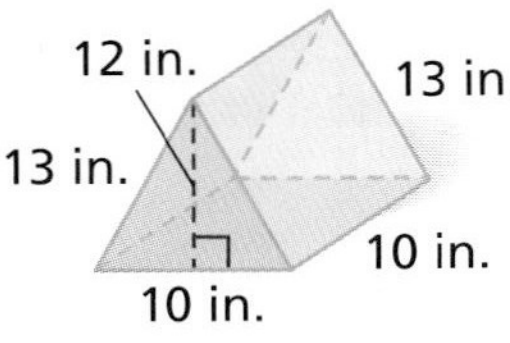

11. 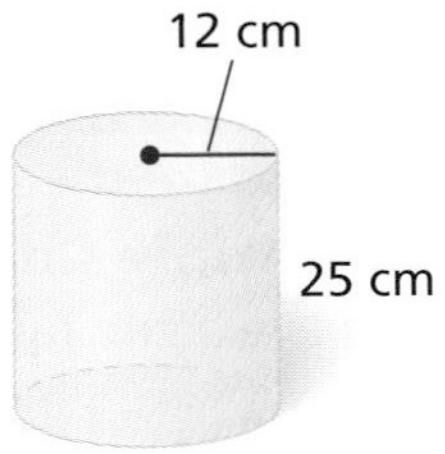

12. The surface area of a cylinder is 1,620 m^2. Its volume is about 1,130 m^3. What are the surface area and volume of a similar cylinder that is smaller by a scale factor of $\frac{1}{9}$? Round to the nearest tenth, if necessary.

13. The surface area of a prism is 142 in^2. Its volume is about 105 in^3. What are the surface area and volume of a similar prism that is larger by a scale factor of 6? Round to the nearest tenth, if necessary.

History LINK

Natalie and Rebecca are making a scale model of the *Titanic* for a history class project. Their model is smaller by a scale factor of $\frac{1}{100}$. For Exercises 14–17, express your answers in both centimeters and meters. Use the conversion chart at right if needed.

METRIC CONVERSIONS	
1 m = 100 cm	1 cm = 0.01 m
1 m^2 = 10,000 cm^2	1 cm^2 = 0.0001 m^2
1 m^3 = 1,000,000 cm^3	1 cm^3 = 0.000001 m^3

14. The length and height of the *Titanic* are shown in the drawing above. What are the length and height of the students' scale model?

15. On the students' model, the diameter of the outer propellers is 7.16 cm. What was the diameter of these propellers on the ship?

16. The surface area of the deck of the students' model is 4,156.75 cm^2. What was the surface area of the deck of the ship?

17. The volume of the students' model is about 127,426 cm^3. What was the volume of the ship?

These are propellers from the *Olympic*, the *Titanic*'s sister ship. They are identical to those that were on the *Titanic*.

Test Prep and Spiral Review

18. Multiple Choice The surface area of a prism is 144 cm^2. A similar prism has a scale factor of $\frac{1}{4}$. What is the surface area of the similar prism?

Ⓐ 36 cm^2 Ⓑ 18 cm^2 Ⓒ 9 cm^2 Ⓓ 2.25 cm^2

19. Gridded Response A cube has a volume of 64 in^3. A similar cube has a volume of 512 in^3. What is the scale factor of the larger cube?

Determine whether the ratios are proportional. (Lesson 5-4)

20. $\frac{7}{56}, \frac{35}{280}$ **21.** $\frac{12}{20}, \frac{60}{140}$ **22.** $\frac{9}{45}, \frac{45}{225}$ **23.** $\frac{5}{82}, \frac{65}{1,054}$

24. Name the polygon that has ten angles and ten sides. (Lesson 8-5)

Technology LAB 10-5

Explore Changes in Dimensions

Use after Lesson 10-5

go.hrw.com
Lab Resources Online
KEYWORD: MS7 Lab10

You can use a spreadsheet to explore how changing the dimensions of a rectangular pyramid affects the volume of the pyramid.

Activity

1 On a spreadsheet, enter the following headings:
Base Length in cell A1,
Base Width in cell B1,
Height in cell C1, and
Volume in cell D1.

In row 2, enter the numbers 15, 7, and 22, as shown.

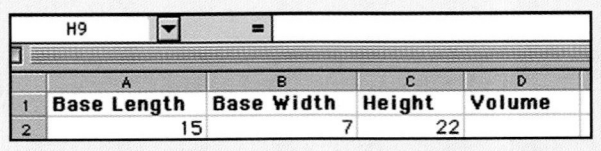

H9 =

	A	B	C	D
1	Base Length	Base Width	Height	Volume
2	15	7	22	

2 Then enter the formula for the volume of a pyramid in cell D2. To do this, enter **=(1/3)*A2*B2*C2.** Press **ENTER** and notice that the volume is 770.

SUM ✕ ✓ = =(1/3)*A2*B2*C2

	A	B	C	D	E
1	Base Length	Base Width	Height	Volume	
2	15	7	22	=(1/3)*A2*B2*C2	

3 Enter 30 in cell A2 and 11 in cell C2 to find out what happens to the volume when you double the base length and halve the height.

C23 =

	A	B	C	D
1	Base Length	Base Width	Height	Volume
2	30	7	11	770

Think and Discuss

1. Explain why doubling the base length and halving the height does not change the volume of the pyramid.
2. What other ways could you change the dimensions of the pyramid without changing its volume?

Try This

1. Use a spreadsheet to compute the volume of each cone. Use 3.14 for π.
   a. radius = 2.75 inches; height = 8.5 inches
   b. radius = 7.5 inches; height = 14.5 inches
2. What would the volumes in problem 1 be if the radii were doubled?

READY TO GO ON?

Quiz for Lessons 10-4 Through 10-5

10-4 Surface Area of Prisms and Cylinders

Find the surface area of the prism formed by each net.

1.

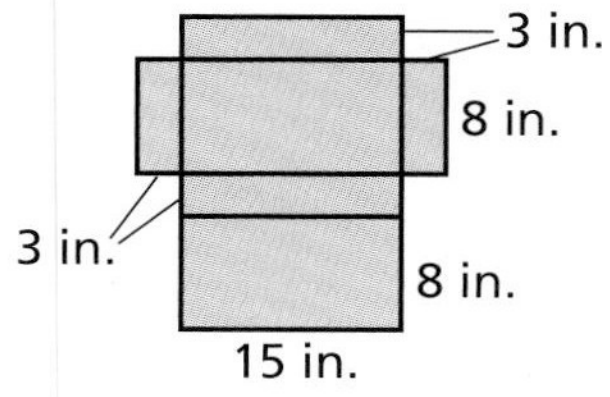

2.

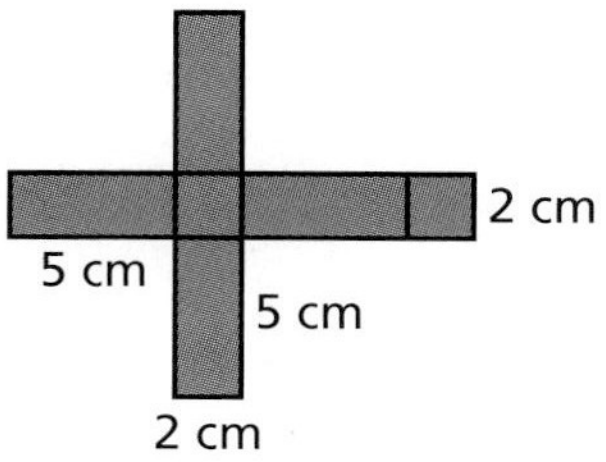

Find the surface area of the cylinder formed by each net to the nearest tenth. Use 3.14 for π.

3.

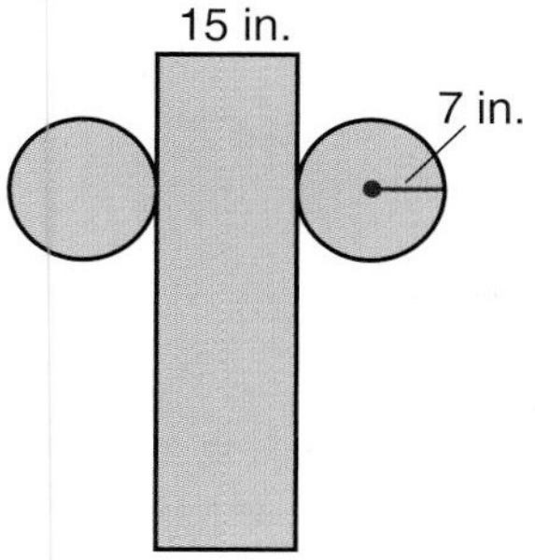

4.

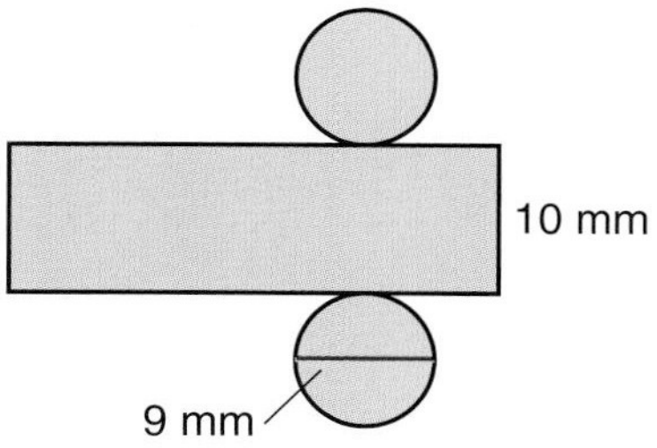

5. The diagram shows a drink can with a drink cooler covering the lower base and part of the curved surface of the can. About how much surface area, in square centimeters, of the drink can is covered by the drink cooler?

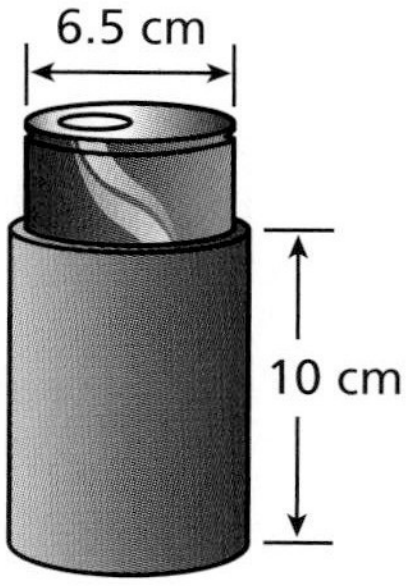

10-5 Changing Dimensions

6. The surface area of a rectangular prism is 45 ft^2. What is the surface area of a similar prism that is larger by a scale factor of 3?
7. The surface area of a cylinder is 109 cm^2. What is the surface area of a similar cylinder that is smaller by a scale factor of $\frac{1}{3}$?
8. The volume of a container is 3,785 in^3. A second container is larger by a scale factor of 4. Estimate how many more gallons the larger container holds. (*Hint:* There are 231 in^3 in 1 gallon.)

MULTI-STEP TEST PREP

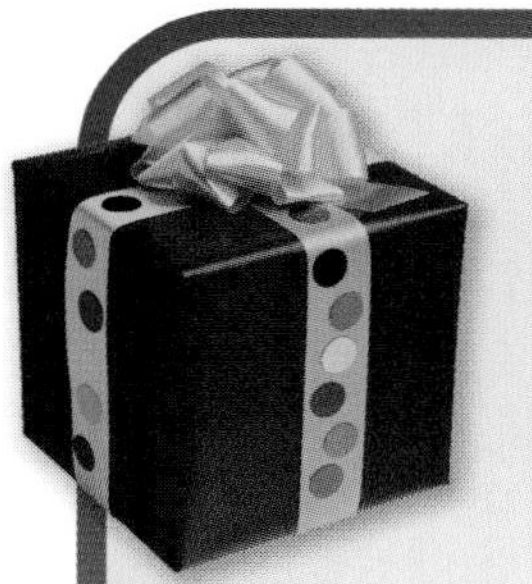

It's a Wrap! Kim and Miguel are raising money for their school track team by running a gift-wrapping service at the mall. Customers can also have their gifts boxed for shipping. Kim and Miguel have rolls of gift wrap, shipping boxes, cardboard, and packing peanuts.

1. A customer wants to wrap and ship a gift that is in the shape of a rectangular prism. The dimensions of the gift are 10 in. by 15 in. by 4 in. How many square inches of wrapping paper are needed to wrap the gift?
2. Kim chooses a shipping box that is 18 in. by 12 in. by 6 in. After the gift is placed inside the box, she will fill the empty space with packing peanuts. How many cubic inches of packing peanuts will Kim need? Explain.
3. Another customer wants to ship a large cone-shaped art piece made out of recycled glass. The figure shows the dimensions of the conic art. Miguel decides to use poster board to make a cylindrical container that is just large enough to hold the art. How much poster board will he need?

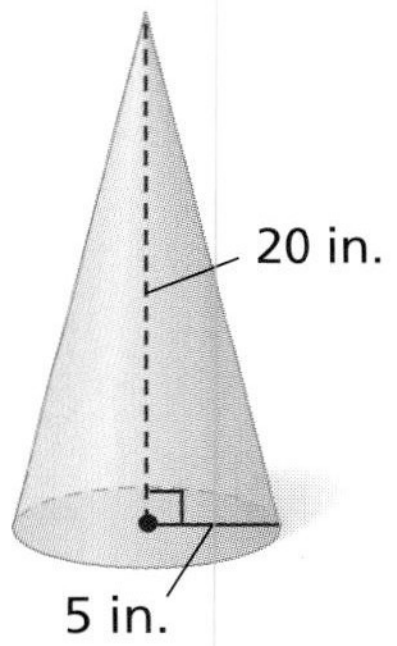

4. Once the conic art is placed in the cylindrical container, how many cubic inches of packing peanuts will be needed to fill the empty space?

EXTENSION Cross Sections

Learn to sketch and describe cross sections of three-dimensional figures.

Vocabulary

cross section

When a three-dimensional figure and a plane intersect, the intersection is called a **cross section**. A three-dimensional figure can have many different cross sections. For example, when you cut an orange in half, the cross section that is exposed depends on the direction of the cut.

EXAMPLE 1 Identifying Cross Sections

Identify the cross section that best matches the given figure.

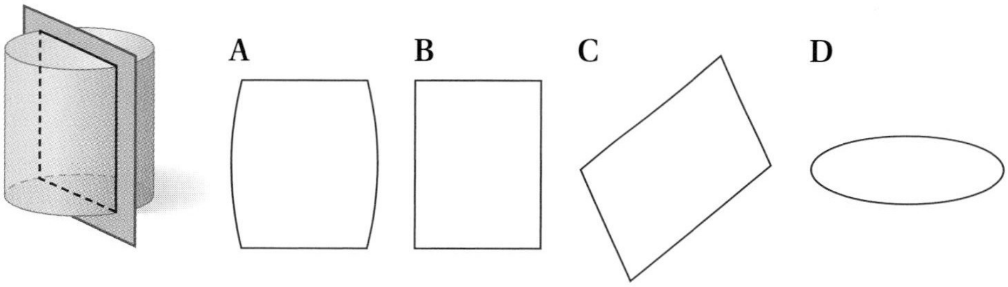

The bases of the cylinder are parallel, so the cross section must contain a pair of parallel lines. The bases of the cylinder meet the lateral surface at right angles, so the cross section must contain right angles. The best choice is **B**.

EXAMPLE 2 Sketching and Describing Cross Sections

Sketch and describe the cross section of a cone that is cut parallel to its base.

The base of a cone is a circle. Any cross section made by cutting the cone parallel to the base will also be a circle.

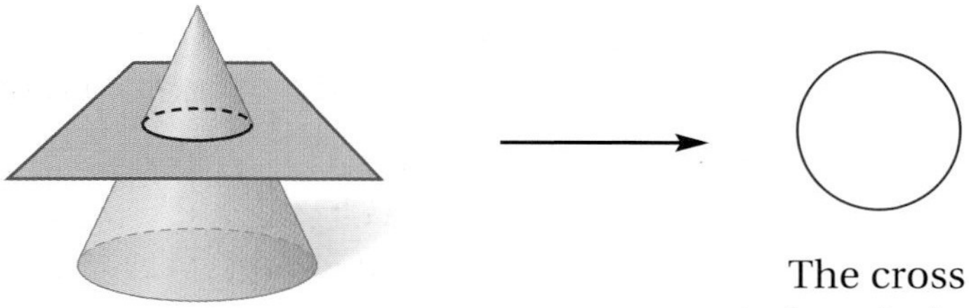

The cross section is a circle.

You can form three-dimensional figures by translating or rotating a cross section through space.

EXAMPLE 3 Describing Three-Dimensional Figures Formed by Transformations

Describe the three-dimensional figure formed by rotating an isosceles triangle around its line of symmetry.

Draw an isosceles triangle and its line of symmetry. Visualize rotating the triangle through space around the line. The resulting three-dimensional figure is a cone.

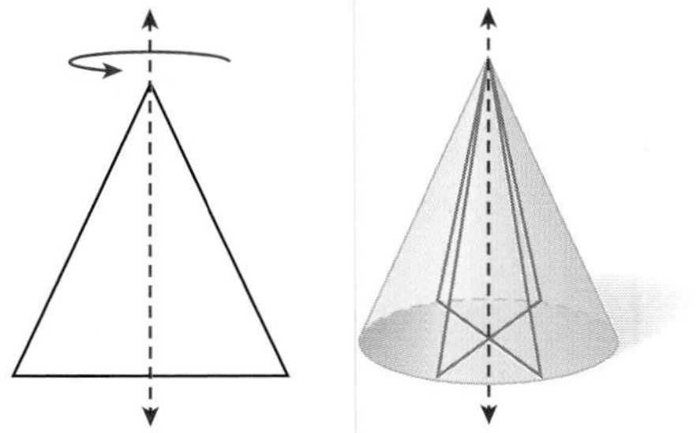

EXTENSION Exercises

1. Identify the cross section that best matches the given figure.

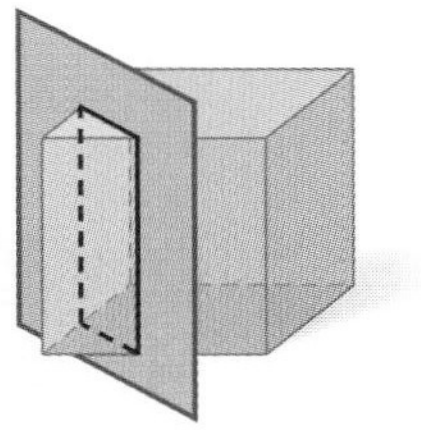

Ⓐ  Ⓑ  Ⓒ 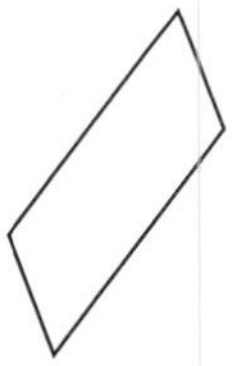 Ⓓ 

Sketch and describe each cross section.

2. a cylinder that is cut parallel to its bases
3. a cube that is cut parallel to one of its faces

Describe the three-dimensional figure formed by each transformation.

4. a rectangle that is rotated around a line of symmetry
5. a circle that is translated perpendicularly to the plane in which it lies (*Hint:* Imagine lifting a circle that is lying on a table straight upward.)
6. A sculptor has a block of clay in the shape of a rectangular prism. She uses a piece of wire to cut the clay, and the resulting cross section is a square. Make a sketch showing the prism and how the sculptor may have cut the clay.

Game Time

Blooming Minds

Students in the Agriculture Club at Carter Middle School are designing a flower bed for the front of the school. The flower bed will be in the shape of the letter *C*. After considering the two designs shown below, the students decided to build the flower bed that required the least amount of peat moss. Which design did the students choose? (*Hint:* Find the volume of each flower bed.)

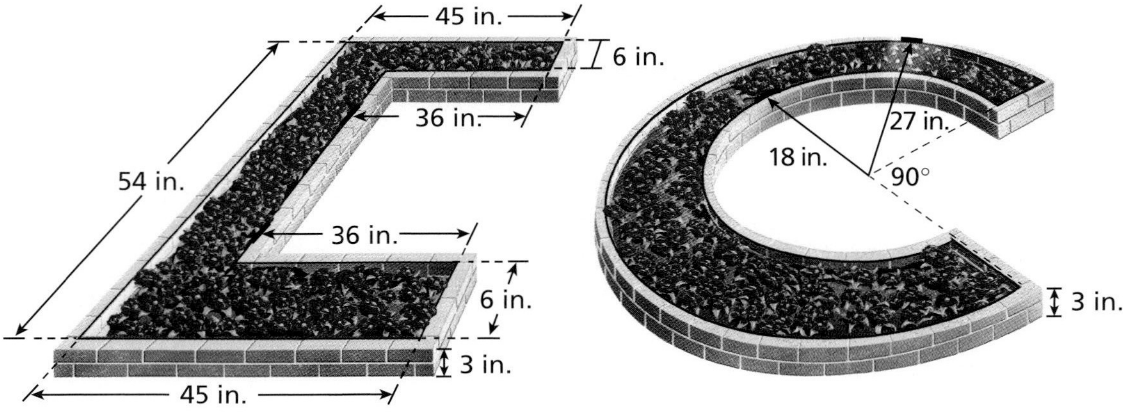

Magic Cubes

Four magic cubes are used in this fun puzzle. A complete set of rules and nets for making the cubes can be found online. Each side of the four cubes has the number 1, 2, 3, or 4 written on it. The object of the game is to stack the cubes so that the numbers along each side of the stack add up to 10. No number can be repeated along any side of the stack.

go.hrw.com
Game Time Extra
KEYWORD: MS7 Games

It's in the Bag!

FOLDNOTES

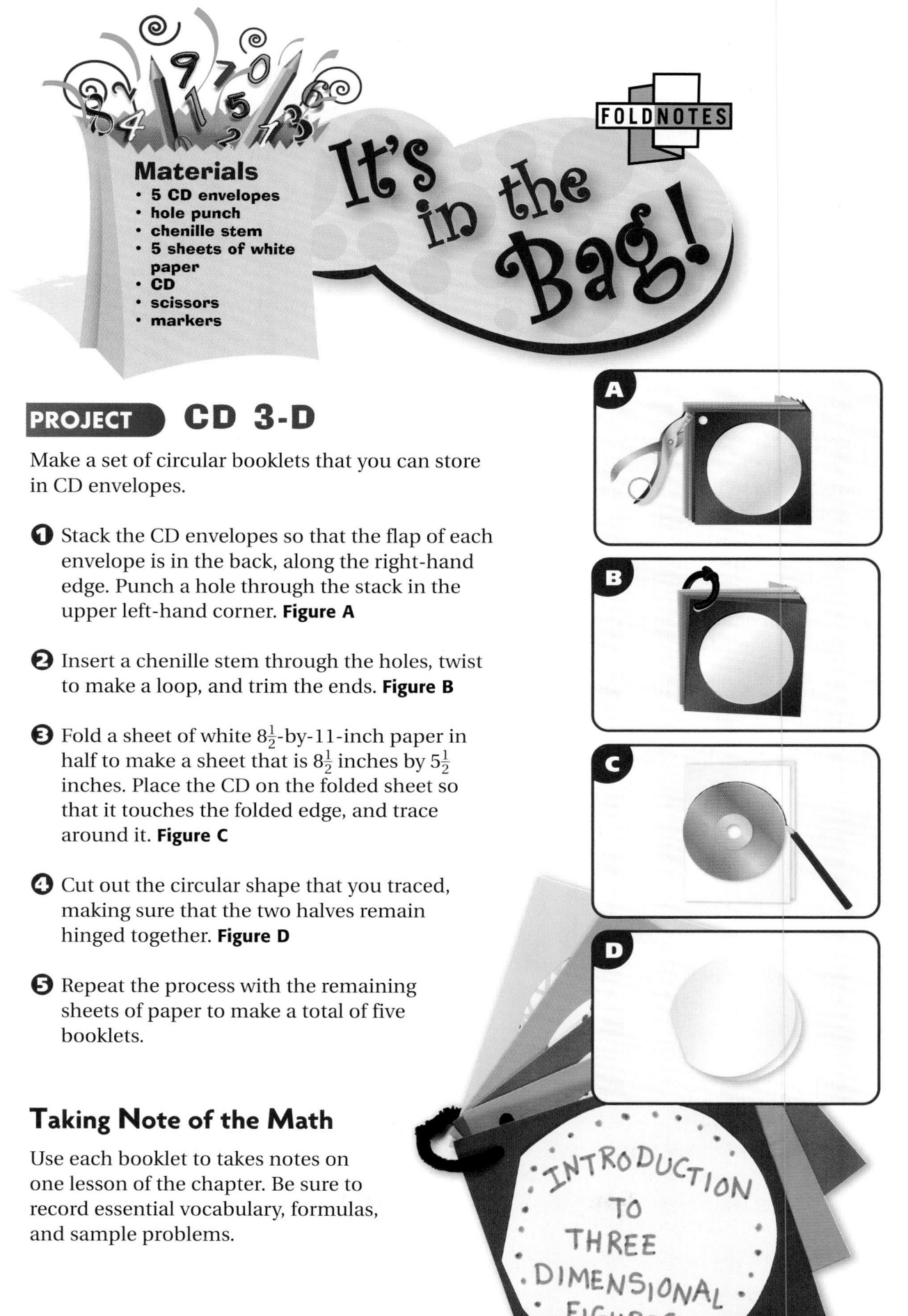

Materials
- 5 CD envelopes
- hole punch
- chenille stem
- 5 sheets of white paper
- CD
- scissors
- markers

PROJECT CD 3-D

Make a set of circular booklets that you can store in CD envelopes.

1. Stack the CD envelopes so that the flap of each envelope is in the back, along the right-hand edge. Punch a hole through the stack in the upper left-hand corner. **Figure A**

2. Insert a chenille stem through the holes, twist to make a loop, and trim the ends. **Figure B**

3. Fold a sheet of white $8\frac{1}{2}$-by-11-inch paper in half to make a sheet that is $8\frac{1}{2}$ inches by $5\frac{1}{2}$ inches. Place the CD on the folded sheet so that it touches the folded edge, and trace around it. **Figure C**

4. Cut out the circular shape that you traced, making sure that the two halves remain hinged together. **Figure D**

5. Repeat the process with the remaining sheets of paper to make a total of five booklets.

A

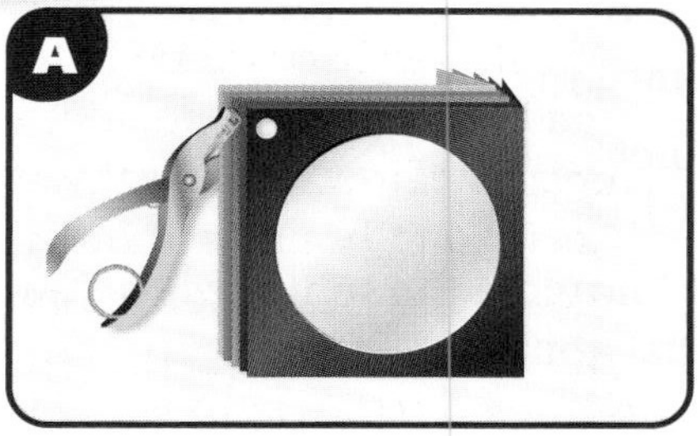

B

C

D

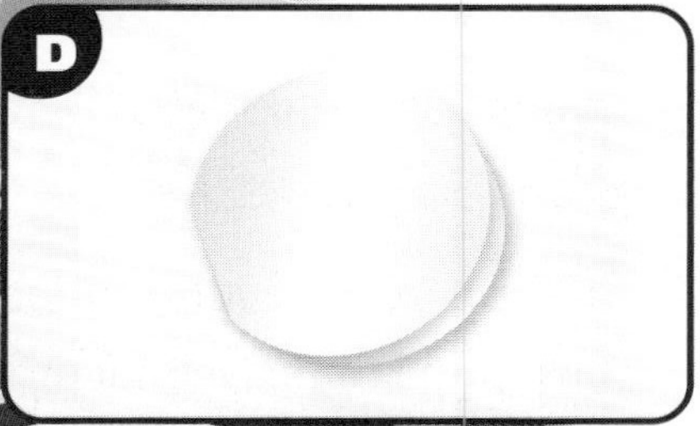

Taking Note of the Math

Use each booklet to takes notes on one lesson of the chapter. Be sure to record essential vocabulary, formulas, and sample problems.

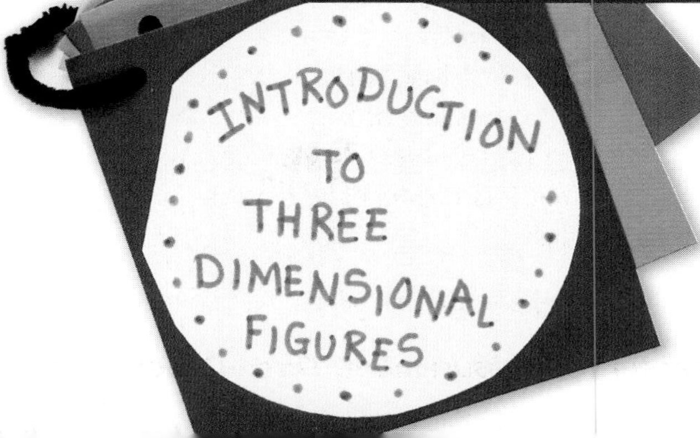

CHAPTER 10

Study Guide: Review

Vocabulary

Complete the sentences below with vocabulary words from the list above.

1. A(n) ___?___ has two parallel, congruent circular bases connected by a curved surface.

2. The sum of the areas of the surfaces of a three-dimensional figure is called the ___?___.

3. A(n) ___?___ is a three-dimensional figure whose faces are all polygons.

4. A(n) ___?___ has one circular base and a curved surface.

10-1 Introduction to Three-Dimensional Figures (pp. 580–583)

EXAMPLE

■ **Name the figure.**

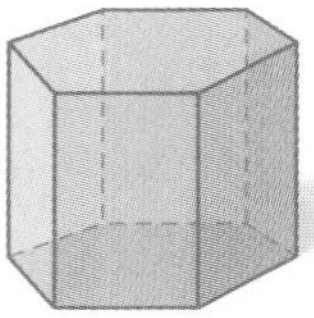

There are two bases that are hexagons.

The figure is a hexagonal prism.

EXERCISES

Name each figure.

5. 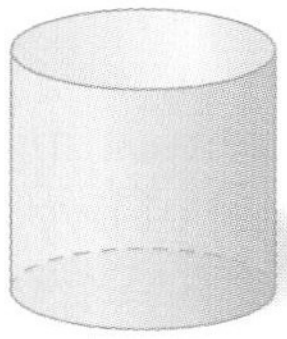

6. 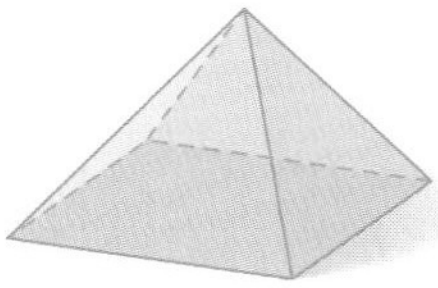

7. 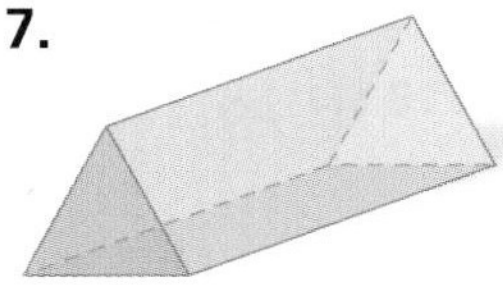

8. 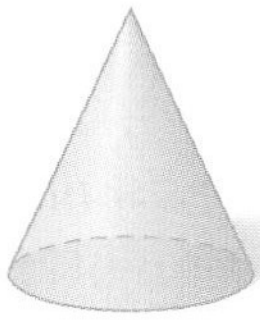

Study Guide: Review

10-2 Volume of Prisms and Cylinders (pp. 586–589)

EXAMPLE

■ **Find the volume of the prism.**

$V = Bh$

$V = (15 \cdot 4) \cdot 9$

$V = 540$

The volume of the prism is 540 ft^3.

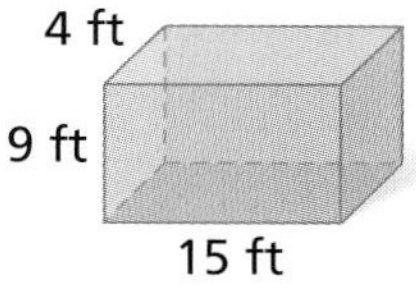

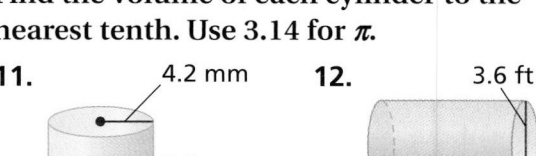

■ **Find the volume of the cylinder to the nearest tenth. Use 3.14 for π.**

$V = \pi r^2 h$

$V \approx 3.14 \cdot 3^2 \cdot 4$

$V \approx 113.04$

The volume is about 113.0 cm^3.

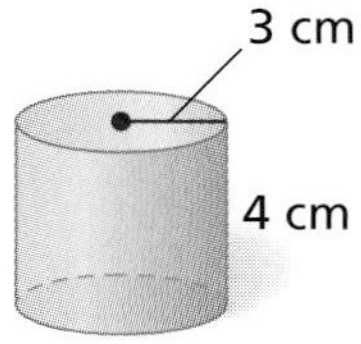

EXERCISES

Find the volume of each prism.

9.

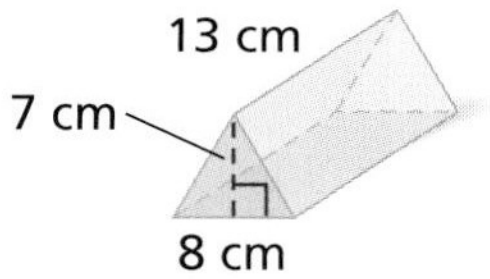

10.

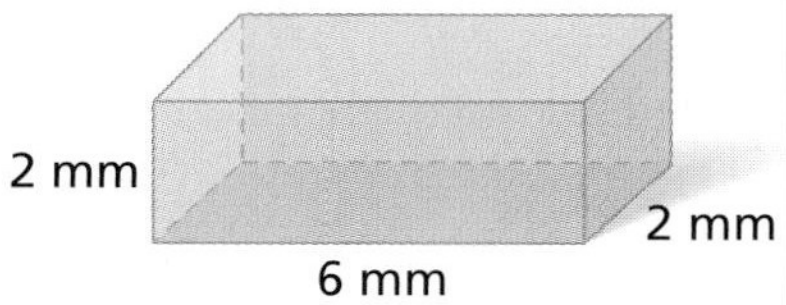

Find the volume of each cylinder to the nearest tenth. Use 3.14 for π.

11.

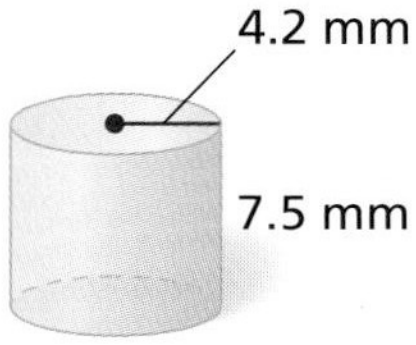

12.

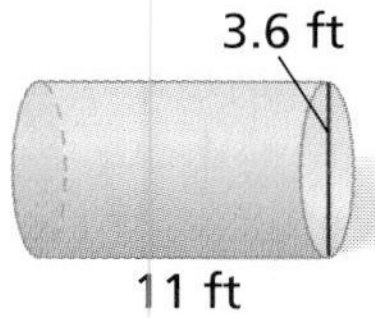

10-3 Volume of Pyramids and Cones (pp. 590–593)

EXAMPLE

■ **Find the volume of the pyramid.**

$V = \frac{1}{3} Bh$

$V = \frac{1}{3} \cdot (5 \cdot 6) \cdot 7$

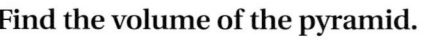

$V = 70$

The volume is 70 m^3.

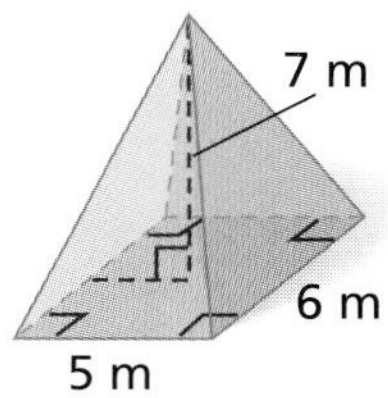

■ **Find the volume of the cone to the nearest tenth. Use 3.14 for π.**

$V = \frac{1}{3} \pi r^2 h$

$V \approx \frac{1}{3} \cdot 3.14 \cdot 4^2 \cdot 9$

$V \approx 150.72$

The volume is about 150.7 ft^3.

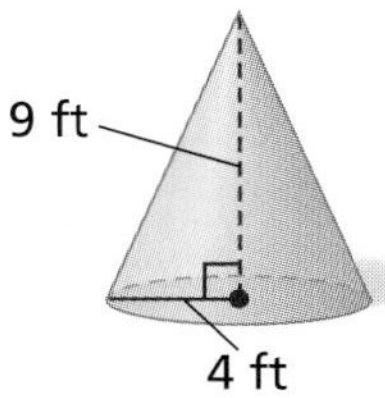

EXERCISES

Find the volume of the pyramid.

13.

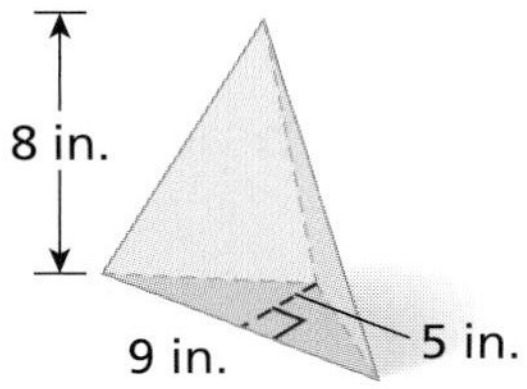

Find the volume of the cone to the nearest tenth. Use 3.14 for π.

14.

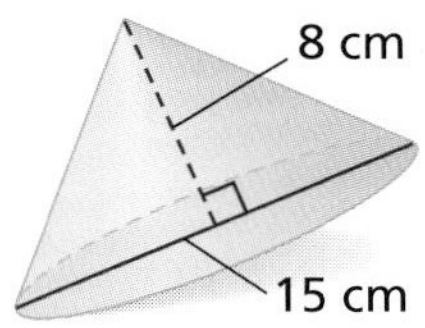

10-4 Surface Area of Prisms and Cylinders (pp. 597–601)

EXAMPLE

■ **Find the surface area of the rectangular prism formed by the net.**

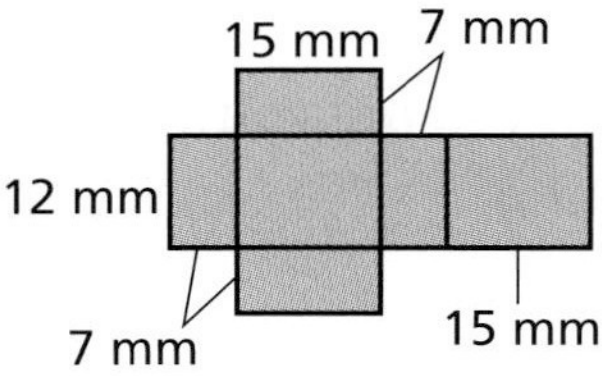

$S = 2\ell w + 2\ell h + 2wh$

$S = (2 \cdot 15 \cdot 7) + (2 \cdot 15 \cdot 12) + (2 \cdot 7 \cdot 12)$

$S = 738$

The surface area is 738 mm^2.

EXERCISES

Find the surface area of the rectangular prism formed by each net.

15.

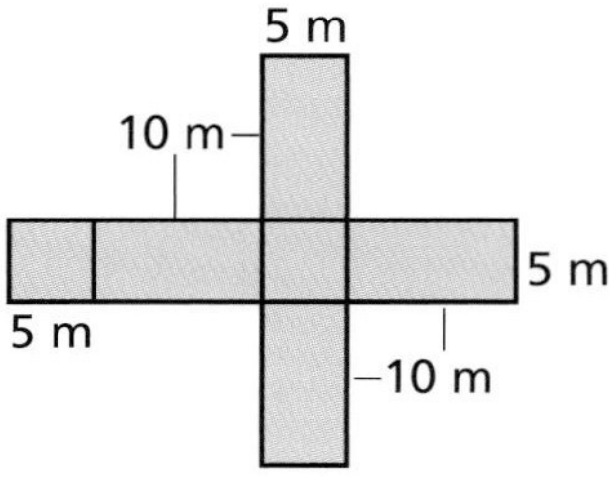

16.

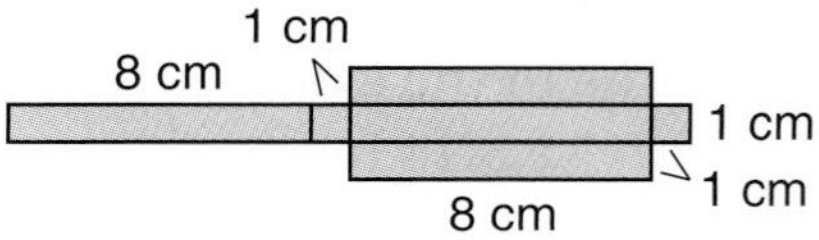

■ **Find the surface area of the cylinder formed by the net to the nearest tenth. Use 3.14 for π.**

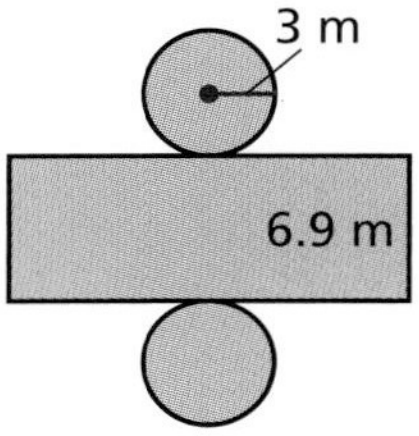

$S = 2\pi r^2 + 2\pi rh$

$S \approx (2 \cdot 3.14 \cdot 3^2) + (2 \cdot 3.14 \cdot 3 \cdot 6.9)$

$S \approx 186.516$

The surface area is about 186.5 m^2.

Find the surface area of the cylinder formed by the net to the nearest tenth. Use 3.14 for π.

17.

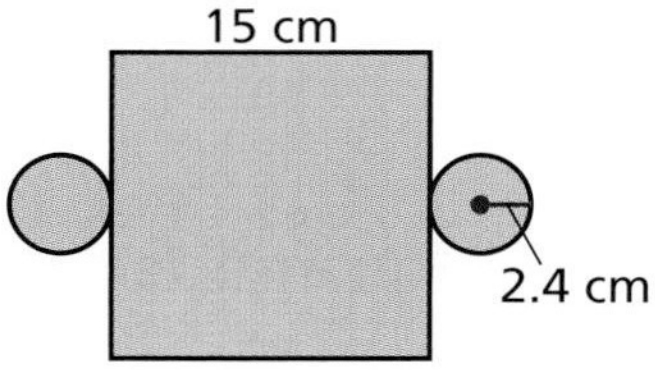

10-5 Changing Dimensions (pp. 604–608)

EXAMPLE

■ **The surface area of a rectangular prism is 32 m^2, and its volume is 12 m^3. What are the surface area and volume of a similar rectangular prism that is larger by a scale factor of 6?**

$S = 32 \cdot 6^2$

$= 1{,}152$

$V = 12 \cdot 6^3$

$= 2{,}592$

The surface area of the larger prism is 1,152 m^2. Its volume is 2,592 m^3.

EXERCISES

18. A cylinder has a surface area of 13.2 in^2. What is the surface area of a similar cylinder that is larger by a scale factor of 15?

19. A refrigerator has a volume of 14 ft^3. What is the volume, to the nearest tenth, of a similar refrigerator that is smaller by a scale factor of $\frac{2}{3}$?

CHAPTER TEST

CHAPTER 10

Classify each figure as a polyhedron or not a polyhedron. Then name the figure.

1. 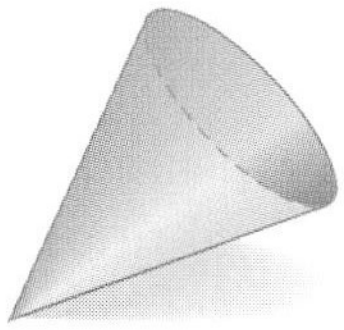

2. 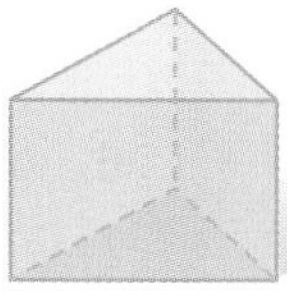

3. 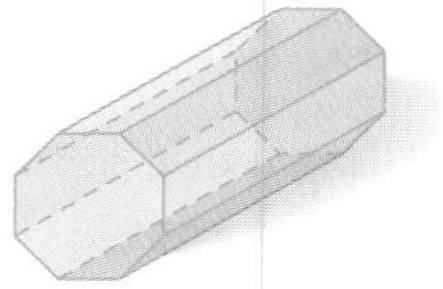

4. 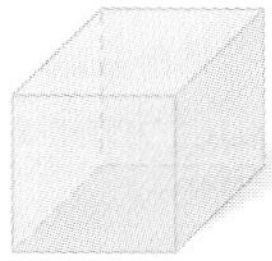

5. 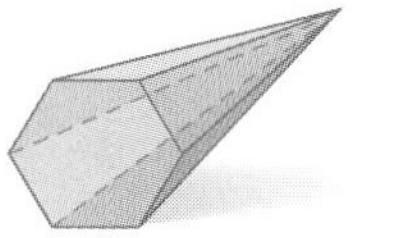

6. 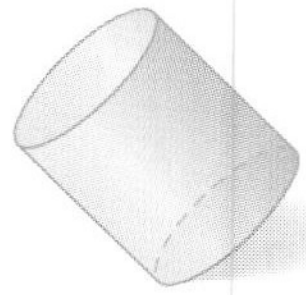

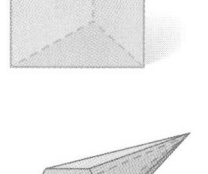

Find the volume of each figure to the nearest tenth. Use 3.14 for π.

7. 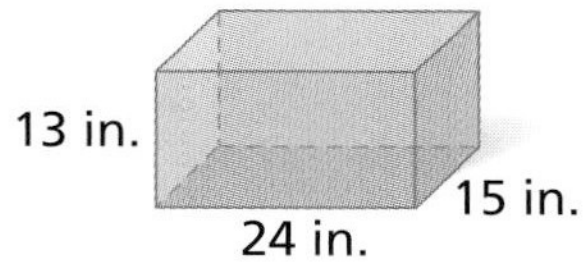

8. 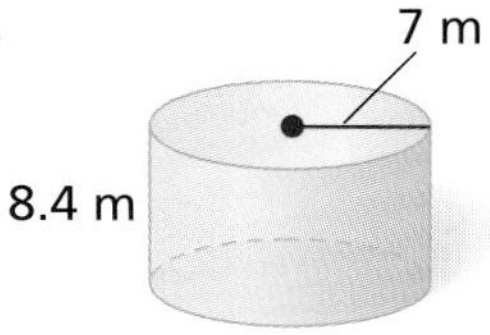

9. 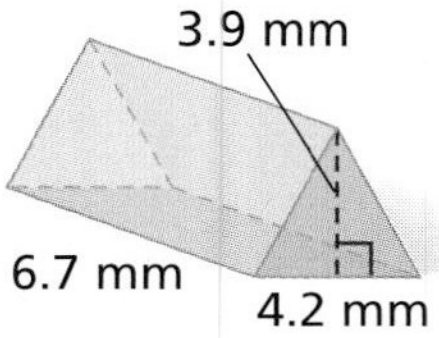

10. 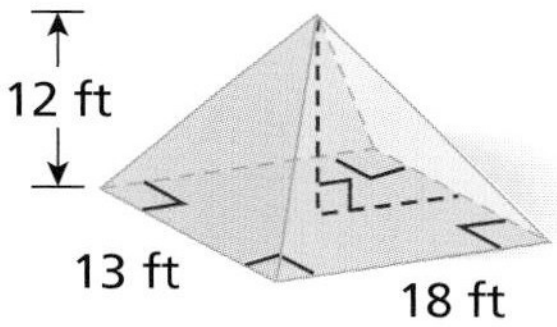

11. 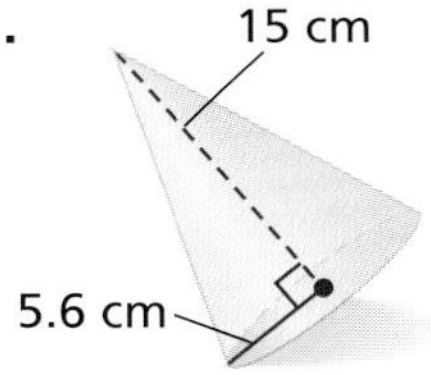

12. 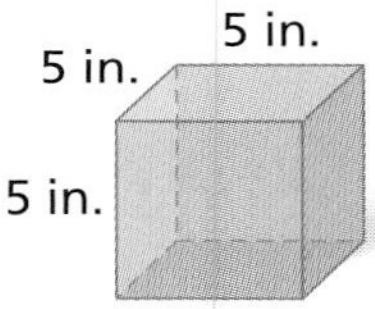

Find the surface area of each figure to the nearest tenth. Use 3.14 for π.

13. 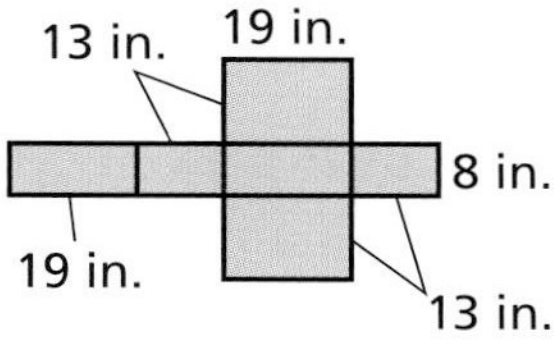

14. 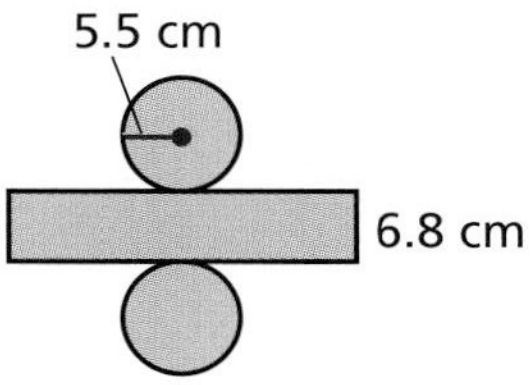

15. 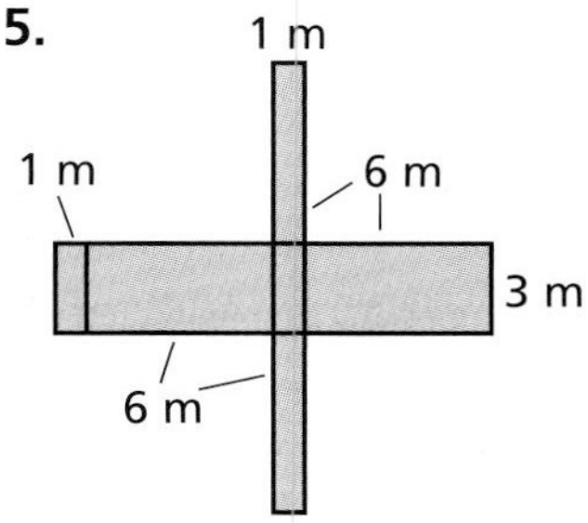

16. The surface area of a rectangular prism is 52 ft^2. What is the surface area of a similar prism that is larger by a scale factor of 7?

17. The volume of a cube is 35 mm^3. What is the volume of a similar cube that is larger by a scale factor of 9?

18. The volume of a flowerpot is 7.5 cm^3. What is the volume, to the nearest hundredth, of a similar flowerpot that is smaller by a scale factor of $\frac{1}{2}$?

Chapter Test

CHAPTER 10

STANDARDIZED TEST PREP

go.hrw.com
State Test Practice Online
KEYWORD: MS7 TestPrep

Cumulative Assessment, Chapters 1–10

Multiple Choice

1. What value represents the median of the data set?

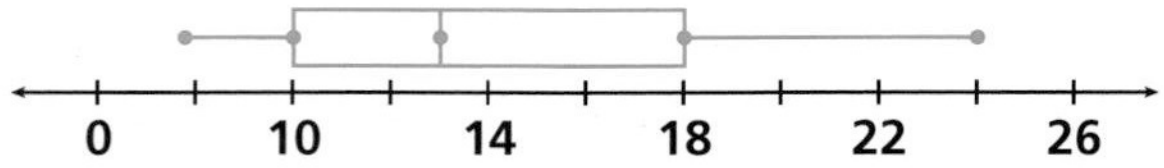

Ⓐ 7 Ⓑ 10 Ⓒ 13 Ⓓ 18

2. How much less is the area of the triangle than the area of the rectangle?

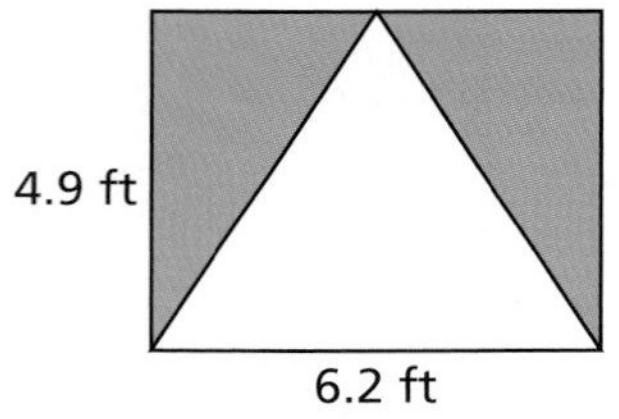

Ⓕ 15.19 ft^2 Ⓖ 30.38 ft^2 Ⓗ 9.61 ft^2 Ⓙ Not here

3. A rectangular tank has a height of 9 meters, a width of 5 meters, and a length of 12 meters. What is the volume of the tank?

Ⓐ 540 m^3 Ⓑ 180 m^3 Ⓒ 45 m^2 Ⓓ 26 m^2

4. What is 140% of 85?

Ⓕ 11.9 Ⓖ 119 Ⓗ 1,190 Ⓙ 11,900

5. Clay jumps rope at an average rate of 75 jumps per minute. How long does it take him to make 405 jumps if he does not stop?

Ⓐ 5 min Ⓑ $5\frac{1}{10}$ min Ⓒ $5\frac{2}{5}$ min Ⓓ $5\frac{5}{6}$ min

6. A cell-phone company is tracking the sales of a particular model of phone. The sales at one store over six months are shown in the graph. What is the approximate percent increase in sales of Model B phones from October to November?

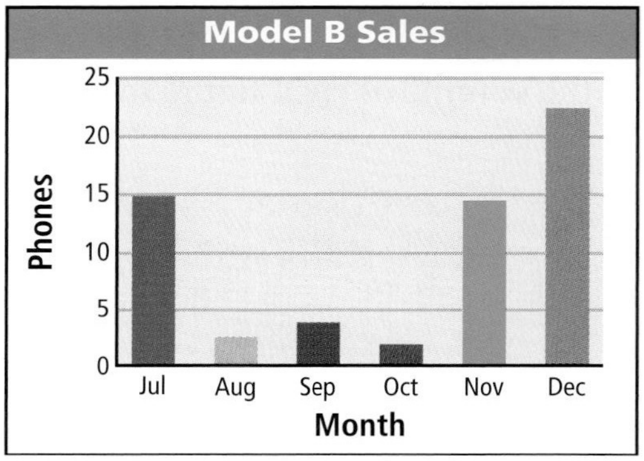

Ⓕ 40% Ⓖ 400% Ⓗ 4,000% Ⓙ 4%

7. What is the decimal equivalent of $4\frac{4}{5}$?

Ⓐ 4.45 Ⓑ 4.54 Ⓒ 4.8 Ⓓ 24.5

8. The circumference of the given cylinder is 6 in. What additional information is needed to find the volume of the cylinder?

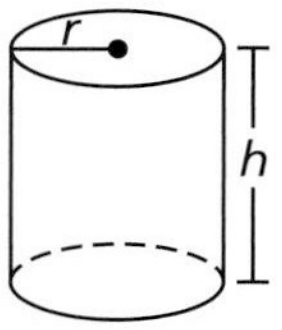

Ⓕ diameter Ⓖ area of base Ⓗ height Ⓙ radius

Standardized Test Prep

9. The straw has a diameter of 0.6 cm. What is the surface area of the straw?

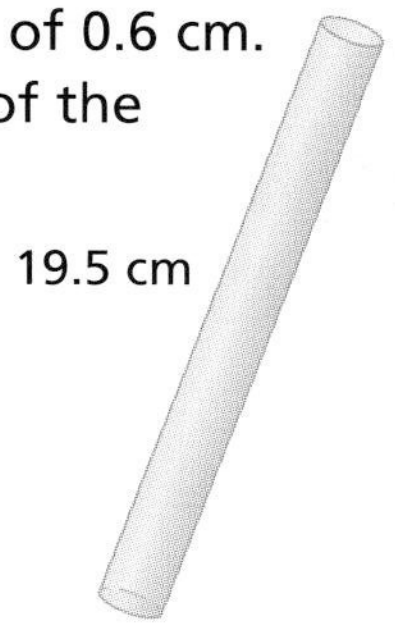

Ⓐ 11.7 cm^2

Ⓑ 5.5 cm^2

Ⓒ 37.3 cm^2

Ⓓ 36.7 cm^2

10. Find the volume of the cylinder to the nearest tenth. Use 3.14 for π.

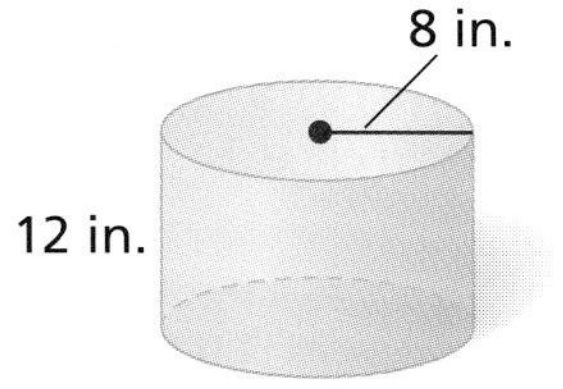

Ⓕ 602.9 in^3 Ⓗ $1{,}205.8 \text{ in}^3$

Ⓖ $3{,}215.4 \text{ in}^3$ Ⓙ $2{,}411.5 \text{ in}^3$

HOT TIP! **Make sure you use the correct units of measure in your responses. Area has square units, and volume has cubic units.**

Gridded Response

11. A cone-shaped cup has a radius of 4 in. and a volume of 256 in^3. What is the height, in inches, of the cup? Round your answer to the nearest tenth.

12. The legs of a right triangle measure 9 units and 12 units. How many units long is the hypotenuse?

13. What is the greatest common factor of 180, 16, and 48?

14. What is the smallest whole-number value of x that makes the value of the expression $-15x + 30$ greater than 0?

15. Angle A and angle B are vertical angles. If angle A measures 62°, what is the degree measure of angle B?

Short Response

16. The surface area of a cylinder is 66 ft^2.
    a. Find the surface area of a larger similar cylinder with a scale factor of 4.
    b. Explain how the surface area changes when the dimensions are decreased by a factor of $\frac{1}{4}$.

17. A polyhedron has two parallel square bases with edges 9 meters long and a height of 9 meters. Identify the figure and find its volume. Show your work.

18. What is the base length of a parallelogram with a height of 8 in. and an area of 56 in^2?

Extended Response

19. Use the figure for the following problems. Round your answers to the nearest hundredth, if necessary. Use 3.14 for π.

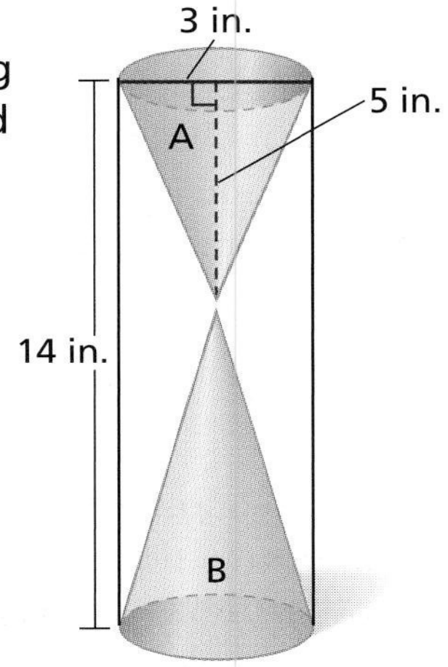

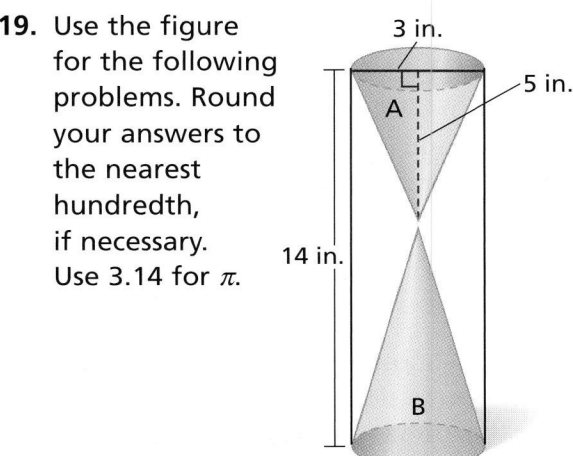

    a. What three-dimensional shapes make up the sculpture?
    b. What is the combined volume of figures A and B? Show your work.
    c. What is the volume of the space surrounding figures A and B? Show your work and explain your answer.

Problem Solving on Location

NEW JERSEY

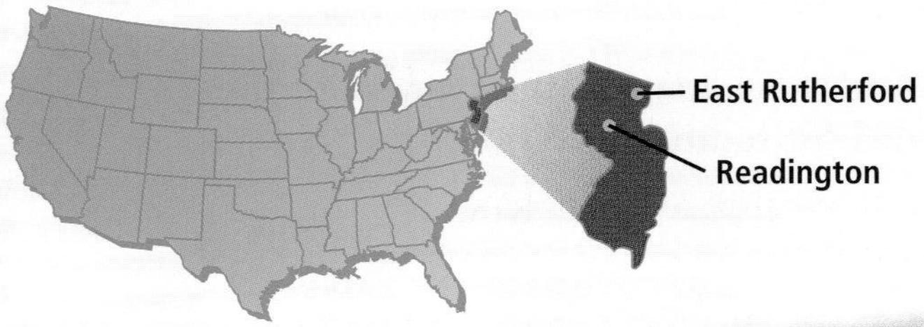

The Meadowlands Sports Complex

In the early 1970s, construction began on a sports and entertainment facility in East Rutherford, New Jersey. Today, the 700-acre Meadowlands Sports Complex includes a football stadium, an arena, and a racetrack. The complex attracts more than 6 million visitors per year.

Choose one or more strategies to solve each problem.

1. The Meadowlands' stadium and arena both have rectangular video screens. The length of the arena's screen is 36 feet less than the length of the stadium's screen. The stadium's screen has an area of 1,392 square feet and a height of 24 feet. What is the length of the arena's screen?

For 2 and 3, use the table.

2. Rectangular tarps protect the football field during bad weather. Each sheet is 60 feet long and 40 feet wide. How many sheets are needed to cover the field without overlap?

3. For a special presentation, a narrow red carpet is placed around the perimeter of the basketball court. The carpet is also placed diagonally from each corner of the court to the opposite corner. To the nearest foot, how much carpeting is needed?

Court and Field Dimensions

	Length (ft)	Width (ft)
Football Field	360	160
Basketball Court	94	50

Draw a Diagram
Make a Model
Guess and Test
Work Backward
Find a Pattern
Make a Table
Solve a Simpler Problem
Use Logical Reasoning
Act It Out
Make an Organized List

✪ The New Jersey Festival of Ballooning

Every summer, the skies over Readington, New Jersey, are filled with gigantic birthday cakes, sneakers, and polar bears. This unusual sight is part of the New Jersey Festival of Ballooning, a three-day event featuring more than 100 hot air balloons from all over the country.

Choose one or more strategies to solve each problem.

1. The 2005 festival included a balloon shaped like a rectangular prism. The balloon weighed 10 pounds for each foot of its height. The balloon's length was 78 feet, its width was 29 feet, and its volume was 119,886 cubic feet. How much did the balloon weigh?

2. A clown balloon flew at an altitude of 980 feet. A dragon balloon flew 620 feet below the clown balloon. A race car balloon cruised at an altitude of 530 feet. What was the vertical distance between the dragon and the race car? Which balloon was higher?

3. Only one of the balloons shown on the graph came from New Jersey. Use the graph and the following information to determine which balloon came from New Jersey.
   - The height of the balloon from New Jersey was greater than the median height of the balloons.
   - The balloon shaped like an eagle came from Wisconsin.
   - The balloon with a height of 112 feet came from Arizona.

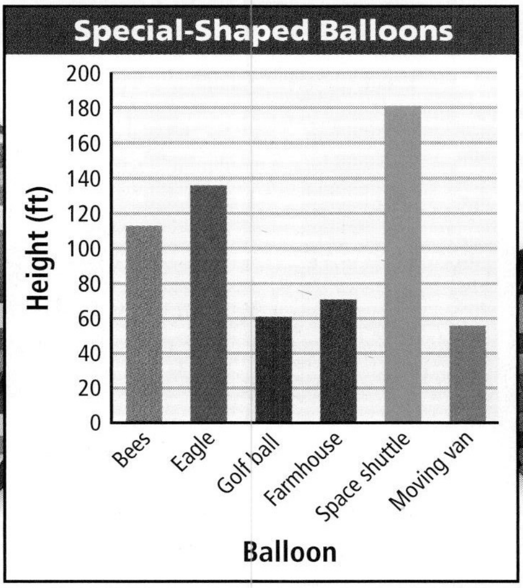

CHAPTER

11

Probability

go.hrw.com
Chapter Project Online
KEYWORD: MS7 Ch11

Career Demographer

Demographers study people: their numbers, how old they are, where they live, with whom they live, where they are moving, and more. They examine how age affects buying habits, which occupations are most popular, how people are affecting the natural environment, and many other behavioral data.

Businesses use demographers to analyze how products are used. The table lists the countries with the highest per capita mobile-phone use. Who might be interested in this kind of demographic information?

Countries with Highest per Capita Mobile-Phone Use

Country	Mobile Phones per 100 People
Finland	67.8
Norway	62.7
Sweden	59.0
Italy	52.2

ARE YOU READY?

Vocabulary

Choose the best term from the list to complete each sentence.

composite number
even number
odd number
percent
prime number
ratio

1. A(n) __?__ is a comparison of two quantities by division.
2. A(n) __?__ is an integer that is divisible by 2.
3. A(n) __?__ is a ratio that compares a number to 100.
4. A(n) __?__ is a number greater than 1 that has more than two whole number factors.
5. A(n) __?__ is an integer that is not divisible by 2.

Complete these exercises to review skills you will need for this chapter.

Simplify Fractions

Write each fraction in simplest form.

6. $\frac{6}{9}$ **7.** $\frac{12}{15}$ **8.** $\frac{8}{10}$ **9.** $\frac{20}{24}$

10. $\frac{2}{4}$ **11.** $\frac{7}{35}$ **12.** $\frac{12}{22}$ **13.** $\frac{72}{81}$

Write Fractions as Decimals

Write each fraction as a decimal.

14. $\frac{3}{5}$ **15.** $\frac{9}{20}$ **16.** $\frac{57}{100}$ **17.** $\frac{12}{25}$

18. $\frac{3}{25}$ **19.** $\frac{1}{2}$ **20.** $\frac{7}{10}$ **21.** $\frac{9}{5}$

Percents and Decimals

Write each decimal as a percent.

22. 0.14 **23.** 0.08 **24.** 0.75 **25.** 0.38

26. 0.27 **27.** 1.89 **28.** 0.234 **29.** 0.0025

Multiply Fractions

Multiply. Write each answer in simplest form.

30. $\frac{1}{2} \cdot \frac{1}{4}$ **31.** $\frac{2}{3} \cdot \frac{3}{5}$ **32.** $\frac{3}{10} \cdot \frac{1}{2}$ **33.** $\frac{5}{6} \cdot \frac{3}{4}$

34. $\frac{5}{14} \cdot \frac{7}{17}$ **35.** $-\frac{1}{8} \cdot \frac{3}{8}$ **36.** $-\frac{2}{15} \cdot \left(-\frac{2}{3}\right)$ **37.** $\frac{1}{4} \cdot \left(-\frac{1}{6}\right)$

CHAPTER 11

Study Guide: Preview

Where You've Been

Previously, you

- found experimental and theoretical probabilities of compound events.
- used organized lists and tree diagrams to find the sample space of an experiment.
- found the probability that an outcome will not occur.

In This Chapter

You will study

- finding experimental and theoretical probabilities, including those of dependent and independent events.
- using lists and tree diagrams to find combinations and all possible outcomes of an experiment.
- using the Fundamental Counting Principle and factorials to find permutations.

Where You're Going

You can use the skills learned in this chapter

- to determine the effect of chance in games that you play.
- to predict the outcome in situations involving sports and weather.

Key Vocabulary/Vocabulario

combination	combinación
dependent events	sucesos dependientes
event	suceso
experiment	experimento
experimental probability	probabilidad experimental
independent events	sucesos independientes
outcome	resultado
probability	probabilidad
sample space	espacio muestral
theoretical probability	probabilidad teórica

Vocabulary Connections

To become familiar with some of the vocabulary terms in the chapter, consider the following. You may refer to the chapter, the glossary, or a dictionary if you like.

1. An *experiment* is an action done to find out something you do not know. Why can we call flipping a coin, rolling a number cube, or spinning a spinner an **experiment**?
2. Several outcomes, or sometimes just one outcome, make up an *event*. For example, rolling an even number and choosing a challenge card can make up an event in a board game. What is another **event** that can occur when you play board games?
3. The word *depend* comes from the Latin word *dependēre,* meaning "to hang or to be attached." How might the probabilities of **dependent events** be linked?

Reading and Writing Math

Reading Strategy: Read Problems for Understanding

To best understand a word problem, read it once to note what concept is being reviewed. Then read the problem again, slowly and carefully, to identify what the problem is asking. As you read, highlight the key information. When dealing with a multi-step problem, break the problem into parts and then make a plan to solve it.

23. Architecture The steeple on a building is a square pyramid with base area 12 square feet and height 15 feet. How many cubic feet of concrete was used to make the pyramid?

Step	Question	Answer
Step 1	What concept is being reviewed?	• finding the volume of a pyramid
Step 2	What are you being asked to do?	• Find the number of cubic feet of concrete used to make the steeple.
Step 3	What is the key information needed to solve the problem?	• The steeple is a square pyramid. • The base area of the pyramid is 12 square feet. • The height of the pyramid is 15 feet.
Step 4	What is my plan to solve this multi-part problem?	• Use the formula for finding the volume of a pyramid: $V = \frac{1}{3}Bh$. • Substitute the values for the base area and the height into the formula. • Solve for V.

Try This

For each problem, complete each step in the four-step method described above.

1. Which has a greater volume: a square pyramid with a height of 15 feet and a base with a side length of 3 feet or a cube with a side length of 4 feet?
2. At a party, each child receives the same number of party favors. There are 16 kazoos, 24 snappers, 8 hats, and 32 pieces of gum. What is the greatest number of children that may be at the party?

11-1 Probability

Learn to use informal measures of probability.

Vocabulary
- experiment
- trial
- outcome
- event
- probability
- complement

An activity involving chance, such as rolling a number cube, is called an **experiment**. Each repetition or observation of an experiment is a **trial**, and each result is an **outcome**. A set of one or more outcomes is an **event**. For example, rolling a 5 (one outcome) can be an event, or rolling an even number (more than one outcome) can be an event.

The **probability** of an event, written *P*(event), is the measure of how likely the event is to occur. Probability is a measure between 0 and 1, as shown on the number line. You can write probability as a fraction, a decimal, or a percent.

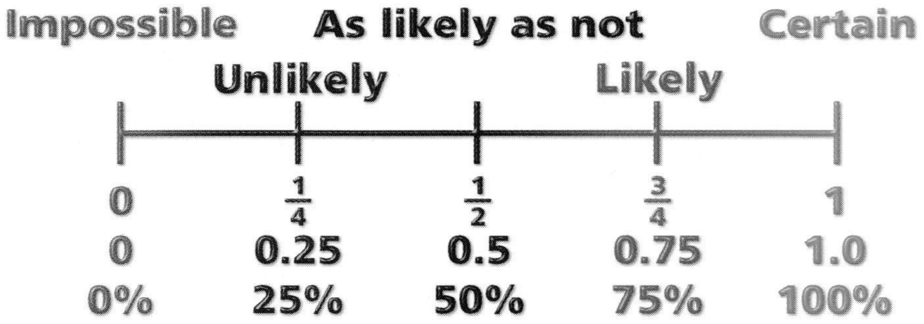

EXAMPLE 1 **Determining the Likelihood of an Event**

Determine whether each event is impossible, unlikely, as likely as not, likely, or certain.

A **rolling an even number on a number cube**

There are 6 possible outcomes:

Even	*Not* Even
2, 4, 6	1, 3, 5

Half of the outcomes are even.

Rolling an even number is as likely as not.

B **rolling a 5 on a number cube**

There are 6 possible outcomes:

5	*Not* 5
5	1, 2, 3, 4, 6

Only one outcome is a five.

Rolling a 5 is unlikely.

When a number cube is rolled, either a 5 will be rolled or it will not. Rolling a 5 and not rolling a 5 are examples of *complementary events*. The **complement** of an event is the set of all outcomes that are *not* the event.

Because it is certain that either an event or its complement will occur when an activity is performed, the sum of the probabilities is 1.

$$P(\text{event}) + P(\text{complement}) = 1$$

EXAMPLE 2 Using Complements

A bag contains 6 blue marbles, 6 red marbles, 3 green marbles, and 1 yellow marble. The probability of randomly drawing a red marble is $\frac{3}{8}$. What is the probability of not drawing a red marble?

$$P(\text{event}) + P(\text{complement}) = 1$$

$$P(\text{red}) + P(\text{not red}) = 1$$

$$\frac{3}{8} + P(\text{not red}) = 1 \qquad \textit{Substitute } \tfrac{3}{8} \textit{ for } P(\text{red}).$$

$$-\frac{3}{8} \qquad = -\frac{3}{8} \qquad \textit{Subtract } \tfrac{3}{8} \textit{ from both sides.}$$

$$P(\text{not red}) = \frac{5}{8} \qquad \textit{Simplify.}$$

The probability of not drawing a red marble is $\frac{5}{8}$.

EXAMPLE 3 *School Application*

Eric's math teacher almost always gives a pop quiz if the class did not ask many questions during the lesson on the previous class day. If it is Monday and no one asked questions during class on Friday, should Eric expect a pop quiz? Explain.

Since Eric's teacher often gives quizzes on days after few questions were asked, a quiz on Monday is likely.

Think and Discuss

1. Describe an event that has a probability of 0% and an event that has a probability of 100%.

2. Give an example of a real-world event and its complement.

11-1 Exercises

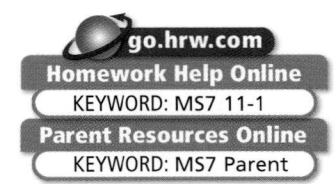

go.hrw.com
Homework Help Online
KEYWORD: MS7 11-1
Parent Resources Online
KEYWORD: MS7 Parent

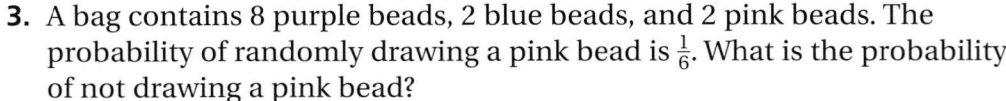

GUIDED PRACTICE

See Example 1

Determine whether each event is impossible, unlikely, as likely as not, likely, or certain.

1. rolling a number greater than 5 with a number cube
2. drawing a blue marble from a bag of black and white marbles

See Example 2

3. A bag contains 8 purple beads, 2 blue beads, and 2 pink beads. The probability of randomly drawing a pink bead is $\frac{1}{6}$. What is the probability of not drawing a pink bead?

See Example 3

4. Natalie almost always sleeps in on Saturday mornings when she does not have to work. If it is Saturday morning and Natalie does not have to work, how likely is it that Natalie will sleep in?

INDEPENDENT PRACTICE

See Example 1

Determine whether each event is impossible, unlikely, as likely as not, likely, or certain.

5. randomly drawing a red or pink card from a deck of red and pink cards
6. flipping a coin and getting tails
7. rolling a 6 on a number cube five times in a row

See Example 2

8. The probability of rolling a 5 or 6 with a number cube is $\frac{1}{3}$. What is the probability of not rolling a 5 or 6?
9. The probability of randomly drawing a green marble from a bag of green, red, and blue marbles is $\frac{3}{5}$. What is the probability of randomly drawing a red or blue marble?

See Example 3

10. Tim rarely spends more than 30 minutes watching TV in the afternoon. If Tim began watching TV at 4:00 P.M., would you expect that he is still watching TV at 5:00 P.M? Explain.

PRACTICE AND PROBLEM SOLVING

Extra Practice
See page 748.

A bag contains 12 red checkers and 12 black checkers. Determine whether each event is impossible, unlikely, as likely as not, likely, or certain.

11. randomly drawing a red checker
12. randomly drawing a white checker
13. randomly drawing a red or black checker
14. randomly drawing a black checker
15. **Exercise** Luka almost always jogs in the afternoon when the weather is not cold or rainy. The sky is cloudy and the temperature is 41°F. How likely is it that Luka will jog this afternoon?

16. **Life Science** A researcher's garden contains 900 sweet pea plants. More than 700 of the plants have purple flowers and about 200 have white flowers. Would you expect that one plant randomly selected from the garden will have purple or white flowers? Explain.

17. **Life Science** Sharks belong to a class of fishes that have skeletons made of cartilage. Bony fishes, which account for 95% of all species of fish, have skeletons made of bone.

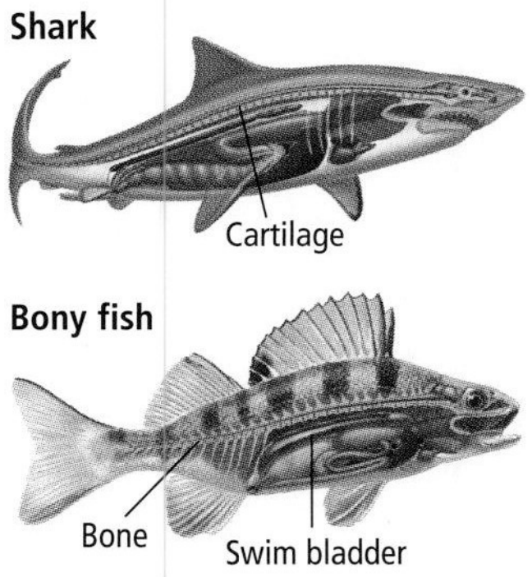

   a. How likely is it that a fish you cannot identify at a pet store is a bony fish? Explain.
   b. Only bony fishes have swim bladders, which keep them from sinking. How likely is it that a shark has a swim bladder? Explain.

18. **Earth Science** The graph shows the carbon dioxide levels in the atmosphere from 1958 to 1994. How likely is it that the level of carbon dioxide fell from 1994 to 2000? Explain.

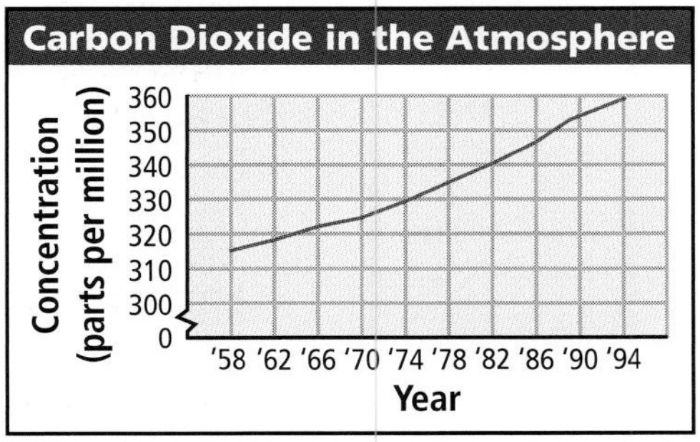

19. **Write a Problem** Describe an event that involves rolling a number cube. Determine the likelihood that the event will occur.

20. **Write About It** Explain how to tell whether an event is as likely as not.

21. **Challenge** A bag contains 10 red marbles and 8 blue marbles, all the same size and weight. Keiko randomly draws 2 red marbles from the bag and does not replace them. Will Keiko be more likely to draw a red marble than a blue marble on her next draw? Explain.

Test Prep and Spiral Review

22. **Multiple Choice** **Which percent best shows the probability that Kito will randomly draw an even number from five cards numbered 2, 4, 6, 8, and 10?**

   Ⓐ 75% Ⓑ 25% Ⓒ 50% Ⓓ 100%

23. **Short Response** Describe an event that is likely to happen.

24. The sales tax on a $45 DVD player is $3.38. What is the sales tax rate to the nearest tenth of a percent? (Lesson 6-5)

Calculate. Use the correct number of significant digits in each answer. (Lesson 9-1)

25. $8.4 + 2.97$ 26. $6.53 + 18$ 27. $7 - 3.6$

28. $12 \cdot 203$ 29. $14.3 \cdot 10.6$ 30. $7.0 \div 6.22$

11-2 Experimental Probability

Learn to find experimental probability.

Vocabulary

experimental probability

During hockey practice, Tanya made saves on 15 out of 25 shots. Based on these numbers, you can estimate the probability that Tanya will make a save on the next shot.

Experimental probability is one way of estimating the probability of an event. The **experimental probability** of an event is found by comparing the number of times the event occurs to the total number of trials. The more trials you have, the more accurate the estimate is likely to be.

EXPERIMENTAL PROBABILITY

$$\text{probability} \approx \frac{\text{number of times the event occurs}}{\text{total number of trials}}$$

EXAMPLE 1 *Sports Application*

Writing Math

"P(event)" represents the probability that an event will occur. For example, the probability of a flipped coin landing heads up could be written as "P(heads)."

Tanya made saves on 15 out of 25 shots. What is the experimental probability that she will make a save on the next shot? Write your answer as a fraction, as a decimal, and as a percent.

$$P(\text{event}) \approx \frac{\text{number of times the event occurs}}{\text{total number of trials}}$$

$$P(\text{save}) \approx \frac{\textbf{number of saves made}}{\textbf{total number of shots attempted}}$$

$= \frac{15}{25}$ *Substitute data from the experiment.*

$= \frac{3}{5}$ *Write in simplest form.*

$= 0.6 = 60\%$ *Write as a decimal and as a percent.*

The experimental probability that Tanya will make a save on the next shot is $\frac{3}{5}$, or 0.6, or 60%.

EXAMPLE 2 *Weather Application*

For the past three weeks, Karl has been recording the daily high temperatures for a science project. His results are shown below.

Week 1	Temp (°F)
Sun	76
Mon	74
Tue	79
Wed	80
Thu	77
Fri	76
Sat	75

Week 2	Temp (°F)
Sun	72
Mon	79
Tue	78
Wed	79
Thu	77
Fri	74
Sat	73

Week 3	Temp (°F)
Sun	78
Mon	76
Tue	77
Wed	75
Thu	79
Fri	77
Sat	75

A **What is the experimental probability that the temperature will be above 75°F on the next day?**

The number of days the temperature was above 75°F is 14.

$$P(\text{above } 75°\text{F}) \approx \frac{\text{number of days above } 75°\text{F}}{\text{total number of days}}$$

$$= \frac{14}{21} \qquad \textit{Substitute data.}$$

$$= \frac{2}{3} \qquad \textit{Write in simplest form.}$$

The experimental probability that the temperature will be above 75°F on the next day is $\frac{2}{3}$.

B **What is the experimental probability that the temperature will not be above 75°F on the next day?**

$$P(\text{above } 75°\text{F}) + P(\text{not above } 75°\text{F}) = 1 \qquad \textit{Use the complement.}$$

$$\frac{2}{3} + P(\text{not above } 75°\text{F}) = 1 \qquad \textit{Substitute.}$$

$$-\frac{2}{3} \qquad = -\frac{2}{3} \qquad \textit{Subtract } \tfrac{2}{3} \textit{ from both sides.}$$

$$P(\text{not above } 75°\text{F}) = \frac{1}{3} \qquad \textit{Simplify.}$$

The experimental probability that the temperature will not be above 75°F on the next day is $\frac{1}{3}$.

Think and Discuss

1. **Describe** a real-world situation in which you could estimate probability using experimental probability.
2. **Explain** how experimental probability could be used for making predictions.

11-2 Exercises

go.hrw.com
Homework Help Online
KEYWORD: MS7 11-2
Parent Resources Online
KEYWORD: MS7 Parent

GUIDED PRACTICE

See Example 1

1. During archery practice, Teri hits the target on 14 out of 20 tries. What is the experimental probability that she will hit the target on her next try? Write your answer as a fraction, as a decimal, and as a percent.

See Example 2

2. **Government** A reporter surveys 75 people to determine whether they plan to vote for or against a proposed amendment. Of these people, 65 plan to vote for the amendment.
   a. What is the experimental probability that the next person surveyed would say he or she plans to vote for the amendment?
   b. What is the experimental probability that the next person surveyed would say he or she plans to vote against the amendment?

INDEPENDENT PRACTICE

See Example 1

3. **Sports** Jack hit a baseball on 13 out of 30 tries during practice. What is the experimental probability that he will hit the ball on his next try? Write your answer as a fraction, as a decimal, and as a percent.
4. Cam hit the bull's-eye in darts 8 times out of 15 throws. What is the experimental probability that Cam's next throw will hit the bull's-eye?

See Example 2

5. For the past two weeks, Benita has been recording the number of people at Eastside Park at lunchtime. During that time, there were 50 or more people at the park 9 out of 14 days.
   a. What is the experimental probability that there will be 50 or more people at the park during lunchtime on the fifteenth day?
   b. What is the experimental probability that there will not be 50 or more people at the park during lunchtime on the fifteenth day?

PRACTICE AND PROBLEM SOLVING

Extra Practice
See page 748.

6. **Recreation** While bowling with friends, Alexis rolls a strike in 4 out of the 10 frames. What is the experimental probability that Alexis will roll a strike in the first frame of the next game?
7. Jeremiah is greeting customers at a music store. Of the first 25 people he sees enter the store, 16 are wearing jackets and 9 are not. What is the experimental probability that the next person to enter the store will be wearing a jacket?
8. During the month of June, Carmen kept track of the birds she saw in her garden. She saw a blue jay on 12 days of the month. What is the experimental probability that she will see a blue jay on July 1?
9. **Critical Thinking** Claudia finds that the experimental probability of her cat waking her between 5:00 A.M. and 6:00 A.M. is $\frac{8}{11}$. About what percent of the time does Claudia's cat not wake her between 5:00 A.M. and 6:00 A.M.?

Earth Science LINK

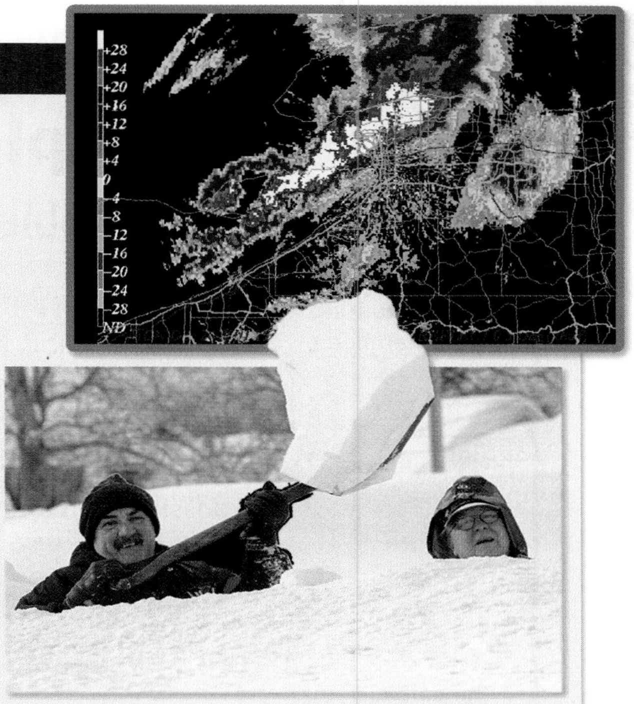

10. **Multi-Step** The stem-and-leaf plot shows the depth of snow in inches recorded in Buffalo, New York, over a 10-day period.

Stems	Leaves
7	9 9
8	
9	1 1 1 1 8 8
10	
11	8
12	
13	0

Key: 7|9 means 7.9

a. What is the median depth of snow for the 10-day period?

b. What is the experimental probability that the snow will be less than 6 in. deep on the eleventh day?

c. What is the experimental probability that the snow will be more than 10 in. deep on the eleventh day?

11. The table shows the high temperatures recorded on July 4 in Orlando, Florida, over an eight-year period.

a. What is the experimental probability that the high temperature on the next July 4 will be below 90°F?

b. What is the experimental probability that the high temperature on the next July 4 will be above 100°F?

Year	Temp (°F)	Year	Temp (°F)
1994	86.0	1998	96.8
1995	95.0	1999	89.1
1996	78.8	2000	90.0
1997	98.6	2001	91.0

Source: Old Farmers' Almanac

12. **Challenge** A toy company finds that the experimental probability of manufacturing a defective balance ball is $\frac{3}{50}$. About how many defective balls are likely to be in a batch of 1,800 balls?

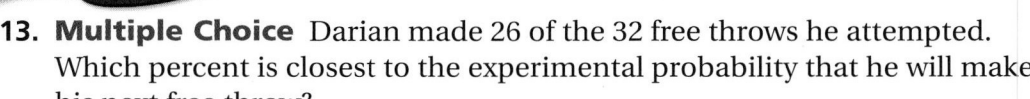

TEST PREP and Spiral Review

13. **Multiple Choice** Darian made 26 of the 32 free throws he attempted. Which percent is closest to the experimental probability that he will make his next free throw?

Ⓐ 50% Ⓑ 60% Ⓒ 70% Ⓓ 80%

14. **Multiple Choice** Survey results show that cheese is the favorite pizza topping for 18 out of 24 people. Which percent is closest to the experimental probability that a person's favorite pizza topping will NOT be cheese?

Ⓕ 25% Ⓖ 33% Ⓗ 40% Ⓙ 75%

15. How many days are equal to 360 hours? (Lesson 5-6)

Compare. Write <, >, or =. (Lesson 6-2)

16. $\frac{3}{5}$ ■ 62% 17. 2.4 ■ $\frac{12}{5}$ 18. 0.04 ■ $\frac{3}{10}$ 19. 8.2 ■ 82%

11-3 Make a List to Find Sample Spaces

Problem Solving Skill

Learn to use counting methods to determine possible outcomes.

Vocabulary

sample space

Fundamental Counting Principle

Because you can roll the numbers 1, 2, 3, 4, 5, and 6 on a number cube, there are 6 possible outcomes. Together, all the possible outcomes of an experiment make up the **sample space**.

You can make an organized list to show all possible outcomes of an experiment.

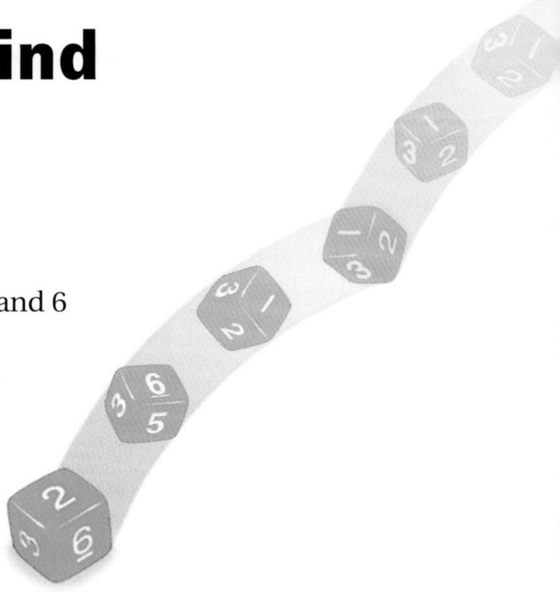

EXAMPLE 1 PROBLEM SOLVING APPLICATION

PROBLEM SOLVING

Lucia flips two quarters at the same time. What are all the possible outcomes? How many outcomes are in the sample space?

1 Understand the Problem

Rewrite the question as a statement.

- Find all the possible outcomes of flipping two quarters, and determine the size of the sample space.

List the **important information:**

- There are two quarters.
- Each quarter can land heads up or tails up.

2 Make a Plan

You can make an organized list to show all the possible outcomes.

3 Solve

Quarter 1	Quarter 2
H	H
H	T
T	H
T	T

Let H = heads and T = tails.

Record each possible outcome.

The possible outcomes are HH, HT, TH, and TT. There are four possible outcomes in the sample space.

4 Look Back

Each possible outcome that is recorded in the list is different.

When the number of possible outcomes of an experiment increases, it may be easier to track all the possible outcomes on a tree diagram.

EXAMPLE 2 Using a Tree Diagram to Find a Sample Space

Ren spins spinner A and spinner B. What are all the possible outcomes? How many outcomes are in the sample space?

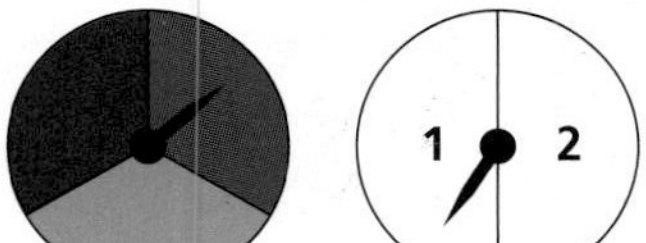

Make a tree diagram to show the sample space. List each color from spinner A. Then for each color, list each number from spinner B.

Red		Blue		Green		*Spinner A outcomes*
1	2	1	2	1	2	*Spinner B outcomes*
R, 1	R, 2	B, 1	B, 2	G, 1	G, 2	*All possible outcomes*

There are six possible outcomes in the sample space.

In Example 1, there are two outcomes for each coin, so there are four total outcomes.

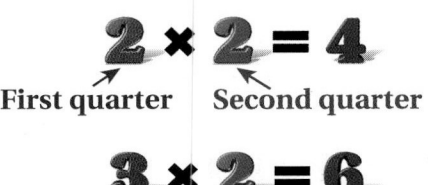

$$2 \times 2 = 4$$
First quarter, Second quarter

In Example 2, there are three outcomes for spinner A and two outcomes for spinner B, so there are six total outcomes.

$$3 \times 2 = 6$$
Spinner A, Spinner B

The **Fundamental Counting Principle** states that you can find the total number of outcomes for two or more experiments by multiplying the number of outcomes for each separate experiment.

EXAMPLE 3 *Recreation Application*

In a game, each player rolls a number cube and spins a spinner. The spinner is divided into thirds, numbered 1, 2, and 3. How many outcomes are possible during one player's turn?

The number cube has 6 outcomes. *List the number of outcomes*
The spinner has 3 outcomes. *for each separate experiment.*

$6 \cdot 3 = 18$ *Use the Fundamental Counting Principle.*

There are 18 possible outcomes during one player's turn.

Think and Discuss

1. **Compare** using a tree diagram and using the Fundamental Counting Principle to find a sample space.
2. **Find** the size of the sample space for flipping 5 coins.

11-3 Exercises

go.hrw.com
Homework Help Online
KEYWORD: MS7 11-3
Parent Resources Online
KEYWORD: MS7 Parent

GUIDED PRACTICE

See Example 1

1. Enrique tosses a coin and spins the spinner at right. What are all the possible outcomes? How many outcomes are in the sample space?

See Example 2

2. An ice cream stand offers cake cones, waffle cones, or cups to hold ice cream. You can get vanilla, chocolate, strawberry, pistachio, or coffee flavored ice cream. If you order a single scoop, what are all the possible options you have? How many outcomes are in the sample space?

See Example 3

3. A game includes a number cube and a spinner divided into 4 equal sectors. Each player rolls the number cube and spins the spinner. How many outcomes are possible?

INDEPENDENT PRACTICE

See Example 1

4. At noon, Aretha can watch a football game, a basketball game, or a documentary about horses on TV. At 3:00, she can watch a different football game, a movie, or a concert. What are all the possible outcomes? How many outcomes are in the sample space?
5. A spinner is divided into fourths and numbered 1 through 4. Jory spins the spinner and tosses a coin. What are all the possible outcomes? How many outcomes are in the sample space?

See Example 2

6. Berto tosses a coin and spins the spinner at right. What are all the possible outcomes? How many outcomes are in the sample space?

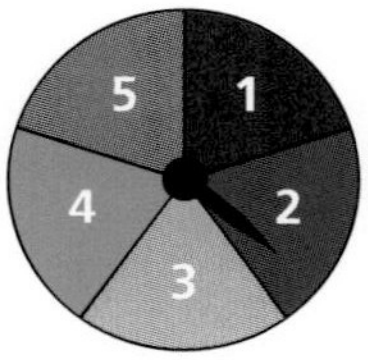

7. For breakfast, Clarissa can choose from oatmeal, cornflakes, or scrambled eggs. She can drink milk, orange juice, apple juice, or hot chocolate. What are all the possible outcomes? How many outcomes are in the sample space?

See Example 3

8. A pizza shop offers thick crust, thin crust, or stuffed crust. The choices of toppings are pepperoni, cheese, hamburger, Italian sausage, Canadian bacon, onions, bell peppers, mushrooms, and pineapple. How many different one-topping pizzas could you order?

PRACTICE AND PROBLEM SOLVING

Extra Practice
See page 748.

9. Andie has a blue sweater, a red sweater, and a purple sweater. She has a white shirt and a tan shirt. How many different ways can she wear a sweater and a shirt together?
10. **Critical Thinking** Suppose you can choose a ball that comes in three colors: blue, red, or green. Make a tree diagram or a list of all the possible ways to choose 2 balls if you are allowed to choose two of the same color.

LINK **Health**

The American Heart Association recommends that people exercise for 30–60 minutes three or four times a week to maintain healthy hearts.

11. **Health** For each pair of food groups, give the number of possible outcomes if one item is chosen from each group.
    a. group A and group B
    b. group B and group D
    c. group A and group C

Group A	Group B	Group C	Group D
milk cheese yogurt	beef fish poultry	bread cereal pasta rice	vegetables fruit

12. **Health** The graph shows the kinds of classes that health club members would like to see offered.
    a. If the health club offers the four most popular classes on one day, how many ways could they be arranged?
    b. If the health club offers each of the five classes on a different weekday, how many ways could they be arranged?

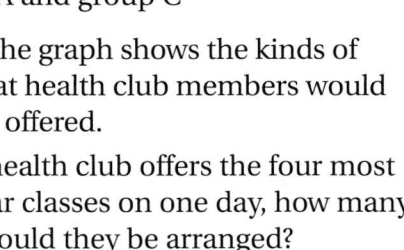

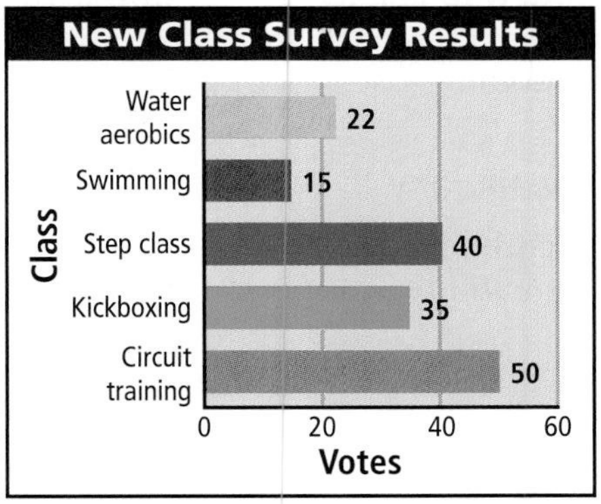

13. **Recreation** There are 3 trails from the South Canyon trailhead to Lake Solitude. There are 4 trails from Lake Solitude to Hidden Lake. How many possible routes could you take to hike from the South Canyon trailhead to Hidden Lake that pass Lake Solitude?

14. **What's the Question?** Dan has 4 face cards and 5 number cards. He shuffles the cards separately and places each set in a separate pile. The answer is 20 possible outcomes. What is the question?

15. **Write About It** Explain how to determine the size of the sample space when you toss three number cubes at the same time.

16. **Challenge** Suppose you flip a penny, a nickel, and a dime at the same time. What are all the possible outcomes?

Test Prep and Spiral Review

17. **Multiple Choice** Amber rolls two number cubes. How many outcomes are possible?

    (A) 6 (B) 12 (C) 24 (D) 36

18. **Extended Response** A sandwich shop offers 3 choices of breads: white, rye, or garlic; 2 choices of cheese: American or Swiss; and 4 choices of meats: beef, turkey, ham, or pork. List the possible choices for a sandwich with 1 bread, 1 cheese, and 1 meat. How many possible choices are there?

Write each fraction as a percent. (Lesson 6-2)

19. $\frac{1}{8}$ 20. $\frac{3}{4}$ 21. $\frac{2}{5}$ 22. $\frac{3}{10}$

23. Find the volume of a cylinder with diameter 8 in. and height 14 in. Use $\frac{22}{7}$ for π. (Lesson 10-2)

11-4 Theoretical Probability

Learn to find the theoretical probability of an event.

Vocabulary

theoretical probability

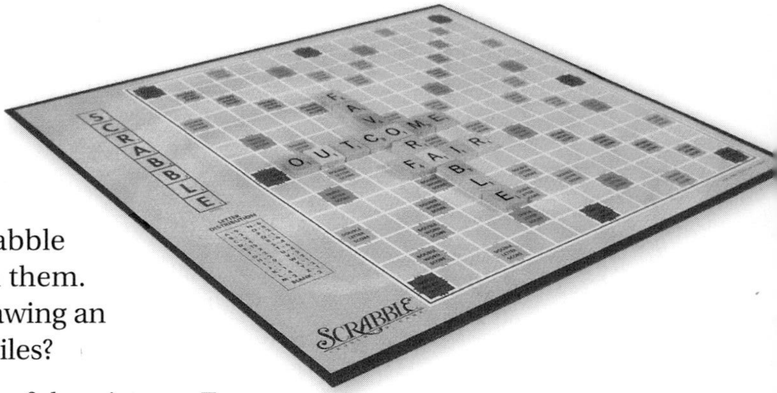

In the game of Scrabble®, players use tiles bearing the letters of the alphabet to form words. Of the 100 tiles used in a Scrabble game, 12 have the letter *E* on them. What is the probability of drawing an *E* from a bag of 100 Scrabble tiles?

To determine the probability of drawing an *E*, you can draw tiles from a bag and record your results to find the experimental probability, or you can calculate the *theoretical probability*. **Theoretical probability** is used to find the probability of an event when all outcomes are equally likely.

THEORETICAL PROBABILITY

$$\text{probability} = \frac{\text{number of ways the event can occur}}{\text{total number of equally likely outcomes}}$$

If each possible outcome of an experiment is equally likely, then the experiment is said to be fair. Experiments involving number cubes and coins are usually assumed to be fair.

EXAMPLE 1 Finding Theoretical Probability

Find the probability of each event. Write your answer as a fraction, as a decimal, and as a percent.

A **drawing one of the 12 *E*'s from a bag of 100 Scrabble tiles**

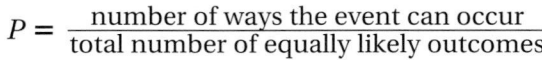

$$P = \frac{\text{number of ways the event can occur}}{\text{total number of equally likely outcomes}}$$

$P(E) = \dfrac{\textbf{number of } E\textbf{'s}}{\textbf{total number of tiles}}$ *Write the ratio.*

$= \dfrac{12}{100}$ *Substitute.*

$= \dfrac{3}{25}$ *Write in simplest form.*

$= 0.12 = 12\%$ *Write as a decimal and as a percent.*

The theoretical probability of drawing an E is $\frac{3}{25}$, 0.12, or 12%.

Find the probability of each event. Write your answer as a fraction, as a decimal, and as a percent.

B **rolling a number greater than 2 on a fair number cube**

There are four favorable outcomes: 3, 4, 5, and 6.

There are six possible outcomes: 1, 2, 3, 4, 5, and 6.

$$P(\text{greater than 2}) = \frac{\text{number of ways the event can occur}}{\text{total number of equally likely outcomes}}$$

$= \frac{4}{6}$ *Write the ratio.*

$= \frac{2}{3}$ *Write in simplest form.*

$\approx 0.667 \approx 66.7\%$ *Write as a decimal and a percent.*

The theoretical probability of rolling a number greater than 2 is $\frac{2}{3}$, or approximately 0.667, or approximately 66.7%.

EXAMPLE 2 *School Application*

There are 11 boys and 16 girls in Mr. Ashley's class. Mr. Ashley has written the name of each student on a craft stick. He randomly draws one of these sticks to choose a student to answer a question.

A **Find the theoretical probability of drawing a boy's name.**

$$P(\text{boy}) = \frac{\text{number of boys in class}}{\text{total number of students in class}}$$

$$P(\text{boy}) = \frac{11}{27}$$

B **Find the theoretical probability of drawing a girl's name.**

$P(\text{boy}) + P(\text{girl}) = 1$ *Substitute $\frac{11}{27}$ for P(boy).*

$\frac{11}{27} + P(\text{girl}) = 1$

$-\frac{11}{27} \quad = -\frac{11}{27}$ *Subtract $\frac{11}{27}$ from both sides.*

$P(\text{girl}) = \frac{16}{27}$ *Simplify.*

Remember!

The sum of the probabilities of an event and its complement is 1.

Think and Discuss

1. **Give an example** of an experiment in which all of the outcomes are not equally likely. Explain.
2. **Describe** how the probability in Example 2 can be affected if Mr. Ashley does not draw randomly from the craft sticks.

11-4 Exercises

go.hrw.com
Homework Help Online
KEYWORD: MS7 11-4
Parent Resources Online
KEYWORD: MS7 Parent

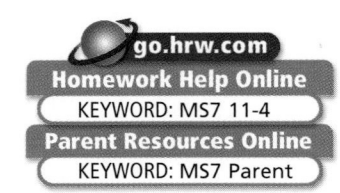

GUIDED PRACTICE

See Example 1

Find the probability of each event. Write your answer as a fraction, as a decimal, and as a percent.

1. randomly choosing a red marble from a bag of 15 red, 15 blue, 15 green, 15 yellow, 15 black, and 15 white marbles
2. tossing 2 fair coins and both landing heads up

See Example 2

A set of cards includes 15 yellow cards, 10 green cards, and 10 blue cards. Find the probability of each event when a card is chosen at random.

3. yellow
4. green
5. not yellow or green

INDEPENDENT PRACTICE

See Example 1

Find the probability of each event. Write your answer as a fraction, as a decimal, and as a percent.

6. randomly drawing a heart or a club from a shuffled deck of 52 cards with 13-card suits: diamonds, hearts, clubs, and spades
7. randomly drawing a purple disk from a game with 13 red, 13 purple, 13 orange, and 13 white disks of the same size and shape
8. randomly drawing one of the two blank Scrabble tiles from a complete set of 100 Scrabble tiles

See Example 2

Sifu has 6 girls and 8 boys in his karate class. He randomly selects one student to demonstrate a self-defense technique. Find the probability of each event.

9. selecting a girl
10. selecting a boy

PRACTICE AND PROBLEM SOLVING

Extra Practice
See page 748.

Find the probability of each event when two fair number cubes are rolled.

11. $P(\text{total of } 3)$
12. $P(\text{total of } 7)$
13. $P(\text{total of } 4)$
14. $P(\text{total of } 2)$
15. $P(\text{total of } 9)$
16. $P(\text{total of } 13)$
17. $P(\text{total} > 8)$
18. $P(\text{total} \leq 12)$

A spinner is divided equally into 10 sectors. The numbers 1 through 5 are each placed in two different sectors. Find the probability of each event.

19. $P(3)$
20. $P(\text{greater than } 3)$
21. $P(\text{less than } 3)$
22. $P(5)$
23. $P(8)$
24. $P(\text{less than } 6)$
25. $P(\text{greater than or equal to } 4)$
26. $P(\text{less than or equal to } 2)$

Recreation The table shows the approximate number of visitors to five different amusement parks in the United States in one year. Find the probability that a randomly selected visitor to one of the amusement parks visited the parks listed in Exercises 27 and 28. Write each answer as a decimal and as a percent.

Amusement Parks	Number of Visitors
Disney World, FL	15,640,000
Disneyland, CA	13,680,000
SeaWorld, FL	4,900,000
Busch Gardens, FL	4,200,000
SeaWorld, CA	3,700,000

27. Disney World

28. a park in California

29. Gardening A package of mixed lettuce seeds contains 150 green lettuce seeds and 50 red lettuce seeds. What is the probability that a randomly selected seed will be a red lettuce seed? Write your answer as a percent.

30. Choose a Strategy Francis, Amanda, Raymond, and Albert wore different-colored T-shirts. The colors were tan, orange, purple, and aqua. Neither Raymond nor Amanda ever wears orange, and neither Francis nor Raymond ever wears aqua. Albert wore purple. What color was each person's T-shirt?

31. Write About It Suppose the probability of an event happening is $\frac{3}{8}$. Explain what each number in the ratio represents.

32. Challenge A spinner is divided into three sectors. Half of the spinner is red, $\frac{1}{3}$ is blue, and $\frac{1}{6}$ is green. What is the probability that the spinner will land on either red or green?

Test Prep and Spiral Review

33. Multiple Choice Renae spins the spinner at right. What is the probability that the spinner will land on the number 4?

Ⓐ $\frac{5}{8}$

Ⓑ $\frac{2}{7}$

Ⓒ $\frac{50}{91}$

Ⓓ $\frac{1}{4}$

34. Gridded Response There are 4 red marbles, 6 green marbles, and 2 yellow marbles in a bag. A marble is drawn at random. What is the probability that the marble will NOT be yellow?

35. Find the area of the trapezoid shown. (Lesson 9-4)

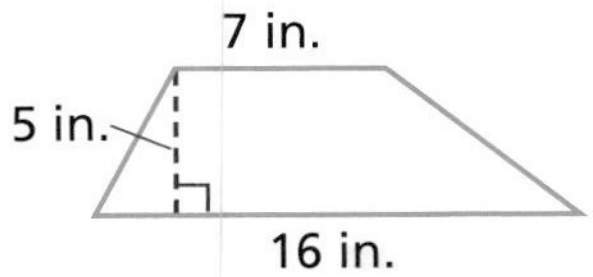

36. Dora is buying one flavor of frozen yogurt. She can choose from two sizes, small and large, and four flavors: berry swirl, vanilla, peach, and lime. How many possible choices are there? (Lesson 11-3)

Hands-On LAB 11-4

Experimental and Theoretical Probability

Use with Lesson 11-4

go.hrw.com
Lab Resources Online
KEYWORD: MS7 Lab11

REMEMBER

- The experimental probability of an event is the ratio of the number of times the event occurs to the total number of trials.
- The theoretical probability of an event is the ratio of the number of ways the event can occur to the total number of equally likely outcomes.

Activity 1

1. Write the letters *A, B, C,* and *D* on four slips of paper. Fold the slips in half and place them in a bag or other small container.

2. You will be choosing these slips of paper without looking. Predict the number of times you expect to choose *A* when you repeat the experiment 12 times.

3. Choose a slip of paper, note the result, and replace the slip. Repeat this 12 times, mixing the slips between trials. Record your results in a table like the one shown.

Outcome	Number of Times Chosen
A	//
B	////
C	𝍸
D	/

4. How many times did you choose *A*? How does this number compare to your prediction?

5. What is the experimental probability of choosing *A*? What is the theoretical probability of choosing *A*?

6. Combine your results with those of your classmates. Find the experimental probability of choosing *A* based on the combined results.

Think and Discuss

1. How is the experimental probability of choosing *A* based on the combined results different from the experimental probability of choosing *A* based on the results of your own experiment?
2. How many times would you expect to choose *A* if you repeat the experiment 500 times?

Try This

1. What is the theoretical probability of choosing *A* from five slips of paper with the letters *A, B, C, D,* and *E*?
2. Predict the number of times you would expect to choose *A* from the five slips in problem 1 if you repeat the experiment 500 times.

Activity 2

1. Write the letters *A, B, C,* and *D* and the numbers 1, 2, and 3 on slips of paper. Fold the slips in half. Place the slips with the letters in one bag and the slips with the numbers in a different bag.

2. In this activity, you will be choosing one slip of paper from each bag without looking. What is the sample space for this experiment? Predict the number of times you expect to choose *A* and 1 (*A*-1) when you repeat the experiment 24 times.

3. Choose a slip of paper from each bag, note the results, and replace the slips. Repeat this 24 times, mixing the slips between trials. Record your results in a table like the one shown.

Outcome	Number of Times Chosen
A-1	/
A-2	~~////~~
A-3	//
B-1	/

4. How many times did you choose *A*-1? How does this number compare to your prediction?

5. Combine your results with those of your classmates. Find the experimental probability of choosing *A*-1 based on the combined results.

Think and Discuss

1. What do you think is the theoretical probability of choosing *A*-1? Why?
2. How many times would you expect to choose *A*-1 if you repeat the experiment 600 times?
3. Explain the difference between the experimental probability of an event and the theoretical probability of the event.

Try This

1. Suppose you toss a penny and a nickel at the same time.
   a. What is the sample space for this experiment?
   b. Predict the number of times you would expect both coins to land heads up if you repeat the experiment 100 times.
   c. Predict the number of times you would expect one coin to land heads up and one coin to land tails up if you repeat the experiment 1,000 times.
2. You spin the spinner at right and roll a number cube at the same time.
   a. What is the sample space for this experiment?
   b. Describe an experiment you could conduct to find the experimental probability of spinning green and rolling a 4 at the same time.

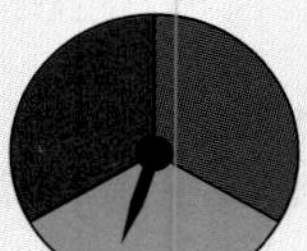

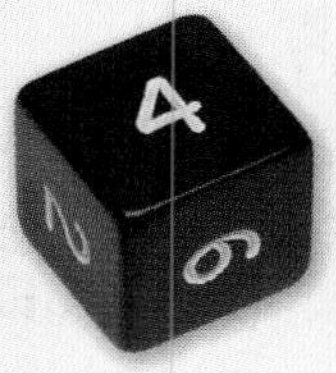

CHAPTER 11

READY TO GO ON?

SECTION 11A

Quiz for Lessons 11-1 Through 11-4

11-1 Probability

Determine whether each event is impossible, unlikely, as likely as not, likely, or certain.

1. rolling 2 number cubes and getting a sum of 2
2. guessing the answer to a true/false question correctly
3. drawing a black marble from a bag containing 2 blue, 3 yellow, and 4 white marbles
4. The probability of Ashur's soccer team winning its next game is $\frac{7}{10}$. What is the probability of Ashur's team not winning the next game?

11-2 Experimental Probability

5. Carl is conducting a survey for the school paper. He finds that 7 students have no pets, 15 have one pet, and 9 have at least two pets. What is the experimental probability that the next student Carl asks will not have a pet?
6. During her ride home from school, Dana sees 15 cars driven by men and 34 cars driven by women. What is the experimental probability that the next car Dana sees will be driven by a man?

11-3 Make a List to Find Sample Spaces

7. Shelly and Anthony are playing a game using a number cube and a nickel. Each player rolls the number cube and flips the coin. What are all the possible outcomes during one turn? How many outcomes are in the sample space?

8. A yogurt shop offers 4 different flavors of yogurt and 3 different fruit toppings. How many different desserts are possible if you can choose one flavor of yogurt and one topping?

11-4 Theoretical Probability

A spinner with 10 equal sectors numbered 1 through 10 is spun. Find the probability of each event. Write your answer as a fraction, as a decimal, and as a percent.

9. $P(5)$
10. $P(\text{prime number})$
11. $P(\text{even number})$
12. $P(20)$
13. Sabina has a list of 8 CDs and 5 DVDs that she would like to buy. Her friends randomly select one of the items from the list to give her as a gift. What is the probability Sabina's friends will select a CD? a DVD?

Ready to Go On?

Focus on Problem Solving

Understand the Problem

• **Identify important details**

When you are solving word problems, you need to identify information that is important to the problem. Read the problem several times to find all the important details. Sometimes it is helpful to read the problem aloud so that you can hear the words. Highlight the facts that are needed to solve the problem. Then list any other information that is necessary.

Highlight the important information in each problem, and then list any other important details.

1. A bag of bubble gum has 25 pink pieces, 20 blue pieces, and 15 green pieces. Lauren selects 1 piece of bubble gum without looking. What is the probability that it is not blue?

2. Regina has a bag of marbles that contains 6 red marbles, 3 green marbles, and 4 blue marbles. Regina pulls 1 marble from the bag without looking. What is the probability that the marble is red?

3. Marco is counting the cars he sees on his ride home from school. Of 20 cars, 10 are white, 6 are red, 2 are blue, and 2 are green. What is the experimental probability that the next car Marco sees will be red?

4. Frederica has 8 red socks, 6 blue socks, 10 white socks, and 4 yellow socks in a drawer. What is the probability that she will randomly pull a brown sock from the drawer?

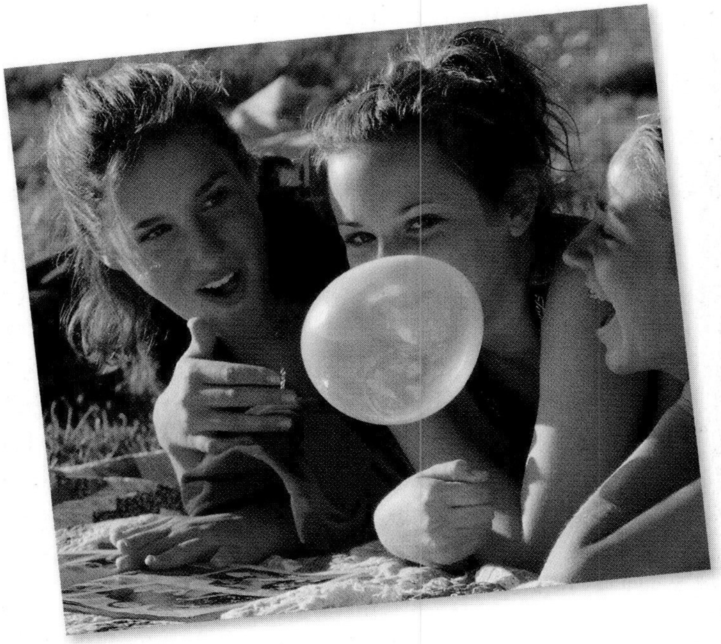

5. During the first 20 minutes of lunch, 5 male students, 7 female students, and 3 teachers went through the lunch line. What is the experimental probability that the next person through the line will be a teacher?

11-5 Probability of Independent and Dependent Events

Learn to find the probability of independent and dependent events.

Vocabulary

independent events

dependent events

Raji and Kara must each choose a topic from a list of topics to research for their class. If Raji's choice has no effect on Kara's choice and vice versa, the events are *independent.* For **independent events**, the occurrence of one event has no effect on the probability that a second event will occur.

If once Raji chooses a topic, Kara must choose from the remaining topics, then the events are *dependent.* For **dependent events**, the occurrence of one event *does* have an effect on the probability that a second event will occur.

EXAMPLE 1 Determining Whether Events Are Independent or Dependent

Decide whether each set of events is independent or dependent. Explain your answer.

A **Erika rolls a 3 on one number cube and a 2 on another number cube.**

Since the outcome of rolling one number cube does not affect the outcome of rolling the second number cube, the events are independent.

B **Tomoko chooses a seventh-grader for her team from a group of seventh- and eighth-graders, and then Juan chooses a different seventh-grader from the remaining students.**

Since Juan cannot pick the same student that Tomoko picked, and since there are fewer students for Juan to choose from after Tomoko chooses, the events are dependent.

To find the probability that two independent events will happen, multiply the probabilities of the two events.

Probability of Two Independent Events

$$P(A \text{ and } B) = P(A) \cdot P(B)$$

Probability of both events — *Probability of first event* — *Probability of second event*

EXAMPLE 2 Finding the Probability of Independent Events

Find the probability of flipping a coin and getting heads and then rolling a 6 on a number cube.

The outcome of flipping the coin does not affect the outcome of rolling the number cube, so the events are independent.

$P(\text{heads and } 6) = P(\text{heads}) \cdot P(6)$

$= \frac{1}{2} \cdot \frac{1}{6}$ *There are 2 ways a coin can land and 6 ways a number cube can land.*

$= \frac{1}{12}$ *Multiply.*

The probability of getting heads and a 6 is $\frac{1}{12}$.

To find the probability of two dependent events, you must determine the effect that the first event has on the probability of the second event.

Probability of Two Dependent Events

$$P(A \text{ and } B) = P(A) \cdot P(B \text{ after } A)$$

Probability of both events — *Probability of first event* — *Probability of second event given that A has occurred*

EXAMPLE 3 Finding the Probability of Dependent Events

Mica has five \$1 bills, three \$10 bills, and two \$20 bills in her wallet. She picks two bills at random. What is the probability of her picking the two \$20 bills?

The first draw changes the number of bills left, and may change the number of \$20 bills left, so the events are dependent.

$P(\text{first } \$20) = \frac{2}{10} = \frac{1}{5}$ *There are two \$20 bills out of ten bills.*

$P(\text{second } \$20) = \frac{1}{9}$ *There is one \$20 bill left out of nine bills.*

$P(\text{first } \$20\text{, then second } \$20) = P(A) \cdot P(B \text{ after } A)$

$= \frac{1}{5} \cdot \frac{1}{9}$

$= \frac{1}{45}$ *Multiply.*

The probability of Mica picking two \$20 bills is $\frac{1}{45}$.

Think and Discuss

1. **Compare** probabilities of independent and dependent events.
2. **Explain** whether the probability of two events is greater than or less than the probability of each individual event.

11-5 Exercises

go.hrw.com
Homework Help Online
KEYWORD: MS7 11-5
Parent Resources Online
KEYWORD: MS7 Parent

GUIDED PRACTICE

See Example 1 **Decide whether each set of events is independent or dependent. Explain your answer.**

1. A student flips heads on one coin and tails on a second coin.

2. A student chooses a red marble from a bag of marbles and then chooses another red marble without replacing the first.

See Example 2 **Find the probability of each set of independent events.**

3. a flipped coin landing heads up and rolling a 5 or a 6 on a number cube

4. drawing a 5 from 10 cards numbered 1 through 10 and rolling a 2 on a number cube

See Example 3

5. Each day, Mr. Samms randomly chooses 2 students from his class to serve as helpers. There are 15 boys and 10 girls in the class. What is the probability that Mr. Samms will choose 2 girls to be helpers?

INDEPENDENT PRACTICE

See Example 1 **Decide whether each set of events is independent or dependent. Explain your answer.**

6. A student chooses a fiction book at random from a list of books and then chooses a second fiction book from those remaining.

7. A woman chooses a lily from one bunch of flowers and then chooses a tulip from a different bunch.

See Example 2 **Find the probability of each set of independent events.**

8. drawing a red marble from a bag of 6 red and 4 blue marbles, replacing it, and then drawing a blue marble

9. rolling an even number on a number cube and rolling an odd number on a second roll of the same cube

See Example 3

10. Francisco has 7 quarters in his pocket. Of these, 3 depict the state of Delaware, 2 depict Georgia, 1 depicts Connecticut, and 1 depicts Pennsylvania. Francisco removes 1 quarter from his pocket and then removes a second quarter without replacing the first. What is the probability that both will be Delaware quarters?

PRACTICE AND PROBLEM SOLVING

Extra Practice
See page 749.

11. An even number is chosen randomly from a set of cards labeled with the numbers 1 through 8. A second even number is chosen without the first card being replaced. Are these independent or dependent events? What is the probability of both events occurring?

12. On a multiple-choice test, each question has five possible answers. A student does not know the answers to two questions, so he guesses. What is the probability that the student will get both answers wrong?

13. **Business** The graph shows the dogs bathed at a dog-grooming business one day. What is the probability that the first two dogs bathed were large dogs?

14. **Write a Problem** Describe two events that are either independent or dependent, and make up a probability problem about them.

15. **Write About It** At the beginning of a game of Scrabble, players take turns drawing 7 tiles. Are drawing *A*'s on the first two tiles dependent or independent events? Explain.

16. **Challenge** Weather forecasters have accurately predicted rain in one community $\frac{4}{5}$ of the time. What is the probability that they will accurately predict rain two days in a row?

TEST PREP and Spiral Review

17. **Multiple Choice** A bag contains 5 red marbles and 5 purple marbles. What is the probability of drawing a red marble and then a purple marble, without replacing the first marble before drawing the second marble?

Ⓐ $\frac{2}{9}$ Ⓑ $\frac{5}{18}$ Ⓒ $\frac{1}{3}$ Ⓓ $\frac{1}{2}$

18. **Short Response** José has 3 brown socks, 5 blue socks, and 6 black socks in his sock drawer. He picked one sock and then another sock out of the drawer. Are the events independent or dependent? Explain your answer. What is the probability that he will pick 2 black socks?

19. Fritz jogged $1\frac{3}{4}$ mi on Monday, $2\frac{1}{2}$ mi on Wednesday, and 3 mi on Friday. How many miles did he jog altogether on these days? (Lesson 3-9)

Given the radius or diameter, find the circumference and area of each circle to the nearest tenth. Use 3.14 for π. (Lessons 9-2 and 9-5)

20. $r = 6.5$ in. 21. $d = 15.7$ ft 22. $r = 7$ cm

11-6 Combinations

Learn to find the number of possible combinations.

Vocabulary

combination

Mrs. Logan's students have to read any two of the following books.

1. *The Adventures of Tom Sawyer,* by Mark Twain
2. *The Call of the Wild,* by Jack London
3. *A Christmas Carol,* by Charles Dickens
4. *Treasure Island,* by Robert Louis Stevenson
5. *Tuck Everlasting,* by Natalie Babbit

How many possible *combinations* of books could the students choose?

A **combination** is a grouping of objects or events in which the order does not matter. For example, a student can choose books 1 and 2 or books 2 and 1. Since the order does not matter, the two arrangements represent the same combination. One way to find all possible combinations is to make a table.

EXAMPLE 1 Using a Table to Find Combinations

How many different combinations of two books are possible from Mrs. Logan's list of five books?

Begin by making a table showing all of the possible groupings of books taken two at a time.

	1	2	3	4	5
1		1, 2	1, 3	1, 4	1, 5
2	2, 1		2, 3	2, 4	2, 5
3	3, 1	3, 2		3, 4	3, 5
4	4, 1	4, 2	4, 3		4, 5
5	5, 1	5, 2	5, 3	5, 4	

Because order does not matter, you can eliminate repeated pairs. For example, 1, 2 is already listed, so 2, 1 can be eliminated.

	1	2	3	4	5
1		1, 2	1, 3	1, 4	1, 5
2	~~2, 1~~		2, 3	2, 4	2, 5
3	~~3, 1~~	~~3, 2~~		3, 4	3, 5
4	~~4, 1~~	~~4, 2~~	~~4, 3~~		4, 5
5	~~5, 1~~	~~5, 2~~	~~5, 3~~	~~5, 4~~	

There are 10 different combinations of two books on Mrs. Logan's list of five books.

You can also use a tree diagram to find possible combinations.

EXAMPLE 2 PROBLEM SOLVING APPLICATION

PROBLEM SOLVING

As a caterer, Cuong offers four vegetable choices: broccoli, squash, peas, and carrots. Each person can choose two vegetables. How many different combinations of two vegetables can a person choose?

1 Understand the Problem

Rewrite the question as a statement.

- Find the number of possible combinations of two vegetables a person can choose.

List the **important information:**

- There are four vegetable choices in all.

2 Make a Plan

You can make a tree diagram to show the possible combinations.

3 Solve

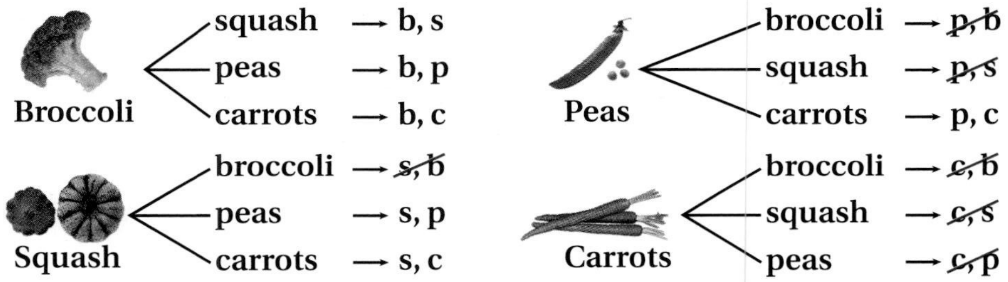

The tree diagram shows 12 possible ways to combine two vegetables, but each combination is listed twice. So there are $12 \div 2 = 6$ possible combinations.

4 Look Back

You can check by making a table. The broccoli can be paired with three other vegetables, squash with two, and peas with one. The total number of possible pairs is $3 + 2 + 1 = 6$.

Think and Discuss

1. **Describe** how to use a tree diagram to find the number of combinations in Example 1.
2. **Describe** how combinations could help you find the probability of an event.

11-6 Exercises

go.hrw.com
Homework Help Online
KEYWORD: MS7 11-6
Parent Resources Online
KEYWORD: MS7 Parent

GUIDED PRACTICE

See Example 1

1. If you have an apple, a pear, an orange, and a plum, how many combinations of 2 fruits are possible?
2. How many 3-letter combinations are possible from *A, E, I, O,* and *U*?

See Example 2

3. Robin packs 2 jars of jam in a gift box. She has 5 flavors: blueberry, apricot, grape, peach, and orange marmalade. How many different combinations of 2 jars can she pack in a box?
4. Eduardo has 6 colors of fabric: red, blue, green, yellow, orange, and white. He plans to make flags using 2 colors. How many possible combinations of 2 colors can he choose?

INDEPENDENT PRACTICE

See Example 1

5. A restaurant allows you to "build your own burger" using a choice of any 2 toppings. The available toppings are bacon, grilled onions, sautéed mushrooms, Swiss cheese, and cheddar cheese. How many burgers with 2 different toppings could you build?
6. Jamil has to do reports on 3 cities. He can choose from Paris, New York, Moscow, and London. How many different combinations of cities are possible?

See Example 2

7. A florist can choose from 6 different types of flowers to make a bouquet: carnations, roses, lilies, daisies, irises, and tulips. How many different combinations of 2 types of flowers can he choose?
8. How many different 2-member tennis teams can be made from 7 students?

PRACTICE AND PROBLEM SOLVING

Extra Practice
See page 749.

9. At Camp Allen, campers can choose 2 out of 8 free-time activities. Use the chart to find the number of possible combinations of 2 activities.

Free-Time Activities	
hiking	volleyball
mosaics	rafting
tennis	pottery
painting	swimming

10. Rob, Caryn, and Sari are pairing up to play a series of chess matches. In how many different ways can they pair up?
11. Gary has to write biographies about 2 historical figures. He can choose from Winston Churchill, Dr. Martin Luther King, Jr., and Nelson Mandela. How many different combinations of 2 biographies can Gary write?
12. Trina wants to select 3 of Ansel Adams's 5 "surf sequence" photos to hang on her wall. How many possible combinations are there?

Art LINK

13. Ms. Frennelle is teaching her art history class about famous impressionist painters. She asks her students to choose 2 artists from among Renoir, Monet, Manet, Degas, Pissarro, and Cassatt, and to find information about at least one painting made by each artist. How many possible pairs of artists can be chosen from the six painters?

The White Water Lilies, 1899, by Claude Monet

Woman with a Pearl Necklace in a Loge, 1879, by Mary Cassatt

14. **Multi-Step** The graph shows the number of paintings by artists of different nationalities displayed in an art book. In how many ways can you combine 4 paintings by Chinese artists?

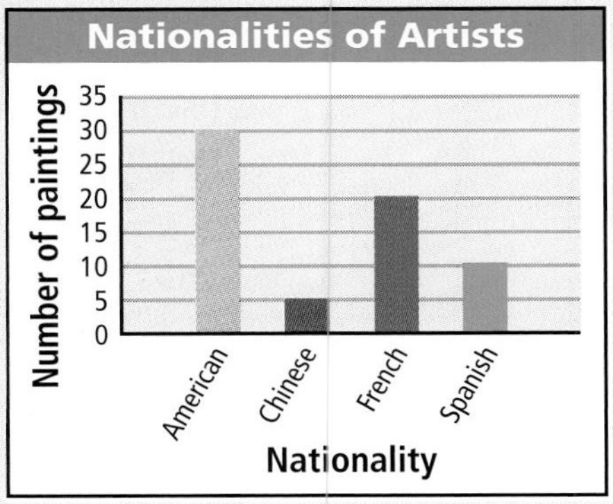

15. **Challenge** A gallery is preparing a show by a new artist. The gallery has enough space to display 7 pieces of art. The artist has prepared 4 paintings and 5 sculptures. How many distinct combinations of the artist's works are possible?

go.hrw.com
Web Extra!
KEYWORD: MS7 Art

TEST PREP and Spiral Review

16. **Multiple Choice** How many different 2-person teams can be made from 5 people?

Ⓐ 10 Ⓑ 20 Ⓒ 24 Ⓓ 36

17. **Gridded Response** How many 2-letter combinations are possible from the letters *A, B, C, D, E,* and *F*?

Estimate each square root to the nearest whole number. (Lesson 9-7)

18. $\sqrt{76}$ 19. $\sqrt{31}$ 20. $\sqrt{126}$ 21. $\sqrt{55}$

Decide whether each set of events is independent or dependent. Explain your answer. (Lesson 11-5)

22. A student is chosen at random from a list. A second student is chosen from the same list.

23. A girl chooses a piece of fruit from one bin. A boy then chooses a piece of fruit from a different bin.

11-7 Permutations

Learn **to find the number of possible permutations.**

Vocabulary
permutation
factorial

The conductor of a symphony orchestra is planning a concert titled "An Evening with the Killer B's." The concert will feature music by Bach, Beethoven, Brahms, and Bartok. In how many different orders can the conductor arrange the music of the four composers?

An arrangement of objects or events in which the order is important is called a **permutation**. You can use a list to find the number of permutations of a group of objects.

EXAMPLE 1 Using a List to Find Permutations

In how many different orders can the conductor arrange the music composed by Bach, Beethoven, Brahms, and Bartok?

Use a list to find the possible permutations.

Let 1 = Bach, 2 = Beethoven, 3 = Brahms, and 4 = Bartok.

1-2-3-4 1-2-4-3 1-3-2-4 1-3-4-2 1-4-2-3 1-4-3-2	*List all permutations beginning with 1.*	2-1-3-4 2-1-4-3 2-3-1-4 2-3-4-1 2-4-1-3 2-4-3-1	*List all permutations beginning with 2.*
3-1-2-4 3-1-4-2 3-2-1-4 3-2-4-1 3-4-1-2 3-4-2-1	*List all permutations beginning with 3.*	4-1-2-3 4-1-3-2 4-2-1-3 4-2-3-1 4-3-1-2 4-3-2-1	*List all permutations beginning with 4.*

There are 24 permutations. Therefore, the conductor can arrange the music by the four composers in 24 different orders.

You can use the Fundamental Counting Principle to find the number of permutations.

EXAMPLE 2 Using the Fundamental Counting Principle to Find the Number of Permutations

Remember!

The Fundamental Counting Principle states that you can find the total number of outcomes by multiplying the number of outcomes for each separate experiment.

Three students have agreed to serve in leadership positions for the Spanish Club. In how many different ways can the students fill the positions of president, vice-president, and secretary?

Once you fill a position, you have one less choice for the next position.

There are 3 choices for the first position.
There are 2 remaining choices for the second position.
There is 1 remaining choice for the third position.

$3 \cdot 2 \cdot 1 = 6$ *Multiply.*

There are 6 different ways that 3 students can fill the 3 positons.

A **factorial** of a whole number is the product of all the whole numbers except zero that are less than or equal to the number.

"3 factorial" is $3! = 3 \cdot 2 \cdot 1 = 6$

"6 factorial" is $6! = 6 \cdot 5 \cdot 4 \cdot 3 \cdot 2 \cdot 1 = 720$

You can use factorials to find the number of permutations.

EXAMPLE 3 Using Factorials to Find the Number of Permutations

Helpful Hint

You can use a calculator to find the factorial of a number. To find 5!, press 5 MATH PRB 4:! ENTER ENTER.

There are 9 players in a baseball lineup. How many different batting orders are possible for these 9 players?

Number of permutations $= 9!$

$= 9 \cdot 8 \cdot 7 \cdot 6 \cdot 5 \cdot 4 \cdot 3 \cdot 2 \cdot 1$

$= 362{,}880$

There are 362,880 different batting orders for 9 players.

Think and Discuss

1. **Evaluate** how the permutations are listed in Example 1. Why is it important to follow a pattern?
2. **Explain** why 8! gives the number of permutations of 8 objects.

11-7 Exercises

go.hrw.com
Homework Help Online
KEYWORD: MS7 11-7
Parent Resources Online
KEYWORD: MS7 Parent

GUIDED PRACTICE

See Example 1

1. In how many ways can you arrange the numbers 1, 2, 3, and 4 to make a 4-digit number?

See Example 2

2. Find the number of permutations of the letters in the word *quiet.*

See Example 3

3. Sam wants to call 6 friends to invite them to a party. In how many different orders can he make the calls?
4. Seven people are waiting to audition for a play. In how many different orders can the auditions be done?

INDEPENDENT PRACTICE

See Example 1

5. In how many ways can Eric, Meera, and Roger stand in line?

See Example 2

6. Find the number of ways you can arrange the letters in the word *art.*

See Example 3

7. How many permutations of the letters *A* through *J* are there?
8. In how many different ways can 8 riders be matched up with 8 horses?

PRACTICE AND PROBLEM SOLVING

Extra Practice
See page 749.

Determine whether each problem involves combinations or permutations. Explain your answer.

9. Choose five books to check out from a group of ten.
10. Decide how many ways five people can be assigned to sit in five chairs.
11. Choose a 4-digit PIN using all of the digits 3, 7, 1, and 8.
12. **Sports** Ten golfers on a team are playing in a tournament. How many different lineups can the golf coach make?
13. Carl, Melba, Sean, and Ricki are going to present individual reports in their Spanish class. Their teacher randomly selects which student will speak first. What is the probability that Melba will present her report first?
14. Using the digits 1 through 7, Pima County is assigning new 7-digit numbers to all households. How many possible numbers can the county assign without repeating any of the digits in a number?
15. How many different 5-digit numbers can be made using the digits 6, 3, 5, 0, and 4 without repetitions?
16. In how many different orders can 12 songs on a CD be played?
17. **Multi-Step** If you have 5 items, and you can fit 3 of them on a shelf, how many choices do you have for the first item on the shelf? for the second item? for the third item? How many different orders are possible for the 3 items chosen from 5 items?

18. **Health** A survey was taken to find out how 200 people age 40 and older rate their memory now compared to 10 years ago. In how many different orders could interviews be conducted with people who think their memory is the same?

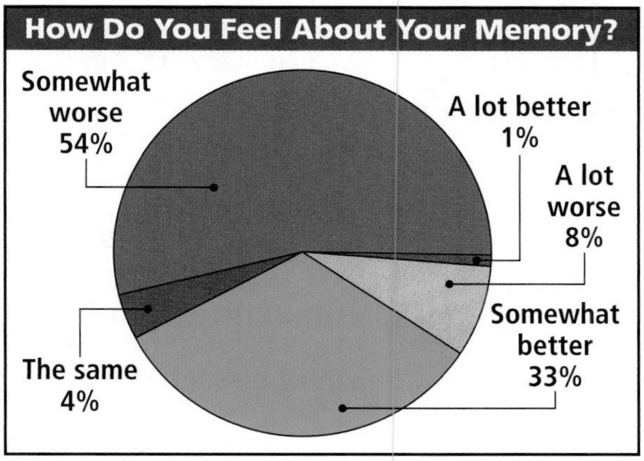

LINK — Literature

Since its initial publication in 1868, *Little Women*, by Louisa May Alcott, has never been out of print. It has been translated into at least 27 languages.

go.hrw.com
Web Extra!
KEYWORD: MS7 Alcott

19. **Literature** The school library has 13 books by Louisa May Alcott. Merina wants to read all 13 of them one after another. Write an expression to show the number of ways she can do that.

20. Use the letters *A, D, E, R.*
   a. How many permutations of the letters are there?
   b. How many arrangements form English words?

21. Josie and Luke have 3 sunflowers and 4 bluebonnets. Josie selects a flower at random. Then Luke chooses a flower at random from the remaining flowers. What is the probability that Josie picks a sunflower and Luke chooses a bluebonnet?

22. **What's the Error?** A student was trying to find 5! and wrote the equation $5 + 4 + 3 + 2 + 1 = 15$. Why is this student incorrect?

23. **Write About It** Explain the difference between combinations of objects and permutations of objects. Give examples of each.

24. **Challenge** Evaluate $\frac{11!}{3!(11-3)!}$.

Test Prep and Spiral Review

25. **Multiple Choice** Which expression can you use to find the number of 5-digit passwords you can make using the digits 1, 3, 5, 7, and 9, if you do not repeat any of the digits?

   (A) $9 + 7 + 5 + 3 + 1$
   (B) $9 \cdot 7 \cdot 5 \cdot 3 \cdot 1$
   (C) $5 + 4 + 3 + 2 + 1$
   (D) $5 \cdot 4 \cdot 3 \cdot 2 \cdot 1$

26. **Gridded Response** A school play has seven different characters. In how many different ways can seven students be assigned to the roles?

27. Use the Pythagorean Theorem to find the missing measure in the triangle at right. Round to the nearest tenth. (Lesson 9-8)

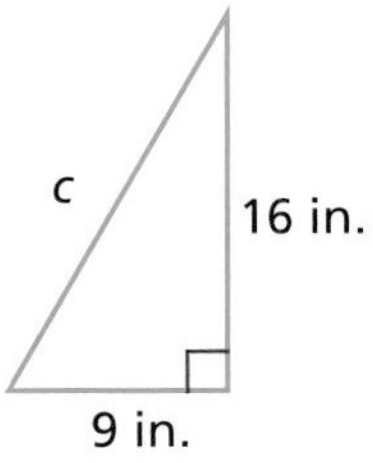

28. Margaret is traveling. She can bring two of her 9 favorite books with her. How many different combinations of 2 books can she bring? (Lesson 11-6)

READY TO GO ON?

Quiz for Lessons 11-5 Through 11-7

11-5 Probability of Independent and Dependent Events

Decide whether each set of events is independent or dependent. Explain.

1. Winny rolls two number cubes and gets a 5 on one and a 3 on the other.
2. A card with hearts is drawn from a full deck of cards and not replaced. Then a card with clubs is drawn from the same deck.

A bag contains 8 blue and 7 yellow marbles. Use this information for Exercises 3 and 4.

3. Find the probability of randomly drawing a blue marble and then randomly drawing a yellow marble without replacing the first marble.
4. Find the probability of randomly drawing a blue marble and then randomly drawing another blue marble after replacing the first marble.

5. Marcelo has six \$1 bills, two \$5 bills, and one \$10 bill in his pocket. He selects two of the bills at random. What is the probability that Marcelo picks one \$5 bill and the \$10 bill?

11-6 Combinations

6. Kenny wants the guests to have 2 juice options at his party. There are 8 different juices that he has to choose from. How many different ways can Kenny choose 2 different juices?
7. Find the number of different ways that 2 out of 12 students can volunteer to organize a class party.
8. A restaurant offers entrees with a choice of 2 side dishes. How many combinations of 2 sides are available from a list of 9 side dishes?

11-7 Permutations

9. Four swimmers are chosen to swim in a relay race. How many orders of the 4 swimmers are possible for the relay race?
10. Six students have volunteered to help with the Spring Fest. In how many ways can these six students be assigned the following positions: concession stand, dunking booth, face-painting booth, fishing pond, ring toss, and haystack hunt?
11. Employees on the second floor have been given five 1-digit numbers from which to create a 5-digit passcode to unlock a color copier. From how many different passcodes can they choose if the passcode cannot have repeated numbers?

MULTI-STEP TEST PREP

The Life of the Party Chantal has a party-planning business. She organizes, caters, and runs parties. Chantal sometimes uses probability when planning party activities.

1. Chantal often prepares a Prize Walk for her parties. Guests walk along a circular path with spaces numbered 1 through 24, and Chantal randomly calls out one of the numbers. If someone is standing on that number, he or she wins a prize. What is the probability that someone will win a prize if 8 people are playing? if 10 people are playing?
2. How many people must play the Prize Walk so that the probability of someone winning a prize is at least 0.75?
3. Chantal plans to play two rounds of the Prize Walk at an upcoming party. All 24 guests will participate in both rounds. Chantal is concerned that the same person will win both times. How likely is this? Is the probability greater than or less than 1%? Explain.
4. Chantal will bring six different prizes to the party. How many different combinations of two prizes can be chosen by the Prize Walk winners?
5. Chantal gives away T-shirts at her parties to advertise her business. Use the table to find how many different styles of T-shirts are available.

T-Shirt Options	
Sizes	S, M, L, XL
Colors	Blue, white, red
Sleeves	Long, short

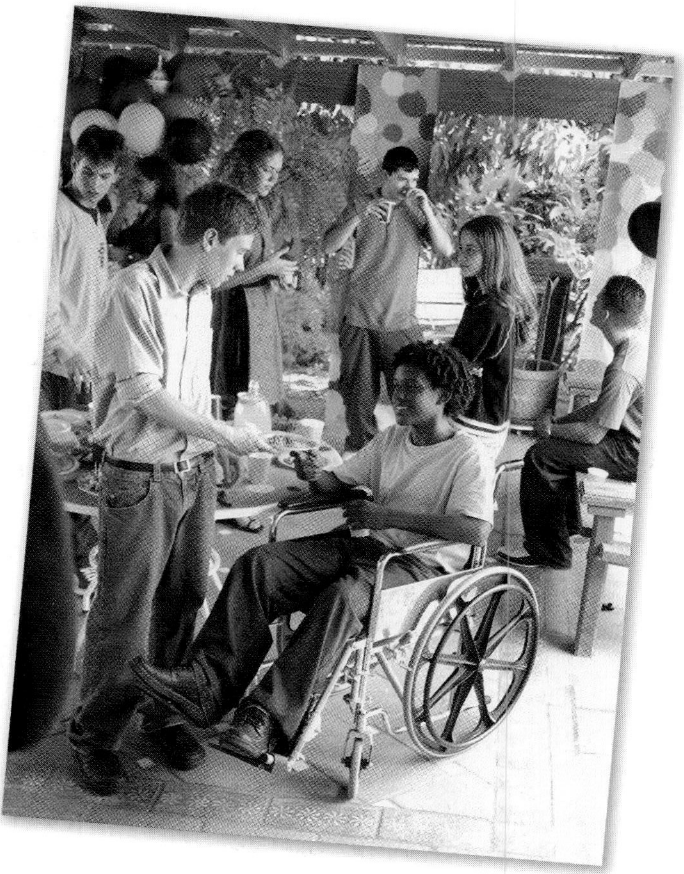

Game Time

Buffon's Needle

If you drop a needle of a given length onto a wooden floor with evenly spaced cracks, what is the probability that it will land across a crack?

Compte de Buffon (1707–1788) posed this geometric probability problem. To answer his question, Buffon developed a formula using ℓ to represent the length of the needle and d to represent the distance between the cracks.

$$\text{probability} = \frac{2\ell}{\pi d}$$

To re-create this experiment, you need a paper clip and several evenly spaced lines drawn on a piece of paper. Make sure that the distance between the lines is greater than the length of the paper clip. Toss the paper clip onto the piece of paper at least a dozen times. Divide the number of times the paper clip lands across a line by the number of times you toss the paper clip. Compare this quotient to the probability given by the formula.

The other interesting result of Buffon's discovery is that you can use the probability of the needle toss to estimate *pi*.

$$\pi = \frac{2\ell}{\text{probability} \cdot d}$$

Toss the paper clip 20 times to find the experimental probability. Use this probability in the formula above, and compare the result to 3.14.

Pattern Match

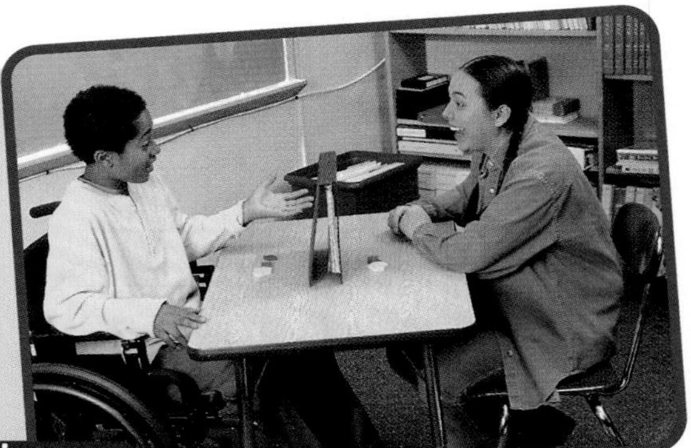

This game is for two players. Player A arranges four different pattern blocks in a row out of the view of player B. Player B then tries to guess the arrangement. After each guess, player A reveals how many of the blocks are in the correct position without telling which blocks they are. The round ends when player B correctly guesses the arrangement.

A complete set of game pieces are available online.

go.hrw.com
Game Time Extra
KEYWORD: MS7 Games

It's in the Bag!

FOLDNOTES

Materials
- card stock
- ruler
- scissors
- tape
- business cards

PROJECT The Business of Probability

Make a holder for business cards. Then use the business cards to take notes on probability.

1. Cut a piece of card stock to $7\frac{1}{2}$ inches by $4\frac{1}{2}$ inches. Fold the card stock in thirds and then unfold it. **Figure A**

2. Cut out a trapezoid that is about $\frac{1}{2}$-inch tall from one end of the card stock as shown. **Figure B**

3. Cut off about $\frac{1}{2}$ inch along the other end of the card stock. Then cut the corners at an angle. **Figure C**

4. Fold up the bottom section of the card stock and tape the edges closed. **Figure D**

A
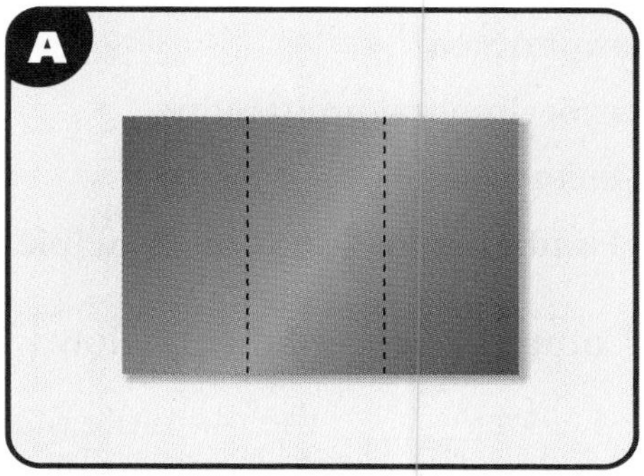

B
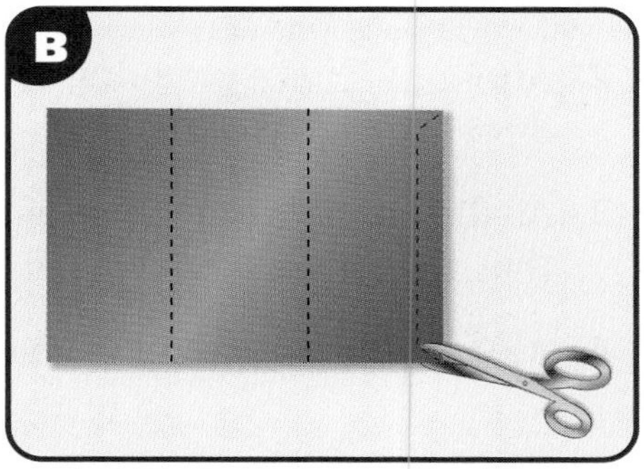

C
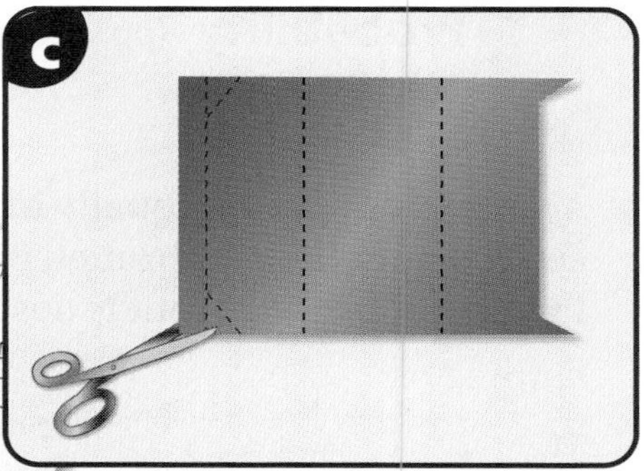

D
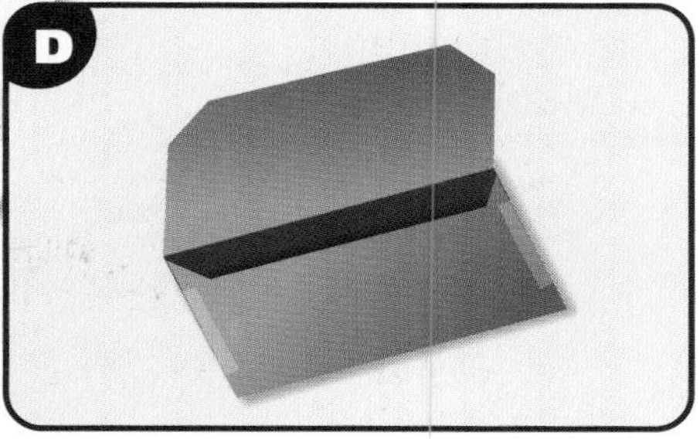

Taking Note of the Math

Use the backs of business cards to take notes on probability. Store the business cards in the holder that you made. Write the name and number of the chapter on the flap of the holder.

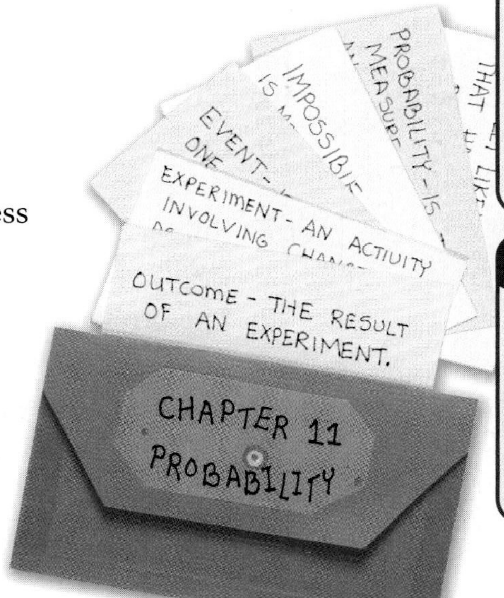

CHAPTER 11

Study Guide: Review

Study Guide: Review

Vocabulary

Complete the sentences below with vocabulary words from the list above.

1. For ___?___, the outcome of one event has no effect on the outcome of a second event.
2. A(n) ___?___ is a grouping of objects or events in which order does not matter.
3. All the possible outcomes of an experiment make up the ___?___.
4. A(n) ___?___ is a result of an experiment.

11-1 Probability (pp. 628–631)

EXAMPLE

■ **A spinner is divided equally into 8 sectors numbered 1 through 8. The likelihood of each event is described.**

landing on:	
0	impossible
5	unlikely
an even number	as likely as not
a number less than 7	likely
100	impossible

EXERCISES

Determine whether each event is impossible, unlikely, as likely as not, likely, or certain.

5. rolling a sum of 12 with two number cubes
6. rolling a sum of 24 with two number cubes
7. The probability of rain is 20%. What is the probability of no rain?
8. The probability of the football team winning its last game is $\frac{1}{5}$. What is the probability of the team not winning the last game?

11-2 Experimental Probability (pp. 632–635)

EXAMPLE

- **Of 50 people surveyed, 21 said they liked mysteries better than comedies. What is the probability that the next person surveyed will prefer mysteries?**

$P(\text{mysteries}) = \dfrac{\text{number who like mysteries}}{\text{total number surveyed}}$

$P(\text{mysteries}) = \dfrac{21}{50}$

The probability that the next person surveyed will prefer mysteries is $\frac{21}{50}$.

EXERCISES

Sami has been keeping a record of her math grades. Of her first 15 grades, 10 have been above 82.

9. What is the probability that her next grade will be above 82?

10. What is the probability that her next grade will not be above 82?

11-3 Make a List to Find Sample Spaces (pp. 636–639)

EXAMPLE

- **Anita tosses a coin and rolls a number cube. How many outcomes are possible?**

The coin has 2 outcomes. The number cube has 6 outcomes. *List the number of outcomes.*

$2 \cdot 6 = 12$ *Use the Fundamental Counting Principle.*

There are 12 possible outcomes.

EXERCISES

Chen spins each of the spinners once.

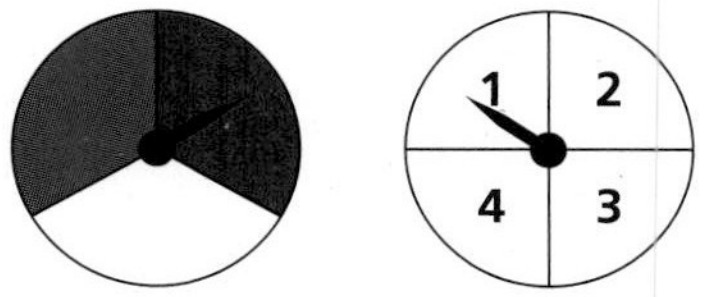

11. What are all the possible outcomes?

12. How many outcomes are in the sample space?

11-4 Theoretical Probability (pp. 640–643)

EXAMPLE

- **Find the probability of drawing a 4 from a standard deck of 52 playing cards. Write your answer as a fraction, as a decimal, and as a percent.**

$$P(4) = \frac{\text{number of 4's in deck}}{\text{number of cards in deck}}$$
$$= \frac{4}{52}$$
$$= \frac{1}{13}$$
$$\approx 0.077 \approx 7.7\%$$

EXERCISES

Find each probability. Write your answer as a fraction, as a decimal, and as a percent.

13. There are 9 girls and 12 boys on the student council. What is the probability that a girl will be chosen as president?

14. Anita tosses 3 coins. What is the probability that each coin will land tails up?

15. Jefferson chooses a marble from a bag containing 6 blue, 9 white, 3 orange, and 11 green marbles. What is the probability that he will select a green marble?

11-5 Probability of Independent and Dependent Events (pp. 648–651)

EXAMPLE

■ **There are 4 red marbles, 3 green marbles, 6 blue marbles, and 2 black marbles in a bag. What is the probability that Angie will pick a green marble and then a black marble without replacing the first marble?**

$P(\text{green marble}) = \frac{3}{15} = \frac{1}{5}$

$P(\text{black after green}) = \frac{2}{14} = \frac{1}{7}$

$P(\text{green, then black}) = \frac{1}{5} \cdot \frac{1}{7} = \frac{1}{35}$

The probability of picking a green marble and then a black marble with no replacement is $\frac{1}{35}$.

EXERCISES

16. There are 40 tags numbered 1 through 40 in a bag. What is the probability that Glenn will randomly pick a multiple of 5 and then a multiple of 9 without replacing the first tag?

17. Each letter of the word *probability* is written on a card and put in a bag. What is the probability of picking a vowel on the first try and again on the second try if the first card is replaced?

11-6 Combinations (pp. 652–655)

EXAMPLE

■ **Tina, Sam, and Jo are trying out for the 2 lead parts in a play. In how many ways can they be chosen for the parts?**

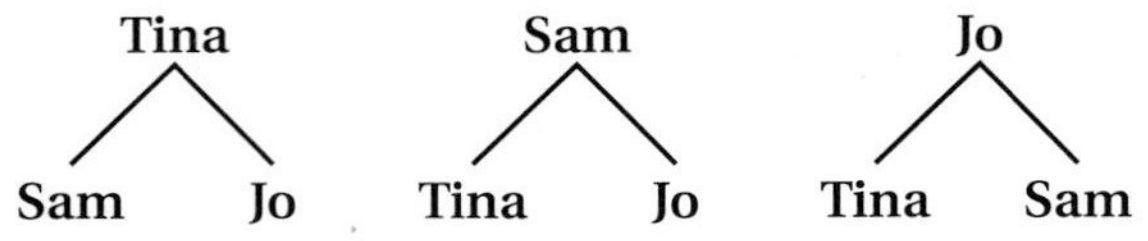

There are 6 possible ways the students can be chosen for the parts.

EXERCISES

18. How many ways can you select 2 pieces of fruit from a basket of 5 pieces?

19. How many 2-person groups can be chosen from 7 people?

20. How many combinations of 2 balloons can be chosen from 9 balloons?

11-7 Permutations (pp. 656–659)

EXAMPLE

■ **How many different four-digit numbers can you make from the numbers 2, 4, 6, and 8 using each just once?**

There are 4 choices for the first digit, 3 choices for the second, 2 choices for the third, and 1 for the fourth.

$4 \cdot 3 \cdot 2 \cdot 1 = 24$

There are 24 different four-digit numbers.

EXERCISES

21. How many different batting orders are possible for 10 players on a league softball team?

22. How many different ways can you arrange the letters in the word *number*?

23. In how many ways can Tanya, Rika, Andy, Evan, and Tanisha line up for lunch?

CHAPTER TEST

A box contains 3 orange cubes, 2 white cubes, 3 black cubes, and 4 blue cubes. Determine whether each event is impossible, unlikely, as likely as not, likely, or certain.

1. randomly choosing an orange or black cube
2. randomly choosing a white cube
3. randomly choosing a purple cube
4. Simon tosses a coin 20 times. The coin lands heads up 7 times. Based on these results, how many times can Simon expect the coin to land heads up in the next 100 tosses?
5. Emilio spins a spinner that is divided into 8 equal sectors numbered 1 through 8. In his first three spins, the spinner lands on 8. What is the experimental probability that Emilio will spin a 10 on his fourth spin?
6. A brand of jeans comes in 8 different waist sizes: 28, 30, 32, 34, 36, 38, 40, and 42. The jeans also come in three different colors: blue, black, and tan. How many different combinations of waist sizes and colors are possible?
7. Greg is planning his vacation. He can choose from 3 ways to travel—train, bus, or plane—and four different activities—skiing, skating, snowboarding, or hiking. What are all the possible outcomes? How many different vacations can Greg plan?

Rachel spins a spinner that is divided into 10 equal sectors numbered 1 through 10. Find each probability. Write your answer as a fraction, as a decimal, and as a percent.

8. P(odd number)
9. P(composite number)
10. P(number greater than 10)

Find the probability of each event.

11. spinning red on a spinner with equally sized red, blue, yellow, and green sectors, and flipping a coin that lands tails up
12. choosing a card labeled *vanilla* from a group of cards labeled *vanilla, chocolate, strawberry,* and *swirl,* and then choosing a card labeled *chocolate* without replacing the first card
13. How many ways can 2 students be chosen from 10 students?
14. How many ways can you choose 2 different snacks from a menu of raisins, oranges, yogurt, apples, crackers, nuts, and grapes?
15. Timothy wants to arrange his 6 model cars on a shelf. How many ways can he arrange them?
16. How many ways can you choose a 7-letter password from 7 different letters if the letters cannot repeat?

TEST TACKLER

Standardized Test Strategies

All Types: Use a Diagram

Sometimes drawing a diagram helps you solve a problem. When a diagram is given with a test item, use it as a tool. Get as much information from the drawing as possible. Keep in mind that diagrams are not always drawn to scale and can be misleading.

EXAMPLE 1

Multiple Choice What is the probability of flipping a coin and getting tails, and then rolling an even number on a number cube?

Ⓐ $\frac{1}{2}$ Ⓒ $\frac{1}{6}$

Ⓑ $\frac{1}{4}$ Ⓓ $\frac{1}{12}$

You can create a tree diagram to determine the sample space.

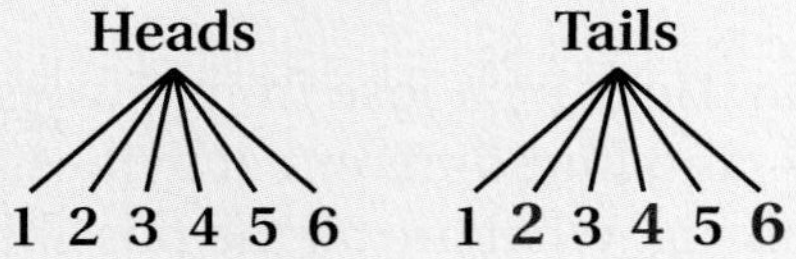

There are 12 possible outcomes but only 3 ways getting tails and an even number can occur. So the probability is $\frac{3}{12}$, or $\frac{1}{4}$, which is answer choice B.

EXAMPLE 2

Short Response Find the volume and surface area of the cylinder, and round your answers to the nearest tenth. Use 3.14 for π.

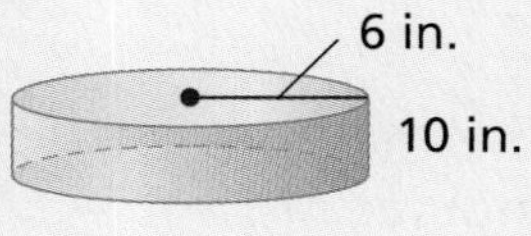

In the diagram, it appears that the radius is greater than the height. Remember that the scale of a diagram can be misleading. Rely on the information shown, and substitute the given values into each formula.

$V = \pi r^2 h$ $SA = 2\pi r^2 + 2\pi rh$

$V = \pi(6)^2(10)$ $SA = 2\pi(6)^2 + 2\pi(6)(10)$

$V = 360\pi$ $SA = 226.08 + 376.8$

$V \approx 1{,}130.4 \text{ in}^3$ $SA \approx 602.9 \text{ in}^2$

HOT TIP! If you are having trouble understanding a test item, draw a diagram to help you answer the question.

Read each test item, and answer the questions that follow.

Item A
Multiple Choice The volume of a box is 6,336 cm^3. The width of the box is 16 cm, and the height is 18 cm. What is the length of the box?

Ⓐ 396 cm
Ⓒ 220 cm
Ⓑ 22 cm
Ⓓ 11 cm

1. What information about the box is given in the problem statement?
2. Sketch a diagram to help you answer the question. Label each side with the correct dimensions.
3. How does the diagram help you solve the problem?

Item B
Multiple Choice Janet spins two spinners at the same time. One spinner is divided into 3 equal sectors, labeled 1, 2, and 3. The second spinner is divided into 3 equal sectors, labeled A, B, and C. What is the probability that the spinners will land on 1 and A or 1 and C?

Ⓕ $\frac{1}{3}$
Ⓗ $\frac{1}{9}$
Ⓖ $\frac{2}{3}$
Ⓙ $\frac{2}{9}$

4. Make a tree diagram to determine the sample space. Then count the ways getting 1 and either A or C can occur.
5. Explain which answer choice is correct.
6. How does the tree diagram help you solve the problem?

Item C
Short Response Which two vats hold the same amount of liquid? Explain.

Vat A
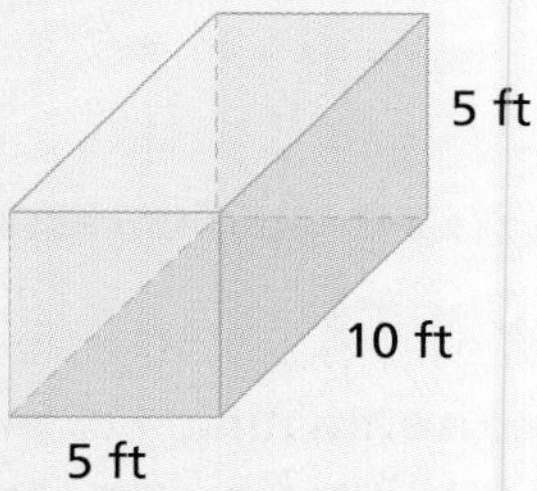

Vat B
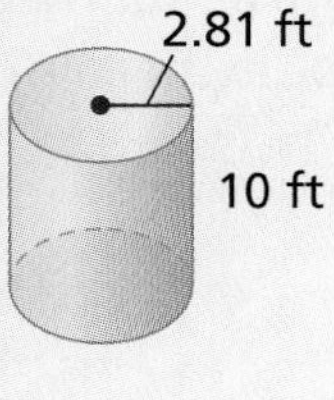

Vat C
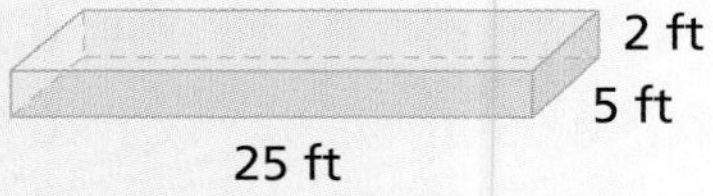

7. Explain why you cannot determine the answer by comparing the scale of each diagram.
8. What formulas do you need to find the answer?
9. Explain which two vats hold the same amount of liquid.

Item D
Gridded Response Determine the surface area in square meters of a rectangular prism that has a length of 13 m, a width of 10 m, and a height of 8 m.

10. How do you determine the surface area of a rectangular prism?
11. Create a net for this prism and label it with the correct dimensions.
12. Use the net from problem 11 to find the surface area of the prism.

STANDARDIZED TEST PREP

go.hrw.com
State Test Practice Online
KEYWORD: MS7 TestPrep

Cumulative Assessment, Chapters 1–11

Multiple Choice

1. In a box containing 115 marbles, 25 are blue, 22 are brown, and 68 are red. What is the probability of randomly selecting a blue marble?

Ⓐ $\frac{115}{25}$ Ⓒ $\frac{5}{23}$

Ⓑ $\frac{22}{115}$ Ⓓ Not here

2. Convert 805 centimeters to meters.

Ⓕ 80.5 m Ⓗ 0.0805 m

Ⓖ 8.05 m Ⓙ 0.00805 m

3. What is the value of $(-8 - 4)^2 + 4^1$?

Ⓐ −143 Ⓒ 145

Ⓑ 0 Ⓓ 148

4. The graph shows a town's high temperatures over a 5-day period. What was the average high temperature over these 5 days?

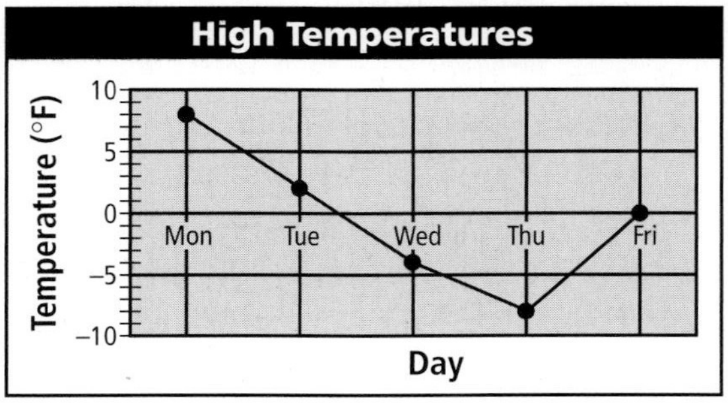

Ⓕ −0.4°F Ⓗ 0.4°F

Ⓖ 4.4°F Ⓙ −4.4°F

5. The fraction $\frac{3}{5}$ is found between which pair of fractions on a number line?

Ⓐ $\frac{7}{10}$ and $\frac{3}{4}$ Ⓒ $\frac{2}{5}$ and $\frac{1}{2}$

Ⓑ $\frac{2}{7}$ and $\frac{8}{11}$ Ⓓ $\frac{1}{3}$ and $\frac{5}{13}$

6. Stu wants to leave a 15% tip for his dinner that cost $13.40. About how much tip should Stu leave?

Ⓕ $1.50 Ⓗ $2.00

Ⓖ $1.75 Ⓙ $2.50

7. What is $2\frac{5}{12} \times \frac{12}{7}$?

Ⓐ $\frac{5}{7}$ Ⓒ $2\frac{17}{19}$

Ⓑ $2\frac{5}{7}$ Ⓓ $4\frac{1}{7}$

8. Find the surface area of the rectangular prism.

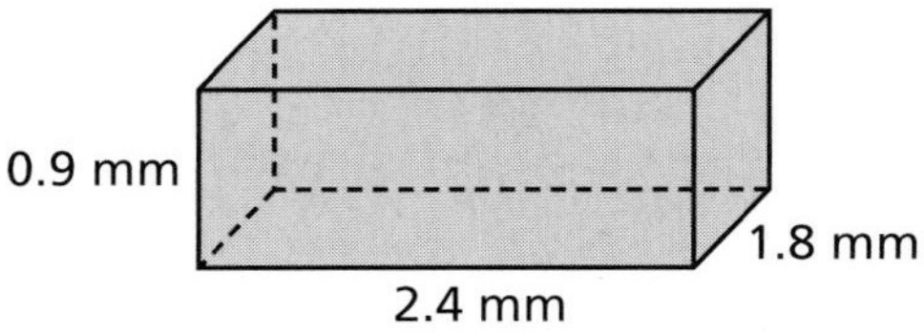

Ⓕ 8.1 mm^2 Ⓗ 15.84 mm^2

Ⓖ 16.2 mm^2 Ⓙ 3.888 mm^2

9. A triangle-shaped wheat field has an area of 225 ft^2. What is the length of the hypotenuse to the nearest tenth?

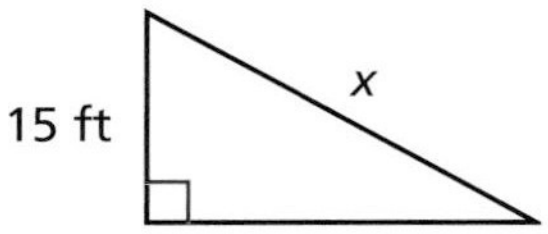

Ⓐ 30 ft Ⓒ 45 ft

Ⓑ 33.5 ft Ⓓ 224.5 ft

10. Which number is NOT expressed in scientific notation?

Ⓕ 7×10^5 Ⓗ 0.23×10^9

Ⓖ 1.9×10^1 Ⓙ 9.2×10^{25}

11. Five of the angles in a hexagon measure 155°, 120°, 62°, 65°, and 172°. What is the measure of the sixth angle?

Ⓐ 115° Ⓒ 180°

Ⓑ 146° Ⓓ 326°

HOT TIP! Probability can be expressed as a fraction, decimal, or percent.

Gridded Response

Use the following graph for items 12 and 13.

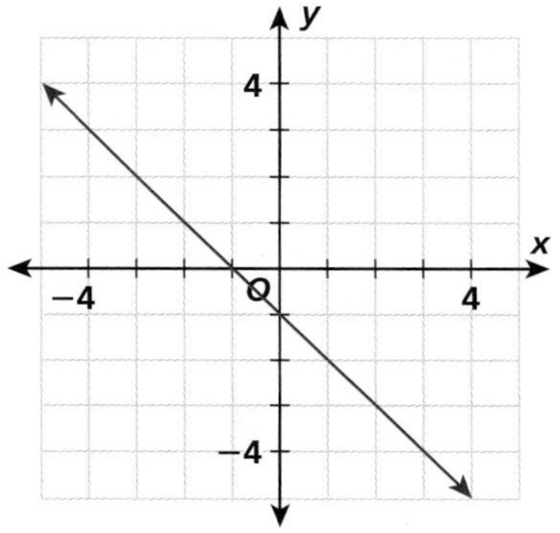

12. Find the y-coordinate of the point on the line whose x-coordinate is -1.

13. Determine the value of y when $x = -6$.

14. Anji bought 4 shirts for \$56.80. She later bought a shirt for \$19.20. What was the mean cost of all the shirts in dollars?

15. Find 4!.

16. Rosa has a coupon for 60% off the before-tax total of two pairs of shoes. The first pair of shoes is marked \$45, and the second pair is marked \$32. What is Rosa's total cost, in dollars, after a 5.5% sales tax is added?

17. What is the value of x? $12 = x - \frac{2}{3}$

Short Response

18. The diameter of the larger circle is 36 in., and the radius of the smaller circle is 6 in.

What is the ratio of the smaller circle's area to the larger circle's area written to the nearest whole percent?

19. Rhonda has 3 different-color T-shirts—red, blue, and green—and a pair of blue jeans and a pair of white jeans. She randomly chooses a T-shirt and a pair of jeans. What is the probability that she will pair the red T-shirt with the white jeans? Show how you found your answer.

20. Write $\frac{5}{6}$ and $\frac{3}{4}$ as fractions with a common denominator. Then determine whether the fractions are equivalent. Explain your method.

Extended Response

21. A bag contains 5 blue blocks, 3 red blocks, and 2 yellow blocks.

a. What is the probability that Tip will draw a red block and then a blue block at random if the first block is replaced before the second is drawn? Show the steps necessary to find your answer.

b. What is the probability that Tip will draw a red block and then a blue block at random if the first block is not replaced before the second is drawn? Show your work.

c. Explain how your answers to parts **a** and **b** are affected by whether or not the first block is replaced.

Standardized Test Prep

CHAPTER 12

Multi-Step Equations and Inequalities

go.hrw.com
Chapter Project Online
KEYWORD: MS7 Ch12

Altitudes of Artificial Satellites

Satellite	Altitude (km)
Sputnik	245
Skylab	270
Mir	390
International Space Station	420

Career *Satellite Engineer*

Artificial satellites were born with the launch of *Sputnik* on October 4, 1957. The 84 kg ball with a 56 cm diameter circled Earth every 35 minutes and signified the beginning of changes in the way people live. Today, there are over 2,500 satellites orbiting Earth.

Satellite engineers work on satellite design, construction, orbit determination, launch, tracking, and orbit adjustment. Satellites can monitor weather, crop growth, and natural resources and communicate this information using television, radio, and other communication signals. Satellites can even directionally guide people who have GPS (Global Positioning System) devices.

ARE YOU READY?

Vocabulary

Choose the best term from the list to complete each sentence.

1. __?__ are mathematical operations that undo each other.
2. To solve an equation you need to __?__.
3. A(n) __?__ is a mathematical statement that two expressions are equivalent.
4. A(n)__?__ is a mathematical statement that two ratios are equivalent.

isolate the variable

equation

proportion

inverse operations

expression

Complete these exercises to review skills you will need for this chapter.

Add Whole Numbers, Decimals, Fractions, and Integers

Add.

5. $24 + 16$	**6.** $-34 + (-47)$	**7.** $35 + (-61)$	**8.** $-12 + (-29) + 53$
9. $2.7 + 3.5$	**10.** $\frac{2}{3} + \frac{1}{2}$	**11.** $-5.87 + 10.6$	**12.** $\frac{8}{9} + \left(-\frac{9}{11}\right)$

Evaluate Expressions

Evaluate each expression for $a = 7$ and $b = -2$.

13. $a - b$	**14.** $b - a$	**15.** $\frac{b}{a}$	**16.** $2a + 3b$
17. $\frac{-4a}{b}$	**18.** $3a - \frac{8}{b}$	**19.** $1.2a + 2.3b$	**20.** $-5a - (-6b)$

Solve Multiplication Equations

Solve.

21. $8x = -72$	**22.** $-12a = -60$	**23.** $\frac{2}{3}y = 16$	**24.** $-12b = 9$
25. $12 = -4x$	**26.** $13 = \frac{1}{2}c$	**27.** $-2.4 = -0.8p$	**28.** $\frac{3}{4} = 6x$

Solve Proportions

Solve.

29. $\frac{3}{4} = \frac{x}{24}$	**30.** $\frac{8}{9} = \frac{4}{a}$	**31.** $-\frac{12}{5} = \frac{15}{c}$	**32.** $\frac{y}{50} = \frac{35}{20}$
33. $\frac{2}{3} = \frac{18}{w}$	**34.** $\frac{35}{21} = \frac{d}{3}$	**35.** $\frac{7}{13} = \frac{h}{195}$	**36.** $\frac{9}{-15} = \frac{-27}{p}$

CHAPTER 12

Study Guide: Preview

Where You've Been

Previously, you

- solved one-step equations.
- read, wrote, and graphed inequalities on a number line.
- solved one-step inequalities.

In This Chapter

You will study

- solving two-step and multi-step equations and equations with variables on both sides.
- reading, writing, and graphing inequalities on a number line.
- solving one-step and two-step inequalities.
- solving equations for a variable.

Where You're Going

You can use the skills learned in this chapter

- to solve problems in the physical sciences that involve comparing speeds, distances, and weights.
- to make decisions when planning events.
- to evaluate options when distributing budget funds.

Key Vocabulary/Vocabulario

algebraic inequality	desigualdad algebraica
compound inequality	desigualdad compuesta
inequality	desigualdad
solution set	conjunto solución

Vocabulary Connections

To become familiar with some of the vocabulary terms in the chapter, consider the following. You may refer to the chapter, the glossary, or a dictionary if you like.

1. What does the word *inequality* mean? How might an **inequality** describe a mathematical relationship? Give an example using numbers.
2. An example of an algebraic equation is $x + 3 = 8$. How do you think $x + 3 = 8$ would change if you were to write it as an **algebraic inequality** instead of as an equation?
3. A compound sentence is made up of two or more independent clauses joined by the words *and* or *or*. What do you think a **compound inequality** might be?
4. A solution of an equation is a value that makes the equation true. For example, $x = 5$ is a solution of $x + 3 = 8$. A set is a group of “items,” such as people or numbers, that have a characteristic in common. What do you think a **solution set** might be?

CHAPTER 12

Reading and Writing Math

Study Strategy: Prepare for Your Final Exam

Math is a cumulative subject, so your exam will cover all of the material you have learned from the beginning of the course. Being prepared is the key for you to be successful on your exam.

2 weeks before the final exam

- **Review lesson notes and vocabulary.**
- **Look at previous exams and homework. Rework problems that I answered incorrectly or that I did not complete.**
- **Make a list of all formulas, rules, and important steps.**
- **Create a practice exam using problems from the book that are similar to problems from the previous tests.**

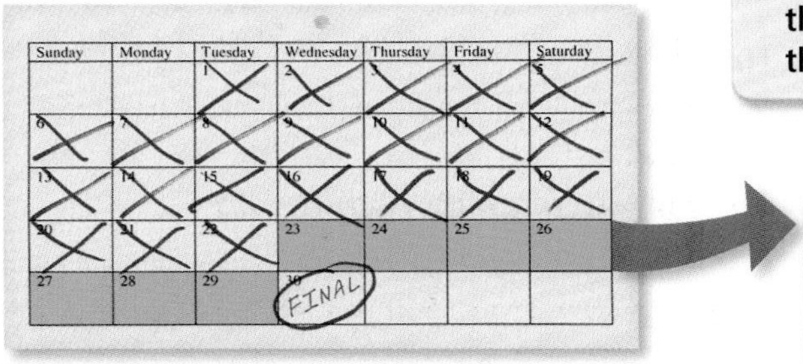

1 week before the final exam

- **Take the practice exam and check it. For each problem I miss, find two or three similar problems and work those.**
- **Look over each chapter's Study Guide: Review.**
- **Quiz a friend or myself on the formulas and major points from my list.**

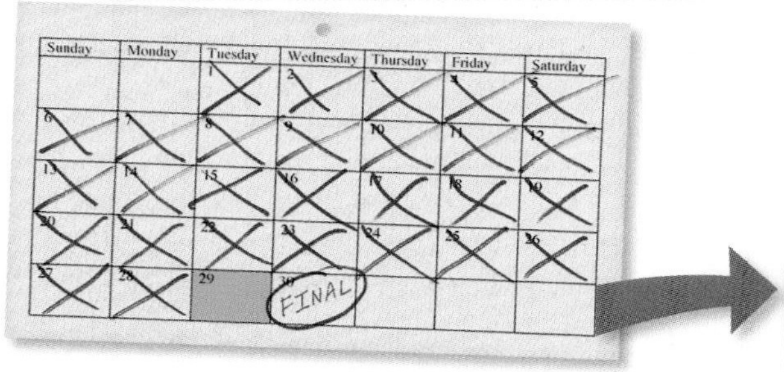

1 day before the final exam

- **Make sure I have pencils and a calculator. (Check the batteries!)**
- **Review any problem areas one last time.**

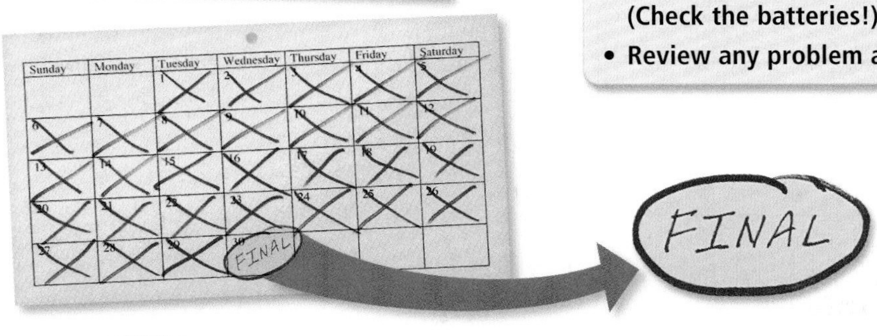

Try This

1. Create a timeline that you will use to study for your final exam.

Hands-On LAB 12-1

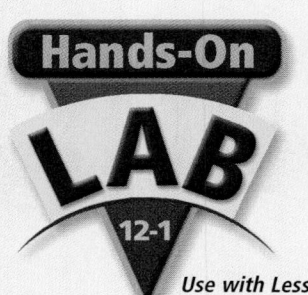

Model Two-Step Equations

Use with Lesson 12-1

go.hrw.com
Lab Resources Online
KEYWORD: MS7 Lab12

KEY

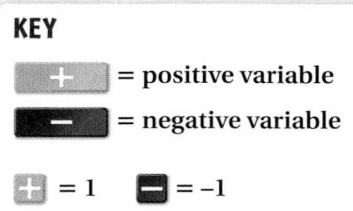

 = positive variable

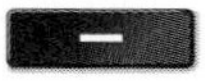 = negative variable

 = 1  = –1

REMEMBER

-  +  = 0
-  +  = 0
- In an equation, the expressions on both sides of the equal sign are equivalent.

In Lab 2-5, you learned how to solve one-step equations using algebra tiles. You can also use algebra tiles to solve two-step equations. When solving a two-step equation, it is easiest to perform addition and subtraction before multiplication and division.

Activity

1 Use algebra tiles to model and solve $2p + 2 = 10$.

$2p + 2 = 10$

Model the equation.

$$\begin{array}{rcr} 2p + 2 & = & 10 \\ -\,2 & & -\,2 \\ \hline 2p \quad & = & 8 \end{array}$$

Remove 2 yellow tiles from each side of the mat.

$$\frac{2p}{2} = \frac{8}{2}$$

Divide each side into 2 equal groups.

$p = 4$

The solution is $p = 4$.

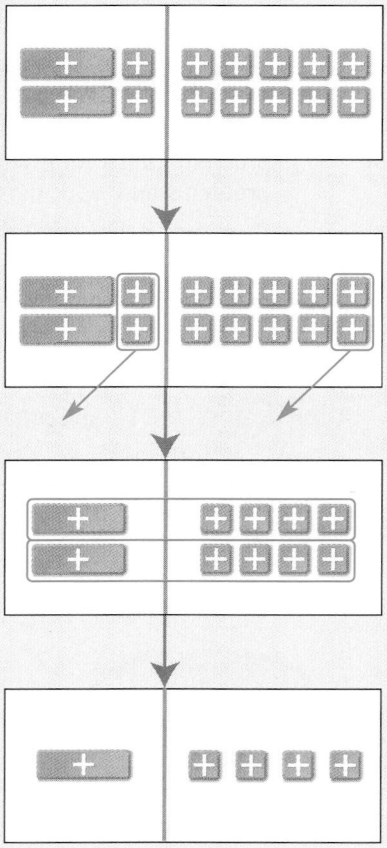

2 Use algebra tiles to model and solve $3n + 6 = -15$.

$3n + 6 = -15$

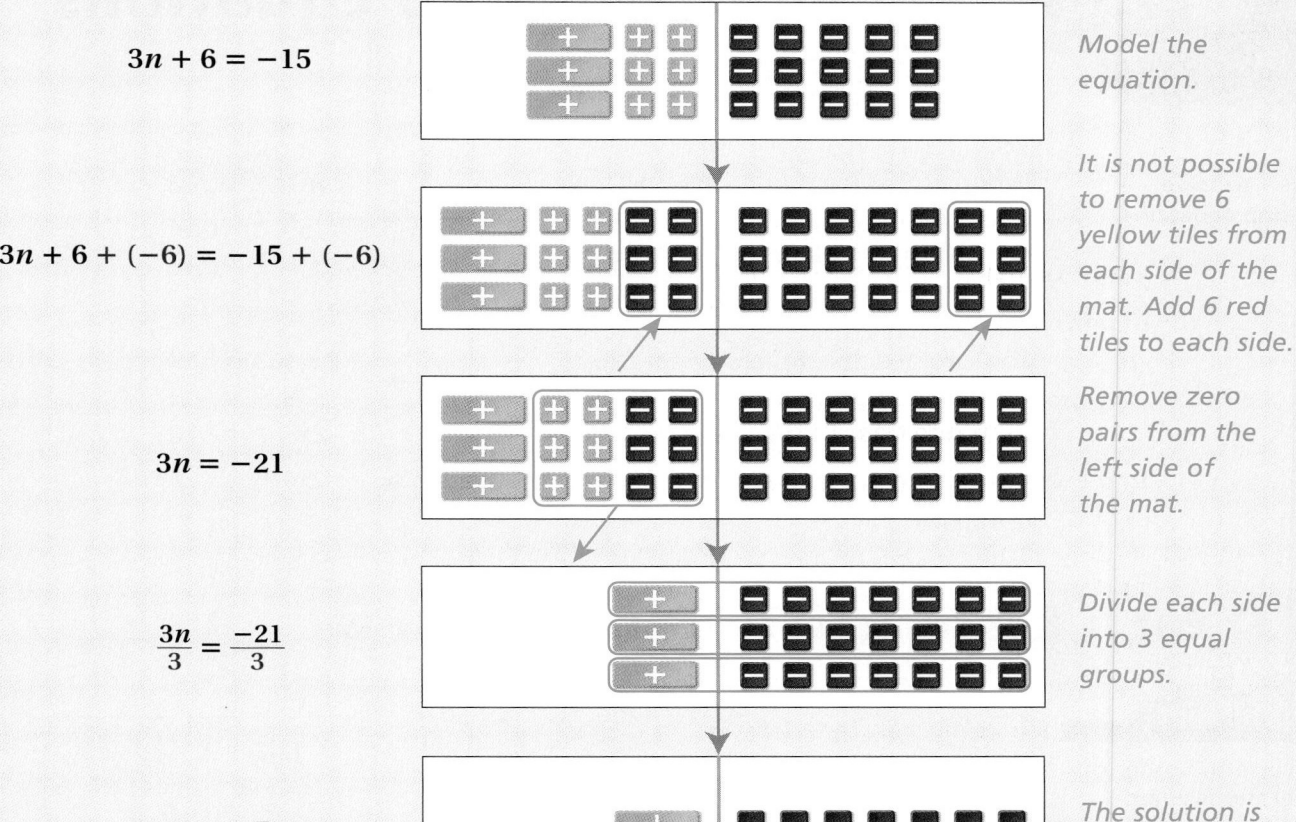

Model the equation.

$3n + 6 + (-6) = -15 + (-6)$

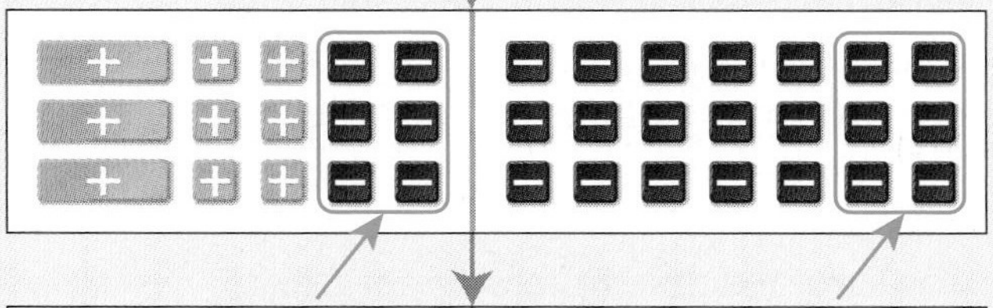

It is not possible to remove 6 yellow tiles from each side of the mat. Add 6 red tiles to each side.

$3n = -21$

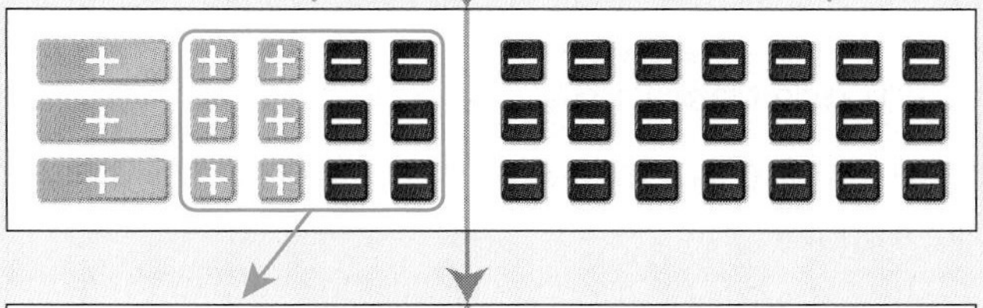

Remove zero pairs from the left side of the mat.

$\frac{3n}{3} = \frac{-21}{3}$

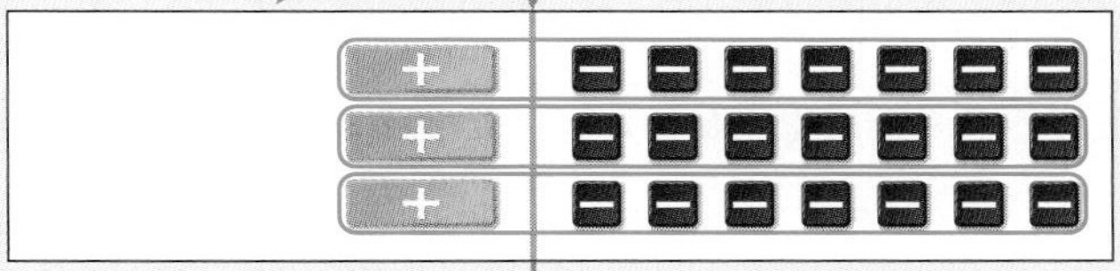

Divide each side into 3 equal groups.

$n = -7$

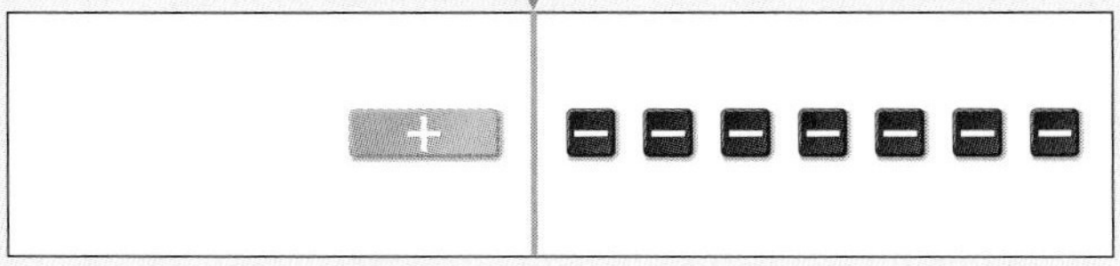

The solution is $n = -7$.

Think and Discuss

1. When you add a value to one side of an equation, why do you also have to add the same value to the other side?
2. When you solved $3n + 6 = -15$ in the activity, why were you able to remove six yellow unit tiles and six red unit tiles from the left side of the equation?
3. Model and solve $3x - 5 = 10$. Explain each step.
4. How would you check the solution to $3n + 6 = -15$ using algebra tiles?

Try This

Use algebra tiles to model and solve each equation.

1. $4 + 2x = 20$
2. $3r + 7 = -8$
3. $-4m + 3 = -25$
4. $-2n - 5 = 17$
5. $10 = 2j - 4$
6. $5 + r = 7$
7. $4h + 2h + 3 = 15$
8. $-3g = 9$
9. $5k + (-7) = 13$

12-1 Solving Two-Step Equations

Learn to solve two-step equations.

When you solve equations that have one operation, you use an inverse operation to isolate the variable. →

$$\begin{array}{rcr} n + 7 &=& 15 \\ -\ 7 & & -\ 7 \\ \hline n &=& 8 \end{array}$$

You can also use inverse operations to solve equations that have more than one operation. →

$$\begin{array}{rcr} 2x + 3 &=& 23 \\ -\ 3 & & -\ 3 \\ \hline 2x &=& 20 \end{array}$$

Use the inverse of multiplication to isolate x. →

$$\frac{2x}{2} = \frac{20}{2}$$

$$x = 10$$

EXAMPLE 1 Solving Two-Step Equations Using Division

Helpful Hint

Reverse the order of operations when solving equations that have more than one operation.

Solve.

A $2n + 5 = 13$

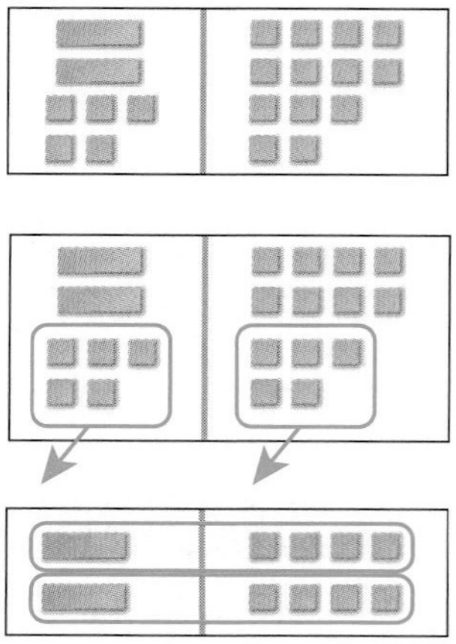

$$\begin{array}{rcr} 2n + 5 &=& 13 \\ -\ 5 & & -\ 5 \\ \hline 2n &=& 8 \end{array}$$

Subtract 5 from both sides.

$$\frac{2n}{2} = \frac{8}{2}$$

$$n = 4$$

Divide both sides by 2.

B $19 = -3p - 8$

$$\begin{array}{rcr} 19 &=& -3p - 8 \\ +\ 8 & & +\ 8 \\ \hline 27 &=& -3p \end{array}$$

Add 8 to both sides.

$$\frac{27}{-3} = \frac{-3p}{-3}$$

Divide both sides by −3.

$$-9 = p$$

Check

$19 = -3p - 8$

$19 \stackrel{?}{=} -3(-9) - 8$ *Substitute −9 for p.*

$19 \stackrel{?}{=} 27 - 8$

$19 \stackrel{?}{=} 19$ ✔ *−9 is a solution.*

EXAMPLE 2 Solving Two-Step Equations Using Multiplication

Solve.

A $8 + \frac{m}{4} = 17$

$$\begin{aligned} 8 + \frac{m}{4} &= 17 \\ -8 \quad &\quad -8 \quad \text{Subtract 8 from both sides.} \\ \frac{m}{4} &= 9 \\ (4)\frac{m}{4} &= (4)9 \quad \text{Multiply both sides by 4.} \\ m &= 36 \end{aligned}$$

B $3 = \frac{u}{6} - 12$

$$\begin{aligned} 3 &= \frac{u}{6} - 12 \\ +12 \quad &\quad +12 \quad \text{Add 12 to both sides.} \\ 15 &= \frac{u}{6} \\ (6)15 &= (6)\frac{u}{6} \quad \text{Multiply both sides by 6.} \\ 90 &= u \end{aligned}$$

EXAMPLE 3 *Fitness Application*

A new one-year membership at Vista Tennis Center costs $160. A registration fee of $28 is paid up front, and the rest is paid monthly. How much do new members pay each month?

registration fee	plus	monthly cost	is	$160

Let m represent the monthly cost.

$28	+	12*m*	=	$160

$$\begin{aligned} 28 + 12m &= 160 \\ -28 \quad &\quad -28 \quad \text{Subtract 28 from both sides.} \\ 12m &= 132 \\ \frac{12m}{12} &= \frac{132}{12} \quad \text{Divide both sides by 12.} \\ m &= 11 \end{aligned}$$

New members pay $11 per month for a one-year membership.

Fitness LINK

Labeled "the sport for a lifetime," tennis is played by people of all ages. Some tennis matches may take just minutes to complete, while others take hours or even days!

Think and Discuss

1. **Explain** how you decide which inverse operation to use first when solving a two-step equation.
2. **Tell** the steps you would follow to solve $-1 + 2x = 7$.

12-1 Exercises

go.hrw.com
Homework Help Online
KEYWORD: MS7 12-1
Parent Resources Online
KEYWORD: MS7 Parent

GUIDED PRACTICE

See Example 1

Solve.

1. $3n + 8 = 29$
2. $-4m - 7 = 17$
3. $2 = -6x + 4$

See Example 2

Solve.

4. $12 + \frac{b}{6} = 16$
5. $\frac{y}{8} - 15 = 2$
6. $10 = -8 + \frac{n}{4}$

See Example 3

7. A coffee shop sells a ceramic refill mug for $8.95. Each refill costs $1.50. Last month Rose spent $26.95 on a mug and refills. How many refills did she buy?

INDEPENDENT PRACTICE

See Example 1

Solve. Check each answer.

8. $5x + 6 = 41$
9. $-9p - 15 = 93$
10. $-2m + 14 = 10$
11. $-7 = 7d - 8$
12. $-7 = -3c + 14$
13. $12y - 11 = 49$

See Example 2

Solve.

14. $24 + \frac{h}{4} = 10$
15. $\frac{k}{5} - 13 = 4$
16. $-17 + \frac{q}{8} = 13$
17. $24 = \frac{m}{10} + 32$
18. $-9 = 15 + \frac{v}{3}$
19. $\frac{m}{-7} - 14 = 2$

See Example 3

20. Each Saturday, a gym holds a 45-minute yoga class. The weekday yoga classes last 30 minutes. The number of weekday classes varies. Last week, the yoga classes totaled 165 minutes. How many weekday yoga classes were held?

PRACTICE AND PROBLEM SOLVING

Extra Practice
See page 750.

Translate each equation into words, and then solve the equation.

21. $6 + \frac{m}{3} = 18$
22. $3x + 15 = 27$
23. $2 = \frac{n}{5} - 4$

Solve.

24. $18 + \frac{y}{4} = 12$
25. $5x + 30 = 40$
26. $\frac{s}{12} - 7 = 8$
27. $-10 + 6g = 110$
28. $-8 = \frac{z}{7} + 2$
29. $46 = -6w - 8$
30. $15 = -7 + \frac{r}{3}$
31. $-20 = -4p - 12$
32. $\frac{1}{2} + \frac{r}{7} = \frac{5}{14}$

33. **Consumer Math** A long-distance phone company charges $1.01 for the first 25 minutes of a call, and then $0.09 for each additional minute. A call cost $9.56. How long did it last?

34. The school purchased baseball equipment and uniforms for a total cost of $1,836. The equipment cost $612, and the uniforms were $25.50 each. How many uniforms did the school purchase?

Health LINK

35. If you double the number of calories per day that the U.S. Department of Agriculture recommends for children who are 1 to 3 years old and then subtract 100, you get the number of calories per day recommended for teenage boys. Given that 2,500 calories are recommended for teenage boys, how many calories per day are recommended for children?

As a service to health-conscious customers, many grocery stores have installed scanners that calculate the total number of calories purchased.

36. According to the U.S. Department of Agriculture, children who are 4 to 6 years old need about 1,800 calories per day. This is 700 calories more than half the recommended calories for teenage girls. How many calories per day does a teenage girl need?

37. Hector consumed 2,130 calories from food in one day. Of these, he consumed 350 calories at breakfast and 400 calories having a snack. He also ate 2 portions of one of the items shown in the table for lunch and the same for dinner. What did Hector eat for lunch and dinner?

Calorie Counter

Food	Portion	Calories
Stir-fry	1 cup	250
Enchilada	1 whole	310
Pizza	1 slice	345
Tomato soup	1 cup	160

38. **Challenge** There are 30 mg of cholesterol in a box of macaroni and cheese. This is 77 mg minus $\frac{1}{10}$ the number of milligrams of sodium it contains. How many milligrams of sodium are in a box of macaroni and cheese?

go.hrw.com
Web Extra!
KEYWORD: MS7 Health

Test Prep and Spiral Review

39. **Multiple Choice** For which equation is $x = -2$ a solution?

Ⓐ $2x + 5 = 9$ Ⓑ $8 = 10 - x$ Ⓒ $\frac{x}{2} + 3 = 2$ Ⓓ $-16 = -4x - 8$

40. **Short Response** A taxi cab costs $1.25 for the first mile and $0.25 for each additional mile. Write an equation for the total cost of a taxi ride, where x is the number of miles. How many miles can be traveled in the taxi for $8.00?

Identify the three-dimensional figure described. (Lesson 10-1)

41. 6 rectangular faces

42. 1 hexagonal base and 6 triangular faces

Find the volume of each figure to the nearest tenth. Use 3.14 for π. (Lesson 10-2)

43. cylinder with radius 5 cm and height 7 cm

44. triangular prism with a base with area 18 in^2 and height 9 in.

12-2 Solving Multi-Step Equations

Learn to solve multi-step equations.

Jamal owns twice as many comic books as Levi owns. If you add 6 to the number of comic books Jamal owns and then divide by 7, you get the number of comic books Brooke owns. Brooke owns 30 comic books. How many comic books does Levi own? To answer this question, you need to set up an equation that requires more than two steps to solve.

EXAMPLE 1 Combining Like Terms to Solve Equations

Solve $7n - 1 - 2n = 14$.

$$
\begin{aligned}
7n - 1 - 2n &= 14 \\
5n - 1 &= 14 && \textit{Combine like terms.} \\
+1 \quad &\quad +1 && \textit{Add 1 to both sides.} \\
5n \quad &= 15 \\
\frac{5n}{5} &= \frac{15}{5} && \textit{Divide both sides by 5.} \\
n &= 3
\end{aligned}
$$

You may need to use the Distributive Property to solve an equation that has parentheses. Multiply each term inside the parentheses by the factor that is outside the parentheses. Then combine like terms.

EXAMPLE 2 Using the Distributive Property to Solve Equations

Remember!

The Distributive Property states that $a(b + c) = ab + ac$. For instance, $2(3 + 5) = 2(3) + 2(5)$.

Solve $3(z - 1) + 8 = 14$.

$$
\begin{aligned}
3(z - 1) + 8 &= 14 \\
3(z) - 3(1) + 8 &= 14 && \textit{Distribute 3 on the left side.} \\
3z - 3 + 8 &= 14 && \textit{Simplify.} \\
3z + 5 &= 14 && \textit{Combine like terms.} \\
-5 \quad &\quad -5 && \textit{Add } -5 \textit{ to both sides.} \\
3z \quad &= 9 \\
\frac{3z}{3} &= \frac{9}{3} && \textit{Divide both sides by 3.} \\
z &= 3
\end{aligned}
$$

EXAMPLE 3 PROBLEM SOLVING APPLICATION

PROBLEM SOLVING

Jamal owns twice as many comic books as Levi owns. Adding 6 to the number of comic books Jamal owns and then dividing by 7 gives the number Brooke owns. Brooke owns 30 comic books. How many does Levi own?

1 Understand the Problem

Rewrite the question as a statement.

- Find the number of comic books that Levi owns.

List the **important information:**

- Jamal owns 2 times as many comic books as Levi owns.
- The number of comic books Jamal owns added to 6 and then divided by 7 equals the number Brooke owns.
- Brooke owns 30 comic books.

2 Make a Plan

Let c represent the number of comic books Levi owns. Then $2c$ represents the number Jamal owns, and $\frac{2c+6}{7}$ represents the number Brooke owns, which equals 30. Solve the equation $\frac{2c+6}{7} = 30$ for c.

3 Solve

$$\frac{2c+6}{7} = 30$$

$$(7)\frac{2c+6}{7} = (7)30$$ *Multiply both sides by 7 to eliminate fractions.*

$$2c + 6 = 210$$

$$2c + 6 - \mathbf{6} = 210 - \mathbf{6}$$ *Subtract 6 from both sides.*

$$2c = 204$$

$$\frac{2c}{\mathbf{2}} = \frac{204}{\mathbf{2}}$$ *Divide both sides by 2.*

$$c = 102$$

Levi owns 102 comic books.

4 Look Back

Make sure that your answer makes sense in the original problem. Levi has 102 comic books. Jamal has $2(102) = 204$. Brooke has $\frac{204+6}{7} = 30$.

Think and Discuss

1. **List** the steps required to solve $-n + 5n + 3 = 27$.
2. **Describe** how to solve the equations $\frac{2}{3}x + 7 = 4$ and $\frac{2x+7}{3} = 4$. Are the solutions the same or different? Explain.

12-2 Exercises

go.hrw.com
Homework Help Online
KEYWORD: MS7 12-2
Parent Resources Online
KEYWORD: MS7 Parent

GUIDED PRACTICE

See Example 1

Solve.

1. $14n + 2 - 7n = 37$
2. $10x - 11 - 4x = 43$
3. $1 = -3 + 4p - 2p$

See Example 2

4. $12 - (x + 3) = 10$
5. $15 = 2(q + 4) + 3$
6. $5(m - 2) + 36 = -4$

See Example 3

7. Keisha read twice as many books this year as Ben read. Subtracting 4 from the number of books Keisha read and dividing by 2 gives the number of books Sheldon read. Sheldon read 10 books. How many books did Ben read?

INDEPENDENT PRACTICE

See Example 1

Solve.

8. $b + 18 + 3b = 74$
9. $10x - 3 - 2x = 4$
10. $18w - 10 - 6w = 50$
11. $19 = 5n + 7 - 3n$
12. $-27 = -3p + 15 - 3p$
13. $-x - 8 + 14x = -34$

See Example 2

14. $2(x + 4) + 6 = 22$
15. $1 - 3(n + 5) = -8$
16. $4.3 - 1.4(p + 7) = -9.7$
17. $1.8 + 6n - 3.2 = 7.6$
18. $0 = 9\left(k - \frac{2}{3}\right) + 33$
19. $6(t - 2) - 76 = -142$

See Example 3

20. Abby ran 3 times as many laps as Karen. Adding 4 to the number of laps Abby ran and then dividing by 7 gives the number of laps Jill ran. Jill ran 1 lap. How many laps did Karen run?

PRACTICE AND PROBLEM SOLVING

Extra Practice
See page 750.

Solve.

21. $\frac{0.5x + 7}{8} = 5$
22. $4(t - 8) + 20 = 5$
23. $63 = 8w + 2.6 - 3.6$
24. $17 = -5(3 + w) + 7$
25. $\frac{\frac{1}{4}a - 12}{8} = 4$
26. $9 = -(r - 5) + 11$
27. $\frac{2b - 3.4}{0.6} = -29$
28. $8.44 = \frac{34.6 + 4h}{5}$
29. $5.7 = -2.5x + 18 - 1.6x$

30. **Consumer Math** Three friends ate dinner at a restaurant. The friends decided to add a 15% tip and then split the bill evenly. Each friend paid \$10.35. What was the total bill for dinner before tip?

31. Ann earns 1.5 times her normal hourly pay for each hour that she works over 40 hours in a week. Last week she worked 51 hours and earned \$378.55. What is her normal hourly pay?

32. **Geometry** The base angles of an isosceles triangle are congruent. The measure of each of the base angles is twice the measure of the third angle. Find the measures of all three angles.

33. Consumer Math Patrice used a \$15 gift certificate when she purchased a pair of sandals. After 8% sales tax was applied to the price of the sandals, the \$15 was deducted. Patrice had to pay a total of \$12 for the sandals. How much did the sandals cost before tax?

34. Physical Science To convert temperatures between degrees Celsius and degrees Fahrenheit, you can use the formula $F = \frac{9}{5}C + 32$. The table shows the melting points of various elements.

a. What is the melting point in degrees Celsius of gold?

b. What is the melting point in degrees Celsius of hydrogen?

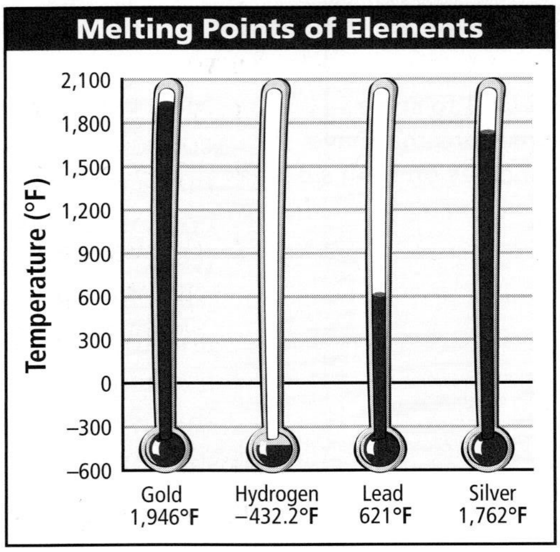

35. On his first two social studies tests, Billy made an 86 and a 93. What grade must Billy make on the third test to have an average of 90 for all three tests?

36. What's the Question? Three friends shared a taxi ride from the airport to their hotel. After adding a \$7.00 tip, the friends divided the cost of the ride evenly. If solving the equation $\frac{c + \$7.00}{3} = \$11.25$ gives the answer, what is the question?

37. Write About It Explain why multiplying first in the equation $\frac{2x - 6}{5} = 2$ makes finding the solution easier than adding first does.

38. Challenge Are the solutions to the following equations the same? Explain.

$$\frac{3y}{4} + 2 = 4 \text{ and } 3y + 8 = 16$$

Test Prep and Spiral Review

39. Multiple Choice Solve $\frac{2x - 2}{4} = 7$.

Ⓐ $x = 15$ Ⓑ $x = 18$ Ⓒ $x = 20$ Ⓓ $x = 21$

40. Multiple Choice For which equation(s) is $x = 3$ a solution?

I $2x - 5 + 3x = 10$ **II** $\frac{-x + 7}{2} = 2$ **III** $\frac{-4x}{6} = 2$ **IV** $6.3x - 2.4 = 16.5$

Ⓕ I only Ⓖ I and II Ⓗ I, II, and III Ⓙ I, II, and IV

Find the volume of each figure to the nearest tenth. Use 3.14 for π. (Lesson 10-3)

41. a cone with diameter 6 cm and height 4 cm

42. a triangular pyramid with height 7 in. and base area 18 in^2

Solve. (Lesson 12-1)

43. $6x - 4 = 2$ **44.** $7 = -y + 4$ **45.** $5 + \frac{z}{2} = -9$ **46.** $12 - 6d = 54$

12-3 Solving Equations with Variables on Both Sides

Learn to solve equations that have variables on both sides.

Mari can rent a video game console for \$14.49 per week or buy a rebuilt one for \$72.45. The cost of renting a game is \$7.95 per week. How many weeks would Mari have to rent both the game and the console to pay as much as she would if she had bought the used console and rented the game instead?

Problems such as this require you to solve equations that have the same variable on both sides of the equal sign. To solve this kind of problem, you need to get the terms with variables on one side of the equal sign.

EXAMPLE 1 Using Inverse Operations to Group Terms with Variables

Group the terms with variables on one side of the equal sign, and simplify.

A $6m = 4m + 12$

$6m = 4m + 12$

$6m - 4m = 4m - 4m + 12$ *Subtract 4m from both sides.*

$2m = 12$ *Simplify.*

B $-7x - 198 = 5x$

$-7x - 198 = 5x$

$-7x + 7x - 198 = 5x + 7x$ *Add 7x to both sides.*

$-198 = 12x$ *Simplify.*

EXAMPLE 2 Solving Equations with Variables on Both Sides

Solve.

A $5n = 3n + 26$

$5n = 3n + 26$

$5n - 3n = 3n - 3n + 26$ *Subtract 3n from both sides.*

$2n = 26$ *Simplify.*

$\frac{2n}{2} = \frac{26}{2}$ *Divide both sides by 2.*

$n = 13$

Solve.

B $19 + 7n = -2n + 37$

$19 + 7n = -2n + 37$	
$19 + 7n + \mathbf{2n} = -2n + \mathbf{2n} + 37$	*Add 2n to both sides.*
$19 + 9n = 37$	*Simplify.*
$19 + 9n - \mathbf{19} = 37 - \mathbf{19}$	*Subtract 19 from both sides.*
$9n = 18$	*Simplify.*
$\frac{9n}{\mathbf{9}} = \frac{18}{\mathbf{9}}$	*Divide both sides by 9.*
$n = 2$	

C $\frac{5}{9}x = \frac{4}{9}x + 9$

$\frac{5}{9}x = \frac{4}{9}x + 9$	
$\frac{5}{9}x - \mathbf{\frac{4}{9}x} = \frac{4}{9}x - \mathbf{\frac{4}{9}x} + 9$	*Subtract $\frac{4}{9}x$ from both sides.*
$\frac{1}{9}x = 9$	*Simplify.*
$(\mathbf{9})\frac{1}{9}x = (\mathbf{9})9$	*Multiply both sides by 9.*
$x = 81$	

EXAMPLE 3 *Consumer Math Application*

Mari can buy a video game console for $72.45 and rent a game for $7.95 per week, or she can rent a console and the same game for a total of $22.44 per week. How many weeks would Mari need to rent both the video game and the console to pay as much as she would if she had bought the console and rented the game instead?

Let w represent the number of weeks.

$22.44w = 72.45 + 7.95w$	
$22.44w - \mathbf{7.95w} = 72.45 + 7.95w - \mathbf{7.95w}$	*Subtract 7.95w from both sides.*
$14.49w = 72.45$	*Simplify.*
$\frac{14.49w}{\mathbf{14.49}} = \frac{72.45}{\mathbf{14.49}}$	*Divide both sides by 14.49.*
$w = 5$	

Mari would need to rent the video game and the console for 5 weeks to pay as much as she would have if she had bought the console.

Think and Discuss

1. Explain how you would solve $\frac{1}{2}x + 7 = \frac{2}{3}x - 2$.

2. Describe how you would decide which variable term to add or subtract on both sides of the equation $-3x + 7 = 4x - 9$.

12-3 Exercises

go.hrw.com
Homework Help Online
KEYWORD: MS7 12-3
Parent Resources Online
KEYWORD: MS7 Parent

GUIDED PRACTICE

See Example 1

Group the terms with variables on one side of the equal sign, and simplify.

1. $5n = 4n + 32$
2. $-6x - 28 = 4x$
3. $8w = 32 - 4w$

See Example 2

Solve.

4. $4y = 2y + 40$
5. $8 + 6a = -2a + 24$
6. $\frac{3}{4}d + 4 = \frac{1}{4}d + 18$

See Example 3

7. **Consumer Math** Members at the Star Theater pay \$30.00 per month plus \$1.95 for each movie. Nonmembers pay the regular \$7.95 admission fee. How many movies would both a member and a nonmember have to see in a month to pay the same amount?

INDEPENDENT PRACTICE

See Example 1

Group the terms with variables on one side of the equal sign, and simplify.

8. $12h = 9h + 84$
9. $-10p - 8 = 2p$
10. $6q = 18 - 2q$
11. $-4c - 6 = -2c$
12. $-7s + 12 = -9s$
13. $6 + \frac{4}{5}a = \frac{9}{10}a$

See Example 2

Solve.

14. $9t = 4t + 120$
15. $42 + 3b = -4b - 14$
16. $\frac{6}{11}x + 4 = \frac{2}{11}x + 16$
17. $1.5a + 6 = 9a + 12$
18. $32 - \frac{3}{8}y = \frac{3}{4}y + 5$
19. $-6 - 8c = 3c + 16$

See Example 3

20. **Consumer Math** Members at a swim club pay \$5 per lesson plus a one-time fee of \$60. Nonmembers pay \$11 per lesson. How many lessons would both a member and a nonmember have to take to pay the same amount?

PRACTICE AND PROBLEM SOLVING

Extra Practice
See page 750.

Solve. Check each answer.

21. $3y + 7 = -6y - 56$
22. $-\frac{7}{8}x - 6 = -\frac{3}{8}x - 14$
23. $5r + 6 - 2r = 7r - 10$
24. $-10p + 8 = 7p + 12$
25. $9 + 5r = -17 - 8r$
26. $0.8k + 7 = -0.7k + 1$
27. A choir is singing at a festival. On the first night, 12 choir members were absent, so the choir stood in 5 equal rows. On the second night, only 1 member was absent, so the choir stood in 6 equal rows. The same number of people stood in each row each night. How many members are in the choir?
28. **Consumer Math** Jaline can purchase tile at a store for \$0.99 per tile and rent a tile saw for \$24. At another store, she can borrow the tile saw for free if she buys tile there for \$1.49 per tile. How many tiles must she buy for the cost to be the same at both stores?

The figures in each pair have the same perimeter. Find the value of each variable.

29.

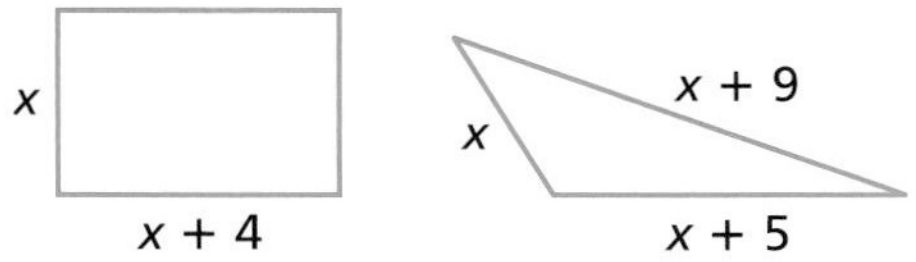

30.

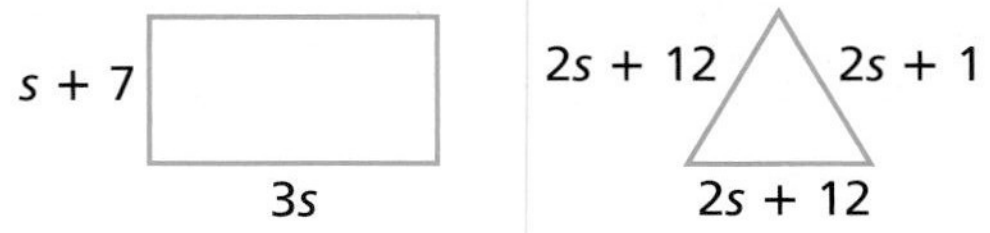

LINK

Recreation

The first indoor rock-climbing gym was built in 1987. Today, indoor rock-climbing gyms exist around the world and include ice-climbing and portable walls.

31. Recreation A rock-climbing gym charges nonmembers \$18 per day to use the wall plus \$7 per day for equipment rental. Members pay an annual fee of \$400 plus \$5 per day for equipment rental. How many days must both a member and a nonmember use the wall in one year so that both pay the same amount?

32. Multi-Step Two families drove from Denver to Cincinnati. After driving 582 miles the first day, the Smiths spread the rest of the trip equally over the next 3 days. The Chows spread their trip equally over 6 days. The distance the Chows drove each day was equal to the distance the Smiths drove each of the three days.

a. How many miles did the Chows drive each day?

b. How far is it from Denver to Cincinnati?

33. What's the Error? To combine terms in the equation $-8a - 4 = 2a + 34$, a student wrote $-6a = 38$. What is the error?

34. Write About It If the same variable is on both sides of an equation, must it have the same value on each side? Explain your answer.

35. Challenge Combine terms before solving the equation $12x - 4 - 12 = 4x + 8 + 8x - 24$. Do you think there is just one solution to the equation? Why or why not?

Test Prep and Spiral Review

36. Multiple Choice For which equation is $x = 0$ NOT a solution?

Ⓐ $3x + 2 = 2 - x$ Ⓑ $2.5x + 3 = x$ Ⓒ $-x + 4 = 3x + 4$ Ⓓ $6x + 2 = x + 2$

37. Extended Response One calling plan offers long-distance calls for \$0.03 per minute. Another plan costs \$2.00 per month but offers long-distance service for \$0.01 per minute. Write and solve an equation to find the number of long-distance minutes for which the two plans would cost the same. Write your answer in a complete sentence.

The lengths of two sides of a right triangle are given. Find the length of the third side to the nearest tenth. (Lesson 9-8)

38. legs: 12 cm and 16 cm **39.** leg: 11 ft; hypotenuse: 30.5 ft

Solve. (Lesson 12-2)

40. $10x + 4 - 3x = -10$ **41.** $1.3y + 2.7y - 5 = 3$ **42.** $5 = \frac{4z - 6}{2}$

CHAPTER 12

READY TO GO ON?

SECTION 12A

Quiz for Lessons 12-1 Through 12-3

12-1 Solving Two-Step Equations

Solve.

1. $-4x + 6 = 54$

2. $15 + \frac{y}{3} = 6$

3. $\frac{z}{8} - 5 = -3$

4. $-33 = -7a - 5$

5. $-27 = \frac{r}{12} - 19$

6. $-13 = 11 - 2n$

7. $3x + 13 = 37$

8. $\frac{p}{-8} - 7 = 12$

9. $\frac{u}{7} + 45 = -60$

10. A taxi service charges an initial fee of \$1.50 plus \$1.50 for every mile traveled. A taxi ride costs \$21.00. How many miles did the taxi travel?

12-2 Solving Multi-Step Equations

Solve.

11. $\frac{3x - 4}{5} = 7$

12. $3(3b + 2) = -30$

13. $-12 = \frac{15c + 3}{6}$

14. $\frac{24.6 + 3a}{4} = 9.54$

15. $\frac{2b + 9}{11} = 18$

16. $13 = 2c + 3 + 5c$

17. $\frac{1}{2}(8w - 6) = 17$

18. $\frac{1.2s + 3.69}{0.3} = 47.9$

19. $\frac{1}{2} = \frac{5p - 8}{12}$

20. Peter used a \$5.00 gift certificate to help pay for his lunch. After adding a 15% tip to the cost of his meal, Peter still had to pay \$2.36 in cash. How much did Peter's meal cost?

21. A group of 10 friends had lunch together at a restaurant. The meal cost a total of \$99.50, including a 15% tip. How much was the total bill for lunch before tip?

12-3 Solving Equations with Variables on Both Sides

Solve.

22. $12m = 3m + 108$

23. $\frac{7}{8}n - 3 = \frac{5}{8}n + 12$

24. $1.2x + 3.7 = 2.2x - 4.5$

25. $-7 - 7p = 3p + 23$

26. $-2.3q + 16 = -5q - 38$

27. $\frac{3}{5}k + \frac{7}{10} = \frac{11}{15}k - \frac{2}{5}$

28. $-19m + 12 = -14m - 8$

29. $\frac{2}{3}v + \frac{1}{6} = \frac{7}{9}v - \frac{5}{6}$

30. $8.9 - 3.3j = -2.2j + 2.3$

31. $4a - 7 = -6a + 12$

32. One shuttle service charges \$10 for pickup and \$0.10 per mile. Another shuttle service has no pickup fee but charges \$0.35 per mile. Find the number of miles for which the cost of the two shuttle services is the same.

Focus on Problem Solving

Solve

• **Write an equation**

When you are asked to solve a problem, be sure to read the entire problem before you begin solving it. Sometimes you will need to perform several steps to solve the problem, and you will need to know all of the information in the problem before you decide which steps to take.

Read each problem and determine what steps are needed to solve it. Then write an equation that can be used to solve the problem.

1. Martin can buy a pair of inline skates and safety equipment for $49.50. At a roller rink, Martin can rent a pair of inline skates for $2.50 per day, but he still needs to buy safety equipment for $19.50. How many days would Martin have to skate in order to pay as much to rent skates and buy safety equipment as he would have to pay to buy both?

2. Christopher draws caricatures at the local mall. He charges $5 for a simple sketch and $15 for a larger drawing. In one day, Christopher earned $175. He drew 20 simple sketches that day. How many larger drawings did he make?

3. Book-club members are required to buy a minimum number of books each year. Leslee bought 3 times the minimum. Denise bought 7 more than the minimum. Together, they bought 23 books. What is the minimum number of books?

4. Coach Willis has won 150 games during his career. This is 10 more than $\frac{1}{2}$ as many games as Coach Gentry has won. How many games has Coach Gentry won?

5. The perimeter of an isosceles triangle is 4 times the length of the shortest side. The longer sides are 4.5 ft longer than the shortest side. What is the length of each side of the triangle?

6. Miss Rankin's class has raised $100.00 for a class trip. The class needs to collect a total of $225.00. How many $0.50 carnations must the class sell to reach its goal?

12-4 Inequalities

Learn to read and write inequalities and graph them on a number line.

Vocabulary

inequality

algebraic inequality

solution set

compound inequality

An **inequality** states that two quantities either are not equal or may not be equal. An inequality uses one of the following symbols:

Symbol	Meaning	Word Phrases
$<$	Is less than	Fewer than, below
$>$	Is greater than	More than, above
$\leq$	Is less than or equal to	At most, no more than
$\geq$	Is greater than or equal to	At least, no less than

EXAMPLE 1 Writing Inequalities

Write an inequality for each situation.

A **There are at least 25 students in the auditorium.**

number of students ≥ 25 *"At least" means greater than or equal to.*

B **No more than 150 people can occupy the room.**

room capacity ≤ 150 *"No more than" means less than or equal to.*

An inequality that contains a variable is an **algebraic inequality**. A value of the variable that makes the inequality true is a solution of the inequality.

An inequality may have more than one solution. Together, all of the solutions are called the **solution set**.

You can graph the solutions of an inequality on a number line. If the variable is "greater than" or "less than" a number, then that number is indicated with an open circle.

This open circle shows that 5 is not a solution.

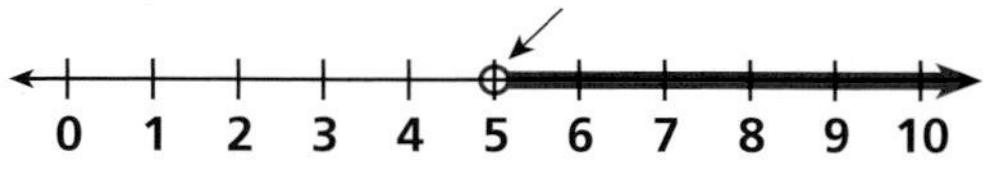

$a > 5$

If the variable is "greater than or equal to" or "less than or equal to" a number, that number is indicated with a closed circle.

This closed circle shows that 3 is a solution.

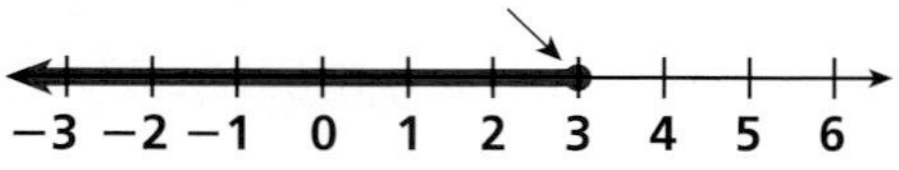

$b \leq 3$

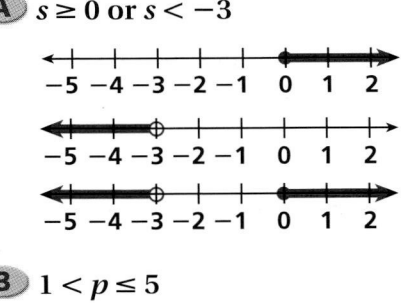

EXAMPLE 2 Graphing Simple Inequalities

Graph each inequality.

A $x > -2$

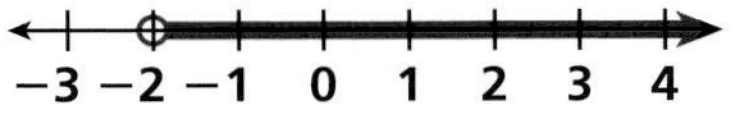

Draw an open circle at −2. The solutions are values of x greater than −2, so shade to the right of −2.

B $-1 \geq y$

Draw a closed circle at −1. The solutions are −1 and values of y less than −1, so shade to the left of −1.

Writing Math

The compound inequality $-2 < y$ and $y < 4$ can be written as $-2 < y < 4$.

A **compound inequality** is the result of combining two inequalities. The words *and* and *or* are used to describe how the two parts are related.

$x > 3$ or $x < -1$	$-2 < y$ and $y < 4$
x is either greater than 3 or less than −1.	*y is both greater than −2 and less than 4. y is between −2 and 4.*

EXAMPLE 3 Graphing Compound Inequalities

Graph each compound inequality.

A $s \geq 0$ or $s < -3$

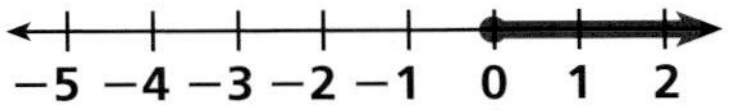

Graph $s \geq 0$.

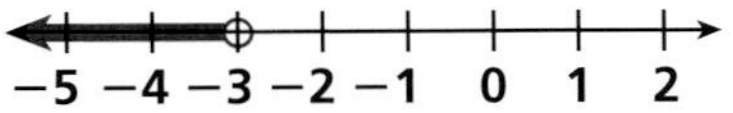

Graph $s < -3$.

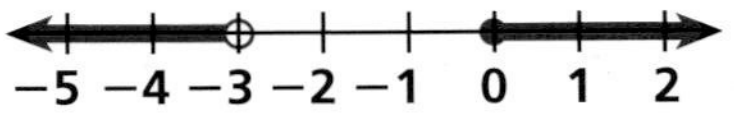

Combine the graphs.

Reading Math

$1 < p$ is the same as $p > 1$.

B $1 < p \leq 5$

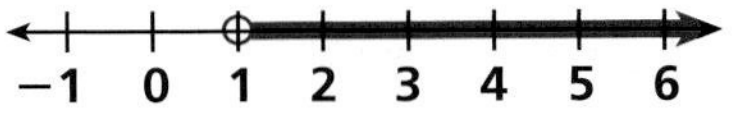

Graph $1 < p$.

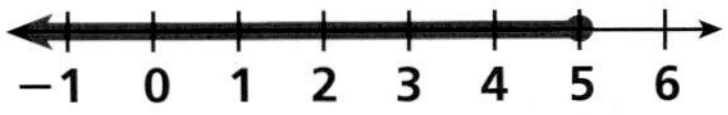

Graph $p \leq 5$.

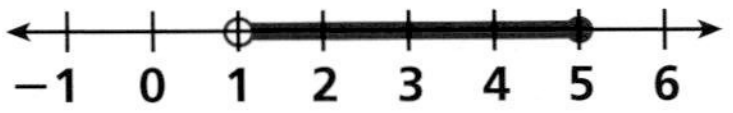

Graph the common solutions.

Think and Discuss

1. **Compare** the graphs of the inequalities $y > 2$ and $y \geq 2$.
2. **Explain** how to graph each type of compound inequality.

12-4 Exercises

go.hrw.com
Homework Help Online
KEYWORD: MS7 12-4
Parent Resources Online
KEYWORD: MS7 Parent

GUIDED PRACTICE

See Example 1 **Write an inequality for each situation.**

1. No more than 18 people are allowed in the gallery at one time.
2. There are fewer than 8 fish in the aquarium.
3. The water level is above 45 inches.

See Example 2 **Graph each inequality.**

4. $x < 3$ 5. $\frac{1}{2} \geq r$ 6. $2.8 < w$ 7. $y \geq -4$

See Example 3 **Graph each compound inequality.**

8. $a > 2$ or $a \leq -1$ 9. $-4 < p \leq 6$ 10. $-2 \leq n < 0$

INDEPENDENT PRACTICE

See Example 1 **Write an inequality for each situation.**

11. The temperature is below 40°F.
12. There are at least 24 pictures on the roll of film.
13. No more than 35 tables are in the cafeteria.
14. Fewer than 250 people attended the rally.

See Example 2 **Graph each inequality.**

15. $s \geq -1$ 16. $y < 0$ 17. $n \leq -3$
18. $2 < x$ 19. $-6 \leq b$ 20. $m < -4$

See Example 3 **Graph each compound inequality.**

21. $p > 3$ or $p < 0$ 22. $1 \leq x \leq 4$ 23. $-3 < y < -1$
24. $k > 0$ or $k \leq -2$ 25. $n \geq 1$ or $n \leq -1$ 26. $-2 < w \leq 2$

PRACTICE AND PROBLEM SOLVING

Extra Practice
See page 751.

Graph each inequality or compound inequality.

27. $z \leq -5$ 28. $3 > f$ 29. $m \geq -2$
30. $3 > y$ or $y \geq 6$ 31. $-9 < p \leq -3$ 32. $q > 2$ or $-1 > q$

Write each statement using inequality symbols.

33. The number c is between -2 and 3. 34. The number y is greater than -10.

Write an inequality shown by each graph.

35. 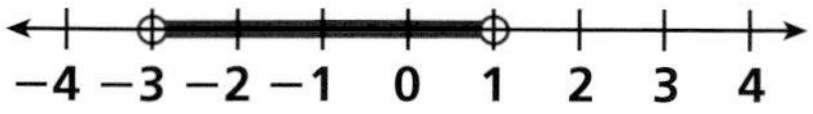

36. 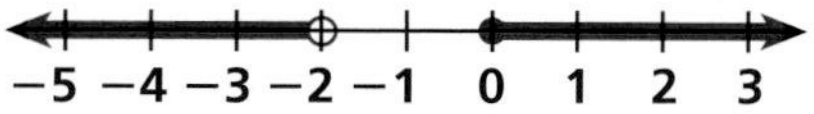

Earth Science LINK

The portion of the earth's surface that lies beneath the ocean and consists of continental crust is the continental margin. The continental margin is divided into the continental shelf, the continental slope, and the continental rise.

37. The continental shelf begins at the shoreline and slopes toward the open ocean. The depth of the continental shelf can reach 200 meters. Write a compound inequality for the depth of the continental shelf.

38. The continental slope begins at the edge of the continental shelf and continues down to the flattest part of the ocean floor. The depth of the continental slope ranges from about 200 meters to about 4,000 meters. Write a compound inequality for the depth of the continental slope.

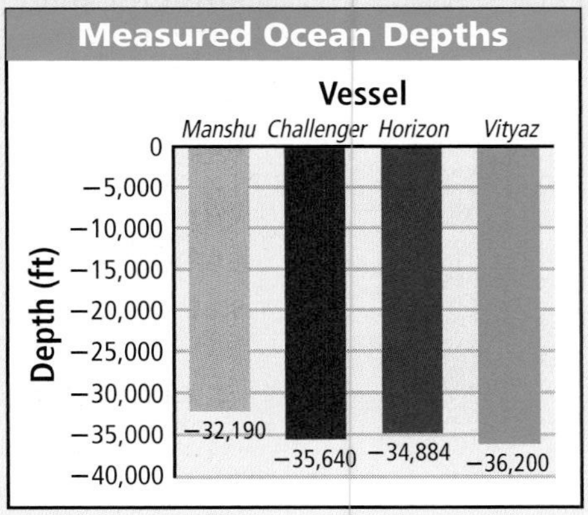

39. The bar graph shows the depth of the ocean in various locations as measured by different research vessels. Write a compound inequality that shows the ranges of depth measured by each vessel.

40. **Challenge** Water freezes at 32°F and boils at 212°F. Write three inequalities to show the ranges of temperatures for which water is a solid, a liquid, and a gas.

Deep Flight is designed to explore the ocean in underwater flights.

Test Prep and Spiral Review

41. **Multiple Choice** Which inequality represents *a number that is greater than −4 and less than 3*?

Ⓐ $-4 \geq n \geq 3$ Ⓑ $-4 < n < 3$ Ⓒ $-4 > n > 3$ Ⓓ $-4 \leq n \leq 3$

42. **Multiple Choice** Which inequality is shown by the graph?

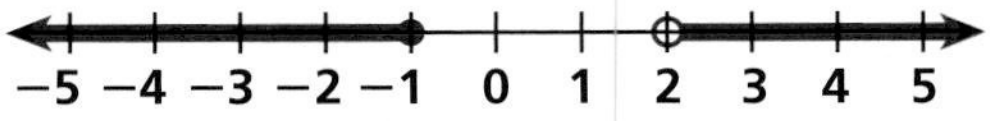

Ⓕ $x < -1$ or $x \leq 2$ Ⓖ $x < -1$ or $x \geq 2$ Ⓗ $x \leq -1$ or $x < 2$ Ⓙ $x \leq -1$ or $x > 2$

43. Mateo drove 472 miles in 8 hours. What was his average rate of speed? (Lesson 5-2)

Solve. (Lesson 12-3)

44. $10x + 4 = 6x$ **45.** $3y + 8 = 5y - 2$ **46.** $1.5z + 3 = 2.7z - 4.2$

12-5 Solving Inequalities by Adding or Subtracting

Learn to solve one-step inequalities by adding or subtracting.

Weather conditions can change rapidly. In some areas, people may wear T-shirts and shorts one day and need a warm coat the next day.

Sunday's high temperature was 72°F. This temperature was at least 40°F higher than Monday's high temperature. To find Monday's high temperature, you can solve an inequality.

When you add or subtract the same number on both sides of an inequality, the resulting statement will still be true.

$$\begin{array}{rcr} -2 & < & 5 \\ \underline{+7} & & \underline{+7} \\ 5 & < & 12 \end{array}$$

You can find solution sets of inequalities the same way you find solutions of equations, by isolating the variable.

EXAMPLE 1 Solving Inequalities by Adding

Solve. Then graph each solution set on a number line.

A $x - 12 > 32$

$$\begin{array}{rcr} x - 12 & > & 32 \\ \underline{+12} & & \underline{+12} \\ x & > & 44 \end{array}$$

Add 12 to both sides.

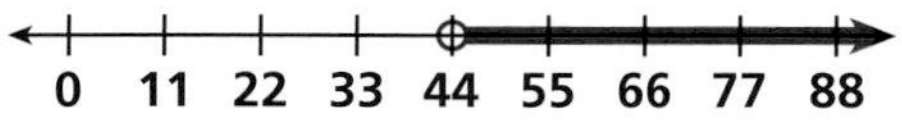

Draw an open circle at 44. Solutions are values of x greater than 44, so shade to the right of 44.

B $-14 \geq y - 8$

$$\begin{array}{rcr} -14 & \geq & y - 8 \\ \underline{+8} & & \underline{+8} \\ -6 & \geq & y \end{array}$$

Add 8 to both sides.

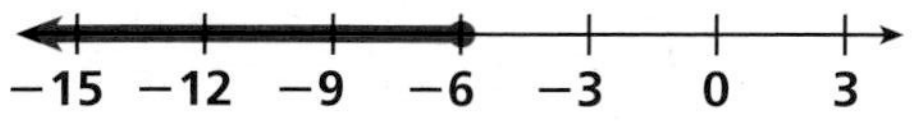

Draw a closed circle at −6. Solutions are −6 and values of y less than −6, so shade to the left of −6.

You can check the solution to an inequality by choosing any number in the solution set and substituting it into the original inequality.

EXAMPLE 2 Solving Inequalities by Subtracting

Solve. Check each answer.

A $c + 9 < 20$

$$\begin{aligned} c + 9 &< 20 \\ -9 \quad & \;\; -9 \\ c &< 11 \end{aligned}$$ *Subtract 9 from both sides.*

Check

$c + 9 < 20$

$0 + 9 \overset{?}{<} 20$ *0 is less than 11. Substitute 0 for c.*

$9 \overset{?}{<} 20$ ✔

B $-2 < x + 16$

$$\begin{aligned} -2 &< x + 16 \\ -16 \quad & \quad\; -16 \\ -18 &< x \end{aligned}$$ *Subtract 16 from both sides.*

Check

$-2 < x + 16$

$-2 \overset{?}{<} 0 + 16$ *0 is greater than −18. Substitute 0 for x.*

$-2 \overset{?}{<} 16$ ✔

> **Helpful Hint**
> When checking your solution, choose a number in the solution set that is easy to work with.

EXAMPLE 3 *Weather Application*

Sunday's high temperature of 72°F was at least 40°F higher than Monday's high temperature. What was Monday's high temperature?

Sunday's high	was at least	40°F higher than		Monday's high.
72	$\geq$	40	+	t

$$\begin{aligned} 72 &\geq 40 + t \\ -40 \quad & \;\; -40 \\ 32 &\geq t \\ t &\leq 32 \end{aligned}$$

Subtract 40 from both sides.

Rewrite the inequality.

Monday's high temperature was at most 32°F.

Think and Discuss

1. **Compare** solving addition and subtraction equations with solving addition and subtraction inequalities.
2. **Describe** how to check whether −36 is a solution of $s - 5 > 1$.

12-5 Exercises

go.hrw.com
Homework Help Online
KEYWORD: MS7 12-5
Parent Resources Online
KEYWORD: MS7 Parent

GUIDED PRACTICE

See Example 1

Solve. Then graph each solution set on a number line.

1. $x - 9 < 18$
2. $y - 11 \geq -7$
3. $4 \geq p - 3$

See Example 2

Solve. Check each answer.

4. $n + 5 > 26$
5. $b + 21 \leq -3$
6. $9 \leq 12 + k$

See Example 3

7. **Weather** Yesterday's high temperature was 30°F. Tomorrow's weather forecast includes a high temperature that is no more than 12°F warmer than yesterday's. What high temperatures are forecast for tomorrow?

INDEPENDENT PRACTICE

See Example 1

Solve. Then graph each solution set on a number line.

8. $s - 2 > 14$
9. $m - 14 < -3$
10. $b - 25 > -30$
11. $c - 17 \leq -6$
12. $-25 > y - 53$
13. $71 \leq x - 9$

See Example 2

Solve. Check each answer.

14. $w + 16 < 4$
15. $z + 9 > -3$
16. $p + 21 \leq -4$
17. $26 < f + 32$
18. $65 > k + 54$
19. $n + 29 \geq 25$

See Example 3

20. Clark scored at least 12 points more than Josh scored. Josh scored 15 points. How many points did Clark score?

21. **Life Science** Adriana is helping track bird populations. She counted 8 fewer birds on Tuesday than on Thursday. She counted at most 32 birds on Thursday. How many birds did Adriana count on Tuesday?

PRACTICE AND PROBLEM SOLVING

Extra Practice
See page 751.

Solve.

22. $k + 3.2 \geq 8$
23. $a - 1.3 > -1$
24. $c - 6\frac{1}{2} < -1\frac{1}{4}$
25. $-20 \geq 18 + m$
26. $4 < x + 7.02$
27. $g + 3\frac{2}{3} < 10$
28. $-109 > r - 58$
29. $5.9 + w \leq 21.6$
30. $n - 21.6 > 26$
31. $-150 \leq t + 92$
32. $y + 4\frac{3}{4} \geq 1\frac{1}{8}$
33. $v - 0.9 \leq -1.5$

34. **Consumer Math** To get a group discount for baseball tickets, Marco's group must have at least 20 people. The group needs at least 7 more people to sign up. How many have signed up so far?

35. It costs \$0.25 per word to put a classified ad in the newspaper. Mila cannot spend more than \$20 on an ad. How many words can she have in the ad?

36. Transportation The *shinkansen*, or bullet train, of Japan travels at an average speed of 162.3 miles per hour. It has a top speed of 186 miles per hour. At most, how many more miles per hour can the train travel beyond its average speed before it reaches its maximum speed?

LINK

Life Science

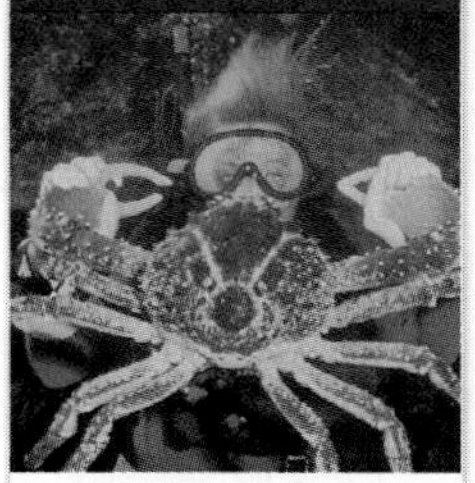

One of the largest giant spider crabs on record weighed 41lb and had a claw span of 12 ft 2 in.

go.hrw.com
Web Extra!
KEYWORD: MS7 Crab

37. Life Science The giant spider crab, the world's largest crab, lives off the southeastern coast of Japan. Giant spider crabs can grow as much as 3.6 meters across. A scientist finds one that could still grow another 0.5 m across. How wide is the giant spider crab that he found?

38. The line graph shows the number of miles Amelia rode her bike in each of the last four months. She wants to ride at least 5 miles more in May than she did in April. At least how many miles does Amelia want to ride in May?

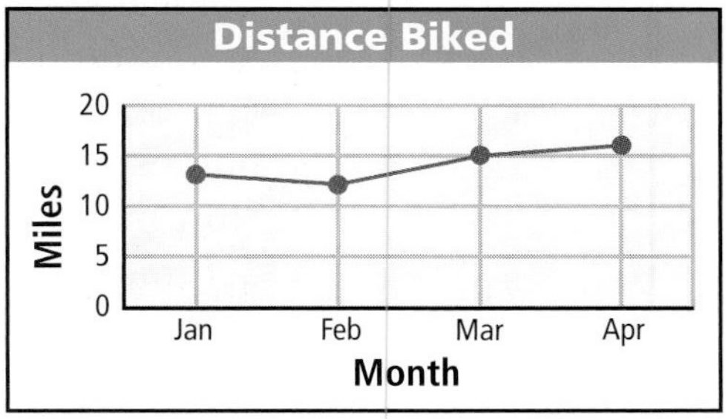

39. Physical Science The average human ear can detect sounds that have frequencies between 20 hertz and 20,000 hertz. The average dog ear can detect sounds with frequencies of up to 30,000 hertz greater than those a human ear can detect. Up to how many hertz can a dog hear?

40. Choose a Strategy If five days ago was the day after Saturday, what was the day before yesterday?

41. Write About It Explain how to solve and check the inequality $n - 9 < -15$.

42. Challenge Solve the inequality $x + (4^2 - 2^3)^2 > -1$.

Test Prep and Spiral Review

43. Multiple Choice Which inequality has the following graphed solution?

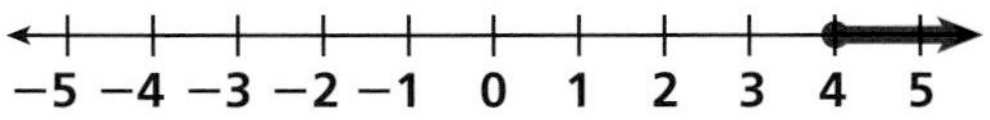

(A) $x - 2 \geq -2$ (B) $x + 3 \geq 7$ (C) $x - 3 \leq 1$ (D) $x + 5 < 9$

44. Short Response The highest-paid employee at the movie theater is the manager, who earns $10.25 per hour. The lowest-paid employees earn $3.90 less per hour than the manager. Write and graph a compound inequality to show all the other hourly wages earned at the movie theater.

The surface area of a prism is 16 in^2. Find the surface area of a similar prism that is larger by each scale factor. (Lesson 10-5)

45. scale factor = 3 **46.** scale factor = 8 **47.** scale factor = 10

48. Find the probability of flipping a coin and getting tails and then rolling a 2 on a number cube. (Lesson 11-5)

12-6 Solving Inequalities by Multiplying or Dividing

Learn to solve one-step inequalities by multiplying or dividing.

During the spring, the Schmidt family sells watermelons at a roadside stand for \$5 apiece. Mr. Schmidt calculated that it cost \$517 to plant, grow, and harvest the melons this year. How many melons must the Schmidts sell in order to make a profit for the year?

Problems like this require you to multiply or divide to solve an inequality.

When you multiply or divide both sides of an inequality by the same positive number, the statement will still be true. However, when you multiply or divide both sides by the same *negative* number, you need to reverse the direction of the inequality symbol for the statement to be true.

$-4 < 2$	$-4 < 2$
$(3)(-4) < (3)(2)$	$(-3)(-4) > (-3)(2)$
$-12 < 6$	$12 > -6$

EXAMPLE 1 Solving Inequalities by Multiplying

Solve.

A $\frac{x}{11} < 3$

$$\frac{x}{11} < 3$$

$$(11)\frac{x}{11} < (11)3 \quad \textit{Multiply both sides by 11.}$$

$$x < 33$$

B $4.8 \le \frac{r}{-6}$

$$4.8 \le \frac{r}{-6}$$

$$(-6)4.8 \ge (-6)\frac{r}{-6} \quad \textit{Multiply both sides by −6, and reverse the inequality symbol.}$$

$$-28.8 \ge r$$

EXAMPLE 2 Solving Inequalities by Dividing

Solve. Check each answer.

A $4x > 9$

$4x > 9$

$\frac{4x}{4} > \frac{9}{4}$ *Divide both sides by 4.*

$x > \frac{9}{4}$, or $2\frac{1}{4}$

Check

$4x > 9$

$4(3) \overset{?}{>} 9$ *3 is greater than $2\frac{1}{4}$. Substitute 3 for x.*

$12 \overset{?}{>} 9$ ✔

B $-60 \geq -12y$

$-60 \geq -12y$

$\frac{-60}{-12} \leq \frac{-12y}{-12}$ *Divide both sides by −12, and reverse the inequality symbol.*

$5 \leq y$

Check

$-60 \geq -12y$

$-60 \overset{?}{\geq} -12(10)$ *10 is greater than 5. Substitute 10 for y.*

$-60 \overset{?}{\geq} -120$ ✔

EXAMPLE 3 *Agriculture Application*

It cost the Schmidts $517 to raise watermelons. How many watermelons must they sell at $5 apiece to make a profit?

To make a profit, the Schmidts need to earn more than $517. Let w represent the number of watermelons they must sell.

$5w > 517$ *Write an inequality.*

$\frac{5w}{5} > \frac{517}{5}$ *Divide both sides by 5.*

$w > 103.4$

The Schmidts cannot sell 0.4 watermelon, so they need to sell at least 104 watermelons to earn a profit.

Think and Discuss

1. **Compare** solving multiplication and division equations with solving multiplication and division inequalities.
2. **Explain** how you would solve the inequality $0.5y > 4.5$.

12-6 Exercises

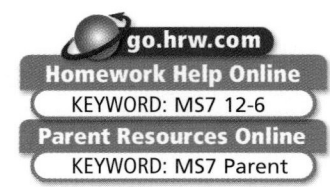

go.hrw.com
Homework Help Online
KEYWORD: MS7 12-6
Parent Resources Online
KEYWORD: MS7 Parent

GUIDED PRACTICE

See Example 1

Solve.

1. $\frac{w}{8} < -4$
2. $\frac{z}{-6} \geq 7$
3. $-4 < \frac{p}{-12}$

See Example 2

Solve. Check each answer.

4. $3m > -15$
5. $11 > -8y$
6. $25c \leq 200$

See Example 3

7. It cost Deirdre $212 to make candles. How many candles must she sell at $8 apiece to make a profit?

INDEPENDENT PRACTICE

See Example 1

Solve.

8. $\frac{s}{5} > 1.4$
9. $\frac{m}{-4} < -13$
10. $\frac{b}{6} > -30$
11. $\frac{c}{-10} \leq 12$
12. $\frac{y}{9} < 2.5$
13. $\frac{x}{1.1} \geq -1$

See Example 2

Solve. Check each answer.

14. $6w < 4$
15. $-5z > -3$
16. $15p \leq -45$
17. $-9f > 27$
18. $20k < 30$
19. $-18n \geq 180$

See Example 3

20. Attendance at a museum more than tripled from Monday to Saturday. On Monday, 186 people went to the museum. How many people went to the museum on Saturday?
21. It cost George $678 to make wreaths. How many wreaths must he sell at $15 apiece to make a profit?

PRACTICE AND PROBLEM SOLVING

Extra Practice
See page 751.

Solve.

22. $\frac{a}{65} \leq -10$
23. $0.4p > 1.6$
24. $-\frac{m}{5} < -20$
25. $\frac{2}{3}y \geq 12$
26. $\frac{x}{-9} \leq \frac{3}{5}$
27. $\frac{g}{2.1} > 0.3$
28. $\frac{r}{6} \geq \frac{2}{3}$
29. $4w \leq 1\frac{1}{2}$
30. $-10n < 10^2$
31. $-1\frac{3}{5}t > -4$
32. $-\frac{y}{12} < 3\frac{1}{2}$
33. $5.6v \geq -14$
34. A community theater group produced 8 plays over the last two years. The group's goal for the next two years is to produce at least $1\frac{1}{2}$ times as many plays as they did in the two previous years. How many plays does the group want to produce in the next two years?
35. Tammy is going to a family reunion 350 miles away. She plans to travel no faster than 70 miles per hour. What is the least amount of time it will take her to get there?

36. Social Studies Of the total U.S. population, about 874,000 people are Pacific Islanders. The graph shows where most of these Americans live.

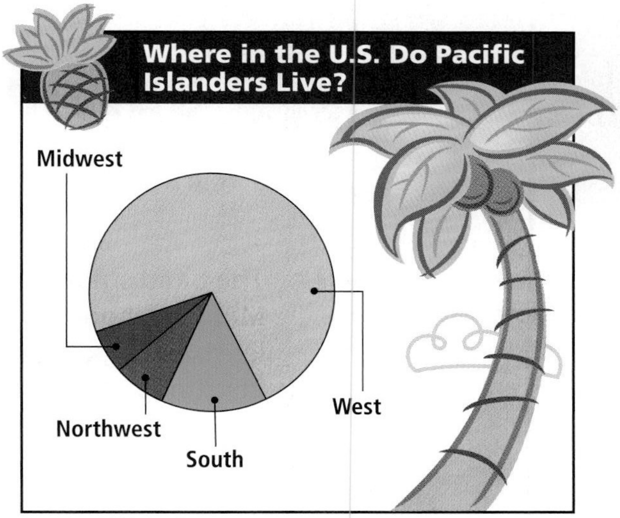

Source: USA Today

a. According to the graph, less than 10% of Pacific Islanders live in the Midwest. How many Pacific Islanders live in the Midwest?

b. According to the graph, between 10% and 20% of Pacific Islanders live in the South. How many Pacific Islanders live in the South?

37. Seventh-graders at Mountain Middle School have sold 360 subscriptions to magazines. This is $\frac{3}{4}$ of the number of subscriptions that they need to sell to reach their goal and to beat the eighth grade's sales. How many total subscriptions must they sell to reach their goal?

38. Recreation Malcolm has saved \$362 to spend on his vacation. He wants to have at least \$35 a day available to spend. How many days of vacation does Malcolm have enough money for?

39. Write a Problem Write a word problem that can be solved using the inequality $\frac{x}{2} \geq 7$. Solve the inequality.

40. Write About It Explain how to solve the inequality $\frac{n}{-8} < -40$.

41. Challenge Use what you have learned about solving multi-step equations to solve the inequality $4x - 5 \leq 7x + 4$.

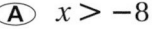

Test Prep and Spiral Review

42. Multiple Choice Solve $\frac{x}{4} > -2$.

Ⓐ $x > -8$ Ⓑ $x < -8$ Ⓒ $x < 8$ Ⓓ $x > 8$

43. Gridded Response It cost John and Jamie \$150 to grow tomatoes. They sell each tomato for \$0.50. How many tomatoes must they sell to make a profit?

44. In 16 tries, Sondra made 9 baskets. What is the experimental probability that Sondra will make a basket the next time she tries? (Lesson 11-2)

Solve. (Lesson 12-5)

45. $x - 3 < -2$ **46.** $-6 < y + 4$ **47.** $z - 1 \geq 4$ **48.** $t - 12 \leq 8.4$

12-7 Solving Two-Step Inequalities

Learn **to solve simple two-step inequalities.**

The band students at Newman Middle School are trying to raise at least $5,000 to buy new percussion instruments. They already have raised $850. How much should each of the 83 band students still raise, on average, to meet the goal?

When you solve two-step equations, you can use the order of operations in reverse to isolate the variable. You can use the same process when solving two-step inequalities.

EXAMPLE 1 Solving Two-Step Inequalities

Solve. Then graph each solution set on a number line.

A $\frac{x}{5} - 15 < 10$

$\frac{x}{5} - 15 < 10$

$\underline{+15} \quad \underline{+15}$ *Add 15 to both sides.*

$\frac{x}{5} < 25$

$(5)\frac{x}{5} < (5)25$ *Multiply both sides by 5.*

$x < 125$

B $42 \leq \frac{y}{-9} + 30$

$42 \leq \frac{y}{-9} + 30$

$\underline{-30} \quad \underline{-30}$ *Subtract 30 from both sides.*

$12 \leq \frac{y}{-9}$

$-9(12) \geq (-9)\frac{y}{-9}$ *Multiply both sides by −9, and reverse the inequality symbol.*

$-108 \geq y$

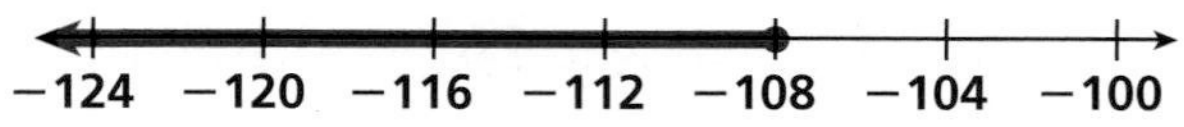

> **Remember!**
> Draw a closed circle when the inequality includes the point and an open circle when it does not include the point.

Solve. Then graph each solution set on a number line.

C $3x - 12 \geq 9$

$3x - 12 \geq 9$

$+12 \quad +12$ *Add 12 to both sides.*

$3x \geq 21$

$\frac{3x}{3} \geq \frac{21}{3}$ *Divide both sides by 3.*

$x \geq 7$

D $10 > -4y + 6$

$10 > -4y + 6$

$-6 \quad -6$ *Subtract 6 from both sides.*

$4 > -4y$

$\frac{4}{-4} < \frac{-4y}{-4}$ *Divide both sides by −4, and reverse the inequality symbol.*

$-1 < y$

EXAMPLE 2 *School Application*

The 83 members of the Newman Middle School Band are trying to raise at least $5,000 to buy new percussion instruments. They have already raised $850. How much should each student still raise, on average, to meet the goal?

Let d represent the average amount each student should still raise.

$83d + 850 \geq 5{,}000$ *Write an inequality.*

$-850 \quad -850$ *Subtract 850 from both sides.*

$83d \geq 4{,}150$

$\frac{83d}{83} \geq \frac{4{,}150}{83}$ *Divide both sides by 83.*

$d \geq 50$

On average, each band member should raise at least $50.

Think and Discuss

1. **Tell** how you would solve the inequality $8x + 5 < 20$.
2. **Explain** why the *greater than or equal to* symbol was used in the inequality in Example 2.

12-7 Exercises

go.hrw.com
Homework Help Online
KEYWORD: MS7 12-7
Parent Resources Online
KEYWORD: MS7 Parent

GUIDED PRACTICE

See Example 1

Solve. Then graph each solution set on a number line.

1. $5x + 3 < 18$ **2.** $-19 \geq \frac{z}{7} + 23$ **3.** $3y - 4 \geq 14$

4. $\frac{m}{4} - 2 > -3$ **5.** $42 \leq -11p - 13$ **6.** $\frac{n}{-3} - 4 > 4$

See Example 2

7. Three students collected more than \$93 washing cars. They used \$15 to reimburse their parents for cleaning supplies. Then they divided the remaining money equally. How much did each student earn?

INDEPENDENT PRACTICE

See Example 1

Solve. Then graph each solution set on a number line.

8. $5s - 7 > -42$ **9.** $\frac{b}{2} + 3 < 9$ **10.** $19 \leq -2q + 5$

11. $-8c - 11 \leq 13$ **12.** $\frac{y}{-4} + 6 > 10$ **13.** $\frac{x}{9} - 5 \leq -8$

14. $\frac{r}{-2} - 9 > -14$ **15.** $44 \geq 13j + 18$ **16.** $\frac{d}{13} - 12 > 27$

See Example 2

17. Rico has \$5.00. Bagels cost \$0.65 each, and a small container of cream cheese costs \$1.00. What is the greatest number of bagels Rico can buy if he also buys one small container of cream cheese?

18. The 35 members of a drill team are trying to raise at least \$1,200 to cover travel costs to a training camp. They have already raised \$500. How much should each member still raise, on average, to meet the goal?

PRACTICE AND PROBLEM SOLVING

Extra Practice
See page 751.

Solve.

19. $32 \geq -4x + 8$ **20.** $0.5 + \frac{n}{5} > -0.5$ **21.** $1.4 + \frac{c}{3} < 2$

22. $-1 < -\frac{3}{4}b - 2.2$ **23.** $12 + 2w - 8 \leq 20$ **24.** $5k + 6 - k \geq -14$

25. $\frac{s}{2} + 9 > 12 - 15$ **26.** $4t - 3 - 10t < 15$ **27.** $\frac{d}{2} + 1 + \frac{d}{2} \leq 5$

28. Mr. Monroe keeps a bag of small prizes to distribute to his students. He likes to keep at least twice as many prizes in the bag as he has students. The bag currently has 79 prizes in it. Mr. Monroe has 117 students. How many more prizes does he need to buy?

29. Manny needs to buy 5 work shirts that are each the same price. After he uses a \$20 gift certificate, he can spend no more than \$50. What is the maximum amount that each shirt can cost?

30. **Business** Darcy earns a salary of \$1,400 per month, plus a commission of 4% of her sales. She wants to earn a total of at least \$1,600 this month. What is the least amount of sales she needs?

31. **Multi-Step** The bar graph shows how many students from Warren Middle School participated in a reading challenge each of the past four years. This year, the goal is for at least 10 more students to participate than the average number of participants from the past four years. What is the goal for this year?

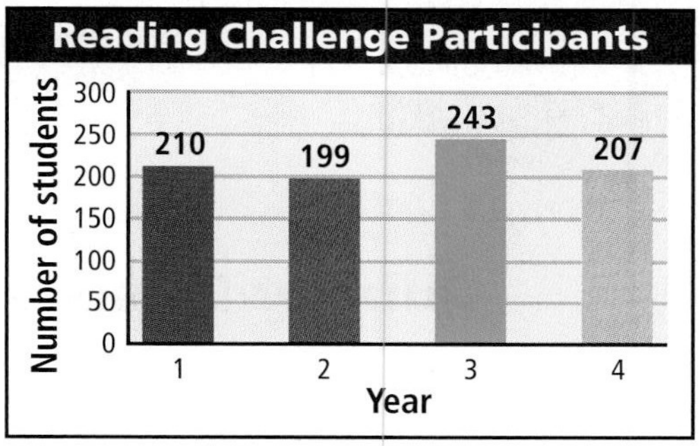

32. **Consumer Math** Michael wants to buy a belt that costs $18. He also wants to buy some shirts that are on sale for $14 each. He has $70. At most, how many shirts can Michael buy together with the belt?

33. **Earth Science** A granite rock contains the minerals feldspar, quartz, and biotite mica. The rock has $\frac{1}{3}$ as much biotite mica as quartz. The rock is at least 30% quartz. What percent of the rock is feldspar?

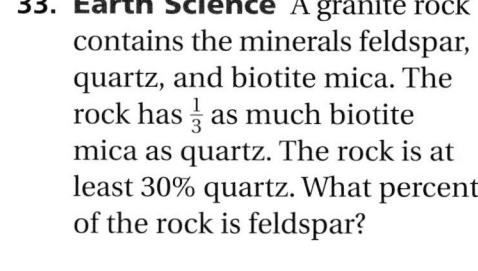

34. **What's the Error?** A student's solution to the inequality $\frac{x}{-9} - 5 > 2$ was $x > 63$. What error did the student make in the solution?

35. **Write About It** Explain how to solve the inequality $4y + 6 < -2$.

36. **Challenge** A student scored 92, 87, and 85 on three tests. She wants her average score for five tests to be at least 90. What is the lowest score the student can get, on average, on her fourth and fifth tests?

Test Prep and Spiral Review

37. **Multiple Choice** Which inequality has the following graphed solution?

Ⓐ $2x - 5 > 1$ Ⓑ $-x + 3 < 6$ Ⓒ $3x - 12 < -3$ Ⓓ $-5x - 2 > -13$

38. **Gridded Response** Gretta earns $450 per week plus a 10% commission on her sales. How much must she sell to earn at least $650 per week?

39. Jamie flips a coin and rolls a number cube. How many outcomes are possible? (Lesson 11-3)

Solve. (Lesson 12-6)

40. $6x > -24$ 41. $-4x < -20$ 42. $-3x \geq 18$ 43. $\frac{x}{3} + 6 \leq 11$

READY TO GO ON?

Quiz for Lessons 12-4 Through 12-7

12-4 Inequalities

Write an inequality for each situation.

1. Gray has at least 25 blue T-shirts.
2. The room can hold no more than 50 people.

Graph each inequality.

3. $b > -1$
4. $5 \leq t$
5. $-3 \geq x$

Graph each compound inequality.

6. $5 \geq p$ and $p > -1$
7. $-8 > g$ or $g \geq -1$
8. $-4 \leq x < 0$

12-5 Solving Inequalities by Adding or Subtracting

Solve. Then graph each solution set on a number line.

9. $28 > m - 4$
10. $8 + c \geq -13$
11. $-1 + v < 1$
12. $5 \leq p - 3$
13. $-8 > f + 1$
14. $-7 - w < 10$
15. A group of climbers are at an altitude of at most 17,500 feet. They are on their way to the top of Mount Everest, which is at an altitude of 29,035 feet. How many more feet do they have left to climb?

12-6 Solving Inequalities by Multiplying or Dividing

Solve. Check each answer.

16. $-8s > 16$
17. $\frac{x}{-2} \leq 9$
18. $-7 \leq \frac{b}{3}$
19. $\frac{c}{-3} \geq -4$
20. $28 > 7h$
21. $6y < -2$

12-7 Solving Two-Step Inequalities

Solve. Then graph each solution set on a number line.

22. $2x - 3 > 5$
23. $3 \geq -2d + 4$
24. $3g - 2 - 10g > 5$
25. $14 < -4a + 6$
26. $3.6 + 7.2k < 25.2$
27. $3z - 2 \leq 13$
28. A concert is being held in a gymnasium that can hold no more than 450 people. The bleachers seat 60 people. There will also be 26 rows of chairs set up. At most, how many people can sit in each row?
29. The 23 members of the Westview Journalism Club are trying to raise at least $2,100 to buy new publishing design software. The members have already raised $1,180. How much should each student still raise, on average, to meet the goal?

MULTI-STEP TEST PREP

CHAPTER 12

Classy Music Ricky is learning to play the guitar and is thinking about taking classes at one of the schools listed in the table.

1. Last year, Ricky spent \$590 on guitar lessons. If he takes classes at Main Street Music and spends the same amount this year, how many classes can he take?

2. How many classes would Ricky have to take in order for the cost at Main Street Music to be the same as the cost at SoundWorks?

School	Cost of Lessons
Main Street Music	Annual registration fee: \$50 \$12 per class
SoundWorks	Annual registration fee: \$14 \$16.50 per class
Town Hall	No annual registration fee \$18 per class

3. Ricky plans to buy a new guitar this year. He expects to pay \$139 for it. His total budget for the guitar and the classes is \$600. Write and solve an inequality to find the maximum number of classes Ricky will be able to take if he goes to Main Street Music and stays within his budget.

4. Write and solve inequalities to find the maximum number of classes Ricky will be able to take with a \$600 budget if he goes to the other schools. Assuming the three schools are equal in other respects, which of the schools should he choose? Why?

EXTENSION

Solving for a Variable

Learn to solve formulas with two or more variables for one of the variables.

The highest recorded speed of a magnetically elevated vehicle was achieved by the MLX01 on the Yamanashi Maglev Test Line in Japan. At its top speed, the MLX01 could travel the 229 miles from Tokyo to Kyoto in less than an hour.

The formula *distance* = *rate* · *time* ($d = rt$) tells how far an object travels at a certain rate over a certain time. In an equation or a formula that contains more than one variable, you can isolate one of the variables by using inverse operations. Recall that you cannot divide by a variable if it represents 0.

The MLX01 attained the record speed of 343 miles per hour in January 1998.

EXAMPLE 1 Solving for Variables in Formulas

Solve $d = rt$ for r.

$d = rt$

$\frac{d}{t} = \frac{rt}{t}$ *Divide both sides by t to isolate r.*

$\frac{d}{t} = r$

EXAMPLE 2 *Physical Science Application*

How long would it take the MLX01 to travel 1,029 mi if it travels at a speed of 343 mi/h?

First solve the distance formula for t because you want to find the time. Then use the given values to find t.

$d = rt$

$\frac{d}{r} = \frac{rt}{r}$ *Divide both sides by r to isolate t.*

$\frac{d}{r} = t$

$\frac{1{,}029}{343} = t$ *Substitute 1,029 for d and 343 for r.*

$3 = t$

It would take the MLX01 3 hours to travel 1,029 miles.

EXTENSION

Exercises

Solve each equation for the given variable.

1. $A = bh$ for h

2. $A = bh$ for b

3. $C = \pi d$ for d

4. $P = 4s$ for s

5. $V = Bh$ for B

6. $d = 2r$ for r

7. $xy = k$ for y

8. $A = \ell w$ for w

9. $W = Fd$ for F

10. $I = Prt$ for P

11. $C = 2\pi r$ for r

12. $A = \frac{1}{2}bh$ for h

13. $V = \frac{1}{3}Bh$ for h

14. $K = C + 273$ for C

15. $E = Pt$ for t

16. $D = \frac{m}{v}$ for v

17. $F = ma$ for a

18. $P = VI$ for I

19. $r = \frac{V}{I}$ for V

20. $I = Prt$ for r

21. $P = 2\ell + 2w$ for ℓ

22. $V = \pi r^2 h$ for h

23. Physical Science The formula $E = mc^2$ tells the amount of energy an object at rest has. In the equation, E stands for the amount of energy in joules, m stands for the rest mass in kilograms of the object, and c is the speed of light (approximately 300,000,000 meters per second). What is the rest mass of an object that has 90,000,000,000,000 joules of energy?

THE FAR SIDE® By GARY LARSON

"*Now* that desk looks better. Everything's squared away, yessir, squaaaaaared away."

24. Physical Science The Kelvin scale is a temperature scale. To convert between the Celsius temperature scale and the Kelvin temperature scale, use the formula $C = K - 273$, where C represents the temperature in degrees Celsius and K represents the temperature in kelvins. Use the formula to convert 38°C to an equivalent Kelvin temperature.

25. Physical Science Density is mass per unit volume. The formula for density is $D = \frac{m}{v}$, where D represents density, m represents mass, and v represents volume. Find the mass of a gear with a density of 3.75 g/cm^3 and a volume of 20 cm^3.

26. What is the height of the cone if its volume is 8,138.88 ft^3? Use 3.14 for π.

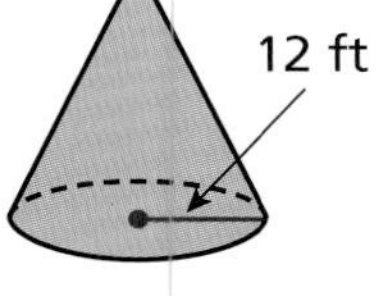

Game Time

Flapjacks

Five pancakes of different sizes are stacked in a random order. How can you get the pancakes in order from largest to smallest by flipping portions of the stack?

To find the answer, stack five disks of different sizes in no particular order. Arrange the disks from largest to smallest in the fewest number of moves possible. Move disks by choosing a disk and flipping over the whole stack from that disk up.

Start with a stack of five.

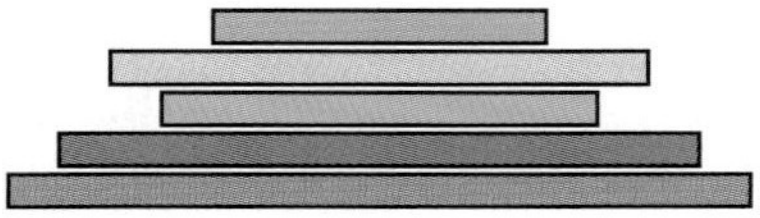

Flip the stack from the second disk up.

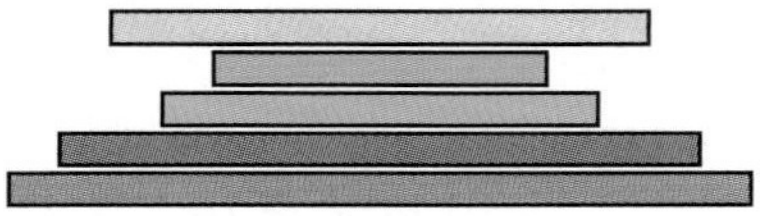

Now flip the stack from the third disk up.

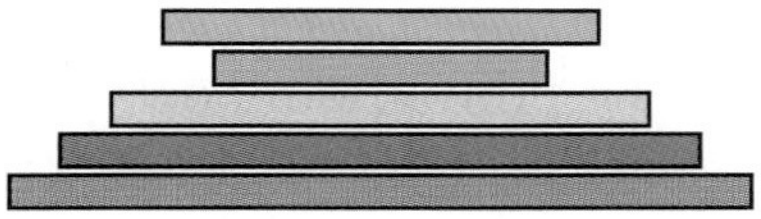

Finally, flip the stack from the second disk up.

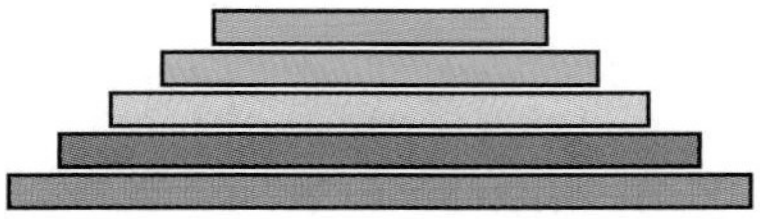

At most, it should take $3n - 2$ turns, where n is the number of disks, to arrange the disks from largest to smallest. The five disks above were arranged in three turns, which is less than $3(5) - 2 = 13$. Try it on your own.

Leaping Counters

Remove all but one of the counters from the board by jumping over each counter with another and removing the jumped counter. The game is over when you can no longer jump a counter. A perfect game would result in one counter being left in the center of the board.

A complete copy of the rules and a game board are available online.

go.hrw.com
Game Time Extra
KEYWORD: MS7 Games

It's in the Bag!

FOLDNOTES

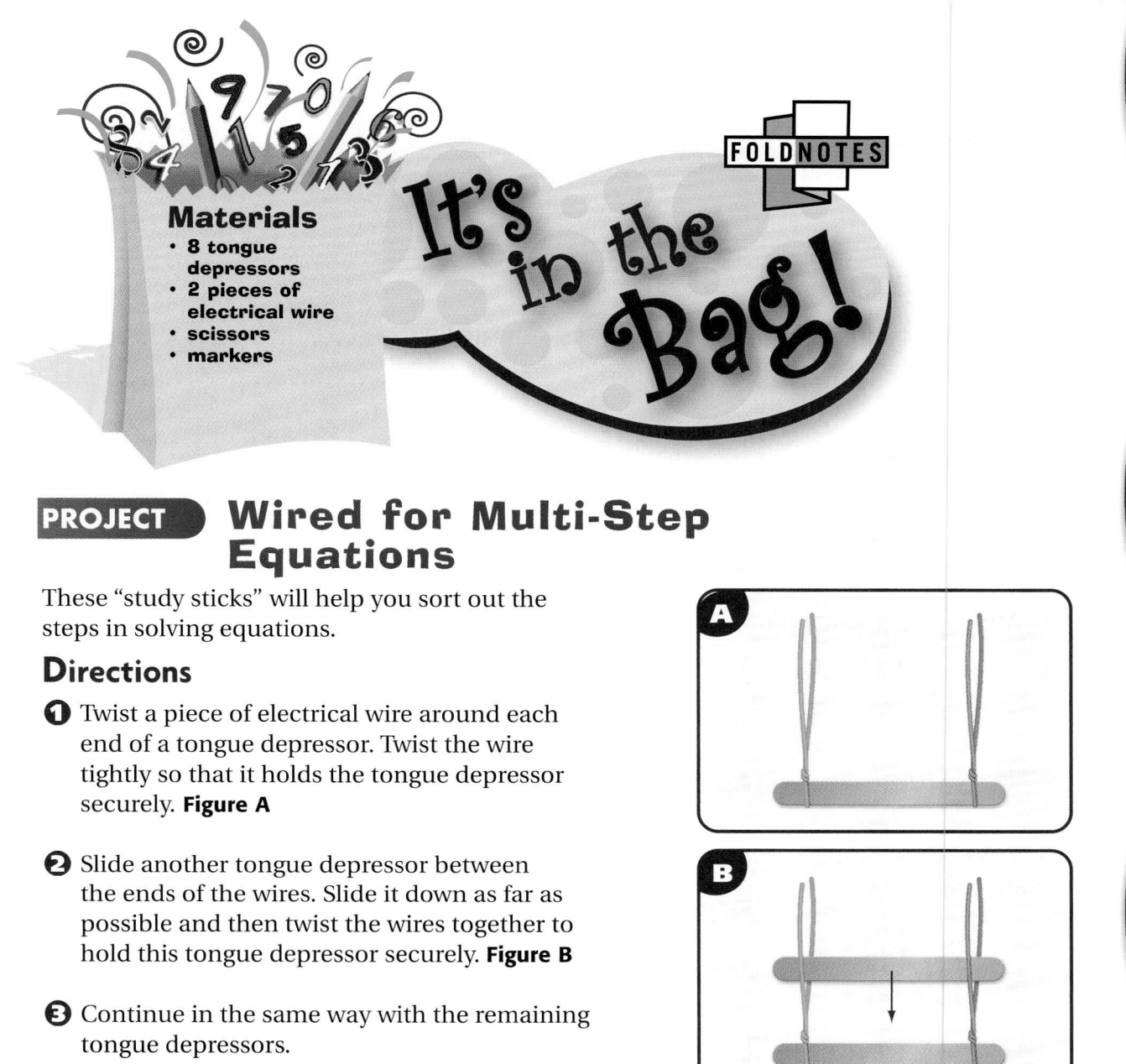

Materials
- **8 tongue depressors**
- **2 pieces of electrical wire**
- **scissors**
- **markers**

PROJECT Wired for Multi-Step Equations

These "study sticks" will help you sort out the steps in solving equations.

Directions

1. Twist a piece of electrical wire around each end of a tongue depressor. Twist the wire tightly so that it holds the tongue depressor securely. **Figure A**

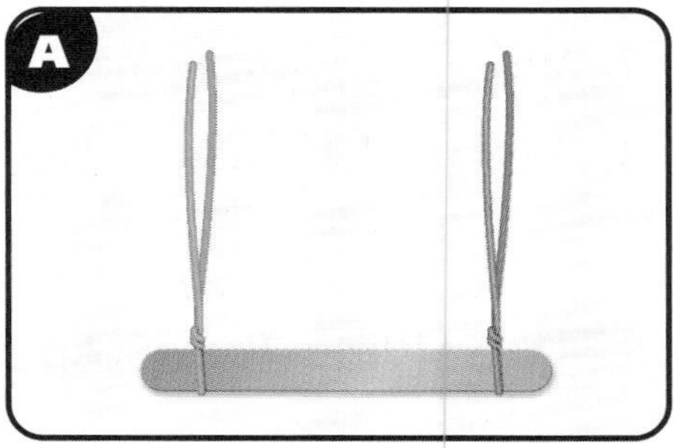

2. Slide another tongue depressor between the ends of the wires. Slide it down as far as possible and then twist the wires together to hold this tongue depressor securely. **Figure B**

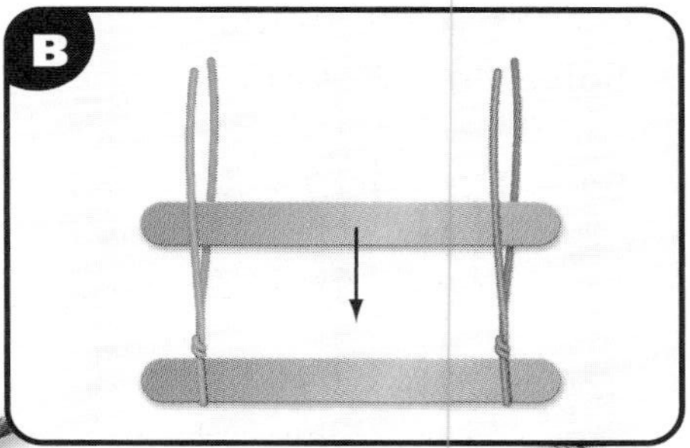

3. Continue in the same way with the remaining tongue depressors.

4. Twist the wires together at the top to make a handle. Trim the wires as needed.

Taking Note of the Math

Write the title of the chapter on the top tongue depressor. On each of the remaining tongue depressors, write the steps for solving a sample multi-step equation.

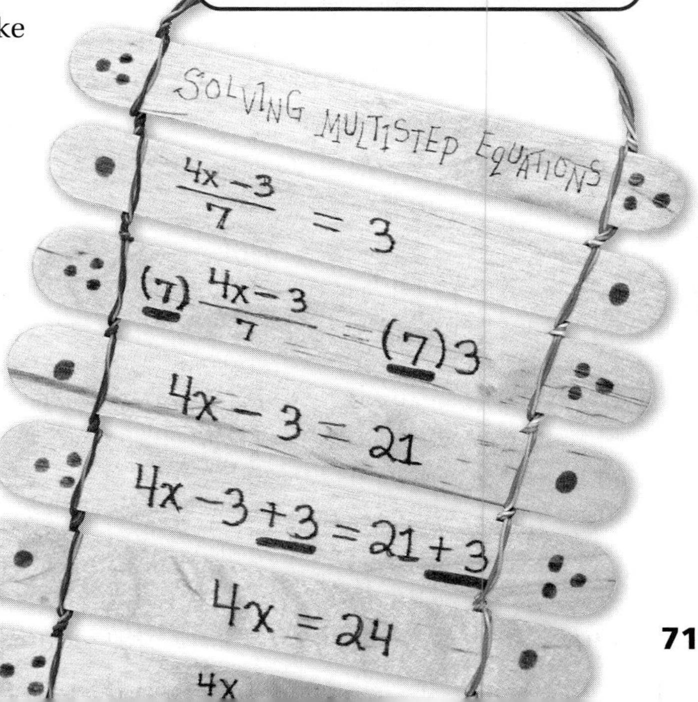

SOLVING MULTISTEP EQUATIONS
4x − 3 / 7 = 3
(7) 4x − 3 / 7 = (7)3
4x − 3 = 21
4x − 3 + 3 = 21 + 3
4x = 24
4x

CHAPTER 12

Study Guide: Review

Vocabulary

Complete the sentences below with vocabulary words from the list above.

1. A(n) ___?___ states that two quantities either are not equal or may not be equal.
2. A(n) ___?___ is a combination of more than one inequality.
3. Together, the solutions of an inequality are called the ___?___.

12-1 Solving Two-Step Equations (pp. 678–681)

EXAMPLE

■ **Solve $6a - 3 = 15$.**

$$6a - 3 = 15$$

$$6a - 3 + 3 = 15 + 3 \quad \textit{Add 3 to both sides.}$$

$$6a = 18$$

$$\frac{6a}{6} = \frac{18}{6} \quad \textit{Divide to isolate the variable.}$$

$$a = 3$$

EXERCISES

Solve.

4. $-5y + 6 = -34$
5. $9 + \frac{z}{6} = 14$
6. $-8 = \frac{w}{-7} + 13$

12-2 Solving Multi-Step Equations (pp. 682–685)

EXAMPLE

■ **Solve $\frac{4x - 3}{7} = 3$.**

$$\frac{4x - 3}{7} = 3$$

$$(7)\frac{4x - 3}{7} = (7)3 \quad \textit{Multiply.}$$

$$4x - 3 = 21$$

$$4x - 3 + 3 = 21 + 3 \quad \textit{Add 3 to both sides.}$$

$$4x = 24$$

$$\frac{4x}{4} = \frac{24}{4} \quad \textit{Divide both sides by 4.}$$

$$x = 6$$

EXERCISES

Solve.

7. $7a + 4 - 13a = 46$
8. $9 = \frac{6j - 18}{4}$
9. $\frac{8b - 5}{3} = 9$
10. $52 = -9 + 16y - 19$
11. Noelle biked twice as many miles as Leila. Adding 2 to the number of miles Noelle biked and dividing by 3 gives the number of miles Dani biked. Dani biked 18 miles. How many miles did Leila bike?

12-3 Solving Equations with Variables on Both Sides (pp. 686–689)

EXAMPLE

■ **Solve $8a = 3a + 25$.**

$$8a = 3a + 25$$
$$8a - \mathbf{3a} = 3a - \mathbf{3a} + 25 \quad \text{Subtract.}$$
$$5a = 25$$
$$\frac{5a}{5} = \frac{25}{5} \quad \text{Divide.}$$
$$a = 5$$

EXERCISES

Solve.

12. $-6b + 9 = 12b$

13. $5 - 7c = -3c - 19$

14. $18m - 14 = 12m + 2$

15. $4 - \frac{2}{5}x = \frac{1}{5}x - 8$

12-4 Inequalities (pp. 692–695)

EXAMPLE

Write an inequality for each situation.

■ **You have to be at least 17 years old to drive a car in New Jersey.**
age of driver ≥ 17

■ **Graph $x < -1$.**

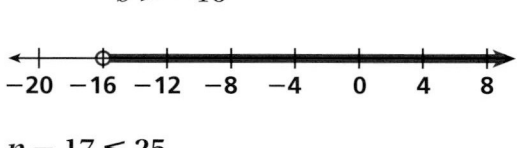

EXERCISES

Write an inequality for each situation.

16. A bridge's load limit is at most 9 tons.

17. The large tree in the park is more than 200 years old.

Graph each inequality.

18. $y \geq 3$

19. $-2 \leq k < -1$

12-5 Solving Inequalities by Adding or Subtracting (pp. 696–699)

EXAMPLE

Solve. Graph each solution set.

■ $\mathbf{b + 6 > -10}$

$$b + 6 > -10$$
$$b + 6 - 6 > -10 - 6$$
$$b > -16$$

■ $\mathbf{p - 17 \leq 25}$

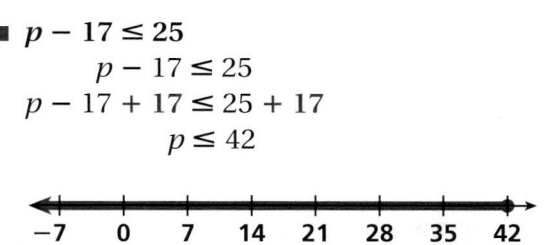

$$p - 17 \leq 25$$
$$p - 17 + 17 \leq 25 + 17$$
$$p \leq 42$$

EXERCISES

Solve. Graph each solution set.

20. $r - 16 > 9$

21. $-14 \geq 12 + x$

22. $\frac{3}{4} + g < 8\frac{3}{4}$

23. $\frac{5}{6} > \frac{2}{3} + t$

24. $7.46 > r - 1.54$

25. $u - 57.7 \geq -123.7$

26. The Wildcats scored at least 13 more points than the Stingrays scored. The Stingrays scored 25 points. How many points did the Wildcats score?

27. Gabe saved \$113. This amount was at least \$19 more than his brother saved. How much money did Gabe's brother save?

Study Guide: Review

12-6 Solving Inequalities by Multiplying or Dividing (pp. 700–703)

EXAMPLE

Solve.

- $\frac{m}{-4} \geq 3.8$

$\frac{m}{-4} \geq 3.8$

$(-4)\frac{m}{-4} \leq (-4)3.8$ *Multiply and reverse the inequality symbol.*

$m \leq -15.2$

- $8b < -48$

$8b < -48$

$\frac{8b}{8} < \frac{-48}{8}$ *Divide both sides by 8.*

$b < -6$

EXERCISES

Solve.

28. $\frac{n}{-8} > 6.9$

29. $-18 \leq -3p$

30. $\frac{k}{13} < -10$

31. $-5p > -25$

32. $2.3 \leq \frac{v}{1.2}$

33. $\frac{c}{-11} < -3$

34. It cost Carlita \$204 to make beaded purses. How many purses must Carlita sell at \$13 apiece to make a profit?

12-7 Solving Two-Step Inequalities (pp. 704–707)

EXAMPLE

Solve. Graph each solution set.

- $\frac{k}{3} - 18 > 24$

$\frac{k}{3} - 18 > 24$

$\frac{k}{3} - 18 + 18 > 24 + 18$

$\frac{k}{3} > 42$

$(3)\frac{k}{3} > (3)42$

$k > 126$

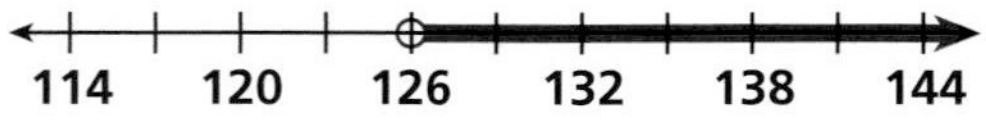

- $-5b + 11 \leq -4$

$-5b + 11 \leq -4$

$-5b + 11 - 11 \leq -4 - 11$

$-5b \leq -15$

$\frac{-5b}{-5} \geq \frac{-15}{-5}$

$b \geq 3$

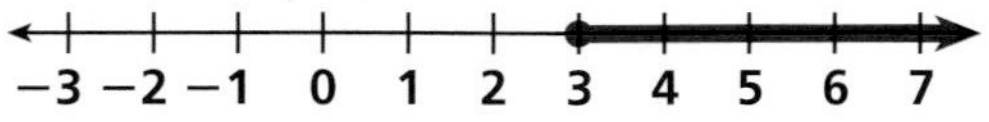

EXERCISES

Solve. Graph each solution set.

35. $-7b - 16 > -2$

36. $3.8 + \frac{d}{5} < 2.6$

37. $15 - 4n + 9 \leq 40$

38. $\frac{y}{-3} + 18 \geq 12$

39. $\frac{c}{3} + 7 > -11$

40. $32 \geq 4x - 8$

41. $18 + \frac{h}{6} \geq -8$

42. $14 > -2t - 6$

43. $-3 < \frac{w}{-4} + 10$

44. $\frac{y}{7} + 3.9 \leq 8.9$

45. Luis has \$53.55. T-shirts cost \$8.95 each, and a belt costs \$16.75. How many T-shirts can Luis buy if he also buys a new belt?

46. Clay, Alberto, and Ciana earned more than \$475 by teaching swimming lessons together. After paying the \$34 pool fee, they divided their earnings equally. How much money did each teacher earn?

CHAPTER TEST

Solve.

1. $3y - 8 = 16$
2. $\frac{x}{3} + 12 = -4$
3. $\frac{a}{6} - 7 = -4$
4. $-7b + 5 = -51$
5. $\frac{5y - 4}{3} = 7$
6. $8r + 7 - 13 = 58$
7. $6 = \frac{12s - 6}{5}$
8. $8.7 = \frac{19.8 - 4t}{3}$
9. $-14q = 4q - 126$
10. $\frac{5}{6}p + 4 = \frac{1}{6}p - 16$
11. $9 - 6k = 3k - 54$
12. $-3.6d = -7d + 34$
13. The bill for the repair of a computer was \$179. The cost of the parts was \$44, and the labor charge was \$45 per hour. How many hours did it take to repair the computer?
14. Members of the choir are baking cookies for a fund-raiser. It costs \$2.25 to make a dozen cookies, and the choir's initial expenses were \$15.75. They sell the cookies for \$4.50 a dozen. How many dozen do they have to sell to cover their costs?

Write an inequality for each situation.

15. You must be more than 4 ft tall to go on the ride.
16. You cannot go more than 65 miles per hour on Route 18.

Graph each inequality.

17. $a < -2$
18. $-5 < d$ and $d \leq 2$
19. $c > -1$ or $c < -5$
20. $b \geq 3$

Solve. Then graph each solution set on a number line.

21. $n + 8 < -9$
22. $n - 124 > -59$
23. $-40 > \frac{x}{32}$
24. $-\frac{3}{4}y \leq -12$
25. Rosa wants to save at least \$125 to buy a new skateboard. She has already saved \$46. How much more does Rosa need to save?
26. Gasoline costs \$2.75 a gallon. At most, how many gallons can be bought for \$22.00?

Solve. Then graph each solution set on a number line.

27. $m - 7.8 \leq 23.7$
28. $6z > -2\frac{2}{3}$
29. $\frac{w}{-4.9} \leq 3.4$
30. $-15 < 4a + 9$
31. $2.8 - \frac{c}{4} \geq 7.4$
32. $\frac{d}{5} - 8 > -4$
33. The seventh-grade students at Fulmore Middle School are trying to raise at least \$7,500 for the local public library. So far, each of the 198 students has raised an average of \$20. How much more money must each seventh-grader collect, on average, to reach the goal?

STANDARDIZED TEST PREP

go.hrw.com
State Test Practice Online
KEYWORD: MS7 TestPrep

Cumulative Assessment, Chapters 1–12

Multiple Choice

1. Nolan has 7 red socks, 3 black socks, 10 white socks, and 5 blue socks in a drawer. If Nolan chooses one sock at a time and puts the sock immediately on his foot, what is the probability that he will choose 2 white socks?

   (A) $\frac{3}{20}$ (C) $\frac{2}{5}$
   (B) $\frac{4}{25}$ (D) $\frac{19}{25}$

2. Of the 10,500 books in the school library, $\frac{2}{5}$ of the books are fiction. Given that 30% of the remaining books are biographies, how many books are biographies?

   (F) 4,200 (H) 1,260
   (G) 2,940 (J) 1,890

3. There are 126 girls and 104 boys attending a luncheon. Each person at the luncheon writes his or her name on a piece of paper and puts the paper in a barrel. One name is randomly selected from the barrel to win a new MP3 player. What is the probability the person selected is male?

   (A) 45.2% (C) 82.5%
   (B) 54.8% (D) Not here

4. A trapezoid has two bases, b_1 and b_2, and height h. For which values of b_1, b_2, and h is the area of the trapezoid equal to 16 in^2?

   (F) $b_1 = 8$ in., $b_2 = 4$ in., $h = 2$ in.
   (G) $b_1 = 5$ in., $b_2 = 3$ in., $h = 4$ in.
   (H) $b_1 = 2$ in., $b_2 = 8$ in., $h = 6$ in.
   (J) $b_1 = 2$ in., $b_2 = 4$ in., $h = 4$ in.

5. Between which two integers does $-\sqrt{32}$ lie?

   (A) -2 and -3 (C) 0 and -1
   (B) -5 and -6 (D) -7 and -8

6. Two of the angles of this triangle measure 36°. Which of the following descriptions best classifies this triangle?

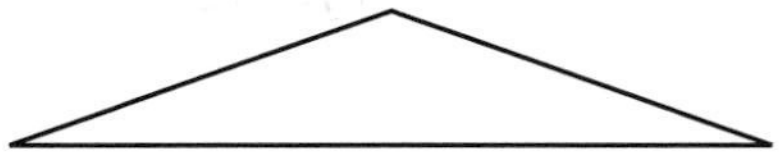

   (F) Isosceles, obtuse (H) Right, acute
   (G) Obtuse (J) Equilateral

7. Martha buys a surfboard that costs \$450 for 40% off. How much money does she save?

   (A) \$243 (C) \$24
   (B) \$162 (D) \$17

8. The total number of students in seventh grade at Madison Middle School is expected to increase by 15% from year three to year four. What will enrollment be in year four?

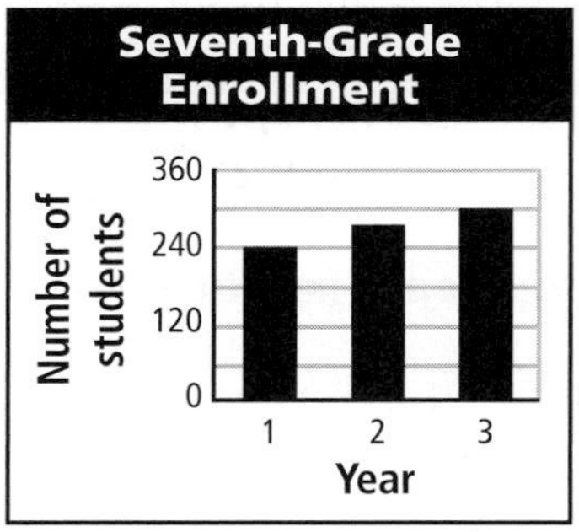

   (F) 42 (H) 345
   (G) 295 (J) 238

9. Calculate 16.0 ft − 9.03 ft. Use the correct number of significant digits in your answer.

(A) 7.0 ft (C) 6.97 ft

(B) 7 ft (D) 6 ft

10. Which rational number is greater than $-3\frac{1}{3}$ but less than $-\frac{4}{5}$?

(F) −0.4 (H) −0.19

(G) $-\frac{22}{5}$ (J) $-\frac{9}{7}$

11. Becky tutors third-graders two days after school each week. She saves $\frac{3}{5}$ of her earnings. What percent of her earnings does Becky save?

(A) 35% (C) 60%

(B) 45% (D) 70%

HOT TIP! Create and use a number line to help you order rational numbers quickly.

Gridded Response

12. What is the next term in the sequence? −3, −1, 1, 3, 5, . . .

13. Fiona has 18 coins, consisting of quarters and dimes, in her pocket. She has 6 more dimes than quarters. How many quarters does she have?

14. Freddy counted the number of bats he saw each night for one week. What is the median of the data set?

Number of Bats Spotted
42, 21, 36, 28, 40, 21, 31

15. Solve for y. $3y + 17 = -2y + 25$

16. What is the probability of flipping a coin and getting tails and then rolling a number greater than or equal to 4 on a 6-sided number cube? Write your answer as a decimal.

Short Response

17. Solve the inequality $-7y \geq 126$ and then graph the solution set on a number line. Is zero part of the solution set? Explain.

18. Nine less than four times a number is the same as twice the number increased by 11. What is the number?

   a. Write the above statement as an equation.

   b. Solve the equation.

19. Hallie is baking 5 batches of brownies for the bake sale. Each batch requires $1\frac{2}{3}$ cups of flour. Hallie has $8\frac{1}{4}$ cups of flour. Does she have enough flour to make five batches? Explain your answer.

Extended Response

20. Tim and his crew trim trees. They charge a service fee of $40 for each job, plus an hourly rate.

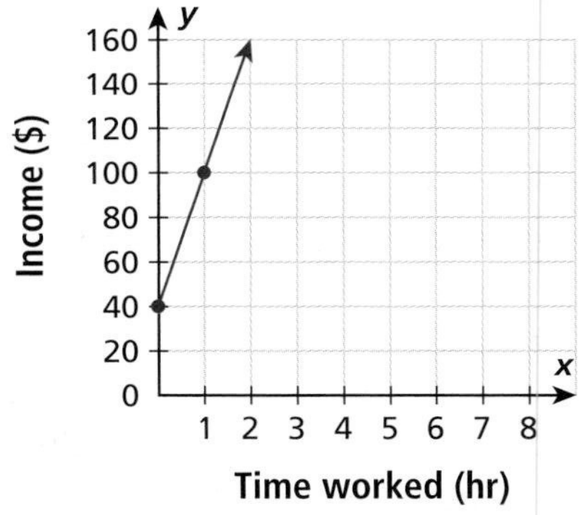

   a. Use the graph to determine the crew's hourly rate. Explain how you found your answer.

   b. Write an equation to find y, the crew's income for x hours of work.

   c. How many hours did Tim's crew work if they earned $490? Show your work.

Standardized Test Prep

Problem Solving on Location

SOUTH CAROLINA

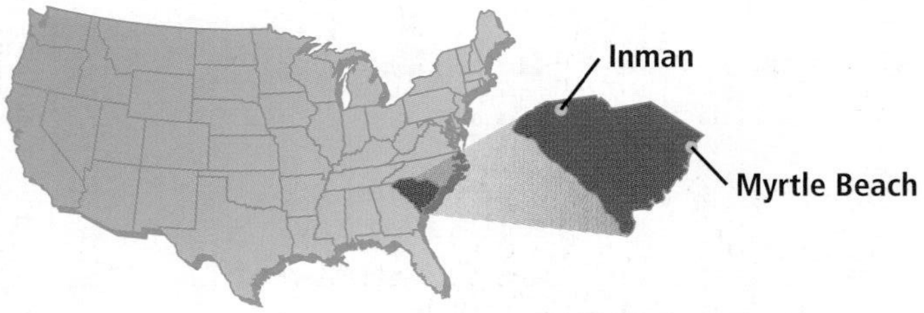

Hollywild

Many film stars live in Hollywood, but when the movie star is an Asian elephant named Donna, you can find her at Hollywild. Located in Inman, South Carolina, Hollywild houses almost 500 rare and exotic animals. Residents of Hollywild have appeared in more than 60 feature films!

Choose one or more strategies to solve each problem.

1. Adult tickets for Hollywild cost $9, and children's tickets cost $7. A group of visitors spends a total of $69 for tickets. There are twice as many children as adults in the group. How many adults and how many children are in the group?

For 2 and 3, use the table.

2. A trainer keeps track of the total amount of dog food used at Hollywild. On the day she begins tracking, 1,000 pounds of dog food have already been consumed. How many more days will it be until the total amount of dog food consumed is greater than 4,200 pounds?

3. In the most recent food shipment to Hollywild, there were 630 pounds of peanuts. How long has it been since the food shipment was delivered if only 180 pounds of peanuts remain?

Daily Food Consumption at Hollywild

Type of Food	Amount (lb)
Raw Meats	250
Hay	2,000
Fruits and Vegetables	300
Peanuts	50
Dog Food	250

Problem Solving Strategies

- Draw a Diagram
- Make a Model
- Guess and Test
- Work Backward
- Find a Pattern
- Make a Table
- Solve a Simpler Problem
- Use Logical Reasoning
- Act It Out
- Make an Organized List

✪ Family Kingdom

Family Kingdom, in Myrtle Beach, South Carolina, is home to the state's only wooden roller coaster as well as its tallest Ferris wheel. The amusement park's popular water park section offers a slide with a 185-foot drop.

Choose one or more strategies to solve each problem.

1. Family Kingdom has two go-kart tracks, six thrill rides, and three water flumes. Jessica wants to go on one of each type of ride. In how many different ways can she choose her three rides?

For 2–4, use the table.

2. Zack is 50 inches tall. He goes on all the rides that he is permitted to ride according to the table. In how many different orders can he go on these rides?
3. Donnell is 54 inches tall. He chooses two of the rides that he is permitted to ride according to the table. How many different combinations of two rides are possible?
4. Sonia went on three different rides and used a total of 14 tickets. Which rides did she choose?

Rides at Family Kingdom

Ride	Number of Tickets	✓ = Visitors this tall may ride.			
		42 in.	46 in.	50 in.	54 in.
Bumble Bee	2	✓	✓		
Flying Dragon	2	✓	✓		
Bumper Boats	4		✓	✓	✓
Carousel	4	✓	✓	✓	✓
Go-Karts	5				✓
Canoes	2	✓	✓		
Log Flume	6	✓	✓	✓	✓
Berry-Go-Round	2	✓	✓	✓	✓

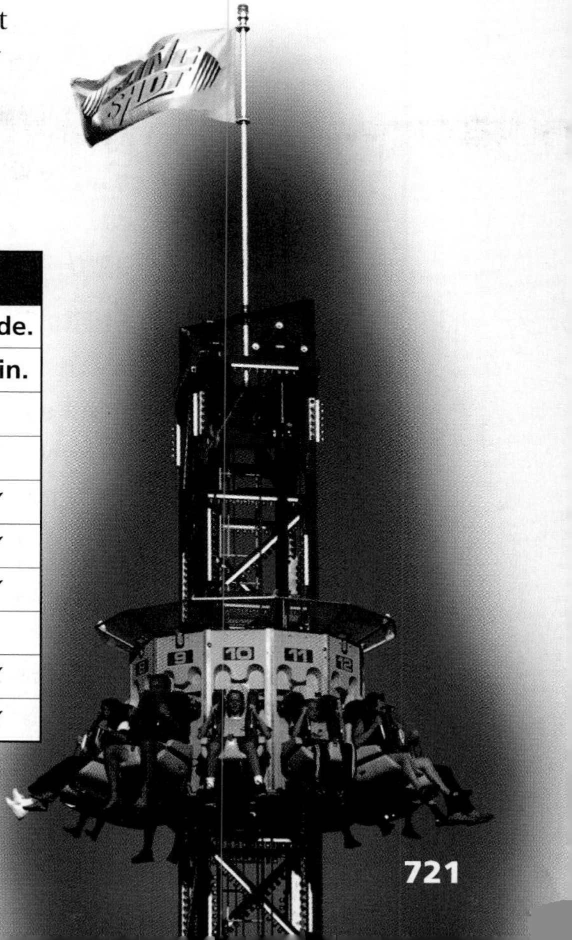

Student Handbook

Extra Practice ■ Chapter 1

LESSON 1-1

Identify a possible pattern. Use the pattern to write the next three numbers.

1. 13, 21, 29, 37, ■, ■, ■, . . .
2. 7, 8, 10, 13, ■, ■, ■, . . .
3. 165, 156, 147, 138, ■, ■, ■, . . .
4. 19, 33, 47, 61, ■, ■, ■, . . .

Identify a possible pattern. Use the pattern to draw the next three figures.

5.

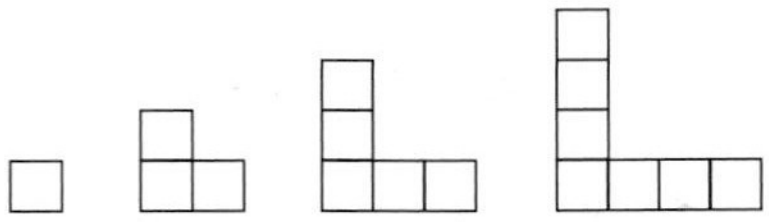

6.

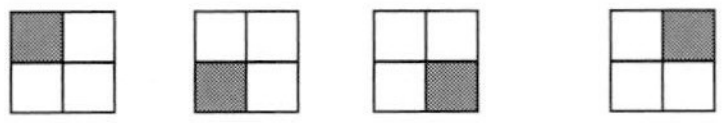

7. Make a table that shows the number of dots in each figure. Then tell how many dots are in the fifth figure of the pattern. Use drawings to justify your answer.

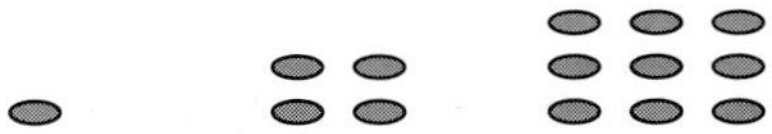

Figure 1 Figure 2 Figure 3

LESSON 1-2

Find each value.

8. 5^3
9. 7^3
10. 5^5
11. 6^5
12. 4^1
13. 8^2
14. 12^2
15. 100^3

Write each number using an exponent and the given base.

16. 121, base 11
17. 4,096, base 4
18. 216, base 6
19. 1,296, base 6
20. 256, base 2
21. 8,000, base 20
22. Maria decided to donate $1.00 to her favorite charity the first week of the month and to double the amount she donates each week. How much will she donate the sixth week?

LESSON 1-3

Choose the most appropriate metric unit for each measurement. Justify your answer.

23. The distance from home plate to first base
24. The height of a telephone pole
25. The mass of a marble
26. The capacity of a baby bottle

Convert each measure.

27. 8.9 m to millimeters
28. 56 mg to grams
29. 900 mL to liters
30. 2 L to milliliters
31. 150 m to kilometers
32. 0.002 kg to milligrams
33. Anthony and Melinda are drinking apple juice. Anthony has 300 mL left and Melinda has 0.09L. Who has the greater amount of juice? Use estimation to explain why your answer makes sense.

Extra Practice ■ Chapter 1

LESSON 1-4

Multiply.

34. $24 \cdot 10^3$

35. $20 \cdot 10^5$

36. $318 \cdot 10^3$

37. $2{,}180 \cdot 10^4$

38. $2{,}508 \cdot 10^5$

39. $5.555 \cdot 10^6$

Write each number in scientific notation.

40. 387,000

41. 2,056,000

42. 65,400,000

43. 1,560

44. 7,000,000,000

45. $206.7 \cdot 10^3$

46. The distance from the Earth to the moon is about 2.48×10^5 miles. Write this distance in standard form.

47. New York City is about 1.0871×10^4 km from Tokyo, Japan. London, England, is about 9.581×10^3 km from Tokyo. Which city is closer to Tokyo?

LESSON 1-5

Simplify each expression.

48. $9 \div 3 + 6 \cdot 5$

49. $16 + (20 \div 5) - 3^2$

50. $(6 - 3)^3 \div 9 + 7$

51. $(4 \cdot 9) - (9 - 3)^2$

52. $5 + 9 \cdot 2^2 \div 6$

53. $6{,}842 - (5^3 \cdot 5 \cdot 10)$

54. Charlotte bought 4 shirts and 3 pairs of pants. She got the pants at a discount. Simplify the expression $4 \cdot 32 + 3 \cdot 25 - (3 \cdot 25) \div 5$ to find out how much she paid for the clothes.

LESSON 1-6

Tell which property is represented.

55. $9 \cdot 2 = 2 \cdot 9$

56. $9 + 0 = 9$

57. $12 \cdot 1 = 1 \cdot 12$

58. $1 \cdot (2 \cdot 3) = (1 \cdot 2) \cdot 3$

59. $xy = yx$

60. $(x + y) + z = x + (y + z)$

Simplify each expression. Justify each step.

61. $5 + 6 + 19$

62. $5 \cdot 10 \cdot 2$

63. $3 \cdot (5 \cdot 9)$

64. $(25 \cdot 8) \cdot 4$

65. $30 + (121 + 39)$

66. $125 \cdot (2 \cdot 3)$

Use the Distributive Property to find each product.

67. $8 \cdot (2 + 10)$

68. $3 \cdot (19 + 4)$

69. $(10 - 2) \cdot 7$

70. $15 \cdot (13 - 8)$

71. $(47 + 88) \cdot 4$

72. $5 \cdot (157 - 45)$

LESSON 1-7

Evaluate each expression for the given value of the variable.

73. $8k - 7$ for $k = 4$

74. $9n + 12$ for $n = 6$

75. $12t - 15$ for $t = 4$

76. $v \div 5 + v$ for $v = 20$

77. $3r - 20 \div r$ for $r = 5$

78. $5x^2 + 3x$ for $x = 3$

LESSON 1-8

Write each phrase as an algebraic expression.

79. 12 less than a number

80. the quotient of a number and 8

81. add 7 to 8 times a number

82. 6 times the sum of 13 and a number

83. A music store sells packages of guitar strings. David bought s strings for \$24. Write an algebraic expression for the cost of one string.

LESSON 1-9

Simplify. Justify your steps using the Commutative, Associative, and Distributive Properties when necessary.

84. $5b + 3t + b$

85. $t + 3b + 3t + 3b + x$

86. $8g + 3g + 12$

87. $3u + 6 + 5k + u$

88. $11 + 5t^2 + t + 6t$

89. $y^3 + 3y + 6y^3$

90. Write an expression for the perimeter of the given figure. Then simplify the expression.

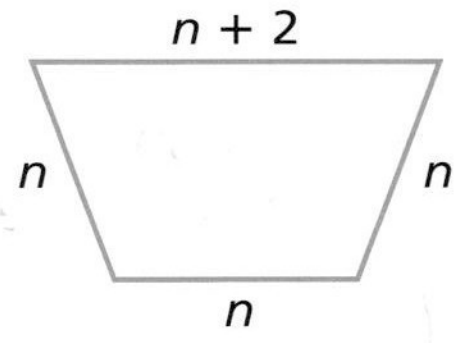

LESSON 1-10

Determine whether each number is a solution of $17 = 45 - j$.

91. 31

92. 28

93. 14

94. 22

Determine whether each number is a solution of $x + 23 = 51$.

95. 42

96. 31

97. 19

98. 28

99. Dano has 87 CDs. This is 12 more than Megan has. The equation $87 = c + 12$ can be used to represent the number of CDs that Megan has. Does Megan have 99, 85, or 75 CDs?

LESSON 1-11

Solve each equation. Check your answer.

100. $n - 22 = 16$

101. $y + 27 = 42$

102. $x - 81 = 14$

103. $t - 32 = 64$

104. $z + 39 = 72$

105. $a + 43 = 61$

106. Raquel is hiking a 9 mile trail in the Grand Canyon. She has already hiked 4 miles. How much farther does she have to hike?

LESSON 1-12

Solve each equation. Check your answer.

107. $20 = s \div 3$

108. $12y = 84$

109. $15 = \frac{n}{9}$

110. $\frac{m}{36} = 12$

111. $144 = 3p$

112. $72j = 360$

113. Adam is saving to buy a computer that costs \$400 before school starts. If school starts in 8 weeks, how much will he need to save per week in order to have enough money?

Extra Practice ■ Chapter 2

LESSON 2-1

Use a number line to order the integers from least to greatest.

1. 5, −3, −1, 2, 0 **2.** −4, −1, 3, 1, 4 **3.** −5, 0, −3, 2, 4

Use a number line to find each absolute value.

4. $|-22|$ **5.** $|9|$ **6.** $|-13|$ **7.** $|21|$

LESSON 2-2

Find each sum.

8. $8 + (-4)$ **9.** $-3 + (-6)$ **10.** $-5 + 9$ **11.** $-7 + (-2)$

Evaluate $c + d$ for the given values.

12. $c = 5, d = -9$ **13.** $c = 12, d = 9$ **14.** $c = -7, d = -2$ **15.** $c = -16, d = 8$

16. The temperature in Pierre at 8:00 A.M. was −33°F. It rose 20°F in 9 hours. What was the temperature at 5:00 P.M.?

LESSON 2-3

Find each difference.

17. $6 - (-3)$ **18.** $-4 - (-8)$ **19.** $2 - 7$ **20.** $3 - (-4)$

Evaluate $a - b$ for each set of values.

21. $a = 5, b = -8$ **22.** $a = -12, b = -6$ **23.** $a = 6, b = 13$ **24.** $a = 9, b = -17$

25. The highest mountain in the continental United States is Mount McKinley at about 20,320 feet. Death Valley, California, is the lowest point at about 282 feet below sea level. What is the difference between the highest and lowest points in the United States?

LESSON 2-4

Find each product or quotient.

26. $-9 \div 3$ **27.** $8 \cdot (-3)$ **28.** $16 \div 4$ **29.** $-7 \cdot 3$

30. $-2 \cdot 9$ **31.** $15 \div (-5)$ **32.** $6 \cdot 7$ **33.** $-72 \div (-12)$

34. A submarine descends below the ocean's surface at a rate of 75 feet per minute. How many feet below the ocean's surface will the submarine be in 12 minutes?

LESSON 2-5

Solve each equation. Check your answer.

35. $n - 25 = -18$
36. $y + (-13) = 61$
37. $21 = \frac{s}{4}$
38. $15y = -45$
39. $\frac{k}{-18} = 2$
40. $h - (-7) = -42$
41. $6 = \frac{z}{9}$
42. $68 = 4 + p$

43. Martin deposited \$76 and withdrew \$100 from his bank account. He now has \$202 in his account. How much money did he start with?

LESSON 2-6

Write the prime factorization of each number.

44. 78
45. 144
46. 96
47. 95
48. 176
49. 156
50. 336
51. 675
52. 888
53. 2,800
54. 780
55. 682

LESSON 2-7

Find the greatest common factor (GCF).

56. 6, 15
57. 18, 27
58. 26, 65
59. 60, 25
60. 84, 48
61. 90, 34
62. 49, 56
63. 36, 120
64. 30, 75
65. 32, 68
66. 81, 75
67. 30, 70, 65, 100
68. 21, 77
69. 64, 84, 120
70. 20, 40, 80, 140
71. 49, 98

72. José is making identical gift bags to sell at his concert. He has 51 CDs and 34 copies of his book. What is the greatest number of gift bags José can make using all of the CDs and all of the books?

LESSON 2-8

Find the least common multiple (LCM).

73. 12, 15
74. 30, 12
75. 16, 32
76. 25, 40
77. 30, 75
78. 12, 64
79. 15, 50
80. 15, 30, 50, 100
81. 21, 28
82. 15, 22, 30
83. 20, 40, 80, 120
84. 42, 90

85. Kanisha shoots a basket every 7 seconds. Thomas shoots a basket every 12 seconds. They begin at the same time. How many seconds will have passed when they next shoot a basket at the same time?

Extra Practice ▪ Chapter 2

LESSON 2-9

Find a fraction equivalent to the given number.

86. $\frac{1}{5}$ **87.** $7\frac{2}{3}$ **88.** 96 **89.** $\frac{50}{13}$

Determine whether the fractions in each pair are equivalent.

90. $\frac{2}{7}$ and $\frac{3}{4}$ **91.** $\frac{4}{6}$ and $\frac{12}{18}$ **92.** $\frac{7}{8}$ and $\frac{20}{24}$ **93.** $\frac{5}{12}$ and $\frac{15}{36}$

Write each improper fraction as a mixed number. Write each mixed number as an improper fraction.

94. $\frac{19}{5}$ **95.** $\frac{23}{8}$ **96.** $3\frac{4}{5}$ **97.** $2\frac{13}{15}$

LESSON 2-10

Write each fraction as a decimal. Round to the nearest hundredth, if necessary.

98. $\frac{4}{5}$ **99.** $\frac{6}{8}$ **100.** $\frac{57}{15}$ **101.** $-\frac{75}{10}$

Write each decimal as a fraction in simplest form.

102. 0.85 **103.** −0.04 **104.** 0.875 **105.** 2.6

106. Brianna sold 84 of the 96 CDs that she brought to sell at her concert. What portion of the CDs did she sell?

107. Jacob used 44 of the 60 pages in his journal. What portion of the pages did he use? Write your answer as a decimal rounded to the nearest hundredth.

LESSON 2-11

Compare the fractions. Write $<$ or $>$.

108. $\frac{8}{13}$ ▒ $\frac{5}{13}$ **109.** 0.82 ▒ 0.88 **110.** $-\frac{8}{9}$ ▒ $-\frac{11}{12}$ **111.** −1.024 ▒ 1.007

Order the numbers from least to greatest.

112. 0.5, 0.58, $\frac{6}{13}$ **113.** 2.7, 2.59, $2\frac{7}{12}$ **114.** −0.61, −0.55, $-\frac{9}{15}$

Extra Practice ▪ Chapter 3

Extra Practice

LESSON 3-1

Estimate by rounding to the nearest integer.

1. $145.2 \cdot 6.7$ **2.** $26.23 + 201.86$ **3.** $438.57 - 129.39$ **4.** $55.72 \div 7.48$

5. $-5.87 \cdot 7.39$ **6.** $54.51 + 135.47$ **7.** $-87.23 - 32.62$ **8.** $63.38 \div 4.77$

9. Caden has $48.50. He thinks he can buy three CDs for $16.99 each. Use estimation to check whether his assumption is reasonable.

LESSON 3-2

Add or subtract. Estimate to check whether each answer is reasonable.

10. $8.79 + 45.63$ **11.** $-7.85 - (-34.7)$ **12.** $43.67 - 14.81$ **13.** $-18 + (-7.32)$

14. $34.43 + (-62.57)$ **15.** $-8.26 + 7.4$ **16.** $-8.75 - 5.43$ **17.** $-35.4 - (-24.08)$

18. Zoe gets to work in 25.5 minutes and gets home from work in 37.5 minutes. How much time does she spend commuting each day?

LESSON 3-3

Multiply. Estimate to check whether each answer is reasonable.

19. $4.3 \cdot 2.8$ **20.** $-3.38 \cdot 0.8$ **21.** $-8 \cdot (-0.07)$ **22.** $7.59 \cdot (-36)$

23. $-67.4 \cdot (-8.7)$ **24.** $5.66 \cdot (-16.34)$ **25.** $-43.9 \cdot (-4.7)$ **26.** $73.3 \cdot 6.85$

27. Griffin works after school and on weekends. He worked 18.5 hours last week and gets paid $7.90 per hour. How much did he earn last week?

LESSON 3-4

Divide. Estimate to check whether each answer is reasonable.

28. $32.8 \div (-4)$ **29.** $-10.5 \div 4$ **30.** $-25.6 \div 8$ **31.** $-69.6 \div (-6)$

32. $63.5 \div (-2)$ **33.** $36.6 \div 6$ **34.** $-62.8 \div 8$ **35.** $56.05 \div 2$

36. Robert is considering purchasing a bike on the internet. The four bikes he has found are priced $79.15, $101.25, $94.18, and $130.62. What is the average price of these bikes?

Extra Practice ■ Chapter 3

LESSON 3-5

Divide. Estimate to check whether each answer is reasonable.

37. $16.9 \div (-1.3)$ **38.** $74.25 \div 6.6$ **39.** $-4.8 \div 0.12$ **40.** $-0.63 \div (-0.7)$

41. $-36.04 \div 4.24$ **42.** $34.672 \div (-4.4)$ **43.** $-128.685 \div 37.3$ **44.** $-231.28 \div (-41.3)$

45. The diameter of a northern red oak tree grows an average of 0.4 inches per year. At this rate, how long will it take the tree's diameter to grow to 24.8 inches?

LESSON 3-6

Solve.

46. $4.7 + s = 9$ **47.** $t - 1.35 = -22$ **48.** $-4.8 = -6x$ **49.** $9.6 = \frac{v}{8}$

50. $-6.5 + n = 5.9$ **51.** $x - 1.07 = -8.5$ **52.** $-6.2y = -21.08$ **53.** $\frac{r}{13} = 3.25$

54. Billy worked 7.5 hours and earned $56.70. What is Billy's hourly wage?

55. A single movie ticket costs $7.25. The Brown family consists of Mr. and Mrs. Brown, Amy, and her two brothers. What does it cost the Brown family to go to the movies together?

56. The same cereal costs $3.99 per box at one store, $3.25 per box at another store, and $3.59 per box at a third store. What is the average price per box of the cereal?

LESSON 3-7

Estimate each sum, difference, product or quotient.

57. $\frac{3}{8} + \frac{5}{6}$ **58.** $\frac{7}{8} - \frac{1}{6}$ **59.** $5\frac{3}{4} + 2\frac{3}{8}$ **60.** $6\frac{2}{3} - 2\frac{1}{6}$

61. $4\frac{7}{12} + 2\frac{3}{8}$ **62.** $\frac{7}{16} - 2\frac{3}{4}$ **63.** $8\frac{9}{10} + 1\frac{1}{9}$ **64.** $3\frac{2}{5} - 1\frac{4}{7}$

65. A stock's price in July was $\$19\frac{3}{8}$ and its price in October rose to $\$27\frac{1}{8}$. Estimate the difference between the price in July and the price in October.

LESSON 3-8

Add or subtract. Write each answer in simplest form.

66. $\frac{1}{4} + \frac{1}{3}$ **67.** $\frac{3}{11} - \frac{3}{22}$ **68** $-\frac{3}{6} + \frac{2}{3}$ **69.** $-\frac{1}{4} - \frac{7}{10}$

70. $\frac{3}{7} + \frac{5}{9}$ **71.** $\frac{7}{8} - \frac{2}{3}$ **72.** $\frac{7}{12} + \frac{5}{6}$ **73.** $\frac{4}{5} - \frac{9}{10}$

74. Jacob and Julius spent $\frac{1}{4}$ hour swimming, $\frac{1}{10}$ hour eating a snack, and then $\frac{1}{2}$ hour hiking. How long did these activities take Jacob and Julius?

LESSON 3-9

Add or subtract. Write each answer in simplest form.

75. $9\frac{7}{8} - 4\frac{1}{4}$ **76.** $3\frac{1}{2} + 2\frac{3}{4}$ **77.** $9\frac{5}{6} - 6\frac{1}{3}$ **78.** $5\frac{7}{12} + 2\frac{5}{8}$

79. $7\frac{1}{4} - 3\frac{2}{3}$ **80.** $4\frac{2}{3} + 3\frac{7}{8}$ **81.** $8\frac{2}{5} - 3\frac{9}{10}$ **82.** $3\frac{7}{8} + 4\frac{3}{5}$

83. The average male giraffe is about $17\frac{1}{2}$ feet tall. One of the giraffes at the zoo is $18\frac{1}{8}$ feet tall. How much taller is the giraffe at the zoo than the average male giraffe?

LESSON 3-10

Multiply. Write each answer in simplest form.

84. $\frac{2}{3} \cdot 12\frac{3}{4}$ **85.** $3\frac{2}{9} \cdot \frac{1}{2}$ **86.** $\frac{5}{7} \cdot 4\frac{3}{8}$ **87.** $5\frac{2}{3} \cdot \frac{7}{12}$

88. $4\frac{3}{5} \cdot 3\frac{2}{3}$ **89.** $3\frac{1}{3} \cdot 2\frac{5}{6}$ **90.** $2\frac{1}{4} \cdot 3\frac{3}{4}$ **91.** $4\frac{1}{5} \cdot 5\frac{1}{12}$

92. Mary is $2\frac{1}{2}$ times as old as Victor. If Victor is $7\frac{1}{2}$ years old, how old is Mary?

LESSON 3-11

Divide. Write each answer in simplest form.

93. $\frac{7}{8} \div \frac{5}{6}$ **94.** $\frac{7}{12} \div \frac{7}{8}$ **95.** $\frac{2}{3} \div \frac{2}{5}$ **96.** $2\frac{1}{4} \div \frac{1}{2}$

97. $5\frac{7}{8} \div \frac{5}{6}$ **98.** $3\frac{3}{4} \div 1\frac{1}{4}$ **99.** $2\frac{5}{6} \div 4\frac{1}{3}$ **100.** $5\frac{2}{3} \div 2\frac{1}{2}$

101. Each serving of chicken weighs $\frac{1}{3}$ pound. Melanie bought 12 pounds of chicken for a party. How many servings does she have?

LESSON 3-12

Solve. Write each answer in simplest form.

102. $\frac{1}{3} + s = \frac{2}{5}$ **103.** $t - \frac{3}{8} = -\frac{5}{6}$ **104.** $-\frac{5}{6} = -\frac{1}{3}x$ **105.** $\frac{2}{3}w = 240$

106. $-\frac{5}{8} + n = \frac{5}{6}$ **107.** $x - \frac{5}{8} = -\frac{5}{8}$ **108.** $-\frac{2}{3}y = -\frac{3}{4}$ **109.** $\frac{r}{6} = \frac{1}{8}$

110. Jorge owns $1\frac{3}{4}$ acres of land. Juanita, his neighbor, owns $2\frac{2}{3}$ acres. How many acres do they own in all?

111. Kyra uses $2\frac{1}{4}$ feet of ribbon to wrap each of the identical fruit baskets that she sells. How many baskets can she wrap with a 144-foot roll of ribbon?

Extra Practice ■ Chapter 4

LESSON 4-1

Plot each point on a coordinate plane. Identify the quadrant that contains each point.

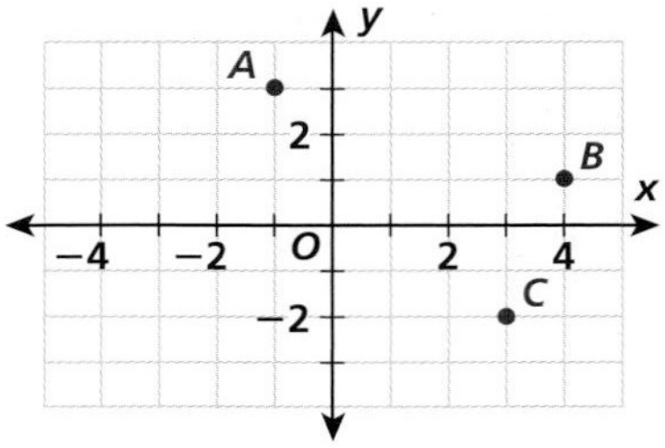

1. $M(-1, 1)$ 2. $N(4, 4)$ 3. $Q(3, -1)$

Give the coordinates of each point.

4. A 5. B 6. C

LESSON 4-2

Write the ordered pairs from each table.

7.

x	1	2	3	4
y	0	1	2	3

8.

x	5	10	15	20
y	−1	−1	−1	−1

9.

x	2	4	6	8
y	−3	−2	−1	0

Write and graph the ordered pairs from each table.

10.

x	1	2	3	4
y	−3	−2	−1	0

11.

x	0	2	4	6
y	−1	0	1	2

12.

x	−2	−1	0	1
y	3	3	3	3

13. The table shows the total cost of buying different numbers of bottles of water. Graph the data to find the cost of buying 10 bottles of water.

Number of Bottles	1	2	3	4
Total Cost ($)	1.75	3.50	5.25	7.00

LESSON 4-3

14. Abby rode her bike to the park. She had a picnic there with friends before biking home. Which graph best shows the situation?

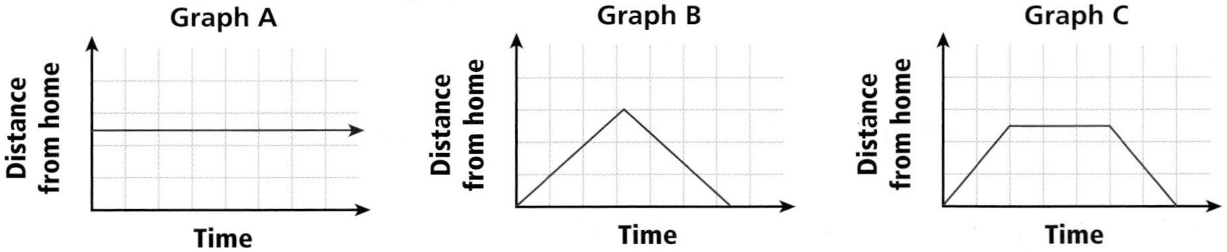

15. Mallory and her sister Jamie walked to a restaurant near their house and had lunch. They then walked to the pool across the street and went for a swim. Their mom picked them up from the pool and drove them home. Sketch a graph to show the distance that the two sisters traveled compared to time.

16. Jose is selling tins of popcorn to make money for a school fund-raiser. Each tin of popcorn sells for $12. Draw a graph to show his possible income from sales.

Extra Practice ▪ Chapter 4

LESSON 4-4

Find the output for each input.

17.

Input	Rule	Output
x	$3x - 1$	y
−2		
0		
2		

18.

Input	Rule	Output
x	$4x^2$	y
1		
3		
5		

Make a function table, and graph the resulting ordered pairs.

19. $y = 2x - 5$

Input	Rule	Output	Ordered Pair
x	$2x - 5$	y	(x, y)
0			
1			
2			

20. $y = x^2 - 1$

Input	Rule	Output	Ordered Pair
x	$x^2 - 1$	y	(x, y)
0			
1			
2			

LESSON 4-5

Tell whether each sequence of y-values is arithmetic or geometric. Then find y when $n = 5$.

21.

n	1	2	3	4	5
y	−4	0	4	8	■

22.

n	1	2	3	4	5
y	2	4	8	16	■

Write a function that describes each sequence.

23. 5, 6, 7, 8, . . . **24.** −4, −3, −2, −1, . . . **25.** 1, 8, 27, 64, . . . **26.** 2, 5, 10, 17, . . .

27. Tim wants to increase the number of miles he runs each week. His plan is to run 10 miles the first week, 12 miles the second week, 14 miles the third week, and 16 miles the fourth week. Write a function that describes the sequence, and then use the function to predict how many miles Tim will run during the eighth week.

LESSON 4-6

Graph each linear function.

28. $y = 2x + 2$ **29.** $y = x - 3$ **30.** $y = -x + 2$

31. The outside temperature is increasing at the rate of 6°F per hour. When Reid begins measuring the temperature, it is 52°F. Write a linear function that describes the outside temperature over time. Then make a graph to show the temperature over the first 3 hours.

Extra Practice ▪ Chapter 5

LESSON 5-1

One day, a veterinarian saw 20 cats and 30 dogs. Write each ratio in all three forms. Make sure each ratio is in simplest form.

1. cats to dogs **2.** dogs to cats **3.** cats to animals

4. A compact car gets 135 miles per 5 gallons of gas. A midsize car gets 210 miles per 10 gallons of gas. Which car gets more miles per gallon?

LESSON 5-2

5. Jamie's family drives 350 miles to her grandparents' house in 7 hours. What is their average speed in miles per hour?

6. A store sells milk in 3 sizes. The 128 fl oz container costs $4.59, the 64 fl oz container costs $3.29, and the 32 fl oz container costs $1.99. Which size milk has the lowest price per fluid ounce?

LESSON 5-3

Tell whether the slope is positive or negative. Then find the slope.

7.

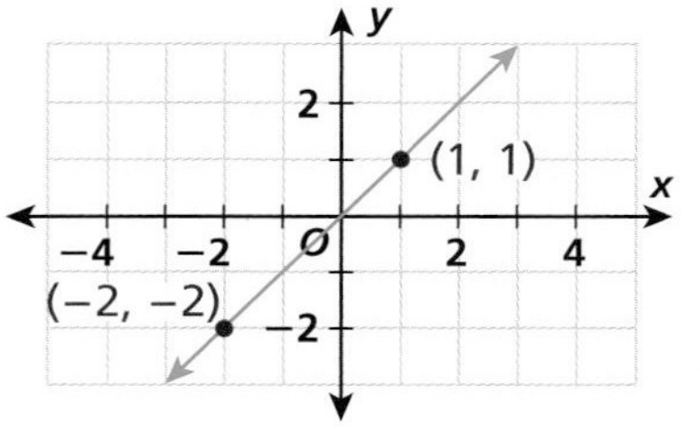

8.

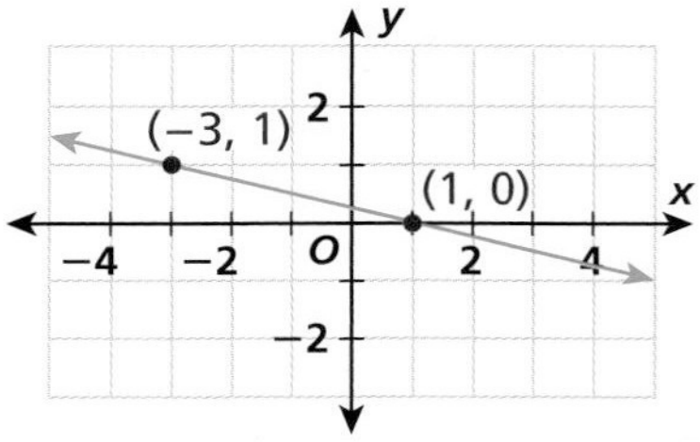

Use the given slope and point to graph each line.

9. $\frac{1}{2}$; (2, 1) **10.** $-\frac{2}{3}$; (4, 1) **11.** $-\frac{4}{5}$; (−2, −3) **12.** 3; (1, −3)

LESSON 5-4

Determine whether the ratios are proportional.

13. $\frac{25}{40}, \frac{30}{48}$ **14.** $\frac{32}{36}, \frac{24}{28}$ **15.** $\frac{5}{6}, \frac{15}{18}$ **16.** $\frac{21}{49}, \frac{18}{42}$

Find a ratio equivalent to each ratio. Then use the ratios to write a proportion.

17. $\frac{72}{81}$ **18.** $\frac{15}{40}$ **19.** $\frac{24}{32}$ **20.** $\frac{5}{13}$

LESSON 5-5

Use cross products to solve each proportion.

21. $\frac{8}{n} = \frac{12}{18}$ **22.** $\frac{4}{7} = \frac{p}{28}$ **23.** $\frac{u}{14} = -\frac{21}{28}$ **24.** $\frac{3}{21} = \frac{t}{49}$

25. $\frac{y}{35} = \frac{63}{45}$ **26.** $-\frac{6}{n} = -\frac{48}{12}$ **27.** $\frac{32}{x} = \frac{52}{117}$ **28.** $\frac{56}{80} = \frac{105}{m}$

29. The ratio of a person's weight on Earth to his weight on the Moon is 6 to 1. Rafael weighs 90 pounds on Earth. How much would he weigh on the Moon?

Extra Practice ▪ Chapter 5

LESSON 5-6

Choose the most appropriate customary unit for each measurement. Justify your answer.

30. the weight of 6 crackers
31. the capacity of a pond
32. the capacity of a baby's bottle
33. the length of a marathon

Convert each measure.

34. 8 pt to cups
35. 5 ft to inches
36. 6.5 lb to ounces

37. The directions on Brant's protein powder say to mix four scoops with 16 ounces of milk to make a protein drink. If Brant has a quart of milk, how many protein drinks can he make?

LESSON 5-7

Use the properties of similarity to determine whether the figures are similar.

38.

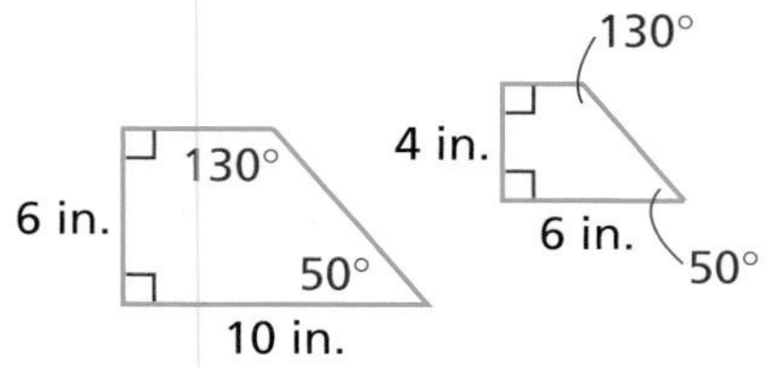

39.

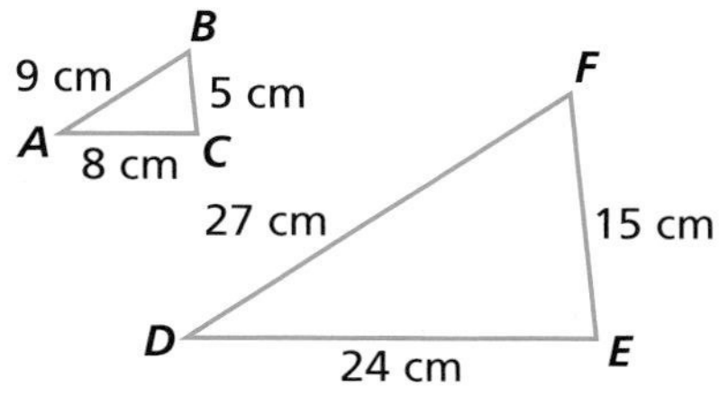

LESSON 5-8

Find the unknown length. $\triangle XYZ \sim \triangle RQS$ and $\square ABCD \sim \square KLMN$.

40.

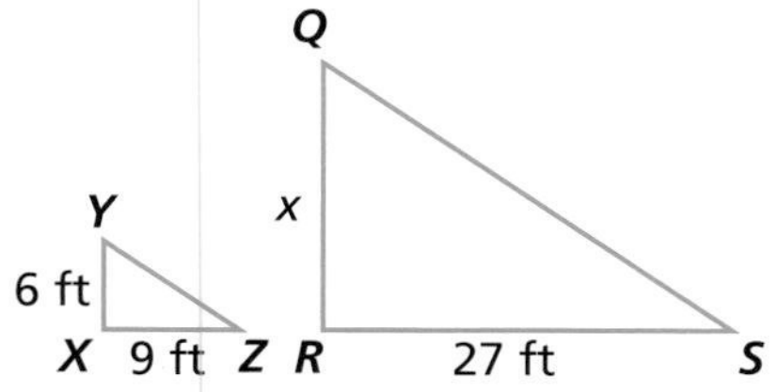

41.

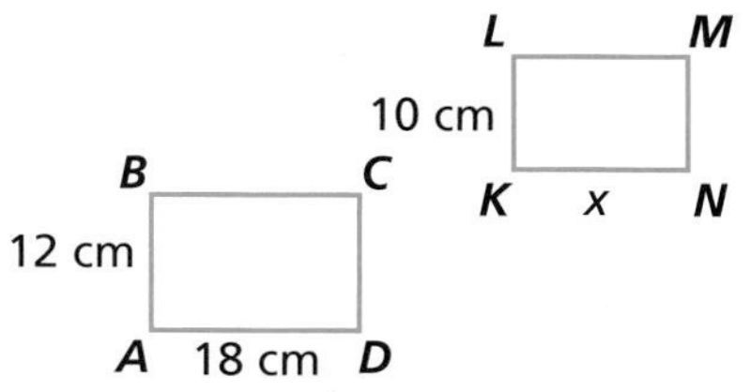

42. A 5-foot-tall girl casts a 7-foot-long shadow. A nearby telephone pole casts a 35-foot-long shadow. What is the height of the telephone pole?

LESSON 5-9

43. A scale model of the Empire State Building is 3.125 feet tall with a scale factor of $\frac{1}{400}$. Find the height of the actual Empire State Building.

44. Kira is drawing a map with a scale of 1 inch = 30 miles. The actual distance from Park City to Gatesville is 80 miles. How far from the dot for Gatesville should Kira draw the dot for Park City?

Extra Practice ■ Chapter 6

LESSON 6-1

Write the percent modeled by each grid.

1. 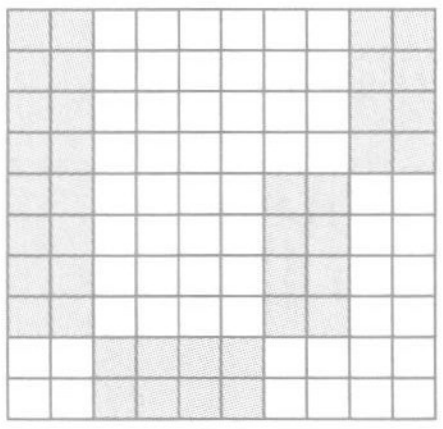

2. 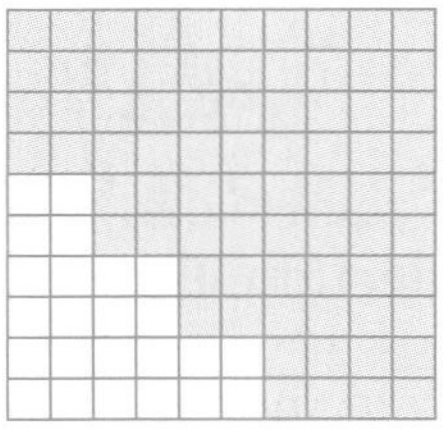

3. 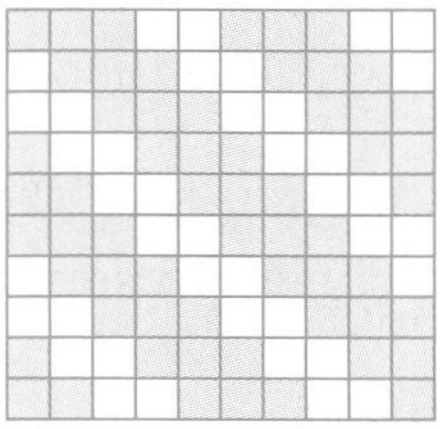

Write each percent as a fraction in simplest form.

4. 14% **5.** 110% **6.** 20% **7.** 9%

Write each percent as a decimal.

8. 27% **9.** 7% **10.** 125% **11.** 0.53%

LESSON 6-2

Write each decimal as a percent.

12. 0.06 **13.** 0.54 **14.** 1.69 **15.** 42.0 **16.** 0.898

Write each fraction as a percent.

17. $\frac{15}{34}$ **18.** $\frac{29}{86}$ **19.** $\frac{33}{44}$ **20.** $\frac{61}{91}$ **21.** $1\frac{2}{5}$

Decide whether using pencil and paper, mental math, or a calculator is most useful when solving the following problem. Then solve.

22. Tyler wants to donate 49% of his 50 stuffed animals to the children's hospital. About how many stuffed animals will he donate?

LESSON 6-3

Use a fraction to estimate the percent of each number.

23. 48% of 200 **24.** 27% of 76 **25.** 65% of 300 **26.** 15% of 15

27. Kel has $25 to spend on a pair of jeans. One pair is on sale for 30% off the regular price of $29.99. Does she have enough money to buy the jeans? Explain.

Use 1% or 10% to estimate the percent of each number.

28. 21% of 88 **29.** 19% of 109 **30.** 2% of 56 **31.** 48% of 200

32. Last year, Maria's retirement fund lost 19%. If the fund was worth $18,000 at the beginning of the year, how much money did she lose?

33. Every year, about 300 movies are made. Only 13% are considered to be hits. About how many movies are considered hits in a year?

Extra Practice ■ Chapter 6

LESSON 6-4

Find the percent of each number. Check whether your answer is reasonable.

34. 35% of 80 **35.** 55% of 256 **36.** 75% of 60 **37.** 2% of 68

38. 17% of 51 **39.** 0.5% of 80 **40.** 1% of 8.5 **41.** 1.25% of 48

42. Ryan bought a new CD holder for his car. He can fit only 60 of his CDs in the holder. This represents 60% of his collection. How many CDs does Ryan have?

LESSON 6-5

Solve.

43. What percent of 150 is 60? **44.** What percent of 140 is 28?

45. What percent of 120 is 24? **46.** What percent of 88 is 102?

47. 24 is 60% of what number? **48.** 9 is 15% of what number?

49. Thomas bought a desk with a retail sales price of $129 and paid $10.32 sales tax. What is the sales tax rate where Thomas bought the desk?

50. The sales tax on a $68 hotel room is $7.48. What is the sales tax rate?

LESSON 6-6

Find each percent of change. Round answers to the nearest tenth of a percent, if necessary.

51. 54 is increased to 68. **52.** 90 is decreased to 82. **53.** 60 is increased to 80.

54. 76 is decreased to 55. **55.** 75 is increased to 120. **56.** 50 is decreased to 33.

57. Abby's Appliances sells DVD players at 7% above the wholesale cost of $89. How much does the store charge for a DVD player?

58. A market's old parking lot held 48 cars. The new lot holds 37.5% more cars. How many parking spaces are on the new lot?

59. A regular bag of potato chips contains 12 ounces. A jumbo bag of chips contains $166\frac{2}{3}\%$ more chips. How many ounces does the jumbo bag contain?

LESSON 6-7

Find each missing value.

60. $I = \square$, $P = \$500$, $r = 5\%$, $t = 1$ year **61.** $I = \$30$, $P = \square$, $r = 6\%$, $t = 2$ years

62. $I = \$168$, $P = \$800$, $r = \square$, $t = 3$ years **63.** $I = \$48$, $P = \$300$, $r = 8\%$, $t = \square$

64. Shane deposits $600 in an account that earns 5.5% simple interest. How long will it be before the total amount is $699?

Extra Practice ■ Chapter 7

LESSON 7-1

The table shows the number of points a player scored during the last ten games of the season.

Game Date	Points	Game Date	Points
Feb 7	36	Feb 25	18
Feb 14	34	Feb 27	31
Feb 18	27	Mar 1	43
Feb 20	46	Mar 3	42
Feb 23	32	Mar 4	28

1. Make a cumulative frequency table of the data.
2. Make a stem-and-leaf plot of the data.
3. Make a line plot of the data.

LESSON 7-2

Find the mean, median, mode, and range of each data set.

4. 13, 8, 40, 19, 5, 8
5. 21, 19, 23, 26, 15, 25, 25

Identify the outlier in each data set. Then determine how the outlier affects the mean, median, and mode of the data. Then tell which measure of central tendency best describes the data with and without the outlier.

6. 23, 27, 31, 19, 56, 22, 25, 21
7. 66, 78, 57, 87, 66, 59, 239, 84

LESSON 7-3

8. The table shows the populations of four countries. Make a double-bar graph of the data.

Country	1998 Population (millions)	2001 Population (millions)
Tunisia	9.3	9.7
Syria	15.3	16.7
Turkey	64.5	66.5
Algeria	30.1	31.7

9. The list below shows the scores on a history quiz. Make a histogram of the data.

   87, 92, 75, 79, 64, 88, 96, 99, 69, 77, 78, 78, 88, 83, 93, 76

LESSON 7-4

The circle graph shows the results of a survey of 100 people from Iran who were asked about their ethnic backgrounds. Use the graph for Exercises 10–12.

Ethnic Groups of Iran

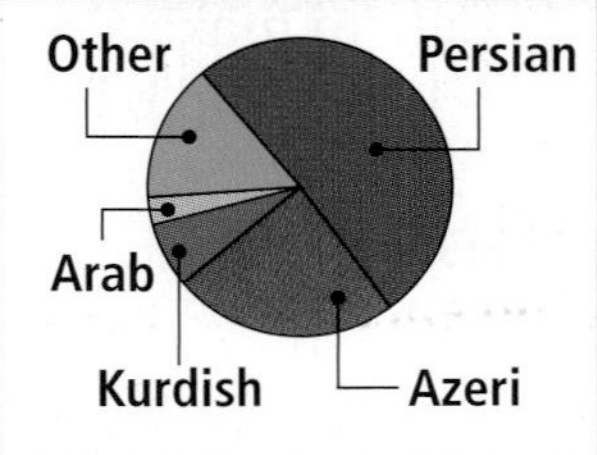

10. Which ethnic group is the second largest?
11. Approximately what percent of the people are Persian?
12. According to the survey, 3% of the people are Arab. How many of the people surveyed are Arab?

Decide whether a bar graph or a circle graph would best display the information. Explain your answer.

13. the number of guitars sold compared with the number of drum sets sold for the year 2002
14. the average temperature for each day of one week

Extra Practice ■ Chapter 7

Extra Practice

LESSON 7-5

15. Use the data to make a box-and-whisker plot. 22, 41, 39, 27, 29, 30, 40, 61, 25, 28, 32

LESSON 7-6

The table shows the number of students Karen tutored during certain months. Use the table for Exercises 16 and 17.

Month	Students
Jan	5
Mar	8
May	9
Jul	12
Sep	14
Nov	18

16. Make a line graph of the data. Use the graph to determine during which months the number of students increased the most.

17. Use the graph to estimate the number of students Karen tutored during the month of October.

LESSON 7-7

Choose the type of graph that would best represent each type of data.

18. the number of participants in a hole-in-one contest for the last 10 years

19. the prices of the five top-selling MP3 players

LESSON 7-8

Determine whether each sample may be biased. Explain.

20. A bank asks the first 10 customers that enter in the morning if they are satisfied with the bank's customer service.

21. Members of a polling organization survey 1,000 residents by randomly choosing names from a list of all residents.

LESSON 7-9

22. The table shows the average number of points per game that Michael Jordan scored during each season with the Chicago Bulls. Use the data to make a scatter plot. Describe the relationship between the data sets.

Year	Points	Year	Points
1990	33.6	1994	26.9
1991	31.5	1995	30.4
1992	30.1	1996	29.6
1993	32.6	1997	28.7

LESSON 7-10

Explain why each graph could be misleading.

23.

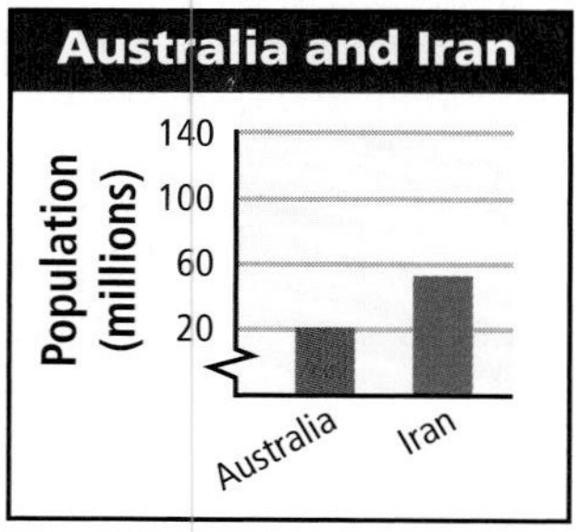

24.

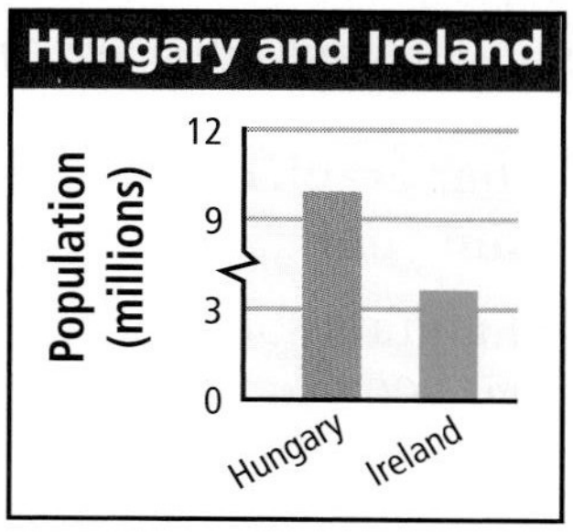

Extra Practice ▪ Chapter 8

LESSON 8-1

Identify the figures in the diagram.

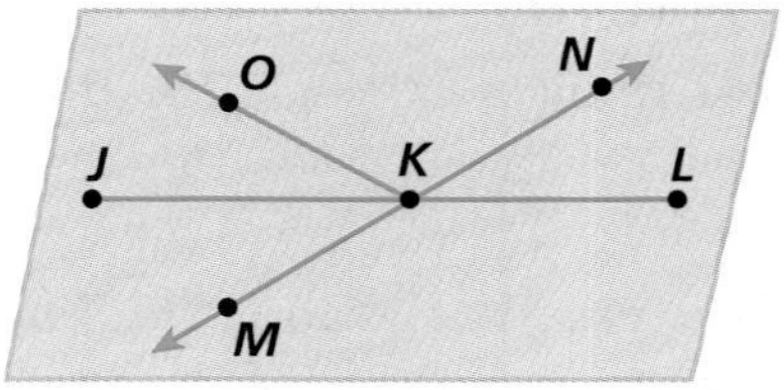

1. three points
2. a line
3. a plane
4. three rays
5. three line segments

6. Identify the line segments that are congruent in the figure.

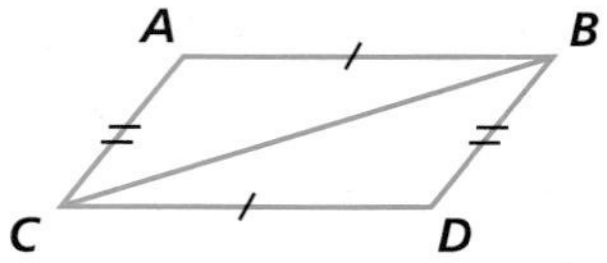

LESSON 8-2

Tell whether each angle is acute, right, obtuse, or straight.

7. 

8. 

9. 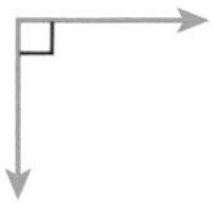

10. 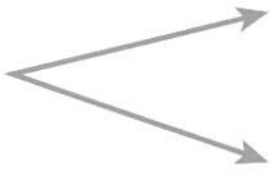

Use the diagram to tell whether the angles are complementary, supplementary, or neither.

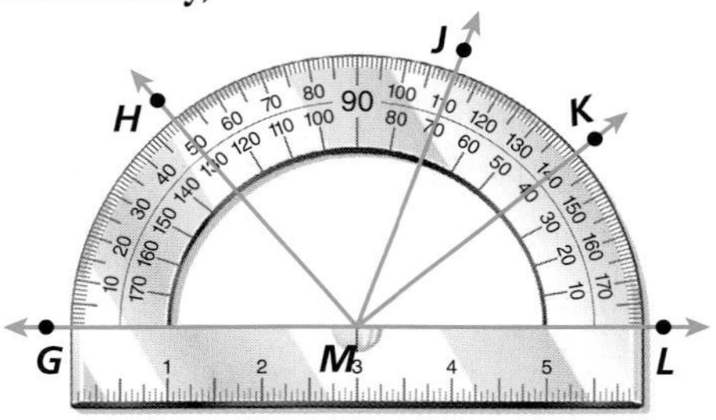

11. $\angle GMH$ and $\angle HMJ$
12. $\angle HMJ$ and $\angle JMK$
13. $\angle LMK$ and $\angle GMK$
14. $\angle JMK$ and $\angle KML$
15. Angles Q and S are complementary. If $m\angle Q$ is 77°, what is $m\angle S$?
16. Angles M and N are supplementary. If $m\angle M$ is 17°, what is $m\angle N$?

LESSON 8-3

Tell whether the lines appear parallel, perpendicular, or skew.

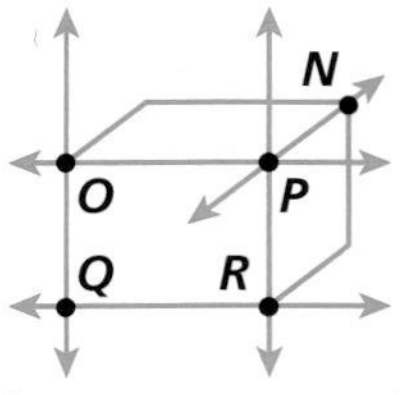

17. $\overleftrightarrow{PN}$ and $\overleftrightarrow{QR}$
18. $\overleftrightarrow{OQ}$ and $\overleftrightarrow{QR}$
19. $\overleftrightarrow{OP}$ and $\overleftrightarrow{QR}$
20. $\overleftrightarrow{PN}$ and $\overleftrightarrow{OQ}$

Line $j \parallel$ line k. Find the measures of each angle.

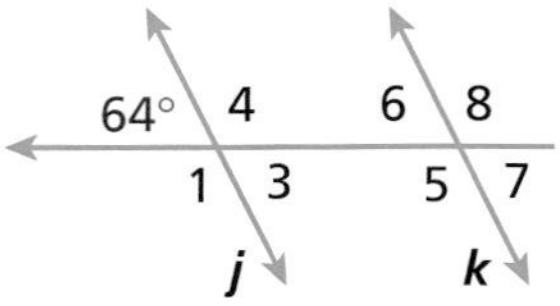

21. $\angle 1$
22. $\angle 3$
23. $\angle 8$

Extra Practice ■ Chapter 8

LESSON 8-4

Name the parts of circle *I*.

24. radii **25.** diameters **26.** chords

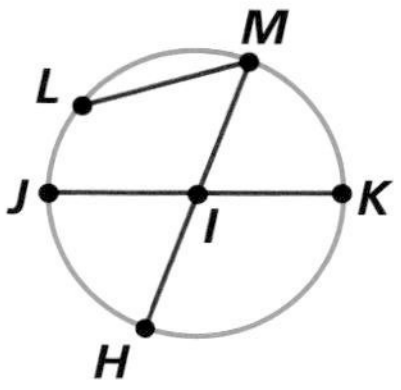

LESSON 8-5

Determine whether each figure is a polygon. If it is not, explain why not.

27.
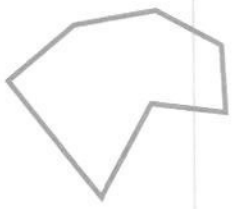

28.
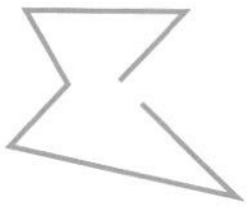

29.

Name each polygon.

30.
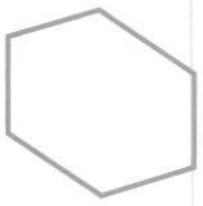

31.
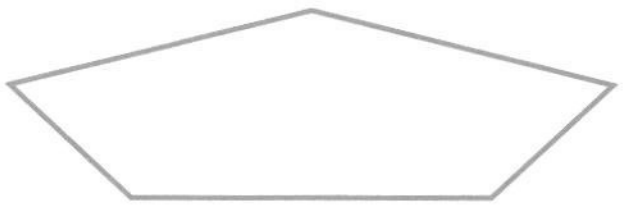

32.
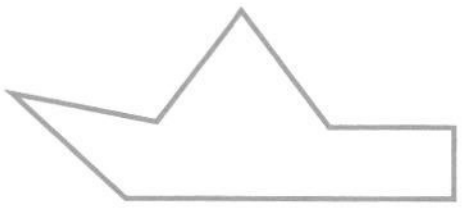

LESSON 8-6

Classify each triangle according to its sides and angles.

33.

34.
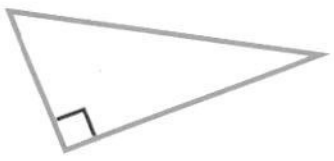

35.

36.
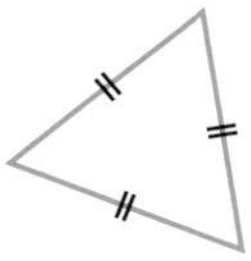

LESSON 8-7

Give all of the names that apply to each quadrilateral. Then give the name that best describes it.

37.
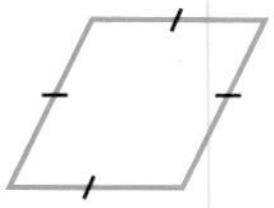

38.

39.

40.
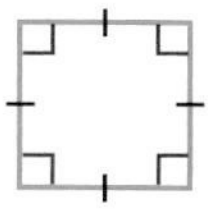

LESSON 8-8

Find the unknown angle measure in each triangle.

41.
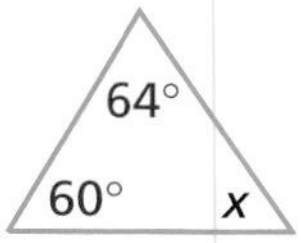

42.
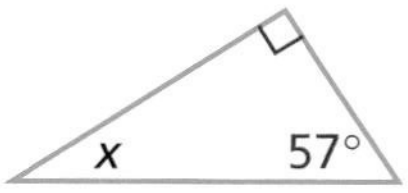

43.
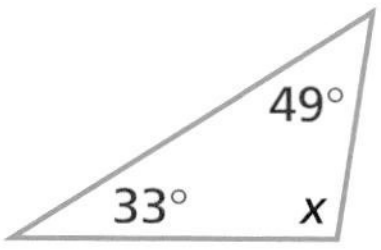

44.
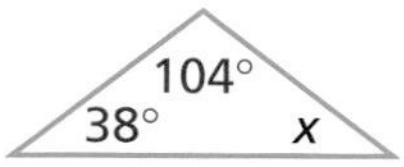

Divide each polygon into triangles to find the sum of its angle measures.

45.

46.
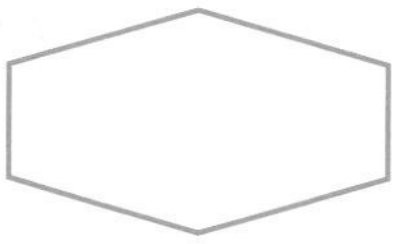

47.
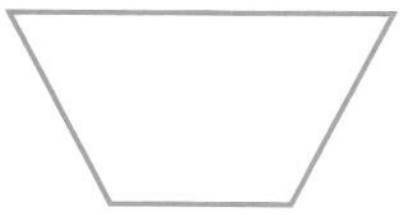

48.

Extra Practice ■ Chapter 8

LESSON 8-9

Determine whether the triangles are congruent.

49.

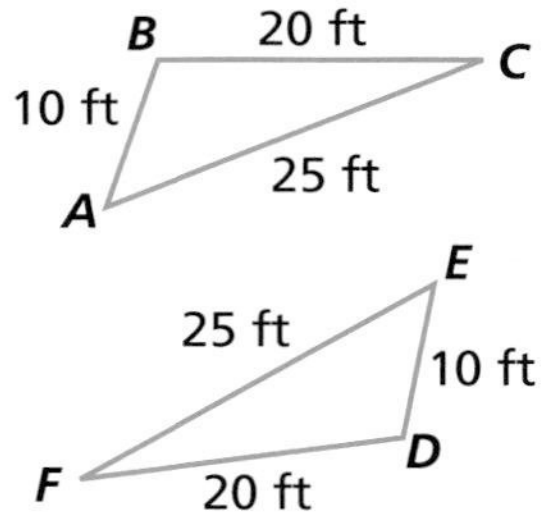

50.

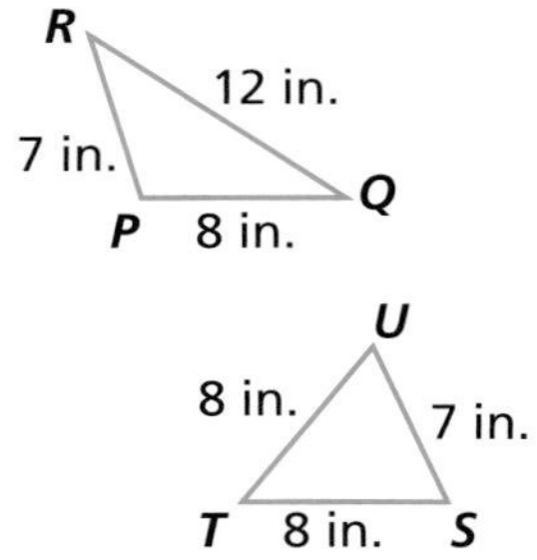

51.

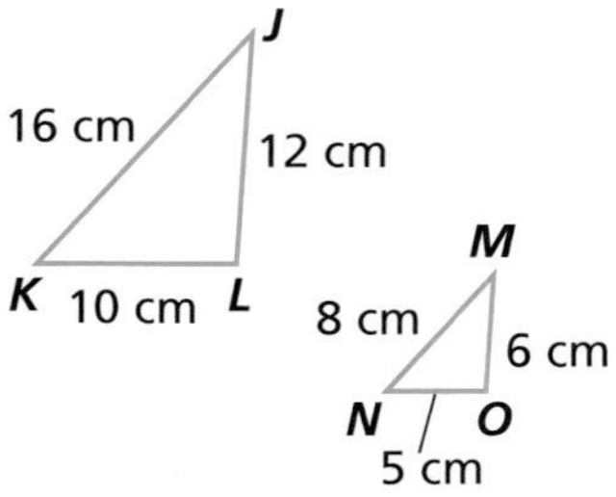

Determine the missing measure(s) in each set of congruent polygons.

52.

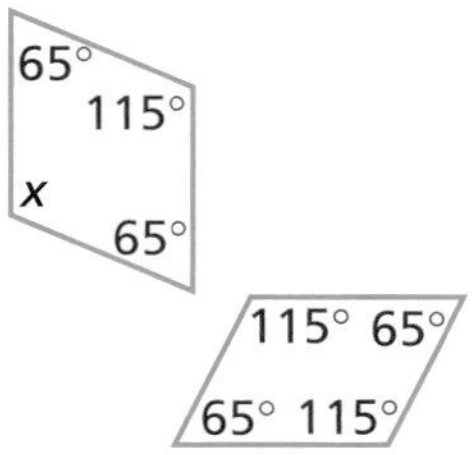

53.

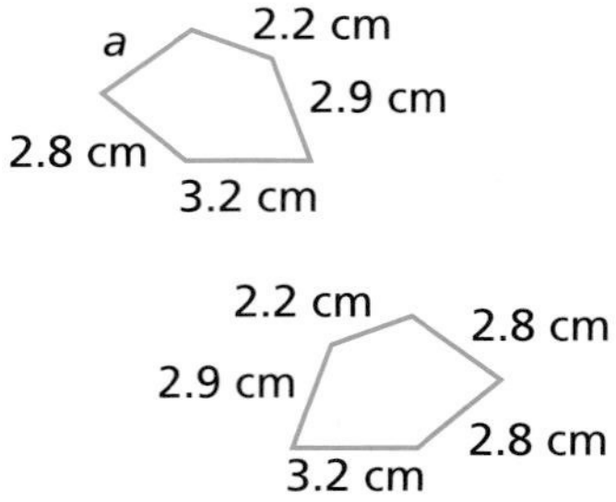

54.

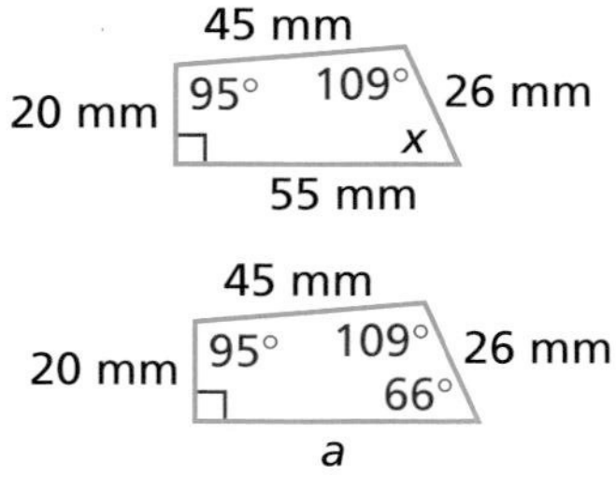

LESSON 8-10

Graph each transformation.

55. Rotate $\triangle PQR$ 90° counter-clockwise about vertex R.

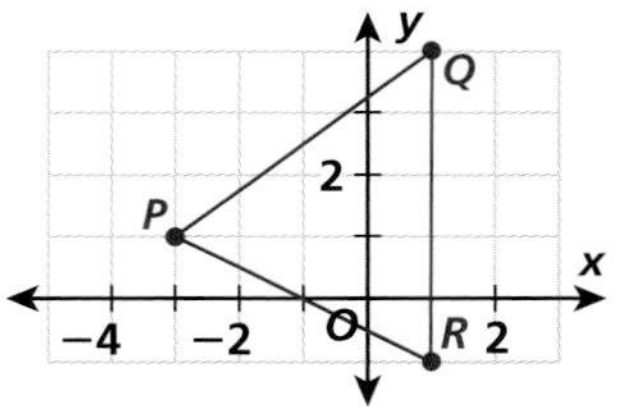

56. Reflect the figure across the y-axis.

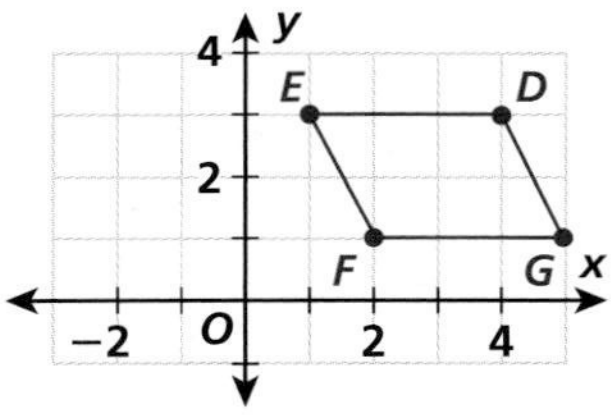

57. Translate $\triangle RST$ 3 units right and 3 units down.

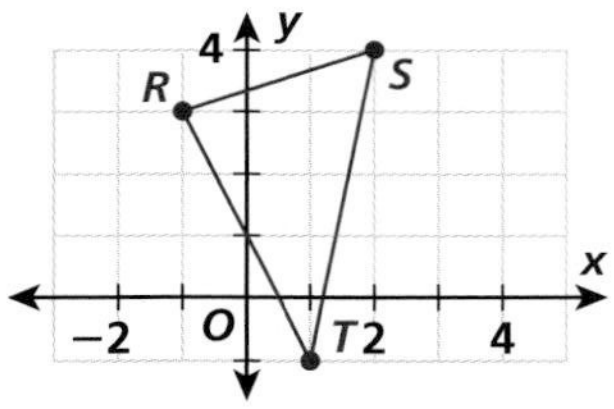

LESSON 8-11

Decide whether each figure has line symmetry. If it does, draw all the lines of symmetry.

58.

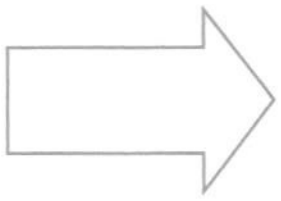

59.

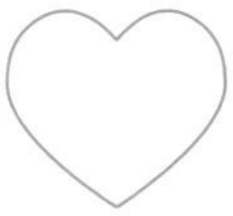

60.

Tell how many times each figure will show rotational symmetry within one full rotation.

61.

62.

63.

Extra Practice ▪ Chapter 9

LESSON 9-1

Choose the more precise measurement in each pair.

1. 2 ft, 23 in. **2.** 8.1 m, 811 cm **3.** $6\frac{5}{16}$ m, $6\frac{3}{8}$ m

Calculate. Use the correct number of significant digits in each answer.

4. $7.02 + 6.9$ **5.** $12 - 5.88$ **6.** $9.20 \div 3.5$ **7.** $3.6 \cdot 1.8$

LESSON 9-2

Find each perimeter.

8.
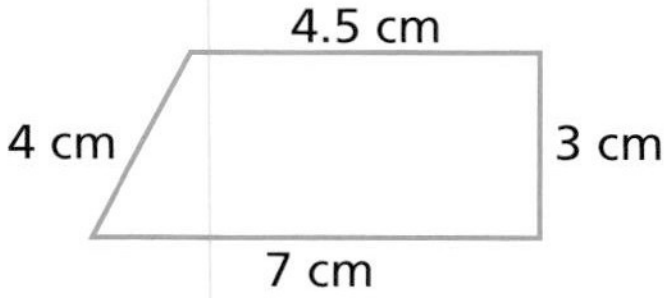

9.
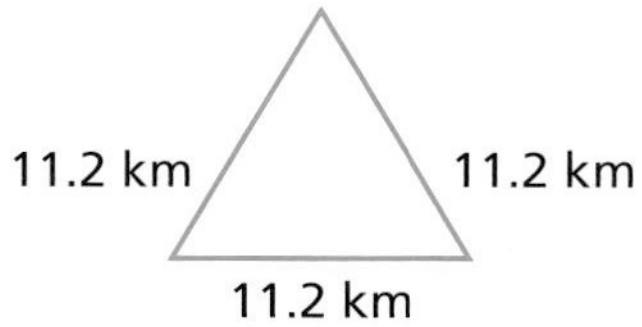

10.
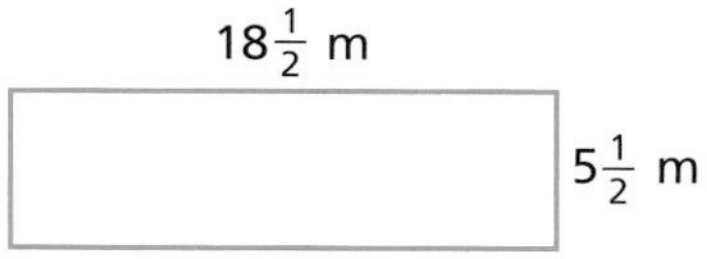

Find the circumference of each circle to the nearest tenth. Use 3.14 or $\frac{22}{7}$ for π.

11.
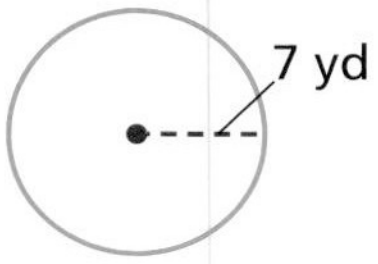

12.
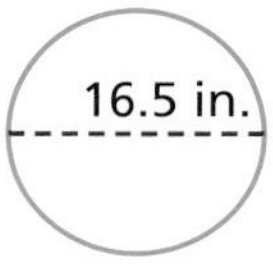

13.
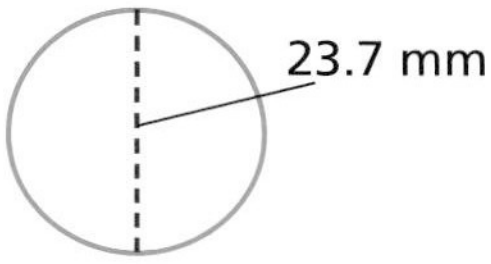

LESSON 9-3

Find the area of each rectangle or parallelogram.

14.
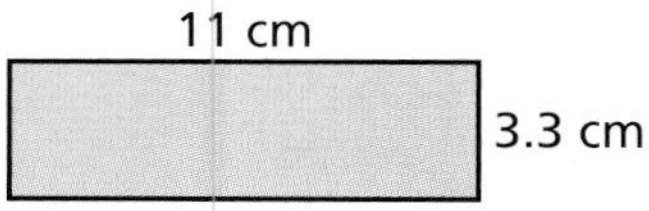

15.
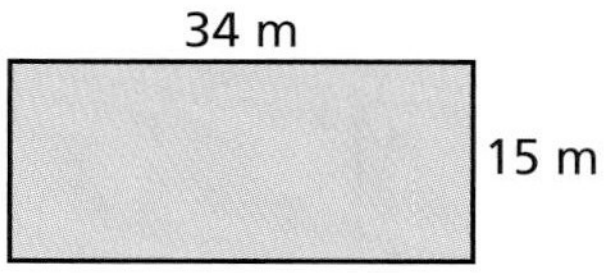

16.
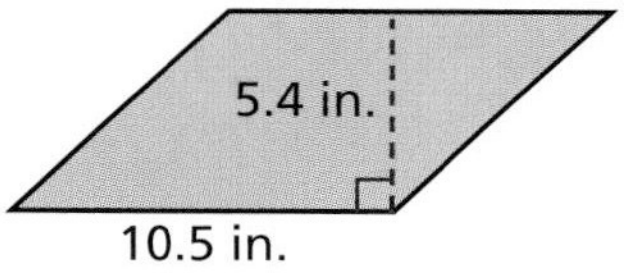

17. Harry is using 16 Japanese tatami mats to cover a floor. Each mat measures 3 feet by 2 feet. What is the total area that will be covered by the mats?

LESSON 9-4

Find the area of each triangle or trapezoid.

18.
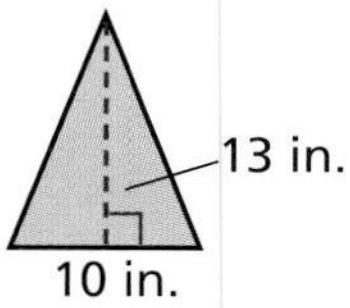

19.
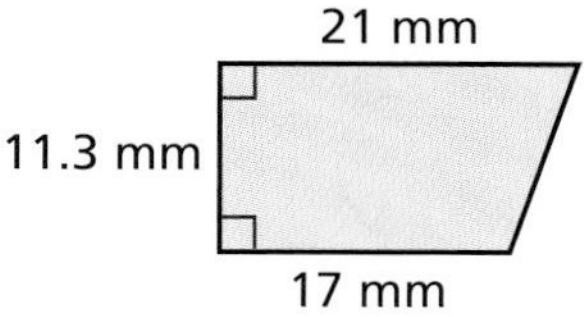

20.
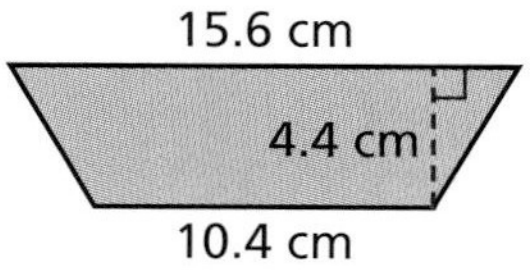

LESSON 9-5

Find the area of each circle to the nearest tenth. Use 3.14 for π.

21.
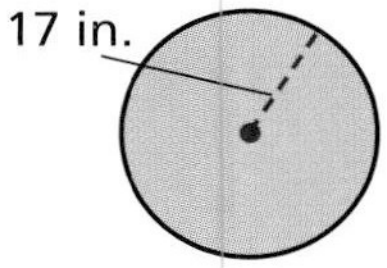

22.
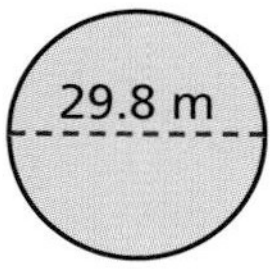

23.
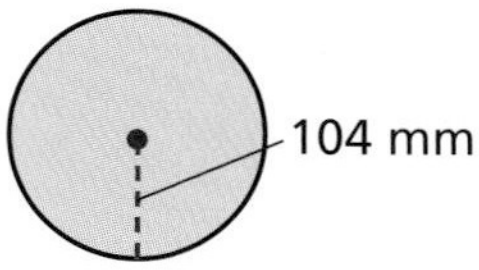

Extra Practice ■ Chapter 9

LESSON 9-6

Estimate the area of each figure. Each square represents 1 ft^2.

24. 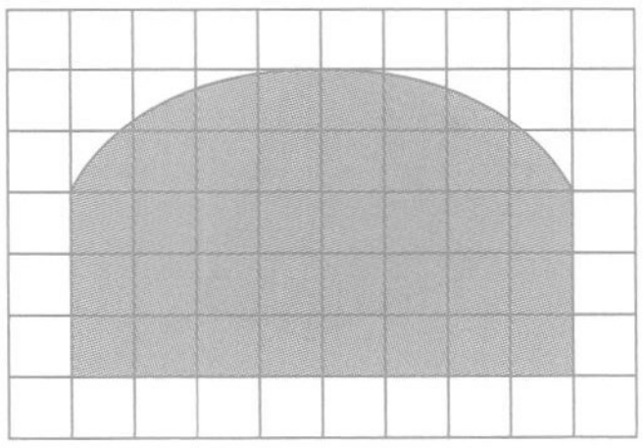

25. 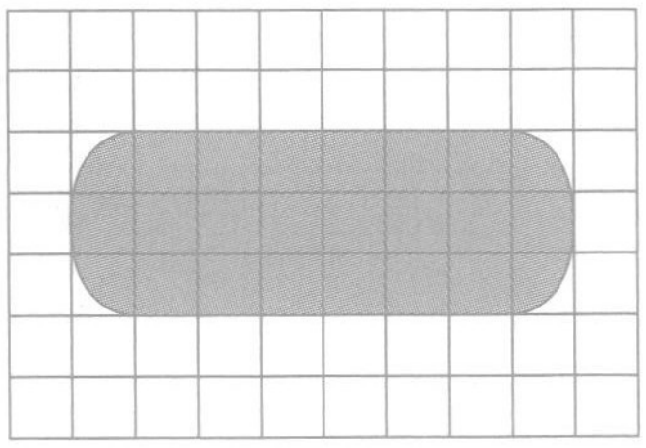

Find the area of each figure. Use 3.14 for π.

26. 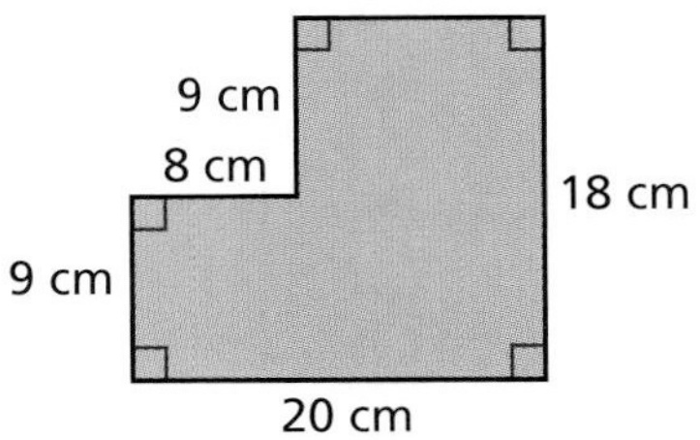

27. 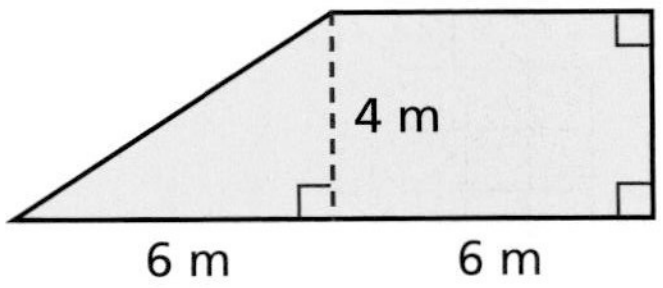

28. 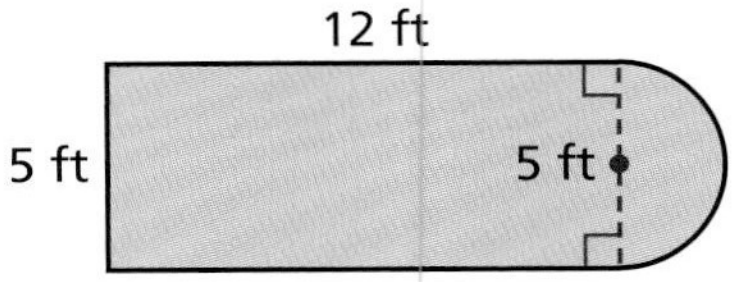

LESSON 9-7

Find each square or square root.

29. 13^2 **30.** $\sqrt{196}$ **31.** $\sqrt{625}$ **32.** 60^2

Estimate each square root to the nearest whole number. Use a calculator to check your answer.

33. $\sqrt{10}$ **34.** $\sqrt{18}$ **35.** $\sqrt{53}$ **36.** $\sqrt{95}$

37. $\sqrt{152}$ **38.** $\sqrt{221}$ **39.** $\sqrt{109}$ **40.** $\sqrt{175}$

41. A square painting has an area of 2,728 square centimeters. About how long is each side of the painting? Round your answer to the nearest centimeter.

LESSON 9-8

Use the Pythagorean Theorem to find each missing measure.

42. 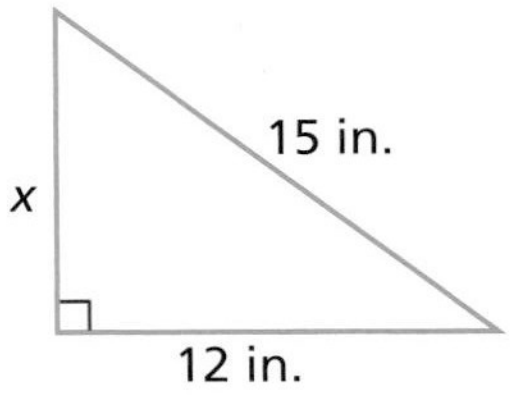

43. 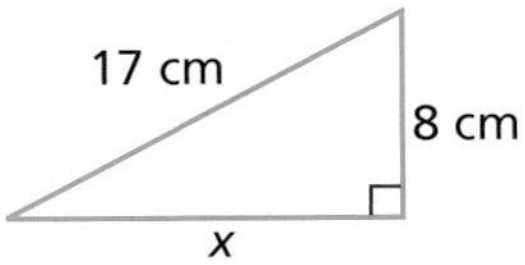

44. 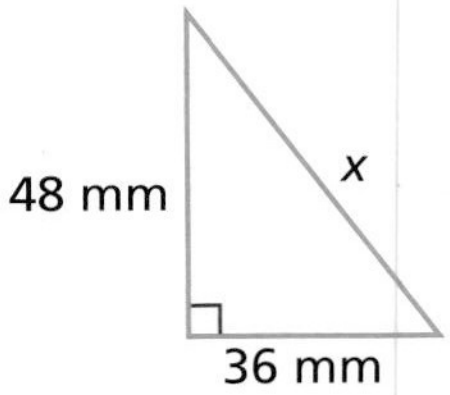

45. Ricky rides his bike 25 miles south and then turns east and rides another 25 miles before he stops to rest. How far is Ricky from his starting point? Round your answer to the nearest tenth.

Extra Practice ■ Chapter 10

LESSON 10-1

Identify the bases and faces of each figure. Then name the figure.

1.

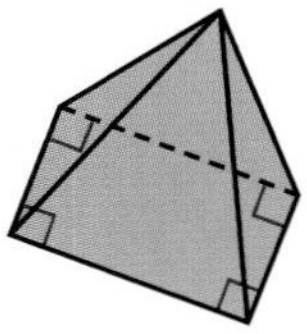

2.

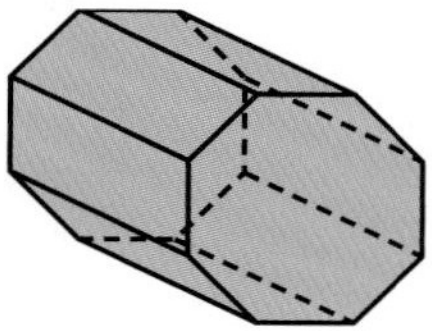

3.

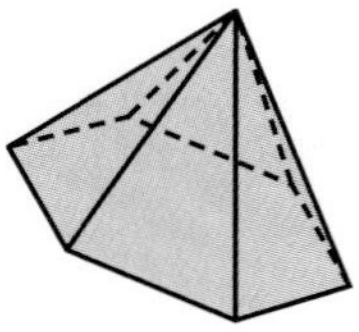

LESSON 10-2

Find how many cubes each prism holds. Then give the prism's volume.

4.

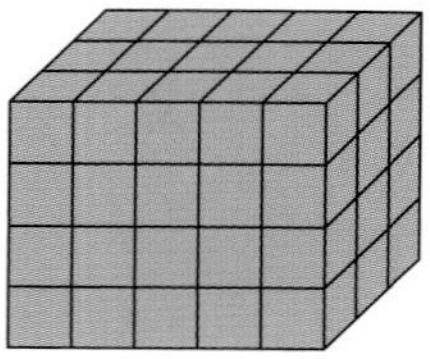

5.

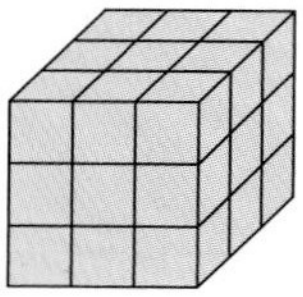

6.

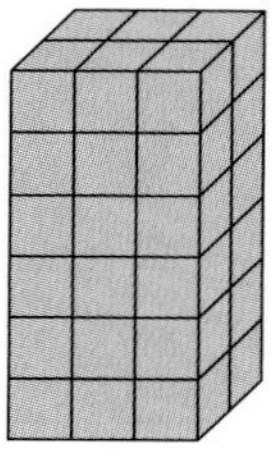

7. The back of a moving van is shaped like a rectangular prism. It is 24 ft long, 7 ft wide, and 8 ft high. Find the volume of the moving van.

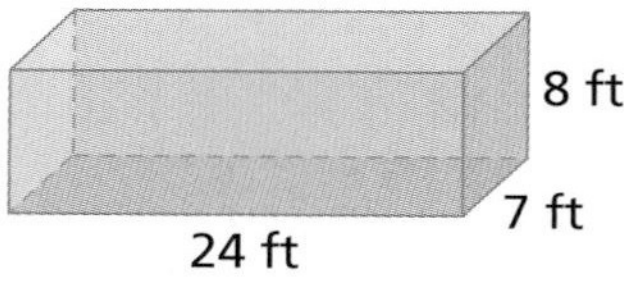

8. A drum is shaped like a cylinder. It is 12.5 in. wide and 8 in. tall. Find its volume. Use 3.14 for π.

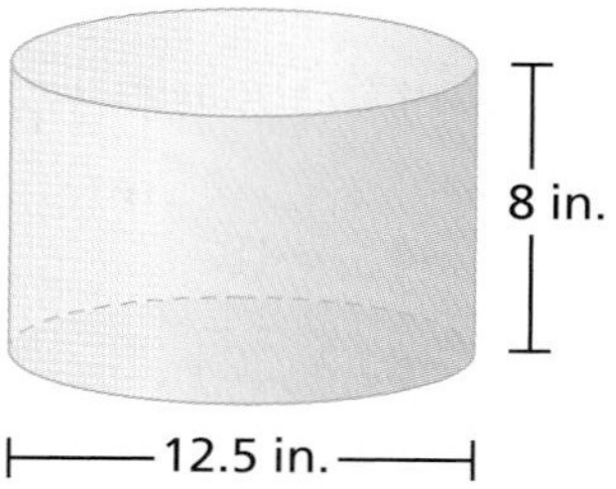

LESSON 10-3

Find the volume of each pyramid to the nearest tenth. Estimate to check whether the answer is reasonable.

9.

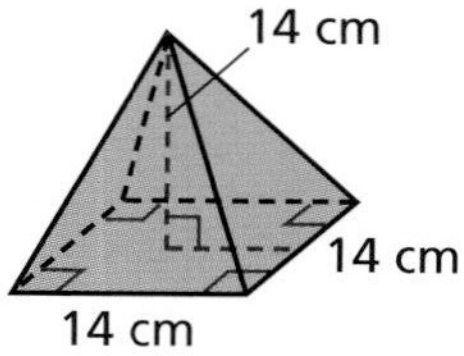

10.

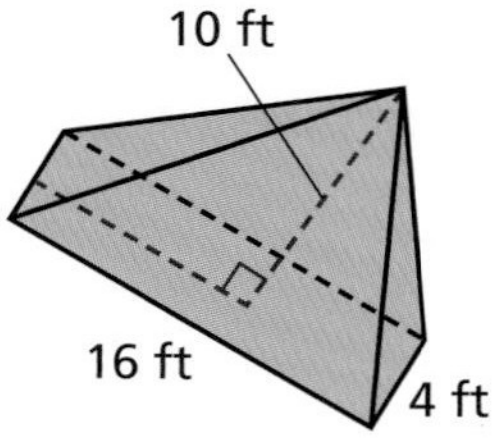

11.

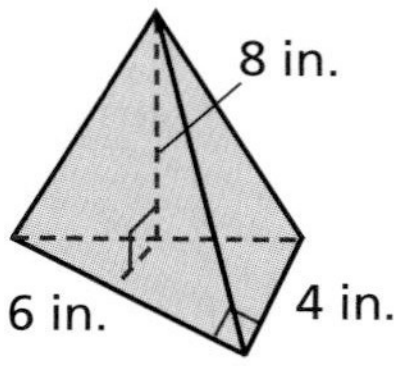

Find the volume of each cone to the nearest tenth. Use 3.14 for π. Estimate to check whether the answer is reasonable.

12.

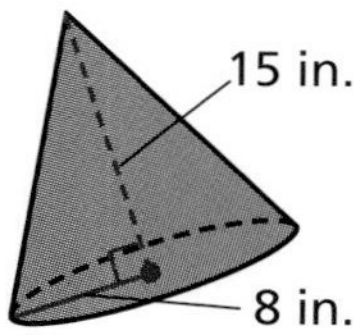

13.

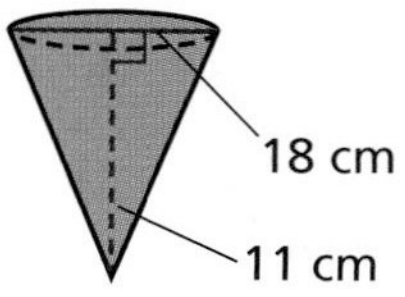

14.

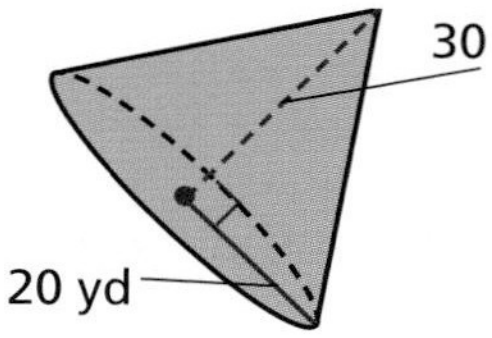

Extra Practice ■ Chapter 10

LESSON 10-4

Find the surface area of the prism formed by each net to the nearest tenth.

15.

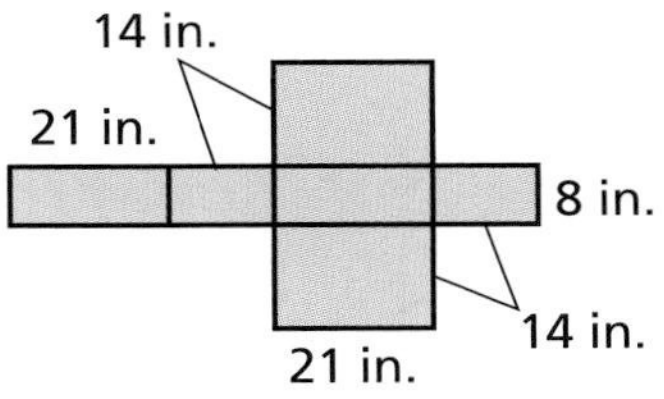

16.

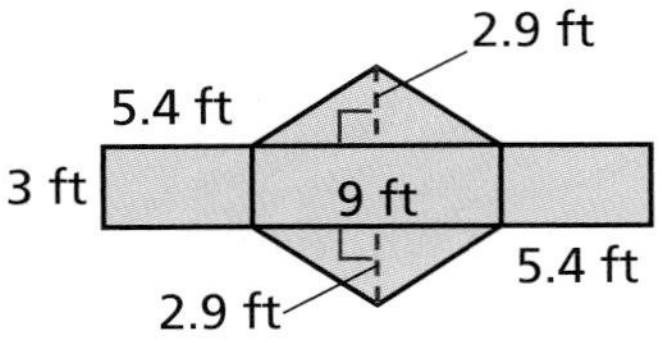

17.

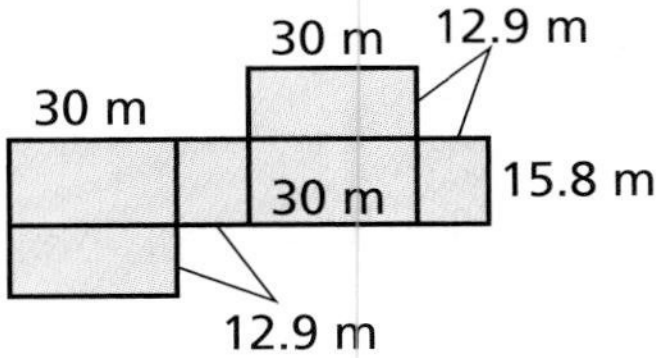

Find the surface area of the cylinder formed by each net to the nearest tenth. Use 3.14 for π.

18.

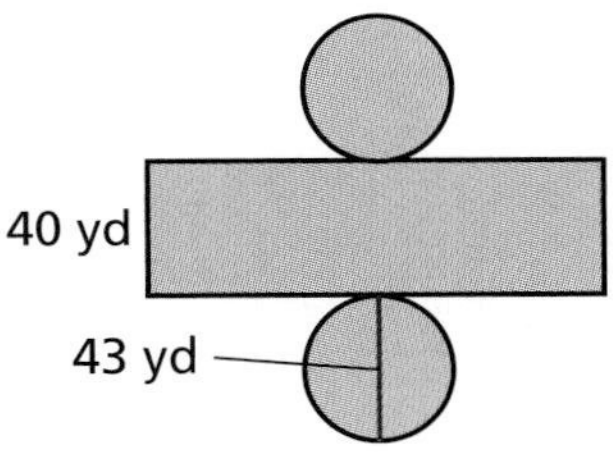

19.

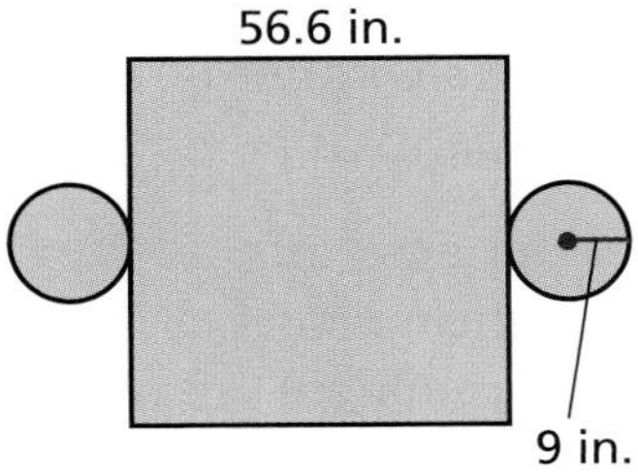

20.

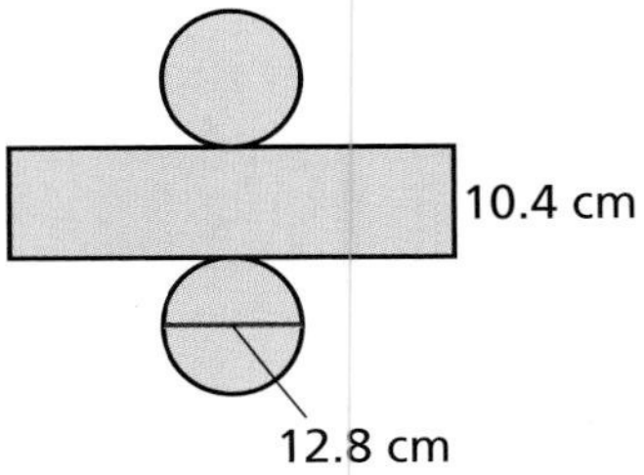

21. An 8 in. tall candle is cylindrical and has a 3 in. wide ribbon around it. What percent of the total surface area of the candle is covered by the 3 in. wide ribbon? Use 3.14 for π. Round your answer to the nearest tenth.

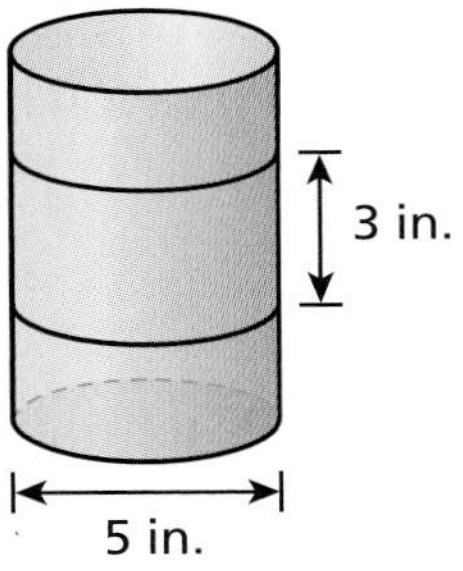

LESSON 10-5

22. The surface area of a cylinder is 49 m^2. What is the surface area of a similar cylinder that is larger by a scale factor of 6?

23. The surface area of a garden is 36 ft^2. What is the surface area of a similar garden that is smaller by a scale factor of $\frac{1}{4}$?

24. The surface area of a hexagonal prism is 65 cm^2. What is the surface area of a similar prism that is larger by a scale factor of 8?

25. The volume of a cube is 50 cm^3. What is the volume of a similar cube that is larger by a scale factor of 7?

26. An oil drum has a volume of 513 cm^3. What is the volume of a similar oil drum that is smaller by a scale factor of $\frac{1}{3}$?

Extra Practice ■ Chapter 11

LESSON 11-1

Determine whether each event is impossible, unlikely, as likely as not, likely, or certain.

1. flipping a coin and getting heads twelve times in a row
2. drawing a green bead from a bag of white and red beads
3. The probability of rolling a 2 on a number cube is $\frac{1}{6}$. What is the probability of not rolling a 2?

LESSON 11-2

4. Bess bowls a strike on 6 out of 15 tries. What is the experimental probability that she will bowl a strike on her next try? Write your answer as a fraction, as a decimal, and as a percent.
5. For the past 10 days, a city planner has counted the number of northbound cars that pass through a particular intersection. During that time, 200 or more cars were counted 9 out of 10 days.
   a. What is the experimental probability that there will be 200 or more northbound cars passing through the intersection on the eleventh day?
   b. What is the experimental probability that there will not be 200 or more northbound cars passing through the intersection on the eleventh day?

LESSON 11-3

6. Ronald flips a coin and rolls a number cube at the same time. What are all the possible outcomes? How many outcomes are in the sample space?
7. For lunch, Amy can choose from a salad, a taco, a hamburger, or a fish fillet. She can drink lemonade, milk, juice, or water. What are all the possible outcomes? How many outcomes are in the sample space?
8. A café makes 23 flavors of ice cream. You can get each flavor in a waffle cone, a sugar cone, a cake cone, or a cup. How many outcomes are possible?

LESSON 11-4

Find the probability of each event. Write your answer as a fraction, as a decimal, and as a percent.

9. rolling a number less than 5 on a fair number cube
10. randomly drawing a pink sock out of a drawer of 6 pink, 4 black, 8 white, and 2 blue socks all of the same size

Extra Practice ■ Chapter 11

There are 12 boys and 14 girls in Mr. Grimes' class. Each student turns in an essay. Find the theoretical probability of each event when Mr. Grimes randomly selects an essay.

11. selecting a boy's essay

12. selecting a girl's essay

LESSON 11-5

Decide whether each set of events is independent or dependent. Explain your answer.

13. Mr. Fernandez's class contains 14 boys and 16 girls. Mr. Fernandez randomly picks a boy and a girl to represent the class at the school spelling bee.

14. Mrs. Rogers's class received new math books. Mrs. Rogers selects a student to hand out the new books. She also picks a second student to collect the old books.

15. There are 52 playing cards in a standard card deck. Alex draws a card and holds onto it while Suzi draws a card.

Find the probability of each set of independent events.

16. flipping 2 coins at the same time and getting heads on both coins

17. drawing a 3 from 5 cards numbered 1 through 5 and rolling an even number on a number cube

LESSON 11-6

18. Venus has decided to have a 2-color paint job done on her car. There are 6 paint colors from which to choose. How many combinations of 2 colors are possible?

19. Philip has 5 different coins. How many combinations of 3 coins can he make from the 5 coins?

20. A juice bar offers 8 different juices. You and a friend want to each try a different blend. How many different combinations of 2 juices are possible?

LESSON 11-7

21. In how many different ways can Ralph, Randy, and Robert stand in line at the movie theater?

22. Roseanne and Rita join Ralph, Randy, and Robert at the movie theater. In how many different ways could they all stand in line?

23. Doris has a $1 bill, a $2 bill, a $5 bill, a $10 bill, a $20 bill, and a $50 bill. In how many different ways can she arrange them in a stack?

24. In how many different ways can 5 students be matched up with 5 mentors?

Extra Practice ■ Chapter 12

LESSON 12-1

Solve. Check each answer.

1. $4c - 13 = 15$
2. $3h + 14 = 23$
3. $-5j - 13 = 22$
4. $\frac{e}{7} + 2 = 5$
5. $\frac{m}{6} - 3 = 1$
6. $\frac{x}{3} + 5 = -13$
7. If you multiply the number of DVDs Sarah has by 6 and then add 5, you get 41. How many DVDs does Sarah have?

LESSON 12-2

Solve.

8. $2w - 11 + 4w = 7$
9. $7v + 5 - v = 11$
10. $-7z + 4 - z = -12$
11. $\frac{5x - 7}{3} = 15$
12. $2t - 7 - 5t = 11$
13. $\frac{6t + 8}{5} = 2$
14. $12a - 3 - 8a = -1$
15. $\frac{2.9h - 5.1}{2} = 4.7$
16. $\frac{3s - 14}{4} = 4$
17. $\frac{10 - 4t}{8} = -12$
18. Erika has received scores of 82, 87, 93, 95, 88, and 90 on math quizzes. What score must Erika get on her next quiz to have an average of 90?

LESSON 12-3

Group the terms with variables on one side of the equal sign, and simplify.

19. $6a = 4a - 8$
20. $3d - 5 = 7d - 9$
21. $-2j + 6 = j - 3$
22. $7 + 5m = 2 - m$

Solve.

23. $7y - 9 = -2y$
24. $2c - 13 = 5c + 11$
25. $\frac{2}{5}g + 9 = -6 - \frac{6}{10}g$
26. $7d + 4 = 8 - d$
27. $-3p + 8 = -7p - 12$
28. $1.2k + 2.3 = -0.5k + 7.4$
29. Roberta and Stanley are collecting signatures for a petition. So far, Roberta has twice as many signatures as Stanley. If she collects 30 more signatures, she will have 4 times as many signatures as Stanley currently has. How many signatures has Stanley collected?
30. Gym members pay $3 per workout with a one time membership fee of $98. Nonmembers pay $10 per workout. How many workouts would both a member and a nonmember have to do to pay the same amount?

Extra Practice ■ Chapter 12

LESSON 12-4

Write an inequality for each situation.

31. The cafeteria could hold no more than 50 people.

32. There were fewer than 20 boats in the marina.

Graph each inequality.

33. $y < -2$ **34.** $f \geq 3$ **35.** $n \leq -1.5$ **36.** $x > 4$

Graph each compound inequality.

37. $1 < s < 4$ **38.** $-1 \leq v < 2$ **39.** $w < 0$ or $w \geq 5$ **40.** $-3.5 \leq y < -2$

LESSON 12-5

Solve. Then graph each solution set on a number line.

41. $c - 6 > -5$ **42.** $v - 3 \geq 1$ **43.** $w - 6 \leq -7$ **44.** $a - 2 \leq 5$

Solve. Check each answer.

45. $q + 3 \leq 5$ **46.** $m + 1 > 0$ **47.** $p + 7 \leq 4$ **48.** $z + 2 \geq -3$

49. By Saturday night, 3 inches of rain had fallen in Happy Valley. The weekend forecast predicted at least 8 inches of rain. How much more rain must fall on Sunday for this forecast to be correct?

LESSON 12-6

Solve. Check each answer.

50. $\frac{a}{5} \leq 4.5$ **51.** $-\frac{v}{2} > 2$ **52.** $\frac{x}{3.9} \geq -2$ **53.** $-\frac{c}{4} < 2.3$

54. $13y < 39$ **55.** $2t \leq 5$ **56.** $-7r > 56$ **57.** $3s \geq -4.5$

58. The local candy store buys candy in bulk and then sells it by the pound. If the store owner spends $135 on peppermints and then sells them for $3.50 per pound, how many pounds must he sell to make a profit?

LESSON 12-7

Solve. Then graph each solution set on a number line.

59. $\frac{m}{3} - 1 \leq 2$ **60.** $7.2x - 4.8 > 24$ **61.** $-5.5h + 2 < 13$

62. $-1 - \frac{s}{3.5} \geq 1$ **63.** $-\frac{w}{1.5} - 8 \leq -10$ **64.** $4j - 6 > 16$

65. $5 - 2u < 15$ **66.** $\frac{r}{7} - 1 \geq 0$ **67.** $5 - \frac{m}{9} \leq 17$

68. Jill, Serena, and Erin are trying to earn enough money to rent a beach house for a week. They estimate that it will cost at least $1,650. If Jill has already earned $600, how much must each of the others earn?

Draw a Diagram

When problems involve objects, distances, or places, you can **draw a diagram** to make the problem easier to understand. You can use the diagram to look for relationships among the given data and to solve the problem.

Problem Solving Strategies

Draw a Diagram	Make a Table
Make a Model	Solve a Simpler Problem
Guess and Test	Use Logical Reasoning
Work Backward	Act It Out
Find a Pattern	Make an Organized List

A bald eagle has built a nest 18 feet below the top of a 105-foot-tall oak tree. The eagle sits on a limb 72 feet above the ground. What is the vertical distance between the eagle and its nest?

Understand the Problem

Identify the important information.

- The height of the tree is 105 feet.
- The eagle's nest is 18 feet from the top of the tree.
- The eagle is perched 72 feet above the ground.

The answer will be the vertical distance between the eagle and its nest.

Make a Plan

Use the information in the problem to **draw a diagram** showing the height of the tree and the locations of the eagle and its nest.

Solve

To find the height of the nest's location, subtract the distance of the nest from the top of the tree from the height of the tree.

105 feet − 18 feet = 87 feet

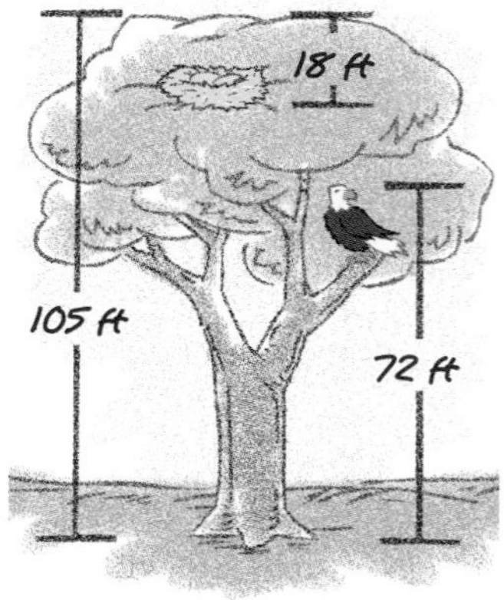

To find the vertical distance from the eagle to its nest, subtract the height of the eagle's location from the height of the nest's location.

87 feet − 72 feet = 15 feet

The vertical distance between the eagle and its nest is 15 feet.

Look Back

Be sure that you have drawn your diagram correctly. Does it match the information given in the problem?

PRACTICE

1. A truck driver travels 17 miles south to drop off his first delivery. Then he drives 19 miles west to drop off a second delivery, and then he drives 17 miles north to drop off another delivery. Finally, he drives 5 miles east for his last delivery. How far is he from his starting point?

2. A table that is standing lengthwise against a wall is 10 feet long and 4 feet wide. Sarah puts balloons 1 foot apart along the three exposed sides, with one balloon at each corner. How many balloons does she use?

Make a Model

When problems involve objects, you can **make a model** using those objects or similar objects. This can help you understand the problem and find the solution.

Problem Solving Strategies

Draw a Diagram	Make a Table
Make a Model	Solve a Simpler Problem
Guess and Test	Use Logical Reasoning
Work Backward	Use a Venn Diagram
Find a Pattern	Make an Organized List

A company packages 6 minipuzzles in a decorated 4 in. cube. They are shipped to the toy store in cartons shaped like rectangular prisms. Twenty cubes fit in each carton. If the height of each carton is 8 in., what are possible dimensions of the carton?

Understand the Problem

Identify the important information.

- Each cube is 4 inches on a side.
- Twenty cubes fit in one carton.
- The height of the carton is 8 inches.

The answer is the dimensions of the carton.

Make a Plan

You can use 20 cubes to **make a model** of cubes packed in a carton. Record possible values for length and width, given a height of 8 in.

Solve

Begin with a carton that is 8 in., or 2 cubes, high. Use all 20 cubes to make a rectangular prism.

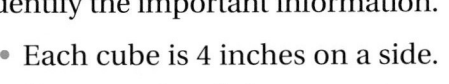

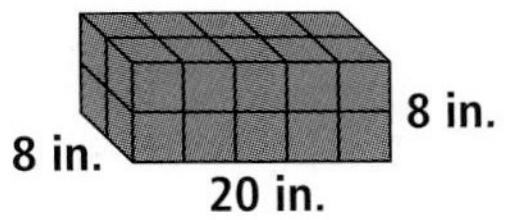

Possible dimensions of the carton are 20 in. × 8 in. × 8 in.

Look Back

The volume of each carton should equal the volume of the 20 cubes.

Volume of cartons: 8 in. × 20 in. × 8 in. = 1,280 in^3

Volume of 1 cube: 4 in. × 4 in. × 4 in. = 64 in^3

Volume of 20 cubes: 20 × 64 = 1,280 in^3

1,280 in^3 = 1,280 in^3 ✔

PRACTICE

1. Give two sets of possible dimensions of a rectangular prism made up of twenty 1-inch cubes.

2. John uses exactly eight 1-inch cubes to form a rectangular prism. Find the length, width, and height of the prism.

Guess and Test

If you do not know how to solve a problem, you can always make a **guess.** Then **test** your guess using the information in the problem. Use what you find out to make a second guess. Continue to **guess and test** until you find the correct answer.

Problem Solving Strategies

- Draw a Diagram
- Make a Model
- **Guess and Test**
- Work Backward
- Find a Pattern
- Make a Table
- Solve a Simpler Problem
- Use Logical Reasoning
- Act It Out
- Make an Organized List

Shannon used equal numbers of quarters and nickels to buy an embossing template that cost $1.50. How many of each coin did she use?

Understand the Problem

Identify the important information.

- Shannon used equal numbers of quarters and nickels.
- The coins she used total $1.50.

The answer will be the number of quarters and the number of nickels Shannon used.

Make a Plan

Start with an educated **guess** in which the numbers of quarters and nickels are the same. Then **test** to see whether the coins total $1.50.

Solve

Make a first guess of 4 quarters and 4 nickels, and find the total value of the coins.

Guess: 4 quarters and 4 nickels
Test: $(4 \times \$0.25) + (4 \times \$0.05) = \$1.00 + \$0.20 = \$1.20$

$1.20 is too low. Increase the number of coins.

Guess: 6 quarters and 6 nickels
Test: $(6 \times \$0.25) + (6 \times \$0.05) = \$1.50 + \$0.30 = \$1.80$

$1.80 is too high. The number of each coin must be between 4 and 6. So Shannon must have used 5 quarters and 5 nickels.

Look Back

Test the answer to see whether the coins add up to $1.50.
$(5 \times \$0.25) + (5 \times \$0.05) = \$1.25 + \$0.25 = \$1.50$ ✓

PRACTICE

1. The sum of Richard's age and his older brother's age is 63. The difference between their ages is 13. How old are Richard and his brother?
2. In the final game of the basketball season, Trinka scored a total of 25 points on 2-point shots and 3-point shots. She made 5 more 2-point shots than 3-point shots. How many of each did she make?

Work Backward

Some problems give you a sequence of information and ask you to find something that happened at the beginning. To solve a problem like this, you may want to start at the end of the problem and **work backward.**

Problem Solving Strategies

Draw a Diagram	Make a Table
Make a Model	Solve a Simpler Problem
Guess and Test	Use Logical Reasoning
Work Backward	Act It Out
Find a Pattern	Make an Organized List

Tony is selling dried fruit snacks to help raise money for a new school computer. Half of the fruit snacks in the bag are apricots. Of the rest of the fruit snacks, half of them are bananas, and the other 8 are cranberries. How many fruit snacks are in the bag?

Understand the Problem

Identify the important information.

- Half of the fruit snacks are apricots.
- Half of the remaining fruit snacks are bananas.
- The final 8 fruit snacks are cranberries.

The answer will be the total number of fruit snacks in the bag.

Make a Plan

Start with the 8 cranberries, and **work backward** through the information in the problem to the total number of fruit snacks in the bag.

Solve

There are 8 cranberries. — 8

The other half of the remaining fruit snacks are bananas, so there must be 8 bananas. — $8 + 8 = 16$

The other half of the fruit snacks are apricots, so there must be 16 apricots. — $16 + 16 = 32$

There are 32 fruit snacks in the bag.

Look Back

Using the starting amount of 32 fruit snacks, work from the beginning of the problem following the steps.

Start: 32
Half of 32: $32 \div 2 = 16$
Half of 16: $16 \div 2 = 8$
Minus 8: $8 - 8 = 0$ ✓

PRACTICE

1. In a trivia competition, each finalist must answer 4 questions correctly. Each question is worth twice as much as the question before it. The fourth question is worth $1,000. How much is the first question worth?

2. The Ramirez family has 5 children. Sara is 5 years younger than her brother Kenny. Felix is half as old as his sister Sara. Kaitlen, who is 10, is 3 years older than Felix. Kenny and Celia are twins. How old is Celia?

Find a Pattern

In some problems, there is a relationship between different pieces of information. Examine this relationship and try to **find a pattern.** You can then use this pattern to find more information and the solution to the problem.

Problem Solving Strategies

Draw a Diagram	Make a Table
Make a Model	Solve a Simpler Problem
Guess and Test	Use Logical Reasoning
Work Backward	Act It Out
Find a Pattern	Make an Organized List

John made a design using hexagons and triangles. The side lengths of each hexagon and triangle are 1 inch. What is the perimeter of the next figure in his design?

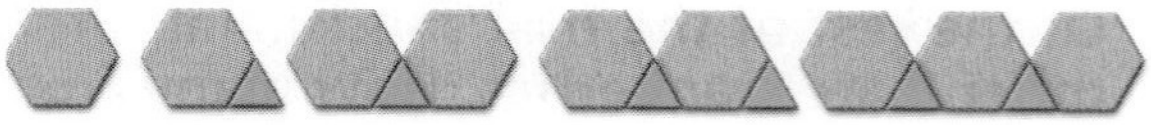

Understand the Problem

Identify the important information.

- The first 5 figures in the design are given.
- The side lengths of each hexagon and triangle are 1 inch.

The answer will be the perimeter of the sixth figure in the design.

Make a Plan

Try to **find a pattern** in the perimeters of the first 5 figures. Use the pattern to find the perimeter of the sixth figure.

Solve

Find the perimeter of the first 5 figures.

Figure	Perimeter (in.)	Pattern
1	6	
2	7	6 + 1 = 7
3	11	7 + 4 = 11
4	12	11 + 1 = 12
5	16	12 + 4 = 16

The pattern appears to be add 1, add 4, add 1, add 4, and so on. So the perimeter of the sixth figure will be 16 + 1, or 17.

Look Back

Use another strategy. **Draw a diagram** of the sixth figure. Then find the perimeter.

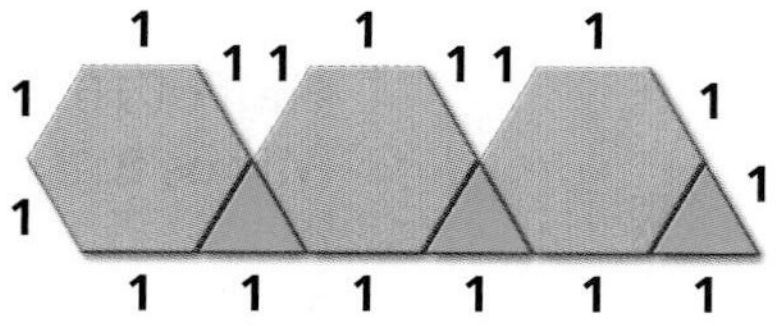

PRACTICE

Describe the pattern, and then find the next number.

1. 1, 5, 9, 13, 17, . . .

2. 1, 4, 16, 64, 256, . . .

Make a Table

When you are given a lot of information in a problem, it may be helpful to organize that information. One way to organize information is to **make a table.**

Problem Solving Strategies

Draw a Diagram	**Make a Table**
Make a Model	Solve a Simpler Problem
Guess and Test	Use Logical Reasoning
Work Backward	Act It Out
Find a Pattern	Make an Organized List

On November 1, Wendy watered the Gribbles' yard and the Milams' yard. If she waters the Gribbles' yard every 4 days and the Milams' yard every 5 days, when is the next date that Wendy will water both yards?

Understand the Problem

Identify the important information.

- Wendy waters the Gribbles' yard every 4 days and the Milams' yard every 5 days. She watered both yards on November 1.

The answer will be the next date that she waters both yards again.

Make a Plan

Make a table using X's to show the days that Wendy waters each yard. Make one row for the Gribbles and one row for the Milams.

Solve

Start with an X in both rows for November 1. For the Gribbles, add an X on every fourth day after November 1. For the Milams, add an X every fifth day after November 1.

Date	1	2	3	4	5	6	7	8	9	10	11	12	13	14	15	16	17	18	19	20	21
Gribble	X				X				X				X				X				X
Milam	X					X					X					X					X

November 21 is the next date that Wendy will water both yards.

Look Back

The sum of 1 and five 4's should equal the sum of 1 and four 5's.

$1 + 4 + 4 + 4 + 4 + 4 = 21 \qquad 1 + 5 + 5 + 5 + 5 = 21$ ✓

PRACTICE

1. Jess, Kathy, and Linda work on the math club's newspaper. One is the editor, one is the reporter, and one is the writer. Linda does not participate in sports. Jess and the editor play tennis together. Linda and the reporter are cousins. Find each person's job.

2. A toll booth accepts any combination of coins that total exactly \$0.75, but it does not accept pennies or half dollars. In how many different ways can a driver pay the toll?

Solve a Simpler Problem

Sometimes a problem may contain large numbers or require many steps to solve. It may appear complicated to solve. Try to **solve a simpler problem** that is similar to the original problem.

Problem Solving Strategies

Draw a Diagram	Make a Table
Make a Model	**Solve a Simpler Problem**
Guess and Test	Use Logical Reasoning
Work Backward	Act It Out
Find a Pattern	Make an Organized List

Lawrence is making touch pools for a project about sea creatures. The pools are squares that will be arranged side by side. The side of each pool is a 1-meter-long piece of wood. How many meters of wood does Lawrence need to complete 20 square sections of pool?

Understand the Problem

Identify the important information.

- Each square side is a 1-meter-long piece of wood.
- There are 20 square sections set side by side.

The answer will be the total meters of wood needed.

Make a Plan

You could sketch all 20 pools and then count the number of meters of wood. However, it would be easier to first **solve a simpler problem**. Start with 1 square pool, and then move on to 2 and then 3. Then look for a way to solve the problem for 20 pools.

Solve

The first pool requires 4 sides to complete. After that, only 3 sides are needed for each pool.

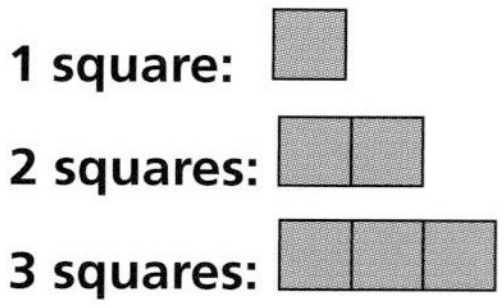

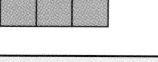

Notice that 1 pool requires 4 meters of wood, and the 19 other pools require 3 meters of wood each. So $4 + (19 \times 3) = 61$. The pools require 61 meters of wood.

Number of Squares	Number of Meters
1	$4(1) = 4$
2	$4 + (1 \times 3) = 7$
3	$4 + (2 \times 3) = 10$
4	$4 + (3 \times 3) = 13$

Look Back

If the pattern is correct, Lawrence would need 16 meters of wood for 5 pools. Complete the next row of the table to check this answer.

PRACTICE

1. The numbers 11; 444; and 8,888 all contain repeated single digits. How many numbers between 10 and 1,000,000 contain repeated single digits?

2. How many diagonals are there in a dodecagon (a 12-sided polygon)?

Use Logical Reasoning

Sometimes a problem may provide clues and facts that you must use to find a solution. You can **use logical reasoning** to solve this kind of problem.

Problem Solving Strategies

Draw a Diagram	Make a Table
Make a Model	Solve a Simpler Problem
Guess and Test	**Use Logical Reasoning**
Work Backward	Act It Out
Find a Pattern	Make an Organized List

Jennie, Rachel, and Mia play the oboe, the violin, and the drums. Mia does not like the drums, and she is the sister of the oboe player. Rachel has soccer practice with the person who plays the drums. Which instrument does each person play?

Understand the Problem

Identify the important information.

- There are three people, and each person plays a different instrument.

Make a Plan

Start with clues given in the problem, and **use logical reasoning** to determine which instrument each person plays.

Solve

Make a table. Make a column for each instrument and a row for each person. Work with the clues one at a time. Write "Yes" in a box if the clue reveals that a person plays an instrument. Write "No" in a box if the clue reveals that a person does not play an instrument.

a. Mia does not like the drums, so she does not play the drums.

b. Mia is the sister of the person who plays the oboe, so she does not play the oboe.

	Oboe	Violin	Drums
Jennie			
Rachel			No
Mia	No		No

c. Rachel has soccer practice with the person who plays the drums, so she does not play the drums.

Jennie must play the drums, and Mia must play the violin. So Rachel must play the oboe.

Look Back

Compare your answer to the clues in the problem. Make sure none of your conclusions conflict with the clues.

PRACTICE

1. Kent, Jason, and Newman have a dog, a fish, and a hamster, though not in that order. Kent's pet does not have fur. The owner of the hamster has class with Jason. Match the owners with their pets.

2. Seth, Vess, and Benica are in the sixth, seventh, and eighth grades, though not in that order. Seth is not in seventh grade. The sixth-grader has band with Benica and the same lunchtime as Seth. Match the students with their grades.

Act It Out

Some problems involve actions or processes. To solve these problems, you can **act it out.** Actively modeling the problem can help you find the solution.

Problem Solving Strategies

Draw a Diagram	Make a Table
Make a Model	Solve a Simpler Problem
Guess and Test	Use Logical Reasoning
Work Backward	**Act It Out**
Find a Pattern	Make an Organized List

Ana, Ben, Cleo, and Diego are in a chess club. To choose the president, they write their names on slips of paper and choose one name at random. Then they choose another name to be the vice president. How many different outcomes are possible?

Understand the Problem

Identify the important information.

- There are four students: Ana, Ben, Cleo, and Diego. One student will be the club's president and another will be the club's vice president.

The answer will be the number of different ways students can be chosen to be the president and vice president.

Make a Plan

Act it out to list all the possible outcomes. Then count the number of outcomes.

Solve

Write the students' names on index cards. Choose pairs of index cards to be the president and the vice president. Write down the results and continue the process until all of the possible outcomes have been listed.

Pres.	Ana	Ana	Ana	Ben	Ben	Ben
Vice Pres.	Ben	Cleo	Diego	Ana	Cleo	Diego
Pres.	Cleo	Cleo	Cleo	Diego	Diego	Diego
Vice Pres.	Ana	Ben	Diego	Ana	Ben	Cleo

There are 12 possible different outcomes.

Look Back

Check to see that you have listed all of the possible outcomes and make sure that no outcome is listed more than once.

PRACTICE

1. Joe has five font choices: Times, Arial, Eras, Gigi, and Onyx. How many different ways can he use one font for a Web site and another for a menu?

2. Mike, Jennifer, Ashley, and Kendall stand side-by-side for a photo. How many different ways can the four friends stand next to each other?

Make an Organized List

In some problems, you will need to find out exactly how many different ways an event can happen. When solving this kind of problem, it is often helpful to **make an organized list**. This will help you count all the possible outcomes.

Problem Solving Strategies

Draw a Diagram	Make a Table
Make a Model	Solve a Simpler Problem
Guess and Test	Use Logical Reasoning
Work Backward	Act It Out
Find a Pattern	**Make an Organized List**

A spinner has 4 different colors: red, blue, yellow, and white. If you spin the spinner 2 times, how many different color combinations could you get?

Understand the Problem

Identify the important information.

- You spin the spinner 2 times.
- The spinner is divided into 4 different colors.

The answer will be the total number of different color combinations the spinner can land on.

Make a Plan

Make an organized list to determine all the possible different color outcomes. List all the different combinations for each color.

Solve

First consider the color red. List all the different outcomes for the color red. Then consider blue, adding all the different outcomes, then yellow, and finally white.

Red	Blue	Yellow	White
RR	BB	YY	WW
RB	BY	YW	
RY	BW		
RW			

So there are 10 possible different color combinations.

Look Back

Make sure that all the possible combinations of color are listed and that each set of colors is different.

PRACTICE

1. The Pizza Planet has 5 different choices of pizza toppings: ham, pineapple, pepperoni, olive, and mushroom. You want to order a pizza with 2 different toppings. How many different combinations of toppings can you order?

2. How many ways can you make change for a fifty-cent piece by using a combination of dimes, nickels, and pennies?

Skills Bank Review Skills

Place Value

You can use a place-value chart to help you read and write numbers.
The number 213,867 is shown.

Hundred Thousands	Ten Thousands	Thousands	Hundreds	Tens	Ones
2	1	3	8	6	7

EXAMPLE

Use the chart to determine the place value of each digit.

A 2
The 2 is in the hundred thousands place.

B 8
The 8 is in the hundreds place.

PRACTICE

Determine the place value of each underlined digit.

1. 543,2$\underline{0}$1 **2.** 23$\underline{9}$,487 **3.** 7$\underline{3}$0,432 **4.** $\underline{4}$,382,121

Compare and Order Whole Numbers

You can use place values from left to right to compare and order numbers.

EXAMPLE

Compare and order from least to greatest: 42,810; 142,997; 42,729; 42,638.

Start at the leftmost place value.

There is one number with a digit in the greatest place. It is the greatest of the four numbers.

Compare the remaining three numbers. All values in the next two places, the ten thousands and thousands, are the same.

In the hundreds place, the values are different. Use this digit to order the remaining numbers.

42,810
142,997
42,729
42,638

42,638; 42,729; 42,810; 142,997

PRACTICE

Compare and order the numbers in each set from least to greatest.

1. 2,564; 2,546; 2,465; 2,654

2. 6,237; 6,372; 6,273; 6,327

3. 132,957; 232,795; 32,975; 31,999

4. 9,614; 29,461; 129,164; 129,146

Read and Write Decimals

When reading and writing a decimal, you need to know the place value of the digit in the last decimal place. Also, when writing a decimal in word form remember the following:

- "and" goes in place of the decimal for numbers greater than one.
- a hyphen is used in two-digit numbers, such as twenty-five.
- a hyphen is used in two-word place values, such as ten-thousandths.

EXAMPLE

Write 728.34 in words.

The 4 is in the hundredths place, so 728.34 is written as "seven hundred twenty-eight and thirty-four hundredths."

PRACTICE

Write each decimal in words.

1. 17.238 **2.** 9.0023 **3.** 534.01972 **4.** 33.00084 **5.** 4,356.67

Rules for Rounding

To round a number to a certain place value, locate the digit with that place value, and look at the digit to the right of it.

- If the digit to the right is 5 or greater, increase the number you are rounding by 1.
- If the digit to the right is 4 or less, leave the number you are rounding as it is.

EXAMPLE

A **Round 765.48201 to the nearest hundredth.**

765.4<u>8</u>201 *Locate the hundredths place.*

The digit to the right is less than 5, so the digit in the rounding place stays the same.

765.48

B **Round 765.48201 to the nearest tenth.**

765.<u>4</u>8201 *Locate the tenths place.*

The digit to the right is greater than 5, so the digit in the rounding place increases by 1.

765.5

PRACTICE

Round 203.94587 to the place indicated.

1. hundreds place **2.** hundredths place **3.** thousandths place

4. tens place **5.** ones place **6.** tenths place

Properties

Addition and multiplication follow certain rules. The tables show basic properties of addition and multiplication.

Addition Properties	
Commutative:	$a + b = b + a$
Associative:	$(a + b) + c = a + (b + c)$
Identity Property of Zero:	$a + 0 = a$
Inverse Property:	$a + (-a) = 0$
Closure Property:	The sum of two real numbers is a real number.

Multiplication Properties	
Commutative:	$a \times b = b \times a$
Associative:	$(a \times b) \times c = a \times (b \times c)$
Identity Property of One:	$a \times 1 = a$
Inverse Property:	$a \times \frac{1}{a} = 1$ if $a \neq 0$
Property of Zero:	$a \times 0 = 0$
Closure Property:	The product of two real numbers is a real number.
Distributive:	$a(b + c) = a \times b + a \times c$

The following properties are true when a, b, and c are real numbers.

Substitution Property: If $a = b$, then a can be substituted for b in any expression.

Transitive Property: If $a = b$ and $b = c$, then $a = c$.

PRACTICE

Name the property represented by each equation.

1. $8 + 0 = 8$

2. $(9 \times 3) \times 7 = 9 \times (3 \times 7)$

3. 3×5 is a real number

4. $7 \times 345 = 345 \times 7$

5. $2(3 + 5) = 2 \times 3 + 2 \times 5$

6. $15 \times \frac{1}{15} = 1$

7. $3.6 + 4.4 = 4.4 + 3.6$

8. $\frac{3}{4} \times \frac{4}{4} = \frac{3}{4}$

9. $18 + (-18) = 0$

10. $(5 + 17) + 23 = 5 + (17 + 23)$

Overestimates and Underestimates

An **overestimate** is an estimate that is greater than the actual answer.
An **underestimate** is an estimate that is less than the actual answer.

EXAMPLE 1

Give an overestimate for each expression.

A $124 + 371$

$124 + 371 \approx 130 + 380$
≈ 510

B $316 \div 12$

$316 \div 12 \approx 320 \div 10$
≈ 32

EXAMPLE 2

Give an underestimate for each expression.

A $64 - 12$

$64 - 12 \approx 60 - 15$
≈ 45

B $28 \cdot 8$

$28 \cdot 8 \approx 25 \cdot 8$
≈ 200

PRACTICE

Give an overestimate and underestimate for each expression.

1. $224 + 545$
2. $756 + 142$
3. $643 - 104$
4. $2{,}456 - 435$
5. 13×17
6. 7×85
7. $261 \div 9$
8. $85 \div 34$

Compatible Numbers

You can use compatible numbers to estimate products and quotients. Compatible numbers are close to the numbers in the problem and can help you do math mentally.

EXAMPLE

Estimate each product or quotient.

A $327 \cdot 28$

Compatible numbers

$327 \cdot 28 \approx 300 \cdot 30$
$\approx 9{,}000$ ← *Estimate*

B $637 \div 8$

Compatible numbers

$637 \div 8 \approx 640 \div 8$
≈ 80 ← *Estimate*

PRACTICE

Use compatible numbers to estimate each product or quotient.

1. $42 \cdot 7$
2. $3{,}957 \div 23$
3. $5{,}169 \cdot 21$
4. $813 \div 8$
5. $78 \cdot 42$
6. $1{,}443 \div 7$
7. $98 \cdot 48$
8. $3{,}372 \div 415$
9. $58 \cdot 9$
10. $27{,}657 \div 67$

Multiply and Divide by Powers of Ten

When you *multiply* by powers of ten, move the decimal point one place to the right for each zero in the power of ten. When you *divide* by powers of ten, move the decimal point one place to the left for each zero in the power of ten.

EXAMPLE

Find each product or quotient.

A **0.37 · 100**

$0.37 \cdot 100 = 0.37$

$= 37$

B **43 · 1,000**

$43 \cdot 1{,}000 = 43.000$

$= 43{,}000$

C **0.24 ÷ 10**

$0.24 \div 10 = 0.24$

$= 0.024$

D **1,467 ÷ 100**

$1{,}467 \div 100 = 1467.$

$= 14.67$

PRACTICE

Find each product or quotient.

1. 10×8.53
2. 0.55×10^4
3. $48.6 \times 1{,}000$
4. $2.487 \div 1{,}000$
5. $6.03 \div 10^3$

Multiply Whole Numbers

When you multiply two whole numbers, think of the second number's expanded form, and multiply by each value.

EXAMPLE

Find the product of 621 · 485.

Step 1: Think of 485 as 4 hundreds, 8 tens, and 5 ones. Multiply 621 by 5 ones.	**Step 2:** Multiply 621 by 8 tens.	**Step 3:** Multiply 621 by 4 hundreds.	**Step 4:** Add the partial products.
621 × 485 3,105 ← 5 × 621	621 × 485 3,105 49,680 ← 80 × 621	621 × 485 3,105 49,680 248,400 ← 400 × 621	621 × 485 3,105 49,680 + 248,400 **301,185**

$621 \cdot 485 = 301{,}185$

PRACTICE

Multiply.

1. 493×37
2. 539×82
3. 134×145
4. 857×662
5. $1{,}872 \times 43$
6. $5{,}849 \times 67$
7. $36{,}735 \times 28$
8. $121{,}614 \times 58$

Divide Whole Numbers

EXAMPLE

Find the quotient of 5,712 ÷ 28.

Step 1: Write the first number inside the long division symbol, and write the second number to the left of the symbol. Divide by the number outside the symbol. $\begin{array}{r} 2 \\ 28\overline{)5712} \end{array}$ *28 cannot go into 5, so try 57.*	**Step 2:** Multiply 28 by 2, and place the product under 57. Subtract and bring down the next digit of the dividend. $\begin{array}{r} 20 \\ 28\overline{)5712} \\ -56\downarrow \\ \hline 11 \\ -0\downarrow \\ \hline 112 \end{array}$ *28 cannot go into 11, so put a 0 in the quotient, and bring down the 2.*	**Step 3:** Divide 112 by 28. Multiply 28 by 4 and place the product under 112. Subtract. $\begin{array}{r} 204 \\ 28\overline{)5712} \\ -56 \\ \hline 11 \\ -0 \\ \hline 112 \\ -112 \\ \hline 0 \end{array}$

PRACTICE

Divide.

1. 23,148 ÷ 18
2. 5,772 ÷ 37
3. 56,088 ÷ 41
4. 34,540 ÷ 55
5. 68,894 ÷ 74
6. 143,296 ÷ 32
7. 398,736 ÷ 72
8. 566,746 ÷ 79

Divisibility Rules

A number is divisible by another number if the quotient is a whole number with no remainder.

A number is divisible by . . .	Divisible	Not Divisible
2 if the last digit is an even number.	13,776	4,221
3 if the sum of the digits is divisible by 3.	327	97
4 if the last two digits form a number divisible by 4.	3,128	526
5 if the last digit is 0 or 5.	9,415	50,501
6 if the number is divisible by 2 and 3.	762	62
9 if the sum of the digits is divisible by 9.	21,222	96
10 if the last digit is 0.	1,680	8,255

PRACTICE

Determine whether each number is divisible by 2, 3, 4, 5, 6, 9, or 10.

1. 324
2. 501
3. 200
4. 812
5. 60
6. 784
7. 351
8. 3,009
9. 2,345
10. 555,555

Factors

A **factor** of a number is any number that divides into it without leaving a remainder.

EXAMPLE

List all the factors of 28.

The possible factors are whole numbers from 1 to 28.

$1 \cdot 28 = 28$ *1 and 28 are factors of 28.*

$2 \cdot 14 = 28$ *2 and 14 are factors of 28.*

$3 \cdot ? = 28$ *No whole number multiplied by 3 equals 28, so 3 is not a factor of 28.*

$4 \cdot 7 = 28$ *4 and 7 are factors of 28.*

$5 \cdot ? = 28$ *No whole number multiplied by 5 equals 28, so 5 is not a factor of 28.*

$6 \cdot ? = 28$ *No whole number multiplied by 6 equals 28, so 6 is not a factor of 28.*

The factors of 28 are 1, 2, 4, 7, 14, and 28.

PRACTICE

List all the factors of each number.

1. 10 **2.** 8 **3.** 18 **4.** 54 **5.** 27 **6.** 36

Roman Numerals

In the Roman numeral system, numbers do not have place values to show what they represent. Instead, numbers are represented by letters.

I = 1 V = 5 X = 10 L = 50 C = 100 D = 500 M = 1,000

The values of the letters do not change based on their place in a number.

If a numeral is to the right of an equal or greater numeral, add the two numerals' values. If a numeral is immediately to the left of a greater numeral, subtract the numeral's value from the greater numeral.

EXAMPLE

A Write CLIV as a decimal number.

$$\begin{aligned} \text{CLIV} &= \text{C} + \text{L} + (\text{V} - \text{I}) \\ &= 100 + 50 + (5 - 1) \\ &= 154 \end{aligned}$$

B Write 1,109 as a Roman numeral.

$$\begin{aligned} 1{,}109 &= 1{,}000 + 100 + 9 \\ &= \text{M} + \text{C} + (\text{X} - \text{I}) \\ &= \text{MCIX} \end{aligned}$$

PRACTICE

Write each decimal number as a Roman numeral and each Roman numeral as a decimal number.

1. XXVI **2.** 29 **3.** MCMLII **4.** 224 **5.** DCCCVI

Binary Numbers

Computers use the **binary number system.** In the binary, or base-2, system of numbers, numbers are formed using the digits 0 and 1. Each place in a binary number is associated with a power of 2. Binary numbers are written with the subscript *two* so that they are not confused with numbers in the decimal system.

The binary number 1101_{two} can be thought of as

$(1 \cdot 2^3) + (1 \cdot 2^2) + (0 \cdot 2^1) + (1 \cdot 2^0)$.

Binary Place Value

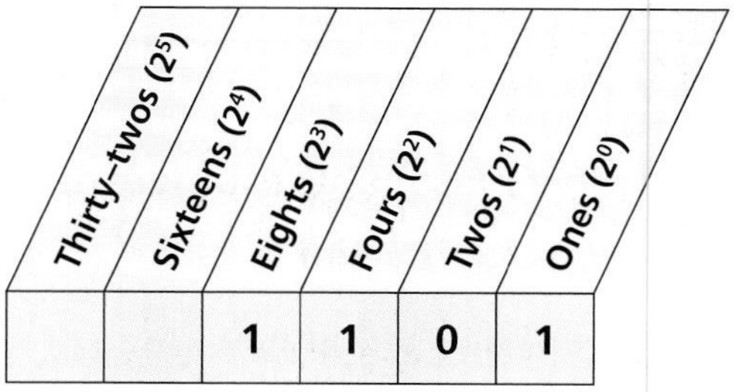

You can use the expanded form of 1101_{two} to find the value of the number as a decimal, or base-10, number.

$$(1 \cdot 2^3) + (1 \cdot 2^2) + (0 \cdot 2^1) + (1 \cdot 2^0) = (1 \cdot 8) + (1 \cdot 4) + (0 \cdot 2) + (1 \cdot 1)$$
$$= 8 + 4 + 0 + 1$$
$$= 13$$

So $1101_{two} = 13_{ten}$.

EXAMPLE

Write each binary number as a decimal number.

A $\mathbf{101110_{two}}$

$$101110_{two} = (1 \cdot 2^5) + (0 \cdot 2^4) + (1 \cdot 2^3) + (1 \cdot 2^2) + (1 \cdot 2^1) + (0 \cdot 1)$$
$$= 32 + 0 + 8 + 4 + 2 + 0$$
$$= 46$$

B $\mathbf{10001_{two}}$

$$10001_{two} = (1 \cdot 2^4) + (0 \cdot 2^3) + (0 \cdot 2^2) + (0 \cdot 2^1) + (1 \cdot 1)$$
$$= 16 + 0 + 0 + 0 + 1$$
$$= 17$$

PRACTICE

Write each binary number as a decimal number.

1. 100_{two} **2.** 110_{two} **3.** 101_{two} **4.** 1100_{two} **5.** 1011_{two}

6. 11011_{two} **7.** 11110_{two} **8.** 101010_{two} **9.** 111111_{two} **10.** 100111_{two}

Estimate Measurements

You can use benchmarks to estimate with metric and customary units.

1 meter (m)	Width of a doorway	**1 centimeter (cm)**	Width of a large paper clip
1 liter (L)	Water in a 1-quart bottle	**1 milliliter (mL)**	Water in an eyedropper
1 gram (g)	Mass of a dollar bill	**1 kilogram (kg)**	Mass of 8 rolls of pennies
30°C (Celsius)	Temperature on a hot day	**0°C (Celsius)**	Temperature on a freezing day

EXAMPLE 1

Choose the most reasonable estimate of the height of the ceiling in your classroom.

A 30 cm B 3 m C 30 m D 30,000 cm

The most reasonable estimate is 3 m.

Length	Temperature	Capacity
1 inch (in.)—about the length of a small paper clip **1 foot (ft)**—about the length of a standard sheet of paper **1 yard (yd)**—about the width of a doorway	**32°F** (Fahrenheit)—water freezes **70°F**—air on a comfortably warm day **90°F**—air on a hot day **212°F**—boiling water	**1 fluid ounce (fl oz)**—amount of water in two tablespoons **1 cup (c)**—amount of water held in a standard measuring cup **1 pint (pt), 1 quart (qt), 1 gallon (gal)**—Think about containers of water at a store.

EXAMPLE 2

Choose the most appropriate estimate.

A **the length of a classroom**

A 30 in. B 30 ft C 30 yd

The most appropriate estimate is 30 ft.

B **a temperature for wearing a T-shirt**

A 20°F B 40°F C 80°F

The most appropriate estimate is 80°F.

PRACTICE

Choose the most reasonable estimate.

1. the temperature on a warm day

A −22°C B 22°C C 68°C

2. the capacity of a kitchen sink

A 12 mL B 1,200 mL C 12 L

Choose the most appropriate estimate.

3. the capacity of a tall drinking glass

A 1 pt B 4 qt C $\frac{1}{2}$ gal

4. a temperature for wearing a warm coat

A 20°F B 60°F C 80°F

5. the temperature of a cup of hot cocoa

A 32°F B 120°F C 250°F

6. the width of a pizza box

A 18 in. B 8 ft C 2 yd

Relate Metric Units of Length, Mass, and Capacity

A cube that has a volume of 1 cm^3 has a capacity of 1 mL. If the cube were filled with water, the mass of the water would be 1 g.

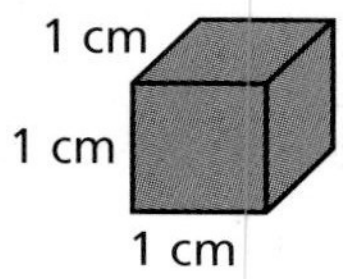

EXAMPLE

Find the capacity of a 50 cm × 60 cm × 30 cm rectangular box. Then find the mass of the water that would fill the box.

Volume: 50 cm × 60 cm × 30 cm = 90,000 cm^3

Capacity: 1 cm^3 = 1 mL, so 90,000 cm^3 = 90,000 mL, or 90 L.

Mass: 1 mL of water has a mass of 1 g, so 90,000 mL of water has a mass of 90,000 g, or 90 kg.

PRACTICE

Find the capacity of each box. Then find the mass of the water that would fill the box.

1. 2 cm × 5 cm × 8 cm
2. 10 cm × 18 cm × 4 cm
3. 8 cm × 8 cm × 8 cm
4. 10 cm × 10 cm × 10 cm
5. 15 cm × 18 cm × 16 cm
6. 23 cm × 19 cm × 11 cm

Pictographs

Pictographs are graphs that use pictures to display data. Pictographs include a key to tell what each picture represents.

EXAMPLE

How many students chose tacos as their favorite lunch?

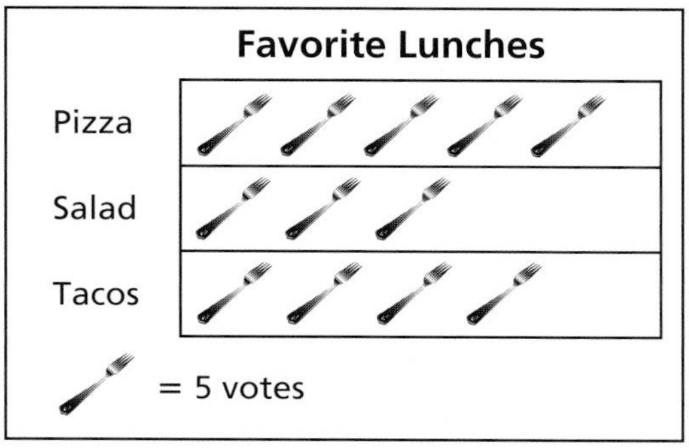

Each (fork) stands for 5 students.

There are 4 (fork) in the row for tacos.

4 × 5 = 20

So 20 students chose tacos as their favorite lunch.

PRACTICE

Use the pictograph for Exercises 1–3.

1. How many bicycles were rented in May?
2. How many more bicycles were rented in June than in April?
3. How many bicycles were rented altogether from April through June?

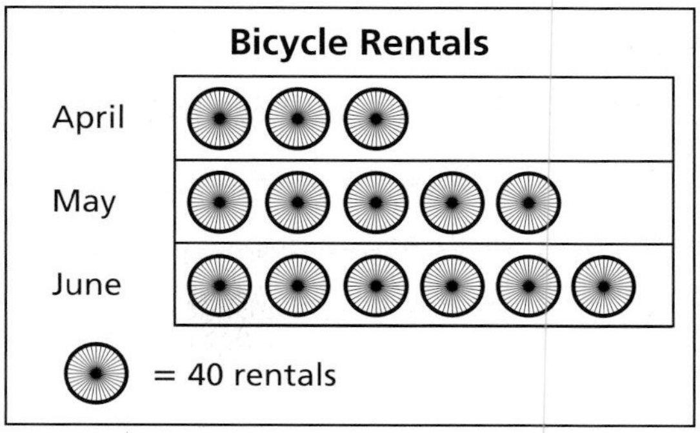

Probability of Two Disjoint Events

In probability, two events are considered to be **disjoint** if they cannot happen at the same time. Examples of disjoint events are getting a 5 or a 6 on a single roll of a 1–6 number cube. To find the probability that either one or the other of two disjoint events will occur, add the probabilities of each event occurring separately.

EXAMPLE

Find the probability of each set of disjoint events.

A rolling either a 5 or a 6 on a 1–6 number cube

$$\begin{aligned} P(5 \text{ or } 6) &= P(5) + P(6) \\ &= \frac{1}{6} + \frac{1}{6} \\ &= \frac{2}{6} \\ &= \frac{1}{3} \end{aligned}$$

The probability of rolling a 5 or a 6 on a 1–6 number cube is $\frac{1}{3}$.

B choosing either an *A* or an *E* from the letters in the word *mathematics*

$$\begin{aligned} P(A \text{ or } E) &= P(A) + P(E) \\ &= \frac{2}{11} + \frac{1}{11} \\ &= \frac{3}{11} \end{aligned}$$

The probability of choosing an A or an E is $\frac{3}{11}$.

PRACTICE

Find the probability of each set of disjoint events.

1. tossing a coin and getting heads or tails
2. spinning red or green on a spinner that has four equal sectors colored red, green, blue, and yellow
3. drawing a black marble or a red marble from a bag that contains 4 white marbles, 3 black marbles, and 2 red marbles
4. choosing either a boy or a girl from a class of 13 boys and 17 girls
5. choosing either A or E from a list of the five vowels
6. choosing either a number less than 3 or a number greater than 12 from a set of 20 cards numbered 1–20

Inductive and Deductive Reasoning

You use **inductive reasoning** when you look for a pattern in individual cases to draw conclusions. Conclusions drawn using inductive reasoning are sometimes like predictions. They may be proven false.

You use **deductive reasoning** when you use given facts to draw conclusions. A conclusion based on facts must be true.

EXAMPLE

Identify the type of reasoning used. Explain your answers.

A ***Statement:* A number pattern begins with 2, 5, 8, 11, . . .**

***Conclusion:* The next number in the pattern will be 14.**

This is inductive reasoning. The conclusion is based on the pattern established by the first four terms in the sequence.

B ***Statement:* It has rained for the past three days.**

***Conclusion:* It will rain tomorrow.**

This is inductive reasoning. The conclusion is based on the weather pattern over the past three days.

C ***Statement:* The measures of two angles of a triangle are 30° and 70°.**

***Conclusion:* The measure of the third angle is 80°.**

This is deductive reasoning. Since you know that the measures of the angles of a triangle have a sum of 180°, the third angle of this triangle must measure 80° ($30° + 70° + 80° = 180°$).

PRACTICE

Identify the type of reasoning used. Explain your answers.

1. *Statement:* Shawna has received a score of 100 on the last five math tests.
   Conclusion: Shawna will receive a score of 100 on the next math test.
2. *Statement:* The mail has arrived late every Monday for the past 4 weeks.
   Conclusion: The mail will arrive late next Monday.
3. *Statement:* Three angles of a quadrilateral measure 100°, 90°, and 70°.
   Conclusion: The measure of the fourth angle is 100°.
4. *Statement:* Perpendicular lines AB and CD intersect at point E.
   Conclusion: Angle AED is a right angle.
5. *Statement:* A pattern of numbers begins 1, 2, 4, . . .
   Conclusion: The next number in the pattern is 8.
6. *Statement:* Ten of the first ten seventh-grade students surveyed listed soccer as their favorite sport.
   Conclusion: Soccer is the favorite sport of all seventh-graders.

Skills Bank

Make Conjectures

Conjecture is another word for conclusion. Conjectures in math are based on observations and in some cases have not yet been proven to be true. To prove that a conjecture is false, you need to find just one case, or *counterexample,* for which the conclusion does not hold true.

EXAMPLE 1

Test each conjecture to decide whether it is true or false. If the conjecture is false, give a counterexample.

A **The sum of two even numbers is always an even number.**

An even number is divisible by 2. The sum of two even numbers can be written as $2m + 2n = 2(m + n)$, which is divisible by 2, so it is even. The conjecture is true.

B **All prime numbers are odd.**

The first prime number is 2, which is an even number. The conjecture is false.

EXAMPLE 2

Formulate a conjecture based on the given information. Then test your conjecture.

$1 \cdot 3 = 3$ $\quad 3 \cdot 5 = 15$ $\quad 5 \cdot 7 = 35$ $\quad 7 \cdot 9 = 63$

Conjecture: The product of two odd numbers is always an odd number.

An odd number does not have 2 as a factor, so the product of two odd numbers also does not have 2 as a factor. The conjecture is true.

PRACTICE

Test each conjecture to decide whether it is true or false. If the conjecture is false, give a counterexample.

1. The sum of two odd numbers is always an odd number.
2. The product of two even numbers is always an even number.
3. The sum of twice a whole number and 1 is always an odd number.
4. If you subtract a whole number from another whole number, the result will always be a whole number.
5. If you multiply two fractions, the product will always be greater than either fraction.

Formulate a conjecture based on the given information. Then test your conjecture.

6. $12 + 21 = 33$ $\quad 13 + 31 = 44$ $\quad 23 + 32 = 55$ $\quad 17 + 71 = 88$
7. $15 \times 15 = 225$ $\quad 25 \times 25 = 625$ $\quad 35 \times 35 = 1{,}225$

Trigonometric Ratios

You can use ratios to find information about the sides and angles of a right triangle. These ratios are called *trigonometric ratios,* and they have names, such as **sine** (abbreviated *sin*), **cosine** (abbreviated *cos*), and **tangent** (abbreviated *tan*).

The **sine** of $\angle 1 = \sin \angle 1 = \dfrac{\text{length of side opposite } \angle 1}{\text{length of hypotenuse}} = \dfrac{a}{c}$.

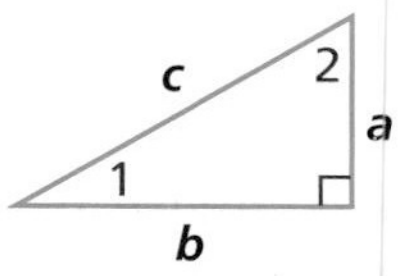

The **cosine** of $\angle 1 = \cos \angle 1 = \dfrac{\text{length of side adjacent to } \angle 1}{\text{length of hypotenuse}} = \dfrac{b}{c}$.

The **tangent** of $\angle 1 = \tan \angle 1 = \dfrac{\text{length of side opposite } \angle 1}{\text{length of side adjacent to } \angle 1} = \dfrac{a}{b}$.

EXAMPLE 1

Find the sine, cosine, and tangent of $\angle J$.

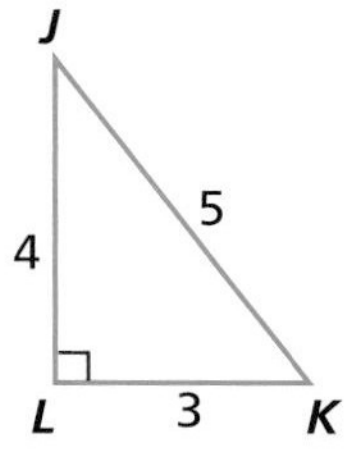

$\sin \angle J = \dfrac{LK}{JK} = \dfrac{3}{5}$

$\cos \angle J = \dfrac{JL}{JK} = \dfrac{4}{5}$

$\tan \angle J = \dfrac{LK}{JL} = \dfrac{3}{4}$

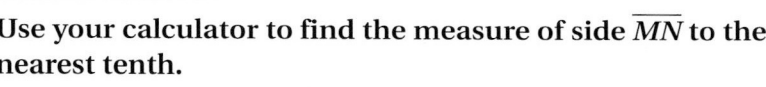

EXAMPLE 2

Use your calculator to find the measure of side $\overline{MN}$ to the nearest tenth.

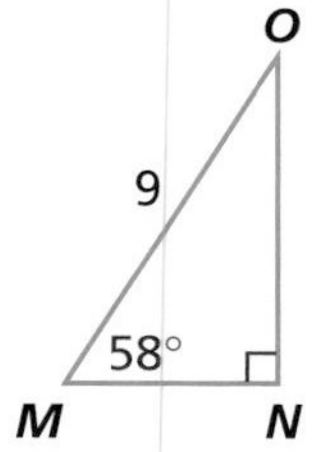

Side $\overline{MN}$ is adjacent to the 58° angle. The length of the hypotenuse is given. The ratio that uses the lengths of the adjacent side and the hypotenuse is cosine.

$\cos (58°) = \dfrac{MN}{9}$ *Write the ratio that is equal to the cosine of 58°.*

$9 \cdot \cos (58°) = MN$ *Multiply both sides by 9.*

9 [×] [COS] 58 [ENTER] *Use your calculator.*

$MN = 4.8$

PRACTICE

Find the sine, cosine, and tangent of each angle.

1. $\angle D$
2. $\angle F$

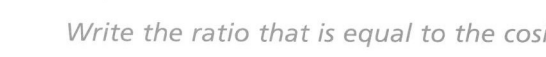

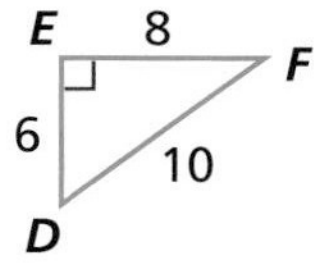

Use your calculator to find the measure of each side, to the nearest tenth.

3. $\overline{QR}$
4. $\overline{PR}$

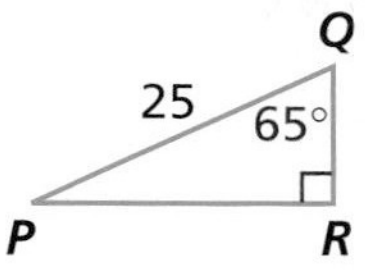

Cube Roots

The volume of the cube at right is $5 \cdot 5 \cdot 5 = 5^3 = 125$. The expression 5^3 is read "5 cubed." Finding a **cube root** is the inverse of cubing a number. The symbol $\sqrt[3]{\ }$ means "cube root." For example, $\sqrt[3]{125} = 5$. You can use a calculator to estimate cube roots.

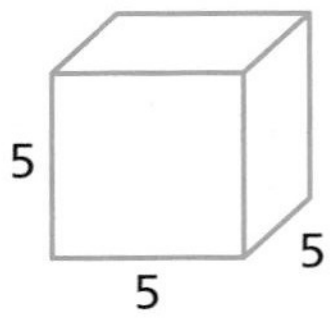

EXAMPLE

Use your calculator to find $\sqrt[3]{43}$ to the nearest tenth.

Press MATH and select 4: $\sqrt[3]{\ }$ (from the menu.) Then enter 43) ENTER .

$\sqrt[3]{43} \approx 3.5$

PRACTICE

Use your calculator to find each cube root to the nearest tenth.

1. $\sqrt[3]{30}$ **2.** $\sqrt[3]{68}$ **3.** $\sqrt[3]{100}$ **4.** $\sqrt[3]{3}$ **5.** $\sqrt[3]{260}$ **6.** $\sqrt[3]{1{,}255}$

Properties of Exponents

Recall that $8^2 = 8 \cdot 8$ and $8^5 = 8 \cdot 8 \cdot 8 \cdot 8 \cdot 8$. Therefore, $8^2 \cdot 8^5 = (8 \cdot 8) \cdot (8 \cdot 8 \cdot 8 \cdot 8 \cdot 8) = 8^7$. Also, $\frac{8^5}{8^2} = \frac{8 \cdot 8 \cdot 8 \cdot 8 \cdot 8}{8 \cdot 8} = 8 \cdot 8 \cdot 8 = 8^3$.
These examples can help you understand the following properties.

- To multiply powers with the same base, keep the base and add the exponents.
- To divide powers with the same base, keep the base and subtract the exponents.

EXAMPLE

Multiply or divide. Write the answer as a power.

A $3^4 \cdot 3^9$

$= 3^{4+9}$ *Add the exponents.*

$= 3^{13}$

B $\frac{10^9}{10^5}$

$= 10^{9-5}$ *Subtract the exponents.*

$= 10^4$

PRACTICE

Multiply or divide. Write the answer as a power.

1. $4^8 \cdot 4^2$ **2.** $7^{12} \cdot 7^{12}$ **3.** $5^6 \cdot 5$ **4.** $x^4 \cdot x^5$

5. $\frac{5^8}{5^2}$ **6.** $\frac{12^{10}}{12^5}$ **7.** $\frac{7^{15}}{7^2}$ **8.** $\frac{b^{10}}{b^7}$

Absolute Value of Real Numbers

The absolute value of a number is its distance from 0 on the number line. The symbol for absolute value is | |. Note that an absolute value can never be negative.

EXAMPLE

Find the absolute value of each real number.

A 2.7

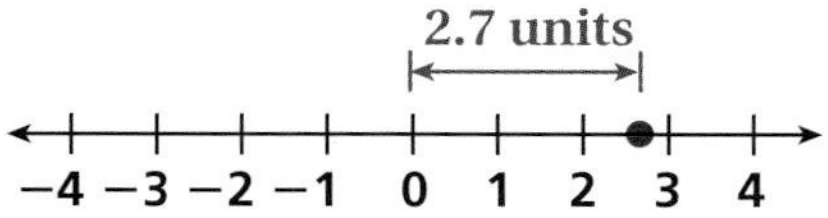

$|2.7| = 2.7$

B $-\pi$

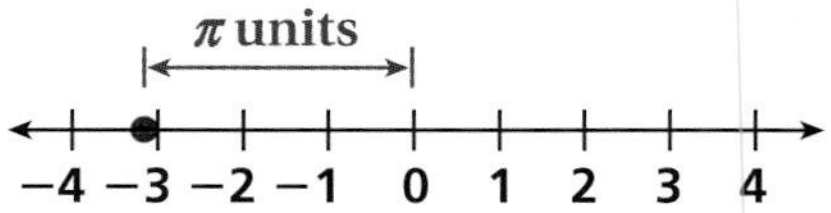

$|-\pi| = \pi$

PRACTICE

Find the absolute value of each real number.

1. $-\frac{3}{4}$ **2.** 5.8 **3.** −6.05 **4.** $\sqrt{3}$ **5.** $-\sqrt{10}$ **6.** $3\frac{5}{8}$

Polynomials

A **monomial** is a number or a product of numbers and variables with exponents that are whole numbers. The expressions $2n$, x^3, $4a^4b^3$, and 7 are all examples of monomials. The expressions $x^{1.5}$, $2\sqrt{y}$, and $\frac{3}{m}$ are not monomials.

A **polynomial** is one monomial or the sum or difference of monomials. Polynomials can be classified by the number of terms. A monomial has one term, a **binomial** has two terms, and a **trinomial** has three terms.

EXAMPLE

Classify each expression as a monomial, a binomial, a trinomial, or not a polynomial.

A $43h + 14b$

binomial — *The expression is a polynomial with 2 terms.*

B $3x^2 - 4xy + \frac{3}{x}$

not a polynomial — *There is a variable in a denominator.*

PRACTICE

Classify each expression as a monomial, a binomial, a trinomial, or not a polynomial.

1. $5a^3 + 6a^2 - 3$ **2.** $4xy^2$ **3.** $7b + \frac{1}{b^2}$

4. $6c^2d - 4$ **5.** $2x - 3y + 1$ **6.** $-12x^3y^4z^2$

Networks and Paths

A **network** is a set of points and a set of line segments or arcs that connect the points. The points of a network are called **vertices**. The line segments or arcs connecting the vertices are called **edges**.

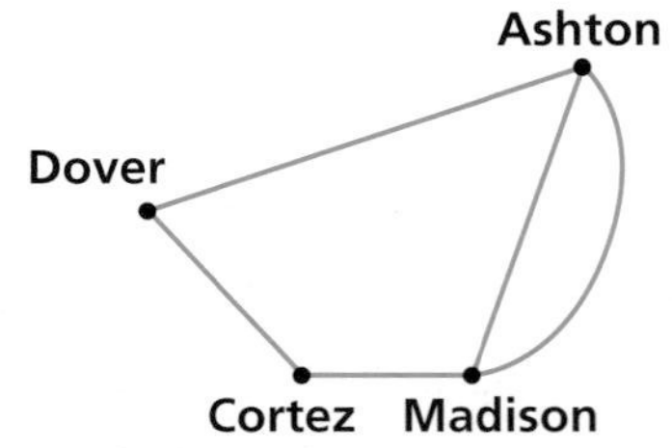

The network at right represents the roads connecting four towns. The network has four vertices and five edges.

A **path** is a way to travel around a network by moving along the edges from one vertex to another. In a simple path, no vertex is visited more than once.

EXAMPLE

Determine the number of simple paths from vertex *A* to vertex *B*.

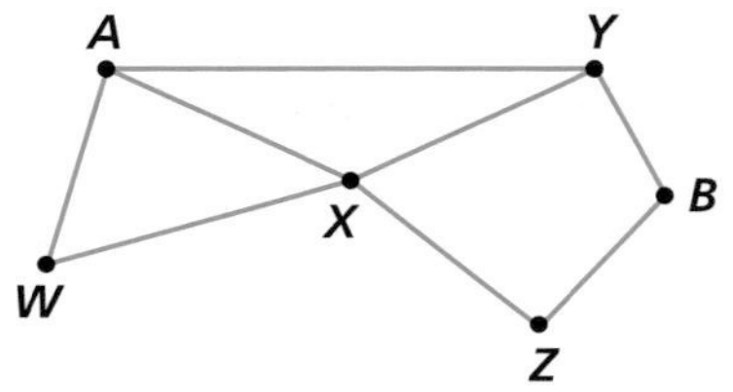

Make an organized list of the simple paths.

A-Y-B

A-Y-X-Z-B

A-X-Y-B

A-X-Z-B

A-W-X-Y-B

A-W-X-Z-B

There are 6 simple paths.

PRACTICE

Determine the number of simple paths from vertex *A* to vertex *B*.

1.
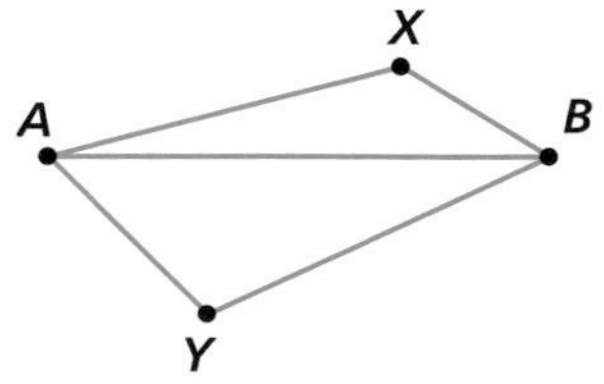

2.
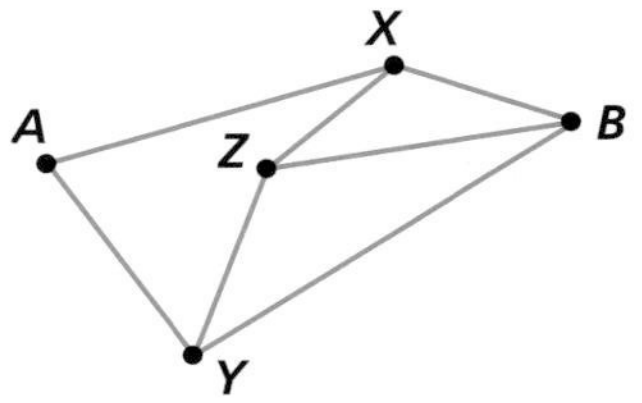

3.
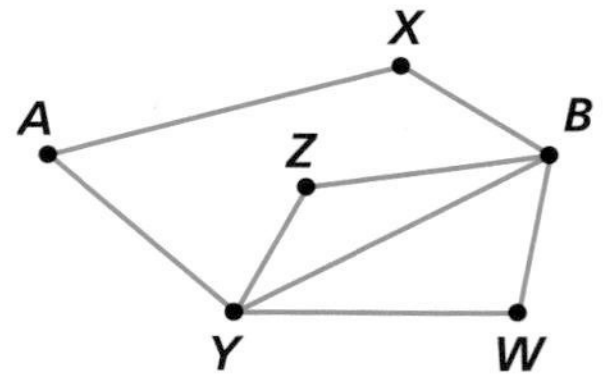

4.
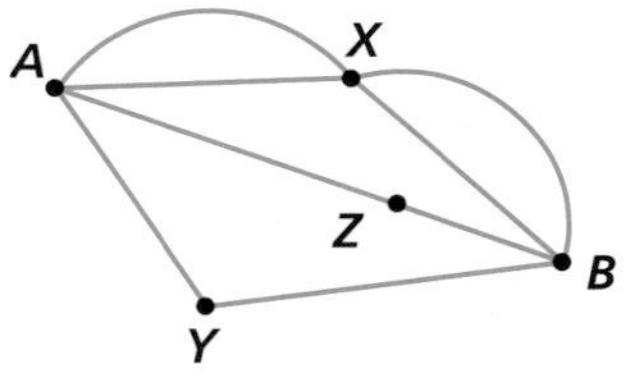

Skills Bank

Half-life

Some atoms give off energy by emitting particles from their centers, or nuclei. The ability of these atoms to release nuclear radiation is called *radioactivity,* and the process is called *radioactive decay.*

Half-life is the amount of time it takes for one-half of the nuclei of a radioactive sample to decay. The half-life of an element can range from less than a second to millions of years.

EXAMPLE 1

The half-life of sodium-24 is 15 hours. If a sample of sodium-24 contains $\frac{1}{8}$ of its original amount, how old is the sample?

Every 15 hours, $\frac{1}{2}$ the sample decays.

Fraction of Sample	1	$\frac{1}{2}$	$\frac{1}{4}$	$\frac{1}{8}$
Time	0 hours	15 hours	30 hours	45 hours

The sample is 45 hours old.

EXAMPLE 2

The half-life of phosphorous-24 is 14.3 days. How much of a 6-gram sample will remain after 42.9 days?

Time	0 days	14.3 days	28.6 days	42.9 days
Amount of Sample (g)	6	3	1.5	0.75

After 42.9 days, 0.75 g of phosphorous-24 will remain.

PRACTICE

1. The half-life of cobalt-60 is 5.26 years. If a sample of cobalt-60 contains $\frac{1}{4}$ of its original amount, how old is the sample?
2. The half-life of sodium-24 is 15 hours. How much of a 9.6-gram sample will remain after 60 hours?
3. Iodine-131 has a half-life of 8.07 days. How much of a 4.4 g sample will there be after 40.35 days?
4. A sample of bismuth-212 decayed from 18 g to 1.125 g in 242 minutes. What is the half-life of bismuth-212?

pH Scale

An acid is a compound that produces hydrogen ions in solution. A base is a compound that produces hydroxide ions in solution. Chemists use the **pH scale** to measure how acidic or basic a solution is.

The range of the pH scale for a solution is 0 to 14. A solution with a pH below 7 is acidic. A solution with a pH above 7 is basic. A solution with a pH of 7 is neutral—that is, it has an equal number of hydrogen and hydroxide ions.

The pH numbers are related by powers of 10.

A pH of 6 is 10 times more acidic than a pH of 7.

A pH of 8 is 10 times more basic than a pH of 7.

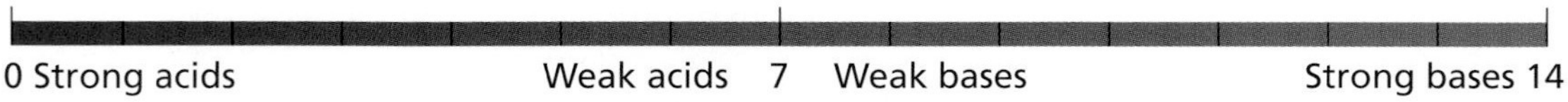

EXAMPLE 1

Solution A and solution B have the same volume. Solution A has a pH of 2, and solution B has a pH of 4. How much more acidic is solution A than solution B?

Since $4 - 2 = 2$ and $10^2 = 100$ solution A is 100 times more acidic than solution B.

EXAMPLE 2

Solution C and solution D have the same volume. Solution C has a pH of 13, and solution D has a pH of 8. How much more basic is solution C than solution D?

Since $13 - 8 = 5$ and $10^5 = 100{,}000$ solution C is 100,000 times more basic than solution D.

PRACTICE

1. Solution E and solution F have the same volume. Solution E has a pH of 5, and solution F has a pH of 1. How much more basic is solution E than solution F?
2. Solution G and solution H have the same volume. Solution G has a pH of 9, and solution H has a pH of 8. How much more basic is solution G than solution H?
3. Solution K and solution J have the same volume. Solution J has a pH of 7, and solution K has a pH of 5. How much more acidic is solution K than solution J?
4. Solution M and solution L have the same volume. Solution L has a pH of 14, and solution M has a pH of 7. How much more basic is solution L than solution M?

Richter Scale

The magnitude of an earthquake is a measure of the amount of energy the earthquake releases. The **Richter scale** is used to express the magnitude of earthquakes. This scale uses the counting numbers. Each number represents a magnitude that is 10 times stronger than the magnitude represented by the previous number.

You can relate Richter scale numbers to the exponents in powers of 10.

$10^1 = 10$ $10^2 = 100$ $10^3 = 1{,}000$ $10^4 = 10{,}000$ $10^5 = 100{,}000$

Just as 10^2 is 10 times 10^1, an earthquake with a magnitude of 2 on the Richter scale is 10 times stronger than an earthquake with a magnitude of 1.

EXAMPLE 1

An earthquake has a magnitude of 5 on the Richter scale. How much stronger is it than an earthquake with a magnitude of 2?

$10^5 = 100{,}000$ and $10^2 = 100$
Since 100,000 is 1,000 times 100, 10^5 is 1,000 times 10^2.

An earthquake with a magnitude of 5 is 1,000 times stronger than an earthquake with a magnitude of 2.

EXAMPLE 2

An earthquake had a magnitude of 3. If the earthquake had been 10,000 times stronger, what would its magnitude have been?

$10^3 = 1{,}000$
$1{,}000 \cdot 10{,}000 = 10{,}000{,}000 = 10^7$

The earthquake would have had a magnitude of 7.

PRACTICE

1. How many times stronger is an earthquake with a magnitude of 3 than an earthquake with a magnitude of 1?
2. How many times stronger is an earthquake with a magnitude of 6 than an earthquake with a magnitude of 3?
3. An earthquake has a magnitude of 2. How many times stronger would the earthquake have to be to have a magnitude of 6?
4. An earthquake has a magnitude of 3. How many times stronger would the earthquake have to be to have a magnitude of 9?
5. An earthquake had a magnitude of 5. If the earthquake had been 1,000 times stronger, what would its magnitude have been?
6. An earthquake had a magnitude of 4. If the earthquake had been 100,000 times stronger, what would its magnitude have been?

Surface Area to Volume Ratios

A surface area to volume ratio is a ratio that compares the surface area and volume of a solid. You can use the surface area to volume ratio of a solid to find the surface area of the solid if you know its volume, or to find the volume of the solid if you know its surface area.

EXAMPLE 1

Find the surface area to volume ratio of the cube.

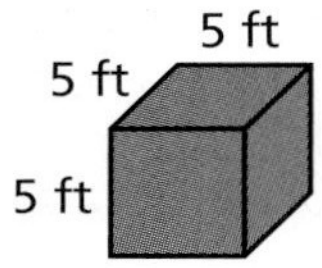

$$\text{surface area} = 2\ell w + 2\ell h + 2wh$$
$$= (2 \cdot 5 \cdot 5) + (2 \cdot 5 \cdot 5) + (2 \cdot 5 \cdot 5)$$
$$= 150$$

$$\text{volume} = \ell wh$$
$$= 5 \cdot 5 \cdot 5$$
$$= 125$$

$$\frac{\text{surface area}}{\text{volume}} = \frac{150}{125}$$
$$= \frac{6}{5} \quad \textit{Simplify.}$$

The surface area to volume ratio is $\frac{6}{5}$.

EXAMPLE 2

Find the surface area of a cube that has a volume of 64 cubic units and a surface area to volume ratio of $\frac{3}{2}$.

$\frac{3}{2} = \frac{\text{surface area}}{64}$	*Write a proportion.*
$2 \cdot \text{surface area} = 3 \cdot 64$	*Find the cross products.*
$2(\text{surface area}) = 192$	*Multiply.*
$\text{surface area} = 96$	*Divide both sides by 2.*

The surface area of the cube is 96 square units.

PRACTICE

Find the surface area to volume ratio of each solid.

1.

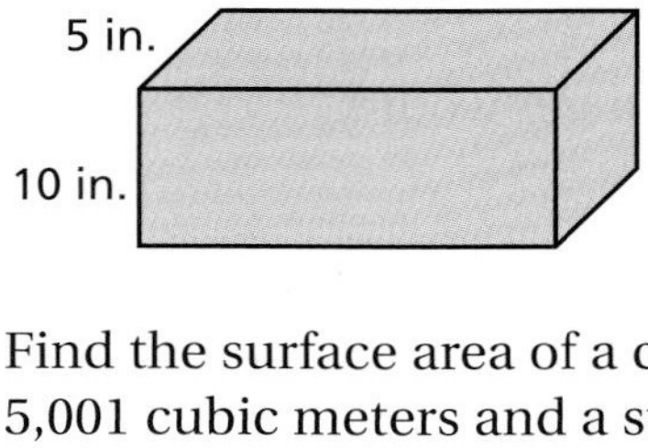

2.

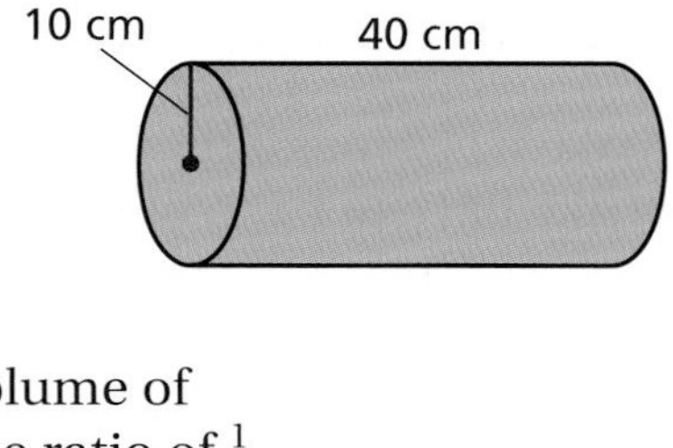

3. Find the surface area of a cylinder that has a volume of 5,001 cubic meters and a surface area to volume ratio of $\frac{1}{3}$.

4. Find the volume of a cylinder that has a surface area of 11,781 square feet and a surface area to volume ratio of $\frac{231}{500}$.

Quadratic Relationships

Quadratic relationships involve one squared value related to another value. An example of a quadratic relationship is shown in the equation $a = x^2 + 5$. If you know the value of one variable, you can substitute for it in the equation and then solve to find the second variable.

EXAMPLE

The distance d in feet that an object falls is related to the amount of time t in seconds that it falls. This relationship is given by the equation $d = 16t^2$.

What distance will an object fall in 3 seconds?

$d = 16t^2$ *Write the equation.*
$d = 16 \cdot (3)^2$ *Substitute 3 for t.*
$= 144$ *Simplify.*

The object will fall 144 feet in 3 seconds.

PRACTICE

A small rocket is shot vertically upward from the ground. The distance d in feet between the rocket and the ground as the rocket goes up can be found by using the equation $d = 128t - 16t^2$, where t is the amount of time in seconds that the rocket has been flying upward.

1. How far above the ground is the rocket at 1 second and at 2 seconds?
2. Did the rocket's distance change by the same amount in each of the first 2 seconds? Explain.
3. When the rocket is returning to the ground, the distance that the rocket falls is given by the equation $d = 16t^2$. If the rocket hits the ground 4 seconds after it starts to return, how far up did it go?
4. As the rocket falls to the ground, does it fall the same distance each second? Explain.

The graph for $y = x^2$ is shown at right. Use the graph for problems 5–7.

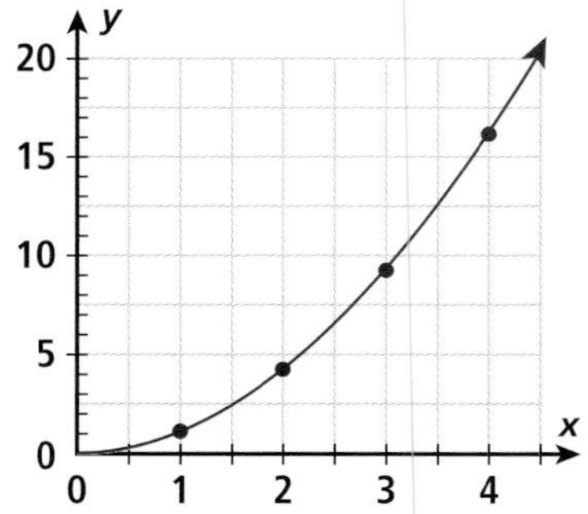

5. Find the value of y for $x = 1, 2, 3, 4$, and 5.
6. Does y increase by the same amount for each value of x? Explain.
7. How would the part of the graph from $x = 5$ to $x = 6$ compare to the part of the graph from $x = 4$ to $x = 5$?

Selected Answers

Chapter 1

1-1 Exercises

1. Add 8 to get the next number **3.** Subtract 9 to get the next number **5.** Equilateral triangles each divided into six congruent triangles with a pair of opposite congruent triangles shaded in two different colors so that the shaded pairs rotate clockwise from each equilateral triangle to the next **7.** 10 green triangles **9.** Divide by 4 to get the next number **11.** Add 23 to get the next number **13.** Regular heptagons sliced into 7 triangles with one triangle shaded in each figure. In each successive figure the shaded triangle rotates clockwise 4 triangles. **15.** 7, 23, 39, 55, 71 **17.** 50, 48, 44, 38, 30 **19.** Multiply by 4 to get the next number **21.** Add 8 to get the next number **23.** 134 **31.** 51 **33.** 90 **35.** 2,020 **37.** 100 **39.** 1,000 **41.** 23,100

1-2 Exercises

1. 32 **3.** 36 **5.** 1,000,000 **7.** 4^2 **9.** 10^2 **11.** 121 **13.** 512 **15.** 81 **17.** 5 **19.** 125 **21.** 9^2 **23.** 4^3 **25.** 2^5 **27.** 40^2 **29.** 10^5 **31.** 3^4 **33.** 8^2 **35.** 5^4 **37.** $<$ **39.** $<$ **41.** $>$ **43.** $>$ **45.** \$21.87 **47.** To simplify a power, do not multiply the base and the exponent. The exponent tells you how many times to multiply the base by itself. **49.** $4 \cdot 3^3 = 108$ stars **51.** 10^1, 33, 6^2, 4^3, 5^3 **53.** 0, 18^0, 2, 16^1, 3^4 **55.** 1^0, 8^1, 9, 3^3, 2^5 **61.** F **63.** 88 **65.** 63 **67.** Subtract 9 **69.** Multiply by 3

1-3 Exercises

1. kilograms **3.** centimeters **5.** 12,000 g **7.** 0.07 cm **9.** Monday **11.** milligrams **13.** centimeters **15.** 0.0014 km **17.** 3,550 mm **19.** 199.5 cm **21.** 2,050,000 L **23.** 0.37 cm **25.** $=$ **27.** $<$ **29.** $<$ **31.** Mona Lisa **33.** 1,120 mm **35.** 0.0008 kg **37.** Red Bat **39.** 1 kg **43.** C **45.** Subtract 3 to get the next number **47.** Add 1, then 2, then 3, and so on **49.** 81 **51.** 128 **53.** 81

1-4 Exercises

1. 1,500 **3.** 208,000 **5.** 3.6×10^6 **7.** 8.0×10^9 **9.** 2,000,000,000,000,000,000,000 **11.** 2,100 **13.** 2,500,000 **15.** 268,000 **17.** 211,500,000 **19.** 4.28×10^5 **21.** 3.0×10^9 **23.** 5.2×10^1 **25.** 8.9×10^6 **27.** 367,000 **29.** 4 **31.** 340 **33.** 540,000,000 **35.** no **37.** yes **39.** 9.8×10^8 feet per second **41.** 1.83×10^8 years **45.** C **47.** 5^4 **49.** 2^9 **51.** 1.7 km

1-5 Exercises

1. 47 **3.** 23 **5.** 4 **7.** \$280 **9.** 42 **11.** 15 **13.** 73 **15.** 588 **17.** \$139 **19.** 18 **21.** 20 **23.** 1 **25.** $>$ **27.** $>$ **29.** $=$ **31.** $4 \cdot (8 - 3) = 20$ **33.** $(12 - 2)^2 \div 5 = 20$ **35.** $(4 + 6 - 3) \div 7 = 1$ **37.** \$82 **39a.** $4 \cdot 15$ **39b.** $2 \cdot 30$ **39c.** $4 \cdot 15 + 2 \cdot 30 + 6$ **43.** C **45.** D **47.** 729 **49.** 27 **51.** 612,000 **53.** 59,000,000 **55.** 191

1-6 Exercises

1. Assoc. Prop. **3.** Comm. Prop. **5.** Assoc. Prop. **7.** 33 **9.** 1,100 **11.** 47 **13.** 18 **15.** 44 **17.** 48 **19.** Ident. Prop. **21.** Assoc. Prop. **23.** Ident. Prop. **25.** 1,600 **27.** 900 **29.** 163 **31.** 135 **33.** 25 **35.** 92 **41.** 220 ft^2 **43.** 9,000 **45.** 17,500 **47.** 15 **49.** 0 **51.** 8 **53.** 2 **59.** H **61.** 6^2 **63.** 3^2 **65.** 19 **67.** 3

1-7 Exercises

1. 12 **3.** 20 **5.** 8 **7.** 19 **9.** 22 **11.** 5 **13.** 11 **15.** 24 **17.** 12 **19.** 41 **21.** 75 **23.** 10 **25.** 22 **27.** 24 **29.** 13 **31.** 31 **33.** \$4.50 **35.** 86°F **41.** H **43.** 6.21×10^7 **45.** 8×10^5 **47.** 68 **49.** 87

1-8 Exercises

1. $7p$ **3.** $\frac{n}{12}$ **5.** $\$5 \div n$, or $\frac{5}{n}$ **7.** $5 + x$ **9.** $n \div 8$ **11.** $3y - 10$ **13.** $5 + 2t$ **15.** $\frac{23}{u} - t$ **17.** $2(y + 5)$ **19.** $35(r - 5)$ **21.** $65{,}000 + 2b$ **23.** 90 divided by y **25.** 16 multiplied by t **27.** the difference between 4 times p and 10 **29.** the quotient of m and 15 plus 3 **31.** $15y + 12$ **37.** $(104 \div 19 \cdot 2)x$; \$426 **39.** 5 **41.** 35

1-9 Exercises

1. $6b$ and $\frac{b}{2}$ **3.** $8x$ **5.** There are no like terms. **7.** b^6 and $3b^6$ **9.** m and $2m$ **11.** $8a + 2b$ **13.** $3a + 3b + 2c$ **15.** $3q^2 + 2q$ **17.** $2n + 3a + 3a + 2n + 5$ **19.** $27y$ **21.** $2d^2 + d$ **23.** no like terms **25.** no like terms **27.** expression $4n + 5n + 6n = 15n$ **29a.** $21.5d + 23d + 15.5d + 19d$ **b.** \$750.50 **c.** the amount Brad earned in June **31.** $23x^2$ **35.** J **37.** $<$ **39.** $<$ **41.** 51 **43.** 159

1-10 Exercises

1. no **3.** yes **5.** situation A **7.** no **9.** yes **11.** no **13.** situation B **15.** yes **17.** yes **19.** no **21.** yes **23.** yes **25.** $10{,}500 + d = 14{,}264$ **29.** A **31.** 1.085×10^7 **33.** 9.04×10^8 **35.** Identity Property of Addition

1-11 Exercises

1. $r = 176$ **3.** $x = 88$ **5.** $f = 9$ **7.** 14 yd **9.** $t = 82$ **11.** $b = 67$ **13.** $k = 123$ **15.** $w = 43$ **17.** $s = 45$ **19.** $j = 76$ **21.** $q = 99$ **23.** 38 mi **25.** $p = 10$ **27.** $b = 52$ **29.** $a = 45$ **31.** $c = 149$ **33.** $m = 199$ **35.** $s = 159$ **37.** $x = 839$ **39.** $w = -229$ **41a.** $315 - x = 65$ **b.** $50x = 250$ **47.** D **49.** $17 - k$ **51.** $12 + 5n$ **53.** $8 + 11t$

1-12 Exercises

1. $s = 847$ **3.** $y = 40$ **5.** $c = 32$ **7.** 9 people **9.** $k = 1{,}296$ **11.** $c = 175$ **13.** $m = 306$ **15.** $p = 21$ **17.** $a = 2$ **19.** $d = 45$ **21.** $g = 27$ **23.** $m = 110$ **25.** $x = 7$ **27.** $b = 62$ **29.** $f = 20$ **31.** $a = 36$ **33.** $d = 42$ **35.** $r = 307$ **37.** $7 + n = 15$ **39.** $12 = q - 8$ **41.** 2 toys **43.** 13,300 **47.** C **49.** 23 **51.** no **53.** $j = 242$ **55.** $a = 47$

Chapter 1 Study Guide: Review

1. exponent; base **2.** numerical expression **3.** composite number **4.** algebraic expression **5.** Add 4 to get the next number **6.** Add 20 to get the next number **7.** Add 7 to get the next number **8.** Multiply by 5 to get the next number **9.** Subtract 4 to get the next number **10.** Subtract 7 to get the next number **11.** 81 **12.** 10 **13.** 128 **14.** 1 **15.** 121 **16.** 18,000 **17.** 0.72 **18.** 5,300 **19.** 6 **20.** 14,400 **21.** 1,320 **22.** 220,000,000 **23.** 340 **24.** 560,000 **25.** 780 **26.** 3 **27.** 103 **28.** 5 **29.** 67 **30.** Comm. Prop. of Add. **31.** Identity Prop. of Add. **32.** Distributive Property **33.** 19 **34.** 524 **35.** 10 **36.** $4 \div (n + 12)$ **37.** $2(n - 11)$ **38.** $10b^2 + 8$ **39.** $15a^2 + 2$ **40.** $x^4 + x^3 + 6x^2$ **41.** yes **42.** no **43.** no **44.** 8 **45.** 32 **46.** 18 **47.** 112 **48.** 72 **49.** 9 **50.** 98 **51.** 13 **52.** 17 h

Chapter 2

2-1 Exercises

5. > **7.** < **9.** −5, −3, −1, 4, 6 **11.** −6, −4, 0, 1, 3 **13.** 8 **15.** 10 **21.** > **23.** < **25.** −9, −7, −5, −2, 0 **27.** 16 **29.** 20 **31.** < **33.** = **35.** = **37.** = **39.** Aug, Jul, Sep, Jun, Apr, Mar, Oct **41.** −29 **45.** decreased by about 9% **51.** H **53.** 1.67 m **55.** 10,300 mL **57.** 112 **59.** 170

2-2 Exercises

1. 12 **3.** −2 **5.** 15 **7.** −15 **9.** −12 **11.** −20 **13.** −9 **15.** 13 **17.** 7 **19.** −17 **21.** −19 **23.** −16 **25.** −88 **27.** −55 **29.** −14 **31.** −13 **33.** −13 **35.** −26 **37.** 14 **39.** > **41.** > **43.** > **45.** Cody's balance is reduced by $24. **47.** −16 **49.** 3 **51.** 4,150 ft **57.** F **59.** 2 **61.** 4 **63.** > **65.** >

2-3 Exercises

1. −3 **3.** 6 **5.** −4 **7.** −10 **9.** 7 **11.** −14 **13.** −5 **15.** 8 **17.** 12 **19.** 16 **21.** −17 **23.** 8 **25.** 50 **27.** 18 **29.** 16 **31.** −5 **33.** −20 **35.** 83°F **37.** −14 **39.** −2 **41.** 2 **43.** 16 **45.** −27 **47.** −17 **49.** −13, −17, −21 **51.** 1,234°F **53.** 265°F **57.** $m + n$ has the least absolute value **59.** 3 **61.** 19 **63.** 24

2-4 Exercises

1. −15 **3.** −15 **5.** 15 **7.** −15 **9.** −8 **11.** 4 **13.** 7 **15.** −7 **17.** −450 feet **19.** −10 **21.** −12 **23.** 48 **25.** 35 **27.** 7 **29.** −8 **31.** −9 **33.** −9 **35.** −40 **37.** −3 **39.** 50 **41.** −3 **43.** 30 **45.** −42 **47.** −60 ft **49.** less **51.** more **53.** 1 **55.** −12 **57.** 1,400 **59.** 11 **63.** C **65.** $x + 6$ **67.** $2d - 4$ **69.** 5 **71.** −2

2-5 Exercises

1. $w = 4$ **3.** $k = -7$ **5.** $y = -30$ **7.** This year's loss is $57 million. **9.** $k = -3$ **11.** $v = -4$ **13.** $a = 20$ **15.** $t = -32$ **17.** $n = 150$ **19.** $l = -144$ **21.** $y = 100$ **23.** $j = -63$ **25.** $c = 17$ **27.** $y = -11$ **29.** $w = -41$ **31.** $x = -58$ **33.** $x = 4$ **35.** $t = 9$ **37.** 3 mi **39.** $-13 + p = 8$ **41.** $t - 9 = -22$ **43.** oceans or beaches **49.** H **51.** multiply by 2 **53.** > **55.** < **57.** =

2-6 Exercises

1. prime **3.** prime **5.** 2^4 **7.** 3^4 **9.** $2 \cdot 3^2$ **11.** $3^2 \cdot 5$ **13.** $2 \cdot 5^3$ **15.** $2^2 \cdot 5^2$ **17.** $3^2 \cdot 71$ **19.** $2^3 \cdot 5^3$ **21.** prime **23.** prime **25.** composite **27.** composite **29.** $2^2 \cdot 17$ **31.** $2^3 \cdot 3 \cdot 5$ **33.** $3^3 \cdot 5$ **35.** $2 \cdot 7 \cdot 11$ **37.** $2^5 \cdot 5^2$ **39.** 5^4 **41.** $3^2 \cdot 5 \cdot 7$ **43.** $3^3 \cdot 7$ **45.** $2 \cdot 11^2$ **47.** $11 \cdot 17$ **49.** $5^2 \cdot 7^2$ **51.** $2^3 \cdot 3^2 \cdot 5$ **53.** 3^2 **55.** 5^2 **57.** 2^4 **59a.** $2 \cdot 32$ **b.** one **61.** 7 **63.** 4 or 8 people **67.** B **69.** $2^3 \cdot 3 \cdot 5$ **71.** 587 **73.** 14,800,000 **75.** $y = 1$ **77.** $x = 0$

2-7 Exercises

1. 6 **3.** 12 **5.** 4 **7.** 12 kits **9.** 12 **11.** 11 **13.** 38 **15.** 2 **17.** 26 **19.** 3 **21.** 1 **23.** 2 **25.** 22 **27.** 40 **29.** 1 **31.** 7 **33.** 3 **35.** 13 **37.** 7 shelves **39a.** 7 students **b.** 5 cookies **45.** B **47.** 13 **49.** 81 **51.** −5 **53.** 2 **55.** 7^2 **57.** 2^2

2-8 Exercises

1. 28 **3.** 48 **5.** 45 **7.** 24 min **9.** 24 **11.** 42 **13.** 120 **15.** 80 **17.** 180 **19.** 360 **21.** 60 min **23.** 12 **25.** 132 **27.** 90 **29.** 12 **31.** 144 **33.** 210 **35.** yes **37.** no **41.** C **43.** $5c - 2$ **45.** $7u + 3v - 4$ **47.** 4 **49.** 15

2-9 Exercises

9. no **11.** yes **13.** $3\frac{3}{4}$ **15.** $1\frac{4}{13}$ **17.** $\frac{31}{5}$ **19.** $\frac{38}{5}$ **29.** yes **31.** yes **33.** yes **35.** no **37.** $6\frac{1}{3}$ **39.** $7\frac{4}{11}$ **41.** $\frac{128}{5}$ **43.** $\frac{29}{3}$ **45.** No **51.** $\frac{11}{2}$ **53.** $\frac{141}{21}$ **55.** $\frac{573}{50}$ **57.** $\frac{12}{20}, \frac{6}{10}$ **59.** $\frac{9}{5}, \frac{72}{40}$ **61.** $8\frac{1}{3}$ ft **63.** $3\frac{1}{2}$ ft **65.** $\frac{150}{4}$ **69.** C **71.** $1\frac{1}{3}$ cups of flour **73.** $y = 12$ **75.** $z = 80$ **77.** 45 **79.** 168

2-10 Exercises

1. 0.57 **3.** 1.83 **5.** 0.12 **7.** 0.5 **9.** $\frac{1}{125}$ **11.** $-2\frac{1}{20}$ **13.** 0.720 **15.** 6.4 **17.** 0.88 **19.** 1 **21.** 1.92 **23.** 0.8 **25.** 0.55 **27.** $\frac{1}{100}$ **29.** $-\frac{2}{25}$ **31.** $\frac{61}{4}$ **33.** $8\frac{3}{8}$ **35.** 8.75 **37.** $5\frac{5}{100}$ **39.** $\frac{307}{20}$ **41.** 4.003 **43.** yes **45.** no **47.** yes **49.** no **51.** $17\frac{9}{10}, 18\frac{1}{20}, 18\frac{1}{25}, 18\frac{11}{20}$ **55.** D **57.** no **59.** yes **61.** $\frac{13}{4}$ **63.** $\frac{25}{4}$

2-11 Exercises

1. $<$ **3.** $<$ **5.** $<$ **7.** $>$ **9.** 2.05, 2.5, $\frac{13}{5}$ **11.** $<$ **13.** $>$ **15.** $>$ **17.** $>$ **19.** $>$ **21.** $<$ **23.** $<$ **25.** $\frac{5}{8}$, 0.7, 0.755 **27.** 2.05, $\frac{21}{10}$, 2.25 **29.** $-2.98, -2\frac{9}{10}$, 2.88 **31.** $\frac{3}{4}$ **33.** $\frac{7}{8}$ **35.** 0.32 **37.** $-\frac{7}{8}$ **39.** Saturn (0.69), Jupiter and Uranus (1.32) **41.** sloths **47.** J **49.** $>$ **51.** $>$ **53.** 169 **55.** 57

Chapter 2 Study Guide: Review

1. rational number; integer; terminating decimal

2. improper fraction, mixed number **3.** $>$ **4.** $<$

5.

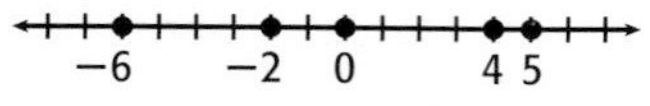

6.

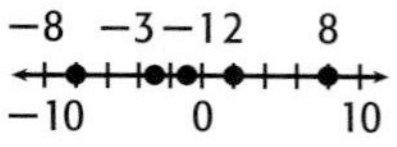

7.

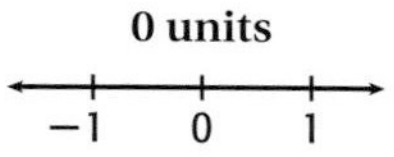

8.

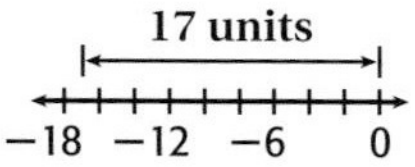

9.

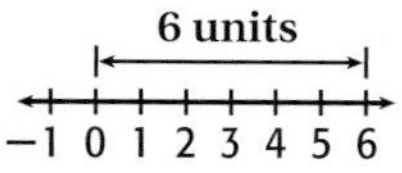

10. −3 **11.** 1 **12.** −56 **13.** 9 **14.** 14 **15.** −6 **16.** 6 **17.** −9 **18.** −1 **19.** −9 **20.** −50 **21.** 3 **22.** 16 **23.** −2 **24.** −12 **25.** −3 **26.** 10 **27.** 14 **28.** −26 **29.** 72 **30.** 13 **31.** −4 **32.** −105 **33.** −19 **34.** 21 **35.** 16 **36.** $2^3 \cdot 11$ **37.** 3^3 **38.** $2 \cdot 3^4$ **39.** $2^5 \cdot 3$ **40.** 30 **41.** 3 **42.** 6 **43.** 40 **44.** 60 **45.** 32 **46.** 27 **47.** 90 **48.** 12 **49.** 315 **50.** $\frac{21}{15}$ **51.** $\frac{19}{6}$ **52.** $\frac{43}{4}$ **53.** $3\frac{1}{3}$ **54.** $2\frac{1}{2}$ **55.** $2\frac{3}{7}$ **56.** Possible answer: $\frac{8}{9}, \frac{24}{27}$ **57.** Possible answer: $\frac{42}{48}, \frac{7}{8}$ **58.** Possible answer: $\frac{16}{21}, \frac{96}{126}$ **59.** $\frac{1}{4}$ **60.** $-\frac{1}{250}$ **61.** $\frac{1}{20}$ **62.** 3.5 **63.** −0.06 **64.** 0.6 **65.** $<$ **66.** $>$ **67.** $>$ **68.** $<$ **69.** $-0.55, \frac{6}{13}, \frac{1}{2}$, 0.58

Chapter 3

3-1 Exercises

1. 63 **3.** 2 **5.** −225 **7.** no **9.** 92 **11.** 8 **13.** 55 **15.** 5 **17.** −120 **19.** 9 **21.** −7 **23.** −59 **25.** −90 **27.** −36 **29.** 11 **31.** −98 **33.** 225 **35.** 13 **37.** about 8 weeks **39.** approximately 5 gallons **41.** about 30 AU **47.** J **49.** −3 **51.** 22 **53.** −11

3-2 Exercises

1. 21.82 **3.** 12.826 **5.** 1.98 **7.** 1.77 **9.** \$37.2 billion **11.** 18.97 **13.** −25.52 **15.** 10.132 **17.** −15.89 **19.** 9.01 **21.** 16.05 **23.** 5.1 **25.** 22.77 **27.** 77.13 g **29.** −4.883 **31.** 14.33 **33.** 1.92 **35.** 30.12 **37.** −1.26 **39.** −3.457 **41.** You must keep the place value units together. **43.** 1915 **49.** G **51.** $y = 15$ **53.** $p = 39$ **55.** 22 **57.** 42

3-3 Exercises

1. −3.6 **3.** 0.18 **5.** 2.04 **7.** −0.315 **9.** 334.7379 miles **11.** 0.35 **13.** 3.2 **15.** −20.4 **17.** 9.1 **19.** 4.48 **21.** 2.814 **23.** −9.256 **25.** 6.161 **27.** 5.445 mi **29.** 0.0021 **31.** 0.432 **33.** −2.88 **35.** 1.911 **37.** 0.351 **39.** 0.00864 **41.** 28.95 in. of mercury **43.** −8.904 **45.** −0.027 **47.** 1,224.1152 **53.** 11.3 mi **55.** $5 \cdot 7$ **57.** 2^6 **59.** 8.57 **61.** −3.74 **63.** 19.71 **65.** −68.868

3-4 Exercises

1. 6.14 3. −3.09 **5.** 0.017 **7.** \$5.54 **9.** −8.9 **11.** −8.92 **13.** −4.8 **15.** 2.04 **17.** 1.13 **19.** −3.07 **21.** \$9.75 **23.** 1.56 **25.** 4.19 **27.** −2.8 **29.** −1.91 **31.** −0.019 **33.** 0.18 **35.** 262.113 **37.** 1985 **39.** 14.53 million people **45.** C **47.** \$9.93 **49.** 1 **51.** 8 **53.** 5 **55.** 2.116 **57.** 18.2055

3-5 Exercises

1. 0.9 **3.** 4.6 **5.** −3.2 **7.** 2.5 **9.** −16 **11.** −4.8 **13.** 28 mi/gal **15.** −0.12 **17.** −14 **19.** 4.2 **21.** 47.5 **23.** 4 **25.** −48.75 **27.** 2.4 min **29.** 22.5 **31.** −0.4 **33.** 25 **35.** 20 **37.** 4.5 **39.** 6.4 **41.** 2,500 years **43.** 11 years **45.** 363.64 days **47.** A **49.** $9\frac{1}{3}$ **51.** $3\frac{2}{5}$ **53.** 5.05 **55.** −2.7

3-6 Exercises

1. $w = 7$ **3.** $k = 24.09$ **5.** $b = 5.04$ **7.** $t = 9$ **9.** \$4.25 **11.** $c = 44.56$ **13.** $a = 5.08$ **15.** $p = -53.21$ **17.** $z = 16$ **19.** $w = 11.76$ **21.** $a = -74.305$ **23.** \$7.50 **25.** $n = -4.92$ **27.** $r = 0.72$ **29.** $m = -0.15$ **31.** $k = 0.9$ **33.** $t = 0.936$ **35.** $v = -2$ **37.** $n = 12.254$ **39.** $j = 11.107$ **41.** $g = 0.5$ **43.** \$171 **45a.** 148.1 million **b.** between English and Italian **49.** C **53.** 6.0×10^6 **55.** 1.5 **57.** 3 **59.** 9

3-7 Exercises

1. about 4 feet **3.** 0 **5.** 2 **7.** 3 **9.** 48 **11.** 1 **13.** $2\frac{1}{2}$ **15.** $\frac{1}{2}$ **17.** $11\frac{1}{2}$ **19.** 6 **21.** 30 **23.** 2 **25.** 30 **27.** $\frac{1}{2}$ **29.** 24 **31.** −8 **33.** 4 **35.** $10\frac{27}{28}$ **37.** $5\frac{1}{2}$ **39.** \$14 **41.** greater **43.** 2 m **47.** J **49.** $x = 27$ **51.** $m = 13$ **53.** $x = 6.5$ **55.** $q = -1.5$

3-8 Exercises

1. $\frac{1}{3}$ **3.** $\frac{3}{7}$ **5.** $\frac{1}{2}$ **7.** $\frac{19}{24}$ **9.** $\frac{1}{12}$ **11.** $\frac{1}{2}$ **13.** $\frac{3}{5}$ **15.** $\frac{2}{3}$ **17.** $\frac{1}{5}$ **19.** $\frac{1}{4}$ **21.** $\frac{3}{4}$ **23.** $-\frac{1}{6}$ **25.** $\frac{8}{15}$ **27.** $\frac{1}{6}$ mi **29.** $\frac{13}{18}$ **31.** $\frac{4}{5}$ **33.** $-\frac{1}{12}$ **35.** 1 **37.** $-\frac{1}{20}$ **39.** $\frac{14}{15}$ **41.** $\frac{41}{63}$ **43.** $\frac{41}{45}$ **45.** 0 **47.** $\frac{9}{120}$ **49.** $\frac{5}{6}$ hour **51.** $\frac{13}{24}$ mi **53.** Cai **55.** $\frac{3}{8}$ lb of cashews **59.** B **61.** 1 **63.** 6 **67.** 11

3-9 Exercises

1. $5\frac{1}{6}$ **3.** $6\frac{5}{8}$ **5.** $7\frac{3}{4}$ **7.** $5\frac{1}{3}$ **9.** $4\frac{9}{40}$ **11.** 15 **13.** $5\frac{2}{3}$ **15.** $6\frac{4}{5}$ **17.** $11\frac{7}{15}$ **19.** $\frac{6}{7}$ **21.** $5\frac{1}{4}$ **23.** $2\frac{7}{20}$ **25.** $\frac{9}{10}$ **27.** $15\frac{8}{15}$ **29.** $13\frac{5}{6}$ **31.** $6\frac{5}{24}$ **33.** $\frac{5}{6}$ **35.** $4\frac{1}{6}$ **37.** $10\frac{1}{24}$ **39.** < **41.** > **43.** $4\frac{5}{8}$ cups **45.** $117\frac{1}{3}$ mi **47.** the waterfall trail **51.** D **53.** 6 **57.** $\frac{3}{4}$ **59.** $1\frac{5}{36}$

3-10 Exercises

1. $2\frac{1}{2}$ hr **3.** $\frac{2}{5}$ **5.** −9 **7.** $\frac{12}{5}$ **9.** −20 **11.** $1\frac{2}{3}$ tsp **13.** $\frac{1}{2}$ **15.** 4 **17.** $\frac{1}{4}$ **19.** $-\frac{5}{9}$ **21.** $\frac{222}{5}$ **23.** $17\frac{1}{2}$ **25.** $\frac{7}{3}$ **27.** $8\frac{1}{4}$ **29.** $\frac{155}{42}$ **31.** $\frac{1}{3}$ **33.** $-\frac{1}{6}$ **35.** $\frac{1}{12}$ **37.** $\frac{1}{5}$ **39.** $\frac{7}{10}$ **41.** $\frac{1}{5}$ **43.** 1 **45.** 3 **47.** 5 **49.** 6 **51.** 1 **53.** $2\frac{1}{12}$ lb **55.** $11\frac{1}{3}$ mi **59.** B **61.** −7, −3, 0, 4, 5 **63.** −9, −4, −1, 1, 9 **65.** $1\frac{5}{12}$ **67.** $2\frac{5}{24}$

3-11 Exercises

1. 18 **3.** $\frac{3}{32}$ **5.** $\frac{1}{4}$ **7.** 2 **9.** 3 capes **11.** 18 **13.** $-4\frac{3}{8}$ **15.** $\frac{1}{27}$ **17.** −40 **19.** $\frac{5}{14}$ **21.** −14 **23.** $\frac{88}{7}$ **25.** $-9\frac{4}{5}$ **27.** 6 pieces **29.** $5\frac{2}{5}$ **31.** 2

33. $\frac{8}{147}$ **35.** $-\frac{16}{25}$ **37.** $\frac{18}{25}$ **39.** $\frac{21}{2}$ **41.** $\frac{1}{3}$ **43.** −1 **45.** 87 hamburger patties **47.** 11 in. **49.** 7 circles **51.** D **53.** 22 **55.** 24 **57.** 24 **59.** $-8\frac{1}{10}$ **61.** $-1\frac{11}{12}$

3-12 Exercises

1. $a = \frac{3}{4}$ **3.** $p = \frac{3}{2}$ **5.** $r = \frac{9}{10}$ **7.** $1\frac{1}{8}$ c **9.** $t = \frac{5}{8}$ **11.** $x = \frac{53}{24}$ **13.** $y = \frac{7}{60}$ **15.** $w = \frac{1}{2}$ **17.** $z = \frac{1}{12}$ **19.** $n = 1\frac{23}{25}$ **21.** $t = \frac{1}{4}$ **23.** $w = 6$ **25.** $x = \frac{3}{5}$ **27.** $n = \frac{12}{5}$ **29.** $y = \frac{1}{2}$ **31.** $r = \frac{1}{77}$ **33.** $h = -\frac{1}{12}$ **35.** $v = \frac{3}{4}$ **37.** $d = 14\frac{17}{40}$ **39.** $11\frac{3}{16}$ **41.** 15 million species **43.** 48 stories **49.** G **51.** 3, 3.02, $3\frac{2}{10}$, 3.25 **53.** −1 **55.** 21

Chapter 3 Study Guide: Review

1. compatible numbers **2.** reciprocals **3.** 110 **4.** 5 **5.** 75 **6.** 4 **7.** about 20 weeks **8.** 27.88 **9.** −51.2 **10.** 6.22 **11.** 52.902 **12.** 14.095 **13.** 35.88 **14.** 3.5 **15.** −38.7 **16.** 40.495 **17.** 60.282 **18.** 77.348 **19.** −18.81 **20.** 2.3 **21.** −4.9 **22.** 0.08 **23.** −5.8 **24.** −1.65 **25.** 3.4 **26.** 4.5 **27.** −1.09 **28.** −15.4 **29.** −500 **30.** 2 **31.** 4 **32.** $x = -10.44$ **33.** $s = 107$ **34.** $n = 0.007$ **35.** $k = 8.64$ **36.** $e = -5.05$ **37.** $w = -3.08$ **38.** 24 **39.** −8 **40.** 3 **41.** 1 **42.** 30 **43.** 3 **44.** about 5 laps **45.** $\frac{5}{12}$ **46.** $\frac{17}{20}$ **47.** $\frac{5}{11}$ **48.** $\frac{1}{9}$ **49.** $6\frac{5}{24}$ **50.** $3\frac{1}{3}$ **51.** $6\frac{1}{4}$ **52.** $1\frac{5}{12}$ **53.** $7\frac{1}{2}$ **54.** $1\frac{21}{25}$ **55.** $17\frac{17}{63}$ **56.** $6\frac{1}{4}$ **57.** $\frac{4}{75}$ **58.** $\frac{2}{15}$ **59.** 1 **60.** $1\frac{11}{12}$ **61.** $1\frac{2}{3}$ **62.** $\frac{1}{15}$ **63.** $1\frac{5}{7}$ **64.** $\frac{13}{28}$

Chapter 4

4-1 Exercises

1. I **3.** III

5–7.

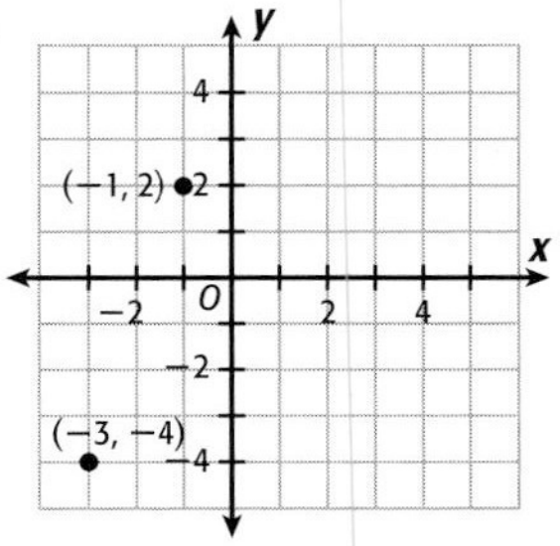

9. (6, −3) **11.** (−4, 0) **13.** I **15.** IV

17–19.

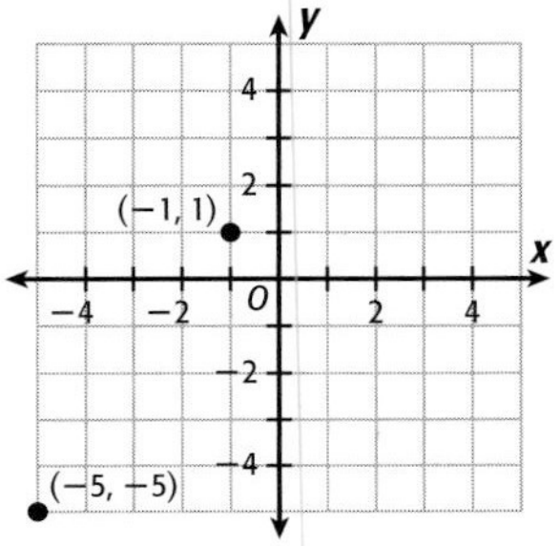

21. (−4, 4) **23.** (−5, −4) **25.** (5, 6)

27.

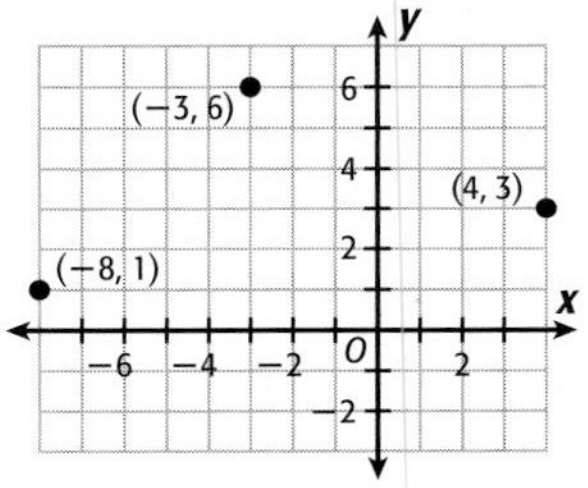

29. triangle; Quadrants I and II **31.** III **33.** (12, 7) **39.** B **41.** 12 **43.** 37 **45.** −87 **47.** $1\frac{1}{2}$ **49.** $\frac{5}{6}$

4-2 Exercises

1. (1, 1) **3.** (−2, 0)

5.

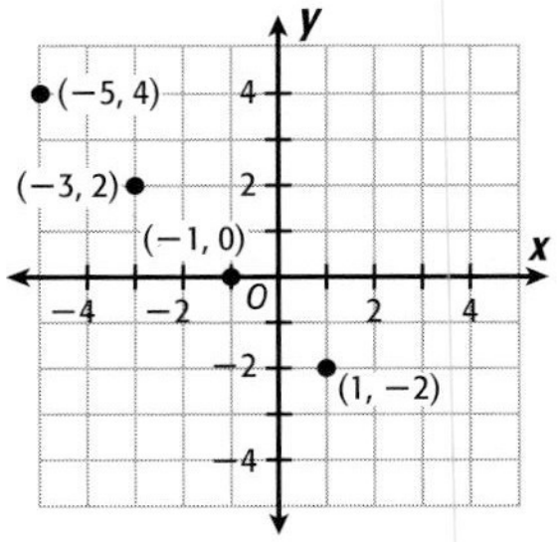

7.

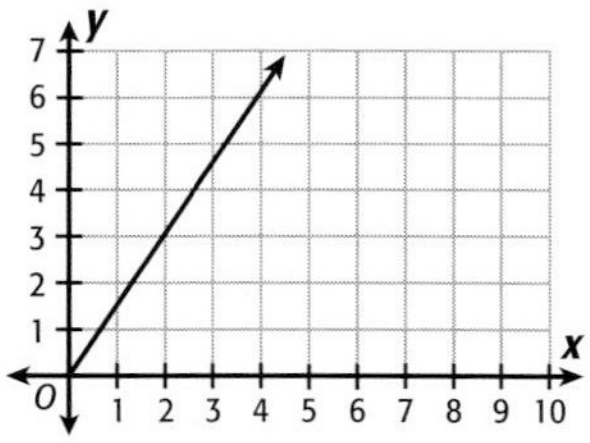

9. (−2, 0), (0, −1), (4, −2), (6, −3)

11.

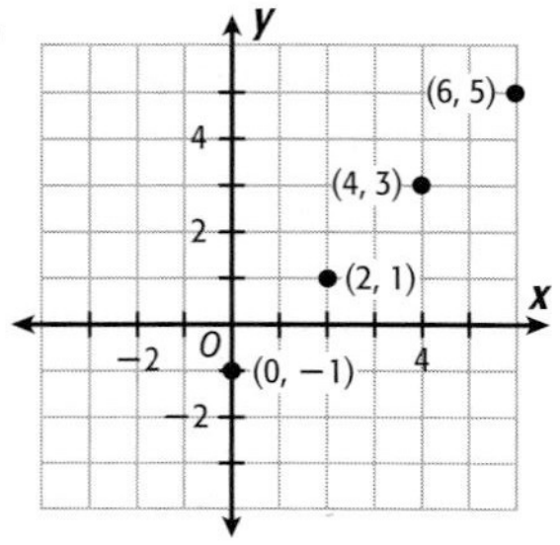

13.

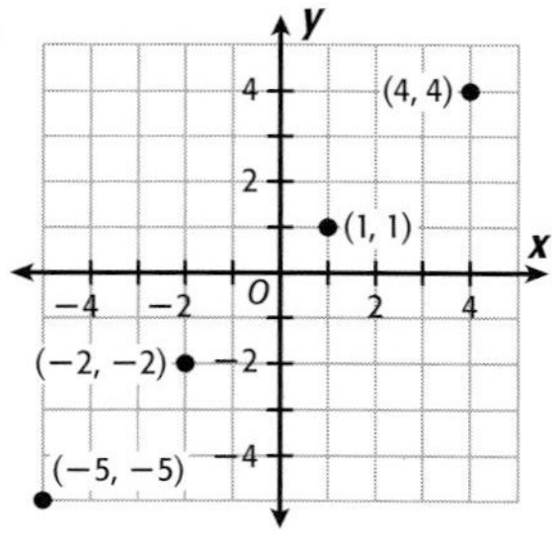

21. −6.3 **23.** −12.35 **25.** $16\frac{1}{3}$
27. $7\frac{33}{40}$

4-3 Exercises

1. A **3.** B **17.** 3 **19.** 0 **21.** 3
23. 3 **25.** (1, 4)

4-4 Exercises

1. −5, 1, 3 **3.** 50, 2, 18

5.

x	−1	0	1	2
y	3	2	3	6

7. −7, 1, 8

9.

x	−1	0	1	2
y	$-\frac{1}{2}$	0	$\frac{1}{2}$	1

11a. $y = x - 11.66$ **17.** J
19. −1 **21.** $x = 6$ **23.** $y = 4\frac{1}{2}$

4-5 Exercises

1. arithmetic **3.** $y = 3n$
5. $y = n - 1$ **7.** $y = 195n$
9. arithmetic **11.** $y = 7n$
13. $y = 20n$ **15.** $y = n + 0.5$
17. multiply 35 by n
19. add $\frac{1}{2}$ to n **21.** divide n by 3
23. $y = n - 0.5$ **25.** $y = 3n + 2$
27. $y = 2n - 1$ **29.** $y = 2^n$
35. 10,000,000 **37.** 1 **39.** 200
41. 105

4-6 Exercises

1.

Input	Rule	Output	Ordered Pair
x	*x* + 3	*y*	(*x*, *y*)
−2	−2 + 3	1	(−2, 1)
0	0 + 3	3	(0, 3)
2	2 + 3	5	(2, 5)

3. $y = 750x$

5.

Input	Rule	Output	Ordered Pair
x	*x* − 1	*y*	(*x*, *y*)
3	3 − 1	2	(3, 2)
4	4 − 1	3	(4, 3)
5	5 − 1	4	(5, 4)

7.

Input	Rule	Output	Ordered Pair
x	2*x* + 3	*y*	(*x*, *y*)
−2	2 (−2) + 3	−1	(−2, −1)
−1	2 (−1) + 3	1	(−1, −1)
0	2 (0) + 3	3	(0, 3)

9. 8,100 cm
15. Simon calculated the y-coordinates incorrectly in the function table. **17.** −1.3
19. As time passes, the distance increases at a steady rate.
21. $y = 2n - 4$

Chapter 4 Study Guide: Review

1. sequence **2.** function
3. linear function
4–7.

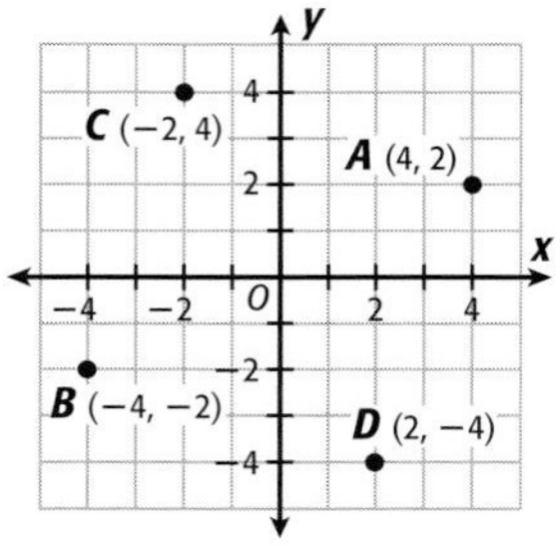

8. (2, −1) **9.** (−2, 3)
10. (1, 0) **11.** (−4, −2)

12.

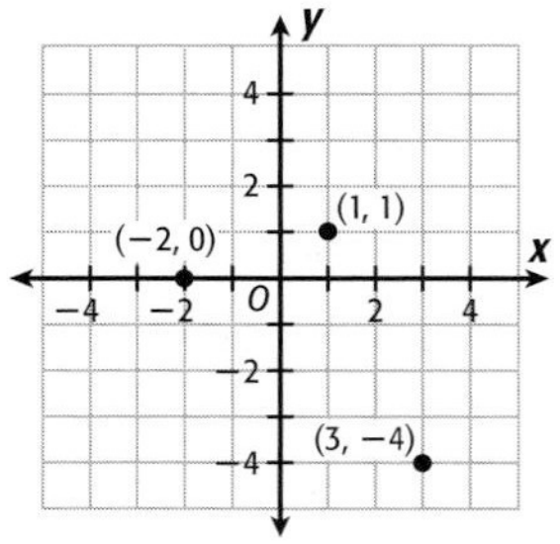

13.

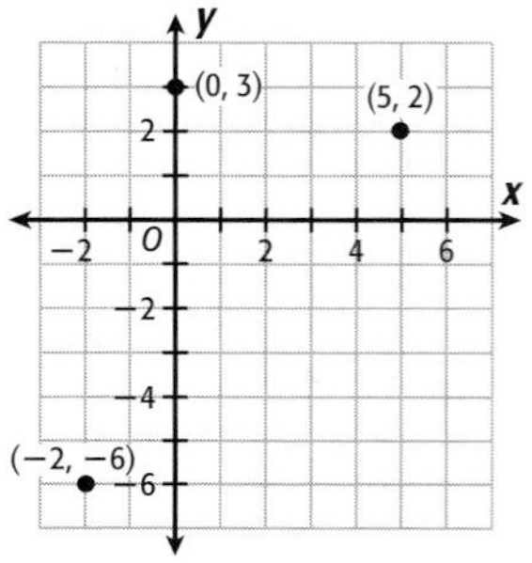

14.

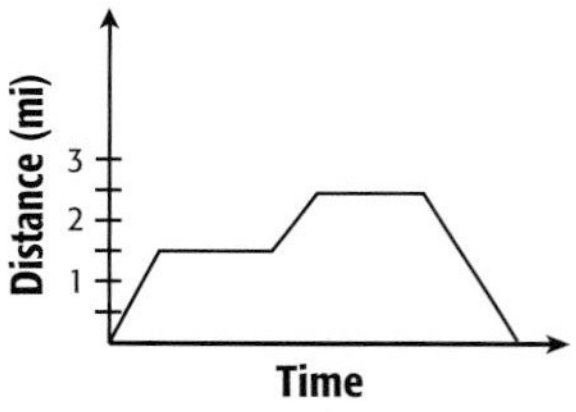

15.

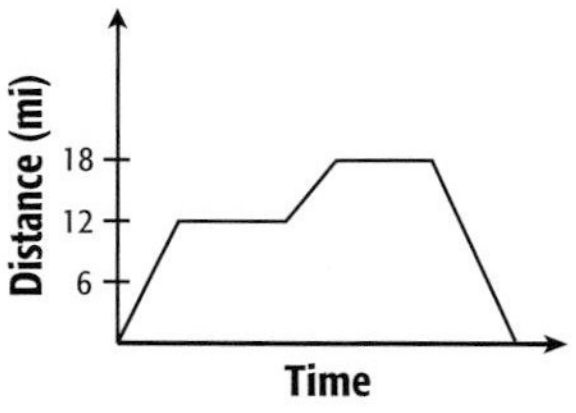

16.

Input	Rule	Output
x	$x^2 - 1$	*y*
−2	$(-2)^2 - 1$	3
3	$(3)^2 - 1$	8
5	$(5)^2 - 1$	24

17. geometric **18.** arithmetic;
19. $y = 25n$ **20.** $y = n - 4$
21. $y = 3n - 7$ **22.** $y = 2n + 2$
23.

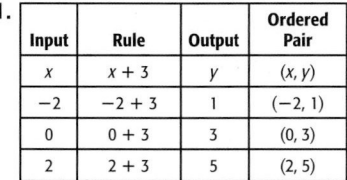

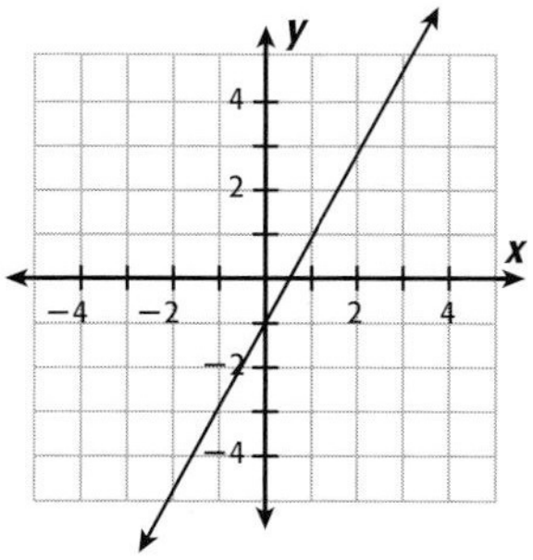

24.

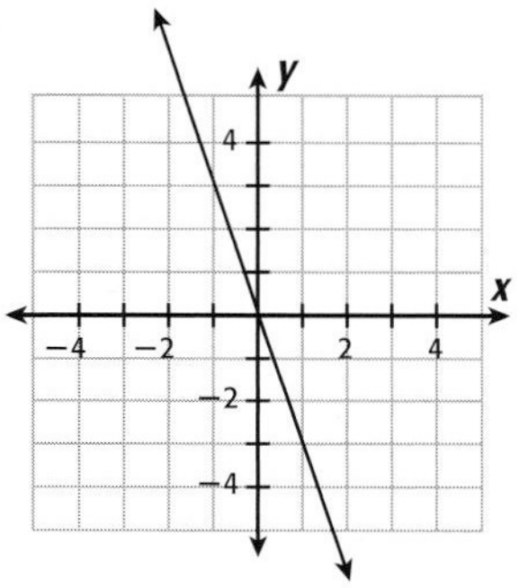

25.

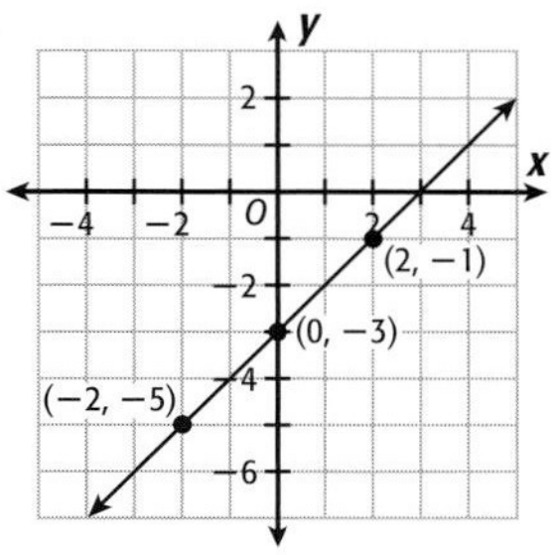

26.

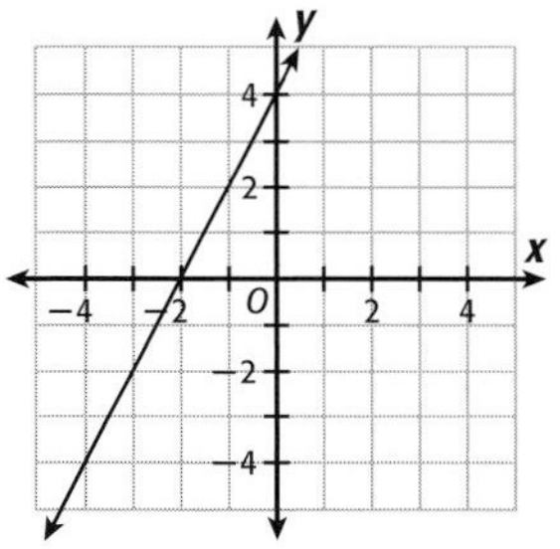

27.

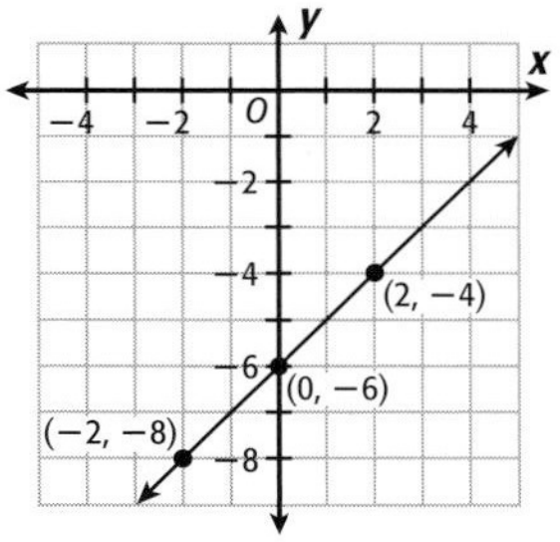

28.

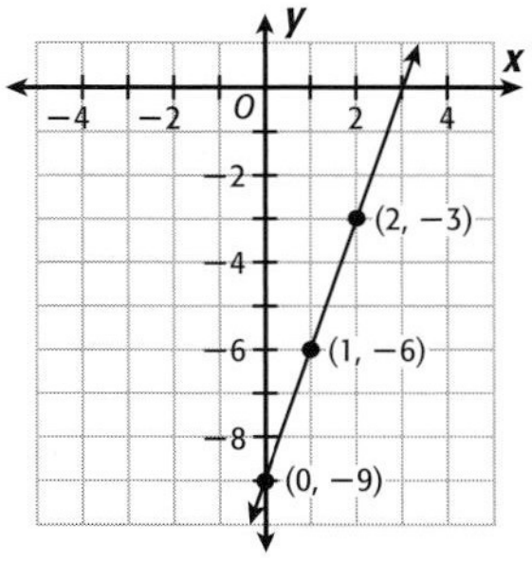

Chapter 5

5-1 Exercises

1. $\frac{10}{3}$, 10 to 3, 10:3 **3.** $\frac{3}{1}$ or 3 to 1 or 3:1 **5.** $\frac{25}{30}$, 25 to 30, 25:30, or $\frac{5}{6}$, 5 to 6, 5:6 **7.** $\frac{30}{15}$, 30 to 15, 30:15, or $\frac{2}{1}$, 2 to 1, 2:1 **9.** $\frac{4}{1}$ or 4 to 1 or 4:1 **11.** group 1 **13.** 2:1; $\frac{2}{1}$, 2 to 1 **15.** 4:1, $\frac{4}{1}$, 4 to 1 **17.** 4:3, $\frac{4}{3}$, 4 to 3 **21.** Pancakes: $\frac{4}{3}$; biscuits: $\frac{1}{2} = \frac{6}{3}$; the biscuits have a greater ratio of mix to milk. **23.** $y = 7.2$ **25.** Quadrant IV

5-2 Exercises

1. 83.5 mL per min **3.** 458 mi/h **5.** \$7.75 per h **7.** about 74.63 mi/h **9.** 3 runs per game **11.** \$115 per ft^2 **13.** 13 songs per CD **15.** 54 words per min **17.** 0.25 s per floor **19.** \$2.16 per lb **21.** 11 m per s **23.** 0.04 mi per min **25.** 0.32 in. per min **27.** $\frac{1{,}026 \text{ students}}{38 \text{ classes}}$; 27 students per class **29.** \$3.55, \$3.70; $\frac{\$28.40}{8 \text{ yd}}$ is the better buy. **31.** \$0.11 per min, \$0.08 per min; 800 minutes of phone time for \$62.99 is the better buy. **33.** 287, 329, 611, (France, Poland, Germany) **37.** D **39.** $<$ **41.** $>$

5-3 Exercises

1. positive; 1

3.

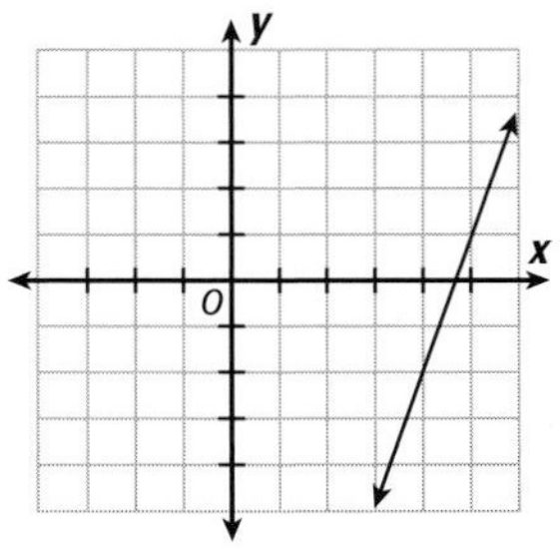

5.

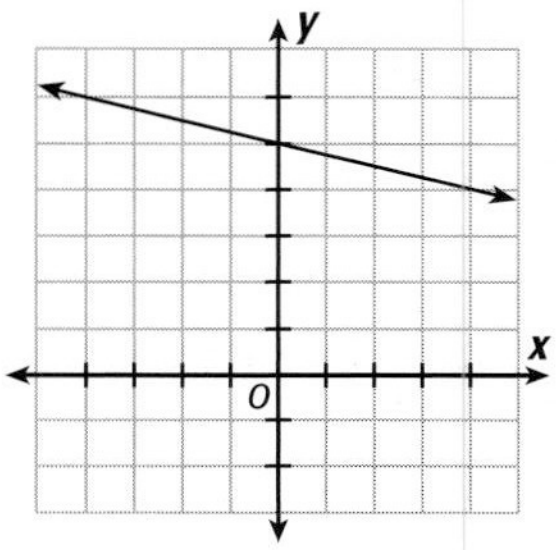

7. constant **9.** constant **11.** negative; −3

13.

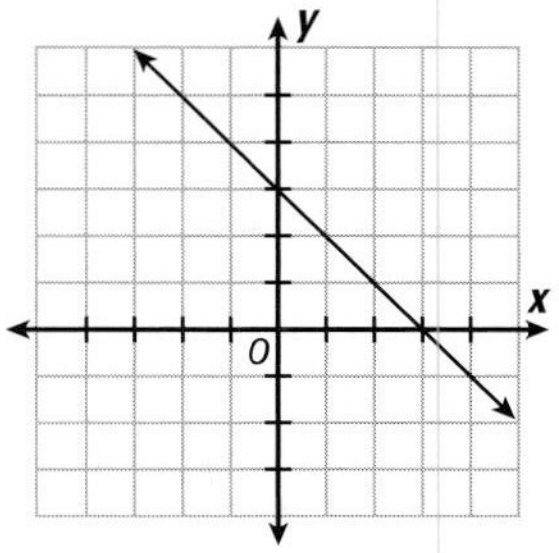

15.

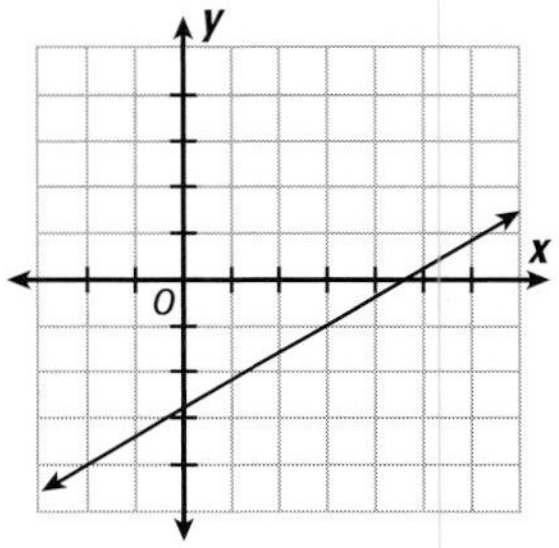

17. constant **19.** variable **21.** −7 **23.** −3 **25.** $\frac{3}{2}$ **29.** The y-value decreased. **33.** B **37.** 125 **39.** 100,000 **41.** add $\frac{3}{2}$ to n; $\frac{9}{2}$, 6, $\frac{15}{2}$

5-4 Exercises

1. yes **3.** yes **5.** yes **7.** no **13.** no **15.** no **17.** no **19.** no **29.** 3, 24, 15 **39a.** $\frac{1 \text{ can}}{4 \text{ hours}}$ **b.** No, $1{:}4 = x{:}2{,}080$; the class recycled 520 cans. **41.** 1:2 = 2:4, 2:1 = 4:2, 1:1 = 2:2, 1:1 = 4:4, 2:2 = 4:4 **43a.** 8:5 **b.** Mill Pond and Clear Pond **49.** H **51.** −3.75 **53.** −76.25

55.

Input	Rule	Output	Ordered Pair
x	$-x + 3$	y	(x, y)
−2	−(−2) + 3	5	(−2, 5)
−1	−(−1) + 3	4	(−1, 4)
0	−(0) + 3	3	(0, 3)
1	−(1) + 3	2	(1, 2)
2	−(2) + 3	1	(2, 1)

57.

Input	Rule	Output	Ordered Pair
x	$-3x + 4$	y	(x, y)
-2	$-3(-2) + 4$	10	$(-2, 10)$
-1	$-3(-1) + 4$	7	$(-1, 7)$
0	$-3(0) + 4$	4	$(0, 4)$
1	$-3(1) + 4$	1	$(1, 1)$
2	$-3(2) + 4$	-2	$(2, -2)$

5-5 Exercises

1. $x = 60$ **3.** $m = 16.4$ **5.** 3 lb **7.** $h = 144$ **9.** $v = 336$ **11.** $t = 36$ **13.** $n = 22\frac{2}{5}$ **15.** 227 grams **29.** 25 paper clips **31.** about 23 **33.** $\frac{4}{10} = \frac{6}{15}$ **35.** $\frac{3}{75} = \frac{4}{100}$ **37.** $\frac{5}{6} = \frac{90}{108}$ **39.** 105 oxygen atoms **45.** $\frac{4}{6}$ **47.** -20 **49.** 64 mi/h **51.** \$9.50/h

5-6 Exercises

1. Feet; the width of a sidewalk is similar to the length of several sheets of paper. **3.** Tons; the weight of a truck is similar to the weight of several buffalo. **5.** 48 qt **7.** 4.5 lb **9.** 27 fl oz **11.** Inches; the wingspan of a sparrow is similar to the length of several paper clips. **13.** Feet; the height of an office building is similar to the length of many sheets of paper. **15.** 3 mi **17.** 75 in. **19.** $>$ **21.** $<$ **23.** $>$ **25.** $<$ **27.** $<$ **29.** 2.4 mi **31.** 8 c, 5 qt, 12 pt, 2 gal **33.** 12,000 ft, 2.5 mi, 5,000 yd **35.** 9.5 yd, 380 in., 32.5 ft **37.** 46,145 yd **39.** The object that you are measuring will contain fewer of the larger units, so it makes sense to divide to get a smaller value for the measure. **43.** A **45.** \$139 **47.** no **49.** no

5-7 Exercises

1. similar **3.** similar **5.** not similar **7.** similar **9.** no **11.** similar **13.** yes **15.** yes **17.** no **19.** no **23.** C **25.** $-10\frac{1}{2}$ **27.** $\frac{3}{2}$

5-8 Exercises

1. $a = 22.5$ cm **3.** 28 ft **5.** $x = 13.5$ in. **7.** 3.9 ft **9.** 21 m **11.** 1.8; 1.5 **15.** B **17.** $18 \cdot y$ **19.** $12 \div z$ **21.** inches

5-9 Exercises

1. $\frac{1}{14}$ **3.** 67.2 cm tall, 40 cm wide **5.** $\frac{1}{15}$ **7.** 135 in. **9.** 16 in. **11.** 75 cm; 141 cm; 240 cm **13.** 2 in. **15.** about 25 mi **17.** 1 mi = 0.25 ft or 1 ft = 4 mi **19.** C **21.** 0.054, 0.41, $\frac{4}{7}$ **23.** $\frac{7}{11}$, 0.7, $\frac{7}{9}$ **25.** 0.06 **27.** 2.7

Extension

1. $\frac{1\text{ ft}}{12\text{ in.}}$ **3.** $\frac{1\text{ hr}}{60\text{ min}}$ **5.** $64\text{ oz} \cdot \frac{1\text{ lb}}{16\text{ oz}} = 4\text{ lb}$ **7.** $3.5\text{ qt} \cdot \frac{2\text{ pt}}{1\text{ qt}} = 7\text{ pt}$ **9.** $\frac{\$1.75}{1\text{ ft}} \cdot \frac{3\text{ ft}}{1\text{ yd}} = \frac{\$5.25}{1\text{ yd}}$ **11a.** 0.615 Earth years **b.** 4.9 Venus years **13.** \$225

Chapter 5 Study Guide: Review

1. similar **2.** ratio; unit rate **3.** scale factor **4.** $\frac{7}{15}$, 7 to 15, 7:15 **5.** red to blue **6.** 6 ft per s **7.** 109 min per h **8.** \$2.24, about \$2.14; $\frac{\$32.05}{15\text{ gal}}$ **9.** 32 dollars per g, 35 dollars per g; $\frac{\$160}{5\text{g}}$ **10.** variable **11.** constant; $\frac{1}{4}$ **12.** $\frac{9}{27} \neq \frac{6}{20}$ **13.** $\frac{15}{25} \neq \frac{20}{30}$ **14.** $\frac{21}{14} = \frac{18}{12}$ **15.** Possible answer: $\frac{10}{12} = \frac{30}{36}$ **16.** Possible answer: $\frac{45}{50} = \frac{90}{100}$ **17.** Possible answer: $\frac{9}{15} = \frac{27}{45}$ **18.** $n = 2$ **19.** $a = 6$ **20.** $b = 4$ **21.** $x = 66$ **22.** $y = 10$ **23.** $w = 20$ **24.** 2 pints **25.** 3,000 pounds **26.** 2.5 miles **27.** not similar **28.** similar **29.** $x = 100$ ft **30.** about 8 ft **31.** 12.1 in. **32.** 163.4 mi

Chapter 6

6-1 Exercises

1. 79% **3.** 50% **5.** $\frac{41}{50}$ **7.** $\frac{19}{50}$ **9.** 0.22 **11.** 0.0807 **13.** 0.11 **15.** 45% **17.** $\frac{11}{20}$ **19.** $\frac{83}{100}$ **21.** $\frac{81}{100}$ **23.** 0.098 **25.** 0.663 **27.** 0.027 **29.** 0.44 **31.** 0.105 **33.** $<$ **35.** $<$ **41.** Sean's team **43.** 12 **45.** $3\frac{1}{2}$

47–49.

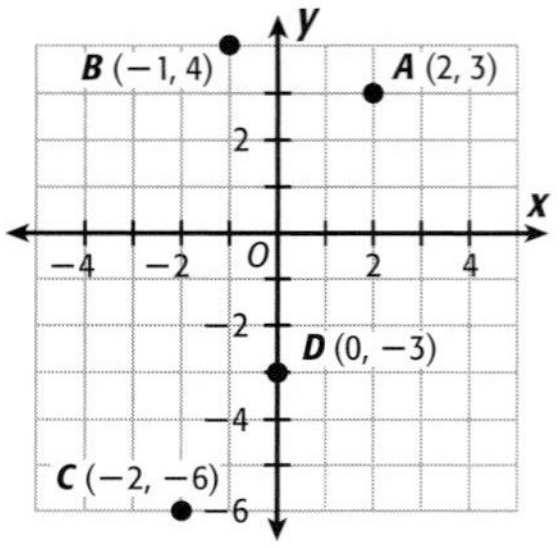

6-2 Exercises

1. 60% **3.** 54.4% **5.** 8.7% **7.** 12% **9.** 17.5% **11.** mental math; 40% **13.** 83% **15.** 8.1% **17.** 75% **19.** 37.5% **21.** 46.7% **23.** $>$ **25.** $<$ **27.** 10% **31.** D

33.

x	y
-2	-8
-1	-3
0	2
1	7
2	12

35.

x	y
-2	$-\frac{8}{3}$
-1	$-\frac{10}{3}$
0	-4
1	$-\frac{14}{3}$
2	$-\frac{16}{3}$

6-3 Exercises

5. Yes; 35% of \$43.99 is close to $\frac{1}{3}$ of \$45, which is \$15. Since \$45 − \$15 = \$30, Darden will have enough money. **19.** Fancy Feet **37.** about 26 oz **39.** about 2% more **49.** 1.2 **51.** 0.375

6-4 Exercises

1. 24 **3.** 20 **5.** 8 **7.** 423 **9.** 171 students **11.** 11.2 **13.** 3,540 **15.** 0.04 **17.** 18 **19.** 13 **21.** 1.74 **23.** 39.6 **25.** 12.4 **27.** 6 **29.** 4.5 **31.** 11.75 **33.** 5,125 **35.** 80 **37.** 120 **39.** 0.6% **41.** 4.2%

Selected Answers

43. $4.80 **45.** 2.25 g **47.** 0.98
53. C **55.** $1.75 per lb **57.** 1.25%
59. 38.9% **61.** 40.7%

6-5 Exercises

1. 25% **3.** 60 **5.** 18% **7.** 50 **9.** 8%
11. $33\frac{1}{3}$% **13.** 300% **15.** 225
17. 100% **19.** 30 **21.** 22 **23.** 55.6%
25. 68.8 **27.** 77.5 **29.** 158.3
31. 5% **33.** You use the number 100 in a proportion to solve a percent problem. *Percent* means "per hundred." **35.** 45 pieces
37. How many laps is the race?
39. She needs to make more than $275,000 per month in sales.
41. 75 **43.** 3.56 **45.** 3.2 **47.** 6.6
49. 66.64

6-6 Exercises

1. 28% **3.** 16.1% **5.** $8.60, $34.39
7. 37.5% **9.** 22.2% **11.** $9.75, $55.25 **13.** 100% **15.** 43.6%
17. 30 **19.** 56.25 gal **21.** $48.25
23a. $41,500 **b.** $17,845 **c.** 80.7%
25. about 8,506 trillion Btu **27.** A
29. $\frac{29}{9}$ **31.** $\frac{29}{4}$ **33.** $\frac{73}{3}$ **35.** 3.25 lb

6-7 Exercises

1. $I = \$24$ **3.** $P = \$400$ **5.** just over 4 yr **7.** $I = \$3,240$ **9.** $P = \$2,200$
11. $r = 11\%$ **13.** almost 9 yr
15. $5,200 **17.** $212.75 **19.** 20 yr
21. $4 **23.** high yield CD: gain $606; Dow Jones: loss $684; a difference of $1,290 **29.** just over $2\frac{1}{2}$ yr **31.** 29.9% **33.** 93.2%

Chapter 6 Study Guide: Review

1. interest; simple interest; principal **2.** percent of increase
3. percent of decrease **4.** percent
5. 0.78 **6.** 0.40 **7.** 0.05 **8.** 0.16
9. 0.65 **10.** 0.89 **11.** 60%
12. 16.7% **13.** 6% **14.** 80%
15. 66.7% **16.** 0.56% **17.** Possible answer: 8 **18.** Possible answer: 90
19. Possible answer: 24
20. Possible answer: 32
21. Possible answer: 40
22. Possible answer: 3
23. Possible answer: $3 **24.** 68
25. 24 **26.** 4.41 **27.** 120 **28.** 27.3
29. 54 **30.** about 474 **31.** 125
32. 8% **33.** 12 **34.** 37.5% **35.** 8
36. 27.8% **37.** 7.95% **38.** 50%
39. 14.3% **40.** 30% **41.** 83.1%
42. 23.1% **43.** 75% **44.** $36.75, $208.25 **45.** $7.80 **46.** $I = \$15$
47. $t = 3$ years **48.** $I = \$243$
49. $r = 3.9\%$ **50.** $P = \$2,300$
51. 7 years **52.** 9 years, 3 months

Chapter 7

7-1 Exercises

1. 6 **3.** 15 **5.** 3 **7.** 4; 31 **9.** B
11. Guyana and Suriname; Colombia **19.** $8.50 per hour
21. 16 points per game

7-2 Exercises

1. 20; 20; 5 and 20; 30 **3.** median
5. 83.3; 88; 88; 28 **7.** mean and median **9.** 151 **11.** 9; 8; 12 **17.** B
19. almost 4.5 years

7-3 Exercises

1. grapes **3.** about 15 pounds
5.

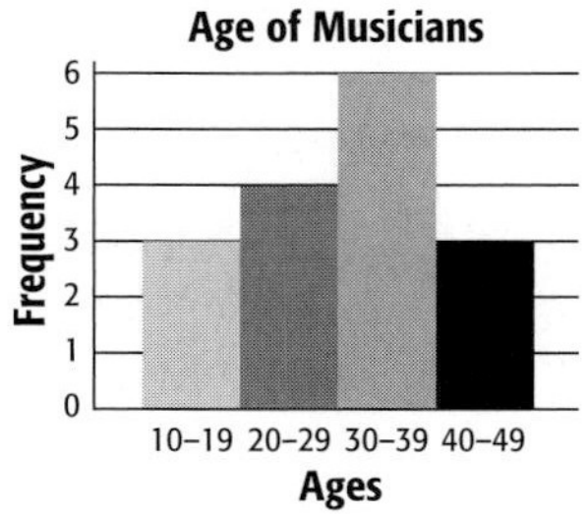

7. about 27 inches
9.

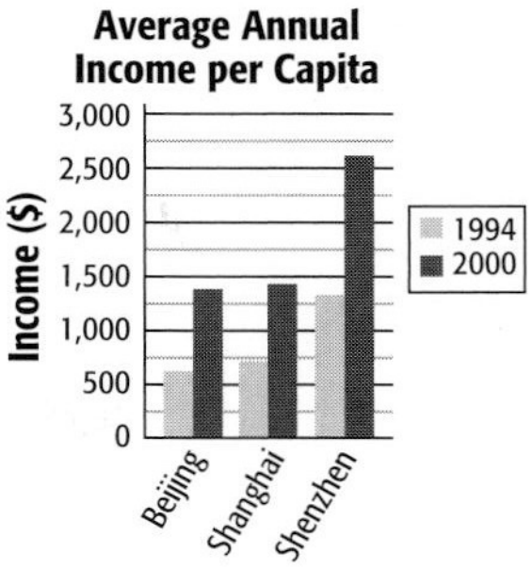

11.

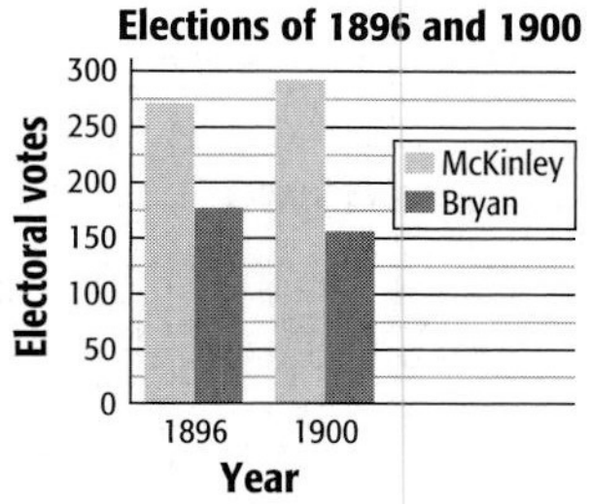

13. 29 **17.** H **19.** no **21.** yes
23. 23.5; 23.5; 15; 19

7-4 Exercises

1. outdoor **3.** $50,000 **5.** circle graph **7.** 30% **9.** circle graph
11. Asia, Africa, North America, South America, Antarctica, Europe, Australia **13.** about 25%
19. about 150 **21.** > **23.** =

7-5 Exercises

1. The range is 16, the interquartile range is 11, the lower quartile is 35 and the upper quartile is 36.
3. airplane B **5.** The range is 16, the interquartile is 12, the lower quartile is 73, and the upper quartile is 85. **7.** city A **11.** the range **19.** 15 **21.** $3.75

7-6 Exercises

1. 1990–1995
3.

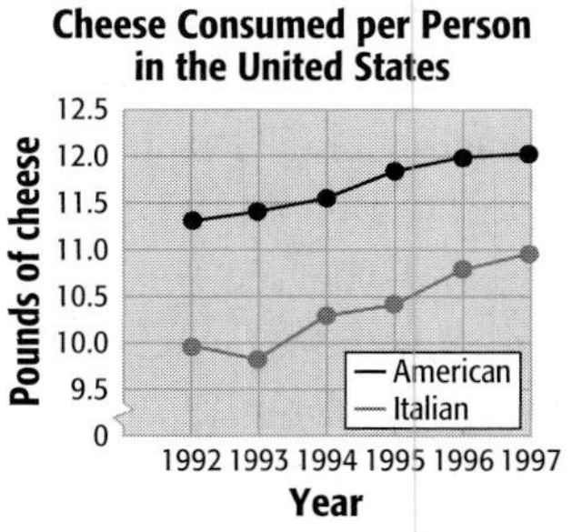

5. 1990–1995
7.

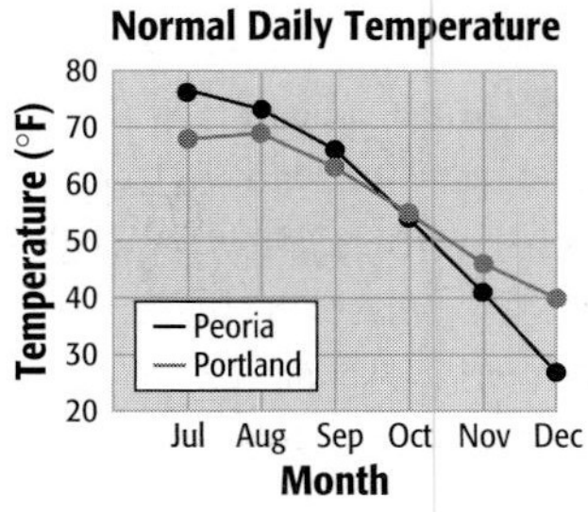

9b. about 3,400 **17.** 136%
19. 55%

7-7 Exercises

1. bar graph **3.** line graph
5. line plot or stem-and-leaf plot
15. circle graph **19.** 90%
21. 40.6%

7-8 Exercises

1. Daria's method **3.** biased
5. Vonneta's method **7.** not biased
9. entire population **11.** entire population **17.** B **19.** 0.52 **21.** 1.1
23. 5.5 **25.** 0.41

7-9 Exercises

1. The heart rate decreases as the weight increases. **3.** positive correlation **5.** The capacity increases with time. **7.** negative correlation **9.** no correlation
11. no correlation **17.** 75.6 **19.** 3.5

7-10 Exercises

1. graph A **3.** The vertical axis does not begin with zero, so differences in scales appear greater. **5.** The scale of the graph is not divided into equal intervals, so differences in sales appear less than they actually are. **7.** The graphs do not use the same scale, so it looks as though September had fewer sales than October, which is not true; redraw the graphs using the same scale.
15. $x = \frac{1}{6}$ **17.** $x = -\frac{11}{24}$
19. negative correlation

Chapter 7 Study Guide: Review

1. population; sample **2.** mean
3. histogram; bar graph
4. negative correlation

5.

	Frequency	Cumulative Frequency
0–9	1	1
10–19	3	4
20–29	3	7
30–39	2	9

6.

Stems	Leaves
0	8
1	4 6 9
2	5 7 9
3	2 5

Key: 1|4 means 14

7.

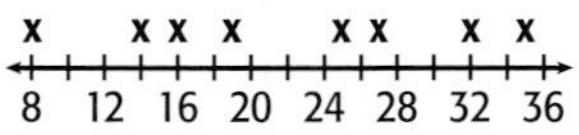

8. The stem-and-leaf plot is the best display of the data, because it is easy to see the distribution of all of the data values. **9.** 4; 4; 2 and 5; 8 **10.** 302; 311.5; 233 and 324; 166 **11.** 43; 46; none; 166

12.

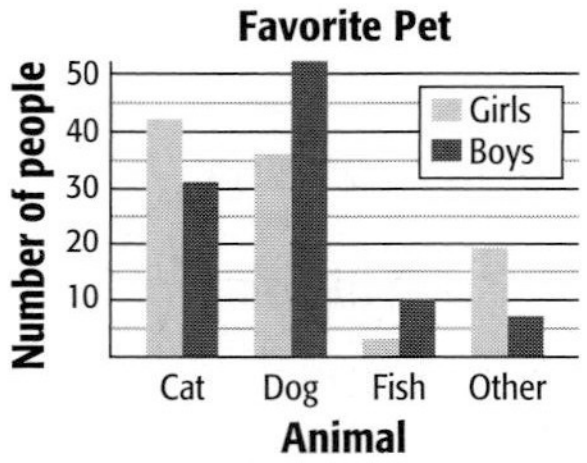

13. yellow **14.** 35 people

15.

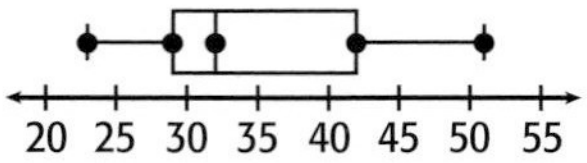

16. 11.5

17.

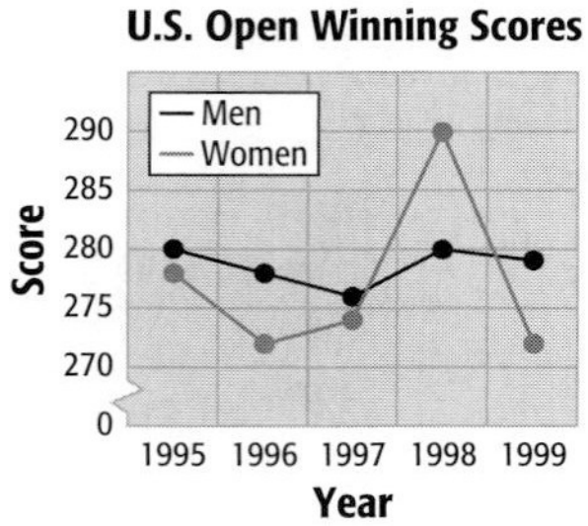

18. line graph **19.** bar graph
20. 2,500 is a reasonable estimate based on the data. **21.** positive correlation **22.** yes

Chapter 8

8-1 Exercises

1. *Q, R, S* **3.** plane *QRS* **5.** $\overline{QU}$, $\overline{RU}$, $\overline{SU}$ **7.** *D, E, F* **9.** plane *DEF*
11. *DE, ED, DF* **21.** C **23.** 16
25. −7 **27.** 29.4% **29.** 83.3%

8-2 Exercises

1. right angle **3.** straight angle
5. complementary
7. complementary **9.** 61° **11.** right angle **13.** complementary
15. supplementary **17.** 95°
19. supplementary; 152°
21. supplementary; 46° **23a.** right angles **b.** about 39°N, 77°W **27.** C
29. 5.6; 6; 6; 5 **31.** 38; 38; 41; 34

8-3 Exercises

1. parallel **3.** perpendicular
5. 115° **7.** skew **9.** parallel
11. 150° **13.** parallel
15. supplementary; adjacent
17. 45° **19.** sometimes **21.** always
23a. They are perpendicular.
b. transversal **c.** They are corresponding angles. **29.** F
31. −1.75 **33.** complementary; 31° **35.** complementary; 65°

8-4 Exercises

1. $\overline{OQ}$, $\overline{OR}$, $\overline{OS}$, $\overline{OT}$ **3.** $\overline{RT}$, $\overline{RS}$, $\overline{ST}$, $\overline{TQ}$ **5.** $\overline{CA}$, $\overline{CB}$, $\overline{CD}$, $\overline{CE}$, $\overline{CF}$ **7.** $\overline{GB}$, $\overline{BF}$, $\overline{DE}$, $\overline{FE}$, $\overline{AE}$ **9.** 10 cm **11.** 133.2°
13. 60° **17.** C **19.** 45 **21.** 1
23. E, F, H, M, N, Z

8-5 Exercises

1. no **3.** no **5.** quadrilateral
7. square **9.** triangle **11.** no
13. pentagon **15.** heptagon
17. pentagon **21.** 16-gon **23.** A
25. $y = 3n + 1$ **27.** $y = n + 1.3$
29. 20.3 **31.** 25.9%

8-6 Exercises

1. isosceles right **3.** isosceles acute **5.** scalene right **7.** equilateral acute **9.** scalene **11.** isosceles **13.** right **15.** 8 in., isosceles **17.** isosceles acute **19.** scalene right **21.** isosceles triangle **23.** isosceles acute **27.** B **29.** $-0.4, \frac{3}{7}, 1\frac{3}{10}, 2.3$ **31.** quadrilateral

8-7 Exercises

1. parallelogram **3.** parallelogram, rhombus; rhombus **5.** not possible **7.** parallelogram **9.** parallelogram; rhombus; rhombus **11.** parallelogram, rectangle; rectangle

13.

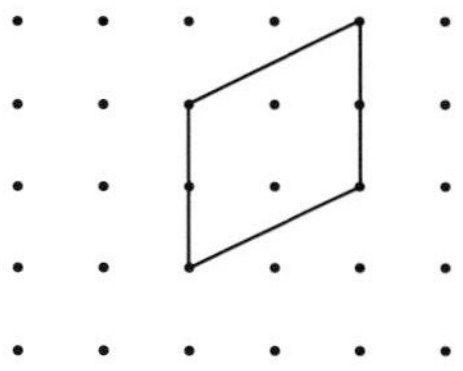

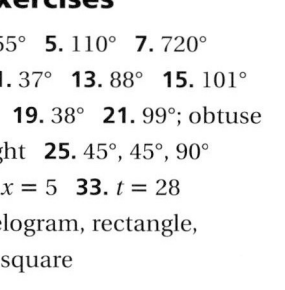

15. parallelogram, rectangle, rhombus, square **17.** parallelogram, rhombus, rectangle, square **19.** true **21.** true **23.** false **25.** 1 triangle, 1 pentagon, and 2 trapezoids **31.** C

33.

Stems	Leaves
1	8
2	8
3	3, 4
4	0, 3, 4, 9
5	7, 7

35. acute **37.** obtuse

8-8 Exercises

1. 77° **3.** 55° **5.** 110° **7.** 720° **9.** 360° **11.** 37° **13.** 88° **15.** 101° **17.** 1,080° **19.** 38° **21.** 99°; obtuse **23.** 90°; right **25.** 45°, 45°, 90° **29.** B **31.** $x = 5$ **33.** $t = 28$ **35.** parallelogram, rectangle, rhombus, square

8-9 Exercises

1. the triangles on the game board and the holes on the game board **3.** the bowling pins **5.** no **7.** 2.5 **9.** the triangles in the kite's design **11.** no **13.** 80°; 8 cm **15.** the lengths of all the sides **17.** the lengths of adjacent sides in each rectangle **19.** 40 m **25.** G

27–29.

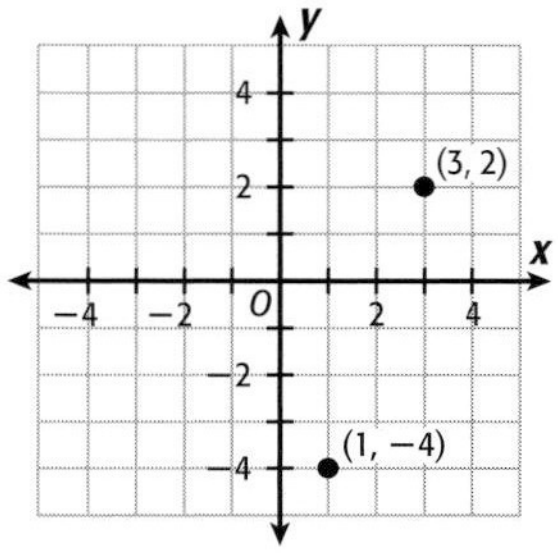

31. 25°; obtuse **33.** 90°; right

8-10 Exercises

1. rotation

3.

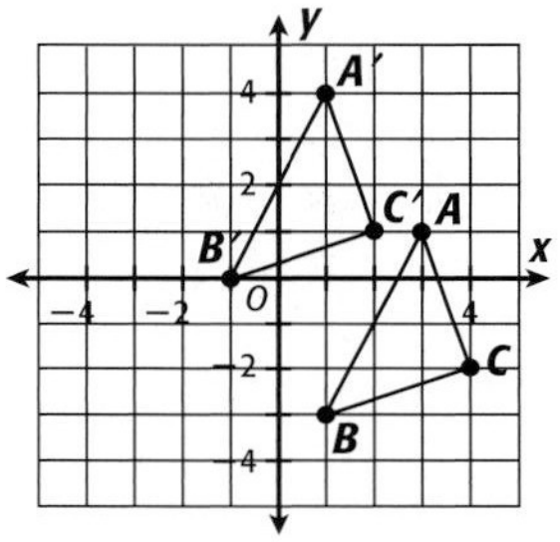

5.

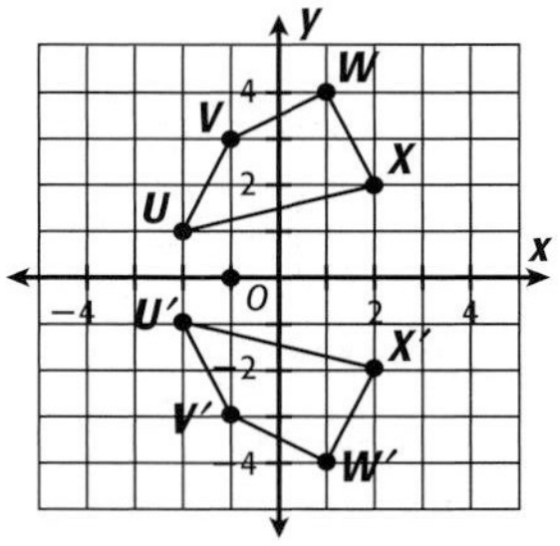

7.

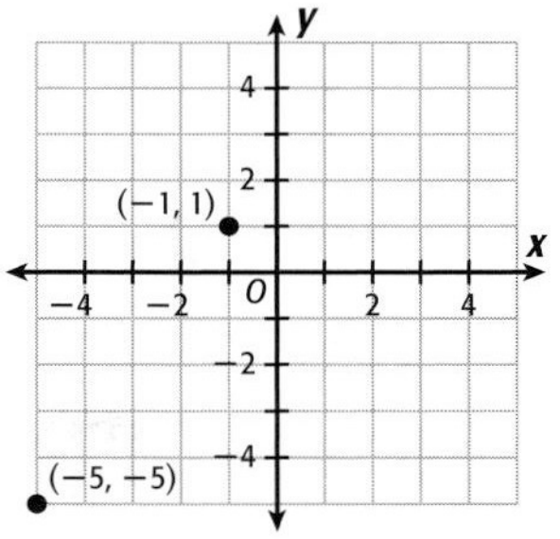

9. translation

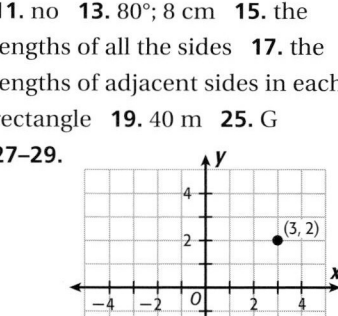

11.

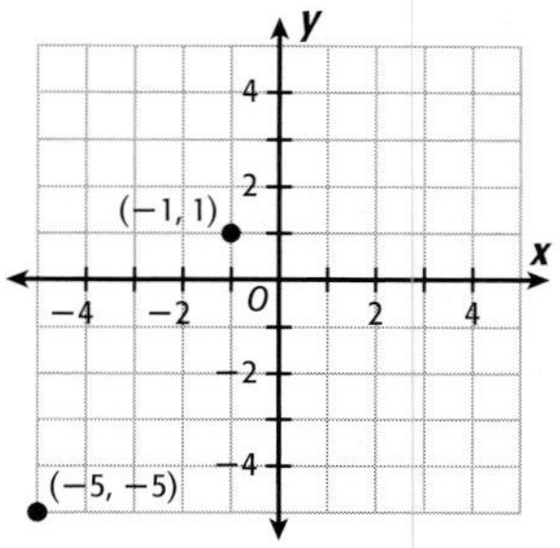

13.

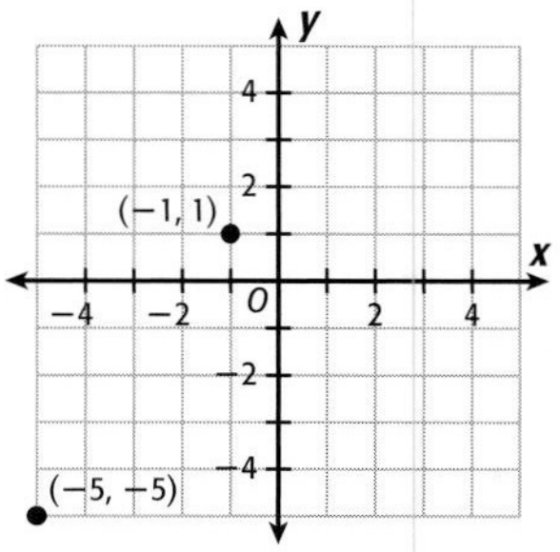

17. A **19.** 38 **21.** 3 m

8-11 Exercises

1. The figure has 5 lines of symmetry. **3.** The figure has 4 lines of symmetry. **5.** none **7.** 6 times **9.** 3 times **11.** The figure has 6 lines of symmetry. **13.** none **15.** The flag has 2 lines of symmetry. **17.** 8 times **19.** regular nonagon **21.** yes; yes **27.** 8 **29.** $J'(3, -1)$, $K'(3, 3)$, $L'(3, -6)$

Extension

1. no

3.

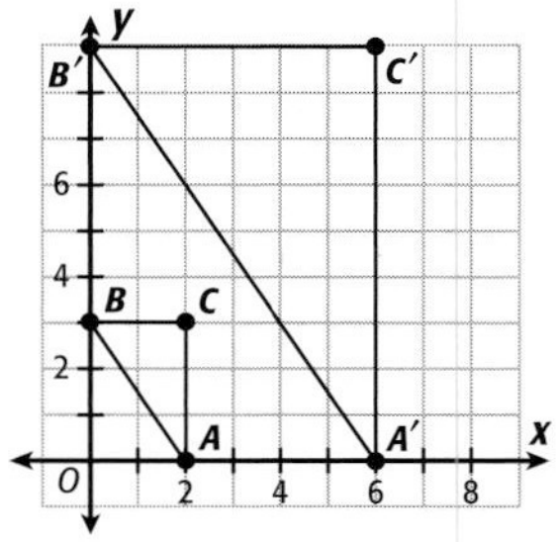

5.

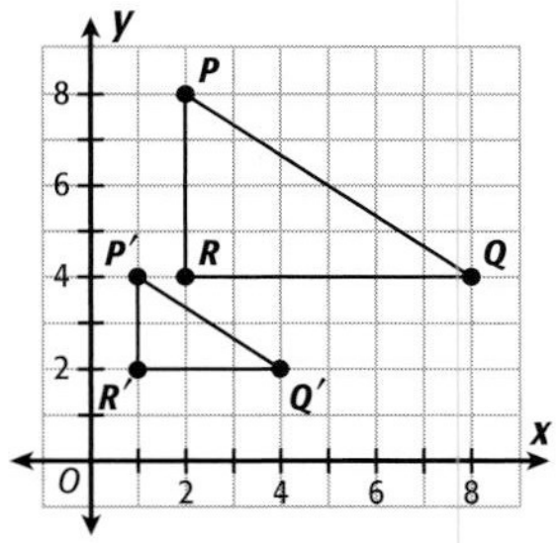

Chapter 8 Study Guide: Review

1. acute or isosceles **2.** parallel lines **3.** chord **4.** *D, E, F* **5.** $\overleftrightarrow{DF}$ **6.** plane *DEF* **7.** $\overrightarrow{ED}, \overrightarrow{FD}, \overrightarrow{DF}$ **8.** $\overline{DE}, \overline{DF}, \overline{EF}$ **9.** acute **10.** straight **11.** skew **12.** parallel **13.** $\overline{HF}, \overline{FI}, \overline{FG}$ **14.** $\overline{GI}$ **15.** $\overline{HI}, \overline{GI}, \overline{GJ}, \overline{JI}$ **16.** Yes; it is a square since all sides are congruent and all angles are congruent. **17.** No; all sides are not congruent. **18.** equilateral acute **19.** scalene right **20.** parallelogram, rhombus **21.** parallelogram, rectangle **22.** 53° **23.** 101° **24.** 133°

25.

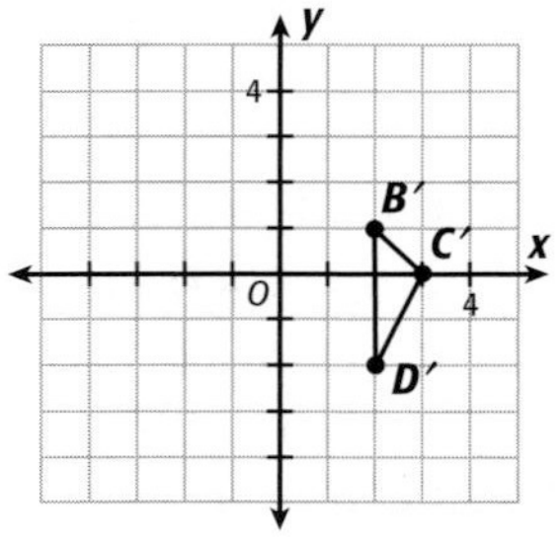

26. 1 vertical line through the center of the flag

Chapter 9

9-1 Exercises

1. 4 ft **3.** $5\frac{1}{4}$ in. **5.** 1 **7.** 12 **9.** 7 **11.** 25 **13.** 11 in. **15.** 14.2 km **17.** 2.8 m **19.** 1 **21.** 6 **23.** 3 **25.** 15.1 **27.** 1 **29.** 18.0 **31.** 1,800 **33.** 2.3 **35.** 300 **37.** foot **39.** milliliter **41.** 180,000 **43.** 280 **45.** 21.8 **49.** 6 servings of fruit **51.** D **53.** no correlation **55.** positive correlation **57.** No

9-2 Exercises

1. 18 m **3.** 32 ft **5.** 20 m **7.** 37.7 m **9.** 132 in. **11.** 48 cm **13.** 44 m **15.** 8 ft **17.** 110 cm **19.** 32.0 in. **21.** 2.8 m; 5.7 m **23.** 5.3 in.; 33.3 in. **25.** 1.98 m **27.** 141 mi **29.** 96 ft **33.** D **35.** 90 **37.** 16.2 **39.** 9.1 **41.** 140

9-3 Exercises

1. 33.6 ft^2 **3.** 147.6 cm^2 **5.** 48 in^2 **7.** 28.6 m^2 **9.** 84 ft^2 **11.** 107.52 in^2 **13.** 6 m^2 **15.** 31.98 cm^2 **17.** 72 yd^2 **19.** 192 cm^2 **21.** 14 $units^2$ **23.** 18 $units^2$ **25a.** 713 in^2 **b.** 108 in. **c.** 1,073 in^2 **27.** $w = 14$ cm **31.** C **33.** acute **35.** straight **37.** 36 in. **39.** 38 cm

9-4 Exercises

1. 28 $units^2$ **3.** 39.2 $units^2$ **5.** 64 m^2 **7.** 50,830 mi^2 **9.** 7.5 $units^2$ **11.** 330 yd^2 **13.** 22.5 cm^2 **15.** 4.5 cm **17.** 22 in. **19.** 15 $units^2$ **21.** 12 $units^2$ **23.** 5,830 mi^2 **25a.** 6,800 mi^2 **b.** 181.7 **29.** 9 $units^2$ **31.** 52° **33.** 99°

9-5 Exercises

1. 78.5 in^2 **3.** 314 yd^2 **5.** 154 in^2 **7.** 28.3 in^2 **9.** 32.2 yd^2 **11.** 616 cm^2 **13.** 17,662.5 mi^2 **15.** 28.3 cm^2 **17.** 56.5 in.; 254.3 in^2 **19.** 40.2 cm; 128.6 cm^2 **21.** $r = 1$ ft **23.** 27,450.7 ft^2 **29.** A **31.** 135° **33.** 45° **35.** 14

9-6 Exercises

1. 28 ft^2 **3.** 224 ft^2 **5.** 38 ft^2 **7.** 25 ft^2 **9.** 84.56 m^2 **11.** 46 cm^2 **13.** 24 ft^2; 30 ft **15.** 255.25 m^2; 65.7 m **17.** 10 **21.** B **23.** 57° **25.** 30° **27.** 706.5 m^2 **29.** 254.3 in^2

9-7 Exercises

1. 16 **3.** 81 **5.** 20 **7.** 12 **9.** 4 **11.** 9 **13.** 11 mi **15.** 256 **17.** 121 **19.** 4 **21.** 21 **23.** 6 **25.** 10 **27.** 13 **29.** 15 **31.** 32 cm **33.** 20 **35.** 39 **37.** 12 **39.** 1 **41.** 192 **43.** 15 m **45.** 6 ft **47.** 28 in. **49.** 36 ft **55.** F **57.** scalene **59.** isosceles **61.** 78.5 cm; 490.6 cm^2

9-8 Exercises

1. 20 m **3.** 24 cm **5.** 30 yd **7.** 16 in. **9.** 9.4 ft **11.** 24.5 m **13.** 22.5 in. **15.** yes **17.** 19,153 m^2 **19.** 269.1 cubits **21.** 68.8 m **23.** 9.8 **25.** 90° **27.** 30° **29.** 8 **31.** 5

Extension

1. irrational **3.** rational **5.** irrational **7.** rational **9.** irrational **11.** rational

13.

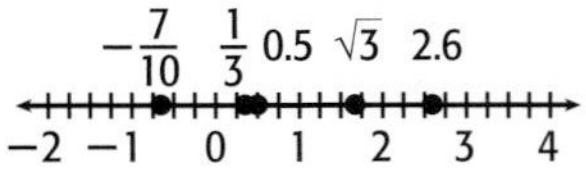

15.

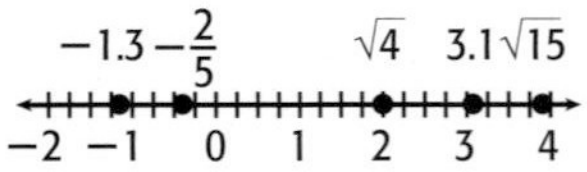

17. 5 and 6 **19.** 3 and 4 **21.** 9 and 10 **23.** 8 and 9

Chapter 9 Study Guide: Review

1. hypotenuse **2.** circumference **3.** precision **4.** square root **5.** 3 significant digits **6.** 5 significant digits **7.** 1 significant digit **8.** 2 significant digits **9.** 4 significant digits **10.** 4 significant digits **11.** 83 m **12.** 81.4 cm **13.** 40.8 ft **14.** 49.0 in. **15.** 50.74 cm^2 **16.** 826.2 yd^2 **17.** 72 in^2 **18.** 266 in^2 **19.** 108.75 cm^2 **20.** 50 yd^2 **21.** 2,163 in^2 **22.** 36.3 m^2 **23.** 226.9 ft^2 **24.** 254.64 in^2 **25.** 34.31 ft^2 **26.** 21 m^2 **27.** 5 **28.** 10 **29.** 10 **30.** 12 **31.** 16 ft **32.** 34 cm **33.** 60 ft **34.** 2 m **35.** 60 mm

Chapter 10

10-1 Exercises

1. pentagon; pentagonal pyramid **3.** triangle; triangular prism **5.** polyhedron; hexagonal pyramid **7.** triangle; triangular pyramid **9.** hexagon; hexagonal pyramid **11.** not polyhedron; cylinder **13.** square prism **15.** triangular pyramid **19.** rectangular pyramid **21.** cylinder **23.** A **25.** 1 **27.** 2 **29.** 100 oz for $6.99 is better

10-2 Exercises

1. 24 cubes; 24 cubic units **3.** 36 cubes; 36 cubic units **5.** 1,000 mm^3 **7.** 75.4 cm^3 **9.** 60 cubes; 60 cubic units **11.** 192 ft^3 **13.** 13.44 in^3 **15.** 288 m^3 **17.** 47.25 ft^3 **21.** B **23.** $40.25 **25.** line graph

10-3 Exercises

1. 10 ft^3 **3.** 32 m^3 **5.** 16.7 in^3 **7.** 176 in^3 **9.** 1,350 mm^3 **11.** 2,375.3 cm^3 **13.** 93.3 ft^3 **15.** 32 in^3 **17a.** 3 **b.** 167.5 in^3 **c.** 502.4 in^3 **d.** yes **25.** parallelogram **27.** 110 ft^3

10-4 Exercises

1. 286 ft^2 **3.** 244.9 cm^2 **5.** about 24.2% **7.** 1,160 ft^2 **9.** 188.4 cm^2 **11b.** 158.0 cm^2 **c.** 85.4 cm^2 **17.** 628 **19.** 79° **21.** 224 in^3

10-5 Exercises

1. 93.6 cm^2 **3.** 33,750 in^3 **5.** 223.84 in^2 **7.** 8.2 cm^3 **9.** 58,750 ft^2; 937,500 ft^3 **11.** 1,460,125 cm^2; 56,250,000 cm^3 **13.** 5,112 in^2; 22,680 in^3 **15.** 716 cm; 7.16 m **17.** 127,426,000,000 cm^3; 127,426 m^3 **19.** 2 **21.** no **23.** no

Extension

1. D **5.** cylinder

Chapter 10 Study Guide: Review

1. cylinder **2.** surface area **3.** polyhedron **4.** cone **5.** cylinder **6.** rectangular pyramid **7.** triangular prism **8.** cone **9.** 364 cm^3 **10.** 24 mm^3 **11.** 415.4 mm^3 **12.** 111.9 ft^3 **13.** 60 in^3 **14.** 471 cm^3 **15.** 250m^2 **16.** 34 cm^2 **17.** 262.3 cm^2 **18.** 2,970 in^2 **19.** 4.1 ft^3

Chapter 11

11-1 Exercises

1. unlikely **3.** $\frac{5}{6}$ **5.** certain **7.** unlikely **9.** $\frac{2}{5}$ **11.** as likely as not **13.** certain **15.** not likely **17a.** It is very likely. **b.** It is impossible. **23.** It is likely that a test will be given over this chapter. **25.** 11.4 **27.** 3 **29.** 152

11-2 Exercises

1. 70% **3.** 43% **5a.** $\frac{9}{14}$ **5b.** $\frac{5}{14}$ **7.** $\frac{2}{5}$ **9.** $\frac{2}{5}$ **11a.** 9.1 in. **b.** 0 **c.** $\frac{1}{5}$ **15.** F **17.** $<$ **19.** $<$

11-3 Exercises

1. H1, H2, T1, T2; 4 **3.** 24 **5.** 1H, 1T, 2H, 2T, 3H, 3T, 4H, 4T; 8 **7.** 12 **9.** 6 **11a.** 9 outcomes **b.** 6 outcomes **c.** 12 outcomes **13.** 12 **17.** D **19.** 12.5% **21.** 40% **23.** 704 in^3

11-4 Exercises

1. 17% **3.** $\frac{3}{7}$ **5.** $\frac{2}{7}$ **7.** 25% **9.** $\frac{3}{7}$ **11.** $\frac{1}{18}$ **13.** $\frac{1}{12}$ **15.** $\frac{1}{9}$ **17.** $\frac{5}{18}$ **19.** $\frac{1}{5}$ **21.** $\frac{2}{5}$ **23.** 0 **25.** $\frac{4}{5}$ **27.** 37% **29.** 25% **33.** D **35.** 57.5 in^2

11-5 Exercises

1. independent **3.** $\frac{1}{6}$ **5.** $\frac{3}{20}$ **7.** independent **9.** $\frac{1}{4}$ **11.** dependent **13.** $\frac{12}{145}$ **17.** B **19.** $6\frac{3}{4}$ **21.** 49.3 ft; 193.5 ft^2 **22.** 44 cm; 153.9 cm^2

11-6 Exercises

1. 6 **3.** 10 **5.** 10 **7.** 20 **9.** 28 **11.** 3 **13.** 15 **17.** 15 **19.** 6 **21.** 7 **23.** independent

11-7 Exercises

1. 24 **3.** 720 **5.** 6 **7.** 3,628,000 **9.** combinations **11.** permutations **13.** $\frac{1}{4}$ **15.** 120 **17.** $5 \times 4 \times 3 = 60$ **19.** 13! **21.** $\frac{2}{7}$ **25.** D **27.** 18.4 in.

Chapter 11 Study Guide: Review

1. independent events **2.** combination **3.** sample space **4.** outcome **5.** unlikely **6.** impossible **7.** 80% **8.** $\frac{4}{5}$ **9.** $\frac{2}{3}$ **10.** $\frac{1}{3}$ **11.** R1, R2, R3, R4, W1, W2, W3, W4, B1, B2, B3, B4 **12.** 12 possible outcomes **13.** 43% **14.** 12.5% **15.** 38% **16.** $\frac{4}{195}$ **17.** $\frac{16}{121}$ **18.** 10 ways **19.** 21 committees **20.** 36 combinations **21.** 3,628,800 ways **23.** 720 ways **23.** 120 ways

Chapter 12

12-1 Exercises

1. $n = 7$ **3.** $x = \frac{1}{3}$ **5.** $y = 136$ **7.** 12 refills **9.** $p = -12$ **11.** $d = \frac{1}{7}$ **13.** $y = 5$ **15.** $k = 85$ **17.** $m = -80$ **19.** $m = -112$ **21.** 6 more than a number divided by 3 equals 18; $m = 36$. **23.** 2 equals 4 less than a number divided by 5; $n = 30$. **25.** $x = 2$ **27.** $g = 20$ **29.** $w = -9$ **31.** $p = 2$ **33.** 120 min **35.** 1,300 calories **37.** 2 slices of pizza for lunch and again for dinner **39.** C **41.** rectangular prism **43.** 549.5 cm^3

12-2 Exercises

1. $n = 5$ **3.** $p = 2$ **5.** $q = 2$ **7.** 12 books **9.** $x = \frac{7}{8}$ **11.** $n = 6$ **13.** $x = -2$ **15.** $n = -2$ **17.** $n = 1.5$ **19.** $t = -9$ **21.** $x = 66$ **23.** $w = 8$ **25.** $a = 176$ **27.** $b = -7$ **29.** $x = 3$ **31.** $6.70 **33.** $25 **35.** 91 **39.** A **41.** 37.7 cm^3 **43.** $x = 1$ **45.** $z = -28$

12-3 Exercises

1. $n = 32$ **3.** $12w = 32$ **5.** $a = 2$ **7.** 5 movies **9.** $-8 = 12p$ **11.** $-6 = 2c$ **13.** $6 = \frac{1}{10}a$ **15.** $b = -8$ **17.** $a = -0.8$ **19.** $c = -2$ **21.** $y = -7$ **23.** $r = 4$

Selected Answers

25. $r = -2$ **27.** 67 members **29.** $x = 6$ **31.** 3 days **37.** $0.03m = 2 + 0.01m$; $m = 100$; 100 minutes makes the cost for long distance from both plans equal. **39.** 28.4 ft **41.** $y = 2$

12-4 Exercises

1. number of people ≤ 18
3. water level > 45
5. 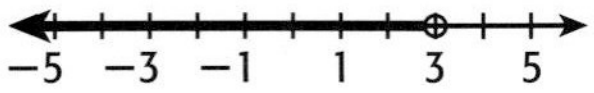

7. 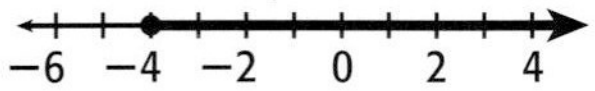

9. 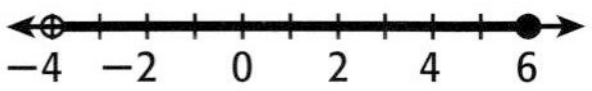

11. temperature < 40
13. number of tables ≤ 35
15. 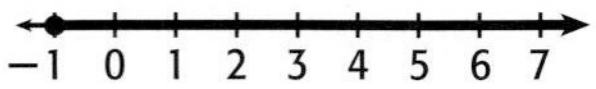

17. 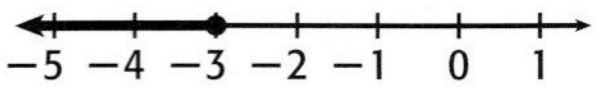

19. 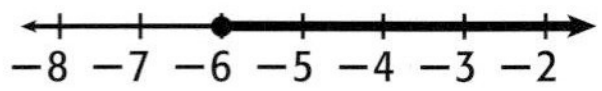

21. 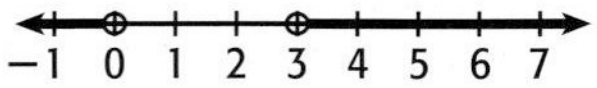

23. 

25. 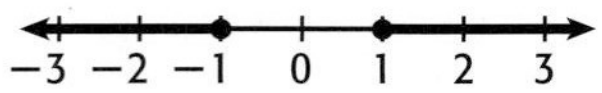

27. 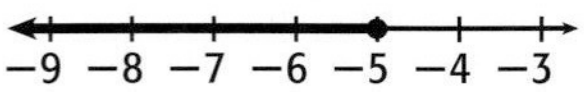

29. 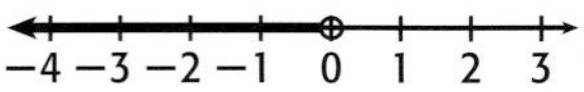

31. 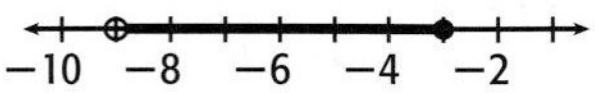

33. $-2 < c < 3$ **35.** $-3 < x < 1$ **37.** $-200 \leq$ depth ≤ 0 **39.** $0 \geq$ *Manshu* depth measurement $\geq -32{,}190$ ft; $0 \geq$ *Challenger* depth measurement $\geq -35{,}640$ ft; $0 \geq$ *Horizon* depth measurement $\geq -34{,}884$ ft; $0 \geq$ *Vityaz* depth measurement $\geq -36{,}200$ ft **41.** B **43.** 59 m/h **45.** $y = 5$

12-5 Exercises

1. $x < 27$ **3.** $p \leq 7$ **5.** $b \leq -24$ **7.** no more than 42°F **9.** $m < 11$ **11.** $c \leq 11$ **13.** $x \geq 80$ **15.** $z > -12$ **17.** $f > -6$ **19.** $n \geq -4$ **21.** at most 24 birds **23.** $a > 0.3$ **25.** $m \leq -38$ **27.** $g < 6\frac{1}{3}$ **29.** $w \leq 15.7$ **31.** $t \geq -242$ **33.** $v \leq -0.6$ **35.** no more than 80 **37.** at most 23.7 mi/h **39.** up to 50,000 hertz **43.** B **45.** 144 in^2 **47.** 1,600 in^2

12-6 Exercises

1. $w < -32$ **3.** $p < 48$ **5.** $y > -\frac{11}{8}$ or $-1\frac{3}{8}$ **7.** at least 27 candles **9.** $m > 52$ **11.** $c \geq -120$ **13.** $x \geq -1.1$ **15.** $z < \frac{3}{5}$ **17.** $f < -3$ **19.** $n \leq -10$ **21.** at least 46 wreaths **23.** $p > 4$ **25.** $y \geq 18$ **27.** $g > 0.63$ **29.** $w \leq \frac{3}{8}$ **31.** $t < \frac{5}{2}$ **33.** $v \geq -2.5$ **35.** 5 hours **37.** at least 480 subscriptions **43.** 301 **45.** $x < 1$ **47.** $z \geq 5$

12-7 Exercises

1. $x < 3$ **3.** $y \geq 6$ **5.** $p \leq -5$ **7.** more than \$26 each **9.** $b < 12$ **11.** $c \geq -3$ **13.** $x \leq -27$ **15.** $j \leq 2$ **17.** at most 6 bagels **19.** $x \geq -6$ **21.** $c < 1.8$ **23.** $w \leq 8$ **25.** $s > -24$ **27.** $d \leq 4$ **29.** \$14 **31.** at least 225 students **33.** at most 60% **37.** B **39.** 12 **41.** $x > 5$ **43.** $x \leq 15$

Extension

1. $h = \frac{A}{b}$ **3.** $d = \frac{C}{\pi}$ **5.** $B = \frac{V}{h}$ **7.** $y = \frac{k}{x}$ **9.** $F = \frac{W}{d}$ **11.** $r = \frac{C}{2\pi}$ **13.** $h = \frac{3V}{B}$ **15.** $t = \frac{E}{P}$ **17.** $a = \frac{F}{m}$ **19.** $V = r\ell$ **21.** $\ell = \frac{(P - 2w)}{2}$ **23.** 0.001 kg **25.** 75 g

Chapter 12 Study Guide: Review

1. inequality **2.** compound inequality **3.** solution set **4.** $y = 8$ **5.** $z = 30$ **6.** $w = 147$ **7.** $a = -7$ **8.** $j = 9$ **9.** $b = 4$ **10.** $y = 5$ **11.** 26 mi **12.** $b = \frac{1}{2}$ **13.** $c = 6$ **14.** $m = \frac{8}{3}$ or $2\frac{2}{3}$ **15.** $x = 20$ **16.** weight limit ≤ 9 tons **17.** age > 20
18. 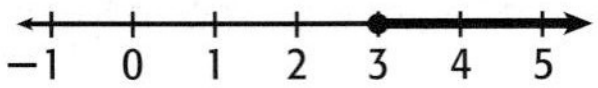

19. 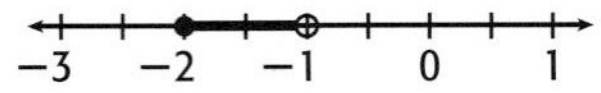

20. $r > 25$ **21.** $x \leq -26$ **22.** $g < 8$ **23.** $t \leq \frac{1}{6}$ **24.** $9 > r$ **25.** $u \geq -66$ **26.** at least 38 points **27.** at most \$94 **28.** $n < -55.2$ **29.** $p \leq 6$ **30.** $k < -130$ **31.** $p < 5$ **32.** $v \geq 2.76$ **33.** $c > 33$ **34.** at least 16 purses **35.** $b < -2$ **36.** $d < -6$ **37.** $n \geq -4$ **38.** $y \leq 18$ **39.** $c > -54$ **40.** $x \leq 10$ **41.** $h \geq -156$ **42.** $-10 < t$ **43.** $52 > w$ **44.** $y \leq 35$ **45.** at most 4 T-shirts **46.** at least \$147

Glossary/Glosario

go.hrw.com
Multilingual Glossary Online
KEYWORD: MS7 Glossary

A

ENGLISH	SPANISH	EXAMPLES
absolute value The distance of a number from zero on a number line; shown by | |. (p. 77)	**valor absoluto** Distancia a la que está un número de 0 en una recta numérica. El símbolo del valor absoluto es | |.	$\|5\| = 5$ $\|-5\| = 5$
accuracy The closeness of a given measurement or value to the actual measurement or value. (p. 518)	**exactitud** Cercanía de una medida o valor a la medida o valor real.	
acute angle An angle that measures less than 90°. (p. 448)	**ángulo agudo** Ángulo que mide menos de 90°.	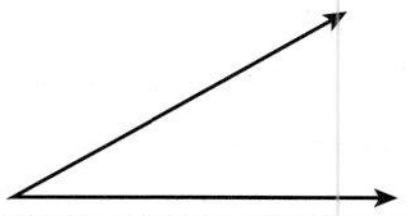
acute triangle A triangle with all angles measuring less than 90°. (p. 470)	**triángulo acutángulo** Triángulo en el que todos los ángulos miden menos de 90°.	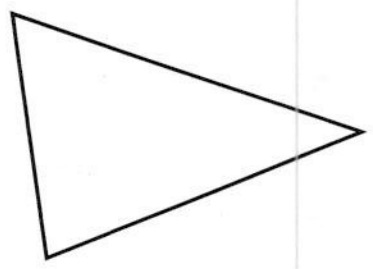
addend A number added to one or more other numbers to form a sum.	**sumando** Número que se suma a uno o más números para formar una suma.	In the expression $4 + 6 + 7$, the numbers 4, 6, and 7 are addends.
Addition Property of Equality The property that states that if you add the same number to both sides of an equation, the new equation will have the same solution. (p. 52)	**Propiedad de igualdad de la suma** Propiedad que establece que puedes sumar el mismo valor en ambos lados de una ecuación y el enunciado seguirá siendo verdadero.	$x - 6 = 8$ $\underline{+6} \quad \underline{+6}$ $x = 14$
Addition Property of Opposites The property that states that the sum of a number and its opposite equals zero.	**Propiedad de suma de los opuestos** Propiedad que establece que la suma de un número y su opuesto es cero.	$12 + (-12) = 0$
additive inverse The opposite of a number.	**inverso aditivo** El opuesto de un número.	The additive inverse of 5 is -5.
adjacent angles Angles in the same plane that have a common vertex and a common side. (p. 453)	**ángulos adyacentes** Ángulos en el mismo plano que están uno al lado del otro y comparten un vértice y un lado.	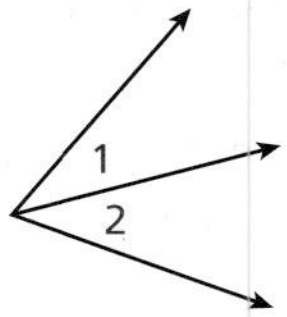 $\angle 1$ and $\angle 2$ are adjacent angles.
algebraic expression An expression that contains at least one variable. (p. 34)	**expresión algebraica** Expresión que contiene una o más variables.	$x + 8$ $4(m - b)$

ENGLISH	SPANISH	EXAMPLES
algebraic inequality An inequality that contains at least one variable. (p. 692)	**desigualdad algebraica** Desigualdad que contiene una o más variables.	$x + 3 > 10$ $5a > b + 3$
angle A figure formed by two rays with a common endpoint called the vertex. (p. 448)	**ángulo** Figura formada por dos rayos con un extremo común llamado vértice.	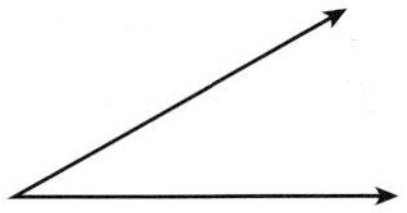
arc A part of a circle named by its endpoints. (p. 460)	**arco** Parte de un círculo que se nombra por sus extremos.	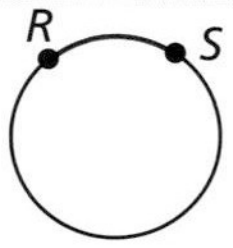
area The number of square units needed to cover a given surface. (p. 530)	**área** El número de unidades cuadradas que se necesitan para cubrir una superficie.	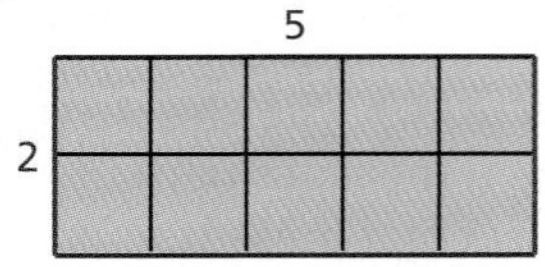 The area is 10 square units.
arithmetic sequence A sequence in which the terms change by the same amount each time. (p. 242)	**sucesión aritmética** Una sucesión en la que los términos cambian la misma cantidad cada vez.	The sequence 2, 5, 8, 11, 14 . . . is an arithmetic sequence.
Associative Property of Addition The property that states that for all real numbers *a, b,* and *c,* the sum is always the same, regardless of their grouping. (p. 28)	**Propiedad asociativa de la suma** Establece que para todos los números reales *a, b* y *c,* la suma siempre es la misma sin importar cómo se agrupen.	$2 + 3 + 8 = (2 + 3) + 8 =$ $2 + (3 + 8)$
Associative Property of Multiplication The property that states that for all real numbers *a, b,* and *c,* their product is always the same, regardless of their grouping. (p. 28)	**Propiedad asociativa de la multiplicación** Establece que para todos los números reales *a, b* y *c,* el producto siempre es el mismo sin importar cómo se agrupen.	$2 \cdot 3 \cdot 8 = (2 \cdot 3) \cdot 8 = 2 \cdot (3 \cdot 8)$
asymmetry Not identical on either side of a central line; not symmetrical. (p. 494)	**asimetría** Ocurre cuando dos lados separados por una línea central no son idénticos; no simétricos.	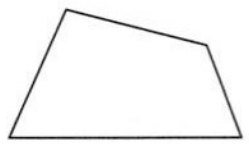 The quadrilateral has asymmetry.
axes The two perpendicular lines of a coordinate plane that intersect at the origin. (p. 224)	**ejes** Las dos rectas numéricas perpendiculares del plano cartesiano que se intersecan en el origen.	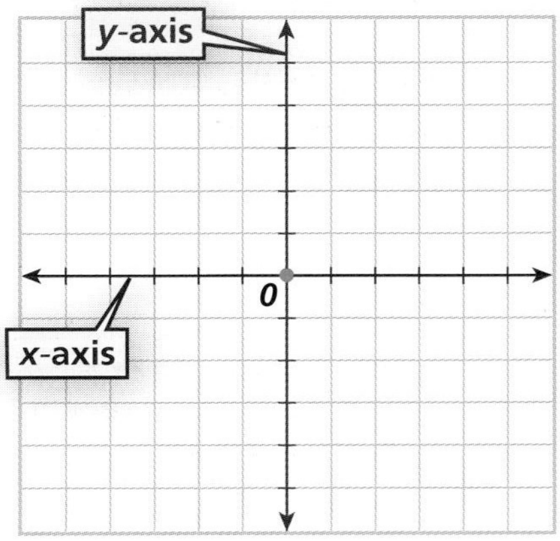

ENGLISH	SPANISH	EXAMPLES
B		
bar graph A graph that uses vertical or horizontal bars to display data. (p. 386)	**gráfica de barras** Una gráfica que muestra los datos con líneas verticales u horizontales.	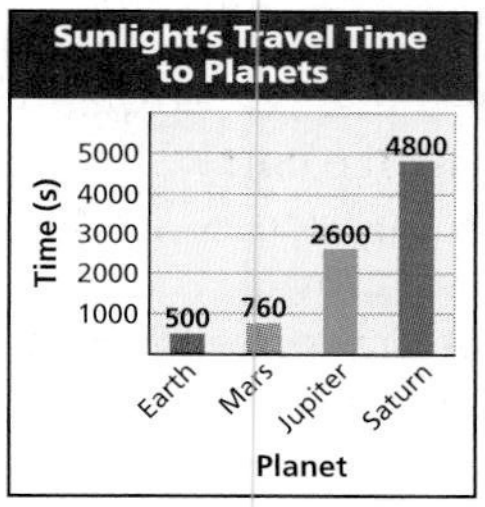
base-10 number system A number system in which all numbers are expressed using the digits 0–9. (p. 15)	**sistema de base 10** Sistema de numeración en el que todos los números se expresan con los dígitos 0–9.	
base (in numeration) When a number is raised to a power, the number that is used as a factor is the base. (p. 10)	**base (en numeración)** Cuando un número se eleva a una potencia, el número que se usa como factor es la base.	$3^5 = 3 \cdot 3 \cdot 3 \cdot 3 \cdot 3$; 3 is the base.
base (of a polygon) A side of a polygon.	**base (de un polígono)** Un lado de un polígono.	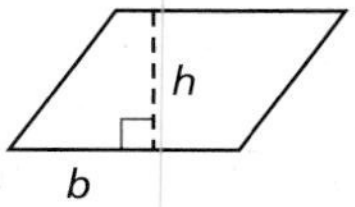
base (of a three-dimensional figure) A face of a three-dimensional figure by which the figure is measured or classified. (p. 580)	**base (de una figura tridimensional)** Cara de una figura tridimensional a partir de la cual se mide o se clasifica una figura.	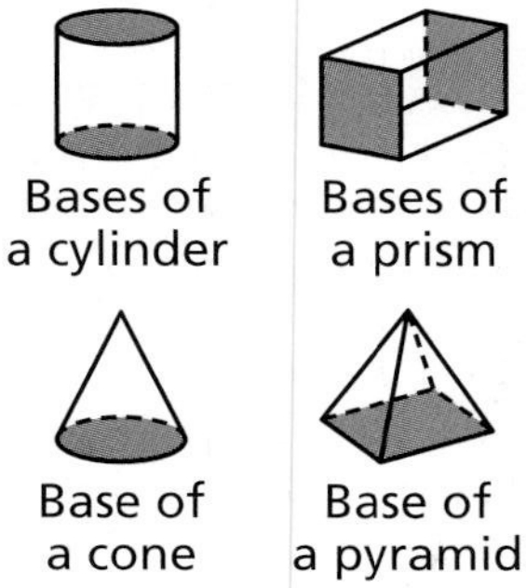
binary number system A number system in which all numbers are expressed using only two digits, 0 and 1. (p. 769)	**sistema de números binarios** Sistema de numeración en el que todos los números se expresan por medio de dos dígitos, 0 y 1.	
bisect To divide into two congruent parts. (p. 456)	**trazar una bisectriz** Dividir en dos partes congruentes.	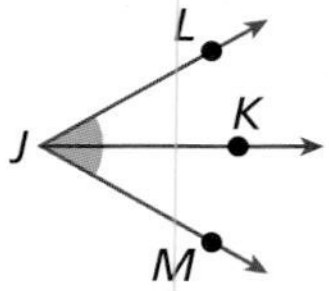 $\overrightarrow{JK}$ bisects $\angle LJM$.
biased sample A sample that does not fairly represent the population. (p. 413)	**muestra no representativa** Muestra que no representa de forma justa la población.	

ENGLISH	SPANISH	EXAMPLES

box-and-whisker plot A graph that displays the highest and lowest quarters of data as whiskers, the middle two quarters of the data as a box, and the median. (p. 394)

gráfica de mediana y rango Gráfica que muestra los valores máximo y mínimo, los cuartiles superior e inferior, así como la mediana de los datos.

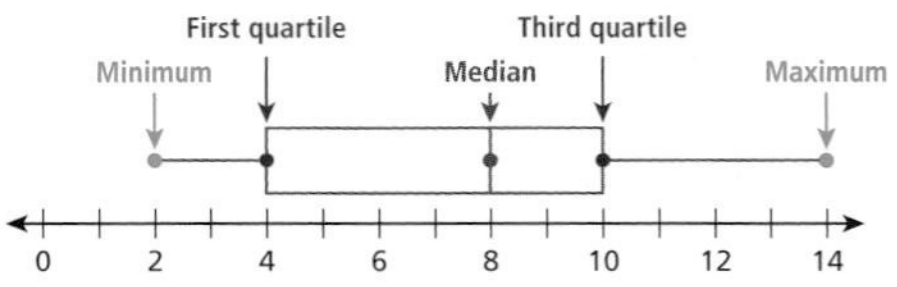

break (graph) A zigzag on a horizontal or vertical scale of a graph that indicates that some of the numbers on the scale have been omitted. (p. 422)

discontinuidad (gráfica) Zig-zag en la escala horizontal o vertical de una gráfica que indica la omisión de algunos números de la escala.

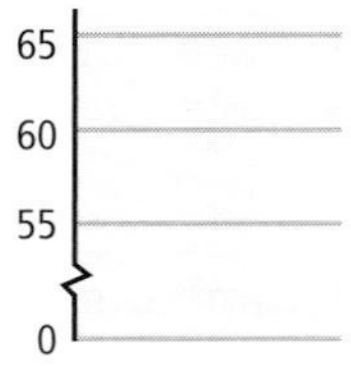

C

capacity The amount a container can hold when filled.

capacidad Cantidad que cabe en un recipiente cuando se llena.

A large milk container has a capacity of 1 gallon.

Celsius A metric scale for measuring temperature in which 0°C is the freezing point of water and 100°C is the boiling point of water; also called *centigrade*.

Celsius Escala métrica para medir temperatura, en la que 0° C es el punto de congelación del agua y 100° C es el punto de ebullición. También se le llama *centígrado*.

center (of a circle) The point inside a circle that is the same distance from all the points on the circle. (p. 460)

centro (de un círculo) Punto interior de un círculo que se encuentra a la misma distancia de todos los puntos de la circunferencia.

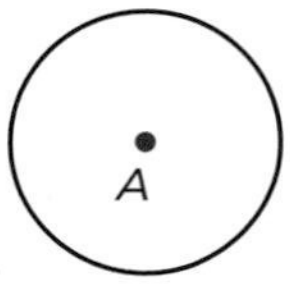

center (of rotation) The point about which a figure is rotated. (p. 495)

centro (de rotación) Punto alrededor del cual se hace girar una figura.

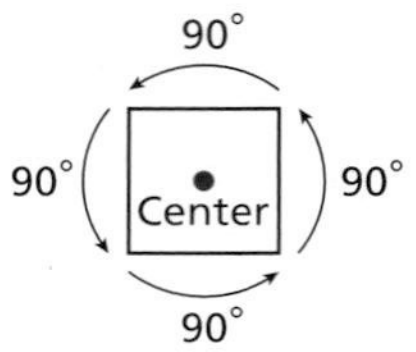

central angle of a circle An angle with its vertex at the center of a circle. (p. 461)

ángulo central Ángulo cuyo vértice se encuentra en el centro de un círculo.

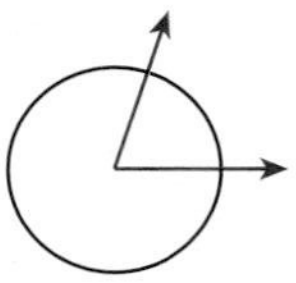

certain (probability) Sure to happen; having a probability of 1. (p. 628)

seguro (probabilidad) Que con seguridad sucederá. Representa una probabilidad de 1.

chord A line segment with endpoints on a circle. (p. 460)

cuerda Segmento de recta cuyos extremos forman parte de un círculo.

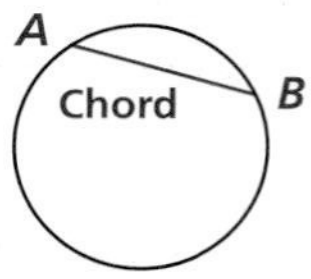

circle The set of all points in a plane that are the same distance from a given point called the center. (p. 460)

círculo Conjunto de puntos en un plano que se encuentran a la misma distancia de un punto llamado centro.

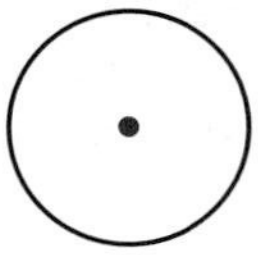

ENGLISH	SPANISH	EXAMPLES
circle graph A graph that uses sectors of a circle to compare parts to the whole and parts to other parts. (p. 390)	**gráfica circular** Gráfica que usa secciones de un círculo para comparar partes con el todo y con otras partes.	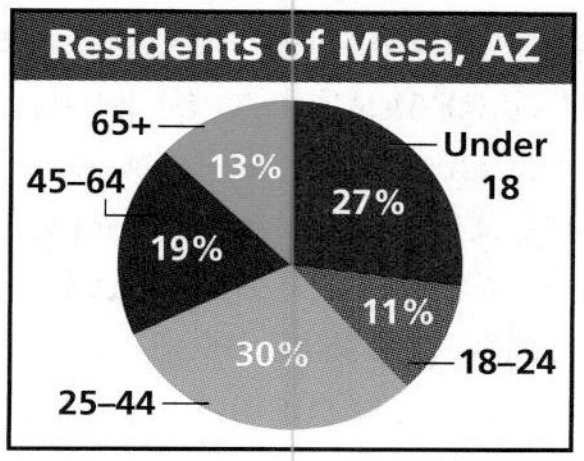
circumference The distance around a circle. (p. 525)	**circunferencia** Distancia alrededor de un círculo.	
clockwise A circular movement to the right in the direction shown.	**en sentido contrario a las manecillas del reloj** Movimiento circular en la dirección que se muestra.	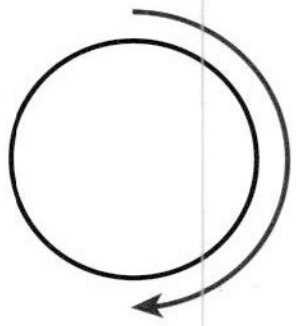
coefficient The number that is multiplied by the variable in an algebraic expression. (p. 42)	**coeficiente** Número que se multiplica por la variable en una expresión algebraica.	5 is the coefficient in 5*b*.
combination An arrangement of items or events in which order does not matter. (p. 652)	**combinación** Agrupación de objetos o sucesos en la cual el orden no es importante.	For objects *A, B, C, and D,* there are 6 different combinations of 2 objects: *AB, AC, AD, BC, BD, CD.*
common denominator A denominator that is the same in two or more fractions.	**común denominador** Denominador que es el mismo en dos o más fracciones.	The common denominator of $\frac{5}{8}$ and $\frac{2}{8}$ is 8.
common factor A number that is a factor of two or more numbers.	**factor común** Número que es factor de dos o más números.	8 is a common factor of 16 and 40.
common multiple A number that is a multiple of each of two or more numbers.	**común múltiplo** Número que es múltiplo de dos o más números.	15 is a common multiple of 3 and 5.
Commutative Property of Addition The property that states that two or more numbers can be added in any order without changing the sum. (p. 28)	**Propiedad conmutativa de la suma** Establece que sumar dos o más números en cualquier orden no altera la suma.	$8 + 20 = 20 + 8$
Commutative Property of Multiplication The property that states that two or more numbers can be multiplied in any order without changing the product. (p. 28)	**Propiedad conmutativa de la multiplicación** Establece que multiplicar dos o más números en cualquier orden no altera el producto.	$6 \cdot 12 = 12 \cdot 6$
compatible numbers Numbers that are close to the given numbers that make estimation or mental calculation easier. (p. 150)	**números compatibles** Números que pueden reemplazar a otros en un problema por ser más fáciles de usar para hacer estimaciones o cálculos mentales.	To estimate 7,957 + 5,009, use the compatible numbers 8,000 and 5,000: 8,000 + 5,000 = 13,000.

ENGLISH	SPANISH	EXAMPLES
complement All the ways that an event can not happen. (p. 629)	**complemento** Todas las maneras en que no puede ocurrir un suceso.	When rolling a number cube, the complement of rolling a 3 is rolling a 1, 2, 4, 5, or 6.
complementary angles Two angles whose measures add to 90°. (p. 448)	**ángulos complementarios** Dos ángulos cuyas medidas suman 90°.	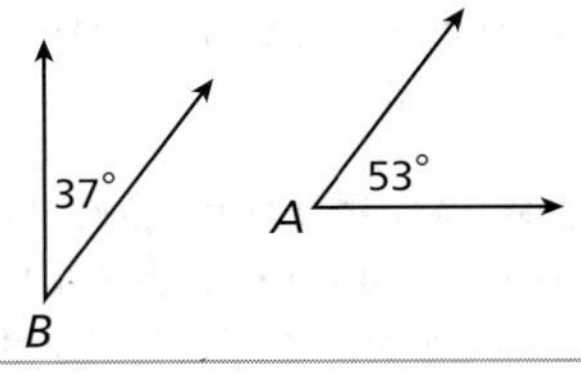
composite number A number greater than 1 that has more than two whole-number factors. (p. 106)	**número compuesto** Número mayor que 1 que tiene más de dos factores que son números cabales.	4, 6, 8, and 9 are composite numbers.
compound event An event made up of two or more simple events.	**suceso compuesto** Suceso que consta de dos o más sucesos simples.	Rolling a 3 on a number cube and spinning a 2 on a spinner is a compound event.
compound inequality A combination of more than one inequality. (p. 693)	**desigualdad compuesta** Combinación de dos o más desigualdades.	$-2 \leq x < 10$
cone A three-dimensional figure with one vertex and one circular base. (p. 581)	**cono** Figura tridimensional con un vértice y una base circular.	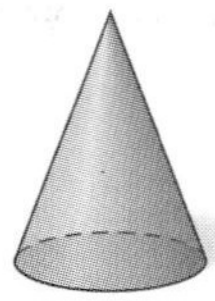
congruent Having the same size and shape. (p. 443)	**congruentes** Que tiene la misma forma y tamaño.	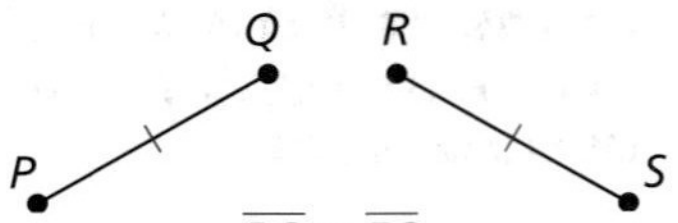 $\overline{PQ} \cong \overline{RS}$
congruent angles Angles that have the same measure. (p. 453)	**ángulos congruentes** Ángulos que tienen la misma medida.	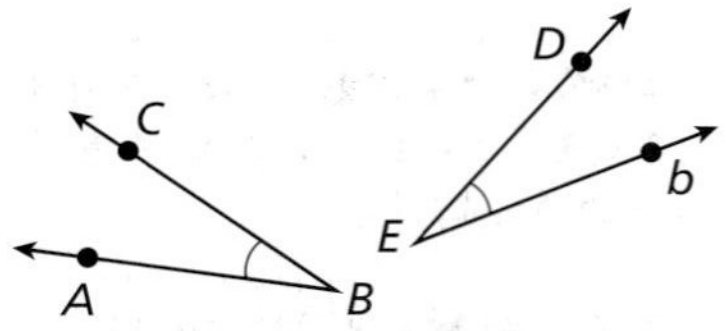 $\angle ABC \cong \angle DEF$
constant A value that does not change. (p. 34)	**constante** Valor que no cambia.	3, 0, π
convenience sample A sample based on members of the population that are readily available. (p. 412)	**muestra de conveniencia** Una muestra basada en miembros de la población que están fácilmente disponibles.	
coordinate plane (coordinate grid) A plane formed by the intersection of a horizontal number line called the x-axis and a vertical number line called the y-axis. (p. 224)	**plano cartesiano (cuadrícula de coordenadas)** Formado por la intersección de una recta numérica horizontal llamada eje de las x y otra vertical llamada eje de las y.	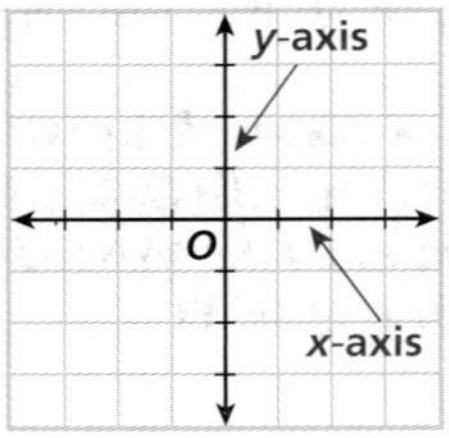

ENGLISH	SPANISH	EXAMPLES
coordinate One of the numbers of an ordered pair that locate a point on a coordinate graph. (p. 224)	**coordenada** Uno de los números de un par ordenado que localizan un punto en un plano cartesiano.	
correlation The description of the relationship between two data sets. (p. 417)	**correlación** Descripción de la relación entre dos conjuntos de datos.	
corresponding angles (for lines) A pair of angles formed by a transversal and two lines. (p. 453)	**ángulos correspondientes (en líneas)** Par de ángulos formados por dos líneas cortadas por una tercera.	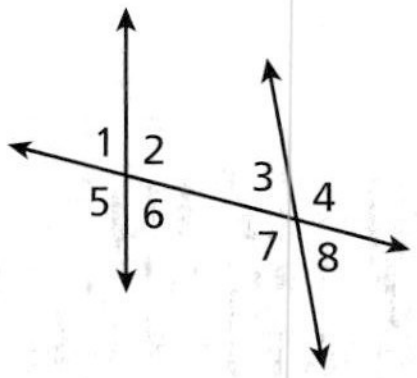 $\angle 1$ and $\angle 3$ are corresponding angles.
corresponding angles (in polygons) Matching angles of two or more polygons. (p. 300)	**ángulos correspondientes (en polígonos)** Ángulos que se localizan en la misma posición relativa en dos o más polígonos.	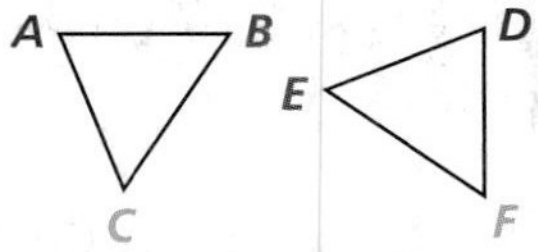 $\angle A$ and $\angle D$ and are corresponding angles.
corresponding sides Matching sides of two or more polygons. (p. 300)	**lados correspondientes** Lados que se localizan en la misma posición relativa en dos o más polígonos.	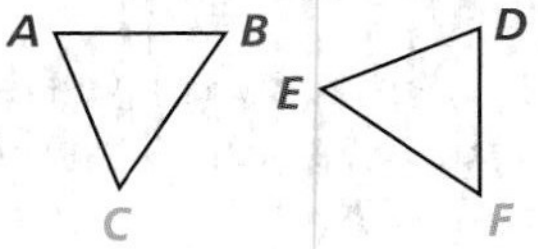 $\overline{AB}$ and $\overline{DE}$ are corresponding sides.
counterclockwise A circular movement to the left in the direction shown.	**en sentido de las manecillas del reloj** Movimiento circular hacia la derecha en la dirección que se indica.	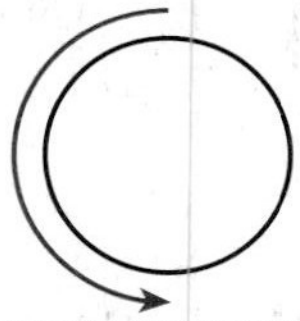
counterexample An example that shows that a statement is false. (p. 774)	**producto cruzado** Multiplicación cruzada de los numeradores y denominadores de dos razones.	
cross product The product of numbers on the diagonal when comparing two ratios. (p. 287)	**contraejemplo** Ejemplo que demuestra que un enunciado es falso.	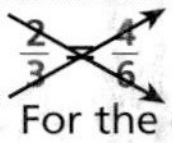 For the proportion $\frac{2}{3} = \frac{4}{6}$, the cross products are $2 \cdot 6 = 12$ and $3 \cdot 4 = 12$.
cube (geometric figure) A rectangular prism with six congruent square faces.	**cubo (figura geométrica)** Prisma rectangular con seis caras cuadradas congruentes.	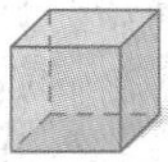
cube (in numeration) A number raised to the third power.	**cubo (en numeración)** Número elevado a la tercera potencia.	$5^3 = 5 \cdot 5 \cdot 5 = 125$
cumulative frequency The frequency of all data values that are less than or equal to a given value. (p. 376)	**frecuencia acumulativa** Muestra el total acumulado de las frecuencias.	

Glossary/Glosario

ENGLISH	SPANISH	EXAMPLES
customary system of measurement The measurement system often used in the United States. (p. 292)	**sistema métrico de medición** Sistema decimal de pesos y medidas empleado universalmente en las ciencias y comúnmente en todo el mundo.	inches, feet, miles, ounces, pounds, tons, cups, quarts, gallons
cylinder A three-dimensional figure with two parallel, congruent circular bases connected by a curved lateral surface. (p. 581)	**cilindro** Figura tridimensional con dos bases circulares paralelas y congruentes, unidas por una superficie lateral curva.	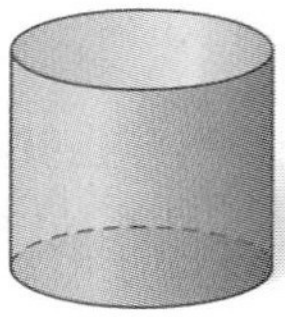

D

ENGLISH	SPANISH	EXAMPLES
decagon A polygon with ten sides. (p. 467)	**decágono** Polígono de 10 lados.	
decimal system A base-10 place value system.	**sistema decimal** Sistema de valor posicional de base 10.	
deductive reasoning Using logic to show that a statement is true. (p. 773)	**razonamiento deductivo** Uso de lógica para demostrar que un enunciado es verdadero.	
degree The unit of measure for angles or temperature. (p. 448)	**grado** Unidad de medida para ángulos y temperaturas.	
denominator The bottom number of a fraction that tells how many equal parts are in the whole.	**denominador** Parte de abajo de una fracción que indica las partes en que se divide el entero.	$\frac{3}{4}$ ← denominator
dependent events Events for which the outcome of one event affects the probability of the second event. (p. 648)	**sucesos dependientes** Sucesos en el que el resultado del primero afecta el del segundo.	A bag contains 3 red marbles and 2 blue marbles. Drawing a red marble and then drawing a blue marble without replacing the first marble is an example of dependent events.
diameter A line segment that passes through the center of a circle and has endpoints on the circle, or the length of that segment. (p. 460)	**diámetro** Segmento de recta que pasa por el centro de un círculo y tiene sus extremos en la circunferencia, o bien la longitud de ese segmento.	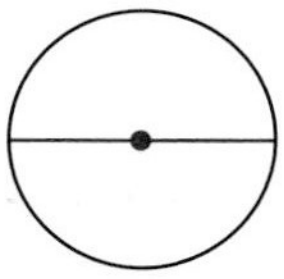
difference The result when one number is subtracted from another.	**diferencia** El resultado de restar un número de otro.	In $16 - 5 = 11$, 11 is the difference.
dimension The length, width, or height of a figure.	**dimensión** Longitud, anchura o altura de una figura.	

ENGLISH	SPANISH	EXAMPLES
Distributive Property The property that states if you multiply a sum by a number, you will get the same result if you multiply each addend by that number and then add the products. (p. 29)	**Propiedad distributiva** Establece que si multiplicas una suma por un número, obtendrás el mismo resultado que si multiplicas cada sumando por ese número y luego sumas los productos.	$5(20 + 1) = 5 \cdot 20 + 5 \cdot 1$
dividend The number to be divided in a division problem.	**dividendo** Número que se divide en un problema de división.	In $8 \div 4 = 2$, 8 is the dividend.
divisible Can be divided by a number without leaving a remainder. (p. 766)	**divisible** Que se puede dividir entre un número sin dejar residuo.	18 is divisible by 3.
Division Property of Equality The property that states that if you divide both sides of an equation by the same nonzero number, the new equation will have the same solution. (p. 56)	**Propiedad de igualdad de la división** Propiedad que establece que puedes dividir ambos lados de una ecuación entre el mismo número distinto de cero, y el enunciado seguirá siendo verdadero.	$4x = 12$ $\frac{4x}{4} = \frac{12}{4}$ $x = 3$
divisor The number you are dividing by in a division problem.	**divisor** El número entre el que se divide en un problema de división.	In $8 \div 4 = 2$, 4 is the divisor.
double-bar graph A bar graph that compares two related sets of data. (p. 386)	**gráfica de doble barra** Gráfica de barra que compara dos conjuntos de datos relacionados.	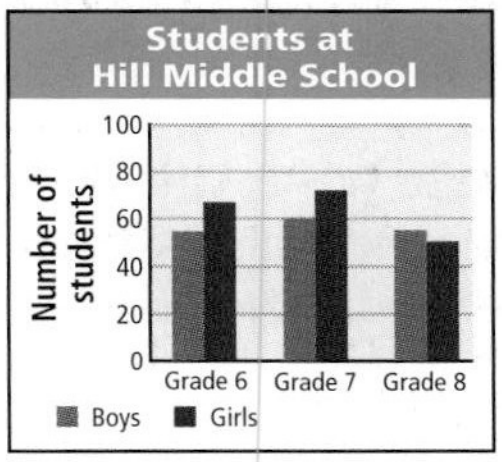
double-line graph A line graph that shows how two related sets of data change over time. (p. 403)	**gráfica de doble línea** Gráfica lineal que muestra cómo cambian con el tiempo dos conjuntos de datos relacionados.	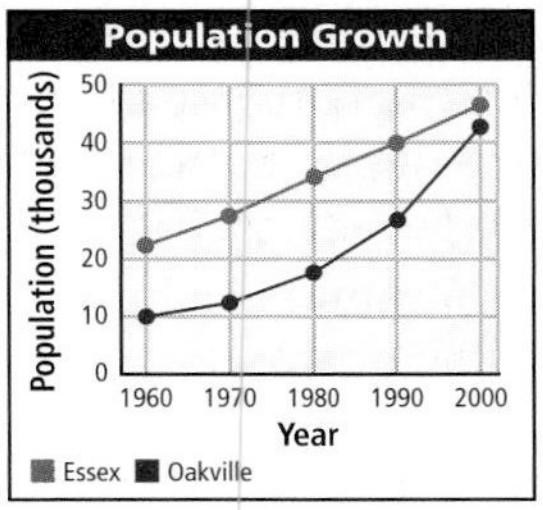

E

ENGLISH	SPANISH	EXAMPLES
edge The line segment along which two faces of a polyhedron intersect. (p. 580)	**arista** Intersección de dos caras de un poliedro.	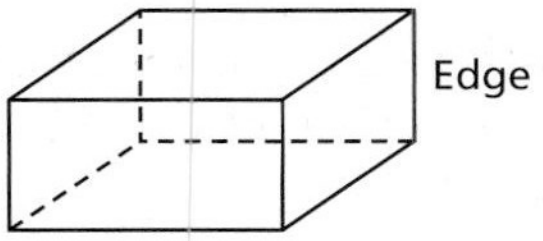
endpoint A point at the end of a line segment or ray.	**extremo** Punto al final de un segmento de recta o rayo.	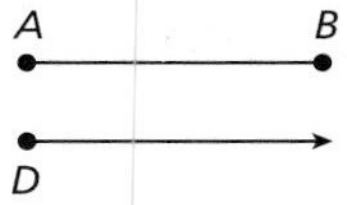

ENGLISH	SPANISH	EXAMPLES
equally likely outcomes Outcomes that have the same probability. (p. 628)	**igualmente probable (resultados)** Resultados que tienen la misma probabilidad de ocurrir.	
equation A mathematical sentence that shows that two expressions are equivalent. (p. 46)	**ecuación** Enunciado matemático que indica que dos expresiones son equivalentes.	$x + 4 = 7$ $6 + 1 = 10 - 3$
equilateral triangle A triangle with three congruent sides. (p. 470)	**triángulo equilátero** Triángulo con tres lados congruentes.	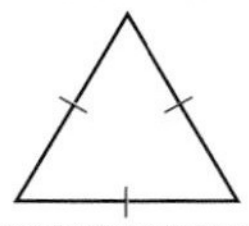
equivalent Having the same value.	**equivalentes** Que tienen el mismo valor.	
equivalent fractions Fractions that name the same amount or part. (p. 120)	**fracciones equivalentes** Fracciones que representan el mismo valor.	$\frac{1}{2}$ and $\frac{2}{4}$ are equivalent fractions.
equivalent ratios Ratios that name the same comparison. (p. 283)	**razones equivalentes** Razones que representan la misma comparación.	$\frac{1}{2}$ and $\frac{2}{4}$ are equivalent ratios.
estimate (n) An answer that is close to the exact answer and is found by rounding, or other methods.	**estimación (n)** Solución aproximada a la respuesta exacta que se obtiene mediante el redondeo u otros métodos.	
estimate (v) To find an answer close to the exact answer by rounding or other methods.	**estimar (v)** Hallar una solución aproximada a la respuesta exacta mediante el redondeo u otros métodos.	
evaluate To find the value of a numerical or algebraic expression. (p. 34)	**evaluar** Hallar el valor de una expresión numérica o algebraica.	Evaluate $2x + 7$ for $x = 3$. $2x + 7$ $2(3) + 7$ $6 + 7$ 13
even number An integer that is divisible by two.	**número par** Número entero divisible entre 2.	2, 4, 6
event An outcome or set of outcomes of an experiment or situation. (p. 628)	**suceso** Resultado o conjunto de resultados posibles de un experimento o situación.	When rolling a number cube, the event "an odd number" consists of the outcomes 1, 3, and 5.
expanded form A number written as the sum of the values of its digits.	**forma desarrollada** Número escrito como suma de los valores de sus dígitos.	236,536 written in expanded form is 200,000 + 30,000 + 6,000 + 500 + 30 + 6.
experiment In probability, any activity based on chance, such as tossing a coin. (p. 628)	**experimento** En probabilidad, cualquier actividad basada en la posibilidad, como lanzar una moneda.	Tossing a coin 10 times and noting the number of "heads"

ENGLISH	SPANISH	EXAMPLES
experimental probability The ratio of the number of times an event occurs to the total number of trials, or times that the activity is performed. (p. 632)	**probabilidad experimental** Razón del número de veces que ocurre un suceso al número total de pruebas o a las veces que se realiza el experimento.	Kendra attempted 27 free throws and made 16 of them. Her experimental probability of making a free throw is $\frac{\text{number made}}{\text{number attempted}} = \frac{16}{27} \approx 0.59$.
exponent The number that indicates how many times the base is used as a factor. (p. 10)	**exponente** Número que indica cuántas veces se multiplica la base por sí misma.	$2^3 = 2 \cdot 2 \cdot 2 = 8$; 3 is the exponent.
exponential form A number is in exponential form when it is written with a base and an exponent.	**forma exponencial** Se dice que un número está en forma exponencial cuando se escribe con una base y un exponente.	4^2 is the exponential form for $4 \cdot 4$.
expression A mathematical phrase that contains operations, numbers, and/or variables.	**expresión** Enunciado matemático que contiene operaciones, números y(o) variables.	$6x + 1$

F

face A flat surface of a polyhedron. (p. 580)	**cara** Lados planos de un poliedro.	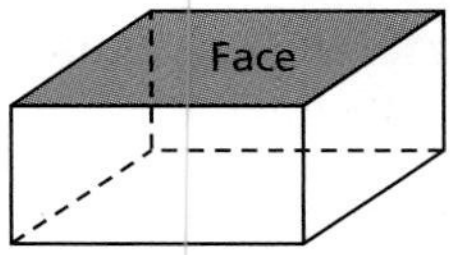
factor A number that is multiplied by another number to get a product. (p. 106)	**factor** Número cabal que se multiplica por otro para hallar un producto.	7 is a factor of 21 since $7 \cdot 3 = 21$.
factor tree A diagram showing how a whole number breaks down into its prime factors. (p. 106)	**árbol de factores** Diagrama que muestra cómo se descompone un número cabal en sus factores primos.	12 / \ $3 \cdot 4$ / \ $2 \cdot 2$ $12 = 3 \cdot 2 \cdot 2$
factorial The product of all whole numbers except zero that are less than or equal to a number. (p. 657)	**factorial** El producto de todos los números cabales menores o iguales a un número, excepto cero.	4 factorial $= 4! = 4 \cdot 3 \cdot 2 \cdot 1$
Fahrenheit A temperature scale in which 32°F is the freezing point of water and 212°F is the boiling point of water.	**Fahrenheit** Escala de temperatura en la que 32° F es el punto de congelación del agua y 212° F es el punto de ebullición.	
fair When all outcomes of an experiment are equally likely, the experiment is said to be fair. (p. 640)	**justo** Se dice de un experimento donde todos los resultados posibles son igualmente probables.	
first quartile The median of the lower half of a set of data; also called *lower quartile*. (p. 394)	**primer cuartil** La mediana de la mitad inferior de un conjunto de datos. También se llama cuartil inferior.	

ENGLISH | **SPANISH** | **EXAMPLES**

formula A rule showing relationships among quantities.

fórmula Regla que muestra relaciones entre cantidades.

$A = \ell w$ is the formula for the area of a rectangle.

---

fraction A number in the form $\frac{a}{b}$, where $b \neq 0$.

fracción Número escrito en la forma $\frac{a}{b}$, donde $b \neq 0$.

---

frequency table A table that lists items together according to the number of times, or frequency, that the items occur. (p. 376)

tabla de frecuencia Manera de organizar los datos de acuerdo con el número de veces que aparece cada valor.

Data set: 1, 1, 2, 2, 3, 4, 5, 5, 5, 6, 6, 6, 6

Frequency table:

Data	1	2	3	4	5	6
Frequency	2	2	1	1	3	4

---

function An input-output relationship that has exactly one output for each input. (p. 238)

función Regla que relaciona dos cantidades de forma que a cada valor de entrada corresponda exactamente un valor de salida.

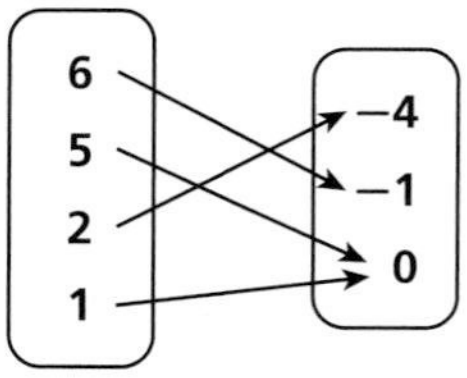

---

function table A table of ordered pairs that represent solutions of a function. (p. 238)

tabla de función Tabla de pares ordenados que representan soluciones de una función.

x	3	4	5	6
y	7	9	11	13

Fundamental Counting Principle If one event has m possible outcomes and a second event has n possible outcomes after the first event has occurred, then there are $m \cdot n$ total possible outcomes for the two events. (p. 637)

Principio fundamental de conteo Si un suceso tiene m resultados posibles y un segundo suceso tiene n resultados posibles, después de ocurrido el primer suceso, entonces hay $m \cdot n$ resultados posibles en total para los dos sucesos.

There are 4 colors of shirts and 3 colors of pants. There are $4 \cdot 3 = 12$ possible outfits.

G

geometric sequence A sequence in which each term is multiplied by the same value to get the next term. (p. 242)

sucesión geométrica Una sucesión en la que cada término se multiplica por el mismo valor para obtener el siguiente término.

The sequence 2, 4, 8, 16 . . . is a geometric sequence.

---

graph of an equation A graph of the set of ordered pairs that are solutions of the equation. (p. 248)

gráfica de una ecuación Gráfica del conjunto de pares ordenados que son soluciones de la ecuación.

---

greatest common factor (GCF) The largest common factor of two or more given numbers. (p. 110)

máximo común divisor (MCD) El mayor de los factores comunes compartidos por dos o más números cabales.

The GCF of 27 and 45 is 9.

ENGLISH	SPANISH	EXAMPLES

H

ENGLISH	SPANISH	EXAMPLES
height In a pyramid or cone, the perpendicular distance from the base to the opposite vertex. (p. 590)	**altura** En una pirámide o cono, longitud de un segmento de recta perpendicular que va de la base y al vértice opuesto.	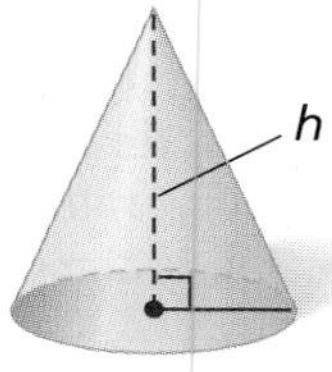
In a triangle or quadrilateral, the perpendicular distance from the base to the opposite vertex or side.	En un triángulo o cuadrilátero, longitud de un segmento de recta perpendicular que va de la base de la figura al vértice o lado opuesto.	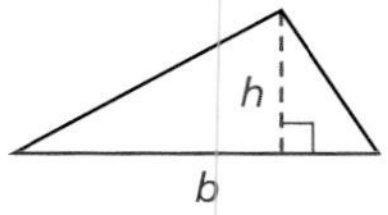
In a prism or cylinder, the perpendicular distance between the bases.	En un prisma o cilindro, la distancia perpendicular entre las bases.	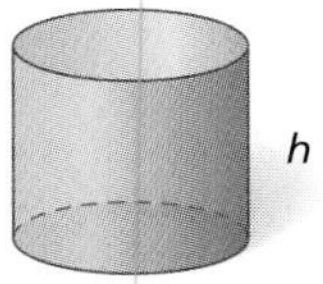
heptagon A seven-sided polygon. (p. 467)	**heptágono** Polígono de siete lados.	
hexagon A six-sided polygon. (p. 467)	**hexágono** Polígono de seis lados.	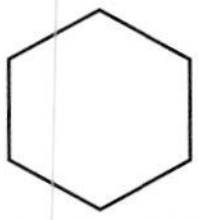
histogram A bar graph that shows the frequency of data within equal intervals. (p. 387)	**histograma** Gráfica de barras que muestra la frecuencia de los datos en intervalos iguales.	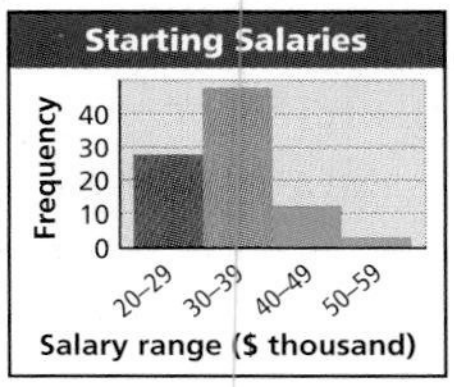
hypotenuse In a right triangle, the side opposite the right angle. (p. 556)	**hipotenusa** En un triángulo rectángulo, el lado opuesto al ángulo recto.	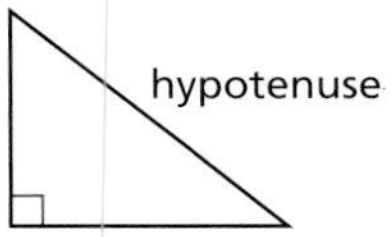

I

ENGLISH	SPANISH	EXAMPLES
Identity Property of One The property that states that the product of 1 and any number is that number. (p. 28)	**Propiedad de identidad del uno** Propiedad que establece que el producto de 1 y cualquier número es ese número.	$3 \cdot 1 = 3$ $-9 \cdot 1 = -9$
Identity Property of Zero The property that states that the sum of zero and any number is that number. (p. 28)	**Propiedad de identidad del cero** Propiedad que establece que la suma de cero y cualquier número es ese número.	$5 + 0 = 5$ $-4 + 0 = -4$
image A figure resulting from a transformation. (p. 488)	**imagen** Figura que resulta de una transformación.	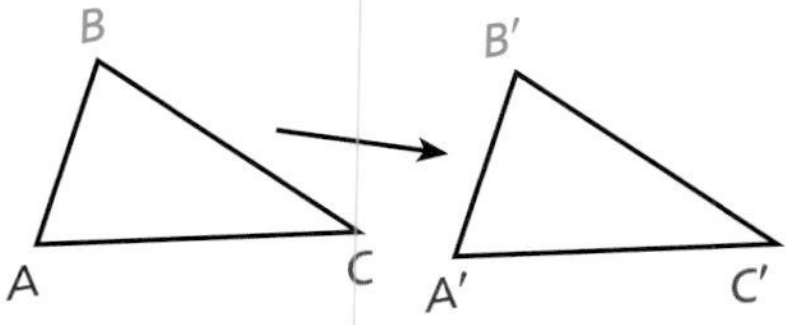

ENGLISH	SPANISH	EXAMPLES
impossible (probability) Can never happen; having a probability of 0. (p. 628)	**imposible (en probabilidad)** Suceso cuya probabilidad de ocurrir es 0.	
improper fraction A fraction in which the numerator is greater than or equal to the denominator. (p. 121)	**fracción impropia** Fracción en la que el numerador es menor que el denominador.	$\frac{5}{5}$ $\frac{7}{4}$
independent events Events for which the outcome of one event does not affect the probability of the other. (p. 648)	**sucesos independientes** Sucesos en que el resultado del primer suceso no influye en la probabilidad de que ocurra el segundo suceso.	A bag contains 3 red marbles and 2 blue marbles. Drawing a red marble, replacing it, and then drawing a blue marble is an example of independent events.
indirect measurement The technique of using similar figures and proportions to find a measure. (p. 304)	**medición indirecta** Técnica que usa figuras semejantes y proporciones para hallar la medida de un objeto que no se puede medir en forma directa.	
inductive reasoning Using a pattern to make a conclusion. (p. 773)	**razonamiento inductivo** Uso de un patrón para sacar una conclusión.	
inequality A mathematical sentence that shows the relationship between quantities that are not equivalent. (p. 692)	**desigualdad** Enunciado matemático que muestra una relación entre cantidades que no son equivalentes.	$5 < 8$ $5x + 2 \geq 12$
input The value substituted into an expression or function. (p. 238)	**valor de entrada** Valor que usa para sustituir una variable en una expresión o función.	For the function $y = 6x$, the input 4 produces an output of 24.
integers The set of whole numbers and their opposites. (p. 76)	**enteros** Conjunto de todos los números cabales y sus opuestos.	$\ldots -3, -2, -1, 0, 1, 2, 3, \ldots$
interest The amount of money charged for borrowing or using money, or the amount of money earned by saving money. (p. 356)	**interés** Cantidad de dinero que se cobra por el préstamo o uso del dinero, o la cantidad que se gana al ahorrar dinero.	
interquartile range The difference between the upper and lower quartiles in a box-and-whisker plot. (p. 395)	**rango entre cuartiles** La diferencia entre los cuartiles superior en inferior en una gráfica de mediana y rango.	Lower half Upper half 18, (23), 28, 29, (36), 42 ↑ Lower quartile ↑ Upper quartile Interquartile range: 36 − 23 = 13
intersecting lines Lines that cross at exactly one point.	**líneas secantes** Líneas que se cruzan en un solo punto.	
interval The space between marked values on a number line or the scale of a graph.	**intervalo** El espacio entre los valores marcados en una recta numérica o en la escala de una gráfica.	

ENGLISH	SPANISH	EXAMPLES
inverse operations Operations that undo each other: addition and subtraction, or multiplication and division. (p. 52)	**operaciones inversas** Operaciones que se anulan mutuamente: suma y resta, o multiplicación y división.	Addition and subtraction are inverse operations: $5 + 3 = 8$; $8 - 3 = 5$ Multiplication and division are inverse operations: $2 \cdot 3 = 6$; $6 \div 3 = 2$
irrational number A number that cannot be expressed as a ratio of two integers or as a repeating or terminating decimal. (p. 562)	**número irracional** Número que no puede expresarse como una razón de dos enteros ni como decimal periódico o cerrado.	$\sqrt{2}$, π
isolate the variable To get a variable alone on one side of an equation or inequality in order to solve the equation or inequality. (p. 52)	**despejar la variable** Dejar sola la variable en un lado de una ecuación o desigualdad para resolverla.	$\begin{aligned} x + 7 &= 22 \\ -7 &\quad -7 \\ x &= 15 \end{aligned}$
isosceles triangle A triangle with at least two congruent sides. (p. 470)	**triángulo isósceles** Triángulo que tiene al menos dos lados congruentes.	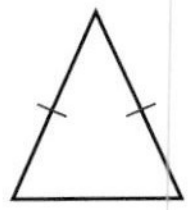

L

ENGLISH	SPANISH	EXAMPLES
least common denominator (LCD) The least common multiple of two or more denominators.	**mínimo común denominador (mcd)** El múltiplo común más pequeño de los denominadores.	The LCD of $\frac{3}{4}$ and $\frac{5}{6}$ is 12.
least common multiple (LCM) The smallest number, other than zero, that is a multiple of two or more given numbers. (p. 114)	**mínimo común múltiplo (mcm)** El menor de los números, diferente de cero, que es múltiplo de dos o más números.	The LCM of 10 and 18 is 90.
legs In a right triangle, the sides that include the right angle; in an isosceles triangle, the pair of congruent sides. (p. 556)	**catetos** En un triángulo rectángulo, los lados adyacentes al ángulo recto. En un triángulo isósceles, el par de lados congruentes.	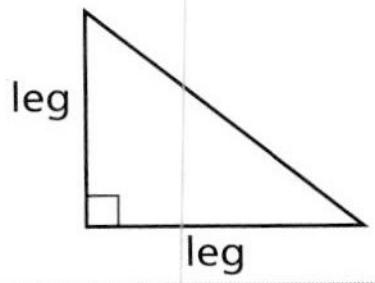
like terms Two or more terms that have the same variable raised to the same power. (p. 42)	**términos semejantes** Dos a más términos que contienen la misma variable elevada a la misma potencia.	In the expression $3a + 5b + 12a$, $3a$ and $12a$ are like terms.
line A straight path that extends without end in opposite directions. (p. 442)	**línea** Trayectoria recta que se extiende de manera indefinida en direcciones opuestas.	
line graph A graph that uses line segments to show how data changes. (p. 402)	**gráfica lineal** Gráfica que muestra los datos mediante segmentos de recta.	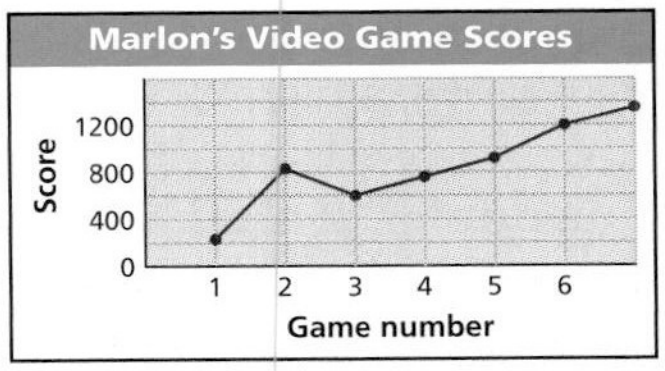

ENGLISH	SPANISH	EXAMPLES
line of reflection A line that a figure is flipped across to create a mirror image of the original figure. (p. 488)	**línea de reflexión** Línea sobre la cual se voltea una figura para crear una imagen de espejo de la figura original.	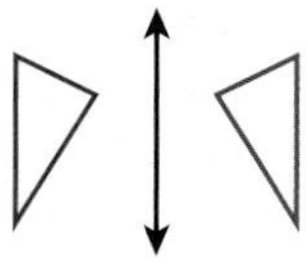 Line of reflection
line of symmetry The imaginary "mirror" in line symmetry. (p. 494)	**eje de simetría** El "espejo" imaginario en la simetría axial.	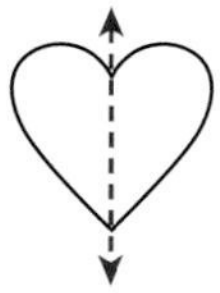
line plot A number line with marks or dots that show frequency. (p. 377)	**diagrama de acumulación** Recta numérica con marcas o puntos que indican frecuencia.	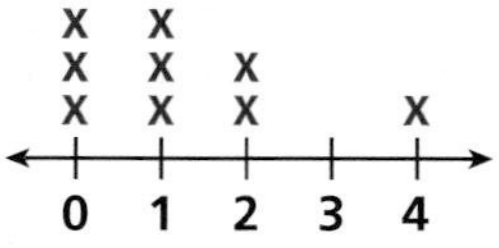 Number of pets
line segment A part of a line between two endpoints. (p. 443)	**segmento de recta** Parte de una línea con dos extremos.	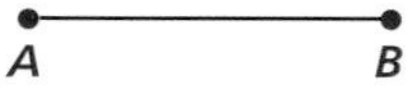
line symmetry A figure has line symmetry if one-half is a mirror-image of the other half. (p. 494)	**simetría axial** Una figura tiene simetría axial si una mitad es imagen de espejo de la otra mitad.	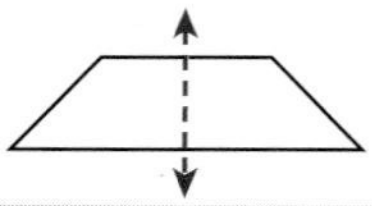
linear equation An equation whose solutions form a straight line on a coordinate plane. (p. 248)	**ecuación lineal** Ecuación cuyas soluciones forman una línea recta en un plano cartesiano.	$y = 2x + 1$
linear function A function whose graph is a straight line. (p. 248)	**función lineal** Función cuya gráfica es una línea recta.	$y = x - 1$ 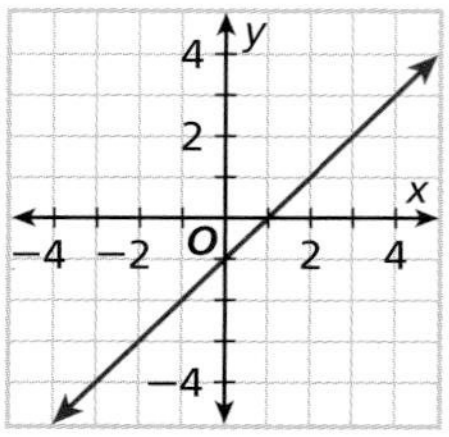
lower quartile The median of the lower half of a set of data. (p. 394)	**cuartil inferior** La mediana de la mitad inferior de un conjunto de datos.	Lower half Upper half 18, (23,) 28, 29, 36, 42 ↑ Lower quartile

M

ENGLISH	SPANISH	EXAMPLES
mean The sum of the items in a set of data divided by the number of items in the set; also called average. (p. 381)	**media** La suma de todos los elementos, dividida entre el número total de elementos en el conjunto de datos. También se le llama promedio.	Data set: 4, 6, 7, 8, 10 Mean: $\frac{4+6+7+8+10}{5} = \frac{35}{5} = 7$
measure of central tendency A measure used to describe the middle of a data set; the mean, median, and mode are measures of central tendency. (p. 381)	**medida de tendencia dominante** Medida empleada para describir la parte media de un conjunto de datos; la media, la mediana y la moda son medidas de tendencia dominante.	

ENGLISH	SPANISH	EXAMPLES
median The middle number, or the mean (average) of the two middle numbers, in an ordered set of data. (p. 381)	**mediana** Es el valor intermedio, o la media (el promedio), de los dos valores intermedios en un conjunto de datos ordenados de menor a mayor.	Data set: 4, 6, 7, 8, 10 Median: 7
metric system of measurement A decimal system of weights and measures that is used universally in science and commonly throughout the world. (p. 292)	**sistema métrico de medición** Sistema decimal de pesos y medidas empleado universalmente en las ciencias y comúnmente en todo el mundo.	centimeters, meters, kilometers, grams, kilograms, milliliters, liters
midpoint The point that divides a line segment into two congruent line segments.	**punto medio** El punto que divide un segmento de recta en dos segmentos de recta congruentes.	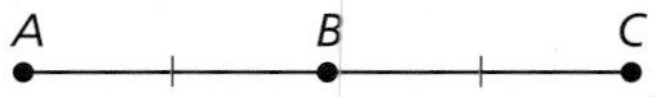
mixed number A number made up of a whole number that is not zero and a fraction. (p. 121)	**número mixto** Número que contiene un número cabal mayor que cero y una fracción.	$5\frac{1}{8}$
mode The number or numbers that occur most frequently in a set of data; when all numbers occur with the same frequency, we say there is no mode. (p. 381)	**moda** Valor o valores más frecuentes en un conjunto de datos; si todos los números aparecen con la misma frecuencia, no hay moda.	Data set: 3, 5, 8, 8, 10 Mode: 8
multiple The product of any number and any nonzero whole number is a multiple of that number. (p. 114)	**múltiplo** El producto de cualquier número y un número cabal es un múltiplo del número.	30, 40, and 90 are all multiples of 10.
Multiplication Property of Equality The property that states that if you multiply both sides of an equation by the same number, the new equation will have the same solution. (p. 56)	**Propiedad de igualdad de la multiplicación** Propiedad que establece que puedes multiplicar ambos lados de una ecuación por el mismo número y la ecuación resultante tendrá la misma solución.	$\frac{1}{3}x = 7$ $(3)(\frac{1}{3}x) = (3)(7)$ $x = 21$
Multiplication Property of Zero The property that states that for all real numbers a, $a \times 0 = 0$ and $0 \times a = 0$. (p. 764)	**Propiedad de multiplicación del cero** Propiedad que establece que para todos los números reales a, $a \cdot 0 = 0$ y $0 \cdot a = 0$.	$6 \cdot 0 = 0$ $-5 \cdot 0 = 0$
mutually exclusive Two events are mutually exclusive if they cannot occur in the same trial of an experiment. (p. 772)	**mutuamente excluyentes** Dos sucesos son mutuamente excluyentes cuando no pueden ocurrir en la misma prueba de un experimento.	

N

ENGLISH	SPANISH	EXAMPLES
negative correlation Two data sets have a negative correlation, or relationship, if one set of data values increases while the other decreases. (p. 417)	**correlación negativa** Dos conjuntos tienen correlación, o relación, negativa, si los valores de un conjunto de datos aumentan a medida que los valores del otro conjunto disminuyen.	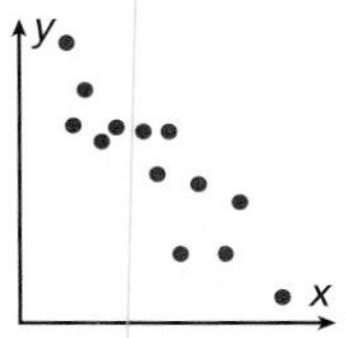

ENGLISH	SPANISH	EXAMPLES

negative integer An integer less than zero. (p. 76)

entero negativo Entero menor que cero.

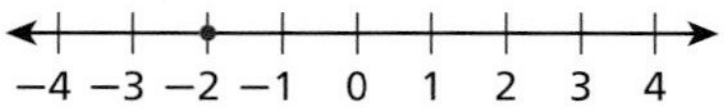

−2 is a negative integer.

net An arrangement of two-dimensional figures that can be folded to form a polyhedron. (p. 597)

plantilla Arreglo de figuras bidimensionales que se doblan para formar un poliedro.

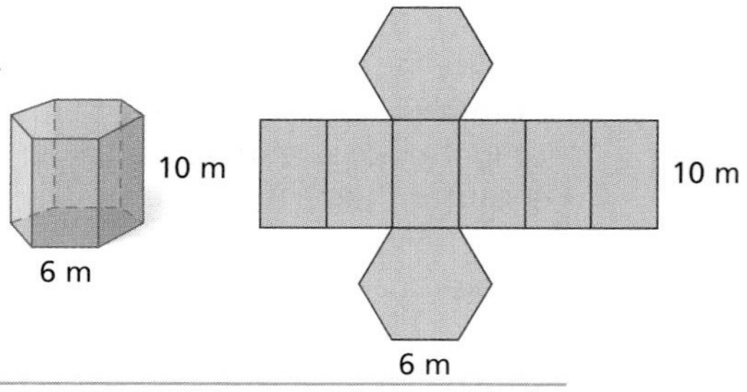

no correlation Two data sets have no correlation when there is no relationship between their data values. (p. 417)

sin correlación Caso en que los valores de dos conjuntos de datos no muestran ninguna relación.

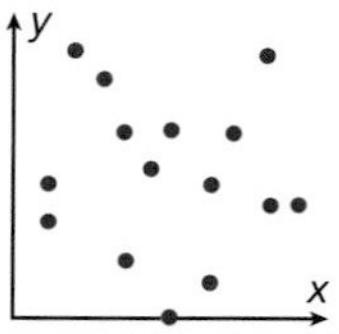

nonlinear function A function whose graph is not a straight line. (p. 254)

función no lineal Función cuya gráfica no es una línea recta.

nonterminating decimal A decimal that never ends. (p. 562)

decimal no cerrado Decimal que nunca termina.

numerator The top number of a fraction that tells how many parts of a whole are being considered.

numerador El número de arriba de una fracción; indica cuántas partes de un todo se están considerando.

$\frac{4}{5}$ ← numerator

numerical expression An expression that contains only numbers and operations. (p. 23)

expresión numérica Expresión matemática que incluye sólo números y símbolos matemáticos de operación.

$(2 \cdot 3) + 1$

O

obtuse angle An angle whose measure is greater than 90° but less than 180°. (p. 448)

ángulo obtuso Ángulo cuya medida es mayor de 90° pero menor de 180°.

obtuse triangle A triangle containing one obtuse angle. (p. 470)

triángulo obtusángulo Triángulo que tiene un ángulo obtuso.

octagon An eight-sided polygon. (p. 467)

octágono Polígono de ocho lados.

odd number An integer that is not divisible by two.

número impar Entero que no es divisible entre 2.

opposites Two numbers that are an equal distance from zero on a number line; also called *additive inverse.* (p. 76)

opuestos Dos números que están a la misma distancia de cero en una recta numérica. También se le llaman *inversos aditivos.*

5 and −5 are opposites.

ENGLISH	SPANISH	EXAMPLES
order of operations A rule for evaluating expressions: first perform the operations in parentheses, then compute powers and roots, then perform all multiplication and division from left to right, and then perform all addition and subtraction from left to right. (p. 23)	**orden de las operaciones** Regla para evaluar expresiones: primero se hacen las operaciones entre paréntesis, luego se hallan las potencias y raíces, después todas las multiplicaciones y divisiones de izquierda a derecha y, por último, todas las sumas y restas de izquierda a derecha.	$3^2 - 12 \div 4$ $9 - 12 \div 4$ Evaluate the power. $9 - 3$ Divide. 6 Subtract.
ordered pair A pair of numbers that can be used to locate a point on a coordinate plane. (p. 224)	**par ordenado** Par de números que sirven para localizar un punto en un plano cartesiano.	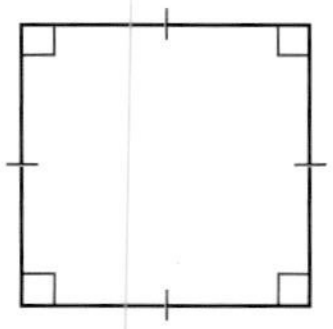 The coordinates of *B* are (−2, 3).
origin The point where the *x*-axis and *y*-axis intersect on the coordinate plane; (0, 0). (p. 224)	**origen** Punto de intersección entre el eje de las *x* y el eje de las *y* en un plano cartesiano: (0, 0).	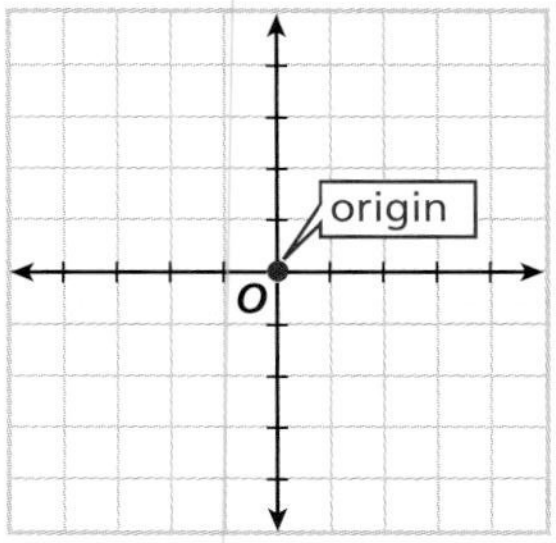
outcome A possible result of a probability experiment. (p. 628)	**resultado** Un posible resultado de un experimento de probabilidad.	When rolling a number cube, the possible outcomes are 1, 2, 3, 4, 5, and 6.
outlier A value much greater or much less than the others in a data set. (p. 382)	**valor extremo** Valor mucho mayor o mucho menor que los demás de un conjunto de datos.	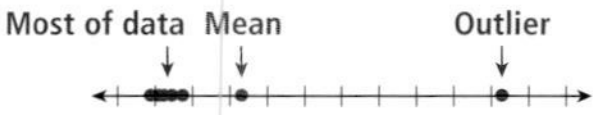
output The value that results from the substitution of a given input into an expression or function. (p. 238)	**valor de salida** Valor que resulta de la sustitución de un valor de entrada determinado en una expresión o función.	For the function $y = 6x$, the input 4 produces an output of 24.
overestimate An estimate that is greater than the exact answer.	**estimación alta** Estimación mayor que la respuesta exacta.	100 is an overestimate for the sum 23 + 24 + 21 + 22.

P

parallel lines Lines in a plane that do not intersect. (p. 452)	**líneas paralelas** Líneas que se encuentran en el mismo plano pero que nunca se intersecan.	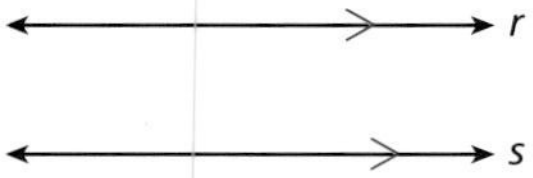
parallelogram A quadrilateral with two pairs of parallel sides. (p. 474)	**paralelogramo** Cuadrilátero con dos pares de lados paralelos.	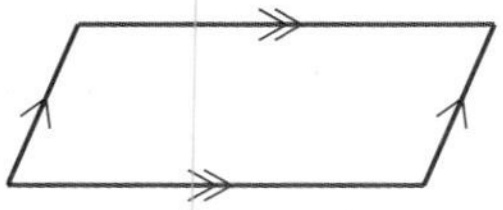

ENGLISH | **SPANISH** | **EXAMPLES**

pentagon A five-sided polygon. (p. 467)

pentágono Polígono de cinco lados.

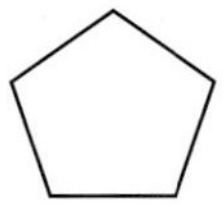

---

percent A ratio comparing a number to 100. (p. 330)

porcentaje Razón que compara un número con el número 100.

$45\% = \frac{45}{100}$

---

percent of change The amount stated as a percent that a number increases or decreases. (p. 352)

porcentaje de cambio Cantidad en que un número aumenta o disminuye.

---

percent of decrease A percent change describing a decrease in a quantity. (p. 352)

porcentaje de disminución Porcentaje de cambio en que una cantidad disminuye.

An item that costs \$8 is marked down to \$6. The amount of the decrease is \$2 and the percent of decrease is $\frac{2}{8} = 0.25 = 25\%$.

---

percent of increase A percent change describing an increase in a quantity. (p. 352)

porcentaje de incremento Porcentaje de cambio en que una cantidad aumenta.

The price of an item increases from \$8 to \$12. The amount of the increase is \$4 and the percent of increase is $\frac{4}{8} = 0.5 = 50\%$.

---

perfect square A square of a whole number. (p. 550)

cuadrado perfecto El cuadrado de un número cabal.

$5^2 = 25$, so 25 is a perfect square.

---

perimeter The distance around a polygon. (p. 524)

perímetro Distancia alrededor de un polígono.

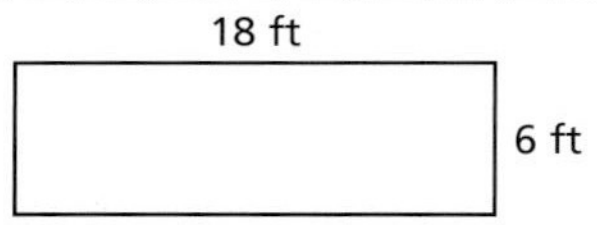

perimeter = $18 + 6 + 18 + 6 = 48$ ft

---

permutation An arrangement of items or events in which order is important. (p. 656)

permutación Arreglo de objetos o sucesos en el que el orden es importante.

For objects *A, B,* and *C,* there are 6 different permutations, *ABC, ACB, BAC, BCA, CAB, CBA.*

---

perpendicular bisector A line that intersects a segment at its midpoint and is perpendicular to the segment. (p. 456)

mediatriz Línea que cruza un segmento en su punto medio y es perpendicular al segmento.

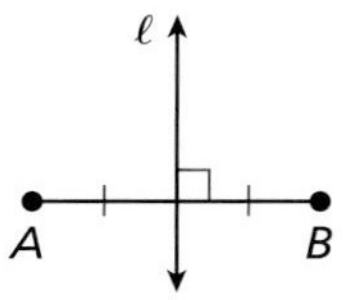

---

perpendicular lines Lines that intersect to form right angles. (p. 452)

líneas perpendiculares Líneas que al intersecarse forman ángulos rectos.

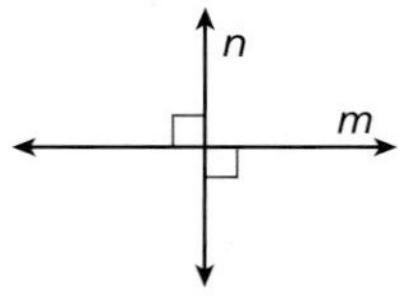

---

pi (π) The ratio of the circumference of a circle to the length of its diameter; $\pi \approx 3.14$ or $\frac{22}{7}$. (p. 525)

pi (π) Razón de la circunferencia de un círculo a la longitud de su diámetro; $\pi \approx 3.14$ ó $\frac{22}{7}$.

---

plane A flat surface that extends forever. (p. 442)

plano Superficie plana que se extiende de manera indefinida en todas direcciones.

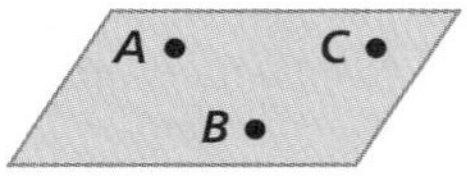

plane *ABC*

ENGLISH	SPANISH	EXAMPLES
point An exact location in space. (p. 442)	**punto** Ubicación exacta en el espacio.	*P* • point *P*
polygon A closed plane figure formed by three or more line segments that intersect only at their endpoints (vertices). (p. 466)	**polígono** Figura plana cerrada, formada por tres o más segmentos de recta que se intersecan sólo en sus extremos (vértices).	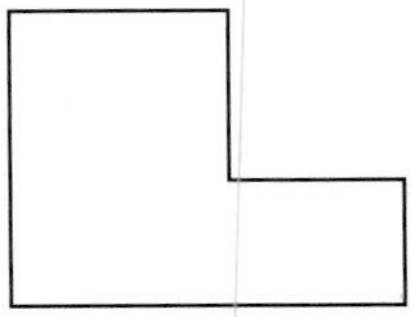
polyhedron A three-dimensional figure in which all the surfaces or faces are polygons. (p. 580)	**poliedro** Figura tridimensional cuyas superficies o caras tienen forma de polígonos.	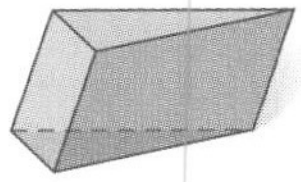
population The entire group of objects or individuals considered for a survey. (p. 412)	**población** Grupo completo de objetos o individuos que se desea estudiar.	In a survey about the study habits of middle school students, the population is all middle school students.
positive correlation Two data sets have a positive correlation, or relationship, when their data values increase or decrease together. (p. 417)	**correlación positiva** Dos conjuntos de datos tienen una correlación, o relación, positiva cuando los valores de datos de ambos conjuntos aumentan o disminuyen al mismo tiempo.	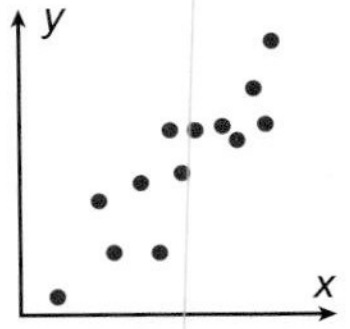
positive integer An integer greater than zero. (p. 76)	**entero positivo** Entero mayor que cero.	
power A number produced by raising a base to an exponent. (p. 10)	**potencia** Número que resulta al elevar una base a un exponente.	$2^3 = 8$, so 2 to the 3rd power is 8.
precision The level of detail of a measurement, determined by the unit of measure. (p. 518)	**precisión** Detalle de una medición, determinado por la unidad de medida.	A ruler marked in millimeters has a greater level of precision than a ruler marked in centimeters.
prime factorization A number written as the product of its prime factors. (p. 106)	**factorización prima** Proceso de escritura de un número como el producto de sus factores primos.	$10 = 2 \cdot 5$ $24 = 2^3 \cdot 3$
prime number A whole number greater than 1 that has exactly two factors, itself and 1. (p. 106)	**número primo** Número cabal mayor que 1 que sólo es divisible entre 1 y entre él mismo.	5 is prime because its only factors are 5 and 1.
principal The initial amount of money borrowed or saved. (p. 356)	**capital** Cantidad inicial de dinero depositada o recibida en préstamo.	
prism A polyhedron that has two congruent polygon-shaped bases and other faces that are all parallelograms. (p. 580)	**prisma** Poliedro con dos bases congruentes con forma de polígono y caras con forma de rectángulos.	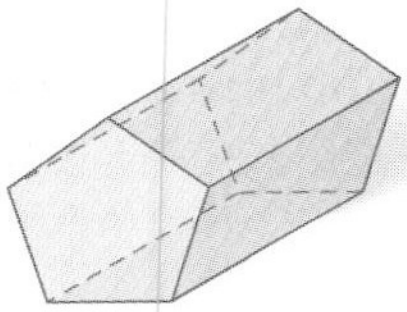
probability A number from 0 to 1 (or 0% to 100%) that describes how likely an event is to occur. (p. 628)	**probabilidad** Un número entre 0 y 1 ó 0% y 100% que describe qué tan probable es un suceso.	A bag contains 3 red marbles and 4 blue marbles. The probability of randomly choosing a red marble is $\frac{3}{7}$.

ENGLISH	SPANISH	EXAMPLES

product The result when two or more numbers are multiplied.

producto Resultado de multiplicar dos o más números.

---

proper fraction A fraction in which the numerator is less than the denominator.

fracción propia Fracción en la que el numerador es menor que el denominador.

$\frac{3}{4}, \frac{1}{13}, \frac{7}{8}$

---

proportion An equation that states that two ratios are equivalent. (p. 283)

proporción Ecuación que establece que dos razones son equivalentes.

$\frac{2}{3} = \frac{4}{6}$

---

protractor A tool for measuring angles. (p. 448)

transportador Instrumento para medir ángulos.

---

pyramid A polyhedron with a polygon base and triangular sides that all meet at a common vertex. (p. 580)

pirámide Poliedro cuya base es un polígono y tiene caras triangulares que terminan en punta.

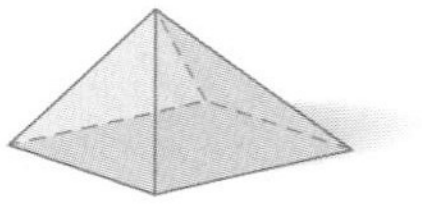

Pythagorean Theorem In a right triangle, the square of the length of the hypotenuse is equal to the sum of the squares of the lengths of the legs. (p. 556)

Teorema de Pitágoras En un triángulo rectángulo, la suma de los cuadrados de los catetos es igual al cuadrado de la hipotenusa.

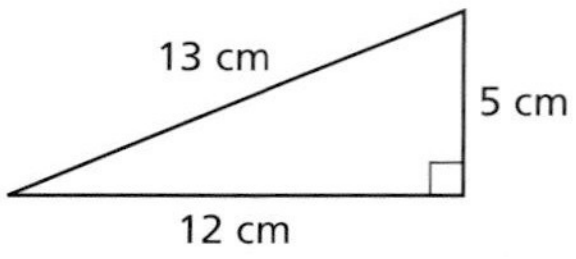

$5^2 + 12^2 = 13^2$

$25 + 144 = 169$

Q

quadrant The x- and y-axes divide the coordinate plane into four regions. Each region is called a quadrant. (p. 224)

cuadrante El eje de las x y el eje de las y dividen el plano cartesiano en cuatro regiones. Cada región recibe el nombre de cuadrante.

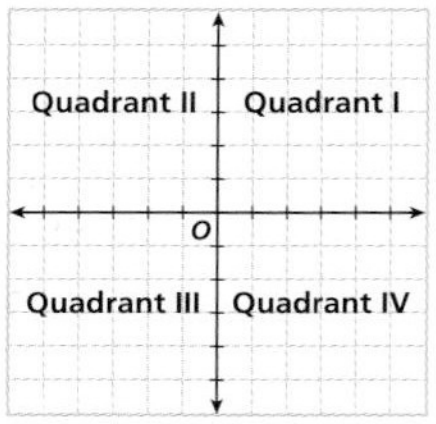

---

quadratic function A function of the form $y = ax^2 + bx + c$, where $a \neq 0$. (p. 783)

función cuadrática Función escrita en la forma $y = ax^2 + bx + c$, donde $a \neq 0$.

$y = 2x^2 - 12x + 10$,
$y = 3x^2$

---

quadrilateral A four-sided polygon. (p. 467)

cuadrilátero Polígono de cuatro lados.

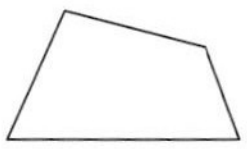

---

quartile Three values, one of which is the median, that divide a data set into fourths. See also *first quartile, third quartile.* (p. 394)

cuartiles Se trata de tres valores, uno de los cuales es la mediana, que dividen en cuartos un conjunto de datos. Ver también *primer cuartil, tercer cuartil.*

---

quotient The result when one number is divided by another.

cociente Resultado de dividir un número entre otro.

In $8 \div 4 = 2$, 2 is the quotient.

ENGLISH	SPANISH	EXAMPLES

R

ENGLISH	SPANISH	EXAMPLES
radical sign The symbol $\sqrt{}$ used to represent the nonnegative square root of a number. (p. 550)	**símbolo de radical** El símbolo $\sqrt{}$ con que se representa la raíz cuadrada no negativa de un número.	$\sqrt{36} = 6$
radius A line segment with one endpoint at the center of a circle and the other endpoint on the circle, or the length of that segment. (p. 460)	**radio** Segmento de recta con un extremo en el centro de un círculo y el otro en la circunferencia. También se llama radio a la longitud de ese segmento.	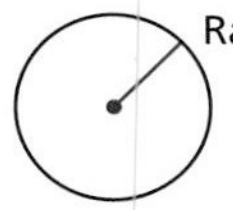
random sample A sample in which each individual or object in the entire population has an equal chance of being selected. (p. 412)	**muestra aleatoria** Muestra representativa que da a cada miembro de una población la misma oportunidad de ser elegido.	Mr. Henson chose a random sample of the class by writing each student's name on a slip of paper, mixing up the slips, and drawing five slips without looking.
range (in statistics) The difference between the greatest and least values in a data set. (p. 381)	**rango (en estadística)** Diferencia entre los valores máximo y mínimo de un conjunto de datos.	Data set: 3, 5, 7, 7, 12 Range: $12 - 3 = 9$
rate A ratio that compares two quantities measured in different units. (p. 274)	**relación** Comparación de dos cantidades expresadas con unidades diferentes.	The speed limit is 55 miles per hour, or 55 mi/h.
rate of interest The percent charged or earned on an amount of money; see *simple interest.* (p. 356)	**tasa de interés** Porcentaje que se cobra por una cantidad de dinero prestada o que se gana por una cantidad de dinero ahorrada; ver *interés simple.*	
ratio A comparison of two quantities by division. (p. 270)	**razón** Comparación de dos cantidades mediante una división.	12 to 25, 12:25, $\frac{12}{25}$
rational number Any number that can be expressed as a ratio of two integers. (p. 129)	**número racional** Número que se puede escribir como una razón de dos enteros.	6 can be expressed as $\frac{6}{1}$. 0.5 can be expressed $\frac{1}{2}$.
ray A part of a line that starts at one endpoint and extends forever. (p. 443)	**rayo** Parte de una línea que inicia en un extremo y se extiende de manera indefinida.	
real number A rational or irrational number.	**número real** Número racional o irracional.	
reciprocal One of two numbers whose product is 1; also called *multiplicative inverse.* (p. 200)	**recíproco** Uno de dos números cuyo producto es igual a 1. También se llama *inverso multiplicativo.*	The reciprocal of $\frac{2}{3}$ is $\frac{3}{2}$.
rectangle A parallelogram with four right angles. (p. 474)	**rectángulo** Paralelogramo con cuatro ángulos rectos.	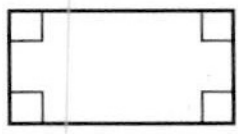

ENGLISH	SPANISH	EXAMPLES

rectangular prism A polyhedron whose bases are rectangles and whose other faces are parallelograms. (p. 580)

prisma rectangular Poliedro cuyas bases son rectángulos y sus caras tiene forma de rectángulos.

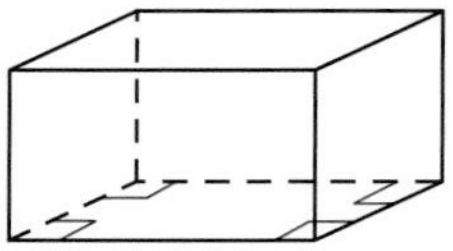

reflection A transformation of a figure that flips the figure across a line. (p. 488)

reflexión Transformación que ocurre cuando se voltea una figura sobre una línea.

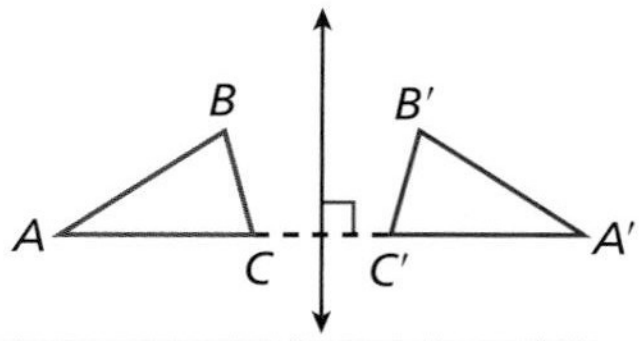

regular polygon A polygon with congruent sides and angles. (p. 467)

polígono regular Polígono con lados y ángulos congruentes.

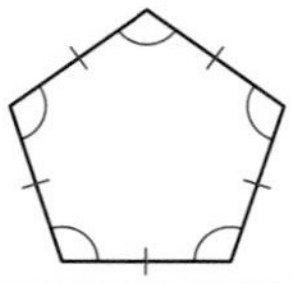

repeating decimal A decimal in which one or more digits repeat infinitely. (p. 124)

decimal periódico Decimal en el que uno o más dígitos se repiten de manera indefinida.

$0.757575\ldots = 0.\overline{75}$

rhombus A parallelogram with all sides congruent. (p. 474)

rombo Paralelogramo en el que todos los lados son congruentes.

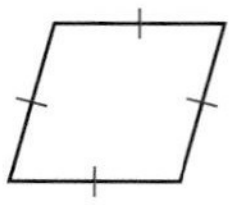

right angle An angle that measures 90°. (p. 448)

ángulo recto Ángulo que mide exactamente 90°.

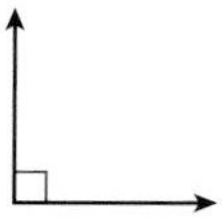

right triangle A triangle containing a right angle. (p. 470)

triángulo rectángulo Triángulo que tiene un ángulo recto.

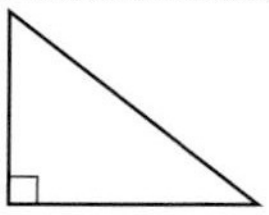

rise The vertical change when the slope of a line is expressed as the ratio $\frac{\text{rise}}{\text{run}}$, or "rise over run." (p. 278)

distancia vertical El cambio vertical cuando la pendiente de una línea se expresa como la razón $\frac{\text{distancia vertical}}{\text{distancia horizontal}}$, o "distancia vertical sobre distancia horizontal".

For the points $(3, -1)$ and $(6, 5)$, the rise is $5 - (-1) = 6$.

rotation A transformation in which a figure is turned around a point. (p. 488)

rotación Transformación que ocurre cuando una figura gira alrededor de un punto.

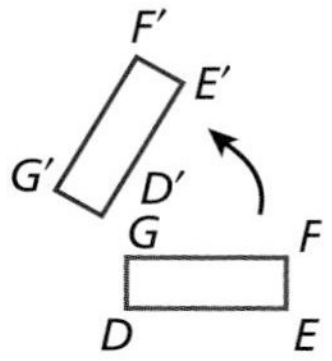

rotational symmetry A figure has rotational symmetry if it can be rotated less than 360° around a central point and coincide with the original figure. (p. 495)

simetría de rotación Ocurre cuando una figura gira menos de 360° alrededor de un punto sin dejar de ser congruente con la figura original.

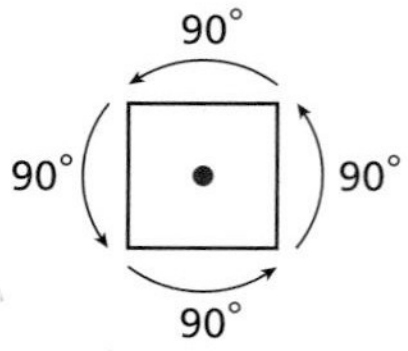

rounding Replacing a number with an estimate of that number to a given place value.

redondear Sustituir un número por una estimación de ese número hasta cierto valor posicional.

2,354 rounded to the nearest thousand is 2,000, and 2,354 rounded to the nearest 100 is 2,400.

ENGLISH	SPANISH	EXAMPLES
run The horizontal change when the slope of a line is expressed as the ratio $\frac{\text{rise}}{\text{run}}$, or "rise over run." (p. 278)	**distancia horizontal** El cambio horizontal cuando la pendiente de una línea se expresa como la razón $\frac{\text{distancia vertical}}{\text{distancia horizontal}}$, o "distancia vertical sobre distancia horizontal".	For the points (3, −1) and (6, 5), the run is 6 − 3 = 3.

S

ENGLISH	SPANISH	EXAMPLES
sales tax A percent of the cost of an item, which is charged by governments to raise money.	**impuesto sobre la venta** Porcentaje del precio de un artículo que los gobiernos cobran para recaudar fondos.	
sample A part of the population. (p. 412)	**muestra** Parte del grupo o población que se desea estudiar.	In a survey about the study habits of middle school students, a sample is a survey of 100 randomly-chosen students.
sample space All possible outcomes of an experiment. (p. 636)	**espacio muestral** Conjunto de todos los resultados posibles de un experimento.	When rolling a number cube, the sample space is 1, 2, 3, 4, 5, 6.
scale The ratio between two sets of measurements. (p. 308)	**escala** La razón entre dos conjuntos de medidas.	1 cm:5 mi
scale drawing A drawing that uses a scale to make an object smaller than or larger than the real object. (p. 308)	**dibujo a escala** Dibujo que usa una escala para que un objeto se vea proporcionalmente mayor o menor que el objeto real al que representa.	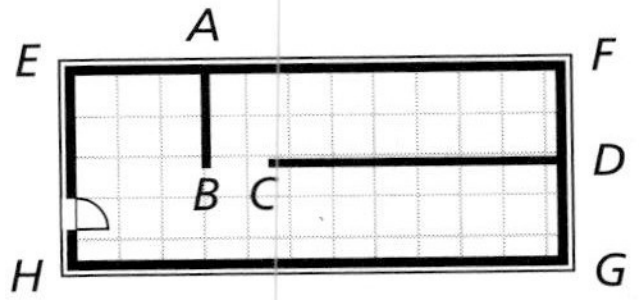 A blueprint is an example of a scale drawing.
scale factor The ratio used to enlarge or reduce similar figures. (p. 308)	**factor de escala** Razón que se usa para agrandar o reducir figuras semejantes.	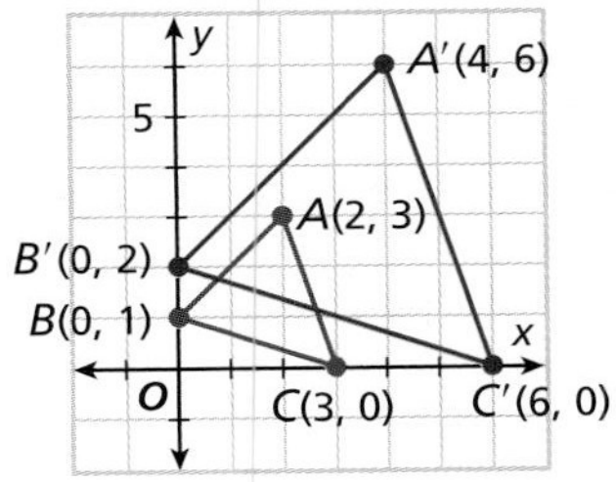 Scale factor: 2
scale model A proportional model of a three-dimensional object. (p. 308)	**modelo a escala** Modelo proporcional de un objeto tridimensional.	
scalene triangle A triangle with no congruent sides. (p. 470)	**triángulo escaleno** Triángulo que no tiene lados congruentes.	

ENGLISH	SPANISH	EXAMPLES
scatter plot A graph with points plotted to show a possible relationship between two sets of data. (p. 416)	**diagrama de dispersión** Gráfica de puntos que se usa para mostrar una posible relación entre dos conjuntos de datos.	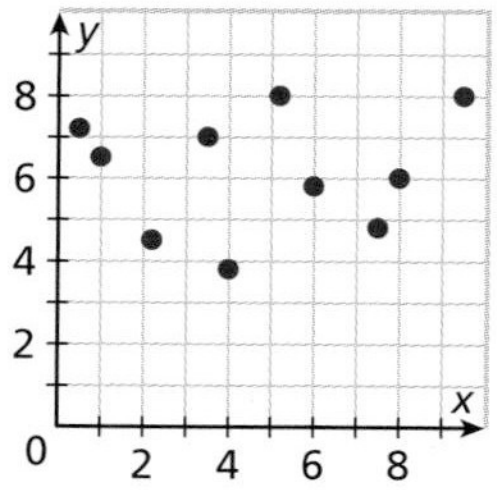
scientific notation A method of writing very large or very small numbers by using powers of 10. (p. 18)	**notación científica** Método abreviado que se usa para escribir números muy largos o muy pequeños usando potencias de 10.	$12{,}560{,}000{,}000{,}000 = 1.256 \times 10^{13}$
second quartile The median of a set of data. (p. 394)	**segundo cuartil** Mediana de un conjunto de datos.	
sector A region enclosed by two radii and the arc joining their endpoints. (p. 461)	**sector** Región encerrada por dos radios y el arco que une sus extremos.	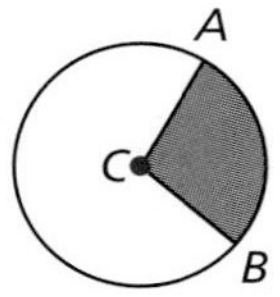
sector (data) A section of a circle graph representing part of the data set. (p. 390)	**sector (datos)** Sección de una gráfica circular que representa una parte del conjunto de datos.	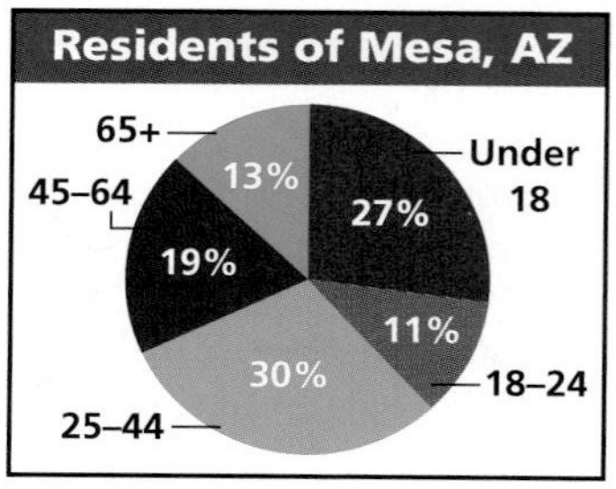 The circle graph has 5 sectors.
segment A part of a line between two endpoints. (p. 442)	**segmento** Parte de una línea entre dos extremos.	
sequence An ordered list of numbers. (p. 242)	**sucesión** Lista ordenada de números.	2, 4, 6, 8, 10, ...
side A line bounding a geometric figure; one of the faces forming the outside of an object. (p. 466)	**lado** Segmento de recta que delimita las figuras geométricas; una de las caras que forman la parte exterior de un objeto.	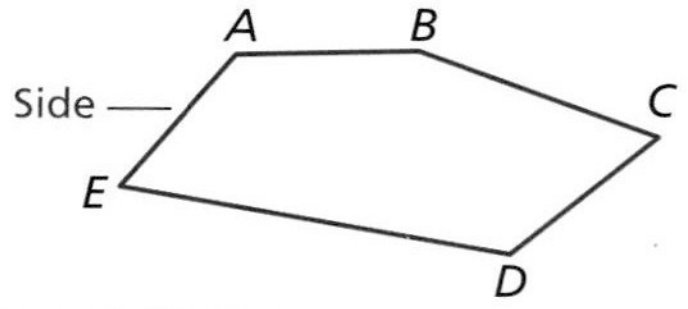
Side-Side-Side (SSS) A rule stating that if three sides of one triangle are congruent to three sides of another triangle, then the triangles are congruent. (p. 484)	**Lado-Lado-Lado (LLL)** Regla que establece que dos triángulos son congruentes cuando sus tres lados correspondientes son congruentes.	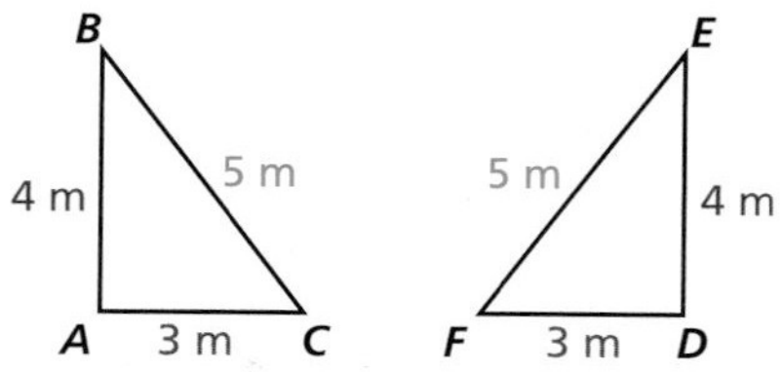 $\triangle ABC \cong \triangle DEF$
significant digits The digits used to express the precision of a measurement. (p. 518)	**dígitos significativos** Dígitos usados para expresar la exactitud de una medida.	0.048 has 2 significant digits. 5.003 has 4 significant digits.

ENGLISH	SPANISH	EXAMPLES

similar Figures with the same shape but not necessarily the same size are similar. (p. 300)

semejantes Figuras que tienen la misma forma, pero no necesariamente el mismo tamaño.

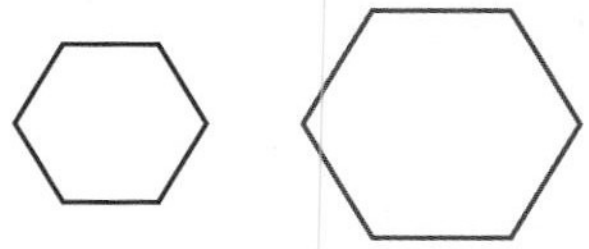

---

simple interest A fixed percent of the principal. It is found using the formula $I = Prt$, where P represents the principal, r the rate of interest, and t the time. (p. 356)

interés simple Un porcentaje fijo del capital. Se calcula con la fórmula $I = Crt$, donde C representa el capital, r, la tasa de interés, y t, el tiempo.

\$100 is put into an account with a simple interest rate of 5%. After 2 years, the account will have earned
$I = 100 \cdot 0.05 \cdot 2 = \$10$.

---

simplest form A fraction is in simplest form when the numerator and denominator have no common factors other than 1.

mínima expresión Una fracción está en su mínima expresión cuando el numerador y el denominador no tienen más factor común que 1.

Fraction: $\frac{8}{12}$
Simplest form: $\frac{2}{3}$

---

simplify To write a fraction or expression in simplest form.

simplificar Escribir una fracción o expresión en su mínima expresión.

---

skew lines Lines that lie in different planes that are neither parallel nor intersecting. (p. 452)

líneas oblicuas Líneas que se encuentran en planos distintos, por eso no se intersecan ni son paralelas.

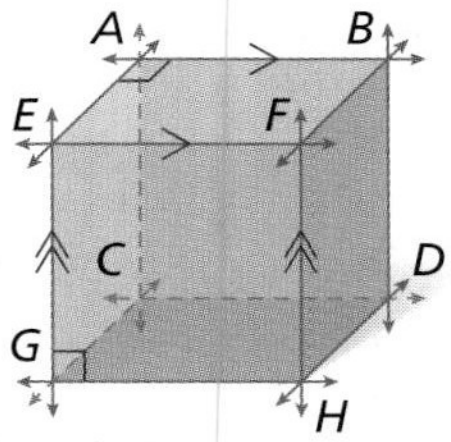

$\overleftrightarrow{AE}$ and $\overleftrightarrow{CD}$ are skew lines.

---

slope A measure of the steepness of a line on a graph; the rise divided by the run. (p. 278)

pendiente Medida de la inclinación de una línea en una gráfica. Razón de la distancia vertical a la distancia horizontal.

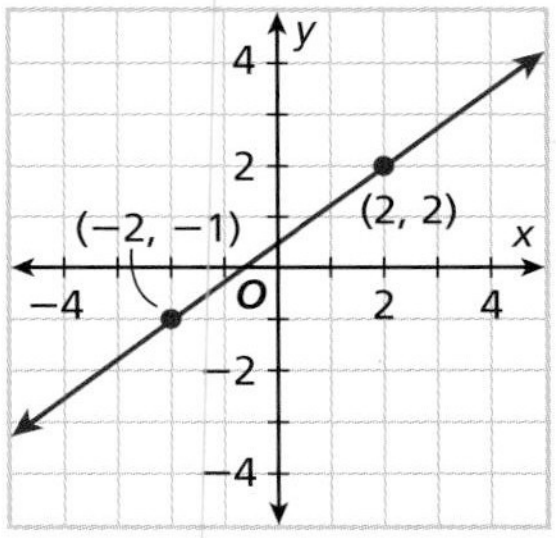

Slope $= \frac{\text{rise}}{\text{run}} = \frac{3}{4}$

---

solid figure A three-dimensional figure. (p. 586)

figura sólida Figura tridimensional.

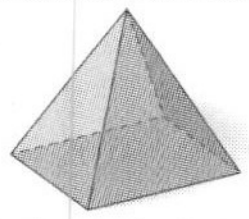

---

solution of an equation A value or values that make an equation true. (p. 46)

solución de una ecuación Valor o valores que hacen correcta una ecuación.

Equation: $x + 2 = 6$
Solution: $x = 4$

---

solution of an inequality A value or values that make an inequality true. (p. 692)

solución de una desigualdad Valor o valores que hacen correcta una desigualdad.

Inequality: $x + 3 \geq 10$
Solution: $x \geq 7$

---

solution set The set of values that make a statement true. (p. 692)

conjunto solución Conjunto de valores que hacen verdadero un enunciado.

Inequality: $x + 3 \geq 5$
Solution set: $x \geq 2$

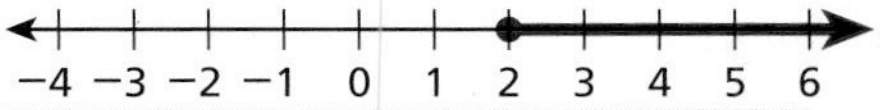

---

solve To find an answer or a solution. (p. 110)

resolver Hallar una respuesta o solución.

ENGLISH	SPANISH	EXAMPLES

square (geometry) A rectangle with four congruent sides. (p. 474)

cuadrado (en geometría) Rectángulo con cuatro lados congruentes.

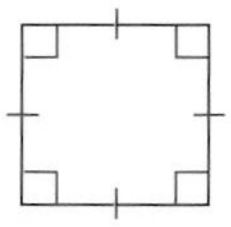

---

square (numeration) A number raised to the second power. (p. 550)

cuadrado (en numeración) Número elevado a la segunda potencia.

In 5^2, the number 5 is squared.

---

square number The product of a number and itself. (p. 550)

cuadrado de un número El producto de un número multiplicado por sí mismo.

25 is a square number.
$5 \cdot 5 = 25$.

---

square root One of the two equal factors of a number. (p. 550)

raíz cuadrada Uno de los dos factores iguales de un número.

$16 = 4 \cdot 4$ and $16 = -4 \cdot -4$, so 4 and -4 are square roots of 16.

---

standard form (in numeration) A way to write numbers by using digits. (p. 65)

forma estándar (en numeración) Una manera de escribir números usando dígitos.

Five thousand, two hundred ten in standard form is 5,210.

---

stem-and-leaf plot A graph used to organize and display data so that the frequencies can be compared. (p. 377)

diagrama doble de tallo y hojas Gráfica que muestra y ordena los datos por valor posicional, de modo que se puedan comparar las frecuencias.

Stem	Leaves
3	2 3 4 4 7 9
4	0 1 5 7 7 7 8
5	1 2 2 3

Key: 3|2 means 32

---

straight angle An angle that measures 180°. (p. 448)

ángulo llano Ángulo que mide exactamente 180°.

---

substitute To replace a variable with a number or another expression in an algebraic expression.

sustituir Reemplazar una variable por un número u otra expresión en una expresión algebraica.

Subtraction Property of Equality The property that states that if you subtract the same number from both sides of an equation, the new equation will have the same solution. (p. 53)

Propiedad de igualdad de la resta Propiedad que establece que puedes restar el mismo número en ambos lados de una ecuación y la ecuación resultante tendrá la misma ecuación.

$$\begin{array}{rcr} x + 6 & = & 8 \\ -\ 6 & & -\ 6 \\ \hline x & = & 2 \end{array}$$

---

sum The result when two or more numbers are added.

suma Resultado de sumar dos o más números.

The sum of 6 + 7 + 1 is 14.

---

supplementary angles Two angles whose measures have a sum of 180°. (p. 448)

ángulos suplementarios Dos ángulos cuyas medidas suman 180°.

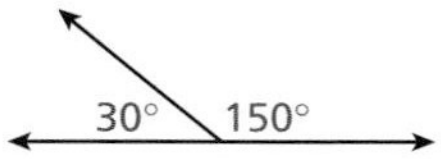

---

surface area The sum of the areas of the faces, or surfaces, of a three-dimensional figure. (p. 597)

área total Suma de las áreas de las caras, o superficies, de una figura tridimensional.

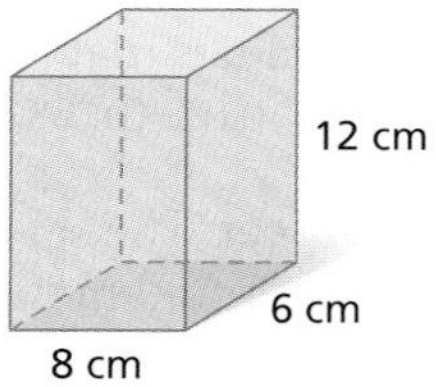

Surface area = 2(8)(12) + 2(8)(6) + 2(12)(6) = 432 cm^2

ENGLISH | **SPANISH** | **EXAMPLES**

T

term (in an expression) The parts of an expression that are added or subtracted. (p. 42)

término (en una expresión) Las partes de una expresión que se suman o se restan.

$3x^2 + 6x - 8$ (Term, Term, Term)

---

term (in a sequence) An element or number in a sequence. (p. 242)

término (de una sucesión) Elemento o número de una sucesión.

5 is the third term in the sequence 1, 3, 5, 7, 9, . . .

---

terminating decimal A decimal number that ends or terminates. (p. 124)

decimal cerrado Decimal con un número determinado de posiciones decimales.

6.75

---

tessellation A repeating pattern of plane figures that completely covers a plane with no gaps or overlaps. (p. 498)

teselado Patrón repetido de figuras planas que cubren totalmente un plano sin traslaparse ni dejar huecos.

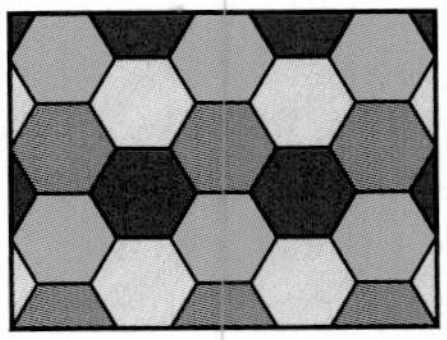

---

theoretical probability The ratio of the number of equally likely outcomes in an event to the total number of possible outcomes. (p. 640)

probabilidad teórica Razón del número de resultados igualmente probables al número de resultados posibles.

When rolling a number cube, the theoretical probability of rolling a 4 is $\frac{1}{6}$.

---

third quartile The median of the upper half of a set of data; also called *upper quartile.* (p. 394)

tercer cuartil La mediana de la mitad superior de un conjunto de datos. También se llama *cuartil superior.*

---

transformation A change in the position or orientation of a figure. (p. 488)

transformación Cambio en el tamaño o la posición de una figura.

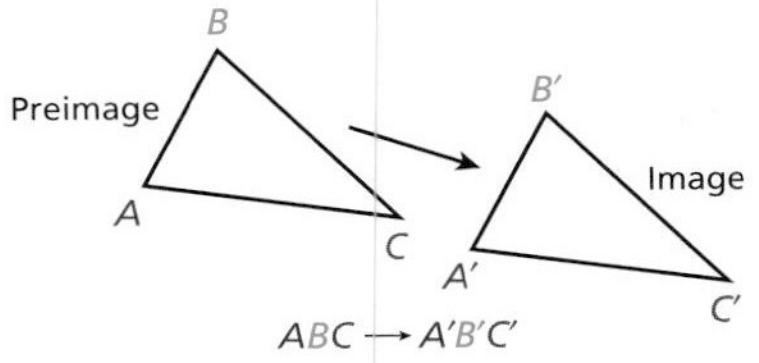

---

translation A movement (slide) of a figure along a straight line. (p. 488)

traslación Desplazamiento de una figura a lo largo de una línea recta.

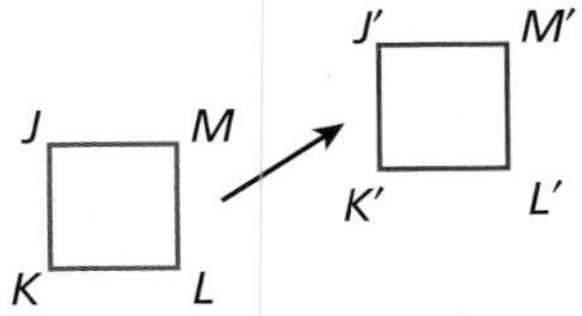

---

transversal A line that intersects two or more lines. (p. 453)

transversal Línea que cruza dos o más líneas.

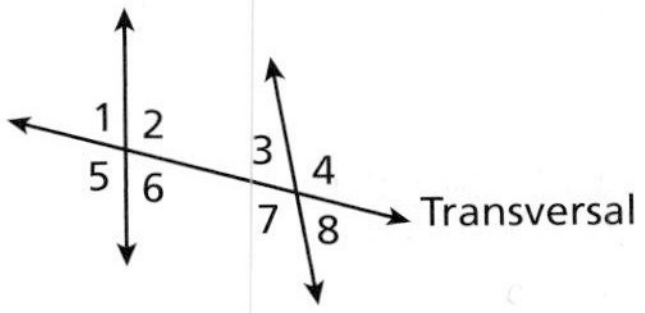

---

trapezoid A quadrilateral with exactly one pair of parallel sides. (p. 474)

trapecio Cuadrilátero con un par de lados paralelos.

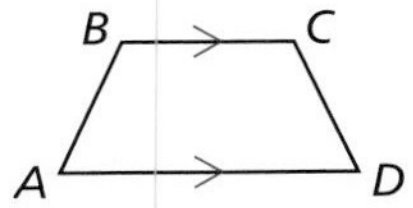

ENGLISH	SPANISH	EXAMPLES
tree diagram A branching diagram that shows all possible combinations or outcomes of an event. (p. 637)	**diagrama de árbol** Diagrama ramificado que muestra todas las posibles combinaciones o resultados de un suceso.	
trial In probability, a single repetition or observation of an experiment. (p. 628)	**prueba** En probabilidad, una sola repetición u observación de un experimento.	When rolling a number cube, each roll is one trial.
triangle A three-sided polygon. (p. 467)	**triángulo** Polígono de tres lados.	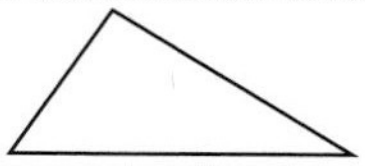
Triangle Sum Theorem The theorem that states that the measures of the angles in a triangle add to 180°.	**Teorema de la suma del triángulo** Teorema que establece que los ángulos de un triángulo suman 180°.	
triangular prism A polyhedron whose bases are triangles and whose other faces are parallelograms. (p. 580)	**prisma triangular** Poliedro cuyas bases son triángulos y sus demás caras tienen forma de rectángulos.	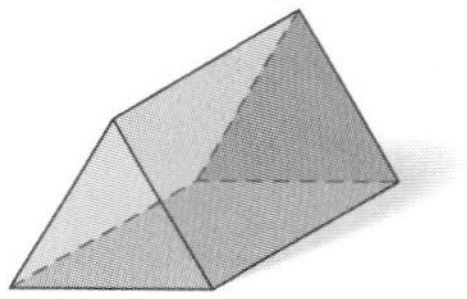

U

ENGLISH	SPANISH	EXAMPLES
underestimate An estimate that is less than the exact answer.	**estimación baja** Estimación menor que la respuesta exacta.	
unit conversion The process of changing one unit of measure to another. (p. 314)	**conversión de unidades** Proceso que consiste en cambiar una unidad de medición en otra.	
unit conversion factor A fraction used in unit conversion in which the numerator and denominator represent the same amount but are in different units. (p. 314)	**factor de conversión de unidades** Fracción que se usa para la conversión de unidades, en donde el numerador y el denominador representan la misma cantidad pero están en unidades distintas.	$\frac{60 \text{ min}}{1 \text{ h}}$ or $\frac{1 \text{ h}}{60 \text{ min}}$
unit price A unit rate used to compare prices.	**precio unitario** Tasa unitaria que sirve para comparar precios.	
unit rate A rate in which the second quantity in the comparison is one unit. (p. 274)	**tasa unitaria** Una relación en donde la segunda cantidad de comparación es la unidad.	10 cm per minute
upper quartile The median of the upper half of a set of data. (p. 394)	**cuartil superior** La mediana de la mitad superior de un conjunto de datos.	Lower half Upper half 18, 23, 28, 29, (36,) 42 ↑ Upper quartile

ENGLISH	SPANISH	EXAMPLES

V

variable A symbol used to represent a quantity that can change. (p. 34)

variable Letra o símbolo que representa una cantidad que puede cambiar.

In the expression $2x + 3$, x is the variable.

Venn diagram A diagram that is used to show relationships between sets.

diagrama de Venn Diagrama que sirve para ilustrar las relaciones entre conjuntos.

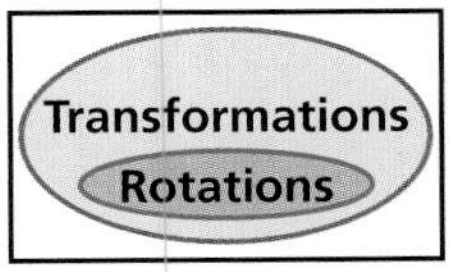

verbal expression A word or phrase. (p. 38)

expresión verbal Palabra o frase.

vertex On an angle or polygon, the point where two sides intersect. (p. 448)

vértice En un ángulo o polígono, el punto de intersección de dos lados.

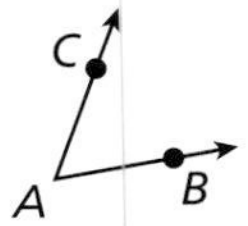

A is the vertex of $\angle CAB$.

vertical angles A pair of opposite congruent angles formed by intersecting lines. (p. 453)

ángulos opuestos por el vértice Par de ángulos opuestos congruentes formados por rectas secantes.

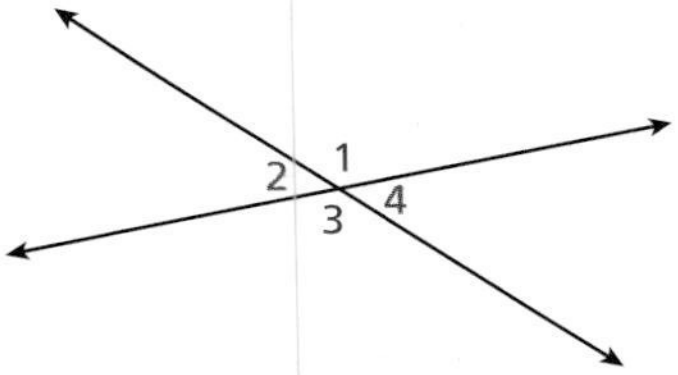

$\angle 1$ and $\angle 3$ are vertical angles.
$\angle 2$ and $\angle 4$ are vertical angles.

volume The number of cubic units needed to fill a given space. (p. 586)

volumen Número de unidades cúbicas que se necesitan para llenar un espacio.

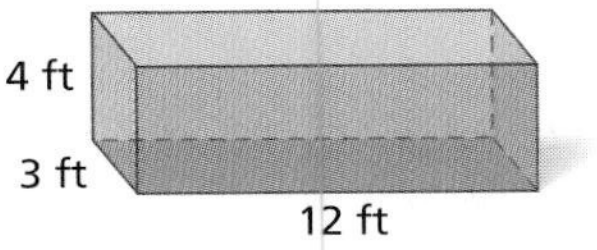

Volume $= 3 \cdot 4 \cdot 12 = 144\ ft^3$

X

***x*-axis** The horizontal axis on a coordinate plane. (p. 224)

eje de las *x* El eje horizontal del plano cartesiano.

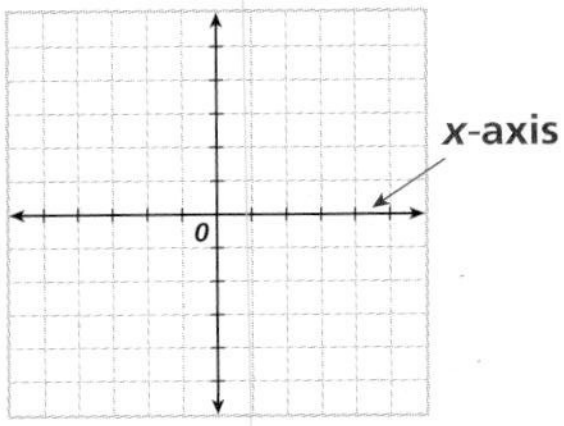

ENGLISH	SPANISH	EXAMPLES
***x*-coordinate** The first number in an ordered pair; it tells the distance to move right or left from the origin, (0, 0). (p. 224)	**coordenada *x*** El primer valor en un par ordenado; indica la distancia que debes avanzar hacia la izquierda o la derecha desde el origen, (0, 0).	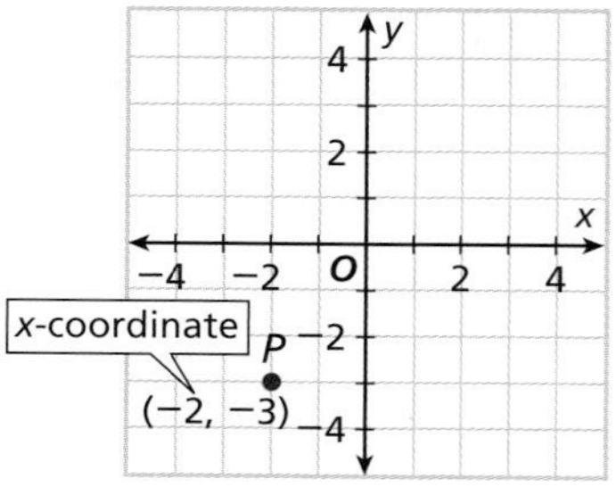

Y

***y*-axis** The vertical axis on a coordinate plane. (p. 224)	**eje de las *y*** El eje vertical del plano cartesiano.	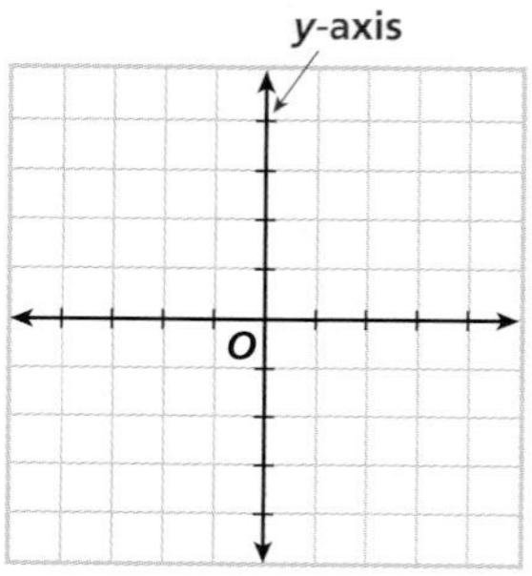
***y*-coordinate** The second number in an ordered pair; it tells the distance to move up or down from the origin, (0, 0). (p. 224)	**coordenada *y*** El segundo valor de un par ordenado; indica la distancia que debes avanzar hacia arriba o abajo desde el origen, (0, 0).	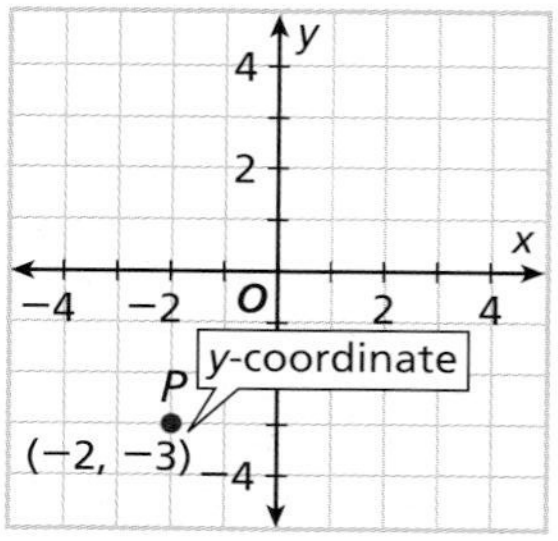

Index

A

B

C

D

Index

T

Credits

Staff Credits

Bruce Albrecht, Margaret Chalmers, Justin Collins, Lorraine Cooper, Marc Cooper, Jennifer Craycraft, Martize Cross, Nina Degollado, Lydia Doty, Sam Dudgeon, Kelli R. Flanagan, Mary Fraser, Stephanie Friedman, Jeff Galvez, José Garza, Diannia Green, Jennifer Gribble, Liz Huckestein, Jevara Jackson, Kadonna Knape, Cathy Kuhles, Jill M. Lawson, Peter Leighton, Christine MacInnis, Rosalyn K. Mack, Jonathan Martindill, Virginia Messler, Susan Mussey, Kim Nguyen, Matthew Osment, Theresa Reding, Manda Reid, Patrick Ricci, Michael Rinella, Michelle Rumpf-Dike, Beth Sample, Annette Saunders, John Saxe, Kay Selke, Robyn Setzen, Patricia Sinnott, Victoria Smith, Jeannie Taylor, Ken Whiteside, Sherri Whitmarsh, Aimee F. Wiley, Alison Wohlman

Photo Credits

Chapter 1: 2, (bkgd), © AFP/CORBIS; 2, (br), David Gamble/Sygma; 6 (tr), © Royalty Free Corbis; 11, (cl), © AFP/CORBIS; 13, (tl), Bruce Iverson; 13, (tr), Bruce Iverson; 13, (bl), Bruce Iverson; 13, (br), Bruce Iverson; 14 (tr), Yoshikazu Tsuno/AFP/GettyImages; 17 (cl), National Geographic/GettyImages; 18 (tr), © Bill Frymire/Masterfile 105, (b), Sam Dudgeon/HRW/Sheet music courtesy Martha Dudgeon.; 26 (br), Sam Dudgeon/HRW; 33 (bc), EyeWire - Digital Image copyright © (2004) EyeWire; 34 (t), Everett Collection; 34 (b), Frederic De Lafosse/Sygma; 34 (c), Ulvis Alberts/Motion Picture & Television Photo Archive; 38 © David Allan Brandt/Getty Images/Stone; 41 (l), Photo Researchers, Inc.; 42 (tr), Digital Vision/GettyImages; 45 Courtesy of the National Grocers Association Best Bagger Contest; 46 (tr), Peter Van Steen/HRW; 47 (r), Sam Dudgeon/HRW/Courtesy Fast Forward Skate Shop, Austin, TX; 47 (l), Sam Dudgeon/HRW/Courtesy Fast Forward Skate Shop, Austin, TX; 49 (br), James Urbach/SuperStock; 57 © Reuters NewMedia Inc./CORBIS; 61 (cr), PhotoDisc/GettyImages; 62 (cl), © Jenny Thomas/HRW; 62 (cr), © Jenny Thomas/HRW; 62 (b), © Jenny Thomas/HRW **Chapter 2:** 72 (br), © Jay Ireland & Georgienne E. Bradley; 72 (bkgd), Tom Pantages Photography; 76 (br), Chuck Nicklin/Al Giddings Images, Inc.; 76 (tl), NATALIE B. FORBES National Geographic Image Collection; 79 (l), © Neil Rabinowitz/CORBIS; 82 ©2001 Jay Mallin; 85 (l), © Lee Foster/Words & Pictures/PictureQuest; 91 (t), © CORBIS; 95 © W. Faidley/WeatherStock; 97 © Ann Purcell; Carl Purcell/Words & Pictures/PictureQuest; 110 (tr), Sam Dudgeon/HRW; 111 (tr), Victoria Smith/HRW; 111 (cr), Victoria Smith/HRW; 113 (l), Collection Walker Art Center, Minneapolis Gift of Fredrick R. Weisman in honor of his parents, William and Mary Weisman, 1988; 117 (t), © D. Donne Bryant/DDB Stock Photo/All Rights Reserved; 117 (b), Erich Lessing/Art Resource, NY; 119 (b), Lisette LeBon/SuperStock; 120 Victoria Smith/HRW; 123 (l), Michael Rosenfeld/Stone/Getty Images; 124 (tr), © Tim Johnson/Reuters/CORBIS; 127 (t), Image Copyright © Digital Vision; 127 (c), © Underwood & Underwood/CORBIS; 131 (l), © Buddy Mays/CORBIS; 136 (br), © Jenny Thomas/HRW; 137 (br), Sam Dudgeon/HRW; 144 (cr), © Carl A. Stimac/The Image Finders; 145 (tr), Stone/GettyImages; 145 (b), © Royalty-Free/CORBIS; 145 (b), PhotoDisc/GettyImages; 145 (b), © Royalty-Free/CORBIS; 145 (b), PhotoDisc/Getty Images **Chapter 3:** 146 (b), Jenny Thomas/HRW; 146 (bkgd), © Brian Leatart/FoodPix; 150 Richard Nowitz/Photo Researchers, Inc.; 153 (l), © Paul Almasy/CORBIS; 154 © Lynn Stone/Index Stock Imagery/PictureQuest; 157 (l), AP Photo/The Fresno Bee, Richard Darby/Wide World Photos; 166 (tr), Darren Carroll/HRW; 173 © Galen Rowell/CORBIS; 174 (tr), Sam Dudgeon/HRW; 175 Victoria Smith/HRW/Courtesy Oshman's, Austin, TX; 177 (l), © Gail Mooney/CORBIS; 179 (b), Ken Karp/HRW; 180 (tr), © Jeffrey L. Rotman/CORBIS; 189 (l), © Gallo Images/CORBIS; 189 (r), G.K. & Vikki Hart/Getty Images; 190 (tr), Dorling Kindersley/GettyImages; 190 (tr), Botanica/GettyImages; 193 (l), © Michael John Kielty/CORBIS; 196 (tr), © Glen Allison/Alamy Photos; 201 (l), Hulton Archive by Getty Images; 203 (r), Victoria Smith/HRW; 203 (tl), Richard Heinzen/SuperStock; 204 Peter Van Steen/HRW/Courtesy Russell Korman Fine Jewelry, Austin, TX; 205 © Charles O'Rear/CORBIS; 209 (tl), PhotoDisc/GettyImages; 209 (cr), © Charles O'Rear/CORBIS; 210 (b), © Jenny Thomas/HRW; 211 (br), Sam Dudgeon/HRW **Chapter 4:** 220 (bkgd), © Kelly-Mooney Photography/CORBIS; 220 (br), Roberto Borea/AP/Wide World Photos; 227 (l), © Stock Trek/PhotoDisc/Picture Quest; 228 (tr), Anna Zieminski/AFP/GettyImages; 235 (r), John Langford/HRW; 235 (l), John Langford/HRW; 237 (b), © Michael T. Sedam/CORBIS; 238 Stamp Designs © 1994 32À Rube Goldberg's Inventions (Scott # 3000f) United States Postal Service, Displayed with permission. All rights reserved. Written authorization from the Postal Service is required to use, reproduce, post, transmit, distribute, or publicly display these images. © Rube Goldberg, Inc.; 242 (t), © Helen Norman/CORBIS; 242 (bl), © John Kaprielian/Photo Researchers, Inc.; 242 (bc), © John Pointer/Animals Animals/Earth Scenes; 242 (r), © ChromaZone Images/Index Stock Imagery/PictureQuest; 245 (t), RO-MA Stock/Index Stock Imagery, Inc.; 245 (inset), RO-MA Stock/Index Stock Imagery, Inc.; 248 Scott Vallance/VIP Photographic Associates; 251 (l), © Ron Kimball Studios; 253 (b), Digital Vision/GettyImages; 257 (br), Sam Dudgeon/HRW; 264 (br), Image Bank/GettyImages; 264 (cr), © Bettmann/CORBIS; 265 (cr), Mark Maziarz/ParkCityStock.com; 265 (b), © 2007 James Kay—NOTE:2007 refers to publication year-change if necessary **Chapter 5:** 266 (bkgd), Ship model by Jean K. Eckert/Photo Courtesy of ©The Mariners' Museum, Newport News, Virginia; 266 (b), Gordon Chibroski/Press Herald/AP/Wide World Photos; 270 (tr), Darren Carrol/HRW; 273 (bc), © Chris Mellor/Lonely Planet Images; 273 (t), © Gavin Anderson/Lonely Planet Images; 283 Victoria Smith/HRW; 284 James L. Amos/SuperStock; 286 (cr), © Lynda Richardson/Corbis; 287 (tr), © Ralph A. Clevenger/CORBIS; 292 (tr), Photonica/GettyImages; 297 (b), Sam Dudgeon/HRW; 300 Peter Van Steen/HRW; 304 © Francis E. Caldwell/Affordable Photo Stock; 308 (t), Sam Dudgeon/HRW/Courtesy Chuck and Nan Ellis; 308 Victoria Smith/HRW; 309 Van Gogh Museum, Amsterdam/SuperStock; 311 (t), Library of Congress; 311 (b), Library of Congress; 311 (c), Victoria Smith/HRW; 311 (t-frame), ©1999 Image Farm Inc.; 317 (br), Sam Dudgeon/HRW; 317 (br), Sam Dudgeon/HRW **Chapter 6:** 326 (bkgd), © Mark E. Gibson Photography; 326 (br), Victoria Smith/HRW; 330 (tr), © Louie Psihoyos/Corbis; 345 (cl), © Tim Graham/Alamy; 346 (tr), © Buddy Mays/CORBIS; 352 (tr), Sam Dudgeon/HRW; 361 (tl), © Hemera Technologies/Alamy; 361 (br), Getty Images/Taxi; 363 (br), Sam Dudgeon/HRW; 363 (br), Sam Dudgeon/HRW; 370 (cr), Hulton Archive/GettyImages; 370 (bc), Indranil Mukherjee/AFP/GettyImages; 370 (cl), © Underwood & Underwood/Corbis; 371 (b), Photograph by Kurt Stepnitz/(c)Michgan State University; 371 (cr), Courtesy Michigan State University; 371 (cr), Courtesy Michigan State University **Chapter 7:** 372 (bkgd), © Sam Fried/Photo Researchers, Inc.; 372 (br), Victoria Smith/HRW; 376 Courtesy IMAX Corporation; 381 © CORBIS; 383 (l), © James L. Amos/CORBIS/Collection of The Corning Museum of Glass, Corning, New York; 385 © Karl Weatherly/CORBIS; 388 (tr), PhotoDisc - Digital Image copyright © 2004 PhotoDisc; 388 (tl), PhotoDisc - Digital Image copyright © 2004 PhotoDisc; 389 (cl), © David J. & Janice L. Frent Collection/CORBIS; 389 (tl), © CORBIS; 389 (cr), © CORBIS; 389 (bl), © David J. & Janice L. Frent Collection/CORBIS; 390 (br), © Kathy deWet-Oleson/Lonely Planet Images; 390 (bl), © Jeffrey L. Rotman/CORBIS; 391 (l), © Ron Sanford/Photo Researchers, Inc.; 392 (t), Sam Dudgeon/HRW; 394 (tr), Image Bank/GettyImages; 401 (b), © Stephen Frink/Index Stock Imagery/PictureQuest; 402 (c), SuperStock; 402 (l), SuperStock; 402 (r), SuperStock; 405 SuperStock; 408 (tr), © V. Brockhaus/zefa/CORBIS; 412 (b), Victoria Smith/HRW; 412 (tr), © Randy M. Ury/CORBIS; 415 (tl), FlyBase/Dr. F. R. Turner; 419 © Ecoscene/CORBIS; 423 (r), © James A. Sugar/CORBIS; 427 (br), © Richard Hutchings/PhotoEdit; 427 (bc), © Thinkstock/Alamy; 429 (br), Sam Dudgeon/HRW **Chapter 8:** 438 (bkgd), © 2002 Bruno Burklin/Aerial Aesthetics; 438 (br), © Stone/Getty Images/Stone; 442 The Art Archive / Private Collection / Harper Collins Publishers/© 2004 Artists Rights Society (ARS), New York/ADAGP, Paris; 444 Science Kit & Boreal Laboratories; 445 (t), © Burstein Collection/CORBIS/© 2004 Mondrian/Holtzman Trust/Artists Rights Society (ARS), New York; 445 (b), Copyright Tate Gallery, London, Great Britain/Art Resource, NY/© 2004 Artist Rights Society (ARS), New York/Pro Litteris, Zurich; 452 © Gisela Damm/eStock Photogarphy/PictureQuest; 455 (l), John Burke/SuperStock; 459 (br), © Robert Landau/Corbis; 460 (t), © Archivo Iconografico, S.A./CORBIS; 460 (b), © Archivo Iconografico, S.A./CORBIS; 466 © Gianni Dagh Orti/CORBIS; 469 (t), John Warden/SuperStock; 469 (tc), © Roman Soumar/CORBIS; 469 (b), © Jacqui Hurst/CORBIS; 473 (r), © Craig Aurness/CORBIS; 474 (tr), UW/Mary Levin; 477 (l), © Bob Krist/CORBIS; 481 (t), © CORBIS; 483 (b), © Craig Aurness/CORBIS; 488 (tr), Matthew Stockman/GettyImages; 494 (tr), Steve Vidler/SuperStock; 495 (tr), © Arthur Thévenart/CORBIS; 495 (c), © Karen Gowlett-Holmes; 497 © Nigel J. Dennis/Photo Researchers, Inc.; 497 (b), © William Panzer/Stock Connection/PictureQuest; 498 (t), Symmetry Drawing E121 by M.C. Escher © 2004 Cordon Art B. V. - Baarn - Holland. All rights reserved.; 499 (t), Symmetry Drawing E25 by M.C. Escher © 2004 Cordon Art B. V. - Baarn - Holland. All rights reserved.; 505 (br), Sam Dudgeon/HRW; 505 (br), Sam Dudgeon/HRW; 512 (cr), AP Photo/Tom E. Puskar; 512 (bl), GettyImages; 513 (cr), Longwood Gardens/L. Albee; 513 (b), Longwood Gardens/L. Albee **Chapter 9:** 514 (bkgd), © Mark E. Gibson c/o MIRA; 518 (t), Photo by Randall L. Ricklefs /McDonald Observatory; 518 (b), Sam

Dudgeon/HRW; 524 (tr), Reportage/Getty Images; 527 (cr), NOAA Costal Services Center; 530 (t), © Nik Wheeler/CORBIS; 533 (cr), © Christie's Images/CORBIS/ © 2004 Banco de México Diego Rivera & Frida Kahlo Museums Trust. Av. Cinco de Mayo No. 2, Col. Centro, Del. Cuauhtémoc 06059, México, D.F./Reproducción autorizada por el Instituto Nacional de Bellas Artes Y Literatura; 539 (tl), © Carl & Ann Purcell/CORBIS; 541 (tr), Photo © Stefan Schott/Panoramic Images, Chicago 1998; 547 (b), © TONY FREEMAN/PhotoEdit; 551 (cr), © Johathan Blair/CORBIS; 553 (tl), Digital Image copyright © 2004 Karl Weatherly/PhotoDisc; 557 (tr), © K. H. Photo/International Stock/ImageState; 559 (t), © Lary Lee Photography/CORBIS; 559 (bkgd), Corbis Images; 561 (tl), PhotoDisc/Getty Images; 561 (br), © Center for Ecoliteracy/Tyler; 561 (b), The Edible Schoolyard (c) 2005; 564 (br), Jenny Thomas/HRW; 565 (br), Sam Dudgeon/HRW; 565 (br), Sam Dudgeon/HRW
Chapter 10: 574 (bkgd), © Arvind Garg/CORBIS; 574 (br), Victoria Smith/HRW; 583 (tr), © Charles & Josette Lenars/CORBIS; 583 (cl), © Kevin Fleming/CORBIS; 583 (tl), Steve Vidler/SuperStock; 583 (cr), R.M. Arakaki/Imagestate; 589 (r), Sam Dudgeon/HRW; 589 (tl), © Natalie Fobes/CORBIS; 590 (t), Peter Van Steen/HRW; 595 (b), Sam Dudgeon/HRW; 597 (tr), Peter Van Steen/HRW; 601 (cr), PhotoDisc - Digital Image copyright © 2002 PhotoDisc
604 (tc), Peter Van Steen/HRW; 604 (tc), Peter Van Steen/HRW; 606 (tr), © Michael Newman/PhotoEdit; 608 (t), Hahn's Titanic Plans by Robert Hahn; 608 (cr), HARLAND & WOLFF PHOTOGRAPHIC COLLECTION, © NATIONAL MUSEUMS & GALLERIES OF NORTHERN IRELAND, ULSTER FOLK AND TRANSPORT MUSEUM.; 611 (tl), PhotoDisc/Getty Images; 612 (tr), Stephanie Friedman/HRW; 614 (br), Jenny Thomas/HRW; 615 (br), Sam Dudgeon/HRW; 622 (cr), Joseph R. Melanson of skypic.com; 622 (br), Bill Kostroun, Stringer/AP; 623 (br), © LMR Group/Alamy; 623 (tr), Festival of Ballooning, Inc. **Chapter 11:** 624 (bkgd), © Getty Images/Stone; 624 (br), Victoria Smith/HRW; 628 (tr), Peter Van Steen/HRW; 631 (tr), REUTERS/Gary Wiepert /NewsCom; 632 (tr), © V. C. L. Tipp Howell/Getty Images/Taxi; 635 (tr), Courtesy of National Weather Service, NOAA; 636 (tr), Peter Van Steen/HRW; 636 (tr), Peter Van Steen/HRW; 639 (tl), © Tom & Dee Ann McCarthy; 640 (b), Sam Dudgeon/HRW/SCRABBLE® is a trademark of Hasbro in the United States and Canada. © 2002 Hasbro, Inc. All Rights Reserved.; 640 (tr), Victoria Smith/HRW/SCRABBLE® is a trademark of Hasbro in the United States and Canada. © 2002 Hasbro, Inc. All Rights Reserved.; 640 (br), Victoria Smith/HRW/SCRABBLE® is a trademark of Hasbro in the United States and Canada. © 2002 Hasbro, Inc. All Rights Reserved.; 646 (cr), Digital Image copyright © 2004 EyeWire; 647 (cr), © Left Lane Productions/CORBIS; 648 (tr), © Dennis Degnan/CORBIS; 650 (b), Sam Dudgeon/HRW; 650 (b), Sam Dudgeon/HRW; 650 (b), Sam Dudgeon/HRW; 650 (b), Sam Dudgeon/HRW; 652 (tr), © Stone/GettyImages; 653 (c), © Stockbyte; 653 (c), © Royalty-Free/CORBIS; 653 (c), © Royalty-Free/CORBIS; 653 (c), © Corbis Images/HRW Image Library; 655 (tc), Pushkin Museum of Fine Arts, Moscow, Russia/SuperStock ; 655 (tr), © Philadelphia Museum of Art/CORBIS; 656 (tr), © Lebrecht Music and Arts Photo Library/Alamy 659 (l), Photofest; 661 (tl), Thinkstock/Getty Images; 662 (cr), Sam Dudgeon/HRW; 662 (br), Ken Karp/HRW; 663 (bc), Sam Dudgeon/HRW **Chapter 12:** 672 (b), NASA; 672 (bkgd), NASA; 679 (cl), Image Bank/Getty Images; 681 (cr), Sam Dudgeon/HRW; 681 (cartoon), CLOSE TO HOME © 1994 John McPherson. Reprinted with Permission of UNIVERSAL PRESS SYNDICATE. All rights reserved.; 686 (tr), (c) Masterfile (Royalty-Free Div.); 689 The Holland Sentiel, Barbara Beal/AP/Wide World Photos; 691 (br), Victoria Smith/HRW; 695 (t), U.S. Geological Survey Western Region Costal and Marine Geology; 695 (b), James Wilson/Woodfin Camp & Associates; 696 (tr), Victoria Smith/HRW; 699 (tl), © Al Grotell 1990; 700 (tr), Spencer Tirey/AP/Wide World Photos; 704 (tr), © Tony Freeman/Photo Edit; 707 (cr), Dr. E. R. Degginger/Color-Pic, Inc.; 707 (cr), Sam Dudgeon/HRW; 707 (cr), Dr. E. R. Degginger/Color-Pic, Inc.; 707 (cr), Pat Lanza/Bruce Coleman, Inc.; 709 (tl), © Dinodia Images/Alamy; 709 (cr), © Rolf Bruderer/Corbis; 710 (tr), © Michael S. Yamashita/CORBIS; 711 (cartoon), The Far Side ® by Gary Larson © 1985 FarWorks, Inc. All Rights Reserved. Used with permission.; 712 (br), Randall Hyman/HRW; 713 (br), Sam Dudgeon/HRW; 720 (cr), © Hollywild Animal Park; 720 (bl), © Hollywild Animal Park; 721 (cr), Courtesy of Family Kingdom; 721 (br), Courtesy Chance Rides Manufacturing.

Art Credits

Chapter 1: 10 (tr), Stephen Durke; 10 (c), NETS; 19 (tc), Greg Geisler; 21 (tr), Argosy; 23 (tr), Cameron Eagle ; 37 (c), Argosy (table); 41 (tr), Greg Geisler; 41 (tr), Jeffrey Oh; 49 (tr), Mark Heine; 55 (tr), Jeffrey Oh; 56 (c), Greg Geisler; 56 (tr), Greg Geisler; 59 (cr), Stephen Durke/Washington Artists; 62 (tr), Lori Bilter; 63 (cr), Leslie Kell **Chapter 2:** 75 (c), Argosy; 79 (tr), Argosy; 82 (tr), Argosy; 85 (c), Mark Heine; 88 (tr), Kent Leech; 103 (cr), Argosy; 109 (tc), Mark Heine; 109 (cr), Jeffrey Oh; 113 (tr), Mark Heine; 121 (bl), Greg Geisler; 123 (cr), Argosy; 128 (tr), Bob Burnett; 131 (cr), Argosy; 135 (tl), David Clegg; 135 (cr), David Clegg; 137 (cr), Leslie Kell; 136 (tr), John Etheridge **Chapter 3:** 153 (tr), Argosy; 154 (cl), Greg Geisler; 161 (cr), Cameron Eagle; 163 (tr), Argosy; 169 (tr), Argosy; 183 (c), Jeffrey Oh; 186 (tr), Stephen Durke; 199 (tr), Argosy; 201 (cr), Jeffrey Oh; 207 (tr), Argosy (graph) ; 209 (b), Argosy; 210 (tr), Ann Flowers; 211 (cr), Leslie Kell **Chapter 4:** 227 (c), Ortelius Design; 232 (tr), Cindy Jeftovic; 237 (cr), James Hindermeier; 249 (c), David Clegg; 253 (tl), Argosy; 253 (cr), Kevin Rechin; 256 (tr), John Etheridge; 305 (tl, tr), Stephen Durke/Washington Artists; 257 (cr), Leslie Kell; 265 (c), Argosy **Chapter 5:** 269 (tl), David Clegg; 269 (br), David Clegg; 270 (tc), NETS; 274 (tr), Kevin Rechin; 305 (cr), Jeffrey Oh; 306 (cr), Jeffrey Oh; 306 (br), Jeffrey Oh; 306 (tr), Mark Heine; 306 Jeffrey Oh; 307 (tl, tr), Jeffrey Oh; 308 (cr), John White/The Neis Group; 313 (tl), David Clegg; 313 (cr), David Clegg; 313 (b), David Clegg; 314 (tc), NETS; 317 (cr), Leslie Kell **Chapter 6:** 352 (c), NETS; 361 (c), NETS; 361 (c), NETS; 363 (cr), Leslie Kell **Chapter 7:** 379 (tc), Argosy; 380 (cr), Jeffrey Oh; 383 (cr), Jeffrey Oh; 386 (bl), Boston Graphics; 388 (bc), Argosy(chart)/Cindy Jeftovic (Illustration); 390 (c), Argosy; 403 (cr), Ortelius Design; 416 (tc), David Clegg **Chapter 8:** 429 (cr), Leslie Kell; 448 (tr), Fian Arroyo; 449 (cr), Ortelius Design; 461 (cr), Stephen Durke/Washington Artists; 462 (br), Cindy Jeftovic; 463 (cr), Stephen Durke/Washington Artists; 481 (cr), John Etheridge; 501 (tl), David Clegg; 501 (cr), Argosy; 501 (b), David Clegg; 505 (cr), Leslie Kell **Chapter 9:** 521 (tr), Argosy; 534 (tr), Cindy Jeftovic; 535 (br), John White/The Neis Group; 536 (cr), John White/The Neis Group; 536 (br), John White/The Neis Group; 537 (cr), John White/The Neis Group; 538 (tr), Argosy; 550 (tr), Greg Geisler; 556 (tr), NETS; 558 (cr), Jane Sanders; 559 (cr), Nenad Jakesevic; 561 (cr), Argosy; 564 (tr), John Etheridge; 565 (cr), Leslie Kell **Chapter 10:** 593 (tr), Jane Sanders; 598 (c), Argosy; 601 (tr), David Fischer; 605 (c), Bernadette Lau; 614 (c), James Hindermeier; 614 (tr), Cindy Jeftovic; 615 (cr), Leslie Kell **Chapter 11:** 629 (br), John Etheridge; 637 (cr), NETS; 643 (tr), Argosy; 648 (bc), Greg Geisler; 649 (c), Greg Geisler; 662 (tr), Cindy Jeftovic; 663 (cr), Leslie Kell **Chapter 12:** 682 (tr), Steward Lee; 683 (tr), Steward Lee; 685 (tr), Argosy; 703 (tr), John Etheridge; 712 (tr), Cindy Jeftovic; 713 (cr), Leslie Kell

Table of Measures

METRIC	CUSTOMARY

Metric

Length

1 kilometer (km) = 1,000 meters (m)
1 meter = 100 centimeters (cm)
1 centimeter = 10 millimeters (mm)

Capacity

1 liter (L) = 1,000 milliliters (mL)

Mass and Weight

1 kilogram (kg) = 1,000 grams (g)
1 gram = 1,000 milligrams (mg)

Customary

Length

1 mile (mi) = 5,280 feet (ft)
1 yard (yd) = 3 feet
1 foot = 12 inches (in.)

Capacity

1 gallon (gal) = 4 quarts (qt)
1 quart = 2 pints (pt)
1 pint = 2 cups (c)
1 cup = 8 fluid ounces (fl oz)

Mass and Weight

1 ton (T) = 2,000 pounds (lb)
1 pound = 16 ounces (oz)

TIME

1 year (yr) = 365 days
1 year = 12 months (mo)
1 year = 52 weeks (wk)
1 week = 7 days
1 day = 24 hours (hr)
1 hour = 60 minutes (min)
1 minute = 60 seconds (s)

Formulas

Perimeter

Square	$P = 4s$
Rectangle	$P = 2\ell + 2w$ or $P = 2(\ell + w)$
Polygon	$P =$ sum of the lengths of the sides

Circumference

Circle	$C = 2\pi r$ or $C = \pi d$

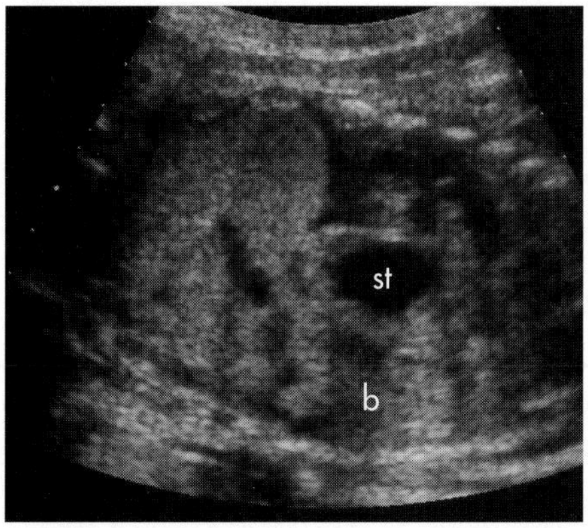

Figure 39-19 Longitudinal image of a 25-week fetus with a large left-side hernia. The stomach *(st)* and bowel *(b)* are seen within the thoracic cavity.

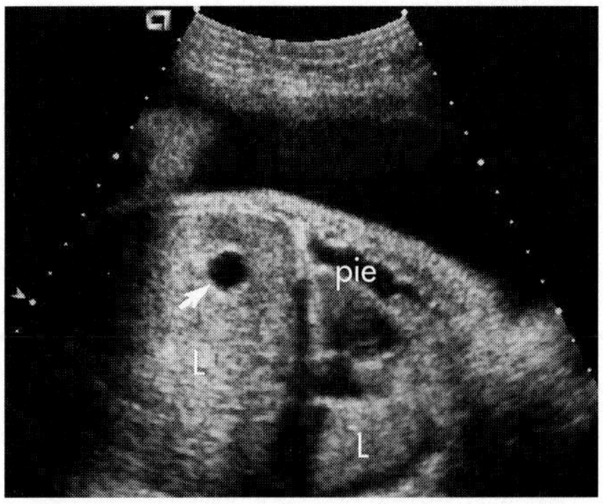

Figure 39-20 Longitudinal scan of the right sided diaphragmatic hernia; the liver *(L)* is seen in the thoracic cavity. Pleural effusion *(ple)* is present. The gallbladder *(arrow)* is seen within the liver.

may communicate with the pericardial sac.[7] In anteromedial defects the heart may be normally positioned and surrounded by pleural fluid, and the fetal stomach may be located in its normal position in the abdomen (Figure 39-20). Thinning of the diaphragm (eventration) may give rise to sonographic characteristics similar to those of diaphragmatic hernias.[7]

The amniotic fluid may be normal unless the bowel is obstructed–with resulting polyhydramnios. The placenta is normal; the abdominal circumference will be abnormally small. Careful scanning prior to 18 weeks of gestation is important to identify the normal contour of the diaphragm in the sagittal and coronal views. A small defect may not show abnormalities early in the gestational period.

The prognosis is poor for the fetus if the congenital diaphragmatic hernia is detected before birth; if the presence of the stomach is found in the chest, especially if it is dilated; if the left heart is underdeveloped or if congenital heart disease is present.[13] The primary cause of death is pulmonary hypoplasia. If the diagnosis is made prior to 25 weeks of gestation and the development of polyhydramnios is present, the survival rate is low.

Frequently associated abnormalities include cardiac (20%), and central nervous system malformation (30%), renal anomalies, vertebral defects, pulmonary hypoplasia, and facial clefts. In addition, chromosome abnormalities (trisomy 18 and 21) have also be associated with diaphragmatic hernia.

It is important to note that when a diaphragmatic hernia is present, the stomach may not be filled when there is concomitant oligohydramnios or if the fetus is swallowing abnormally. The only clue to a diaphragmatic hernia in this situation may be evidence of a solid mass in the chest. Peristalsis within the herniated intestines confirm the diagnosis.

When the sonographer is unable to demonstrate the stomach bubble in the normal anatomic location after repeated observations, a search for a diaphragmatic hernia should be attempted.

Lung and mediastinal masses, in particular cystic adenomatoid malformations, may be difficult to distinguish from diaphragmatic hernias. The normally positioned peritoneal organs should aid in differentiating these two conditions.

At birth, the majority of infants with congenital diaphragmatic hernia have pulmonary hypoplasia and secondary respiratory insufficiency. There is a high mortality rate (75%) because of the increased frequency of coexisting fatal congenital anomalies.

Fetal surgery for diaphragmatic hernia. Attempts to surgically correct diaphragmatic hernias have been investigated in animal models.[9] Correction of this defect in utero may allow for normal development of the lungs, thereby preserving lung tissue and preventing pulmonary hypoplasia.

ACKNOWLEDGMENT

The author acknowledges the contribution of Kara Mayden Argo to this chapter in the fourth edition of this book.

REVIEW QUESTIONS

1. What are the normal sonographic features of the thoracic cavity?
2. How is fetal respiration determined on ultrasound?
3. Describe the sonographic features of:
   a. pulmonary hypoplasia
   b. bronchogenic cyst
   c. hydrothorax
   d. bronchopulmonary sequestration
   e. cystic adenomatoid malformation
   f. diaphragmatic hernia
4. How can the sonographer distinguish between CAM, sequestration, and a diaphragmatic hernia?

REFERENCES

1. Besinger RE, Compton AA, Hayashi RH: The presence or absence of fetal breathing movements as a predictor of outcome in preterm labor, *Am J Obstet Gynecol* 157:753, 1987.
2. Bromley B, Benacerraf B: Unilateral lung hypoplasia: report of three cases, *J Ultrasound Med* 16:599, 1997.
3. Bromley B, and others: Fetal lung masses: prenatal course and outcome, *J Ultrasound Med* 14:927, 1995.
4. Budorick NE and others: Spontaneous improvement of intrathoracic masses diagnosed in utero, *J Ultrasound Med* 11:653, 1992.
5. Callen P: *Ultrasonography in obstetrics and gynecology,* Philadelphia, 1994, WB Saunders.
6. Chitkara U and others: Prenatal sonographic assessment of the fetal thorax: normal values, *Am J Obstet Gynecol* 156:1069, 1987.
7. Comstock CH: The antenatal diagnosis of diaphragmatic hernia, *J Ultrasound Med* 5:391, 1986.
8. Graham D, Sanders RC: Sonographic evaluation of the fetal chest. In Sanders RC, editor: *The principles and practice of ultrasonography in obstetrics and gynecology,* ed 3, Norwalk, Conn, 1985, Appleton-Century-Crofts.
9. Harrison MR, Golbus MS, Filly RA: Congenital diaphragmatic hernia. In Harrison MR, Golbus MS, Filly RA, editors: *The unborn patient,* Orlando, Fla, 1984, Grune and Stratton.
10. Johnson A and others: Ultrasonic ration of fetal thoracic to abdominal circumference: an association with fetal pulmonary hypoplasia, *Am J Obstet Gynecol* 157:764, 1987.
11. Mayden KL and others: The antenatal, sonographic detection of lung masses, *Am J Obstet Gynecol* 148:349, 1984.
12. Moore KL: *Before we are born,* ed 3, Toronto, 1989, WB Saunders.
13. Nyberg DA, Mahony BS, Pretorius DH, editors: *Diagnostic ultrasound of fetal anomalies: text and atlas,* St Louis, 1990, Mosby.
14. Rodeck CH and others: Long-term in utero drainage of fetal hydrothorax, *N Engl J Med* 319:1135, 1988.
15. Romero R and others: Antenatal sonographic findings of extralobar pulmonary sequestration, *J Ultrasound Med* 1:131, 1982.
16. Stocker JT and others: Congenital cystic adenomatoid malformations of the lung, *Hum Pathol* 8:155, 1977.
17. Vintzileos AM and others: Comparison of six different ultrasonographic methods for predicting lethal fetal pulmonary hypoplasia, *Am J Obstet Gynecol* 161:606, 1989.

BIBLIOGRAPHY

Graham D and others: Prenatal diagnosis of cystic adenomatoid malformation of the lung, *J Ultrasound Med* 1:9, 1982.

Romero R and others: Prenatal diagnosis of congenital anomalies, Norwalk, Conn, 1988, Appleton & Lange.

Sanders RC, editor: *Clinical sonography: a practical guide,* ed 3, Boston, 1998, Little, Brown.

Sharland GK and others: Prognosis in fetal diaphragmatic hernia, *Am J Obstet Gynecol* 166:9, 1992.

Teixeira J and others: Abdominal circumference in fetuses with congenital diaphragmatic hernia: correlation with hernia content and pregnancy outcome, *J Ultrasound Med* 16:407, 1997.

CHAPTER **40**

Fetal Echocardiography

Sandra L. Hagen-Ansert

Objectives

- Learn about the embryology of the fetal heart
- Understand the circulation of the fetal heart
- Discuss how the fetal circulation differs from the neonatal circulation
- Describe the risk factors that may lead to congenital heart disease
- Identify the type of transducer to use for the fetal echo
- Understand how to evaluate the fetus with two-dimensional, motion mode (M-mode), pulsed Doppler, and color flow Doppler imaging
- Discuss the sonographic characteristics necessary to obtain before the fetal echo
- Describe the normal anatomy seen in the four-chamber and long and short axis views of the heart
- Discuss the "criss-cross" view of the heart
- List the echocardiographic findings in common forms of congenital heart disease (septal defects, right and left ventricular disturbances, great vessel anomalies, and fetal cardiac arrhythmias)

KEY TERMS

atrial fibrillation - condition in which the atria beat more than 400 beats per minute and the ventricular rate is 120 to 200 beats per minute

atrial septal defect - communication between the right and left atrium that persists after birth

atrioventricular block - blockage that occurs when the transmission of the electrical impulse from the atria to the ventricles is blocked (may be 2:1 or 3:1 block)

atrioventricular node - areas of cardiac muscle that receives and conducts the cardiac impulse

atrioventricular septal defect - defect that occurs when the endocardial cushion fails to fuse in the center of the heart
bicuspid aortic valve - two leaflets instead of the normal three leaflets with asymmetric cusps
bulbus cordis - primitive chamber that forms the right ventricle
cardiomyopathy - disease of the myocardial muscle layer of the heart that causes the heart to dilate secondary to regurgitation and also affects cardiac function
cardiosplenic syndromes - sporadic disorders characterized by a symmetric development of normally asymmetric organs or organ systems
coarctation of the aorta - discrete or long segment narrowing in the aortic arch, usually at the level of the left subclavian artery near the insertion of the ductus arteriosus
complete atrioventricular septal defect - large ventricular and atrial septal defect with a single, undivided, free-floating leaflet that stretches between both ventricles
critical aortic stenosis - abnormal thickening and closure of the aortic leaflets in the second or third trimester causes the left ventricle to "balloon" from increased pressure; leads to heart failure and, if severe, fetal demise
double outlet right ventricle - ventricular septal defect with the overriding aorta directed more to the right ventricular outflow tract than the left (more than 50% override toward the right)
ductus arteriosus - communication between the pulmonary artery and descending aorta that closes after birth
Ebstein's anomaly - abnormal apical displacement of the septal leaflet of the tricuspid valve
ectopia cordis - condition in which the ventral wall fails to close and the heart develops outside the thoracic cavity
foramen ovale - also termed fossa ovale; opening between the free edge of the septum secundum and the dorsal wall of the atrium
hypoplastic left heart - underdevelopment of the mitral valve, left ventricle, and aorta
hypoplastic right heart - underdevelopment of the tricuspid valve, right ventricle, and pulmonary artery
incomplete atrioventricular septal defect - membranous septal defect, abnormal tricuspid valve, primum atrial septal defect, and cleft mitral valve
inferior vena cava - venous return into the right atrium of the heart along the posterior lateral wall
infracristal septal defect - defects found below the crista supraventricularis ridge in the membranous or muscular area
left atrium - filling chamber of the heart
left ventricle - pumping chamber of the heart
main pulmonary artery - main artery that carries blood from the right ventricle to the lungs
mitral atresia - thickened, underdeveloped mitral apparatus
mitral regurgitation - failure of the leaflets to close completely, allowing blood to leak backward into the left atrium
mitral valve - atrioventricular valve between the left atrium and left ventricle
patent ductus arteriosus - open communication between the pulmonary artery and descending aorta that does not constrict after birth
premature atrial and ventricular contractions - fetal cardiac arrhythmia resulting from extra systoles and ectopic beats
pulmonary stenosis - thickening and narrowing of the pulmonic cusps; causes blood to back up into the right ventricle and atrium
pulmonary veins - four pulmonary veins bring blood from the lungs back into the posterior wall of the left atrium; there are two upper (right and left) and two lower (right and left) pulmonary veins
rhabdomyoma - benign cardiac tumor of the heart that is associated with tuberous sclerosis
right atrium - filling chamber of the heart
right ventricle - pumping chamber of the heart
septum primum - first part of the atrial septum to grow from the dorsal wall of the primitive atrium; fuses with the endocardial cushions
septum secundum - grows into the atrium to the right of the septum primum
single ventricle - condition in which there are two atria with one ventricle
sinoatrial node - forms in the wall of the sinus venosus near its opening into the right atrium
subvalvular aortic stenosis - occurs when a membrane is formed beneath the aortic leaflets and causes left ventricular outflow obstruction
superior vena cava - venous return from the head and upper extremities into the upper posterior medial wall of the right atrium
supracristal septal defect - refers to a high membranous septal defect just beneath the pulmonary orifice
supraventricular tachyarrhythmias - abnormal cardiac rhythms above 200 beats per minute with a normal sinus conduction rate of 1:1
tetralogy of Fallot - membranous ventricular septal defect, overriding of the aorta, and pulmonary stenosis
transposition of the great arteries - occurs when the truncus arteriosus fails to complete its rotation during the first trimester and causes the pulmonary artery to arise from the left ventricle and the aorta to arise from the pulmonary artery (blue baby at birth)
tricuspid atresia - underdevelopment of the tricuspid valve (usually associated with hypoplasia of the right ventricle and pulmonary stenosis)
tricuspid valve - atrioventricular valve found between the right atrium and right ventricle

truncus arteriosus - common arterial trunk that divides into the aorta and pulmonary artery
ventricular septal defect - communication between the right and left ventricles

---

The continued development and improvement of high-resolution, real-time sonography has enabled the sonographer to visualize cardiac activity with transvaginal transducers early in the first trimester with detailed visualization of all the anatomic structures of the fetal heart better imaged in the second and third trimesters. This ability to visualize cardiac anatomy has aided in the prenatal diagnosis of congenital heart disease. The incidence of congenital heart disease is about 8%, or 30,000 infants per year in the United States.[2] Ultrasound enables the sonographer and clinician the opportunity to image the small cardiac structures and to obtain hemodynamic information from the fetal heart.

Conditions such as small defects, abnormal size or location of cardiac structures, arrhythmias, or abnormal cardiac function may all be observed with fetal echocardiography. The information obtained about congenital heart defects is usually managed through a team effort, including the pediatric cardiologist, geneticist, cardiovascular surgeon, and imaging specialists, to allow the patient to make educated decisions regarding the opportunities and outcomes of her fetus with a congenital heart defect.

Improvement of high-resolution transducers has permitted good visualization of even the smallest structures within the fetal cardiac chambers. These transducers and dedicated cardiac instrumentation, complete with motion mode (M-mode), two-dimensional, color, and Doppler capabilities, enable the sonographer to perform a complete fetal echocardiogram on obstetric patients in their 16th week of pregnancy until the time of delivery. Although fetal heart motion may be seen within the gestational sac as early as 4 to 5 weeks of gestation, structural information is better seen at 14 to 16 weeks of gestation, with detailed information shown after 18 weeks of gestation.

Fetal echocardiography has been a tremendous clinical aid for the high-risk obstetric patient (Box 40-1). The ability to map normal cardiac structures and function in a patient who has had a previous child with congenital heart disease has been a great aid in relieving the stress of the pregnancy. In addition, if a congenital heart condition is found, arrangements may be made to deliver the patient in a facility with the appropriate staff to manage such a neonate. The addition of Doppler and color flow imaging has aided the diagnosis of congenital heart disease and has helped us understand the flow dynamics in the fetus. These two modalities, Doppler and color flow imaging, are used with discretion in the fetus with congenital heart disease.

BOX 40-1 SONOGRAPHIC PITFALLS FOR CARDIAC ANOMALIES

ECHOGENIC FOCI IN VENTRICLE
- Measures 1 to 4 mm
- Bright, echogenic without distal shadow; usually in left ventricle
- Frequency 0.15% to 20%; related to image quality
- May be caused by bright chordae tendineae, papillary muscle (mineralization or calcification), or ischemia or may be idiopathic
- Increased finding in trisomies 13 (39%) and 21 (16%); normal, 2%

SMALL PERICARDIAL EFFUSION
- Hypoechoic area in peripheral part of myocardium; 2-mm separation normal
- May be abnormal if less than 2 mm, but surrounds heart; could be associated with hydrops
- May occur secondary to indomethacin—closes patent ductus arteriosus
- Pulmonary effusion associated with coxsackievirus, cytomegalovirus, parvovirus, human immunodeficiency virus, intrauterine growth restriction (IUGR), aneuploidy (trisomy 21)

MILD VENTRICULAR SIZE DISCREPANCY
- Four-chamber view shows right ventricle slightly larger than left
- Smaller left ventricle may represent early sign of coarctation (sensitivity 50% to 62% in detection of coarctation)
- Coarctation false positive likely in third trimester based on ventricular disproportion
- Look for predominate left to right flow through patent ovale
- Measure aorta, arch, descending aorta
- Small left ventricle may represent ductus-dependent lesion
  - Interrupted aortic arch
  - Anomalous pulmonary venous return
- Enlarged right ventricle resulting from pulmonary valve atresia, stenosis, or regurgitation
- IUGR may cause ventricular disproportion (increased placenta vascular resistance with polycythemia and hypervolemia resulting from chronic hypoxia may produce volume and pressure overload and dilation of the right ventricle)

Data from Brown DL: *Semin Ultrasound CT MRI* 19(4)329, 1998.

EMBRYOLOGY OF THE CARDIOVASCULAR SYSTEM

A single major error in the genetic constitution is the basis of congenital malformations. Human teratogens produce or raise the incidence of congenital malformations; 7% are caused by environmental agents or teratogens. A spontaneous abortion usually occurs if the genetic malformation is severe.

The most sensitive period for cardiac development is $3\frac{1}{2}$ to $6\frac{1}{2}$ weeks. The cardiovascular system is the first organ system to reach a functional state; by the end of the 3rd week, circulation of blood has begun and the heart begins to beat in the 5th week.

DEVELOPMENT OF BLOOD VESSELS

The primitive heart is a tubular structure that forms like a large blood vessel from the mesenchymal cells in the car-

diogenic area of the embryo. Paired endocardial heart tubes develop before the end of the 3rd week and begin to fuse to form the primitive heart.

The circulation of blood starts by the end of the 3rd week as a tubular heart begins to beat. The embryo obtains sufficient nourishment during the 2nd week of development by diffusion of nutrients from maternal blood flow. The vascular system begins during the 3rd week in the wall of the yolk sac, the connecting stalk, and the chorion. The blood vessels begin to develop 2 days later. Blood islands are formed; cavities develop in the islands to form primitive blood cells and vessels. These primitive vessels form a vascular network in the wall of the yolk sac. Blood vessels form in the mesenchyme associated with the connecting stalk and chorion. Blood vessels also form in the embryo toward the end of the 3rd week and join to form a continuous system of vessels on each side.

Blood vessels from the embryo join those on the yolk sac, connecting stalk, and chorion to form a primitive cardiovascular system (Figure 40-1).[5] The cardinal veins return blood from the embryo, and the vitelline veins return blood from the yolk sac. The umbilical veins return oxygenated blood from the placenta (only one umbilical vein persists). Two dorsal aortas fuse in the caudal half of the embryo to form a single dorsal aorta. Blood formation in the embryo begins at the 5th week.

AORTIC ARCHES

Each branchial arch is supplied by an aortic arch (Figure 40-2). The arteries to the fifth pair are rudimentary or absent. The third pair of aortic arches becomes the common carotid artery and the proximal parts of the internal carotid arteries. The left fourth arch forms part of the arch of the aorta. The right fourth arch forms the proximal part

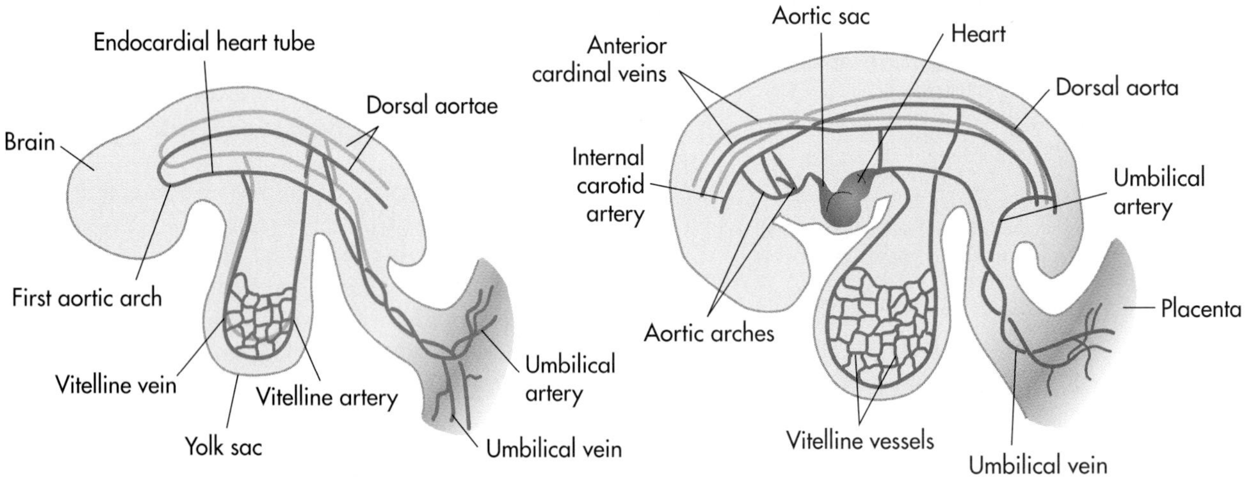

Figure 40-1 Drawing of the cardiovascular system in a 26-day-old embryo. The two endocardial heart tubes have fused to form a tubular heart ring. The umbilical vein carries oxygenated blood and nutrients to the embryo from the placenta.

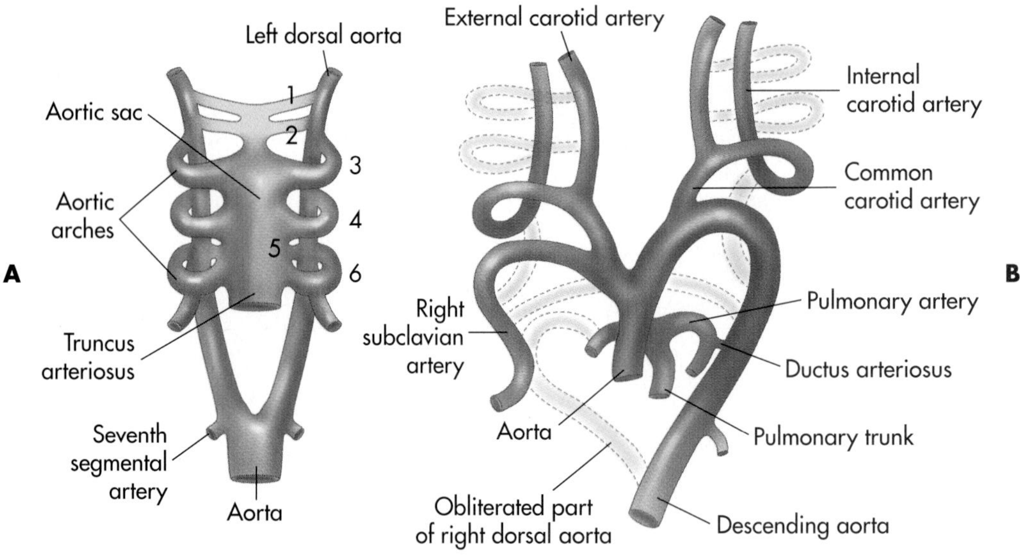

Figure 40-2 Drawing of the aortic arches in a 6-week embryo **(A)** and in an 8-week embryo **(B).**

of the right subclavian artery. The right sixth aortic arch becomes the right pulmonary artery. The left sixth aortic arch forms the left pulmonary artery and the ductus arteriosus (Box 40-2).

DEVELOPMENT OF THE HEART

The heart tube grows rapidly, bending on itself because it is fixed at its cranial and caudal ends. The bending forms a U-shaped bulboventricular loop. The sinus venosus is initially a separate chamber that opens into the **right atrium** (Figure 40-3).

Right Atrium. The left horn of the sinus becomes the coronary sinus. The right horn is incorporated into the wall of the right atrium (forms a smooth portion of the adult right atrial wall). The right half of the primitive atrium persists as the right auricle.

Left Atrium. The **left atrium** is formed by incorporation of the primitive pulmonary vein. As the atrium grows, parts of this vein and its branches are absorbed. Four pulmonary veins eventually enter the left atrium from the lungs. The smooth wall of the left atrium is from the absorbed pulmonary vein. The left auricle is from the primitive heart.

Four-Chambered Heart. During the 4th and 5th weeks of fetal development the division of the four chambers occurs.

Division of the Atrioventricular Canal. Endocardial cushions develop in the atrioventricular region of the heart. The cushions grow toward each other and fuse to divide the atrioventricular canal into right and left canals.

Division of the Primitive Atrium. The **septum primum** grows from the dorsal wall of the primitive atrium and fuses with the endocardial cushions (Figure 40-4, *A* and *B*). Before the fusion of the septum primum a com-

BOX 40-2 CARDIAC DEVELOPMENT

- *Sinus venosus:* The caudal region of the primitive heart, which receives all blood returning to the heart from common cardinal veins, vitelline veins, and umbilical veins
- *Primitive atrium:* Develops into the right and left atria
- *Primitive ventricle:* Develops into the left ventricle
- *Bulbus cordis:* Develops into the right ventricle
- *Truncus arteriosus:* Dilates to form the aortic sac from which the aortic arches arise

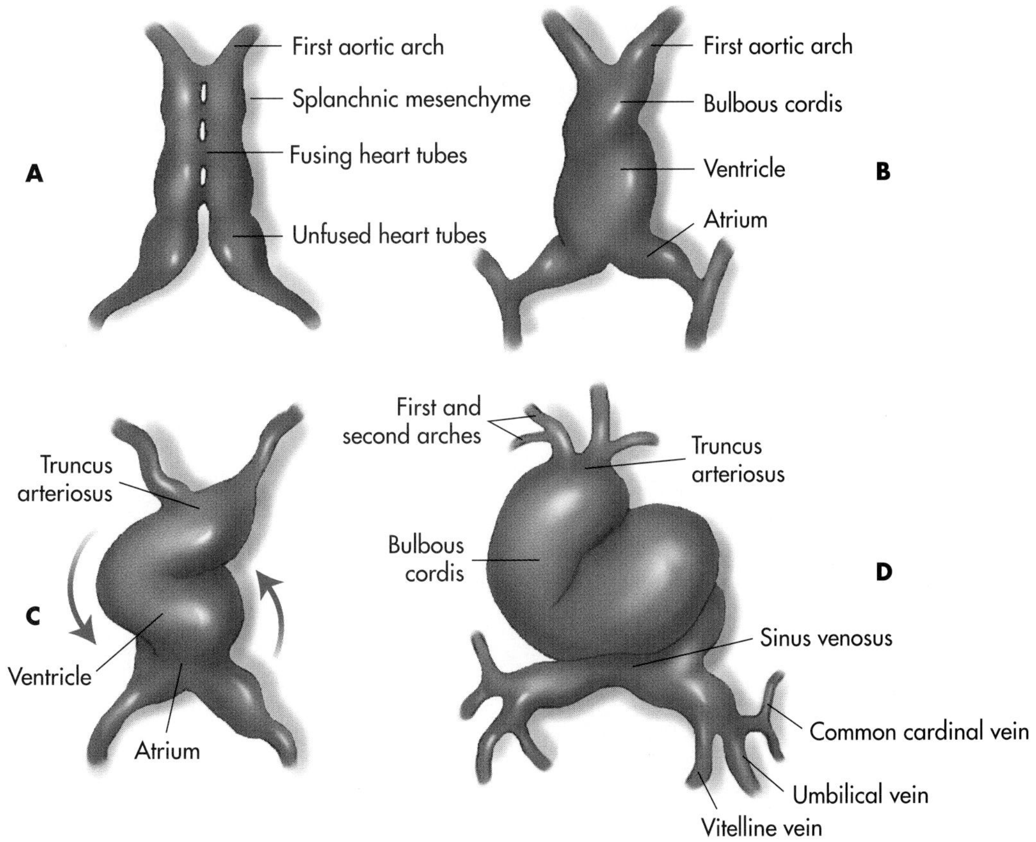

Figure 40-3 Drawings of the heart during the 4th week of development. The paired endocardial heart tubes **(A)** gradually fuse to form a single tubular heart **(B).** The fusion begins at the cranial end of the tubes and extends caudally until a single tubular heart is formed. As the heart elongates, it bends on itself **(C),** forming an S-shaped heart **(D).**

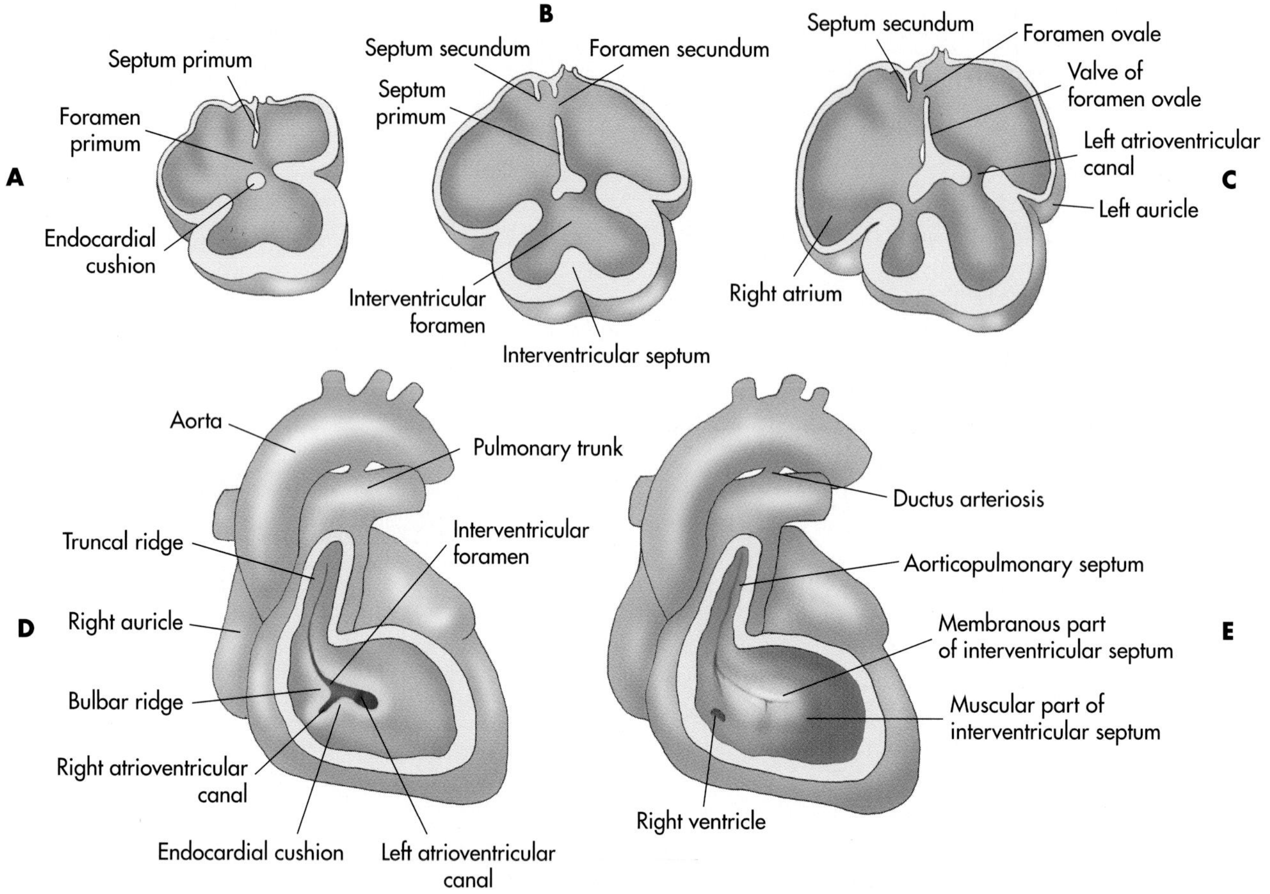

Figure 40-4 Drawings of the developing heart illustrating partitioning of the primitive atrioventricular canal, atrium, and ventricle. **A, B,** and **C,** Frontal sections of the embryonic heart during the 4th week. **D,** (5 weeks) and **E,** (7 weeks) show schematic drawings of the heart illustrating closure of the interventricular foramen and formation of the interventricular septum. Note that the interventricular foramen is closed by tissues from three sources.

munication exists between the right and left halves of the primum atrium through the ostium primum or foramen primum. As the septum primum fuses with the endocardial cushions (obliterating the foramen primum), the superior part of the septum primum breaks down, creating an opening called the *foramen secundum* (see Figure 40-4, *A* and *B*). As this foramen develops, another membranous fold, the **septum secundum,** grows into the atrium to the right of the septum primum. The septum secundum overlaps the foramen secundum, the opening of the septum primum. There is also an opening between the free edge of the septum secundum and the dorsal wall of the atrium–the **foramen ovale** (Figure 40-4, *C*).

Formation of the Ventricles. The **left ventricle** is formed from the primitive vein. The right ventricle is formed from the **bulbus cordis.** The interventricular septum begins as a ridge in the floor of the primitive ventricle and slowly grows toward the endocardial cushions (see Figure 40-4, *B* and *C*). Until the 7th week, the right and left ventricles communicate through a large interventricular foramen. Closure of the interventricular foramen results in formation of the membranous part of the interventricular septum.

Partitioning of Bulbus Cordis and Truncus Arteriosus. The division of this part of the heart results from the development and fusions of the truncal ridges and bulbar ridges (Fig. 40-4, *D* and *E*). Fused mesenchymal ridges form the aorticopulmonary septum, which divides the **truncus arteriosus** and bulbus cordis into the ascending aorta and pulmonary trunk.

Development of the Conducting System of the Heart. The **sinoatrial node** forms in the wall of the sinus venosus, near its opening into the right atrium; later it is incorporated into the right atrium with the right horn of the sinus venosus. The **atrioventricular node** and bundle are derived from cells in the walls of the sinus venosus and atrioventricular canal.

FETAL CIRCULATION

Blood flow in the fetus varies in two respects from the neonatal stage (Figure 40-5). Communication is open between the right and left sides of the heart through the **fossa ovale,** as well as between the aorta and the pulmonary artery via the **ductus arteriosus.** It is useful to

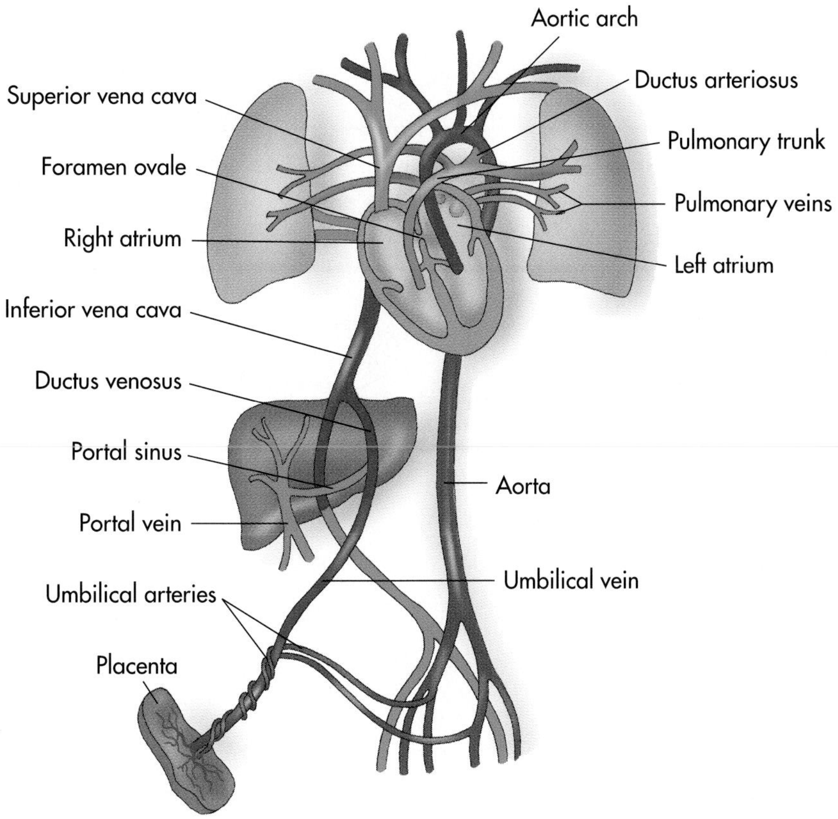

Figure 40-5 Fetal circulation.

know these important communications to appreciate the fetal physiology of the cardiac structures.

Before birth the oxygenated blood is given to the fetus by way of the umbilical vein from the placenta to the heart. Approximately half of the blood passes through the hepatic sinusoids, whereas the remainder bypasses the liver to go through the *ductus venosus* into the inferior vena cava. Blood flows from the **inferior vena cava** and **superior vena cava** and enters the **right atrium.** Blood in the right atrium is less oxygenated than blood in the umbilical vein.

A small amount of oxygenated blood from the inferior vena cava is diverted by the *crista dividens* and remains in the right atrium to mix with deoxygenated blood from the superior vena cava and *coronary sinus.* Some of the blood from the inferior vena cava is directed by the lower border of the *septum secundum* (the crista dividens) through the *foramen ovale* into the **left atrium.**

The blood in the right atrium flows through the three leaflet **tricuspid valve** into the ***right ventricle*** and leaves the right ventricle through the **main pulmonary artery.** This artery bifurcates into right and left pulmonary artery branches that lead to their respective lungs. However, most of this blood passes through the connection of the *ductus arteriosus* into the *descending aorta;* only a very small amount goes to the lungs.

The blood mixes with a small amount of deoxygenated blood as it returns from the lungs via the four **pulmonary veins** into the left atrium. The pulmonary veins enter the posterior of the left atrium. The four veins are named according to their locations, that is, right upper, left upper, right lower, and left lower. The blood then flows from the left atrium into the **left ventricle** through the bicuspid **mitral valve** and leaves the heart through the *ascending aorta.* The head, neck, and upper torso of the fetus are fed via the three branches off the ascending aorta. These branches are the innominate, left carotid, and left subclavian arteries. The rest of the mixed blood in the descending aorta passes into the umbilical arteries and is returned to the placenta for reoxygenation. The remainder of the blood circulates through the lower part of the body.

After birth the circulation of the fetal blood through the placenta ceases, and the neonatal lungs begin to function. The fetal cardiac structures no longer needed are the foramen ovale, the ductus arteriosus, the ductus venosus, and the umbilical vessels (Figure 40-6).

Omission of the placental circulation causes an immediate fall of blood pressure in the newborn's inferior vena cava and right atrium. As the lungs expand with air, there is a fall in the pulmonary vascular resistance. This causes an increase in pulmonary blood flow and a progressive thinning of the walls of the pulmonary arteries. Thus the pressure in the left atrium becomes higher than that in the right atrium. This causes the foramen ovale to close. With time, complete closure of the foramen occurs from adhesion of the septum primum to the left margin of the sep-

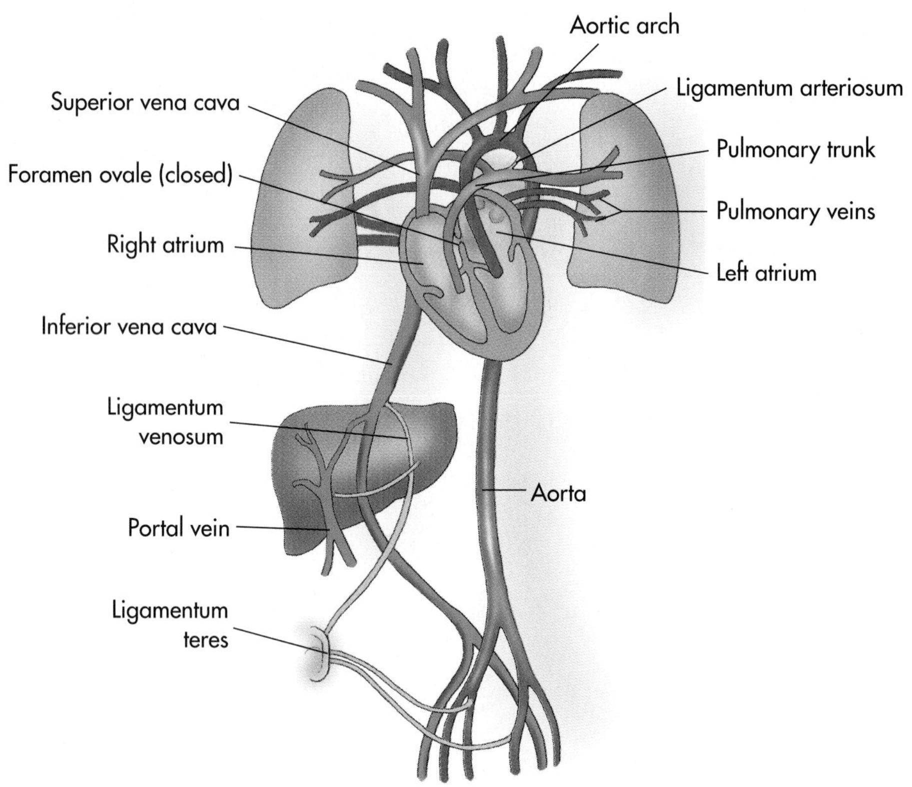

Figure 40-6 Neonatal circulation.

tum secundum. The septum primum forms the floor of the fossa ovalis. The lower edge of the septum secundum forms the limbus fossae ovalis, which demarcates the former cranial boundary of the foramen ovale.

The ductus arteriosus usually constricts shortly after birth (usually within 24 to 48 hours), once the left-sided pressures exceed the right-sided pressures. Often there is a small shunt of blood from the aorta to the pulmonary artery until these pressures adjust to neonatal life. The ductus turns into the ligamentum arteriosum in the neonate. If this communication persists, it is called a **patent ductus arteriosus.** This ligament passes from the left pulmonary artery to the arch of the aorta.

The umbilical arteries also constrict after birth to prevent blood loss from the neonate. The umbilical vein may remain patent for some time after birth.

The normal fetal heart rate is between 120 and 160 beats per minute. In the first trimester of pregnancy the heart rate begins around 90 beats per minute and increases to 170 beats per minute before returning to a normal rate and sinus rhythm. If the heart rate is too slow (less than 60 beats per minute), it is called *bradycardia;* a heart rate over 200 beats per minute is termed *tachycardia.*

RISK FACTORS INDICATING FETAL ECHOCARDIOGRAPHY

Specific risk factors indicate that the fetus is at a higher than normal risk for congenital heart disease and warrant a fetal echocardiogram. These may be divided into the following three categories: fetal risk factors, maternal risk factors, and familial risk factors (Box 40-3).[1]

BOX 40-3 INDICATIONS FOR FETAL ECHOCARDIOGRAPHY

FETAL INDICATIONS
Polyhydramnios (1.5%)
Nonimmune hydrops (7.5%)
Arrhythmias (23%)

FETAL ABNORMALITIES AND DYSMATURITY (11%)
Extracardiac abnormalities
Chromosome abnormalities
Intrauterine growth restriction

FETAL RISK FACTORS

Fetal risk factors include the presence of intrauterine growth restriction, cardiac arrhythmias, abnormal amniocentesis indicating a trisomy, abnormal amniotic fluid collections, abnormal heart rate, and other anomalies as detected by the sonogram, such as hydrops fetalis.

MATERNAL RISK FACTORS

Maternal risk factors include the previous occurrence of congenital heart disease in siblings or parents; a maternal disease known to affect the fetus, such as diabetes mellitus or connective tissue disease (e.g., lupus); and maternal use of drugs such as lithium or alcohol (Box 40-4).

BOX 40-4 MATERNAL INDICATIONS

MATERNAL DISEASE AFFECTING THE FETUS (7%)
Diabetes
Lupus erythematosus
Infections during pregnancy

MATERNAL INGESTIONS OF DRUGS OR TERATOGENS (4.5%)
Alcoholism
Drug exposure during pregnancy

BOX 40-5 FAMILIAL INDICATIONS

Familial history of congenital heart disease (44%)

FAMILIAL RISK FACTORS

Familial risk factors include genetic syndromes or the presence of congenital heart disease in a previous sibling (Box 40-5). The recurrence risk cited given a sibling with one of the most common cardiovascular abnormalities (ventricular septal defect, atrial septal defect, patent ductus arteriosus, tetralogy of Fallot) varies from 2.5% to 3%.[1] Similar data given one parent with a congenital heart defect suggest that for the common defects listed the recurrence risk ranges from 2.5% (atrial septal defect) to 4% (ventricular septal defect, patent ductus arteriosus, tetralogy of Fallot).[1]

HEART RATE

A very slow fetal heart rate, under 80 beats per minute, places the fetus at high risk of associated heart disease; fetal echocardiography should be performed to rule out the presence of a structural heart defect.[4] The association of complete heart block with structural cardiac defects appears to have a poor prognosis, presumably because of their adverse interaction and the atrioventricular valve regurgitation that commonly complicates the condition.[4] The connective tissue disorder, that is, systemic lupus erythematosus, is associated with heart block and pericardial effusion.

BEYOND THE FOUR-CHAMBER VIEW

TRANSDUCER REQUIREMENTS

The ideal transducer for fetal echocardiography is a multifrequency transducer that can be quickly and easily changed from a low to a high frequency. This is especially useful when the baby is located in a position far from the transducer face or when a lower-frequency Doppler signal is needed to obtain a high-velocity flow profile.

The following guidelines may be used in selecting the proper multihertz transducer for the fetal echocardiogram:

1. A 5.0-MHz transducer or higher with a medium focus is generally ideal for the typical pregnancy in a small to average-size patient in the second trimester.
2. A 3.5-MHz transducer with a medium to long focus may be used on patients of average to large build and on patients in the third trimester.
3. A 2.25-MHz transducer with medium to long focus is used for the obese patient in the second or third trimester.
4. The higher-frequency transvaginal probe is useful when the fetus is directed in a transverse lie. The probe is placed transabdominally in the mother's umbilicus with gentle pressure and angled toward the fetal heart.
5. The size of the transducer varies. The early second trimester fetus may be adequately imaged with a curved array transducer; however, some laboratories prefer the small-sector, high-frequency probe.

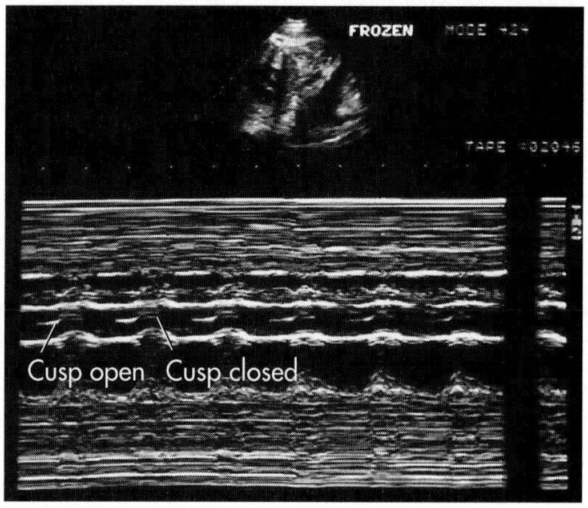

Figure 40-7 M-mode of the aorta and left atrial cavity. Time is depicted along the horizontal axis *(dots along the top of the image)*. The distance between two dots represents 1 second. Distance is located along the vertical axis. The aorta is shown as the two parallel lines moving as a "unit" through systole (pumping) and diastole (resting). The aortic cusps open and remain open during ventricular diastole. The left atrial cavity is shown posterior to the aorta. The left atrial wall motion may be seen within the left atrial cavity.

INSTRUMENTATION

Other features useful on the ultrasound equipment include the following: cine-loop feature that allows imaging of the heart in frame-by-frame analysis, videotape or disk recordings for later playback or comparison evaluation, high-power resolution zoom capability, simultaneous M-mode with range expansion (for cardiac arrhythmias), simultaneous Doppler capability with pulsed and continuous wave (to record high-velocity flows), and color Doppler.

MOTION MODE IMAGING

Motion mode (M-mode) is used to evaluate cardiac motion. Once the two-dimensional image is made, a single vertical line of information can be obtained from the face of the transducer through the fetal cardiac structures. This image is electronically rotated 90 degrees so the depth of the image is along the vertical axis and the time display is shown along the horizontal axis (Figure 40-7). Acquisition of heart wall motion, septal and valve movement, and cavity size may be easily obtained from this technique. Heart rate is measured by counting the number of beats

that occur within a specific time frame, usually over 1 second. If 2.5 beats were shown in a 1-second time period, the heart rate would be 2.5 beats × 60 seconds = 150 beats per minute (Table 40-1).

PULSED DOPPLER IMAGING

Pulsed Doppler demonstrates the direction and characteristics of blood flow within the fetal heart and great vessels and allows the qualitative and quantitative definition of flow disturbances such as those that occur with valvular stenotic or regurgitant lesions.[4] Doppler uses the principle of the Doppler shift or sound waves reflected from the red blood cells within the fetal heart; if the cells are moving toward the transducer, the pitch increases; if the cells are traveling away, the pitch is decreased. On the spectral display, the flow is displayed above (toward) or below (away) from the baseline. The sample volume may be gated or moved to the area of interest to record the optimum signal as the transducer is parallel to the flow of blood (Figure 40-8).

Higher levels of ultrasound energy are used with Doppler, and although no harmful effects have been reported on the fetal heart, it is recommended by the American Institute of Ultrasound in Medicine (AIUM) to keep the Doppler ultrasonic energy at or below 100 mW/cm^2 spatial peak-temporal average, and Doppler interrogation should be limited to as short a time as possible (Table 40-2).[4]

COLOR FLOW DOPPLER

Color flow Doppler may help in detecting flow disturbances and flow direction (to see if vessels or chambers are patent) and should be integrated into the fetal echocardiogram. Color Doppler flow mapping is a multigated Doppler technique in which sampling along all the scan lines and depths in the field occurs simultaneously. Color displays are usually oriented so that flow toward the transducer is projected in shades of red and orange, and flow away is projected in cool colors of blues. Disturbed flow is seen as a mixture of red, orange, and yellow or blues and greens.

TABLE 40-1 NORMAL FETAL M-MODE CARDIAC MEASUREMENTS

Weeks of gestation	Cardiac Structure LV/RV	IVS	AO/PA	LA
20	6	1.5	4	5
22	8	1.7	4.8	6
24	9	2	5	6.5
28	10	2.3	6	8
32	12	3	7	10
36	14	3.5	8	11
40	16	3.8	9	12.5

AO, Aorta; *IVS*, interventricular septum; *LA*, left atrium; *LV*, left ventricle; *PA*, pulmonary artery; *RV*, right ventricle.

THREE-DIMENSIONAL IMAGING

Clinical investigation of three-dimensional echocardiography has been performed both with and without cardiac gating. The gated acquisition showed improved resolution of structures compared with the nongated acquisition. Clarity of images is still the primary problem in this technique, because the fetal heart is beating so quickly and the volume is so small to acquire enough data points to display an image better than the current real-time two-dimensional images.

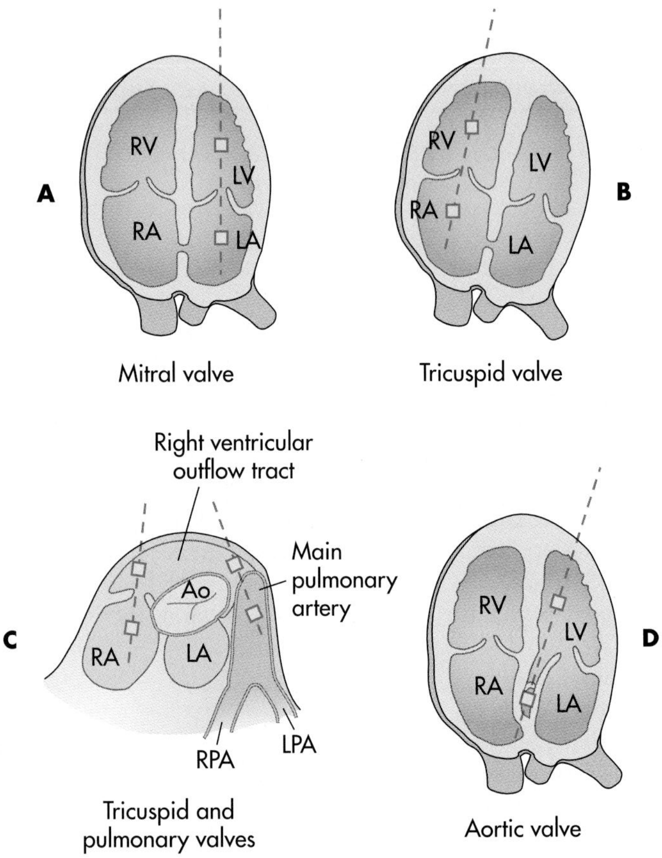

Figure 40-8 Pulsed Doppler sample volume placement for fetal echo. **A** and **B,** The four-chamber view is ideal to sample the velocity flow patterns of the mitral and tricuspid valves. The sample volume is initially placed at the annulus of the valve. To record regurgitation the volume is moved into the atrial chamber; to record inflow of the valves the sample volume is moved into the ventricular cavity. *LA,* Left atrium; *LV,* left ventricle; *RA,* right atrium; *RV,* right ventricle. **C,** The high short-axis view is best to obtain velocities from the tricuspid and pulmonary valves. The same procedure is used for the tricuspid valve as described in the four-chamber view. To record flow in the main pulmonary artery the sample volume is placed at the level of the cusps and then moved back into the right ventricular outflow tract, then into the main pulmonary artery to look for abnormal flow patterns. *AO,* Aorta; *LPA,* left pulmonary artery; *RPA,* right pulmonary artery. **D,** The five-chamber view is good to record velocity flow in the left ventricular outflow tract and the ascending aorta. The sample volume should be placed below the aortic leaflets in the left ventricular outflow tract and then slowly moved through the cusps into the ascending aorta to see flow velocities.

FETAL ULTRASOUND LANDMARKS

In most cases the obstetric patient has had a previous ultrasound and is referred for a dedicated or "target" fetal echocardiographic examination. Generally a dedicated fetal echocardiographic study may take from 30 to over 60 minutes, depending on the type of pathologic condition present.

The cardiac sonographer must know certain characteristics that will help in the cardiac evaluation. (The reader is referred to Chapter 28 for illustration of these normal structures.)

The fetal survey should demonstrate the following structures before focusing on the fetal heart:

1. The position of the fetus (vertex, breech, transverse).
2. The position of the fetal thorax (spine up or down; determine right side and left side).
3. The position of the fetal stomach (right or left).
4. The location of the apex of the heart (left, right, or midline) (Figure 40-9).
5. The location of the fetal abdominal aorta and inferior vena cava (aorta left, close to spine, inferior vena cava right and elevated from spine).
6. The position of the fetal placenta (anterior placenta may cause noise that interferes with visualization of the cardiac structures if the thorax is adjacent to the placenta).
7. The biparietal diameter and/or femur length for measurement correlation.

TABLE 40-2 NORMAL DOPPLER MEASUREMENTS (PEAK SYSTOLE)

Mitral valve	40-60-80 cm/sec
Tricuspid valve	45-65-87 cm/sec
Aortic valve	40-60-100 cm/sec
Pulmonic valve	25-55-80 cm/sec
Foramen ovale	20-30 cm/sec
Aortic arch, level of ductal insertion	120-150 cm/sec

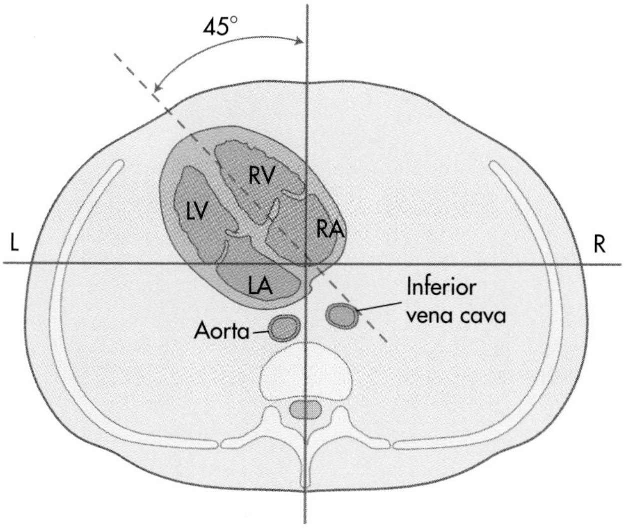

Figure 40-9 Measurement of the cardiac axis from a four-chamber view plane of the fetal chest. *LA,* left atrium; *LV,* left ventricle; *RA,* right atrium; *RV,* right ventricle. The apex of the heart should not exceed a 45-degree angle from the line drawn perpendicular to the fetal spine.

Technical difficulties in obtaining an adequate image include the following problems: decreased amniotic fluid (oligohydramnios), unusual fetal position (spine up, transverse, or low lie in the maternal pelvis), and maternal obesity. The diabetic mother is generally more difficult to scan; these patients image best in the middle of the second trimester, between 20 and 22 weeks of gestation.

When the fetus is in a difficult-to-image position, the sonographer may ask the mother to get up, use the rest room, walk the hall for a few minutes, or do "toe touches" or jumping jacks to encourage the fetus to change positions. This technique usually works.

ECHOCARDIOGRAPHIC EVALUATION OF THE FETUS

A normal cardiac study should include the following views: four-chamber, outflow tracts, and oblique long-axis view for the aortic arch and ductus arteriosus.

FOUR-CHAMBER VIEW

The four-chamber view is probably one of the easiest views to demonstrate cardiac anatomy (Box 40-6). Remember, the fetal heart lies in a horizontal position within the thorax and the apex of the heart (the left ventricle) is directed toward the left hip (Figure 40-10). The transducer is angled in a cephalic direction through the fetal liver, which serves as a good window to visualize cardiac structures.

The sonographer should note the relative size and function of the atria and inflow ventricular cavities (see Figure 40-10, *D* and *E*). The right heart is slightly larger in utero than the left heart. The right and left sides may be identified by the opening flap of the patent foramen ovale; in utero the foramen opens toward the left atrium; after birth the pressure in the left heart forces the foramen to close. Failure to close results in an atrial septal defect. The moderator band can also be used to identify the right ventricle. It stretches horizontally across the right ventricle near the apex. The right ventricle is also more trabeculated than the left ventricle at the apex.

BOX 40-6 FOUR-CHAMBER VIEW ANATOMY

- Right atrium and ventricle (with moderator band)
- Tricuspid valve
- Left atrium and ventricle
- Mitral valve
- Interventricular septum
- Interatrial septum
- Foramen ovale
- Pulmonary veins as they enter the left atrium

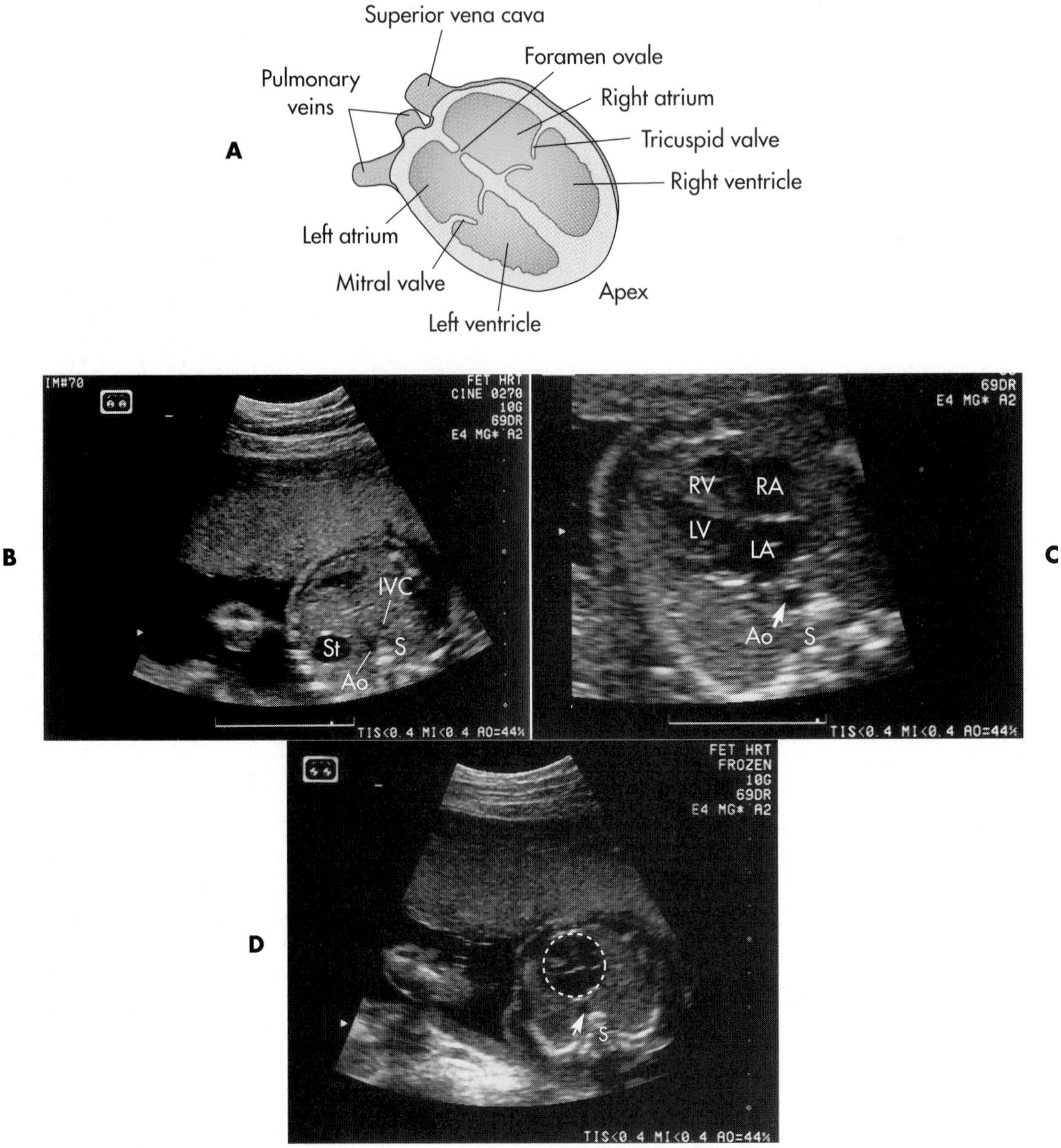

Figure 40-10 **A,** The normal fetal heart lies horizontal in the fetal thorax, with the apex pointing to the left hip. The four-chamber view shows the superior vena cava as it enters the right atrium. The two upper pulmonary veins enter the left atrium. The foramen ovalae opens into the left atrium during fetal life. **B,** Transverse view of the 18-week fetus. The fetus is vertex with the spine *(S)* posterior, aorta *(Ao),* and anterior and inferior vena cavas *(IVC)* anterior and to the right; the stomach *(St)* lies to the left. **C,** As the transducer is angled cephalad, the four-chamber view of the heart is seen within the thorax. The spine *(S)* is posterior with the aorta *(arrow),* anterior to the spine. The left atrium lies directly anterior to the aorta. *LA,* Left atrium; *LV,* left ventricle; *RA,* right atrium; *RV,* right ventricle. **D,** Four-chamber view of the heart with a normal axis.

The position of the mitral and tricuspid leaflets (atrioventricular leaflets) should be assessed. Normally the tricuspid valve is located just slightly inferior to the mitral valve.

The left atrial cavity is generally about the same size as the right atrial cavity and is hypoechoic. The four pulmonic veins enter into the posterior wall of the left atrium. The right upper enters into the medial/posterosuperior wall; the left upper enters into the lateral/posterosuperior wall; the left lower enters the lateral inferior wall; and the right lower enters the medial inferior wall (see Figure 40-10, *F*). On the four-chamber view all the pulmonary veins are imaged except for the right lower vein.

The inferior and superior vena cava may be seen to enter the right atrium. The inferior vena cava enters the pos-

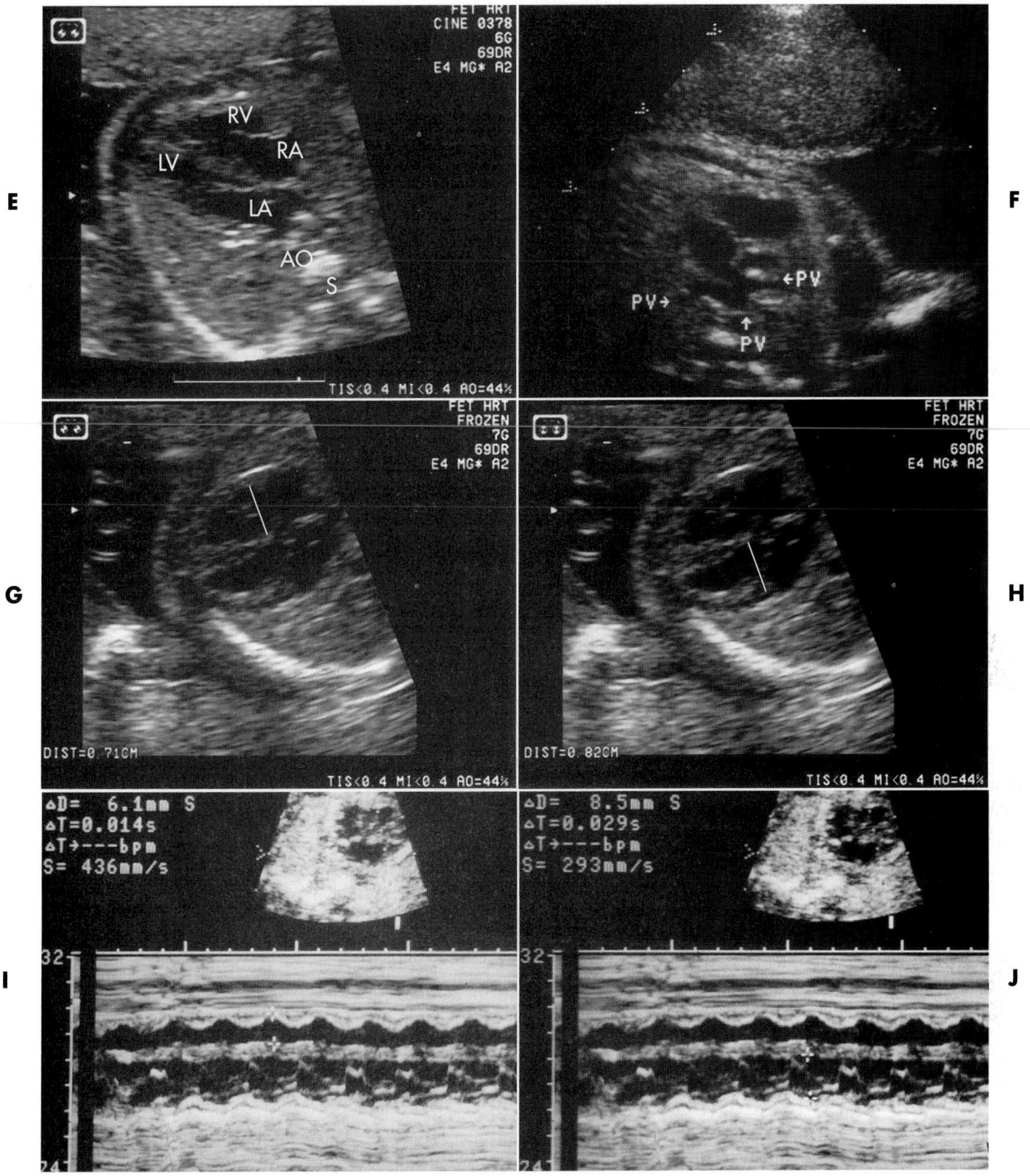

Figure 40-10, cont'd. **E,** *AO,* Aorta; *LA,* left atrium; *LV,* left ventricle; *RA,* right atrium; *RV,* right ventricle; *S,* Spine. **F,** Three of the four pulmonary veins *(PV)* enter the left atrial cavity. Measurements of the left ventricle **(G)** and right ventricle **(H)** are made on two-dimensional views at the level of the mitral annulus. **I,** M-mode measurements may also be made at the level of the annulus for the RV and LV **(J)**.

terior wall along the inferior lateral margin; the superior vena cava enters the medial posterosuperior wall.

The right and left ventricular width measurements are performed in the four-chamber view at the level of the atrioventricular annulus. The sonographer should clean up the image as much as possible for this measurement by turning the gain down. The right ventricle is measured from the lateral wall, across the level of the tricuspid annulus, to the midportion of the septum (see Figure 40-10, *G*). The left ventricle is measured from the midportion of the septum, across the level of the mitral annulus, to the endocardial surface of the lateral wall of the ventricle (see Figure 40-10, *H*). Normal values have been established to correspond to appropriate gestational ages. At 18 weeks of gestation the ventricles should each measure approximately 6 mm.

If any abnormality exists in the atrioventricular valves or if the atria are enlarged, the four-chamber view is excellent to record Doppler tracings of blood flow (Figure 40-11). The transducer should be parallel to the four-chamber view, with the cursor placed at the level of the

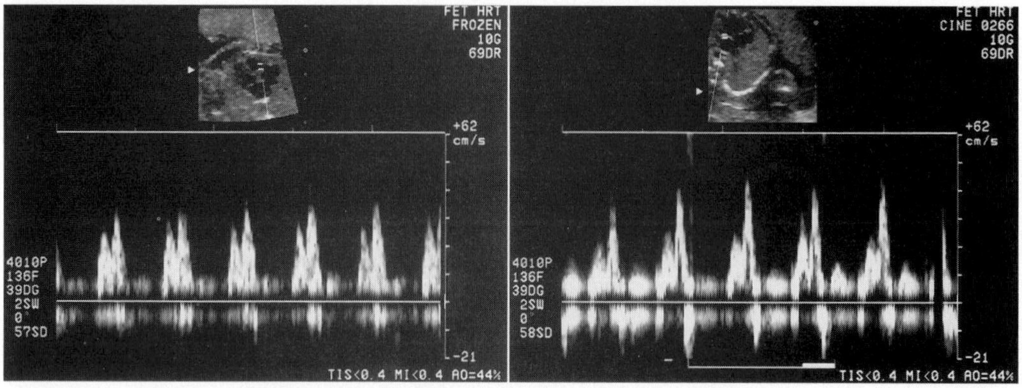

Figure 40-11 Normal Doppler flow patterns made in the four-chamber view of the mitral **(A)** and tricuspid **(B)** leaflets. The smaller first peak is the *"e"* wave; the second higher peak is the *"a"* wave.

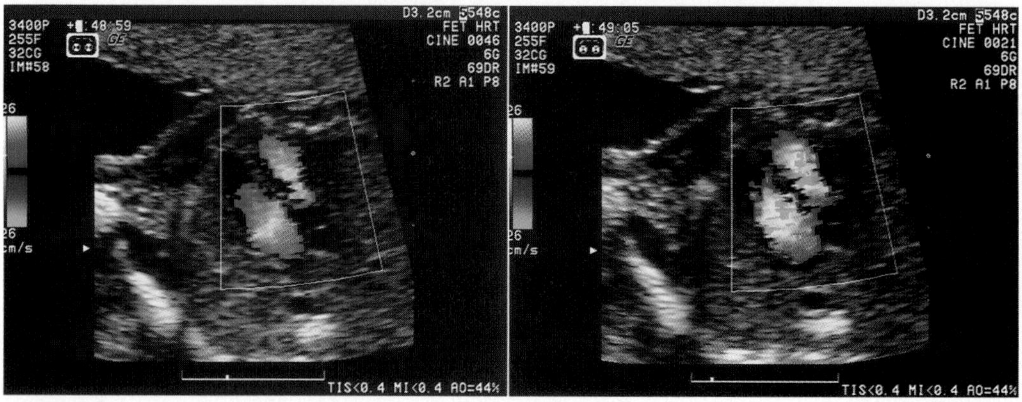

Figure 40-12 Color Doppler inflow patterns of the normal heart in a four-chamber view. **A** corresponds to early diastole at the *"e"* wave (early inflow filling of the ventricle), and **B** represents the *"a"* wave.

annulus and slowly moved into the ventricular cavity to record atrioventricular inflow patterns. To record regurgitation of the atrioventricular valves, the cursor is slowly moved into the atrial cavity to map the flow pattern and assess flow dynamics. Normally there is no backward flow through the orifice. The sonographer can assess the atrial size as an additional determinant of the presence of regurgitation.

The atrioventricular valves have a "double peak" of blood flow on the Doppler tracing. The first peak, e, is termed the *passive filling phase* (this increases with fetal breathing and with gestational age). This peak is smaller than the second peak because the fetal heart is less compliant than the neonatal heart. The second, taller peak, a, is termed the *active atrial phase.* In later pregnancy the e point equals or exceeds the a point on the Doppler tracing as the pressure on the left side exceeds the right-side pressure. The mean tricuspid valve velocity is 65 cm per second; the mean mitral valve velocity is 60 cm per second.[3]

Color flow Doppler (Figure 40-12, *A* and *B*) may be useful in demonstrating the amount and path of regurgitation. A multicolored jet would be present in the atrial cavity posterior to the atrioventricular valve. Remember the pressures in the fetal heart are different than after birth; therefore the color and Doppler flow patterns will not be truly representative of the velocities obtained after birth.

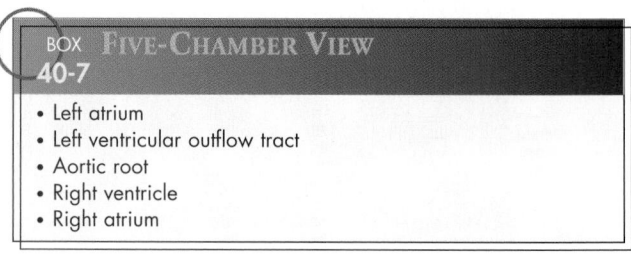

BOX 40-7 FIVE-CHAMBER VIEW

- Left atrium
- Left ventricular outflow tract
- Aortic root
- Right ventricle
- Right atrium

LEFT AND RIGHT VENTRICULAR OUTFLOW TRACTS

Five-Chamber View. Aortic flow may be recorded in the "five"-chamber view (Box 40-7); to obtain this view, the transducer should be angled slightly anterior from the four-chamber view to include the left ventricular and aortic outflow tract (Figure 40-13). Doppler flow patterns of the aorta are recorded with the transducer again parallel to flow and the cursor placed first at the level of the aortic cusps and then moved into the ascending aorta. The mean velocity in the aorta is 60 cm per second.

A

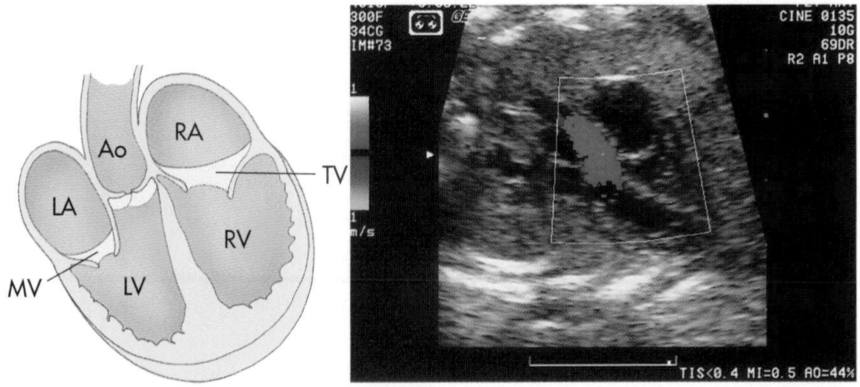

B

Figure 40-13 Aortic outflow is shown in red in this four-chamber view. *Ao,* Aorta; *LA,* left atrium; *LV,* left ventricle; *MV,* mitral valve; *RA,* right atrium; *RV,* right ventricle; *TV,* tricuspid valve.

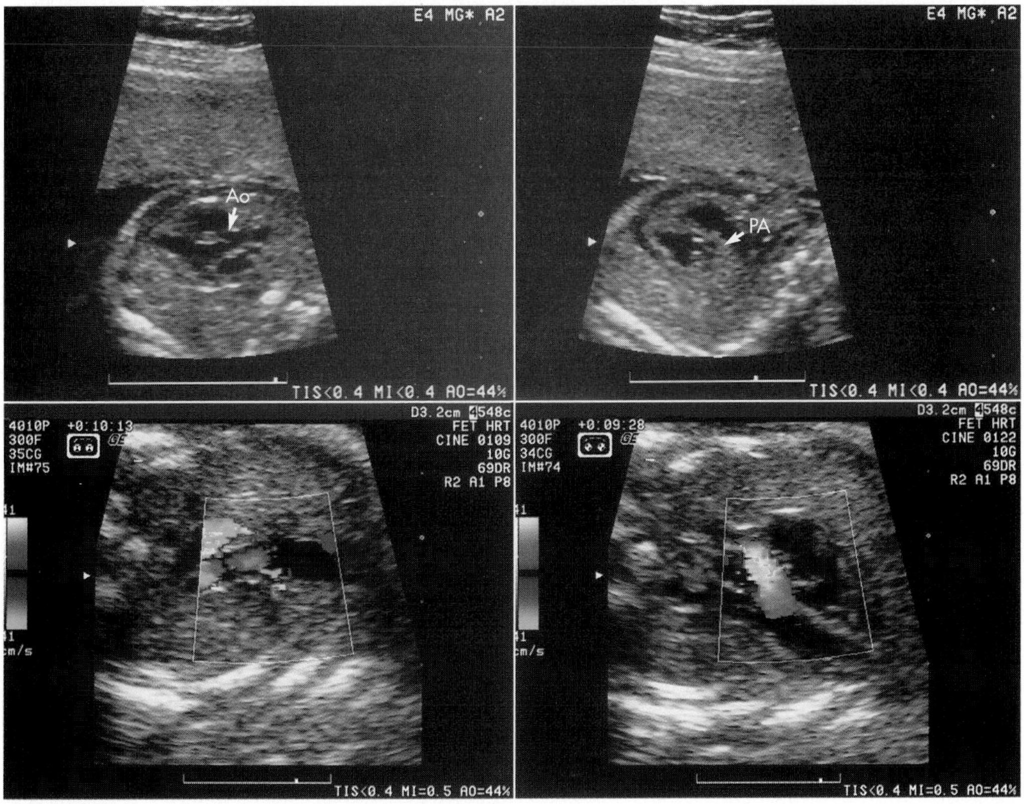

A

B

Figure 40-14 **A,** Criss-cross view of the heart shows the aorta *(Ao)* posterior in continuity with the ventricular septum. The transducer is angled medial and anterior to image the pulmonic artery *(PA).* **B,** Color Doppler image of the pulmonary artery outflow is blue as it leaves the right ventricular cavity. The aortic outflow is red as the blood leaves the left ventricle.

Criss-cross View. As the transducer is angled from the aorta, slightly to the left, the pulmonary artery may be seen as it arises from the right ventricular outflow tract (Figure 40-14). The pulmonary artery normally is anterior and to the left of the aorta. This "sweep" from the aorta to the pulmonary artery is called the criss-cross view and allows the sonographer to see the normal relationship of the great arteries to one another (Box 40-8). Pulmonary flow patterns may be obtained in this view if the cursor is parallel with the flow. The cursor is moved into the main pul-

BOX 40-8 CRISS-CROSS VIEW OF GREAT ARTERIES

- Sweep from aorta (located posterior) to pulmonic vessel (located anterior)
- Left ventricular outflow tract
- Right ventricular outflow tract

A

B

C

D

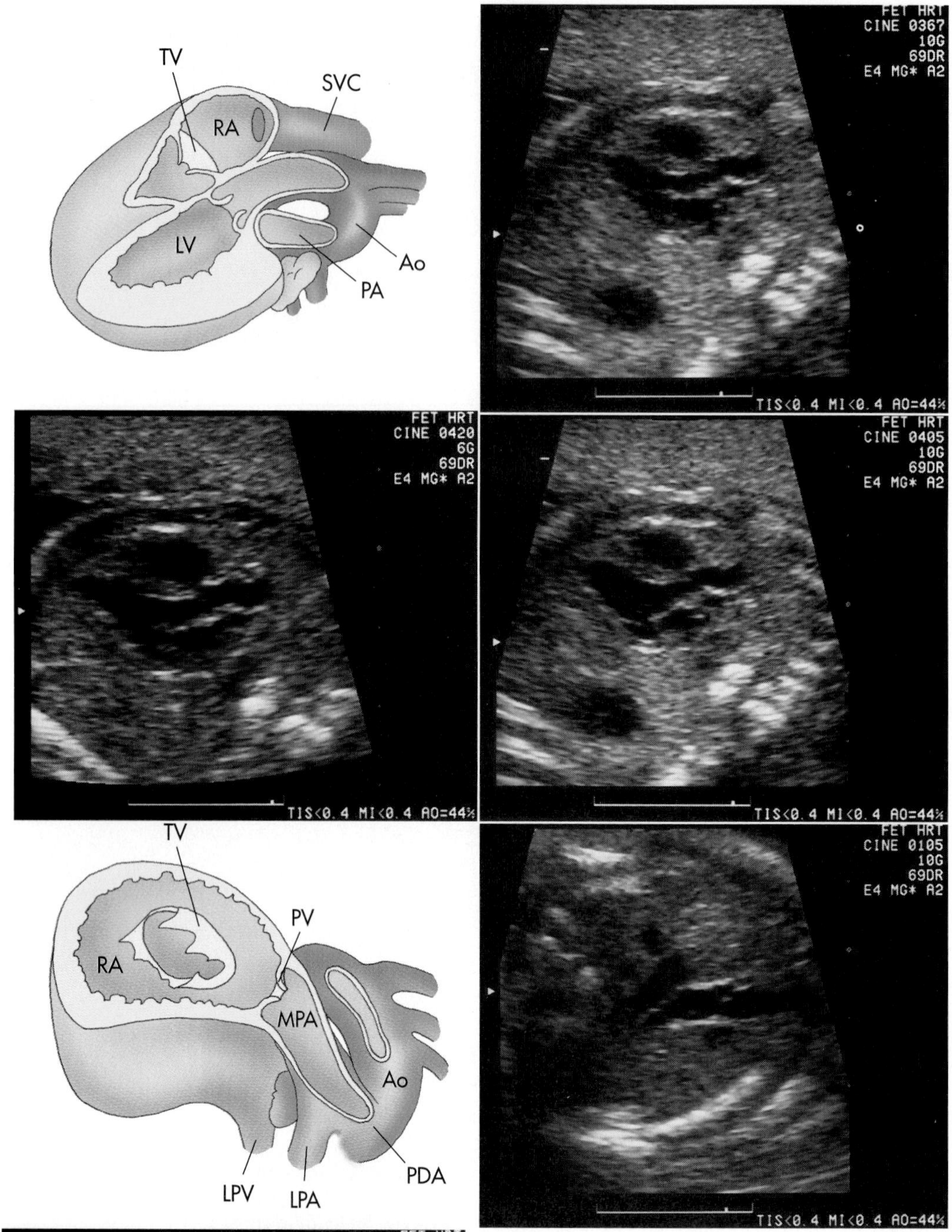

E

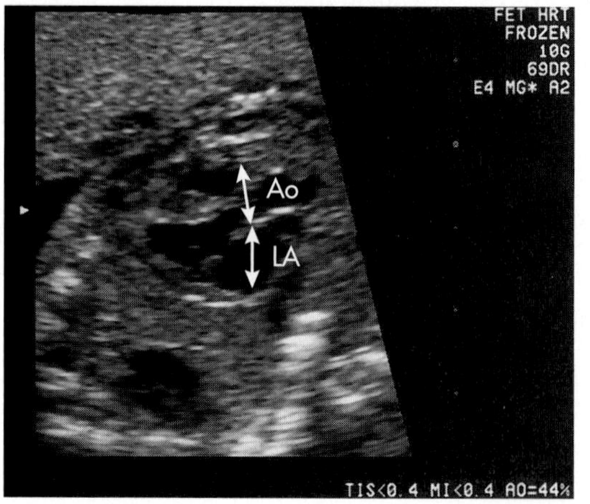

Figure 40-15 **A,** Long-axis view of the left ventricular outflow tract shows the crescent right ventricle, the interventricular septum and its continuity with the anterior wall of the aorta, and the posterior wall of the aorta with its continuity with the anterior leaflet of the mitral valve. The fetal echo was imaged at early diastole, mitral valve open fully, aortic valve closed. **B,** Mid-diastole, mitral valve begins to close. **C,** End-diastole, mitral valve closed, aortic valve opens. **D,** As the transducer is angled medial and slightly anterior, the right ventricular outflow tract with the pulmonary artery *(PA)* is seen on the fetal echo. *Ao,* Aorta; *LPA,* left pulmonary artery; *LPV,* left pulmonary vein; *MPA,* main pulmonary artery; *PDA,* posterior descending artery; *PV,* pulmonary valve; *TV,* tricuspid valve. **E,** The size of the aorta *(Ao)* and left atrium *(LA)* may be measured in this long-axis view.

BOX 40-9 LONG-AXIS VIEW

- Right ventricle
- Interventricular septum
- Left ventricle
- Mitral valve leaflets
- Aorta with aortic cusps
- Left atrium

BOX 40-10 SHORT-AXIS VIEW

- Right ventricular outflow tract
- Pulmonary cusps
- Main pulmonary artery
- Right and left pulmonary arteries
- Aorta with cusps
- Left atrial cavity

monary artery to record the flow patterns. The mean velocity in the pulmonary artery is 55 cm per second.

Long-Axis View. In the long-axis view (Figure 40-15, *A* and *B*) the sizes of the right and left ventricles as well as the left atrial cavity should be assessed to obtain an overview of cardiac disease and contractility (Box 40-9). The left atrial cavity in this view is generally about the same size as the aorta and is hypoechoic. The crescent-shaped right ventricle is anterior to the left ventricle.

The thickness of the interventricular septum may be assessed from the parasternal long axis view when the transducer is perpendicular to the septum. The septum is divided into membranous and muscular segments. The membranous portion is located just inferior to the aorta. This part of the septum is the last to develop and is very thin and must be examined in several planes to evaluate its inflow and outflow sections. The inflow membranous septum is best seen on the apical four-chamber view at the level of the atrioventricular valves, whereas the outflow may be seen on the long-axis view.

The septum thickens along its muscular component, which makes up the remaining two thirds of the septum. The septum and the posterior left ventricular wall are generally the same thickness at the end of ventricular systole. Normal septal thickness should correspond to the gestational age; a good rule of thumb to remember is that the second-trimester septum should measure about 2 to 2.5 mm and the third-trimester septum should measure under 4 mm. If the septum measures over 5 mm, septal hypertrophy or concentric ventricular hypertrophy should be considered.

On the long-axis view (see Figure 40-15, *C*) the continuity of the right side of the septum with the anterior wall of the aortic root is important to rule out the presence of a membranous ventricular septal defect (VSD), conal truncal abnormality (such as truncus arteriosus), endocardial cushion defect, or tetralogy of Fallot. A very small VSD may not be visualized at this stage, depending on the resolution of the equipment and quality visualization of the fetus. Generally the septal defect must be at least half the size of the aortic diameter to be imaged by ultrasound. Multiple septal defects may be difficult to image in the second trimester.

As the transducer is angled slightly anterior and medial from the aortic root, the right ventricular outflow tract may be imaged (see Figure 40-15, *E* and *F*). The pulmonary artery is slightly wider at its origin than the aorta.

The size of the aorta should be assessed. A gestational age of 20 weeks would show a normal aortic measurement of 4 mm. The aortic cusp motion should be assessed on the long and short-axis views (see Figure 40-15, *G*). Normally the three cusps open in systole to the full extent of the aortic root and close in a midposition in diastole. The cusps do not "flop" into the left ventricular outflow tract, as is sometimes seen to varying degrees with a bicuspid or unicuspid valve. The aortic root should be anechoic from its base throughout the arch and descending aorta. The presence of interluminal echoes with dilation may indicate some degree of aortic stenosis (with poststenotic dilation). The presence of a membrane inferior to the aortic cusps may indicate subvalvular aortic obstruction.

Short-Axis View. Once the long-axis view has been obtained, the transducer is rotated 90 degrees to the transverse or short-axis view (Box 40-10). Generally the transducer is angled in a cephalic direction to make this a high parasternal short-axis view (Figure 40-16, *A*). The structures listed in Box 40-10 should be visualized.

The high short-axis is the view we use to measure the diameter of the pulmonary artery and the aorta (see Figure 40-16, *B*). It is also important to visualize the bifurcation of the main pulmonary artery into the right and left pulmonary arteries to demonstrate the normal relationship of the pulmonary artery as it lies anterior and to the left of the aorta. On the short-axis view, normally the right ventricular outflow tract and pulmonary artery "drape" anterior to the circular aorta (see Figure 40-16, *A*). The great vessels are measured two-dimensionally at the level of the semilunar cusps. At 20 weeks of gestation both arteries should measure approximately 4 mm each.

The trileaflet aortic cusps may be visualized in this short-axis view. A two-leaflet or **bicuspid aortic valve** appears as two cusps with or without eccentric closure, depending on the equal distribution of cusp tissue.

Pulmonic flow patterns are obtained parallel to flow in the high short-axis plane with the Doppler cursor at the level of the pulmonic cusps. The cursor is moved into the main pulmonary artery to map any changes in the flow pattern. The mean velocity in the pulmonary artery ranges from 60 to 80 cm per second; when the cursor reaches the level of ductal insertion, near the left pulmonary branch artery, the flow dramatically increases to nearly double the velocity in the main pulmonary artery (150 cm per second) (Figure 40-16, *C*).

A

B

C

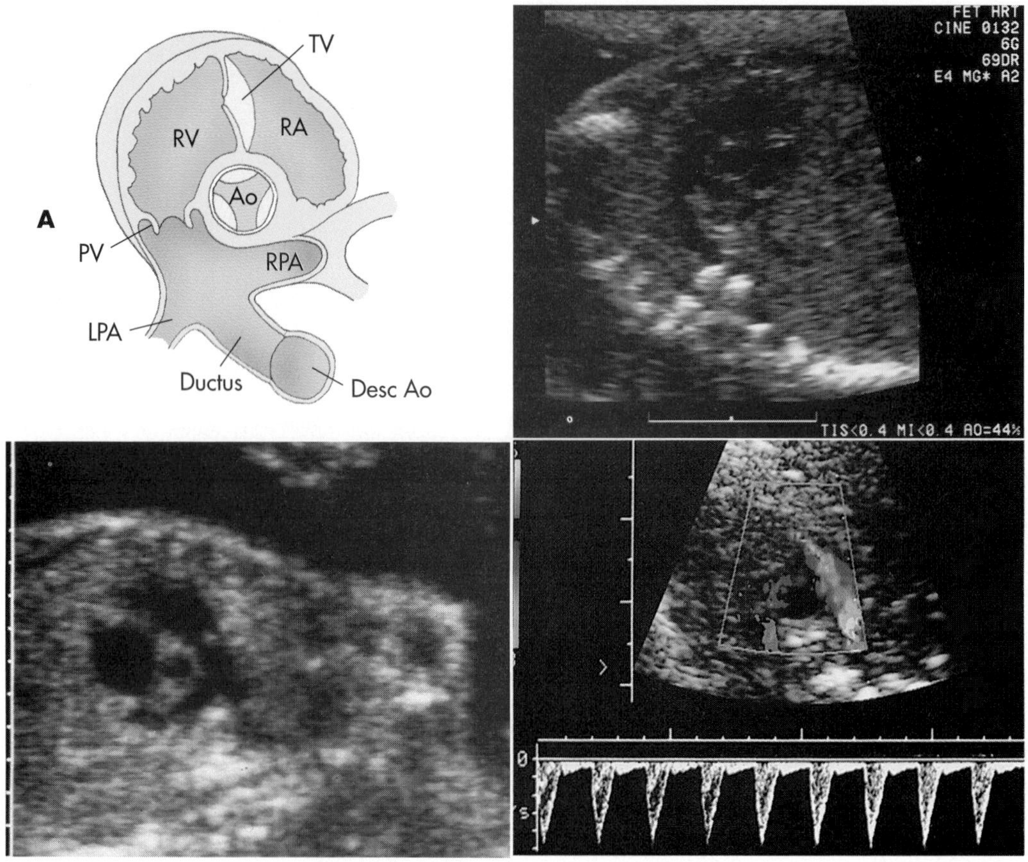

Figure 40-16 **A,** High, short-axis view of the great vessels. The right ventricular outflow tract wraps anterior to the aorta. The pulmonary artery arises from the right ventricle and bifurcates into right and left branches. The ductal insertion occurs midway between the bifurcation of the pulmonary vessels. Measurement of the great vessel diameters may be made at the level of the cusps. *Ao,* Aorta; *Desc Ao,* descending aorta; *LPA,* left pulmonary artery; *PV,* pulmonary vein; *RA,* right atrium; *RPA,* right pulmonary artery; *RV,* right ventricle; *TV,* tricuspid valve. **B,** Normal relationship of the pulmonary artery (tubular) with the bifurcation into right and left pulmonary arteries as it lies anterior to the aorta. **C,** Color Doppler shows the increased velocity in the main pulmonary artery *(blue)* at the ductal insertion *(yellow). AO,* Aorta; *PA,* pulmonary artery.

Ductal and Aortic Arch Views: Oblique Long Axis

With careful angulation of the transducer to an oblique longitudinal plane, the root of the aorta, the ascending aorta, the arch, and the descending aorta may be assessed (Figure 40-17). The sonographer may find the fetal spine in the sagittal plane and angle slightly inward toward the left chest to search for the descending aorta and arch. The tubular dimension of this vessel should be somewhat uniform as one follows the aorta from its base into the thorax and abdomen. As the sonographer carefully sweeps back and forth, the inner core should be anechoic. The three head and neck branch arteries (innominate, carotid, and left subclavian) may be seen to arise from the perfect curve of the aortic arch as they ascend into the fetal head. The sonographer should be able to demonstrate the "candy cane" appearance of the ascending aorta, arch, and descending aorta in one image plane.

A second "arch-type" pattern (which appears as large as the aorta) is shown as the transducer is angled inferior from the aortic arch. This represents the patent ductus arteriosus, a communication between the pulmonary artery and the aorta that is patent during fetal life but closes shortly after birth. The ductus is slightly larger than the aortic arch and has a sharper angle ("hockey stick") as it drains into the descending aorta (Figure 40-18). The ductus does not have arterial structures arising from its wall as the aorta does.

FETAL ECHOCARDIOGRAPHIC FINDINGS IN COMMON FORMS OF CONGENITAL HEART DISEASE

The most common type of congenital heart disease is the ventricular septal defect, followed by atrial septal defects and **pulmonary stenosis** (Table 40-3).

Environmental factors influence congenital heart disease. Chromosomal abnormalities also have a high association with congenital heart disease. Fetuses with trisomy

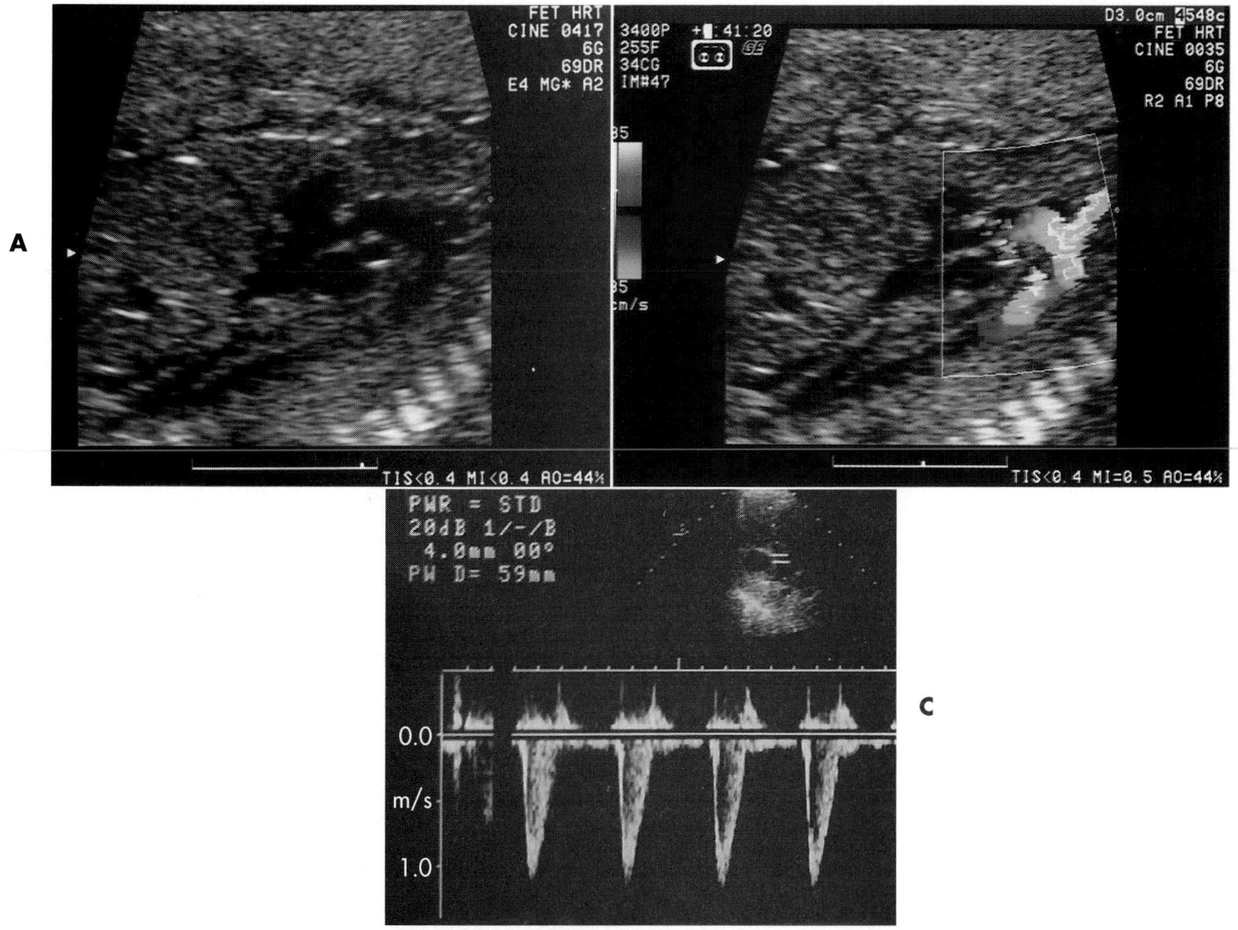

Figure 40-17 Normal gray-scale **(A)** and color Doppler **(B)** images of the ascending aorta, arch, and descending aorta. The left subclavian is one of the three vessels that arise from the arch of the aorta and is well seen on the color image. **C,** Normal velocity in the aorta.

21 have a 50% incidence of congenital heart disease, specifically endocardial cushion defects. Fetal echocardiography can help to establish the presence and severity of congenital heart disease.

The following congenital heart diseases are discussed in this chapter: septal defects, right heart disease, left heart disease, great vessel anomalies, other cardiac anomalies, and fetal arrhythmias.

SEPTAL DEFECTS

Atrial Septal Defect. **Atrial septal defects** are not always recognized during fetal life unless part of the intra-atrial septum is missing. The foramen ovale remains open in the fetal heart until after birth, and the pressures change between the right and left heart to force the foreman to close completely. Failure of the foramen to close may result in atrial septal defect, secundum type (Box 14-11).

Ultrasound findings. The area of the foramen ovale is thinner in the fetus than the surrounding atrial tissue; therefore with echocardiography it is prone to signal dropout, particularly in the apical four-chamber view when the transducer is parallel to the septum. Any break in the atrial septum in this view must be confirmed by the short-axis or "subcostal" view (the transducer is inferior to the heart and angled cephalad in a transverse or short-axis plane), in which the septum is more perpendicular to the transducer. Because of beam-width artifacts, the edges of the defect may be slightly blunted and appear brighter than the remaining septum.

In utero the natural flow is right to left across the foramen (as the pressures are slightly higher on the right). A small reversal flow may be present. The foramen should flap into the left atrial cavity. The flap should not be so large as to touch the lateral wall of the atrium; when this redundancy of the foramen occurs, the sinoatrial node may become agitated in the right atrium and cause fetal arrhythmias. The sonographer should be sure to sweep inferior to superior along the atrial septum to identify the three parts of the septum: the primum septum, fossae ovalis, and septum secundum.

Secundum atrial septal defect. The most common atrial defect is the secundum atrial septal defect, which oc-

curs in the area of the fossa ovalis. Usually an absence of the foramen ovale flap is noted, with the fossa ovalis opening larger than normal.

Ultrasound findings. Doppler tracings of the septal defect with the sample volume placed at the site of the defect show a right-to-left flow with a velocity of 20 to 30 cm per second. Color flow Doppler is performed in the apical four-chamber and subcostal views and may be useful to outline the size and direction of flow as it crosses the foramen ovale (Figure 40-19, *B*). The flow patterns of the mitral and tricuspid valves are slightly increased with the elevated shunt flow.

Sinus venosus septal defect. The sinus venosus atrial septal defect is technically more difficult to visualize with echocardiography. This defect lies in the superior portion of the atrial septum, close to the inflow pattern of the superior vena cava.

Ultrasound findings. Sinus venosus septal defects are best visualized with the subxiphoid four-chamber view. If signs of right ventricular volume overload are present, with no atrial septal defect obvious, care should be taken to study the septum in search of a sinus venosus type of defect. Partial anomalous pulmonary venous drainage of the right pulmonary vein is usually associated with this type of defect; thus it is important to identify the entry site of the pulmonary veins into the left atrial cavity. Color flow mapping is useful in this type of problem because it allows the sonographer to actually visualize the venous return to the left atrium and a flow pattern crossing into the right atrial cavity.

Ventricular Septal Defect. **Ventricular septal defect** is the most common congenital lesion of the heart, accounting for 30% of all structural heart defects. The septum is divided into two basic segments: the membranous and muscular areas (Figure 40-20). There are a number of sites where ventricular septal defects may occur within the septum. Muscular defects occur lower in the septum, usually are very small, and may be multiple. Often smaller defects will close spontaneously shortly after birth.

Ultrasound findings. This type of defect is difficult to image with echocardiography.

A

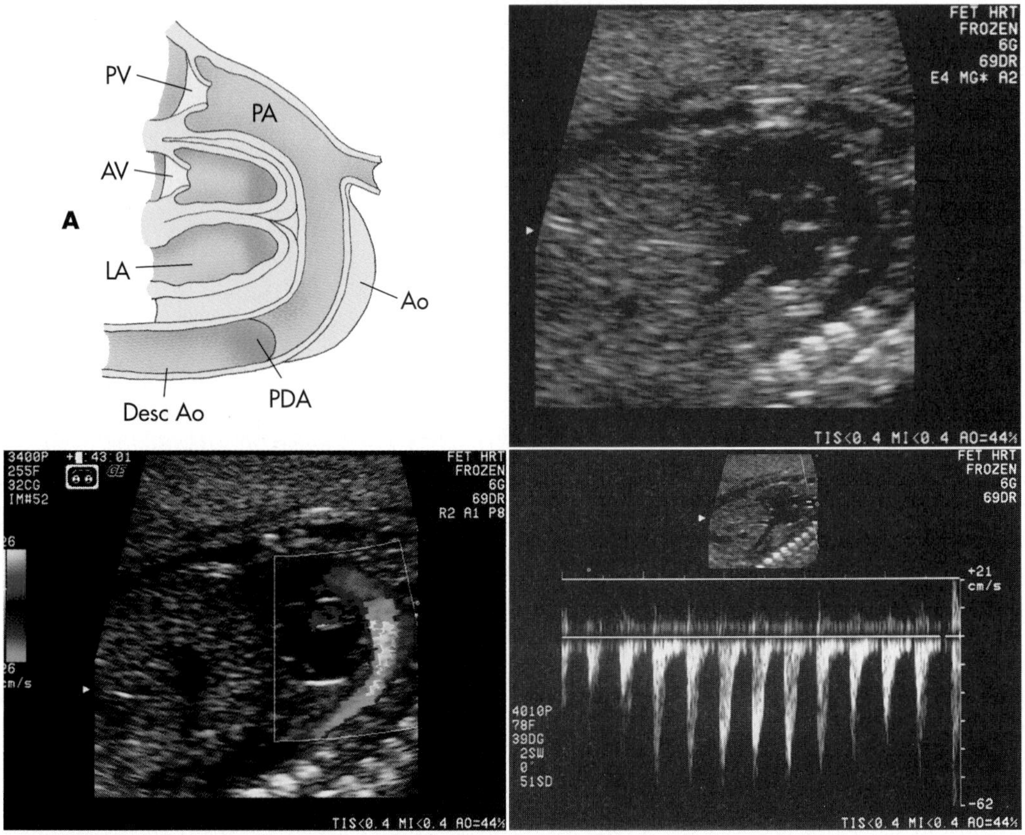

B C

Figure 40-18 The ductal arch is found slightly inferior to the aortic arch. **A,** The short-axis view shows the main pulmonary artery and ductal arch as it empties into the descending aorta. *Ao,* Aorta; *AV,* aortic valve; *Desc Ao,* descending aorta; *LA,* left atrium; *PA,* pulmonary artery; *PDA,* patent ductus arteriosus; *PV,* pulmonary valve. **B,** Color shows the increased velocity *(yellow)* at the level of the ductus. **C,** Pulsed Doppler flow velocity shows the normal pattern of 50 cm per second in the main pulmonary artery. This velocity may more than double at the level of the ductal insertion.

TABLE 40-3 DISTRIBUTION OF TYPES OF CONGENITAL HEART DISEASE AMONG AFFECTED LIVE-BORN INFANTS

Condition	Percentage (%)
Ventricular septal defect	30
Pulmonary stenosis	7
Secundum atrial septal defect	7
Coarctation of the aorta	6
Aortic stenosis	5
Tetralogy of Fallot	5
Transposition of the great arteries	5
Atrioventricular defects	3
Hypoplastic right ventricle	2
Hypoplastic left ventricle	1
Total anomalous pulmonary veins	1
Truncus arteriosus	1
Single ventricle	0.3
Double-outlet right ventricle	0.2
Miscellaneous	17

Data modified from Hoffman C: *Am J Cardiol* 42:641, 1978.

BOX 40-11 ATRIAL SEPTAL DEFECTS (FIGURE 40-19, *A*)

- *Secundum type:* Occurs in the area of the foramen ovale.
- *Sinus venosus type:* Located in the most superior portion of the atrial septum and usually associated with partial anomalous pulmonary venous drainage.
- *Primum type:* Located just superior to the atrioventricular ring and usually associated with a cleft mitral valve leaflet.

Membranous septal defect. The (perimembranous) ventricular septal defect may be classified as membranous, muscular, aneurysmal, or supracristal (see Figure 40-21, *A*).

Ultrasound findings. The significant anatomic landmark is the crista supraventricularis ridge. The defect lies either above or below this ridge. Defects that lie above are called **supracristal.** These defects are located just beneath the pulmonary orifice so that the pulmonary valve forms part of the superior margin of the interventricular communication. Defects that lie below the crista are called **infracristal** and may be found in the membranous or muscular part of the septum. These are the most common defects. The lesion may be partially covered by the tricuspid septal leaflet, and care must be taken to carefully evaluate this area with Doppler and color-flow tracings. The membranous defect is found just below the aortic leaflets; sometimes the aortic leaflet is sucked into this defect (Figure 40-21, *B*).

The presence of an isolated ventricular septal defect in utero usually does not change the hemodynamics of the fetus. Defects smaller than 2 mm are not detected by fetal echocardiography. Care must be taken in the four-chamber view to carefully sweep the transducer posterior (to record the inlet part of the septum) to anterior (to record the outlet part of the septum).

Ventricular septal defects may close with the formation of aneurysm tissue that is commonly found along the right side of the septal defect. These aneurysms generally protrude into the right heart in one of the following three directions: (1) above the tricuspid valve and into the right atrium, (2) directly into the septal leaflet of the tricuspid valve, or (3) below the tricuspid leaflets and into the right ventricular cavity. Usually these aneurysms are small, but when they become large, obstruction may occur in the right ventricular outflow tract.

A

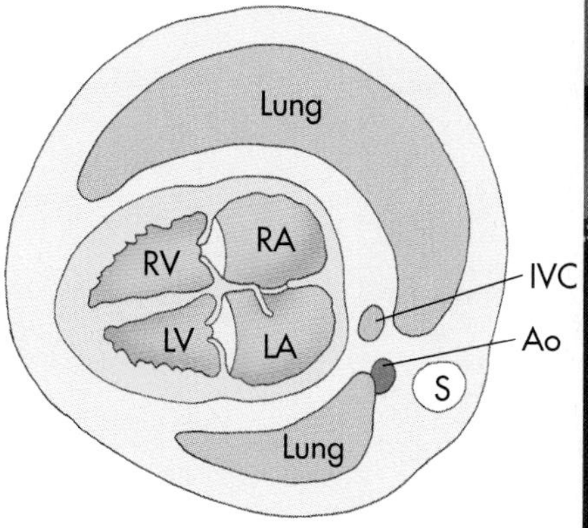

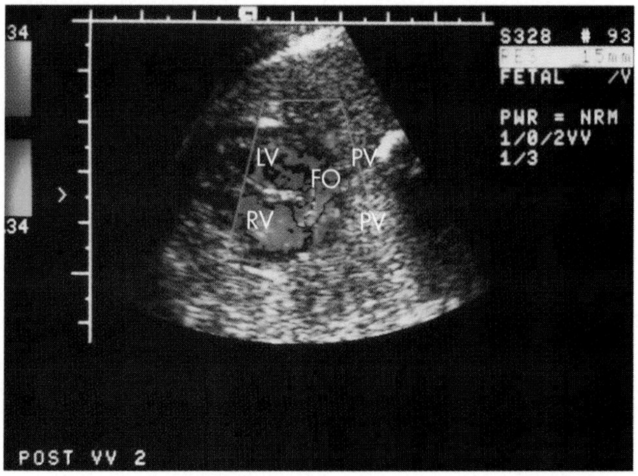

B

Figure 40-19 **A,** The most common type of atrial septal defects occurs in the area of the fossa ovalis, known as the secundum defect. *Ao,* Aorta; *IVC,* inferior vena cava; *LA,* left atrium; *LV,* left ventricle; *RA,* right atrium; *RV,* right ventricle. **B,** In the fetus, normal flow should occur at the level of the foramen ovale *(FO)*. *PV,* pulmonary vein.

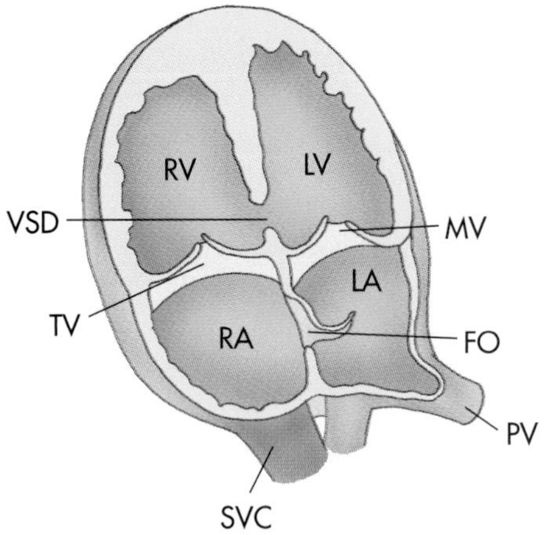

Figure 40-20 The membranous septal defect is shown in this four-chamber view. This is located in the inflow of the ventricles. The muscular defect in this four-chamber view may be large, small, or multiple along the thicker part of the septum. *FO,* Foramen ovale; *LA,* left atrium; *LV,* left ventricle; *MV,* mitral valve; *PV,* pulmonary vein; *RA,* right atrium; *RV,* right ventricle; *SVC,* superior vena cava; *TV,* tricuspid valve; *VSD,* ventricular septal defect.

Muscular defect. A less common infracristal defect is located in the muscular septum. These defects may be large or small, or they may be multiple fenestrated holes (Figure 40-21, *B* and *C*). The multiple defects are more difficult to repair, and their combination may have the same ventricular overload effect as a single large communication. Small muscular defects are usually found in the neonatal stage and often close spontaneously.

The prognosis is good for a patient with a single ventricular septal defect. However, the association of other cardiac anomalies, such as tetralogy of Fallot, single ventricle, transposition of the great arteries, and endocardial cushion defect, is increased when a ventricular septal defect is found.

One study reported that 40% of ventricular septal defects are closed within 2 years of life and that 60% close by 5 years. The incidence of closure for membranous defects is 25% by 5 years and that of muscular defects is 65% by 5 years.

Ultrasound findings. The best echocardiographic views to image the septal defect in the outflow tract are the long-axis, short-axis, and five-chamber views; the septal defect in the inflow tract is best seen on the four-chamber view.

Evaluation of shunt flow and direction is made with color flow mapping. Remember that pressures between the

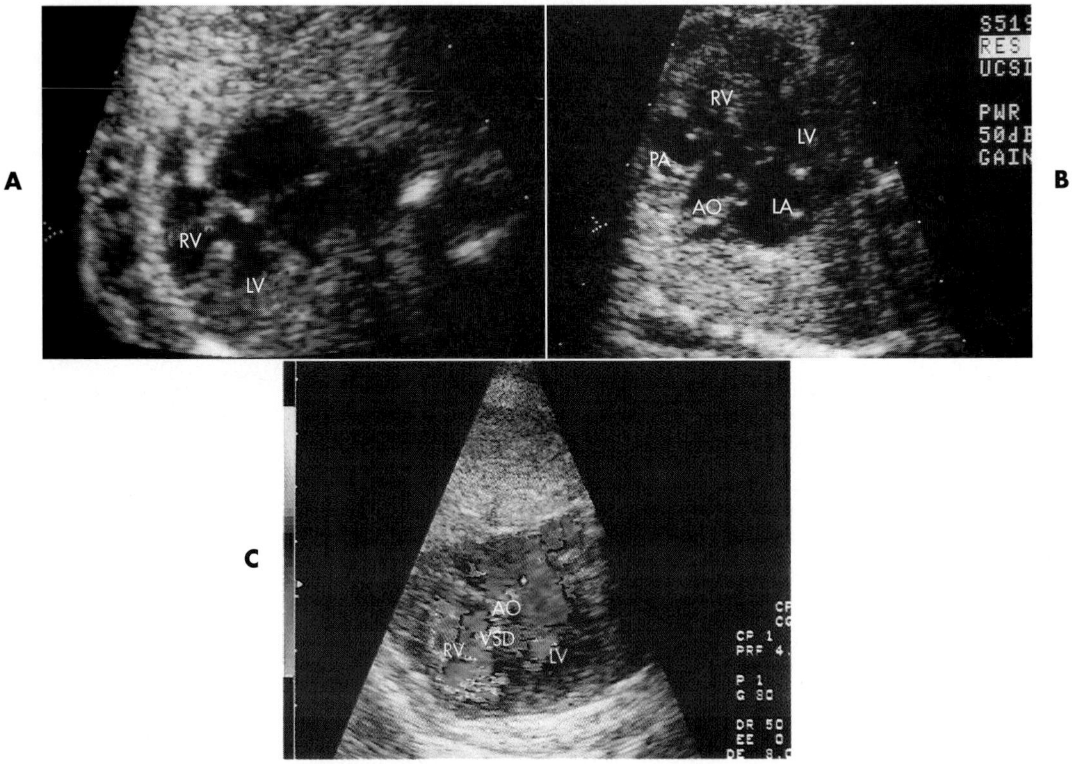

Figure 40-21 Ventricular septal defects. **A,** Large isolated membranous septal defect shown in this four-chamber view. The edges of the defect are slightly brighter than the rest of the septum. *LV,* left ventricle; *RV,* right ventricle. **B,** A patient with trisomy 18 shows a large septal defect involving the membranous and muscular areas. *AO,* Aorta; *PA,* pulmonary artery; *LA,* left atrium. **C,** Color doppler is helpful when the ventricular septal defect *(VSD)* is large enough to allow cross-over of flow from the higher-pressured right heart into the left heart.

right and left heart are almost the same in utero, so a small defect will probably not show a velocity change. If the defect is large, the sample volume should be placed alongside the defect in the left ventricle to see the jet flow.

Atrioventricular Septal Defect. The endocardial cushion defect is also called *ostium primum atrial septal defect, atrioventricular canal malformation, endocardial cushion defect,* and ***atrioventricular septal defect (AVSD)*** (Figure 40-22). These defects are subdivided into complete, incomplete, and partial forms.

Incomplete atrioventricular septal defect. The failure of the endocardial cushion to fuse is termed an **incomplete atrioventricular septal defect.** This condition results in a membranous ventricular septal defect, abnormal tricuspid valve, primum atrial septal defect, and cleft mitral valve (Figure 40-23). A cleft mitral valve means that the anterior part of the leaflet is divided into two parts (medial and lateral). When the leaflet closes, blood leaks through this hole into the left atrial cavity. The leaflet is usually somewhat malformed, further causing regurgitation into the atrium. In addition, there is a communication between the left ventricle and right atrium (left ventricular to right atrial shunt) because of the absent primum atrial septum and membranous interventricular septum. The ventricular septal defect occurs just below the mitral ring and is continuous with the primum atrial septal defect.

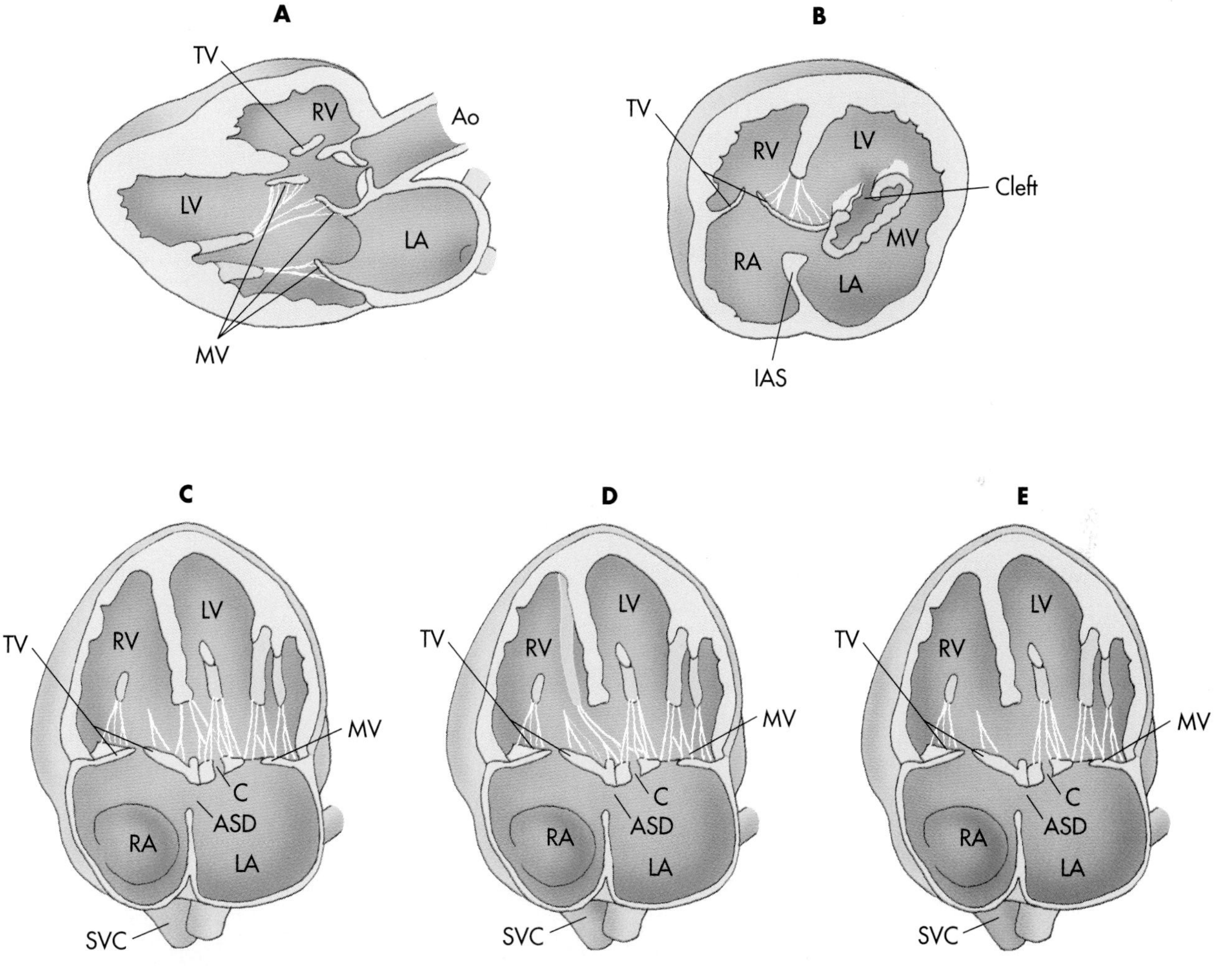

Figure 40-22 Atrioventricular septal defect. **A,** Long-axis view shows the discontinuity of the anterior leaflet of the mitral valve with the posterior wall of the aorta. The membranous septal defect is seen. *Ao,* Aorta; *LA,* left atrium; *LV,* left ventricle; *MV,* mitral valve; *RV,* right ventricle; *TV,* tricuspid valve. **B,** Short-axis through the atrioventricular valves shows the cleft in the anterior leaflet of the mitral valve *(MV).* The primum septal defect is seen. *IAS,* Interarterial septum. **C,** Four-chamber view showing the Rastelli type A large defect in the center (crux) of the heart. The membranous and primum septal defects are seen with the cleft mitral valve. There is a common leaflet from the anterior mitral leaflet to the septal tricuspid leaflet. *ASD,* Atrial septal defect; *SVC,* superior vena cava. **D,** Rastelli type B defect shows the chordal attachments from the medial portion of the cleft mitral leaflet related to the papillary muscle on the right side of the septal defect. **E,** Rastelli type C defect shows a free-floating common atrioventricular leaflet *(C),*

Complete atrioventricular septal defect. The endocardial defect may be further classified into Rastelli types A, B, and C. Types A and B are characterized by insertion of the chordae from the cleft mitral and tricuspid valve into the crest of the ventricular septum or a right ventricular papillary muscle (Figure 40-24). Type C is the most primitive form and is called **complete atrioventricular septal defect.** This defect has a single, undivided, free-floating leaflet stretching across both ventricles. An M-mode sweep from the mitral to the aortic valves would show the anterior mitral leaflet swinging through the ventricular septal defect in continuity with the tricuspid valve. The tricuspid valve is said to cap the mitral valve. The anterior and posterior leaflets are on both sides of the interventricular septum, causing the valve to override or straddle the septum. This is a much more complex abnormality to repair because the defect is larger and the single atrioventricular valve is more difficult to manage clinically, depending on the amount of regurgitation present. Complete AVSDs are frequently associated with malpositions of the heart (mesocardia and dextrocardia) and atrioventricular block (secondary to distortion of the conduction tissues).

AVSDs are frequently associated with other cardiac defects, including truncoconal abnormalities, coarctation of the aorta, and pulmonary stenosis or atresia. There is an increased incidence of Down syndrome (50% of trisomy 21 babies have congenital heart disease) and asplenia and polysplenia syndromes.

Occasionally, complete absence of the interatrial septum is noted in the fetal four-chamber view. With color flow the entire atria are completely filled throughout systole and diastole. This is termed *common atria.*

With a partial AVSD the fetus has only some of the above findings, usually an absent primum atrial septum and a cleft mitral valve.

Ultrasound findings. Echocardiographically the ideal views are the long-axis, short-axis (to search for abnormalities in the atrioventricular valves, such as presence of cleft), and four-chamber views (to search for chordal attachment, overriding, or straddling of the valves). The crux of the heart is carefully analyzed by sweeping the trans-

A

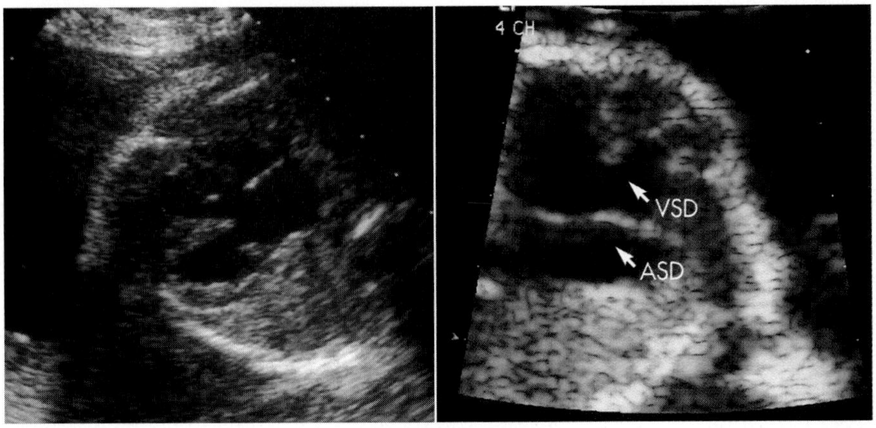

B

Figure 40-23 Atrioventricular septal defect. **A,** A patient with trisomy 21 had 2:1 heart block secondary to the complete atrioventricular septal defect that included the membranous and atrial septae. **B,** A patient with trisomy 21 had a huge atrioventricular defect. The membranous and part of the muscular septum is not present *(VSD);* the primum septum is also absent *(ASD).*

A

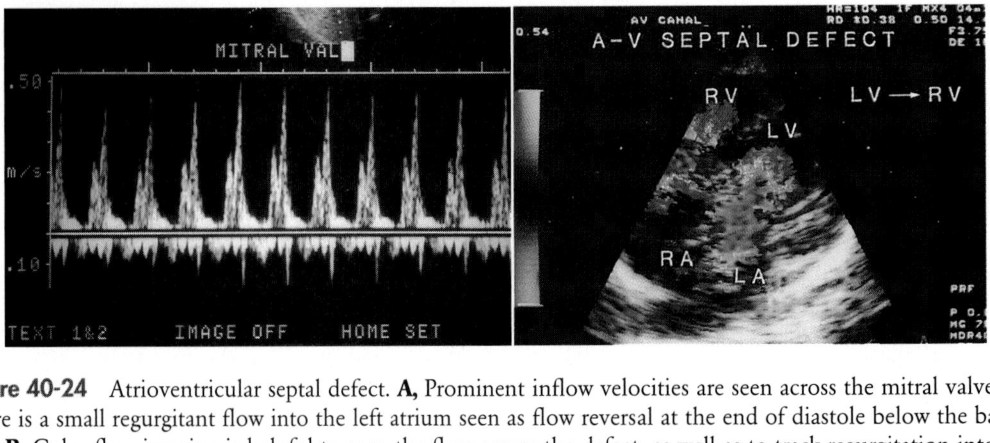

B

Figure 40-24 Atrioventricular septal defect. **A,** Prominent inflow velocities are seen across the mitral valve. There is a small regurgitant flow into the left atrium seen as flow reversal at the end of diastole below the baseline. **B,** Color flow imaging is helpful to map the flow across the defect, as well as to track regurgitation into the atria. *LA,* Left atrium; *LV,* left ventricle; *RA,* right atrium; *RV,* right ventricle.

ducer anterior to posterior to record the outlet and inlet portions of the membranous septum.

Doppler and color flow techniques are extremely useful in determining the direction and degree of regurgitation present in the atrioventricular valves and the direction of shunt flow (increased right heart pressure causes a right ventricular to left atrial shunt in the fetus).

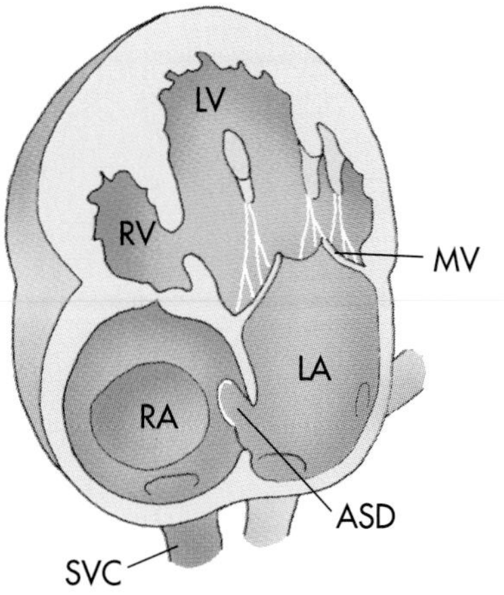

Figure 40-25 The hypoplastic right ventricle and immobile echogenic tricuspid valve apparatus are key factors in the four-chamber view in the patient with tricuspid atresia. The right atrium *(RA)* is enlarged. *ASD,* atrial septal defect; *LA,* left atrium; *LV,* left ventricle; *MV,* mitral valve; *RV,* right ventricle; *SVC,* superior vena cava.

RIGHT VENTRICULAR DISTURBANCES

Abnormalities that affect primarily the right side of the heart are listed as inflow or outflow tract disturbances. Each lesion is presented along with technical advice on how to obtain the ideal fetal cardiac image.

Right Ventricular Inflow Tract Disturbances

Tricuspid atresia. **Tricuspid atresia** is the interruption of the growth of the tricuspid leaflet that begins early in cardiac embryology. This interruption involves the growth of the tricuspid apparatus, causing the valve to be hypoplastic or atretic.

In tricuspid atresia the inflow portion of the right ventricle has failed to form, and a membrane or dimple in the floor of the right atrium represents the position where the tricuspid valve should have originated (Figure 40-25). A ventricular septal defect may be present to help shunt blood into the hypertrophied right ventricle. The right ventricular outflow tract and pulmonary artery are generally diminished in size.

Ultrasound findings. Echocardiographically, the tricuspid valve is best visualized on the four-chamber view (Figure 40-26). The findings in tricuspid atresia are a large dilated left ventricular cavity with a small, underdeveloped

A

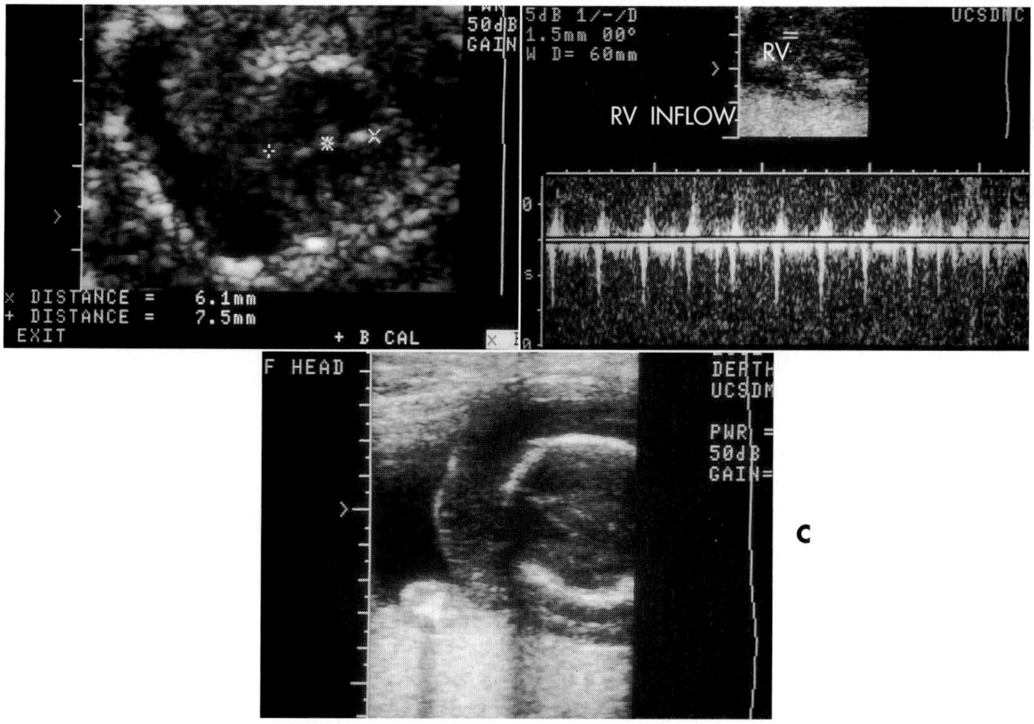

B

C

Figure 40-26 Tricuspid atresia. **A,** This patient presented in her 22nd week with the fetus demonstrating asymmetry of the ventricles. The annulus of the tricuspid valve was echogenic and immobile. The right ventricle was smaller than the left ventricle. The right atrium was enlarged. **B,** Pulsed Doppler imaging shows decreased inflow through the immobile tricuspid valve. There is mild to moderate tricuspid regurgitation seen at the end of diastole as flow reversal below the baseline. **C,** The patient developed severe hydrops with edema surrounding the scalp and abdomen, pleural effusion, and ascites.

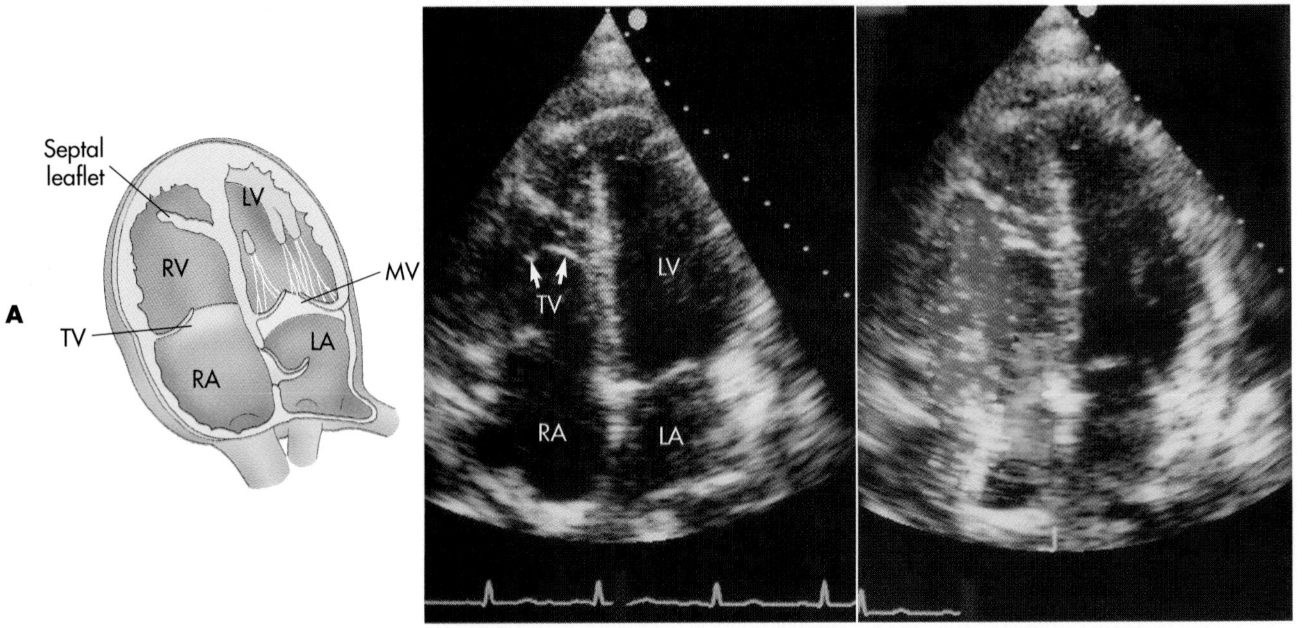

Figure 40-27 **A,** Four-chamber view of Ebstein's anomaly shows the septal leaflet of the tricuspid valve *(TV)* inferiorly displaced from its normal insertion point. The right atrium *(RA)* is markedly enlarged. *LA,* Left atrium; *LV,* left ventricle; *MV,* mitral valve; *RV,* right ventricle. **B,** Inferior displacement of the tricuspid valve into the apex of the right ventricle. This valve is usually dysplastic and regurgitation is present.

right ventricular cavity. The echogenic tricuspid annulus is seen with no valvular movement. The mitral valve is clearly the dominant atrioventricular valve. On the long- and short-axis views, the right ventricle is seen as a slitlike cavity just anterior to the interventricular septum.

Color flow imaging shows the incoming blood entering the right atrium and crossing over the patent foramen ovale to enter the left heart. If no blood flow passes the tricuspid orifice, then pulmonary stenosis is present. However, if a ventricular septal defect is present, the blood flows from the high-pressured left ventricle across the defect into the hypertrophied right ventricle and out the pulmonary outflow tract.

Ebstein's anomaly of the tricuspid valve. **Ebstein's anomaly** is an abnormal displacement of the septal leaflet of the tricuspid valve toward the apex of the right ventricle (Figure 40-27, *A*). Tricuspid valvular tissue may adhere directly to the ventricular endocardium or may be closely attached to the ventricular wall by multiple, anomalous, short chordae tendineae. The portion of the right ventricle underlying the adherent tricuspid valvular tissue is quite thin and functions as a receiving chamber analogous to the right atrium. This is referred to as the *atrialized chamber* because it registers a right atrial pressure pulse.

The anterior leaflet of the tricuspid valve is the least affected of the three leaflets. The septal and posterior leaflets show the greatest deformity, and the posterior cusp may be rudimentary or entirely absent. The right atrium is usually massively dilated. Often these patients have an incompetent or fenestrated foramen ovale or a secundum atrial septal defect.

The abnormal function of the right heart is related to the following three factors: (1) the malformed tricuspid valve, (2) the "atrialized" portion of the right ventricle, and (3) the reduced capacity of the pumping portion of the right ventricle.

Ultrasound findings. Echocardiographically, there is apical displacement of the septal leaflet of the tricuspid valve with resultant insufficiency (as seen on the apical four-chamber view) (Fig. 40-27, *B*). The atrialized right ventricle is well seen. Generally, right ventricular dysfunction is present, which results in an overload pattern of wall motion with paradoxical or anterior septal motion in systole. This right ventricular overload also shows flattening of the septum when viewed in the short-axis plane.

Doppler tracings are useful to record the amount of insufficiency present from the abnormal tricuspid valve. The sample volume should be placed at the annulus of the tricuspid valve and then mapped through the atrialized right ventricle into the right atrial cavity to record the maximum jet of insufficiency. One should note how far the regurgitant jet extends as well as the width of the jet to determine the degree of insufficiency.

Right Ventricular Outflow Tract Disturbance. The normal pulmonic valve comprises three semilunar cusps that open in systole and close completely in diastole just like the aortic cusps. These cusps are best imaged in the high short-axis plane or right long-axis plane of the right ventricular outflow tract.

Hypoplastic right heart. There are several forms of **hypoplastic right heart syndrome:** pulmonary atresia with

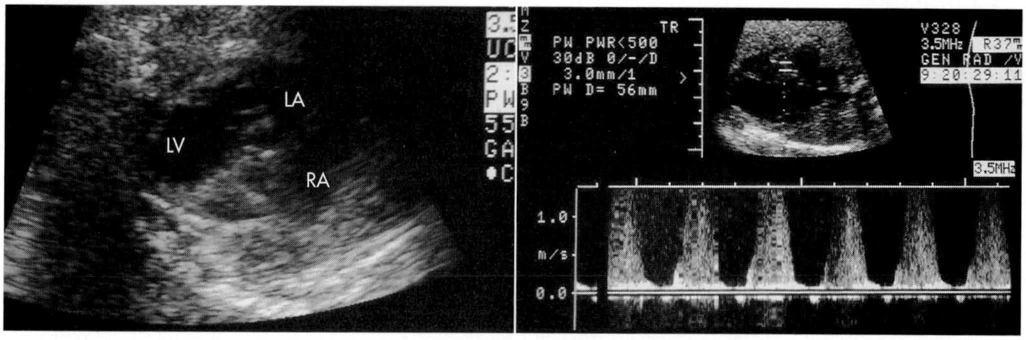

Figure 40-28 Hypoplastic right heart. Asymmetry of the ventricles **A,** with severe tricuspid regurgitation into the right atrium *(RA)* **(B).** *LA,* Left atrium; *LV,* left ventricle.

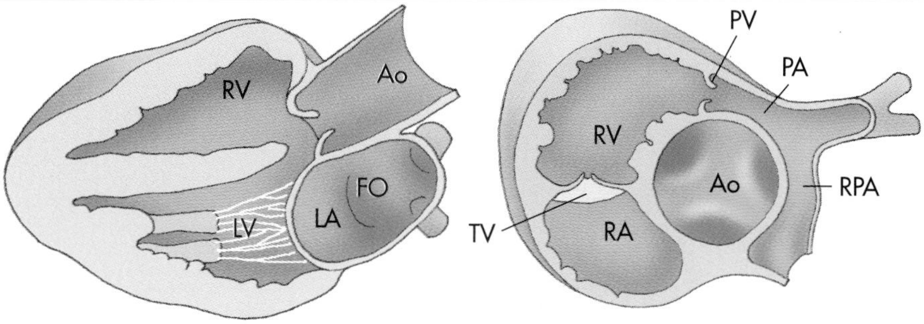

Figure 40-29 Tetralogy of Fallot. **A,** Long-axis view of the enlarged aorta *(Ao)* as it overrides the interventricular septum. The amount of aortic enlargement depends on the degree of pulmonary stenosis or atresia present. *FO,* Foramen ovale; *LA,* left atrium; *LV,* left ventricle; *RV,* right ventricle. **B,** Short-axis view of the small pulmonary artery *(PA)* displaced anteriorly by the enlarged aorta *(Ao). PV,* Pulmonary valve; *RA,* right atrium; *RPA,* right pulmonary artery; *TV,* tricuspid valve.

an intact interventricular septum, pulmonary valve fusion with an intact interventricular septum and atrial septal defect, or pulmonary atresia with a normal aortic root diameter.

The right heart is underdeveloped because of obstruction of the right ventricular outflow tract secondary to pulmonary stenosis. The tricuspid valve is small and the pulmonary infundibulum is atretic (see Figure 40-25).

Ultrasound findings. The sonographer must be careful not to call a hypoplastic right heart a hypoplastic left heart (which may be a lethal situation) (Figure 40-28). Careful assessment of the situs of the fetus, great vessel relationships, and trabeculation pattern helps the sonographer determine right from left heart (the right heart is more trabeculated than the left). Care must also be taken to avoid mistaking the papillary muscle for the septum when a large membranous defect is present. In a fetus with a single ventricle (and essentially a hypoplastic right heart), it may be easy to confuse a large papillary muscle with the septum. In this case, it would be difficult to figure out the great vessel origin. A single ventricle usually has an associated transposition of the great arteries with a small pulmonary artery and large aorta.

Tetralogy of Fallot. **Tetralogy of Fallot** is the most common form of cyanotic heart disease. The severity of the disease varies according to the degree of pulmonary stenosis present; the more stenosis, the greater the cyanosis. It is possible to have a mild form of pulmonary stenosis and not have any cyanosis after birth.

Tetralogy of Fallot has the following four characteristics (Figure 40-29):

1. High, membranous ventricular septal defect
2. Large, anteriorly displaced aorta, which overrides the septal defect
3. Pulmonary stenosis
4. Right ventricular hypertrophy (not seen in fetal life; occurs after birth when pulmonary stenosis causes increased pressures in the right ventricle)

A large septal defect with mild to moderate pulmonary stenosis is classified as acyanotic disease, and a large septal defect with severe pulmonary stenosis is considered cyanotic disease ("blue baby" at birth).

Other congenital cardiac malformations may occur in patients with pulmonic stenosis and ventricular septal defect, including the following:

- Right aortic arch
- Persistent left superior vena cava
- Anomalies of the pulmonary artery and its branches
- Absence of the pulmonary valve
- Incompetence of the aortic valve
- Variations in coronary arterial anatomy

A B C

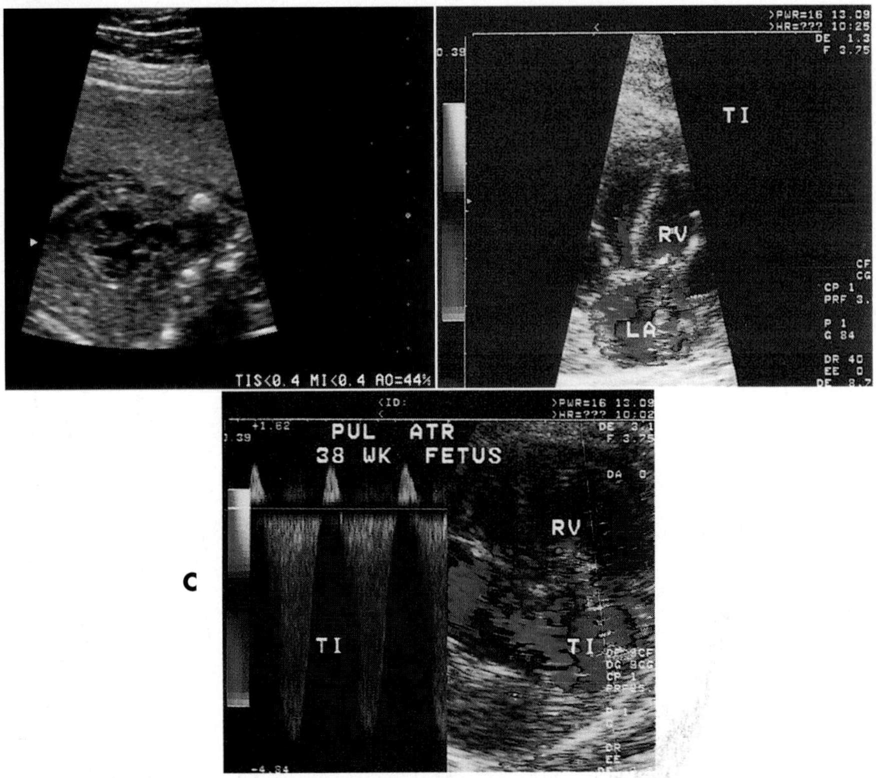

Figure 40-30 Tetralogy of Fallot. **A,** Long-axis of the heart shows the aorta as it overrides the septum. **B,** Pulmonary stenosis may cause severe tricuspid regurgitation into the right atrium as the blood flow is obstructed in the right ventricular outflow tract. *LA,* Left atrium. **C,** Pulmonary atresia with tricuspid insufficiency (TI) is the most severe form of stenosis. *RV,* Right ventricle.

The prognosis for a fetus with tetralogy of Fallot is quite good with surgical intervention. One of the first surgical approaches was developed to obviate the underperfusion of the lungs. The Blalock-Taussig shunt was performed to anastomose the subclavian artery to the pulmonary artery.

The prognosis of tetralogy of Fallot with pulmonary atresia or an absent pulmonary valve does not show such a dramatic improvement (Figure 40-30, *A*). The absent pulmonary valve may cause congestive heart failure in the fetus. Aneurysmal dilation of the pulmonary artery and its branches may be a cause of pulmonary distress.

Ultrasound findings. Echocardiographically, the demonstration of tetralogy of Fallot is distinguished on the parasternal long-axis view (see Figure 40-30). The large aorta overrides the ventricular septum. If the override is greater than 50%, the condition is called a **double-outlet right ventricle** (both great vessels arise from the right heart). A septal defect is present; the size may vary from small to large. The parasternal short-axis view shows the small, hypertrophied right ventricle (if significant pulmonary stenosis is present). The pulmonary artery is usually small, and the cusps may be thickened and domed or difficult to image well.

A sample volume should be made in the high parasternal short-axis view to determine the turbulence of the right ventricular outflow tract and pulmonary valve stenosis (see Figure 40-30, *C*). Color flow is very helpful in this condition to actually delineate the abnormal high-velocity pattern and to direct the sample volume into the proper jet flow. If the ventricular septal defect is large, increased flow is seen in the right heart (increased tricuspid velocity, right ventricular outflow tract velocity, and increased pulmonic velocity). The best view for imaging the subvalvular portion of the right ventricular outflow tract is obtained with the subcostal short-axis plane. This view allows extensive visualization of the subpulmonary area so often affected in tetralogy of Fallot. In the fetus the pulmonic obstructive flow patterns are not as pronounced as in the neonatal period.

Pulmonic stenosis. In **pulmonic stenosis** the abnormal pulmonic cusps become thickened and domed during diastole.

Ultrasound findings. The domed effect is not quite as noticeable on the fetal echocardiogram, but with careful evaluation the thickness of the cusp may be compared with that of the aortic cusp. An M-mode image may be made through the area to further define cusp mobility and thickness. As with the aortic cusps, multiple degrees of stenosis and atresia may develop in the right ventricular outflow tract. The more atretic the cusp, the more hypoplastic the pulmonary artery becomes. Critical pulmonary atresia may be very difficult to image in the early

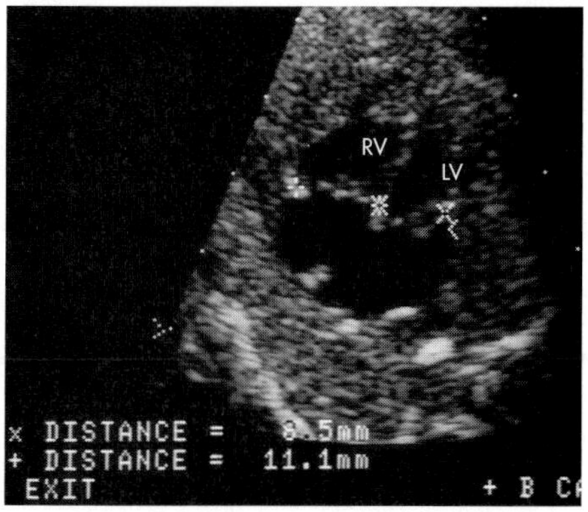

Figure 40-31 Mitral atresia. Four-chamber view shows a thickened, immobile mitral leaflet with a small left ventricular cavity. Mitral regurgitation was present. *LV,* Left ventricle; *RV,* right ventricle.

second-trimester fetus because the pulmonary outflow becomes so hypoplastic that it is difficult to recognize.

When pulmonary stenosis is associated with another cardiac anomaly, such as transposition, double-outlet right ventricle, or tetralogy of Fallot, it becomes even more difficult to diagnose. Secondary findings of dilation of the right ventricular cavity and right atrial cavity (secondary to tricuspid insufficiency) usually lead the investigator to the principal cause of the right heart overload (pulmonic stenosis.

Color flow Doppler evaluation of the velocity is useful not only to assess the degree of obstruction but also to monitor the fetus in terms of following the course of disease (see Figure 40-30, *B*).

Subpulmonic stenosis. Subpulmonic stenosis occurs when a membrane or muscle bundle obstructs the outflow tract into the pulmonary artery.

Ultrasound findings. If the right ventricular outflow tract can be imaged adequately, the actual obstruction may be imaged. The Doppler and color flow pattern shows a turbulent obstructive pattern just before the pulmonary cusps. The velocity would not be as high as in the neonatal period but would measure at least 1.8 to 2 m per second.

Supravalvular pulmonic stenosis. Supravalvular pulmonic stenosis is an abnormal narrowing in the main pulmonary artery. It usually is associated with Williams' syndrome and is hereditary.

Ultrasound findings. The parasternal short-axis view is best to image this condition. Prominent, dilated right and left pulmonary branch arteries may be present. Again, color flow would show a turbulent high-velocity flow pattern across the narrowed vessel.

Left Ventricular Disturbances

Abnormalities that affect primarily the left side of the heart are listed as inflow or outflow tract disturbances. Each of these lesions is presented along with technical advice on how to obtain the ideal fetal cardiac image.

Left Ventricular Inflow Tract Disturbance. In normal cardiac development the endocardial cushion forms the anterior and posterior mitral apparatus with chordae tendineae attached to two papillary muscles on the left side of the heart. When this development is interrupted in the first trimester, the mitral valve apparatus may not fully develop, causing mitral stenosis or a hypoplastic left heart.

Ultrasound findings. The mitral valve should be evaluated from at least two cardiac windows, the long-axis and the four-chamber views. The long-axis view allows the examiner to evaluate the mobility of the anterior and posterior mitral valve leaflets as they open into the left ventricular cavity. The four-chamber view allows comparison of the placement of the mitral valve with the normal, slightly apical displacement of the tricuspid valve. It also allows observation of the pliability of the thin leaflets as they open in diastole and close in systole. The ideal Doppler waveform should be recorded from this apical position.

Mitral atresia. In a fetus with **mitral atresia** or congenital mitral stenosis the examiner sees a thickened mitral orifice with restriction of leaflet amplitude. The left ventricular cavity is reduced in volume because of decreased inflow (Figure 40-31). The myocardial thickness is increased (secondary to increased left ventricular pressure overload) if associated aortic atresia is present.

Ultrasound findings. Color Doppler can be very helpful to determine how much, if any, mitral inflow is present. The apical four-chamber view is again best to obtain this assessment.

Mitral regurgitation. In fetal life the presence of **mitral regurgitation** is probably from a cleft mitral valve (endocardial cushion defect) or a congenital mitral stenosis. In the presence of mitral regurgitation the left atrial cavity would become enlarged because of the leakage of blood from the defective mitral valve.

Ultrasound findings. The color Doppler flow pattern of disturbed flow in the left atrial cavity would be seen on the apical four-chamber and probably on the parasternal long-axis view.

Left Ventricular Outflow Tract Disturbance. The normal aortic valve comprises three semilunar cusps that open in systole and close completely in diastole. The cusps are best imaged in the long-axis and short-axis planes. The aortic root is measured in the short axis plane as the transducer bisects the right ventricular outflow tract, the pulmonary artery, and the aortic root.

Ultrasound findings. Normal Doppler flow is recorded in the aortic outflow tract (either from an five-chamber view or a modified long- or short-axis view).

Bicuspid or unicuspid valve. If the development is interrupted during the first trimester, the three aortic cusps may not fully separate. In this instance the valve may be a unicuspid valve with a central opening and aortic stenosis or a **bicuspid** (two-leaflet) valve with asymmetric cusps.

Ultrasound findings. In this case the raphe between the cusp tissue has not separated; thus the leaflet opens

asymmetrically and may show "doming" on the parasternal long-axis view. In the fetus a bicuspid valve may be difficult to image at 18 weeks but should be well visualized in the late second trimester at 27 weeks.

Critical aortic stenosis. Critical aortic stenosis signifies end-stage left ventricular dysfunction. At some point in the second or third trimester an infection or other viral process has caused the aortic leaflet to thicken and close prematurely. The fetus shows a normal ascending and descending aorta with abnormal opening of the aortic cusps. The enlarged, dysfunctional left ventricle then "billows" from the increased pressure in the ventricle because the left ventricular outflow tract is blocked (Figure 40-32, *A*). The ventricular walls would be thin and bulge into the right ventricular cavity. The parasternal long-axis and apical four-chamber views are the most helpful to image this disease.

Ultrasound findings. Color flow helps to assess the severity of the stenosis to determine how much, if any, blood is flowing through the stenotic aortic leaflets (Figure 40-32, *B*).

Subvalvular or supravalvular aortic stenosis. Subvalvular aortic stenosis occurs when a membrane covers the left ventricular outflow tract (Figure 40-33, *A* and *B*). Supravalvular aortic stenosis is a narrowing of the ascending aortic root.

Supravalvular aortic stenosis may be related to the Williams' syndrome (Figure 40-34). Subaortic stenosis has been described in patients with Turner's syndrome, Noonan's syndrome, and congenital rubella.

Ultrasound findings. The left ventricular outflow tract should be carefully evaluated in the parasternal long axis, apical five-chamber, and aortic arch views to image this thin membrane. The Doppler view shows increased velocity across the obstructive membrane, whereas color flow imaging shows increased turbulence at the area of narrowing.

Coarctation of the aorta. **Coarctation of the aorta** is a discrete shelf-like lesion present in the isthmus of the arch or, more commonly, at the site of the ductal insertion near the left subclavian artery (Figure 40-35, *A*). The coarctation may be discrete, long-segment, or tubular.

Intracardiac associated malformations are present in 90% of cases. These include aortic stenosis, aortic insufficiency, septal defects, transposition of the great arteries, truncus arteriosus, and double-outlet right ventricle. In Turner's syndrome, coarctation of the aorta and ventricu-

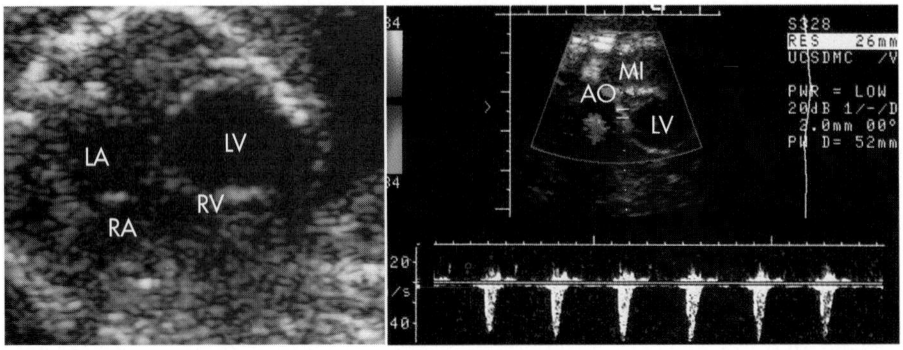

Figure 40-32 Critical aortic stenosis. **A,** Critical aortic stenosis appears in the second or third trimester. The four-chamber view shows a dilated left ventricular cavity (assumes the shape of a balloon). The ventricle is tense and quickly becomes noncompliant. *LA,* Left atrium; *LV,* left ventricle; *RA,* right atrium; *RV,* right ventricle. **B,** Color Doppler imaging shows aortic insufficiency *(blue)* and mitral insufficiency *(MI, red)*. *AO,* Aorta; *LV,* left ventricle.

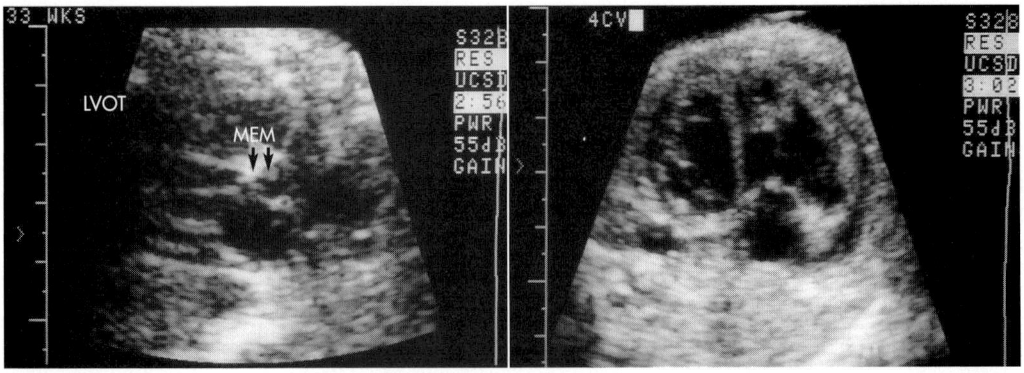

Figure 40-33 Submembranous aortic obstruction. **A,** Long-axis view of the ascending aorta and left ventricle shows the thick membrane *(MEM, arrows)* that is located above the aortic cusps to cause obstruction to the left ventricular outflow tract *(LVOT)*. **B,** This outflow obstruction causes the left ventricle to enlarge, as seen on this four-chamber view, and go into failure. A small pericardial effusion is seen around the heart.

lar septal defects are the most common cardiac defects found.

Ultrasound findings. If a bicuspid aortic valve is suspected, the aortic arch should be carefully searched for a narrowing or coarctation of the aorta. There is a 25% association of bicuspid aortic valves in fetuses with coarctation of the aorta. It is important to keep in mind that coarctation may be difficult to evaluate in the fetus because the ductus arteriosus is patent, so some of the blood may flow into the arch during fetal life (see Figure 40-35, *B*). Once

A

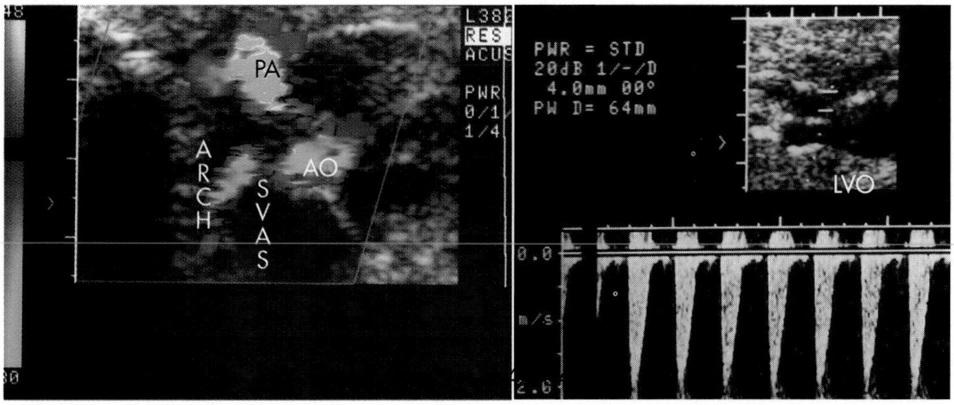

B

Figure 40-34 Supravalvular aortic stenosis. **A,** Long-axis view of the ascending aorta *(AO)* and arch with the supravalvular narrowing *(SVAS)*. *PA,* Pulmonary artery. **B,** Doppler velocities measure 200 cm per second, well above the normal range.

A

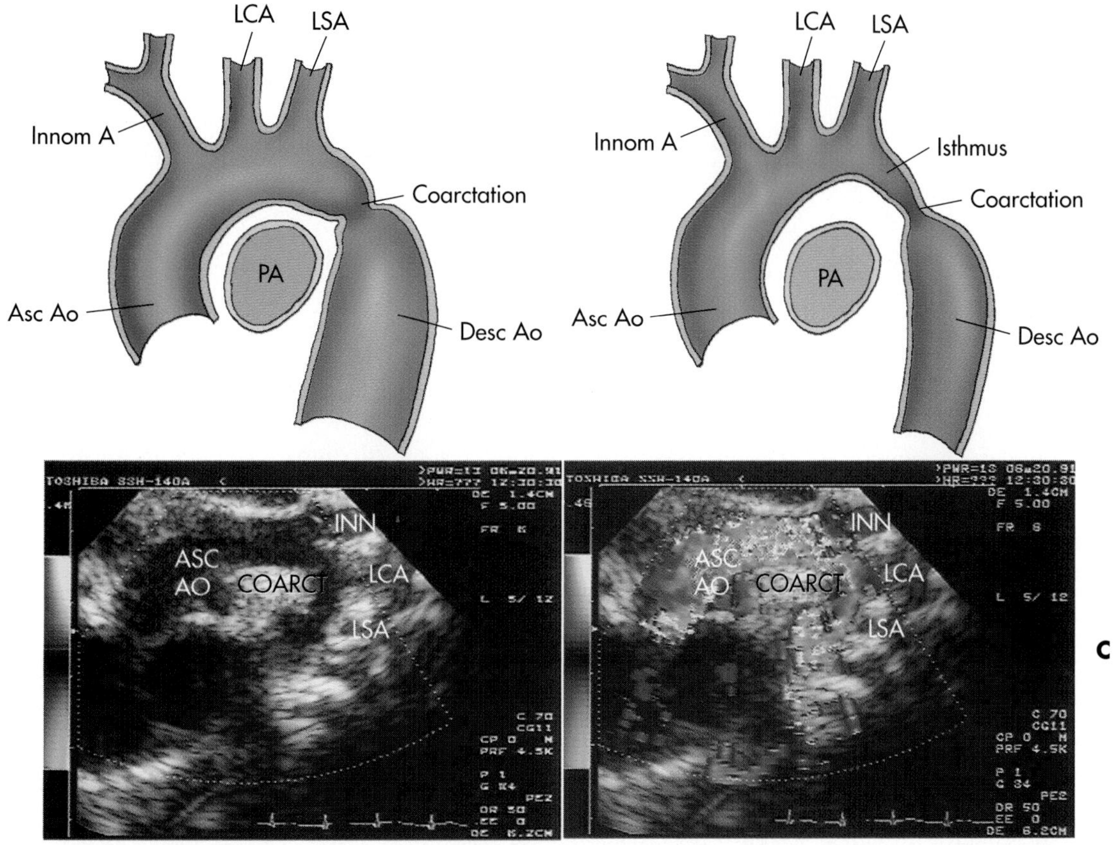

B

C

Figure 40-35 Coarctation of the aorta occurs just inferior to the insertion of the left subclavian artery *(LSA)*. The coarctation may be discrete **(A)** with mild poststenotic dilation in the fetus. This narrowing usually is near the point of ductal insertion. *Asc Ao,* Ascending aorta; *INN,* innominate artery; *LCA,* left carotid artery. **B,** A long-segment narrowing of the isthmus is more likely to be found by echocardiography. **C,** A discrete narrowing was found in this 32-week fetus. Long-axis view of the aortic arch shows the narrowing at the level of the left subclavian artery. Pulsed Doppler imaging recorded velocities of 190 cm per second. *COARCT,* Coarctation, *INN,* innominate artery.

the fetus is delivered and the ductus closes, however, the narrowed portion of the arch becomes evident.

Aortic atresia or hypoplastic left heart syndrome. **Hypoplastic left heart syndrome** is characterized by a small, hypertrophied left ventricle with aortic and/or mitral dysplasia or atresia (Figure 40-36). This syndrome has been found to be an autosomal-recessive condition. If a couple has had one child with hypoplastic left heart syndrome, the recurrence is 4%; if two births have been affected, recurrence increases to 25%.

Although the cause of the hypoplastic left heart is unknown, it is thought to be decreased filling and perfusion of the left ventricle during embryologic development. It also may be associated with premature closure of the foramen ovale. When this closure occurs, the blood cannot cross the foramen to help the left ventricle grow. The real-time image shows a reduction in the size of the foramen ovale (the foramen should measure at least 0.6 multiplied by the diameter of the aortic root). Premature closure of the foramen would also show increased velocities across the interatrial septum (around 40 to 50 cm per second).

The right ventricle supplies both the pulmonic and systemic circulations. The pulmonary venous return is diverted from the left atrium to the right atrium through the interatrial communication. Through the pulmonary artery and ductus arteriosus the right ventricle supplies the descending aorta, along with retrograde flow to the aortic arch and the ascending aorta. Overload on the right ventricle may lead to congestive heart failure in utero with the development of pericardial effusion and hydrops.

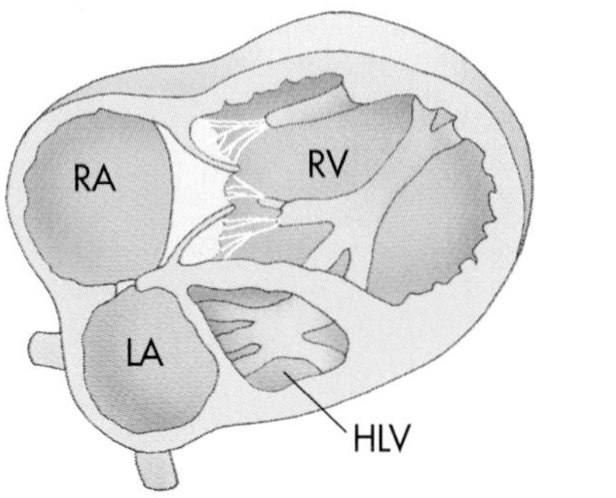

Figure 40-36 Hypoplastic left heart syndrome is characterized by a small, hypertrophied left ventricle *(HLV)* with aortic and/or mitral atresia. *LA,* Left atrium; *RA,* right atrium; *RV,* right ventricle.

Ultrasound findings. A fetus with major disturbance to the development of the mitral valve or aortic valve shows dramatic changes in the development of the left ventricle. The amount of hypoplasia depends on when the left-sided atresia developed in the valvular area (Figure 40-37). If the mitral atresia is the cause, the blood cannot fill the left ventricle to provide volume, and thus the aortic valve becomes atretic as well, with concentric hypertrophy of the small left ventricular cavity. If the cause is aortic stenosis, the myocardium shows extreme hypertrophy from the increased pressure overload (Figure 40-38).

M-mode imaging may be used to further define the ventricular disproportion. The sonographer must be aware that even in normal fetuses, the M-mode and real-time measurements of the ventricles depend totally on the position of the fetus, position of the transducer, and angle of the cursor. Therefore it is important to make sure the transducer is directly perpendicular to the right and left ventricles before making an M-mode measurement. This measurement is always slightly smaller than the real-time direct measurement because the detail of the endocardium is seen better on the M-mode than on the real-time image.

The prognosis for a fetus with a hypoplastic left heart is not good. This syndrome is responsible for 25% of cardiac deaths in the neonatal period. The surgeon Norwood has developed a series of surgical repairs for the hypoplastic left heart patient. His repairs are based on the development of the aorta and aortic arch. Initial palliative procedures are done, including atrial balloon septostomy, banding of the pulmonary artery (to protect the potential volume overload to the lungs), and creation of an aortopulmonary shunt. The modified Fontan surgical procedure is done to connect the left atrium to the tricuspid valve and the right atrium to the pulmonary artery. Norwood's challenge is to rebuild the hypoplastic aorta to im-

A

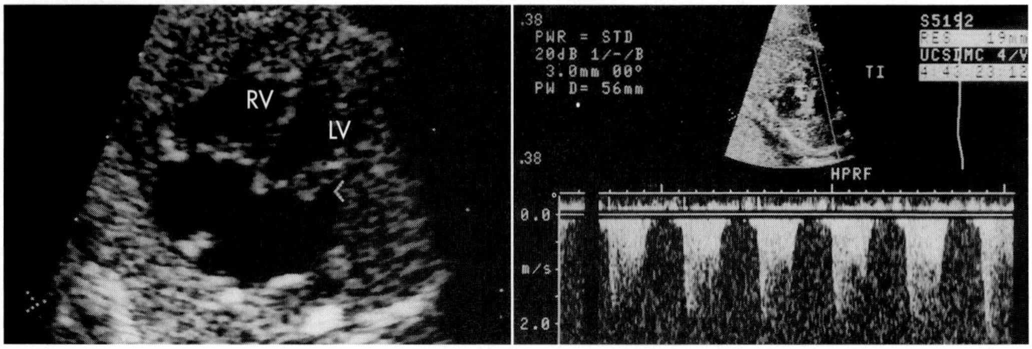

B

Figure 40-37 Hypoplastic left heart. **A,** Four-chamber view shows asymmetry between the right *(RV)* and left *(LV)* ventricles. The aorta and ascending aorta were also hypertrophied. **B,** Backflow of pressures from the left ventricular outflow obstruction results in severe tricuspid regurgitation.

prove blood flow into the left ventricle. Cardiac transplantation is another alternative for these patients.

GREAT VESSEL ABNORMALITIES

Great vessel abnormalities include interruption in the spiraling that occurs during early embryonic development. These anomalies include complete transposition of the great arteries, corrected transposition of the great arteries, and truncus arteriosus.

Transposition of the Great Arteries. **Transposition of the great arteries** is an abnormal condition that exists when the aorta is connected to the right ventricle and the pulmonary artery is connected to the left ventricle (Figure 40-39). The atrioventricular valves are normally attached and related. This occurs because of an abnormal completion of the "loop" in embryology. The great vessels originate as a common truncus and undergo rotation and spiraling; if this development is interrupted, the great arteries do not complete their spiral and thus transposition occurs. Usually the aorta is anterior and to the right of the pulmonary artery. Less frequently, the two arteries are side by side or the aorta is posterior.

In the fetal heart, no hemodynamic compromise is seen in the fetus when the great arteries are transposed. The problems occur in the neonatal period when there is inadequate mixing of oxygenated and unoxygenated blood.

The prognosis for a neonate with transposition of the great arteries is quite good with surgical intervention. The survival rate is 92% at 1 year with surgical correction. Survival depends on other cardiac anomalies that may also be present.

Other associated cardiac anomalies include atrial septal defects, anomalies of the atrioventricular valves, and underdevelopment of the right or left ventricles.

Ultrasound findings. The parasternal short-axis view is the key view to image the great arteries and their normal relationship (Figure 40-40). The right ventricular outflow tract, pulmonary artery, and bifurcation should be seen anterior to the aorta in the parasternal short axis view. In transposition this relationship is not present; it is impossible to demonstrate the bifurcation of the pulmonary artery because the aorta would be the anterior vessel. Sometimes the double circles of the great arteries can be seen in this view.

On the modified long-axis view the normal criss-cross pattern (Figure 40-41) obtained from a normal fetal echocardiogram occurs when the transducer is swept from the left ventricular outflow tract anterior and medial into the right ventricular outflow tract. In a fetus with transposition this criss-cross sweep of the great arteries is not possible.

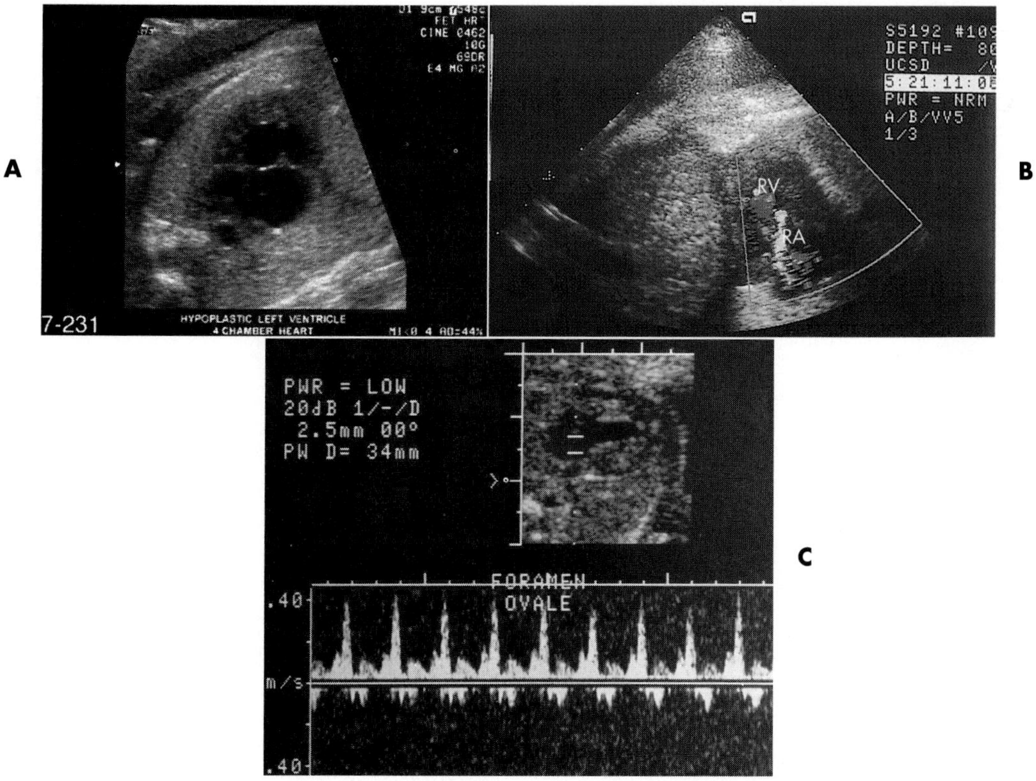

Figure 40-38 Hypoplastic left heart. **A,** Small hypertrophied left ventricle is shown in this four-chamber view. **B,** Color Doppler imaging helps to define if any inflow is going into the left ventricle or how much tricuspid regurgitation is present. *RA,* Right atrium; *RV,* right ventricle. **C,** Flow across the foramen ovale may be increased with restriction of the flap of the foramen.

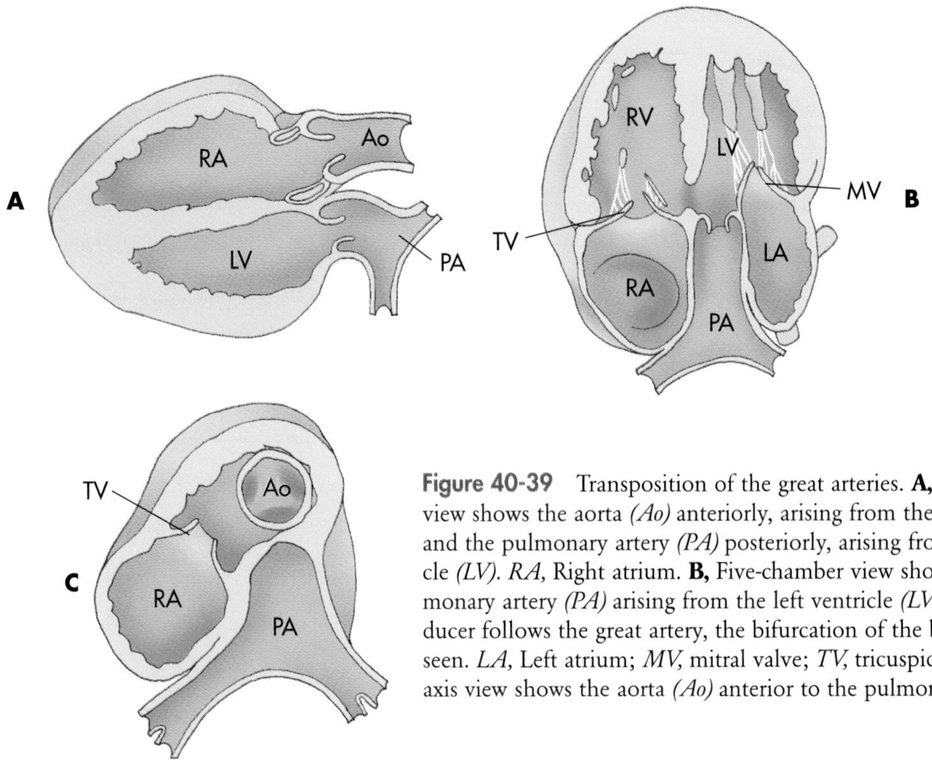

Figure 40-39 Transposition of the great arteries. **A,** Four-chamber view shows the aorta *(Ao)* anteriorly, arising from the right ventricle, and the pulmonary artery *(PA)* posteriorly, arising from the left ventricle *(LV)*. *RA,* Right atrium. **B,** Five-chamber view shows the pulmonary artery *(PA)* arising from the left ventricle *(LV)*; as the transducer follows the great artery, the bifurcation of the branch arteries is seen. *LA,* Left atrium; *MV,* mitral valve; *TV,* tricuspid valve. **C,** Short-axis view shows the aorta *(Ao)* anterior to the pulmonary artery *(PA)*.

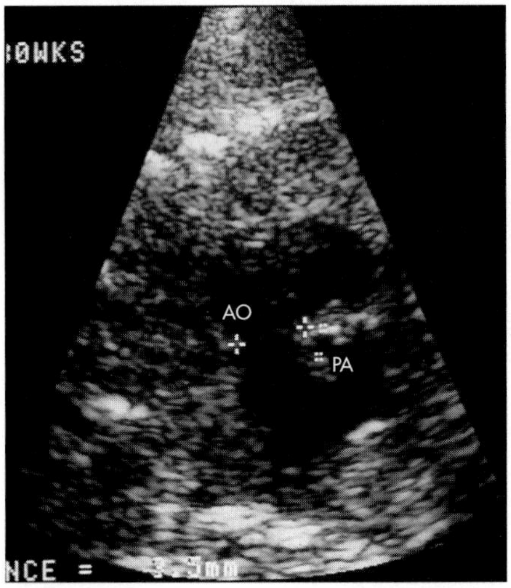

Figure 40-40 Short-axis view shows the dilated aorta *(AO)* anterior to the hypertrophied pulmonary artery *(PA)* in this patient with transposition.

The parallel great arteries are sometimes seen in this view as they both arise from the ventricles.

Corrected Transposition of the Great Arteries. Corrected transposition is a cardiac condition in which the right atrium and left atrium are connected to the morphologic left and right ventricle, respectively, and the great arteries are transposed. Therefore these two defects essentially cancel each other out without hemodynamic consequences.

Ultrasound findings. Corrected transposition is associated with malpositions of the heart and sometimes with situs inversus. A ventricular perimembranous septal defect may be present in half of the fetuses. The pulmonary artery may be seen to override the septal defect, with pulmonary stenosis in 50%. Abnormalities of the atrioventricular valves, such as an Ebstein type of malformation and straddling of the tricuspid valve, may be present. Atrioventricular heart block may also be recorded.

Truncus Arteriosus. **Truncus arteriosus** is a complex congenital heart lesion in which only one great artery arises from the base of the heart (Figure 40-42). From this single great artery arise the pulmonary trunk, the systemic arteries, and the coronary arteries. This defect occurs in the early embryologic period when the conotruncus fails to separate into two great arteries. The conus corresponds to the middle third of the bulbus cordis. It gives rise to the outflow tract of both ventricles and to the muscular portion of the ventricles located between the atrioventricular and semilunar valves. The truncus is the distal part of the bulbus cordis. This structure rotates and divides into the two great semilunar valvular structures that represent the aortic and pulmonic leaflets. Failure of the bulbus to divide causes a single great artery with multiple cusps within.

Associated anomalies include mitral atresia, atrial septal defect, univentricular heart, and aortic arch abnormalities. In the neonatal stage the prognosis is poor for truncus arteriosus.

Ultrasound findings. The fetal echo shows an abnormal, large, single great vessel arising from the ventricles (Figure 40-43). Usually an infundibular ventricular septal defect is present. Significant septal override is present. The truncal valve is usually dysplastic, thick, and domed. Mul-

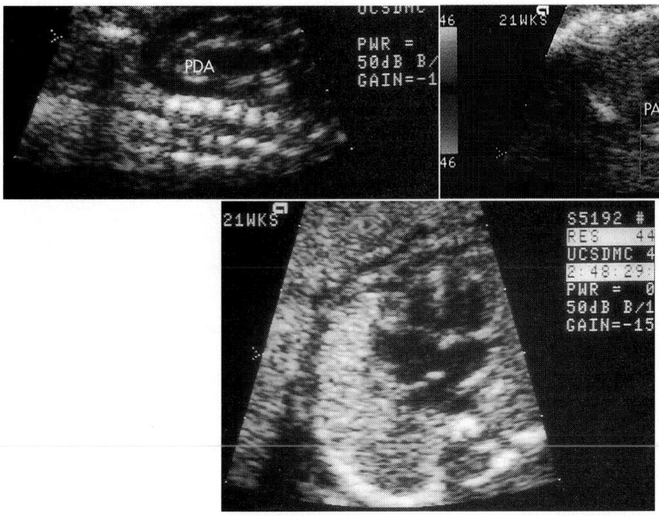

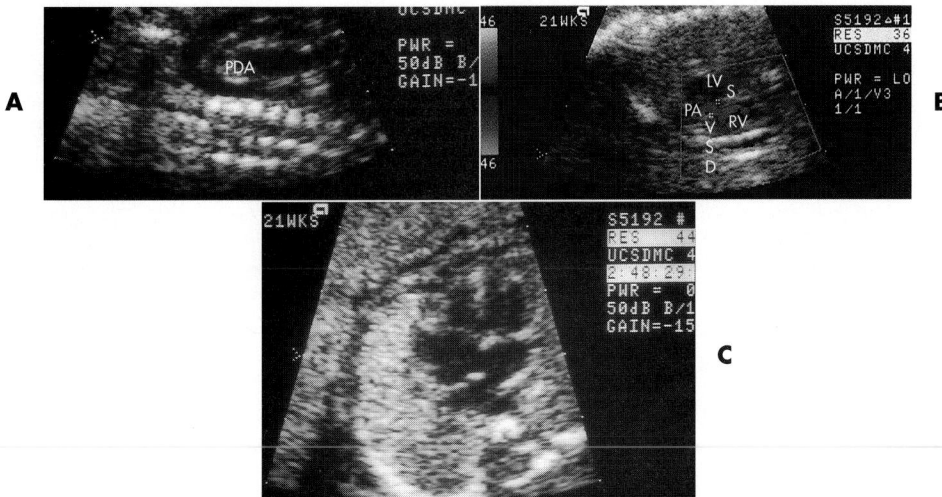

Figure 40-41 Transposition of the great arteries. **A,** Long-axis view of the aorta as it arises from the anterior right ventricle. *PDA,* Patent ductus arteriosus. **B,** A ventricular septal defect *(VSD)* is usually present in the fetus with transposition of the great vessels. *LV,* Left ventricle; *PA,* pulmonary artery; *RV,* right ventricle; *S,* septum. **C,** Four-chamber view shows the membranous septal defect.

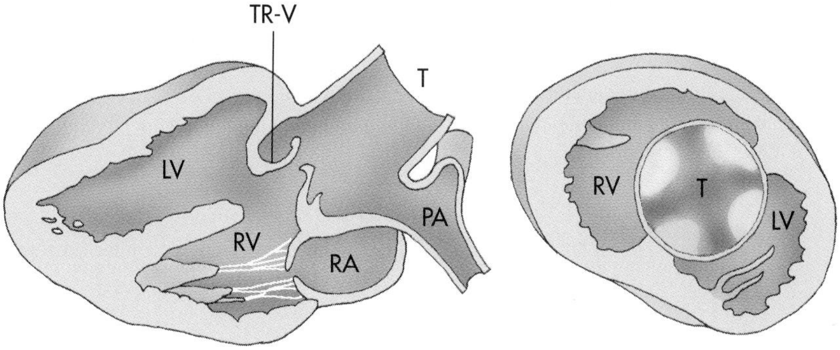

Figure 40-42 Truncus arteriosus results when the aorta and pulmonary arteries *(PA)* fail to complete their rotations and divisions early in development. A single large great artery is shown as it arises from the center of the heart on the long-axis view **(A).** *LV,* Left ventricle; *RA,* right atrium; *RV,* right ventricle; *T,* truncus; *TR-V,* truncal valve. The short-axis view **(B)** shows the single great artery with multiple cusps within.

tiple cusps are seen within the great artery. If truncal regurgitation is present the prognosis is grim; the fetus usually develops congestive heart failure, pericardial effusion, and hydrops. Truncus arteriosus may be difficult to separate from a severe tetralogy of Fallot with pulmonary atresia (small pulmonary artery and large aorta overriding septal defect).

OTHER CARDIAC ANOMALIES

Single Ventricle. **Single ventricle** is a congenital anomaly in which there are two atria but only one ventricular chamber, which receives both the mitral and tricuspid valves (Figure 40-44). Both valves are patent, so mitral and tricuspid atresia are excluded. (Occasionally the mitral and tricuspid valves join to form a common atrioventricular valve.)

Ultrasound findings. The most common form of a single ventricle heart is a morphologic left ventricle with a small outlet chamber that represents the infundibular portion of the right ventricle. The right or left atrioventricular connection may be absent and the great arteries may be transposed, with the aorta arising above the small outlet chamber. If transposition is present, the pulmonary artery lies posterior to the aorta. The infundibulum lies at the base of the ventricle, communicating with the aorta above and the single ventricle below. If the great vessels are normal, the infundibulum communicates with the pulmonary trunk. The outlet chambers may be left-side and anterior or right-side and anterior, but they commonly lie high on the cardiac silhouette.

Pulmonary stenosis may or may not coexist. If present, the pulmonary stenosis is usually valvular or subvalvular. The pulmonary trunk is usually slightly smaller than the aortic trunk.

The four-chamber view is the most useful window in delineating the cardiac anatomy (Figure 40-45). The prominent papillary muscles should not be confused with

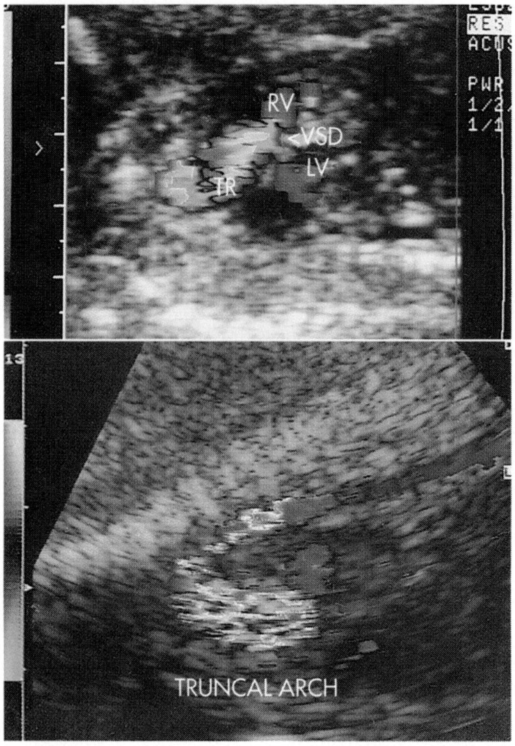

Figure 40-43 Color Doppler imaging demonstrates the single large vessel arising from both ventricles. The multiple cusps within the large vessel may be deformed and dysplastic, resulting in moderate to significant aortic insufficiency. *LV,* Left ventricle; *RV,* right ventricle; *TR,* tricuspid regurgitation; *VSD,* ventricular septal defect.

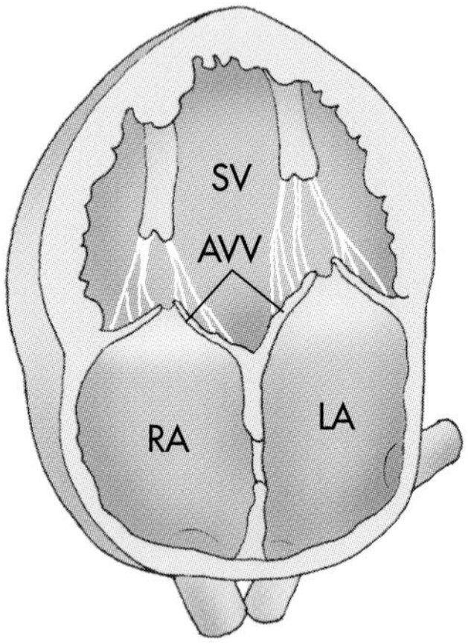

Figure 40-44 "Three"-chamber view shows a single inflow cavity (single ventricle *[SV]*). Two atrial cavities and atrioventricular valves *(AVV)* are present. *LA,* Left atrium; *RA,* right atrium.

the interventricular septum. In a single ventricle the papillary muscles may be quite prominent. With careful transducer angulation, the chordal structures may be traced to these structures for correct delineation. The right ventricle may be just a slitlike cavity as seen on the apical four-chamber view. The position of the great arteries should be assessed, and the aorta and pulmonary arteries should be delineated clearly. Regurgitant jets may be associated with

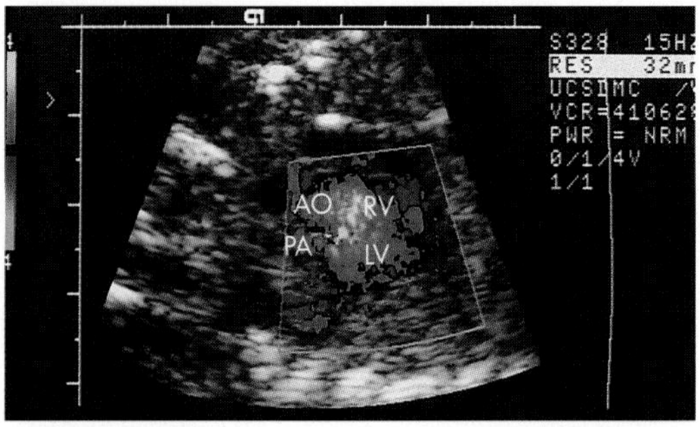

Figure 40-45 Color flow image demonstrates complete filling of the essentially "single ventricle" in a patient with transposition of the great arteries and a huge ventricular septal defect. *AO,* Aorta; *LV,* left ventricle; *PA,* pulmonary artery; *RV,* right ventricle.

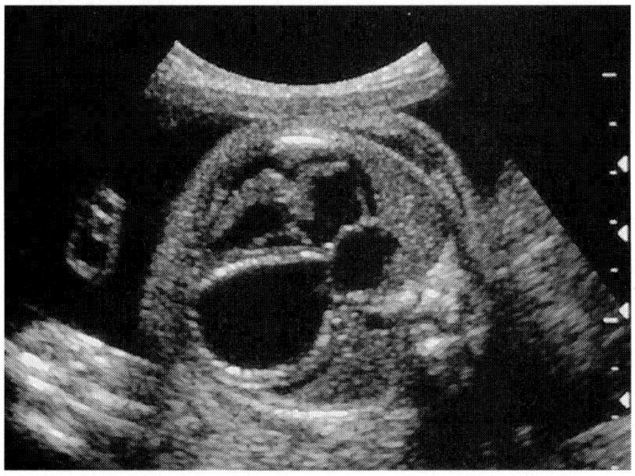

Figure 40-46 Four-chamber view of the heart shows dilation of all four chambers. Regurgitation was present in the mitral and tricuspid valves.

abnormal chordal connections of the atrioventricular valves. Doppler evaluation of these valves is useful in depicting any regurgitation present. Color flow imaging is especially useful in outlining the direction of jet flow for proper Doppler evaluation.

Cardiomyopathy. **Cardiomyopathy** involves a disease of the myocardial tissue in the heart. This disease process is caused by several problems, including exposure to a virus (coxsackie or mumps) or bacteria leading to an infection that causes a cardiomyopathy. Another cause may be errors of metabolism. Endocardial fibroelastosis has also been associated with cardiomyopathies and hypoplastic left-heart syndrome. Asymmetric septal hypertrophy (as seen in patients with hereditary idiopathic subaortic stenosis) and concentric hypertrophy as seen in some uncontrolled diabetic mothers have been reported.

Myocarditis is characterized by necrosis and destruction of myocardial cells, as well as an inflammatory infiltrate. In a viral cardiomyopathy, all four chambers are dilated, with thinning of the myocardial walls (Figure 40-46). Gross valvular regurgitation is present from the stretched mitral and tricuspid anulus. The cardiac function is decreased severely, leading to congestive heart failure and death.

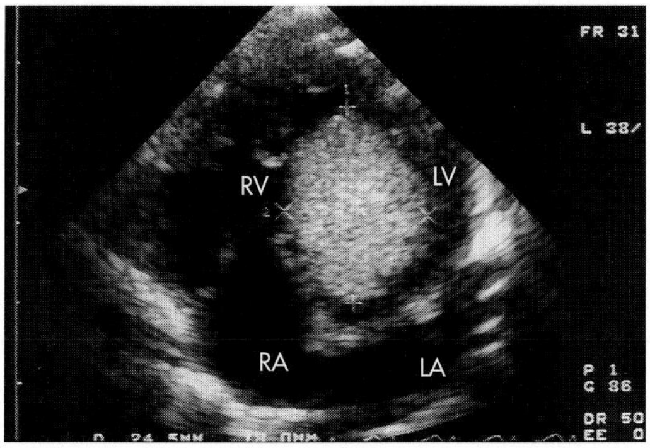

Figure 40-47 Four-chamber view of a fetus with a huge rhabdomyoma completely filling the left ventricular cavity. *LA*, Left artery, *LV*, left ventricle, *RA*, right artery, *RV*, right ventricle.

The general prognosis for a fetus with evidence for a cardiomyopathy is very poor. Serial fetal echoes are performed to monitor chamber size, regurgitation, and contractility.

Total Anomalous Pulmonary Venous Return. The four pulmonary veins normally return blood into the left atrium from the lungs. When this fails to occur, the condition is termed total anomalous pulmonary venous return (TAPVR). The venous return may be totally into the right atrium or into a "common chamber" posterior to the left atrium, into the superior or inferior vena cava, or into the left subclavian vein, azygos vein, or portal vein. The venous drainage may be total or partial.

Ultrasound findings. In the fetus, TAPVR may not be evident unless the pulmonary veins are carefully recorded. The sonographer may image an enlarged right atrial cavity with the atrial septum bulging into the small left atrium. The normal pulmonary veins are seen on the four-chamber view. The right upper vein is seen near the base of the heart at the level of the septum secundum, the left upper vein is seen at the lateral atrial wall near the base of the heart, and the left lower vein is seen just above the atrioventricular junction, along the lateral atrial wall. The right lower vein is not routinely imaged in a four-chamber view. Color Doppler imaging may help identify these venous structures.

TAPVR should be suspected in all cases of atrioventricular septal defects and in asplenia and polysplenia syndromes. The prognosis is poor, with 75% dying within the first year after birth if no surgery is performed. Reconstruction of the pulmonary venous drainage into the left atrium has shown very promising survival results.

Cardiac Tumors. Cardiac tumors of the heart are very unusual. Most of these tumors are benign and isolated. The most common tumors are rhabdomyoma (58%) and teratoma (20%), followed by fibroma, myxoma, hemangioma, and mesothelioma. Less than 10% of cardiac tumors are malignant.

Rhabdomyomas tend to be multiple and involve the septum. This tumor is associated with tuberous sclerosis (50% to 86%) (Figure 40-47).

The fetus becomes symptomatic when the tumor is large and causes obstruction to the outflow tract, leading to congestive heart failure, pericardial effusion, hydrops, and death. The prognosis depends on the size of the tumor, its location, and its histologic type.

Ultrasound findings. If this mass is suspected, the sonographer should also look for associated tumor mass abnormalities in the kidneys and fetal head. The teratoma may be intrapericardial and extracardiac. The fibroma tumors account for 12% of all cardiac tumors in the neonate. This tumor is pedunculated and may calcify.

The fetal echo shows the tumor best in the four-chamber view. Close analysis should be made to search for regurgitation and obstruction. The right and left ventricular outflow tracts should be carefully studied with Doppler to record velocities in the subvalvular and supravalvular area. Serial evaluation may be made with fetal echocardiography to follow the ventricular function and Doppler flow patterns.

Cardiosplenic Syndromes. Cardiosplenic syndromes are sporadic disorders characterized by a symmetric development of normally asymmetric organs or organ systems. The cardiosplenic syndromes are subdivided into asplenia and polysplenia syndromes. These two conditions are characterized by lack of the normal asymmetry of the visceral organs. The trunk tends to have two halves that are mirror images of one another. Generally speaking, asplenia is a condition of bilateral right-sidedness and polysplenia is bilateral left-sidedness.

In a fetus with asplenia the following anomalies have been seen: the spleen is absent; the lungs are bilaterally trilobed with morphologic right bronchi on both sides; the liver is central; the stomach may be right, left, or central; the gut is malrotated; the superior vena cava is bilateral; the inferior vena cava lies to the right or left of the spine; and the aorta and cava are seen on the same side of the spine (instead of the aorta on the left and the cava on the right).

There is a high association between asplenia and congenital heart disease. Total anomalous pulmonary venous return was seen in nearly all patients, atrioventricular septal defect in 85%, single ventricle in 51%, transposition of the great arteries in 58%, and pulmonary stenosis or atresia in 70%. In less than half the patients, dextrocardia was present. Asplenia syndrome is twice as common in males.

Polysplenia syndrome is characterized by two or more spleens on both sides of the mesogastrium. Bilateral morphologic left lungs and bronchi are found in 68% of patients. The liver and stomach are on the right or left, malrotation of the bowel is found in 80%, bilateral superior vena cava is seen in half the fetuses, and the inferior vena cava is absent in 70% (blood is drained by the azygos vein, which may be on the right or left).

Cardiac malformations are frequent but not as common as with asplenia. The most common lesions found are TAPVR (70%), dextrocardia, atrial septal defect, AVSD, transposition of the great arteries, and double-outlet right ventricle.

The prognosis of this disease depends on the severity of the cardiac lesion. Surgical intervention has increased the survival rate.

Ultrasound findings. The recognition of the cardiosplenic syndrome relies on the demonstration of both the abnormal relationship between the abdominal organs and the associated cardiac deformities. The abdominal situs must be determined clearly, with the stomach on the left, heart apex to the left, aorta on the left, and inferior vena on the right, to rule out a cardiosplenic syndrome.

Ectopia Cordis. **Ectopia cordis** is a heart lesion that results from an abnormal development of the primitive heart outside the embryonic disc in the early stage of development (Figure 40-48).

Associated anomalies include facial and skeletal deformities, ventral wall defects, and central nervous system malformations (meningocele and cephalocele). Cardiac anomalies include tetralogy of Fallot and transposition of the great arteries. The prognosis is very poor for this fetus.

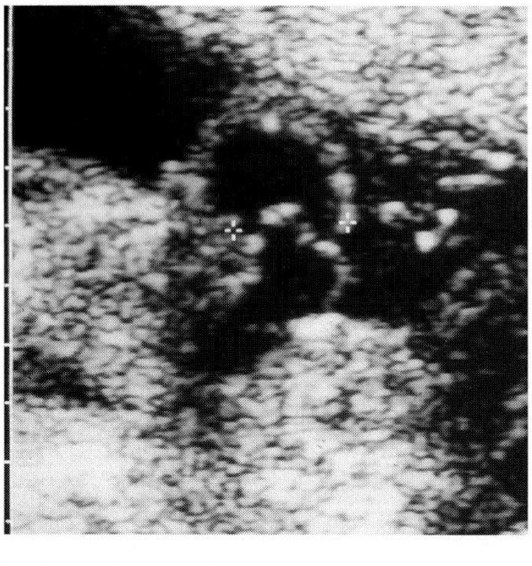

Figure 40-48 A fetus with pentology of Cantrell (multiple midline defects) including ectopia cordis. The heart was completely outside the thoracic cavity.

FETAL CARDIAC ARRHYTHMIAS

The fetal heart undergoes multiple changes during the embryologic stages. One of these stages is the progression of the cardiac electrical system, which matures to cause a normal sinus rhythm in the cardiac cycle. It is not uncommon during the course of a fetal echocardiogram to see the normal fetal heart rate decelerate from 150 beats per minute to a bradycardia stage (under 55 beats per minute), or even to pause for a few seconds. This may happen if the baby is lying on the umbilical cord or if the transducer pressure is too great. The fetus should be given a recovery time to bring the heart rate to a normal sinus rhythm. This is usually done by changing the position of the mother or releasing the pressure from the transducer.

Other changes in rhythm patterns seen during fetal development may result from premature atrial and ventricular contractions, supraventricular tachycardia, tachycardia, or atrioventricular block (Table 40-6).

Premature Atrial and Ventricular Contractions. **Premature atrial** and **ventricular contractions,** commonly called **PACs** and **PVCs,** arise from the electrical impulses generated outside the cardiac pacemaker (sinus node). The sinus node is located along the lateral right atrial wall. It is not clearly understood why some patients develop these ectopic premature contractions. Some investigators have tried to link them to increased amounts of caffeine, alcohol, or smoking, but none of our patients with PACs have these associations. An increased redundancy of the flap of the foramen ovale has been noted in these patients. The flap is larger than seen in the normal fetus and appears to swing with a great excursion from the left atrium into the right atrial cavity, touching the right atrial node.

The patient is usually referred for a fetal cardiac arrhythmia as heard on the routine obstetric examination by Doptone or auscultation. These techniques provide information about the ventricular rate only. To adequately assess the fetal rhythm the ventricular and atrial rates must be analyzed simultaneously.

The atrium and ventricle may both experience extrasystoles and ectopic beats to give rise to complex echo patterns. The PACs may either be conducted to the ventricles or blocked, depending on the moment of the cardiac cycle in which they occur (Figure 40-49). Repeated PACs may lead to an increased or decreased ventricular rate. A

TABLE 40-4 SONOGRAPHIC PITFALLS FOR ARRHYTHMIAS

Heart Rate	Rhythm	Features: Atrial to Ventricular Association
40-60	Complete heart block	A-V dissociation
60-90	Atrial bigeminy	Every other atrial impulse blocked
80-110	Sinus bradycardia	Normal A-V conduction
105-185	Normal sinus rhythm	Normal A-V conduction
180-210	Sinus tachycardia	Normal A-V conduction
150-220	Ventricular tachycardia	A-V dissociation or 1:1 V-A conduction
180+	SVT (ectopic)	1:1 A-V conduction, incessant
220-260	SVT (reentrant)	A-V conduction with sudden onset and cessation
150-600	Atrial flutter	1:1 A-V conduction or 2:1, 3:1, 4:1 A-V block
Any rate	Ectopy or blocked atrial PVCs	Frequent or occasional PACs conducted

A-V, Atrioventricular; *PACs,* premature atrial contractions; *PVCs,* premature ventricular contractions; *SVT,* supraventricular tachycardia.

blocked PAC must be differentiated from an atrioventricular block. This distinction relies on the demonstration of an atrial contraction that appears prematurely. PVCs are characterized by a PVC that is not preceded by an atrial contraction.

Ultrasound findings. The sonographer can help sort out the rhythm with M-mode and real-time ultrasound. To record the atrial and ventricular rates simultaneously, the four-chamber heart must be perpendicular to the transducer. The M-mode beam must dissect the ventricle and atria of the heart. It does not matter if the right heart or left heart is more anterior. The best area to record atrial motion is usually just superior to the atrioventricular junction along the lateral wall of the atria. The atrial pattern appears to move with a box-type motion. The ventricular rate is best recorded at the level of the atrioventricular valve and is seen to move as a smooth, uniform, well-defined pattern.

If the sonographer cannot obtain adequate images from the four-chamber view, the parasternal short axis view may be used. The M-mode beam should be directed through the right atrial wall, aortic cusps, or the left atrial wall and aortic cusps. As the aorta moves in an anterior direction, the aortic cusps open in systole and close in diastole. Thus the aortic leaflets may signify the ventricular systolic event, whereas the atrial wall signifies the atrial event.

The M-mode should be expanded to its full extent to clearly see the movement of the atrial and ventricular walls. Changes in the atrioventricular valve patterns are also noted in patients with arrhythmias. Doppler imaging of the atrioventricular valves demonstrates whether regurgitation is present during the disturbance in rhythm.

Patients with PACs and PVCs are assured that this development is a normal benign condition resulting from the immaturity of the electrical conduction system of the heart. This pattern is not associated with other cardiac anomalies.

Supraventricular Tachyarrhythmias. **Supraventricular tachyarrhythmias** include abnormal rhythms above 200 beats per minute with a conduction rate of 1:1 (Figure 40-50). These rhythm disturbances may be paroxysmal supraventricular tachycardia, paroxysmal atrial tachycardia, atrial flutter, or atrial fibrillation. In atrial flutter the atrial rate is recorded at 300 to 460 beats per minute with a normal ventricular rate. **Atrial fibrillation** shows the atria to beat at more than 400 beats per minute with a ventricular rate of 120 to 200 beats per minute.

Supraventricular tachycardia occurs by automaticity or reentry mechanisms. In cases of automatic induced tachyarrhythmias an irritable ectopic focus discharges at a high frequency. The reentry mechanism consists of an electrical impulse reentering the atria, giving rise to repeated electrical activity. Reentry may occur at the level of the sinoatrial node, inside the atrium, at the atrioventricular node, and in the His-Purkinje system. Reentry may also occur along an anomalous atrioventricular connection, such as the Kent bundle in the Wolff-Parkinson-White (WPW) syndrome.

Supraventricular tachycardia is the most frequent arrhythmia caused by atrioventricular nodal reentry, occurring in 1 in 25,000 births. Viral infections or hypoplasia of the sinoatrial tract may trigger supraventricular tachycardia.

Ultrasound findings. The finding of supraventricular tachycardia in a fetus is an emergency situation. The fetus should be scanned immediately to assess signs of heart rate, ventricular and atrial size, amount of regurgitation present, ventricular function, and presence of pericardial effusion and hydrops (Figure 40-51). With supraventricular tachycardia the fetus develops suboptimal filling of the ventricles, decreased cardiac output, and right ventricular volume overload leading to subsequent congestive heart failure.

Other cardiac anomalies associated with supraventricular tachycardia are atrial septal defects, mitral valve disease, cardiac tumors, and WPW syndrome.

Atrial flutter and fibrillation often alternate and are thought to result from a mechanism similar to that found in supraventricular tachycardia. Atrial flutter and fibrillation have been described in patients with WPW syndrome, cardiomyopathies, and thyrotoxicosis.

The fetus with this arrhythmia is usually admitted into the hospital and medically treated with antiarrhythmic drugs to control the ventricular rate, with the goal of converting the

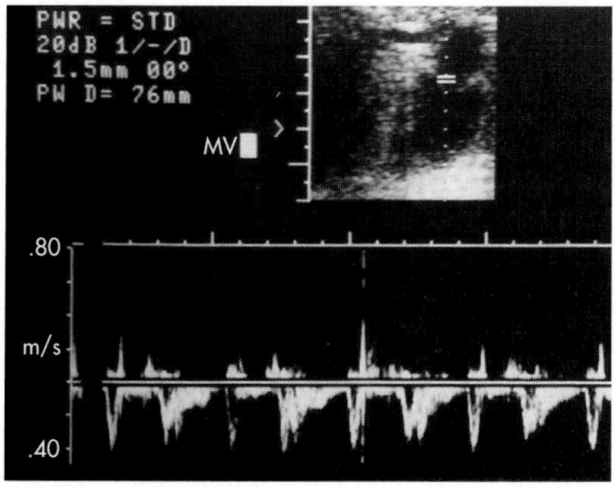

Figure 40-49 Fetus with premature atrial contractions. The fetus had normal cardiac anatomy.

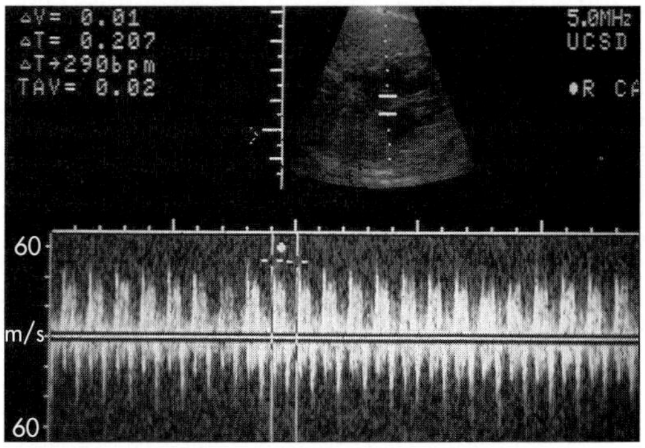

Figure 40-50 Fetus with supraventricular tachycardia showed normal conduction with a heart rate of over 220 beats per minute.

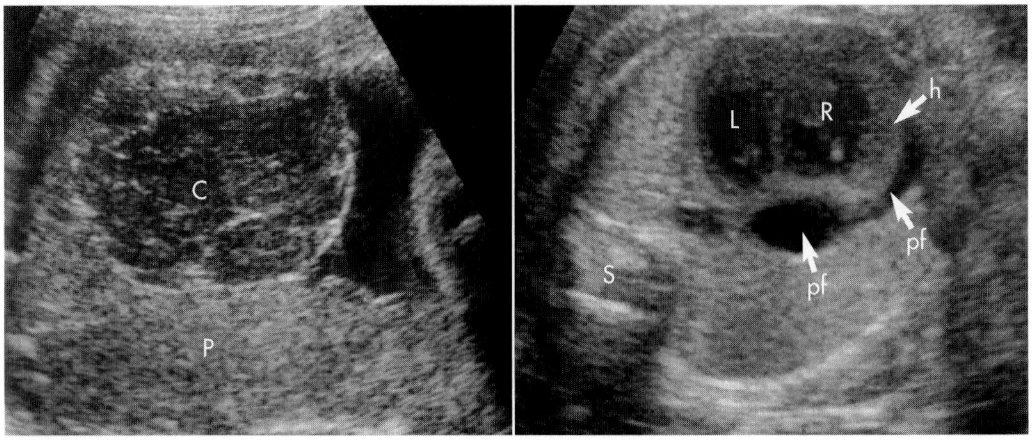

Figure 40-51 Pericardial effusion *(pf)* may be present if the arrhythmia is significant (i.e., supraventricular tachycardia). The fetus cannot withstand rapid changes in cardiac activity without developing signs of heart failure. *C,* Fetal head; *h,* heart; *L,* liver; *P,* placenta; *R,* right ventricle; *S,* spine.

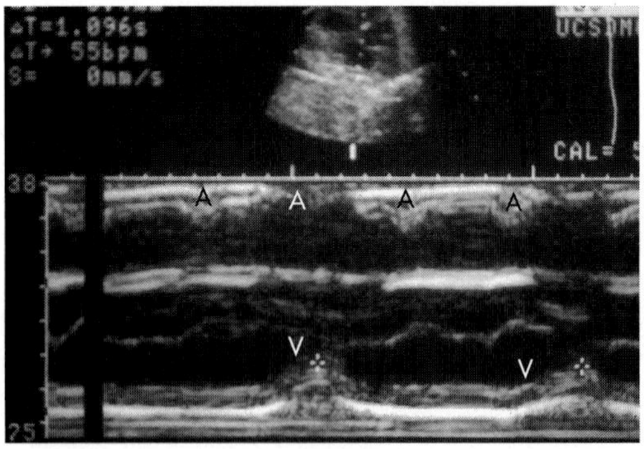

Figure 40-52 Mother with systemic lupus erythematosus presented at 20 weeks of gestation because of a "slow heart rate." The fetus was in 2:1 heart block with the atria beating twice as fast as the ventricle; every other beat was conducted. *A,* atrium; *V,* ventricle.

rate into normal sinus rhythm. Fetal echocardiography may be clinically useful in monitoring these patients' recovery.

Atrioventricular Block. When the transmission of the electrical impulse from the atria to the ventricles is blocked, the condition is called an **atrioventricular block.** Normally the atria fill in ventricular diastole and empty in ventricular systole. Just before ventricular systole occurs, the pressure in the atria is at its peak (this corresponds to the p wave on the ECG). The QRS complex signifies the onset of ventricular systole, causing the pressure from the atria to open the atrioventricular valves so the left ventricle may fill. If this electrical process is blocked, the blood remains in the atria and does not cause the atrioventricular valves to open so blood can fill the ventricular cavities. This condition may be attributed to immaturity of the conduction system, absence of connection to the atrioventricular node, or an abnormal anatomic position of the atrioventricular node. The fetus may have a first-, second-, or third-degree heart block.

The fetus with a third-degree atrioventricular block has been found to have associated structural anomalies, including corrected transposition, univentricular heart, cardiac tumors, and cardiomyopathies. Patients with a connective tissue disorder, such as lupus erythematosus, have also been found to develop heart block.

First- and second-degree atrioventricular blocks are not associated with any significant hemodynamic disturbance. A complete heart block may result in bradycardia, leading to decreased cardiac output and congestive heart failure during fetal life.

Ultrasound findings. The fetal M-mode echocardiogram should be performed after the normal anatomic cardiac anatomy has been demonstrated (Figure 40-52). As described in the supraventricular tachycardia section, the four-chamber and parasternal short axis views are best used to record atrial and ventricular events simultaneously.

First-degree heart block is not seen in the fetus, since the heart rate and rhythm are normal. The blockage of a normal atrial impulse can be diagnosed by demonstrating a normally timed atrial contraction that is not followed by a ventricular contraction.

Second- and third-degree heart blocks are defined by observing the relationship between the atrial and ventricular rates. In second-degree Mobitz type I block, only a few atrial impulses are not conducted; in Mobitz type II block, a submultiple of atrial impulses is transmitted. In complete heart block, atrial and ventricular rates are independent of each other, with the atrial rate slower. The fetus becomes symptomatic when the cardiac output is decreased and congestive heart failure develops.

REVIEW QUESTIONS

1. Describe the fetal circulation pathway.
2. How is fetal circulation different from neonatal circulation?

3. Name five risk factors in each of the following categories: fetal, maternal, familial.
4. What transducer is best to use for a fetal echocardiogram?
5. Describe the normal approach to a fetal cardiac ultrasound study.
6. Name and describe the routine views used in the fetal cardiac study.
7. Name the three types of septal defects that may occur in the fetus.
8. What is the most common septal defect?
9. Describe the abnormalities found in Ebstein's anomaly.
10. How does a hypoplastic right heart develop?
11. Describe the four findings in tetralogy of Fallot.
12. What is the difference between tetralogy of Fallot and double-outlet right ventricle?
13. Define the types of pulmonic stenosis present in the fetus. Describe the echocardiographic features of each type.
14. Describe the Doppler technique for defining mitral regurgitation.
15. What is the difference between a normal aortic valve, aortic atresia, aortic stenosis, and a bicuspid aortic valve?
16. Define the patterns of coarctation of the aorta and the appearance seen on the fetal echo.
17. What is hypoplastic left heart syndrome?
18. Describe the difference between transposition of the great arteries and corrected transposition.
19. What is truncus arteriosus?
20. Describe the echocardiographic findings in a fetus with cardiomyopathy.
21. Define the pathway the pulmonary veins may take if they do not drain into the left atrial cavity.
22. Name three benign cardiac tumors and their echocardiographic appearance.
23. What is the significance of PACs or PVCs? How frequently do they occur? What is the M-mode technique used to record the abnormalities?
24. Describe the supraventricular tachyarrhythmia rhythm. How is it different from PACs and PVCs?
25. What are the problems associated with a complete atrioventricular heart block?

REFERENCES

1. Allen L: *Manual of fetal echocardiography,* London, 1986, MTP Press Limited.
2. Beeby AR and others: Reproducibility of ultrasonic measurement of fetal cardiac haemodynamics, *Br J Obstet Gynaecol* 98:807, 1991.
3. Brand JM, Friedberg DZ: Spontaneous regression of a primary cardiac tumor presenting as fetal tachyarrhythmias, *J Perinatol* 12:48, 1992.
4. Callan NA and others: Fetal echocardiography: indications for referral, prenatal diagnoses, and outcomes, *Am J Perinatol* 8:390, 1991.
5. Moore KL: *The developing human,* Philadelphia, 1991, WB Saunders.

BIBLIOGRAPHY

Allan LD, Sharland G, Tynan MJ: The natural history of the hypoplastic left heart syndrome, *Int J Cardiol* 25:341, 1989.

Bharati S and others: In utero echocardiographic diagnosis of premature closure of the foramen ovale with mitral regurgitation and large left atrium, *Am Heart J* 122:597, 1991.

Bromley B and others: Fetal echocardiography: accuracy and limitations in a population at high and low risk for heart defects, *Am J Obstet Gynecol* 166:1473, 1992.

Bronshtein M, Siegler E, Eshcoli Z, Zimmer EZ: Transvaginal ultrasound measurements of the fetal heart at 11 to 17 weeks of gestation, *Am J Perinatol* 9:38, 1992.

Brown DL: Borderline findings in fetal cardiac sonography, *Semin Ultrasound CT MRI* 19(4):329, 1998.

Brown DL and others: The peripheral hypoechoic rim of the fetal heart, *J Ultrasound Med* 8:603, 1989.

Callan NA, Kan JS: Prenatal diagnosis of tetralogy of Fallot with absent pulmonary valve, *Am J Perinatol* 8:15, 1991.

Callen, PC: *Ultrasonography in obstetrics and gynecology,* ed 3, Philadelphia, 1994, WB Saunders.

Chobot V and others: Prenatal detection of restrictive foramen ovale, *J Am Soc Echocardiogr* 3:15, 1990.

Comstock C: Normal fetal heart axis and position, *Obstet Gynecol* 70:2, 87.

Comstock CH and others: Pulmonary-to-aorta diameter ratio in the normal and abnormal fetal heart, *Am J Obstet Gynecol* 165:1038, 1991.

Copel J, Pilu G, Kleinman CS: Congenital heart disease and extracardiac anomalies: associations and indications for fetal echocardiography, *Am J Obstet Gynecol* 154:1121, 1986.

Copel JA, Hobbins JC, Kleinman CS: Doppler echocardiography and color flow mapping, *Obstet Gynecol Clin North Am* 18:845, 1991.

Cyr D and others: A systematic approach to fetal echocardiography using real-time/two-dimensional sonography, *J Ultrasound Med* 5:343, 86.

Davidson SR and others: Fetal heart rate variability and behavioral state: analysis by power spectrum, *Am J Obstet Gynecol* 167:717, 1992.

DeVore GR: The aortic and pulmonary outflow tract screening examination in the human fetus, *J Ultrasound Med* 11:345, 1992.

DeVore GR and others: Fetal echocardiography: normal anatomy as determined by real-time–directed M-mode ultrasound, *Am J Obstet Gynecol* 144:249, 1982.

Dolkart LA, Reimers FT: Transvaginal fetal echocardiography in early pregnancy: normative data, *Am J Obstet Gynecol* 165:688, 1991.

Fabbri EL, Hamner LH III: Congenital complete heart block associated with maternal anti-Ro antibody: a case report, *J Perinatol* 12:225, 1992.

Gembruch U and others: Color Doppler flow mapping of fetal heart, *J Perinatal Med* 19:27, 1991.

Geva T and others: Cardiac rhabdomyoma: rare cause of fetal death, *Chest* 99:139, 1991.

Goldstein SR: Significance of cardiac activity on endovaginal ultrasound in very early embryos, *Obstet Gynecol* 80:670, 1992.

Groves AM and others: Cardiac tumours in intrauterine life, *Arch Dis Child* 67:1189, 1992.

Ho SY and others: Disposition of the atrioventricular conduction tissues in the heart with isomerism of the atrial appendages: its relation to congenital complete heart block, *J Am Coll Cardiol* 20:904, 1992.

Hornberger LK and others: Tricuspid valve disease with significant tricuspid insufficiency in the fetus: diagnosis and outcome, *J Am Coll Cardiol* 17:167, 1991.

Kachalia P and others: In utero sonographic appearance of the atrial septum primum and septum secundum, *J Ultrasound Med* 10:423, 1991.

Mellick JD, Radford DJ, Galbraith AJ: Fetal echocardiography in the diagnosis of congenital heart disease, *Aust Paediatr J* 25:356, 1989.

Morin LR : Prenatal diagnosis of left ventricular false tendon, *Acta Obstet Gynecol Scand* 68:463, 1989.

Phillipos EZ, Robertson MA, Still DK: Prenatal detection of foramen ovale obstruction without hydrops fetalis, *J Am Soc Echocardiogr* 3:495, 1990.

Rane HS, Purandare H: Fetal echocardiography in normal pregnancies: a basis for prenatal detection of cardiac malformations, *Indian Pediatr* 27:729, 1990.

Reed KL: Cyanotic disease in the fetus, *J Am Soc Echocardiography* 3:9, 1990.

Reed KL: Introduction to fetal echocardiography, *Obstet Gynecol Clin North Am* 18:811, 1991.

Reed KL and others: Human fetal tricuspid and mitral deceleration time: changes with normal pregnancy and intrauterine growth retardation, *Am J Obstet Gynecol* 161:1532, 1989.

Reed KL and others: Cardiac Doppler flow velocities in human fetuses, *Circulation* 73:41, 1986.

Respondek A and others: Echocardiographic evaluation of fetal arrhythmias, *Kardiol Pol* 33:136, 1990.

Respondek M and others: 2D echocardiographic assessment of the fetal heart size in the 2nd and 3rd trimester of uncomplicated pregnancy, *Eur J Obstet Gynecol Reprod Biol* 44:185, 1992.

Rizzo G, Arduini D, Romanini C: Accelerated cardiac growth and abnormal cardiac flow in fetuses of type I diabetic mothers, *Obstet Gynecol* 80:369, 1992.

Roberts DJ, Genest D: Cardiac histologic pathology characteristic of trisomies 13 and 21, *Hum Pathol* 23:1130, 1992.

Romero R and others: *Prenatal diagnosis of congenital anomalies,* East Norwalk, Conn, 1988, Appleton & Lange.

Sahn DJ and others: Quantitative real-time cross sectional echocardiography in the developing normal human fetus and newborn, *Circulation* 62:3, 1980.

Santulli TV Jr: Fetal echocardiography: assessment of cardiovascular anatomy and function, *Clin Perinatol* 17:911, 1990.

Schmidt KG and others: Echocardiographic evaluation of dilated cardiomyopathy in the human fetus, *Am J Cardiol* 63:599, 1989.

Sharland GK, Chita SK, Allan LD: The use of colour Doppler in fetal echocardiography, *Int J Cardiol* 28:229, 1990.

Sharland GK, Chita SK, Allan LD: Tricuspid valve dysplasia or displacement in intrauterine life, *J Am Coll Cardiol* 17:944, 1991.

Shaw CT: Polysplenia in a fetus with bradycardia from 26 to 36 weeks' gestation, complex cardiac malformations, and heart block, *J Am Osteopath Assoc* 90:1100, 1990.

Shime J and others: Two-dimensional and M-mode echocardiography in the human fetus, *Am J Obstet Gynecol* 143:178, 1983.

Silver MM, Laxer RM, Laskin CA, et al: Association of fetal heart block and massive placental infarction due to maternal autoantibodies, *Pediatr Pathol* 12:131, 1992.

Silverman NH, Schmidt KG: Ventricular volume overload in the human fetus: observations from fetal echocardiography, *J Am Soc Echocardiography* 3:20, 1990.

Sutton MS and others: Assessment of right and left ventricular function in terms of force development with gestational age in the normal human fetus, *Br Heart J* 66:285, 1991.

Swartjes JM and others: Quantitated fetal heart rhythm at 20, 32 and 38 weeks of gestation and dependence on rest-activity patterns, *Early Hum Dev* 28:27, 1992.

Tan J and others: Cardiac dimensions determined by cross-sectional echocardiography in the normal human fetus from 18 weeks to term, *Am J Cardiol* 70:1459, 1992.

Tulzer G and others: Doppler echocardiography of fetal ductus arteriosus constriction versus increased right ventricular output, *J Am Coll Cardiol* 18:532, 1991.

Ursell PC and others: Growth of the great vessels in the normal human fetus and in the fetus with cardiac defects, *Circulation* 84:2028, 1991.

Vaha-Eskeli K and others: Doppler flow measurement of uterine and umbilical arteries in heat stress during late pregnancy, *Am J Perinatol* 8:385, 1991.

van der Mooren K, Barendregt LG, Wladimiroff JW: Fetal atrioventricular and outflow tract flow velocity waveforms during normal second half of pregnancy, *Am J Obstet Gynecol* 165:668, 1991.

van der Mooren K, Barendregt LG, Wladimiroff JW: Flow velocity wave forms in the human fetal ductus arteriosus during the normal second half of pregnancy, *Pediatr Res* 30:487, 1991.

Vergani P and others: Screening for congenital heart disease with the four-chamber view of the fetal heart, *Am J Obstet Gynecol* 167:1000, 1992.

Wenink AC: Quantitative morphology of the embryonic heart: an approach to development of the atrioventricular valves, *Anat Rec* 234:129, 1992.

Wilson AD, Rao PS, Aeschlimann S: Normal fetal foramen flap and transatrial Doppler velocity pattern, *J Am Soc Echocardiogr* 3:491, 1990.

Wladimiroff JW and others: Normal fetal Doppler inferior vena cava, transtricuspid, and umbilical artery flow velocity waveforms between 11 and 16 weeks' gestation, *Am J Obstet Gynecol* 166:921, 1992.

Wladimiroff JW and others: Normal fetal cardiac flow velocity waveforms between 11 and 16 weeks of gestation, *Am J Obstet Gynecol* 167:736, 1992.

CHAPTER 41

The Fetal Anterior Abdominal Wall

Sandra L. Hagen-Ansert

OBJECTIVES

- Describe the embryology of the abdominal wall
- Differentiate among an omphalocele, gastroschisis, and an umbilical hernia
- List the sonographic findings in a fetus with an omphalocele
- List the sonographic findings in a fetus with a gastroschisis
- Describe limb–body wall defects, cloacal exstrophy, and pentalogy of Cantrell

KEY TERMS

amniotic band syndrome - rupture of the amnion that leads to entrapment or entanglement of the fetal parts by the "sticky" chorion

Beckwith-Wiedemann syndrome - group of disorders having in common the coexistence of an omphalocele, macroglossia, and visceromegaly

cloacal extrophy - defect in the lower abdominal wall and anterior wall of the urinary bladder

encephalocele - protrusion of the brain through a cranial fissure

exencephaly - abnormal condition in which the brain is located outside the cranium

gastroschisis - opening in the layers of the abdominal wall with evisceration of the bowel (and occasionally the stomach and genitourinary organs)

limb–body wall complex - anaomaly with large cranial defects, facial cleft, large body wall defects, and limb abnormalities

omphalocele - develops when there is a midline defect of the abdominal muscles, fascia, and skin that results in herniation of intraabdominal structures into the base of the umbilical cord.

pentalogy of Cantrell - rare anomaly with five defects: omphalocele, ectopic heart, lower sternum, anterior diaphragm, and diaphragmatic pericardium

scoliosis - abnormal curvature of the spine

Ultrasound has proven to be a very effective tool in determining anterior abdominal wall defects in utero. These defects occur during the first trimester as the midgut elongates and migrates into the umbilical cord. The midgut usually returns into the abdominal cavity by the 11th week of gestation. When this fails to occur, an abdominal wall defect is formed. The two most common defects are omphalocele and gastroschisis. Less common defects are ectopia cordis, limb-body wall complex, cloacal exstrophy, and allantoic cyst.

EMBRYOLOGY OF THE ABDOMINAL WALL

The embryo is a flat disk consisting of three layers: ectoderm, mesoderm, and endoderm by the end of the 5th week of development. In the 6th week a process called *folding* helps the embryo transform itself into a cylindrical shape and becomes a critical process in the closure of the abdominal wall.[6]

As the embryo folds at the cranial end, the base of the yolk sac is partially incorporated as the foregut, which later develops as the pharynx, lower respiratory system, esophagus, stomach, duodenum (proximal to the opening of the bile duct), liver, pancreas, gallbladder, and biliary duct system.[6]

The growth of the neural tube causes the embryo to fold at the caudal end, incorporating part of the yolk sac as the hindgut, which turns into the cloaca. It also causes the connecting stalk (located at the tail) to move to the ventral surface of the embryo, incorporating the allantois into the umbilical cord. The derivatives of the hindgut are the distal part of the transverse colon, the descending colon, the sigmoid colon, the rectum, the superior portion of the anal canal, the epithelium of the urinary bladder, and most of the urethra (Figure 41-1).

The sides of the embryo fold, leading to the formation of the lateral and anterior abdominal wall. The midgut is the primordium of the small intestines (including most of the duodenum), cecum, vermiform appendix, ascending colon,

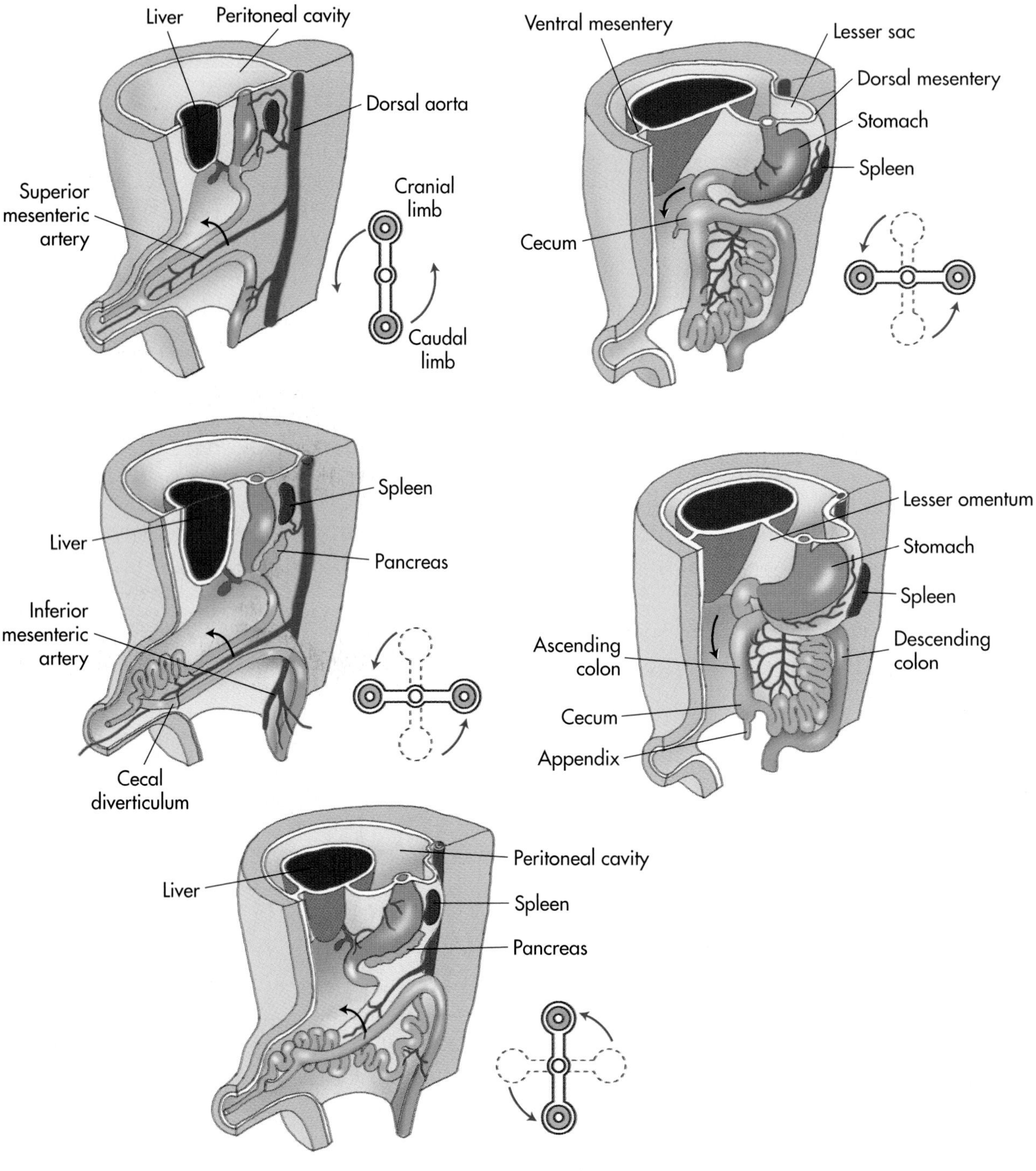

Figure 41-1 Development and rotation of the midgut from the sixth to eleventh week. The midgut is the primordium of the small intestines, cecum, appendix, ascending colon, and right half to two thirds of the transverse colon. The connection of the yolk sac and body stalk will form the umbilical cord at the ventral region of the embryo.

and the right half to two thirds of the transverse colon.[6] The connection of the yolk sac and body stalk will form the umbilical cord at the ventral region of the embryo. Expansion of the amniotic cavity will cover the umbilical cord by the amnion. Fusion of the midline begins during the 7th week of development and is completed by the 8th week.

The umbilical veins drain the placenta, body stalk, and the evolving abdominal wall. During the 7th week the hepatic bud enlarges, and an atrophy of the right umbilical vein occurs. The proximal portion of the left umbilical vein between the subhepatic portion and the common cardinal vein also atrophies. Branches of the aorta now replace the nutritive function of the umbilical veins with respect to the developing abdominal wall. The superior mesenteric artery is formed from the right omphalomesenteric artery.

Umbilication hernia of the bowel occurs during the 8th week of development as the midgut extends to the extraembryonic coelom in the proximal portion of the umbilical cord.[6] The midgut grows faster than the abdominal cavity at this stage because of the increased size of the liver and kidneys. Thus the herniation develops. The intestines return to the abdominal cavity by the 12th week of gestation.

ABNORMALITIES OF THE ANTERIOR ABDOMINAL WALL

Abdominal wall defects cause distortion of the normal contour of the ventral or anterior surface of the fetal abdomen. There are three common abdominal wall defects: **omphalocele,** umbilical hernia (a form of omphalocele), and **gastroschisis** (Box 41-1).

The incidence of omphalocele is roughly 1 in 4000 live births.[8] Rarer abdominal wall defects include ectopia cordis, pentalogy of Cantrell, limb–body wall complex, amnion rupture sequence, and bladder and cloacal exstrophy. Overall, gastroschisis has an incidence of 12 per 10,000 although only rarely are affected infants born to older mothers.[2,10] The role of the perinatal team is to distinguish among these lesions because clinical management, associated anomalies, delivery, and postnatal surgical survival vary, depending on the specific type of abdominal wall defect.

OMPHALOCELE

During the eighth to 12th weeks of development, the fetal bowel normally migrates into the umbilical cord from the abdominal cavity. This normal embryologic herniation of the bowel permits the development of the intraabdominal organs and allows necessary bowel rotation. Because of the lack of space within the abdominal cavity and the large fetal liver and kidneys, the bowel is forced from the abdomen and into the extraembryonic coelom of the umbilical cord. This herniation permits the bowel to rotate around the superior mesenteric artery. These herniated loops of bowel normally return and rotate into position within the abdominal cavity by the 12th week of pregnancy. When bowel loops fail to return to the abdomen, a bowel-containing omphalocele occurs (Figure 41-2).[2,10]

BOX 41-1 DIFFERENTIATION OF OMPHALOCELE FROM GASTROSCHISIS

The sonographer should investigate the following to differentiate an omphalocele from a gastroschisis:

- Look for the presence of a membrane; gastroschisis does not have one.
- Look at the umbilical cord; the cord goes through the omphalocele—it usually is to the right of the gastroschisis.
- Determine which organs are eviscerated.
- Determine if the bowel is normal in texture.
- Look for other anomalies; omphalocele has a higher percentage of chromosome abnormalities.

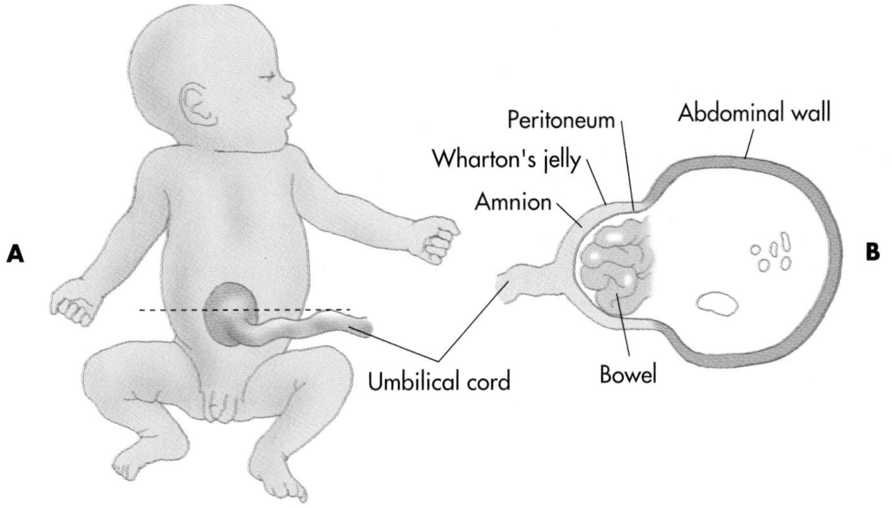

Figure 41-2 Typical features of bowel-containing omphalocele (intracorporeal liver) shown on external examination **(A)** and on cross-sectional view, **(B).**

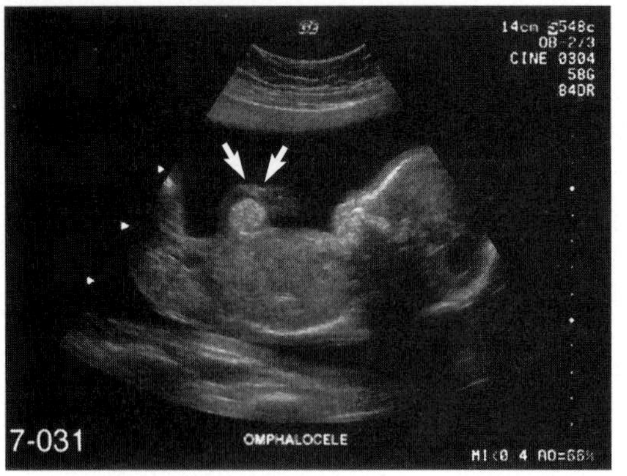

Figure 41-3 Longitudinal image of a 14-week-old fetus showing a small omphalocele with its covering membrane *(arrows)* projecting from the umbilical area.

An omphalocele develops when there is a midline defect of the abdominal muscles, fascia, and skin that results in herniation of intraabdominal structures into the base of the umbilical cord (Figure 41-3). This herniation is covered by a membrane that is composed of amnion and peritoneum. The alpha-fetoprotein (AFP) level may be slightly elevated or within normal limits. The omphaloceles are characterized as two types: (1) those that contain the liver within the sac and (2) those that contain a variable amount of bowel, but no liver.

Fetuses with omphaloceles that contain only bowel have a higher risk for chromosomal abnormalities and other anomalies (Figures 41-4 and 41-5). Omphaloceles with bowel develop because the intestine fails to return to the abdomen (primitive body stalk remains).[3] Liver omphaloceles represent a developmental defect in abdominal wall closure.[6] This type of omphalocele affects the ab-

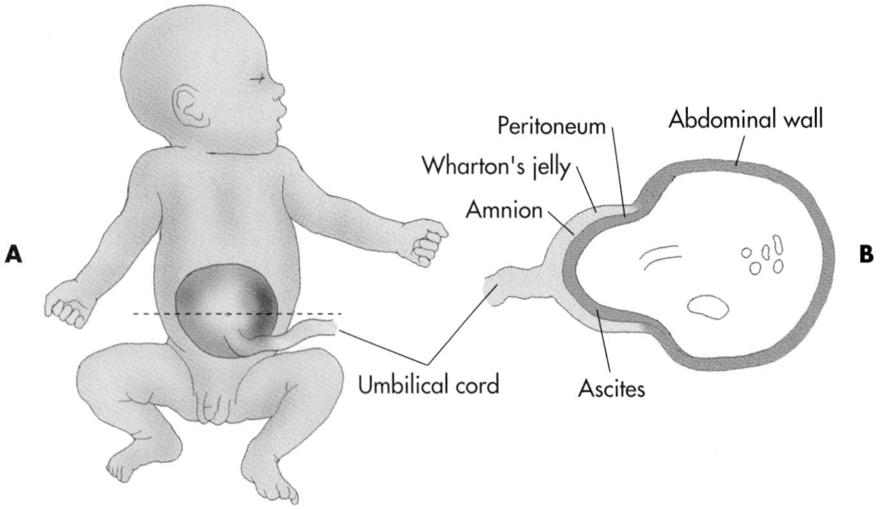

Figure 41-4 Typical features of liver-containing omphalocele shown on external examination **(A)** and on cross-sectional view **(B).**

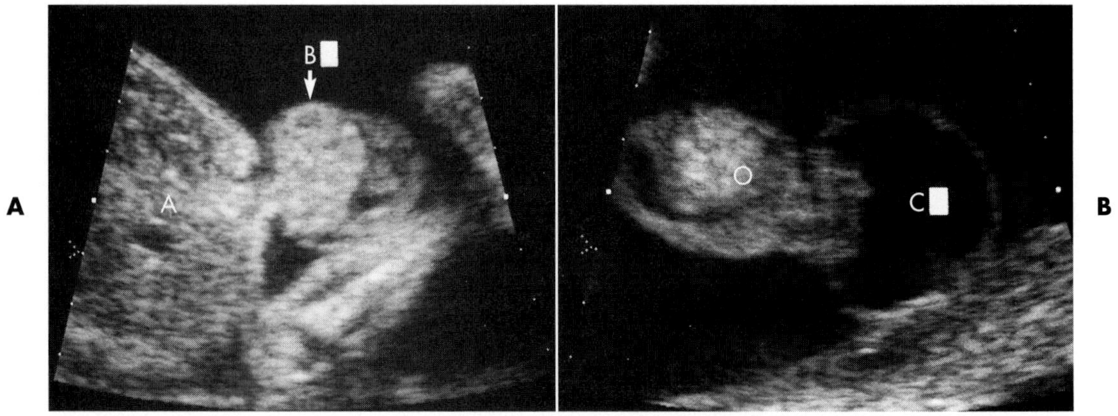

Figure 41-5 **A,** Bowel omphalocele *(B)* in a fetus with trisomy 18. *A,* Abdomen. **B,** In the same fetus an umbilical cord cyst *(C)* is noted coursing distally into the omphalocele *(O).* Other anomalies observed included a strawberry-shaped cranium (see Figure 30-32), hypoplastic cerebellum, nuchal fold, and esophageal atresia. Additionally, a large atrial septal defect, hypoplastic left ventricle, single umbilical artery, and hydramnios were found.

dominal wall muscles, fascia, and skin. Liver omphaloceles may contain bowel and demonstrate a relatively large abdominal wall defect in comparison to the abdominal diameter (Figures. 41-6 and 41-7).

The prognosis for infants with omphalocele varies according to the extent of the primary defect and associated structural and chromosomal abnormalities. Perinatal mortality approaches 80% when more than one fetal abnormality exists, and almost all infants die when there is a chromosomal or major heart defect. Without other anomalies, the mortality rate is approximately 10% with an isolated omphalocele.

The mode of delivery for fetuses with omphalocele varies according to the type of omphalocele and other anomalies. The obstetrician may elect vaginal delivery when a chromosomal abnormality and other major anomalies predict no chance for survival.

Ultrasound findings. The sonographic signs of omphalocele are as follows:

- Central abdominal wall defect with evisceration of the bowel or a combination of liver and bowel into the base of the umbilical cord. Color flow imaging may aid in viewing the continuity of the umbilical cord into the omphalocele. The stomach may be involved (Figure 41-8). Bowel omphaloceles appear echogenic and must be distinguished from umbilical hernia (covered by skin and fat).
- Membrane composed of peritoneum and amnion forms the omphalocele sac encasing the herniated organs.
- Umbilical hernias may be confused with liver omphaloceles; however, a normal cord insertion suggests hernia (Figure 41-9).
- Ascites may coexist with omphalocele.
- Hydramnios are found in one third of fetuses.
- Associated anomalies (50% to 70%) include complex cardiac disease (30% to 50%) and gastrointestinal, neural tube, and genitourinary tract anomalies (Polycystic kidneys with a small omphalocele may indicate trisomy 13.) (Figure 41-10).
- Omphaloceles may occur concurrently with diaphragmatic hernia.
- Chromosomal anomalies occur in 35% to 60%. Most common are trisomies 13 and 18. Omphalocele may be found with trisomy 21, Turner's syndrome, and triploidy.
- When scoliosis is found, consider limb-body wall complex (or body-stalk anomaly), a lethal disorder, which also includes severe cranial defects (acrania, encephalocele), facial clefts, ex-

A 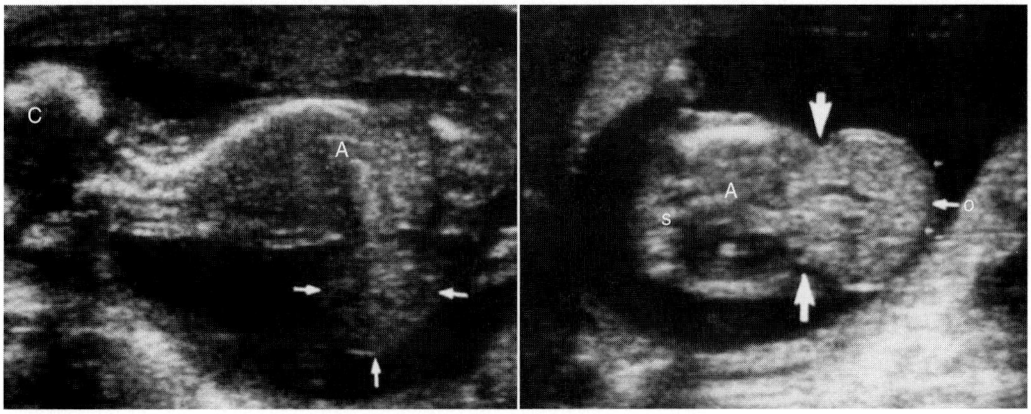 B

Figure 41-6 **A,** Sagittal scan in an 18-week-old fetus in a spine-up position with a mass herniating from the anterior abdominal wall representing an omphalocele *(arrows)*. *A,* Abdomen; *C,* cranium. **B,** In the same fetus, in a transverse direction, herniation of the liver into the omphalocele *(o)* is observed. Note the portal vessel within the liver. *A,* Abdomen; *large arrows,* first border of omphalocele; *s,* spine.

A 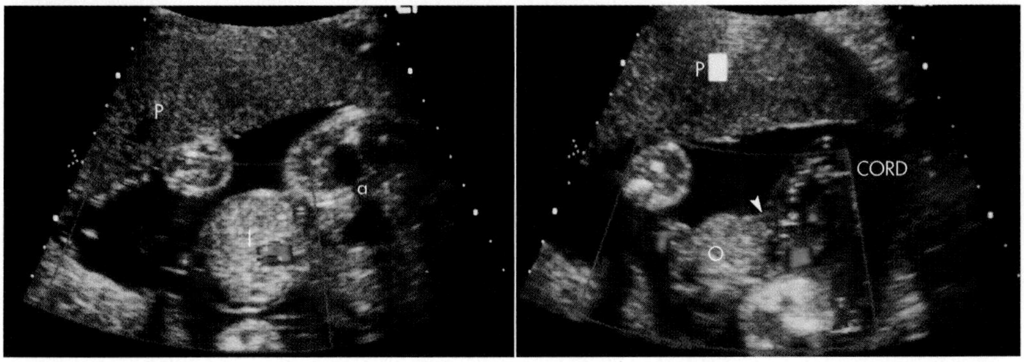 B

Figure 41-7 **A,** Color flow imaging of a liver-filled omphalocele in a 26-week-old fetus showing hepatic vessel flow within the herniated liver. *a,* Abdomen; *P,* placenta. **B,** In the same fetus, color enhancement aids in the confirmation of the cord vessels entering the base of the omphalocele *(O, arrow); P,* placenta. No other anomalies were found and the karyotype was normal.

A
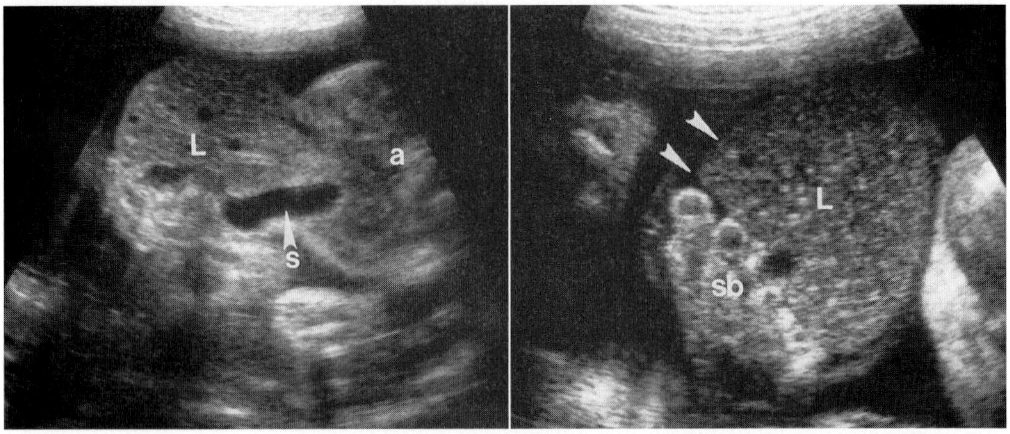

B

Figure 41-8 **A,** Large, liver-filled *(L)* omphalocele shown in a 27-week-old fetus. This omphalocele also contained a portion of the stomach *(S)* and small bowel. *a,* Abdomen. The karotype was normal and no other sonographic anomalies were detected. **B,** In the same fetus, small bowel *(sb)* and ascites *(arrows)* are shown. Surgical repair of the omphalocele was successful after birth. *L,* Liver.

A
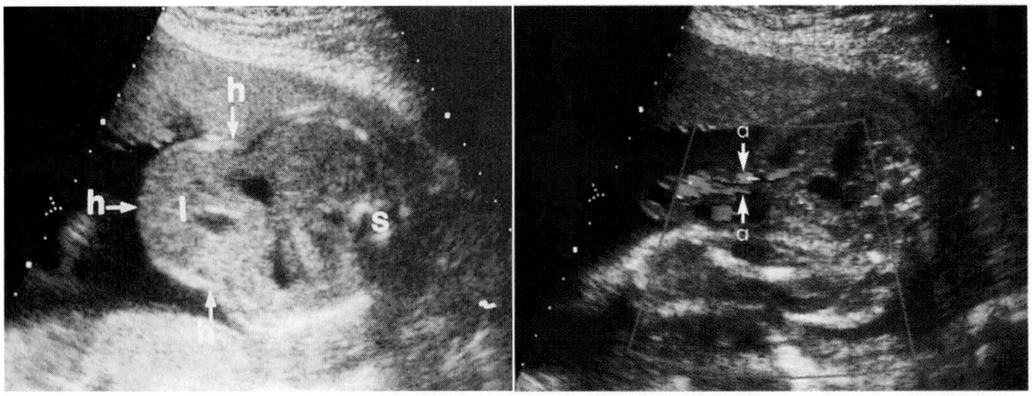

B

Figure 41-9 **A,** Umbilical hernia *(h; arrows)* observed in a fetus with Carpenter's syndrome (acrocephalopolysyndactyly). *l,* Liver; *s,* spine. **B,** In the same fetus, at the cord insertion level, using color imaging, the umbilical arteries are observed entering the abdomen in a normal location. This excludes the diagnosis of omphalocele. *a,* Artery.

A
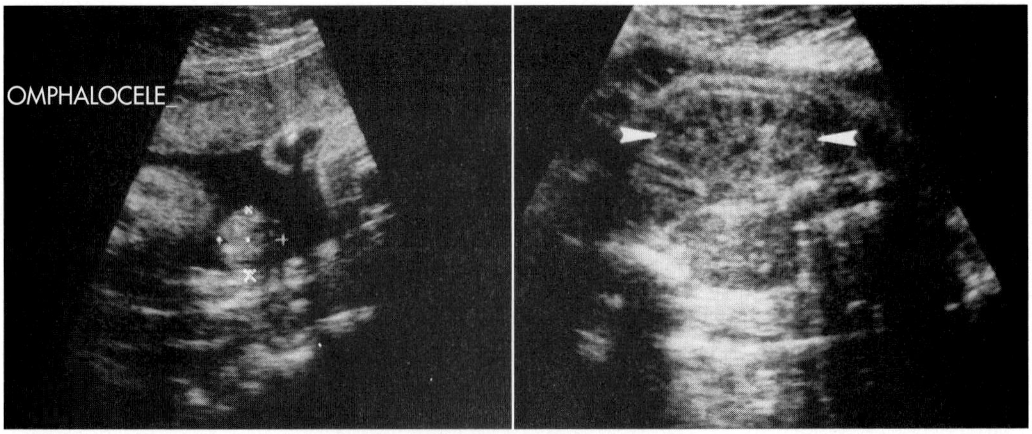

B

Figure 41-10 **A,** Bowel-filled omphalocele (2 mm) *(calipers)* in a 27-week-old fetus. **B,** In the same fetus, enlarged polycystic kidneys *(arrows)* were observed bilaterally. Oligohydramnios, an 8-mm nuchal fold, cerebellar hypoplasia, and enlarged cisterna magna with Dandy-Walker malformation and asymmetry of the heart were found. Genetic amniocentesis was declined. Intrauterine growth restriction was apparent by 33 weeks of gestation. Trisomy 13 was suspected. Neonatal karyotype after birth confirmed the diagnosis of trisomy 13 with translocation. The infant died within 1 hour of birth.

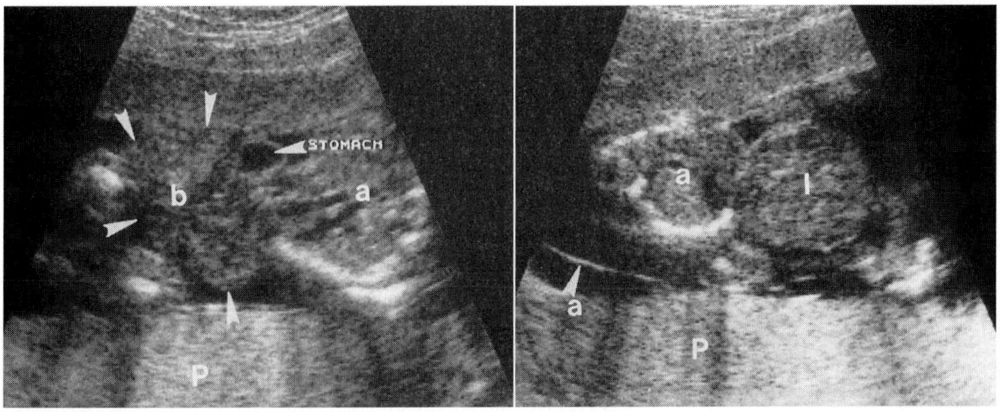

Figure 41-11 **A,** Early amnion rupture sequence or body stalk anomaly in a 17-week-old fetus revealing extensive herniation of the abdominal organs. The *stomach* and bowel *(b)* are eviscerated. *a,* Abdomen; *P,* placenta. **B,** In the same fetus, herniation of the liver *(l)* is noted. Note the amniotic band *(a, arrow)* outlined within the amniotic cavity. Amniocentesis revealed a chromosomally normal infant. *a,* Abdomen.

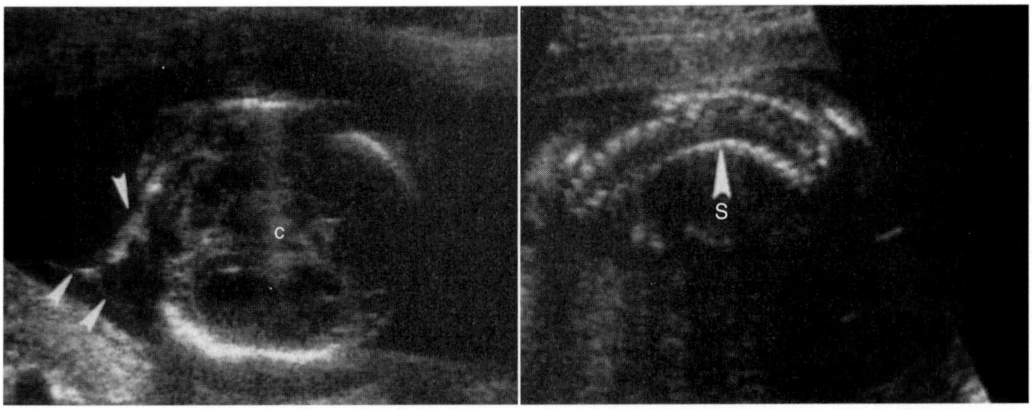

Figure 41-12 **A,** In the fetus depicted in Figure 41-11, amniotic bands *(arrows)* are shown adhering to the cranium *(c).* **B,** In the same fetus, scoliosis *(s)* is demonstrated. The fetus delivered prematurely at 29 weeks of gestation because of premature rupture of the membranes. Autopsy revealed posterior scalp defects with attachment of amniotic bands. Low-set ears and posteriorly rotated ears, bilateral cleft lip and palate, absent toes unilaterally, constriction ring of the thumb and first finger of one hand, and bilateral simian creases were found. The abdominal wall defect included herniation of the stomach, intestine, liver, and two spleens. A wide midline defect that was continuous with the cord was found. Scoliosis was also confirmed.

tensive abdominal wall defect of the chest, and abdomen and limb defects. Abnormal fusion of the amnion and chorion extends as a sheet from the cord and adheres to the fetus and placenta (Figures 41-11 and 41-12).

- Amniotic band syndrome may represent a milder form of limb–body wall complex and may be predicted by amniotic bands (fibrous tissue strands) that entangle or amputate fetal parts.[5,7] Facial clefts, asymmetric encephaloceles, constriction or amputation defects of the extremities, and clubfoot deformities are common findings. Uterine sheets (synechiae) should not be confused with amniotic bands.
- Pentalogy of Cantrell is considered when a large omphalocele, diaphragmatic hernia, ectopia cordis (evisceration of heart), and other heart defects are observed (Figures 41-13 and 41-14).[2]
- Consider bladder or cloacal exstrophy when a low omphalocele is observed. Other anomalies may include anal atresia, spina bifida, and lower limb defects.
- When organomegaly and macroglossia are observed, Beckwith-Wiedemann syndrome is suspected (occurs in 12% of infants with omphalocele).

GASTROSCHISIS

Gastroschisis is an opening in the layers of the abdominal wall with evisceration (herniation) of the bowel and, infrequently, the stomach and genitourinary organs (Figure 41-15). It is thought that gastroschisis is a consequence of atrophy of the right umbilical vein or a disruption of the omphalomesenteric artery.[1,6] Gastroschisis defects are usually not known to be genetically transmitted, although the recurrence risk for gastroschisis has been estimated at 3.5%.[7]

Gastroschisis defects are small (2 to 4 cm in size) and are located next to the normal cord insertion. In the ma-

jority of cases, the defect is positioned to the right of the umbilical cord. The insertion of the umbilical cord is normal in fetuses with gastroschisis (Figures 41-16 and 41-17). Small bowel is always found in the herniation.

Other organs that may be involved in the herniation include the large bowel, the stomach, occasionally portions of the genitourinary system, and rarely the liver.

Alpha-fetoprotein levels are significantly higher in gastroschisis compared with omphalocele because of the exposed bowel. The occurrence of gastroschisis is 1.75 to 2.5 in 10,000 live births.[2] It has been found more frequently in males.

Although coexisting anomalies are rare with gastroschisis, associated gastrointestinal problems may be of considerable medical consequence to the infant. This defect prevents the occurrence of normal bowel rotation, and intestinal atresia or stenosis may ensue because of ischemia (compression of mesenteric vessels or bowel torsion).[6] Ischemia may cause bowel perforation or meconium peritonitis. In several neonatal studies, over half of the infants with gastroschisis in which ischemia and gangrene of the bowel were present subsequently died.[6]

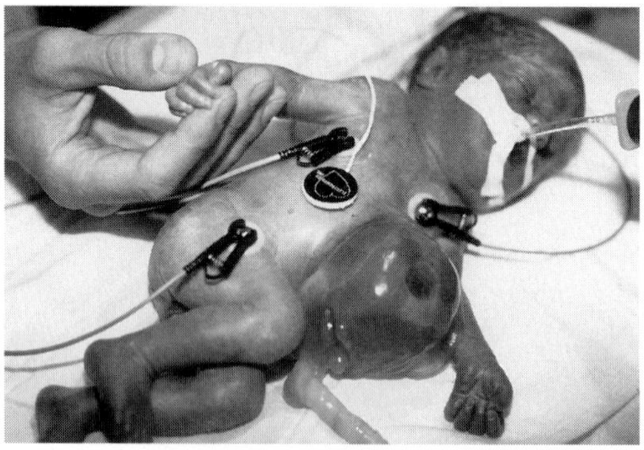

Figure 41-13 Neonate depicted in Figure 41-14 with diaphragmatic hernia and omphalocele.

The obstetrician usually prefers to deliver the infant by cesarean section to avoid bowel damage and contamination from a vaginal delivery. The prognosis for the infant with uncomplicated gastroschisis is excellent. Surgical repair usually occurs within hours of delivery; with extensive defects, reconstruction is performed in stages using Silastic sheets.

Ultrasound findings. The sonographer may be able to detect gastroschisis after 12 weeks of gestation. The patient usually has a markedly elevated maternal serum AFP level. As the sonographer evaluates the area of umbilical cord insertion, multiple loops of bowel (small bowel and often colon) may be seen outside the abdominal cavity in the area of the cord. The cord is normally inserted into the abdominal wall, and the defect is most always to the right of the umbilical cord insertion. The edges of the bowel are irregular and free floating without a covering membrane, as is seen with omphalocele. Ascites is not present in the abdominal cavity.

The sonographic appearance of gastroschisis is as follows:

- Right paraumbilical defect of abdominal wall, rarely a left-side defect (Figure 41-18).
- Free-floating herniated small bowel. Large bowel, stomach, gallbladder, urinary bladder, and pelvic organs may be involved. When organs other than small or large bowel are seen body stalk anomalies should be suspected.[4]
- Herniated bowel may be mildly dilated with bowel wall thickening (chemical peritonitis because of irritation by urine within amniotic fluid) (Figure 41-19).
- Markedly dilated bowel may suggest infarction or bowel atresia (Figure 41-20).
- Hydronephrosis, bladder deviation (Figure 41-21), and exstrophy (Figure 41-22) may be observed.

A

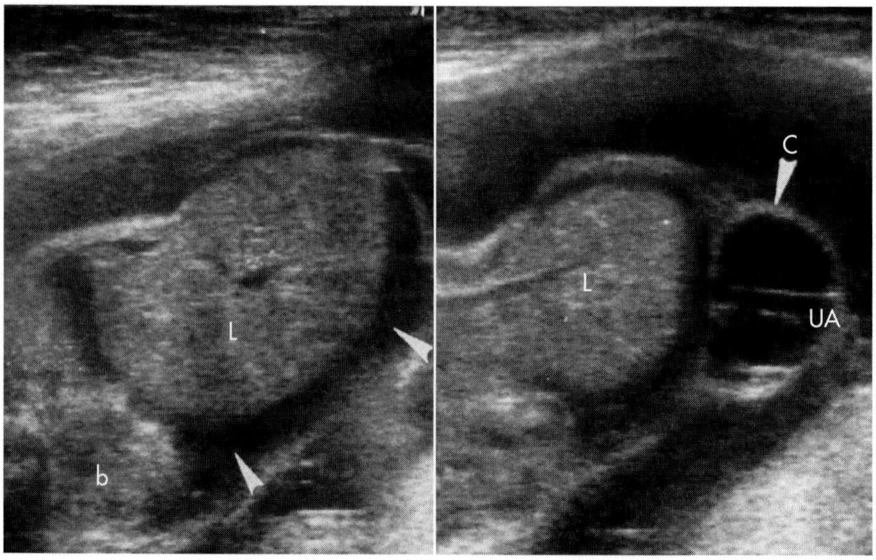

B

Figure 41-14 **A,** In the fetus shown in Figure 41-13 a coexisting liver-filled omphalocele *(L)* and ascites *(arrows)* are observed. Displaced bowel in chest *(b)*. **B,** In the same fetus, umbilical cord dilation *(c)* at the base of the omphalocele is demonstrated. *ua,* Umbilical artery.

- Consider amniotic band syndrome amputations when clefting of the face and/or encephalocele is found. Severe body wall defects may be seen in gastroschisis with secondary band formation (Figures 41-23 to 41-25).

AMNIOTIC BAND SYNDROME

The **amniotic band syndrome** is the rupture of the amnion, which leads to entrapment or entanglement of the fetal parts by the "sticky" chorion. This may cause amputation or defects in random sites. Early entrapment by the bands may lead to severe craniofacial defects and internal malformations. Late entrapment leads to amputations or limb restrictions. The prevalence of this syndrome is low, occurring in 7.8 in 10,000 births. Anomalies associated with amniotic band syndrome include anomalies of the limbs, cranium, face, thorax, spine, abdominal wall (gastroschisis, omphalocele, bladder exstrophy), and the perineum.

BECKWITH-WIEDEMANN SYNDROME

Beckwith-Wiedemann syndrome is a group of disorders having in common the coexistence of an omphalocele,

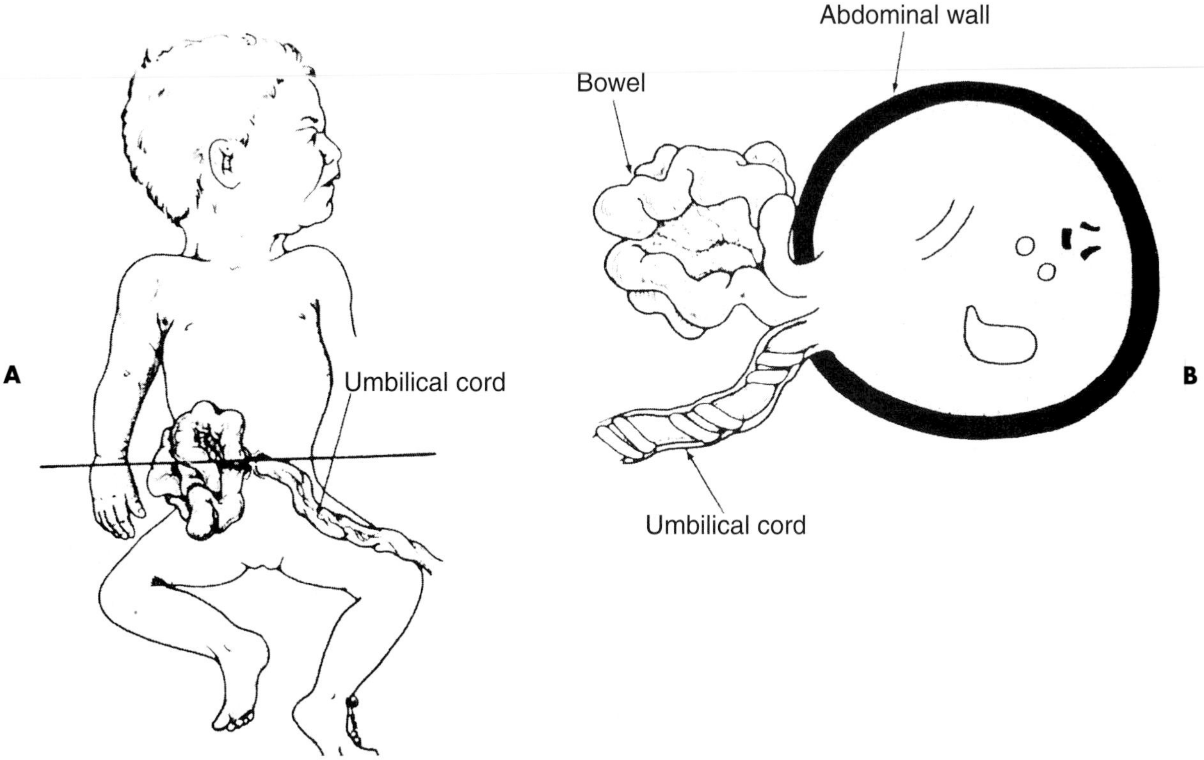

Figure 41-15 Typical features of gastroschisis shown on external examination **(A)** and cross-sectional view **(B).**

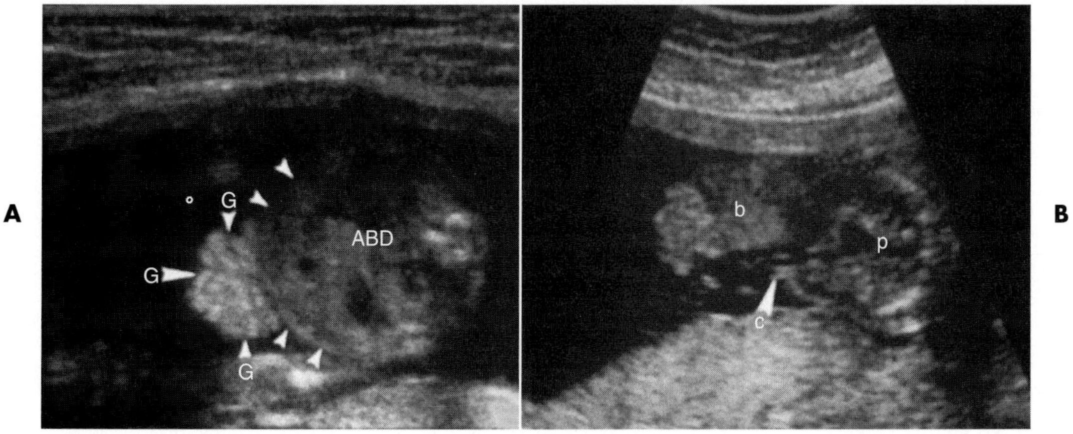

Figure 41-16 **A,** Appearance of a gastroschisis *(G)* in a 19-week-old fetus with elevation of materal serum alpha-fetoprotein. Note the typical appearance of herniated, free-floating bowel loops. *ABD,* Abdomen; *arrowheads,* anterior abdominal wall. **B,** In the same fetus a normal cord insertion *(c)* is shown with herniated bowel *(b)*. *p,* Pelvis.

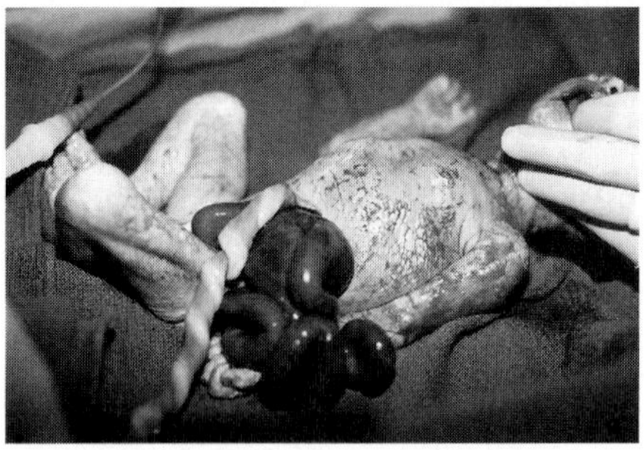

Figure 41-17 Neonate with left-side gastroschisis shown in Figure 41-19, **A.** Note the insertion of the cord to the right of the defect.

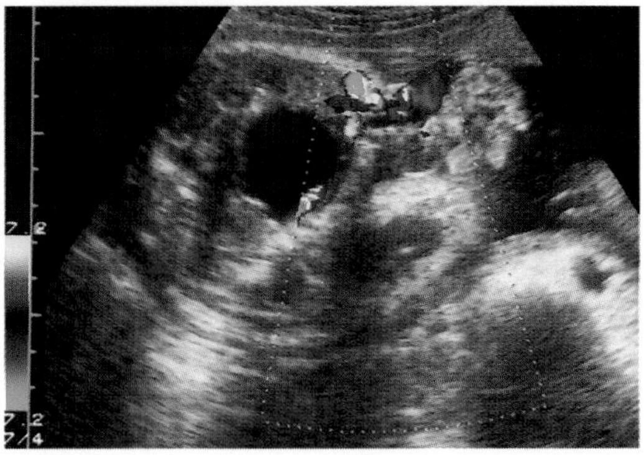

Figure 41-18 Transverse image of a 22-week fetus with a moderate-size gastroschisis; the umbilical cord is well seen with color as it enters to the right of the defect.

A

B

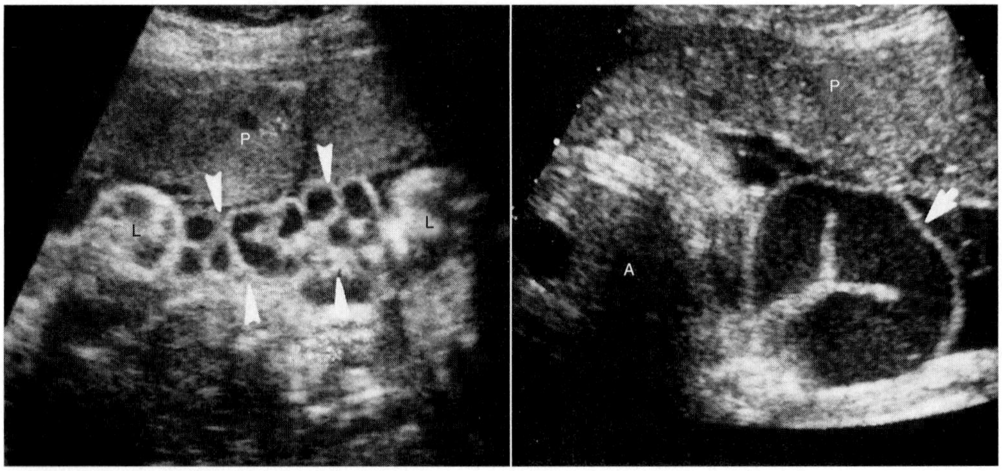

Figure 41-19 **A,** Gastroschisis showing herniated bowel *(arrows)* in the amniotic cavity. Cesarean section was performed at 36 weeks of gestation because of a nonreactive nonstress test with variable decelerations and absent breathing. A small-for-gestational age infant with a left-side gastroschisis was delivered. *L,* Limb; *P,* placenta. **B,** Isolated bowel segment *(arrow)* observed in another fetus with gastroschisis at 29 weeks of gestation. Bowel dilation (29 mm) and obstruction (meconium ileus) are shown. Note the haustral markings within the obstructed bowel. *A,* Abdomen, *p,* placenta.

A

B

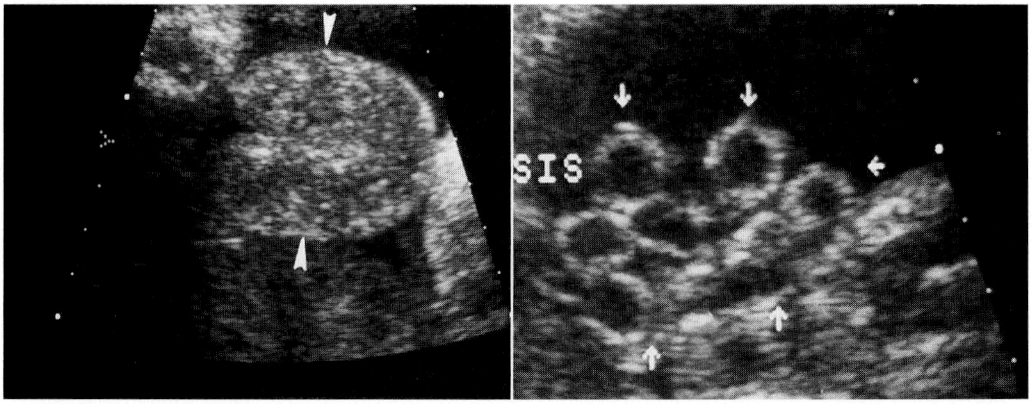

Figure 41-20 **A,** Herniated large intestine *(arrows)* with meconium at 34 weeks of gestation in a fetus with gastroschisis. Note the dilated bowel, which measured 20 mm in diameter. **B,** In the same fetus, portions of the small bowel *(arrow)* are observed with mild dilation.

A

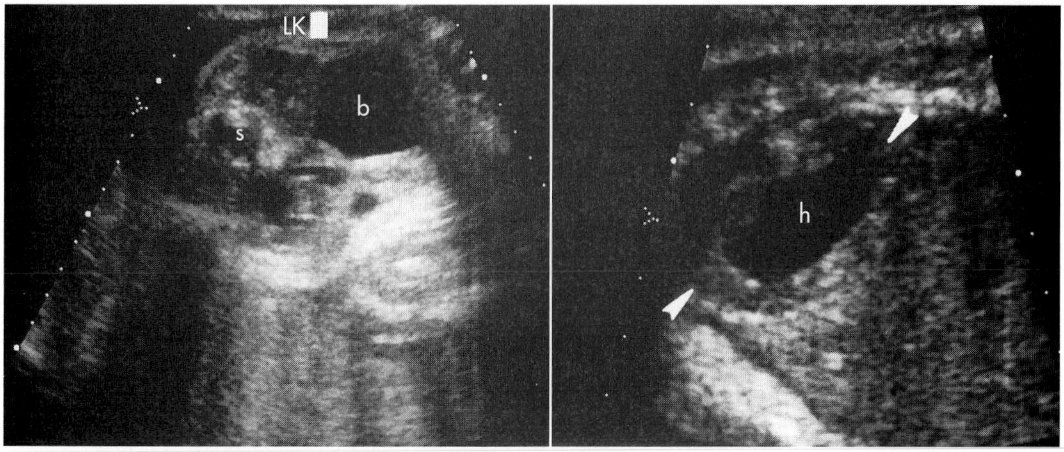

B

Figure 41-21 In a fetus with gastroschisis, concommitant anomalies were detected and included **(A)** deviation of the bladder **(B)** and unilateral hydronephrosis *(h, arrows)*. *LK,* Normal left kidney; *s,* spine.

A

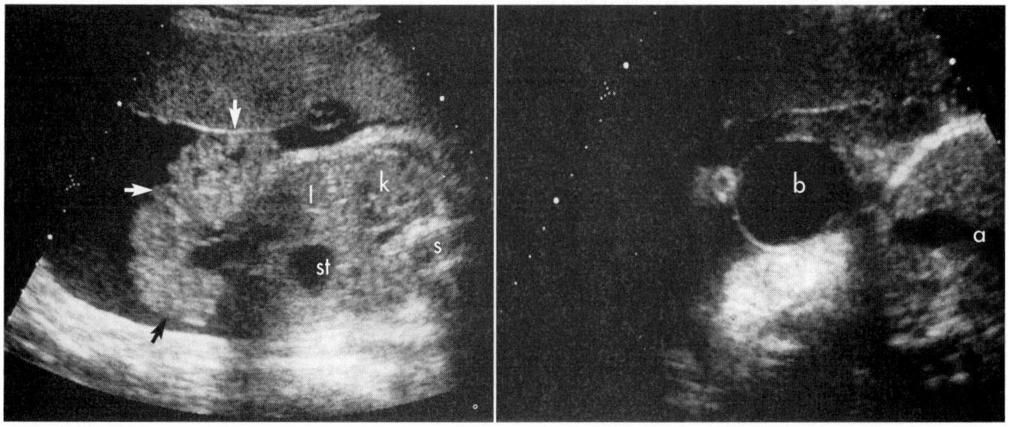

B

Figure 41-22 **A,** Gastroschisis *(arrows)* evident in a 34-week-old fetus in a transverse view. Note the intraabdominal position of the stomach *(st)*, liver *(l)*, and kidney *(k)*. *s,* Spine; **B,** In the same fetus, note that the bladder *(b)* is herniated from the pelvis (exstrophy). The uterus and ovaries were also found to be herniated from the pelvis after delivery. Congenital microcolon was also found. *a,* Abdomen.

A

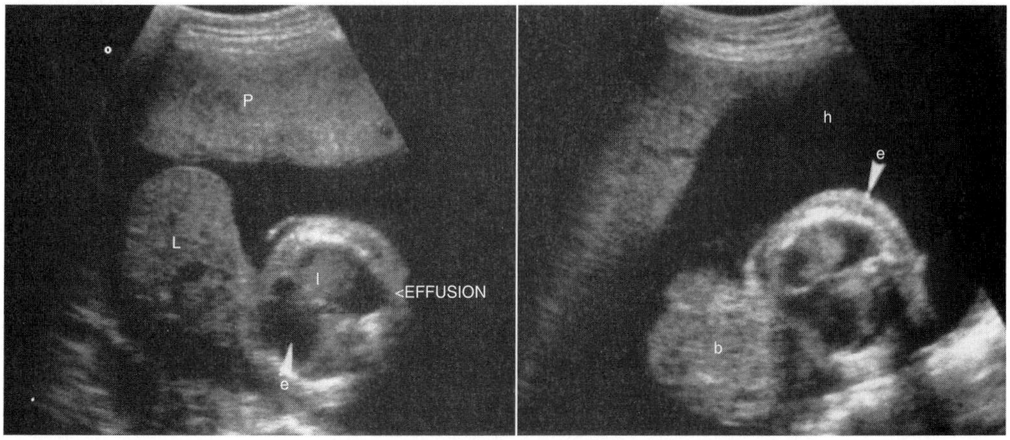

B

Figure 41-23 Gastroschisis with secondary amniotic bands shown in a 28-week-old fetus. Eviscerated liver *(L)* and bowel *(b)* are documented. Bilateral pleural effusions *(arrows)* and soft tissue edema *(e)* in **B** are apparent. Note the hydramnios *(h)*. *l,* Lung; *P,* placenta.

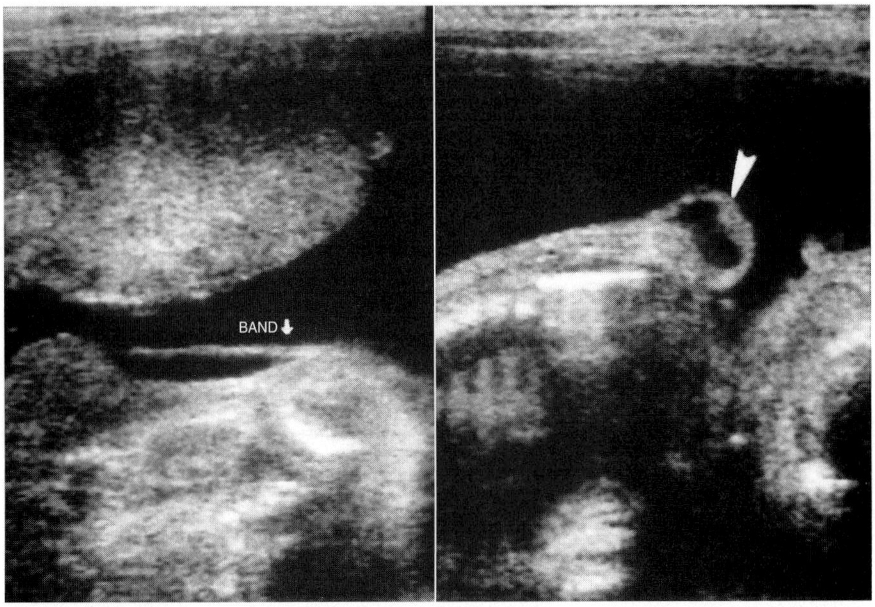

Figure 41-24 In the fetus depicted in Figure 41-23, multiple amniotic bands *(band)* **(A)** were found adhering to the abdomen with attachment to the shoulder *(arrow)* in **(B).** Normal chromosomes were found by amniocentesis. Amniotic fluid alpha-fetoprotein was extremely elevated (175 MOM) with positive acetylcholinesterase. The fetus was delivered at 28 weeks of gestation because of worsening hydrops. No resuscitative measures were undertaken. Autopsy findings revealed a right paraumbilical gastroschisis with eventration of the liver and intestine. Intestinal malrotation and small-bowel obstruction were found. Moderate fetal hydrops with bilateral pleural effusions and pulmonary hypoplasia were noted. An amniotic band or peritoneal band extended from the liver to the thumb. The defect was consistent with a gastroschisis occurring early in embryogenesis because of the intestinal malrotation with secondary amniotic band rupture.

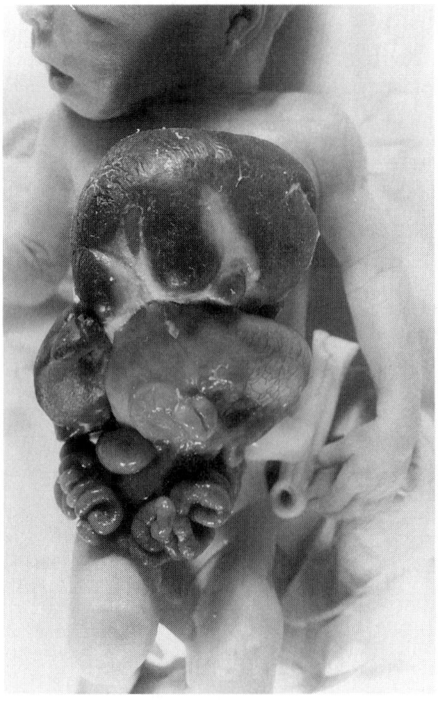

Figure 41-25 Neonate depicted in Figures 41-23 and 41-24 with gastroschisis and secondary amniotic band rupture.

macroglossia, and visceromegaly. Most of the cases are sporadic.

CLOACAL EXSTROPHY

Bladder exstrophy is characterized by a defect in the lower abdominal wall and anterior wall of the urinary bladder. The everted bladder becomes exposed on the lower abdominal wall. The anomaly may be mild or severe (accompanied by an omphalocele, inguinal hernia, undescended testes, and anal problems). Cloacal exstrophy is rare and occurs early in development with involvement of the primitive gut.

Ultrasound findings. On ultrasound examination, the normal urinary bladder is not visible. Instead, a soft tissue mass, representing the exposed bladder mucosa, may be seen on the surface of the lower abdominal wall. In addition, an anterior abdominal wall defect may be the primary ultrasound finding of cloacal exstrophy.

PENTALOGY OF CANTRELL

The **pentalogy of Cantrell** is rare and is the association of two major defects: an omphalocele and an ectopic heart. The three other anomalies are the result of these defects, involving a defect in the lower sternum, the anterior diaphragm, and the diaphragmatic pericardium.

Ultrasound findings. On ultrasound examination, the heart may be seen to lie outside the normal thoracic cavity or bulge through the defective sternum. It is common to see pericardial and pleural effusions. A differential diagnosis includes body stalk anomaly, amniotic band syndrome, or isolated ectopia cordis. The prognosis depends on many factors, including the extent of the defect and the size of the thoracic cavity allowing surgical intervention to place the heart back into the chest.

LIMB–BODY WALL COMPLEX

The **limb–body wall complex** anomaly is associated with large cranial defects (**exencephaly** or **encephalocele**); facial cleft; body wall defect involving the thorax, abdomen, or both; and limb defects. Other anomalies include **scoliosis** and various internal malformations. The limb–body wall complex occurs with the fusion of the amnion and chorion; the amnion does not cover the umbilical cord normally, but extends as a sheet from the margin of the cord and is continuous with both the body wall and the placenta. Left-side body wall defects are three times more common than right-side defects.

Ultrasound findings. On ultrasound examination the defects are large, involving the abdomen and thorax. The eviscerated organs form a complex, bizarre-appearing mass entangled with membranes. The umbilical cord is short and adherent to the placental membranes.

ACKNOWLEDGMENT

The author acknowledges the previous contribution of Kara Mayden Argo to this chapter in the fourth edition of this book.

REVIEW QUESTIONS

1. Discuss herniation of the bowel during the first trimester.
2. Name the common abdominal wall defects.
3. Describe the difference between a bowel-filled and a liver-filled omphalocele.
4. How does an omphalocele differ from gastroschisis on ultrasound?
5. Which anomalies are commonly associated with omphalocele?
6. What is Pentalogy of Cantrell?
7. Describe the limb–body wall complex.

REFERENCES

1. Arey LB: The vascular system. In Arey LB, editor: *Developmental anatomy,* ed 7, Philadelphia, 1974, WB Saunders.
2. deVries PA: The pathogenesis of gastroschisis and omphalocele, *J Pediatr Surg* 15: 245, 1980.
3. Langman J: Caudal part of the foregut. In Langman J, editor: *Medical embryology,* Baltimore, 1975, Williams and Wilkins.
4. Lindfors KK, McGahan JP, Walter JP: Fetal omphalocele and gastroschisis: pitfalls in sonographic diagnosis, *Am J Roentgenol* 147:797, 1986.
5. Miller ME and others: Compression-related defects from early amnion rupture: evidence for mechanical teratogenesis, *J Pediatr* 98:292, 1981.
6. Moore KL, editor: *The developing human: clinically oriented embryology,* ed 4, Philadelphia, 1988, WB Saunders.
7. Nakayama DK: Management of the fetus with an abdominal wall defect. In Harrison MR, Golbus MS, Filly RA, editors: *The unborn patient: prenatal diagnosis and treatment,* Orlando, Fla, 1984, Grune & Stratton.
8. Nyberg DA, Mahony BS, Pretorius DH, editors: *Diagnostic ultrasound of fetal anomalies: text and atlas,* St Louis, 1990, Mosby.
9. Torfs CP, Curry CJR: Familial cases of gastroschisis in a population based registry, *Am J Med Genet* 45:465, 1993.
10. Torfs CP, Curry CJR, Roeper P: Gastroschisis, *J Pediatr* 116:1, 1990.

BIBLIOGRAPHY

Callen DW, editor: *Ultrasonography in obstetrics and gynecology,* ed 3, Philadelphia, 1995, WB Saunders.

Raynor BD, Richards D: Growth retardation in fetuses with gastroschisis, *J Ultrasound Med* 16:13, 1997.

Sanders RC, editor: *Clinical sonography: a practical guide,* ed 3, Boston, 1998, Little, Brown.

CHAPTER 42

The Fetal Abdomen

Sandra L. Hagen-Ansert

Objectives

- List the differences between the fetal and adult abdomen
- Describe the development of the digestive system
- Detail the malformations of the midgut
- Describe the sonographic findings of the fetal gastrointestinal system
- Describe normal development of the stomach and the importance of its sonographic visualization
- Detail the fetal hepatobiliary system
- Describe situs inversus
- List the abnormalities of the gastrointestinal tract and their sonographic findings

KEY TERMS

anorectal atresia - complex disorder of the bowel and genitourinary tract
asplenia - no development of splenic tissue
choledochal cyst - cystic growth of the common bile duct
cholelithiasis - gallstones
cystic fibrosis - mucous buildup within the lungs and other areas of the body
duodenal atresia - complete blockage at the pyloric sphincter
duodenal stenosis - narrowing of the pyloric sphincter
esophageal atresia - congenital hypoplasia of the esophagus; usually associated with a tracheoesophageal fistula
esophageal stenosis - narrowing of the esophagus, usually in the distal third segment
gastroschisis - abnormality of the abdominal wall in which the bowel without a covering membrane protrudes outside of the wall
haustral folds - found within the colon
hemopoiesis - formation of blood
Hirschsprung's disease - megacolon
jejunoileal atresia - blockage of the jejunum and ileal bowel segments that appears as multiple cystic structures within the fetal abdomen
Meckel's diverticulum - remnant of the proximal part of the yolk stalk
meconium ileus - small-bowel disorder marked by the presence of thick echogenic meconium in the distal ileum
omphalocele - abnormality of the abdominal wall in which bowel and liver, both covered by a membrane, protrude outside the wall

partial situs inversus - condition in which only the heart or the abdominal organs are reversed (dextrocardia or liver on the left, stomach on the right)
peristalsis - movement of the bowel
polysplenia - more than one spleen; associated with cardiac malformations
pseudoascites - sonolucent band near the fetal anterior abdominal wall seen in the fetus over 18 weeks (does not outline the falciform ligament or bowel as ascites will)
situs inversus - heart and abdominal organs are completely reversed.
VACTERL - vertebral defects, heart defects, renal and limb abnormalities

The fetal abdominal organs, liver, biliary system, spleen, stomach, kidneys, and colon, are well formed by the second trimester. The following differences between the fetal and adult abdomen have been noted[6]:

- The umbilical arteries and veins provide important anatomic landmarks for fetal abdominal anatomy and measurements.
- The ductus venous is patent and serves as a conduit between the portal veins and systemic veins.
- The proportions of the fetal body differ from those in the adult; the fetal abdomen is larger compared with body length, and the liver occupies a larger volume of the fetal abdomen.
- The fetal pelvic cavity is small; therefore the urinary bladder, ovaries, and uterus lie in the abdominal cavity.
- The apron of the greater omentum is small, contains little fat, and remains unfused in the fetus. Fetal ascites may therefore separate the omental leaves.

EMBRYOLOGY OF THE DIGESTIVE SYSTEM

The primitive gut forms during the 4th week of gestation as the dorsal part of the yolk sac is incorporated into the embryo during folding. The primitive gut is divided into three sections: foregut, midgut, and hindgut.[14]

THE FOREGUT

The derivatives of the foregut are the pharynx, lower respiratory system, esophagus, stomach, part of the duodenum, liver and biliary apparatus, and pancreas.

Esophagus. The esophagus is short in the beginning, but it rapidly lengthens as the body grows, reaching its final length by the 7th week. The *tracheoesophageal septum* partitions the trachea from the esophagus. **Esophageal atresia,** usually associated with a tracheoesophageal fistula, results from abnormal deviation of the tracheoesophageal septum in a posterior direction. When this occurs, amniotic fluid cannot pass to the intestines for absorption and hydramnios results.

Esophageal stenosis is the narrowing of the esophagus, usually in the distal third portion. This occurs from incomplete recanalization of the esophagus during the 8th week of development.

Stomach. The stomach appears as a fusiform dilatation of the caudal part of the foregut (Figure 42-1). During the 5th and 6th weeks the dorsal border (greater curvature) grows faster than the ventral border (lesser curvature). The stomach is suspended from the dorsal wall of the abdominal cavity by the dorsal mesentery or dorsal mesogastrium. The dorsal mesogastrium is carried to the left during rotation of the stomach and formation of a cavity known as the omental bursa or lesser sac of peritoneum.

The lesser sac communicates with the main peritoneal cavity or greater peritoneal sac through a small opening, called the epiploic foramen.

Duodenum. The duodenum develops from the caudal part of the foregut and cranial part of the midgut (see Figure 42-1). The two parts grow rapidly and form a C-shaped loop that rotates to the right, where it comes to lie primarily in the retroperitoneum. The junction of the two embryonic parts of the duodenum in the adult is just distal to the entrance of the common bile duct. The duodenum is supplied by branches of the celiac trunk and the superior mesenteric artery.

During the 5th and 6th weeks, the lumen of the duodenum becomes partly or totally occluded (depending on the proliferation of its lining of epithelial cells). Normally, the duodenum is recanalized by the end of the 8th week. Partial or complete failure of this process results in either **duodenal stenosis** (narrowing) or **duodenal atresia** (blockage). Usually the third or fourth parts of the duodenal are affected.

Liver and Biliary System. The liver, gallbladder, and biliary ducts arise as a bud from the most caudal part of the foregut in the 4th week (see Figure 42-1). The hepatic diverticulum grows between the layers of the ventral mesentery, where it rapidly enlarges and divides into two parts. The liver grows rapidly and intermingles with the vitelline and umbilical veins, divides into two parts, and fills most of the abdominal cavity. The large cranial part is the primordium of the parenchyma of the liver. The small caudal part gives rise to the gallbladder and cystic duct.

The hemopoietic cells, Kupffer cells, and connective tissue cells are derived from the mesenchyme in the septum transversum. The septum transversum is a mass of mesoderm between the pericardial cavity and the yolk stalk. It forms a major part of the diaphragm and the ventral mesentery.

Hemopoiesis (blood formation) begins during the 6th week and accounts for the large size of the liver between the 7th and 9th weeks of development. By the 12th week, bile formation by the hepatic cells has begun.

Extrahepatic biliary atresia. Blockage of the bile ducts results from their failure to recanalize following the solid

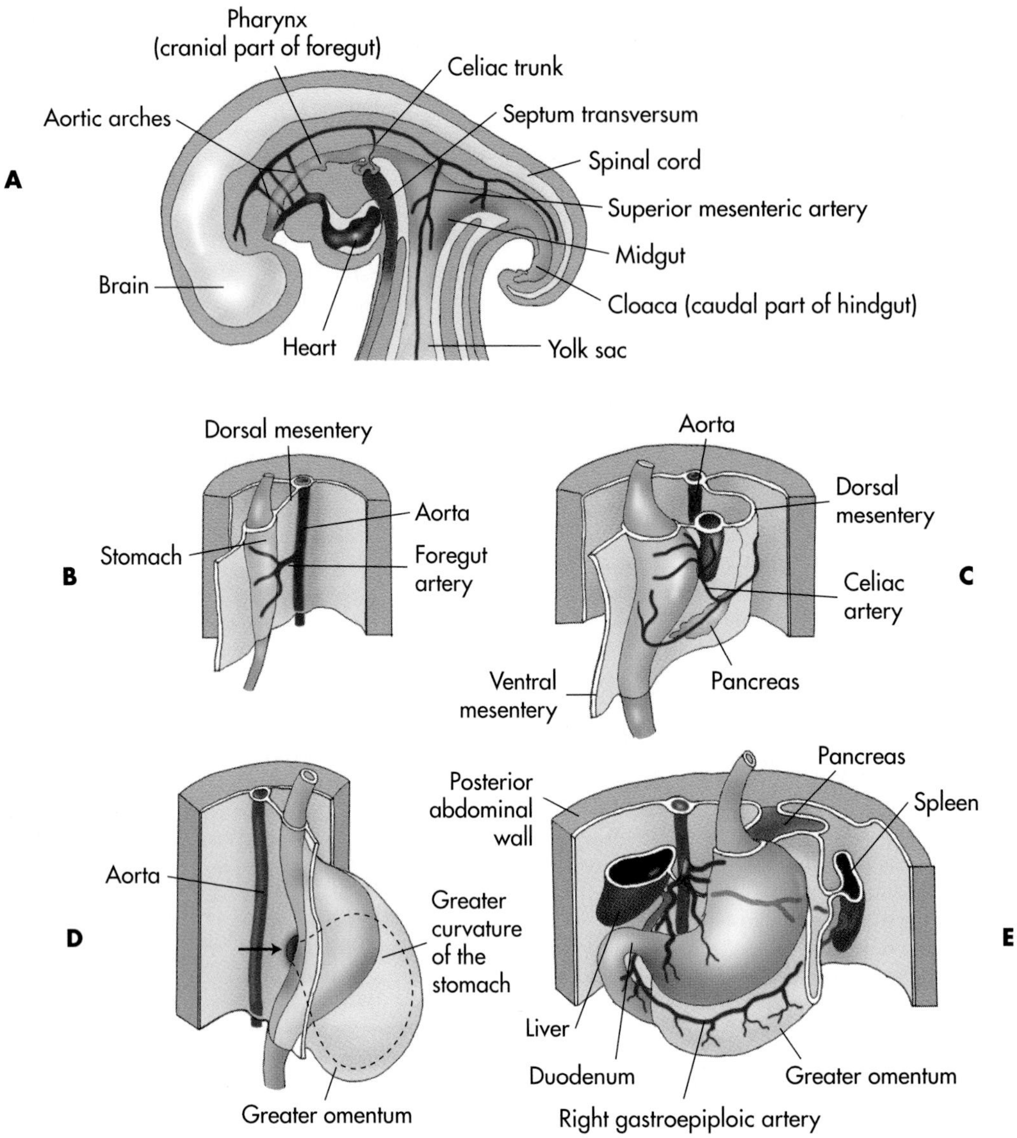

Figure 42-1 Development of the digestive system. **A,** Four weeks. **B,** Five weeks. **C,** Six weeks. **D** to **E,** Development of stomach. Seven weeks.

stage of their development. This malformation may also result from interference with the blood supply of the ducts resulting from infection during the fetal period.

Pancreas. The pancreas develops from the dorsal and ventral pancreatic buds of the endodermal cells that arise from the caudal part of the foregut (see Figure 42-1). When the duodenum grows and rotates to the right, the ventral bud is carried dorsally and fuses with the dorsal bud. The ducts of the two pancreatic buds join. The combined duct becomes the main pancreatic duct that opens with the bile duct into the duodenum. The proximal part of the duct may persist as the accessory pancreatic duct.

Spleen. The spleen is a lymphatic organ that is derived from a mass of mesenchymal cells located between the layers of the dorsal mesogastrium (see Figure 42-1). The spleen is lobulated in the fetal period.

THE MIDGUT

The derivatives of the midgut are the small intestines (including most of the duodenum), the cecum and veriform appendix, the ascending colon, and most of the transverse colon. All of these structures are supplied by the superior mesenteric artery.

The midgut is suspended from the abdominal wall by an elongated dorsal mesentery. It communicates with the yolk sac via the yolk stalk. While the midgut lengthens and forms a midgut loop, it herniates outside the abdomen into the proximal part of the umbilical cord. Usually by the 10th or 11th week, this midgut herniation returns to the abdomen and undergoes further rotation resulting

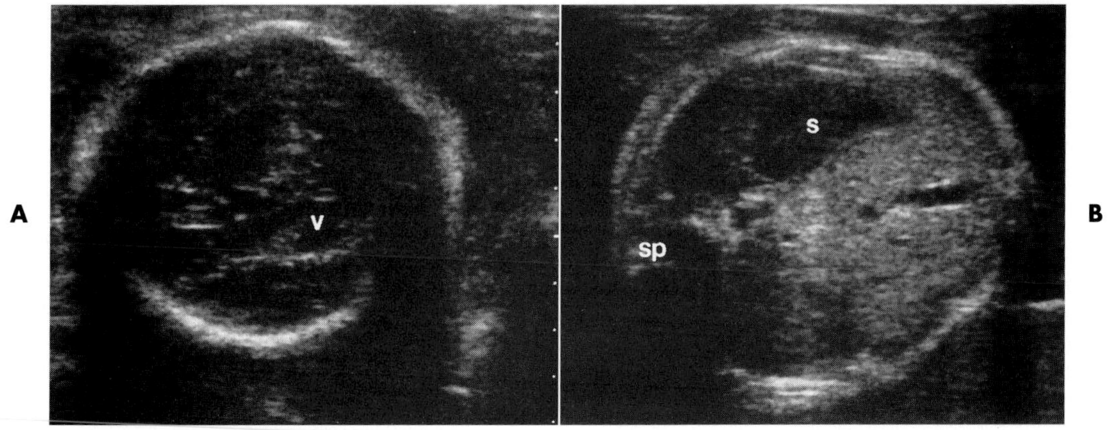

Figure 42-2 A 32-week fetus with microcephaly. **A,** Small head and ventricle *(v)*. **B,** transverse image at the level of the stomach *(s)* and spine *(sp)*.

from the decrease in size of the liver and kidneys and the growth of the abdominal cavity.

After the intestines return to the abdominal cavity, they enlarge, lengthen, and assume their final positions. Their mesenteries are pressed against the posterior abdominal wall. At this time, the ascending and descending colon become retroperitoneal. Likewise, the duodenum and most of the pancreas also become retroperitoneal. At the same time, the small intestines form a new line of attachment that extends from where the duodenum becomes retroperitoneal to the ileocecal junction. The mesentery of the transverse colon fuses with the dorsal mesogastrium to form the posterior wall of the inferior part of the omental bursa. The sigmoid colon retains its mesentery, but it is shorter than in the early fetus.

Malformations of the Midgut

Omphalocele and Gastroschisis. Omphalocele and gastroschisis occur when the midgut fails to return to the abdominal cavity from the umbilical cord during the 10th week. In an **omphalocele,** coils of intestine protrude from the umbilicus and are covered by a transparent sac of amnion. The umbilical cord pierces the central part of the omphalocele. Conversely, a **gastroschisis** is a condition in which the bowel and/or organs are free floating from the midline defect. The gastroschisis is usually located to the right of the umbilical cord.

Umbilical Hernia. When the intestines return normally to the abdominal cavity and then herniate either prenatally or postnatally through an inadequately closed umbilicus, an umbilical hernia forms. The hernia differs from an omphalocele in that the protruding mass (omentum or loop of bowel) is covered by subcutaneous tissue and skin.

Meckel's Diverticulum. Meckel's diverticulum is the most common malformation of the midgut. A **Meckel's diverticulum** is a remnant of the proximal part of the yolk stalk that fails to degenerate and disappear during the early fetal period. It is usually a small fingerlike sac, about 5 cm long, that projects from the border of the ileum.

The Hindgut

The derivatives of the hindgut are the left part of the transverse colon, the descending colon, the sigmoid colon, the rectum, the superior portion of the anal canal, the epithelium of the urinary bladder, and most of the urethra. All of these structures are supplied by the inferior mesenteric artery.

SONOGRAPHY OF THE ABDOMINAL CAVITY

The sonographer needs to carefully evaluate the gastrointestinal system during each routine scan. Clear definition of the stomach, liver and vascular structures, cord insertion, small bowel, and colon should be identified by the sonographer.

Gastrointestinal System

Stomach. The stomach should be identified as a fluid-filled structure in the left upper quadrant. Most fetuses older than 14 to 16 weeks should have fluid in their stomachs (Figure 42-2). If no fluid is apparent, the stomach should be reevaluated in 20 to 30 minutes to rule out the possibility of a central nervous system problem (swallowing disorders), obstruction, oligohydramnios, or atresia. Esophageal anomalies are the least common problems for nonvisualization of the stomach.

The fluid within the stomach should be anechoic in the normal fetus. Walker and others have reported the demonstration of hematoma formation within the fetal stomach secondary to placental abrutpion.[22] The presence of an echogenic mass in the fetal stomach in a patient who demonstrates clinical or sonographic evidence of placental abruption should raise the possibility of hematoma formation associated with an intraamniotic hemorrhage.[22]

Abdominal Circumference. The abdominal circumference is measured at the level of the portal sinus and the umbilical portion of the left portal vein ("hockey stick" appearance on the sonogram) (Figure 42-3). Be careful to avoid oblique scanning of the abdomen that may lead to an incorrect diameter-circumference measurement. The abdomen should be round, not oval. The pressure of the transducer should not compress the abdominal cavity.

Umbilical Cord Insertion. In the fetus, the umbilical vein courses cephalically in the free, inferior margin of the falciform ligament.[7] It joins the umbilical portion of the left portal vein at the caudal margin of the left intersegmental fissure of the liver (Figure 42-4). The insertion of the umbilical cord must be imaged with color because it inserts both into the fetal abdomen and into the placenta. Visualization of the umbilical cord insertion site must be made to rule out the presence of an omphalocele, gastroschisis, hernia, or mass formation. After birth, the umbilical vein collapses and ultimately becomes the ligamentum teres hepatis.[7]

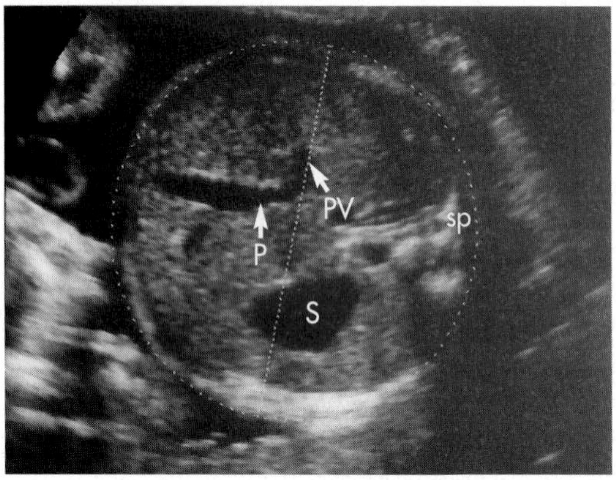

Figure 42-3 The abdominal circumference is measured from a transverse image at the level of the portal sinus *(P)* and the umbilical portion of the left portal vein *(PV)*. The stomach *(S)* is seen posterior; the spine *(sp)* is at 3 o'clock.

Bowel. Movement of the gastric musculature begins in approximately the 4th to 5th month of gestation. In the second trimester, this movement and fetal swallowing result in the delivery of increased amniotic fluid volume distally into the small bowel and colon where fluid and nutrients are reabsorbed.[11] After the 15th to 16th week, meconium begins to accumulate in the distal part of the small intestine as a combination of desquamated cells, bile pigments, and mucoproteins.[5]

In early gestation (10 to 20 weeks), the small bowel lumen is quite difficult to demonstrate.[16] The region of the small bowel can be seen because it is slightly hyperechoic, compared with the liver, and may appear "masslike" in the abdomen and pelvis (Figure 42-5). The hyperechoic appearance could be secondary to reflections from the walls of collapsed loops of small bowel or from mesenteric fat between the loops.[16] This hyperechoic appearance of the small bowel persists throughout the pregnancy. As the pregnancy progresses, the hyperechoic area becomes less prominent and the small bowel is located more centrally in the abdomen than the colon. After 27 weeks, **peristalsis** of normal small bowel is increasingly observed. The normal diameter of the small bowel lumen is less than or equal to 6 mm.

The colon is seen near the end of the second trimester as a long tubular hypoechoic structure with well-defined walls. The **haustral folds** of the colon help to differentiate it from the small bowel.[16] In early gestation, haustral folds appear as thin linear echoes within the lumen of the colon; later, the colon diameter increases and the folds become longer and thicker. Normal measurements of the colon diameter are 14 to18 mm at term.[6] The colon is more peripheral than the small bowel. Hypoechoic echoes from the meconium may be seen within the lumen. The colon does not have peristalsis like the small bowel does.

After 14 weeks of gestation, lipid is absorbed from the fetal colon, and the remaining contents collect in the colon as meconium.[16] In all fetuses in one study, the meconium within the lumen of the colon appeared hypo-

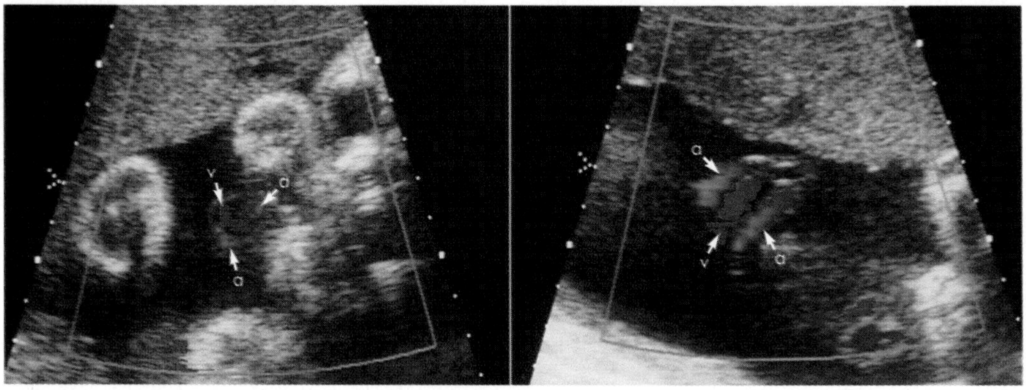

Figure 42-4 **A,** Color representation of the paired umbilical arteries *(a, blue)* and single umbilical vein *(v, red)* in a 30-week fetus viewed in a transverse plane. **B,** Sagittal view of the umbilical arteries *(a, blue)* and umbilical vein *(v, red)*. Color flow imaging may highlight vessels that may not be obvious because of fetal position, oligohydramnios, and congenital anomalies.

echoic relative to the fetal liver and in comparison with the bowel wall.[16] The meconium increased slightly in echogenicity while the fetus grew near term.

HEPATOBILIARY SYSTEM

Liver. The fetal liver is relatively large compared with the other intraabdominal organs. It accounts for 10% of the total weight of the fetus at eleven weeks and 5% of the total weight at term.[6] The hepatic veins and fissures are formed by the end of the first trimester (Figure 42-6).

Gallbladder. The normal gallbladder may be seen sonographically after 20 weeks of gestation. Both the gallbladder and portal-umbilical vein appear as oblong fluid-filled structures on the transverse view of the fetal abdomen through the liver (Figure 42-7). The gallbladder is distinguished by its location to the right of the portal-umbilical vein and as an oblong, more oval structure than the "tubular" intrahepatic umbilical vein.[6]

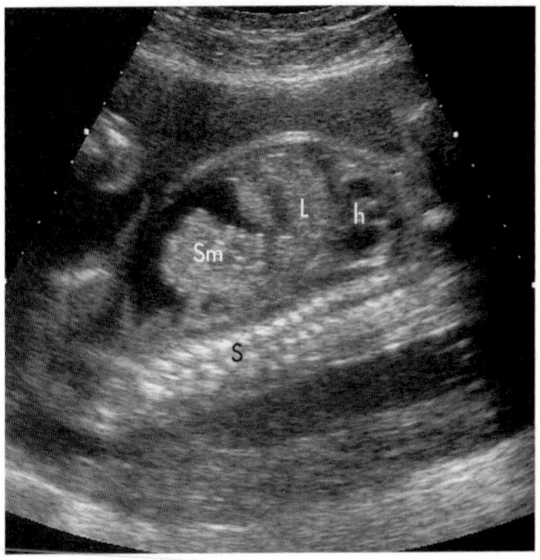

Figure 42-5 Longitudinal scan of the 23-week fetus with abdominal ascites surrounding the small bowel *(Sm)*. *h,* Heart; *L,* liver; *S,* spine.

A
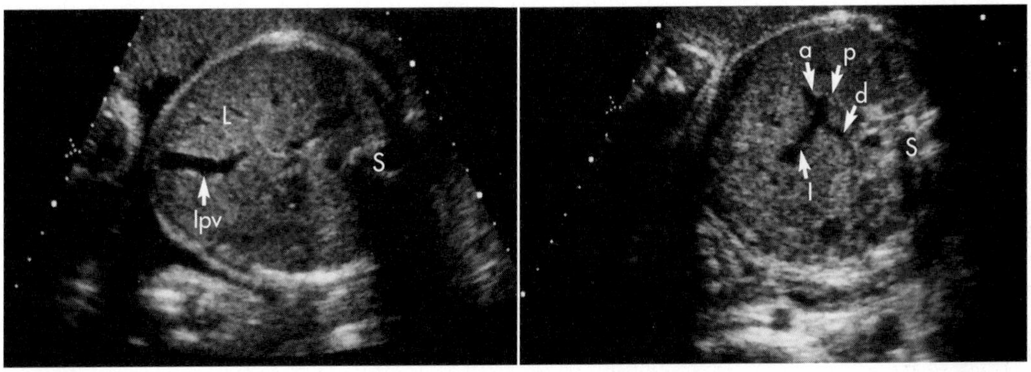

B

Figure 42-6 **A,** Transverse section of the liver in a 31-week fetus outlining the course of the left portal vein *(lpv)* at its entrance into the liver *(L)* from the fetal umbilical cord insertion. The left portal vein ascends upward and into the liver tissue *(L)*. *S,* Spine. **B,** The left portal vein *(l)* is shown to bifurcate into the portal sinus, right anterior *(a)*, and right posterior *(p)* portal veins. The ductus venosus *(d)* is observed before its drainage into the inferior vena cava. *S,* Spine.

A
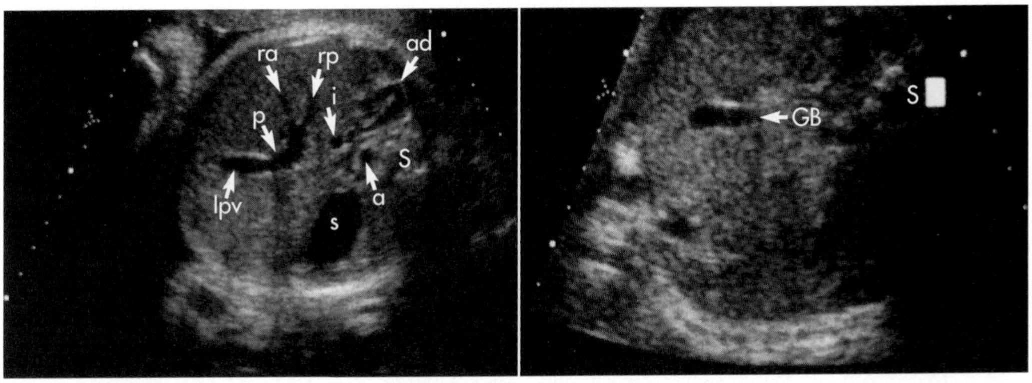

B

Figure 42-7 **A,** Transverse section of the liver and related structures in 32-week fetus showing the left portal vein *(lpv)* coursing into the portal sinus *(p)*. Then blood then moves into the right anterior *(ra)*, and right posterior *(rp)*, portal veins and ductus venosus (see Figure 42-6, *B*). The right adrenal gland *(ad)*, fluid-filled stomach *(s)*, aorta *(a)*, and inferior vena cava *(i)*, are shown. *S,* Spine. **B,** The gallbladder *(GB)* is viewed in the right upper quadrant of the abdomen in a 32-week fetus. The teardrop shape of the gallbladder should be distinguished from the left portal vein. *S,* Spine.

Pancreas. The normal fetal pancreas has been seen in utero but is more difficult to routinely recognize because of the lack of fatty tissue within the gland. It lies in the retroperitoneal cavity anterior to the superior mesenteric vessels, aorta, and inferior vena cava (Figure 42-8).

Spleen. The spleen is homogeneous in texture, similar in echogenicity to the kidney and slightly less echogenic than the liver. It increases in size during gestation.

ABNORMALITIES OF THE HEPATOBILIARY SYSTEM

Anomalies of the liver, gallbladder, pancreas, and spleen are rare. Detection of abnormal morphology is beneficial, because many lesions may be undetected in the newborn period.

LIVER

The fetal liver, although involved in several congenital anomalies (diaphragmatic hernia, omphalocele), is rarely affected by isolated hepatic lesions. Liver parenchymal cysts and hemangiomas of the liver have been reported.[17] The liver enlarges in fetuses with Rh-immune disease in response to increased hematopoiesis (red blood cell production in the liver).

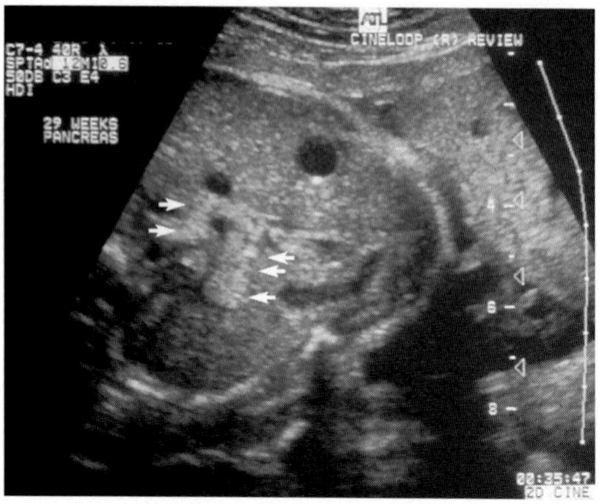

Figure 42-8 Transverse image of the fetal abdomen. The fetal spine is shown at 8 o'clock with the pancreas just anterior *(arrows).*

Liver tumors, hamartoma, and hepatoblastoma, are uncommon and may be observed prenatally. Other tumors seen on ultrasound include hepatic teratoma, adenoma, or metastases from neuroblastoma. Another rare tumor, hemangioendothelioma is the most common, symptomatic, vascular hepatic tumor of infancy and may cause nonimmune hydrops in the fetus.

Ultrasound findings. Most of these tumors appear as hypoechoic solid masses within the liver, although cystic component has also been reported as mixed with the solid mass. About 5% of benign and malignant liver tumors are calcified.

Liver calcification may be observed as an isolated focus. This calcification is usually a benign finding; rarely, it may be a hemangioma, multiple foci secondary to infection (transplacental infections, cytomegalovirus, toxoplasmosis), or hepatic necrosis from ischemia. If multiple calcifications are seen within the liver, other organs such as the brain and spleen may also be affected.

SITUS INVERSUS

Situs inversus may present as a total reversal of the thoracic and abdominal organs or as a partial reversal (mirror image of some organs). Partial situs inversus is a more severe disorder and may develop in two different combinations of organ reversals. In partial situs inversus, the stomach may or may not be reversed. Asplenia occurs with absence of the spleen, abnormal positioning of the liver and gallbladder (more midline position), and abnormal positioning of the aorta and inferior vena cava on the same side. Polysplenia is represented as a transposition of the liver and stomach, absence of the gallbladder, and disruption of the inferior vena cava. At least two spleens are present along the greater curvature of the stomach (which is on the right side). Heart block is common in polysplenia syndrome.

The cause of situs inversus is unclear, but it is thought to occur early in embryogenesis before normal laterality determination (before 3 weeks). Cardiac malformations are particularly common (99%) in asplenia syndrome and are

A

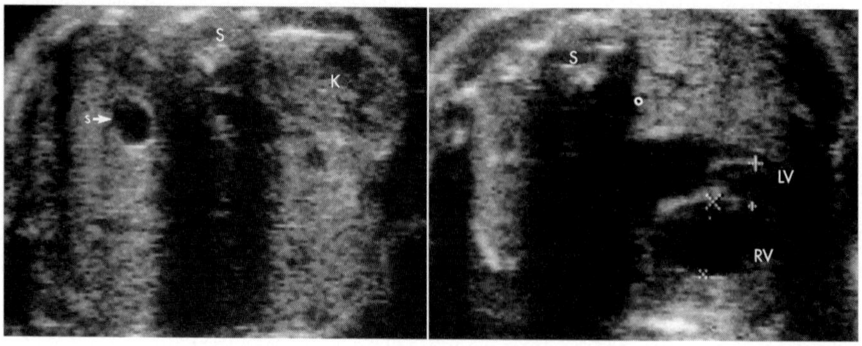

B

Figure 42-9 **A,** Partial situs inversus observed in a transverse spine-up position. The stomach *(S with arrow)* was found on the right side of the abdomen. *K,* Kidney. **B,** In the same fetus a hypoplastic left ventricle *(LV)* is shown. Other findings included bilateral liver, a left-side inferior vena cava, and a right-side descending aorta, right gallbladder, double inlet right ventricle *(RV),* common atrioventricular valve, atrial septal defect, and one outflow vessel (pulmonary artery).

seen with less frequency in polysplenia syndrome (90%).[15] Cardiac defects include endocardial cushion defects, hypoplastic left heart (Figure 42-9), and transposition of the great vessels.

The infant with total situs inversus usually has a normal outcome. About 20% may have Kartagener's syndrome (immotile cilia, bronchiectasis). The mortality rate for partial situs inversus is extremely high with death occurring in 90% to 95% with asplenia syndrome and 80% with polysplenia syndrome.[15]

Ultrasound findings. Sonographically, the following signs may be observed:

- Total situs inversus (right-side heart axis and aorta; transposition of liver, stomach, and spleen; left-side gallbladder).
- Partial situs inversus (right-side stomach, left-side liver). Dextrocardia with normal stomach position (see previous section).
- Other anomalies to check for include gastrointestinal, genitourinary, and neural tube defects.

PSEUDOASCITES

A sonolucent band near the fetal anterior abdominal wall is commonly identified during routine obstetric examinations in the fetus over 18 weeks of gestation. This band results from normal musculature surrounding the abdominal wall. True ascites is identified within the peritoneal recesses while pseudoascites is always confined to an anterior or anterolateral aspect of the fetal abdomen.[12] Also pseudoascites never outlines the falciform ligament, while true ascites does (Box 42-1).[12]

BOX 42-1 CAUSES OF ASCITES

- Immune or nonimmune hydrops
- Genitourinary
- Gastrointestinal
- Liver
- Cardiac
- Infections
- Metabolic storage disorders
- Idiopathic

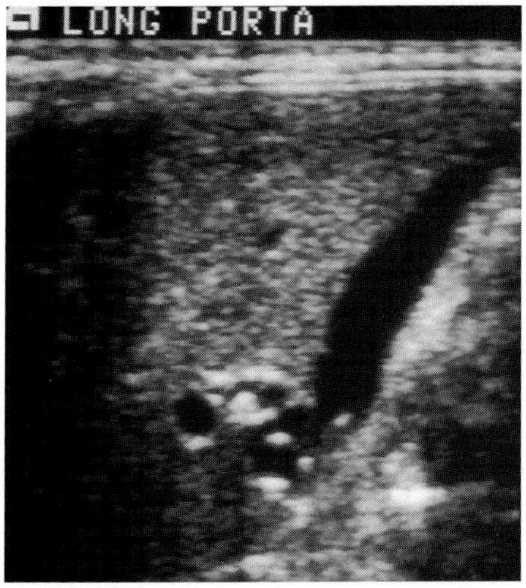

Figure 42-10 Sagittal scan of a neonate with gallstones. Small calcifications with shadowing were seen in the fetal ultrasound in the gallbladder.

GALLBLADDER

Anomalies of the gallbladder may be detected using prenatal sonographic techniques. **Cholelithiasis** (gallstones) may be identified in the fetus when calcifications are found within the gallbladder.[1] These gallstones resolve spontaneously in utero or in the childhood period (Figure 42-10).

A **choledochal cyst** (dilation of the common bile duct) may be diagnosed when a cystic mass is identified adjacent to the fetal stomach and gallbladder (Box 42-2).[8]

Choledochal cysts may be confused with malformation of the stomach or bowel or duodenal atresia.[20] The sonographer should remember the gallbladder is more anterior than the duodenum and thus a cystic mass attached to the bile duct near the gallbladder would make the mass more likely a choledochal cyst. Choledochal cysts may be associated with intermittent biliary obstruction and severe biliary cirrhosis; therefore early diagnosis is important.[6]

PANCREAS

The pancreas is difficult to routinely visualize in utero. Pancreatic cysts may appear as midline cystic masses in the fetal abdomen.

SPLEEN

Evaluation of the fetal spleen for exclusion of splenic anomalies is possible. Asplenia (absence of the spleen) may be amenable to antenatal identification, and in association with congenital heart disease the polysplenia-asplenia syndrome should be considered.

Congenital splenic cysts are rare but have been reported in utero. Enlargement of the spleen (splenomegaly) may be seen on the ultrasound examination. The spleen, like the liver, may enlarge in fetuses with Rh-immune disease. Nomograms are available to detect hepatomegaly and splenomegaly.[19]

ABNORMALITIES OF THE GASTROINTESTINAL TRACT

The majority of gastrointestinal malformations are correctable after birth; consequently, recognition of a gastrointestinal anomaly before delivery may avoid the com-

BOX 42-2 SONOGRAPHIC CRITERIA FOR CHOLEDOCHAL CYST

- Close proximity of the cyst to the neck of the gallbladder
- An ovoid right upper quadrant cyst with an entering bile duct
- A cyst and gallbladder that enlarge as gestation progresses
- Absence of peristaltic activity in the cyst

From Schwartz and others: Choledochal cyst in a second trimester fetus, *J Diagn Med Sonogr* 1:10, 1989.

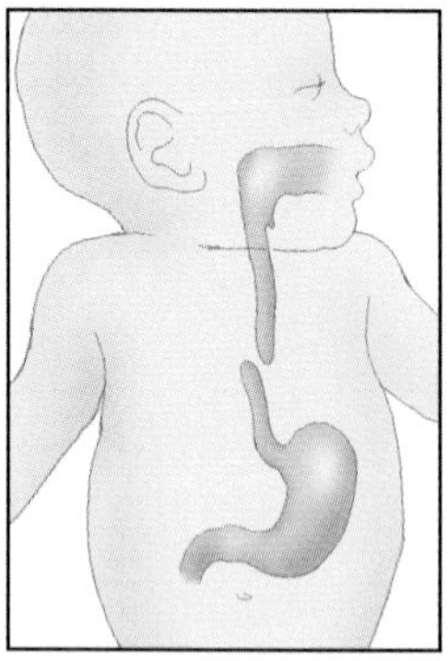

Figure 42-11 Esophageal atresia is a congenital blockage of the esophagus. The primary sonographic findings are polyhydramnios and an absence of the stomach bubble.

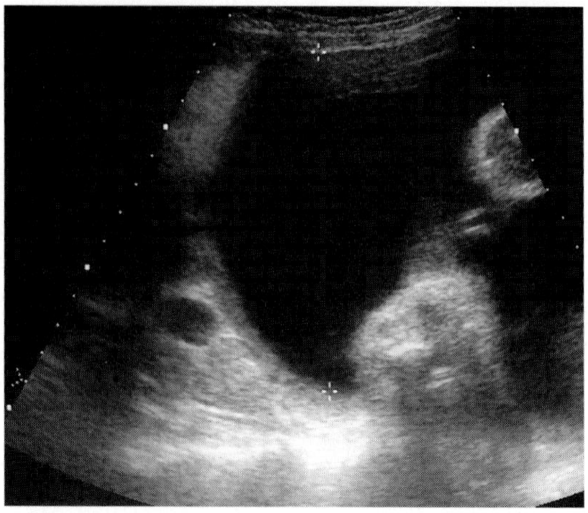

Figure 42-12 Longitudinal scan of a patient who had polyhydramnios. This quadrant of fluid measured over 10 cm, which alone qualifies for an abnormal collection of fluid. The fetus did not show a stomach bubble and was diagnosed with esophageal atresia.

BOX 42-3 CAUSES OF NONVISUALIZATION OF THE STOMACH

- Esophageal atresia or tracheoesophageal fistula
- Diaphragmatic hernia
- Facial cleft
- Central nervous system disorder
- Other swallowing disorders
- Oligohydramnios from other causes

BOX 42-4 ATRESIAS

- Develop when a portion of the bowel grows and infarcts; occurs anywhere in the gastrointestinal tract
- Polyhydramnios on ultrasound

plications of dehydration, bowel necrosis, and respiratory difficulties that occur when these lesions are unsuspected before delivery (Box 42-3).[2]

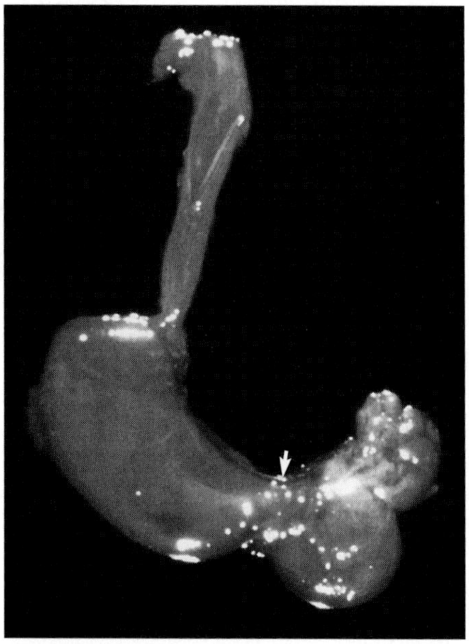

Figure 42-13 Gross specimen showing duodenal atresia from a neonate with trisomy 21 (Down syndrome). Note the narrowing at the duodenum *(arrow)*.

ESOPHAGUS, STOMACH, AND DUODENUM

The normal upper esophagus may be seen after amniotic fluid is swallowed. This fluid passes from the esophagus into the fetal stomach. Obstruction of the normal swallowing sequence may occur because of an atretic or obstructive process. A membrane covers the lumen and intestinal loops enlarge above the obstruction; and bowel loops below the atresia are narrowed (stenotic). This enlargement of the bowel proximal to the obstruction is readily apparent on ultrasound.[8] Blockage results in the back-up of amniotic fluid and hydramnios.

Esophageal atresia is a congenital blockage of the esophagus resulting from the faulty separation of the foregut into its respiratory and digestive components (Figure 42-11) (Box 42-4).[3,4] The most common form occurs in conjunction with a fistula communicating between the trachea and esophagus (tracheoesophageal fistula), that allows the passage of amniotic fluid into the stomach. Gastric secretions may contribute to stomach fluid. In some instances, however, a fistula is not present and fluid will not reach the stomach; hence the stomach will not be visualized by ultrasound. The combination of polyhydramnios and an absent stomach over repeated studies may be suggestive of esophageal atresia. Esophageal atresia will not be diagnosed in the majority of cases because of a tracheoesophageal fistula.

Esophageal atresia occurs in 1 in 2500 live births. The sonographer may observe the absent stomach and hydramnios (Figure 42-12). However, in more than half of the cases, the stomach is present because a fistula is usually

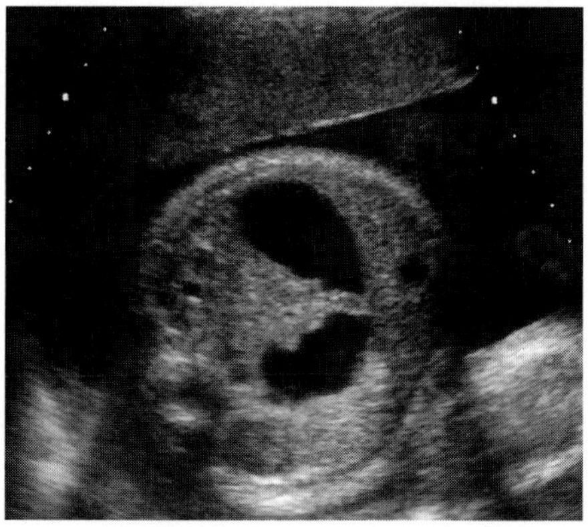

Figure 42-14 Transverse image of the fetal abdomen showing two large echo-free structures that communicated on real-time imaging. The patient had duodenal atresia.

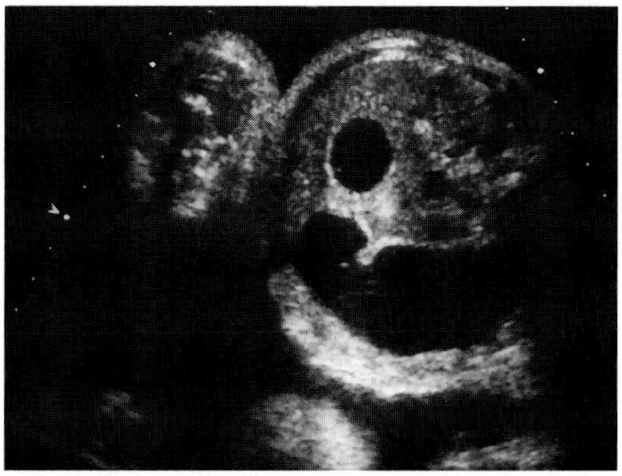

Figure 42-15 This 24-week fetus had trisomy 21. The transverse abdomen showed a very dilated stomach with communication into a smaller sac. Thirty percent of trisomy 21 pregnancies will also have duodenal atresia.

BOX 42-5 CAUSES OF DOUBLE BUBBLE

- Duodenal atresia
- Duodenal stenosis
- Annular pancreas
- Ladd's bands
- Proximal jejunal atresia
- Malrotation
- Diaphragmatic hernia

present that leads to fluid filling the stomach.[18] Hydramnios may exist from impaired reabsorption of swallowed fluid and may be associated with esophageal atresia, but it usually does not develop until the third trimester.[6] The upper neck sign has been observed as an additional finding in a patient with esophageal atresia.[13] A fluid-filled, blind-ending esophagus during fetal swallowing has been noted in a 22-week fetus.[13]

Coexisting anomalies are common in 50% to 70% of fetuses with esophageal atresia. The most commonly observed anomaly is anorectal atresia (others include vertebral defects, heart defects, and renal and limb anomalies **[VACTERL]**). Growth restriction is present in 40% of the cases. Chromosomal trisomies (18 and 21) are reported in association.[18] Survival depends on the presence of associated congenital anomalies.

Duodenal atresia is a blockage of the duodenal lumen by a membrane that prohibits the passage of swallowed amniotic fluid (Figure 42-13). Atresia or narrowing of the bowel segment below the obstruction occurs. In duodenal atresia the amniotic fluid fails to move beyond the obstruction, and consequently, amniotic fluid backs up in the duodenum and stomach.

Ultrasound findings. Two echo-free structures (stomach and duodenum) are found in the upper fetal abdomen and communicate. This sonographic appearance is termed the double bubble sign (Figure 42-14) (Box 42-5). Hydramnios is almost always seen with duodenal atresias later in pregnancy. Most cases of duodenal atresia are found distal to the ampulla and often coexist with annular pancreas.

About 30% of fetuses with duodenal atresia have trisomy 21 (Down syndrome) (Figure 42-15). Cardiovascular anomalies are frequent, and therefore fetal echocardiography is invaluable in excluding cardiac lesions. Anomalies occur in approximately 50% of infants with duodenal atresia. Genitourinary anomalies (horseshoe kidney, ectopic kidneys) may coexist with this condition. Other gastrointestinal abnormalities, such as imperforate anus and atresia of the small bowel, may be present.[10] Esophageal atresia may also be found.

Symmetric growth restriction commonly occurs in fetuses with duodenal atresia.[9] Amniotic fluid alpha-fetoprotein values are commonly elevated in fetuses with duodenal atresia caused by faulty swallowing. Infants with duodenal atresia require immediate surgery after birth to connect the stomach to the jejunum thus bypassing the obstruction.

BOWEL

Jejunoileal atresia or stenosis occurs in 1 in 3000 live births and is thought to be secondary to a vascular accident, sporadic, or secondary to volvulus or gastroschisis. Various fetal malformations may also occur with maternal drug usage (Table 42-1). The entire length of the bowel is subject to obstruction. Blockage of the jejunum and ileal bowel segments (jejunoileal atresia or stenosis) appears as multiple cystic structures (more than two) within the fetal abdomen. Because these structures are high in the abdomen, hydramnios may be present. The general rule is the more distal the obstruction, the less severe the hydramnios, and the later it will develop.[6] The causes of fetal small-bowel obstruction include malrotation, atresias, volvulus, peritoneal bands, and cystic fibrosis. The dilated bowel loops may be isolated or may be associated with other anomalies, ascites, or meconium peritonitis.

Table 42-1 Potential Fetal Malformations Associated With Maternal Drug or Chemical Use

Drug	Fetal Malformations
Acetaminophen overdose	Polyhydramnios
Clomiphene	NTDs, microcephaly, syndactyly, clubfoot, polydactyly, esophageal atresia
Coumadin	NTDs, cardiac defects, scoliosis, skeletal deformities, nasal hypoplasia, stippled epiphyses, chondrodysplasia punctata, short phalanges, toe defects, incomplete rotation of gut, IUGR, bleeding
Disulfiram	Vertebral fusion, clubfoot, radial aplasia, phocomelia, tracheoesophageal fistula
Fluorouracil of lungs	Radial aplasia, absent thumbs, aplasia of esophagus and duodenum, hypoplasia
Oral contraceptives	NTDs, cardiac defects, vertebral defects, limb reduction, IUGR, tracheoesophageal malformation
Phenothiazines	Microcephaly, syndactyly, clubfoot, omphalocele
Phenylephrine	Eye and ear abnormalities, syndactyly, clubfoot, hip dislocation, umbilical hernia

From Nyberg DA, Mahony BS, Pretorius DH: *Diagnostic ultrasound of fetal anomalies: text and atlas,* St Louis, 1990, Mosby.
IUGR, Intrauterine growth restriction; *NTDs,* neural tube defects.

A

B

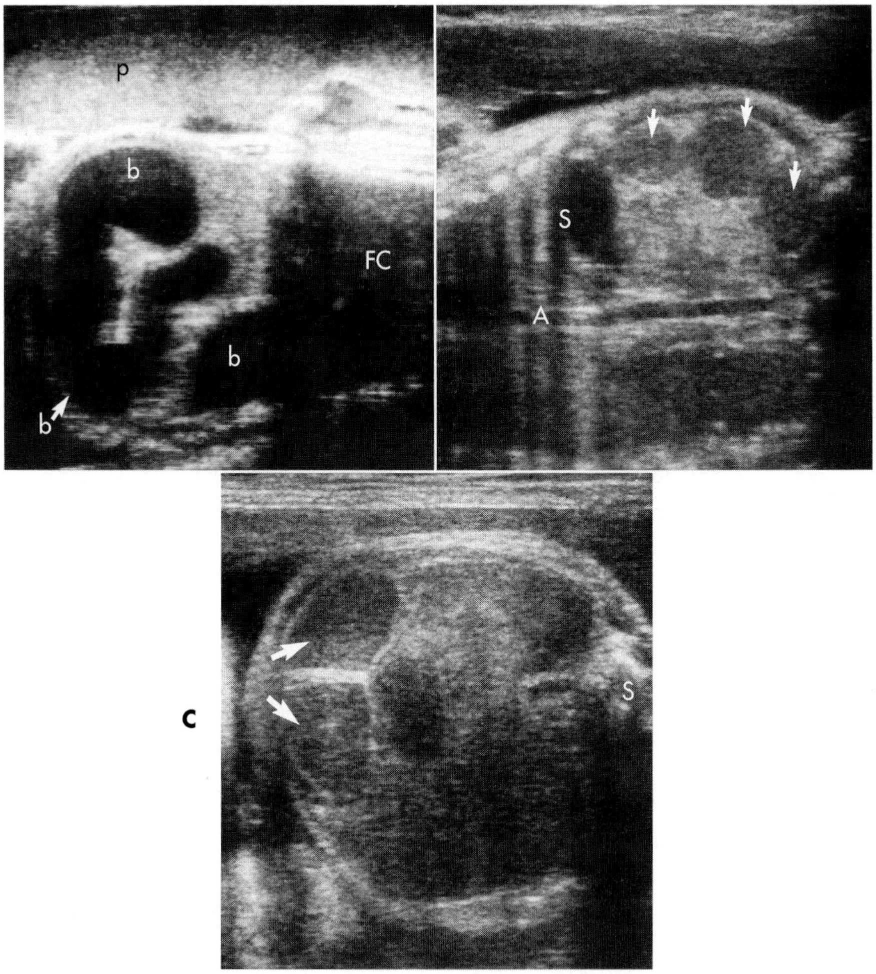

C

Figure 42-16 **A,** Bowel obstruction secondary to gastroschisis. Note the tubular shape of the cystic bowel loops *(b). FC,* Fetal chest; *P,* placenta. **B,** Bowel obstruction in a fetus with cystic fibrosis at 36 weeks of gestation. Note that the bowel loops in this case are filled with meconium *(arrows)* rather than cystic, as in **A.** *A,* Aorta; *S,* stomach. **C,** In the fetus shown in **B,** echo-filled bowel loops are viewed in a transverse direction *(arrows). S,* Spine.

A 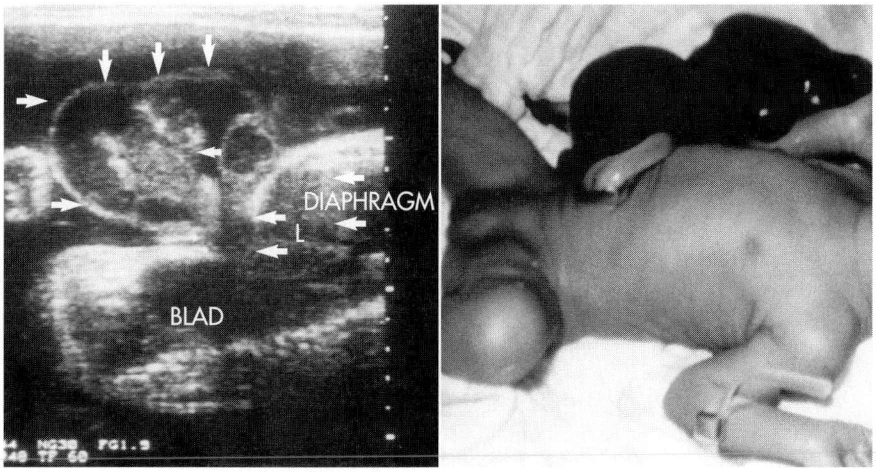 B

Figure 42-17 **A,** Sagittal scan demonstrating anterior abdominal wall defect with protrusion of the entire small bowel in a fetus with a gastroschisis *(arrows)*. Note the obstructed (cystic) components of small bowel. *L,* Liver. **B,** Gastroschisis defect in same patient after birth. Note the normal cord insertion.

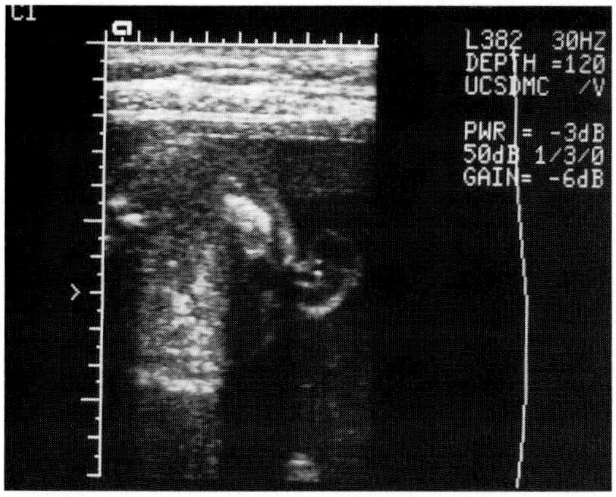

Figure 42-18 Meconium accumulates in the fetal bowel in the second trimester and is seen sonographically as echogenic reflections (notice shadowing) within the peristaltic small bowel.

Ultrasound findings. Sonographically, intestinal obstructions appear as cystic bowel loops that are discontinuous with the stomach (Figure 42-16). It is important to remember that bowel loops may be identified in the third trimester of pregnancy. One study reported that the normal fetal colon progressively increased in diameter after 23 weeks of gestation, although it never exceeded 18 mm in a preterm fetus.[15] Fetal intestinal obstruction should be suspected when clear cystic structures are found in the pelvis. In some instances, echoes within the bowel may be identified in intestinal obstructions but may also represent normal meconium patterns (see Figure 42-16). Vascular restriction may lead to obstruction secondary to a gastroschisis (Figure 42-17).

Meconium ileus is a small-bowel disorder marked by the presence of thick meconium in the distal ileum. Meconium ileus is the earliest manifestation of cystic fibrosis occurring in 10% to 15% of patients and is the third most common form of neonatal bowel obstruction after atresia and malrotation.[10] Most cases of meconium ileus occur in newborns with cystic fibrosis. Infants with **cystic fibrosis** have multiple medical problems, including pancreatic disease and respiratory problems resulting from long-standing lung disease. Cystic fibrosis is an autosomal-recessive condition.

Meconium begins to accumulate in the fetal bowel in the second trimester, at which time it can be seen on sonography as tiny echogenic reflections within the peristaltic small bowel (Figure 42-18). Because the colon does not exhibit peristalsis in utero, the meconium remains suspended at the rectum. The anal sphincter prevents the passage of meconium (meconium plug) into the amniotic fluid unless the fetus is stressed or traumatized.

Ultrasound findings. With meconium ileus, the ileum dilates because of impacted meconium (which appears echogenic) (Figure 42-19). Increased production of mucus by the gastrointestinal organs and electrolyte imbalance explains the overproduction of meconium (characteristic of cystic fibrosis). It is important to realize that the normal small bowel may appear echogenic during the second trimester of pregnancy. Other fetal conditions have been associated with echogenic small bowel (cytomegalovirus and trisomy 21).[15] Meconium peritonitis may occur secondary to perforation of obstructed bowel. An inflammatory response occurs because of leakage of the bowel contents, which may cause fibrosis of tissue and calcifications. A pseudocyst may develop because of chronic meconium peritonitis (Box 42-6).

Other Small Bowel Obstructions. Rarer small-bowel obstructions, chloridorrhea (life-threatening diarrhea in the newborn), and megacystis-microcolon intestinal hypoperistalsis syndrome (absence of peristalsis) may be observed during pregnancy. In the latter, bladder dilation and hydronephrosis are characteristic findings in predominantly female fetuses. Amniotic fluid volume is typically

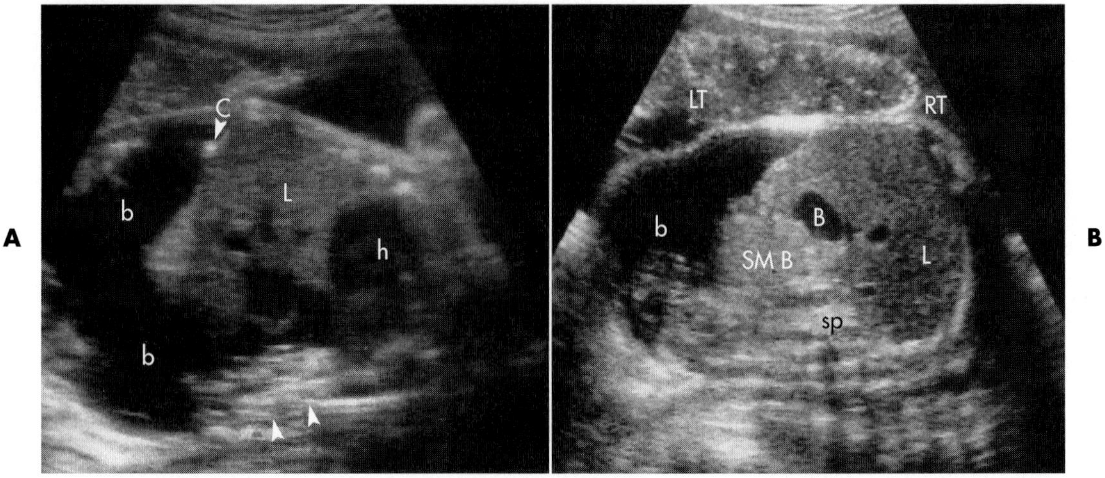

Figure 42-19 **A,** Meconium peritonitis secondary to bowel obstruction is shown with an irregular appearance of the bowel *(b)* in the lower pelvis extending upward toward the chest in a 30-week fetus. Calcifications *(C)*, are observed in several locations. Clumping of bowel was observed *(arrows)*. Meconium peritonitis with bowel perforation was suspected. There was a moderate increase in the amniotic fluid volume by 33 weeks of gestation. *h,* Heart; *L,* Liver. **B,** In the same fetus, transverse view showing bowel dilation *(b)* in a spine-down position. Note the normal-appearing small bowel *(SM B)*. *L,* Liver; *LT,* left side of abdomen; *RT,* right side of abdomen; *S,* stomach. At birth the neonate was diagnosed with meconium ileus and peritonitis necessitating an ileostomy. At 2 months of age, the infant was discharged on normal formula feedings. Cystic fibrosis was suspected.

BOX 42-6 PITFALLS IN THE DIAGNOSIS OF MECONIUM ILEUS

- Significant dilation of the meconium-filled ileum in meconium ileus can simulate colon in morphology and location especially in the presence of the expected microcolon.
- More proximal small bowel can retain the expected features of active peristalsis and fluid-filled contents and the discrepancy in caliber between proximal and distal small bowel should not distract the sonologist from the diagnosis of small-bowel obstruction or meconium ileus.

From Goldstein RB, Filly RA, Callen PW: Sonographic diagnosis of meconium ileus in utero, *J Ultrasound Med* 6:663, 1987.

normal to increased. Obstruction may also be present when gastroschisis is present (see Figure 42-17). Obstructions of the large intestine diagnosed prenatally include anorectal atresia and Hirschsprung's disease.

Anorectal atresia. **Anorectal atresia** presents as a complex disorder of the bowel and genitourinary tract. Imperforate anus (a finding in anorectal atresia) is a disorder that occurs when a membrane covers the anus prohibiting the expulsion of meconium. Anorectal atresia may present as part of the VACTERL association or in caudal regression. The prognosis is poor with anorectal atresia because of associated anomalies. Incontinence of both bowel and bladder is common in the infant.

Ultrasound findings. Anorectal atresia may be diagnosed sonographically by observing dilated colon and calcified meconium. Amniotic fluid is typically normal or may be decreased when there are associated renal problems.

Hirschsprung's disease. **Hirschsprung's disease** (megacolon) is a congenital disorder in which there is abnormal innervation of the large intestine.[15]

Ultrasound findings. This condition is difficult to diagnose prenatally but may be suspected when dilated bowel loops are observed.[21]

Meconium peritonitis. **Meconium peritonitis** is a condition that may arise when the fetus has a sterile chemical peritonitis secondary to in utero bowel perforation. Hydramnios is present in 65% of the fetuses with meconium peritonitis. A complication may result in the formation of a meconium pseudocyst as the inflammatory reaction seals the perforation.

Ultrasound findings. On ultrasound examination, calcifications are seen on the peritoneal surfaces or in the scrotum via the processus vaginalis. The ascitic fluid may also be echogenic. It is unusual to see calcification in the meconium ileus in a fetus with cystic fibrosis.

Ascites. True ascites in the fetal abdomen is always abnormal. In the fetus, the ascitic fluid collects between the two leaves of unfused omentum, resulting in a cystlike appearance in the abdomen (Figure 42-20). The prognosis is poor in nonimmune hydrops. Other conditions that may cause ascites to develop include bowel perforation or urinary ascites secondary to bladder rupture.

Ultrasound findings. Ascites usually outlines the falciform ligament and umbilical vein. When ascites is associated with hydrops fetalis, pleural effusions, and pericardial effusion, integumentary edema will often be observed.

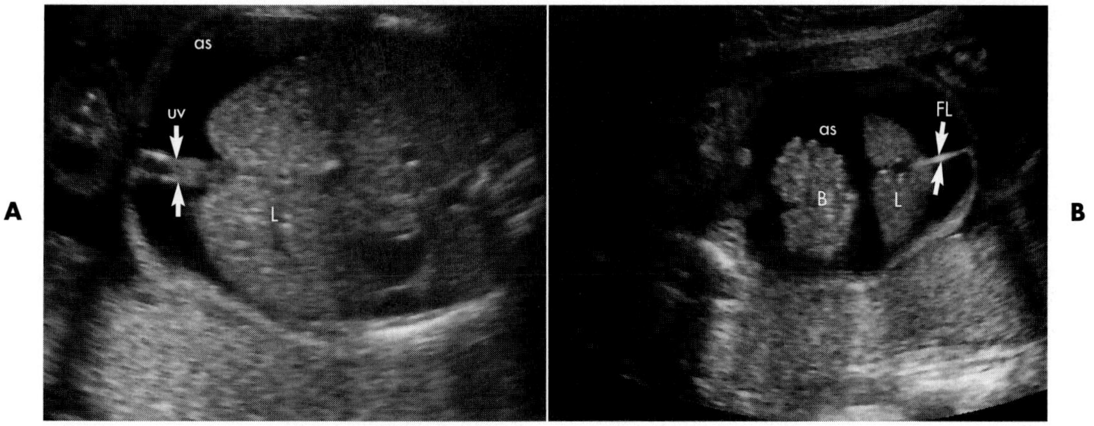

Figure 42-20 **A,** Fetal ascites *(as)* surrounds the umbilical vein *(uv)*. *L,* liver. **B,** Ascites *(as)* completely surrounds the liver *(L)* and falciform ligament *(FL)*. *B,* Bowel.

BOX 42-7 ABDOMINAL CYSTIC MASS

It is important for the sonographic team to determine:

1. The precise location of the mass
2. The size of the mass
3. Resultant compression of other organ systems (hydronephrosis, hydroureter, fetal hydrops)

MISCELLANEOUS CYSTIC MASSES OF THE ABDOMEN

Cystic masses of the lower fetal abdomen may be observed prenatally (Box 42-7). As demonstrated previously, cystic dilations of many organ systems may occur during the fetal period.

When a cystic mass is discovered, attempts should be made to determine the characteristics of the mass. A description of the mass should include the components of the structure, such as: (1) an echo-free versus an echo-filled mass, (2) presence or absence of septations, and (3) coexisting fetal anomalies. The investigator should systematically investigate all abdominal organ systems to determine the anatomic origin of the mass. The hepatic system (liver, gallbladder, spleen, and pancreatic areas) should be evaluated, as well as the gastrointestinal system (esophagus, stomach, intestines) and genitourinary system (kidneys, ureters and bladder).

Occasionally, cysts arise from the urachus (dilation of remnant allantoic stalk between umbilicus and bladder), fetal ovary or omentum. Ovarian and omental cysts are generally isolated and well circumscribed. Determination of the fetal gender is beneficial when an ovarian mass is suspected. If abdominal masses are large, they may occupy the entire lower fetal pelvis, making a specific intrauterine diagnosis impossible.

ACKNOWLEDGMENT

The author recognizes the previous contribution of Kara Mayden Argo to this chapter in the fourth edition of this book.

REVIEW QUESTIONS

1. Describe the differences between the fetal and adult abdomen.
2. Describe the malformations of the hindgut and midgut.
3. What is the sonographic appearance of the stomach?
4. How is the abdominal circumference obtained?
5. How is the gallbladder localized on ultrasound?
6. What anomalies are seen in the fetal liver?
7. What is situs inversus?
8. How may situs inversus be prenatally detected?
9. What anomalies are seen in the fetal gallbladder?
10. Describe the normal sonographic findings of the small bowel and colon.
11. What are the sonographic features of esophageal atresia, duodenal atresia, meconium ileus, meconium peritonitis, and anorectal atresia?
12. What is pseudoascites?

REFERENCES

1. Beretsky I, Lankin DH: Diagnosis of fetal cholelithiasis using real time high resolution imaging employing digital detection, *J Ultrasound Med* 2:381, 1983.
2. Berkowitz RL and others: Fetal urinary tract obstruction: what is the role of surgical intervention in utero? *Am J Obstet Gynecol* 144:367, 1982.
3. Bovicelli L and others: Prenatal diagnosis and management of fetal gastrointestinal abnormalities, *Semin Perinatol* 7:109, 1983.
4. Bowie JD: Sonography of fetal abdominal abnormalities. In Sanders RC, editor: *The principles and practice of ultrasonography in obstetrics and gynecology,* ed 3, Norwalk, Conn, 1985, Appleton-Century-Crofts.

5. Bustamante S, Koldovsky O: Synopsis of development of the main morphological structures of the human gastrointestinal tract. In Lebenthal E, editor: *Textbook of gastroenterology and nutrition in infancy,* New York, 1981, Raven Press.
6. Callen DW, editor: *Ultrasonography in obstetrics and gynecology,* ed 2, Philadelphia, 1988, WB Saunders.
7. Chinn DH, Filly RA, Callen PW: Ultrasonic evaluation of fetal umbilical and hepatic vascular anatomy, *Rad* 144:153, 1982.
8. Elrad H and others: Prenatal diagnosis of choledochal cyst, *J Ultrasound Med* 4:553, 1985.
9. Fakhry J and others: Fetal gastric pseudomasses, *J Ultrasound Med* 6:177, 1987.
10. Goldstein RB, Filly RA, Callen PW: Sonographic diagnosis of meconium ileus in utero, *J Ultrasound Med* 6:663, 1987.
11. Grand RI, Watkins JB, Torti FM: Development of the human gastrointestinal tract, *Gastroenterology* 70:790, 1976.
12. Hashimoto BE, Filly RA, Callen PW: Fetal pseudoascites: further anatomic observations, *J Ultrasound Med* 5:151, 1986.
13. Kalache KD and others: The upper neck pouch sign: a prenatal sonographic marker for esophageal atresia, *Ultrasound Obstet Gynecol* 11:138, 1998.
14. Moore KL, editor: *The developing human: clinically oriented embryology,* ed 4, Philadelphia, 1988, WB Saunders.
15. Nyberg DA, Mahony BS, Pretorius DH, editors: *Diagnostic ultrasound of fetal anomalies: text and atlas,* St Louis, 1990, Mosby.
16. Parulekar, SG: Sonography of normal fetal bowel, *J Ultrasound Med* 10:211, 1991.
17. Platt LD and others: Antenatal diagnosis of a fetal liver mass, *J Ultrasound Med* 2:521, 1983.
18. Pretorius DH and others: Tracheoesophageal fistula in utero (twenty-two cases), *J Ultrasound Med* 6:509, 1987.
19. Schmidt W and others: Sonographic measurements of the fetal spleen, *J Ultrasound Med* 4:667, 1985.
20. Schwartz H and others: Choledochal cyst in a second trimester fetus, *J Diagn Med Sonogr* 1:10, 1989.
21. Vermesh M and others: Prenatal sonographic diagnosis of Hirschprung's disease, *J Ultrasound Med* 5:37, 1986.
22. Walker JM, Derguson DD: The sonographic appearance of blood in the fetal stomach and its association with placental abruption, *J Ultrasound Med* 7:155, 1988.

BIBLIOGRAPHY

Callen PW and others: Ultrasonographic evaluation of fetal paranephric pseudocysts, *J Ultrasound Med* 2:309, 1983.

Gross BH, Callen PW, Filly RA: Ultrasound appearance of fetal greater omentum, *J Ultrasound Med* 1:67, 1982.

Hill LM, Breckle R, Avant RF: Sonographic findings associated with a sterile fetal appendiceal abscess, *J Ultrasound Med* 1:257, 1982.

Jackson GH and others: Sonography of combined esophageal and duodenal atresia, *J Ultrasound Med* 2:473, 1983.

Lince DM and others: The clinical significance of increased echogenicity in the fetal abdomen, *Am J Roentgenology* 145:683, 1985.

Nancarrow PA and others: Fibroadhesive meconium peritonitis: in utero sonographic diagnosis, *J Ultrasound Med* 4:213, 1985.

Nyberg DA and others: Dilated fetal bowel: a sonographic sign of cystic fibrosis, *J Ultrasound Med* 6:257, 1987.

Nyberg DA and others: Fetal bowel: normal sonographic findings, *J Ultrasound Med* 6:3, 1987.

Pretorius DH, Meier PR, Johnson ML: Diagnosis of esophageal atresia in utero, *J Ultrasound Med* 2:475, 1983.

Richards DS, Cruz AC, Dowdy KA: Prenatal diagnosis of fetal liver calcifications, *J Ultrasound Med* 7:691, 1988.

Roberts AB, Mitchell JM, Pattison NS: Fetal liver length in normal and isoimmunized pregnancies, *Am J Obstet Gynecol* 161:42, 1989.

Sanders RC, editor: *Clinical sonography: a practical guide,* ed 3, Boston, 1998, Little, Brown.

CHAPTER 43

The Fetal Genitourinary System

Sandra L. Hagen-Ansert

OBJECTIVES

- Discuss the development of the urogenital system
- Describe the ultrasound appearance of the fetal kidneys and bladder
- Detail the complications of renal agenesis
- Describe the sonographic findings in polycystic disease
- Differentiate multicystic dysplastic kidney from polycystic disease
- Distinguish between pyelectasis and calyectasis
- Detail the sonographic findings in ureterovesical junction obstruction and posterior urethral valves
- Describe prune-belly syndrome
- Detail the development of the genital system
- List the congenital malformations of the genital system

KEY TERMS

bicornuate uterus - duplication of the uterus (two horns and one vagina)

calyectasis - rounded calyces with renal pelvis dilation measuring greater than 10 mm in the anteroposterior direction

crossed renal ectopia - occurs when the kidney is located on the opposite side of its ureteral orifice

cryptorchidism - failure of the testes to descend into the scrotum

extrophy of the bladder - protrusion of the posterior wall of the urinary bladder, which contains the trigone of the bladder and the ureteric orifices

fetal hydronephrosis - dilated renal pelvis

hermaphroditism - condition in which both ovarian and testicular tissues are present

horseshoe kidney - forms when the inferior poles of the kidney fuse while they are in the pelvis

hydrometrocolpos - collection of fluid in the vagina and uterus

hydroureters - dilated ureters

hypospadias - abnormal congenital opening of the male urethra on the undersurface of the penis

infantile polycystic kidney disease - autosomal recessive disease that affects the fetal kidneys and liver; the kidneys are enlarged and echogenic on ultrasound

multicystic dysplastic kidney disease - multiple cysts replace normal renal tissue throughout the kidney; usually causes renal obstruction

ovarian cyst - may be found in the fetus; results from maternal hormone stimulation and is usually benign

pelvic kidney - occurs when the kidney does not migrate upward into the retroperitoneal space

posterior urethral valve - occurs only in male fetuses; is manifested by the presence of a valve in the posterior urethra

Potter's syndrome - characterized by renal agenesis, oligohydramnios, pulmonary hypoplasia, abnormal facies and malformed hands and feet

prune-belly syndrome - dilatation of the fetal abdomen secondary to severe bilateral hydronephrosis, and fetal ascites; fetus also has oligohydramnios and pulmonary hypoplasia

pyelectasis - dilated renal pelvis measuring 5 to 9 mm in the anteroposterior direction

renal agenesis - renal system fails to develop

unicornuate uterus - anomaly of the uterus in which only one horn and tube develop

ureteropelvic junction - most common site of obstruction; junction of the ureter entering the renal pelvis

ureterovesical junction - junction where the ureter enters the bladder

urethral atresia - this condition causes a massively distended bladder (prune belly)

uterus didelphys - double uterus and double vagina

Prenatal ultrasound has the capability of diagnosing many genitourinary system anomalies. In the presence of oligohydramnios the sonographer should carefully search the renal areas and bladder to determine if obstruction is present that may lead to the diminished production of amniotic fluid. On the other hand, abnormalities of the genitourinary system may be discovered incidentally during the complete obstetric ultrasound evaluation (Table 43-1). A complete examination includes evaluation of both kidneys, documentation of the urinary bladder, and assessment of amniotic fluid.

EMBRYOLOGY OF THE UROGENITAL SYSTEM

The urinary and genital systems develop from the intermediate mesoderm that extends along the length of the dorsal body wall of the embryo. The excretory ducts of both systems initially enter a common cavity called the cloaca.[14]

While development continues, the overlapping of the two systems is well seen in males. The mesonephric duct first serves as a urinary duct, and later is transformed into the main genital duct, the vas deferens.[14] The ureter develops from a small bud and develops later in the adult male. The urinary and genital organs discharge their secretions through a canal in the penis known as the spongy urethra.

While the embryo bends and folds in the horizontal plane during the 4th week, the intermediate mesoderm forms a longitudinal mass on both sides of the aorta called the urogenital ridge. Both the urinary and genital systems develop in these ridges. The nephrogenic cord gives rise to the urinary system and the gonadal ridge gives rise to the genital system.[14]

The urinary system begins development first. The urinary system consists of two kidneys that excrete urine; the ureters, which transport urine to the urinary bladder; and the urethra, through which the urine is discharged to the exterior.

DEVELOPMENT OF THE KIDNEYS

There are three sets of excretory organs that develop in the embryo; only the third set remains as the permanent kidneys (Figure 43-1). The permanent kidneys (metanephros) begin to develop early in the 5th week although they do not begin to function and produce urine until around the 11th week (end of the first trimester).[14] Urine formation continues to fill the amniotic cavity throughout fetal life. The kidneys do not function in utero because the placenta eliminates waste from the fetal blood.

TABLE 43-1 POTENTIAL UROGENITAL FETAL MALFORMATIONS ASSOCIATED WITH MATERNAL DRUG OR CHEMICAL USE

Drug	Fetal Malformations
Amitriptyline	Micrognathia, limb reduction, swelling of hands and feet, urinary retention
Amobarbital	NTDs, cardiac defects, severe limb deformities, congenital hip dislocation, polydactyly, clubfoot, cleft palate, ambiguous genitalia, soft tissue, deformity of neck
Caffeine	Musculoskeletal defects, hydronephrosis
Cocaine	Spontaneous abortion, placental abruption, prematurity, IUGR, possible cardiac defects, skull defects, genitourinary anomalies
Imipramine	NTDs, cleft palate, renal cysts, diaphragmatic hernia
Sulfonamide	Limb hypoplasia, foot defects, urethral obstruction

Modified from Nyberg DA, Mahony BS, Pretorius DH: *Diagnostic ultrasound of fetal anomalies: text and atlas,* St Louis, 1990, Mosby.
NTDs, Neural tube defects.

The permanent kidneys develop from two different sources: (1) the metanephric diverticulum or ureteric bud and (2) the metanephric mesoderm (Figure 43-2). The ureteric bud gives rise to the ureter, renal pelvis, calyces, and collecting tubules. The collecting tubule is also derived from the ureteric bud. The major and minor calyces are developed from these collecting tubules.

The ends of the tubules form metanephric vesicles. The ends of these tubules are invaginated by an ingrowth of the fine blood vessels, the glomerulus, to form a double-layered cup called the glomerular capsule or Bowman's capsule.[14] The renal corpuscle (glomerulus and capsule) and its associated tubules form a nephron. Each distal convoluted tubule contacts an arched collecting tubule, and then the tubules become confluent, forming a uriniferous tubule. Each uriniferous tubule consists of two parts: a nephron and a collecting tubule.

The kidneys initially lie very close together in the pelvis. Gradually they migrate into the abdomen and become separated from one another. They normally complete this migration by the 9th week of gestation.[14] In some cases, one of the kidneys may remain in the pelvic cavity while the other migrates into the posterior flank of the abdomen. On ultrasound, the identification of a **pelvic kidney** may be seen with adequate bladder dilation and may appear in the females as a pelvic mass.

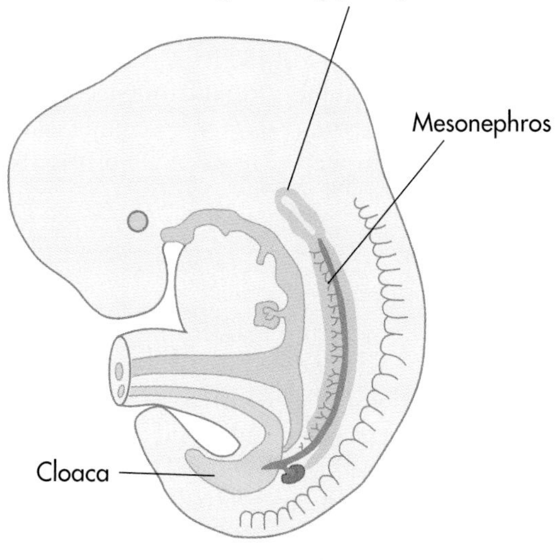

Figure 43-1 Five-week embryo showing three sets of kidneys that developed in the embryo. The pronephros is rudimentary and nonfunctional. The mesonephros functions for two weeks and then degenerates. The metanephros develops into the permanent kidney.

The arterial vascular supply to the kidneys comes from the arteries that arise from the aorta. Usually these vessels disappear when the kidneys ascend, but some of them may persist accounting for the variations one may find in the renal arteries. At least 25% of adult kidneys have two to four renal arteries.

The fetal kidneys are subdivided into lobes that may be separated by grooves. This lobulation usually diminishes by the end of the fetal period, but in some cases the lobes may still be noticeable by the end of the neonatal period. In adolescent and adult patients, persistence of the fetal lobulation and groove may be seen on ultrasound as an echogenic triangular notch along the anterior wall of the right kidney.

Congential Malformations of the Kidneys

Complete absence of the kidneys is known as **renal agenesis.** This condition occurs when the ureteric buds fail to develop or when they degenerate before they can induce the metanephric mesoderm to form nephrons.[14] Because the uriniferous tubules develop from two different sources, the failure of the tubules to join results in congenital polycystic disease of the kidneys.

Division of the ureteric bud at an early stage results in a double or divided kidney**.** The ureteral bud closest to the sinus drains the lower renal pole and enters the bladder at the trigone, where the ureter drains the upper pole while it enters the bladder in a more medial and caudal position (ectopic ureter). The lower pole is more prone to reflux and the upper pole more prone to obstruction. The hydronephrotic, nonfunctioning upper pole may cause downward displacement of the lower pole calyces.

A **horseshoe kidney** forms when the inferior poles of the kidney fuse while they are in the pelvis. This fusion may occur in 1 to 4 in 1000 births and is two to three times more common in males.

Another variation from the horseshoe kidney may result in **crossed renal ectopia** and abnormal renal posi-

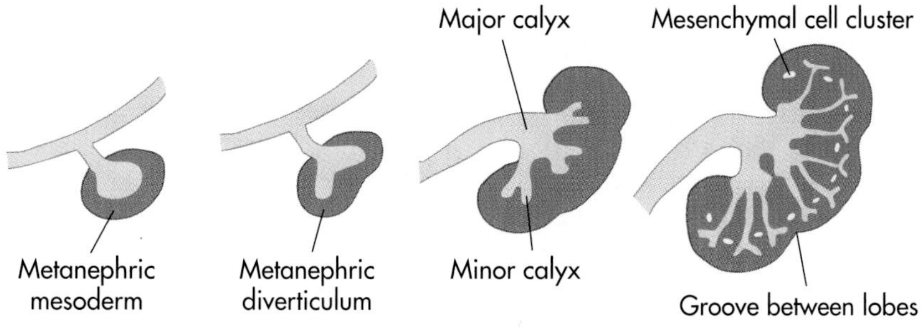

Figure 43-2 Developing kidney in weeks 5 through 8.

tion. In this case, the kidney is located on the opposite side of its ureteral orifice. Crossed renal ectopia usually affects the left kidney going toward the right and is inferior to the normal kidney. This is more common in males.

DEVELOPMENT OF THE URINARY BLADDER

The fetal urinary bladder is derived from the hindgut derivative known as the urogenital sinus (see Figure 43-1). The caudal ends of the mesonephric ducts open into the cloaca, and parts of them are gradually absorbed into the wall of the urinary bladder. This development causes the ureters (derived from the ureteric buds) and the mesonephric ducts to enter the bladder separately.

While the kidneys migrate upward, the orifices of the ureters move cranially and the primordia of the ejaculatory ducts (derived from the mesonephric ducts) move toward one another and enter the prostatic part of the urethra.

Exstrophy of the Bladder. Exstrophy of the bladder occurs primarily in males and the incidence is 1 in 50,000 births. It is characterized by the protrusion of the posterior wall of the urinary bladder, which contains the trigone of the bladder and the ureteric orifices. Exstrophy of the bladder is caused by the defective closure of the inferior part of the anterior abdominal wall during the 4th week of gestation. As a result of this defect, no muscle or connective tissue forms in the anterior abdominal wall to cover the urinary bladder and therefore the bladder is formed external to the abdominal wall.

DEVELOPMENT OF THE URETHRA

The epithelium of the female urethra and most of the epithelium of the male urethra is derived from the endoderm of the urogenital sinus.

DEVELOPMENT OF THE PROSTATE GLAND

The prostate gland is an auxiliary genital gland that is derived from evaginations of the epithelium of the prostatic portion of the urethra that penetrates the surrounding mesenchyme. The urethral and paraurethral glands in the female are comparable with the prostate gland.

THE URACHUS

Early in development the urinary bladder is continuous with the allantois. The allantois regresses to become a fibrous cord known as the urachus. This cord, or ligament, extends from the apex of the bladder to the umbilicus. If the lumen of the allantois persists while the urachus forms, a urachal fistula develops, which causes urine to drain from the bladder to the umbilicus.[14] If only a small part of the lumen of the allantois persists, it is called a **urachal cyst.** If a larger portion of the lumen persists, it may cause a urachal sinus to develop that may open at the umbilicus or into the urinary bladder.

BOX 43-1 RENAL ABNORMALITIES

- Renal agenesis
- Multicystic renal dysplasia
- Congenital hydronephrosis
- Renal duplication
- Pelvic kidney
- Horseshoe kidney
- Infantile polycystic kidney disease
- Adult polycystic kidney disease
- Meckel-Gruber syndrome

ABNORMALITIES OF THE URINARY TRACT

Renal malformations may be divided into two categories: (1) those involving congenital malformation and (2) those resulting from an obstructive process (Box 43-1). The consequences of renal malformations vary depending on the type of lesion and extent of obstruction. Amniotic fluid volume is a significant factor in predicting outcome.

The recognition of urinary tract anomalies is of significant clinical concern because several fetal conditions are incompatible with life. In unilateral obstructions of the urinary tract, early delivery of the fetus is often warranted to salvage the normal kidney. Intrauterine decompression of an obstructed urinary tract (posterior urethral valve syndrome) has been performed to relieve the obstruction and allow expansion of the lungs to prevent pulmonary hypoplasia.[8] Recognition of lethal or treatable renal anomalies is necessary to ensure appropriate clinical and therapeutic management.

Amniotic fluid is a critical marker in the assessment of renal function. The fetal kidneys begin to excrete urine after the 11th week but do not become the major contributor of fetal urine (hence, amniotic fluid volume) until 14 to 16 weeks of pregnancy. Therefore the observation of normal amniotic fluid volume before this time will not exclude the possibility of renal agenesis (absent kidneys).

In fetuses with severe renal disease, amniotic fluid is reduced, and in the most severe malformations it is virtually absent. When severe oligohydramnios is found, usually both kidneys or ureters and the urethra are malformed. Unilateral obstructions may yield a normal amount of amniotic fluid because the contralateral kidney produces urine. Conversely, hydramnios may be present with some renal disorders, such as mesoblastic nephroma and unilateral renal obstruction. It is important to identify the fetal bladder early in the ultrasound examination to make sure adequate fluid is present. If no bladder is seen, the sonographer should reevaluate the bladder at the end of the examination. It usually takes at least 30 minutes to fill and empty the fetal bladder.

It is important to determine whether the pathology is unilateral (implies ureteral bud defect with good prognosis) or bilateral. When bilateral, decide if the condition is

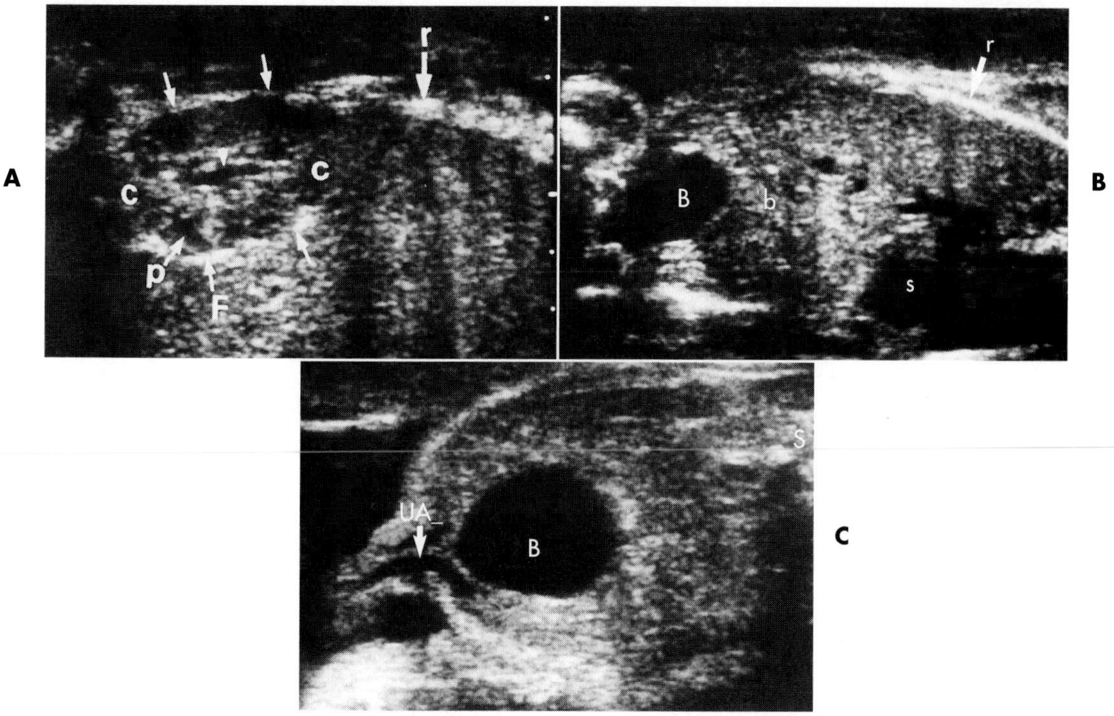

Figure 43-3 **A,** Longitudinal image of the kidney in a 37-week fetus revealing the renal cortex *(c)* pelvis *(arrowhead),* and pyramids *(p).* The kidney is marginated by the capsule of the kidney *(arrows),* which is sonographically enhanced because of perirenal fat *(F). r,* Rib. **B,** Sagittal view of the fluid-filled bladder *(B)* in the pelvis. Note the more cephalic location of the stomach *(s)* in the upper abdomen. *b,* Bowel, *r,* rib. **C,** Transverse view of the bladder *(B)* with demonstration of the umbilical arteries *(UA)* as they course around the bladder after exiting the umbilical cord. *S,* Spine.

asymmetric (dissimilar abnormal patterns for each kidney) or symmetric (same abnormal pattern for both kidneys; this may imply a genetic condition, such as autosomal-recessive infantile polycystic kidney or multicystic dysplastic kidney disease).

SONOGRAPHIC EXAMINATION OF THE URINARY TRACT

The sonographer should be familiar with several important concepts when evaluating the fetal urinary tract. The fetal kidneys and bladder may be seen by 15 weeks of gestation. By 25 weeks it is possible to distinguish the renal cortex from the medulla, outline the renal capsule clearly, and see a central echogenic area in the renal sinus region.[3]

The kidneys should be evaluated by assessing their anatomy, texture, and size. Normal anatomic structures of the kidney include the relatively homogeneous renal cortex and parenchyma, echogenic pyramids and calyces, and anechoic renal pelvis (Figure 43-3). Kidney texture that appears significantly enhanced (echogenic) should be a cause for concern.

Marked deviations of anatomy should alert the sonographer to investigate the urinary tract more extensively. It is important to remember that a small amount of urine may be seen in the renal pelvis in the normal fetus, measuring in its anterior-posterior diameter less than 5 mm. This should not be misinterpreted as an abnormal collection of urine within the renal pelvis, **pyelectasis** (5 to 9mm), or **calyectasis,** rounded calyces with renal pelvis dilation (greater than10 mm), which may lead to severe hydronephrosis (Figure 43-4). A renal pelvis diameter, measured in an anteroposterior direction in a transverse plane that exceeds 10 to 15 mm is considered abnormal.[10]

The effect of maternal hydration on the fetus has been evaluated by many investigators. One study reported that maternal hydration influences fetal renal diameter.[4] The larger fetal renal diameters seen in the hydrated group supported physiologic theories that the effects of maternal hydration on amniotic fluid volume are partially mediated via fetal urine production. Another study showed no significant change in the degree of fetal renal pyelectasis before and after maternal hydration.[1]

The size of the fetal kidneys may be assessed by measuring the length, width, and height of the kidney (Table 43-2).[13] The length of the kidney closely correlates with the gestational age of the fetus.

The normal fetal ureters are usually unobserved because they measure less than 1 mm in diameter. When the ureters are pathologically dilated, they become visible as tortuous cystic masses in the midportion of the lower fetal pelvis. Abnormally dilated ureters are referred to as **hydroureters** and may be traced into the kidney and bladder (Figure 43-5).

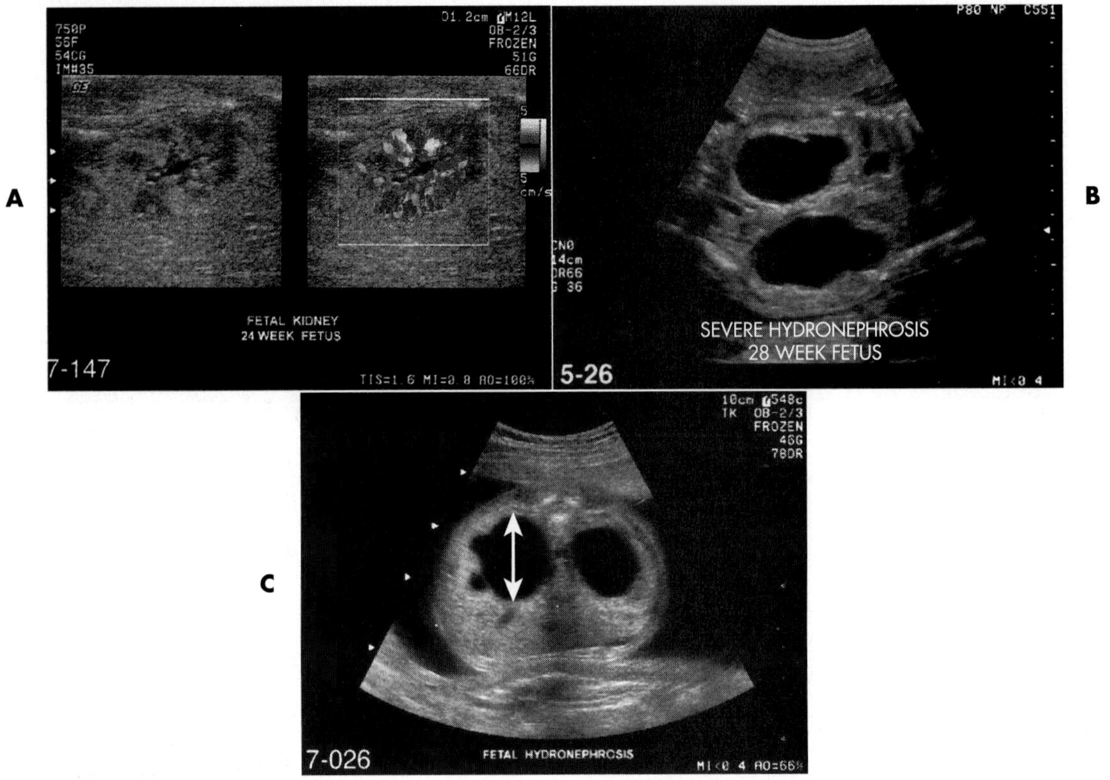

Figure 43-4 **A,** Sagittal view of normal fetal kidneys with a small separation in the renal pelvis measuring less than 1 to 2 mm. Color flow shows the tremendous vascularity of the renal parenchyma. Sagittal **(B)** and transverse **(C)** view of the severe hydronephrosis. The separation of the collecting system may be measured on the transverse anterior-posterior scan *(arrow).*

TABLE 43-2 NORMAL SIZE VALUES OF KIDNEY DIMENSIONS

	Kidney thickness (mm)			Kidney width (mm)			Kidney length (mm)			Kidney volume (cm³)		
Age (weeks)	5th	50th	95th	5th	50th	95th	5th	50th	95th	5th	50th	95th
16	2	6	10	6	10	13	7	13	18	—	0.4	2.6
17	3	7	11	6	10	14	10	15	20	—	0.6	2.8
18	4	8	12	6	10	14	12	17	22	—	0.7	2.9
19	5	9	13	7	10	14	14	19	24	—	0.9	3.1
20	6	10	13	7	11	15	15	21	26	—	1.1	3.3
21	6	10	14	8	12	15	17	22	28	—	1.4	3.6
22	7	11	15	8	12	16	19	24	29	—	1.7	3.9
23	8	12	16	9	13	17	21	26	31	—	2.1	4.3
24	9	13	17	10	14	18	22	28	33	0.3	2.5	4.7
25	10	14	18	11	15	19	24	29	34	0.8	3.0	5.2
26	11	15	19	12	16	19	25	31	36	1.3	3.5	5.7
27	11	15	19	12	16	20	27	32	37	1.9	4.1	6.3
28	12	16	20	13	17	21	28	33	38	2.5	4.7	6.9
29	13	17	21	14	18	22	29	35	40	3.2	5.4	7.6
30	14	18	22	15	19	23	31	36	41	3.9	6.1	8.3
31	14	18	22	16	20	24	32	37	42	4.6	6.8	9.0
32	15	19	23	17	20	24	33	38	43	5.4	7.5	9.7
33	16	20	23	17	21	25	34	39	44	6.1	8.3	10.5
34	16	20	24	18	22	26	35	40	45	6.8	9.0	11.2
35	17	21	25	18	22	26	35	41	46	7.4	9.6	11.8
36	17	21	25	19	23	27	36	41	47	8.1	10.2	12.4
37	18	22	26	19	23	27	37	42	47	8.6	10.8	13.0
38	18	22	26	19	23	27	37	43	48	9.0	11.2	13.4
39	19	23	27	19	23	27	38	43	48	9.4	11.6	13.8
40	19	23	27	19	23	27	38	44	49	9.6	11.8	14.0

From Romero R and others: *Prenatal diagnosis of congenital anomalies,* Norwalk, Conn, 1988, Appleton and Lange.

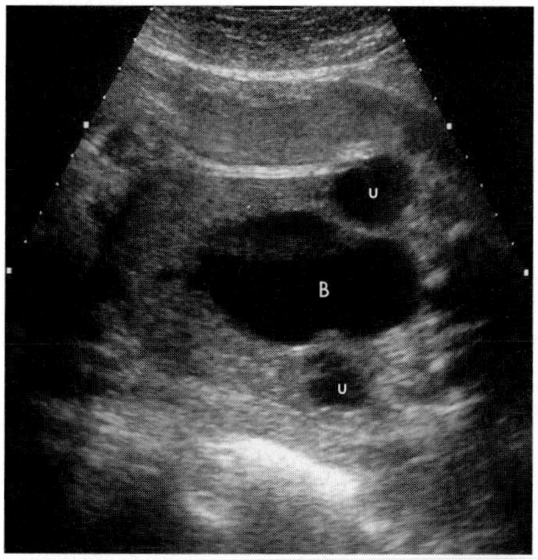

Figure 43-5 Coronal view of the fetal abdomen and pelvis demonstrates a huge urinary bladder *(B)* with extension into the ureters *(u)* in a fetus with bladder outlet obstruction.

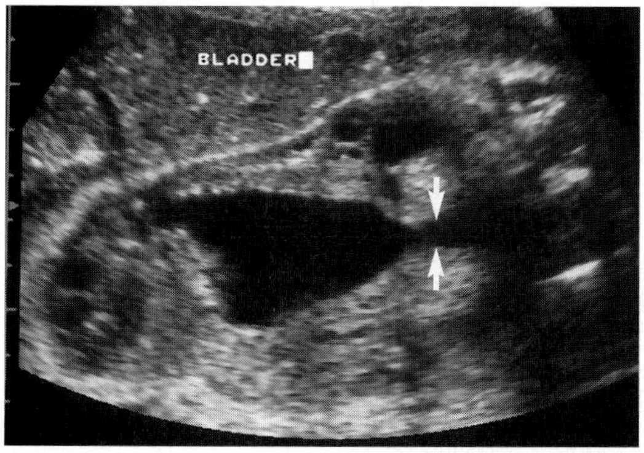

Figure 43-6 Coronal view of the dilated bladder and urethra *(arrows)* in the same patient as seen in Figure 43-5.

BOX 43-2 SONOGRAPHIC FINDINGS IN RENAL AGENESIS

- Severe oligohydramnios after 13 to 15 weeks menstrual age
- Persistent absence of urine in fetal bladder
- Failure to visualize kidneys (use color flow to outline renal arteries)
- Abnormally small thorax

The fetal bladder is normally visualized in all fetuses. If the bladder appears too large, it should be evaluated again at the end of the study (assuming the examination takes at least 45 to 60 minutes) to see if normal emptying has occurred.

Failure to observe the bladder may indicate a severe renal abnormality when accompanied by oligohydramnios. The bladder wall should be thin in a normal fetus. When obstruction occurs at the level of the urethra, the bladder wall becomes hypertrophied. The presence of ureteral jets may be assessed in the fetus to rule out obstruction. Color Doppler is focused over the area of the bladder, near the base, and the presence of ureteral jets streaming into the bladder over time indicates the ureter is not obstructed.

The urethra, like the ureters, is usually unidentifiable in the normal fetus. Dilation of the posterior urethra is highly suspicious for an obstructive process such as posterior urethral valve syndrome (Figure 43-6).

Obstructions of the urinary system may originate anywhere along the urinary tract. The consequences of an obstruction depend on the origin of the blockage. For example, in fetuses with complete posterior urethral valve obstruction, urine is unable to pass through the urethra and into the amniotic fluid. Consequently, urine backs up in the posterior urethra, bladder, ureters, and often extends to the kidneys (hydronephrosis).

ABNORMALITIES OF KIDNEY DEVELOPMENT

A renal malformation may represent a serious or life-threatening condition. Renal agenesis and infantile polycystic kidney disease are fetal conditions incompatible with life. Multicystic dysplastic kidneys, when bilateral, result in immediate neonatal death. Recognition of these fetal disorders is crucial in the antenatal period. The clinician will be able to provide information distinguishing lethal conditions from those with good outcomes.

Renal Agenesis. Renal agenesis means the virtual absence of the kidneys (Box 43-2). Bilateral agenesis occurs in 1 in 3000 to 1 in 10,000 births. The male to female ratio is 2.5:1. In this disease, the kidneys and bladder are not visualized sonographically (Figure 43-7). Amniotic fluid is absent or severely decreased (oligohydramnios) because urine is not produced. The combination of the above findings is highly suggestive of this lethal disorder. It is important to remember that in the early stages of renal agenesis, amniotic fluid may be visible because it is produced from other fetal sources. In renal agenesis the adrenal glands may be large and may mimic the kidneys.

Fetal anomalies found in association with renal agenesis include cardiac defects and musculoskeletal disorders (sirenomelia, absent radius and fibula, anomalies of the digits, sacral agenesis, diaphragmatic hernia and cleft palate). Central nervous system anomalies include hydrocephalus, meningocele, cephalocele, holoprosencephaly, anencephaly, and microcephaly. Gastrointestinal anomalies include duodenal atresia, imperforate anus, tracheoesophageal fistula, malrotation, and omphalocele. The sonographer should understand that most of these malformations will be undetected prenatally because of poor visualization resulting from anhydramnios (complete lack of amniotic fluid).

Ultrasound findings. The lower fetal pelvis should be carefully searched when the kidneys cannot be found in their normal locations. Ectopic kidneys should be considered when the kidneys are not located in a retroperitoneal location.

Unilateral renal agenesis occurs in 1 in 500 to 1 in 1000 births and therefore is more common than bilateral disease. Unilateral agenesis may be associated with uterine anomalies in females and testicular hypoplasia, agenesis, or hypospadias in males. The contralateral kidney may be hy-

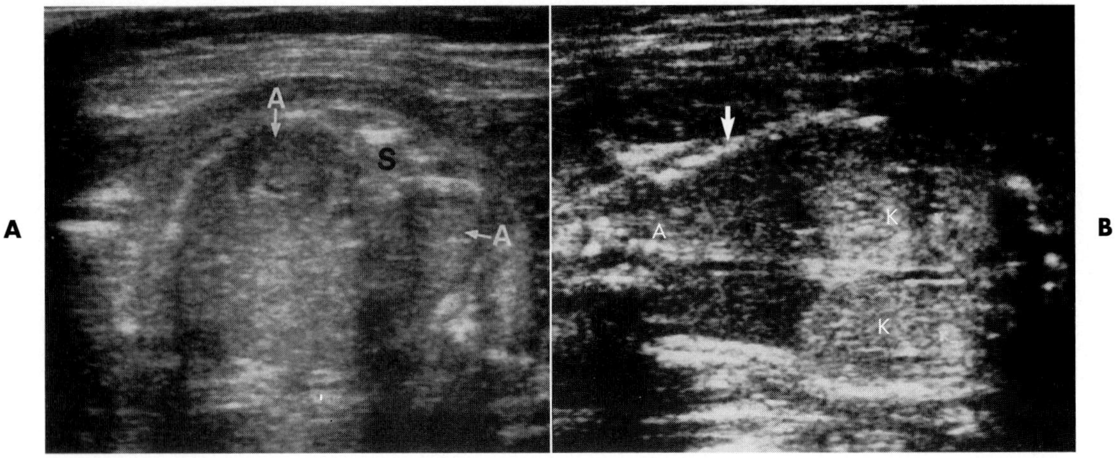

Figure 43-7 **A,** Renal agenesis in a 29-week fetus showing enlarged adrenal glands *(A)* occupying the renal spaces. Oligohydramnios and an absent bladder confirmed the diagnosis. **B,** Infantile polycystic kidney disease shown with enlarged and dense kidneys *(K)*. Note the enhanced transmission of sound through the kidneys because of the dilated cystic tubules. Oligohydramnios and absent bladder were coexisting findings.

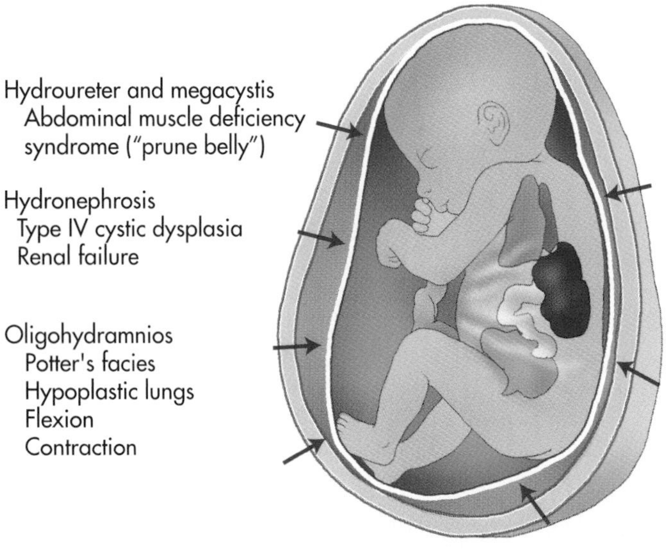

Figure 43-8 Schematic of Potter sequence and the consequences of fetal urethral blockage.

pertrophied to compensate for the absent kidney. With a normal contralateral kidney, adequate amounts of amniotic fluid are produced and chances for survival are excellent.

Amniotic fluid may be normal in a fetus with bilateral renal agenesis when esophageal atresia and tracheoesophageal fistula are present.

Potter's Syndrome. **Potter's syndrome** occurs in 3 in 10,000 births. It is characterized by renal agenesis, oligohydramnios, pulmonary hypoplasia, abnormal facies, and malformed hands and feet (Figure 43-8). The oligohypoplastic lung complex is also seen in other genitourinary malformations such as renal hypoplasia, cystic dysplasia, posterior urethral valves, and prune-belly syndrome. Intrauterine shunting may reduce renal damage and the devastating effects of oligohydramnios.

Potter described the classifications of cystic renal anomalies[16]:

Type 1: Autosomal recessive (AR) infantile polycystic kidney disease
Type 2: Renal agenesis, multicystic kidneys, renal dysplasia
Type 3: Autosomal dominant (AD) polycystic kidney disease
Type 4: Renal dysplasia, obstructive kidney disease

Infantile Polycystic Kidney Disease. Infantile polycystic kidney disease (IPKD) is an autosomal-recessive disorder (25% chance of recurrence) that affects the fetal kidneys and liver. This disease has varying presentations and affects 2 in 100,000 births. Most commonly, abnormal kidneys may be found in association with liver cysts. The most severe forms of IPKD are those found prenatally (Box 43-3).

In the most severe cases of IPKD, renal failure occurs with oligohydramnios and an absent urinary bladder.[17] In some cases the kidneys are so massive that they fill the entire abdomen. In view of the high recurrence rate and dismal prognosis in severe IPKD, recognition of this defect is important. IPKD may occur as part of a genetic syndrome such as Meckel-Gruber syndrome. The intrauterine diagnosis of IPKD should only be considered when the following characteristics are found[17]:

- Family history of IPKD
- Enlarged kidneys on both sides
- Highly echogenic kidney texture
- Significant oligohydramnios
- Inability to identify the fetal bladder

Renal hyperplasia has also been associated with Beckwith-Wiedemann syndrome, along with omphalocele, macroglossia, gigantism, medullary dysplasia, adrenal cytomegaly, pancreatic islet-cell hyperplasia, facial nevus flammeus, and hypoglycemia.[19]

Ultrasound findings. In this disease the collecting tubules of the kidney are microscopically dilated. By ultrasound, individual cysts are not identified; instead the kidneys are massively enlarged because of hundreds of dilated tubules (Figure 43-7). Enlargement of the kidneys may not occur until the 24th week of gestation; therefore serial studies of at-risk fetuses are recommended.[17] Enhanced renal tissue echogenicity is characteristic because of the multiple interfaces created by the dilated cystic tubules.

BOX 43-3 SONOGRAPHIC FINDINGS IN INFANTILE POLYCYSTIC KIDNEY DISEASE

- Progressive renal enlargement
- Echogenic renal parenchyma
- Empty bladder and oligohydramnios

BOX 43-4 SONOGRAPHIC FINDINGS IN ADULT POLYCYSTIC KIDNEY DISEASE

- Large kidneys with hyperechoic parenchyma
- Size may be asymmetric
- Genetic link

Adult Polycystic Kidney Disease. Autosomal-dominant (adult) polycystic kidney disease may be diagnosed in a fetus when there is a family history of polycystic kidneys, liver, or both (Box 43-4). The fetal kidneys appear large and echogenic, and rarely, cysts may be observed prenatally. Amniotic fluid volume is normal. Conversely, visualization of bilateral enlargement of the kidneys may prompt a renal and liver work-up in the parents to exclude this disorder.

Bilateral renal enlargement may be found in association with a syndrome, such as Beckwith-Wiedemann syndrome, in which visceromegaly of many organs is present (Figure 43-9).

Multicystic Dysplastic Kidney Disease. The third nonobstructive renal disease is **multicystic dysplastic kidney disease** (Box 43-5). In this condition, renal tissue is replaced by cysts of varying sizes that are found throughout the kidney (Figures 43-10 and 43-11). Kidney borders are difficult to define because of the distorted renal outline. The affected kidney is nonfunctional. When a multicystic kidney has been identified, a careful search for anomalies of the opposite kidney should be undertaken.

BOX 43-5 SONOGRAPHIC FINDINGS IN ADULT MULTICYSTIC DYSPLASTIC KIDNEY

- Multiple noncommunicating cysts of variable size
- No distinct renal pelvis
- No distinct renal parenchyma
- Renal size may be normal, hypoplastic, or enlarged
- Severe oligohydramnios if bilateral

A

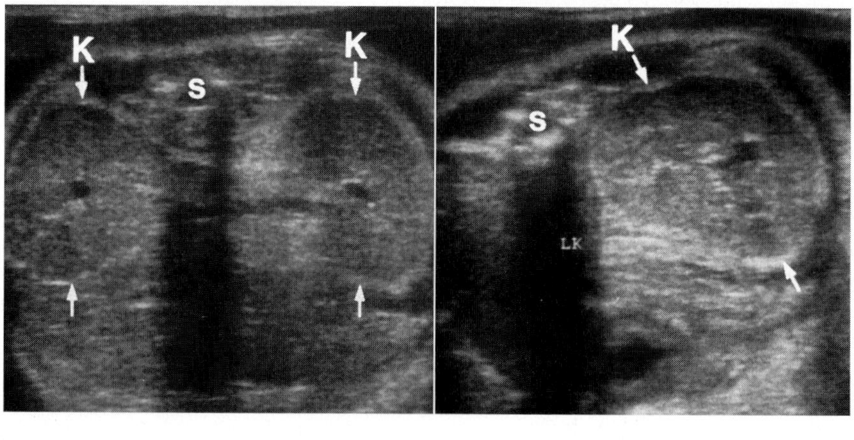

B

Figure 43-9 **A,** Bilateral renal enlargement of the kidneys *(K, arrows)* in a 32-week fetus with Beckwith-Wiedemann syndrome (congenital visceromegaly of organs, which may present with or without an omphalocele). Both kidneys occupy more than half of the abdomen. *s,* Spine. **B,** In the same fetus a sagittal view shows an enlarged left kidney *(K, arrow).*

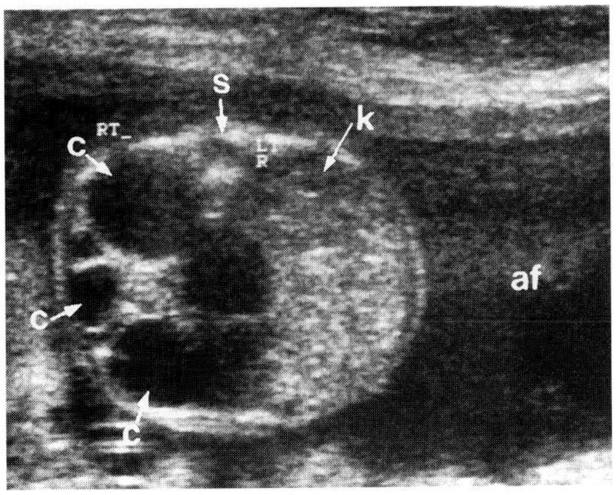

Figure 43-10 Unilateral multicystic kidney *(arrows)* in a 21-week fetus. Note the varying sizes of the cysts *(c)* and the normal contralateral kidney *(k)*. Amniotic fluid *(af)* is normal because of the functioning unaffected kidney. *RT*, Right, *s*, spine.

When both kidneys are found to be multicystic, and oligohydramnios and an absent bladder are expected, a lethal condition exists for the neonate. The prognosis for infants with multicystic kidney disease varies based on the prenatal findings. Figure 43-12 illustrates several presentations of multicystic dysplastic kidney disease. For example, when one kidney is multicystic and the other absent, the infant will not survive. Many syndromes are associated with cysts of the kidneys. The reader is referred to sources in the reference list for a comprehensive listing of associated syndromes.[15]

Associated anomalies include encephalocele suggestive of Meckel-Gruber syndrome in the presence of bilateral renal cystic disease, polydactyly, and severe oligohydramnios. Multicystic kidney disease may also be associated with ureteral atresia.

Ultrasound findings. A multicystic kidney must be distinguished from hydronephrosis and calyceal dilation. Se-

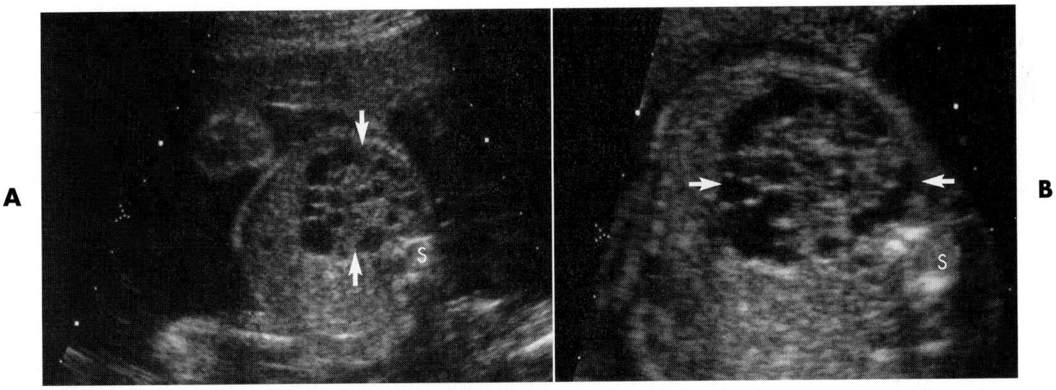

Figure 43-11 **A,** Unilateral dysplastic multicystic kidney *(arrows)* in a 25-week fetus. The contralateral kidney appeared normal with adequate amniotic fluid volume. A single umbilical artery was identified. *S*, Spine. **B,** In the same fetus, a magnified view of the dysplastic kidney *(arrows)*.

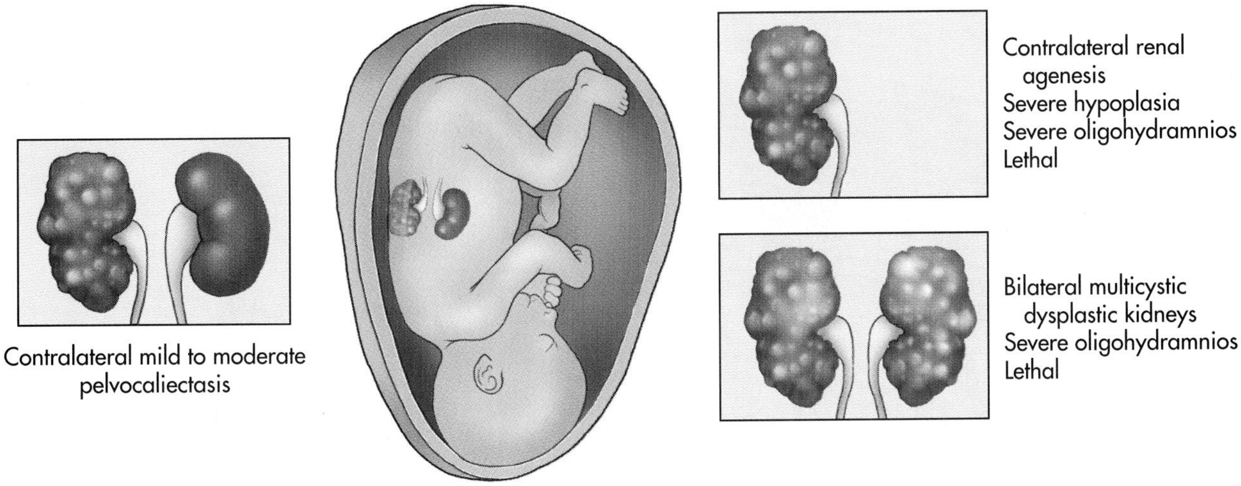

Figure 43-12 Multicystic dysplastic kidney disease may be unilateral, bilateral, or associated with contralateral renal agenesis. Although the affected kidney typically produces very little urine, it may change in size throughout gestation. Because the contralateral kidney is the only potentially functional kidney, it must be examined carefully.

rial scans are often requested to follow the function of the normal kidney. Hydronephrosis of the functioning kidney may warrant early delivery. Remember when the fetal bladder is visualized and the amount of amniotic fluid is normal, renal function of the unaffected kidney is present. When oligohydramnios is found, pursuit of other renal malformations should ensue.

OBSTRUCTIVE URINARY TRACT ABNORMALITIES

The urinary tract may be obstructed at the junction of the ureter entering the renal pelvis **(ureteropelvic junction)** or at the junction of the ureter where it enters the bladder **(ureterovesical junction)** or at the level of the urethra **(megacystis).**

Hydronephrosis. Fetal hydronephrosis is the most common fetal anomaly. The sonographic appearance of urinary tract obstruction varies depending on the site and extent of blockage (Box 43-6). Dilation of the renal pelvis (hydronephrosis) occurs in response to a blockage of urine at some junction in the urinary system. This blocked urine is unable to pass the obstruction. Urine is continually produced and will back up into the kidney. Hydronephrosis commonly occurs when there is an obstruction in the ureter, bladder, or urethra. Hydronephrosis is generally the end result of an obstruction at a lower level in the urinary tract.

Ultrasound findings. The ultrasound appearance of hydronephrosis varies according to the severity of the underlying obstruction. The dilated renal pelvis, which often communicates with the calyces (caliectasis), is centrally located and distended with urine (Figure 43-13). The remaining renal tissue may be identified in all but the most severe cases of hydronephrosis.

BOX 43-6 SONOGRAPHIC FINDINGS IN HYDRONEPHROSIS

- Anteroposterior renal pelvic diameter greater than 5 to 10 mm
- Rim of renal parenchyma preserved
- Calyceal distention with central pelvis communication

Renal dysplasia often occurs and represents cystic changes within the renal tissue (Figure 43-14). Several obstructive patterns may be observed. The sonographic team should attempt to define the severity of the cystic changes affecting the kidney.

Fetal hydronephrosis may occur as a unilateral or bilateral process. Unilateral renal hydronephrosis commonly results from an obstruction at the junction of the renal pelvis and the ureter. This is called a **ureteropelvic junction obstruction.**

Ureteropelvic junction. Ureteropelvic junction obstruction is the most common reason for hydronephrosis in the neonate. Only half of these disorders are found during early childhood; therefore early prenatal detection may improve long-term renal function. The causes of ureteropelvic junction obstructions are abnormal bends or kinks in the ureter, adhesions, abnormal valves in the ureter, abnormal outlet shape at the ureteropelvic junction, or absence of the longitudinal muscle that is imperative to the normal excretion of urine from the kidney.[15]

Uteropelvic junction obstruction is usually a unilateral defect, and amniotic fluid remains normal because of the normal contralateral kidney. Bilateral ureteropelvic junction obstruction is uncommon. Anomalies associated with this disorder may involve the presence of a urinoma, which presents as a large cyst that is in contact with the spine (Figure 43-15). Urinary ascites may also be a complicating feature of ureteropelvic junction obstruction.

Ultrasound findings. Sonographically, there is a collection of urine located medially within the renal pelvis that communicates with the calyces (caliectasis) (Figures 43-16 and 43-17). The ureter, bladder, and amniotic fluid are usually normal. Ureteropelvic junction obstruction may be severe.

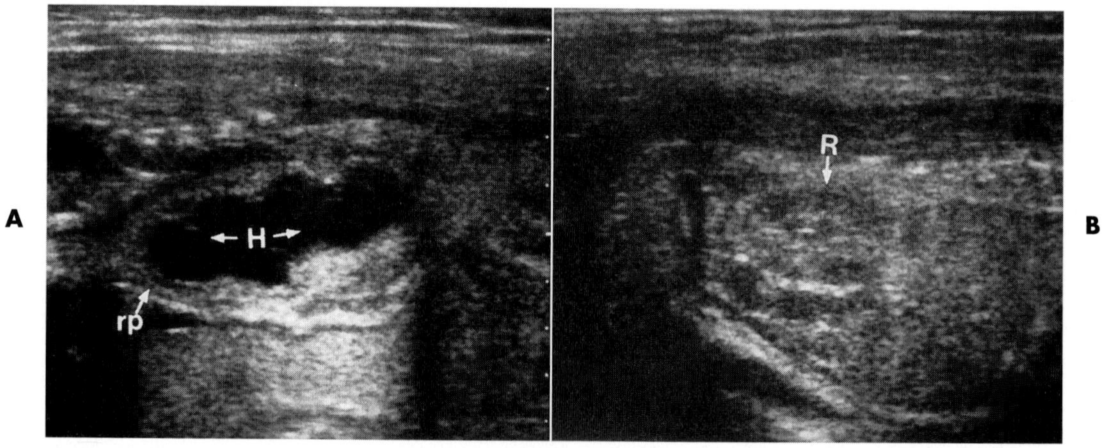

Figure 43-13 **A,** Unilateral ureteropelvic junction obstruction showing collection of urine within the renal pelvis communicating with the renal calyces (hydronephrosis *[H]*). It is important to study the remaining renal parenchyma *(rp)* for pathologic changes. **B,** In the same fetus the contralateral kidney is normal. *R,* Renal architecture.

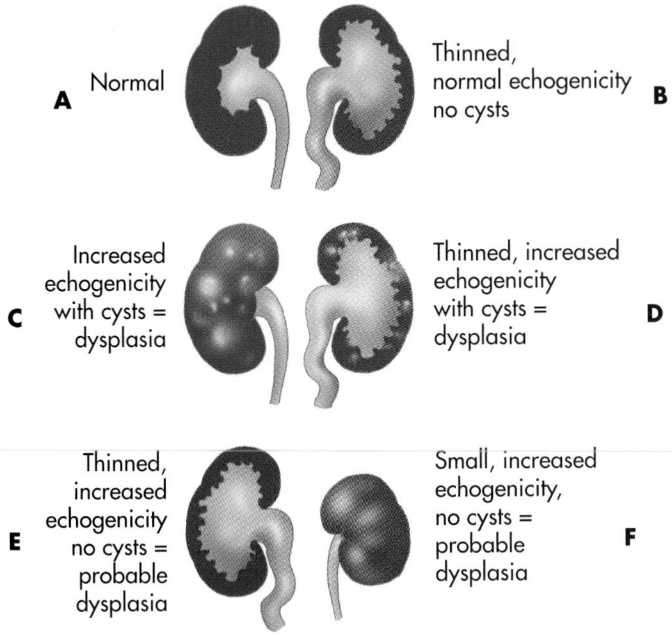

Figure 43-14 Renal parenchymal responses to obstruction. **A,** In distal urinary tract obstruction without reflux the kidney may remain normal. **B,** Pyelocaliectasis may thin the renal parenchyma. **C,** Cystic dysplasia may occur with renal cysts and fibrosis (increased echogenicity) and cease to function (lack of pyelocaliectasis). **D,** Cystic dysplasia may occur with persistent pyelocaliectasis. **E,** Increased renal echogenicity with visible cysts suggests but is not diagnostic of dysplasia. **F,** A small, echogenic kidney without pyelocaliectasis is also suggestive but not diagnostic of dysplasia.

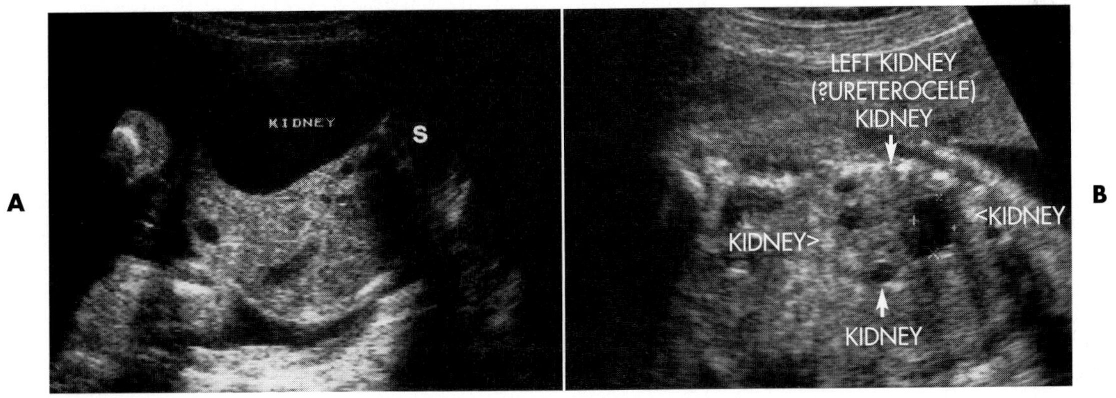

Figure 43-15 **A,** Massively dilated renal pelvis *(kidney)* shown in a transverse plane in a 28-week fetus. *S,* Spine. **B,** In the same fetus at 30 weeks of gestation, the renal cyst ruptured, with only a small, upper-pole cyst *(calipers)* evident. A urinoma was suspected.

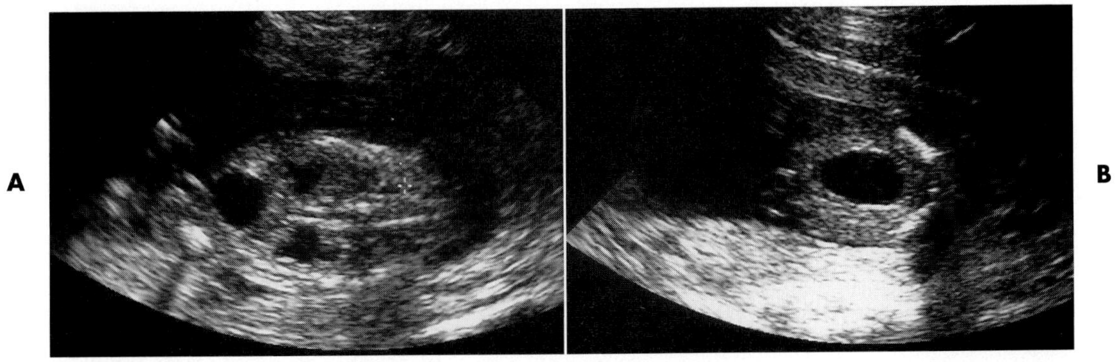

Figure 43-16 **A,** Coronal scan of a 20-week fetus with moderate hydronephrosis and a prominent bladder. **B,** The bladder remained dilated after 45 minutes, suggesting an outlet obstruction.

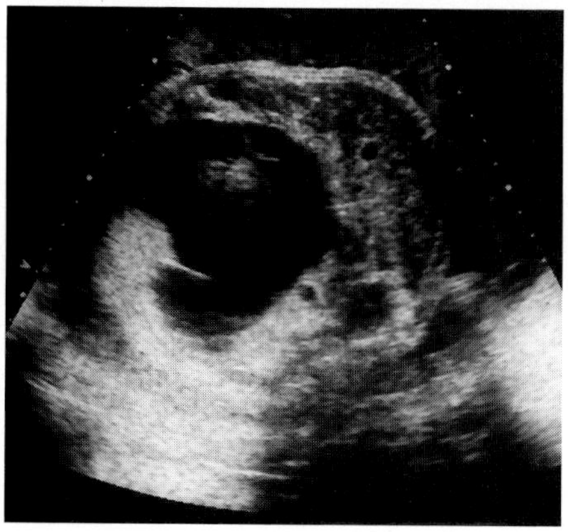

Figure 43-17 Transverse image of a fetal kidney that has severe unilateral hydronephrosis. The renal parenchyma is no longer visible.

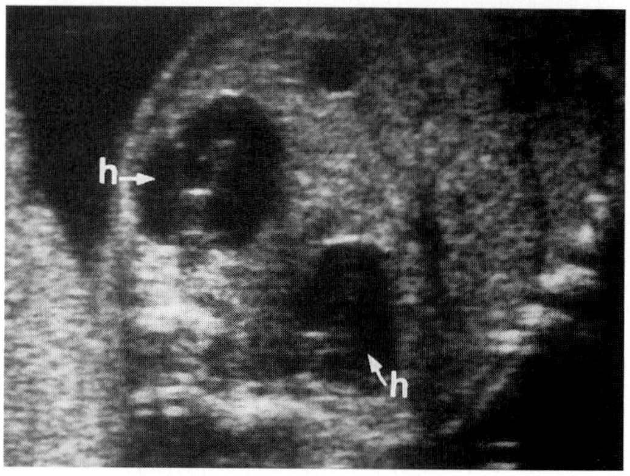

Figure 43-18 Bilateral megaureters (hydroureters) *(h)* noted in an axial pelvic view. Partial blockage to the posterior urethra was found after birth.

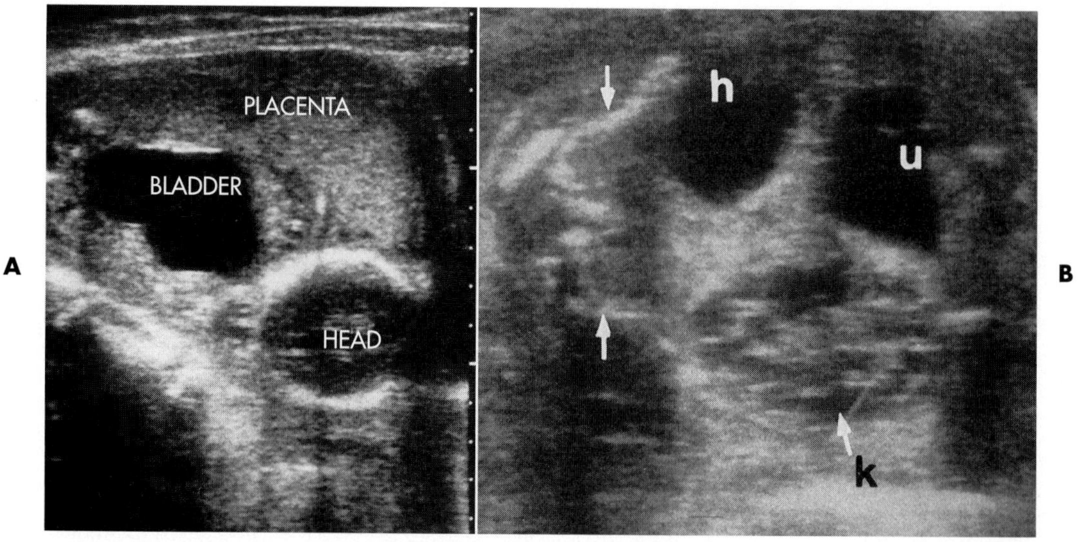

Figure 43-19 **A,** Posterior urethral valve syndrome in a 17-week fetus showing abnormally distended bladder with a key-hole urethra. Note the significant lack of amniotic fluid. **B,** In the same fetus at 21 weeks of gestation a small thoracic cavity *(arrows),* hydronephrosis *(h),* hydroureter *(u),* and enlargement and mild hydronephrosis of the contralateral kidney *(k)* are noted.

Ureterovesical Junction Obstruction. Ureterovesical junction obstruction commonly presents with dilation of the ureter (megaureter). Megaureter may result from a primary ureteral defect (stenotic ureteral valves or fibrosis) or occur secondary to obstruction at another level (causing reflux or backward flow of urine) (Figure 43-18).

Ultrasound findings. Other defects, such as duplication of the renal collecting system, are common and may be diagnosed prenatally. When a dilated upper renal pole is observed with a normal lower pole, an obstructed duplicated collecting system may be indicated. This defect may result from an ectopic ureterocele within the bladder causing obstruction of the upper pole of the kidney.

Posterior Urethral Valves. Posterior urethral valve obstruction results in hydronephrosis, hydroureters, or dilation of the bladder and posterior urethra (Figures 43-19 and 43-20). Cystic dysplasia and poor renal function are suggested when sodium, chloride, and osmolality are unusually elevated.[15]

Ultrasound findings. This entity occurs only in male fetuses and is manifested by the presence of a valve(s) in the posterior urethra. As a result, urine is unable to pass through the urethra and into the amniotic fluid. This obstruction causes a back-up of urine in the bladder, ureter and, in the most severe cases, the kidneys. Severe oligohydramnios is a classic finding in the complete obstruction form (Box 43-7).

When these sonographic signs occur in the female fetus, abnormalities of the sacrum (caudal regression anomalies) and megacystis-microcolon intestinal hypoperistalsis syndrome should be considered.

Fetal renal function may be assessed by aspirating urine from an obstructed bladder (Figures 43-21 and 43-22).

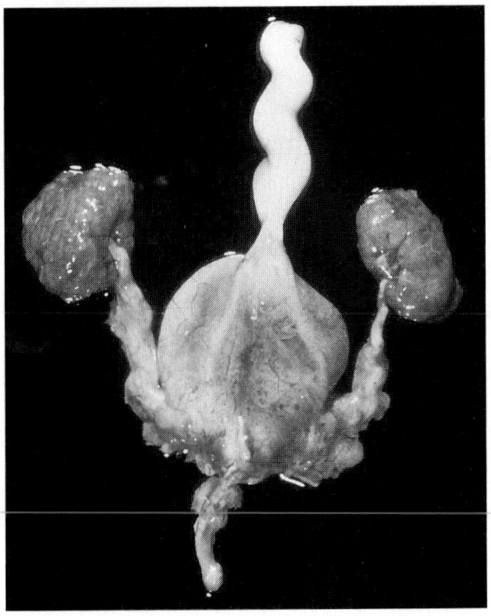

Figure 43-20 Pathologic specimen of obstructed urinary tract showing bladder enlargement, hydroureters, and bilateral hydronephrosis in posterior urethral valve syndrome.

BOX 43-7 SONOGRAPHIC FINDINGS OF POSTERIOR URETHRAL VALVE OBSTRUCTION

- Dilated bladder (thickening of the bladder wall)
- Dilated posterior urethra (keyhole appearance)
- Oligohydramnios
- Hydroureters
- Hydronephrosis and dysplasia
- Fetal ascites (some cases)
- Distension of fetal abdomen (urethral obstruction malformation complex/prune-belly syndrome)
- Male fetus

From Hobbins JC and others: *Am J Ostet Gynecol* 148:868, 1984.

A

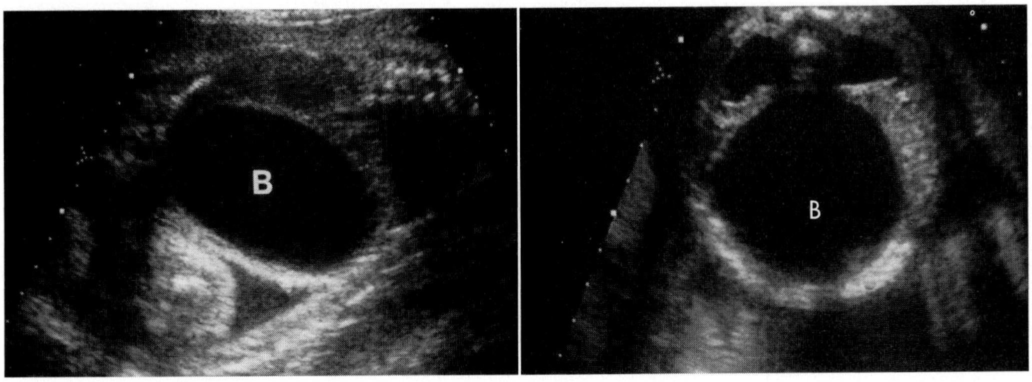

B

Figure 43-21 Massively enlarged bladder *(B)* in a 28-week fetus in both sagittal **(A)** and transverse **(B)** views. Bilateral hydronephrosis (*right* and *left*) is evident. Amniotic fluid volume was increased.

A

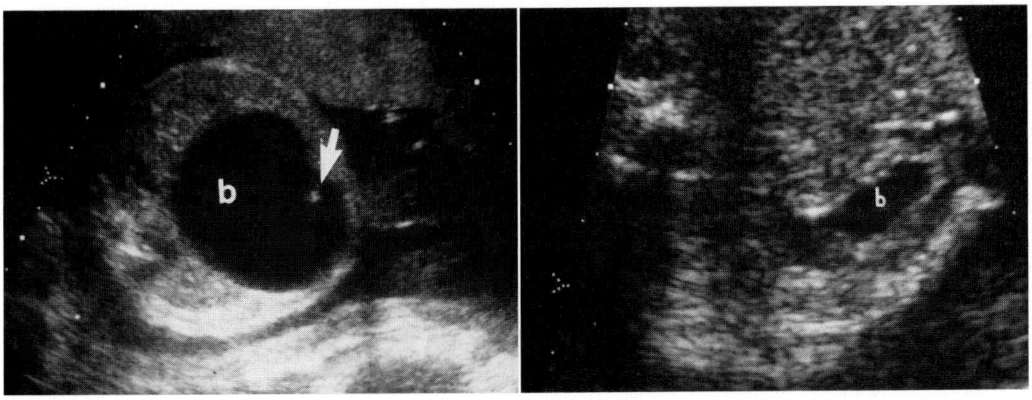

B

Figure 43-22 **A,** In the fetus shown in Figure 43-21, bladder aspiration was performed to assess kidney function. Note the needle *(arrow)* within the bladder *(b)*. **B,** After urine aspiration, decompression of the bladder *(b)* occurred. Note the thickened bladder wall. Laboratory analysis of osmolality, sodium, potassium, and chloride indicated favorable renal function. Bilateral reflux was diagnosed after birth.

Intermittent posterior urethral valve obstruction may occur with a normal amount of amniotic fluid (Figs. 43-23 and 43-24). Diminishing fluid volume and increased hydronephrosis may prompt early delivery.

Prune-Belly Syndrome. Prune-belly syndrome may be called the urethral obstruction malformation complex. The condition consists of cryptorchidism, agenesis of abdominal wall muscle, megaureters, and bladder outlet obstruction caused by urethral anomalies such as atresia, stenotic valves, or diverticulum.

Ultrasound findings. Sonographic findings in prune-belly syndrome include oligohydramnios, mild to severe bilateral hydronephrosis, fetal ascites, and hypoplastic lungs. The abdomen is extremely distended compared with the small thoracic cavity. The dilated ureters and bladder appear as numerous cystic lesions within the distended abdominal cavity.

Fetal Surgery in Obstructive Uropathy. The prognosis of posterior urethral valve syndrome is invariably fatal, but in selected fetuses with documented normal renal function, placement of an indwelling bladder shunt to relieve the obstruction has improved chances for survival in some cases (Figure 43-25).[11] This shunt drains the blocked urine into the amniotic fluid, allowing the fetal lungs to develop. When the urinary tract is completely blocked, severe oligohydramnios and the Potter sequence occur.[5]

Other Urinary Anomalies. Rare disorders, such as **urethral atresia,** may cause a massively dilated bladder (prune belly) (Figures 43-26 and 43-27). Duplication of the renal complexes and ectopic ureteroceles may be detected. Dilation of the ureters may occur as isolated lesions (primary megaureters), resulting from atresia of the distal ureter.[6] The disorders are generally associated with adequate to increased amounts of amniotic fluid and a normal bladder. Infre-

A

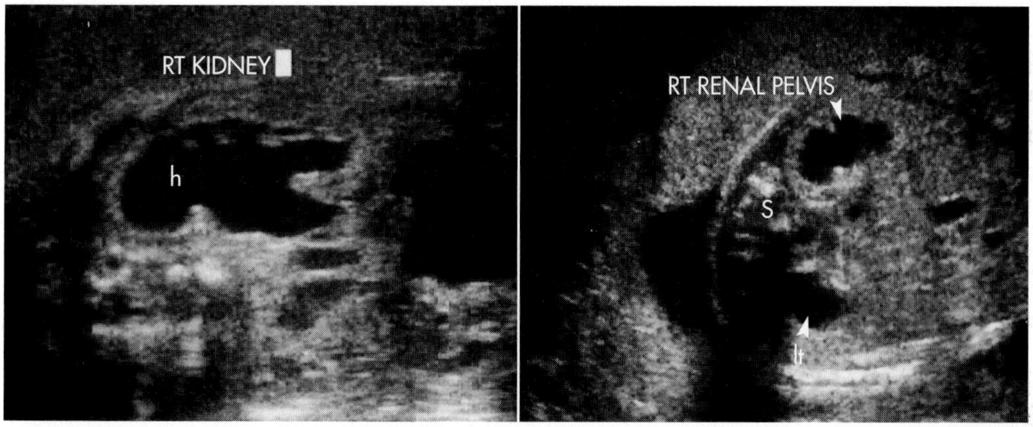

B

Figure 43-23 Bilateral posterior urethral valve syndrome shown in a 24-week fetus with severe hydronephrosis *(h)* of the right kidney in a male fetus in both sagittal **(A)** and transverse **(B)** views. *lt,* Left kidney; *S,* spine.

A

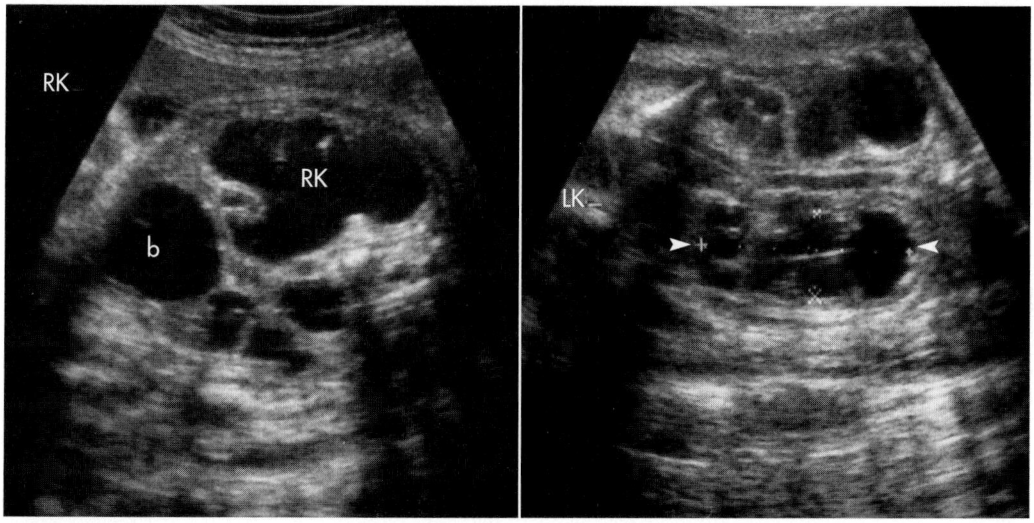

B

Figure 43-24 In the fetus shown in Figure 43-23 the hydronephrotic right kidney *(RK)* is shown in **A** and the opposite kidney is shown in a coronal view **(B),** with hydronephrosis *(LK).* Amniotic fluid volume was normal. At 32 weeks of gestation, worsening hydronephrosis prompted early delivery. After birth, the right kidney did not function and the left kidney had reasonable function. The child, however, awaits a renal implant. *b,* Bladder.

quently, renal pelvis hydronephrosis may occur. The antenatal diagnosis of crossed renal ectopia (both kidneys fused on one side) has been reported.[9] Failure to identify a kidney should prompt the sonographer to check for this condition, as well as pelvic kidneys (located ectopically in the pelvis), unilateral renal agenesis, or horseshoe kidneys. Horseshoe kidneys are normal in location (one on each side).

Tumors of the fetal kidney are rare.[7] Masses in the kidney should be suspected when the contour of the kidney is distorted or replaced by a mass and the pelviocalyceal echoes are absent.

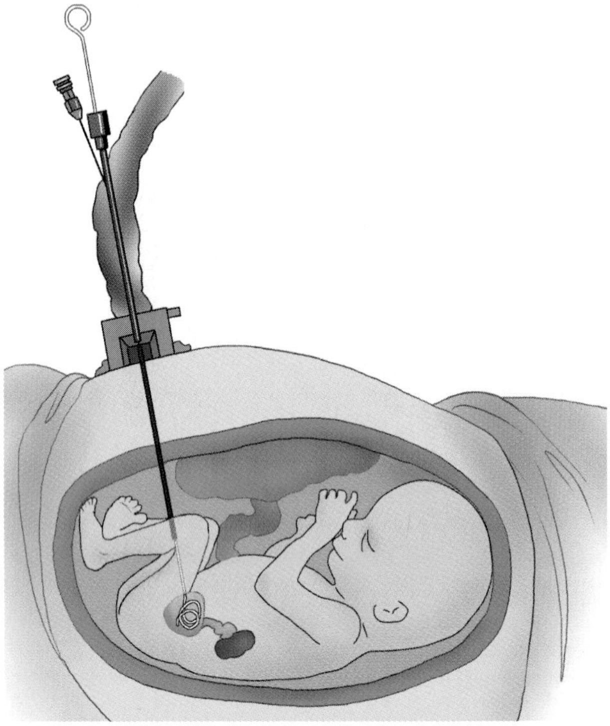

Figure 43-25 Schematic showing initial steps in a bladder shunt procedure.

The most common renal tumor is a mesoblastic nephroma that is a hamartoma (Figure 43-28). A hamartoma is a collection of oddly arranged tissue indigenous to the area. Mesoblastic nephroma are sonographically observed as large, single, solid masses originating from the kidney. Hydramnios is a typical manifestation. The opposite kidney is usually normal and therefore, with surgical removal of the affected kidney, prognosis is excellent.

Ultrasound findings. An adrenal tumor, neuroblastoma, may be observed prenatally above the kidney. These tumors have varying echo patterns and are associated with liver and placental metastasis. The prenatal diagnosis of nephroblastomatosis (premalignant precursor of Wilms' tumor) has been reported.[2] Bilateral renal enlargement with calcifications with shadowing was observed.

THE GENITAL SYSTEM

The sex of the fetus is determined at the time of fertilization; however, there is no morphologic indication of gender until the 7th week of development (Figure 43-29). Early embryogenesis shows similar development in both sexes. The gonads are derived from the gonadal ridges and are the first parts of the genital system to undergo development. As the genital ridge enlarges and frees itself from the mesonephros by developing a mesentery, the male ridge becomes the mesorchium and the female the mesovarium. At the same time, the coelomic epithelium that covers the primitive gonads proliferates and forms the cords of cells, called primary sex cords, that grow into the mesenchyme of the developing gonads. The primordial germ cells originate in the wall of the yolk sac and migrate into the embryo and enter the primary sex cords to give rise to the ova and sperm.

DEVELOPMENT OF THE EXTERNAL GENITALIA

Although the early development of the external genitalia is similar for both sexes, distinguishing sexual characteristics begin during the 9th week and external genital organs are fully differentiated by the 12th week of gestation (Figure 43-30).

A

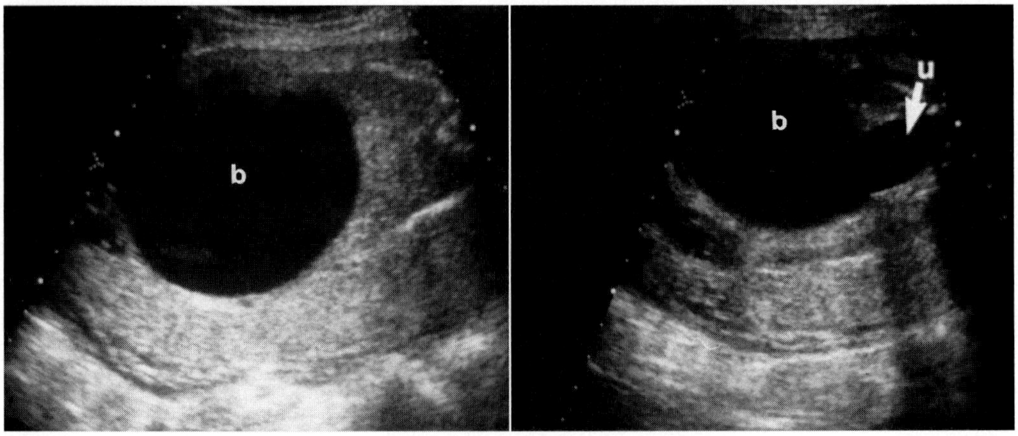

B

Figure 43-26 **A,** Urethral atresia shown with massively dilated bladder *(b)* in a 24-week fetus. **B,** In the same fetus, urethral dilation *(u)* is evident at a lower level. *b,* Bladder.

A

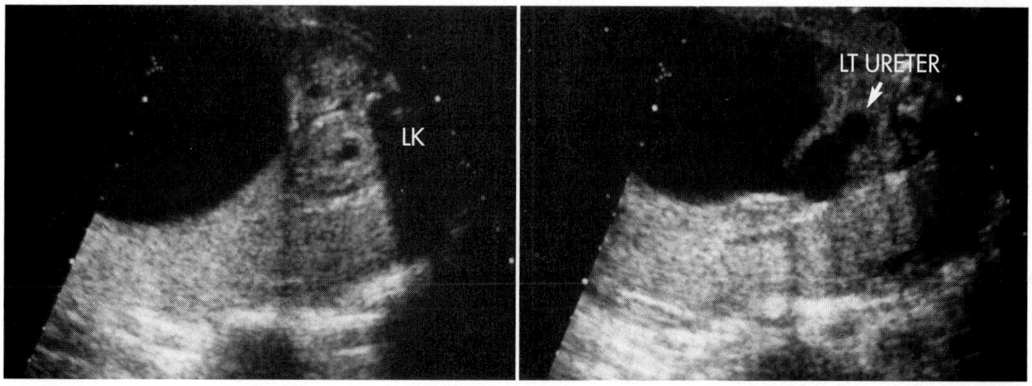

B

Figure 43-27 **A,** In the fetus shown in Figure 43-26, transverse views reveal a normal-appearing left kidney *(LK)*. **B,** In the same fetus a left unilateral hydroureter is shown. Severe oligohydramnios was found. Spontaneous labor occurred at 32 weeks of gestation and urethral atresia was confirmed. The infant died shortly after birth.

A

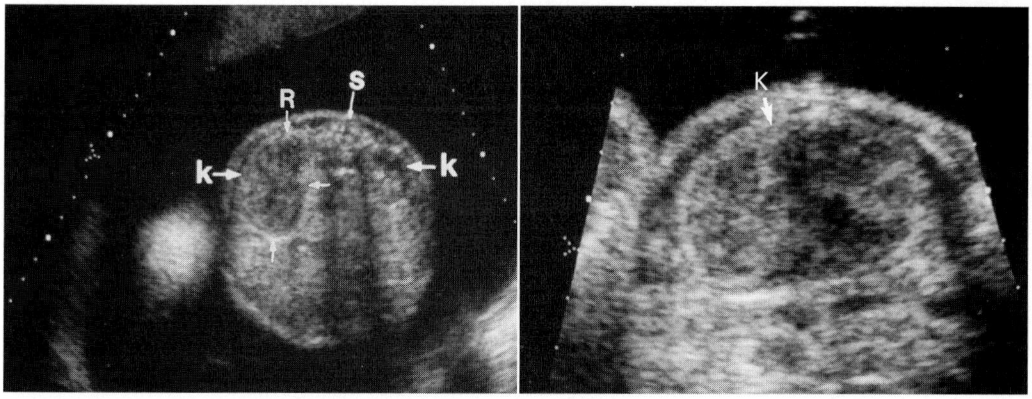

B

Figure 43-28 **A,** Mesoblastic nephroma in a 32-week fetus showing obvious enlargement of the right kidney *(k, arrows) (R)* compared with the left kidney *(k)*. Hydramnios was observed. *S,* Spine. **B,** In the same fetus the encapsulated and solid appearance of the nephroma *(K)* was observed. The nephroma was removed within a few days after birth.

A

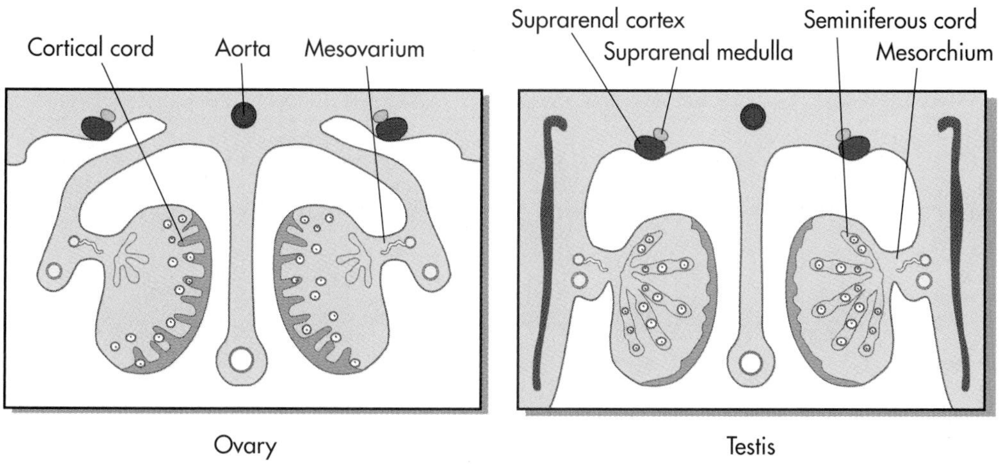

B

Figure 43-29 Development of the female **(A)** and male **(B)** gender at 7 weeks.

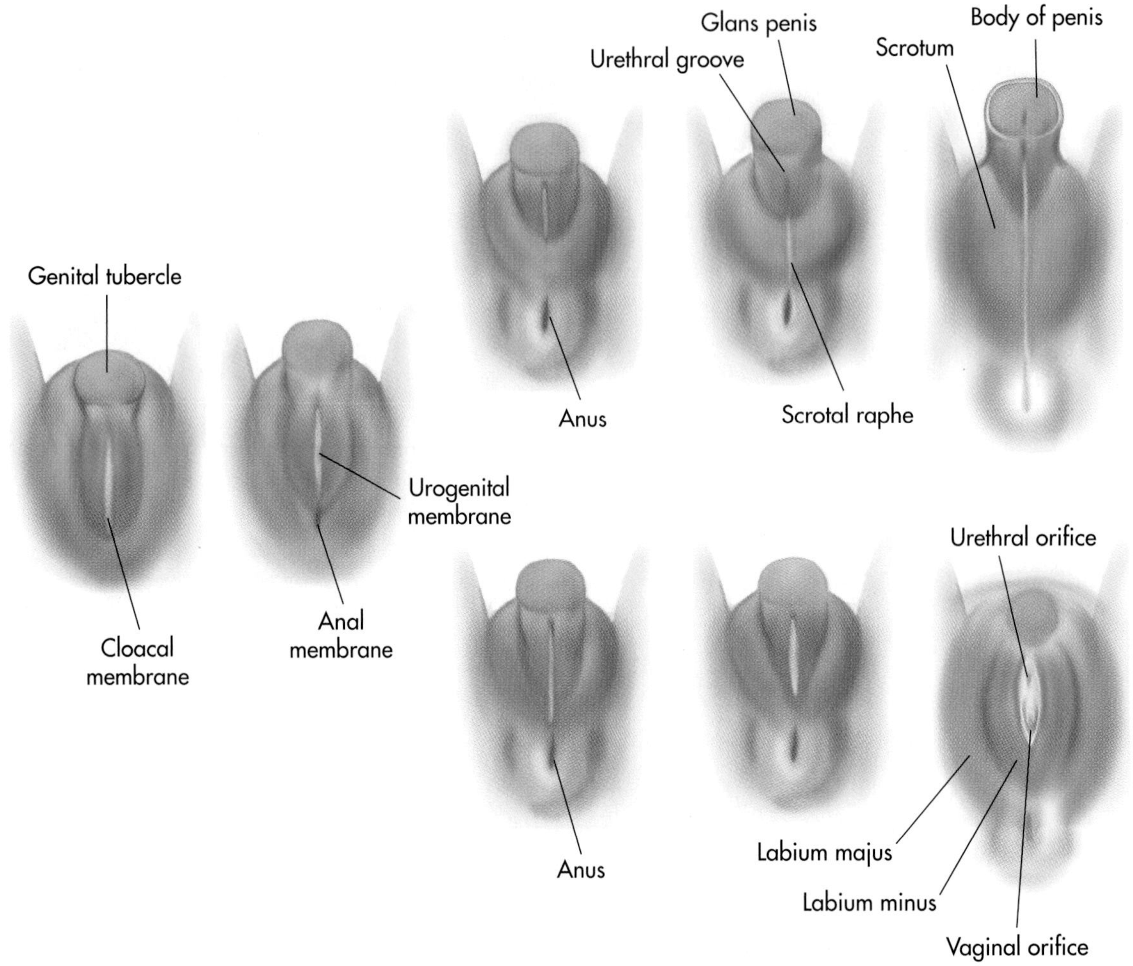

Figure 43-30 Sexual characteristics begin during the 9th week and are fully differentiated by the 12th week.

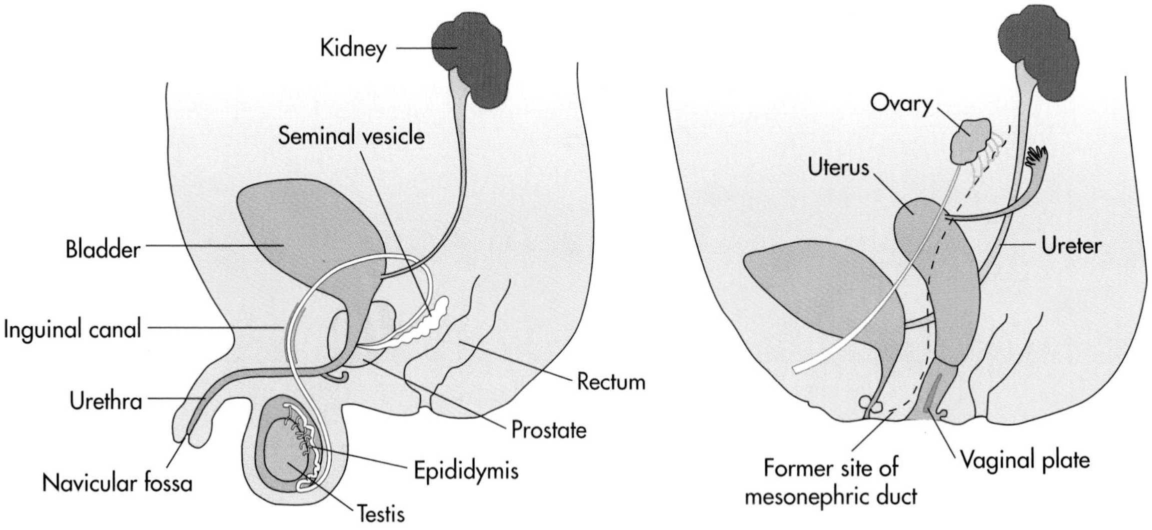

Figure 43-31 Hormonal changes cause further development of the male and female reproductive systems.

In the 4th week, a genital tubercle develops at the cranial end of the cloacal membrane. Labioscrotal swellings and urogenital folds develop on either side of this membrane. The genital tubercle elongates to form a phallus, which is similar in both sexes.

Development of the Male External Genitalia. The fetal testes produce androgens that cause the masculinization of the external genitalia. The phallus elongates to form the penis. The urogenital folds fuse on the ventral surface of the penis to form the spongy urethra (Figure 43-31). The labioscrotal swellings grow toward the median plane and fuse to form the scrotum. The line of fusion of the labioscrotal folds is called the scrotal raphe.

Development of the Female External Genitalia. Both the urethra and vagina open into the urogenital sinus, the vestibule of the vagina. The urogenital folds become the labia minora, the labioscrotal swellings become the labia majora, and the phallus becomes the clitoris.

CONGENITAL MALFORMATIONS OF THE GENITAL SYSTEM

Although congenital malformations of the genital organs are rare, the sonographic team may be requested to determine the gender of the fetus when a gender-linked disorder is considered (i.e., hemophilia or aqueductal stenosis).[12] Because these conditions usually occur in male fetuses, identification of male genitalia aids in counseling and diagnostic testing (Figure 43-32). Likewise, the demonstration of abnormal fetal genitalia may be indicative of syndromes of the endocrine and genital systems (Figure 43-33).[13]

HYPOSPADIAS

Incomplete fusion of the urogenital folds may cause abnormal openings of the urethra along the ventral aspect of the penis. This disorder occurs in one in every 300 infants. The abnormal urethral orifice may be near the glans penis (*glandular hypospadias*). The other type of hypospadias is

A

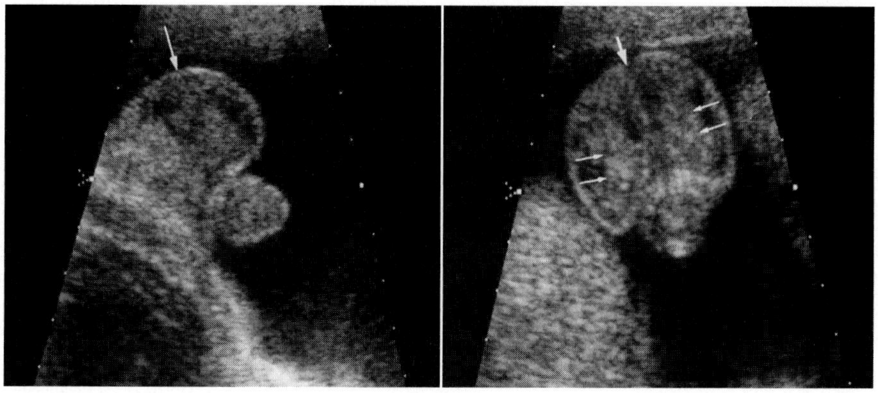

B

Figure 43-32 **A,** Male genitalia in a 40-week fetus showing the scrotum *(arrow)* and phallus. **B,** Coronal view of the male genitalia outlining descended testicles *(double arrows)* within the scrotum. Note the scrotal septum *(thick arrow)* and phallus.

A

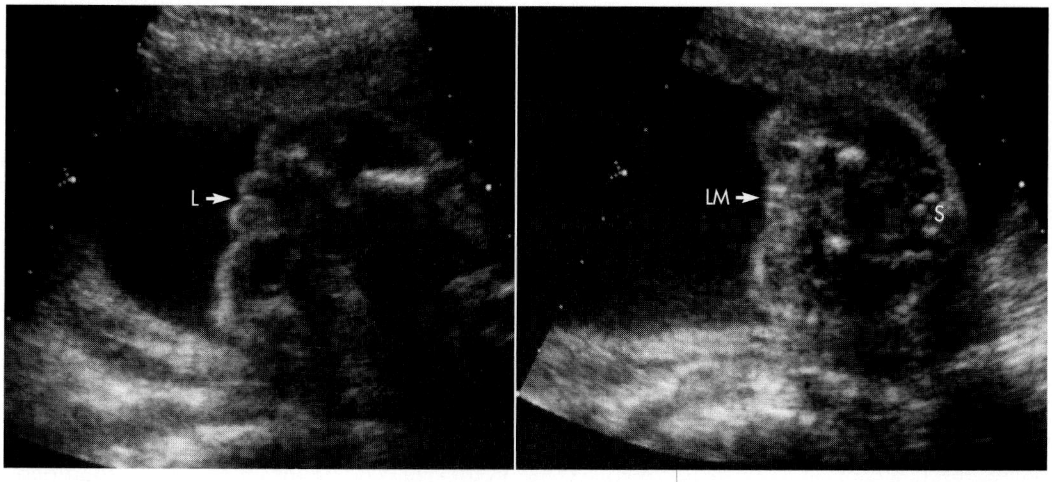

B

Figure 43-33 **A,** Female genitalia viewed axially in a 23-week fetus showing the typical appearance of the labia majora *(L)*. **B,** In the same fetus the labia minora *(LM)* are represented as linear structures between the labia majora.

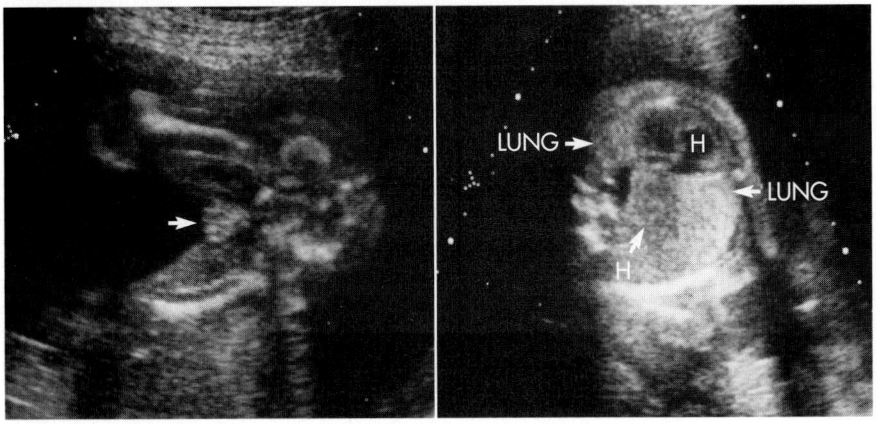

Figure 43-34 **A,** Ambiguous genitalia in a fetus with Simpson-Golabi-Behmel syndrome. Labia *(arrow)* were observed in this fetus with a male karyotype. Other multiple anomalies included an umbilical hernia, hydronephrosis, a 12-mm nuchal fold, and a right diaphragmatic hernia (shown in **B**). *H,* Heart.

called *penile hypospadias.* This disorder results from defective closure of the urogenital folds causing the urethra to open on the ventral surface of the body of the penis.

Malformations of the Uterus and Vagina

The formation of the uterus is dependent on the fusion of two paramesonephric ducts (mullerian ducts). If this fusion is incomplete, various forms of duplication of the uterus and/or vagina may occur.[14] Complete failure of the fusion will give rise to a duplication of the entire female genital tract, **uterus didelphys** (double uterus and double vagina). Duplication of the uterus **(bicornuate uterus)** with one vagina may also occur. If only one paramesonephric duct develops, a **unicornuate uterus** (single uterine tube and horn) is formed. (See Chapter 46.)

Hydrocele

Hydrocele occurs in the male fetus and is seen as an accumulation of serous fluid surrounding the testicle resulting from a communication with the peritoneal cavity.[13] Lesions may occur as unilateral or bilateral and are generally benign.

Descent of the Gonads

The gonads eventually descend from the abdomen to the pelvis. While this occurs a diverticulum of the peritoneum, the processus vaginalis, protrudes through the anterior abdominal wall to form the primordium of the inguinal canal. The processus vaginalis is attached to a ligament that extends from the caudal pole of the gonad to the labioscrotal swelling.

In the male, the testes remain near the deep inguinal rings until the 28th week. They descend through the inguinal canals and enter the scrotum before birth. Failure to complete this descent results in undescended testes, **cryptorchidism.** The distal part of the processes vaginalis persists as the tunica vaginalis of the testis.

In the female, the ligament attaches to the uterus to form the ovarium ligament and the round ligament. The processus vaginalis completely obliterates.

Ambiguous Genitalia

This condition occurs when errors are made determining male or female sexuality, **hermaphroditism.** True hermaphroditism is a rare condition in which both ovarian and testicular tissues are present. The internal and external genitalia are variable. Most fetuses will have a normal karyotype, but some are mosaics (46,XX/46,XY). The sonographer must be careful diagnosing ambiguous genitalia because penile and clitoral size may vary in the normal fetus. Determination of fetal gender may be critical in establishing a correct diagnosis (Figure 43-34).[15]

Female Pseudohermaphrodites. The female fetus with pseudohermaphroditism has a 46,XX karyotype. The most common cause is congenital virilizing adrenal hyperplasia that causes masculinization of the external genitalia (enlarged clitoris, abnormalities of the urogenital sinus, and partial fusion of the labia majora).

Male Pseudohermaphrodites. The male fetus with pseudohermaphroditism has testes and a 46,XY karyotype. There is variable external and internal genitalia depending on the development of the penis and genital ducts.

Other Pelvic Masses

Hydrometrocolpos. Hydrometrocolpos is a collection of fluid in the vagina and uterus. Hydrometrocolpos in conjunction with a double uterus and septated vagina (vagina divided by a septum into two components) has been described.[18] The fluid collection may be so large that it extends into the abdominal cavity or may cause compression of the ureters and hydronephrosis of the kidneys.

Ultrasound findings. On ultrasound examination hydrometrocolpos appears as a hypoechoic "cysticlike" mass posterior to the bladder in the area of the uterus. These masses may be predominantly cystic, may contain midlevel echoes, or may have fluid-debris levels.[18] Echoes within these masses may result from mucous secretions.

Ovarian Cyst. An ovarian cyst may also occur in the female fetus. The ovarian mass results from maternal hormonal stimulation and is usually benign. Differential considerations would include a mesenteric cyst, urachal cyst or an enteric duplication.

Ultrasound findings. The ovarian cyst often appears multiseptated and bilateral. The mass may twist on itself and may lead to torsion, rupture, or intestinal obstruction.

ACKNOWLEDGMENT

The author recognizes the previous contribution from the fourth edition contribution of Kara Mayden Argo to this chapter.

REVIEW QUESTIONS

1. What is Bowman's capsule?
2. How does a pelvic kidney form?
3. Describe the congenital malformations of the kidneys.
4. What is exstrophy of the bladder?
5. Discuss the difference between pyelectasis and calyectasis.
6. What are the sonographic characteristics of:
   a. bilateral and unilateral renal agenesis?
   b. infantile and adult dominant polycystic kidney disease?
   c. multicystic kidney disease?
7. What are the effects of severe obstruction on the urinary tract?
8. Describe the difference between ureteropelvic, ureterovesical, and posterior urethral valve obstruction.
9. What is the Potter sequence?
10. What are the common abnormalities of the genitalia?
11. Discuss the sonographic findings in male versus female genitalia.

REFERENCES

1. Allen KS and others: Effects of maternal hydration on fetal renal pyelectasis, *Radiology* 163:807, 1987.
2. Ambrosino MM and others: Prenatal diagnosis of nephroblastomatosis in two siblings, *J Ultrasound Med* 9:49, 1990.
3. Arger PH and others: Routine fetal genitourinary tract screening, *Radiology* 156:485, 1985.
4. Babcook CJ and others: Effect of maternal hydration on mild fetal pyelectasis *J Ultrasound Med* 17:539, 1998.
5. Berkowitz RL and others: Fetal urinary tract obstruction: what is the role of surgical intervention in utero? *Am J Obstet Gynecol* 144:367, 1982.
6. Dunn V, Glasier CM: Ultrasonographic antenatal demonstration of primary megaureters, *J Ultrasound Med* 4:101, 1985.
7. Ehman RL, Nicholson SF, Machin GA: Prenatal sonographic detection of congenital mesoblastic nephroma in a monozygotic twin pregnancy, *J Ultrasound Med* 2:555, 1983.
8. Golbus MS and others: In utero treatment of urinary tract obstruction, *Am J Obstet Gynecol* 142:383, 1982.
9. Greenblatt AM and others: In utero diagnosis of crossed renal ectopia using high-resolution real-time ultrasound, *J Ultrasound Med* 4:105, 1985.
10. Grignon A and others: Urinary tract dilatation in utero: classification and clinical applications, *Radiology* 160:645, 1986.
11. Harrison MR, Golbus MS, Filly RA: Congenital hydronephrosis. In Harrison MR, Golbus MS, Filly RA, editors: *The unborn patient: prenatal diagnosis and management,* Orlando, Fla, 1984, Grune & Stratton.
12. Hobbins JC and others: Antenatal diagnosis of renal anomalies with ultrasound: obstructive uropathy, *Am J Obstet Gynecol* 148:868, 1984.
13. Jeanty P, Romero R, editors: *Obstetrical ultrasound,* New York, 1984, McGraw-Hill.
14. Moore, KL: *Before we are born,* ed 3, Toronto, 1989, WB Saunders.
15. Nyberg DA, Mahony BS, Pretorius DH, editors: *Diagnostic ultrasound of fetal anomalies: text and atlas,* St Louis, 1990, Mosby.
16. Potter EL: Bilateral absence of ureters and kidneys: a report of 50 cases, *Obstet Gynecol* 25:3, 1965.
17. Romero R and others: The diagnosis of congenital renal anomalies with ultrasound. II, Infantile polycystic kidney disease, *Am J Obstet Gynecol* 150:259, 1984.
18. Russ PD and others: Hydrometrocolpos, uterus didelphys and septate vagina: an antenatal sonographic diagnosis, *J Ultrasound Med* 3:371, 1984.
19. Weinstein L, Anderson C: In utero diagnosis of Beckwith-Wiedemann syndrome by ultrasound, *Radiology* 134:474, 1980.

BIBLIOGRAPHY

Anderson N and others: Detection of obstructive uropathy in the fetus: predictive value of sonographic measurements of renal pelvic diameter at various gestational ages, *Am J Roentgenol* 164:719, 1995.

Bobrowski RA and others: In utero progression of isolated renal pelvis dilation, *Am J Perinatol* 14:423,1997.

Callen DW, editor: *Ultrasonography in obstetrics and gynecology,* ed 3, Philadelphia, 1995, WB Saunders.

Curtis MR and others: Prenatal ultrasound characterization of the suprarenal mass: distinction between neuroblastoma and subdiaphragmatic extralobar pulmonary sequestration, *J Ultrasound Med* 16:75, 1997.

DeVore GR: The value of color Doppler sonography in the diagnosis of renal agenesis, *J Ultrasound Med* 14:443, 1995.

Dremsek PA and others: Renal pyelectasis in fetuses and neonates: diagnostic value of renal pelvis diameter in pre- and postnatal sonographic screening, *Am J Roentgenol* 168:1017, 1997.

Fong KW and others: Fetal renal cystic disease: sonographic-pathologic correlation. *Am J Roentgenol* 146:767, 1986.

Hadlock FP and others: Sonography of fetal urinary tract anomalies, *Am J Roentgenol* 137:261, 1981.

Hayden SA and others: Posterior urethral obstruction: prenatal sonographic findings and clinical outcome in fourteen cases, *J Ultrasound Med* 7:371, 1988.

Jeanty P and others: Measurement of fetal kidney growth on ultrasound, *Radiology* 144:159, 1982.

Lewis E and others: Real-time ultrasonographic evaluation of normal fetal adrenal glands, *J Ultrasound Med* 1:265, 1982.

Montemarano H and others: Bladder distention and pyelectasis in the male fetus: causes, comparisons, and contrasts, *J Ultrasound Med* 17:743, 1998.

CHAPTER 44

The Fetal Skeleton

Charlotte G. Henningsen

OBJECTIVES

- Describe in detail the embryology of the skeleton
- Describe the variety of musculoskeletal anomalies that can occur in the fetus
- Differentiate sonographically between the most common skeletal dysplasias
- List limb abnormalities and the anomalies that are associated with specific defects

KEY TERMS

achondrogenesis - lethal autosomal-recessive short-limb dwarfism marked by long bone and trunk shortening, decreased echogenicity of the bones and spine, and "flipperlike" appendages

achondroplasia - a defect in the development of cartilage at the epiphyseal centers of the long bones producing short, square bones

craniosynostosis - early ossification of the calvarium with destruction of the sutures; hypertelorism frequently found in association; sonographically, the fetal cranium may appear brachycephalic

heterozygous achondroplasia - short-limb dysplasia that manifests in the second trimester of pregnancy; conversion abnormality of cartilage to bone affecting the epiphyseal growth centers; extremities are markedly shortened at birth with a normal trunk and frequent enlargement of the head

homozygous achondroplasia - short-limb dwarfism affecting fetuses of achondroplastic parents

hypophosphatasia - congenital condition characterized by decreased mineralization of the bones resulting in "ribbonlike" and bowed limbs, underossified cranium, and compression of the chest; early death often occurs

osteogenesis imperfecta - metabolic disorder affecting the fetal collagen system that leads to varying forms of bone disease; intrauterine bone fractures, shortened long bones, poorly mineralized calvaria, and compression of the chest found in type II forms

polydactyly - anomalies of the hands or feet in which there is an addition of a digit; may be found in association with certain skeletal dysplasias

thanatophoric dysplasia - lethal short-limb dwarfism characterized by a marked reduction in the length of the long bones, pear-shaped chest, soft-tissue redundancy, and frequently clover-leaf skull deformity and ventriculomegaly

EMBRYOLOGY

The majority of the musculoskeletal system forms from the primitive mesoderm arising from mesenchymal cells that are the embryonic connective tissues.[14] These cells arise from different regions of the body. The vertebral column and ribs arise from the somites, and the limbs arise from the lateral plate mesoderm. The formation of the

head is more complex in that the cranial bones that form the roof and base of the skull arise from mesenchymal cells of the primitive mesoderm, but the facial bones actually arise from mesenchymal cells arising from the neural crest, which is ectodermal in origin.[7] The skeleton initially appears as cartilaginous forms that then undergo ossification.

Limb development begins the 26th or 27th day after conception with the appearance of upper limb buds. Lower extremity development begins 2 days later. Although the stages of development for the upper and lower extremities are the same, lower extremity development continues to lag behind that of the upper extremities.[14] Initially the limbs have a paddle shape with a ridge of thickened ectoderm, known as the apical ectodermal ridge, at the apex of each bud. Digital rays begin to differentiate from the apical ectodermal ridge around day 41 through a process of cell death of the ridge between the digits.[7,14] The fingers are distinctly evident by day 49, although they are still webbed, and by the 8th week of development the fingers are longer. The development of the feet and toes is essentially complete by the 9th week, although the soles of the feet are still turned inward at this time.[14]

Anomalies of the skeletal system often result from genetic factors, though etiology may be unknown or the result of environmental factors, possibly including drug or mechanical effects.

ABNORMALITIES OF THE SKELETON

Skeletal dysplasia is the term used to describe abnormal growth and density of cartilage and bone. Dwarfism occurs secondary to a skeletal dysplasia and refers to a disproportionately short stature. There are over 100 types of skeletal dysplasias, and not all of them are amenable to sonographic detection. The perinatal team may be able to isolate a skeletal dysplasia when abnormal skeletal structures are observed, such as bone shortening or hypomineralization.

Some skeletal dysplasias are incompatible with life. The lethal forms characteristically are extremely severe in their prenatal appearance, as with severe micromelia. Nonlethal skeletal dysplasias tend to manifest in a milder form. The sonographer should become familiar with the sonographic characteristics of the more common skeletal dysplasias that can be diagnosed in utero.

There are multiple anomalies of the musculoskeletal system that may be identified with ultrasound. Many of these osteochondrodysplasias have similar features, although often there are distinguishing features that can lead to a diagnosis. A list of short-limb skeletal dysplasias, ultrasound characteristics, and their distinguishing features are listed in Table 44-1.

SONOGRAPHIC EVALUATION OF SKELETAL DYSPLASIAS

The patient whose fetus is at risk for a skeletal dysplasia is commonly referred to a maternal-fetal center for genetic counseling and a targeted ultrasound. Although many skeletal dysplasias are inherited, sporadic occurrences and new mutations do occur, so it is important to screen for skeletal dysplasias as part of every obstetric ultrasound examination. The majority of prenatally diagnosed skeletal dysplasia occurs in association with polyhydramnios or other fetal anomalies or when there is a risk for recurrence.

When a skeletal dysplasia is suspected, the protocol of the obstetric ultrasound examination should be adjusted to include the following criteria:

1. Assess limb shortening. All long bones should be measured. A skeletal dysplasia is suspected when limb lengths fall more that 2 standard deviations below the mean (Tables 44-2 and 44-3).
2. Assess bone contour. Thickness, abnormal bowing or curvature, fractures, and a ribbonlike appearance should be noted.
3. Estimate degree of ossification. Decreased attenuation of the bones with decreased shadowing suggests hypomineralization. Special attention should be focused toward this assessment of the cranium, spine, ribs, and long bones.
4. Evaluate the thoracic circumference and shape. A long, narrow chest or a bell-shaped chest may be indicative of specific dysplasias.
5. Survey for coexistent hand and foot anomalies such as talipes and polydactyly.
6. Evaluate the face and profile for facial clefts, frontal bossing, micrognathia, hypertelorism, and other facial anomalies that may be associated with skeletal dysplasias.
7. Survey for other associated anomalies such as hydrocephaly, heart defects, and nonimmune hydrops.

The manifestation of skeletal dysplasias varies based on the specific dysplasia. Long bones are affected in different patterns (Figure 44-1) according to the dysplasia. Rhizomelia is shortening of the proximal bone segment (humerus and femur). Mesomelia refers to shortening of the middle segments (radius/ulna and tibia/fibula). Micromelia describes the shortening of the entire extremity. Sonographic examination of the long bones should include an assessment to define whether there is segmental shortening or micromelia, because this will aid in the diagnosis.

THANATOPHORIC DYSPLASIA

Thanatophoric dysplasia is the most common lethal skeletal dysplasia and occurs in 1 in 10,000 births (Figure 44-2).[20] The term *thanatophoric* comes from the Greek word *thanatophoros,* which means death bearing.[20] The two main subdivisions of thanatophoric dysplasia are types I and II. Type I is characterized by short, curved femurs and flat vertebral bodies. Type II is characterized by straight, short femurs, flat vertebral bodies, and a cloverleaf skull. Most cases of thanatophoric dysplasia are sporadic occurrences; however, type II may be inherited in an autosomal recessive fashion.[9,18]

The prognosis for thanatophoric dysplasia is extremely grim. It is considered a lethal anomaly, with most infants dying shortly after birth as a result of pulmonary hypoplasia, which results from the narrow thorax.

TABLE 44-1 OSTEOCHONDRODYSPLASIA FINDINGS

Anomaly	Ultrasound Findings	Distinguishing Characteristics
Thanatophoric dysplasia	Severe micromelia Macrocephaly Cloverleaf skull Narrow thorax	Cloverleaf skull
Anomaly	**Ultrasound Findings**	**Distinguishing Characteristics**
Achondrogenesis	Severe micromelia Macrocephaly Poor ossification of spine, skull Short thorax	Decreased ossification Severity of limb shortening
Anomaly	**Ultrasound Findings**	**Distinguishing Characteristics**
Achondroplasia	Rhizomelia Macrocephaly Trident hands	Rhizomelic shortening Trident hands
Anomaly	**Ultrasound Findings**	**Distinguishing Characteristics**
Camptomelic dyplasia	Hypoplastic fibulas Long bone bowing Micrognathia Small thorax Talipes	Fibula hypoplasia Bowing affects lower extremities
Anomaly	**Ultrasound Findings**	**Distinguishing Characteristics**
Osteogenesis imperfecta (type II)	Severe micromelia Generalized hypomineralization Narrow thorax Multiple fractures	Normal head size Hypomineralization of skull Multiple fractures
Anomaly	**Ultrasound Findings**	**Distinguishing Characteristics**
Short-rib polydactyly syndrome	Micromelia Narrow thorax Facial cleft Polydactyly	Facial anomalies Polydactyly
Anomaly	**Ultrasound Findings**	**Distinguishing Characteristics**
Hypophosphatasia	Mild limb shortening Narrow thorax Limb fractures and bowing	Hypomineralization of skull Fractures

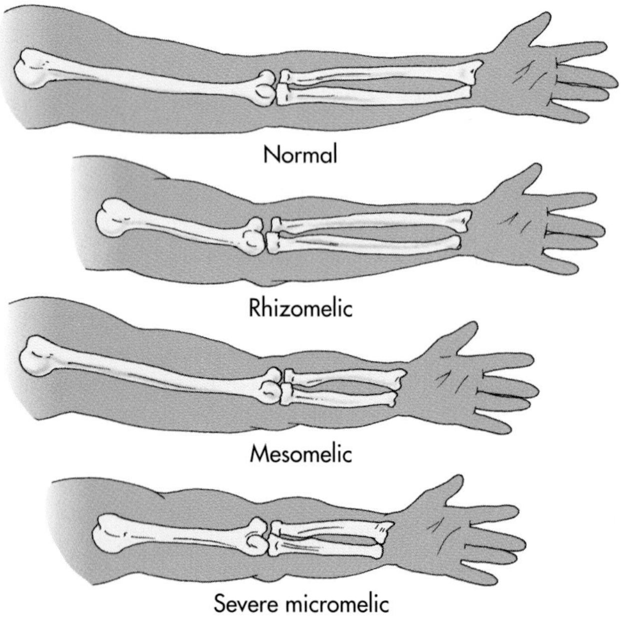

Figure 44-1 Varieties of short-limb dysplasia according to the affected bones. Rhizomelic dysplasia is characterized by shortening of the proximal long bones (humerus and femur). Mesomelic dysplasia is described as shortening of the distal extremities (radius/ulna and tibia/fibula). Severe micromelia produces shortening of both proximal and distal extremities.

TABLE 44-2 LENGTH OF THE BONES OF THE LEG: NORMAL VALUES

Week No.	Tibia Percentile 5th	Tibia Percentile 50th	Tibia Percentile 95th	Fibula Percentile 5th	Fibula Percentile 50th	Fibula Percentile 95th
12	—	7	—	—	6	—
13	—	10	—	—	9	—
14	7	12	17	6	12	19
15	9	15	20	9	15	21
16	12	17	22	13	18	23
17	15	20	25	13	21	28
18	17	22	27	15	23	31
19	20	25	30	19	26	33
20	22	27	33	21	28	36
21	25	30	35	24	31	37
22	27	32	38	27	33	39
23	30	35	40	28	35	42
24	32	37	42	29	37	45
25	34	40	45	34	40	45
26	37	42	47	36	42	47
27	39	44	49	37	44	50
28	41	46	51	38	45	53
29	43	48	53	41	47	54
30	45	50	55	43	49	56
31	47	52	57	42	51	59
32	48	54	59	42	52	63
33	50	55	60	46	54	62
34	52	57	62	46	55	65
35	53	58	64	51	57	62
36	55	60	65	54	58	63
37	56	61	67	54	59	65
38	58	63	68	56	61	65
39	59	64	69	56	62	67
40	61	66	71	59	63	67
	mm	mm	mm	mm	mm	mm

From Jeanty P, Romero R, editors: *Obstetrical ultrasound.* New York, 1984, McGraw Hill.

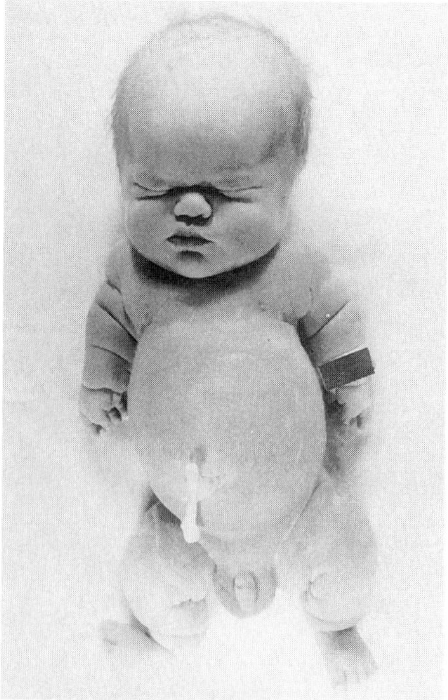

Figure 44-2 Thanatophoric neonate.

Ultrasound findings. The sonographic features of thanatophoric dysplasia include the following:

- Severe micromelia (Figure 44-3, A and B), especially of the proximal bones (rhizomelia)
- Cloverleaf deformity, Kleeblattschadel skull, occurs in 14% of thanatophoric fetuses as a result of premature craniosynostosis[20]
- Narrow thorax with shortened ribs (Figure 44-3, C and D)
- Protuberant abdomen
- Frontal bossing (bulging forehead)
- Hypertelorism (widely spaced eyes)
- Flat vertebral bodies (platyspondyly)

Other sonographic findings that may be associated with thanatophoric dysplasia include severe polyhydramnios, hydrocephalus, and nonimmune hydrops.

ACHONDROPLASIA

Achondroplasia is the most common nonlethal skeletal dysplasia and occurs in 5 to 15 of every 10,000 births, with a reported incidence of 1 in 66,000 births in the United States.[11,18] It results from decreased endochondral bone

TABLE 44-3 LENGTH OF THE BONES OF THE ARM: NORMAL VALUES

		Ulna Percentile				Radius Percentile		
Week No.		5th	50th	95th		5th	50th	95th
12	:	—	7	—	:	—	7	—
13	:	5	10	15	:	6	10	14
14	:	8	13	18	:	8	13	17
15	—:—	11	16	21	—:—	11	15	20
16	:	13	18	23	:	13	18	22
17	:	16	21	26	:	14	20	26
18	:	19	24	29	:	15	22	29
19	:	21	26	31	:	20	24	29
20	:	24	29	34	:	22	27	32
21	:	26	31	36	:	24	29	33
22	:	28	33	38	:	27	31	34
23	:	31	36	41	:	26	32	39
24	:	33	38	43	:	26	34	42
25	—:—	35	40	45	—:—	31	36	41
26	:	37	42	47	:	32	37	43
27	:	39	44	49	:	33	39	45
28	:	41	46	51	:	33	40	48
29	:	43	48	53	:	36	42	47
30	:	44	49	54	:	36	43	49
31	:	46	51	56	:	38	44	50
32	:	48	53	58	:	37	45	53
33	:	49	54	59	:	41	46	51
34	:	51	56	61	:	40	47	53
35	—:—	52	57	62	—:—	41	48	54
36	:	53	58	63	:	39	48	57
37	:	55	60	65	:	45	49	53
38	:	56	61	66	:	45	49	54
39	:	57	62	67	:	45	50	54
40	:	58	63	68	:	46	50	55
		mm	mm	mm		mm	mm	

From Jeanty P, Romero R, editors: *Obstetrical ultrasound.* New York, 1984, McGraw-Hill.

formation, which produces short, squat bones.[6,10] It is the result of a spontaneous mutation in 80% of cases, but can also be transmitted in an autosomal fashion.[8]

The prognosis for achondroplasia depends on the form. **Heterozygous achondroplasia** has a good survival rate with normal intelligence and a normal lifespan.[17] Health problems may include neurologic complications that may require orthopedic or neurologic surgical intervention.[3] **Homozygous achondroplasia** is considered lethal (with the sonographic findings also more severe, including a narrow thorax), with most infants dying shortly after birth from respiratory complications.

Ultrasound findings. The sonographic features of achondroplasia may not be evident until after 22 weeks of gestation, when biometry becomes abnormal.[3] Ultrasound findings include the following:

- Rhizomelia
- Macrocephaly
- Trident hands (short proximal and middle phalanges)[6,11]
- A depressed nasal bridge
- Frontal bossing
- Mild ventriculomegaly may be identified

ACHONDROGENESIS

Achondrogenesis is a rare, lethal skeletal dysplasia occurring in 2.8 per 100,000 births.[22] It is caused by cartilage abnormalities that result in abnormal bone formation and hypomineralization. The two types of achondrogenesis are types I (Parenti-Fraccaro) and II (Langer-Saldino), with 80% of cases of achondrogenesis falling into the type II category.[6] Most cases of achondrogenesis are inherited in an autosomal-recessive manner.

The prognosis for achondrogenesis is grim. It is a lethal abnormality with infants either being stillborn or dying shortly after birth from pulmonary hypoplasia.[3]

Ultrasound findings. The sonographic features of achondrogenesis include the following:

- Severe micromelia
- Decreased or absent ossification of the spine
- Macrocephaly
- Short trunk
- Short thorax and short ribs
- Micrognathia
- Polyhydramnios
- Hydrops possibly identified

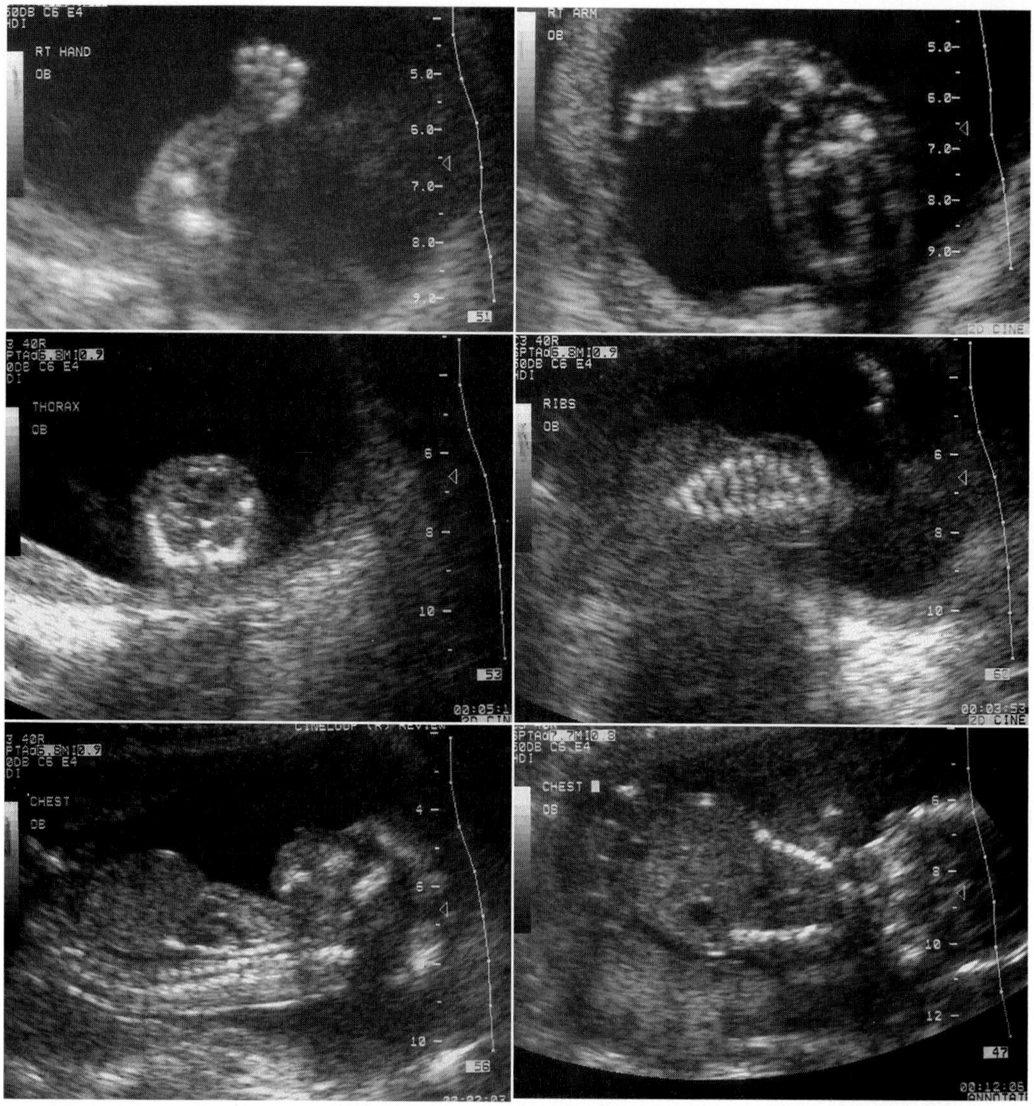

Figure 44-3 Lethal skeletal dysplasia consistent with thanatophoric dysplasia at a gestational age of 18 weeks, 1 day. **A** and **B,** The right arm demonstrates micromelia. The lower extremities were also short, with the femurs measuring gestational age 14 weeks. **C,** The thorax was very narrow. **D,** The ribs were short. The abdomen was protuberant **(E)** and compared with the narrow thorax **(F)** gives the appearance of a "champagne cork."

OSTEOGENESIS IMPERFECTA

Osteogenesis imperfecta is a disorder of collagen production leading to brittle bones; manifestations in the teeth, skin, and ligaments; and blue sclera. The incidence of osteogenesis imperfecta is 1 in 20,000 to 30,000 births.[5] There are four classifications, types I to IV. Types I and IV are the mildest forms, and it would be unlikely that a diagnosis would be made in utero. Types I and IV are transmitted in an autosomal dominant fashion. Type III is a severe form that may be transmitted in an autosomal-dominant or autosomal-recessive manner. Type II (Figure 44-4) is considered the most severe form of osteogenesis imperfecta, having a lethal outcome. It has a prevalence of 1 in 60,000 births and is inherited in autosomal dominant or recessive fashion or may result from a spontaneous mutation.[3,6,11]

The prognosis for osteogenesis imperfecta depends on the type. Children with types I and IV may have multiple fractures during childhood and may be short. Type I children may also suffer with kyphoscoliosis and deafness. Because of the severity of the brittle bones and multiple fractures, osteogenesis imperfecta type III may produce significant handicaps with progressive deformities of the long bones and spine.[6] Infants with type II usually die shortly after birth because of respiratory complications.

Ultrasound findings. The sonographic features of osteogenesis imperfecta type II include the following:

- Generalized hypomineralization of the bones, especially the calvarium (Figure 44-5)
- Multiple fractures of the long bones, ribs, and spine (Figure 44-6)
- Narrow thorax (Figure 44-5, A)
- Micromelia (Figure 44-7)

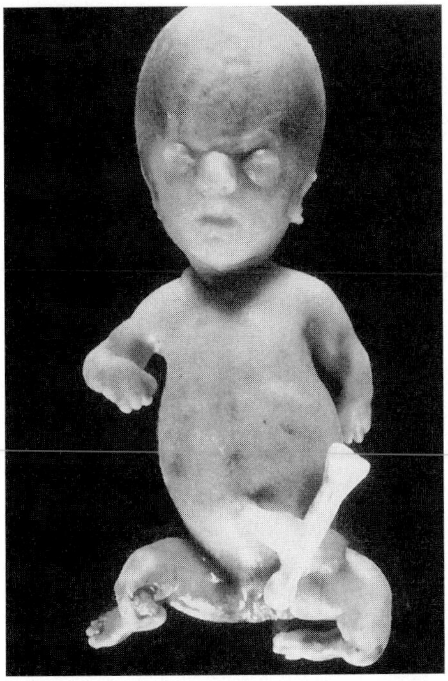

Figure 44-4 Postmortem photograph of neonate with osteogenesis imperfecta (type II).

In addition to these findings, because of the hypomineralization of the calvarium, brain structures are clearly visualized. The calvarium will also be compressible.[23] The multiple fractures that have occurred during the course of pregnancy may leave the bones bowed, thickened, and sharply angulated.[3,6] Polyhydramnios may also be evident.

The sonographic features of osteogenesis imperfecta type III are similar to those of type II, though it is less severe.

CONGENITAL HYPOPHOSPHATASIA

Congenital **hypophosphatasia** is a condition that presents with diffuse hypomineralization of the bone caused by an alkaline phosphatase deficiency. The occurrence rate is 1 per 100,000 births. It is an inherited condition transmitted in an autosomal-recessive manner.[6,15]

Congenital hypophosphatasia is a lethal disorder, with death usually occurring shortly after birth as a result of respiratory complications.

Ultrasound findings. The sonographic features of congenital hypophosphatasia include the following:

- Diffuse hypomineralization of the bones
- Moderate to severe micromelia
- Extremities that may be bowed, fractured, or absent

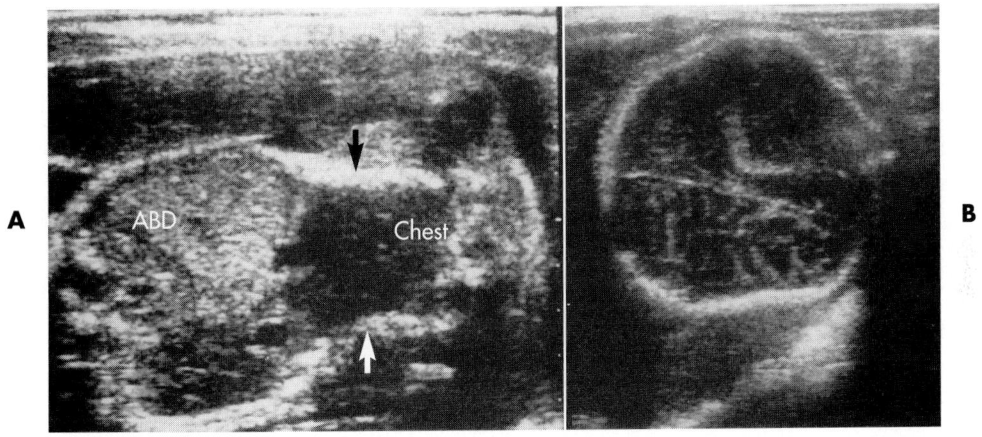

Figure 44-5 **A,** In the fetus shown in Figure 44-7 with osteogenesis imperfecta (type II), a small thoracic cavity *(arrows)* is shown. *ABD,* Abdomen. **B,** In the same fetus, hypomineralization of the skull is evident. Note the improved resolution of brain anatomy because of the lack of calvarial calcification.

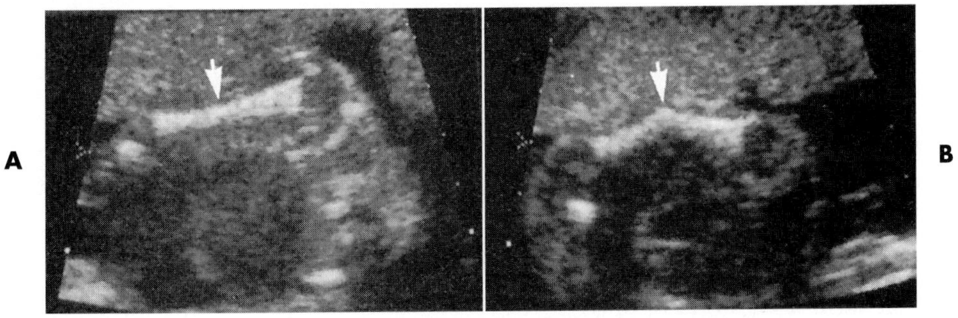

Figure 44-6 Images of both femurs in a 22-week fetus. **A,** The femur *(arrow)* is normal compared with **B,** in which a femoral fracture *(arrows)* is shown. Other long bones appeared normal in length and contour. There was hypomineralization of the spine. Osteogenesis imperfecta type I or IV is considered.

- Poorly ossified cranium with well-visualized brain structures
- Small thoracic cavity[3,15]

DIASTROPHIC DYSPLASIA

Diastrophic dysplasia is a very rare disorder characterized by micromelia, talipes, cleft palate, micrognathia, scoliosis, short stature, earlobe deformities, and hand abnormalities (Figure 44-8). It is inherited in an autosomal-recessive pattern.[3,13,18]

The prognosis for diastrophic dysplasia is variable. There is an increase in infant mortality because of respiratory complications related to the micrognathia and kyphoscoliosis. This is not a lethal disorder, with most patients having a normal life span and normal intelligence. Adult height is usually under 4 feet, and orthopedic abnormalities can cause significant handicaps.[3,15,18]

Ultrasound findings. The sonographic features of diastrophic dysplasia include the following:

- Micromelia (Figure 44-9)
- Talipes
- Fixed abducted thumb (hitchhiker thumb; see Figure 44-9, B).[6,18]
- Scoliosis

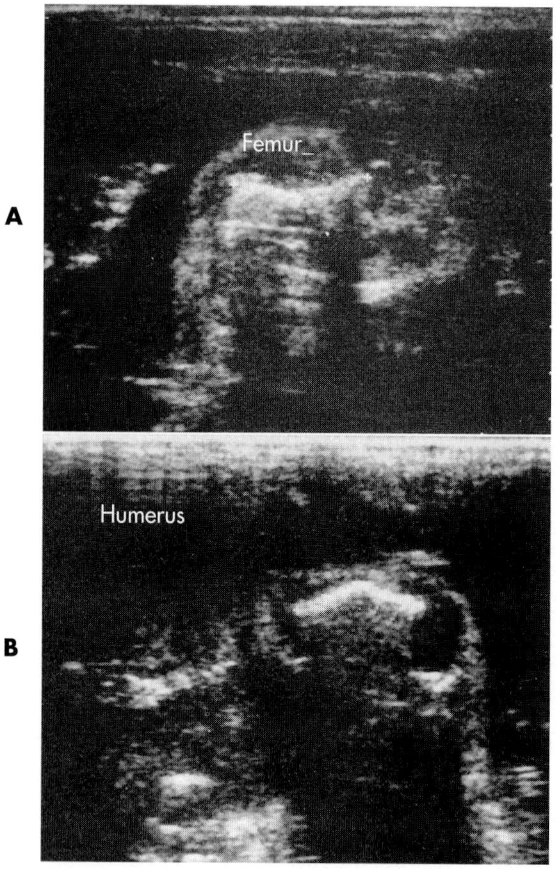

Figure 44-7 **A,** Marked micromelia in a 30-week fetus with osteogenesis imperfecta (type II). The femur measured 29 mm (normal for 30 weeks is 57 mm). **B,** In the same fetus a humeral fracture is shown. Humeral length measured 27 mm (normal for 30 weeks is 51 mm).

- Talipes (clubfoot)
- Micrognathia (small chin)
- Cleft palate

CAMPTOMELIC DYSPLASIA

Camptomelic (bent bone) dyplasia is a group of lethal skeletal dysplasias that are characterized by bowing of the long bones. Most cases occur as a spontaneous mutation, but camptomelic dysplasia is also inherited in an autosomal-recessive pattern.

Camptomelia dysplasia is considered a lethal anomaly with most infants dying in the neonatal period because of pulmonary hypoplasia. Infants surviving the neonatal period usually die within the first year of life and suffer with respiratory and feeding problems, are developmentally delayed, and are mentally retarded.[3,18]

Ultrasound findings. The sonographic features of camptomelic dysplasia include the following:

- Bowing of the long bones with the lower extremities affected most severely (Figures 44-10 and 44-11).
- Small thorax
- Hypoplastic fibulas
- Hypertelorism
- Cleft palate
- Micrognathia
- Talipes (Figures 44-12 and 44-13)
- Ventriculomegaly
- Hydronephrosis[18,19]

ROBERTS' SYNDROME

Roberts' syndrome is a rare condition characterized by phocomelia and facial anomalies. Roberts' syndrome is an autosomal-recessive disorder; it is also known as a pseudothalidomide syndrome.[3]

The prognosis for Roberts' syndrome is poor. Stillbirth and infant mortality are common. Survivors are growth restricted and have severe mental retardation.[3,6]

Ultrasound findings. The sonographic features of Roberts syndrome include the following:

- Phocomelia with the upper extremities more severely affected
- Bilateral cleft lip and palate
- Hypertelorism

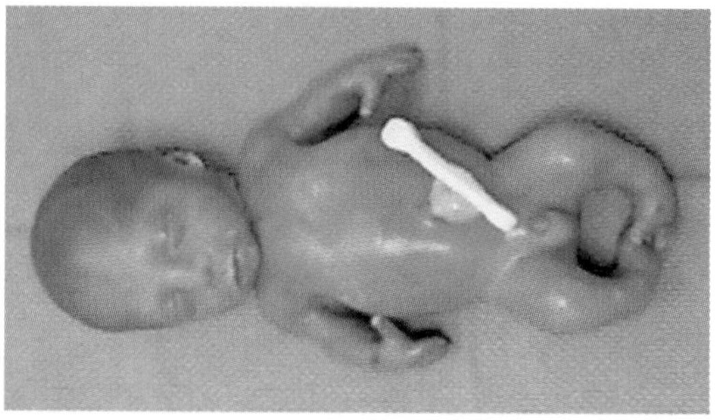

Figure 44-8 Postmortem photograph of a fetus with diastrophic dysplasia. (Courtesy Armando Fuentes, MD, Director, Maternal Fetal Medicine at Florida Hospital Medical Center, Orlando, Fla.)

A

B

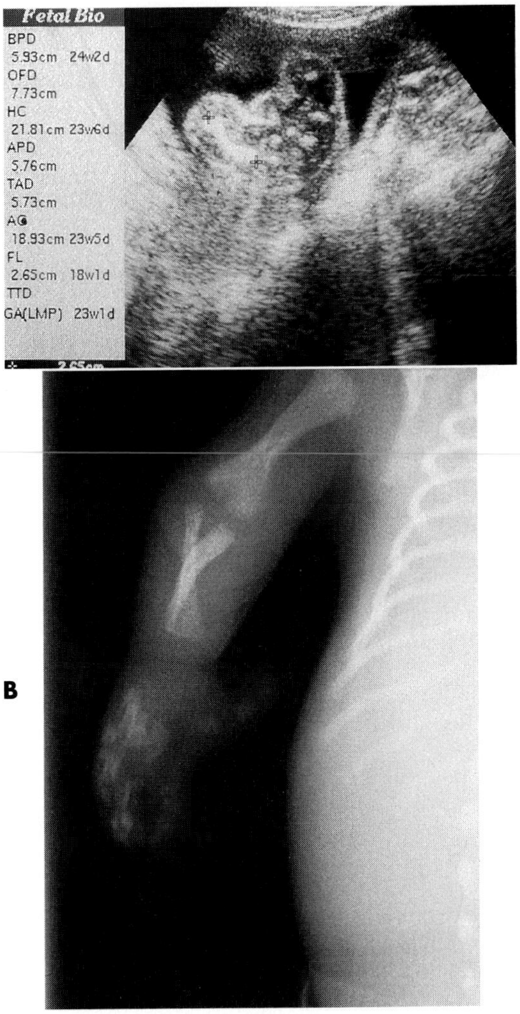

Figure 44-9 Diastrophic dysplasia imaged at 23 weeks and 1 day. **A,** Micromelia is demonstrated in this femur measuring 18 weeks, 1 day. The thoracic circumference was also small. **B,** Postmortem radiograph demonstrates the "hitchhiker thumb."

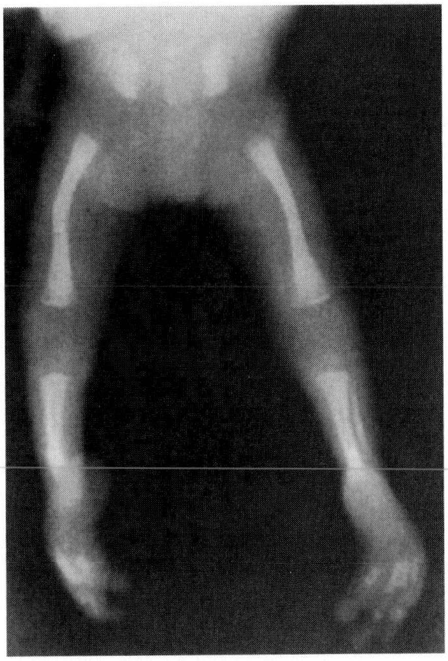

Figure 44-11 Radiograph of neonate shown in Figures 44-10, 44-12, and 44-13 with camptomelic dysplasia and Swyer syndrome. Note the hypoplastic cervical vertebrae, normal ribs, elongated clavicles, and hypoplastic distorted scapulae. The upper extremity bones are normal. The lower extremity deformities include anterior lateral bowing of the femurs at the midshaft; both tibias are short with sharp anterior bowing at midshaft with mild bowing at the distal ends. The fibulas are hypoplastic and bowed. Minimal ischial ossification and absent mineralization of the pubic bone are shown.

A

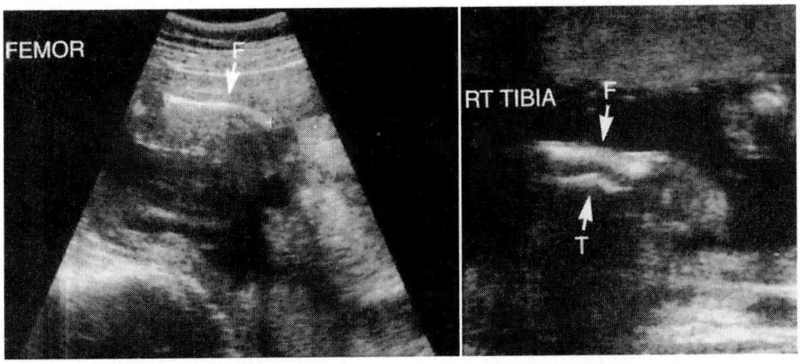

B

Figure 44-10 **A,** Camptomelic dysplasia and Swyer syndrome in a 20-week fetus with femoral bowing *(F)* found bilaterally. The femoral lengths were normal. **B,** In the same fetus, the tibias *(T)* were short and hypoplastic with sharp anterior bowing of the midshaft of the bone. Distal bowing was also observed. The fibulas *(F)* were hypoplastic and bowed. The upper extremities were normal in length without bowing or **angulation.** Bilateral hydronephrosis was observed. Examination of the neonate and radiologic findings (see Figure 44-11) confirmed the diagnosis of camptomelic dysplasia. Gonadal dysgenesis (female internal and external genitalia with a male karyotype) was consistent with Swyer syndrome. The neonate had other characteristic signs of the disorder, including tall and narrow hypomineralized ischial bones, absent pubic bone ossification, receding chin, hypoplastic cervical vertebra, elongated clavicles, hypoplastic scapulae, and flexion abnormalities of the feet.

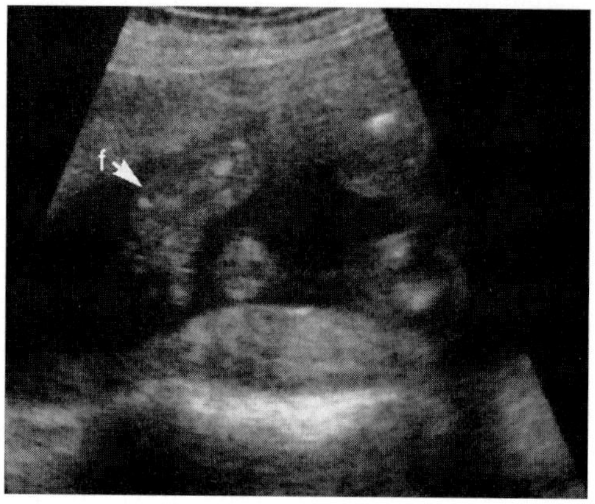

Figure 44-12 In the fetus with camptomelic dysplasia and Swyer syndrome, as shown in Figures 44-10, 44-12, and 44-13, abnormal plantar flexion of the feet is shown. The feet *(f)* are markedly supinated with curvature to the soles of the feet. The toes are plantar flexed with the great toes separated by flexion.

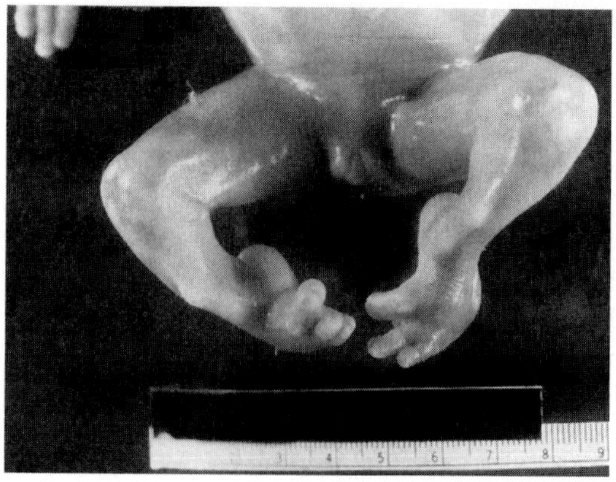

Figure 44-13 Postmortem photograph of neonate shown in Figures 44-10, 44-11, and 44-12, with camptomelic dysplasia and Swyer syndrome. Note the markedly angulated lower legs with protrusion of the tibia anteriorly at the midshaft. The fibulas were hypoplastic and bowed. The feet, as shown in Figure 44-12, are abnormally rotated with prominent heels (rocker-bottom foot).

- Microcephaly
- Cardiovascular, renal, and gastrointestinal anomalies may be identified[16]

SHORT-RIB POLYDACTYLY SYNDROME

Short-rib **polydactyly** syndrome is a lethal skeletal dysplasia characterized by short ribs and polydactyly. There are four types of this dysplasia, which is inherited in an autosomal-manner. Type I is also known as Saldino-Noonan syndrome, type II is also known as Majewski syndrome, and type III is known as Naumoff syndrome. Type IV, Beemer-Langer dysplasia, was included in this group of short-rib dysplasias in the 1992 International Classification of Osteochondrodysplasias.[8]

Short-rib polydactyly syndrome is considered a lethal anomaly. Most infants die shortly after birth as a result of pulmonary hypoplasia.

Ultrasound findings. Common sonographic features of short-rib polydactyly syndrome include the following:

- Narrow thorax with short ribs
- Polydactyly
- Micromelia
- Midline facial cleft [3,8]

Other sonographic findings associated with short-rib dysplasias include anomalies of the central nervous system, cardiovascular system, and genitourinary tract. Polyhydramnios may also be identified.[8] Saldino-Noonan and Naumoff syndromes are usually not associated with cleft lip and palate, and polydactyly may not always be present in Beemer-Langer dysplasia.[3,8]

JEUNE SYNDROME

Jeune syndrome, also known as asphyxiating thoracic dysplasia, is a skeletal dysplasia characterized by a very narrow thorax. The prevalence of Jeune syndrome is 1 in 70,000 births, and it is inherited in an autosomal-recessive manner.[6,15] There is a range of severity with the most severe form resulting in death because of pulmonary hypoplasia, which results from the narrow thorax.

Ultrasound findings. The sonographic features of Jeune syndrome include the following:

- Small thorax
- Rhizomelia
- Renal dysplasia
- Polydactyly (14%)[6,15]

ELLIS-VAN CREVELD SYNDROME

Ellis–van Creveld syndrome is also known as chondroectodermal dysplasia. The prevalence is 1 in 200,000 births, with an increased frequency in the Amish community. It is inherited in an autosomal-recessive pattern.

Ellis–van Creveld syndrome may also present with a narrow thorax, which affects the prognosis by causing pulmonary hypoplasia, causing death in up to one half of cases. Survivors are short and have normal intellect.[3]

Ultrasound findings. The sonographic features of Ellis–van Creveld include the following:

- Limb shortening
- Polydactyly
- Heart defects (50%)[3,6]

CAUDAL REGRESSION SYNDROME/SIRENOMELIA

Caudal regression syndrome includes a range of malformations from sacral agenesis to sirenomelia, in which there is fusion of the lower extremities. The overall incidence of caudal regression syndrome is unknown; however, the incidence of sirenomelia is reported to be 1 in 60,000 births, with a male prevalence of 3 to 1.[1]

The etiology of caudal regression syndrome is not completely understood, although it has been associated with diabetes. Genetic factors have also been linked with this disorder. Vascular hypoperfusion is thought to be a causative

factor in sirenomelia with a single umbilical artery commonly associated that may divert blood flow to the caudal end. Sirenomelia is also associated with monozygotic twinning, with an incidence 100 times greater than in singleton gestations.[1]

The prognosis for caudal regression syndrome depends on the severity and the associated anomalies. Neuro-urologic and orthopedic evaluations with their intervention can help to reduce and correct deformities and minimize handicaps. Sirenomelia is considered a lethal anomaly because of the severe renal anomalies that result in oligohydramnios and pulmonary hypoplasia.[1,3]

Ultrasound findings. Sonographic features of caudal regression syndrome include the following:

- Sacral agenesis (Figure 44-14)
- Talipes
- Abnormal lumbar vertebrae, pelvic abnormalities, and contractures or decreased movement of the lower extremities may also be seen[3]

Sonographic features of sirenomelia include the following:

- Variable fusion of the lower extremities (Figure 44-15)
- Bilateral renal agenesis
- Oligohydramnios
- Single umbilical artery[1,3]

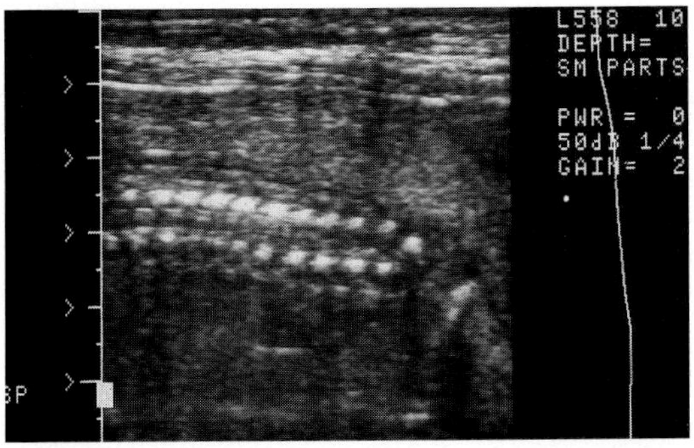

Figure 44-14 Sacral agenesis noted at 21 weeks of gestation. Note the lack of tapering usually seen in the lumbosacral area.

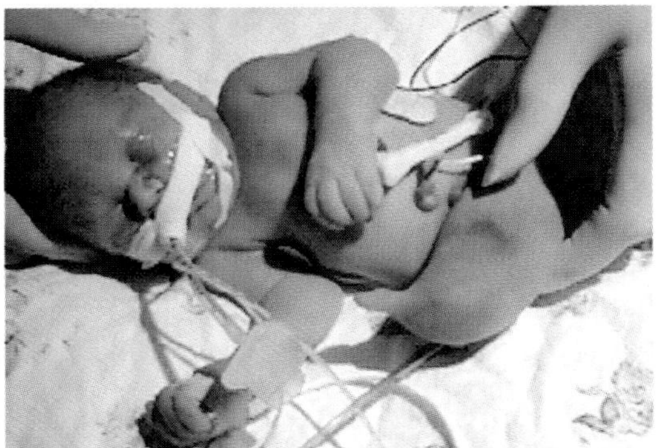

Figure 44-15 A neonate with sirenomelia. Note the fusion of the lower extremities. There was also bilateral renal agenesis, and the infant died shortly after birth. This was a twin pregnancy, and the other infant was normal. (Courtesy Armando Fuentes, MD, Director, Maternal Fetal Medicine at Florida Hospital Medical Center, Orlando, Fla.)

Other anomalies that may be associated with caudal regression syndrome and sirenomelia include anal atresia, heart defects, and gastrointestinal and genitourinary anomalies. When severe oligohydramnios is present, a confident diagnosis with ultrasound may be difficult. Amnioinfusion and magnetic resonance imaging may be used to evaluate the severity of anomalies.[1]

VACTERL Association

The VACTERL association is a group of anomalies that may occur together. In this sporadic group of anomalies, *V*ertebral defects, *A*nal atresia, *C*ardiac anomalies, *T*racheo*E*sophageal fistula, *R*enal anomalies, and *L*imb dysplasia may occur in combination. For the VACTERL association to be considered, three features must be identified. A single umbilical artery has also been noted in association with VACTERL.[4]

Postural Anomalies

The normal development of the fetus requires movement. There are multiple events that can cause a decrease in fetal movement, including oligohydramnios, multiple gestations, and congenital uterine anomalies. Decreased movement may also be due to an abnormality of the fetal nerves, connective tissues, or musculature. These fetal conditions may not only cause a decrease or absence of fetal movement, but they may also result in abnormal contractures and postural deformities.

Arthrogryposis Multiplex Congenita. Arthrogryposis multiplex congenita is a condition marked by severe contractures of the extremities because of abnormal innervation and disorders of the muscles and connective tissues. It represents a group of disorders that may be inherited in an autosomal-dominant or autosomal-recessive pattern or may be X-linked.

Ultrasound findings. The sonographic findings for arthrogryposis include the following:

- Rigid extremities
- Flexed arms
- Hyperextension of the knees
- Clinched hands
- Talipes

Polyhydramnios or oligohydramnios may accompany this anomaly as can anomalies of the central nervous system. Other defects that may be associated include facial and renal anomalies.[3,15]

Lethal Multiple Pterygium Syndrome. Lethal multiple pterygium syndrome is characterized by webbing across the joints and multiple contractures. It is usually inherited in an autosomal-recessive fashion.

Ultrasound findings. The sonographic findings for pterygium syndrome include the following:

- Limb contractures
- Webbing across joints
- Cystic hygroma

Micrognathia, hydrops, and polyhydramnios are also associated with this syndrome.

Pena-Shokeir Syndrome. Pena-Shokeir syndrome is characterized by abnormal joint contractures, facial abnormalities, polyhydramnios, intrauterine growth restriction, and pulmonary hypoplasia. This syndrome may be inherited in an autosomal-recessive manner or as a sporadic occurrence.

Ultrasound findings. The sonographic findings of Pena-Shokeir (Figure 44-16) include the following:

- Limb abnormalities such as contractures, clinched hands, and talipes
- Facial abnormalities, including micrognathia, and cleft palate

Polyhydramnios and hydrops may also be identified.[3,6]

MISCELLANEOUS LIMB ABNORMALITIES

Hand and foot abnormalities may occur with skeletal dysplasias, as part of a chromosomal syndrome, or as an isolated event. Amputation defects may be identified as total or partial absence and may be associated with amniotic band syndrome. Congenital absence of one or more extremities (amelia) may be observed prenatally (Figure 44-17).

Hand anomalies may include missing digits, fused digits (syndactyly, Figure 44-18) or a split hand (lobster-claw deformity, Figure 44-19). Extra digits (polydactyly) may be isolated or part of a syndrome or chromosomal anomaly (Figures 44-20 to 44-22). Overlapping digits (clinodactyly) and clinched hands may also be a feature of a syndrome or chromosomal anomaly.[6]

Radial ray defects include hypoplasia or aplasia of the radius and thumb. Radial ray defects are associated with chromosomal anomalies such as trisomies 13 and 18 and the VACTERL association. Numerous syndromes have also presented with an absent or hypoplastic radius and thumb, including Holt-Oram syndrome and thrombocytopenia with absent radii (TAR) syndrome (Figure 44-23).[15]

Clubfoot, also known as talipes, describes deformities of the foot and ankle. It occurs in approximately 1 in 400

A B

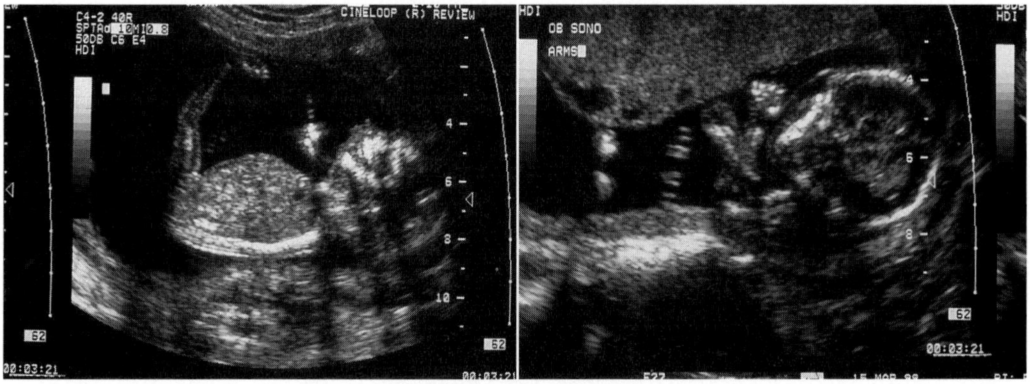

Figure 44-16 An ultrasound at 19 weeks of gestation revealed rigid legs with the knees hyperextended **(A)**. **B,** The arms were contracted and crossed over the chest with hands clenched. Polyhydramnios and micrognathia were also noted. The primary diagnosis was Pena-Shokeir syndrome.

A B

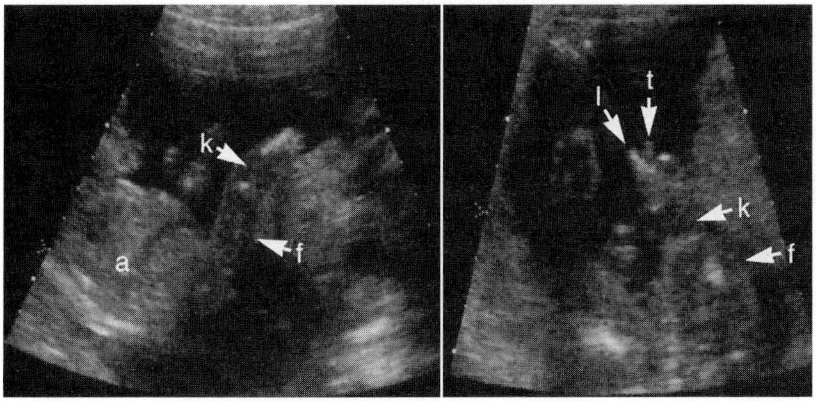

Figure 44-17 **A,** Partial amelia (absence) of the lower extremity. The femur *(f)* is observed without evidence of a lower leg or foot. *a,* Abdomen; *k,* knees. **B,** In the same fetus, magnified view of distal extremity anomaly. Note the single short bone in the lower leg *(l)* and single toe *(t)* protruding from the defect. All other extremities were of normal length and appeared anatomically normal. There were no amniotic bands observed. These findings were confirmed after birth. *f,* Femur; *k,* knee.

A

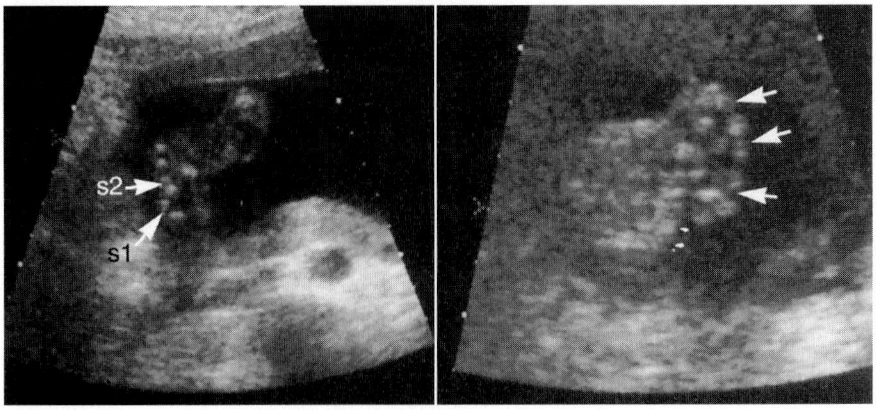

B

Figure 44-18 **A,** Polysyndactyly in a fetus with Carpenter syndrome. There was webbing (syndactyly) of the first and second toes *(s1)* and of the third and fourth toes *(s2)*. Six toes were present (polydactyly). **B,** In the same fetus, scans of the toes *(arrows)* show malalignment of the phalanges. Other ultrasound findings included craniosynostosis, ventriculomegaly, and umbilical hernia.

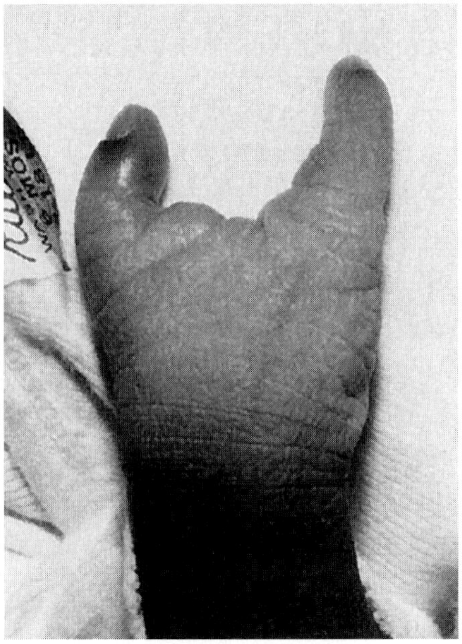

Figure 44-19 Pathologic specimen showing a split-hand deformity (ectrodactyly).

A

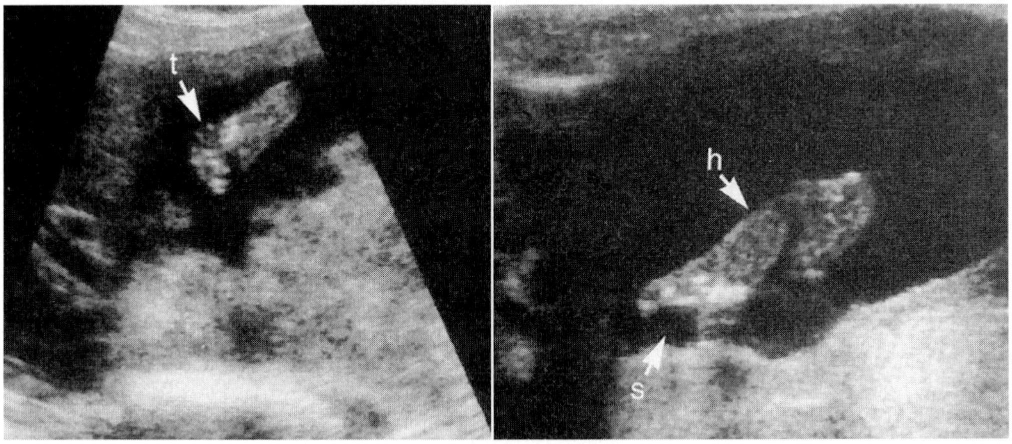

B

Figure 44-20 **A,** Polydactyly of a foot in a fetus with trisomy 18. *t,* Toes. **B,** In the same fetus the other foot was split (ectrodactyly). Note the splaying of the toes *(s)* and malalignment of the metatarsals. Coexisting anomalies included a septal cardiac defect, bilateral choroid plexus cysts, hydramnios, and growth restriction. Autopsy was declined. *h,* Heel.

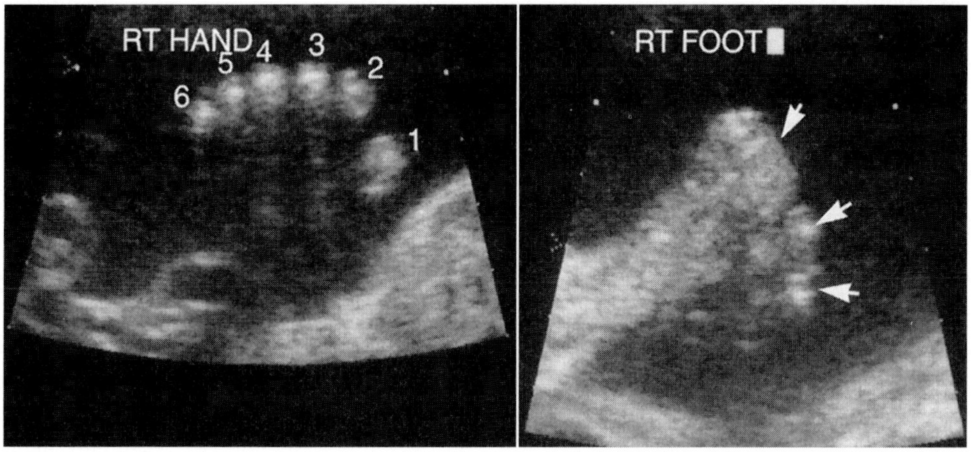

Figure 44-21 **A,** Polydactyly (six fingers) in a 26-week fetus with multiple congenital anomalies, including micromelic dwarfism and semilobar holoprosencephaly. A normal karyotype was found by amniocentesis, but genetic evaluation after birth suggested pseudotrisomy 13 (an autosomal-recessive condition). **B,** In the same fetus, duplication of the great toe *(arrows)* is shown.

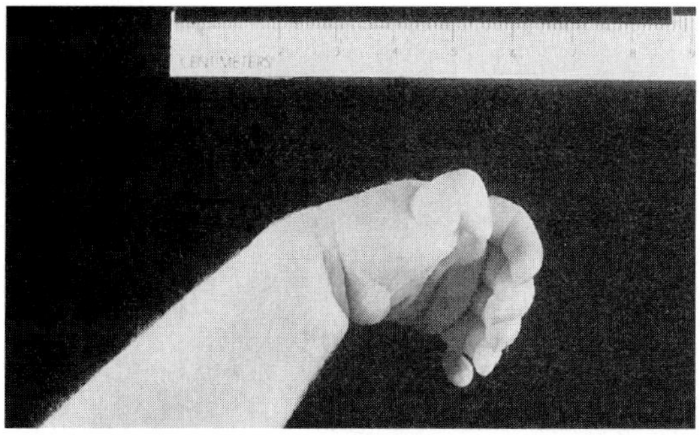

Figure 44-22 Polydactyly of a hand shown in a neonate.

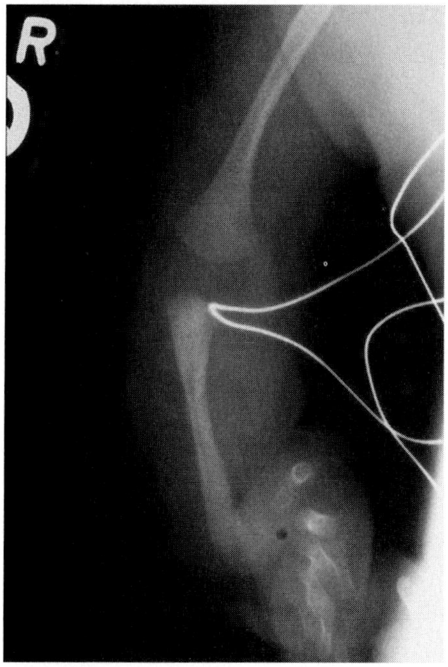

Figure 44-23 A radiograph of a neonate with thrombocytopenia with absent radii (TAR) syndrome. Note the absence of the radius in the arm and the turned-back hand.

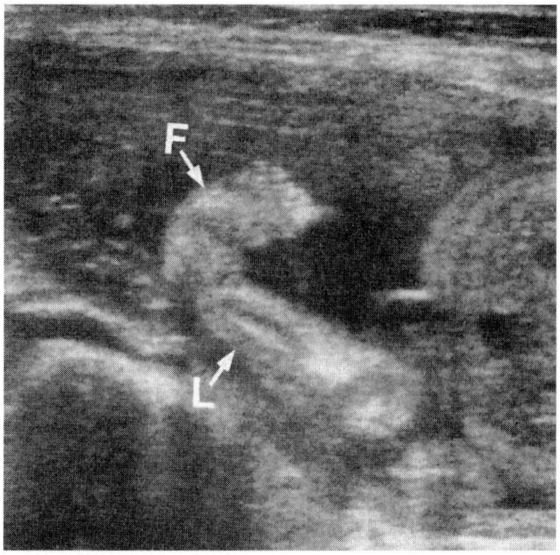

Figure 44-24 Clubfoot identified during a basic scan in a 19-week fetus. Other anomalies included cystic hygroma, ventriculomegaly, and ascites. Note the medial inversion of the foot *(F)* in relationship to the lower leg *(L)*.

live births. There is a male predominance, and slightly more than half of the cases of clubfoot are unilateral.[12]

The majority of cases of talipes are idiopathic and isolated findings. Talipes may be associated with chromosomal anomalies, syndromes, musculoskeletal disorders, and spina bifida. It has also been associated with exposure to tubocurarine, sodium aminopterin, and lead poisoning.[2] Clubfoot has also been identified with oligohydramnios and in multiple gestations. Because of the numerous anomalies that may be identified, karyotyping should be offered.[21]

Clubfoot may be identified sonographically when there is persistent abnormal inversion of the foot perpendicular to the lower leg (Figure 44-24).

Rocker-bottom foot is characterized by a prominent heel and a convex sole. It has been associated with multiple syndromes and chromosomal anomalies, especially trisomy 18.[18]

REVIEW QUESTIONS

1. What are the sonographic features of thanatophoric dysplasia and achondrogenesis, and how would you differentiate between the two?
2. Which types of osteogenesis imperfecta are the most severe, and how would you identify this disorder with ultrasound?
3. What are the types of short-rib polydactyly syndrome, and what are the sonographic findings?
4. Discuss the various types of limb abnormalities and the anomalies that could be associated with them.
5. Discuss how you would differentiate between achondrogenesis and osteogenesis imperfecta type II.

REFERENCES

1. Adra A and others: Cadal regression syndrome: etiopathogenesis, prenatal diagnosis, and perinatal management, *Obstet Gynecol Surv* 49:508, 1994.
2. Bar-Hava I and others: Caution: prenatal clubfoot can be both a transient and a late-onset phenomenon, *Prenat Diagn,* 17:457, 1997.
3. Benacerraf BR: *Ultrasound of fetal syndromes,* Philadelphia, 1998, WB Saunders.
4. Berman MC, Cohen HL: *Obstetrics and gynecology,* ed 2, Philadelphia, 1997, JB Lippincott.
5. Bulas DI and others: Variable prenatal appearance of osteogenesis imperfecta, *J Ultrasound Med,* 13:419, 1994.
6. Callen PW: *Ultrasonography in obstetrics and gynecology,* ed 3, Philadelphia, 1994, WB Saunders.
7. Carlson BM: *Human embryology and developmental biology,* ed 2, St Louis, 1999, Mosby.
8. Den Hollander NS and others: Early transvaginal ultrasonographic diagnosis of Beemer-Langer dysplasia: a report of two cases, *Ultrasound Obstet Gynecol* 11:298, 1998.
9. Fleischer AC and others: *Sonography in obstetrics and gynecology: principles and Practice,* ed 5, Stamford, 1996, Appleton & Lange.
10. Goodman RM, Gorlin RJ: Genetic syndromes: skeletal dysplasias. In *The malformed infant and child: an illustrated guide,* New York, 1983, Oxford University Press.
11. Guzman ER and others: Prenatal ultrasonographic demonstration of the trident hand in heterozygous achondroplasia, *J Ultrasound Med,* 13:63, 1994.
12. Kyzer SP, Stark SL: Congenital idiopathic clubfoot deformities, *AORN J* 61:492, 1995.
13. Makitie O, Kaitila I: Growth in diastrophic dysplasia, *J Pediatr* 130:641, 1997.
14. Moore KL, Persaud TVN, Shiota K: *Color atlas of clinical embryology,* Philadelphia, 1994, WB Saunders.
15. Nyberg DA, Mahony BS, Pretorius DH, editors: *Diagnostic ultrasound of fetal anomalies: text and atlas,* St Louis, 1990, Mosby.
16. Paladini D: Prenatal ultrasound diagnosis of Roberts syndrome in a family with negative history, *Ultrasound Obstet Gynecol* 7:208, 1996.
17. Patel MD, Filly RA: Homozygous achondroplasia: US distinction between homozygous, heterozygous, and unaffected fetuses in the second trimester, *Radiology* 196:541, 1995.
18. Sanders RC and others: *Structural fetal anomalies: the total picture,* St Louis, 1996, Mosby.
19. Sanders RC and others: Osteogenesis imperfecta and camptomelic dysplasia: difficulties in prenatal diagnosis, *J Ultrasound Med,* 13:691, 1994.
20. Schild RL and others: Antenatal sonographic diagnosis of thanatophoric dysplasia: a report of three cases and a review of the literature with special emphasis on the differential diagnosis, *Ultrasound Obstet Gynecol* 8:62, 1996.
21. Shipp TD, Benacerraf BR: The significance of prenatally isolated clubfoot: is amniocentesis indicated? *Am J Ostet Gynecol* 178:600, 1998.
22. Tongsong T, Srisomboon J, Sudasna J: Prenatal diagnosis of Langer-Saldino achondrogenesis, *J Clin Ultrasound* 23:56, 1995.
23. Wax JR, Smith JF, Floyd, RC: Lethal osteogenesis imperfecta: second trimester sonographic diagnosis in a twin gestation, *J Ultrasound Med* 13:711, 1994.

PART IX

Foundations of Gynecology

CHAPTER 45

Normal Anatomy and Physiology of the Female Pelvis

Sandra L. Hagen-Ansert

OBJECTIVES

- Name the pelvic landmarks
- Describe the muscles of the pelvic cavity
- Discuss the pelvic organs and their function
- Describe the development of the ovum and its passage from the ovary into the uterus
- Describe the ligaments of the uterus and ovaries
- Discuss the follicular development process
- Define about the function of the corpus luteum

KEY TERMS

anteverted - refers to the position of the uterus when the fundus is tipped slightly forward

coccygeus muscles - form the floor of the pelvis

false (major) pelvis - portion of the pelvis found above the brim of the pelvis; that portion of the abdominal cavity cradled by the iliac fossae

follicle-stimulating hormone (FSH) - hormone produced in the pituitary gland that influences the ovaries

iliacus muscle - paired muscles that form the lateral wall of the pelvis

levator ani muscles - form the floor of the pelvis

menarche - refers to the onset of menstruation

menopause - cessation of menstruation

menses - monthly flow of blood from the endometrium

mesosalpinx - free margin of the upper portion of the broad ligament where the oviduct is found

obturator internus muscle - arises from the anterolateral pelvic wall surrounding the obturator foramen to insert on the greater trochanter of the femur

piriformis muscle - arises from the sacrum between the pelvic sacral foramina and the gluteal surface of the ilium

premenarche - time period in young girls before the onset of menstruation

psoas major muscle - begins at the hilum of the kidneys and extends inferiorly along both sides of the spine into the pelvis

rectouterine pouch (pouch of Douglas) - area in the pelvic cavity between the rectum and the uterus that is likely to accumulate free fluid

retroverted - refers to the position of the uterus when the fundus is tipped posteriorly

true (minor) pelvis - found below the brim of the pelvis; the cavity of the minor pelvis is continuous at the pelvic brim with the cavity of the major pelvis

---

The understanding of the anatomy and physiology as it relates to the female pelvis is very important for the sonographer to build a foundation before learning pathophysiology. There are many pelvic landmarks, ligaments, and muscular structures within the pelvis that help the sonographer differentiate the normal reproductive organs from muscular and vascular structures.

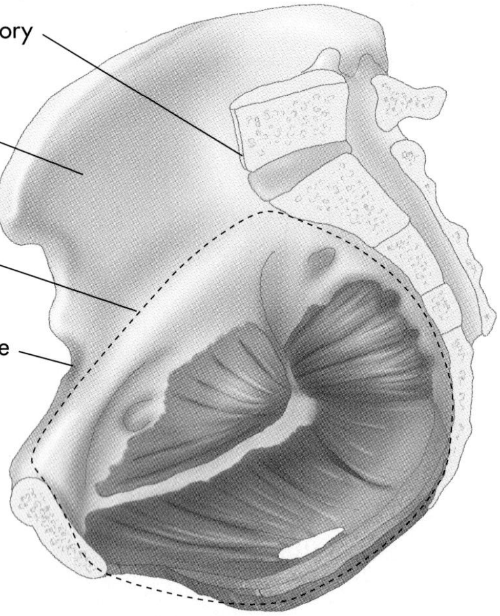

Figure 45-1 Lateral diagram of the pelvis. The true pelvis is the inferior-most portion of the body cavity and is separated from the false pelvis by the iliopectineal line and the sacral promontory.

The bladder is the best sonographic window the sonographer can use in transabdominal scanning. The adequate filling of the bladder may make the difference between a high-quality scan or the inability to visualize any reproductive organs. On the other hand, overfilling of the bladder may cause compression of the pelvic organs.

When transvaginal ultrasound is used to evaluate the pelvic structures, the patient is able to empty her bladder completely before the introduction of the special transducer into the vaginal canal. The uterus and iliac vessels are now used as the primary landmark to image the pelvic organs.

This chapter presents the primary muscular structures and pelvic ligaments the sonographer should know to perform an adequate pelvic ultrasound examination.

PELVIC LANDMARKS: BONY PELVIS

Anatomically, the pelvis is divided by an oblique line that separates the greater (false) and lesser (true) pelvis. This pelvic brim passes through the prominence of the sacrum to the superior margin of the pubic symphysis. The greater pelvis is cephalic to this brim and communicates with the abdomen cephalically and with the lesser pelvis caudally (Figure 45-1). The lesser pelvis represents the area caudal to the pelvic brim.[2]

PELVIC CAVITY AND PERINEUM

The pelvic cavity is that part of the abdominal cavity found below the pelvic brim (Figure 45-2 and Box 45-1). The posterior wall is formed by the sacrum and coccyx. The piriformis and coccygeus muscles overlie the sacrum and coccyx. Along the lateral margins of the pelvic cavity lie the hip bones, which are covered by the obturator internus muscles. The lower margin of the pelvic floor is formed by the levator ani and coccygeus muscles. The re-

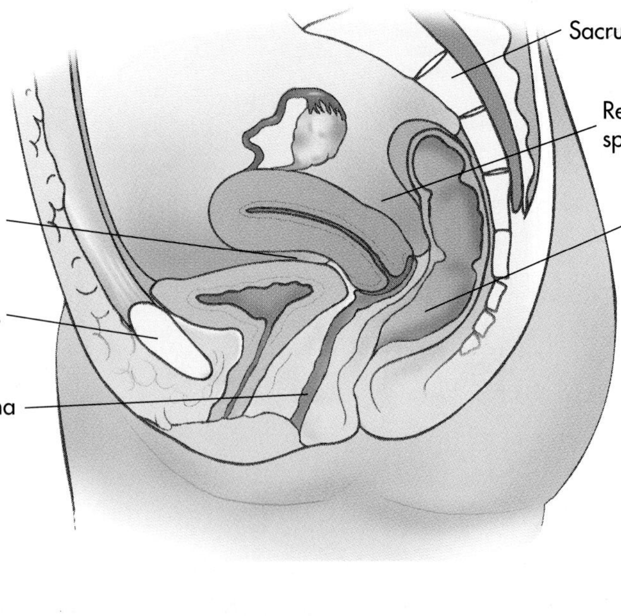

Figure 45-2 The lowest part of the peritoneal cavity is the rectouterine pouch (also known as the pouch of Douglas).

BOX 45-1 PELVIC CAVITY

- *Posterior:* Occupied by rectum, colon, and ileum
- *Anterior:* Bladder, ureters, ovaries, fallopian tubes, uterus, and vagina

BOX 45-2 PELVIC MUSCLES

- *Psoas major:* Lumbar spine to anterior side wall
- *Iliacus:* Forms pelvic side wall
- *Piriformis:* Sacrum to posterior pelvis
- *Obturator internus:* Forms pelvic floor (diaphragm)
- *Coccygeus:* Forms pelvic floor (diaphragm)

gion above the pelvic diaphragm is the pelvic cavity; the smaller area below the pelvic floor is the perineum. The lowest part of the peritoneal cavity is the rectouterine pouch (pouch of Douglas).

MUSCLES OF THE PELVIS

There are several primary muscle groups in the pelvis that the sonographer should be able to identify as landmarks to help distinguish the reproductive organs (Box 45-2). The psoas major muscle extends from the abdominal cavity into the pelvic cavity from the lateral margins of the lumbar spine to the anterior side wall (Figure 45-3). The iliacus is closely related to the psoas major muscle as it forms the pelvic side wall.

The piriformis and obturator internus muscles pass out from the pelvis through the sciatic foramina to become attached to the greater tuberosity of the femur (Figure 45-4).

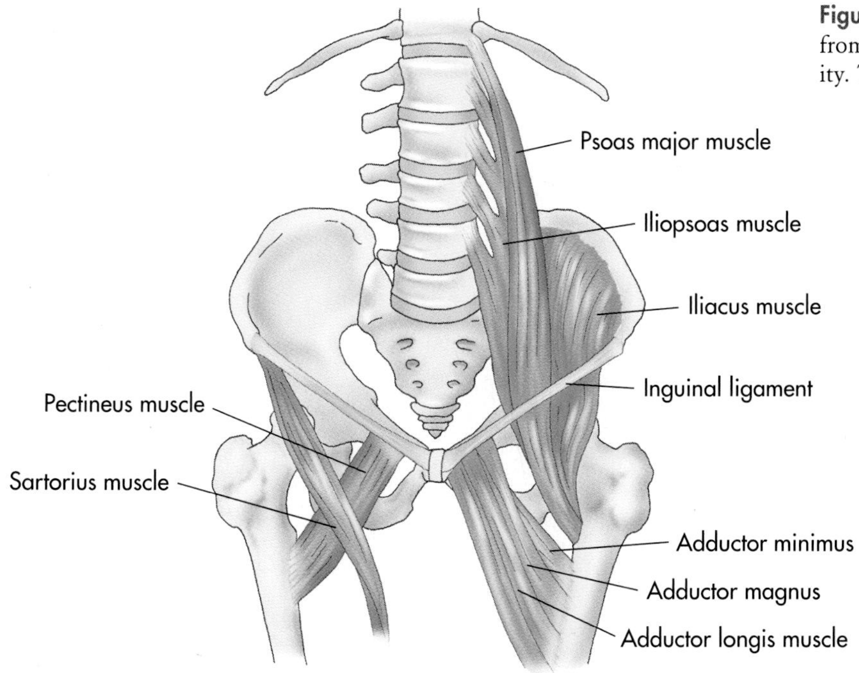

Figure 45-3 The psoas major muscle extends from the abdominal cavity into the pelvic cavity. The iliacus forms the pelvic side wall.

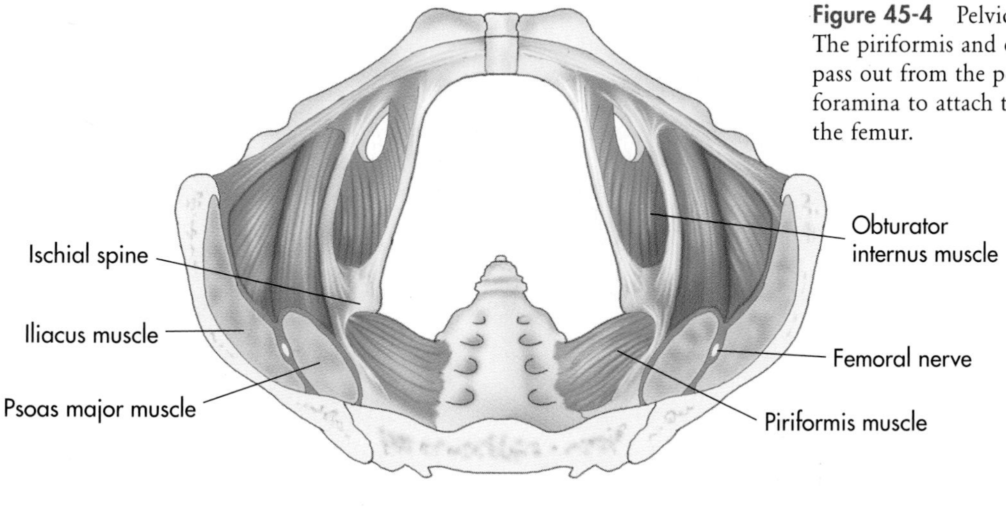

Figure 45-4 Pelvic cavity viewed from above. The piriformis and obturator internus muscles pass out from the pelvis through the sciatic foramina to attach to the greater tuberosity of the femur.

The coccygeus muscle is the muscular part of the sacrospinous ligament and forms the posterior part of the pelvic diaphragm; the anterior part of the diaphragm is formed by the levator ani muscles (Figure 45-5). In addition to forming the floor of the pelvis, the levator ani muscles also have an important role in rectal and urinary continence and maintain the position of the uterus and vagina.

PELVIC VASCULATURE

The common iliac artery provides blood to the pelvic cavity through the external and internal iliac arteries (Figure 45-6 and Box 45-3). The external iliac artery and vein course along the pelvic brim. The internal iliac artery runs down into the pelvis on the posterior wall to

Figure 45-5 The floor of the pelvis is formed by the coccygeus and levator ani muscles.

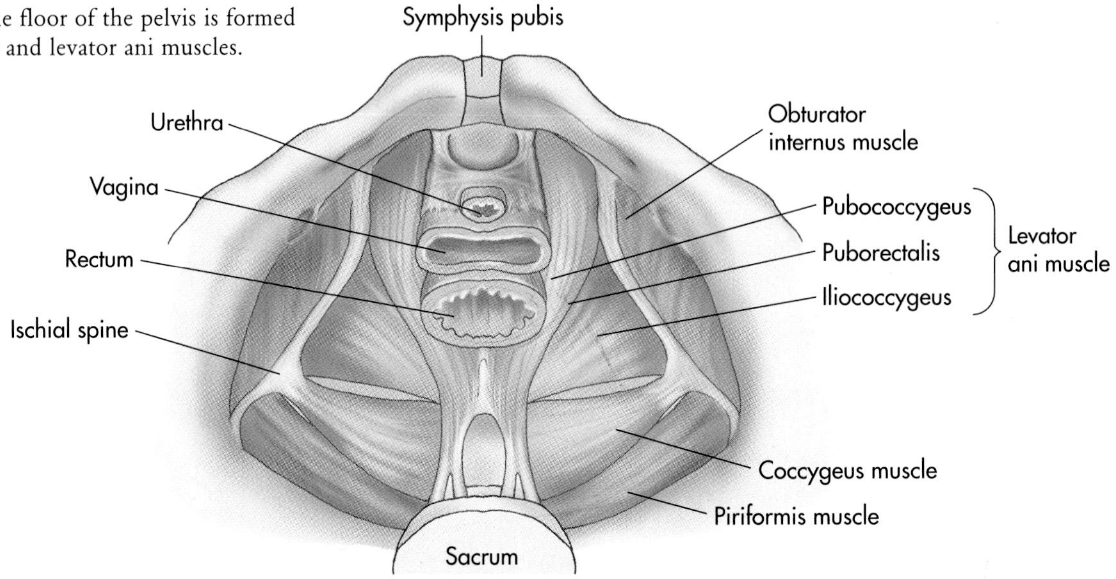

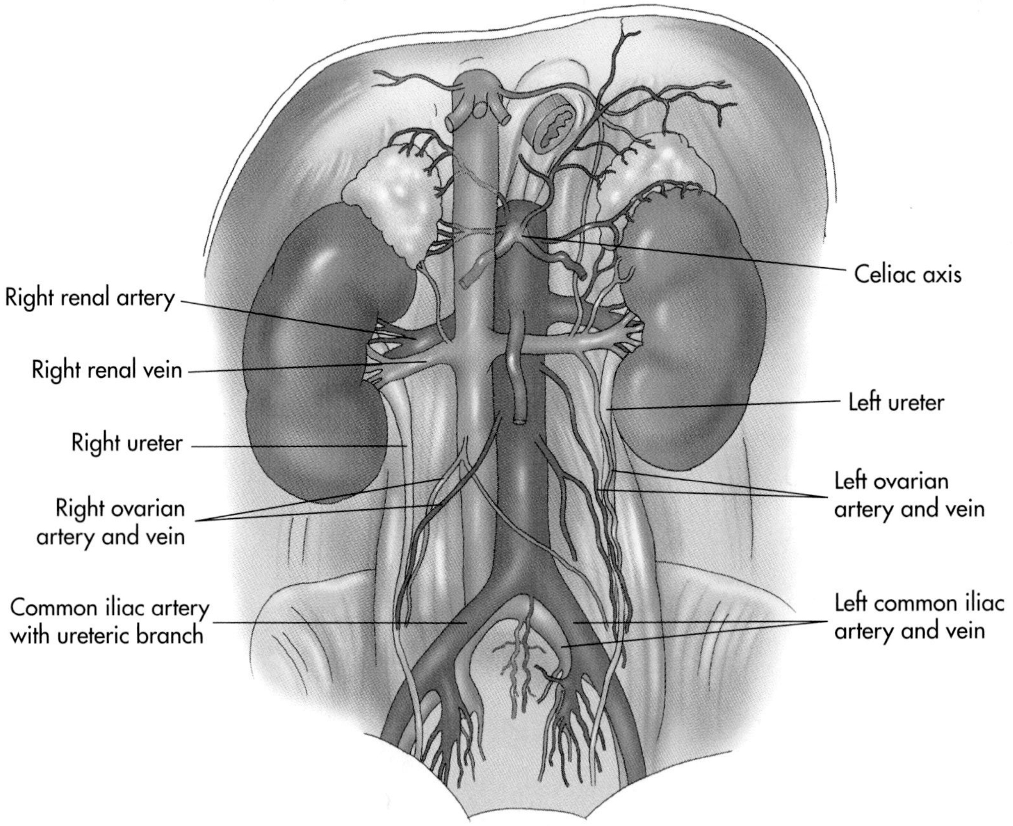

Figure 45-6 The blood supply to the pelvic cavity is through the external and internal iliac arteries; the iliac veins drain the pelvis. The ureter enters the pelvis as it courses anteriorly to the internal iliac artery to empty into the posterior base of the bladder.

provide multiple branches to the pelvic structures. The ureter also enters the pelvis as it courses anterior to the internal iliac artery to empty into the posterior base of the bladder.

Blood is supplied to the uterus from the uterine artery arising from the internal iliac artery. From the internal iliac artery, the uterine artery courses medially over the ureter in the base of the broad ligament to the uterus at the cervical level. It is tortuous and spirals up the sides of the uterus with many anastomotic sites giving off branches and blood supply (Figure 45-7).

The vagina has two sources of blood supply. The anterior surface of the vagina and the cervix are supplied with blood from a branch off the uterine artery before it reaches the uterus. The posterior surface of the vagina is supplied with blood from a branch off the internal iliac vessel.[1]

The ovary receives its blood supply from the aorta. The ovarian arteries also have a tortuous course from the lateral posterior border of the ovary to anastomose with the uterine artery in the broad ligament adjacent to the cornual area (see Figure 45-7). This is considered the ovarian branch of the uterine artery, which is the most consistent and successful area for assessing ovarian Doppler flow.

BLADDER AND URETERS

The bladder is located in the anterior segment of the pelvic cavity, posterior to the pubic symphysis (Box 45-4). The function of the bladder is to collect and store urine until it empties through the urethra (Box 45-5). When the bladder is empty or slightly filled, it remains entirely within the pelvis; as it becomes distended, it rises up behind the lower anterior abdominal wall and pushes the peritoneum away from the wall.

The internal organs of the female pelvis consist of two ovaries and fallopian tubes, a uterus, and the vagina. The external genitalia include the mons pubis, labia majora, labia minora, clitoris, bulb of the vestibule, greater vestibular glands, and vestibule of the vagina.

BOX 45-3 VESSELS OF THE PELVIC CAVITY

- *External iliac arteries:* Medial psoas border
- *External iliac veins:* Medial and posterior to the artery
- *Internal iliac arteries:* Posterior to ureters and ovaries
- *Internal iliac veins:* Posterior to arteries
- *Uterine arteries and veins:* Broad ligaments
- *Ovarian arteries:* Suspensory ligaments

BOX 45-4 BLADDER

- *Apex:* Located posterior to pubic bones
- *Base:* Anterior to vagina, superior surface related to uterus
- *Neck:* Rests on upper surface of urogenital diaphragm; inferolateral surfaces relate to retropubic fat, obturator internus and levator ani muscles, and pubic bone

BOX 45-5 URETER

- Crosses pelvic inlet anterior to bifurcation of common iliac artery
- Runs anterior to internal iliac artery and posterior to the ovary
- Runs anterior and medially under the base of the broad ligament where it is crossed by the uterine artery
- Runs anterior and lateral to the vagina to enter the bladder

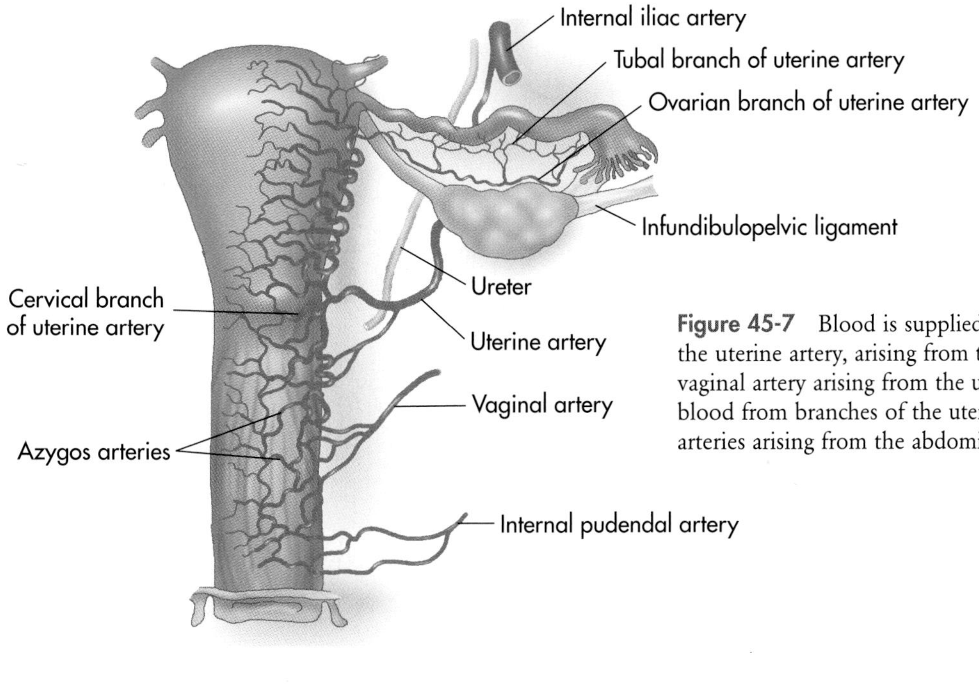

Figure 45-7 Blood is supplied to the uterus and vagina from the uterine artery, arising from the internal iliac artery and the vaginal artery arising from the uterine artery. The ovaries receive blood from branches of the uterine artery and from the ovarian arteries arising from the abdominal aorta.

BOX 45-6 Vagina, Urethra, and Fornix

- Extends upward and backward from the vulva
- Upper half lies above pelvic floor
- Lower half lies within perineum
- Area of vaginal lumen surrounding the cervix is divided into four fornices
- Arterial supply is from vaginal and uterine arteries; drains into the internal iliac vein

Vagina

The vagina is a muscular tube composed of primarily smooth muscle with some skeletal muscle fibers at the lower end (Box 45-6). It measures about 10 cm in length. The vagina lies anterior to the rectum and anal canal and posterior to the pubic symphysis, urinary bladder, and urethra (Figure 45-8). It is the passageway for the products of the menstrual cycle and is easily distensible (especially during childbirth). The vagina has a mucous membrane lining

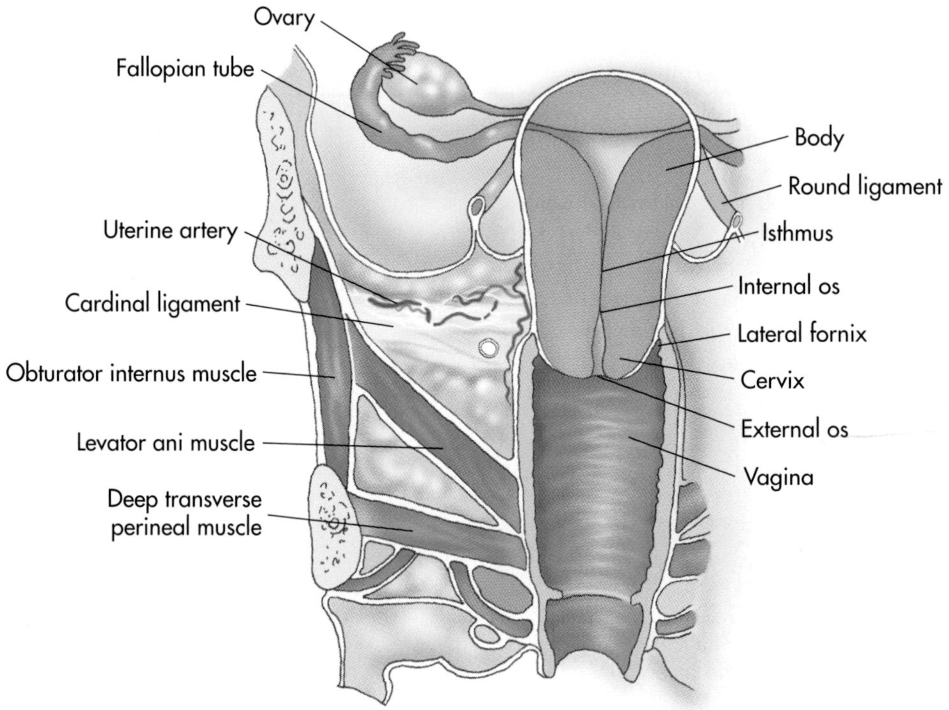

Figure 45-8 Coronal view of the vagina, cervix, and uterus.

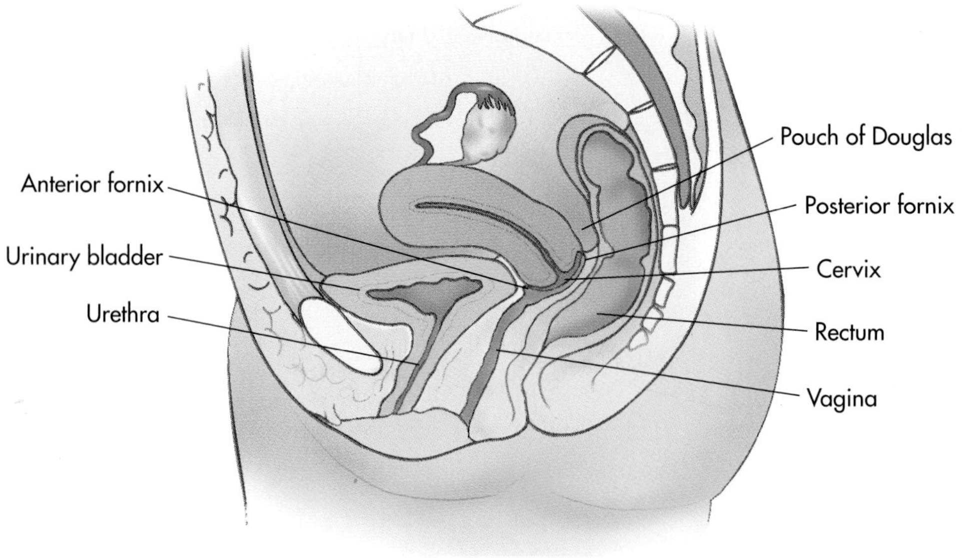

Figure 45-9 Lateral view of the pelvis demonstrating the relationship of the anterior and posterior fornices to the cervix and vagina.

its muscular walls to receive secretions from the vaginal wall and the mucous glands of the cervix and vestibular glands (during sexual excitement).

URETHRA

The urethra is located in the lower part of the anterior vaginal wall. The opening (the external urethral meatus) is anterior to the opening of the vagina.

FORNIX

The fornix is found at the upper end of the vagina, near the external cervix. The fornix is further classified into an anterior and a posterior segment (Figure 45-9). The posterior part of the fornix is covered on the pelvic cavity side by the peritoneum; instruments that are directed into the area of the cervix may be misdirected and perforate the posterior fornix, causing the instruments to enter into the peritoneal cavity and risk peritonitis.

UTERUS

ANATOMY AND PHYSIOLOGY

The uterus becomes the largest organ in the normal female pelvis when the urinary bladder is empty (Box 45-7). It is a mobile, hollow, muscular, pear-shaped structure partially covered by peritoneum. The normal menarchal uterus measures about 7.5 cm long, 5 cm wide, and 2.5 cm thick (Box 45-8 and Table 45-1).

BOX 45-7 UTERUS

- Hollow, pear-shaped organ
- Divided into fundus, body, and cervix
- Usually anteflexed and anteverted
- Covered with peritoneum except anteriorly below the os where peritoneum is reflected onto bladder
- Supported by levator ani muscles and pelvic fascia
- Round ligament keeps uterus in position

BOX 45-8 UTERINE SIZE

- *Prepubertal:* 3 cm long by 0.5 to1.0 cm wide
- *Menarcheal:* 8 cm long by 4 cm wide
  With multiparity: Increases size by 1.2 cm
- *Postmenopausal:* 3.5 to 5.5 cm long by 1 to 2 cm wide

The uterus is composed of the asternal layer or serous coat, the middle layer or muscular coat, and the internal mucous layer (Figure 45-10). The external layer, the peritoneum, surrounds the uterus except where the bladder lays against it at the cervical-vaginal connection. The middle layer, the myometrium, composes the majority of the uterus. It is primarily smooth muscle that is longitudinal and circular (Box 45-9). The inner layer, the endometrium, is lined by a thin, smooth mucous membrane. This membrane is contiguous with the lining of the vagina.[3] The inner lining of the body of the uterus varies in appearance and histologic structure, depending on the period of life in which it is studied.

The uterus consists of the fundus or most upper portion, the body or central area (Box 45-10), and the cervix (Box 45-11), or the lower cylindric portion that joins the uterus to the vagina (see Figure 45-10).[3] At the lateral borders of the fundus are the cornua, where the fallopian tubes are attached to the uterine cavity. The central cavity is a potential space allowing for the dynamic changes during the normal menstrual cycle and pregnancy. The upper portion of the cervix is constricted by the internal os and the lower portion by the external os.

The uterus is supported in its midline position by paired broad ligaments, round ligaments, and uterosacral ligaments, as well as other lesser ligaments (Figure 45-11 and Box 45-12).[3,9] The broad ligaments are a double fold of peritoneum and provide bilateral support for the uterus. They attach to the lateral walls of the pelvis, surrounding the fallopian tubes, round ligaments, ovary, parovarium, connective tissue, unstriped muscular fiber, blood vessels, and nerves. The upper edge of the broad ligament encloses the fallopian tube as it extends from the cornua of the uterus.

The round ligaments occupy space between the layers of broad ligament and occur in front of and below the fallopian tube. These two cords commence on each side of the superior aspect of the uterus and course upward and lateral to the inguinal canal and the labia majora. The uterosacral ligaments originate laterally at the level of the internal os of the cervix and pass downward along the sides of the rectum extending to the third and fourth bones of the sacrum.[3]

TABLE 45-1 UTERINE SIZE

	Length (cm)	Width (cm)	AP (cm)	Volume (ml)	Cervix/ corpus ratio
Adult (nulliparous)	6-8	3-5	3-5	30-40	1:2
Adult (parous)	8-10	5-6	5-6	60-80	1:2
Postmenopausal	3-5	2-3	2-3	14-17	1:1

From Warwick W, editor: *Gray's anatomy,* New York, 1994, Churchill-Livingstone.

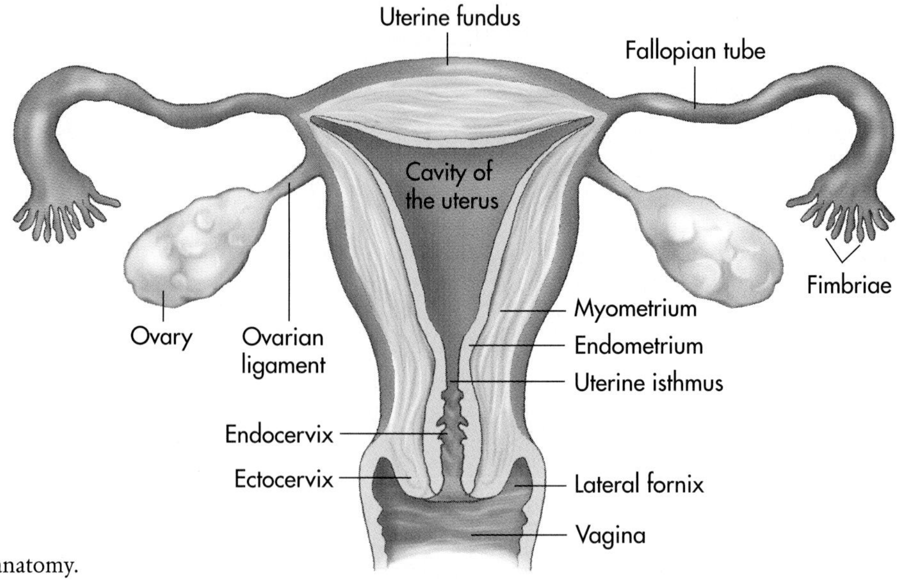

Figure 45-10 Normal female pelvic anatomy.

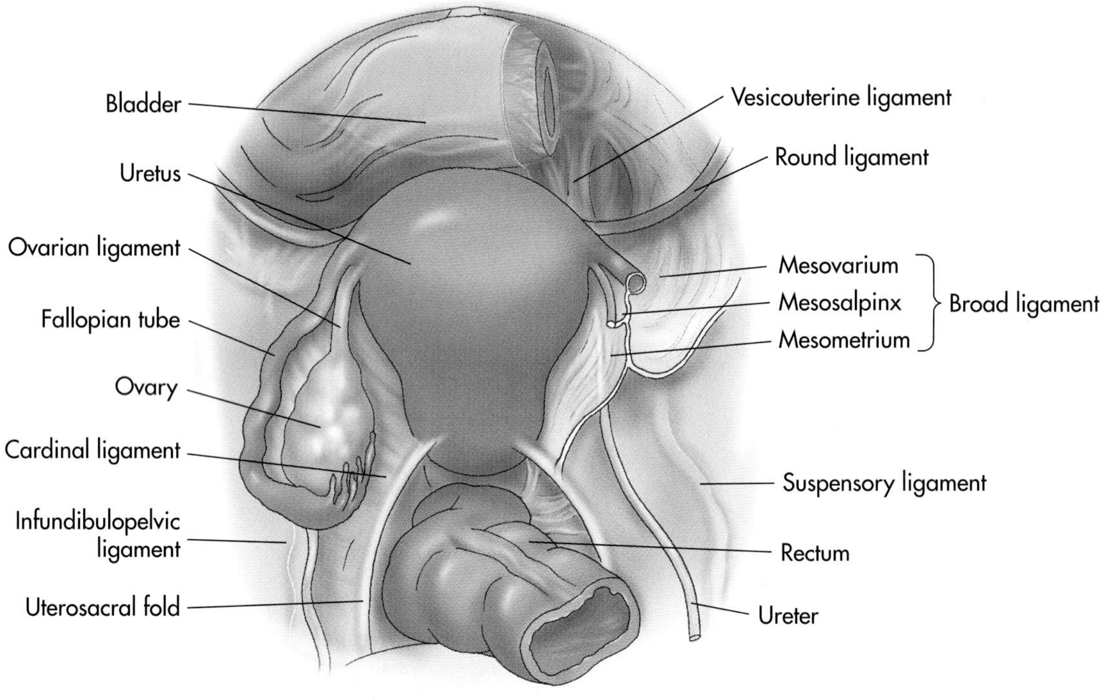

Figure 45-11 View of the pelvic cavity from above, looking inferior, showing the attachment of the round ligament and broad ligament to the uterus.

BOX 45-9 Myometrium and Endometrium

- *Myometrium:* Muscular middle layer of the uterus composed of thick, smooth muscle supported by connective tissue
- *Endometrium:* Mucous membrane of the uterine body

BOX 45-11 Cervix

- Canal communicates with uterine cavity by the internal os; the vagina by the external os

BOX 45-10 Body of the Uterus

- Related anteriorly to the uterovesical pouch and the superior surface of the bladder
- Related posteriorly to the rectouterine pouch (of Douglas), the ilium, and colon
- Lateral to the broad ligament and uterine vessels
- Funnel shaped on coronal plane; a "slit" on sagittal

BOX 45-12 Uterine Ligaments

- *Broad:* Lateral aspect of uterus to pelvic wall; ovary attached via mesovarium
- *Suspensory:* Ovary to pelvic wall
- *Round:* Fundus to anterior pelvic side walls
- *Ovarian:* Ovary to uterus

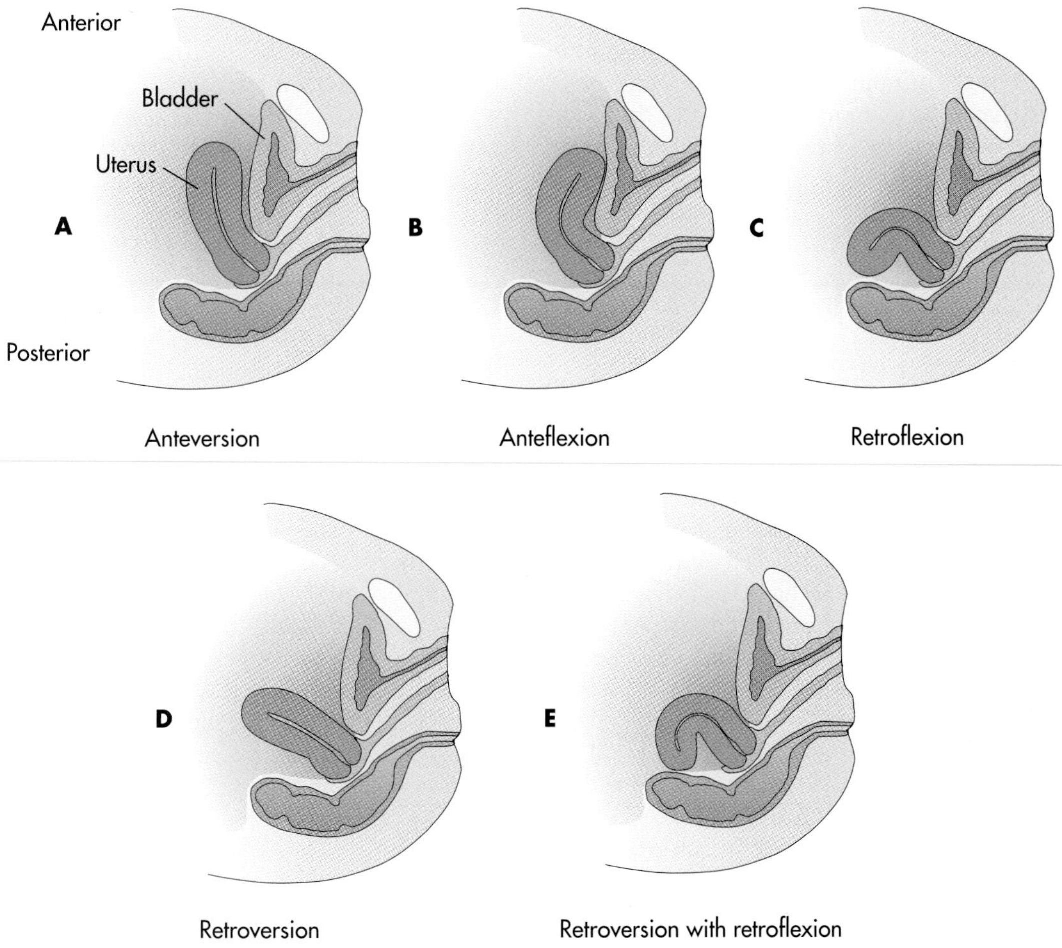

Figure 45-12 The uterine cavity may be found in one of several positions: **A,** Anteversion (tipped forward). **B,** Anteflexion (tipped forward at the cervix). **C,** Retroflexion (tipped backward at the cervix). **D,** Retroversion (tilted posterior). **E,** Retroversion with retroflexion (tipped backward and posterior).

BOX 45-13 UTERINE POSITION

- *Midline anteversion:* Most common; degree of anteversion is bladder distention dependent
- *Right or left:* Normal variant in absence of pelvic masses
- *Retroverted:* Entire organ displaced posteriorly
- *Retroflexed:* Body displaced with respect to cervix

POSITIONS OF THE UTERUS

The body of the uterus is normally "bent" forward, or anteflexed, to make a slight angle with the cervix. The cervix makes a similar angle with the vagina, also called **anteverted** (Figure 45-12 and Box 45-13). In some females the uterus tips backward rather than forward, becoming "retroverted" and/or retroflexed. The broad ligaments and round ligaments help somewhat to hold the uterus in position. In addition, there are condensations of connective tissue under the peritoneum in the region of the cervix of the uterus and fornix of the vagina. Those condensations are known as the lateral ligaments, cervical ligaments, and cardinal ligaments. The ligaments passing on either side of the rectum are uterosacral ligaments. The clinical condition of "prolapse" of the uterus is found when these ligaments are stretched or abnormal.

ENDOMETRIUM

ANATOMY AND PHYSIOLOGY

The endometrium consists primarily of two layers: the functional layer (zona functionalis) and the deep basal layer (zona basalis). The functional layer is a superficial layer of glands and stroma. The basal layer is a thin layer of the blind ends of endometrial glands that regenerates new endometrium after menses.[6] It is well known that the endometrium of the uterus changes dynamically in response to cyclic hormonal flux.[1]

FALLOPIAN TUBES

ANATOMY

After evaluation of the uterus and cervix is complete, the adnexa are interrogated. It is important to assess the fallopian tube (uterine tube) in its normal and pathologic

states (Box 45-14). The normal fallopian tube is about 12 cm in length and 1 to 4 mm in diameter.[7,8] It is difficult to distinguish from the surrounding ligaments and vessels. The tubes lies above the uteroovarian ligaments, the round ligaments, and tuboovarian vessels. It is contained in a special fold of the broad ligament called the **mesosalpinx,**[3] which is attached to the part of the ligament near the ovary. Doppler imaging may help distinguish vessels from tubes. The fallopian tube has three anatomic parts(the infundibulum (distal), ampulla (mid), and isthmus (proximal) (Figure 45-13).[1]

OVARIES

Ovarian Ligaments

Originating bilaterally at the cornua of the uterus are the ovarian ligaments, the uterine tube, and the round ligaments of the uterus. The ovary is attached to the broad ligament via the mesovarium and to the lateral pelvic wall via the suspensory ligament. The area of broad ligament superior to the mesovarium is called the mesosalpinx (see Figure 45-11).[1,9]

Position and Size of the Ovaries

The ovaries are almond-shaped structures, each measuring about 3 cm long (Table 45-2 and Box 45-15). They usually lie near the cornua of the uterus, along the side wall of the pelvis, suspended from the back of the broad ligament of the uterus in a fold of peritoneum called the mesovarium. The ovaries are usually medial to the external iliac vessels and anterior to the ureter. The blood supply to the ovary is from the ovarian artery, which arises from the abdominal aorta near the renal artery. Early embryologic development shows the ovary to develop high on the posterior abdominal wall and then migrates into the pelvis, retaining its original blood supply (Box 45-16).

BOX 45-14 Fallopian Tubes

- *Infundibulum:* Funnel-shaped lateral tube that projects beyond the broad ligament to overlie the ovaries; "free edge" of the funnel has fimbriae—(fingerlike projectors draped over the ovary
- *Ampulla:* Widest part of the tube where fertilization occurs
- *Isthmus:* Hardest part; lies just lateral to the uterus
- *Interstitial:* Pierces the uterine wall
- *Length:* 12 cm; supplied by ovarian arteries and veins

Cortex and Medulla

The ovary consists of the outer region or cortex, which surrounds the central medulla, and the cortex consists primarily of follicles in varying stages of development. It is covered by a layer of dense connective tissue, the tunica albuginea, and a thin single layer of cells, the germinal epithelium. The central medulla is composed of connective tissue containing blood, nerves, lymphatic vessels, and some smooth muscle at the region of the hilum.[9]

The ovaries produce the reproductive cell, the ovum, and two known hormones: estrogen, secreted by the follicles, and progesterone, secreted by the corpus luteum (Figure 45-14). These hormones are responsible for producing and maintaining secondary gender characteristics, for preparing the uterus for implantation of the fertilized ovum, and for development of the mammary glands.[9]

Follicular Development

A female's reproductive years begin around age 11 to 13 years at the onset of menstruation, and terminate around age 50 years when menstruation ceases. During these years, once a month an ovum is released from one of the two ovaries. This process is known as ovulation. It is speculated that the ovum release alternates between the two ovaries. All ova begin development in embryonic life and remain in suspended animation until the onset of menses begins. Some of the ova will mature and be discharged from the ovaries on a monthly basis, and others die without coming to anything.

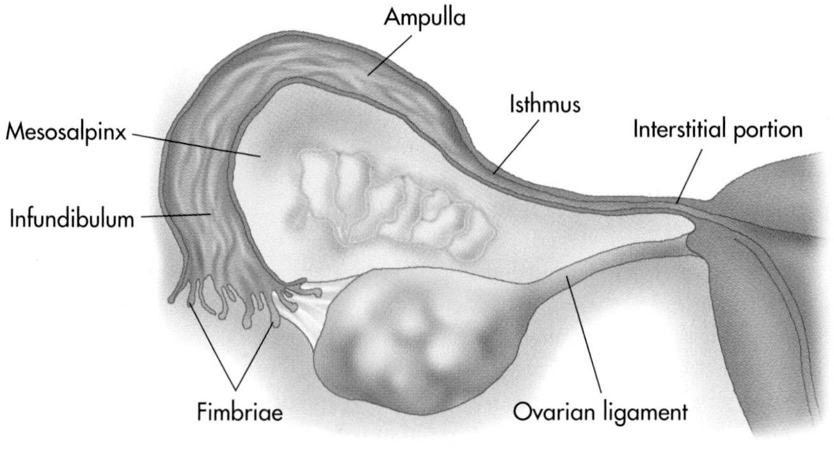

Figure 45-13 Diagram of the fallopian tube showing the fimbriae, infundibulum, ampulla, isthmus, and interstitial parts.

TABLE 45-2 NORMAL OVARIAN VOLUME BY MENSTRUAL STATUS

Group	Mean volume (cm^3)	Standard deviation	No. of ovaries	95% confidence interval (cm^3)*
Premenarchal	3.0	2.3	32	0.2 to 9.1
Menstruating	9.8	5.8	866	2.5 to 21.9
Postmenopausal	5.8	3.6	100	1.2 to 14.1

From Cohen HL, Tice HM, Mandel FS: *Radiology* 177:189, 1990.
*Calculated on the basis of cube root values, then transformed back to cubic centimeters.

BOX 45-15 OVARIES

- Almond shaped
- Attached to back of the broad ligament by mesovarium; sometimes called suspensory ligament of the ovary
- Lies in ovarian fossa
- Fossa is bounded by external iliac vessels, ureter, and obturator nerve
- Receives blood from ovarian artery
- Blood drained by ovarian vein into inferior vena cava on right; on left by ovarian vein into left renal vein

BOX 45-16 VARIABLE POSITIONS

- Direct relationship to internal iliac vein
- Ellipsoid shape with long axis vertical
- Location variable, especially after pregnancy

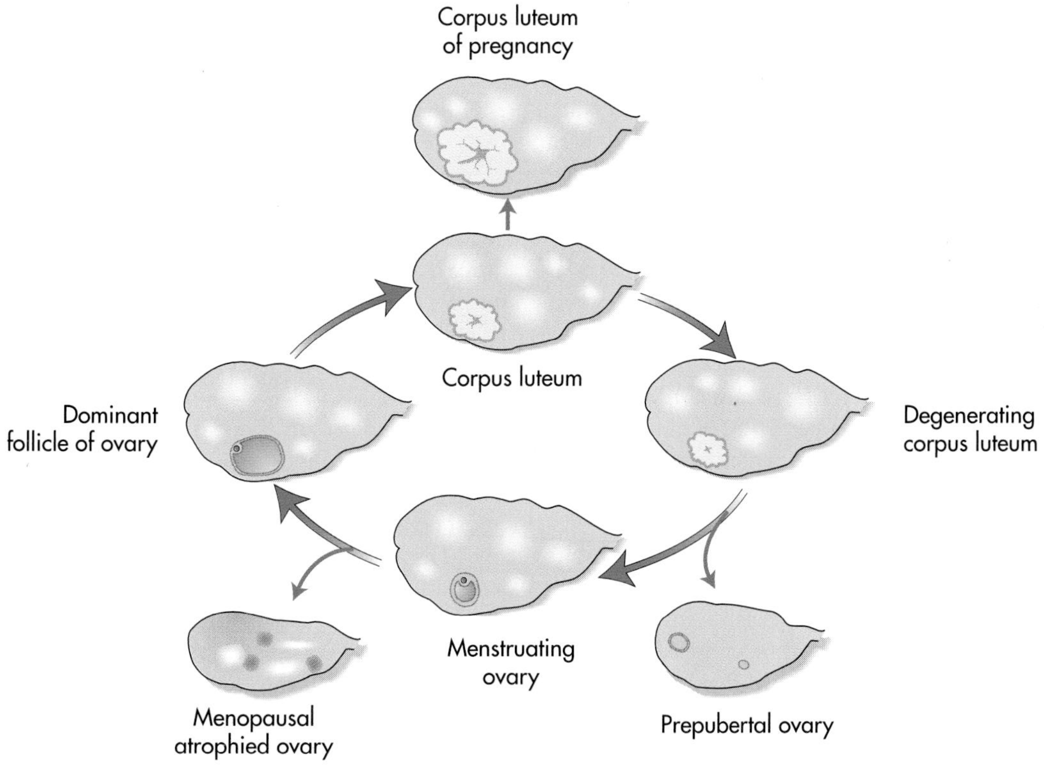

Figure 45-14 Diagram of cyclic changes of the normal ovary. The prepubertal ovary may contain small follicles. The menstruating ovary contains several primary follicles that begin the process of growth and development. One follicle becomes the dominant follicle because the pituitary gland produces follicle-stimulating hormone *(FSH)*. The dominant follicle *(ova)* fills with fluid and begins to secrete estrogen. The estrogen level increases, which inhibits further production of FSH. The pituitary then begins the secretion of luteinizing hormone. This luteinizing surge causes ovulation. The collapsed follicle lining begins to multiply and create the corpus luteum. The corpus lutem secretes both progesterone and estrogen. If pregnancy occurs, the corpus luteum continues to grow and secrete progesterone and estrogen to support the pregnancy up to 3 months. If pregnancy does not occur, the corpus luteum degenerates. Because of the decrease in progesterone and estrogen, menstruation occurs and the cycle repeats itself.

BOX 45-17 THE CYCLE

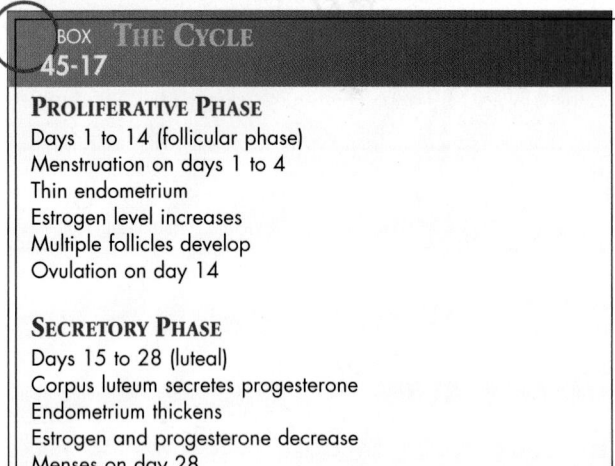

PROLIFERATIVE PHASE
Days 1 to 14 (follicular phase)
Menstruation on days 1 to 4
Thin endometrium
Estrogen level increases
Multiple follicles develop
Ovulation on day 14

SECRETORY PHASE
Days 15 to 28 (luteal)
Corpus luteum secretes progesterone
Endometrium thickens
Estrogen and progesterone decrease
Menses on day 28

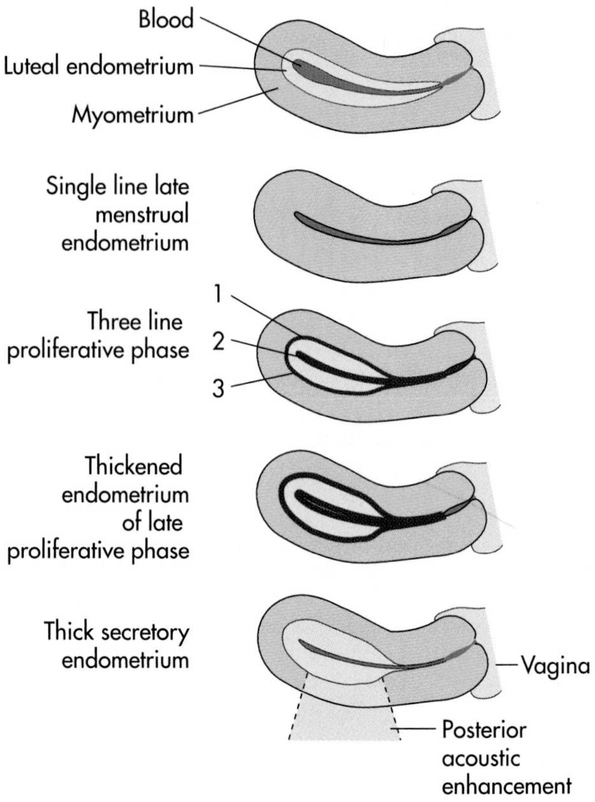

Figure 45-15 Changes in the endometrium.

THE OVARIAN CYCLE

Menstrual status is described using the terms **premenarche, menarche,** and **menopause** (Box 45-17). Premenarche is the physiologic status of prepuberty, the time before the onset of menses. Menarche is the state after reaching puberty in which menses occur normally every 27 to 28 days. Menopause is when menses have ceased permanently.

The cyclic changes of the uterus throughout the menstrual cycle correlate with the interactions of hormones from the ovaries and hormones from the pituitary gland. The typical cycle is identified and described in three phases (Figure 45-15). The menstrual phase is approximately days 1 to 4. The ovaries contain many primary follicles to begin the process of growth and development.

At the same time the uterus is shedding the superficial layer of the endometrium, known as the menses. The proliferative or follicular phase is approximately days 5 to 14. The ovarian follicles are under the influence of a hormone produced in the pituitary gland known as **follicle-stimulating hormone (FSH)** and begin a period of rapid growth. The ova grows, fills with fluid, and begins to secrete estrogen. Although many follicles may be present, only one usually reaches maturity each month.

The estrogen level reaches a point at which it inhibits further production of FSH. The pituitary then begins secreting luteinizing hormone. This shift in hormones causes ovulation at about day 14 of the cycle. Ovulation is the release of an egg from the ruptured mature follicle. At the same time the uterus reacts to the increase of estrogen, causing the superficial layer of the endometrium to regenerate and grow.

The secretory phase extends from approximately day 15 to day 29 (to the onset of menses). The collapsed follicle lining begins to multiply and create the corpus luteum, or yellow body. The corpus luteum secretes both progesterone and estrogen. As the progesterone level increases, the endometrium prepares to accept a fertilized egg. If fertilization does not occur, the corpus luteum degenerates. Because of the decreased progesterone and estrogen levels, menstruation occurs and the cycle begins again. If fertilization and implantation occur, the corpus luteum continues to secrete progesterone and estrogen for approximately 3 more months until the placenta takes over.

RECTOUTERINE RECESS AND BOWEL

It is normal to observe an accumulation of free fluid throughout the menstrual cycle in the rectouterine recess and cul-de-sac (see Figure 45-2).[4,6,8,10] This region is the most posterior and dependent region of the peritoneal cavity.[6] The greatest quantity of free fluid in the cul-de-sac occurs after the mature follicle ruptures.[5] This does not always indicate ovulation. If the fluid contains blood or pus, pathology may be present, such as a ruptured cyst, ascitic fluid, a ruptured corpus luteum cyst, ectopic pregnancy, or pelvic inflammatory disease.[8]

REVIEW QUESTIONS

1. Describe the bony landmarks of the pelvis.
2. Discuss the anatomic landmarks of the perineum.
3. Describe the exact location of the following muscles: psoas, iliacus, piriformis, obturator internus, coccygeus, and levator ani.
4. What is the course of the ureter as it relates to the iliac vessels?

5. List the female reproductive organs.
6. Describe the layers of the uterus.
7. What are the normal uterine positions?
8. Discuss the function of the broad and round ligaments of the uterus.
9. Describe the location and relationship of surrounding structures of the fallopian tubes.
10. What are the three anatomic areas of the fallopian tubes?
11. What are the two regions of the ovary?
12. What are the functions of the ovary?
13. What is the best landmark for the ovary?
14. How is the ovary measured and the volume calculated?
15. What vessels are routinely evaluated in the female pelvis using Doppler imaging?
16. Describe the ovarian cycle.
17. What is the significance of the rectouterine recess and bowel?

REFERENCES

1. Anderson JE: *Grant's atlas of anatomy,* ed 8. Baltimore, 1983, Williams and Wilkins.
2. Kurtz AB, Rifkin MD: *Ultrasonography in obstetrics and gynecology,* Philadelphia, 1983, WB Saunders.
3. Crocco JA: Introduction. In Gray H: *Gray's anatomy,* ed 15, New York, 1977, Bounty Books.
4. Davis JA, Gosink BB: Fluid in the female pelvis: cyclic patterns, *J Ultrasound Med* 5:75, 1986.
5. Grunfeld L and others: High resolution endovaginal ultrasonography of the endometrium: a noninvasive test for endometrial adequacy, *Obstet Gynecol* 78:200, 1991.
6. Lyons EA, Gratton D, Harrington C: Transvaginal sonography of normal pelvic anatomy, *Radiol Clin North Am* 30:663, 1992.
7. Nyberg D and others: *Transvaginal ultrasound,* St Louis, 1992, Mosby.
8. Rosen DJD and others: Transvaginal ultrasonographic quantitative assessment of accumulated cul-de-sac fluid, *Am J Obstet Gynecol* 166:542, 1992.
9. Thomas CL, editor: *Taber's cyclopedic medical dictionary,* ed 4, Philadelphia, 1982, FA Davis.
10. Timor-Tritsch IE, Rottem S: Transvaginal ultrasonographic study of the fallopian tube, *Obstet Gynecol* 70:424, 1987.

BIBLIOGRAPHY

Evers JLH, Heineman MJ: *Gynecology: a clinical atlas,* St Louis, 1990, Mosby.

Parsons AK, Ryva JC: Gynecologic ultrasound. In Hagen-Ansert S, editor: *Textbook of diagnostic ultrasonography,* ed 3, St Louis, 1989, Mosby.

Tesser FN and others: Endovaginal sonographic diagnosis of dilated fallopian tubes, *Am J Roentgenol* 153:523, 1989.

CHAPTER 46

Embryogenesis and Pediatric and Congenital Anomalies

Sandra L. Hagen-Ansert

OBJECTIVES

- Discuss the development of the ovaries
- Describe when external genitalia may be seen by ultrasound
- Detail the sonographic findings in pediatric gynecology
- Differentiate between the müllerian anomalies that may occur in the uterus
- Define the sonographic findings of a bicornuate, didelphys, and septate uterus
- Discuss the findings in ambiguous genitalia
- Describe the characteristics of precocious puberty

KEY TERMS

bicornuate uterus - duplication of the uterus and sometimes cervix
hematometrocolpos - blood-filled vagina and uterus
hydrocolpos - fluid-filled vagina
hydrometrocolpos - fluid-filled vagina and uterus
unicornuate uterus - anomaly of the uterus in which only one horn develops
uterus didelphys - complete duplication of the uterus, cervix, and vagina
vagina atresia - failure of the vagina to develop

The development of the female genital system and the role embryology plays in congenital abnormalities of the female reproductive tract are presented in this chapter. Frequently, uterine anomalies are associated with abnormalities of the urinary tract.

Both transabdominal and transvaginal sonography are important in these evaluations. Transabdominal imaging furnishes a survey of anatomy, whereas endovaginal imaging provides better characterization of internal architecture of anatomical structures.[3]

EMBRYOLOGY OF THE FEMALE GENITAL TRACT

Development of the Gonads

The first parts of the genital system to develop are the gonads. The gonads arise from the parts of the urogenital ridges, gonadal ridges. This ridge enlarges and frees itself from the mesonephros by developing a mesentery that becomes the mesovarium. At the same time, the coelomic epithelium covering the gonadal ridges grows and forms cords of cells, called primary sex cords, that grow into the mesenchyme of the developing gonads.[4] The primordial germ cells originate in the wall of the yolk sac and migrate into the embryo and enter the primary sex cords to give rise to the ova.

Development of the Ovaries

In embryos with a double "X" chromosome, differentiation of the gonads occurs later than in the males.[4] The primary sex cords converge to form a network of canals called the rete ovarii, which soon disappears with the primary sex cords. At the same time, the surface epithelium of the developing ovary gives rise to secondary sex cords, or corti-

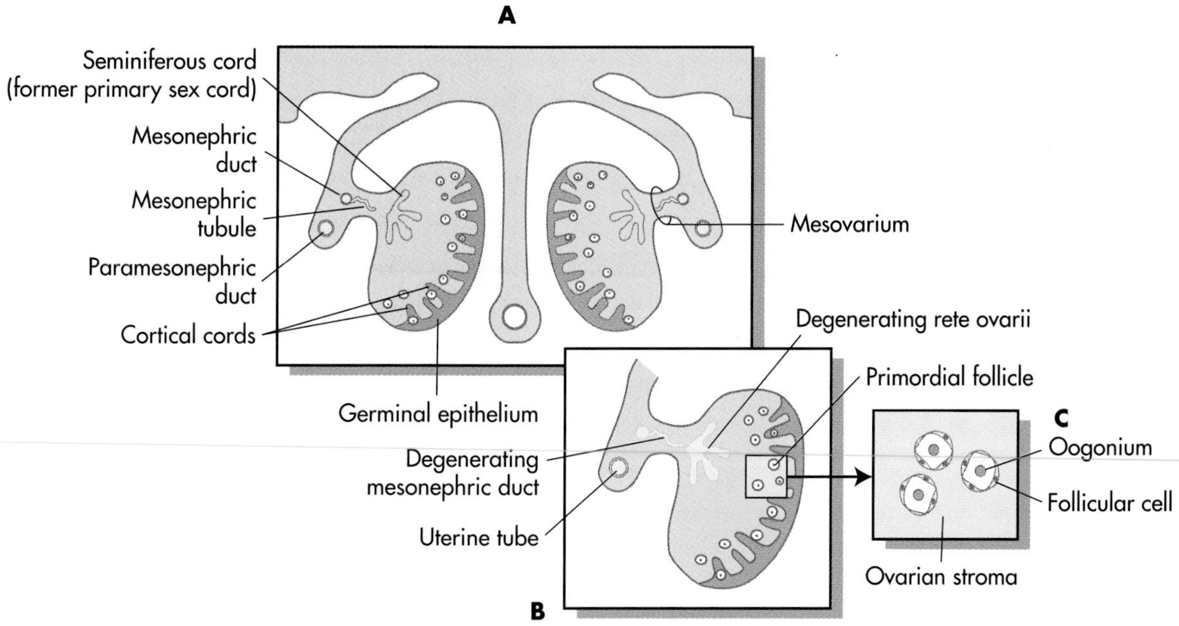

Figure 46-1 **A,** Fetus at 12 weeks of gestation shows the ovary beginning to develop. **B,** Ovary at 20 weeks, showing the primordial follicles formed from the cortical cords. **C,** Section from the ovarian cortex of a 20-week fetus showing three primordial follicles.

cal cords (Figure 46-1). As these cords grow in the ovary, primordial germ cells are incorporated into them. At about 16 weeks of gestation, the cortical cords break up into isolated cell clusters called primordial follicles, each of which contains an oogonium derived from the primordial germ cell. Each oogonium is surrounded by a layer of flattened follicular cells derived from the surface epithelial cells in the cortical cord. The oogonia multiply rapidly by mitosis, producing thousands of these primitive germ cells. Before birth, all oogonia enlarge to form primary oocytes and most of them have entered the first meiotic prophase, but this process remains in an arrested state until puberty.

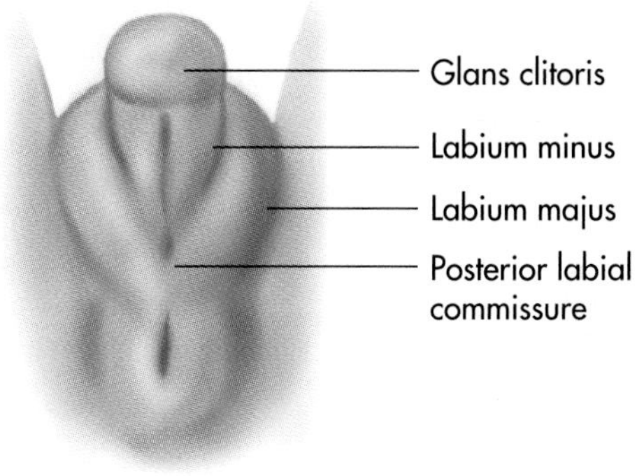

Figure 46-2 Development of the female external genitalia at 11 weeks.

DEVELOPMENT OF THE GENITAL DUCTS

All embryos have identical pairs of genital ducts. The female or *paramesonephric ducts* (see Figure 46-1) develop into the female reproductive system.[4] During the indifferent state of sexual development, both pairs of genital ducts are present. Even though the genetic sex of an embryo is determined at fertilization by the kind of sperm that fertilizes the ovum, there are no morphologic indications of maleness or femaleness until the 7th week.

DEVELOPMENT OF THE FEMALE GENITAL DUCTS

The paramesonephric ducts form most of the female genital tract.[4] Their cranial parts form the uterine tubes and their caudal parts fuse to form the uterovaginal primordium or canal, which develops into the uterus and part of the vagina. Contact of the uterovaginal primordium with the urogenital sinus induces paired endodermal outgrowths, called sinovaginal bulbs, to form. These bulbs fuse to form a solid vaginal plate. The central cells of this plate break down to form the vagina; the peripheral cells form the vaginal epithelium.

DEVELOPMENT OF THE EXTERNAL GENITALIA

Early in development, both sexes appear similar until the 9th week of gestation.[4] External organs are fully developed by the 12th week. Both the urethra and vagina open into the urogenital sinus, which becomes the vestibule of the vagina. The urogenital folds become the labia minora, the labioscrotal swellings become the labia major, and the phallus becomes the clitoris (Figure 46-2).

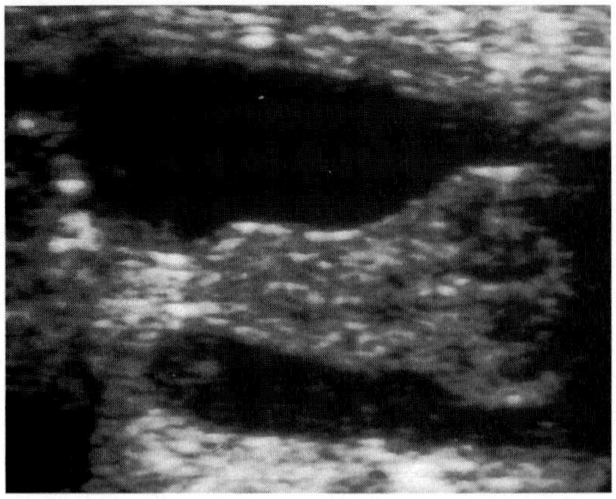

Figure 46-3 Neonatal uterus well seen within the pelvic cavity with ascitic fluid surrounding the teardrop-shaped uterine wall. The cervix consumes the majority of the total uterine length at this stage.

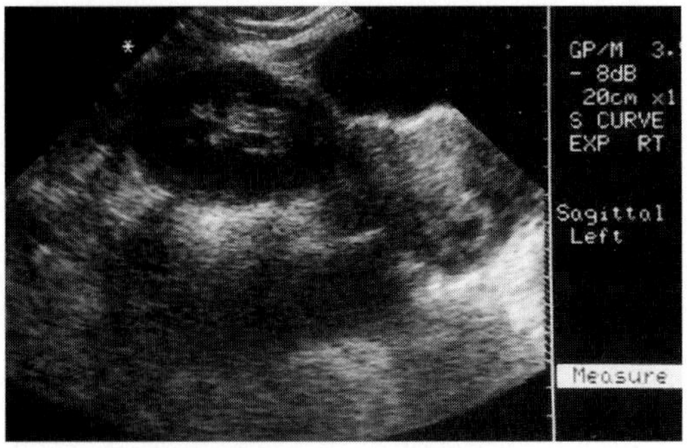

Figure 46-4 A pelvic kidney is seen adjacent to the bicornuate uterus on this sagittal transabdominal scan.

PEDIATRIC GYNECOLOGIC SONOGRAPHY

The sonographic evaluation of the neonatal and pediatric pelvic cavity requires a distended urinary bladder because only the transabdominal ultrasound technique is used. The evaluation of ovarian size is most accurate when the volume is determined by using the prolate-ellipse formula:

$$\text{Volume in cubic centimeters} = \text{Length} \times \text{Height} \times \text{Width} \times 0.523$$

The mean ovarian volume is stable up to 5 years of age and ranges from 0.75 to 0.86 cm^3. Ovarian volume gradually increases until puberty is reached. Usually the ovarian texture is homogeneous; however, small follicles may be seen with ultrasound.

The normal uterus is a small tubular structure measuring 2.3 to 4 cm in length and 0.8 to 2.1 cm in width. The cervical width measures 0.8 to 2.2 cm. The endometrium is usually visualized in the neonatal and pediatric patient as an echogenic line; a quarter of the neonates may show some endometrial fluid. The maternal hormones stimulate the initial size of the uterine cavity after birth; as these hormones decrease, so does the uterine size. The uterus assumes a teardrop shape, with the cervix consuming more area than the uterus (Figure 46-3).

The uterus increases in size after the age of 7, with the greatest increase in size occurring after the onset of puberty, when the fundus becomes much larger than the cervix.

CONGENITAL MALFORMATIONS OF THE GENITAL SYSTEM

UTERUS

The definitive diagnosis and classification of a congenital anomaly of the uterine cavity requires the visualization of the uterine cavity or cavities and the serosal margin(s). Before ultrasound, hysterosalpingography with laparoscopy was used to define the uterine cavity. Now with transabdominal and transvaginal ultrasound, the uterine cavities may be defined. A newer technique of injecting a small amount of contrast material into the cavity further differentiates the uterine cavity and septae.

Congenital Anomalies. The uterus provides the endometrial canal for the site of implantation and growth for the intrauterine pregnancy. Developmental problems, interference with blood supply, or distortion of the uterine cavity may result in infertility or spontaneous abortion. Congenital uterine abnormalities occur in approximately 0.5% of women and are associated with an increased incidence of abortion and other obstetric complications.[6]

Patients may be asymptomatic, or they may have pelvic pain, history of infertility problems, early pregnancy loss (spontaneous abortion), or premature deliveries.

The uterus and upper third of the vagina are derived from the embryonic müllerian (paramesonephric) ducts. These ducts must elongate, fuse, and form lumens between the 7th and 12th weeks of embryonic development. When this sequence fails to occur, one of the following three types of mullerian abnormalities results: improper fusion, incomplete development of one side, or incomplete vaginal canalization.[3,4]

Ultrasound findings. If müllerian anomalies are encountered, the kidneys should be examined for ipsilateral renal agenesis or morphologic abnormalities (Figure 46-4), because these conditions are commonly associated with mullerian anomalies.[2] Uterine malformations may be suspected on the basis of abnormal configuration of the uterus on pelvic sonograms.

Müllerian Anomalies. The congenital abnormalities have been classified into six groups based on their prognosis for future fertility and their surgical correction (Figure 46-5).[7]

Class I. Segmental müllerian agenesis or incomplete vaginal canalization, is suspected when a young girl reaches puberty without menstruation. This condition produces a transverse vaginal septum or vaginal atresia. **Vaginal atresia** is diagnosed by the development of **hydrocol-**

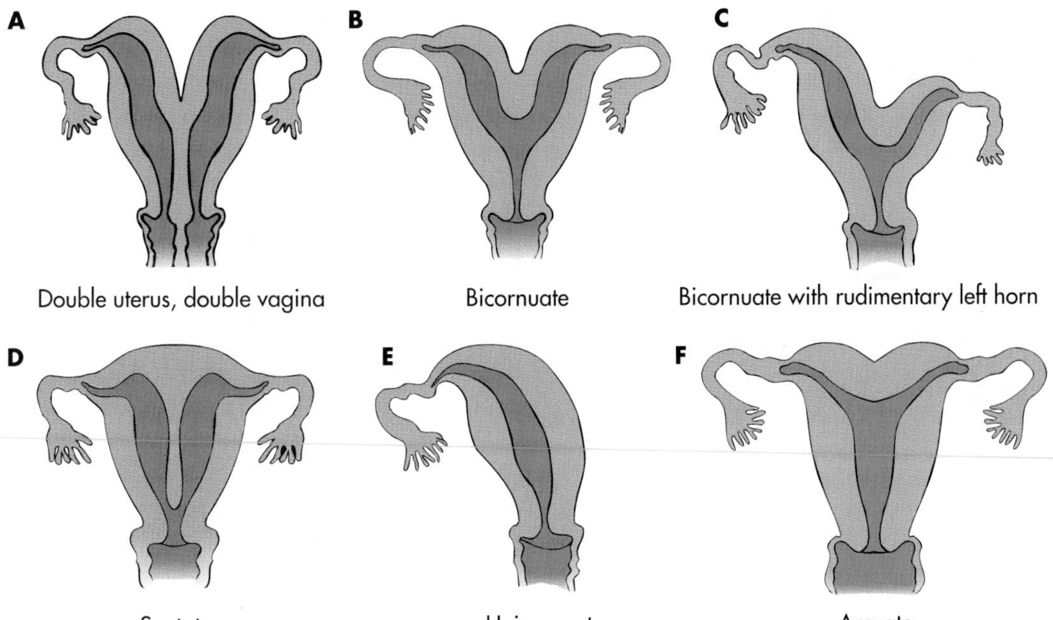

Figure 46-5 Congenital uterine abnormalities. **A,** Uterus didelphys: double uterus. **B,** Bicornuate uterus. **C,** Bicornuate uterus with a rudimentary left horn. **D,** Septate uterus. **E,** Unicornuate uterus. **F,** Arcuate uterus.

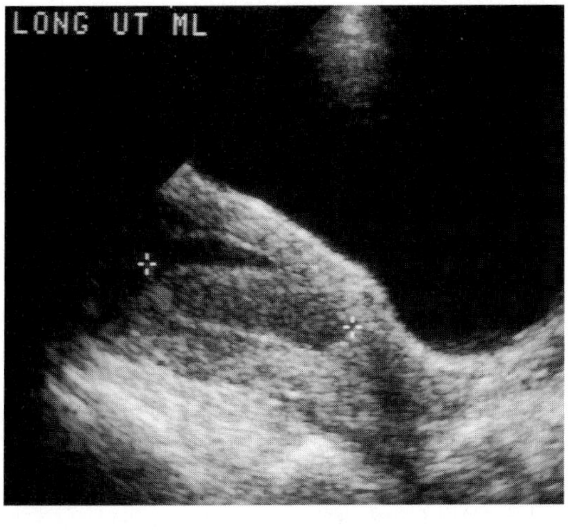

Figure 46-6 Transabdominal image along the midline of the pelvic cavity shows the distended urinary bladder anterior to the uterine cavity. A complex area within the endometrial canal represents both blood and fluid in the uterus and vagina (hematometrocolpos).

pos (fluid-filled vagina), **hydrometrocolpos** (fluid-filled vagina and uterus), or **hematometrocolpos** (blood-filled vagina and uterus) (Figure 46-6).

Ultrasound findings. On sonographic examination the cervix may be absent with or without blood in the uterine and/or cervical cavities. This condition either presents in the neonatal period as a large cystic pelvic-abdominal mass because of stimulation from maternal hormones or is discovered at puberty.[1] These findings also result from an imperforate hymen.

Class II. **Unicornuate uterus** is related to infertility and pregnancy loss.

Ultrasound findings. Sonography demonstrates a uterus that is long and slender ("cigar"-shaped) and deviated to one side. Usually, renal agenesis is apparent on the contralateral side. This is difficult to differentiate from the normal uterus by sonography but is suspected when the uterus appears small and laterally positioned.

Classes III through V. Classes III through V are more difficult to diagnose because they all have two uterine cavities, and their correct classification and treatment depend on the appearance of the external contour of the uterine fundus.[7] In the nonpregnant state a congenital malformation is often difficult to demonstrate and may mimic a fibroid.

CLASS III. **Uterus didelphys** is a complete duplication of the uterus, cervix, and vagina. This condition is not usually associated with fertility problems and does not generally require treatment.

Ultrasound findings. Sonography detects two endometrial echo complexes, which are best demonstrated during the secretory phase of the menstrual cycle when the endometrium is most prominent.[5] Then the external contour of the uterus is helpful in distinguishing between the septate and the bicornuate uterus.

CLASS IV. **Bicornuate uterus** is a duplication of the uterus and sometimes the cervix (Figure 46-7). This bilobed uterine cavity has wide-spaced cavities, a low incidence of fertility complications, and is usually not treated. The exception is when one of the horns is rudimentary and noncommunicating. If an embryo implants in this rudimentary cavity, it may grow until about 12 to16 weeks,

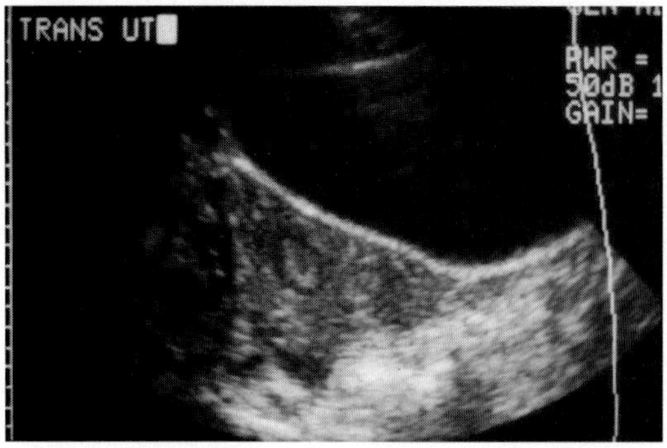

Figure 46-7 Transabdominal image of the bicornuate uterus showing two endometrial canals within the bilobed uterine horns.

when rupture of the uterine cavity occurs. In many cases the bicornuate uterus is diagnosed incidentally in early pregnancy, when a gestational sac is present in one horn and decidual reaction in the other.

Class V. Class V involves a septate uterus in which two uterine cavities are seen, closely spaced, with one fundus and sometimes two cervical canals or a vaginal septum. This condition has the highest incidence of fertility problems, and the septum may be hysteroscopically removed.

Class VI. Class VI is related to the exposure to the drug diethylstilbestrol (DES) in utero.

Ultrasound findings. The uterus is normal in size and shape externally; however, the cavity is T-shaped with an irregular contour. This condition may be difficult to diagnose with ultrasound.

Ambiguous Genitalia

The embryo has the potential to develop as a male or female. Errors in sexual development result in ambiguous genitalia or hermaphroditism. True hermaphrodites have both ovarian and testicular tissues. The internal and external genitalia are variable, although most true hermaphrodites have a 46,XX karyotype, but some are mosaics (46,XX/ 46,XY).[4]

Female pseudohermaphrodites have a 46,XX karyotype. The most common cause is congenital virilizing adrenal hyperplasia. An increased production of androgens leads to masculinization of the external genitalia (enlarged clitoris, abnormalities of the urogenital sinus, and partial fusion of the labia majora).

The external genitalia may also be masculinized by androgenic hormones that reach it via the placenta from the maternal circulation.[4] These hormones may be present in excessive amounts if the mother's suprarenal cortices are overactive or if she has received hormone therapy involving androgenic substances.

Ultrasound findings. Ultrasonography may be helpful in identifying the uterus and ovaries in utero or in neonates with ambiguous genitalia, although in many in utero cases it can be difficult if a clear image cannot be made of the genital area. Sex assignment is based on results of karyotype analysis, gonadal biopsy, and knowledge of genital anatomy.

Precocious Puberty

True precocious puberty is isosexual and characterized by the early development of gonads and secondary sex characteristics with ovulation before 8 years of age. Both estrogen and gonadotropin levels are increased. This abnormality may be caused by idiopathic activation of the hypothalamic-pituitary-gonadal axis or lesions of the pituitary gland or hypothalamus.

Ultrasound findings. Ultrasound is used to determine the volume and size of the ovaries, uterus, and cervix, and to exclude an ovarian neoplasm.

REVIEW QUESTIONS

1. At what gestational age may the fetal sex be determined?
2. Discuss the development of the female external genitalia.
3. List the six different types of mullerian abnormalities that may develop in the uterus and vagina.
4. Describe the sonographic findings in congenital anomalies of the uterus.
5. What factors must be present to diagnose ambiguous genitalia?
6. What are the sonographic findings in precocious puberty?

REFERENCES

1. Blask ARN, Sanders RC, Gearhart JP: Obstructed uterovaginal anomalies: demonstration with sonography. I, Neonates and infants, *Radiology* 179:79, 1991.
2. Fried AM and others: Congenital uterine anomalies associated with renal agenesis: role of gray scale ultrasonography, *Am J Roentgenol* 131:973, 1978.
3. Mendelson B and others: Endometrial abnormalities: evaluation with transvaginal sonography, *Am J Roentgenol* 150:139, 1988.
4. Moore KL: *The developing human,* Philadelphia, 1982, WB Saunders.
5. Nicolini V and others: Can ultrasound be used to screen uterine malformations? *Fertil Steril* 47:89, 1987.
6. Pennes DR, Bowerman RA, Silver TM: Congenital uterine anomalies and associated pregnancies: findings and pitfalls of sonographic diagnosis, *J Ultrasound Med* 4:531, 1985.
7. Thurmond AS: Imaging of infertility and mullerian abnormalities: women's imaging symposium, San Diego, Calif, 1991, University of California at San Diego.

BIBLIOGRAPHY

Malini S, Valdes C, Malinak LR: Sonographic diagnosis and classification of anomalies of the female genital tract, *J Ultrasound Med* 3:397, 1984.

Reuter KL, Daly DC, Cohen SM: Septate versus bicornuate uteri: errors in imaging diagnosis, *Radiology* 172:749, 1989.

Weir J, Murray AD: *Mosby's atlas and text of clinical imaging,* St Louis, 1998, Mosby.

CHAPTER 47

The Sonographic Evaluation of the Female Pelvis

Sandra L. Hagen-Ansert

OBJECTIVES

- Demonstrate how to take a patient history pertinent to the ultrasound examination
- Define the terms *premenarche, menarche,* and *menopause*
- Describe the sonographic technique to evaluate the uterus and adnexal area
- Distinguish when it is appropriate to do a transabdominal scan and/or transvaginal scan
- Name the contraindications for transvaginal sonography
- Describe the disinfectant technique for transducers
- Discuss the difference between longitudinal, sagittal, transverse, and coronal planes
- Describe the scan orientation for transabdominal and transvaginal ultrasonography
- Name the important muscles in the pelvic cavity
- Discuss quantitative Doppler measurements
- Define the sonographic appearance of the uterus and adnexal area

KEY TERMS

arcuate vessels - small vessels found along the periphery of the uterus

coronal - refers to a horizontal plane through the longitudinal axis of the body to image structures from anterior to posterior

endometrium - inner lining of the uterine cavity that appears echogenic to hypoechoic on ultrasound, depending on the menstrual cycle

internal os - inner surface of the cervical os

menarche - state after reaching puberty in which menses occur normally every 27 to 28 days

menopause - when menses have ceased permanently

myometrium - middle layer of the uterine cavity that appears very homogeneous with sonography

Pourcelot resistive index - Doppler measurement that takes the highest systolic peak minus the highest diastolic peak divided by the highest systolic peak

premenarche - time before the onset of menses

proliferative phase - days 5 to 9 of the menstrual cycle; endometrium appears as a single thin stripe with a hypoechoic halo emcompassing it; creates the "three-line sign"

pulsatility index (PI) - Doppler measurement that uses peak systole minus peak diastole divided by the mean

S/D ratio - difference between peak systole and peak diastole

sagittal - refers to a vertical plane through the longitudinal axis of the body that divides it into two portions

secretory phase (early) - days 10 to 14 of the menstrual cycle; ovulation occurs; the endometrium increases in thickness and echogenicity

secretory (luteal) phase - days 14 to 28 of the menstrual cycle; the endometrium is at its greatest thickness and echogenicity with posterior enhancement

sonohysterography - technique that uses a catheter inserted into the endometrial cavity with the insertion of saline solution or contrast medium to fill the endometrial cavity for the purpose of demonstrating abnormalities within the cavity or uterine tubes

---

Ultrasonography has proved to be an important diagnostic tool for the evaluation of pelvic diseases in the adult and pediatric populations. The noninvasive nature of sonography with its high-resolution imaging capabilities and ability to separate fluid from soft tissue structures within the pelvis in multiple imaging planes has proved clinically useful to evaluate pelvic anatomy.

In the pediatric population, transabdominal ultrasound is used in a variety of clinical circumstances to evaluate the presence of ambiguous genitalia, pelvic masses, and disorders of puberty and to further evaluate pelvic or lower abdominal pain that may result from appendicitis.

The size, location, contour, vascularity, and physiologic state of pelvic organs are easily obtained using both transabdominal and transvaginal ultrasound, and it complements the clinical evaluation and the process of forming a diagnosis.

PATIENT PREPARATION AND HISTORY

A complete history is critical to adequately correlate ultrasound findings with the proper differential. It is important for the sonographer to use a routine patient questionnaire requesting the following information: last menstrual period, gravidity, parity, physiologic menstrual status, hormone regimen, symptoms, history of cancer, family history of cancer, past surgeries, laboratory tests, pelvic examination findings, and previous ultrasound findings.

The patient's menstrual status is described by using the terms **premenarche, menarche,** and **menopause.** Premenarche is the physiologic status of prepuberty, the time before the onset of menses. Menarche is the state after reaching puberty in which menses occur normally every 27 to 28 days. Menopause is when menses have ceased permanently.

AMERICAN COLLEGE OF RADIOLOGY STANDARD FOR THE PERFORMANCE OF ULTRASOUND EXAMINATION

The American College of Radiology Standard for the Performance of Ultrasound Examination of the Female Pelvis[1] has defined these guidelines when performing a pelvic ultrasound examination. Ultrasound examination of the pelvis should be performed only when there is a valid medical reason, and the lowest possible ultrasonic exposure settings should be used to gather the necessary information. All relevant structures should be identified by the transabdominal or transvaginal approach; in some cases, both techniques will be used. Standards regarding qualifications of personnel, protocols, documentation, equipment, quality control, and quality improvement are presented.

SONOGRAPHIC TECHNIQUE

The complete ultrasound examination of the pelvis uses both the transabdominal and transvaginal approaches (Box 47-1). The transabdominal technique provides an opportunity to survey the pelvic anatomy and pathology. Further investigation with high-resolution transvaginal scanning follows the transabdominal examination after the patient has emptied her bladder completely.

TRANSABDOMINAL ULTRASONOGRAPHY

It is optimal to perform both transabdominal and transvaginal procedures unless either technique is contraindicated. The transabdominal technique may be contraindicated or limited with patients who are unable to fill their urinary bladders, are obese, have a retroverted uterus, or

BOX 47-1 UTERUS

- Vagina and uterus serve as anatomic landmarks
- Document the following:
  - Uterine size, shape, and orientation
  - Endometrium
  - Myometrium
  - Cervix
- Vagina serves as a landmark for the cervix and lower uterine segment
- Uterine length measured in the long axis from the fundus to the cervix
- Anteroposterior depth of the uterus measured in the long axis from its anterior to posterior walls, perpendicular to the length
- Width measured from the transaxial or coronal view
- Cervical diameters (length and width) can be obtained
- Endometrium analyzed for thickness and echogenicity
- Myometrium and cervix evaluated for contour changes, echogenicity, and masses

ADNEXA (OVARIES AND FALLOPIAN TUBES)

- Ovaries should be identified anterior to the internal iliac (hypogastric) vessels
- Document the following:
  - Size, shape, contour, and echogenicity
  - Position relative to the uterus
- Ovarian size determined by measuring the length in the long axis with the anteroposterior dimension measured perpendicular to the length
- Ovarian width measured in the transaxial or coronal view
- Ovarian volume may be calculated

CUL-DE-SAC

- Evaluate cul-de-sac for the presence of free fluid or a mass
- If a mass is detected, document its size, position, shape, echocardiographic pattern (cystic, solid, or complex), and relationship to the ovaries and uterus
- Differentiate normal loops of bowel from a mass

have pelvic masses lying posterior in the pelvis (which are distant from the focal zone).[7]

The transabdominal technique requires the urinary bladder to be adequately filled. Instruction should be given to the patient to drink at least 32 oz of fluid 1 hour before examination time and not to empty her bladder before the scheduled appointment. The full bladder displaces bowel and "flattens" the anteflexed uterus slightly so it is more perpendicular to the transducer angle. The distended bladder also becomes an acoustic window to view pelvic anatomy and pathology. The bladder is considered optimally full when it covers the fundus of the normal-sized uterus (Figure 47-1), although an overdistended bladder may compress, distort, and displace anatomy beyond the focal zone of the transducer (Figure 47-2).

In most average-size patients the anatomic survey is usually performed with at least a 3.5 to 5.0 MHz curved linear array transducer. If the ovaries lie anteriorly, the use of a higher-frequency transducer may be preferred. If the patient is obese, the lower-frequency transducer may be used.

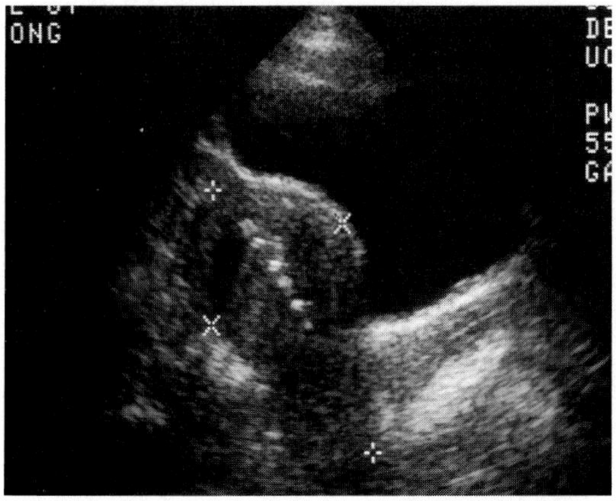

Figure 47-1 Sagittal image of the distended urinary bladder covering the fundus of the uterus. The intrauterine contraceptive device is seen within the endometrial cavity as bright linear reflectors. The cervix is seen posterior to the angle of the bladder; the vagina is the tubular structure posterior to the bladder.

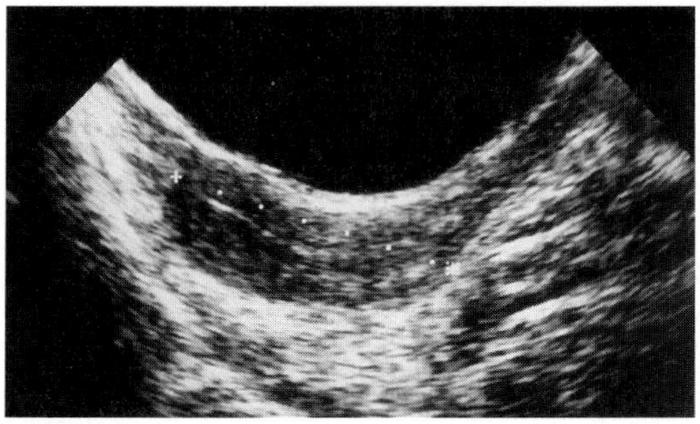

Figure 47-2 Sagittal image of an overdistended bladder compressing the uterine cavity.

The sonographer should carefully explain the examination to the patient after the clinical history has been taken. The patient should be told that the pelvic ultrasound examination is performed in two parts; the first is the transabdominal approach, in which the transducer is carefully scanned across her lower abdomen after warm gel has been applied, and the second is the transvaginal approach that is similar to a pelvic examination. The sonographer should tell the patient she is able to empty her bladder completely after the first part of the examination is completed. After receiving a brief explanation of the entire ultrasound examination, the patient is placed in the supine position. The patient should be examined expeditiously in both the longitudinal and transverse planes of the uterus and adnexa–remember her bladder is very full!

Anatomic orientation is correct for longitudinal scans (Figure 47-3) when the left side of the screen represents cephalic anatomy (toward the patient's head) and the right side of the screen represents caudal anatomy (toward the patient's feet). After the longitudinal orientation has been established, the transducer is turned counterclockwise 90 degrees to perform the transverse images, and the left side of the screen should correlate with the right side of the patient (Figure 47-4).

Documentation should be methodical and become routine for viewing by both the sonographer and the physician. A routine image protocol consists of longitudinal and transverse scans of the uterus (to include the **myometrium** and **endometrium**), cervix, rectouterine recess (cul-de-sac), right adnexa, and left adnexa (Box 47-2). Measurements of normal structures and pathology are made in the length, width, and depth dimensions. Additional information may be obtained by the Doppler evaluation of all pelvic pathology. If pathology is present, documenta-

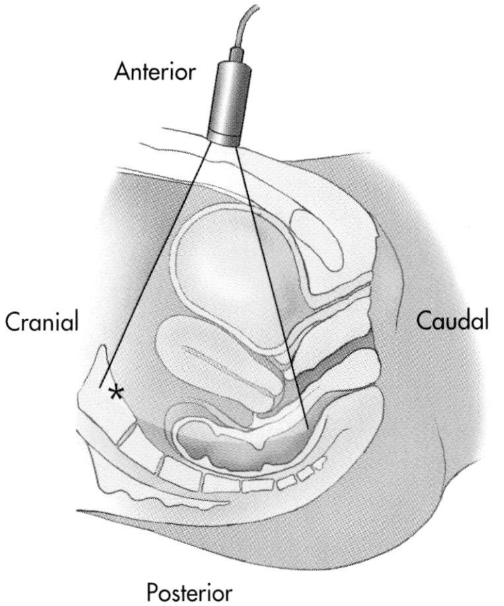

Figure 47-3 Longitudinal plane is oriented with the patient's head toward the left of the image and the feet to the right.

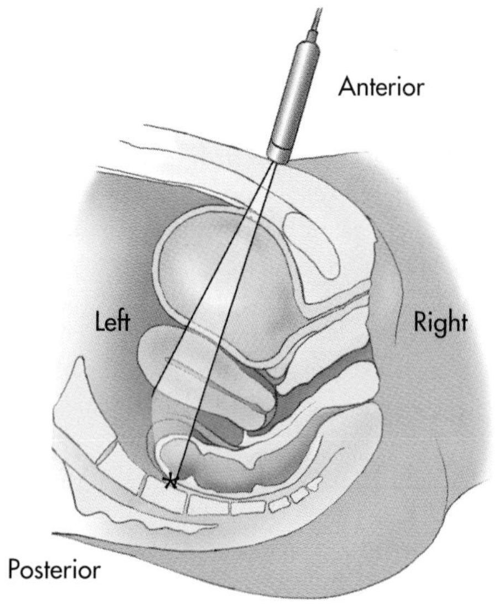

Figure 47-4 Transverse plane is 90 degrees to the longitudinal plane. The right of the patient is located on the left of the image.

BOX 47-2 TRANSABDOMINAL PELVIC ULTRASOUND PROTOCOL

Survey the pelvic area before images are made.

LONGITUDINAL

Midline: Distended urinary bladder, uterus, endometrium, cervix, vagina (Figure 47-5)
Measure length of uterus from the fundus to the cervix
Angle right of midline: Bladder, uterus, area of right ovary (Figure 47-6)
Angle left of midline: Bladder, uterus, area of left ovary (Figure 47-7)
Look at both right and left adnexal areas in true pelvis (iliacus muscle is lateral border)

TRANSVERSE

Low: Distended urinary bladder, vagina, cervix
Mid: Bladder, body of uterus, endometrium; look for ovaries (Figure 47-8)
High: Fundus of uterus, endometrium; look for ovaries lateral to cornu of uterus

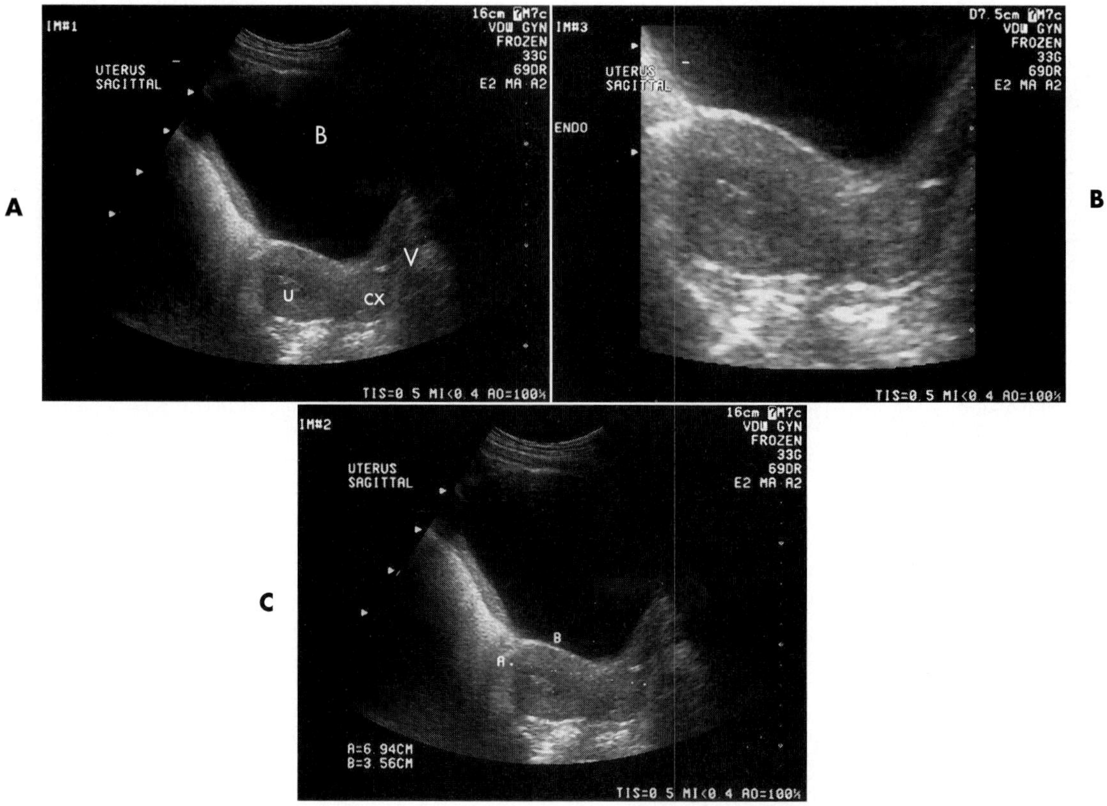

Figure 47-5 **A,** Sagittal midline image of the pelvic cavity demonstrates the urinary bladder *(B),* uterus *(u),* cervix *(cx),* and vagina *(V).* **B,** The image is magnified to better view the myometrium and endometrial canal within the uterus. **C,** Measurements of the length *(A)* and anteroposterior *(B)* dimension of the uterus are shown.

tion of the right upper quadrant (Morison's pouch and subphrenic area) and bilateral renal areas must be obtained. The evaluation of these areas demonstrates the presence or absence of free fluid, hydronephrosis, or anatomic variants related to pelvic findings.

TRANSVAGINAL ULTRASONOGRAPHY

Transvaginal ultrasonography adds more information because the transducer is of a higher frequency and closer to the field of view, and this is often the preferred method of evaluation.[6,7,24] Transvaginal scanning is a routine proce-

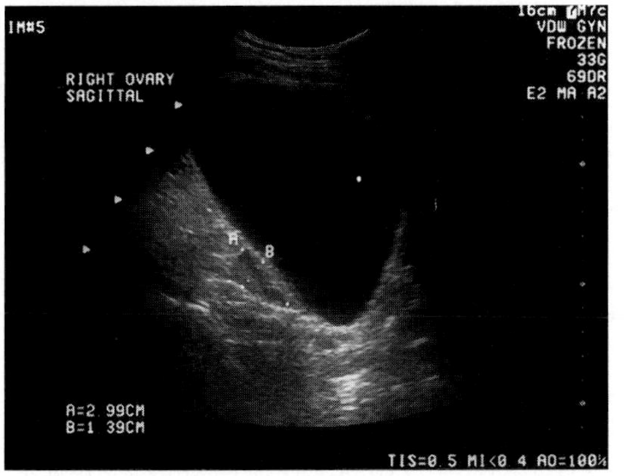

Figure 47-6 Sagittal image to the right of midline shows the bladder with the right ovary posterior. The ovarian length *(A)* and depth *(B)* are measured.

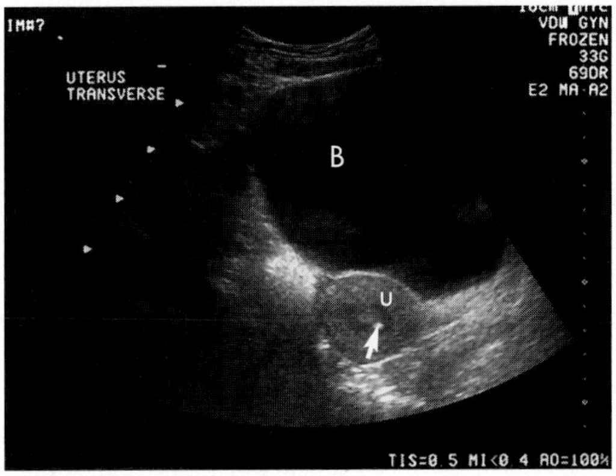

Figure 47-8 Transverse image of the bladder *(B)* with the uterus *(u)* posterior. The endometrial cavity *(arrow)* is well seen in the center of the uterine cavity.

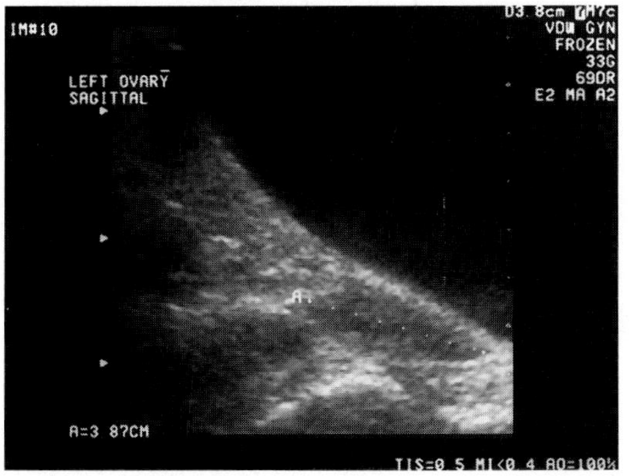

Figure 47-7 Sagittal image to the left of midline shows the left ovary posterior to the urinary bladder. The lenth *(A)* is measured.

dure that accompanies the transabdominal examination unless it is contraindicated. Contraindications include patient refusal, lack of patient tolerance (usually secondary to intense pelvic pain), and age (both premenarcheal and menopausal). Evaluation with transvaginal scanning is exempted with patients who have an intact hymen or a small vaginal canal.[7]

The advantages of transvaginal ultrasonography include the following: the patient is allowed to have an empty bladder; the ability to evaluate gaseous, obese, and difficult patients; and high tissue characterization of the pelvic organs.[16] The high-resolution capability results from use of high-frequency transducers ranging from 5 to 10 MHz. The primary disadvantage or limitation of high-frequency transvaginal ultrasound is the limited field of view (usually less than 6 cm from the transducer surface).[12,16]

Patient Instructions. After the transabdominal study is completed, the patient is asked to empty her bladder completely. If the bladder is very full from all the fluids ingested before the examination, the patient may void and think the bladder is "empty" because it had been difficult to hold so much urine during the transabdominal examination. Ask the patient to wait a few seconds after the bladder has been emptied and try to void again–this technique is usually successful in completely emptying the bladder. This is also an opportune time to reiterate the transvaginal procedure, obtain a verbal consent, and answer any questions the patient may have. It is suggested that either another sonographer or a physician chaperone be present when the transvaginal procedure is performed.

Disinfectant Technique. The use of an intracavitary device requires the prevention of cross-contamination between patients. The transducer should be soaked in a disinfectant between uses for at least the minimum recommended amount of time. Most disinfectants are glutaraldehyde based, and care should be taken when handling these caustic and toxic chemicals.[15] Each transducer manufacturer usually specifies the amount of time and the brand of disinfectant recommended.

After the transducer has been soaked in a Cidex-type solution for at least 10 minutes, it is important to rinse the transducer with water and dry it before applying the coupling gel and protective condom. Careful examination for air trapped under the condom and subsequent removal prevent artifacts. The final step of transducer preparation is adding sterile lubrication to the outer surface. If the examination is performed on an infertility patient, the use of water to lubricate the transducer is preferred, because water does not have a negative effect on sperm mobility.[7]

Scanning Planes. When inserting the transducer in the sagittal plane, the flat part of the transducer is along the top surface of the handle so the beam is projected in the midline anteroposterior aspect of the body. This is termed **sagittal** throughout this chapter. From the sagittal plane, the transducer is limited in motion because of the vagina. True parasagittal planes are never obtained, but angulation from this central point is considered sagittal imaging

(Figure 47-9). The transducer is then rotated 90 degrees counterclockwise to obtain **coronal** images (Figure 47-10). True anatomic coronal images are not obtainable.

Scan Orientation. Currently, the most accepted method of orientation used during transvaginal scanning is such that the left side of the screen corresponds to the cephalad and right side of the patient and the right side of the screen to the caudal and left side of the patient.[9] This method of orientation is the same as for radiograph and conventional ultrasound. Residual fluid in the bladder is a helpful orientation landmark and should always appear in the right upper corner of the screen in the sagittal plane. Thus the cervix would also be seen in the right side of the screen while the fundus of the uterus is found in the left side of the screen.

Scan Technique. The patient is asked to undress from the waist down, given a gown, and placed in the lithotomy position with her buttocks elevated with several folded sheets. The elevation is necessary to provide adequate mobility of the transducer handle. The patient's anxiety may be reduced if the transducer is shown to her and she is assured that the transducer is inserted only a few centimeters. The insertion of the transducer into the vaginal vault should be in real time so the sonographer may watch the anatomy as it appears to ensure proper orientation. It should not be inserted beyond the external cervical os. To maintain patient dignity and privacy, the patient should be properly draped and all practitioners who will be observing the examination should be present at its beginning.

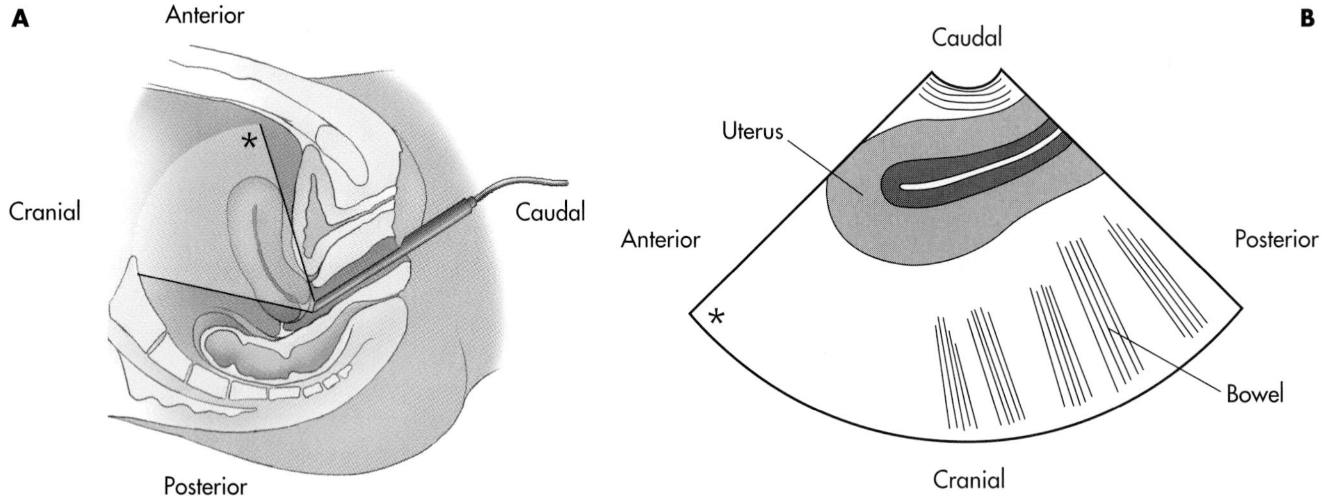

Figure 47-9 **A,** Transvaginal sagittal plane. The notch of the transducer is along the top surface of the handle so the beam is projected in the midline anteroposterior aspect of the body. **B,** The bladder is emptied, so only the uterine cavity and endometrial canal are seen.

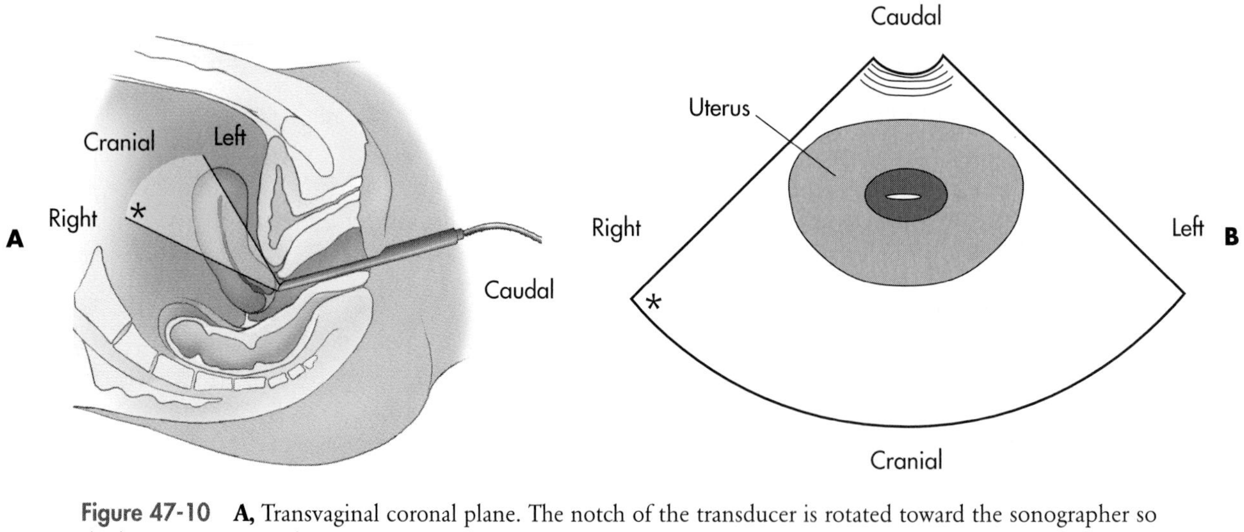

Figure 47-10 **A,** Transvaginal coronal plane. The notch of the transducer is rotated toward the sonographer so the beam may image the uterus in a coronal view. **B,** Coronal view of the uterus with the endometrial canal centrally located.

Scan Protocol. The protocol to follow should be methodical and expeditiously evaluated. The uterus, cervix, rectouterine recess, and bilateral adnexa should be documented in sagittal and coronal planes. Additional views of pathology or areas indicated should be obtained and measured in three dimensions.

The transvaginal scanning process involves three basic maneuvers of the transducer: insertion or withdrawal, angulation or tilting, and rotation (Box 47-3).[11,15,23,24] Varying the depth of the transducer may optimize the imaging of a structure in that field of view.

It is often necessary to advance the transducer angling anterior to visualize the fundus and withdraw angling posterior to see the cervix and rectouterine recess (Figure 47-20). Angulation and tilting of the transducer directs the sound beam to visualize the adnexa in an oblique sagittal plane. Applying pressure (either by the sonographer or the patient) to the outer abdominal wall often displaces bowel and helps delineate the borders of ovaries.

Rotating the transducer 360 degrees is possible. When the transducer is rotated 90 degrees from the sagittal plane, image orientation represents the coronal plane. The sonographer should check the orientation to guarantee that the left side of the screen represents the right side of the patient. If the uterus is retroverted, better resolution is obtained by inverting the transducer 180 degrees. The image is inverted to properly document the retroverted uterus. It is also helpful to rotate the transducer 180 degrees in the coronal plane to better image the left ovary (it is necessary to change the orientation on the screen to indicate the left ovary is on the right of the screen).

BOX 47-3 Transvaginal Scanning Pelvic Protocol

Survey the pelvic area before images are made.

Sagittal: Uterus

Image the uterus from cervix to fundus, endometrial cavity: measure the long axis (Figure 47-11).
Angle slowly to right of uterus.
Angle slowly to left of uterus.
Pull probe out slightly to image cervix (Figure 47-12).

Coronal: Uterus

Rotate transducer 90 degrees; image uterine fundus, body, and cervix with endometrial canal (Figure 47-13).
Look for free fluid surrounding uterine cavity (Figure 47-14).

Sagittal: Ovaries

Follow the fundus of the uterus to the area of the cornu to image the ovaries; the internal iliac vessels serve their posterior border (Figures 47-15 and 47-16). Color imaging may be used to separate vascular structures from the ovary. Look for follicles surrounding the periphery of the ovary.
Measure long axis (Figure 47-17).

Coronal: Ovaries

Rotate transducer 90 degrees once sagittal plane of ovary is obtained (Figure 47-18).
Measure width and depth (Figure 47-19).

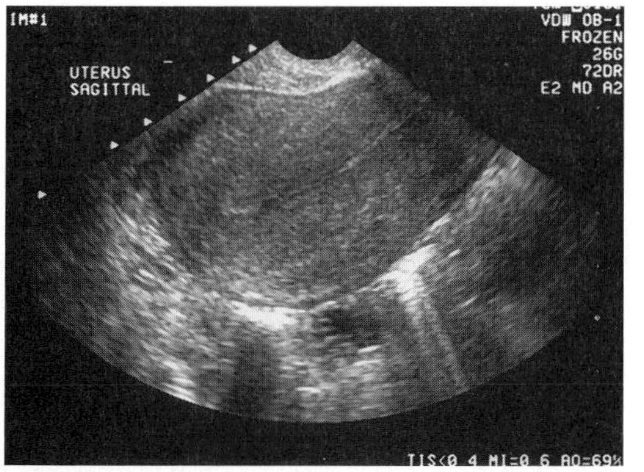

Figure 47-11 Transvaginal sagittal view of the uterus. The rounded fundus is shown toward the left of the image with the endometrial stripe running through the middle of the uterine cavity.

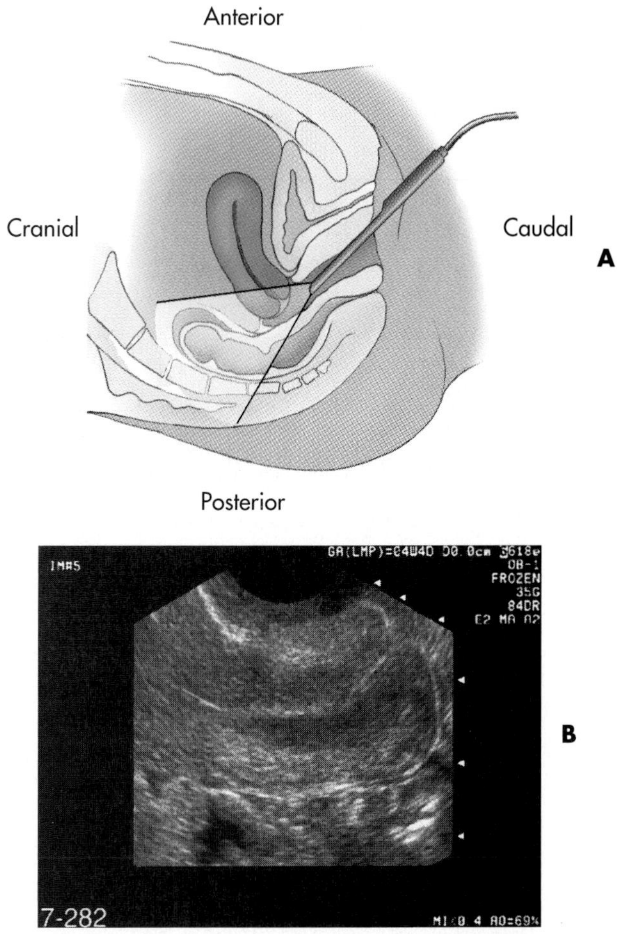

Figure 47-12 **A,** Illustration of the transvaginal probe angled more posteriorly (the handle moves up) to image the cervical area. **B,** Transvaginal sagittal view of the cervix.

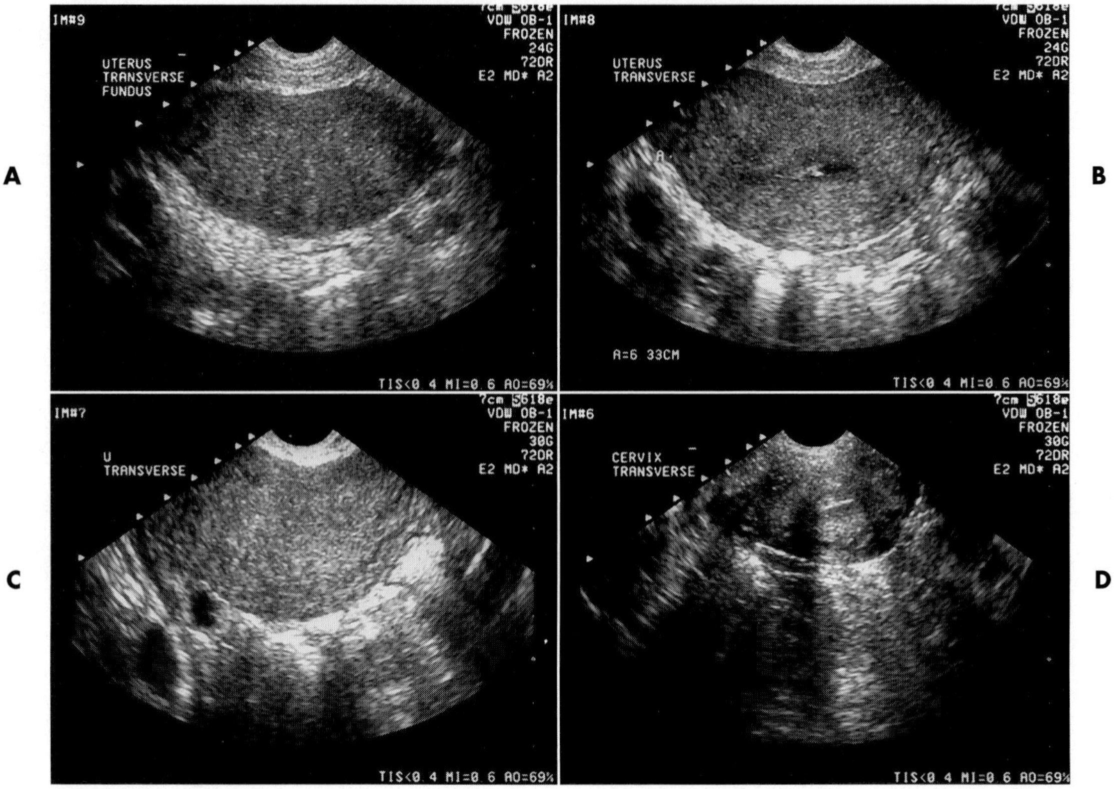

Figure 47-13 Transvaginal coronal view of the fundus body **(A),** with a small amount of fluid in the endometrial cavity (**B** and **C**), lower uterine segment **(D),** and cervix of the uterus.

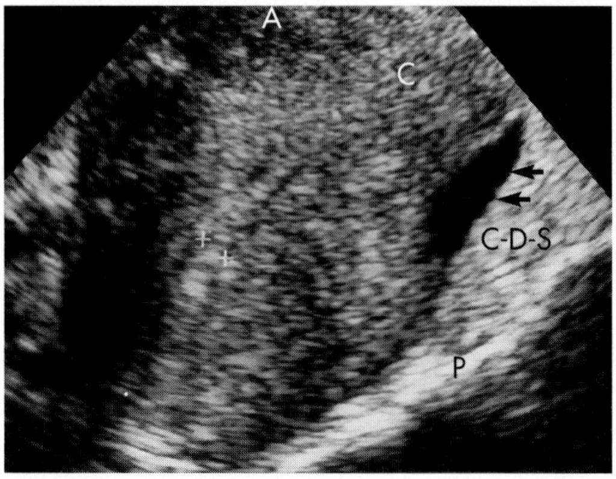

Figure 47-14 Transvaginal sagittal uterus with posterior angulation to best visualize the cervix, *C* and cul-de-sac *(C-D-S).* Free fluid *(arrows)* is present and normal throughout the menstrual cycle. *A,* Anterior; *P,* posterior.

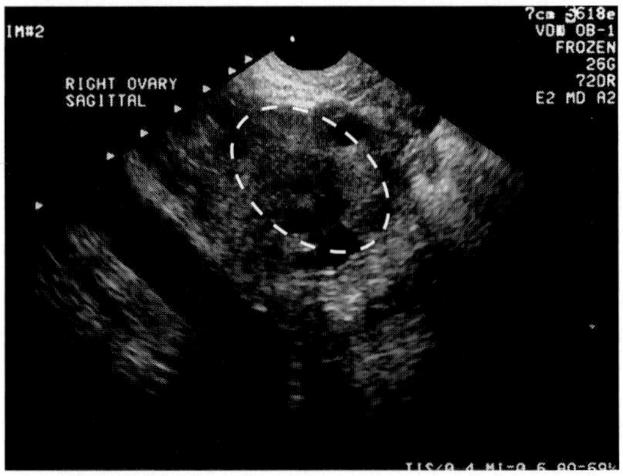

Figure 47-15 Transvaginal sagittal view of the right ovary with multiple follicles.

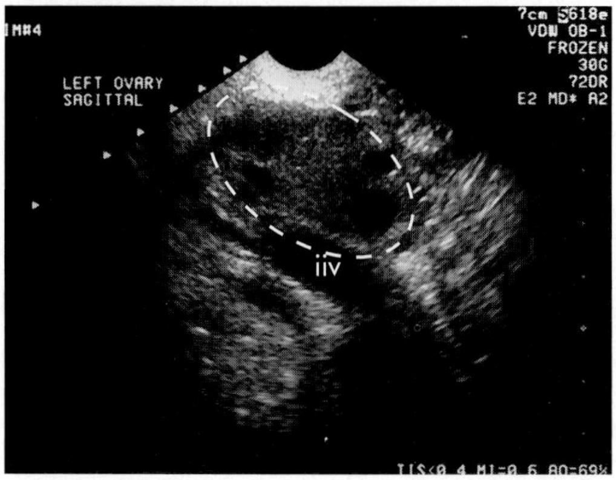

Figure 47-16 Transvaginal sagittal view of the left ovary as it lies anterior to the internal iliac vein *(iiv).*

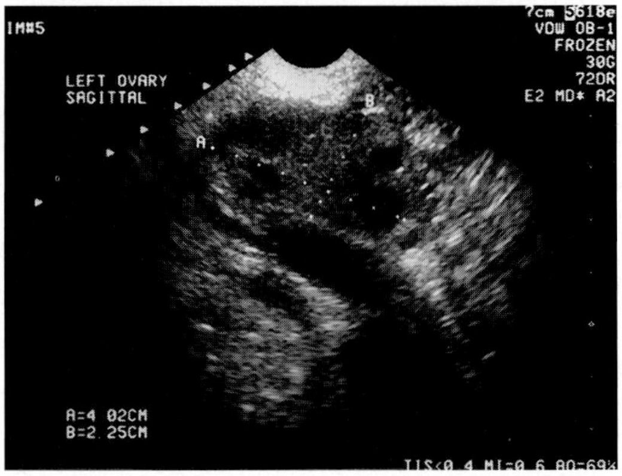

Figure 47-17 Measurements of the ovary are made along the length *(A)* and anteroposterior *(B)* dimensions.

A

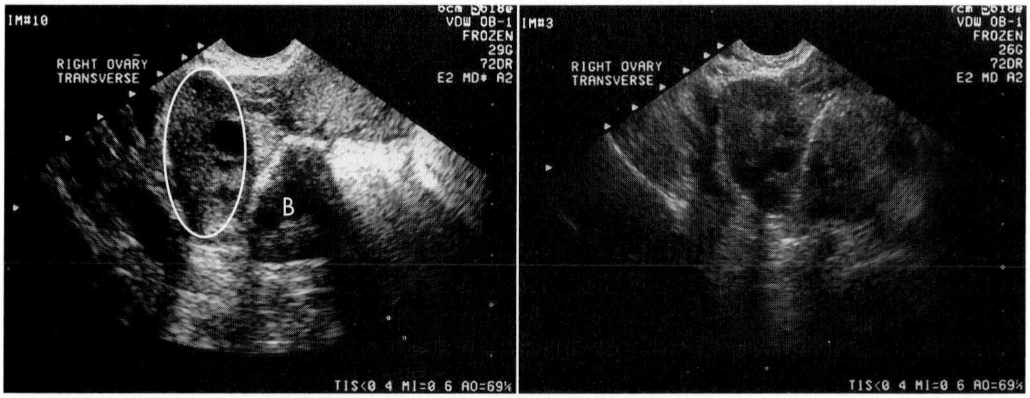

B

Figure 47-18 **A,** Transvaginal coronal view of the right ovary. Bowel *(B with shadowing)* is seen lateral to the ovary. **B,** Slight compression of the abdominal wall (with the transducer) may cause the bowel to move from the sight of view to better delineate the ovary.

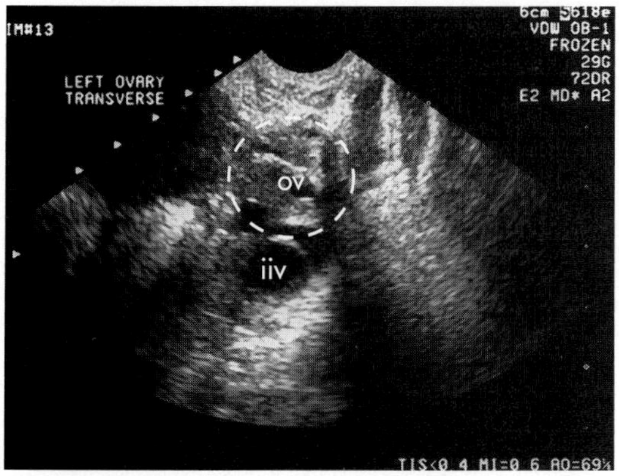

Figure 47-19 Transvaginal coronal view of the left ovary *(ov)* anterior to the internal iliac vein *(iiv).*

A

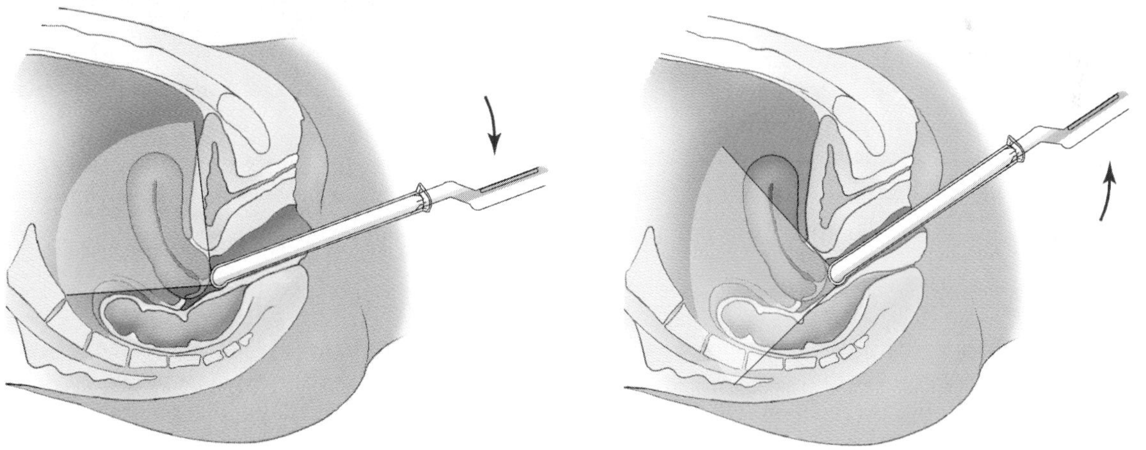

B

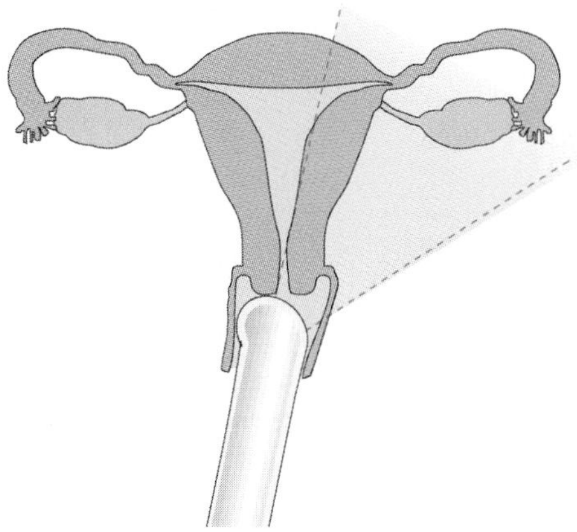

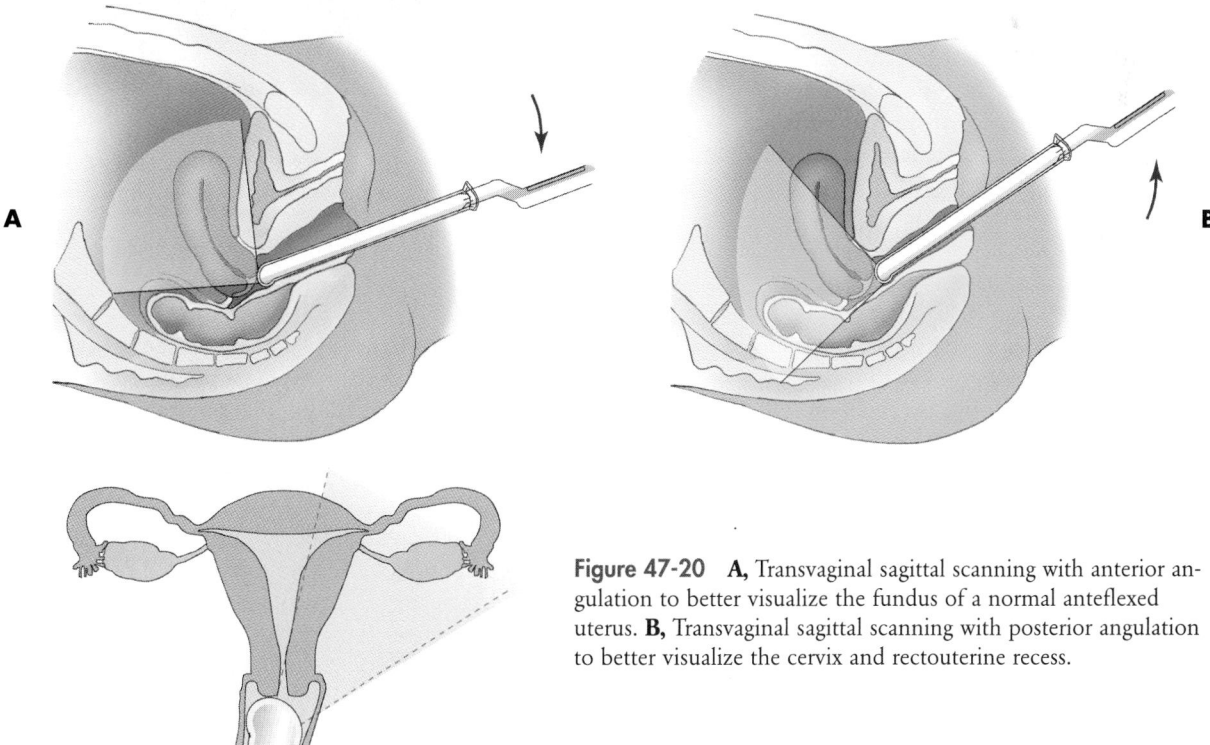

Figure 47-20 **A,** Transvaginal sagittal scanning with anterior angulation to better visualize the fundus of a normal anteflexed uterus. **B,** Transvaginal sagittal scanning with posterior angulation to better visualize the cervix and rectouterine recess.

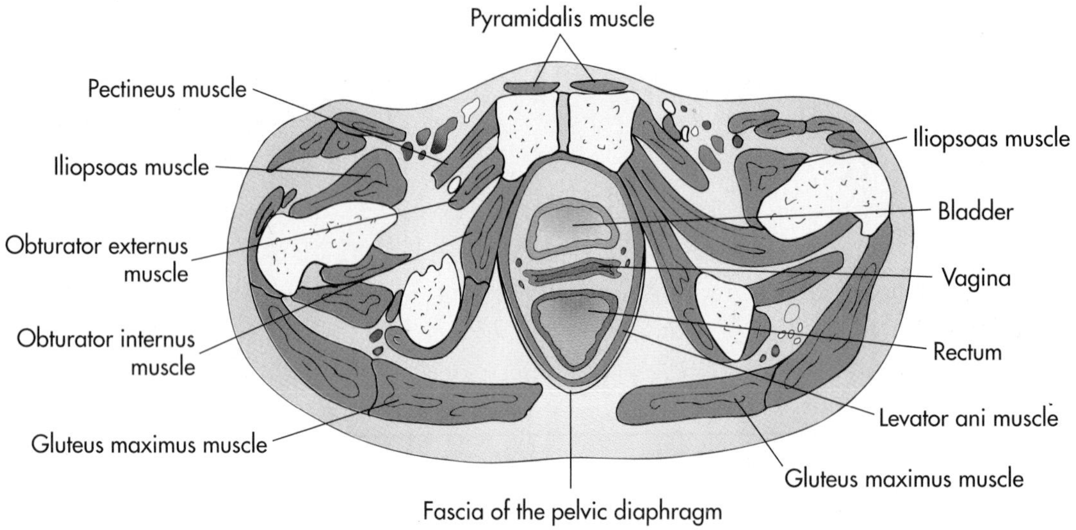

Figure 47-21 The bladder serves as an acoustic window to image the muscles of the pelvis.

SONOGRAPHIC EVALUATION OF THE PELVIS

BONY PELVIS

Ultrasound is essentially reflected by bone. The contrast between the sound impedance of bone and that of soft tissue produces a bright echo from which emanates an acoustic shadow.[20] The bony pelvis resembles a ring or funnel in shape. Anteriorly, the pubic symphysis is formed by the articulation of the pubic bones with each other. The transabdominal study is begun just superior or cephalad to this midline landmark. Posteriorly, the connection between the os ilium and the sacrum is formed by the sacroiliac joint on either side.[10] Sonographically, the sacrum may appear as a bright line with an overlying bowel shadow. This is much more apparent in infants, children, and thin patients.

MUSCLES OF THE PELVIS

The filled urinary bladder displaces bowel and acts as an acoustic window for evaluating three major groups of muscles.[12] Pelvic muscles may be mistaken for ovaries, fluid collection, or masses. A symmetric bilateral arrangement indicates that they are muscles (Figure 47-21). The rectus abdominis muscles insert on the pubic rami and are paired parasagittal straps in the abdominal wall. These muscles are best visualized with the use of at least a 5-MHz curved linear transducer; they appear as hypoechoic fascia with echogenic striations. The rectus sheath separates the sonographic appearance of the rectus abdominis muscle from surrounding fat and bowel as a bright linear echogenic reflector (Figure 47-22).

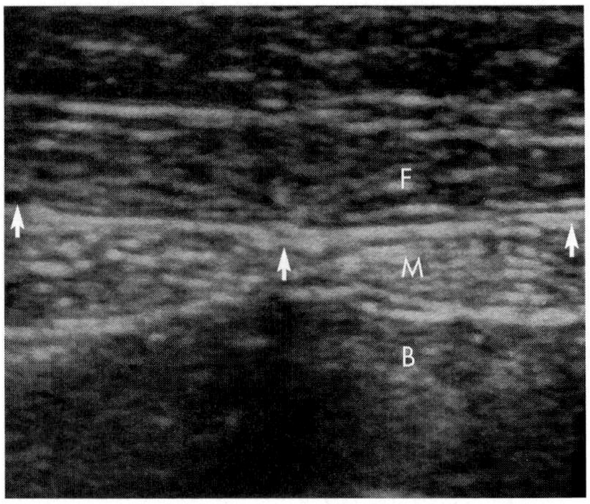

Figure 47-22 The rectus abdominis muscle is visualized with a 5 MHz linear transducer. *Arrows* represent the rectus sheath, which separates the muscle *(M)* from surrounding fat *(F)* and bowel, *(B)*.

Obturator Internus Muscle. In the lesser or true pelvis, the urinary bladder, reproductive organs, levator ani, and obturator internus muscles can be identified. Sonographically, sections of the obturator internus muscle are best visualized in the transverse plane with cephalic angulation of the transducer at the symphysis pubis. It is hypoechoic, ovoid, and surrounded by the obturator fascia, which serves as a tendinous attachment for the levator ani muscle (Figure 47-23).

Pelvic Floor Muscles. The levator ani muscle is best visualized sonographically in a transverse plane with caudal angulation at the most superior aspect of the bladder. It is a hypoechoic, hammock-shaped area that is medial, caudal, and posterior to the obturator internus (Figure 47-24). The two other muscles of the lesser pelvis, the coccygeus and piriformis, are located deep, cranially, and posteriorly. They are not routinely visualized on ultrasound examination and are not distinguished from other surrounding muscles.

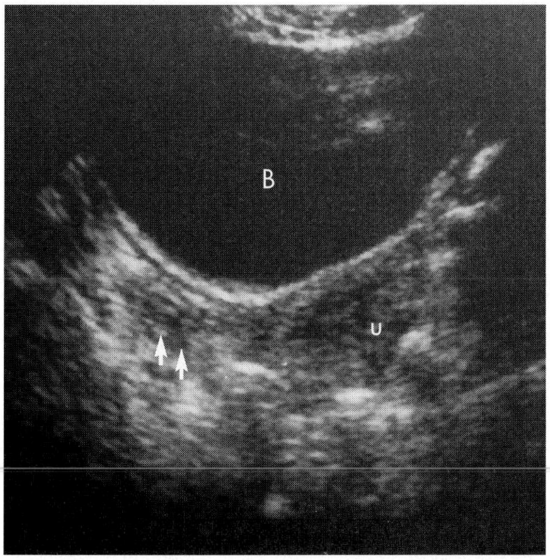

Figure 47-23 The obturator internus muscle *(arrows)* is visualized with the transabdominal sector transducer as hypoechoic-ovoid muscles lateral to the bladder *(B)*. Angle the transducer through a distended bladder from the contralateral side to demonstrate these muscles. *u,* Uterus.

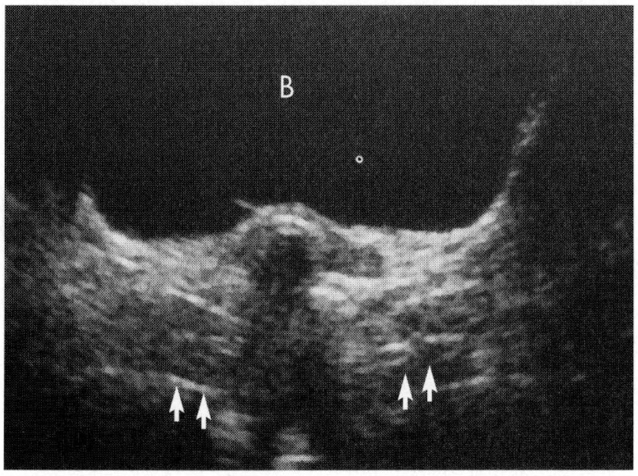

Figure 47-24 The levator ani muscle *(arrows)* is visualized with the transabdominal sector transducer as hypoechoic, hammock-shaped muscles medial, caudal, and posterior to the obturator internus. Angle from the most superior aspect of the urinary bladder *(B)* caudally to demonstrate these muscles.

Iliopsoas Muscle. In the greater, or false, pelvis, the iliopsoas muscles can be seen. The iliopsoas muscle is a combination of the iliacus muscle and the psoas major. The psoas major originates bilaterally at the paravertebral lumbar region and courses caudally. The iliacus muscle is contiguous with and arises posterior to the psoas major at the level of the superior two thirds of the iliac fossa. Together, they form the iliopsoas muscle, which continues in the caudal direction, coursing anterolaterally to its insertion on the lesser trochanter of the femur.[4]

The sonographic appearance of this muscle varies greatly depending on its development. On ultrasound examination the iliopsoas muscle is discretely marginated and hypoechoic (Figure 47-25). The separation of the iliacus and psoas muscles can often be determined by the bright echogenic line representing the interposed fascial sheath. Both longitudinal and transverse images may be obtained through the urinary bladder midline with lateral angulation. Transvaginally, the positions of these muscles are deep and beyond the field of view.

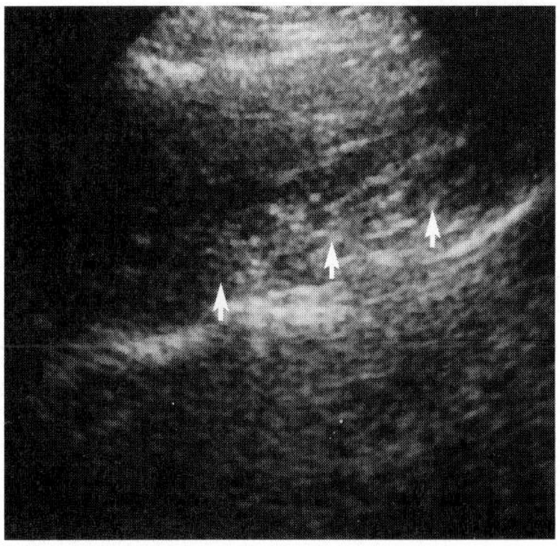

Figure 47-25 Sagittal image of the iliopsoas muscle *(arrows)*.

PELVIC VASCULARITY

Pelvic vascularity can easily be evaluated using real-time and Doppler imaging. The use of color Doppler technique permits the vessel to be localized, allows the sample gate to be placed exactly in the area of interest, and reduces examination time. The quantitative waveform is displayed and analyzed in one of the following indices:

A/B ratio (A equals peak systolic and B equals end diastolic)
Pourcelot resistive index (A – B/A)
Pulsatility index (A – B/mean)

Because the Doppler velocities are assessed as ratios, the waveform values are angle-independent.

Imaging both transabdominally and transvaginally, the internal iliac vessel can almost always be visualized and used as a landmark for the lateral pelvic wall and ovary. These vessels are commonly seen lateral and deep to the ovary (Figure 47-26). The internal iliac vessel has classic characteristic blood flow, demonstrating parabolic flow with an even distribution of velocities throughout the waveform.[14] The pulsatility and slow movement of blood flow can often be appreciated on gray-scale imaging. It is important to differentiate the vessels from an ovarian cyst because of its proximity. If uncertain, the sonographer can use Doppler technique or turn on the structure to elongate a vessel into a tube.

The veins are of large size and course along the uterus with the arteries.[2] To assess the uterine vessels, the sonographer interrogates just lateral to the cervix and lower uterine segment at the level of the **internal os.** Uterine flow in the nonpregnant female usually shows a resistive pattern with a resistive index (RI) of 0.88 in the **proliferative phase,** decreasing slightly beginning the day before ovulation.[14]

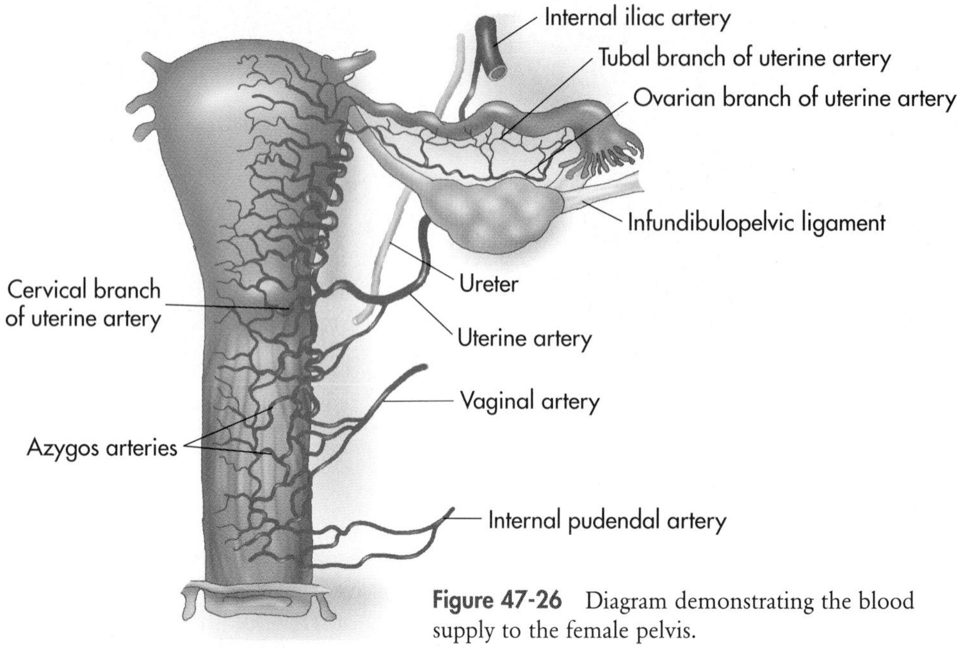

Figure 47-26 Diagram demonstrating the blood supply to the female pelvis.

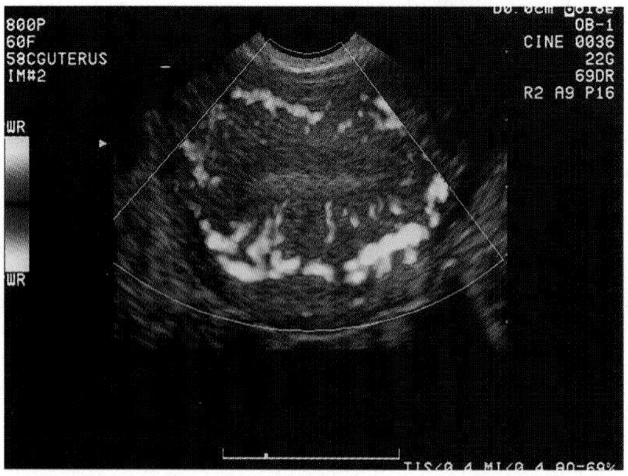

Figure 47-27 Transvaginal coronal view of the uterus with color Doppler that outlines the vascularity of the uterine cavity. The arcuate arteries are in the periphery of the uterine myometrium.

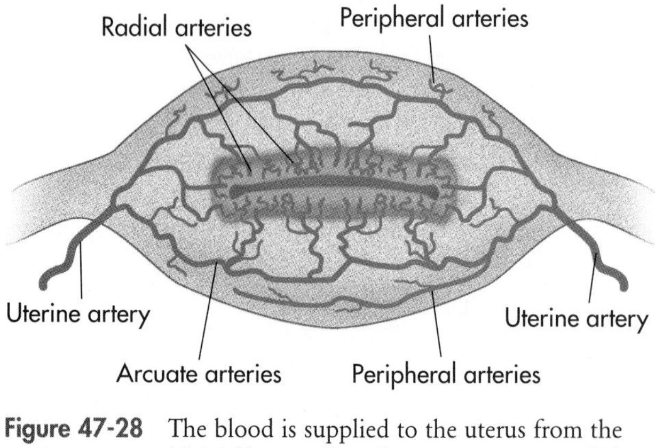

Figure 47-28 The blood is supplied to the uterus from the uterine artery, which bifurcates into the arcuate artery, radial arteries, and peripheral arteries. These vessels are very tortuous and have many anastomotic sights.

The vagina has two sources of blood supply. The anterior surface of the vagina and cervix is supplied with blood from a branch off the uterine artery before it reaches the uterus. The posterior surface of the vagina is supplied with blood from a branch off the internal iliac vessel (see Figure 45-26).[2]

The ovary receives its blood supply from the aorta. The ovarian arteries also have a tortuous course from the lateral posterior border of the ovary to anastomose with the uterine artery in the broad ligament adjacent to the cornual area (see Fig. 47-26). This is considered the ovarian branch of the uterine artery, which is the most consistent and successful area for assessing ovarian Doppler flow. The blood flow of the functional ovary varies cyclically. A low-velocity, highly resistive flow pattern is shown during the follicular phase of the menstrual cycle. At ovulation the maximal velocity increases and the RI decreases. The RI reaches 0.44 ± 0.004, and 4 to 5 days later it rises slightly before menstruation.[14] The nonresistive flow pattern during ovulation probably results from the neovascularization of the follicle and subsequent corpus luteum.[14] A normal pregnancy causes persistent low-resistive corpus luteal flow throughout the first trimester.

UTERUS

The myometrium of the uterus should have a homogeneous echotexture with smooth-walled borders. Any areas of increased or decreased echotexture should be noted and measured. The normal **arcuate vessels** are often seen in the periphery of the uterus and should not be mistaken for pathology (Figure 47-27). These vessels bifurcate into radial branches, which supply blood throughout the uterus (Figure 47-28). These vessels are most often demonstrated between 1 and 3 weeks after the onset of the last menses. Just before the onset of menses and during menses, these ves-

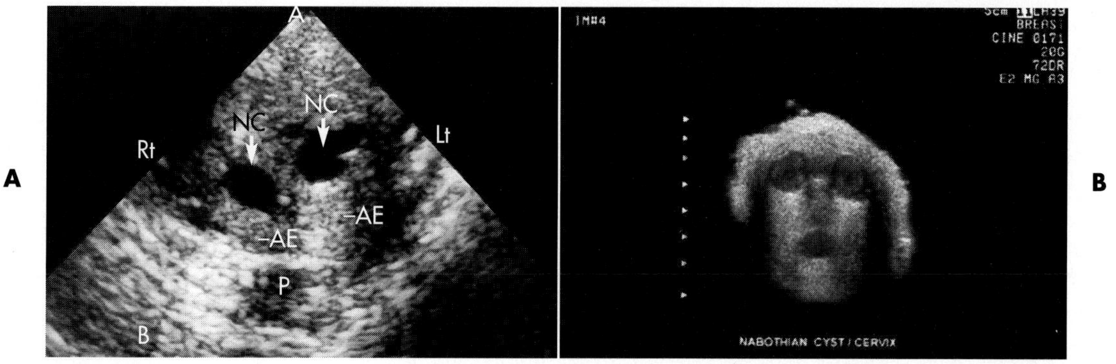

Figure 47-29 **A,** Transvaginal midline coronal view of the cervix with Naboth's cysts. Naboth's cysts are often multiple and demonstrated in the coronal plane. *A,* Anterior; *AE,* acoustic enhancement; *B,* bowel; *Lt,* left side of patient; *NC,* Naboth's cyst; *P,* posterior; *Rt,* right side of patient. **B,** Transvaginal coronal view of the cervical area demonstrating multiple nabothian cysts.

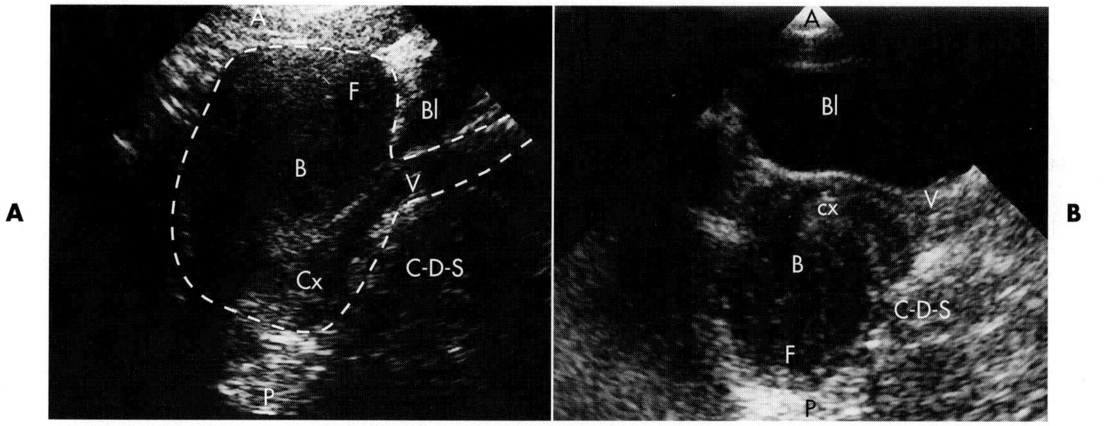

Figure 47-30 **A,** Transabdominal longitudinal scan of an anteflexed uterus. Anteflexion is abnormal bending-forward of part of an organ. *A,* Anterior; *B,* body of uterus; *Bl,* bladder; *C-D-S,* cul-de-sac; *Cx,* cervix of uterus *F,* fundus of uterus; *P,* posterior; *V,* vagina. **B,** Transabdominal longitudinal scan of a retroflexed uterus. Retroflexion is abnormal backward-bending of part of an organ. *A,* Anterior; *B,* body of uterus; *Bl,* bladder; *C-D-S,* cul-de-sac; *cx,* cervix of uterus; *F,* fundus of uterus; *P,* posterior; *V,* vagina.

sels are less apparent. The vasodilating actions of estrogens on the uterus during midcycle and the vasoconstricting hormonal influences during the late luteal phase before menses explain the normal dynamic changes of these vessels.[12,19] The bladder should appear anechoic.

The body of the uterus is separated from the cervix by the isthmus at the level of the internal os and is identified by the narrowing of the canal.[12] Tissue echogenicity surrounding the cervical canal should appear homogeneous. One can frequently visualize a cervical inclusion cyst (Naboth's cyst) near the endocervical canal. These are generally less than 1 to 2 cm wide and are anechoic smooth-walled structures with acoustic enhancement posteriorly; they are of no clinical significance (Figure 47-29).[15,19]

Both the transabdominal and the transvaginal examinations use the uterus as a central landmark to orient the sonographer. When using the transvaginal technique, the best landmark is the bladder. It should appear anechoic in the upper left of the screen, which demonstrates proper sagittal orientation and displays the variable positions of the uterus–anteflexed uterus, retroflexed uterus, anteverted uterus, and retroverted uterus. Anteflexion is an abnormal bending forward of part of an organ, and retroflexion is a bending or flexing backward (Figure 47-30).[22]

The uterus may also be positioned to the left or right. In this instance the sonographer should rotate the transducer and use the centrally positioned cervix to elongate the contiguous endometrial stripe of the uterus. It is often difficult to include both the fundal and cervical ends of the uterus on the same image using transvaginal scanning. New technology and design of transducers have increased the degrees of arc of the sector beam area and provide a wider field of view. Generally, by withdrawing the transducer, the cervical end can be included.

Transabdominally, the retroverted or retroflexed uterus often appears as a mass in the rectouterine space.[3] It is best

evaluated with transvaginal scanning. Rotation of the transducer 180 degrees may help. As discussed earlier, it is necessary to use all three motions of the transvaginal transducer to optimize the image.

Transvaginal evaluation of the cervix and rectouterine recess is superior to the transabdominal technique. While inserting or withdrawing the transducer into or from the vaginal fornix about 2 to 3 cm from the external os, the cervix is posterior to the anechoic bladder. Improved visualization may require posterior angulation if the uterus is anteverted and anterior angulation if the uterus is retroverted.

The transabdominal technique is the best way to measure the cervical-fundal dimension of the uterus in the longitudinal plane. Oblique angulation may be needed to elongate and measure the entire length of the longitudinal plane of the uterus. Its length is always measured from the distal end of the fundus to the distal end of the cervix (Figure 47-31). The size of the uterus depends on the patient's age and parity.

Either transabdominal or transvaginal scanning technique may be used to measure the width and anteroposterior dimensions of the uterus (Figure 47-32). Because of the proximity of the uterus to the broad ligament and surrounding vessels, it may be difficult to delineate the lateral borders of the uterus. Color Doppler technique or changing post-processing controls may help delineate these borders.

Neonatally, the uterus is pear-shaped secondary to maternal hormonal stimulation (Figure 47-33). Prepubertally, the cervix occupies two thirds of the uterine length and the uterus is about 1 to 3 cm in length and 0.5 to 1 cm in width and diameter (Figure 47-34). The nulliparous cervix occupies

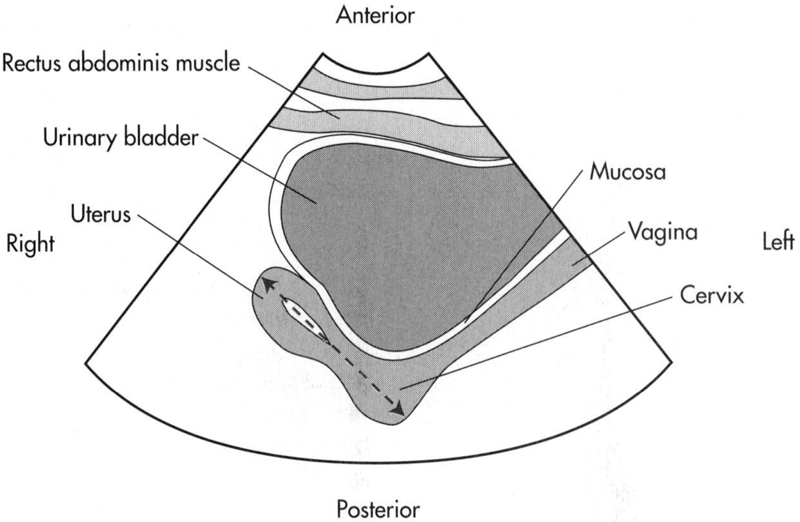

Figure 47-31 The length of the uterus is measured on the longitudinal image from the fundus to the cervix.

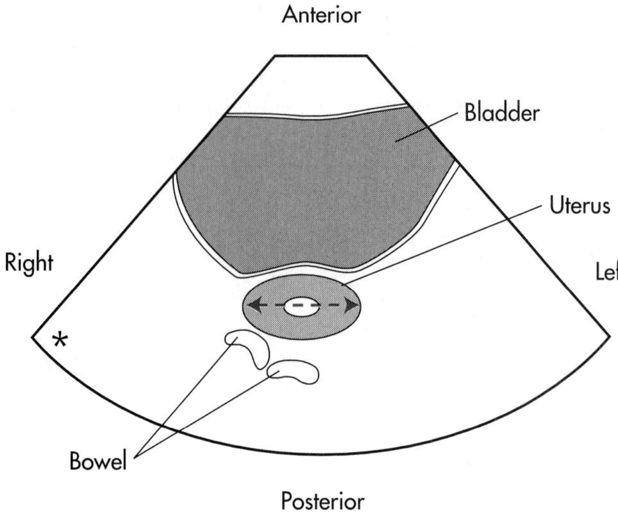

Figure 47-32 The width of the uterus is measured on the transverse image at the widest diameter of the body.

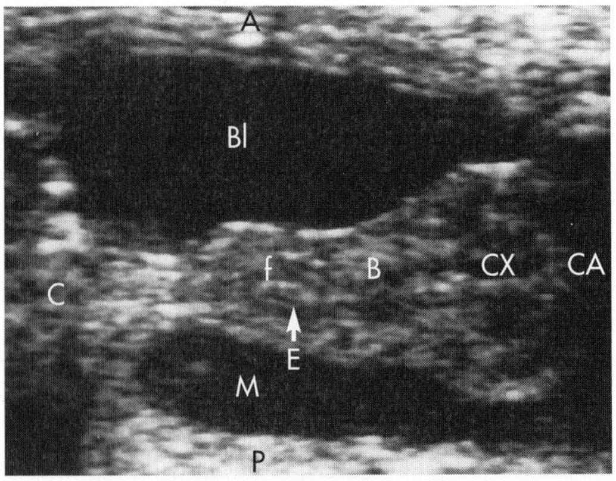

Figure 47-33 Transabdominal sagittal scan of a 1-day-old neonatal uterus. The cervix occupies two thirds of the entire uterine length secondary to maternal hormonal stimulation. *A,* Anterior; *B,* body of uterus; *Bl,* bladder; *C,* cephalic; *CA,* caudal; *CX,* cervix of uterus; *E,* endometrial canal; *f,* fundus of uterus; *M,* meconium; *P,* posterior.

one third of the uterine length and is about 6 to 8 cm in length and 3 to 5 cm in width and diameter–add 2 cm for multiparous dimensions. The postmenopausal cervix occupies one third of the uterine length. The uterus is about 3 to 5 cm in length and 2 to 3 cm in width and diameter.

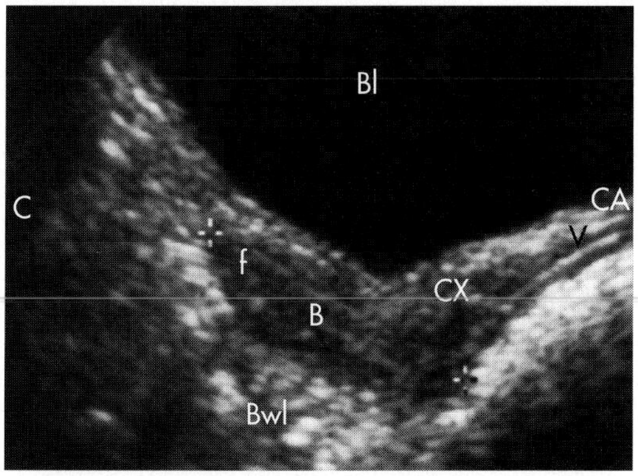

Figure 47-34 Transabdominal sagittal scan of a 6-year-old prepubertal uterus. The cervix occupies two thirds of the entire uterine length but loses the pear shape of a neonatal uterus. *B,* body of uterus; *Bl,* bladder; *Bwl,* bowel; *C,* cephalic; *CA,* caudal; *CX,* cervix of uterus; *f,* fundus of uterus; *V,* vagina.

Sonographic images of the endometrium disclose a characteristic appearance at each phase of the menstrual cycle (see Figure 45-15). To optimally visualize and delineate the endometrium, transvaginal scanning is performed.

ENDOMETRIUM

During menstruation (days 1 to 4) the endometrium appears as a hypoechoic central line representing blood and tissue. This is surrounded by a hyperechoic endometrial echo. If menstrual flow is heavy, the entire endometrial cavity can appear anechoic (Figure 47-35). During this phase of early menses, acoustic enhancement posterior to the endometrium may appear as it does in the luteal phase, but to a lesser degree. As menses progress (days 3 to 7), the hypoechoic echo that represented blood disappears.

In the proliferative phase (days 5 to 9) the endometrium appears as a single thin stripe (the endometrial cavity) with a hypoechoic halo (the functionalis) encompassing it, creating the three-line sign (Figure 47-36). The thin surrounding hyperechoic layer of endometrium represents the basalis. In the **secretory phase (early)** (days 10 to 14), ovulation occurs. The endometrium increases in thickness and echogenicity, representing the basalis that progresses and inundates the entire endometrium (Figure 47-37).[13]

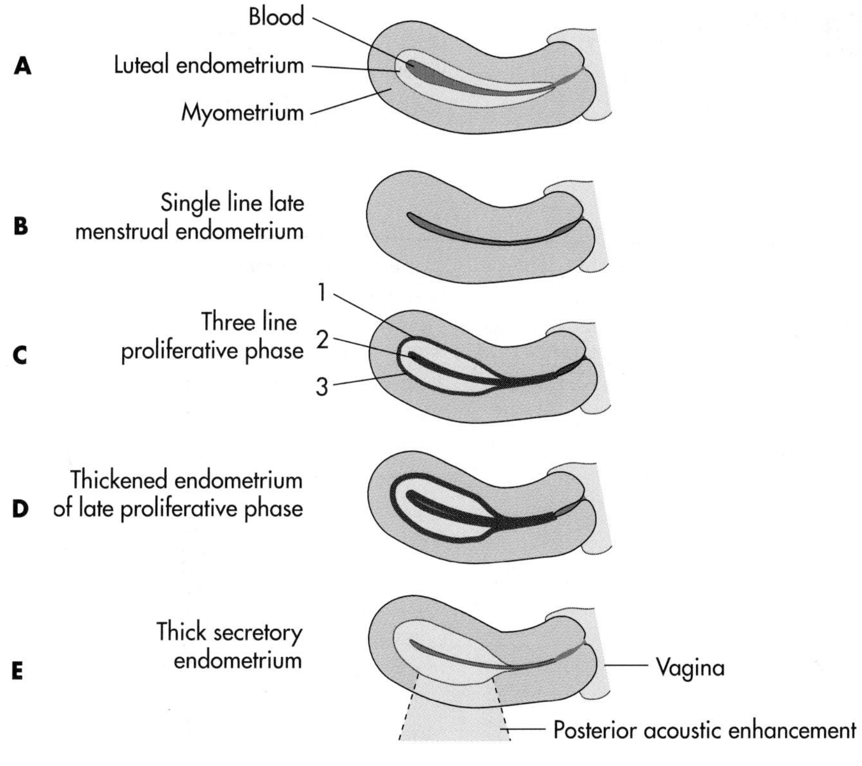

Figure 47-35 Endometrial changes through a normal menstrual cycle. **A,** Endometrium (days 1 to 4) of early menses. The hypoechoic central cavity represents blood and tissue. This is surrounded by a hyperechoic endometrial echo. **B,** Endometrium (days 3 to 7) as menses progress. The hypoechoic area that represented blood is sloughed. **C,** Proliferative phase (days 5 to 9) endometrium presents as the three-line sign. The thin endometrial center cavity is surrounded by a hypoechoic halo (the functionalis). The thin surrounding echogenic layer represents the basalis. **D,** The endometrium of the late proliferative phase (days 10 to 14) increases in thickness and echogenicity, representing the basalis. **E,** The secretory endometrium is at its greatest thickness and echogenicity with posterior acoustic enhancement.

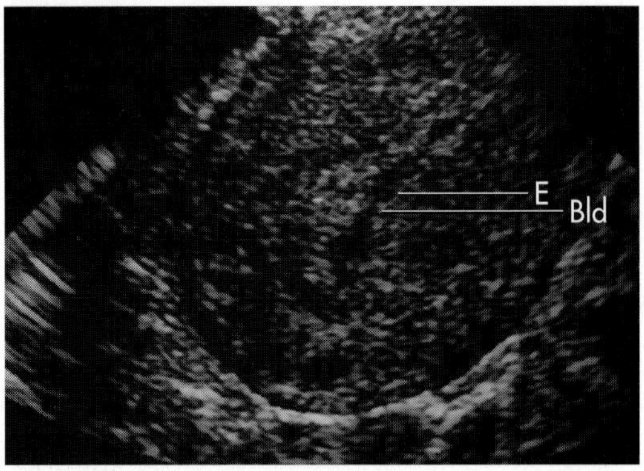

Figure 47-36 Transvaginal scan of the endometrium during menses (see Figure 47-35 correlation). *Bld,* Blood and tissue; *E,* endometrial echo.

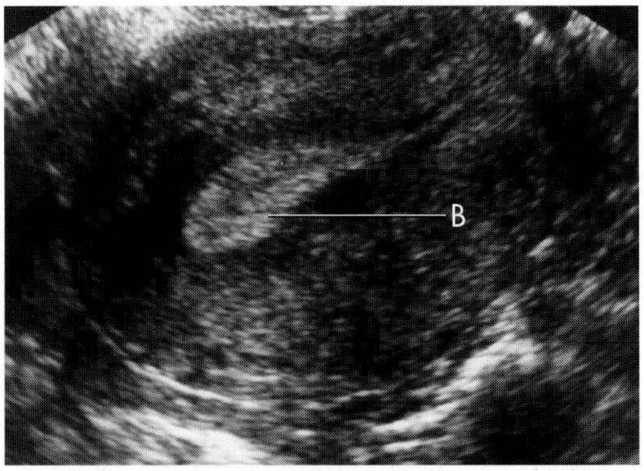

Figure 47-38 Transvaginal scan of the endometrium during late proliferative (early secretory) phase (see Figure 47-35 correlation). *B,* Basalis.

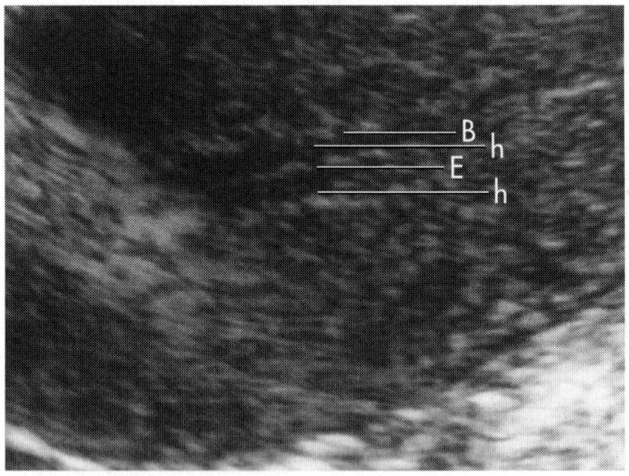

Figure 47-37 Transvaginal scans of the endometrium during proliferative phase (see Figure 47-35 correlation). *B,* Echogenic basalis; *E,* endometrial echo; *h,* halo (functionalis).

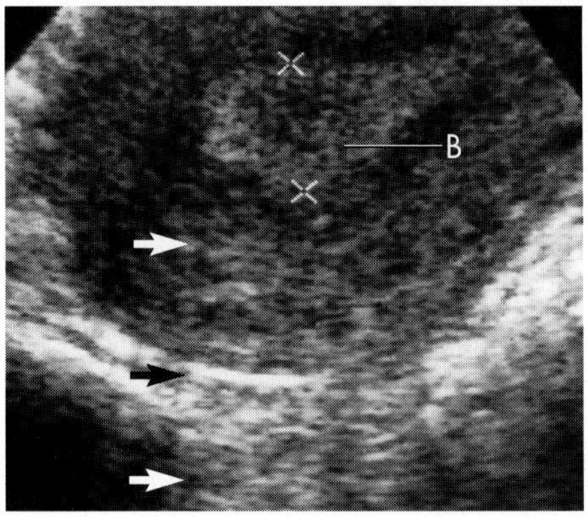

Figure 47-39 Transvaginal scan of the endometrium during the secretory phase (see Figure 47-35 correlation). The basalis *(B)* is at its greatest thickness and echogenicity with posterior acoustic enhancement *(arrows).*

During the **secretory (luteal) phase** the endometrium is at its greatest thickness and echogenicity with posterior enhancement (Figure 47-38).[9,13] The posterior enhancement is thought to be attributable to the increased vascularity of the endometrium.[10]

The endometrial thickness is measured from the highly reflective interface of the endometrium and myometrium in the sagittal view. This sonographic measurement includes both the anterior and posterior layers of the endometrium (Figure 47-39). The surrounding hypoechoic area and fluid within the endometrial cavity are not included in the measurement (Figure 47-40).[18] With the use of electronic calipers and transvaginal scanning, measurements of endometrial thickness have been found to be within 1 mm of measurements from pathology examinations.[3]

In all stages of a female's life the normal measurement of the endometrium varies depending on hormonal status. As an infant, the endometrium may appear thick and echogenic because of maternal hormonal stimulation.[7] In the menstruating stage the endometrium varies between 4 and 12 mm.[7] During menopause the endometrial size varies depending on which hormone regimen is followed. The literature conflicts as to what the normal cut-off measurement is for the nonhormonally stimulated endometrium. The range clinically accepted as being normal is between 4 and 10 mm (Figure 47-41).

If no hormonal replacement therapy is being used, the endometrium should remain unstimulated and less than 8 mm.[21] At present, multicentered postmenopausal endometrial studies are being performed across the country in hopes that ultrasound can indicate when an endometrium needs further investigation. Currently, curettage is the gold standard used to distinguish benign from malignant endometrium.[13] It is hoped that ultimately ultrasound may minimize unnecessary invasive procedures.

Fallopian Tubes

In the transverse view transabdominally or the coronal view transvaginally the fallopian tube region can be followed laterally from either side of the cornua at the fundal level of the uterus to the ovaries. The high resolution of transvaginal scanning allows improved visualization of the

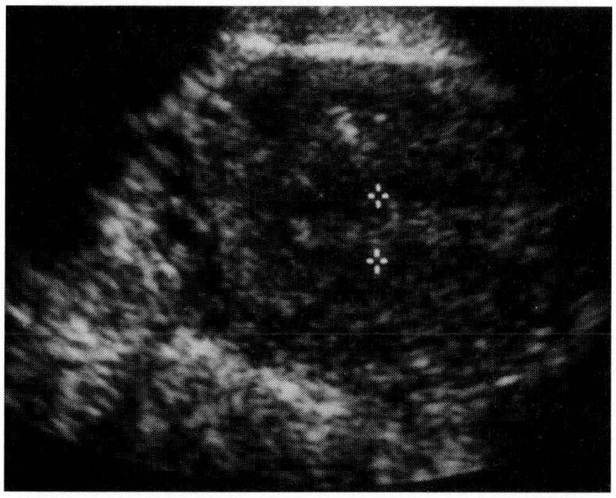

Figure 47-40 Transvaginal sagittal uterus. The endometrial measurement includes both the anterior and posterior layers of the endometrium. The hypoechoic area surrounding the endometrium is not included.

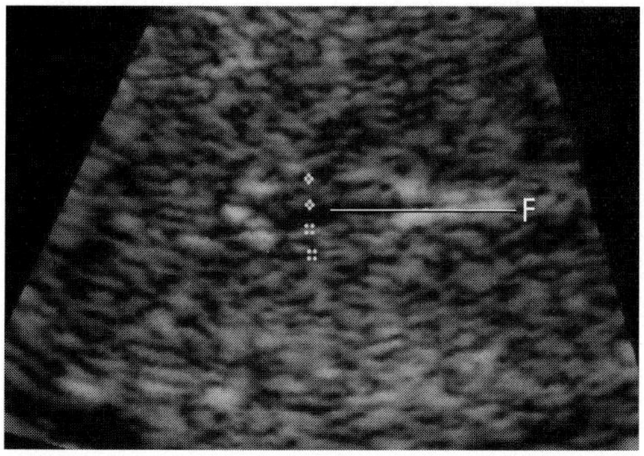

Figure 47-41 Transvaginal sagittal uterus. Fluid that is within the endometrial cavity is excluded from the measurement. Measure the anterior and posterior layers separately and add together. *F,* Fluid.

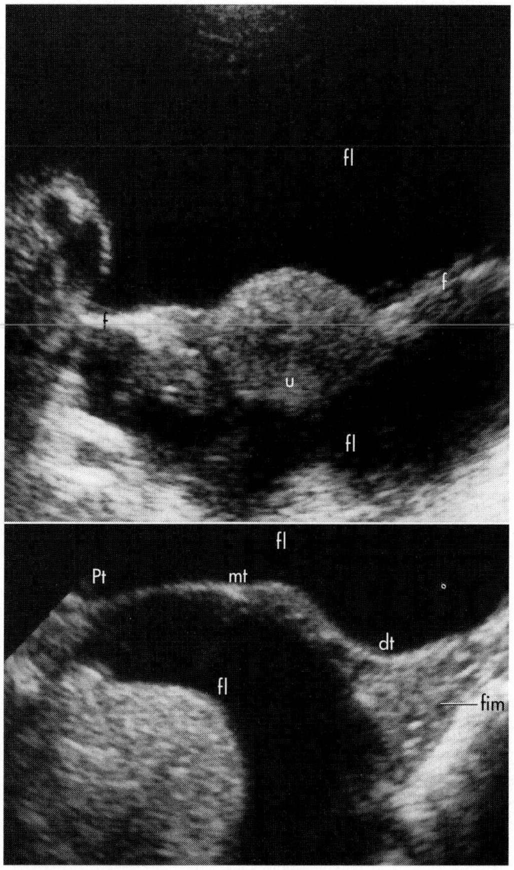

Figure 47-42 **A,** Transabdominal transverse scan of uterus and fallopian tubes. *f,* Fallopian tube; *fl,* free-fluid. *u,* uterus. **B,** Transvaginal coronal scan of fallopian tube surrounded by free fluid within peritoneum. *dt,* Distal tube; *fim,* fimbriae; *fl,* free fluid; *mt,* mid (ampulla) tube; *Pt,* proximal (isthmus) tube.

fallopian tube. It is not unusual to visualize the region of the proximal tube and surrounding ligaments.[15] If the tubes are distended with or surrounded by a sufficient amount of fluid, they can be easily outlined by the contrasting fluid.[9,19,23] The patient is placed in reverse Trendelenburg position to use any fluid in the peritoneum as a contrast agent (Figure 47-42).

OVARY

The sonographic approach to evaluate the ovary is often initially performed transabdominally. The transabdominal approach is especially important when the ovary is in an obscure location so as to determine a general location to interrogate transvaginally. Transabdominal evaluation is also necessary to evaluate a large adnexal mass and determine its origin. The ovary is very mobile and can move considerably in the pelvis, depending on bladder volume. To better characterize the ovary and its contents and to visualize ovaries that are nonvisible transabdominally, transvaginal scanning is superior.

Typically, the ovary is located just lateral to the uterus and anteromedial to the internal iliac vessels, which can be used as a landmark to localize the ovary. The contralateral side of the bladder is used as a window when scanning transabdominally. Transvaginally, the ovaries are easiest to locate in the coronal plane lateral to the cornua. However, it is not uncommon to find the ovaries located above the uterus or posterior in the rectouterine cul-de-sac area.

Sonographically, the normal ovary appears as an ovoid homogeneous echodensity; follicular cysts are often present (see Figure 45-13). The best sonographic marker for the ovary is identification of a follicular cyst, which has the classic appearance of being thin walled and anechoic with through-transmission posteriorly (Figure 47-43). The nor-

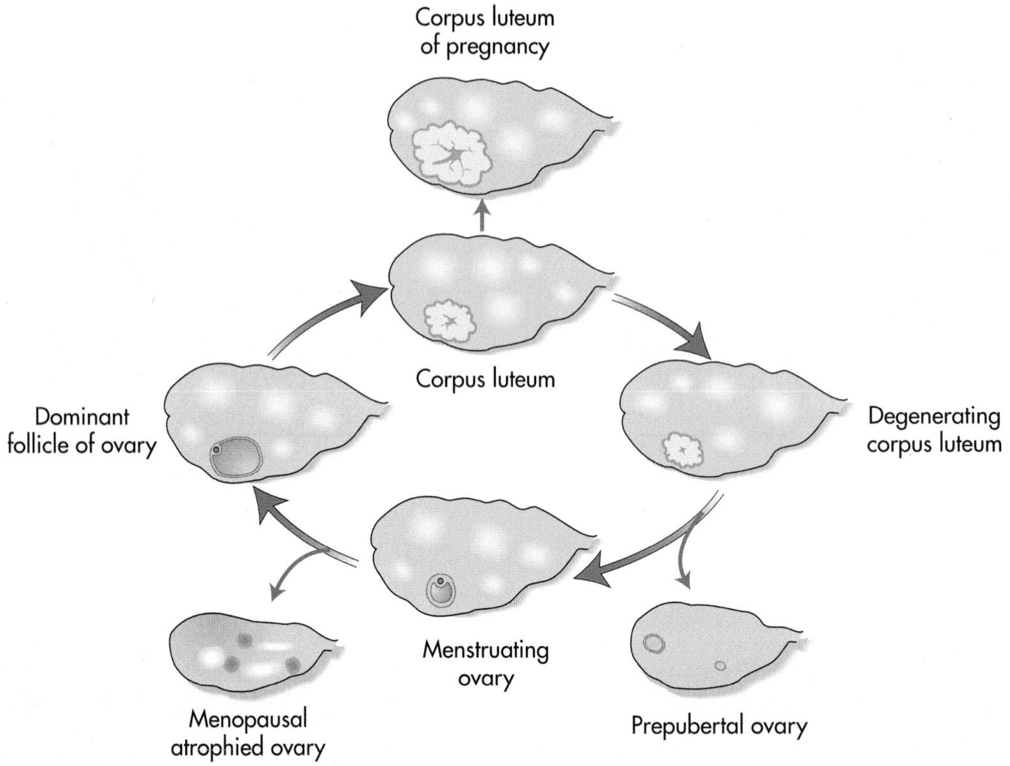

Figure 47-43 Diagram of cyclic changes of the normal ovary. The prepubertal ovary may contain small follicles. The menstruating ovary contains several primary follicles that begin the process of growth and development. One follicle becomes the dominant follicle because the pituitary gland produces follicle-stimulating hormone (FSH). The dominant follicle (ova) fills with fluid and begins to secrete estrogen. The estrogen level increases, which inhibits further production of FSH. The pituitary then begins the secretion of luteinizing hormone. This luteinizing surge causes ovulation. The collapsed follicle lining begins to multiply and create the corpus luteum. The corpus luteum secretes both progesterone and estrogen. If pregnancy occurs, the corpus luteum continues to grow and secrete progesterone and estrogen to support the pregnancy up to 3 months. If pregnancy does not occur, the corpus luteum degenerates. Because of the decrease in progesterone and estrogen, menstruation occurs and the cycle repeats itself.

mal range in diameter of a mature graafian follicle is 1.8 to 2.4 cm.[13] These cysts may be present in normal premenarchal, menstruating, and menopausal ovaries (Figure 47-44).

The ovary is measured in the sagittal or longitudinal plane at its longest length and anteroposterior dimension (Figure 47-45). In transverse or coronal scans the width is measured at the widest point. With the use of color Doppler technique, a vessel and a cyst can easily be distinguished. The volume of the ovary is calculated using the formula for a prolate ellipse: 0.523 = Length × Thickness × Width.[5,17,19,25] Cohen's study demonstrates the mean ovarian volumes, standard deviations, and 95% confidence intervals for groups separated by menstrual status. This study suggests that the normal measurement for ovaries is larger than previously reported in the literature. The mean volume for a premenarchal ovary is 3.0 cm^3, for a normal menstruating ovary 9.8 cm^3, and for a menopausal ovary 5.8 cm^3.[5]

Rectouterine Recess and Bowel

Gas- and fluid-filled bowel loops are poorly defined, echo-free mobile structures that usually demonstrate peristalsis under observation. Solid material in the bowel is hyperechoic and may produce shadowing, as does gas (Figure 47-46). Empty bowel can look like an irregular bull's eye with a thin, sharp, hypoechoic outline on cross section. When rectal gas obscures the cul-de-sac and it is necessary to differentiate a mass from bowel, a saline or water enema may delineate the rectosigmoid, posterior uterus, and cul-de-sac in a transabdominal view.

Fluid-filled small bowel loops can appear cystic but are easily identified by their swirling activity demonstrated on real-time imaging. Fluid may accumulate in the small bowel with rapid oral hydration. A transvaginal search for ovaries is often aided by the movements of bowel outlining the ovary. Immobile, dilated, or distorted bowel should be further investigated.

Hysterosalpingosonography

Sonohysterography involves the instillation of sterile saline solution into the endometrial cavity. The patient is prepared in the same manner as would be used for a pelvic examination. A sterile speculum is inserted by the physician and the cervix is cleansed with an antiseptic so-

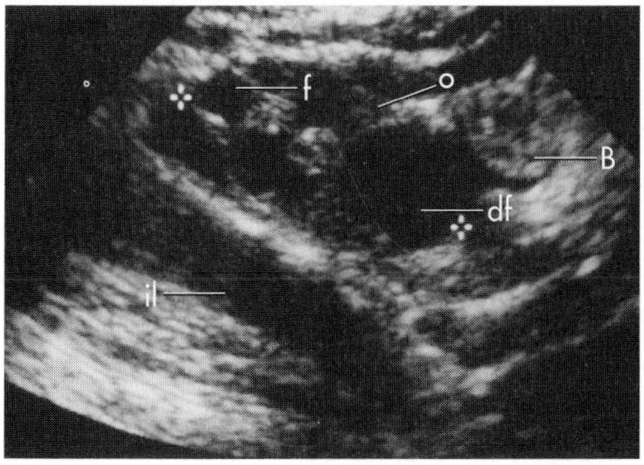

Figure 47-44 Transvaginal sagittal scan of right ovary. Follicles within the ovary and iliac vessels lateral to the ovary serve as excellent landmarks. *B,* Bowel; *df,* dominant follicle; *f,* follicle; *il,* iliac vessel; *o,* ovary.

A

B

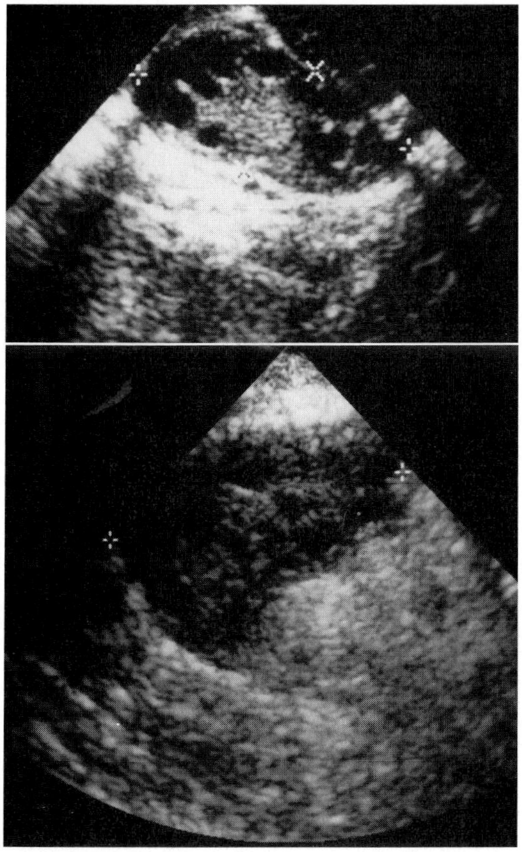

Figure 47-45 **A,** Transvaginal sagittal ovarian measurement. Calipers are placed at the longest length and anteroposterior thickness of the ovary. **B,** Transvaginal coronal ovarian measurement. Calipers are placed at the widest width of the ovary.

lution. A very small catheter filled with saline solution or contrast medium (Albunex) is inserted into the uterine cavity to the level of the uterine fundus. The speculum is removed with the catheter in place and the transvaginal transducer is inserted into the vagina. The tip of the catheter may be localized on ultrasound, and then sterile

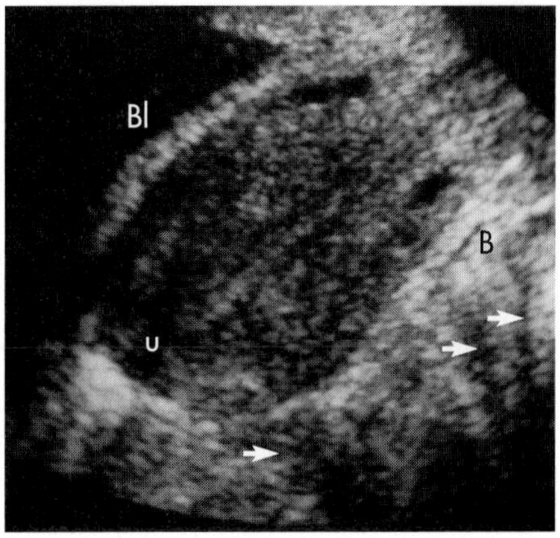

Figure 47-46 Transvaginal sagittal uterus *(u). B,* Bowel. Peristalsis is often observed in the cul-de-sac. Solid material in bowel is hyperechoic and produces shadows posteriorly *(arrows).* The bladder *(Bl)* is always oriented in the upper left corner.

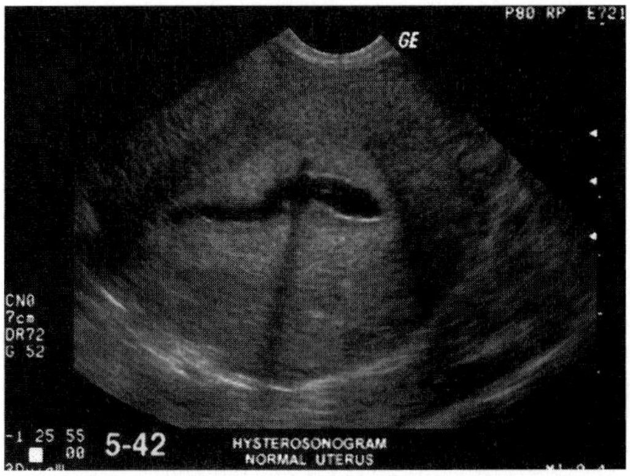

Figure 47-47 Transvaginal hysterosonogram of the uterus with a small amount of saline solution injected into the endometrial cavity.

saline solution is slowly injected into the cavity under sonographic evaluation.

The uterus is surveyed with ultrasound in sagittal and coronal planes to delineate the entire endometrial cavity (Figure 47-47). This technique is clinically useful to outline the endometrial cavity to determine the presence of polyps, tumors, or hyperplasia. In addition, the cornu of the uterus may be demonstrated with the interstitial area of the fallopian tube. The examination is contraindicated in patients with pelvic inflammatory disease.

REVIEW QUESTIONS

1. Before a pelvic ultrasound, what pertinent information should be requested from the patient?
2. What is the purpose of a full bladder when using the transabdominal scanning technique?
3. What are the contraindications for transvaginal ultrasound?
4. Describe the proper transvaginal transducer preparation before each examination.

5. When using the transvaginal scanning technique, what labeling terms are used to represent the scanning planes?
6. What are the three major muscle groups in the female pelvis that are visualized by ultrasound?
7. What is the best way to visualize the rectus abdominis muscles? How do they appear sonographically?
8. What three layers compose the uterus?
9. What are the three anatomic areas of the uterus?
10. What blood vessels are routinely visualized within the myometrium of the uterus?
11. What is the best landmark for orientation in the female pelvis when using transvaginal sonography?
12. How is the uterus properly measured?
13. In a normal anteflexed uterus, visualization of the cervix is optimized by what angulation of the transvaginal transducer?
14. What are the two layers of the endometrium? What are their functions?
15. Describe the changes of the endometrium throughout the normal menstrual cycle.
16. How is the endometrium properly measured?
17. When is it normal to visualize free fluid in the rectouterine recess and cul-de-sac area? At what point is the free fluid greatest in quantity?
18. What is another name for the uterine tubes?
19. Describe the location and relationship of surrounding structures of the fallopian tubes.
20. What are the three anatomic areas of the fallopian tubes?
21. What are the two regions of the ovary?
22. What are the functions of the ovary?
23. What is the best landmark for the ovary?
24. How is the ovary measured and the volume calculated?
25. What vessels are routinely evaluated in the female pelvis using Doppler imaging?

REFERENCES

1. ACR standard for the performance of ultrasound examination of the female pelvis, *ACR Res* 37, 1995.
2. Anderson JE: *Grant's atlas of anatomy,* ed 8, Baltimore, 1983, Williams and Wilkins.
3. Arger PH: Transvaginal ultrasound in postmenopausal patients, *Radiol Clin North Am* 30:759, 1992.
4. Kurtz AB, Rifkin MD: *Ultrasonography in obstetrics and gynecology,* Philadelphia, 1983, WB Saunders.
5. Cohen HL, Tice HM, Mandel FS: Ovarian volumes measured by US: bigger than we think, *Radiology* 177:189, 1990.
6. Coleman BG and others: Transvaginal and transabdominal sonography: prospective comparison, *Radiology* 168:639, 1988.
7. Crocco JA: Introduction. In Gray H: *Gray's anatomy,* ed 15, New York, 1977, Bounty Books.
8. Debose TJ, Hill LW, Hennigan HW: Sonography of arcuate uterine blood vessels, *J Ultrasound Med* 4:229, 1985.
9. Dodson MG: *Transvaginal ultrasound,* New York, 1991, Churchill Livingstone.
10. Evers JLH, Heineman MJ: *Gynecology: a clinical atlas,* St Louis, 1990, Mosby.
11. Fleischer AC and others: Transvaginal scanning of the endometrium, *J Clin Ultrasound* 18:337, 1990.
12. Goldstein SR: Incorporating endovaginal ultrasonography into the overall gynecologic examination, *Am J Obstet Gynecol* 162:625, 1990.
13. Greimanis MG, Jones AF: Transvaginal ultrasonography, *Radiol Clin North Am* 30:955, 1992.
14. Hackeloer BJ: Ultrasonic demonstration of follicular and corpus luteum development, *Appl Radiol Ultrasound,* pp. 169-176, Nov/Dec, 1979.
15. Kurjak A, Zalud I: Doppler and color flow imaging In Nyberg and others, editors: *Transvaginal ultrasound,* St Louis, 1992, Mosby.
16. Lyons EA, Gratton D, Harrington C: Transvaginal sonography of normal pelvic anatomy, *Radiol Clin North Am* 30:663, 1992.
17. Mendelson EB and others: Gynecologic imaging: comparison of transabdominal and transvaginal sonography, *Radiology* 166:321, 1988.
18. Munn CS and others: Ovary volume in young and premenopausal adults: US determination, *Radiology* 159:731, 1986.
19. Nasri MN and others: The role of vaginal scan in measurement of endometrial thickness in postmenopausal women, *Br J Obstet Gynaecol* 98:470, 1991.
20. Nyberg D and others: *Transvaginal ultrasound,* St Louis, 1992, Mosby.
21. Parsons AK, Ryva JC: Gynecologic ultrasound. In Hagen-Ansert S, editor: *Textbook of diagnostic ultrasonography,* ed 3, St Louis, 1989, Mosby.
22. Thomas CL, editor: *Taber's cycloped medical dictionary,* ed 4, Philadelphia, 1982, FA Davis.
23. Timor-Tritsch IE, Rottem S: Transvaginal ultrasonographic study of the fallopian tube, *Obstet Gynecol* 70:424, 1987.
24. Timor-Tritsch IE and others: The technique of transvaginal sonography with the use of a 6.5 MHz probe, *Am J Obstet Gynecol* 158:1019, 1988.
25. Varner E and others: Transvaginal sonography of the endometrium in postmenopausal women, *Obstet Gynecol* 78:195, 1991.
26. Winer-Muram HT and others: The sonographic features of the peripubertal ovaries, *Adolesc Pediatr Gynecol* 2:160, 1989.

BIBLIOGRAPHY

Andreotti RF and others: Endovaginal and transabdominal sonography of ovarian follicles, *J Ultrasound Med* 8:555, 1989.

Davis JA, Gosink BB: Fluid in the female pelvis: cyclic patterns, *J Ultrasound Med* 5:75, 1986.

Granberg S and others: Endometrial thickness as measured by endovaginal ultrasound for identifying endometrial abnormality, *Am J Obstet Gynecol* 164:47, 1991.

Grunfeld L and others: High resolution endovaginal ultrasonography of the endometrium: a noninvasive test for endometrial adequacy, *Obstet Gynecol* 78:200, 1991.

PART X

Gynecologic Pathophysiology

CHAPTER 48

Pelvic Infections and Inflammatory Disease

Sandra L. Hagen-Ansert

Objectives

- List the causes of pelvic inflammatory disease
- List the risk factors for pelvic inflammatory disease
- Describe the complications of inflammation of the fallopian tubes
- Describe the sonographic findings of salpingitis, pyosalpinx, and tuboovarian abscess
- List the locations of endometrial implants in the body
- Describe the sonographic findings in endometrioma
- Discuss the development of endometritis in the postpartum patient
- Describe the sonographic findings of adenomyosis
- Discuss the role of ultrasound in pelvic inflammatory disease

KEY TERMS

adenomyosis - benign invasive growth of the endometrium into the muscular layer of the uterus

endometrioma - localized tumor of endometriosis most frequently found in the ovary, cul-de-sac, rectovaginal septum, and peritoneal surface of the posterior wall of the uterus

endometriosis - occurs when functioning endometrial tissue invades sites outside the uterus

endometritis - infection within the endometrium of the uterus

hydrosalpinx - fluid within the fallopian tube

myometritis - infection within the myometrium of the uterus

oophoritis - infection within the ovary

parametritis - infection within the uterine serosa and broad ligaments

pelvic inflammatory disease (PID) - all-inclusive term that refers to all pelvic infections (endometritis, salpingitis, hydrosalpinx, pyosalpinx, and tuboovarian abscess)

pyosalpinx - retained pus within the inflamed fallopian tube

salpingitis - infection within the fallopian tubes

tuboovarian abscess (TOA) - infection that involves the fallopian tube and the ovary

---

Pelvic inflammatory disease (PID) and endometriosis are diffuse disease processes of the female pelvic cavity that display very different clinical presentations and pathologies. Early in the disease the clinical presentation is nonspecific: endometriosis may mimic functional bowel disease, and PID may mimic functional bowel disease.[7]

PID is a inclusive term that refers to all pelvic infections (i.e., endometritis, salpingitis, hydrosalpinx, pyosalpinx, and tuboovarian abscess). The infection occurs bilaterally and may be found in the endometrium (endometritis), the uterine wall (myometritis), the uterine serosa and broad ligaments (parametritis), the ovary

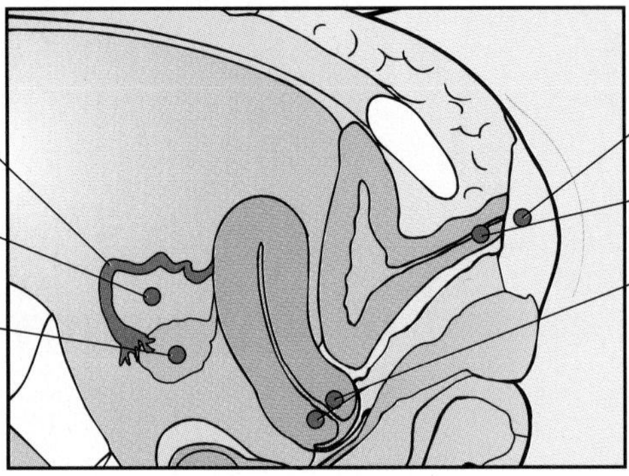

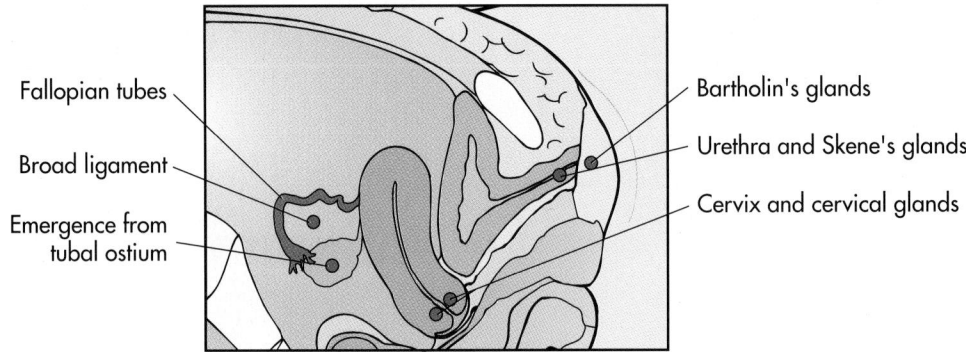

Figure 48-1 Pelvic inflammatory disease may be found in the endometrium, the uterine wall, the uterine serosa and broad ligaments, the ovary, and the fallopian tubes.

(oophoritis), and the most common location, the oviducts (salpingitis) (Figure 48-1).

PELVIC INFLAMMATORY DISEASE

The occurrence of PID is becoming more common. PID occurs in 10% of women during reproductive age (17% in African Americans) and affects 1 million American women each year. Risk factors include early sexual contact, multiple sexual partners, history of sexually transmitted disease, and douching. The causes of PID vary from sexually transmitted diseases (gonorrhea and chlamydia), abscess collections that have ruptured into the pelvis, intrauterine contraceptive device (IUD), to postabortion complications. PID is almost always found as a bilateral collection of fluid and pus within the pelvic cavity. Clinically, patients may have intense pelvic pain and a history of infertility. A vaginal discharge may be present with abnormal bleeding. A large palpable mass is usually present. The patient diagnosed with PID has an increased risk of ectopic pregnancy. Differential diagnosis may include hematoma, dermoid cyst, ovarian neoplasm, or endometriosis (Box 48-1).

The bacterial infection may arise from *Chlamydia trachomatis* and *Neisseria gonorrhea.* Other bacteria that have been found in PID patients include aerobes *(Streptococcus* sp., *Escherichia coli, Haemophilus influenzae),* anaerobes *(Bacteroides, Peptostreptococcus,* and *Peptococcus* spp.*), Mycobacterium tuberculosis, Actinomycetes* sp. in IUD users, and Herpesvirus hominis type 1.

Although sexual transmission is the most common form of infection, other routes of infection are possible. The string from the IUD may be a route for bacterial infection to invade the cervix. Other types of invasive instrumentation procedures in the pelvic cavity may also leave the route more accessible for bacterial invasion. The infection is spread via the mucosa of the pelvic organs through the cervix into the uterine endometrium (endometritis), out the fallopian tubes (salpingitis) to the area of the ovaries and peritoneum. As the tube becomes obstructed, a pyosalpinx develops.

BOX 48-1 PELVIC INFLAMMATORY DISEASE

- Inflammatory disease (acute or chronic); infection spreads to pelvis
- Large, palpable, bilateral complex mass; ovary may be seen separate from mass
- Free fluid in cul-de-sac
- Doppler image shows increased vascularity and diastolic flow
- Associated with infertility and endometritis

FALLOPIAN TUBES

Ultrasound findings. The normal fallopian tube generally is not visualized with ultrasound unless fluid surrounds it. If outlined by ascitic fluid, it is a 1-cm-thick tortuous structure. The normal lumen is usually not well visualized. If fluid, pus, or products of conception fill the tube, detection is easier (Figure 48-2). If the lumen is outlined and shows irregularity and multiple diverticula, a pathologic state is probable. The dilated tube may show a pointed beak at the swollen end of the tube near the isthmus where the tube enters the uterus. When a large tubular structure is present in the pelvis, color flow Doppler sonography is helpful in distinguishing a dilated fallopian tube from a dilated pelvic vein (Box 48-2).

SALPINGITIS, HYDROSALPINX, AND PYOSALPHINX

Salpingitis is an inflammation of a fallopian tube. This condition may be acute, subacute, or chronic. Clinical signs may range from asymptomatic to pelvic fullness or discomfort, or a low-grade fever. An obstructed tube filled with serous secretions is a hydrosalpinx; this can occur as a result of PID, endometriosis, or postoperative adhesions.

The differential diagnosis for hydrosalpinx would include fluid-filled bowel (watch for peristalsis in the bowel, or change the patient's position to see change in fluid pattern), dilated distal ureter, omental cyst, ovarian cyst, or tuboovarian abscess (Box 48-3).

Ultrasound findings. The sonographer should be sure not to confuse the dilated tube with a dilated ureter or

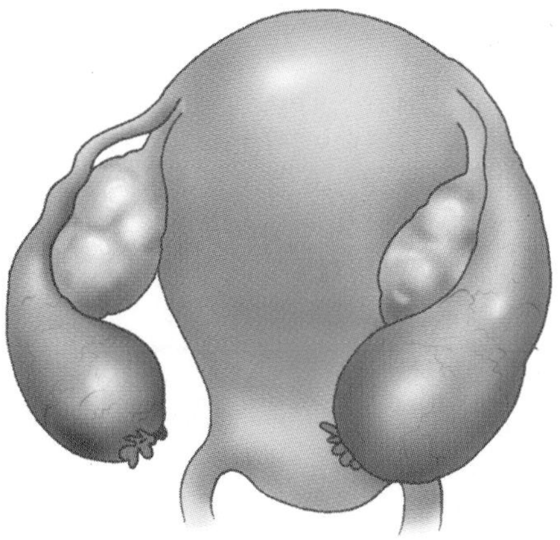

Figure 48-2 Salpingitis is an inflammation of the fallopian tubes that causes nodular dilation. This infection may be unilateral or bialteral.

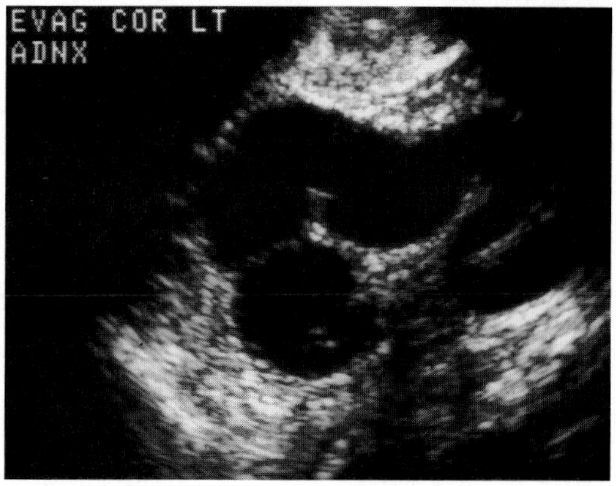

Figure 48-3 Transvaginal coronal image of the very dilated fallopian tube. When swollen with fluid, the tube bends and curls in the adnexal area.

BOX 48-2 SONOGRAPHIC FINDINGS OF PELVIC INFLAMMATORY DISEASE

- *Endometritis:* Thickening or fluid in the endometrium
- *Periovarian inflammation:* Enlarged ovaries with multiple cysts, indistinct margins
- *Salpingitis:* Nodular thickening, irregularity of tube with diverticula
- *Pyosalpinx or hydrosalpinx:* Fluid-filled irregular fallopian tube with or without echoes
- *Tuboovarian abscess:* Complex mass with septations, irregular margins, and internal echoes; usually in cul-de-sac

Data from Fedele L and others: *Am J Obstet Gynecol* 167:603.

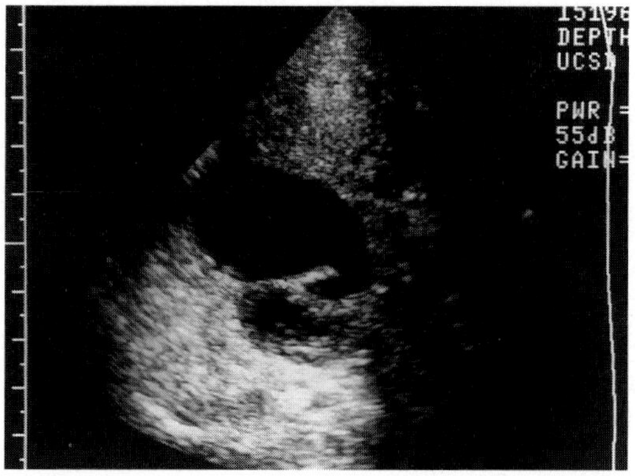

Figure 48-4 Transvaginal coronal image of a patient with acute salpingitis. The wall appears slightly thickened and very dilated.

BOX 48-3 HYDROSALPINX

- Occluded tube at fimbrial and cornual site; filled with serous secretions
- Occurs secondary to PID
- Walls become thin (secondary to dilation)
- Appearance of multicystic or fusiform mass
- Must be able to follow dilated tubes on ultrasound
- Usually bilateral; ampullary portion of tube more dilated than interstitial part

prominent vessel. The sonographer can try to follow the dilated fallopian tube as it enters the cornu of the uterus (at the fundus). Careful oblique angulations of the transducer are necessary to trace the pathway of the tube. Hydrosalpinx presents as echogenic fluid or fluid-fluid levels (Figure 48-3). Acute salpingitis is evident as a thick-walled nodular hyperemic tube (Figure 48-4). Pyosalpinx is retained pus in the tube with inflammation. In addition to hydrosalpinx or pyosalpinx, sonographic findings of PID include fluid in the cul-de-sac (Figure 48-5), mild uterine enlargement, and endometrial fluid or thickening.[12]

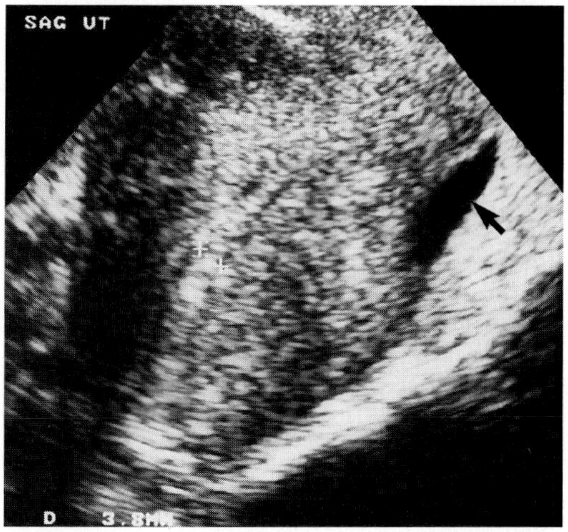

Figure 48-5 Free fluid. Sagittal view of the uterus in an asymptomatic, postmenopausal female demonstrates a small fluid collection *(arrow)* posterior to the uterus.

The unhealthy dilated tubes usually surround the ovaries like two crescents of ring sausage encircling the posterior surface of the uterus and filling the cul-de-sac. The walls of the tubes are thickened and nodular. The ovaries may be difficult to delineate because of surrounding tissue, edema, and pus. Severe and chronic pyosalpinges often contain thick, echogenic mucoid pus, which does not transmit sound as well as serous fluid or blood. Infection can obscure normal tissue planes, making anatomy unclear. Severe pain requires gentle use of ultrasound probes in acute PID, and in some cases a full bladder for transabdominal study is intolerable.

Tuboovarian Abscess

The adhesive, edematous, and inflamed serosa may further adhere to the ovary and/or other peritoneal surfaces, which distorts anatomy. This causes a further loculation of pus known as a **tuboovarian abscess (TOA).** This may be unilateral abscess or bilateral and appears as a complex mass in the posterior cul-de-sac.

The tuboovarian complex or abscess does not behave as a true abscess and usually responds well to antibiotic treatment without the need for surgical drainage.

Ultrasound findings. Serial ultrasound images during treatment allow observation of resolution and can indicate which patients need prolonged intravenous antibiotics and which patients may benefit more from removal of the involved tissue.

A pelvic abscess is usually a complex mass in the cul-de-sac that distorts pelvic anatomy (Figure 48-6). It can involve the ovary alone or the fallopian tube and ovary as a TOA. TOA appears as a complex hypoechoic adnexal mass with septations, irregular margins, and fluid-debris levels. The ovaries are often difficult to recognize as separate from the mass because of surrounding tissue, edema, and pus (Figure 48-7). As noted, TOAs usually are bilateral (Figure 48-8) but may be unilateral if an IUD is present. Sonographic guidance is used to assist in percutaneous or transvaginal drainage and thus hasten recovery.[1,9]

Peritonitis

Involvement of the bladder, ureter, bowel, and adenxal area may become infected.

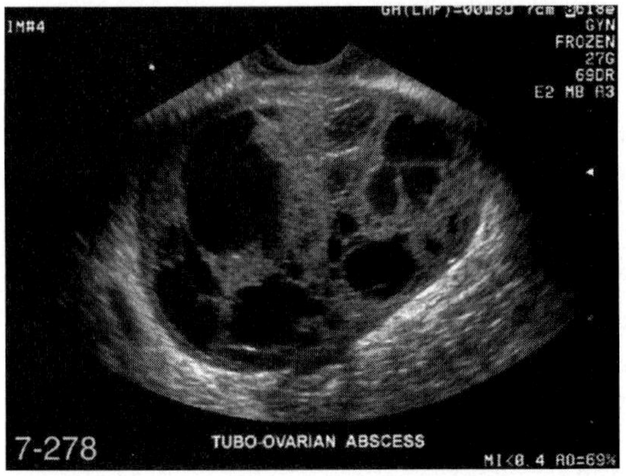

Figure 48-7 Transvaginal image in a 27-year-old female who presented with fever and intense pelvic pain shows a huge complex collection within the adnexal area consistent with a tuboovarian abscess.

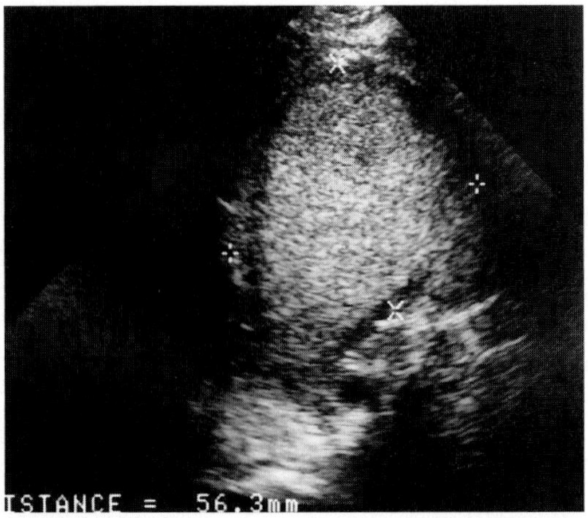

Figure 48-6 Pelvic abscess. Transvaginal sagittal view of the cul-de-sac demonstrates a 6-cm complex fluid collection in a 37-year-old intravenous drug abuser with multiple complex fluid collections in the pelvis. This abscess was drained transvaginally.

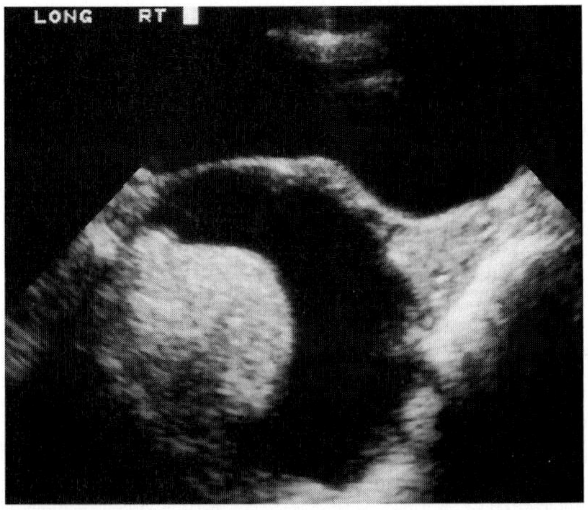

Figure 48-8 A 23-year-old female came to the emergency department with fever, vaginal discharge, and acute pelvic pain that persisted for 3 days. The transabdominal sagittal image shows the full bladder with the tubular vagina just posterior. The large complex tuboovarian abscess has both cystic and solid components and has pushed the uterus *(not seen)* away from the midline.

Ultrasound findings. If the abscess collection has gas-forming bubbles within, it may be difficult to delineate well with sonography because the beam is reflected from the area of interest. The sonographer should look for loculated areas of fluid within the pelvis, the paracolic gutters, and mesenteric reflections.

ENDOMETRIOSIS

Endometriosis is a common condition in which functioning endometrial tissue is present outside the uterus. Usually the ectopic tissue is found on the ovaries, the external surface of the uterus, and scattered over the peritoneum, especially in the dependent parts of the pelvis (Figure 48-9). The endometrial implants may be present in almost any area of the body. This condition has been found to occur in 1% to 7% of American women and affects women during their reproductive years. The endometrial tissue cyclically bleeds and proliferates as stimulated by hormonal influence. Clinical symptoms include (1) painful periods or intercourse and (2) infertility secondary to adhesions and fibrosis. Differential diagnosis would include hemorrhagic ovarian cyst, TOA, cystic ovarian neoplasm, solid ovarian tumor, or ectopic pregnancy.

Ultrasound findings. Two types of endometriosis have been described: diffuse and localized. The diffuse form is difficult to recognize with sonography because the implants are so small. The diffuse form leads to disorganization of the pelvic anatomy with an appearance similar to PID (Figure 48-10) or chronic ectopic pregnancy.[2]

ENDOMETRIOMA

Endometriosis also occurs in a localized form, known as an endometrioma. Clinically, patients are asymptomatic.

Ultrasound findings. An endometrioma often appears as a well-defined predominately cystic mass with transabdominal ultrasound, but with transvaginal ultrasound, uniform internal echoes are usually seen.[8] The most common presentation is of a "chocolate cyst" with low-intensity echoes and acoustic enhancement (Figure 48-11). Other appearances include an enlarged polycystic ovary with a thick wall and internal septations or a cyst with fluid-debris levels (because of different degrees of organization of the hemorrhage).

ENDOMETRITIS

Endometritis most often occurs in association with PID, in the postpartum state, or following instrumentation invasion. In patients with pelvic infection the uterus is the route for infection to the tubes and adnexa. Postpartum patients may develop endometritis (Figure 48-12) after prolonged labor, vaginitis, premature rupture of the membranes, or retained products of conception.[7] Clinically the patient has intense pelvic pain.

Ultrasound findings. Sonographically, the endometrium appears prominent, irregular, or both, with a small amount of endometrial fluid. Pus may be demonstrated in the cul-de-sac as echogenic particles. Enlarged ovaries with multiple cysts and indistinct margins may be seen secondary to periovarian inflammation.[6] Dilation of the fallopian tube should be distinguished from fluid-filled bowel by gentle compression on the pelvic wall to look for peristalsis or movement in the bowel lumen. Gas bubbles are present in rare cases; however, these also are seen in normal postpartum patients. In the immediate postpartum period the presence of retained tissue is difficult to distinguish from inflammatory debris or blood clots.

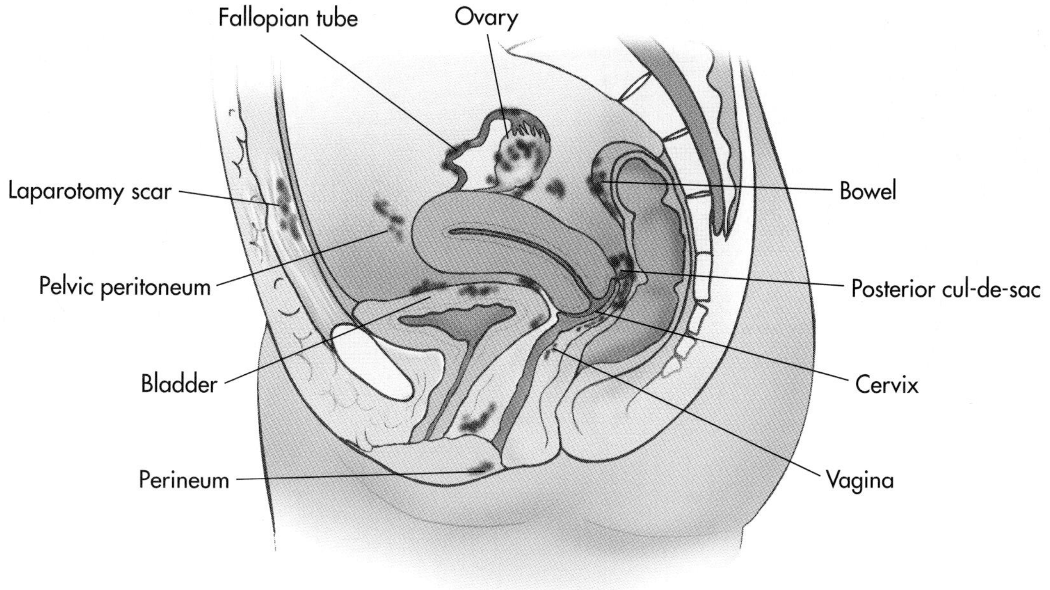

Figure 48-9 Possible pelvic sites of endometriosis.

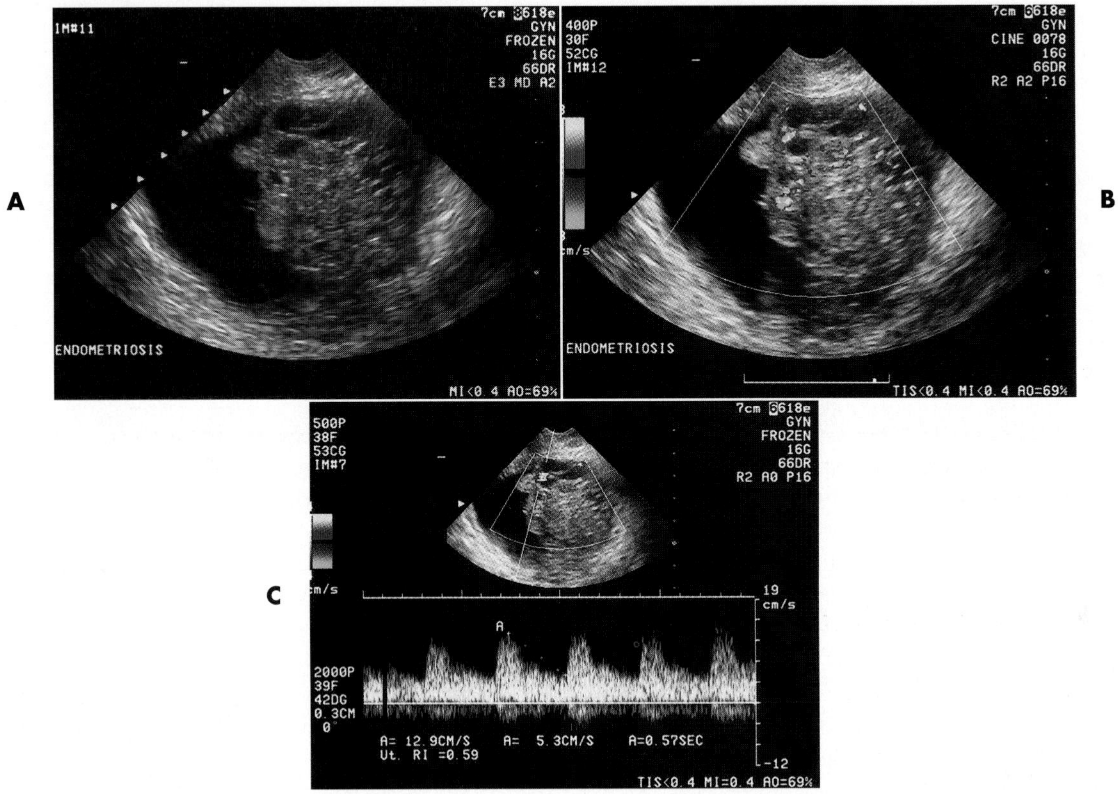

Figure 48-10 A 34-year-old female with pelvic fullness. **A,** The transvaginal coronal image shows a complex mass in the right adnexal area. **B,** Color Doppler imaging shows increased flow from the bleeding within the tissue. **C,** The spectral Doppler tracing shows a low-resistance flow pattern.

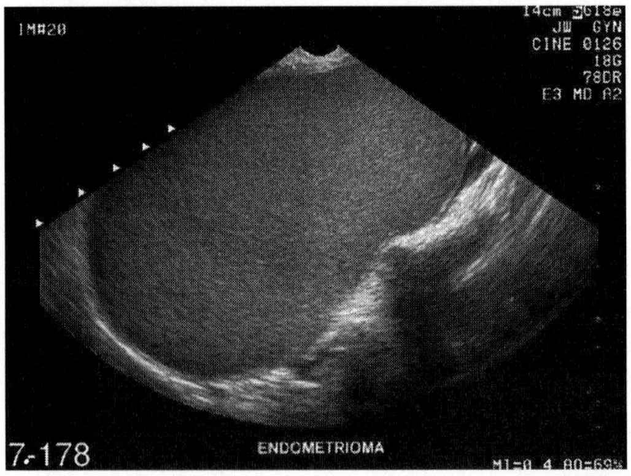

Figure 48-11 An endometrioma is a well-defined homogeneous mass with low-intensity echoes and acoustic enhancement.

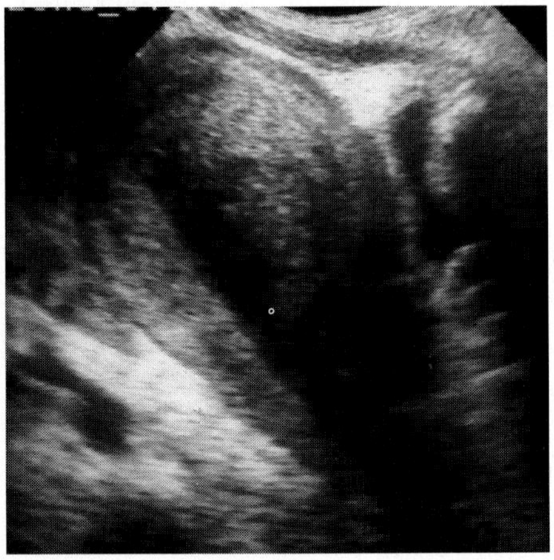

Figure 48-12 The enlarged uterus with an edematous complex endometrium in a patient who came 10 days postoperatively with intense pelvic pain. She was diagnosed with endometritis.

ADENOMYOSIS

Adenomyosis is the ectopic occurrence of nests of endometrial tissue within the myometrium and is more extensive in the posterior wall. Adenomyosis is commonly a diffuse disease with global infiltration of the endometrium; on occasion, adenomyosis may be focal with discrete masses or adenomyomas in the wall of the uterus.[5]

The etiology of this disease may arise from multiple pregnancies and deliveries with subsequent uterine shrinking. Elevated estrogen levels may also promote the growth of myometrial islands of endometrial tissue.[5] Clinically,

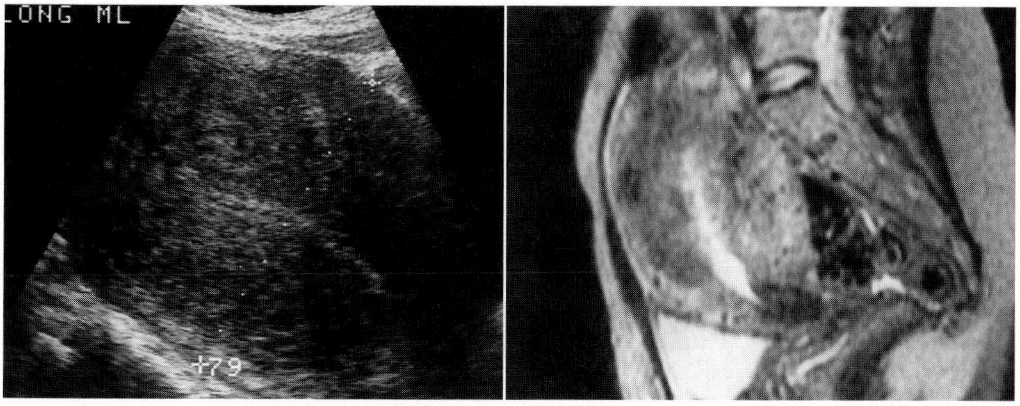

Figure 48-13 Adenomyosis. **A,** Transvaginal view of the uterus demonstrates an enlarged heterogeneous uterus. **B,** Magnetic resonance imaging shows an enlarged uterus with heterogeneous decreased signal intensity throughout the myometrium.

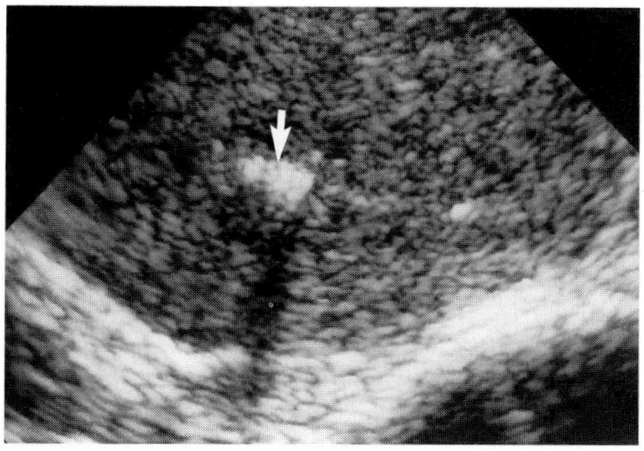

Figure 48-14 Transvaginal sagittal view of the uterus in a different patient demonstrates endometrial calcification *(arrow)* with shadowing. This woman had a history of previous dilation and curettage.

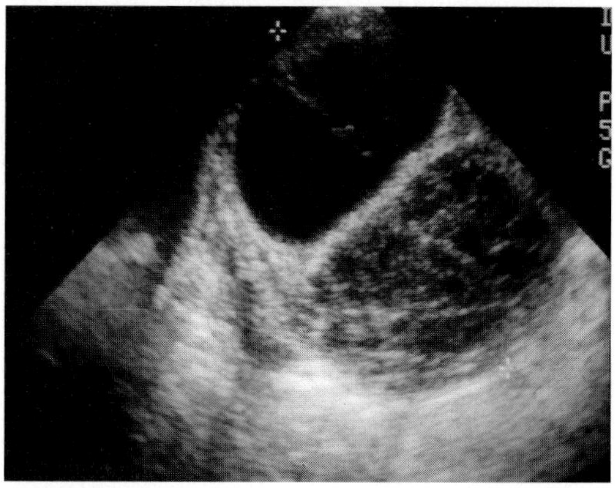

Figure 48-15 Transvaginal sagittal image in a 24-year-old female who had pelvic pain. A complex mass was seen in the right adnexal secondary to a hemorrhagic corpus lutein cyst.

the patient presents in middle age with heavy, painful menses and uterine enlargement. Treatment may be local excision of the affected area or hysterectomy if the symptoms are severe.

Ultrasound findings. Sonographically the diagnosis of adenomyosis may be difficult. The most common finding of extensive adenomyosis is diffuse uterine enlargement.[6] There may be thickening of the posterior myometrium, with the involved area being slightly more anechoic than normal myometrium.[6] Hemorrhage in islands of endometrial tissue appears as small hypoechoic myometrial cysts.[14] Adenomyosis is not reliably diagnosed by ultrasonography, but is well characterized by magnetic resonance imaging (MRI) (Figure 48-13).

Calcifications resulting from prior instrumentation are seen along the inner myometrium and cervix (Figure 48-14). Localized adenomyomas may be seen by transvaginal sonography as inhomogeneous, circumscribed areas in the myometrium, having indistinct margins and containing anechoic lacunae.[6] They may be difficult to distinguish from leiomyomas, and these two conditions frequently occur together.[10]

COMPLEX MASSES

Any simple cyst that hemorrhages may appear as a complex mass (Figure 48-15). In patients of reproductive age the classic differential diagnosis of a complex adnexal mass is ectopic pregnancy, endometriosis, and PID. Dermoids and other benign tumors can appear in a similar fashion.

INTERVENTIONAL ULTRASOUND

Transabdominal or transvaginal guidance is used for aspiration of benign-appearing cysts. Transvaginal drainage is helpful in TOAs, other pelvic abscesses such as appendicitis and diverticulitis, and drainage of postoperative fluid collections (Figure 48-16).[9,13] Transrectal drainage is used for deep pelvic abscesses.[3] Transvaginal

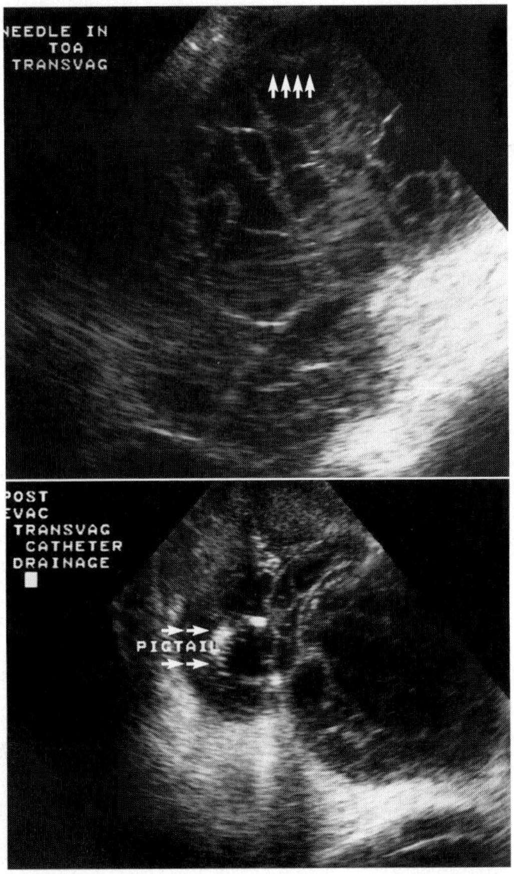

A
B

Figure 48-16 Hematometra in a 23-year-old woman 4 weeks after a dilation and curettage. **A,** Transabdominal longitudinal view of the uterus demonstrates a central fluid collection with a fluid debris level *(arrows).* **B,** Transvaginal image in the same patient again demonstrates the pigtail catheter *(arrows).* The fluid is monitored by ultrasound guidance.

ultrasonography also is used to biopsy benign and malignant solid pelvic masses[4] and to drain recurrent malignant collections.

POSTOPERATIVE USES OF ULTRASOUND

Pain and masses after pelvic surgery can indicate complications such as postoperative bleeding, hematomas, or abscess formation. Postoperative masses are not always dangerous. More than one surgeon has made the diagnosis of severely distended bladder by ordering an ultrasound for a postoperative pelvic mass. Ultrasound can be used to demonstrate these fluid collections and to visualize the operative site. The ability to palpate specific structures with the transvaginal probe and avoid the abdominal wound are valuable in determining the site of pain in a postoperative pelvis. Resolving hematomas (1 week after surgery) often appear to be of a solid consistency and can be followed as they shrink.

Ultrasonically guided needle drainage of abscesses and stable hematomas, either through the abdominal wall or the vagina, is diagnostic and therapeutic. Recurrent tumor masses may be biopsied in a similar fashion. The transvaginal ultrasound and needle guide make entering the anterior or posterior cul-de-sacs safer and easier for pelvic fluid aspiration, biopsies, or radiation needle placement.

An expert combination of transvaginal and transabdominal techniques is essential as new gynecologic applications of ultrasound continue to be found in screening, diagnosis, and therapy of pelvic pathology in female fetuses, children, and adults.

REVIEW QUESTIONS

1. What is pelvic inflammatory disease?
2. Describe the risk factors that lead to pelvic infection.
3. Describe the clinical findings in patients with pelvic inflammatory disease.
4. Discuss the routes of infection to the pelvis.
5. List the sonographic findings of pelvic inflammatory disease.
6. What is the difference between hydrosalpinx and pyosalpinx?
7. Describe the findings in a tuboovarian abscess.
8. What is endometriosis?
9. Describe the sonographic findings in an endometrioma.
10. Why do postpartum patients develop endometritis?
11. What is adenomyosis?
12. Discuss the role of ultrasound in the postoperative patient.

REFERENCES

1. Abbitt PL, Goldwag S, Urbanski S: Endovaginal sonography for guidance in draining pelvic fluid collections, *Am J Roentgenol* 154:849, 1990.
2. Athey PA, Diment DD: The spectrum of sonographic findings in endometriomas, *J Ultrasound Med* 8:487, 1989.
3. Bennett JD and others: Deep pelvic abscesses: transrectal drainage with radiologic guidance, *Radiology* 185:825, 1992.
4. Burkman RT: Association between intrauterine contraceptive device and pelvic inflammatory disease, *Obstet Gynecol* 57:269, 1981.
5. Callen P: *Ultrasonography in obstetrics and gynecology,* ed 3, Philadelphia, 1994, WB Saunders.
6. Fedele L and others: Transvaginal ultrasonography in the differential diagnosis of adenomyoma versus leiomyoma, *Am J Obstet Gynecol* 167:603, 1992.
7. Hall, R: Pelvic inflammatory disease and endometriosis. In Berman MC, Cohen HL, editors: *Obstetrics & gynecology,* ed 2, Philadelphia, 1997, JB Lippincott.
8. Kupfer MC, Schwimer SR, Lebovic J: Transvaginal sonographic appearance of endometriomata: spectrum of findings, *J Ultrasound Med* 11:129, 1992.
9. Nosher JL, Winchman HK, Needell GS: Transvaginal pelvic abscess drainage with US guidance, *Radiology* 165:872, 1987.
10. Patten RM and others: Pelvic inflammatory disease: endovaginal sonography with laparoscopic correlation, *J Ultrasound Med* 9:681, 1990.

11. Seidler DS and others: Uterine adenomyosis: a difficult sonographic diagnosis, *J Ultrasound Med* 6:345, 1987.
12. Swayne LC, Love MB, Karasick SR: Pelvic inflammatory disease: sonographic-pathologic correlation, *Radiology* 151:751, 1984.
13. vanSonnenberg E and others: US-guided transvaginal drainage of pelvic abscesses and fluid collections, *Radiology* 181:53, 1991.
14. Walsh JW, Taylor KJW, Rosenfield AT: Gray scale ultrasonography in the diagnosis of endometriosis and adenomyosis, *Am J Roentgenol* 132:87, 1979.

BIBLIOGRAPHY

Bernaschek G, Deutinger J, Kratochwil A: *Endosonography in obstetrics and gynecology,* Berlin, 1990, Springer-Verlag.

Bohlman ME, Ensor RE, Sanders RC: Sonographic findings in adenomyosis of the uterus, *Am J Radiol* 148:765, 1987.

Carlson JA Jr and others: Clinical and pathologic correlation of endometrial cavity fluid detected by ultrasound in the postmenopausal patient, *Obstet Gynecol* 77:119, 1991.

Cotran RS, Kumar V, Robbins SL: *Robbins' pathologic basis of disease,* Philadelphia, 1989, WB Saunders.

Kurjak A, Zalud I, Alfirevic Z: Evaluation of adnexal masses with transvaginal color ultrasound, *J Ultrasound Med* 10:295, 1991.

Laing FC and others: Ultrasonic demonstration of endometrial fluid collections unassociated with pregnancy, *Radiology* 137:471, 1980.

Najarian KE, Kurtz AB: New observations in the sonographic evaluation of intrauterine contraceptive devices, *J Ultrasound Med* 5:205, 1986.

Radecki PD and others: Inflammatory diseases. In Friedman AC and others, editors: *Clinical pelvic imaging: CT, ultrasound and MRI,* St Louis, 1990, Mosby.

Senanayake P, Kramer DG: Contraception and the etiology of pelvic inflammatory disease: new perspective, *Am J Obstet Gynecol* 138:82, 1980.

Timor-Tritsch IE, Rottem S: Transvaginal ultrasonographic study of the fallopian tube, *Obstet Gynecol* 70:424, 1987.

Togashi K and others: Enlarged uterus: differentiation between adenomyosis and leiomyoma with MR imaging, *Radiology* 171:531, 1989.

CHAPTER 49

Uterine Anomalies

Sandra L. Hagen-Ansert

OBJECTIVES

- Describe the location of a Gartner's duct cyst and a nabothian cyst
- Discuss the clinical signs of a cervical polyp
- List the different locations where a leiomyoma is found
- Describe the sonographic findings in a leiomyoma
- List the causes of calcification within the uterine cavity
- Describe how to measure the endometrial thickness and the normal measurements for the various menstrual phases
- Define endometrial hyperplasia
- Distinguish endometrial hyperplasia from carcinoma
- Describe the role Doppler has in evaluating pathologic conditions in the pelvis
- Differentiate between the types of intrauterine contraceptive devices and describe their sonographic appearance
- Describe the sonographic appearance of an ectopic pregnancy

KEY TERMS

adenomyosis - benign invasive growth of the endometrium that may cause heavy, painful menstrual bleeding

cervical polyp - hyperplastic protrusion of the epithelium of the cervix; may be broad based or pedunculated

cervical stenosis - acquired condition with obstruction of the cervical canal

ectopic pregnancy - pregnancy occurring outside the uterine cavity

endometrial carcinoma - presents with abnormal thickening of the endometrial cavity; usually presents with irregular bleeding in perimenopausal and in postmenopausal women

endometrial hyperplasia - results from estrogen stimulation to the endometrium without the influence of progestin; frequent cause of bleeding (especially in postmenopausal women)

endometrial polyp - pedunculated or sessile well-defined mass attached to the endometrial cavity

endometritis - infection within the endometrium of the uterus

Gartner's duct cyst - small cyst within the vagina

intramural leiomyoma - most common type of leiomyoma; deforms the myometrium

intrauterine contraceptive device (IUD) - device inserted into the endometrial cavity to prevent pregnancy

leiomyoma - most common benign gynecologic tumor in women during their reproductive years

nabothian cyst - benign tiny cyst within the cervix

submucosal - type of leiomyoma found to deform the endometrial cavity and cause heavy or irregular menses

subserosal - type of leiomyoma that may become pedunculated and appear as an extrauterine mass

Ultrasonography is traditionally applied in the female pelvis to delineate the size, texture, vascularity, and structure of pelvic anatomy. The examination may also supply information on the morphology of malfunctioning organs that seem normal on pelvic examination. Small, nonpalpable submucosal myomas or polyps may cause abnormal bleeding. The localization of intrauterine contraceptive devices (IUD) may be assessed by pelvic ultrasound examination. The homogeneity of the myometrium is assessed, and the thickness of the endometrial cavity is measured, in addition to the length and width of the uterus and cervix. Newer techniques in hysterosalpingography include the use of ultrasonography to follow the placement of the catheter within the endometrial canal. Both transabdominal and transvaginal sonography are important in these evaluations. Transabdominal imaging furnishes a survey of anatomy, whereas transvaginal imaging provides better characterization of internal architecture of the vagina, cervix, and uterus.

PATHOLOGY OF THE CERVIX AND THE VAGINA

BENIGN CONDITIONS

The cervix may be a challenge to obtaining good sonographic images unless transvaginal ultrasound is used. The cervix lies posterior to the bladder between the lower uterine segment and the vaginal canal. If the patient's hips are elevated (with folded sheets) before the insertion of the vaginal probe, the sonographer will have better access to imaging the cervical area. After the uterine cavity has been examined, the probe should be slowly pulled back to image the internal and external cervical os. In the sagittal view the handle of the transducer is slowly moved upward to better image the cervix (see Chapter 47).

The most common finding with sonography is the presence of **nabothian cysts** (Figure 49-1) that result from chronic cervicitis and are seen frequently in middle-age women. This cyst results from an obstructed and dilated transcervical gland and is also called an epithelial inclusion cyst. On ultrasound examination, they appear as discrete, round, fluid-filled anechoic cysts, usually measuring less than 2 cm, along the cervical canal; they may be multiple (Box 49-1).

Clinical findings of irregular bleeding may be the result of **cervical polyps.** This benign condition arises from the hyperplastic protrusion of the epithelium of the endocervix or ectocervix.[8] Chronic inflammation is the most likely factor. The polyps may be pedunculated, projecting out of the cervix, or broad based. Usually women in late middle age are more likely to develop polyps.

A small percentage of leiomyomas originate in the cervix (Figure 49-2). When the fibroids are small, the patient is asymptomatic; however, as the mass enlarges, bladder or bowel obstruction may result. The fibroid may be pedunculated (Figure 49-3) and prolapse into the vaginal canal.

Cervical stenosis is an acquired condition with obstruction of the cervical canal at the internal or external os resulting from prior instrumentation, childbirth, surgery, cancer, or irradiation. The menopausal patient may be asymptomatic even though the stenosis can produce a distended, fluid-filled uterus (Figure 49-4). Premenopausal patients may experience oligomenorrhea or amenorrhea with cramping or dysmenorrhea.[8]

BOX 49-1 NABOTHIAN CYSTS

- Benign cysts in cervix
- Chronic inflammatory retention cysts
- Asymptomatic

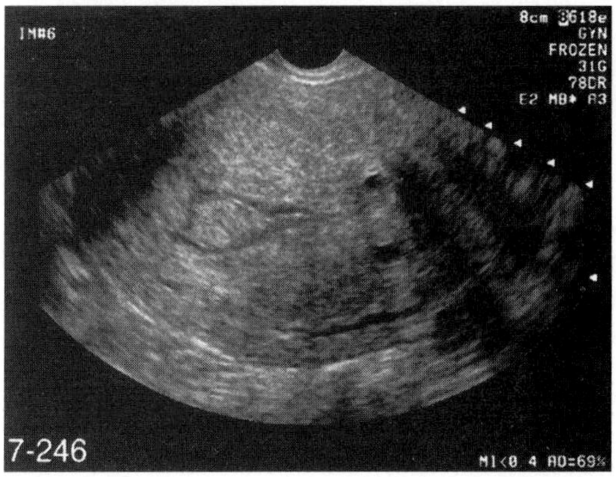

Figure 49-1 Transvaginal sagittal image of the cervix shows multiple very small nabothian cysts just inferior to the endometrial cavity in the center of the cervix with increased through-transmission beyond. The areas of shadowing represent poor contact or air bubbles between the transducer and the vaginal wall.

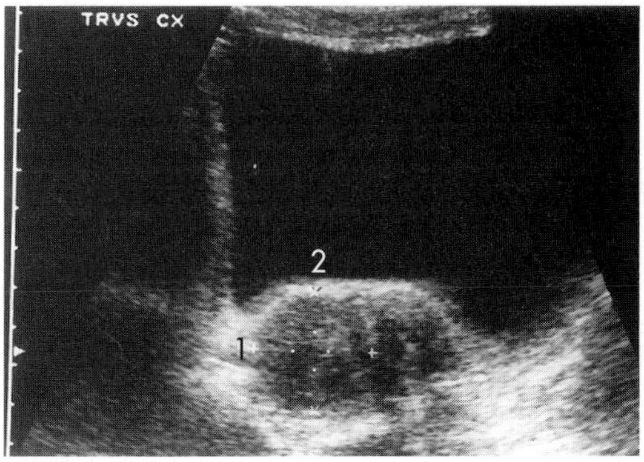

Figure 49-2 Transabdominal transverse view of the cervix reveals a 3-cm cervical fibroid.

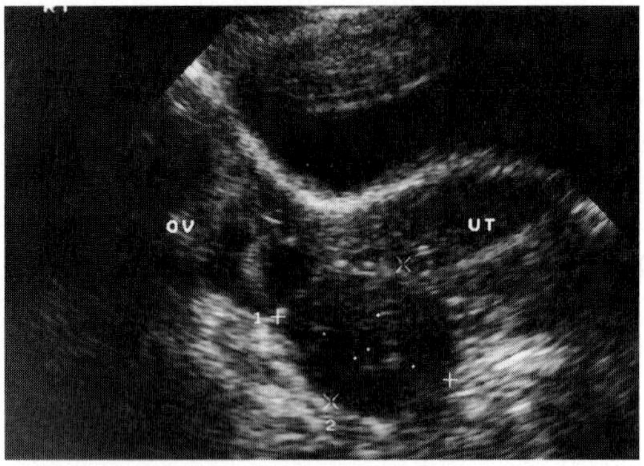

Figure 49-3 Transabdominal view of the uterus *(UT)* and ovary *(OV)* with a 4-cm hypoechoic pedunculated fibroid *(mass outlined by calipers)*. The pedicle is not visible on this image.

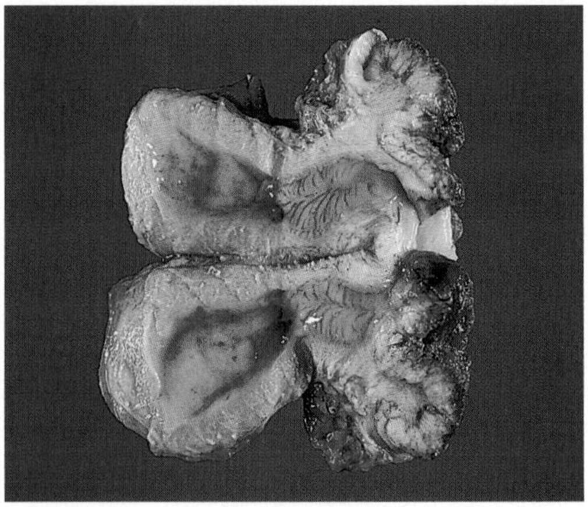

Figure 49-5 Gross pathologic findings of cervical squamous cell carcinoma.

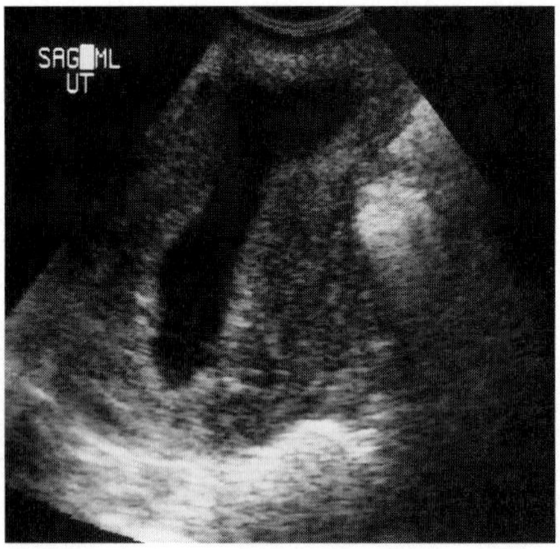

Figure 49-4 A 63-year-old asymptomatic woman on cyclic hormone replacement therapy demonstrates a large endometrial fluid collection. She underwent dilation for cervical stenosis, and bloody fluid was drained.

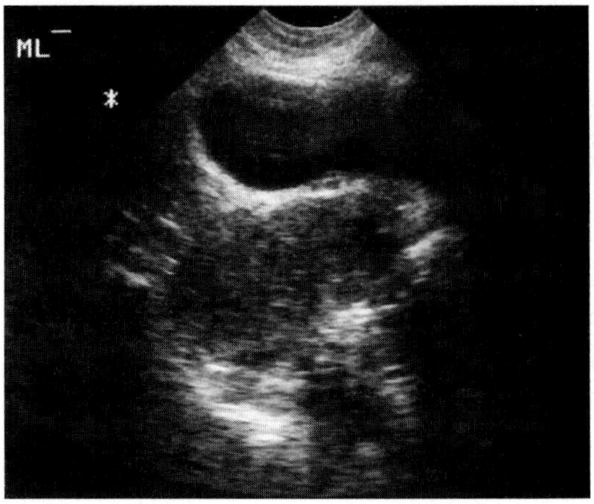

Figure 49-6 Transabdominal image of the distended urinary bladder and lower uterine segment. The cervical area is enlarged and hypoechoic with decreased through-transmission. The patient was found to have cervical carcinoma at surgery.

BOX 49-2 CERVICAL CARCINOMA

- Affects women of menstrual age
- *Clinical:* Vaginal discharge or bleeding
- *Sonography:* Retrovesical mass, obstruction of ureters, invasion of bladder

Cervical Carcinoma

Advanced cervical cancer is usually evident clinically (Box 49-2 and Figure 49-5). Transvaginal and transrectal ultrasonography demonstrate bladder, ureteral, vaginal, and rectal involvement and thus are used in staging cervical cancer.[2,10,11,22] Areas of increased echogenicity or hypoechoic areas with an irregular outline signify changes compatible with cervical carcinoma (Figure 49-6).

Transrectal ultrasonography is used in some centers to evaluate tumor size and depth of cervical infiltration. However, transvaginal ultrasonography is more sensitive in evaluating the extent of vaginal infiltration and helps diagnose local spread from cervical carcinoma or primary vaginal carcinoma.[3] Transonography is thus very helpful in staging the contiguous spread of cervical carcinoma and is better than computerized tomography (CT) or magnetic resonance imaging (MRI) in this respect. However, CT and MRI are superior for evaluating lymphatic spread for staging.[2]

Ultrasonic guidance is also helpful in guiding biopsies of the cervix and vagina.[3]

The Vaginal Cuff

A vaginal cuff is seen in hysterectomy patients after surgery. The upper size limit of a normal vaginal cuff is 2.1 cm.[38] If the cuff is larger than this or contains a well-defined mass or areas of high echogenicity, it should be regarded with suspicion for recurrence of malignancy.[37] Nodular areas in the vaginal cuff may reflect postradiation fibrosis.[37]

DIFFERENTIAL DIAGNOSIS LISTS Box 49-3

ENLARGED UTERUS
Pregnancy
Postpartum
Leiomyoma

UTERINE TUMOR
Leiomyoma
Carcinoma

THICKENED ENDOMETRIUM
Endometrial hyperplasia
Retained products of conception
Inflammatory disease
Endometrial carcinoma

ENDOMETRIAL FLUID
Endometritis
Retained products of conception
Pelvic inflammatory disease
Cervical obstruction

ENDOMETRIAL SHADOWING
Gas (abscess)
Intrauterine device
Calcified fibroids or vessels
Retained products of conception

THE VAGINA

Occasionally, sonography is used to characterize a vaginal mass, such as a **Gartner's duct cyst.** These are the most common cystic lesions of the vagina and usually are found incidentally during sonographic examination. Obstruction of the uterus and/or the vagina may result in an accumulation of fluid (hydrometra), blood (hematometra), or pus (pyometra).

Vaginal adenocarcinoma and rhabdomyosarcoma appear as solid masses, occasionally with areas of necrosis.[42]

PATHOLOGY OF THE UTERUS

Common differential considerations for the uterus are seen in Box 49-3.

LEIOMYOMAS

Leiomyomas, commonly called myomas or fibroids, are the most common gynecologic tumors, occurring in approximately 20% to 50 % of women of reproductive age.[8] They are most frequently diagnosed in premenopausal women over age 30 and in younger African-American women.

The tumor arises from the smooth muscle of the uterine wall and consists of a whorled, spherical configuration of myometrial tissue that can degenerate into a number of different histologic subtypes (Figure 49-7). The tumors consist of nodules of myometrial tissue and are usually multiple. The myoma is encapsulated (Figure 49-8) with a pseudocapsule and separates easily from the surrounding myometrium.[8] With atrophy and vascular compromise, fibrotic changes and degeneration of the myomas occur.[8] Liquefaction, necrosis, hemorrhage, and ultimate calcification may take place.[8]

Hyalinization (development of an albuminoid mass in a cell or tissue) occurs most often, making the myomas appear more lucent (hypoechoic) than myometrium. Ten percent of myomas contain calcification, and a similar number have areas of hemorrhage. Other fibroids contain tissue that has undergone necrosis and liquefaction and become myxoid in texture.[12] The tumor usually does not become malignant; however, it is sensitive to estrogen and may increase in size during pregnancy.[37] After menopause, with the regression of estrogen stimulation, the tumor becomes smaller but does not entirely disappear.

Clinically myomas cause uterine irregularity and enlargement with the sensation of pelvic pressure and sometimes pain. Patterns of irregular bleeding, menometrorrhagia, or heavy menstrual bleeding, menorrhagia, are the primary clinical problems with myomas.

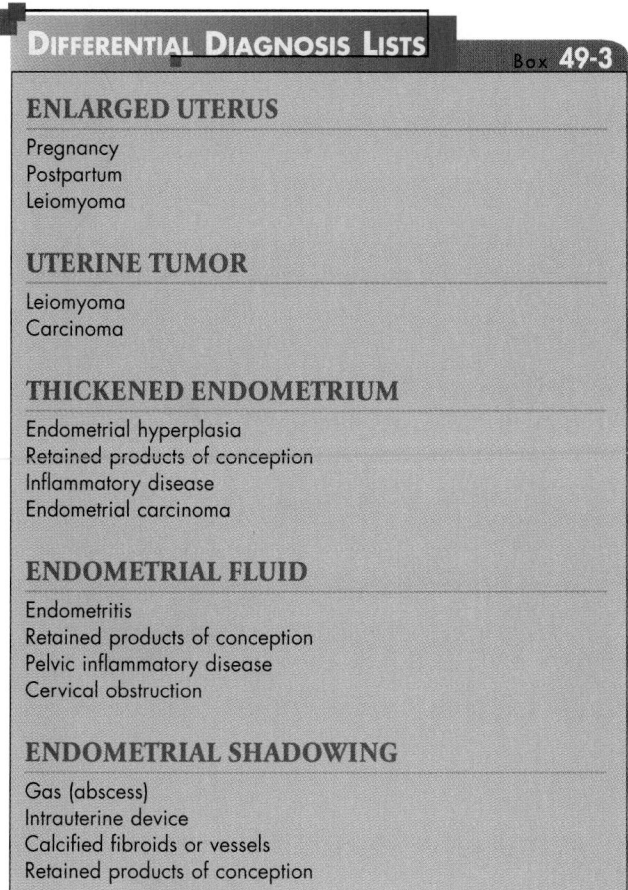

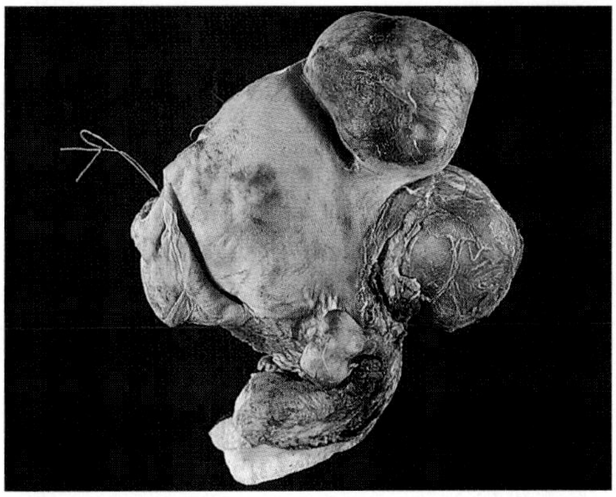

Figure 49-7 Gross pathologic findings of the uterine cavity with multiple subserosal fibroid tumors arising from its walls.

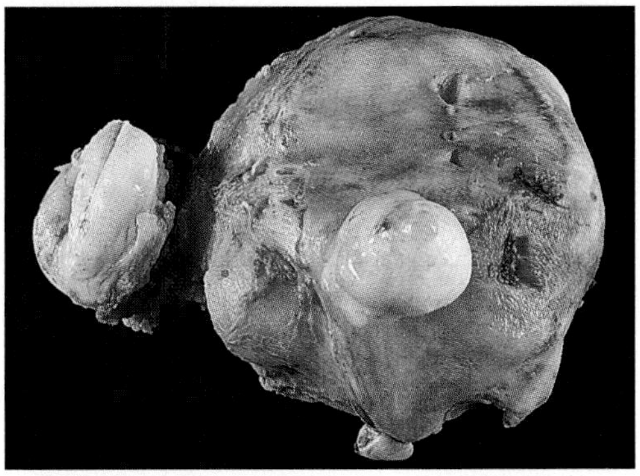

Figure 49-8 Gross pathologic findings of the uterus with the encapsulated leiomyoma in the submucosal area.

BOX 49-4 Characteristics of Leiomyomas

- Most common pelvic tumor
- Smooth muscle cell composition
- Fibrosis occurs after atrophic or degenerative changes
- Degeneration occurs when fibroids outstrip their blood supply; calcification
- May be pedunculated
- *Clinical:* Enlarged uterus, profuse and prolonged bleeding, pain

BOX 49-5 Uterine Locations of Leiomyomas

Submucosal
Erode into endometrial cavity—heavy bleeding; infertility

Intramural
May enlarge to cause pressure on adjacent organs; infertility

Subserosal
May enlarge to cause pressure on adjacent organs

The tumor may contribute to infertility by distorting the fallopian tube or endometrial cavity; if located in the lower uterine segment, the tumor may interfere with normal vaginal delivery. Because of the increased estrogen during pregnancy, the tumor grows and may bleed within, causing pain (Box 49-4).

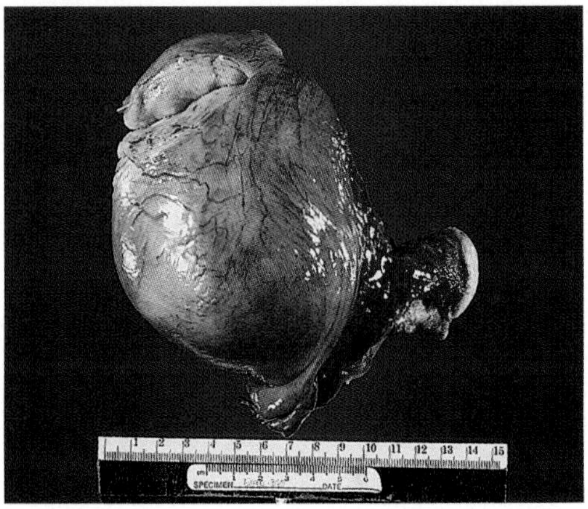

Figure 49-9 Gross pathologic findings of a pedunculated subserosal fibroid of the uterus.

A B

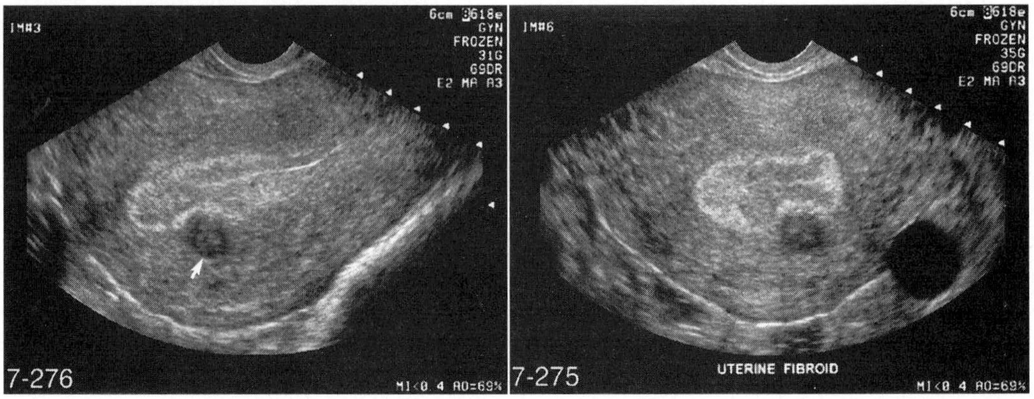

Figure 49-10 Sagittal **(A)** and coronal **(B)** transvaginal images of the uterus with a small submucosal fibroid indenting the endometrial cavity *(arrow).* A follicular cyst is seen along the posterior border slightly compressing the uterine wall.

A B

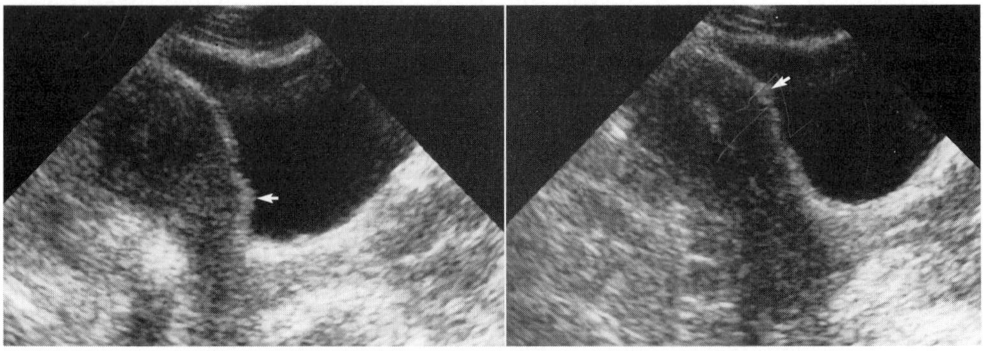

Figure 49-11 **A** and **B,** Transabdominal longitudinal views of the uterus reveal subtle fibroids *(arrows).* These slightly echogenic masses distort the contour between the bladder and the uterus.

Leiomyomas can affect any portion of the uterine wall; however, the tumor may also be uncommonly found in the lower uterine segment, the cervix, and in the broad ligament. Leiomyomas are **submucosal** (deforming the endometrial cavity and causing irregular or heavy menstrual bleeding); **intramural** (deforming the myometrium, the most common type); or **subserosal** (sometimes becoming pedunculated and appearing as extrauterine masses) (Box 49-5 and Figure 49-9).

The signs and symptoms of leiomyomas depend on their size and location. Submucosal myomas may erode into the endometrial cavity and cause irregular or heavy bleeding, which may lead to anemia (Figure 49-10).[8] Fertility may be affected by submucosal or intramural fibroids, which may impede sperm flow, prevent adequate implantation, or cause recurrent miscarriages.

Uncommonly, a pedunculated subserosal lesion develops a long stalk and is migratory; it can implant into the blood supply of the broad ligament, omentum, or the bowel mesentery. Transvaginal sonography is often helpful in showing the uterine origin of the mass. Occasionally, a pedunculated fibroid becomes adherent to surrounding structures and develops an auxiliary blood supply.

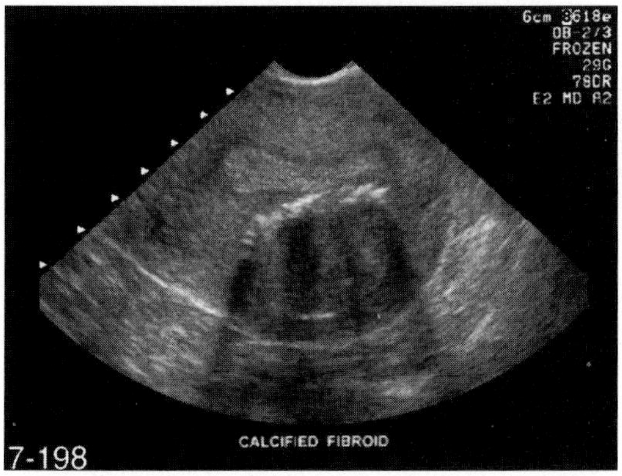

Figure 49-12 Transvaginal image of the uterine cavity with a large calcified fibroid posterior to the endometrium producing multiple shadows.

Ultrasound findings. The earliest sonographic finding of fibroids is demonstrated uterine enlargement with a heterogeneous texture. The sonographer should also look for contour distortion along the interface between the uterus and the bladder (Figure 49-11). The myoma alters the normal homogeneous myometrial texture pattern. Discrete fibroids usually are hypoechoic but can be hyperechoic if they contain dense fibrous tissue. Bright clusters of echoes occur with calcific deposits and produce typical distal acoustic shadowing (Figure 49-12). If extensive calcification is present, the uterus and adnexa are difficult to image because of shadowing. In such cases, transvaginal imaging is helpful in visualizing the ovaries. Fibroids as small as 0.5 cm can be detected by transvaginal sonography and their relationship to the endometrial cavity defined precisely.[29] Larger fibroids cause heterogeneous uterine enlargement and are better outlined by transabdominal sonography.

The ultrasound study should include measurement of the uterus in three dimensions: (1) cervix to fundus, (2) widest transverse diameter at fundus, and (3) widest anteroposterior diameter (Figure 49-13). The texture of the myoma (calcific, complex, or anechoic), size, and location are described. Individual myomas are measured if they are discrete. The shape of the endometrial stripe and its thickness are also described; alterations in endometrial border will be evident if a myoma is present (Figure 49-14). This is especially important in women with a history of abnormal bleeding. A measurement of more than 6 mm in the follicular phase or more than 5 mm in untreated menopausal women implies hyperplasia or endometrial cancer. Both of these conditions can be associated with myomas. Blood debris and polyps can artifactually widen the endometrium; therefore diagnosis of the cause of abnormal bleeding requires endometrial biopsy.

Cystic degeneration of fibroids causes lucencies that are well visualized with transvaginal sonography.[38] Cystic degeneration often occurs during pregnancy and causes pain.[18,29] Color Doppler sonography shows thin vessels with low-velocity flow within myomas. In cases of cystic

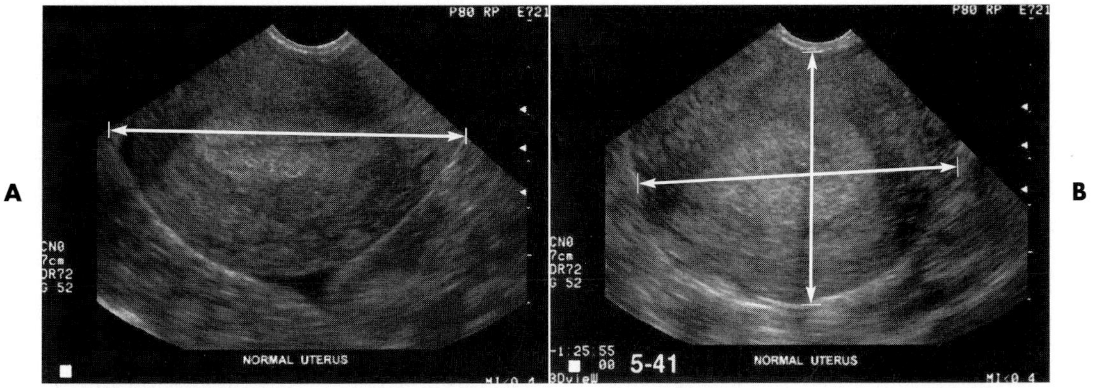

Figure 49-13 Transvaginal images of the uterus for measurement. **A,** Sagittal image should measure the uterus at the longest point from the fundus to the cervix. **B,** Coronal image at the level of the fundus measures the anteroposterior dimension and the width of the uterus.

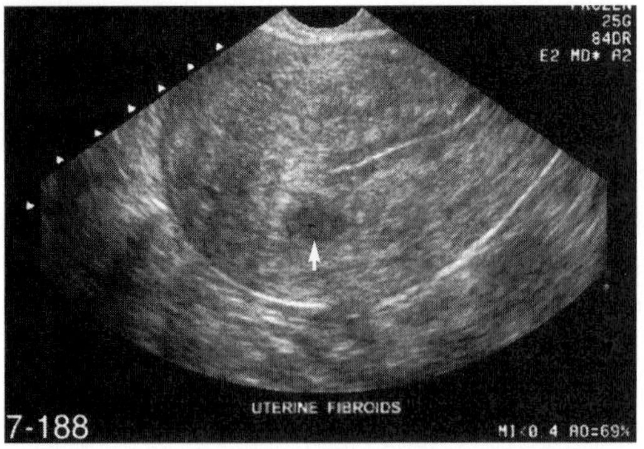

Figure 49-14 Transvaginal sagittal image of the uterus with a small fibroid tumor *(arrow)* just posterior to the endometrial stripe. The tumor is not large enough to displace the endometrium.

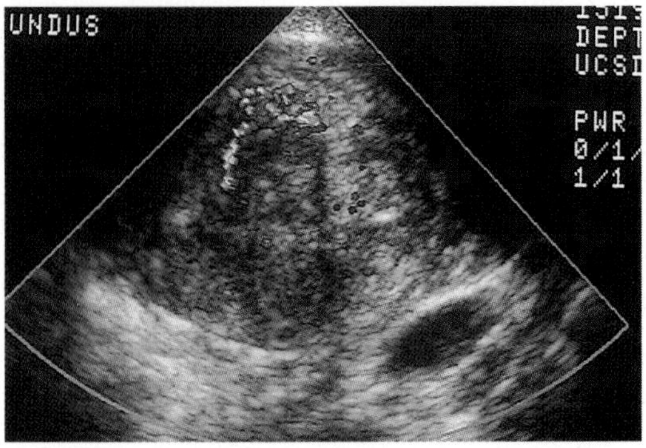

Figure 49-15 Transvaginal sagittal image of the uterus in a pregnant women with a 13-cm fibroid. No flow within the fibroid was seen on color Doppler imaging.

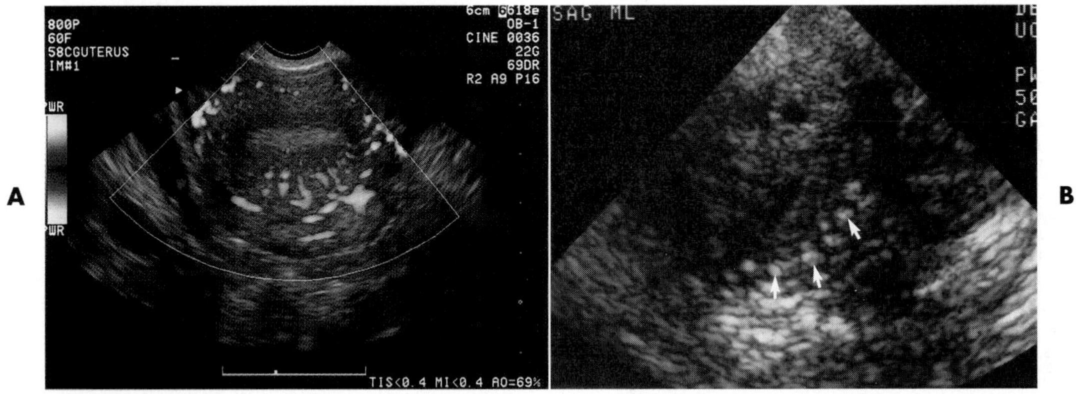

Figure 49-16 **A,** Color Doppler image of normal arcuate artery flow within the periphery of the uterus. **B,** Transvaginal sagittal view of the uterus demonstrates multiple echogenic foci in the region of the arcuate vessels. These are consistent with arcuate artery calcifications *(arrows).*

degeneration, these vessels with low flow velocity are not seen (Figure 49-15).

Although ultrasonography is used to identify fibroids in women with abnormal bleeding, uterine enlargement, or infertility, MRI is more sensitive in evaluating the location, size, and number of fibroids.

Adenomyosis

Adenomyosis causes heavy painful menses. Histologically, the condition is characterized by nests of endometrial tissue within the myometrium.

Ultrasound findings. On ultrasound examination, extensive adenomyosis appears as diffuse uterine enlargement.[39] Hemorrhage in islands of endometrial tissue appears as small myometrial cysts.[46] Adenomyosis is not reliably diagnosed by ultrasonography but is well characterized by MRI.[42]

Uterine Calcifications

Fibroids are the most common cause of uterine calcifications. A less common cause is arcuate artery calcification in the periphery of the uterus (Figure 49-16). These calcifications are thought to occur as a consequence of cystic medial necrosis within these vessels[13] and indicate underlying disease, such as diabetes mellitus, hypertension, and chronic renal failure.[35]

Ultrasound findings. Calcifications resulting from prior instrumentation are seen along the inner myometrium and cervix.[7]

Uterine Leiomyosarcoma

Sarcomas make up less than 5% of uterine malignancies (Figure 49-17). The tumor is derived from smooth muscle in the wall of the uterus (the same as leiomyomas) and is thought to arise from preexisting leiomyoma (Box 49-6).

Ultrasound findings. On ultrasound examination, sarcomas resemble fibroids or endometrial carcinoma with features of solid or mixed solid and cystic texture.[20] Clinically, enlargement of a fibroid in the perimenopausal or postmenopausal patient raises concern about the development of a malignant sarcoma.

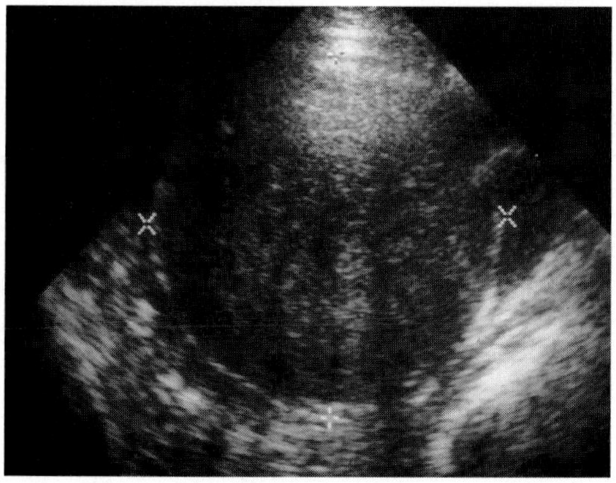

Figure 49-17 A 61-year-old woman with lower abdominal "fullness" and frequency of urination. Transvaginal ultrasound showed a large heterogeneous mass in the uterus. A large leiomyosarcoma was found at surgery.

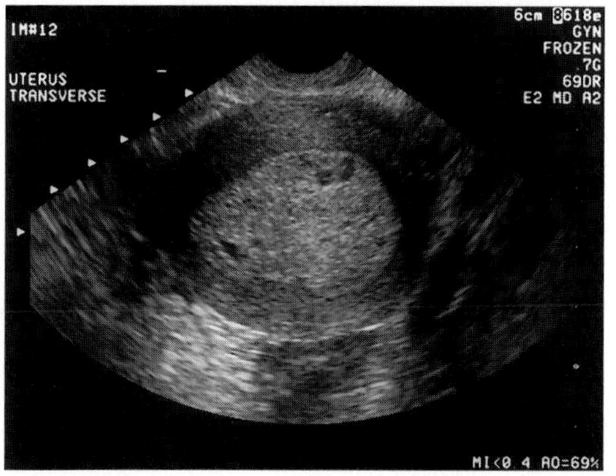

Figure 49-18 Transvaginal coronal image of the uterus with a very prominent endometrium measuring more than 23 mm. On biopsy the patient had endometrial hyperplasia.

BOX 49-6 LEIOMYSARCOMA

- Rare, solid tumor arising from the myometrium or endometrium
- Commonly in fundus of uterus
- Can affect any age
- Rapid growth
- *Sarcoma botryoides:* Very rare condition in children characterized by grapelike clusters of tumor mass

TABLE 49-1 ENDOMETRIAL THICKNESS RELATED TO PHASES OF MENSTRUAL CYCLE

Phase of Menstrual Cycle	Endometrial Thickness* (mm)
Menstrual	2-3
Early proliferative	4-6
Periovulatory	6-8
Secretory	8-15

Data from Goldberg BB, Kurtz AB: *Ultrasound measurements,* St Louis, 1990, Mosby.
*Measured as full thickness, anteroposterior (AP), from outer border to outer border of hypoechoic interfaces

BOX 49-7 ENDOMETRIAL HYPERPLASIA

- Follows prolonged endogenous or exogenous estrogenic stimulation
- May be precursor of endometrial cancer
- *Sonography:* Abnormal thickening of endometrium

PATHOLOGY OF THE ENDOMETRIUM

The endometrium is the landmark for the identification of the uterus. It is recognized as a central hyperechoic stripe or band, with the echogenicity being judged relative to the outer two thirds of the myometrium. The endometrium is surrounded by a hypoechoic layer of myometrium. Progressive thickening and increased reflectivity of the endometrium occurs in the majority of patients until it is shed during menstruation.[14] In the immediate preovulatory and postovulatory periods (2 days), an additional inner hypoechoic layer appears secondary to edema.

The endometrium should be measured perpendicular to the long axis of the uterus (Table 49-1). The hypoechoic halo surrounding the endometrium should not be included in the measurement because this represents the inner compact layer of myometrium. Fluid, if present, should not be included in endometrial measurements (see Table 49-1).

An abnormally thick endometrium results from a variety of conditions, including early intrauterine pregnancy, gestational trophoblastic disease, endometrial hyperplasia, secretory endometrium, estrogen replacement therapy, polyps, and endometrial carcinoma.*

ENDOMETRIAL HYPERPLASIA

Endometrial hyperplasia is caused by unopposed estrogen. It appears as thickening of the endometrium (Box 49-7). In premenopausal women, if the endometrium measures more than 14 mm (double thickness), hyperplasia is suggested (Figure 49-18). In asymptomatic postmenopausal women, 8 mm (double thickness) is the upper limit of normal.[13,36,38] However, women on sequential estrogen and progesterone replacement regimens may have endometrial thickness up to 15 mm during the estrogen phase; the thickness decreases after progesterone is added. Ideally, a woman using sequential hormones should be studied at the beginning or end of her hormone cycle, when the endometrium is theoretically at its thinnest (Figure 49-19). Common hormonal regimens in menopausal women can be seen in Box 49-8.

*References 9, 12, 15, 17, 23, 25, 31.

A

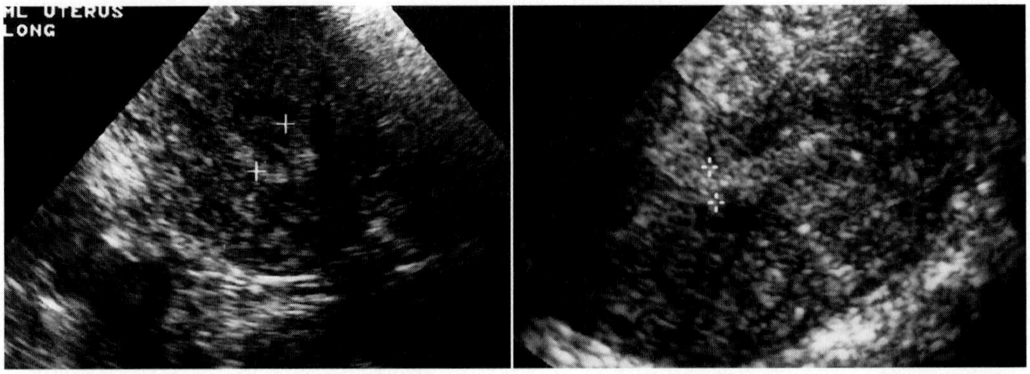

B

Figure 49-19 Normal variation in endometrial thickness from cyclic hormone replacement in a 62-year-old woman. **A,** Day 9, three-layer endometrium, 10 mm thick. **B,** Day 3, 4-mm-thick endometrium. Women taking sequential hormones should be examined after the progesterone phase of the cycle, when the endometrium is theoretically at its thinnest. (From Levine D, Gosink BB. In Nyberg DA and others, editors: *Transvaginal ultrasound,* St Louis, 1992, Mosby.)

BOX 49-8 Common Hormonal Regimens in Menopausal Women

1. **No Hormones**
2. **Unopposed estrogen** (usually Premarin): These women generally have had hysterectomies; if uterus is intact, unopposed estrogen is associated with increased risk for endometrial hyperplasia or carcinoma.
3. **Continuous/combined estrogen and progesterone** (Premarin and Provera): This combination produced endometrial atrophy after 3 to 6 months. Usually there is no risk of endometrial cancer; however, women may have "breakthrough" bleeding during the month and/or annoying progesterone side effects (i.e., irritability, depression, bloating, breast tenderness).
4. **Sequential estrogen and progesterone** (Premarin first half then Provera second half of month): Women have predictable withdrawal bleeding at end of each month.

In the United States, regimens 2 and 4 are most commonly used.

Beneficial Effects

Estrogen

Alleviates menopausal symptoms (hot flashes, night sweats, painful intercourse)
Reduces risk of osteoporosis, vertebral and hip fractures
Reduces risk of heart attacks, strokes

Progesterone

Produces endometrial atrophy, reduces risk of endometrial hyperplasia/cancer

Negative Effects

Estrogen

Increases risk of endometrial hyperplasia/ cancer

Progesterone

Increases risk of breast cancer?
Irritability, depression, breast tenderness in some women

Endometrial Polyps

Endometrial polyps usually are asymptomatic but may cause uterine bleeding. They typically cause diffuse or focal endometrial thickening.[23]

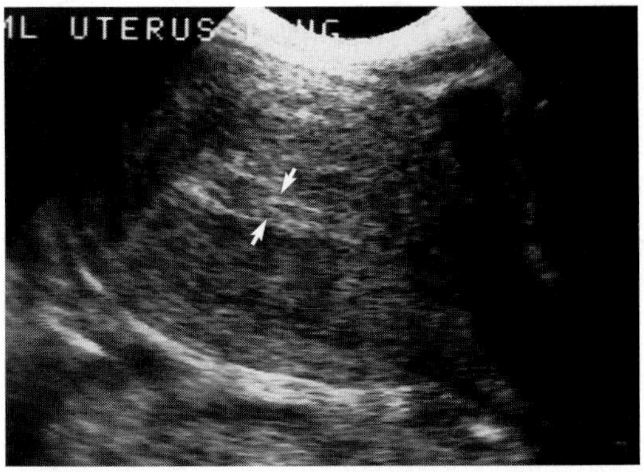

Figure 49-20 Endometritis in a 31-year-old woman. A transvaginal sagittal view of the uterus 3 days postpartum demonstrates a slightly irregular endometrium *(arrows).*

Ultrasound findings. They appear as either cysts or dense masses in the endometrial cavity. Individual polyps are better visualized when outlined by intracavitary fluid.

Endometritis

Endometritis most often occurs in association with pelvic inflammatory disease, but it also occurs postpartum.

Ultrasound findings. On ultrasound examination the endometrium appears prominent, irregular, or both (Figure 49-20) with a small amount of endometrial fluid.[23,27] Gas bubbles are present in rare cases; however, these also are seen in normal postpartum patients.[43] In the immediate postpartum period the presence of retained tissue is difficult to distinguish from inflammatory debris or blood clots.[19,28]

Synechiae

Intrauterine synechiae are found in women with a prior history of uterine curettage or spontaneous abortion.

Ultrasound findings. Ultrasonography may demonstrate bright echoes within the endometrial cavity in this condition.[33] These are more easily seen in the gravid uterus.

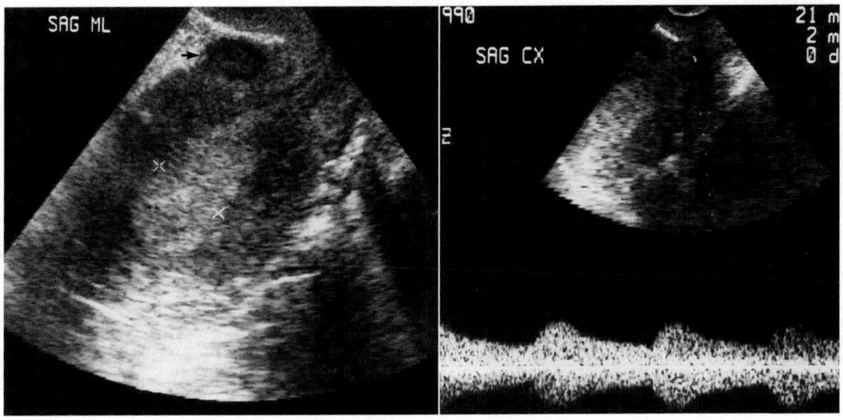

Figure 49-21 Endometrial carcinoma in a 52-year-old woman. **A,** Sagittal view of the uterus demonstrates a 2-cm-thick endometrium. A small myoma *(arrow)* is also present. **B,** Doppler examination of the uterine artery shows abnormal increased diastolic flow (resistive index, 0.5).

BOX 49-9 ENDOMETRIAL CARCINOMA

- Associated with estrogen stimulation
- *Clinical:* Postmenopausal bleeding
- *Sonography:* Prominent endometrial complex; enlarged uterus with irregular areas of low-level echoes

ENDOMETRIAL CARCINOMA

Most endometrial malignancies are adenocarcinomas occurring in perimenopausal and postmenopausal patients with irregular bleeding. The earliest change of **endometrial carcinoma** is a thickened endometrium (Figure 49-21). An abnormally thick endometrium also is associated with endometrial hypertrophy and polyps.[23]

Recent studies of patients with postmenopausal bleeding show that an endometrial thickness (double layer) less than 5 mm reliably excludes significant endometrial abnormality. At present, most investigators believe biopsies should be performed for all symptomatic patients. In the future, however, transvaginal ultrasonography may be used to follow symptomatic patients with normal endometrial thickness for whom biopsy is contraindicated or who do not wish to undergo an invasive procedure.

Although increased endometrial thickness is an early finding in endometrial carcinoma, enlargement with lobular contour of the uterus and mixed echogenicity are correlated with more advanced stages of the disease.[23] The risk of malignancy increases with the presence of a large endometrial fluid collection or clinical symptoms, such as abdominal pain or bleeding.[5,32,37]

Ultrasound findings. Transvaginal examination is helpful in screening for early changes of endometrial hyperplasia or carcinoma by accurately measuring endometrial thickness.

Demonstration of myometrial invasion is clear evidence for endometrial carcinoma. Transvaginal ultrasonography demonstrates myometrial invasion as thickening and irregularity of the central endometrial interface with echogenic or hypoechoic patterns combined with infiltration of hyperdense structures in the myometrium (Box 49-9).[16,37] The level of invasion (superficial versus deep) also can be detected by transvaginal ultrasonography,[13,37] although MRI is slightly more sensitive.[21] Magnetic resonance imaging is also valuable in evaluating extrauterine extension and involvement of lymph nodes.

DOPPLER EVALUATION

Doppler ultrasonography of the uterine artery may help distinguish benign from malignant endometrial thickening. Pulsed Doppler is used to evaluate the resistive index (RI = Systolic − Diastolic/Systolic) or pulsatility index (PI = Systolic − Diastolic/Mean). The technique of this examination is discussed in Chapter 47. Low-resistance flow (RI<0.4) has been found in patients with endometrial carcinoma and high-resistance flow (RI>0.5) in normal postmenopausal women. If a pulsatility index is used, the cutoff is 1. Intratumoral neovascularity is a more sensitive marker of endometrial carcinoma than resistive index alone.[26]

SMALL ENDOMETRIAL FLUID COLLECTIONS

Small endometrial fluid collections also occur with ectopic pregnancy, endometritis (see Figure 25-14, *B*), degenerating fibroids, and recent abortion (Figure 49-22).[27]

Ultrasound findings. Transvaginal sonography, with its improved resolution, sometimes shows tiny endometrial fluid collections not seen on transabdominal scans. These small endometrial fluid collections (less than 2 ml) are common in women during the menstrual phase of the cycle. They are seen in postmenopausal women,[24,46] especially during the menstrual phase in women taking sequential hormones.

In a uterus with a fluid collection the anteroposterior diameter of the fluid should be subtracted from the endometrial measurement for a true assessment of endometrial thickness.

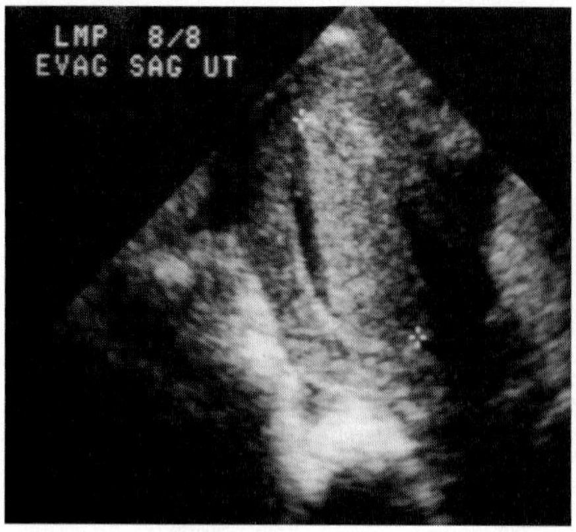

Figure 49-22 Transvaginal image in a 23-year-old woman after a dilation and curettage demonstrates a central fluid collection with a fluid debris level representing a hematometra.

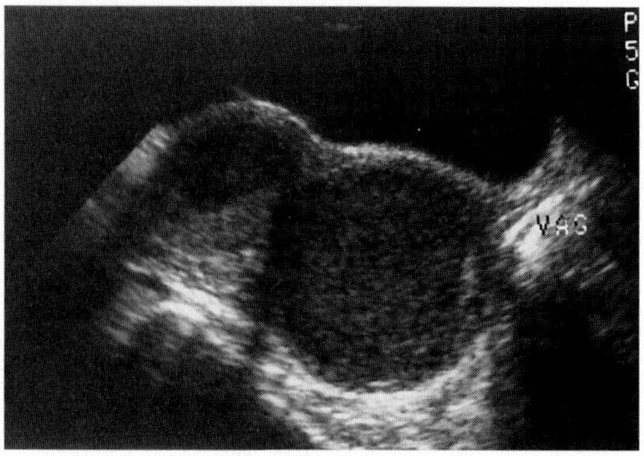

Figure 49-23 Large endometrial fluid collection. Transvaginal ultrasound image of obstructed right horn of a bicornuate uterus. This 63-year-old asymptomatic woman, placed on cyclic hormone replacemnt therapy, demonstrates a large endometrial fluid collection. She subsequently underwent dilation for cervical stenosis, and bloody fluid was drained. Biopsy was unremarkable. (From Levine D, Gosink BB. In Nyberg DA, and others, editors: *Transvaginal ultrasound,* St Louis, 1992, Mosby.)

LARGE ENDOMETRIAL FLUID COLLECTIONS

Large endometrial fluid collections should be regarded with suspicion. They result from pyometra or hematometra in women who have cervical stenosis from prior irradiation for gynecologic malignancies, or they are caused by uterine, cervical, tubal, or ovarian carcinoma.[1,27,38] Hyperplasia and polyps also cause endometrial fluid collections,[16] so these collections indicate increased risk of endometrial carcinoma. However, large amounts of endometrial fluid also are associated with benign conditions, such as congenital anomalies (Figure 49-23) or cervical stenosis from prior instrumentation or childbirth.[32]

The patient typically complains of abdominal pain and has a globular abdominal mass. She usually has little or no vaginal bleeding. The presence of fever suggests infection of the blood collection. In simple hematometra the uterine cavity returns to normal promptly after dilation and curettage. Pyometra (pus in the uterus) is more likely to occur with uterine cancer.

Abnormal development of the vagina or uterus may result in a cystic uterine or vaginal collection of mucus in children. When menstruation begins, the collection consists of blood.

Ultrasound findings. The sonographic picture of large endometrial fluid collections is that of a centrally cystic, round, moderately enlarged uterus.

INTRAUTERINE CONTRACEPTIVE DEVICES

LOST INTRAUTERINE DEVICE

Intrauterine contraceptive devices (IUDs) are placed in the uterine cavity during menses and provide reliable birth control. Proper placement is verified by weekly digital palpation of the string in the cervix, performed by the patient. If the string is not felt in the cervix, the IUD may have been expelled or, more likely, the string retracted into the uterus. A sensitive urine pregnancy test is performed. If it is negative, the gynecologist explores the uterine cavity with a sterile hooked probe. If no IUD or string is found or if the pregnancy test is positive, an ultrasound examination is performed.

Ultrasound findings. Straight-shafted IUDs form solid lines demonstrated by careful longitudinal and transverse examinations of the uterus. Lippes loop appears as dotted lines because the ultrasound beam transects the parallel segments.[8] An analysis of in vivo and in vitro transabdominal images of the four types of IUDs previously used in the United States found that the shafts of all of them appeared as a double line because of entrance-exit reflections of sound waves when scanned perpendicular to the uterine cavity with high-resolution equipment.[8] Posterior shadowing occurs when the ultrasound beam is entirely interrupted. This requires that the scanning plane be placed perpendicular to the IUD.

The Copper 7 is shaped like a 7, with a copper wire spiraled around the vertical shaft. The Tatum T and Progestasert are T-shaped (Figure 49-24), and the Lippes loop is serpentine. The notorious Dalkon Shield, which caused a number of serious complications and is rarely found in situ anymore, is a small, flat disk with hooks around the periphery. Occasionally a thick midcycle endometrium obscures the bright IUD echo when transabdominal ultrasonography is used. If no intrauterine IUD is identified on ultrasound examination and the pregnancy test is negative, a thin metal probe is inserted into the uterine cavity to mark it, and abdominal x-ray films are obtained to search for the IUD in an extrauterine location (Figure 49-25). Perforation of the uterus by an IUD almost always occurs at the time of insertion. The displaced IUD may not be suspected until an abscess or painful bowel involvement occurs.

When a pregnancy is present, either transabdominal or transvaginal ultrasound examination demonstrates both

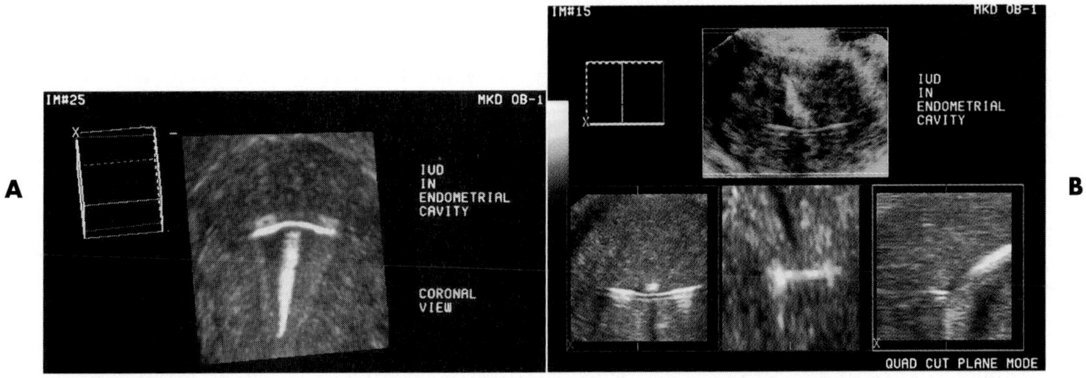

Figure 49-24 **A,** Three-dimensional reconstruction of a safety coil intrauterine contraceptive device located within the uterine cavity. **B,** X, Y, and Z axes of the IUD.

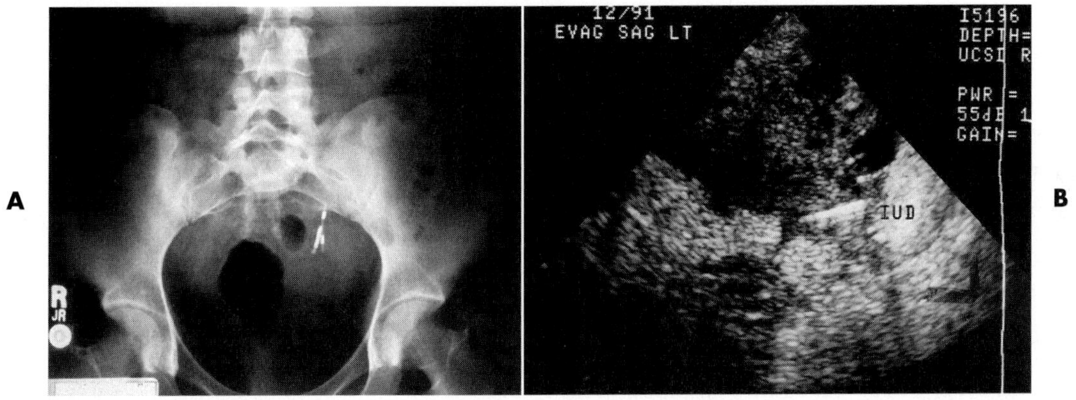

Figure 49-25 Extrauterine location of IUD in a 25-year-old woman with abdominal pain. Patient was unable to feel the string of the IUD. **A,** Plain film of the abdomen shows the extrauterine location of the IUD. **B,** Left parasagittal view demonstrates a linear echogenic focus consistent with the IUD located outside the uterus.

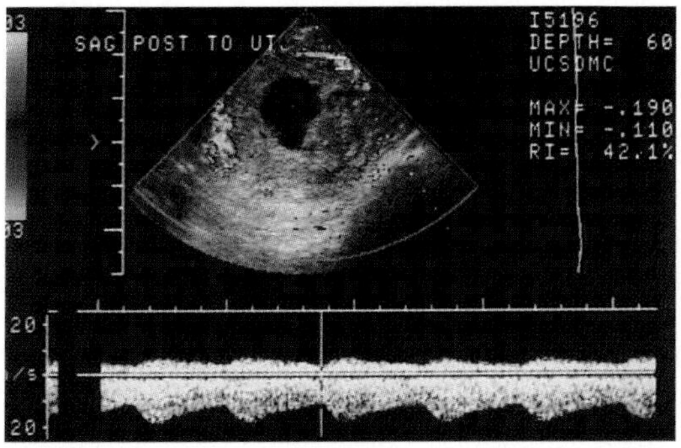

Figure 49-26 A 26-year-old woman came to the emergency department because of bleeding, and a positive pregnancy test. The ultrasound study showed an empty uterus with an adnexal mass. Color Doppler examination showed increased vascularity consistent with an ectopic pregnancy.

gestational age and the location of the IUD. Occasionally a string is visible in the external os of a pregnant uterus. Approximately 50% of pregnancies abort on extraction of the IUD. With transvaginal scanning the location of the IUD can be detected relative to the sac, and it may be possible to predict which pregnancy will be disrupted. Intrauterine contraceptive devices are always external to fetal membranes.

Patients with IUDs are at increased risk for ectopic pregnancy and pelvic inflammatory disease. In these women, tuboovarian abscess (TOA) may be unilateral; in the more common situation, it is bilateral.[6,40]

ECTOPIC PREGNANCY

Ultrasound findings. The diagnosis of **ectopic pregnancy** is greatly simplified by the use of pelvic ultrasound examination and beta-human chorionic gonadotropin (beta-hCG) levels. With transvaginal transducers, tubal anatomy is substantially clarified, as are early ($4\frac{1}{2}$ weeks) intrauterine gestational sacs (Figure 49-26). This enables early identification of ectopic pregnancies and prevention of tubal rupture with more selective use of surgery. The "discriminatory zone" of beta-hCG for the transvaginal probe is about 1000 mIU/ml (second IS) compared with 6500 mIU/ml (IRP) originally described for transabdominal ultrasound examination. At that level, an identifiable gestational sac or chorionic cavity is always seen in a normal intrauterine pregnancy. If the uterine cavity appears

empty with a thick endometrial stripe, a pregnancy must be sought in the tubes or elsewhere.

To reiterate, very early pregnancy is best diagnosed with transvaginal ultrasound examination. There are virtually no technical limitations imposed by patient size or uterine retroversion. The scanner should always be alert for free fluid in the abdomen or the adnexal mass of an ectopic pregnancy. If the uninvolved tube is full of blood, it can be difficult to distinguish which tube carries the conceptus.

It is important to examine the ovaries carefully, because a ruptured, bleeding corpus luteum can produce symptoms similar to a ruptured ectopic pregnancy. Frequently women with normal early intrauterine pregnancies have unilateral discomfort from a normal cystic corpus luteum. The rare occurrence of simultaneous intrauterine and ectopic pregnancy has been reported to be increasing. This tends to happen more often in patients who are undergoing infertility treatments.

A gestational sac and heartbeat are only occasionally seen within the tube. The criteria for ectopic pregnancy include (1) absence of an intrauterine sac with a serum beta-hCG of more than 1500 mIU/ml (IRP) or 1000 mIU/ml (2nd IS) and (2) an adnexal mass and free fluid in the abdomen.

ACKNOWLEDGMENT

The author acknowledges the previous contribution of Deborah Levine, MD, to this chapter.

REVIEW QUESTIONS

1. Discuss the development of leiomyomas, their ultrasonic appearance, their sensitivity to estrogen stimulation, and their classification.
2. What is adenomyosis?
3. Describe endometrial hyperplasia. What effect does hormone replacement have on the endometrium?
4. How are endometrial polyps best imaged?
5. What is the ultrasound appearance of endometritis?
6. Discuss endometrial carcinoma and its ultrasound findings.
7. Name the causes of fluid collections seen within the endometrial cavity.
8. What is the role of Doppler examination of the uterine artery in distinguishing benign from malignant endometrial thickening?
9. Name the common intrauterine contraceptive devices and their ultrasonic appearance.
10. What is the appearance of cervical carcinoma on ultrasound examination?
11. How does a Gartner's duct cyst appear on ultrasound examination? Where is it found?
12. When is the fallopian tube best seen on ultrasound examination?

REFERENCES

1. Aartsen EJ: Fluid detection in the uterus during and after irradiation for carcinoma of the cervix: clinical implications, *Eur J Surg Oncol* 16:42, 1990.
2. Bernaschek G and others: *Endosonography in obstetrics and gynecology,* Berlin, 1990, Springer-Verlag.
3. Bernaschek G and others: Endosonographic staging of carcinoma of the uterine cervix, *Arch Gynecol* 239:21, 1986.
4. Blask ARN and others: Obstructed uterovaginal anomalies: demonstration with sonography. I, Neonates and infants, *Radiology* 179:79, 1991.
5. Breckenridge JW and others: Post-menopausal uterine fluid collection: indicator of carcinoma, *Am J Roentgenol* 139:529, 1982.
6. Burkman RT: Association between intrauterine contraceptive device and pelvic inflammatory disease, *Obstet Gynecol* 57:269, 1981.
7. Burks DD and others: Uterine inner myometrial echogenic foci: relationship to prior dilatation and curettage and transcervical biopsy, *J Ultrasound Med* 10:487, 1991.
8. Callen PW and others: Intrauterine contraceptive devices: evaluation by sonography, *Am J Roentgenol* 135:797, 1980.
9. Carlson JA Jr and others: Clinical and pathologic correlation of endometrial cavity fluid detected by ultrasound in the postmenopausal patient, *Obstet Gynecol* 77:119, 1991.
10. Chambers CB and others: Ultrasonographic evidence of uterine malignancy in the postmenopausal uterus, *Am J Obstet Gynecol* 154:1194, 1986.
11. Cobby M and others: Magnetic resonance imaging, computed tomography and endosonography in the local staging of carcinoma of the cervix, *Br J Radiol* 63:673, 1990.
12. Cotran RS and others: *Robbins pathologic basis of disease,* Philadelphia, 1989, WB Saunders.
13. Fleischer AC and others: Transvaginal scanning of the endometrium, *J Clin Ultrasound* 18:337, 1990.
14. Goldberg BB and others: *Ultrasound measurements,* St Louis, 1990, Mosby.
15. Goldstein SR and others: Endometrial assessment by vaginal ultrasonography before endometrial sampling in patients with postmenopausal bleeding, *Am J Obstet Gynecol* 163:119, 1990.
16. Gordon AN and others: Preoperative assessment of myometrial invasion of endometrial adenocarcinoma by sonography (US) and magnetic resonance imaging (MRI), *Gynecol Oncol* 34:175, 1989.
17. Granberg S and others: Endometrial thickness as measured by transvaginal ultrasonography for identifying endometrial abnormality, *Am J Obstet Gynecol* 164:47, 1991.
18. Gross BH and others: Sonographic features of uterine leiomyomas: analysis of 41 proven cases, *J Ultrasound Med* 2:401, 1983.
19. Grunfeld L and others: High-resolution transvaginal ultrasonography of the endometrium: a noninvasive test for endometrial adequacy, Obstet *Gynecol* 78:200, 1991.
20. Hata K and others: Sonographic findings of uterine leiomyosarcoma, *Gynecol Obstet Invest* 30:242, 1990.
21. Hricak H and others: Endometrial carcinoma staging by MR imaging, *Radiology* 162:297, 1987.
22. Innocenti P and others: Staging of cervical cancer: reliability of transrectal US, *Radiology* 185:201, 1992.

23. Johnson MA and others: Abnormal endometrial echoes: sonographic spectrum of endometrial pathology, *J Ultrasound Med* 1:161, 1982.
24. Karasick S and others: Imaging of uterine leiomyomas, *Am J Roentgenol* 158:799, 1992.
25. Kupfer MC and others: Transvaginal sonographic appearance of endometriomata: spectrum of findings, *J Ultrasound Med* 11:129, 1992.
26. Kurjak A and others: The characterization of uterine tumors by transvaginal color Doppler, *Ultrasound Obstet Gynecol* 1:50, 1991.
27. Laing FC and others: Ultrasonic demonstration of endometrial fluid collections unassociated with pregnancy, *Radiology* 137:471, 1980.
28. Lee CY, Madrazo B, Drukker BH: Ultrasonic evaluation of the postpartum uterus in the management of postpartum bleeding, *Obstet Gynecol* 58:227, 1981.
29. Lev-Toaff AS and others: Leiomyomas in pregnancy: sonographic study, *Radiology* 164:375, 1987.
30. Lin MC and others: Endometrial thickness after menopause of hormone replacement, *Radiology* 180:427, 1991.
31. Lyons EA and others: Characterization of subendometrial myometrial contractions throughout the menstrual cycle in normal fertile women, *Fertil Steril* 55:85, 1991.
32. McCarthy KA and others: Postmenopausal endometrial fluid collection: always an indicator of malignancy? *J Ultrasound Med* 5:647, 1986.
33. Mendelson B and others: Endometrial abnormalities: evaluation with transvaginal sonography, *Am J Roentgenol* 150:139, 1988.
34. Narjarian KE, Kurtz AB: New observations in the sonographic evaluation of intrauterine contraceptive devices, *J Ultrasound Med* 5:205, 1986.
35. Occhipinti K and others: Sonographic appearance and significance of arcuate artery calcification, *J Ultrasound Med* 10:97, 1991.
36. Osmers R and others: Vaginosonography for early detection of endometrial carcinoma? *Lancet* 335:1569, 1990.
37. Rosati P and others: Longitudinal evaluation of uterine myoma growth during pregnancy: a sonographic study, *J Ultrasound Med* 11:511, 1992.
38. Schoenfeld A and others: Transvaginal sonography in postmenopausal women, *J Clin Ultrasound* 18:350, 1990.
39. Scott WW Jr and others: The obstructed uterus, *Radiology* 141:767, 1981.
40. Seidler DS and others: Uterine adenomyosis: a difficult sonographic diagnosis, *J Ultrasound Med* 6:345, 1987.
41. Senanayake P and others: Contraception and the etiology of pelvic inflammatory disease: new perspective, *Am J Obstet Gynecol* 138:82, 1980.
42. Siegel MJ: Pediatric gynecologic sonography, *Radiology* 179:593, 1991.
43. Togashi K and others: Enlarged uterus: differentiation between adenomyosis and leiomyoma with MR imaging, *Radiology* 171:531, 1989.
44. Varner RE and others: Transvaginal sonography of the endometrium in postmenopausal women, *Obstet Gynecol* 78:195, 1991.
45. Wachsberg RH and others: Gas within the endometrial cavity at postpartum US: a normal finding after spontaneous vaginal delivery, *Radiology* 183:431, 1992.
46. Walsh JW and others: Gray scale ultrasonography in the diagnosis of endometriosis and adenomyosis, *Am J Roentgenol* 132:87, 1979.

CHAPTER 50

Ovarian Anomalies

Sandra L. Hagen-Ansert

OBJECTIVES

- Describe the effect of hormones on the ovarian cycle
- Define the characteristics of the simple ovarian cyst
- Discuss the sonographic findings of the common cystic and the complex ovarian masses
- Discuss the sonographic findings of the common solid ovarian masses
- Describe a functional ovarian cyst
- List the characteristics found in polycystic ovarian disease
- Discuss the benign pelvic masses found in neonates and adolescent girls
- Describe the sonographic findings in ovarian neoplasms
- Differentiate between mucinous and serous types of tumors
- Discuss the sonographic findings in a dermoid tumor
- Define the Doppler parameters used in ovarian torsion
- Discuss the role of ultrasonography with infertility patients

KEY TERMS

androgen - substance that stimulates the development of male characteristics, such as the hormones testosterone and androsterone

corpus luteum cyst - a small endocrine structure that develops within a ruptured ovarian follicle and secretes progesterone and estrogen

cystadenocarcinoma - a malignant tumor that forms cysts

cystadenoma - a benign adenoma containing cysts
dermoid - benign tumor comprised of hair, muscle, teeth, and fat
endometriosis - occurs when functioning endometrial tissue invades other sites outside the uterus
estrogen - the female hormone produced by the ovary
follicular cyst - benign cyst within the ovary that may occur and disappear on a cyclic basis
functional cyst - results from the normal function of the ovary
Meigs' syndrome - benign tumor of the ovary associated with ascites and pleural effusion
mucinous cystadenocarcinoma - malignant tumor of the ovary with multilocular cysts
mucinous cystadenoma - benign tumor of the ovary that contains thin-walled multilocular cysts
ovarian carcinoma - malignant tumor of the ovary that may spread beyond the ovary and metastasize to other organs via the peritoneal channels
ovarian torsion - partial or complete rotation of the ovarian pedicle on its axis
paraovarian cyst - cystic structure that lies adjacent to the ovary
polycystic ovarian disease - endocrine disorder associated with chronic anovulation
serous cystadenocarcinoma - most common type of ovarian carcinoma; may be bilateral with multilocular cysts
serous cystadenoma - second most common benign tumor of the ovary; unilocular or multilocular
simple ovarian cyst - smooth, well-defined cystic structure that is filled completely with fluid
theca-lutein cysts - multilocular cysts that occur in patients with hyperstimulation (hydatidiform mole and infertility patients)

Ultrasonography is clinically useful to characterize adnexal masses, evaluate abnormal bleeding, assess infertility, monitor follicular growth, perform transvaginal needle aspiration and biopsy, and screen for ovarian carcinoma. Both transabdominal and transvaginal sonography are important in these evaluations. Transabdominal imaging furnishes a global survey of anatomy, whereas transvaginal imaging provides better characterization of internal architecture of the ovary, vascular anatomy, and adnexal area.[37] It is important to note that information from the clinical pelvic examination is required for optimal interpretation of the ultrasound studies, thus necessitating good communication between the referring physician and the sonologist.

A woman will ovulate nearly 400 times in her reproductive cycle, and a quarter of a million follicles will be stimulated to varying degrees over this time. It is not surprising that such a dynamic organ as the ovary can form over 100 different types of tumors, both benign and malignant. These masses are described on ultrasound examination as primarily cystic, complex, or predominantly solid; however, the final diagnosis is left to the pathologist. Precise diagnosis on the basis of ultrasonography alone is usually impossible. The primary role of sonography is to indicate the need for surgical or medical intervention.

SONOGRAPHIC EVALUATION OF THE OVARIES

Simple Cystic Masses

The ovary's function is to mature oocytes until ovulation, under the influence of luteinizing hormone and follicle-stimulating hormone from the pituitary. At the same time the ovary synthesizes **androgens** (male hormones) and converts them to **estrogens** (female hormones). Finally, it produces progesterone after ovulation to sustain early pregnancy until the placenta can do so at 10 to 12 weeks of gestation.

Usually only one follicle enlarges from 3 mm to approximately 24 mm over about 10 days in the mid- and late-follicular phases of the cycle. This is followed by ovulation. The resulting corpus luteum or an abnormal unruptured follicle can persist as a webbed cystic structure from 1 to 10 cm in size. These so-called functional cysts may produce discomfort and/or delayed menses but can be observed to regress within 8 weeks with serial ultrasound studies. If a cyst greater than 6 cm persists more than 8 weeks, surgical intervention is usually considered necessary.

Ultrasonically guided needle aspiration has become popular for deflating recurrent **simple ovarian cysts** in carefully selected cases. The majority of ovarian masses are simple cysts, most of which are benign. Sonographic criteria for a simple cyst include a thin smooth wall, anechoic contents, and acoustic enhancement (Figure 50-1, *A*). In premenopausal women these cysts usually are functional. The differential considerations of simple adnexal cysts include functional cyst, paraovarian cyst, cystadenoma, cystic teratoma, endometrioma, and rarely tuboovarian abscess (TOA) (Box 50-1).

Complex Masses

Any simple cyst that hemorrhages may appear as a complex mass (Box 50-2). In patients of reproductive age the classic differential considerations of a complex adnexal mass are ectopic pregnancy, endometriosis, and pelvic inflammatory disease (PID) (Figure 50-1, *B*). Dermoids and other benign tumors can appear in a similar fashion.

Solid Tumors

Mixed solid to cystic ovarian masses are typical of all the epithelial ovarian tumors; the most common are the serous types: the **cystadenoma** and **cystadenocarcinoma** (Figure 50-1, *C*). During the peak fertile years only 1 in 15 is malignant; this ratio becomes 1 in 3 after age 40.

The more sonographically complex the tumor, the more likely it is to be malignant, especially if associated

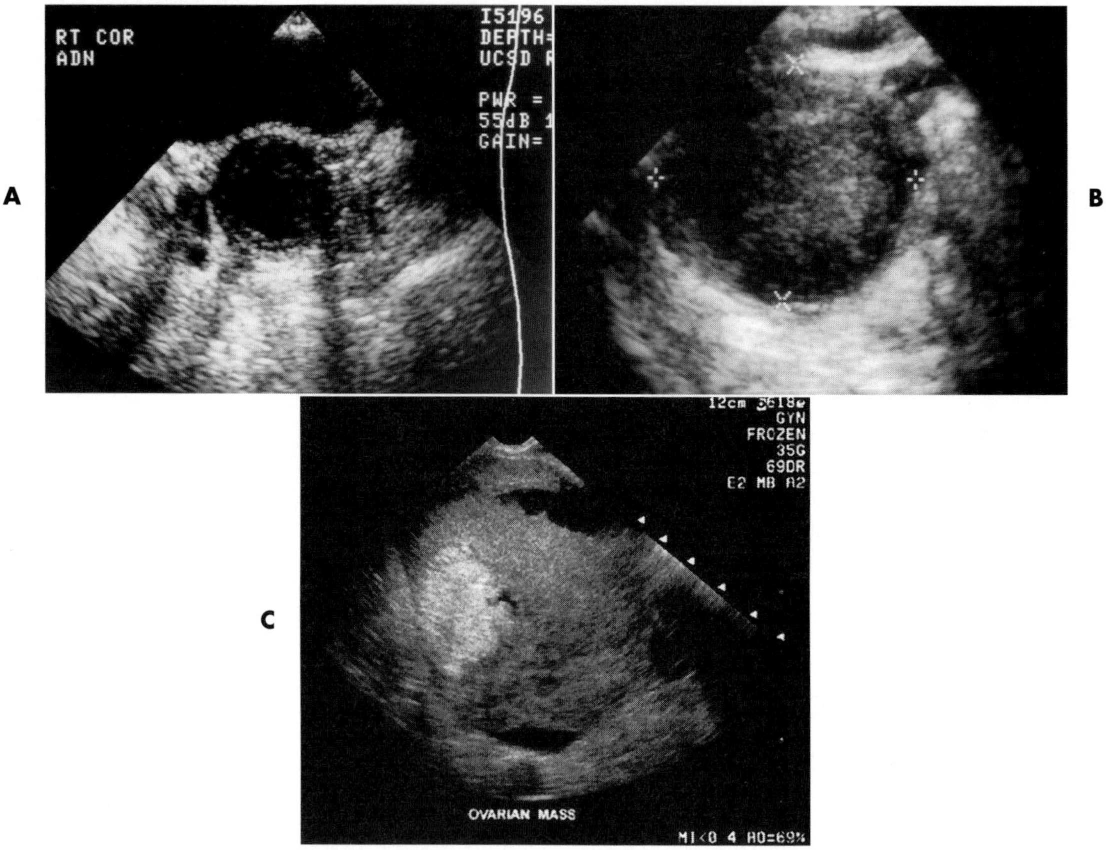

Figure 50-1 **A,** Simple ovarian cyst. Transvaginal coronal image of the corpus luteum cyst (just posterior to the bladder) in the right adnexal area. The cyst is well defined and anechoic, with increased through-transmission. **B,** Complex ovarian cyst. Transvaginal coronal image of a simple cyst that has hemorrhaged; this mass had resolved spontaneously when the patient was rescanned 2 weeks later. The borders of the mass are well defined; there are low-level internal echoes within the mass. On real-time imaging, swirling of these echoes could be seen. **C,** Solid mass. Transvaginal sagittal image of a large, solid ovarian mass in a 56-year-old woman. The mass has irregular borders with a heterogenous texture and decreased through-transmission.

Box 50-1 Common Cystic or Complex Ovarian Mass

- Follicular cyst
- Corpus luteum cyst of pregnancy
- Cystic teratoma
- Paraovarian cyst
- Hydrosalpinx
- Endometrioma (low-level echoes)

Box 50-2 Common Complex Masses

- Cystadenoma
- Dermoid cyst
- Tuboovarian abscess
- Ectopic pregnancy
- Granulosa cell tumor

with ascites. The epithelium of serous tumors is tubal in type, and there may be one or multiple cysts. One fourth of them are bilateral, and most occur in women over age 40. They are large and often fill the pelvic cavity.

Box 50-3 Common Solid Masses

- Solid teratoma
- Adenocarcinoma
- Arrhenoblastoma
- Fibroma
- Dysgerminoma
- Torsion

The differential considerations of a solid-appearing adnexal mass include pedunculated fibroid, dermoid, fibroma, thecoma, granulosa cell tumor, Brenner tumor, and metastasis. Tuboovarian abscess, ovarian torsion, hemorrhagic cysts, and ectopic pregnancy also may appear solid. Solid adnexal masses are often difficult to diagnose because normal ovarian size varies widely. Therefore many authors suggest that an ovary with a volume twice that of the opposite side be considered abnormal.[8,20,22] When a solid mass is found, care should be taken to identify a connection with the uterus to differentiate an ovarian lesion from a pedunculated fibroid (Box 50-3).

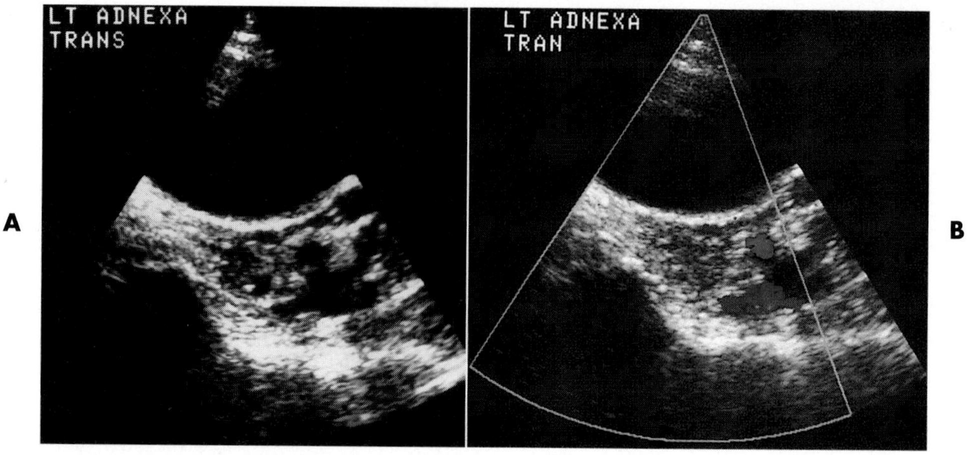

Figure 50-2 Usefulness of color Doppler to distinguish cysts from vessels. **A,** Transabdominal transverse view of the left adnexa demonstrates multiple hypoechoic regions adjacent to the adnexa. **B,** Color Doppler demonstrates flow within these areas consistent with vessels.

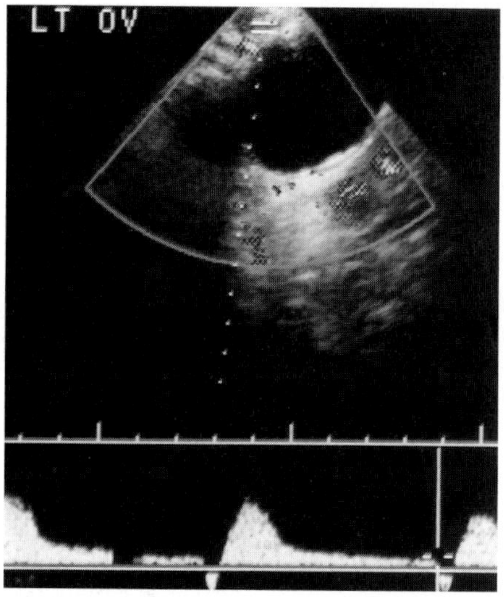

Figure 50-3 Simple cyst. Coronal view of the right ovary in an asymptomatic 52-year-old woman demonstrates a 3-cm simple cyst. Ovarian artery Doppler shows a normal resistive pattern with low diastolic flow. (From Levine D, Gosink BB. In Nyberg DA and others, editors: *Transvaginal ultrasound,* St Louis, 1992, Mosby.)

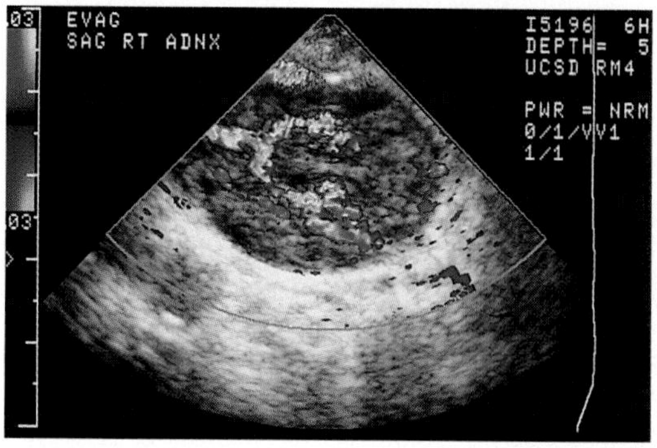

Figure 50-4 Transvaginal color Doppler view of the right adnexa in a woman during the luteal phase. Note the prominent flow to the ovary during this phase of the cycle.

DOPPLER OF THE OVARY

When any abnormality of the ovary is detected, including a cyst, Doppler examination should be performed. In the case of cysts, color Doppler is helpful in differentiating a potential cyst from adjacent vascular structures (Figure 50-2). Color also can be used to localize flow for pulsed Doppler, which should be obtained on all ovarian masses. Pulsed Doppler interrogation of the adnexal branch of the uterine artery, the ovarian artery, or intratumoral flow is performed to determine the resistive index (RI) (RI = Systolic – Diastolic/Systolic) or pulsatility index (PI) (PI = Systolic – Diastolic/Mean) (Figure 50-3). Patients with normal menstrual cycles are best scanned in the first 10 days of the cycle; this avoids confusion with normal changes in intraovarian blood flow, because high diastolic flow occurs in the luteal phase (Figure 50-4).[50]

A debate in literature exists regarding the value of an RI in distinguishing between benign and malignant adnexal masses. The largest study in the literature uses a cutoff of greater than 0.4 as a normal RI in a nonfunctioning ovary.[29] Other investigators employ a PI of greater than 1 as normal.[4,17] Intratumoral vessels, low-resistance flow, and absence of a normal diastolic notch in the Doppler waveform are all signs that are worrisome for malignancy[17,28]; however, abnormal waveforms can be seen in inflammatory masses, metabolically active masses (including ectopic

pregnancy), and corpus luteum cysts.[16] The most significant problem in the use of an RI is that it is not a sensitive indicator of malignancy. One recent study found a low RI in only 25% of malignant lesions.[31]

BENIGN ADNEXAL CYSTS

FUNCTIONAL OVARIAN CYSTS

Functional cysts result from the normal function of the ovary (Figure 50-5). They are the most common cause of ovarian enlargement in young women. Functional cysts include follicular cysts, corpus luteum cysts, and hemorrhagic cysts. Hormonal therapy is sometimes administered to suppress a cyst. Most cysts measure less than 5 cm in diameter and regress during the subsequent menstrual cycle. A follow-up ultrasound examination in 6 weeks usually documents change

FOLLICULAR CYSTS

A **follicular cyst** occurs when a mature follicle fails to ovulate or involute (Box 50-4). These cysts are usually unilateral and less than 2 cm in size, but they can be as large as 20 cm in diameter. They regress spontaneously.[21,42]

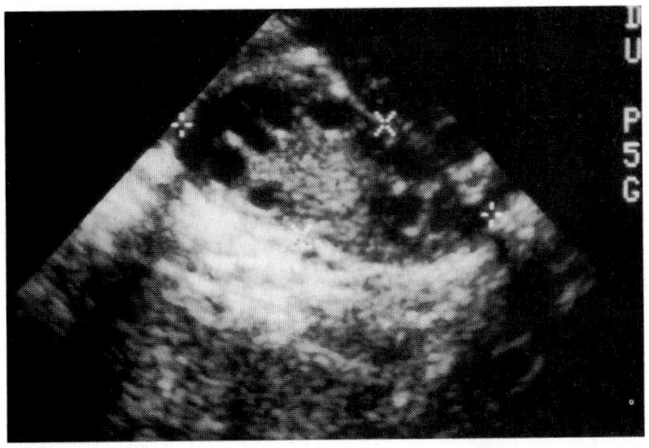

Figure 50-5 Transvaginal sagittal image of the right ovary with normal follicles surrounding the periphery of the ovary. The prominent follicles make it easier to identify the ovary; if not present, color Doppler imaging should be used to separate normal vasculature from ovarian tissue.

CORPUS LUTEUM CYSTS

Corpus luteum cysts result from failure of absorption or excess bleeding into the corpus luteum. These cysts usually are less than 4 cm in diameter (Figure 50-6). They are prone to hemorrhage and rupture. The presenting feature is often pain. Corpus luteum cysts are particularly common during the first trimester of pregnancy, when maximum size is reached by 10 weeks, and resolution occurs by 16 weeks (Box 50-5).

BOX 50-4 FOLLICULAR CYSTS

- Occur when a dominant follicle does not succeed in ovulating and remains active though immature
- Usually unilateral
- Thin-walled, translucent, watery fluid, may project above or within surface of the ovary
- May grow 1 to 8 cm
- Usually disappear spontaneously by resorption or rupture
- *Clinical:* Asymptomatic to dull, adnexal pressure and pain, abnormal ovarian function, torsion of the ovary resulting in severe pain
- *Sonography:* Simple cyst

BOX 50-5 CORPUS LUTEUM CYSTS

- Result from hemorrhage within a persistently mature corpus luteum
- Filled with blood and cystic fluid
- May grow 1 to 10 cm in size
- May accompany intrauterine pregnancy (IUP)
- *Clinical:* Irregular menstrual cycle, pain, mimic ectopic pregnancy, rupture
- *Sonography:* "Cystic" type lesion; may have internal echoes secondary to hemorrhage

A

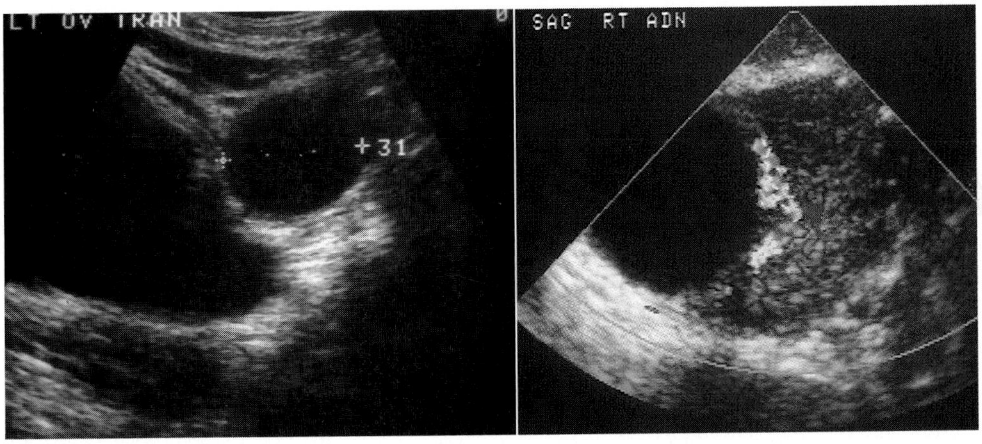

B

Figure 50-6 Hemorrhagic corpus luteum cyst. Transabdominal, **A,** and transvaginal, **B,** views of the right adnexa demonstrate a 3.5-cm cystic mass with internal echoes. The acoustic enhancement posterior to this mass confirms the cystic nature of this mass.

Ultrasound findings. Because of the hemorrhagic nature of these cysts, they usually appear as a complex mass with central blood clot and echogenic septations. This appearance is difficult to distinguish from ectopic pregnancy and endometriosis.

Duplex Doppler reveals prominent diastolic flow in corpus luteum cysts. This low-velocity waveform is present throughout the luteal phase of the cycle.[50]

POLYCYSTIC OVARIAN DISEASE

Polycystic ovarian disease, which includes Stein-Leventhal syndrome (infertility, oligomenorrhea, and hirsutism), is an endocrinologic disorder associated with chronic anovulation (Box 50-6). Pathologically, the ovaries contain an increased number of follicles.

Ultrasound findings. On ultrasound examination, the ovaries appear normal or enlarged with echogenic stroma (Figure 50-7).[39] The number of small follicles is often increased bilaterally (>1 cm), usually to more than five in each ovary.[24,38,39,49] Transvaginal ultrasonography is more sensitive for detecting these small follicles than is transabdominal scanning.[48]

PARAOVARIAN CYSTS

Paraovarian cysts account for approximately 10% of adnexal masses (Box 50-7). They arise from the broad ligament and usually are of mesothelial or paramesonephric origin.[1]

BOX 50-6 POLYCYSTIC OVARIAN DISEASE

- Stein-Leventhal syndrome
- Bilaterally enlarged polycystic ovaries
- Occurs in late teens through twenties
- May have endocrine imbalance
- Spectrum of ultrasound appearances
- *Clinical:* Amenorrhea, obesity, infertility, hirsutism
- *Sonography:* Multiple tiny cysts around the periphery of the ovary; ovary may be normal size or enlarged

Ultrasound findings. Paraovarian cysts have thin, deformable walls that are not surrounded by ovarian stroma. They are difficult to distinguish from ovarian cysts. Paraovarian cysts can become large, extending into the upper abdomen, but rarely are patients symptomatic. Paraovarian cysts can also arise anywhere in the adnexal structures, and if they fill the pelvis their point of origin may not be clear (Figure 50-8). Their size does not change with the hormone cycle.

THECA-LUTEIN CYSTS

Theca-lutein cysts appear as large, bilateral, multiloculated cystic masses. They are associated with high levels of human chorionic gonadotropin (hCG). They are seen most frequently in association with gestational trophoblastic disease (30%). Similar cysts occur in normal pregnancies, especially multiple gestations, and in some patients being treated with infertility drugs, particularly Pergonal (Box 50-8).

BOX 50-7 PARAOVARIAN CYSTS

- Usually simple
- Can bleed or torse
- Wolffian duct remnants
- Ten percent of all adnexal masses
- Located in broad ligament
- *Clinical:* Asymptomatic
- *Sonography:* Simple cyst adjacent to ovary

BOX 50-8 THECA-LUTEIN CYSTS

- Large, bilateral, multiloculated cysts
- Associated with high levels of human chorionic gonadotropin
- Seen in 30% of patients with trophoblastic disease
- *Clinical:* Nausea and vomiting
- *Sonography:* Multilocular cysts in both ovaries

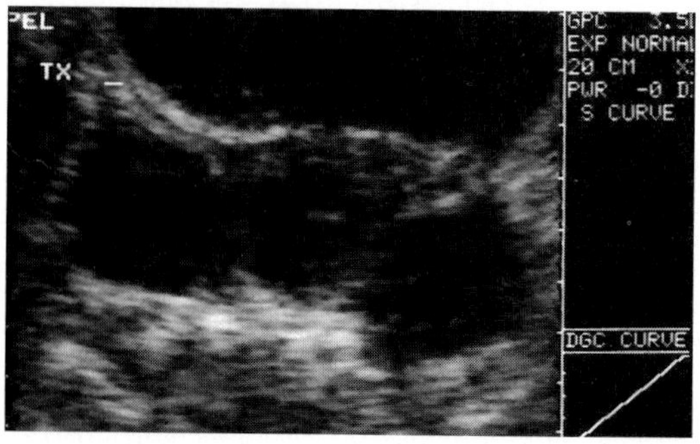

Figure 50-7 Polycystic ovaries. Transabdominal transverse image of the enlarged ovaries as they lie adjacent to the uterine cavity and posterior to the bladder.

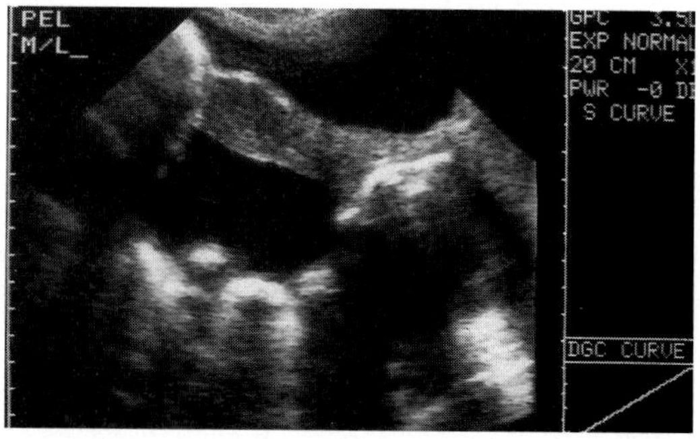

Figure 50-8 Parovarian cyst. Transabdominal longitudinal scan of the parovarian cyst seen posterior to the uterus and bladder. Anterior reflections from the bowel loops are shown posterior to the cyst.

A

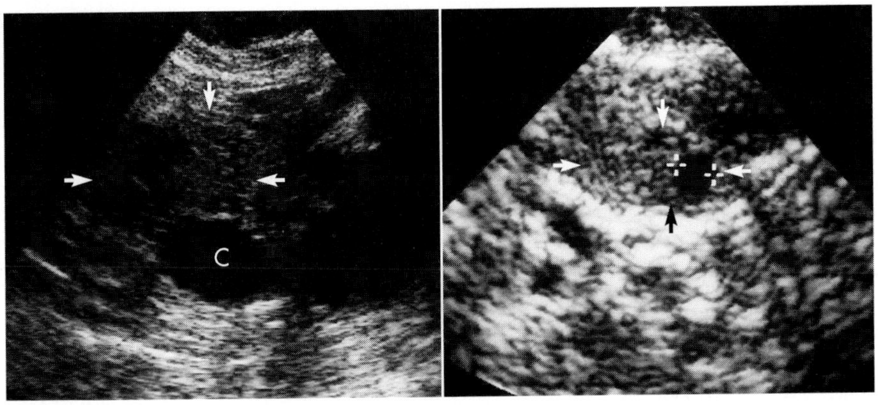

B

Figure 50-9 Disappearing ovarian cyst. **A,** Transverse view of the left ovary in a 63-year-old woman demonstrates a 4.7-cm simple cyst *(C).* **B,** Follow-up examination 6 months later shows near-complete resolution of the cyst, now 0.3 cm. *Arrows* indicate the margins of the left ovary. (From Levine D, Gosink BB. In Nyberg DA and others, editors: *Transvaginal ultrasound,* St Louis, 1992, Mosby.)

FLUID COLLECTIONS IN ADHESIONS

Fluid collections in adhesions can create cystic structures of odd shapes throughout the abdomen. Omental cysts tend to be higher in the abdomen, and urachal cysts are midline in the anterior abdominal wall peritoneum above the bladder.

Any tumor may have cystic elements, and the songrapher should demonstrate if the tumor is a "simple" cyst or a complex mass.

BENIGN CYSTS IN FETUSES AND ADOLESCENTS

Small simple cysts (1 to 7 mm) normally occur in fetuses and newborn girls because of stimulation by maternal hormones.[36] In premenarchal girls, small follicles (<9 mm) are common.[9,37] Larger cysts also are seen in otherwise healthy premenarchal girls.[9] These may be followed closely if they are regressing, as long as the child's growth and development appear normal. Occasionally, ovarian cysts produce symptoms of precocious puberty in young girls.[46] These may arise spontaneously, or in association with other hormonal derangements.

SIMPLE CYSTS IN POSTMENOPAUSAL WOMEN

Palpable ovaries in postmenopausal women are of concern.[3] However, the cause of ovarian enlargement is often a simple adnexal cyst. In postmenopausal women, small (up to 3 cm) simple cysts of the ovaries are seen in approximately 15% of patients. These cysts commonly change in size and often disappear completely (Figure 50-9).

Because 85% to 90% of ovarian malignancies are epithelial in origin and most are cystic, the occurrence of any ovarian cyst in a postmenopausal woman has, in the past, been considered abnormal and an indication for surgery.[35] However, several retrospective studies have evaluated simple ovarian cysts and have concluded that simple cystic lesions of the ovary, especially cysts less than 5 cm in diameter, are not likely to be malignant. Some recommend that if the resistive index is normal (>0.4), these simple adnexal cysts be followed sonographically rather than surgically removed.

The serum cancer antigen 125 (CA 125) level also is of value, because it is elevated in over 80% of epithelial ovarian cancers. When combined with sonography, CA 125 levels increase the effectiveness of screening for ovarian cancer.[13]

ENDOMETRIOSIS

Endometriosis is a common condition in which functioning endometrial tissue is present outside the uterus. Usually the ectopic tissue is found on the ovaries, the external surface of the uterus, and scattered over the peritoneum, especially in the dependent parts of the pelvis. The endometrial tissue cyclically bleeds and proliferates. In the diffuse form, this leads to disorganization of the pelvic anatomy with an appearance similar to pelvic inflammatory disease (PID) or chronic ectopic pregnancy.[2]

Two possible explanations for the cause of endometriosis are presented. The first is that the chronic reflux of menstrual fluid through the tubes and into the pelvis, which may in some women produce implantation and proliferation of endometrial cells with cyclic bleeding. The second theory involves the evolution of endometrial activity in susceptible cells that retain the embryonic capacity to differentiate in response to chronic irritation (for example by menstrual fluid) or to hormonal stimulation. The resulting tissue bleeds and proliferates in response to cyclic hormones, producing pain, scarring, and distortion of adherent pelvic organs and endometrium-lined collections of blood known as endometriomas in the ovary. These may become moderately enlarged and may create a surgical emergency by rupturing or by causing the ovary to twist on the vessels that supply it (torsion).

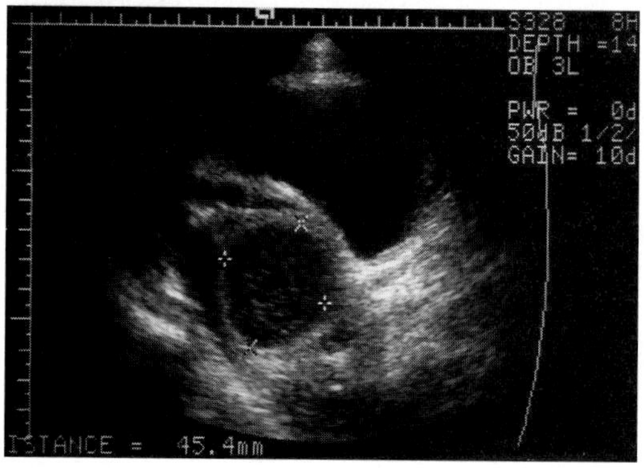

Figure 50-10 Endometrioma. A well-defined mass with homogeneous low-level echoes is seen in this 43-year-old woman.

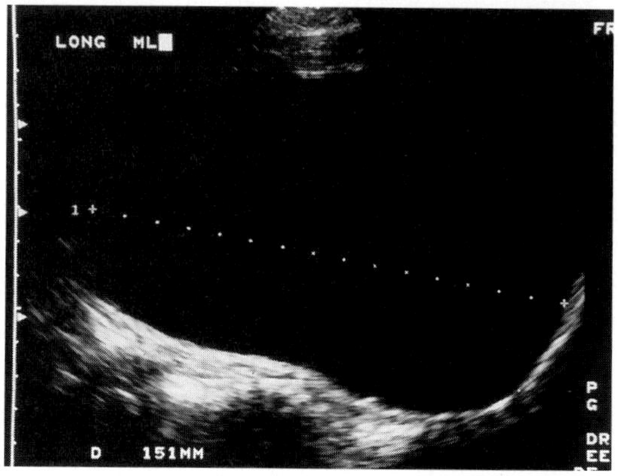

Figure 50-11 Mucinous cystadenoma. A 37-year-old woman presented with pelvic pressure and fullness. A large pelvic mass was found on pelvic examination. The ultrasound image shows a huge "cystic"-appearing mass with smooth borders extending beyond the patient's umbilicus.

BOX 50-9 MUCINOUS CYSTADENOMA

- Unusually large (15 to 30 cm)
- Most common cystic tumor
- Usually unilateral
- Cyst filled with sticky, gelatin-like material
- Multilocular cystic spaces
- Benign type more common than malignant
- *Clinical:* Pressure, pain, increased abdominal girth
- *Sonography:* Simple or septate thin-walled multilocular cysts

Ultrasound findings. Endometriosis may appear as bilateral or unilateral ovarian cysts with patterns ranging from anechoic to solid, depending on the amount of blood and its organization (Figure 50-10). The ovaries are typically adherent to the posterior surface of the uterus or stuck in the cul-de-sac and may be intimately associated with the rectosigmoid colon and difficult to define. Obscured organ borders and multiple irregular cystic masses are also suggestive of either disseminating cancer or pelvic infection, and the clinical picture and serial sonographic studies determine when and if exploratory surgery is indicated.

OVARIAN NEOPLASMS

Mixed cystic and solid masses are the most frequent presentation of the common epithelial tumors of the ovary.

Ultrasound findings. Ultrasonography can describe morphologic characteristics of the tumor but cannot (with the exception of dermoid cysts) distinguish benign from malignant tumors.[7] Simple cysts are probably benign, whereas cysts with thick septations and solid elements are frequently malignant.[33] Abnormal tumor vascularity and RI or PI are also worrisome for malignancy. Ascites, extension to adjacent organs, peritoneal implants, lymphadenopathy, and hepatic metastases support the diagnosis of malignant disease.

EPITHELIAL TUMORS

Of the epithelial tumors, 70% are benign and 30% malignant. The two most common types are serous and mucinous tumors. The benign or low-malignancy potential form is termed ***adenoma*** and the malignant form is termed ***adenocarcinoma.*** The prefix ***cyst*** is added if the lesion is cystic, and *fibroma* is added if the tumor is more than 50% fibrous.

Some investigators believe that benign-appearing tumors (which are anechoic, thin walled, have no septation, and are acoustically enhanced) can be aspirated safely.[6,19] Others believe that cystadenomas have a low malignancy potential and that any persistent cyst greater than 5 cm should be removed surgically.[27]

Ultrasound findings. Serous and mucinous tumors can be very large. They often fill the pelvis and extend into the abdomen.

MUCINOUS CYSTADENOMA

Mucinous cystadenoma is a type of epithelial tumor that is lined by the mucinous elements of the endocervix and bowel. When benign, it is a mucinous cystadenoma; when malignant, it is a cystadenocarcinoma. This type of tumor is usually found in a woman between the ages of 13 and 45 years old.

Ultrasound findings. In 75% of patients with mucinous tumors, ultrasonic examination shows simple or septate thin-walled multilocular cysts (Figure 50-11). They often contain internal echoes with compartments differing in echogenicity. These tumors are large, measuring 15 to 30 cm in diameter, and weigh more than 100 pounds. They usually are benign and unilateral (Box 50-9).

MUCINOUS CYSTADENOCARCINOMA

Mucinous cystadenocarcinoma is usually bilateral when malignant (Box 50-10). Ten percent occur in menopausal women. These tumors can also become very large and are

more likely than the benign form to rupture. If they rupture, they are associated with pseudomyxoma peritoneum. This causes loculated ascites with mass effect.

Ultrasound findings. On ultrasound examination, the mucoid ascites appears as hypoechoic fluid with bright punctate echoes. Malignant cysts tend to have thick, irregular walls and septations (Figures 50-12 and 50-13).

Serous Cystadenoma

Serous cystadenoma is the second most common benign tumor of the ovary (after the dermoid cyst) and represents 20% of all benign ovarian neoplasms. This tumor is usually unilateral (7% to 30% are bilateral) (Box 50-11).

Ultrasound findings. Serous tumors are usually unilocular or multilocular (Figure 50-14). Their size is smaller than the mucinous cysts (up to 20 cm); borders are irregular with a loss of capsular definition. Multilocular cysts contain a small amount of solid tissue in chambers of varying size with occasional internal septum or mural nodules.

Serous Cystadenocarcinoma

Serous cystadenocarcinoma constitutes 60% to 80% of all ovarian carcinomas. More than half of these tumors are bilateral (50% to 70%).

Ultrasound findings. Serous cystadenocarcinomas are smaller than mucinous cysts; borders are irregular with a loss of capsular definition (Box 50-12). The tumor may be accompanied by bilateral ovarian enlargement. Multilocular cysts contain chambers of varying size with septated, internal papillary projections. Calcifications may be present. Solid elements or bilateral tumors suggest malignancy (Figure 50-15). Ascites forms secondary to peritoneal surface implantation. The tumor may spread to the lymph nodes (e.g., periaortic, mediastinal, supraclavicular).

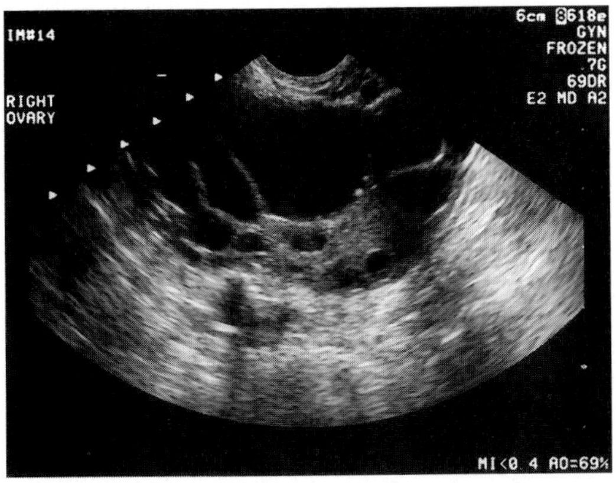

Figure 50-12 Mucinous cystadenocarcinoma. A large septated mass with thick, irregular walls was found in this 33-year-old woman.

Box 50-10 Mucinous Cystadenocarcinoma

- Bilateral
- May occur in menopausal women (10%)
- Large, likely to rupture—ascites
- *Clinical:* Pelvic pressure, pain when ruptured
- *Sonography:* Ascites appears as hypoechoic fluid with bright punctate echoes; thick, irregular walls and septations

Box 50-11 Serous Cystadenoma

- Usually unilateral
- Smaller than mucinous cysts
- Multilocular cysts with septations
- *Clinical:* Pelvic pressure, bloating
- *Sonography:* Multilocular cyst—may have nodule

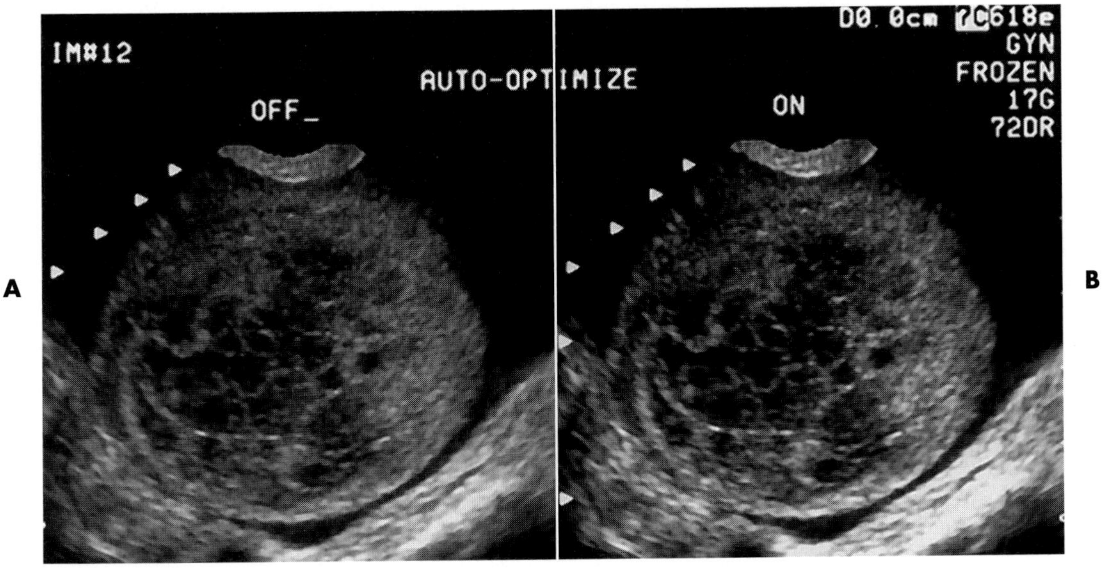

Figure 50-13 Mucinous cystadenocarcinoma. Adjustments in equipment focus may help the sonographer determine the thickness of the septations within the large ovarian mass.

OTHER EPITHELIAL TUMORS

Less common varieties of epithelial tumors are endometrioid, clear cell, Brenner, and undifferentiated carcinoma. The Brenner tumor is found in 1.5% to 2.5% of patients; peak age ranges from 40 to 70 years.

Ultrasound findings. These types of epithelial tumors cannot be distinguished sonographically; however, they are found unilaterally and are benign. They are usually small and unilateral and have calcifications.

GERM CELL TUMORS

Germ cell tumors include teratoma, dysgerminoma, embryonal cell carcinoma, choriocarcinoma, and transdermal sinus tumor. With the exception of teratomas, all are rare. They often occur as mixed tumors with elements of two or three varieties of germ cell tumors. They are associated with elevated alpha-fetoprotein (AFP) and hCG levels.[5] This tumor usually is found in adolescents.

Clinical symptoms include pelvic and/or abdominal pain and a palpable mass (average diameter is 15 cm).

Ultrasound findings. The germ cell tumor is usually unilateral; 40% of tumors will calcify. The tumor ranges in texture from homogeneously solid (3%), predominantly solid (85%), to predominantly cystic (12%).

TERATOMA

Dermoid Tumors. **Dermoid** tumors are the most common ovarian neoplasm, constituting 20% of ovarian tumors. Up to 20% are bilateral. About 80% occur in women of childbearing age.

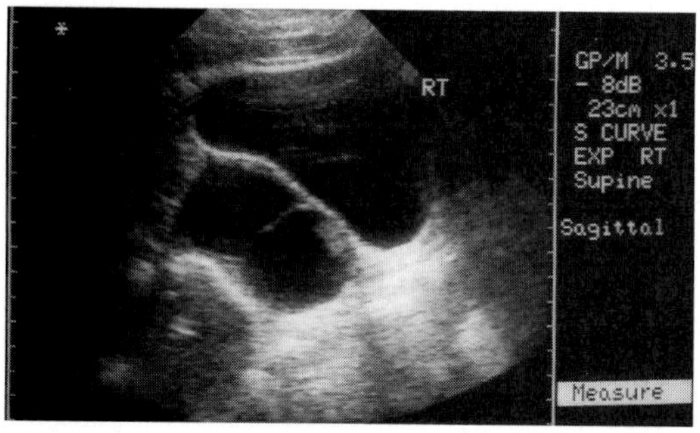

Figure 50-14 Serous cystadenoma. Multilocular mass with septations is seen in this ovarian mass posterior to the bladder.

BOX 50-12 SEROUS CYSTADENOCARCINOMA

- External papillary mass adhesions and infection lead to bilateral involvement
- Loss of capsular definition and tumor fixation; calcifications
- Peritoneal implants; ascites; metastases to omentum, lymph nodes, liver, and lungs
- Clinical: Pelvic fullness, bloating
- Sonography: Cystic structure with septations and/or papillary projections; internal and external papillomas usually present

A

B

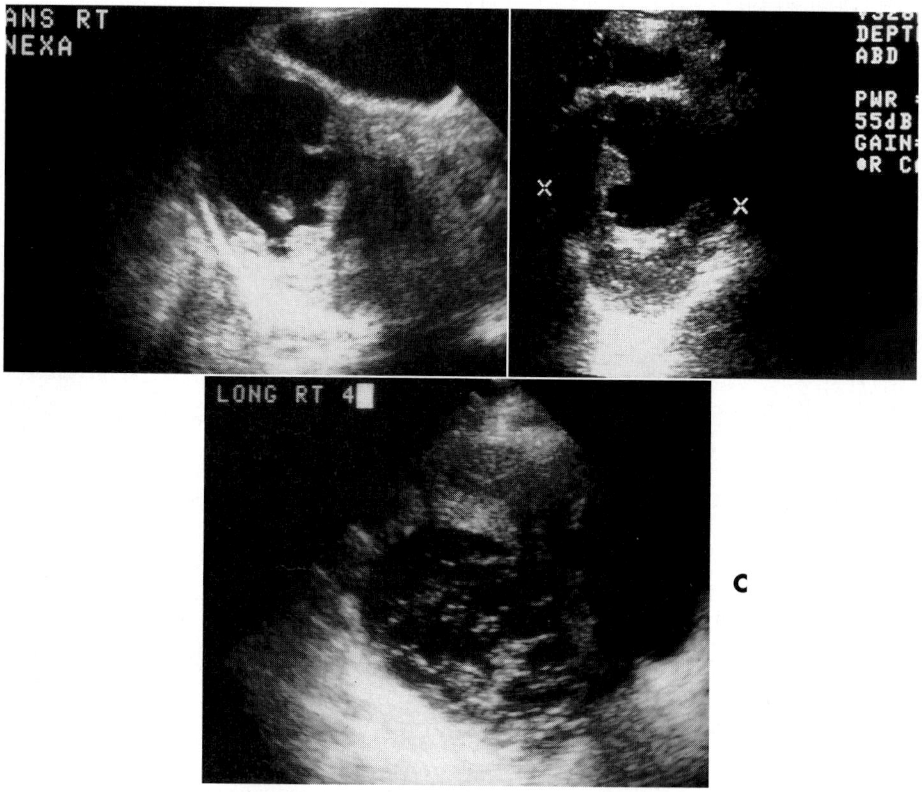

C

Figure 50-15 Serous cystadenocarcinoma. **A** and **B,** A 14-cm mass was found in a 62-year-old woman. This mass had papillary projections within. **C,** In another patient the ovarian mass showed multiple thick septations within. Massive ascites was seen throughout the pelvic cavity.

A rare dermoid that is composed of thyroid tissue is termed a struma ovarii (thyroid tissue) and may produce unsuppressible thyrotoxicosis. Malignant degeneration into squamous cell carcinoma frequently occurs in teratomas, usually in older women.

Ultrasound findings. Dermoids have a spectrum of sonographic appearances, depending on which elements (ectoderm, mesoderm, or transderm) are present. Teeth, bones, and fat can be seen on plain films (Box 50-13). Clinical findings include abdominal mass and/or pain secondary to torsion or hemorrhage.

Ultrasonography demonstrates a completely cystic mass, a cystic mass with an echogenic mural nodule (Figure 50-16, *A*), a fat-fluid level (Figure 50-16, *B*), high-amplitude echoes with shadowing (e.g., teeth or bone), or a complex mass with internal septations (Figure 50-16, *C* and *D*). Echogenic dermoids often are confused with bowel. If a palpable pelvic mass is present that is not identified on ultrasonography, an echogenic dermoid must be considered. Indentation on the bladder wall will be a clue that a mass is present. The calcification within the pelvic cavity is also shown on the radiograph (Figure 50-17).

BOX 50-13 Dermoid Tumors

- Size ranges from small to 40 cm
- Unilateral, round to oval mass
- Contains fatty, sebaceous material, hair, cartilage, bone, teeth
- *Clinical:* Asymptomatic to abdominal pain, enlargement and pressure; pedunculated, subject to torsion
- *Sonography:* Cystic/complex/solid mass, echogenic components; acoustic shadowing

Immature and Mature Teratomas

Immature teratomas occur in girls and young women 10 to 20 years of age. These are rapidly growing, solid malignant tumors with many tiny cysts (Figure 50-18). AFP is elevated in 50% of patients. The tumor is unilateral and small in size, although it may grow to a larger dimension.

Ultrasound findings. On ultrasound examination the texture of immature teratomas ranges from cystic to complex; the teratoma usually is solid with internal echoes.

Dysgerminoma

Dysgerminoma is a rare malignant tumor that is unilateral (more than 83%). An entirely solid ovarian mass in a woman less than 30 years of age is usually a dysgerminoma.

Ultrasound findings. Dysgerminoma is a hyperechoic solid mass with areas of hemorrhage and necrosis on ultrasound examination. It may show a speckled pattern of calcifications. In a postmenopausal patient a fibroma or thecoma is most likely.

STROMAL TUMORS

Sex cord–stromal tumors typically are solid adnexal masses. This category includes granulosa cell tumor, thecoma, fibroma, and Sertoli-Leydig cell tumors. Thecomas and fibromas are the most common of these. They are benign solid hypoechoic adnexal masses that occur in middle-age women.

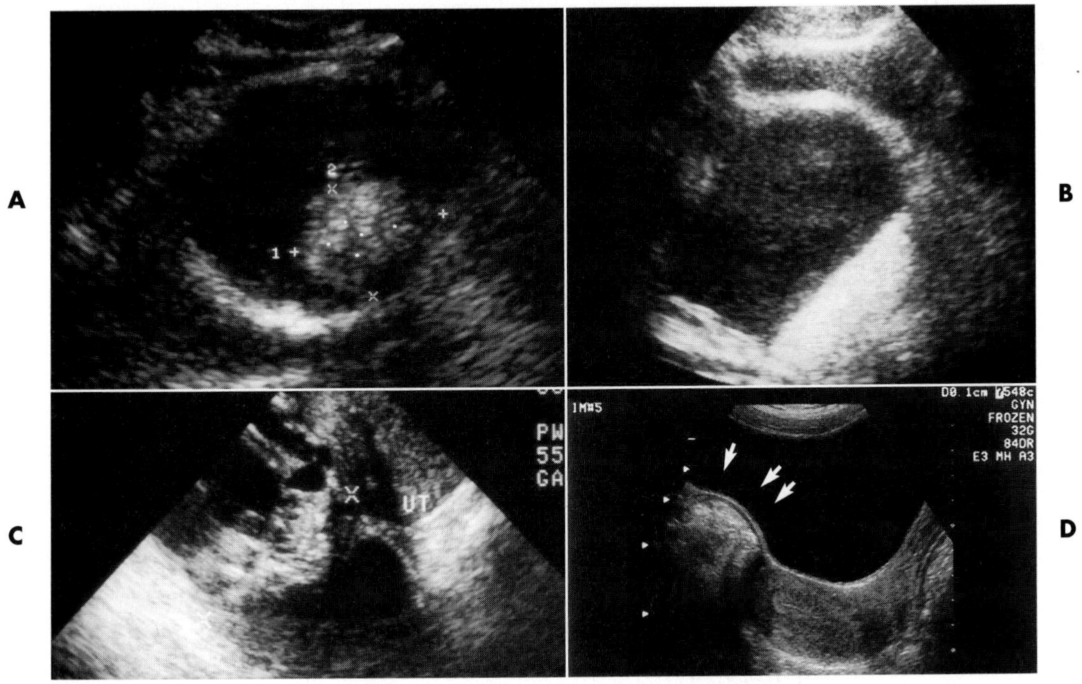

Figure 50-16 Dermoid tumor. Spectrum of appearances on ultrasound examination. **A,** Cystic dermoid with an echogenic mural nodule. **B,** Cystic dermoid with a fat-fluid level. **C,** Complex pattern of a dermoid tumor. *UT,* Uterus. **D,** Calcification and shadowing are shown in this dermoid tumor as it indents the bladder wall *(arrows).*

Ultrasound findings. Stromal tumors are often so hypoechoic as to appear cystic, but there is lack of through-transmission.[3,47]

FIBROMA

Fibroma is a rare tumor that may be associated with massive ascites and pleural effusion and is then referred to as **Meigs' syndrome.** The tumor in found in postmenopausal women. Clinical signs include lack of symptoms if the tumor is small; if large, increasing pressure and pain are apparent.

Ultrasound findings. Fibromas are usually unilateral (90%), and their size ranges from small to melon size. The larger tumors are pedunculated and prone to torsion (Figure 50-19).

GRANULOSA

A granulosa is a feminizing neoplasm composed of cells resembling the graafian follicle. It is the most common hormone-active estrogenic tumor of the ovary but is rarely found (1% to 3%). It is more common after menopause (50%) but is also seen in the reproductive age (45%) and in adolescence (5%). Clinical symptoms may include precocious puberty or vaginal bleeding and full breasts. Pain, pressure, and fullness may also be present. The tumor may twist on itself to cause torsion or rupture, leading to Meigs' syndrome. Malignant transformation is rare, but when it occurs the lesion spreads via the lymphatics and bloodstream.

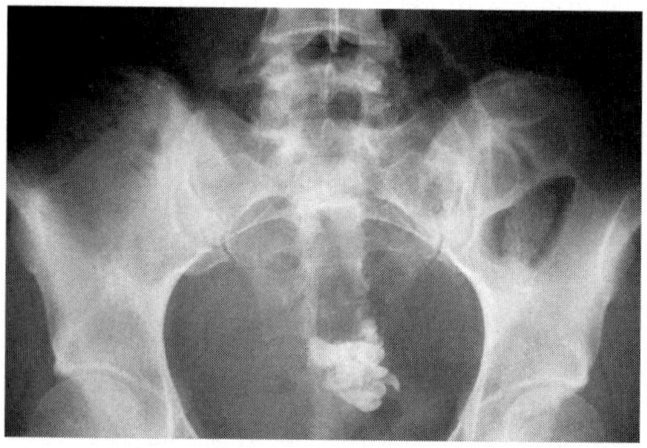

Figure 50-17 Radiograph of a 17-year-old girl with a calcified dermoid tumor shown within the pelvic cavity.

Ultrasound findings. On ultrasound examination a mass without torsion is similar to an endometrioma with low-level homogenous echoes (Figure 50-20); if torsion occurs, a multilocular cyst containing blood or fluid is seen. The size may range up to 40 cm in diameter; the mass is usually unilateral. Endometrial glandular hyperplasia may be apparent.

ARRHENOBLASTOMA

Arrhenoblastoma is a masculinizing ovarian tumor that occurs in females 15 to 65 years with a peak incidence at 25 to 45 years. Clinical features are the same as for other pelvic masses, with the addition of amenorrhea and infertility. This mass may experience malignant transformation in 22% of patients.

Ultrasound findings. The tumor is a solid mass with cystic components; it is lobulated and well encapsulated. In 95% of patients the mass is unilateral, and the size ranges from 2 to 30 cm.

METASTATIC DISEASE

The ovary is a common site of metastasis from carcinoma of the bowel (Krukenberg's tumor), breast, and endometrium and from melanoma and lymphoma.

Ultrasound findings. Metastatic disease to the ovaries frequently is bilateral and is often associated with ascites (Figure 50-21). Metastases are usually completely solid or solid with a "moth-eaten" cystic pattern.[45]

OVARIAN CARCINOMA

Every year **ovarian carcinoma** kills more women than cancer of the uterine cervix and body combined. In the United States, 15,000 women die from this disease annually, and approximately 1 in 70 women develop the disease. Ovarian carcinoma is the leading cause of death from gynecologic malignancy in the United States. About 80% of cases involve women over 50 years of age, with the risk of cancer increasing with age. New chemotherapeutic and

A

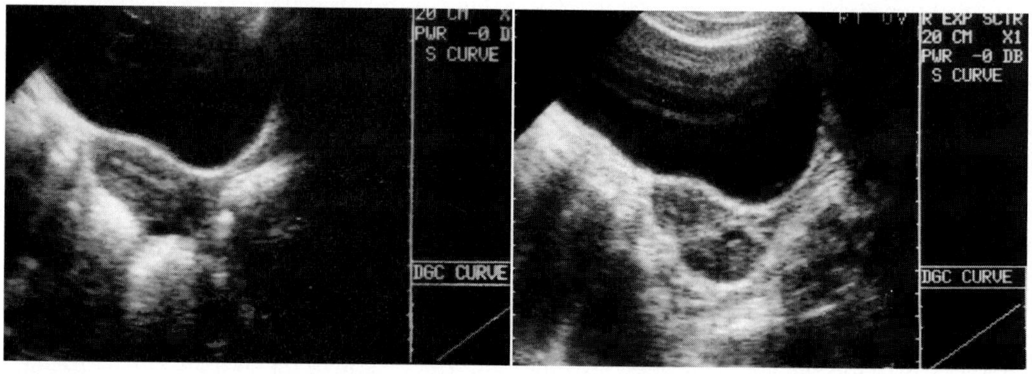

B

Figure 50-18 Teratoma. A small, solid mass was incidentally found posterior to the uterus in this 2-year-old girl. **A,** Transabdominal, midline (bladder and uterus). **B,** Midline, slightly to the left, to show the uterus and teratoma in the area of the left ovary.

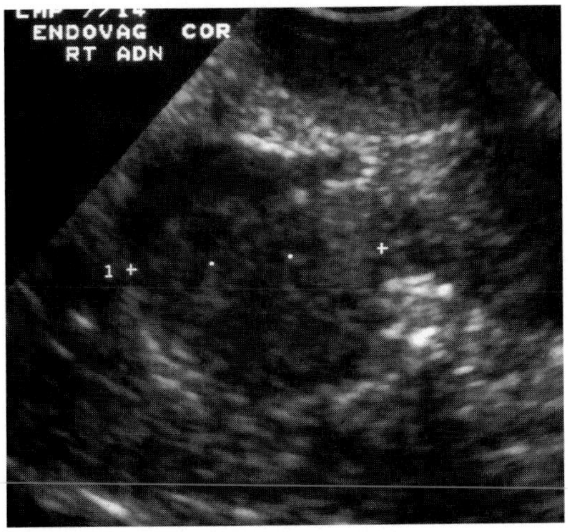

Figure 50-19 Fibroma. A 65-year-old woman presented with fullness in her abdomen. A homogeneous, well-defined mass was found in the right ovary. At surgery an endometrioid cyst adenofibroma was removed.

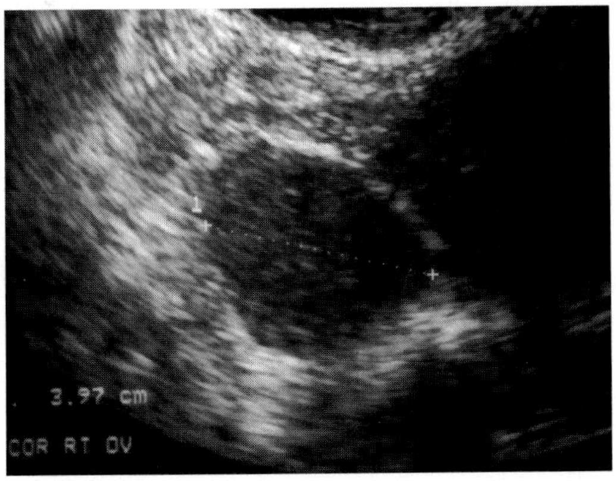

Figure 50-20 Granulosa. A 46-year-old woman was found to have a grapefruit-size mass on pelvic examination. The ultrasound image showed a well-defined, homogeneous mass in right ovary, which was surgically removed.

surgical techniques have done little to decrease mortality. The 5-year survival rate is between 20% and 40% overall (stages I through IV).

The primary clinical problem with this disease is the asymptomatic and undetectable nature of the cancer in the earliest stages. Often the patient will seek medical attention after ascites has initiated abdominal distention. The 5-year survival for stage IV ovarian cancer is 5%; stage I tumors diagnosed early and confined to the capsule show a survival of 90% at 5 years.

The strongest risk factor is a family history of ovarian or breast cancer. Women with carcinoma of the breast have increased risk of developing ovarian cancer, and women with ovarian cancer are three to four times more likely to develop breast cancer. Other risk factors include nulliparity, infertility, uninterrupted ovulation, and late menopause.

Clinical symptoms include vague abdominal pain, swelling, indigestion, frequent urination, constipation, and

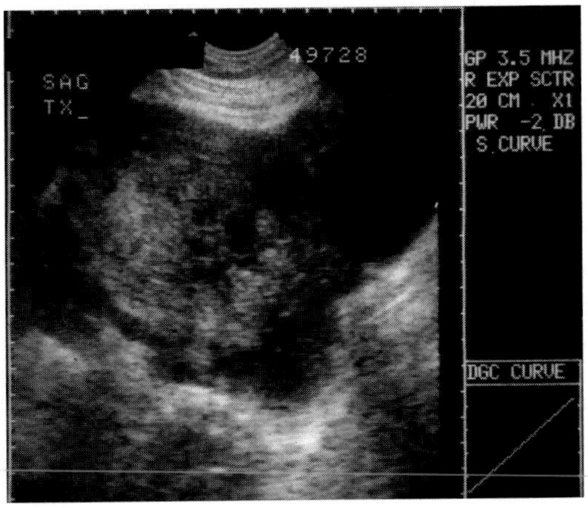

Figure 50-21 Metastatic disease. A complex, solid-appearing mass was found in this 42-year-old woman 6 months after she was diagnosed with adenocarcinoma of the colon.

weight change (ascites). Over 70% of the women first seen by their doctor are in their advanced stages of the disease. Although the median age of diagnosis is 63 years, the peak age ranges between 55 and 59 years, although it may also affect women in their forties.

Ovarian cancer[10] arises primarily from epithelial tumors (60% to 70%): serous cystadenocarcinoma (50%), endometrioid tumor similar to endometrial adenocarcinoma (15% to 30%), mucinous cystadenocarcinoma (15%), clear cell carcinoma (5%), Brenner tumor (2.5%), or undifferentiated tumor (less than 5%). Germ cell tumors contribute 15% to 30% of the malignancies and are more common in girls and young women (age 4 to 27 years): mature teratoma, dysgerminoma, immature teratoma, transdermal sinus tumor, malignant mixed germ cell tumor, choriocarcinoma, or embryonal carcinoma. Metastases (5% to 10%) and stromal tumors (5%) are the remaining tumors that contribute to ovarian cancer.

On laparotomy, the cancer is classified into one of the following stages[10]:

STAGE I: Limited to ovary
- a Limited to one ovary
- b Limited to two ovaries
- c Positive peritoneal lavage (ascites)

STAGE II: Limited to pelvis
- a Involvement of uterus/ fallopian tubes
- b Extension to other pelvic tissues
- c Positive peritoneal lavage (ascites)

STAGE III: Limited to abdomen–intraabdominal extension outside pelvis/ retroperitoneal nodes/ extension to small bowel/ omentum

STAGE IV: Hematogenous disease (liver parenchyma)/ spread beyond abdomen

The treatment for ovarian carcinoma includes surgery and chemotherapy initially, followed by a second laparotomy in 6 months and follow-up CA 125 blood tests and computerized tomography (CT) scans.

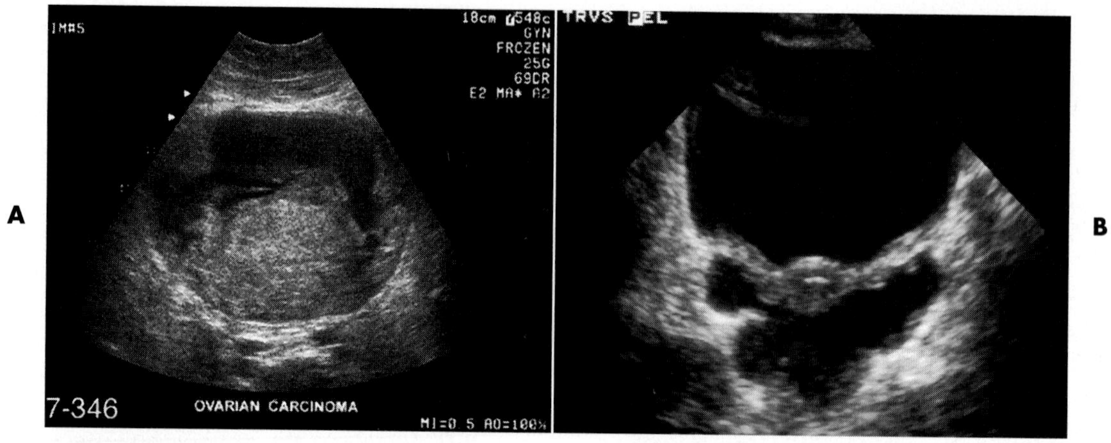

Figure 50-22 Ovarian carcinoma. **A,** A large, solid mass was found in the left adenxa in this 49-year-old woman whose presenting symptom was a palpable mass. **B,** Complications of advanced stages of ovarian carcinoma lead to malignant ascites. This transabdominal transverse image shows the distended urinary bladder anterior to the uterus as it is surrounded by massive ascites.

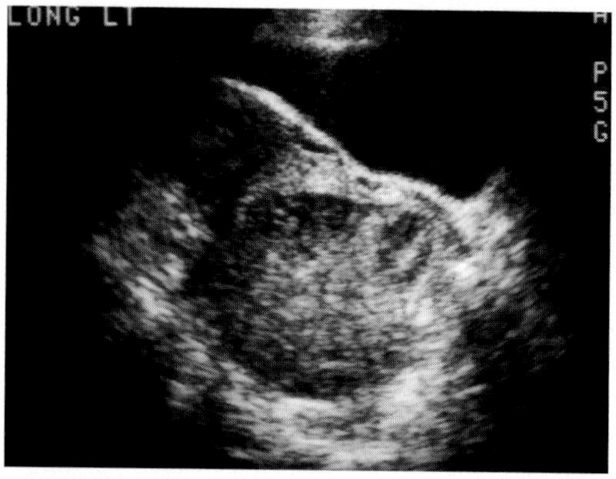

Figure 50-23 Ovarian torsion. Transabdominal view of the distended bladder lying anterior to the enlarged ovary in this 5-day-old girl. Decreased Doppler flow was apparent during the real-time examination.

The CA 125 test is a serum marker for ovarian cancer; it is elevated in over 80% of epithelial ovarian cancers. It has not been found effective as a screening tool because only 50% of stage I malignant ovarian tumors have CA 125 levels higher than 35 U/ml, and the method has a high false-positive rate that is attributed to nonmalignant gynecologic disease. Levels of CA 125 may be elevated in benign conditions such as endometriosis, pelvic inflammatory disease, uterine fibroids, pregnancy, and in other types of cancer not arising from the ovaries.

Ultrasound findings. Ultrasound screening finds adnexal cysts in 1% to15% of postmenopausal women; only 3% of ovarian cysts less than 5 cm are malignant; therefore a cyst greater than 5 cm is recommended to be surgically removed. In the postmenopausal woman, the ovaries are enlarged; if a mass is seen, it may be mixed texture to solid with papillae within (Figure 50-22). Doppler examination shows a low-resistive pattern. Extension beyond the ovary into the omentum, peritoneum, or liver metastases should be evaluated. Malignant ascites may also be present.

BOX 50-14 OVARIAN TORSION

- Usually associated with a mass
- Hypoechoic, enlarged ovary, with or without peripheral follicles
- Absent blood flow on Doppler examination
- Free fluid in cul-de-sac
- Surgical emergency

OVARIAN TORSION

Torsion of the ovary is caused by partial or complete rotation of the ovarian pedicle on its axis. Torsion usually occurs in childhood and adolescence and is common in association with adnexal masses. Clinical features include severe lower abdominal pain, nausea, vomiting, and fever. A palpable mass is felt in over 50% of patients. The right ovary is three times more likely to torse than the left.

Ovarian torsion produces an enlarged edematous ovary, usually greater than 4 cm in diameter.[25] The classically described appearance is of multiple tiny follicles around a hypoechoic mass, but the most common presentation is that of a completely solid adnexal mass (Figure 50-23). Free fluid often is present in the pelvis. Doppler examination usually reveals absent blood flow to the torsed ovary (Box 50-14); however, a recent case report describes normal blood flow to torsed ovaries.[41] This is thought to be the result of the dual blood supply of the ovary or because of venous thrombosis, leading to symptoms before arterial thrombosis occurs.

OTHER PELVIC MASSES

Not all pelvic masses are gynecologic in origin. Pelvic kidneys, omental cysts, distended impacted feces in the rectosigmoid colon, a distended bladder, hydroureters, colonic cancer or masses, diverticular abscesses, and retroperitoneal masses can all be identified by ultrasound examination. The

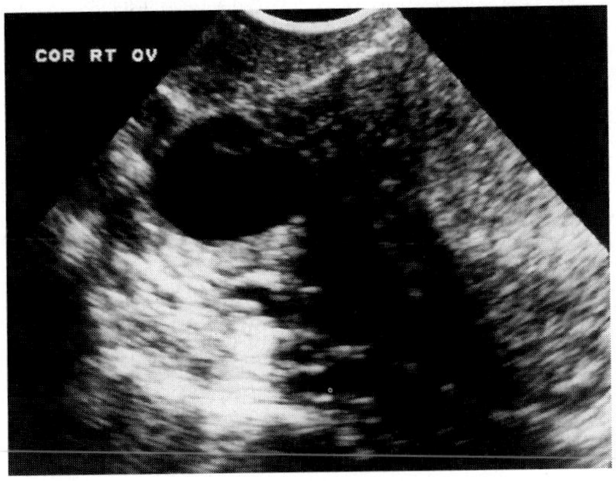

Figure 50-24 Cumulus oophorus. Transvaginal coronal view of the right ovary demonstrates a dominant follicle (26 mm) with a cumulus oophorus seen along its anterior margin.

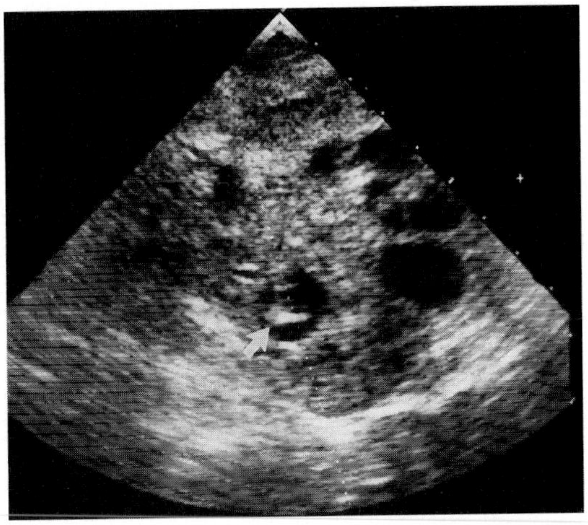

Figure 50-25 A needle tip is seen in one follicle along a biopsy guideline during transvaginal ovum aspiration under ultrasound guidance. (Courtesy HH Vander Kolk and RD Visscher.)

location, size, consistency, and source of adnexal masses can be defined by a flexible combination of transvaginal and transabdominal scanning. It is of key importance to try to distinguish solid ovarian masses from pedunculated myomas by identifying the uterine connection and searching for an ovary. Any fluid present in the pelvis can be used to outline dependent portions of the pelvic organs by tilting the patient, using a transvaginal approach, or both. Large palpable tumors rising out of the pelvis are best viewed with transabdominal technique.

Ultrasound examination is useful in defining symptomatic or palpable masses, as described previously. It allows the surgeon to observe functional-appearing cysts without resorting to immediate surgery and to plan strategy for surgical exploration and treatment when necessary. Obvious signs of malignancy, such as sonolucent liver metastases or nodular peritoneum outlined by ascites, assist in preoperative assessment. With current equipment, excellent resolution is available, and the experienced sonographer may frequently identify the tumor by its texture if the clinical context is understood. However, histologic diagnosis is the job of the pathologist.

ULTRASONOGRAPHY AND INFERTILITY

Ovarian scanning throughout the menstrual cycle is used to monitor follicle development during spontaneous or induced ovulation. This aids in timing insemination and medication[12] and in diagnosis of ovulatory malfunction.[12,26,32] Transvaginal color Doppler also is used to assess follicular development by demonstrating blood flow parameters.[14] Transvaginal sonography can be used to detect luteal phase abnormalities by identifying a functioning corpus luteum (with high diastolic flow) and a secretory transmetrium.[15]

Tubal obstruction is a factor in 20% to 40% of cases of female infertility. This is caused by adhesions from previous surgery, endometriosis, infection, or a ruptured appendix. Ultrasonically monitored fluid infusion compares favorably with x-ray hysterosalpingography in identifying occluded fallopian tubes.[11,40]

In vitro fertilization and embryo transfer are used to establish pregnancy in women without tubal function. Hyperstimulation of the ovaries with clomiphene, human menopausal gonadotropins, or gonadotropin-releasing hormone is instituted after menses and continued for 7 to 10 days with frequent ultrasonic monitoring of follicular growth. Follicles enlarge from a diameter of 3 to 5 mm at the end of menses to over 20 mm 10 days later (just before ovulation).

Before ovulation, the cumulus oophorus is seen on the wall of the clear spherical follicle as a 1- to 3-mm bleb (Figure 50-24). Human chorionic gonadotropin is administered when several follicles have reached a size of 16 mm or greater, and final oocyte maturation then occurs.

The follicles are aspirated with ultrasonic guidance (Figure 50-25).[18,30,44] The oocytes are incubated and inseminated, and fertilized ova are then inserted through the cervix into the uterus. Ultrasonography aids intrauterine transfer of the embryos to avoid trauma and to direct placement in the endometrial cavity. After 3 weeks, ultrasonography is used to detect a gestational sac.

The technique of ovarian stimulation with medications is used in patients who fail to ovulate spontaneously (Figure 50-26).[23,43] If in vitro fertilization is not planned, a less intensive hormone regimen is used with sonographic monitoring to avoid excessive or inadequate stimulation. Complications of ovulation induction include multiple gestation and ovarian hyperstimulation syndrome.

Hyperstimulation syndrome can be diagnosed and followed sonographically. Its most severe form occurs when the ovaries continue to enlarge rapidly after ovulation, sometimes reaching 20 to 30 cm in diameter. Massive fluid shifts produce ascites, hypovolemia, and hemoconcentration, which can result in blood clot formation, hypercoag-

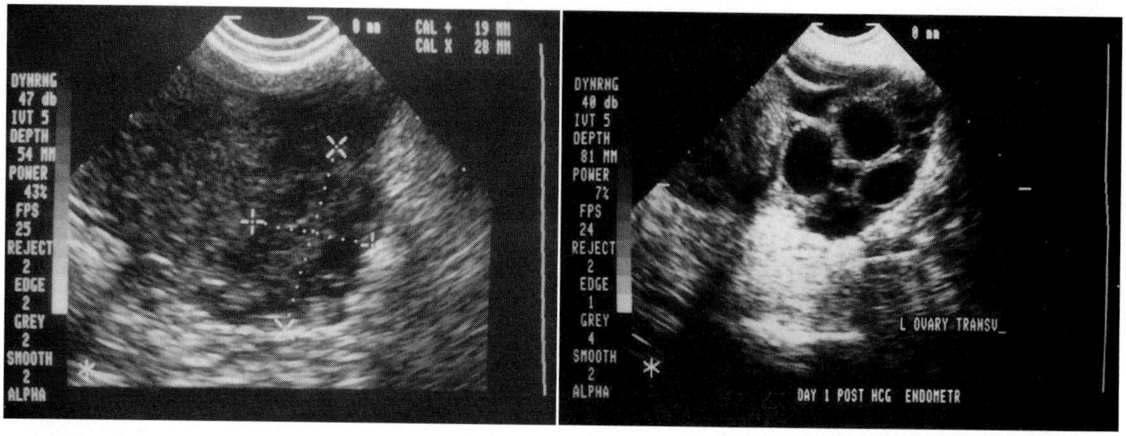

Figure 50-26 **A,** Normal ovary outlined by calipers, measuring 1.9-2.8 cm. **B,** The same ovary, 10 days later, after stimulation with human chorionic gonadotropin.

ulability, or renal failure. Any trauma, including pelvic examination, could rupture the fragile ovaries and produce hemorrhage.

The syndrome is more likely to occur in polycystic ovaries and with pregnancy. It does not occur if the ovulatory dose of hCG is withheld. Sonographic evidence of more than two or three stimulated follicles causes many clinicians to withhold hCG. Gentle serial sonographic examinations provide information that is preventive, diagnostic, and helpful in following the progress of the syndrome when physical palpation is unwise.

REVIEW QUESTIONS

1. Describe the sonographic features of cystic ovarian lesions.
2. Name four common cystic ovarian masses.
3. Discuss how a cystic mass can become complex.
4. List four common solid ovarian masses.
5. What is the role of Doppler in the evaluation of the ovary?
6. Describe the development of corpus luteum cysts.
7. Discuss the cause and appearance of theca-lutein cysts.
8. What is Stein-Leventhal syndrome? What are the complications of this disease?
9. Postmenopausal women may develop ovarian enlargement. What are the causes of such enlargement?
10. List the common benign cysts found in adolescent girls.
11. Name the most common types of epithelial tumors of the ovary.
12. Discuss ovarian carcinoma and the role of ultrasound examination in its detection.
13. What is the most common ovarian neoplasm?
14. Describe the sonographic findings in a dermoid tumor.
15. The ovary is a common site of metastasis from which organs or tumors?
16. What is Meigs' syndrome?
17. List the risk factors of ovarian carcinoma.
18. Describe the clinical signs of ovarian carcinoma.
19. Discuss the sonographic findings in a patient with ovarian carcinoma.
20. Describe the appearance of ovarian torsion on ultrasound examination.
21. Discuss the role of ultrasound examination in the infertility patient.

REFERENCES

1. Athey PA and others: Sonographic features of parovarian cysts, *Am J Roentgenol* 144:83, 1985.
2. Athey PA and others: Sonography of ovarian fibromas/thecomas, *J Ultrasound Med* 6:431, 1987.
3. Barber HRK and others: The postmenopausal palpable ovary syndrome, *Obstet Gynecol* 38:921, 1971.
4. Bourne T and others: Transvaginal colour flow imaging: a possible new screening technique for ovarian cancer, *Br Med J* 299:1367, 1989.
5. Brammer HM III and others: From the archives of the AFIP: malignant germ cell tumors of the ovary: radiologic-pathologic correlation, *Radiographics* 10:715, 1990.
6. Bret PM and others: Transvaginal US-guided aspiration of ovarian cysts and solid pelvic masses, *Radiology* 185:377, 1992.
7. Buy J-N and others: Epithelial tumors of the ovary: CT findings and correlation with US, *Radiology* 178:811, 1991.
8. Campbell S and others: Real-time ultrasonography for determination of ovarian morphology and volume: a possible early screening test for ovarian cancer? *Lancet* 1:425, 1982.
9. Cohen HL and others: Ovarian cysts are common in premenarchal girls: a sonographic study of 101 children 2-12 years old, *Am J Roentgenol* 159:89, 1992.
10. Dahnert W: *Radiology review manual,* ed 3, Baltimore, 1996, Williams and Wilkins.
11. DeCherney AH, Romero R, Polan ML: Ultrasound in reproductive endocrinology, *Fertil Steril* 37:323, 1982.
12. Eissa MF and others: Characteristics and incidence of dysfunctional ovulation patterns detected by ultrasound, *Fertil Steril* 47:603, 1987.

13. Finkler NJ and others: Comparison of serum CA 125, clinical impression, and ultrasound in the preoperative evaluation of ovarian masses, *Obstet Gynecol* 72:659, 1988.
14. Fleischer AC: Ultrasound imaging-2000: assessment of utero-ovarian blood flow with transvaginal color Doppler sonography: potential clinical applications in infertility, *Fertil Steril* 55:684, 1991.
15. Fleischer AC, Kepple DM, Vasquez J: Conventional and color Doppler transvaginal sonography in gynecologic infertility, *Radiol Clin North Am* 30:693, 1992.
16. Fleischer AC and others: Assessment of ovarian tumor vascularity with transvaginal color Doppler sonography, *J Ultrasound Med* 10:563, 1991.
17. Fleischer AC and others: Color Doppler sonography of benign and malignant ovarian masses, *Radiographics* 12:879, 1992.
18. Gonen Y and others: Transvaginal ultrasonically guided follicular aspiration: a comparative study with laparoscopically guided follicular aspiration, *J Clin Ultrasound* 18:257, 1990.
19. Granberg S and others: Comparison of transvaginal ultrasound and cytological evaluation of cystic ovarian tumors, *J Ultrasound Med* 10:9, 1991.
20. Granberg S and others: A comparison between ultrasound and gynecologic examination for detection of enlarged ovaries in a group of women at risk for ovarian carcinoma, *J Ultrasound Med* 7:59, 1988.
21. Hall DA: Sonographic appearance of the normal ovary, of polycystic ovary disease, and of functional ovarian cysts, *Semin Ultrasound* 4:149, 1983.
22. Hall DA and others: Sonographic visualization of the normal postmenopausal ovary, *J Ultrasound Med* 5:9, 1986.
23. Haning RV and others: Ultrasound evaluation of estrogen monitoring for induction of ovulation with menotropins, *Fertil Steril* 37:627, 1982.
24. Hann LE and others: Polycystic ovarian disease: sonographic spectrum, *Radiology* 150:531, 1984.
25. Helvie MA and others: Ovarian torsion: sonographic evaluation, *J Clin Ultrasound* 17:327, 1989.
26. Hilgers TW and others: Assessment of the empty follicle syndrome by transvaginal sonography, *J Ultrasound Med* 11:313, 1992.
27. Hurwitz A and others: The management of persistent clear pelvic cysts diagnosed by ultrasonography, *Obstet Gynecol* 72:320, 1988.
28. Kurjak A and others: New scoring system for prediction of ovarian malignancy based on transvaginal color Doppler sonography, *J Ultrasound Med* 11:631, 1992.
29. Kurjak A and others: Evaluation of adnexal masses with transvaginal color ultrasound, *J Ultrasound Med* 10:295, 1991.
30. Lenz S and others: Ultrasonically guided percutaneous aspiration of human follicles under local anesthesia, *Fertil Steril* 38:673, 1982.
31. Levine D and others: Sonography of adnexal masses: poor sensitivity of resistive index for identifying malignant lesions, *Am J Roentgenol* 162:1355, 1994.
32. Marinbo AO and others: Real time pelvic ultrasonography during the periovulatory period of patients attending an artificial insemination clinic, *Fertil Steril* 37:633, 1982.
33. Meire HB and others: Distinction of benign from malignant ovarian cysts by ultrasound, *Br J Obstet Gynaecol* 85:893, 1978.
34. Mendelson B and others: Gynecologic imaging: comparison of transabdominal and transvaginal sonography, *Radiology* 166:321, 1988.
35. Moyle JW and others: Sonography of ovarian tumors: predictability of tumor type, *Am J Roentgenol* 141:985, 1983.
36. Nussbaum AR and others: Neonatal ovarian cysts: sonographic-pathologic correlation, *Radiology* 168:817, 1988.
37. Orsini LF and others: Pelvic organs in premenarchal girls: real-time ultrasonography, *Radiology* 153:113, 1984.
38. Orsini LF and others: Ultrasonic findings in polycystic ovarian disease, *Fertil Steril* 43:709, 1985.
39. Pache TD and others: How to discriminate between normal and polycystic ovaries: transvaginal US study, *Radiology* 183:421, 1992.
40. Randolph JR and others: Comparison of real-time ultrasonography, hysterosalpingography, and laparoscopy/hysteroscopy in the evaluation of uterine abnormalities and tubal patency, *Fertil Steril* 46:828, 1986.
41. Rosado WM and others: Adnexal torsion: diagnosis by using Doppler sonography, *Am J Roentgenol* 159:1251, 1992.
42. Rottem S and others: Classification of ovarian lesions by high-frequency transvaginal sonography, *J Clin Ultrasound* 18:359, 1990.
43. Sallam HN and others: Monitoring gonadotropin therapy by real-time ultrasonic scanning of ovarian follicles, *Br J Obstet Gynaecol* 89:155, 1982.
44. Schulman JD and others: Outpatient in vitro fertilization using transvaginal ultrasound guided oocyte retrieval, *Obstet Gynecol* 69:665, 1987.
45. Shimizu H and others: Characteristic ultrasonographic appearance of the Krukenberg tumor, *J Clin Ultrasound* 18:697, 1990.
46. Siegel MJ: Pediatric gynecologic sonography, *Radiology* 179:593, 1991.
47. Stephenson WM and others: Sonography of ovarian fibromas, *Am J Roentgenol* 144:1239, 1985.
48. Takahashi K and others: Transvaginal ultrasound is an effective method for screening in polycystic ovarian disease, *Gynecol Obstet Invest* 30:34, 1990.
49. Yeh HC and others: Polycystic ovarian disease: US features in 104 patients, *Radiology* 163:111, 1987.
50. Zalud I and others: The assessment of luteal blood flow in pregnant and nonpregnant women by transvaginal color Doppler, *J Perinat Med* 18:215, 1990.

CHAPTER 51

Ultrasound Evaluation of Gestational Trophoblastic Disease

Sandra L. Hagen-Ansert

OBJECTIVES

- Define gestational trophoblastic disease
- Differentiate between a complete and partial molar pregnancy
- Recognize the clinical signs and symptoms of a molar pregnancy
- Describe the sonographic findings in a molar pregnancy
- Discuss the findings in an invasive molar pregnancy
- Detail the differential considerations for a molar pregnancy

KEY TERMS

choriocarcinoma - malignant invasive form of gestational trophoblastic disease

complete mole - has only trophoblastic parts without a fetus; forms when the sperm fertilizes an empty egg

gestational trophoblastic disease - tumors arising from the placental chorionic villi

hydatidiform mole - benign form of gestational trophoblastic disease

invasive mole - tumor that penetrates into and through the uterine wall

partial mole - develops when two sperm fertilize an egg

theca-lutein cysts - appear as multiple cysts within each ovary; complication of hyperstimulation

---

Tumors arising from the placental chorionic villi are generically termed **gestational trophoblastic disease.** Gestational trophoblastic neoplasia is a proliferative disease of pregnancy related to the trophoblast that may present as a relatively benign form, a **hydatidiform mole,** or as a more malignant form, an invasive mole or **choriocarcinoma.** In a normal pregnancy, the trophoblast infiltrates the maternal tissues, invades the vessels, and can be transported to the lungs.[12] The chorion and amnion are derived from the trophoblast as it attaches to the maternal wall. Abnormal proliferation of the trophoblast leads to the development of a molar pregnancy.

Ultrasound examination has the ability to image the abnormal tissue growth within the uterus, and in combination with the patient's clinical symptoms and laboratory findings, to provide differential considerations for the evaluation and management of the patient. If molar disease is present, ultrasound studies may be used to follow the patient's progress after aggressive treatment has been initiated.

The spectrum of gestational trophoblastic disease includes hydatidiform mole, invasive mole, and choriocarcinoma. Each of these tumors will be discussed with its sonographic and Doppler findings.

HYDATIDIFORM MOLE

The **hydatidiform mole** is the most common and benign of the trophoblastic diseases (Box 51-1). It occurs in 1 in 1200 to 1 in 2000 pregnancies in the United States.[16] A

higher incidence is reported in women in Europe, Asia, and Mexico. Maternal age has been a factor in molar pregnancies; women near the end of their reproductive years have a higher incidence of developing the disease. Women who have had a previous molar pregnancy are at a higher risk of having another pregnancy with trophoblastic disease. However, this risk decreases if a normal pregnancy has followed a molar pregnancy.[3]

TYPES OF MOLES

There are two types of molar pregnancy, **complete mole** and **partial mole.** A complete molar pregnancy has only trophoblastic placental parts with no fetal parts; it forms when the sperm fertilizes an empty egg.[9] Because the egg is empty, no embryo is formed. The placenta continues to grow and produces human chorionic gonadotropin (hCG), so the patient has pregnancy-like symptoms. A partial mole develops when two sperm fertilize an egg. Instead of forming twins, the pregnancy is interrupted, and an abnormal fetus with an abnormal placenta develops. Often, the fetus dies in utero because of triploidy, but the trophoblastic tissue continues to grow and develops into a molar pregnancy.

The "classic" or complete mole has 46,XX as the chromosome pattern. This results from the fertilization of an egg with an absent or inactivated nucleus by haploid sperm that duplicates to a normal diploid number.[3,7] The other type of mole is 46,XY. This results from the fertilization of the egg with an absent nucleus by two different haploid sperm.[3,7] There is no fetal development in a complete molar pregnancy. The placenta is entirely replaced by the invasive trophoblastic tissue proliferation.

CLINICAL SIGNS AND SYMPTOMS

The most classic clinical presentation is vaginal bleeding. The patient usually is in her late first trimester or early second trimester, with rapid enlargement of the uterus and very high hCG levels. The sonographer must be aware that twin pregnancies may also have similar findings, uterine enlargement and high hCG levels; however, the hCG level is markedly elevated in molar pregnancies. Extreme nausea and projectile vomiting (hyperemesis gravidarum) often accompany this disease because the hCG level is severely elevated (greater than 100,000 mIU/ml). The patient may show signs of toxemia or hyperthyroidism or go into respiratory failure.

PATHOPHYSIOLOGY

The explanation for the pathophysiology of a hydatidiform mole is that the chorionic villi of a blighted ovum in a missed abortion persist and continue to undergo hydatid swelling. This accounts for the characteristic vesicular appearance of the swollen chorionic villi but not for the primary pathologic feature of trophoblastic proliferation.[3]

When the molar tissue is examined pathologically, several characteristics are apparent: (1) marked edema and engorgement of the chorionic villi, (2) disappearance of villus blood vessels, (3) proliferation of the lining trophoblast of the chorionic villi, and (4) absence of fetal tissue.[1] The primary problem is the proliferation of the lining trophoblast of chorionic villi within the uterus.[4]

In 80% of patients initially diagnosed as having hydatidiform mole, the disease will follow a benign course, with resolution after evacuation. However, in 12% to 15% of patients, invasive mole develops, and in 5% to 8%, metastatic choriocarcinoma develops.[3]

BOX 51-1 HYDATIDIFORM MOLE

- Benign
- *Incidence:* 1 per 1200 to 1 per 2000 pregnancies
- *Age:* End of reproductive years
- *Previous mole:* Increases risk

SONOGRAPHIC EVALUATION

In the first trimester the sonographic appearance of a molar pregnancy may simulate a blighted ovum or threatened abortion. If the pregnancy is early, the sonographer may note the thickened, less echogenic myometrial tissue surrounding the more echogenic complex mass in the endometrial cavity (Figure 51-1). There may not be a characteristic appearance of swollen vesicles at this time. Doppler and color flow Doppler would show low impedance, indicating a high-flow state with increased systolic and diastolic frequencies throughout the mass.

The sonographer should also look for the presence of theca-lutein cysts in the presence of a molar pregnancy because the incidence ranges from 20% to 50% in this disease (Figure 51-2). The ovaries may be displaced in a cephalic direction, away from their normal location near the cornu of the uterine cavity. Their appearance is easy to see because the ovaries are enlarged with multilocular cysts. It should be noted that it takes at least 2 to 4 months after the molar tissue is evacuated for the ovaries to return to normal size.

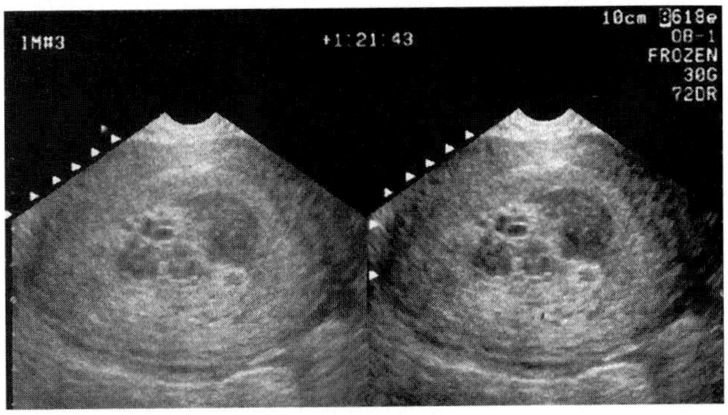

Figure 51-1 A 25-year-old woman came to the emergency department with a history of nausea and vomiting for the last 7 days. Her human chorionic gonadotropin levels were markedly elevated, and she had been bleeding the last 24 hours. The transvaginal ultrasound examination showed an enlarged uterus completely filled with small vesicles, which were thought to represent a molar pregnancy. No intrauterine pregnancy was seen.

The sonographer should look for elevated hCG levels, note the patient's clinical symptoms (nausea, vomiting, uterus too large for dates), and if a gestational sac is not well seen with a yolk sac or embryo, consider the possibility of an ectopic pregnancy, a missed abortion, or a molar pregnancy (Box 51-2).

In the second trimester, sonography may show a large echogenic soft-tissue mass that fills the entire uterine cavity. The engorged villi become cystic cavities scattered throughout the uterine cavity, ranging in size from 1 to 2 mm to 2 to 3 cm.[3]

Complications of Molar Pregnancy

Complications may range from hemorrhage, anemia, and rupture of **theca-lutein cysts** to invasive mole or choriocarcinoma (Box 51-3). The multiple cystic type of structures from the trophoblastic invasion of the villi may hemorrhage and develop anechoic regions throughout the molar tissue. Anemia may develop secondary to the blood loss because many patients have excessive vaginal bleeding. Theca-lutein cysts may rupture or hemorrhage to cause further bleeding. The patient may develop pulmonary embolization or edema. And finally, the patient could progress to an invasive mole or choriocarcinoma with distant metastasis.

BOX 51-2 Sonographic Findings in Molar Pregnancy

- Large echogenic soft tissue mass within uterine cavity
- Numerous small cystlike spaces within mass
- *First trimester:* Blighted ovum or threatened abortion
- Check hCG level
- *Doppler:* Low-impedance, high-flow state with high systolic and diastolic frequencies

BOX 51-3 Complications of Molar Pregnancy

- Hemorrhage
- Anemia
- Rupture of theca-lutein cysts
- Invasive mole
- Choriocarcinoma

VARIATIONS OF MOLAR PREGNANCY

Coexistant Mole and Fetus

The sonographer must differentiate a viable fetus and coexistant mole from a hydropic degeneration of the placenta or an incomplete molar pregnancy. The occurrence of a normal conception with a coexistent complete hydatidiform mole in a twin pregnancy is extremely rare, with fewer than 30 cases reported in the literature (Figure 51-3).

Incomplete or Partial Mole

Incomplete or partial mole results when the chromosomes consist of one set of maternal and two sets of paternal chromosomes (i.e., 69,XXX, 69,XXY, or 69,XYY), resulting from fertilization of the normal ovum by two haploid sperm. The placenta is enormous (measuring more than 5 cm in anteroposterior diameter) and contains multiple cystic spaces scattered throughout the molar tissue. A deformed gestational sac may be present.[2,7] Other problems may result in a growth-restricted fetus with triploidy.[5,7]

Ultrasound findings. On ultrasound examination an intrauterine pregnancy is found with the abnormal placenta. The fetal growth may be abnormal (intrauterine growth restriction), and an amniocentesis may be ordered to see if a triploidy component is present.

INVASIVE MOLAR PREGNANCY

The **invasive mole,** or chorioadenoma destruens, is more common than choriocarcinoma. Invasive moles penetrate into and even through the uterine wall (Figure 51-4). They may also embolize through vessels to distant locations but do not grow within the vessels; that is, they are locally invasive but do not metastasize. The pathologic features of invasive mole are (1) extensive local invasion, (2) excessive trophoblastic proliferation, and (3) preservation of the villous pattern.[3] The difference between an invasive mole

A B

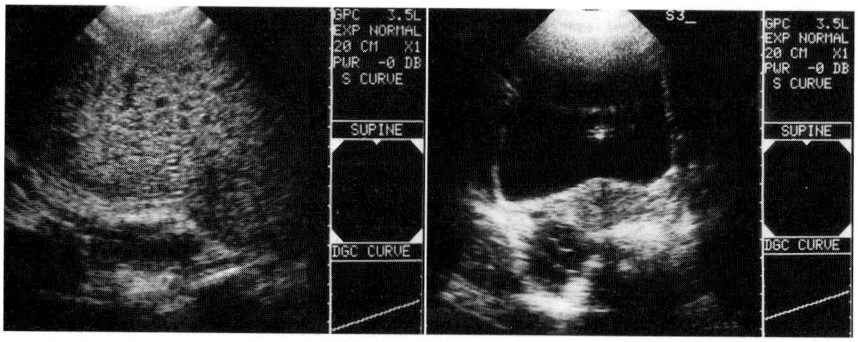

Figure 51-2 **A,** A patient in her 15th week of pregnancy came to the clinician with size larger than dates. The ultrasound examination showed an enlarged uterus completely filled with grapelike clusters. **B,** Evaluation of both ovaries demonstrated enlargement with multiple septations, suggesting the presence of bilateral theca-lutein cysts with the molar pregnancy.

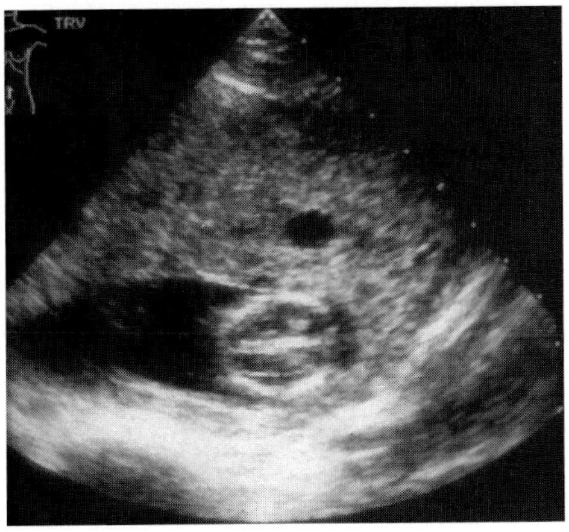

Figure 51-3 Image of a molar pregnancy with a rare coexistent fetus.

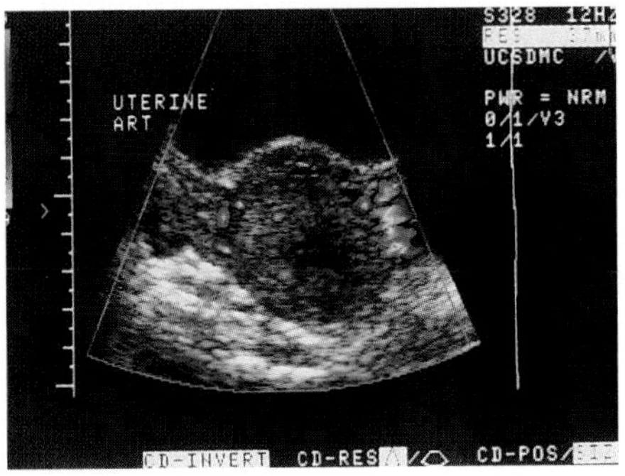

Figure 51-4 A 24-year-old woman presented with hyperemesis in her first trimester. The hCG levels were markedly elevated. The transabdominal scan showed a molar pregnancy with increased flow around the periphery. The patient was taken to surgery, where an invasive mole was found.

and choriocarcinoma is the preservation of the villous pattern in invasive molar disease. If molar tissue is found, the uterus is evacuated; 2% to 4% may require chemotherapy after evacuation.

This disease is considered benign if it is confined to the uterus. However, when there is uterine penetration or proliferation, there is a danger that hemorrhage may occur–resulting in death. The molar tissue may also invade the parametrial tissues, adjacent organs, and blood vessels.[4,12] In addition, it may embolize to the distant organs of the lung and brain.

CHORIOCARCINOMA

Choriocarcinoma is the most malignant and invasive form of trophoblastic disease. It occurs in 1 in 30,000 to 1 in 40,000 pregnancies.* At least half of the cases are preceded by a hydatidiform molar pregnancy.[8,11,14,16] It has been reported that 3% to 5% of all molar pregnancies result in choriocarcinoma.[2,3,7] The other cases of choriocarcinoma show that 25% occur after an abortion, 22% after a normal pregnancy, and 3% after an ectopic pregnancy.[3]

Choriocarcinoma is a purely cellular lesion defined histologically by the absence of formed villi and the invasion of the myometrium by abnormal proliferating trophoblast.[3]

Vaginal bleeding is the most common presenting symptom, secondary to the hemorrhage and necrosis of the invasive process. Patients who have metastatic involvement may have further complications, depending on the tumor location; lung metastasis may produce cough or shortness of breath, liver metastasis may cause abdominal pain or jaundice, and brain metastasis may lead to confusion, seizure, or coma.

Ultrasound findings. On ultrasound evaluation, the sonographer will note the focal echogenic myometrial nodules. The proliferative process lies close to the endometrial canal and may extend deep into the myo-metrium.[2,6,10,17] The multiple lesions may vary in their sonographic presentation from solid and uniformly echogenic to complex and multicystic. The tissue necrosis with hemorrhage presents as thick, irregular cavities within the solid tumor mass.[7,10] The sonographer should look for extension outside of the uterine cavity as a complex pelvic mass.

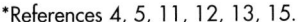

*References 4, 5, 11, 12, 13, 15.

DOPPLER EVALUATION

In an invasive molar pregnancy, there is hypervascularity of the invasive trophoblast. The uterine spiral arteries feed directly into the engorged spaces that communicate with draining veins.[5,7] Functional arteriovenous shunts produce abnormal uterine hypervascularity with high-velocity, low-impedance flow. The resistive index (RI) is less than 0.5 (the normal RI is 0.7). The peak systolic index, or highest velocity, measures greater than 50 cm per second.[7]

Differential considerations for abnormal hypervascular Doppler patterns may include missed abortion, retained products of conception, ectopic pregnancy, pelvic inflammatory disease, pelvic abscess, degenerating fibroids, and ovarian neoplasms.[7]

DIFFERENTIAL CONSIDERATIONS

Previous literature about trophoblastic disease encompassed many other diseases beyond gestational trophoblastic neoplasia, such as hydropic degeneration or partial moles (Box 51-4). Hydropic degeneration of the placenta occurs in 1% to 3% of pregnancies. The chorionic villi become engorged, but there is no proliferation of the lining trophoblast or the chorionic villi. It may be difficult to separate from a molar pregnancy or missed abortion, but the sonographer should check the hCG levels to distinguish between these conditions.[3]

BOX 51-4 DIFFERENTIAL CONSIDERATIONS

- Hydropic degeneration of the placenta
- Necrotic leiomyoma

Cystic degeneration of a fibroid with a pregnancy may also cause some confusion in the diagnosis of a molar pregnancy. However, it is rare to find a coexisting pregnancy with a molar pregnancy, which can occur in an abnormal twin gestation.[6] Again, abnormal hCG levels would not be elevated in a degenerating fibroid tumor.

TREATMENT

Treatment of molar pregnancy involves complete evacuation and removal of all molar tissue. The surgeon performs curettage of the endometrium to determine if there is invasion of the myometrium. At pathologic examination 80% of moles are considered complete and 95% of partial moles are benign.[8,11] A baseline chest x-ray examination is performed to rule out metastases, followed by computerized tomography of the head, chest, abdomen, and pelvis.

The patient is categorized into one of two groups: (1) low risk, which includes low levels of hCG, absence of metastasis, and no prior molar pregnancy; and (2) high risk, which includes high levels of the blood pregnancy test, metastasis to distant sites, and prior molar pregnancy. The low-risk patients are treated with chemotherapy and carefully followed after therapy is completed until the hCG levels return to normal. The high-risk patients require aggressive chemotherapy treatment and may also require surgery or radiation therapy to control the disease. Chemotherapy is used if there are signs of distant metastases to the lung, brain, liver, gastrointestinal tract, kidney, or skin.[7]

The patient is closely followed by the oncologist at 6- to 12-month intervals with x-ray examination and laboratory analysis of hCG levels (which should fall to normal within 10 to 12 weeks after removal of the tumor). The patient is further counseled to avoid becoming pregnant for at least 1 year following chemotherapy. These patients are at increased risk of recurrence and may be followed with pelvic ultrasound examinations during future pregnancies.

REVIEW QUESTIONS

1. Name the benign and malignant forms of gestational trophoblastic disease.
2. What is the most common benign trophoblastic disease?
3. Name the risks associated with molar pregnancy.
4. Discuss the two types of molar pregnancies.
5. Describe the clinical symptoms of a molar pregnancy.
6. List the sonographic and Doppler findings in a molar pregnancy.
7. What are the complications of a molar pregnancy?
8. Discuss the course of choriocarcinoma.
9. Discuss how the sonographer could differentiate between a molar pregnancy, hydropic degeneration of the placenta, and a necrotic fibroid tumor.

REFERENCES

1. Benirschke K and others: *Pathology of the human placenta,* ed 3, New York, 1995, Springer-Verlag.
2. Berkowitz RS and others: Evolving concepts of molar pregnancy, *J Reprod Med* 36(1):40, 1991.
3. Callen PW: Ultrasonography in evaluation of gestational trophoblastic disease. In Callen PW, editor: *Ultrasonography in obstetrics and gynecology,* ed 3, Philadelphia, 1994, WB Saunders.
4. Crum CP: Female genital tract. In Ramzi S and others, editors: *Robbins' pathologic basis of disease,* ed 5, Philadelphia, 1994, WB Saunders.
5. DiSaia PJ and others: *Clinical gynecologic oncology,* ed 5, St Louis, 1997, Mosby.
6. Fleischer AC and others: Sonographic patterns in trophoblastic diseases, *Radiology* 126:215, 1978.
7. Fraser-Hill MA and others: Gestational trophoblastic neoplasia. In Rumack CM, Charboneau JW, Wilson SR, editors: *Diagnostic ultrasound,* ed 2, St Louis, 1998, Mosby.
8. Goldstein DP, Berkowitz RS: Current management of complete and partial molar pregnancy, J *Reprod Med* 39(3): 201, 1994.
9. Hill A: http://www.obgyn.net/women/articles/molarpre_dah.htm, Accessed 1999.
10. Magii G and others: Transvaginal ultrasonography in persistent trophoblastic tumor, *Am J Obstet Gynecol* 169(5):1218, 1993.
11. O'Quinn AG and others: Gestational trophoblastic diseases. In Decherney AH, Pernoll ML, editors: *Current obstetric and gynecologic diagnosis and treatment,* ed 8, East Norwalk, Conn, 1994, Appleton & Lange.
12. Paradinas FJ: Pathology and classification of trophoblastic tumors. In Knapp RC, Berkowitz R, editors: *Gynecologic oncology,* ed 2, New York, 1992, Churchill Livingstone.
13. Redline RW and others: Pathology of gestational trophoblastic disease, *Semin Oncol* 22(2):96, 1995.
14. Rice LW and others: Pathologic features of sharp curettings in complete hydatidiform mole: predictors of persistent gestational trophoblastic disease, *J Reprod Med* 36(1):17, 1991.
15. Sand PK and others: Repeat gestational trophoblastic disease, *Obstet Gynecol* 63:140, 1984.
16. Semer DA and others: Gestational trophoblastic disease: epidemiology, *Semin Oncol* 22(2):109, 1995.
17. Soper JT: Identification and management of high-risk gestation trophoblastic disease, *Semin Oncol* 22(2):172, 1995.

GLOSSARY

abdominal aortic aneurysm - permanent localized dilation of an artery, with an increase in diameter of 1.5 times its normal diameter.
abdominal circumference (AC) - measurement at the level of the stomach, left portal vein, and left umbilical vein.
abruptio placenta - premature detachment of the placenta from the maternal wall.
abscess - localized collection of pus.
absorption - process of nutrient molecules passing through wall of intestine into blood or lymph system.
accessory spleen - results from the failure of fusion of separate splenic masses forming on the dorsal mesogastrium; most commonly found in the splenic hilum or along the splenic vessels or associated ligaments.
achondrogenesis - lethal autosomal-recessive short-limb dwarfism marked by long bone and trunk shortening, decreased echogenicity of the bones and spine, and "flipper-like" appendages.
achondroplasia - a defect in the development of cartilage at the epiphyseal centers of the long bones producing short, square bones.
acini cells - cells that perform exocrine function.
acinus (acini) - glandular (milk producing) component of the breast lobule (see terminal ductal-lobular unit, or TDLU). Each breast contains hundreds of lobules that each contain one or a few small glands (acini) along with the surrounding stromal connective tissue elements, the small ducts, a variable amount of fat, and Cooper's ligaments. The TDLU (a terminal duct and its corresponding acinus) is the site of origin of nearly all pathologic processes of the breast.
acoustic impedance - measure of a material's resistance to the propagation of sound; expressed as the product of acoustic velocity of the medium and the density of the medium ($Z = pc$).
acrania - condition associated with anencephaly in which there is complete or partial absence of the cranial bones.
acrocephalopolysyndactyly - congenital anomaly characterized by a peaked head and webbed fingers and toes.
Addison's disease - condition caused by hyposecretion of hormones from the adrenal cortex.
adenoma - tumor of the glandular tissue.
adenomatous hyperplasia - see multinodular hyperplasia.
adenomyomatosis - small polypoid projections.
adenomyosis - benign invasive growth of the endometrium that may cause heavy, painful menstrual bleeding.
adenopathy - enlargement of the lymph nodes.
adenosis - disease of the glands. In the breast, overgrowth of the stromal and epithelial elements of the small glands (acini) within the breast lobule. Adenosis is one component of fibrocystic condition, recognized by characteristic histopathologic changes in a breast biopsy specimen. Adenosis can exist by itself or in conjunction with other manifestations of fibrocystic condition, such as fibrosis (e.g., sclerosing adenosis combines adenosis with surrounding fibrosis) and is often mistaken for possible breast cancer.
adrenal hemorrhage - hemorrhage that occurs when the fetus is stressed during a difficult delivery or a hypoxic insult.
afferent arteriole - arteriole that carries blood into the glomerulus of the nephron.
alimentary canal - also known as the gastrointestinal tract; includes the mouth, pharynx, esophagus, stomach, duodenum, and small and large intestine.
allantoic duct - elongated duct that contributes to the development of the umbilical cord and placenta during the first trimester.
alobar holoprosencephaly - most severe form of holoprosencephaly characterized by a single common ventricle and malformed brain; orbital anomalies range from fused orbits to hypotelorism, with frequent nasal anomalies and clefting of the lip and palate.
alpha-fetoprotein (AFP) - protein manufactured by the fetus, which can be studied in amniotic fluid and maternal serum. Elevations of alpha-fetoprotein may indicate fetal anomalies (neural tube, abdominal wall, gastrointestinal), multiple gestations, or incorrect patient dates. Decreased levels may be associated with chromosomal abnormalities.
amaurosis fugax - transient partial or complete loss of vision in one eye.
American College of Radiology (ACR) - a national professional organization of physicians who specialize in radiology. Agency that first began voluntary accreditation of facilities performing screening mammography and that created the BI-RADS system of reporting and classifying mammograms that were later made mandatory by federal legislation (Mammography Quality Standards Act of 1994).
amniocentesis - aspiration of a sample of amniotic fluid through the mother's abdomen for diagnosis of fetal maturity and/or disease by assay of the constituents of the fluid.
amnion - smooth membrane enclosing the fetus and amniotic fluid; it is loosely fused with the outer chorionic membrane.
amniotic band syndrome - rupture of the amnion that leads to entrapment or entanglement of the fetal parts by the "sticky" chorion.

amniotic bands - multiple fibrous strands of amnion that develop in utero that may entangle fetal parts to cause amputations or malformations of the fetus.
amniotic cavity - cavity in which the fetus exists that forms early in gestation and surrounds the embryo; amniotic fluid fills the cavity to protect the embryo and fetus.
amniotic fluid - produced by the umbilical cord and membranes, the fetal lung, skin, and kidney.
amniotic fluid index (AFI) - sum of the four quadrants of amniotic fluid. The uterus is divided into four quadrants; each "quadrant" is evaluated with the transducer perpendicular to the table in the deepest vertical pocket without fetal parts; the four quadrants are added together to determine the amniotic fluid index.
amplitude - strength of the ultrasound wave measured in decibels.
ampulla of Vater - small opening in the duodenum in which the pancreatic and common bile duct enter to release secretions.
amylase - enzyme secreted by the pancreas to aid in the digestion of carbohydrates.
amyloidosis - metabolic disorder marked by amyloid deposits in organs and tissue.
anaplastic carcinoma - rare, undifferentiated carcinoma occurring in middle age.
androgen - substance that stimulates the development of male characteristics, such as the hormones testosterone and androsterone.
anechoic - without echoes; simple cyst on ultrasound should be anechoic.
anembryonic pregnancy (blighted ovum) - ovum without an embryo.
anencephaly - neural tube defect characterized by the lack of development of the cerebral and cerebellar hemispheres and cranial vault; this abnormality is incompatible with life.
angle of incidence - angle at which the ultrasound beams strikes the interface between two types of tissue.
angle of reflection - the amplitude of the reflected wave depends on the difference between the acoustic impedances of the two materials forming the interface.
anomaly - an abnormality or congenital malformation.
anophthalmia - absent eyes.
anophthalmos - absence of one (cyclops) or both eyes.
anorectal atresia - complex disorder of the bowel and genitourinary tract.
anterior cerebral artery (ACA) - smaller of the two terminal branches of the internal carotid artery.
anterior communicating artery (AcoA) - a short vessel that connects the anterior cerebral arteries at the interhemispheric fissure.
anterior pararenal space - space located between the anterior surface of the renal fascia and the posterior area of the peritoneum.
anterior tibial artery - artery that begins at the popliteal artery and travels down the lateral calf in the anterior compartment to the level of the ankle.
anterior tibial veins - veins that drain blood from the dorsum of the foot and anterior compartment of the calf.
anteverted - position of the uterus when the fundus is tipped slightly forward.
antiradial - plane of imaging on ultrasound of the breast that is perpendicular to the radial plane of imaging. The radial plane of imaging uses the nipple as the center point of an imaginary clock face imposed on the breast, such that the radial 12 o'clock plane is a line extending upward toward the top of the breast. Similarly, the radial 9 o'clock plane extends straight out to the right aspect of the breast, and so on. Three-dimensional measurements of a breast mass can be recorded using sagittal transverse or radial/antiradial planes.
aorta - largest arterial structure in the body; arises from the left ventricle of the heart to supply blood to the head, upper and lower extremities, and abdominopelvic cavity by descending into the abdominal cavity to branch into iliac vessels at the level of the umbilicus.
apex - inferior region of the prostate.
apex - the ventricles of the heart come to a point called the *apex;* normally the apex is directed toward the left hip.
aphasia - inability to communicate by speech or writing.
apical - position of the transducer located over cardiac apex (at the point of maximal impulse).
apocrine metaplasia - in the breast, an increase in the number and activity of the lining cells of the breast acini (glands). These lining cells normally secrete only a small amount of fluid in the nonlactating breast. Fluid production can often increase with apocrine metaplasia, which is one of the conditions thought to be responsible for the formation of benign fluid-filled breast cysts.
appendicitis - inflammation of the appendix.
appendicolith - echogenic structure within the appendix.
aqueductal stenosis - blockage of the duct connecting the third and fourth ventricles.
arcuate arteries - arteries that lie at the bases of the medullary pyramids and appear as echogenic structures.
arcuate vessels - small vessels found along the periphery of the uterus.
arcuate arteries - small vessels found at the base of the renal pyramids.
areola - the pigmented skin surrounding the breast nipple.
Arnold-Chiari malformation - defect in which the cerebellum and brainstem are pulled toward the spinal cord (banana sign); frontal bossing, or "lemon head," is also evident on ultrasound.
arteries - vascular structures that carry blood away from the heart.
arteriosclerosis - thickening and hardening of arterial walls.
arteriovenous fistula - communication between an artery and vein.
ascites - accumulation of serous fluid in the peritoneal cavity.
asphyxiating thoracic dystrophy - significantly narrow diameter of the chest in a fetus.

asplenia - no development of splenic tissue.
asymptomatic - without symptoms.
ataxia - impaired ability to coordinate movement, especially disturbances of gait.
atrial fibrillation - condition in which the atria beat more than 400 beats per minute and the ventricular rate is 120 to 200 beats per minute.
atrial septal defect - communication between the right and left atrium that persists after birth.
atrioventricular valve - valve located between the atria and ventricle.
atrioventricular block - block of transmission of the electrical impulse from the atria to the ventricles (may be 2:1 or 3:1 block).
atrioventricular node - area of specialized cardiac muscle that receives the cardiac impulse from the sinoatrial node and conducts it to the atrioventricular bundles.
atrioventricular septal defect - defect that occurs when the endocardial cushion fails to fuse in the center of the heart.
atrium (trigone) of the lateral ventricles - the ventricle is measured at this site (junction of the anterior, occipital, and temporal horn) on the axial view.
attenuation - reduction in the amplitude and intensity of a sound wave as it propagates through a medium; attenuation of ultrasound waves in tissue is caused by absorption and by scattering and reflection.
atypical hyperplasia - abnormal proliferation of cells.
atypical lobular hyperplasia (ALH) - see atypical hyperplasia and lobular neoplasia.
augmentation - increase in blood flow velocity with distal limb compression or with the release of proximal limb compression.
autoimmune hemolytic anemia - anemia caused by antibodies produced by the patient's own immune system.
axial plane - placement of the transducer above the ear (above the canthomeatal line).
axilla - armpit.
axillary artery - continuation of the subclavian artery.
axillary vein - vein that begins where the basilic vein joins the brachial vein in the upper arm and terminates beneath the clavicle at the outer border of the first rib.
banana sign - the shape of the cerebellum when a spinal defect is present (cerebellum is pulled downward into the foramen magnum).
bare area - area superior to the liver that is not covered by peritoneum so inferior vena cava may enter the chest.
base - superior region of the prostate.
basilar artery - artery formed by the union of the two vertebral arteries.
basilic vein - vein that originates on the small finger side of the dorsum of the hand.
battledore placenta - marginal or eccentric insertion of the umbilical cord into the placenta.
Beckwith-Wiedemann syndrome - group of disorders having in common the coexistence of an omphalocele, macroglossia, and visceromegaly.
beneficence - quality or state of being beneficent (doing good, such as performing acts of kindness).
benign prostatic hypertrophy - enlargement of the glandular component of the prostate.
bicornuate uterus - duplication of the uterus (two horns and one vagina).
bicuspid aortic valve - two leaflets instead of the normal three leaflets with asymmetric cusps.
bilirubin - yellow pigment in bile formed by the breakdown of red blood cells.
biophysical profile (BPP) - assessment of fetus to determine fetal well-being; includes evaluation of cardiac Non-Stress Test, fetal breathing movement, gross fetal body movements, fetal tone, and amniotic fluid volume.
biparietal diameter (BPD) - measurement of the fetal head at the level of the thalamus and cavum septum pellucidum.
blood urea nitrogen (BUN) - laboratory measurement of the amount of nitrogenous waste, along with creatinine; waste products accumulate in the blood when kidneys malfunction.
body of the pancreas - located in the midepigastrium anterior to the superior mesenteric artery and vein, aorta, and inferior vena cava.
bowel herniation - extrusion of the bowel outside the abdominal cavity; during the first trimester normally occurs between 8 and 12 weeks.
Bowman's capsule - the cup-shaped end of a renal tubule enclosing a glomerulus; site of filtration of the kidney; contains water, salts, glucose, urea, and amino acids.
brachial artery - continuation of the axillary artery.
brachycephaly - fetal head is elongated in the transverse diameter and shortened in the anteroposterior diameter.
brain stem - comprises the midbrain, pons, and medulla oblongata.
branchial cleft cyst - remnant of embryonic development that appears as a cyst in the neck.
Braxton-Hicks contractions - spontaneous painless uterine contractions described originally as a sign of pregnancy; they occur from the first trimester to the end of pregnancy.
breast - differentiated apocrine sweat gland with a functional purpose of secreting milk during lactation.
breast cancer (breast carcinoma) - breast cancer involves two main types of cells: ductal and lobular. Ductal cancer, accounting for approximately 85% of the breast cancer cases, also includes many subtypes, such as medullary, mucinous, tubular, apocrine, or papillary types. In addition, very early or preinvasive breast cancer is generally ductal in type. This preinvasive breast cancer is also called *in situ, noninvasive,* or *intraductal* breast cancer. Another commonly used term for this early type of cancer is *ductal carcinoma in situ,* or *DCIS.*
breast cancer screening - screening for breast cancer involves annual screening mammography (starting at age 40), monthly breast self-examination (BSE), and self breast examination (SBE).
Breast Imaging Reporting and Data System (BI-RADS) - trademark system created by the American College of Radiology (ACR) to standardize mammographic reporting

terminology, categorize breast abnormalities according to the level of suspicion for malignancy, and facilitate outcome monitoring. This system of classification of breast imaging results has now been made a mandatory part of mammogram reports by federal legislation (Mammography Quality Standards Act of 1994).
breast self-examination (BSE) - procedure in which a woman examines her breasts for evidence of change that could indicate malignancy; part of breast cancer screening. Every woman is encouraged to perform breast self-examination monthly starting at age 20. BSE is usually best performed at the end of menses.
breech - indicates the fetal head is toward the fundus of the uterus.
bronchogenic cyst - most common lung cyst detected prenatally.
bronchopulmonary sequestration - extra pulmonary tissue is present within the pleural lung sac (intralobar) or connected to the inferior border of the lung within its own pleural sac (extralobar).
bruit - noise caused by tissue vibration produced by turbulence.
Budd-Chiari syndrome - thrombosis of the hepatic veins.
bulbus cordis - primitive chamber that forms the right ventricle.
bulk modulus - amount of pressure required to compress a small volume of material a small amount.
bull's eye (target) lesion - hypoechoic mass with echogenic central core (abscess, metastases).
calcitonin - a thyroid hormone that is important for maintaining a dense, strong bone matrix and regulating the blood calcium level.
caliectasis - rounded calyces with renal pelvis dilation measuring greater than 10 mm in the anteroposterior direction.
calyx - part of the collecting system adjacent to the pyramid that collects urine and is connected to the major calyx.
capillaries - minute vessels that connect the arterial and venous systems.
cardiac orifice - entrance of the esophagus into the stomach occurs at the cardiac orifice.
cardiomyopathy - disease of the myocardial muscle layer of the heart that causes the heart to dilate secondary to regurgitation and also affects cardiac function.
cardiosplenic syndromes - sporadic disorders characterized by a symmetric development of normally asymmetric organs or organ systems.
caudal pancreatic artery - branch of the splenic artery that supplies the tail of the pancreas.
caudal regression syndrome - lack of development of the lower limbs (may occur in the fetus of a diabetic mother).
caudate lobe - small lobe of the liver situated on the posterosuperior surface of the left lobe; the ligamentum venosum is the anterior border.
caudate nucleus - area of the brain that forms the lateral borders of the anterior horns, anterior to the thalamus.
cavernous transformation of the portal vein - periportal collateral channels in patients with chronic portal vein obstruction.
cavum septum pellucidum - prominent structure best seen in the midline filled with cerebrospinal fluid in the premature infant.
cebocephaly - form of holoprosencephaly characterized by a common ventricle, hypotelorism, and a nose with a single nostril.
celiac axis - first major anterior artery to arise from the abdominal aorta inferior to the diaphragm; it branches into the hepatic, splenic, and left gastric arteries.
central zone - portion of the prostate that surrounds the urethra; site of benign prostatic hypertrophy.
cephalic vein - vein that begins on the thumb side of the dorsum of the hand.
cephalocele - protrusion of the brain from the cranial cavity.
cerebellum - area of the brain that lies posterior to the brainstem below the tentorium.
cerebral vasospasm - vasoconstriction of the arteries.
cerebrum - two equal hemispheres; largest part of the brain.
cervical polyp - hyperplastic protrusion of the epithelium of the cervix; may be broad based or pedunculated.
cervical stenosis - acquired condition with obstruction of the cervical canal.
cervix - inferior segment of the uterus; more that 3.5 cm long during normal pregnancy, decreases in length during labor.
cholangitis - inflammation of the bile duct.
cholecystectomy - removal of the gallbladder.
cholecystitis - acute or chronic inflammation of the gallbladder.
cholecystokinin - hormone secreted into the blood by the mucosa of the upper small intestine; stimulates contraction of the gallbladder and pancreatic secretion of enzymes.
choledochal cyst - cystic growth of the common bile duct that may cause obstruction.
choledocholithiasis - stones in the bile duct.
cholelithiasis - gallstones.
cholesterosis - variant of adenomyomatosis; cholesterol polyps.
choriocarcinoma - malignant invasive form of gestational trophoblastic disease.
chorion - cellular, outermost extraembryonic membrane, composed of trophoblast lined with mesoderm; it develops villi about 2 weeks after fertilization, is vascularized by allantoic vessels a week later, gives rise to the placenta, and persists until birth.
chorion frondosum - the portion of the chorion that develops into the fetal portion of the placenta.
chorionic cavity - surrounds the amniotic cavity; the yolk sac is between the chorion and amnion.
chorionic plate - that part of the chorionic membrane that covers the placenta.

chorionic villi - vascular projections from the chorion.
choroid plexus - echogenic cluster of cells important in the production of cerebrospinal fluid that lie along the atrium of the lateral ventricles.
chorion frondosum - portion of the chorion that develops into the fetal portion of the placenta.
circle of Willis - vascular network at the base of the brain.
circummarginate placenta - condition in which the chorionic plate of the placenta is smaller than the basal plate, with a flat interface between the fetal membranes and the placenta.
circumvallate placenta - condition in which the chorionic plate of the placenta is smaller than the basal plate; the margin is raised with a rolled edge.
cistern - reservoir for cerebrospinal fluid.
claudication - walking-induced muscular discomfort of the calf, thigh, hip, or buttock.
clinical breast examination (CBE) - examination of the breast by a health care provider; part of breast cancer screening. Every woman is encouraged to have a thorough CBE in conjunction with her routine health care assessment. Between ages 20 and 40, CBE is advised every 3 years. From age 40 on, CBE should be performed by the woman's regular health care provider annually.
cloacal exstrophy - defect in the lower abdominal wall and anterior wall of the urinary bladder.
C-loop of the duodenum - forms the lateral border of the head of the pancreas.
coarctation of the aorta - discrete or long segment narrowing in the aortic arch, usually at the level of the left subclavian artery near the insertion of the ductus arteriosus.
coccygeus muscles - muscles that form the floor of the pelvis.
collateral circulation - circulation that develops when normal venous channels become obstructed.
collateral vessels - ancillary vessels that develop when portal hypertension occurs.
color flow mapping (CFM) - ability to display blood flow in multiple colors depending on the velocity, direction of flow, and extent of turbulence.
column of Bertin - bands of cortical tissue that separate the renal pyramids; a prominent column of Bertin may mimic a renal mass on sonography.
common bile duct - duct that extends from the point where the common hepatic duct meets the cystic duct; drains into the duodenum after it joins with the main pancreatic duct.
common carotid artery (CCA) - artery that rises from the aortic arch to supply blood to the head and neck.
common duct - refers to common bile or hepatic ducts when cystic duct is not seen.
common femoral arteries - arteries originating from the iliac arteries and seen in the inguinal region into the upper thigh.
common femoral vein - vein formed by the confluence of the profunda femoris and the superficial femoral vein; also receives the greater saphenous vein.
common hepatic artery - artery arising from the celiac trunk to supply the liver.
common hepatic duct - bile duct system that drains the liver into the common bile duct.
common iliac arteries - a division of the abdominal aorta at the level of the umbilicus to supply blood to the lower extremities.
common iliac vein - vein formed by the confluence of the internal and external iliac veins.
complete abortion - complete removal of all products of conception, including the placenta.
complete atrioventricular septal defect - large ventricular and atrial septal defect with a single, undivided, free-floating leaflet that stretches between both ventricles.
complete mole - trophoblastic parts without a fetus; forms when the sperm fertilizes an empty egg.
confidentiality - the nondisclosure of certain information except to another authorized person.
confluence of the splenic and portal veins - junction of the splenic and portal veins that occurs in the midabdomen and serves as the posterior border of the pancreas.
congenital bronchial atresia - pulmonary anomaly that results from the focal obliteration of a segment of the bronchial lumen.
congenital mesoblastic nephroma - most common benign renal tumor of the neonate and infant.
conjoined twins - monozygotic twins physically joined by varying degrees; condition that occurs when the division of the egg occurs after 13 days.
continuous wave probe - probe with which sound is continuously emitted from one transducer and continuously received by a second transducer.
Cooper's ligaments - connective tissue septae that connect perpendicularly to the breast lobules and extend out to the skin; are considered to be the fibrous "skeleton" supporting the breast glandular tissue.
coronal - horizontal plane through the longitudinal axis of the body to image structures from anterior to posterior.
coronal plane - transducer is perpendicular to the anterior fontanelle in the coronal axis of the head.
corpus callosum - prominent group of nerve fibers that connect the right and left sides of the brain; found superior to the third ventricle.
corpus luteum - yellow body formed from the Graafian follicle after ovulation that produces estrogen and progesterone.
corpus luteum cyst - small endocrine structure that develops within a ruptured ovarian follicle and secretes progesterone and estrogen. It may persist until the 20th to 24th week of pregnancy.
cortex - outer parenchyma of an organ. Liver cortex is thin in the neonate, with echogenicity similar or slightly greater than that of the normal liver parenchyma.
cran- - helmet; *cranial:* pertaining to the portion of the skull that surrounds the brain.
craniosynostoses - premature closure of the cranial sutures.

creatinine (Cr) - a product of metabolism; laboratory test measures the ability of the kidney to get rid of waste; waste products accumulate in the blood when the kidneys are malfunctioning.
critical aortic stenosis - abnormal thickening and closure of the aortic leaflets in the second or third trimester causes the left ventricle to "balloon" from increased pressure.
Crohn's disease - inflammation of the bowel, accompanied by abscess and bowel wall thickening.
crossed renal ectopia - condition that occurs when the kidney is located on the opposite side of its ureteral orifice.
crown-rump length (CRL) - most accurate measurement for determining gestational age in the first trimester.
crus of the diaphragm - muscular structure in the upper abdomen at the level of the celiac axis.
cryptorchidism - failure of the testes to descend into the scrotum; testicles remain within the abdomen or groin and fail to descend into the scrotal sac.
crystal - special material in the ultrasound transducer that has the ability to convert electrical impulses into sound waves.
culling - process by which the spleen removes nuclei from the red blood cells as they pass through.
Cushing's syndrome - condition caused by hypersecretion of hormones from the adrenal cortex.
cycle - measurement of the vibration of the crystal in frequency per second.
cyclopia - severe form of holoprosencephaly characterized by a common ventricle, fusion of the orbits with one or two eyes present, and a proboscis (maldeveloped cylindrical nose).
cyst - fluid-filled sac of variable size.
cyst aspiration - common breast procedure (both diagnostic and interventional) that involves placing a needle through the skin of the breast into a cystic mass and pulling fluid out of the cystic mass through the needle. In the case of a palpable cyst, this procedure can be performed in a physician's office. In the case of a small, complex, or nonpalpable cyst, image guidance (usually with ultrasound) can be used to facilitate the aspiration.
cystadenocarcinoma - a malignant tumor that forms cysts.
cystadenoma - benign adenoma containing cysts.
cystic adenomatoid malformation - abnormality in the formation of the bronchial tree with secondary overgrowth of mesenchymal tissue from arrested bronchial development.
cystic duct - duct that connects the gallbladder to the common hepatic duct.
cystic fibrosis - inherited disorder of the exocrine glands; symptoms include mucous build up within the lungs and other areas of the body.
cystic hygroma - increase in size of the jugular lymphatic sacs because of abnormal development.
cystic hygroma - dilation of jugular lymph sacs (may occur in axilla or groin) because of improper drainage of the lymphatic system into the venous system. Large, septated hygromas are frequently associated with Turner's syndrome, congestive heart failure, and death of the fetus in utero; isolated hygromas may occur as solitary lesions at birth.
cystic medial necrosis - weakening of the arterial wall.
Dandy-Walker syndrome - displacement of the fourth ventricle, often accompanied by hydrocephalus.
decibel (dB) - unit used to quantitatively express the ratio of two amplitudes or intensities; decibels are not absolute units, but express one sound level or intensity in terms of another or in terms of a reference (e.g., the amplitude 10 cm from the transducer is 10 dB lower than the amplitude 5 cm from the transducer).
decidua basalis - the part of the decidua that unites with the chorion to form the placenta.
decidua capsularis - the part of the decidua that surrounds the chorionic sac.
deep femoral vein - vein that travels with the profunda femoris artery to unite with the superficial femoral vein to form the common femoral vein.
deep venous thrombosis (DVT) - blockage of the venous circulation (upper or lower) by a blood clot.
DeQuervain's thyroiditis - inflammatory condition of the thyroid, sometimes occurring after a viral respiratory infection.
dermoid - benign tumor comprised of hair, muscle, teeth, and fat.
diagnostic breast imaging - also called "consultative," "workup," or "problem-solving" mammography or breast imaging. This type of breast imaging examination is more intensive than routine screening mammography. Diagnostic breast imaging is usually directed toward a specific clinical symptom of possible breast cancer, or an abnormal finding on a screening mammogram. The goal of diagnostic breast imaging is to categorize the abnormality according to the level of suspicion for cancer (see BI-RADS).
diamniotic - multiple pregnancy with two amniotic sacs.
diaphragmatic hernia - opening in the pleuroperitoneal membrane that develops in the first trimester.
diastole - part of the cardiac cycle in which the ventricles are filling with blood; the tricuspid and mitral valves are open during this time.
dichorionic - multiple pregnancy with two chorionic sacs.
diffuse hepatocellular disease - disease that affects hepatocytes and interferes with liver function.
diffuse nontoxic goiter - condition that occurs as a compensatory enlargement of the thyroid gland resulting from thyroid hormone deficiency; also known as colloid goiter.
diplopia - double vision.
dissecting aneurysm - tear in the intima and/or media of the abdominal aorta.
dizygotic - twins that arise from two separately fertilized ova.
dolichocephaly - fetal head is shortened in the transverse plane and elongated in the anteroposterior plane.
Doppler effect - change in the frequency of a sound wave when either the source or the listener are moving relative to one another; the difference between the received echo frequency and the frequency of the transmitted beam is

the Doppler shift; pulsed wave Doppler is used in most fetal examinations; this means the transducer has the ability to send and receive Doppler signals.
Doppler shift in frequency - change in frequency as red blood cells move from a lower-frequency sound source at rest toward a higher-frequency sound source; change in frequency.
Doppler sample volume - the sonographer selects the exact site to record Doppler signals and sets the sample volume (gate) at this site.
dors- - back; *dorsal:* position toward the back of the body.
dorsal pancreatic artery - branch of the splenic artery that supplies the body of the pancreas.
dorsalis pedis artery - continuation of the anterior tibial artery on the top of the foot.
double decidual sac sign - interface between the decidua capsularis and the echogenic, highly vascular endometrium.
double outlet right ventricle - ventricular septal defect with the overriding aorta directed more to the right ventricular outflow tract than the left (more than 50% override toward the right).
dromedary hump - normal variant that occurs on the left kidney as a bulge of the lateral border.
duct of Santorini - small accessory duct of the pancreas found in the head of the gland.
duct of Wirsung - largest duct of the pancreas that drains the tail, body, and head of the gland; it joins the common bile duct to enter the duodenum through the ampulla of Vater.
ductus arteriosus - communication between the pulmonary artery and descending aorta that closes after birth.
ductus venosus - fetal vein that connects the umbilical vein to the inferior vena cava and runs at an oblique axis through the liver.
duodenal atresia - complete blockage at the pyloric sphincter.
duodenal bulb - first part of the duodenum.
duodenal stenosis - narrowing of the pyloric sphincter.
dynamic range - ratio of the largest to smallest signals that an instrument or component of an instrument can respond to without distortion.
dysarthria - difficulty with speech because of impairment of the tongue or muscles essential to speech.
dysphagia - inability or difficulty in swallowing.
Ebstein's anomaly - abnormal apical displacement of the septal leaflet of the tricuspid valve.
eclampsia - coma and seizures in the second- and third-trimester patient secondary to pregnancy-induced hypertension.
ectopia cordis - condition in which the ventral wall fails to close and the heart develops outside the thoracic cavity.
ectopic kidney - kidney located outside of the normal position, most often in the pelvic cavity.
ectopic pregnancy - pregnancy occurring outside the uterine cavity.
ectopic ureterocele - ectopic insertion and cystic dilation of distal ureter of duplicated renal collecting system; occurs more commonly in females (on left side).
efferent arteriole - arteriole that supplies the peritubular capillaries of the kidneys, which also supply the convoluted tubules.
ejaculatory ducts - ducts that connect the seminal vesicle and the vas deferens to the urethra at the verumontanum.
electrocardiography - study of the heart's electrical activity.
embryo - conceptus to the end of the ninth week of gestation.
embryologic age (conceptual age) - age since the date of conception.
embryonic period - time between 6 and 12 weeks.
encephalocele - protrusion of the brain through a cranial fissure.
endocardium - inner layer of the heart wall.
endocrine - process of cells that secrete into the blood or lymph circulation that has a specific effect on tissues in another part of the body.
endometrial carcinoma - condition that presents with abnormal thickening of the endometrial cavity; usually presents with irregular bleeding in perimenopausal and postmenopausal women.
endometrial hyperplasia - condition that results from estrogen stimulation to the endometrium without the influence of progestin; frequent cause of bleeding (especially in postmenopausal women).
endometrial polyp - pedunculated or sessile well-defined mass attached to the endometrial cavity.
endometrioma - localized tumor of endometriosis most frequently found in the ovary, cul-de-sac, rectovaginal septum, and peritoneal surface of the posterior wall of the uterus.
endometriosis - condition that occurs when functioning endometrial tissue invades sites outside the uterus.
endometritis - infection within the endometrium of the uterus.
endometrium - inner lining of the uterine cavity that appears echogenic to hypoechoic on ultrasound, depending on the menstrual cycle.
epicardium - outer layer of the heart wall.
epididymis - anatomic structure that lies posterior and lateral to the testes in which the spermatozoa accumulate.
epididymitis - infection and inflammation of the epididymis.
epigastrium - area between the right and left hypochondrium that contains part of the liver, duodenum, and pancreas.
epignathus - teratoma located in the oropharynx.
epiploic foramen - opening to the lesser sac.
epitheliosis - overgrowth of cells lining the small ducts of the terminal ductal-lobular unit; one of the common components of most varieties of fibrocystic condition.
erythroblastosis fetalis - hemolytic disease marked by anemia, enlargement of liver and spleen, and hydrops fetalis.

erythrocyte - red blood cell.
esophageal atresia - congenital hypoplasia of the esophagus; usually associated with a tracheoesophageal fistula.
esophageal stenosis - narrowing of the esophagus, usually in the distal third segment.
estimated fetal weight (EFW) - estimation based on incorporation of all fetal growth parameters (biparietal diameter, head circumference, abdominal circumference, femur and humeral length).
estrogen - the female hormone produced by the ovary.
ethics - discipline dealing with what is good and bad and with moral duty and obligation.
euthyroid - refers to a normal functioning thyroid gland.
exencephaly - abnormal condition in which the brain is located outside the cranium.
exocrine - process of secreting outwardly through a duct to the surface of an organ or tissue or into a vessel.
exophthalmia - abnormal protrusion of the eyeball.
exstrophy of the bladder - protrusion of the posterior wall of the urinary bladder, which contains the trigone of the bladder and the ureteric orifices.
external carotid artery (ECA) - smaller of the two terminal branches of the common carotid artery.
external iliac vein - vein that drains the pelvis along with the internal iliac vein.
extrahepatic - outside the liver.
falciform ligament - ligament that attaches the liver to the anterior abdominal wall and undersurface of the diaphragm.
false (major) pelvis - portion of the pelvis found above the brim of the pelvis; that portion of the abdominal cavity cradled by the iliac fossae.
false knots of the umbilical cord - condition that occurs when blood vessels are longer than the cord; they fold on themselves and produce nodulations on the surface of the cord.
false pelvis - portion of the pelvic cavity that is above the pelvic brim, bounded posteriorly by the lumbar vertebrae, laterally by the iliac fossae and iliacus muscles, and anteriorly by the lower anterior abdominal wall.
falx cerebri (interhemispheric fissure) - echogenic fibrous structure separating the cerebral hemispheres
febrile - has a fever.
fecalith - calculus that may form around fecal material associated with appendicitis.
femoral veins - upper part of the venous drainage system of the lower extremity that empties into the inferior vena cava at the level of the diaphragm.
femur length (FL) - measurement from the femoral head to the distal end of the femur.
fetal cystic hygroma - malformation of the lymphatic system that leads to single or multiloculated lymph-filled cavities around the neck.
fetal hydronephrosis - dilated renal pelvis.
fetus papyraceous - fetal death that occurs after the fetus has reached a certain growth that is too large to resorb into the uterus.
fever - elevation of normal body temperature (above 98.6° F).
fibroadenoma - most common benign solid tumor of the breast, consisting predominantly of fibrous and epithelial (adenomatous) tissue elements. These masses tend to develop in young women (even teenagers), tend to run in families, and can be multiple. The usual appearance of a fibroadenoma is a benign-appearing mammographic mass (round, oval, or gently lobular and well circumscribed) with a correlating sonographic mass that is well defined and demonstrates homogeneous echogenicity.
fibrocystic condition (FCC) - also called *fibrocystic change* or *fibrocystic breast,* this condition represents many different tissue processes within the breast that are all basically normal processes that over time can get exaggerated to the point of causing symptoms or mammographic changes that raise concern for breast cancer. The main tissue processes are adenosis, epitheliosis, and fibrosis. These processes can cause symptoms such as breast lumps and pain. These processes can cause mammographic changes such as cysts, microcalcifications, distortion, and masslike densities. Pathologic changes of fibrocystic condition include apocrine metaplasia, microcystic adenosis, blunt ductal adenosis, epithelial ductal hyperplasia, lobular hyperplasia, and sclerosing adenosis. Only a few fibrocystic tissue processes are associated with an increased risk of subsequent development of breast cancer. These include atypical ductal hyperplasia and lobular neoplasia (formerly called lobular carcinoma in situ).
focal zone - the region over which the effective width of the sound beam is within some measure of its width at the focal distance.
follicle-stimulating hormone (FSH) - hormone produced in the pituitary that influences the ovaries.
follicular carcinoma - occurs as a solitary mass within the thyroid gland.
follicular cyst - benign cyst within the ovary that may occur and disappear on a cyclic basis.
fontanelle - soft space between the bones; the space is usually large enough to accommodate the ultrasound transducer until the age of 12 months.
foramen of Bochdalek - type of diaphragmatic defect that occurs posterior and lateral in the diaphragm; usually found in the left side.
foramen of Morgagni - diaphragmatic hernia that occurs anterior and medial in the diaphragm and may communicate with the pericardial sac.
foramen ovale - opening between the free edge of the septum secundum and the dorsal wall of the atrium; also termed *fossa ovale.*
four chamber - view that transects the heart approximately parallel with dorsal and ventral surfaces of body.
frame rate - rate at which images are updated on the display; dependent on frequency of the transducer and depth selection.
frequency - number of cycles per second that a periodic event or function undergoes; number of cycles completed

per unit of time; the frequency of a sound wave is determined by the number of oscillations per second of the vibrating source.
frontal bossing - slight indentation of the frontal bones of the skull; also known as "lemon head."
functional cyst - cyst resulting from the normal function of the ovary.
fusiform dilation - enlargement with tapering at both ends.
gain - measure of the strength of the ultrasound signal; can be expressed as a simple ratio or in decibels; overall gain amplifies all signals by a constant factor regardless of the depth.
gallbladder - storage pouch for bile.
Gartner's duct cyst - small cyst within the vagina.
gastrin - endocrine hormone released from the stomach (stimulates secretion of gastric acid).
gastroduodenal artery - branch of the common hepatic artery that supplies the stomach and duodenum.
gastrophrenic ligament - ligament that helps support the greater curvature of the stomach.
gastroschisis - congenital fissure that remains open in the wall of the abdomen just to the right of the umbilical cord; bowel and other organs may protrude outside the abdomen from this opening.
gastroschisis - opening in the layers of the abdominal wall with evisceration of the bowel (and occasionally the stomach and genitourinary organs).
gastrosplenic ligament - one of the ligaments between the stomach and spleen that helps hold the spleen in place.
gastrocnemius veins - paired veins that lie in the medial and lateral gastrocnemius muscles and terminate into the popliteal vein.
Gaucher's disease - one of the storage diseases in which fat and proteins are deposited abnormally in the body.
germinal matrix - fragile periventricular tissue (includes the caudate nucleus) that easily bleeds in the premature infant.
Gerota's fascia - another term for the renal fascia; the kidney is covered by the renal capsule, perirenal fat, Gerota's fascia, and pararenal fat.
gestational age - age of embryo since the date of conception.
gestational sac - structure that is normally within the uterus that contains the developing embryo.
gestational sac diameter - measurement used in the first trimester to estimate appropriate gestational age with menstrual dates.
gestational trophoblastic disease - trophoblastic tissue that has overtaken the pregnancy and has propagated throughout the uterine cavity; these tumors arise from the placental chorionic villi.
glomerulus - part of the filtration process in the kidney.
glucagon - hormone that stimulates the liver to convert glycogen to glucose; produced by alpha cells.
goiter - any enlargement of the thyroid, focal or diffuse, regardless of cause.
Graves' disease - syndrome characterized by a diffuse toxic goiter, ophthalmopathy, and cutaneous manifestations.
gravidity - total number of pregnancies.
gray scale - B-mode scanning technique that permits the brightness of the B-mode dots to be displayed in various shades of gray to represent different echo amplitudes.
greater omentum - double fold of the peritoneum attached to the duodenum, stomach, and large intestine; helps support the greater curve of the stomach; known as the "fatty apron."
greater sac - primary compartment of the peritoneal cavity; extends across the anterior abdomen from the diaphragm to the pelvis.
greater saphenous vein - originates on the dorsum of the foot and ascends anterior to the medial malleolus and along the anteromedial side of the calf and thigh; joins the common femoral vein in the proximal thigh.
growth-adjusted sonar age (GASA) - method whereby the fetus is categorized into small, average, or large growth percentile.
gutters - most dependent areas in the flanks of the abdomen and pelvis where fluid collections may accumulate.
gynecomastia - hypertrophy of residual ductal elements that persist behind the nipple in the male, causing a palpable, tender lump. There is generally no lobular (glandular) tissue in the male. A breast mass resulting from gynecomastia must be distinguished from male breast cancer.
Hartmann's pouch - small part of the gallbladder that lies near the cystic duct where stones may collect.
Hashimoto's thyroiditis - chronic inflammation of the thyroid (goiter).
haustra - normal segmentation of the wall of the colon.
head of the pancreas - portion of the pancreas that lies in the C-loop of the duodenum; the gastroduodenal artery is the anterolateral border and the common bile duct is the posterolateral border.
Heister's valves - tiny valves found within the cystic duct.
hemangioma of the cord - vascular tumor within the umbilical cord.
hematocele - blood within the sac surrounding the testes.
hematometrocolpos - blood-filled vagina and uterus.
hematopoiesis - blood-cell production.
hemiparesis - unilateral partial or complete paralysis.
hemoglobin - oxygen-binding protein found in red blood cells.
hemolytic anemia - anemia resulting from hemolysis of red blood cells.
hemopoiesis - formation of blood.
hemorrhage - collection of blood
hemosiderin - pigment released from hemoglobin process.
hepatic artery (HA) - common hepatic artery arises from the celiac trunk and courses to the right of the abdomen and branches into the gastroduodenal artery and proper HA.
hepatic flexure - point at which the ascending colon arises from the right lower quadrant to bend at this point to form the transverse colon.

hepatic veins - largest tributaries that drain the liver and empty into the inferior vena cava at the level of the diaphragm.
hepatocellular disease - disease of the liver cells or hepatocytes.
hepatofugal - flow away from the liver.
hepatopetal - flow toward the liver.
hermaphroditism - condition in which both ovarian and testicular tissues are present.
hertz (Hz) - unit for frequency, equal to 1 cycle per second.
heterotopic pregnancy - simultaneous intrauterine and extrauterine pregnancy.
heterozygous achondroplasia - short-limb dysplasia that manifests in the second trimester of pregnancy; conversion abnormality of cartilage to bone affecting the epiphyseal growth centers; extremities are markedly shortened at birth with a normal trunk and frequent enlargement of the head.
hilus - area of kidney where vessels, ureter, and lymphatics enter and exit.
Hirschsprung's disease - congenital megacolon.
holoprosencephaly - congenital defect caused by an extra chromosome which causes a deficiency in the forebrain.
homeo- - same.
homeostasis - maintenance of a stable internal environment.
homozygous achondroplasia - short-limb dwarfism affecting fetuses of achondroplastic parents.
horseshoe kidney - congenital malformation in which both kidneys are joined together, most commonly at the lower poles.
human chorionic gonadotropin (hCG) - hormone within the maternal urine and serum; hCG is elevated during pregnancy; laboratory test that indicates pregnancy when values are elevated.
humeral length - measurement from the humeral head to the distal end of the humerus.
hydatidiform mole - benign form of gestational trophoblastic disease in which there is partial or complete conversion of the chorionic villi into grapelike vesicles; villia are avascular and there is trophoblastic proliferation; condition may result in malignant trophoblastic disease.
hydranencephaly - congenital absence of the cerebral hemispheres because of an occlusion of the carotid arteries; midbrain structures are present, and fluid replaces cerebral tissue.
hydrocele - fluid within the sac surrounding the testes.
hydrocephalus - ventriculomegaly in the neonate; abnormal accumulation of cerebrospinal fluid within the cerebral ventricles, resulting in compression and frequently destruction of brain tissue.
hydrocolpos - fluid-filled vagina.
hydrometrocolpos - collection of fluid in the vagina and uterus.
hydronephrosis - dilation of the renal collecting system.
hydrops - massive enlargement of the gallbladder.
hydrops fetalis - fluid occurring in at least two areas in the fetus: pleural effusion, pericardial effusion, ascites, or skin edema.
hydrosalpinx - fluid within the fallopian tube.
hydroureters - dilated ureters.
hyperechoic - echo texture that is more echogenic than the surrounding tissue. Hyperechoic masses in the breast are nearly always benign.
hyperemesis gravidarum - excessive vomiting that leads to dehydration and electrolyte imbalance.
hyperglycemia - uncontrolled increase in glucose levels in the blood.
hyperlipidemia - congenital condition in which there are elevated fat levels that may cause pancreatitis.
hyperplasia - enlargement of the adrenal glands.
hypertelorism - abnormally wide-spaced orbits usually found in conjunction with congenital anomalies and mental retardation.
hypertension - elevation of maternal blood pressure that may put fetus at risk.
hyperthyroidism - overactive thyroid gland.
hypertrophic pyloric stenosis (HPS) - thickened muscle in the pylorus that prevents food from entering the duodenum; occurs more frequently in males.
hyperventilation - deficiency of carbon dioxide.
hypochondrium - area of the duodenum in the upper zone on both sides of the epigastric region beneath the cartilages of the lower ribs.
hypoechoic - echo texture that is less echogenic than the surrounding tissue. Most solid breast masses (including cancer) are hypoechoic.
hypoglycemia - deficiency of glucose in the blood.
hypophosphatasia - congenital condition characterized by decreased mineralization of the bones resulting in "ribbonlike" and bowed limbs, underossified cranium, and compression of the chest; early death often occurs.
hypoplastic left heart - underdevelopment of the mitral valve, left ventricle, and aorta.
hypoplastic right heart - underdevelopment of the tricuspid valve, right ventricle, and pulmonary artery.
hypospadias - abnormal congenital opening of the male urethra on the undersurface of the penis.
hypotelorism - abnormally closely spaced orbits; association with holoprosencephaly, chromosomal and central nervous system disorders, and cleft palate.
hypothyroidism - underactive thyroid gland.
hypoventilation - abnormal condition of the respiratory system of insufficient ventilation resulting in an excess of carbon dioxide.
ileus - dilated loops of bowel without peristalsis; associated with various abdominal problems, including pancreatitis, sickle cell crisis, and bowel obstruction.
iliac arteries - arteries that originate from the bifurcation of the aorta at the level of the umbilicus.
iliacus muscle - paired muscles that form the lateral wall of the pelvis.

incompetent cervix - cervix dilation that can result in the membranes bulging and rupturing so that fetus drops out; occurs silently in the second trimester.
incomplete abortion - retained products of conception.
incomplete atrioventricular septal defect - membranous septal defect, abnormal tricuspid valve, primum atrial septal defect, and cleft mitral valve.
infantile polycystic kidney disease - autosomal recessive disease that affects the fetal kidneys and liver; the kidneys are enlarged and echogenic on ultrasound.
inferior mesenteric artery (IMA) - artery that arises from the anterior aortic wall at the level of the third or fourth lumbar vertebra to supply the left transverse colon, descending colon, sigmoid colon, and part of the rectum.
inferior mesenteric vein - vein that drains the left third of the colon and upper colon and joins the splenic vein.
inferior vena cava - largest venous abdominal vessel, formed by the union of the common iliac veins; supplies the right atrium of the heart along the posterior lateral wall.
informed consent - consent to surgery by a patient or to participation in a medical procedure or experiment by a subject after achieving an understanding of what is involved.
infracristal septal defect - defects found below the crista supraventricularis ridge in the membranous or muscular area.
infiltrating (invasive) ductal carcinoma - cancer of the ductal epithelium; most common general category of breast cancer, accounting for approximately 85% of all breast cancers. This cancer usually arises in the terminal duct in the terminal ductal-lobular unit.
inguinal ligament - ligament between the anterior superior iliac spine and the pubic tubercle.
innominate artery - first branch artery from the aortic arch.
innominate veins - veins that follow these courses: on the right, courses vertically downwards to join the left innominate vein below the first rib to form the superior vena cava; on the left, courses from left chest beneath the sternum to join the right innominate vein; the left innominate vein is longer than the right.
insulin - hormone that allows circulating glucose to enter tissue cells; failure to produce insulin results in diabetes mellitus.
interface - surface forming the boundary between media having different properties.
internal carotid artery - larger of the two terminal branches of the common carotid artery that arises from the common carotid artery to supply the anterior brain and meninges.
internal os - inner surface of the cervical os.
interstitial pregnancy - pregnancy occurring in the cornu of the uterus.
intertubercular plane - lowest horizontal line joins the tubercles on the iliac crests.
intrahepatic - within the liver.
intramural leiomyoma - most common type of leiomyoma; deforms the myometrium.
intraperitoneal - within the peritoneal cavity.
intrauterine contraceptive device (IUD, IUCD) - device inserted into the endometrial cavity to prevent pregnancy.
intrauterine growth restriction (IUGR) - decreased rate of fetal growth, usually a fetal weight below the tenth percentile for a given gestational age; may be symmetric (all growth parameters are small) or asymmetric (maybe caused by placental problem; head measurements correlate with dates; body disproportionately smaller); formerly referred to as intrauterine growth retardation.
intussusception - bowel prolapses into distal bowel (telescoping) and is then propelled in an antegrade fashion.
invasive mole - tumor that penetrates into and through the uterine wall
ischemic rest pain - critical ischemia (lack of blood) of the distal limb when the patient is at rest.
islets of Langerhans - portion of the pancreas that has an endocrine function and produces insulin, glucagon, and somatostatin.
isoechoic - echo texture that resembles the surrounding tissue. Isoechoic masses can be difficult to identify.
isthmus - small piece of thyroid tissue that connects the lower lobes of the gland.
IUP - intrauterine pregnancy.
jaundice - excessive bilirubin accumulation causes yellow pigmentation of the skin; first seen in the whites of the eyes.
jejunoileal atresia - blockage of the jejunum and ileal bowel segments that appears as multiple cystic structures within the fetal abdomen.
junctional fold - small septum within the gallbladder, usually arising from the posterior wall.
juxtathoracic - near the chest wall (thorax).
kilohertz (kHz) - 1000 Hz.
Klatskin's tumor - cancer at the bifurcation of the hepatic ducts; may cause asymmetric obstruction of the biliary tree.
large for gestational age (LGA) - fetus measures larger than would be expected for dates (diabetic fetus).
lateral arcuate ligament - thickened upper margin of the fascia covering the anterior surface of the quadratus lumborum muscle.
left atrium - filling chamber of the heart.
left crus of the diaphragm - tendinous connection of the diaphragm that arises from the sides of the bodies of the first two lumbar vertebrae.
left gastric artery - artery that arises from the celiac axis to supply the stomach and lower third of the esophagus.
left hypochondrium - left upper quadrant of the abdomen that contains the left lobe of the liver, spleen, and stomach.
left lobe of the liver - lobe that lies in the epigastrium and left hypochondrium.
left portal vein - the main portal vein branches into the left and right portal veins to supply the liver.
left renal artery - artery that arises from the posterolateral wall of the aorta directly into the hilus of the kidney.

left renal vein - leaves the renal hilum, travels anterior to the aorta and posterior to the superior mesenteric artery to enter the lateral wall of the inferior vena cava.
left ventricle - pumping chamber of the heart.
leiomyoma - most common benign gynecologic tumor in women during their reproductive years.
lemon sign - seen on sonography, sign of frontal bones collapsing inward; occurs with spina bifida.
lesser omentum - membranous extension of the peritoneum that suspends the stomach and duodenum from the liver; helps to support the lesser curvature of the stomach.
lesser sac - peritoneal pouch located behind the lesser omentum and stomach.
lesser saphenous vein - vein that originates on the dorsum of the foot and ascends posterior to the lateral malleolus and runs along the midline of the posterior calf; vein terminates as it joins the popliteal vein.
leukocyte - white blood cell; primary function is to defend the body against infection.
leukocytosis - increase in the number of leukocytes.
leukopenia - abnormal decrease of white blood corpuscles; may be drug induced.
levator ani muscles - a pair of muscles that form the floor of the pelvis.
lienorenal ligament - ligament between the spleen and kidney that helps hold the spleen in place and supports the greater curvature of the stomach.
ligamentum teres - termination of the falciform ligament; seen in the left lobe of the liver.
ligamentum venosum - transformation of the ductus venosus in fetal life to closure in neonatal life. It separates left lobe from caudate lobe; shown as echogenic line on the transverse and sagittal images.
limb–body wall complex - anomaly with large cranial defects, facial cleft, large body wall defects, and limb abnormalities.
linea alba - fibrous band of tissue that stretches from the xiphoid to the symphysis pubis.
linea semilunaris - line that extends from the ninth costal cartilage to the pubic tubercle
lipase - pancreatic enzyme that acts on fats; enzyme is elevated in pancreatitis and remains increased longer than amylase.
liver function tests - specific laboratory tests that look at liver function (aspartate or alanine aminotransferase, lactic acid dehydrogenase, alkaline phosphatase, and bilirubin).
lobular carcinoma in situ (LCIS) - see lobular neoplasia
lobular neoplasia - term preferred by many authors to replace LCIS (not considered a true cancer nor treated as such) and atypical hyperplasia.
long axis - plane that transects heart perpendicular to dorsal and ventral surfaces of body and parallel with long axis of heart.
loop of Henle - portion of a renal tubule lying between the proximal and distal convoluted portions; reabsorption of fluid, sodium, and chloride occurs in the proximal convoluted tubule and the loop of Henle.
lower uterine segment - thin expanded lower portion of the uterus at the junction of the internal os and sacrum that forms in the last trimester of pregnancy.
lymph - alkaline fluid found in the lymphatic vessels.
lymphangiectasia - dilation of a lymph node.
lymphoma - malignancy that primarily affects the lymph nodes, spleen, or liver.
macrocephaly - enlargement of the fetal cranium as a result of ventriculomegaly.
macroglossia - hypertrophied tongue.
macrosomia - birth weight greater than 4000 g or above the 90th percentile for the estimated gestational age; these infants have fat deposition in the subcutaneous tissues
main lobar fissure - boundary between the right and left lobes of the liver; seen as hyperechoic line on the sagittal image extending from the portal vein to the neck of the gallbladder.
main portal vein - vein formed by union of the splenic vein and superior mesenteric vein; enters the liver at the porta hepatis.
main pulmonary artery - main artery that carries blood from the right ventricle to the lungs.
major calyces (also known as the infundibulum) - area of the kidneys that receives urine from the minor calyces to convey to the renal pelvis.
malpighian corpuscles - small, round, deep red bodies in the cortex of the kidney, each communicating with a renal tubule.
mammary layer - middle layer of the breast tissue (one of three layers recognized on breast ultrasound between the skin and the chest wall) that contains the ductal, glandular, and stromal portions of the breast.
Marfan's syndrome - hereditary disorder of connective tissue, bones, muscles, ligaments, and skeletal structures.
maternal serum alpha-fetoprotein (MSAFP) - antigen present in the fetus; the maternal serum is tested between 16 and 18 weeks of gestation to detect abnormal levels.
maximum or **deep vertical pocket** - method to determine the amount of amniotic fluid; pocket less than 2 cm may indicate oligohydramnios; greater than 8 cm indicates polyhydramnios. This method is used more often in multiple gestation pregnancy.
McBurney's point - site of maximum tenderness in the right lower quadrant; usually with appendicitis.
mean velocity - velocity based on the time average of the outline velocity (maximum velocity envelope).
Meckel's diverticulum - congenital sac or blind pouch found in the lower portion of the ileum; a remnant of the proximal part of the yolk stalk.
meconium ileus - small-bowel disorder marked by the presence of thick echogenic meconium in the distal ileum.
medial arcuate ligament - thickened upper margin of the fascia covering the anterior surface of the psoas muscle. It connects the medial borders of the two diaphragmatic crura as they cross anterior to the aorta.

mediastinum testis - linear structure within the midline of the testes.
medulla - central tissue of the adrenal gland that secrets epinephrine and norepinephrine.
medulla (also known as the pyramid) - inner portion of the renal parenchyma that contains the loop of Henle.
medullary carcinoma - neoplastic growth that accounts for 10% of thyroid malignancies.
medullary pyramids - large and hypoechoic in the neonate.
megahertz (MHz) - 1,000,000 Hz.
Meigs' syndrome - benign tumor of the ovary associated with ascites and pleural effusion.
membranous or velamentous insertion of the cord - insertion of the cord into the membranes before it enters the placenta.
menarche - onset of menstruation; state after reaching puberty in which menses occur normally every 27 to 28 days.
meninges - linings of the brain.
meningocele - open spinal defect characterized by protrusion of the spinal meninges.
meningomyelocele - open spinal defect characterized by protrusion of meninges and spinal cord through the defect, usually within a meningeal sac.
menopause - cessation of menstruation.
menses - monthly flow of blood from the endometrium.
menstrual age - gestational age of the fetus determined from the first day of the last normal menstrual period (LMP) to the point at which the pregnancy is being assessed.
mesentery - a fold from the parietal peritoneum that attaches to the small intestine anchoring it to the posterior abdominal wall.
mesosalpinx - free margin of the upper portion of the broad ligament where the oviduct is found.
mesothelium - tissue that lines the body cavities of the embryo, part of which develops into the peritoneum.
meta- - change.
metabolism - physical and chemical changes that occur within the body.
metastatic disease - tumor that develops away from the site of the organ; most common form of neoplasm of the liver; most common primary sites are colon, breast, and lung.
microcephaly - head smaller than the body.
micrognathia - abnormally small chin; commonly associated with other fetal anomalies.
microphthalmos - small eyes.
middle cerebral artery (MCA) - large terminal branch of the internal carotid artery.
midline echo complex (the falx) - widest transverse diameter of the skull; proper level to measure the biparietal diameter.
minor calyces - area of the kidneys that receives urine from the renal pyramids; form the border of the renal sinus.
mitral atresia - thickened, underdeveloped mitral apparatus.
mitral regurgitation - failure of the leaflets to close completely, allowing blood to leak backward into the left atrium.
mitral valve - atrioventricular valve between the left atrium and left ventricle.
molar pregnancy - also known as gestational trophoblastic disease; abnormal proliferation of trophoblastic cells in the first trimester.
monoamniotic - multiple pregnancy with one amniotic sac.
monochorionic - multiple pregnancy with one chorionic sac.
monozygotic - twins that arise from a single fertilized egg that divides to produce two identical fetuses.
Morison's pouch - right posterior subphrenic space that lies between the right lobe of the liver, anterior to the kidney and right colic flexure, where fluid may lie or an abscess may develop.
MSD - mean sac diameter.
mucinous cystadenocarcinoma - malignant tumor of the ovary with multilocular cysts.
mucinous cystadenoma - benign tumor of the ovary that contains thin-walled, multilocular cysts
mucosa - mucous membrane; thin sheet of tissue that lines cavities of the body that open to the outside; it is the first layer of bowel.
multicystic dysplastic kidney disease (MCDK) - multiple cysts replace normal renal tissue throughout the kidney; usually causes renal obstruction; most common cause of renal cystic disease in the neonate; may have contralateral ureteral pelvic junction obstruction.
multinodular goiter - nodular enlargement of the thyroid associated with hyperthyroidism.
Murphy's sign - positive sign implies exquisite tenderness over the area of the gallbladder upon palpation.
muscularis - third layer of bowel.
myocardium - thickest muscle in the heart wall.
myometritis - infection within the myometrium of the uterus.
myometrium - middle layer of the uterine cavity that appears very homogeneous with sonography.
nabothian cyst - benign tiny cyst within the cervix.
neck of the pancreas - small area of the pancreas between the head and the body; anterior to the superior mesenteric vein.
neonate - infant during the early newborn period.
neoplasm - refers to any new growth (benign or malignant).
nephroblastomatosis - abnormal persistence of fetal renal blastema (potential to develop into Wilms' tumor).
nephron - functional unit of the kidney; includes a renal corpuscle and a renal tubule.
neuroblastoma - malignant adrenal mass that is seen in pediatric patients.
nonimmune hydrops (NIH) - group of conditions in which hydrops is present in the fetus but not a result of fetomaternal blood group incompatibility.
nonpalpable - cannot be felt on clinical examination; nonpalpable breast mass is one that is usually identified on screening mammogram and is too small to be felt as a breast lump on BSE or CBE.

nonresistive - vessels that have high diastolic component and supply organs that need constant perfusion (internal carotid artery, hepatic artery, and renal artery).
Non-Stress Test (NST) - test that utilizes Doptone (a brand of Doppler instrumentation used in obstetric examinations) to record the fetal heart rate and its reactivity to the stress of uterine contraction.
normal situs - indicates normal position of the abdominal organs (liver on right, stomach on left, heart apex to the left).
nuchal cord - condition that occurs when the cord is wrapped around the fetal neck.
nuchal lucency - increased thickness in the nuchal fold area in the back of the neck associated with trisomy 21.
obstructive disease - blockage of bile excretion within the liver or biliary system.
obturator internus muscle - arises from the anterolateral pelvic wall surrounding the obturator foramen to insert on the greater trochanter of the femur.
oculodentodigital dysplasia - underdevelopment of the eyes, fingers, and mouth.
oligohydramnios - insufficient amount of amniotic fluid
-ology - study of; *physiology:* study of body functions.
omphalocele - anterior abdominal wall defect in which abdominal organs (liver, bowel, stomach) are atypically located within the umbilical cord and protrude outside the wall; highly associated with cardiac, central nervous system, renal, and chromosomal anomalies. It develops when there is a midline defect of the abdominal muscles, fascia, and skin.
omphalomesenteric cyst - cystic lesion of the umbilical cord.
oophoritis - infection within the ovary.
ophthalmic artery - first branch of the internal carotid artery.
osteogenesis imperfecta - metabolic disorder affecting the fetal collagen system that leads to varying forms of bone disease; intrauterine bone fractures, shortened long bones, poorly mineralized calvaria, and compression of the chest found in type II forms.
ovarian carcinoma - malignant tumor of the ovary that may spread beyond the ovary and metastasize to other organs via the peritoneal channels.
ovarian cyst - cyst of the ovary that may be found in the fetus; results from maternal hormone stimulation and is usually benign.
ovarian torsion - partial or complete rotation of the ovarian pedicle on its axis.
Paget's disease of the breast - surface erosion of the nipple that results from direct invasion of the skin of the nipple from underlying breast cancer.
palpable - can be felt on clinical examination; palpable breast lump is one that is identified on CBE or BSE.
pampiniform plexus - multiple veins that drain the testicles; when a varicocele is present, dilation and tortuosity may develop.
pancreatic ascites - fluid accumulation caused by a rupture of a pancreatic pseudocyst into the abdomen; free-floating pancreatic enzymes are very dangerous to surrounding structures.
pancreatic duct - duct that travels horizontally through the pancreas to join the common bile duct at the ampulla of Vater.
pancreatic pseudocyst - "sterile abscess" collection of pancreatitis enzymes that accumulate in the available space in the abdomen (usually in or near the pancreas).
pancreaticoduodenal arteries - arteries that help supply blood to the pancreas along with the splenic artery.
pancreatitis - inflammation of the pancreas; may be acute or chronic.
papillary carcinoma - most common form of thyroid malignancy.
paralytic ileus - dilated, fluid-filled loops of bowel without peristalsis secondary to obstruction, decreased vascularity, or abnormal metabolic state.
parametritis - infection within the uterine serosa and broad ligaments.
paraovarian cyst - cystic structure that lies adjacent to the ovary.
parasternal - transducer placement over the area bounded superiorly by left clavicle, medially by sternum, and inferiorly by apical region.
pariet- - wall; *parietal membrane:* membrane that lines the wall of a cavity.
parietal peritoneum - layer of the peritoneum that lines the abdominal wall.
parity - number of live births.
partial mole - condition that develops when two sperm fertilize an egg.
partial situs inversus - reversal of the heart or the abdominal organs (dextrocardia or liver on the left, stomach on the right).
patent ductus arteriosus - open communication between the pulmonary artery and descending aorta that does not constrict after birth.
peau d'orange - French term that means "skin of the orange"; descriptive term for skin thickening of one breast that, on clinical breast examination, resembles the skin of an orange. Such an appearance can result from an inflammatory breast condition (mastitis), simple edema, or skin involvement from underlying breast cancer.
pelv- - basin; *pelvic cavity:* basin-shaped cavity enclosed by the pelvic bones.
pelvic inflammatory disease (PID) - all-inclusive term that refers to all pelvic infections (endometritis, salpingitis, hydrosalpinx, pyosalpinx, and tuboovarian abscess).
pelvic kidney - location of the kidney when the kidney does not migrate upward into the retroperitoneal space.
pelviectasis - dilated renal pelvis measuring 5 to 9 mm in the anteroposterior direction.
pentalogy of Cantrell - rare anomaly with five defects: omphalocele, ectopic heart, lower sternum, anterior diaphragm, and diaphragmatic pericardium.
perforating veins - veins that connect the superficial and deep venous systems.

pericardium - sac surrounding the heart, reflecting off the great arteries.
period - duration of a single cycle of a periodic wave or event.
peripheral occlusive arterial disease - narrowing or stenosis of the peripheral arteries.
peripheral zone - posterior and lateral aspect of the prostate.
perirenal space - located directly around the kidney; completely enclosed by renal fascia.
peristalsis - rhythmic dilatation and contraction of the gastrointestinal tract as food is propelled through it.
peritoneal cavity - potential space between the parietal and visceral peritoneal layers.
peritoneal recess - slitlike spaces near the liver; potential space for fluid to accumulate.
peritonitis - inflammation of the peritoneum.
periventricular leukomalacia - echogenic white matter necrosis best seen in the posterior aspect of the brain or adjacent to the ventricular structures.
peroneal veins - veins that drain blood from the lateral lower leg.
phagocytosis - process by which cells engulf and destroy microorganisms and cellular debris; "cell-eating"; for example, the red pulp destroys the degenerating red blood cells.
phenylketonuria (PKU) - hereditary disease caused by failure to oxidize an amino acid (phenylalanine) to tyrosine, because of a defective enzyme; if PKU is not treated early, mental retardation can develop.
pheochromocytoma - benign adrenal tumor that secretes hormones that produce hypertension.
phlegmasia alba dolens - swollen, painful white leg.
phlegmasia cerulea dolens - swollen, painful cyanotic leg.
phrenocolic ligament - one of the ligaments between the spleen and splenic flexure of the colon.
phrygian cap - gallbladder variant in which part of the fundus is bent back on itself.
piezoelectric effect - generation of electric signals as a result of an incident sound beam on a material that has piezoelectric properties; in the converse (or reverse) piezoelectric effect, the material expands or contracts when an electric signal is applied.
piriformis muscle - muscle that arises from the sacrum between the pelvic sacral foramina and the gluteal surface of the ilium.
pitting - process by which the spleen removes abnormal red blood cells.
placenta - organ of communication (nutrition and products of metabolism) between the fetus and the mother; forms from the chorion frondosum with a maternal decidual contribution.
placenta accreta - growth of the chorionic villi superficially into the myometrium.
placenta increta - growth of the chorionic villi deep into the myometrium.
placenta percreta - growth of the chorionic villi through the myometrium.
placenta previa - placental implantation that encroaches upon the lower uterine segment; the placenta comes first and bleeding is inevitable.
placental grade - technique of grading the placenta for maturity.
placental grading - arbitrary method of classifying the maturity of the placenta with a grading scale of 0 to 3.
placental insufficiency - abnormal condition of pregnancy manifested by a restricted rate of fetal and uterine growth. One or more placental abnormalities cause dysfunction of maternal-placental or fetal-placental circulation.
placental migration - movement of the placenta as the uterus enlarges the placenta; a low-lying placenta may move out of the uterine segment in the second trimester.
pleur- rib; *pleural membrane:* membrane that encloses the lungs within the rib cage.
pleural effusion (hydrothorax) - accumulation of fluid within the thoracic cavity.
polycystic kidney disease - poorly functioning enlarged kidneys.
polycystic ovarian disease - endocrine disorder associated with chronic anovulation.
polycythemia - excess of red blood cells.
polycythemia vera - chronic, life-shortening condition of unknown etiology involving bone marrow elements; characterized by an increase in red blood cell mass and hemoglobin concentration.
polydactyly - anomalies of the hands or feet in which there is an addition of a digit; may be found in association with certain skeletal dysplasias.
polyhydramnios - excessive amount of amniotic fluid (>20 cm).
polyp - small, well-defined soft tissue projection from the gallbladder wall.
polysplenia - condition where there is more than one spleen; associated with cardiac malformations.
popliteal artery - artery that begins at the opening of the adductor magnus muscle and travels behind the knee in the popliteal fossa.
popliteal vein - vein that originates from the confluence of the anterior tibial veins and posterior and peroneal veins.
porta hepatis - central area of the liver where the portal vein, common duct, and hepatic artery enter.
portal confluence - see confluence of the splenic and portal veins.
portal vein - vein formed by the union of the superior mesenteric vein and splenic vein near the porta hepatis of the liver.
portal venous hypertension - results from intrinsic liver disease; may cause flow reversal to the liver, thrombosis of the portal system, or cavernous transformation of the portal vein.
portal-splenic confluence - junction of the splenic and main portal vein; posterior border of the body of the pancreas.

posterior arch vein - main tributary of the greater saphenous vein.
posterior cerebral artery (PCA) - artery that originates from the terminal basilar artery and courses anteriorly and laterally.
posterior communicating artery (PcoA) - courses posteriorly and medially from the internal carotid artery to join the posterior cerebral artery.
posterior pararenal space - space found between the posterior renal fascia and the muscles of the posterior abdominal wall.
posterior tibial veins - veins that originate from the plantar veins of the foot and drain blood from the posterior lower leg.
posterior urethral valve - the presence of a valve in the posterior urethra; occurs only in male fetuses; most common cause of bladder outlet obstruction in the male neonate.
postterm - fetus born later than the 42-week gestational period.
Potter's syndrome - condition characterized by renal agenesis, oligohydramnios, pulmonary hypoplasia, abnormal facies and malformed hands and feet.
Pourcelot resistive index - Doppler measurement that takes the highest systolic peak minus the highest diastolic peak divided by the highest systolic peak.
preeclampsia - complication of pregnancy characterized by increasing hypertension, proteinuria, and edema.
premature atrial and ventricular contractions - fetal cardiac arrhythmia resulting from extra systoles and ectopic beats.
premature rupture of the membranes (PROM) - may lead to premature delivery or infection.
premenarche - time period in young girls before the onset of menstruation.
preterm - fetus born earlier than the normal 38- to 42-week gestational period.
primary yolk sac - first site of formation of red blood cells that will nourish the embryo.
profunda femoris artery - artery posterior and lateral to the superficial femoral artery.
projectile vomiting - condition found in pyloric stenosis in the neonatal period; after drinking the infant experiences projectile vomiting secondary to the obstruction.
proliferative phase - days 5 to 9 of the menstrual cycle; endometrium appears as a single thin stripe with a hypoechoic halo encompassing it; creates the "three-line sign."
prune-belly syndrome - dilation of the fetal abdomen secondary to severe bilateral hydronephrosis, and fetal ascites; fetus also has oligohydramnios and pulmonary hypoplasia.
pseudoaneurysm - perivascular collection (hematoma) that communicates with an artery or a graft and has the presence of pulsating blood entering the collection.
pseudoascites - sonolucent band near the fetal anterior abdominal wall seen in the fetus over 18 weeks (does not outline the falciform ligament or bowel as ascites will).
pseudogestational sac - decidual reaction that occurs within the uterus in a patient with an ectopic pregnancy.
psoas major muscle - begins at the level of hilum of the kidneys and extends inferiorly along both sides of the spine into the pelvis.
pulmonary embolism - blockage of the pulmonary circulation by a thrombus or other matter; may lead to death if blockage of pulmonary blood flow is significant.
pulmonary hypoplasia - small, underdeveloped lungs with resultant reduction in lung volume; secondary to prolonged oligohydramnios or as a consequence of a small thoracic cavity.
pulmonary stenosis - thickening and narrowing of the pulmonic cusps; causes blood to back up into the right ventricle and atrium.
pulmonary veins - four pulmonary veins bring blood from the lungs back into the posterior wall of the left atrium; there are two upper (right and left) and two lower (right and left) pulmonary veins
pulsatility index (PI) - Doppler measurement that uses peak systole minus peak diastole divided by the mean.
pulse duration - measure of the ring-down (an artifact that occurs when the ultrasound transducer strikes the ribs) time of a transducer after excitation.
pulsed wave transducer - single crystal that sends and receives sound intermittently; a pulse of sound is emitted from the transducer, which also receives the returning signal.
pyloric canal - canal located between the stomach and duodenum.
pyogenic - pus producing.
pyogenic abscess - pus-forming collection of fluid.
pyosalpinx - retained pus within the inflamed fallopian tube.
pyramidal lobe - lobe of the thyroid gland that is present in small percentage of patients; extends superiorly from the isthmus.
pyramids - area of the kidneys that convey urine to the minor calyces.
radial - descriptive term used to denote area of the breast relative to a clock.
radial artery - artery that begins at the brachial artery bifurcation.
reactive hyperemia - alternative method to stress the peripheral arterial circulation.
real-time - ultrasound instrumentation that allows the image to be displayed many times per second to achieve a "real-time" image of anatomic structures and their motion patterns.
rectouterine pouch (pouch of Douglas) - area in the pelvic cavity between the rectum and the uterus that is likely to accumulate free fluid.
rectus abdominis muscle - muscle of the anterior abdominal wall.
rectus sheath hematoma - hemorrhage within the anterior rectus sheath muscle usually secondary to trauma.
red pulp - tissue composed of reticular cells and fibers (cords of Billroth); surrounds the splenic sinuses.
refraction - change in the direction of propagation of a sound wave transmitted across an interface where the speed of sound varies.

renal agenesis - interruption in the normal development of the kidney resulting in absence of the kidney; may be unilateral or bilateral.
renal artery - artery that arises from the posterolateral wall of the aorta, travels posterior to the inferior vena cava to supply the kidney.
renal capsule - first layer adjacent to the kidney that forms a tough, fibrous covering.
renal corpuscle - part of the nephron that consists of Bowman's capsule and the glomerulus.
renal hilum - area in the midportion of the kidney where the renal vessels and ureter enter and exit.
renal pelvis - area in the midportion of the kidney that collects urine before entering the ureter.
renal sinus - central area of the kidney that includes the calyces, renal pelvis, renal vessels, fat, nerves, and lymphatics.
renal vein thrombosis - obstruction of the renal vein resulting in kidney becoming enlarged and edematous.
resistive index - peak systole minus peak diastole divided by peak systole (S-D/S 5 RI); an RI of 0.7 or less indicates good perfusion; an RI of 0.7 or higher indicates decreased perfusion.
resolution - ability of the transducer to distinguish between two structures adjacent to one another.
respect for autonomy - relation to or concern with self-governing or self-directing freedom and especially moral independence.
respiratory phasicity - change in blood flow velocity with respiration.
reticuloendothelial cells - certain phagocytic cells (found mainly in the liver and spleen) make up the reticuloendothelial system (RES), which plays a role in the defense against infection and synthesis of blood proteins and hemopoiesis.
retromammary layer - deepest of the three layers of the breast noted on breast ultrasound. The retromammary layer is predominantly fatty and can be thin. The retromammary layer separates the active breast glandular tissue from the pectoralis fascia overlying the chest wall muscles.
retroperitoneum - space behind the peritoneal lining of the abdominal cavity.
retroverted - refers to the position of the uterus when the fundus is tipped posteriorly.
Rh blood group - system of antigens that may be found on the surface of red blood cells. When the Rh factor is present, the blood type is Rh positive; when the Rh antigen is absent, the blood type is Rh negative. A pregnant woman who is Rh negative may become sensitized by the blood of an Rh positive fetus. In subsequent pregnancies, if the fetus is Rh positive, the Rh antibodies produced in maternal blood may cross over the placenta and destroy fetal cells, causing erythroblastosis fetalis.
rhabdomyoma - benign cardiac tumor of the heart that is associated with tuberous sclerosis.
right atrium - filling chamber of the heart.
right crus of the diaphragm - arises from the sides of the bodies of the first three lumbar vertebrae.
right gastric artery - artery that supplies the stomach.
right hepatic artery - artery that supplies the gallbladder via the cystic artery.
right hypochondrium - right upper quadrant of the abdomen that contains the liver and gallbladder.
right lobe of the liver - largest of the lobes of the liver.
right portal vein - the main portal vein branches into the right and left portal veins to supply the lobes of the liver.
right renal artery - artery that arises from the posterolateral wall of the aorta and travels posterior to the inferior vena cava to enter the hilum of the kidney.
right renal vein - vein that leaves the renal hilum to enter the lateral wall of the inferior vena cava.
right ventricle - pumping chamber of the heart that sends blood into the pulmonary artery.
rugae - inner folds of the stomach wall.
S/D ratio - difference between peak systole and peak diastole.
saccular aneurysm - localized dilatation of the vessel.
sagittal plane - vertical plane through the longitudinal axis of the body that divides it into two portions.
salpingitis - infection within the fallopian tubes.
scoliosis - abnormal curvature of the spine.
scrotum - dependent sac containing the testes and epididymis.
secondary yolk sac - sac formed at 23 days when the primary yolk sac is pinched off by the extra embryonic coelom.
secretin - hormone released from small bowel as antacid; stimulates secretion of bicarbonate.
secretory (luteal) phase - days 14 to 28 of the menstrual cycle; the endometrium is at its greatest thickness and echogenicity with posterior enhancement.
secretory phase (early) - days 10 to 14 of the menstrual cycle; ovulation occurs; the endometrium increases in thickness and echogenicity.
semilunar valve - valve located in the aortic or pulmonic artery.
seminal vesicles - reservoirs for sperm located posterior to the bladder.
sepsis - spread of an infection from its initial site to the bloodstream.
septicemia - infection in the blood.
septum primum - first part of the atrial septum to grow from the dorsal wall of the primitive atrium; fuses with the endocardial cushions.
septum secundum - part of the atrial septum that grows into the atrium to the right of the septum primum.
serosa - fourth layer of bowel; thin, loose layer of connective tissue, surrounded by mesothelium covering the intraperitoneal bowel loops.
serous cystadenocarcinoma - most common type of ovarian carcinoma; may be bilateral with multilocular cysts.
serous cystadenoma - second most common benign tumor of the ovary; unilocular or multilocular.

INDEX

Page numbers in boldface type are in Volume Two.

velocity envelope - trace of the peak velocities as a function of time.
ventricular septal defect - communication between the right and left ventricles.
ventriculitis - inflammation or infection of the ventricles that appears as echogenic linear structures along the gyri; may also appear as focal echogenic structures within the white matter.
ventriculomegaly - abnormal accumulation of cerebrospinal fluid within the cerebral ventricles resulting in dilation of the ventricles; compression of developing brain tissue and brain damage may result; commonly associated with additional fetal anomalies.
vertebral artery - branches of the subclavian artery that merge to form the basilar artery.
vertex - position of fetus with head down in the uterus.
vertigo - sensation of having objects move about the person or sensation of moving around in space.
verumontanum - junction of the ejaculatory ducts with the urethra.
villi - inner folds of the small intestine.
visceral peritoneum - layer of peritoneum that covers the abdominal organs.
vital signs - medical measurements used to ascertain how the body is functioning.
wall echo shadow (WES) sign - sonographic pattern found when the gallbladder is packed with stones.
wandering spleen - spleen that has migrated from its normal location in the left upper quadrant.
wave - propagation of energy that moves back and forth or vibrates at a steady rate.
wavelength - distance over which a wave repeats itself during one period of oscillation.
Wharton's jelly - myxomatous connective tissue that surrounds the umbilical vessels and varies in size.
white blood cells - cells that defend the body by destroying invading microorganisms and their toxins.
white pulp - tissue composed of lymphatic tissue and lymphatic follicles.
Wilms' tumor - most frequent malignant tumor in the neonate and infant.
yolk sac - circular structure seen between 4 and 10 weeks that supplies nutrition to the fetal pole (the developing embryo); it lies within the chorion outside the amnion.
yolk stalk - the umbilical duct connecting the yolk sac with the embryo.
zygote - fertilized ovum resulting from union of male and female gametes.

TIPS - transjugular intrahepatic portosystemic shunt.
-tomy - cutting; *anatomy:* study of structure, which often involves cutting or removing body parts.
transducer - any device that converts signals from one form to another.
transitional zone - prostate area that is located on both sides of the proximal urethra and ends at the level of the verumontanum.
transorbital window - transducer placement on the closed eyelid.
transposition of the great arteries - failure of the truncus arteriosus to complete its rotation during the first trimester; causes the pulmonary artery to arise from the left ventricle and the aorta to arise from the pulmonary artery (blue baby at birth).
transpyloric plane - horizontal plane that passes through the pylorus, the duodenal junction, the neck of the pancreas, and the hilum of the kidneys.
transtemporal window - transducer placement on the temporal bone cephalad to the zygomatic arch anterior to the ear.
transvaginal transducer - high-frequency transducer that is inserted into the vaginal canal to obtain better definition of first-trimester pregnancy.
transverse lie - description of the fetus lying transversely (horizontally) across the abdomen.
tricuspid atresia - underdevelopment of the tricuspid valve (usually associated with hypoplasia of the right ventricle and pulmonary stenosis).
tricuspid valve - atrioventricular valve found between the right atrium and right ventricle.
trimester - pregnancy is divided into three 13-week segments called *trimesters.*
true (minor) pelvis - found below the brim of the pelvis; the cavity of the minor pelvis is continuous at the pelvic brim with the cavity of the major pelvis.
true knots of the umbilical cord - knots formed when a loop of cord is slipped over the fetal head or shoulders during delivery.
truncus arteriosus - common arterial trunk that divides into the aorta and pulmonary artery.
tuboovarian abscess (TOA) - infection that involves the fallopian tube and the ovary.
tunica adventitia - outer layer of the vascular system.
tunica albuginea - membrane surrounding the testicle.
tunica intima - inner layer of the vascular system.
tunica media - middle layer of the vascular system; veins have thinner tunica media than arteries.
tunica vaginalis - membrane lining the inner wall of the scrotum; hydroceles may develop between the tunica albuginea and tunica vaginalis.
Turner's syndrome - congenital endocrine disorder caused by failure of the ovaries to respond to pituitary hormone stimulation; cystic hygroma often seen.
twin-to-twin transfusion - monozygotic twin pregnancy with single placenta and arteriovenous shunt within the placenta; the donor twin becomes anemic and growth restricted with oligohydramnios; the recipient twin may develop hydrops and polyhydramnios.
umbilical cord - connecting lifeline between the fetus and placenta; it contains two umbilical arteries and one umbilical vein encased in Wharton's jelly.
umbilical herniation - failure of the anterior abdominal wall to close completely at the level of the umbilicus.
uncinate process - small, curved tip of the pancreatic head that lies posterior to the superior mesenteric vein.
unicornuate uterus - anomaly of the uterus in which only one horn and tube develop.
ureteropelvic junction - junction of the ureter entering the renal pelvis; most common site of obstruction.
ureteropelvic junction obstruction - most common neonatal obstruction of the urinary tract; results from intrinsic narrowing or extrinsic vascular compression.
ureterovesical junction - junction where the ureter enters the bladder.
ureters - retroperitoneal structures that exit the kidney to carry urine to the urinary bladder.
urethra - small, membranous canal that excretes urine from the urinary bladder.
urethral atresia - lack of development of the urethra; condition causing a massively distended bladder (prune belly).
urinary amylase - pancreatic enzyme that remains elevated longer than serum amylase in patients with acute pancreatitis.
urinary bladder - muscular retroperitoneal organ that serves as a reservoir for urine.
urinoma - cyst containing urine.
uterine synechiae - scars within the uterus secondary to previous gynecological surgery.
uterovesical space - anterior pouch between the uterus and bladder.
uterus didelphys - complete duplication of the uterus, cervix, and vagina.
VACTERL - **v**ertebral abnormalities, **a**nal atresia, **c**ardiac abnormalities, **t**racheo**e**sophageal fistula, and **r**enal and **l**imb abnormalities.
vagina atresia - failure of the vagina to develop.
valvulae conniventes - normal segmentation of the small bowel.
varicocele - dilated veins caused by obstruction of the venous return from the testicle.
varicose veins - dilated, elongated, tortuous superficial veins.
vas deferens - tube that connects the epididymis to the seminal vesicle.
vasa previa - condition that occurs when the umbilical cord vessels cross the internal os of the cervix.
veins - collapsible vascular structures that carry blood back to the heart.
velocity - speed of the ultrasound wave; determined by tissue density.

submucosal leiomyoma - type of leiomyoma found to deform the endometrial cavity and cause heavy or irregular menses.
suboccipital window - window formed when the transducer is placed on the posterior aspect of the neck inferior to the nuchal crest.
subphrenic - below the diaphragm.
subserosal - type of leiomyoma that may become pedunculated and appear as an extrauterine mass.
subvalvular aortic stenosis - formation of a membrane beneath the aortic leaflets causes left ventricular outflow obstruction.
succenturiate placenta - one or more accessory lobes connected to the body of the placenta by blood vessels.
sulcus - groove on the surface of the brain that separates the gyri.
superficial femoral artery - artery that courses the length of the thigh through Hunter's canal and terminates at the opening of the adductor magnus muscle.
superficial femoral vein - vein that originates at the hiatus of the adductor magnus muscle in the distal thigh and ascends through the adductor (Hunter's) canal.
superficial inguinal ring - triangular opening in the external oblique aponeurosis.
superior mesenteric artery - artery that arises inferior to the celiac axis to supply the proximal half of the colon and the small intestine.
superior mesenteric vein - vein that drains the proximal half of the colon and small intestine, travels vertically (anterior to the inferior vena cava) to join the splenic vein to form the portal veins.
superior vena cava - vessel receiving venous return from the head and upper extremities into the upper posterior medial wall of the right atrium.
superior vesical arteries - after birth the umbilical arteries become the superior vesical arteries.
supracristal septal defect - high membranous septal defect just beneath the pulmonary orifice.
suprasternal - transducer placement in the suprasternal notch.
supraventricular tachyarrhythmias - abnormal rhythms above 200 beats per minute with a normal sinus conduction rate of 1:1.
systemic lupus erythematosus (SLE) - inflammatory disease involving multiple organ systems; fetus of a mother with SLE may develop heart block and pericardial effusion.
systole - part of the cardiac cycle in which the ventricles are pumping blood through the outflow tract into the pulmonary artery or the aorta.
systolic to diastolic (S/D) ratio - Doppler determination of the peak systolic velocity divided by the peak diastolic velocity.
tail of the pancreas - tapered end of the pancreas that lies in the left hypochondrium near the hilus of the spleen and upper pole of the left kidney.
target (donut) sign - characteristic of gastrointestinal wall thickening consisting of an echogenic center and a hypoechoic rim; frequently associated with sectional areas of the gastrointestinal tract; the muscle is hyperechoic, and the inner core is hypoechoic.
tentorium - "tent" structure in the posterior fossa that separates the cerebellum from the cerebrum.
teratoma - solid tumor.
terminal ductal-lobular unit (TDLU) - smallest functional portion of the breast involving the terminal duct and its associated lobule containing at least one acinus (tiny milk-producing gland). The TDLU undergoes significant monthly hormone-induced changes and radical changes during pregnancy and lactation. The TDLU is the site of origin of nearly all significant pathological processes involving the breast, including all elements of fibrocystic condition, fibroadenomas, and in situ and invasive breast cancer (both lobular and ductal).
testicle - male gonad that produces hormones that induce masculine features and production of spermatozoa.
tetralogy of Fallot - a congenital anomaly consisting of four defects: membranous ventricular septal defect, overriding of the aorta, right ventricular hypertrophy, and pulmonary stenosis.
thalamus - portion of the midbrain that serves as two landmarks for the sonographer that abut both sides of the third ventricle.
thalassemia - group of hereditary anemias occurring in Asian and Mediterranean populations.
thanatophoric dysplasia - lethal short-limb dwarfism characterized by a marked reduction in the length of the long bones, pear-shaped chest, soft-tissue redundancy, and frequently clover-leaf skull deformity and ventriculomegaly.
theca-lutein cysts - multilocular cysts that occur in patients with hyperstimulation (hydatidiform mole and infertility patients); appear as multiple cysts within each ovary; complication of hyperstimulation.
thoracic outlet syndrome - changes in arterial blood flow to the arms related to intermittent compression of the proximal arteries.
thyroglossal duct cyst - congenital anomaly that presents in the midline of the neck anterior to the trachea.
thyroiditis - inflammation of the thyroid.
thyroid-stimulating hormone (TSH) - hormone secreted by the pituitary gland that stimulates the thyroid gland to secrete thyroxine and triiodothyronine
tibial-peroneal trunk - arterial branch that exits after the anterior tibial artery and bifurcates into the posterior tibial artery and the peroneal artery.
time gain compensation (TGC) - also referred to as *depth gain compensation;* ability to compensate for attenuation of the transmitted beam as the sound wave travels through tissues in the body; usually, individual pod controls allow the operator to manually change the amount of compensation necessary for each patient to produce a quality image.

serum amylase - pancreatic enzyme that is elevated during pancreatitis.
short axis - plane that transects heart perpendicular to dorsal and ventral surfaces of body and perpendicular to long axis of heart.
sickle cell anemia - inherited disorder transmitted as an autosomal recessive trait that causes an abnormality of the globin genes in hemoglobin.
sickle cell crisis - condition in sickle cell anemia in which the malformed red cells interfere with oxygen transport, obstruct capillary blood flow, and cause fever and severe pain in the joints and abdomen.
simple ovarian cyst - smooth, well-defined cystic structure that is filled completely with fluid.
single umbilical artery - condition of one umbilical cord instead of two; it has a high association with congenital anomalies.
single ventricle - condition in which there are two atria with one ventricle.
sinoatrial node - forms in the wall of the sinus venosus near its opening into the right atrium.
situs inversus - heart and abdominal organs are completely reversed.
sludge - low-level echoes found along the posterior margin of the gallbladder; move with change in position.
small for gestational age (SGA) - fetus measures smaller than would be expected for dates.
soleal sinuses - large venous reservoirs that lie in the soleus muscle and empty into the posterior tibial or peroneal veins.
sonohysterography - technique that uses a catheter inserted into the endometrial cavity with the insertion of saline solution or contrast medium to fill the endometrial cavity for the purpose of demonstrating abnormalities within the cavity or uterine tubes.
spatial pulse length - spatial extent of an ultrasound pulse burst.
Spaulding's sign - overlapping of the skull bones; occurs in fetal death.
specific gravity - aboratory tests that measure how much dissolved material is present in the urine.
spectral analysis waveform - graphic display of the flow velocity over period of time.
spectral broadening - change in the spectral width that increases with flow disturbance.
spermatocele - cyst within the vas deferens containing sperm.
spherocytosis - condition in which erythrocytes assume a spheroid shape; hereditary.
sphincter of Oddi - small muscle that guards the ampulla of Vater.
spina bifida - neural tube defect of the spine in which the dorsal vertebrae (vertebral arches) fail to fuse together, allowing the protrusion of meninges and/or spinal cord through the defect; two types exist: spina bifida occulta (skin-covered defect of the spine without protrusion of meninges or cord) and spina bifida cystica (open spinal defect marked by sac containing protruding meninges and/or cord).
spina bifida occulta - closed defect of the spine without protrusion of meninges or spinal cord; alpha-fetoprotein analysis will not detect these lesions.
splaying - widening.
splenic agenesis - complete absence of the spleen.
splenic artery - one of the three vessels that arise from the celiac axis to supply the spleen, pancreas, stomach, and greater omentum; forms the superior border of the pancreas.
splenic flexure - the transverse colon travels horizontally across the abdomen and bends at this point to form the descending colon.
splenic hilum - site where vessels and lymph nodes enter and exit the spleen; located in the middle of the spleen.
splenic sinuses - long, irregular channels lined by endothelial cells or flattened reticular cells.
splenic vein - vein that drains the spleen; travels horizontally across the abdomen (posterior to the pancreas) to join the superior mesenteric vein to form the portal vein; serves as the posterior medial border of the pancreas.
splenomegaly - enlargement of the spleen.
spontaneous - flow is present without augmentation.
-stasis - standing still; *homeostasis:* maintenance of a relatively stable internal environment.
strabismus - eye disorder in which optic axes cannot be directed to the same object
subclavian artery - artery that originates at the inner border of the scalenus anterior and travels beneath the clavicle to the outer border of the first rib to become the axillary artery.
subclavian steal syndrome - symptoms of brain stem ischemia associated with a stenosis or occlusion of the left subclavian, innominate, or right subclavian artery proximal to the origin of the vertebral artery.
subclavian vein - continuation of the axillary vein.
subcostal - placement of the transducer located near body midline and beneath costal margin.
subcutaneous layer - most superficial of the three layers of the breast identified on breast ultrasound, the subcutaneous layer is mainly fatty; it is located immediately beneath the skin and superficial to the mammary layer. The subcutaneous layer can be very thin and difficult to recognize.
subependyma - fragile area beneath the ependyma that is subject to bleed in the premature infant.
subhepatic - inferior to the liver.
subjective assessment of fluid - sonographer surveys uterine cavity to determine visual assessment of amniotic fluid present
submandibular window - window formed when transducer is placed at the angle of the mandible and angled slightly medially and cephalad toward the carotid canal.
submucosa - one of the layers of the bowel, under the mucosal layer; contains blood vessels and lymph channels.

M

P

S

U